ISBN 978-0-266-01641-0
PIBN 10961239

AMERICAN DRUGGIST

AND

PHARMACEUTICAL RECORD,

A Semi-monthly Illustrated
Journal of Practical Pharmacy.

CASWELL A. MAYO, Ph.G.,
EDITOR

THOMAS J. KEENAN,
ASSOCIATE EDITOR.

Volume XLVIII. January to June, 1906.

NEW YORK:
PUBLISHED BY AMERICAN DRUGGIST PUBLISHING CO., 62 TO 68 WEST BROADWAY.

1906.

INDEX TO VOLUME XLVIII.

AMERICAN DRUGGIST

and PHARMACEUTICAL RECORD

PHILADELPHIA. NEW YORK, JANUARY 8, 1906. CHICAGO

ISSUED SEMI-MONTHLY BY

AMERICAN DRUGGIST PUBLISHING CO.,

62-68 WEST BROADWAY, NEW YORK.

CHICAGO, 221 Randolph St. PHILADELPHIA, 3718 Walnut St.

A. R. ELLIOTT, President.

CASWELL A. MAYO, Ph.G. .... Editor.
THOMAS J. KEENAN .... Associate Editor.

ROMAINE PIERSON .... Manager Chicago Office.

$1.50 a year. 15 cents a copy.

ADVERTISING RATES QUOTED ON APPLICATION.

THE AMERICAN DRUGGIST AND PHARMACEUTICAL RECORD is issued on the second and fourth Mondays of each month. Changes of advertisements should be received ten days in advance of the date of publication.

Remittances should be made by New York exchange, post office or express money order or registered mail. If checks on local banks are used 10 cents should be added to cover cost of collection. The publishers are not responsible for money sent by unregistered mail, nor for any money paid except to duly authorized agents. All communications should be addressed and all remittances made payable to American Druggist Publishing Co., 62-68 West Broadway, New York.

Entered at New York as Second-Class Matter.

TABLE OF CONTENTS.

EDITORIAL COMMENT.

GET A PHARMACOPŒIA, OR BE DENIED A STORE LICENSE. The report of the annual meeting of the New York State Board of Pharmacy, which is printed elsewhere, should be of the highest interest to every practicing pharmacist in this State, and to these a careful perusal of it is commended. Most pharmacists are doubtless aware of the fact that the board has authority to adopt rulings calculated to strengthen the law and make easier its enforcement. Rule No. 20, the substance of which is given in our report, provides that no license shall be issued for any store which is not equipped with a copy of the latest revised edition of the Pharmacopœia. The board has authority to enforce this ruling, and pharmacists who are not possessed of the book would do well to get one at once. The board does not insist that the Pharmacopœia itself shall form part of the store's furniture—the board will be satisfied if a book embodying the Pharmacopœia in its contents is used; so that the possession of any of the Dispensatories or reference books containing the text of the latest revised edition of the Pharmacopœia will be regarded as a compliance with the ruling.

BULLETIN A. PH. A. At the Atlantic City meeting of the American Pharmaceutical Association steps were taken for the establishment of a monthly bulletin for the publication of association news, reports of officers, council motions, etc. The first number of the *Bulletin* was received the first of the year. It presents a very creditable appearance, both as regards form and typography. The pages are of equal size with those of the annual volume of Proceedings—namely, 6 x 9 inches, and the quality of paper is good. No. 1 contains a salutatory by the editor (C. S. N. Hallberg), the address of President Beal (11 pages), followed by the report of the committee on the address, the report of the Committee on National Legislation, and other committee reports. We do not doubt but that the *Bulletin* will admirably serve its purpose, reawakening interest in the affairs of the association on the part of the members and acquainting non-members with the aims and objects of the national organization. The association is distinctly to be congratulated on its choice of an editor for the *Bulletin*. Professor Hallberg has been actively identified with pharmacy and pharmaceutical journalism for a number of years, and there are few pharmaceutical journalists who are able to wield so trenchant and convincing a pen.

THE "AMERICAN DRUGGISTS' SYNDICATE." Inquiries continue to reach us regarding the aim, objects, purpose and responsibility of a concern styling itself the American Druggists' Syndicate, a concern with which, by the way, we feel it well to say again that the AMERICAN DRUGGIST has no connection. The syndicate is seeking to interest retail druggists in a scheme for the manufacture and sale of a new line of proprietary medicines, to be sold in competition with the products of the old line manufacturers. The avowed business of the syndicate has been set forth at different times in the columns of the AMERICAN DRUGGIST, particularly in the issues of August 28, page 115, and November 13, page 275, of this year. But beyond what the organizer, Charles H. Goddard, formerly of San Francisco, has chosen to reveal in interviews with our reporter we know really very little and do not feel warranted in saying anything regarding either the ability of the syndicate to carry out its promises or its responsibility generally. While the syndicate has declared its intention of marketing its products under the Direct Contract Serial Numbering Plan, the impression prevails in some quarters that it was organized to offset the operations of the N. A. R. D. by providing retailers with a line of proprietary remedies which could be sold independently of the old line manufacturers and jobbers who are tied up with the N. A. R. D. It may be also well to add that the directors of the syndicate are intimately connected with the association of large cutting druggists in New York: in fact they are the most active spirits in this association, and from this fact readers should be able to draw their own conclusions.

CLEMMONS PARRISH. A mere news item recording the passing of Clemmons Parrish, of Brooklyn, from active pharmaceutical life would convey little meaning to the average reader. The name Parrish is, however, still one to conjure with in American pharmacy. Parrish's chemical food is still prescribed by physicians and used by the laity, more perhaps in England than in America nowadays, but there are pharmacists living hereabouts who pride themselves on their ability to turn out a syrup of phosphate of iron equal to that produced by the famous Philadelphia professor of pharmacy whose name is known in connection with this article in all civilized countries. Professor Parrish's son, Clemmons, has conducted a pharmacy in Brooklyn for upward of 20 years, and he had the reputation among physicians of being a careful and experienced dispenser who took a pride in his work. Certain physical disabilities have rather interfered with active prosecution of work on his part of late years, and having recently received a satisfactory offer for his business he closed with it and now intends to take his ease away from the trials and exactions of active store life. The transfer takes place this month. Because he never identified himself prominently with association work Clemmons Parrish was seldom heard of in pharmaceutical politics, but his contributions to pharmacy were of as solid a nature as those of many of the more pushing members of the craft, and his abstention from association discussions cannot be considered as other than a loss to the associations, for he has a mind richly stored with the lore of his craft. He was assisted in the active management of the store by his wife, whose attention to details of a business nature relieved Mr. Parrish of many annoyances, while Mrs. Parrish's charming manner and sociable disposition helped not a little to make Parrish's pharmacy a pleasant place to visit. We can only wish his successor an equal share of the confidence of customers and patrons with that enjoyed by Mr. Parrish.

Grocers' Drugs Adulterated.

We publish in another column a summary of the report of the New York State Board of Pharmacy which druggists would do well to study carefully, as it contains material which can with much advantage be utilized by the druggist for advertising purposes in a perfectly legitimate manner.

The trade in cream tartar, spices and what are generally looked upon as "grocers' drugs" really belongs to the retail druggist and not to the grocer. The public has gradually come to look to the grocer for a number of the household drugs and chemicals, largely because they fear that they will pay higher prices for goods bought from the pharmacist than for the same goods bought from the grocer. But as a matter of fact they do not buy the same goods from the grocer. What they do buy from the grocer is adulterated goods bearing the same name. This fact cannot be too strongly dwelt upon by the enterprising druggist who wishes to get back some of the trade in spices and what might be termed domestic chemicals. The statistics of the New York State Board of Pharmacy, which we publish, can be used by our readers as a perfectly legitimate argument against their customers dealing with grocers when in need of spices, cream tartar, borax, etc.

The masses of dry statistics which are published from time to time by the various boards of pharmacy frequently contain valuable and interesting matter of this kind, and the discriminating reader will nearly always find something in the array of figures given in the annual reports of these bodies which will give him food for thought and not infrequently material for furthering his commercial interests.

The too strict adherence to routine work of prosecuting druggists on the part of the Board of Pharmacy without attention to such collateral work as the conservation of the purity of drugs tends to beget a feeling of irritation among the unthinking pharmacists, who are inclined to look upon the board as a source of persecution rather than as a body charged with the elevation and conservation of the calling in which the pharmacist is engaged. It is fortunate therefore that the New York State Board has found some scope for its energies which must benefit the pharmacist commercially as well as tend toward the elevation of his calling.

The Massachusetts Board has also found an opportunity to exercise its powers in behalf of pharmacists generally, and as will be seen by reference to the annual report of that board, which is also summarized in our news columns, that body proposes to put a stop to the incursions of the grocer into the field of pharmacy, which has been made possible by the too liberal interpretation of the term "domestic drugs."

A Foreign Market for Our Manufactures.

Nature has been generous to the people of America and the people have displayed a commendable skill and activity in the utilization of the natural advantages with which they are surrounded. With a view to stimulating domestic manufactures of all kinds a tariff has been imposed upon goods of foreign manufacture which has protected our "infant industries" from competition from foreign manufacturers. The home market thus guaranteed them has grown so rapidly as to supply an outlet for our manufactures which has hitherto been satisfactory so long as the country generally is in a prosperous condition. In times of financial depression the manufacturer has been compelled to shut down. Now, however, the capacity of our manufacturers has about caught up with the demands of the home market and it is becoming more and more necessary for us to look abroad for a possible outlet for our surplus goods. Moreover, as the total volume of our manufactures increases the problem of tiding over any period of financial depression grows increasingly important and increasingly difficult.

Other manufacturing nations after protecting their own home markets are reaching out vigorously for the world trade. Our own national policy has been declared by our activity in securing a guarantee of the open door to trade in China and Manchuria. John Hay's vigorous policy in foreign affairs showed his keen perception of our need for a foreign outlet for our manufactures and his strong determination to secure it so far as it could be secured by diplomatic means. But all that diplomacy can do is to secure an opening for our goods on equal terms with the other manufacturers of the world. When the diplomat has done this his function ceases and the further responsibility rests with the manufacturer and the merchant, but neither manufacturer nor merchant in America is yet trained to take advantage of the openings which have been secured for them by the diplomat.

We have so often dwelt upon the need for a careful study of foreign markets and foreign methods that we should hesitate to recur to the subject save for the timeliness of the remarks made in some recent addresses to the Sphinx Club, which are reported in another column. These speakers urge the American manufacturer to undertake a personal study of foreign markets and foreign methods. American manufacturers have so long been protected from competition with foreign manufacturers by the tariff that they underrate their competition and overrate American ingenuity. Foreign trade cannot be built up in a day. As aptly stated by Mr. Moore to the Sphinx Club, "the Yankee expects to drop into a town one day and to leave it the next with orders for his goods just as he does here in the United States." This is impossible. The people must be studied, their needs learned, their prejudices catered to and whims gratified. If they want goods packed in a certain way the man who would trade with them must pack them that way. The man who pays has a right to choose, and if our manufacturers will not comply with the requirements of the foreign buyers, however absurd they may appear to us, others will. Now in this era of unexampled prosperity is the time when our manufacturers should cast an anchor to windward and provide for an outlet in foreign markets which will serve to tide them over that period of depression which we hope will be long delayed, but which will surely come some day.

(Written for the American Druggist.)

PRESCRIPTION TALK.

By J. T. Pepper.

The usual sign, ℞, is absent from prescription No. 1, reproduced herewith, but we must take it for granted that it is there. I think it is quite easy to make out the first word as "Acid." The next word is not so easy, but the first letter is a capital "B," and the next letters are "oric," making the word "Boric." The quantity required is 6 drachms. The first letter of the second line is a capital "A," and the next letter is "q," the two forming the contraction "Aq," for "Aquæ." The next word is "Camphoræ." The abbreviation commencing the next line is "Aq." You can compare it with the "Aq" just above and decide upon that for a fact. The next two words are not so easy. But by comparing these letters with other letters that you are sure of you may arrive at a conclusion that is perfectly satisfactory. The letter "m," for minims, next to the "X" at the end of the line, you are sure is correct. Then compare that "m" with the letter at the first of the second word and I think that you will decide that it is an "m" also and then trace out the following letters, "enthæ," and you get the word "menthæ." The next little word of three letters is "pip," although the dot over the "i" is carried along nearly to the "m" for minims. The contraction "pip" stands for "piperitæ." The next line is "Aq," add to one fluid ounce. The directions are in plain enough English.

The druggist who gave me this prescription told me that

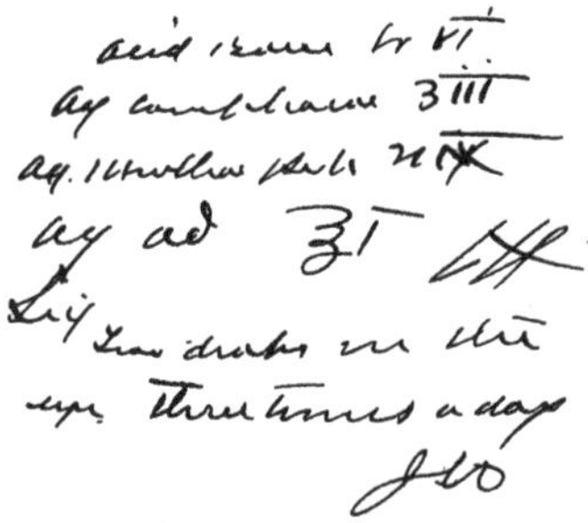

Prescription No. 1.

when it was presented at his drug store for dispensing neither he nor his partner nor any of the clerks were able to decipher "menthæ pip.," but were obliged to communicate with the physician in order to find out for what he intended these words to stand.

The physician was very pleasant over the matter and told a story of a lawyer who wrote out some advice for a client. The client when he reached home tried to read the advice that the lawyer had given, but was unable to make out a word of the writing, so next day he took the paper back to the lawyer, who was unable to read his own writing of the day before, but advised his client to take the written advice to his druggist, saying that druggists were used to reading the bad writing of physicians, and that he would likely be able to read this.

So the client took the written advice to the druggist, who looked at it knowingly for a few minutes, disappeared behind the dispensing case, and shortly reappeared with a bottle of medicine which he presented to the lawyer's client with a demand for $1.00.

In prescription No. 2, the first part calls for a pill. The word "case" might be taken for "cat-c," meaning "cathartic," that is, taking "cat," and the rest for the word "cathartic," as understood, finishing with a final "c." But I think that this is intended for the word "cascara," and that a compound pill of cascara is desired by the physician. The number required is 16. The "sig." or directions are "one or two for a dose." The little word "for" is contracted so much that the letter "o" is not seen at all. The word for "dose" is not

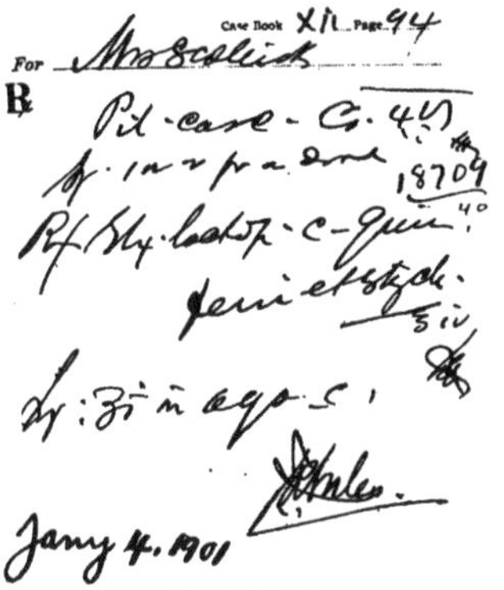

Prescription No. 2.

very distinctly written either. The first letter is "d," and the third one "s," while the last one looks like an "e"; we may suppose that the second letter is "o," and so make the word "dose."

The second prescription on prescription No. 2 is not very difficult. Notice the second sign "℞" instead of the Latin

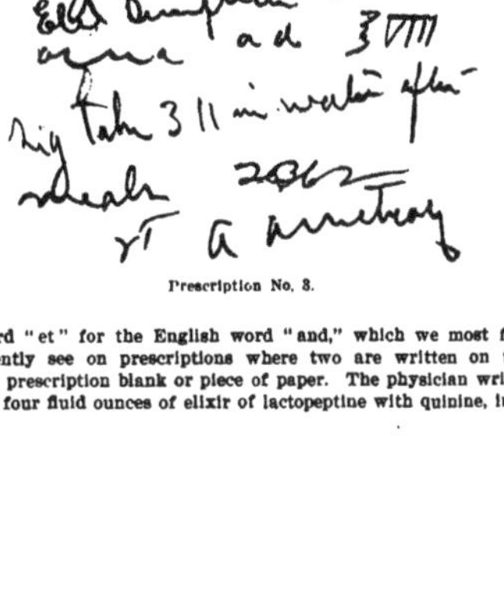

Prescription No. 3.

word "et" for the English word "and," which we most frequently see on prescriptions where two are written on the one prescription blank or piece of paper. The physician writes for four fluid ounces of elixir of lactopeptine with quinine, iron, and strychnine. The letter "c" stands for the Latin preposition *cum*, meaning "with." Notice also how the "c" and "y" are run together in the contracted word "strych." The dose is quite plainly one drachm or one teaspoonful. How is it to be taken? The answer is "*in aq.*," *in aqua*, in water. When is it to be taken, or how often? and the answer is, "*a. c.*," *ante cibos*, before meals. The directions to write on the label are then: *One teaspoonful in water before meals.*

Prescription No. 3 presents no difficulties, but is worth considering on account of the different appearance it presents to the usual run of prescriptions. I think it can all be read easily by anyone. Notice how the sign for drachm is made. If you saw it anywhere else but on a prescription you would say it was the figure 3. Also notice that there is no dot above the Roman numerals, but they are plainly made and there is no doubt as to the quantity desired by the prescriber.

SOME INTERESTING PRESCRIPTIONS.

At the November meeting of the Liverpool Chemists' Association Harold Wyatt presented some interesting prescriptions followed by comments on methods of dispensing them:

I.

℞ Cocainæ puræ..........................gr. i.
Paraffin. liquid..........................f. ʒij.

The cocaine is soluble at the temperature of a water bath, but comes out on cooling. Most authorities state that cocaine is soluble in liquid paraffin to the extent of "about 1 in 100." This depends upon the sample of liquid paraffin, for there are plenty falling within the B. P. description which will not dissolve and keep in solution the cocaine in greater proportion than 1 in 150. To overcome this separation on cooling a little olive oil, in which cocaine is ten times more soluble than in liquid paraffin, is recommended.

II.

℞ Acid. sulph. dil....................min. xxx.
Quin. sulph..............................gr. x.
Pot. chloratis............................ʒij.
Liq. ammon. acet. fort. (1-7)..............ʒiv.
Sp. ætheris nit...........................ʒvi.
Tinct. hyoscyami.........................ʒiv.
Aqua....................................ad ℥vi.

M. ft. Mist.

The solution of ammonium acetate must be distinctly acid or there will be a precipitate of quinine hydrate and acetate formed. The relatively low solubility of the potassium chlorate hastens the separation of quinine acetate. If sodium chlorate be used this removes another disturbing influence.

III.

℞ Quin. sulph.............................gr. i.
Butyl chloral hydrat.....................gr. i.
Ext. nucis vom...........................gr. ½.
Ext. gelsemii............................gr. ¼.
Pil. rhei comp...........................gr. ½.

M. ft. pil. Mitte xxiv.

Not having any extract of gelsemium, the author had evaporated ʒij of a good fluid extract to the consistence of a soft extract by means of a water bath, and took enough of this to make the quantity of mass desired, using as excipient enough alcohol with 20 grains of licorice powder to give firmness and toughness.

IV.

℞ Bismuth subnitrat.........................ʒij.
Acid. hydrocyan. dil...................min. xxx.
Sp. chloroformi...........................ʒiij.
Mucilaginis tragacanthæ...................ʒi.
Aquæ anethi.............................ad ℥vi.

M. ft. Mist.

It was found necessary to use ʒvi. mucilage of acacia to suspend the bismuth, owing to the tragacanth producing a gelatinous precipitate with the bismuth subnitrate. In dispensing such a prescription one should use mucilage of acacia freshly made from the powdered gum; take care to always dilute the mucilage with half the menstruum, and pour into the bottle first; and, thirdly, add the bismuth subnitrate, well elutriated with the menstruum, in successive and small portions to the mucilage in the bottle. The bismuth remains suspended, and when it settles a slight shake will diffuse it again. As Mr. Cowley pointed out, the trouble with bismuth subnitrate and oxychloride is invariably caused by hydrolysis, and if this be got over as soon as possible by well rubbing the salt with the water, the mixture will not change after it has left the dispenser's hands.

V.

℞ Sodii salicylatis.........................ʒij.
Sp. etheris nitrosi.......................ʒiv.
Sp. chloroform............................ʒiij.
Aquæ destill............................ad ℥vi.

M. ft. Mist.

A dark orange-red color was caused in this by the action of the nitrous acid on the sodium salicylate, an unavoidable change, and one the prescriber might have rendered unnoticeable by prescribing compound infusion of gentia or other infusion to mask the color.

THE ANALYSIS OF POWDERED EXTRACT OF NUX VOMICA.

For the analysis of both solid and liquid extracts of nux vomica, Bird's[1] method of extraction has answered admirably in the hands of Walter H. Lenton, who described his experiments at a meeting of the Liverpool Chemists' Association on December 14, 1905, reported in the *Pharmaceutical Journal* for December 23, as follows:

With the powdered extract I have not been so successful, and have generally found that a more or less persistent emulsion or jelly is formed. The following method has been worked out on somewhat similar lines to the process referred to above, using a hydro-alcoholic solvent for the powder, and shaking out with a mixture of ether and chloroform:

Powdered extract of nux vomica	Gm.	2
Ether, 0.720	Cc.	10
Chloroform	Cc.	10
Alcohol, 90 per cent	Cc.	5
Strong solution of ammonia	Cc.	3
Distilled water	Cc.	5

Place the ether and chloroform in a dry separator and add the powder. Next add the alcohol and solution of ammonia and shake well. Finally add the water and shake vigorously for about a minute; allow to separate, and draw off the ether-chloroform layer into another separator and agitate well with 5 Ml. of solution of ammonium carbonate (1 in 10), as recommended in Bird's process. Separate and repeat the agitation with another 5 Ml. of solution of ammonium carbonate and draw off the washed ether-chloroform layer into a clean separator, preserving the two wash liquors separately for subsequent washings.

To the alkaline mother-liquor add ether and chloroform (10 Ml. of each), agitating and separating as before, and washing the ether-chloroform solution with the reserved wash-liquors.

Repeat the extraction and washings a third time.

Extract the mixed ether-chloroform solutions and proceed as usual for strychnine determinations.

Personally, I prefer Bird's method of precipitation as being very convenient and reliable. At all events, whatever the details of manipulation, the process of separation should be carried out by precipitation by potassium ferrocyanide, as not only has this method official sanction, but has been shown by Farr and Wright[2] and Bird to give concordant results, when carried out under well-defined conditions of temperature, etc. My own experience is in entire accordance with this.

The new U. S. P. uses the nitric acid separation, which is practically Gordin's[3] modification of Keller's process. As far as my experience goes, the results obtained by the nitric acid separation are somewhat erratic, and are certainly not comparable with the figures yielded by the ferrocyanide method.

At a meeting of the Society of Public Analysts on June 7, Mr. Howard showed that, by conducting the separation with a

[1] Analysis of Nux Vomica, P. J., XI (4), 574, and "Year Book, 1901."
[2] "Year-Book, 1900," p. 440.
[3] Compare abstract, "Year-Book of Pharmacy, 1903."

small amount of nitric acid, and at 0 degree C., exact results could be obtained; but above this temperature errors occurred. I mention this point because I know several pharmacists use this method because it is simpler of execution than the official one, and I think it would be well to have a general expression of opinion on the matter, as it is of considerable importance to the working pharmacist and public analyst alike.

METHOD FOR THE ANALYSIS OF EMULSIONS.[1]

By L. F. Kebler and Geo. W. Hoover,

of the Drug Laboratory, Bureau of Chemistry, U. S. Department of Agriculture,

Washington, D. C.

An examination of the literature shows that little has been done on the analysis of emulsions, and such results as are recorded are restricted almost exclusively to the determination of the fatty portion. While codliver oil and other fatty bodies are considered the essential constituents of emulsions, there is no gainsaying the fact that there are numerous other important medicinal agents which exert a beneficial effect, and harmful agents may at times be present. In arriving at the value of an emulsion these agents must be taken into consideration and the emulsifying agent may or may not serve the function of a nutritive.

That this portion of analytical chemistry has been so much neglected is surprising in view of the fact that emulsions are so extensively used, not only by physicians, but also by the laity, in many forms of diseases.

The first available results were recorded by H. Leffman and W. Beam,[2] who reported the per cent. of fat found by them in ten American emulsions. The authors stated that the most approved methods in use for fat extraction in milk analysis were employed by them. H. W. Schimpf[3] estimates the oil by a modification of the well-known Adams' method, extracting by means of ether or benzin with a Soxhlet apparatus. Schimpf also used a specially devised apparatus, whereby the fatty portion is extracted directly from the emulsion by means of the above-named solvents. In our experience these solvents with some emulsions fail to remove all of the fat by this method. In 1899 A. Schneegans[4] communicated the following method for determining the amount of fats in emulsion: Mix 300 parts of the emulsion with 50 parts each of coarse *sand* and *kaolin*, evaporate to dryness, with occasional stirring, and toward the end of the operation add 50 parts of dry sodium sulphate. The residue thus obtained is powdered, transferred to an extraction apparatus, extracted with ether, the ether evaporated and the residual oil weighed. In the case of emulsions prepared with egg-yolk, simple shaking out with ether may be resorted to after heating the emulsion for a short time at 100 degrees C. to coagulate the albumin. It must be remembered, however, that egg-yolk contains fat and lecithin, both of which are removed by the above solvent, and will be weighed as fat unless proper provisions are made. Mr. Schneegans places the average amount of these two products in the yolk of the average egg at about 6 Gm. The fat alone of egg-yolk approximates 20 per cent.

This paper deals only with the analytical side, and includes more or less complete identification and determination of inorganic substances, volatile matter, fatty bodies, alcohol, benzoates, salicylates, saccharin, sugar, enzymes and emulsifying agents.

This method employed by us is as follows:

DETERMINATION OF ASH.

This is accomplished by weighing out from 5 to 6 Gm. of emulsion, previously well agitated, in a platinum dish and incinerating in a muffle furnace. The resulting ash, if sufficient in amount, is then examined for the presence of inorganic bodies by the conventional methods. Those most likely to be present in emulsions are compounds of sodium, potassium, iron, calcium, manganese and phosphatic material. The presence of a phosphate might indicate any of the following phosphorus-bearing organic compounds, such as lecithin, phosphates, hypophosphites or glycerophosphates. Whichever may be present in the original compound must be determined by examination of the aqueous portion of the emulsion. The method for separating the same will be detailed later. The amount and kind of ash may give some indication as to the presence or absence of gum acacia.

ESTIMATION OF TOTAL VOLATILE MATTER.

Into the bottom of an ordinary leaden bottle-cap place a layer of purified and ignited asbestos and dry to constant weight at 110 degrees C. On to the layer of asbestos place from 5 to 6 Gm. (accurately weighed) of the emulsion, previously well agitated. Transfer the leaden cap and contents to a vacuum apparatus which carries a vacuum of about 550 mm. (22 inches) at a temperature of approximately 70 degrees C. The drying is continued for eight to ten hours, or until constant weight is maintained. This not only gives the amount of moisture, but also includes bodies volatile under the above conditions, including alcohol and certain flavoring agents. The above procedure prevents any material oxidation of the component constituents of the emulsion, which is an important desideratum.

ESTIMATION OF FAT.

After determining the volatile matter as outlined above the leaden caps and asbestos are cut into pieces of suitable size and transferred to a Knorr extraction apparatus, which consists of a condenser, extraction tube and flask. In this apparatus the use of stopples and ground-glass joints is entirely dispensed with. There is only one connection and that is between the condenser and flask, which is sealed by a layer of mercury. The condenser does not need to be described in detail. The extraction tube rests on the neck of the extraction flask, being supported by three projecting glass nipples. Near the bottom it is provided with a perforated platinum disk, which serves the purpose of holding a layer of prepared asbestos. The layer of asbestos is placed into the extraction tube, on top of the perforated platinum disk, in a pulpy, moist condition to the depth of about ¼ inch, by means of a vacuum. The extraction tube and contents are then dried at about 110 degrees C. The material in the extraction tube is then treated with ether of U. S. P. quality from 10 to 14 hours, or until complete extraction is insured. The ether is then completely evaporated at water-bath temperature and the amount of ether extractive calculated from data in hand. The residue left in the above tubes, after treating with ether, can now be examined to advantage by means of the microscope.

DETECTION OF CERTAIN EMULSIFYING AGENTS.

It is quite possible that the mucilages have been so prepared as to destroy all possible clues to their origin, but in many cases there are frequently left some particles which will indicate their nature. A few starch grains are sufficient to identify gum tragacanth. A few fragments of plant tissue may be sufficient to establish the source from which the emulsifying agent has been obtained. Microchemical tests may also indicate the presence of dextrine and certain mucilaginous bodies. The amount and kind of ash left on incineration also gives evidence as to the presence or absence of acacia.

DETECTION OF ALL BODIES SOLUBLE IN THE AQUEOUS MENSTRUUM EMPLOYED.

It was found by experiment that when emulsions in general are submitted to the process commonly known as "centrifuging" they are separated into two distinct layers, the upper consisting of the fatty and the lower of the aqueous portion. From this the suggestion presented itself that if we could construct an apparatus which would permit the use of a separatory funnel in place of the ordinary test-tube it would render the separation of the two layers into which emulsions are converted by centrifuging a very easy matter, and would simplify future

[1] Presented at the Atlantic City meeting of the American Pharmaceutical Association, 1905.

[2] Med. News, 1892, 60, 577.

[3] Am. Drug., 1894, 25, 425.

[4] J. Pharm. Elsass-Loth., 1897, 24, 321.

analytical operations very materially. An apparatus was accordingly brought into play which exactly fitted the conditions. It consists of an electrical centrifugal, carrying a frame of suitable size, which will hold an ordinary 75 Cc. conical separatory funnel. We have met with only one emulsion, which will be described later, that could not be separated by this means. The process in general from this point is as follows:

Into two separatory funnels of suitable size place about equal amounts of the emulsion. Place both into the centrifuge and whirl a sufficient time to bring about the desired separation, which usually requires from 15 minutes to 1 hour. The aqueous menstruum is then withdrawn and submitted to such testing as may be necessary. In this manner we are able not only to separate emulsions thoroughly so as to simplify analysis, but the fatty portion is left in its original condition, so that it can be extracted by means of the immiscible solvents and identified.

REACTION OF EMULSION.

This can be determined by testing the aqueous layer obtained in the above operation by immersing strips of red and blue litmus paper.

DETERMINATION OF ALCOHOL.

Separate a given volume or weight of the emulsion by centrifuging as indicated above, withdraw the aqueous portion and place same in distilling flask. To the fatty residue in the funnel add another portion of water, approximately equal to the amount of material withdrawn, agitate thoroughly, centrifuge, withdraw the clear layer and place it into the distilling flask used above. The latter operation can be repeated a second and a third time, but in practice it has been found that one extraction in addition to the first separation is sufficient to obtain all the alcohol in the emulsion. The aqueous portions contained in the distilling flask are now treated in the usual manner for determining alcohol—namely, render alkaline with sodium carbonate and add a small amount of tannin to prevent frothing. The mixture is then submitted to distillation, and the amount distilled should be exactly equal to the amount of original emulsion employed. By determining the specific gravity of the distillate at the recognized temperature and referring to an alcohol table the per cent. of alcohol can readily be deduced.

DETECTION OF ENZYMES.

Centrifuge any suitable quantity of the emulsion, withdraw the lower aqueous portion and test for the presence of pancreatin and pepsin by the official method of the eighth revision of the Pharmacopœia. It is also advisable to test for the presence of pancreatin by the method of 1890 Pharmacopœia. The methods at present available for detecting and identifying enzymes are far from satisfactory. Many disturbing factors present themselves, but with the scheme in hand the difficulties are no greater than they are in this field exclusive of emulsions. There may be other enzymes added that have the power of converting starch, and thus make it difficult for the analyst to decide whether or not pancreatin is present. It also frequently happens that the aqueous portion of the emulsion as withdrawn above contains products which will prevent the usual starch-iodine reaction used in determining whether or not the starch has been converted into sugars. The chemicals especially conspicuous are the hypophosphites. It will be necessary for us to extend this line of research, but for the present time it is proper to say that when these disturbing factors are absent and a starch-converting enzyme is present there is little difficulty in ascertaining this fact, and if some of these disturbing elements are present and the starch-iodine reaction is obtained under proper testing, it is evidence that no starch-converting enzyme is present.

DETERMINATION OF SUGARS.

The sugars present may be sucrose, glucose, maltose and lactose. Separate the emulsion as outlined above and determine the sugars in the separated aqueous portion by the methods usually employed for determining sugars. Methods for determining sucrose and glucose will be found in "Bul. Bur. Chem.," 65, pp. 84 and 85, respectively. The most suitable methods available for determining lactose will be found in "Bul. Bur. Chem.," 46, p. 40, and maltose is best determined by method given in Wiley's Principles and Practice of Agricultural Analysis, III., 265.

DETECTION OF SALICYLIC ACID AND SALICYLATES.

Determine the reaction of the aqueous solution prepared by the above centrifugal method from about 50 Cc. of the emulsion. If acid, render slightly alkaline with sodium carbonate, shake out with ether and discard the ethereal solution. This removes any disturbing oily matter that may be present in the aqueous solution left from the emulsion. Now render this aqueous solution distinctly acid with sulphuric acid and again shake out with ether. The ethereal solution is now evaporated in a porcelain dish, the residue taken up with a small amount of water, and two or three drops of a 0.5 per cent. solution of ferric alum added in such a way that the two solutions come together slowly. If salicylic acid or a salicylate is present there will be developed a purple or violet color, depending on the amount present.

DETECTION OF BENZOIC ACID AND BENZOATES.

Separate emulsion by centrifugal. Extract aqueous portions as directed under salicylic acid. Confirm the presence of benzoic acid by method outlined in "Bul. Bur. Chem.," 65, 89.

DETECTION OF SACCHARIN.

If, after evaporating the ethereal solution obtained as directed above for detecting salicylic acid and taking up the residue in water, the latter possesses a distinctly sweet taste, the indication is that saccharin is present. This chemical in the absence of salicylic acid is tested for in the following manner: Separate the aqueous portion of the emulsion by means of the centrifuge, proceed as directed under salicylic acid, evaporate the ethereal solution in a silver dish, take up the residue with 5 Cc. of water, add 1 Gm. sodium hydroxide, evaporate to dryness and finally heat for 20 minutes at 210 to 215 degrees C. This procedure will convert the saccharin into a salicylate. The fused mass is taken up with water, acidulated with sulphuric acid, and the presence of salicylic acid determined as directed above for detecting this chemical.

In case salicylic acid is present proceed as directed under salicylic acid until the residue is obtained in the porcelain dish. Dissolve this residue in 10 Cc. of water, add 2 Cc. of 35 per cent. sulphuric acid, bring the mixture to boiling, add drop by drop a 5 per cent. solution of potassium permanganate to slight excess, cool the solution, add about 1 Gm. of sodium hydroxide, and proceed from this point as directed under saccharin in the absence of salicylic acid.

VOLATILE MATTER EXCLUSIVE OF WATER AND ALCOHOL.

The volatile bodies liable to be present are the essential oils and petroleum. The former can usually be identified either by the odor of the emulsion itself or after distillation in connection with the estimation of alcohol.

INORGANIC BODIES.

These can readily be tested for by the conventional methods in the aqueous portion separated by the centrifugal, and details for this purpose are not necessary.

NITROGEN.

Nitrogenous bodies are frequently employed in the preparation of emulsions, and the determination of nitrogen may serve a useful purpose. A considerable percentage of nitrogen will undoubtedly point to the presence of such compounds as casein and egg albumin. The Kjeldahl-Gunning method is best suited for this purpose.

LECITHIN.

This compound is present in emulsions made with egg-yolk, and the best way of determining whether it is present or not is to ash the ether extractive obtained by the method outlined above and test for the presence of phosphates. Under these conditions if a phosphate is present the indications are that lecithin is present.

ANALYTICAL RESULTS.

In order to definitely ascertain whether the scheme originally outlined would give satisfactory results a number of emulsions of known composition were prepared according to the directions of the U. S. Pharmacopœia and the National Formulary. The percentage composition of these emulsions was based on weight.

Actual composition of codliver oil emulsions prepared according to the eighth revision of the U. S. Pharmacopœia and the National Formulary, with modifications:

Serial number.	Emulsifying agent.	Per cent. moisture.	Per cent. oil.	Per cent. solids.
1,010	Acacia	37.75	43.71	18.54
1,011	Irish moss	45.47	46.07	8.46
1,012	Yolk of egg	34.38	44.52	21.10
1,013	Dextrin	38.49	43.75	17.76
1,014	Tinct. quillaja	47.18	44.69	8.13
1,015	Acacia	49.77	32.63	17.60
1,016	Irish moss	56.16	35.65	8.19
1,017	Yolk of egg	42.17	35.70	22.13
1,018	Dextrin	44.53	35.93	19.55
1,019	Tinct. quillaja	56.03	35.84	8.13
1,020	Acacia	48.22	36.22	15.56
1,021	Acacia	48.22	36.22	15.56
1,022	Acacia	48.60	36.50	14.90
1,023	Acacia	36.70	45.04	18.26

The above emulsions vary from the authority cited in the following points:

No. 1,018 contains 100 Cc. of simple syrup in place of 125 Cc.

Nos. 1,015 to 1,019 contain 100 Cc. less per liter of oil than No. 1,010.

No. 1,023 was prepared according to the directions of the eighth revision of the U. S. Pharmacopœia, and Nos. 1,020, 1,021 and 1,022 were this same emulsion reduced by the addition of definite quantities of water and whisky so as to lower the percentage content of the other constituents.

The above emulsions are representative of those commonly met with in practice. In addition to these a number of the well known emulsions on the market were purchased and submitted to examination, with the following results:

ent. There are a number of cases where the differences amount to 2 per cent., but this we believe is largely due to errors of manipulation, because we find that it is very important to exercise care in securing an average sample by thorough agitation previous to weighing off, and it was found by practice to be best to place approximately the desired quantity in a weighing flask and agitate same thoroughly before a sample is taken, and this precaution is to be again observed when a duplicate is taken from the same bottle.

With a single exception all of the emulsions examined were either acid or neutral. One was distinctly alkaline, requiring 0.9 Gm. of pure sulphuric acid to neutralize the alkalinity of 100 Cc. This is a very unusual emulsion, as will be seen later on.

The amount, physical appearance and composition of the ash are all useful aids in arriving at the probable nature of the medicinal chemicals employed, and in the absence of these the nature of the emulsifying agent may be indicated. As will be seen, the per cent. of ash in the emulsions prepared with Irish moss, dextrin and quillaja is very low. Acacia emulsions run a little higher in ash. Very little weight can be attached to these ash determinations when inorganic chemicals are present in the emulsions.

The amount of volatile matter obtained is closely in accord with the amount that is known to be present. In the case of a petroleum emulsion purchased on the market the figures show that the usual method employed for determining moisture will not apply. This can be readily seen at a glance at the table.

Table Embodying Analytical Results of Emulsions.

Serial number.	Reaction to litmus.	Per cent. of ash.	Per cent. volatile matter in 550 Mm. vacuum at 68-70 degrees C.	Per cent. ether extract, chiefly fat.	Fat by saponification method.	Emulsifying agent.	Solids. (By difference.)	Remarks.
1,010	Acid.	0.356	37.18	42.27	42.5	Acacia.	20.55	
1,011	Acid.	0.023	43.24	47.89	45.0	Irish moss.	8.87	
1,012	Acid.	....	31.52	54.87	....	Yolk of egg.	13.61	
1,013	Acid.	0.027	37.88	44.79	....	Dextrin.	17.33	
1,014	Acid.	0.020	45.13	45.47	44.0	Tinct. quillaja.	9.40	Alcohol present.
1,015	Acid.	0.333	47.11	33.18	32.5	Acacia.	19.71	
1,016	Acid.	....	54.08	39.06	....	Irish moss.	6.86	
1,017	Acid.	....	39.37	41.94	....	Yolk of egg.	18.69	
1,018	Acid.	....	44.66	36.04	33.5	Dextrin.	19.30	
1,019	Acid.	....	55.59	36.60	....	Tinct. quillaja.	7.81	Alcohol present.
1,020	Acid.	0.310	44.99	34.99	34.0	Acacia.	20.02	Alcohol 5.68 per cent.
1,021	Acid.	....	46.89	36.38	....	Acacia.	16.73	
1,022	Acid.	....	44.55	35.63	....	Acacia.	19.82	Alcohol 6.71 per cent.
1,023	Acid.	0.337	37.21	45.19	42.5	Acacia.	17.60	
1,024	Acid.	0.038	45.03	39.22	39.0	Egg.	15.75	Alcohol 8.02 per cent.
1,025	Acid.	1.750	42.33	43.14	33.0	Not known.	14.53	Phosphatic emulsion.
1,026	Acid.	2.033	56.07	30.71	32.0	Not known.	13.22	Claims presence of vegetable oils and hypophosphites.
1,027	Acid.	0.180	45.04	39.30	38.0	Egg.	15.66	
1,028	Alkaline.	2.240	50.18	38.51	38.0	Not known.	11.31	
1,029	Acid.	2.660	42.94	24.50	30.0	Not known.	32.56	Petroleum compounds present.
1,030	Acid.	0.620	30.52	44.41	46.0	Not known.	25.07	
1,031	Acid.	0.262	23.65	51.81	40.0	Not known.	24.54	Claims to contain salts of calcium and manganese.
1,032	Neutral.	0.068	53.26	39.12	38.0	Not known.	7.62	
950	Acid.	0.325	55.33	30.00	....	Not known.	14.67	No saponifying enzyme present.
952	Acid.	0.210	58.03	38.67	38.5	Not known.	3.30	Salicylic acid present, but no pancreatin.

An examination of the above tables shows that the method outlined above for extracting the fatty portion with ether is satisfactory, excepting in the case of the egg emulsions. There seems to be a disturbing factor somewhere which has not been located at present. It was at first thought that the discrepancy was traceable to the presence of glycerin in the glyconin, but an examination along this line indicates that this is correct only to a small degree. A sample of glyconin was treated as directed for the estimation of fats in the method described above, and the ether removed only 14.54 per cent. While this indicates that something has been removed from the glyconin aside from fat, the total percentage is not sufficient to account for the discrepancies present in several of the egg emulsions.

The method employed for the determination of volatile matter is not applicable to emulsion 1,029, which is a petroleum product. The high percentage of volatile matter is undoubtedly due to the volatilization of the petroleum products of the emulsion. This is emphasized by the fact that when the amount of fat is determined by the saponification method the percentage of fat indicated to be present is materially in excess of that removed by the ether.

Aside from the egg emulsion and the petroleum emulsion the various figures obtained on analysis correspond closely with those which represent the amount of material known to be present. The ether extracted was 24.5 per cent., whereas the amount of fat found to be present by the saponification method amounted to 30 per cent. The difference between these two figures may undoubtedly be attributed to the loss of certain volatile petroleum products during the process of drying.

When it was observed that the ether extracted a larger amount of material than was known to be present in the emulsion that could be extracted with ether it was deemed desirable to determine the actual amount of fat by other methods. The method at present largely used for the determination of fatty products is the well known Babcock test. It was found, however, that this method could only be utilized after some experimentation with the emulsions in hand—that is, no set procedure could be outlined by means of which the Babcock method could be applied to all emulsions. If the details were worked out for an acacia emulsion, the same amounts of the various reagents could not be used for an egg or a dextrin emulsion. It was readily seen from this that the Babcock method would not be applicable in practice, because the nature of the emulsifying agents and other ingredients is generally not known. After some experimentation it was found that the fat in all emulsions could readily be determined by the saponification method and the use of the centrifuge. The process as used for obtaining the results recorded in the paper is as follows:

Into a Babcock cream-test bottle place 9 Gm. of the emulsion to be examined. Add 10 Cc. of a saturated aqueous solution of potassium hydroxide. Heat on the steam bath for about 15 minutes and add cautiously, drop by drop, 15 Cc. of 75 per cent. sulphuric acid. This will neutralize the excess of alkali and liberate the fat which is now to be brought to the surface by centrifuging for five minutes. Then add enough hot water to bring the top of the contents of the bottle up to the neck, and centrifuge again for two minutes. After the second centrifuging add sufficient hot water to raise the fat to within about ½ inch of the top of the flask, centrifuge again for one minute, remove the bottle and read off the per cent. of fat as indicated by the scale on the neck of the bottle. The readings were made at about 75 degrees C. This scale is made for use with 18 Gm. of material, and inasmuch as only 9 Gm. were used in the above operation it will be necessary to multiply the percentage indicated by the scale by two.

On comparing the results obtained by the ether-extraction method and the saponification method, it will be found that they run closely parallel, excepting in those cases where it has been found that a disturbing factor exists. This is particularly shown in the case of emulsion No. 1,029, and was known to exist in the case of egg emulsions, but this fact we were not able to show because of the loss of the egg emulsions before this method could be applied. The saponification method also reveals the fact that there is something present in emusions Nos. 1,025, 1,031 and 1,032 which vitiates the ether extractive. Exactly what the difficulty is has not been made out.

The solids being taken by difference, naturally show any inequality that might be present in any part of the analytical work. In those emulsions, however, where the exact amount of solid material present was known, the amount obtained by difference is very well in accord with that actually present.

Before concluding it is necessary to say that in the case of only one emulsion was the method as outlined above impracticable, and that was No. 1,028. After working with it unsuccessfully for a considerable length of time, Mr. Schulz, of this laboratory, noticed that the label on the bottle containing this emulsion directed an unusual amount of caution to prevent the emulsion from freezing, which would destroy it, and from this observation he hit upon the idea that by freezing the emulsion it might be possible to separate it into two layers, as had been the case with other emulsions. After a trial experiment he found that such a procedure would bring about the desired results. In order to separate this emulsion it is therefore necessary to first freeze it, then warm to about 60 degrees C., and centrifuge as directed with the other emulsions.

Mr. Schulz did all of the work connected with the Babcock method, and made all of the fat determinations by the saponification method recorded in this paper.

Anaesthesin.—Further work has been done with anæsthesin since the publication of a note on this new drug in this column in a recent issue. According to von Noorden, anæsthesin is the para-amidobenzoic ether, or the ethylic ether of para-amidobenzoic acid (*Berliner klinische Wochenschrift*, Nov. 17, 1902). It is manufactured by the Hoechst Farbenfabriken under the name of Ritsert Anæsthesin. Ritsert prepared it in 1890 and recognized its value as a local anæsthetic, but the product attracted little attention, as at that time every one was looking for substitutes for cocaine soluble in water. Anæsthesin was again brought into prominence when the advantages of a dry anæsthetic like orthoform were recognized. Anæsthesin is a white, odorless powder, tasteless, but producing a numbness on being applied to the tongue, almost insoluble in cold water, but soluble to some extent in hot water. It is easily soluble in alcohol, ether, chloroform, acetone, fats and oils and miscible without decomposition with fatty substances. The symptoms evoked by too large doses resemble those of excessive doses of phenacetin and are more pronounced when the drug is administered dissolved in oil.

The New Remedies Compendium and Prices Current is printed in this number. See last advertising pages.

HOW TO BECOME A BETTER QUALIFIED PHARMACIST.

By F. J. Butler, Ph.G.

Pontiac. Ill.

Many pharmacists depend too much upon the manufacturing chemists, and when an emergency presents itself and they are called upon to prepare a prescription containing some solid extract, chemical or drug seldom used or carried by the ordinary druggist they are at a loss to know what to do. A druggist should be well qualified in this line and be able to come to his own relief by meeting the emergency and manufacturing the drug in his own laboratory.

HOW TRADE IS LOST.

They not only lose custom but also the confidence of their customers by saying: "We do not have one of the ingredients, therefore we cannot fill this prescription." The customer leaves with the impression that the druggist is incompetent, or he will say: "Mr. —— is certainly not an up-to-date pharmacist, for he could not fill my prescription."

WHAT TO DO.

These unqualified druggists should lose no time in preparing themselves by a few moments' diligent study every day. They should secure some of the books used in the chemical and pharmaceutical laboratories of the colleges of pharmacy and learn to make many chemicals and preparations.

HOW I DO IT.

I have had many prescriptions handed me by customers who had tried the nearest drug stores and had been told that they were unable to fill the prescription because they did not have some of the ingredients or "were just out of the same."

One case that I will mention was a prescription calling for ointment of lead iodide, handed to me by a physician. He was unable to obtain it in the city, but I told him to wait a few minutes and I would make it. As we had no lead iodide in stock I had to make it. I prepared two solutions, one of potassium iodide and another of lead acetate, and poured the last named solution into the first. In this way a copious yellow precipitate of lead iodide was obtained. This I collected on a paper filter, washed it with water and weighed a sufficient amount of it to make the ointment.

Another case was of a prescription calling for six or seven solid extracts. The customer asked me if I could fill it, and I told him that I didn't have three of the extracts, but had the fluid extracts and would make them in a few minutes if he could wait. He looked at me in a rather surprised way and said that he had called at three or four other pharmacies without getting what he wanted.

Taking three evaporating dishes, I poured a quantity of the fluid extracts in each and applied a gentle heat, which soon drove off the menstruum, leaving the desired solid extracts, which enabled me to fill the prescription.

In these and in many other instances I have gained the confidence of many new customers who otherwise would still be patronizing "the nearest drug store."

Malayan Citronella Oil.

In the Chemist and Druggist for October 4, p. 608, reference was made to the manufacture of citronella oil on the Kellas Estate, Perak. This oil has been examined at the Imperial Institute, and Professor Dunstan gives the following figures for it, compared with Java and Ceylon oils:

	Kellas	Java.	Ceylon.
Sp. gr.	0.8948 at 15° C.	0.892	0.908
Refractive index.	1.4858 at 24° C.	....	....
Optical rotation (100 mm.) tube	1.34′ at 24° C.	0° 50′ to 2° 26′	9° 36′
Solubility in 80 p. c. alcohol. .	1 in 1 or more vols.	1 in 1 or more vols.	1 in 1 vol. becoming cloudy on further addition.
Geraniol	32.7 per cent.	31.9 to 38.1 p. c.	32.9 per cent.
Citronella (by difference)	55.3 per cent.	50.4 to 55.3 p. c.	28.2 per cent.

These results show that the Kellas oil more nearly, in composition, approximates to Java oil than to that produced in Ceylon.

OXYMEL SCILLAE.[1]

By A. C. Abraham, F.C.S., F.I.C.

Many chemists have examined squill, but their results do not appear to agree to such an extent as to justify one in speaking with any confidence about them. One thing, however, seems clear, and that is that the active principles are glucosides and one at least of them is a bitter principle easily decomposed by heat. This latter point should be specially borne in mind. Perhaps few preparations in the present British Pharmacopœia show a greater lack of the practical pharmacist in the composition of their formulæ than does oxymel of squill. In the old London Pharmacopœia of 1763 it was ordered to be made by boiling 3 pounds of honey with 2 pounds of vinegar of squill until reduced to a syrupy consistence; in the P. L. 1851 by boiling 50 fluid ounces of vinegar of squill to 12 fluid ounces and adding to 60 ounces of melted honey. In the British Pharmacopœia, 1867, the older process was employed, but the quantities were varied; a pint of vinegar of squill being employed and 2 pounds of honey, and to ensure uniformity the evaporation was to be carried on until the specific gravity was 1.32. The evaporation was also to be conducted on a water bath instead of by boiling. This process remained unaltered in the Pharmacopœia of 1885. In 1898, however, the process was altered. To avoid the evaporation the squill, which is ordered simply to be bruised, is macerated with a quantity of acetic acid and water, from which is produced a much more concentrated vinegar of squill than the article previously employed. It is as a matter of fact practically twice the strength of ordinary acetum scillæ. The object of this variation is entirely to avoid evaporation.

The old process of boiling together honey and vinegar of squill would probably, if not certainly, result in a considerable alteration of the active principles, and the modified process of the 1867 and 1885 Pharmacopœias would perhaps produce the same result. According to the 1898 process, however, as no heating is employed, the final product will contain, even after it has been kept for a considerable period, the unaltered constitutents. It is therefore quite a different medicine from that made under the 1885 process, although, curiously enough, the name and the dose remain exactly the same. What should we think of a dispenser who substituted in a prescription, say, sodium acetate for bicarbonate without consulting the writer of the prescription or even taking the trouble to tell the prescriber that he had altered it? That is what the Pharmacopœia has in effect done, without even, so far as I can find, any evidence that the unaltered principles are better for the purposes for which oxymel of squill is employed than the products of its decomposition which hitherto had been used. Moreover, the Pharmacopœia does not even state in a footnote that, owing to the process of manufacture having been altered, the preparation is different from what it was in previous Pharmacopœias. Yet it undoubtedly is different, and very different; and some who have been in the habit of using the older kind notice the difference and will not have it. It may be thought that my objection to a change of this kind being made in such a way as not to call the attention of prescribers to the fact that they had a new article to deal with is somewhat fanciful, but I think a careful consideration of the facts will convince any one that this is not the case. Squill is, especially at times, a powerful and dangerous poison, probably due to the bitter principle, and it therefore behoves us to be very careful how we vary from official directions as to the manufacture of its preparations. An inquest was held in, I think, Leeds, some years since which to my mind strongly emphasizes this, and I may say that although up to that time I had always been in the habit of making syrup of squill with as little heat as possible, or practically none, I have been very careful since to give it the gentle heat that the Pharmacopœia mentions, as even this difference in treatment makes a distinct difference in the product. From a strictly pharmaceutical point of view, however, a much more serious objection can be taken to the present process than the one which I have mentioned. It is the great variation in strength, which is not only possible, but which undoubtedly exists. The directions of the Pharmacopœia are as follows:

Digest the squill for seven days in a mixture of the acetic acid and distilled water, press strongly, filter, mix the product, which should measure approximately 10 fluid ounces, with about 27 fluid ounces of the clarified honey, or sufficient to produce oxymel of squills having the s. g. 1.320.

These directions are palpably bad, because it is clear that the weaker and lower the specific gravity of the vinegar of squill which is prepared by the process given the greater will be the quantity of honey required to raise the specific gravity to the required figure. No doubt the author of this process was quite unaware how great the variation might be, and it is difficult to see how the variation which exists actually occurs. To show how it works out in practice we will suppose that we are working on eight times the quantities mentioned in the Pharmacopœia, and assuming that the honey is specific gravity 1.450, and that we obtain 80 fluid ounces of filtrate from the acetum scillæ (which is the Pharmacopœia assumption), I find it almost invariably necessary to use 14 pounds of honey, whereas the Pharmacopœia indicates that about 19 pounds 9½ ounces (equal to 216 fluid ounces) will be required, and Mr. Brown reckons that 20 pounds will be needed for this quantity.

The following experiments were made to test this point accurately:

Three different quantities of squill were taken. A was dried and passed through a 20 sieve; B was merely dried and bruised; while C was simply bruised without drying. The details of this experiment are shown in the following table:

		Sp. Gr. of liquid.	Liquid expressed.	Quantity used.	Honey theory.	Honey used.	Normal acid for 2 fl. dr.	Sp. Gr. of product.
A	Per 20 sieve......	1.080	20	18	48¾	50¾	2.6	1.320
B	Dried and bruised.	1.082	20¼	18	47¾	49¾	2.5	1.320
C	Undried bruised...	1.077	20¾	18	48¾	51	2.65	1.320

A sample from stock (specific gravity 1.320) (D) required 2.8 of normal acid, and four purchased samples required (E) 3.3, (F) 1.8, (G) 1.7 and (H) 1.6, the first two being specific gravity 1.325 and 1.32.

It will be seen that although the sample put through the 20 sieve has a higher specific gravity than that merely bruised, the sample which was dried and merely bruised has a still higher gravity, no doubt due to the fact that by avoiding the sifting it was less exposed to the air, and therefore absorbed less water. Upon the whole, however, it will be seen that these samples very closely agree in all respects. The amount of acid present in them is practically identical, and contrasts remarkably with the figures obtained from purchased samples, which, however, from their great variation can hardly be accepted as samples of the B. P. preparation, but had been made by the 1885 B. P. process. The conclusions to which I think we are entitled to come when we consider the facts are:

1. The Pharmacopœia is not justified in vitally altering the composition of a remedy which has for hundreds of years been of practically the same composition, without altering its name.

2. If the Pharmacopœia is right in altering the composition, the commercial article certainly to a large extent is not made in conformity with it.

3. The Pharmacopœia process requires radically altering in the following ways: The squill should be put through a No. 20 sieve, which will ensure its being practically dry. The honey should be of a fixed weight, and the vinegar of squill should be evaporated on a water bath, say, to half, before mixing with the honey.

Cresol Solution.—M. Paul Adam (*Journal de pharamcie et de chimie*) gives particulars of some experiments he has been making in devising a cresol disinfectant which shall be cheap, of small volume, and mix with cold water. Soap and alkali carbonates do not give good results in this experimenter's hands; it requires too much soap to make a solution that will mix with water without separation of flakes. Equal parts of cresol and 30 per cent. solution of caustic soda boiled together give a satisfactory result. One part of this solution is diluted with 100, 200 or 300 parts of water, according to requirements.

[1] Read before the Liverpool Chemists' Association.

INCOMPATIBLE QUININE MIXTURE.[1]

By Joseph Tait, Ph.C.

This communication gives the results of an inquiry regarding the following prescription:

℞ Quin. sulph....................gr. xviij.
Acd. sulph. dil.......................ʒiij.
Potass. iodid.........................ʒij.
Aquam ....ad ℥vi.

When dispensed with different commercial samples the mixture varies from pale straw to a yellowish color, but in a few hours throws down a reddish-brown precipitate, which gradually changes into a brownish-black. The inquiry was designed to account for the incompatibility and ascertain whether it could be avoided.

It is known that in mixtures like the foregoing there may be separation of reddish-brown quinine, iodo-hydriodide or brownish-black herapathite (quinine iodo-sulphate). It was suggested that the precipitation might be due to a minute trace of nitric acid in the sulphuric acid employed. Such a contamination does undoubtedly readily cause separation of free iodine and consequent precipitation.

To determine whether this was the cause of the trouble attention was directed to the sulphuric acid used in dispensing the prescription. On applying the usual ferrous sulphate test for nitric acid the result was negative. When tested, however, by Lunge's diphenylamine reaction very distinct evidence of a nitrogen acid was obtained. Lunge's reagent is prepared by dissolving 0.5 Gm. of diphenylamine in 100 Ml. of pure concentrated sulphuric acid and adding 20 Ml. of water. In applying the test about 1 Ml. of the sample is placed in a test tube and covered with an equal quantity of the diphenylamine solution. If a nitrogen acid is present there is formed at the junction of the liquids a bright blue-colored ring, and the reaction is exceedingly delicate. A dilute sulphuric acid made from this sample gave just perceptibly the characteristic blue reaction, showing that it was near the limit of delicacy of Lunge's test—namely, 1 part of nitric acid in 5,000,000.

Ferric and selenic salts, which are possible contaminations of sulphuric acid, also give the blue reaction with diphenylamine. The absence of the latter was proved by Dragendorff's codeine test, in which a few drops of the sample are added to a solution of codeine in sulphuric acid, when a green coloration is at once produced in the presence of a trace of selenium. Potassium ferrocyanide and potassium sulphocyanate indicated a trace of iron. Evidently, however, the reaction with ferric salts is not so delicate as with nitric acid, as it was found, by a blank experiment, that the trace of iron present in the acid was not sufficient to give the blue reaction. It is evident, therefore, that the indication of the test pointed to a trace of nitrogen acid, and consequently the sulphuric acid might be the source of the trouble.

It was found, however, that on using a specially redistilled sulphuric acid, proved to be free from nitrogen acids by Lunge's test, and the ordinary commercial pure potassium iodide, there was an immediate separation of free iodine, and in a few hours a brownish precipitate fell and after a time changed into the brownish-black precipitate which gave rise to the inquiry. The decomposition, therefore, does not appear to indicate necessarily any contamination of the sulphuric acid with nitrogen acids.

It was observed that the potassium iodide crystals were slightly moist, and on dissolving a little and testing for iodate with tartaric acid and starch, distinct evidence of slight contamination was obtained. On washing these crystals with water and dissolving, practically no evidence of iodate was obtained. This may indicate that in presence of moisture an originally iodate-free potassium iodide may become contaminated through slow oxidation of the exposed surface. This indicated that the potassium iodide might be the cause of the difficulty.

On using Merck's extra pure potassium iodide, giving no reaction with tartaric acid and starch, and nitrogen-free redistilled sulphuric acid, however, it was found that the mixture became very slightly yellow at once, and after standing some hours the reddish-brown precipitate had formed and gradually passed into the brownish-black herapathite as in the other cases. From this it is clear that the result is not necessarily due to contamination of either the sulphuric acid or the potassium iodide.

Experiment indicated that the quinine sulphate played no part in the reaction beyond supplying the material for the formation of herapathite with the liberated iodine. The sulphuric acid reacting with the potassium iodide liberates hydriodic acid, which speedily decomposes into water and free iodine. The latter reacts with the quinine sulphate to form ultimately herapathite, which is iodo-sulphate of quinine. The mixture must therefore be described as quite incompatible, as it stands, from a chemical point of view. The prescription may be dispensed with water from which dissolved oxygen has been expelled by boiling, and such a mixture, kept securely corked, has remained clear for a considerable time. On exposure to air, however, decomposition at once sets in, and therefore this remedy is impracticable.

Several experiments were made, such as adding citric acid and an alkaline citrate, but these were unavailing. On adding about 2 per cent. of hypophosphorous acid, sp. gr. 1.136, to the mixture, it was found that only a very faint yellow color was developed, and it has not increased, and the mixture remains perfectly clear after standing for several days. On substituting 0.7 per cent. of sodium hypophosphite for the hypophosphorous acid an equally satisfactory result was obtained, and this latter is suggested as a means of overcoming the incompatibility.

It may be mentioned that the method of mixing the ingredients had no influence on the final result. Of course, the sodium hypophosphite must be added to the potassium iodide solution before adding the acid solution of quinine sulphate.

During these experiments eight commercial samples of what was supplied as pure potassium iodide were examined and only two gave no coloration on the addition of starch and tartaric acid. One of the two, labeled "extra pure," was exposed to the air for two days. It was then deliquesced and its solution at once gave a distinct blue with starch and tartaric acid.

Seven samples supplied as pure sulphuric acid were examined, and all of them, except one, indicated traces of nitrogen acids with Lunge's test, some of them very distinctly. All the samples but one gave indication of a trace of iron with potassium ferrocyanide, but even this one gave a faint indication with potassium sulphocyanate. The latter, therefore, appears to be a more reliable and delicate test than the former. Only one sample of acid gave the nitrous reaction with ferrous sulphate. The absence of selenium was proved in every case, and in no case was the iron in sufficient proportion to react with Lunge's test.

[1] Communicated to the Pharmaceutical Society of Great Britain, at an evening meeting in Edinburgh, on Wednesday, December 20, 1905, and reprinted from the *Pharmaceutical Journal* for December 23, 1905.

Iron Tropon.—Brownish powder; albuminoid food preparation, composed of tropon (pure albumen) and iron in an assimilable form. Contains 2½ per cent. of iron. Used as a tonic food in treatment of anæmia, chlorosis, impoverished conditions of the system generally and in convalescence.

Incompatibility of Boric Acid and Sodium Salicylate.—If boric acid and sodium salicylate are mixed together in powder form the mixture becomes moist and unsuitable for use as a powder. The change appears to be due to a combination taking place with elimination of water, sodium borosalicylate, $BO_4(C_6H_4COONa)_n$ being formed.—P. Planès, *Bull. de Pharm. de S. E.* through *Apoth. Ztg.* and *Phar. Jour.*

VENUS TOILET CREAM.

Mucilage quince seed (thick)............℥vi.
Glycerite starch ....℥i.
Rose water ....℥i.
Tinct. benzoin ....gtt. xv.

Add the benzoin to the rose water, agitating thoroughly, and mix with the remaining ingredients. Put up in 4-ounce toilet cream bottles; label and cap; sells for 25 cents.

Cream of Current Literature

A summary of the leading articles in contemporary pharmaceutical periodicals.

Mercuran.—Mercuran is an ointment containing 50 per cent. of mercury in goose oil, made by the Eusoma Pharmaceutical Company, of Cincinnati. The advantages claimed are: Rapid absorption, ease of application, and that it is a soothing and non-irritating preparation. It is prescribed in soft gelatin capsules, each containing 61.73 grains of mercuran.

Aldol.—Aldehyde, when allowed to remain in contact for several days with hydrochloric acid, condenses and forms aldol, or beta-oxybutyric aldehydes. Aldol is a thick, odorless liquid, soluble in 2 parts of water and in ether and alcohol. When exposed to the air it gradually crystallizes, forming a polymer called paraldol. According to Camurri (*Pharmaceutische Zeitung*, 1905, page 729), aldol can be used as a hypnotic.

Cocaine Formate.—Vigier announced to the Therapeutic Society of Paris, at its meeting in November, 1905, that he was about to publish his researches on cocaine formate, which he declared to be a very soluble and very stable salt, which presents several advantages over the already known salts of cocaine. Vigier got his idea for the compound from the preparation of quinine formate by Lacroix, which was recently announced.

Urocitral Not a True Salt.—Urocitral is a combination of sodium citrate with theobromine, which is asserted by the makers to contain 40 per cent. of theobromine. Zernik (*Apothcker Zeitung*, 1905, page 779) has analyzed the substance and found both theobromine and sodium citrate present, but he found only 13.9 per cent. of theobromine. Zernik furthermore states that urocitral does not correspond with the formula indicated by the makers, but is a mixture of various double salts.

A New Preparation for Dyeing and Bleaching the Hair.—A new German patent has been issued for a hair dye which is said to be "relatively" nonpoisonous and which does not irritate the skin. The preparation is made by the Aktiengesellschaft für Anilinfabrikation of Berlin. The hair is first treated with a dilute alcoholic slightly alkaline solution of naphthylendiamine, and then washed with an oxidizing solution. The result is a blond or light brown tint, which resists the influence of light, of water and of the substances ordinarily used in washing the hair.

Iodan.—Iodan is a permanent solution of free iodine, 25 per cent., in goose oil, according to the formula of Dr. E. H. Shield, of Cincinnati, and made by the Eusoma Pharmaceutical Company of that city. The liquid portion of goose fat obtained in the manufacture of mercuran is employed in the solvent. Iodan should be non-irritating to the skin or mucous membrane, readily assimilable when used internally or absorbable when externally applied. For internal use iodan is prescribed in capsules of 5 and 10 minims; the former containing 1.25 grains of iodine, the latter 2.5 grains of iodine. Of the smaller 2 to 10 capsules, and of the larger 4 to 6 capsules, may be given daily. For external use it is put up in 1 ounce glass stoppered bottles.

Distinction Between Bombay and Banda Mace.—F. Utz recommends the color reaction described by Pritchard for distinguishing Bombay mace from Banda mace. Bombay mace is colored red under the influence of a 1 per cent. soda solution, while the mace of Banda does not give this color reaction. The best way of performing this test (*Journal de Pharmacie de Chimie*, November 16, 1905) is the method recommended by Busse, which consists in moistening strips of filter paper in an infusion of the mace in the alkaline solvent. These strips are then dried and if the Banda mace is perfectly pure, the filter paper remains entirely colorless, while if Bombay mace is present it is colored a deep orange. In this way we can recognize 5 per cent. of the Bombay mace added to the mace from Banda.

Formicin.—Formaldehyde-acetamide, obtained by the action of acetamide on formaldehyde or its polymers, has been introduced into medicine as a powerful antiseptic. In consequence of the marked hygroscopic properties of the crystalline compound it is put on the market in the form of a syrupy liquid of the specific gravity 1.240 to 1.260. It is miscible with water, alcohol and chloroform in all proportions and forms a fairly permanent emulsion with oil. It has a slight amine odor, a feeble acid reaction and slightly bitter taste. It does not affect metals. In aqueous solution is begins to decompose, liberating formaldehyde at about 25 degrees C., and is rapidly decomposed on boiling. It has been used as a surgical disinfectant, being applied in the form of tepid 2 per cent. solution. (*Pharm. Centralh.*, 46, 776, through *Phar. Jour.*)

A New Preparation of Camphor and Caffeine for Hypodermic Injection.—Claret presented to the Société de Thérapeutique, in Paris (*Bulletin Commercial*, November, 1905), a new formula for hypodermic injections containing both camphor and caffeine. There is often occasion to use these two drugs simultaneously for stimulating a patient. It is very difficult to prepare a solution which would contain the two ingredients mentioned and the physician has been obliged to use them in separate solutions. Claret suggests the following method of preparation: To 3 cubic centimeters of pure sterilized glycerin, add 1 cubic centimeter of the following solution: Caffeine, and sodium salicylate, of each 0.25 gramme; distilled water, enough to make 1 cubic centimeter. To the mixture, add 1 gramme (or 1.25 cubic centimeters) of spirit of camphor. Each 5 cubic centimeters of this solution will contain 0.25 gramme of caffeine and 0.10 gramme of camphor,—the usual doses of these drugs. The solution keeps perfectly clear for several months.

The Serum Treatment of Typhoid Fever.—Chantemess, who studied the subject experimentally for some years, has communicated his results to the Medical Congress at Cairo, Egypt. The first experiments of Chantemess with his serum showed a diminution in the typhoid mortality of his cases to 6 per cent., whereas the mortality of typhoid patients in the Paris hospitals at the time was 19.3 per cent. His serum is both an antitoxic and antibacillary, besides being an excitant of phagocytosis. It is in the latter role that Chantemess considers it is strongest. In order that this effect be obtainable it is necessary that the lymphoid and myeloid systems should not be too profoundly poisoned, but should be capable of responding to the stimulus of the serum upon cellular activity. For this reason it is best to give the serum early in the disease. The weaker the patient the smaller should be the dose used, and if the patient is in an advanced stage of typhoid it is better to give him small doses, gradually increasing so as to tide him over the dangerous part of the disease. The serum treatment of typhoid fever, which increases phagocytosis, can be given with the hydrotherapeutic treatment, as the two methods fortify each other.

Solurol, a New Remedy for Gout.—Zucker (*Pharmaceutische Zentralhalle*, Sept. 14, 1905) describes solurol (thyminic acid), a new preparation used in the treatment of gout, as a yellowish brown, almost tasteless powder, soluble in water and having a slight acid reaction. According to Minkowski, solurol, or thyminic acid, has the formula:

$$C_{16}H_{26}N_4O_{12}2P_2O_5$$

It has the property of dissolving its own weight of uric acid at a temperature of 20 degrees C. Uric acid, as is known, requires 1,600 parts of cold water to keep it in solution. The solvent property of solurol for urea is doubled at the temperature of the blood, which is 37 degrees C. The solvent properties of this product can be tested by preparing a slightly alkaline solution of uric acid in a test tube, using a very small amount of uric acid. In another test tube a slightly larger amount of solurol is dissolved in water, and equal parts of the solutions are mixed with a third tube and shaken. If the mixture be rendered acid it will be found that the uric acid remains in solution. If the test tube in which the remaining uric acid is in solution be then filled with water and its contents rendered slightly acid the uric acid contained in it will be precipitated. (See also AMERICAN DRUGGIST, vol. xlvii, pp. 69, 295, 317.)

Self-Opening Papers for Powders.—A new form of papers for powders has been placed on the market recently by a German firm (Hammer & Vorsak), who are also manufacturers of machines for compressing tablets, etc. The idea of the new powder papers is to make them perfectly hygienic and easy to handle. These powder papers come (*Pharmazeutische Post*, December 10, 1905) in sets, already folded, and are pasted together in such a way that when the outermost paper is pulled upon the paper next following opens itself, so that it may be filled with the necessary amount of powder. The custom of blowing into folded powder papers before filling them with a powder is one that prevails generally in Germany, but that should not be tolerated in a pharmacy, whether the powders are made at the prescription counter before the eyes of the public or are filled in a back room of the establishment. The necessary number of powder papers are counted from the package of ready-made papers and are separated from the package by means of a small spatula. The papers are then filled in the usual way, save that by pressure of the fingers each paper is opened widely enough to admit the powder. The powder papers are separated by drawing the spatula between them from below upward, and they are closed in the usual manner. These powder papers are manufactured now with the printed name of the firm and the manufacturers have devised a machine which prints, folds and pastes the papers.

Some Practical Tests for Hydrogen Dioxide.—Schmatolla (*Pharmazeutische Zeitung*, 1905, page 641) describes some simple tests for the purity of hydrogen dioxide. In these days, when so many impure products are found in the market, a few tests of this sort will be found convenient at times for distinguishing the article of real merit from those which have merit only in the advertisements. The acidity of a sample may be determined quantitatively by using Congo-red as an indicator. Ten cubic centimeters of hydrogen dioxide solution are treated with three or four drops of a solution of Congo-red, of 1 per cent. strength. The sample, if pure, will become colored red on the addition of ten drops of lime water, corresponding to 0.25 gramme of decinormal potassa solution. When hydrochloric acid is present hydrogen dioxide cannot be used and the sample should be rejected. One-tenth of 1 per cent. of hydrochloric acid suffices to give the dioxide an odor of chlorine. To test for this impurity, 10 cubic centimeters of the hydrogen dioxide solution are treated with 25 drops of diluted sulphuric acid, half a gramme of crystalline ferric sulphate and with five cubic centimeters of decinormal silver nitrate solution. The amount of silver which remains in solution is then titrated with ammonium sulphocyanide. A red color which persists should develop after the use of not less than 4.6 cubic centimeters of ammonium sulphocyanide solution. Schmatolla also describes a reaction for the detection of traces of hydrogen dioxide. This is a very sensitive reaction, and serves to detect one milligramme of hydrogen dioxide per litre of solution. Two hundred cubic centimeters of the suspected solution are treated with from five to ten drops of diluted sulphuric acid, and from five to ten drops of 1 per cent. cobalt nitrate solution. A blue color appears distinctly if potassa solution be added to this mixture drop by drop, if a trace of hydrogen peroxide is present.

The Cause of the Red Color of Carbolic Acid.—Kübl (*Pharm. Zeitung*, November 29, 1905), studies the interesting question as to the cause of the red color of carbolic acid which has puzzled so many chemists in the past and which has not been very thoroughly investigated as yet. The author reminds us that the red color of carbolic acid which is acquired by this substance on standing for some time finds its analogue in the discoloration of aniline, which becomes discolored much more rapidly than does phenol. The experiments of the author were conducted upon a small scale, for the reason that only 100 grammes of red carbolic acid were available at the time. Fifty grammes of phenol was rectified in a retort. A colorless phenol was distilled, remaining a violet reddish mass in the retort. On heating this residue in a watch crystal for a little while, the phenol was completely evaporated, the residue consisting of a small amount of a violet reddish substance. This residue was not soluble in water. Upon warming it with a solution of ferric chloride, and after evaporating it upon the water bath, a residue remained which was at first slightly reddish in color, while the pure carbolic acid that had been distilled off showed a dark violet color under the same conditions. A solution of phenol in ammonia was colored green on standing, after the addition of hydrogen peroxide. The violet reddish mass was not soluble in dilute ammonia, and the latter did not become discolored in any way upon the addition of hydrogen peroxide. A solution of the residue in concentrated sulphuric acid did not become colored on the addition of sodium nitrite.

The reddish mass gave all the characteristic reactions of carbolic acid. The author concludes that some coloring matter is developed in phenol on standing, but the exact nature of this coloring matter can only be discovered by studying the exact composition of the residue and comparing its molecular composition with that of phenol.

A New Way of Using Iodoform. — Bianchi (*Boll. Chim. Farm.*, 1905, Nov. 20) describes a new method of introducing iodoform into the system by applying it to the skin and allowing it to be absorbed. It is well known that iodoform acts somewhat in the manner of iodine, only less severely, for it is less irritating, and relieves pain. Unfortunately it cannot be used very readily in the place of iodine, where the action of iodide is desired, inasmuch as it is not absorbed by the unbroken skin, and therefore cannot be used in the form of inunctions. The author tried to obviate this difficulty by preparing a solution of iodoform which is absorbed by the skin. He gives the following formula for this solution:

Pure caustic potash in powder....	35.0 parts.
Distilled water	25.0 parts.
Pure oleic acid..................	50.0 parts.
Sublimed iodine	30.0 parts.
Alcohol, 95 per cent.............	30.0 parts.

The iodoform in this mixture is prepared extemporaneously in the following way: The powdered potash and the water are mixed in a glass-stoppered flask, the oleic acid is then added and the mixture is thoroughly shaken. Then the iodine and the alcohol are added and the heat which develops during the various reactions is sufficient to produce a uniform mixture of all the ingredients. The flask must be constantly and slowly shaken from time to time until the contents become colorless. Iodine is then added in small amounts, just as is done in preparing iodoform, until the mixture no longer becomes decolorized. The remaining excess of iodine is then removed by means of the potash. The mixture is allowed to cool and to stand for several days and a slight precipitate is removed by decantation. The product is filled into dark bottles. The result is a yellow syrupy fluid which smells of iodoform and which is miscible with water, with alcohol, ether, chloroform, volatile oils, etc., and also with glycerin, oils and fats, creosote, etc. This mixture does not contain any free iodine, nor does it develop any free iodine from standing, as may be seen from the fact that its solutions with chloroform do not become affected by light or air. This mixture of iodoform and soap can therefore be used as an application to the healthy skin for the purpose of producing the effects of iodine without producing the irritation caused by it. The author states that it is absorbed.

A Welcome Visitor

Inclosed please find check to cover two years' subscription to your valuable paper. It is a welcome fortnightly visitor which is always a satisfaction to read. With best wishes for the new year, MAYO & WEAVER.

COLUMBUS, MISS., December 30, 1905.

Queries and Answers

We shall be glad, in this department, to respond to calls for information on all pharmaceutic matters.

"Species."—E. B. asks what should be dispensed when laxative species is asked for. He adds: "I have also had inquiry for breast tea and I should like you to inform me what I am to supply for this."

It is evident that our correspondent is not in possession of a copy of the National Formulary, for if he would have consulted the index of that work he would have found the formulas asked for. These preparations are not called for so frequently now as they were a few years ago, the advance of popular education and the more general dissemination of knowledge bearing on medical subjects having educated the people to higher things in laxative medication (?). Teas of this description are, however, occasionally called for in the cities as well as in outlying districts, and it may be that they will be retained in the next revision of the National Formulary. For the benefit of our subscriber we reprint the formulas below:

Laxative Species.

Senna, cut	16 parts.
Elder flowers	10 parts.
Fennel, bruised	5 parts.
Anise, bruised	5 parts.
Potassium bitartrate, in fine powder	4 parts.

Moisten the senna with a little water, then sprinkle over it as uniformly as possible the potassium bitartrate. When it has become dry mix it lightly and uniformly with the other ingredients.

Pectoral Species or Breast Tea.

Althæa, peeled	8 parts
Coltsfoot leaves	4 parts
Peeled Russian licorice	3 parts
Anise	2 parts
Mullein flowers	2 parts
Orris root	1 part

Cut, bruise and mix them.

Emollient Species.

Althæa leaves,
Mallow leaves,
Melilot tops,
Matricaria,
Flaxseed................of each equal parts.

Reduce them to a coarse powder, and mix uniformly.

Calisaya Elixir.—R. F. writes: "I have made several attempts to reproduce the calisaya elixir made by the elder Hegeman, of New York, but something has always gone wrong and I have not succeeded in obtaining the delicate flavor which characterized the Broadway elixir. Can you suggest a formula?"

The formula referred to has become pretty well known of late years. It is believed to call for the following ingredients:

Tinct. aurantii cort.	℥ss.
Olei aurantii	♏iv.
Olei cassiæ	♏ij.
Olei anisi	♏ij.
Olei coriandri	♏ij.
Olei rosæ	♏ij.
Olei myristicæ	♏ij.
Ext. vanillæ	℥ss.
Syrup simplicis	℥xiiss.
Alcoholis	℥viij.
Acid citric	gr. x.
Quin. sulph.	gr. xxxij.
Cinchonin. sulph.	gr. xvi.
Precipitated calcium phosphate	℥ss.
Aquæ	q. s. ad ℥xxxij.

M.

In preparing this elixir it is best to make a solution of the citric acid in the water and dissolve in this the cinchona salts. Dissolve the oils in alcohol and to this add the tincture of orange peel and extract of vanilla; then mix both solutions and triturate the resulting mixture with the precipitated calcium phosphate; finally filter the product through a wetted filter.

Lotio Alba.—R. F. P. writes: "Please advise me by return mail what *Lotio Alba* is. If a patented product, please advise me of address of makers."

Lotio alba is one of the oldest and best known preparations in hospital dispensing practice. What is usually put up under this name is a solution of sulphurated potash and zinc sulphate in water in the following proportions:

Zinci sulphatis	ʒi
Potassæ sulphuratæ	ʒi
Aquæ ad	℥iv

M.

A compound white lotion is also known. This is made by mixing 90 grains of precipitated sulphur with 4 ounces of the simple white lotion of the above formula.

The druggist who is handed a prescription for lotio alba will do well to dispense the product made by the first formula. A different preparation bearing the name lotio alba is put up in the dispensary of Bellevue Hospital, and the formula as given in the Bellevue Hospital Formulary reads as follows:

Zinci oxidi	ʒij
Liq. plumbi subacetatis	fl ʒiij
Glycerini	fl ʒiv
Liq. calcis	q.s.ad.fl ℥iv

We do not know what induced the editor of the formulary to apply the title long used for a different preparation to a mixture of the character of this one dispensed at Bellevue Dispensary, except that he was influenced by the fact of its color and was perhaps ignorant of the established use of this title for a totally different compound. Unless the physician specifically designated the Bellevue Dispensary formula, the simple solution of zinc sulphate and sulphurated potash should be sent out.

Production and Market Price of Carbon Dioxide.—F. M. A.—Carbon dioxide or carbonic acid is no longer made solely by the decomposition of marble dust or of whiting with sulphuric acid, though this means is still employed for producing the acid when an article of notable purity is required. Some producers of gas depend on natural sources for the supply of the acid, there being extensive plants in the neighborhood of Saratoga Springs where the gas is collected and liquified under pressure. Most breweries have plants for the collection of carbon dioxide from the fermenting worts, the Pabst Brewing Company, Milwaukee, being among the first to collect and utilize carbon dioxide in this way. The acid can be produced at a cost of about 2 cents a pound, but the method of putting it up and transporting it adds to the cost so that large consumers—users of, say, 2,500 pounds a week—are required to pay at least 8 cents, while in ordinary lots 8 cents a pound is paid.

Correspondence.

A College Requirement for New Jersey.

To the Editor:

Sir,—Although not a member of the New Jersey Pharmaceutical Society (though I hope to join it some day), I suggest that a special meeting be called, the object being to amend the pharmacy law so as to require applicants appearing before the State Board to be graduates of a bona-fide college of pharmacy. We can do some good pharmaceutical reform work now, as we have an able champion of our interests in the Legislature in the person of G. Roeber, Ph.G., N. Y. C. P., 1881, of Newark, Essex County, who would no doubt introduce in the present Legislature any just bill if requested to do so. This is the era of reformation. Let us elevate our profession by all means.

JOHN PFEIFFER, PH.G., N. Y. C. P., 1881.

NEWARK, N. J., January 2.

Under this head will appear suggestions and plans for increasing trade, advertising experiences, information, and notes of interest useful to the pharmacist in the preparation of his advertising matter. Specimens of current advertising will be reproduced, with suggestive analysis and criticism, and queries relative to advertising matters will be answered. To avoid delay address communications to the Department of Business Building, AMERICAN DRUGGIST, 66 West Broadway, N.Y.

SUCCESS IN BUSINESS.

By J. A. Wilson,
Baltimore.

As druggists are often compelled to begin and carry on business with a very limited capital it behooves them to study how best to succeed. The road to success is open to all, and although it may seem easy it is in reality much the reverse. Success is not a phantom, to be secured by luck alone, but it is the outcome of close attention, energy, enterprise, enthusiasm, tact and a firm determination against failure.

In business the expenditure of capital is an absolute necessity and requires very close and careful attention. Of course a sufficient and varied assortment of staple and salable goods must be bought and always kept on hand, and it is in buying that the druggist must exercise most care. A "want book" should be kept always close at hand, the demands of patrons which you are unable to supply being noted therein. Buy in limited quantities, as money is frequently wasted in buying too much that is unsalable. Price-lists are valuable agencies in business. Through them you can keep posted as to prices and discounts and thus buy in a way to net the greatest profits. It is well to have regular houses at which to buy, but if you find that you can occasionally buy to better advantage elsewhere do so. An occasional change will show your dealers that you are independent.

Use energy in frequently scrutinizing your books, your debts, your clerks and your system. Balance your books every month and begin the new month with the determination to increase your profit column. Discount your bills, as by so doing you effect a great saving. Make a deposit in the bank each month, no matter how small, and keep your check stubs made out and numbered to correspond with checks. Don't put this off until you have forgotten the amount, the number and the date. Keep the respect of your clerks by being industrious, honest and sober. Show them that with you business comes first, while pleasure is but a secondary consideration. Examine your system and if it is not a good one change it, improve on it, try another.

You are in business not merely to make a living but to get a good financial return for your efforts. Let your business activities then equal and even surpass those of your competitors.

Arrange your stock often and properly, so that it may always appear to advantage. In the placing of stock have all of one class of goods together; this will prevent that motley and unattractive appearance so often seen in stores and will prove a great convenience to you.

Never talk failure nor look on the dark side of things, as this is not the way to succeed. The man who succeeds is he who does not wait for the opportunity that never comes, but who strikes out boldly for himself, and with undaunted energy overcomes every obstacle that may seem in his way. An independent, self-reliant, enterprising man who sees success ahead is the man who reaches it. Many business men become chronic grumblers and fault-finders, never seeing success in anything. A gloomy, melancholy disposition retards advancement, and it is impossible for such people to prosper. Be enthusiastic; look on the bright side of things. The world likes sunny, buoyant, hopeful people. Let your establishment be dominated by a bright, sunshiny atmosphere, of which you are the center.

Some one has said that tact is better than talent. However that may be in the professional world, it is more than certain that tact is truly an essential to the merchant. Tact in dealing with customers, employees, wholesale men and drummers; tact in talking politics, religion and current events.

If we examine the cause of all the failures in the world we shall see that a lack of determination was more often responsible than a lack of property. Nothing can keep a man down when he possesses determination and grit. Have a firm determination, then, to succeed and to make every dollar of your capital tell. Read your drug journal and spare no honest means to reach the goal to which all your efforts should be directed—success.

Clipped from Current Advertising.

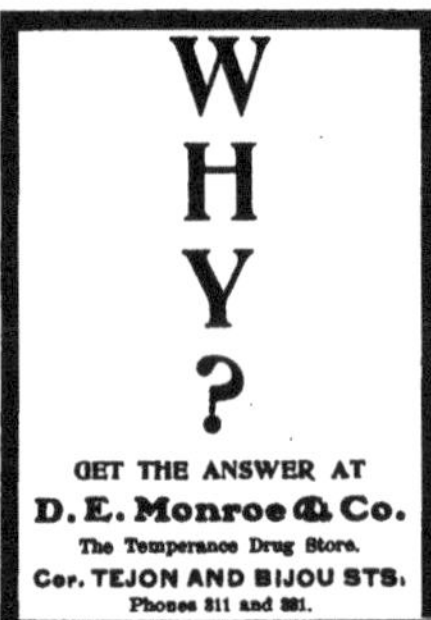

WHY waste space with such conundrums? WHY not *advertise?*

Take Nobody's Word,

Not Even Ours.

Test "Menk's Cpd. Syr. of Hypophosphites"

Yourself. Convince yourself, then tell others the wonderful, peculiar power that belongs to Menk's Hypophosphites.

Its Menk's Hypophosphites

That makes one hungry.

Its Menk's Hypophosphites

That makes one enjoy life.

Its Menk's Hypophosphites

That builds up and makes strong. It is a powerful nutrient tonic, reconstructor and digestant.

But don't take our word for it. Get a bottle of Menk's Hypophosphites and let it convince you—65c. a bottle.

Menk's Pharmacy

Good Ad.—Bad Display.

NEW YORK STATE BOARD OF PHARMACY MEETS.

New Officers Elected and Much Business of Importance to Druggists Transacted—Grocery Drugs and Spices Make a Bad Showing in Report of Committee on Adulteration and Substitution.

The annual meeting of the New York State Board of Pharmacy was held at the capitol in Albany on January 1. The meeting was convened in one of the Senate committee rooms by President Charles B. Sears, at 10 o'clock a.m. Prior to organizing and electing new officers of the board for 1906, the retiring board of officers received committee reports and closed up the year's business by adjusting the finances, settling accounts, etc. Two new members made their appearance at the meeting, namely, John C. Krieger, of Salamanca, who was chosen last year to fill the vacancy in the Western Branch caused by the retirement of Alfred M. Palmer, of Olean, and John Hurley, of Little Falls, who succeeded George H. Merritt, of Newburg, in the Middle Branch. There was no change in the Eastern Branch, Dr. George C. Diekman having been chosen to succeed himself at the last election.

THE NEW OFFICERS.

After the selection of a temporary chairman and secretary the board went on with the election of officers for the ensuing year, the following being chosen:

President, C. O. Bigelow, New York.

Secretary-treasurer, Warren L. Bradt, Albany.

The law provides for two officers only, but by a ruling of the board two additional officers, a first vice-president and a second vice-president, are chosen annually. This allows for rotation in the office of president, it being understood that the first vice-president is the nominee for president at the next election. A Buffalo man will be president next year, as George Reimann, of Buffalo, was made first vice-president. Judson B. Todd, of Ithaca, was named second vice-president. One vote was missing in the election of officers, Herbert M. Groves, of Batavia, being absent on account of sickness.

During a short intermission the several branches of the board were reorganized. The Eastern, or New York City, Branch, remains as before, C. O. Bigelow being re-elected chairman, and Joseph Weinstein, secretary. In the Middle Branch, Judson B. Todd was chosen chairman in place of George H. Merritt, who failed of election last year; Warren L. Bradt, general secretary, remains secretary of the Middle Branch, according to a provision in the law. In the Western Branch, S. A. Grove, of Buffalo, retired as chairman, in favor of H. M. Groves, of Batavia.

Secretary-Treasurer's Report.

The annual report of the secretary-treasurer was submitted by Mr. Bradt and adopted. The text of the report follows:

ALBANY, N. Y., January 1, 1906.

Number of Store Certificates Issued.

	Pharmacies.	Drug Stores.	Permits.
Eastern Branch	2,413	2	14
Middle Branch	1,419	12	625
Western Branch	402	4	77
Total	4,234	18	716

Number of Apprentices Registered.

	Male.	Female.
Eastern Branch	115	8
Middle Branch	103	6
Western Branch	33	5
Total	251	14

Number of Former Board Certificates Exchanged for All State Certificates.

	Pharmacists.	Druggists.
Eastern Branch	52	..
Middle Branch	24	2
Western Branch	9	2
Total	85	4

Number of Duplicate Certificates Issued in Lieu of Those Lost or Destroyed.

Eastern Branch	1
Middle Branch	2
Western Branch	4
Total	7

Number of Substitute Certificates Issued in Lieu of Those Lost or Destroyed.

Eastern Branch	..
Middle Branch	9
Western Branch	7
Total	16

Examination Report.

Eastern Branch.

	Pharmacist.	Druggist.	Total.
Number of applications for examination received	115	2	117
Examined for Middle Branch	5	..	5
Examined for Western Branch	1	..	1
Number of applications withdrawn	1	..	1
Number of individuals examined, including re-examinations	230	2	232
Passed	192	2	194
	Male.	Female.	Total.
Number of licenses granted	189	5	194

Middle Branch.

	Pharmacist.	Druggist.	Total.
Number of applications for examination received	17	20	37
Examined for Eastern Branch	..	..	..
Examined for Western Branch	..	..	..
Number of applications withdrawn	..	..	..
Number of individuals examined, including re-examinations	54	23	77
Passed	37	19	56
Rejected	17	4	21
	Male.	Female.	Total.
Number of licenses granted	55	1	56

Western Branch.

	Pharmacist.	Druggist.	Total.
Number of applications for examination received	30	48	78
Examined for Eastern Branch	..	..	..
Examined for Middle Branch	..	..	..
Number of applications withdrawn	1	1	2
Number of individuals examined, including re-examinations	75	60	135
Passed	49	43	92
Rejected	26	17	43
	Male.	Female.	Total.
Number of licenses granted	89	8	92

Number of Examinations Held in 1905.

New York	3
Brooklyn	3
Albany	5
Rochester	5
Buffalo	5
Total	21

Meetings Held by General Board.

Albany	January 2-3
Saratoga	June 26

Meetings Held by Branches.

	Eastern.	Middle.	Western.
Examination meetings	6	5	6
Executive meetings	13	..	..
Special meetings	1	..	15

Report of Committees on Inspection, Complaints and Prosecutions for the Year Ending December 30, 1905.

Number of Stores Inspected.

	Pharmacies.	General stores.	Towns & cities visited.
Eastern Branch	2,709	...	...
Middle Branch	...	...	...
Western Branch	169	190	...

Number of Samples Collected.

	Collected.	Assayed.	Found standard or nearly so.	Deficient.
Eastern Branch	2,968	...	...	...
Middle Branch	831	...	...	...
Western Branch	417	407	354	58

Prosecutions.

Criminal Prosecutions.

	Convictions.	Acquittals.	Pending.	Fines collected.
Eastern Branch	...	...	1	...
Middle Branch	...	...	...	...
Western Branch	...	...	...	...

Civil Prosecutions.

	Convictions.	Acquittals.	Pending.	Fines collected.
Eastern Branch	95	8	40	$2,936
Middle Branch	1	...	...	50
Western Branch	...	...	1	...

Cases Settled Out of Court.

	Pharmacists.	Other dealers.	Fines collected.
Eastern Branch	207	42	$7,716
Middle Branch	38	14	1,975
Western Branch	14	12	975

[It should be stated here that a large proportion of the sums collected in fines came from painters, general dealers and others found violating the law, and not from pharmacists.]

Financial Statement of the Branches for the Year 1905.

Receipts.

	Eastern.	Middle.	Western.
Examination fees	$1,160.00	$270.00	$540.00
Pharmacy registrations	4,826.00	2.840.00	804.00
Drug store registrations......	4.00	24.00	8.00
Permits	70.00	3,125.00	388.00
Apprentice registrations	59.00	54.50	19.00
Exchange of certificates	52.00	26.00	11.00
Engrossing certificates	26.00	12.50	5.50
Duplicate certificates	2.00	4.00	6.50
Substitute certificates	....	13.50	10.50
Fines collected	10,652.00	2,025.00	975.00
Examining candidates for other branches	30.00	15.00	....
Interest on deposits..........	94.90	29.49	8.78
Surplus from 1904...........	8,594.36	....	....
Total	$25,570.26	$8,438.99	$2,776.28

Expenditures.

	Eastern.	Middle.	Western.
New York College of Pharmacy	$5,284.62	....	....
Brooklyn College of Pharmacy	3,547.74	....	....
Secretary's salary	2,000.00	$1,800.00	$500.00
Inspectors' salaries	1,440.00	875.00	225.00
Inspectors' expenses	549.64	2,076.28	409.75
Rent	....	120.00	60.00
Secretary's surety bond.......	10.00	10.00	10.00
Per diems paid to members...	540.00	580.00	580.00
Members' traveling and hotel expenses	....	1,584.86	361.69
Legal expenses	2,574.79	612.21	103.60
Postage	177.25	252.00	64.00
Office and general expenses...	605.35	476.01	166.80
Paid other branches for examining candidates	15.00	5.00	5.00
Returned fees	10.00	70.00	15.00
Analyses	2,855.28	10.00	256.50
Quota to General Board......	2,700.00	....	....
Deficit for 1904.............	....	5.01	70.55
Surplus	3,260.59	....	....
Total	$25,570.26	$8,476.37	$2,827.89
Deficiency	....	37.38	51.61

Per Diems Paid to Members.

	General Board.	Branch.	Total days.
Eastern Branch.			
Clarence O. Bigelow....................	10	20	30
George C. Diekman.....................	5	25	30
William Muir	7	23	30
Frederic P. Tuthill.....................	10	20	30
Joseph Weinstein	4	20	24
Middle Branch.			
Charles B. Sears........................	7	23	30
Byron M. Hyde..........................	6	24	30
George H. Merritt......................	5	25	30
Judson B. Todd.........................	7	23	30
Warren L. Bradt	9	21	30
Western Branch.			
Willis G. Gregory......................	7	23	30
Alfred M. Palmer.......................	8	22	30
S. A. Grove............................	7	23	30
Herbert H. Groves......................	5	21	26
George Reimann	2	27	29

Financial Statement of the New York State Board of Pharmacy for the Year Ending December 30, 1905.

Receipts.

Balance from 1904..................................	$894.94
Received from Western Branch (draft of 1904)......	650.00
Received from Eastern Branch......................	2,700.00
Interest on deposits................................	2.52
Total	$4,247.46

Expenditures.

Postage		$177.10	
Engrossing		216.50	
Legal expenses		10.00	
Secretary's salary		500.00	
Stationery and printing, including office supplies, stationery, printing of applications and certificates of all kinds and examination questions		689.46	
General expenses		773.98	
Rent		120.00	
Per diems paid to members:			
Clarence O. Bigelow................	$50		
George C. Diekman.................			
William Muir			
Frederic P. Tuthill.................			
Joseph Weinstein			
Charles B. Sears...................			
Byron M. Hyde.....................			
George H. Merritt..................			
Judson B. Todd....................			
Warren L. Bradt...................			
Willis G. Gregory..................			
Alfred M. Palmer..................	.00		
S. A. Grove.......................	[illegible]		
Herbert M. Groves.................	25.00		
George Reimann	10.00—	495.00	
Members' traveling and hotel expenses:			
Clarence O. Bigelow................	$94.00		
George C. Diekman.................	59.00		
William Muir	74.00		
Frederic P. Tuthill.................	109.00		
Joseph Weinstein	59.00		
Charles B. Sears...................	96.00		
Byron M. Hyde.....................	67.00		
George H. Merritt	47.50		
Judson B. Todd....................	72.00		
Warren L. Bradt	69.00		
Willis G. Gregory	138.00		
Alfred M. Palmer..................	86.00		
S. A. Grove	72.00		
Herbert M. Groves	72.00		
George Reimann	70.00—	1,179.50	
Total		$4,166.54	
Cash on hand December 30, 1905........		80.92	
			$4,247.46

WARREN L. BRADT, Secretary-Treasurer.

THE LABELING OF POISONS IN ORIGINAL PACKAGES.

A number of communications were read and discussed. The question of retailers dispensing original packages of poisonous preparations without affixing a poison label to the container was settled by permitting retailers to attach the required label to the paper wrapper surrounding the bottle or package. An opinion bearing on this was obtained from the board's attorney, who decided that the practice, which had prevailed for some time with the druggists of the State, was permissible. Another matter which engaged the attention of the members was the proposed transfer of corrosive sublimate from schedule B to schedule A. It developed, however, that the board has no authority to take articles from the schedules, so that if corrosive sublimate were to be included in schedule A it would still have to remain in schedule B. Among several amendments to the pharmacy law which the board will endeavor to get through the legislature this year, with the help of the State Pharmaceutical Association, this will be one.

Adulteration and Substitution.

Dr. George C. Diekman, chairman of the Committee on Adulteration and Substitution of the Eastern Branch, submitted the following report covering the work performed by his committee during the past year: In all 2,746 samples were collected from pharmacists and others doing business within the territory over which this branch of the board has jurisdiction. These samples were submitted to the chemist of the branch for analyses, and reports on 2,655 samples were received from him, 91 samples remaining unanalyzed. These samples were collected by the inspectors of the board from stores located in every part of the territory embraced in the Eastern section. In each instance a portion of the sample, duly sealed, was left in possession of the person from whom purchased.

A comparison of this report with that for the year 1904 shows that while a greater number of samples were collected, the deviations from the pharmacopœial requirements of strength and purity are steadily on the decrease.

The following detailed tabulation of the results of analyses was given:

	Standard.	Not Standard.	Number Examined.
[1] Tincture of iodine	512	72	584
Camphor liniment	353	61	414
Solution of magnesium citrate	352	49	401
Chloroform liniment	269	24	293
[2] Spirit of camphor	252	23	275
Tincture of arnica	220	9	229
Tincture of benzoin	131	4	135
Bay rum	65	11	76
[3] Cream of tartar	41	17	58
Soap liniment	49	4	53
Solution of hydrogen dioxide	42	4	46
Tincture of nux vomica	21	3	24
Tincture of opium	9	4	13
Essence of ginger	13	0	13
Essence of peppermint	1	0	1
Belladonna ointment	12	0	12
Tincture of cinchona	9	0	9
Syrup of ipecac	7	0	7
Codliver oil	7	0	7
Pepsin	5	0	5
Totals	2,370	285	2,655

Total number of samples collected and analyzed, 2,655

Total number of samples found standard		2,370
Total number of samples found deficient		285
Totals	2,655	2,655

Per cent. of deficient samples, 10.74.

Total number of samples containing wood alcohol, 79, or 2.97 per cent. of total number analyzed.

Comparison with 1904 Report.

Per cent. of deficient samples, 1904	12.63
" " " " 1905	10.74
Per cent. decrease	1.89
Per cent. of samples containing wood alcohol, 1904	5.51
" " " " " " 1905	2.97
Per cent. decrease	2.54

In proceeding against violators of the law for the sale of articles below the required standard of strength, the board has found that the courts would not sustain it in the contention that separate fines could be collected for two or more offenses committed in one day. The law at present reads that any person violating the section in question shall forfeit $25 "for *every* such violation." The board will endeavor to secure the insertion of the words "each and" before *every* in the words previously quoted. It is also contemplated to strike out from subdivision 3 of section 196 the words "knowingly, wilfully or fraudulently," to meet some legal technicality which the board has had to contend with in prosecuting offenders.

An effort is to be made by the board through an amendment to the law to place wood alcohol among the poisons listed in schedule B, there being some conflict of opinion among lawyers as to whether the board had power to add wood alcohol to the list without authority of the Legislature.

Doctor Taylor, of the State Education Department, appeared before the board and read the minutes of the Ad Interim of the pharmacy council of the Board of Regents. The adoption of these minutes places Scio College, Ohio, among the recognized colleges of pharmacy in this State. The report covered practically the same ground as described in the AMERICAN DRUGGIST for November 13, 1905, page 276. The business of Monday's session was conducted in two sittings, the first lasting from 10 till 12 and the second from 2.30 till 5.

Important Ruling at Tuesday's Session.

The board met in the same place on Tuesday at 10 a. m. At this sitting definite action was taken in the matter of allowing druggists to label original packages of poisonous preparations by pasting the poison label over the waxed paper wrapper in which the package is sent out by the manufacturer.

STORES MUST BE EQUIPPED WITH THE LATEST PHARMACOPŒIA.

The board adopted a new and important ruling which will be known as Rule No. 20. This provides that no store license will be issued to any pharmacist applying for the same who fails to give satisfactory proof to the board that he is in possession of the latest revised edition of the United States Pharmacopœia, or of some work which embodies the latest revised edition of the United States Pharmacopœia in its contents.

At the suggestion of Doctor Muir a committee was appointed to wait on Governor Higgins, both to pay the respects of the board and to get the Governor's views on the wisdom of introducing the proposed amendments to the pharmacy law at this session of the legislature. On this committee were appointed C. O. Bigelow, William Muir, Willis G. Gregory and Judson B. Todd. The committee reported later that the Governor had received them very cordially, showed much interest in their talk and assured them that the proposed amendments met with his approval. One of the amendments not mentioned above provides increased remuneration for the members of the board. At present members are allowed $5 for each day actually engaged in the performance of services as a member, and it is provided that no member shall receive more than $150 in any one year, together with his necessary expenses and disbursements. By the proposed amendment members shall be entitled to $10 per day, the minimum amount allowed to members of every other State board.

Sundry other business of a routine nature was transacted, after which the board adjourned to meet with the State Pharmaceutical Association in Niagara Falls next year.

The National Wholesale Druggists' Association.

Washington has been selected as the next place for the meeting of the National Wholesale Druggists' Association and the new Willard Hotel as the headquarters. The date chosen is the second Tuesday of October.

---

[1] Tincture of iodine, number of samples analyzed 584
Deficient 72

(a) Wood alcohol	8
(b) Wood alcohol and strength	10
(c) Strength alone	54
Total	72

[2] Spirits of camphor, number of samples analyzed 275
Found deficient 23

(a) Wood alcohol	5
(b) Wood alcohol and strength	4
(c) Strength alone	14
Total	23

[3] Cream of tartar, number of samples analyzed 58
Found deficient 17

Samples purchased from pharmacists	30
Samples purchased from general dealers	28
Total	58
Found deficient (pharmacists)	0
Found deficient (general dealers) (60.71 per cent.)	17
Total	17

A NATIONAL LEAGUE OF BUYING CLUBS.

Representatives of Co-operative Drug Buying Associations Meet and Form a National Organization—Disposition Evinced to Cultivate Friendly Relations with Manufacturers.

Representatives of the principal co-operative drug buying associations, irreverently known in some quarters as "buying clubs," came together for a conference in the Hotel Astor, New York, on Wednesday evening, January 3. Some ten cities were represented and the total attendance was 12. It was purely a business meeting and was not either preceded or followed by anything in the way of luncheon or dinner. Those present were evidently animated by a desire to establish the friendliest relations with the proprietary interests, and contrary to what was expected by those who had been "tipped off" about the meeting, no antagonistic spirit made itself felt during the entire proceedings. It was decided to form a national organization of co-operative companies and a committee was formed for this purpose to report with a constitution and articles of incorporation some time during the month. The gratifying announcement was made that no company which had made a practice of selling to cutters or otherwise demoralizing prices would be admitted to membership.

The fact that a meeting was to take place was kept very quiet, but many of the wholesale houses were aware of the movement. One of the leading wholesale druggists of this city said that such a plan was bound to prevail in the end. He said there was more of a disposition on the part of the manufacturers to deal directly with the consumer, and in some instances large houses have issued circulars to the trade announcing that a saving of 40 per cent. could be made by dealing direct, since they had dispensed with salesmen and had no outside expenses. Continuing, he said: "We are manufacturers as well as jobbers, but we experience considerable trouble in selling the goods of other houses who compel us to live up to their contract, while they at the same time are dealing directly with the people whom we are refusing to have any business with. A change is bound to come. It may not be for five years and it may be longer, but it will come."

This shows the feeling of some jobbers.

THE ILLINOIS PHARMACY LAW EXPOUNDED.

The Illinois Board Issues an Explanation of the Law—Temporary Absence Defined—The Status of the Pharmacopoeia Defined—Poison Law Will Be Enforced.

We print below a copy of a letter which is being sent by F. C. Dodds, of Illinois, secretary of the Board of Pharmacy of the State of Illinois, to every registered pharmacist in the State, calling attention to the provisions of the pharmacy law that are not clearly understood by all druggists and other matters of importance to them. The letter is being sent out with the annual certificates. The letter reads as follows:

STATE OF ILLINOIS.—BOARD OF PHARMACY.

OFFICE OF THE SECRETARY.

To the Registered Pharmacists of Illinois:

I am directed by the State Board of Pharmacy to call your attention to the following provisions of the Pharmacy Law and other matters of importance to registered pharmacists.

TEMPORARY ABSENCE.

Section 1 provides that every drug store in the State must be under the direct charge of a registered pharmacist. A slight exception is made in section 6, which provides that any assistant pharmacist shall have the right to act as clerk or salesman in a drug store or pharmacy during the "temporary absence" of the registered pharmacist.

The board construes the words "temporary absence" to mean that *the assistant pharmacist may have charge of the store only while the registered pharmacist has gone to his meals, or any other like necessary duty requiring no more time than is generally so consumed.*

APPRENTICE REGISTRATION.

Section 7 of the law is in regard to the registration of apprentices. It is as follows:

"It shall be the duty of registered pharmacists who take into their employ an apprentice for the purpose of becoming a pharmacist to require said applicant to at once apply to said Board of Pharmacy for registration as apprentice, and the said Board of Pharmacy shall have the right to require such an examination as shall establish the educational qualifications of the applicant, *and the date of experience required of applicants for assistant or registered pharamcist shall be computed from the date of registration as apprentice.* The Board of Pharmacy shall furnish proper blanks for this purpose and issue a certificate of registration as a registered apprentice upon the payment of $2."

You will observe that it is the duty of a registered pharmacist who takes into his employ an apprentice for the purpose of becoming a pharmacist to at once apply to the State Board of Pharmacy for his registration as an apprentice. It is also of great interest to the apprentice to become registered at the earliest moment possible, since under the law *the drug store experience required of applicants for assistant pharmacist or registered pharmacist commences with the date of apprentice registration.*

A certificate as a registered apprentice does not give authority to the holder thereof to compound, recommend, dispense or sell drugs, medicines or poisons, *except under the immediate supervision of a registered pharmacist,* and must not be construed to empower the holder thereof to exercise the duties of a registered pharmacist or assistant pharmacist, nor to conduct a drug store during the absence of the registered pharmacist. If a registered apprentice is left in charge of a drug store it is a clear violation of the pharmacy law.

EXPOSE YOUR CERTIFICATE.

Section 8 provides that every certificate of registration shall be conspicuously exposed in the pharmacy or drug store to which it applies. Any person violating this provision is liable, upon conviction thereof, to pay a penalty of not less than $25 nor more than $50.

This provision applies to the certificate of every registered pharmacist, every assistant pharmacist and every registered apprentice, and the board especially requests a proper compliance with it.

Section 8 also provides that the name of the registered pharmacist who conducts a drug store or pharmacy shall be conspicuously displayed over the door or department. A proper compliance with this provision is also requested.

LABELS.

Section 12 refers to labels. It is as follows:

"No person shall sell at retail any drug, medicine or poison without affixing to the box, bottle, vessel or package containing the same a label bearing the name of the article, distinctly shown, with the name and place of business of the registered pharmacist from whom the article was obtained: Provided, nothing in this section shall apply to the sale of patent or proprietary medicines when sold in original packages, nor with the dispensing of physicians' prescriptions. Any person failing to comply with the requirements of this section shall be liable to a penalty of $5 for any and every offense."

This means that a printed, written or stamped label or tag must be affixed to every box, bottle, vessel or package containing any drug, medicine or poison. The label or tag should give the name and place of business of the registered pharmacist from whom the article was obtained.

You will observe that this section does not apply to the sale of patent or proprietary medicines when sold in original packages, nor to the dispensing of physicians' prescriptions.

ADULTERATION AND SUBSTITUTION.

Section 14 refers to adulterations and substitutions and provides a penalty of $50, together with all costs and expenses, for adulterating or altering any drug, medicine, chemical or pharmaceutical preparation, or substituting one material for another.

According to a recent opinion of the Attorney-General of the State, the 1890 edition of the U. S. Pharmacopœia will remain the standard of purity until the 1900 U. S. Pharmacopœia is adopted by legislative enactment.

The Board is determined to protect the honest, law-abiding druggists against the unscrupulous competition of the druggists who substitute and adulterate their preparations. You have nothing to fear if your preparations are according to either the 1890 or 1900 Pharmacopœia. If they are not according to either, you are liable to prosecution.

COCAINE.

Section 14b relates to the sale of cocaine. It provides among other things that the certificate of a pharmacist who has been twice convicted for its illegal sale *shall* be revoked.

The board wants to impress upon you the fact that this provision applies to all pharmacists, and that the certificate of a *clerk* may be revoked the same as the certificate of the *proprietor* of a drug store.

POISONS.

Sections 62 and 63 of the Criminal Code refer to the sale of poisons. These sections are as follows:

Section 62. "Every druggist or other person who shall sell and deliver any arsenic, strychnine, corrosive sublimate, prussic acid or other substance or liquid usually denominated as poisonous, without having the word "Poison" written or printed upon the label attached to the phial or parcel in which such drug is contained, or shall sell and deliver any drug or medicine other than upon the prescription of a physician, without having the name of such drug or medicine printed or written upon the label attached to the phial or parcel containing the same, shall be fined not exceeding $25."

Section 63. "If any druggist or other person sells or gives away any arsenic, strychnine, corrosive sublimate or prussic acid, without the written prescription of a physician, and fails to keep a record of the date of such sale or gift, the article and amount thereof sold or given away, and the person to whom delivered, he shall be fined not exceeding $50 for each neglect. Whoever purchases any such poison and gives a false or fictitious name shall be punished in the same manner."

Your attention is called particularly to the requirements of the above sections.

VIOLATIONS OF LAW.

If you know of any violations of the Pharmacy Law please notify the Board of Pharmacy at once. All correspondence concerning violations will be regarded as strictly confidential. We are making a determined effort to stop violations of the law and need your assistance.

CHANGE OF ADDRESS.

If you change your address at any time during the year please notify this office at once, in order that we may change our registration books accordingly and that mail from this office may reach you promptly.

DEATHS.

Please notify this office of the death of any registered pharmacist or assistant pharmacist occurring within your knowledge during the year, giving the date thereof, if possible.

Yours respectfully, F. C. DODDS, Secretary.

SUITS AGAINST CUTTERS.

Paris Medicine Company Sues Hegeman Corporation—Wells & Richardson Company Proceed Against Abraham & Straus.

Suit has been brought by the Paris Medicine Company, manufacturer of Laxative Bromo Quinine, to restrain the Hegeman Corporation of New York from selling Laxative Bromo Quinine at less than the established price. The bill of complaint contains the usual statements regarding the restraining of the defendants from corrupting the agents of the plaintiff. The case will be tried in the United States Circuit Court for this district and it is expected to be brought to a speedy trial.

The case of Wells & Richardson Company against Abraham & Straus, Brooklyn, was up last week before Judge Thomas in the United States Court for Brooklyn, when briefs were submitted by the attorneys for the plaintiff and the defendant. Frank F. Reed, of Chicago, appeared for Wells & Richardson Company and E. Wise submitted a brief in behalf of the defendants.

BILLS OBJECTED TO.

Virginia Drug Clerks Oppose Measures Favored by the State Association.

The drug clerks holding membership in the Virginia Association of Registered Drug Clerks, with branches in the cities of Richmond, Lynchburg, Manchester, Danville and Portsmouth, are in an angry mood over the proposed amendment to the pharmacy law of Virginia drafted by the Virginia Pharmaceutical Association, which reads as follows:

Any registered pharmacist having in his employment and under his training a clerk not under 18 years of age, who has had at least two years of experience in his drug store, pharmacy, or pharmaceutical department and who proposes to qualify himself as a registered pharmacist, may, by application to said board and by offering satisfactory evidence of said clerk's age, experience and purpose, as above required, and by paying a fee of $5, have the said clerk duly registered as his apprentice in pharmacy, for a period not exceeding three years and for the business of said pharmacist at a place particularly designated, and upon such application and evidence the said board, making proper record thereof, shall grant to such pharmacist a permit authorizing said pharmacist in his discretion and upon his own responsibility to allow the said clerk, as an apprentice in pharmacy for the period and at the place aforesaid, to be in the sole management and control of the said drug store, pharmacy or pharmaceutical department for not more than six consecutive days at any one time and for not more than 30 days in the aggregate during any year.

The said permit shall be returned to said board for cancellation at the expiration of said three years, or whenever the said apprentice before the expiration of said three years shall cease to do business for said pharmacist at the said designated place, and for the failure to so return to said board the said permit, the said pharmacist shall be deemed guilty of a misdemeanor and upon conviction thereof shall be fined not less than $10 nor more than $100.

The drug clerks insist that under this amendment it would be possible for a druggist who had a negro porter in his store for a term of two years to have him registered as an apprentice, and they object strenuously to this, saying it would be an end to the business so far as a registered white clerk is concerned.

OPPOSITION TO A PATENT MEDICINE BILL.

Opposition to the so-called Patent Medicine bill has also developed. The text of this bill reads:

Before any patent or proprietary medicine may be sold or offered for sale in this State the proprietor, owner or seller thereof shall make written application to the Board of Pharmacy of this State for the privilege, and shall file with said board ample specimens or samples of said medicines, an affidavit showing the ingredients of said medicines, with description of the packages in which it is sold, together with the directions and advertisements thereof, if any, and shall pay to said board for each medicine a fee of not less than $5 nor more than $50, the amount of the fee to be determined by the board in its discretion, upon considering the selling price and profitable sales of said medicine; and shall obtain from the said board a certificate, as provided in the next section of this act, and if the same medicine contains alcohol, cocaine, opium or any poison, then the said applicant shall file with said board an affidavit showing the respective portions of the several ingredients of said medicine. As a further condition of selling or offering for sale a patent or proprietary medicine containing alcohol, cocaine, opium or any poison, the said board, if it deems it best, may require the formula showing the ingredients and the proportions thereof to be shown conspicuously by label or otherwise on each package of said medicine.

THE NAVAL HOSPITAL CORPS.

Review of Its Work During the Past Seven Years—The Surgeon-General Recommends Reorganization—Increased Number of Warrant Officers Advocated.

The annual report of the Surgeon-General of the United States Navy contains the following interesting references to the Naval Hospital Corps:

The Naval Hospital Corps was authorized by act of Congress approved June 17, 1898, and has existed as an organization for seven years. During this period much has been accomplished in securing to the service a competent and efficient body of men. The desire of the bureau has been to secure for service in this corps, which forms a part of the enlisted force of the navy, men of sobriety, reliability, and intelligent aptitude, and it is gratifying to report the fact that the work and conduct of the corps is commendable.

During the past year demands for the detail of members of the corps for duty at naval hospitals, dispensaries, naval stations, marine detachments, recruiting offices, and for service on board vessels in commission have been met with considerable embarrassment, and there should be material increase in the number of these grades to supply the needs of the service. Careful study of the present condition of the hospital corps and of the future needs of the service has satisfied the bureau that in order to place it in efficient condition, and to retain in the service desirable men in the lower ratings for a longer period than one enlistment, it is imperatively necessary to effect a reorganization whereby greater inducements than the law now permits may be offered. It is discouraging to note that very few of the men in the two lower ratings enlist for a second term.

PERSONNEL OF THE CORPS.

At present the corps is composed of 25 pharmacists, 207 hospital stewards, 240 hospital apprentices, first class, and 264 hospital apprentices. The pay allowed by present law for the hospital stewards is $60 per month; for hospital apprentices, first class, $30, and for hospital apprentices, $20. Unless there is a reasonable prospect for advancement with increase of pay for the men, particularly for those in the ratings of hospital apprentice, and hospital apprentice, first class, it will be impossible to keep the corps recruited with desirable, experienced and trained men.

TRAINED NURSES.

The hospital apprentice, first class, represents the trained nurse of the navy, and he, after being qualified for this rating, is not satisfied with the pay given, and usually will not remain in the service unless further promotion before the expiration of the term of his enlistment to the higher rating of hospital steward, with attendant increase of pay, is assured, but will seek the more lucrative employment and greater comforts of life to be found ashore. The result is that the trained men are not held for the service, and under existing conditions it will be impossible to secure permanently for the medical establishment of the navy a thoroughly competent nursing staff of men.

UNJUST DISCRIMINATION.

The pay of hospital stewards having been fixed by the act of Congress organizing the hospital corps, the men of this rating are deprived of the benefits of the executive order of

June 26, 1903, increasing the pay of all other chief petty officers of the navy who have qualified after examination for permanent appointment. Thus placed at a disadvantage, as compared with other chief petty officers of the service, hospital stewards are dissatisfied. Moreover, as the number in the grade of pharmacist is limited to 25, the chance of promotion to the warrant grade for any individual is very small. It is apparent that the inducements offered are not sufficient to cause the most desirable members of the hospital corps to remain permanently attached to the naval service. Unless reorganization is effected a permanent corps of trained men will not be secured. The number of pharmacists allowed by law is 25, and with this small number there is little hope for the more ambitious and useful men in the lower ratings to secure ultimate advancement to the warrant grade.

NO HOPE FOR COMMISSIONS.

Moreover, the pharmacists are placed at a disadvantage in reference to other warrant officers of the Navy, as there exists no provision for their promotion to commissioned rank, as obtains for other warrant officers of the navy. Thus hampered by unsatisfactory provisions of the law, it long since became apparent to the bureau that it is idle to expect to retain in the hospital corps the men who have been carefully trained for service requirements and whose attachment to the service was most desirable and necessary in the care and treatment of the sick.

The bureau, in the two preceding annual reports and on other occasions, has earnestly represented that it was necessary to reorganize and increase the efficiency of the hospital corps, and these recommendations have met with the approval of the department, which has urgently recommended favorable action thereon by Congress. After thorough investigation of the subject, a favorable report was submitted by the Naval Committee of the House on a bill incorporating the recommendations of the bureau, but it failed of consideration and final action during the last Congress. The necessity for the reorganization of the hospital corps, heretofore recommended, still exists, and the bureau again earnestly recommends that request be made for prompt consideration of this important matter by Congress, as it is vital to the efficiency of the medical establishment of the navy.

REORGANIZATION BILL APPROVED BY THE SURGEON-GENERAL.

An organization that will meet present needs and permit of ready expansion in the event of war and secure an efficient hospital corps for the navy, is, in the opinion of the bureau, provided for in House bill No. 12646, third session, Fifty-eighth Congress, which contains the following provisions:

First, that the hospital corps of the navy shall consist of chief pharmacists; pharmacists; chief baymen; baymen, first class; baymen, second class, and baymen apprentices. Second, that the number of chief pharmacists and pharmacists on the active list shall not exceed 50 in all, the chief pharmacists and pharmacists to be appointed by the President and have the status of warrant officers, and that the provisions of law regulating the promotion, pay and allowances, and rights of warrant officers set forth in Section 12 of the act approved March 3, 1899, known as the "personnel act," shall extend to and include all chief pharmacists and pharmacists of the hospital corps. Also that vacancies in the grade of pharmacists shall be filled from men holding the rating of chief baymen, subject to such examination as may be prescribed by the Secretary of the Navy, and that no pharmacist shall be promoted to the rank of chief pharmacist until he shall have passed an examination as to his mental, moral, physical and professional fitness, before a board of officers, in accordance with regulations prescribed by the Secretary of the Navy. Third, that as many chief baymen, baymen, first class, baymen, second class, and baymen apprentices shall be enlisted as, in the judgment of the secretary of the navy, may be necessary, and that enlisted men of the navy and marine corps shall be eligible for transfer to the hospital corps. Fourth, that all necessary hospital and ambulance service at naval hospitals, naval stations, navy yards, and marine barracks, and on vessels of the navy and fish commission, shall be performed by members of the hospital corps, and that the corps shall be permanently attached to the medical department of the navy and shall be included in the effective strength of the navy and be counted as part of the enlisted force provided by law, to be subject to the rules for the government of the navy. Fifth, that the pay of chief baymen shall be $70 per month, except when serving under acting appointments, when it shall be $60 per month; for baymen, first class, $50 per month; for baymen, second class, $35 per month, and for baymen apprentices $20 per month, with such an increase on account of length of service as is allowed other enlisted men of the navy, and that all benefits given by existing law or that shall hereafter be allowed to other warrant officers and enlisted men of the navy shall hereafter be allowed in the same manner to warrant officers and enlisted men of the hospital corps of the navy.

BUSINESS METHODS IN NEW ENGLAND.

Recollections of a Summer's Trolley Tour—Painting the Town—Effect of the Trolley on Advertising Methods.

(*Special Correspondence.*)

The electric roads with which this country is so thickly gridironed afford an easy, rapid and pleasant means of observing the business methods pursued in sparsely settled districts by the drug trade. Such an opportunity was an interesting incident in a summer's holiday, during which a portion of the line running between Lewiston and Bath, Maine, was traversed. While the stocks of country stores and those of some small cities would perhaps not pass muster in the large centers, yet the side lines and outside issues are not more numerous than those of the modern city establishments, and for the dollars the city chap cannot excel his country brother in keenness.

PAINT POT AND BRUSH.

At Lisbon Walter S. Cole, registered pharmacist, looks after the welfare of the inhabitants of that town with a varied stock well adapted to country needs. On the trip from Lisbon Falls to Brunswick it was in evidence by various landscape disturbances that some of the druggists at the latter place had confidence in the paint pot and brush, for such signs as "Deprean's Pharmacy" and "Deprean's Reliable Drug Store, Brunswick, Maine," were noticed. The public was also admonished to "Go to Wilson's Pharmacy, Brunswick, Maine." Arriving at Brunswick, both of these stores, judging from outside appearances, were neatly arranged. The Wilson establishment looked as though recently from the painter's hand and bore many signs calling attention to the "reliable" specialties. P. J. Meserve has on a prominent corner of the same street on which the above stores are located an establishment of inviting appearance.

AN ENTERPRISING ADVERTISER IN BATH.

Proceeding from Brunswick to Bath one who attempts to read all of the drug signs will find ocular excitement galore and at the same time be impressed with the thought that a certain Dougherty of Bath is attempting to corner all of the fences, ledges and trees by the wayside. But in this effort Mr. Dougherty is not alone, for other Bath druggists are engaged in the same publicity game; the former's output and put-up is, however, most extensive—in fact, he seems insatiable. To him the thoroughfare traversed by the electrics have limitations and when the cars approach the steam railroad lines it is noted that the fences belonging to the latter corporation bear Dougherty's handiwork. For fence, store and board signs he evidently believes in black background and white for letters. He also uses tin signs tacked on trees, the background being yellow and the lettering black. Here are some of the Dougherty signs which he who runs (or rides) may read: "Trade with Dougherty, the Drug Man," "Dougherty's Drug Store" and the above with the addition "Honest Goods"; "Trade with the People—Dougherty's Drug Store"; "Dougherty's Up-to-Date Store"; "Dougherty for Low Prices"; "Dougherty, the Leading Drug Man"; "Bath's Leading Druggist, Dougherty," with the Hub baseball localism, "'Nuf ced." Upon some of the small wooden signs used by Mr. Dougherty a small mortar and pestle are painted, and these read: "Dougherty Prescriptions Carefully Compounded." A. Hallet & Co. also use roadway signs to a marked extent. They choose blue and white for colors and the mortar and pestle figure extensively in their signs. One sign reads: "A Hallet & Co., Bath Maine. Everything the latest. Patent Medicines." Another states: "Graduates in Pharmacy,

A. Hallet & Co." One sign was a round wooden affair, with the inevitable blue background and white letters.

Swett & Co. is another firm using this idea and some of the signs are of the shape of a large wooden mortar. This appears upon one: "Swett & Co., Prescriptions, Books and Stationery."

Webber, also of Bath, is not wholly devoted to inconspicuousness, for as the car dashed down a slope it was noticed that the green of the opposite hillside was disturbed by a dash of brown which bore the information that there were "Drugs at Webber's, 94 Front Street, Bath, Maine."

The extent to which this method of advertising is carried is no doubt due to the advent of electricity as a means of locomotion, which with the frequent trips and low fares makes the city easily and cheaply accessible to the country resident, thereby greatly increasing the population from which the druggists can draw revenue.

THE SIGNS OF BATH.

Bath has a population of approximately 10,000. One of the first stores noted on Front street was that of Leonard & Mitchell, "pharmacists." Swett & Co., "drugs and medicines," were nearby. This store bore an abundance of yellow and black signs and an attempt was being made to push sales of soda water and root beer. Before one window a sidewalk display of periodicals was being made. Attention is directed to another store by a marble slab in the brick sidewalk, in which is chiseled "A. Hallet & Co., Pharmacy." The proprietor of this establishment is F. C. Cox, Ph.G. (M. C. P., '89), and one of his clerks is the genial W. C. Temple, an M. C. P. student of a few years ago. "John D. Foster & Co.," "Foster's Drug Store; Prescriptions Accurately Dispensed," are signs to be noted on another store. "Anderson's Drug Store" has the "Agency for Huyler's Chocolates and Bon-Bons." Webber's drug store is another establishment also on Front street. At Webber's drug store a drive on cigars, tobacco and patents was being made. That of David T. Dougherty is on one of the principal streets running back from the Kennebec. Mr. Dougherty is a Ph.G. of the M. C. P. brand. On his store appears "Prescription Pharmacist and Drugman." He was featuring his soda drinks by attractive fountain signs.

The window displays were characterized by sameness and an absence of anything unique. Package cigars and patent medicines were predominating features. A window of one store was devoted to an exhibit from a correspondence school. The window shows did not keep pace with the roadside energy above noted.

Severe Examinations.

We have had some complaints from different sections of the State, says the *Midland Druggist*, in regard to the rigid examinations of the State Board of Pharmacy. At the last examination of the Ohio board, out of a class of 113 applicants only 10 were granted certificates. The burden of the complaint from the trade is that their apprentices are becoming discouraged because of their failure to pass the examinations and are quitting the business, and that such severe tests are not any more necessary now than 5, 10 or 15 years ago.

Without any wish to criticise our friends we are compelled to take exception to this statement. It is the consensus of opinion that no art, trade or profession has taken greater strides forward or been more thoroughly revolutionized than has that of pharmacy during the last 12 or 15 years—and the end is not yet.

With these changes in the very life of the profession has come the necessity for higher standards in the laws regulating the practice of pharmacy, and what is more important, higher standards of education. So keenly has this necessity been felt that a prerequisite law has been passed in several States, the general requirements have been raised in many others, and still others are contemplating similar steps in the near future.

If the profession demands a higher education, how can the result be secured other than by raising the entrance requirements of colleges and State boards? How could the State boards show that their applicants possessed the necessary qualifications in any other way than by a rigid test?

Perhaps the greatest change has taken place in the chemistry of our pharmaceuticals, and this branch seems to be the stumbling block of the applicant in his examinations. The average druggist may say that advanced chemistry is not necessary in the drug store now, since the larger proportion of drugs and chemicals come into the drug store ready for the prescription. This is all true enough so far as the manufacture of the chemicals is concerned, but if the clerk has not the necessary qualifications to understand the chemistry of these various preparations is he competent to fill a physician's prescription for them? Is he to be trusted to do the compounding—avoiding incompatibles—and to correct the errors likely to creep into the busy physician's prescription? Were these examinations made lax or the method of grading less careful and the country flooded with a lot of incompetent clerks the first to decry such a state of affairs would be the proprietors of retail drug stores.

It is true the securing of competent clerks in this State has become very difficult. The really competent men are being retained in their present positions by more attractive salaries, and with the number of registered men not located actually less than formerly it simply leaves the proprietor to employ assistants and apprentices, many of whom are neither morally nor mentally fit for the business.

If the advanced requirements of State boards and colleges can be made the means for weeding out such men from the profession and the interval of a year or two can be tided over until the colleges can turn out the requisite number of men fully competent to pass the rigid examinations of State boards the reformation of another side of the business will have been completed.

DR. ALEXANDER TSCHIRCH,

Vice-President of the Swiss Pharmacopœia Revision Committee.

Dr. Tschirch, whose scholarly work on the medicinal and economic plants of India is well-known to pharmacognoscists, delivered an address on "The Pharmacopœia as the Mirror of Its Time" at the last meeting of the Swiss Apothecaries' Society, and in sending a copy of it to the AMERICAN DRUGGIST he inclosed a recent portrait of himself, which we have pleasure in reproducing herewith for the benefit of the many admirers of his work in the ranks of pharmacy.

New Year's Luncheon at the New York Drug and Chemical Club.—The Western Wing.

New Year's Luncheon at the New York Drug and Chemical Club.—The Southern Wing.

David E. Green Goes with Seabury & Johnson.

It was rumored in the drug market last week that S. H. Black, of Bauer & Black, had left Chicago and formed a connection with the firm of Seabury & Johnson and that David E. Green, jr., a son-in-law of Mr. Seabury, was to assume the general management of the firm with the opening of the year.

When George J. Seabury was seen by a representative of the AMERICAN DRUGGIST in regard to this rumor he denied that Mr. Black was to join the firm, branding it as a falsehood. "Not while I have anything to say in the matter," he added, bringing his jaws together with a snap in his emphatic way. As to Mr. Green, Mr. Seabury said that he had been contemplating taking on Mr. Green in some administrative capacity for some time past, but there were obstacles in the way. "While Mr. Green's father was alive I counseled him to stick to the gum business and assist his father in its management," said Mr. Seabury, "and now that his father is dead and it has been decided to discontinue the gum business he is free to come with us as a member of the managing staff under my direction." Mr. Seabury said that additional help was needed in the office as the business was constantly expanding and several of the staff had been overworked of late.

An Almond Trust.

The United States Consul at Malaga, Spain, reports that a syndicate which will probably control the almond market has been formed by the seven principal Malaga exporters. The syndicate will have to do only with the purchase of the almonds from the growing districts and will not intervene with respect to the ultimate sales to European and American buyers. Each local exporting house will retain its identity and business will be conducted along lines followed in past seasons. The purpose of the trust is to reduce first-cost prices and to eradicate certain alleged abuses heretofore practised by local speculators and brokers.

What It Was They Heard.

On a recent visit to Baltimore, Bishop Rowe of Alaska told the following good story: "I had recently to make a visit to a tribe of Indians far from the places where the white men go. Only a very few of the tribe had ever seen white men. One of the members of our party had with him a phonograph. He thought it would amuse the Indians, and so brought it out. They gathered around it in wonder, and spent some time looking at it from every direction. At last the old chief got down on his knees and peered into it. He raised himself, threw his arm out with a sweeping gesture and said, 'Ugh! canned white man.'"—*Harper's Magazine.*

The Farewell Banquet of the Drug Club.

The final festival occasion of the Drug Club—or more accurately speaking the Drug and Chemical Club—in its old quarters took the form of a special luncheon on Saturday, December 30. The rooms were appropriately decorated with Christmas greens and were filled to overflowing with members who enjoyed thoroughly the excellent music, which was furnished by a Mexican orchestra, as well as the luncheon itself. After luncheon a very interesting vaudeville entertainment was given on a temporary stage, erected in a room adjoining the Drug Club in the new building. The prospects of the club are brighter than ever, and it is expected when it moves into its new quarters, which will be much more commodious than those now occupied, the rooms will be quite as well filled as at present. The members of the Entertainment Committee are to be congratulated upon the eminent success of the last function of the club in its old quarters. We present herewith two views of the members at luncheon.

DIED.

CALKINS.—In Elmira, N. Y., on Tuesday, December 12, William H. Calkins, in the seventy-first year of his age.

DRUMMOND.—In Massies Mill, Va., on Wednesday, December 20, D. Aubrey Drummond, in the thirty-sixth year of his age.

DWYER.—In Ansonia, Conn., on Sunday, December 24, Edward J. Dwyer.

GRIFFITH.—In Oil City, Pa., on Tuesday, December 26, Frederick T. Griffith, in the thirty-ninth year of his age.

PROUT.—In New Orleans, La., on Wednesday, December 20, Dr. William David Prout, in the eighty-fourth year of his age.

SANDT.—In Martin's Creek, Pa., on Saturday, December 23, Warren Sandt, in the thirtieth year of his age.

SMITH.—In Easthampton, Mass., on Friday, December 22, Charles J. Smith, in the seventy-first year of his age.

STORIE.—In Dayton, Tenn., on Sunday, December 17, John M. Storie, in the thirty-ninth year of his age.

J. B. KENNARD.

J. B. Kennard, one of the oldest and most popular pharmacists in South Baltimore, Md., was stricken with paralysis on November 24 and died December 3 at his home, 1137 Light street. He was found lying on the floor in a semiconscious condition by a patron and did not fully regain his senses. Mr. Kennard was born in Delaware, but had lived in this city nearly 50 years. The drug store at the address given had been conducted by him for about 25 years. At the beginning of the Civil War he offered his services as a pharmacist to the Confederate army and served through the conflict. It is said that during the last three years of his life he never left the store for any purpose except to enter the dwelling part of the house. He was especially popular with the children of the neighborhood. His second wife and three children by the first survive.

HERMAN BEHRENS.

Herman Behrens, president of the Behrens Drug Company, Waco, Texas, died in that city December 17, after a short illness. He was born in Germany in 1852 and was thus in the fifty-fourth year of his age. He was connected with the drug business in Paris, Texas, for several years before he removed to Waco. In Waco he formed a partnership with a Mr. Moser, the firm name being Behrens & Moser. The Behrens Drug Company was formed in 1891 and Mr. Behrens was made president, an office which he held up to the time of his death. The deceased is survived by his wife and daughter, an aged mother and two brothers and one sister who make their home in Germany.

Greater New York News.

Ira M. Clark, the local representative of the Paris Medicine Company, has returned to New York after a visit to headquarters in St. Louis. Mr. Clark is stopping at the Herald Square Hotel.

J. I. Maggio, Phar.D., has purchased the pharmacy at 507 Spring street, West Hoboken, N. J., and will conduct it as the Red Cross Drug Store. The store has been entirely restocked and it is Dr. Maggio's intention to cultivate a prescription trade especially, though he is alive to the advertising value of staple articles and advertises these at low figures.

F. W. Fink, formerly a partner in the firm of Lehn & Fink, this city, spent a few days in New York last week. On Wednesday, January 3, he made a final trip to the West to settle his business affairs there preparatory to removing East again. Mr. Fink intends to take up his residence in New York as soon as he is able to dispose of his business interests in Wisconsin.

The pharmacy of I. Leaf, at 449 Nepperhan avenue, Yonkers, N. Y., has passed into the possession of Robert Jacobson, who has had charge of the prescription department of the Liberty Pharmacy in Yonkers for several years past. Mr. Jacobson has put in a new stock of drugs and chemicals and made a number of other improvements calculated to make his pharmacy a popular one.

An important meeting of the Westchester County Pharmaceutical Association is scheduled to take place Wednesday, January 10. The headquarters of this association are in Yonkers and it is here that the meeting will be held. Some startling developments are expected. It is announced quietly that the members of the eastern branch of the State Board of Pharmacy have been invited to attend the meeting and explain some actions of theirs to which the druggists of Westchester County have taken exception.

Dr. R. G. Eccles, accompanied by his wife, expects to start in July for two tours around the world. The first takes in Manchuria, Japan, Corea, China, Philippine Islands, Siam, Burmah, India, Ceylon, Egypt, Holy Land, Turkey, Greece, Morocco, Spain and Portugal, to Great Britain, where he will arrive in July, 1907. From a point in the British Isles he will make his start for his second tour, which takes in Central Africa, Australia, New Zealand, Van Dieman's Land and South America. He will return to New York July, 1908.

A meeting of the General Committee of the Metropolitan Association of Retail Druggists will be held this evening at the College of Pharmacy, 115 West Sixty-eighth street. This committee is composed of the New York district leaders in the N. A. R. D. organization and the meeting is preliminary to the annual meeting of the association, which takes place next Friday. At this meeting officers will be elected for the ensuing year and considerable business of direct importance to the retail druggists of New York will be transacted. A cordial invitation has been extended to the members of the local associations and the trade generally to attend, and it is hoped the meeting will be a large and enthusiastic one.

Lehn & Fink to Build.

Lehn & Fink, wholesale druggists and manufacturing chemists, 120 William street, New York, have been compelled, by increasing business, to secure additional premises to serve as a laboratory and drug mill, and a plot of ground has been secured on Irving street, between Columbus and Van Brunt avenues, South Brooklyn, on which a warehouse and factory of fireproof construction with modern equipment will be erected. The removal of the laboratory from William street will give the firm increased warehouse facilities there and afford increased room for the different departments. The new buildings will comprise one of 4 stories for the manufacture of chemicals and pharmaceuticals, one of 2 stories to contain the engines, boilers, dynamos and drug mills and a third building of 4 stories to accommodate the perfumery department, packing rooms, storage, etc. The factory will be convenient and easily accessible to the wharfs and steamship lines, as it is situated midway between South Ferry and Hamilton Ferry, about a block from the New York Dock Company's terminal.

"Syd." Carragan Guest of Honor.

Sydney H. Carragan, manager of the traveling force of the Eastern branch of Parke, Davis & Co., was the guest of honor at a dinner party the Saturday before Christmas at which he was presented with a handsome scarf pin consisting of an Oriental pearl surrounded with diamonds. The affair came off at the New York Drug and Chemical Club and the presentation speech was made by W. P. Rich, one of the firm's New Jersey representatives, who lauded Mr. Carragan in the most eloquent terms. Frank Cuddy, one of the New York City representatives, acted as toastmaster and he made so many humorous allusions as to disconcert Mr. Rich, who forgot the lines of his presentation speech in laughing at Mr. Cuddy's

Sydney H. Carragan at His Desk.

sallies. Mr. Carragan had arranged to leave for his former home in Saratoga on the 3.40 o'clock train the same afternoon, but the dinner was prolonged until 6 o'clock and it was twenty-four hours later before he could get away. Mr. Carragan is keeping bachelor hall at present with one of his sons, as Mrs. Carragan is enjoying herself in Europe. She started on the return voyage on January 3, sailing in the S. S. Baltic of the White Star line. During her stay abroad she visited the British Isles and the Continent of Europe, spending the last fortnight very pleasantly in Paris.

OHIO.

A Substantial Business Doing in Holiday Goods—The New U. S. P. and the State Laws—A Successful Woman Pharmacist.

(From our Regular Correspondent.)

Cleveland, January 5.—Retail druggists in this city have been doing a good holiday business and believe the next three weeks will be busy ones. There is an exceptionally good demand for novelties and all the goods which drug houses carry for the holiday trade. This applies to stores in the residence district as well as those in the downtown section. In the regular drug line they report conditions good in every way. While there has not been an abnormal amount of sickness in the city the fall weather, with all its changes, has made a good sale for drugs. Patents are doing very well and the prescription business is very satisfactory.

That druggists in the smaller towns of the State are doing well is attested by the liberal orders received at the wholesale houses. So far as the holiday goods go these are largely filling in, but in the regular trade the demand has been good. It is believed that the aggregate of business transacted over the territory covered from Cleveland will be larger than a year ago, although that was considered a good year.

A WOMAN PHARMACIST.

The Standard Drug Company some time ago published a picture of Miss M. Louise Carroll, their pharmacist, in the store in the Schofield Building, with an article regarding rarity of women pharmacists. Miss Carroll graduated at the Cleveland School of Pharmacy in the class of 1896, and has had several years' practical experience. Miss Carroll's presence as a prescription pharmacist is said to have attracted much business to the new store.

OHIO NEWS NOTES.

A. F. Conrad has purchased the Woodland Park Pharmacy, 1007 Kinsman street, this city.

W. H. Tissot, formerly of Wellington, has succeeded E. C. Linden at the corner of Balton avenue and Prospect street.

Isa Leist, formerly of Napoleon, Ohio, has purchased the store of G. W. Glines on Franklin Circle.

J. P. Emrich, a druggist at Nottingham, just east of Cleveland, has been elected Mayor of the village.

The Owl Drug Company, of Defiance, has been incorporated with a capital stock of $10,000 by W. S. Shelly, R. W. Wortman, S. F. Shelly, C. M. Harrison and H. R. Dithner.

The Gleim & Selzer Drug Company, of Cleveland, has been incorporated by John C. Gleim, Eugene R. Selzer, Calvin Haas, H. A. Beckett and L. M. McGrath, to take over the business of the firm of Gleim & Selzer, who owned a store on the Public Square and one on Superior street. The capital stock is $40,000.

North Carolina Board of Pharmacy.

At a meeting of the North Carolina Board of Pharmacy, held in Raleigh, November 21, 1905, the following named candidates for license to practice pharmacy passed successful examinations: H. M. Bell, Windsor; Warren H. Biggs, Williamston; M. N. Bogart, Washington; Walter Buhmann, Greensboro; J. E. Burton, High Point; E. S. Cook, Goldsboro; J. S. Hall, Fayetteville; S. P. Fletcher, Harrisonburg, Va.; H. M. Harper, Richmond, Va.; A. K. Hardee, Benson; W. A. Jetton, Davidson; Dr. A. A. Kent, Lenoir; T. G. Levister, Raleigh; G. F. McGee, Greensboro; J. M. Monger, Sanford; E. G. Mullen, Charlotte; L. G. O'Brien, Winston; R. H. Parker, Durham; E. F. Redding, Asheboro; C. A. Ring, High Point; R. B. Suggs, Belmont; J. N. Thomas, Warrenton; F. L. White, Mebane; J. H. Eaton (colored), Winston; F. W. McNair (colored), Greensboro.

The next meeting of the board will be held at Wrightsville, June 12, 1906, at 9 A. M.

Indicative Faces.

Physiognomists are agreed that where affections of the brain exist the upper third of the face is altered in appearance, in diseases of the chest the middle third, in diseases of the abdominal region the lower third.

WESTERN NEW YORK.

Business for the Holidays Satisfactory—Buffalo College to Drop Age Limit for Graduates—Expansion of the Drug Merchants' Exchange—Depressing Effects of Good Weather.

(From our Regular Correspondent.)

Buffalo, January 5.—The holiday season was as kind to the Buffalo retail druggist as it has been of late. The big trade in specialties not drugs that used to be a great part of the business of the end of the year, is no longer looked for, so nobody is disappointed. There is always an increase of the sale of perfumes, candies and the like, and that is about the extent of the holiday trade since the major portion of it was snatched away from the druggist by the department store a dozen or more years ago. The year has been a fair one, better than the year before, and the promise is of some further improvement the present year, if only because the price cutter is not raging at present and promises to remain quiet for a while. As a rule the legitimate trade of the druggist is increasing, not because there is more sickness, but—except with the poor, who can go to the dispensary—medicines, especially of a certain sort, are something of a luxury and so regarded.

DO NOT NEGLECT THE SHOW WINDOW.

The calculating druggist is always a man of whom the trade can learn something. One of the Buffalo retailers who always knows at the end of the month how many prescriptions he has made up and how much has been sold generally and tries to learn the reason for any increase or falling off, said the other day that he was at a loss to know why a neighbor retailer of his never made any use of his windows for display. The store was on a corner and well situated for anything of the sort, yet the windows were made a mere catch-all for this or that. "My window space is small," said he, "and yet we lately made a display of cough drops in one window and in three days sold 200 quarter-pound packages of them, not to mention a stack of 5-cent chocolates which were put in there also." The retail druggist in a big city is very much circumscribed, but he is not entirely shut away from the streets, and his grasp of the whole situation ought to be complete.

AGE LIMIT ON GRADUATION MAY BE DROPPED.

The Buffalo College of Pharmacy is on the point of dropping the age limit in the matter of graduation. It was borrowed from the medical colleges, apparently, and there was once a good reason for it, as a diploma was all that was required to practice, but now the State requires a further examination in each case and fixes the age limit itself, so there is no need of the college withholding a diploma any longer. The authorities are agreed that it is useless.

DRUG MERCHANTS' EXCHANGE DEVELOPING A BIG BUSINESS.

The Buffalo Drug Merchants' Exchange has been called together to provide an increase of capital, which means that there are more druggists seeking membership with no stock to turn over to them. The plan makes every member a stockholder, and forbids the sale of the individual stock to any but the company. In case a member withdraws from the company, dies or goes out of business, his stock is at once bought by the company. Nobody is eligible to membership but retail druggists, and even these are ruled out if they do a jobbing business also. The company has been so successful that it has brought practically all the Buffalo retailers into line, besides quite a good many outside of the city. The capital stock has been only $15,000, but will probably be doubled now. This very modest beginning has surprised everybody by its capacity for growth, and the members now see in it the nucleus of a big jobbing house under a reorganization and ample stock in the not very distant future. Before this can be done the plan of operation will have to be changed, especially as no sales are now made to nonmembers. Buffalo has not been successful in its effort to multiply wholesale drug stores, and this may be the way of doing it.

GOOD WEATHER A BAD THING—FOR SOME.

It is odd that there should be so much difference in the drug business owing to mere locality in a single town. The outlying member of the trade is now complaining that the weather was too good through the holidays, so that the people all went down for everything, buying their drugs and medicines with the rest. The single-line dealers, as the outlying druggists call themselves, always suffer whenever there is an even chance of getting into the big stores, but let the weather turn hot or stormy and the thin wall thus built up between the center and the suburbs is very plainly visible.

THE BUFFALO DRUGGISTS' BOWLING CLUB

is still meeting with unusual success, but the word is that there is plenty of enjoyment at home yet, and no effort has been made to try titles with any other clubs. One member says that the boys have not got their eye on the alley yet, as they should to make it easy for them to down other bowlers, so they will spend some time yet getting into form. They usually come out ahead when they get ready to play.

THE NATIONAL CIGAR STANDS COMPANY.

The Buffalo retail druggists are considerably interested in the effort of the National Cigar Stands Company to establish itself in the city. The cigar cases are distributed by the Cahoon-Lyon Drug Company, which is said to be interested in the company. There is some difference of opinion as to the propriety of going into the plan, but those who are against it are merely wondering if the distributers, who are in the downtown cut-price district, are likely to devise anything that will benefit the rest of the trade. To this it is remarked that the test of the pudding is in the eating. A dinner was given to the retail druggists a short time ago, and of the 40 guests present all who expressed an opinion spoke in favor of the plan. One good point about it is that the cases will not be given to any one out of the drug trade.

SHORT WESTERN NEW YORK DRUG NOTES.

R. K. Smither is fitting up his new drug store on upper Main street, Buffalo, and will soon be in occupation. Everybody says that it is going to be a fine store, and will line up well with his two others in the city.

Horace P. Hayes, since selling his Main street drug store in Buffalo, has gone to the Isle of Pines to look after his property there. It was his company that precipitated Government action turning the island over to Cuba, much to the harm of the company's interests.

E. W. Brainerd, of South Park avenue, Buffalo, has sold his drug store to Chauncey Terwilliger, a licensed pharmacist, who has been for some time in Government employ in Panama, and before that time was at the Craig Colony at Sonyea, N. Y.

J. H. Hilligas, who has two drug stores in the Elmwood avenue district of Buffalo, has sold the one at the Potomac avenue corner to M. E. Lipman, a graduate of the Philadelphia College of Pharmacy, who formerly traveled for Meinecke & Co.

The traveling drug salesman is for the moment a pretty nearly minus quantity, as he is home eating turkey and resuming his acquaintance with his family. Some Buffalo retail druggists report that they have not seen any of the fraternity for weeks. A good year to them when they resume their travels.

BUFFALO DRUGGISTS' CHANGES.

Fire in the Carmichael flats on the 16th threatened the Rano drug store, but was put out before it was reached.

Charles de Chiara, druggist on the Terrace, is opening a second store on Canal street, in the Italian district also.

There are to be two new drug stores on the corner of Delaware avenue and Chippewa street. Some time ago Harry Wise, who keeps a restaurant on one corner, announced that a stock of drugs would be put in soon, and now C. E. Clark, the Clinton street druggist, has rented the opposite corner.

W. C. Dambach, for a long time occupying the upper end of the downtown trade district, being obliged to move next spring on account of the store being made part of a bank, has bought the store of H. P. Hayes, ½ mile further up the street, and is already in possession. Mr. Hayes still has two stores on the lower East Side.

NEW ENGLAND.

Improved Conditions in Bay State Pharmacy—Reciprocity and Registration—Full Drug Stocks Carried by Grocers—Annual Report of the Board of Pharmacy—Members' Night at the Boston Association—Unexpected Results of the Enforcemen of the Screen Law.

(From our Regular Correspondent.)

Boston, January 3.—The twentieth annual report of the Board of Pharmacy, just issued, contains recommendations of importance. The board finds evidence of improvement in the practice of pharmacy in this State and asserts that candidates are giving more attention to the study of the subject and that a larger percentage is successful from the examination standpoint.

RECIPROCAL REGISTRATION PROPOSED.

They recommend that the law be so changed that certificates from other States may be accepted as evidence of qualification to practice pharmacy in this commonwealth, providing that in the examination of the applicant he received 5 per cent. more than the minimum per cent. required here. The section dealing with co-partnership has been found unsatisfactory and the board's desire is to have this feature so changed that a registered pharmacist should have at least an unincumbered financial interest of $500 in a co-partnership with persons not registered pharmacists. The 15 day limitation, after which complaints cannot be made to the board against druggists alleged to have violated the law, is deemed an unwise limitation. The board suggests the removal of this time limit so that complaint may be made after conviction by a court of competent jurisdiction.

A CLEAR DEFINITION OF THE TERM "DOMESTIC REMEDIES" NEEDED.

It has been found that many grocers carry an assortment of drugs which would favorably compare with that of some drug stores and a close legal definition of what constitutes "non-poisonous domestic remedies" is recommended. The poison law and care of purity of drugs, now in charge of the Board of Health, should come under the jurisdiction of the Board of Pharmacy.

They also make a plea for an increase in salary, stating that the salaries now received do not pay for the extra clerks employed in the stores while the employers are attending to State business.

Regret is expressed for the resignation during the year of President George M. Hoyt, and congratulations for the quick filling of the vacancy by the choice of Charles F. Ripley, of Taunton.

There are 1,515 stores in the State. There were 27 stores closed during the year, 24 druggists convicted in court, one found not guilty, one imprisoned and $675 in fines imposed.

MEMBERS' NIGHT AT THE BOSTON ASSOCIATION.

The December meeting of the Boston Druggists' Association was held at Young's Hotel on the 26th inst. It was announced as "members' night" and the speaker of the evening was William W. Bartlet, Ph.G. His topic was "A Trip to the Pacific Coast." He described the homes of the prehistoric Cliff Dwellers of southern Colorado, and exhibited photographs and pottery specimens. He charmed his hearers with the verbal description of the trip from the Atlantic to the Pacific and was given much applause and a vote of thanks. Arrangements for the annual dinner will be made by a committee consisting of the president, treasurer and secretary. A committee on nomination of officers was appointed as follows: Charles F. Cutler, William F. Sawyer and Joel S. Orne. President Flynn began preparations at once for the meeting of this month and all indications point to its being a history making gathering.

THE SCREEN LAW AS APPLIED TO DRUG STORES.

Much dissatisfaction has been expressed over the enforcement or interpretation recently placed upon the screen law in its application to the drug trade and from the discussion which it has entailed it is certain that some attempt will be made at the coming legislative session to either bring about its repeal or modify its provisions so that at least the displaying of goods in a drug store window will not be deemed a law-breaking act. Nearly 20 Hub druggists surrendered their licenses rather than remove their goods from their windows. This act in itself cannot fail to have beneficial influence upon public sentiment outside of the question in point, for it has proved a complete boomerang to those carping laymen whose creed was that all drug stores to succeed must sell liquor. With this idea in the minds of many it can be readily seen that the giving up of the licenses was the cause of much discussion. In fact it proved a sensation not secondary to the preliminary rumor of the up-to-date manner in which it was said, and now proved, that the authorities were to read this section.

GOOD FELLOWSHIP REIGNED.

Thirty officers and salesmen attended a dinner, held by manufacturers of soda fountain supplies on December 29, at the American House. J. W. Moore presided, and speeches were made by J. W. Moore, M. E. Murray, F. L. Miller, A. R. Curtice and George F. Claridge. Good fellowship was the spirit of the occasion. The speakers touched informally on business conditions, salesmanship, fair competition and the history of soda water.

CANADIAN NEWS NOTES.

(*From our Regular Correspondent.*)

The monthly report of the Canadian Department of Trade and Commerce for September, 1905, just issued, shows the value of drugs, dyes, chemicals and medicines imported for home consumption to be $461,638, as compared with $436,423 in September, 1904. Importations from the United States were $263,906 in September, 1905, as against $262,816 in the corresponding month of 1904. Exports of drugs, dyes, chemicals and medicines of home produce amounted to $78,986, of which $59,821 went to the United States, as against total shipments of $70,757 and American shipments of $38,582 in September, 1904.

The Eastern Drug Company has been incorporated with head office at Montreal and a capital of $75,000, the incorporators being Fabian Duffy, Louis Gosselin, Thomas J. Coulter, James Trickey and George Boon.

D. H. Ross, Canadian commercial agent for Australia, reports to the Department of Trade and Commerce concerning eucalyptus oil, which has an increasing popularity as a household remedy for rheumatism, pulmonary troubles, etc., and an embrocation for muscular complaints. The volume of trade is comparatively small as yet but it is increasing, and when its value is more generally known a considerably greater demand must result. Mr. Ross believes that it would be a profitable line for the wholesale drug trade in Canada to investigate, particularly in the better qualities, and that an extensive introduction of eucalyptus oil would result in a satisfactory business.

At the sittings of the Canadian Tariff Commission, at Quebec, on December 28, the Paint and Varnish Association asked for the imposition of a duty of 30 per cent. on paints, equivalent to the duty on white lead.

The drug store of F. P. Reynolds, St. Thomas, Ont., was entered by burglars on the night of December 21 and a large number of articles stolen.

A fire occurred in the Standard Chemical Works, Deseronto, Ont., on December 27, owing to the ignition of waste gasoline, which spread to the acetate room. Though the flames had made considerable headway they were got under control by the fire department with comparatively small loss.

The license inspector of Winnipeg has been instructed to prosecute any druggist found retailing goods other than drugs after 6 o'clock p.m., except on Saturday.

J. Skeith, druggist, Montreal, has disposed of his business to J. H. Howell.

G. McGillivray, druggist, of Sydney, N. S., is offering to compromise with his creditors at 50 cents on the dollar.

PENNSYLVANIA.

A Good Year's Business Closed—General Cutting Imminent—The Pre-requisite Law Goes Into Force—Plans of the P. A. R. D.

(*From our Regular Correspondent.*)

Philadelphia, January 5.—The wholesale business last year exceeded that of any other period. All the wholesale houses here have had good years and their losses have been comparatively few. Some of them have added greatly to their plants and are now in a position to do a much larger business. There has been a merger of several firms but in almost every case the consolidation has increased the output and made it possible to employ a greater force. During the past year several of the large houses have extended their business into territory which has heretofore been shut to them. The Southern business is larger than ever and Philadelphia drug houses have secured a good foothold in that section of the country. The general prosperity throughout the country has been of great good to all retailers and wholesalers. The improvements made by the retail druggists have been on a larger scale and many of the stores here are considered the finest in the country.

THE RESULT OF THE LODER SUIT

has created considerable uneasiness among the retail druggists in this city. A number of them have begun to mark down proprietary articles to meet the prices made by Loder and it is understood that within the next few weeks the cutting will be general. Several of the large retail druggists are now having a new price list prepared and when they are ready it is said they will show that many goods can be purchased at a much lower figure than is now quoted.

THE GRADUATE REQUIREMENT GOES INTO FORCE.

The new graduate pre-requisite law went into effect on January 1. From now on all applicants for permission to practice the drug profession will have to be graduates of some reputable college of pharmacy. It is believed that this will in a great measure prohibit the acceptance of druggists who have a superficial knowledge of the business and at the same time it will cause a greater number to take a regular pharmacy course in a reputable college. Naturally this law is approved by the Faculty of the College of Pharmacy as this college had considerable to do with getting the measure through the last legislature.

PLANS FOR ACTIVE WORK BY P. A. R. D.

There is to be renewed activity in the Philadelphia Retail Drug Association this year. Plans have been made to make this association more of a power than ever before. The set back given by the Loder decision has only been temporary and the members have flocked around the officers and promised their support, both financial and influential. The case is to be carried to a higher court and the officers believe that the decision of the lower court will be reversed. Every effort is to be made to get the retail druggists who are not members to come into the association and within the next few months it is thought the membership will be greatly increased. The meetings are more largely attended and there is an increased interest taken in the various subjects that are brought up. It is the intention to have some special subject at each meeting so that a free discussion can be indulged in.

PHILADELPHIA NEWS NOTES.

W. E. Kline will open a new store at Fifteenth and Tasker streets. He has handsomely fitted it up and it will be one of the finest in that section of the country.

A new drug store is to be opened at Thirteenth street and Fairmount avenue. This is a new locality and for some time there have been rumors that one would be started up.

On December 29 an explosion occurred in the establishment of Powers & Weightman and as the result Joseph Wilcox was dangerously burned about the face and arms and legs. Several other men were also injured in the explosion. The exact cause for the accident is not known outside of the fact that a carboy of fluid exploded.

THE SOUTH.

Chemists Ask for Tax-Free Alcohol—Good Trade for the Holidays—Turkey for Travelers—Dollar for Every Orphan.

(From our Regular Correspondent.)

New Orleans, La., January 2, 1906.—An important step was taken yesterday by the Bureau of Chemistry in the American Association of Science, in session in this city, when a resolution was unanimously adopted calling for the abolition of the tax on alcohol used in the manufacture of drugs and other necessities. This question has been agitated for some time, and it was the opinion of the members present yesterday when the resolution was adopted that the removal of the tax on ethyl alcohol would be advantageous and of benefit to all concerned. Much discussion was brought out on the question, and the resolution was finally decided upon. This matter is of vital interest to the drug trade because of the large quantity of alcohol used in the manufacture of drugs.

HOLIDAY TRADE GOOD.

The holidays, with their accompanying bustle and rush, have had a good effect on the trade here and in the last few days conditions have been very satisfactory. All of the houses have been carrying on a good holiday business, and in the city and country the indications are that the trade has shaken off the depression which was evident some time ago.

A CHRISTMAS SPREAD.

The usual Christmas spreads to its office forces and traveling men were given last week by Parke, Davis & Co., the big New Orleans branch of the concern presenting its men with a spread which was among the best they had ever sat down to. Wednesday night the office force, both young women and men, were entertained in the big offices in Camp street, and there were given all kinds of good things. Mr. Steiner, the able manager, ably acquitted himself as a host, and made the evening very pleasant for his subordinates.

TRAVELERS DINE AND TALK.

The following night the travelers were gathered at the Hotel de la Louisiane, and there ate, drank and made merry until the early morning hours. The *menu* was excellent, and the food and wine were enjoyed to the fullest extent. S. G. Steiner, the manager of the New Orleans branch, was called upon to answer the toast, "Our Representatives," and in doing so complimented the men on their excellent work during the year. He hoped they would do as well during the 12 months to come. Others who answered toasts were: "Louisiana," E. W. Gitskey; "The New Orleans Branch," Dr. S. S. Coleman; "Mississippi," W. R. Ellis; "Our Jobbing Friends," Thomas Booth; "Texas," W. N. Forbes; "The Crescent City, the Future Business Center of the United States," A. E. Breslin; "The Medical Profession," W. H. West; "The Ladies," F. T. Glasscock; "Alabama Against the World," B. D. Turner; "Benedicts," F. J. Offer; "Our Future," W. A. Doyle; "Our Past," P. S. Freret; "Our President, Theodore Roosevelt," R. H. Grimes; "Our Retail Friends," W. J. Patterson; "Our House," W. H. Voerg; "Our Dental Friends," C. C. Reeves; "The South, This Fair Land of Ours," Lawton Miller; "The North," Dr. J. M. Vance, and "The Press," Dr. C. V. Unsworth.

THE PARKER-BLAKE COMPANY ENTERTAINS.

Last Thursday night in the big banquet hall of the St. Charles Hotel the Parker-Blake Company, the big wholesale drug house of this city, banqueted its officers, traveling men, city salesmen and office and store forces. All were brought together to have a good time, and they succeeded in doing so. The room was prettily decorated, and everything was as tastefully arranged as could be desired. C. C. Johnston, treasurer of the company, attended to the details of the affair.

S. D. Pursell was made toastmaster, and he called upon J. M. Parker to answer the first toast, which was "To the President of the United States." Arthur D. Parker, president of the Parker-Blake Company, followed, and made a strong plea to his city salesmen to enlist the sympathy of the druggists in the movement to prevent the use of pharmaceutical specialties which interfere with the druggists in conducting their legitimate business. Mr. Parker touched on the good fellowship existing among his employees, and expressed the hope that this condition would continue to prevail. He thanked the men for the work they had done in the year.

Mr. Johnston spoke for the press of the city, and A. P. Irwin, of Clinton, La., spoke for the out-of-town trade. Max Samson was heard from on the local dealers, and W. F. Dent on the drummers. H. C. Mackie and James Cullen also delivered toasts.

The drummers presented resolutions of thanks and appreciation to the firm for treatment accorded them in the year.

The officers of the company follow: A. D. Parker, president; John M. Parker, vice-president; Percy H. Brown, secretary; C. C. Johnston, treasurer.

THE WEST.

Operations of the Chicago Drug Syndicate—One Hundred Stores Under One Head—Promoter Joins the C. R. D. A. and Promises Price Protection—To Do Its Own Jobbing.

(From our Regular Correspondent.)

Chicago, January 4.—The operations of the new syndicate which has started out to buy 100 drug stores in Chicago are attracting much attention. The syndicate is being operated by Marcus Pollasky, a former corporation attorney, who has opened an office at 55 South Water street, in the same building where the distributing office of the United Cigar Stores is located. President Avery, of the C. R. D. A., says that Mr. Pollasky is for price protection and organization and that he will work in harmony with the C. R. D. A. Mr. Pollasky has joined the association and has paid his dues. In an interview the promoter said that he did not intend to cut prices and that it was on that account he bought no stores inside "the loop." The following bit of philosophy is credited to Mr. Polalsky: "There is money in the drug business or there wouldn't be so many in it." He has evidently found some who are willing to get out of it, for he has bought the following stores already: R. E. Rhode, 504 North Clark street; Aldine Pharmacy, 3645 Cottage Grove avenue; Fred. A. Thayer, 572 West Madison; E. von Herman, 226 Thirty-first street; Henson & King, 3654 Cottage Grove avenue; Edward T. Richards, 2300 Cottage Grove avenue; Herman Fry, 1100 North Halsted street; H. Foersterling, 396 Wells street; Joseph F. Forbrich, 301 Thirty-fifth street. Of course such extensive operations have stirred up the local trade. The promoters take the view that they can buy in large quantities, discount the bills and obtain the best prices. The syndicate will have a wholesale establishment of its own at 55-57 South Water street. This will be used as a sore of clearing house, from which the big chain of stores in all sections of the city will be supplied. There is some skepticism in regard to the successful issue of the plan for operating of drug stores through managers has not invariably proved profitable. Mr. Pollasky says that great attention will be paid to neatness, order and high-class fixtures. The Ideal Drug Company is the name of the corporation and each store is to bear the same title.

CHICAGO NOTES.

The Board of Pharmacy will meet in Chicago on January 16.

Alex. Harris has been chosen as one of the board of directors of the new Bank of America, in which a large number of druggists are interested. The bank is now open for business.

A lecture on "The N. A. R. D., Its Past, Present and Future," was delivered before the senior class of the Chicago College of Pharmacy recently by Major P. E. Holp.

William J. Smith, who was a confidential bookkeeper for the Robert Stevenson Drug Company for 12 years, has been arrested on a charge of forgery. Smith admits having taken in the neighborhood of $3,000, which he says went to loan sharks. Smith made it a practice to borrow on his salary and then says he plundered from his employers in order to prevent being garnisheed. George E. Krolage, who formerly worked for the same firm, was sentenced to Joliet not long ago on a similar charge.

The Drug and Chemical Market

The prices quoted in this report are those current in the wholesale market, and higher prices are paid for retail lots. The quality of goods frequently necessitates a wide range of prices.

Condition of Trade.

NEW YORK, January 6, 1906.

The demand for drugs and chemicals fell off slightly the past fortnight, the situation being dominated by conditions always felt at the holiday season. Some improvement in demand became manifest toward the close of last week and dealers are anticipating an increase in the volume of business as the month progresses, cheerful expressions being heard on all sides relative to the trade prospects. As for the year just closed its record has been a peculiarly satisfactory one and jobbers and importers unite in satisfactory references to the large volume of profitable business which was transacted. Regarding prices, there is a generally firm feeling, though several important declines have been announced, alcohol being fractionally lower and iodine preparations marking a much sharper decline. Refiners have again marked up the price of camphor and acetanilid is dearer. Among other important price changes is an advance in manufacturers' quotations on castor oil. The principal fluctuations of the period under review are tabulated below:

HIGHER:	LOWER:
Camphor,	Alcohol,
Acetanilid,	Opium,
Lemon oil,	Iodine preparations,
Orange oil,	Lycopodium,
Styrax,	Prickly ash bark,
Castor oil,	White pine bark,
White arsenic,	Citronella oil,
Chinese cantharides,	Bleached calamus root.
Pink root,	
Squill root,	
Orris root, Florentine,	
Blue vitriol.	

Drugs.

Acetanilid has been advanced by the manufacturers owing to the higher cost of crude material and the new range is 23c to 24c.

Alcohol is lower in sympathy with freer offerings in the West, and producers now quote on the basis of $2.49 to $2.51 for grain, the usual rebate being allowed. (Readers are kindly asked to make this correction in Original Package Prices.)

Amyl acetate is held with increased firmness owing to scarcity of crude material both here and abroad, and manufacturers now quote at an advance to $1.25 to $1.50 as to quantity and quality.

Balm of Gilead buds are easier owing to offerings of new crop, and sales on spot are making at 38c to 40c.

Balsam copaiba, Central American, is selling fairly in small lots at steady prices, or, say, 30c to 31c; Para is held with firmness under the influence of light supplies and 37c to 40c is generally named.

Balsam fir is taken rather sparingly by the trade, but values are firmly maintained at $3.00 to $3.10 for Canada and 70c to 80c for Oregon, as to quality and quantity.

Balsam Peru is dull and the market is well sustained under the influence of light stocks at 37c to 40c.

Balsam tolu is finding a moderate jobbing outlet, but important demand is absent; sales at 21c to 22c.

Barks.—Bayberry is in light supply and wanted, with 13c to 14c named as to holder. Cascara sagrada is without change of consequence either as regards price or demand; holders remain firm in their views at 13c to 14c. Cottonroot is quiet, though holders are firm in their views at 9c to 10c. Cramp is steadily held and supplies are available in a limited way only at 79c. Sassafras is in good seasonable demand and values are steadily maintained at 12c to 15c. White pine offers a shade easier, the revised quotations showing a decline to 4½c to 5c. Wild cherry has been in good seasonable demand and a moderate trade is reported at the ruling quotation of 69c.

Burgundy pitch is held with more firmness and we hear of several large sales at the inside price of 4¼c.

Cacao butter is meeting with a steady inquiry and the limited available supply of Dutch is held at 28½c.

Cantharides, Chinese, are higher owing to diminished supplies and an improved consuming inquiry, with holders holding 55c to 57½c.

Cocaine is in good demand and values are firmer in sympathy with the tenor of advices from abroad regarding the crude material. While $3.25 is yet named for bulk an advance would surprise no one.

Codliver oil is dull and neglected, there being nothing like the usual seasonable demand; some of the more desirable brands are offering at $24.00, without, however, stimulating the demand.

Colocynth apples are quiet, but we have no quotable change in price to report, Trieste being still held at 30c to 32c and Spanish at 25c to 26c, as to quality and quantity.

Cuttlefish bone, Trieste, is finding a moderate jobbing outlet and values are steadily maintained at 16c to 16½c for prime.

Ergot has shown no activity since our last, but prices are nominally steady on the basis of 45c to 50c for either Russian or Spanish.

Haarlem oil is firmer, owing to scarcity and higher import cost; dealers now ask at an advance to $3.25.

Iodine preparations are uniformly lower in consequence of the decline in the cost of crude iodine. The revised range is as follows: Ammonium iodide, $3.45 to $3.50; bismuth subiodide, $3.25; iodine resublimed, $2.70 to $2.75; iodoform, $3.00 to $3.05; iron iodide, $2.50; iron iodide syrup, 20c to 22c; mercury iodide, green, $1.95 to $2.00; mercury iodide, red, $2.20 to $2.25; mercury iodide, yellow, $1.95 to $2.00; potassium iodide, $2.05 to $2.10; sodium iodide, $2.60 to $2.65.

Juniper berries are held with increased confidence, owing to scarcity of supplies, but the demand is limited at the moment, and prices do not vary from 4½c to 4¾c.

Lycopodium is in better supply and this, coupled with a lessened inquiry, has influenced holders to reduce quotations to the range of 54c to 55c.

Menthol is meeting with a limited inquiry only, and holders are seeking to urge the distribution by naming lower prices; cases offer at $2.30, while up to $2.40 is named for broken lots, though most sales are making at $2.35.

Opium has remained dull and values have further weakened, with $3.00 now named as an open quotation for broken cases, while broken lots are obtainable at $3.05. Powdered is held and selling at $3.50 to $3.52½.

Quinine has undergone no change of importance during the interval and the market is dull, with manufacturers quoting on the old basis of 19c for bulk in 100-oz. tins; second hands continue to quote 18c to 18½c for Java and German respectively.

Saffron of the different varieties is maintained in steady position, American being quoted at $1.15 to $1.20 and Valencia and Alicante at $5.00 to $6.00, as to quality.

Senna leaves, Alexandria, continue inquired for, most of the demand being for sifted, which is quoted at 5¾c to 6c.

Chemicals.

Acids, mineral, are irregular and unsettled owing to the disruption of the agreement among manufacturers and the fact that the market at present is an open one; muriatic is quoted at 1¼c to 1¾c; nitric, 4c to 5c, and sulphuric at 1c to 1¾c.

Ammonium muriate is in light supply and values are well sustained at 5⅞c to 6½c for white grain, 6c to 6½c for rough grain and 9¼c to 9¾c for lump.

Arsenic, white, is scarce and wanted, and holders of the limited available supply have marked up the inside price to 5½c.

Blue vitriol is higher in sympathy with the strong position of raw material and manufacturers hold carload lots at 5.90c up to 6¼c being named for lesser quantities.

Citric acid is in moderate demand, with the market firm and sales making at 38c to 38½c, for barrels and kegs respectively.

Epsom salts is generally held at 90c. in carload lots, while sales in jobbing quantities are making at $1.15.

Iodine.—The revised schedule of prices on iodine and its preparations is given in the preceding column under Drugs.

Oxalic acid is held with increased firmness, some dealers having marked up their quotations to 5¼c to 5½c.

Essential Oils.

Anise is in good jobbing request and the market is well sustained at the previous range of $1.30 to $1.35.

Cassia remains quiet but steady at 80c to 85c, for 75 to 80 per cent. oil.

Citronella is a shade easier and spot oil in drums is held and selling at 34c.

Messina essences are held with increased firmness in sympathy with the strong tenor of advices from primary sources of supply, and quotations show an advance of 2½c in lemon and 10c in sweet orange; bergamot is held and selling at $2.15 to $2.30.

Peppermint has ruled quiet in the interval since our last report, buyers appearing to hesitate about stocking up at the present range, though holders remain firm in their views. Bulk is quoted at $2.40 to $2.50 and HGH at $3.10 to $3.15, as to seller and quantity.

Rose is firmer in sympathy with advices from primary markets, and recent sales were at $4.25 to $4.50.

Wintergreen, natural, meets with very little attention, but we hear of occasional sales within the quoted range of $1.65 to $2.00.

Gums.

As told in our review of the Conditions of Trade, refined camphor has marked another advance, the range for barrels and cases now standing at 88c to 88½c, though second hands offer at a fractional reduction. Aloes maintains its steady position, Barbadoes being yet quoted at 14c to 16c, Cape at 8c to 10c and Curacao at 6¼c to 6½c. Benzoin is quiet, but the market appears sustained at 32c to 35c for Sumatra and 40c to $1.00 for Siam. Chicle has regained some of its steadiness, but supplies continue to offer at 35c to 36c.

Roots.

Calamus has sold down to 23c for bleached during the interval and the market is easier in tone, though for prime grades 25c is an inside quotation.

Dandelion, German, of the new crop, has arrived and supplies are offered more freely at the range of 7½c to 8c.

Golden seal is not inquired for to any extent and the quoted range of 58c to 60c is largely nominal.

Ipecac, Carthagena, continues in demand and values are steadily maintained at $1.75 and upward, as to quality and quantity.

Jalap is not inquired for to any extent and values show no change from 9½c to 11c.

Orris, Florentine, is held with increased firmness and we hear of numerous sales at 5½c to 6½c.

Squill has developed an upward movement and values show an advance to 8c, the previous quotation being 4½c.

Seeds.

There is little of special interest to report in the general line of druggists' seeds. Celery offers with increased freedom and values are fractionally lower, 7½c to 7¾c being now named as to quantity. Russian hemp is in better supply and values have dropped a notch or two, the range of quotations standing at 3¾c to 4c. Sunflower has developed increased firmness owing to scarcity, and for the limited available supply holders ask 4½c to 5c. Russian anise is easier to the extent that holders will release supplies at 6½c to 7c.

Rubber Growing in Siam.

United States Consul-General Nash, Bangkok, Siam, reports that the cultivation of rubber in Siam has only recently been started, some thousands of plants having been set out as an experiment. These plants of the Para variety (*Hevea brasiliensis*) are said to be doing exceedingly well, although I believe they have had no especial care, but have been planted indiscriminately in various places and under varying conditions of moisture, sun, etc. It is still too soon to tell what the ultimate result of this venture will be, but I am of the opinion that it will prove highly successful. There is, however, one thing to fear—namely, the new so-called disease, which I hear has developed in the Para rubber plantations of the Malay Peninsula. I can learn nothing definite about this pest, except that it attacks the leaves and is very destructive. I am inclined to the opinion that it is caused by the larvæ of some insect.

In this connection it may be interesting to note two of the rubber producing plants indigenous to Siam. The more important of these is the *Ficus elastica*, so much used in the United States for ornamental purposes, and found in large quantities in the Siamese jungle and throughout India and Indo-China generally.

Rubber is collected from these trees by the simple process of making longitudinal scarifications in the bark, from which the coagulated milk is taken in long strips. It is said that a plant six years old will yield 4 pounds of rubber annually of a quality which could be sold in London at about 90 cents per pound, but this price appears to me to be a trifle exaggerated.

The other rubber producing plant of known commercial value is a creeper of great size, probably one of the *Urceola* (either *U. esculenta* or *U. elastica*), although from certain descriptions I am sometimes inclined to believe it to be a *Willughbeia*. It is most difficult to obtain any reliable information on the subject, from a botanical point of view, and it is quite possible that both are indigenous to Siam. These creepers, whatever they may be, yield a fair quality of rubber, produced by cutting them into sections 2 or 3 feet long and collecting the juice, which is subsequently boiled for a moment in water and immediately coagulates into a viscous mass, which has to be dried by smoking over a fire before it can be handled. The bark is also used, and upon being pounded and boiled gives about 10 per cent. of a rather inferior rubber.

F. V. JOHNSON,
President St. Louis Retail Druggists' Association and better known as the "No More Gray Hair" man from St. Louis.

Opportunities *for* Export Trade

PANAMA WAKES UP.

Fast Becoming Americanized—Many Changes Wrought by the Canal Commission—Modern Business Methods Introduced—Trade Benefited by Stable Government.

(*From our Traveling Correspondent.*)

Panama, October 19.—Visiting this city of 35,000 inhabitants after an absence of 15 months has shown us almost as remarkable changes as we see in New York City before and after the Subway.

Panama now has electric lights, water works and sewerage system, built by the United States Government, and an ice plant. Shall we make it more modern to your views when we say that two of the leading drug stores have given orders for the installation of the latest type American soda fountains? Asking a prominent pharmacist the other day as to methods of advertising to bring in sales on a new remedy now being placed before the people of the Republic, brought the reply, "You can safely employ American methods in getting the trade here, for the people have really changed entirely within the last two years, and they are now as susceptible to the methods you employ to create sales as though our city was situated in your own country."

IMPROVED BUSINESS TONE.

The entire business tone has so greatly improved and the general confidence which prevails is so sound that you are given instructions to ship promptly instead of as formerly, "hold until we see how the Government decides." Foreign goods are now being crowded to one side of the market, and with the reduction of freight rates, which it is hoped will be followed by a more satisfactory delivery of merchandise in the markets of Panama, will enable American exporters to have Panama trade as their very own.

THE PANAMA RAILROAD CONGESTED.

The greatest drawback to trade now comes from the abominable service given by the Panama Railroad, whose time for the delivery of freight from the Atlantic port of Colon over to Panama, though but 47 miles, requires more time by double or treble than from the house in New York to Colon.

Every one dealing with Panama must have heard of the freight blockade at Colon, but it is difficult to realize until you see for yourself that mountains of freight lie upon the docks at Colon waiting transportation across the Isthmus, and a score or more of carpenters are working day and night repairing broken cases, barrels, etc., and trying their best to make shape of some sort out of the mess. 'Tis in these immense piles that your lost shipment lies and your customers won't get relief for months to come, regardless of the many promises.

A HIGH RATE OF DUTY ON ESSENCES.

Duties on goods entering from the United States are generally placed at 10 per cent. of the net invoice value, while the duties on essences for liquors have been placed at an extremely high figure to try and prohibit the manufacture of liquors on the isthmus. It will therefore require caution in making out the consular declarations not to place an essence of some of the fruit flavors simply under the head of essences, for this will surely cause the higher duties.

THE DRUG STORES OF PANAMA.

The drug business, wholesale and retail, in Panama is controlled by about eight firms, among whom we find Sr. Y Preciado, the head of the "Botica El Globo," who established himself in business in Panama in 1882 and is now the owner of five drug stores in the Republic—three in the city of Panama, one in David and one in Colon. Being probably the largest importer of drugs in the Republic he buys annually in the foreign markets to the extent of $150,000, and which is divided between Germany, France, United States, England and Italy, with a small portion from Spain. They are now going to install in the Botica a new prescription department for which they have purchased an entire new equipment, and will have the fittings of mahogany.

Panama from Deck of a Steamer.

AMERICAN SODA FOUNTAINS.

The drug stores of Sr. Arturo Kohpoke and of Sr. Manuel Espinosa are soon to be equipped with the finest models of American Soda Fountain Company apparatus, and the progressive manner in which these stores follow modern business methods is well exemplified, not only in their recent installations, but their fairness in considering any sound business scheme presented to them.

The portion of the drug trade taken up with prescriptions is largely handled by Cermelli Hnos.

AMERICAN DRUGGIST

and PHARMACEUTICAL RECORD

PHILADELPHIA. NEW YORK, JANUARY 22, 1906. CHICAGO

ISSUED SEMI-MONTHLY BY

AMERICAN DRUGGIST PUBLISHING CO.

62-68 WEST BROADWAY, NEW YORK.

CHICAGO, 221 Randolph St. PHILADELPHIA, 3718 Walnut St.

A. R. ELLIOTT, President.

CASWELL A. MAYO, Ph.G. .... Editor.
THOMAS J. KEENAN .... Associate Editor.

ROMAINE PIERSON .... Manager Chicago Office.

$1.50 a year. 15 cents a copy.

ADVERTISING RATES QUOTED ON APPLICATION.

THE AMERICAN DRUGGIST AND PHARMACEUTICAL RECORD is issued on the second and fourth Mondays of each month. Changes of advertisements should be received ten days in advance of the date of publication.

Remittances should be made by New York exchange, post office or express money order or registered mail. If checks on local banks are used 10 cents should be added to cover cost of collection. The publishers are not responsible for money sent by unregistered mail, nor for any money paid except to duly authorized agents. All communications should be addressed and all remittances made payable to American Druggist Publishing Co., 62-68 West Broadway, New York.

Entered at New York as Second-Class Matter.

TABLE OF CONTENTS.

EDITORIAL COMMENT.

THE NAVAL PHARMACIST. Pharmacy fares somewhat better in our navy than in our army, for in the navy the pharmacist ranks as a warrant officer. It is gratifying to note, however, that the Surgeon-General of the navy is not yet satisfied, and as may be seen by the excerpt from his annual report printed in our last issue he asks for an increase in the number of pharmacists ranking as warrant officers and for better pay for the lower grade of the naval hospital corps. It would seem that the better the pharmacist is known the more he is appreciated. The army authorities are apparently still guided by General Sternberg's dictum, "We have no use for pharmacists in the army."

N. A. R. D. EXECUTIVE TO MEET. The semiannual meeting of the Executive Committee of the National Association of Retail Druggists is scheduled to take place in Chicago on February 12, when it is expected that a readjustment of views regarding the operation of the tripartite plan will be discussed. While the verdict in the Loder suit handed down recently in Philadelphia appeared to bear hardly upon the plan, it is felt by the active workers in the association that the tripartite principle cannot be dropped, as the co-operation of all three branches of the trade is necessary to the success of any movement for the regulation of prices on proprietary medicines. The action taken by the committee will be awaited with much interest in the trade generally.

CRIMINAL SUBSTITUTION. Just where the picking of other people's brains becomes actually indictable is not clearly defined in the Penal Code. There is no sort of justification for the practice of palming off an imitation article when a proprietary medicine is called for, but it is unfortunately true that the custom prevails among certain unscrupulous pharmacists. The searing of the commercial conscience through crookedness of this kind cannot be compensated for by the satisfaction of gains not obtained along straight lines, for the same expenditure of brain power in the direction of evolving a new idea would have resulted in a greater measure of success than it is possible to attain by the imitation of some other fellow's idea. Let us have a square deal!

PRESCRIPTION REGULATIONS IN HONDURAS. In a recent Consular report attention is called to the fact that in Honduras the prescriber is required to write his prescriptions in the language of the people—Spanish. The vexed questions of copies and of refilling are both cared for by specific regulation. We are told that "all prescriptions that are filled must be sealed and numbered with a number corresponding to that of the register kept by the pharmacist, returning to the interested party the original prescription or a sealed and numbered copy of the same." The refilling of a prescription is specifically prohibited save on express orders from the prescriber, who is required to state in the order for refilling how often it shall be refilled. Our neighbors to the South cannot complain of any lack of definiteness in their regulations.

MAKESHIFT METHODS. The appearance in our Paris contemporary, the *Répertoire de pharmacie*, of an article describing a rapid method for the preparation of tincture of opium prompts us to enter an earnest protest against the tendency to employ short cuts for the preparation of galenical compounds of the importance of tincture of opium. The author's method is to dissolve extract of opium in sufficient hot distilled water to reduce the alcohol in the extract from 90 to 60 degrees. The mixture is allowed to cool and afterward is filtered to remove the slight deposit which is necessarily formed. It is only in extreme emergencies, such as would scarcely arise under ordinary circumstances, that it should be permitted to the pharmacist to make tincture of opium in any other way than that prescribed by the Pharmacopœia. Such tinctures as those of opium, digitalis, aconite and nux vomica should be held sacred against the encroachments and unscientific tinkering of the few pharmacists who employ makeshift methods of the French kind.

Pharmacists as Perfumers.

In an interesting address delivered before the College of Pharmacy of the City of New York on last Tuesday evening Mr. Burr presented an idea which, it seems to us, promises much for the future of perfumery in the United States. He made the criticism that American perfumery lacked in originality, that American perfumers were prone to be copyists rather than originators, and in partial explanation of that fact suggested the need for a more intimate knowledge of the technical aspects of perfumery than is possessed by the majority of those engaged in the practical aspects of this work.

As a correct basis for the making of a good perfumer there must be a thorough familiarity with the basic materials entering into the manufacture of perfumes. This knowledge should go further than a mere superficial acquaintance with the physical characteristics of the materials and must embrace a scientific knowledge of the chemical constituents and of the behavior of the material under varying conditions and with different solvents. Added to this basis of accurate scientific knowledge there must be an artistic instinct, of a character allied to that which enables the painter to reproduce on canvas an idealized transcript of nature. Mr. Burr has lofty aspirations for the American perfumer and has happily set forth the peculiar combination of knowledge and special gifts required to produce this American perfumer of the future.

The College of Pharmacy embraces in its curriculum just that kind of training which is needed as a basis for the production of the perfumer. It teaches the student the sources, the characteristics and the properties, both physical and chemical, of the material which the perfumer uses. It is true that this teaching does not embrace all the perfumer's material, but what is more important than the mere knowledge attained in the school is that the students of pharmacy are taught how to learn and how to apply learning. We heartily commend Mr. Burr's suggestion and second his hope that from among the many graduates of pharmacy who go out into the world each year there may be some whose inclinations may lead them to a systematic study of the perfumer's art and who may be so informed with the artistic spirit as to be able to utilize to the best end the information and the methods learned in the College of Pharmacy.

No profession has wholly fulfilled its mission when its members fail to make themselves felt in lines allied to their calling. Rich and profitable as is the field of pharmacy, it is well that the teachers imbue their pupils with that breadth of insight, with that aspiration which will lead them to face life with an open mind and enable them to grasp special opportunities which may present themselves for the use of their learning in fields outside the immediate limits of pharmacy. Such a field is offered in the art of perfumery, and we commend to our younger readers some attention to this field as offering a possible outlet for special qualifications of taste and artistic instinct which but few can possess, but which, when possessed and when reinforced by proper training, can be utilized to the best possible advantage.

The Military Pharmacist.

In our issue for December 25 we presented a paper which had been read before the American Pharmaceutical Association on The Pharmacist in the Civil War and some comments on this paper, which took the form of a plea for the recognition of pharmacy in the army. With the statement that the army had no use for pharmacists, Surgeon-General Sternberg some years ago dismissed very cavalierly the recommendation of President McKinley, or, rather, indorsement by President McKinley of a recommendation that pharmacists be appointed with the rank of commissioned officers.

We are pleased to see that the attitude of the military authorities on this head has changed materially, for Major J. R. Kean, Surgeon United States Army, assistant to the Surgeon-General, writes us a letter in which he admits that the army could with advantage use the services of half a dozen pharmaceutical chemists and of a like number of medical storekeepers, though he strenuously objects to the establishment of so elaborate a corps as was proposed in our editorial article. This letter from Major Kean, which is published in another column, takes up the subject in a way which makes it deserving of attention and which shows that he has given the subject some degree of study, which is more than can be said of some of the communications on this subject which have emanated from the office of the Surgeon-General in the past.

Major Kean states that the temporary deficiences in the medical supply at Tampa and Jacksonville and in Cuba were due to defective transport arrangements, and that since the transport service is not under the control of the Medical Department, but under the Quartermaster's Department, this difficulty would not have been helped by the existence of a pharmaceutical corps organized along the lines proposed by the AMERICAN DRUGGIST. This difficulty in the transport system has long been a weak spot in the organization of the Medical Department, and the defense in this respect is a sound one, though there is some question whether there would not have been a greater provision shown by a regularly organized pharmaceutical corps, which would have foreseen and provided against the blocking of transportation by having medical supplies on the ground in advance.

While the evidence presented before the Dodge Commission as to the abundance of supplies will probably have to be accepted as conclusive, it is not at all in consonance with statements made to the editor of the AMERICAN DRUGGIST at Montauk Point by the individual members of the corps charged with the duty of furnishing medical supplies. One member of the hospital corps, who is no longer in the service, gave to the editor the details of his own duties in making good the temporary deficiency. It is possible that he may have exaggerated this deficiency, but his statements bore all the impress of truth. As to the question of mortality in the army corps the official statistics must be accepted as final.

But our interest in the question is one of principle rather than of detail. We wish to have the pharmacist recognized as an "officer and a gentleman" by giving him a commission. If the service can be helped by the employment of "half a dozen pharmaceutical chemists and a like number of storekeepers," as Major Kean says, then by all means let us have this number. Their appointment will concede the principle for which we have long fought. If after they have been installed and their duties outlined it should be found necessary to increase the corps we would then have the advantage of their experience as a guide.

(Written for the American Druggist.)

THE SYSTEMATIC AMENDMENT OF AMERICAN PHARMACY.

By Oscar Oldberg.
Northwestern University.

I.

The prosperity of pharmacy and pharmacists depends largely upon the condition of pharmaceutical education; but, for forty years the educational conditions of the occupation of pharmacy in our country have been growing more and more unsatisfactory. Pharmacy legislation has been prolific but grotesquely crude. Pharmacy schools have increased, but attendance at these schools is purely voluntary and small. The calibre of the material gathered into the drug stores, and out of which the pharmacists of the next generation must be fashioned, is growing poorer. No wonder the older pharmacists and other thoughtful friends of pharmacy are becoming alarmed.

Laws and rules fixing the prerequisites to the licensing of pharmacists are the topic of the day. Existing conditions are such that they might well lead one to feel that any change must necessarily be an improvement. But there is danger in such a feeling. There is no convincing evidence that the measures so far taken or proposed are the results of careful study of the problem in all its bearings.

The discouraging diversity of opinion indicates that the only hope of rational and safe progress must rest upon a sufficient restudy of the whole question. An attempt to recount the more important features of the problem before us is here presented, which I hope may serve as a stimulus to active participation in the movement by those competent and sufficiently experienced to lead in it. Let us try to determine just what we ought to have and what we can get, and also to discover what we ought to avoid.

The Boards of Pharmacy have shown that they appreciate the great desirability of more uniform requirements for the licensing of pharmacists in order that an interchange of State certificates of registration may be rendered possible. But an approach to uniformity is impossible unless we have some definite standards in view.

We must keep clearly in mind the primary object of the regulation of the practice of pharmacy, the conditions which govern that occupation, the means by which the object sought may best be accomplished, and how to bring order out of the present chaos instead of making matters worse.

PRESENT CONDITION OF PHARMACY IN AMERICA.

The Pharmacopœia of the United States is abreast of those of other countries. Much scientific work is being done by members of the American Pharmaceutical Association. A large number of individual American pharmacists take pride in their occupation and conduct pharmacies in which professional work is done *secundum artem*. In fact, if we look for them we shall find some pharmacies as nearly free from commercialism as any that ever existed.

Our pharmaceutical manufacturers are second to none in the world and produce preparations showing remarkable perfection of finish.

But we also find the other extreme—too many drug stores that are in no sense pharmacies, druggists that have no knowledge of pharmacy, too ignorant to ever acquire any such knowledge, and opposed to any change for the better—men who have no thought for anything higher than pecuniary gain.

We have several very efficient pharmaceutical schools, but we also have some without any equipment, with wholly unfit teachers, and evidently conducted primarily, if not solely, for the private profit of their owners or for other selfish ends.

The most absorbing topics of discussion among druggists today are purely commercial. Their only right to distinction from other merchants is generally neglected and often treated with contempt by them.

Well trained pharmacists are, indeed, indispensable to the welfare of the people, but the unsatisfactory condition of pharmaceutical education, the dominant air of commercialism that pervades most of the drug stores, and the utter indifference, if not actual hostility, toward education displayed by many druggists are so conspicuous as to place the whole profession in a false light.

In no other country is the legally established standard of education for pharmacy so low as it is in America. Fortunately for the people, a large number of our pharmacists still continue to be better educated than the law requires them to be. But the drug business has undergone great changes in the past generation.

Druggists complain that there is no professional, technical or scientific work for them to do. They say that physicians have almost ceased to write prescriptions for pharmacists to dispense. But is not that our own fault? What have we pharmacists done to remedy this state of things? Is it not a fact that practically no effort whatever has been made by the great body of druggists to demonstrate to the medical profession and the public that the occupation and services of pharmacists are necessary to civilization and entitled to respect, confidence and support?

DISPENSING PHYSICIANS AND PRESCRIBING PHARMACISTS.

It is contrary to wise public policy to permit physicians to dispense or pharmacists to prescribe. The selling of medicines by the prescribers and the prescribing of medicines by the dispensers cannot but have an immoral tendency. The separation of pharmacy from medicine was a decided step forward in civilization. There must be no retrogression. But when a physician writes a prescription he writes it for a particular occasion and not to be abused, and physicians complain that their prescriptions are refilled without authority and otherwise abused. They further declare that they are themselves more competent to safely dispense medicines than some of the druggists with whom they come in contact. Are these accusations against the druggist entirely devoid of truth? In States where the law does not enjoin upon the druggist a degree of special training, such as tends to render his peculiar technical services a safeguard against danger, the restriction of the practice of pharmacy to his hands is without warrant.

THE NATURE OF THE PRESCRIPTION.

A physician's prescription is simply his order to any qualified and licensed pharmacist to prepare and dispense what is prescribed. It is not the property of the patient. The patient compensates the physician for diagnosis, advice and treatment, but the prescription is simply a detail incident to the treatment. The patient does not buy and the physician does not sell prescriptions. When the pharmacist has carried out the directions given in the prescription he may properly retain the latter in his possession on the ground that it is an order to him. But the pharmacist has no right to dispense it more than once unless expressly authorized by the writer of it to do so; he has no right to dispense it at all if to his knowledge it is to be used for any other person than the one for whom it was prescribed, or for some purpose other than that for which it was intended by the prescriber, nor has he any right to dispense it so long after its date that it is evidently doubtful whether the prescriber still desires it to be filled. Do all druggists respect these self-evident rights of the prescriber? Is it not a fact that physicians have some cause for complaint as well as the pharmacists? If so steps should be taken to establish a better understanding between physicians and pharmacists.

WHY INCREASED EDUCATIONAL REQUIREMENTS ARE NOW NECESSARY FOR PHARMACY.

Scientific progress in pharmacy has been great. All recent pharmacopœias show it plainly. Compare them with the pharmacopœias of 30 years ago and be convinced. There has been very great progress also in scientific medicine. Yet the educational status of the pharmacist has not advanced.

It is the duty of every pharmacist to understand the pharmacopœia and to observe its requirements. But the understanding of pharmacopœias of this age requires a technical education, such as has never yet been insisted upon in our country, although it is compulsory in nearly every other civilized portion of the world. A person who cannot understand the pharmacopœia is clearly not a reasonably well educated pharmacist.

With the increasing number of organic chemical compounds now used in the treatment of disease a knowledge of organic chemistry is required of the up to date pharmacist, such as was never before called for. You may say that many of the new so-called "synthetics" are of doubtful value or even worse; my answer is that if pharmacists generally were better educated and able to do their part toward establishing the truth about the "new remedies," the worthless ones would be more rapidly weeded out and a far less number of fraudulent new "discoveries" and nostrums would be brought forth. But the really valuable organic chemicals are many.

The medical schools are of a high grade. How can the pharmacist hold his own unless he is able to discuss intelligently with the physician the pharmacy of the modern materia medica?

The pharmacist of to-day must demonstrate that he is able to contribute his special share toward safer and more efficient medication. He must show that he possesses the ability to furnish uniform and reliable medicines; that he knows how to examine and verify their quality and strength; that he knows how to preserve them from change, and that he performs his duty faithfully. He must understand the processes of assay described in the pharmacopœia.

In short, he must be a really competent pharmacist. If he is not, why should he not be abolished? If he is merely a buyer and seller of drugs and medicines he has absolutely no right that any other merchant does not possess in equal degree.

Disaster to the profession of pharmacy will surely come sooner or later unless there shall be a change for the better, and that speedily.

THE PHARMACY LAWS.

Safety to the public is the object of the regulation of the practice of pharmacy by law.

The greatest attainable degree of security against the dangers which necessarily attend the preparation and dispensing of medicines can be achieved in no other way than by restricting the practice of pharmacy to persons whose training renders them fit to perform these important and responsible services with intelligence, efficiency and seasoned reliability.

In return for the protection enjoyed by the people through the pharmacy laws is given to the qualified pharmacist the sole right to dispense medicines. Here we have then a mutual agreement, a contract between the public and the pharmacist. The terms are necessarily dictated by the public, but it is nevertheless a binding contract.

There are many pharmacists who do not consider their exclusive privilege a valuable one. Their opinion, however, does not change the terms of their contract with the people, nor does it alter the fact that no person enters upon that contract except of his own free will.

But the exclusive right to his own occupation, which the pharmacist possesses, is valuable. It is worth more than it costs him. The price consists of the acquirement of sufficient education to perform his duty properly, faithful service to the community and the expense of the machinery by which the pharmacy law is enforced. Every citizen, however, is in duty bound to perform his uses in the world properly and faithfully, so that really all that the pharmacist pays for his special privilege is his registration fee and annual fee for the renewal of his license.

Should the pharmacist not fulfill his part of the contract he thereby forfeits his rights under it, and it is certain that if the degeneration of pharmacy goes on and the people or the medical profession shall become convinced that the pharmacist is not sufficiently educated, not faithful to his trust, not safe, there will follow not an abrogation of the contract, but a new specification of its terms which will enforce better education, greater faithfulness, greater safety—terms which will probably prove to be more onerous to the pharmacist if framed without his willing co-operation than they will be as long as he continues to take the initiative himself.

No druggist should ever forget that his special license, which distinguishes him from the grocer, the liquor dealer, the tobacconist, the general dealer, refers solely to his services to the community as a dispenser and preparer of medicines. In his capacity as a pharmacist he is incidentally protected against general and excessive competition; but as a dealer in general merchandise, such as patent medicines, cigars, toilet articles, books, stationery and any other articles not of a pharmaceutical character, he stands in precisely the same position as other nontechnical shop keepers of whatever kind.

When the druggist, in his endeavors to extend his purely commercial business, permits himself to minimize or neglect his really pharmaceutical work he is digging his own grave.

DEFECTS OF AMERICAN PHARMACY LAWS.

American pharmacy laws and regulations are mostly burlesque.

In Maryland a pharmacy law was passed applying to all parts of the State except Talbot County. This would seem to indicate that it is not impossible that the next step might be to extend the operation of the law to such towns of Talbot County as may not object to it, while continuing the exemption in towns that do object.

In one State, located in the extreme northwest corner of the United States, the Board of Pharmacy has declared a quarantine against the rest of our common country, for under the discretionary powers conferred by the law the board has found it best to establish a geographical standard of excellence and finds no school of pharmacy satisfactory unless it is situated within the boundaries of that State. One would naturally expect more liberal ideas in educational affairs.

In countries where the regulation of pharmacy has been gradually perfected through centuries no person is permitted to enter a drug store as an apprentice unless his preliminary education is at least equal to that attained by a completed high school course.

In our country, on the contrary, we have some pharmacy laws from which it may be plainly inferred that 14 years is a suitable age at which to undertake the task of learning the serious and responsible duties of pharmacy.

Not one of our State laws prescribes any qualifications for apprentices. The boards of pharmacy in three States prescribe one year's high school work as a preliminary to examination for license—not for apprenticeship.

One State orders one year's high school work as a preliminary to special education in a pharmacy school.

In most civilized countries no person is allowed a license to practice pharmacy as a principal unless he has satisfactorily completed a systematic course of special college education prescribed for that purpose and occupying his whole time and attention through at least two years of from seven to nine months each. In our country, so far, only three States demand any special college training for pharmacy—New York, Pennsylvania and Wisconsin—and they have established these requirements within the last two years.

In other countries it rarely, if ever, happens that any one can become a duly authorized principal or manager of a pharmacy at as early an age as 21 years.

In some of our States the law declares that boys may open and conduct drug stores on their own account three years before they have attained the age of legal responsibility.

Several pharmacy laws order that graduates of all pharmaceutical schools requiring four years' drug store experience as a prerequisite to graduation shall be registered and licensed without question, while graduates of all other schools of pharmacy must undergo examination; and yet several of the schools not requiring drug store experience for graduation are superior to several of the schools that do require it.

Several pharmacy laws authorize the boards of pharmacy to issue licenses to practice pharmacy to persons without a day's actual experience, the passing of the board examination being the sole prerequisite.

In States where the pharmacy laws order that graduates of schools of pharmacy shall be licensed without examination, nothing has been done to prevent the licensing of the graduates of unfit institutions masquerading under the name of schools of pharmacy.

The defects in our American pharmacy laws are not chargeable to the boards of pharmacy. Those laws are the work of our legislators. If the committees to which such laws are referred, and by which they are considered and reported back for adoption or rejection (or for further amendment or mutilation), would only call into consultation with them some men of experience and capacity familiar with the real requirements of pharmacy, the results would undoubtedly be much more satisfactory. Pharmacy boards and pharmaceutical associations should watch legislation carefully, and should always send able, level-headed representatives to the seat of government whenever pharmaceutical legislation is on foot, to try to protect the people and the profession against unwise measures. I fear there is much truth in the complaint, often heard, that such matters are either wholly neglected or that the men selected to look after them are not men of sufficient strength and ability to accomplish much. The result is necessarily that the legislators, who know little or nothing about the whole question, must either do nothing or proceed blindly.

(*To be continued.*)

PERFUMERY MATERIALS, NATURAL AND ARTIFICIAL.[1]

By Edwin H. Burr,

New York.

Inasmuch as there are no rules for the guidance of the manufacturing perfumer for the artistic combination of odorous materials, he must of necessity be dependent upon his imagination and inspiration, and upon the full realization of this fact will depend his success. The French manufacturers have long since comprehended this fact, which is without question the reason why French perfumes have attained such preeminence the world over. In America the spirit of commercialism has to a great degree crushed and hampered this artistic spirit, and if any words, work or influence of mine can arouse, encourage and stimulate the independent and original artistic spirit in American perfumery and thereby pave the way for greater commercial success for the American perfumer, I shall be more than compensated for all my efforts in this direction. In addition to the artistic spirit and inspiration necessary to the successful composition of perfumes it is always most important, yes, absolutely essential, that the manufacturing perfumer must have the most intelligent and comprehensive knowledge of all the materials entering into such compositions, and in this direction I am satisfied that the educated pharmacist possesses qualifications which specially suit him for this work. In fact, it is my opinion that the best perfumes of the future will be found among the educated pharmacists of the country.

THE INDUSTRY OF NATURAL PERFUMES

has existed in France for ages. It is localized in the Department of the Alpes-Maritimes and, in the case of certain special products, in some of the neighboring departments. Its center is Grasse, where the factories are collected which are fed by the floral plantations of the district. Grasse and its district are placed, as regards climate, in an exceptional situation. Its inhabitants, who have been able to create this industry there and who, whatever may be said, have always kept it in line with the march of ideas and of improvements in the methods of working and appliances, will not easily allow themselves to be despoiled of the supremacy they have acquired. An industry, which prepares products such as those which I am going to show you, is neither stationary nor in decay. The considerable development and the remarkable progress of the method of volatile solvents in the south of France is a manifest proof of the care with which the perfumers of the Alpes-Maritimes are constantly seeking to improve their products. Grasse supplies the perfumery trade with products extracted from the flowers which grow upon its soil; the rose, orange flower, violet, jasmin, cassie mimosa and tuberose. It is impossible for me to enter into details as to the processes employed for this extraction, but I may briefly outline them as follows. They are three in number:

DISTILLATION WITH STEAM.

The first, the most ancient, is distillation with steam. It is practiced to-day with highly perfected apparatus, heated by steam. It yields essential oils, which are generally oily liquids

General View of the City of Grasse.

almost insoluble in water, which do not always resemble exactly the perfume of the flower, but which, nevertheless, possess special properties, mainly of tenacity, which cause them to enter into all the preparations of perfumery.

THE USE OF FIXED SOLVENTS.

The second process for the extraction of the perfume of flowers involves the use of fixed solvents. This process has also been practised for a very long time. It consists in placing the flowers in contact with fatty bodies, either solid or liquid, which absorb the perfume. There are thus obtained pomades or perfumed fats, which are then carefully exhausted with alcohol, which extracts the perfume and which can then be utilized by the perfumer. Lard is generally employed as the solid fatty body; it is melted and mixed with the flowers. After remaining for some time in contact, the perfumed fat is separated from the exhausted flowers by filtration and pressure. Several successive macerations are performed with fresh flowers. This is the process of hot maceration. In the case of jasmin and tuberose, the flowers are placed in contact with

Gathering Violets Near Grasse.

the fat at the ordinary temperature in wooden frames having glass bottoms on which the fat or oil, held by a coarse cloth, is spread. This is the process of cold enfleurage.

THE USE OF VOLATILE SOLVENTS.

The third process involves the use of volatile solvents and is more modern than the preceding. Its origination is attributed to a chemist named Robiquet. After numerous experiments the manufacturers of Grasse succeeded, a short time ago, in completely solving the problem of extracting faithfully

[1] Read before the College of Pharmacy of Columbia University, January 16, 1906. See page 47.

with all their characteristics the subtle aromas of flowers. The "párfums solides" thus extracted by digestion of the flowers with light petroleum spirit and evaporation of the latter under vacuum, occur in the form of waxy masses, frequently colored. As a matter of fact, the solvent becomes charged not only with the odoriferous matter, but also with vegetable fatty matters similar to beeswax and with coloring matters. Manufacturers who have succeeded particularly in this branch of the industry have conceived the idea of preparing in a more utilizable from the odorous bodies thus extracted. Their "essences liquides," a collection of which I place before you, contain the same quantity of perfume as an equal weight of the "parfume solide." Proceeding further, they have prepared, by methods which are not divulged, the actual odorous matter of the flower, without any vehicle. Here you see a collection of these absolute flower essences. Some of them have a considerable intrinsic value. The absolute flower essence of violet costs no less than 15,000 francs per kilogram.

Gathering Orange Blossoms in Grasse.

TROPICAL PRODUCTS.

Side by side with these products yielded by French soil the perfumer also employs a multitude of materials imported from abroad, which are mostly derived from the Far East. I will mention the essential oils of Mexican linalœs, of the female rosewood of Guiana, those of ylang-ylang from the Philippines and cananga from Java, the various oils from the British Indies, the various oils of cinnamon from China and Ceylon and of cloves and patchouly. For the majority of these products we are indebted to the British colonies.

ARTIFICIAL PERFUMES.

It would be most interesting to follow from the beginning the wonderful development of these products, but the limited time at my disposal forbids it. Neither am I capable nor would I think of attempting such a scientific problem before this company of gentlemen, all of whom know infinitely more of chemistry and chemical problems than I do. However, I am perfectly safe in saying that synthesis commences where analysis leaves off, and that the former is dependent upon the progress of the latter. The manufacturer of artificial perfumes to-day is aiming at a two-fold object. First, the reproduction of the natural perfumes by means of chemical methods and, second, the preparation of products possessing odors hitherto unknown, which may add new notes to the scale at the disposal of the perfumer, and it may be said that at the present time they are chiefly concerned in extending the series of perfumes without striving after an absolute imitation of nature's products. From this point of view the industry of artificial perfumes is capable of a very great development, for the reason that it thus adds great and useful support to the originality of the perfumer. At first, the question presented itself as to whether the discovery of chemical perfumes was not likely to paralyze the development of the natural perfùme industry. On the contrary, the prosperity of the industry of natural raw materials has not ceased to increase since the introduction of artificial perfumes. The only consequence, fortunately, has been a formidable increase in the production of perfumery. Thanks to the chemical products, the perfumer and the soap manufacturer have been enabled to turn out articles at very low prices, which have immediately found a new clientele. One of the most prominent characteristics of the social history of our time has been the progress of the lower classes towards a comfort, one may say a luxury, hitherto reserved only for the privileged class. This tendency is found in a particularly marked degree so far as the use of the products of perfumery is concerned. At the present day the poorest artisan uses scented soap, which he can procure at a trifling price. The use of eau de Cologne, aromatic vinegars, toilet waters and handkerchief scents has become general. This increase of production has taken place owing to the employment of artificial products, which place at the disposal of the perfumer, at a moderate price, a considerable strength of perfume, but at the same time and in a perfectly parallel manner, the consumption of natural products has increased, a fact which is easily understood.

The definite chemical product cannot, in any case, suffice for the composition of an harmonious perfume. The conjoint use of natural products, in however small a quantity, is necessary. In support of my statement I may quote some typical examples. Since the discovery of vanillin, vanilla has always been cultivated, the importation has not diminished and prices have been maintained. Artificial vanillin has found an enormous outlet in confectionery for flavoring the products of everyday sale, while the manufacture of high class articles has continued to utilize the vanilla pod. Nearer home, it might have been thought that the discovery of ionone would be likely to ruin the cultivation of the iris and the violet. It has been found necessary, on the contrary, to extend considerably the cultivation of the flower, and the manufacturers of the natural product have had a difficulty in supplying the demand. The reason is that the employment of ionone, enabling the perfumer to reproduce the aroma of the flower with greater facility, has led to the creation of a multitude of articles which have enjoyed and still enjoy a well deserved vogue. Now ionone alone cannot be employed for making up these articles; it has to be combined with tincture of orris root, violet and various other natural products, the consumption of which has increased in consequence. I might further quote the case of musk, neither the consumption nor the price of which has decreased since the appearance of Baur's musk.

Sorting Roses for Perfume Making at Grasse.

I will now speak of a few of the principal artificial products.

ARTIFICIAL MUSK.

A very long time ago it was noticed that the nitration of certain bodies yielded products endowed with a faint, musk-like odor. None of the substances so described obtained any employment in perfumery. In 1888 A. Baur took out a patent for a substitute for musk, obtained by nitrating butyl-toluene.

IONONE.

The chemical history of ionone falls into the chapter opened up ten years ago, which contains a multitude of facts concerning the history of linalool, gernaiol and citral. Discovered in

1898 by Tiemann, it is derived from citral, an aldehyde contained in the essential oils of lemon and lemongrass. Citral when shaken with acetone in the presence of a weak alkaline agent, such as baryta water, yields by Claisen's reaction a

A Jasmine Field Near Grasse.

ketone possessing three double bonds. This ketone possesses no characteristic odor. When heated with a dilute acid, such as sulphuric acid, it undergoes a peculiar isomeric change into the geranic series; the chain is closed and ionone is obtained. This componnd possesses such favorable properties that it was immediately adopted with enthusiasm by the perfumery trade. Indeed, in a state of extreme dilution it evolves a very characteristic odor of violets.

VANILLIN.

The synthetical reproduction of vanillin, the predominant odorous principle of the vanilla pod, is due to the work of Tiemann and his collaborators. After experiments of little practical interest performed with coniferin, the preparation of vanillin really entered the industrial arena in 1876, when Tiemann and Nagai established the fact that it could be produced by the oxidation of acetyl-eugenol by potassium permanganate. The second step in advance effected in this manu-

Gathering Tuberoses at Grasse.

facture was the discovery by Tiemann, in 1890, of isoeugenol. Now the production of vanillin is an immense industry and the price of the product under the influence of active competition has fallen to an astonishingly low figure.

While it is true that artificial perfumes have done much in extending the demand for perfumes among the humbler classes of society, yet it must be added that these artificial perfumes are not used exclusively for the preparation of cheap perfumes. They also have a place in fine perfumery, and skillfully used they are capable of increasing the beauty of the sweetest perfumes and developing their originality, on the express condition that they are accompanied by a large proportion of natural products; consequently it is impossible at the present time to conceive the employment of one class of products to the exclusion of the other. In fact the introduction of the artificial perfumes has increased instead of diminished the demand for the natural perfumery product.

REMEDIES OF YE OLDEN TIMES.

"Kronos," in the *Pharmaceutical Journal*, gives some specimens of ancient remedies. The oldest formula he has met with for

UNGUENTUM POPULEUM

in the "Pharmacopœa Amstelredamensis," published in 1630, reads as follows:

℞ Oculorum, *seu* Gemmarum Populi recentium, Libras tres. Axungiæ porcinæ recentis insulsæ, Libras sex.
Gemmæ Populi contundantur & macerentur in Axungia, donec sequentes herbæ collectæ fuerint.

℞ Herb. Bardanæ,
Herb. Hyoscyami.
Herb. Lactucæ,
Herb. Mandragoræ,
Herb. Papaveris nigri,
Herb. Sempervivi majoris,
Herb. Sempervivi minoris,
Herb. Solani,
Herb. Violarum,
Herb. Umbilici Veneris, *aut* Portulacæ,
Cymarum rubi tenerrimarum ana Manipulos duos.
Quæ contusæ Axungia & Oculis Populi coquantur ad consumptionem humiditatis: fiatque s. a. Unguentum.

Salmon's formula (1683) contained very similar ingredients, but in addition he ordered a considerable quantity of opium (℥vi. to lb. viii. of lard), which he recommended to be dissolved in vinegar, or spirit of wine, and inspissated before adding to the other ingredients. This preparation was a powerful sedative, and of such a different nature from the official Unguentum Populeum that it ought not to have been prescribed under the same name.

OLEUM POPULEUM.

Besides the Poplar Ointment there was in general use an oil made from poplar buds in this manner:

Buds of poplars ....p. iii.
Rich white wine ....p. iiij.
Sweet oyl ....p. viij.

First bruise the buds and infuse them in the wine and oyl seven days, then boyl and press out.

OIL OF PETRE.

This has been a medicinal agent as long as it has been known. Its virtues are not the result of modern discovery, although its vices may have been more manifest to some of us since the invention of motor-cars. A seventeenth-century writer says of it that "Oleum Petrae, or Rock Oyl, is a liquamen or fat flowing from rocks and stones, it is hot and dry, digests, dissolves, is Cephalick, Arthritick, Anodyne, and of thin parts. It comforts and strengthens the Nerves and Brain, consolidates Wounds and heals them. The spirit thereof helps ulcerated kibes and chilblains, being applyed with Spirit of Wine. It is extraordinary good against Convulsions, Palsies, Numbness, and fits of the Mother." Pomet and Lemery wrote of it in similar terms. But this rock oil was not necessarily the only article to which the name of "Oil of Petre" was applicable, as we find there was a balsamic oil, used for internal and external application, which bore the name of "Oyl of Peter de Ebano" (Oleum Balsami Petri de Ebano). This is the recipe for it:—

℞ of Myrrh, Aloes, Spicknard, Dragon's Blood, Frankincense, Mumany, Opopoynax, Carpo Balsam, Bdellium, Ammoniacum, Scarcocolla, Saffron, Mastich, Gum Arabick, liquid Storax, Labdanum, Castor ana ℨij.: Musk ʒss.: Turpentine the weight of them all: being bruised and beaten let them be mixt and distilled in B.M. (*balneum mariae*).

The dose of it was from 6 to 15 or 20 drops. Besides curing wounds "it cures the Palsey and all the Vices of the Nerves: helps the Palpitation and Trembling of the Heart as also Swooning fits. . . . . It takes away Sadness and Melancholy."

POPYLION.

From a very quaint book published 250 years ago the following recipe for making Popylion, or Populion is given. This article was evidently used as a variant on the Unguentum Populeum and the Oleum Populeum.

To Make Popylion.

Take the buds of the Popler Tree, pure water, take Henbane, take Plantane, take Morell, take Orpen, take Houslike, take Sempervive, take Endine, take Violets, take Watercreases, take Dayses the white and red, take Ribwort, take Stonecrop, take Aragon, take Tonnow.

POMANDERS.

The decadents of modern life differ in one respect at least from those of former ages; they are not so much given to the affectation of perfumes. The lady, however, still carries her sachet powder, but she does not prepare it herself, as did her ancestors, neither does she know that the practice is merely a modification of that of carrying pomanders. The pomander was a perfumed ball hung around the neck or waist. The word is probably of French origin—*pomme d'ambre*, an apple of amber. Amber signified in this case the Oriental amber or ambergris, if we may judge from this recipe published with several other similar ones in 1655:

To make a costly Pomander or counterfeit Amber.

Take a quarter and a halfe of Amber, and a quarter of Musk, and beat them in a Morter with gum Dragagante dissolved in Rose-water, but you must make it thick, then take it in the palm of your hand, your hand being anoynted first with oile of Beniamyn, or in some sweet oile cleaving to your hands, and so Oile it round like balls, and put them on a string, and let them dry betwixt two papers and wrap them up close.

PERFUME FOR GLOVES.

It rarely happens that our customers bring their gloves to our establishments to have them perfumed. There are not a few pharmacists still living who will remember that this was not an uncommon practice some years ago. The gloves were laid in boxes containing sachet powders, and were not, as in olden days, directly treated with perfumes. What our ancestors thought requisite even in the stern days of Cromwell was of a much more elaborate nature:

To Perfume Gloves.

Take Damask water two or three peniworth and put it in a pewter dish, and lay the Gloves in it one night, and one day, with a little turning now and then that they may be thoroughly wet. Then take them out and put in your bosome two or three days till they be drye, then take one ounce and a halfe of cloves beaten in fine pouder, and put it into the same water, stir them together, and lay it upon the Gloves, and wet the Gloves therewith, and dry them as before. Then take Storax liquida a great weight, and halfe a pound of Almondes or more, and an ounce and a halfe of Beniamyn in fyne powder, and mingle them together in a Morter, and anoynt thy gloves therewith. Then take Muske four or five graines, and mix it with a drop or two of good Damaske water. And grind it small, and lay it with your finger upon the turning down of the Gloves, and so drye them alwayes in your bosome.

OIL OF SWALLOWS.

In the poorer districts of town and country alike the people still cling tenaciously to remedies the names of which have lost their meaning. Two of the commonest of these are the oil of swallows, and the oil of bricks. I have a rare volume entitled "Natura Exenterata" containing many quaint recipes, and from it the following method of making oil of swallows is taken:—

Oyle of Swallows.

Take young Swallows, beat them feathers and all, and take a handfull of the crops of Rosemary, of Lavender Cotton, of Strawberry leaves and strings and all, of each a handfull, beat the herbs and swallows together, and put to them a quantity of May butter, boyl them in an earthen pot, stop it close, and let it stand nine daies, then boyl it again, and strain it, and put it into a glass.

Confounding a Name.

We would suggest to the editor of *Meyer Brothers' Druggist* the wisdom of preceding his customary telegram of congratulation to State associations assembled in annual convention with a printed form of title, for State association secretaries seem to be shockingly ignorant of the real name of the journal and frequently confound it with a firm name, as in the case of the secretary of the North Dakota association, who renders it "Meyer Brothers, druggists."

REACTIONS OF SOME NEW REMEDIES.

The behavior of certain medicinal chemicals of recent introduction with reagents is described in an article by L. Rosenthaler in the *Deutsch-Amerikanische Apotheker Zeitung*, which is translated in *Merck's Report* as follows:

Acetanilide gives with Millon's reagent a yellowish-green color which gradually changes into orange and finally into a dark brown. The liquid remains clear. (Compare phenacetin.)

Acoin.—The precipitate which forms with bromine water appears first green, but soon turns to brown, and then quickly to violet.

Anæsthesin.—Its solution in glacial acetic acid gives with lead peroxide a red color. On dissolving it in concentrated sulphuric acid, the addition of a drop of nitric acid develops a yellowish-green color. On diluting the solution with water and supersaturating with sodium-hydroxide solution, the color is changed to red.

Arrhenal dissolved in water gives with a solution of stannous chloride in hydrochloric acid a precipitate which is at first whitish, but soon darkens to a violet color, and for some time remains suspended in the liquid (colloidal arsenic?); the precipitate deposits in the form of brownish-black flocks, and finally again goes into solution.

Aspirin is dissolved with the aid of aqueous solution of sodium carbonate until the solution reacts slightly acid or is neutral. Ferric chloride added to the solution develops in it a light-brown precipitate; copper sulphate affords a brownish-green precipitate.

Bismuth subgallate, when heated with concentrated sulphuric acid, becomes violet. The reaction is caused by the gallic acid.

Epicarin.—A dark-green color is developed when epicarin is dissolved in concentrated sulphuric acid and a drop of formaldehyde added.

Guaiacol carbonate.—On adding a 0.5 per cent. solution of sodium nitrite to a solution of guaiacol carbonate in concentrated sulphuric acid, a reddish-violet color develops.

Iodol, when heated with a solution of sodium hydroxide and then with chloroform, colors the aqueous liquid violet, while the chloroform gradually acquires a deep violet-red color.

Lactophenin.—The alcoholic solution gives with ferric chloride a brownish-red color.

Mesotan gives with concentrated sulphuric acid a deep red color, and at the same time colored clots appear in the liquid. (The action is caused by the coexistence of salicylic acid and formaldehyde in the liquid.)

Alphanaphtol.—When alphanaphtol is heated with a little formaldehyde and hydrochloric acid until the condensation product acquires a reddish tint, the liquid develops a blue or bluish-green color on adding sodium-hydroxide solution, and red flocks separate when an acid is added. The addition of a sodium-hydroxide solution redissolves the precipitate, and the solution again acquires a blue color. Betanaphtol also gives with hydrochloric acid and formaldehyde a red condensation product, but the liquid remains colorless on adding sodium-hydroxide solution.

Neuronal.—An aqueous solution of neuronal gives with Nessler's reagent an immediate whitish precipitate; if first heated with sodium-hydroxide solution, however, the precipitate does not appear.

Nirvanin.—The orange-colored liquid which is formed after a few minutes by the action of nitric acid (sp. gr. 14) upon nirvanin, becomes brownish-red or blood-red on supersaturation with sodium-hydroxide solution.

Orexine.—The solution in concentrated sulphuric acid, on adding a drop of nitric acid, becomes green, with a reddish margin occasionally. On adding water and supersaturating with sodium-hydroxide solution, a yellow precipitate develops in the yellow liquid.

Orthoform new, when treated as detailed under orexine with sulphuric acid, nitric acid, and sodium-hydroxide solution, gives on adding the nitric acid a reddish or bluish-violet color, becoming red on the addition of sodium-hydroxide solution. The solution of orthoform in glacial acetic acid gives with lead peroxide a beautiful green color.

Phenacetin with Millon's reagent gives a color gradually deepening to an intense violet, which after a short time passes into a brownish-red and finally into a light brown. In the liquid are found yellowish crystals of nitrophenacetin. This reaction takes place similarly with other phenetidid, for instance, lactophenin, citrophen, and phenetidin citrate, give with Millon's reagent an immediate violet color.

Pyramidon.—In an aqueous solution of pyramidon there appears, on adding a little iodopotassium iodide, a dark (brown or blackish) precipitate which soon dissolves, while the liquid takes on a violet color. On again cautiously adding iodopotassium iodide, the reactions can be repeated till finally, when sufficient reagent is added, the precipitate is permanent.

Saccharin.—Sprinkle some saccharin 300 times sweeter than sugar upon a solution of alphanaphtol in concentrated sulphuric acid; first the saccharin, and then the liquid, becomes violet. Saccharin 500 times sweeter than sugar gives a reaction so slight that it can hardly be noticed. It cannot consequently be a question of the reaction of the saccharin, but of one of its impurities, most probably parasulphaminbenzoic acid. With a preparation of this acid at the disposal of the author, the reaction was indeed very sharp. The violet color produced with alphanaphtol and sulphuric acid can serve as a proof of the presence of parasulphaminbenzoic acid, and, by means of a colorimetric comparison, it could also serve for the quantitative determination, provided carbohydrates, which also give with alphanaphtol and sulphuric acid a similar color, are excluded.

Tannoform.—On shaking tannoform with water and overlaying the mixture on concentrated sulphuric acid, there develops a bluish-green ring, the color of which gradually passes over into the sulphuric acid.

Vioform.—The alcoholic solution affords with ferric chloride a green color; this color is also afforded with Millon's reagent.

Yohimbine, when dissolved in concentrated sulphuric acid, gives on the addition of nitric acid blue and green streaks, and the liquid finally becomes yellowish. When dissolved in Millon's reagent, the liquid becomes immediately a dark brown-red.

The Peroxides of the Alkali Earths.

A valuable contribution to our knowledge of the peroxides of the alkali earths was made at this month's meeting of the Society of Chemical Industry, held at the Chemists' Club, 108 West Fifty-fifth street, New York, last Friday evening, the authors of the paper being Dr. Richard von Foregger, of the Roessler & Hasslacher Chemical Company, and Dr. Herbert Philipp.

Numerous compounds are known for their oxidizing properties, instances being bichromates, permanganates, hydrogen dioxide, the halogens, etc., but their application is restricted, while the peroxides of the alkali earths are capable of liberating their available oxygen readily, leaving behind either an inert solid residue, or a soluble salt of a harmless nature.

Calcium peroxide is described in the text books as a product obtained by the action of hydrogen dioxide on lime water. It occurs in fine needle-like crystals of a bulky nature. Dr. von Foregger, who read the paper, gave an intimate account of the chemistry of the substance, which he said was the most stable of the peroxides of the alkali earths. It has the advantage over calcium permanganate of being nonhygroscopic, while a sulphuric acid solution of this yields nothing but nascent oxygen, or hydrogen dioxide, with calcium sulphate as a by product. Strontium peroxide, dehydrated, contains 85 per cent. of strontium dioxide, the remainder being strontium hydrate. Like calcium peroxide it is very stable in a dry atmosphere even at high temperatures and can be heated up to 150° C. without loss of available oxygen. Magnesium peroxide was described as a white amorphous powder which the authors think is in reality perhydrate of magnesium, and that obtainable in the European and American markets is a compound of both, accompanied with water of crystallization. Magnesium peroxide is soluble in 14,550 parts of water at 20° C. Suspended in water it liberates its available oxygen more quickly than does zinc peroxide, but slower than calcium or strontium peroxides. It reacts with acids and certain organic matter in a similar way to the other peroxides. Zinc peroxide differs from calcium and strontium peroxide in having no water of crystallization and in the fact that it forms no perhydrate. In constitution it is believed to be a mixture of zinc peroxide (averaging 50 per cent.), zinc hydrate and free moisture. It forms a dense yellowish-white powder of strong antiseptic properties, with the advantage over other antiseptics of being odorless and non-irritant.

Dr. von Foregger gave an interesting account of the application of the peroxides in the industries. Calcium peroxide has been found a splendid bleaching agent for oils. Its use as a preservative of food substances has been suggested. All that was said about the application of calcium peroxide applied as well, the authors said, to magnesium peroxide, but the latter had the added advantage of being capable of internal administration, its main value in the latter use consisting of its pronounced metabolism and as an internal disinfectant. Strontium peroxide has been recommended as a basis of oxygenated tooth powders, on account of its solubility in water without the aid of acids. The buccal secretions being alkaline in reaction, a peroxide requiring the intervention of an acid to decompose it would be ineffective.

In closing Dr. von Foregger suggested the use of calcium peroxide as a preservative of milk. Milk so treated would obviate the necessity of the use of lime water as an adjuvant in infant feeding. Milk treated with calcium peroxide would, he said, bear in itself the prevention of abnormal fermentation.

An interesting feature of the meeting was a paper on the Cuban Sugar Industry, with illustrations, by W. D. Horne.

Syrup of Bromoform for Whooping Cough.—The following formula is given in a recent number of the *Bulletin Général de thérapeutique* for a compound syrup of bromoform:

Bromoform	Gm.	1
Codeine	Gm.	0.5
Tincture of aconite root (French)	Gm.	10
Alcohol	Gm.	40
Syrup of cherry laurel	Gm.	250
Syrup of tolu	Gm.	250
Syrup of Dessartz (see below)	Gm.	450

A tablespoonful of this syrup contains 0.02 Gm. of bromoform and 0.01 Gm. of codeine. The syrup of Dessartz, which is not familiar to American readers, is also known as the compound syrup of ipecac, or as the pectoral syrup of Dessartz. It is composed as follows:

	Parts.
Ipecac	30
Senna	100
Thyme	30
Red poppy	125
Magnesium sulphate	100
White wine	750
Orange flower water	750
Sugar, a sufficient quantity.	

The ipecac and the senna should be macerated in the wine for twelve hours, and the product strained and filtered. The residue is mixed with the other ingredients, and 3,000 parts of boiling water poured upon the mixture, which is infused for six hours, strained and expressed. The product is mixed with the vinous solution, and the orange flower water containing the magnesium sulphate is added. To 100 parts of this mixture 190 parts of sugar are added, and a syrup is made by simple solution on the water bath. This syrup is an old and well tried remedy for whooping cough in children, the dose of which is from 30 to 60 Gms. daily, according to Dorvault ("L'Officine," ninth edition, 1875, page 862).

Cream *of* Current Literature

A summary of the leading articles in contemporary pharmaceutical periodicals.

Capsic Acid, the Active Principle of Pimenta.—Gabriel de la Puerta (*Anales de la Sociedad Española de fisica y quimica*, 1905, November 23) discovered the irritant principle of pimeta, which he has named capsic acid. This principle has never been obtained before in the pure state. Capsicine, discovered by Braconnot, is not a definite substance, while Thresch's capsaicine does not present the characters of an acid. According to De la Puerta, capsic acid is obtained by triturating the seeds and macerating them in alcohol at 70 degrees, evaporating the product upon the water bath, and thus obtaining a yellowish mass partly soluble in water, the solutions having an acid reaction. This solution is precipitated with sulphuretted hydrogen, and by filtering the liquid and evaporating it on the water bath capsic acid is obtained. It occurs in the pericarp of pimenta, as well as in the seed. The drug contains 0.8 per cent. of this acid.

A Rapid Method for Preparing Paregoric.—Forget (*Répertoire Pharmacie*, December, 1905, p. 534) suggests the following method of preparing the elixir of paregoric of the French Codex, without being obliged to delay the process for several days by macerating the ingredients, as the French formula prescribes. The United States Pharmacopœia VIII requires three days' maceration of all the ingredients, followed by filtration and the addition of diluted alcohol. The French author takes the necessary amounts of benzoic acid, of oil of anise and of camphor, and dissolves them in 890 Gms. of 90 per cent. alcohol. He next dissolves 3 Gms. of the extract of opium (not employing the powdered opium, as prescribed in the U. S. P.) in 260 Gms. of hot distilled water. To this solution he adds the alcoholic solution mentioned above, allows the mixture to cool, and filters. The preparation keeps without any deposit forming. The gist of this formula, therefore, is the employment of the extract of opium in place of the powdered opium, thus obviating the necessity for macerating.

The Freezing Point of Codliver Oil.—Barthe (*Bulletin des sciences pharmacologique*, October, 1905) insists upon the value of the freezing point of codliver oil as an aid in the recognition of the best kinds of oil, and thinks that the pharmacopœias should define a definite freezing point for codliver oil as a part of the official requirements. He gives the results of his observations upon two samples of codliver oil, having been attracted to this problem by the experience of Moreau and Bietrix, who showed that a perfectly pure codliver oil may become clouded in winter, owing to the fact that it has not been subjected to a preliminary cooling and filtration. The reactions which have been recommended hitherto as indicative of strict purity in codliver oil are not very exact, and in commerce the usual test has been permanent clearness of the oil at 0 degree C. Since the researches of the two French observers named have shown that perfectly pure oil may become clouded at a low temperature this test obviously no longer obtains. According to Barthe, codliver oil exposed for three hours to form 4.5 to 3.5 degrees C. becomes slightly clouded. At 2 degrees, with an exposure of two hours, the first sample examined became completely solid. This same oil when immersed in melting ice at zero for an hour became completely solid at the end of that time, while at —1 degree C. it became solid at the end of five minutes. Cryoscopy (determining the freezing point with a Beckmann apparatus) showed that this oil becomes cloudy at —2 degrees C., and does not freeze until a temperature of —6 degrees is reached.

The second sample did not freeze until the thermometer fell to —6.9 degrees C., but became a solid block at the end of an hour when exposed to the temperature of melting ice at zero for that length of time, after it had been subjected to a succession of lower temperatures for varying periods of time. This shows therefore that under certain conditions genuine codliver oil can become solid at zero C. The commission at present revising the Codex might well look into this matter and determine the method of employing the freezing test for detecting impure codliver oils.

Practical Points in Testing for Albumin in the Urine.—Jacquemet (*Dauphiné médical*, 1905, Nos. 3, 4 and 5) gives an interesting summary of the precautions to be taken for testing for albumin in the urine and of the sources of error that obtain in the use of the various reagents. A very frequent cause of error is the presence of urates, especially the acid urate of sodium, when present in a quantity exceeding 60 or 70 Cc. per liter. The urates cause confusion in all cases in which nitric, citric, acetic and other acids are employed, and also in the use of potassium ferrocyanide, ammonium sulphate, etc. We must remember, however, that deposit of urates dissolves on gently heating. The only way to avoid all errors is to eliminate the uric acid from the sample. This may be done by adding ammonium chloride to the amount of 30 or 35 per cent. and allowing the urine to stand for half an hour, whereupon the usual reagents can be tried without being interfered with by the ammoniacal salt. Two exceptions, however, obtain to this rule—namely, Esbach's solution and potassium ferrocyanide—both of which are interfered with by the presence of the ammonium salts. In the use of the nitric acid test (Heller's) the source of error next in importance to that entailed by the presence of urates is the existence of albumose in the urine. The precipitate which results should be always decanted with pipette, and is soluble upon the application of heat in contact with the precipitate of albumin. Another important source of error is the presence of "resins" such as that of sandal wood, copaiba, turpentine, etc., which form a ring in the nitric acid test. The presence of these resins should therefore be excluded.

Fluid Extract of Licorice.—Pégurier (*Bulletin des Sciences Pharmacologique*, October, 1905) suggests to the commission at present engaged in revising the French Codex the introduction of fluid extract of glycyrrhyza, in addition to those already decided upon. This extract is used a great deal in England and in the United States for sweetening mixtures or for masking the bitter taste of drugs. The Russian Pharmacopœia adds a certain amount of the extract of licorice to the fluid extract of buckthorn, and, according to Pégurier, licorice extract could be advantageously added to the fluid extract of cascara sagrada in such a manner as to obtain a mixture containing equal parts of each of these extracts. The fluid extract of licorice is also useful for masking the taste of golden seal, and Pégurier suggests the addition of two parts of the licorice extract to one part of that of golden seal. Pégurier prefers the method of preparation of the fluid extract of licorice prescribed in the British Pharmacopœia. One kilo of the coarsely powdered root is macerated for 24 hours in two kilos. of distilled water, and the product is filtered and expressed; to the residue a second quantity of two kilos. of distilled water is added and is allowed to remain in contact for six hours. The liquid is again filtered and expressed, and the two portions are mixed, heated to 100 degrees C. strained, and concentrated until the cooled liquid has a specific gravity of 1,200. To this alcohol is added to the amount of one-quarter of the volume of the liquid, and after standing for 24 hours, the extract is filtered. The author does not state his reasons for preferring the British formula to the American, which employs glycerin and ammonia as important ingredients in the menstruum and in which also distillation plays a part.

Queries and Answers

We shall be glad, in this department, to respond to calls for information on all pharmaceutic matters.

Cough Syrup.—C. H. S. asks for the formula of a cough syrup, "something that is pleasant to take and keeps well."

The simplest form of cough syrup of good keeping quality is syrup of wild cherry containing ammonium chloride in the dose of 2½ grains to each teaspoonful. Most of the other compounds contain ingredients that are prone to undergo fermentation. However, the range of cough syrups and mixtures so-called is wide and varied. From "The Pharmaceutical Journal Formulary" we quote the following as examples of recent invention:

I.

Ipecacuanha wine	fl. ounce 1
Spirit of anise	fl. drachm 1
Syrup	fl. ounce 16
Syrup of squill	fl. ounce 8
Tincture of tolu	fl. drachms 4
Distilled water, enough to make	fl. ounces 30

II.

Heroin	grains 6
Aromatic sulphuric acid	fl. ounces 1½
Concentrated acid infusion of roses	fl. ounces 4
Distilled water	fl. ounces 5
Glycerin	fl. ounces 5
Oxymel of squill	fl. ounces 10

III.

Glycerin	fl. ounces 2
Fluid extract of wild cherry	fl. ounces 4
Oxymel	fl. ounces 10
Syrup	fl. ounces 10
Cochineal, a sufficient quantity.	

IV.

Chlorodyne	fl. ounces 4
Ipecacuanha wine	fl. ounces 2
Syrup of black currant	fl. ounces 4
Syrup of squill	fl. ounces 4
Syrup of balsam of tolu a sufficient quantity to produce	fl. ounces 20

V.

Ipecacuanha wine	fl. ounces 4
Oxymel of squill	fl. ounces 6
Syrup of red poppy	fl. ounces 4
Chloroform water	fl. ounces 4

VI.

Clarified honey	ounce 1
Oxymel of squill	fl. ounce 1
Compound tincture of gentian	minims 15
Syrup	fl. ounce 1
Syrup of balsam tolu	fl. ounce 1
Syrup of white poppies (B. P. 1885)	fl. ounce 1

The average dose of these syrups is a teaspoonful.

Massage Cream.—M. L. asks for the formula of a modern massage cream and begs us not to refer him to back numbers.

The basis of the modern massage cream is casein, as we have previously pointed out. Casein is now produced very cheaply in the powdered form, and by treatment with glycerin and perfumes it is possible to turn out a satisfactory cream. The following formulas are suggested:

I.

Casein, dried	℥i
Boric acid	ʒss
Glycerin	♏lxxv
Water	q. s.
Carmine solution, N. F., enough to color.	

Perfume either with oil of bitter almond or extract of vanilla.

II.

Casein, dried	ʒi
Boric acid	gr. v
Glycerin	♏x
Carmine solution, N. F.	q. s.
Oil of bitter almond	q. s.

Kierstedt's Ointment.—A subscriber desires the formula for this ointment and we should be obliged if any reader would kindly supply it.

A Question of Quantity.—H. writes: "To settle an argument between a physician and myself would you be good enough to state the correct interpretation of the subjoined prescription? Does it call for a mixture measuring 1½ ounces, or a mixture measuring 8 ounces? The prescriber asserts that '*q. s. ad* 1½ oz.' would also mean 8 ounces. He argues that *ad* ℥iss means to add sufficient to make up 1½ ounces of the last two ingredients, which would make the complete mixture measure 8 ounces. What is your decision?"

The prescription submitted by our correspondent reads as follows:

℞ Acid nitromuriatic	℥ss
Tr. nuc. vom	ʒij
Tr. gent. co. } Tr. cinchon. }	āā ad ℥iss
M. Sig.: ʒi t.i.d.	

Appended to the copy of the prescription is an inquiry by the pharmacist as to whether *aa ad* without the contraction *q. s.* stands for the same thing as *q. s. ad.*

The prescription as written calls for a mixture measuring 1½ ounces, but this is not what the prescriber evidently intended, for unless we have confounded the symbol ʒ with ℥, and the copyist strong nitromuriatic acid with diluted nitromuriatic acid, the dose of acid is excessive, amounting as it does to 20 minims, which would be a pretty stiff dose of the diluted acid. We should say that the physician intended to prescribe 1½ ounces each of the tinctures of gentian and cinchona to make a mixture measuring ℥iij ℥vi, but he did not write the prescription in such a way as to obtain this. In regard to the question whether *aa ad*, without the contraction *q. s.*, stands for the same thing as *q. s. ad.*, the first contraction may be translated "of each to," while the second with *ad* followed by a period may be taken to mean "add a sufficient quantity," the amount being indicated by the symbol and quantity expressed.

Dealers in Chamois Scraps.—F. P. B. writes: "Please be good enough to give the names of a few of your advertisers of whom we could purchase scraps of chamois skin. Upon receipt of same we will be pleased to take up correspondence with them."

Chamois scraps can be purchased from any large dealer in chamois skins, such as Smith, Kline & French Company, Philadelphia. No individual firms making a specialty of chamois scraps advertise in the columns of the AMERICAN DRUGGIST, but dealers known to us who make a specialty of selling scraps and odd pieces of chamois skin are Louis Dejonge & Co., 73 Duane street, New York, and D. Davis & Sons, 148 William street, New York.

Nonsecret Toilet Preparations.—A. H. L. asks for the name and addresses of any reliable firms that put up toilet preparations in boxes, bottles or jars, bearing labels supplied by retailers.

We suppose that any firm manufacturing nonsecret preparations would be in a position to supply the wants of our correspondent, and would suggest his communicating with firms like Frederick Stearns & Co., Detroit, Mich., or the Manhattan Drug Company, 11 Warren street, New York.

The Varieties of Sarsaparilla.—According to M. Fleury, professor of *materia medica* at Rennes (*Union pharmaceutique*, December, 1905, page 532), the commercial varieties of sarsaparilla are extremely limited, and practically the only variety which is met with ordinarily is that known as Tampico sarsaparilla. This sarsaparilla is distinguished from the Vera Cruz variety by the shape of the endoderm cells, which are not shaped like horseshoes, but have square, rectangular or triangular forms. Fleury also found that the varieties of sarsaparilla could be distinguished by the shape of the starch grains in the plant. [The United States Pharmacopœia recognizes four varieties of sarsaparilla, including the dried root, known commercially as Honduras sarsaparilla, which is obtained from *Smilax officinalis*, Kunth.]

Book Reviews.

VORSCHRIFTENBUCH FUER DROGISTEN. Die Herstellung der gebräuchlichten Handverkaufsartikel. Von G. A. Buchheister. Fünfte, vermehrte Auflage. Berlin: Verlag von Julius Springer. 1905. [Paper, 8 marks; sheep, 9 marks, 20 pfennig.]

In this book of 500 pages, inclusive of index, formulas are given for nearly every possible preparation demanded of the pharmacist who aims to supply the public with pharmaceutical specialties, as well as household and other remedies of his own make. Veterinary remedies and cattle medicines are considered and the formulas are admirably selected, though only a little over four pages are given up to *Tierheilmittel*, as against 79 pages of information concerning the manufacture of dietetic and nutritive compounds, which include notes on the preparation of fruit syrups and wines, as well as curry powder, soy and the numerous "bitters" for which Germany is famed. The bitters include such widely different compounds as *Boonekamp of Magbitter*, *Angostura-Bitter* and *Getreidekümmel, Berliner*, to say nothing of *Kümmel, Danziger* and *Schweizer Absinth*. The list of punch essences (*Punschextrakte*) in this department is bewildering. They range from *Punschextrakt von Rum, ordinär*, through *besser* and *mittelfein* to *Tee-Punschextrakt, Kaiserpunsch* and *Kardinal-Punschextrakt*, and pass on to processes for the fabrication of artificial rums, *arraks* and *Kognaks*. Cosmetics occupy considerable space, as they do in all collections of pharmaceutical formulas, the chapter taking some 97 pages. The formulas start with the simpler complexion washes and run into almond meals and pastes, through toilet vinegars, cold creams and pomades to soaps and soap powders. Then follow face powders and theatrical rouges, the rest of the chapter being given up to preparations for the hair, like the old fashioned pomades, mustache waxes, brilliantine, shampoos, hair restorers, invigorators, dyes and depilatories. The entire range is fully covered even to bleaches. Tooth powders and mouth washes complete the chapter. Listerine is included among the dentifrices and the formula given is certain to astonish the Americans owners of the trademark by its simplicity. The German formula constructor is truly a daring individual! Lacquers and varnishes receive adequate mention and the formulas are well constructed. The chapter on inks is very complete and informing, containing formulas for nearly every known variety of ink. Insecticides and vermin poisons are adequately treated, formulas being given for the most approved destroyers of bugs, rats, mice, moles, crows, foxes, martens and polecats. The chapter concludes curiously with formulas for scented baits for otters, fish and crabs. Photographic formulas and hints in developing make up a useful chapter, which brings the volume to a close. We have no hesitation in saying that the pharmacist who is possessed of a copy of "Buchheister's Formulary" need never be at a loss to supply any specialty asked of him.

A MANUAL OF PHARMACY FOR MEDICAL STUDENTS. By M. F. De Lorme, M.D., Ph.G., Instructor in Materia Medica and Pharmacy, Long Island College Hospital, etc. New York: The John C. Lindsay Company, 1905.

The neglect of pharmacy in medical colleges has been the subject of frequent comment in medical journals. The failure of the colleges to include a satisfactory course in pharmaceutical dispensing in their curricula has also been discussed by the medical societies. The growing tendency of physicians to prescribe the ready-made preparations of manufacturing pharmacists has been often deplored, but notwithstanding this no systematic effort has been made to remedy matters. In the Long Island College Hospital—the name under which the only medical college in Brooklyn is known—special attention seems to be paid to the study of pharmacology and the prescribing and dispensing of medicines. It is gratifying to note and record this fact. Dr. De Lorme's little book is well calculated to make the student of medicine familiar with the Pharmacopœia and with the galenical preparations in common use. It is purely a medical student's compendium, intended to give him the information needed by the practicing physician in the application of his knowledge of therapeutics. The manual contains a number of illustrative prescriptions, and it is to be presumed that the student will receive practical instruction in the compounding of these prescriptions, and by laboratory exercises and recitations receive a grounding in the art of prescribing sufficient to guard him against many of the common errors which tax the patience and the ingenuity of the pharmacist.

The book is of handy size, being adapted to fit the coat pocket, and the interleaving in the second section should prove a convenience to the student.

The proofreading of the book has been evidently neglected, for typographical errors abound. This is no reflection on the author, who should have been spared the appearance of errors of this kind, which belong to the purely mechanical part of the building of a book.

THE PRACTICE OF PHARMACY. A Treatise on the Modes of Making and Dispensing Official, Unofficial and Extemporaneous Preparations, with Descriptions of Medicinal Substances, Their Properties, Uses and Doses. Intended as a Hand-book for Pharmacists and Physicians and a Text-book for Students. Fourth edition. By Joseph P. Remington, Ph.M., Phar.D., F.C.S., chairman of the Committee of Revision of the Pharmacopœia of the United States of America; Professor of Theory and Practice of Pharmacy, and Director of the Pharmaceutical Laboratory in the Philadelphia College of Pharmacy. Philadelphia: J. B. Lippincott Company, 1906.

This new revised edition of Remington's well-known "Practice of Pharmacy" is distinguished by numerous improvements, which extend even to details of typography. De Vinne type has been substituted for the antique full faced type employed in the preceding edition, and the work has been improved in other mechanical features to make it more easy of reference and agreeable to the eye. The order of the book has not been changed, though the several divisions of the work have been remodeled and new illustrations of autograph prescriptions and new cuts of apparatus have been added. A valuable feature of the work for pharmacy students are the tables of official and unofficial substances and preparations. Among the unofficial preparations most of the newer remedies are included, and such as may not be found listed there find place in the glossary at the end of the volume. Each chapter is followed by a list of questions, the answers to which are given in an appendix. The questions bearing on the introductory chapter are, however, omitted in the fourth edition.

Professor Remington appears to prefer the abbreviation, "U. S. P. (8th Rev.)" for the purpose of quoting the title of the Eighth Decennial Revision of the United States Pharmacopœia, but we think the purpose would be just as well served if the abbrevation, "U. S. P., VIII," were used.

We have referred to the more agreeable appearance of the volume. This has been obtained largely, as stated, by the use of modern type, but the quality of the paper has also been improved, a whiter stock being employed, which, together with a blacker ink, makes the illustrations stand out better. The number of *fac-simile* prescriptions has been considerably increased.

Textbooks may come and textbooks may go, but Remington's "Practice" is destined to remain the standard for pharmacy students for many years to come.

Correspondence.

In Full Harmony with the N. A. R. D.

To the Editor:

Sir,—My attention is particularly called to one of the leading editorials in your valuable publication, entitled "The American Druggists' Syndicate," and fully appreciating your reputation for fairness, I feel sure that the article is inspired by a misunderstanding of the purpose of our organization and the personnel of its members.

Of course, I do not expect your publication to in any way vouch for the success of this enterprise, for such would be entirely unreasonable, but I do sincerely wish to correct the impression which the article states is prevailing that the object of this association is to offset the operations of the N. A. R. D. by providing the retailers with a line of proprietary remedies which could be sold independently of the old line jobbers.

Such an impression could only prevail among those who know absolutely nothing whatever about our plan. Our object is to work in perfect harmony with the N. A. R. D., as shown by the bona-fide stand taken by the directors in their resolution providing that all goods shall be marketed under a Direct Contract Serial Numbering Plan.

I, personally, without the assistance of any individual druggist, had the organization of this association well on the road to success before any of the gentlemen who now help to make up the directorate were invited or had any knowledge that they would be invited to act for the association in an official capacity, and the majority of the board of directors, consisting of fifteen members, are now and always have been actively associated with the N. A. R. D. E. L. Weston, of Syracuse, chairman of our finance committee, is well known as one of the most active and ardent supporters of the N. A. R. D. in the State of New York.

In fact, out of our 980 members, over 800 are either active members or in sympathy with the N. A. R. D. and its plan. This I will be glad to prove to you or anyone interested in the matter, by the signed statements of the members attached to suggestion blanks, which were filled out by them at my request, to be used as a guide by the directors at their first meeting, when the plan of marketing our products was decided upon.

While some of the gentlemen who consented to act on the directorate of this association are connected with institutions not affiliated with the N. A. R. D., I know that not one of them personally is opposed to that popular retail organization, and I also know that not one of them sought a position on this directorate. They only accepted after being assured that their services were desired by almost a unanimous vote of those who had subscribed for stock, and I don't believe that the members will ever have cause to regret their selection, for which I personally feel very grateful.

In conclusion, I can best illustrate how unfair that impression you refer to is when I assure you that I can convince you or any representative who will do us the honor of calling at our offices, that there is not 5 per cent. of the stock of this association held by any person or persons identified with any interests opposed to the N. A. R. D., and further, that no stockholder of this syndicate, except myself, owns more than one membership consisting of ten shares.

I hope that to carry out your usual policy of fairness, you will give this correction the publicity accorded to the article referred to, which reflected upon the honesty of the intention governing the organization of this syndicate.

C. H. Goddard, Secretary.

1 Madison Avenue, New York, January 12, 1906.

An Improvement in the Nomenclature of the Metric System.

The use of the metric system in the prescribing and dispensing of medicines has hitherto presented one or two difficulties which may have hindered its wider adoption, says the *Lancet*. In the metric system of measures the smallest subdivision of the measure of capacity is the millilitre, or as it has erroneously been called, the cubic centimetre. It is the one-thousandth part of the litre, and is equivalent to about 17 minims. The term cubic centimetre denotes, strictly speaking, a measure of volume, and as applied to a measure of capacity it is inappropriate, just as would be the case in the Imperial system if the term cubic feet were substituted for gallons. A practical disadvantage that is met with in the metric system lies in the relative magnitude of the smallest measure, the millilitre. This has been overcome to some extent by using decimal fractions of the millilitre. Thus, the dose of oil of copaiba is from 0.3 to 1.2 Mm., a quantity which does not convey to the mind so definite an impression as five to 20 minims, its Imperial equivalent. In order to simplify matters the suggestion has been made to the editor of *The Pharmaceutical Journal* that the millilitre should be known as the "mil," the one-tenth part of a millilitre as the "decimil," and the one-hundredth part of a millilitre as the "centimil." The actual values of these new terms will be better understood in the form of a table of suggested metric apothecaries' measure:

1 Centimil	= 0.00001 litre	=	0.1689 minim.
1 Decimil	= 0.0001 "	=	1.6894 minims.
1 Mil or Millilitre.	= 0.001 "	=	16,941 minims.
1 Centilitre	= 0.01 "	=	2.8157 fluid drachms.
1 Decilitre	= 0.1 "	=	3.5196 fluid ounces.
1 Litre		=	1.7598 pints.

The minim is equal to nearly six centimils, the fluid drachm to rather more than three and a half mils, the fluid ounce to nearly three centilitres, and the pint to nearly 57 centilitres, thus:

1 Minim	= 5.9192 centimils.
1 Fluid drachm	= 3.5515 mils.
1 Fluid ounce	= 2.8412 centilitres.
1 Pint	= 0.5682 litre.
1 Gallon	= 4.5459 litres.

The proposal to provide convenient subsidiary names for the 1.0, 0.1 and 0.01 millilitre with a view to promote the ready use of the metric system in prescribing and dispensing, was approved by the Council of the Pharmaceutical Society and submitted to Dr. Donald MacAlister for the consideration of the British Pharmacopœia Committee. This council agreed to support the suggestions and communicated its views to the Warden of the Standards. Mr. Chaney, superintendent of the Standards Department, warmly took the matter up and brought it to the notice of the Comité International des Poids et Mesures, with the result that this committee also accepted the proposition as useful in Great Britain. Measures and pipettes graduated to decimils and centimils are now obtainable, and as the Board of Trade has officially recognized the new terms prescribers will find no practical difficulty in employing the metric system. Thus in the case of oil of copaiba the dose as expressed by the metric system is 3 to 12 decimils. In actual practice the centimil will be found too small a quantity to be measured, but it is useful in calculations. It should be noted that one-half a decimil is equivalent to one standard drop from a pipette made to deliver 20 drops to one gramme of distilled water at 150 degrees C. The opponents of the metric system have laid emphasis on the danger there is of misplacing the decimal point. This objection does not now hold good in the case of the measures of capacity. There is little chance of a voluntary acceptance by the medical profession of the metric system. We are still accustomed to think in Imperial terms, a fact which should gratify a prominent British statesman. But if the compilers of the next edition of the British Pharmacopœia go a step further than the compilers of the 1898 edition, by inserting only the metric system of weights and measures, perhaps prescribers and dispensers would universally adopt it. The simplification of calculations of strengths and doses would alone afford sufficient reason for its early adoption. Thus, the exact amount of the potent ingredient in one dose of a given preparation may be calculated almost at a glance, whereas by the present system a laborious calculation is often required. Again, minute fractional parts of a grain convey only an indefinite meaning, but by the metric system the doses of potent preparations would be expressed in milligrammes; the dose of sulphate of physostigmine would then become 1 to 3 Mg., instead of 1-60 to 1-20 grain. Now that bottles and measures graduated by the metric system are easily obtainable, and the metric system, with the convenient new terms, mil, decimil and centimil have been officially recognized, there is no practical hindrance to a wider use of the metric system in medicine.

Red Cabbage as an Indicator.—Recently E. Fuld (*Münchener medicinische Wochenschrift*) recommended the coloring matter contained in red cabbage as an indicator in neutralization titrations. Claiming priority, P. Krebitz (*Seifensiederzeitung*) stated that he has used this indicator for more than a year. W. A. Puckner states (*Pharmaceutical Review*, January, 1905) that twenty years ago, when he was a student at the Chicago College of Pharmacy, Professor N. Gray Bartlett proposed the use of this coloring matter as an indicator in the volumetric estimation of acids and bases. The indicator when used in rather large amounts imparts a blue color to neutral solutions, turns red with acids and green with alkalies and in lecture demonstrations was used effectively to distinguish between acid, neutral and alkaline solutions.

MILITARY PHARMACISTS.

The Assistant Surgeon-General Opposes "American Druggist" Plans —Conceded Need for a Few Skilled Pharmacists—Dr. Payne Supports a Plan for a Pharmaceutical Corps—George J. Seabury Enters the Arena.

The efforts heretofore put forth to interest the military authorities in any plan providing for military pharmacists of commissioned rank have usually been met with either a chilly silence or with the mere negative assurance that the army has no need for pharmacists. The editorial article which appeared in our issue of December 25 on this subject in conjunction with a paper by the editor, which had been read before the Historical Section of the American Pharmaceutical Association, brought forth a letter from the office of the Surgeon-General of the army, which, while in pronounced opposition to our plan, shows a wholly different spirit from that which permeated that office. Major Jefferson R. Kean, the author of the letter, is assistant to the Surgeon-General, and since his communication is signed with his official title it is to be presumed that the opinions expressed meet with the approval of his superior officers. Editorial comment on this letter appears in another column. The letter from Major Kean follows:

SMALL NEED FOR MILITARY PHARMACISTS.

To the Editor:

Sir,—I have read with interest the editorial in your issue of December 25, entitled "Wasted Experience," and also the paper in the same number, "The Military Pharmacist in the Civil War." You will doubtless be willing to believe that there may be something which can be said in mitigation of your rather sweeping criticism of existing methods of medical supply in the army, and it is the purpose of this letter to say that something, and to state briefly what are the existing methods and what has been, in fact, the teaching of military experience. Of the 586 articles on the general supply table of the Army Medical Department 204, or not quite 35 per cent., are medicines and disinfectants, while the other 65 per cent. consists of furniture, bedding, clothing, hospital stores, instruments, appliances, dressings and miscellaneous articles. With regard to the latter, a surgeon who has had practical experience of their use in hospitals is probably the best judge of their quality and suitability. As to drugs, none are purchased until samples of the delivery have been analyzed by the accomplished chemist of the laboratory of the Surgeon General's Office and their purity thus assured. There is no difficulty in securing in this way any amount of medicines which may be required and, in point of fact, to keep the non-medicinal supplies up to standard is much more difficult.

In time of war the difficulty is not with the purchase of medical supplies, but with their transportation and prompt delivery at the front. This is by regulations delegated to the Quartermaster's Department and is the weak point of the system, transportation being the great and controlling factor of army administration on which depends the issue of battles and campaigns. Abundant medical supplies were taken to Santiago, but the troops lacked them because no means were provided for unloading them from the transports and transporting them to the front, and they were mostly brought back to the home ports untouched. The temporary deficiencies at Tampa and Jacksonville were due to defective transporting arrangements, causing delays in forwarding and confusion in locating medical supplies among the miles of freight cars.

It is difficult to see how these conditions would be improved by adding to the army even "148 pharmacists, officers ranging from colonel down to second lieutenant." The evidence of the surgeons at Montauk as brought out before the Dodge Commission shows that there was from the beginning a lavish abundance of medicines at that camp. And it is time to recognize (now that our national attack of hysteria has passed) that our soldiers, in spite of their grave infection with yellow fever and tropical malaria, did not "perish like flies." The total mortality from disease of the Fifth Army corps (Shafter's), from its organization at Tampa to its disbandment at Montauk, was just 400.

The European armies have pharmacist officers in their medical service because, in times past, before the development of the great establishments of modern manufacturing chemists, the pharmacists of the army manufactured its medicines and surgical dressings. This is still done by them to a large extent, whereas, in the United States, we find it from every point of view preferable to buy our supplies, from quinine pills to first aid dressings, from the great and reliable firms which have sprung up all over the land as a result of our national development. In the same way our Ordnance Department finds it preferable to buy powder rather than to manufacture it. This is a policy which the AMERICAN DRUGGIST will certainly not disapprove.

It does not take more than half a dozen officers, whether surgeons or pharmacists, to purchase the medical supplies of the army, and the drugs are—thanks to the skill and enterprise of our manufacturing pharmacists—for the most part in forms ready for convenient administration, so if a numerous corps of pharmacists were added to the army, no responsible duties could be found in which to employ them unless by the establishment of great government factories for the manufacture of medical supplies for the army. What else can we do with the 148 pharmacist officers which, Mr. Editor, you generously allow us? The great German Army with its 23 army corps has only 49 pharmaceutists permanently belonging to the military establishment, re-enforced by some 250 one-year volunteers (conscripts), yet they employ them for many purposes with which in our army the Medical Department has nothing to do, such as the analysis of foods and beverages. With all their wealth of conscripted *personnel* they do not find need of the services of even a one-year volunteer to a garrison of less than 1,800 men. The United States Army numbers two scant army corps and has only three garrisons as large as 1,800 men.

It is certain that the Medical Department could make good use of half a dozen pharmaceutical chemists and a like number of medical storekeepers, but 148, ranging from colonel to second lieutenant, would be surely an *embarras de richesse.*

Very respectfully,

J. R. KEAN,

Major, Surgeon U. S. Army,

Assistant to the Surgeon General.

War Department,
Office of the Surgeon General,
Washington, January 6, 1906.

THE "ARMY AND NAVY REGISTER'S" VIEWS.

A copy of Major Kean's letter to the editor of the AMERICAN DRUGGIST must have been furnished to the *Army and Navy Register*, for we find it published in full in that journal for January 13, together with the following editorial comment:

There is during a session of Congress no escape from unusual bills, the enactment of which would produce no other effect than needlessly increasing Governmental expenditure. It will be recognized at once that to this class belongs the proposition, evidently originating with and certainly advocated by the *American Druggist and Pharmaceutical Record*. An article and an editorial in a recent issue of that valuable representative journal are devoted to the subject of military pharmacists and argue in favor of a corps of pharmacists, consisting of nearly 150 officers, whose rank shall be from colonel down to second lieutenant, the senior member to have the additional title of "pharmacist general." The proposition is based on the far-fetched theory that the deaths during the war with Spain might have been prevented in a large measure had there been a corps of pharmacists. It is very properly pointed out in a letter reproduced elsewhere—written by Major J. R. Kean, United States army, assistant to the Surgeon-General, and addressed to the editor of the *American Druggist*—that there is no warrant for saying that our soldiers at Montauk "perished like flies." That is a fiction which has been too long endured and, as the army surgeon remarks, it is time to establish the truth. As a matter of fact, "the total mortality from disease in the Fifth Army Corps fro mits organization at Tampa to its disbandment at Montauk was just 400." Whatever failure occurred at Tampa and Jacksonville in the medical service and whatever was subject to criticism in the same department while our troops were in Cuba were due to lack of transportation at a time and in a country where the facilities were impeded beyond any relief which the most experienced army quartermasters could afford.

There is no question of the value of pharmacists and the medical department, as is stated in Major Kean's letter, could make good use of some six pharmaceutical chemists and as many medical storekeepers. Beyond that the pharmacists of the projected corps would be an incumbrance and an extravagance. We imagine that the firms which manufacture medical supplies, of which the Government buys a large quantity for its military and naval services, will not relish the movement inaugurated by the *American Druggist* to impose upon the army medical department 149 pharmaceutical officers of rank from colonel down to second lieutenant. There would be one direct result at least: that of the establishment of Government plants to produce the medical supplies which are now purchased under contract.

DR. PAYNE SUPPORTS THE AMERICAN DRUGGIST'S PLAN.

Dr. George F. Payne, of Atlanta, Ga., a former president of the American Pharmaceutical Association, and who was for many years chairman of the committee of the American Pharmaceutical Association on the status of the pharmacists in the service of the United States, writes a letter supporting the views of the AMERICAN DRUGGIST as follows:

DR. PAYNE HAS LIVELY HOPES FOR THE FUTURE OF THE MILITARY PHARMACIST.

To the Editor:

Sir,—I have just read with a great deal of interest in the December number of the AMERICAN DRUGGIST the article on "The Military Pharmacist in the Civil War." In the last paragraph of the article you refer to the work of the American Pharmaceutical Association and suggest that if it had been along the line of securing pharmacists independent of the present hospital stewards, it would have been more successful. I wish to say as chairman of that committee that we took up this feature of the case on several occasions with the Surgeon-General of the United States Army, but the answers were practically of the same character and each amounted to stating that there was no need of pharmacists in the United States Army, as pharmacy was a very small part of the work of the present hospital steward, as his pharmaceutical duties were chiefly the counting out of ready-made tablets and the handling of other ready-made preparations.

It might be interesting to the pharmacists of the United States to see some of this correspondence, but I think we have shown the spirit in which these suggestions were made in one or two of our reports. It would be much more satisfactory to the hospital stewards for us to work in touch with them for further advancement and their aid and suggestions would be very valuable, but this, it has been found, is very difficult to secure on account of the peculiarly handicapped position in which the army hospital steward is placed. I have come to the conclusion that the surest way to get pharmacy properly recognized in the army is to have a separate corps of pharmacists independent of the present hospital stewards, as you suggest. It will probably take a big fight, however, to bring the Surgeon-General of the army over to our way of thinking, but I believe the advance which has been accomplished in the navy and marine hospital service can be accomplished in the army also. Our committee has taken some active steps in this direction and we believe that this condition of affairs which you suggest will eventually be brought about.

When we consider what has already been accomplished in the navy and in the marine hospital service we have every reason to feel encouraged for active work in regard to the status of the pharmacists in the army. In the navy we have practically secured commissions and good salaries, and but for the interpretation of one of the acts in a way adverse to the naval pharmacists they would be enjoying at present the rank of ensign and commissions, as they have been made warrant officers and if given the full rights of other warrant officers they would now have the rank of ensign without further legislation. The Surgeon-General has taken up the matter of securing legislation to accord to the present pharmacists of the navy who are warrant officers *all* of the privileges of other warrant officers and we think commissions will be secured within the next few months. They would have been secured last year but for there being a deficit in the treasury and anything carrying an appropriation which could be deferred to a later date was left to be taken up at a later period. The bill no doubt would have passed early in the last session, but it was found necessary to change the wording of the bill to meet certain conditions and it got placed later down on the list than would have otherwise been the case. The Surgeon-General went before the Naval Committee and made a strong argument in favor of the bill, and I am confident it will pass at the present session of Congress.

In the name of pharmacy I wish to thank you for your continued interest in this work. You were among the first to help us in labor when so many thought it was useless to even make an effort.

Yours sincerely,

GEORGE F. PAYNE.

ATLANTA, GA., January 2, 1906.

GEORGE J. SEABURY TAKES UP THE TASK OF SECURING RECOGNITION FOR THE PHARMACIST.

George J. Seabury, of New York, who has been the New York member of Dr. Payne's committee for many years and who this year succeeds Dr. Payne as chairman, has written a letter on the subject of the status of the military pharmacist to a member of the United States Senate, from which we take the following excerpts:

THE AMERICAN PHARMACEUTICAL ASSOCIATION AND THE GOVERNMENT PHARMACIST.

To the Editor:

Sir,—I have pleasure in sending you herewith a list of the names of the committee of the American Pharmaceutical Association on the status of the pharmacist. This committee has been formed for success, and will not surrender until we succeed. We may have to bide a wee, but when the plan of action is once resolved upon, we propose to fight it out, not only all Summer, but all Spring, Autumn and Winter as well.

I enclose you a letter sent to the United States Senator who will have charge of our interests. I have corresponded with him and will, when I see him personally, draw up our plan of action. We will not proceed on any guerilla legislation, but tack our bill to one that will concern the reformation of the medical service, where it belongs by proper classification. Will keep you posted when we start in for victory. We will be content with nothing less—the rank and pay will be fought for the entire service—no discrimination in any branch. With a "Happy New Year," I remain,

Yours truly,

GEORGE J. SEABURY, Chairman.

NEW YORK, January 3, 1906.

COMMITTEE ON STATUS OF PHARMACISTS IN THE ARMY, NAVY AND PUBLIC HEALTH AND MARINE HOSPITAL SERVICE OF THE UNITED STATES.

George J. Seabury, chairman, New York.

MEMBERS AT LARGE.

Prof. James H. Beal, Pennsylvania.

Dr. George F. Payne, Georgia.

Lucien B. Hall, Ohio, president National Wholesale Druggists' Association.

M. T. Breslin, Louisiana, president National Association of Retail Druggists.

Members of general committee, the presidents of State Associations:

State and name.	State and name.
Alabama, E. H. Cross.	Nebraska, Niels P. Hansen.
Arizona, Harry Brisley.	Nevada, Jos. M. Taber.
Arkansas, W. H. Skinner.	New Hampshire, Albert J. Weeks,
California, J. H. Dawson.	New Jersey, Wm. M. Davis.
Colorado, Chas. J. Clayton.	New Mexico, Geo. A. Morris.
Dist. of Columbia, S. L. Hilton.	New York, J. A. Lockie.
Connecticut, J. A. Hodgson.	North Carolina, T. R. Hood.
Delaware, Joseph P. Williams.	North Dakota, H. H. Bateman.
Florida, Thomas Clarke.	Ohio, Z. T. Baltzly.
Georgia, Max Morris.	Oklahoma, A. B. Clark.
Idaho, David E. Smithson.	Oregon, B. F. Jones.
Illinois, Christian Garver.	Pennsylvania, D. J. Thomas.
Indiana, Harry E. Glick.	Rhode Island, John E. Groff.
Iowa, Geo. M. Pedersen.	South Carolina, C. A. Milford.
Kansas, Carl Engel.	South Dakota, W. F. Michel.
Kentucky, C. A. Leathers.	Tennessee, T. J. Shannon.
Louisiana, C. D. Sauvinet.	Texas, J. P. Hayter.
Maine, A. W. Meserve.	Utah, F. C. Schramm.
Maryland, M. A. Toulson.	Vermont, F. W. Mitchell.
Massachusetts, Peter McCormick.	Virginia, T. A. Miller.
Michigan, J. O. Schlotterback.	Washington, P. Jensen.
Minnesota, Chas. H. Huhn.	West Virginia, C. G. Buchanan.
Mississippi, Anthony Fly.	Wisconsin, H. L. Schulz.
Missouri, J. F. Llewellyn.	Wyoming, R. L. Newman.
Montana, Fred. A. Woehner.	Indian Territory, Thomas Shackle.

THE LETTER TO THE UNITED STATES SENATOR.

Below is a copy of the letter referred to above by Mr. Seabury:

Dear Senator:

In September last I accepted the chairmanship of the American Pharmaceutical Associations' Committee on the status of pharmacists in the Army and Navy in particular and extended it to the National Guard and Marine Hospital Service as well. You know something about the latter since you interested yourself in its behalf, but we have not gone far enough.

In his message the President referred to our lack in the medical department. I endorse many of his observations and criticisms of the quality and capacity of physicians at present in the government service and think he might have gone just one step further and made the same remarks apply to the practitioners in pharmacy.

When we asked Surgeon-General O'Reilly to send a representative to our last meeting in Atlantic City to represent the hospital stewards, he replied, that he regretted to say that we had no pharmacists in the army; he was therefore unable to send a representative—an admission that will spur on our committee. However the government was not unrepresented since General Wyman sent us a most worthy representative of the profession from the Marine Hospital Service.

When Governor of the State of New York the President signed a bill making the hospital steward in the National Guard a first lieutenant, though a year afterwards he was reduced to his former non-commissioned officer's position to conform with the regulations of the regular establishment. We want him reinstated through new army medical regulations with rank and pay of an officer.

It will be my duty to see you and I will be armed with proper documents and will ask you to act as the medium of our pleadings to have our professional brethren promoted to the rank and pay of an officer. I am not sure that we will ask for a captaincy or first lieutenancy, but officer he must be at proper compensation; he is entitled to this distinction by training, deportment and mental capacity, whether he be an Army pharmacist, Naval apothecary, Marine hospital service pharmacist or National Guard hospital steward. He enjoys an officer's position in all the advanced and well regulated armies of the world, the German, French, Russian and Japanese. The highest officer on the German apothecary staff has the rank of a colonel and so on down to the lowest grades of officers.

There is no sound reason why pharmacists should be discriminated against in their demand for equal rank and pay with the allied professions, whether it be medicine, veterinary practice or dentistry. In fact the studies of the pharmacist of to-day are more complex than those of any other single profession.

I have organized my committee and will be ready to work at any time. This committee will also suggest to the government that it owes to the nation and to our soldiers and sailors that they appoint as hospital stewards, naval apothecaries or hospital pharmacists, only those having a college education or certificates from a State Board of Pharmacy. Our soldiers and sailors are worthy of the best service at the command of the profession to compound and dispense their medicines and deadly drugs. It is economy for the government to keep our forces in good health wherever they may be. In war the pharmacist temporarily supplants the disabled physician.

Another point that favors this movement is that to-day the college curriculum has been extended to four years with entrance qualifications equal to those of the highest colleges, especially in the College of the City of New York. Our sister-colleges are not far behind. The pharmacist is the practical copartner of the physician and equals him in point of responsibility. His life work is even more exacting—if I may so define it, it is a life of slavery to both professions.

This letter is longer than I contemplated writing when addressing you, but I thought it would relieve you from a tedious interview when I made a personal application. You can think it over at your leisure and then when I visit you, you can get rid of me in record time.

I herewith enclose a list of our committee as formed for Victory and, let us hope, not for Defeat.

Very truly yours,

George J. Seabury, Chairman.

New York, January 6, 1906.

SPECIAL MEETING OF THE VIRGINIA ASSOCIATION.

Attitude of the Association on Legislative Matters Referred—Bill Requiring Filing of Proprietary Formulas Held Up—Virginia Apprentice Bill Disapproved.

Richmond, Va., January 12.—By practically unanimous vote the Virginia Pharmaceutical Association, in special session held in this city on January 3, rejected both the so-called pharmacy bill and the proposed measure designed to regulate the sale of patent and proprietary medicines in the State, and referred the entire matter to committees, which will not report until after the General Assembly has adjourned.

CHARACTER OF THE BILLS.

At its last regular meeting the association indorsed the bills, one legalizing the employment of a registered apprentice pharmacist under 18 years of age, who may be left in management of the business, and the other providing that the proprietor of any patent medicine should make written application to the Board of Pharmacy for the privilege of selling it, and should file with the board an affidavit showing the ingredients of the medicine and a description of the package in which it is sold, together with the directions and advertisements. The resolution calling for the introduction of the Patent Medicine bill was adopted by a vote of 10 to 9.

OPPOSITION DEVELOPS.

Recently a strong movement in opposition to these bills developed. Meetings were held in this city by the druggists, and the drug clerks as well, and an organized fight began. Twelve members of the Virginia Pharmaceutical Association, which had indorsed the bills, signed a request for a special session, and the body was called to meet in this city. The session began at 10.30 o'clock in the auditorium of the Medical College of Virginia, with about 40 members present, including druggists from Richmond, Lynchburg, Newport News, Portsmouth and other cities. T. A. Miller, of this city, presided, and C. W. Fleet, of Lynchburg, acted as secretary.

ANIMATED DISCUSSION.

Practically the entire session was devoted to a consideration of the bills. The discussion was very animated, but the final action is said to have been almost unanimous. Various suggestions were made, with the result that the association ultimately rescinded its former action and rejected both bills. Two committees were appointed, one for each bill, to report at the next annual meeting, which will be held in July, after the General Assembly has adjourned. This practically leaves the entire matter in abeyance until the Legislature of 1908. The committee to consider the Patent Medicine bill consists of E. D. Taylor, T. W. Chelf and Gordon Blair, all of this city. Its report, if it makes one at all, will be diametrically opposed to the bill as proposed. The committee on the Apprentice bill is composed of Polk Miller, T. N. Curd and Gordon Blair, all of this city. It will likely recommend a bill with the features objectionable to the drug clerks eliminated.

Syracuse Druggists to Celebrate.

The Syracuse Druggists' Association is to hold its annual outing at Long Branch on January 25. The attendance will include all druggists in the county, with their wives and friends, and dinner will be served promptly at 8 o'clock, after which bowling, dancing and cards will give all a chance for a sociable time. The committee has secured a prize for each person in attendance and also grand prizes for bowling, whist, pedro and dancing.

THE PERFUME INDUSTRY DISCUSSED AT THE COLLEGE OF PHARMACY.

The Flower Industry of Grasse—The Invention of Synthetic Perfume Material Increases the Demand for the Natural Product—Nominating Committee Appointed.

President Nicholas Murray Butler held an informal reception in the office of the secretary of the Department of Pharmacy of the University on the evening of Tuesday, January 16, on the occasion of the regular quarterly meeting of the College of Pharmacy. Many of the older members of the college were in attendance and met President Butler for the first time and were uniformly impressed with his cordiality and by the prompt and energetic manner in which he took up the business before the college.

THE NOMINATING COMMITTEE.

After the reading of the minutes of preceding meeting President Butler asked for the reading of the minutes of the transactions of the Board of Trustees during the interval which had occurred since the last meeting. These transactions were largely routine in their character and required no action upon the part of the college. The president announced the following members as constituting the Nominating Committee who were charged with the presentation of a list of nominees for the offices of the college to be presented at the annual meeting, which occurs in March. The names of the members of the committee follow: Ewen McIntyre, Adolph Henning, Oscar Goldmann, Charles S. Erb, Gustavus Balser, John R. Caswell and F. O. Collins.

MR. BURR'S ADDRESS.

This being the only business before the college the meeting adjourned, after which Edwin H. Burr, the American representative of Roure, Bertrand Fils, of Grasse, France, delivered an address on Perfumery Materials. A full report of the address appears in another column, together with reproductions of a few of the numerous attractive lantern slides showing various aspects of the perfume industry in and around Grasse, which were used by the lecturer to illustrate his remarks. Mr. Burr was listened to with marked attention both by the members of the college and by the members of the senior class, who were present by special invitation.

A VOTE OF THANKS.

At the conclusion of the address Albert L. Plaut moved that the thanks of the college be extended to Mr. Burr for his interesting and instructive address. In seconding this motion Caswell A. Mayo said that he wished particularly to congratulate the members of the senior class upon this opportunity to have their attention directed to a field which offered remarkable openings for such men as had the special qualifications and attainments required to win success in it. He said that in discussing the subject of the lecture before the meeting Mr. Burr had pointed out as his particular reason for desiring to lay before the college such information as he possessed concerning the perfume industry the fact that American perfumers lacked somewhat of that artistic instinct backed up by a thorough and basic knowledge of materials which had enabled the French perfumer to take the first rank in the markets of the world. Mr. Burr, he said, believed that the ranks of pharmacy were the source from which expert perfumers should spring. The colleges of pharmacy gave the necessary preliminary education along scientific lines and inculcated the scientific spirit necessary to a proper study of perfumery material. It was to be hoped that among the thousands of young men who were being educated in pharmacy from year to year there might be some few who in conjunction with the knowledge acquired at the schools might have those peculiar gifts of sense and artistic taste necessary to develop the highest type of perfumer. Mr. Mayo congratulated the members of the senior class upon this opportunity to learn something of perfumery materials, and said he hoped that among them there might be some one who could fulfill the ideal set up by Mr. Burr to his own great pecuniary gain, to the honor of American perfumery and to the credit of American pharmacy.

The thanks of the college were extended to Mr. Burr by rising vote.

A collation was served for the senior class in the pharmacognosy room and for the members of the college in the library.

BOSTON DRUGGISTS ELECT OFFICERS.

Closing of a Successful Year by the Boston Association of Retail Druggists—An Annual Ball Decided Upon—New Officers—A Life Membership for Mr. Canning, the Retiring President.

(*From our Regular Correspondent.*)

Boston, January 17.—The annual meeting of the Boston Association of Retail Druggists was held at the Massachusetts College of Pharmacy, January 10, President Canning in the chair. Forty-eight members were present. The reports of the secretary and treasurer were read and approved. The treasurer reported $2,221.11 on hand.

The Executive Committee reported, recommending the more extensive use of the National Association of Retail Druggists' cost mark on prescriptions; second, that the dues remain the same as last year; third, that Stephen F. Chamberlain be elected to membership. The recommendations were all adopted. The Auditing Committee reported the books as correctly kept. The annual report of the secretary was read and placed on file. President Canning gave the summary of the work accomplished during the year.

On motion of Mr. Wheeler, the motion of Mr. Finneran, which was laid on the table at the last meeting, was amended to the effect that the elections in the various auxiliaries should take place within fifteen days after date of annual meeting, instead of seven. This was voted.

BOSTON DRUGGISTS TO DANCE.

On motion of Mr. Ernst, it was voted that an annual ball be held not later than March 1.

A letter from the National Association of Retail Druggists' headquarters, with bill for one third of the annual dues, was read. On motion, it was voted that the bill be referred to a committee of three, consisting of the president, secretary and treasurer, who were to be authorized to send the amount when collected.

The election of officers was as follows: President, Prof. Elie H. LaPierre; first vice-president, J. Arthur Bean; second vice-president, John J. Tobin; treasurer, John G. Godding; secretary, Charles H. Davis.

On motion of Mr. Ernst, it was voted that Mr. Canning, the retiring president, be accorded a life membership. He was also given a rising vote of thanks for his services.

Mr. Brown, of Brighton, reported on the good work done in Auxiliary 12. Upon motion of Mr. Tobin, it was voted that the books kept by the secretaries of the different auxiliaries be withdrawn as superfluous.

On motion of Mr. Finneran, it was voted that the Executive Committee comprise the Schedule Committee, with full power to act until the new committee is appointed.

After an interesting discussion of the liquor law as pertaining to druggists, it was voted, on motion of Mr. Canning, that the Legislative Committee be instructed to work for the repeal of that part of the screen law that relates to druggists. On motion of Mr. Tobin, it was voted that flowers be sent to Miss Sumner, one of the lady members, who recently met with an accident.

It was moved by Mr. Ernst that the Boston Association of Retail Druggists be incorporated under the laws of Massachusetts. This, as amended by Mr. Canning to the effect that the matter be left to the officers of the association, with full powers to act, was voted.

Frank W. Dallinger, of Cambridge, gave an interesting illustrated lecture on his hot soda urn, with samples of his product.

METROPOLITAN ASSOCIATION MEETS.

Annual Meeting of the Local Branch of the N. A. R. D.—Harmony Prevailed Contrary to Expectations—Action Taken and Officers Elected.

Those who went to the annual meeting on Friday night, January 12, of the Metropolitan Association of Retail Druggists expecting to see a stormy session were disappointed in this respect. Prior to the meeting it had been whispered around that some members had brought their 'axes" with them and were going to use them quite freely; that the meeting would be marked by some pretty plain talk and that there would be a lively debate over some features of the local situation. But nothing of that sort happened. If any member of the association took his "axe" with him, he kept it well out of sight. The meeting, which was held at the New York College of Pharmacy, and which lasted from about 9.30 p. m. until midnight, proved perfectly harmonious from beginning to end without one discordant note. It was a veritable lovefeast.

When President Anderson called the meeting to order there were about 60 members present; this number was increased to about 75 as the meeting progressed. Following the roll call of officers, president Anderson called vice-president Lauer to the chair, while he made his annual address; Mr. Lauer was not present then, neither were the two other vice-presidents—Peter Diamond or A. G. Searles. He finally asked Jacob Diner to preside temporarily. In his address president Anderson dwelt at some length upon price demoralization in the retail drug trade, particularly in Greater New York. It was, he said, an evil which affected all three branches of the drug trade, the manufacturer, jobber and retailer, and he pointed out how necessary it was to have perfect co-operation among all these interests if they hoped to accomplish the desired results. Of the Direct Contract Serial Numbering Plan, President Anderson said among other things:

"It rises so far above all other plans that have been suggested or tried that its general introduction by the individual proprietor should not be interfered with by connecting it in any way with those plans that fail to give results, are illegal or benefit one branch of the trade alone. It is a plan involving the legal rights and the will of the individual proprietor and compliance with the same by those who desire to act as his wholesale or retail distributing agents, and I believe the time has come for each local association affiliated with the N. A. R. D. and the N. A. R. D. in turn to leave no room for doubt as to their true position on this subject and at the same time cut off the possibility of misrepresentations by those whose selfish interests would retard or prevent the general acceptance of the plan by declaring that we want the direct contract serial number plan only and the friendship and co-operation of the proprietor will be measured by his acceptance or rejection of the same. And in this connection I recommend that the N. A. R. D. reaffirm its faith in an allegiance to the direct contract serial numbering plan as the only plan that will produce desired results, and call upon each manufacturer of proprietary remedies to market his products on that plan.

"I further recommend that this association suggest to its members the advisability of refusing to become distributing agents for any new proprietary remedy not marketed on the direct contract serial number plan.

LOCAL CONDITIONS.

"It is less than one year since this association took up the work of assisting in the great movement for better conditions in the retail drug trade. We very wisely decided to confine our efforts principally to making a success of the direct contract serial number plan, and while I realize that local conditions must be changed somewhat before full success can be claimed for our undertaking, sufficient progress has been made to demonstrate the practicability and power of the D. C. S. N. plan, and a continuation of our efforts cannot fail to accomplish all we started out to do.

"Our constituents must bear in mind the many obstacles to be overcome in a great commercial center like New York and the time required in order to bring about a condition that will conform to the provisions of the new plan.

"Many doubtful retailers had to be convinced, wholesalers who did not believe there was anything in it and that it would soon blow over shown that it was full and secure and had come to stay, and the deliberate and determined opposers hunted out and dealt with.

"Unnumbered goods that were on the market before the proprietor put his plan in effect have caused much trouble and delay, but the supply of these is now practically exhausted, and thus one by one the difficulties are disappearing and the issue is narrowing down to a contest with a few who apparently are determined to exhaust every means before giving in and accepting the new regulations and increased profits.

"One of the most encouraging things in the situation to-day is the interest and activity of each proprietor who is marketing his products on the direct contract serial number plan. They are all here and treating violations and evasions of their contracts in a most consistent and determined manner, and with our support and co-operation success will surely crown their efforts. We all realize the importance and necessity of the work our association has undertaken. We have faith in the plans under which we are operating, and now all that is needed is a little patience, sufficient backbone to stand up and combat difficulties, and untiring efforts in the interest of those proprietors who have come to our rescue and replaced promises that were weak and unfruitful with acts that are sincere, strong and beneficial.

"We cannot do too much to show our appreciation of their efforts, and I recommend that this association request its members to give the products of all D. C. S. N. proprietors a most prominent place in their stores and by frequent window displays, free distribution of advertising matter and personal suggestions, cause them to feel the true value of the retailer's friendship and co-operation.

FINANCES.

"The financing of any organization is an important item. The uncertainty as to membership made our estimate of last year's income and expense a matter of speculation, but I believe the report of the treasurer will show that we figured closely, and our income has been at least sufficient to pay all moneys due the N. A. R. D. for dues, organizers' services, etc., and the ordinary running expenses of the association, except a salary for the secretary, which has never been fixed, Secretary Swann having done all the work of that office, and it has not been small by any means, without compensation.

"In reviewing the work before us I have tried to figure how small a burden we can place upon our members and still pay expenses, and inasmuch as we must pay $4 to the N. A. R. D. for each member, and organization work should be continued in order to strengthen our association as much as possible, I recommend that the dues for the coming year be $8 per member.

CONCLUSION.

"In conclusion I want to assure you of my appreciation of the honor conferred on me by my election as the first president of the M. A. R. D., extend my thanks to the other officers for the assistance they have rendered to the members of the executive and general committees, for their interest and encouragement, and express the hope that my successor may receive the same loyal support from all and the M. A. R. D. with increased strength and power may become a greater factor in the work for the benefit of the retail drug trade than its most ardent supporters have hoped it might be."

A committee of three, consisting of Messrs. Rosenzweig, Montgomery and Bischoff, was appointed to consider and report upon the recommendations in the president's address.

S. V. B. Swann then reported as secretary. Regarding the membership he said that on March 28, 1905, there were about 400 members; since then the number steadily increased up to November of last year, very few new members having joined the association during that and the succeeding month. The membership at present, he said, stood as follows:

Member in boroughs of Kings and Richmond who have paid $7.50	120
Members in boroughs of Kings and Richmond who have paid less than $7.50	227

Members in Borough of Manhattan who have paid less than $7.50	425
Members in Borough of Manhattan who have paid $7.50	247
Total	1,069

This total membership represents 75 per cent. of the retail drug trade of Greater New York, and shows an increase in membership of more than 600 since the association was organized. Secretary Swann then read the minutes of the meetings of the executive committee and also of the last meeting of the general committee, held at Allaire's, 192 Third avenue, Monday, January 8. What took place at that meeting may be briefly summarized as follows: The general committee refused to accept the resignation of the Staten Island auxiliary and also refused to take favorable action on the "open market" resolution adopted at a previous meeting of the Kings County Pharmaceutical Society. The Staten Islanders claimed that the only relief they had obtained was a schedule adopted last summer which the N. A. R. D. was unable to enforce for them. That was the reason they wished to withdraw from the local branch of the national association. A communication on this subject from Thomas V. Wooten left the matter entirely in the hands of the M. A. R. D. Secretary Swann was instructed by the general committee to inform the Staten Island contingent that the M. A. R. D. could not accept their resignation for the reason that it recognizes only individuals and not districts. It also developed at the meeting of the general committee that upon the request of president Anderson the two organizers had been withdrawn from this city, because of the lack of funds with which to pay them. The committee endorsed this action. On the question of buying clubs, Mr. Wooten said he had no intention of interfering.

On motion the secretary's report was received.

Treasurer Rosenzweig reported that the total receipts up to and including January 12, 1906, were $2,269.75; the total disbursements were $2,226.10, leaving a balance in the treasury of $58.65.

The matter of the Kings County "open market" resolution then came up. The resolution as passed by the Kings County Society read as follows:

Resolved, That it is the sense of the Kings County Pharmaceutical Society that the Metropolitan Association of Retail Druggists, through the N. A. R. D., shall request all manufacturers to market their goods on the Direct Contract Serial Numbering Plan, and that those who do not adopt this plan be requested to sell their goods in the New York market without regard to the rebate plan or tripartite agreement, providing such sale does not interfere with existing arrangements in other parts of the country.

Mr. Rehfus then offered a substitute resolution as follows:

Resolved, That we request all manufacturers of proprietary remedies to market their products on the direct Contract Serial Numbering Plan, and we request those who do not to give to all retail druggists of this city the same privileges in buying as may be accorded the large dealers, brokers or other buyers of their products.

After some discussion in which Reuben R. Smith, Jacob Diner and others participated, this substitute resolution, seconded by Mr. Diner, was unanimously adopted, and the subject which many had expected would precipitate a hot discussion was meekly and harmoniously settled.

Mr. Montgomery, for the special committee that had been appointed to secure representation for pharmacists on the City Board of Health, reported. He said that a joint committee representing the various pharmaceutical associations had waited on Health Commissioner Darlington and had submitted arguments in favor of having pharmacists represented on the advisory board of the Health Department. Commissioner Darlington, he said, did not think it necessary to have a pharmacist on the general advisory board, but the Commissioner said he had been thinking seriously of asking some pharmacists to act as an advisory board on all matters of the department affecting the drug trade. He accordingly requested the delegation to name some ten pharmacists from whom say five could be selected to act as such a board. Mr. Montgomery said that had been done and the list of names had been mailed to Commissioner Darlington.

RECOMMENDATIONS ADOPTED.

The report of the committee on the president's recommendations was then received and unanimously adopted. The recommendations follow:

"We reaffirm our faith in the Direct Contract Serial Numbering Plan. The evidence of the success of the plan is so fully illustrated to our satisfaction by the action of the several proprietors marketing their goods in this manner that we urge our members to use their utmost efforts for furthering this plan.

"We advise our members to refuse to put any new preparations on sale unless they are marked under the D. C. S. N. plan.

"We recommend that the dues of $8 for the ensuing year may be divided into two parts whenever the payment of the whole at one time would be impracticable."

The matter of the status of pharmacists in the army and navy was brought up, and on motion of Mr. Bischoff the Metropolitan Association "endorsed the movement to elevate the position of pharmacists in the army and navy."

Mr. Bohan, of the N. A. R. D. staff, was reappointed as an organizer in this city.

TALKS BY VISITORS.

President Anderson then called on some of the visitors at the meeting for remarks. The first one to respond to this invitation was Dr. Leed, president of the Eye-Fix Company. He said that his company had had great success with the D. C. S. N. plan. The next speaker was Mr. Weil, of the wholesale firm of Britt, Loeffler & Weil; he congratulated the association on the work already accomplished. The jobbing trade, he said, would give all the support it possibly could, and it would not be the jobbers' fault if the movement did not succeed. At any time that the M. A. R. D. is in need of assistance, the jobbing trade, he said, will be ready to give it.

JOBBERS ARE PLAYING FAIR.

Mr. DeShetley, manager of the N. A. R. D.'s Department of the East, spoke on the strength of the M. A. R. D. organization. A very good showing had been made, he said, in view of the demoralized conditions at the start. The West Side of the city was well organized, but much remained to be done on the East Side. He referred to a conference which he, John C. Gallagher and two others had had recently with representatives of the local jobbing trade. The jobbers gave assurances of assisting the movement in every possible way. "The jobbers are playing fair," said Mr. DeShetley, "and are for the retailer, and we are friends of the jobber if the jobber is our friend." He spoke of the work being done by the Department of the East. "The department is here to stay," he continued, "and will gladly assist every retailer in Greater New York at any and all times."

Among others who made remarks were Harry B. Mason, associate editor of the *Bulletin of Pharmacy*, Detroit; Messrs. Bellaire and Bohan, N. A. R. D., organizers; Mr. Davis, of Westchester County; Mr. Maas, of the East New York district, and Mr. Adams, N. A. R. D. organizer in New Jersey.

THE NEW OFFICERS.

The election of officers for the ensuing year was then taken up. President Anderson declined re-election. On motion of Mr. Diner, a rising vote of thanks was tendered to Dr. Anderson for his untiring efforts in behalf of the association and the able manner in which he had performed the duties of president. Mr. Diner then proposed Reuben R. Smith for president. There were no other nominations and one ballot was cast by the secretary for Mr. Smith. The following officers and trustees were then named, there being no contest in any office and one ballot being cast for the nominee in each case:

For first vice-president, Jacob Diner, of Manhattan.

For second vice-president, O. C. Kleine, of Brooklyn.

For third vice-president, W. F. Maas, of Brooklyn.

For secretary, S. V. B. Swann, of Manhattan.

For treasurer, A. H. Bischoff, of the Bronx.

For trustees, Messrs. Alpers, Lauer, Rafter and Diamond, of Manhattan; Messrs. Kunkle and Heimmerzheim, of Kings, and Louis Axt, of Staten Island.

After the installation of the new officers and trustees, the meeting adjourned.

MANHATTAN DRUGGISTS MEET.

Advisory Board of Pharmacists for the Health Department—Commissioner Darlington's Official Recognition Gratifies Members of the Manhattan Association—An Address by Harry B. Mason.

Routine matters were about the only business transacted at the regular monthly meeting of the Manhattan Pharmaceutical Association's meeting last Monday night. President Alpers was in the chair and there were about twenty members present. After the reading and approving of the minutes as read by Secretary Swann (who was complimented on the complete nature of same) Treasurer Hitchcock reported that $11.25 had been received in dues since the previous meeting; the disbursements had been $97. The balance on hand was reported as $101.85.

Mr. Searles, for the Legislative Committee, reported that nothing had so far developed in the State Legislature of any direct interest to pharmacists, and he hoped that this state of affairs would continue.

RECOGNITION FOR PHARMACISTS.

Dr. Alpers, as chairman of the special committee appointed to secure representation for pharmacists on the advisory board of the City Health Department, reported that joint meetings had been held with delegates from the various pharmaceutical associations, at which the subject had been thoroughly discussed. A sub-committee was appointed and conferred with Health Commissioner Darlington, placing before him the request of the drug trade. The Commissioner did not think it advisable or necessary to have a pharmacist as a member of the advisory board, but he favored the creation of an advisory board composed of pharmacists which could be consulted in all health board matters pertaining to pharmacy. Commissioner Darlington asked the committee to send him names of pharmacists for such a board, and accordingly the committee forwarded the following names: C. O. Bigelow, William C. Alpers, Felix Hirsemann, William Muir and B. H. Bernstein.

"I believe we should all be gratified with this official recognition," said Dr. Alpers; "it is a matter for congratulation, and I believe that gradually the profession of pharmacy will be looked upon in a much broader light than it has been in the past."

INVITED TO THE ALUMNI BALL.

A communication was read from the Alumni Association of the New York College inviting the members of the Manhattan Association to attend the annual Alumni ball, which is to be held on February 7 at the Crystal Palace.

Mr. Hitchcock, for the committee in charge of the pamphlet which will contain data on the new United States Pharmacopœia, reported progress.

President Alpers then introduced Harry B. Mason, associate editor of the *Bulletin of Pharmacy*, Detroit, who delivered an address on

"THE TWO LEGISLATIVE QUESTIONS OF THE HOUR."

Mr. Mason said that "wise legislation, effective legislation, the legislation which accomplishes results, is simply the crystallization into written law of the unwritten dictates of public sentiment." He dwelt at some length upon legislation in general, and then divided his subject into two chief movements now manifesting themselves in pharmaceutical legislation—namely, graduation prerequisite laws and antinarcotic legislation. Among other things, he said:

GRADUATION PREREQUISITE LAWS.

Just at present we are entering upon a new legislative movement—that for making graduation in pharmacy compulsory—and there is danger that we may proceed with too much haste. New York blazed the path of the bold and ambitious pioneer two years ago, and won historic credit for herself by enacting the first graduation prerequisite law. Pennsylvania was quick to follow in her footsteps; the Wisconsin Board promptly established the graduation requirement on its own initiative. Hawaii had previously enacted the Beal model law containing the graduation provision. Minnesota endeavored to secure a prerequisite measure, but her bill was defeated at the eleventh hour by a deputation of pharmacists themselves. During the last year association after association in the various States has resolved to tread the new path, and we need not be surprised if a number of graduation prerequisite bills appear here and there before different legislatures within the next few weeks.

The new gospel has found wide acceptance. It is in the air. Enthusiastic zealots and supporters are everywhere to be found. But we need to be careful. We need to go slow. The opposition which the Minnesota measure encountered furnishes clear evidence of at least one State that is not yet ready for the step. The rank and file of pharmacists themselves must gradually come to realize the necessity of prerequisite legislation before it can be successfully accomplished. If we push it through in defiance of their wishes and in spite of their opposition we shall certainly find it robbed largely of its strength, and we need not be surprised if we wake up some morning and discover that it has been repealed and that the cause has been given a setback from which it will not speedily recover. A year ago opposition developed against the New York law in the center of the State, and it cannot be gainsaid that the statute would have been in serious danger but for the strong sentiment which existed in its favor—a sentiment which had been slowly developing throughout the State during the years that the subject of prerequisite legislation was being discussed and agitated among you.

I believe absolutely in the wisdom and necessity of the graduation prerequisite movement. I am convinced that the public welfare demands it, and that incidentally it will result in vital benefit to the material no less than to the professional welfare of pharmacy itself. But I desire the progress of the movement so much that I am anxious to see it realized in the right and permanent way. Some States—a very few—are doubtless ripe for prerequisite legislation immediately. In the majority of States, however, even if laws were passed, and even if they were not afterward repealed, they would inevitably be enforced in a manner which would put a premium upon cheap and inferior education, and which would cause a horde of mushroom colleges to spring into existence and lower the tone of pharmaceutical training.

SIX NECESSARY FEATURES OF ANTI-NARCOTIC LAWS.

After somewhat extended study and observation, I am led to the conclusion that an anti-narcotic law should contain the following features:

1. It should, of course, confine sales to physicians' prescriptions, forbid "repeats," the presentation of copies, and provide for the proper filing of all prescriptions.

2. It should involve the sale not merely of one or two narcotics, but of the several substances used by drug habitues to any considerable extent. The A. Ph. A. model law mentions cocaine, heroin, alpha or beta cocaine, opium, morphine, chloral hydrate, salts or compounds of these, and preparations containing more than specified amounts of them. It has been discovered in Illinois that to prohibit the sale of cocaine simply is but to increase the sale of morphine. In Ohio, where the law mentions nothing but "cocaine," and not even the salts of this alkaloid, it has been found difficult to secure convictions.

3. The law should by clear inference or direct statement involve the sale of proprietary preparations containing more than permissible quantities of narcotics. Certain snuffs have made cocaine habitues by the score and have also perpetuated the vice.

4. The enforcement of the law must be placed specifically in the hands of some definite officer or board or court. The omission of this principle has made dead letters of at least two or three laws.

5. The physician as well as the pharmacist should be punished. In some instances laws have been nullified by the acts of unprincipled physicians in writing prescriptions *ad libitum*. Important as this principle is, however, it was recognized in only two of the six laws enacted last year—those of Texas and Minnesota.

6. The law should provide penalties severe enough to act as deterrents. In Ohio, where until recently only a small fine was imposed, it was found that cocaine sellers were not disturbed in the least, since with sales amounting in many instances to $15 or $20 a day they could laugh at such light punishment. Much the same experience has been had in several other States.

To this list of provisions should perhaps be added that which the Illinois pharmacists propose to insert in their new law and which may also be found in the statute enacted last year in Missouri—namely, power to examine the books of any jobber in order to secure confirmatory evidence against a violator.

With the exception of this last provision all in the foregoing list are to be found in the model anti-narcotic law drafted by Professor Beal some years ago at the request of the American Pharmaceutical Association. The model is unquestionably an admirable measure, and there can be no doubt that it represents the best wisdom of the hour on this important subject. That it should be made the basis of all new anti-narcotic legislation is clear, not only because of its excellence, but because *the acts of the various States must be uniform so far as possible if the conditions are to be coped with successfully and if the law of one State is not to some extent to nullify that of another.*

Summing up these suggestions for an anti-narcotic law, I would repeat that the A. Ph. A. model should be used with the possible addition of a provision giving the right to examine the books of the jobbers, suggested by the experience in Illinois, and with the imposition of more severe penalties than the model provides—jail imprisonment for either the first or second offense and suspension or revocation of license for either the second or third offense. The model provides for jail imprisonment for the third offense and does not, as has been explained, provide at all for the revocation or suspension of licenses.[1] The question of proper penalties is a vital one, for several laws have been found practically worthless because the punishment has been insufficient.

Wholesalers Dine and Confer.

There have been several interesting gatherings of the wholesale trade in New York during the past fortnight. At an informal dinner given in the Waldorf-Astoria, on January 10, Albert Plaut, of Lehn & Fink, entertained W. J. Walding, of Toledo; W. A. Hover, of Denver; Frank A. Faxon, of Kansas City; James W. Morrisson, of Chicago; Mahlon N. Kline, of Philadelphia; Clayton F. Shoemaker, of Philadelphia; John N. Carey, of Indianapolis; M. Cary Peter, of Louisville; Samuel E. Strong, of Cleveland, and Lucius B. Hall, of Cleveland.

On the same day the Committee on Suits of the N. W. D. A. met and adopted a course of action with regard to suits against members of the association. The legal expenses incurred by members in cases brought against them because of their support of N. W. D. A. principles will hereafter be borne by the association, though in cases in which damages are awarded the damages must be paid by the individual defendants against whom the verdict is given.

Thomas H. Potts, of Philadelphia, attended the meeting as the representative of the National Association of Retail Druggists, accompanied by John C. Gallagher, of Jersey City; Charles Rehfuss, of Philadelphia, and William DeShetley, manager of the New York office of the N. A. R. D.

The organization of wholesale druggists known as the Metropolitan Drug Club entertained the visiting jobbers at the Drug and Chemical Club on Thursday. President William P. Ritchie had to leave early and his place was taken by Albert Plaut, who toasted the visitors and put forward John N. Carey, chairman of the Committee on Proprietary Goods of the N. W. D. A., as the next president of the association, at the same time naming Dr. W. J. Schieffelin to succeed Mr. Carey as chairman of the Committee on Proprietary Goods.

Fort Worth Druggists Elect Officers.

Fort Worth, Texas, January 9.—The Fort Worth Retail Druggists' Association held its annual meeting last evening at the Delaware Hotel and elected officers, who are as follows: C. B. Ambrose, president; R. M. Anderson, first vice-president; R. Haddaway, second vice-president; H. F. Lackey, secretary, and John R. Parker, treasurer.

He Decided Not to Open It.

Caller—I was thinking about opening a drug store in this neighborhood. Do you think one is needed around here?

Resident—Great idea. There's no place within ten blocks where a man can buy stamps or see the city directory.

[1] At a conference just held in Chicago in the interests chiefly of the Proprietary Association of America, and attended by representatives of this association and of the A. Ph. A., the N. A. R. D. and the N. W. D. A., the A. Ph. A. model anti-narcotic bill was so modified as to provide for the imposition of the revocation penalty for the third offense.

BOARD OF TRADE DRUG SECTION.

Annual Meeting and Election of Officers—Section Will Oppose the Heyburn Pure Food Bill—Customs Delays.

The annual meeting of the Drug Trade Section of the New York Board of Trade and Transportation was held at the rooms of the board on Thursday, January 18, when new officers were elected for the ensuing year, and action was taken on a number of matters presented to the board. The Committee on Legislation was instructed to oppose the Heyburn Pure Food bill and any similar measure containing provisions objectionable to the interests of the drug trade.

A report was read from the Committee of Jobbing Druggists showing that the past year had been prosperous and that many trade abuses had been corrected.

John H. Stallman called the attention of the section to the fact that certain drugs are being ordered to the appraiser's stores and held there by the customs authorities for an indefinite time. In some instances, Mr. Stallman said, the goods were detained from three to four weeks, greatly inconveniencing the importers. He said detentions of Mexican sarsaparilla had resulted in sending much of the merchandise to European ports. A committee was named to investigate the alleged delays.

The annual election of officers resulted as follows: Chairman, Charles S. Littell; vice-chairman, Philip S. Tilden; treasurer, William A. Hamann, and secretary, William F. McConnell. James H. Taft & Co. and the Carl H. Schultz Company were elected to membership.

Appraiser Whitehead, when asked about the alleged delays in drug imports, said he knew of no unusual delays. He said samples of drugs are taken to the United States laboratory for tests, and that if the examination showed impurities it was probable the corresponding goods on the docks would be ordered into the appraiser's warehouse for scrutiny. In such instances, the appraiser declared, he was only carrying out the provisions of the treasury regulations.

KINGS COUNTY SOCIETY.

Topics Discussed at the Regular Monthly Meeting—New Telephone Company Makes a Bid for Business—Telephone Committee of the Society Asked to Confer—Health Commissioner Does Not Want a Pharmacist on the Advisory Board.

The January meeting of the Kings County Pharmaceutical Society was held at the Brooklyn College of Pharmacy on the 9th inst. President Paradis occupied the chair and Secretary Hegeman recorded. An application for membership was received from Arthur Worthington, and the following candidates proposed at the previous meeting were balloted for and declared elected, after the usual formalities: John J. Cizmowski, George Arthur Deitz, jr., Dudley G. Worden, George V. Dressner, Antonino Virdone, Samuel Grant, W. J. N. Brandenberg, Frank M. Byrne, Isidor Hirsch, Thomas Lamb, Alfred T. Wood and John J. Fenton.

Dr. P. W. Ray, treasurer, reported a balance in the treasury of the college of $4,839.21 and in the society's treasury of $221.02.

The annual meeting of the New York State Board of Pharmacy was reported at length by Dr. William Muir, after which announcement was made of the forthcoming annual meeting of the M. A. R. D., when the secretary was instructed to notify all members of the Kings County Pharmaceutical Society to attend.

The privileges of the floor were given to L. J. Lewis, a representative of the Great Eastern Telephone Company, who addressed the members briefly, telling them that his concern would put in telephones at one-half the price per year now charged. He made the request that members sign the contract of his company. A committee, consisting of Adrian Paradis, J. G. Wischert and William Muir, was appointed to look into the matter and report at the next meeting.

Harry B. Mason, associate editor of the *Bulletin of Phar-*

macy, of Detroit, was introduced by President Paradis, and expressed the good wishes of the pharmacists of his city. He paid several compliments to the society, saying among other things that the members of the Kings County Pharmaceutical Society were always to be found in the front ranks when there was fighting to be done for the elevation of pharmacy and the pharmacist.

J. H. Rehfuss made a report for the committee which waited on Health Commissioner Darlington in regard to the appointment of a pharmacist on the Advisory Board of the Health Department. No appointment had yet been made, he said, and it was doubtful if pharmacists would be named for the place. Dr. Muir said he didn't think it would be prudent to have a representative on the board, even should Commissioner Darlington desire it, because in such a case all business men would think their lines should have a representative on the board and complications would perhaps arise.

WESTCHESTER COUNTY DRUGGISTS.

Officers Elected—Westchester Wants Board Recognition.

The twenty-third annual meeting of the Westchester County Pharmaceutical Association, which was held at the Park Hill Inn, Yonkers, on Wednesday, January 10, was one of the largest in the history of the association. The discussion relative to legislative matters and the question of getting representation on the State Board of Pharmacy were the principal topics, and a committee of five, consisting of J. M. McCullough, of White Plains; F. C. Koch, of Mamaroneck; W. J. Townsend, of Ossining; Geo. B. Wray, of Yonkers, and U. Wiesendanger, of Yonkers, was appointed by the president to look into the matter. The committee was given power to use whatever means were considered best to accomplish the desired end.

The retiring president, F. C. Koch, of Mamaroneck, in his annual address spoke at some length on the future conditions to be encountered by the retail druggist in the handling of patents that will require a liquor license.

OFFICERS ELECTED.

The election of officers for the ensuing year resulted in the choice of the following: President, John T. Davis, of Yonkers; vice-presidents, Fred Lent, of Peekskill, and U. Wiesendanger, of Yonkers; treasurer, J. B. Sackett, of Tarrytown (his eighteenth year); secretary, H. R. Safford, of Yonkers.

A number of applications for membership were received. This association has always been a staunch adherent of the N. A. R. D., and pays $1 of each members' dues in that body. J. D. Bellair, representing the N. A. R. D., was present, and spoke in a convincing and forceful manner on the good work accomplished by the organization.

During the dinner hours, Bert K. Forest, of Brooklyn, entertained the association with humorous stories and popular songs, and Wm. Walsh, of Yonkers, played selections on the piano.

The County Association on this occasion was the guest of the Yonkers Drug Association. The next meeting will be held at the City Club, Mt. Vernon, Wednesday, April 11.

Kennebec Valley Druggists Elect Officers.

Augusta, Maine, January 12.—A largely attended meeting of the Kennebec Valley Druggists' Association was held Thursday afternoon in the rooms at Hotel North, and the following officers were elected to serve the ensuing year: President, John Coughlin, of Augusta; vice-president, Chester H. Beane, of Gardiner; secretary, H. Leroy Simpson, of Waterville; treasurer, Percy W. Means, of Augusta. The above were also elected members of the Executive Committee, with the addition of J. F. Young.

Following the business meeting a fine banquet was served.

The following members of the association were in attendance: John Coughlin, Percy Means, T. P. Kenney, Harry E. Goodrich, Charles B. Murphy, Willis R. Partridge and Horace E. Bowditch, of Augusta; Chester H. Beane, of Gardiner; J. F. Young, of Hallowell, and H. Leroy Simpson, W. G. Bell, John D'Orsay and John Davieau, of Waterville.

RHODE ISLAND PHARMACISTS IN SESSION.

Officers Elected at the Annual Meeting—Prof. John E. Groff, President.

The attendance at the annual meeting of the Rhode Island Pharmaceutical Association, which was held in Providence on Wednesday, January 10, was disappointingly small and most of the time of the meeting was occupied with the discussion of proposed changes in the pharmacy law. The chairman of the committee appointed last year to investigate the matter and bring about the passage of a new law was not present, but the topic was discussed by members. Most of the chairmen of committees were absent. The secretary reported a membership of 159. Two members died during the last year and two were elected to membership. The election of officers resulted as follows: President, John E. Groff. Vice-presidents—Providence County, G. A. Gladding; Washington County, A. B. Collins; Newport County, J. T. Wright; Kent County, S. W. Hines; Bristol County, W. H. Buffington. Secretary, Charles H. Daggett; treasurer, E. T. Colton; Executive Committee, H. A. Pearce (chairman), E. W. Vars and A. A. Johnson, jr.

The society voted to pay the treasurer $20 per annum and to make a contribution toward the Procter monument at Washington, the amount to be decided upon later.

That National Association of Buying Clubs.

It is reported that the members of the various retail drug clubs who brought about the meeting of co-operative drug companies in New York recently are quietly at work organizing drug companies throughout the country. It is the intention, it is said, to establish co-operative buying clubs in at least fifty of the leading cities of the United States. Each company will be managed by its own directors and officers, but there will later on be a company organized to do the purchasing for all members of the association.

The new association which is to be formed will consist solely of the members of the co-operative drug companies throughout the United States and will be in many respects similar to the National Wholesale Druggists' Association. Since the meeting in New York the committee has received assurances from many cities that were unrepresented. Within a short time there is to be another meeting of the co-operative drug companies, at which it is believed definite plans will be presented for the formation of the new association.

DIED.

ATTON.—In Toledo, Ohio, on Thursday, December 28, 1905, Charles R. Atton, aged thirty-two years.

BRADSHAW.—In Huntsville, Ala., on Friday, January 5, Robert Bradshaw.

CLARK.—In New York, on January 6, Henry A. Clark.

DOVOIS.—In New York, on Thursday, January 11, Ernest Dovois.

GEIGER.—In Alexandria, La., on Friday, January 5, Henry Geiger, aged thirty-seven years.

PIQUETT.—In Baltimore, Md., on Thursday, December 28, 1905, Dr. John P. Piquett, aged fifty-six years.

SPACKMAN.—In Hamilton, Canada, on Tuesday, January 2, George W. Spackman, aged forty-one years.

SWIFT.—In Salt Lake City, Utah, on Saturday, December 30, 1905, C. D. Swift.

TOWNSEND.—In Albany, N. Y., on Thursday, December 28, 1905, John de Peyster Townsend, aged sixty-six years.

YOCKEY.—In Worthington, Ind., on Friday, December 29, 1905, James A. Yockey, aged thirty-seven years.

Greater New York News.

President Calvin Hotchkiss, of the H. G. Hotchkiss Essential Oil Company, Lyons, N. Y., was in town last week.

R. R. Boggs has been engaged by Lehn & Fink to handle their sundry line in Philadelphia, Baltimore and Washington.

N. Nicolai, one of Parke, Davis & Co.'s foreign representatives, sailed recently for Europe on a business trip. He went to London and from there he will go to the Continent.

H. C. Fick, who represents Lehn & Fink in Wisconsin and Minnesota, has returned to that territory, after a two weeks' visit made by him and his wife in New York.

P. E. Hall, auditor of Parke, Davis & Co., returned recently on the steamship Baltic from London, where he went in the interest of the firm. After a brief stay here he left for Detroit.

H. G. Polson, manager of the Canadian branch of Magnus & Lauer at Kingston, Ont., has returned to that place after a short stay in this city. He was accompanied here by Mrs. Polson.

At the regular meeting of the Society of Chemical Industry, held in the Chemists' Club last Friday evening, Prof. Charles Baskerville, of the College of the City of New York, delivered a lecture on the "Uses of the Rare Earths."

Mrs. Sydney H. Carragan returned to New York on the steamship Baltic last week from a tour of the British Isles and the Continent of Europe. P. E. Hall, auditor of Parke, Davis & Co., of Detroit, and Mrs. Hall, were Mrs. Carragan's traveling companions.

The firm of Charles Pfizer & Co. has been reorganized, Charles Pfizer, Jr., having withdrawn as president. The firm is now officered by Emil Pfizer, president; William H. Erhart, vice-president; John Anderson, treasurer, and Franklin Black, secretary.

Recent visitors to New York included Clinton E. Worden, president of the National Pharmacy Company, of San Francisco; Frederick H. Stearns, president of Frederick Stearns & Co., of Detroit; T. B. Glazebrook, of the Tilden Company, New Lebanon, N. Y., who is manager of the St. Louis office; S. J. Tilden, New Lebanon, N. Y., and Harry B. Mason, of Detroit.

M. J. Breitenbach, of the M. J. Breitenbach Company, spent the holidays at his old home near Brunswick, Ga. It is always a pleasure to meet and talk with Mr. Breitenbach after one of his regular visits to the Southland, for his darkey tales and reminiscences of wild turkey shooting are interesting in an unusual degree.

Henry A. Clarke, one of the New York City representatives of Parke, Davis & Co., was found dead on a side track of the Third Avenue Elevated Road near the 177th street station on Saturday, January 6. It is believed that the deceased met his death by accident, though the police were unable to account for the manner of his death. Mr. Clarke lived at 2209 Cambreling avenue, the Bronx, and was well known to the retail trade of this city.

Joseph L. Lemberger, of Lebanon, Pa., president of the American Pharmaceutical Association, was registered as a guest at the Drug and Chemical Club of this city last week. Mr. Lemberger, who is treasurer of the Board of Foreign Missions of the Reformed Church in America, was in the city in attendance on a conference of treasurers of various foreign mission boards. Mr. Lemberger took occasion to call on several of the active members of the association, who are engaged in committee work, and confer with them on association affairs.

The Drug Trade Bowling Association resumed its tournament on Monday evening, January 8, after the holiday interval. Teams representing the following firms participated: Merck & Co., Lanman & Kemp, Roessler & Hasslacher Chemical Company, Seabury & Johnson, Whitall-Tatum Company, and the Dodge & Olcott Company. The Roessler & Hasslacher and Dodge & Olcott teams won two games each. The Whitall-Tatum team lost both of its games, thus placing the Parke, Davis & Co. team in the lead in the series. The Merck & Co. bowlers lost one game and forfeited one. The Lanman & Kemp and the Seabury & Johnson teams each won and lost a game. The highest score of the evening—214, was made by Mr. Ruddiman, of Dodge & Olcott.

New York Druggists and Telephones.

In the New York Business Telephone Directory, covering the boroughs of Manhattan and the Bronx, there are, at a rough estimate, about 36,850 names. Of these, something like 1,150 are of retail druggists. But this three per cent. does not begin to represent the relative importance of the druggists to the telephone company. A more numerous class of 'phone users is made up of physicians. Perhaps there are 4,000 telephones in physicians' offices in the two boroughs, but these are for the use of the physicians, while the druggists' 'phones are for the use of the public. The 1,150 druggists' 'phones yield the company a large income from tolls. There are public 'phones in saloons, too, but these have a rather restricted field of usefulness at all times, and are closed to the public, or are supposed to be, on Sundays, election day, and after 1 o'clock at night. Apartment house 'phones are used by residents in the apartment house, but not by the general public, and the same holds good to a limited extent as to hotel 'phones. Pay 'phones are to be found in cigar stores and confectionery shops, but these are by no means so numerous or so well distributed as drug stores. In other words, the telephone company reaps its rich harvest through the druggists.

Perhaps there are druggists in this city who regard the telephone company's charges as too high, its service not always what it ought to be, its treatment of themselves not uniformly courteous, or even just.

Whom have they to blame for this?

If the 1,150 druggists in Manhattan and the Bronx, and their brothers in the other three boroughs of this city, who are not satisfied with the telephone situation would stop appointing committees to stand with hat in hand outside the doors of the telephone company's offices, craving a hearing, and would rise as one man and remove the instruments from their stores, the telephone bosses would go to them and beg them to put the 'phones back on any terms which they might name.

The druggist is a "good thing"; he is being ground to powder between the telephone monopoly on the one side and the public who uses him as a free convenience on the other.

There is such a thing as riding a willing horse to death; but the horse which permits such treatment deserves to be classed with another species of the genus equus which is distinguished by its harsh bray and long ears.

Druggists have the power to dictate terms to the telephone companies. In other towns they have exercised this power. Perhaps in no other large city in the country are the druggists so imposed upon by telephone owners as are the druggists of New York. The company is not to blame, as things go in this get-rich-quick day; it is not conducting an eleemosynary institution—only druggists do that. The average New York druggist is so busy working to pay rent on a store to be shared with him (rent free) by the telephone company, and to pay for a directory to be shared with him (also free) by every other business man and private individual in the block, that he thinks he has "no time to read the journals" or to go to the association meetings to learn what druggists in other towns have done to free themselves from the nuisances which beset them.

One trouble with New York is that it is so well satisfied with the fact that it *is* New York that it refuses to learn valuable lessons from Kansas City and other "provincial" municipalities.

The ass that patiently staggers under an onerous burden excites one's pity but hardly one's admiration.—*Druggists' Circular.*

Brooklyn High School's Encouraging Move.

The Boys' High School, of Brooklyn, evening class department, has circularized the druggists of Brooklyn calling their attention to the courses in physiology, hygiene and anatomy which are open to prospective pharmacy students. The pharmacists addressed are asked to bring the matter to the attention of their apprentices, as any student attending 85 out of 100 evening classes and passing a satisfactory examination is entitled to an affidavit to that effect from the principal of the High School, and such affidavit forwarded to the Regents of the University of the State of New York entitles the holder to a credit of six Regents' counts. The course is a free one, and, as will be seen, its successful completion leaves the student in possession of one-half of the Regents' counts required by the prerequisite law pertaining to pharmacy.

Annual Ball of the N. Y. C. P. Alumni.

The Alumni Association of the College of Pharmacy of the City of New York will hold its eleventh annual concert and ball at the Grand Central Palace, New York, on Wednesday evening, February 7. Under the chairmanship of Fred Borggreve, who is the president of the association, the affair promises to be one of the most successful events in the annals of the alumni association, as special talent has been engaged to make the concert feature a success. A prima donna, well known to lovers of opera, will be the soloist, and Crowley's Eighth Regiment Band will render the musical programme during the evening. The hall is to be specially decorated for the occasion and a large attendance is expected. Mr. Borggreve is determined that the concert and ball shall be conducted with the utmost decorum, and no misconduct of any kind will be tolerated. On this account members will be induced to bring their wives, sweethearts and sisters and thus swell the gathering of alumni and alumnæ.

Ball of the German Apothecaries' Society.

Although the attendance was not as large as expected, the fifty-fifth annual ball of the German Apothecaries' Society, held at the Harlem Casino on Thursday night, January 11, proved a most enjoyable affair. The hall was quite elaborately decorated with bunting and the society's banners, while above the stage was the lettering "1851—N. Y. D. A. V.—1906" in red, white and blue electric bulbs. Music was furnished by A. Lederhaus' orchestra, and after a preliminary concert of appropriate music, the ball proper was opened with the grand march, led by President and Mrs. Felix Hirseman. Supper was served between 2 and 3 A. M., President Hirseman presiding. The president's speech of welcome was followed by a toast to the ladies by Mr. Lehman, who also read a toast he had prepared on sociability. It was almost daylight when the last dance was finished. The committees in charge of the affair were: Floor, R. S. Lehman, chairman; S. V. B. Swann, H. F. Albert, August Diehl, Bruno Dauscha, Charles W. Dietz and George Leinecker. Reception, Felix Hirseman, chairman; C. F. Schleussner, Paul Gebicke, H. Imhof and C. E. Kessler. Press, Hugo Kantrowitz, chairman; George Huether, C. F. Klippert and O. A. Leister.

State and National Authorities Co-operating on Liquor Problem.

The Excise Commissioner of the State of New York states that the department is continuing its efforts to prohibit the sale of certain proprietary medicines which, although being sold as medicines, are almost wholly alcoholic unless the vendors pay the same tax as is required for the sale of any other liquors.

The department has laid before the United States Commissioner of Internal Revenue the result of investigations concerning proprietary medicines sold in this State, and the Government is now co-operating with the department to facilitate its efforts in compelling the vendors of said proprietary medicines not only to pay the necessary tax, but to apprise the public of the absolute ingredients of these so-called medicines.

EXTENSION OF P. D. & CO.'S CRUDE DRUG DEPARTMENT.

New Premises Acquired on the Water Front—Convenient to the Shipping Wharves and the Wholesale Market.

The Eastern branch of Parke, Davis & Co., at 91 Maiden lane, New York, has been compelled by the growth of its crude drug department to acquire additional premises for the housing of supplies, and extensive warehouses at 292, 293, 294 and 295 South street, with an extension to and access at 573, 575, 577 and 579 Water street, have been secured. The building, which has a six-story frontage on South street and a two-story extension on Water street, equipped with three fast freight elevators, will be used for the storage of crude drugs in original packages, such as gums, barks, roots, herbs and seeds, and the building being conveniently located near the terminals of the great shipping lines it is expected that deliveries will be greatly facilitated by the change. This department of Parke, Davis & Co.'s immense business has flourished greatly under the management of W. B. Kaufman, who will enter on the 24th year of his connection with the firm next month. The firm is now the largest importer of gum arabic and gum tragacanth in America. It is understood that that portion of the Maiden lane establishment now given over to crude drugs will be turned into a show room and sampling office.

P.-W.-R. Company Removes.

It was with something of a shock that our market reporter saw last week the removal notice on the closed doors of the offices so long occupied by the firm of Powers-Weightman-Rosengarten Company, at 56 Maiden lane, opposite the Seabury Building. The firm now occupies its own building, at 145 and 147 Front street. The new building is of typical Philadelphia architecture, the front being of red brick with massive stone columns and foundations, while the interior gives one the impression of great height and depth. It is a Colonial structure and the interior decorations are in harmony; a balcony runs along two sides of the wall, and the railings are painted white, of a refreshingly clear and cool tint; a touch of green here and there carries out the idea of the Colonial architecture and again suggests Philadelphia. The building contains 35,000 feet of floor space and has five floors in front and six in the rear. The receiving and shipping departments open on Maiden lane at No. 158. The affairs of the New York office are presided over by Charles A. Loring, a quiet, reserved gentleman, of most engaging personality, who gives one the impression of being alive with business, while still sparing a moment to chat affably with callers. Mr. Loring was formerly connected with Lehn & Fink, and before his promotion represented the old firm of Powers & Weightman on the road as a traveling salesman. He came from Boston to take charge of the New York office. Mr. Perry still retains his connection with the firm, but the state of his health prevents him taking the active part he once did in the affairs of the New York office. He drops in for an hour or so every day to keep in touch with things.

Now the Drug and Chemical Club.

At a special meeting of the Drug Trade Club, held on December 12 at 1.30 P.M., the name of the Drug Trade Club was changed to that of the Drug and Chemical Club. A resolution was adopted giving the Board of Governors power to carry out the desired change.

The Manufacturing Chemists' Registration Bureau.

The following title has been received for registration in the Manufacturing Chemists' Registration Bureau:

Syrup Euphorbia Compound............Parke, Davis & Co.

WESTERN NEW YORK.

Improvement in the Price Situation—Many New Stores Opening—Registration by the Board Simplified.

(*From our Regular Correspondent.*)

Buffalo, January 17.—There is some difference of report as to the trade finding its way into the Buffalo retail drug stores just now, some finding it good, others poor and still others medium, the last probably being pretty nearly correct. The winter is mild, but the weather is not usually much of a guide in the matter. The notion that more drugs and medicines are bought in bad or unseasonable weather than any other does not prove true generally.

THE PRICE SITUATION.

It is improving so fast—which means that the agreement is held so firmly—that it is about time to advance the prices of the old cut list a little more. The plan has been to begin with only a slight advance from the bottom prices and then add a little now and then, as the patient seems to be able to stand it, until the top is reached, the top always being the highest point that the situation seems to be likely to stand. One or two advances of the sort have already been made since the first scale was issued.

At the same time it is not expected that the old full prices can be obtained by this sliding scale plan. It is likely that the manufacturers would be satisfied considerably short of the full price. All the retail druggist is looking out for is the margin between the wholesale and the retail price of the cut-price articles, and he is not a very close friend of the manufacturer. He predicts that the ascendancy of the proprietary is about at an end and he looks on such a decline as a throwing off of a sort of imposition on him.

NEW STORES AND CHANGES.

It appears that the Buffalo retail druggist is getting perniciously active again, for the number of new stores reported and the number changing hands of late has been much larger than for a long time past. It is such a "neat" and fetching business that the public will always drop into it liberally, so long as a living can be made at it.

THE BUFFALO DRUGGISTS' BOWLING CLUB

still comes in for all possible amount of enthusiasm on the part of the members. It takes only a word to any of them to bring out a flow of eloquence concerning the high character of the sport at the Friday meetings.

THE WESTERN BRANCH OF THE STATE BOARD OF PHARMACY

is active in the main just now in getting in the store registries, which are much more easily obtained now than they used to be. There are about 400 stores in the eight counties making up the district and fully three-quarters of the list was in by the middle of January.

It used to be a hard job to complete the list, and when the law was new the board was as easy about the registry as possible, so it happened that a few, and usually the very same few, took advantage of the leeway allowed and were months behind the time set for completing the list. It happened also that the delinquents were practically all in Buffalo, where it was handy to comply with the law. After a while, when it was seen that the delinquents were a mere group who were pleasing themselves in doing as they liked, steps were taken to make them come in.

Complaint was made informally to the district attorney, who merely asked for the list. He had had experience in that line, and said that a letter from him to small lawbreakers often went as far as a court indictment would. He was right. No sooner had he informed the good people that he had hold of the case than they fell over each other to get in, and they remembered the warning next year.

There will be a regular examination held by the board in February, and then Secretary Reimann of the Western branch will take advantage of the interval that follows and make a trip to California.

NEW ENGLAND.

The License Question to the Fore in Haverhill—Druggists Must Not Advertise Liquors—A Sunday Liquor Raid—Pharmacy Board Agent Becomes Chief of Police—Investigating Quality of Olive Oil.

(*From our Regular Correspondent.*)

Boston, January 17.—While Boston druggists have been busy discussing the screen law their Haverhill brethren have had the license question forcibly presented to them. Some of the druggists of that city have been advertising their stock of liquors, and this questionable proceeding has incurred for those adopting this method the displeasure of the License Commission. This opposition of the commissioners was made manifest by their serving notices upon the druggists to appear before them and receive instructions as to the conduct of their places.

RAIDED FOR SELLING ON SUNDAY.

Pending this conference the police, on Sunday, January 7, raided the store of Henri Prevost & Co., River street, and cleaned out their entire stock of liquors, including ale, wine, whiskey and brandy. This seizure is said to have been the first interference with Sunday drug store trade in this city for years and is viewed as a "crusade" upon the part of the commission.

Apropos of the screen law it is possible that Mayor Fitzgerald, who is to be a guest of the Boston Druggists' Association at their annual dinner, may upon that occasion state his views upon this subject.

CHIEF OF POLICE.

That the mill grinds slowly but surely is demonstrated by the history of Simeon B. Harris, who for many years was agent for the State Board of Pharmacy. Mr. Harris' methods, while keeping him constantly in the foreground, were of the mailed fist order, and as a consequence numerous protests were lodged with the Board of Pharmacy. Not long ago he was allowed to take his departure from the employ of the board. But this did not end his public career, for he has recently been offered a position of greater prominence and his name was placed in nomination by the mayor of Malden for chief of police of that city.

LOOK TO THE QUALITY OF YOUR OLIVE OIL.

Bay State druggists should have an eye to the quality of their supply of olive oil, if for no other reason than because the analysts of the State Board of Health are making examinations of this commodity. A number of samples recently tested proved to be cotton seed oil. The last monthly report of the board shows the examination of 99 samples of drugs, of which 17 were found to vary from the legal standard. The adulterated drugs were: Ether, Aqua Ammonia, Cera Flava, Extractum Zingiberaś Fluidum, Oleum Limonis, Spiritus Camphoræ, Syrupus and Tinctura Iodi.

THE T. METCALF COMPANY REORGANIZED.

The T. Metcalf Company has just reorganized under the laws of this State with a capital of $100,000, divided into 1,000 shares of $100 each. The concern has been conducting business for some years past under a State of Maine incorporation. The present officers are as follows: Frank A. Davidson, Ph.G., president and treasurer; Edward F. Varney, Ph.G., clerk; Frank A. Davidson, Ph.G., Edwin W. Shedd, Ph.G., and Michael F. Lyons, Ph.G., directors.

MERE MENTION.

Lighting a leaking oil stove was the cause of a recent fire in the store of John J. Kingsley, Prospect street, Waltham. The blaze caused a damage of $1,500. While endeavoring to extinguish the fire Mr. Kingsley was burned about the arms and hands.

The stamp tax law was recently declared unconstitutional.

William F. Sawyer, secretary of the Board of Pharmacy, is being initiated into jury work. His speciality is criminal cases. He endeavored to convince the judge that he was needed elsewhere, but that official had no sympathy with this line of thought and so Mr. Sawyer acts as a sifter of evidence for a month or more.

PENNSYLVANIA.

Renewed Activity of the Philadelphia Association of Retail Druggists—Judge Holland at One Time a Druggist—Officers Elected—Hope for Reversal on Law Points in the Loder Suit—Cut Rate Prices Proposed by the Association—Philadelphia Association of Retail Druggists in Flourishing Condition.

(*From our Regular Correspondent.*)

Philadelphia, January 17.—There was an old-time "rally around the flag" meeting of the Philadelphia Association of Retail Druggists at the regular monthly meeting on January 5. It seemed that the members turned out in force to assist the officers in upholding the affairs of the association. Since the Loder verdict there has been considerable talk about the usefulness of the association being at an end and there were rumors that many were to resign. These reports naturally gave the officers and those who have the good will of the association at heart some apprehension, but after the meeting all gloomy views were cast aside and it is now believed that the association is stronger than ever and those who have not taken any prominent part will come forward and in many ways endeavor to make it stronger than ever. It was expected that there were to be a number of resignations, but on the contrary there were only two, and they were members who had not taken much interest in the affairs of the retailers and never paid much attention to what was going on.

Since the Loder verdict there have been about six resignations. This, it is said, tends to show how the members feel. Besides being a harmonious meeting the attendance was the largest in the history of this body and there was the best of feeling displayed. The Loder suit has not by any means come to an end. A new trial has been asked for and the matter is now being held under advisement by Judge Holland. By the way, this Judge, it is said, was at one time a druggist, and on this account the members of the association as well as the wholesale druggists feel that when it comes to the points of law that the contention of the association will be upheld. The learned counsel for the retail association is said to have stated that he is willing to stake his reputation on the outcome and that when it comes to deciding the points of law the verdict of the lower court will be set aside. Instead of gloom permeating the affairs of the Philadelphia Retail Druggists' Association the future is brighter than ever.

OFFICERS ELECTED.

There were many speeches made by prominent druggists and the election of officers for the ensuing year took place. The following officers were elected: President, Charles Rehfuss; first vice-president, Thomas H. Potts; second vice-president, William E. Lee; third vice-president, A. T. Pollard; recording secretary, N. A. Cozzins; financial secretary, C. W. Shull; treasurer, G. W. Fehr. The dues for the coming year were fixed at $8. This is the same as last year, and there was no objection to the amount. Besides receiving the resignation of two members there were four new members admitted.

A NEW PRICE-LIST DISCUSSED.

On Friday last there was a special meeting of the association to take action on a new price-list. This is the first official move on the part of the association to take any retaliatory action against those who are classed as retail cutters. It was agreed to formulate a new list, so that the retail druggists could meet the competition of those who have not agreed to the prices set by the association. It is understood that the fight is now on in earnest and every effort is to be made to either meet the prices quoted by Loder or to make lower ones. The outcome is awaited with considerable interest. One of the leading retail druggists in the city said the fight should go further than to compete with those who have not agreed to the prices set by the retail association. He contended that the few sales made by the average druggist were nothing as compared to what the department stores are doing. He said: "I do not as a rule mind what the druggists quote, but when the department stores make a reduction I very often meet it, and in this way am forced to sell much lower than would be the case if I had to meet the competition of the retail druggist." Although this druggist said he would not pay any attention to what Loder did, as his business amounted to over $1,000,000 a year, while the latter was only $75,000, he will nevertheless abide by the action of the Philadelphia Association of Retail Druggists and in every way do all that he can to assist that body. It is believed that the retail association in this city is much stronger to-day than any time in its history and that its future is much brighter than ever before. All the members are working in harmony and it is expected that considerable will be accomplished this year which will be of immense value to the members of the association and all the retail druggists throughout the State of Pennsylvania.

OHIO.

Trade in Proprietaries Good—Wholesalers All Satisfied—The Revocation of Licenses for Cocaine Sales—Candy as a Side Line.

(*From our Regular Correspondent.*)

Cleveland, Ohio, January 17.—Market conditions in this city are considered very good for the first of the year by druggists generally. The prescription business has been good, notwithstanding the fact that the health office reports are not showing up especially bad. The very mild weather that has prevailed, however, has been conducive to minor complaints, which are as good for the druggists as the more serious ailments. The trade in patents has been equally as good as at any other time in the year. Medicines that are recommended for cold and catarrhal troubles have had an especially good sale. Business in sundries and novelties has also been good. The wholesale houses say that the year has started out well with them and they expect it to be as good as any they have ever had. The large houses here are constantly adding to their stock of preparations manufactured in the house and are gaining a large business on them. They take special care to have them as nearly perfect in compounding as possible and because of this are very successful with them.

UNITED CIGAR STORES COMPANY TO BUY AND TO BUILD.

Financiers interested in the United Cigar Stores Company have taken a long lease on the Forest City Hotel property, facing on the public square, and have given notice that they will take advantage of a clause in the lease and purchase the property within five years. It is their intention to erect a large and finely equipped hotel on the land. The company now has a store in the corner room of the present building on Superior avenue and the square. Another store is located on Euclid avenue in space formerly occupied by Deutsch's drug store. This last move would indicate that the company intended to gain a permanent foothold in the city. Property has been purchased in several other large cities, but this is said to be the first hotel property acquired.

NO RETROACTIVE ACTION BY THE BOARD.

According to reports from Columbus the State Board of Pharmacy will not revoke the licenses of the six druggists convicted of selling cocaine illegally. The convictions were brought about before the opinion of the attorney general on the subject was received and they have decided that such a move on their part would be retro-active and possibly not legal. The opinion of the attorney general will be made use of in reference to any cases that may come up in the future.

CANDY AS A SIDE LINE.

A new candy counter case has been put in the Marshal cut-rate store on the corner of Superior street and the square. Many of the stores are making a specialty of candies now. Some of them handle no goods of fine quality, while others keep both fine grades and goods that sell at popular prices. Cleveland seems to be keeping pace with the remainder of the United States in the consumption of sweets, and the investment in a candy department is no doubt a paying addition to any store. Some of them make handsome window displays of their box candies and these attract a good trade.

The Drug and Chemical Market

The prices quoted in this report are those current in the wholesale market, and higher prices are paid for retail lots The quality of goods frequently necessitates a wide range of prices.

Condition of Trade.

NEW YORK, January 20, 1906.

Business during the interval since our last report has been of a rather limited character, the demand being chiefly for jobbing quantities, and buyers showing no disposition to anticipate the probable requirements of the future by speculative purchases. At present values the market is firm in tone and where advances have taken place they have been for the most part in favor of buyers, though some of the staple products, like glycerin, cream tartar, tartaric acid and quinine, show fluctuations to a lower range. Camphor continues to advance in price, owing to the higher cost of crude gum. The decline in quinine did not come as a surprise, the lower values for bark at recent auctions having prepared the trade to some extent for the reduction. The principal fluctuations of the interval are tabulated below:

HIGHER.	LOWER.
Camphor,	Cream tartar,
Castor oil,	Tartaric acid,
Squills,	Glycerin,
Tannic acid,	Clove oil,
Snake root,	Quinine,
Arsenic,	Corrosive sublimate,
Quicksilver,	Juniper berries,
Haarlem oil,	Peppermint oil,

Drugs.

Alcohol, grain, is meeting with about the usual jobbing demand, with a fair outlet into the usual channels of consumption, and is noted at the lower range of values established recently—namely, $2.47 to $2.49, as to terms. Wood does not improve in demand, but the market is well sustained at the range of 70c to 75c for 95 per cent. and 97 per cent. respectively.

Amyl acetate has advanced in the interval, owing to slowness of delivery causing temporary scarcity; $1.50 to $1.60 now named, as to quantity.

Arnica flowers are selling fairly in small lots from jobbers' hands, who quote 9c to 10c, as to quantity and quality.

Balsam copaiba, Central American, is offered with some reserve, owing to scarcity, and 30c to 31c is named; Para is held with increased confidence and 37c to 40c represents the range.

Balsam Peru is given very little consideration, though the market appears well sustained at the previous range of $1.00 to $1.10.

Balsam tolu has continued in good seasonable demand and the prices are well sustained at 21c. to 22c.

Barks.—Bayberry continues to offer at 12c to 14c, but sales are making in a limited way only. Cascara sagrada is held with firmness and the sales were at the former range of 5½c to 9c as to quality and quantity. Cottonroot is held with increased confidence, and most holders are firm in their views at 9c to 10c. Wild cherry is scarce and wanted, and holders generally quote at an advance to 6c to 10c, as to quality and quantity. Sassafras has developed a slightly upward tendency, with nothing offering at under 12c, while 15c is named for prime goods; there is some scarcity of spot supplies, which influences holders to offer sparingly.

Belladonna leaves remain quiet, though holders are firmer in their views, owing to scarcity of supplies both here and at primary sources; recent sales were at 10c to 11c.

Buchu leaves, short, have met with a more active inquiry since our last, and holders are firmer in their views, the reports of crop shortage influencing them to name 18c for the better grades and 17c for yellowish.

Cacao butter is maintained in steady position, with prime Dutch brands quoted at 28c and Van Houten's and Cadbury's at 29½c.

Cantharides are slow of sale, but holders are firm in their views and the market is generally well maintained, with Chinese offering in a limited way at 52½c, though 55c to 56c is more generally quoted; Russian are held and selling at $1.25 to $1.30.

Castor oil has been advanced by the refiners, the revised range standing at 11½c to 12½c for No. 1 in barrels and 12c to 13c in cases; 10¾c to 11¾c for No. 3 in barrels and 11¼c to 12½c for cases, according to size of order.

Codliver oil is dull for the season, there being only a limited jobbing demand at previous prices, or, say, $24.00 to $28.00 for Norwegian, as to brand, and $24.00 to $25.00 for Newfoundland.

Cuttlefish bone is meeting with about the usual jobbing demand and values are steadily maintained on the basis of 16c to 16½c for Trieste, 12c to 15c for French and 40c to 70c for jewelers', as to quality and quantity.

Ergot is slow of sale, but the market is fairly firm in tone; Russian is held at 43c to 45c, and Spanish at 45c to 50c.

Glycerine is a shade easier owing to competition among manufacturers; sales of C. P. at 11½c to 11¾c in drums or barrels and 12½c to 12¾c in cans, according to quantity.

Haarlem oil is in reduced supply, and the limited available stock is closely concentrated, with holders asking $3.25 to $3.50.

Juniper berries are in better supply and easier, with goods available at 4¼c to 4½c.

Lycopodium is fractionally lower, holders apparently seeking to increase the distribution at a concession from previous prices, for we hear of sales at 53c to 54c.

Menthol has been irregular and unsettled, and the tone of the market is easier at a reduction to $2.50 to $2.40.

Opium remains quiet and prices are somewhat easier, with cases quoted at $2.97½, while broken packages range from $3.00 to $3.02½. Powdered is unchanged at $3.50 to $3.52½.

Quinine was reduced in price on the 13th inst. and the demand showed immediate improvement. The decline followed the announcement of lower prices for bark at the Amsterdam auction. The announcement of the decline caused little comment, as it had been expected for some time. The inside price now stands at 17c for bulk in 100-oz. tins, and several large transactions are reported at this figure, together with some development of speculative interest. Second hands do not quote at under manufacturers' prices.

Saffron, American, continues in active demand and the tone of the market is firmer, with some holders asking up to $1.30, though a limited quantity still offers at $1.20.

Saw palmetto berries continue held and selling in a jobbing way at 15c to 20c.

Spermaceti is moving into firmer position in sympathy with the situation at producing points; supplies in refiners' hands are said to be limited. Sales during the interval were at 27c for block and 28c for cases.

Sugar of milk has recovered a trifle and the lowest inside quotation is now 14c.

Tannic acid has been advanced by the manufacturers, who now name 58c to 60c, or 10c above the former price.

Tonca beans continue in fair, moderate inquiry, and values are well sustained at 65c to 67½c for Angostura, 18c to 20c for Para and 30c for crystallized Surinam.

Vanilla beans are held with increased firmness, owing to the stronger tenor of advices from primary sources. Whole Mexican are held at $2.75 to $6.50, cut Mexican at $1.75 to $2.00, Bourbon at $1.00 to $3.00 and Tahiti at 45c to $1.00.

Chemicals.

Arsenic, white, is scarce and wanted. Holders display unusual firmness and name 6½c to 7c, but little is available even at this figure.

Blue vitriol is firmly sustained on the basis of 5.90c for car lots.

Bleaching powder is without quotable change. The demand is somewhat limited at the present, owing to the fact that larger buyers and consumers are kept supplied by contract deliveries. The jobbing demand is being met at 1¼c and upward, as to quantity and terms.

Brimstone, crude seconds, has continued in good request, but spot supplies are ample and values are steady at the previous range of $22.12½ to $25, as to quantity, terms, etc.

Bromine and bromides are attracting some attention in view of a statement made in the *Frankfurter Zeitung* for December 22, which in translation reads as follows:

"We hear that at the meeting of the members of the bromine convention, held in Leopoldshall on the 21st inst., the difference between the several members could not be settled in a satisfactory way. It is therefore to be expected that the prices for bromine preparations will be lowered, but it is uncertain whether the convention will, notwithstanding this reduction, go out of existence."

Chlorate of potash is slow of sale, but the market maintains its steadiness in the face of light stock, the range for crystals and powdered being 9½c to 9¾c and 9¾c to 10c respectively.

Corrosive sublimate, granular and powdered, has been reduced 2c per lb., and manufacturers now quote on the basis of 70c for lump, crystals, granular and powdered; lump being unchanged in price.

Cream tartar is fractionally lower, manufacturers having reduced the prices of powdered to 22¾c to 23c as to quantity.

Tannic acid was advanced 10c per lb. on the 15th instant, and the change is noted under Drugs.

Tartaric acid has been offering more freely from second hands of late with the result of forcing down prices, and the revised quotations for powdered are 28c to 28½c as to quantity and ¼c per lb. less for crystals.

Essential Oils.

Anise is jobbing slowly, but the price is well maintained at $1.30 to $1.35.

Camphor has dropped a notch or two in the interval and quotations for Japanese are now 17½c to 18c.

Cassia maintains its steadiness in view of conditions prevailing in the primary market, and quotations are unchanged at 80c to 85c for 75 and 80 per cent. respectively.

Cedar leaf is more freely inquired for and holders offer with reserve at the current range of 60c to 65c.

Citronella has developed increased firmness, though quotations are nominally unchanged, recent sales being at 34c to 35c.

Clove has reacted slightly since our last and now offers more freely at the range of 85c to 87½c for cans, and 87½ to 90c for bottles.

Messina essences generally show an advancing tendency and bergamot is now quoted at $2.15 to $2.30 and sweet orange at $2 to $2.25, as to quality and quantity. Lemon has hardened in the interval and quotations have been advanced, up to 75c being asked by some holders.

Peppermint has been in good export inquiry during the interval since our last report and the market is firmly maintained at the range of $3.10 to $3.20 for HGH, according to quantity and seller; bulk is steady, but unchanged, at $2.30 to $2.40.

Sassafras is in limited supply and some dealers ask up to 28c for artificial.

Wintergreen is in more abundant supply, both on spot and at producing points, and recent sales of natural were at $1.50 to $1.75.

Gums.

Apart from another sharp advance in the price of refined camphor none of the other articles in this department has attracted much attention. An advance of 3c in camphor quotations was announced on the 9th inst., bringing the range to 91c to 91½c for barrels and cases respectively. Curacao aloes are scarce and wanted, and values are firmly maintained at 6¼c to 6½c; Barbadoes is well maintained at 14c to 16c for gourds. Asafœtida is selling in a small jobbing way only at nominally unchanged quotations. Arabic sorts are maintained with increased firmness under the influence of light stocks, and 6½c to 11c is generally named. Chicle is well held at current quotations, or, say, 35c to 36c. Gamboge in a small way is realizing 85c to 90c for pipe.

Roots.

There have been few changes of consequence to report in this market. Transactions are largely confined to jobbing sales and speculation is an absent feature. Burdock is held with increased firmness at 12c, with sales at this figure. Elecampane has been advanced to 4¾c to 5c in consequence of improved conditions at primary sources. Ipecac shows a fractional decline, recent sales being at $1.70. Golden seal offers a shade more freely at $1.30. Squill continues in upward tendency, owing to scarcity and a fairly good demand; quotations at the close were 8½c to 9c. Pink is in light supply and wanted at 50c. Sarsaparilla, Mexican, is dull and easier at 10¾c. Mandrake is generally held at 4½c, but a firm bid on a quantity lot would shade this figure. Senega is moving into firmer position and a large sale is reported at 57c.

Seeds.

Anise, Italian, is meeting with a fair jobbing inquiry, with sales at 8½c to 10c, as to quantity; Russian in a jobbing way realizes 6½c to 7c, while Star is maintained at 20c to 21c. Asparagus has met with considerable inquiry of late, and prices are higher, owing to scarcity; recent sales were at 11c to 12c.

Celery has developed increased firmness, quotations showing an advance to 7¾c to 8c.

Hemp, Russian, has receded from its previous firm position, and quotations show a reduction to 3½c to 3¾c.

Sunflower continues scarce and 4¾c to 5c is named in most quarters.

Wormseed, Levant, is held with increased firmness and 17½c to 20c is now named, the higher range being prompted by scarcity.

INDIANA NEWS NOTES.

In the list of taxpayers on ten thousand or more dollars' worth of real and personal property in Marion County (Indianapolis), taken from the treasurer's books, now being prepared for the year 1905 by the County Auditor, the following drug firms of Indianapolis are included: The Eli Lilly & Co., manufacturers, $225,000; the Kiefer Drug Company, wholesale druggists, $99,500; Mooney, the Mueller Drug Company, wholesale druggists, $65,000; the Pitman-Myers Company, manufacturers, $14,500; the Daniel Stewart Company, wholesale druggists, $102,100; Ward Bros. Drug Company, wholesale druggists, $51,650, and the Winona Mineral Water Company, $10,000.

The rigid enforcement of the pharmacy statute in Indiana is causing druggists all over the State to draw heavily on the schools of pharmacy for competent employees. Consequently the classes of pharmacy schools in the State are being crowded with young men who aspire to become proficient in that line of work. Recently the newly organized school of pharmacy at the Winona Technical Institute organized a two years' course, and already 59 students are enrolled. The department of pharmacy at this school has more students enrolled than has any other department. It is said this is due largely to the strict examination which drug clerks must pass before they are allowed to go behind a prescription case. A permit from the State Board, costing $3, is demanded of each student, the money going to defray the expenses of detecting clerks and employees who are evading the law. However, drug men who are in favor of rigidly enforcing the law are of the opinion that $3 is not a large enough fee, and they will petition the next General Assembly to increase the price of these certificates.

AMERICAN DRUGGIST

and PHARMACEUTICAL RECORD

PHILADELPHIA. NEW YORK, FEBRUARY 12, 1906. CHICAGO

ISSUED SEMI-MONTHLY BY

AMERICAN DRUGGIST PUBLISHING CO.,

62-68 West Broadway, New York.

CHICAGO, 221 Randolph St. PHILADELPHIA, 3713 Walnut St.

A. R. ELLIOTT, President.

CASWELL A. MAYO, Ph.G....................Editor.
THOMAS J. KEENAN................Associate Editor.

ROMAINE PIERSON...........Manager Chicago Office.

$1.50 a year. 15 cents a copy.

ADVERTISING RATES QUOTED ON APPLICATION.

The American Druggist and Pharmaceutical Record is issued on the second and fourth Mondays of each month. Changes of advertisements should be received ten days in advance of the date of publication.

Remittances should be made by New York exchange, post office or express money order or registered mail. If checks on local banks are used 10 cents should be added to cover cost of collection. The publishers are not responsible for money sent by unregistered mail, nor for any money paid except to duly authorized agents. All communications should be addressed and all remittances made payable to American Druggist Publishing Co., 62-68 West Broadway, New York.

Entered at New York as Second-Class Matter.

TABLE OF CONTENTS.

EDITORIAL COMMENT.

One Man and His Ways. In more ways than one, C. H. McConnell, president of the Economical Drug Company, of Chicago, is an unique figure in the retail drug world. Although he pretends to no knowledge of pharmacy he is the proprietor of and conducts one of the most strictly pharmaceutical stores in the United States, putting up 400 to 500 prescriptions daily and selling no soda water and no cigars. Without any pretence of being a professional man he has not hesitated to discourage the use of proprietary medicines, and has gone to the extent of printing circulars warning customers against the use of certain patent medicines containing alcohol or cocaine, and of handing out one of these circulars with each of the bottles sold. He first declined to sell a catarrh snuff containing cocaine, but finding that this did not stop the sale he again put it in stock, and with each bottle sold handed the customer a circular setting forth the dangerous contents of the patent medicine and the risk of acquiring a habit from its use. Now Mr. McConnell has set aside $26,000 worth of common stock, one-fourth of the whole, to be given to employees who have been five years in his service, the stock being paid for out of the annual dividends, which have been fixed at 40 per cent., though the earnings have really exceeded this figure. Would that we had more such figures in pharmacy!

An Investment for the Drug Clerk. Mr. Greaven, widely known as the manager of Perry's pharmacy in the Pulitzer Building, is impressed by long experience with the necessity of the study of languages on the part of pharmacy students, and he has given expression to this in a letter to the editor which is printed elsewhere. The cosmopolitan character of New York's population makes it incumbent upon the prescription pharmacist to know something of the languages of continental Europe. The young clerk should be encouraged to occupy his spare moments in the study of German or French, and if Italian could be added so much the better. It is expected, of course, that the competent prescriptionist possesses a knowledge of Latin. Education of a higher order is the demand of the times and the acquirement of skill in languages should not interfere with the business education of the pharmacist. Time and money spent in acquiring a knowledge of German alone will be well spent. As an investment it is better than putting money in a savings bank, for it will bring returns throughout a lifetime of a character such as would be impossible from a mere monetary investment.

Growth in the Prescribing of Proprietaries. A quiet inquiry conducted by the American Druggist has revealed the fact that contrary to expectations aroused by the crusade of the American Medical Association against proprietary medicinal compounds, the number of such compounds prescribed by physicians was greater during 1905 than in the year preceding. One out of five prescriptions are, according to one of our correspondents, "wholly or in part for factory-made preparations." Some of our readers in certain localities appear to be singularly favored, one pharmacist who does a considerable prescription business in one of the chief cities in Connecticut not having been called upon to put up a dozen special preparations in a year, though he enjoys a larger share of the prescription trade of his city than any of his competitors. Reports from Boston, Philadelphia, Chicago and the metropolitan district of New York indicate that the custom of prescribing proprietary preparations by physicians has grown steadily year by year and the rate of increase has been greatest during 1905. This would seem to indicate one of two things, either that *The Journal of the American Medical Association* is without influence in the larger cities, or that it has no circulation in them.

The Legislative Situation.

A good deal of space in our news columns is taken up with reference to proposed legislation affecting pharmacy. The agitation against the indiscriminate sale of medicinal preparations of secret formula has reached the point where it finds expression in legislative measures intended to cure the evils surrounding the sale of these remedies.

It is to the credit of the American Pharmaceutical Association that the first step in the direction of regulating the sale of narcotic drugs and preparations was taken by that body, and our readers will recall the able report made by Hy. P. Hynson, of Baltimore, as chairman of the Committee on Narcotic Drugs, appointed at the meeting of the American Pharmaceutical Association in St. Louis in 1901. This committee, which was appointed to study the subject of drug addictions with a view of checking the evil, collected a mass of valuable statistics, which resulted in the drafting of what is known as the "Model Anti-Narcotic Law." This model has been of service, and has been adopted by two State bodies as a basis for legislation governing the sale of narcotics.

The attitude of the American Pharmaceutical Association toward this question has been adopted by the more progressive and intelligent section of the drug trade generally. It is, of course, preferable to have any legislation affecting the drug trade emanate from the trade itself, than to have it come from alien and possibly inimical sources. It is better for the drug trade as well as the public that practically all legislation affecting pharmacy and imposing restrictions upon it in the interest of the public welfare has come from within the ranks of the craft. The history of pharmaceutical legislation shows clearly the lofty aspirations which have moved the leaders in pharmacy to undertake pharmaceutical legislation. It is well, therefore, that the regulation of the proprietary medicine business should also have the benefit of the advice and the experience of the American Pharmaceutical Association, and it is with pleasure that we present to our readers the draft of the measure which was formulated at Chicago last month at a joint conference attended by representatives of the four national bodies of the drug trade, namely, the American Pharmaceutical Association, the National Wholesale Druggists' Association, the National Association of Retail Druggists and the Proprietary Association of America. The text of the special bill proposed for the State of New York by a volunteer committee, of which Dr. William J. Schieffelin is a prominent member, and the text of the measure which *The Ladies' Home Journal* has placed before the public are also given.

While the measure proposed by the joint conference may not be ideal, it is the result of a careful study of the situation by competent experts who are thoroughly familiar with all the practical aspects of the questions involved. While not imposing impossible conditions, the enactment of this measure would, in our opinion, go far toward remedying the evils which have been so freely ventilated of late in the public press.

One objection which applied to all anti-narcotic legislation thus far proposed is that none of the measures which we have seen provides for future additions to the list of narcotic drugs. This phase of the subject has been discussed at meetings of the American Pharmaceutical Association on various occasions, and it seems to be one which it is impossible to meet in any practicable way.

The measure proposed by *The Ladies' Home Journal* provides for the publication of the complete working formula of every "patent" or proprietary medicine. This, it seems to us, is wholly unnecessary from the point of view of protecting the public. An attempt to accomplish the same purpose is made in the New York bill in so far as the public safety demands such a protection by the requirement to print on the container the name of any narcotic drug or chemical (the names being given in the bill), "or any other hypnotic, anæsthetic, analgetic, or cardiac, circulatory, respiratory or nerve depressant," which may be contained in the preparation, together with a statement as to the exact proportion of such ingredients as may be contained in the preparation. This provision comes as near to providing for possible additions to the list of narcotics as anything which we have yet seen, and it is open to criticism on the ground that the widest difference of opinion would be found to exist among experts as to what really constitute "a hypnotic, anæsthetic, analgetic, or cardiac, circulatory, respiratory or nerve depressant." In fact, this difference of opinion on the part of experts is the stumbling block in the formulation of any measure intended to provide for additions to our materia medica.

In connection with this, the statement of Governor Higgins, of New York, in regard to the insurance situation, that what was needed was legislation that is drastic but practicable, radical but sane; that what was wanted were laws drafted in a courageous but not in a hysterical spirit, is worth remembering. Governor Higgins' formula would seem to be well adapted to pharmaceutical and narcotic legislation.

New York a Storm Center.

The pharmaceutical pot is fairly a-boil in New York at the present time, and, from the pharmacist's point of view, the city is the storm center of the country. First in importance would appear to be the formation of the United Chemists' Company with a capitalization of $10,000,000, whose promoters are quite convinced that they can effect a revolution in retail drug trade methods. The chief promoter of this enterprise observes a strange reticence regarding the real aim and objects of the company, and the uneasy feeling has been allowed to grow among those interested in the welfare of pharmacy that drug stores are to be operated in connection with the tobacconist shops of the United Cigar Stores Company, the president to be, and principal promoter of, the United Chemists' Company being president of the United Cigar Stores Company.

Much of the speculation in regard to the probable operations of the new drug store combine is silly and utterly unworthy of serious attention. Some news agency has evidently been at work in the collection of salable "copy" to credulous country newspapers, for we have been deluged with reports from all parts of the country in which newspapers are named as authority for statements respecting the purchase of drug stores in the respective localities by the new drug trust, whose charter, it may be well to state, confines its operations to the cities of New York, Chicago and Philadelphia. Another wild rumor has connected the United Chemists' Company with the United Drug Company and the United Cigar Stores Company with the National Cigar Stands Company and the American Tobacco Company. For much of the misinformation regarding the new company which has been circulated through the press of the country the promoter himself is largely responsible, for he has been offered the opportunity to declare his intentions through reputable trade periodicals and he has declined to take advantage of the offer. All the information at present obtainable from officers of the new concern through personal interviews with them is published elsewhere in this issue of the AMERICAN DRUGGIST.

As part of the seething and fermenting of the pharmaceutical melange the discussion at a recent meeting of the New York Academy of Medicine of the question of adulterated drugs deserves mention. In this case a departure was made from the customary point of attack on pharmacists, for it was the wholesalers who had to bear the brunt of assault. Particulars of the meeting are contained in our news columns along with many other matters of interest to the trade.

(Written for the American Druggist.)

OXYGEN TOILET PREPARATIONS.

BY RICHARD VON FOREGGER, PH.D.

New York.

The appearance on the market lately of a number of oxygen products leads us to speculate on the various uses to which they might be put.

There is no doubt that the cosmetic trade will be one of the first to benefit by these new products, the importance of which is indicated by the word "oxygen." It is not incorrect to say that the words "oxygen" and "ozone" have already gained some importance in this trade; but, indeed, almost without exception, in name alone. A number of preparations, ointments, lotions, powders, etc., pretend to indicate by their trade name, their relationship to this all-important element, oxygen, the value of which has been recognized; is known to the public and its suggestion is, on this account, calculated to attract the user.

So far there is, to our knowledge, only one toilet preparation on the market which claims the name of an oxygen preparation with full right, and that is "Calox," the oxygen tooth powder. It is a dentifrice containing calcium peroxide, liberating in its use active oxygen, which disinfects and bleaches. It is a splendid preparation, gaining daily in reputation with both the medical profession and the public.

We predict that this marks only the beginning of the era of oxygen preparations; there is a strong demand for more. We need an oxygen talcum powder, an oxygen face cream, an oxygen skin bleach, a nail bleach, and a harmless fluid oxygen disinfectant.

To accomplish this we now have besides the calcium peroxide a sodium perborate, a zinc perborate, and a zinc peroxide; all of which, according to their properties, will serve for the useful putting up of the various preparations.

WHAT IS SODIUM PERBORATE?

Let us first ask What is sodium perborate? It is a powder which produces upon its solution in water hydrogen peroxide of variable strength. It is a powder which, in contact with moisture or with skin secretions, produces nascent oxygen. It is therefore a concentrated form of hydrogen peroxide. As it also exerts all the properties of potassium permanganate, excepting the toxic irritating and color effects, it might be called a white and nonirritating potassium permanganate. These properties are suggestive for the man who knows, but there is still more worth mentioning.

As seen, perborate offers the advantage that it is soluble in water and liberates its oxygen quicker than the other peroxides, by mere contact with moist substances. In addition it has the property of being stable and, to use a paradoxical expression, is chemically elastic. Exposed to humid air it will attract moisture; it will gain in weight and in volume, and lose both when exposed to dry air, without having lost any of its strength in available oxygen. It is particularly noted that the powder offers no chance of explosion or combustion. In this property of the stability of an oxygen powder lies the secret of its superiority over simple peroxide of hydrogen, which begins to lose its strength for the time it is made, and decomposes so rapidly under certain conditions, that an explosion may occur.

It will be recognized at once that with a powder which enables us to make our own hydrogen peroxide solutions, of any strength and at any time and place, by simply dissolving it in water, we have a means which will work safely, without loss or unnecessary expense, without risk or danger, in any climate and at any distance from civilization. Tropical countries, the surgeon in the field and the pioneer of civilization will profit greatly from it.

This chemical—$NaBO_3 + 4H_2O$—is of mild alkaline reaction and neutralizes acids. If used in a talcum powder it will prove of threefold benefit. (1) Its oxygen disinfects and destroys putrefaction; (2) the alkaline base neutralizes the acidity of perspiration; (3) it is a perfect deodorant.

AN A1 TALCUM POWDER.

These three properties are only mentioned in addition to the ordinary effects of talcum powders, which, naturally, the oxygenated powder also includes. We recommend the following formula for an A1 talcum powder:

Talci	94 parts
Perborate	5 parts
Violet (Trol-D)	1 part

In order to obtain an efficient skin bleach the perborate has to be applied in a larger proportion. It must be understood right here, that there is a vast difference between this preparation, to be used as a skin bleach, and the numerous preparations which so far flood the market.

If we are candid we have to confess that all our present preparations act corrosively upon the skin, and that their so-called bleaching effect is based merely on the effect of the destruction of sound tissue.

Perborate is a mild, soothing and refreshing bleach, whose action is not confined to the surface of the skin. Oxygen, which is essential to the life of cells, is absorbed by the same, in its active state, and the result is a strengthening of the living tissue, and the rejuvenescence of the skin, besides the bleaching effect.

AS A NAIL BLEACH.

The fine bleaching effect of sodium perborate is quickly manifested in its use as a nail bleach. Peroxide of hydrogen, which is known to us as a hair bleach, is not advisable for use in the line of manicuring as it is always acid in reaction and, therefore, does not possess the quality of saponifying the fatty secretions of the skin, but sodium perborate dissolves fats and acts as a bleach almost instantaneously at the same time.

Place one-half teaspoonful of the powder in a small dish and add six teaspoonfuls of lukewarm water, to form a milky liquid. Apply the liquid to your finger nails with a nail brush and rub for a few minutes, whereupon the nails are bleached and the surrounding skin is rendered elastic and soft.

The same results are obtained by simply holding the fingers in the solution for a few minutes or by applying the dry powder with a moistened brush on the wet fingers.

OXYGENATED NAIL POWDER.

Perborate as an ingredient of a nail polish will act as a slow bleach and add to the lustre of the nails, as here, again, it will absorb fatty substances, which are the cause of dullness.

Putty powder	Gm. 30
Sodium perborate	Gm. 2
Carmin	Gm. 1
Perfume	q. s.

OXYGENATED HAND CLEANER.

A good and wholesome hand cleaner in powder form is made up in the following way:

	Parts.
Castile soap, finely powdered	30
Pumice, in the finest powder form	3
China clay	45
Sodium perborate	22

AS A REMEDY FOR SWEATY FEET.

To conclude this brief exposition of the many uses of sodium perborate, we will refer to a method which is frequently used for the treatment of hyperhidrosis of the feet, by potassium permanganate. A 1 to 3 per cent. solution of this chemical is used as a foot bath, and for a dusting powder 20 per cent. permanganate is mixed with talcum. The permanganate in decomposing forms manganous salts, or black manganese oxide, an irritating and toxic substance. If, as happens with the above disease, sore spots occur inflammation and blood poisoning may result.

It is obvious that no such action would take place with the perborate treatment, the same having all the effects of permanganate, without the coloring, and without the least irritation. It should not be overlooked that the boric base of perborate assists the antiseptic action of the nascent oxygen and that it is one of the most popular healing and soothing agents.

For the treatment of hyperhidrosis of the feet, then, we

recommend a daily foot bath with a 2 per cent. perborate solution, and a dusting powder of the following composition:

Sodium perborate ....Gm. 15
Zinc peroxide ....Gm. 10
Talcum ....Gm. 75

This brings us to the employment of zinc peroxide, which is another subject in itself.

(*Written for the American Druggist.*)

THE SYSTEMATIC AMENDMENT OF AMERICAN PHARMACY.

By Oscar Oldberg,
Northwestern University.

(*Continued from page 33.*)

II.

The Three Recognized Grades of Workers in Pharmacy.

There are in all countries not less than three grades of workers in pharmacies—namely: 1, principals; 2, clerks, and 3, apprentices. All of these three grades are recognized everywhere except in our own country.

The laws of Illinois and New York are the only ones making any mention of apprentices.

Seventeen American pharmacy laws prescribe certain qualifications for principals or so-called registered pharmacists, while ignoring the clerks or assistants. But it ought to be evident to any thoughtful person that no proper systematic regulation of the practice of pharmacy and the qualifications of pharmacists is possible without making due distinction between apprentices, clerks and principals. To establish but one standard of education for all who do any pharmaceutical work necessitates making that standard so low that there will still be a plentiful supply of clerks. It pulls the standard down to the level of a barely qualified clerk.

It has been argued that because the clerk prepares medicines for the sick to as great an extent as his employer, he must, therefore, be as well educated. This argument is clearly fallacious. It is true that every person employed in compounding and dispensing medicines must be competent to do so, be he employer or employee, but owners and managers of pharmacies have other duties and responsibilities which their employees cannot have.

A higher education should justly be demanded of the principal because he is responsible for the identity, quality and reliability of all the medicinal materials in the shop; it is his duty to direct and supervise the work of his employees, and he is legally answerable to the public for the management of his whole establishment, which must be so conducted that the public is properly served and its welfare safeguarded.

Clerks or assistants, on the other hand, are responsible only for their own individual work as practical dispensers. They are not responsible for the acts of their employers whose agents they are, and must perform their duties under whatever conditions their employers see fit to impose. They are not really "in charge" even when their employer is temporarily absent, because they are still but agents, and have no control over the character of the medicines and materials supplied by the principals.

They must know the art of dispensing, but they are not called upon to exercise the special knowledge, skill, experience and executive ability which are necessary in procuring, examining and preserving the medicinal supplies. They are always clerks or agents, not principals.

With regard to the beginners or apprentices it is worth while to remember that to insure a satisfactory standard of education and professional fitness at the top it is obviously necessary to begin properly at the bottom. Silver spoons cannot be made of lead. Apprentices in pharmacy must be *fit to learn*, otherwise their apprenticeship or "practical experience" must be a farce or perhaps a tragedy.

INTERSTATE COMPLICATIONS.

When a licensed pharmacist moves across the State line he may cease to be a pharmacist in the eyes of the law. If he be a licensed assistant pharmacist in one State his license becomes useless whenever he sees fit to migrate to a State in which no distinction is made between principals and clerks.

One State proceeds on the principle that the dispensing clerk must be the equal of his employer in education and experience. Another State holds the licensed clerk so far inferior to the principal that he must perform his duties only under the personal supervision of the superior registered pharmacist, except when the latter is eating or sleeping.

As the apprentice or beginner cannot be abolished without pharmaceutical race suicide, the difference between the apprentice and the licensed dispensing clerk in any State where the latter cannot be permitted to do any pharmaceutical work except under immediate supervision must be the difference between tweedledum and tweedledee.

NECESSARY QUALIFICATIONS.

These should include:

For apprentices: Sufficient age and general education to render the beginner, whether at the school of pharmacy or in the drug store, a fit student or learner.

For clerks: Sufficient age, study and shop experience to make the student or apprentice a safe clerk and practical dispenser.

For principals: Sufficient age, special training in a pharmaceutical school and shop experience to make the clerk a competent principal, who may be safely licensed to conduct a pharmacy.

All of these qualifications must be determined or verified by the respective State governments through their boards of pharmacy, and should in no particular be relegated to the colleges or schools of pharmacy, or to other parties.

THE BOARDS HAVE AMPLE POWER.

The Board of Pharmacy of any State is a part of the machinery of the State government. It is or ought to be independent of all outside influences. Its acts should be governed only by the law, the objects of the law and by enlightened public opinion. Its first duty is to the people.

The boards are doing much to secure fair results under even the worst of pharmacy laws. But they can do much more, and will surely do so, when they realize that they will be sustained by public opinion, and they will be so sustained if their acts are reasonable and right.

Insistence upon trifling minor details which cause friction, hardships or annoyance to applicants for license without any corresponding gain to the public should be carefully avoided. Reasonableness is perfectly compatible with the objects to be accomplished.

Many druggists insist that the boards of pharmacy can do nothing except to carry out the literal and specific mandates of the law in the easiest and most inert way. In fact, they expect the boards to study out how little it is possible to do and to do just that little and no more. But the boards cannot even then get along without exercising discretionary powers not specifically prescribed in the letter of the law. They are all necessarily exercising such powers extensively and at all times. Failure to do so would certainly render the law nugatory, as we may prove by a process of *reductio ad absurdum*.

Nearly all pharmacy laws prescribe a certain amount of practical experience in pharmacy as a prerequisite to registration and license, omitting to specify the conditions under which that experience must be acquired in order to satisfy the objects in view.

But the boards should certainly not accept as sufficient any drug store experience which in their judgment can be of no value. Drug store experience gained between the ages of 9 and 13, for instance, could not be counted without utter disregard of the law's intent. Neither can the board take cognizance of any drug store experience had by any person so illiterate as to be unable to read or write. Nor is one day's work or three days or a few evenings a week in a drug store for a year one year's drug store experience.

Evidently then the board *must* adopt some definite rules on these points. They must draw the line somewhere, and it is their duty to do so in a manner that will insure the ends sought by the law and prevent flagrant evasions.

Most of the pharmacy laws require that the qualifications of candidates for license shall be determined by examination. But the scope and character of that examination are necessarily left to the discretion of the board. Evidently the board has the power and is in duty bound to include in that examination whatever will best serve to bring out the real facts as to the fitness of the candidate to be a pharmacist.

In the absence of any rules definitely fixing the preliminary education of the candidate the board must make its examination not only a test of the pharmaceutical knowledge and skill of the candidate, but also of his general education. All boards do this after a fashion, because gross ignorance incidentally shown by the candidate must debar him from registration unless they should proceed on the extraordinary theory that fitness for the profession of pharmacy is quite compatible with gross ignorance and altogether undisciplined mental faculties.

We expect pharmacists and embryo pharmacists to prove that their mental machinery is something more than mere memory, imitation, instinct and guessing.

Evidently the line must be drawn somewhere, and the boards of pharmacy must do the drawing. The question is simply, Where is the line to be drawn? At present we are absolutely without any definite standard in nearly every State. Are we to continue in that condition? If not, then let the boards act.

If boys of 14 years who have had only six years in the primary schools are good enough material to make pharmacists of without further scholastic training let us have that plainly understood. If a completed high school course is required let that be the rule. If a part of the high school course is sufficient the amount required should be defined.

The board has the power to decide according to its judgment.

The Board of Pharmacy clearly has the power to decide whether or not the candidate for license shall be required to furnish evidence of the reasonableness of his claim to fitness for the practice of pharmacy.

A person who has never made any serious effort to master any of the subjects which make up the scientific technical art of pharmacy can have no right to any consideration of such a claim. His application to be examined upon subjects he never studied is clearly an insult to the board.

Every pharmacist of ordinary education and intelligence knows that to learn chemistry, pharmacognosy and pharmacy without systematic study is quite impossible. The candidate should accordingly be required to prove that he has, in fact, given these subjects such study in such a way and for such a period of time that it is at least possible that he may know enough about them. Here again the question is, Where shall the line be drawn?

There has never been any difficulty in fixing definite educational requirements for medicine, law, dentistry and veterinary medicine. In what does pharmacy differ from these?

There is no reason why the boards of pharmacy should not at once prescribe a definite course of special training in a pharmaceutical school as prerequisite to registration and license. There is abundant reason why they should do so. One of the many reasons why they should do it is the fact that laboratory methods and practice are in this day and generation absolutely necessary to any substantial course of training in chemistry, pharmacognosy and pharmacy, as well as in medicine and many other branches, and laboratory courses are quite impossible except in properly equipped schools.

If the boards of pharmacy shall decide that laboratory training is superfluous, then let them say so. If not, then let it be decided how much laboratory work must be required. The boards have ample power to prescribe whatever they may deem necessary.

The only limitations upon the discretionary powers of the boards of pharmacy consist of the self evident facts that they have no right to prescribe conditions that are clearly unreasonable, and *no right to license persons who are unfit.*

Additional legislation is not needed. Amendments to existing pharmacy laws are unnecessary. Common sense is sufficient. The boards have ample power. Responsibility for existing evils must rest with those who are alone competent to remedy them.

WHAT WE OUGHT TO HAVE.

What we ought to have is a definite consistent practical system adapted to our conditions and just to all concerned.

We should have a definite standard in view which we ought to gradually work up to and which can be attained within a reasonable time, and we should do nothing that may obstruct our journey toward that goal. We should at once begin making some progress in that direction. The prerequisites which we should look forward to should ultimately include high school graduation and a full two years' course in a good pharmacy school. How many years will be required to accomplish this we do not know, but it is a reasonable ideal and we should begin at once to strive for it.

What we should do immediately is to adopt: (1) One year's high school work as a minimum of general education required for admission to apprenticeship in pharmacy or to a school of pharmacy, the age of 17 years to be also required as a minimum for beginners; (2) the minimum age of 20 years for licensed assistants, together with either two years' drug store training and one year in a school of pharmacy, or three years' drug store training and an examination designed to test the candidates' qualifications as a *practical dispenser and clerk;* (3) the minimum age of 21 for pharmacists (principals), together with not less than two years' shop training, a two years' course in a school of pharmacy and an examination designed to test the candidate's fitness to properly *conduct a pharmacy.*

The total period of training should occupy three years for assistants and four years for principals.

The pharmaceutical schools should adapt their courses to whatever system the boards may adopt. If the plan here suggested should be the one adopted, then the schools should do all that can be done to include in their first year's curriculum the work best adapted to help produce intelligent and efficient practical dispensers to serve as clerks or assistant pharmacists.

It is sad but notoriously true that the young rarely prepare themselves in a substantial way for their life occupation in any line except under compulsion unless they are wise enough to believe that "it pays."

We should have thousands practicing medicine without any education were it not for the fact that the law forbids it. We do have thousands of persons practicing pharmacy who have no education because the law does not forbid it.

Whatever may be the rules and prerequisites adopted for the profession of pharmacy, they should be consistent with each other and with the end sought. They are not so now.

SUGGESTED STANDARD FOR SCHOOLS.

In order to render the system effective it is clearly necessary to prescribe certain standards of efficiency which the schools must observe in order to receive recognition at the hands of the boards. These standards should include:

Entrance requirements in harmony with the conditions prescribed for license; reasonably sufficient equipment; a reasonably sufficient corps of competent teachers; the length of the college course should include not less than 50 weeks of active work; the total amount of college instruction (lectures, recitations and laboratory work) should be not less than 1500 hours from matriculation to graduation, and *not less than 1000 hours laboratory work should be required.*

THE AGE AND PRELIMINARY EDUCATION PROPOSED FOR APPRENTICES AND STUDENTS.

The new "prerequisite law" of New York, which is the most intelligent, comprehensive and admirable pharmacy law in our country, prescribes one year of high school work or its equivalent for admission to the colleges. The boards of pharmacy of Ohio, South Dakota and Wisconsin have declared for the same requirement as a minimum of preliminary general education for pharmacy and the American Pharmaceutical Association has also evidenced its approval of it. Twenty-two of the twenty-five members of the American Conference of Pharmaceutical Faculties have already adopted this entrance requirement—several of them since the New York law was passed. This modicum of general education is a very low standard, but, all things considered, it seems to be all that stands a fair chance of present adoption and acquiescence. Now, let us see what this minimum requirement means.

The public schools, throughout the United States must, of course, be almost exclusively depended upon for this preliminary education. Whatever differences there may be between the schools of one State and those of another it is altogether out of the question to take such differences into serious consideration at this early stage of educational reform in pharmacy.

In order to be able to make substantial progress we must begin by establishing a foothold. If we waste our time straining at gnats the camels will surely continue to choke us. We must adopt means which are ready for us, easily applied, not burdensome.

AGES OF GRAMMAR AND HIGH SCHOOL GRADUATES.

The age of graduates of the elementary schools (grammar schools) in Chicago, in 1904, was as follows:

Below 13 years, 11; 13 years, 262; 14 years, 1589; 15 years, 3229; 16 years, 2248; 17 years, 813; 18 years, 144; above 18 years, 24; total, 8320.

The age of the graduates of the high schools was:

Under 18 years, 77; 18 years, 256; 19 years, 350; 20 years, 178; 21 years, 44; over 21 years, 18; total, 923.

It will be seen that only about 11 per cent. of the grammar school graduates *finished* the high school course. A much large proportion, of course, attended high school one or two years.

I am informed by excellent authority that these figures represent very nearly the conditions in all large States where the public schools are reasonably well provided for. From these figures it is apparent that the rule adopted by the authorities of the State of New York under the new prerequisite law establishing 17 years as the minimum age for admission to a pharmaceutical school is consistent with the preliminary education requirement. Long experience has convinced me that students with less general education than that represented by one year's high school work, or its equivalent, are rarely able to make their college work in pharmacy successful even if 20 years of age.

THE IRREDUCIBLE MINIMUM.

The preliminary education now required for admission to a medical school of good repute is not less than high school graduation. Next year the dental schools will require the same preparatory education. Must the occupation of the pharmacist be considered so far inferior that eight or ten years less of preparatory general and special school training is sufficient for it? Is it unreasonable to propose that the pharmacist shall be not more than five and one-half years behind the physicians in education? Or, are we to believe that there is something about young men who take up pharmacy that enables them to learn chemistry and pharmacognosy and pharmacy at an earlier age and with less preliminary mental equipment than is deemed requisite for similar grades of study in a medical school?

Is American pharmacy so much simpler than that of other countries that four years' less preparation before beginning to learn it is enough? Or are our boys so much smarter that they can, after only six or eight years of primary school education, accomplish in less than two years what the Germans, Austrians, Swiss, Scandanavians, etc., are not allowed to try to do in less than six or seven years after high school graduation? Those are the questions for us to answer.

I am one of those who believe that it would be a disgrace for us not to adopt at least the age of 17 and one year's completed high school work as the irreducible minimum of entrance conditions. No boy with less education, or under 17 years of age, should be recognized as a student of pharmacy or an apprentice in a drug store entitled to any credit for his work or time toward fulfillment of the conditions upon which he must base his claim to obtain a license as an assistant pharmacist or pharmacist.

Apprentices and clerks in drug stores do not go back to school to mend their deficient preliminary general education. It would be absurd to adopt any system based upon the expectation that they will do so.

People generally believe that *some* education is necessary to become a pharmacist, and they open their eyes in astonishment when informed how little is actually required by law.

EVIDENCE ON WHICH BOARDS SHOULD REGISTER APPRENTICES.

The principals of public high schools will undoubtedly furnish to the state boards of pharmacy and to the colleges of pharmacy the necessary reports required to verify the attendance of the candidate and show his standing in every study. These reports should be accepted without question. To require further evidence on the points involved would be purely supererogatory, at least at this stage.

The evidence, then, upon which the board of pharmacy ought to issue certificates of registration to apprentices should consist of: (1) Authentic official certificates of actual regular attendance for one year at a high school or academy, or evidence of equivalent preliminary education; (2) satisfactory outcome of an examination in arithmetic conducted at or near the home town of the candidate, if such an examination is deemed necessary, the questions being furnished by the Board of Pharmacy and the examination papers returned to the board; (3) such additional evidence of general fitness and good character as the board may require, if any.

The colleges of pharmacy should be satisfied with the same kind of evidence for admission. But it must be clearly understood that the only object of the preliminary education is to put the student's mental machinery in reasonably effective working order.

MENTAL EFFICIENCY SHOULD BE THE STANDARD.

Proficiency in the particular studies embodied in the programme of the work of the public school is not the chief end of the schooling; for it makes comparatively little difference what the studies are if the result is healthy, all around, mental growth.

Proficiency in history, geography, Latin and some other branches is not necessary for the purpose of learning chemistry, pharmacognosy and pharmacy. But these or other studies are necessary to the scheme of general training of the boy.

The student's fund of common knowledge gained in school is valuable, to be sure, but we can afford to take his possession of some such knowledge for granted if he has really attended school the prescribed length of time and has satisfactory credentials showing that he was a good scholar. To ask him questions in Board of Pharmacy examinations about the capitals of different States, etc., is wholly unnecessary.

The mental efficiency which is the result of his school training is the thing sought. For this reason an examination cannot take the place of the schooling itself. If it be thought impracticable to prescribe both, then a definite amount of high school work without any entrance examination for either apprenticeship or college admission must be preferable to any examination without the prescribed schooling.

A small number of young men with exceptionally good natural ability and perseverence, but without education, have made and may still make a success of their careers. But that is no reason for ignoring the fact that 99 per cent. of the ill equipped must fail. Many of the men with only a grammar school education who have become successful pharmacists heretofore had far better advantages than are enjoyed by the apprentices of to-day. The drug store of to-day is more strenuous and more mercantile.

(*To be continued.*)

Readers are invited to scrutinize carefully the New Remedies Compendium and Prices Current which appears in this issue. In no other periodical is the information regarding characteristics, uses, prices and form of container so full or so trustworthy.

THE STANDPOINT OF THE MANUFACTURER OF SPECIAL AND PROPRIETARY PREPARATIONS.[1]

By Frédéric S. Mason, M. P. S.

I address this meeting with some hesitation because I am connected with the manufacture of proprietary remedies. Perhaps I may, however, claim your indulgence when I say that I am also a pharmacist and have long been in contact with physicians in such capacity in Europe, where the relations between the physician and pharmacist are more cordial than in this country.

The Medico-Pharmaceutical League has, I believe, the very laudable object of bringing about similar close relations here, and I can assure you that such relations are very beneficial not only to the pharmacist but also to the physician. From actual experience in Paris, I am able to affirm that the very best professional men consult the pharmacist on new remedies, posology and especially on convenient methods of formulating, and are guided by their advice, looking to the pharmacist as an authority on such matters. How rarely this confidence is shown here we all know. In Europe physician and pharmacist complement each other, for each in his sphere is a specialist and jealousy is eliminated, since the physician is prohibited by law from dispensing, while the pharmacist does not prescribe over the counter. By specialization the best results are obtained in every calling, even in the manufacture of proprietary remedies.

Specialization in the manufacture of pharmaceutical products is just as legitimate as in medicine or surgery, and you will be ready to admit the value of the experienced and skillful specialist in the latter fields. With the manufacturer of pharmaceutical preparations, "neither wise men nor fools work well without proper tools," and in saying this I do not depreciate the skill of my confreres, the retail pharmacists, or their ability to make good preparations, but they will agree with me that some preparations are valuable for which they have neither the time, the experience nor the manufacturing facilities; hence the physician is justified in using such remedies which have proved reliable, under the signature of a reputable firm or a trade marked name, and which are better than extemporized substitutes.

PROPRIETARIES ABROAD.

This is so fully recognized abroad that a majority of continental prescriptions call for proprietary remedies which have acquired a reputation for excellence; and we find such specialization among a number of small dispensing retail pharmacists as well as amongst the large manufacturers. In reply to this, it may be opposed that there are firms whose special mission is the substitution or imitation of proprietary remedies, who are fully as competent as the manufacturers of pharmaceuticals, and who are possessed of the capital, brains and apparatus for the purpose of so doing. But while ethical preparations bear the formula (qualitative and quantitative), and an analysis will determine the accuracy of such alleged formula, manufacturers generally have some "tour de main," some pharmaceutical "trick," if I may so express it, which has warranted the investment of money and which only special knowledge and experience acquire, which give them special claim to recognition. Besides, what guarantee has the physician in using a so-called "less expensive" substitute, as compared with the original preparation, when the maker of the substitute has no reputation to sustain? Finally, there is not even "money" economy to the patient—the final interest concerned in the use of the substitute.

I know of one popular preparation which is imitated by more than twenty firms who make it their business to reproduce anything which becomes popular and who have procured the special plant necessary for its preparation. Yet I do not believe these firms are making money, for competition has cut the price down nearly to the cost of production, and I am inclined to believe that more of the original preparation is still sold than of all the imitations, which are often dispensed, unless original bottles are ordered by the physician.

THE REASON FOR THE EXISTENCE OF THE PROPRIETARY.

A specialty or proprietary which can be easily compounded or manufactured by any competent pharmacist has no reason to exist, and indeed few of them do, whatever you may say to the contrary. A special preparation must have a *raison d'etre*, and manufacturers are generally too shrewd business men to invest money in promoting the sale of anything which is easily reproduced. I have been intimately conected with the manufacturing of special pharmaceuticals for the last twenty-five years and think I am correct in saying that it would be difficult to find any new remedy or preparation which attained popularity with the medical profession which has not had behind it the brains and capital of manufacturers.

SOME HISTORICAL NOTES.

Going back as far as 1820, I would give as an example, one of our most popular drugs, quinine, first isolated by Pelletier, who founded the firm with which I am connected. To-day, one can hardly conceive it possible that this drug would not have found its place in the treatment of diseases alone and unaided; nevertheless it was the financial interest behind it which brought it quickly to the front rank. Otherwise, it might have remained a chemical curiosity for years before attaining the position it holds to-day, and this is one of a dozen valuable medicines, which the persistent efforts of some one firm has brought to the notice of the medical profession.

My pharmaceutical friends probably know of some scores of valuable remedies which have been brought to notice by isolated members of the profession, but, which having no powerful commercial interest behind them, have been relegated to the shelves of museums, and the experiments made with them forgotten, because there was no way of holding the business created.

In the manufacture of chemicals and pharmaceutical preparations, with the constant advances that are made from every standpoint, and with the critical, discriminating study to which they are increasingly submitted, the unethical, the inferior, the objectionable, will be gradually eliminated and die a natural death.

We are all familiar with the fact of the formation of a Council on Chemistry and Pharmacy by the American Medical Association, which has set itself to the task of eliminating the ethical from the unethical preparations, and incorporating them in a book of "new and unofficial remedies," a sort of extra pharmacopœia, and we have seen another movement in the public press with the object of suppressing quackery and protecting the public from the wiles of the advertiser of secret nostrums, which foreshadows future legislation, to control to some extent the use of nostrums. In this connection it would appear that the physician should co-operate with the pharmacist, and the large manufacturing chemists who have rendered valuable service in the past. The American Medical Association has very rightly expressed the opinion that it is equally derogatory to the professional character for physicians to dispense or promote the use of secret remedies, and its Council on Chemistry and Pharmacy is ambitious to go even further and are making, perhaps, rather excessive demands on manufacturers, since the latter are desired to sanction the application of synonymous Latin names to their products, which would be liable to confuse physicians. Such synonymous pseudo-scientific appellations applied to proprietary remedies would thus become semi-official, and it is unlikely that manufacturers of even the most ethical therapeutic agents will acquiesce in these exaggerated requirements of the council, who in the frenzy of their zeal for putting down the sale of secret nostrums, are liable to discourage honest manufacturers, who have given their time, money and energy to help the physician in the production of the best modern therapeutic agents, and who naturally consider that they have some claim to furnish the products on which they stake their reputation. Therefore, to accept without protest, synonymous pseudo-scientific Latin names, would be an injustice to themselves as well as to the medical profession.

I sympathize with the doctor in his difficulty in differentiating the ethical from the unethical amongst the immense number of new therapeutic agents, which we bring to his notice, but it would appear to me to be a mistake to follow the Council on Chemistry and Pharmacy in prescribing proprietary preparations under the proposed synonymous titles, for those given

[1] Read at a meeting of the Medico-Pharmaceutical League, January 23, 1906.

..ie makers who have selected distinctive names to the best their judgment, under all the conditions to be dealt with.

THE DIFFERENCE IN THE STATUS OF THE GALENICAL AND OF THE CHEMICAL PROPRIETARY.

Those chemicals which can be patented have doubtless ample protection, since even if they are prescribed under synonymous terms they cannot be supplied except by those holding the patent, but in the case of galenical preparations, which require equal skill, experience and especial appliances, the only protection the manufacturer and physician have against substitution is its trade name.

The present situation for the best of manufacturers of pharmaceuticals is thus in a measure perplexing and, indeed, unjust. Doubtless grave abuses of the good faith of physicians have been committed, but care should be taken, in this crusade for crushing the unethical, that the work and business of those who conform to ethical rules be not hampered and, above all, be not unjustly prejudiced. I believe that the profession generally are not in sympathy with extreme views, since we all recognize that the manufacturer has certain rights which cannot be ignored.

Within the last ten years great progress on ethical lines has been made among manufacturers, as can be seen by comparison of the advertisements in the medical journals, for the best of us now give the exact composition, although we may not fully explain the *modus operandi* of the manufacture of our products, which is of no importance to the physician, and is the business asset of the manufacturer, which he is not willing to abondon, since he considers this his right. You are all familiar with the detail man and the samples which come by mail and other methods of reaching the physician, but few of you probably realize how often the manufacturer is unsuccessful in these efforts, although most of you imagine we make huge profits. I am in a position to say from actual knowledge of the inside of many manufacturing houses that this is much exaggerated, even in cases where millions are supposed to have been made, and I venture to say that the lucky ones who succeed would have much greater profits on their investment in any other commercial venture. You must all recognize that the attempt to introduce new remedies cheaply is impossible to-day, and I do not know of a single case of a proprietary remedy for physicians' use which has become profitable in less than five years, and many largely prescribed by physicians are not so after even ten years.

Preparations which do not succeed must not always be blamed on the manufacturer; those which succeed the best are not often the ethical and scientific, and I could give several examples of valuable remedies which have been commercial failures, owing to the manufacturer overestimating the intelligence or desire to learn of the rank and file of physicians.

I will not discuss here the views of the therapeutic nihilist, for discussion as to possibility of using less variety of drugs is out of place, but certainly a number of empirical formulæ could be dropped from our pharmacopœias, many of which have only a hoary reputation founded on the opinions of our ancestors to recommend them. New remedies only obtain official recognition long after those who have made them popular have done the work, and to curtail progress on these lines by discouraging new remedies would be absurd.

The claim that the physician becomes, in the phrases dear to the *Journal of the American Medical Association*, the "unpaid peddler" of the manufacturer is often advanced, but physicians should not lose sight of the fact that the patient does not want to know simply what remedy to use for his troubles. He consults his physician, just as he does his lawyer, on some special condition of the present. He wants a diagnosis of his case and advice on diet, and, if necessary, to get a prescription to suit the *present* condition, and the remedy prescribed is only intended (just as the diet and other details) for the present. One might just as well object that because the physician recommends a voyage and certain kinds of food, that the patient will forever after follow this advice. If the patient is such a fool as to take bicarbonate of soda, bromides or a proprietary remedy because his doctor once recommended it, it is his own lookout. I think patients begin to understand that self-medication is a mistake, and that they rarely consult a physician just to know once and for all to learn what medicine to take, for the prescription is only a small part of the duty of the medical profession.

The patient is just as likely to say "Dr. So-and-so recommended me to take quinine the last time I had chills and fever," as he would if the doctor had ordered some special proprietary remedy in which he had confidence and believed to be better than what he could prescribe extemporarily.

I am opposed to the sale of dangerous remedies and self-medication generally, but we should also remember that the public of the United States have been educated by the newspapers to use drugs, which are not necessarily harmful, and which it would be extremely difficult to prevent, and I do not think that we; any of us, desire to see conditions obtain here as in Germany, where, in order to get the simplest remedy, it is necessary to consult a physician and obtain a prescription.

In speaking of manufacturers of proprietary remedies, I wish it distinctly understood that I am referring to manufacturers of pure chemicals used in medicines and to special preparations sold exclusively on physicians' prescriptions, and of which the composition and quantities are made known to the physician and pharmacist.

I wish to say a word here with regard to the dispensing of remedies by physicians themselves, that this condition appears to me to be a deplorable one. While it may be necessary for the prescriber to dispense his own drugs sometimes, the habit is a retrograde one. It was abandoned in Europe and in this country long ago, but the question is again becoming a burning one in certain sections. Some physicians claim it is an advantage to dispense themselves rather than prescribe, in order to prevent substitution by the unscrupulous pharmacist and also to keep the public from refilling prescriptions without again consulting them.

Are physicians, however, justified in considering the average pharmacist unreliable and unscrupulous? Are not the medical profession largely responsible for the pharmacist of the United States occupying the low position he does to-day? Has not the qualified pharmacist been forced by the growing habit of physicians' self-dispensing to give the greater part of his attention to selling cigars, soda water, tooth brushes, and everything but his legitimate calling of filling prescriptions? I think I am not exaggerating when I say that the business of the average pharmacist is not more than one-fifth of legitimate prescription filling. It appears to me a somewhat selfish position on the physicians' part to wish to conceal from their patients what they are taking, and it is not likely to elevate them in public esteem.

In conclusion, these few somewhat disconnected remarks will, I trust, be received with indulgence, for they are given with the hope that the physician, the dentist, the dispensing pharmacist and the manufacturing chemist will all see that they have mutual interests and can find a common ground of sympathy in discussion.

THE PROPRIETARY MEDICINE FROM THE PHARMACIST'S STANDPOINT.[1]

By P. J. Diner.

To understand thoroughly the present "proprietary medicine" we must trace it back to the original medicine man. In ancient times the priests or holy men attended to the healing of the sick. By laying on of hands, incantations and magic, combined with copious draughts of infusions and decoctions, the devil, who caused the disturbance in the patient, was driven out. As a side issue, these holy men handled "charms" to ward off disease and did quite a little business through the sale of love potions. That the vegetable kingdom furnished its share of the charms is well established, and even as recently as last week I sold five cents' worth of "star anise" to a clairvoyant, who told me that each "star" would charm $5 from some fool.

[1] Read at a meeting of the Medico-Pharmaceutical League, January 23, 1906.

We see, therefore, that the art and science of medicine included not only the diagnosis of diseases, but also embraced the gathering of herbs and their preparation and dispensing for medicinal and other purposes. The gradual advance in medicine finally resulted in a separation of pharmacy from medicine, and it became the "handmaiden" of medicine. The discovery of alkaloids and active principles put pharmacy on a new basis again, and it became impossible for the apothecary to manufacture everything he needed in his own pharmacy. This developed the "manufacturing chemist." We now have the functions of the original medicine man divided between three branches: the physician, the pharmacist, the manufacturing chemist.

About this time a number of medicine men developed formulæ for the treatment of certain diseases, and we see these preparations named after them, as, for instance, Huxham's Tincture of Bark, Griffith's Mixture, Lugol's Solution, etc. So far, so good.

But the human mind was ever so constituted that it could not view success without envy. The success gained by some of the manufacturing chemists by reason of original discoveries immediately brought on such a flood of so-called proprietary preparations that pharmacy sank from the position of handmaiden of medicine to that of servant girl of the manufacturer. No professional pharmacist objects to dispensing preparations which are the outcome of discovery or original research. But when he is called upon to dispense any of the numberless St. Louis chemicals, when a physician wants him to act as his private dividend developer by dispensing the original discov- ... of concerns in which he is interested, then the professional ... of the pharmacist rises up and revolts.

... the eyes of the professional pharmacist, the physician ...ibing any of these preparations is either an ignoramus ... charlatan, or both, mostly both. The pharmacist is com...elled by law to be thoroughly familiar with the drugs he dispenses, and to examine them for purity, etc. The "caveat emptor" of ordinary commerce is changed into "caveat vendor" in the case of pharmacy. With chemicals, even of those protected by patent, which are really scientific discoveries, he can easily assume responsibility. Chemical tests are at his command. But what can he do with preparations which never had a chemical test, and never could have a chemical test, because they are mechanical mixtures, and because the manufacturers can and do change their composition at will. The M.D. who prescribes these preparations is on a par with the customer who buys Lydia Pinkham's, or Father John's, with this difference: that the layman who takes the statements of the manufacturer for truth pays for it himself, while the doctor makes the patient pay for it, and often gets a little rake off from the manufacturer in the shape of discount.

Let us now view the effect which the prescribing of such remedies has on the three classes most affected.

First comes the physician. After the detail man or the manufacturer's ad. has insulted the M.D.'s intelligence by telling him what to prescribe, the manufacturer proceeds to separate the doctor from his patients in a most ingenious manner. He tells the M.D. that to insure the genuineness of the preparation he must write for an original bottle. Right here he undermines his friend, the M.D., for before very long the article has been so well introduced by the aid of the guileless M.D. that the people buy it over the counter without paying the M.D. his fee for recommending it. This is the financial phase for the M.D.

There is also another phase. When the M.D. has become accustomed to let the detail man think for him, he has given up medicine thinking altogether. His first impulse after diagnosing a case is to call for some proprietary remedy, irrespective of what its actual constituents may be, without regard to idiosyncrasies in the patient and without the possibility of knowing what secondary effects that particular dope may produce. Often he is puzzled by what he supposes to be newly developed symptoms, which are nothing less than after effects from some of the constituents of the (to him) unknown remedy. The effect on the patient is a matter not to be lightly passed over. We pharmacists often have occasion to judge it.

I will relate an incident which happened not long ago in my store. A lady brought in a prescription asking for a proprietary tablet whose chemical test consists of the monogram on top. After receiving the medicine she opened the box, and on discovering that the tablets were old friends of hers, which she had been buying in 25-cent boxes over the counter, she said some very uncomplimentary things about the M.D., and wound up by declaring that hereafter she would consult a doctor who wrote "real medicine." The evil of self-medication is largely due and directly attributed to the prescribing of proprietary preparations by the M.D.

To compel the druggist to dispense preparations of this ilk, is to rob him financially and to insult him professionally. He is compelled to stock up on 40 to 50 acetanilid preparations, the numberless bromide mixtures, the legion of dope cure-alls, and simply because the physician is too indolent or too ignorant to compose his own prescriptions.

That there are a number of valuable preparations of proprietary origin, nobody will deny. That the M.D. has a right to use them in his daily practice is equally true, but it is up to the physician to differentiate between an ethical proprietary and a fake with a high-sounding name, and when in doubt there is always at the command of the practicing physician that great and, alas, often neglected, book, the United States Pharmacopœia.

Mr. Fairchild's Views.

B. T. Fairchild said he had listened with interest to the sketch Mr. Diner had given of the evolution by which we had to-day the three distinct professions—the physician, the dispensing pharmacist and the manufacturing pharmacist and chemist. He thought that the present agitation, both in the public and medical press—the exposure and condemnation of "fake" medicines and "fake" testimonials—would certainly result in a great public benefit.

Alluding to the work of the American Medical Association by its Council on Medicine and Pharmacy, in undertaking certain regulations and requirements for new and nonofficial remedies, he said that all the agitation and movements for reform were inevitably accompanied to a certain extent by impracticable ideas and advocated with an excess of zeal. Consequently there had naturally at the outset arisen many matters which required conference and a better understanding on the part of all interested, and that in conference with the manufacturers there had been shown, he thought, a disposition to make concessions and receive suggestions modifying the position which had been necessarily tentatively taken and in regard to matters not vital to the main object to be accomplished. He said he wished to speak only of one or two aspects of the question in this regard, viz., about trademarks and patented processes. Admitting and recognizing, indeed as every one must, the really marvelous advances which had been made in pharmacy and which should be attributed, as a whole, to the manufacturer, he said that it was very significant and important to note that all this work, all over the world, had been done by people who had found it necessary to adopt trademarks in their business; that it was an inevitable and wholly beneficial and appropriate thing, and he thought that there were no manufacturers of modern and original products who had not found it necessary to adopt the trademark, which certainly was advantageous to every possible good interest concerned. He especially spoke of the fallacious idea which had been so much insisted upon, viz., that a trademark gave certain rights to the manufacturer of any particular article or product; he said it was, on the contrary, clearly a fact that it gave no right or property except that of the trademark itself, and thus the identity of the product—that is to say, the particular product placed upon the market under any particular name.

The whole tenor of Mr. Fairchild's remarks was to the effect that all this agitation and movement as regards every interest, including the public, would crystallize into a form which would undoubtedly be of very material and very distinct progress and benefit.

THE LATEST REMEDIES.

(*Continued from Vol.* XLVII, *No.* 10, *p.* 295.)

Acetysal is a trade name adopted for acetylsalicylic acid, as made by G. and R. Fritz, Vienna.

Aethrol is a name applied to a series of water-soluble antiseptic and cosmetic preparations which find a wide range of usefulness, being employed for spraying in sick rooms and for rendering the hands aseptic and as a mouth wash. Aethrol can be combined with eau de cologne, eucalyptol, peppermint and other flavoring agents. It is also put up in powder form, *e. g.*—aethrol powder B is a borax compound for the bath and toilet. It is made and marketed by H. Noerdlinger, Flörsheim on Main, Germany.

Alcho is the name used by A. Gawalowski to designate the aluminum carbonate prepared by him and already described.

Aldol is a colorless liquid of characteristic odor and sweetish taste, soluble in two parts of water and in corresponding portions of ether and alcohol. When exposed to the air it gradually crystallizes, forming a polymer called paraldol. Chemically aldol is an aldehyde corresponding to butanediol. To make it a cold mixture of ethyl aldehyde and diluted hydrochloric acid is set aside until the whole assumes a yellow color. After then neutralizing with sodium bicarbonate, the mixture is shaken with ether and the aldol finally obtained by evaporating the ether in a vacuum. It is said to possess hypnotic properties and has been used in the treatment of insomnia.

Anticilloids are urethral bougies composed of oil of theobroma containing 10 per cent. of protargol. Used as a prophylactic against gonorrhœa.

Antidiabetic is the name given by the maker, W. M. Stock, Düsseldorf, Germany, to a mixture composed of aqueous fluid-extract of Senecio Fuchsi,. 97.78 per cent.; salicylic acid, 0.2 per cent. (as a preservative); trypsin, 0.02 per cent., and 2 per cent. of an alkali, the nature of which is not disclosed. It is given in doses of one tablespoonful three times daily after meals.

Antisudor is a disinfectant solution in which salicylic acid is present, but no formaldehyde. As its name implies, it is used as a remedy against excessive perspiration, being applied as a paint over the parts affected twice daily and allowed to dry. It should not be confounded with antisudorin, previously described. Made by C. Fr. Hausmann, St. Gall, Switzerland.

Antitaenin is a preparation of pumpkin seed which is put up in tablet form as a remedy against intestinal worms by K. Habben, Mülhausen, Thuringia, Germany.

Antitranspirin is the name applied to an external application for the relief of excessive perspiration of bromidrosis. It is said to consist of a 5 per cent. solution of formaldehyde perfumed with spirit of lavender.

Apicin, the chief constituent of which is calcium guaiacolphosphate, and which is used in the treatment of pulmonary disorders, is marketed as a chocolate covered pastil by the makers, G. and R. Fritz, Vienna.

Arsenferratose is a compound of ferratin, 5 per cent., and arsenic trioxide, 0.003 per cent., in organic combination.

Benzoyl peroxide is the name of an anæsthetic antiseptic preparation which has been made by Hynson, Westcott & Co., Baltimore, in an experimental way for one of the faculty of Johns Hopkins University. It is a white crystalline substance, only sparingly soluble in water, but easily so in alcohol. With oils, 2 or 3 per cent. solutions may be readily obtained. When applied locally it produces slight anæsthesia, and hence its use has been suggested in burns, which are said to heal rapidly under its influence, while the pain is quickly relieved. Benzoyl peroxide is obtained by the action of sodium peroxide on benzoyl chloride.

Bioforin is described as a granulated powder consisting of calcium glycerophosphate, Gm. 50; extract of cinchona, Gm. 10; chocolate, flavored with vanilla, Gm. 40; extract of kola, Gm. 20; extract of coca, Gm. 5, and sugar, Gm. 875.

Bromotan, which is chemically methylene bromtannin urea, occurs as a brownish white powder without taste or odor. It is said to be efficacious applied as a 10 per cent. dusting powder or 10 per cent. ointment in skin eruptions, itching, rash, etc. Marketed by Arnold Voswinkel, Berlin, Germany.

Butipyrine is a new name for trigemine, a compound of butylchloral hydrate with pyramidon, which is used as an antineuralgic. (See Tregenim.)

Cidrase is the dried yeast of cider of the apple. It occurs as a granular powder, having the characteristic flavor of apples and a slightly acid taste. Cidrase is said to contain an unusually active oxydase and it is to this that its efficacy in the treatment of gouty and rheumatic affections is attributed. It is given in doses of 0.5 Gm. three to six times daily in slightly sweetened water.

Dericin [Name adopted for pure floricin, which see.] is a thick, pale yellow oil obtained from castor oil, which has been used in the treatment of tuberculosis combined with antiseptic oils. It can be used as a vehicle for hypodermic injections containing eucalyptol, menthol, etc. Compounds of dericin are known as dericinates.

Diabeteserine is a combination of eserine and Trunececk's serum put up in two strengths. Diabeteserine I contains the salts of Trunececk's serum and 0.07 per cent. of eserine salicylate; two tablets contain 0.0005 Gm. of eserine salicylate and the salts of 100 Cc. of blood serum. Diabeteserine II is diabeteserine I with the addition of 0.0118 per cent. of atropine, two tablets containing 0.0001 Gm. of atropine. The tablets are manufactured by W. Natterer, Munich.

Dichondra brevifolia, in the form of a glycerin solution of the extract of the seed and stems of the plant, has been recommended by an Armenian physician as a remedy for diphtheria, applied to the diphtheritic membrane on a pledget of cotton.

Diethylbarbituric acid is another name for veronal, a hypnotic drug which is marketed in the United States by Merck & Co. under the name veronal, and by the Continental Color Works (formerly the Farbenfabriken of Elberfeld Company) under both names. (Veronal, it will be recalled, is the shorter trade name of diethylmalonylurea.) (See Proponal.)

Dispnon tablets have been introduced as a remedy for asthma and shortness of breath. Each tablet contains diuretine, Gm. 0.25; agurine, Gm. 0.10, and extract of guebracha, 0.10. The dose is two tablets three times daily.

Dolonephran is a preparation used by dentists and surgeons as a local anæsthetic. It consists of a combination of alypin and suprarenin. Made and marketed by Chemical Institute, 55 Koniggrätzerstrasse, Berlin.

Epiosin, which is chemically N-methyldiphenylenimidazol, occurs as glistening prismatic crystals, soluble in water, alcohol and chloroform. It is analgetic and hypnotic, but must be administered with care, as it is slightly toxic. It is given in doses of 0.05 Gm. twice daily, preferably in milk on account of its bitter taste.

Ergogenine Joachim is described as a roborant and recommended in anæmia, neurasthenia, etc. It is marketed as a syrup and in capsules. Its composition is a secret of the manufacturer, Oscar vom Schoor, Antwerp.

Eucodeine is the brommethylate of codeine, having the same sedative properties of codeine without the latter drug's tendency to induce clonic convulsions. It is a crystalline powder, soluble in water, which is used in the treatment of bronchitis and phthisis as a sedative and analytic in doses of Gm. 0.2 to Gm. 0.3. Marketed by G. D. Riedel, Berlin.

Fagacid is a resin-like substance obtained from beechwood tar. It forms a black, glistening mass of tarry odor and taste, fairly soluble in absolute alcohol and in solutions of caustic alkalies and alkali carbonates. It is less soluble in ether, benzin, chloroform and oil of turpentine, and completely insoluble in water and weak acids. It is used as an internal antiseptic, and for the preparation of soaps, plasters, dressings, etc. In antiseptic energy a 2 per cent. solution of fagacid is said to be the equal of a 5 per cent. solution of carbolic acid. Manufactured by Dr. H. Noerdlinger, Flörsheim on Main.

Floria kresol is the latest German name for a compound of the three cresols contained in tar oil. It probably corresponds to the cresole of U. S. Pharmaeopœia VIII. Manufactured by H. Noerdlinger, Flörsheim on Main.

Floricin is a name applied to an oil obtained from castor oil by a special process. Floricin oil in contrast to castor oil saponifies readily with dilute solutions of alkali carbonates. The soaps thus prepared are adapted for the purposes of rendering certain substances more soluble in water, as, for instance, volatile oils, phenols, resins, etc. Two varieties of floricin oil are marketed—pure and commercial. The first named is the only oil used for medicinal purposes, and as the name floricin might be easily confounded with phloridzin, the pure oil has been named dericin and compounds of the oil are known as dericinates.

Formicine is formaldehyde-acetamide, and is produced by the action of formaldehyde on acetamide. It possesses powerful antiseptic properties, and has been recommended as a succedaneum for iodoform, applied in 5 per cent. solution, bandages, etc. It is marketed as a syrup liquid, the crystals being very hygroscopic. Manufactured by Kalle & Co., Biebrich on Main.

Formacetone is the name of a French disinfectant preparation, the composition of which is not stated. Marketed by Eugene Fournier, Paris.

Fortose is a nutritive preparation consisting chiefly of hæmialbumose obtained from meat. It dissolves readily in water, yielding a tasteless and odorless solution which is well borne by the stomach. Marketed by Brückner, Lampe & Co., Berlin.

Gadose is an ointment vehicle composed of animal fats, which is capable of hydration to the extent of 25 per cent. It is made by G. and R. Fritz, Vienna.

Gasterogen is a compound of the peptic juice of the dog's stomach and tonics like condurango bark, cinchona and rhubarb. Manufactured by Weydenberg Laboratory, Berlin.

Glycolytic substance (*organa glycolytica auf deutsch*) consists of a mixture of dried heparon and muscolon used in diabetes. Made by Fabrik Rhenania, Aachen.

Gouttine is another and later name for citarin (sodium anhydromethylene citrate), introduced as a remedy for gout Manufactured by G. & R. Fritz, Vienna.

Haemoquinine is a preparation of the peptonates of iron and manganese with quinine.

Haemostasin is the name of a substance obtained from the suprarenal gland of the sheep which is said to be identical with adrenalin. It is manufactured by the Serum and Impf. Institute, Bern, and is marketed in powder form and in solution, 1 : 1000.

Heparon is a new organotherapeutic substance obtained by the action of pancreatic juice on ox liver. It is said to be useful in diabetes by its action in aiding the liver to split up grape sugar. Made by the Fabrik Rhenania, Aachen.

Hysterol is the name applied to bornyl valerate, put up in gelatin pearls containing 0.25 Gm. each, by G. Pohl, Schönbaum, Danzig.

Ibogaine is an alkaloid obtained from the roots of *Tabernanthe iboga*. It forms amber colored crystals, which readily form salts on treatment with acids. It possesses feeble local anæsthetic properties and acts as a nervous stimulant like caffeine. It is said to be useful in the treatment of nervous prostration following influenza.

Ichthyolidin is a piperazin ichthyol compound which forms an amorphous powder with a slight tarry odor and bitter taste. It is insoluble in water. Used in treatment of the uric acid diathesis. Manufactured by Cordes, Hermanni & Co., Hamburg.

Ichthyomenthol is the name of an alcoholic solution of ichthyol, menthol, methyl salicylate and aromatic oils which is recommended for the external treatment of myalgia and rheumatic pains.

Iodoglycine is stated to be a mixture of aluminum silicate, iodine and glycerin, which is used, spread on linen or gauze, as an application to ulcers of the leg and in the treatment of bronchial troubles in children to exclude the air.

Kasucolum is a recently coined trade term for potassium guaiacolsulphonate, also known as thiocol.

Krelution is a cresol soap solution made by a special process so that it contains 66 per cent. of meta an dpara cresol. It is intended for use in antiseptic surgery and in the treatment of certain skin diseases. Manufactured by H. Noerdlinger, Flörsheim on Main.

Kremulsion is an emulsion of resin soap and cresol which is recommended as a sheep dip and as a veterinary antiseptic. Made by H. Noerdlinger, Flörsheim on Main.

Lactoserve is a prepared nutrient for infants, obtained by souring pasteurized milk with a pure culture of lactic acid bacteria, evaporating to dryness and mixing it with sugar, flour and vegetable albumin in definite proportions. Mixed with water lactoserve furnishes an emulsion resembling buttermilk. It is made by Boehringer & Loetine, Mannheim, Germany, and New York.

La Zima is the name of a preparation recommended for the treatment of biliary calculus, which is said to consist of sodium chlorate, carduus marinus, taraxacum, nasturtium, cinchona, and a liver ferment obtained from the livers of animals affected with gallstone. Made by Aktien Gesellschaft La Zima, Montreux.

Lecin is an iron albuminate compound which is said to contain in each liter 200 Gm. of egg albumin, 5 to 6 Gm. of iron in chemical combination, 80 Gm. of sugar and 150 Gm. of alcohol, together with flavoring essences. Manufactured by Hirschapotheke, Hannover, Germany.

Lenicet is a condensed anhydrous basic form of aluminum acetate. It is a fine, voluminous, white powder of faint acetous odor, insoluble in water, but soluble in dilute inorganic acids and solutions of caustic alkalies. It is a compound of 1 molecule of aluminum with 2 molecules of acetic acid. In hyperhidrosis it is used as a dusting powder for its drying properties in dilutions of 10 to 15 per cent. with talcum, and as ointment paste or compress in the antiseptic treatment of ulcers and wounds in similar dilutions. Manufactured by R. Reiss, Berlin.

Leprine or **Leprotine**, as it is variously designated, is an antitoxin prepared from the lepra bacillus, which is used in the treatment of leprosy by subcutaneous injection in doses of 10 Cc.

Letalbin is a compound of lecithin and albumin which is prescribed as a tonic in the same way as lecithin and the glycerophosphates.

Musculon is an organotherapeutic substance prepared from muscular tissue by digestion with pancreatic juice. It is stated to have the property of aiding the liver in the splitting up of grape sugar. Made by Fabrik Rhenania, Aachen.

Nalicin is the name of a local anæsthetic in use by German dentists. It is said to consist of a mixture of 1 per cent. spirit of nitroglycerin; 1 per cent. cocaine hydrochloride with compound spirit of thymol; alcohol, sodium chloride, phenol, formaldehyde and water. It is made by A. Kirsch, Wiesdorf on Rhine.

Novocaine is para-amido-benzoyl-diethylamine-ethanol mono-chlorhydride, a new substitute for cocaine. It forms crystalline needles which are readily soluble in water. It is stated to be less toxic than cocaine. It has been used in solutions of 0.25 Gm. novocaine in 50 or 100 Gm. physiologival salt solution with 5 to 10 drops of 1 : 1000 adrenalin solution as a local anaesthetic. Manufactured by Farbwerke Vorm. Meister Lucius & Brüning, Höchst on Main.

(*To be continued.*)

Cream *of* Current Literature

A summary of the leading articles in contemporary pharmaceutical periodicals.

Aspidium Spinulosum in Tapeworm.—Laurent found that *Aspidium spinulosum*, a fern quite common in Finland, is just as useful in the treatment of tapeworm as *Aspidium Filix-mas*. The dose is 4 grammes of the ethereal extract of the root of *Aspidium spinulosum*.—*Répertoire de therapeutique*.

The Treatment of Frostbites.—The following treatment for frostbites is given in a recent number of the *Répertoire de therapeutique* (December, 1905, p. 204). The frozen hands are dipped into a bath consisting of a decoction of walnut leaves and then dried and rubbed with spirit of camphor. They are then dusted with the following powder:

Bismuth salicylate .... 10 Gm.
Starch .... 90 Gm.
Mix.

In the evening the fingers are rubbed with a solution of equal parts of glycerin and rosewater, to which is added one-tenth of one per cent. of tannin. The hands are then again dusted with the powder.

The Largest Flower in the World.—Until recently the largest flower in the world was thought to be one of the *Rafflesiæ*, which grow in Java and Sumatra as parasites upon the roots of tropical trees in the virgin forests of those countries. According, however, to a German periodical (*Sudd. Apoth. Zeitung*, 1905, p. 222) one of the *Aroideæ* which grows upon Sumatra is the plant that produces the largest flower in the world. A single leaf of this plant may have a circumference of 15 metres, while the stem of a leaf forms a column 3.5 metres in height and 0.9 metres in circumference. The flower when in full bloom presents the shape of a mammoth funnel, light green or white in color and 1.20 metres in diameter. The interior of this is of the color of red wine and is velvety to the touch. The pistil is of a yellow creamy color, is 1.5 metres in height, and has a penetrating odor.

The Cultivation of Asparagus.—It is important in cultivating asparagus to produce as thick a stalk as possible. We know that some plants produce very thin stalks, while others produce the desirable variety. Nothing can be done to promote this end by manuring, but one can tell, the *Pharmazeutische Zentralhalle* says, from the appearance of a one-year-old plant whether thin or thick stalks will grow. The one-year-old plant which has thick and widely spreading roots and a few thick buds should be planted in preference to that which has thin, deeply penetrating roots and thin pointed buds. The latter variety of plants should be destroyed. In the second year the difference between the plants that produce thick stalks and those that give rise to thin ones, are more or less obliterated, and so it is important to select with great care for further cultivation from among the one-year-old plants.

Acidol, a Substitute for Hydrochloric Acid in the Treatment of Dyspeptic Conditions.—Flatow (*Presse médicale*, quoted in *L'Union pharmaceutique*, December, 1905, p. 536) recommends acidol or betine hydrochloride, a by-product of the manufacture of beet sugar, as a substitute for hydrochloric acid in the treatment of stomach diseases. It contains 25 per per cent. of hydrochloric acid, and it is said that acidol gives up HCl more rapidly than the official hydrochloric acid. Flatow has used the new remedy for two years with considerable success, and considers its agreeable taste as a marked advantage. It can be administered with or without pepsin in the form of tablets or pills, and can be kept in this form indefinitely without decomposing. If the observations of Flatow are confirmed by further experience, acidol may prove a valuable addition to pepsin tablets, which, on account of their stability and convenient form, present an excellent way of treating dyspeptic symptoms, especially in persons who travel.

Rice Oil.—At the Food Experiment Station in Audubon Park, a suburb of New Orleans, investigations have been carried on to determine the value of an oil expressed from rice, and it was shown that the reason for the aversion of cattle to this food product lay in the acidity of the oil which it contains. This acidity is the result of the action of a ferment contained in the oil, in virtue of which ferment the neutral glyceride is decomposed into glycerin and fatty acids. The oil exerts a laxative effect upon the animals, and it is therefore necessary to destroy the ferment by heating the fodder to a temperature of 200 degrees F. or higher.

So successful has been the manufacture of rice oil that a special concern (The Lawrence Feed Company) has been organized in Crowley, Louisiana, for the purpose of manufacturing the oil on a large scale, thus creating a new industry. The decomposition of the oil takes place very quickly after the rice has been mashed and the oil, therefore, always contains free acid. For this reason rice oil can neither be employed as a table oil nor for lubrication. On account of its semi-liquid condition, it is not adapted for the manufacture of oil paints, but offers an excellent material for making candles and soap, although it contains a smaller percentage of glycerin than the neutral vegetable oils.

Considered from an industrial viewpoint, the manufacture of rice oil will probably never form an important industry in the United States, for the entire rice crop of the State of Louisiana is capable of furnishing only about half a million gallons of the oil, and this crop constitutes about 60 per cent. of the entire production of rice of this country. Some interest in this oil has been evinced in Europe and samples of it have been sent to various countries. There is always a possibility that further uses may be found for an oil that exists in so nutritive a product as rise, and experiments looking to that end are now under way at the experiment station named.

Solutions of Apomorphine for Hypodermic Use.—Baroni (*Bolletino Chimico Farmaceutico*, 1905, p. 597) reminds us of the difficulty of preparing neutral, colorless or slightly greenish solutions of apomorphine hydrochloride for hypodermic use. Even if a chemically pure apomorphine be used, the solution has a tendency to turn green. A solution to which a faint trace of hydrochloric acid has been added until a weak acid reaction was produced was sterilized and sealed in tubes, but turned an emerald green, which changed to violet after a few days, and finally turned brown. In spite of these changes in color its properties remained the same. The addition of acid, even in traces, to these solutions is very injurious, inasmuch as the skin and tissues under it may be irritated by these acids. An attempt to avoid the change of color by depriving the solution of air by running a current of carbonic acid gas through it, proved a failure, although the color that appeared was not so marked as ordinarily. The author recommends the use of neutral solutions, sterilized by boiling, and sealed in neutral glass, but he also advises that these solutions be prepared only when they are needed.

Method of Preparing the Ointment of the Yellow Oxide of Mercury.—Pinchbeck (*Pharmaceutical Journal*, 1905, p. 359) offers the following suggestions as to the best method of preparing a perfect ointment of the yellow mercuric oxide. The yellow oxide is now preferred to the red, especially in ointments intended for the eye, for the reason that its chemical activity is far greater. Unfortunately the yellow oxide is not stable, but changes under the influence of light and moisture, and especially has a tendency to lump into masses that are difficult to divide by trituration, and which, when they are applied to the eye, are very irritant.

A number of writers have recommended that the freshly

precipitated yellow oxide be employed in making the ointment, the precipitation being effected by the addition of solution of potassium hydroxide to mercuric chloride (in the U. S. P. sodium hydroxide is used as the precipitant instead of potassium). According to Schweissinger, it is best to wash the precipitate thoroughly and to remove the water by a suction filter, the precipitate being then mixed with the ointment base. According to Knapp, the water which adheres to the precipitate can be removed by displacement by means of alcohol and ether, while the residue can be mixed with petrolatum which should be heated so as to evaporate the ether. Unfortunately, as Schand has shown, alcohol and ether decompose yellow mercuric oxide.

The following method is, therefore, recommended by Pinchbeck: The oxide should be precipitated in a dark room, such as a photographer's development room; it should be washed thoroughly by repeated decantation, and should be poured upon a muslin filter, the washing being continued until the residue is perfectly neutral in reaction. The powder is then dried carefully at low temperature over a water-bath and the ointment base then incorporated. Some base which can be mixed with water should be selected, as the precipitate contains a certain amount of water at best. The ointment-base should be soft and should melt at the temperature of the body, but should not be subject to changes due to the weather. The following formula is recommended by Pinchbeck:

Yellow mercuric oxide....from	0.10 to 1 Gm.
Anhydrous lanolin	1 Gm.
White paraffin	10 Gm.

This ointment is very smooth, perfectly stable, and does not change on exposure to light.

Assay of Coca Leaves.—The following method is that employed in determining the value of Java coca leaves at the Haarlem Colonial Museum:—30.5 Gm. of the dry, finely powdered leaves is heated on a water bath at about 80 degrees C., under a reflux condenser, for two hours with 300 Cc. of alcohol, 90 per cent., the weight of the flask and contents, having previously been noted. After cooling, the quantity of alcohol lost is made up, and 150 Cc. (equivalent to 15 Gm. of leaves) is filtered off and the filtrate distilled. The residue is then heated on the water bath, with constant agitation, allowed to cool, and filtered from the insoluble residue, which is washed with tepid water and bulked with the first filtrate through the same filter, until about 60 Cc. have been collected. This filtrate is shaken out with two portions each of 30 Cc. of ether, which are rejected; the aqueous liquid is then made alkaline with ammonia and shaken out with three successive 30 Cc. of ether. The bulked ether solutions are then distilled from a tared flask. The residue is heated in the drying oven, a strong current of air, dried by previously traversing a calcium chloride tube, being aspirated through the flask during this drying. This removes a volatile base with a strong tobacco-like odor. The amorphous straw-yellow residue is then dissolved in a little 1 per cent. sulphuric acid solution, the acid liquid is again made alkaline with ammonia, and the shaking out with ether repeated. After removing the solvent by distillation the residue is dried for three hours and weighed, after cooling in the desiccator. Young leaves which contained, when fresh, 72 per cent. of moisture, gave, when dried, 6.4 per cent. of ash, 8.6 per cent of water, and gave by the above process a mean of 2.02 per cent. of total alkaloid. Old leaves, containing in the fresh state 59 per cent. of moisture, gave, when dry, 8.2 per cent. of ash, 9.1 per cent. of moisture, and only 0.78 per cent. of total alkaloid, confirming the fact that the young leaves yield at least twice as much alkaloid as those of older growth. Java coca leaves are found to be particularly rich in alkaloids. Selected apical leaves were found to yield 2.1 per cent. of alkaloids; those from the base of the plant 1.2 per cent. As the process of drying and storing causes a marked diminution of the alkaloidal contents, this figure cannot be expected in the commercial article; but this should not assay below 0.6 to 0.7 per cent. The above gravimetric method is stated to be preferable to any volumetric process, for the latter give uncertain and variable results.—M. Greshoff (*Apoth. Zeit.*, 1905, 20, 291).

Some Incompatibilities of the Newer Remedies.—Formerly it was a much simpler matter to grasp the principles underlying the various incompatibilities which occurred in dispensing, but nowadays with the advent of the numerous newer remedies the task of avoiding incompatibilities has become a far more complicated one. In the following brief summary are given some of the more common incompatibilities of modern pharmacy:

A favorite method nowadays with some physicians is to prescribe a large variety of drugs in wafers. Many remedies, however, are unsuitable for dispensing in wafers because they are deliquescent and soften the wafers. Among these are sodium bromide, calcium chloride, strontium chloride, chloral, glycerophosphates, piperazine, and the dry vegetable extracts from drugs obtained by dessication *in vacuo*. Iodides should not be prescribed in wafers as they decompose or change color.

Some of the pharmaceutical incompatibilities are due to the fact that the mixture of some solids produces a liquid. Thus, camphor mixed with naphthol makes a liquid, while antipyrine and sodium salicylate give rise to a semi-liquid, pasty mass. Antipyrine gives also an oily liquid with chloral, beta-naphthol, salol, resorcin, phenol, pyrogallol, thymol and urethane.

Acetanilid is incompatible with chloral, thymol, resorcin and menthol. Betanaphthol should not be mixed with antipyrine, camphor, menthol, phenol and urethane. Camphor should not be dispensed with betanaphthol, chloral, exalgine, menthol, phenol, pyrogallol, resorcin, salol, thymol and urethane. Camphor bromide is incompatible with chloral, phenol, salol and thymol.

Chloral is incompatible with acetanilid, camphor, camphor bromide, exalgine, menthol, methacetine, phenacetine, phenol, salol, thymol and urethane.

Exalgine is incompatible with chloral, naphthol, menthol, phenol, pyrogallol, resorcin, salol, thymol, and salicylic acid.

Menthol cannot be mixed with naphthol, chloral, phenol, pyrogallol, resorcin, salol, thymol and urethane.

Sodium salicylate should not be dispensed with antipyrine and phenol. Phenacetin, with naphthol, chloral and phenol. Phenol with antipyrine, naphthol, camphor bromide, camphor, chloral, exalgine, menthol, methacetine, sodium salicylate, pyrogallol, resorcin, salol, thymol and urethane.

Pyrogallol is incompatible with antipyrine, camphor, exalgine, menthol and phenol. Resorcin with acetanilid, camphor bromide, exalgine, naphthol, menthol, methacetine, phenol and urethane.

Salol with antipyrine, camphor, camphor bromide, chloral exalgine, phenacetine, pyrogallol and thymol. Thymol is incompatible with acetanilid, antipyrine, camphor, chloral, exalgine, menthol, phenol, salol and urethane.

Urethane should not be dispensed with antipyrine, naphthol, camphor, chloral, exalgine, phenol, pyrogallol, resorcin, salicylic acid, salol or thymol.

Great care should be taken in preparing mixtures of syrups containing gum acacia with certain phenol derivatives and synthetics. Incompatibilities are apt to occur as the result of the presence of oxidizing ferment or oxydase in the gum, in virtue of which chemical changes take place either resulting in a precipitation or a change of color. Witness, for example, the following combination which we find in an article by Tanzi, quoted in *Répertoire de thérapeutique:*

Pyramidon	0.20 Gm.
Sodium bromide	0.25 Gm.
Syrup of gum acacia............	130. Gm.

This mixture at once turns a bluish-violet, then violet, then pink and after a few hours becomes yellow. Syrup of gum acacia gives a blue color with guaiacum resin; a pink color turning black with phenol, a violet color and later a blue precipitate with alphanaphthol; a grayish white opacity with beta-naphthol, a yellowish-brown color and a garnet precipitate with pyrocatechin; a white precipitate with vanillin; and a deposit of white crystals of oxy-morphine with morphine hydrochloride. Syrup of gum acacia is also incompatible with eserine, adrenalin, syrup of tar, and the liquid preparations of aloes.

Queries and Answers

We shall be glad, in this department, to respond to calls for information on all pharmaceutic matters.

The Preparation of Lecithin.—C. D. C.—Lecithin is made commercially from the yolk of egg by fractional extraction with ether, the yoke being treated with ether until no more pigment is taken up. The ethereal extracts are then united, the ether is distilled off and the oil filtered off at the temperature of the body. The yellow, frothy material which remains on the filter is dissolved in as little ether as possible and precipitated with acetone until the wash acetone dissolves no more cholesterin. The residue is again dissolved in a small amount of ether or benzol. To this solution an excess of absolute alcohol is added, when, on standing, a white amorphous substance separates out. After filtration the pure lecithin can then be obtained by dissolving off the alcohol and ether. Obtained in this way lecithin is a yellowish-white, waxy, hygroscopic solid, soluble in ether and in alcohol, and which swells in contact with water.

Formulas of Proprietary Remedies.—In response to queries from various sources regarding the composition of Gowan's Pneumonia Cure, Glyco-Thymoline and Doctor Miles' Nervine, we have to say that it is not our practice to guess at the ingredients of proprietary remedies. To the correspondent who asks us to make an analysis for which he would be willing to pay the answer is made that we do not conduct an analytical department for the examination of remedies of the character mentioned in his letter.

Cheltenham Sauce.—C. D. L. writes: "Kindly publish a formula for the old English Cheltenham Sauce."

It is likely that our correspondent has confounded the word "sauce" with salt, for we are unable to place "The Old English Cheltenham Sauce," though Cheltenham Salts is a preparation with which we are very familiar. The formula for the latter varies, the following being an accepted one in England:

Ferrous sulphate	1 grain.
Sodium chloride	20 grains.
Sodium sulphate	240 grains.
Magnesium sulphate	132 grains.

Mix.

An effervescing Cheltenham Salts is also used and has the following composition:

Tartaric acid, dried	25 parts.
Ferrous tartrate	1 part.
Seidlitz mixture	120 parts.

Mix.

Turbid Burrows' Solution.—C. R. says he has made solution of aluminum acetate according to the National Formulary and something went wrong with it, for in about a week a flocculent precipitate formed which made it impossible to pour the solution from the bottle.

This should not take place if the directions of the Formulary are properly observed and the right ingredients are used. It is possible that our correspondent has made the mistake of using the ordinary alum of the Pharmacopœia, which is a mixture of aluminum and potassium sulphate. He should be careful to satisfy himself that he is using aluminum sulphate and not ordinary alum.

Kiersted's Ointment.—P. kindly advises us that this ointment is a proprietary article owned and manufactured by C. N. Crittenton Company.

Reng.—C. B. writes: "Would you please inform me where I can purchase some Reng, the leaves of the indigo plant. I have tried several firms who make a specialty of handling botanic drugs, but without success."

There are a great many varieties of indigo, but the leaves of the true indigo, *Indigofera tinctoria*, should not be difficult to obtain. Try Parke, Davis & Co. It is the first time we have seen the word "Reng" applied to indigo leaves.

Spontaneous Combustion of Cottonroot Bark?—Joe Jacobs, of Atlanta, Ga., has called our attention to what appears to be a case of spontaneous combustion of ground cottonroot bark. It appears that a barrel of the ground bark received recently by the Jacobs Pharmacy Company emitted a peculiar odor, which suggested that the bark had been ground in a green condition and was fermenting. The barrel and contents were left in the basement over night and the following day they were discovered in flames, having apparently taken fire from spontaneous combustion. Fortunately the fire was seen early and extinguished by one of the employees with a chemical extinguisher which stood nearby. Mr. Jacobs would like to know if a similar occurrence has ever been noticed or if it is something entirely new in the way of spontaneous combustion.

The Incompatibilities of Iron Compounds.—C. A. B. writes: "Would you please say which numbers of the AMERICAN DRUGGIST contain prescriptions which owe their incompatibility to the formation of insoluble iron compounds?"

Instances of the kind mentioned by our correspondent are numerous in the literature of pharmacy and there is scarcely an article on the subject of incompatible combinations of drugs which does not include reference to some incompatible iron compound. A valuable article on Incompatibility in Theory and Practice, by J. P. Gilmour, was published in the AMERICAN DRUGGIST for March 13, 1905. If information is wanted regarding specific iron incompatibilities we shall be glad to give attention to any inquiry received.

Baume or Beaume.—O. R. writes: "Would you please inform me as to the proper spelling of the name of the inventor of the instrument for determining the specific gravity of liquids. Is it Baumé or Beaumé?"

The inventor of the hydrometer in general use by chemists was Antoine Baumé, not Beaumé. He was a chemist and pharmacist of considerable scientific renown, being the author in 1784 of a treatise on The Theory and Practice of Pharmacy. (*Eléments de pharmacie théorique et pratique.*) A few years earlier he published a Manual of Chemistry. Doctor Baumé was born at Senlis, France, February 26, 1728, and died October 15, 1804. He was apprenticed to an apothecary in Compiegne when ten years old and at the age of 17 he removed to Paris and entered the celebrated pharmacy of Geoffroy. At the age of 24 he was graduated Master of Pharmacy with high distinction. He wrote many scientific treatises, including interesting monographs on crystallization, fats, sulphur, opium, mercury, boric acid, platinum, quinine, etc.

Various Tanno-Organic Compounds.—Combinations of tannin with the extracts of various animal organs have been prepared and introduced (*Pharmazeutische Zeitung* through *Merck's Report*). The active constituents of these preparations, and which may be designated as organic enzymes, pass through the stomach unacted upon, and decompose only in the intestines, where they develop their effects. Among the preparations made are the following: *Heparon* made from the liver of cattle, together with pancreas, greatly increases the power of the liver to decompose grape sugar. *Musculon*, similarly made from the muscular tissue of cattle and pancreas, also effects the decomposition of grape sugar. *Organa glycolytica* is a mixture of the dried heparon and musculon, and the tannin compounds is designated as *trion;* this is believed to be an excellent antidiabetic. *Ovaron* is a tannin compound of ovarial substance. *Teston* is prepared from the testicles of steers. *Thyron* is obtained from the *thyroid* glands of pigs, and *Splenon* from the spleens of pigs. All these tannin-compounds are said to act like the simple organic preparations. They are marketed in the form of powder, and in tablets each containing 0.1 gramme of the active substance.

Correspondence.

Drug Clerks Should Study Foreign Languages.

To the Editor:

Sir,—The attention of druggists, and especially of drug clerks, should be directed to the advantages accruing from a study of the German, French and Italian languages. In our metropolitan city prescriptions are received which give the directions (or *Signatura*) in different languages, depending upon the nationality of the physician, and it would be a great advantage if drug clerks were able to decipher and write the directions in the language in which they are written. It is true that a limited number of prescription clerks are able to do this, but I am convinced that the majority are not. If you would point out in the AMERICAN DRUGGIST the advantages to be gained from a study of foreign languages, and the small amount of time it would require to become familiar with them through systematic study, I am sure you would confer a great benefit on many aspiring clerks. D. A. GREAVEN.

PERRY'S PHARMACY, NEW YORK, January 19, 1906.

Guessing at Prescriptions.

To the Editor:

Sir,—In your issue of January 8 J. T. Pepper, under Prescription Talk, gives fac-similes of four prescriptions, with comments on each. I will take prescription No. 1 as an example. Mr. Pepper proceeds with his analysis as follows: "I think it is quite easy to make out the first word as 'Acid.' The next word is not so easy, but the first letter is a capital B, and the next letters are 'oric,' making the word Boric. The quantity required is 6 drachms. The first letter on the second line is a capital 'A,' and the next letter is 'q,' the two forming the contraction 'Aq.' for 'Aquæ,'" and so Mr. Pepper continues to tell what he thinks each sign, letter and word means, until he reaches the final "ad (to) 1 fluid ounce."

If Mr. Pepper offers this batch of prescriptions, with his analysis, as a curiosity, I have no comment to make, but if his article was written with the hope that it might be instructive, I believe that he should have been more specific and given the method by which he arrived at his conclusions. He says the first letter is a B. How does he know it is a B, and how does he know that the next letters are "oric"? If it is all so plain that he can read it without expressing a doubt, then there is no occasion for putting it under the dissecting knife; if there is a doubt, then he should not name it so positively without giving his reasons. He says "the quantity required is 6 drachms." How did he arrive at that? I should have *guessed* it 6 grains. If it is 6 drachms, as Mr. Pepper positively states, how did he obtain solution of 6 drachms of boric acid in one ounce of water?

It looks as if Mr. Pepper may have done some guessing, and that is just the point upon which I wish to touch. I know that some pharmacists pride themselves on their ability to decipher any kind of an old scrawl, but the practice should not be encouraged. A man who is thoroughly up in his business may "keep safe" and his errors may do no harm, but that is no argument in favor of the practice. If a prescription is carelessly written, and cannot be thoroughly understood, the pharmacist should have the courage to return it to the physician for interpretation; there is no other safe way.

A pharmacist should never receive instruction as a guesser; he should be taught to be positive, not "think," but know.

A. H. MALONEY.

CAMDEN, N. Y.

Our Past a Guarantee of the Future.

Inclosed please find check, payment in full for subscription for 1906. Best wishes for the continued prosperity in the future, which I feel sure your past record insures.

WM. O. FRAILEY.

LANCASTER, PA., February 2, 1906.

The Ready Made Cut in Drug Advertising.

Among all the shortcomings of retail drug advertising nothing perhaps is a more discouraging feature than the syndicate cut: its trail is over everything, and its absurdity is appalling, or would be if it were not so funny.

The experienced advertising man, if he is conscientious, says the editor of *The New Idea*, usually writes his copy first, makes it strong enough to stand alone without any illustration and then plans his illustration to strengthen the advertisement. To write an advertisement to fit an illustration pre-supposes that it doesn't matter much what one says anyway, which is about as complete a reversal of sound advertising tenets as one could imagine.

The man who takes a syndicate-cut service, however, never knows just what he is going to write about till his proofsheet arrives, whereupon he selects a cut that he thinks may be made to "do," and endeavors to drag in, as by the hair, some allusion to the part of his business that he wants to advertise.

And while we may treat the subject rather lightly it is no laughing matter to the advertiser—for while other people have the privilege of laughing at it, he is the man who has to pay the bill. Not only does it represent a loss of money to him for the cost of the space, it represents also a loss of opportunity worth a great deal more than the money.

A QUESTION OF STYLE.

Here is a cut used in a soda advertisement last July—1905, mind you. Now as you may not be up on such things ask your wife's opinion of the style of the ladies' hats and the cut of their sleeves. She will tell you that they reached the zenith of their popularity in 1894, and if you were to use such a cut in one of your ads it would probably cost you a $20 hat as the price of relief from her apt but irritating remarks about the attractiveness of your advertising to the stylish women who trade at your store. The soda fountain is apparently automatic, as no dispenser is in sight: we may well suppose, however, that he deserted his post of duty as soon as possible after serving the fair ones, to test his eyesight by such familiar devices as counting fingers, etc., and thereby assure himself that he was not dreaming when this vision of the past appeared before him.

As a puller of soda trade something better might be evolved.

NOT JOB'S.

The doleful title of this cut has no reference to the trials of Job, or at least if it has the druggists who use it in various parts of the country have wrenched it from its original context and now employ it as a startling introduction to the bold declaration that "Many Trials will prove that our drug store is the best place for you to trade!" or something to that effect.

It must be somewhat discouraging to the man who has been considering the advisability of transferring his patronage to this advertiser to learn that "many trials" will be required to demonstrate the wisdom of such a course. Similarly this does not appear to be a very effective appeal to the satisfied customers of other stores and therefore it appears to *The New Idea* to be a rather dangerous advertisement:

POSSESS YE YOUR SOULS IN PATIENCE.

Observe, gentle reader, the look of resignation on the face of the young woman who is patiently waiting for the prescription to be filled. She said in an unguarded moment that she would wait for the medicine, and now she has been there 45 minutes, but it is not ready yet. Hubby is always cross, too, if his luncheon is not ready promptly at 12, and next time she will go to a store that is either quicker about its prescription work or else insists on delivering the medicine when there is likely to be a delay.

Waiting for a prescription is usually a trying experience. The time always seems twice as long as it is, and most people feel like using harsh language—except, of course, the ladies—when reminded of such an experience. Therefore, don't remind them of it. Show a delivery boy spinning along on his wheel, instead, if you want to show anything.

THE ACME OF PERFECTION.

We are not exactly sure what it is that deserves the encomium, "Acme of Perfection," which this cut so gracefully (?) brings to our attention. At first we thought it was a brand of flour stamped on the barrel ends so conspicuous in the illustration. This, however, seems to be fallacious, for the advertisement says nothing about flour, or, indeed, about the cut at all, which is probably wise. Next to the wisdom of omitting such a meaningless cut, comes the discernment which leads to its being ignored.

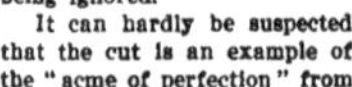

It can hardly be suspected that the cut is an example of the "acme of perfection" from either a mechanical, artistic, or commercial standpoint. And a wise druggist will not be likely to claim that much for his store—since that is a good deal to claim. If he did claim it no one would believe it.

DOGS NOT ALLOWED.

The patrons of one drug store at least were no doubt greatly relieved to learn that there is no danger of finding a young dog swimming around in the tonic prescribed by the doctor, although the druggist modestly takes no credit to himself for any extra care to avoid such an undesirable complication; it being a mere matter of physical impossibility for a twelve-pound dog to fall through the opening of a small-necked funnel, there can certainly be no harm in allowing him to lie down in the funnel, even though the latter is still over an open bottle of—presumably—medicine.

It may be that there are certain whimsical folk, who are finicky enough to think that a dog has no business in the prescription department of a drug store; and others who think that even if the dog has the run of the store to this extent, it is hardly worth advertising as a drawing card; so it might be well to concede the point and omit the dog hereafter.

A DEATH BED SCENE.

One of the most fetching things that has been sent in lately is this death bed scene, rendered doubly pathetic by being inserted upside down. After gazing in mute but terrible anguish upon it for a moment we saw the words "Recovery is Doubtful," and next the name of the druggist in display type, who is suspected of having brought about this catastrophe. But stay—that cannot be! And on reading the fine type carefully, we find that the druggist proves an excellent alibi, it having developed that recovery is doubtful unless the "drugs" came from his store.

Our art critic being absent, we shall say nothing as to perspective, foreshortening, light and shade, and the respective merits of the Dutch and Flemish schools. We desire, however, to call attention to the right hand of the prospective widow, evidently modeled after a mason's trowel. Note its exquisite expression! Though struggling nobly to hide her grief, her hand trembles, and the artist has reproduced it beautifully. The doctor has broken the patient's wrist in trying to feel his pulse, and may soon be defendant in a malpractice suit. The nurse is evidently making a rapid mental calculation of the amount of her bill, while the young heir of the family title has such a broad smile on his face at the thought of how he will make the old man's money fly that you can almost make out the gold filling in his left lower wisdom tooth. As we remarked before, for pathos and true artistic feeling, this is indeed a masterpiece.

RECOVERY IS DOUBTFUL
if the quality of the
DRUGS and MEDICINES

But it is not good advertising: we don't want the idea of death associated with our store. Let it stand for life and happiness, comfort and convenience, aye, and a little luxury now and then.

A MARINE OUT OF PLACE.

By way of variety, let us consider this marine; so realistic is it that you wish you had your rubbers on, lest the water splash over your shoes.

And what flight of imagination could bring about any connection between the drug business and this surf-bathing exhibition, unless it be that both parties here represented are in a fair way to catch severe colds?

TO ATTRACT ATTENTION IS NOT ALL OF ADVERTISING.

Nearly always the vile cheap cuts that disfigure retail drug advertising are used through a misconception of their mission and usefulness. "They attract attention" is what their promoters claim for them. This may be true, but it does not necessarily make them valuable. One might easily attract attention by wearing a red flannel shirt with his evening clothes, yet it would reflect seriously on his good taste, at least, and perhaps on his good sense as well.

Cut out the bum cuts. Make your copy strong enough to stand alone. Tell the public interesting timely facts about your store. Make your store *worth* telling about first though, if you have any doubt on that point. Don't treat the drug business as a joke to be mixed up with meddlesome pups, crawling over the funnels, nor as a lugubrious death bed proposition. Straight, clean business talk will do the work, will increase people's respect for your store and for the drug business and will please you yourself so much better than the crude caricatures that grossly libel your business at your expense, that you will wonder why any one ever used them.

WINTER WINDOW DISPLAYS.

The recent cold snap—about the first taste of real winter weather New York has had this season—brought out many timely window displays in pharmacies of cough drops, rock candy, licorice gum drops and remedies for coughs and colds. In many of these displays, particularly where cough drops are featured, the old but effective method of showing the goods dumped carelessly from a pail, barrel or some such container on to the floor of the window has been adopted. One window uptown, for instance, shows licorice gum drops rolling from a barrel and covering the front part of the window, while other windows contain white and brown rock candy, cherry and other cough drops in open wooden boxes or loose in the window.

FOR CHAPPED LIPS AND HANDS.

It would be hard to make a window display which in beautiful blending and harmonizing of colors and in the arrangement of goods could excel that of the W. B. Riker & Sons Company, in one of its windows in the store at Twenty-third street and Sixth avenue. The article featured was the firm's violet cerate. On a raised platform, or pedestal, at back of the window in the center was a large wax doll. The doll's dress consisted entirely of bunches of violets. The outstretched hand offered a package of violet cerate. The cerate is put up in white glass containers tied with narrow violet ribbon, which formed a pleasing contrast with the white containers. The goods were symmetrically arranged and cards telling about the merits of the cerate and giving the price plainly were placed in a conspicuous position. At the store of the same company at 771 Broadway, this same article was featured in another way. The window contained a large frame with sloping sides inclosing a changeable mirror; the frame, covered with white cloth, held packages of the cerate. The mirror alternately reflects a picture of a young woman having blemishes removed from her face by a cupid mounted on a ladder. Bunches of violets were scattered among the goods, which were neatly arranged in the window.

A DISPLAY OF RUBBER GOODS.

The Kalish pharmacy, at Fourth avenue and Twenty-third street, had an attractive window display last week of rubber goods, consisting principally of hot water bags and syringes. In the center of the window was suspended an immense water bag about 4 feet long, which of course arrested the attention of the passerby. The window was filled, but not crowded, with various articles of the kinds mentioned. Some crude rubber was also shown, and there was an exhibit showing all the parts and pieces cut and ready to be put together to make a hot water bag. The same store recently had a very good soap display in one of its windows. It was a Russian violet perfumed soap, and the predominating tints in the display were violet, blue and gold. The soap is done up in blue wrappers with gold lettering. Some of the cartons were uncovered; others were not. Bunches of violets were scattered freely about the window. The floor of the window was covered with white and green crepe paper. In the background were two large horseshoes covered with green velvet and on these were attached cartons of the soap. The whole display was very effective.

AN UNUSUAL DISPLAY.

A rather unusual window exhibit was seen recently in the window of a Sixth avenue pharmacy. It consisted of a patent folding bath cabinet. The lamp for generating the vapor, the screens to surround the bather, and printed instructions were shown in one part of the window, while in one corner were the screens set up and joined. Over the top of these screens is seen the face of the wax image of a lady. A card explains the purpose of the outfit and gives the price.

SOUVENIR CARD DISPLAY.

An unusually attractive display of souvenir post cards was shown in the window of Kneuper's City Hall Pharmacy last week. The cards, which were exceptionally good, were shown in three large frames, each frame holding some eight or nine rows. Scenes of points of interest, pictures of theatrical artists, prominent men and reproductions of well-known paintings appeared on the cards. The effectiveness of the display was enhanced by a large illuminated sign suspended from the top of the window.

THE LEGAL REGULATION OF PROPRIETARY MEDICINES.

Many Bills from Many Sources—Text of the Bill Devised at a Joint Conference of the Four National Associations—The Ladies' Home Journal Bill—Special Bill Prepared by a Volunteer Committee in New York.

The agitation of the question of narcotics, which was begun some four years ago by the American Pharmaceutical Association at St. Louis and which led to the formulation of the Beal Anti-Narcotic Law, has gradually spread until under the influence of the attacks on proprietary medicines by the *Ladies' Home Journal*, *Colliers' Weekly* and similar publications a host of legislative enactments have been proposed as a means for remedying the evils surrounding the sale of proprietary medicines of secret composition.

At the invitation of the Committee on Legislation of the American Pharmaceutical Association a conference was held in Chicago last December between delegates representing the American Pharmaceutical Association, the Proprietary Association of America, the National Wholesale Druggists' Association and the National Retail Druggists' Association. While these delegates were not empowered to commit the associations which they represented to the indorsement of the results of the conference, they succeeded in agreeing upon a draft of two bills, which are presented below in full.

The delegates who drafted the bills are Albert E. Ebert, Chicago, of the American Pharmaceutical Association; J. M. Good, St. Louis, of the National Association of Retail Druggists; M. N. Kline, Philadelphia, of the National Wholesale Druggists' Association, and John W. Kennedy, Chicago, of the Proprietary Association of America.

The following is the text of the two measures:

ANTI-NARCOTIC BILL.

A BILL

To Provide Against the Evils Resulting From the Traffic in Certain Narcotic Drugs, and to Regulate the Sale Thereof.

Be it Enacted by the General Assembly of the State of ——————.

SECTION 1. That it shall be unlawful for any person, firm or corporation to sell, furnish or give away any cocaine, alpha or beta eucaine, opium, morphine, heroin, chloral hydrate or any salt or compound of any of the foregoing substances, or any preparation or compound containing any of the foregoing substances, or their salts or compounds, except upon the original written order or prescription of a lawfully authorized practitioner of medicine, dentistry or veterinary medicine, which order or prescription shall be dated and shall contain the name of the person for whom prescribed, or if ordered by a practitioner of veterinary medicine shall state the kind of animal for which ordered, and shall be signed by the person giving the prescription or order. Such written order or prescription shall be permanently retained on file by the person, firm or corporation who shall compound or dispense the articles ordered or prescribed, and it shall not be again compounded or dispensed, except upon the written order of the original prescriber for each and every subsequent compounding or dispensing. No copy or duplicate of such written order or prescription shall be made or delivered to any person, but the original shall at all times be open to inspection by the prescriber and properly authorized officers of the law.

Provided, however, that the above provisions shall not apply to preparations containing not more than two grains of opium or not more than one-fourth grain of morphine, or not more than one-fourth grain of heroin, or not more than one-eighth grain of cocaine, or not more than one-eighth grain of alpha or beta eucaine, or not more than ten grains of chloral hydrate, in one fluid-ounce, or if a solid preparation, in one avoirdupois ounce. Provided also that the above provisions shall not apply to preparations containing opium and recommended and sold in good faith for diarrhœa and cholera, each bottle or package of which is accompanied by specific directions for use, and a caution against habitual use, nor to powder of ipecac and opium commonly known as Dover's Powder, nor to liniments or ointments when plainly labeled "for external use only." And provided further that the above provision shall not apply to sales at wholesale by jobbers, wholesalers and manufacturers to retail druggists or qualified physicians, or to each other, nor to sales at retail by retail druggists to regular practitioners of medicine, dentistry or veterinary medicine, nor to sales made to manufacturers of proprietary or pharmaceutical preparations for use in the manufacture of such preparations, nor to sales to hospitals, colleges, scientific or public institutions.

Sec. 2. It shall be unlawful for any practitioner of medicine, dentistry, or veterinary medicine to furnish to or to prescribe for the use of any habitual user of the same any cocaine, heroin, alpha or beta eucaine, opium, morphine, chloral hydrate, or any salt or compound of any of the foregoing substances, or any preparation containing any of the foregoing substances or their salts or compounds. And it shall also be unlawful for any practitioner of dentistry to prescribe any of the foregoing substances for any person not under his treatment in the regular practice of his profession, or for any practitioner of veterinary medicine to prescribe any of the foregoing substances for the use of any human being.

Provided, however, that the provisions of this section shall not be construed to prevent any lawfully authorized practitioner of medicine from furnishing or prescribing in good faith for the use of any habitual user of narcotic drugs who is under his professional care such substances as he may deem necessary for their treatment, when such prescriptions are not given or substances furnished for the purpose of evading the provisions of this act.

Sec. 3. Any person who shall violate any of the provisions of this act shall be deemed guilty of a misdemeanor, and upon conviction for the first offense shall be fined not less than $25.00 nor more than $50.00, and upon conviction for a second offense shall be fined not less than $50.00 nor more than $100.00, and upon conviction for a subsequent offense shall be fined not less than $100.00 nor more than $200.00, and shall be imprisoned in the county jail for not more than six months and if a licensed pharmacist, physician, dentist or veterinary surgeon, his license shall be revoked. It shall be the duty under this act of all judges of the courts of common pleas in this State, at every regular term thereof, to charge all regularly impanelled grand juries to diligently inquire into and investigate all cases of the violation of the provisions of this act and to make a true presentment of all persons guilty of such violations. It shall be the duty of the Board of Pharmacy to cause the prosecution of all persons violating the provisions of this act. No prosecution shall be brought for the sale of any patent or proprietary medicine containing any of the drugs or preparations hereinbefore mentioned until the Board of Pharmacy shall certify that such medicine contains any of the said drugs or preparations in excess of the maximum percentages hereinbefore mentioned.

Sec. 4. In any proceedings under the provisions of this act the charge may be brought against any or all of the members of a partnership, or against the directors or executive officers of a corporation, or against the agent of any person, partnership or corporation.

Sec. 5. All laws and parts of laws in conflict with this act are hereby repealed.

Sec. 6. This act shall take effect and be in force from and after the .... day of ....19...

THE PROPRIETARY MEDICINE BILL.

A BILL

To Regulate the Sale of Certain Proprietary Medicines.

Be It Enacted, etc.

SECTION 1. Any proprietary medicine which contains a percentage of alcohol greater than is reasonably necessary for the extraction and dissolving of the active constituents of the drugs used in the preparation of said medicine or to prevent the precipitation of such active constituents or to preserve the medicine from fermentation or freezing, shall be deemed to be an intoxicating liquor and shall be sold only under the provisions of the law regulating the sale of intoxicating liquors. Provided that this act shall not be construed to apply to preparations compounded according to any formula embraced in the United States Pharmacopœia or the National Formulary, when sold under a title recognized by the said United States Pharmacopœia, or National Formulary.

Sec. 2. No prosecution shall be brought for the sale of any proprietary preparation in violation of the provisions of this act unless the Board of Pharmacy shall, after due investigation, certify that such proprietary preparation contains alcohol in a percentage greater than the limit fixed by Section 1.

A LOCAL LAW FOR NEW YORK STATE.

A volunteer committee composed of leading New Yorkers in various lines met recently at the residence of Dr. William Jay Schieffelin and prepared a measure governing the labeling of proprietary medicines, the main features of which are included in the following excerpts:

AN ACT to amend the public health law by providing for the proper labeling of proprietary and other medicines containing alcohol and narcotic drugs, and for the inspection, analysis and regulation of the manufacture and sale of the same.

The people of the State of New York, represented in the Senate and Assembly, do enact as follows:

SECTION 1. Chapter six hundred and sixty-one of the laws of eighteen hundred and ninety-three, entitled "An Act in Relation to the Public Health, Constituting Chapter Twenty-five of the General Laws," is hereby amended by inserting therein a new article, to be Article XIV, and to read as follows:

ARTICLE XIV.

PROPRIETARY AND OTHER MEDICINES.

SECTION 225. Manufacture and Sale of Certain Medicines Prohibited Unless Properly Labeled.—No person shall manufacture, sell or offer or expose for sale any proprietary or patent medicine or other medicinal preparation containing alcohol, opium or any of its preparations, its alkaloids or their derivatives, strychnine, digitalis, chloroform, cannabis indica, chloral or any of its derivatives, cocaine or any of its salts, eucaine or any of its salts, acetanilid, antipyrine, bromoform, exalgine, holocain, phenacetin, phenocoll, sulphonal, trional, veronal or any other hypnotic, anæsthetic, analgesic or cardiac, circulatory, respiratory or nerve depressant, unless the same shall have plainly and conspicuously stamped or printed on the bottle, box or receptacle containing the same or on the label affixed thereto, and also on the outside wrapper or package, if any, and also on the inside wrapper and all circulars accompanying said medicine or medicinal preparation and relating to it, if any, a true statement of the percentage of alcohol and the percentage or portion or proportion of each of the above mentioned or described drugs contained in each box, bottle, receptacle or package of such medicine or medicinal preparation. Such information shall be stamped or printed in antique or gothic type, easily to be read, of a size not smaller than that known as ten point, and so displayed as to be conspicuous.

Where alcohol is used as a solvent or preservative, or for any other purpose, it is to be deemed as contained in the medicine or medicinal preparation within the meaning of this act, and the drugs above specified shall be described by their common, or English, names.

Sec. 226. Definition.—The term "medicinal preparation" as used in this article shall be deemed to include every preparation or combination or mixture of drugs or of drugs with substances which are not drugs, when such preparation, combination or mixture purports to have medicinal properties or to be a remedy or mixture or cure or food, or is intended to be used for medicinal effects or for the cure, alleviation or prevention of disease.

Sec. 227. Application of This Article.—The provisions of this article shall not apply to preparations intended solely for external use, whenever the label plainly indicates that the preparation is to be used externally, and is not to be used internally, nor to the dispensing of medicinal compounds on prescriptions by registered physicians, nor to preparations listed in the Pharmacopœia of the United States and the official Pharmacopœias of other nations, the National Standard Dispensatory and United States Dispensatory or the National Formulary, unless sold under a proprietary name.

Sec. 228. Statements on the Label to Constitute a Warranty.—The label placed on a proprietary or patent medicine or other medicinal preparation by the manufacturer, as required by this act, shall be a warranty of the truth and accuracy of the statements contained therein, and the absence of any statement on such label shall constitute a warranty by the manufacturer that such medicine or medicinal preparation contains none of the drugs mentioned or described in section 225 of this article. Any person injured by reason of the failure of a manufacturer to comply with the provisions of this act shall have cause of action against the manufacturer, and may recover both actual and exemplary damages.

Section 229 defines the duties of the State Department of Health in respect to proprietary and other medicines, and provides for the appointment of additional inspectors, chemists and analysts, and gives the board power to adopt such measures and regulations as may be necessary to enforce the law.

Section 230 provides for the analyses of proprietary and other medicines, the taking, keeping, registering and testing of samples, etc.

The last three sections are as follows:

Sec. 231. Penalties. Subdivision 1.—Any person violating any provision of this article shall be guilty of a misdemeanor, and shall be punished for each offense by a fine of not less than fifty dollars nor more than two hundred and fifty dollars, or by imprisonment for not less than ten days nor more than one hundred days, or by both fine and imprisonment, in the discretion of the court.

Subdivision 2. Any person violating any provision of this article, in addition to and irrespective of the punishment hereinbefore provided, shall forfeit to the State Department of Health the sum of fifty dollars for every such violation, except that where said violation occurs in a city of the first class, said forfeiture of fifty dollars shall be to the Department of Health of said city. The said amount may be sued for and recovered in the name of said State department, or where the violation occurs in a city of the first class, by the Department of Health thereof, and shall be paid to the said State or city department, as the case may be, to be applied to the running expenses of said department, together with the costs, and a reasonable allowance in the discretion of the court to reimburse the said department for the expenses incident to such suit and recovery, not exceeding two hundred and fifty dollars.

Sec. 232. Analysis as Evidence.—In any suit or prosecution under this article a copy of the analysis of the State Department of Health or of the analysis of the Department of Health in a city of the first class, of a sample of a medicine or medicinal preparation manufactured, sold or offered or exposed for sale under the same name and purporting to be of the same manufacture as the medicine or medicinal preparation in question, in such suit or prosecution, duly certified by the commissioner or by the secretary of said State or city Department of Health, to be a true copy thereof, shall be presumptive evidence in all courts and places of the percentage of alcohol, and the percentage or proportion of each of the other drugs named or described in section 225 of this article, if any, contained in the said medicine or medicinal preparation. Provided that where the analysis has been made by a city Department of Health it shall be certified by the commissioner or by the secretary of said department that said analysis was made by an analyst, chemist or officer of said department in like manner as in section 230 of this article provided for analysis by the State Department of Health.

Sec. 2. This act shall take effect October first, nineteen hundred and six, except that section 229 hereof shall take effect immediately.

The committee which is responsible for this local measure comprises representatives of the leading civic organizations in this city. Among the members of the committee are Dr. Wm. Jay Schieffelin, of Schieffelin & Co.; Dr. Charles F. Chandler, dean of the School of Mines of Columbia University, and Professor of Organic Chemistry in the New York College of Pharmacy; Dr. Charles Baskerville, Professor of Chemistry in the College of the City of New York; Dr. Charles L. Dana, president of the New York Academy of Medicine; Dr. Thomas Darlington, Commissioner of Health of New York City; Mrs. Russell Sage, William A. Jenner, V. Everit Macy, James A. Talcott, the Rev. Dr. William R. Huntington, of Grace Church; William T. Wardwell, Seth Low, the Rev. Charles L. Thompson, Dr. W. Gilman Thompson, A. Alexander Smith, James A. McCorkle, Alexander Lamber, Dr. Francis P. Kinnicut, Dr. Charles G. Kerley, Dr. Glentworth R. Butler, Dr. Joseph B. Bryant, Dr. Robert Abbey, Dr. Edward G. Janeway, James Speyer, Dr. Virgil P. Gibney, Dr. Charles M. Dowd, Dr. Francis Delafield, Dr. M. F. Crandall, Prof. Graham Lusk, the Rev. D. Stewart Dodge, the Rev. Dr. Stires, of St. Thomas' Church, and many others. The committee was organized by Albert Manierre, of Manierre & Manierre, attorneys, of 31 Nassau street.

THE LADIES' HOME JOURNAL BILL.

The Ladies' Home Journal devotes three pages in its February issue to proprietary medicines, and proposes the enactment of the following bill:

AN ACT

to Regulate the Manufacture and Sale of "Patent" and "Proprietary" Medicines.

Be it enacted by the Legislature of the State of ....

Section 1. Each package, bottle, box or other parcel containing what is commonly known as a "patent" or "proprietary" medicine of any kind or in any form, intended for internal consumption by human beings, other than a medicine specially compounded upon the written order or prescription of a physician duly authorized to practice his profession in this State, which shall be hereafter manufactured within this State, or which shall be hereafter manufactured without this State and exposed or offered for sale, or sold or given away, or otherwise disposed of, within this State, shall have both on the outside wrapper of such package, bottle, box or other parcel, and also on the label affixed to such package, bottle, box or other parcel, in plain English, printed in black letters on white paper, of a size not smaller than of type eight point, so called, a complete schedule showing all the ingredients contained in such "patent" or "proprietary" medicine, and the exact proportions of each ingredient thereof.

Sec. 2. Whenever any such "patent" or "proprietary" medicine shall contain more than eight per cent. of ethyl alcohol, or more than one-twenty-fifth of one per cent. of morphine, heroin, cocaine or of the salts or equivalents or derivatives of the same or any of them, or more than one-fourth of one per cent. of chloral hydrate, or any quantity of belladonna, cotton-root, ergot, or other abortifacient, there shall be printed in plain English, in red letters of a size not smaller than eight point, so called, on white paper, in addition to the schedule of ingredients hereinbefore required, both on the outside wrapper of the package, bottle, box or other parcel containing the same, and also on the label affixed to such package, bottle, box or parcel, a notice reading as follows:

"This package (or bottle or box or parcel as the case may be) contains (here give the name and proportion or percentage of the drug as the case may be), and is therefore under the Act of the Legislature of the State of..............., marked

"POISON,"

and also the single separate word "POISON," which shall be printed separately on a line by itself, in bold-face type, and in letters not less than one-quarter of an inch high.

Sec. 3. The Board of Health of this State is hereby empowered, immediately upon the passage of this act and from time to time thereafter, to make, or cause to be made, a chemical analysis of "patent" or "proprietary" medicines, manufactured, or exposed or offered for sale, or sold or given away, or otherwise disposed of, within this State, for internal consumption by human beings, other than those specially compounded upon a physician's written prescription as aforesaid. If any such analysis shall show that there has been, with respect to any such "patent" or "proprietary" medicine, a failure to comply with the requirements of this act, said board shall at once notify the District Attorney of any county in this State in which the said "patent" or "proprietary" medicine is manufactured, or exposed or offered for sale, or sold or given away, or otherwise disposed of, whose duty it shall be to prosecute the person, firm or corporation so violating the provisions hereof.

Sec. 4. Any changes, either in the ingredients or in the proportions or percentages of the ingredients in any such "patent" or "proprietary" medicine manufactured within this State, shall be at once reported by the manufacturer thereof to the Board of Health of this State.

Sec. 5. Any person, firm or corporation who shall manufacture, or expose or offer for sale, or sell, or give away, or otherwise dispose of, any such "patent" or "proprietary" medicine within this State in violation of the provisions of this act, or any of them, shall be guilty of a misdemeanor and on conviction thereof shall be punishable therefor by a fine of not less than fifty dollars ($50), nor more than five hundred dollars ($500), or imprisonment for not less than thirty (30) days nor more than six (6) months, or both.

Sec. 6. All acts or parts of acts inconsistent herewith are hereby repealed.

Sec. 7. This act shall take effect on the .... day of ...., 1906.

Sale of Intoxicating Proprietaries Illegal in Arkansas.

The Arkansas State Board of Pharmacy has issued a circular to the druggists of the State embracing the following opinion from the Attorney General:

Office of Attorney-General,
Robert L. Rogers, Attorney-General; G. W. Hendricks, Assistant.
LITTLE ROCK, ARK., January 17, 1906.

Dr. J. W. Biedelman, Secretary State Board of Pharmacists, City.

DEAR SIR,—We have your letter of the 15th inst., in which you call our attention to a report of the case of Steele vs. The State of Arkansas, which was affirmed by the Supreme Court on last Saturday, and reported in Sunday's *Arkansas Gazette*, as being a conviction in "violation of the Liquor law" in selling a bottle of a certain proprietary preparation, and asking us what particular article this man had sold in violation of law, in order that you may in a circular letter give the result of this decision to the various druggists over the State, in order that they may be protected.

This "certain proprietary preparation" is not so generally described in the decision, but the decision says: "Appellant sold to one Kelley a certain compound called Pe-ru-na." Why the newspaper described this in such general terms and avoided using the term Pe-ru-na, will be perhaps understood by all those familiar with the contracts newspapers are compelled to make for advertising this article, if they make any contracts at all. In this instance in which the newspaper failed to reflect the truth of this decision sufficiently to enable the druggists to protect themselves from violations of the law, the issuance of this circular by you is quite commendable and will doubtless be appreciated by the druggists.

This is a sweeping decision and will not only apply to Pe-ru-na, but to any other preparation which may intoxicate. The court in this decision said: "It is unlawful to sell the same even though the seller do so thinking, in good faith, that it is to be used as a medicine." To sustain a conviction it is only necessary to show that the article was intoxicating, and that it was sold without license.

As stated by us in a previous letter to you, under the Blind Tiger Act of 1883, the possession of a United States Liquor License is made prima facie evidence of the guilt of the party owning or controlling the house. This provision of the law will be of considerable interest to those druggists who contemplate taking out United States Revenue License in compliance with the recent Internal Revenue Department order, taking effect April 1, 1906.

Yours very truly,
ROBERT L. ROGERS,
Attorney-General.

In calling attention to the above from the highest legal authority in the State, the Board believed it to be a duty to advise the druggists to be exceedingly careful in the sale of anything that may be used as an intoxicant—unless they possess all the licenses—State, county, city, as well as U. S. Internal Revenue.

George Merrell Made a Trustee of the Cincinnati Sinking Fund.

The Mayor of Cincinnati has appointed George Merrell, president of the William S. Merrell Chemical Company, a trustee of the sinking fund for a term of four years. Mr. Merrell was nominated for City Treasurer on the Democratic ticket, but declined to run. He is a native of Cincinnati and was educated in the public schools of that city, entering business in 1853. Mr. Merrell is a member of the oldest lodge of Masons in Ohio.

JOBBERS AND RETAILERS CONFER.

A Great Meeting Under Auspices of the Metropolitan Association—Mr. Plaut for the Jobbers Is Interrogated by Ex-President Anderson of the N. A. R. D.—Dr. Schieffelin Explains His Anti-Narcotic Bill.

Retail and wholesale druggists of this city now understand each other much better than they ever did before. The differences which, for the past month or two, have disturbed both branches of the drug trade here were threshed out at a joint meeting of retailers and jobbers held at the New York College of Pharmacy on Friday evening, January 26. While it was officially a meeting of the General Committee of the N. A. R. D., with well-known jobbers and others as guests, it was a notable gathering of men prominent in organization work. Among those present were Albert Plaut, of Lehn & Fink; Dr. William Jay Schieffelin, of Schieffelin & Co.; Frank E. Holliday, of the N. W. D. A.; John C. Gallagher, of Jersey City, formerly a member of the Executive Committee of the N. A. R. D.; William De Shetley, manager of the N. A. R. D.'s Department of the East; Clarence O. Bigelow, W. C. Anderson, former president of the N. A. R. D. and of the M. A. R. D.; Dr. William Muir and Felix Hirseman. There were in all some forty or fifty persons present.

The respective merits of the D. C. S. N. and tripartite plans were discussed at great length. It was one of the most open, frank and candid discussions of the questions involved that ever took place in the drug trade of this city. Everyone who participated in the debate spoke his mind freely and plainly, and while the arguments at times were perhaps somewhat heated, good feeling and fellowship prevailed throughout; every speaker was earnest and sincere and expressed his loyalty to the common cause.

AT THE OPENING OF THE MEETING.

The business meeting proper was called to order about 9.15 o'clock P. M., in the library of the college, President Reuben R. Smith being in the chair. After the minutes had been approved as read, Treasurer Bischoff reported a balance in the treasury of $278.65. Reports were then called for from various districts. The Hudson River Branch and the Bronx Association, it was stated, were doing all in their power to educate the physicians on the N. S. P. and National Formulary preparations. Jacob Diner said that in the 22d district this work is already yielding good financial returns. On Mr. Diner's suggestion, it was decided to unite the fourth and sixth districts with the second district, and the appointment of a special committee to organize that territory was authorized.

J. H. Morey said he thought it would be a great help if the minutes of the meetings were printed and distributed among the members. This is done in other large cities, he said, with good results. The sentiment of the meeting favored this plan as a valuable suggestion, and it was referred to the Executive Committee. President Smith then announced that there were a number of guests present, representing jobbing and other interests, and he took pleasure in introducing as the first speaker Albert Plaut, whom he referred to as the representative of the jobbers.

MR. PLAUT'S POSITION.

At the outset Mr. Plaut made it plain that he had come not as a representative of jobbing interests, but merely as an individual, and that he had intended simply to take part in the discussion. He said he did not represent the Metropolitan Association of Jobbers; he merely wished to become familiar with the work being done by the retailers. He had been under the impression, he continued, that the retailers did not take sufficient interest in organization work; in this he found he had been mistaken and was agreeably surprised. He said he was a strong believer in the value of co-operation; he was a labor union man in his views, and great good could come from organization if properly carried on. Co-operation is the watchword of the day, and as an illustration of its value he cited what had been accomplished in recent years among peasants in Ireland in the dairy industry. In the scheme successfully worked out there he said that profits were sought through full selling prices on a co-operative basis, rather than by effecting petty economies in buying; "no buying clubs over there," he remarked, rather significantly.

IT IS UP TO THE RETAILERS.

Mr. Plaut urged the retailers to do more than merely pay their dues; they should work individually, call on their neighbors, etc.; "you can't press the button and expect the N. A. R. D. to do the rest," said he; "don't wait for the other fellow to act." Mr. Plaut said he was much interested in the work being done by retailers to educate physicians to prescribe more U. S. P. and N. F. preparations; he spoke of the tendency of physicians to write fewer prescriptions and to prescribe proprietary preparations, of the danger of their becoming "rusty" in the matter of materia medica and therapeutics. Of late years, he continued, too much attention has been given to so-called patent medicines. It was most important, he said, for the retail druggist to bring the ethical side of his profession to the front.

AS TO LEGISLATION,

he said that it was commendable if of the right kind; for instance, it was right and proper to urge laws to curb the sale of nostrums, etc., and to protect the public against incompetent druggists; but he advised retailers not to be too eager to rush to Albany or Washington to oppose bills that contain clauses which seem inimical to their interests.

THE TWO PLANS.

Mr. Plaut then plunged into the subject of the direct contract serial numbering and tripartite plans. "I was one of the four," said he, "who opposed the D. C. S. N. plan to the last; I have been converted to that plan and now I am a firm believer in it, but not for New York. It has been a success in smaller cities and towns, but a failure here. The fault lies partly with the manufacturer, but mostly with the retailers. The jobbers, who have been much abused, are about the only ones who have remained steadfast and who have stood up religiously for the direct contract serial numbering plan. They are turning down orders daily because the orders are so large that they are evidently meant for cutters. Only to-day an order for five gross of Bromo Laxative Quinine, accompanied by a certified check, was turned down by three jobbers, notwithstanding the fact that the retailer's name appeared on the retail agency lists. New York jobbers have succeeded in having some 20 odd retailers, who were known to be violating contracts, removed from the lists, and we have more names in the refrigerator. There is great need of purging these lists; the manufacturers want them purged, and the local retail associations ought to assist in this purging process."

MULTITUDINOUS NEW REMEDIES.

In the early part of the meeting some one had spoken upon the necessity of having all new remedies marketed under the direct contract serial numbering plan. "That is not good business," said Mr. Plaut. "Lately we have been simply swamped with all sorts of new remedies and preparations, and almost every manufacturer uses the argument that he is going to market the new goods under the D. C. S. N. plan. This new remedy feature of the drug business is becoming a nuisance, and we are obliged to refuse to take the new goods even on consignment."

PROFITS ON PROPRIETARIES.

Mr. Plaut said that the patent medicine trade was but a small part of the business of the average retail pharmacy; entirely too much attention, he said, was paid to patent medicines; the profits, too, from "patents" were very small. He then took up the old tripartite plan.

"If you were familiar with the operation of the tripartite plan," said he, "you would not decry it. It has done more to prevent price cutting and to bring about present conditions in the drug trade than any other plan. The Roanoke list has worked wonders. Let us urge the tripartite manufacturers to adopt the D. C. S. N. plan. Don't throw out the tripartite plan. Don't make the alternative of D. C. S. N. plan or nothing. We have succeeded in getting a number of proprietors to stop selling direct to retailers.

JOBBERS WANT TO CO-OPERATE.

"The jobbers' association," he continued, "wants to co-operate with you. It is often said that the jobber or middleman will soon be extinct. That may apply to the candy business, the shoe or meat trade, but never to the drug business; there the jobber is indispensable. He cannot prosper unless the retailer does, and the manufacturer cannot successfully market his goods without the help of the wholesaler. The interests of one branch are identical with those of every other branch."

Upon the conclusion of his remarks Mr. Plaut was greeted with much applause.

MR. DINER ASKS SOME POINTED QUESTIONS.

Jacob Diner then made one of his forceful and characteristic speeches. He asked some very pointed questions. So long as no definite price is stipulated, such as is provided under the D. C. S. N. plan, how can it be determined, he inquired, whether a man is a cutter or not? A retail price, he declared, is a necessary adjunct to the tripartite plan. We, as retailers, are not entitled to the 5 per cent. discount, we do not ask it; but we must make a living profit, and *the only way we can do it is at the selling end and through the direct contract plan!* The jobber can help us by absolutely insisting on the plan. Eliminate direct buying, put every retailer on an equal buying basis, and you will solve half the problem." Mr. Diner's eloquent plea was roundly applauded.

MR. PLAUT REPLIES.

Mr. Plaut, to whom Mr. Diner's remarks were really addressed, said he did not claim that the tripartite agreement was the equal of the D. C. S. N. plan. The former, he said, had undoubtedly done much good in the past, and tripartite goods should not be thrown out pending their being placed on a better plan, such as the D. C. S. N. The jobbers, he said, would heartily support all efforts to bring such goods under the D. C. S. N. system.

The next speaker was Mr. Holliday. He declared that the local jobbers' association was formed solely for the purpose of maintaining proprietors' contracts. He asserted that goods are now sold to the retail drug trade of the country on equal terms. Ninety per cent. of the jobbers of the United States are ready to adopt the D. C. S. N. plan on all goods that have a general sale; but the jobber has no voice in the making of the direct contracts; all pressure on the manufacturer must come from the retailer."

A BITTER ATTACK ON THE TRIPARTITE PLAN.

Dr. Anderson, the next speaker, bitterly attacked the tripartite plan. He was frequently interrupted by applause and by questions from Mr. Plaut.

"Mr. Plaut has said more against the direct contract plan than for it," he began. "The question to be settled here in New York is between these two plans. I fail to see the evidence of co-operation, which the jobbers speak of and which they ask."

"What do you want us to do that we are not now doing?" inquired Mr. Plaut.

"Do with the D. C. S. N. plan what you did with the tripartite plan when it was endorsed by the retailers. You tried to induce everybody to adopt it and the retailers stood back of you. The tripartite agreement has now been declared a failure, has it not?"

"Only in certain sections," replied Mr. Plaut, "it has been a success all over the West."

"Then why did retailers come from all over the West to Boston to demand the D. C. S. N. plan?" Loud applause greeted this rejoinder by Dr. Anderson. "Wherever it is a success," he continued, "don't interfere with it; but don't bring it to New York to oppose the D. C. S. N. plan. The only way of attaining success is through a system of tracing and a contract whereby a violator can be reached through the courts. Instead of putting the tripartite plan above the direct contract plan, let the wholesalers join the retailers absolutely in supporting the D. C. S. N. plan, and success will soon be assured."

Dr. Anderson sat down amid tremendous applause.

D. C. S. N. PLAN FAVORED BY JOBBERS.

Mr. Plaut then said: "Because we claim good for an old plan does not mean that we do not favor the new plan, which has proven itself better. We favor it as superseding the old plan; but don't pour out dirty water before you have clean."

Mr. Holliday coincided with this view. Dr. Schieffelin remarked that at a recent dinner of jobbers all of the seventeen present had indorsed the D. C. S. N. plan.

John C. Gallagher, of Jersey City, the last speaker, reminded the druggists that they would never get contracts from proprietors until they refused to handle or to give window displays to unprotected goods. "The only way the proprietors, jobbers and retailers can get along," said he, "is by getting together just like this and having a 'show-down.'"

DR. SCHIEFFELIN'S ANTI-NARCOTIC BILL.

In the course of the meeting Dr. Schieffelin read the draft of a cocaine bill, which would soon be sent to the Legislature. The measure, he said, was a compromise between the views of the church and temperance people and the Board of Halth; it was to be introduced to anticipate legislation which might be much less reasonable. The sentiment of the meeting seemed to be rather against the bill.

DRUG STORE TELEPHONES.

The association unanimously adopted the following resolution:

WHEREAS, The New York and New Jersey Telephone Company contemplates on or before July 1, 1906, making a flat rate in each borough of Greater New York of five cents for a single call in each of the said boroughs, and

WHEREAS, Such rate has already been established in the Borough of the Bronx, therefore, be it

Resolved, That the New York and New Jersey Telephone Company be requested that before making such flat rate of five cents for a single call in each borough of Greater New York a slot machine be placed in each pharmacy of a member of the M. A. R. D., and be it further

Resolved, That from all moneys taken in the said slot machines, a deduction of 40 per cent. be allowed the pharmacy wherein such slot machines be located, and be it further

Resolved, That a copy of these resolutions be forwarded to the New York and New Jersey Telephone Company and to the Telephone Committee of the National Association of Retail Druggists, calling upon the parties herein mentioned that such requests be granted and the efforts of the N. A. R. D. Telephone Committee be directed toward securing for the members of the M. A. R. D., such concessions.

Secretary Swann was voted a salary on the basis of 50 cents a member. As there are more than 1,200 members, this means a salary at present of about $600 per year for his services as secretary to the M. A. R. D.

MANAGER DE SHETLEY IS PLEASED.

Mr. De Shetley, who was largely instrumental in bringing about the joint conference of jobbing and retail interests, expressed himself as much pleased with what had been accomplished, and said that he hoped to have one or two jobbers present at future meetings of the Metropolitan Association. The meeting adjourned about 1 A. M.

Physicians, Pharmacists and Proprietors Discuss Proprietary Medicines.

A special meeting of the New York County Medico-Pharmaceutico League was held at the Hotel Astor on Tuesday night, January 30, to discuss the proprietary medicine question.

The remarks made by Frederic S. Mason, B. F. Fairchild and P. J. Diner at the meeting appear on pages 66 and 67 of this issue.

Dr. William J. Robinson, speaking for the physicians, stated his own views in the matter, which were set forth in a paper read before the American Medical Association at the New Orleans meeting two years ago, which paper was, he thought, the beginning of the present campaign of that association, a campaign which had gone further in some directions that was desirable for the good of medicine.

SQUIBB'S NEW SELLING PLAN.

No Direct Sales to Physicians—Jobbers Benefited by the Change—Detail Man Eliminated.

E. R. Squibb & Sons, the well-known manufacturing chemists of this city, recently completed arrangements for distributing their products on a new basis. The new system, or plan, was adopted after a conference held here between the Pharmaceutical Committee of the National Wholesale Druggists' Association and the firm of Squibb & Sons. By its terms the leading wholesale druggists of the country agree to keep regularly in stock a full line of the Squibb preparations and to supply same to the retail trade at the Squibb terms. The jobbers are to receive a suitable compensation. The Squibb company on its part agrees not to sell direct to physicians, but will supply only the trade, thus eliminating practically the detail man. Furthermore, the company declares it will not establish branch houses throughout the country; the wholesaler will become the legitimate distributor to the retail trade of the company's products, while retail druggists are assured that they will all stand on an equal footing before the jobber and that physicians can obtain their supplies on better terms from the retailers than from the jobber or manufacturer. The company has issued the following circular to the drug trade:

To the Drug Trade:

The prices of all our products are regularly published in Squibb's Materia Medica. Our prices are uniform throughout the United States and are calculated as low as the quality furnished permits. The trade receives the following discounts:

A trade discount of 10 per cent. on all orders of less than $25 net and 1 per cent. for cash within ten days.

A trade discount of 10 per cent. and 5 per cent. on orders amounting to $25 net or over, but less than $50 net.

A trade discount of 10 per cent. and 10 per cent. on orders amounting to $50 net or over, but less than $100 net.

A trade discount of 10 per cent. and 15 per cent. on orders amounting to $100 net or over. And on such lots a cash discount of 5 per cent. for remittances received within ten days from date of invoice will be granted.

We pay freight on all shipments of not less than $25 net in value and aggregating at least 100 pounds in weight, but only one-half of express and postage charges.

In order to place our products at the lowest possible cost within easy reach of every pharmacist we have arranged for a service through the wholesale trade which will insure throughout the country a most convenient, prompt and economical distribution. The wholesalers have agreed to supply all the Squibb products, everywhere in the United States, at our own terms as stated. They will endeavor to meet every demand as it comes to them and keep a complete assortment of our line, thereby saving the pharmacist trouble, expense and delay.

The prices published in Squibb's Materia Medica are net to physicians, and in order to protect the pharmacist in his dealings with physicians we shall not permit ourselves or the wholesale trade or physicians' supply houses to sell to physicians at better prices than those published by us.

The pharmacist is the natural purveyor to the physician and he should be enabled to furnish to the physician whatever supplies the latter may require, at the lowest possible cost. Our new plan and terms make this possible.

We feel confident that our sincere desire to serve the best interests of the pharmaceutical and medical professions will be appreciated and will still further extend the growing preference for the Squibb label.

E. R. SQUIBB & SONS.

January 15, 1906.

MR. WEICKER SAYS THE PLAN MEETS WITH FAVOR.

To a representative of the AMERICAN DRUGGIST Theodore Weicker, president of E. R. Squibb & Sons, said:

"Our new plan seems to meet with general favor in the trade. The retailers, I think, will appreciate what we are trying to do for them. As for the jobber, he is the legitimate distributer and is entitled to fair compensation for his services as such. It is far better all around for the retailer to get his supplies from the natural and proper source—namely, the jobber—and by eliminating the detail man, who heretofore has sought individual orders from physicians, we will be relieved of considerable expense and inconvenience. The new plan seems to be for the best interest of all concerned."

Under the plan both jobbers and physicians' supply houses are restrained from selling at less than list price to physicians, though retailers are not so restrained. This discrimination will, it is hoped, have the effect of bringing the retailer into closer relation with physicians, even where physicians dispense their own medicines.

At a recent meeting of the Metropolitan Drug Club (the new association of local jobbers) Mr. Weicker was the guest of honor. The new Squibb plan was discussed by the wholesalers and was favorably commented on.

RETAIL PHARMACIES UNDER A TRUST.

President of the United Cigar Stores Company Starts a Chain of Pharmacies—Ominous Outlook for the Small Retailer.

The incorporation in New Jersey, on January 24, of the United Chemists Company, with a capitalization of $10,000,000, for the establishment of a chain of retail pharmacies in the leading cities of the country, to be operated like the United Cigar Stores, has created a flurry of excitement in the trade. A reporter of the AMERICAN DRUGGIST, who started out to investigate the purposes of the company, ascertained that the four pharmacies in this city formerly owned by William Wilson, had been acquired by the new corporation. This was admitted by Robert H. Sherlock, personal counsel for President George H. Whelan, of the United Cigar Stores Company, who is president of the United Chemists Company. Mr. Sherlock did not wish the reporter to leave with the impression that Mr. Whelan was to retain his connection with the United Cigar Stores Company, or to operate the two in common. He said that Mr. Whelan had indicated to him his intention of resigning from the presidency of the cigar combine.

Mr. Sherlock is full of the possibilities of the new company, which he believes will revolutionize retail pharmacy in the same way as the cigar stores company has revolutionized the cigar business. He referred to the improved *morale*, the lessened hours of work, better salaries, and the interest in the business which the cigar store clerks are favored with since the operation of the trust stores, and said that similar conditions would result from the drug combine.

When seen again shortly before the AMERICAN DRUGGIST was put to press, Mr. Sherlock referred our representative to Michael Whelan, a brother of the cigar stores president, who is also interested in the drug corporation, but is almost equally reticent in giving any details about the proposed operation of the drug stores already purchased and about to be acquired.

"I am inclined to believe that the United Chemists Company has already disclosed too much about its plans," said Michael Whelan when seen in his offices at 111 Broadway. "The fact that the new corporation intends to establish several stores in all of the leading cities in the East has been officially announced, and this should be enough information to make public at the present time. I cannot state positively, even if I desired to do so, whether it is the company's intention to buy or control stores in Washington, D. C., or Boston or Newark, for its plans do not yet include the establishment of stores in any other cities besides New York, Philadelphia and Chicago. Great progress has already been made. The company will be conducted in accordance with the general principles of the United Cigar Stores Company, but I cannot tell just what these principles are in detail. As soon as the corporation is prepared to give out a statement on these points all its plans will be made public. I cannot even tell when my brother expects to resign as president of the United Cigar Stores Company, and I refuse to say anything more at present."

When asked if the corporation proposed to inaugurate a system of cut rates on proprietary remedies and drugs Mr. Whelan refused to make any definite reply, but asserted that this subject as well as all others would be considered and commented upon in the public statement which the company will issue later.

The fact that Mr. Sherlock has become suddenly silent in regard to the United Chemists Company's plans makes his former remarks of even greater interest to the drug trade. As mentioned above, Mr. Sherlock, after telling of George J. Whelan's intention to resign from the presidency of the Cigar Stores Company within the near future to assume his new duties as head of the drug combine, denied the report that the drug and cigar stores of both companies would be run in connection with each other like a combination of interests actually owned and operated by the Cigar Stores Company or its parent organization, the American Tobacco Company. At the same time Mr. Sherlock announced the purchase of the Wilson drug stores and added that options had been secured on several other retail drug stores in this city, saying that it was the intention of the United Chemists Company to improve the condition of the drug stores by adopting methods similar to those of the cigar company. These methods of improving the condition of the cigar stores, he explained, had included the employment of a more experienced and skillful class of clerks and salesmen at considerably higher salaries than those now prevailing in most city stores, the giving of an interest in the business to the most competent salesmen by means of stock transfers or purchases on the installment plan, and a provision for the care and treatment of employees who might be ill at any time while in the employ of the company.

If, as is generally believed in local drug circles, the United Chemists Company is planning to adopt a general scheme of price cutting, which is also included in the fundamental principles of the United Cigar Stores Company, the new corporation is likely to experience some trouble in obtaining its supplies because of the existence of the tripartite selling and price maintaining agreement between the National Association of Retail Druggists, the National Wholesale Druggists' Association and the Proprietary Association of America, which is now being strengthened and enlarged in such a manner that the purchase of goods by price cutting retailers will soon become even more difficult.

No information in relation to the plans of the United Chemists Company for evading this difficulty is obtainable from George J. Whelan, his brother, Michael, or Mr. Sherlock. At the main offices of the United Cigar Stores Company, at 141 West Seventeenth street, the president of that corporation refuses to be interviewed on this matter, referring everything to Michael Whelan, who, with Mr. Sherlock, also refuses to discuss this point.

It is suggested in some quarters that the new corporation might avoid trouble by manufacturing a large proportion of the goods which it proposes to sell, but if the company wishes to compete with other stores in the sale of proprietary remedies it is difficult to understand how it will surmount this barrier.

The manager of William Wilson's pharmacy on Liberty street declined to give any information regarding the reported transfer of the Wilson pharmacies to the United Chemists Company, and he appeared to be chagrined over the fact that the news of the transfer had leaked out, though Mr. Sherlock was quite ready to make the announcement to the press.

It is believed that the leading men in the tobacco trust, who have made such a success of the United Cigar Stores Company, are anxious to repeat their experiment in the drug business, and that the bulk of the necessary capital will come from this quarter. The names given in the incorporation papers are Jacob Fischel, 765 Broad street, Newark; Morris Klein, 135 East 115th street, and J. Wesel Parker, 236 West 146th street, New York. The company's charter permits it to operate only in cities of 1,000,000 or more population, which restricts its territory to New York, Chicago and Philadelphia. Mr. Sherlock denied that there were any business arrangements with the new company and the United Cigar Stores Company.

The Ichthyol Trademark.

The Federal Tribunal of Lausanne, Switzerland, recently gave its decision in an appeal against the decision of the Court of Appeal of Berne in the action brought by the Ichthyol Company, Hamburg, proprietor of the trademark "Ichthyol," to prohibit Luedy & Co., Burgdorf, from infringing the trademark, and particulars are given in *The Chemist and Druggist* for January 13. The Lausanne Court rejected the defendants' appeal and confirmed the former judgment, which ordered that the defendant firm should no longer use for its products names containing in any way the characteristic word "Ichthyol." It was proved that the trademark "Ichthyol" is the legitimate property of the Ichthyol Company and that only this company is able to supply the sulphur preparation known under the name "Ichthyol." The defendants had pretended to supply the same preparation as supplied by the Ichthyol Company, but the court stated that their product differed essentially in composition from the genuine article.

PARIS MEDICINE COMPANY SUES BALTIMORE CUTTERS.

Retailers Abandon the Task of Price Regulation and Proprietors Take It Up—First Step Taken by Laxative Bromo Quinine Makers.

(*From our Regular Correspondent.*)

Baltimore, February 8.—As a result of the price demoralization which followed the action of the Baltimore Retail Druggists' Association in withdrawing the established minimum price list on proprietaries and patent medicines and throwing the town wide open, and the consequent cutting of prices on goods included in the Direct Contract and Serial Numbering Plan, suits were docketed last Tuesday by the Paris Medicine Company, of St. Louis and London, against the Read Drug and Chemical Company, Lexington and Howard streets; Klingel's Pharmacy on West Lexington street, near Liberty; L. H. Sprague, Liberty and Fayette streets; John K. Wiley, 430 South Broadway, and August Kach, 1470 William street, and Judge Wickes, in the Circuit Court, issued an order requiring them to show cause in five days why they should not be restrained from obtaining the preparation from wholesale druggists and retail druggists who have entered into contracts with the Paris Medicine Company, in violation of these contracts, and from advertising and selling the medicine when obtained in this manner.

This move is the outcome of the efforts made in the past by the Retail Druggists' Association to stop price cutting on the part of a limited number of pharmacists who persist in violating schedules and agreements. When the association found that it was not making any headway in its campaign against demoralization it served notice on the manufacturers that they would have to take matters into their own hands. The proprietors of various preparations subsequently sent agents here to gather evidence, and the suits followed.

The bill of complaint alleges that because of the great demand for the goods of the complainant in pharmacies, some stores, in order to attract customers through their advertisements, cut the price of the preparation, and in this way procure the trade of persons thus attracted for other articles, thereby cheapening and injuring the reputation of the medicine. The bill then alleges that, in order to secure a uniform price, the Paris Medicine Company entered into contracts with the jobbers whereby the latter were not to sell the goods except to such retailers as would in turn execute a written contract directly with the Paris Medicine Company under which they agreed not to sell the medicine for less than 25 cents. The bill further alleges that the defendants "collusively and fraudulently" procured various retail druggists and dealers to enter into these retail agency contracts for the purpose of obtaining the preparation, which was then turned over to the druggists sued in violation of the contract. An injunction is asked to restrain these druggists from obtaining the preparation by inducing wholesalers or retailers to violate their contracts with the owners of the formula.

Syracuse Druggists Have a Country Supper.

The Syracuse Druggists' Association gave an "old fashioned country supper" at Long Branch, near Syracuse, on January 25, which was a pronounced success, being attended by upwards of 130 ladies and gentlemen. President W. B. Bissell occupied the seat at the head of the table and introduced the speakers, among whom were President J. A. Lockie, of the State Pharmaceutical Association, Buffalo; A. J. Horlick, of Horlick's Food Company, Racine, Wis., and Frank S. Gardner, of Baldwinsville. Mr. Lockie made one of his characteristic speeches and referred among other things to the progress of the N. A. R. D. work. He interlarded the serious portion of his speech with numerous funny stories which created considerable mirth. Frank S. Gardner, chairman, and the rest of the committee having charge of the arrangements for the dinner and entertainment are deserving of much credit for the successful outcome of the affair. Among the traveling men who contributed to the evening's entertainment were Charles L. Pettis, of Solon Palmer, and Bob. Service, of Lazelle, Dalley & Co.

ALUMNI BALL A GREAT SUCCESS.

Unprecedented Attendance and Gayest of Events.

The Alumni Association of the College of Pharmacy of the City of New York conducted a most successful concert and ball in the Grand Central Palace, Lexington avenue, on Wednesday evening, February 7. This was the eleventh annual ball, and both by attendance and general success it eclipsed any previous event. The two college societies, or Greek letter fraternities, the Phi Chi and Kappa Psi, respectively, were more in evidence than ever before and contributed greatly to the evening's entertainment. The Phi Chi's occupied a box which was gaily decorated with the pennants of the society and the society's insignia was picked out in electric lights in front of the box. Among the members who occupied the box were W. J. Sabine, W. J. Hall, C. W. Holzhauer, C. K. Brown, W. P. Maher, F. L. Everson, W. J. Becker, of Amsterdam; Dr. F. A. Leslie, H. Dingler, Lloyd Record, Sayville; A. J. Bauer, F. N. Pond, Nelson S. Kirk, H. A. Herold and John Sullivan, of Utica; H. Crowe, of Englewood, N. J. The ladies in the box were S. Strauss, A. E. Kerber, K. C. Reckelman, C. A. Brown, S. Eller, B. Thode, L. Donihee, E. Bonn, F. Kiernan, Rae Safier, M. M. Kenna, R. L. Frisbie, Theresa Driscoll, Irene Dainhee, Rose M. Strauss, Anna E. Driscoll, Bessie Brown, Margaret Coleman, L. L. Beach, Eugenie Doyle, Agnes Doyle and Henrietta Hyer.

The programme, which was arranged by President Fred Borggreve and Henry J. Binder, Jr., chairman of the Executive Committee, included a preliminary concert consisting of five numbers. Crowley's Eighth Regiment Band furnished the music and Miss Madeline Bourdette sang and responded to an encore. The dance programme was lengthy, including some twenty-four waltzes, two-steps and lanciers, but it was all thoroughly enjoyed, the pleasure of the evening being heightened by the services of the band, which was heard between the dances in promenade music. The attendance numbered about 1,200 and the dancing continued until half past three o'clock next morning.

The success of the ball crowns a very successful administration of alumni affairs under the presidency of Mr. Borggreve, whose popularity was attested by the presence of a large number of representative pharmacists, nearly all of the local societies and colleges allied to pharmacy having one or more members on the floor or in the boxes. The opportunity thus afforded for the members of different societies to meet and exchange ideas was improved to the utmost and many a pleasant reunion took place. The college is evidently greatly advantaged by the work of the Greek letter societies, whose members were conspicuous on the dance floor by their distinctive silken sashes and the badges of their fraternity displayed on the coat lapel. The Phi Chi society held an election of officers last week, when the following were chosen: E. E. Driscoll, W. C. C.; E. U. Bock, V. C. C.; W. G. Sabine, W. K. of R. S.; W. P. Maher, W. K. F.; V. L. Peirce, W. P.; E. A. Grogan, M. A.; C. T. Maloney, Historian.

New Committee Appointments of the N. W. D. A.

President Lucian B. Hall has named the following chairmen of committees for the ensuing year: Adulterations, W. B. Robeson; arrangements and entertainments, Edgar D. Taylor; commercial travelers, A. B. Stewart; credits and collections, Charles F. Cutler; drug market, I. Frank Stone; fire insurance, George W. Lattimer; fraternal relations, John A. Burgess; legislation, M. N. Kline; membership, A. J. More; memorials of deceased members, Charles W. Whittlesey; paints, oils and glass, Henry W. Evans; passenger rates and routes, Romaine Pierson; proprietary goods, John N. Carey; relations with local associations, city and interstate, Charles S. Martin; trade marks, A. J. Horlick; transportation, Courtney H. West, special committee on census of 1910, Albert Plaut; special committee on box and cartage, J. C. Eliel; special committee of commercial travelers, W. A. Conner; special committee on paris green, H. B. Fairchild; special committee on pharmaceuticals and plasters, William J. Walding; special committee on suits against members, M. N. Kline; sub-committee on legislation to confer with other associations, M. N. Kline.

OPPOSE THE AMERICAN DRUGGISTS' SYNDICATE.

Metropolitan Association of Retail Druggists Issues a Card Advising Members to Have Nothing to Do with the Syndicate —Mr. Goddard's Comment.

Members of the Metropolitan Association of Retail Druggists received a postal card in their mail last week reading as follows:

M. A. R. D.

Firmly believing in the "Square Deal" and "equal opportunities for all," we suggest that members of the M. A. R. D. have nothing whatever to do with the American Druggists' Syndicate and its contracts until such time as further information is obtainable.

Fraternally yours,

S. V. B. SWANN, Secretary.

R. R. SMITH, President.

MR. GODDARD DISCUSSES MOTIVES.

C. H. Goddard, the secretary of the American Druggists' Syndicate, was seen by a representative of the AMERICAN DRUGGIST and expressed the opinion that the card was the work of some individual or individuals who did not have the true interests of retail druggists at heart. He said that of the 1,200 retail druggists who are members of the American Druggists' Syndicate, at least 1,000 of them are stanch supporters of the N. A. R. D. and its principles. Continuing, he said:

"The motive prompting those responsible for the postal card is a mystery which may perhaps be explained by competitive manufacturers. The American Druggists' Syndicate since its inception has endeavored to comply fully with both the letter and spirit of the N. A. R. D., fully approving the legitimate efforts of the association in the interests of the retail druggists.

"We expect attacks to be inspired by jealous manufacturers, and perhaps some wholesale houses who fear legitimate competition, but we hardly expected it from an organization to which over 90 per cent. of our members belong, and the purposes of which are in a measure identical with ours, and I personally cannot help but feel that at the next meeting of the N. A. R. D. official action will be taken and a rebuke offered for that which, I am informed, is the unauthorized action of the officers."

When asked if he had anything to add to the statement made in the postal card Secretary Swann replied in the negative, except to say that the matter had been fully discussed by the officers at a special meeting and that the text of the card had been approved by the association's counsel.

Adulterated Drugs from New York Wholesalers.

At a recent meeting of the New York Academy of Medicine Dr. Herman M. Biggs, of the Health Department, charged the wholesale druggists of New York City with general and gross adulterations. Out of thirty-five different drugs examined eight samples of each drug are being obtained from the largest New York drug houses. According to the chemist of the Health Department the following were some of the faults found:

Of ground aconite root, which is supposed to be 60-mesh fine, a large amount was retained in a 20-mesh sieve. Color ranged from dark yellow to brown. Some of the samples had no odor of aconite. The extracts made from the samples varied from 34½ per cent., which is about standard, down to 28 per cent.

Of powdered belladonna leaf only 60 per cent. met the sieve test, some being retained in a 20-mesh sieve, some at 60-mesh and some at 80-mesh, 100-mesh being standard. Color and odor were uniform. Alkaloidal strength varied, one sample showing 0.35, one 0.212, another 0.14 and another 0.069. Powdered and ground belladonna root samples showed great variability in size of granules, color varying from brownish white to dark gray, the belladonna odor being very slight in some, others having a woody odor. The total alkaloidal strengths shown in four samples of the ground were 0.39, 0.407, 0.263, and 0.356, and in the powdered, 0.41, 0.358, 0.325 and 0.429.

Ground and powdered digitalis leaves were found to be much too coarse as a rule, color varying from light olive green (perfect) to greenish drab. Only two of the eight samples had a pronounced digitalis odor, the rest having only slight and musty odors.

Only two samples of saffron were purchased, from two different houses; one sample was very fine. The other sample had only 23 per cent. of saffron petals, the rest being aniline-dyed petals of magnolia and uncolored foreign material.

Powdered rhubarb was found to be very much adulterated in most of the samples. According to the chemist of the board the above results were characteristic of the results of the examinations of lobelia, strophanthus, senna, cinchona, licorice, larkspur and the other drugs examined. In no instance was it found that the various samples gathered from any one house were uniformly bad, both good and bad samples being found in each house purchased from.

An Emphatic Denial.

The most explicit denial was made by L. K. Liggett, president of the United Drug Company, when he was asked as to the truth of a report that the National Cigar Stands Company, an associated concern of the United Drug Company, was connected in some way with the American Tobacco Company. The rumor received circulation in a contemporary periodical through the publication of an anonymous letter, which purported to come from a shareholder in the United Drug Company. When seen by a representative of the AMERICAN DRUGGIST Mr. Liggett at first declined to discuss the subject, saying that as the communication was an anonymous one it would not be proper for him to dignify it with any attention. He stopped long enough, however, to deny in the most emphatic way that the United Drug Company or the National Cigar Stands Company had any connection, near or remote, directly or indirectly, with the American Tobacco Company. George C. Lyon, of the well known retail firm of Hall & Lyon, Providence, and of the Cahoon-Lyon Drug Company, Buffalo, and who is a director in the United Drug Company, was present while Mr. Liggett was being interviewed and signified his willingness to be quoted. He stigmatized the story connecting the National Cigar Stands Company and Mr. Liggett with the American Tobacco Company as a pure fabrication; in his own words, "a damned lie."

DIED.

BOOTH.—In Rochester, N. Y., on Monday, February 8, Charles M. Booth, aged seventy-five years.

DOWLING.—In Meridian, Miss., on Thursday, January 18, W. A. Dowling, aged twenty-four years.

GLASS.—In Atlanta, Ga., on Saturday, January 20, C. B. Glass, aged nineteen years.

HALLIDAY.—In Essex, Conn., on Sunday, January 21, William Halliday, aged fifty-eight years.

HISCOX.—In Patchogue, L. I., on Thursday, January 26, David Hiscox, aged sixty-seven years.

HODGES.—In Ellicott City, Md., on Wednesday, January 17, Dr. William E. Hodges, aged seventy-six years.

HOLLERBACH.—In New Orleans, La., on Thursday, January 18, J. F. Hollerbach, aged fifty-nine years.

HOOKER.—In Longmeadow, Springfield, Mass., on Friday, January 19, John Hooker, aged seventy-nine years.

HUNTSMAN.—In Langhorne, Bucks County, Pa., on Saturday, January 27, Howard D. Huntsman, aged forty-five years.

LOOMIS.—In Cincinnati, Ohio, on Friday, February 2, E. E. Loomis.

LYON.—In Chicago, Ill., on Tuesday, January 16, Dr. George G. Lyon, aged forty-five years.

MCPHERSON.—In New York, on Friday, January 26, William F. McPherson, aged sixty-six years.

OVERHOLT.—In Baltimore, Md., on Wednesday, January 25, William T. Overholt, aged sixty years.

RAMLER.—In Richmond, Ind., on Sunday, January 21, Joseph H. Ramler, aged seventy-five years.

RIETZ.—In Duluth, Minn., on Monday, January 15, Rev. Louis Rietz, aged fifty-seven years.

Greater New York News.

C. E. Spurge, chemist of the Ozone-Vanillin Company, Niagara Falls, came here a few days ago on a short business trip.

W. P. Ungerer, of this city, and wife have gone to Summerville, N. C., for the balance of the winter.

Frederick Dowsey, of Washington, D. C., has purchased the S. S. Hayden Pharmacy, at Great Neck, L. I.

The Heffley Drug Company, of Babylon, L. I., has opened a pharmacy at Hicksville and put W. C. Bradley in charge as manager.

Louis C. Dickert, formerly proprietor of the pharmacy at Greene and Stuyvesant avenues, Brooklyn, has given up his store there and moved to Lynbrook, L. I.

Martin Arneman, N. Y. C. P. '88, formerly in business at Eighth avenue and Thirty-eighth street, Manhattan, is now conducting a prospering pharmacy at College Point, L. I.

Dr. E. M. Houghton, bacteriologist of Parke, Davis & Co., Detroit, was in town recently and visited the company's local branch.

Lester H. Carragan, of the traveling staff of Parke, Davis & Co., left for Havana on January 19 to reassume his duties in the Havana office of the company.

The New York office of the Powers-Weightman-Rosengarten Company was favored recently with a visit from A. G. Rosengarten, treasurer of the company.

The Roessler & Hasslacher Chemical Company has been appointed agent for the sale of Dr. Schaeffer's saccharine, manufactured at Maywood, N. J.

The next examination by the Eastern Branch of the New York State Board of Pharmacy will be held at the Brooklyn College of Pharmacy on Wednesday, February 21.

The fifth regular meeting of the New York Section of the American Chemical Society was held on Friday, February 9, at 8.15 P. M., in the Assembly Hall of the Chemists' Club, 108 West Fifty-fifth street.

G. C. Eliel, of the Lyman-Eliel Drug Company, Minneapolis, made a brief visit here accompanied by Mrs. Eliel. They sailed on the steamship Princess Irene for a tour of the Mediterranean.

The new addition to the Woodbridge Building, 100 William street, is rapidly nearing completion. The Roessler & Hasslacher Chemical Company expects to move into its new quarters in the annex in a few days.

J. A. Leverty, of Bridgeport, Conn., was elected treasurer of the Connecticut Pharmacy Commission on January 16. The next meeting of the board for the examination of candidates for licenses will take place in Hartford March 6.

At a meeting of the Riker's Drug Stores Company held at 456 Fulton street, Brooklyn, on January 23, the following officers were elected: President, W. C. Bolton; vice-president, J. H. Marshall; treasurer, E. D. Cahoon; assistant treasurer and general manager, A. H. Cosden; secretary, John J. Haigney.

Colonel E. W. Fitch is anything but superstitious. He entertained a party of thirteen at dinner in the Café Martin on January 13, the guests being Harry B. Mason, P. E. Hall, Dr. J. Takamine, C. N. Brunn, H. R. Saunders, W. McKay, D. A. Lyle, G. R. Tompkins, H. Turrell, W. J. Carr, J. Burnside, E. Plummer and S. H. Carragan.

C. C. and Marion Speiden have become associated with the firm of Innis & Co., and a new firm is to be incorporated as Innis, Speiden & Co., to deal in chemicals, dyestuffs, etc., at 181 Front street. The directors of the new company will be the Messrs. Speiden and Geo. V. Sheffield, who for some years has been connected with Innis & Co.

The firm of E. J. Bush & Co., essential oil distillers, with offices in New York, has made some notable additions to its staff of representatives, Thomas Wynn, formerly with A. Klipstein & Co., and J. W. McKnight, formerly with Proctor & Gamble, having been added to the force of traveling representatives in the West. Edward Long, sales manager of the New York office, attended to the arrangements while in Chicago ar . St. Louis last month.

M. J. Breitenbach and Martin H. Smith, the first named of Pepto-Mangan fame and the second of Glyco-Heroin, spent a short time recently at Hillsmere on the Chesapeake Bay, with the Shooters' Shoot Club, an organization of New Yorkers who go in for duck shooting. Mr. Breitenbach and Mr. Smith are kind to their friends, and more than one brace of ducks have reached New York since the shooting began.

The programme for the evening included the presentation of the Nichols Medal to Marston Taylor Bogert by the president of the American Chemical Society, W. F. Hillebrand, and the presentation of papers by H. W. Wiley on The Stimulus of Research; by H. C. Sherman and R. H. Williams on The Osazone Test for Glucose and Fructose, as Influenced by Dilution and by the Presence of Other Sugars; and by F. D. Dodge on Some Derivatives of Citronellal.

Floyd Holiday, until lately employed as prescription clerk in the pharmacy of the H. Cassebeer Drug Company, Columbus avenue and Seventy-second street, is missing and friends and police of the city are trying to ascertain his whereabouts. Mr. Holiday left the store on Monday, January 22, for the purpose of filling a small bill of sale for his employer, but he never arrived at his destination, and it is feared that he may have met with foul play. Mr. Holiday is 50 years old.

Lowe Brothers, proprietors of the pharmacy at Central avenue, Far Rockaway, have purchased the old established business of George L. Peck, on Fulton street, Jamaica, L. I. Peck's "Hall of Pharmacy," as it was styled, was for many years one of the landmarks of Jamaica. After 50 years of active business life Mr. Peck disposed of his pharmacy to David L. Van Nostrand and Charles E. Twombly, who in turn sold out to Lowe Brothers, as stated.

The Bronx Pharmaceutical Association will hold its annual ball on February 22. An interesting feature of the event will be a journal of some 60 odd pages issued by the association. The affair will take place in Morrisania Hall, 170th street and Third avenue. Keating's band has been engaged to furnish the music. The Entertainment Committee, which consists of A. Allison, chairman; Albert Bischoff and Louis Weiner, is sparing no effort to make the association's first ball a decided success.

At the recent annual meeting of the New York Consolidated Drug Company the following officers were elected: President, R. C. Werner, Brooklyn; vice-president, George Leinecker, New York; secretary, George Kleinan, New York; treasurer and manager, Felix Hirseman, New York; directors, W. C. Alpers, S. V. B. Swann, George Leinecker, Felix Hirseman and George Kleinan, New York; R. C. Werner and August Diehl, Brooklyn. Mr. Hirseman's salary as manager was increased from $2,000 to $2,500 a year.

The State Board of Pharmacy are hot on the trail of manufacturers who, it is claimed, are violating the New York State Pharmacy law in regard to the labeling of poisons. Sales have been discovered of ¼-grain morphine tablets bearing no poison label, and other cases just as serious have been found. The board is about to investigate several tablets, as well as some of the preparations now on the market, which should be up to the U. S. P. standard, but which, it has been discovered, are below that standard. Some of these have already been analyzed and have been found to be below the required strength.

Among the out of town visitors to the local drug trade recently, many of whom registered at the Drug and Chemical Club, were: G. P. Finnigan, Geneva, N. Y.; Warren L. Bradt, secretary of the New York State Board of Pharmacy, Albany; J. L. Lemberger, president of the American Pharmaceutical Association, Lebanon, Pa.; R. E. Burdick, Cleveland; F. C. Schapper, Chicago; E. C. and J. R. True, Auburn, Maine; A. C. Sturtevant, Boston; D. E. and F. M. Breinig, New Milford, Conn.; A. W. Clarke, Utica, N. Y.; G. W. Lukens, Philadelphia; J. T. Monfort, Cincinnati; J. Farnell, Glasgow, Scotland; H. G. Thresher and W. A. Copeland, Providence, R. I.; G. K. Webster, North Attleboro, Mass.; H. C. Smith, Buffalo; H. D. Martin, St. Louis; C. J. Robb, Toledo, Ohio; R. A. Parke, Cleveland; D. L. Ross, Chicago; J. H. McGuinness, Waterbury, Conn., and William Beal, Wilmington, Del.

Hundredth Anniversary of Colgate & Co.

The firm of Colgate & Co. celebrated the hundredth anniversary of the founding of the concern on January 20 by a banquet and entertainment in the Grand Central Palace, which was attended by upward of 1,000 members of the factory and office staff. Austin Colgate presided, and the seat of honor was occupied by Richard M. Colgate, senior member of the firm. Other members of the firm present were Gilbert Colgate, Sidney M. Colgate and Russell Colgate. Several foreign representatives attended, G. H. Weyand being there from the Argentine Republic, W. A. Chipman, from Australia; W. G. M. Sheppard, from Canada, and E. Bourdois, from France. The reminiscences of some of the older employees, represented respectively by Ira T. Fortmeyer and Patrick Madden, who have been with the concern fifty years, were most interesting. Some interesting souvenirs of the firm were exhibited, included among them being the mortar in which was mixed the first cake of modern toilet soap. Messrs. Fortmeyer and Madden were presented with gifts of $250 each, being $5 for each year of service, and a pro-rata amount was distributed among the other employees. The foundation of the firm of Colgate & Co. dates from 1806, when the office and residence of William Colgate were at 6 Dutch street.

WESTERN NEW YORK.

Drugs Pretty Active—Price Schedule Maintained—Physicians to Manufacture Pharmaceuticals—The Prerequisite.

(*From our Regular Correspondent.*)

Buffalo, February 7.—Most of the Buffalo retailers agree that business in the city drug stores has not gone to pieces in the way it has in the dry goods and clothing establishments. Soda water has never sold so well in winter before, for January was several degrees warmer on the average than it has been before in the history of the weather bureau. There has been no particular ailment to send people after drugs, but there is money to spend, and the idea that much that is sold by a druggist is in the nature of a luxury, is gaining ground. It would go much further if city druggists would only copy the theater people and put their windows full of the display part of their goods. Buffalo is not enterprising in that respect, especially in the drug trade.

ADVERTISING SCHEDULE PRICES.

There is no complaint of price cutting. There is evidence of some activity in the advertising of specialties by certain downtown stores, always at very low prices, but it is found that the prices named are always schedule and nothing else. It seems to have been found that there is no need of cutting the price, just to set off an advertisement. The display can be made just as well without.

DOCTORS FORM CO-OPERATIVE COMPANY.

An evidence of the tendency of things pharmaceutical is noted in the report that F. W. Beck, for 16 years with Stoddart Brothers, and a licensed pharmacist, of course, has taken a position with the new Alpha Chemical Company, of Buffalo. This is said to be a combination of doctors, or their representatives, for the manufacture of specialties needed in their practice, being merely another step in the general move to hang up the patent medicine man. The city is full of such companies, from the Empire State Drug Company down, all manufacturing goods, not to throw on the open market so much as to supply a certain trade that the company can control, in which case the business done can be reckoned up almost exactly before starting in.

SUICIDES USE CARBOLIC ACID.

There is a growing uneasiness on the part of Buffalo druggists—which appears to be shared elsewhere—over the many suicides by means of carbolic acid. Buffalo has had over a dozen such cases in a month, and steps are to be taken at once to see what can be done about it. There is no city ordinance on the subject, but some other cities have them, and an effort will be made, probably through the retail association, to correct the evil.

THE ADULTERATED FOODS.

Dr. Herbert M. Hill, city chemist of Buffalo, who is also at the head of the chemistry departments of the colleges of Pharmacy and Medicine of the University of Buffalo, is at work on adulterated foods. He has already brought out a test for foreign sweets in maple sugar, which seems to be all that is desired. He works on the principle that the difference between maple, cane and beet sugar lies all in the different mineral constituents, which the maple tree, the sugar cane and the sugar beet take up from the soil in their sap. It is noted that the authorities are now on the right road in the pure food movement. They do not say what an article shall contain, but that the label shall tell the truth as to what it does contain. Then let people eat glucose for sugar and cotton seed oil for lard, and oleomargarine for butter if they want to.

THE WORKING OF THE PREREQUISITE LAW.

Secretary Reimann, of the western branch of the State Board of Pharmacy, has been asked, oddly enough, very often lately what he thinks of the Prerequisite Pharmacy law. As he is the father of the law it is hardly to be expected that he will condemn it, but it may be that he is expected to be acquainted with the working of the law for a year, so that he can give additional reasons for supporting it. He declares that it has been quite as successful as he expected. The opposition to it has apparently disappeared, for all possible chance was given to those who might wish to come in under the old law, by extra examinations and second examinations when the first was not successful. There will be plenty of young men willing to go through a pharmacy college for their licenses to fill all the vacant places in the drug stores, which will very materially raise the standard of excellence.

THE BUFFALO DRUG MERCHANTS' EXCHANGE

has been incorporated under the same name, with $30,000 capital stock. The move has been made on account of the increase of business, and the demand for a larger membership. There are 100 members now, nearly all Buffalo druggists, and no sales are made to non-members. Dr. W. G. Gregory has been the president for several years.

NEW ENGLAND.

Officers for the B. A. R. D.—The Mayor Dines with the Druggists—Action on Patent Medicines to Be Delayed—A Hearing on February 27—Charges Against Metcalf & Co.—A Human Bar.

(*From our Regular Correspondent.*)

Boston, February 7.—The annual meeting of the Boston Druggists' Association was held at Young's Hotel on the evening of January 23. Reports were made by the secretary and treasurer; that of the latter showing a balance on hand of over $3,300. Harry C. Wiggins, of the Eastern Drug Company, was elected to membership. The election of officers resulted as follows: President, William W. Bartlet; treasurer, Geo. H. Ingraham; secretary, James O. Jordan. Executive Committee, Cornelius P. Flynn, chairman; Fred A. Hubbard, Joel S. Orne, Geo. L. Roskell, William D. Wheeler, Geo. W. Cobb, and James F. Finneran. Membership Committee, Amos K. Tilden, chairman; Henry Canning, John G. Godding, Frank A. Davidson, and William F. Sawyer.

THE ANNUAL DINNER.

At the annual dinner which followed President Flynn presided. There was a large attendance and he had for guests Hon. John F. Fitzgerald, Mayor of Boston, and Hon. Jeremiah J. McCarthy, Surveyor of the Port. Mr. McCarthy spoke first, being followed by Mayor Fitzgerald, who aroused his hearers to enthusiasm and was the recipient of a vote of thanks. Other speakers were President-elect W. W. Bartlet, W. F. Sawyer, Secretary of the Board of Pharmacy, Hon. Wm. J. Bullock and Hon. Gorham D. Gilman. All of the speakers spoke adversely of the screen law as now interpreted and Mr. Sawyer gave an account of the recent doings of the pharmacy board. Retiring President Flynn covered himself with glory in this final effort. Music was supplied by Astrella Brothers' orchestra.

SUBJECTS DISCUSSED.

A conference of druggists was held in this city February 1, and important action taken in legislative matters. As an outcome there will be a united effort of the different associations in this State on trade matters. Among the subjects discussed was the attempt aimed at regulating the percentage of alcohol in patent medicines. The Board of Pharmacy's recommendation that it be given charge of the inspection of drugs was warmly endorsed and it is stated that it will have the support of every druggist in the State. It was the sentiment of those present that the U. S. P., which the State Board of Health now uses as a standard, is so technical that it is impossible to keep some drugs up to its standards, and that the deviations are too insignificant to endanger public health. Another matter discussed was the present application of the screen law, which was bitterly denounced. Concerning the patent medicine bill it was recommended that no action be taken by the legislature until the Government had completed its analysis of patent medicines and had announced which were to be handled as alcoholic beverages.

A HEARING ON ALCOHOLIC PROPRIETARIES AND NARCOTICS.

W. W. Bartlet, Ph. G., will have charge of bills and hearings. One will be held on February 27, on the sale of cocaine and regulation of percentage of alcohol.

Some of those present at this meeting were: President W. W. Bartlett and Charles F. Cutler, of the Boston Druggists' Association; President E. H. La Pierre, Charles H. Davis, Mr. Finneran and H. Canning, of the Boston Association of Retail Druggists; Chairman Amos K. Tilden, Senator William J. Bullock and Charles Carter, of Lowell, of the committee on legislation of the State Pharmaceutical Association, and C. H. Packard, of the National Association of Retail Druggists.

METCALF & CO. CHARGED WITH SALE OF ADULTERATED DRUGS.

An indictment was returned at the last sitting of the grand jury charging the T. Metcalf Company with having sold adulterated olive oil, brandy and extract of vanilla. The evidence was furnished by the agents of the State Board of Health. A plea of not guilty has been entered by defendants' counsel. The U. S. P. standards were used with the olive oil and brandy and the label upon the vanilla mixture did not comply strictly with the law.

ILLEGAL LIQUOR SALES IN DRUG STORES.

Much space has recently been given in the public press to specific instances of the connection of druggists with the liquor traffic. The store of John F. Hurley, twice mayor of Salem, was raided on two occasions. On the last visit a human bar was unearthed, a man in the rear room having 10 half-pint bottles around his waist. This man was arrested. On Sunday, January 21, three New Bedford stores were visited. At the Michand Company's store none of the ardent was found, but at McMurray's and the store of Theophile Lebeau liquor was seized and arrests made. Alleyn E. Howe and his clerk, Charles Hines, Stoughton, were recently before the court charged with violating the liquor law. A Rockport druggist has just paid a fine for the illegal sale of liquor.

ALUMNI DANCE.

A reception and dance was held by the A. A. M. C. P. at Huntington Hall on the evening of February 5. President Thompson was in charge of the arrangements with the able assistance of Vice-President Tripp and Treasurer Acheson. The dancing was continued until midnight, the Salem Cadet orchestra furnishing the music. The matrons were: Mrs. P. B. Thompson, Mrs. A. H. Tripp, Mrs. F. S. Schmidt, Mrs. E. H. LaPierre, Mrs. W. R. Acheson.

TALKED ABOUT.

The store of Jaynes & Company, South and Summer streets, was the scene of a recent fire. The blaze was soon under control and the main damage was by water.

PENNSYLVANIA.

Price Schedule Will Be Adhered To—Drug Trust Rumors—Renewed Interest in the Local Association—Officers of the Drug Exchange.

(From our Regular Correspondent.)

Philadelphia, February 7.—On January 19 a special meeting of the Philadelphia Association of Retail Druggists was held at the College of Pharmacy. Rumors that an effort would be made to do away with the schedule of price on proprietary articles and give every member the privilege of affixing his own price, served to bring out a large attendance. It was expected that the association would withdraw its schedule of prices on proprietary articles and permit the members of the association to cut prices at will. However, after a full discussion, the following resolution was adopted:

Whereas, The establishing and maintaining of a minimum selling retail price on proprietary articles being of essential benefit to the public and to the interests of the retail druggists; be it

Resolved, That the Philadelphia Association of Retail Druggists retains its schedule as a guide to the minimum seling price of proprietary articles, and requests its members not to violate the same.

A THREE HOURS' DEBATE.

There are many druggists in this city that are advocating the meeting of the cutters on their own ground and the selling of proprietary articles at prices even lower than are now asked, while others representing the more conservative element have advocated adherence to the minimum price agreed to by the Retail Druggists' Association. While the resolution was passed unanimously, it required nearly three hours before a vote was taken. Considerable discussion was indulged in, and it was not until T. H. Potts, ex-president of the association, announced that the status of the body was exactly the same as it was before the Loder decision, that the air was sufficiently cleared to warrant action being taken on the resolution. The passing of the resolution means, that, while the druggist can charge whatever he may please for proprietary articles, he is expected not to go below the minimum price agreed upon by the association.

THE REGULAR MONTHLY MEETING

of the Philadelphia Retail Drug Association, which was held on February 2, was largely attended and the discussions were entered into with considerable spirit. Since the Loder verdict it seems as if the members are rallying around the officials and are taking a more active part in the affairs of the association. For the time being there is talk of the members dropping out, and every effort is now being made to secure new ones. At this meeting an additonal one was elected, and it is understood that at the next there will be several more. The association now numbers over 450, which, considering the set-back it has had owing to the Loder fight, is considered a very good showing.

Nearly all the prominent druggists in the city are members, and the few who are not are generally working in harmony with the association. Owing to the prices of the St. Louis goods not being maintained, it has caused some hardship among the loyal members of the association who will not violate their pledges, so while they are maintaining rates they are not only losing business but are not able to compete with the druggists who are not bound by any promises. At the meeting this question was freely discussed, and an effort is now being made by the St. Louis manufacturers, the Pain Medicine Co., to remedy the evil by having all houses maintain their prices. This is all that can be done at the present time. The Loder suit has had some depressing effect and has caused many of the druggists to think that they were "up against it," but it is the opinion of the officers of the association that this will blow over in the course of time.

THE RUMORS OF A TRUST IN RETAIL STORES.

The retail drug trade is considerably exercised over the report that the same element that controls the United Cigar Stores Company will open at least one hundred stores in this city. There are rumors galore about this new venture. A drug company has been chartered in New Jersey with a capital of $10,000,000, and it is said that the corporation proposes to control 100 drug stores each in Philadelphia, New York and Chicago. In connection with the rumors of breaking into the drug business it is said that an offer has been made to George B. Evans & Co., of this city, for the purchase of his stores. The price being set for the good will alone at $500,000. This offer, it is reported, has been refused. The new trust has not given up hope of securing these stores, and it is claimed that negotiations are still pending. It is said that Harvey K. Fenner, who has conducted the drug store at Broad street and Columbia avenue for many years, has been served with notice that at the expiration of his lease it will not be renewed. There are two rumors in connection with this notice, one is that the United Gas Improvement Company, which owns the building, desires it for its own use, and the other report is that the store has been leased to the same parties that are connected with the United Cigar Stores Company, for a drug store.

NOT ROOM FOR A HUNDRED NEW STORES.

All these reports are causing worriment to the retail drug trade. While it is believed that the average druggist can hold his own trade and that the backers of the new drug combine will find it difficult to run a line of drug stores profitably, it is thought that any reduction in price will be an incentive to the purchaser to patronize the new store. However, it will be very difficult for 100 new drug stores to exist in this city. Many that are now in operation are not paying, and if a cut-throat business were indulged in, a number would be forced to the wall. The wholesale dealers do not apprehend any difficulty and they are of the opinion that the new company is really in the nature of a threat to compel the druggists to handle the combine's cigars.

A BIRTHDAY CELEBRATION.

M. N. Kline, on February 6, celebrated the anniversary of his birth. Mr. Kline is in a quandary. He does not know whether to say he is 60 years of age or 59 years old. He says he was born in 1846, and he was not a year old until the following year. This would make him 59 years old. He and Harry B. French had quite an argument on the matter. Mr. Kline would like to know just how old he is. He would be pleased to hear from his many friends. The question is whether a man born in 1846 is 59 or 60 years of age.

OFFICERS OF THE DRUG EXCHANGE.

At the annual election of the Philadelphia Drug Exchange, the following officers were elected: President, Charles E. Hires; vice-president, Richard V. Mattison, M.D.; secretary, William Gullagher; treasurer, Edward H. Hance. Directors, Edward J. Lavino, Adolph W. Miller, M.D.; Mahlon N. Kline, Clayton F. Shoemaker, John Fergusson, Walter B. Smith, A. Robinson McIlvaine and Adam Pfromm.

PHILADELPHIA NEWS ITEMS.

The regular monthly meeting of the Board of Trustees, of the Philadelphia College of Pharmacy, was held on February 6. It was said that nothing but routine business was transacted.

C. J. Peacock, who formerly conducted the drug store at 2012 South Tenth street, will open a new store at Germantown and Erie avenues.

C. A. Eckles has purchased the private residence at the south-west corner of Broad street and Erie avenue, which he will convert into a drug store.

Mr. Franciscus, who recently closed his drug store on Lancaster avenue, will open a new store at the north-east corner of Broad and Walnut streets. This is where the famous "yellow mansion" stood for so many years.

Mahlon N. Kline, of the firm of Smith, Kline & French Company, has been elected president of the Trades' League, of this city. Mr. Kline takes considerable interest in anything pertaining to the welfare of this city. He is one of the Mayor's advisors, and, besides, is a leader in all movements which are of advantage to the business men of Philadelphia.

The affairs of the College House, of the Philadelphia College of Pharmacy, are now in a settled condition and about 50 of the students have returned. To make it pleasant for the boarders a series of Saturday evening talks are to be held. Arrangements are being made with prominent men to address the boys on that night.

THE WEST.

To Increase Druggists' Liquor Licenses—A Warning to Wholesalers Regarding the D. C. S. N. Plan—To Prevent Over Crowding A Peace Conference.

(From our Regular Correspondent.)

Chicago, February 7.—A step forward in the campaign for higher saloon licenses was taken at the meeting of the City Council last evening. This action is of especial interest to druggists because a similar campaign to increase the license fee of drug stores has been started. The original demand for a $1,000 saloon license was started because of the necessity for better police protection. In order to increase the city's income so that this could be done the higher license plan was evolved. In order to escape carrying the entire burden the saloon men demanded that money be raised by increasing the tax on drug stores. This movement is already well under way. At present the druggists pay $25 for a government license and $5 for police inspection of the liquor register. It is proposed to tax them $250 for the benefit of the city.

FEAR FOR THE RESULTS.

It is recalled that the C. R. D. A. came into existence 25 years ago because of a similar situation. It is feared that if the $250 license plan is adopted that it will undo much of the work accomplished during this time, because many druggists are likely, in a spirit of retaliation, to begin illicit sales of drinks.

VIOLATING THE D. C. S. N. PLAN.

At the annual meeting of the C. R. D. A. attention was called to the fact that some of the Chicago wholesalers are violating the direct contract serial numbering plan. The following resolution was adopted:

"*Resolved*, That the attitude of some of the wholesale druggists of Chicago toward the direct contract serial numbering plan is discreditable in the highest degree to these jobbers, because it seems to prove beyond question that their professions of devotion to the welfare of their retail customers are not sincere;

"*Resolved*, That the secretary of this association is instructed to send to *N. A. R. D. Notes* for publication all instances coming under his observation where wholesale drug houses or their representatives speak disparagingly of the direct contract serial numbering plan, or those proprietors who have adopted the plan, so that the retail druggists of Chicago may know beyond a doubt who it is that is interfering with the success of the plan and preventing its adoption by other proprietors."

Since then Secretary Yeomans has issued an open letter in which he says information has reached him that two of the five wholesale drug houses in Chicago are "declining to sign the D. C. S. N. wholesale contracts that are presented to them and are in every possible way doing what they can to discourage the adoption of the plan." Mr. Yeomans offers them one more chance and threatens them with publicity in case the matter is carried further.

Active efforts are being made to prevent the opening of new stores in localities that are already crowded, because of the peril that a druggist runs of losing all of the work expended during many years in building up a trade. A campaign has been begun, for the purpose of finding out what wholesalers will aid the retailers in their efforts to prevent over crowding.

NUTRIOLA COMPANY PRESIDENT SENTENCED TO PENITENTIARY.

Judge Bethea of the United States District Court sentenced Edward F. Hanson, president of the Nutriola Company, to one year in the penitentiary and fined him $5,000 yesterday for sending objectionable literature advertising his concern through the United States mails. The case will be appealed.

Hanson formerly was mayor of a small town in northern Maine. He came to Chicago and organized the Nutriola Company. Complaints reached the Post Office Department that the company's advertising matter was objectionable and that Hanson had made misrepresentations in disposing of stock in his company.

CORNELIUS P. VAN SCHAICK.

Inspector Ketcham recently secured the issuance of an order prohibiting mail from being delivered to the Nutriola Company.

HE CARRIED HIS OWN FIRE ESCAPE.

James I. Gulick, Western representative of Ed. Pinaud & Co., recently achieved fame by escaping from the fifth floor of a burning hotel in Minneapolis by means of a simple rope fire escape which he always carried with him for the past five years. Mr. Gulick was in very close quarters and believes that he would have undoubtedly lost his life but for the fact that he had this fire escape in his possession.

THE CHICAGO OFFICE OF THE COCA COLA COMPANY LEADS.

E. C. Reese, manager of the Chicago office of the Coca Cola Company, is receiving the congratulations of the other branches of the company, as he increased his business 61 per cent. in 1905, beating the record even of the parent house in Atlanta. The Chicago branch manufactured last year 293,625 gallons of Coca Cola, the total output of the company for the year being 1,548,888 gallons, an increase of 37 per cent. over the amount manufactured in 1904.

A PEACE CONFERENCE.

Cornelius P. Van Schaack held what he facetiously termed a "peace conference" on Saturday evening, January 27, which was attended by 20 leading members of the drug trade. Of what happened the half will never be told, for the affair was conducted literally sub rosa, the roses in this case being an enormous bunch of American beauties which hung above the entrance to the dining room. Appropriate music was furnished by a quartette of Afro-Americans. The dinner cards were floral names divided in half, each half being printed on a separate card thus: Lily—of the valley. Regrets were received from L. A. Becker, who was in New York, and from Frank L. E. Gauss, who was in Wheeling, W. Va. Such meagre details of the affair as have leaked out in spite of the seal of the roses indicate that the occasion was one unique in its enjoyability.

NOTES.

The Christenson pharmacy at 800 West North avenue has been purchased by W. Amundsen.

E. R. Wolfner has sold his store at 351 South Clark street to J. X. Rivard, Loomis and Harrison streets.

The Social Drug Club's annual ball and banquet is to take place on the evening of Washington's Birthday.

More efforts made by the Ideal Drug Company to buy local drug stores have proved failures, and there are some who believe the entire plan will finally fall through.

It is said that representatives of the Chicago Telephone Company have offered 'phones at a straight rate of $85 a year if the Illinois Manufacturers' Association will let up on the fight to have the present yearly toll reduced.

Efforts at "scalping" among real estate agents have caused indignation among Chicago druggists. One druggist lost a long established stand because he was out bid by representatives of a cigar combine. He was told that he could oust some other druggists from their stands if he would only raise their offers on rentals.

All of the retiring officers were re-elected at the annual meeting of the United States Pharmacal Company. The annual report showed a satisfactory condition and indicated the probability of future development.

W. C. Hayhurst has been appointed manager of the St. Louis branch of Parke, Davis & Co., taking effect February 1, to succeed C. F. Allen. Mr. Hayhurst has been connected with Parke, Davis & Co. for the past ten years, having been associated with their Chicago branch for seven years under J. E. Bartlett, and was subsequently transferred as assistant manager to the New Orleans branch for one year, and has had charge of the city department of the St. Louis branch for the past two years.

The Illinois Board.

At the meeting of the Illinois State Board of Pharmacy, in Springfield, on January 16 and 17, 9 of the 19 applicants for registered pharmacist and 7 out of a class of 12 candidates for assistant pharmacist passed successful examinations. Their names follow:

Registered Pharmacists.—Oskar Adler, Chicago; Francis E. Bird, Quincy; E. W. Bothe, Chicago; W. I. Burns, Harvel; Earl W. Cutler, Abingdon; C. A. Demes, Chicago; Herman H. Diesner, Chicago; Wm. V. Dufner, Peoria, and Wm. Shaw, Chicago.

Assistant Pharmacists.—Jennie M. Duncan, Ottawa; Howard W. Duncan, Mattoon; Roy C. Fritts, Metropolis; John O. Gottrick, jr., Knoxville; R. E. Hattan, Galesburg; James O. Kelley, McLeansboro, and Robert McEvoy, Mound City.

The board will hold a meeting in Chicago at the Hampden Building, corner Thirty-ninth street and Langley avenue, on Tuesday, February 20, for the examination of applicants who have not heretofore passed the preliminary test required by the board. An examination will be held the following day for applicants who have already passed the preliminary test. The new Pharmacopœia will be used hereafter in all examinations.

Mr. Horton Retires from the Firm of Faxon, Horton & Gallagher.

The partnership heretofore existing between Frank A. Faxon, James C. Horton and John A. Gallagher, doing business under the firm name of Faxon, Horton & Gallagher, wholesale druggists, at the northwest corner of Eighth street and Broadway, Kansas City, Mo., has been dissolved by mutual consent, James C. Horton retiring. The business will be continued by Frank A. Faxon and John A. Gallagher, under the firm name of Faxon & Gallagher, and they have assumed all liabilities of the firm of Faxon, Horton & Gallagher, and all accounts, notes and assets of every name and nature, due and to become due, to the firm of Faxon, Horton & Gallagher, are to be paid to their successors, Faxon & Gallagher.

James C. Horton has issued the following statement in connection with the announcement of his retirement: "Having sold my interest in the business of Faxon, Horton & Gallagher to my partners, Messrs. Faxon and Gallagher, I beg to add to the formal notice of the dissolution of our partnership my grateful appreciation of the many favors received from our friends in the trade who have given us their loyal support, and if, in retiring from the business, a personal allusion will be pardoned, I can hardly find words to express the high regard in which I shall always hold my friends, Mr. Frank A. Faxon and Mr. John A. Gallagher, with whom I have been so long and so pleasantly associated, each year only increasing my confidence and my esteem."

Opportunities *for* Export Trade

(Written for the American Druggist.)

TRADE CONDITIONS IN ECUADOR.

By John Maxwell Draper.

Few foreign markets present such an interesting and profitable field for the American exporter as does the Republic of Ecuador. We possess an advantage over European exporters in being so much nearer, and with good shipping facilities we are able to land our goods in Guayaquil sometimes in two months' less time than is required to land shipments from Europe. This brings to our markets many orders and increases the good business relations between buyer and seller.

INADEQUATE TRANSPORTATION FACILITIES ACROSS THE ISTHMUS.

Ecuador bought more goods in the past year from the United States than from any other country, but complains most bitterly of the abominable service rendered by the Panama Railroad and steamship Company during the last eight months. Druggists of this republic not only have to pay a higher freight rate from New York to Guayaquil than from New York to Lima, Peru, or even to Valparaiso, Chile, though fully two weeks nearer our country, but in addition must endure the hardships of having their orders delayed in Colon sometimes three and four months, through the inadequate service rendered by the Panama Railroad, where a veritable mountain of freight awaits forwarding to Panama for transshipment to Ecuador, Peru and Chile.

View of City of Guayaquil and River Guayaquil, Principal Port of Entry for Ecuador

THE UNITED STATES A FAVORITE MARKET.

In the report of the Chamber of Commerce of Guayaquil, for the year ending April, 1905, we find that the total of imports of drugs and medicines amount to about $157,000 gold; and perfumes, toilet powders, etc., $46,000 gold. Of the markets which supply these totals, France stands at the head, with the United States second; then follow Germany, England, Italy and Spain.

Of the total imports of Ecuador during the year, which amounted to some $7,000,000 gold, at least $2,400,000 came from the United States; and of the total imports entering the republic, almost nine-tenths enter through the port of Guayaquil. The next port along the coast of importance for its imports is Manta, followed by Bahia, Esmeraldas and Puerto Bolivar.

IMPORTANT NEW TARIFF REGULATION.

The new tariff which went into effect on the first of January, 1906, should be well noted by all foreign houses and exporters, for the changes are of great importance. Heretofore, marking the gross weight in kilos on each case served the purpose of the customs authorities, as duties were levied on the gross weight; but in the new tariff both the gross and the net weight must be marked, as under the new tariff they now levy duty on the net weight of many articles.

THE REGULATION OF FORMULAS OF PATENT MEDICINE.

Next of interest is the new law stating that all medicines which do not bear upon the label of the bottle the formula, must pay a duty amounting to about $1 gold per kilo (2 1-5 lbs.). This will make the cost of some proprietary remedies almost prohibitive. This tax can be avoided, however, where the formula is known, or where it is registered in Quito. The general opinion is that the law will be strictly observed for a while, but that later on will be allowed to fall into disuse and gradually die. While no similar law has been really passed in the country before, many others of the sort have been broached, but never put into effect. Among the special changes we notice that all medicines whose formula is known or registered shall pay a duty of about 50 cents gold per kilo, *net weight*. Other special duties follow:

Emulsion of codliver oil, reduced to about	10 cents per kilo.
Medicinal wines, such as wine of codliver oil, etc	12 cents per kilo.
Dentifrices in paste, powder or liquid	30 cents per kilo.
Perfumed soaps	30 cents per kilo, net weight.
Extracts of perfumes and perfumery in general	60 cents per kilo.
Hypodermic syringes	40 cents, net weight.

Guayaquil, with its 60,000 inhabitants, supports about 15 drug stores, and of these about five are of importance to the exporter.

THE LEADING FIRMS OF GUAYAQUIL.

During the past year the most notable change among these firms has been the purchase of the Botica del Comercio, by O.

R. G. Blom, who was associated with Sr. Holger Glaesel in the Drogueria Alemana for the past six years. The Botica and Drogueria Alemana is now conducted under the sole name of Sr. Holger Glaesel. Mr. Glaesel is well known among New

Botica y Drogueria Alemana, Guayaquil, Ecuador, Sr. Holger Glaesel, Proprietor.

York houses and confines his purchases there to two or three of the larger firms. At present the bulk of his purchases is made in Europe, France and England standing ahead of the United States. Next year he contemplates enlarging his store

Sr. O. R. G. Blom, Owner of the Botica del Comercio, Guayaquil; a Very Enterprising German Pharmacist.

to double its present size, and the installation of a handsome soda fountain of American make will be among the improvements which he will make.

With the Botica del Comercio under its new management, its owner, O. R. G. Blom, has given to Guayaquil one of the most up-to-date pharmacies to be met with along the coast, and through his progressiveness it has become one of the leading stores of Ecuador. Mr. Blom is now forty years of age and is

Interior View of the Botica del Comercio, Guayaquil, Ecuador, O. R. G. Blom, Proprietor.

a graduate of the University of Copenhagen (1885). He went to Ecuador in 1893 and took the examinations in Quito in 1895 and was named Professor in Chemistry by the University of Quito. Most of his purchases are made in the United States, and he is quite American in his methods of doing business.

A WHOLESALE BUSINESS.

Sres. J. C. Muñoz & Cia., of the Botica Ecuatoriana, enter largely into the wholesale business with the interior, and their name is very well known there. They buy in large quantities and supply the smaller dealers. In their retail department they were the first to instal an American soda fountain. This is but one instance of their modern methods of doing business.

Drogueria Ecuatoriana, Guayaquil, Ecuador; Sres. J. C. Muñoz & Co., Proprietors.

Few firms enjoy the reputation for business integrity which this house has, and it is very highly recommended.

Proceeding two squares further along the Malecon we find the Botica La Marina of Sres. Pazmiño y Garcia. Their large business differs materially from that of almost all the other drug stores in the city. They have no prescription trade, nor do they want it, but with their location directly in the Market they have built up a general drug business that many American firms would be proud to have. Their purchases in the United States are confined mostly to one large firm in New York City.

Don Cárlos López Lascano conducts the Droguería of his name which has been established since 1880 and which has a large retail and wholesale drug trade. Closely identified with the progress and study of pharmacy, he has been for the past twenty-five years a professor in the faculty of medicine of the University of Guayaquil. Of his purchases the United States and France receive the major part.

Señor Flores Ontaneda is also closely identified with the professional side of pharmacy and has a very high standing as a pharmacist.

The Botica de la Merced of Sr. Tarquinio J. Viteri, is among the smaller stores of the city, but Sr. Viteri acts as agent for the forwarding of merchandise, etc., to the firm of Viteri & Cornejo, of Quito. Sr. Viteri, of this latter firm, is his brother.

The Botica Rocafuerte of Drs. Manrique y Chiriboga is more of a prescription store for the doctors than a drug store in general.

The Botica del Pueblo, Botica Central, Botica del Globo and Botica del Progreso, are among the other drug stores found in Guayaquil.

COMMERCIAL CONDITIONS IN THE INTERIOR OF ECUADOR.

This republic, whose coast line extends along the west coast of South America from latitude 2 north to latitude 4 south, is bounded on the north by Colombia, on the south by Peru and on the west by Brazil. Extending inland from the Pacific Ocean one may travel 700 miles before reaching the boundary of Brazil. In order to see the interior of this republic, with its two million inhabitants, I left Guayaquil one Friday morning at six o'clock. After being carried across and up the River Guayaquil some three miles I arrived at Duran and, taking a narrow gauge railroad, began my journey inland. For five hours the road ran through forests of the most beautiful tropical verdure, with palms of every variety, tall imperial bamboo trees, from which are constructed all the houses in Guayaquil, and creeping vines so thickly entwined as to make it impossible even to see very far among the trees. These scenes followed one another until nearly eleven o'clock, when the road began to climb the Andes, and soon the passengers were able to look down upon this sea of greenness, much more beautiful than one can describe. Following the road, we stopped about two o'clock in the afternoon at a tiny station called Alausi, and five minutes later were told that because of a large washout ahead we must wait here until the following day. There we spent among the clouds one of the most bitter, cold nights one could imagine, and this after leaving a tropical city early that morning. The next afternoon we resumed our journey and arrived at Riobamba in the evening. We were obliged to wait here three days for the next stage running to my destination, Quito.

Riobamba has about 35,000 inhabitants, but, strange to say, has no bank. The drug stores are as follows: Botica Inglesa, Botica de la Union, Botica del Comercio and Botica del Sr. Mariano Prado Orrego.

THE CITY OF QUITO.

Quito lies 10,000 feet above Guayaquil, and the climate is very bracing. I left Riobamba by stage for Quito, and after two days of hard travel arrived at the capital of the republic.

Quito has about 80,000 inhabitants and until three years ago had but three drug stores, but the good trade attracted others, and to-day there are eight stores to supply the trade. This is, of course, the cause of much complaint among the older stores, but with only eight pharmacies to this population they are not overdoing matters.

With the completion of the railroad from Guayaquil to Quito, which, it is expected, will be finished next year, Quito will enter into the foreign commercial world as a much larger buyer than ever. Heretofore her purchases were largely made in Guayaquil, and it required some three weeks or perhaps a month to bring freight from the coast to Quito. Here is established the celebrated University of Quito, which, with its schools of medicine, pharmacy, law, etc., gives to the city, aside from its great historical interests, a name to be envied by many other countries.

The city lies almost on the line of the equator, but its great altitude of 10,000 feet above the sea gives it one of the most delightful climates to be found in the world. Consumptive patients from the coast cities go there to be cured, and from there those suffering from rheumatism go to Guayaquil to be relieved by the warmer climate.

The most notable of the drug stores of Quito is that of Don Antonio Mortensen, namely, the Botica Alemana, which, with its branch store, does by far the largest share of the drug business in and around Quito. Sr. Mortensen, who is also a graduate of Copenhagen, came to Quito in the early nineties and seven years later became the owner of his present business, which has gone on increasing year by year under his care. He is a professor in the University of Quito. Aside from the drug business he is interested in many other lines. The new automobile stage route from Quito to Riobamba is his latest enterprise. His business record is rated very high.

Sr. Antonio Mortensen, Proprietor of the Botica Alemana, Quito, Ecuador.

The death of Sr. M. Barriga has left the widow, Sra. Clothilde de Barriga, as present owner of the Botica Nacional, and the store is being conducted in the same careful manner as heretofore.

The Botica Inglesa of Sr. Manuel Zaldumbide enjoys a very large trade and is well rated.

Stres. Viteri y Cornejo of the Botica Americana are large buyers of American goods and have a well-established business.

The new Botica del Comercio of Dr. Florentino Uribe, which was opened this fall, has the most modern equipment of any store in Quito, and the staff of clerks is comprised of men of excellent standing. Preparations for the opening of this pharmacy were carefully made for two years and nothing was left undone to make it a modern drug store in every respect. Its owner enjoys an excellent reputation and is very partial to the American market.

The Botica de Guayas of Sres. Molina Buchell and Botica Central of Sr. Alejandro Cartegenova are among the drug stores in Quito.

Botica del Mariano Prado Orrego, Riobamba, Ecuador.

The city possesses but one bank, namely, Sucursal de Banco Comercial y Agricola. Shipments for the interior are made to the customer's agent in Guayaquil, who re-forwards the merchandise to the buyer.

In the city of Latacunga the Botica of Dr. Subia Urvia is the only one worthy of note.

My journey inland took me but half way across the country —to the edge of civilization. Further eastward the Indians are about the only inhabitants. To the south is Cuenca, a city of 35,000 inhabitants, two days' journey by mules, and some distance further, about three days' journey, is Loja. Along the coast northward from Guayaquil are the small cities of Manta, Bahia and Esmeraldas, of which places I shall write later.

The Drug and Chemical Market

The prices quoted in this report are those current in the wholesale market, and higher prices are paid for retail lots
The quality of goods frequently necessitates a wide range of prices.

Condition of Trade.

NEW YORK, February 10.

Business during the interval since our last report has been moderately active, the demand for seasonable articles being especially good, with more inquiry for round lots, though jobbing parcels continue to receive the larger share of attention. Shipments of cinchona bark have been lighter than for some time past, and increased interest has been extended to quinine, with the result that manufacturers have advanced prices of sulphate and the minor salts. The market for bromides is very unsettled and lower prices are quoted on the three principal salts. Opium is characterized by continued absence of important demand, and the market is weak and lifeless, though prices are nominally unchanged. Ipecac has weakened in the interval, as has menthol, and lower prices are quoted on both articles. Powdered white arsenic has developed increased strength owing to scarcity, and quotations are higher. Ergot has weakened and is now quoted at a lower range. The tone of the market continues steady, and, with the exception of quinine, speculation is still an absent feature. The character of the weather has been unfavorable to the sale of purely winter specialties, such as codliver oil, but in other lines a good steady trade has been the rule. The price fluctuations are for the most part unimportant, though we have to record a sharp advance in santonin and another rise in camphor.

HIGHER.	LOWER.
Quinine,	Bromides,
Camphor,	Ergot,
Santonin,	Opium,
Arsenic,	Menthol,
Cacao butter,	Iron and quinine citrates,
Squills,	Golden seal,
Saffron, American,	Sarsaparilla, Mexican,
Peppermint oil,	Ipecac,
Citronella oil,	Juniper berries,
Pink root,	Guarana,
Amyl acetate,	Balm of Gilead buds,
Carbolic acid,	Lycopodium,
Gum mastic,	Canary seed.
Stearic acid.	

Drugs.

Alcohol continues inquired for, and about the usual distribution is passing out into consuming channels, at steady values, or, say, $2.47 to $2.49 for grain, and 70c to 75c for wood.

Balm of Gilead buds are not inquired for, and holders are more free to sell in view of the near approach of new crop; quoted at 35c to 38c.

Balsam copaiba is selling fairly in small lots from jobbers, with values well sustained at 37c to 40c for Para, and 30c to 31c for Central American.

Balsam fir, Canada, continues held and selling at the recently established higher range of $3.00 to $3.10; Oregon is dull, and the market is easy at 65c to 80c.

Balsam Peru is taken rather sparingly by the trade, and holders offer more freely at a decline to 95c to $1.00.

Barks.—Bayberry is held with increased confidence, and little is available at the inside price of 12c. Cascara sagrada is offered with less reserve at the more or less nominal quotation of 5½c to 9c, as to quality and quantity. Cramp is selling in a limited way at 7c to 9c. Cotton root is held less firmly, and the range has dropped to 8½c to 9½c. Sassafras is in good seasonable demand, and the tone of the market is firm at 14c. Wahoo is scarce and values are firmly maintained, with up to 60c paid for small lots. Wild cherry is not meeting with the inquiry usual at this season, but values are maintained at 6c to 9c, as to quality and quantity.

Buchu leaves, short, continue scarce and wanted, and holders are firm in their view at 16½c to 19c, as to quality and quantity.

Cacao butter is in moderately active demand, and the tone of the market is steady at 28c to 29½c, as to brand.

Cantharides remain quiet, but values are steady at 55c to 56c for Chinese and $1.20 to $1.25 for Russian.

Cannabis indica has weakened a trifle in the interval, quotations showing a reduction to 95c to $1.00.

Castor oil is passing out in moderate volume into channels of consumption at previous prices, or, say, 11c to 12c for No. 1 in barrels, and 10¼ to 11¼ for No. 3; cases command an advance of ½c over these prices.

Coca leaves continue in moderately active demand, and values are well sustained at 17c to 19c for Truxillo and at 30c to 32c for Huanuco.

Codliver oil is finding sale in a jobbing way only, and the market is somewhat depressed, though $23.00 to $27.00 is yet quoted as to brand and seller. It is intimated in some quarters that forward shipments of new oil are offered at a figure which would bring the cost here to $21.00.

Cuttlefish bone is finding a good jobbing outlet, with quotations maintained at 16c to 16½c for fine Trieste, 12c to 12½c for French, 70c for jewelers' large, and 40c to 50c for small.

Ergot is quiet and easier in sympathy with conditions at primary points, 38c to 42c being now named as to quantity and quality. Demand is inactive at the moment.

Haarlem oil is in better supply, and the former quotation of $3.25 inside has dropped to $3.00.

Iron and quinine citrates, including the strychnine preparation, have declined in the interval, and the revised quotations are $1.15 to $1.20 for iron and quinine citrate and $1.65 to $1.70 for iron, quinine and strychnine citrate.

Juniper berries have attracted more attention since our last, and a good jobbing demand is experienced at 4c to 4¼c.

Menthol is slow of sale and the tone of the market is easier at $2.20. The recent break in the weather will probably stimulate demand and some holders are governing themselves accordingly, turning down orders at under $3.00.

Opium meets with very little inquiry and the market retains its dull and lifeless appearance, a decline of 2½c since our last having failed to stimulate the demand; broken lots are held at $2.97½ to $3.00, while cases offer at $2.95. Powder is quoted nominally at $3.45 to $3.50.

Quinine has recovered its tone under the influence of light shipments of bark and an active demand for the salt. Foreign manufacturers advanced quotations 1c on the 7th instant, restoring the price to the previous basis of 18c for bulk in 100-oz. lots; domestic makers followed suit, and second hands were quoting at manufacturers' prices at the close, though previous to the advance some heavy sales were made at 17c. The minor preparations of quinine are correspondingly higher, being now quoted as follows: Alkaloid, 30c; acetate, 35c; arsenate, 31c; bimuriate, 29c; do with urea, 40c; bitartrate, 25c; borate, 28c; citrate, 28c; bromide, 25c; muriate, 25c; ferrocyanide, 29c; iodide, 37c; hypophosphite, 30c; lactate, 30c; phosphate, 27c; salicylate, 25c; tannate, 19c; valerianate, 29c; do powdered, 31c.

Santonin is higher, manufacturers having advanced quotations in the interval to $9.50 to $9.70 for crystals, as to quantity, and $9.70 to $9.90 for powdered, the inside figures being for 25 lb. lots. The manufacture of santonin is a Russian monopoly, and the advance is attributed to the disturbed conditions of affairs in Russia.

Tonka beans are dull and featureless; Angostura quoted at 65c to 70c, Surinam at 25c to 30c and Para at 17½c to 20c.

Vanilla beans are quiet, but quotably unchanged at $2.75 to $6.50 for whole Mexican, $1.75 to $2.00 for cuts, $1.00 to $3.00 for Bourbon, and 45c to $1.00 for Tahiti.

Vanillin has been in good demand, with sales within the quoted range of 32c to 40c as to quantity and seller.

Chemicals.

Amyl acetate has advanced in the interval in sympathy with conditions abroad affecting the crude material; quoted $1.50 to $1.60.

Arsenic, white, has developed increased strength since our last owing to scarcity. The spot supply is almost exhausted and dealers decline to shade 12c. A sale of a consignment afloat was made at this figure.

Blue vitriol offers in a limited way from second hands at 5⅝c, but manufacturers' quotations remain at 5.90c.

Brimstone, crude seconds, is without special variation, the tone of the market being steady at the previous range of $22.12½ to $22.62½.

Bromine and bromide salts are irregular and unsettled. Potash is freely offered at 15c, and it is said that a firm offer of about 1c under that figure would be accepted, though we hear of no sale at less than 15c to 16c. Ammonium and sodium bromides are correspondingly lower, 23c being named for the former and 21c for the latter.

Carbolic acid is in less abundant supply and holders of the limited stock in drums have advanced quotations to 14½c to 15½c.

Chlorate potash is maintained firmly at the recently established range of 9½c to 9¾c for crystal and 9¾c to 10c for powdered, in jobbing quantities.

Citric acid is maintained in firmer position and holders are not free sellers at the present range of 38c to 38½c, the tendency of values being upward.

Copperas is in moderately active demand and we hear of sales at 57½c to 62½c for barrels and bags, respectively.

Cream tartar is inactive, but there appears no pressure to sell below 22½c to 22¾c for crystals and 22¾c to 23c for powdered.

Saltpetre is a shade easier and quotations have been marked down to 4¼c to 4⅜c for crude, as to quality.

Stearic acid is firmer and the revised quotations are 9c to 9½ for single press, 10c to 10½c for double and 11½c to 12c for extra quality.

Zinc oxide has developed increased firmness, quotations for G. S. and R. S. having been advanced to 8c, 8½c and 7½c to 7⅞c, respectively; domestic is unchanged at 5c to 5½c.

Zinc sulphate has advanced owing to scarcity, the revised quotation standing at 2½c to 2¾c.

Essential Oils.

Anise is meeting with increased inquiry, but the prices show no change from the previous range of $1.35 to $1.37½.

Bergamot and other Messina essences are maintained firmly, bergamot being quoted at $2.20 to $2.30, lemon at 60c to 75c and sweet orange at $2.00 to $2.25.

Cajuput has been moderately active since our last, though we hear of a sale at a concession on the quoted figures. The inside quotation is now 50c.

Cassia, in common with other Chinese oils, is held with increased firmness, though prices are nominally unchanged at 77½c to 85c for 75-80 per cent.

Citronella has attracted unusual attention since our last, and values have jumped from 34c to 40c and 42c. Great difficulty in obtaining unadulterated oil is reported, and offers of shipments from Ceylon are said to be unobtainable, though rumors are also current of a combination of the principal shippers to maintain prices.

Pennyroyal is firmer, quotations for prime American having been advanced to $1.25 to $1.30.

Peppermint is developing increased strength, and holders show no disposition to shade $3.10 to $3.20 for HGH, while bulk oil is firmly maintained at $2.40 to $2.60.

Gums.

There have been no new developments in the market for mucilaginous and medicinal gums since our last report, save for camphor, which has marked another advance, bringing the current quotation to 94c to 94½c, the higher figure being named for cases. Curacao aloes continues scarce and firm at 6c to 6¼c, and Barbadoes is steady at 14c to 15c. Arabic sorts are in moderate demand, with the sale at 6½c to 11c. Gamboge is held and selling in a jobbing way at 85c to 90c. Asafœtida is dull and neglected, though quotations are nominally unchanged. Mastic is scarce and wanted, and quotations have been advanced to 48c to 50c. Myrrh is held more firmly at 25c.

Roots.

Little of new interest has developed in the market for roots, the demand seldom rising above jobbing proportions for any variety. Ipecac continues on the downward grade and recent sales were at $1.50 to $1.55, the two varieties commanding the same price. Russian musk is a shade lower, being offered at 13c to 14c, while pink is fractionally higher at 60c. Mexican sarsaparilla continues to reflect an easy undertone and quotations have been further reduced to 9½c to 9¾c. Senega is generally quoted at 57c to 58c, but important demand is lacking. Golden Seal is not inquired for to any extent and spot quotations have been reduced to $1.35 to $1.30.

Seeds.

Anise, Italian, is jobbing in a moderately active way at 8½c to 10c.

Canary, Smyrna, is lower in sympathy with corresponding conditions at primary sources, and we hear of sales at 4c to 4¼c.

Caraway is maintained steadily at 66¼c.

Celery is held less firmly, owing to lack of demand, and holders offer more freely at 7½c to 7⅝c.

Fennel, German, has weakened in the interval under the influence of slow demand and somewhat freer offering, and the revised quotations are 9c to 10c.

New Crop Digitalis.

Lehn & Fink, 120 William street, New York, have announced that they received the new crop digitalis direct from Stafford, Allen & Sons, Limited, of London, England. This concern have large farms in Bedfordshire, near Ampthill, where they grow medicinal drugs under the very best conditions for a production of the highest quality drugs. In the production of their drugs full recognition is given to the fact that much of the activity of the drugs depends upon the care with which the leaves are handled. In the case of digitalis the leaves are stripped from the plant immediately after collection, the sound leaves are sorted out, put on trays, carried to the drying room and ultimately packed in tins such as is illustrated herewith. Across the cover of the tin is placed the special label of the company.

In a drug like digitalis the utmost reliance has to be placed on the preparation of the dried herb, and really no druggist or pharmacist should employ digitalis leaves in the preparation of infusions or tinctures which he has not himself prepared, or which do not come from very reliable sources, as through want of an active preparation much harm may be done to a patient. It is, therefore, a druggist's absolute duty to insure that his foxglove leaves have been carefully dried and carefully stored. This should be done regardless of the price of the leaves, for careful cultivation and drying of the leaves, of course, entails much more labor and expense, but to know that digitalis comes from an absolutely reliable source is a better assurance of an active preparation than a doubtful physiological test, which the druggist cannot himself control.

AMERICAN DRUGGIST

and PHARMACEUTICAL RECORD

?HIA. NEW YORK, FEBRUARY 26, 1906. CHICAGO

ISSUED SEMI-MONTHLY BY

.AN DRUGGIST PUBLISHING CO.,

62-68 West Broadway, New York.

.GO, 221 Randolph St. PHILADELPHIA, 3718 Walnut St.

A. R. ELLIOTT, President.

CASWELL A. MAYO, Ph.G....................Editor.
THOMAS J. KEENAN................Associate Editor.

ROMAINE PIERSON...........Manager Chicago Office.

$1.50 a year. 15 cents a copy.

ADVERTISING RATES QUOTED ON APPLICATION.

The American Druggist and Pharmaceutical Record is issued on the second and fourth Mondays of each month. Changes of advertisements should be received ten days in advance of the date of publication.

Remittances should be made by New York exchange, post office or express money order or registered mail. If checks on local banks are used 10 cents should be added to cover cost of collection. The publishers are not responsible for money sent by unregistered mail, nor for any money paid except to duly authorized agents. All communications should be addressed and all remittances made payable to American Druggist Publishing Co., 62-68 West Broadway, New York.

Entered at New York as Second-Class Matter.

TABLE OF CONTENTS.

EDITORIAL COMMENT.

Watch the Legislature. Some extremely ill advised movements are under way for the purpose of letting down the bars in country districts against the sale of drugs and medicines in general stores, and it behooves everybody who is concerned in the control of the sale of narcotics and poisons to protest vigorously against any attempts to make it easy for incompetent persons to deal out habit-forming drugs or poisons. One of the amendments proposed in a bill fathered by Assemblyman Lupton seems to be in the interest of jobbing druggists, for it seeks to remove the restriction in section 199 of the State pharmacy law against the sale of medicines or poisons at wholesale to consumers. Other proposed amendments would make it possible for general dealers to set up at country crossroads stores for the retailing of drugs and medicines. While we naturally view with disfavor any outside interference with the pharmacy law our opposition to several measures now under discussion in the Legislature is not based on this, but arises from a proper interest for the public, who will in the end be sufferers by any weakening of the pharmacy law.

A Model Pharmacy Law for the District of Columbia. No pun is intended in the statement that pharmacy in a measure has come into its own. The passage in the House of Representatives of the Babcock bill (H. R. 8,997) for the regulation of the practice of pharmacy and the sale of poisons in the District of Columbia is something on which the pharmacists of Washington, D. C., are to be distinctly congratulated, for the bill in question was framed by the pharmacists of the district and it includes a section prohibiting the sale of narcotic drugs which is in effect the antinarcotic law advocated by the American Pharmaceutical Association. While the law is intended primarily to regulate the sale of poisons and to control the sale of narcotics, its general features are very comprehensive, including as it does a general pharmacy law providing rules for the admission to and the regulation of the practice of pharmacy. A most important section of the new law, which met with considerable opposition, specifically provides that the superintendent of police and the corporation counsel of the District of Columbia are charged with its enforcement, and upon complaint by proceedings in court the commissioners of pharmacy have power to revoke licenses. A novelty in pharmacy laws provides that courts having jurisdiction are directed to "charge regularly their grand juries to investigate alleged violations." Senator Gallinger, of New Hampshire, has charge of the measure in the Senate and has already moved its advancement, so that its passage and final enactment seem assured.

The Responsibility of the Pharmacist. Some of our French contemporaries have been re-enunciating a principle of law, as applied to the pharmacist, which has been long recognized in English law—that is, that the pharmacist owning the store is responsible for the acts of his assistants. One of the Paris courts, the 11th Chamber of the Seine Tribunal, has declared that the pharmacist is legally responsible for everything which takes place in his store. The case arose out of the preparation of a prescription for 20 pills, in which the dispenser made the mistake of reading it as a *talis dosis* prescription. The prescription was prepared by an apprentice, who failed to realize the large amount of arsenic and strychnine which it contained. The pharmacist himself was held culpable and sentenced to imprisonment for six days in addition to a fine of 100 francs. The physician was held equally guilty with the pharmacist, there being some ambiguity in the directions to the pharmacist, and he and the pharmacist were sentenced conjointly to pay a fine of 500 francs and costs. An appeal from this decision was not sustained.

Faults of Our Educational System.

We present in this issue the last installment of a paper by Prof. Oscar Oldberg, of Chicago, in which he has undertaken to set forth concisely the evils besetting the professional side of pharmacy and to formulate plans for the elimination of the evils indicated.

While we are unable to agree with much that Professor Oldberg has to say regarding the degradation of pharmacy, there is enough ground for criticism in existing conditions to warrant a careful study of those conditions, with a view to their amelioration. The spread of education has established higher standards in all lines of endeavor, and pharmacy is no exception. We require much more of pharmacists now than ever before, and if the particular standards are open to criticism, this is an error of judgment of the individuals charged with their formulation.

There is so much of new knowledge to be acquired by the children of to-day that pedagogues are prone to err in the direction of giving to their pupils a smattering of all knowledge, rather than to endeavor to make them masters of a few basic studies upon which the later and fuller education of the pupil can be grounded.

The complaint is made by board of pharmacy examiners that our high school graduates are unable to solve the ordinary problems in simple arithmetic which are daily presented at the prescription counter, and unfortunately the records of our examining bodies, whether of schools or of State boards, tend to bear out this charge.

The explanation is simple and the remedy may be easily pointed out, though it will probably never be applied. When the pupil graduates from the grammar school he generally has a fair grounding in the basic principles of arithmetic. Upon entering the high school he is immediately confronted with higher mathematical problems, by which we mean the study of algebra and geometry. After absorbing a smattering of these he gets no more mathematics, devoting the time which should be spent in a thorough drilling in arithmetic to obtaining a smattering of languages—French, German and Latin—studying at the same time zoology, botany, drawing, ancient and modern history, physics, chemistry, international law, psychology and English literature, not to mention a half dozen other special studies which may at the moment be the fashion among pedagogues.

The observer is tempted to believe that the teacher is more interested in being able to present a high sounding curriculum for the admiration and envy of his colleagues than in turning out pupils who have learned that most important thing of all—namely, how to study.

It is manifestly impossible within the compass of the few years which can be allotted to grammar school and to high school for the pupil to cover the whole field of knowledge. The one important thing which can be taught is how to study. If the pupil is made to learn a few things and learn each one of them thoroughly he is prepared to go on after leaving school and apply to any special studies which he may wish to take up the same methods which have made him a master of the few primary studies, a thorough mastery of which is essential as a basis for all education.

Where a pupil has given two hours a week for ten months to German and during the next ten months is required to give that time to French, it is not to be expected that the average boy of 16 or 17 will learn enough of the language to be of any use to him. He acquires merely a smattering, which is practically useless and gained at a serious sacrifice of his ideals as to methods of study.

The young men who graduate from our colleges or so-called universities are inclined to sneer at the comparatively elementary curriculum of the schools at Annapolis and West Point, but the difference between the graduates of these institutions and those of our colleges is that the West Pointer and the Annapolis man know what they know thoroughly, and have had it so drilled into them that they cannot forget it. They may be lacking in some of the educational frills, but in the basic studies they are so thoroughly grounded that in later life their knowledge is always available.

What we need in our educational institutions everywhere is just such thoroughness in a few elementary studies, leaving to postgraduate work that specialization which is necessary in most cases, and abandoning the futile effort which is now made to crowd into four years of high school a complete compendium of all the knowledge that the world is heir to.

It is in our public common school system that the reforms must begin.

The Stevens Bill Should Be Amended.

The bill introduced in the Senate of the State of New York by Mr. Stevens, and intended to regulate the manufacture, sale and labeling of drugs and proprietary medicines, should receive the closest scrutiny of the legislative committees of the various local associations as well as of the committee of the State association. The bill was, it is generally understood, prepared by the New York Health Department with the advice and assistance of a self-constituted committee of physicians and chemists, and we have yet to hear that a single pharmacist was consulted in regard to the measure until it had been presented for passage in the Legislature and had reached the committee stage. The Kings County Pharmaceutical Society, ever alert to detect and head off movements in pharmacy not initiated by pharmacists, and which appear but calculated to add to the burdens under which pharmacists now conduct business in this State, made prompt objection to the measure. The objection of the druggists of Brooklyn was based chiefly on that provision of the bill which takes from the Board of Pharmacy and places with the Health Department certain supervisory powers. As pharmacists our Brooklyn brethren are quite justified in the stand which they have taken. The legislative committee of the Manhattan Pharmaceutical Association appear to be indifferent to the maintenance of the integrity of the Board of Pharmacy, for when the question of opposing the Stevens bill on this and other grounds was discussed at this month's meeting it found only a few supporters. The Manhattan druggists have, however, asked for a change in the bill on a different account. Objection was made and sustained to the enumeration in the bill of certain medical terms referring to symptoms which presupposed on the part of the pharmacist a knowledge both of pharmacodynamics and therapeutics, which is not possessed by physicians themselves. Not a day passes but what some new remedy is launched on the market of which pharmacists know little beyond what the manufacturers are pleased to tell in their advertising circulars, and of which physicians are even less well informed. The bill should certainly be amended in this particular and undoubtedly will be when the weakness of the paragraph containing the descriptions of drug action which are intended to place certain drugs in the list of poisons are better understood by those responsible for it.

THE ÆSTHETICS OF PHARMACEUTICAL DISPENSING.[1]

By Hy. P. Hynson, Ph.G.,
Baltimore, Md.

Before we begin to discuss the actual compounding of prescriptions I should like to make a few remarks regarding a phase of dispensing which, in my opinion, has not received quite the attention it deserves, especially from a commercial point of view. I refer to that which, I think, may be properly styled the æsthetics of dispensing, and to make this reference more distinctive and more certain in its application I will venture to draw an easily visible line between the appearance of things that are dependent upon strictly pharmaceutical manipulations and the appearance that is dependent upon general æsthetic laws, which are not necessarily attached to pharmaceutical study.

It is the habit of some enthusiastically impractical persons to regard only that which is impracticable and ultra useful as scientific, and to such individuals it does not appear creditable that good results can be obtained either through the application of common sense principles or from the acceptance of laws established by repeated experiences. Yet, with this school of philosophers well in mind, I am firm in the belief, as heretofore expressed, that our pharmacists are generally well enough trained in that which is usually understood as the science of pharmacy and also in the art of pharmacy, excepting in the particular field to which I seek to draw your attention. I refer to containers, style of labels, the writing of labels, the copying of prescriptions and the corking, capping and wrapping of prescriptions.

The mere mentioning of these subjects may, I fear, put me in an unenviable light before you and bring to your minds only the commonplace—the seemingly unimportant. I assure you I am by no means unmindful of your regard and respect, yet as sensitive as I confess myself to be I am perfectly willing to hazard any reputation I may have if I may but seriously interest you in what careful observation leads me to believe, is one of the greatest deficiencies in pharmaceutical practice to-day.

I am quite confident that no little of the success attained and much of the reputation enjoyed by our more prominent pharmacists has been won by unusual attention to details in the finishing of prescriptions that are regarded by many as non-essential, and think over it as much as I may, view it from as many points as I possibly can, it still remains a positive conviction that much of the study of our students goes for naught because they have not been impressed by the commercial value of a more æsthetical practice. The canvas is strong and strongly framed; carefully selected colors are on it in abundance, but truth and taste and touch are missing.

Is it not true in other phases of living that all values above those based upon the demands of actual necessity are rated by the standards established by our more æsthetic senses? Is it not true that the relative beauty of an object makes it more or less precious than another, and that the particular things which appeal to our more æsthetic tastes are the ones that win our greatest tribute? If all this is true regarding other lines of commerce, why should it not apply quite as pertinently to prescription pharmacy?

This commercial value is made strikingly apparent when contemplating two apartment houses now in course of construction in new Baltimore. Equally well located, of equal size and offering apparently equal accommodations and conveniences, the suites in one will rent for $450 to $900, while in the other they are eagerly sought for at rentals running from $2,000 to $3,500. The difference is due simply to the fact that the builder of one refuses to lay sufficient sacrifice upon beauty's altar and must needs violate all of beauty's laws, while tthe other, paying ample tribute, is able to meet the requirements of good taste and refinement. Many of us pay this tribute, sometimes lavishly, on account of our stores, in their fixtures and furnishings. No doubt these expenditures in time and thought and money are wisely made, but are we quite consistent? Do all use time and thought and money to produce the same effects upon our products, especially prescriptions? Does it occur to many of us that a large percentage of our patrons, possibly the majority, never enter our stores? Certainly many do not, while they are taking our medicines. Comparatively few of the physicians whose prescriptions we fill have ever seen the costly fixtures and elaborate decorations of our establishments. Nurses, who have no little influence with their patients, seldom, if ever, visit the store to which they send much trade. Patients, physicians and nurses alike have much more to do with our containers, their labels and wrappings, have them in sight so much that it would seem wise for us to try by every means in our power to favorably impress them through the appearance of our packages and labels.

The details to which I would call your special attention are a part of a pharmacist's technics and bear much the same relationship to his knowledge of chemistry, physics and materia medica as the technics of the modern surgeon bear to the latter's knowledge of anatomy, physiology and pathology. The one is as important and as necessary, relatively, as the other. The standing and success of the pharmacist are as dependent upon his technics as are those of the surgeon.

The importance of this subject impels me to strive to present it carefully, and, as far as I am able, fundamentally and systematically, for in no other way do I believe it will be helpfully understood. It is knowledge based on sound principles, elastic enough to meet the varying tests to which it may be put. To some of you I fear I must say you are inclined always to underestimate that with which you have most to do. "Familiarity breeds contempt" is one of the very truest of true proverbs. It was by dint of much effort that we slowly, very slowly, acquired the power of speech and became possessed of a limited vocabulary, and because we can make ourselves understood, or think we are understood, we rate talking as quite simple. It is only when we have compared our abilities in this direction with those of one whom we know to be cultured that we begin to understand how much there is yet to win and how little we really know about such a commonplace thing as fair speech, and then, when we begin to study and continue to study how to talk, we realize with singular surprise how intricate and how very interesting this every day matter has become. The proposition that it is only through and by the eager contemplation of a subject or object that we discover whatever is hidden within it of worth, of comfort and of beauty is indeed trite, but needs to be stated to make positive the necessity for study along the lines indicated.

It must be granted, however, that the possession of sufficient knowledge in detail to meet any exigency is as utterly impossible in this phase of dispensing as in any other; fundamental knowledge is what we must have. It is what some call talent or knack—that which by fortunate circumstances or accident some learned and learned to value very early, even before they knew what it was. It is with laws and principles that we must become familiar. Fortunate, indeed, then are those of you who, without thought or application, are possessed of a knowledge of the essential principles of beauty, who without penalty of mortifying experience recognize true order and who, missing the shame of many mistakes, know what is pleasingly appropriate.

Our efforts, if this be true and we would produce the really beautiful (that which pleases and continues to please the senses), must be directed toward the production of the useful, the true, the well ordered and the appropriate; these are the essentials and they must be characteristic of our offerings. There may be doubt as to their application, and you must bear with me a few minutes more while I try to make this clear.

One prescription is for 1 ounce of potassium bromide, which is directed to be dissolved at once in a pint of water. Another is for an equal amount of the same substance, a half teaspoonful of which, you see, is to be taken in a wineglass full of water. The last mentioned should undoubtedly be dispensed in a well stoppered, wide mouthed bottle, while the former as certainly should not, because the bottle would be useless, extravagant and in appropriate. A neat package, using first parchment or

[1] Read at the February meeting of the Manhattan Pharmaceutical Association.

waxed paper and then white paper or an envelope, would be more appropriate for the first. I cannot persuade myself that a glass stoppered bottle is either useful or appropriate for chalk or bismuth mixtures, while I would be equally as much offended to see even diluted acids dispensed in corked bottles. Ordinarily, rubber stoppers are hideously ugly to me, but they look particularly attractive in bottles containing fluid extract of cascara or compound tincture of benzoin, because they are the only stoppers that can be invariably removed from the containers of such substances; in such instances they are useful and appropriate.

It is difficult to believe that either the physician who writes a prescription or the party who pays for its compounding contemplated that its container should be made the carrier of a direct advertisement. That is not for what it was properly intended, and the larger the space taken for advertising purposes on either label or bottle the greater the violation of the true purposes of both. It is quite right that our names and addresses should appear sufficiently large to be easily read—this might be useful for obvious reasons—but why we should be so particular about calling attention to the fact that we are pharmaceutical chemists and not shoemakers, reliable druggists and not indifferent grocers, does not appear. When descriptive reference is useful or necessary then it should by all means be used, as on envelopes in which prescriptions are delivered and on address tags. Nor do I believe we should make our labels the carriers of questionable art productions. Whether they represent bridal bouquets, funeral wreaths, the head of Minerva or a Japanese fishing scene I cannot see the use of these or why they are appropriate. Yet any of them, no matter how objectionable in the abstract, may become acceptable if consistently adopted as personal insignia or as trademarks; they then become useful, appropriate, true.

We shall have but little difficulty in pointing out the application of the rule of order. It is in order and quite necessary that the figures, called letters, we use in writing should be distinctly made, so they may be easily distinguished from each other; it is also in order that the letters of the different classes should be uniform in size and that those which extend below the line should be of the same length below as a similar letter would be above. If we will clearly follow these very simple rules of *order* our writing will undoubtedly be easily read, useful and attractive. Great variation brings great disorder.

I believe if by some transformation you and I should become laymen and have a child ill we would not be pleased, if, when we were about to administer the little one's medicine, we had to look through an inch or more of some pharmacist's card and then meet a lot of numbers, followed by a more mysterious arrangement of these—if not 4-11-44, perhaps 4-11-05—after which the directions, more or less crowded, might be discovered. This surely is not orderly. It may be that appropriateness should sacrifice something to proportion or balance and a label might possibly be more attractive with the name at top and address below, but there can be no good excuse offered for giving both the greater prominence. The rule of order is important. First should come the name of the patient, followed by directions for use; the doctor's name upon whose authority the directions are given; the date—using name of month, not numerals—then *your* number list, next to or with your card.

Trusting I have shown how the fundamental laws of beauty, more or less intense, may be applied to all these things, I seek now to prove by the specimens I offer that these laws are not followed, that the better principles of ornamentation are generally violated and that more attention to these details would enhance the commercial value of our various attainments, both scientific and technical.

These specimens are not selected; they are all I have been able to collect since I decided to discuss this subject about a month ago. Neither do they, as you will see, exempt any locality; they are from North and South, East and West, and the Central districts included. They represent no particular school nor class; neither must they be considered to represent the parties whose names appear upon the labels. They represent individual dispensers whose identity I do not know, else I would not show them. And, lastly, they do not represent the collections of a fault finder, who is trying to destroy, but they are the efforts of a devoted friend, trying to make our faults plain that we may by united effort correct them and thereby, if we may, raise pharmacy to a higher plane of usefulness and honor.

[Professor Hynson then exhibited on the blackboard various prescriptions which illustrated the several points brought out in his paper. These prescriptions will be presented in a later issue. Our report of the meeting is printed elsewhere.]

(*Written for the American Druggist.*)

THE SYSTEMATIC AMENDMENT OF AMERICAN PHARMACY.

By Oscar Oldberg.
Northwestern University.

(*Concluded from page 64.*)

III.

EXAMINATION HAS BECOME A FETISH.

One of the strangest and most mischievous peculiarities of our pharmacy laws and the manner of their execution has been the exaggerated importance attached to the "examination." Examinations have their uses. They are something more than a necessary evil. But when they are exalted to the degree of all-sufficiency it is, indeed, time to call a halt.

Actual training and study constitute the real preparation for pharmacy as well as for all other technical and professional work. This preparation is the substance; the examination is but one of the means by which the sufficiency of that preparation may be tested *if the examination is conducted in a masterly way.*

We may to a certain extent recognize the substance from its shadow; but in the absence of any evidence that the substance ever had any existence it would seem to be vain to attempt to photograph it. It is much easier to find out whether or not the candidate has actually made any serious effort to master his task than it is to determine how well he succeeded.

If the girl has no hands it is not necessary to place her at a piano to find out that she cannot play.

In two of our States the laws do not prescribe any kind of training either in the shop or in the school; any candidate who may pass the examination held by the Board of Pharmacy must be licensed. It would be very much better to require definite courses of study and training to be proved by certificates satisfactory to the board and to drop the examination.

Common sense would seem to dictate that the candidate should be required to first comply with reasonable regulations fixing in definite terms the training which he must have, and when he has shown that these prescribed terms have been met he should then, and not until then, be permitted to take the examination.

More than three-fourths of the candidates examined by the boards of pharmacy are men who never attended any pharmaceutical school, men whose shop training is mostly commercial and who have given little or no attempt to study of any kind, except cramming.

One of the most difficult problems a conscientious teacher in any school has to solve is how to conduct examinations so that they will fairly show the student's real condition and progress. A teacher who comes in personal contact with the student almost daily and observes his habits and work can form a far more accurate estimate of his ability and worth from that personal contact with him than from any final examination. A teacher of experience knows very well that even the most carefully conducted examination is frequently disappointing in that its results do not reflect the truth. The best men, of course, always pass and the worst fail, but in all those cases the examination is to the teacher superfluous. Good students may make a very poor showing, and very poor students sometimes make a good showing in examinations.

When the candidates are utter strangers to the examiners

the results are by no means reliable except as to the best and the worst of the examinees. If an examination is sufficient, why require any drug store experience whatever? Let us be reasonable!

If absolute proof of the weakness of the system of determining the qualifications of pharmacists, physicians, dentists, etc., by examination *alone* were needed, it could be furnished by the teachers of the colleges in overwhelming abundance. Actual and sufficient special training for pharmacy is *the real requisite, and of that training laboratory instruction and practice and sufficient drug store experience* are the most important features. Both should count fully as much as the examination.

In one examination recently held by a board of pharmacy over 90 per cent. of the candidates failed. As that board is probably one of the most efficient in the country it is evident that the whole system is wrong and that probably 75 per cent. of the candidates should never have been admitted to the examination.

Experience and observation convince me that thoroughly competent examiners are not born such: they must not only be well endowed naturally and have a thorough education, both general and special, but they must besides have abundant practice before they can become really intelligent, practical, reliable and fair examiners. Several years' active experience is usually required to learn to do that work well.

Pharmacists long in active business, when well educated, should make the best examiners in such subjects as the proper reading of prescriptions, the ability to detect serious errors in them, the computation of doses and other every day problems in pharmaceutical arithmetic, and the candidate's ability to prepare medicines and to compound or dispense prescriptions in a workmanlike way. But they are rarely competent to prepare the questions and rate the answers for examinations in the scientific principles upon which pharmacy rests, such as chemistry, etc. Only the least competent board members are likely to dispute that fact, and the very best of them will freely admit its truth because it is palpable. Men may be most reliable, skilled and excellent pharmacists and yet be quite incompetent examiners. It is not their business to be examiners. I have the highest respect for the able practical men usually selected to serve as board members, and when I assert that they are not competent to be examiners in chemistry I am not in the slightest degree questioning their professional education and skill, but simply stating a proposition that ought to be perfectly self-evident even if actual results were wanting to prove it. It simply must be so, and it is so.

The boards should of course never surrender the direction of their examinations to others, but they certainly should employ specialists experienced in holding examinations to prepare the questions and rate the answers in all subjects included in their examinations except the oral and practical tests on dispensing. They can in most States have the services of the teachers in the colleges without cost.

The only objection I have heard against utilizing the services of the teachers of the pharmaceutical schools is that there is danger that those teachers may be too lenient in rating the papers of their own pupils and unfair in the opposite direction to the pupils or graduates of rival schools. But the candidates can be numbered, their papers also numbered, and their names known only to the board members.

The board examinations of candidates for license to be assistant pharmacists should cover only such subjects as are indispensable to the makeup of a practical dispenser. The board examinations for pharmacists to be given the authority to conduct pharmacies as principals should include all that is necessary to the proper interpretation and observance of all the directions and requirements of the pharmacopœia.

The character of the examination should, moreover, be such as not to defeat its own ends. It should include nothing that does not have a real and important bearing upon the question of the fitness of the candidate to practice his occupation. The inability of the candidate to state the boiling point of mercury, the melting point of silver nitrate, the number of wines in the pharmacopœia, the name of the family to which the plant belongs from which a certain drug is obtained, and other facts which no sensible pharmacist attempts to remember, does not prove him to be incompetent, and his ability to remember such facts does not prove him competent.

A graduate fresh from college is, of course, much less competent and reliable than the same graduate several years later, if he continues in active practice. But a perfectly competent man may undoubtedly fail in the board examination after having been out of college for a year or more unless that examination is rational.

It would seem to be most suitable that the board examinations of candidates for license as assistants should include: Elementary inorganic chemistry, weights and measures and pharmaceutical arithmetic, elementary materia medica, doses, pharmaceutical processes and manipulations, pharmaceutical preparations, the general character, scope and functions of the pharmacopœia, and dispensing.

The board examinations of candidates for license to conduct pharmacies as principals should include in addition: Pharmacognosy, applied pharmaceutical chemistry, organic chemistry, drug assaying, and elementary therapeutics.

Whatever may be the scope of the examinations of the boards, the subjects covered should be definitely fixed, and a sufficiently explicit syllabus thereof should be published for the information of all concerned. In fact *all* laws, rules and regulations adopted by the boards (except such as concern only the board members and their employees) should be promulgated and accessible to all who are interested in them. Any other course is disorderly.

THE RELATIONS AND RESPECTIVE FUNCTIONS OF THE BOARDS AND COLLEGES.

The boards of pharmacy are charged with the enforcement of the law. They have the power to prescribe proper standards and enforce obedience to them. The pharmaceutical schools are bound to recognize the authority of the boards. Jealousy and want of mutual respect and confidence between the boards and the schools would be supercilious, senseless and puerile, and sure to defeat all efforts at progress. Boards and schools need each other. They are both engaged in promoting decent pharmaceutical education. They should get together and confer about the means by which the objects of the pharmacy laws can best be gained.

The schools are utterly helpless without the aid of the law and the boards, for if they should establish higher entrance requirements than those made obligatory by law or by the rules of the boards under the law, the doors of many of the best pharmacy schools would certainly have to be closed for want of sufficient classes to keep them alive.

The educational requirements for admission to the schools of pharmacy are now fixed *by the druggists*, for the students of these schools nearly all must come from the drug stores, and a large proportion of the boys now taken into drug stores to learn the business are not even grammar school graduates. The boards alone can remedy this crying evil.

One school of pharmacy which recently increased its entrance requirements immediately suffered an anticipated loss of students, resulting in a diminution of revenue amounting to several thousand dollars. Those students doubtless entered other schools of pharmacy where the entrance conditions were lower. Entrance requirements must, therefore, be made compulsory by the boards, both for admission to pharmacy schools and to the drug stores. Otherwise, the efforts of the schools to advance the educational standards must be defeated.

If the pharmaceutical college training is made compulsory as a prerequisite to final registration and license to conduct pharmacies, there would possibly be a sufficient increase of attendance at the schools of pharmacy on that account to offset the loss resulting from increased entrance requirements. All that the schools of pharmacy should be expected to do is to give good and sufficient courses of instruction, to admit no students whose age and general education do not conform to the requirements fixed by the boards, and to maintain proper standards and methods in their work.

In order to get a clear idea of the respective functions of

boards and schools it is necessary to brush away some of the old cobwebs. Graduation from a school of pharmacy can never mean anything more than that the graduate has successfully completed the courses in the school from which he graduated, and that his character and conduct were such as to justify his graduation. It cannot mean that the graduate is in all respects qualified to practice pharmacy, for no school can take the place of the pharmacy board.

The claim that the college of pharmacy can or should verify the quality and quantity of the shop training of any person is inadmissible, first, because the school has no power to compel sufficient evidence, and, secondly, because the board, which has that power, is specifically charged with that duty, so that any attempt of the school to perform this function is not only superfluous and futile, but a clear case of gratuitous meddling with the duties of the board.

On the other hand, the boards should not interfere with the schools any further than is necessary to the satisfactory fulfillment of the duty which the schools alone can perform.

The boards of pharmacy should not impose upon the schools the duty of requiring drug store experience as a prerequisite to graduation, and discriminate between the schools that require it and those that decline to accept any responsibility so clearly foreign to their legitimate functions. Dread of the board examination drives numerous students to the colleges that require drug store experience for graduation and who require it for just that purpose, and that dread drives the boys away from schools often for better that do not require drug store work.

Neither should the boards prescribe the age to be required for graduation.

A demand that the pharmaceutical schools shall require the age of 21 years before graduation must be regarded as educationally a blunder, for if the school can admit a student at "17 years" to take a "two years' course" it not only can but should confer upon him the diploma which constitutes the evidence of his having successfully accomplished his task as soon as he has done so, for the diploma evidences nothing more, and nothing can be gained by compelling him to wait for it for a period of two years. If he is fit to begin his course and to continue it to the end he is also quite as fit to graduate immediately as at any later date, and to withhold the diploma is to inflict a useless annoyance and disappointment.

NO HARDSHIPS IMPOSED BY PREREQUISITE LAWS AND RULES.

An unwritten law prevents retroactive legislation in this country. Our laws and regulations are not so framed as to infringe upon individual rights already specifically conferred and exercised. When our pharmacy laws were originally passed all druggists and drug clerks in business were undisturbed. The same principle undoubtedly will continue to prevail in any further legislation fixing the educational requirements for pharmacy. No person already licensed can be or will be deprived of any privilege he possesses.

The reform movement in pharmaceutical education does not, either directly or indirectly, impose any burden or injustice upon any one. On the contrary, it adds increased value to the rights already conferred upon those who are registered or licensed and at the same time extends to all persons to be licensed under the new requirements benefits and rights worth much more than the price exacted.

After generations of neglect it is not to be expected that we shall suddenly and recklessly disturb the existing order of things, to the serious disadvantage of the druggists and their clerks, or of the public whom they serve. To close the door of advancement against those already engaged in the occupation of pharmacy would certainly not be sane reform.

SCARCITY OF DRUG CLERKS.

Strong objections to higher requirements for license have been made on the ground that the supply of apprentices and clerks is already insufficient and that this practical difficulty must be aggravated by establishing higher standards of education. But as the apprentices and clerks we have are not to be disturbed we find upon reasonably careful consideration of the matter that the effect of the proposed reforms will really be to relieve the strain, if there be any.

It is proposd to raise the requirements for license to own and operate a pharmacy. The direct effect will be to lessen competition by checking the increase of pharmacies. We may well cite the conditions in Illinois to illustrate this proposition.

The Board of Pharmacy of Illinois reported in 1904 that the total registration included:

4,801 pharmacists,
891 assistant pharmacists,
3,289 apprentices.

There are 2,768 drug stores in that State.

These figures are astonishing. They ought to be about as follows:

3,300 registered pharmacists, instead of 4,801.
3,400 registered assistant pharmacists, instead of only 891, and 3,000 apprentices.

The excessive number of registered pharmacists is due to the ease with which full registration can be secured. This statement is not to be construed as in any way a criticism of the board or its examinations. It is simply the inevitable result of not requiring any systematic special course of education as a prerequisite to the examination for the highest grade of pharmacists.

What is the result of having 2,000 more registered pharmacists than drug stores? A constant and usually irresistible temptation to those 2,000 men to start drug stores of their own just as soon as they can possibly do so, with or without capital. This "wide open" policy is bad for the public, bad for the trade, bad for the ambitious young man who cannot wait until he has acquired sufficient experience and capital to insure reasonable hope of success in his enterprise.

Every clerk who starts a new drug store diminishes the supply of clerks, but increases the demand for them.

Is there any wonder that the drug business is demoralized and that clerks are scarce?

The right remedy for the scarcity of drug clerks and apprentices is not to take into the drug stores an increasing number of apprentices of a low grade, to be railroaded into the station of full fledged pharmacists and employers, but to stop creating an excessive number of principals and to extend the privileges and widen the sphere of work of the clerks, so as to make them more contented with their position, and to cease compelling employers to either have full-fledged registered pharmacists for clerks or hire costly substitutes whenever they have occasion to absent themselves from their stores for a day or two.

As long as there is but one grade of licensed pharmacists in any State that State will surely suffer from a multiplication of drug stores far beyond reasonable limits, and the superfluous drug stores will be of such a class that they will do more harm than good to the community.

Absolutely nothing else can degrade pharmacy so effectually, rapidly and permanently as the unchecked introduction of unfit boys as apprentices. The scarcity of fit apprentices cannot under any circumstances justify the employment of unfit ones.

But, instead of growing better, the material has been constantly getting worse, on account of the increasing competition in business and the failure of employers to render the conditions of employment more satisfactory to the employees.

The occupation of pharmacy is by no means inviting to intelligent, ambitious, fairly well educated and self-respecting young men under existing conditions. A large number of the better class of drug clerks are deserting their occupation on account of unnecessarily disagreeable surroundings and because they find that so many of their fellow clerks are of a low grade of intelligence and education.

Many a time have I heard fathers and sons, who had entertained the thought that pharmacy must be a desirable occupation, summarily dismiss that thought upon being informed of the low educational requirements for it.

Other occupations are sought by high school boys. But as other occupations pay no better, offer no better inducements, except as to personal surroundings, *and are overcrowded*, it is easy enough to remedy the difficulties complained of in pharmacy if we will only be reasonable.

THE DANGER FROM ILLITERATE CLERKS.

I am sure the better grade of druggists of to-day would resent any suggestion that the undisciplined boys now taken into pharmacies to learn the business are fit to be their successors. But to some of the employers "any old thing" (pardon the slang) seems to be good enough lumber to make druggists out of in these times, and when once taken into the drug store the cheap child labor thus introduced yields a large per cent. of worthless clerks, beyond redemption in education or morals.

Every insufficiently educated boy in the drug store is, however, looked upon as having an inalienable right to advance in the profession until he wrenches a license from the Board of Pharmacy by a stroke of luck, by cribbing, or sheer persistence, which finally induces the board to pass him in order to get rid of him, and in time he becomes a proprietor and in his turn introduces a lot of other equally unfit candidates for pharmaceutical honors. It requires only from four to six years to make a proprietor out of the apprentice, and the unfit apprentices are rapidly coming to the surface as still more unfit pharmacists.

LET TECHNICAL SERVICES BE TREATED WITH MORE RESPECT.

The present system requires to be radically changed. Instead of admitting to apprenticeship the cheap labor employed to do the rough work, and unfit to do any other, let it be thoroughly understood that only those who possess reasonably hopeful educational qualifications are or can be recognized as apprentices. Let the recognized apprentices understand from the beginning that their duties, responsibilities and professional prospects are serious and entitled to some respect, and give to them some of the duties now reserved for assistant pharmacists. Such treatment will have a tendency to make them self-respecting and more thoughtful. Let any apprentice who may mistakenly acquire exaggerated notions of his own importance be summarily dismissed; but let the fit ones feel that they are not mere bottlewashers, even if they do wash bottles.

Let the assistant pharmacists, too, understand that they are not so inferior to registered pharmacists that they may not be trusted to dispense medicines without having the registered pharmacist nearby to look over their shoulders. They are trusted now during the "temporary absence" of the registered pharmacist to put up prescriptions. They do as a matter of fact put up prescriptions every day in the presence of the principal without supervision. They are or should be competent practical dispensers. Let them be trusted accordingly. They should not have the right to take or have real or permanent charge of a pharmacy, but I fail to see why they should not go on performing their duties for a whole week or month in the absence of their employer. Assistant pharmacists in other countries are not looked upon as incompetent to perform any and all technical duties about the pharmacy whether the proprietor is present or not; but they are *not* permitted to be managers or principals, and when temporarily alone in the pharmacy the assistant pharmacist is certainly not in any true sense in charge of the establishment or the manager of it.

It is inconsistent to hold the registered assistant pharmacist competent to compound and dispense medicines during meal hours, but not at other times, or that he is quite qualified to do any of the work in the pharmacy without the presence of the principal for half a day, but suddenly becomes incompetent and disqualified whenever the principal's absence is prolonged beyond that half-day. I am quite unable to discover any good reason why the proprietor of a drug store should not be allowed to leave his store for even a month if he has a trusted registered assistant pharmacist to attend to the work during his absence in accordance with his directions. Common sense would seem to indicate that the difference between the principal and the clerk is great enough to require recognition without reducing the clerk to a nonentity and the principal to a slave who cannot get needed rest to enable him to do his duty more efficiently and to have a reasonable share of the enjoyments of life. If these facts were recognized it would be far better for all concerned, including the public.

There is nothing to hinder any druggist from employing any kind of help, such as store boys, porters, purely mercantile salesmen, bookkeepers, etc., who are not registered apprentices or pharmacists, to render any service other than that of preparing and dispensing medicines; but no person should be permitted to participate in the pharmaceutical work unless licensed to do so.

There would be no scarcity of clerks under the conditions described. It would be quite as easy for the boards of pharmacy to prevent abuses under such a system as under the present one.

Let pharmacy be redeemed and protected.

(*Written for the American Druggist.*)

ADULTERATED MILK SUGAR.

By E. H. Gane, Ph.C.

Milk sugar, whether of domestic or foreign origin, is usually of good quality and has rarely been subject to adulteration. Recently, however, a product has been offered to the trade as pure milk sugar, which is grossly adulterated. The adulterant is a fine grade of glucose, known commercially as confectioner's grape sugar, or starch sugar. The same firm that offers the mixture of glucose and milk sugar also offers a product under the name of "Pure Lactose Sugar," which consists wholly of grape sugar or glucose.

The adulterated article is offered at a price somewhat under the market price of pure milk sugar, although worth considerably less, and its detection is fortunately easy for the retail druggist, who is most likely to be imposed upon by this sophistication.

The simplest test is based upon the solubility of the substance in water. Pure milk sugar is only soluble in six to seven parts of water at ordinary temperatures, while the adulterated article is much more soluble, the glucose or grape sugar being easily soluble in an equal quantity of water. This furnishes a ready means of distinguishing between the pure lactose and the so-called "lactose sugar." Further, the adulterated article is easily recognized by its taste, which is characteristic of the commercial glucose and lacks the "sandy" feel on the tongue of pure milk sugar.

The adulteration is a particularly mean one, when we consider the fact that one of the principal uses of milk sugar is as an ingredient of infants' food.

Treatment of a Common Cold.

Dr. F. P. Atkinson writes to the *British Medical Journal* stating that for the ordinary cold in the head his experience is that the quickest result is obtained by giving 30 minims of spt. æther nit. and 30 drops of spt. ammon. aromat. in 1 oz. of water, repeating the dose in two hours, and then every four hours. Three or four doses are generally sufficient to put a stop to the discharge. Should the discharge be thick when first seen, then a snuff composed of 1 grain of cocaine, 2 grains of menthol and 100 grains of boric acid quickly effects a rapid cure. When the cold has run down into the trachea, as shown by the tickling of the throat whenever a long breath is taken, then a mixture of liq. ammon. acet. ʒij., spt. æther, nit. mx., in 1 oz. of water, every four hours, rapidly gives the required relief.

The *Chemist and Druggist*, which prints the foregoing, says it can indorse Dr. Atkinson's remarks in regard to the spirit of ammonia and nitrous ether mixture. Whenever one feels the shivering symptoms of a chill the mixture has a wonderful effect in restoring warmth and bodily comfort, and shivering symptoms rapidly disappear. The spirit of nitrous ether should be recent, and a pleasant draught is made by addition of aq. chlorof.:

Spt. æther. nit. .... ʒss.
Spt. ammon. aromat. .... ʒss.
Aq. chlorof. ad .... ℥j.
Fiat haustus.

This dose can be taken every half hour for four doses. Then allow an hour to elapse before going to bed, and take another dose.

A New Idea in Bottle Seals.

On January 2d there was issued a patent, No. 809,011, on a new form of bottle seal which promises to be available in many directions in the drug trade. As shown by the accompanying illustration, which is reproduced from the patent specifications, the essential feature of the patent consists in two slides fitting into slots on opposite sides of the neck of the bottle. These slots have projecting flanges which retain the slide in place. The interior of the slide is provided with a notch which engages a hook on the end of a metal strap which reaches across the top, confining the cork. The slides being wedge shape cannot be pushed upward, and the slot engaging the hook on the end of the strap prevents their being shoved downward without breaking the projecting glass flanges on the neck of the bottle which retain the slot in place. The result of this is that the bottle is practically non-refillable. The seal being a portion of the strap which reaches across the top of the cork must be cut in order to open the bottle, and even when this is done the slides will be retained in place, unless they are forced out by breaking the retaining

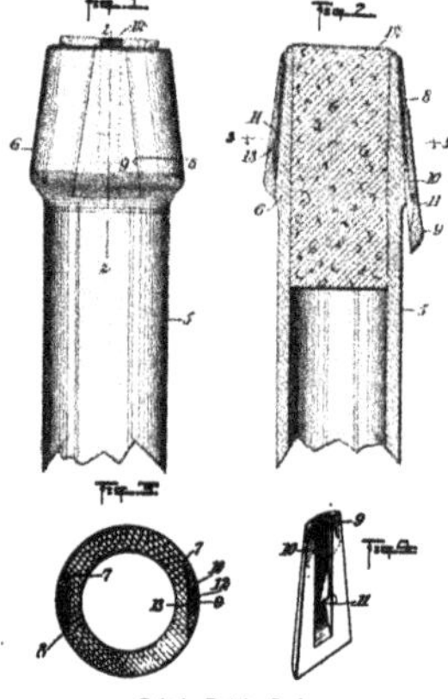

Prier's Bottle Seal.

flanges. When this is done the bottle is no longer available and the customer cannot fail to see that the seal has been tampered with.

Andrew E. Prier, of Richmond, Staten Island, N. Y., who is the inventor and owner of the patent, suggests that the seal will solve the rather troublesome question of returns of empty magnesium citrate bottles. These bottles are now brought back to the druggist, who is, through force of custom, compelled to redeem them at a loss to himself and with considerable danger that his patrons may be poisoned by the retention of some poisonous substance in the bottle, for the public is very careless in matters of this kind. Mr. Prier suggests that if his improved bottle seal is used the druggist can readily show to the customer who returns the bottle that it is no longer available for its original use and that therefore the druggist cannot be expected to pay for it. The additional cost involved in use of the seal would be a very small fraction of a cent when once these bottles are placed in the market in the regular channel.

Another field of usefulness is in the seal of proprietary liquids of all kinds, whether medicines or liquors, as the use of this seal makes refilling of the bottle practically impossible.

American Methods of Teaching Chemistry Condemned.

Professor Wilhelm Ostwald, of Leipzig University, who is now acting as visiting professor of chemistry at Harvard University, and Dr. Harry P. Morse, professor of physics at Harvard, were the guests at the bi-monthly meeting of the Massachusetts Schoolmasters' Club, at a meeting held in Boston on December 23, and they discussed before the members the subject of "The Relation of the New Chemistry to Elementary Teaching."

Both speakers were inclined to discard the method of teaching chemistry which prevails almost universally in this country. Professor Ostwald took delight in scoffing at the atomic theory, and said that if it was to be mentioned at all in a lesson in chemistry it might be referred to historically as something which was once believed.

TEACHING MUST BE POPULARIZED.

Professor Ostwald said one of the problems of all education was how to make the subject of science palatable to the average small boy. Yet it could be done, he asserted, and he cited the widespread interest that was aroused by the discovery of radium. He said that very often teachers used the day before a holiday for an experiment in chemistry which would serve to entertain the class, and then after the holiday returned to the old book method of teaching chemistry, often using hypotheses which are mentioned in the book, but which are never found in common experience. He recommended using the popular experiment almost altogether, and to teach chemistry by showing the common and simple relation between things rather than by urging the mastery of certain fixed and disconnected rules. To show the relation of things was the most effective way, he said.

"It is impossible to teach chemistry from beginning to end, as is attempted in most of the text books, without accidentally meeting with something we don't know about or where it exists, except that it exists in the book.

DO AWAY WITH HYPOTHESES.

"The main reason for changing the present way of teaching chemistry is to get rid of the hypotheses, and to compile generalizations from the facts before us. If you can't show the boy in his hand what it is desired for him to learn, or put it before his eyes so he can see the meaning of it and the relation to other things, little good is being gained by merely memorizing the rule or the hypothesis."

Dr. Morse told of his own experience in studying chemistry and of the great array of facts regarding the subject which he had successfully memorized. Later, in attending a course of lectures on chemistry at Leipzig, he found fellow students who had not only been studying chemistry for a much shorter period and who knew far fewer facts relating to the subject than he did, but who were able to do much better work than himself. The reason, Dr. Morse said, was that instead of attempting to memorize separated facts, they were trained to learn the relation between the facts. A relation in itself is not harder to learn than the two facts which form the relation. The most general principles are the easiest to learn. The hardest are those which are least different from the general principles.

He said: "After an experience of 20 years in studying chemistry, I believe I could safely forget nearly all the facts which I was required in school to memorize, provided I remembered the fundamental relations which hold them together."

Artificial Essence of Banana.—According to Gioli (*Revue Internationale des Falsifications*, June, 1905), a soluble combination of saccharine is offered for sale in some places as essence of banana. This product is a syrupy fluid which at first tastes bitter and afterwards sweet. It contains 54 per cent. of saccharine and a base similar to pyridine. The compound burns, leaving but a slight residue of ash and gives the reactions of the alkaloids. When treated with an alkali, the odor of pyridine is developed. When mineral acids are added they precipitate saccharine which can be dissolved in ether and isolated.

Georgia Board Questions.

The following questions were given by the Georgia State Board of Pharmacy at the examination held in Atlanta, November 18, 1905:

Pharmacy.

1. Name the best solvent for (*a*) chloral hydrate, (*b*) chlorate potash, (*c*) sulphur, (*d*) reduced iron.

2. Define: (*a*) sublimation; (*b*) percolation.

3. Describe the process of making chalk mixture, U. S. P.

4. How can the following be made to dissolve in water: (*a*) bichloride mercury, (*b*) iodine?

5. Give the English name for: (*a*) pearl ash, (*b*) natrium iodide, (*c*) crab's eye, (*d*) violet potash.

6. Tell in grains the amount of carbolic acid contained in each dose of the following prescription:

℞ Acid. carbolic 1.0
Tr. lobelia 2.0
Syr. pruni. virg., q. s. 125.0
M. et. sig.—4 Cc. every three hours.

7. What three methods of preparation are employed in making ointments? Give an example of each.

8. How many grains of cocaine hydrochloride are required to make 100 Cc. of a 2 per cent. solution?

9. Convert 100 degrees C. into degrees Fahrenheit. (Show all the figures on your paper.)

10. On what four conditions does the solubility of a solid depend?

Chemistry and Toxicology.

1. Define inorganic and organic chemistry.

2. Name the halogens and give their symbols.

3. (*a*) Why is phosphorus kept under water? (*b*) Mention some of the chemical properties and some of the uses of phosphorus.

4. What is a salt?

5. Define a normal salt; acid salt; basic salt, and a double salt.

6. Define (*a*) hygroscopic. (*b*) efflorescence.

7. What is the difference between sulphur lotum and sulphur præcipitatum?

8. Why should alkaloids and alkalies be avoided in mixtures?

9. What are some of the symptoms in belladonna poisoning and what is the treatment for same?

10. Name two poisonous gases and treatment for same.

Materia Medica.

1. State difference between corm and root; (*a*) give example of each.

2. Define the terms annual, biennial and perennial as applied to herbaceous stems; (*a*) mention an official herb, bark, flower, seed, leaf.

3. What four official preparations are obtained from the sheep; (*a*) their therapeutic uses; (*b*) average dose of those for internal administration.

4. What is the principal constituent of clove oil, rosemary oil, santal oil, eucalyptus oil?

5. Give the U. S. P. description of vanilla; (*a*) to what family does it belong; (*b*) its habitat, constituents and uses?

6. Cinchona: to what family does it belong; (*a*) what per cent. total alkaloids does it contain; (*b*) its original source; (*c*) state briefly the process of obtaining quinine sulphate from cinchona; (*d*) what is the average wholesale market price of quinine sulphate?

7. Oleum olivæ: what is its natural order and common name; (*a*) with what is it usually adulterated; (*b*) give a simple test for their detection; (*c*) its principal use and dose.

8. Digitalis: give common name and uses; (*a*) its chief constituents; (*b*) which is the diuretic principle; (*c*) which official preparation is best for diuretic action; (*d*) dose of the powder?

9. What is the common or commercial name for acetphenetidinum, phenyl salicylas, sulphonmethanum, sulphonethylmethanum, hexamethylenamina?

10. Identify five specimens of crude drugs.

Prescriptions and Doses.

What are the common names of the following: (*a*) Acetphenetidinum; (*b*) sulphonethylmethanum; (*c*) sulphonmethanum; (*d*) chromii trioxidum; (*e*) arseni trioxidum?

2. Give the strength and average dose of tincture of aconite, U. S. P., 1900.

3. What is the strength and average dose of tincture of veratrum veride, U. S. P., 1900?

4. State the adult dose, number of drops and weight in grains in fluid drachm of: (*a*) chloroform; (*b*) tr. opium; (*c*) tr. nux vomica.

5. What is the average dose of the following: (*a*) morphinæ sulphas; (*b*) strychninæ nitras; (c) acidum hydrocyanicum dilutum; (*d*) oleoresina aspidii?

6. State the quantity of water and potassium iodide used in making an ounce of saturated solution.

7. Outline the process of manufacturing spirit of mindererus, stating the strength of the acid used, why this product should always be dispensed fresh and the average dose of same.

8. What is the strength, average dose and medicinal properties of Tinctura Gambir Composita and what tincture does this replace of the Pharmacopœia of 1890.

9. Criticise the following prescriptions:

I.

℞ Ammonium bromide. }
Sodium bromide } ......āā.......... ʒij
Caffeine citrate .... gr.x.
Codeine sulphate .... gr.iv.
Elx. Lacto pepsin........................ ℥iv.
Dose, one teaspoonful.

II.

℞ Morphine sulph. .... gr.xviij
Quinine sulph. .... gr.i.
Salol }
Phenacetin } .... āā. ....gr.xij
M. Ft. caps. No. 6.
Sig—One every 3 or 4 hours.

Dispensing.

I.

℞ Pulveris opii .... 3.000.
Aquæ fervidæ .... 12 Cc.
Alcoholis .... 12 Cc.
Alcoholis diluti .... q. s. ad 30 Cc.
Prepare properly, filter and pass enough diluted alcohol through filter to make up to 30 Cc.
Label: Laudanum.

II.

℞ Acidi salicylici .... gr. lxxx.
Glycerini .... fl. ℥ss.
Sodii bicarbonatis .... q. s.
Aquæ .... ad fl. ℥i.
M. Signa: Cochleare parvum t. i. d.

III.

℞ Olei theobromatis .... 8.000.
Pulveris opii .... 0.300.
M. Ft. suppositorum in numero iv. (Rectal.)

IV.

℞ Potassii permanganatis........................ gr. xx.
Ft. pil. No. x.

V.

℞ Pulveris ipecacuanhæ .... gr. ij.
Pulveris opii .... gr. ij.
Pulveris sacchari lactis........................ gr. xvj.
M. Div. in chart., No. ij.

QUESTIONS TO BE ANSWERED.

(A) How would you dispense the following so as to get the proper amount of hyoscyamine sulphate in each pill, using ordinary balances and ordinary prescription weights? And how would you manage to obtain a convenient pill?

℞ Hyoscyaminæ sulphatis .... gr. 1-50.
Ft. pil. No. ij.

(B) How would you dispense the following so as to get the proper amount of each ingredient in the prescription?

℞ Aconitinæ .... gr. 1-100.
Ol. limonis .... m. 1-10.
Alcoholis .... fl. ℥i.
Misce.

The Latest Remedies.

(Continued from page 69.)

Nucleogen is a compound of nucleinic acid with iron and arsenic. It is marketed in tablet form with 0.05 Gm. of the nuclein-iron-arsenic to the dose; and in solution for hypodermic use, each Cc. of which contains 0.1 Gm. The preparation is stated to be a general tonic. Manufactured by Hugo Rosenberg, Berlin.

Paranephrin is one of the lengthening list of vasoconstrictors obtained from the suprarenal glands, of which adrenalin is the type. It is said to be less toxic than other suprarenal preparations. It is marketed as a powder and in the form of a sterilized 1 : 1000 solution in 0.6 per cent. sodium chloride.

Parisol is a condensation product of formaldehyde and saponified naphtha quinones, which is recommended as a non-toxic antiseptic. Manufactured by Bense & Eicke, Embeck, Germany.

Phagocytin is a sterilized solution of sodium nucleinate intended for hypodermic use in the treatment of lowered conditions of the nervous system. Each Cc. contains 0.05 Gm. of the salt. Marketed by Hugo Rosenberg, Berlin.

Piperazine monomethylarsinate is made by dissolving one molecular weight of piperazine in cold 90 per cent. alcohol, and adding to this solution a solution of two molecular weights of monomethylarsinic acid in 90 per cent. alcohol.

Pittylene is a condensation product of pine tar and formaldehyde, which forms a fine brown powder of a strong tarry odor. It is readily soluble in alkaline solutions, alcohol, chloroform, collodion and acetone. It is used in the treatment of chronic eczema, combined with zinc-starch paste and glycerin.

Proponal is an improved veronal, being dipropylbarbituric acid. It forms colorless crystals which are soluble in 70 parts of boiling water and in 1640 parts of cold water. It is administered in doses of 0.15 Gm., 0.2 Gm. and 0.5 Gm. A quiet sleep follows in from 15 to 40 minutes after taking. Manufactured by Farbenfabriken vorm. Friedrich Bayer & Co., Elberfeld, and E. Merck, Darmstadt; marketed by the Continental Color Works and Merck & Co., New York.

Protosal is the salicylic acid ester glycerin formaldehyde compound. It is an oily liquid, used as an embrocation in rheumatic affections, combined with alcohol or olive oil.

Purgella is a phenolphthalein compound recommended as a laxative. It is said to consist of phenolphthalein, 0.25 Gm.; sodium tartrate, 75 Gm.; sodium bicarbonate, 25 Gm.; fruit oleosaccharate, 100 Gm., and tartaric acid, 27.4 Gm. Manufactured by Hesse & Goldstaub, Hamburg.

Quinine formate has been introduced into medicine in two forms—neutral and basic—and they are said to be particularly adapted for hypodermic use. Solutions of formic acid and the formates have acquired a vogue of late as rejuvenators. The basic quinine formate is soluble in 5 parts of cold water.

Pararegulin is an emulsionized mixture of liquid paraffin combined with 10 per cent. of aqueous extract of cascara sagrada. It is marketed in gelatin capsules containing 3 Gm. by Chemische Fabrik, Helfenberg. (See Regulin.)

Radiophor is a radio-active mass of a special shape intended for introduction under the skin for the application of radio-activity to diseased organs or parts. It is made and marketed by P. Beiersdorf & Co., Hamburg.

Regulin is a combination of agar agar with cascara sagrada. Acting on the theory that when any substance is added to the diet which will render the fæces more voluminous and richer in water, agar agar was tried, and found efficacious. As a stimulant to the lower intestines 25 per cent. of fluid extract of cascara sagrada was added and regulin resulted. It is made by the Chemische Fabrik, Helfenberg.

Ovaron is an organotherapeutic preparation made by treating the active constituent of the ovaries with tannin so as to produce a substance which is not affected by the gastric juice and will be absorbed in the intestinal tract. Put up in tablets containing 01. Gm. of active substance by the Fabriken Rhenania, Aachen.

Santyl is a salicylic acid ester compound of santalol, the alcohol of sandal oil. It forms an oily liquid which is used like gonosan and gonosol in the treatment of gonorrhœa, in doses of 30 droops, three times daily. Manufactured by Knoll & Co.

Silver iodide has been recently put forward as a remedy for gastralgia, syphilis and urethritis. It is a voluminous yellow powder used internally in the treatment of syphilis in pills containing 0.005 Gm. each, and externally as an injection in 5 to 10 per cent. solutions.

Solulorol (thyminic acid; nucleotin-phosphoric acid) is a yellowish brown amorphous powder, which is recommended as a uric acid solvent in the treatment of gout. It is put up in tablets containing 0.25 Gm. each by Max Elb, Dresden. Consult also AMERICAN DRUGGIST for August 14, 1905, p. 69; November 27, 1905, p. 295; December 11, 1905, p. 317.

Splenon. What is said under teston applies to splenon, except that the latter is prepared from pig spleen.

Strychnine antitoxine is obtained, like the antitoxine of morphine, from animals which have been habituated to large doses of strychnine and are thus immune to the toxic effects of the drug.

Suprarenal tonogene is a solution of suprarenal extract, 0.1 Gm.; chloretone, 0.5 Gm.; sodium chloride, 0.7 Gm., dissolved in water, 100 Gm., which is marketed by Apotheker Richter, Budapest.

Tannalborin is a grayish brown powder consisting of a compound of aluminum subgallate with 10 per cent. of sodium borate. It is not soluble to any extent in water or alcohol. It is chiefly intended for veterinary use in the treatment of diarrhœa in foals and pigs, the dose being a teaspoonful to a tablespoonful.

Teston is prepared from steer testicles and manufactured and put on the market in the same way as ovaron, which see.

Theranol. See thermiol.

Thermiol is the correct name of a preparation consisting of a 25 per cent. solution of sodium phenylpropiolate which has been incorrectly designated theranol in various journals. It is used in pulmonary tuberculosis and affections of the throat as an inhalation in the form of 1 to 3 per cent. solutions. Prepared by Dr. T. Schuchardt Chemische Fabrik, Görlitz.

Thymidol is methylpropyl-phenol menthol made of thymol and menthol by a patented process. It finds use in the preparation of antiseptic mouth washes and toothpastes. It is made by Hesse & Goldstaub, Hamburg.

Turicin is a chemical combination of tannin and glutenin, which forms a fine flesh colored powder without special odor or taste; insoluble in water, alcohol and diluted acids, but soluble in dilute alkali solutions. Being resistant to the action of the gastric juice and affected only by the alkaline fluids of the intestines, it is recommended for use in the treatment of diarrhœa, accompanied by intestinal catarrh. Manufactured by Blattman & Co., Waedensville, Switzerland.

Vitose is a name applied to a new ointment base, which is described as a glycerin-oil-albuminate (*Glycerin Oelalbuminat*). It is an odorless ointment vehicle without any tendency to rancidity, which is miscible with glycerin, water, oil and other fats. Mixed with an equal weight of glycerin and perfumed vitose cream is formed, which is used as a cosmetic and application to the hair. Made by J. E. Stroschein, Berlin.

Urea diethylmalonate is one of several chemical titles for veronal.

Urgosan is a preparation of gonosan and hexamethylenetetramin put up in gelatin capsules containing 0.3 gm. of the former and 0.15 gm. of the latter. It is used in the treatment of inflammation of the bladder, following gonorrhœal infection of the urinary tract. Made by J. D. Riedel, Berlin.

Veratrol is the shorter name adopted by E. Merck, Darmstadt, for pyrocatechindimethylether, a succedaneum for guaiacol. It forms a liquid, insoluble in water, but soluble in alcohol, ether and fatty oils. It is used externally as a liniment in intercostal neuralgia, and internally in doses of two drops in gelatin capsules, three times daily in pulmonary tuberculosis.

Cream of Current Literature

A summary of the leading articles in contemporary pharmaceutical periodicals.

Liquid Iodoform.—Biachi (*Bolletino Chimico Farmaceutico*, 1905, No. 44) suggests the preparation of a "liquid" iodoform which has the advantage of easily penetrating into the tissues. Thirty-five parts of caustic potassa are dissolved in twenty-five parts of water, and to the solution are added fifty parts of oleic acid and thirty parts of alcohol, 95 per cent. To this mixture thirty parts of sublimed iodine are added gradually, shaking from time to time. The mixture is now heated, and when the entire amount of iodine has become absorbed, a little more iodine is added, so that the mixture will assume a slightly brownish color. A few drops of a solution of potassa are next added until the mixture becomes decolorized. After a few days, during which the mixture is allowed to stand in a dark place, the supernatant liquid is decanted. This liquid is syrupy in consistence, yellowish in color and has the odor of iodoform. It is miscible with water, alcohol, ether, chloroform, carbon disulphide, volatile oils, fixed oils, benzol, glycerin, etc. This liquid iodoform may also be employed as a solvent for guaiacol and other drugs. When applied to the skin it is rapidly absorbed, and iodine is found in the urine a few hours after it has been applied.

Sodium Chloride Solution as a Reagent.—Tralapatani (*Bulletin de Pharmacie et de Chimie de Roumanie*, 1905) calls attention to the manifold uses of a saturated solution of sodium chloride as a reagent. The solution, with the addition of acetic acid, precipitates albumoses in the urine, the precipitate dissolving when the mixture is heated and forming again on cooling. Interesting reactions are also obtained with a saturated solution of sodium chloride and the salts of quinine or quinidine, naphthylamine, hydrochloride and dimethylamine. Each of these substances, however, has a different effect upon the reagent, so that it may serve to differentiate between the members of the group. Thus, with quinine hydrobromide or with quinidine sulphate, the solution gives rise to an amorphous precipitate is once redissolved it does not crystallize again on cooling. thyamine hydrochloride one obtains a crystalline precipitate abundant in quantity, but slightly soluble in acetic acid in the cold, though freely soluble with the aid of heat. When this precipitate is once redissolved it does not crystallize again on colling. With dimethylamine a crystalline precipitate is formed which is insoluble in the cold, soluble with the aid of heat in acetic acid, but crystallizes again on cooling. It is distinguished from the precipitate produced by albumoses through the fact that the latter is amorphous. The saturated solution of sodium chloride also furnishes a means for differentiation between ethylamine, diethylamine and triethylamine. With the first of these no precipitate occurs, with the second a precipitate is thrown down in the cold, while with the third no precipitate occurs, but the addition of acetic acid gives rise to a precipitate.

The Flow of Resin.—Tschirch (*Archiv. der Pharmazie*, 1905, p. 81) has made an interesting study of the secretion of resin in resin-bearing trees which have been incised intentionally or wounded accidentally. These injuries not only increase the amount of resin in plants which are normally provided with secretory apparatus, but even cause a secretion in plants, such as *Styrax benzoin*, which are devoid of this apparatus. The author experimented for six years upon four species of *Coniferæ* which furnish ordinary turpentine. As the result of these experiments he concluded that any injury which affects the cambium produces a resinous flow. He divides the secretion thus obtained into two parts: The primary secretion, which follows immediately upon the injury, lasting but a short time and consisting in the emptying of normally existing reservoirs; and the secondary secretion derived from newly-formed receptacles which is pathological. The newly formed excretory apparatus form a network of anastomosing receptacles, which open at the surface of the wound and occupy the ligneous tissue, but do not form in the bark; even the youngest of these newly-formed canals contains resin. This secondary flow occurs in summer, usually three or four weeks after the wound has been inflicted, and ends at the close of the season by the healing of the wound, which becomes covered with a solid mass of resin. This takes place annually, and the amount of resin produced is proportionate to the size of the wound and the duration of the irritation. A variety of methods of wounding these trees has been tried, including superficial injuries produced by scraping the bark; burns, which destroy the cambium without previously removing the bark, and incised wounds of various types.

The Treatment of Burns.—The old method of treating burns with carron oil is gradually becoming obsolete, although frequent calls for this time-honored preparation still occur in every drug store. In a summary on the treatment of burns in *Répertoire de therapeutique* (December, 1905, p. 262) we find the following useful hints: The modern treatment of all burns begins with a most careful antisepsis, by means of which we avoid the suppuration which formerly was regarded as a necessary part of the evolution of burns. In order to obtain absolute cleanliness, surgeons in severe cases of burns now very frequently give chloroform and wash the injury with soapsuds and, if necessary, with a brush. Blisters that have opened are carefully cut away, while those that have remained intact are left alone. The next thing to do is to apply a treatment which will favor the healing of the burn and also relieve pain. A wet compress soaked in a saturated solution of potassium nitrate produces a lowering of the local temperature of the burn, and thus relieves pain. The solution may also be used in the form of a prolonged bath for two or three hours. If necessary morphine must be administered in small doses to relieve pain and later stimulants and tonics are indicated.

Ichthyol or thiol are useful local applications which may be applied in the liquid state, or else mixed with equal parts of talcum and bismuth nitrate. The most approved modern healing agent in burns is picric acid. The only limitations for this remedy being that it is not applicable in children, and that it is not suitable for deep burns with eschars, nor in old suppurating burns. The reason for this is that picric acid may be toxic in the young and that it is primarily a drying application, while deep burns with sloughs require the wet treatment.

The method of using picric acid is as follows: After having disinfected the parts with the aid of soap and water, alcohol and ether, and having washed them with a weak solution of mercuric chloride, as well as having attended to the blisters, the parts are immersed for from one-half to three-quarters of an hour in a solution of twelve parts of picric acid to 1,000 parts of water. Finally, the parts are dressed with gauze pads soaked in the picric acid solution, over which is placed some absorbent cotton and a bandage. An important rule is that no rubber sheeting or gutta-percha tissue should be used over the compress, because this would keep up the moisture of the dressing, while picric acid is essentially a dry dressing. The compress should be allowed to remain for six or eight days, when healing will have progressed sufficiently and when the gauze will be found adhering to the burn. In order to remove the gauze the parts should be immersed for ten minutes in a hot picric acid solution and the dressing should be renewed. A further detail of interest is the question of removing picric acid stains from the hands. In order to avoid these stains the hands may be anointed with petrolatum before touching picric acid, but if they are stained they should be washed in a saturated solution of lithium carbonate or sodium borate, or simply in water to which an alkali, like ammonia, has been added.

Queries and Answers

We shall be glad, in this department, to respond to calls for information on all pharmaceutic matters.

Show Globe Colors.—" J. F." and others: The following are approved formulas:

AMETHYSTINE.

Sodii salicylatis ....Gr. x.
Tinct. ferri chlor........................ʒss.
Aquæ ....Cong. iiss.

Dissolve the salicylate in the water and add the tincture.

BLUE.

Cupri sulphatis ....℥iv.
Aquæ ammoniæ........................q. s.
Aquæ ....Cong. iiss.

Dissolve the copper sulphate in 40 ounces of water and add ammonia water cautiously until the precipitate first formed is redissolved; then add the rest of the water.

GREEN.

Nickel sulphate ....℥iij.
Sulphuric acid ....℥vi.
Water ....Cong. iiss.

Dissolve the nickel sulphate in the water and add the acid, stirring constantly. Allow to deposit and decant.

GARNET RED.

Potassium bichromate ....℥xvi.
Sulphuric acid ....℥xvi.
Water ....Cong. iiss.

Dissolve the bichromate in the water, then add the acid gradually, stirring all the time.

ROSE RED.

Cudbear ....℥ij.
Water ....℥x.

Macerate for a day or two, filter and add to the water until the desired shade is produced; then add to each gallon—

Stronger ammonia water........................℥ss.

ORANGE.

Potassii bichromatis ....℥xvi.
Acid nitrici ....℥viij.
Aquæ destillata ....Cong. iiss.

Dissolve the potassium bichromate in the water and add the acid.

Cement for Wedgewood Mortars.—" D. B.": Numerous formulas are extant for cements to unite fractured mortars, but the most satisfactory of all consists of equal parts of gutta percha and shellac, fused together to a fluid consistency in an iron pot. The fractured surfaces must be strongly heated, a little of the cement applied and the pieces brought together under pressure. Mixtures of calomel and acacia mucilage and of fresh white of egg with finely powdered quicklime are favored by some pharmacists as cements for porcelain and composition mortars. The first named is made by incorporating a sufficient quantity of calomel with acacia mucilage to form a thin paste. It is applied to the dried surfaces of the fractures, the pieces being afterward brought together and maintained in position by means of a string tightly wound around the mortar or by the imposition of weights or pressure. The quicklime cement is made by mixing quickly one part of quicklime, one part of water, two parts of fresh egg albumen (white) and applying at once to the fractured surfaces, which must be immediately brought into apposition and retained there until the cement sets.

A preparation having a great vogue in China for the repair of broken porcelain, faïence, stoneware, etc., is said to be made as follows:

	Parts.
Slaked lime, finely powdered..............	54
Alum, powdered	6
Oxblood, fresh, well beaten..............	40

According to the source from which this formula is taken, the ingredients are mixed and stirred until a homogeneous creamy mass is obtained. As a possible improvement on this formula we would suggest the use of unslaked lime (finely powdered quicklime) and the serum of oxblood after the fibrin has been removed by whipping.

Blackboard Paint.—" E. I. C.": We have had no experience with the paint made from the following formula, but the ingredients mixed in the proportions named should form a satisfactory surface. We take the recipe from MacEwan's "Pharmaceutical Formulas":

Shellac ....℥iv.
Lampblack ....℥ij.
Emery powder ....℥i.
Ultramarine ....℥i.
Alcohol ....℥iiss.

Dissolve the shellac in the alcohol; place the lampblack, emery and ultramarine on a cheese-cloth strainer, pour on part of the shellac solution, stirring constantly and gradually adding the rest of the solution until all of the powders have passed through the strainer.

To Detannate Tincture of Cinchona.—" C. F." asks us to give him a process for detannating tincture of cinchona which will not affect the other constituents of the tincture. Our correspondent is referred to that necessary book for pharmacists, the National Formulary, where it will be learned that detannated tincture of cinchona is made by shaking 8 fluid ounces of fluid extract of cinchona with 8 ounces of moist ferric hydrate freshly prepared, shaking well, filtering through cotton and washing the filter with 16 ounces of diluted alcohol.

To Make One Gallon of Toilet Cream.—" B. M. C." writes: "Kindly publish a formula for making one gallon of toilet cream containing tragacanth, glycerin, quince seed, tincture of benzoin, boric acid and distilled water; also give directions for compounding."

It is not customary to combine tragacanth with quince in a toilet cream, glycerite of starch being considered superior to tragacanth in association with quince. We suggest the following formulas, No. 1 being the one desired and No. 2 a starch-quince combination:

Quince seed ....℥iss.
Tragacanth ....ʒss.
Boric acid ....ʒss.
Glycerin ....Oiss.
Alcohol ....℥viij.
Distilled water ....Ovi.
Tincture of benzoin........................Mxv.
Perfume, q. s. to suit.

Dissolve the acid in the glycerin and add the water. In this macerate the quince seed and tragacanth for several days, shaking frequently until the mucilages are thoroughly diffused. The quince seed should first be broken in a mortar, care being taken not to crush or powder the dark outer coating of the seed. After the mucilage is formed strain through cheese cloth or coarse calico with pressure; lastly add the tincture of benzoin and the perfume (about 4 drachms of eau de cologne is suggested), which have been previously mixed with the alcohol.

II.

Quince seed........................℥iiss.
Boric acid ....ʒi.
Glycerin ....Oij.
Carbolic acid (95 per cent.)........................ʒij.
Glycerite of starch........................℥xxx.
Alcohol ....Oij.
Oil of lavender........................ʒij.
Cologne water ....℥iv.

Dissolve the boric acid in the water and macerate the quince seed in the solution for three hours; press the mucilage through a straining cloth and add the carbolic acid, glycerin and glycerite of starch and mix well. Dissolve the oil of lavender and cologne water in the alcohol, add the solution to the mucilage and mix thoroughly.

PURE FOOD BILL PASSED.

Comprehensive Definitions of Drugs Retained—Sale of Imitations Prohibited—Variations from U. S. P. Strength Permissible if Stated on the Label—Power Vested in Bureau of Chemistry.

(*From our Regular Correspondent.*)

Washington, February 22.—After debate covering the major portion of ten days the Heyburn Pure Food bill passed the Senate of the United States yesterday afternoon by a vote of 63 to 4. The four Senators voting in opposition stated that their opposition was due to the centralization of power in the hands of the Bureau of Chemistry of the Agricultural Department, which is a feature of the bill.

That portion of the measure which most nearly affects the drug trade is contained in sections 6 and 9. Section 6 defines the term drug as including "all medicines and preparations recognized in the United States Pharmacopœia or National Formulary for internal and external use; also any substance intended to be used for the cure, mitigation or prevention of disease." Section 9 defines adulteration, and states that a drug shall be deemed to be misbranded "if it be an imitation or offered for sale under the name of another article," or if the label shall contain any statement which shall be false or misleading as to the constituents of the contents of the package.

We present below an abstract of the measure, reproducing in full those parts which bear particularly on the drug business.

Section 1 provides that it shall be unlawful to manufacture, sell or deliver in any Territory of the United States or to ship into any Territory of the United States or from one State to another any article of food, drug, medicines or liquors which is adulterated or misbranded, or which contains any poisonous or deleterious substance within the meaning of this act, section 4 providing that this shall mean "added poisonous or deleterious substances or ingredients injurious to human health when used or prescribed in the usual manner of use of such article," and prescribes a fine of not more than $500 or imprisonment for not more than one year for infraction of the law.

Section 2 provides among other things that the officers of any corporation guilty of transgressing the law shall be personally liable for such transgression.

Section 3 provides that the Secretary of the Treasury, Secretary of Agriculture and the Secretary of Commerce and Labor shall make uniform rules and regulations for the collection and examination of samples.

Section 4 provides that the samples collected are to be examined by the Bureau of Chemistry of the Department of Agriculture and that where the sample appears to be adulterated the Secretary of Agriculture shall give notice to the offenders, who shall be given an opportunity for defense in the United States Court, and that only after final judgment in the United States Court can the results of the examination be made public.

Section 5 provides the United States District Attorney shall bring prosecutions on the complaint of the Secretary of Agriculture or of any health officer or agent of any State, Territory, district or insular possession.

DEFINITION OF THE TERM DRUG.

Section 6 reads as follows:

Sec. 6.—That the term "drug" as used in this act shall include all medicines and preparations recognized in the United States Pharmacopœia or National Formulary for internal and external use; also any substance intended to be used for the cure, mitigation or prevention of diseas.

Sections 7 and 8 define the terms food and liquor.

DEFINITION OF ADULTERATION AND MISBRANDING.

Section 9 provides that for the purpose of this Act any article shall be deemed to be adulterated:

In case of drugs:

First. If, when any drug is sold under or by a name recognised in the United States Pharmacopœia or National Formulary, it differs from the standard of strength, quality or purity, as determined by the test laid down in the United States Pharmacopœia or National Formulary official at the time of investigation: Provided, That no drug defined in the United States Pharmacopœia or National Formulary shall be deemed to be adulterated under this provision if the standard of strength, quality or purity be plainly stated upon the bottle, box or other container thereof, although the standard may differ from that determined by the test laid down in the United States Pharmacopœia or National Formulary.

Second. If its strength or purity fall below the professed standard or quality under which it is sold.

That such drug shall be deemed to be misbranded:

First. If it be an imitation of or offered for sale under the name of another article.

Second. If the package containing it, or its label, shall bear any statement as to its constituent ingredients or the substances contained therein, which statement shall be false or misleading in any particular, or if the same is falsely branded as to the country, State or Territory, or place therein, in which it is manufactured or produced, or if the contents of the original package shall have been removed, in whole or in part, and other contents shall have been placed in such package.

The remainder of this section defines in detail the application of the law to confectionery, food and liquors.

GUARANTY AS A PROTECTION FOR THE RETAILER.

Section 10 reads as follows:

Sec. 10. That no dealer shall be prosecuted under the provisions of this act when he can establish a guaranty signed by the wholesaler, jobber, manufacturer or other party residing in the United States, from whom he purchases such articles, to the effect that the same is not adulterated or misbranded within the meaning of this act, designating it such article. Said guaranty, to afford protection, shall contain the name and address of the party or parties making the sale of such articles to such dealer, and in such case said party or parties shall be amenable to the prosecutions, fines and other penalties which would attach in due course to the dealer under the provisions of this act.

Section 12 provides that refusal to furnish samples shall constitute a misdemeanor. Section 18 provides for the confiscation of articles coming within the provisions of the law. Section 16 provides that the act shall take effect on July 1, 1906.

PHILADELPHIA COLLEGE OF PHARMACY.

Prof. Coblentz Discusses the Chemistry of the U. S. P.—Dr. Lowe Talks on U. S. P. Doses—Mr. Wilbert Reviews Pharmaceutical Advances.

The regular monthly pharmaceutical meeting of the Philadelphia College of Pharmacy was held on Tuesday afternoon, February 20, with Prof. Samuel P. Sadtler in the chair.

Prof. Virgil Coblentz, of the College of Pharmacy of the City of New York, gave a series of Comments on the Chemicals of the Eighth Decennial Revision of the United States Pharmacopœia. Professor Coblentz described the manner in which the revision work was carried on, and then considered some of the special features of the new Pharmacopœia pertaining to the inorganic chemicals. Among these were the purity rubric, time-limit test for heavy metals, elimination of the flame test for the presence or absence of sodium salts; the elimination of tests for innocuous impurities, as of chlorides, sulphates, sodium or calcium in the salts of the alkalies; precautions to be observed in the estimation of the organic salts of the alkalies. In considering the special tests for arsenic, Dr. Coblentz said that "while absolute purity is neither attainable nor desirable, yet under no circumstances should considerations of commercial advantage as to the cheapness or the convenience of manufacturers defer us from guarding most carefully public health and safety." He said: "While 1 part of arsenic in 10,000 parts of chemical is permissible in all chemicals which are given in moderate doses, yet there are instances in which it is evidently excessive, as in sodium phosphate, sodium sulphate and sulphur, which are usually given in large doses, frequently extending over considerable periods of time." Dr. Coblentz stated that he considered the modified Gutzeit test for arsenic as especially adapted to pharmaceutical work.

Dr. Clement B. Lowe read a paper on Doses in the United States Pharmacopœia.

M. I. Wilbert, Ph. M., read a paper on Recent Advances in Pharmacy, in which he called attention to the efforts now being made to eliminate charlatanry and fraud from the practice of medicine and pharmacy.

The Manufacturing Chemists' Registration Bureau.

The following titles have been received for registration by the Manufacturing Chemists' Registration Bureau: Almarosa and Diastase Potent, by Nelson, Baker & Co., Detroit, Mich.; American Girl and Zira, by Frederick Stearns & Co., Detroit, Mich.

JOINT MEETING OF THE EXECUTIVE COMMITTEES OF THE N. A. R. D. AND THE N. W. D. A.

The Details Arranged for Enforcement of the Reciprocity Plan—Utmost Harmony Prevails—Chicago Jobbers in Line—N. A. R. D. to Meet in Atlanta October 22—Banquets to Cement Good Feeling.

(From our Regular Correspondent.)

CHICAGO, February 22.—One result of the joint meeting of the executive committees of the National Association of Retail Druggists and the National Wholesale Druggists' Association, which was held in Chicago, February 12 to 16, was the decision of the jobbers to aid the retailers in inaugurating immediately a determined campaign to induce all manufacturers to join in the Direct Contract and Serial Numbering Plan and insist upon the strict observance of the terms of agreement, hitherto known as the tripartite plan, but hereafter to be called the reciprocity plan, for the proper marketing of all proprietary remedies and patented drugs.

PROPRIETORS URGED TO ADOPT D. C. S. N. PLAN.

It was unanimously agreed at a conference of the Executive Committee of the National Association of Retail Druggists on the second day of the meeting that it would be advisable to send out agents to urge the proprietors who are not already interested in the direct contract and serial numbering plan to join in the work of persuading others to pledge themselves to the agreement. Another interesting feature of the meeting, all the sessions of which were held in the Auditorium Annex, was the fact that the jobbers appeared more willing than ever before o work in harmony with the retailers in the performance of both the D. C. and S. R. and reciprocity plans.

The reason for changing the name of the latter plan was due to the belief that the word tripartite suggested an iron clad trust agreement and that it would be more advisable to give the scheme a more euphonistic title. The main provisions of the plan, however, as far as they affect the marketing of goods by the manufacturer, jobber and retailer, remain the same.

The retailers also decided at the Chicago meeting to use drastic measures in insuring the scrupulous observance of this plan by listing any dealer who fails to live up to the terms of the reciprocity plan as an aggressive cutter.

CHICAGO JOBBERS IN LINE.

An amicable conference with the Chicago jobbers was held by a subcommittee of the N. A. R. D. at the conclusion of the joint conference of the N. A. R. D. and the N. W. D. A. executive committees, Tuesday afternoon, February 13. After discussing existing difficulties, the retail men found that the Chicago jobbers were ready to assist them in their efforts to enforce both plans. The N. A. R. D. Executive Committee discussed questions and details on Wednesday and again on Thursday until late in the evening, when the meeting was finally adjourned.

CHICAGO RETAILERS AND JOBBERS CONFER.

A second conference on disputed questions was held between the members of the Chicago Association of Retail Druggists Executive Committee and the Chicago jobbers on Thursday afternoon, but no further action was taken.

N. A. R. D. TO MEET IN ATLANTA.

The next meeting of the National Association of Retail Druggists will be held in Atlanta, Ga., about October 22, almost immediately after the meeting of the National Wholesale Dealers' Association, which will be held in Washington on October 8.

Representatives of the retailers who were present at the meeting were: Simon N. Jones, of Louisville; M. T. Voegeli, of Minneapolis; J. A. Lockie, of Buffalo; Lewis C. Hopp, of Cleveland; W. D. Wheeler, of Boston, and Thomas H. Potts, of Philadelphia, all of whom composed the Executive Committee of the N. A. R. D., and John G. Gallagher, of 466 Grove street, Jersey City.

Among the wholesale representatives were M. N. Kline, of Philadelphia; Albert Plaut, of New York; M. Cary Peter, of Louisville; Frank A. Faxon, of Kansas City; W. J. Walding, of Toledo; Theodore F. Meyer, of St. Louis, and John W. Morrison, of Chicago, all members of the Executive Committee of the N. W. D. A., as well as F. E. Hollidy, vice-chairman of the Proprietary Committee of the N. W. D. A., and Joseph E. Toms, secretary of the N. W. D. A.

TIME FOR BANQUETS BETWEEN SESSIONS.

Although a considerable amount of business was transacted every day at the meeting, entertainment features were not lacking. A. J. Horlick entertained both retailers and jobbers Monday evening before the meeting began, while on Tuesday evening the Executive Committee of the Chicago Association of Retail Druggists tendered a banquet to both national Executive Committees at Vogelsang's. At this banquet Charles A. Avery presided as toastmaster, while President M. T. Breslin, Thomas Voegeli, T. H. Potts and Simon N. Jones delivered addresses. A. H. Beardsley, of the Dr. Miles Medical Company, also gave a dinner to the N. A. R. D. Executive Committee, and other retailers on Wednesday evening, at the Stratford Hotel.

LABEL LAWS ALL OVER THE UNITED STATES.

Bills Introduced in Various States to Label Proprietary Medicines—Features of the Various Measures—Much Diversity of Opinion.

Many druggists in this State are expressing their decided disapproval of the provisions contained in the Stevens bill, which has been drafted to amend the public health law relative to the proper labeling of proprietary and other medicinal preparations containing alcohol, narcotic or other potent drugs and providing for the inspection, analysis and regulation of their manufacture and sale. The main objection to this proposed measure, in the opinion of most of its opponents, is that the necessity for labeling the amount of alcohol contained in most preparations might tend to check the sale of the liquid, although the presence of a small amount of alcohol is absolutely necessary for the proper preservation of the medicine. The idea of compelling manufacturers of proprietary remedies virtually to publish their formulas is also repellant to most dealers. Many cough medicines, moreover, most dealers contend, would not sell as freely if it was publicly advertised that they contained necessary narcotics. The fact that a bill similar to the Stevens measure will become effective in the District of Columbia on April 1 affords no reason, according to dealers in this State, why the proposed bill should be enacted in New York.

In the State of New Jersey, also, the drug trade is greatly exercised over the announcement that Senator Johnson Cornish, of Warren County, has introduced into the Legislature a bill requiring that all packages which contain proprietary medicines shall have a label attached showing in detail the ingredients of the medicine. The object of this bill, says Senator Cornish, is to prevent the use of alcohol and drugs of various characters in alleged "cure-alls," many of which, he asserts, are injurious to such an extent that their sale should be prohibited. Naturally the drug trade of New Jersey has the same objections to this measure that many New York State dealers have to the Stevens bill.

The Oliver bill, which was introduced in the New York State Legislature on January 22, providing for "the proper labeling of poisonous articles," is for similar reasons believed to contain more harm than good.

Members of the Schenectady Retail Druggists' Association are planning to modify the liquor tax license of $450, which was recently imposed upon the majority of the druggists in that city as the result of an investigation made by the State Excise Department special agents. George E. Duryea, J. T. Lyons and Rudolph Kellar have been appointed as a special committee to confer with Assemblyman Wemple and Senator Brackett for the purpose of fixing the price of the license at a fair figure and also to see what can be done to recover a portion of the sums already collected.

In Louisiana, another patent medicine restriction bill, prepared by Mr. Lockwood, of Copiah, La., is also attracting widespread attention. This measure, which is a modified form of a former bill, provides that it shall be required of all manufacturers of proprietary medicines to label their preparations intended for internal consumption which "contain more than 8 per cent. of ethyl alcohol or more than one-twenty-fifth of 1 per cent. of morphine, heroin, cocaine or salts or equivalents or derivatives of the same or any of them" and several similar poisons.

THE PROPRIETARY ARTICLES TRADE ASSOCIATION OF CANADA.

A Large Meeting—The Association Growing—To Combat Attacks Against Patent Medicines.

(*From our Regular Correspondent.*)

Toronto, Canada., Feb. 15.—The annual convention of the Proprietary Articles Trade Association of Canada opened at the St. Lawrence Hall, Montreal, on February 12, with a large attendance. President Henry Miles, of Leeming, Miles & Co., occupying the chair. Those present included the following: Arthur C. Fowler, Paris Medicine Company; Henry G. Polson, Polson Company; A. P. Raid, F. W. Schumacker and H. H. Hersby, Peruna Drug Mfg. Company; Thomas Reid, Wingate Chemical Company; John Mackenzie, Dr. Williams Medicine Company; D. Watson, Liquozone Company; R. R. Land, D. Kilmer Company; J. A. McKee, Dodds Medicine Company; F. H. Worthington, Wood Medicine Company; J. H. Mackenzie, Northrup & Lyman Company; N. G. Hargin, Centaur Company; Thomas Brady, Wells, Richardson Company; Brent Good, Carter Medicine Company; L. S. Levee, Dr. T. A. Slocum, Limited; W. J. Edmanson, Edmanson, Bates & Co.; E. T. Milburn, T. Milburn & Co., and W. H. Gore, Lydia Pinkham Company.

TO OPPOSE ANTI-PATENT MEDICINE AGITATION.

L. S. Levee, Toronto, secretary-treasurer, presented his annual report, which contained a recommendation that special articles should be prepared for general circulation through the medium of the newspaper press, pointing out the absurdity of the position assumed by physicians who posed as public benefactors.

The report was adopted and a resolution in accordance with its suggestion as to combating through the press the claims of the medical men who opposed the use of patent medicines.

OFFICERS ELECTED.

The following officers were elected: President, David Watson, Montreal; vice-president, J. A. Mackenzie, Brockville; secretary-treasurer, L. S. Levee, Toronto. Board of Control—J. A. McKee, Toronto; J. H. McKinnon, Toronto; E. T. Milburn, Toronto; N. G. Hargin, Montreal; W. J. Edmanson, Toronto; Thomas Brady, Montreal, and Henry Miles, Montreal.

Retiring President Miles was elected honorary president in place of the late Senator Fulford. It was decided that the next annual convention should be held in Toronto.

A banquet was held on the evening of the 12th, which was attended by many distinguished guests in addition to the members of the association.

Senator Dandurand, referring to the question of legislation, said that it might be advisable to have a board of experts appointed to whom all formulas should be submitted, but he did not sympathize with the proposition to have the formula printed on each bottle, as he believed that the men who had spent years in securing an article that would benefit the public should reap the reward of their labors.

Brent Good, of the Carter Medicine Company, New York, took a strong stand in opposition to any legislation which would compel proprietors to publish their formulas. A formula, he said, was private property and was entitled to protection as such. The people had not demanded this legislation.

H. B. Ames, M. P. P., expressed the hope that American medicine proprietors would come over and establish their factories in Canada.

F. H. Mathewson, president of the Montreal Board of Trade, spoke of the favorable conditions which existed in Canada. Owing to the general prevalence of prosperity, business had never been on a sounder basis than at present.

Other speakers were: J. A. McKee, J. A. Mackenzie, F. T. Schumacker, Henry Lyman, Thomas Brady, W. H. Gore and David Watson.

A COMPREHENSIVE PHARMACY LAW FOR THE DISTRICT OF COLUMBIA.

The A. Ph. A. Antinarcotic Bill Adopted—The Poison Regulations Laid Down—Modern Features of the Bill.

What is known as the Babcock-Gallinger bill has been enacted by both the House and the Senate and now awaits the signature of the President. This measure provides for the regulation of the practice of pharmacy in the District of Columbia.

THE ANTINARCOTIC FEATURES OF THE MEASURE.

Besides providing for the appointment of a Board of Pharmacy and administration of its affairs, the bill contains a section which is practically a duplicate of the antinarcotic bill drawn up by a committee of the American Pharmaceutical Association and approved by that organization at the Kansas City meeting in 1904. The section in question reads as follows:

"Sec. 11. That it shall be unlawful for any person, by himself, or by his servant or agent, or as the servant or agent of any other person, or of any firm or corporation, to sell, furnish or give away any cocaine, salts of cocaine or preparation containing cocaine or salts of cocaine; morphine, salts of morphine or preparation containing morphine or salts of morphine; or any opium or preparation containing opium; or any chloral hydrate or preparation containing chloral hydrate, except upon the original written order or prescription of a lawfully authorised practitioner of medicine, dentistry or veterinary medicine, which order or prescription shall be dated and shall contain the name of the person for whom prescribed, or, if ordered by a practitioner of veterinary medicine, shall state the kind of animal for which ordered, and shall be signed by the person giving the order or prescription. Such order or prescription shall be, for a period of three years, retained on file by the person, firm or corporation who compounds or dispenses the article ordered or prescribed, and it shall not be compounded or dispensed after the first time, except upon the written order of the original prescriber: Provided, however, That the above provisions shall not apply to preparations containing not more than two grains of opium, or not more than one-quarter grain of morphine, or not more than one-quarter grain of cocaine, or not more than two grains of chloral hydrate in the fluid ounce, or, if a solid preparation, in one avoirdupois ounce: Provided, also, That the above provisions shall not apply to preparations sold in good faith for diarrhea and cholera, each bottle or package of which is accompanied by specific directions for use and caution against habitual use, nor to liniments or ointments sold in good faith as such when plainly labeled 'for external use only,' nor to powder of ipecac and opium, commonly known as Dover's powder, when sold in quantities not exceeding twenty grains: And provided further, That the above provisions shall not apply to sales at wholesale by jobbers, manufacturers and retail druggists to retail druggists, hospitals, colleges and scientific or public institutions."

TO REGULATE THE SALE OF POISONS.

Another feature of the bill is a section providing in detail for the restriction of sale of poison in the District. This phase of the subject is covered by section 13, which is printed below:

"Sec. 13. That it shall be unlawful for any person to sell or deliver to any other person any of the following described substances, or any poisonous compound, combination or preparation thereof, to wit: The compounds of salts of antimony, arsenic, barium, chromium, copper, gold, lead, mercury, silver and zinc; the caustic hydrates of sodium and potassium, solution of water of ammonia, methyl alcohol, paregoric, the concentrated mineral acids, oxalic and hydrocyanic acids and their salts, yellow phosphorus, Paris green, carbolic acid, the essential oils of almonds, pennyroyal, tansy, rue and savin; croton oil, creosote, chloroform, cantharides or any aconite, belladonna, bitter almonds, colchicum, cotton root, cocculus indicus, conium, cannabis indica, digitalis, ergot, hyoscyamus, ignatia, lobelia, nux vomica, physsostigma, phytolacca, strophanthus, stramonium, veratrum viride or any of the poisonous alkaloids or alkaloidal salts derived from the foregoing, or any other poisonous alkaloids or their salts, or any other virulent poison, except in the manner following, and, moreover, if the applicant be less than eighteen years of age, except upon the written order of a person known or believed to be an adult.

"It shall first be learned, by due inquiry, that the person to whom delivery is about to be made is aware of the poisonous character of the substance, and that it is desired for a lawful purpose, and the box, bottle or other package shall be plainly labeled with the name of the substance, the word 'poison,' the name of at least one suitable antidote, when practicable, and the name and address of the person, firm or corporation dispensing the substance. And before delivery be made of any of the foregoing substances, excepting solution or water of ammonia, and sulphate of copper, there shall be recorded in a book kept for that purpose the name of the article, the quantity delivered, the purpose for which it is to be used, the date of delivery, the name and address of the person for whom it is procured, and the name of the individual personally dispensing the same; and said book shall be preserved by the owner thereof for at least three years after the date of the last entry therein: Provided, however, That the foregoing provisions shall not apply to articles dispensed upon the order of persons believed by the dispenser to be lawfully authorised practitioners of medicine, dentistry or veterinary surgery: Provided, also, That when a physician writes upon his prescription a request that it be marked or labeled 'poison,' the pharmacist shall, in the case of liquids, place the same in a colored glass, roughened bottle, of the kind commonly known in trade as a 'poison bottle,' and, in the case of dry substances, he shall place a poison label upon the container: Provided further, That the record of sale and delivery above mentioned shall not be required of manufacturers and wholesalers who shall sell any of the foregoing substances at wholesale to licensed pharmacists, but the box, bottle or other package containing such substances, when sold at wholesale, shall be properly labeled with the name of the substance, the word 'poison' and the name and address of the manufacturer or wholesaler: Provided further, That it shall not be necessary, in sales either at wholesale or retail, to place a poison label upon, nor to record the delivery of, the sulphide of antimony or the oxide or carbonate of zinc, or of colors ground in oil and intended for use as paints, or calomel, or paregoric when sold in quantities not over two fluid ounces; nor, in the case of preparations containing any of the substances named in this section, when a single box, bottle or other package, or when the bulk of one-half fluid ounce, or the weight of one-half avoirdupois ounce, does not contain more than an adult medicinal dose of such substance; nor, in the case of liniments or ointments, sold in good faith as such, when plainly labeled 'for external use only'; nor in the case of preparations put up and sold in the form of pills, tablets or lozenges, containing any of the substances enumerated in this section and intended for internal use, when the dose recommended does not contain more than one-fourth of an adult medicinal dose of such substance.

"For the purpose of this and of every section of this act, no box, bottle or other package shall be regarded as having been labeled 'poison' unless the word 'poison' appears conspicuously thereon, printed in plain, uncondensed gothic letters in red ink."

THE BOSTON ASSOCIATION.

A New England Headquarters Asked For—Eighteen Different Measures Affecting Pharmacists—To Repeal Screen Law—Antinarcotic Legislation.

(From our Regular Correspondent.)

BOSTON, February 17.—The monthly meeting of the Boston Association of Retail Druggists was held at the Massachusetts College of Pharmacy building on the evening of February 14, President La Pierre in the chair. Secretary Davis and Treasurer Godding submitted reports. The latter showed a cash balance of $1,090.83.

URGING $2, $4, $8 PRICE.

Chairman Ernst for the Executive Committee offered these resolutions, all of which were adopted: Urging upon manufacturers the importance of placing their goods upon a $2, $4 and $8 basis; advocating an N. A. R. D. headquarters for New England at Boston to be in charge of Mr. Keiser and assistants, and proposing for membership Charles H. Knott and J. A. Munkley.

LEGISLATIVE MATTERS.

Chairman Canning, of the Legislative Committee, reported eighteen bills before the Legislature of more or less importance to the trade. Two of these measures were proposed by the B. A. R. D., one of which restricted the sale of cocaine, the other excepting sixth-class license holders from the screen law. Mr. Canning gave the particulars of some of the objectionable measures and stated it as his belief that the poison bills would create conditions not intended. By enumerating substances like alcohol and cocaine the sale of certain preparations would be increased rather than lessened. He suggested that druggists urge upon legislators and others the importance of awaiting the outcome of the government's plan with preparations containing liquors and which were used as beverages under the guise of medicines.

President La Pierre cautioned the members against giving away compounds containing cocaine while urging legislation upon this subject.

Chairman Tobin for the Entertainment Committee advocated postponing the proposed ball until next fall, as there was insufficient time for preparation before March 1.

The Incorporation Committee reported progress and stated that a special meeting would be held at the earliest possible date to adopt the plan.

A copy of the souvenir engravings of thanks now being sent to those who assisted in making the N. A. R. D. convention a success was shown by Mr. Nute.

AT WORK ON THE SCHEDULE.

Mr. Ernst for the Executive Committee reported that all possible consideration is being given the subject of a schedule. Mr. Canning discussed the subject of a schedule in counter goods like that published by the N. A. R. D. It was voted to refer the matter to the Executive Committee, the latter to report at the next regular meeting. The members were urged to forward to Mr. Keiser memoranda of the articles which in their opinion should be upon the schedule.

CATALOGUING STOCK.

Frank F. Ernst, Ph. G., then gave an account of the method by which he catalogued goods in his stores, and Prof. La Pierre spoke adversely of the U. S. P. kaolin test for the detection of coloring matter in whisky. The speakers were each given a rising vote of thanks.

STANDING COMMITTEES.

President La Pierre has appointed the following standing committees for 1906:

LEGISLATIVE.—Henry Canning, chairman; C. Herbert Packard, J. F. Finneran, I. P. Gammon, F. F. Ernst.

TELEPHONE AND PRESS.—H. O. Nute, chairman; J. F. Finneran, G. L. Burroughs, C. G. Harring, C. P. Flynn.

COMMERCIAL INTEREST.—S. V. Rintels, chairman; A. E. Lynch, J. J. Mahoney, Frank Tucker, F. W. Archer.

RECEPTION.—C. Herbert Packard, chairman; W. D. Wheeler, W. C. Durkee, J. S. Woodrow, T. T. Reed.

MEMORIAL.—W. C. Durkee, chairman; Henry Canning, A. P. Fairbanks, L. D. Drury, S. T. Jeffers.

BY-LAWS.—W. D. Wheeler, chairman; J. W. McDermott, F. W. Connolly, Silas McVey, E. F. Varney.

AUDITING.—J. A. Bean, chairman; S. A. D. Sheppard, J. J. Naughton.

ENTERTAINMENT.—P. J. McCormick, chairman; Paul C. Klein, A. H. Tripp, J. J. Tobin, C. A. Stover, J. M. O'Brien, J. A. Tupper, E. G. Bossom, E. W. Shedd, W. A. Howe, J. R. Sawyer, M. J. Coleman.

FINANCE.—F. F. Ernst, chairman; W. D. Wheeler, L. W. Griffin, C. A. Stover, T. R. Grimes.

THE AMERICAN PHARMACEUTICAL ASSOCIATION.

A Local Branch Formed in Chicago—Growing Interest in the Plan—To Discuss Nostrums.

Acting on the recommendation of the committee on local organization, adopted at the annual meeting, members in Chicago and other pharmacists interested in the objects and purposes of the A. Ph. A. gathered in the Northwestern University Building, Tuesday evening, January 16. The meeting was called to order by Oscar Oldberg, who congratulated those present on their evident interest in the object of the call by braving the inclement weather.

C. S. N. Hallberg was elected temporary chairman and C. M. Snow secretary. The chairman reviewed recent efforts to increase the usefulness of the A. Ph. A., and the desirability of increasing the membership. Expressions of similar views were heard from nearly every one present, some regretfully admitting that while they realized that they had indirectly been benefited by the work of the association they had never been able to attend the annual meetings and, therefore, had not become members. With a local branch society holding monthly meetings they would gladly join the association.

Among those present who participated in the discussion were the following: Retail pharmacists, Messrs. Adamick, H. Fry, Klenze, Martin and Miss Stahl; hospital pharmacists, Messrs. Backer and von Zelinski, Misses Pierce and Stimson; U. S. P. H. and Marine Hospital Service, L. L. Watters; manufacturing pharmacists, Mr. Koch; Physicians, Dr. A. W. Baer; Northwestern University School of Pharmacy, Messrs. Oldberg, Gordin, Miner, Patterson, Pond, Oglesby, Clothier and Harrison; University of Illinois School of Pharmacy, Messrs. Hallberg, Day and Snow.

Messrs. Hallberg, Patterson and Snow were formed a Committee on Permanent Organization and Programme, to report at the next meeting, Northwestern University Building, Tuesday, February 13, at 8 P. M.

The second meeting of the Chicago branch convened Tuesday, February 13, at 8 P.M., in the Northwestern University Building.

Despite the most inclement night of the year, 24 persons were in attendance. Mr. Hallberg, temporary chairman, convened the meeting and announced having received regrets of inability to be present from Leo Eliel, South Bend, and W. O. Gross, Ft. Wayne. F. W. Meissner, Jr., La Porte, Ind., graced the occasion with his presence. Secretary Snow read the report of the Committee on Permanent Organization. The draft of the Declaration and By-Laws was read and after considerable discussion was unanimously adopted as amended on motion of Mr. Oldberg, seconded by Miss Stahl.

After some discussion it was decided that no provision be made for dues to the branch, the fee of $1 received by the secretary out of the annual contribution of $5 for every application for membership being sufficient to defray all necessary expenses of the branch, comprising printing and postage.

Mr. Oldberg introduced the Committee on Public Relations of the Chicago Medical Society, comprising Drs. C. S. Bacon and F. X. Walls, president and secretary, respectively, of the society, and Commissioner of Health, Dr. Whalen. They addressed the meeting relative to the work of the Chicago Medical Society in securing better laws for the regulation of pure food and drugs and restrictions on proprietary medicines. They hoped to have the active co-operation and support of the Pharmaceutical Association.

Responses were made by Messrs. Oldberg, Meissner, Day, Klenze, Misses Stahl, Stimson and the chairman, all of whom expressed pleasure that the medical profession had awakened to the desirability, if not necessity, of turning to the pharmacists for aid in these endeavors, which could only be mutually advantageous and of great benefit to the public.

The election of officers resulted in the following:

President, Oscar Oldberg; first vice-president, Herman Fry; second vice-president, F. W. Meissner, Jr.; third vice-president, Amanda W. Stahl; secretary-treasurer, W. B. Day. Chairmen of committees: Membership, C. M. Snow; education, and legislation, C. W. Patterson; practice, M. A. Miner; medical relations, C. S. N. Hallberg; public relations and publicity, E. D. Irvine.

The next meeting, to be held on March 18 at the same place and hour, will be devoted to a symposium on proprietary medicines. Prominent physicians will be present.

The following applications for membership were received from pharmacists in Chicago: Charles H. Avery, Otto E. Bruder, John J. Boehm, George Bollinger, Albert Henry Clark, Wm. Theo. Klenze, Edward H. Ladish, Albert Geo. Manns, Geo. M. Porter, Marvin Bird, Cleo Rounds, Julia Runkel, Charlotte E. Stimson, Otto G. Stolz, Wm. George Valentine, Cornelius Van Schaack and Mark Henry Watters.

J. Uri Lloyd Off for the Orient.

Prof. John Uri Lloyd, of Cincinnati, the widely known chemist and author, sailed from New York with his wife and two daughters for Naples on the steamship *Celtic* on February 17. In a personal letter to the editors of the AMERICAN DRUGGIST he says:

"When this letter reaches you I shall be on my way to the Orient, where I shall remain for the next four to six months. I write you not only to extend my good will, but to say that in case any of our friends inquire about me, by correspondence or at the State meetings, I will be obliged if you will give them my regards, together with a statement as concerns my absence.

"For the first time I have the opportunity of studying subjects that are of interest and value in foreign countries, but in this instance the opportunity presented me is such as to lead me to hope that the time spent will not be wasted."

From earlier correspondence with Professor Lloyd we are able to say that from Naples he intends to take steamer for Smyrna, and meet Prof. T. H. Norton, U. S. consul at that port and former professor at the University of Cincinnati. He will then make a tour of Turkey and Arabia under the auspices of the Smithsonian Institution and the Department of Agriculture, of Washington, D. C. He carries credentials both from the institution and the department. The letter of introduction supplied by the Smithsonian Institution reads as follows:

SMITHSONIAN INSTITUTION, WASHINGTON, D. D.

To the Correspondents of the Smithsonian Institution, Washington, District of Columbia:

I have the honor to introduce to you Dr. John Uri Lloyd, of Cincinnati, O., the well-known botanist and a valued friend of this institution.

Dr. Lloyd is visiting Turkey, Arabia and the countries bordering on the Mediterranean for the purpose of carrying on scientific botanical investigations, and any assistance or personal courtesy that you may be able to extend to him will be highly appreciated by the Smithsonian Institution.

Professor Lloyd intends to call upon United States Consuls in the line of his travels and will study the natural products of the countries he visits.

THE MANHATTAN ASSOCIATION

Approves a Modified Formula-on-the-Label Bill—Professor Hynson, of Baltimore, the Lecturer of the Evening—Talks on the Æsthetics of Pharmacy—Dispensing Difficulties Discussed.

The presence of Prof. Hy. P. Hynson, of Baltimore, was responsible for an unusually large attendance at the regular monthly meeting of the Manhattan Pharmaceutical Association, which was held in the main lecture hall of the New York College of Pharmacy, Monday evening, February 19. The announcement that Professor Hynson would address the members on The Æsthetics of Pharmacy had attracted many of the older members, including Ewen McIntyre, Oscar Weissman, W. H. Ebbitt and F. O. Collins, while the audience was further augmented by the presence of many of the senior class.

President Alpers opened the meeting at 9.15 o'clock and after the reading of the minutes of the preceding meeting by the secretary he called for reports from the various committees. The only report forthcoming was one from Arthur C. Searles, chairman of the Committee on Legislation. Mr. Searles called attention to Assembly bill No. 218, which had been introduced by Mr. Oliver and which provided for the placing of a red poison label with skull and crossbones on the container of any drug or chemical which is recognized as a poison by the standard authors.

Mr. Searles also referred in a general way to a measure which had been introduced in the Assembly providing that upon the affidavit of parents that they had scruples against vaccination children might be admitted to the public schools without a vaccination certificate.

Mr. Searles then read portions of Assembly bill No. 258, introduced by Mr. Stevens, which provided for the labeling of proprietary remedies containing narcotic drugs or alcohol. The text of this measure is printed in full in the AMERICAN DRUGGIST for February 12, page 76. The essential features are contained in the following excerpts:

Section 225. No person shall manufacture, sell or offer or expose for sale or give away any proprietary medicine or other medicinal preparation containing alcohol, opium or any of its preparations, its alkaloids or their derivatives, strychnine, digitalis, chloroform, cannabis indica, chloral or any of its derivatives, bromides, cocaine or any of its salts, eucaine or any of its salts, acetanilid, antipyrine, bromoform, exalgine, holocain, phenacetin phenocoll, sulphonal, trional veronal or any other hypnotic anæsthetic, analgesic or cardiac, circulatory, respiratory or nerve depressant, unless the same shall have plainly and conspicuously stamped or printed on the bottle, box or receptacle containing the same or on the label affixed thereto, and also on the outside wrapper or package, if any, and also on the inside wrapper and on all circulars accompanying said medicine or medicinal preparation and relating to it, if any, a true statement of the percentage of alcohol and the percentage or proportion of each of the other above-mentioned or described drugs contained in each bottle, box, receptacle or package of such medicine or medicinal preparation. Such information shall be stamped or printed in antique or gothic type, easily to be read, of a size not smaller than that known as ten-point, and so displayed as to be conspicuous. Where alcohol is used as a solvent or preservative, or for any other purpose, it is to be deemed as contained in the medicine or medicinal preparation within the meaning of this act, and the drugs above mentioned or specified shall be described by their common, or English, names.

Sec. 226. The term medicinal preparation as used in this article shall be deemed to include every preparation or combination or mixture of drugs, or of drugs with substances which are not drugs, when such preparation, combination or mixture purports to have medicinal properties or to he a remedy or medicine or cure or food, or is intended to be used for medicinal effects or for the cure, alleviation or prevention of disease.

Sec. 227. The provisions of this article shall not apply to preparations intended solely for external use, whenever the label plainly indicates that the preparation is to be used externally, and is not to be used internally, nor to the dispensing of medicinal compounds on prescriptions by registered physicians, nor to preparations listed in the Pharmacopœia of the United States and the official Pharmacopœias of other nations, the National Standard Dispensatory and United States Dispensatory or the National Formulary, unless sold under a proprietary name.

Sec. 228. The label placed on a proprietary or patent medicine or other medicinal preparation by the manufacturer, as required by this act, shall be a warranty of the truth and accuracy of the statements contained therein, and the absence of any statement on such label shall constitute a warranty by the manufacturer that such medicine or medicinal preparation contains none of the drugs mentioned or described in section 225 of this article. Any person injured by reason of the failure of a manufacturer to comply with the provisions of this act shall have cause of action against the manufacturer and may recover both actual and exemplary damages.

The chairman stated that a hearing was to be given on this bill at Albany on February 21 and that the Committee on Legislation would like to be instructed as to the attitude to be assumed by them in the matter.

In response to a request for information Secretary Swann stated that the bill had the endorsement of the County Medical

Society, the Women's Christian Temperance Union and a number of civic organizations and prominent citizens.

After some discussion a motion that the committee be instructed to oppose the measure was defeated and the committee was instructed to advocate its passage, with the proviso that it should first be amended, if possible, by the insertion of a clause providing that a certain minimum proportion be specified for the various narcotic drugs and alcohol which it may be permissible to use without having any specification as to their presence printed on the label. The committee was also instructed to endeavor to secure the elision of the clause in the measure referring to "any other hypnotic and anæsthetic, analgesic, cardiac, circulatory, respiratory or nerve depressant." The deletion of this clause was proposed on the ground that it was so vague and general as to render the pharmacist liable in many cases in which he might have good grounds to think himself safe. It was also suggested that the opinions of experts would differ so materially in the application of the definitions as to make their presence in the measure conducive to endless litigation.

AMERICAN DRUGGISTS' SYNDICATE METHODS CONDEMNED.

J. Diner presented resolutions condemning the methods pursued by the American Druggists' Syndicate in their advertising propaganda as being calculated to disturb the friendly relations between the pharmacist and the physician. He stated that the advertising circulars distributed by the American Druggists' Syndicate contained copies of prescriptions which the laity were advised to use under varying conditions, thus usurping the functions of the physician. The resolution advised the members to refrain from encouraging the syndicate in any way, and were adopted as read after the assurance from Mr. Diner that they had received the sanction of the counsel of the association.

The application for membership of John Whitehill, of Hegeman & Co., was referred to the Committee on Membership for investigation.

THE ÆSTHETIC ASPECTS OF PHARMACEUTICAL DISPENSING.

The routine business of the meeting having been disposed of President Alpers introduced Prof. Hy. P. Hynson, of Baltimore, as the guest of the evening.

Professor Hynson said that in coming from the village of Baltimore, which had been recently all but wiped out in a fire, to the metropolis of New York with some ideas on dispensing he felt as though he were doing the hazardous thing of carrying coals to Newcastle, but he was consoled with the thought that the people of Newcastle would not know what kind of coals they had if they did not see others. He referred in a humorous way to the visit of one representative of New York to Baltimore who had discoursed learnedly on the metric system without carrying conviction, and of another who had told the Baltimore pharmacists a great deal about the relation of chemical constitution to physiological action. One of the listeners to this latter lecture, whose name was not mentioned, though it might be known to the members of the senior class, had said that what was interesting was not new and what was new was uninteresting. Mr. Hynson also took one or two other good natured flings at men prominent in pharmacy with whom he differed on various points. He then proceeded to read the address, which appears in full in another column.

DISPENSING PROBLEMS DISCUSSED.

At the close of his formal address, in the course of which Mr. Hynson showed a number of boxes and bottles bearing labels which he used to illustrate the various points made by him, he then dealt with some prescription problems, observing that the discussion of prescription problems had been a hobby of his for many years, and he looked upon such discussions somewhat in the nature of a pharmaceutical clinic and believed that they were as essential to the development of the best in pharmacy as the clinic made for the development of the best in medicine. Mr. Hynson had a number of specimens of prescriptions taken from prescription files, copies of which he exhibited, making remarks in passing upon the special features involved. Copies of the prescriptions shown, together with the comments on them, with be given in a later issue.

On motion of Mr. Diner, seconded by Ewen McIntyre, a rising vote of thanks was passed to Professor Hynson, who made suitable acknowledgment. In speaking to the motion the venerable Mr. McIntyre cheered the guest of the evening by telling him that he (Mr. McIntyre) had started to learn the business when New York had only a population of 250,000; since that the population had been depleted by two big fires, and there was consequently hope for Baltimore.

BROOKLYN DRUGGISTS SET AGAINST LOCALS.

Declare Themselves Opposed to Organizations on the District Plan, and Say They'll Have Nothing but D. C. S. N.—Metropolitans Told to Set Their Own House in Order.

The February meeting of the Kings County Pharmaceutical Society was unusually interesting owing to the discussion of bills in the Legislature pertaining to pharmacy, the operation of the different price protection plans and the attitude of the N. A. R. D. on the subject of organizing Brooklyn into districts, without regard to the position of the Kings County Pharmaceutical Society as the oldest and strongest pharmaceutical association in the county. A firm stand was taken against the proposition to district Brooklyn after the Manhattan plan, and the action of some druggists in Greenpoint who had asked to be organized in this way was shown to be taken under a misapprehension. One of the Greenpoint leaders admitted that a mistake had been made which he would endeavor to have rectified.

Dr. William Muir, chairman of the Legislative Committee, reported on several bills which were being pressed for passage in the State Legislature. Previous to this, however, Secretary Hegeman read the minutes of the preceding meeting and Treasurer Ray reported a surplus of $8,359.40 in the treasury of the college and a balance of $402.30 in that of the society. Dr. Muir described the provisions of Assembly bill No. 291, introduced by Mr. Santee, which is in effect the original anti-cocaine bill fathered by the New York State Pharmaceutical Association. The general provisions of this bill were approved. Objection was made to a bill amending the pharmacy act so as to permit more than one dealer in rural districts to sell drugs and medicines for terms of one year on payment of an annual fee of $3.00. The preparations sold in this way must bear the label of a licensed pharmacist.

Senator Stevens's bill, No. 258, which ostensibly provides for the labeling of proprietary and other medicinal preparations and for the inspection, analysis and regulation of the manufacture and sale of the same, was disapproved by the committee on the ground that it takes from the Board of Pharmacy certain powers now vested in it. At the hearing on the Stevens bill in Albany last Wednesday Dr. Muir was present to oppose its passage in behalf of the Kings County Pharmaceutical Society. A bill introduced in the Assembly by Mr. Oliver, No. 218, which provides for the placing of a red poison label with skull and cross bones and the naming on the label of two antidotes, was opposed chiefly for the reason that it provides for the labeling of "any drug or chemical which is recognized as a poison by the standard authors." This was characterized as a weakness in the measure which would lead to endless litigation, especially when it was remembered that some standard German authors had declared distilled water to be a poison. The committee was instructed to oppose the bill. Senator Hill, of Buffalo, is to introduce the various amendments to the pharmacy law which were decided upon at the last annual meeting of the State Board of Pharmacy, which were described in the AMERICAN DRUGGIST for January 8 at page 17.

On motion of Dr. Muir $50 was appropriated as a contingency fund for the National Formulary Committee.

President Paradis asked for the reports of the Committee on Papers who were to award prizes for papers presented by members during the preceding year. Chairman Rosenzweig stated that three prizes of $25.00, $15.00 and $10.00 respectively had been offered. Only two of the papers submitted had been found worthy of prizes and the first and second prizes were awarded to Dr. I. V. S. Stanislaus and Thomas J. Keenan, the first prize of $25.00 going to the first named for his paper on The Ipecac Root of the Pharmacopœia, printed in the AMERICAN DRUGGIST for December 25 at page 350, and the second prize to Mr. Keenan for his paper on Radium and Its Properties, printed in the AMERICAN DRUGGIST for April 24, 1905, at page 225.

Oscar C. Kleine gave an account of the proceedings at the meeting of the Metropolitan Association of Retail Druggists and this led to a free discussion of the movement to organize the Brooklyn territory into districts. Dr. Anderson said that the whole trouble arose from the fact that the officers of the Metropolitan Association of Retail Druggists had forgotten that their association had such a thing as a constitution and by-laws. By-law No. 11, of the M. A. R. D., distinctly excepts Brooklyn, Queens and Richmond boroughs from district organization under the Manhattan plan. If, he said, the metropolitan association would meet and change its by-laws and then send organizers into Brooklyn to disrupt the present organization all right, but it would have a bad effect. If the Kings County Society were to be recognized as the head of the district in Brooklyn there would be no objection, but there was no demand on the part of Brooklyn druggists for the organization of locals. Dr. Anderson said some harsh things about the M. A. R. D. The organization served as an excuse for supporters of the tripartite plan and merely enabled Mr. Holliday and his friends the jobbers to cast discredit on the direct contract and serial numbering plan. He advised the metropolitan association to set its own house in order before meddling with Brooklyn, for out of twenty-two districts in Manhattan and the Bronx, only two organizations were alive.

J. T. McLeod, a member of the Queens county branch, agreed to all that Dr. Anderson had said. He was sure that some misrepresentation had been practiced and that the druggists of Greenpoint were not responsible for the signatures attached to the petition for the organization of the local in that district or failed to realize what was intended by their action.

Dr. Muir said he believed in supporting the N. A. R. D. to the utmost extent. Druggists had been benefited by the association and it was incumbent upon the members to pay their dues promptly.

W. F. Maas advocated the formation of a few locals in Brooklyn, pleading that benefit would be sure to result, but in this he was not supported.

On the motion of T. H. Rehfuss a resolution was passed declaring that the Kings County Pharmaceutical Society was opposed to any plan other than the D. C. S. N. plan and that the Kings County Pharmaceutical Society should be allowed to remain as one district. Dr. Anderson was elected a delegate to the meeting of the general committee of the N. A. R. D.

District captains to carry on organization work were elected as follows: William C. Anderson, chairman; O. B. Deakyne, Albert Fischer, C. L. Gesell, Charles Heimerzheim, Andrew E. Hegeman, W. F. Maas, T. F. Raymow, J. H. Rehfuss, Benjamin Rosenzweig, A. Braunstein, W. H. Bussenschutt, L. Freidman, Otto Raubenheimer and Oscar C. Kleine.

The secretary having asked the members to submit copies of difficult prescriptions for comment A. E. Marsland responded with the following:

℞ Iodi }
Tannin } ....āā 0.50
Syrup rhataniæ 25.00
Syrup simplicis, ad...................225.00

The peculiarity of this prescription lay in the directions for its preparation. The iodine and tannin were to be mixed with 20 Cc. of water and the mixture then evaporated to 5 Cc. and added to the syrup of rhatany. A few of the members who discussed the prescription were of opinion that the prescriber intended his patient to get an iodo-tannic syrup resembling the well-known French preparation.

Before adjourning a motion was adopted to continue the Committee on Papers and set aside $50.00 to be awarded in three prizes to the authors of the best papers presented during the ensuing session.

The Merrell Drug Company and the Moffit & West Drug Company Consolidate.

(*Special to the American Druggist.*)

St. Louis, February 23.—The J. S. Merrell Drug Company has bought out the Moffit & West Drug Company and the business of the two concerns will be consolidated.

THREE NEW BILLS IN THE LEGISLATURE.

A Summary of Proposed Measures Affecting Pharmacists.

Three new bills of considerable interest to the drug trade have just been presented in the New York State Senate and Assembly. Two of them, which are believed to be likely to work an injury to the retail druggists in small townships or villages, are called the Coggeshall and Lupton bills. The Coggeshall bill in the Senate provides for the sale of the ordinary nonpoisonous remedies by owners of stores other than drug stores at any point where there is a distinct hamlet or incorporated villages of the fourth class not having therein or within three miles thereof a regularly licensed pharmacy or drug store. The permit for such sale of drugs by other than regular licensed pharmacists is to be secured according to this measure by any resident of said village who retails some kind of merchandise in a store as a business who shall present the affidavit of any reputable practicing physician of the same or an adjoining town to the effect that he has known the person for three years and knows that he has had experience in dealing in drugs and can be safely trusted to traffic in the same. These permits shall be granted, says the bill, to all persons applying therefor in any given place or village until three such permits are in force in one hamlet or village and may be granted in excess of that number in the discretion of the said division of the State Board of Pharmacy.

The second and similar measure, known as the Lupton bill, is now pending before the Assembly and provides for the sale of a larger class of drugs. The Lupton bill also permits the granting of a permit to a storekeeper other than a drug store within two instead of three miles from a regularly licensed pharmacy, and also provides that any division of the State Board of Pharmacy shall grant the permits to one or more residents.

The third measure, which is known as the Hill bill, has been introduced into the State Senate and provides several amendments to the laws governing the State Board of Pharmacy. The first amendment is that the members shall meet on the first Tuesday in January of every year, instead of on the first Monday, as heretofore, and the second amendment provides that each member shall receive $10 a day for his services instead of $5, as formerly. The fourth amendment eliminates the words of intent in providing for the punishment for falsifying or adulterating drugs, as it has been found to be very difficult if not practically impossible to secure a conviction when it is necessary to prove that the dealer "knowingly, willfully or fraudulently" committed such a misdemeanor. The fourth amendment provides that where more than one article is sold or dispensed at the same time each article sold in violation of or contrary to the provision of this act shall constitute a separate offense, the several penalties for which may be recovered in one and not several actions, as heretofore the case.

Tariff War with Germany Averted.

The German Reichstag has passed through the second reading a bill providing for the extension of reciprocal tariff rates to the United States until June 30, 1907. This averts a tariff war which would have been precipitated by the enactment of a new tariff law last year by Germany, which goes into effect on March 1, this year, and which would have imposed almost prohibitory tariffs on American agricultural products and on certain of our manufactures. Strong representations having been made by our Secretary of State on the subject the German Government introduced a measure granting the German conventional tariff to the United States for the period expiring June 30, 1907.

MARYLAND DRUGGISTS OPPOSE LABEL BILLS.

All of Section of the Drug Trade Unite in Opposing Labeling Bills—Joint Conference of All Branches of the Trade.

(*From our Regular Correspondent.*)

Baltimore, February 21.—Manufacturers of pharmaceuticals and representatives of the Maryland College of Pharmacy, the Maryland Pharmaceutical Association and wholesale as well as retail druggists assembled in one of the parlors of the Eutaw House on the 14th inst. to protest against the Godwin and the Bryan bills now pending in the Legislature. The former provides that all proprietary and patent medicines are to have the formulas printed upon the wrapper or label, and that any compound containing more than 8 per cent. of ethyl alcohol or more than 1-25 of 1 per cent. of morphine, heroin or cocaine or any of their derivatives, or more than ¼ of 1 per cent. of chloral hydrate or any quantity of belladonna, cotton root, ergot or other abortifacient, shall have the fact plainly printed on the label in red letters. The Bryan bill, which was drafted by the State's Attorney-General after the death of a child from some soothing syrup, specifies that every preparation which contains drugs in dangerous quantities shall be labeled "poison." Addresses were made at the meeting by Edward M. Parrish, of the Caffeeno Company; Harry Hines, of the Emerson Drug Company; A. C. Meyer, manufacturer of Dr. Bull's Cough Syrup; Dr. A. J. Corning, president of the Baltimore Retail Druggists' Association; R. E. Lee Williamson, of Williamson & Watts, and Dr. John G. Beck, manager of the Calvert Drug Company. It was resolved to ask the Legislative Committee on Hygiene to set a date for a hearing at which the arguments of the druggists in opposition can be presented. On this occasion two delegates from each of the divisions represented at the meeting are to go to Annapolis and offer arguments. It was also determined to raise no money whatever for the purpose of lobbying against the proposed measures, the druggists being of the opinion that the matter ought to be fought out on its own merits. Frank A. Baily, of James Baily & Son, presided at the meeting.

The bills were also discussed on the 17th inst. before a meeting of physicians at McCoy Hall, Johns Hopkins University. The medical profession generally favors the measures. State Senator J. Charles Linthicum presided at this meeting, and the speakers were Dr. William S. Thayer and Dr. W. Harvey Wiley, from the Department of Agriculture at Washington.

Rumors That Standard Oil is to Enter the Drug Field.

Rumors are afloat in Chicago that the Standard Oil Company is about to operate actively in drugs and will shortly erect a laboratory for the manufacture of pharmaceuticals that will rival the great establishment of Parke, Davis & Co., in Detroit. Efforts made in this city to verify the rumor met with failure. When the Bolton Drug Company, of Brooklyn, was interrogated in the matter it scoffed at the notion of the thing. Mr. Bolton was in Chicago last week, the manager of the Bolton Drug Company said, and arranged for the opening of a branch warehouse to serve as a distributing center for the preparations made and marketed by the United Drug Company, but the Standard Oil Company had no relation to the United Drug Company. It is likely that the rumor originated through Mr. Bolton's visit to Chicago.

Obituary.

CORNELIUS P. DOHME.

Cornelius P. Dohme, a member of the firm of Sharp & Dohme, manufacturers of pharmaceuticals and extracts, at Howard and Pratt streets, Baltimore, died on the evening of the 16th inst. after an illness of six months. Mr. Dohme was born 67 years ago in Germany and came to the United States as far back as 1852. About 1882 he became a partner of the firm of Sharp & Dohme, which his brother, Louis Dohme, had founded in 1860, together with A. P. Sharp. In 1866 another brother, Charles E. Dohme, was admitted into the business. The manufacture of pharmaceuticals was then hardly more than in its infancy, but the firm recognized its possibilities and engaged in the enterprise, with most gratifying success. For a number of years Mr. Cornelius P. Dohme was at the head of the pill department, his thoroughness and sound attainments being an important factor in the success of the house. He continued active until a short time ago. Personally he was of a most amiable disposition, which quality won him a host of friends.

EDWARD T. DOBBINS.

Following a fall on the icy pavement in front of his late home, 1808 South Rittenhouse Square, on February 12, Edward Tonkin Dobbins, a member of the John Wyeth & Bro. Chemical Company, died on February 17 at the University Hospital. In falling, Mr. Dobbins broke one of his hip bones. Soon after he was carried into his house Dr. J. William White recommended his removal to the University Hospital, where he and Dr. A. C. Wood attended him, while Dr. Alfred Stengel was called in for consultation. Every effort was made to prevent his sinking under the shock, as he was over 65 years old. He failed to rally, however, and, although given the best medical and surgical atention of the city, he died on February 17. Mr. Dobbins was one of the best-known business men in Philadelphia. His connection with the Wyeth firm began in 1865, and until recent years he took an active part in the conduct of the company. He was a member of the Union League and the Philadelphia Country Club and a trustee of the Philadelphia College of Pharmacy.

PETER ROSS LANCE.

Peter Ross Lance, one of the most widely known men in the drug trade in the United States, died at his late residence in this city, at 12.45 on Sunday afternoon, February 18, after a short illness, said to have been brought about by an accident while returning from a recent trip. Mr. Lance was born in Londonderry, Ohio, about 60 years ago, in which place he spent the major part of his early life. His business career was started with John D. Parks, of Cincinnati, with whom he gained a good general knowledge of the requirements of the druggists through the Middle West, which knowledge he made use of in the wider field to which his work extended when he became connected with the house of William R. Warner & Co., of Philadelphia. About 30 years ago he was made their general or chief traveler, which position he continued to fill to within a few days of his death. Mr. Lance not only occupied the position as chief traveler, but his advice was frequently sought and acted upon in matters pertaining to the policy of the house, and his cheerfulness, encouragement and wise counsel will be missed not only by his employers, but by the druggists throughout the country as well, as he was known and consulted by many. He was of a retiring disposition, generous to a fault to those with whom he was intimate, and his loss will be greatly felt.

DIED.

COLLINS.—In Dorchester, Mass., on Thursday, February 8, Joseph Collins.

GRIESEMER.—In Allentown, Pa., on Tuesday, February 6, James A. Griesemer, aged 30 years.

JOHNSON.—In St. Louis, Mo., on Sunday, February 11, Carston P. Johnson, aged 72 years.

MATTISON.—In Plainfield, N. J., on Monday, February 12, Judge William E. Mattison.

PRICE.—In Davenport, Ia., on Thursday, February 8, Dr. J. F. Price, aged 76 years.

ROBERTS.—In Columbus, O., on Tuesday, February 6, Charles F. Roberts.

YATES.—In Ada, O., on Monday, February 12, Samuel Yates, aged 32 years.

Greater New York News.

Warren L. Bradt, of Albany, general secretary of the New York State Board of Pharmacy, has been confined to his home with a severe attack of grip during the past week, but is now recovering speedily.

Among the out of town visitors to the local drug trade recently, many of whom registered at the Drug and Chemical Club, were: John M. Ross, Prescott, Arizona; O. J. Standt, Philadelphia, and C. R. Meredith, Fargo, North Dakota.

C. R. Meredith, who visited the local manufacturing drug trade during the last week, is president of the Meredith Drug Company of Fargo, N. D., a newly incorporated wholesale house, for which he bought an extensive line of drugs, proprietary remedies and fancy goods.

Col. E. W. Fitch, who has been manager of the New York office of Parke, Davis & Co., has announced his determination to retire from active business, and to that end has resigned his position with Parke, Davis & Co., but will retain the management until his successor is appointed. His retirement will cause regret among a large circle of warm friends.

At the regular annual meeting of the governors of the New York Drug and Chemical Club, held in the rooms of that organization on Thursday afternoon, February 15, the former officers were re-elected, as follows: J. L. Hopkins, president; William S. Gray, vice-president; Harry Hall, secretary, and Alexander Robb, treasurer. These officers will continue their duties during the current year.

At the recent meeting of the Phi Chi Fraternity, Gamma Chapter, Charles K. Brown, of Deposit, was elected a delegate to attend the meeting of the Grand Chapter, which is to be held in Chicago from February 22 to 24. Mr. Brown is a Ph.C. man, having taken the university course, and his name will be familiar to many of the old members of the trade as having been borne by his father, who was a member of the State Board of Pharmacy from 1885 to 1890.

A regular meeting of the New York Retail Druggists' Association was held January 26, at Odd Fellows' Hall, with President L. Marmor in the chair. During the absence of Secretary Diamond Mr. Epstein recorded the minutes, but Mr. Diamond appearing later the minutes of the previous meeting as well as the minutes of the meeting of the Executive Committee were read and approved.

For the Legislative Committee Mr. Diamond reported on proposed legislation affecting the sale of poisons. The recommendation of the Executive Committee to engage a legal representative was discussed and approved. A committee was appointed, consisting of Peter Diamond, I. Lewine and A. Bokshitzky, for that purpose, with instructions to report at the next regular meeting of the association. It was also decided to hold the meetings of the association alternately below Fourteenth street and in Harlem.

A special meeting of the Drug Trade Section of the New York Board of Trade and Transportation will be held Monday afternoon, February 26, for the purpose of discussing the merits of the Stevens and Santee bills, which are now pending in the State Senate and Assembly. The former measure was to have been opposed by members of the legislative committees representing the State, Kings County and Manhattan Pharmaceutical Associations and German Apothecary Society at the hearing before the Senate Health Committee set for Wednesday, February 21, but the Santee bill would have received the support of these organizations had not the hearing been postponed.

April 26 has been selected as the date for the graduating exercises of the School of Pharmacy of Columbia University, which will as usual be held at Carnegie Hall. The committee of the college in charge of the exercises has succeeded in securing a promise from Jules M. Mayer, Attorney General of the State of New York, to deliver the address to the graduating class. Mr. Mayer's reputation as an orator is such as to warrant the guests on that occasion in expecting a most admirable address. The Seventh Regiment Band will furnish music for the occasion, and it is expected that President Nicholas Murray Butler will preside.

Much sympathy has been shown in the wholesale drug and proprietary trade for Ed. G. Wells, whose wife, Mary A. Orr, died at the Hotel Buckingham, Fifth avenue and Fiftieth street, this city, on Wednesday, February 14, in the fifty-ninth year of her age. Mrs. Wells, who was the daughter of Robert and Elizabeth Orr, was born in New York, and was almost as well known to the manufacturers of proprietary articles throughout the country as is her bereaved husband. She was a woman of refined appearance and altogether captivating personality, and Mr. Wells, who was a most devoted husband, is prostrated with grief over her loss. The AMERICAN DRUGGIST joins Mr. Wells' many friends in the trade in expressions of sympathy and condolence.

No Hearings Last Week.

The proposed hearings on the Stevens and Oliver bills, now pending before the New York State Senate and Assembly, which were to have been held on Wednesday, February 21, in the rooms of the respective health committees of the Senate and Assembly in Albany, have both been postponed. Because of the fact that State Senator Tully was unable to attend the scheduled committee hearing on the Stevens bill, all action in regard to this measure was adjourned until another hearing could be fixed. Dr. William Muir, representing the legislative committee of the New York State Pharmaceutical Association and chairman of the legislative committee of the Kings County Pharmaceutical Society; A. C. Searles, chairman of the legislative committee of the Manhattan Pharmaceutical Association, and George Kleinau, representing the State Pharmaceutical Association and chairman of the legislative committee of the German Apothecaries' Society, were present on the day of the proposed hearings to represent the wishes of the drug trade in regard to both bills, but when it was discovered that no hearing could be held on the Stevens bill, Dr. Muir requested Assemblyman Whitney, chairman of the committee in charge of the Oliver bill, that consideration of this measure also be laid over until another hearing should be set. Although it was generally expected that a hearing would also be held on the Santee bill, no mention of this measure was made by its promoters, and it is now believed that it will not be brought up again for some time.

The Bowling Scores.

The latest results of the bowling tournament now being conducted under the auspices of the Wholesale Drug Trade Bowling Association, of New York, in the Albion Alleys, 117 West Twenty-third street, show the Parke, Davis & Co. team still in the lead, but closely pressed by the Dodge & Olcott and Seabury & Johnson bowlers. At the session held Monday evening, February 19, the Dodge & Olcott team won two games and the Colgate & Co. men also added two victories to their credit. The Seabury & Johnson contingent likewise won another game and lost one, while the Sharp & Dohme twirlers were also victorious in a hotly contested trial of skill, though they also lost another game. The Roessler & Hasslacher knights of the pin lost two games and the Bruen, Ritchey & Co. ball rollers were compelled to forfeit their two scheduled contests because of the fact that they did not have enough members on hand to compose a team. As the great contest is now only half concluded, it is likely that many changes will be made in the standing of the clubs before the grand prizes are awarded to the successful teams and the bowlers possessing the highest individual scores. From present appearances, however, it seems likely that J. Ruddiman, of Dodge & Olcott, will capture the first individual score honors, as his 253 record has not yet been equalled. At the bowling last Monday night he rolled only 212, but as this was the highest point reached by any of the contestants it looks as though the honors would be easy for Ruddiman. Details of the last six games show the following team scores: First game, Dodge & Olcott, 811; Roessler & Hasslacher, 772. Second game, Dodge & Olcott, 779; Sharp & Dohme, 664. Third game, Sharp & Dohme, 808; Roessler & Hasslacher, 670. Fourth game, Colgate & Co., 830; Seabury & Johnson, 826. Fifth game, Colgate & Co., 815; Bruen, Ritchey & Co., 426. Sixth game, Seabury & Johnson, 826; Bruen, Ritchey & Co., 486.

WESTERN NEW YORK.

Uneasiness in the Retail Trade—Druggists Divided on the Published Formula Question—A Negative Law Proposed—Carbolic Acid Sales.

(*From our Regular Correspondent.*)

Buffalo, February 20.—"Trade is good" was the ready reply of a leading down-town Buffalo retail druggist who keeps about as close tab on his sales as any of them. It may sometimes serve little more than to satisfy one's curiosity to figure up every day the results of business as compared with last month or last year, but there would be fewer failures in the land if it were oftener done, for a sudden decline or a steady falling behind is often discovered and fixed up when it can be located in time. A Buffalo merchant some time ago ran behind seriously and was not able to find out why till he learned that a confidential clerk had been taking a good part of the receipts to himself for some years.

NO TROUBLE WITH PRICE CUTTERS.

There is any amount of unrest in the Buffalo drug trade, but it is of a character that is of more general interest than the mere matter of cutting prices down town. In passing it may be said that the price cutter is still on his very best behavior, and though there is any amount of temptation to throw out display advertising for the early spring trade with drugs as the chief attraction there is no sign of it yet. The big advertisements come out, but the great price reductions are all according to the general schedule. And everybody, including the public, is satisfied.

THE LABELING OF PROPRIETARIES.

One source of uneasiness comes from the cloud of bills in the Legislature providing for wearing your heart on your sleeve, otherwise putting the exact formula on the outside of all preparations, from a tooth powder to Paris green. It cannot be maintained that the public is very much worried about the matter, even if the sensational papers are at the bottom of the movement, just because they want to keep up the fun of "roasting" some one, even if they do have to make money out of it incidentally. Some of the druggists are preparing to fight the entire movement, as radically wrong and monumentally impudent, but others see two pretty good reasons, to them, for favoring the idea in a way. They very well know that a certain very bad class of preparations can be driven out of the trade by a proper sort of law, and they are not against forging another nail for the coffin of the patent medicine business at the same time. Said a Buffalo retailer, who can generally see through a millstone, even if the hole is small, "What is needed is a negative law. We all very well know that there are harmful things going into certain preparations. They may contain cocaine, or morphine or some of the other habit-forming poisons and should never be tolerated a minute. What I should like to see is a law providing that labels shall state that there are no such injurious ingredients in the preparation. The list is small, perhaps not more than a dozen, and it would then all be easy. Nobody would feel it a hardship to conform with such a law, but if I must state exactly what I put into a wash for chapped hands or a new perfume I am prepared to fight the entire bill." So far nothing has been done, as the Legislature is a very slow body and may not be very dangerous in any direction this year.

REGULATING CARBOLIC ACID SALES.

Then there is the question of a city ordinance for the regulation of the sale of carbolic acid. The Pharmaceutical Association is not doing anything about it, as Health Commissioner Greene has taken it up and will look after it. He proposes to forbid the sale of anything more than a 5 per cent. solution without a physician's prescription and to insist on a registry. It is now proposed to include cocaine.

BUFFALO CHANGES.

The sensation of the moment in Buffalo retail drug circles is the prospective sale of Dr. Willis G. Gregory's Genesee Pharmacy to the Cahoon-Lyon Drug Company, whose extensive store is nearly half a mile further down town. The sale has not yet been completed, but is expected to go through in a day or two. That is all that the doctor can say about it at present. He was not inclined to say anything about it, but the report was out and he found it necessary to admit that negotiations were pending. It is expected that the purchasers will run both stores and that Dr. Gregory will locate elsewhere, as he does not intend to retire from the business.

Herbert M. Groves, member of the State Board of Pharmacy, who lately sold his store in Batavia to his clerks, is in Buffalo looking for a residence store. He has not been very well since getting up from his attack of typhoid fever, but after one slight relapse is again apparently recovered.

NEW ENGLAND.

College Work to Count as Experience—Forger of Orders for Narcotics Punished—Druggist Wins Suit—Theodore Metcalf Company Fined.

(*From our Regular Correspondent.*)

Boston, February 21.—The Board of Pharmacy held three examinations last month, granting certificates to the following successful candidates: William E. Boyle, Amesbury; William J. Charles, Lee; Timothy J. Dooley, Springfield; Thomas F. Grady, Providence, R. I., and Hermon O. Webster, Auburndale. Secretary W. F. Sawyer reports that a change has been made in the qualification for examination. It was voted to apply half the time spent in a recognized college of pharmacy to a deficiency of three years of practical experience in a retail drug store.

A DANIEL COME TO JUDGMENT.

Mr. Harris, the new Chief of Police of Malden and former agent of the Board of Pharmacy, has taken a stand upon the subject of selling poisons which is unique and should be satisfactory to druggists. He recently caused the arrest of a man for obtaining poison from several drug stores in that city by signing doctors' prescriptions with fictitious names. He carried a doctor's prescription book with him, and testimony was produced to the effect that he had received cocaine from more than a dozen druggists in Malden.

On trial the prisoner admitted that he was an occasional user of cocaine and was addicted to the morphine habit. Chief Harris stated that while at the police station drugs had to be administered to the prisoner and that upon examination the region of his heart was found perforated from cocaine injections. The man was found guilty and sentenced to pay a fine of $50; in default of payment, he was obliged to go to jail.

ACQUITTED ON THE CHARGE OF MAKING AN ERROR.

James E. Boyd, 295 Main street, Charlestown, is being sued by a former customer for $2,000 damages. The purchaser alleges that his messenger was sent to Boyd's store for a certain brand of salts and that saltpetre was given instead. This being taken by the complainant, caused him "financial loss and physical distress." Boyd avers that it was the boy's mistake, as he asked for "peter salt"; also that the package was plainly labeled. The court decided in Mr. Boyd's favor.

THEODORE METCALF COMPANY PLEAD GUILTY.

The last monthly report of the State Board of Health shows the examination of 93 drugs, of which number 26 varied from the legal standard. The adulterated drugs included ammonia water, lemon and olive oils, spirits of camphor, capsicum, whiskey and tincture of iodine. Five dealers were fined during the month for the sale of adulterated olive oil and one for the sale of tincture of iodine of low strength. Recently the board has given much attention to the examination of olive oil, and many of these samples contain considerable amounts of cottonseed oil. Brandies and whiskies are also being tested. Several samples have been found artificially colored and with residues largely sugar. Recently upon complaint of the board, the Theodore Metcalf Company pleaded *nolo contendere* to the indictment charging it with the sale of impure olive oil, vanilla and brandy and was fined $50 on each count.

PENNSYLVANIA.

Prerequisite Law Goes Into Effect—Rumors of Drug Trust Cause No Disturbance Locally—Retailers Prosper.

(*From our Regular Correspondent.*)

PHILADELPHIA NEWS ITEMS.

Philadelphia, February 20.—John Q. Rogers, of the firm of Chapman & Rogers, perfumers, is lying dangerously ill at his home in this city. Mr. Rogers has been sick for the past three months and his condition has now become serious.

On February 19 Torrey & Alexander held religious services in the large room of the Philadelphia College of Pharmacy. These evangelists are now holding forth in this city and during the midday they visit some of the leading colleges. The meeting at the Philadelphia College of Pharmacy was largely attended, there being about 250 students present, besides a number of other people.

Frank G. Rohrman, president of the Philadelphia Wholesale Drug Company, Limited, had to go home from his office on February 20 on account of illness. Mr. Rohrmann has never been very strong since his last illness and it is hoped that this recent attack is only a slight indisposition.

Considerable interest is being manifested by the graduates of pharmacy in regard to the next meeting of the Pennsylvania pharmaceutical examining board. Under the new laws in relation to these examinations no one but a graduate from a reputable college of pharmacy can make application for this examination who desires to become a manager. On March 17 an examination will be held in Philadelphia alone and on May 19th an examination will be held in Harrisburg and Pittsburg at the same time. The new law does not apply to applicants who are desirous of obtaining a qualified assistant certificate providing they have served the requisite time under a competent druggist, which is two years.

DRUG TRUST RUMORS SCARE NO ONE.

Although there are rumors in regard to the new drug corporation which was recently chartered at Trenton being after drug stores in this city, so far little credence can be given to the report. Those who are in a position to know of such a movement say that they have not been advised of any definite offers having been made for drug stores here and they are of the opinion that the men who are back of this new company will find it entirely different from running a drug store as compared with the selling of cigars. The drug stores in this city have not taken the cigars of the United Cigar Stores Company, and although every effort has been made to get them to handle the goods of this company so far little headway has been made. There are several independent cigar manufacturers in this city whose cigars the druggists prefer handling to those kept in stock by the United Cigar Stores Company.

On February 23 the evidence submitted in the Loder suit, which amounts to volumes, is to be presented to court. The lawyers for the defendants feel satisfied that they will win in their effort to have the verdict of the jury set aside. It is understood that no matter what decision is given the case will be taken to the Court of Appeals. Not only the druggists are desirous of having an opinion rendered on this suit which will be final, but the manufacturers are as anxious to know what to do in this matter as their customers are.

Forgetful of the sad experiences of others, Jerry Higgins, an engineer and night watchman in the pharmaceutical establishment of Boericke & Tafel, 125 South Eleventh street, sought to find a gas leak with the aid of a lighted lamp. The explosion which followed was one of terrific proportions. The leak of gas was found in the cellar and when Mr. Higgins' light came sufficiently near to it the force blew out the glass front of the pharmacy store, the windows of the cellar and raised the pavement some inches. What it did to Higgins he can't remember. But the report of the explosion was heard for some distance away, and when people rushed into the cellar, after a fire alarm had been sent in, the engineer was found unconscious in a corner, but eventually recovered. The partial wrecking of the drug store was the only damage, that being estimated at about $250.

MARYLAND.

Patent Medicine and Anti-Narcotic Legislation—Officers for the Wedgewood Club—The Spanish Edition—Dr. Dohme in Paris.

(*From our Regular Correspondent.*)

Baltimore, February 20.—There are pending in the Legislature two bills which affect the drug trade throughout the State. One of these was introduced by State Senator Godwin and provides that the manufacturers of all patent or proprietary medicines shall print on the wrappers or labels of such preparations a formula of the ingredients contained in the medicine. Violations are to be punished by fine. If the compound contains opium or other toxic substance in dangerous quantities, the word "Poison" is also to appear. The measure was suggested by the death of a three-year-old child which had been dosed with a preparation known as "Kopp's Baby Friend." The coroner decided that the medicine had caused death.

THE ANTI-NARCOTIC BILL.

Another bill was prepared by State Attorney General Bryan, and prohibits the sale of cocaine, morphine and other habit forming drugs except on the prescription of a practicing physician, and then only once unless the doctor in attendance orders the medicine renewed. This latter measure is deemed by many druggists entirely too sweeping in its provisions, since it could be made to include even paregoric and laudanum. The present law is admittedly too lax and wholly ineffective. It requires druggists to keep a register of all sales of poisons, but provides no machinery for its enforcement and leaves the way open for all manner of evasions. The proposed corrective of existing statutory insufficiencies, however, in the opinion of not a few pharmacists, goes too far in the other direction and would tend to restrict unduly the sale of preparations in general use. The Legislative Committee of the Maryland Pharmaceutical Association will be asked to visit Annapolis and oppose the measure.

THE WEDGEWOOD CLUB.

The social features which usually distinguish the sessions of the Wedgewood Club were dispensed with at the meeting held in the Hotel Caswell, January 25, which was also the annual gathering, because of the death on the previous Tuesday of August Schrader, one of the most popular members, at his residence, 2920 Elliott street. The meeting was turned into a memorial event and resolutions of regret and condolence were adopted, Dr. John F. Hancock, A. J. Corning, John B. Thomas and J. Edwin Hengst being appointed a committee to attend the funeral. The club elected Owen C. Smith secretary and Charles Morgan treasurer. Ernest E. Quandt, John G. Beck and J. Edwin Hengst were chosen members of the Executive Committee. Mr. Schrader was 51 years old, came here from Germany and had been in the drug business for 30 years. The Maryland College of Pharmacy was represented at the funeral by Charles H. Ware, Louis Schulze, John C. Muth and Henry P. Hynson.

THE PHARMACEUTICAL JOURNAL CLUB

held its regular meeting on January 25 at the house of L. A. Beck, of Waverly, a suburb, who gave a talk on the manner of making and using acetylene gas. He illustrated his talk with practical experiments and showed, by means of microphotographic slides and a lantern, the projecting power of acetylene light. Dr. E. F. Kelly, Dr. Joel Barnet and Dr. W. J. Lowrey, Jr., were appointed a committee on honorary members. After the scientific and business part of the programme the members were entertained by Mr. Beck.

Trademark Rights to Phenacetine Will Be Claimed After Expiration of the Patent.

The Farbenfabriken, of Elberfeld, state that they propose to vigorously assert their claims to trademark rights in the word Phenacetine after the expiration of the patent. It is reported that the price will be cut down very close to the manufacturing cost as soon as the patent expires in March.

OHIO.

A Bill Regulating the Sale of Narcotics Introduced—Formulas of Proprietary Remedies to Appear on the Label—Officers Elected by the Columbus Pharmacal Company.

(*From our Regular Correspondent.*)

Cleveland, February 21.—Druggists report buisness in good condition here, with a fair amount of prescription trade. The reports of the Health Department indicate that there has been an increase in sickness, due largely to the warm weather of the past two or three months, and druggists have profited to a certain extent by this. In sundries the trade has been very good. Wholesale houses also report a good business in all their departments, as well as in the miscellaneous goods they handle.

TO PRINT FORMULÆ ON PROPRIETARIES.

Senator Vanover, of Wayne County, introduced in the Legislature a bill requiring the formula to be printed on all bottles or packages of patent medicines sold in the State. This kind of a bill has been brought before several General Assemblies heretofore, but has always been killed. But this bill goes further and says that all preparations containing ethyl, alcohol, morphine, heroine, cocaine, chloral hydrate, belladonna, ergot, cotton root and other drugs of a like nature. If present in certain defined quantities, the label must contain that fact in red ink and the word "poison" in quarter-inch letters must be placed on it. Violations of the law are punishable with a fine of from $50 to $500 and a term of imprisonment not exceeding six months.

TO PROHIBIT THE SALE OF NARCOTICS, SAVE ON PRESCRIPTION.

Another bill, introduced by Representative Spicer, prohibits the sale of morphine except upon the prescription of a physician.

PATENT MEDICINE LEGISLATION.

The Criswell patent medicine bill, introduced in the Legislature some time ago, has been referred to the Committee on Medical Jurisprudence in the House, and the general belief seems to be that it will not see daylight again. The vote on the reference was unanimous. However, Representative Grover has introduced another bill that will require manufacturers using alcohol, cocaine, opium or other narcotics to state the fact on the labels of the packages.

A PREREQUISITE LAW FOR OHIO.

An amendment to the present pharmacy law has been drawn by Attorney Frank H. Freericks, who is attorney for the State Association, which is expected to raise the standard of pharmacists.

The amendment provides that no candidate can take the pharmacist examination after January 1, 1908, unless he is a graduate of some college or school of pharmacy, and also provides that registered pharmacists from other States may without examination register as assistant pharmacists in Ohio.

CHANGES IN THE CIGARETTE LAW.

Considerable contention has been aroused in the Legislature over the McFadden anticigarette bill, which a few days ago passed the House of Representatives. In its original form the bill prohibited the sale and use of cigarettes in the State, but it was amended so as to include only the sale of the articles. Manufacturers in Ohio may continue their business and wholesale houses may carry them, but they must not sell them within the borders of the State. Dealers, under this law, must dispose of their cigarettes, including all component parts, by June 20, when the law would go into effect. It is expected that a fight will be made against it in the Senate.

THE UNITED CHEMISTS COMPANY.

Cleveland druggists are discussing a telegram received from New York the latter part of the week stating that the United Chemists Company, known here as the drug trust, is looking for a location in this city. It is also said that these people are also looking for locations in Pittsburg and Cincinnati. W. G. Marshal, who operates a number of stores here on an independent basis, says the company has looked over the ground here with a view to securing stores, but that it has been beaten at its own game. He declares that neither he nor any of the other independent dealers will make a compromise, although he says that they are discriminated against in some things.

DIRECTORS OF THE PHARMACAL COMPANY.

At the annual election of the stockholders of the Columbus Pharmacal Company, Columbus, the following directors were chosen: W. T. Wells, W. H. Grigsby, A. W. Connor, W. B. Beebe, C. E. Munson, Foster Copeland and A. McConnell. The directors organized by electing W. T. Wells president and general manager; W. H. Grigsby, vice-president, and A. W. Connor, secretary. The past year has been very satisfactory, according to the reports of the officers.

A SCARCITY OF DRUG CLERKS.

Retail druggists in Cleveland and various other places have been complaining of late of the scarcity of clerks. Many of the stores have been unable to secure sufficient help. It is said that some of the drug clerks have deserted the business and gone into other lines of work. Then the examinations have been rather difficult of late and but few have passed. The usual supply of fresh men are, therefore, not on the market.

PARK LOSES A POINT.

In the case of S. B. Hartman, of Columbus, Ohio, maker of Peruna, against the J. D. Park & Sons Company, of Cincinnati, Federal Judge Cochran has overruled the demurrer of the defendants. Dr. Hartman manufactures certain medicines which are bottled and labeled to sell at a certain price. He makes contracts with those who purchase the goods to sell them at the prices fixed. Certain cut-rate druggists have been able to purchase these medicines through some of the wholesale houses and put them on the market at cut rates. Dr. Hartman brought the suit to prevent this firm from cutting the prices. It is claimed that this firm secured the goods in this way, defaced the labels on the bottles and sold them at a cut rate. Dr. Hartman, if sustained in his contentions, will establish that a manufacturer has a right to contract with retailers to take his goods and sell them at a price equal to or above any minimum he may fix.

OHIO NEWS NOTES.

S. D. Yates, a druggist of Ada, died on February 12.

A. L. Stevenson has opened a new store at Bryan, south of Toledo.

The Gem Pharmacy Company has purchased the business of I. H. McGoughey at Lorain.

A. J. Preisendorfer has succeeded Phillips & Walters in the drug business at Shelby.

The style of the firm name of S. S. Bacon & Co., Ottawa, has been changed to Robenault & Butler, but no change has taken place in the personnel.

A. B. Maumhart, a druggist at Vermillion, was married on the afternoon of February 19 to Miss Effie C. Washburn, of Axtel. The wedding took place at the home of the bride and was attended by close friends.

A. J. Cromwell and E. A. Cook, druggists and prominent business men of Chardon, were arrested a few days ago on the charge of selling liquor illegally. M. C. Flanavan, of Cleveland, is said to have brought the charges.

CLEVELAND NOTES.

Henry Polack has sold his store on Scovill avenue to Alexander Skinner.

W. M. Hinson is now traveling for Benton, Hall & Co. in the territory formerly covered by E. O. Van Gorder, who resigned to go into the shoe business in this city.

Edward Beckenbach & Co., who have been in business for several years on Superior avenue, near the corner of Seneca street, will move to 418 Prospect avenue about April 1.

An explosion of oxygen tanks in the medical and surgical supply store of H. H. Hessler & Co., 437 Superior avenue, February 19, wrecked the room and damaged a large portion of the goods. The building took fire, but the department soon had this under control. H. H. Hessler and D. S. Hitchcock, of the firm, were badly bruised, and one or two other persons were slightly injured.

THE WEST.

Druggists Lose Through Bank of America—Prosecution Hinted At—Creelman Said to Have Wrecked the Institution—N. A. R. D. to Meet in Atlanta—Drug Store Opened With a Banquet

(*From our Regular Correspondent.*)

Chicago, February 21.—The collapse of the Bank of America has caused heavy loss to about 180 local druggists who were stockholders. These men became owners of stock because of their desire to reap the benefits from branches of the bank to be opened in their stores. It was necessary to be a stockholder in order to become an agent for receiving deposits. The collapse was due to the fact that F. E. Creelman, head and front of the enterprise, proved to be a disciple of high finance. His operations are believed to have netted him about $193,000. The money went out largely in the form of loans to Creelman's lumber enterprises, for he was heavily interested in that business. It is said that few of the other officers of the bank were experienced in that line of activity and that Creelman had things his own way. There is now talk of prosecuting the officers because of the alleged facts that their stock was not paid for and also because they are charged with irregularities in regard to loans. Some time ago the directors became aware that all was not right with regard to Creelman and they demanded that he make good the amounts loaned him. He agreed to do so within ten days, but the exposure and failure came before the expiration of that time. The savings depositors were saved from loss by the action of Attorney Clarence S. Darrow, who paid them the amounts of their deposits, about $25,000. This action of course saves the druggists trouble. The crash was most unfortunate, as it is said the bank was prospering and that its business was growing rapidly. Had the officers been experienced bankers it is probable the trouble would have been averted. The local association refused to indorse the plan when it was first broached, the members being told that they must act on their own responsibility.

N. A. R. D. TO MEET IN ATLANTA.

Atlanta has been chosen as the next meeting place for the N. A. R. D. This decision was reached at the meeting of the Executive Committee, which has just taken place. A number of routine matters were disposed of during the course of the sessions. A delegation of jobbers conferred with the committee in regard to the relations of the two branches of the trade and matters likely to cause friction were adjusted. The seven members of the committee were all present. In addition there were at the sessions Charles H. Avery, first vice-president; John C. Gallagher, of Jersey City, a member of the Committee on National Legislation, and F. W. Meissner, of La Porte, Ind., former committeeman. At the close of the meeting it was given out that there had been little done that could be given out as of interest to the general public. Further details appear in another column.

WESTERN BRANCH OF UNITED DRUG COMPANY OPENED.

The official opening of the Western branch of the United Drug Company, of Boston, and of the National Cigar Stands Company, of New York, is to be made the occasion for a large gathering of friends and stockholders of the enterprises. The opening is to take place February 28. Several hundred stockholders are expected and there will be about two carloads of visitors from the East among them. There will be a luncheon at Rector's and a banquet at the Auditorium in the evening. The headquarters of the Western branch are to be at 45 and 47 Randolph street. An interesting feature of the main offices will be the largest and finest cigar humidor ever built.

L. K. Liggett, president of the United Drug Company, of Boston, is in this city to arrange for the opening of their new branch at 45 Randolph street. The stockholders of the Middle West meet this week to outline the policy for the coming year. The Eastern delegation left New York Monday, the 19th, in two cars attached to the Twentieth Century New York Central-Lake Shore 18-hour train. These people selected this route, as they claim the best was none too good for them, and they figured that time was money.

CHICAGO NEWS NOTES.

The entire plant of S. H. Gernder and of the concerns in which he is interested is to be moved to Richmond, Va.

Governor Deneen has not yet made appointments to fill the vacancies on the Board of Pharmacy of Illinois.

George R. Baker has opened a new store at Montrose and Evanston avenues.

E. R. Wolfner, who formerly was located at Clark and Harrison streets, has gone to New York to manage the drug department of the Siegel store.

The $250 license proposition is still before a council committee. The plan to tax druggists this amount in case they wish to sell liquor is being fought as hard as possible and the result is still uncertain. Some of the politicians and the saloon interests are said to be determined to "soak" the druggists.

The Executive Committee of the N. A. R. D. was entertained at lunch last week by the local druggists at Vogelsang's restaurant and thirst quenching emporium. The visitors were treated to a ride on the water wagon. One of them said afterward that he came near offering prayer.

The Medical Society had an enthusiastic meeting recently and passed resolutions in favor of U. S. P. preparations as against proprietary remedies. It has been suggested that this action offers an opportunity for the druggists to join issues with the physicians in driving in a nail for the U. S. P. preparations.

W. C. Bolton, President of the Riker Drug Stores, of New York and Brooklyn, was a guest at the Chicago Drug Club last week. Stephen Hexter, who is president and manager of the Public Drug Company, had him in charge. Mr. Bolton came to the city to attend the meeting and banquet of the United Drug Company. He is an active worker in this organization.

Chas. L. Gleeson, of the P. E. Anderson Company, was in Chicago in the middle of February. He had a large order book in one pocket and a supply of lead pencils, and was very busy with the jobbers here, booking carload orders. He had just been making his quarterly round of the circuit, touching St. Louis, Kansas City, St. Paul and was headed for the East. The smile that he wore indicated that the trip has been most satisfactory.

A Cashier's Chair.

A cashier's chair designed along entirely new lines is being placed on the market by the A. H. Andrews Company, metal furniture manufacturer, 174-176 Wabash avenue, Chicago, Ill. As will appear from an examination of the accompanying illustration, several excellent features are incorporated in its make-up which differ greatly from the ordinary idea. The framework is made from Bessemer steel rods, twisted and interwoven into rigid form. The woodwork can be supplied in either oak or birch, or mahogany finish if preferred. All the metal work is beautifully plated and given a Japanese copper finish. Attention is drawn to the adjustable curved spring back and seat, which insure the maximum comfort for the cashiers, as they can be arranged to meet their individual requirements. The footrest being metal cannot be worn through, nor will the chair lose any of its rigidity from constant use. The manufacturers claim, on account of the construction, a cleaner and more satisfactory chair than any other on the market, there being no parts which are liable to injury from misuse or other causes. This chair is made in two heights, 24 inch and 28 inch, and is guaranteed for ten years. Besides this chair the company makes a full line of metal furniture for general purposes. Catalogues and other information will be furnished upon request.

THE SOUTH.

Levy & Bros. Absorb the Druggists' Sundries Company—Annual Meeting of the Drug Clerks—Officers Elected—Registered by the Board of Pharmacy.

(*From our Regular Correspondent.*)

New Orleans, La., February 19.—The Druggists' Sundries Company, a $25,000 corporation organized in this city some months ago, is now being liquidated with a view to having it made part of the big stationery house of Joseph Levy & Bros., which will devote a good part of its establishment to a druggists' sundries department. The merging of the two concerns was made simply because of the fact that the Levys were interested largely in the Druggists' Sundries Company. Sylvan Levy and Joseph Levy, of Levy & Bros., were president and vice-president, respectively, of the Sundries concern, and B. I. Blum was the secretary and treasurer. All of the business handled by the Druggists' Sundries Company will be taken charge of by the druggists' sundries department of Joseph Levy & Bros.

THE DRUG CLERKS' ASSOCIATION IN A FLOURISHING CONDITION.

Before a large number of the association's members the retiring officers of the Retail Drug Clerks' Association read annual reports of progress made by the association and then assisted at the installation of the newly elected organization officials. The meeting took place at the College of Pharmacy, February 7. One of the most important suggestions made in the annual report of the retiring president, Eugene H. Daste, was that the association immediately proceed about securing permanent headquarters.

The various annual reports showed the association's affairs to be in excellent condition and stated also that the finances had never before been in better shape. These facts were brought out not only in Mr. Daste's report, but also in the annual statement of Arnold Troxler, the retiring secretary.

OFFICERS ELECTED.

These are the names of the new officers installed: A. J. Ferry, president; Louis Gouaux, first vice-president; Van A. Woods, second vice-president; William M. Avery, secretary; Ed. Koeckert, treasurer; Harry Code, grand marshal; R. L. Bacas, sergeant-at-arms. After the installation a smoker was held.

REGISTERED IN LOUISIANA.

F. C. Godbold, member of the Examining Board of the State Board of Pharmacy, has given out the following names of successful candidates for certificates in the examinations of February 2 and 3:

Registered pharmacists—H. J. Lagarde, Thibodaux; Henry Walsche, E. L. King, P. D. O'Donnell, W. J. Gagnet and Walter Payton, of New Orleans; W. H. Wellman, of Shreveport, and M. B. Main, of New Iberia.

Assistants—J. J. Dubourg, Union Port Office; C. A. Desport, J. C. Richards, E. B. Scott, E. J. Maguire, of New Orleans; R. H. Chargois, of Lafayette; A. J. Laiche, of Lutcher.

Twenty-four applicants were examined and of these the above were successful. The members who conducted the examinations were F. C. Godbold, William M. Levy, Adam Wirth and C. D. Sauvinet.

NEW ORLEANS NOTES.

A number of prominent local chemists have interested themselves in the New Orleans branch of the American Chemical Society, now in process of organization. It is intended to make this the biggest and best branch of the association in the South.

Trade in New Orleans during the last fortnight or so has been very good, and during the last two months exceptionally so. Reports from the various wholesalers and jobbers show that conditions have been good for the conducting of a profitable business and that they have taken advantage of these opportunities. One wholesale house reports a bigger business for January and February than it has ever before experienced.

The Union Label Drug Store is one of the latest additions to the establishments in Algiers, the Fifth District of New Orleans, which lies directly across the river from the Crescent City. This store has secured a good location and its prospects are flattering.

PACIFIC COAST.

Liquozone Company Compromised with the Board of Health—Growing Gold and Silver—In Favor of Tax Free Alcohol.

(*From our Regular Correspondent.*)

San Francisco, February 16.—The Liquozone Company has agreed with City Attorney W. G. Burke to take a judgment without costs in its suit for $350,000 damages against President Ward of the local Board of Health, now pending in the United States Circuit Court of the Ninth District. The City Attorney advises the board to assent to this course. The grievance of the Liquozone people, it was mentioned in these columns, is the action of the Health Board in attempting to prohibit the sale of its product in this city except it be labeled "poison," a movement which the board itself rescinded later on the advice of the City Attorney.

WANT LOWER TAX ON GRAIN ALCOHOL.

Painters' Union No. 19, of this city, at a recent meeting, resolved to petition Congress for the enactment of a law to provide for the use of alcohol made from domestic grain, the same to be made unfit for beverage, which is desired for use in the painting business as a substitute for wood alcohol. The excessive tax on ethyl alcohol precludes its use at present, and the cheaper methyl spirits which are now used are said to injure the health of the painters.

"GROWS" GOLD AND SILVER IN VALUELESS ORES.

The tranquility of scientific circles on the Pacific Coast was rather abruptly disturbed a few weeks ago by the sudden announcement that a scientist by the name of J. Addison Marshall, an assayer of Sacramento, Cal., had solved the fascinating problem of the artificial production or "growth" of gold. In sensational fashion the newspapers made the bold statement that Marshall had worked out the problem on plain, scientific lines; that he could readily demonstrate the artificial growth of gold from the "elemental crystal," the same as the vegetable develops from the cell, and that he could produce gold from silver and iron, with the incidental production of mercury and copper. Marshall claims that by "chemicalization, melting and parting" ores he can divide them into subatomic particles, and then by a process he calls "growing" form gold and silver. He maintains "beyond the peradventure of a doubt that there is a 'growth' of elements from baser ones in the mineral world akin to growth in animal and vegetable kingdoms. Science has stopped short at chemical elements, but could not analogy indicate that even elements have 'grown' from simpler matter?"

'FRISCO NEWS ITEMS.

Mrs. L. G. Bennett's pharmacy, at 299 Devisadero street, was looted on January 18 by Joe Stanfield, a 16-year-old boy who was employed in the store.

City Attorney Burke has notified the Supervisors that they may make any law they want to regulate the sale of poisons in this city.

Emile Pierron, druggist, at Union and Powell streets, tried to commit suicide on the night of January 31. Only by chance was he discovered, else what is said by his parents to have been an attempt at "experiments with chloroform" would no doubt have killed him. Heavy losses at the races were probably the cause of the incident.

G. H. Dietz, of the Holden Drug Company, Stockton, Cal., was the guest of honor at a banquet given recently by the company to its employees. In addition to the banquet, the employees and members of the Holden Drug Company presented Mr. Dietz with a gold watch, chain and charm. Will Hobin made the presentation speech and Mr. Dietz responded. J. A. Sanford, the manager of the company, presided at the head of the table and Mr. Hobin had the chair at the foot of the table, with Mr. Dietz at his right.

The Drug and Chemical Market

**The prices quoted in this report are those current in the wholesale market, and higher prices are paid for retail lots
The quality of goods frequently necessitates a wide range of prices,**

Condition of Trade.

NEW YORK, February 24, 1906.

Trade during the interval since our last report has been of a light jobbing character only, and we have consequently few price changes of consequence to report. Quinine is unchanged, but the light shipments of bark during the first half of the month have encouraged holders to look for an advance, as light shipments mean higher prices for bark and a corresponding increase in the value of the alkaloid. Makers of citric acid are, according to current report, declining to enter into contracts for future deliveries, and an advance is looked for. Menthol is attracting more attention and values are steadier. Grain alcohol has been reduced in price as a result of a lower market in the West and sugar of milk is offered at a fractionally lower price; but apart from these fluctuations there is comparatively little change in market conditions.

HIGHER.	LOWER.
Carbolic acid,	Alcohol,
Peppermint oil,	Ergot,
Pennyroyal oil,	Codliver oil,
Balsam copaiba,	Opium,
Pink root,	Sugar of milk,
Silver nitrate,	Balm of Gilead buds,
Cuttlefish bone, Trieste,	Arsenic,
Citronella oil,	Cassia buds,
Lemon oil,	Juniper berries,
Cannabis indica,	Carnauba wax.
Corrosive sublimate, powdered,	
Cubeb berries.	

Drugs.

Alcohol has been reduced 2c to correspond with a lower range of prices announced by Western distillers and grain is now quoted at $2.45 to $2.47, and molasses $2.43 to $2.45, as to quantity and terms. Arnica flowers of the new crop are offering from sources of supply at 8½c, though quotations on spot are maintained at 9c to 10c.

Balsam copaiba is in good consumptive demand and Para has advanced owing to scarcity of spot supplies, some holders asking up to 40c. Central American is offered more freely and we hear of sales at 30c to 32c.

Balsam fir, Canada, is without quotable change, holders of the limited available supply continuing to ask $3 to $3.10: Oregon is fairly steady at the previous range of 65c to 80c, as to quality and quantity.

Balsam Peru is well maintained, the quotable range standing at 95c to $1.00, as to size of order.

Balsam tolu continues in good seasonable demand and values are steadily maintained at 21c to 22c.

Barks. Bayberry is meeting with increased inquiry and we hear of sales at 12c to 13c, with up to 14c asked. Cascara sagrada is steady at 5½c to 9c. Cotton root is held and selling fairly at 8½ to 10c. Sassafras is steady at 12c to 15c, as to quality and quantity. Wahoo, bark of root, is extremely scarce, and commands 60c.

Bromide of potash is irregular and unsettled. There were rumors of sales down to 12c, but these could not be verified, and 15c appears to be an inside quotation, though one manufacturer is said to be a seller for export at 14c.

Buchu leaves, short, continue scarce and maintained firmly, with practically no prime green leaf available at the quoted range of 17c to 18c for short and 40c to 45c for long.

Cacao butter is in moderately active demand and values are well sustained at the range of 28½c to 30c for bulk and 34c to 35c for 12-lb. boxes.

Cannabis indica has developed increased strength, owing to the stronger tenor of reports from London, and spot quotations have been advanced to $1.10 for either tops or siftings.

Cantharides are finding a moderate outlet into consumptive channels at unchanged prices, or, say, 52½c to 55c for whole Chinese and $1.20 to $1.25 for Russian.

Chamomile flowers are in demand and steady at 18c to 22c for Roman, 15c to 25c for German and 9c to 11c for Hungarian.

Codliver oil, under more favorable reports of the season's catch, and lack of seasonable demand, is being pressed for sale, with some brands of Norwegian offering at $22, though up to $25 is named for the more desirable brands. New oil for shipment is offered at $21, laid down.

Cubeb berries are in moderately active demand, and price quotations are maintained at the previous range of 8c to 9c for ordinary and 9½ to 10c for XX.

Cuttlefish bone, Trieste, has advanced since our last, the revised quotations for prime being 16½c to 17c. French and jewelers' large are unchanged, at 12c to 12½c for the former and 70c for the latter; small is held and selling at 40c to 50c.

Ergot has developed an easier tendency and is offered at a decline from previous prices, sales of Russian being reported at 35c to 36c and of Spanish at 37c to 38c. The situation at primary markets is not encouraging to holders here, as supplies are said to be accumulating rapidly, and cabled offers have been received at marked concessions.

Eucalyptus leaves have met with a moderate inquiry during the interval and sales to consumers are reported at 4c.

Glycerin is meeting with about the usual inquiry, and the market is unchanged at 11½c to 11¾c and 12½c to 12¾c for C. P. in drums and cases respectively.

Guarana is firmer under the influence of light stocks in this market and reported scarcity at primary sources of supply; quoted 65c to 70c.

Juniper berries have eased off a trifle since our last owing to lack of demand, though reports from primary markets point to a poor crop; sales at the close were at 3⅞c to 4c.

Menthol shows signs of recovery with the disposal of many of the cheaper lots which have been a disturbing factor in the market, but sales are making at the previous range of $2.20 to $2.30, though some dealers hold out for $2.25 inside.

Opium, owing to weaker cable advices and competition among holders, has declined in the interval, cases being offered freely down to $2.87½, while the figure for broken lots has receded to $2.90. Powdered is apparently steady, at $3.40 to $3.45.

Prince's pine has developed considerable firmness of late, owing to increased demand and consequent scarcity; held and selling at 20c.

Quinine maintains its firm position and is in good consuming demand, though speculative interest seems to have been somewhat checked. We hear of several large contract orders at 18c. While bark shipments from Java for the first half of the current month are reported light, they exceed the shipments during the corresponding period of last month, and holders express confidence in the situation. Meanwhile prospective buyers are in the market for round lots at a concession from manufacturers' figures, but second hands are not urging the distribution in this way any more than the manufacturers, and business is somewhat restricted in consequence. Some German is said to be available at 17¾c, but 18c is generally quoted.

Saffron, American, is fairly active in a jobbing way, numerous sales being recorded at $1.25 to $1.30. Valencia is firmly maintained at $7.50 to $8.00 and Alicante at $5 to $6.

Senna leaves, Alexandria, continue in good request, with the bulk of the sales of siftings, for which 5¾c to 6c is paid.

Sugar of milk is in steady demand, and though we hear of a sale of 10 bbls. at 13½c, the general asking price is 14c to 15c.

Vanilla beans continue held and selling at the range of $2.75 to $6.50 for whole Mexican, as to quality and quantity.

Wax, carnauba, is in good demand and, spot supplies being rather limited, quotations have been advanced to 49c to 50c for No. 1, 33½c to 34c for north country and 32c to 33c for No. 3. The market appears to be entirely bare of No. 2. Japan is finding a slow sale at 12c to 12½c.

Chemicals.

Arsenic, white, has attracted great attention since our last. Prices were advanced early in the week, up to 12c being named, but business at the close was done at 9½c, and offers of forward shipment were made at 6½c. Red is held and selling at 6¾c to 7c.

Carbolic acid is firmer under the influence of decreasing spot supplies, and some holders are asking 15c to 16c for crystals in bulk, though 14½c would probably be accepted on a firm bid. Pound bottles are in ample supply and unchanged at 20c to 22c.

Carbonate of potash has weakened in the interval owing to pressure to realize on the part of holders, and 96 to 98 per cent. is quoted nominally at 4¼c to 4¾c.

Chlorate of potash continues scarce on spot, and values are firmly maintained at the range of 9½c to 9¾c for crystals and 9¾c to 10c for powdered.

Citric acid is firmer, but spot prices are as previously quoted, though an advance would occasion no surprise considering the position of the raw material. We quote the range at 38c to 38½c.

Corrosive sublimate, powdered, was advanced 3c per pound on the 19th instant, bringing it up to 73c. Lump crystal and granulated are quoted on the uniform basis of 70c.

Nitrate of silver has marked another advance influenced by a stronger market for the metal, manufacturers now naming 41¾c to 45¼c, as to quantity.

Oxalic acid maintains its firm position and we hear of nothing offering at less than 5½c.

Platinum salts are higher owing to the increased cost of the metal, and double chloride is now quoted at $11 to $12 per oz.

Quicksilver is in good demand and a fair business is passing at current quotations, or say 56c to 58c.

Tartar emetic shows an advancing tendency in sympathy with the crude material, and barrels are now quoted at an advance to 23c to 25c, as to quantity.

Essential Oils.

Anise is in good consuming request and values are well sustained at the range of $1.30 to $1.35, the former for 14 degree and the latter figure for 15 degree test.

Bergamot is quiet, but prices are well maintained at the previous range of $2.15 to $2.30.

Camphor has sold actively during the interval and prices have materially advanced, natural Japanese white being now maintained at 17c to 18c, while ordinary heavy is quoted at 10c to 12c.

Cassia is meeting with a good demand and numerous transactions in a jobbing way are reported at the quoted range of 80c to 85c, as to test.

Citronella is firmer in sympathy with the foreign markets, the oil drums being held by most dealers at 40c, though 38c would buy in a limited way; cans are quoted at 41c to 42c.

Lemon is meeting with increased attention and values are likely to go higher, though competition is active. While some old oil is obtainable at 60c, fresh importations do not offer at under 62½c, with up to 75c asked, according to quality and quantity.

Pennyroyal has advanced in the interval, prime American being now quoted at $1.30 to $1.35, though off grades offer down to $1.20, and some French oil of doubtful botanical source is obtainable at $1.10.

Peppermint continues to attract most attention in the list of essential oils. The lightness of stocks in producing districts, coupled with an active consuming demand, has served to materially strengthen the views of holders, who now name $2.50 to $3 for bulk in tins, while HGH has been marked up by the bottler to $3.25, and cases in a jobbing way command $3.10 to $3.20.

Gums.

Aloes, of the various grades, is meeting with a limited inquiry only, but values are well sustained at the range of 6c to 6¼c for Curacao and 14c to 15c for Barbadoes.

Ammoniac is scarce and wanted, and quotations have been advanced to the range of 15c to 20c, the lower figure being named for mass and the higher for prime free tears.

Arabic sorts are actively inquired for in a jobbing way, and quotations are firmly maintained at 6½c to 11c.

Asafœtida is without change of consequence, either as regards price or demand. Only a limited jobbing demand is experienced at the current range of 14c to 18c for good to prime.

Benzoin (Sumatra) is held with increased firmness in some quarters, and it is difficult to buy at less than 34c, with up to 38c quoted for choice grades.

Camphor maintains its firm position in sympathy with conditions at primary sources of supply, and there is talk of a further advance in values. The demand, considering the present range of values, continues of a satisfactory character and the tone of the market is strong at current quotations of 94c to 94½c for domestic refined in barrels and cases, respectively. Japanese refined in ounces is offering fractionally lower.

Chicle is in good request and the consuming demand for Mexican is being met at 36c to 38c.

Gamboge is not being pressed for sale, and the market has developed a firmer tone as a result of recent reports from primary markets advising scarcity there. Such sales as come to the surface are making at 85c to 90c.

Guaiac, kino and myrrh have sold in seasonable volume during the interval at previous prices, or say, 15c to 25c for guaiac; 25c to 27c for kino, and 23c to 30c for myrrh, as to quality.

Tragacanth has continued in good demand at previous prices, sales of both Aleppo and Turkey being recorded at 30c to 65c and 35c to 80c, respectively, the figures representing a wide range of quality.

Roots.

Burdock is quoted at an advance, owing to the strong tenor of advices from foreign markets; up to 12c to 13c is named.

Culvers offers more freely at a fractional decline, 9c being now named as acceptable.

Ginger, bleached Jamaica, commands slightly higher prices, the popular figure standing at 12c; unbleached shows no change from 9c to 10c.

Golden seal is dull and neglected and quotations are somewhat nominal at $1.25 to $1.30.

Ipecac continues on the downward grade, the latest quotation for both varieties being a fraction lower than previously quoted, with sellers at $1.50 for Rio or Carthagena.

Jalap has hardened in the interval owing to diminishing stocks, and sales at the close were at 10½c to 11c.

Lady's slipper is slow of sale and the market is somewhat easier at the range of 40c to 42c.

Manaca is in better supply and holders are more free to offer at a reduction to 16c to 18c.

Pink is very scarce and holders of the small available supply decline to shade 75c.

Sarsaparilla is fractionally lower, Mexican now offering at 9¼c to 9½c.

Senega is irregular and unsettled. While business might be done at 55c, some dealers quote up to 60c.

Seeds.

Only a limited demand is experienced for the various druggists' seeds and we have no changes of consequence to report in this department.

Hints to Buyers.

Columbian Spirit for external use is in all respects the equal of the finest grain alcohol. The Manhattan Spirit Company, of New York, invites the attention of the drug trade through the AMERICAN DRUGGIST to this fact.

The old English house of W. J. Bush & Co., with branches at 5 Jones lane, New York, and 185 Kinzie street, Chicago, offers to the American drug trade two of its specialties—namely, oil of sandalwood and oil of cloves. This concern can be relied upon for first-class goods through all its long list of essential oils.

The Crandall & Godley Company, of 165 Franklin street, New York, has obtained an enviable reputation for its soda fountain goods, and we take pleasure in inviting the attention of our readers to its advertisement which appears in this issue. The drug trade can confidently look for first-class products and honerable treatment at their hands.

All sorts of chemical and physical apparatus and pharmaceutical and laboratory appliances may be had of Eimer & Amend, of 205 Third avenue, New York. This concern is also a large distributer of medicinal products and chemicals and has made for itself a reputation of supplying the best goods at the lowest prices and of treating its customers with fairness.

Evans' Sons, Lescher & Webb, Limited, of Liverpool and London, and with a branch at 92 William street, New York, are meeting with marked success in the marketing of their British Lanolin, which they are able to sell at so low a price as to make it very attractive to the buyer. Our readers are referred to the advertisement appearing in this issue, in which will be found the price and a special offer concerning free delivery.

Cudahy's Nutritive Beef Extract, which is sold only by the drug trade and is endorsed by leading druggists as one of the best sellers on the market, contains all the nutriment of fresh lean meat scientifically prepared by the Cudahy Packing Company. As mentioned in its advertisement the Cudahy extract is a soluble beef, possessing a fine flavor. It is of uniform quality and guaranteed to keep in any climate.

The absolute purity and excellent flavor of the licorice sticks, paste and lozenges prepared by W. G. Dean & Son, of 361-363 Washington street, New York, furnish sufficient rea-reason for every wholesale and retail druggist to recommend them to his customers. Every stick, package of paste and lozenge made by this firm bears the stamped initials D. & S., so that no counterfeit can be passed off upon dealers who know a good article when they see it.

The "Reliable" and the "Q. S." Carbonators, made by the American Soda Fountain Company, are especially well adapted to the needs of the druggist. If you want a money-saving, reliable, long-life-without-repairs, automatic carbonator just write to it for information. If you're not sure that you want one, but are willing to weigh the facts and to install a carbonator if it will mean larger profits at small initial expense, just send the American Soda Fountain Company, Boston, a card of inquiry.

Careful druggists will do well to heed the constantly reiterated warning of the Fellows Medical Mfg. Company regarding colorable imitations of Fellows' Compound Syrup of Hypophosphites. As this is a standard product of very wide sale it is frequently imitated and the manufacturer is consequently compelled to defend its trademark rights against not only the makers but the sellers of the imitations. Many druggists have got themselves into an annoying and expensive lawsuit by carelessness in this respect, and therefore these repeated warnings are pertinent and useful and will be taken in good part by the more intelligent retail dealers of America.

Fairchild Brothers & Foster have issued a circular to the physicians of Brooklyn stating that substitutes for Fairchild's essence of pepsin have been dispensed upon prescriptions in which essence of pepsin, Fairchild's, has been plainly specified, at the drug store of James G. Brown, 240 Court street, Brooklyn. At the close of their circular the firm said: "In calling your attention to these facts we desire to assure you of our purpose to take every legal means in our power to protect ourselves and all proper interests concerned against this substitution of other products for ours, and we would request that if you have any cause for complaint, after having prescribed Fairchild's essence of pepsin, you will kindly communicate with us."

An opportunity to make a handsome profit in the sale and distribution of post cards containing views of the principal places of interest and attraction in their respectve cities, towns or villages is afforded the retail drug trade by the Albertype Company, of Brooklyn, N. Y., which has an excellent process for reproducing local views upon the ever-popular mailing cards. The Albertype Company, whose advertisement may be noted in this issue of the AMERICAN DRUGGIST, guarantees to make 250 or more handsome reproductions of an original subject, each one as clear and distinct as the subject itself, and each artistically displayed upon a post card at a rate which insures the dealer a good profit.

It will be profitable to druggists to note the series of advertisements which are being run in the farming papers by W. F. Young, P.D.F., of 49 Monmouth street, Springfield, Mass., covering his veterinary remedies, chief among which is Absorbine. This series is published piecemeal in the advertising columns of the AMERICAN DRUGGIST, and one specimen of the kind may be found in this issue. The object of publishing the series is to show the druggists of America just what the manufacturer is doing to stimulate a demand which will be profitable to retail druggists. Druggists who carry the goods in stock would do well to notify Mr. Young of the fact. so that he may file the name of the dealer and refer local purchasers directly to his store.

Clever advertising is now necessary if you would attract attention to and increase the volume of your business in these days of progress along all lines. If you would like to have your name constantly before your customers and likewise add to your list of purchasers a novelty is almost a requisite. The old method of having your name stamped upon the box or package, blown into bottles and printed on wrapping paper has been used a long time. Why not have it printed on wrapping tape? As mentioned in the advertisement in this issue, "Your name on the Wall street tape might mean failure, but your name on Reis Advertising Tape means business success." This new method of advertising is decidedly clever and attractive. Samples and prices will be submitted by G. Reis & Bro., 640 Broadway, New York.

As there is always an ever increasing demand for skilled pharmacists in every large city in the country, it is not surprising to note the growth in student attendance within the last few years at many of the most prominent colleges of pharmacy. A marked example of this increase in the number of undergraduates is characteristic of the history of the Highland Park College of Pharmacy, one of the professional schools of Highland Park College in Des Moines, Iowa, which was founded in 1889 and now numbers among its students almost 400 young men and women every year. The faculty of this college assert that it is the largest of its kind in the West, the attendance this year being the greatest since its establishment. It is claimed that there are twice as many students in this college as in all the other similar institutions in the State of Iowa.

The popularity of the college has been extraordinary from the beginning. Dr. S. R. Macy, dean of the college, was for seven years State chemist for Iowa, and every member of the faculty has had practical experience in a drug store and has completed college courses before taking up instruction with the institution.

The courses offered are thorough and practical, leading to the degrees of Ph.G., Ph.C., Ph.M., Phar.D. and B. S. The directors and faculty assert that the school has unexcelled equipments for high grade pharmaceutical and chemical work, while its laboratories are modern in every respect. The college has received the indorsement of the Iowa State Board of Pharmacy and its graduates are registered without examination at the time of graduation. No entrance examinations are given, but students are privileged to enter any class in which they are able to do satisfactory work. The first term of the third quarter opened on February 20 and the second term will begin April 2. In the fourth quarter the first term opens May 15 and the second term June 19.

Stearns' Private Circulating Library.

The Detroit *News Tribune* of February 11 contains an interesting description and illustration of the circulating library maintained by Frederick Stearns & Co. for their employees. This library contains about 3,000 volumes, devoted to general literature, science and medicine, and about 800 volumes of fiction. The firm also subscribes to every medical and chemical journal of any importance and to about 50 of the best weekly and monthly magazines. Every week from one to three of the best new books are added. On account of the many educational and scientific books it contains the Stearns library has proved of great value to many of the firm's employees.

The New Candy Book.

Have you seen the new advertising offer of the C. I. Hood Company, of Lowell, Mass.? By addressing the concern a supply of these very attractive candy books for counter distribution may be had. Each book will contain the dealer's business card, and as it is something which customers have evinced a marked interest in the advertising should prove of particular profit to the druggist. We invite the attention of our readers to the advertisement in this issue.

New Soda Fountains Big Money Makers.

With the approach of spring druggists would do well to consider the condition of their soda dispensing equipments and discover whether a new fountain would not be advantageous and result in realizing larger profits than are now obtainable with their old apparatus. The popularity of an article is often the surest proof of its excellence, and in view of this fact it is interesting to note that the Herron Soda Fountain Company, of 2509-2517 State street, Chicago, reports an enormous influx of orders for its onyx and marble soda fountains, carbonators and supplies. The Herron Soda Fountain Company reports this avalanche of business as follows: "We are receiving many inquiries from all over this country, Canada and Mexico for our soda fountains and are doing a good mail order business. We find that many people prefer to buy our fountains by mail, for in this way they get the proposition made to them in writing just exactly as they want it and are not influenced by what the salesmen tell them. We have recently placed a very handsome fountain in the store of Messrs. White & Gillis, of Clinton, Ind.; also a very up-to-date apparatus in the store of Richard Voge, at 1499 Ogden avenue, Chicago, besides numerous smaller fountains all over the country. The fountain placed in Mr. Voge's store has brought us many encomiums, people telling us that while it is not the largest fountain in the city it is certainly the handsomest that they have ever seen."

Schieffelin & Co. Agents for New Products.

Schieffelin & Co., 170 William street, New York, announce that they have completed arrangements with the Rufus Crowell Company, of Somerville, Mass., for the selling agency of its following products: Hemapeptone, Hemec Tablets, Colalin and Colalin Laxative, and are prepared to fill all orders and furnish any desired information on these goods with samples and literature. This big wholesale drug house has also secured the sole agency for the Whitlatch extracts of New York and Paris, which are packed in cut glass bottles inclosed in hand embroidered corded silk boxes. Within each bottle is a branch or tiny cluster of the natural flower itself.

A critical publication recently commented upon these extracts, as follows: "A novelty which is the most attractive seen in many a day is this floral extract of the highest class, which is absolutely perfect in delicacy, though with sufficient body to give it lasting strength. The extracts are all prepared from single flower odors, such as violet, lily, rose, orchid and sweet pea, but one never wearies of such perfumes and in the end their natural charm must prevail."

Schieffelin & Co. have also accepted the agency for the Triton effervescent bath salts for the Nauheim treatment, manufactured by the Triton Company, of Saratoga Springs, N. Y. These salts are offered to the trade at $8 per dozen. One dozen weigh, when packed, about 75 pounds, and therefore when ordering explicit shipping directions should be given.

A Price Correction.

A serious error was made in the price quotations on Phenix graduates in the advertisement of the Whitall Tatum Company, published in our last issue. We publish below the correct price list for these handsome and well-made graduates:

APOTHECARIES' FLUID MEASURES.

To deliver.	Per doz.	To deliver.	Per doz.
60 minims	$4.25	6 ounces	$7.00
120 minims	5.00	8 ounces	8.00
½ ounce	4.25	12 ounces	10.00
1 ounce	4.50	16 ounces	12.00
2 ounces	5.40	32 ounces	19.00
3 ounces	5.75	64 ounces	36.00
4 ounces	6.25		

METRIC MEASURE.

To deliver.	Per doz.	To deliver.	Per doz.
5 cc.	$4.00	120 cc.	$7.00
10 cc.	4.50	250 cc.	9.75
15 cc.	4.75	500 cc.	14.75
30 cc.	5.50	1,000 cc.	25.50
60 cc.	5.75		

The above are list prices, from which a discount of 40 per cent. is made to the trade.

Indeed It Does!

"Good wine needs no bush!"

That sentence has a smooth sound, but lacks logic, at least *modern* logic, whatever may have been true in the days when the saw was originated.

Nowadays good wine will lie still and slumber on through the centuries unless somebody does the "bush" trick with it.

The bush that everything needs to-day is spelled A-d-v-e-r-t-i-s-i-n-g. Good wine and good water, good jewelry and good jackknives need advertising to make known their merits to a rushing, bustling world.

Good post cards are, comparatively speaking, easy sellers, yet they "go" more quickly when well displayed on a Souvenir Post Card Rack.

This being true, the wise dealer will seek to make his profits come easier and faster by using the rack to display his card stock.

The Souvenir Post Card Company, 50 Franklin street, New York, are making an inviting offer to druggists, whereby one of the best racks yet made may be had, with 1,200 up-to-date cards, for only $10.

Their advertisement gives details; but the provision, "return cards not wanted," makes it safe to accept the offer without preliminary correspondence. The Souvenir Post Card Company is one of the biggest in the world and none is more reliable.

A Soluble Beef Bonus Offer.

Armour & Co., of Chicago, have instituted a special campaign of advertising on their Soluble Beef and Extract of Beef, and for a limited time will give a 2-ounce jar free with each order for 1 dozen of Armour's Soluble Beef, will give three 2-ounce jars free with each order for 2 dozen Armour's Soluble Beef and with each order for 3 dozen will give six 2-ounce jars free. No more than six jars will be given to any purchaser, however much he may buy. If desired orders may be divided between Armour's Extract of Beef and Armour's Soluble Beef, but only the soluble beef will be given free. We illustrate a package of this herewith. All jobbers are empowered to fill orders on this basis. For further particulars regarding soluble beef address Armour & Co., beef extract department, Chicago, mentioning the AMERICAN DRUGGIST.

AMERICAN DRUGGIST
and PHARMACEUTICAL RECORD

PHILADELPHIA. NEW YORK, MARCH 12, 1906. CHICAGO

ISSUED SEMI-MONTHLY BY

AMERICAN DRUGGIST PUBLISHING CO.

62-68 West Broadway, New York.

CHICAGO, 221 Randolph St. PHILADELPHIA, 3718 Walnut St.

A. R. ELLIOTT, President.

CASWELL A. MAYO, Ph.G. .... Editor.
THOMAS J. KEENAN .... Associate Editor.

ROMAINE PIERSON .... Manager Chicago Office.

$1.50 a year. 15 cents a copy.

ADVERTISING RATES QUOTED ON APPLICATION.

THE AMERICAN DRUGGIST AND PHARMACEUTICAL RECORD is issued on the second and fourth Mondays of each month. Changes of advertisements should be received ten days in advance of the date of publication.

Remittances should be made by New York exchange, post office or express money order or registered mail. If checks on local banks are used 10 cents should be added to cover cost of collection. The publishers are not responsible for money sent by unregistered mail, nor for any money paid except to duly authorized agents. All communications should be addressed and all remittances made payable to American Druggist Publishing Co., 62-68 West Broadway, New York.

Entered at New York as Second-Class Matter.

TABLE OF CONTENTS.

EDITORIAL COMMENT.

AT LAST, A PURE FOOD AND DRUG LAW. At last the long fight is ended, or as good as ended, for the Heyburn Pure Food and Drug bill has been passed in the Senate, and the Hepburn bill now under discussion in the House is well on its way toward acceptance. It is expected that the two bills will be harmonized, the House accepting the Heyburn bill with the incorporation of some of the distinctive features of the Hepburn bill. The new law will bear heavily on any manufacturers of proprietary medicines who make extravagant claims as to the therapeutic efficacy or effects of their products, or indeed any statement regarding the remedy which cannot be proved in court. Manufacturers will, however, be pleased with one provision of the measure, which makes substitution a misdemeanor. On the other hand, many proprietors will have to be more careful than they have been as to the claims made for their preparations, for if fraudulent claims are made the proprietor renders himself amenable to the law. On Wednesday of last week the Hepburn bill was reported favorably from the Committee on Interstate and Foreign Commerce of the House of Representatives, the minority being allowed a week in which to file its views. This means that action on the measure will not be taken until March 15.

IMPOSING ON THE COUNTRY PRESS. The absurd press dispatches which have been appearing of late in the newspapers of nearly every hamlet, village and city in the country regarding the possibility of the United Chemists' Company absorbing some local pharmacy is admirably hit off by our esteemed contemporary, *The Northwestern Druggist*, of Minneapolis, which observes that "it is a poor town that has not seen the approach of the 'drug trust.'" It is evident that the country press has been badly imposed upon by some unscrupulous news agency in this city, which boldly selecting names from a directory of druggists and, intimating in a preliminary dispatch that the firm named was about to be absorbed by the "drug trust," asked if a "story" was wanted. It would seem that most editors snatched eagerly at the bait and thus became responsible for the circulation of a whole lot of nonsense. It looks now as if the United Chemists' Company was to die a-borning, but it should be known that, whether dead or alive, its operations are limited by its charter to the cities of New York, Chicago and Philadelphia.

AGE REQUIREMENT AND STORE EXPERIENCE DISPENSED WITH. The Board of Trustees of the College of Pharmacy of the City of New York have taken an important step in rescinding the rule which required successful students to be twenty-one years of age and possess four years' store experience before graduation. This action was taken, we are informed, with the view of attracting a larger class of university students to the pharmacy course and at the same time to relieve a large number of young men who had passed successful examinations and were deprived of their diplomas either on account of not being of age or not possessing the necessary store experience. As the action of the college authorities has been approved by the Education Department of the State of New York, and that part of the department rules specifying an age limit for graduation has been stricken out, the effect of the action of the college trustees will be instantly felt by graduates of the New York College of Pharmacy whose diplomas have been withheld by reason either of the age or experience requirement. We are asked to announce that the retained diplomas will be delivered to the graduates immediately on application to the secretary of the college. Colleges outside of the State of New York which have not been admitted to registration by the department, or which have been admitted only conditionally, because their requirements for graduation did not include an age limit or store experience, will be greatly interested in this announcement, as they are now entitled to registration, providing they comply with the other requirements of the State Board of Pharmacy and of those of the Education Department.

The Regulation of the Sale of Narcotics.

The agitation which has swept over the country concerning the abuse of narcotic drugs has led to the introduction in many State legislatures of measures which are so absurd as to preclude the possibility of their enforcement, even should any legislature be so fatuous as to enact them. In the course of this agitation the pharmacist has come in for an unusual amount of vituperation from those callow reformers who undertake to set right all the ills that flesh is heir to by legislative enactment of the most drastic character, without due consideration of the circumstances which have led up to the evil which they propose to remedy.

Judging from the tirades which have appeared in various yellow journals and in a few which belong to the type which might be termed a ladylike pink, there is no good druggist except a dead druggist. Under these circumstances it is well for the pharmacist to bear in mind that the American Pharmaceutical Association has long taken an active interest in this question and was the first national body, so far as we can recall, to formulate any definite plan for minimizing this evil.

At the St. Louis meeting of the American Pharmaceutical Association, held in September, 1901, a discussion was held on the growth of the illegitimate use of narcotic drugs, and a committee was appointed to "consider and report upon the acquirement of drug habits in general and on the best method for the legislative regulation of the dangers connected with the use of narcotic drugs." The committee appointed in pursuance of this resolution made a report at the next meeting of the association, submitting statistics which proved the crying need for some legislative enactment. The temper of this committee may best be shown by the following excerpts from the report:

> Many of our correspondents—in fact, the large majority—were jealous of their reputations in this regard, and boldly declared that they were not and could not be made parties to this degradation. Pharmacy is proud of these, and pharmacy honors them. . . . How far the responsibility of jobber and manufacturer extends is not yet settled, but when they know, as they must know, that they, too, are pandering to this most unfortunate, this man-destroying appetite they must indeed have seared consciences to continue to supply this unwarranted demand without protest. Yet the greater responsibility, the responsibility for their sale, rests largely with registered pharmacists, who not only have control but discretionary control. . . . The responsibility is upon us and we must meet it or go down. . . . Through the various State associations, and with the aid of medical bodies, every State legislature should be induced to pass a uniform law, carefully prepared by this association. . . . All persons persistently trading in narcotics to be used by drug habitues should be excluded from pharmaceutical brotherhood.

As a result of this report another committee on the drug habit was appointed, and a committee was also selected to draft a law regulating the sale of narcotic drugs.

Both these committees made reports at the meeting of the association held in Mackinac, in 1903, the report of the Committee on Drug Habit being a voluminous and instructive paper which could be consulted with advantage by many who are interested in this movement but who are probably unaware of the existence of such a body as the American Pharmaceutical Association. The draft of an antinarcotic law which had been submitted and tentatively approved at the Mackinac meeting was submitted in a revised form at the Kansas City meeting, in 1904, and definitely adopted by the association.

This law, which is known generally as the Beal Antinarcotic law, being principally the work of Professor Beal, was used as the basis for the national law recently enacted governing the practice of pharmacy in the District of Columbia. It was also the basis of a bill approved at the Chicago conference of jobbers, proprietors and retailers, held at Chicago on December 28, 1905, and it has been introduced into the legislatures of Maryland and various other States as well.

Pharmacists would do well to direct the attention of those who busy themselves with wholesale attacks upon the drug trade to the facts mentioned, as they prove that pharmacists themselves have not been negligent of their duties in this grave matter, but have taken the initiative and have done so with moderation, with judgment and with discrimination. This measure is one which can be enacted without opposition and enforced without hardship and will accomplish all that it can be hoped to accomplish in this direction.

Discretion in Dispensing.

It will be recalled that in our issue of November 27 last year we printed a number of prescriptions involving points on which there was room for some difference of opinion as to methods of dispensing. These prescriptions were submitted to ten different pharmacists of high standing and in no case was there absolute unanimity of opinion as to the best methods to be followed. In the current number we present another paper along somewhat similar lines, consisting of an abstract of the remarks made by Professor Hynson, of Baltimore, in the course of a recent lecture delivered at the New York College of Pharmacy before the Manhattan Pharmaceutical Association.

Mr. Hynson has aptly termed the study of such prescription problems "a pharmaceutical clinic," as in this way there is brought before the pharmacist prescriptions such as he may with reason look forward to some day having presented to him over the counter. One question which is ever present is, How much discretion is vested in the pharmacist in dispensing prescriptions concerning the interpretation of which there is room for difference of opinion.

In discussing this phase of the prescription problem one of our valued correspondents, Mr. Wilbert, of Philadelphia, urged that on every prescription on which there was a possibility of two interpretations being placed the physician should be consulted. The pharmacist should never take any responsibility on his own shoulders where he could secure an expression of opinion from the writer of the prescription. Mr. Wilbert pointed out that the mere fact that a prescription is capable of two different constructions indicates the necessity for directing the attention of the physician to the need for greater care in writing.

If the druggist should correct what appeared to him to be a palpable error in the prescription the physician might go on indefinitely writing duplicates of this prescription and in every case duplicating the error. If the dispenser, however, directs the attention of the prescriber to the fault in the prescription the prescriber will be in a position to avoid falling into the same error in the future, and the dispenser would thus be conferring a very material benefit on the public, as well as on the physician.

It must be admitted that the primary duty of the pharmacist is to consult the prescriber when in doubt. This is not always feasible, however, and there are also occasions when, though the prescription itself is perfectly clear, there is room for reasonable difference of opinion as to method of dispensing. It is in such cases that the "pharmaceutical clinic" of Mr. Hynson is valuable particularly. We commend to our readers this form of study and should be pleased to receive specimens of difficult and doubtful prescriptions for discussion in future numbers.

PRACTICAL PRESCRIPTION ADVICE.

Professor Hynson's Lecture on Dispensing Problems—Reported by the Editor.

At the February meeting of the Manhattan Pharmaceutical Association, a report of which appeared in the preceding number, Henry P. Hynson, professor of dispensing and commercial pharmacy in the department of pharmacy of the University of Maryland, read a paper on the æsthetic aspects of dispensing. He presented and discussed a number of prescription problems and invited the members to discuss them. The prescriptions exhibited were all taken from prescription files and had been presented for dispensing in the regular way. We print the prescriptions below, together with an abstract of the comment in each case.

I.

Potassii chloratis ....ʒss
Aquæ ....℥ij
Acidi hydrochlorici ....ʒss

II.

Potassii chloratis ....ʒss
Acidi hydrochlorici ....ʒss
Aquæ ....℥ij

Mr. Hynson said that in the second prescription the intention of the prescriber was, he thought, to produce a solution of chlorine water. This would be obtained if the acid was poured directly on the potassium chlorate and the water added in divided portions with frequent shaking so as to dissolve the chlorine formed in the water. While this was not an unusual form of prescription the speaker said he not infrequently found that it had been filled incorrectly by first dissolving the chlorate in the water and then adding the acid.

The first form of prescription indicated that the physician merely wanted an acid solution of the chlorate.

III.

Ichthyolis ....♏iij
Fiat capsula mitte tales XXX.

In this prescription Mr. Hynson said that the catch consisted in the fact that ichthyol contained water and would dissolve the gelatin of the capsules unless it was previously mixed with some absorbent powder. As an absorbent he preferred powdered licorice. President Alpers, who had furnished the prescription from his file, said that in his own establishment powdered marshmallow was used.

IV.

Calomel ....gr. v
Aquæ menth. pip, ...℥ij

Mr. Hynson said that having found this was to be administered internally in teaspoonful doses he suspended the calomel in the water by adding two drachms of powdered acacia to the ounce. Secretary Swann said he had received the same prescription with instructions that it should be shaken before using and should be used as a mouth wash. In this case it being administered in conjunction with the iodides he thought that it was possible that the physician had really wanted black wash. He had not acted on this supposition, however, but had dispensed the mixture exactly as written without the addition of any mucilage and had never heard any criticism on it.

V.

Capsulæ validolis...................āā gr. v.
No. XX.

This prescription Mr. Hynson always puts up in soluble elastic capsules, taking good care to see that each capsule is entirely full. The way he did this was to weigh out the required quantity of validol for one capsule, put this in the capsule, fill up the capsule with a bland oil (he had used almond oil himself), making note of the amount of oil required. The figures gave him the necessary data to act on in adding almond oil to the validol in proper proportions so that each capsule when filled with the mixture would contain precisely the required quantity of validol. Mr. Hynson pointed out that in using an elastic capsule it was quite necessary that the capsule should be entirely full, as otherwise the side would collapse making a very awkward package.

VI.

Sodium glycerophosphatis (Schering)......ʒiv
Tincturæ cardamomi compositi } q. s. ad ℥iij
Aquæ sterilisatæ }

Mr. Hynson said that in this prescription the general understanding would be, he thought, that four drachms of the 75 per cent. solution, which is the form in which glycerophosphate is marketed by Schering, should be dispensed. Where the word Schering was omitted he thought it would be understood that a sufficient quantity of the solution should be used to furnish four drachms of the dry salt.

Discussing this point Mr. Tobin said that he had got into hot water frequently with physicians who had written such prescriptions over the question of whether or not the 50 per cent. solution (it was first put up in a 50 per cent. solution) or whether the dry salt was really meant. For his own part he had always construed the prescription as meaning four drachms of a dry salt and when using a 50 per cent. solution had put in eight drachms of this solution.

Mr. Alpers said that the most interesting point of this prescription was that it was necessary not only to use sterilized water, but to make sure that the receptacle in which the prescription was put up was itself sterilized. Unless this precaution was taken the prescription would keep only a day or two, but where it was taken it would keep several weeks, even though repeatedly opened.

VII.

Zinci sulphatis ....gr. ij
Cocain. hydrochlor.......................gr. ij
Liquor. acidi borici satur...............℥i

Mr. Alpers said if dispensed as written the prescription would be slightly cloudy, whereas if the sulphate was substituted for hydrochloride of cocaine no such cloudiness appeared. Mr. Alpers did not undertake to offer any reason for this difference, but merely stated the fact as one which had been observed and acted upon by him. One of the members of the association suggested that possibly zinc hydrate was formed, though no suggestion was offered as to how this might come about.

VIII.

Capsularum
Extracti nucis vomicæ...................gr. ss
Extracti tincturæ Warburg...............ʒss
No. XX.
S. T. i. d.

Mr. Hynson said that this was a prescription which was frequently presented to the Baltimore pharmacists and that what was wanted was a powdered extract of Warburg's tincture which would represent one-half drachm of the tincture. He said that in his own store he kept powdered extract made by the evaporation of the tincture which bore a known proportion to the tincture and the use of which much facilitated the filling of this prescription.

IX.

Zinci sulphatis
Potassæ sulphuratæ......................āā ℈ij
Glycerini ....♏xx
Spiriti myrciæ ....℥ss
Aquæ ....ad ℥iv
Misce ft. mistura.

Mr. Hynson pointed out that in the above prescription two very different results could be obtained by different methods of dispensing. If the two salts were dissolved separately in water and then mixed and added to the other ingredients a very much more diffused precipitate was obtained, and in this way the odor of sulphureted hydrogen was much less pronounced. By mixing the salts directly with the water and adding the other ingredients a less satisfactory preparation was obtained. Mr. Hynson said that the mixture was a very popular one in Baltimore.

In the discussion which ensued F. O. Collins told an amusing incident. In a copy of a similar prescription which had been handed to him for refilling sulphurated potash was written sulphate of potash and he had hesitated a good deal about which chemical to use. He finally decided to put the prescription up as written, and the user on her return for a refill told Mr. Collins that he and the druggist who had supplied the copy were the only two druggists who had compounded the preparation properly, as she understood what was proper.

X.

Sulphuris præcipitatis ....℈x
Zinci sulphatis ....℈x
Kalii sulphuratæ ....℈x
Aquæ rosæ ....℥iv

In this prescription the best results were obtained by proceeding as in the former prescription and then triturating the sulphur with the precipitate already formed, adding the water gradually, with constant trituration. Mr. Hynson said it was essential to reduce the sulphur to a very fine powder.

XI.

℞ Pulveris opii ....gr. xx
Plumbi acetatis ....ʒss
Aquæ bullientis ....℥iv
M. S. A.
S. Apply to eye.

This prescription is quite an unusual one and the physician who wrote it complained to Mr. Hynson that it was rarely dispensed just as he wanted it. An infusion should be made of the opium with the major portion of the water; the infusion filtered, the lead acetate dissolved in the reserved portion of the water and this solution mixed with the filtered infusion. The result is a mixture containing a fine flocculent precipitate of opium meconate, which is what was intended by the prescriber.

XII.

℞ Potassii chloratis ....ʒi
Tincturæ cinchonæ co.
Tincturæ guaiaci
Mellis ....āā ʒiv
Mucilagonis acaciæ
Aquæ ....āā ʒvi
Misce.

Mr. Hynson said that honey was a favorite substance with him, as so much could be done with it, and it was so valuable under such varying conditions. In the present instance he gave the following directions for dispensing: Dissolve in the full amount of water ordered as much of potassium chlorate as will pass into solution. To the remainder of the potassium chlorate in the form of fine powder add the honey and to this the tincture of guaiac, stirring constantly; then the compound tincture of cinchona and finally the solution of chlorate gradually. The resulting mixture is a pale pink, which sometimes turns to blue through the oxidation of the resin by the chlorate and this will gradually turn to a reddish brown; which variation in color was a frequent cause of concern to the patient. The change in color occurs more certainly if acacia is a constituent of the mixture. Mr. Alpers said it was his practice to rub up the potassium chlorate directly with the honey.

XIII.

℞ Potassii iodidi
Resinæ guaiaci....................āā gr. lxxx
Vini colchici seminis....................℥ss
Aquæ cinnamomæ ....℥ij
Syrupi simplicis..............q. s. ft. ℥vijss
Misce.

Mr. Hynson advised the rubbing of the resin and potassium iodide to a very fine powder and then to triturate with the syrup, lastly adding the wine. In this manner the resin could be separated in fine particles after the iodide was dissolved. No attempt should be made to dissolve a part of the resin in the wine.

XIV.

℞ Sulphuris præcipitatis ....ʒi
Pulveris tragacanthæ ....gr. v
Pulveris camphoræ ....gr. i
Aquæ calcis
Aquæ rosæ....................āā ℥ss
Misce.

Mr. Hynson cited this as a prescription in which too much tragacanth was directed—three grains was quite enough. After powdering the camphor, it and the tragacanth should be triturated with the sulphur, and to this the water should be added *very gradually*. Prepared in this way the sulphur will remain suspended much longer than if the water is added in larger quantities.

XV.

℞ Ammonii carbonatis ....ʒi
Aquæ menthæ ....℥i
Syrupi acaciæ ....℥ij
Tincturæ cinchonæ co....................℥ss
Misce.

Mr. Hynson said that the question of what was meant by "aquæ menthæ" seemed to be a matter of geographical location. He said that in Baltimore it meant generally "green" mint, though he would dispense peppermint. He asked what would be used in New York. The members agreed that in this city where mint was ordered without specification, mentha piperita was invariably understood.

XVI.

℞ Holocain ....gr. ss
Olei ricini....................ʒij
Misce. ft. solutio.
S. eye drops.

Holocain is not soluble in castor oil, but is quite soluble—the hydrochloride—in alcohol. Mr. Hynson used about five drops of alcohol and incorporated the solution with the castor oil.

XVII.

℞ Mentholis
Thymolis ....āā gr. x
Acidi borici ....ʒi
Glycerini ....ʒiij
Aquæ ....q. s. ℥ij
Misce. ft. solutio.
S. use as spray.

Mr. Hynson said wherever borax or boric acid was prescribed together with glycerin in larger quantities than could be otherwise dissolved, the substance should be mixed directly and heated so as to form a boroglyceride which was not only very soluble itself, but possessed a marked solvent action on many substances prescribed with it.

XVIII.

℞ Zinci sulphatis ....gr. i
Sodii biboratis ....gr. vij
Aquæ camphoræ ....ʒij
Aquæ distillatæ ....ad ℥i
S. Three drops in eye twice a day.

The remarks which Mr. Hynson made concerning the preceding prescription were applied to the prescription containing borax, zinc sulphate, etc. He added to this latter prescription 16 to 20 minims of glycerin, adding this directly to the borax and then combining this with the other ingredients. Unless this were done the incompatibility between the zinc sulphate and the borax would result in the formation of a precipitate.

XIX.

℞ Glycothymolini ....℥vi
Acidi borici ....ʒij
Argyrolis ....ʒii
Aquæ ....q. s. ℥iij
Misce. ft. solutio.

This prescription had been the cause of a good deal of trouble and seemed on the face of it to be irreconcilably incompatible. A little study of the situation, however, disclosed the fact that the whole trouble was due to an excess of boric acid, and the only thing to do was to leave out some of the acid. Mr. Hynson emphasized the fact that a knowledge of solubilities was of great advantage to dispensers.

XX.

℞ Creosoti ....gtt. vi
Cocainæ muriatis ....gr. iij
Aquæ calcis ....℥vi
Misce. ft. solutio.

The interesting facts were developed that the alkaloid was dissolved in this case in excess of alkali present. Mr. Hynson also directed attention to a fact which he had observed in course of investigation in connection with the above prescription that on adding lime water to alcohol a cloudiness was formed which was cleared up by the addition of creosote.

XXI.

℞ Zinci sulphatis ....gr. viij
Sodii biboratis ....gr. x
Aquæ ....℥i
Misce. ft. solutio.

A precipitate ordinarily forms in this solution, which can

be prevented if the borax is triturated with a few drops of glycerin.

XXII.

℞ Morphinæ sulphatis ....gr. i
Acidi borici ....gr. v
Sodii biboratis ....gr. x
Aquæ ....℥i
Misce ft. solutio.

The above prescription is another instance where the addition of a small quantity of glycerin serves a good purpose and is open to no objection.

XXIII.

℞ Sodii biboratis ....ʒiv
Sodii bicarbonatis ....ʒiij
Glycerini ....ʒiv
Acidi carbolici ....♏xij
Aquæ ....q. s. ℥vi
Misce ft. solutio.

Glycerin combined with sodium borate sets free some boric acid, which is liable to react with the sodium bicarbonate and cause effervescence; it also assists in the solution of the borax.

XXIV.

℞ Tincturæ ferri chloridi ....ʒss
Acidi phosphorici dil....................ʒss
Spiriti limonis ....ʒij
Syrupi simplicis ....ʒij
Aquæ ....ad ℥iv
Misce.

The amount of spirit of lemon ordered to be added in the above prescription was much more than was needed and very much more than desirable. The only purpose it could possibly serve would be that of a flavoring ingredient. Mr. Hynson had therefore decreased the amount of lemon to the proper proportion of about 10 drops. In commenting on this prescription President Alpers said that he had received a prescription in which two drachms of oil of peppermint had been prescribed in a two ounce mixture. On inquiring of the prescriber he was told that he merely wanted to get the flavor of peppermint and had not any idea that he was prescribing an excessive quantity.

XXV.

℞ Liquoris potassii iodidi saturatis...........℥i
S. Ten drops t. i. d.

Mr. Hynson said that theoretically one could make a 62 per cent. solution of potassium iodide, but practically it was better to look upon a 60 per cent. solution as being a saturated solution. He made it a practice to add five drachms of hot water to an ounce of potassium iodide and when the solution was cold he brought the mixture up to a fluid ounce, thus making a one grain in one minim solution.

XXVI.

℞ Quininæ dihydrochlor................gr. lxxv
Aquæ ....q. s. ad. ʒij
Misce ft. solutio.

Mr. Hynson said that the use of the dihydrochloride would be much more popular if its availability for making a concentrated solution was understood. He had suggested to many physicians who liked to give their quinine in the form of solution that they could dispense a concentrated solution of hydrochloride, leaving the patient to drop the proper quantity into the capsule just before taking it.

XXVII.

℞ Saponis viridis ....℥iij
Spiriti vini rect...................q. s. ℥iv
Misce.

Mr. Hynson said that it was next to impossible to make a solution of this soap unless the soap were first fused by the aid of a gentle heat, and the alcohol then added. By proceeding in this way very satisfactory results were quickly obtained.

XXVIII.

℞ Strychninæ sulphatis ....gr. i
Acidi arseni ....gr. i
Hydrargyri bichloridi...................gr. i
Tincturæ ferri chloridi ....℥i
Misce.

This prescription brought up a wholly new phase of dispensing. Mr. Hynson said that it not infrequently happened that by taking the constituents of a preparation and using them separately one could obtain results which could not be obtained by using the finished preparation as ordered in the prescription. In the present case he took a solution of ferric chloride representing the amount of the solution contained in one ounce of the tincture, dissolved the arsenous acid in it and added this to the mixture after the other ingredients had been dissolved in the alcohol.

XXIX.

℞ Adrenalum ....ʒi
Eucaine β...............................gr. x
Liq. ac. boric. satur.....................℥ij
S. Use in atomizer.

This prescription was written at a time when the dried suprarenal capsules were used and before adrenalin had come into general use. The prescription was dispensed by making a cold infusion of the powdered capsules, filtering and adding the eucaine.

Mr. Hynson said that when the use of the powdered suprarenal capsules was not uncommon he had been called up on the telephone by a fellow pharmacist who asked if he had any suprarenal capsules on hand. Mr. Hynson said he had. His interlocutor then asked what size they were, as the only ones he had on hand were No. 00, which were too large.

XXX.

℞ Ferri redacti
Mangan. dioxid....................āā gr. xiv
Extracti nucis vomicæ ....gr. x
Misce ft. pilulæ xxx.

Mr. Hynson said that here was a case where his "old friend licorice" came into play. There was no powder in his opinion so useful as licorice. In this case it made a good soft mass possible.

Mr. Hynson said that mercury and chalk powder could be made up into pills very readily by the addition of licorice powder to the mass. If an effort was made to work it up into a pill mass without such an addition the mercury would be thrown out.

XXXI.

℞ Pulveris rhei
Sodii bicarbonatis.................āā gr. xxx
Misce ft. pilulæ xij.

Mr. Hynson said that this prescription was one which could cause a good deal of surprise to the unwary one who met it for the first time, for it rose up like a yeast cake owing to the liberation of carbon dioxide. He said the best way to handle it was to make it up rather soft, let the reaction proceed to a finish and then add sufficient licorice to make a firm mass.

Emulsions with Soapbark.

A contributor to the *British Medical Journal* observes that although the emulsifying properties of quillaja are mentioned in every text book yet its advantages do not appear to be generally known or made use of. The following emulsions are, he says, easy to prepare, and remain permanent on the addition of either alkalies or acids:

Concentrated Chloroform Water.

Chloroform ....ʒix
Tinct. of quillaja........................ʒiij
Water to..................................℥x

Concentrated Peppermint Water.

Ol. menth. pip............................ʒiv
Tinct. of quillaja........................ʒij
Water to..................................℥x

Concentrated cinnamom can be prepared in the same way.

Concentrated Camphor Water.

Camphor ....ʒi
Rectified spirit..........................ʒiij
Dissolve, then add:
Tinct. of quillaja........................ʒiss
Water to..................................℥ij

Emulsion of Sandalwood Oil.

Ol. santal................................ʒi
Tinct. of quillaja........................ʒss
Water to..................................℥i

(Written for the American Druggist.)

BOMBAY'S NATIVE DRUGGISTS.

BY FRANK ROSS.

Bombay.

Bombay's landmark, as you approach the gateway of India by sea, the Taj Mahal Palace hotel, Asia's greatest achievement of the kind, stands out and dominates all else in the first view the *voyageur* gets of "beautiful Bombay," and for our purpose offers a striking contrast in splendor to the squalor of the shanties which shelter the native druggists of the city.

Splendidly situated on one of the finest natural harbors of the world, with a population well over a million, and an over seas and local commerce and industry that is going ahead by bounds, Bombay not remotely resembles New York in the limited space it has at disposal on which to build, and in the towering sky scrapers that have in consequence risen on the narrow tongue of land which constitutes the town and island of Bombay, as the only solution of the housing problem.

Taj Mahal Hotel, Bombay.

I have chosen as subject matter for the views set forth rather those businesses round which history builds the birth and growth of the drug business in native hands in Bombay than those which may to-day claim to have a little larger turnover than their older neighbors.

LEADING NATIVE FIRMS.

Tradition as handed down places the name of Nathoo Mooljee & Co. as that of the parent concern; separating in time from this beginning we have Karsondass Nathoo & Co., and Hurjee Mooljee & Co., to-day in turn the oldest and most respected of the crowd of men who adorn their places with the pretentious title "wholesale and retail druggist." The first of these firms can, I think, safely claim to do the largest business in a field in which the stress of competition is yearly growing and already reaches breaking point.

The firm of Hurjee Mooljee & Co. rank as their chief asset the agencies of the well-known American proprietaries, Fellows' Syrup and Perry Davis' Pain Killer, in both of which they do a very large business. Securing these valuable auxiliaries when the native of the land (the greatest drug lover on earth) was being educated into the ways and benefits of tonics and pain balms, they have come along on the flowing tide of prosperity that successive and successful sampling and advertising campaigns have established.

Situated in one of the busiest arteries of traffic, in a congested portion of the city given over to the native dealer and popularly and generally known as "the market," the shops that constitute the drug bazaar of Bombay rub shoulders with each other for more than a thousand yards of the crowded and unwholesome thoroughfare shown in the illustration. The reverse of imposing—dirty, disheveled, unkempt—the external aspect offers no sort of index to the volume and value of the business done. With signboards on which never a penny is spent year in, year out, and that initially came to them gifts at an open door from the great London house of "Burgoyne," which holds the field in all that pertains to the drug and general sundry requirements of the native dealer and physician, the men who to-day constitute the leading native druggists began, I should explain, as youngsters at an age when European children would have reached perhaps the third standard. [About seventh primary grade, American.]

Starting with this decided advantage in the matter of years over his English or American fellow, and with no qualifying examination of any kind to worry about, is it any wonder he is by the time he reaches his eighteenth year an expert and practical craftsman, backing everyday arguments with the artifices, industry and cunning that go to constitute the bazaar man of India?

"PRINCES OF HAGGLERS."

To endeavor to place before you some mind picture of the keenness of the ordinary native of Bombay (as distinct from those princes of hagglers, the dealers) it is a not uncommon practice for a customer bent on striking rock bottom depths for the commodity he is after—be it potassium iodide or Clark's blood mixture—to start at one end of the street with which we are particularly concerned and sail down from door to door discussing and disputing to fractions the price asked till he feels he has indeed got to windward of the last price possible.

It is thus the European marvels at the prices the natives ask for their wares, as compared with the charge made by the British or European shopkeeper for the same article, unmindful of the fact that, whereas the native lives in a plague-ridden hovel five floors up, with little rent and less in the way of personal and household expenses, the European usually has a large rental and expensive staff to maintain, eating into the ratio of profits and prices that have to be charged. It is a curious testimonial to themselves and their distrust of one another that the greatest part of the drug business that is done is done in original London packed ounce, 4-ounce, 8-ounce or pound containers (bottles, pots or tins). Indeed, you conclude that the public confidence in the business honesty of their fellows is a quality very much at a discount in the dealings of one native with another, for the public, mindful of their own weaknesses, give them as it were no opportunity to be tempted into ways that are crooked and profitable by tampering with the contents of bulk parcels of goods. For of these same children of the sun, who have walked calmly through nine years of plague, it is recorded, and pretty well public property, that in the earlier days of the pest, when the death rate was quite appalling and iodoform, salol, phenacetin, strychnine hydrochlor., corrosive sublimate and numerous other drugs sprang into instant demand in quantities that at once exhausted all local stocks and obtainable supplies, it was no uncommon experience to discover iodoform had been diluted down with

Street Scene in Bombay. (Bullock cart in foreground is aerated water delivery cart.)

sulphur sublime, salol and phenacetin with boric acid, strychnine with antifebrin and corrosive sublimate with a special local stone intimately resembling the original.

AN INTERNATIONAL COLLECTION OF DRUGS.

Another factor and large constituent deciding for original bottles and packages is the native medico with his own dispensary (advice free). Of these there are some two hundred forming an important *clientele*. To take a casual inventory of the contents of a native drug shop, one may see ranged round the shelves a perfectly international collection of drugs, patents and sundries—the fine chemicals of Merck, Howard and Homer; galenicals from Dakin, Lorimer, Burgoyne, Southall and Hewlett; cottons and lints from Johnson & Johnson; the specialties of Grimault, of Paris; Serracallo's Austrian tonic wine, proprietary remedies from makers of all shades in Great Britain, McK. & R.'s pills, Stearns' wine of codliver oil and headache cure, Scott's emulsion, a firmly established and freely handled article; Parke, Davis & Co.'s products (adrenalin, trifolium euthymol, cascara evacuant, etc.); the multiple B. W. & Co.'s preparations, Beecham's, Carter's, bile beans, Doan's pills, pink pills; Brand's various dietetic specialties, Eno's, Elliman's, Lemco, Calvert's foods, Scrubb's ammonia, Japanese camphor, celerina, lactopeptine, Angiers emulsion, sen sen, fig syrup, Huxley's syrup, to name a few of the hundreds that line the cases and stand piled around in original boxes, while a journey to the warehouses reveals stocks running from hundredweights of boric acid, naphthalin balls, carbonate of ammonia, etc., to tons of Epsom salt, everything, in fact, that is in any demand from the public being in evidence. Local tastes incline to a famous hair douche produced by a Bombay firm of chemists, Easton's syrup and Parrish's food in 4-ounce bottles, fever and ague mixtures, the chief of these called "Batliwalas," being in very great demand; cough syrups and mixtures have a large vogue, as also have pain removers.

GERMANY'S DIMINISHING TRADE WITH INDIA.

Of the over-sea's contributors to local questions Germany shows a diminished and yearly diminishing head in drugs and galenicals, but more than compensates for loss of ground in these by big business in aniline dyes and adjuncts going direct to the distributers through local agents giving 60 to 90 days' credit.

Hurjee Mooljee & Co.'s Pharmacy in Bombay.

I should explain that things pertaining to pharmacy and associated lines range themselves into classes under various retailers, bottles, jars, soda water bottles (Bombay does an enormous business in aerated waters all the year round) and such like being obtained from men who handle bottles exclusively, acids, bicarbonate of soda, soda water essences, carbonic acid gas and mineral water factory requirements from people dealing in these and associated goods only, soaps, perfumes, children's foods (Mellen's, Neave's, Horlick's, the Allenbury series, etc.), eau de cologne (used very largely by illiterate cultivators for "little Mary" troubles) from provision dealers, indigenous drugs and "simples" from other men.

Karsondass Nathoo & Co.'s Pharmacy in Bombay. (The two ropes dangling in front are hoists by which customers and friends pull themselves into the shop.)

THE AMAZING AMERICAN DRUMMER.

The climate of Bombay being a bar to the strenuous life beloved of your President, the American traveler, with his hustling, tearing methods, when he first strikes India is at once a marvel and an enigma, accustomed as our Aryan brother (the poor heathen in India!) is to amble backward and forward for the best part of a morning over the fraction of an anna, time and hurry being unknown terms in the linguistic existences of these princes of hagglers.

That natives are apt pupils I can best illustrate by the manner in which the drug men have grasped the possibilities of the "own specialties" trade. Starting in a timid way years ago, Bhicka Cullianjee & Co. (to select one example of what is true of all the rest) are to-day the successful manufacturers of half a dozen proprietary remedies having very large sales; indeed it is worthy of note that unlike his English confrère in the old country he does not attempt to pirate some one else's successful idea, but strikes out boldly on his own. Thus, to single out one of the articles put on the market by the firm, "Buckal ointment," a ringworm specific, retailing at annas 4 per pot (eight cents), has now reached a yearly sale of close on to 500 gross, a small army of women workers being employed to fill, label and wrap.

NATIVES GIVING WAY TO MERCHANT HOUSES.

Time was, to turn to another phase of the energies of the small band of men who have made the drug bazaar of Bombay a power in the province, when the export of everything in oils, gums, roots and spices pertaining to their calling passed through their hands, a department that has been of late slowly usurped and taken over by the great merchant houses. The dispensing of prescriptions receives, I find I have omitted to say, but scant attention, except with one or two firms.

Here then I will leave these prodigals of time and artists in discussion, with whom bargaining is a part and parcel of their daily existence, bringing as it does the subtlety of their thousand year old civilization very much to the front, and who have amply earned the encomium of that splendid man, the late Lord Dufferin, who, in speaking of the natives of Kipling's birthplace, said that their "sagacity, industry and enterprise have created a city vying in its prosperity and wealth with any capital that has ever been called into existence by caliph or mogul."

Wisconsin Board Questions.

The following is a specimen set of the questions given by the Wisconsin State Board of Pharmacy:

1. Define (*a*) atom; (*b*) molecule; (*c*) give molecular weight of oil of vitriol (omitting fractions); (*d*) in determining atomic weights, what element is taken as the standard and what is its atomic weight?

2. (*a*) Differentiate between valence and affinity: give an example of each of the following (*b*) univalent, (*c*) bivalent, (*d*) trivalent, (*e*) quadrivalent element; (*f*) is the valence of an element toward hydrogen also its valence toward other elements? If not, illustrate by examples; (*g*) is it constant or variable toward the same element? Give examples.

3. Explain why oxalic acid is used to remove ink stains or iron rust from linen. Why is ammonia used to remove the stains of iodine?

4. (*a*) A solid weighs in air 1,000 grains; by immersion in water it loses four-fifths its weight; what is its specific gravity? show your work. (*b*) How would you determine the specific gravity of a solid insoluble in and lighter than water? Explain briefly the use of the specific gravity bottle.

5. (*a*) Name the ingredients in Fehling's solution; (*b*) for what is it used? (*c*) explain briefly upon what the reaction depends?

6. Define the following terms and give an example of each: (*a*) hydragogue cathartic; (*b*) anodyne; (*c*) escharotic; (*d*) antipyretic; (*e*) expectorant.

7. Give the official Latin title and name the ingredients which enter into a Dover's powder; (*b*) citrine ointment; (*c*) elixir of vitriol; (*d*) Basham's mixture; (*e*) seidlitz powder.

8. Syrup iodide of iron; (*a*) give ingredients which enter into it; (*b*) process of preparation in detail; (*c*) why is the large excess of iron used? (*d*) what precautions are necessary to keep it, and why?

9. (*a*) Name a natural emulsion; (*b*) is linimentum calcis an emulsion? If not, why not? (*c*) give ingredients in linimentum calcis and give a common name.

10. Iodine. (*a*) To what class of elements does it belong? (*b*) how is it found in nature? (*c*) what is the chief source of supply? (*d*) name the official preparations; (*e*) what is the percentage of iodine in liquor iodi compositus? (*f*) what salt is used in the solution and why?

11. (*a*) Name the official plants which belong to the natural order Solonaceæ; (*b*) what are their general medicinal properties taken as a group? (*c*) name two official alkaloids obtained from them and give dose of same.

12. (*a*) What is dialysis? (*b*) how is it accomplished? (*c*) show why the process might be applied in examining the contents of the stomach in case of suspected poisoning; (*d*) in what pharmaceutical preparation is it employed?

13. (*a*) What do you understand by saponification? (*b*) what is the difference between saponification and emulsification? (*c*) what substances may be saponified and what products result? (*d*) name the official preparations prepared by this process.

14. Glycerin: (*a*) what is it chemically? (*b*) how is it obtained? (*c*) what is its specific gravity? (*d*) what impurities is it liable to contain and how would you detect them? (*e*) how would you prepare 1 fluid ounce of a 10 per cent. by weight solution of boric acid in glycerin?

15. Aqua Regia: (*a*) give official Latin title; (*b*) how did it derive its name? (*c*) how is it prepared? (*d*) give chemical properties and dose; (*e*) with what should it never be prescribed and why? (*f*) how should it be kept?

16. (*a*) What is the difference between analysis and synthesis? (*b*) what is a synthetic preparation? (*c*) give two official examples, one a solid and one a liquid.

17. (*a*) Give the common name and state the ingredients contained in Comp. Syr. Squills; (*b*) what official syrup contains aqua ammonia, and why? (*c*) what official syrup contains an official vinegar? (*d*) name an official syrup made from (1) a tincture, (2) a water, (3) a fresh fruit.

18. (*a*) What is the official name of carbolic acid? (*b*) from what is it obtained? (*c*) does it unite with water, and in what proportions? (*d*) how would you distinguish it from creosote? (*e*) give antidotes which should be used in case of poisoning; (*f*) which do you consider the best?

19. Corrosive sublimate: (*a*) give official and chemical names and chemical formula; (*b*) what chemical test would you use to detect the presence of corrosive sublimate in calomel? (*c*) show the reaction by an equation; (*d*) how would you prepare a liter of a-1: 1,000 solution?

20. Give the official Latin title for the following: (*a*) chloric ether; (*b*) Friar's balsam; (*c*) Griffith's mixture; (*d*) tartar emetic; (*e*) black draught; (*f*) spirit of mindererus.

21. Write a prescription calling for at least two solids and two liquids in apothecaries' weights and measures; (*b*) re-write the same prescription in the metric system; (*c*) give directions for taking in Latin.

22. Give official Latin title, botanical origin and natural order of the following: (*a*) thoroughwort; (*b*) cubeb; (*c*) burdock; (*d*) mandrake; (*e*) foxglove.

23. (*a*) What is understood by the term alterative? (*b*) name two alteratives of vegetable origin; (*c*) two not of vegetable origin; (*d*) give an official preparation of salt of each.

24. What is the source and medicinal uses of the following: (*a*) pepsin; (*b*) pancreatin; (*c*) ext. thyroids; (*d*) adrenalin.

25. (*a*) What is toxicology? (*b*) posology? (*c*) a toxin? (*d*) what do you understand by a drug having a cumulative effect?

26. Into what two classes are antidotes divided? Give an example of each. What are the symptoms of poisoning and antidotes for the following: (*a*) strychnine; (*b*) oxalic acid.

27. In relation to the usual dosage by the mouth, what general rule is followed in administering medicine by rectum and hypodermatically? What rule in administering medicine to children?

28. Name two official plants which stimulate the heart's action, giving botanical origin and natural order and name an official preparation of each with dose.

29. Give quantities required to make four av. pounds of tooth powder, prepared from the following formula:

Precipitated chalk	24 parts.
Powdered sugar	4 parts.
Powdered cuttlebone	3 parts.
Powdered borax	1 part.

30. With what provisions of the pharmacy laws of this State will it be necessary for you to conform, if you purchase a store after having been registered?

SPECIMENS.

Identify the sample (1) tincture of hydrastis—give official Latin title; what color should it be? how prepared? percentage strength; name principal constituents; give two common names of drug; what part of plant is used? what are its medicinal properties? give official preparations of the drug. (2) Boric acid—give official Latin title; how obtained? solubility; describe appearance: when ignited what occurs? give chemical formula; has it acid or basic properties? medical properties; with what may it be adulterated? (3) Senna leaves: give official Latin name; make drawing of leaf; botanical name of plants of both varieties; best solvent for extracting virtues of leaf; what would be incompatible with the infusion? what effect has boiling upon the leaves? what effect have acids and alkalies upon the leaves? how would you increase the medical value of leaves? official preparation. (4) Compound powder of jalap: give official Latin title; name ingredients; give botanical name of plant from which drug is derived; to what country is the plant indigenous? what part of the plant is used? best solvent for drug; what are the requirements of the pharmacopœia as to its purity? official preparations of drug; medical properties and dose. (5) Castor oil: give official Latin title; botanical name of plant from which derived; how would you administer a dose of oil? what is considered the best method of obtaining oil? what does it differ from other fixed oils? commercially, what are its uses? how would you emulsify it? does it become rancid? can you prevent it? state how; give medical properties and dose.

PRACTICAL EXAMINATION.

Name........................ Date........................

Normal Urine.

Color.
Odor.
Specific gravity.
Chemical reaction.
Quantity.
Sample of urine, No.
Color.
Odor.
Specific gravity.
Chemical reaction.
Sugar.
Albumin.
Phosphates.
Remarks.
Dispensing.
Prescription heading.
Miscellaneous.
Remarks.

In addition to questions like those given above, the Board also gives each applicant a practical examination in compounding, dispensing and pharmacopœial tests and such oral questions as to thoroughly prove the fitness of the candidate for registration.

Haarlem Oil the Oldest Proprietary in the World.

The true Haarlem Oil which is still made in the city of Haarlem, Holland, is lighter in color and more transparent than the numerous imitations with which the market abounds. The preparation is put up in curious half-ounce bottles wrapped in an ancient hand bill. It has a large sale among sailor folk the world over. In discussing this preparation from the popular point of view *Printers' Ink* says:

Haarlem Oil is a remedy that almost disproves the theory that the sales of a proprietary depend on advertising. For, while nobody in the United States had ever seen an advertisement of Haarlem Oil until recently and it is hardly advertised at all in other countries, there are annual sales of millions of bottles of the preparation all over the world. Its manufacturers in Haarlem, a city in Holland that has been a flourishing commercial center from the twelfth century, now make 40,000,000 bottles a year, it is said, and the output of the genuine is insignificant in comparison with the imitation. Practically every druggist in the United States has his own preparation of Haarlem Oil, and ten bottles of substitute are sold to one of the genuine.

Genuine Haarlem Oil has been made in Holland since the year 1672, when it was discovered by a Dutch physician named Claas Tilly. For 233 years it has been manufactured by his descendants, the present member of the family being C. de Koning Tilly. The little black bottles containing the preparation are put up strangely, no corks being used, but a piece of raw hide tied around the neck that serves the same purpose. It is sold in this country for twenty-five cents a bottle, while a wide sale in the imitation has been built up on the basis of 10 cents.

Of its formula, perhaps the least said the better—it is a family secret and heirloom. Haarlem Oil is a survival of the middle ages that ought to be extremely interesting to the antiquarian. But of the widespread belief of millions of people in its virtues there can be no reasonable doubt. Known popularly as "Dutch Drops," it is valued as a diuretic and really has a specific action as such. But those who purchase the preparation seem to have an almost superstitious faith in its power to ward off contagious diseases, and it is said that by far the greater portion of sales are made, not to people who need a diuretic or any other form of medicine, but who wish to take out a sort of blanket health insurance. A curious circular comes around every bottle of the genuine remedy. Headed by the arms of the Tilly family, it rehearses the virtues of Haarlem Oil in phraseology of two hundred years ago. The typography of the circular leads one to believe that this piece of literature was composed at least a century ago, and while in one place, as a guarantee of good faith, the reader is urged to visit two invalids in the city of Haarlem, Adolp Cornelis Jonkhout and Abraham van Neer, who were miraculously cured of dire ailments by the remedy, there is no doubt that both of these burghers have been dead lo! these many years, in spite of Haarlem Oil. Thackeray mentions Haarlem Oil, and it is said the first settlers in America brought it with them. Furthermore, it is stated that Lewis and Clark never started on an expedition without it and that it has been carried all over the world by explorers and missionaries. It is supposed to be good for the kidneys, bladder, stomach, the nerves, etc., and the directions state that a few drops applied to the eyes will so strengthen sight that spectacles will no' be needed until the age of seventy or eighty. As a matter of fact, the preparation is really of use in decreasing inflammation.

A Philadelphia firm has lately acquired agents' rights to this medicine in the United States, succeeding a firm that never made any attempt to advertise it or counteract sales of imitations. The name, the bottles, the labels and the quaint circular, the arms of the Tilly family and every feature of the remedy except C. de Koning Tilly's signature, have been exactly counterfeited. The new agents are now taking steps to protect their trademarks and have begun a campaign of advertising to kill substitution. Small single column ads ha-e lately appeared in the Philadelphia dailies warning the public to look for the red signature that alone distinguishes the real stuff, but, rather curiously, this advertising, while it increases sales of the genuine, has also helped the imitations, purchasers taking the latter at the lower price under the impression that they are trial sizes.

Haarlem Oil has long had a steady sale among Germans in this country, and indeed among all foreign-speaking people. There is good reason to believe that it is the oldest proprietary remedy in the world, and unless possessing some sterling merit it surely could not have lasted all these years. As the quaint direction-circular says: "This medicine works miracles in everyone who makes use of it, and the Grace of the Omnipotent God is admirably exemplified by it." The circular also has printed, in large letters, the legend, "Medicamentum Gratia Probatum" (remedy approved by Grace). Purchasers frequently ask for the medicine known as "Medicamentum," a query that usually stumps young drug clerks. But old heads in the trade know that Haarlem Oil is meant, and an inquiry for "Medicamentum" indicates a constant purchaser.

THE COMPOSITION OF HAARLEM OIL.

As to what it was originally there is some doubt. One writer says that it was the red oil obtained as a second fraction in the dry distillation of resin; another, that it was made by the dry distillation of a mixture of aloes, myrrh, olibanum, and olive oil; and another, that it was a mixture of balsam of sulphur, oil of turpentine, and Dippel's oil. The last, minus the oleum animalis, is the form generally adopted now, and the following is a translation of directions for making it followed in Denmark and Holland:

Mix in an iron vessel large enough to allow some frothing 4 parts of linseed oil and 1 part of sulphur. Heat to a temperature of 165 degrees C., stirring well all the time, until the mixture drops off the stirrer with a glassy appearance. Remove from the fire and add 15 parts (by weight) of oil of turpentine, and agitate until solution is complete or nearly so. Then filter. The liquid should be limpid and of a brownish-red color.

Of the following formulas only Nos. I and III closely resemble the original. Nos. II. and IV. the strange diversions, which show how things may become altered:

I.

Balsam of sulphur .... ℥i.
Oil of turpentine .... ℥iv.
Mix.

II.

Ol. lini .... ℥xl.
Resin .... lb.j.
Sulphur .... lb.j.
Boil till stringy, remove from the fire and add
Ol. terebinth .... ℥xx.
Liq. ammon. fort .... ♏50.
M.

III.

Balsam of sulphur .... ʒj.
Oil of turpentine .... ℥ij.
Huile de Cade .... ℥iv.
All by weight.
Mix.

IV.

Ol. terebinth .... ʒj.
Tr. guaiac. simp .... ʒj.
Spt. æther. nit .... ʒj.
Ol. succin. rect .... ʒj.
Ol. caryoph .... ʒj.
M.

Baume de Menthol Compose.

The following formula is from the *Apothcker Zeitung*:

Lanolin .... 45 parts.
Yellow wax .... 15 parts.
Menthol .... 15 parts.
Methyl salicylate .... 10 parts.

Warm gently to dissolve and incorporate the 15 parts of water.

Cream of Current Literature

A summary of the leading articles in contemporary pharmaceutical periodicals.

Coloring for Carbolic Acid Obligatory.—Reuter (*Revista de farmacia*, 1905, No. 8) advocates the enactment of a law requiring that all carbolic acid should be colored some uniform color in order to avoid confusion with other liquids resembling it. In some countries tablets of mercuric chloride must be colored blue, or some other color, when offered for sale.

Protosal is another of the numerous substitutes for salicylic acid intended for external application in rheumatism. Protosal is a glycero-formyl salicylic acid ester, and occurs as an oily, colorless fluid, which is readily soluble in ether, alcohol and benzol. Under the action of acids protosal is split up into salicylic acid, glycerin and formaldhyde.

A New Test for Indican in the Urine.—Gruber (*Pharm. Zeitung*, 1905, page 752) suggests a new method of testing for indican in the urine, or rather a variation of the old principle of oxidation with the use of osmic acid. The advantage of this reagent is that it oxidizes indigo very slowly. The urine to be tested is treated with twice its volume of concentrated hydrochloric acid, and then with a few drops of a 1 per cent. solution of osmic acid. If the urine contains indican it almost immediately turns violet, bluish-violet or blue, and traces of indican may be detected by shaking the urine with a few drops of chloroform which dissolves the indigo and which becomes colored blue.

To Test Adrenalin Solutions.—A colorimetric method has been devised for determining the potency of solutions of adrenalin. Owing to the fact that adrenalin solutions quickly lose their strength it is important to have assayed solutions. The method depends upon the color-reaction of adrenalin with a dilute solution of iodine. A standard solution for comparison is prepared by mixing 10 Cc. of a 0.01 per cent. solution of adrenalin with 5 Cc. of a decinormal solution of iodine, and allowing the mixture to stand. The excess of iodine is then taken off by means of a decinormal solution of sodium thiosulphate. This standard solution when diluted with 50 Cc. of distilled water has a pink color, and contains exactly 1 mg. of adrenalin. The sample to be examined is compared as to color with this standard solution. The standard solution must, however, be prepared extemporaneously for each assay, as the color fades when the solution is allowed to stand. A standard coloring has, however, been prepared, which keeps indefinitely by adding some acid to tincture of turmeric and thus producing the red color and then diluting until the exact shade of the standard adrenalin solution is matched.

Prulaurasine, a Glucoside in the Leaves of Cherry Laurel.—Herissey (*Journal de Pharmacie et de Chimie*, January 1, 1906, p. 5) in an exhaustive study on the glucosides of cherry laurel announces the isolation of a new crystalline glucoside to which he has give the name of prulaurasine. This he obtained by soaking the leaves of cherry laurel in boiling distilled water to which a little calcium carbonate had been added. In this way the emulsion of the leaves is destroyed. The leaves are then mashed in a machine, and are again subjected to boiling for a few seconds in the original fluid. After cooling the product is strained, expressed and the liquid cleared with white of egg. The extract is then distilled at low temperature under partial vacuum, and alcohol is added, whereupon a precipitate is formed which is rejected. The remaining liquid is distilled, the residue exhausted with acetic ether five different times with the aid of heat, and the ethereal solutions completely evaporated, the residue being dissolved in water. From this residue the glucoside is extracted in a crystalline mass. In the entire process only neutral solvents are employed. The glucoside crystalizes in small prisms or in needles, is colorless, odorless and has a bitter taste. It is split up by emulsion and rotates polarized light to the left. Prulaurasine should be regarded as an isomer of Fischer's amygdonitril glucoside, and of Bourquelot and Danjou's sambunigrine.

Improved Paraffin Ointment.—William Swan says that the paraffin ointment, British Pharmacopœia, has never been held in great esteem because of its hardness and the difficulty of preparing it free from granules, and carbolic ointment, British Pharmacopœia, has been generally condemned because of the rapidity with which it separates. The following base, capable of as wide an application as the present one, if not wider, is suggested (*Chemist and Druggist*) as a substitute. The chief test of such a base is its relation to carbolic acid: Will it dissolve the acid, and retain it bacteriologically active? The latter part of the question lies chiefly in the province of the bacteriologist, but the great stability of the chemical entities of adeps lanæ would suggest an affirmative answer. The solubility of the acid in the base was confirmed by preparing a solution of adeps lanæ, 1 part in liquid paraffin, British Pharmacopœia, 4 parts, and dissolving in it the acid in the proportion of 1 in 25. No separation took place after standing for several weeks. The following is the formula which I suggest for the base:

Unguentum Paraffini.

Wool-fat	2 parts
Hard paraffin	2 "
Soft paraffin	6 "

Melt together in a shallow dish, and as the liquid cools triturate constantly until, when cold, a uniform plastic ointment is produced.

To prepare carbolic ointment it is simply necessary to place the acid in a mortar, sufficiently warmed, and triturate till cold.

Indestructible Japanese Varnish.

Stevens (*American Journal of Pharmacy*, February, 1906, page 53) gives an interesting study of the chemistry of a Japanese varnish known as ki-urushi. Japanese varnish is almost indestructible, and some varieties have withstood every injurious influence for centuries. Alcohol, ether, acids and alkalies practically do not affect genuine Japanese varnish, although strong acids do so to some extent. The lac industry came to Japan from China in the early part of the third century, and for hundreds of years its method of manufacture and its mode of use remained secret, until in 1873 a great deal of information about this industry was furnished by Rhein, who made a study of the subject. The pure lac comes from a small tree about 15 feet high, which grows wild in both China and Japan, but is also cultivated in those countries. The lac is obtained by making horizontal incisions in the bark and removing the sap from the cuts at intervals of about four days, until the tree is covered with incisions. The raw lac comes in the form of a grayish-white emulsion, which when exposed to air turns brown and later becomes black. It contains a certain amount of bark mixed with it and has to be strained before it can be used. When the season is over the various parts of the tree are soaked in warm water and the sap which exudes is removed from the surface of the water. This is a second grade of the lac and is not as valuable as the first.

The black color of Japanese lac is not due to any artificial admixture but to the presence of a natural enzyme, which acts on the resin under the influence of moisture. After the articles are coated with the varnish they are placed in a room in which wet cloths are hung about.

An interesting feature of Japanese lac is a peculiar kind of poisoning which attacks persons new to working with it. The backs of the hands, the eyelids, the ears, the navel and the lower part of the body become mildly red and swollen and feel hot and itching, especially at night. This lasts two or three days and disappears, but in some cases small boils develop. This poisoning is due to a volatile substance in the lac, although some doubt has been expressed as to this. The poison seems to be very active and cannot be removed by washing with soap and water. To remove it powdered soap, pumice stone and sodium carbonate are used, followed by soap and sand.

Queries and Answers

We shall be glad, in this department, to respond to calls for information on all pharmaceutic matters.

Spring Tonics and Alterative Mixtures.—F. K. S.—A great variety of formulas is extant for preparations variously labeled blood purifiers and alterative compounds, and the simpler these are made the better. It is now generally believed that the condition sometimes referred to as "spring fever" is caused by an acid condition of the blood, which is best remedied by the administration of alkalis in combination with a mild tonic of a vegetable nature, so a simple solution of potassium bicarbonate in compound infusion of gentian is found very efficacious in most cases where the symptoms are accompanied by a pimply skin. Most patrons of drug stores would, however, object to so simple a preparation as this and it appears to be necessary to mix a whole pharmacopœia of botanic drugs in order to produce an effect. As a result we have compounds like the following, which we name for the benefit of our correspondent:

Compound Syrup Sarsaparilla and Stillingia.

Red clover .... ℥vi.
Stillingia .... ℥viij.
Sarsaparilla .... ℥viij.
Prickly ash bark .... ℥ij.
Licorice .... ℥iij.
Coriander .... ℥i.
Anise .... ℥i.
Wintergreen .... ℥i.
Senna .... ℥iv.
Potassium iodide .... ℥iij.
Alcohol (33 1-3 per cent.) .... q. s.

Percolate the coarsely powdered drugs, after maceration for 12 hours, with 33 1-3 per cent. alcohol until 6 pints are obtained; then dissolve 4 pounds sugar in this by agitation; lastly add the potassium iodide and dissolve.

Syrup Red Clover Compound.

Red Clover .... ℥viij.
Stillingia .... ℥iv.
Berberis aquifolia .... ℥ij.
Prickly ash berries .... ℥i.
Burdock root .... ℥iv.
Poke root .... ℥i.
Sarsaparilla .... ℥iv.
Iodide potass .... ℥ij.
Oil wintergreen .... gtt. xxx.
Alcohol (33 1-13 per cent) .... q. s.

After 1 hour's maceration, percolate the powdered drugs to 5 pints; to 6 pounds sugar add the oil of wintergreen, add the iodide of potassium to the percolate, dissolve sugar by percolation and make up to 1 gallon with simple syrup.

But if a really meritorious article is desired a combination of alkalis with a cholagogue must be prepared. This is effected in the following formula:

Potass. bitartratis .... ℥ss.
Potass. bicarb .... ʒiiss.
Ext. podophyll fld .... ʒi.
Ext. sarsaparillæ comp. fld .... ℥iss.
Tinct. card. comp .... ʒij.
Glycerini .... ℥ij.
Aquæ .... q. s. ad Oi.

Dissolve the potassium salts in 8 fluid ounces of water with the aid of a gentle heat, add the remaining ingredients and set aside over night and filter.

A variant of the above used in England contains the following ingredients:

Magnesium sulphate .... ℥ss.
Potassium bicarbonate .... ℥ss.
Potassium iodide .... ʒij.
Alcohol (90 per cent.) .... ʒiv.
Fluid extract of licorice .... ℥i.
Sassafras oil .... Mxx.
Spirit of chloroform .... ʒij.
Burnt sugar .... q. s.
Distilled water .... ℥xx.

M.

Russian Pharmaceutical Journal.—O. R.—The correct address of the drug journal published from St. Petersburg, Russia, is: *Farmazeftitscheski Journal*, No. 31, Wosnessenski Prospect, St. Petersburg, Russia. This journal is received regularly in exchange by the AMERICAN DRUGGIST and is a periodical of considerable interest and value to pharmacists. It has lately issued a comprehensive guide to the newer remedies which will be found very useful to pharmacists who are familiar with the Russian language.

Formulas for Proprietary Articles.—We do not know the composition of seguro, which is presumably a proprietary preparation of secret composition. Any formula for this or a similar preparation which others would give would amount to little more than a guess at the nature of the compound. While we are ready and willing to supply information on any subject of a business, technical or scientific character that pertains to pharmacy, we must ask correspondents not to request the formulas of secret compounds.

The Sale of Alcoholic Proprietary Medicines.—J. W.—The Commissioner of Internal Revenue has ruled that certain proprietary medicines, composed wholly or in part of alcohol, will be subject to tax when sold by druggists and other dealers after April 1, 1906. A number of so-called stomach bitters and tonics have been specifically named by the Commissioner, and in New York the State Commissioner of Excise has brought suit against a firm of druggists on the charge that the firm sold liquor under the name of Pe-ru-na. Testimony in this suit is now being taken in the State of Ohio. This suit is understood to be a test case and the beginning of a stern crusade against so-called patent medicines in which alcohol predominates. Pharmacists will require to exercise care in the sale of proprietary medicines which have been listed by the Internal Revenue Department, at Washington, as liquors subject to the Federal liquor tax. In some Prohibition States the possession of a Federal liquor license is deemed a *prima facie* case of traffic in liquors contrary to the State law.

Indian Soy.—W. B. B. asks us to state the composition of Indian Soy and where it can be obtained.

This sauce may be purchased at any large grocery store. It is prepared by subjecting a mixture of cooked and pulverized soy beans, roasted and pulverized wheat, wheat flour, salt, and water, to fermentation, with rice wine ferment, in casks, for from one and a half to five years. The resulting product is a moderately thick brown liquid, and has an odor and taste not unlike a good quality of wheat extract, though perhaps a trifle more pungent.

The following particulars regarding soy and its manufacture are found in *Pharmaceutical Formulas*: Soy is generally imported from the East. It is made from the seeds of *Glycine soja* (*soya hispida*), which is largely cultivated in China, India and Japan. The seeds or beans are first roasted like coffee, and to this a certain quantity of malted barley (also partially torrified) is added, with a liberal dose of salt and cold water to make the whole into a gruel. This is set aside for some time, then a special ferment is added and the mixture kept for a long time—frequently for three years, if the quality of the product is to be the best. The method of manufacture, so far as the details are concerned, is practically a secret, and as the product cannot be accurately imitated, it is recommended that only the imported soy be used in making sauces. According to *Cooley's Cyclopædia of Practical Receipts*, the soy of the shops is, in nine cases out of ten, a spurious article, made by simply saturating molasses with common salt. A better and a really wholesome imitation is made as follows: Malt syrup, 1 gallon (or 13½ pounds); molasses, 5 pounds; salt, 4¼ pounds; mushroom juice, 40 ounces. Mix with a gentle heat and stir until the union is complete. In a fortnight decant the clear portion.

Correspondence.

Concerning Ready Made Cuts.

To the Editor:

Sir,—The remarks on ready-made cuts, published in a recent issue, awaken a responsive echo in my heart. I know all about it. I have been stuck myself. The ads. didn't fit. They would apply as well to stoves as to drugs. Druggists are the "worst ever" on advertising. You must shock them into a realization that they must advertise, and then as like as not they will do some fool thing, such as was described in the article on "Ready Made Cuts." I know, because I'm one of the fools. I've wasted more good, hard thinking over efforts to make an ad. fit a cut than Rockefeller would in making a million dollars. EBIN R. SMITH.

IPSWICH, MASS., February 15.

The Hospital Stewards and the Proposed Pharmaceutical Corps.

To the Editor:

Sir,—In a recent issue of the AMERICAN DRUGGIST AND PHARMACEUTICAL RECORD, that valuable organ of the profession of pharmacy, there appears some correspondence relative to proposed legislation to organize a corps of pharmacists in the army, navy and marine hospital service, with commissions ranging from lieutenant up; and as a member of a body of men who for 50 years have satisfactorily performed the pharmaceutical duties for the army I wish to raise my feeble voice in protest against the proposed measure.

The views of the office of the Surgeon-General have already been set forth in no uncertain terms in a letter from Major Kean published in your journal. In this letter, if Major Kean does not plainly say as much, he at least leaves a strong impression that the office of the Surgeon-General is satisfied with the manner in which prescriptions have been compounded and supplies cared for in the past and that that official is well content to leave that part of the work in the hands that have for so long and, with modesty we say it, so faithfully performed it.

It is not presumed; it is an assured fact that the Surgeon-General and the entire corps of medical officers under him have the welfare of the service and the best interests of the hospital corps at heart. Times without number our officers have proven their devotion to duty and great solicitude for the welfare of the army by voluntarily relinquishing all that life holds dear, severing tender ties, giving up all that would seem to make life acceptable, cheerfully risking all, even life itself, in efforts to promote the welfare of the army.

The Surgeon-General of the army holds his office not so much by virtue of seniority as by demonstrated fitness for the position, executive ability and desire for the good of the service. He, having as he has before him all available data, must better than any one else know what our army most needs from a medical department point of view, and we feel assured that whenever the needs of the service demand the organization of a corps of pharmacists he (be it the present or some future incumbent) will be the first to recognize such need and will strenuously advocate such legislation as may be required to supply the want.

At present the Surgeon-General is putting forth every effort to secure Congressional action providing for additional medical officers, shortage of which has long been one of the most vexatious problems with which the medical authorities have had to deal, and just at this time, when he is so fully occupied with such weighty matters, it seems to us that the A. Ph. A. should appreciate the fact and at least defer until some more opportune time efforts to have introduced a medical department bill carrying as does this one so large an increase in appropriations.

Nor do we see the need of the commissioned pharmacist; at any rate of any such number as is proposed. As Major Kean has so plainly stated, a very limited number could be utilized, but 148 would be more than enough to allow one to each important post in the army, both at home and in our insular possessions, at which posts it is difficult to determine to just what duties they could be assigned.

DUTIES OF THE HOSPITAL STEWARD.

I for one believe that we, who have for so long compounded the prescriptions of our surgeons, have cared for medical supplies, have worked day and night preparing apparently endless reports and returns, have superintended messes, have preserved discipline in hospitals, have assisted in the instruction of the hospital corps, have administered anæsthetics, assisted in operations, extracted teeth, analyzed urine, assisted in bacteriological and chemical work, have satisfactorily acted in emergencies in the absence of those more competent, and who have, in fact, been assistants to the surgeons, executive officers, first sergeants and jacks of all trades, almost invariably giving full satisfaction, are fully competent to perform the pharmaceutical work required in the army at the present time; and it is doubtful if the proposed officers could for some years to come, if, indeed (not having, as we have, attended for years the school of experience), ever perform the other duties that are ours and uphold as we have done the high standard of excellence that has been attained in that branch of the medical department work.

To consider for a moment the cost of the proposed bill. Even at the lowest rate of pay (second lieutenant, mounted). $1,500 per annum, the expense for pay alone of the 148 men would reach the sum of $220,000 per year, and this in addition to the numerous allowances—quarters, fuel, forage, mileage, etc. Of course if it is intended that these officers replace the present sergeants (first class) of the hospital corps there would be to deduct from the above amount the sum of $162,000, which is the annual pay of the 300 sergeants (first class) in the service. This leaves a total of $58,000 per year which it would cost our Government to effect the change. But to imagine that the 148 new men proposed can do the work now done by 300 trained, experienced sergeants (first class) is folly. If man for man they should prove as efficient it is as much as could be expected.

Therefore they could only replace 148 of us at $79,920 per year, which would under the most favorable circumstances make the additional cost to the Government $140,080, and even then we much doubt if the affairs of the medical department would run as smoothly or the work be done as satisfactorily as under the present arrangement.

One of the to us most striking points in the legislation advocated by the A. Ph. A. is what appears to be rank injustice to the sergeants (first class) now in the army. To quote from Dr. Paynes' letter: "I have come to the conclusion that the surest way to get pharmacy properly recognized in the army is to have a separate corps of pharmacists, independent of the present hospital stewards, as you suggest." From Mr. Seabury's "letter to a Senator" we recall: "The committee will also suggest to the Government that it owes to the nation and to our soldiers and sailors that they appoint as hospital stewards, naval apothecaries or hospital pharmacists only those having a college education or certificates from a State Board of Pharmacy. Our soldiers and sailors are worthy of the best service at the command of the profession to compound and dispense their medicines and deadly drugs."

INJUSTICE TO THE HOSPITAL STEWARD.

Of the about 300 so-called hospital stewards in the army at this time probably 50 per cent. possess the qualifications recommended by Mr. Seabury. Not having the necessary data at hand it is impossible to give the exact percentage, but I believe it to be as stated. A large percentage have reached an age at which they would probably be barred from appointment to a commission if the proposed bill should become a law. Of those not graduates of colleges or holding State board certificates many are married or have reached an age after which men are loath to commence a special course of study of several years' duration. Among this latter class are some of the most efficient sergeants, many of whom with no preliminary training, some with the most rudimentary education, entered the army hospital corps, and by stern devotion to duty, by hard work, by burning the midnight oil as they pored over musty text books, by faithfully discharging the duties that were theirs, have finally raised themselves to their present responsible position.

And since their appointments have they failed in the performance of their duties? Have they been found less proficient because of their lack of preliminary training? Has their conduct been such as to warrant their being replaced by or having commissioned over them men whose only claim to superiority is that they have graduated from some college or have been issued a certificate from some State Board of Pharmacy? I say No! As a body we have a record of which I believe each sergeant (first class) is proud. A glance at court martial records will show how few of us have been guilty of military offenses. A careful perusal of the annual reports of the Surgeon-General will show that where mention has been made of our work the verdict has been flattering. As early as 1886 Lieut.-Col. J. R. Smith, medical department, in writing of the hospital steward, said: "He is a sort of majordomo. He superintends the hospital, administers treatment and dispenses medicines and is of so much value and of so high qualifications that he deserves a better pay and position than he enjoys in the army." (See "Reference Handbook of Medical Sciences," Buck, vol. III, page 107.)

IN PRAISE OF THE HOSPITAL STEWARD.

In "Reference Handbook of Medical Sciences," revised edition, vol. I, pages 483 and 484, we find the following from the pen of Maj. G. E. Bushnell: "No other non-commissioned officer requires so much special knowledge for the proper discharge of his duties or has such a variety of duties to perform as the hospital steward." Further on in the same paragraph we find: "He must be unwearying in his care for the multiplicity of articles embraced under the name of hospital property. He must be an expert pharmacist and have sufficient knowledge of medicine and surgery to be able to act intelligently in emergencies in the absence of the surgeon."

With a record such as ours behind us, with a standard of excellence as high as is ours, we can but feel that the enaction of a law like that proposed would be an unjust discrimination.

Many of us are now old and if, as is feared should the proposed measure become a law, our grade should be abolished or our number decreased many of us would eventually be forced from the service, and that, too, at a time in life which is beyond the age at which men readily find new careers open to them. And even should our corps not be decreased, it would seem unjust to commission over old and tried sergeants men who are ignorant of every detail of the work save pharmacy, who in that branch will probably not be superior in a working knowledge to the sergeants over whom they are placed.

So without underestimating the value of a thorough training in pharmacy, for we would have found such a training of great help to many of us in our preparation for the position we fill, we still believe that men who have satisfied the surgeon-general as to their proficiency in a working knowledge of this important branch of our work and have proven themselves efficient in all other respects should be upheld and not discriminated against as in the proposed legislation.

About a year ago a petition was circulated requesting the surgeon-general to ask for us advanced grade and pay similar to that then enjoyed by our brothers of the navy. I personally signed this petition, but did not anticipate nor do we believe that any sergeant who signed it wished for anything more than was there asked for, and we believe that those in authority fully appreciate the work that has been done by us and will at the proper time give to us such recognition and advancement as they believe we may merit.

We also hope and believe that when the surgeon-general finds that the army is in need of a corps of pharmacists he will at once take steps to have such a corps organized, with whatever rank he thinks proper, which rank we know will be a just one, and that in his recommendation preference will be given to those who have for so long satisfactorily performed the duties of army pharmacists, even though they may not be registered or graduate pharmacists, rather than to those who come with no other qualifications.

J. F. HAMNER,
Sergeant First Class, Hospital Corps, United States Army.
BOISE BARRACKS, IDAHO, February 3, 1906.

Business Building.

A Novel Advertising Idea.

E. B. Heimstreet, who in point of experience is, we believe, the oldest druggist in Janesville, Wis., and whose name is widely known in pharmacy through his services as secretary of the Wisconsin Board of Pharmacy, has recently moved his store to more commodious quarters. He utilized the opportunity by inserting the following advertisement in the local papers on February 12:

> The store now known as Grubb's Grocery Store will be refitted and opened soon. The following will be given for the first correct replies to questions:
> 1. What will the store be? Wins $1.00.
> 2. Who is the proprietor? Wins $1.00.
> 3. What will be the name of the store? Wins $1.00.
> 4. When will it open? Give day, hour and minute. Wins $1.00.
>
> Address replies by postal card to "Guess," care *Gazette*.

He took good care, of course, to prevent the answer to the puzzle becoming known until he was ready to make a formal announcement, which he did through the following advertisement, set in reading notice style, in the newspapers dated February 22:

E. B. Heimstreet to Remove His Store.

Will Occupy the Present Location of the Grubb Produce Company March 1.

A change in business location is to be made March 1 by which E. B. Heimstreet takes possession of the three stores now occupied by the Grubb Produce Company, corner of South Main and Court streets. The room will be refitted into a fine pharmacy and Mr. Heimstreet will make out of it an elegant business place. In order to conduce friendly speculation on several points a list of prizes is to be given for correct replies to questions listed on page four. Mr. Heimstreet leaves the location at 9 North Main street, in which a drug store has been conducted continuously since 1865. Business was first inaugurated by Chas. Colwell and shortly after was taken over by Mr. Heimstreet, who has carried it on since. He is the oldest druggist, in point of business years, in the city, and has had opportunity of watching the city development and many changes as have but few others. Mr. and Mrs. Heimstreet have rented the lower south flat in the La Vista block and will occupy it.

Opportunities Missed by Retailers.

There is something radically wrong with the man who does not advertise nowadays—something wrong with the man and something wrong with his business. He may not realize either, but the fact still remains. The trader who buys and sells in a small town looks upon his situation as a limited field, divided among himself and his competitors. He is wont to say: "Well, I have my share of the trade and I cannot expect more—it is useless for me to advertise." Aside from the fact that this theory is wrong, he forgets, or is ignorant of, one of the great cardinal truths of advertising—namely, that of stimulating trade, of creating new customers.

Let us begin with the druggist. This gentleman has an establishment of more or less magnitude, situated in the central part of the town. On the other side of the street is a rival; up on the next corner is another, while two blocks further south still another active competitor, who bids for trade, but—they all do it the same way. They sit back of their counters and wait for trade to turn up.

In these days of competition the druggist's opportunities are almost limitless. He can no longer confine himself to his originally legitimate business of dispensing of drugs. Physicians have taken the greater bulk of his prescription trade away, and the general public, educated along modern lines, do not rely so much upon the old-time methods of filling the system with drugs. Comparatively speaking, the druggist of 1906 is so in name only. It behooves him then to stir up side lines allied more or less with his profession. Grant that he carries these lines, what then? The small department store and the dry goods store have simply duplicated his stock of goods in the way of toilet accessories, etc., and because of the greater number of customers these latter establishments have they are able to pretty effectually cut off this source of his income.

If the druggist would live he must advertise. He must do it intelligently and copiously. He must use display space in his country papers, not for a standing advertisement, but for special announcements from day to day. Featuring "trade getters," advertising special lines, in brief, taking away from the department store and the dry goods establishment that which is rightfully his—*Ad. Sense.*

UNITED DRUG COMPANY ENTERTAINS OVER TWO HUNDRED DRUGGISTS.

An Enthusiastic Meeting in Chicago—Wise Men from the East via the Twentieth Century Limited—All Is Harmony at the Banquet—Many Leading Druggists Present.

(*From our Regular Correspondent.*)

Chicago, March 1.—For the purpose of demonstrating to the retail druggists of the Central West the advantages to be gained by becoming interested in the marketing of the products of the United Drug Company and the selling agency scheme of the National Cigar Stands Company twelve representatives and associates in these two corporations tendered a luncheon and banquet to more than 200 druggists from Illinois, Indiana, Michigan and Wisconsin in this city on Wednesday afternoon and evening, February 28. The guests of the United Drug Company and National Cigar Stands Company were also invited to witness the opening of the new depot and distributing point for the two concerns, and every effort was made by the representatives of the companies to familiarize the druggists with the objects of the corporations and to correct the mistaken impressions which may have existed among them as a result of the campaign of wholly unjustified abuse which has been conducted by interests inimical to the success of the retail druggist.

From the expressions of most of the guests at the luncheon and banquet it was evident that they all realized the injustice which had been done to both companies, and after the visit to the National Cigar Stands Company's humidors and general offices in this city many of those who had not already accepted an agency indicated their confidence by promptly doing so.

REPRESENTATIVES FROM THE EAST.

The trip of the Eastern representatives to this city, which was conducted by Louis K. Liggett, president of the United Drug Company and National Cigar Stands Company, was made in a special car attached to the Twentieth Century Limited, which left New York City at 3.30 o'clock on Tuesday afternoon, February 27, and arrived in the Windy City at 9.30 A.M. on Wednesday, February 28. Besides Mr. Liggett, who led the hosts of the occasion, the Eastern party included: George M. Gales, vice-president of the National Cigar Stands Company; W. C. Bolton, president of the Riker Drug Stores; Albert E. Siebert, of 49 Wall street, attorney for the U. D. C. and the N. C. S. C.; E. D. Cahoon, treasurer of the William B. Riker Company of New York; John Haigney, of the same company; Edward Dodge, of Buffalo, N. Y.; James Brady, of Fall River, Mass.; Major Hall, of the firm of Hall & Lyons, of Providence, R. I.; Charles E. Ball, of Holyoke, Mass.; Harry Wilson, of the N. C. S. C., and Benjamin B. Hampton, advertising agent, of 7 West Twenty-second street.

LUNCHEON AT THE AUDITORIUM.

A few hours after the arrival of the Eastern contingent the guests of the two companies were invited to luncheon at the Auditorium Annex in this city. The guests sat down to the luncheon at 1 P.M., and left about 3 P.M. to make a tour of inspection at the National Cigar Stands Company's general offices and humidors, at 45 and 47 East Randolph street. The druggists expressed themselves as delighted to note the magnitude of the distributing facilities and the general conduct of the business of the company.

THE BANQUET AT RECTOR'S.

At 6.30 P.M. the guests were invited to the banquet, which was held in Rector's, at which President Liggett and several other representatives of the U. D. C. and N. C. S. C. as well as the retail druggists themselves spoke in most favorable terms of the work of both concerns and the benefits accruing to all who participated in the advantages offered. Mr. Liggett, who was the first after-dinner speaker of the occasion, reiterated the reply to those critics who have asserted that the National Cigar Stands Company was controlled and managed by the American Tobacco Company and the United Cigar Stores Company. He denied in unmeasured terms the statement that the N. C. S. C. had any connection or association whatsoever with the Tobacco Trust, and asserted that the products of the firms composing the trust were by no means handled exclusively by the Cigar Stands Company, which, as a matter of fact, handles just as many independent brands as those turned out or controlled by the Tobacco Trust.

Mr. Liggett also explained that a retail druggist can buy from the N. C. S. C. one single box of cigars at a lower figure than a jobber can buy 1,000 boxes of cigars of corresponding quality.

"There are now almost 1,500 stockholders in the United Drug Company," said Mr. Liggett, "and to all stockholders in the U. D. C. was extended the opportunity of buying as many shares in the N. C. S. C. as they held in the parent company."

Mr. Liggett then denounced the attempts of a certain pharmaceutical periodical to unjustly work an injury to the U. D. C. and N. C. S. C., and, without any justification, persuade all retail druggists to blacklist the enterprises, which actually have been proved of inestimable value to many druggists now interested in the companies.

VIEWS OF A SUBSCRIBER.

Mr. Valentine, a Chicago retail druggist, interrupted the speaker long enough to remark that the person issuing such

LOUIS K. LIGGETT,
President of the United Drug Company.

false statements about the companies needed only enough rope to hang himself and would soon accomplish this end if left alone. He advised that no reply be made to such attacks, as none was necessary.

MANY RETAILERS SPEAK.

Edwin Scholtz, a retail druggist of Denver, Col., then addressed the guests on his favorable experience with the two companies. His remarks were followed by a short address by Thomas Voegeli, of Minneapolis. Louis Ecstein, of Chicago, who is interested in the Public Drug Company of this city, then spoke at length on the merits of the U. D. C. and N. C. S. C. He was followed by Edward Dodge, of the Cahoon-Lyon Drug Company of Buffalo, who also talked about the success of the U. D. C. and N. C. S. C. He reported, and his assertions were subsequently confirmed by other speakers who had the stands of the N. C. S. C. in their stores, that their cigar business had already increased 33 to 75 per cent. President Antram, of the Randolph Paper Box Company, also made a short speech.

Romaine Pierson, Chicago representative of the AMERICAN

DRUGGIST, delivered a felicitous address upon the success of the U. D. C. and N. C. S. C. E. D. Cahoon, treasurer of the Wm. B. Riker & Sons Company; Albert E. Seiber, counsel for the U. D. C.; Ben B. Hampton, the advertising expert of the firm, and William C Batton, secretary of the National Cigar Stands Company, also made addresses.

Among other guests at the banquet were: Charles D. Prutzman, of Muncie, Ind.; W. S. Milliner, of Williamsport, Pa.; P. A. Lignell, of Superior, Wis., and Mayor Van Wart, of Beloit, Wis.

Parke, Davis & Co. Appoint Oscar W. Smith as New York Manager.

The officers of Parke, Davis & Co. have just appointed Oscar W. Smith, until recently manager of the Baltimore branch of the company, to succeed Col. E. W. Fitch as manager of the New York offices at 90 Maiden lane. Mr. Smith has been connected with Parke, Davis & Co. for more than 20 years and has been advanced steadily since he was a youngster of 17 years. Born in Detroit in 1869, he received his early education in the public schools of that city, and in 1886 entered the employ of Parke, Davis & Co. He remained in the Detroit house for ten years and during the last ten years has been manager of the Baltimore branch of that corporation. After being trained in the office work of the Detroit house he was sent on the road as a traveling salesman and was later appointed manager of the travelers by the late William M. Warren, then prominent in the affairs of the company.

Mr. Smith has been very popular in the drug trade of Baltimore and is recognized by all wholesale and retail drug men in this city as a splendid executive for the New York offices. He is a member of the Maryland Club, the Baltimore Yacht Club and several other business and social organizations. He will continue to supervise the affairs of the Baltimore house, although he will naturally make his headquarters in the New York offices.

REGRET AT COLONEL FITCH'S WITHDRAWAL.

Expressions of deep regret are heard on all sides in the wholesale and retail drug trade throughout the country whenever the resignation of Colonel Edward Wright Fitch, head of the New York department of Parke, Davis & Co., is mentioned. The genial and lovable Colonel himself explains his determination to abandon his active and remarkably successful administration of affairs for the purpose of retiring permanently from business and taking a much needed rest by asserting that a stitch in time frequently saves nine. He believes that he needs a long respite from business cares and worries, and his army of friends and admirers realize that he deserves to gratify his wish.

Colonel Fitch has not enjoyed the best of health for some time and upon the advice of his physicians will leave his mantle to the younger shoulders of his newly appointed successor, Oscar W. Smith, formerly manager of the Baltimore house, who will take up the work where the Colonel left off within the ensuing fortnight. Colonel Fitch says he will then leave this city with his wife, his son and two grandchildren and return to his home in Louisville, Ky., where he will remain for several weeks before taking a trip to Pasadena, Cal., in which restful spot he purposes to stay for a long time. It is also the Colonel's intention to travel through England and the Continent of Europe after he feels thoroughly rested from the strain of 38 years in the retail, jobbing and manufacturing drug business.

Born in Indiana, Colonel Fitch was apprenticed early in life in the retail drug store of George Patrick & Co., in Terre Haute, where he learned pharmacy and acquired a love of literature and research, as well as of his chosen profession. At the beginning of the Civil War he enlisted in the Ninety-seventh Indiana Volunteers and later was appointed commissary sergeant. He served in several fierce engagements around Vicksburg and retired from the army as a colonel only when a severe attack of typhoid fever made it impossible for him to continue in military service.

Returning to Patrick & Co., in Terre Haute, he was later associated with the jobbing house of Arthur Peter & Co., of Louisville, Ky., and was a partner in the business until the concern was reorganized. In 1894 he was appointed a special traveling representative of Parke, Davis & Co. and three years later was made manager of the New York branch, with which he has been associated for nine years, during which time the business of the company has more than doubled, involving at the present time many millions of dollars yearly.

Colonel Fitch is a vestryman of All Angels' Church. He is also a member of the New York Yacht Club, the Metropolitan Museum of Art, the American Museum of Natural History, the Torrey Botanical Club and the New York College of Pharmacy. He is likewise a member of the Drug and Chemical Club and was appointed a few years ago chairman of the Drug Trade Section of the New York Board of Trade and Transportation.

MR. SMITH AND COLONEL FITCH.

In addition to his duties as manager of the New York department of Parke, Davis & Co. Colonel Fitch has also had entire charge of the territory embracing Mexico, Cuba, Porto Rico, Central America, South America and the Philippines. It is not a matter of great surprise therefore that he is now desirous of seeking a much-merited rest.

Mr. Swift Gives Banquet to Parke, Davis & Co.'s Men.

Ernest G. Swift, of Detroit, general manager of Parke, Davis & Co., who is now in this city for the purpose of introducing Oscar W. Smith, the new manager of the local offices, to those who will be his associates in 90 Maiden lane, tendered a private banquet on Wednesday evening in the Hotel Astor to several of the company's most popular men. As Col. Edward W. Fitch and Mr. Smith were the guests of honor, the after dinner orations naturally took the form of a farewell to the former manager of the local offices, who has decided to retire from business permanently because of ill health, and a welcome to the newly appointed administrator. Expressions of profound regret were voiced when mention was again made of the colonel's resignation, while best wishes for a pleasant trip to California and a speedy recovery of his former good health were also indorsed by all present at the banquet. Among others who attended the dinner were: W. J. Carr, superintendent of the local offices; Syd. H. Carragan, assistant manager; W. D. Kaufman, Mr. Burnside and Herbert Turrell, head of the special preparation department.

AIN'T DRUGGISTS THE BRUTES?

"Sell Death-Dealing Drugs"—A "Terrible Menace to the Race"—"Frauds" and All that Is Wicked—Yellow Journalism Run Mad.

(From our Regular Correspondent.)

Boston, March 9.—February 27 was sensational day at the State House, with druggists and nostrums for targets. The dictionary was heavily drawn upon for sensational phrasing, in which "death-dealing drugs," "terrible menace" and "frauds" were examples of some of the wild characterizations. It was a money campaign in which these pleaders for legislation were engaged, for one of the daily papers which gave a full account of the hearing was extensively mailed on the evening of its appearance in large numbers to those thought to be in sympathy with these advocates. The wrappers upon these "marked copy" papers bore typewritten addresses, which points strongly to long prior arrangement both as to mailing and printing of this article in the newspaper in question. The attendance was large.

ALCOHOL AND NARCOTICS AIMED AT.

Most of the bills before the committee were of the same general tenor, providing in the main that all proprietary medicines or foods shall have inscribed upon the bottle, package or other receptacle the amount of alcohol, cocaine or other poisonous drugs which they contain; that this label shall be conspicuous, and that for failure to comply with the law in this respect penalties be imposed varying in the different bills from $5 to $1000. The alcohol limit in one of the bills was 3 per cent. Any amount above that was to be stated upon the label.

There was little opposition to placing on the label the percentage of poisonous drugs, exclusive of alcohol, contained in proprietary medicines, although one druggist said that this would increase their sale among "dope fiends," who will stoop to anything to get what they want. The Retail Druggists' Association opposed the bill designed to make known the percentage of alcohol in patent medicines on the ground that many legitimate medicines which require a large percentage of alcohol to make active the drug strength of the medicine would be greatly injured.

C. I. Hood & Co., of Lowell, through their representative, Mr. Taylor, said they had no objection to the passage of the bill and would conform to its provisions if it were adopted. Mr. Taylor said:

C. I. Hood Company will welcome any and all legislation in the interests of pure foods and pure drugs. We certainly will not oppose the passage of any law that will stop or restrict the sale of secret nostrums that contain poisons or other ingredients so compounded as to be injurious to health. We do not wish to be even suspected of believing that the Commonwealth of Massachusetts is to adopt any legislation that can do any harm to our business, and any legislation for the public good most surely has our unqualified support.

If the State deems it wise to require publication of the percentage of alcohol or names of ingredients entering into medicines we will at once cheerfully comply. The amount of alcohol we use is the smallest quantity possible to extract and preserve in liquid form and to convey to the patient the remedial values of the ingredients we use. Hood's Sarsaparilla is so strongly medicinal that no person could possibly obtain anything like the effect of intoxication from it, for the reason that no stomach could retain a quantity large enough.

As to the ingredients, we have no objection to a law compelling the manufacturers of proprietary articles to publish upon their packages the names of the ingredients contained therein. Such legislation will be harmful to fraudulent concerns. When such legislation is passed it should be impossible for dishonest men to successfully sell any inefficacious or possibly health destroying drugs under the name of medicines, and reputable manufacturers of proprietary remedies of true medicinal value will be the gainers.

We have never hesitated to tell any person who asked what the ingredients of Hood's Sarsaparilla are. In fact, we publish the names of the ingredients used. For obvious reasons we have not considered it advisable to publish our working formula. One of these reasons as stated briefly is that our experience and our facilities and the care we exercise enable us to compound and put up our remedy perfectly; and only the man who wishes to imitate or substitute would have any real use for it. Imitations which might be made would be of inferior quality. No imitator wishes to produce the best; his only object being to get money, he would make the cheapest possible mixture. We are willing to submit our working formula if desired to any competent board of experts and we regard the Massachusetts State Board of Pharmacy as being such a board, and we wish to say here that our formulas are just as they have been for many years, not changed nor adapted to meet the exigencies of the present situation.

Our business was started with one preparation, Hood's Sarsaparilla, which had its origin in a physician's prescription about 1873, and it was prescribed for years by the best physicians in Lowell under the name of "Mist. Alter. Comp.," meaning compound alterative mixture. It continues to be prescribed by physicians all over the country. As Hood's Sarsaparilla gained the public confidence and as new avenues were opened we have introduced several other preparations, all of which represent a vast amount of research and experiment. Our laboratory is under the personal supervision of C. I. Hood, whom you probably all know as a thoroughly educated pharmacist, and he is assisted by a regular graduate of the Massachusetts College of Pharmacy.

Our interests in the matter of legislation for the benefit of pure drugs and honest medicines are identical with the interests of the Commonwealth. Thirty years of constant effort to produce the best medicines naturally commits us to this position.

Several doctors favored the proposed legislation, and it was also favored by a large representation of temperance workers representing temperance organizations, although not on temperance grounds. Representative Leonard, of Springfield, spoke for the drug trade and presented a bill in behalf of the Retail Druggists' Association of that city. This dealt with the labeling of powerful drugs in amounts in excess of stated percentages in connection with the word poison.

IT RESEMBLES THE BEAL BILL.

Henry Canning declared that the advertisement of the percentage of cocaine and other drugs in certain remedies would increase their sale largely, because "dope fiends" would buy them simply because of that fact. "We think it is inexpedient to legislate on the alcohol part of this question, because it is being taken care of at Washington in good shape at the present time."

J. F. Finneran said the passage of the alcohol bill would hurt his business, for while it would increase the sale of certain remedies, it would tend to drive away the best class of customers.

Henry D. Smith, of Middleboro, wanted to know the meaning of "patent or proprietary medicines" and was informed that there were no court decisions defining exactly what those terms meant.

W. W. Bartlet, Ph.G., made the closing argument for the druggists, and before doing so created an amusing diversion by swallowing five grains of acetanilid, to prove that the petitioners were exaggerating when they stated that dose was known to prove fatal.

Victor Klotz, of Ed. Pinaud Fame, Dead.

Friends and business associates of Victor Klotz, senior member of the French firm of Victor Klotz & Co., familiarly known as the house of Ed. Pinaud, manufacturing perfumers, with New York offices at 84 Fifth avenue, are grieved to learn of his death, which occurred at his home in Paris. Mr. Klotz was one of the leading perfume manufacturers in France and among the first to introduce a pension system for old employees in his factories and take other steps to ameliorate the condition of all classes of workmen in his employ. He was also interested in many kinds of philanthropy and was an officer in the Legion of Honor. Mr. Klotz's business was founded by Ed. Pinaud, an expert perfumer, who earned a local reputation in the suburbs of Paris, but it was not until after Pinaud's death, when the business passed into Mr. Klotz's hands, that the Pinaud perfumery gained a world-wide reputation. In 1890 Emile Utard was appointed representative of the house for this country, and an office was then opened in Union Square, New York City. In 1903 the present Pinaud Building was erected at Fifth avenue and Fourteenth street. Two sons survive Mr. Klotz.

THE LEGISLATIVE SITUATION.

Review of Bills at Albany—Hearing on Lupton Measure—Santee Bill Reported Favorably—A Crime to Prescribe Proprietaries.

At a hearing before the Assembly committee in charge of the Lupton bill, which was held in Albany on Wednesday, March 7, a committee of three members, representing the New York State Pharmaceutical Association, Kings County Pharmaceutical Society and German Apothecaries' Society, opposed this measure on the ground that its passage would be detrimental to the public health by permitting unskilled merchants to handle drugs which should only be offered for sale by licensed pharmacists.

Dr. William Muir, a member of the Legislative Committee of the State Pharmaceutical Association and chairman of the Legislative Committee of the Kings County Pharmaceutical Society; Warren L. Bradt, secretary of the State Board of Pharmacy and a member of the Legislative Committee of the State Pharmaceutical Association, and George Kleinau, member of the Legislative Committee of the State Pharmaceutical Association and of the German Apothecaries' Society, were the only representatives of the drug interests present at the hearing. All three spoke in opposition of the measure and probably did more to kill the bill than any similar representation could have done owing to their long experience in matters of this kind.

Dr. Muir, who spoke first, urged that the bill be not passed because it would permit grocery, hardware and other general merchants to deal in medicines and drugs which require knowledge to sell. He also showed that the passage of this bill would nullify to a great extent the full power of the State pharmacy law, which prohibits the sale of the drugs specified in the bill by persons without a license.

The bill, as previously mentioned, provides for the granting of permits by the State Board of Pharmacy to all classes of retail merchants situated within a limit of two miles from a licensed pharmacy to deal in many drugs and medicines other than the ordinary household remedies, which they are already permitted to sell. The list of drugs and medicines which the bill proposes to permit unskilled merchants to sell includes ipecac, syrup of squills, syrup of rhubarb, hive syrup, paregoric, tincture of arnica, tincture of iodine, spirit of nitre, camphorated oil, tincture of rhubarb, citrate of magnesia, quinine and seidlitz powders.

The committee did not oppose strongly the provision of the bill that more than one resident of a section two miles from a licensed pharmacy be granted a permit to deal in the above mentioned drugs and medicines, as it believed that if the Board of Pharmacy had the matter under its control its regulation of the number of such permits would prevent a too liberal granting of such privileges.

Dr. Muir and Messrs. Bradt and Kleinau expressed great surprise to note the absence of many representatives of pharmaceutical associations which it was believed would be interested in opposing the passage of the measure.

THE SANTEE COCAINE BILL.

The Santee bill for the regulation of the sale of cocaine has been reported out of the Committee on Health, with the amendment, however, suggested by the Board of Pharmacy and the Drug Trade Section of the New York Board of Trade and Transportation which permits the free sale of such drug by wholesalers to physicians, manufacturers of pharmaceuticals, retail druggists, colleges, hospitals and all other public institutions.

It is reported from Albany that some opposition has developed in Buffalo against the Hill bill, which provides for several inconsequential amendments to the present Board of Pharmacy laws.

A MISDEMEANOR TO PRESCRIBE A PROPRIETARY REMEDY.

Three new bills have been presented to the State Legislature during the past fortnight, two of them by Assemblyman Thompson, of Kings County, and the third by Assemblyman Hartman, of New York. The first of the Thompson measures, known as Assembly Bill 1,006, seeks to make it a misdemeanor for any practicing physician to prescribe to any patient by Latin prescription or otherwise than by its true name any drug, medicine or mixture commonly known as a patent or proprietary medicine. The second Thompson bill, known as Assembly Bill 1,065, provides for an amendment of the public health laws so that manufacturers of a drug, medicine or mixture of drugs, herbs or medicines, commonly known as patent or proprietary medicine, shall be compelled to file in the office of the State Commissioner of Health a verified statement containing the name under which such medicine is to be sold, the place where it is manufactured and an analysis or formula specifying the ingredients thereof and the quantity. Such manufacturers shall also place, according to the provisions of this bill, a label on the bottle or package and on the outside wrapper, such label to contain a statement of the ingredients or formula of the medicine contained therein. In this latter respect it is somewhat like the Stevens and Wainwright bills.

GRADY'S PURE FOOD BILL REVIVED.

The third new measure now pending before the Assembly is known as the Hartman, or Assembly Bill 1,145, which is substantially the same pure food and drug bill promoted by Senator Grady and defeated by the efforts of the Legislative Committee of the State Pharmaceutical Association about a year ago. This measure makes it a misdemeanor to label or brand a drug or food preparation so as to deceive the purchaser or prepare its wrapping, labels and brands in such a way that they represent the drug or food to be a foreign product when it is not so. The bill also makes it a misdemeanor to prepare the package, bottle or wrapper so that it is in imitation either in package or label of another substance of a previously established name which has been trademarked or patented. If the package containing the drug or food or its label shall bear any statement, design or device regarding the ingredients or substances contained therein which shall prove to be false, the bill further provides that such labeling or preparation or the offering for sale by a dealer of such articles shall constitute a misdemeanor. The measure also provides that all food and drug preparations shall be labeled with the formula and percentage of the substances contained therein, and also provides that the person who shall make the complain against the dealer offering such prohibited articles shall be paid one-half of the fine imposed as a penalty upon the conviction of the offender.

The Drug and Chemical Club Prospers.

Jesse L. Hopkins, president of the Drug and Chemical Club of New York has issued an address to the members which shows that the affairs of the club are in a most prosperous condition. The membership on January 1, 1906, included 357 resident and 155 nonresident members, as against 316 resident and 147 nonresident members on the corresponding date of last year, while 42 applications are now awaiting action. The financial statement submitted shows that the receipts for 1905 amounted to $18,644.89 and the expenditures to $12,533.36. The credit balance of $6,111.53, added to the balance carried over from 1904—$5,318.25—gives, after deducting $429.78 for depreciation, a surplus fund of $11,000. It is estimated that $15,000 will be required to fit up the new rooms of the club in the fourteenth, fifteenth and sixteenth stories of the new annex to the Woodbridge Building, which will be ready for the occupancy of the club some time during the current year.

Mr. Hopkins says that "the new home of the Drug and Chemical Club will be superior, in location at least, to that of any downtown club at the present time. It will command a beautiful outlook over the North and East rivers, as well as over the city itself. There will be a lobby entrance, cloak room, toilet and bath rooms, large reception room, buffet, ladies' reception and dressing room, general club dining rooms, ladies' and nonsmoking dining room, with a number of private dining rooms, each accommodating a party of at least 15. There will also be lounging and smoking rooms. The sixteenth floor will be occupied for kitchen purposes, including dining rooms for employees, storerooms and lockers. The rental of the new rooms will be $15,000 per annum."

On April 1 the initiation fee will be increased from $25 to $50, and the members are invited to propose suitable nominees for membership in the club.

Changes in the Firm of Schieffelin & Co.

William Newton Clark, who retired from the directorate of Schieffelin & Co. on March 5, has long been a prominent figure in the wholesale drug field in this city. Mr. Clark is a great grandson of Jacob Schieffelin, the founder of the house, and was born in 1832. He entered the business when 17 years of age, and for 57 years has continued in active work with the concern. In 1865 he became a member of the firm of W. H. Schieffelin & Co., and in 1895, on the death of W. H. Schieffelin, Mr. Clark became the senior partner. In 1903, when the business was incorporated, he was chosen president.

The stockholders, at their annual meeting March 5, 1906, unanimously adopted the following preamble and resolutions:

Whereas, William N. Clark, Esq., president of Schieffelin & Co., this day completes his term as president and declines re-election; therefore be it

Resolved, That we, the stockholders of Schieffelin & Co., express to Mr. Clark our high appreciation of his worth and character and our sense of his great service to our corporation and to the house of Schieffelin & Co. for more than half a century; that we feel that the continued good reputation and high standing of this house are in a large measure due to his efforts and probity.

Resolved, That we regret his determination to retire, but recognise he richly deserves his rest, and we wish him long life and happiness.

Mr. Clark is an elder in the Union Reformed Church and a member of the Board of Foreign Missions, and is president of the Caughnawaugha Club, in the Adirondacks.

His son, Henry Schieffelin Clark, who entered the business in 1877, continues as treasurer of Schieffelin & Co.

William Jay Schieffelin, Ph. D., who was first vice-president of Schieffelin & Co., has been elected president, to succeed Mr. Clark.

Dr. Schieffelin was born in 1866 and, with Henry Schieffelin Clark, represents the fifth generation in the business. Dr. Schieffelin studied chemistry at the School of Mines of Columbia University and at the University of Munich, where his degree of Doctor of Philosophy was obtained. He has been actively associated with Schieffelin & Co. since 1889 and has been particularly active in developing their laboratory products. He is first vice-president of the National Association of Wholesale Druggists, president of the Chemists' Club and vice-president of the New York College of Pharmacy. Dr. Schieffelin is a director of the New York Eye and Ear Infirmary, a trustee of Hampton Institute, treasurer of the Manhattan Trade School and president of the American Church Missionary Society. He has been active in reform politics and served as Civil Service Commissioner in Mayor Strong's adminstration.

Dr. Schieffelin was vice-president of the Society of Chemical Industry and last year was chairman of the New York Section of the American Chemical Society, and has taken a very active part in the affairs of both societies.

Henry S. Livingston, who has been with Schieffelin & Co. since 1881, was elected director and appointed secretary of the company. Mr. Livingston has for many years had the supervision of the propaganda department and has had general charge of the introduction of the laboratory products of the firm. He is widely known in the wholesale drug trade and is personally very popular.

$500 for a Formula.

In the advertising columns of this issue will be found a unique offer, the character of which justifies us in calling attention to it editorially. A responsible business man, whose identity is well known to us, offers to pay the sum of $500 for an acceptable formula for any one of three preparations, and if more than one formula is taken an additional sum of $250 will be paid. There are doubtless a large number of both young and old men among our readers who could compete successfully for the $500 prize, and we can fancy the eagerness with which they will turn to their old books of formulas and debate with themselves as to which of their treasures should be offered. It may be that some skilled pharmacists will set a higher value on the treasures of their formulary books than the amount offered by our advertisers, but it must be conceded that the offer is a liberal one, and the advertiser's pledge to treat communicated formulas as absolutely confidential should be reassuring to any who might hesitate about divulging the secrets of the "back shop."

WHOLESALE DRUGGISTS OPPOSE STEVENS BILL.

Drug Section of Board of Trade Adopts a Resolution of Disapproval—Santee Anticocaine Bill Also Opposed.

Representatives of 82 of the leading manufacturing and wholesale druggists in New York City, who assembled at a special meeting of the Drug Trade Section of the Board of Trade and Transportation, held Thursday afternoon, March 8, in the rooms of that organization, decided at this gathering to oppose the bill now pending in the State Senate, known as the Stevens bill, as well as a similar measure now before the Assembly, known as the Wainwright bill. Both of these measures have been drafted to amend the public health laws by providing for the proper labeling of proprietary and other medicinal preparations containing alcohol, narcotic or other potent drugs with the exact percentage of such ingredients, and also for the inspection, analysis and regulation of the manufacture and sale of the same.

The Drug Trade Section formulated its obections to the bill in a resolution and agreed to send a delegation to the hearing on these measures, which will be held before the respective committees of the Senate and Assembly on March 14.

The resolution adopted by the section follows:

The Drug Trade Section of the New York Board of Trade and Transportation disapproves of Senate bill No. 239 and the like bill in the Assembly, for the reasons that the bill, if passed, will effect not over 50 per cent. of medicines sold; would not be likely to subserve the desired end; would compel the pharmacists to specially label medicines and preparations sold by them for family use, while expressly including the special labeling of medicines of the same character when prescribed by physicians, and would cause great and needless inconvenience to the drug trade.

Resolved, That if further legislation to regulate the sale of narcotics and medicines containing alcohol is deemed desirable or necessary, we strongly recommend and will support bills drawn upon the lines of the model bills prepared by the conference of all branches of the drug trade called by the Legislative Committee of the American Pharmaceutical Association and held in Chicago in December last, which was attended by representatives of the National Association of Retail Druggists and the Proprietary Association of America.

It was also expressly stipulated by the section that acetanilid should be named in the model bill.

At a previous meeting of the Drug Trade Section, held on Monday, February 26, for the purpose of discussing pending legislation, it was decided to accept in its present form Assembly bill No. 291, known as the Santee bill, which purposes to regulate the sale and handling of cocaine. While the section expressed itself as heartily in favor of restricting the sale of the drug to individuals, it believed that this measure, as a law, would hamper manufacturers and other drug interests. It was therefore decided at this meeting to urge the following amendment:

Nor shall this (provision regulating the sale and handling of cocaine) apply to sales to jobbers, retail druggists, hospitals, colleges or scientific or public institutions, manufacturers of proprietary medicines and pharmaceutical preparations, or for use in the manufacture of such preparations.

Though it was expected that the Drug Trade Section would also discuss the merits of the House of Representatives' Pure Food bill, drafted along the lines of the Heyburn bill, which has already been passed by the Senate, no action was taken on this measure at either of its most recent meetings.

Wooten-Lake.

The marriage is announced of Thomas V. Wooten and Mrs. Turner Lake, the ceremony taking place in Chicago on February 24. The bride and bridegroom are so widely known and held in such deserved esteem by a host of pharmacists throughout the country as to assure a flood of congratulations and good wishes from all quarters, in which the AMERICAN DRUGGIST would gladly join. Mrs. Wooten has attended nearly every meeting of the National Association of Retail Druggists since its organization in the capacity of assistant secretary.

Greater New York News.

Eugene Callahan, formerly clerk and salesman in the pharmacy of Starr Bros., of New London, Conn., has just purchased the retail drug business of C. M. Rogers, in that city.

The annual entertainment and ball of the New York Retail Druggists' Association will be held Friday evening, March 16, in Terrace Garden, 145 East Fifty-eighth street, near Third avenue.

L. B. Levey, manager of the San Francisco offices of Magnus & Lauer, Incorporated, visited the local offices of that company, at 257 Pearl street, the first week in March.

Edward Lowell, representing Magnus & Lauer in Mexico, Cuba and South America, has returned to his territory after a brief rest from his duties. He is now in Havana.

W. E. Floods, senior clerk in the Montgomery pharmacy, at Tenth avenue and Twenty-third street, will soon open a new drug store at 1013 Fox street, Borough of the Bronx.

Emil Wetschel, manager of the retail drug store of C. O Talcott, of Glastonbury, Conn., is spending a few days in this city on a business and pleasure trip.

A. and H. Goldwater have purchased the stock and fixtures of Halper's pharmacy, at Lenox avenue and 140th street. The store will hereafter be known as the Goldwater Pharmacy.

L. Frank, formerly a partner in the drug firm of Frank & Schnackenberg, of 426 Pearl street, has purchased the interest of Mr. Schnackenberg in the business and the store will hereafter bear the name of L. Frank. Mr. Schnackenberg has stores in other sections of this city.

The Phi Chi fraternity will hold their annual dinner at Reisenweber's on the evening of March 27. Graduate members who may desire to attend are requested to notify the chairman of the Dinner Committee, so that seats may be reserved. The chairman is Eugene Briscoll, 115 West Sixty-eighth street.

W. H. McCracken, Southern representative of Lehn & Fink, in charge of the marketing of that firm's products in the States of Maryland, North and South Carolina, Georgia and Alabama, has returned to his territory after a visit of a week to the home office. Mr. McCracken's residence is in Selma, Ala.

P. C. Magnus, of Magnus & Lauer, Incorporated, was agreeably surprised on the occasion of his last birthday, on March 1, by being presented with a handsome silver service, the gift of all of the employees, who adopted this method of showing their appreciation of his uniform kindness and consideration to them.

George J. Seabury, of Seabury & Johnson, is beaming with gratification at the knowledge that his pet hobby, the Ship Subsidy bill, has at length been passed by the United States Senate. He is greeting his friends nowadays with the salutation: "Well, I see the Senate has made a present to the country of a world-power merchant marine."

John W. Rossiter, Western representative of the Powers-Weightman-Rosengarten Company, has just returned to his territory after a visit of a few days at the local offices, at 145-147 Front street. Mr. Rossiter stopped at the Philadelphia house on his way back to Chicago, where he makes his headquarters.

Weinpohl, the crack bowler of the Parke, Davis & Co. team, who was recently transferred from the local to the Boston offices of that company, made a flying trip to this city Monday, March 5, in order to play in the latest tournament games with his friends. He returned to Boston late Monday night and was at his desk the following day.

S. V. B. Swann, secretary of the Manhattan Pharmaceutical Association and the Metropolitan Association of Retail Druggists, has sold at public auction the entire stock and fixtures of his retail pharmacy at 918 Sixth avenue and has returned to the wholesale drug business, in which he is now local and traveling salesman for Eli, Lilly & Co., manufacturers of pharmaceuticals, at 203 Fulton street. The property at 918 Sixth avenue in which Mr. Swann's store was located is owned by the Horton Ice Cream Company, of 115 Park row, which since Mr. Swann's retirement from the retail business has leased the premises to the Neergaard Pharmacy, of which Charles Wylie is proprietor.

The first annual ball of the Bronx Pharmaceutical Association was held Thursday evening, February 22, in Zeltner's Morrisania Hall, at Third avenue and 170th street. President A. H. Bischof made the formal address of welcome, and Jacob Diner, first vice-president of the M. A. R. D., spoke in lighter vein. Music for the dancing which followed was supplied by Prof. W. E. J. Keating's band. The Entertainment Committee included A. Allison, chairman; A. H. Bischof, and Louis I. Weiner.

The Brooklyn Pharmaceutical Society, formerly known as the Bushwick Pharmaceutical Society, the local organization of the N. A. R. D. in the northeastern section of the Borough of Brooklyn, held its regularly weekly meeting Monday evening, February 26. At this conference it was decided to make a painstaking investigation of the operation of the Direct Contract Serial Numbering Plan in the section which the society represents and report any discoveries of violation of the agreement at its next meeting.

Recent visitors to New York, most of whom have registered at the New York Drug and Chemical Club, include: William Menhemueller, Wheeling, W. Va.; F. Geiger, Philadelphia; M. Lenz, Garwood, N. J.; W. B. Marsh, Hartford, Conn.; A. C. Sunterant, jr., Boston, Mass.; Mr. Caithness, London, England; W. H. Dubold, Cleveland, Ohio; R. B. Barrison, Staten Island; Calvin Hotchkiss, Lyons, N. Y.; Norman Elliot, Williamsport, Pa.; C. E. Liach, Essex Falls, N. J.; L. M. Rosin, Perth Amboy, N. J.; Steward Flagler, Stroudsburg, and William Knowlton, Cleveland, Ohio.

Though George Kneuper, the well-known and popular proprietor of the City Hall Pharmacy, at 263-264 Broadway, realizes that he will soon be compelled to move, owing to the contemplated demolition of the building in which his store is located in order to make room for the erection of a 12-story structure for Smith, Gray & Co., clothiers, he is now uncertain as to the future location of his business. He says that he has several desirable places in the immediate neighborhood under consideration, but has not yet made up his mind just which one is most advantageous.

The following list of candidates for offices has been submitted by the Nominating Committee of the College of Pharmacy of the City of New York: For president, Nicholas Murray Butler; first vice-president, Charles F. Chandler; second vice-president, William Jay Schieffelin; third vice-president, Herbert D. Robbins; treasurer, Clarence O. Bigelow; secretary, Thomas F. Main; assistant secretary, O. J. Griffin; for trustees to serve three years, Frederick W. Carpenter, Thomas P. Cook, Arthur H. Elliott, Hieronimus A. Herold and Albert Plaut. The election will take place at the annual meeting of the college, to be held March 20 at 8 P. M.

The Powers-Weightman-Rosengarten Company is anxious to correct a mistaken report, published in several of the New York daily newspapers immediately after the fire at 149 Front street on February 21 had gutted the building adjoining its local offices. This report asserted that the fire did considerable damage to its stock and goods, when, as a matter of fact, its goods were not injured either by smoke or flames, as they were in that section of the building farthest removed from the fire in the adjoining structure, which was occupied by A. G. Marshuetz & Co., importers and wholesale dealers in liquors. Some slight damage was done to the party wall of the Powers-Weightman-Rosengarten Company building, but this was immediately repaired.

Benjamin B. Hamlin, jr., formerly manager of the American Peroxide & Chemical Company, has just been elected president and general manager of the Hydrox Chemical Company, of 59-61 Maiden lane, and general manager of the Medical Dioxide Company, which has recently been merged in the Hydrox Company, without, however, losing its identity as a separate and distinct corporation. Mr. Hamlin has also been elected president and manager of the Thymox Company, which is likewise a subsidiary concern of the Hydrox Company. The Medical Dioxide Company, which until recently has had its offices at 90 Maiden lane, and the Thymox Company have just moved into the same offices with the Hydrox Company, which was formerly located at 140 Maiden lane, but is now on the seventh floor of 59-61 Maiden lane.

H. McK. Kirkland has resigned his position as secretary and treasurer of the New York Quinine & Chemical Works, at No. 114 William street, and has also retired from his connection with McKesson & Robbins as superintendent of the local offices at 91 Fulton street. No reason is assigned for Mr. Kirkland's retirement from either of the companies, but it is believed that he intends to engage in some other business. Oscar M. Reed, formerly their credit man, who has been appointed to succeed Mr. Kirkland as superintendent of McKesson & Robbins' local offices, has also been chosen by the directors of the New York Quinine & Chemical Works as secretary of that corporation, while W. E. Titus, formerly collector for McKesson & Robbins and later connected with the credit department of that company, has been appointed treasurer of the New York Quinine & Chemical Works.

Dodge & Olcott Lead in Bowling Tournament.

STANDING OF THE WHOLESALE DRUG TRADE BOWLING TEAMS.

	Won.	Lost.
Dodge & Olcott	16	2
Parke, Davis & Co	14	2
Colgate & Co	10	4
Seabury & Johnson	9	7
Whitall Tatum Company	8	6
Lazell, Dalley & Co	6	10
Sharp & Dohme	6	10
Roessler & Hasslacher	5	9
Lanman & Kemp	5	11
Bruen, Ritchey & Co	3	13
Merck & Co	2	12

By capturing the two most recent games which they played in the bowling tournament of the Wholesale Drug Trade Association of New York the Dodge & Olcott knights of the pin have forged to the front and have now wrested from the Parke, Davis & Co. rollers the position of topliners in the contest. This temporary victory was scored by the Dodge & Olcott contingent at the games held in the Albion alleys, at 117 West Twenty-third street, on Monday evening, March 5, when its members worsted in hotly contested matches both the Parke, Davis & Co. crew and the Lazell, Dalley & Co. club. Although Dodge & Olcott are now leaders in the "tourney," it must be remembered that the Parke, Davis & Co. team has not played as many games as its rival and may still pull out at the top of the heap.

Several splendid individual scores were recorded at the latest contest, Critchley, of the Dodge & Olcott team, making the star performance of the evening with 228 as his mark, and Burgess, of the Parke, Davis & Co. team, scoring second at 227, while Ruddiman, of the Dodge & Olcott group, made 204. Critchley's star play helped to make the Dodge & Olcott team's best score of 957, which is only second to that of the highest team score of 962, which belongs to the Parke, Davis & Co. contingent.

Dodge & Olcott, however, was not the only successful candidate for honors at the latest games, for the Whitall Tatum Company also won two victories, from Lanman & Kemp and Sharp & Dohme. Parke, Davis & Co. lost one game and won one, and Sharp & Dohme made a similar record, while Lazell, Dalley & Co. and Lanman & Kemp lost both of their games. The team scores of the latest games follow: First game: Dodge & Olcott, 957; Parke, Davis & Co., 873. Second game: Parke, Davis & Co., 772; Lazell, Dalley & Co., 722. Third game: Sharp & Dohme, 774; Lanman & Kemp, 661. Fourth game: Whitall Tatum Company, 827; Lanman & Kemp, 749. Fifth game: Whitall Tatum Company, 855; Sharp & Dohme, 787. Sixth game, Dodge & Olcott, 763; Lazell, Dalley & Co., 725.

The Dodge & Olcott and Seabury & Johnson bowlers divided the honors at the tournament games held Monday evening, February 26, by winning both of their match contests. These teams are making steady progress toward the prize winning class; in fact, the Dodge & Olcott contingent swelled their score thereby to 14 games won and only 2 lost, which record places them at the head of the list, though closely pressed by the Parke, Davis & Co.'s knights of the pins, who came in second with a score of 13 to their credit and only 1 to their discredit. The Seabury & Johnson alley chasers also pulled themselves into fourth place by their successes on that night and are likely to work their way further up the ladder if "Mat." Judge continues to roll up his characteristic high scores. Judge carried off the laurels for high record on February 26 with 222 as his mark, while Robertson, of the Dodge & Olcott rollers, was second with 216 to his credit. The Bruen, Ritchey & Co. ball rollers won one game and lost one game, and the Lanman & Kemp crew made a similar record. Merck & Co. lost two games and Lazell, Dalley & Co. also scored two marks on the wrong side of the ledger. The scores recorded in the games follow: First game: Dodge & Olcott, 869; Bruen, Ritchey & Co., 657. Second game: Bruen, Ritchey & Co., 746; Merck & Co., 588. Third game: Seabury & Johnson, 792; Lanman & Kemp, 781. Fourth game: Lanman & Kemp, 813; Lazell, Dalley & Co., 666. Fifth game: Dodge & Olcott, 857; Merck & Co., 413. Sixth game: Seabury & Johnson, 818; Lazell, Dalley & Co., 726.

METROPOLITAN ASSOCIATION MEETS.

In the belief that they will be able to head off the threatened encroachment upon their business by the United Chemists' Company by making a determined resistance before the plans of the big combine have materialized the members of the General Committee of the Metropolitan Association of Retail Druggists have decided to select a committee of three which shall confer with similar committees to be appointed by the presidents of the various district organizations for the purpose of meeting all possible advances of the Chemists' Company. This decision was arrived at by the General Committee of the M. A. R. D. at its meeting in the New York College of Pharmacy Building on Friday evening, March 2, at which gathering it was also deemed advisable to secure the co-operation of the drug clerks in the proposed fight against the $10,000,000 drug combine.

Peter Diamond, vice-president of the M. A. R. D., an active member of the M. A. R. D. General Committee, opened the subject for general discussion, and then, at the request of the chairman, told what he knew of the plans and line of campaign to be adopted by the Chemists' Company.

Col. J. B. Duble, formerly connected with the N. A. R. D. and recently associated with the American Druggists' Syndicate, who was challeneged at a recent meeting of the Eighteenth District of the M. A. R. D. to produce contracts signed by large retail druggists in which these interests promised to observe a minimum price under penalty of a money forfeit, showed the General Committee two such contracts signed by the firm of William B. Riker, Son & Co. and another large retail firm in this city.

Although it was expected that some action would be taken by the General Committee of the M. A. R. D. in relation to the reported failure of the Kings County Pharmaceutical Society to assist the Metropolitan Association in the establishment of new district organizations in the Borough of Brooklyn all criticism of the Kings County Association was checked in its inception by the felicitous remarks made by Prof. W. C. Anderson, president of the K. C. P. S. and delegate of that body at all meetings of the M. A. R. D., who told the General Committee that only the most harmonious relations existed between the two associations. Professor Anderson asserted that the Kings County Society was always pleased to help the M. A. R. D. in the establishment of new district organizations, and further stated that the K. C. P. S. considered itself as a part of the Metropolitan Association. His statement on the attitude of the K. C. P. S. toward the M. A. R. D. was, by motion of the chairman and members of the General Committee, spread upon the minutes of the meeting.

The desirability of having public telephones installed in the retail drug stores in this city was also discussed at the meeting. Secretary S. V. B. Swann reported that the New York & New Jersey Telephone Company had written a letter to the association in which it refused to make any rate discrimination in favor of druggists.

NEW ENGLAND.

Legislators Confer with Druggists—New Ways of Robbing—Wily Schemes of Swindlers—Local Veto on Promiscuous Sampling.

(*From our Regular Correspondent.*)

Boston, March 7.—The February meeting of the Boston Druggists' Association was held at Young's Hotel on February 27, with President Bartlet in the chair. It was a legislative night, with reporters barred, the reason for this being that the guests were members of the Great and General Court, and it was deemed wise not to have the "between ourselves" discussions reach the public. The announced guests were Hon. J. M. Grosvenor, Hon. D. W. Lane, Hon. C. L. Dean and Representative E. F. Leonard. These were the first speakers, and the drug trade may rest assured of fair treatment at the hands of these gentlemen. Several members of the B. D. A. then presented their views upon pending legislation. This list includes G. H. Ingraham, Hon. G. D. Gilman, J. A. Gilman, C. F. Cutler, H. D. Smith, J. F. Finneran and F. A. Hubbard. The result of the evening's discussion cannot fail of being favorable to those interested in the sale of drugs in this State.

A BOGUS EXPRESSMAN CATCHES ONE DEALER NAPPING.

Some of the members of the drug trade in this vicinity are being made the victims of sharp practices, and alertness is required to combat these schemers for unlawful gains. A few days ago a bogus expressman walked into the wholesale store of Gilman Bros., Franklin street, and took a package containing assorted drugs, valued at $15.50. Later in the day he disposed of the contents to B. F. Bradbury, 39 Harrison avenue, for $1.50. Persisting in this plan with other dealers finally caused his arrest.

A TELEPHONE MESSAGE AND A TEN-DOLLAR BILL.

Recently Young & Brown, with stores at Winchester and Brookline, received a telephone message at one of their establishments which purported to come from one of their customers. An order was given the firm with a request that the goods be sent immediately with two $5 bills in exchange for a ten. The firm sent the order by messenger, who, on arriving at the house designated, was met upon the sidewalk by a man, who took the package and money and stated that he would go inside for the $10 bill. This man went around the house and disappeared. Complaint was made to the police, and the trickster has since been apprehended. Jesse W. Sargent, of Malden, also had an unprofitable experience. He received a telephone call stating that the man at the 'phone was a well-known resident of Malden and that he wanted 10 cigars and change for a $10 bill. A boy was sent to the residence and met a man in front of the house, who took the money and cigars, telling the boy to wait a minute. The boy waited half an hour and then reported the matter.

PROMISCUOUS' DISTRIBUTION OF MEDICINE SAMPLES PROHIBITED.

On February 20 the Board of Health of Haverhill issued an order prohibiting the distribution of a medicinal tablet which was being left at houses in that city for advertising purposes. It was held that the tablet would be injurious to children who might get hold of it. This action was taken under an ordinance which the city adopted some years ago.

Registered in New Jersey.

Following is a list of the successful applicants for registration in New Jersey who appeared at the January session of the board of pharmacy:

REGISTERED PHARMACISTS.—Harry J. Abrahams and Morris E. Berkowitz, Newark; Abraham Brodsky, New York; Thomas A. Connor, Bayonne; John H. Crowe, Englewood; C. Maclay Diller, Philadelphia; Charles D. Flynn, New Brunswick; Jacob B. Gollobin, Newark; Philip C. McLaughlin, Camden; Edwin L. Newcomb, Vineland; Henry C. Neer, Park Ridge; Carl W. Poetz, Jersey City; Chester Riland, Rahway; Charles A. Reibel, Elizabeth; George B. Spath, Jersey City.

REGISTERED ASSISTANTS.—Dionisio Capone, Newark; Reese Davis, Elizabeth; Walter A. Gaskill, Atlantic City; Robert J. Lyman, Newark; Eugene A. McAdams, Camden; Jacob Pinkinson, Newark.

The next meeting of the board for the examination of candidates will be held at Trenton on April 19 and 20. Applications should be filed in advance with the secretary of the board, Henry A. Jordan, Bridgeton.

PENNSYLVANIA.

The Largest Class of Applicants on Record—The Patent Medicine Evil—Lees Leads Bowlers.

(*From our Regular Correspondent.*)

Philadelphia, March 7.—This is an era of investigation. The insurance companies and the railroads have for the past few months been undergoing severe trials, and now the doctors have come to the front and taken up nostrums and the patent medicine evils. At a recent meeting of the Acorn Club, in this city, Dr. W. M. L. Coplin, Director of the Department of Health and Charity; Dr. Albert P. Francine and Dr. Augustus A. Eshner were the speakers against the use of nostrums and patent medicine.

SEVEN HUNDRED APPLICANTS EXAMINED.

The result of the first pharmaceutical examination under the new law was announced from the headquarters of the Pharmaceutical Examining Board at Harrisburg on February 27. Out of a total of 701 students that appeared before the board more than 500 were successful. The State Pharmaceutical Board is composed of the following members: President, Lewis Emanuel, of Pittsburg; Charles T. George, of Philadelphia, secretary; W. L. Cliffe, of Philadelphia; Paul W. Houcke, of Shenandoah, and George W. Davis, of Scranton. This was the largest list of applicants that ever appeared before the board and it said to be the largest that has ever appeared in any State of this country. The next examination will be held in this city on March 17 and other examinations will be held simultaneously in Pittsburg and Harrisburg May 17.

WITH THE BOWLERS.

During the summer certain cities swear by their baseball clubs, but there have been no reports of any town turning out with a brass band to welcome the return of the members of the druggists' bowling clubs. There are six clubs in this city and they are plodding slowly along. The J. E. Lee Club is so far in the lead that it will be impossible to catch up with it, even if a racing automobile should be used. However, each Tuesday evening representatives of the six leading wholesale drug houses here gather in the Central Alleys, at Eleventh and Arch streets, and for several hours they endeavor to punch holes in the pins. There is a fair attendance of rooters, but there is not as much interest taken in the games as was the case last year. On March 5 the score was as follows:

	Won.	Lost.	P. C.		Won.	Lost.	P. C.
J. E. Lee	45	9	.833	P. C. P. W.	25	29	.463
Wanderers	26	10	.5[illegible]	P. C. P. Bl.	16	35	.314
S. K. & F. Co.	27	24	.529	W. D. Feldt	14	34	.292

From now on it is said there will be more practice indulged in by the members of the various teams, so that a crack team can be selected to represent this city in the intercity bowling match which is to be held at Atlantic City during the latter part of April or early in May. There will be teams present from New York, Philadelphia and Baltimore. There is plenty of money on hand to bet that our team will win.

PHILADELPHIA NEWS NOTES.

M. N. Kline, of the firm of Smith, Kline & French Company, has returned from Buffalo, where he went to testify in the suit of Pierce against the *Ladies' Home Journal*.

John Quentin Rodgers, of the firm of Chapman & Rodgers, died on February 21. Mr. Rodgers had been ill for several months, and while it was expected that he would not recover, his death, however, was a severe blow to his many friends. He was well known in the drug trade and had a large acquaintance.

J. B. Thompson, formerly of 1933 Tioga street, will shortly open a store in Atlantic City at Pacific and Tennessee avenues.

Mr. Sheldon, who was with the Piso Company, has secured a position with the Bromo Lithia Chemical Company, of this city, and will push these goods to the best of his ability.

William Davis has sold his store in Jenkintown and rumor has it that he will permanently retire from the drug business.

The theatre party which was given by the members of the

OHIO.

Cleveland Jobbers Busy—Columbus Druggists Caught on Cheap Jewelry Schemes—Suits Threatened—To Prohibit the Sale of Tobacco to Minors—The Graduate Pre-Requisite Bill Reported Favorably.

(*From our Regular Correspondent.*)

Cleveland, Ohio, March 7.—The jobbing houses here are struggling with their March business, which is always heavy. They report that it is even heavier this year than usual. However, there has been no complaint since the first of the year over the business that has come to the Cleveland houses. Through their work on special excursions and the plans they have had of getting retailers into the city at low rates business has increased steadily.

VICTIMS OF FAKE JEWELRY SCHEMES.

Columbus druggists are complaining that they have been victimized by a concern that sold them cabinets of cheap jewelry at a pretty high price, holding out that the goods could be easily sold at a good profit. Although the goods were sold them on a five-year guarantee the druggists say that after the articles are used for a month they lose the little wash they have on the outside and show a very poor quality of base metal. The wholesale house generously gave the druggists time on the entire lot and took a series of notes, aggregating $192. If the notes were not paid when due they were notified, but no attempt was made to collect until the last one became due, and then legal process was used in some cases to enforce payment. A suit is now pending against G. W. Racer, and the American Drug Company has been threatened. Both refused to pay for the goods because they alleged that they are not what they were represented to be. Some of the druggists took a smaller lot than those mentioned, but it is said that at least 50 of them were taken in on the offer.

A SUBSTITUTE FOR THE CIGARETTE BILL.

In place of the McFadden Anti-Cigarette bill, which was drastic in its features, a measure has been introduced in the State Senate which prohibits dealers from selling tobacco in any form to persons under 18 years of age and forbids the harboring of boys while they use tobacco.

A PRE-REQUISITE CLAUSE TO TAKE EFFECT 1908.

The Braun Pharmacy bill has been reported favorably by the House Committee and will come up at an early date. The bill provides that after January 1, 1908, all applicants for certificates of pharmacy must be graduates of some recognized school of pharmacy and applicants who fail on the first examination must pay a second fee if they try again. Certificates will be renewed within three years after the expiration, but after the lapse of that time another examination must be taken. Druggists from other States will be admitted to Ohio on the same terms that their own States admit Ohio druggists. Druggists who allow their certificates to expire and go on with their work for 60 days without renewing them will be subject to a fine.

FINED FOR ILLEGAL LIQUOR SALES.

A. J. Cromwell and E. A. Cook, prominent druggists of Chardon, have been fined $50 each by Mayor Bickle on the charge of selling liquor illegally. Motions have been made for a new trial, and if granted a jury will be asked for the next time. Although Chardon has been dry for 18 years, these are the first prosecutions in all that time. W. H. Cromwell, of Parkman, has also been arrested on the same charge.

CLEVELAND NOTES.

August Stern, who already owns four stores in the city, has purchased the business of F. A. Reynolds & Son, at Lake View, the eastern line of the city.

The Standard Drug Company has purchased the store of J. J. Schantz, at the corner of Wade Park avenue and Brookdale street.

THE WEST.

Renewed Agitation of the Cocaine Evil—Unjust Generalizations—The Efforts of the Board Toward Suppressing the Evil—A Thousand-Dollar Liquor License for Drug Stores.

(*From our Regular Correspondent.*)

Chicago, March 7.—The cocaine agitation has broken out afresh, with the result that the agitators have done much injustice to the drug trade in general. A reporter for the *Tribune* visited a tough section of the West Side, that lying between Peoria and Halsted streets, Washington boulevard and Lake street, and succeeded in buying some cocaine. Purchases were made in two drug stores and two saloons. Then the facts, with considerable coloring, were printed as prominently as possible, druggists generally being blamed along with the guilty ones. Those who are really the guilty ones are well known. They have been prosecuted frequently and have been fined time and again, but have often evaded the payment of the fine in one way and another. The State Board of Pharmacy has prosecuted these cases relentlessly. Workers at Hull House Settlement have taken active part in the campaign against the traffic, and the police have occasionally stirred things up. One of the habitual offenders was formally expelled from the C. R. D. A. Yet in spite of all this, a sensation is worked up under the following lurid headlines:

COCAINE BLIGHT RULES UNCURBED.

Traffic in Drug, with All Attendant Horrors, Again Boldly Conducted on the West Side.

Police, Supine, Know It.

Investigators for *The Tribune* Buy "Flake" in Stores and Saloon, Revealing Conditions.

One of the things that hampers those who are trying to stamp out the traffic is that the present law does not cover the sale of eucaine. The effects of eucaine are similar to those of cocaine, yet traffic in this dangerous drug cannot, at present, be easily checked. Efforts are being made to have changes made in the city ordinances so that eucaine will be included among the drugs that cannot be sold to the general public.

A THOUSAND DOLLAR LICENSE PROPOSED.

A fresh blow was aimed at retail druggists at the meeting of the Council Monday evening. Soon after the ordinance placing the license of saloons at $1,000 was passed Alderman Pringle introduced another measure, requiring druggists to pay the same amount. The ordinance is meant only for those who sell liquor. It provides also that the exhibition of spiritous liquors in druggists' windows shall be prohibited. The measure was referred to the License Committee. If it should ever go into effect this ordinance would, of course, be prohibitive in its workings, unless drug stores were converted into saloons, for no druggist could pay $1,000 a year out of the profits of ordinary liquor sales. The other ordinance requiring a $250 license is still sleeping in committee.

The Scholtz Drug Company, of Denver, Col., who installed two years ago a large and elaborate Twentieth Century soda fountain, said to be the finest soda fountain in the entire West, have opened up a branch store in Denver, and the L. A. Becker Company report the sale of a 20-foot Sanitas counter fountain, to be located in the new store.

Henry Huder, a prominent druggist of Indianapolis, Ind., will make extensive improvements within the next 30 days. Mr. Huder was recently in New York investigating soda fountains, and now announces that he has placed his contract with the L. A. Becker Company for a 27-foot Sanitas counter fountain, equipped with "dripless" pumps. We are advised that Mr. Huder's new fountain will be one of the finest in the country and, as a whole, will possess artistic features of extraordinary merit.

NOTES.

The store of F. G. Waiss, at 335 West Harrison street, has been purchased by his clerk, M. M. A. Levering.

Legal action has been taken against a number of telephone subscribers who have put in extension instruments not authorized by the telephone company.

Dr. Alfred Dahlberg, 260 West Madison street, has been arrested on a charge of having sold cocaine to a gang of young thieves.

The Chicago branch of the Woman's Organization, N. A. R. D., held its first meeting at the home of Mrs. Wm. W. Klöre. The next meeting will be at the home of Mrs. S. C. Yeomans, 5543 Wabash avenue.

At its last meeting the Western branch of the American Pharmaceutical Association elected the following officers: President, Oscar Oldberg; first vice-president, Hermann Fry; second vice-president, F. W. Meissner; third vice-president, Amanda W. Stahl; secretary-treasurer, W. B. Day. A delegation was present from the Chicago Medical Society, and Dr. Whalen, Commissioner of Health, also attended. Addresses were made regarding better laws for regulation of pure food and drugs.

Moffitt-West Drug Company Sold to J. S Merrell Company.

As announced in the AMERICAN DRUGGIST for February 26, the business of the Moffitt-West Drug Company, of St. Louis, Mo., has been purchased by the J. S. Merrell Drug Company, of that city, which purchased the entire wholesale stock, business and good will of the former company on February 22, when C. P. Walbridge, president of the Merrell Company, and G. H. West, secretary of the Moffitt-West Company, acted for their respective companies. The value of the Moffitt-West Company's stock is estimated at $300,000.

As soon as an invoice can be taken of the stock in the Moffitt-West Company's store, at Broadway and Clark avenue, it will be moved into the Merrell Company's house, at Fourth and Market streets. Friendly relations have always existed between the officers of both companies and a circular letter has been sent out to the trade by C. P. Walbridge and G. H. West urging that customers of the retiring house patronize the Merrell Company.

Most of the employees of the Moffitt-West Company will be retained by the Merrell Company, but none of the officers of the retiring company will go with it. As no transfer of the capital stock of the Moffitt-West Company has been made, the corporation will soon be liquidated under the terms of a contract whereby its officers agree not to engage in the drug business in St. Louis again.

The Merrell Company has been in the business 61 years and its officers now consist of: C. P. Walbridge, president; H. S. Merrell, first vice-president; G. R. Merrell, second vice-president; E. Bindschadler, secretary, and H. J. Stolle, treasurer. The Moffitt-West Company had a capital stock of $250,000, which was practically held by W. F. Niedringhaus, president of the company, and his family. It began business in 1888.

Virginia News Items.

The Hampton Roads Drug Company (Inc.), of Norfolk, have opened a new drug store at corner of Bowdens Ferry road and Pocahontas avenue, Lambert's Point. J. L. Harward, formerly of Concord, N. C., is in charge.

Mr. Field, formerly of North Carolina, is opening a new store on Main street, Norfolk. Everything is of the latest pattern in fixtures, and he has a very handsome Innovation soda fountain.

Burrow & Martin, of Norfolk, have installed a very handsome Innovation fountain in each of their Main street stores.

The people of Norfolk expect a big boom this season as the result of the Jamestown Exposition, and abundant preparation is being made to slake the thirst of sightseers.

J. F. Newman is fitting up a very attractive store on Duke street, Norfolk. Mr. Newman has been an old-time friend of the AMERICAN DRUGGIST, and we wish him success in his new enterprise.

THE SOUTH.

An Ad. on Wheels—A Big State Meeting Expected—Druggists Enjoy a Theatre Party—Cyclone Hits a Drug Store.

(From our Regular Correspondent.)

New Orleans, La., March 5.—Excepting that the large accumulation of drug stores in the downtown district of the city has started what is to all appearances a cut-rate war there is little out of the ordinary transpiring in New Orleans at present. Many of the establishments are advertising extensively, and the daily papers and street cars are being made use of in this respect. A number of novel schemes are being adopted, and these are attracting considerable attention. For instance, one of the big downtown stores, and incidentally one of the new ones, has a man on skates, dressed in a peculiar costume and carrying the store's name all over his coat. The man is an expert skater and operates along the principal thoroughfares of the downtown district.

PLEADED GUILTY OF PHENACETINE SALES.

David B. Comer, David B. Comer, Sr., and John E. King, the three men who operated the German Chemical Company, and who as the operators of this company used the mails to fraudulently dispose of phenacetine, recently appeared in the United States Court here and withdrew their pleas of not guilty and entered pleas of guilty, as charged. Each was fined $250 and costs.

PREPARING FOR THE STATE MEETING.

Elaborate arrangements for the annual convention of the Louisiana State Pharmaceutical Association are being made, and it is expected that one of the best conventions ever held will take place next month. The local Pharmaceutical Association has its committee at work on a programme, and this, it is understood, will be ready for publication within the next two weeks. There will be many novel features for the entertainment of the delegates, and the business of the convention will be so arranged that the delegates can give a good deal of their time to pleasure.

A THEATRE PARTY FOR OUT-OF-TOWN DRUGGISTS.

Mardi Gras night the Parker-Blake Company, Limited, entertained a party of 75 of its out-of-town friends, most of them retail druggists, at the Crescent Theatre. All of the guests were visitors to the carnival, and with the theatre party the popular drug house put the finishing touches to what had been a pleasant stay for every one of them. All of the boxes of the theatre and several rows of seats were engaged by the company and occupied by its guests. The company was represented by Arthur D. Parker, president; C. C. Johnson, treasurer; P. H. Brown, secretary, and half a dozen salesmen who were in the city. "The Maid and the Mummy" was the attraction and it was thoroughly enjoyed by those who had the good fortune to be the guests of the widely known and popular commercial concern. Among those present were:

H. P. Yough, jr., Ellisville, Miss.; Edw. Belknap, jr., Mary Almindinger, New Orleans; Dr. and Mrs. R. B. Paine, Mrs. Mitchell, Mandeville, La.; Mr. and Mrs. W. A. Caperton, Mr. and Mrs. P. H. Brown, New Orleans; L. B. Baynard, jr., Miss Eugenie Baynard, Dr. T. M. Dupuy, Alexandria; Miss Lester, Miss Corve, Glmtown, Miss.; Mr. and Mrs. O. Eastland, Scooba; E. A. Harper, New Orleans; Mr. and Mrs. C. W. Perkins, Ruston, La.; J. Edward Hanson, J. Edward Hanson, jr., Pass Christian, Miss.; Dr. R. L. Hagaman, Frank H. Hagaman, Centerville, Miss.; Mrs. H. T. Liverman, Mansfield, La.; Miss Magaline, Blackshire, Natchitoches, La.; Mr. and Mrs. Walter Lastrapes, Mr. and Mrs. H. W. Lyle, New Orleans; S. M. Covington, Summit, Miss.; George A. Patterson, Alexandria, La.; P. M. Birmingham, W. M. Fox, Louisville, Miss.; C. M. Leggett, Laurel, Miss.; Dr. L. Lazaro, Washington, La.; J. Moody, M. M. Montgomery, Goodman, Miss.; C. P. McWhorter, Louisville, Miss.

THE JOSH MOORE DRUG COMPANY IN THE PATH OF THE CYCLONE.

In the disastrous cyclone which visited the town of Meridian, Miss., last Friday evening and which killed nearly forty people, besides destroying a large amount of property, the Josh Moore Drug Company, a popular establishment of the town, was damaged to the extent of $2,000. The store of the Moore company was in the path of the cyclone, and it was almost swept away. The company, however, was not one of the heaviest losers.

The Drug and Chemical Market

The prices quoted in this report are those current in the wholesale market, and higher prices are paid for retail lots
The quality of goods frequently necessitates a wide range of prices.

Condition of Trade.

NEW YORK, March 10, 1906.

The movement into consuming channels has been fairly animated since our last report, importers as well as jobbers being favored with liberal orders, though little of new interest has developed. Jobbers report a good, seasonable demand for articles in request during the spring and summer months, and a hopeful feeling prevails regarding the outlook. Price changes of importance include advances in citric acid and acetanilid. Camphor has been further advanced, reaching top-notch figures. Opium is again lower, with a dull and uninteresting market. The various other price changes are noted below:

HIGHER.	LOWER.
Acetanilid,	Opium,
Citric Acid,	Ergot,
Citrates,	Hempseed, Russian,
Peppermint oil,	Glycerin,
Camphor,	Arsenic, white,
Ipecac,	Bayberry bark,
Rhubarb,	Manna, small flake.
Senna leaves, Alexandria,	
Gum gamboge,	
Canary seed,	
Cantharides, Chinese,	
Menthol,	
Oxalic acid.	
Pennyroyal oil,	

Drugs.

Acetanilid has been advanced by the manufacturers to meet the increased cost of raw material, and quotations are now 24c to 25c.

Arnica flowers are meeting with only limited inquiry, but values are apparently steady at 9c to 10c.

Balsam copaiba, Central American, is in good demand and firmly maintained at 29c to 31c; Para is generally quoted at 40c to 42½c.

Balsam Peru is given little consideration; jobbing sales at $1 to $1.05, though 97½c is named as acceptable in some quarters.

Balsam tolu has continued inactive, though without quotable change in price, 20c to 22c being yet named.

Barks.—Cottonroot of the new crop is maintained with firmness at 8½c to 10c, supplies coming in very slowly. Choice grades of sassafras are scarce and wanted, and prime sifted bark is generally held at 14c to 15c. Cascara sagrada has ruled quiet during the week, but quotations show no variation from 5½c to 9c as to quantity and quality. Soap is in demand, and for whole bark 4¾c to 5c is named, while cut is jobbing at 6c to 6½c, though 5½c might buy. Elm is scarce and wanted, and quotations for chip have been advanced to 17c to 18c, with sales reported at the inside figure. Bayberry is in better supply and offered more freely at 12c to 13c.

Buchu leaves, short, are firmer, and recent sales were at an advance to 17½c to 20c, the outside figures being for prime green of recent arrival.

Cacao butter is steadier and recent sales of bulk were at 28¾c to 30c.

Cannabis indica is held with increased firmness owing to stronger cable advices from primary market, but $1.00 to $1.05 will yet buy.

Cantharides, Chinese, is maintained in firm position, the stock being limited and under good control. The principal holder declines to shade 60c, and we hear of sales at 62c. Powdered is also firmer at 60c to 62c.

Chamomile flowers are maintained in steady position on the basis of 18c to 22c for Roman of new crop.

Coca leaves, Huanuco, are without important action; a sale is reported at 27c, but 28c to 30c is generally named.

Codliver oil is dull and neglected and the market retains a quiet appearance at a reduction to $21.00 to $25.00 for Norwegian; a sale of Newfoundland oil is reported at $18.00.

Ergot is lower in sympathy with conditions in European markets, and Russian is obtainable at 30c to 32c and Spanish at 35c to 37c, as to quantity and seller.

Glycerin continues to reflect an easier undertone and C. P. is obtainable at 11¼c to 11½c in drums or barrels and at 12¼c to 12½c for cans.

Guarana is maintained in good position and a fair jobbing inquiry is reported at the range of 55c to 57c.

Haarlem oil is meeting with fair inquiry, but the supply continues limited and holders are firm in their views at $3.00.

Lycopodium is meeting with rather less attention, and unlabeled is easier at 49c, while pollitz is held and selling at 50c to 52c as to quantity.

Menthol has attracted some attention since our last, and values are steadier, at an advance to $2.25 to $2.50. Recent importations from Japan have been heavy, and some in the trade are disposed to discount the recent flurry in the article.

Opium continues extremely dull, with only a moderate jobbing business passing at the present low level of values. Cases are quoted at $2.85 to $2.87½, and up to $2.90 is named for jobbing lots. Powdered is generally quoted at $3.40 to $3.45, as to quantity and quality.

Quinine has developed no feature of consequence, either as regards price or demand, since our last issue, but the tendency of the market appears to favor holders, and manufacturers' prices are well maintained, on the basis of 18c to 21c for both domestic and foreign brands. Java is quoted on a parity with German in second hand.

Senna, whole Alexandria, is scarce and in active request, and the higher range of 20c to 22c is now named, though sales are reported at 19c.

Spermaceti continues in demand, and we hear of numerous sales at 27c to 28c for block and 28c to 29c for case.

Wax, Carnauba, is held with increased firmness, owing to scarcity, one bid of 40¼c for No. 1 in Brazil being turned down. The latest spot quotations were 52c to 53c for No. 1, 47c for No. 2 and 33½c to 34c for No. 3. Ceresin offers more freely, at a reduction to 12½c to 18c for yellow and 13½c to 20c for white. Sesame oil has hardened in value since our last, in sympathy with corresponding conditions at primary sources, and quotations for Jaffa are maintained at 60c to 61c, while choice grades from France are quoted at 85c.

Chemicals.

Alum is meeting with increased inquiry, with plum quoted at $1.75 to $1.85 and ground at $1.85 to $1.90.

Arsenic, white, is fractionally lower, offerings being more free in the absence of demand. We now quote the range at 8c to 10c for powdered on spot, while forward shipments are quoted at 6½c.

Blue vitriol is steady and in moderate request at 5⅝c.

Brimstone has been in increased demand, but the distribution is restricted by a temporary scarcity of stocks caused by a failure to ship promptly from the West. Values are maintained at $22.12½ to $22.62½ as to quantity and terms.

Bromide of potash is held with increased firmness, 16c being now named as inside.

Citric acid is firmer in all markets and domestic manufacturers have advanced quotations 3c per lb., to 41c in bbls. and 41½c in cases. Citric salts are correspondingly higher.

Cream tartar has developed a firmer tone and an early rise in values would occasion no surprise, though previous quotations prevail, or, say, 22¼c to 23⅝c for crystals and 22½c to 23c for powdered.

Iodine preparations are in good demand and values are steadily maintained at the range of $2.70 to $2.75 for resublimed iodine and $3.00 to $3.05 for iodoform and $2.05 to $2.10 for potassium iodide.

Nitrate of silver has been advanced to meet increased cost of bullion and manufacturers now name 42c to 45½c.

Nitrate of soda has developed an upward tendency and the last sales on spot were $2.30, while none is offered to arrive at under $2.25 for 96 per cent. and $2.22½ for 95 per cent.

Oxalic acid is scarce and wanted. The bulk of recent arrivals has gone into channels of consumption on contract orders. For prompt deliveries of German 5¼c is an inside quotation, while 5½c is named for Norwegian.

Platinum chloride has hardened in the interval, the revised quotations of manufacturers being $10.50 to $11.75 per oz., as to quantity.

Prussiate of potash, yellow, has moved into firmer position, due to scarcity of spot supplies, and quotations are now 14¼c to 14½c.

Tartaric acid is maintained at manufacturers' prices, or, say, 27⅝c to 28¼c for crystals and 28c to 28½c for powdered.

Essential Oils.

Anise is held with noticeable firmness, in view of the tenor of cable advices from China, but $1.35 to $1.37½ will yet buy.

Cassia is unchanged from 80c to 82½c and 85c to 87½c for 75 to 80 per cent. and 80 to 85 per cent. tests, respectively.

Citronella is in better supply and offers more freely at the range of 40c to 41c and 41c to 42c for drums and cans respectively.

Clove is firm, in sympathy with the spice, and bottles are quoted at 85c to 87½c, and cans at 82½c to 85c.

Hemlock is in demand and the market is steady upon the basis of 45c to 50c, marking a slight advance.

Messina essences are more generally inquired for and some of the leading brands of lemon and sweet orange are revised in price, lemon being offered at 70c to 72½c and orange at $2.10 to $2.15, these figures showing a fractional decline. The former schedule was considered to be above the prevailing range of quotations.

Pennyroyal of pharmacopœial test is scarce, and for such quality values are firmly maintained at the range of $1.25 to $1.30, though French oil is obtainable at $1.15 to $1.20.

Peppermint is characterized by increased firmness, and both case and bulk oil have moved freely during the interval. The undertone of the market is decidedly stronger, owing to unfavorable reports from producing districts regarding crop prospects. It is reported that a leading house has contracted for Wayne County oil of the new crop, on the basis of $3. Case oil is firmly maintained at $3.20 to $3.35, and bulk at $2.60 to $2.75.

Gums.

Aloes of various grades are steadily held at full previous prices. Most of the demand is for Curacoa, which is held at 5⅛c to 6c, but sales of Barbadoes are reported at 14c to 15c.

Arabic of the various grades continues to receive considerable attention, and a good jobbing trade is reported, at the range of 25c to 35c for first pick, 19c to 23c for second pick, 15c to 17c for third pick and 6½c to 11c for sorts.

Asafœtida is dull and featureless, with quotations maintained at the previous range of 14c to 18c for good to prime.

Camphor continues to occupy the center of the stage, another advance of 2c in American refined being announced on the 26th instant, and it would surprise no one if a $1 basis was reached soon in view of the stringency of crude supplies. Cable advices from Germany showed refined in that market to have advanced to the parity of 98¾c net. The recent advance in this market brings values to the basis of 96c in barrels and 96½c in cases, with only limited offerings at this range.

Chicle has been in good demand during the interval, and we hear of a sale of several carloads of old Progresa at 36c. on spot, but new gum is obtainable at 35c.

Gamboge is maintained in firm position, and whole pipe does not offer at under $1.05, while powdered is maintained at $1.15.

Kino is maintained at 25c to 27c, in view of the limited available supply.

Tragacanth is meeting with a good consumptive demand, and the tendency is higher, if anything, with sales of Aleppo at 30c to 65c, and of Turkey at 35c to 80c, as to quality and quantity.

Roots.

Ginger is held with increasing firmness, bleached Jamaica being maintained at 12c, though good bold natural root is obtainable at 11c to 12c.

Golden seal is reported firmer in primary markets, but little interest is extended on the spot, though holders' ideas are maintained at $1.20 to $1.25.

Helonias is offered more freely owing to lack of inquiry and quotations have been reduced to 40c. to 42c.

Ipecac is attracting most attention and values continue to mount steadily upward, especially for Rio, which is in most demand and held at $1.75 to $1.80; some Carthagena is offering at $1.65, but $1.70 to $1.75 are more popular quotations.

Mandrake continues held at 4¾c to 5¼c, but little interest is extended by buyers.

Orris is higher at primary sources of supply, but spot values are not as yet affected, Florentine remaining at 68c and Verona at 4c to 6c.

Pink is very scarce, and holders of the limited available supply have advanced their price to 80c.

Rhubarb, Chinese, is maintained with strength and confidence, in view of the difficulty of obtaining supplies from the primary market. For high dried 21c to 24c is generally quoted, Canton being maintained at 35c to 40c and Shensi at 65c to 70c.

Sarsaparilla, Mexican, is in improved demand, and some holders have advanced their limit, following a sale of 10 bales at 9⅝c. We quote the range at 9½c to 9¾c.

Senega, Western, is quoted by some dealers at 58c to 60c, the stock being limited, but some holders are free to offer at 57c.

Seeds.

Rather quiet conditions have prevailed in the seed market during the past fortnight. Russian hemp has weakened in the interval, and supplies were obtainable at 2¾c to 3c. Canary is well maintained at the recent advance to 4½c to 4¾c for Smyrna and 4¾c to 5c for Sicily. Wormseed, American, is dull and neglected, with quotations nominal at 7c to 8c, while Russian is in light supply and firm at 17c to 18c. Celery is quiet, but unchanged at 7½c to 7¾c. Foenugreek is higher abroad, and spot quotations are said to be below the parity of value, there being sellers at 2c.

William. B. Riker Dead.

William B. Riker, founder of the Wm. B. Riker & Son Drug Company, died at his home in this city on February 22. Mr. Riker was 85 years old and his death was ascribed solely to old age. He was a native of New York, having been born in Duane street. As a young man he was employed by John Meakin, well known in the drug trade in the early 40's. In 1846 he went into business for himself at 353 Sixth avenue. After a few years he moved to 373 Sixth avenue, where one of the Riker drug stores still is. After years of active service Mr. Riker retired from the business, leaving it in the hands of his only child, William H. Riker. Before retiring, however, he founded the present company, of which Joseph H. Marshall is president.

Opportunities *for* Export Trade

ECUADOR AS A MARKET FOR AMERICAN PRODUCTS.

United States Consul Dietrich, of Guayaquil, replying to inquiries from the managers of the proposed floating exposition

Botica Alemana, Quito, Ecuador; Sr. A. Mortensen, Proprietor.

regarding the character of the markets in Ecuador, writes as follows:

"So far, the main articles of value that are imported from the States that are ready salable products are flour, lard, kerosene and lumber, which of late years have only been imported from the United States. The bulk of the shoes handled here also come from the United States, as well as the majority of nutritious articles and a considerable amount of drugs, paints, oils, candles, thread, cordage, hardware and machinery, wines and liquors. Some American hats are also handled here, but the bulk of them are brought from Europe. As to the class and kind of goods that would be particularly susceptible of display here, I might say all kinds of merchandise, if the quality and price is attractive and interesting to the buyers. That means, of course, that the quality should be equal or superior to the same class of merchandise offered by the European markets. The price must be equally as interesting in order to receive the consideration desired.

"Therefore it is quite natural for the merchants of Ecuador to be interested in all kinds of American merchandise, especially as there are no factories of importance here of any kind. The close competition offered between American and European markets will, to a certain extent, cause the merchants of this country to be more alert and make a more exhaustive investigation of prices and terms offered them. In preparing yourselves to meet competition in this country you will also bear in mind the fact that nearly all the merchants here have from the very beginning of their business career acquired the habit and custom of buying principally from European manufacturers on account of the wide latitude given in paying for their merchandise, and for which reason they are still in close touch with the said manufacturers.

Botica de la Merced, Guayaquil, Ecuador, Tarquinio J. Viteri, Proprietor, Showing the Professors of La Facultad de Medicinia de Guayaquil Making Their Inspection Tour of the Pharmacies.

"The merchants here claim that European manufacturers always extend to them a credit from six to twelve months time without interest, which terms they claim they can never get from manufacturers and jobbers in the States. Therefore, as long as European manufacturers extend more liberal terms for the payment of merchandise than the manufacturers and jobbers of the States are willing to extend, it will certainly be very

Loading and Unloading Boats in the River About Five Miles from Guayaquil, Ecuador.

hard to get these merchants to buy other articles of merchandise in the States than such articles of merchandise that cannot be duplicated or bought for less money in Europe."

Further description of the stores illustrated herewith and details regarding commercial conditions in Ecuador will be found in our issue for February 12.

Stamped Paper in Argentina.

Minister Beaupré, of Argentina, forwards to the State Department a copy of a law of that republic regulating the use of stamped paper and stamps in all commercial transactions, which became operative January 1. By this law substantially every written contract, document or obligation is made subject to stamp taxes, and where money values are stated the stamped paper or stamps required are fixed at about one-tenth of 1 per cent; that is to say, on expressed values from $20 to $100, 10 cents in stamps; from $101 to $200, 20 cents in stamps, and so on, the increase being 10 cents for each $100 or fraction. There are a number of exceptions to this rule, but the rate given will apply to nearly all commercial transactions. Among the exceptions may be noted insurance policies, which must be stamped according to the prescribed schedule providing that policies from $100 to $1,000 shall pay 5 cents; on each $1,000 up to $5,000, 25 cents; from $5,000 to $10,000 a charge of 50 cents; above $10,000 and not above $15,000, 75 cents, and from $15,000 to $20,000, $1. All above that must pay for each additional $5,000, or a fraction thereof, 25 cents.

RUSSIAN PHARMACY.[1]

By D. A. Ruffmann.

Ancient Russia had its national system of medicine, with a very modest stock of remedies. After the conversion to Christianity and the baptism of the Grand Duke Vladimir, the Greek clergy monopolized the healing art, and it was only at the end of the 16th century that foreign doctors first appeared in Moscow. In 1581, at the court of Ivan the Terrible, an Imperial "apteka" (pharmacy or apothecary's shop) was established in Moscow by an Englishman named James Frencham, who was recommended by Queen Elizabeth of England. The necessary materials for the purpose were imported from England.

During the reign of Michail Fedorovitch, in 1620, a Board of Management of Aptekas was instituted, and the pharmacists as well as the doctors were placed under the control of that body. Subsequently it was reorganized and renamed "The Medical Chancery," and finally the "State Medical Administration." The Zar Alexis Michailovitch permitted the opening of a second pharmacy in Moscow, which was named the "New Pharmacy," and another one at Wologda. At the same time three gardens were established by the Crown for the purpose of cultivating medicinal herbs, the work of sorting and collecting which was very often done by people in lieu of paying their taxes.

CHARTER ISSUED BY PETER THE GREAT.

Peter the Great, in striving for the good of his people, did not neglect the apothecaries, who were expected to provide the public with rationally prepared medicine. In 1702 he allowed the establishment of eight apothecary's shops in Moscow, whereby the owners were given great privileges. In the same year Johann Gottfried Gregorius opened the first independent apothecary's shop in the German quarter of the old Russian capital. In 1721 the government assisted apothecaries to open shops in St. Peterburg and in many other Russian towns, on condition that they followed the model of the pharmaceutical establishments of Moscow. The right of dispensing powerful drugs, and of preparing medicines from prescriptions, was con-

Ivan the Terrible, the father of the Russian Empire, and the ruler who caused the first pharmacy to be established in Russia. It was opened by an Englishman in 1581, and the goods for the purpose were imported from London.

ferred exclusively upon these apothecaries. The following is a translation of a charter issued during the reign of Peter the Great:

By the Grace of God, We, the Most Serene and Ruling Great Lord-Zar and Grand Duke Peter Alexejevitch, Autocrat of all the Great, Little and White Russias, etc., etc., etc., have conferred upon the Pharmacist Daniel Gurtschin the right, and by Imperial Charter he is commanded to open an Apteka for the public welfare in the Imperial town of Moscow, in the same style of pharmacy as exists in neighboring lands, whereby he builds his Pharmacy for his own account on the land given him free of charge last year on the Mjasnitzkaja Street, behind the Nicolsk Gates, in the White Town. In this pharmacy he must have a full stock of medicaments, for which he also sends orders beyond the seas. In this Apteka the proprietor is suffering now a great deal from his workmen, who steal the medicaments and sell the same in the green-grocer and other shops, whereas in the charter issued by our Father of sacred memory and everlasting remembrance, the Great Emperor and Autocrat of all the Great, Little and White Russias, the Grand Duke Alexiej Michailovitch, in 1672 on February 28, it was forbidden to sell any elixirs, vodkis, oils and other medicaments from the above-named green-grocer shops, and that anybody carrying on

Peter the Great, who did much to develop Russian pharmacy, and who issued the interesting charter to a Moscow pharmacist that will be found translated and reprinted in the accompanying article.

such trade would be severely punished. Owing to such a trade now being carried on by the named traders, who with the stolen medicaments are only causing great harm to many people, We command Daniel Gurtschin to continue in his endeavors in the keeping of the Apteka and the multiplying of the medicaments, whereby this charter should remain in force for him and his children's children, and that in the above named shops no trade should be carried on in medicaments and ointments, so that the public should not suffer from the unscientific sale of medicaments; and We, the Most Serene and Ruling Great Lord-Zar and Grand Duke Peter Alexejevitch, Autocrat of all the Great, Little and White Russias, etc., etc., hereby confirm having conferred upon the Pharmacist Daniel Gurtschin the charter and commanded him to keep in his Apteka for the sick and suffering healing spirit and vodki and other medical articles, buying the same beyond the seas with his own money, and selling them to all classes of the public at the price according to measure, and after careful examination of the Doctor. If Daniel should need in the making up of his medicaments any Rhine or any other wines, he is to keep such in small quantities for his medicaments only and not for sale in glasses, buckets or casks, and this Rhine or any other wines Daniel is to buy in Archangel or on the Azoff by paying the fixed duties. Any other Russians in the green-grocer and other shops are prohibited to keep or to sell any medicaments, elixirs and oils, and the shops that are situated along the streets of the green-grocer's market, in China Town, White Town and Land Town, from which various classes of people are selling herbs and green stuffs as medicaments, are to be transferred and the owners of those shops are to be exiled. By this present We also command that another 8 Aptekas should be opened in Moscow, and should he, Daniel, not desire for some reason or other to keep his Apteka, but to sell or let it, he can do so by informing the Imperial Chancery. This charter is given to him by the Chancery of Our Zar in the Imperial reigning Capital Moscow, in the 1701st year from our Redeemer Jesus Christ, December 28th, reigning year 81st.

From the Zar's Imperial Chancery,
Sgd. Djak Boris Michailoff.

In 1787 the apothecary's tax, or fixed scale of charges for medicines, was issued. In the reign of Alexander I Russian pharmacy developed more rapidly, inasmuch as a Pharmaceutical Section was then established in connection with the Medico-Surgical Academy. Later on, by order of the Emperor Nicholas I, a university education for managers of apothecary shops was made a compulsory qualification.

THE MONOPOLY GIVEN "PHARMACIES."

From the details set forth below it will clearly be seen why the Russian "pharmacies" have such a monopoly of the pharmaceutical business in that country, and why, in consequence of the peculiar law existing, the so-called "drug stores" are debarred from doing the same kind of business as the "pharmacies."

A pharmacy or "apteka" can be opened and managed in Russia by any one who is a qualified pharmacist, *but* the fol-

[1] From the *Bulletin of Pharmacy* for January, to which we are also indebted for the use of the cuts.

lowing conditions must be observed before the permission to open a pharmacy is given. In St. Petersburg and Moscow a pharmacy can be opened for every 12,000 inhabitants, the number of prescriptions annually for every pharmacy to be not less than 30,000; in all other principal cities of Russia a pharmacy can be opened for every 10,000 inhabitants and 15,000 prescriptions, and in country towns 7,000 inhabitants and 6,000 prescriptions. Taking into consideration the number of inhabitants that are allotted to every pharmacy it is clear why the owners of pharmacies are bound to make large profits.

This management the government finds it necessary to keep up in order to protect the pharmacies from competition and therewith enable them to keep a large store of the best and finest medicaments for the welfare of the public. A Russian pharmacy is allowed to keep and sell every possible existing drug in its pure and mixed state. Foreign ready-made-up medicaments, however, must be allowed by the Government Medical Council to enter the Empire before they can be kept and sold at a pharmacy.

The "drug stores," on the other hand, are permitted to sell only household medicaments, cosmetics, and some ready-made preparations in their original packages. They cannot dispense prescriptions, and there is a list of about a hundred

The Warehouse of Lud. Spiess & Son, Ltd., Warsaw, Manufacturing and Retail Pharmacists.

substances which they cannot sell. This list is too extensive to print, but it contains such articles as:

Vina medicinalia omnia, exceptis vino pepsini et vino chinæ.
Aquæ medicinales, exceptis aqua triplice flor.
Chlorum solutum officinale.
Ferrum carbonicum saccharatum.
Electuaria medicinalia omnia.
Acidum aceticum aromaticum et hydrocyanatum medicinale.
Collodium cantharidatum.
Rhizomata omnia concisa et pulverata omnia, exceptis rhizom. curcumæ pulverato, rhiz. graminis conciso, et rhizom. iridis florentinæ conciso, pulverato et tornato.
Radices omnes concisæ et pulveratæ, exceptis rad. althææ concisa, rad. bardanæ concisa, rad. liquiritiæ concisa, rad. rhei in cabulis, rad. saponariæ concisa, et rad. sarsaparillæ concisa.
Sapo jalapinus.
Suppositoria omnia.
Liquor arsenicalis Fowleri.
Infusa omnia.
Tincturæ omnes.
Pilulæ omnes, exceptis pilulis rhei tornatis.
Antidotum Arsenici.
Sirupi medicinales omnes, exceptis sirupo cerasi, ribis, et rubi idæi.
Aceta: camphoratum, colchici, rubi idæi, scillæ, et digitalis.
Plumbum aceticum solutum.
Cantharides pulveratæ.

SOME UNFORTUNATE CONDITIONS.

With a list of 100 important articles not to be sold in "drug stores," and with the difficulty of having foreign ready-made medicaments enter the country, it is no wonder that the "pharmacists" of Russia have a great monopoly. In spite of this, however, there are very few pharmacists indeed who can boast of having made fortunes. The obtaining of a license for opening a pharmacy is naturally very difficult, on account of the law which prescribes that it can be opened only for every 7,000 to 12,000 inhabitants. The inhabitants in a city do not increase as fast as the number of qualified pharmacists, and therefore the pharmacist who succeeds in getting the license prefers to sell it right out to some one else for a very high amount (50,000 to 100,000 roubles) instead of opening the pharmacy himself. You will seldom find a qualified pharmacist in Russia

Lud. Spiess & Son, Ltd., have three retail pharmacies in different sections of Warsaw. This is one of them, and the others are shown in the next two illustrations.

with such an amount of cash; consequently the money is borrowed, and a high interest is paid for it in the hope that the pharmacy will bring in a good return.

The actual proprietor of the pharmacy is thus in reality not the man who has purchased the license, but the one who has loaned the money; the former works like a slave for the latter, and many, many years pass before he is able to pay off the debt with its high interest. Nowadays, when chemistry, pharmacy, and medicine have far more products than was the case 40 or 50 years ago, a Russian "apteka" that is expected to concoct and mix up all the preparations prescribed by physicians cannot cope with such a task without having large premises, an ample stock of drugs and a large staff of trained pharmacists. This fact our pharmacists lose sight of and blindly pay anything that is demanded for a license. Experience, however, soon shows them that their expenses in keeping up the establishment and paying off the debts with interest are enor-

The Second of the Retail Pharmacies Owned in Warsaw by Lud. Spiess & Son, Ltd.

mous in comparison with the profits, and in consequence they are slowly reaching the end, the beginning of which has already commenced in Russia.

The number of assistants employed in a pharmacy is very small indeed in comparison with the work to be done; the preparations are consequently got up in a hurry, and the exactness of the dose is very doubtful indeed; the quality of the drug leaves much to be desired; the general cleanliness that ought to reign in the pharmacy does not strike one when making a close inspection of things. Keeping up such a system in the "apteka" the proprietor is enabled to cut down expenses; and, to improve his affairs still more, he is constantly pleading before the Medical Council (through the two delegates who represent the pharmacists of Russia at the sittings of the Medical Council) to "shut out" the foreign pharmaceuticals and to wrench from the "drug stores" that bit of limited right which they now possess of selling household and certain other prepared medicaments. The physicians, however, now see that the Russian "apteka" does not answer the present requirements and that the nation is paying far more for a badly prepared medicine in the "apteka" than for a correctly made-up article that hails from an up-to-date laboratory; the young pharmacists working in the "aptekas" are striking for more wages and less work; the "druggists" are expanding their efforts and with every strain of their nerves are proving to the public that they can sell just as good articles as the "pharmacists" and at a far less price; and the Medical Council, consisting of now enlightened men, is only vaguely lending an ear to the monopoly demands of the pharmacists. With this and many other facts the authorities, physicians, and public are now more or less acquainted, and the time is not far distant when the monopoly will be abolished and the pharmaceutical business will be as free as in England, America and France.

THE FAMOUS FERREIN PHARMACY.

Before I finish this article on Russian pharmacy, past and present, let me briefly describe the most famous "apteka" in

The Third of the Retail Pharmacies Owned in Warsaw by Lud. Spiess & Son, Ltd.

the country—the wholesale and retail pharmacy owned by K. I. Ferrein in Moscow. This, indeed, is the largest pharmacy in the world and is not subject to the strictures which have been made against the small "aptekas" in Russia. There are about 200 qualified pharmacists at the "Staro-Nikolskaja Apteka," as this pharmacy is properly called, and not less than half a million prescriptions are dispensed each year. Moscow has 54 other pharmacists, and it is therefore astonishing that such a prescription business is done. The sales in the retail department amount daily to at least $2,000.

The establishment consists of several sections or departments. The analytical department is of the greatest importance in relation to the entire business, inasmuch as it is in this section that the raw materials entering the warehouses of the firm are analyzed to see that their quality is good; and here also are tested the preparations of the chemical laboratory. Besides this, analyses are also made for private persons, of technical products, food stuffs, etc.

In the pharmaceutical department are prepared the so-called galenicals—that is to say, infusions, extracts, plasters, etc. A whole series of distilling retorts are used for preparing spirits, aromatic waters, ethereal oils, etc. In separate rooms, divided off by glass partitions, are prepared the various vegetable oils. Spanish almonds, crushed in a mill with dentated cylinders, are then compressed in a hydraulic press of high pressure for expressing the oil. Then there is the chemical, the cosmetic, the pulverizing and other departments. For the purpose of assisting physicians in making a true diagnosis of disease the histology-bacteriological section of the laboratory examines pathological objects, urine, sputum, etc., and also carries on the pure culture of micro-organisms.

The growing activity of the firm has attracted the attention of the Government, which conferred upon it at the Pan-Russian Exhibition at Nijni-Novgorod the highest award in the form of the right to use the coat of arms of the State.

The firm of Ferrein is now turned into a limited company, the stock of which is held entirely by the members of the family. The company owns the Staro-Nikolskaja Apteka, the laboratory for manufacturing pharmaceutical and chemical products and a immense drug store which is also attached to the pharmacy. Notwithstanding the fact that the laboratory is turning out so many home made products, the firm of Ferrein is still buying enormous quantities of foreign pharmaceuticals and chemicals, which, together with its own wares, it is selling at wholesale and retail to jobbers, pharmacists, druggists and the public direct.

Progress in Porto Rico.

Through the courtesy of G. O'Neil, manager of the Spanish department of Johnson & Johnson, we are enabled to print an illustration of the Farmacia del Carmen, which is the latest addition to the drug stores of Guayama, Porto Rico. Dr. Manuel M. Travieso, the proprietor of this establishment, is one of the best-informed pharmacists on the island. He is young, aggressive and full of new ideas, which he is success-

Farmacia del Carmen of M. Travieso, Calle de Hostos, No. 1, Guayama, Porto Rico.

fully applying to the development of his business. Dr. Travieso has had many years' experience as a clerk in the wholesale establishment of Fidel Guillermety, at San Juan.

Guayama is quite an important city, as it is the headquarters for supplies for a very prosperous territory which surrounds it. Besides several retail stores it contains one wholesale house, that of Julio S. Bruno, who does quite an extensive business. We published an illustration of Mr. Bruno's establishment some years ago.

Hospital Supplies for Syria.

Consul-General Berdnot, of Beirut, Syria, directs the attention of American manufacturers to the fact that Dr. Franklin T. Moore, Syrian Protestant College, Beirut, Syria, desires to enter into correspondence with hardware dealers and makers of hospital supplies with a view to furnishing a women's hospital which is now in course of construction in that city. Dr. Moore will welcome catalogues and price lists of the following articles: Hardware for house furnishing, sterilizing apparatus on large and small scale, elevator, furniture, instruments and operating room appliances, bath tubs, etc.

New Regulations for the Practice of Pharmacy in Argentina.

United States Minister Beaupre has advised the Department of State of the United States that the Argentine Government on September 14 adopted a law regulating the practice of pharmacy within that country. The text of the law follows:

Article 1. After the promulgation of this law only those pharmacists may establish new pharmacies who possess a diploma authorized or revalidated by the National University, and they shall have the effective and personal direction of the same.

Art. 2. For the purpose of the preceding article there shall be considered as the establishment of a new pharmacy every modification in the firm or partnership, as well as the reopening of any pharmacy that may have remained closed for more than thirty days.

Art. 3. The maximum period of four years shall be accorded for the actually existing pharmacies to place themselves within the provisions of the first article.

Art. 4. The qualified pharmacists who may be proprietors of pharmacies before the fifteenth of July of one thousand nine hundred and five, that have passed in the capacity of qualified pharmacists for three consecutive years immediately previous to that date, are qualified to matriculate in the courses in pharmacy of the national universities.

Art. 5. In the case of the death of a pharmacist only his widow or his minor sons shall be allowed to keep open the pharmacy until the termination of the four years, the pharmacy to be directed during this period by a pharmacist.

Art. 6. The pharmacist shall in every case be personally responsible for the purity and legitimacy of the products that he dispenses or that he employs in making his preparations, of whatever origin they may be.

Art. 7. Those who infringe this law and the regulation of the same that may be decreed shall be subject to a fine of one hundred to a thousand pesos, the closing of their establishment, and the suspension from and disqualification for the practice of their profession, according to the gravity and circumstances of the case.

Art. 8. The penalties shall be imposed by the National Department of Hygiene, it being permitted to appeal from its decision within five days to the respective criminal or titular judge.

The sentence shall be executed by the corresponding tribunals.

Art. 9. The Executive, with the intervention of the National Department of Hygiene, shall regulate this law, establishing everything that refers to the conducting of pharmacies, to the preparation and dispensing of drugs, serums, vaccines, and other curative, preventive, or diagnostic agents, decreeing all the measures tending to safeguard the morale of the profession and the public health.

Hints to Buyers.

A special 5 per cent. discount will be given by any wholesale druggist on purchases of Antiphlogistine amounting to $24. This excellent product may be had in four sizes, known as "small," "medium," "large" and "hospital."

The Marvel Syringe is advertised to the trade by the manufacturers in this issue. Of all the syringes of the kind this has proved the most satisfactory to both physician and patient. It is something which the pharmacist is fully warranted in recommending to his customers.

When ordering ointment boxes the purchaser should specify "Mt. Washington," in order to obtain the best article of the kind made in America. The line comprises all sizes, from ¼ ounce to 16 ounce, and is made in black walnut and in silver poplar. Every wholesale druggist carries the line in stock.

Ammonol in powdered and in tablet form and in combination with other drugs is advertised in this issue by the Ammonol Chemical Company, of New York. This stimulant, analgesic, antipyretic product is particularly in demand at this season of the year, when grippe and other kindred ailments are rife.

Uricedin Strochein, the well-known German laxative salt which has done good work as a uric acid solvent, is supplied to the American trade by the Fischer Chemical Importing Company, of 14 Platt street, New York. This concern also imports a line of German chemicals, upon which they have interesting and instructive literature, which will be supplied to the trade upon application.

There is quick money in illustrated post cards if they are bought right and properly displayed. Four special offers are made to the drug trade by Joseph Koehler, department A, 150 Park Row, New York City. Write him for details of these offers. They afford a liberal margin of profit and assurance of quick sales.

C. Le Roy Parker, for five years examiner in the Division of Chemicals and Medicine of the Patent Office, is now junior member of the law firm of Shepherd & Parker, of Washington, D. C., having charge of all matters relating to patents and trademarks on drugs and chemicals. This firm is particularly well fitted to undertake patent and copyright cases involving drugs, chemicals, proprietary medicines, etc.

The advertisement of H. P. Eysenbach on Cresol, found in another column of this issue of the AMERICAN DRUGGIST, should be liberally answered. It is in line with progress and the Pharmacopoeia, and those who have formerly taken advantage of his proposition are more than ordinarily pleased. For full particulars address H. P. Eysenbach, 1251 North Forty-fourth avenue, Chicago.

Syringe boxes of white wood, bass, oak, ash, etc., can be had of the Henry H. Sheip Mfg. Company, of 529 Columbia avenue, Philadelphia. This concern also manufactures all kinds of fancy wood boxes, and its extensive facilities and long experience enable it to turn out first-class goods promptly and at the lowest market prices. Purchasers should obtain samples and estimates from this old and reliable concern before placing orders.

The sale of Sal Hepatica has reached large proportions in the United States owing to the fact that it possesses a combination of tonic, alterative and laxative qualities and is very similar in composition to the celebrated bitter waters of Bohemia, with the addition of lithium and sodium phosphates. It is sold at $2, $4.80 and $10.20 per dozen, according to size, and is carried in stock by all wholesale druggists. The advertisement of the manufacturer, Bristol-Myers Company, of 277 Greene avenue, Brooklyn, will be found in this issue.

The Manufacturing Chemists' Registration Bureau.

The following title has been received for registration by the Manufacturing Chemists' Registration Bureau: Glaseptic Nebulizer, Parke, Davis & Co., Detroit, Mich.

The Quick Sales Route.

The Detroit Show Case Company, 476 West Fort street, Detroit, have in their "Quick Sales" show case one of the most attractive means of displaying goods. Only the finest materials are used in the manufacture of these cases, and the highest degree of mechanical skill and artistic ability is combined in their production. Write the makers for descriptions and prices, mentioning the AMERICAN DRUGGIST.

Armour's Soluble Beef.

A more than satisfactory food for invalids and convalescents who are not able to digest the ordinary food preparations may be found in Armour's Soluble Beef, which is sold exclusively to the drug trade and which meets all requirements of the pure food laws of all States. This preparation may also be used for any purpose for which beef extract is employed. It is wholly free from preservatives of any kind and contains as high as 54 per cent. proteids. The article may be recommended by all druggists as a concentrated form of all nourishing, stimulating and appetizing properties of beef.

National College of Pharmacy to Become a Department of University.

The National College of Pharmacy, of Washington, was incorporated February 13. The college is to affiliate with George Washington University, and the incorporation is under the act of Congress amending the charter of the university. The incorporators are Charles W. Needham, G. G. C. Simms, Samuel L. Hilton, Frank C. Henry, Henry E. Kalusowski, Frank P. Weller, Samuel Waggaman, Walter G. Duckett, W. H. Bradbury, Charles B. Campbell, Herbert C. Easterday, Lewis Flemer and Willard S. Richardson.

AMERICAN DRUGGIST
and PHARMACEUTICAL RECORD

PHILADELPHIA. NEW YORK, MARCH 26, 1906. CHICAGO

ISSUED SEMI-MONTHLY BY

AMERICAN DRUGGIST PUBLISHING CO.,

62-68 West Broadway, New York.

CHICAGO, 221 Randolph St. PHILADELPHIA, 3718 Walnut St.

A. R. ELLIOTT, President.

CASWELL A. MAYO, Ph.G. .... Editor.
THOMAS J. KEENAN .... Associate Editor.

ROMAINE PIERSON .... Manager Chicago Office.

$1.50 a year. 15 cents a copy.

ADVERTISING RATES QUOTED ON APPLICATION.

The American Druggist and Pharmaceutical Record is issued on the second and fourth Mondays of each month. Changes of advertisements should be received ten days in advance of the date of publication.

Remittances should be made by New York exchange, post office or express money order or registered mail. If checks on local banks are used 10 cents should be added to cover cost of collection. The publishers are not responsible for money sent by unregistered mail, nor for any money paid except to duly authorised agents. All communications should be addressed and all remittances made payable to American Druggist Publishing Co., 62-68 West Broadway, New York.

Entered at New York as Second-Class Matter.

TABLE OF CONTENTS.

EDITORIAL COMMENT.

A Newspaper Retraction. A remarkable demonstration of the power of organization has been made by the druggists of Chicago in compelling a local newspaper to make amends for the publication of a cartoon which was regarded as defamatory and insulting. The cartoon is reproduced elsewhere and requires no elaboration on our part. We have not space for the reproduction of the second cartoon, which was printed as an apology for the first, but in it the artist succeeds in portraying some of the trying experiences of the druggist in meeting the exacting demands of customers. An entire page is occupied with reading matter, in which the impositions practiced on the druggist are very fully set forth. The exactions of the stamp customer and of directory and telephone patrons are told in anecdote and illustration under a title extending the entire width of the page and reading: What Would You Do Without the Druggist? The Chicago Retail Druggists' Association continues to give evidence of its active usefulness to the trade which it so ably represents and offers a splendid example for other associations similarly situated.

A Startling Decision. The decision handed down by Judge Macfarlane, of Pittsburgh, in the case of the Dr. Miles Medical Company *vs.* the May Drug Company of Pittsburgh is nothing short of startling, and it does not seem possible that the verdict will be sustained by the higher courts. The plaintiff sought to restrain the defendant from selling the Miles remedies at cut prices, it being asserted that the party from whom the May Drug Company had obtained its supplies had violated its contract. In defense it was urged that the contract was in restraint of trade. This latter contention was brushed aside by the judge, who refused relief to the plaintiff for other reasons, giving utterance to the dictum that the plaintiff had no standing in a court of equity because the business of the plaintiff was "contrary to public policy," inasmuch as the advertisements of the complaining firm contained false statements. This the judge deemed a bar to action on the plaintiff's part. Judge Macfarlane added that "the public health required protection against these preparations ('patent medicines') and that the vender of remedies of unknown ingredients, advertised and sold as remedies for disease, should not be aided by courts of equity." The State of Pennsylvania has been noted in the past for the acumen of its lawyers, and the phrase "it would puzzle a Philadelphia lawyer" is a traditional compliment to the learning of the Quaker City jurists, but a new apothegm will have to be invented to describe the magisterial mind if decisions of the character of that handed down by Judge Macfarlane should become common.

The Pure Food Bill.

The Pure Food bill was referred to the Committee of the House on Interstate and Foreign Commerce on February 22 and was reported out of the committee on March 7 with amendments and committed to the Committee of the Whole House. In its present form this bill embraces the main features of the Senate bill passed on February 21, and it seems probable that the measure will be enacted in substantially the form in which it now stands.

The two essential features in which this measure differs from the Hepburn bill, passed in the previous session of Congress, are the amplification of the term "drug" and the requirement for specification under the heading of misbranding of alcohol, opium and cocaine and other "poisonous substances" on the label.

The measure was discussed at some length in our issue of March 12, page 123. Those features of the law which affect the drug business were printed in the form in which the measure passed the Senate in our issue for February 26, on page 105. None of these have been materially modified in the House measure.

Section 5 of the bill in its present form declares

that the term "drug" as used in this act shall include all medicines and preparations recognized in the United States Pharmacopœia or National Formulary for internal or external use and any substance or mixture of substances intended to be used for the cure, mitigation or prevention of disease of either man or other animals.

In the measures which have been previously proposed the term "drug" was specifically limited to medicines and preparations recognized in the United States Pharmacopœia or National Formulary. Some four years ago, however, a small coterie of men interested in proprietary goods appeared before the Senate and secured the addition of the blanket clause, extending the term so as to include "any substance or mixture of substances intended to be used for the cure, mitigation or prevention of disease of either man or animals."

It is a rather singular turn of fate that since the amplification of this particular clause in the act other clauses have been introduced which make the act quite as objectionable to proprietary medicine dealers as does this clause to the retail druggist. This amplification was made apparently so as to give the proprietor a weapon with which to castigate any one marketing imitations or substitutes and without any consideration of the infinite complications and annoyances to the retail trade which the enforcement of such a law might result in.

The National Wholesale Druggists' Association has put itself on record several times as being opposed to this expanded definition and, it is understood, will vigorously urge a change in this section.

Section 7 states that the term "misbranded" shall be deemed to apply to

all drugs the package or label of which shall bear any statement regarding the ingredients or substances contained in said article, which statement shall be false or misleading in any particular and to any food or drug product which is falsely branded as to the State, Territory or country in which it is manufactured or produced.

In the case of drugs it is also provided that they shall be deemed misbranded—

First, if it be an imitation of or offered for sale under the name of another article. Second, if the contents of the original package shall have been removed, in whole or in part, and other contents shall have been placed in such package, or if it fail to bear a statement on the label of the quantity or proportion of any alcohol therein or of any opium, cocaine or other poisonous substances which may be contained therein.

The representatives of the drug trade interests who are in Washington propose to substitute for the second clause the following words:

Second, if the contents of the original package shall have been removed, in whole or in part, and other contents shall have been placed in such package, or if it fail to bear a statement on the label of the quantity of alcohol therein, where such quantity is in excess of the amount shown to be necessary by the United States Pharmacopœia or the National Formulary as a solvent or preservative of the active constituents of the drugs contained therein and to prevent deterioration by freezing or fermentation; or if it fail to bear a statement on the label of the quantity of any opium, morphine, heroine, cocaine, alpha or beta eucaine or chloral hydrate contained therein; provided that the package contains more than 2 gr. of opium or more than ¼ gr. of morphine, or more than 1-16 gr. of heroine, or more than 1-16 gr. of cocaine, or not more than 1-16 gr. of alpha or beta eucaine, or more than 8 gr. of chloral hydrate in 1 fluid oz., or, if a solid preparation, in 1 avoirdupois oz.

A serious objection which is raised to the second clause of Section 7 is that the presence of a relatively high proportion of alcohol is necessary to preserve any vegetable solution. For instance, no less than 15 per cent. of alcohol is required to satisfactorily preserve so simple a preparation as distilled extract of witch hazel. Hence the proposal on the part of the drug interests to modify this feature of the bill.

The specification in a general way of "other poisonous substance" is so vague that it would be impossible for any manufacturer or dealer to be sure that he was complying with the law. No definition has yet been devised for the term "poisonous substance," which is not open to some criticism and concerning which there is not some different opinion. So far as the members of the drug trade are concerned their efforts will be concentrated on the modification of these two particular clauses in the measure, and there seems to be a reasonable hope that these objectionable clauses will be modified so as not to work a hardship on the trade.

THE INCREASING POPULARITY OF SODA WATER.

In this issue we print a number of valuable contributions on the manufacture of soda fountain syrups, together with hints and suggestions for the serving of fountain beverages, which will repay perusal.

The glittering paraphernalia which decorates the soda counter has come to be regarded by the public as characteristic of the drug store as those more homely insignia of the craft, the mortar and pestle. From the metropolitan fountain of translucent onyx and glittering silver with its accompanying electric fans and beveled-edged mirrors, its white coated knowing and natty attendants and its thousand and one glasses of soda a day to the humble "goose-neck," which, on a lucky day, may be called upon perhaps a score of times, every soda fountain in an American drug store is there as the legitimate outcome of normal trade conditions and, if properly managed, serves a proper purpose.

While it is true that there are a few pharmacies in which the soda fountain has never found a place and where its presence would perhaps work injury instead of benefit, the fact remains that in a majority of instances the introduction of the fountain has not detracted the slightest from the esteem in which the well conducted pharmacy is held by the more scientific and ethical physicians. When properly conducted the sale of soda water is not at all incompatible with the higher pharmacy, and if we read the signs of the times aright, the tendency is in the direction of a more general introduction of soda fountains of ornate and expensive design in those pharmacies from which they have been heretofore excluded. There is room, of course, in every large city for at least one ultra scientific pharmacy modeled somewhat on the German plan, but to make such an establishment a success requires a somewhat rare combination of scientific ability and business acumen.

It is difficult to give any reasonably accurate estimate of the amount of soda water sold in the United States, but it is certainly enormous and the consumption is growing with startling rapidity. In New York a dozen or more pharmacies dispense from 500 to 10,000 glasses of soda water a day during the hot season, and even in cold weather from two to six attendants are kept busy dispensing the many forms of temperance drinks which are sold over the soda counter under the generic name of fountain beverages.

As a minor contribution to the subject it may be remarked that in figuring out the number of glasses of soda water sold at a downtown fountain in New York the gross number of glasses, about 8,000 daily, seemed so large in proportion to the number of draught arms on the fountain, that the suspicion arose that an error had been made. This suspicion was dissipated after a careful count of the number of glasses which one dispenser could hand out in a given period of time. The dispenser was observed without his knowledge and it was found that he would frequently dispense the drinks at the rate of ten glasses a minute. What the soda dispenser might be able to do when working against time it is difficult to say, but we are curious to know, and gladly offer a prize of $5 for the best authenticated record made by any soda water dispenser in the United States during the season of 1906. We should suggest that a record be kept and properly authenticated, of the largest number of glasses of soda water actually dispensed in 15 minutes, the winner of the prize to hold the championship.

NEW PHARMACEUTICAL SOURCES OF OXYGEN.[1]

By Richard von Foregger, Ph. D.

When we speak of oxygen in a medical sense we usually think of the gas compressed in cylinders as used for inhalation purposes. It is only of late that we have begun to hear of pharmaceutical preparations of oxygen in powder form, the characteristic feature of which is the liberation of active oxygen at the point of contact with moisture. We give little consideration to the oxidation processes occurring in various reactions, with substances such as possess no easily liberated oxygen. In referring, for instance, to a chlorine bleach or bleach powder it seldoms occurs to us that the bleaching effect of the material is produced by indirect oxidation; so in considering the purifying and disinfecting properties of formaldehyde it seldom occurs to us that these effects are due to a secondary process of oxidation. Nor do we consider, when speaking of the preservative properties of benzoic acid, that the sterilization produced by this chemical is also due to a secondary autooxidation, though such assertions have been made recently by scientists who have demonstrated the phenomenon both in theory and practice.

SOURCES OF VITAL ENERGY.

It is known, for example, that the intramolecular respiration of cells is due to the action of two enzymes called, respectively, oxydase and peroxydase, the function of these enzymes being connected with the abstraction of active oxygen from water and air. The processes of oxidation occurring in this way lead to the formation of organic matter and are thus sources of vital energy. These secondary processes of autooxidation are believed to be due to the presence of inorganic constituents of alkaline reaction and explain in a measure the rôle played by sodium, magnesium and calcium in the building up of the hæmoglobin of blood and the chlorophyl of plants as well as of nearly all living tissue.

WHY USE SECONDARY OXIDIZERS.

These facts are fundamental and are mentioned because I consider it necessary that the subject I bring before you should be "grabbed by its roots." If by means of a peroxide or a perborate a direct bleaching effect can be secured, why should a chlorine product with its corrosive action be used, which bleaches by a secondary oxidation? The same applies to disinfection by formaldehyde. If the disinfecting action is caused by a secondary oxidation, why should not oxygen be used in its proper form?

Direct oxidation is possible by the use of such compounds as the peroxides of magnesium, calcium, strontium and zinc, and with the perborates of sodium, zinc, calcium and magnesium, not to speak of the latest product—fused sodium peroxide, which has been introduced under the trade name of oxone.

These products resemble each other in that they all possess a certain percentage of available oxygen, which is easily liberated by appropriate treatment, their only points of difference consisting in their solubility in water and the character of the alkali radical. It is important to bear these distinctions in mind if use is to be made of the preparations.

PERBORATES AND PEROXIDES.

Sodium perborate, for example, is easily soluble in water and gives up its oxygen readily in the process. Other perborates and peroxides are not so soluble in water, but readily yield up their content of oxygen on being brought into contact with water. Strontium peroxide and the alkali perborates belong to the last-named class. Another group, the members of which do not dissolve in water and which do not give off their available oxygen at ordinary temperatures, but which are readily soluble in diluted acids, are the peroxides of magnesium, calcium and zinc.

It is important to know what takes place when a peroxide or perborate passes into solution in water and is decomposed. It is generally understood that when a peroxide is dissolved in aqueous or weak acid solutions, hydrogen dioxide is formed, which is true, but we should err in regarding the formation of H_2O_2 as the basis for calculating the various reactions which occur with the use of the peroxides. It has been shown by various authors, among them Boujean (American Druggist, May, 1905), that hydrogen dioxide produced by the decomposition of calcium peroxide is much more efficient than an equal quantity of *Aqua hydrogenii dioxidi*. It is evident that active oxygen is produced by the decomposition of the peroxide in aqueous or weak acid solutions, and if organic substances are present this active oxygen unites with them, and if no organic substance is present the oxygen unites with the water to form hydrogen dioxide.

[1] Read before the Kings County Pharmaceutical Society at the regular monthly meeting, March 13, 1906.

REACTION WITH MAGNESIUM PEROXIDE.

The reaction which takes place when magnesium peroxide is dissolved in water acidulated with citric acid may be used as an illustration:

$2C_6H_5O_7H_3 + 3MgO_2 = (C_6H_5O_7)2Mg_3 + H_2O + 3O$ and $3O + 2H_2O = 2H_2O_2$. Such a mixture of magnesium peroxide and citric acid applied to the sterilisation of drinking water probably acts by the three atoms of active oxygen attacking the bacteria at the moment of liberation to oxidize them and producing carbon dioxide as a final product; the oxygen would not start to combine with the water until after the destruction of the bacteria, hydrogen dioxide being the end product. It would not be correct to assume that free oxygen is evolved during the solution of a peroxide or a perborate, for the peroxide oxygen is probably all absorbed in the reaction.

REACTION WITH SODIUM PERBORATE.

The reaction which takes place when sodium perborate is dissolved in water may be stated thus:

$$NaBO_3 + H_2O = NaBO_2 + H_2O_2 \text{ and } 4NaBO_2 + CO_2 = Na_2B_4O_7 + Na_2B_4O_7 + Na_2CO_3.$$

Sodium metaborate is probably formed first, and the unstable nature of this salt is well known. In contact with the carbon dioxide contained in the water it is transformed into borax and sodium carbonate. It is evident therefore that in a solution of sodium perborate hydrogen peroxide is formed on one side and an alkaline borax on the other. The first reaction is instantaneous and affords an ideal means for the production of solutions of hydrogen dioxide at the time and place of consumption.

CHARACTERISTICS OF SODIUM PERBORATE.

Sodium perborate is soluble in water at the ordinary temperature to the extent of 26 Gm. per liter, while in water heated to a temperature of 30 degrees C. twice the amount, or 50 Gm., will dissolve, which means that up to 5 per cent. solutions of this chemical are possible without the aid of acids, corresponding to 3.5 per cent. solutions of hydrogen dioxide. With the aid of acids solutions of much higher concentrations, or up to 50 volumes, can be obtained. Such solutions are of scientific interest only, as such strong solutions are not required either for bleaching or disinfecting purposes. On account of the slight alkalinity of sodium perborate solutions of this chemical would seem to be more effective than ordinary solutions of hydrogen dioxide.

The following table indicates the amounts of sodium perborate which pass into solution under the application of different temperatures and varying amounts of acids:

Acid (citric or tartaric). 75 c.c.	Temp. of water. (400 c.c.)	Gm. per lt. of solution. Grains.	Solution. Per ct.	Available. oxygen.	Vols. H_2O_2 sol.
————	Ord. temp.	15	1.5	1,050 c.c.	1
————	Ord. temp.	20	2	1,400 c.c.	1.4
————	80° F.	30	3	2,100 c.c.	2
————	95° F.	40	4	2,800 c.c.	3
————	105° F.	50	5	3,500 c.c.	3.5
10 grains	Ord. temp.	60	6	4,200 c.c.	4
25 grains	Ord. temp.	70	7	4,900 c.c.	5
38 grains	Ord. temp.	100	10	7,000 c.c.	7
55 grains	Ord. temp.	140	14	9,800 c.c.	10
140 grains	95° F.	360	36	25 lt.	25
H_2SO_4 66°	Cold.	430	43	30 lt.	30.35
————	Ord. temp.	10	1	700 c.c.	0.7

Between the two groups just mentioned, one of which is soluble and the other insoluble in water, is a third group "partly soluble in water." It is understood, of course, that the expression "solubility" is not quite appropriate from a strictly scientific standpoint, as what takes place in reality is molecular dissociation, in which the greater portion of the base remains undissolved, liberating, however, 1 part of its available oxygen, which is absorbed by the water to form H_2O_2.

YIELD OF OXYGEN FROM MAGNESIUM PERBORATE.

Magnesium and calcium perborate as well as strontium peroxide are included in this group. When magnesium perborate, containing about 10 per cent. available oxygen, is suspended for five minutes in water at a temperature of 20 degrees C. 40 per cent. of its available oxygen passes into solution. With calcium perborate, containing 11 per cent. available oxygen, 80 per cent. of the total available oxygen goes into solution under similar conditions. Strontium peroxide, with about 11 per cent. available oxygen gives up 80 per cent. of oxygen at a temperature of 20 degrees C.

This distinguishing property of certain peroxides and perborates of readily parting with their available oxygen is of great importance, especially when it is taken into account that the reaction differs with the method of application, whether internal or external, the reaction being dependent on the alkalinity or acidity of the body fluids. It is well to bear in mind that the alkali bases of the peroxides and perborates are nontoxic and nonirritating; while some of these products are only adapted for external use others find more suitable employment as internal medicaments. Time and space do not permit of mentioning the entire list of peroxide bodies, so I will make a selection of some characteristic products and comment on their pharmaceutical application.

THE MOST APPROPRIATE FOR INTERNAL USE.

Magnesium peroxide is regarded as the most appropriate for internal use, being considered the most efficient of all as an intestinal disinfectant, and the bactericidal effect of a mixture of magnesium peroxide and citric acid are very pronounced, a 5-grain tablet of such mixture having been found amply sufficient to sterilise a glassful of typhoid contaminated drinking water within the time of its solution, amounting to about one minute. Effervescent magnesium oxycitrate tablets would be a novelty which would take with the medical profession, and the idea is commended to the members of this society. An oxygenated magnesium citrate solution would perhaps appeal more strongly to physicians, since Dr. Wm. H. Park, director of the New York Board of Health Research Laboratory, has established the pronounced bactericidal effect of a compound of magnesium peroxide and citric acid.

THE PREPARATION FOR EXTERNAL USE.

For external use zinc peroxide is most available and of chiefest importance. In this salt we have a highly antiseptic and nonirritating, odorless compound, which, in addition to the well-known soothing properties of zinc oxide, possesses the germicidal properties of active oxygen. Under the name "dermogen" it has been already introduced in the American market as a pure powder, with a peroxide content averaging about 40 per cent. In its concentrated form it is wasteful, and a dusting powder composed of some neutral substance like talcum, or starch, with 20 per cent. of a 55 to 60 per cent. zinc peroxide, would perhaps be more feasible. As compared with hydrogen dioxide, 10 Gm. of zinc dioxide solution would contain 0.821 Gm. of available oxygen, whereas 10 Gm. of a 3 per cent. hydrogen dioxide solution would contain only 0.14 Gm. available oxygen. Zinc peroxide in any case is superior to hydrogen peroxide as a dressing for wounds, since it does not part with its oxygen so readily and is not reduced to water containing irritating if not toxic acids. In addition to its value as a disinfectant, zinc peroxide possesses efficient bleaching and deodorizing properties. The skin secretion being mostly butyric acid, zinc peroxide in contact with this forms zinc butyrate, at the same time liberating free oxygen. A face cream compounded of petrolatum and zinc peroxide exerts a considerable bleaching effect on the skin after a few applications. Mineral fats only should be used in combination with the peroxide, because vegetable fat would react with the oxygen, and the zinc peroxide should not exceed 15 per cent. of the whole where the cream is intended for cosmetic purposes.

USE IN FOOT POWDERS.

In regard to foot powders where the correction of excessive perspiration accompanied by a fetid odor is aimed at zinc peroxide answers admirably. Most of the popular foot powders are nothing but absorbents, and, after being abundantly applied, act as little more than irritating pastes, whereas zinc peroxide exerts a curative action through the liberation of active oxygen within the tissues, restoring them to a healthy condition.

As a skin bleach a combination of zinc peroxide and tannic acid is popular in Europe. The effect upon the skin is said to be very agreeable, inducing the desired change of tint after a few days.

FOR EXTEMPORANEOUS PREPARATION OF H_2O_2.

For the production of solutions of hydrogen dioxide, sodium perborate deserves special attention. Solutions of sodium perborate are quickly made and yield a liquid of an alkaline reaction, the product being harmless and nonirritating. It is frequently prescribed as a nasal douche in the treatment of hay fever and colds and as a gargle for sore throats, a knifepointful of the powder being dissolved in a glassful of lukewarm water. A somewhat stronger solution is applicable for use as a lotion and antiseptic wash for wounds and ulcers. Wounds washed with a solution of sodium perborate and dusted afterward with a zinc peroxide dusting powder would be found to heal satisfactorily. In an article entitled Oxygen Toilet Preparations, printed in the AMERICAN DRUGGIST for August 12, I have given formulas for various preparations of sodium perborate.

FOR TOOTH POWDERS.

A very useful peroxide compound is strontium peroxide, the merits of which are almost unknown to pharmacists, as compared with the other peroxides. Although strontium peroxide is only partially soluble in water, it has the advantage of liberating its oxygen without contact with acids, and I consider this property of great importance in the preparation of tooth powders. There is no doubt but that the addition of an oxygen compound to a tooth powder increases its value considerably, because complete disinfection of the oral cavity is obtained, the teeth being bleached at the same time. It is well known that the buccal secretions are frequently of alkaline reaction, especially in the morning, and the advantage of a peroxide which does not require the interposition of an acid will be apparent.

In these days of stringent pure food and drug laws it is important to avoid the use of substances in cosmetics, face creams, etc., which necessitate the use of the red sign of the skull and crossbones on the label. Corrosive sublimate has been used heretofore as a bleaching agent, but there is nothing that corrosive sublimate will do which zinc peroxide will not do and do better. Zinc peroxide exerts a lasting bleaching and purifying effect, leading to a healthy condition of the skin.

AS A PRESERVATIVE FOR FRUIT SYRUPS.

For the reasons just stated magnesium peroxide should appeal to druggists as an admirable preservative for fruit syrups, displacing salicylic or benzoic acid. Despite all that Dr. R. G. Eccles says in his pamphlet on *Food Preservatives, Their Advantages and Proper Use*, such preservatives are doomed, and his publication is, in my opinion, nothing but the swan song of these cumulative food poisons.

FOR THE EXTEMPORANEOUS PREPARATION OF OXYGEN GAS.

Having referred in rather an abstract way to the application of peroxide compounds, I am fortunate to be able to demonstrate some of the applications of oxygen in a concrete form. I would now call your attention to an interesting preparation called oxone, which is a fused sodium peroxide. The preparations previously mentioned yield active or atomic oxygen in contact with water, either plain or acidulated, but oxone yields molecular oxygen in the form of a gas upon mere contact with water, acting very similarly to calcium carbide, which, upon being immersed in water, yields acetylene gas. Oxygen gas, produced by bringing oxone in contact with water, may be said to be 100 per cent. pure, the average figures being 99.4 per cent. at the outlet of generation, and about 99.7 per cent. after being passed through a wash bottle.

It must be evident to you that a product which furnishes pure oxygen in so simple a manner must be of the greatest utility in therapeutics, where the use of compressed oxygen in heavy cylinders is often cumbersome, if not altogether impracticable. For the extemporaneous preparation of oxygen I have constructed a small portable generator, weighing something between four and five pounds, which when filled with water, after exposing one or two cartridges of oxone, yields about 27 liters of gas per cartridge, the average dose for inhalation.

[Doctor von Foregger here exhibited his apparatus and demonstrated the generation of oxygen from oxone in the usual manner, making lighted cigars glow and otherwise showing the passage of the gas.]

PHARMACEUTICAL FLAVORS AND THEIR USES.[1]

By Wilbur H. Scoville, Ph. G.

Boston, Mass.

We American druggists are prone to boast that we are ahead of the world in the art of pharmacy. It may be true, but I fear that there is a tendency among us to forget many of the small points which help to make the art as well as the science of pharmacy successful. The establishment within recent years of numerous colleges of pharmacy in all sections of this country has undoubtedly assisted materially in raising the standard of the science of pharmacy, but perhaps we have forgotten to pay enough attention to the art, and as it is the art which pays best in the commercial end of the business it is worth while to look into this branch of pharmacy a little more closely. Science is described as a development of truth, but art is the practical application of science or the application of science to a practical end.

THE PROPER USE OF FLAVORS.

In discussing the benefits of practicing the art as well as the science of pharmacy, however, I shall limit my remarks to the proper use of flavors purely from a pharmaceutical point of view. I realize that I myself am only an amateur in the study of proper flavoring, but I have learned from past experience that it is the privilege of an amateur to arouse interest in others, as well as that of an expert.

Now, if you wish to make your own private preparations good sellers, why not begin by making them appear better and taste better? The better they taste and appear the more urgent will be the demand for them. From a commercial viewpoint you can afford to neglect, to some degree, the medicinal and therapeutic effect if you can make your preparations more palatable. The users of your preparations will call for them more frequently because they taste well and look well rather than because they contain the most efficient drugs. Perhaps you never thought of it in this way before, but it is generally true that some flavoring ought to go into all the medicinal preparations which you compound. You might think, for example, that there would be little effect resulting from the use of different flavors in preparing aromatic elixir, but I can show you no less than 30 different effects in 30 different preparations of aromatic elixir, all of them the result of the use of different flavors in varying proportions. Each manipulator makes a little modification in the taste of the finished elixir. Some of the preparations deserve approbation, but others condemnation. In other words, the art of flavoring shows individuality. In these elixirs before me (Professor Scoville pointed to 30 bottles on the table in front of him) some show individuality, but some of them also show carelessness. It is not only necessary to follow the formulas of the Pharmacopœia, it is also necessary to use the best quality of materials, and extra pharmacopœially to use proper flavoring—that is, flavoring most suited to the drugs used. Proper flavoring will make a lot of difference in the taste of the preparation. Stores which are careless about this subject are not likely to be as successful as those which pay attention to these details. The public says of a medicinal preparation: "If it tastes good it must be better than the preparation which tastes disagreeable." Now, knowing that this is the way the consumer regards your preparations, you should take pains in selecting proper flavors.

THE PURPOSE OF FLAVORING.

The purpose of flavoring is to blend the drugs and the flavor, or to render the drugs palatable. It is not the purpose of flavoring to conceal the drug. If you will consider for a moment the composition of a mixture of quinine, sulphuric acid, licorice and water, you will notice that the acid intensifies the taste of the quinine and neutralizes the effect of the licorice. If a preparation contains quinine it must necessarily be bitter. You cannot hope to eliminate wholly this bitter taste. You may modify it, but you cannot expect to get rid of it entirely. Therefore, as a general principle let me assert positively, that *it is better art not to cover up a disagreeable drug but to get it to blend with the flavor used.* If we have in front of us food which does not possess a good flavor, we try to dress it up with something pungent. We try, in other words, to make it agreeable. A chef always wins a good reputation by doing this very thing, why shouldn't the druggist?

In flavoring, moreover, you must first discover whether any one flavor will do the work required of it. A single substance will rarely or never give the best result. In fact, I don't know of a single oil which has a true flavor, all of itself. Even oil of almond hasn't a true almond flavor. It needs another element to make it more apparent. It needs a fixer to hold it. We have many examples of artistic preparations in the Pharmacopœia, but we have become so familiar with them that we do not realize why they are so popular—why they are so artistic. Yet if you will examine them you will see that they have been properly flavored. For example, take the confection of senna. This is an old preparation—so old that it has fallen out of general use. If it were called "Fig Paste," and put up in attractive boxes and packages it would have a wide use. In this preparation we have two drugs—senna and cassia fistula. Now notice how the Pharmacopœia renders the mixture palatable. It uses as a flavoring the fig and the prune. The drug flavor blends with these fruits. The fruits intensify the entire flavor and, to fix that flavor, a little oil of coriander is then used. It must be borne in mind, however, that it is difficult to select a proper fruit flavor in a medicine. A delicate fruit flavor needs something to stimulate the nerves of the mouth and to develop the flavor. At the soda fountain the fruit flavor tastes well because the gas gives it pungency and the cold also helps, but in drugs you cannot get an agreeable effect that way. If, however, you use a little oil of coriander, this will take the place in the orange or lemon oil flavoring of the cold and pungency in the soda water, making it more pleasant to the taste.

WINE TO BRING OUT LEMON AND OIL FLAVORS.

No flavoring varies more widely than do orange and lemon oils. You can't make a chemical examination of all the oils you use, but you can make an examination as to their freshness. For myself, I prefer to use the tincture of fresh orange and lemon peel, but others may find some other way of procuring the pure oils. Even when you have a pure oil, however, you find that the taste is not that of the fresh orange or lemon. But if you will use a little wine, say about one-eighth wine, the wine is not noticeable, when it has been allowed to mellow, while the fruit taste becomes more pronounced and pleasant. Muscatel, Catawba and light white wines will serve this purpose excellently. Any good domestic or commercial wine is equally good. Port wine may also be used if you are willing to have a red color in the mixture. Sweet white wine, however, is the most desirable. Brandy or rum, in great moderation, may also be used to good effect in place of a portion of alcohol. It must be remembered, though, that the wines and liquors must be used in great moderation. While one-eighth of wine doesn't show, a trifle more than this will make the preparation vinous in taste.

FLAVORS FOR ACID MIXTURES.

In acid mixtures the acids naturally predominate. A fruity flavor, such as an orange flavor, blends with a wide variety of acid substances. When brandy is used as a fixer it must be used sparingly or else you will have a brandy flavor. If you use wine flavor in moderation, however, you will notice in tasting the mixture not wine but only the intensified fruit flavor. In the past, acetic ether has been used for the purpose of supply-

[1] An address delivered before the Manhattan Pharmaceutical Association at the regular monthly meeting, March 19, and reported exclusively for the AMERICAN DRUGGIST.

ing a fixer, but acetic ether is not as pleasant to the taste as wine or brandy.

CHLOROFORM FOR ALKALINE MIXTURE.

So much for acid mixtures; now let us consider alkaline mixtures. These are the most difficult mixtures to flavor. I have learned that the best sweetener for alkaline mixtures is chloroform. This may be astonishing to you, but it is true that chloroform does brighten the mixture up and render it more palatable. Licorice is the flavor which is now used more than any other in alkaline mixtures, as the alkali develops the taste of the licorice, but I think that chocolate is better when it can be used. The more alkali there is in chocolate the more definite is the taste of the chocolate. Therefore chocolate and alkali make an excellent combination, especially when you use a little sugar as a sweetener. Salt can also be used, but the mixture must *not* be very sweet to stand the salt.

BROMIDES DIFFICULT TO DISGUISE.

For bromides, and other salts, carbon dioxide is the best flavoring agent. Besides making these preparations palatable it also aids by strengthening their therapeutic effect. Only two flavors appear to blend well with pronounced salty mixtures. These are vanilla and molasses. Vanilla flavoring will conceal the unpleasant taste, and molasses will also be found to be effective. The average person still likes molasses, although the day when we ate molasses on our bread appears to have gone. This is due, however, to the fact that we cannot get the same old-fashioned, pure molasses that we used to produce years ago. Therefore it is now frequently more advantageous to use brown sugar in flavoring. For the non-effervescent and for bitter drugs, however, molasses is better. Syrup of senna, for example, can be made very palatable with brown sugar and so can syrup of tar. The preparation with brown sugar is not colored except by the sugar itself. The brown sugar blends with the tar and the senna better than refined sugar. Chloroform also adds pungency to such preparations and does not remove any of their medicinal features. The sweetness is retained and yet no different or sharp flavor is introduced. It merely brightens up the entire mixture.

THE FLAVORING OF BITTERS.

In the flavoring of bitters there is considerable trouble experienced. The Pharmacopœial tincture of gentian is an instance of artistic pharmacy in the line of aromatic bitters, the aromatics in this case being orange peel and cardamom. When the preparation contains strychnine the mixture can scarcely be made anything but bitter. Malt will go well with bitter drugs, but it is often less efficient than brown sugar. With an unpleasant bitter, like myrrh, a little salt will blend remarkably well, but the mixture must not be made too sweet. Moreover, too much salt must not be used. You must use just enough to brighten the mixture up. Aromatics must be used sparingly. It is always a mistake to attempt to cover up one pungency with another. It is better to work with opposites.

FLAVORS FOR EMULSIONS AND OILS.

In the National Formulary you will note many ways of preparing codliver oil so that the oil may be disguised. When you use aromatics you must use them sparingly. If you use too much of them you get first a pungent flavor and then a disgusting oil flavor, each of them separate and distinct. The French druggists use coffee as a flavoring for oils. I don't know whether this is desirable or not, but it shows that a soft flavor goes well with oils. A licorice emulsion, such as extract of licorice with a little lavender and peppermint in it, is frequently used, but lavender is a rank flavor and must be used sparingly. Oil of neroli is excellent for some combinations. In combination with aromatics like cinnamon, neroli goes extremely well. It pays to get the best quality of neroli. The flavor is more delicate in the best varieties and also more powerful, and in proportion does not cost more. Artificial oil of neroli, however, is often satisfactory. The mixture must not be too aromatic and, as a rule, it musn't be too sweet. It is well worth while to experiment with oil of neroli.

Next to licorice as a flavoring for oils I should put malt. Malt is very mild, but with brandy or chloroform it is very attractive. In France brandy is especially recommended in oil mixtures. Saccharine or sugar can also be used to good advantage. Salt also goes well. Rose flavor is also good and with a little sassafras the rose flavor can be made more pronounced. Heliotropin is sometimes desirable and it tastes about as it smells. It has a flavor like that of almonds but is very persistent, and if you have in your mixture a drug which is very strong you cannot use this flavoring.

There is a very wide field, financially, for the druggist who will experiment along the lines of proper flavoring, and the possibilities are as unlimited as the science of drugs itself. Some of the most successful preparations on the market to-day have become so because their proprietors have experimented with their flavoring until they have given to the preparations an artistic finish. They have no better therapeutic effect than many other unsuccessful preparations, but they possess what the public wants—a pleasant taste—and this can only be achieved by proper flavoring.

The Corpuscular Theory of Matter.[1]

By Prof. J. J. Thompson.

Any new theory of matter must be able to explain all the chemical, optical and electrical properties of matter in a satisfactory manner. According to the new theory, that which we were accustomed to describe as an atom is supposed to be made up of positive and negative electricity, the latter taking the form of extremely small particles known as corpuscles. It was shown originally by Crookes that when an electric discharge is passed through a highly exhausted glass tube a light green fluorescence is produced in the glass immediately opposite the kathode or negative terminal by the impact upon the glass of a beam of luminous rays known as the kathode rays. That these rays were traveling in straight lines was shown by interposing in their path a plate of mica, cut in the form of a cross, when a shadow of the cross was produced upon the glass. By most continental physicists these kathode rays were regarded as vibrations of the ether, whereas English physicists favored the view that they were material particles or corpuscles. The latter theory has since been proved to be correct by the following three facts: First, the rays can be deflected by a magnet; secondly, when diverted against a hollow metal bowl within the vacuum tube the metal was found to assume a negative charge, as shown by connecting it to an electroscope; thirdly, the rays are deflected by electrostatic forces of attraction or repulsion. It has recently been shown by Wehnelt that kathode rays are also produced when calcium or barium oxides are heated to incandescence on a platinum foil in a vacuum. Rays produced in this way and allowed to impinge upon a metallic surface in the vacuum tube are readily shown to be deflected from their normal course in a parabolic orbit. As a result of careful quantitative measurements the velocity of the corpuscles is found to vary in different cases within very wide limits, being influenced both by the shape of the tube and the height of the vacuum. The corpuscles produced from incandescent calcium oxide travel much more slowly than those produced by means of the induction coil. The ratio of the electric charge (e) to the mass (m) of the corpuscles, however, is found to be a constant quality which is independent of their velocity or of the materials of which the electrodes are made or of the nature of the residual gas in the tube. From this it is argued that all substances emit the same corpuscles. This ratio e/m is found to be 1.7×10^7 C.G.S. units—*i. e.*, 1,700 times as great as the corresponding value for the atom of hydrogen in electrolysis, which is 10^4 C.G.S. units. The difference must be attributed to one of two causes—either the corpuscle bears a much greater charge than does the atom of hydrogen in electrolysis, or else its mass is very much less. Since, however, it has been proved by Prof. C. T. R. Wilson that the charges borne by the two are identical, the difference in the magnitude of the ratio e/m must be explained by assuming that the mass of the corpuscle is 1-1700th part of the mass of the atom hydrogen.

[1] An abstract of a lecture delivered at the Royal Institution and printed in the *Pharmaceutical Journal*.

FOUNTAIN BEVERAGES OF TO-DAY.

Review of Conditions and Directions for the Preparation of Soda and Other Drinks and Delicacies.

One would think that in New York novelties in soda fountain beverages would be found in abundance, but the reverse is true, and it is curious to note the lack of invention displayed by metropolitan pharmacists in this regard. What novelties there are appear to have come out of the South or West, and as most local pharmacists adhere to the policy of making their own soda syrups the result can be easily imagined. At a very busy fountain near a very busy thoroughfare we were told that the drinks which were featured by means of small painted signs hanging from the wall of the fountain had not been changed during the past ten years. At another fountain on Broadway at which the daily sales amount to 4,000 or 5,000 glasses nothing new had been offered for four years past. The novelties were mostly confined to egg drinks, as egg lemonade, egg chocolate, egg phosphate, etc. Indeed in New York the soda fountain trade seems to be permitted to drag along on the impetus first given to it.

According to John Teissel, manager of Hegeman & Co.'s soda fountain, the drinks which should always be kept on hand are chocolate, coffee, orange, vanilla, lemon, strawberry, raspberry, morella cherry, root beer and ginger ale. Where any considerable trade is done the list might be extended to include maple, peach, orgeat, wild cherry, grape fruit, sarsaparilla, celery phosphate, apricot and red cherry. Many of the drinks named are also served as phosphates. With those enumerated and the addition of a few tonics, a good headache cure, a good stomachic and bracer, the pharmacist should be well equipped to supply the needs of customers.

The statement in regard to the utter lack of inventiveness in the formulation of soda fountain beverages may perhaps bear modification since W. E. Beall, who has charge of the fountain in the Alper's pharmacy at the corner of Thirty-first street and Broadway, has introduced one or two novelties since his connection with the store. One of these is a fermented milk drink which be has named clabberade, from clabber, the name applied in the South to fermented milk. Other special drinks served at the Alper's fountain, which by the way is a Decker Twentieth Century, are sherry flip, sherry egg nog, spiced milk, coca cola, claret punch, claret cocktail, calisaya cocktail, egg claret, mint claret and hot eye opener, none of these containing any alcohol. Among the sundaes served are tutti frutti, chop suey, walnut, cocoanut, mixed nuts, fresh whole cherry, sliced peaches, fresh strawberry and sliced pineapple. Mr. Beall kindly contributes the following formulas:

HOT CHOCOLATE.

Powdered chocolate	1 lb.
Condensed milk	2 lbs.
Sugar	½ lb.

Thin out to the proper consistency with hot water and serve from a silver pitcher in the proportion of 2 oz. to an 8 oz. cup; top with whipped cream.

COFFEE SYRUP.

Java coffee	¼ lb.
Mocha coffee	¾ lb.
Boiling water	4 pints.

Make by hot percolation, passing the menstruum through the marc several times. Enough sugar should be dissolved in the percolate to make a syrup of the desired consistency. The addition of about 1 oz. of table salt to each gallon of water will be found an effective means of extracting the flavor.

TOMATO BOUILLON.

Canned tomatoes	1 quart.
Extract of beef	3 oz.
Worcestershire sauce	½ oz.
Red pepper	3 grains.
Celery	3 grains.
Salt	3 grains
Tomato catsup	1 quart.

The tomatoes should be cooked and the liquor strained and mixed with the other ingredients. The catsup serves to thicken and give an aromatic and tangy tone.

Notwithstanding the dearth of new ideas in soda fountain beverages we have been able through correspondence to bring together a goodly number of formulas, hints and suggestions for those who are prepared to develop and increase their trade in soda water beverages. As evidence of the lack of novelty the formulas submitted by Mr. Whitehill may be noted. We happen to know that these formulas were used successfully many years ago by one of the leading pharmacists on upper Broadway, and it is noteworthy that they are just as popular to-day as they were when first introduced. To our Western friends we are indebted for the only formulas which possess the merit of freshness and novelty.

There has been a notable increase in the consumption of ice cream, the manager of one large establishment informing us that four times the amount is now dispensed as compared with that sold two or three years ago. The introduction of the sundae is no doubt responsible in a large measure for this, and, speaking of the sundae, our readers will be interested in the explanation of the origin of the name which is offered by our Philadelphia correspondent. If not true, this explanation is surely *ben trovato*. Some readers may, however, be disposed to place more credence in another explanation of the origin of the word which refers it merely to the day on which the delicacy was invented.

Our Chicago correspondent advises us that light luncheons are becoming customary offerings at the soda fountain, these being supplied to patrons of the fountain at cheap rates along with hot drinks. At one fountain hot cakes are served. Many of the larger pharmacies dispense entirely with the soda fountain, by which we mean that no fountain is maintained. There is none in the Economical Drug Company's place, owing to the decided stand taken by Manager McConnell against anything of the kind. The Public Drug Company formerly had a fountain, but it is now no longer to be seen. Notwithstanding exceptions of this kind the druggists of Chicago generally make special efforts to cultivate the trade in fountain beverages and they control the cream of this business.

New York's Busiest Fountain.

One of the busiest soda fountains in New York is to be found in the Hegeman pharmacy, at 200 Broadway. The fountain is 37 feet long and fitted with innumerable faucets for carbonated waters and syrups. It was made for the Hegeman coporation by the Liquid Carbonic Acid Mfg. Company at a cost of $20,000. During the summer as many as 10,000 glasses of fountain beverages are dispensed daily. Even in winter the demand is enormous, the sales averaging 4,000 glasses daily.

In conversation with John Whitehill, assistant manager of Hegeman & Co., many interesting points were gleaned. The trouble with many druggists, according to Mr. Whitehill, is that they regard the soda fountain end of their business with their eyes out of focus. They have a general sort of idea it is a good thing, but they do not get down to hard pan and show their customers what they can do in this respect. Continuing, Mr. Whitehill said:

"As a business proposition the fountain will give as good returns for the money invested as any other portion of the store. The drug store depends entirely on the profits from prescriptions, the sales of drugs, own preparations, toilet goods and receipts of fountain. Its profit on cigars, candies or patent medicines can never pay any more than expenses, unless, perhaps, the druggist be a Hegeman or a Jayne.

"Any druggist who has traveled must marvel at the amount of space and the prominent position which the fountain occupies in the large stores. A fair estimate would be to say that almost 25 per cent. of the floor space is given over to the fountain. The fountains themselves are marvels of construction. The appointments are the best, the products handled are the purest in the market, and the help are in a great measure thoroughly trained in this branch of the business.

"The time is now drawing near when the so-called soda season will be with us, and I have this to say to the druggist with the small fountain—get the right start. Hold a little convention with yourself. With all your knowledge of what goes to make a palatable beverage, make a good start and keep it up all through the hot weather, and when the cool weather comes it will find you well prepared to serve hot beverages as well as the cold.

"Granting a neat fountain, the druggist should have a responsible attendant. An inexperienced and slovenly attendant is always a source of dissatisfaction to customers and a detriment to the increase of the store's general business. Get the best attendant you can afford. Buy the best glasses. A good glass will outlast three or four of the cheap. Get pure concentrated syrup and dilute as wanted. Most of the manufacturers make very good products. Always make your own orange and lemon syrup and ice cream.

"For small stores I recommend the coffee and chocolate syrups as supplied by the manufacturers. I have tried several of them and find them excellent for either hot or cold soda. Large stores can make their own from reliable goods at a much less cost.

"During the season druggists should buy strawberries and raspberries and make their own syrups. Wherever this has been done the soda business has been greatly increased, as there is nothing appeals to a thirsty person like whole fresh fruit in a soda. Keep the syrup as cold as possible. Have a few good tonics, bracers and appetizers always on hand.

"Charge 5 cents for ordinary soda; 10 cents for tonics, etc., and if possible serve your ice cream soda for 5 cents.

"Ice cream soda is profitable at 5 cents when made by the druggist, is one of the best advertising mediums of the modern drug store, and if you give the right drink it is a business bringer to the other parts of the store. I have in mind one druggist in my section whom I advised to charge 5 cents instead of 10 cents for soda. At the end of the year he had taken in more cash at 5 cents a glass than he had in former years at 10 cents and his general business had been increased one-third. This in spite of competition all around him, and the only additional expense was a menu card, on which was printed a list of beverages for the customers' selection."

Mr. Whitehill has been good enough to supply the AMERICAN DRUGGIST with the following formulas, which will be found very satisfactory:

SIMPLE SYRUP.

Loaf sugar.............................8 lbs.
Water.............................1 gallon.

Syrup made from loaf sugar keeps better than that made from ordinary sugar.

EXTRACT OF VANILLA.

Vanilla beans, sliced Mexican............1 lb.
Alcohol (90 per cent.)...............1 gallon.

Pack in percolator after thoroughly moistening; let stand one week, and percolate to 1 gallon.

Hegeman & Co.'s Soda Fountain, New York City.

To make vanilla syrup use 2 ounces of extract to 1 gallon of simple syrup and color with caramel.

SOLUTION OF CITRIC ACID.

Citric acid.............................2 lbs.
Water.............................1 qt.

Dissolve.

TINCTURE OF SAFFRON.

American saffron.......................2 oz.
Diluted alcohol.........................1 pint.

Percolate.

ESSENCE OF SARSAPARILLA.

Gaultheria oil...........................3v
Sassafras oil.............................3v
Deodorized alcohol.......................Oi

To make syrup of sarsaparilla, or root beer syrup, mix 1 ounce of the essence with 1 gallon of syrup and color with ½ ounce of caramel.

COCHINEAL COLOR FOR SYRUP.

Cochineal.

Potassium carbonate....................āā ℥i
Water ....℥viij

Boil for three minutes and add gradually:

Alum, powdered..........................ʒi
Potass. bitartrate......................ʒij

Bring to boiling point; let stand, and filter.

BEEF TEA OR BOUILLON.

Fluid beef (Armour's or Wyeth's).......8 oz.
Extract of spice....................2 drachms.
Table salt..............................2 oz.
Celery salt.........................4 drachms.
Arrowroot ....4 oz.
Tincture of capsicum..................20 min.
Boiling water..........................1 gall.

M.

EXTRACT OF SPICE.

Allspice (pimento)......................2 oz.
Cloves ....1 oz.
Nutmegs ....2 oz.
Mace ....2 oz.
Cassia ....3 oz.
Alcohol ....q. s.

Moisten the mixed drugs with alcohol and percolate until 1 quart of extract is obtained.

TOMATO BOUILLON.

Tomato catsup (any good brand).....1 bottle.
Beef bouillon, enough to make........1 gallon.

M.

GINGER ALE SYRUP.

Fluid extract ginger (soluble)..........20 oz.
Tincture of capsicum....................2 oz.
Essence of lemon........................½ oz.
Solution of citric acid.................4 oz.
Caramel ....1 oz.
Simple syrup........................5 gallons.

M.

COFFEE SYRUP.

Ground coffee (Mocha and Java, p. e.)..5 lbs.

Percolate with 2 gallons of hot water into 12 pounds of sugar and stir until dissolved. Keep on ice.

NECTAR SYRUP.

Extract of vanilla..................3 drachms.
Extract of orange...................1½ drachms.
Pineapple syrup........................1 quart.
Simple syrup..........................2 quarts.

WILD CHERRY SYRUP.

Ground wild cherry.....................2 lbs.
Water ....1 gallon.

Infuse for 24 hours, express and add

Sugar ....9 lbs.

M.

RASPBERRY VINEGAR.

Acetic acid.............................4 oz.
Raspberry syrup.......................1 gallon.

RED ORANGE SYRUP.

French currant syrup..................½ gallon.
Port wine..............................12 oz.
Extract of orange.......................½ oz.
Tincture of cochineal...............4 drachms.

M.

WALL STREET EXQUISITE.

Raspberry syrup........................½ pint.
Pineapple syrup.........................1 pint.
Vanilla syrup...........................½ pint.
Rose water..............................4 oz.

M.

ICE CREAM.—I.

Cream ....14 quarts.
Condensed milk.........................5 quarts.
Sugar ....10 lbs.
Gelatine ....4 oz.
Extract of vanilla......................5 oz.
Hot water...............................1 pint.

Make a solution of the gelatin in the water.

ICE CREAM.—II.

Cream ....10 quarts.
Milk ....5 quarts.
Condensed milk.........................5 quarts.
Sugar ....10 lbs.
Gelatin ....4 oz.
Extract of vanilla......................5 oz.
Hot water...............................1 pint.

Make a solution of the gelatin in the water.

FRENCH CURRANT SYRUP.

French currant juice..................1 bottle.
Citric acid.........................2 drachms.
Caramel ....1 drachm.
Tincture of cochineal...............3 drachms.
Syrup, enough to make...............2 gallons.

M.

LEMON OR ORANGE SYRUP.

Take six oranges or lemons and grate them into 8 pounds of sugar. Squeeze the juice into the mixture of orange and peel and triturate together until well combined; then add 1 gallon of water and agitate until solution is effected; then strain. Add a few drops of tincture of curcuma to deepen the color, if necessary.

ESSENCE OF LEMON.

Lemon oil...............................1 oz.
The peel of one fresh lemon.
Deodorized alcohol.....................15 oz.

Allow to stand one week and filter.

ESSENCE OF ORANGE.

Oil of sweet orange.....................1 oz.
The peel of one fresh orange.
Deodorized alcohol.....................15 oz.

Let stand one week and filter.

Gathered by Our Correspondents.

The services of our regular correspondents here and in other countries were enlisted in the work of spreading before our readers the fullest information regarding the methods of pharmacists who have been successful in building up a profitable soda trade.

The soda fountain has not yet found a home in the Paris pharmacy, and our correspondent at the French capital, who was instructed to investigate the soda trade there, tells the story of an unsuccessful search for information. His experiences in search of a soda fountain are so entertaining and throw such an interesting light on national characteristics, as he recounts them, that we are glad to place them before our readers.

Soda Fountains in Paris Pharmacies.

THE STORY OF AN UNSUCCESSFUL SEARCH.

"A soda fountain in a Paris pharmacy; why, certainly," said my first informant. "There's a very smart one, by a London firm, I'm told, at the Pharmacie Britannique, in the rue Saint-Honoré. I forget the number, but it's at the rue Royale end, a stone's throw from the rue Castiglione, where the English pharmacies are."

I thanked him and followed his instructions. "I suppose it's because I haven't got the number," I said to myself, after staring on both sides of the busy little street in vain, and I went to make inquiries, at a pharmacy, of course. I always make inquiries at a pharmacy, because there you're certain to find some one who is both well informed and obliging, and my pharmacist, an Englishman evidently, was no exception to this well established rule.

"Yes, it was there all right enough," he said. "But it shut up some months ago. Didn't pay."

"And where can I find a pharmacy where there is one?" I asked.

"Not in Paris, so far as I know."

"Don't you think the experiment would succeed?" I inquired, "for the fact that there is a pharmacy about every 50 yards in the rue Saint Honoré may have had something to do with the nonsuccess of our friend here."

"I rather doubt it. You see the conditions are so very different. In the first place look at the room it takes up. You have noticed how small all the drug stores are in this (the Anglo-American) part of Paris. Rents are terribly high, and profits—well, they're not always like the rents, in spite of what outsiders say about us. Then, again, an American drug store or even an English chemist's is much more of a general shop than a Paris pharmacy. Why, Frenchmen are surprised I handle perfumery and hair brushes. You see they expect to find nothing in a pharmacy but actual remedies, and, I was going to say actual invalids or their messengers, quiet and often worried people, who want a discreet private sort of a place, whereas the American drug store, I take it, is more of a public institution and used for dozens of things besides the actual preparation and purchase of medicines."

"Then where do you think soda fountains could be placed in Paris?"

"I'll tell you where there is one. You know Fuller's candy store on the rue Daunou? Go 'round there and see the proprietress. She'll tell you all about it."

"EVERY COUNTRY HAS ITS OWN WAY OF TAKING LIQUID REFRESHMENTS."

I thanked my informant and found the rue Daunou, a little good class street just between the Avenue de l'Opera (which hangs out more Stars and Stripes on the Fourth of July than any other street in Paris) and that ladies' shopping paradise, the rue de la Paix. Madame Margaret was chatty and communicative. "Yes, I've been here eight years, and the fountain 16, I believe, so I should know something about it. My soda customers are mostly ladies—American, and some English. They bring in French friends sometimes who try the soda, but they don't take to it as a rule. I dare say it's partly a question of habit. I fancy, too, that every country has its own way of taking liquid refreshments."

"You mean that here men and women go together to a café, while in America and England you would find ladies at a soda bar or tea shop and the men more in the saloons."

Madame Margaret acquiesced. She had never been to see herself, but she had been told that some of the best cafés in Paris—the Riche, the Grand, and so on—had tried soda fountains and abandoned them. The American custom alone was insufficient to support them, and the French were refractory. Wine was cheap enough over here for every one to drink it, and so on.

"BOISSONS AMERICAINES."

At the Café Royal, in the Boulevard Montmartre, soda fountain beverages are listed in a menu card bearing the title "Boissons Américaines," and the announcement is made that the drinks are given forth (*débitées*) *à la grande soda fontaine* "le président."

The list of *boissons Américaines* include the following, which sell at 40 centimes each:

Eau-de-soda au jus de fruits.

Citron, orange, vanille, ananas fraises, framboisès, pêches, chocolat, café, cerises, cerises sauvag, groseilles, grenadine, orgeat, ginger ale, kola, nectar, prunes, abricots, menthe, cider *Champ guisé*, rose, limonade.

Boissons aux Oeufs.

The following egg drinks are listed at 75 centimes:

Phosphates d'orange aux œufs, phosphates de citron aux œufs, limonade aux œufs, chocolat aux œufs, egg-liqueur, egg royal.

I may add that in one or two good Anglo-American pharmacies in Paris—Swann's, for instance—there is a sort of little table where cooling beverages are placed in summer, so that it is not impossible to get a "soft drink" in a drug store in the French capital. But evidently this is the London (West End) system of a casual convenience for customers and not a great trade like the American soda fountain.

Frenchmen are conservative in most things, but most of all in their eating and drinking habits. I have seen one or two American notions succeed in France in spite of this natural characteristic—one might cite the typewriter, now in ordinary use, and the cash register, which has now found its way into almost every pharmacy—so it is well never to "prophesy unless you know." But the soda fountain is some way off; even the "thin end of the wedge" cannot be said to have as yet been successfully inserted.

Fountain in the Store of George B. Evans, 1106-1108 Chestnut Street, Philadelphia. Length 49 Feet. Constructed of Onyx, Marble and Mahogany. Made by Robert M. Green & Sons

Soda Beverages in Philadelphia.

By our Regular Correspondent.

The contribution of our Philadelphia correspondent will be found a most interesting historical study of the subject, in addition to being a paper crammed with valuable suggestions capable of practical application anywhere. He writes:

To Philadelphia belongs the credit of having manufactured the first soda water in America. About 1807, when this city enjoyed the prestige of being the first city of the United States, as well as having the leading hospital and medical college, Dr. Philip Syng Physick had his attention attracted to the experiments of Joseph Priestly, the great English chemist, in producing a carbonated beverage by pouring water briskly back and forth between two small vessels held in the layer of carbonic acid gas which collects in a brewer's vat. This carbonated water was designed by Priestly as a drink for dyspeptics, his researches having satisfied him that the natural mineral waters at the "spas" of Europe owed their much heralded virtues largely to the presence of carbonic acid gas in solution. Dr. Physick, the Philadelphia surgeon with the marvelously appropriate name, like all progressive medical men, determined to try the Priestly discovery. He called to his aid an equally progressive Philadelphia druggist in the person of Townsend Speakman, who had a pharmacy at 8 South Second street and who had supplied many of the medicines to the Continental armies.

AN IMPROVED METHOD ADOPTED.

The method of obtaining carbonic acid gas from a brewer's vat did not commend itself to these progressive scientists, and Speakman suggested the manufacture of the gas from sulphuric acid and sodium bicarbonate. A local coppersmith constructed an apparatus for the purpose, and the first soda water ever produced in this country was made here. Later on sugar and flavors were added to render the drink more palatable, and John Hart, an apprentice of Speakman, who had married his master's daughter, in accordance with the good old custom, first began the manufacture of these beverages and started selling them. Professor Remington is a descendant of John Hart and, of course, of old Townsend Speakman likewise.

THE INTRODUCTION OF ICE CREAM SODA.

The soda water industry was destined in 1874 to receive another impetus by the invention of ice cream soda by another Philadelphian, Robert M. Green, of the well-known soda fountain firm of Robert M. Green & Sons. This invention paved the way for the "Sundaes," the long line of "spoon novelties," and the many delicious beverages which have gone far to make the soda fountain business the immense industry which it is.

A TIME WHEN HOT DRINKS WERE NOT THOUGHT OF.

There was a time, and it is not very long ago, either, when soda water fountains were considered only a summer necessity. As for using them in winter, such a thing was not thought of. However, all this has been changed. The retail druggist who does a rushing business in ice cold drinks during the summer months does almost as great a trade in the winter by serving hot drinks and special drinks to the thirsty.

It is estimated that about 90 per cent. of the pharmacists in Philadelphia have a soda water fountain in their stores. The revenue from this source varies. In some cases it is said that enough money is taken at the soda water fountain counter to pay the rent of the store and practically all of its running expenses, but cases of this kind are few and far between. A small number of drug stores have a steady soda water trade and the owners are compelled to employ a corps of soda water clerks, who do nothing else but serve the various kinds of drinks that are now concocted.

THE INCREASE IN FANCY DRINKS.

Great progress has been made in the methods of serving soda water. A few years ago the call was for plain soda, with some kind of a simply flavored syrup, which was all that could be secured. Now there is no limit to the kinds of drinks, and the variety is constantly increasing. In some stores from 50 to 75 different kinds of drinks are offered and, strange to say, they are all of a temperance character, though named juleps, cocktails, fizzes and other names familiar to those who are accustomed to patronizing a different kind of a store. But there is a difference in the drinks, as one knows who has tried the experiment.

THE OLD "GOOSE NECK."

From little acorns tall oaks grow, and from the old time "goose neck" there has sprung the elaborate creations of onxy, silver and rare woods, which add so materially to the beauty of the store. In some places the soda water fountains cost more than the fixtures of an old time drug store, and the improvement in the make and style of soda water fountains has by no means reached the end.

Philadelphia boasts of two of the leading soda water fountain manufacturers of the country, Robert M. Green & Sons and the American Soda Fountain Company, which latter concern manufactures under the patents of the old firm of Chas. Lippincott & Co. Although these two firms do a very large business, the fountains in Philadelphia do not by any means tell what these firms have accomplished, for the number of really large and handsome fountains in this city is small as compared with other cities.

WHERE MOST IS SOLD.

The number of glasses dispensed during a day varies. In the stores in the central portion of the city thousands of glasses are dispensed daily, while in those where a fountain is maintained merely as an adjunct the number is considerably less. There are certain sections of the city outside of what is known as the retail business district in which a large business is done, but the big trade is confined to a few who have made the advertising of special drinks a specialty and do so with the knowledge that something new always brings trade.

It is the pharmacy that varies its drinks which does the most business. On Chestnut and Market streets there is considerable competition. Each day a druggist announces that he has a special new drink on sale. It is surprising how many people there are who manage to try the different drinks. It is said that some of the popular drinks were concocted on the spur of the moment. At the present time sundaes are in favor. All the leading stores dispense these compounds, although a different name may be given to them.

ORIGIN OF THE SUNDAE.

It is correct to say that the sundae is the most popular drink this year. As a rule flavors only last a short time, and something new has to be put up to take their places. The sundae came into existence through that necessity which is the mother of so many inventions. It is said that a certain place in New Orleans which was run by a Mr. Sundae did a flourishing soda water trade. On one particular day Mr. Sundae discovered that he was running short of soda water and as the day was warm and the outlook good for a rushing business he was at his wit's end to know what to do. Looking over his stock he discovered that he had a lot of fruit on hand. Then an idea struck him. He crushed the fruit, mixed it with ice-cream, and announced a new soda fountain delicacy. He called it sundae and it sold like the proverbial hot cakes. The fame of the sundae has now spread throughout the length and breadth of the land like many of the other beverages for which the Crescent City is renowned.

WHERE THE LARGEST NUMBER OF GLASSES IS SOLD.

It is believed that the greatest trade in soda water in Philadelphia is divided between the pharmacy of George B. Evans, on Chestnut street, above Eleventh, and the Broad Street Station Pharmacy, conducted by Mr. Stoever. Both of these stores make a specialty of soda water and there is as much attention paid in them to keeping up this department as there is in any other department of the store. Manager Burk, of the Broad Street Station Pharmacy, says 5,000 tickets have been sold in one day. The manager of Evans' store says the largest day's business was when 4,000 drinks were dispensed. Both of these stores average about 2,000 glasses of soda water beverages of some kind or another every day in the year.

WINTER AND SUMMER BUSINESS DOES NOT VARY MUCH.

During the winter months there is not as much soda water drunk as there is when the thermometer is doing its best to escape from the top of the tube. In the winter there is a better demand for fancy and hot drinks, which are generally sold at 10 cents. So while the trade in winter is not as large, there is not much difference in the receipts.

THE LARGEST SODA FOUNTAIN IN PHILADELPHIA.

Outside of some of the department stores the largest soda water fountain in Philadelphia is contained in the drug store of George B. Evans, at 1104 Chestnut street. This fountain is 40 feet long and was manufactured by Robert M. Green & Sons. The soda fountain department in this store is under the supervision of W. S. Stinson. While the fountain is not so showy as some others made by the same firm, the most careful attention was given to its construction so as to assure a perfectly harmonious blending of all the materials used. It is constructed of marble, onxy, silver and mahogony. These materials are arranged so as to give the best effect and produce a striking appearance. To an outsider the interior of this fountain is as Greek to those who have never studied that language. Its distinguishing feature is an apparatus that does away with the slop, which for many years was a drawback to a large soda water trade. Behind this magnificent fountain is a refrigerating plant, or, more properly speaking, the pipes lead to such a plant located in the basement, which keeps the liquids at all times at a certain low temperature.

HOW THE WATER IS COOLED.

The ammonia refrigerating process is used. The ammonia, contained in a steel tank directly under the fountain, passes through a small iron pipe to an expansion valve, where the liquid is converted into a gas. The ammonia passes on into a set of iron coils laid in a steel tank thoroughly insulated, 20 feet high and 5 feet wide on each side. This tank is kept constantly filled with filtered water, and when by starting a motor the ammonia commences to flow the ice begins to form on the iron coils. This gradually cools the water, and when the temperature reaches 33 degrees the ammonia is shut off. The ammonia gas after passing through the ice covered coils enters a compressor just outside the far end of the box, where the fumes are compressed and passed into a condenser; from there, transformed into liquid, it returns to the ammonia tank.

The filtered water cooled in this way is pumped by means of a 1 horse-power driving pump into the tanks of the fountain on the floor above. The coils containing the soda water are located there, while directly below are the porcelain drawer containers which hold the flavors. The water is allowed to pass very slowly through this tank and then it is permitted to perform a double duty—that is, it is made to pass through many feet of iron pipe arranged in coil form along the sides of the refrigerator room, where is kept an extra supply of syrup flavors made from the crushed fruits. In this room are contained the articles which are used by the dispensers above.

Mr. Evans has everything down to a science. No empty glasses are allowed to stand on the counter. As soon as they are emptied they are sent down on dumbwaiters to the basement, where they are thoroughly cleaned. All flavors are made freshly every day. Daily changes are made in dressing the fountain and everything possible is done to attract the customer. From eight to ten men are constantly employed in serving drinks.

THE NUMBER OF DIFFERENT BEVERAGES.

In commenting on the growth of the soda water business Mr. Stinson said he had always about 60 kinds of syrups to draw upon, although at times there were about 100 concoctions. Some of them did not live long, and when it was found there was no demand for a certain drink it was withdrawn. At the present time Mr. Stinson said the big run was on sundaes. There were also such popular drinks as pulp de marron, walnut bisque, hot grape juice, ginger rickey, egg bisque, hot egg phosphate, cherry orangeade, hot malted milk, maple cream puff, egg and chocolate cream puff, egg and coffee, celery egg tonic, nut salad sundae, besides the regular hot drinks that are sought after at this time of the year.

ADVERTISING BY ELECTRIC SIGNS.

To attract attention the names of special drinks are figured in electric signs, which are constantly flashed. The bar is 47 feet long. One of this winter's specialties is egg and milk. The demand for this beverage has been very large, as it is recommended by physicians. It is said it is good for that feeling which comes to some social enthusiasts after a night of hard work in attempting to suppress the liquor traffic.

THE BROAD STREET STATION PHARMACY.

The Broad Street Station Pharmacy is an admirably located stand. Thousands of people pass each day in and out of the station, and many of them stop on their way to quench their thirst. In the summer, from early in the morning until late at night, there is a row of thirsty people three or four deep around this counter. On account of its location it is considered about the best patronized soda water counter in Philadelphia.

Handsome Fountain in the Broad Street Station Pharmacy, Philadelphia.

THE DISPENSING COUNTER

has a total length of 84 feet and is L shaped, the front being constructed of white glass with a black glass surface. The interior working arrangements are entirely of slate, marble, metal, porcelain jars and hard rubber, not a particle of wood entering into its construction. Forty-three 1-gallon syrup jars are distributed in sets along the three fronts of the counter. Three onyx columns support two soda and mineral draft tubes. The work board of metal supports ice cream cabinets and tumbler washers, together with every convenience of arrangement that experience has suggested.

The refrigerator base measures 34 feet in length, of L shape. The front is constructed of white and black glass, similar to the dispensing counter, the doors being of metal and silver plated, with double plate glass panels. In the construction of the refrigerator no wood whatever was used.

Upon the refrigerator stands a magnificent onyx wall fixture. Constructed of the finest peninsula onyx, this fixture is large and massive in appearance and is richly carved. In the corner of the angle is a large grotto, in the back of which mirrors are placed at an angle so as to afford reflections of the illuminated ornamental figure which it holds and to reflect the electric lights. An accurate timepiece surmounts the grotto. In front of each of the large mirrors is placed the onyx hot soda stands, plate glass shelves being placed in front of the small mirrors to permit the display of crystal glasses, fruits, flowers, &c. The fountain in the Broad Street Station Pharmacy is called an Innovation apparatus. It was the original fountain that has revolutionized the methods of dispensing soda and was the result of many years of experience in the designing and construction of soda water apparatus. This fountain was the production of the genius of F. H. Lippincott, and it is believed to be one of the greatest advancements ever made in this line. The fountain is supplied by an automatic generator, which furnishes a constant supply of fresh soda water at the right temperature. Frequent changes in the dressing of the counter are one of the attractions.

HOW JACOBS BROS. ATTRACT THE THIRSTY.

These are not the only stores that do a large soda water business, for Jacob Bros., located on the north side of Chestnut street, west of Tenth, also gets a goodly share of the Chestnut street trade. This store has an up to date fountain and attracts a large number of customers by frequent changes of its soda water displays. In other words, it keeps its patrons guessing what is coming next. In commenting on the success of their soda water fountain Jacob Bros. said:

"The success of a fountain depends largely upon the individuality put into its management. The public wants good goods and good values and an ability to cater to their peculiarities. The training of a druggist is such that he is peculiarly well qualified to attend to the manufacturing and mixing of the various preparations necessary for the successful running of a soda fountain. We practically manufacture all of our own syrups from the fresh fruit. We also preserve in season sufficient fruit of all kinds to run us until the next season's crop is ready. We also make up many mixtures which the individual taste of customers call for, and these are constantly being changed according to the needs of our patrons. Our soda water is manufactured on the premises by an automatic machine as fast as it is consumed, thus avoiding all handling or shifting of tanks. The public wants quick service as well as good goods; therefore everything must be arranged for the economic and quick dispensing of drinks. The question of cleanliness is one of the most important, both in the appearance of the dispensers and in every detail of the fountain. The public wants to be satisfied that what they eat and drink is clean, pure and fresh."

Soda Water Conditions in Buffalo

By our Regular Correspondent.

In a chatty letter our Buffalo correspondent touches on the improved methods of displaying and serving soda as compared with former times, but intimates that there is still room for improvement. His allusion to the question of prices will probably apply to other cities besides Buffalo.

The Buffalo retail druggist believes thoroughly in soda water and is doing what he can, according to his lights, to make a success of that branch of his business. While there are a great many grades of this success, as soda water beverages are sold at all the drug stores as well as at a host of other public places, it may be said that the dispensing of it is pretty generally done in a neat and cleanly manner, and the public is satisfied. There is a very noticeable improvement in the way the drink is handled in late years, though it must be said that there is still plenty of room for more of the same thing.

THE QUESTION OF PRICE.

One of the serious difficulties found in the trade is the two prices asked for perhaps the same beverage. The leading retailers insist that they cannot produce a satisfactory drink for less than 10 cents, though the department stores, all the outlying stores and not a few of the other large downtown stores of any sort, including a few drug stores, sell all drinks at 5 cents. This cuts down the profits very seriously, in one case on account of the light sales and in the other on account of the small margin.

As it looks now there is always to be this difference, for the stores asking the higher price are doing what they can to attract the better part of the public by adding to the value of their drinks. One downtown druggist says that he is doing this by multiplying the variety of his egg drinks and is now able to say that he is selling as many of these 10-cent preparations as of all the rest combined. Of course he is located in the business center or he would not be able to do anything of the sort. There does not seem to be much shifting about of custom and it is a noticeable fact that the more soda water stands the more business.

NOT MANY NEW FLAVORS.

As to new leads in flavors and the like, there is some, but the advances in that line are not great. Probably more than half the flavors sold are chocolate, as it has been found that there is nothing so potent in case of the "all-gone" feeling as a chocolate ice cream soda. It acts as quickly as alcoholic drinks and leaves no sting behind. It is said that Moxie and Coca-Cola have probably come to stay in recent years, but there are plenty of steady soda water drinkers who have yet to taste of either.

There is very little scandal in the Buffalo soda water trade. Occasionally a store goes in for selling something that belongs to the low saloon trade, but the practice is short lived, and if the "fiend" must have cocaine he gets it in some other form.

The introduction of the sundae is credited to the soda water trade, as it goes over that counter and it seems to be very much in favor on the part of the seller, as it affords a third variety after the regular foaming soda and the clearer phosphates, though it really belongs more strictly to the ice cream trade. The pure fruit juices are very wholesome and they have the substance to them that makes it easy to ask a fair price. It is too bad that our coinage forms such a bar to this class of business, for it would otherwise be easy to make prices that stand for values instead of style or locality. Still the customer is usually willing to pay for style, for it suggests neatness, and without at least a fair showing of that the trade is hardly endurable or possible.

HOT DRINKS NOT MUCH IN DEMAND.

As to the hot drinks the dealers say they are here to stay, but they do not by any means take the place of the cold sodas, and their sale is not either large or growing very fast. It used to be the rule to shut up the cold soda fountain in the late fall and not run it through the winter, but the rule is now the opposite, and stores that have a big summer reputation for the drink in summer are always doing a pretty fair business in cold weather.

SODA WATER PAYS THE RENT.

As to the value of a fountain, it is the testimony of a manager of an expensive store downtown that it is not a very hard job to make soda water pay the rent, so it is to be inferred that he is doing it. The thinking public believes in the drink. It is wholesome and it makes against the saloon. There are, of course, people who regard it, or try to do so, as fit only for the weak stomached woman or child, while the brazen throat of the lord of the soil must be treated to some form of alcohol; but that it is a sentiment that is not so common as it used to be.

For this reason it is well to do as much as can be done with the 5-cent soda, for it is in a way as satisfying to the unvitiated palate and stomach as alcoholic drinks are and it can be made to answer the entire purpose of such if it is taken intelligently. So it will be the study to increase the attractiveness and the actual value of the low priced soda, and Buffalo appears to be doing her fair share in the effort.

The Soda Fountain in Canada.

By our Regular Correspondent.

Our correspondent in Toronto remarks: The soda fountain is a comparatively small factor in connection with the retail drug trade in this city. Few of the druggists give much attention to it, and those who do a soda water business are as a rule conservative in their methods and make few changes in their equipment. Some are of opinion that it is either detrimental to a prescription trade or not worth the space and attention that it demands, as compared with the drug trade proper.

The leading drug establishment in which the sale of soda water is made a specialty is the Bingham Pharmacy at 100 Yonge street. In addition to seating accommodation in the front of the store there is a palm room in the rear capable of accommodating 150 persons. A new fountain has been ordered from the American Soda Fountain Company, of Boston. The counter is 30 feet long, of white Italian marble, and the portion of white wood is fitted with cathedral glass domes. An automatic electric carbonator will secure the uniform standard of the soda. As a means of advertising it is proposed when this fountain is installed to offer a first prize of $10 and a second prize of $5 worth of perfumery to the lady suggesting the most appropriate name for the fountain.

George A. Bingham, the proprietor, said that there was a conservative idea among the trade that a fountain injured the drug business. His experience was in the other direction. It brought people to the store and had largely increased his trade. The reason why some druggists did not make it pay was that they did not attend to it properly. The service was often poor and the quality of the drinks inferior. To make it pay it required, close attention to every detail, more especially as regarded cleanliness, attractiveness, quick service and high quality. The pharmacy had a large line of fountain specialties, both for summer and winter, and the returns were steadily increasing.

Henry A. Swan, secretary of the Hooper Company, Limited, 43-45 King street, West, a large and old established house, said that it did a small soda fountain business, but intended to discontinue it, as it thought the space could be utilized to better advantage.

W. H. Lee, of the King Edward Hotel drug store, and 68 Wellesley street, said that he did not consider that the soda fountain injured prescription trade. At the same time the only way to make it remunerative was to go into it thoroughly with an up to date equipment and the best goods. Unless a druggist was prepared to do this he had better leave it alone.

Some Methods in Kentucky.

At last year's meeting of the Kentucky Pharmaceutical Association three helpful papers to the soda water dispenser were read and we have pleasure in reproducing them below in a slightly revised form:

Soda Water: How to Make It Profitable.

By Vernon Driskell.

There is no other one thing in our business that at one and the same time yields so much satisfaction to the customer and profit to the dealer as soda water—if made good. It can be made unprofitable by treating it as a side line of no importance; allowing it to be served by sloppy, inattentive, careless attendants and served in a very uninviting style, so that the soda may be so unsatisfactory that your time and investment might be used to better advantage in some other line—and it had better be used in some other line if you do not make your soda good enough and serve it nice enough to be good advertising for you. It will be advertising of some kind, either good or bad, just as you, or I, make it. There is a something that makes people talk about soda water, and they don't hesitate a minute about testifying to the goodness or badness of it.

Soda water is a side line, but you must put enough enthusiasm back of it to keep your customers from feeling that you feel that way about it. Many customers will catch inspiration and enthusiasm from you and value your soda as you do—but no higher. And to many of your customers soda is apt to taste as your fountain looks; if it looks dirty, the soda is supposed to be dirty; if the fountain is clean, the soda is clean.

Make soda right, serve it right, be attentive and obliging to your customers, satisfy both "crank" and saint and you'll sell more soda water.

When you see that you are selling more soda water, then try to sell still more, and again try still harder, and continually try to sell more soda water.

Pleasant surroundings and proper attention and good soda will sell more soda. Have plenty of chairs, tables, stools, fans, straws, napkins, etc., for comfort, and mirrors, artificial palms, flowers, etc., to please the eye, and good soda to tickle the palate, and you'll sell more soda.

PUSH SPECIALS.

Push a special drink, or flavor, one of your own naming, so your competitor will not steal your thunder, and push it hard, as your leader, by suggesting it when your customers ask, "What have you?" and by advertising in your newspaper and by neat signs placed prominently on fountain and counter. But be sure that your special is a good one—one that is likely to please the greater number of your customers. Possibly it would be better to have two specials, one a sweet drink and the other a phosphate—tastes and desires differ, you know.

Be liberal with ice at all times; you can't make soda too cold.

Don't be too liberal with your syrups, unless your customer desires it. Too much syrup is nauseating to some people, while others want a good deal. The idea is to try to please your customer rather than have a sameness in the quantity of syrup dispensed.

Also don't be too liberal in size of your glasses. Don't try to serve the largest glass of soda ever handed over the counter, but do try to serve the best. A small glass of the best soda is a tempting beverage and will draw more trade, but a large glass of any kind of soda does not leave that "longing-for-more" taste in the mouth.

HOW TO ECONOMIZE ON ICE.

Another saving which adds to profit is to contract early for your entire season's supply of ice; or, better still, if you can't buy ice at a low price, and you live where this is practicable, put up your own ice, either in your own house or a rented one. You can usually rent a house by agreeing to furnish the owner with the ice he will use during the hot season. In small towns where there is no regular ice dealer you can keep a small quantity of surplus ice at your store and let it be known that you will sell 5 and 10 cent lots, and you will sell enough during the summer to pay the cost of filling the icehouse. I have an icehouse that holds 100 tons. The digging, walling and roof cost me $120. It costs about $50 a season to fill it (can you buy your ice for $50?), making a total of $170 that this house and ice cost me the first year. The first season I sold $95 worth of ice, beside having ice to use lavishly at store for fountain and freezing cream and for three homes. Since then I have sold enough ice to more than pay for a two-story warehouse, built over the icehouse, besides having my ice without cost, and when the local lodge and church supper grafters come at me for donations I give them a cold deal—ice. It suits them and it suits me. When the poor get sick I give them ice. So you see ice is good for several things, as well as a cash saver. But if you are afraid of work don't tackle the icehouse proposition. I suggest it as a money saver, but not as a work saver.

Another saving which adds to profit is to freeze your own ice cream. You can make a first-class cream at from 45 to 60 cents a gallon.

Another saving which adds to profit is not to throw away your ice cream or allow it to melt at night. Keep it in a porcelain lined packing can and repack it with ice before closing your store at night; next morning your cream will be as good as ever and ready for the earliest dry throat.

CHARGE YOUR OWN FOUNTAIN.

Another saving which adds to profit is to charge your own fountain. As most of you know, charging outfits can be bought at a small or large price and size, to suit your purse and needs. With them charging your own fountain costs from 25 to 35 cents, as against 75 cents to $1 if others charge them for you. Besides the money saved on the charging you are always prepared for emergencies and leaks. Aside from carrying a few buckets of water, charging your fountains is very little work.

Another saving which adds to profit is to save the gas usually lost when changing fountains. This saving can be made by using a "two-way" cock. This cock allows you to keep two fountains attached all the time, so that the turn of a lever will throw one on and the other off without loss of gas, and it's mighty convenient to have the two fountains attached all the time, so that if one springs a leak or runs empty while serving soda all you have to do is to turn the lever and go on drawing soda from the other fountain.

Profitable Soda Methods.

By Herman H. Koegel.

To succeed with soda you must first of all have absolute cleanliness, pleasant surroundings, plenty of seats, an electric fan, fresh cut flowers and polite clerks. Use only the very best materials; poor flavors are dear at any price. Keep ice cream in perfect condition; never dish it out in a sloppy manner. Use plenty of ice. Keep fountain well filled with both ice and syrups; never tell a customer you are just out of a popular flavor. If a drink served is not satisfactory, throw it away and offer another to replace it; this makes friends. Use either rock candy syrup or simple syrup made by cold percolation. For soda fountain, use seven parts of syrup to one of water; use no eggs, soap bark or gum arabic for foam; with a first-class quality of ice cream it is not necessary. Don't be stingy with your carbonated water; it costs too little, and is what the customer expects in ordering soda water on a hot day. Use thin glasses, light holders, and never run the soda over the glass; it looks bad, besides you may ruin the expensive dress of a lady customer. Do not allow any young men to loaf about the store if you want to build up a paying soda business; their cigarette smoke, and oftentimes the remarks made by them, are not conducive to bring the patronage of the ladies. Take care of the ladies and they will bring their sweethearts, husbands and children, and success will crown your efforts. A little advertising is advantageous, especially when introducing a new drink. Advertise with a one-line ad. in your local paper, or with attractive signs about the fountain, but be brief and to the point.

A FEW HINTS.

Use thin glasses, kept perfectly clean. Use a solution of carbonate of soda, 2 pounds to 1 gallon of water, for cleaning greasy glasses, syrup cans and tumbler brushes; it keeps them perfectly sweet and clean. Never let a customer wait; be prompt in rush hours; put on extra help, and serve people in rotation as they come in. Push plain drinks; be sure and serve them solid and have them very cold. Never put ice in the carbonated water unless the customer requests it. Never argue with a customer; remember there are other fountains as good as yours; it is far better to keep their good will. When your fountain begins to splutter let out gas through vent found on each soda fountain until water flows; if air is in the pipes this will remedy the trouble; if caused by a foreign substance take faucet apart and remove it; uncouple the pipes, if necessary.

Never make up a supply of syrups to last more than two days; chocolate, cream, pineapple and strawberry are liable to ferment unless you add a preservative, which should never be done. Don't use artificial flavors when you can buy the real fruit juices so cheap; there is no excuse for it.

Never hurry a customer, or show that you are in a hurry to serve him or her, or get him or her out; give him or her plenty of time; often a customer buys a glass of soda water to get a chance to sit down and rest.

If you are using a copper drainer, use a solution composed of oxalic acid, 8 ounces, water, 1 gallon; sprinkle powdered pumice stone over drainer, using about 2 ounces of the oxalic acid solution, and scour with a hand scrub until bright, using plenty of water to remove all traces of poison. Keep your silverware bright.

If using crushed fruits, make no more than you can dispose of within two or three days; use half-crushed fruit and half-diluted rock candy syrup. In using concentrated fruit syrups any reliable make will do; go by the directions on the label.

Never place your carbonated bottled waters where the sun will strike them, as they will lose some of the carbonic acid gas and taste flat. In serving phosphates give a 12-ounce glass; don't be stingy with the water, it costs so little, and a customer ordering a plain drink wants water—not fizz.

In serving ice cream or sundaes be as neat as possible; furnish a glass of ice water and a paper napkin with each one; customers appreciate all these little details.

Even though you may not make expenses early or late in the season, you cannot figure on the profits of daily or weekly sales. Follow these rules to the letter and you will possess the secret of how to make soda water profitable.

Essentials of Success in the Sale of Soda Water.

By W. H. Tibbals.

To make the soda water business profitable the pharmacist must be like the successful politician in his efforts—"keep everlastingly at it." I would not recommend, however, that he use as much spirits in dispensing soda as the ordinary politician does in his campaign. To keep everlastingly at it I mean that the druggist must not think that all he has to do is to have a freezer of ice cream made up, a tank of carbonated water attached to the fountain, the syrup cans filled, etc., then sit down and wait for the soda customer to come in; but it is necessary that he should keep his eye on the soda man or young lady dispenser, whichever it may be, and insist on absolute cleanliness, "dispenser included," as this is the first and one of the most important things to be observed.

CLEANLINESS THE KEYNOTE.

Fountain, inside and out, and marble slabs or counter should be kept thoroughly clean; glasses and all silverware used about the fountain should be brilliantly polished. Plenty of clean towels must be kept at hand for this purpose. Do not allow the practice of allowing the soiled glasses to remain on the counter, and finally, when they are removed, merely rinsing them and turning them up on the drainer to be used for the next customer; keep them polished. This cannot be always done, perhaps, during a rush, but can be done at all other times.

In some cases the pharmacist may be able to do a large part of the work about the fountain himself, but if he has to also do considerable of the general work about the store the soda fountain will likely not receive the attention it should have to get the best results. Therefore, in most cases it is the best plan to employ a boy or girl, if not a man, to give most of their time and attention to that part of the business.

The store doors and open windows, if any, should be well screened during the summer season, and an electric or power fan, where the power is available, adds considerably to the attractiveness of the soda department, as well as to the comfort of customers. There is nothing more disgusting to customers than a swarm of flies buzzing around them while drinking soda.

The ice cream should be of good quality, and should be kept solid enough to stand when the carbonated water is drawn upon it. Good syrups and plenty of ice in the fountain are essential. Warm, sloppy soda will not only draw soda trade for your competitor, but will hurt your drug and sundry trade. They will go to him if his soda is better. People who get in the habit of coming to your store for soda will generally get in the habit of buying other articles there.

PUSH FANCY DRINKS.

The soda dispenser should not be satisfied with selling the ordinary 5-cent drinks, if he is unfortunate enough to have to dispense ice cream soda at that price, but should always push two or three good 10-cent fancy drinks, many of which can be found in the different journals. There are generally a few people, even in towns of moderate size, who are willing to part with a 10-cent piece for something out of the ordinary. A few of these sold each day help the profits out considerably. My opinion is that the dispenser does not make the profit he really deserves for his hard work in preparing and serving ice cream soda at 5 cents, and for that reason he should push the drinks on which he can make a better profit.

ADVERTISE, ADVERTISE!

Advertising in this department must not be overlooked. It is not necessary, however, to spend large amounts in newspaper advertising. Occasionally a few locals will do good, but one of the very best and least expensive ways to let the public know what you are serving at your fountain is to hang about your store and at the door cards made with the marking brush and cardboard. A bulletin board on the sidewalk with a slated surface, giving a list of drinks, is another good means of advertising.

INVENT NEW DRINKS.

Soda customers are generally looking for something new in this line. Get up a new drink occasionally, and keep pushing it. If your trade will not justify keeping sherbet or fruit ices every day, have one kind one or two days each week, at least, and make it known by hanging out a card. Lemon, orange and pineapple ices are popular. If your fountain has side draft tubes, they may be used to good advantage for ginger ale, root beer or some similar drinks, which can be made at a small expense where you have a carbonating outfit, which every soda dealer should have. A very good outfit can be bought for $20. There can be enough saved in a short time by carbonating your own soda water to pay for the outfit, besides you are enabled to make and carbonate these side drinks, in which there is a far better margin of profit than in ice cream soda at 5 cents.

ROOT BEER A DRAWING CARD.

A good quality of root beer or ginger ale can be made from extracts, several different brands of which are on the market. We have found a very good way to get these drinks started is to have a circular printed giving a list of the different drinks you are serving, and at the bottom of circular a coupon good for one glass of ginger ale or root beer, good on a certain date or for a number of days. To give away two or three hundred glasses in this way will make more soda customers than twice the cost spent in other advertising.

The man who has several hundred dollars invested in soda apparatus cannot afford to shake lemonade at 5 cents. Make it good and charge 10 cents. Those who know what good lemonade is will prefer to pay you 10 cents rather than buy the 5-cent kind.

Push soda not only in hot weather, but push hot soda in winter. A very good way to get hot soda started is to have menu cards printed and send out to the ladies of your town, announcing that you will serve hot soda free to ladies at a certain time; for instance, from 2 to 5 P. M. on a certain date. Use whipped cream with chocolate and wafers at 10 cents, or plain chocolate may be served at 5 cents.

Do not go into the soda business unless you have a good store of energy and push, but the fountain, if properly managed, will not only yield a profit to the pharmacist, but will make your store a more popular place to trade.

A Handsome Fountain and Some Special Drinks.

By Beaton Drug Company, Omaha, Neb.

The Beaton Drug Company has recently renovated the premises occupied by it at Fifteenth and Farnam streets, Omaha, and popularly known as the Busy Corner Pharmacy. One of the principal attractions of the store is a magnificent onyx soda fountain finished in solid mahogany. The following description of the premises and formulas for some of the beverages dispensed were written especially for the Soda Fountain number of the American Druggist by Mr. Smock, the head dispenser of the Beaton Drug Company:

The Beaton Drug Company has been in business for ten years on the same corner. Recently it has remodeled the store until it now has one of the largest and finest pharmacies in the West. The ceiling is of enameled steel panels, lighted with ten incandescent lamps of 187 candle-power each. Along the center of the ceiling are placed at intervals five electric fans, making the store in summer time one of the coolest places in the city. A vitrous tiled floor in a handsome green and white pattern is kept always clean and shining.

Fifteen tables down the center of the room bear ample evidence to the fact that the drinks served at the handsome new fountain are popular with the people of Omaha; two miniature tables and tiny chairs to match for the little ones are in constant use. Waving palms are arranged about the room in artistic corners and upon the marble soda fountain counter. Along one side of the room are the glass show cases filled with the large variety of sundries which every enterprising druggist keeps nowadays. These cases have glass shelves, which add greatly to their beauty and, moreover, are easily cleaned, for the one aim of this drug store is cleanliness and a perfect sanitary condition.

The soda fountain is the L. A. Becker Twentieth Century Sanitary, made in Chicago. Everything about it is open to the public. There are no closed closets or block tin syrup cans or hiding places of any kind. It is interesting to see this soda fountain in full blast after the theatre of an evening.

Almost as many ice cream drinks are sold in the winter as in the summer; and the way the hot chocolate, hot tomato bisques and egg malts disappear is something startling. The dispensers have everything prepared beforehand as far as possible for the theatre crowd. Four dispensers are employed and, besides, two boys who wait on the tables. Behind the counters stand the china cups in dainty patterns and array. A heaping spoonful of chocolate paste, all ready for the hot milk, is placed in each cup, and a clean crock of puffy, delicious whipped cream stands near, all ready for the finishing touch of rich cream to be added to the steaming hot chocolate. Dozens of these cups are ready for the crowd. The bottle of malted milk is set out handy for the dispensers, and baskets of fresh eggs are at hand under the counter for those who call for egg malts. The syrups for cold drinks are contained in large clean bottles instead of in tin cans. This soda fountain is a marvel in itself. Constructed of marble, onyx and richly grained mahogany, it is as beautiful and artistic an affair in the way of a soda fountain as was ever placed in the West. The counters are of marble, with onyx panels, and the back is of marble, while facing the street at the back are three blocks of French plate mirrors built around three pillars instead of the usual plain back of glass, as seen in most fountains.

This fountain is perhaps the most expensive and complete fountain in the West. With the hot drinks dainty sandwiches and salads are now served, and they have proved very popular with the shoppers and the "after the show" crowds. The following are a few of the popular drinks and sundaes served:

CONEY ISLAND PHOSPHATE.

Pineapple syrup........................1 oz.
Orange syrup...........................1 oz.
Egg 1
Cream ....2 oz.
Phosphate ....1 dash

Shake thoroughly, fill with fine stream, strain and serve with nutmeg.

MAPLE CREMO.

In a large shaking glass put 4 oz. ice cream, 2 oz. maple syrup and 1 oz. plain cream. Shake and when thoroughly shaken fill with fine stream and serve.

RASPBERRY TART.

Raspberry syrup........................2 oz.
Phosphate ....2 dashes
Shaved ice............................½ glass

Soda to fill glass. Top with sliced pineapple and red cherry.

TEJOHN BRACER.

Claret syrup............................1 oz.
Sherry wine.............................1 oz.
Malted milk.....................2 spoonfuls
Egg 1

Shake; add fine stream; strain and serve; nutmeg on top.

CLUBHOUSE SUNDAE.

Cone of ice cream in sundae cup. Pour on top 1 ladleful of chocolate; 1 ladleful of chopped nuts; 1 green cherry and 2 red cherries on each side. Sprinkle over all 1 teaspoonful of malted milk.

CHOP SUEY FOR SUNDAES.

Seeded raisins.........................½ lb.
Shredded cocoanut......................2 oz.
Green cherries.........................4 oz.
Red cherries...........................4 oz.
Sliced pineapple.......................4 oz.
Dates ....4 oz.

Chop and mix; add maple and cherry syrup equal parts to thin enough to serve; 2 oz. port wine and 2 oz. sherry wine adds to the flavor.

Ways of Expanding Soda Trade.

By W. T. O'Connor.

How many druggists with soda fountains in their stores ever do a single thing from one year to the other to boom their soda business? And yet the fountain is one of the main features of the store. In proportion to its size it is often the most expensive of all the fixtures. Grudgingly or otherwise, it must be given a liberal amount of attention. It must be kept clean and shining. Ice has to be bought every day and the syrup tanks frequently refilled. It eats up a very nice amount of your time and should be forced to pay, and pay well, for the expenditure.

Napoleon said that an army traveled upon its stomach. A soda trade will grow upon what is in the fountain. If the contents are good or bad, so the trade will be, according to the proportions of the soda's virtues or deficiencies. The public knows good from bad too well (in some things at least) to make it profitable to try to exploit the inferior. The first requisite is good quality. When the quality is offered that the service is entitled the recompense should be demanded. If the quality and quantity of syrup, cream and soda that is offered entitle the server to charge 10 cents instead of the more common 5 cents, 10 cents should be charged. There is a druggist in Newark, N. J., who makes a feature of his fountain and who charges 10 cents for practically all drinks except phosphates or plain flavors and who fills a 20-foot counter often three deep. There is a large candy store next to him, where the charge is only 5 cents for nearly every drink; still this store is far from doing a business like the druggist. And yet the fountain is an integral part of a candy store.

The drug store window is one of the best mediums for advertising the soda fountain, and in window advertising, as a general rule, one is limited to window cards. Make them as attractive as possible. It is a good plan to try to suggest daintiness all through your soda advertising.

The druggist mentioned above puts a card, illustrated in colors, into his window once or twice a week. Usually they are built around some timely topic. For instance, at the last election the public was advised, with the accompaniment of an appropriate illustration, to pay election bets with Blank's soda. The cards are a feature, and the people who use the street the store is on usually look for them.

The points to bring out in advertising a fountain are: Purity of the syrup, etc., cleanliness and first-class service.

Purity is the most important of the three and furnishes the strongest kind of advertising arguments.

Tell of the care you take to see that every ingredient that goes into the making of the soda is the best that can be obtained. Try to show that it is a vital thing that soda be just as pure as it is possible to make it.

There is so much agitation concerning adulteration that the reading public will easily be persuaded to drink your product if they are persuaded that it is pure.

Second is cleanliness. This means everything, from the spoons to the clerks. Nothing will so neatly and quickly drive away custom as the sight of dirt, and the possibility of absorbing it with a drink that should be a draught of joy. I once saw a soda dispenser remove an embalmed fly from a quantity of syrup that was about to be made into soda. Up to the time of witnessing this interesting operation I thought that I wanted a soda, but I suddenly discovered that it was a cigar that I really did want.

Keep the spoons and all the metal parts shining, the glasses bright and the rest of the fountain spick and span.

All of these make excellent advertising topics. Even without advertising they will create trade.

Most advertising along this line can be aimed at the women folks. On account of their housewifely duties they will readily appreciate the cleanliness that is akin to godliness.

Good service means prompt attention and the mixing of the soda, so that its constituents will appear in their right proportions and not be one part soda and two parts air, is important.

Soda advertising should be seasonable. The foolishness of advertising hot drinks in May is at once apparent. If trade justifies it give patrons the various fresh fruits as they appear on the market, and be the first to do it.

Cards in the lines of trolleys that pass the druggist's door are profitable for promoting sales. They bring the subject to the attention of a possible "absorber" when he is in or approaching your neighborhood, and are therefore very timely.

Inclosure slips will "pull" with that portion of possible patrons that have not acquired the soda habit.

The newspapers will do their full share if a good line of copy is put into them.

Here are some specimen advertisements that can be used for any of the above mediums:

Suggested Soda Water Ads.

A Glass of Soda

to taste right must "balance" properly. There must be the correct amount of syrup and of cream and of soda. This is a thing that is often overlooked, but we give it the deserved attention, and as a result our soda tastes particularly good. This is an indication of the care that we give to details.

Soda Syrup

is the soul of the drink. Good syrup makes soda a thing of joy, while poor syrup, or "varnish," as it has been facetiously called, is a horror.

Every pint of syrup used at our fountain is made by us right on the premises, and we use the best ingredients obtainable. That is why our soda tastes as good at the tenth or twentieth drink as at the first.

The Nectar of the Gods

could not have given more pleasure than one glass of our fine soda.

Besides, where the gods had only one flavor to enjoy, we have ...... for you.

Notice How Spick

and span everything is about our fountain. You cannot see a sign or trace of anything unpleasant. And inside the fountain, and under the counter, everything is as clean as the things in plain sight. Could you ask a better guarantee of goodness?

Perfection

we have been told, is unattainable. But we believe that our soda is as near to that supreme state as it is possible to get. This means that you will find no soda better than that which we dispense. Come in and we will "show you."

The Next Time

that you are thirsty come around and ask us for a glass of ——— soda. We are proud of every flavor in our fountain, but this is our masterpiece. Paper and type cannot do justice to its virtues. You will have to try it to appreciate it.

When You Bet

make our soda the stake and no matter whether you win or lose you will be satisfied, for you will have to treat yourself when you pay the bet to the winner.

One of Our Customers

recently told us that the only reason she did not drink a glass of our soda every time she thought of it was because she could not have it sent through the telephone, and she thought of it entirely too often to come to the store.

We never had a higher compliment paid to our soda than this. If you know nothing about it, it is time to learn.

We Believe

that if burglars should enter our store they would get no further than the fountain. The goodness of the soda would hold them there until the break of day. It ought to be good soda, for no fountain in town gets more attention.

Begin and End Right

Start the holiday with a glass of our soda and end it the same way. Can you think of anything more appropriate or which will round out a day of festivity more seasonably?

Are You Prejudiced

against soda because you have had the bad kind served to you? If you are we can banish all remembrance of your experience with one glass of our soda.

Lay yourself open to conviction.

The Hague Tribunal

would have to go out of existence if we could make enough soda to supply the world. Nothing on earth can promote peace or good feeling better than the contents of our fountain. Come in and be "harmonised."

Some Well-Tried Formulas.

BY ALBERT E. EBERT,

Chicago.

The writer's experience has of late years been limited so far as giving personal attention to the soda fountain is concerned. However, he has always advocated that the syrups which are dispensed should be home made and not purchased from dealers of soda supplies or from manufacturers of rock candy syrup. He has advised the use of a standard, pure granulated sugar, which when made into a syrup is in every respect superior, more satisfactory and less expensive than such as are bought. If the cost of granulated sugar is 6 cents a pound and 12 pounds are used to 1 gallon of water, making nearly 1⅓ gallons of syrup, the cost of the finished product will be about 40 cents a gallon. Rock candy syrup is not usually sold at this figure, and the cost of the same fluctuates in the same ratio as that of sugar. This must be taken into consideration when the price of such syrup is quoted.

The following formula for a chocolate syrup has been very satisfactory to us and has been very popular with our patrons:

CHOCOLATE SYRUP.

Chocolate, Baker's soluble..........6 av. oz.
Oil of cinnamon..........................1 drop
Tincture vanilla.............1 fluid drachm
Sugar, granulated.................32 av. oz.
Boiling water.........................24 fl. oz.
Syrup, enough to make 1 gallon.

In an empty chocolate can we make the mixture of the powdered chocolate and the granulated sugar by shaking the two together. In a vessel having the capacity to hold the finished syrup heat the water to boiling and into this pour the mixture of chocolate and sugar, keeping up the boiling for about five minutes with stirring; now add the syrup, bring to boiling point, add the vanilla and oil of cinnamon; agitate and allow to cool. Keep in dispensing bottles, which should be shaken at times when the syrup is used.

COFFEE SYRUP.

Coffee..............................8 av. oz.
Sugar...............................6 av. lbs.
Tincture of vanilla...........2 fluid drachms
Boiling water.
Soda foam, of each, sufficient.

Moisten the finely ground coffee with boiling water; pack in percolator, let macerate for 15 to 20 minutes; then percolate with boiling water until 32 fluid ounces of percolate are obtained. In this dissolve the sugar and add the vanilla and foam.

JAVA TONIC SYRUP.

Compound tincture of cinchona...6 fluid drachms
Coffee syrup..........................8 fl. oz.
Vanilla syrup.........................4 fl. oz.
Glucose syrup.........................8 fl. oz.
Syrup enough to make 32 fl. oz.

Serve "solid" in 8-ounce glasses, like the phosphates.

WILD CHERRY PHOSPHATE SYRUP.

Syrup of wild cherry, U. S. P.........10 fl. oz.
Cherry juice, German, black..........8 fl. oz.
Glucose syrup.......................12 fl. oz.
Diluted phosphoric acid..............2 fl. oz.
Oil bitter almond....................4 drops
Mix. Serve like the preceding.

The Importance of the Fountain.

BY FRANK A. EPSTEIN,

Boston, Mass.

My drug store in the retail business section of Boston presents some peculiar features that needed special study in order to make the most of opportunities. Every druggist's problem is perhaps a little different from any other, and yet the experience of one may be of help to another.

Of course every druggist takes pride in the quality of his prescription work, and I am no exception to the rule. The successful druggist must keep his stock of drugs always up to standard, and his prescription clerks must be men of skill and experience. Then there are lots of questions always coming up as to what lines of patent medicines to carry, how large a stock to order, how much space to allow to cigars, confectionery, etc.

My store is located on a corner near the Scollay square subway entrance. Lots of people pass the door daily. I didn't want them to *pass by*—I wanted them to *come in*. So I reasoned that it was up to me to hold out some attraction that they couldn't help seeing.

Well, I've got something now that *does* bring them in, that catches their eye, even if they're hurrying to catch a subway car at the rush hour, and that first glance is pretty often followed by a longer look, and then the customer steps in.

What do you think of this picture of my soda fountain? Isn't it honestly something out of the common line of soda fountains? When it is illuminated in the evening it shows up in great style, the light behind the art panels giving the effect of stained glass windows. The onyx columns, the Tiffany shades, the gleam of the electric lights on the cut glass, the big mirrors, with the handsome wall paintings above—all making a magnificent display that no customer can fail to observe.

Of course, I'm not in business for my health, and I didn't pay for all this just for the sake of having an ornamental front in my store. I did it after a good deal of hard thinking as to whether it would *pay* in dollars and cents.

And the results? Here are the facts:

The last year with my old equipment I did a soda business of $8,009.

The first year with the "Innovation" apparatus I did a soda business of $30,000, an increase of 300 per cent.

I aim to serve the best soda in town. Good flavoring, with the genuine fruit taste, goes a long way in making your customer come again for another glass. Then I insist that everything about the fountain shall be kept absolutely clean and sweet, an easy matter with the new construction of this apparatus.

My experience has been that every department in the store helps the other departments. Regular customers for cigars remember my store when they are in need of quinine or cough drops, or when they have a prescription to be filled. The ladies who drop in for candy or soda may be attracted by the sight of perfumes or toilet accessories.

Since the new fountain was installed my drug trade and prescription business has increased 20 per cent. As there has been no change in local conditions or in general store management I attribute this increase solely to the attractiveness of the "Innovation." The American Soda Fountain Company, when the matter of installing a new fountain was first considered, assured me that a really handsome apparatus of the "Innovation" model would prove far more profitable, in proportion to its first cost, than any less expensive apparatus of older style construction. And results have proved that they were right, for my new fountain was a trade winner from the word go.

So much for an aggressive policy in my soda water department, with strict attention to business in *every* department.

Manning's Favorites.

By Raymond Manning,

Manager of the Soda Water Department of the Buntin Drug Company, Terre Haute, Ind.

CREAM DESSERT.

The most delicious dessert ever served is made as follows:

Brazil nuts .... 4 oz.
English walnuts .... 6 oz.
Pecans .... 4 oz.

Chop the kernels finely together; sprinkle over ice cream; add ladies of whipped cream, maple syrup and two cherries.

TURKISH PUNCH.

Raspberry syrup .... 2 oz.
Acid phosphate .... 4 dashes.
Angostura bitters .... 2 dashes.
Soda .... q. s. ad 6 oz.

Use a 10-ounce goblet and float claret wines on top. Decorate with cherries, oranges and a sprig of mint. (15 cents.)

FROZEN MINT CORDIAL.

Spearmint syrup .... 1½ oz.
Acid phosphate .... 2 dashes.
Soda .... q. s. ad 8 oz.

How to serve.—Use an 8-ounce glass. First bruise a sprig of fresh mint in the glass and add syrup. Fill the glass two-thirds with shaved ice and soda q. s. Decorate with a slice of orange, cherries and a sprig of mint. (10 cents.)

BOSTON DESSERT.

Peanuts, finely chopped .... 6 oz.
Cocoanut, shredded .... 3 oz.
Maple syrup .... 6 pts.

Color dark with caramel. Serve over ice cream.

CELERY CORDIAL.

A Bracer.

Syrup .... 1 gallon.
Syrup citric acid .... 1 ounce.
Fluid extract celery .... 2 drams.

Color green. Serve in 8-ounce glasses, with plenty of shaved ice and a slice of orange. (5 cents.)

Epstein's Handsome Fountain, Boston, Mass

ROYAL PHOSPHATES.

Cherry syrup .... 1 ounce.
Acid phosphate .... 2 dashes.
Grape juice .... 1 ounce.

Serve with shaved ice and decorate with oranges and cherries. (5 cents.)

MOCHA SUNDAE.

Ice cream .... 1 dish.
Chopped hickory nuts.
Mocha coffee syrup.
Maraschino cherries.

Very delicious, and a big winner with us. (10 cents.)

OPERA DESSERT.

Ice cream .... 1 dish.
Maraschino cherries.
Whipped cream.
Maple syrup.

(10 cents.)

Old Favorites.

By George W. Hague, Ph. C.

Hempstead, Long Island.

The pharmacist usually experiences little difficulty in devising new drinks and names, the chief difficulty being connected with the improvement of the older popular formulas. There are still many who are unable to prepare a good vanilla syrup or lemon syrup. Soda foam of good foaming quality and harmless character is not always made properly. The best soda foam, in my opinion, is fluid extract gycyrrhiza, U. S. P., 1 drachm to 1 gallon of syrup. This has many advantages over other kinds. Egg albumen has also been used with satisfaction, and here is a good one made from soap bark

QUILLAJA SODA FOAM.

Soap bark .... ℥ij
Alcohol .... ℥ij
Glycerin .... ℥ij
Water, enough to make .... ℥viij

Macerate the bark in 2 ounces of each of the other ingredients and filter after three days, passing enough water through the filter to make 8 ounces. Use 2 drachms of this foam to 1 gallon of syrup.

VANILLA SYRUP.

Ext. vanilla with tonka .... ʒij
Fld. ext. glycyrrhiza .... gtt. xv
Syrup .... Ov

This syrup should not be colored, as the vanilla and foam give it a sufficiently dark color. The amount of vanilla in this syrup is in just the right proportion. I do not care for the U. S. P. tincture of vanilla for soda syrups.

LEMON SYRUP.

Spirits of lemon .... ʒvi
Sat. solu. citric acid .... ʒvi
Soap bark foam .... ʒij
Tinct. curcuma .... gtt. xv
Syrup .... Ov

Mix and filter through sponge to make a clear and sparkling syrup.

COFFEE SYRUP.

Coffee, equal parts, Mocha and Java ...... 1 lb.
Water .... 4½ pints.
Sugar .... 5 lbs.
Caromel .... q. s.

Boil the coffee in the water for 15 minutes, strain through cheesecloth and add enough water through the dregs to make 4½ pints, and color with caramel after dissolving the sugar in the coffee solution. Coffee syrup should be served with plenty of cream.

CHOCOLATE SYRUP.

Powd. chocolate .... 1½ lbs.
Sugar .... 5 lbs.
Table salt .... 10 grains.
Ext. vanilla, with tonka .... 1 oz.

Rub the chocolate into a smooth paste with 1 pint of boiling water; then add remainder of water and the sugar; boil ten minutes with continuous stirring. Add the vanilla and table salt when cold. The table salt is added on the theory that salt in small amounts brings out the flavor of sweets. The chocolate must be boiled to burst the starch granules. About ½ ounce of French brandy added to the above amount gives the syrup a desirable flavor.

ORANGE SYRUP.

Oranges 6
Sugar .... 4 oz.
Syrup to make .... ½ gallon.

Grate the oranges into a large mortar, taking care not to remove any of the white bitter portion; then rub with the sugar. Cut the oranges and squeeze the juice into the mortar; then add enough syrup to make ½ gallon; allow to stand several hours, then strain. As orange syrup is used mostly in the form of phosphates no foam or acid solution is used in this syrup. The secret of a successful orange syrup consists in using plenty of oranges.

GINGER ALE EXTRACT.

Tincture of ginger .... 1 gallon.
Tincture of capsicum .... 7½ oz.
Extract of orange .... 3 oz.
Extract of lemon .... ½ oz.
Caramel .... 5 oz.
Water .... 1½ gallons.
Sugar .... 2 lbs.
Magnesium carbonate .... 1 lb.

Mix and allow to stand 12 hours; shake occasionally and filter.

GINGER ALE SYRUP.

Ginger ale extract .... Oiv
Sat. sol. citric acid .... ℥iss
Syrup q. s. ad .... Ciij

The above formulas are in general use. Below I give a few special formulas which have proven profitable:

MIXED FRUITS.

Orange syrup .... }
Strawberry syrup .... } Of each 1 pint.
Pineapple syrup .... }

ENGLISH BREAKFAST TEA SYRUP.

English breakfast tea .... 1½ oz.
Sugar .... 1 lb.
Boiling water .... 2 pints.

Infuse for 15 minutes; filter, and dissolve the sugar in the filtrate. This drink is served in mineral glasses, with plenty of milk.

APRICOT SYRUP.

French apricots .... 10 lbs.
Sugar .... 25 lbs.
Sat. sol. citric acid .... ½ oz.
Water .... 1½ gallons.

Boil the fruit in the water and strain; then add the sugar and citric acid solution.

SODA MINT MIXTURE.

Sodium bicarbonate .... ℥ij
Sugar .... ʒij
Aromatic spirits ammonia .... Mxx
Peppermint water .... ℥viij

Dose: One or two fluid drachms in a little plain soda. This last formula is hardly entitled to a place with soda syrups, but I give it because I have sold so much of this mixture at the fountain in place of bicarbonate of soda for acid stomachs.

HINTS ON DISPENSING MINERAL AND OTHER BOTTLED WATERS.

By J. B. Moore,

Philadelphia.

In some localities there is a large demand for bottled mineral and drinking waters and other similar goods, and their sale is not alone confined to the wealthier classes.

The corks of these bottles are often difficult to remove, and especially with the means at hand in many families, as the corks are often driven into the necks of the bottles their entire length, not leaving sufficient of the cork projecting for one to take hold of for its removal. It often happens that many of these waters, after long standing, become cloudy and deposit considerable sediment. Now in selling these waters to customers, and especially to your more particular and fastidious ones, it would be a very courteous and pleasing thing to say to them, "Mrs., or Mr. So-and-so, shall I remove the cork for you and replace it with a new one, so that you will have no trouble in opening the bottle?" and if necessary, you might also add, "You see the water is slightly cloudy"; or, "there is a little sediment in it which you don't want to drink; now, if you would like to have me do so, I will filter it for you, and wash out your bottle. It will take me only a few minutes to do it, and if you have not the time to wait I will send it home to you with pleasure, in good condition for use." Your gracious offer will generally be accepted with a smile of kindly appreciation, and you may feel pretty well assured that all the mineral waters that your customer may need in the future will be likely to come from your store, and with them, perhaps, many other articles which he has been accustomed to purchase elsewhere.

The carbonated and effervescent waters of course you cannot very well filter without the escape of much of their gas, but you can kindly offer to remove the cork and replace it with a nicely fitting new one.

This same voluntary tender of kindly service may be made in dispensing extract of malt and many other liquid bottled goods, which you know are difficult and troublesome to open.

In selling all goods of this character you should invariably offer to send them home, and especially if the purchaser be a lady. These little *extra* courtesies, as we might call them, will be appreciated, will redound to your credit, and will tighten your grip upon the confidence and respect of your customer, and perhaps secure from him a voluntary recommendation to others.

Cream of Current Literature

A summary of the leading articles in contemporary pharmaceutical periodicals.

To Prepare Calcined Magnesia.—Morato (*Revista de Farmacia*, 1905, No. 10) analyzed several samples of magnesium oxide bought in the market, and found that the best of these contained only 82 per cent. of true magnesium oxide. In order to obtain a good magnesia Morato advises that purified magnesium carbonate be calcined in a special oven until the loss of carbon dioxide ceases, and then the product should be placed in hermetically sealed boxes. This process gives a magnesia of excellent quality.

The Preparation of Turpentine Liniment.—G. Stein (*Pharmazeutische Zeitung*, 1906, No. 18) gives the following formula for the preparation of a perfectly clear turpentine liniment:

Fused caustic potash	Gm. 40
Water	Gm. 20
Alcohol	Gm. 100
Linseed oil	Gm. 210
Oil of turpentine	Gm. 200

The constituents are gently heated until a clear solution results, and 100 Gm. of water is added until the mixture is completely saponified. The soap thus obtained is dissolved in 330 Gm. oil of turpentine and a perfectly clear liniment is thus prepared.

The Adulteration of Lycopodium.—Gallois (*Journal de pharmacie et de chimie*, March 1, 1906) calls attention to the frequency with which lycopodium is now adulterated, owing to the fact that the genuine article has considerably increased in price. Under the name of "substitute" a powder has been placed on the market for the distinct purpose of adulterating lycopodium. "Substitute" is a rather dark yellow powder, having a grayish tinge, and quite a different feel from that of true lycopodium, and as much as 50 per cent. of this powder can be added to lycopodium without danger of detection, unless a careful examination takes place. "Substitute" burns like lycopodium when thrown into a flame. It is insoluble in water and does not become moistened, just as is the case with lycopodium. In alcohol it partly dissolves, giving rise to a straw colored solution and an insoluble residue which is rather darker than the original powder. It is also partly dissolved in chloroform and in ether, while lycopodium, as we know, resists these solvents. Under the microscope it appears as irregular, transparent granules, with rounded angles, which cannot be confused with the characteristic form of lycopodium. When heated upon a platinum foil this powder does not completely melt, but softens and turns back, giving off white vapors. After combustion it leaves a mineral residue of a red brick color consisting almost entirely of ferric sesqui oxide.

Metallic Copper for Purifying Drinking Water.—Kraemer (*American Journal of Pharmacy*, March, 1906) gives the results of his experiments in regard to the use of copper in the purification of water. For this purpose copper foil, copper sulphate or the salts of copper may be employed. Copper foil is useful in the household when purifying water, while copper sulphate and other salts of copper are useful in disinfecting solutions and in purifying the water in reservoirs. Kraemer found that in water containing the typhoid germ or the colon bacillus these bacteria were destroyed in from two to four hours after the addition of copper foil. On the other hand, when copper foil was not added these germs multiplied rapidly in water for months. It was found, however, that the filtering of contaminated water also was followed by destruction of the germs in from two to four hours. But it seemed that the contact of the water with a copper faucet in the slow process of filtration had much to do with the destruction of the germs.

A very brief period of time was sufficient to destroy typhoid and other germs by means of copper foil. In fact, if the foil was allowed to remain in distilled water for from one to five minutes no live typhoid germs were found within a few hours.

It is a question as to whether the treatment of water with copper has any injurious effect upon persons drinking this water. Professor Kraemer does not think so; as for nearly a year the drinking water in his home has been treated with copper and no ill effects have been noticed. The water so treated is more palatable than boiled water. He makes it a practice to wash vegetables in copper-treated water, or to allow them to soak in a vessel of water containing a strip of clean copper foil for from three to four hours, shaking occasionally.

Mercuric Oxycyanide.—The chemistry and pharmacy of mercuric oxycyanide are comparatively unknown, and so the recent article of Holdermann (*Archiv. für Pharmazie*, 1905, page 600) is of considerable interest, especially as mercuric oxycyanide has been lately used quite extensively as an antiseptic. Holdermann agrees with Richard that the oxycyanide of commerce is in reality pure cyanide, or very slightly basic cyanide containing a small amount of oxide. There is in reality but one real oxycyanide of mercury. He found that in the process of preparing this compound the first crystallization gave oxycyanide, while the subsequent one gave the ordinary cyanide. The usual method of preparing this salt is to saturate a solution of mercuric cyanide with mercuric oxide and to crystallize the product. But by this method one can never combine one molecule of the cyanide with one of the oxide to form one molecule of oxycyanide. If equal molecules of the two constituents be employed a large portion of the oxide remains free and so does a large portion of the cyanide. The following process devised by Holdermann yields 80 per cent. of oxycyanide: First, 13.5 Gm. of mercuric cyanide are powdered and thoroughly mixed with 11.5 Gm. of the yellow oxide. The mixture is placed in a small Erlenmeyer flask, a little water is added and the contents heated for four hours on the water bath. Five hundred Cc. of water is then added, and the whole heated to boiling until the insoluble portion has lost its granular appearance and contains only the powdered oxide. The hot filtered liquid deposits the crystalline oxycyanide on cooling.

The latter is a white crystalline powder, which turns brown on heating, swells and becomes decomposed, leaving a voluminous residue. It is soluble in about 100 volumes of water, more soluble in hot water, but in contact with hot water decomposes to some extent.

How to Tell the Poisonous Mushrooms.—Professor Labesse (*Anjou Médical*, November, 1905) discusses the question as to the popular method of distinguishing poisonous mushrooms from the edible variety. Mushroom poisoning, as we know, is by no means uncommon, and the chief cause thereof is the ignorance of the majority of people as to the poisonous varieties. The best way to avoid this poisoning is to learn to know the edible mushrooms growing in one's neighborhood and never to eat any other varieties but those few whose properties are well known.

It is a popular idea among cooks that poisonous mushrooms blacken gold and silver. As a matter of fact, a mushroom which is decaying blackens silver or gold, while a fresh mushroom, whether poisonous or not, never does so. It is also said that poisonous mushrooms curdle milk. This occurs with both edible and poisonous varieties if a ferment or an acid is contained in the mushroom. A variety of other fallacies are held which have no foundation in fact, as, for example, that an onion will become brown when placed in a pan in which poisonous mushrooms are boiling; that all mushrooms which have pink leaflets are edible; that insects attack only edible mushrooms and that the latter have always an agreeable odor. A most common fallacy is that mushrooms with a firm flesh which breaks and which have a dry skin are good to eat, and that a good mushroom always has an agreeable taste. All these qualities can occur in exceedingly poisonous mushrooms. There are some rules, however, which are useful in distinguishing poisonous from nonpoisonous varieties.

Thus, mushrooms which grow on the wood of Coniferæ are poisonous. Mushrooms growing upon trees should never be eaten. Nor should mushrooms with a blue, violet green or red color be used at the table. Mushrooms with a milky juice should always be rejected, as should also be those growing in shady woods. There is, however, no really absolute method of distinguishing a poisonous mushroom from one fit to eat. A specialized knowledge of the different varieties is the only safe course.

The Detection of Traces of Sugar in Urine.

M. J. Blaise (*Répértoire de pharmacie*, February 10, 1906) presents an interesting study of the difficulties encountered in testing urine for glucose when but minute quantities of this abnormal constituent are present. Most urines containing traces of glucose give a yellowish-green precipitate when boiled with Fehling's solution, and this precipitate remains in suspension in the liquid, thus rendering the recognition of the reaction difficult. Various expedients have been adopted to remedy this, with but little success. Urines rich in glucose give a very distinct precipitate of anhydrous copper oxide, while urines poor in glucose give a precipitate of copper hydroxide. Other urines containing a moderate amount of glucose often give a greenish precipitate which is found on qualitative testing, while with a quantitative test, when the reagent is added drop by drop, the anhydrous oxide is obtained. It seems that the precipitation of the anhydrous oxide from the start is followed by the precipitation of the same form, the anhydrous, throughout the operation. Hence the author conceived the idea that a few Cc. of a solution of glucose of known composition might be added to the Fehling's solution in order to produce a precipitate of anhydrous cupric oxide. Then if glucose was present in the urine the precipitation would go on normally. In urines rich in glucose the addition of a little glucose to the reagent does not modify the result of the direct quantitative test; in fact, this addition facilitates the recognition of the end-reaction.

In urines containing very small amounts of sugar, which give a reddish color to Fehling's solution without producing the precipitate, the simple expedient of adding glucose to the Fehling's solution has relieved the author in many a difficult situation and has allowed him to determine the absence or presence of sugar.

The procedure which he employs is as follows: He mixes 10 Cc. of each of the two solutions composing Fehling's solution, corresponding to 0.05 gm. of glucose, and to the mixture adds 2 Cc. of a solution containing 0.01 gm. of glucose. Instantly, on boiling, there is a precipitate of the anhydrous oxide. The operation is next continued with the urine to be analyzed until the color disappears. The end-reaction can thus be determined just as accurately with a urine containing a minute amount of glucose as with one containing a larger amount. The author concludes that this slight modification of Fehling's method secures the most accurate results possible, results such as can be obtained ordinarily only with the optical methods (polarization).

Pharmacists in the German Army.

Apothecary-Major of the First Class Kopp, in the issue of the *Archives de médicine et de pharmacie militaires* for December, 1905, reviews the status of the pharmacist in the German army. He points out that the pharmaceutical department of the German army was reorganized in 1902. In Germany medical and pharmaceutical students are allowed to perform the military duty which is incumbent upon all able-bodied adolescents of the male sex by volunteering for one year, but before they can claim this privilege they have to produce a certificate of aptitude for military service from a board appointed by the State and must also undertake to equip, to clothe and to maintain themselves at their own expense. Military apothecaries on the permanent list are recruited from these volunteers. When the new organization came into force they were 49 in number, all classed as officers, although their relative rank was not defined, but when the new scheme is completed their strength will be considerably increased.

The official title of the chief of the department is *Oberstabsapotheker* (chief staff Apothecary). He is attached to the medical section of the War Office, where he deals with the technical questions appertaining to his specialty and also controls all military pharmacies whether they belong to the active army or to the reserve.

Next in rank are the *Korpsstabsapotheker* (corps staff Apothecary), 24 in number. One of these officers is attached to each of the 23 army corps into which the German army is divided. Under the orders of the principal medical officer he is responsible for the efficiency and good order of everything connected with his department, his duties including the biannual inspection of every pharmacy in the command, the control of supply and expenditure in these establishments, the auditing of their accounts, the superintendence of subordinates not only with the colors but also in the reserve, and the direction of the analytical laboratory with which every army corps is provided.

The officers of the third grade are designated *Stabsapotheker* (staff Apothecary), and in 1902 they too were 24 in number. The duties of a Stabsapotheker consist in superintending the sanitary depot of the army corps to which he belongs and in managing the pharmacy of the garrison hospital at headquarters.

According to the reorganization decree of 1902 every military hospital with 71 beds and upwards should have a *Stabsapotheker* in charge of its pharmacy, but this part of the scheme has not as yet been carried out.

The pharmaceutical students serving for a year as volunteers are distributed according to requirements among 120 hospitals to the number of 265, some of them doing additional duty in the laboratories and sanitary depots. There are also five more serving in the Kaiser Wilhelm Academy at Berlin under a Korpsstabsapotheker, which brings the total strength up to 270. After serving for six months a volunteer student may be permitted to return to his home in order that he may complete his professional education and obtain a diploma. He then has to resume military duty for a second period of six months and, should he be desirous of joining the permanent branch, must next go through a special course of duty of six weeks' duration to the satisfaction of the principal medical officer. Having passed this test the student has then to go through a course of analytical chemistry, with special reference to water and alimentary substances, in a Government laboratory. The duration of this course is 18 months and at the end of it the candidate has to satisfy a board of examiners.

Ability to carry out analyses was rendered obligatory in 1902 for all the apothecaries who were then serving and all desirous of remaining in the department were obliged to provide themselves with the State diploma.

The relief of military medical officers from more or less uncongenial work in the superintendence of pharmacies is a distinct step in advance, but as yet the reform is incomplete. In all hospitals of less than 71 beds the medical officer is supplied with a limited stock of simple medicaments of which he has to control the distribution. Should more complicated medicine be required he must have recourse to the civilian pharmacy of the locality. In commenting on this article the *Lancet*, of London, says: "The fact that the total strength of the pharmaceutical department of the German army in 1894 was only 217 of all ranks, whereas in 1904 it was 321, is of good augury that in time all military medical officers will be relieved from pharmaceutical duty."

Emulsion of Paraldehyde.

Paraldehyde ....℥i
Tinct. of quillaja..........................♏xx
Water to..............................℥ss or ℥i

Queries and Answers

We shall be glad, in this department, to respond to calls for information on all pharmaceutic matters.

Sticky Fly Paper.—G. C.—A fairly economical method of making sticky fly paper is to take ordinary rough paper, previously glazed with a hot solution of glue or gelatin, and spread upon it a solution of resin in castor oil, made by dissolving about 2 parts of resin in 1 part of oil. A mixture of molasses and glucose, containing 1 part molasses to 3 parts glucose, has also been recommended.

Silver Plating.—D. asks for a formula for silver plating. Silver plating nowadays is done usually by means of a battery and appropriate solutions. The process is known as electroplating. For minor work, covering the worn parts of plated goods, for instance, the following solution may be found useful:

℞		
	Silver nitrate	35 grains.
	Sodium chloride	60 grains.
	Alum	30 grains.
	Cream of tartar	3 drams.
	Water, enough to make	2 ounces.

It is applied with a sponge or rag to the previously well cleaned article by friction.

Home-Made Root Beer.—S. A. asks how he should proceed to make "a good root beer in a concentrated form, for making about 5 gallons at home."

The following is a much used formula which may be concentrated by increasing the amount of barks or decreasing the amount of water: Dissolve molasses, 4 ounces, in boiling water, 12 ounces, and add to the cooled solution 1½ ounces of sarsaparilla root, sassafras bark, wild cherry bark, wintergreen bark and 2½ ounces of fresh yeast, with sufficient water to bring the bulk up to 5 gallons. After this has fermented for 12 hours it can be drawn off and bottled.

Freezing Mixture.—W. E. B.—Pretty specimens of colored and uncolored ice for experimental purposes can be turned by the use of a mixture made from the subjoined formula. Special apparatus is required for the production of ice on a large scale by artificial means. The formula:

Sodium sulphate	6 parts.
Ammonium nitrate	5 parts.
Dilute nitrate acid	4 parts.

This mixture is placed in a large porcelain container into which is set a smaller vessel of the same kind of ware containing the fluid to be frozen.

Hydrochloride and Hydrochlorate.—P. R. asks for an explanation of the varying use of the terms hydrochloride and hydrochlorate, and we cannot do better than reproduce the extremely lucid and accurate explanation offered some time ago by the late Dr. Charles Rice.

It is well known, observed Dr. Rice, that in English nomenclature all salts derived from acids ending in —ic are designated by corresponding terms ending in —ate, thus, sulphate denotes a salt derived from sulphuric acid; nitrate denotes a salt derived from nitric acid; hydrochlorate denotes a salt derived from hydrochloric acid.

In all inorganic salts, it will be remembered, the formation of these compounds is accompanied by the elimination of one or more atoms of hydrogen from the molecule of the acid, the place of the eliminated hydrogen being taken by the basylous radical.

In the salts of alkaloids and similar organic bases the formation of these compounds is not accompanied by the loss of any hydrogen of the acid, the unchanged molecule of which is simply added to the molecule of the organic base.

Attempts were made at different times to distinguish between these two classes of salts by a modification in nomenclature, but no practical result was obtained until the question was more thoroughly discussed and agitated. Prominent attention was drawn to the subject in 1885, when the *Weekly Drug News*, of New York, invited a number of leading chemists to express their views on the relative correctness of the terms "hydrochlorate" and "hydrochloride" of cocaine. The decision in favor of the latter term was almost unanimous. Regret was at the same time expressed that a similar modification of nomenclature could not well be introduced in the cases of salts of oxygenated acids (sulphuric, nitric, &c.), as such terms as "hydrosulphate" would lead to confusion.

Many authors and writers subsequently adopted the nomenclature thus indorsed, and the same has been approved and adopted by the revisers of the United States Pharmacopœia.

In further elucidation of the subject the following account of the formation of salts, being an anonymous contribution to the *Pharmaceutical Record*, for September 15, 1902, will be found of interest and value:

Acids may form salts in two ways, one by substitution and the other by addition.

1. *By substitution.*—All true acids contain replaceable hydrogen. Some contain only one such atom, others two or more. Thus acetic acid ($C_2H_4O_2$) contains only one replacable hydrogen; hypophosphorus acid (H_3PO_2) also only one; citric acid ($C_6H_8O_7$) contains three, &c. When the acid combines with a metal or basylous compound the replacable hydrogen steps out of the molecule of the acid and the metal, or a certain portion of the basylous compound steps in place of it. In the case of a metal the hydrogen escapes (for instance, $Zn + 2HCL = ZnCl_2 + H_2$). But in the case of a basylous compound this itself splits up into portions, which immediately seek and find new mates, being unable to exist in the form in which they were separated. Thus NaOH and HCl form NaCl and H_2O, neither the Na nor the OH of the sodium hydrate being able to remain free under the circumstances. We speak here only of normal salts.

2. *By addition.*—With acids containing replaceable hydrogen this occurs when they combine with a compound substance which cannot split up into portions without losing its individuality. Such compounds are the alkaloids. An alkaloid is an individual which, when once split up, no longer represents the original in its various properties. Quinine ($C_{20}H_{24}N_2O_2$) remains quinine only while its molecule remains intact. When sulphuric acid combines with it the whole molecule of the acid, without any loss of hydrogen, joins the molecule of quinine. If the acid were to lose the hydrogen it would thereby become an unsaturated radical ($''SO_4$), which could itself be saturated only by another unsaturated radical. As no hydrogen, or hydroxyl (OH), or other fraction, can drop out of the molecule of quinine, the latter cannot become an unsaturated radical, and therefore there is nothing which could replace the hydrogen in the acid.

A Good Hair Tonic.—F. K. writes: "Please publish the formula of a good hair tonic, something that is not a 'back number.'"

Perhaps the most up to date and satisfactory application for improving the condition of the hair, preventing dandruff and loss of the follicles is obtained by a combination of chloral hydrate and tannic acid in suitable proportions in solution with perfumed alcohol containing a trace of castor oil. The only objection to a solution of this kind lies in its tendency to stain when dropped on linen. Apart from this, a solution of the following ingredients will be found very effective:

Chloral hydrate	ʒij.
Tannic acid	ʒi.
Tartaric acid	ʒi.
Castor oil	gtt. xij.
Alcohol	℥viij.
Distilled water	℥vss.
Violet extract	ʒss.

Proportions of Ingredients to Be Used in Making Cold Cream.—F. K. asks us to state what proportion of each ingredient should be used in making a cold cream consisting of white wax, spermaceti, liquid petrolatum, borax, water and oil of rose geranium.

The formula suggested by W. C. Alpers and printed at the time in the AMERICAN DRUGGIST dispenses with the spermaceti and calls for 150 parts of white wax, 600 parts of liquid petrolatum, 240 parts of water, 9 parts of borax and 1 part of oil of rose geranum.

The wax is dissolved in the oil with the aid of a gentle heat, the borax being dissolved in the water in another vessel. Both solutions are brought to the same temperature, not exceeding 60 degrees C. (140 degrees F.), when the aqueous solution is poured into the melted wax and petrolatum in a continuous stream. The mixture is stirred gently for a minute or two, the essential oils being added meanwhile. The ointment is poured into jars before it cools and while it is still of a semiliquid consistency.

Prendergast's Pills or Tablets.—The formula for a pill or tablet named after a Dr. Prendergast is desired by a subscriber. Can any reader supply it?

Burrow's Solution.—O. R. writes: "On page 72, AMERICAN DRUGGIST, February 12, solution of aluminum acetate is referred to as Burrow's solution. Permit me to point out that Burrow's solution is more correctly a solution of aluminum and sodium acetate, prepared as follows:

Plumbi acetatis	Gm. 100
Aluminis	Gm. 66
Sodii sulph	Gm. 12
Aquæ	Cc. 800

Dissolve the lead acetate in 300 Cc. of the water, which has been previously boiled and cooled. Dissolve the alum and sodium sulphate in a separate portion of 500 Cc. water; pour the solution first made into the second solution and shake vigorously; set aside and when the solution has fully settled decant the clear supernatant liquid and filter if necessary.

Books on Perfumery.—E. A. B. asks if we can name any other books of reference on the manufacture of perfumery besides Askinson's work.

The more important books dealing with the chemistry and manufacture of perfumery are the works by Piesse and Charabot, named respectively *Chimie des Parfums*, published by J. B. Baillière et fils, Paris, at 4 francs, and *Les Parfums Artificiels*, by the same publishers, at 5 francs. W. L. Scoville, of Boston, is the author of a useful work on *Extracts and Perfumes*, which is published by the Spatula Publishing Company, of that city, at $1.

Alterative Compound.—J. D. S.—A vegetable alterative compound which has had considerable vogue is made as follows:

Bamboo brier root	℥iv
Stillingia	℥iv
Burdock root	℥iv
Poke root	℥iv
Prickly ash bark	℥i
Diluted alcohol	q.s.

Mix the drugs, reduce to fine powder, and extract, using diluted alcohol as a menstrum, by the process of the pharmacopœia, or the National Formulary, or any other suitable process for fluid extracts, the product to measure one pint.

A Question on Deodorized Opium.—A. A. A., Tampico, Mexico, writes: "I made deodorized tincture of opium according to the process of the United States Pharmacopœia and exhausted the remaining opium afterward with diluted alcohol. I wish you to tell me what constituents are contained in the deodorized tincture and what in the percolate obtained afterwards. I note that both liquors have the same color, a light reddish-brown, the first being odorless and the other having a very distinct flavor of opium. Both are equally bitter. How may I utilize the second liquor? Would it form a good addition to rheumatic lotions, etc.? Do any of the constituents of opium remain in the exhausted mass?

This query was submitted to Professor Remington, who, with his customary courtesy, has kindly framed the following reply:

"In reply to your letter I would state that your correspondent failed to entirely exhaust the granulated opium with water. It should have removed the morphine from the opium, and this could be proved by assaying it by the process given. The presence of coloring matter in the residue, as shown by a colored tincture having been obtained with diluted alcohol, would not be conclusive evidence that the opium had not been exhausted of the morphine. If your correspondent obtained morphine, as shown by an assay, from the residue, it would prove that the opium had not been thoroughly exhausted in the first place. The presence of bitterness would not necessarily prove the presence of morphine in the residue, but an assay would. I do not think it would be safe to depend upon the medicinal value of the second liquor obtained, and the latter would always be a vehy uncertain product.—JOSEPH P. REMINGTON."

Correspondence.

Comment on Prescriptions.

To the Editor:

Sir,—I beg leave to make a few comments on some of Professor Hynson's prescriptions as published in the AMERICAN DRUGGIST for March 12.

In prescription No. XVI Mr. Hynson states that he used 5 drops of alcohol to dissolve the holocaine hydrochloride. I think this might be objected to because alcohol, even in small amount, when put into the eye causes a very unpleasant burning sensation. This fact will be best appreciated by any one who ever had a drop of alcohol accidentaly splashed into his eye. I should have rubbed the holocaine to a very fine powder, mixed it with the castor oil and dispensed it with a "shake well" label attached.

The use of glycerin in prescriptions Nos. XVIII, XXI and XXII might also be objected to on the same grounds, but to a much lesser degree. I remember when cocaine first came into use we frequently received prescriptions for eye waters calling for cocaine hydrochloride and sodium borate, in all of which we used boric acid in the place of the sodium borate; this, too, without consulting the prescriber. I would have pursued practically such a course in dispensing the prescriptions above referred to rather than add any glycerin.

In order to test the effect of a small quantity of glycerin on the eye I made the following experiment: I prepared a solution of 20 drops of glycerin and 1 fluid ounce of water and dropped 3 or 4 drops into the right eye of six different people, then using another dropper I dropped 3 or 4 drops of distilled water into the left eye of those same people. Without telling them which dropper had the glycerin solution four of them declared that they observed a slight smarting sensation in the right eye and the other two declared they could not notice any difference. I am inclined to believe that in an inflamed eye a small quantity of glycerin in an eye water would cause a smarting sensation.

I think it is advisable to avoid the use of alcohol or glycerin in eye preparations, certain kinds of injections and in a great many salves and ointments, especially pile ointments.

In prescription No. XXIV if a spirit of lemon (ʒi) is used, prepared from the terpeneless extract of lemon, no difficulty will be experienced. The preparation will have a very pleasant lemon flavor, which will be maintained until the last is used up.

WILLIAM F. KAEMMERER.

COLUMBUS, OHIO, March 18, 1906.

The "Ethical Preparation."

We sometimes read, says the editor of the *New York Medical Journal*, that a certain medicinal preparation is "ethical" and that a certain other one is "unethical." We doubt if, strictly speaking, it is proper to apply either term to an inanimate object like a drug. If we regard ethics as a system by which we ascertain our duty to our fellow men, and in accordance with which we perform that duty, our duties are ethical, inasmuch as they are deduced from ethics, and we ourselves are ethical in so far as we conform to ethics. But in using any drug, no matter what it may be, we neither conform to the requirements of ethics nor violate them. We doubt if even the stiffest of trade unionists would look upon a burglary as venial because the burglar was able to prove that his jimmy bore the union label. It is acts that call for commendation or censure, not the tools with which they are performed.

BOARD OF PHARMACY VS. HEALTH DEPARTMENT.

Power of the New York Board of Health in Relation to the Powers of the Board of Pharmacy Set Forth—A Guarded Opinion in Which Some Interesting Questions Are Raised—Board of Pharmacy Seemingly Has Power to Enforce Health Board's Carbolic Ordinance and Revoke Licenses of Violators—Questions Validity of Pharmacy Board's By-Law No. 33, Regulating Hours of Labor—No Opinion as to the Constitutionality of the Organization of the Board.

The relations of the pharmacy law of the State of New York to the power of the New York Health Department in regard to the regulation of the sale of poisons are succinctly, but comprehensively and interestingly, set forth in an opinion obtained by the Kings County Pharmaceutical Society from the law firm of Perkins & Butler, New York, attorneys to the society. This opinion was read to the members of the society at the March meeting and will undoubtedly attract the interested attention of every pharmacist in the State of New York. The text of the opinion, which is dated March 12, 1906, follows:

THE CARBOLIC ORDINANCE.

In September, 1904, responding to your request for our opinion, we advised you that the Board of Health had the power to enact section 66a of the Sanitary Code of New York City, which reads as follows: "No phenol, commonly known as carbolic acid, shall be sold at retail by any person in the City of New York, except upon the prescription of a physician, when in a stronger solution than 5 per cent."

Upon the question, however, as to the relative powers of the city Board of Health and the State Board of Pharmacy we expressed no opinion, but advised you that, inasmuch as the Board of Health had taken action with reference to the sale of carbolic acid and the Board of Pharmacy had not taken any action, and the Board of Health had power in the premises, the regulation referred to must be obeyed.

The question now recurs, and our opinion is asked with reference to the power of the Board of Health of the city, and particularly in relation to the powers of the Board of Pharmacy. First, as to the Board of Health of New York City.

POWERS DELEGATED TO THE BOARD OF HEALTH.

The Legislature has always exercised a very broad power in enacting laws which are intended to protect the comfort, health and safety of the public, and this power is commonly known as the police power. This power has, so to speak, been delegated to the Board of Health of New York. Every act of the Legislature passed for the purposes mentioned is subject to review by the courts, and the courts will consider and decide whether the health, comfort or safety of the public is reasonably and necessarily protected by the act. If so, the act is valid; if not, it is invalid. The same thing applies in case of an ordinance or regulation in the Sanitary Code. The Sanitary Code has repeatedly received the sanction of the courts and it is recognized by the Greater New York Charter, but every provision in it may be subjected to review by the courts for the purpose of ascertaining whether, in the judgment of the court, it is reasonably intended for the health, comfort or safety of the people of the city. Resting our opinion upon various court decisions, we think that section 66a of the Sanitary Code, above quoted, is valid, as reasonably intended to secure the safety of the public. To the powers of the Board of Health is added the duty, among other things, to enforce all laws relative to the use or sale of poisonous, unwholesome, deleterious or adulterated drugs, medicines or foods. So much as to the powers of the Board of Health. Now as to its organization. It is composed of the Commissioner of Health, the Police Commissioner and the Health Officer of the Port. The Commissioner of Health and the Police Commissioner are appointed by the Mayor, and the Health Officer by the Governor, with the consent of the Senate. Thus, you will see that the majority of the Board of Health is appointed by the Mayor, who is elected directly by the people.

The right of the Legislature to delegate to the city Board of Health the power to legislate, as it has been expressed, is found in a provision of the Constitution requiring the Legislature to provide for the organization of cities, etc., and in another section, referring to the appointment of city officers, hereinafter mentioned. Second, as to the State Board of Pharmacy.

The powers of the State board are given to the board as an entirety, and among them, as you all know, is power to regulate the practice of pharmacy; to regulate the sale of poisons, and to regulate and control the character and standard of drugs and medicines dispensed in this State.

UNIQUE ORGANIZATION OF BOARD OF PHARMACY.

The organization of the Board of Pharmacy is, to say the least, unique. While you are all more or less familiar with the provisions of the statute, we think, for convenience, they had better be summarized here. For convenience we shall term the law the "pharmacy law," but it is not so called in the statute, and is Article XI of the Public Health Law. For the purpose of the pharmacy law the State is divided into three sections by counties. The Eastern, also called New York, section consists of the counties of New York, Kings, Queens, Nassau, Suffolk, Richmond and Westchester; the Western, or Erie, section, consists of the counties of Erie, Niagara, Orleans, Genesee, Wyoming, Allegany, Cattaraugus and Chautauqua; and the Middle, or Albany, section consists of Albany and all other counties not contained in the other two sections.

The board consists of 15 members, five from each of the sections, and it is organized into branches, known as the Eastern, Western and Middle branches. At the elections for members for the Middle section all licensed pharmacists and druggists residing in that section are entitled to vote, whereas in the other two sections not only must the voter be qualified as a licensed pharmacist or druggist, but he must also be a member either of the New York State Pharmaceutical Association or of an incorporated pharmaceutical association or society in one of the counties in the section.

The Constitution, in a section which first provides with reference to the election or appointment of county, city, town and village officers, etc., provides as follows: "All other officers, whose election or appointment is not provided for by this Constitution, and all officers, whose offices may hereafter be created by law, shall be elected by the people, or appointed, as the Legislature may direct."

QUESTION IF BOARD IS UNCONSTITUTIONALLY ORGANIZED.

Now, it is the general rule that the Legislature may not delegate any of its powers, but that rule is subject to exceptions. The Constitution permits the Legislature to confer legislative powers upon county boards of supervisors and city boards of aldermen and health boards, etc. The Legislature may also confer administrative powers upon other officers or boards.

It seems that legislative powers can be delegated only to officers elected or appointed, as provided in the section of the Constitution referred to, and it is obvious that the State Board of Pharmacy, which is not appointed, and which, though elected, is not elected *by the people*, is not chosen in the manner pointed out by that section of the Constitution; but recalling our statement that the organization of the board is unique, we must say that there is no reported decision, so far as we have been able to find, which relates to a body of officers chosen in any manner similar to the method under which the Board of Pharmacy is organized. While, however, it may not be proper for the Legislature to delegate its legislative powers to such a board, yet it is by no means clear that the board has exercised any legislative powers. Probably the Legislature may lawfully confer upon the Board of Pharmacy administrative powers.

It seems to us that the powers of the Board of Pharmacy, which we have mentioned above, namely, those to regulate the practice of pharmacy, the sale of poisons and the character and standard of drugs, etc., may fairly be deemed administrative in view of the other provisions of the act. In the pharmacy law itself the Legislature has in a measure regulated the sale of poisons, and in schedule B of section 198 carbolic acid is mentioned.

WHERE THE HEALTH DEPARTMENT DERIVES ITS POWER.

Furthermore, the Greater New York Charter, from which the Sanitary Code derives its force, is a special act applicable to the city of New York. The pharmacy law is a general law applicable to the State at large. In the case of a special law and a general law relating to the same matter, the rule is that the special law is not superseded or annulled by the general law, in so far as the special law applies in its locality, but that it continues in force there even if its provisions are contrary to the general law, unless the Legislature has expressed a contrary intention. We think that there can be little doubt of the intention of the Legislature as expressed in section 190 of the Pharmacy Law. The Eastern section includes the counties of New York, Kings, Queens and Richmond, which are the counties included in Greater New York. In so far as the Board of Pharmacy may lawfully exercise its powers, we believe it may exercise them within the city of New York, irrespectively and independently of the city Board of Health.

But this might lead to conflicting regulations and wherever two statutes appear to conflict or wherever lawful ordinances or regulations seem to be inconsistent and the question concerning them is presented to the courts, the courts will always seek to reconcile the inconsistent or conflicting provisions if they can be reconciled.

CARBOLIC ORDINANCE MUST BE OBEYED.

The Board of Pharmacy, as we understand it, has not passed any regulation which conflicts with section 66a of the Sanitary Code and that section is not inconsistent with any provision of the statute. It simply makes a physician's prescription a "prerequisite" to the sale of carbolic acid in a solution stronger than 5 per cent. Until it is altered or rescinded, this regulation must be obeyed and while we do note presume to express any opinion as to the duty of the Board of Pharmacy, we should infer that it would be the duty of that board to enforce section 66a of the Sanitary Code and that it has the power to do so—that it has the power to revoke a license for violation of that section.

BOARD MAY MAKE CONTRARY REGULATION IF—

We think also that the powers conferred upon the Board of Pharmacy by the statute are sufficient, and that the territorial jurisdiction of the board is such that the Board of Pharmacy may make a contrary regulation to that which is contained in section 66a of the Sanitary Code, but our opinion on this point is subject to qualification if the Board of Pharmacy is not lawfully organized for the purpose of exercising the necessary power. Upon the question of validity of the organization of the Board of Pharmacy we feel obliged, after careful consideration, to decline to hazard an opinion. It is a question which ought to be submitted to the courts, if it is of sufficient importance, but it could only be submitted in a case arising under the law. This refers to what may be called the legislative powers of the board. Undoubtedly the powers of the board to examine and license, etc., are lawful. We do not find in the by-laws of the board or in its rules, regulations which we think can fairly be called "legislative," but they are all rather administrative, that is, essential to the enforcement of the law, except, however, by-law 33. We have always questioned the validity of the power to regulate the hours of labor, but one part of the law may be invalid and the other parts yet be valid and enforcible.

We regret to feel obliged to withhold any opinion as to the validity of the organization of the board, but it does not appear to us to be a practical question at present, there does not seem to be any occasion to disturb the operations of the board which are beneficial and satisfactory, and we frankly think that the question is one upon which so much may be said on both sides that it must remain open until the courts have decided it. Please bear in mind that we speak not with reference to the administrative, but to what may be called the legislative, powers of the board.

MILES LOSES SUIT IN EQUITY.

Direct Contract Plan Not Illegal—Suit Denied on Ground that Patent Medicine Business Is Contrary to Public Policy—Vender of Proprietary Remedies of Secret Composition Denied Standing.

In denying any standing in courts of equity to makers of proprietary remedies of secret composition Judge James R. Macfarlane, of Pittsburgh, has dealt the most serious blow yet struck at the direct contract and serial numbering plan and also at the patent medicine business generally. The Judge admitted that the contract itself was legal and not in restraint of trade, as it had been said to be, but denied any relief to the plaintiffs, the Dr. Miles Medical Company, on the following grounds:

The enormous business done by the proprietors of medicines and the serious menace which it is to the health and lives of the public requires us to scrutinize carefully the grounds upon which the plaintiff stands, and as it has been shown that it belongs to the reprehensible class we decline to grant a decree.

In his opinion Judge Macfarlane says that it seems clear that the contracts on which the plaintiff asks for an injunction are valid, but that the sale to third parties carries no restriction, and therefore an innocent purchaser may do as he pleases. Judge Macfarlane, however, adds that if the third party conspires to break its accepted contract the party injured can maintain an injunction.

On the argument of the case before the court generally that the vender or manufacturer of a secret formula sold as a proprietary medicine had no standing in a court of equity, Judge Macfarlane says:

On further consideration it is our opinion that the public health required protection against these preparations, and that the vender of remedies of unknown ingredients advertised and sold as remedies for disease should not be aided by courts of equity. If he sees fit to keep them a trade secret and to persuade the public to dose of his mysteries, let him come into chancery. We take judicial notice of the facts of medical science which are known to intelligent persons, although not educated as physicians, but we need not go even so far in finding that plaintiff cannot cure incurable cases.

Aside from the general question of public policy this State has by its statutes regulating the practice attempted to protect the public against charlatans and quacks, and thus declares its public policy that no one may habitually prescribe medicine for the public without certain qualifications. It also by these statutes recognizes the science of medicine and the necessity for a course of study. The plaintiff may not be liable for a violation of these acts, but its business is against public policy. Such methods of doing business do not commend themselves to the conscience of a chancellor. It is no answer that the defendants are also transgressors and may incidentally reap some advantage from our decision.

This answer was handed down by Judge Macfarlane in the Court of Common Pleas in Pittsburgh on March 14 in the case of the Dr. Miles Medical Company against the May Drug Company, of Pittsburgh, the latter concern being prominent cut-rate druggists of that city.

ELECTION AT THE N. Y. COLLEGE OF PHARMACY.

A Paper on Cocaine by Dr. Wm. J. Schieffelin.

As generally expected, the annual election of officers and trustees of the Columbia University College of Pharmacy of the City of New York, which was held Tuesday evening, March 20, in the college building at 115 West Sixty-eighth street, resulted in the re-election of all the former officers and three of the former trustees. Hieronimus A. Herold and Albert Plaut were also selected as trustees to fill the places of Felix Hirseman and Carl Schur. In brief, the entire official ticket received the almost unanimous vote of the 32 members of the college, the only scratching noticeable being in the case of O. J. Griffin, assistant secretary, for whom 29 votes were cast, while three ballots had his name erased.

The officers re-elected for the ensuing year were: Nicholas Murray Butler, president; Charles F. Chandler, first vice-president; William Jay Schieffelin, second vice-president; Herbert D. Robbins, third vice-president; Clarence O. Bigelow, treasurer; Thomas F. Main, secretary, and O. J. Griffin, assistant secretary.

The trustees, elected and re-elected, to serve three years, were: Frederick W. Carpenter, Thomas P. Cook, Arthur H. Elliott, Hieronimus A. Herold and Albert Plaut. The ten other trustees of the college, whose terms expire in 1907 and 1908, respectively, are: Otto P. Amend, Oscar Goldman, Adolph Henning, Gilbert P. Knapp, Charles H. White, William C. Alpers, Max J. Breitenbach, Charles S. Erb, Leo W. Geisler, jr., and Henry Imhof.

Immediately after the election of officers and new trustees, which was concluded about 8.30 P. M., Dr. Schieffelin read an interesting paper on Cocaine, Its Constitution, Synthesis and the Safe Guarding of Its Sale. An abstract of Dr. Schieffelin's paper follows:

The Indians of the Andes, by constantly chewing coca leaves, sustain their strength for long journeys and are able to exert themselves for several days without much, if any, food. This stimulating effect of cocaine is no doubt what is sought and obtained by the victims of the cocaine habit—intensified by the larger doses they employ.

The amount of cocaine in the leaves varies from ½ of 1 per cent. to 1 per cent. The leaves deteriorate on keeping, especially in warm and humid weather. In manufacturing the alkaloid is extracted after the leaves have been made alkaline, or else directly by dilute acid, the subsequent purification being a process involving a number of steps. The non-crystallizable alkaloids are split into ecgonine, which is then benzoylated and methylated.

The chemical constitution of cocaine has only recently been established and the honors for this are again with the German chemists, notably Willstatter. When cocaine is treated with alkalies it is split up into ecgonine, methyl alcohol and benzoic acid. Ecgonine is closely related to tropine, the product resulting from splitting the tropa alkaloids. Tropine has an n-methylpyrolidin ring combined with an n-methylpiperidin ring. Both ecgonine and tropine can be changed into suberone—$C_7H_{12}O$ — which can be made by distilling the calcium salt of suberic acid. Suberon has marked sleep producing and numbing powers. Ecgonine has the same constitutional formula as tropine, except that one atom of hydrogen is replaced by COOH. Ecgonine has no anæsthetic power, nor has it much when the methyl or benzoyl radical alone is added to it—but when both are there the cocaine is both anæsthetic and toxic. Benzoyl, ecgonine and methyl ecgonine are each but one-twentieth as toxic as cocaine.

Cocaine turns the polarized ray to the left, as does ecgonine. The effort to build up cocaine synthetically has led to the production of several substitutes for it of greater or less chemical resemblance to it, the chief ones being eucaine, holocaine, stovaine and alypin. The cocaine synthesized by Willstatter was racemic and had not the same physiological properties as the natural lævo-rotary cocaine.

The annual consumption of cocaine in the United States is between 100,000 and 120,000 ounces. Judging from the ratio of decline of the sale in a locality where a strict cocaine law is enacted and enforced at least 20 per cent. is used for indulgence.

No one should be exposed to the risk of forming the cocaine habit by ignorantly taking a catarrh powder or remedy containing cocaine; the drug should only be sold on prescription and physicians should not be permitted to prescribe it for those having the habit. The sale of it, both wholesade and retail, should be under rigid control and physicians should be taught to use it with the utmost caution, almost with dread.

Routine business of the college was discussed after Dr. Schieffelin had read his paper, and at the conclusion of the meeting a light collation was served in the library of the college building.

CUMBERLAND COUNTY ASSOCIATION PLACES ITSELF ON RECORD.

Opposes Formula Bills Now Before Congress.

The Cumberland County Pharmaceutical Association desires to go on record as heartily favoring legislation for the protection of the public, by regulating the sale of any dangerous proprietary medicines now in the market, and will be glad to support a law compelling the placing on the labels or wrappers of same the name and quantity of any active poisons or narcotics therein contained.

The association believes that the sale of all proprietary medicines may be controlled by a national law, requiring the establishment of a National Medical Council, which shall require every proprietor to submit his working formula before he can be licensed to put his remedy on the market, this council to be authorized to pass judgment on the fitness of every remedy and to suppress such remedies as may be considered unsafe for general use. This association believes that the public will be better protected by forming such a council, to whom all formulas will be submitted, than by a law which will make public property of private formulas, regardless of their merit or medicinal efficiency.

In case a proprietor shall be found guilty of sending out a remedy differing from the formula submitted to the council his license may be revoked for all time, or other penalty may be imposed.

The association also wishes to go on record as opposing the formula bills now being urged upon our national Congress. We regard these bills as unjust to the owners of proprietary articles which by many years' use have been demonstrated to be not only safe but beneficial to humanity. We also consider it oppressive and unfair to every dealer in medicine, on account of the great amount of labor and expense involved in relabeling the medicines already in stock.

Therefore the association desires to urge our representatives in Congress to earnestly oppose such unjust, radical, class legislation, affecting solely as it does the large number of educated, respectable pharmacists throughout our country.

John Williamson, Secretary.

Portland, Me., March 12, 1906.

INTERESTING MEETING IN BROOKLYN.

Members of the Kings County Pharmaceutical Society Listen to Entertaining and Instructive Papers—Dr. R. von Foregger Tells of New Pharmaceutical Sources of Oxygen—Neglected Opportunities in the Drug Business Pointed Out by E. H. Gane—College Debt Will Be Cut $9,000 by Next Meeting—Members Would Like to See the Health Department's Carbolic Ordinance Enforced—Counsel Says Board of Pharmacy Can Do It.

The usual monthly meeting of the Kings County Pharmaceutical Society took place at the Brooklyn College of Pharmacy, 265 Nostrand avenue, on Tuesday afternoon, March 13. The meeting opened at 3 o'clock, with President Adrian Paradis in the chair and Andrew E. Hegeman recording.

Before receiving the reports of officers Alonzo Robbins, who was proposed for membership at the preceding meeting, was balloted for and elected. Treasurer P. W. Ray reported a balance of $216.27 in the treasury of the society and $8,785.66 in that of the college.

Dr. William Muir, chairman of the Committee of Supervision of the College, announced that Prof. G. B. White, of the Hoagland Laboratory, would deliver courses of lectures on bacteriology at the college, to which members of the society were cordially invited. Methods of culture and staining will be described and illustrated by means of lantern slides, and the effects of antiseptics and disinfectants elucidated. The lectures will be given on March 26 and April 2, from 9 a.m. to 12 m. each day.

At this point the welcome announcement was made that the college authorities would be in a position by the next meeting to pay $9,000 of the debt on the college building, which would leave a balance of $8,000 on the entire institution. As the property was valued at $60,000, Dr. Muir remarked that there was no doubt of the financial success of the college, and he referred with pride to the fact.

Reporting for the Legislative Committee, Dr. Muir described the various bills pertaining to pharmacy now under consideration. Some opposition had developed in Buffalo to the proposed amendment to the pharmacy law increasing the per diem payment to members of the Board of Pharmacy from $5 to $10. but this he hoped to overcome. He made mention of the Stevens bill, which he said was a well-intentioned measure, but of impracticable character. He favored a bill to compel the manufacturer of secret compounds to submit formulas to the State Board of Health and take out licenses.

Dr. Muir then read the opinion of counsel on the conflict between the Department of Health and the Board of Pharmacy in regard to the sale of carbolic. After the opinion was read and discussed it was decided to place a copy of it before the State Board of Pharmacy for its information. The board will probably undertake to enforce the Health Department's ordinance, as counsel said the board had power to do so.

Dr. von Foregger was then introduced and described the properties of the peroxides and perborates of the alkalies and alkaline earth metals. The text of his paper is printed elsewhere.

On motion of Mr. Marsland, supported by Dr. Muir and President Paradis, a most hearty vote of thanks was passed to Dr. von Foregger for his instructive and entertaining lecture.

Eustace H. Gane, chairman of the Committee on Publicity of the American Pharmaceutical Association, was then introduced and spoke of Neglected Opportunities in the Drug Business.

In beginning his remarks Mr. Gane observed that the subject uppermost in the mind of the present day pharmacist was undoubtedly the small compensation he received for very exacting work and the necessity of constantly looking for new outlets for increasing his business. There seemed to be a very general impression that pharmacists as a whole have failed to make progress, either along business or scientific lines. As a general proposition he thought it safe to assert that the pharmacist was more likely to be successful along business rather than along scientific lines, and the financial success of the large corporations now engaged in the drug business proved the truth of this assertion. Not every pharmacist, however, was a good business man, and some of the colleges had recognized this fact and added a commercial course to their curricula, a step to be commended in view of the fact that most of the pharmacist's work was purely commercial, and this part should receive attention in institutions that purport to train men to follow the art of pharmacy. With proper training it should necessarily follow that this training should give the pharmacist an advantage over his competitors in the struggle for existence. Too often, however, it did just the opposite, in giving him simply the idea that as a tradesman he was superior to other men in business in more or less allied lines. This, Mr. Gane said, was a great mistake. Pharmacists must remember that pharmacy laws were passed, not for their protection, but for the protection of the public, and unless the pharmacist could convince the public that he was giving them better value he must meet competition from whatever source.

THE VALUE OF SCIENCE AS AN AID TO BUSINESS.

On the subject of the value of science as an aid to business the speaker remarked that pharmacists were not interested in science *per se*, but in the commercial application of it, and he instanced the old English saying about the pestle and mortar being the pharmacist's natural emblem because it connected the man who "pounds" with shillings and pence.

THE OPPORTUNITY OF THE PHARMACIST.

There was no doubt in Mr. Gane's mind that pharmacists had sadly neglected their opportunities in the utilization of their scientific knowledge, and largely owing to the neglect of the leaders in pharmacy to point out the applications of new discoveries and inventions to pharmacy. This neglect had caused many of the legitimate side lines of pharmacy to fall into other hands. The time was, however, ripe for a change in this respect. The agitation for pure food and drugs against nostrums and against inexpert men in all lines of business was the retail pharmacist's opportunity, and with a little aid from his mentors he should not fail to rise to it.

The general public of America know more about medicine and science than the people of any other country, owing to the freedom of the press. Scientific knowledge was no longer confined to the few. The public was becoming more and more interested in scientific subjects, and would be more so from year to year with each new invention and discovery. Somebody must be ready to furnish such scientific information as the public wants and that somebody must be the retail pharmacist.

PHARMACY DEVELOPING ALONG TWO LINES.

Pharmacy, according to Mr. Gane, was developing along two lines, the business and the scientific. Most pharmacists will have perforce to be content with the lesser share, for unless run on generous lines the volume of business would not be sufficient to secure other than a moderate return. Pharmacists accordingly would have to take part of their compensation in the realization of a duty well performed, and in the interest which science always arouses in its devotees. But in doing so pharmacists should guard against holding their knowledge too cheaply and giving all away without adequate return. Much, of course, would depend on environment. Not all businesses are located in centers where science would be of much avail; and the business which needed these adventitious aids most was that situated in residential localities among the more intelligent class, who are too prone to take their custom to the larger business centers, under the erroneous impression that they thereby secure more expert service. Much of the success of the pharmacist in such localities would depend on the impression he made on his neighbors, and this impression could best be made by utilizing his particular expert knowledge.

THE TWO WAYS OF UTILIZING HIS SCIENTIFIC KNOWLEDGE.

Mr. Gane intimated that the pharmacist's scientific knowledge could be utilized in two ways. First, indirectly as an aid to advertising, where the direct return was not always evident, but was none the less sure in the long run, and secondly, as a direct means of increasing business. He illustrated the indirect methods by referring to an incident that came under his notice some time ago. An itinerant quack was lecturing to a street crowd near a prominent center of business and after the manner of his kind drawing horrible pictures of the fearful effects of neglecting to care for one's stomach and blood. The crowd was not much impressed until he commenced to demonstrate the supposed injurious action of the usual drugs upon the human stomach. This was done by exhibiting the action of strong sulphuric acid upon starch and sugar to show the effects of acids, while the effect of adding alkalies was shown by adding a little potassium chlorate to the mixture, which ultimately went up in smoke. The wonderful revivifying effects of the quack's medicine upon the human blood was demonstrated to the amazement of the crowd by the addition of phenolphthalein to an alkali solution, the latter supposed to be the blood of an anæmic person. Sales thereafter were prompt and large. Mr. Gane said he mentioned this incident not to urge his hearers to follow in the quack's footsteps nor to induce them to lower in any way the dignity which rightly surrounded the drug business, but to point out the impression which a modicum of scientific knowledge, even when misdirected, would produce upon the general public. He then instanced a number of ways by which the pharmacist could attract attention to his store. Window displays might include the exhibition of apparatus for the distillation of water, with a working model. The culture of bacteria might be shown in its different stages; all the accessories, such as microscopes, slides and stains, being displayed. Pharmaceutical operations might be conducted in view of the passersby, the process of percolation being especially available for the purpose of display.

Direct methods of utilizing scientific knowledge consisted in taking advantage of new ideas and discoveries. He mentioned the case of an English pharmacist who rented out tubes of radium to physicians at so much per hour.

Oscar C. Kleine, chairman of the Districting Committee, reported, reading a list of the new districts laid out. Several vacancies were announced, and the president was authorized to fill these. Four or five of the district captains who were in attendance at the meeting reported conditions in their territories. It was decided to furnish every member, through the secretary of the association, with a copy of the districts and the names of the captains in charge, so as to facilitate attention to complaints.

Amendments to the constitution of the society and college proposed at the preceding meeting were brought up for passage and adopted by rising votes. The amendments related to the abolishment of the experience and age requirements, and the requirements, eligibility, etc., of candidates for the scholarships recently established.

Registered in North Dakota.

The North Dakota Board of Pharmacy examined the 49 applicants for licenses, and licenses were issued to the following registered pharmacists and assistants, 16 of the former and 4 of the latter, 2 of those registered being ladies:

Hy. L. Claybough, Rolette; Joseph E. Swab, Harvey; Nellie E. McLean, Williston; P. C. Gronvold, Lankin; Harvey H. McDowell, Sawyer; W. F. Moede, Lisbon; Geo. E. Haines, Jr., Towner; Hilden P. Lundin, Fargo; Idion W. Swenson, Lake Park, Minn.; D. K. Bryant, Minot; John J. Flaherty, Linton; A. B. Hermann, Rolette; Robt. C. D. Higgins, Pelican Rapids, Minn.; Lillian V. Jefferson, Souris; Thos. L. Larson, Grand Forks, and Oscar Nelson, Fargo.

Assistants: A. Arnegaard, Northwood; H. E. Hansen, Wimbledon; M. J. Ivec, Dickinson, and George E. Mathews, Minneapolis.

The next meeting of the board will be held in Fargo June 5. Since the last meeting of the board there have been seven prosecutions for violation of the State pharmacy law and it is the intention of the board to keep on waging warfare until every drug store in the State is in charge of a competent person. An instance came to the attention of the board recently where an alleged pharmacist gave out laudanum for paregoric for administration to a child and there were serious results, and it is stated that the end is not yet, as there are very indignant parents and friends to deal with.

THE USE OF ANTISEPTICS IN FOODS CONDEMNED.

Dr. Wiley and Dr. Wood Agree—Antiseptics Used to Overcome Effect of Dirt and Carelessness.

Philadelphia, March 22.—The regular monthly pharmaceutical meeting of the Philadelphia College of Pharmacy was held Tuesday afternoon, March 20, with J. H. Redsecker, Ph. M., of Lebanon, Pa., in the chair.

The meeting was devoted to a symposium on the subject of Antiseptics in Foods. There was a large attendance, among whom were: Chas. T. George, of Harrisburg, president of the Board of Pharmacy; Prof. Louis Emanuel, of Pittsburgh; Joseph L. Lemberger, Lebanon; Franklin M. Apple, George M. Beringer, E. M. Boring, George W. Davis, W. L. Cliffe, Joseph W. England, C. P. Gabell, A. M. Hance, E. H. Hance, J. T. Harbold, Prof. Susannah G. Haydock, Aquila Hoch, Ambrose Hansberger, Henry Kraemer, C. H. La Wall, C. B. Lowe, William McIntyre, Mr. and Mrs. J. C. Peacock, Warren H. Poley, Samuel P. Sadtler, Richard H. Shoemaker, Joseph P. Remington, James T. Shinn, F. P. Stroup, E. F. Cook, C. A. Weidemann, Geo. B. Weidemann, C. B. Vanderkleed and M. I. Wilbert.

Dr. H. W. Wiley, Chief of the Bureau of Chemistry, U. S. Department of Agriculture, read a paper on Antiseptics in Foods, in which he insisted that the use of chemicals for the preservation of food products is totally unnecessary. He said that food could be preserved by sterilization, low temperature and certain curing processes. He said that the general use of preservatives places a premium upon dirt, carelessness and inferiority and endangers health. In the use of chemical preservatives Dr. Wiley said that there was not only danger from the cumulative action of certain chemicals, but also danger from the continuous use of them.

Dr. H. C. Wood, Jr., of Philadelphia, read a paper entitled Is the Use of Food Preservatives Justifiable? in which he said that he desired to be fair to manufacturers, but nevertheless felt that even though the name and amount of the preservative were given on the label the consumer would not be able to judge as to its harmlessness or harmfulness. He was therefore entirely opposed to the use of antiseptics in foods and medicines and urged the members to do all they could to secure the passage of the Pure Food bill now before Congress.

Jobbers Come Out Strongly for D. C. S. N. Plan.

John N. Carey, secretary of the Committee on Proprietary Goods of the National Wholesale Druggists' Association, has issued the following notice to the members, under date of Indianapolis, March 13, 1906:

URGING SUPPORT OF DIRECT CONTRACT AND SERIAL NUMBERING PLAN.

To Proprietors and Wholesale Druggists:

For the past three years this association has gone on record annually in favor of the direct contract and serial numbering plan. The following is a copy of the resolutions unanimously adopted at our last meeting in October, 1905, at New York:

Resolved, That this association again places itself on record as favoring the direct contract and serial numbering plan for articles having an established demand in at least a considerable section of the country, provided that any proprietor adopting the same will allow wholesale druggists additional compensation for the extra labor and expense devolving upon them under this plan; and provided that every such proprietor will first submit his proposed wholesale contract to a sub-committee of five, to be appointed by the chairman of our Committee on Proprietary Goods, of which he shall be chairman, for consideration and approval before the plan is put into effect by the proprietor.

Resolved, That we call the attention of jobbers to the importance and necessity of complying in every particular with the contract terms of the manufacturers who sell their goods on the serial numbering plan. It is absolutely essential that all jobbers should forward to the manufacturers, at such times as they require, the cards containing records of the sales of serially numbered goods, and we earnestly recommend that wholesale druggists take pains to see that this matter is carefully attended to.

The direct contract and serial numbering plan has been in operation on the goods of a number of prominent proprietors for a sufficient length of time to demonstrate conclusively that it is the very best plan yet devised to maintain the prices fixed by the proprietors for the sale of their articles at both retail and wholesale. Indeed, the plan has been successful to a remarkable degree, and it is undoubtedly to the interest of all three branches of the trade to have it extended to proprietary articles generally.

The undersigned recently conferred in person with some members of this committee, and has since received communications from the others in regard to this plan. The members of the committee expressed themselves as being heartily in favor of the plan, and the chairman was authorized to urge its adoption by proprietors, in accordance with the resolutions of the N. W. D. A., as quoted above. It is earnestly hoped that many proprietors will place their preparations on this plan and thus give the greatest possible protection to their distributers, both wholesale and retail.

It goes without saying that a plan which has proven so effective and of such great value to jobbers as well as retailers is entitled to the most hearty support of every wholesale druggist. We therefore confidently bespeak for the manufacturers who adopt this plan the loyal co-operation of the wholesale drug trade, who will thereby give evidence of their active interest in the welfare of their retail customers.

BOSTON DRUG ASSOCIATION INCORPORATED.

Better Prices in Boston—Associated Effort for Protection of Drug Interests—Troublous Times Ahead for Drug Trade.

(From our Regular Correspondent.)

Boston, March 17.—The regular meeting of the B. A. R. D. was held at the M. C. P. Building on the evening of March 14, with President La Pierre in the chair. The secretary and treasurer submitted routine reports.

The Executive Committee made these recommendations which were adopted: That it is inexpedient to adopt a general schedule at this time, but that the auxiliaries are free to adopt any schedules upon which they can agree; that Dr. J. W. Baird be retained as consulting chemist; that the matter of employing legal counsel be referred to the Legislative Committee, this committee to later confer with the representatives of the other organizations of the State, with the end in view of having this counsel supported by all druggists that the present association be absorbed in the newly incorporated Boston Association of Retail Druggists.

FOR THE PROTECTION OF THE TRADES.

Henry Canning spoke on State House affairs. He thought hard work was ahead and that the trade was facing a serious state of affairs. A meeting for the protection of druggists will be held at Young's Hotel later, at which all interested were invited to attend.

The Schedule Committee reported that the increases of the new lists to be out March 22 would be satisfactory.

Secretary Wooten of the N. A. R. D. reported by letter that the plan of a New England headquarters in Boston, with Mr. Keiser in charge, aided by assistants, was being considered.

THE INCORPORATED BODY TO SUCCEED THE ASSOCIATION.

It was then voted to end the life of the B. A. R. D., and to transfer all of the members and records to the newly incorporated Boston Association of Retail Druggists, the charter having just been issued.

Mr. Van Horn of the Perene Company and M. P. Gould of M. P. Gould & Co., then addressed the members.

A WEDDING GIFT FOR MR. AND MRS. WOOTEN.

It was voted on motion of Henry Canning to send a suitable wedding gift to Mr. and Mrs. Thomas V. Wooten of Chicago.

The new price of phenacetine was discussed and care was urged with future sales. Phanacetine was to be sold upon request, but the plan of educating physicians to use the U. S. P. preparation was thought to be a good one.

The Woman's Organization of the N. A. R. D. announced a whist party for March 22, at the Hotel Oxford.

F. M. Furbush then read a paper on Sweet Spirits of Nitre, accompanying it with demonstrations.

The "Chicago Tribune" and the Retail Trade.

We reproduce below a cartoon which appeared in the Chicago *Tribune* and which has created something of a sensation among druggists in the Middle West. The publication of this cartoon seems to have been repented in sackcloth and ashes by the *Tribune* managers, because since its publication the *Tribune* has printed a page devoted to a laudation of the retail druggist, setting forth, by anecdote and illustration, the trying experiences to which the retail druggist is subjected. The cartoon did not even have as excuse the basis of a single sale, for the reporters of the *Tribune* who were sent to buy "flake," a name given by the negroes and habitual users to cocaine, could not

THE MAN WHO

Thinks he is a Christian

But ready to be the most dangerous criminal

obtain any cocaine at all, but did obtain mixtures of eucaine and acetanilid. The injustice of the *Tribune* attack on the druggists of Chicago at large and on the Board of Pharmacy in particular is all the more marked in view of the fact that Chicago was one of the first cities in which the retail druggists took active steps of their own volition to prohibit the indiscriminate sale of cocaine, the Illinois Board of Pharmacy having been particularly active in enforcing the anticocaine laws. It is to be hoped that the *Tribune* will be taught a lesson by which other "yellow journals" will profit, for it is high time that the newspaper press learned that the pharmacist cannot be treated like a yellow dog without cause and with impunity.

The Manhattans Hear Prof. Scoville of Boston.

Prof. Wilbur L. Scoville, of Boston, an active member of the Committee on National Formulary of the American Pharmaceutical Association, delivered before the members of the Manhattan Pharmaceutical Association, who assembled in the New York College of Pharmacy Building, Monday evening, March 19, a most interesting lecture on The Æsthetic Side of Pharmacy. Though the professor's remarks upon this apparently inexhaustible subject were confined almost entirely to the question of proper flavors for medicinal preparations and prescriptions, he also found time to mention briefly the benefits to be derived from the careful observance of other branches of the art as well as the science of pharmacy. It was on the subject of flavors, however, that the lecture was most instructive and likely to prove of incalculable benefit to all retail pharmacists.

Because of the extremely inclement weather the attendance at the meeting was considerably smaller than usual, and in introducing Professor Scoville President Alpers of the association added a graceful apology for the fact that more members were not present to enjoy the lecture. The professor, however, assured President Alpers and the other members that no apology was necessary, as he believed that it was easier to indulge in a heart to heart talk with a few auditors than with a large audience. He then explained that when he accepted the kind invitation of the association to deliver his lecture he was not aware of the fact that Professor Hynson, of Baltimore, had already spoken to the members on a somewhat similar subject, but in view of this fact, he said he would limit his talk, which was to be purely informal and without notes, to the selection of flavors. We print a full report of the address on another page.

An Old Broadway Landmark Moved.

Milhau has moved. This is as much as to say that Trinity has moved or that St. Paul's has moved, for Milhau's drug store has been a fixture longer than anything else on lower Broadway except these two churches and the peaceful cemeteries which surround them, for it was 76 years ago when John, Vicomte de Milhau, after 17 years of successful business life in Baltimore, purchased a lot at 183 Broadway, New York, and there opened a pharmacy in which the highest ideals went hand in hand with the greatest skill. For John Milhau (he had dropped his title) was a man of noble aspirations and was one of the active movers in calling that meeting which resulted in the organization of the American Pharmaceutical Association in 1851. His interest in public affairs had already been shown by his activity in bringing about the incorporation of the New York College of Pharmacy in the year 1831, and in the movement looking toward the protection of our market from the flood of impure drugs of foreign origin, which resulted in the enactment by Congress in 1848 of a law to prevent the importation of fraudulent, adulterated, inferior or deteriorated drugs.

Among the few relics of the early days which are being moved by the present corporation of J. Milhau's Son to the new stand at 205 Broadway is the certificate of membership of John Milhau in the College of Pharmacy of the State of New York, dated May 3, 1838, and signed by Constantine Adamson, president; Oliver Hull, first vice-president; J. Milhau, second vice-president, and James Hart, third vice-president. In view of the hysterical attacks which have been made on the drug trade recently it is interesting to read in this musty old parchment that the College of Pharmacy was instituted "to guard against the abuses in the preparation and the sales of medicines," showing that the pharmacists themselves were the prime movers in the efforts to purify and keep clean the ranks of the retail drug trade. It was in 1869, after 56 years of unbroken and honorable activity, that John Milhau retired, leaving at the head of his business Edward L. Milhau, a worthy son and successor to an able father.

But few are left who knew the elder Milhau, but the younger—and he too is now dead after an honorable business career of 53 years—is remembered by many as a pharmacist of wide and accurate information, of lofty ideals, and a gentle and pleasing personality.

The business was incorporated under the name of J. Milhau's Son in 1898, with Edward L. Milhau as president. Since his death in 1903 the corporation has continued to operate the business with the same executive staff, including many who have been actively engaged in the business for the past 20 or 30 years.

The new building at 205 Broadway, which will be devoted exclusively to the business of J. Milhau's Son, embraces five floors and is being fitted up with a careful view to combination of the most artistic effects and the greatest economy of effort in the conduct of the large and steadily growing business.

A handsome Matthews wall fountain is being fitted for the store by the American Soda Fountain Company, with 36 feet of counter space. The fixtures are in white and gold and elevators connect the five floors.

Hanson Sues Collier's.

The W. T. Hanson Company, of Schenectady, manufacturer of Dr. Williams' Pink Pills for Pale People, has brought suit against the publishers of *Collier's Weekly* for malicious libel, naming damages at $100,000.

Greater New York News.

Luther Hommell, a retail druggist of Saugerties, N. Y., is purchasing pharmaceuticals and toilet supplies in this city.

Ralph P. Hoagland, senior partner in the wholesale drug firm of Hoagland & Mansfield, of Boston, visited the local manufacturing and wholesale houses last week.

E. A. Holton, of Holton & Adams, manufacturers of brushes, at 54 Beekman street, has just returned from a brief business trip to Baltimore and Washington.

William Kirn, of Detroit, Mich., head of the private formula department of Parke, Davis & Co., visited the local offices, at 90 Maiden lane, March 15 to 17.

M. O. Robbins, the retail druggist at 34 Fulton street, Brooklyn, has just sold the fixtures and good will of his store to P. W. Barry.

H. E. Steinhilber, the retail druggist formerly occupying the store at Amsterdam avenue and One Hundred and Forty-fourth street, has moved into new quarters one block farther north at One Hundred and Forty-fifth street.

A theater party is being planned by the members of the Alumni Association of the Brooklyn College of Pharmacy for Thursday evening, April 5. The party will attend the vaudeville performance at the Orpheum Theatre.

A. C. Robertson, traveling representative of the Mallinckrodt Chemical Works in New England and New York State, has just returned to the general offices of that company at 90 William street after a successful trip through his territory.

Hiram Merritt, partner in the wholesale and retail drug firm of Theodore Merritt's Sons, of Newburgh, N. Y., was among the recent prominent visitors to the local wholesale trade.

J. R. Lorah, senior partner in the retail drug firm of J. R. Lorah & Co., of Newport, R. I., spent several days in this city recently and bought a large assortment of drugs, proprietary remedies and toilet articles.

J. Milhau's Son, who is now compelled to move from the old site at 183 Broadway, where the firm has been located for 78 years, because the store has been leased to a haberdashery concern, will enter new quarters, at 205 Broadway, near Fulton street, on March 26.

Frederick Robbins, agent for Parke, Davis & Co. in Cambridge, Mass., has just been transferred to the Maine territory, which he has been anxious to secure for several years. The death of the former agent left the position open. Mr. Robbins will have his headquarters in Bangor.

Congratulations are being heaped upon R. H. Smith, treasurer of the Alfred H. Smith Company, importers of rubber sponges and brushes, at 84 Chambers street, who was married on Tuesday, March 13, to a Brooklyn girl. The happy couple sailed the following day on the steamship Baltic for a three months' tour of continental Europe.

The Kalish pharmacy at Fourth avenue and Twenty-third street will open a branch store on or about April 15 in the Emmet Arcade Building at Madison avenue and Fifty-ninth street, which has just been remodeled. The new store will have two entrances, one on the west side of Madison avenue and the other on Fifty-ninth street.

After spending four months of hard work in the interests of the New York jobbers, Frank E. Holliday, vice-chairman of the Proprietary Goods Committee of the National Wholesale Druggists' Association, has left this city and returned to Indianapolis, Ind., where he will resume his usual duties for the association. Mr. Holliday left town Thursday afternoon, March 8, but expects to return about the middle of April.

C. W. Whittlesey, president of the C. W. Whittlesey Company, a prominent wholesale and retail drug house in New Haven, Conn., visited the local drug trade recently and announced to his friends that he is planning to take a long pleasure trip through the Mediterranean Sea, sailing from Boston on April 10.

A banquet was given on Thursday, March 14, by the residents of the lower East Side to William Cohen, who has been the apothecary of Gouverneur Hospital for the past eleven years and who has recently resigned to accept the appointment of supervising apothecary for the Board of Health of the city of New York.

Ernest Berger, secretary and manager of the newly incorporated Tampa Drug Company, of Tampa, Fla., has been personally buying large supplies in the local wholesale market for his house. Mr. Berger is secretary and treasurer of the National Association of Boards of Pharmacy and secretary-treasurer of the Florida State Board of Pharmacy.

E. T. Mitchell, sales representative of E. J. Hart & Co., of New Orleans, has just been appointed Eastern agent for the leading products of that house, which include "Lac-Bismo," an indigestion cure, and "Alimentary Elixir," a similar proprietary remedy. Mr. Mitchell is now in this city, and it is expected that he will soon establish Eastern headquarters here.

Jesse L. Hopkins, president of the New York Drug Club; William S. Gray, vice-president of that body; Charles A. Schieren, former Mayor of Brooklyn; William A. McCarroll and Louis L. Drake, all of whom represented the club at the National Consular Reform Convention, which was held recently in Washington, D. C., enjoyed the privileges of a private audience with President Roosevelt.

The Brooklyn Pharmaceutical Association, formerly known as the Bushwick Pharmaceutical Society, but now a branch of the Metropolitan Association of Retail Druggists, entertained its members with a vaudeville show and smoker, Wednesday evening, March 7, at Siegmund's Hall, at Hamburg avenue and Woodbine street, Brooklyn. The Entertainment Committee included George A. Grunbok, Jr., chairman; Carl Mittenzweig, Otto Huener, Henry B. Lentz and William G. Turner.

Recent advices from India bring information that Robert Rowlette Martin, general Eastern manager for Frederick Stearns & Co., with headquarters at Bombay, is to take a six months' vacation, the major portion of which he will spend recuperating at the German baths. Mr. Martin has many friends in this country who will regret to learn of the inroads of the tropical climate on his health which have made this vacation a necessity.

The local committee of the New York section of the Society of Chemical Industry tendered a banquet, Saturday evening, March 24, to R. C. Woodcock, honorary treasurer of the section, who has been compelled to resign his office because of his intended return to England. Mr. Woodcock was elected treasurer of the section when it was founded. The members of the New York section decided to substitute the dinner to Mr. Woodcock in place of their regular March meeting.

F. N. Oxley, general sales manager of the Western territory for Seabury & Johnson, paid a visit of several days' duration to the home offices of that firm, at 59 Maiden lane, during the past fortnight, and has just returned to the Chicago offices. Mr. Oxley is one of Seabury & Johnson's most successful salesmen and is said to carry a trunk full of orders back to the firm whenever he returns from his trips. "A bag or a suit case isn't large enough to hold all the new business," is the facetious way he explains the necessity for his order trunk.

Colonel Edward W. Fitch and Mrs. Fitch, who are still in this city, have changed their plans regarding the much-needed and deserved rest which the colonel intended to take after his retirement from the management of the local offices of Parke, Davis & Co. Instead of going immediately to Pasadena, Cal., they have now decided to take a trip through the Mediterranean Sea. They will sail April 3, with Mr. and Mrs. Hartwell, of Louisville, on the steamship Slavonia, and will not return for three months. Upon their return they will go to Louisville, and later it is the colonel's intention to seek the healthful climate of Pasadena.

Members of the Hudson River branch of the Metropolitan Association of Retail Druggists will hold their first joint meeting of physicians and pharmacists in the Harlem Casino at One Hundred and Twenty-fourth street and Seventh avenue on

Thursday evening, March 29, at 9:30 o'clock. The Hudson River branch draws its membership from the large Harlem territory bounded by One Hundred and Twenty-fifth street, Fifth avenue and the Harlem and North Rivers. Arrangements have been made by the reception committee for a light collation to be served at the conclusion of the meeting. William F. Rawlins, of 2539 Eighth avenue, is the secretary of the branch.

When seen by a reporter for the AMERICAN DRUGGIST in his offices in the Metropolitan Building, 1 Madison Square, last Wednesday, C. H. Goddard, secretary of the American Druggists' Syndicate, expressed himself as well pleased with the success of the Syndicate's undertaking. "The noticeably unfair opposition manifested by a few of the local druggists has really been of benefit to us," he said. Unless the opposition can secure some more reasonable argument than it has yet discovered Mr. Goddard thinks there is little danger of the A. D. S. feeling any loss of patronage in this field.

A typical Japanese dinner, in which chop sticks played an important part, was tendered Wednesday evening, March 21, to Oscar W. Smith, the newly-appointed manager of the local offices of Parke, Davis & Co., by Dr. Jokichi Takamine, the well-known Japanese chemist, whose laboratories are located in the Parke, Davis & Co. building. Besides Dr. Takamine and Mr. Smith fourteen other guests, all connected with Parke, Davis & Co., attended the dinner, which was held in the Nippon Club, at 44 West Eighty-fifth street, for the purpose of affording Mr. Smith an opportunity to become better acquainted with all of his new associates.

The work of constructing the new crude drug warehouses of Parke, Davis & Co., at South and Water streets, is progressing rapidly, and the buildings will probably be completed within a week or two. One of the elevators in the main warehouse will be in operation by April 1. These crude drug warehouses are connected with the company's importing department, which is ably managed by W. B. Kaufman. The shipping of drugs on orders from all parts of the country has always been promptly executed by Parke, Davis & Co., but it is expected that the completion of the new warehouses will facilitate such shipments materially, as all the handling of the merchandise will hereafter be conducted under one roof. The new warehouses are located at 573-579 Water street and 292-295 South street.

Dr. William Jay Schieffelin was the principal proponent in the hearing before the New York State Senate Committee on Public Health on the Stevens bill. Samuel Hopkins Adams, Dr. Edward G. Janeway and Dr. Albert T. Weston all appeared in favor of the measure. George L. Douglas appeared in opposition. One of the strongest arguments advanced in opposition to the measure was that it placed more power in the hands of the Board of Health than was contemplated by the Legislature and that the matters concerned should really be in the hands of the Board of Pharmacy. The introducers of the measure have agreed to amendments making it a felony to sell opium or cocaine without a physician's prescription, and a felony for physicians to prescribe either drug unless it should be absolutely necessary for purely medicinal purposes.

William De Shetley, manager of the Eastern territory of the National Association of Retail Druggists, is to have two more organizers to help him in his work. This fact was developed at the meeting of the Executive Committee of the Metropolitan Association of Retail Druggists which was held Friday evening, March 16, in the New York College of Pharmacy Building, when it was decided that the M. A. R. D. would bear the expense of one of the new organizers, while the National Association would pay for the other. It is understood that the new organizers will soon arrive in this city. At this latest meeting of the General Committee of the M. A. R. D. it was also decided to send a remittance of $260 to Chicago as the first instalment on the 1906 dues. A general meeting of the members of the M. A. R. D. will be held April 6.

Oscar C. Kleine, former president of the Kings County Pharmaceutical Society, entertained a number of friends at his residence, 110 Hamburg avenue, Brooklyn, on Friday evening, March 16. Several of the local physicians attended with their wives, and notwithstanding the inclement weather the gathering was a large and representative one. Mr. and Mrs. Kleine are blessed with a talented family, and music was a feature of the evening's entertainment, his daughter, Miss Libbie, presiding at the piano, and his son Charles playing first violin, while a young friend played the clarionet. Mr. Brown, the Long Island representative of Bauer & Black, sang some verses in which his splendid barytone voice was heard at its best. Mr. Kleine is assisted in the management of the pharmacy by his son, Dr. Edward, while his younger son, Martin H., is Brooklyn representative for Eli Lilly & Co.

Recent visitors to New York, many of whom have registered at the New York Drug Club, include: Dr. M. H. Carter, Baltimore, Md.; A. B. Wilson, Philadelphia; I. W. Estes, Morristown, N. J.; Edward B. Creighton, Philadelphia; W. G. Todd, Somers, N. Y.; S. L. Stewart, Boston, M. D. Martin, Indianapolis, Ind.; A. H. Warner, Boston; E. L. E. Drake, Providence, R. I.; B. G. Goodale, Denver, Col.; Charles L. Shanwald, San Francisco, Cal.; E. B. Cooper, Nashville, Tenn.; Judge Pratt Rogers, Denver, Col.; Dr. C. Portius, Cairo, Mich.; A. T. G. Smith, St. Louis, Mo.; W. C. Barry, Danbury, Conn.; H. S. Davis, Chicago; W. H. Rankin, Elizabeth, N. J.; R. L. Bradin, Elizabeth, N. J.; W. L. Mix, New Haven, Conn.; W. B. Duryea, Freehold, N. J.; Theodore L. Bristol, Ansonia, Conn.; W. L. Briner, Princeton, N. J.; Bunting Hankins, Bordentown, N. J.; George M. Carslake, Allentown, N. J.; Charles Stuckert, Trenton, N. J.; Joseph Priest, Princeton, N. J.; George W. Jacques, South Amboy, N. J.; F. H. Slater, Matteawan, N. J.; John D. Case, Somerville, N. J.; R. B. Busby, Philadelphia, Pa.; Charles S. Crosby, Providence, R. I.; E. O. Jadek, Mobile, Ala.; C. J. Wietz, Chicago; J. F. Pacy, Baltimore, Md.; H. D. Page, San Francisco, Cal.; Dun Cameron, London, England.

Dr. W. Gilman Thompson in the course of discussion of the nostrum evil and the narcotic drug habit before the New York section of the American Chemical Society, on March 9, at the Chemists' Club, said that the increased use of nostrums was largely due to the failure of physicians to pay adequate attention to pharmacology and the art of prescribing. Samuel Hopkins Adams, of *Collier's Weekly*, outlined the legislation regarding the publication of formulas in various States and the status of the pure food bills before Congress. Alfred L. Manierre, secretary of the committee for safeguarding the sale of narcotics in New York, presented an outline of the Stevens-Wainwright bill, which is now before the State Legislature. Dr. William J. Schieffelin, president of Schieffelin & Co., said that his interest in regulating the sale of narcotic drugs was due primarily to the fact that he was one of the largest manufacturers of cocaine in the United States, and that having become convinced that at least a considerable proportion of this cocaine was used for illegitimate purposes he felt it his duty to take steps to minimize this illegitimate use of the drug. Caswell A. Mayo outlined the work which had been done by the American Pharmaceutical Association in the direction of regulating the sale of narcotic drugs and recommended that the Beal Model Antinarcotic law be substituted for the Stevens-Wainwright bill. Dr. H. Schweitzer, Prof. Virgil Coblentz and Dr. Charles A. Doremus also took part in the discussion.

Dr. Anderson Did Not Refer to M. A. R. D.

The statement that "Dr. Anderson said some harsh things about the M. A. R. D.," made in the report of the February meeting of the Kings County Pharmaceutical Society, as printed in the AMERICAN DRUGGIST for February 26, p. 110, is denied by Dr. Anderson, who assures us that he had not the M. A. R. D. in mind, but certain individuals. We are glad to print this correction, and trust that Dr. Anderson has not been placed in a wrong light by the erroneous reference.

The Manufacturing Chemists' Registration Bureau.

The following title has been received for registration in the Manufacturing Chemists' Registration Bureau: Nicotox, by Frederick Stearns & Co., Detroit, Mich.

WESTERN NEW YORK.

A New Poison Ordinance Before the City Council—Sale of Strong Carbolic Acid and of Cocaine Prohibited—Surprise at Award in the Pierce Damage Suit.

(From our Regular Correspondent.)

Buffalo, March 20.—The new Buffalo poison ordinance has been arranged by the health commissioner, assisted by leading druggists and doctors, and will no doubt be passed by the city council. It forbids the selling of carbolic acid of more than 5 per cent. strength except on a prescription, and it cuts off cocaine entirely unless ordered by a doctor or a dentist, a provision that is regarded as especially good.

THE BUFFALO COLLEGE OF PHARMACY

is preparing a thorough and exhaustive course in analytical chemistry, to include both qualitative and quantitative laboratory work, and it is hoped that it will be ready to be put into effect next year.

THE FORMULA BILLS FROM THE DRUG TRADE STANDPOINT.

The Buffalo druggists appear to have come to a very rational understanding on the question of legislation in regard to patent medicine formulas. In the first place, they say there should be no action taken on anything but preparations to be taken internally. Of these there is no need of a published formula in full. Let the poisons only be mentioned, and even then there will be no need of mention unless a dose contains more than 25 per cent. of a dose of such poison prescribed in the standard lists. This cuts down the application of the law so that it is not likely to go so far as to do more harm than good. "In other words," said a leading Buffalo druggist, "let us be reasonable."

REGISTRATIONS ALL IN SAVE TWO.

The druggists in the western section of the State have done pretty well this year in responding to the call for registration. Only three stores had to be reported to the authorities, and of these one has settled, with the other two expected to follow. It took a few of this sort to prove the need of pharmacy boards and give them something to do.

THE PIERCE DAMAGE SUIT.

The verdict of $16,000 for Pierce's World's Dispensary Medical Institute in its suit against the *Ladies' Home Journal* is variously regarded in Buffalo, where the case was tried. One druggist told an officer of the Pierce Company that the verdict was too large or too small, he was not prepared to say which. If the verdict is too small to satisfy a libel held by the plaintiff to have cost him $200,000 it shows that the jury did not consider the injury very great, and it also shows a small estimate on the value of a retraction, or at least such a retraction as the *Home Journal* made. One druggist said that a retraction, to be of any account, ought to have appeared in the paper in big letters month after month. Another view of the verdict is that the jurymen were mostly country people, who took $16,000 to be a large sum of money. The Pierce Company will no doubt appeal the case.

THE BUFFALO DRUGGISTS' BOWLING CLUB

is still attracting a host of players, the athletic sports of the summer indulged in by so many appearing to convince them that it pays to keep the muscles up. A handicap prize of an elegant "stein" was lately put up for the largest score made in 12 games. The captain fixed up the handicaps according to rules based on the records of the members and the result was a victory for H. A. Scheck, the Genesee street druggist, with an average of 158. One or two of the "scratch" members have an idea that they might have come in first but for the fact that they were not able to play all the games. It is the plan after the holidays to arrange some games with neighboring cities, for instance, Niagara Falls and Rochester.

The Buffalo Drug Merchants' Exchange will be given a complimentary banquet at the Broezel Hotel on the 28th by the J. Hungerford Smith Fruit Syrup Company of Rochester. It is expected that there will be about 150 guests in attendance, as the ladies are also invited. A fine time is looked for.

NEW ENGLAND.

Phi Chi's Dine—Reciprocity of Registration Legalized—Swindle Works by Telephone—Druggists' Licenses in Prohibition Towns.

(From our Regular Correspondent.)

Boston, March 21.—The annual installation and banquet of Eta Chapter of Phi Chi Fraternity was held at the Copley Square Hotel on the evening of March 8. It was the banner event in the organization's history, the attendance being about 50, and the festivities continued to a late hour. Prof. C. F. Nixon was the toastmaster at the banquet and the speakers were Prof. E. H. Pierre, A. H. Tripp, Ph.G.; S. G. Bixby, Ph.G.; G. B. Gunn, Pharm.D.; Theodore Dangelmayer, Pharm.D.; G. E. Vise, C. R. Varney, E. J. Morris and H. F. Gerald, Ph.G. Music was furnished by I. R. Howatt and W. L. Stokes, who volunteered piano solos, and by an orchestra.

REGISTERED IN NEW ENGLAND.

The Board of Pharmacy recently held three examinations, the dates of which and results follow:

On February 18 nine candidates were examined and the five following were successful:

Eliza G. H. Brackett, West Medford; Edward W. Burke, Natick; John F. Kershaw, North Andover; James T. O'Neill, Boston; Paul V. Rockwood, Keene, N. H.

On February 27 11 candidates were examined and the eight following were successful:

Henry Adams, jr., Springfield; Carl D. Bates, Fitchburg; John C. Brown, New Bedford; Irving R. Howatt, Cambridge; Frank G. Killigrew, Holyoke; Fred C. Locke, Lynn; William L. Stokes, Boston; Percival Stone, Lynn.

On March 6 12 candidates were examined and the two following were successful:

Alfred C. St. Pierre, Taunton; Frank J. Young, Lawrence.

IMPORTANT CHANGES IN THE MASSACHUSETTS LAW.

Important changes have been made in the pharmacy law; these were approved the first of the present month. The Board of Pharmacy may now in its discretion grant certificates of registration to such persons as shall furnish with their application satisfactory proof that they have been registered by examination in some other State: Provided, that such other State shall require a degree of competency equal to that required of applicants in this State. This is an amendment to the present law which has been further changed so that a person who desires to do business as a pharmacist shall, upon payment of $5, be entitled to examination, and if found qualified shall be registered as a pharmacist and shall receive a certificate signed by the president and secretary of said board. Any person who fails to pass such examination shall upon request be re-examined after the expiration of three months at any regular meeting of the board, upon the payment of $3.

A BILL TO PERMIT DRUGGISTS TO SELL LIQUORS IN NO-LICENSE TOWNS.

The question of liquor sales in no-license towns by pharmacists has been considered by the present Liquor Committee, which has just reported a bill providing that in no-license cities and towns the licensing authorities shall permit registered pharmacists to sell intoxicating liquors upon the prescription of a physician, provided that no such prescription shall be refilled. Any pharmacist who shall violate the provisions of this act by filling a prescription more than once, or by failing to keep a record, or by refusing to show the record to a person authorized to see it, shall have his permit revoked and be subject to a penalty of not less than $50, nor more than $100, or by imprisonment for not less than one, nor more than six months.

THE TELEPHONE-CHANGE SWINDLE STILL BEING WORKED.

Druggists should be alive to the telephone game, which is rapidly becoming popular with those who try to get money without working. On the evening of March 19 a man entered the store of Arthur Hudson, Newton, and telephoned to Fred A. Hubbard, another druggist, in the name of Charles Casey, to send goods to the value of $1 to his house.

PENNSYLVANIA.

Active Preparations for the State Meeting—A Possible Candidate for Mayor of Philadelphia—October Applicants to Be Re-examined—Effect of Theft of Board Examination Papers.

(*From our Regular Correspondent.*)

Philadelphia, March 22.—A thorough canvass of the drug trade is being made by officers of the Pennsylvania State Pharmaceutical Association. Every effort is being exerted to secure a large increase in the membership, and it is believed that considerable good will be the outcome of the work which is being done. F. M. Apple, the chairman of the Committee on Membership, has taken a deep interest in this subject, and has sent out broadcast a letter to all druggists who are not members. In this letter he gives reasons why they should become members.

MR. KLINE WOULD MAKE A GOOD MAYOR.

Mahlon N. Kline, the president of the drug house of Smith, Kline & French Company, has greatly endeared himself to the good element of this city for the time and work he has done in taking the affairs of the municipality out of the hands of the gang of politicians that have for so many years been plundering the citizens. There is hardly any doubt that Mr. Kline is one of the busiest men in Philadelphia. He is not only the head of the great drug house, but there is not an important meeting that he is not in some way connected with it. He is the head of the Trades League, holds an important position in the Drug Exchange, is chairman of the Legislative Committee of the N. W. D. A., and besides holds office in a number of other trades organizations. Notwithstanding all these duties he is one of Mayor Weaver's advisers, and there is hardly a day that he does not confer with the Chief Executive of the City of Brotherly Love. Now he has again taken another step upward in the hearts of the people. He has been instrumental in securing the Philadelphia & Western Railroad in petitioning the city for permission to extend its line under certain streets of Philadelphia, the said railroad company agreeing to pay handsomely for its franchise. This move has met with universal approval, and it is safe to say that if Mr. Kline desired it he could have any political position in the gift of the people. There is some talk of making him the next Mayor. This suggestion is a good one, for there would not only be honesty in every form under him, but there would be a head to this city which would have the brains necessary to bring all its good traits to the front.

BOARD EXAMINATION PAPERS SOLD TO APPLICANTS.

On March 17 the Pennsylvania State Pharmaceutical Examining Board held an examination in this city, there being 87 applicants. It was the first examination under the new law held here, and considerable interest is attached to the outcome. At this meeting it was announced that all the successful applicants who took the examination of the State Pharmaceutical Board last October will have to be examined over again before they can obtain their certificates. This announcement has come as a great surprise, and to those who managed to just get through it was a hard blow. The cause for this order is that during the last examination some of the applicants had secured the questions before the board met. A member of the board said the reason for withholding the certificates was that the questions had been obtained in advance by some one who had peddled them out to certain applicants for $50. Shortly after that examination the AMERICAN DRUGGIST made the announcement that a downtown druggist had been caught with the goods on him, and he was arrested and held for trial. It is also stated that the board has received information that certain druggists in this city are practicing medicine and writing prescriptions. The members of the board declare that war will be made on the illegal practice.

BUSINESS BOOMING.

The retail drug business in this city is much better than it has been for years. A prominent wholesale dealer said he believed that there were less bills out now than ever before. This he said means that the retail druggists are not only doing a better business but they are making more money. For the last few months there were less retail stores in trouble and very few were bought in by the wholesale druggists. In some cases stores that have been under the supervision of the wholesale dealers and jobbers have been turned over to the original owners. Bills are being more promptly paid and the orders for drugs and other supplies are much larger. The retail druggists have been doing a large business, as there is considerable sickness in this city, and the number of prescriptions put up has been exceedingly large.

PHILADELPHIA NEWS NOTES.

The Miller Drug Company of Eleventh street, north of Market, Philadelphia, has purchased the Snyder Drug Company, of Lancaster, Pa.

D. E. Bransome has returned from a business trip to Reading.

J. M. Riegel has bought the store at Twenty-first and Clearfield streets that was formerly conducted as Ziegler Pharmacy.

William Bransome, the son of D. E. Bransome, of Johnson & Johnson fame, has secured a position with H. B. Leeds, of Atlantic City.

W. A. Booth, of Booth Brothers, at 504 Arch street, died at his residence in this city on the 16th inst. Mr. Booth was very popular with the trade, and his loss is a severe one.

Henry C. Blair, of Eighth and Walnut streets, has returned from a trip to New York City, where he has been for the past week.

Michael Herr, the druggist at Broad and Girard avenues, died of uræmia at his residence in this city on March 16, after an illness of but eight hours. He leaves a widow and son.

The quarterly report of the Philadelphia Wholesale Drug Company shows that there has been an increase in business of 20 per cent. over the phenomenal business done during the same period last year.

Mr. Cave, who was formerly of the firm of French, Cave & Co., at 429 Arch street, has severed his connection with that firm and entered into partnership with John H. Wood & Co., wholesale druggists, at 112 Market street. The name of the new firm will be Wood, Cave & Co.

Colonel Duble, who was the organizer for the N. A. R. D., has severed his connection with that organization, and is now in this city in the interest of the American Druggists' Syndicate. He reports having obtained many members in this city, and from his account the new concern is doing a fine business.

The question of the P. A. R. D. giving a musical and dance on May 1 is being agitated, and as the association is in need of funds it would seem to be good policy to have it, as it has always been a money maker, besides promoting good fellowship among the members.

The appeal in the Loder case, which was set for March 6, has not come up yet. As it was No. 32 on the list the chances are that it will not come up for argument until some time in April. The druggists feel that they have now a better chance than ever and are quite confident that they will win.

The officers of the State Board of Pharmacy have been making some arrests of those who are running stores without having the necessary legal authority. So far most of the cases are in the Italian settlement in the southern part of the city, but a watchful eye is being kept on all stores that a registered manager be in charge.

A Wholesale House at Tampa.

Tampa, Fla., now boasts its first wholesale drug house in the big corporation recently organized by the Hutchinson-Cotter Drug Company. The store is known as the Hillsborough Drug Store. It is well equipped to do business and its officers are among the very best citizens of the town. Tampa has heretofore been without a wholesale drug house, and this one fills a long felt want. Considerable interest is being manifested throughout this section in the future of the new company, and it is indicated that this will be bright and prosperous. E. D. Berger, the efficient secretary of the Florida Association, is the moving spirit.

MARYLAND.

Opposing Other Drug Bills—Any Legislation Unlikely—A Theatre and Dinner Party—To Form a Local Board of the A. Ph. A.

(*From our Regular Correspondent.*)

Baltimore, March 22.—While the Bryan bill, drafted by the Attorney-General of Maryland, and which aimed to restrict the promiscuous sale of narcotics and habit forming drugs, as well as the Godwin bill, requiring manufacturers of proprietary and patent medicines to print formulas of their preparations on the label or wrapper, have been killed, two other measures now before the General Assembly are hardly more acceptable. One of these is a substitute for the Godwin bill, having been introduced by the same delegate, and being somewhat modified in its provisions. The author asserts that he has met the objections urged against the first measure. The druggists of the State, however, do not take kindly to the substitute, and will arrange to oppose it before the Committee on Hygiene. The other bill was offered by Delegate Blank, of the city delegation, and is said to be virtually the measure now before the New York Legislature. It endeavors to prevent the sale of poisons and narcotics without a prescription from a physician, and the pharmacists say would tend to prevent any one from getting a simple household remedy without a prescription. The bill was alleged to be a compromise between the druggists and physicians, the State Board of Pharmacy having been named a committee on the part of the Maryland Pharmaceutical Association to confer with the doctors and endeavor to reach an agreement. The opponents of the measure assert that the committee saw a few doctors on board the train for Annapolis and then and there agreed to submit the bill as acceptable to all concerned, instead of reporting it first to the druggists and having action taken upon it.

From present indications the outlook for additional pharmacy legislation is not favorable, and it is altogether likely that all measures will fail.

There is also pending a pure food bill, in which, however, the druggists are only indirectly interested.

THE WEDGEWOOD CLUB.

The last meeting of the Wedgewood Club, on the first Thursday evening in March, took the form of a theatre party at the Maryland. But instead of the company taking seats in the auditorium, they were placed at a richly laden board on the mezzanine floor, where they could enjoy good things to eat and still take in some of the performance. The occasion proved to be one of the most successful gatherings held by the club.

BALTIMORE DRUG TRADE BOWLERS.

The season of the Baltimore Drug Trade Bowling Club is practically closed, with the team of James Baily & Son in first place. This quintette early in the season gained such a lead that it could not be overtaken. Baltimore will of course be represented at the contests of the National League, which will take place this year in Atlantic City.

A meeting of members of the American Pharmaceutical Association residing in Maryland and the District of Columbia has been called for the purpose of organizing a local branch, as provided for by the general association, such as has been successfully inaugurated at Chicago. Members are earnestly requested to assemble in the lecture hall of the Dental and Pharmaceutical Building, University of Maryland, Lombard and Greene streets, Baltimore, Saturday afternoon, March 24, promptly at 3 o'clock. An adjourned meeting may be held at the same place in the evening if such be found desirable.

BACK FROM EUROPE.

Dr. A. R. L. Dohme, of Sharp & Dohme, of this city, arrived home on the 14th inst. after a protracted trip to Europe, most of his time having been spent in the laboratories of Paris and London, where he studied the latest processes and products, with a view to introducing some of them in the establishment of Sharp & Dohme. While Dr. Dohme had some recreation, the main object of his trip was work, to which he applied himself faithfully.

NEWS NOTES.

H. B. Gilpin, of Gilpin, Langdon & Co. and the H. B. Gilpin Company, who is traveling in Europe, was last heard of enjoying himself along the shores of the Mediterranean.

Druggist A. B. Lennan, Patterson Park avenue and Monument street, died on March 16. He was only 26 years old, a graduate of the Maryland College of Pharmacy, and is survived by his parents.

Dr. D. M. R. Culbreth, of the faculty of the department of pharmacy, Maryland University, gave a dinner on March 9 to the other members of the faculty and their wives. The company also included Dr. and Mrs. John F. Hancock.

H. W. Troxell, one of the lecturers at the department of pharmacy, University of Maryland, has sold his retail drug store at Fulton and Riggs avenues to H. E. Wilson, who formerly conducted the pharmacy at Gilmor street and Frederick avenue.

OHIO.

The Alcohol Bill Amended Little Likelihood of Further Legislation —Columbus Association Elects Officers.

(*From our Regular Correspondent.*)

Cleveland, March 20.—As the Legislature will adjourn early in April druggists believe that there is an end to all objectional legislation for the present. There are about 600 bills on the calendar, and it will be a hard matter to reach all of them. Because the pharmacal bills are not considered as important as some others it is believed they will be allowed to sleep in the committees, where by hard work they have been kept so far. The bill relating to alcohol in proprietary medicines has been amended so as not to require the amount to be placed upon the label unless it exceeds the quantity sufficient to preserve the other ingredients and keep it from freezing. Even with this change it has not been reported out of the committee and it is thought that it will not be. All the other bills have been gone over by leading druggists and they believe that they are now safe.

THE RETAIL DRUGGISTS' ASSOCIATION OF COLUMBUS has elected the following officers: President, A. W. Kiler; vice-president, F. R. Innis; second vice-president, Robert Sleeman; secretary, F. C. Haney; treasurer, Frank Kerr; executive committee, Elmore Hatton, Charles Sentz, Harvey Miller, Henry Beck, Daniel Magle. The retiring president is H. F. Bradshaw. The wives of the druggists were entertained at a card party after the close of the meeting, which was held at the Hartman Hotel.

FOUND DEAD.

Robert J. McMakin, a retired druggist of Cincinnati, was found dead in his apartments on Hoffner street about two weeks ago. He had been missing for several days, and the other occupants of the house had the door forced. Mr. McMakin's wife died some years ago, and since that time he has lived alone. He was about sixty-five years of age and was well known among the business men of the city. His relatives took charge of the remains and the funeral was held at the home of one of them.

OHIO NEWS NOTES.

Conner Brothers have purchased the business of the late S. D. Yates, at Ada, Ohio.

W. M. Beidler, of Millersburg, has made an assignment for the benefit of creditors.

Harry Mason, a well-known young druggist of Westerville, died on March 16 from organic heart trouble. He had been married but a few months.

Rev. S. P. Long, of the First Lutheran Church, Mansfield, created considerable feeling not long ago, while preaching at the funeral of a druggist, when the local association was present in a body, by saying that he wished the druggists would all put up a Sunday closing sign in their stores and sign it "God."

THE WEST.

Liquor Licenses in Chicago—War Between Druggists and "The Tribune"—The Newspaper Tries to Square Itself—N. A. R. D. Officials Issue Warning Against National Cigar Stands Company.

(*From our Regular Correspondent.*)

CHICAGO, March 22.—A number of druggists attended the meeting of the Telephone Committee of the Common Council last Friday, and as a result the session proved to be lively. Special interest was lent to the hearing because of the effort made by the *Tribune* to prove that druggists are dissatisfied with slot machine 'phones. On account of the manner in which it vilified druggists in the cocaine agitation and also because of its stand in regard to telephones this paper is not popular with the trade at present. Mr. Bodemann went for the *Tribune* rough-shod in his talk at the hearing, and others also freed their minds. All of the best speeches in favor of the slot machines were omitted from this report. In its article the *Tribune* found seventeen druggists who said they were displeased with the slot machine.

NO COCAINE OBTAINABLE.

It has been pointed out that the paper displayed much ingenuity to find these men among 1,000 pleased druggists. The few kickers are put in the light of objecting to profits of only $10 a month, whereas they formerly paid out $12.50 during the same period. Subsequent investigation has shown that in the *Tribune's* recent display of yellow journalism, when it asserted that two purchases of cocaine were made, a serious mistake was made. There was no cocaine purchased; all that was obtained was eucaine, which is not covered by the State law. As has been explained, efforts are being made to have changes made in the law. The inability of reporters to get cocaine really speaks well for the enforcement of the law.

N. A. R. D. officials have issued a warning to members advising them to have nothing whatever to do with the National Cigar Stands Company. Attention is called to the fact that the United Cigar Stores Company is reported to be part of the same scheme, and that "trust" goods are handled. Druggists are warned to stand clear until the situation is better understood. President Avery sent Field Agent White to these people for information. He was refused the desired facts. The officials concluded that there must be something wrong when the cigar people showed themselves afraid to talk. The action of the Eastern Association also had weight here.

UNIVERSITY OF ILLINOIS SCHOOL OF PHARMACY.

Prof. W. A. Puckner has resigned his position as chief chemist of the Searle & Hereth Company and has entered upon his duties as secretary of the Council of Pharmacy and Chemistry of the American Medical Association. He will also be the chemist for the association as soon as the chemical laboratory is established, which will be within a few months. Two interesting special lectures were recently given before the senior class of the school, as a part of the course of lectures on business topics. The first of these was on olive oil, by I. Giles Lewis. Mr. Lewis gave a very instructive talk, referring briefly to the great antiquity of the olive culture, the various commercial grades of the oil, its adulteration and the tests for its purity, its uses as a food and its medicinal value. Specimens of olives and olive oil were shown and attention was called to use of containers of tin, glass, etc. Mr. Lewis thought it a mistake to handle the oil in glass bottles, especially if these were exposed to light, which destroys the delicate flavor of the oil.

DRUGGISTS' PRINTING.

The subject of the second lecture was Druggists' Printing, Labels and Boxes, and the speaker F. H. Hertle. Mr. Hertle's interesting talk was reinforced by the exhibition of a large line of samples. The lecturer referred to the way in which lithographed labels are made, the improvement in taste displayed in the selection of labels and the fact that gaudy and high colored labels for prescriptions are now obsolete. He mentioned also the desirability of avoiding labels having a broad black border as too suggestive of mourning.

CHICAGO NEWS NOTES.

The State Board of Pharmacy will meet in Chicago April 3.

Henry Swannell, former president of the T. Ph. A., is on a long trip in California.

The drug store at 422 West Twelfth street, formerly owned by Henry Langenban, has passed into the control of Lilley Bros.

Fred. Klein has leased the store at the corner of Madison street and Sacramento avenue. He will move his stock there May 1.

The Social Drug Club's annual banquet and ball at the Sherman House proved to be highly successful. There were 320 guests, as compared with 202 last year.

Illinois Board of Health officials are showing great activity of late, their leader being Carl R. Chindblom, attorney. C. R. D. A. officials have announced that they are ready to defend members from unjust prosecution.

About twenty members of the Chicago Veteran Druggists' Association sat down to an informal luncheon at the Union in honor of the birthday of T. N. Jamieson, founder of the organization. President Waltersdorf brought out the toast to the founder of the association. Secretary Bodemann handed in his report on the Waltersdorf banquet, and in accordance with the order of the association this report was passed over to Mr. Waltersdorf.

The Carter Medicine Company Granted Exclusive Rights to the Red Wrapper.

Judge Gildersleeve of the Supreme Court of the State of New York, has handed down a decision in which he decrees that the Carter Medicine Company has the sole and exclusive right to the use of the red colored wrappers and labels upon small round packages of the general size and shape of the package of Carter's Little Liver Pills, containing little liver pills, and to the use upon such wrappers of and labels of the words "Little Liver Pills" printed in black ink.

The case at trial was that of the Carter Medicine Company against Simon Ager, a retail druggist doing business at Howard and Willett streets, in the lower East Side of New York City. The decree of the judge in full is printed below:

At a Special Term, Part IV, of the Supreme Court of the State of New York, held in the Court House in the County of New York on March 13, 1906.

Present: Hon. Henry A. Gildersleeve, Justice.

Carter Medicine Company versus Simon Ager. } Final decree.

Ordered, adjudged and decreed:

That the plaintiff, the Carter Medicine Company, has the sole and exclusive right to the use of red colored wrappers and labels upon small round packages of the general size and shape above described—to wit, about half an inch in diameter and two and one-half inches in length, containing little liver pills, and to the use upon such wrappers and labels of the words "Little Liver Pills," printed in black ink, in connection with the other wording appearing upon the wrappers and labels used by the plaintiff, specimens of which are hereto attached.

Also that the acts of the defendant, Simon Ager, in offering for sale or selling pills in packages of about the same general size and shape as those used by the plaintiff, with the red colored wrappers and labels bearing the words "Little Liver Pills," printed in black ink, and the other wording shown on the specimens hereto attached, were an infringement and violation of the plaintiff's rights aforesaid.

Forever enjoining the said defendant, Simon Ager, his servants and agents, from selling or offering for sale any medicinal preparation except the plaintiff's, put up in a small round package, inclosed in a red colored wrapper and bearing the words "Little Liver Pills," or the other wording aforesaid, and from selling or offering for sale or putting up any pills or other medicinal preparation in packages or wrappers resembling in any manner, in color or otherwise, the package used by the plaintiff, as hereinbefore described, and from making any use of the plaintiff's trade-mark, or the words "Little Liver Pills," either in connection with a red wrapper or in connection with any medicinal preparation except that of the plaintiff.

Directing the said Simon Ager to deliver up to be destroyed all bottles, packages, wrappers, circulars or things in his possession or under his control, bearing the plaintiff's said trade-mark, or the words "Little Liver Pills," and all small round packages of pills contained in red wrappers.

That the plaintiff, the Carter Medicine Company, recover of the defendant, Simon Ager, the sum of fifty dollars as damages, together with the sum of one hundred and fifty-three and 12-100 dollars, for the costs of this action, making in all the sum of two hundred and three and 12-100 dollars, with interest from March 7, 1906, and that the plaintiff have execution therefor.

Dated March 13, 1906.

Enter. H. A. GILDERSLEEVE,
Justice of the Supreme Court of the State of New York.

THE PACIFIC COAST.

Druggists Oppose Antinarcotic Legislation Proposed by Clerks—Still More Stringent Bills in Course of Preparation by Board of Health—Co-ordination of Organization Work—Activity of the Pharmacy Board.

(From our Regular Correspondent.)

PROPRIETORS OPPOSE NARCOTIC LEGISLATION.

San Francisco, Cal., March 17.—Three resolutions to provide against the evils resulting from the "traffic of certain poisons," "narcotic drugs" and wood alcohol, and to regulate the sales thereof, which were fathered by the local Drug Clerks' Association, were turned down by the Supervisors' Hospital and Health Committee on the request of the employing druggists. Because the latter had not been formally consulted in the formulation of the proposed ordinances a committee of the proprietors took what appears to be a pessimistic view of the situation and killed the resolutions. Those objecting to the regulation concerning the sale of cocaine, opium, etc., admitted that the purpose of the ordinance was good, but that "the form was bad;" still what was used is the draft presented by the conference of delegates representing the A. Ph. A., the P. A. A., the N. W. D. A. and the N. A. R. D., held last December in Chicago. No doubt the resolutions would have been adopted and conditions have been materially improved if the proprietors had used their efforts in proposing any desirable changes or additions which might have been overlooked. The Board of Health has in preparation another ordinance which, if it becomes a law, will cover all that was sought to be brought about by the rejected ordinances and considerably more.

LOCAL COMMITTEE, P. C. P. A., ACTIVE.

The Local Committee, in charge of the 1907 meeting of the Pacific Coast Pharmaceutical Association, which was launched at the Lewis and Clark Pharmaceutical Congress last July, composed of J. H. Dawson, chairman; A. S. Musante, secretary; Professors W. M. Searby and J. H. Flint, Dr. Albert Schneider, Val Schmidt and D. M. Fletcher, held their first meeting yesterday. It was decided to invite the State Board of Pharmacy, the local branch of the N. A. R. D. and the Drug Clerks' Association to each send a representative to act as a member of the committee. It was also moved that this committee work with the officers of the California Pharmaceutical Society in the effort of reviving the latter organization, so that the State society may be prepared for the tri-State meeting next year.

BOARD REGISTERS CLERKS AND IS OTHERWISE ACTIVE.

According to present appearances the new Board of Pharmacy is going to establish an enviable record in the prosecution of offenders against the pharmacy law of the State. The best element of the profession is looking with favor upon the seven arrests and four convictions of druggists carrying on stores illegally as well as the prosecution of itinerant venders who do not obey the law that has been brought about through the instrumentality of the board. If the policy outlined by Secretary C. B. Whilden in an interview with the AMERICAN DRUGGIST correspondent be followed, there is no doubt that the best interests of the pharmacists will be served. In the present activity the board is notifying grocery stores and general dealers that they must stop selling "drugs and medicines, such as castor oil, salts, tincture of arnica, quinine," etc. The following is a list of those who were successful in the last examinations held at Los Angeles and San Francisco:

Licentiates.—J. R. Baker, Paul Barsi, W. A. Bennetts, H. D. Morgan, Otto Mausert, E. W. Hubbard, E. R. McCall, Frank T. Wilt, Ernest Forbes, B. Frank Stout, Frank Glando, S. M. Grier, Gordon M. Clarke, Albert G. Knott, R. S. Wait, Leslie E. Gillin, Charles H. Crawford, Angelo Garibaldi, Emily E. Salter, F. Stanley Whitlock, Thomas M. Cummings, Roy Reid Henderson, S. Byron Pretty, William H. Baum, David Roy Douglass, Noble S. Elder, Charles N. Bichard, Arthur H. McCoy, J. C. Peterson, James J. Jennings, Fred. D. Campbell, S. H. Burston, George C. Butler, George H. Dietz, Charles N. Greusel, E. H. Spiering, Lawrence Zembsch, Phillas C. A. Theriault, A. A. B. Schmerker Charles F. Buchanan, Andrew S. Dickson, Will C. Evans, Frank W. Fogwell, Earle D. Gilson, Grace L. Hedges, Melville N. Knoth, Harriett E. Montgomery, Robert H. Lang, John W. Thomas, James R. Pickerill, Leo I. Mulvey, Harry J. Wrede, S. H. Weltman, M. W. Heinrice, Wm. G. Mangold, Guy Felt, W. S. Carpenter, Chas. F. M. Stone, Frank B. Wright, L. F. Bass, Carl M. H. Hagen, Otto A. Hartmann, Frank L. Orr, Andrew J. Gardner, E. W. Woolsey, Adolph Dittmer, W. H. Bedford, Robt. C. Kerntopf, Justin O. Bigelow, Chas. E. Petter, W. T. Aitken, Parley P. Pratt, Omer L. Cole, W. A. Clingen, Louis Dehmel, Edward H. Charette.

Assistants.—F. H. Seery, Rafael G. Dufficy, Niels Jogensen, Walter F. Vaughan, Lester O. Kimberlin, Henry W. Lund, Raymond E. Marden, C. A. Buck, L. M. Grubbs, Wm. S. Carson, Theodore T. Purkett, Ansel Woodworth, G. W. Pfender, Proctor Moulton, H. J. Johnson, J. W. Melvin, Lionel Wachs, J. W. Salter, Roscoe E. Benson, John F. Gates, Frank Monaco, George V. Morrison, Henry J. Laurie, T. S. Whitling, Ralph Harrod Rogers, W. K. Sproule.

The next meeting of the board will be at Los Angeles on April 2, to be followed by one in San Francisco on April 9.

DEPARTMENT OF PHARMACY, UNIVERSITY OF CALIFORNIA.

Dr. Albert Schneider, Professor of Botany, Materia Medica and Pharmacognosy, has accepted the position of the Spreckles Sugar Company, and after the end of the present term will devote most of his time in pathological and physiological research work at Spreckles, near Salinas, Cal. Dr. Schneider will probably retain the Chair of Bacteriology. Although several prominent men of the East have applied for the position the fact that the faculty is in communication with others also makes it impossible to say at present who will succeed Dr. Schneider.

Four lectures of the first annual lecture course on popular subjects given by the faculty and Alumni Association have already been presented, and the remaining two will be delivered at the college on March 22 and April 5.

Zeta chapter of Phi Chi fraternity held its annual dance in the Marble Room of the Palace Hotel on February 20.

THE SOUTH.

Druggists Criticise Telephone Service—To Entertain the State Association.

(From our Regular Correspondent.)

New Orleans, La., March 19, 1906.—A determined effort to secure better telephone service in the city is the object of a movement recently inaugurated by the local druggists' association, and it is believed that within a very short time it will be taken to the National Association of Retail Druggists, in hopes of having that body stamp the movement with its approval and aid in the fight. This matter was broadly discussed at the last meeting of the Orleans Pharmaceutical Association, and the committee which has it in hand was instructed to continue its work. According to the statements of the druggists the present telephone service is wholly inadequate and the conditions are badly in need of improvement. The party line system is very unsatisfactory, and because of the high rates the majority of the druggists are unable to secure other than party line 'phones.

THE STATE MEETING.

Within the next few days the Committee on Entertainment which has in charge the arrangements for the coming convention of the Louisiana State Pharmaceutical Association will make public its report, showing just what sort of a reception the many delegates who attend will be given. The annual meeting of the State association will be held here April 17, 18 and 19, and it is believed a large number of well-known drug men from all parts of the State will attend. It is hinted that the programme of entertainments this year will surpass any other which has ever been issued.

LOUISIANA NEWS NOTES.

W. J. Wendt, who formerly operated an establishment in Magazine street, has bought out Fear's Pharmacy at Philip and Baronne streets.

Otto's Pharmacy at Washington avenue and Magazine street has passed into new hands and will hereafter be known as Caillouette's Pharmacy.

Dr. D. P. Albers has taken over the interests of the Claiborne Pharmacy at Claiborne and Tulane avenues and will henceforth operate that popular establishment.

The Union Label Drug Store in Algiers, across the river from New Orleans, has been succeeded by the Suburban Drug Store, which will be opened for business in a very few days.

E. J. Marion has opened a new store in the big building at Napoleon and St. Charles avenues which was formerly occupied by S. W. Clark & Sons. The location is ideal and Mr. Marion has shown excellent judgment in selecting it.

The Drug and Chemical Market

The prices quoted in this report are those current in the wholesale market, and higher prices are paid for retail lots
The quality of goods frequently necessitates a wide range of prices,

Condition of Trade.

NEW YORK, March 24, 1906.

The volume of trade during the period under review has not been large, the extent of mail orders and inquiries being somewhat light. The expectations of an advance in the price of quinine have been somewhat dashed by the result of the cinchona bark auction at Amsterdam, which was disappointing, a slightly lower unit being reached as compared with the February auction and only about three-quarters of the offerings sold. Unless the demand for quinine shows a material improvement or spot stocks prove lower than generally believed the likelihood of any advance is remote. Notwithstanding the apparent inactivity cheerful expressions are heard on all sides in regard to the trade prospects, and apart from a further fractional decline in opium and an advance in camphor, no very important price changes are to be noted, our list of advances and declines involving principally articles of secondary importance. Menthol has developed rather an unexpected strength and Chinese cantharides have moved into stronger position. The continued firmness in crude gum contributes to a firmer feeling for refined camphor, and the recent sharp advances are said to leave the spot quotations at less than the prices ruling in European markets.

HIGHER.	LOWER.
Camphor,	Opium,
Guarana,	Blue vitriol,
Menthol,	Sodium benzoate,
Ginger, Jamaica,	Codliver oil, Norwegian,
Camphor, monobromated,	Silver nitrate,
Cantharides, Chinese,	Ergot,
Vanilla beans, cut,	Cassia oil,
Oxalic acid,	
Quinine, Java,	
Gamboge,	

Drugs.

Acetanilid has not changed during the interval and the market is firmer if anything at the higher values named in our last report, following an advance in the price of raw material. From 24c to 25c is now asked as to quantity, and we hear of numerous sales within this range.

Alcohol has developed no new feature of interest since our last, the demand continuing of steady proportions, with values well sustained at $2.45 to $2.47. Refined wood is quoted at 70c to 75c for 95 and 97 per cent., respectively.

Ammonia water is irregular and unsettled, owing to competition, and 26 degrees in carboys is now quoted at 5½c to 5¾c, as to quantity.

Balm of Gilead buds have not shown any special activity during the interval, but the market is steady in tone and values are well sustained at 32c to 33c.

Balsam copaiba continues in fair jobbing demand, at unchanged prices, but no large sales are reported; Central American is held at 29c to 30c, and Para at 42½c to 45c, the latter being in very light supply.

Balsam fir, Canada, is taken rather sparingly at present, but prices are well maintained at the range of $3.00 to $3.10 for Canada, and 65c to 67c for Oregon.

Balsam Peru is dull, but prime grades are somewhat scarce and it is doubtful whether $1.05 could be shaded for this variety, though some stock offers at 97½c.

Balsam tolu reflects an easier tone, and offerings are made with less reserve at 20c to 21c.

Barks.—Cottonroot is maintained in steady position at 8½c. to 10c. Bayberry is difficult to obtain at under 13c, though sales have been made during the interval in some instances at 12c. Cascara sagrada is dull and neglected and no 1905 bark seems to be available below 5½c. Sassafras is maintained in steady position and a good consuming inquiry is appearing at the quoted range of 13c to 15c. Wahoo, bark of root, continues to offer at 45c, notwithstanding present scarcity, the early prospect of new crop supplies being in buyer's favor.

Buchu leaves, short, are maintained in steady position, owing to scarcity of spot supply and nothing offers at under 18c to 20c, the outside figure being for prime green. The tenor of advices from primary sources contributes to a firmer feeling on the part of holders, for the new crop is reported a failure.

Camphor, monobromated, has advanced in sympathy with gum camphor, and the revised quotations are $1.50 to $1.60, an advance of 10c per lb.

Cantharides is held with increased firmness owing to scarcity. For the limited available supply, which is under good control, 75c is named, for both whole and powdered.

Cassia buds are given very little consideration, though the market appears well sustained at the point of 18½c to 19½c.

Codliver oil is seasonably dull and quotations are fractionally lower, with Norwegian offering at $20.00 to $27.00 as to brand, quantity and seller. The season's catch of fish announced from Norway on the 19th instant represents the equivalent of 7,700 barrels of oil for Lofoden, and 16,930 barrels for all Norway.

Cuttlefish bone remains quiet, though holders are firm in their views, quotations for prime Trieste being maintained at 16½c to 17c, and French at 12c to 12½c. Supplies of jewelers are scant and prices continue steady, on the basis of 70c for large and 40c to 50c for small.

Ergot has developed an easier turn and there are sellers at 31c to 33c.

Guarana continues held in firm position on spot, and nothing is now available at under 70c to 75c.

Juniper berries are somewhat unsettled owing to offerings of inferior grades from Germany, and supplies are obtainable at 3¾c to 4c.

Lycopodium is slow of sale and offers more freely at 48c to 50c as to brand.

Menthol has developed increased firmness, and an improved inquiry is noted with supplies well maintained at $2.40 to $2.60 for spot goods, though little is offered at the inside figure.

Opium has been characterized by no new developments during the past fortnight. There is little or no demand for the article and the weakening tendency of spot values continues unchecked. Buyers limit their orders to jobbing quantities and values have eased off during the interval to the range of $2.80 to $2.82½ for cases, and $2.82½ to $2.85 for broken packages. Powdered is held and selling at $3.30 to $3.35.

Quinine has not gained in strength since our last, the bark auction at Amsterdam having resulted in a slightly lower unit as noted in our editorial review of the conditions of trade. The average unit paid at the sale last Thursday was 4.18 Dutch cents as against 4.38 Dutch cents paid the month preceding. Only three-quarters of the offerings of 9,865 packages were sold. The expected advance in price of quinine is therefore not likely to materialize unless an improved demand sets in. The spot market meanwhile retains a tame and uninteresting appearance, with manufacturers quoting at the previous range of 18c for bulk for 100-oz tins, while second hands name 17¾c and 17½c as acceptable for German and Java respectively.

Saw Palmetto berries are not coming forward very liberally and the principal holder has advanced the limit to 17c for prime quality. The unfavorable reports regarding the outlook for new crop influences holders to increased firmness.

Vanilla beans, Mexican, have attracted increased attention since our last and first hands are firmer in their views at current quotations of $2.00 to $2.25 for cuts, and $2.75 to $6.50 for whole beans. Tahiti of the new crop are reported scarce owing to damage done by a tornado in the producing districts. While short ordinary beans are still offered at 45c there is a shortage of long length, for which the range extends to $1.25.

Chemicals.

Arsenic, white, is rather weaker in tone and though some of the more favored brands are held at 9c, 6½c is generally named.

Blue vitriol is maintained steadily at 5.80c to 5.95c, the inside figure being for carload lots.

Bromides are tending upward and while 16c is the ruling quotation for potash it is doubtful whether any large quantity could be obtained at this figure, since the outbreak is considered favorable to higher prices.

Calmium, metallic, is reported in active demand and firmer at an advance to $1.25.

Carbolic acid is scarce on spot and values are firmly maintained at the previous range of 14c to 15c for drums, and 20c to 22c for bottles.

Citric acid develops increased strength with the advance of the season and manufacturers' prices are well maintained at the range of 41c to 41½c.

Cream tartar has continued in good request and the market is steady at 22½c to 22¾c for crystals and powdered respectively.

Oxalic acid is in light supply and the market is stronger, with quotations advanced to 5⅜c to 5½c.

Silver nitrate is lower in sympathy with the metal and manufacturer's quotations are easy at 41c to 44½c.

Sodium benzoate is irregular and unsettled owing to competition, with 28c to 31c named for granular as to quality and quantity.

Tartaric acid continues in good jobbing request and the quotations of the market show a slight advance, with crystals and powdered held and selling at 28¼c to 28½c.

Essential Oils.

Anise continues in good demand and values are steadily maintained at the quoted range of $1.30 to $1.35.

Camphor is dull and the market a shade easier at 10c for heavy gravity oil, though natural white is firmly maintained at 17c to 18c.

Citronella has eased off in the interval, some holders offering at 39c, though 40c to 41c is generally named.

Clove is taken rather indifferently by the trade and there is not the response to the conditions governing the market for the spice which was expected, cans being still available at 80c to 82½c and bottles at 82½c to 85c.

Juniper is in better demand and the price of the ordinary grade has been advanced to 70c.

Lemon is irregular and reports are conflicting. We hear of offerings in some quarters at a shade under our quotations, while in others reports of labor troubles in Messina have contributed to a firmer feeling.

Pennyroyal of U. S. P. standard continues in light supply and wanted; French oil answering U. S. P. requirements is held at $1.35 to $1.40.

Peppermint continues in upward tendency under the influence of conditions in primary markets and for prime oil on spot $2.60 is regarded as an inside quotation, though one dealer has announced an advance to $2.70. Case oil is now meeting with a good inquiry for export and steadily maintained at $3.25 to $3.35, as to quantity.

Sassafras, natural, is meeting with increased demand and the current range of 50c to 60c is likely to show an early advance.

Wintergreen is in good seasonable demand, current sales being made at the range of $1.50 to $1.75, though $1.45 will buy in instances.

Gums.

Apart from the somewhat sensational advance in camphor, which brings the quotation for cases up to $1.15, there is little change to report in the condition of other varieties. Gamboge is in reduced supply and higher, with quotations advanced to $1.15 to $1.25 for pipe and Curacao aloes are in moderate demand and steady at 6c to 6¼c.

Roots.

Alkanet in a jobbing way continues to realize 7½c to 8c. Belladonna, German, is offered more freely with sellers at 9c to 10c. Ginger, Jamaica, continues in upward tendency and quotations for natural show a further advance to 13c to 16c, while bleached has sold during the interval at 16c and ground and powdered at 13½c to 14½c.

Ipecac continues firmly maintained at the higher range recently established, there being sales of Rio since our last at $1.75 to $1.80, and of Carthagena at $1.70 to $1.75.

Pink maintained its firm position and nothing seems available at under 80c.

Rhubarb is maintained in firm position and we hear of sales of high dried at 24c.

Sarsaparilla, Mexican, is scarce for prompt delivery and sales are reported at 9⅝c.

Seeds.

The market for druggists' seeds has been quiet since our last, and we have few changes of consequence to report, either as regards price or demand. Decorticated cardomoms are somewhat irregular, there being open quotations at 30c, though 35c is asked in some quarters. Canary is firmly maintained at the recent advance to 4½c to 4⅝c for Smyrna and 4¾c to 5c for Sicily. Celery is quiet, but apparently steady at 7½c to 7¾c. Caraway does not offer with any freedom at less than 6c to 6¼c, but less could probably be done on a firm bid. Russian hemp continues held and selling at 3c to 3¼c.

Gasoline Explosions.

John J. Clark, Fire Marshal for the Borough of the Bronx, New York, is convinced that gasoline, benzin and naphtha are responsible for most of the destruction and loss of life from fires, accidental or incendiary. He believes that business interests demand that increased effort should be made to safeguard by statute the sale of benzin, naphtha, etc. In speaking of this to a representative of the AMERICAN DRUGGIST, Fire Marshal Clark said:

"A label, containing a caution not to handle near an open light, affixed to every package of benzin or gasoline sold for domestic purposes would lessen carelessness in handling it, and to prohibit its use as wash water inside a building might save some property and lives. The only State law which refers to gasoline prohibits its sale for lighting except in streets or in machines buried outside the building. This petroleum product, which continuously gives off a vapor that makes an explosive of the air with which it mixes, is sold as freely as flour. Recently I saw a child get a nickel's worth of gasoline in a liniment bottle which had a rag stopper. Gasoline vapor, unlike all other inflammable gases, sinks in air, spreads over the floor and is drawn up by the current produced by any open light and ignited. Gasoline may be fired by an electric spark due to rubbing fabrics, especially silk, in it."

Arthur A. Stilwell Dead.

Arthur A. Stilwell, widely known as a dealer in essential oils, at 103 William street, died on Tuesday, March 20, at his home, 118 West 121st street. He was fifty-two years old. Mr. Stilwell was a director of the Kress & Owen Company and the Maiden Lane National Bank, and a member of the Harvard Club.

A Busy Pharmacist.

The twelfth annual report of the State Asylum for the Chronic Insane of Pennsylvania bears evidence of beneficent activity of the president of the American Pharmaceutical Association, Joseph L. Lemberger, of Lebanon, who is and has for many years been treasurer of the institution. With over 800 patients in the asylum and an annual expenditure of over $131,000, it will be seen that the office of treasurer is by no means a sinecure.

AMERICAN DRUGGIST
and PHARMACEUTICAL RECORD

PHILADELPHIA. NEW YORK, APRIL 9, 1906. CHICAGO

ISSUED SEMI-MONTHLY BY

AMERICAN DRUGGIST PUBLISHING CO.,

62-68 West Broadway, New York.

CHICAGO, 221 Randolph St. PHILADELPHIA, 3718 Walnut St.

A. R. ELLIOTT, President.

CASWELL A. MAYO, Ph.G. ....Editor.
THOMAS J. KEENAN....................Associate Editor.

ROMAINE PIERSON..........Manager Chicago Office.

$1.50 a year. 15 cents a copy.

ADVERTISING RATES QUOTED ON APPLICATION.

The American Druggist and Pharmaceutical Record is issued on the second and fourth Mondays of each month. Changes of advertisements should be received ten days in advance of the date of publication.

Remittances should be made by New York exchange, post office or express money order or registered mail. If checks on local banks are used 10 cents should be added to cover cost of collection. The publishers are not responsible for money sent by unregistered mail, nor for any money paid except to duly authorized agents. All communications should be addressed and all remittances made payable to American Druggist Publishing Co., 62-68 West Broadway, New York.

Entered at New York as Second-Class Matter.

TABLE OF CONTENTS.

EDITORIAL COMMENT.

American Perfumes. We devote a good deal of space in this issue to a report of the transactions of the Manufacturing Perfumers' Association, an organization which has steadily grown in strength and importance since its foundation in 1894. In order to cope successfully with foreign competition the association means to urge the speedy passage of the Lovering bill for the reduction of the tax on alcohol, which is now under consideration by the Congress. It is a source of pride and gratification to note the steady improvement in the quality of American perfumes and to see how steadily they have grown in popular favor. At the exposition in Jamestown next year an exhibit will be made which will fittingly set forth the great progress which has been made in this industry, and it is certainly to the credit of the Manufacturing Perfumers' Association that such a display is possible. We are sure that the association will make a most creditable showing.

The Pure Food and Drug Bill To-morrow. To-morrow (Tuesday) the Hepburn Pure Food and Drug bill, which is the House substitute for the Hepburn bill in the Senate, will be made a special order of business, and there is a likelihood of its becoming law. The essential features of the bill have been indicated at various times in these columns. The objection of the drug trade has been focused on the paragraph amplifying the meaning of the term "drug" and on the requirement for the specification on the label of the quantity or proportion of alcohol, opium and cocaine, or "other poisonous substances" contained in the preparation sold. At the instance of the drug interests, Representative Loring, of Massachusetts, has introduced an amendment in which provision is made for a more equitable definition of the term misbranding which should appeal to the sense of equity and fairness of Congressmen and be incorporated in the law. The vagueness of the expression "other poisonous substances," as now used in the bill, is too evident for comment.

Fight the Stevens-Wainwright Bill! Active opposition has been at last aroused to the passage in the State Legislature of the Stevens-Wainwright bill. Druggists all over the State are interesting themselves in keeping the bill where it belongs—namely, in committee. Action in opposition to the bill was taken rather late in the day, and for this delay some of the chairmen of the committees on legislation of the various pharmaceutical associations will have to render account. The objectionable character of the measure was evident from the first, and it needed no lawyer to pass upon its inconsistencies and absurdities. The idea of transferring some of the functions of the Board of Pharmacy to the State and local Boards of Health is particularly objectionable. Confusion would be sure to result, and both pharmacists and the public would suffer in the end. It is to be hoped that the united, though belated, opposition of the pharmacists of the State will keep the measure from ever being reported for passage.

Getting Together. Action along the right lines was taken by the Hudson River branch of the Metropolitan Association of Retail Druggists in inviting physicians to attend the meeting and get acquainted with pharmacists. The local members of the medical profession attended the meeting in such numbers as to constitute a majority of those present, and the result of their deliberations cannot but be regarded as most wholesome. A new prescription contract was entered into whereby the pharmacists engaged not to refill prescriptions without the consent of the physician. It is expected that the subject will be taken up by the general association and action taken to remove what has been frequently a source of friction between pharmacists and physicians. If a step further can be taken and the physician be brought to see the unwisdom of office-dispensing the pharmacist will be glad to co-operate to the extent of completely discouraging counter-prescribing. It is an encouraging sign of the times that pharmacists and physicians can be brought together for the friendly discussion of matters affecting their interests; certainly an improvement upon the old bad policy of fighting each other at a distance.

Tax Free Alcohol.

The passage of the bill providing for tax free alcohol for use in the arts seems to be practically assured, so far as the House of Representatives is concerned, and seems likely to pass the Senate, though the ways of the Senate are past finding out. The pharmacist has but little direct interest in the results of the passage of this measure, save as all citizens are interested in a measure which will promote the welfare of the various branches of trade, enable manufacturers in many lines to compete in foreign markets as they have never heretofore been able to do and will make available a new, valuable and economical fuel. While it is impossible to predict with certainty the precise cost of alcohol under the new regulations until after those regulations have been promulgated in detail it seems probable that the wholesale price of the "denatured" spirit will be about 40 cents per gallon, the price depending upon various considerations, among which are the methods which may be prescribed for Governmental supervision of the denaturing process.

Among the memoranda submitted to the Committee on Ways and Means of the House was one presented on behalf of the American Chemical Society by Rufus F. Herrick, in which the practice followed in other countries was gone into in detail. The measure, as approved by the committee, has marked advantages over the laws existing in Great Britain and Germany in that there are no statutory requirements concerning the methods to be pursued in denaturing the alcohol. This gives a very desirable degree of plasticity to the act and would enable the Commissioner of Internal Revenue to adopt regulations suitable for specific cases. In England the alcohol which is put on miscellaneous sale is denatured by the addition of 10 per cent. of crude spirit. This is known as methylated spirit. The addition of 0.375 per cent. petroleum oil to this mixture produces what is known as "mineralized" spirit. Only these two kinds of denatured alcohol may be sold at retail. Manufacturers, however, may under certain regulations use any kind of denaturing agent which they find least objectionable in the production of their particular line of goods, provided that the agent used has been approved by and is applied under the direction of the British revenue authorities.

In Germany 1 part of pyridine bases and 4 parts of wood spirit are mixed, and of this mixture 2½ parts per 100 are added to the alcohol. This is the alcohol used for miscellaneous sale, but other processes are permitted under special regulations applying to particular lines of manufacture.

In addition to this bill providing for denatured alcohol Congress has under consideration a measure reducing the tax from its present rate of about $2.07 per wine gallon of strong alcohol to about $1.35, irrespective of the usage to which the alcohol is to be put. It seems hardly likely that this particular measure will go through.

The Lovering bill, however, which provides for the withdrawal from bond of pure alcohol to be used in the manufacture of preparations for export, seems to have a good chance of being adopted, and its adoption would mean much to our export industries.

Pan-American Railway.

The traveling representative of the AMERICAN DRUGGIST on the west coast of South America has contributed to this issue a paper describing briefly something of his travels through Peru along the line of the great Pan-American Railway, and the photographs taken by him for us will have a special interest to our readers coming as they do just at the time when a series of somewhat similar pictures appear in *Scribner's* as illustrations of an article on the Pan-American Railway published in that magazine for April.

The project for a railway to bring New York into direct communication with Buenos Ayres is aptly termed "the commercial corollary of the Monroe Doctrine," and that such a project is not wholly chimerical is shown by the fact that at the beginning of this year every Central and every South American country, so we are told by Mr. Pepper, "has a definite policy of aiding railway construction as an integral part of the Pan-American system, and some of them, as in the case of Peru and Bolivia, have enacted special legislation. All of them are sympathetic toward an intercontinental trunk line because it coincides with their plans for internal development and external trade."

The distance from New York to Buenos Ayres is about 10,391 miles. Of this, 5,709 miles of railroad are already in operation, 703 miles are under construction and only 3,969 miles remain to be built. The lines under construction are sufficiently advanced to assure us that the journey from New York to Guatemala City may be made without change of cars by the close of 1907, and another year will suffice to complete the line to the city of Salvador in the heart of Central America. Some of the lines which have been built in the Andes are masterpieces of scientific engineering.

The manufacturing pharmacists of the United States should lay their plans now to reap the harvest of trade which will follow the completion of this Pan-American road. Those pioneers who now establish cordial relations with our southern neighbors will be in command of the situation when it becomes possible to ship carload lots direct from New York to Buenos Ayres.

Objectionable Bills in the Legislature.

The introduction of three more bills in the State Legislature since our last issue impels us to again call the attention of the legislative committees of the various associations in this State to the necessity of keeping a watchful eye on the Legislature. All three of the bills are assaults on the integrity of the pharmacy law and should receive the united opposition of organized pharmacy in this State. The apparent object of Assembly bill No. 1464 is to enlarge the list of drugs that may be dealt in by country storekeepers and to remove the restrictions regarding the licensing of country stores in which drugs may be sold.

In the Senate, bill No. 856, introduced by Mr. Page, is an antisubstitution measure, which provides that any person substituting or dispensing a different article for or in lieu of the article prescribed, ordered, required or demanded shall be guilty of a misdemeanor and subject to heavy penalties, especially for second and third offenses.

As the various bills mentioned have been drawn without the advice or consent of the pharmaceutical authorities of this State we deem it our duty to urge pharmacists to write to their Assemblymen and Senators at Albany and urge the defeat of these measures, mentioning them specifically by number.

THE SCOPE AND PURPOSE OF THE DRUG PRESS.[1]

BY PROF. FREDERICK J. WULLING,
Dean of the College of Pharmacy of the University of Minneapolis.

The pharmaceutical press is to the pharmaceutical profession more than what the newspaper is to the public. The news stories in the drug journals constitute a later and less important development of the pharmaceutical press, its original purpose having been to bring prompt information of discovery, inventions and progress in the profession.

Journals were preceded by and really are the outgrowth of the annual and biennial proceedings and transactions of learned bodies. There was a time up to a century or so ago when philosophical and scientific progress and matters connected therewith were communicated to the world solely through associations of learned men, who met usually once a year and either did or did not publish their proceedings. The circulation at that time of information among those interested was a difficult and slow process and to expedite this circulation private enterprise undertook to publish at more frequent intervals matters of a special interest relating to certain departments of knowledge. In this way most of the first philosophical, scientific and technical journals originated or received their incentive.

The pharmaceutical press is and has been on a par with other departments of journalism. It is a faithful servant of the profession, and while its original aim was to chronicle pharmaceutical progress it has grown into the greater field of supplying everything readable of interest to the pharmacist. Its function is not merely to report progress and impart news, but it is distinctively educative; indeed, it is not too much to state that the pharmacist who can intelligently and understandingly read and study the better pharmaceutical journals must be a person of a generous degree of education. The pharmaceutical journals, since they reveal the tendency of pharmaceutical progress, are to many, and should be to all, pharmacists the means of indicating the direction in which they should extend their professional education and training. They really are to the conscientious reader and student a continuous postgraduate course, not only supplying, largely, the text, but indicating directly or indirectly the references to and sources of further elucidation or exhaustive treatment of technical subjects.

Complete sets of bound volumes of the leading pharmaceutical journals and association proceedings, principally in the English, German, and French languages, are the best and most complete records we have of the development and evolution of the later pharmacy and related branches. These volumes offer either in themselves or in the references they contain the most useful field, not only for the research worker in pharmaceutical literature, but also for the laboratory worker, since one who wants to add to the sum of pharmaceutical knowledge must first ascertain all that has already been published on the subject on which he is working.

The pharmaceutical journals bring the professional and related scientific facts of the world to the door of the pharmacist. Many of these facts are not alone for the day, and it would therefore be a mistake to say that the pharmaceutical press is only ephemeral in its uses. While some of the scientific associations compile annual reports on the progress of their respective professions, which summaries they necessarily must glean from current journals and related publications, the references are as a rule brief and only in abstract, and recourse must usually be had by the exhaustive worker to original sources. While these reports are very valuable and have even become indispensable, they obviously do not perform the same functions that the current pharmaceutical periodicals do.

The excellence and the educational value of the pharmaceutical press is due to a large extent to the business, literary and professional ability of the men who manage, edit and write for the many good pharmaceutical periodicals, and in this fact is to be found an added and substantial reason why earnest students of pharmacy should intelligently and regularly read the current literature of their chosen profession.

---

[1] A stenographic abstract of remarks made by Dean Wulling to his classes in the College of Pharmacy of the University of Minnesota.

(Written for the American Druggist.)

THE BOARDS OF PHARMACY MAY PROMOTE PROPER PHARMACEUTICAL EDUCATION.

BY OSCAR OLDBERG.
Northwestern University.

We have in America a surprisingly great number of good pharmaceutical schools—great when we consider the fact that they have always had to struggle along without any encouragement from the pharmacy laws and boards. We have a still greater number of poor schools of pharmacy, because such schools are not only freely permitted to do as they may see fit, but really enjoy certain advantages under the laws which put a premium on inferior education.

No one can justly say that either the laws or the boards intentionally place the best schools at a disadvantage, but the laws are such that in many States an inferior or even fraudulent school may easily thrive at the expense of the efficient and honest institutions.

PREVALENT MISCONCEPTIONS.

The want of information and the consequent misconceptions concerning the pharmaceutical schools are so great and so general that the cause of education must continue to suffer more and more unless a better understanding of the actual facts and conditions in all their bearings can be brought about and proper remedies found for the ills with which we are afflicted. The boards of pharmacy do not seem to have taken up this question at all, or have given scant attention to it.

Any educational institution or department of such institution must be a school of pharmacy, if pharmacy is what it teaches. To me this is a self-evident proposition, and most men will doubtless consider the statement of it superfluous, but the rulings of two or more boards of pharmacy seem to be based upon the assumption that a "college of pharmacy" cannot be a university school and that a university school of pharmacy cannot be a college. One board states that it "recognizes all colleges of pharmacy, but not the departments of pharmacy of the universities." What will that board do when more of the schools of pharmacy named colleges shall have become connected with universities?

Some boards of pharmacy give no recognition to any school of pharmacy of whatever kind and no credit to candidates for any course of education in pharmacy. Other boards recognize all pharmaceutical schools without distinction. Others say they recognize all "reputable colleges" or colleges "in good standing," but fail to define what a reputable school or a school in good standing is. The board of one of the Western States east of the Rocky Mountains declares that it recognizes only the colleges of pharmacy in its own State and "rejects colleges not generally considered up to standard," but the colleges of pharmacy in that State are elsewhere very generally considered to be below the average grade of older pharmaceutical schools. I have often heard the opinion expressed that only the schools under the control of universities merit any consideration, and I have as often heard the opposite view. All of these avowals and opinons are utterly jejune and harmful. Definite tangible facts, rules and conditions should take the place of vague expressions.

FACTORS OF DISCREDIT.

Whenever a board of pharmacy wholly ignores all schools of pharmacy and the special training which such schools furnish it positively casts discredit upon real pharmaceutical education. It cannot be that the pharmacists of our country want the schools of pharmacy abolished or ignored; let us hope that they, instead, want them encouraged, improved, strengthened and "recognized" whenever they comply with certain definite requirements deemed necessary to efficiency.

SOME COLLEGES OF PHARMACY.

A wholesale recognition of all institutions calling themselves colleges or schools or institutes of pharmacy is equally destructive. A year ago I had a list of about 80 such institutions. I thought it complete. To-day, March 3, 1906, at 5 o'clock p.m., I have a list of over 90. I discovered two last week. Do we need them all? Are they all efficient and honest? What is the use of mincing words? We all know that some of them have no equipment of any kind. Some have no laboratory facilities. The principal teachers of some of them would not be regarded as competent to fill the most subordinate positions in the faculties of the really good schools. Several are owned and operated by men who are neither educators nor pharmacists and for no other purpose than to produce dividends on the capital invested—schools in which the teachers are the cheapest than can be had and the hired men of the owner, who is the only real authority directing the work and conferring degrees. Some conduct their courses of instruction, knowingly or ignorantly, in utter disregard of recognized correct principles of pedagogy. Some apparently have no reason for existence except to satisfy the vanity of the incompetents who figure as their professors, often without pay. Some have absolutely no educational entrance requirements, while others demand high school graduation for admission. The amount of actual work done in the pharmaceutical school varies from 500 hours or less to 2,400 hours or more from matriculation to graduation, and the actual school days in the whole course for graduation vary from 150 or less to 350 or more.

AS TO FINANCIAL PROFIT.

The worst schools produce profits. The best schools nearly always show financial deficits at the end of every year and would inevitably have to close their doors were it not for endowments, bequests, appropriations, annual incomes derived from properties, or the fact that they are fortunate enough to be well housed without payment of rent, or because of several of these advantages combined.

To carry on a really efficient school of pharmacy requires more money than the tuition fees ever amount to, unless the classes are unusually large, and yet we have many schools without any resources whatever except the tuition fees and with less than half the number of students necessary to make a good school self-supporting. I know of no good school of pharmacy that does not need all of its income for its legitimate educational purposes.

Present conditions actually foster institutions that ought not to be permitted to exist and which certainly could not continue to exist if the boards of pharmacy would establish proper and definite rules and standards ~~which all~~ schools must live up to in order to be entitled to recognition, and then give real and substantial recognition to those that comply with those rules and standards and refuse to give any countenance to all others.

Several States authorize the licensing of graduates of pharmacy without examination. It is evident that unless the boards of pharmacy of those States prescribe proper standards to which the schools must conform there is nothing to prevent the increase and prosperity of sham schools.

FRAUDULENT METHODS OF ESTIMATING "DRUG STORE EXPERIENCE."

Many States authorize the boards of pharmacy to deduct from the drug store experience required for license the time of attendance at a pharmaceutical school. Here again the fraudulent, dishonest or worthless schools have a harvest wherever the boards fail to discriminate.

In States where the laws contain the absurd provision that graduates of all schools of pharmacy requiring four years' drug store experience for graduation shall be entitled to be licensed without examination, there seems to be nothing to hinder Smith, Jones & Co. from starting in the business of manufacturing graduates in pharmacy with (or even without) the four years' experience, a business which may well be made to pay handsomely, for the number of young men who fear the State board examination more than the smallpox is great, and if they have graduated from a college that requires four years' drug store experience they may be registered and licensed without any further question, without reference to the kind and amount of learning they absorbed at the "college" or how much time was required to secure a diploma. Unless the boards of pharmacy adopt some means of preventing the multiplication of diploma mills stimulated by these remarkable conditions I cannot see how the good schools of pharmacy that honestly believe that drug store experience should be a prerequisite to graduation can continue that requirement. It is evident to me that when the law contains this proviso and the Board of Pharmacy fails to interpret it in a rational way, it is nothing short of a travesty upon justice, common sense and the actual intent of every pharmacy law. If the graduate of a school that does require drug store experience for graduation must be licensed without examination, while the graduates of other schools are not entitled to that right, then it is the drug store experience and not the special education that counts, and since the special education does not count, there can be no difference between a graduate and a nongraduate.

Several of the schools of pharmacy that require drug store experience for graduation are those in which the programme of instruction requires only three days' attendance weekly. Schools giving a full programme of instruction, occupying the student's whole time, rarely require it. In other words, the schools not requiring drug store attendance for graduation are generally giving far more substantial courses of instruction.

EFFECT ON EDUCATION.

Let us see how the prevailing practice affects education. A student attends a school of pharmacy three days weekly for 50 weeks, and he is employed in a drug store the rest of his time. He can usually count all of this time toward the fulfillment of the legal requirements for license. Therefore he can get his license in four years from the time he enters the drug store. Another student attends a school of pharmacy where concurrent drug store work is impossible, because his time is all advantageously occupied upon his studies, and he takes a full two years' course. This student cannot complete the required drug store experience and the college course, too, in less than 5½ years. In other words, he is punished for taking a more substantial course by being made to wait 1½ years longer for his license! The graduate who may have had less than 800 hours' instruction at the school is rewarded by receiving his license in four years, and in some States without examination, while he who may have had over 2,000 hours' instruction in two full university years is punished by being compelled to wait 1½ years longer before he is placed on an equality before the law with the less well trained man.

SOMETHING TO BE THANKFUL FOR.

Perhaps we should be thankful that the law does not really forbid systematic special education for pharmacy. As the laws stand and are enforced we surely have little else to be thankful for in that direction.

I have also seen deplorably inferior, if not dishonest, schools of pharmacy actually advertise that they not only prepare candidates for the State board examinations and guarantee success, but that they are recommended by boards of pharmacy or by individual board members.

A SUGGESTION FOR BOARD MEMBERS.

Members of the boards of pharmacy should visit the pharmaceutical schools and see for themselves what they are—not as mere chance visitors having but a general interest in them and in a hurry to end their visit, but as official inspectors, with all their eyes and ears open. They will find themselves most heartily welcomed by all honest schools. As they cannot visit all schools of pharmacy, especially as some of them may not be readily accessible by modern means of transportation, let them select a few representative ones, good and bad, and see those thoroughly, get acquainted with their teachers, hear a lecture or two, see the classes at work in the laboratories, etc. It may surprise them to find what a variety there is of these institutions and how easily all that there is of any one of several smaller ones may be stowed away in any one of several of the score of rooms of the larger schools.

The pharmaceutical schools will be just what the boards of pharmacy see fit to make them.

I have heard many board members condemn in unmeasured terms the frauds and shams called colleges and schools and institutes of pharmacy that are springing up everywhere. Why do not the boards refuse to recognize them? All that is necessary is to formulate satisfactory standards of efficiency which all schools must live up to.

PROPOSED BOARD STANDARDS.

The least that any board of pharmacy should do in this respect would be to order, perhaps:

1. A school of pharmacy in order to receive recognition must be a regularly incorporated or chartered educational institution or a department of such an institution, and must be governed by persons not exercising ownership in the school or deriving personal profit from the proceeds of its operation.

2. It must possess an equipment for its pharmaceutical courses to the value of at least $5,000, exclusive of its quarters.

3. It must give reasonably adequate courses of instruction in the subjects usually taught in pharmaceutical schools, which subjects shall include at least pharmacy, chemistry and materia medica.

4. It must have not less than three teachers, of sufficient education, special training and experience, and at least one of these teachers shall have had not less than five years' experience in pharmacy.

5. The obligatory courses for graduation shall include not less than 500 hours of lectures and recitations and not less than 1,000 hours of laboratory instruction, and shall extend over not less than 50 weeks of regular attendance.

6. The courses of instruction must be given in proper logical sequence, according to approved educational methods.

7. The entrance requirements shall include a preliminary general education of not less than one year of satisfactorily completed high school work or its full equivalent of studies of similar grade in academies or other schools or colleges.

The foregoing proposed requirements are surely moderate enough. The suggested minimum value of the equipment is that adopted by the State Board of New York. The minimum number of hours of instruction is that now given by more than a dozen schools.

The preliminary education suggested (one year of high school work) is that prescribed by law in New York, and by rule of the boards of pharmacy of Ohio, Wisconsin and South Dakota. This or more is required by 22 of the schools of pharmacy which are members of the American Conference of Pharmaceutical Faculties and by several other pharmacy schools besides.

THE CRISIS HAS COME.

At this time, when the medical profession is so vigorously exposing the evils of proprietary preparations and all ready-made mixtures which have been so largely prescribed by physicians, when the American Medical Association is spending much time, labor and money to the same end, and when medical men are declaring that they will hereafter write prescriptions, not for such ready-made preparations, but for the pharmacopœial medicines and others not covered by patents, secrecy or doubt, and when the doctors are ready to make use of the services of the pharmacist again, it behooves the latter to do all that he can to prove his title to the privilege of being the only legally qualified compounder and dispenser. Better pharmaceutical education should be made general and should be systematically enforced. The boards can do it. No one else can.

The Nobel Prizes.

The award of the Nobel prizes for 1905 have been as follows: The prize for physics to Prof. Phillip Lenard, of Kiel University, for his important works on cathode rays; the prize for chemistry to Prof. Adolf von Bayer, of the University of Munich, for the development in organic chemistry and chemical industry resulting from his works on organic coloring matters and hydroaromatic compounds; and the medical prize to Dr. Robert Koch for his works and discoveries in connection with tuberculosis. In addition to a handsome sum of money, each prize is accompanied by an illuminated diploma and a gold medal with an appropriate inscription.

American Sulphur in France.

The first shipment (3,000 tons) of American sulphur was despatched from Louisiana to Marseilles last October. A prosperous future seems to await this new development of American enterprise, for France yearly needs some 90,000 tons of sulphur, mostly for her vineyards. About one-third is ground and sold as powder, the rest refined to "flowers of sulphur." More than half the French imports in this line pass by the ports of Cette and Marseilles. Raw sulphur enters France duty free. The refined article pays $6 per ton (general tariff), or $4.50 minimum tariff.

THE ADULTERATION OF CHEMICALS.[1]

By L. F. Kebler.

Some one has said that the finding of adulterations is numerous only because people are looking for them. The principle underlying this statement is applicable to a vast majority of human achievements. The sluggard finds nothing, his coffers are usually empty, and the world is no better for his having lived in it. In order to arrive at a proper understanding of the amount of adulteration in chemicals it will be necessary to clearly set forth what is meant by adulteration. If we mean gross, deliberate adulteration, not including what is commonly known as substitution, the amount is comparatively small, but if we are to understand that it includes all chemicals which do not comply with the standards set by competent authorities, or which fall below the professed standards under which they are sold, the per cent. will mount considerably.

The day of gross and deliberate sophistications is largely a thing of the past, unless the reprehensible practice known as substitution be construed as having taken their place, but we still meet with them occasionally. For example, thymol replaced in part or as a whole by sodium sulphate crystals; acetyl isoeugenol, the antecedent of vanillin, delivered for vanillin; calcium phosphate replaced in part by calcium carbonate; various mixtures consisting of starch, calcium acid phosphate and calcium sulphate sold for cream of tartar; washing soda for borax; coumarin mixed with acetanilid, and potassium bromide used to fill orders for potassium iodide. The above examples represent adulterations met with before the goods reached the hands of the retailer. These frauds are frequently traceable to brokers, but manufacturers and wholesalers are not entirely free from taint. Adulterations of the above character, practiced by manufacturers, jobbers, brokers and wholesalers, do not amount to 1 per cent.

Chemicals that fall below recognized standards, or below the professed standards under which they are sold, in my experience, approximate 25 per cent. By recognized standards are meant such as are set by Krauch's book on the *Testing of Chemical Reagents*, the United States, British and German Pharmacopœias and such self-imposed standards as are found on the labels of various manufacturers. Some one may say that the first book enumerated was written to favor a certain brand of chemicals and the pharmacopœias are unreasonable. In reply to such a statement I only need to say that in my experience there are several brands of chemicals that conform to the requirements laid down in Krauch's book as well as does the brand alluded to, and the requirements for chemicals of the pharmacopœias enumerated are not so unreasonable as we are ofttimes led to believe by the manufacturer. It would be absurd to claim perfection for these books, but to deny their high value and great utility would be to discredit a large field of science. As a matter of fact, many manufacturers label their chemicals by designations which clearly mean that the contents of the packages comply with these unreasonable standards, or fill orders which call for goods conforming with these standards. Chemicals marked C. P. ought certainly to comply with the requirements laid down by the U. S. Pharmacopœia.

The claim is frequently presented that the impurities present are so small in amount, or are of such a harmless nature, that they could neither act injuriously or deteriously nor materially influence the physiological effects. If every analyst were permitted to decide whether or not impure chemicals were injurious or deleterious, or would give the results desired by the physician, there would be an endless amount of confusion and disagreement. The analyst usually has little difficulty in deciding whether a given impurity will be likely to impair his analytical results and can act accordingly, but he is naturally not competent to say to what extent small amounts of noxious bodies or greater quantities of supposedly inactive substances will influence therapeutic activity. The numerous legislative acts which fix standards for medicinal agents bear testimony to this end.

[1] Contribution No. 10 from the Drug Laboratory, Bureau of Chemistry, U. S. Department of Agriculture, presented at the Atlantic City meeting of the American Pharmaceutical Association.

I shall now take up a few cases from experience that illustrate this phase of the subject. Sulphuric acid, C. P., contaminated with lead sulphate; hydrochloric acid, U. S. P., containing free chlorine; ammonium hydroxide, U. S. P., mixed with pyridin bodies, calcium compounds, and a heavy sediment—a very interesting chemical to use either for medicinal purposes or in analysis. Ethyl ether, U. S. P., 1890, for anæsthesia, found to contain aldehydic and disagreeable-smelling foreign bodies, was highly acid and totally unfit for any use, yet the manufacturers contended that they tested their ether, and such a product could not have left their factory. This kind of talk may work with some, but it did not fit the case in hand, and the manufacturer ultimately "made good." Some manufacturers will contend that the pharmacopœial requirements are too rigid. Let me tell you there is plenty of ether produced every day that will comply with this standard. It is impossible to exercise too much care with an article that is used daily to keep unfortunate patients hovering on the brink of the grave. Ethyl acetate marked U. S. P. I have found to contain from 65 to 80 per cent. of pure material, and incidental impurities of all kinds, from fertilizer extractive odors up. I regret to see that the eighth revision of the Pharmacopœia has lowered the percentage purity of the article. There is no trouble in producing a 98 per cent. pure article at a cost equal to the present price of alcohol. Sodium phosphate, U. S. P., granular and crystals, was contaminated with arsenical compounds. It seems as if the reprehensible practice of selling a medicinal chemical used as liberally as sodium phosphate, poisoned by arsenic, had been often enough referred to, but there is considerable on the market at present fit only for fertilizing purposes. The iodides and bromides notoriously fall below the present standards. It is seldom that these valuable chemicals are what they should be. There is no difficulty in making them of proper quality. Manganese dioxide, C. P., containing impurities soluble in water and testing only 70 per cent. pure. There is an abundance of commercial manganese dioxide which will test from 80 to 90 per cent. pure. Lithium citrate, U. S. P., 1890, containing from 11 to 20 per cent. of water of crystallization. The Pharmacopœia (1890) recognized the anhydrous salt only. No one can supply the standard product and compete with such misrepresentations. A large proportion of the samples of calomel examined contained traces of corrosive sublimate. It can be made without the presence of this impurity. Glycerin, both C. P. and U. S. P., seldom complies with the recognized standard. Formerly it was mixed with an undue amount of arsenical compounds, but these dangerous impurities have been largely reduced to proper limits within the past few years. There is considerable hydrogen peroxide on the market that does not conform to the proper standard and the statements made about stability read well on the label, but too much faith should not be placed in such statements. Almost all of the potassium cyanide labeled as C. P. and U. S. P., consists of mixtures of sodium and potassium cyanides. Manufacturers and dealers are well aware of this, yet most of them continue to label it in the above manner and some label it "potassium cyanide, 98-100 per cent. pure." Sodium hydroxide, labeled "free from aluminum, nitrogen and sulphur," contains all these impurities. Potassium permanganate and magnesium oxide represented as being free from sulphur were both contaminated with this impurity. Copper sulphate, labeled "C. P., strictly iron-free," was not in accordance with the facts. Numerous additional examples could be cited, but the above should certainly be ample to remove any doubt. Furthermore, they do not represent a single sample only, but from 50 pounds to tons.

Much has been published about adulterated chemicals and chemicals of inferior quality, but little has been placed on record which gives any idea where the trouble is and to what extent it prevails before these chemicals reach the hands of retailers and consumers. Dr. D. Base, in a paper presented to this association last year, gave data which represented drugs examined under conditions similar to those enumerated above. Deliberate adulteration to the extent of 1.7 per cent. was detected, and after making extremely liberal allowances for the small quantities of impurities, he says: "Twenty-six samples (out of 115, or 22.6 per cent.) were unsatisfactory, chiefly because of the failure on the part of the manufacturers to sufficiently purify the drugs to meet the official demands and to a less degree because of a deficiency in strength." Dr. R. Hunt, in discussing the above, spoke of a recent examination of some 200 chemicals and, while only thirty-six (or about 20 per cent.) came up absolutely to the standards of the Pharmacopœia, there was not one where the impurity could be declared injurious. Dr. C. E. Caspari, in a paper presented before a recent meeting of the Missouri State Pharmaceutical Association, gave his finding on eight much used chemicals, including bromides, iodides, calomel, bismuth subnitrate and sodium salicylate, and the per cent. of inferiority varied from 50 to 100. The results of these workers clearly show that my findings of chemicals under conditions herewith set forth are better than the average, and the above representation of chemicals that fall below the standard is quite conservative.

I have had little experience with the quality of chemicals supplied by retailers; neither do the various published reports permit of fair and just deductions. It is therefore difficult for me to give even an approximate idea as to the amount of chemicals supplied by retailers that fall below recognized standards or below the professed standards under which they are sold, but it is quite certain that the chemicals handled by retailers are not superior to their sources of supply, and there is no gainsaying the fact that some chemicals are adulterated in some quarters by retailers.

Color Reactions of Asaprol.—Asaprol (calcium betanaphtholmonosulphonate) is often used as a food preservative, and a number of tests have been devised for its detection. Some of these are as follows: On adding a few drops of formaldehyde solution and of sulphuric acid to a little asaprol solution, a bright green fluorescence results. On heating with sodium persulphate a greenish yellow color is produced, which changes to a brown-green, and then to a brown-orange. Sulphomolybdic acid gives on heating a greenish-yellow color which changes to a dark blue. (*Journal de pharmacie et de Chimie*, 1905, page 422).

Doses in the New U. S. Pharmacopoeia.—An interesting analytical study of the doses given in the new edition of the U. S. Pharmacopœia by M. I. Wilbert, of Philadelphia, is continued in the February number of the *American Journal of Pharmacy*. This is the second time in the history of the Pharmacopœia that doses have been expressed in connection with the descriptions of drugs and preparations. In the first revision of the book, which appeared in New York in 1830, a range of dosage was indicated, while in the present edition only the average adult dose has been given. In this revision the doses of all drugs and preparations intended for internal use have been given, the list including 752 articles. Twelve drugs have two doses mentioned.

The smallest official dose is of crystalline aconitine—namely, 0.00015 Gm. The next smallest is that of 0.0003 Gm. for strophanthin. The largest dose of a solid substance is for the bulky drug, pepo—30 Gm. The largest dose for an official preparation is that of solution of magnesium citrate, which is officially dosed at 300 Cc. Wilbert is inclined to criticise the Revision Committee for having adopted such unwieldy quantities in the metric system as 3, 8, etc., Gm., instead of 5 Gm., 10 Gm., etc. The figure 1 Gm. and 1 Cc., however, occurs quite frequently among the doses given in the book. In giving doses by measure the Revision Committee has accepted 0.05 Cc. as the equivalent for one minim, which is of course only approximate. On the other hand, in giving doses by weight the committee has deemed it best to be more exacting, and has adopted 0.065 Gm. as the equivalent of one grain. Elsewhere 0.01 Gm. is given as the equivalent of one-fifth of a grain, and one-half of this amount, 0.005 Gm., as the equivalent of one-tenth of a grain.

The author thinks that while the Committee on Revision has succeeded in giving us a practical solution of the much-dreaded problem of official doses, and while it has also contributed materially toward advancing the use of the metric system in this country, it has not altogether been successful in the selection of quantities indicative of approximate metric doses.

Cream *of* Current Literature

A summary of the leading articles in contemporary pharmaceutical periodicals.

Santyl.—Another substitute for santal oil has been placed on the market under the name of santyl. It is described as the neutral salicylic ester of santalol, and is an almost odorless and tasteless fluid, the dose of which is about 30 drops daily. It is said not to disturb the stomach, nor to irritate the kidneys as sandalwood oil does.

Protosal a New Salicylic Compound.—Protosal is a complex ether of glycerin which, under the influence of acids and of dilute alkalis, decomposes into glycerin, formaldehyde and salicylic acid. It occurs as a colorless oily liquid, soluble in alcohol, ether, chloroform, benzin, castor oil, etc., less easily in oil of sesame and in olive oil. According the Laggnard (*Journal de pharmacie et de chimie*, March, 1906, page 295) it is used in the form of applications locally in equal parts of protosal and olive oil, to which 10 per cent. of alcohol had been added. Twelve hours after the first application salicylic acid will be found in the urine of the patient. The applications are not irritant, and have been used with success in the treatment of rheumatic pains.

Proponal a Homologue of Veronal.—The list of hypnotics grows steadily in length and complexity, and one of the newest is proponal, a homologue of veronal, which has just had time to become fairly well known. Proponal is simply a purified dipropylbarbituric acid prepared by Fischer and von Mering in the course of their researches on barbituric acids. Proponal occurs in the form of colorless, fusible crystals, soluble in 70 parts of boiling water, and 1,640 parts of cold water. The dose ranges from 0.15 to 0.50 grammes, and the remedy is said to be an excellent hypnotic. Being easily soluble in alkalies, it is readily absorbed by the intestines, so that its action is very prompt. It is given in powders or in alcoholic solution.—*Journal de pharmacie et de chimie*, 1906, March, page 294.

Soaps for Cleansing Fabrics.—The German soap journal, *Seifenfabrikant*, gives the following formulæ for the manufacture of soaps for cleansing fabrics, etc.: White benzin soap is prepared by mixing thoroughly 57.6 kilos of olein and 6.8 kilos of water of ammonia of the specific gravity of 0.910. The resulting soap preparation can be dissolved in benzin, to yield a clear solution. It should not be heated in the process of mixing. Powdered benzin soap is prepared by mixing 56.8 kilos of stearin and 6.8 kilos of ammonia water of the same specific gravity as given above, cooling and powdering the mass. Liquid benzin soap is prepared in two qualities. The first, known as quality A, is used for the removal of stains which cannot be removed by benzin alone. It does not produce any grease spots nor does it fade the fabrics. Quality B serves to remove all impurities from the material in the cleaning vat, and is added to the benzin. It prevents the impure products from adhering to the material to be cleansed. Soap A is prepared by mixing 100 kilos of acetic ether with 6 kilos of soft soap. Soap B is made by mixing 30 kilos of 60 per cent. alcohol and 10 kilos of Marseilles soap. To this mixture are added benzin, 100 kilos; benzole, 20 kilos, and olein, 10 kilos.

Hydrogen Dioxide as a Preservative of Milk: Its Detection.—Paul Adam (*Journal de pharmacie et de chimie*, March, 1906, page 263) sums up his study of the detection of hydrogen dioxide in milk as follows: Raw fresh milk in which there is no hydrogen dioxide when treated with hydrogen dioxide and guaiacol turns a garnet-red; with paraphenylenediamine it turns blue, and in the presence of aldehydes decolorizes methylene blue. Decomposed or stale milk does not give the first two reactions mentioned, but decolorizes Schardinger's reagent. The latter consists of a concentrated alcoholic solution of methylene blue, 5 Cc.; formaldehyde, 5 Cc., and distilled water, 190 Cc. Raw milk which contains hydrogen dioxide gives the color reaction with guaiacol, or with paraphenylenediamine, but does not decolorize Schardinger's reagent. Raw milk which had been treated with hydrogen dioxide, but which no longer contains this substance, gives the same reactions as pure milk if hydrogen dioxide be added to it. Unless the milk has decomposed, however, it does not decolorize Schardinger's reagent. Boiled milk gives none of these reactions. The conclusion to be drawn from these reactions is that the reducing ferment of milk is destroyed by the oxidizing agent.

Detection of Diacetic Acid in the Urine.—Aceto-acetic or diacetic acid ($C_4H_{10}O_3$) may be present in the urine in considerable quantity, especially when there is an excess of acetone present. The presence of this substance is usually a serious symptom in diabetes and fevers. The ordinary method of detecting this interesting substance in the urine is that of Von Jaksch, by the addition of ferric chloride solution to produce a deep Bordeaux-red color. A new method of detecting aceto-acetic acid has, however, been devised by Riegler (*Münchener Medizinische Wochenschrift*, 1905, page 29), which is as follows: Fifteen Cc. of the urine and 2 Cc. of a 10 per cent. solution of hydriodic acid are shaken with chloroform. If aceto-acetic acid is absent the chloroform will take up the color of iodine from the hydriodic acid. If diacetic acid is present in the urine the chloroform will not change color. The reaction therefore involves a negative color change. A modification of this test has been introduced by Lindemann: Instead of hydriodic acid a solution of potassium iodide and iodine is used (Lugol's solution) together with a little acetic acid. The latter is added to render the reagent acid. Five drops of acetic acid to 10 Cc. of urine usually prove sufficient for this purpose. The solution of iodine is composed of 1 Gm. of iodine, 2 Gm. of potassium iodide, and 100 Cc. of water. Five drops of this solution and 5 drops of acetic acid are added to the sample of urine measuring 10 Cc. The mixture is then shaken with chloroform. If the latter remains colorless aceto-acetic acid is present in the urine.

Collection and Preparation of the Tonka Bean.—André, in his work, "A Naturalist in the Guineas," gives an interesting account of the Tonka bean, of which the following extract is contained in the *Pharmaceutical Journal:* The tree which furnishes the Tonka bean (*Coumarouna orata Aubl.*) grows in various parts of tropical America. The beans from Para are, however, less valuable than those from the regions supplied by the rivers Caura and Cuchivero. The region between these two rivers where are found rocky heights measuring from 3,000 to 4,000 feet, is the true home of this tree. The gathering of these beans is rather an exhausting occupation, as the trees often occur quite a distance apart. In Venezuela the tree is called "sarrapia," and the laborêrs engaged in gathering the beans are called "sarrapieros." These arrive at Caura at the beginning of February, often from a great distance—usually from Ciudad Bolivar. A variety of parrots cause a great deal of damage to these trees during the months of October and November, when the beans are still small and green. The fruit of sarrapia is like a small melon, and is eaten by the natives. The sarrapieros break the fruit between two stones and remove the single bean which it contains. The beans are then dried in the sun on large blocks of granite called "laja." The crop is gathered in by the end of May or the beginning of June and the beans in their dried state are sent to Bolivar city or to Trinidad, where they are subjected to a process of crystallization. This is done by filling casks with the beans up to within a foot of the brim. Then rum is poured in, to the brim, and the cask is covered with canvas. After 24 hours the rum is drawn off and the fruit is dried in the free air. When thus removed from these casks the beans are black and swollen, but after they have dried their surface shows the presence of shining white crystals, so that when they are ready for packing they look as if they had beeen powdered with sugar. When they are dry they look cracked and wrinkled. A tax of 25 centesimos is levied in Venezuela for the exportation of Tonka beans.

Cultivation of Cinchonas in the United States.—Albert Schneider, in an address read before the Lewis and Clark Pharmaceutical Congress, reviewed the subject of cinchona cultivation in various countries, and pointed out the possibilities for such a cultivation in the United States, especially on the Pacific Coast. The cultivation of cinchona in other countries than Peru has been pursued only within comparatively recent times. The first attempts were made by the Dutch who succeeded in cultivating the plant in Java in 1854. In 1860 the British Government made its first attempts to cultivate in India plants obtained by Markham in Bolivia, together with plants and seeds from the Dutch plantations in Java and New Granada. The first British plantation was established in the southwestern portion of the Madras Presidency, among the Nilgiri hills. The bark began to appear in the London market in 1867, and has been sold there ever since.

The question of cultivating cinchona in this country came up soon after it was evident that the Dutch and the English had so well succeeded in growing this valuable drug in their respective colonies. In 1879, at the suggestion of W. Weaver, at that time in Bogota, attempts were made to cultivate cinchonas in California. These experiments were conducted under the direction of the University of California, and the plants were obtained from the English plantations in India. These experiments showed that it was very difficult to cultivate cinchonas under ordinary conditions. Proper hothouses and proper conditions of drainage were lacking at the time, and most of the test plants perished, *C. succirubra* being apparently the most hardy species. The great enemy of the cinchonas seemed to be frost, which killed them rapidly even when it occurred in the slightest degree. There are regions in California, however, the climate of which is very similar to that of the Andes, and theoretically cinchona should grow in these regions. But it seems that very slight variations in temperature are sufficient to interfere with the growth of these plants, and it is possible, as Dr. Rusby unhesitatingly states, that cinchona cannot be cultivated anywhere within the limits of this country. Success, however, is not out of the question, in view of the encouragement already received in previous tests. Schneider suggests that large quantities of the more hardy species be planted in seeds obtained from Java, India, or Jamaica. These should be sown in mat-covered or glass-covered cold frames, filled with a compost of a turfy mixture of loam and peat, to which has been added a little sand and charcoal. The bottom temperature should be kept at about 60 degrees F. The plants will not germinate so readily in hot beds. The soil should be kept well moistened, but not wet. The seedlings should be kept under glass in beds of suitable size for two or three years, at a temperature of 50 to 60 degrees, with moist air. Santa Barbara County is probably the most suitable locality for these experiments.

Problem Prescriptions.

At a recent meeting of the Edinburgh Chemists', Assistants' and Apprentices' Association William Duncan, Ph. C., F.C.S., contributed a series of notes and queries.

The first was in regard to a precipitate in a pigment containing solution of corrosive sublimate, glycerin and cocaine hydrochloride. Mr. Duncan explained that the corrosive sublimate precipitates alkaloids. The second query referred to the following mixture, in which a voluminous olive-green precipitate weighing 1½ grain occurs:

Ferri et quin. cit........................ℨij
Tr. nucis vom..............................ℨj
Tr. rhei co...................................ℨj
Aquam ad...................................℥viij

It consists of resins of the nux vomica and traces of quinine tannate. Asked "What is magnes. carb.?" Mr. Duncan traced the evolution of the B. P. names and said he would dispense the heavy carbonate. The fourth query was about a solution of 4 grains of iodine in 1 oz. of glycerin, and it was explained that it does not require the addition of potassium iodide. The fifth query was in respect to the following emulsion, which resembles the "mist. rachitis" of the Sick Children's Hospital Pharmacopœia:

Ol. morrhuæ.............................℥ij
Syr. calc. lact. phosph....................℥j
Liq. calcis...................................℥j
Sodii hypophosph....................gr. xxx
Ol. cassiæ.................................♏ij
Pulv. acaciæ...............................q.s.
Glycerin ....ℨiv

A fair product is obtained by dissolving the hypophosphite in the mixed syrup, glycerin and lime water. With a portion of this make a mucilage of 2 dr. pulv. acaciæ and emulsify the oils little by little, thinning with the mixture as required. The emulsion separates slightly in time, but if more gum be used it is unmanageably thick.

In a mixture of liq. hydrarg. perchlor., liq. Donovan. and water, equal parts, red iodide of mercury is precipitated through interaction of mercuric iodide with arsenious iodide and hydriodic acid. A mixture containing bismuth salicylate, sodium iodide, syrup of codeine, tragacanth and water undergoes some change which Mr. Duncan could not definitely determine. The next query was about the following prescription:

Aspirin ....ℨij
Potassii iodidi.............................ℨij
Glycerin ....℥ss
Aquam ad...................................℥vj

Here the acetylsalicylic acid, reacting with potassium iodide, forms hydriodic acid, which by absorption of oxygen liberates iodine.

A mixture containing calcined magnesia and ferrous sulphate changes in color, due to formation of ferrous hydroxide and gradual oxidation of this to a darker color.

He thought it advantageous to add a suspending agent to a mixture of equal parts of tr. quin. ammon. and aq. aurant. flor., otherwise the quinine hydrate becomes crystalline and adheres to the glass.

Liq. bismuthi..............................℥iij
Magnes. sulph..............................℥j
Sod. salicyl..................................ℨij
Syr. aurant...................................℥j
Aq. menth. pip. ad........................℥xij

Sod. salicyl..................................ℨiv
Caffein. cit............................gr. xxiv
Tr. capsici................................♏xxx
Spt. chlorof................................♏xxx
Inf. gentian. ad.............................℥iv

In regard to the first of these prescriptions the querist said a precipitate is formed, but Mr. Duncan had been unable to get one, and suggested that the liq. bismuthi should be examined to see if it contained excess of alkali. If so, magnesium hydrate might be precipitated. Salicylic acid is precipitated in the second prescription and the precipitation cannot be prevented. He then dealt with the bursting of a bottle containing the following mixture:

Tr. digitalis..................................ℨj
Tr. hyoscyami...............................ℨj
Spt. æther. nit..............................ℨiv
Inf. caryoph. ad.............................℥vj

The bursting he believed to be due to the action of the nitrous acid in the spirit of nitre on the tannin of the infusion, and proved this by stating that an infusion detannated with isinglass gives no trouble.

To dissolve old rubber the following process is employed: The material is shredded finely and then heated, under pressure, for several hours, with a strong solution of caustic soda. All cloth, paint, glue, fillers, etc., in the rubber is disintegrated, but the rubber is not affected. The mass is then washed repeatedly with water, to remove all alkali, and the resultant pure rubber may then be formed into sheets.

Queries *and* Answers

We shall be glad, in this department, to respond to calls for information on all pharmaceutic matters.

Solubility of Phenols in Sodium Salicylate Solutions.—R. S.—The solvent action of concentrated solutions of sodium salicylate on phenols and phenol derivatives is a matter of record. Carbolic acid solutions may be made as concentrated as 80 per cent. by first dissolving the acid in a concentrated solution of sodium salicylate, and a solution of this strength is not caustic. Creosote, menthol, thymol, etc., show similar solubility; the volatile oils are also freely soluble in a solution of sodium salicylate, but owing to their variable chemical composition not in all proportions.

Paper Bottles for Milk.—G. B., Italy, who makes inquiry regarding milk bottles made of paper, is advised that there is no such thing on the market for fresh milk in this country. A number of attempts have been made to manufacture such bottles and various methods have been devised, but up to the present time no reliable process has been provided. We have made inquiries in several directions and beyond ascertaining that a paper box or carton is made for dried milk powder we have not learned of any bottle made of paper for fluid milk. Perhaps some of our readers may know more of the subject.

Books for the Pharmacist.—E. M. y S., Mexico, asks us to name "the best book for making pharmaceutical preparations and the best book for compounding medical formulas."

Our correspondent's query is somewhat vague, but we suppose that it is a formulæ book and a work on dispensing which he is in search of. Of formulæ books the best are represented by the Standard Formulary, by Ebert and Hiss, published by G. P. Englehard & Co., Chicago, at $4, and Pharmaceutical Formulas, by MacEwan, published by *The Chemist and Druggist*, London, and sold in this country by McKesson & Robbins, New York, at $2.50. The same publishers put out a work on the Art of Dispensing, which will perhaps meet the second inquiry. It is supplied, postpaid, by McKesson & Robbins for $2. The National Formulary, published by the American Pharmaceutical Association, is an indispensable work for the pharmacist. The third edition is nearly ready and can be obtained, when published, through the secretary of the association, Charles Caspari, jr., Baltimore, Md. An American work on the subject of prescription compounding is The Art of Compounding, by Prof. Wilbur L. Scoville, which is published by P. Blakiston, Son & Co., at $2.50. A reference book, which should be in the possession of every pharmacist is The Extra Pharmacopœia, by Martindale and Westcott, published by H. K. Lewis, 136 Gower street, W. C., London, which is delivered, postpaid, for $2.68. Any of the books named may be obtained through the American Druggist Publishing Company.

Prendergast's Pills or Tablets.—Several correspondents have kindly volunteered information regarding the composition of these pills or tablets. The pills are used in the treatment of diarrhœa and contain the following ingredients:

Bismuth salicylate	gr. i.
Salol	gr. ss.
Calomel	gr. 1-40
Tinct. opii camph.	♏ij.
Mist. cret. arom.	q. s.
Ol. cinnam.	q. s.

M. fiat pil. No. 1.

One correspondent advises us that he has experienced considerable difficulty in obtaining the tablets, which are made by a firm in Jersey City, N. J.

Extract of Lemon.—G. M. asks us to publish a formula for extract of lemon which will yield a good, up-to-date product.

Parrish's formula has never been surpassed. It calls for a mixture of freshly grated lemon peel, lemon oil and alcohol. The peel should be grated carefully so that none of the white interior portion is scraped off and the lemon oil should be of the freshest. Deodorized alcohol should, of course, be used. the formula follows:

Lemon oil	℥viij.
Lemon peel	℥iv.
Diluted alcohol	Cong. i.

Mix the oil and peel with seven pints of deodorized alcohol, then add a mixture of water and alcohol, one pint, in such proportions that the mixture will be only slightly clouded; let it stand seven days and filter for use.

Extract of Vanilla.—G. M.—One of the most satisfactory formulas known to us is that communicated by Oscar Kalish, of New York, at one of the stated meetings of the New York College of Pharmacy. The first step in the process is to secure a prime quality of vanilla bean. The beans must be divided into small pieces of three-quarters to one inch in length, and longitudinally, by means of an herb cutter. The formula and directions for the preparation of the extract reads as follows:

Vanilla beans, Mexican	3½ av. lb.
Granulated sugar	7 av. lb.
Deodorized alcohol	4 gals.
Water	3 gals.

Upon the cut beans contained in a porcelain jar is poured seven pints of boiling water. The jar is then covered and allowed to stand for 24 hours, the object of this maceration being to bring the bean as nearly as possible to its natural green state. After this maceration the supernatant liquor is poured off and the beans transferred to a machine which will cut or grind them up as finely as possible—a sausage cutter serves the purpose best, and, preferably, one in the form of a chaser consisting of four steel disks revolving about a block of wood. It is important that the beans should not be brought into contact with iron. The finely ground vanilla is transferred to a porcelain jar and seven pounds of granulated sugar is added to it, followed by the liquid with which it had been previously macerated and eight additional pints of water. The mixture is stirred frequently during 24 hours, after which one gallon of deodorized alcohol is added and the whole allowed to macerate for seven days, when another gallon of alcohol is added, maceration continued for a week and four pints more of alcohol added. Filtration is to be avoided. Up to the addition of the last four pints of alcohol the liquid has a turbid appearance, but the alcohol finally added precipitates the albumen, leaving a clear solution. The mixture now formed is allowed to macerate 30 more days and at the expiration of this time the whole is transferred to a Squibb's percolater, which is covered with a muslin diaphragm. After the liquid with which the vanilla has been standing has passed through, continue the percolation with a menstruum consisting of nine pints of water and 12 pints of alcohol. The percolate will be found an excellent extract of vanilla. There is no method to be followed which will yield a satisfactory product in a few days, and the pharmacist must anticipate his wants at least sixty days in advance.

His Favorite Medium.

I have been one of your readers several years and am always interested in your editorial comments, as well as the other contents of the DRUGGIST. A word about advertising. After having been in business fourteen years and tried all kinds of advertising and spent hundreds of dollars in country signs, etc., I am thoroughly convinced that the newspaper is the medium to get at the *people* in a small city. I always watch for the AMERICAN DRUGGIST to get pointers for my ads. Wishing you a prosperous new year, I remain,

L. B. SWETT, Ph. G.,
Massachusetts College, 1890.

BATH, MAINE, January 13.

Business Building.

(Written for the American Druggist.)

TWO MONEY MAKERS.

BY C. P. C. TIMMERMAN.

A good hair tonic and a toilet cream are specialties which if properly advertised and pushed are money makers.

Most every druggist has his own make of these preparations, but if he does not then I would advise him to put them up. Any number of good formulas may be obtained through the AMERICAN DRUGGIST for such preparations. The best size of container for the hair tonic is a two and a half or three ounce bottle (toilet water shape), which may be retailed for twenty-five cents, this size of hair tonic not being on the market, to my knowledge. The toilet cream may be put up in the same size and shape of bottle to retail at from fifteen to twenty-five cents. Fifteen cents would be a suitable retail price for this article, since it can be made very cheaply.

The next step is to introduce them, and one method which I have used successfully is to have printed signs about 12 x 14, reading somewhat like the specimens shown herewith:

25c. Try 25c.

Summers's Hair Tonic

Cleans the Scalp

and

Makes the Hair Grow

Ask the Barber for a Free Trial

15c. Summers's 15c.

Witch Hazel Cream

For

Chapped Hands, Face and Lips

Delightful After Shaving

Ask the Barber for a Free Trial

Display one each of these signs in about twenty-five barber shops, and if a small shop leave a bottle each of your hair tonic and toilet cream; if a large shop two bottles of each, or so that a bottle can be placed at about every other chair. Then ask the barbers to use them on customers and tell them about the preparations. Make an arrangement with the barbers whereby if they are the means of sending customers to you or sell it in the shop you will allow them 20 per cent. for their trouble. By getting them to talk about the preparations and recompensing them for their trouble the druggist is enabled to introduce his own preparations easily, and at the same time secure the trade of the barber.

MANUFACTURING PERFUMERS MEET.

Members a Unit for Reduction of Tax on Alcohol—To Boom American Perfumes.

By far the most important feature of the twelfth annual convention of the members of the Manufacturing Perfumers' Association of the United States, which was held in the Hotel Astor on Tuesday, Wednesday and Thursday, April 3, 4 and 5, was the passing of a resolution whereby the leading perfume makers in this country agreed to inaugurate a general campaign for educating the American consumer in the superiority of the American perfumes over the foreign products. As an initial step in this direction, the members of the association decided to appropriate a sum of money not to exceed $800, to be used in disseminating the information concerning the excellence of American perfumes through the medium of newspapers and magazines, such information to be prepared in the form of news items. The members of the association also recommended that the Executive Board consider the advisability of establishing at the exposition to be held in Jamestown, Va., the first public exhibition of American perfumes, by means of which they expect to spread still further the merits of the American products, which enjoy the advantage of being exempt from the 66 per cent. tariff paid by foreign perfumers.

THE ALCOHOL TAX.

Many other subjects of general interest to the perfumery world and especially to American manufacturers were also discussed at the various sessions of the convention and resolutions, embodying the sentiments and proposed action of the members in relation to pending legislation, were likewise passed. Among these resolutions was one proposed by Henry Dalley, chairman of the Legislative Committee, recommending that the association again place itself on record as favoring all legislation looking toward the removal of the tax on alcohol used in the perfumery industry, and, in particular, as urging the Commissioner of Internal Revenue to exercise certain restrictions in regulating the capacity of the stills to be used by manufacturers of denatured alcohol, which in accordance with the terms of House of Representatives Bill 8453, to be passed by that body within a few days, is exempt from all duty. Though the denatured alcohol bill only indirectly affects the perfume trade, the association deemed it advisable to recommend to the Committee on Ways and Means that Commissioner Yerkes limit the minimum capacity of all denatured alcohol stills to 250 wine gallons, and also that the expense of the administration of this law be borne by the Bureau of Internal Revenue and not by the manufacturers. This resolution met with unanimous approval and was passed by the association members, who also passed another resolution declaring themselves in favor of the Lovering bill, now before the House of Representatives, which provides for a tax on alcohol in its pure state, amounting to only 70 cents per gallon. As pure alcohol is the only kind now used by perfumers as the foundation for their odors and extracts, the bill providing for some relief in the Internal Revenue tax on such spirits is naturally of primal importance to the American perfume makers.

ELABORATE PROGRAMME OF ENTERTAINMENT.

The business of the convention, however, did not occupy all the time, for several elaborate entertainments had been planned for the members by the entertainment committee composed of W. G. Ungerer, of this city, chairman; H. O. Brawner, of Baltimore; Florence Fox, of Philadelphia; Monroe P. Lind, of Philadelphia, and John Blochi, of Chicago. This committee arranged for a theatre party on Tuesday evening, when all the members attending the convention, with their wives, sisters and daughters, went in a body to the Hippodrome. To the entertainment committee, moreover, the members owed the delightful banquet and vaudeville entertainment, which was held in the big ball room in the Hotel Astor on Thursday evening, as the concluding feature of the convention.

THE BUSINESS SESSIONS.

More than 40 active and associate members of the asso-

Photographed by the George R. Lawrence Co.

Banquet of American Perfumers' Association.

ciation attended the opening session of the convention, which was held, like all the other sessions, in the small ball room at the Astor. The first gathering was called at 1 o'clock Tuesday afternoon, when a light luncheon was served. The business meeting began at 2 o'clock and lasted until 4 o'clock, when an adjournment was taken until 11 o'clock on Wednesday morning. This second session lasted until 1 o'clock, when adjournment was taken for luncheon. The third session began at 2 o'clock in the afternoon of the same day and the fourth and fifth sessions were held in the morning and afternoon of Thursday, from 11 to 1 and from 2 to 4 o'clock, respectively. President D. H. McConnell, Secretary Frank B. Marsh, and Treasurer Richard Hudnut were present at all the sessions.

Mr. McConnell opened the first session by reading his report, which contained no special recommendations, but endorsed the reports of all the committees. The president laid great stress in his report upon the necessity for concerted action by all the members of the association, praising what had already been accomplished and expressing the conviction that every one connected with the association would continue to further its interests in every way possible.

Secretary Marsh then reported that the membership of the association amounted to 97 active and associate members, representing the leading perfume manufacturers in all the principal cities in the country. Though there were 125 members last year, the secretary explained that, with the present 50 active and 47 associate members, the association was accomplishing as much as it could with a larger membership.

The report of Treasurer Hudnut was more than satisfactory, showing that the general receipts during the past year had steadily increased, so that the sum in the treasury afforded an ample guarantee of the prosperous financial condition of the organization. Reports from the Committee on Legislation, Entertainment, Membership, Freight and Transportation, Trade Interests, Fraternal Relations, Importations and Undervaluation of Foreign Goods were also read and approved, as was also the report of Theodore Ricksecker, chairman of the Executive Board. All the reports except that of the treasurer were referred to the Committee on Resolutions, which in turn made its reports on Wednesday morning and afternoon.

MADE HONORARY MEMBERS.

James E. Davis, of Detroit, chairman of the Committee on Resolutions, opened the business of the Wednesday morning session by proposing an amendment to the constitution of the association whereby the terms of service for the members of the Executive Board should be increased from one year to three years. This amendment was unanimously passed. Mr. Davis then proposed that Harry S. Woodward and Sturgis Coffin, two former active members of the association, be made honorary members, and, as there was no provision in the constitution for honorary members, Mr. Davis proposed the addition of a third class, to be known as honorary, and also that "any individual, who shall have been actively engaged in furthering and promoting the interests of the association, shall be eligible and may be elected to honorary membership." Mr. Davis also proposed another amendment relative to honorary membership, whereby there should be no dues or assessments for such members. The amendments were unanimously carried and Mr. Woodward and Mr. Coffin were thereupon elected honorary members.

A resolution congratulating Colgate & Co. on the occasion of the celebration of their centennial in the perfume business was also unanimously passed by the members after it had been prepared in proper form by Messrs. Dalley, Wright and Ricksecker.

J. Clifton Buck, chairman of the Freight and Transportation Committee, then presented a resolution expressing disapproval of the system of mileage issued by the Pennsylvania Railroad, on the ground that the railroad demands a deposit of $10 on every mileage book issued, and does not return this deposit until the covers of the book are sent back to the company. Mr. Buck asserted that the railroad had constantly on hand at least $500,000 in deposits of this character. The members readily passed the resolution disapproving the company's rebate system, which has already been condemned by similar associations of manufacturers and merchants.

FOR AN EDUCATIONAL CAMPAIGN.

When the reports of the Committee on Resolutions were called for Mr. Dalley recommended that the association pass resolutions favoring legislation looking for the relief of the tax on alcohol used in the perfumery industry as contained in both House Bill 8453 and the Lovering bill. When this resolution had been drafted by Messrs. Dalley and Ingram, it was adopted by the members without one dissenting vote. Mr. Davis thereupon proposed the campaign of educating the public in the merits of American perfumes and Mr. Ricksecker suggested the subscription of the sum of not more than $300, for the publication of articles on this subject, and also proposed the inauguration of the public exhibition of American perfumes at the 1907 exposition to be held in Jamestown, Va., in celebration of the three hundredth anniversary of the landing of Captain John Smith and John Rolf. As previously mentioned, both resolutions were approved and passed.

A resolution expressing the deep regret of the association on the death of C. L. Cotton, head of the C. L. Cotton Perfume and Extract Company, of Earlville, N. Y., was also passed and a memorial was drafted to that effect.

Resuming their discussion on the inauguration of a campaign of education in American perfumes, the delegates opened their business session Thursday morning by voting to empower the Executive Board to expend the $300 to be appropriated for newspaper and magazine items at their own discretion. They also referred to the Executive Board the advisability of makign a public exhibition of their products at the exposition to be held at Jamestown, Va.

The Committee on Trade Interests and Fraternal Relations presented a resolution whereby all names of new perfumes, toilet waters, etc., should be submitted to it, so that if any of the names submitted are similar to those already used by other manufacturers they may be immediately rejected. The resolution also provided that the use of the names of flowers should be prohibited, and that all new names should hereafter be published, either in a well established trade journal or in a publication to be prepared and edited by the association itself.

The Committee on Importations and Undervaluations announced that it had discovered no evidence of undervaluation on any imported goods.

UNIFORM TERMS AND DISCOUNTS.

The Committee on Trade Interests then submitted for the approval of the members several agreements for the proper preparation and sale of their products. The Executive Board was instructed to submit the agreements to all the active members of the association for their approval by signature. In the event of unanimous approval, the agreements, which are as follows, will become binding:

First. We hereby agree not to offer our products at terms exceeding 60 days, or 2 per cent. off for cash in 10 days.

Second. We hereby agree to date all bills from time of shipment.

Third. We hereby agree not to put foreign labels upon goods of domestic manufacture.

Fourth. We hereby agree to affix a label to each bottle of bulk extract (so-called) stating that any person refilling this bottle or substituting for the contents thereof any other perfume will be prosecuted to the full extent of the law.

At the Thursday afternoon session Mr. Davis called upon Mr. Ingram to discuss the parcels post question. Mr. Ingram, who was thoroughly acquainted with every phase of the Henry bill, known as House of Representatives bill 4,549, explained it in detail, and suggested that a committee be appointed to investigate the parcels post bill and associate itself with similar committees which may be appointed by other manufacturers' associations. The suggestion was adopted.

The following nominees were elected to office for the ensuing year: President, D. H. McConnell, New York; first vice-president, J. Clifton Buck, Philadelphia; second vice-president, Frederick F. Ingram, Detroit; secretary, Frank B. Marsh; treasurer, William Bradley, Philadelphia.

The members of the Executive Board elected for the ensuing year were: Henry Dalley, New York; Alfred Wright, Rochester, and Gilbert Colgate, New York. Benjamin I. Mott had previously been chosen to fill the place on the Executive Board left vacant by the resignation of Sturgis Coffin, and J. Clifton Buck had been selected to fill the place of Herman Tappan, resigned.

MEMBERS IN ATTENDANCE.

Among the local and out-of-town active members of the Perfumers' Association who attended the convention were: D. R. Bradley and William A. Bradley, of D. R. Bradley & Son, this city; A. B. Calisher, of A. B. Calisher & Co., this city; Gilbert Colgate, of Colgate & Co., this city; F. C. De Callant, of the Cotton Perfume and Extract Company, Earlville, N. Y.; Theodore D. Williams, of the Crescent Perfume Company, Rochester, N. Y.; J. Clifton Buck, of French, Cave & Co., Philadelphia; D. H. McConnell and A. D. Henderson, of Goetting & Co., this city; Richard A. Hudnut, of R. Hudnut's Pharmacy, this city; Frederick F. Ingram, of F. F. Ingram & Co., Detroit; Henry Dalley and Henry A. Dalley, of Lazell, Dalley & Co., this city; Joseph A. Brohel, of R. H. Macy & Co. and Abraham & Straus, this city; James E. Davis, of the Michigan Drug Company, Detroit; N. Calisher, of Oakley & Co., this city; Theodore Ricksecker and Frank B. Marsh, of the Theodore Ricksecker Company, this city; John J. Haigney, of William B. Riker & Son Company, this city; S. S. West and William H. Hyde, of the Abner Royce Company, Cleveland, Ohio; George Selick, of G. H. Selick, this city; Frederick K. Stearns, of Frederick Stearns & Co., Detroit.

The associate members at the convention were: Carl Buedingen, of the Buedingen Mfg. Company, Rochester, N. Y.; Christian G. Euler, of Antoine Chiris, Grasse, France; P. R. Dreyer, of the P. R. Dreyer Company, this city; Alexander Goldman, of Alexander Goldman, this city; T. H. Grossmit, of T. H. Grossmit, this city; Richard F. Fischer, of Heine & Co., this city; W. G. Ungerer, of Ungerer & Co., this city, and Jeancard Fils, Cannes, France; H. O. Brawner, of Swindell Brothers, Baltimore, and Louis E. Elldrot, of the William Thompson & Norris Company, this city.

THE BANQUET.

The final function of the meeting was the banquet held in the main banquet hall of the Hotel Astor on Thursday evening. The dinner was served at round tables, and, following the precedent of the previous year, there was no speechmaking. At one end of the room was a raised platform on which a vaudeville performance was given after the dinner, music being furnished during the dinner by the Metropolitan Colored Quartette. The cover of the menu was particularly attractive, consisting of a reproduction of a beautiful painting by Georges Picard entitled "Perfume," which is in the new Hotel Belmont. The committee having charge of the banquet consisted of W. G. Ungerer, chairman, New York; H. O. Brawner, Baltimore; Monroe P. Lind, Philadelphia; Hurlburt W. Smith, Oswego, N. Y., and Florence Fox, Philadelphia. We reproduce herewith a photograph of the diners taken by the George R. Lawrence Company, 1368 Broadway. During the course of the dinner a rising vote of thanks was extended by the diners to Mr. Ungerer and his associates for the entertainment which had been so elaborately extended to the members during their stay in the city.

THE REVENUE TAX UPON ALCOHOLIC PROPRIETARIES.

Peruna Formula Revised and Peruna Taken from the Black List—When Druggists Must Take Out Retailers' License—State to Fo'low Government Lead.

It will be remembered that the United States Bureau of Internal Revenue announced that, beginning with April 1, the following proprietary preparations would be looked upon as alcoholic beverages within the meaning of the Internal Revenue law and that a special United States retail liquor dealers' license would be required of all persons selling them at retail, the wholesalers' license required of them who sold them at wholesale:

Atwood's La Grippe Specific, Cuban Gingeric, De Witt's Stomach Bitters, Dr. Bouvier's Buchu Gin, Dr. Fowler's Meat and Malt, Duffy's Malt Whiskey, Gilbert's Rejuvenating Iron and Herb Juice, Hostetter's Stomach Bitters, Kudros, Peruna and Rockcandy Cough Cure.

PERUNA OFF THE BLACK LIST.

Since publication of this list a new formula has been adopted for Peruna, which took effect on December 1, 1905. The new product was analyzed and passed upon favorably by Dr. Virgil Coblentz, professor of chemistry in the New York College of Pharmacy. The Peruna Company notified Commissioner Yerkes of the change in the product on December 30, 1905, and also told him that the new preparation could be produced in several drug stores in the city of Washington. The new wrappers on Peruna, Dr. Hartman also said, contained a special notice of the revision of the formula and label. Commissioner Yerkes on January 5, 1906, consented to have the new product analyzed by the chemist of the Bureau of Internal Revenue. This analysis was made by the internal revenue chemist and the product was then submitted to the Secretary of the Treasury and by his direction to the Surgeon General of the Public Health and Marine Hospital Service. On March 15 the Surgeon General declared that the new preparation, which had been examined and analyzed by the director of the hygienic laboratory and certain of his assistants, had been found to contain drugs of such a character and in sufficient quantity to warrant its being considered as a medicine and to inhibit its use as a beverage. Two days after the receipt of this report Commissioner Yerkes withdrew the new Peruna from the list of alcoholic compounds, with the understanding, however, that any supplies of the old product which may still be in existence and exposed for sale shall render the seller subject to the special liquor tax of the Internal Revenue Department.

LICENSE NOT REQUIRED OF RETAILERS GENERALLY.

First Deputy Collector David S. Wendel, when interviewed recently in the office of the Collector of Internal Revenue for the Second District of New York, said that Commissioner Yerkes would add from time to time other medicinal remedies containing a large percentage of alcohol to the list now subject to the special liquor tax, but that up to date any licensed pharmacist or other merchant might sell proprietary remedies which have not yet been listed, although they may appear to contain as much alcohol as those which are now listed. A regularly licensed pharmacist, he added, may also sell liquors upon the written prescription of a regularly licensed physician, signed by such physician, without being subject to the Government special liquor tax, and such a regularly licensed pharmacist may also sell such medicinal remedies as spirits of camphor, tincture of iodine or any other tinctures, although they contain a larger percentage of alcohol, because such preparations are medicinal and not beverages. If, however, a licensed pharmacist wishes to sell alcohol for medicinal or mechanical purposes but not as a beverage, without a prescription, he must pay the Government $25 special retail liquor dealer's tax in addition to paying the New York State excise tax of $7.50 which is specially provided for licensed pharmacists.

THE ATTITUDE OF THE STATE EXCISE COMMISSIONER.

Commissioner P. W. Cullinan, head of the New York State Department of Excise, has agreed not to anticipate United States Commissioner of Internal Revenue Yerkes in bringing suit against any druggist or other dealer in proprietary remedies on the ground that such person is selling alcoholic compounds which have not yet been listed by the Internal Revenue Department. Commissioner Cullinan will, however, continue to prosecute any dealers who do not pay the "trafficking in liquors" tax as well as the Government special liquor tax when selling the compounds now on the list of Commissioner Yerkes. It is generally understood that the New York Excise Department began its crusade against sellers of alcoholic compounds for the purpose of arousing the Internal Revenue Department to similar action, but now that the Government has prepared its first list of alcoholic preparations which are subject to both Government and State taxation, and purposes to add to this list other alcoholic compounds, the State Excise Department is willing to follow the lead of the Government department and attend only to the enforcement of the existing liquor tax law of this State.

TAX-FREE ALCOHOL FOR THE ARTS.

Alcohol for Medicinal Purposes Specifically Excluded from Benefit—Administrative Details Left to Executive Authorities—Bill Reported Favorably in the House—Good Prospects for Passing Senate.

Washington, April 3.—After a most thorough and exhaustive investigation the Committee on Ways and Means of the House of Representatives has made a favorable report on a bill providing for the use of denatured alcohol in the arts, but especially excluding from the benefits of the measure alcohol to be used in "liquid medicinal preparations." The text of the essential portions of the act follows:

A Bill for the withdrawal from bond, tax-free, of domestic alcohol when rendered unfit for beverage or liquid medicinal uses by mixture with suitable denaturing materials.

Section 1. Be it enacted by the Senate and House of Representatives of the United States of America in Congress assembled, that from and after three months from the passage of this act domestic alcohol of such degree of proof as may be prescribed by the Commissioner of Internal Revenue and approved by the Secretary of the Treasury, may be withdrawn from bond without the payment of internal revenue tax, for use in the arts and industries, and for fuel, light and power; provided said alcohol shall have been mixed in the presence and under the direction of an authorised Government officer, before withdrawal from the bonded warehouse, with denaturing material suitable to the use for which the alcohol is withdrawn, but which destroys its character as a beverage and renders it unfit for liquid medicinal purposes. The character and quality of the said denaturing material and the conditions upon which said alcohol may be withdrawn free of tax shall be prescribed by the Commissioner of Internal Revenue, who shall, with the approval of the Secretary of the Treasury, make all necessary regulations for carrying into effect the provisions of this act.

Sec. 2. That any person who uses alcohol withdrawn from bond under the provisions of section 1 of this act for manufacturing any beverage or liquid medicine preparation, or knowingly sells any beverage or liquid medicinal preparation made in whole or in part from such alcohol, or knowingly violates any of the provisions of this act, shall for the offense be fined not more than $5000 or be imprisoned not more than five years, or both; provided, that manufacturers employing processes in which alcohol, used free of tax under the provisions of this act, is expressed or evaporated from the articles manufactured, shall be permitted to recover such alcohol and to have such alcohol restored to a condition suitable solely for re-use in manufacturing processes, under such regulations as the Commissioner of the Internal Revenue, with the approval of the Secretary of the Treasury, shall prescribe.

Section 3 appropriates the sum of $25,000 for the payment of the expenses involved in the administration of the law and exempts appointees made under the law from the Civil Service rules for the term of two years.

Among the numerous memorials presented in favor of the measure was one by Mahlon N. Kline, chairman of the Committee on Legislation of the National Wholesale Druggists' Association, in which were enumerated a large number of the many chemicotechnical industries in which the introduction of tax-free alcohol would be of very material advantage.

The industries referred to included the manufacture of aniline dyes, hats, electrical apparatus, transparent soap, all kinds of fancy woodwork, including furniture, pencils, toys, etc., smokeless powder, brass goods, incandescent mantels, photographic material, celluloid and similar substances, ether and organic chemicals.

The investigations and reports made to the committee embrace a very full account of the method in use in Germany, England and other European countries in the denaturing of alcohol, which has resulted in the very widespread use of alcohol for chemical purposes and has built up, notably in Germany, an immense sale for small motors propelled by alcohol.

The Lovering bill providing for a reduction of the tax on pure alcohol to 70 cents per gallon has also received favorable consideration and may possibly pass.

VIGOROUS OBJECTION TO THE STEVENS BILL.

Measure Favored by Dr. Schieffelin Opposed by Wholesale and Retail Druggists.

Decided opposition to the amended Stevens-Wainwright bill, which provides for the labeling of proprietary and other medicinal preparations containing alcohol, narcotic and other potent drugs and for the inspection, analysis and regulation of the manufacture and sale of the same has arisen among the members of the Drug Trade Section of the New York Board of Trade and Transportation. This body of drug interests, which includes in its membership such prominent manufacturers and wholesalers as Thomas F. Main, president of the Tarrant Company, secretary of the New York College of Pharmacy and president of the N. W. D. A.; Albert Plaut, member of the firm of Lehn & Fink and trustee of the College of Pharmacy; Charles S. Littell and Thomas P. Cook, placed itself on record at its regular meeting, held Wednesday afternoon, March 28, as unanimously disapproving of the provisions of the labeling measure now before the State Senate and the similar measure before the State Assembly, and as especially opposed to the amendments which have just been framed in the Assembly bill, whereby extraordinary powers have been conferred upon the departments of health in cities of the first class for the regulation of the sale, conditions of sale and labeling of the preparations in question.

The local Drug Trade Section has also determined to fight the bill, through its Legislative Committee, on the ground that it will entail an enormous expense to the State and upon the druggists and manufacturers affected. In order to embody all of their objections to the bills and enlist in their opposition to the measure the Senators and members of the Assembly from their home districts, the members of the section adopted at their meeting a resolution, copies of which will be sent to the members of the Legislature and to Governor Higgins, in the hope that they may obtain assistance in preventing the passage of the bill in its present form. The resolution adopted and unanimously passed by the section follows:

"*Whereas*, At the meeting of the Drug Section of the New York Board of Trade and Transportation, held March 8, 1906, resolutions were passed disapproving of the Stevens-Wainwright bill, and

"*Whereas*, The bill in its amended form (1722 Assembly) is still more objectionable, owing to the addition of Section 231, conferring extraordinary powers on the departments of health in cities of the first class, under which said departments are to regulate the sale, conditions of sale and labeling of all proprietary and medicinal preparations, being powers far in excess of those of the original measure, and

"*Whereas*, The bill, if passed, would entail an enormous expense to the State without compensating advantages to the public; would place wholesale druggists in cities of the first class at a serious disadvantage, as compared with those doing business in other cities and in other States; would vest a power in a few hands, which could and doubtless would be used as a means of oppression and to destroy legitimate branches of business; therefore be it

"*Resolved*, That the Legislative Committee of this section be directed to use all legitimate means to prevent the passage of Assembly Bill 1722, and that copies of these resolutions be sent to members of the Legislature and Governor of this State, and be it further

"*Resolved*, That members of the section be requested to use their influence with the Senators and members of Assembly from their districts to defeat the measure."

The amendments, which have just been made to the Wainwright bill and which will also be added to the Stevens bill, include the addition to the list of proprietary and medicinal preparations already prohibited, unless properly labeled, of "any other hypnotic, anæsthetic, analgetic or cardiac, circulatory, respiratory or nerve depressant" and also stipulate that the percentage or proportion of each of these additional drugs shall also be printed upon the label of the bottle or package.

The new amendment, which is considered most objectionable by the Drug Section reads in full as follows:

"Local departments of health in cities of the first class shall have power from time to time to adopt such ordinances to form a part of the sanitary codes of said cities, and make such regulations in addition to the provisions of this article as may seem necessary to enforce or facilitate the enforcement of this article; and such local departments of health are hereby also authorized and empowered to adopt such ordinances and make such regulations as to the sale of *proprietary and medicinal preparations and the conditions under which the same may be sold*, and the labeling thereof as they shall deem necessary for the protection of the public."

The very suggestion that such powers as these, which are now possessed by the State Board of Pharmacy, should be virtually taken away from that body, to be vested in the departments of health in the principal cities of this State, is deemed most objectionable, as it is generally felt that, inasmuch as the State Board of Pharmacy has the right to license pharmacists, it should also exercise exclusively the right to punish the offenders of any State laws.

Mr. Main, although unable to attend the hearing on the Stevens bill, which was recently held before the Senate Committee on Public Health, forwarded on that occasion a statement of his principal reasons for opposing the bill. These reasons, which are also shared by most of the members of the Drug Trade Section, can be briefly summarized as follows:

First—The bill, if passed, will entail a large expense upon the druggist and manufacturer.

Second—It will place no restriction whatever upon the physician nor on the sale of the most dangerous compounds, provided that they bear the special label.

Third—It will entail an untold but undoubtedly heavy expense upon the State, with the prospect of actually increasing the sale of the compounds of narcotic drugs for illegitimate purposes and with but the most remote chance of in any way promoting public health or safety.

M. D.'S AND PH. G.'S CEMENT FRIENDSHIP.

Hudson River Branch of M. A. R. D. Favors Adoption of Non-Refilling Prescription Contract.

Never before in the history of pharmacy have more amicable relations been established between druggist and doctor than prevailed at the joint meeting of pharmacists and physicians, held under the auspices of the Hudson River or Twenty-second District Branch of the Metropolitan Association of Retail Druggists in the Harlem Casino on Thursday evening, March 29. One specially noticeable feature of this occasion was the fact that the physicians who attended the meeting outnumbered the pharmacists themselves, for, while 36 members of the Twenty-second District Branch and four non-member druggists were present to welcome the representatives of the medical fraternity, no less than 45 M. D.'s gathered at the place of rendezvous for the purpose of becoming more intimately acquainted with the knights of the pestle and mortar.

The Hudson River pharmacists were more than willing to meet the medical practitioners half-way when the M. D.'s presented for their approval the new prescription contract, which has proved of great benefit to the doctors of Philadelphia, where it has been generally adopted by the retail druggists. This new prescription contract is printed upon the reverse side of a small square of cardboard which contains on its face the usual blank space for a doctor's prescription. The contract provides that the patient, for whom the doctor has prescribed, shall not have the prescription on the face of the card refilled, except with the consent of the physician whose name appears at the top of card. Realizing that many persons frequently use the same prescription for any illness, in total ignorance of the therapeutic effect of the drugs called for, the members of the Hudson River Branch of the M. A. R. D. were quite willing to relinquish the practice of refilling prescriptions repeatedly.

DODGE & OLCOTT AND PARKE, DAVIS & CO. TIE IN BOWLING TOURNAMENT.

Standing of Teams in Wholesale Drug Trade Bowling Association.

	Won.	Lost.
Dodge & Olcott	16	4
Parke, Davis & Co	16	4
Colgate & Co	15	5
Whitall, Tatum Company	14	6
Seabury & Johnson	13	7
Lazell, Dalley & Co	8	12
Sharp & Dohme	8	12
Roessler & Hasslacher	8	12
Lanman & Kemp	7	13
Bruen, Ritchey & Co	4	16
Merck & Co	2	18

The Parke, Davis & Co. knights of the pin have succeeded in tieing with the Dodge & Olcott rollers for first honors and the silver trophy cup in the great bowling tournament of the Wholesale Drug Trade Bowling Association of New York. In two fiercely contested games with the Bruen, Ritchey & Co. and the Lanman & Kemp teams the Parke, Davis & Co. experts proved themselves the unquestioned victors at the latest, and supposedly the last, set of games, which were played at the Albion alleys, 117 West Twenty-third street, on Monday evening, April 2. With 16 games to their credit and only 4 to their discredit, the Parke, Davis & Co. men have pulled themselves up to the standing of the hitherto presumptive winners of the tournament, and the final struggle for first place will be fought out in a contest between these two teams at the Albion alleys on Monday evening, April 9.

The Parke, Davis & Co. crackerjacks, it will be remembered, won the trophy cup last year and it is therefore likely that they will put up a hard fight with the Dodge & Olcott contingent before they express willingness to surrender this emblem of prowess on the alleys. The victory in this two-sided contest will lie in the winning of two out of three games. There is no question about third honors, however, as the Colgate & Co. rollers have cinched the place immediately below that of the two tied teams, and interest in the tournament now centers only upon the coming battle royal of the Dodge & Olcott and Parke, Davis & Co. crews.

At the latest contest of the teams the Whitall, Tatum Company as well as the Parke, Davis & Co. men also won both of their games, while the Lanman & Kemp, Colgate & Co. and Lazell, Dalley & Co. teams each scored one victory and one defeat, but the Bruen, Ritchey & Co. and Merck & Co. alley dodgers both registered two defeats.

The high individual scores recorded at this contest included that of Terry, of the Whitall, Tatum Company team, who reached 233, with 7 strikes and 2 spares, and that of "Lou" Burgess, of the Parke, Davis & Co. contingent, who chalked up 223 as his mark, with 5 strikes and 5 spares. Gemmel, of the Lanman & Kemp team, also made 206, with 4 strikes and an equal number of spares.

To "Lou" Burgess, moreover, belongs the distinction of having made the highest average among the individual records during the entire tournament. His average score is 184 7/[illegible], while that of J. Ruddiman, of the Dodge & Olcott team, is 181 14/[illegible]. "Mat" Judge, of the Seabury & Johnson crew, also made his mark in the average score contest by reaching 180 11/[illegible].

The team scores of the latest games follow: First game—Parke, Davis & Co., 912; Bruen, Ritchey & Co., 779. Second game—Parke, Davis & Co., 945; Lanman & Kemp, 864. Third game—Lanman & Kemp, 778; Bruen, Ritchey & Co., 678. Fourth game—Whitall, Tatum Company, 893; Colgate & Co., 771. Fifth game—Lazell, Dalley & Co., 648; Merck & Co., 624. Sixth game—Colgate & Co., 857; Merck & Co., 597.

By winning its games with the Lazell, Dalley & Co. and Roessler & Hasslacher rollers at the contest held Monday evening, March 26, the Colgate & Co. contingent tied with the Parke, Davis & Co. crew for second place in the bowling tournament of the Wholesale Drug Trade Bowling Association of New York. The big silver cup, which has reposed peacefully on the shelf over Dr. Carr's desk in the Parke, Davis & Co. offices for almost a year, trembled on its lofty perch at the thought of the hot finish which the tournament was likely to have. With two games yet to play, the Parke, Davis & Co. knights of the pin still had a chance to tie with the Dodge & Olcott men, who held the lead with 16 games to their credit and only 4 to their discredit, while the Colgate & Co. rollers were offered a similar opportunity.

In the March 26 contest Seabury & Johnson also won both of its games, while Lazell, Dalley & Co. and Sharp & Dohme each scored one victory and one defeat. Roessler & Hasslacher accepted with good grace two defeats, and Merck & Co., the tail-enders, also lost two games. No especially brilliant individual records were made, but Oldershaw, of the Colgate & Co. team, marked up 191 as his score, while Mr. Colgate himself reached 189, and Gooding, of Lazell, Dalley & Co., touched 186.

The team scores in detail were as follows: First game—Seabury & Johnson, 700; Sharp & Dohme, 662. Second game—Seabury & Johnson, 816; Merck & Co., 579. Third game—Sharp & Dohme, 665; Merck & Co., 588. Fourth game—Colgate & Co., 874; Lazell, Dalley & Co., 781. Fifth game—Lazell, Dalley & Co., 784; Roessler & Hasslacher, 692. Sixth game—Colgate & Co., 857; Roessler & Hasslacher, 813.

New York Branch of Parke, Davis & Co. Wins Intercity Cup.

Bowling enthusiasts in the local offices of Parke, Davis & Co. are rejoicing over their victory in the Intercity bowling match, in which they competed with the star rollers of the Detroit, Chicago, New Orleans and Kansas City offices of that company. The teams representing each of the competing offices rolled their games in their respective cities on Saturday afternoon and evening, March 31, and the results of their prowess in alley work were sent by telegraph to the captains of the respective teams. The team representing the local offices of Parke, Davis & Co. held their pin knocking session on Saturday afternoon of the above mentioned date in the Albion alleys, at 117 West Twenty-third street, where Messrs. Bruun, Burgess, Conway, Blake and Carr upheld the honors of the New York branch by chalking up a grand total of 4,366 in five trials of their skill. The Detroit, or home office, team, which bowled its scores in the evening, made the second best showing, by rolling up 4,348. The special silver trophy cup, which was given last year by the officers of the corporation to the Detroit office bowlers, as the winners of the 1905 intercity contest, will now be forwarded to the local office victors without delay.

A Thomas S. Weigand Scholarship.

In commemoration of the fifty years of active service in behalf of the Philadelphia College of Pharmacy which have been rendered by Thos. S. Wiegand it is proposed to establish a scholarship to be known by his name. To effect this it is needful that at least $3,000 be raised, which will secure a full course of instruction in all the regular branches and some extra practice in the laboratories.

More than one-fourth of this amount has been contributed, so that it will require but moderate contributions to effect this object. The interest of this amount will enable the college to sustain the scholarship in perpetuity.

To carry out this scheme, an appeal is made by the committee, not only to the alumni of the Philadelphia College, but to all who are interested in the welfare of pharmacy and the promotion of pharmaceutical education. The plan appeals with peculiar emphasis to every alumnus of the institution, for the figure of Mr. Wiegand looms large in the memory of everyone who calls the Philadelphia College of Pharmacy his alma mater, for his uniform kindness and courtesy have done much to make thousands of awkward and shy freshmen feel at home in the institution.

All drafts, money orders or checks should be made payable to the order of George M. Beringer, Treasurer Wiegand Scholarship Fund, Philadelphia College of Pharmacy, 145 North Tenth street, Philadelphia.

A Retail Druggist Gives to His Employees Stock Worth $250,000.

C. H. McConnell, president of the Economical Drug Company of Chicago, has recently set aside one-fourth of the $100,000 of common stock of his company to be given to employees who have been in the employ of the company for five years or more. This has been divided into lots ranging from $500 for the porter to $10,000 for the manager. As the stock pays a dividend of 40 per cent., the gift is really worth very much more than the face value, and according to Wall Street usage would be reckoned at ten times the face value. While the stock is to be turned over to the employees, each one is expected to pay for his stock at the face value from his dividends, but since only two and a half years would be required to do this, this requirement is by no means a hardship.

Mr. McConnell has built up a most remarkable business in the fifteen years or so since he established his store in the heart of the downtown district of Chicago. Owing to the concentration of the offices of physicians in the center of Chicago there are probably 1,000 physicians located within a few blocks of his store, and as a result he does a prescription business ranging from 400 to 600 prescriptions a day. He began with the sale of soda water and cigars, but eventually got rid of both of these side lines, believing that they were detrimental rather than beneficial to his legitimate drug business.

Prior to his undertaking the establishment of this company he had been engaged in an entirely different line of trade, and even now makes no pretense of any knowledge of pharmacy, intrusting all purely pharmaceutical matters to his expert pharmaceutical staff.

Notwithstanding his purely commercial training he has taken a remarkable stand in his attitude toward patent medicines. He has never permitted his employees to endeavor to sell anything except what is called for. Most cut rate druggists insist upon their salesmen making an effort to substitute when cut rate patents are asked for. This Mr. McConnell has never permitted in his establishment. He had, however, a disagreement with one firm, and when it was officially stated, by the United States Government, that a preparation made by this firm contained a large percentage of alcohol, he instructed each salesman to state that fact in making sales of that particular remedy, and he used his show windows to advertise the fact. In the same way he has endeavored to discourage the sale of catarrh snuff containing cocaine by wrapping up with each bottle of such remedy a statement of the results of analyses made by the chemist of the Board of Health, and warning the purchaser against the danger incurred by the use of the remedy.

Mr. McConnell is a firm believer in having the best help and paying an adequate remuneration. He has invariably advanced the wages of his clerks from time to time as he thought advancement was deserved, without waiting to be asked, and by giving a certain small commission on amount of sales made has given a special incentive to each employee to exert himself to the utmost at all times. One result of this liberal policy is shown in the fact that the number of sales made by each of his salesmen exceed by 25 to 50 per cent. the number of sales made by men employed in the same capacity in other stores of the same character. His latest move in giving his employees one-fourth of the common stock of the company is exactly in line with his previous record as an employer.

Mr. McConnell's health has of late not been particularly robust, and he sailed from New York last week for a seven months' tour through the West Indies and Central America. He has taken long vacations every summer during the last four or five years and finds that the loyalty of his employees is such that his business never suffers by his absence.

American Medical Association Invites Drug Exhibits.

Manufacturing and proprietary drug interests have been invited to exhibit their products at the annual convention of the American Medical Association, which will be held in Boston, on June 5, 6, 7 and 8. It is announced that the character of the claims made for the exhibits will be carefully scrutinized by the council on pharmacy and chemistry of the Association.

Obituary.

ROBERT OGDEN DOREMUS, M.D., LL.D.

Dr. Robert Ogden Doremus, the eminent chemist, educator and inventor, died at his home in this city on March 22. Born in New York January 11, 1824, Dr. Doremus lived to witness the marvelous growth of his native city from the time when he made his home in the old residence building at the northwest corner of Broadway and Cortlandt street up to the present time, when the population of the city exceeds 4,000,000. On his father's side Dr. Doremus was a direct descendant of Anneke Jans, one of the most notable of the early Dutch settlers; while his mother was the granddaughter of Robert Ogden, one of the founders of Princeton University. His father, Thomas C. Doremus, was the senior member of the firm of Doremus, Suydam & Nixon, then the largest wholesale mercantile firm in the country, with offices and warerooms at the southwest corner of Liberty and Nassau streets.

Dr. Doremus entered Columbia College after completing his school education in 1838, but remained there only a short time, changing to the New York University, of which his father was a founder. He graduated from this institution in 1842 with a degree of A.B. Three years later he took the degree of A.M., and graduated from the medical department in 1850, after pursuing a full course in medicine. In 1871 he received the honorary degree of LL.D. from his *alma mater*.

Dr. Doremus always evinced the greatest interest in pharmacy, and his communications to the AMERICAN DRUGGIST on the subject of restricting the sale of carbolic acid will be fresh in the minds of our readers. It was in the newly established College of Pharmacy that he began his career as a public lecturer, about 1849. In 1850 he helped to found the New York Medical College, where he equipped a chemical laboratory, the first in this country in which students could, and were required to, study chemistry practically. Later he was instrumental in founding the Long Island College Hospital and the Bellevue Hospital Medical College, and he occupied the chair of chemistry and toxicology in both institutions. In the early days when efforts were first made to regulate the practice of pharmacy in this city and a Board of Examiners of Druggists and Prescription Clerks was formed, Dr. Doremus was chosen president, holding the office until a change in the statutes placed it in the hands of a new Board of Pharmacy.

He attained great fame in forensic chemistry, his first notable case establishing a precedent which has been followed ever since in the employment of chemical experts by the district attorney. When asked to make a toxicological analysis of the remains of the wife of James Stephens, who was suspected of being poisoned, he insisted upon having a special laboratory, with dissecting room, new apparatus, and the assistance of a coworker. His demands were acceded to. The present law which makes the expenses of experts a charge on the county when the expert is employed by the coroner, with the consent of the Comptroller and a Justice of the Supreme Court, was the outcome of representations made by Dr. Doremus. As a member of the Medical Advisory board of the Board of Health, in 1865, he was called upon to devise means of disinfecting a vessel which had arrived at Quarantine with an epidemic of cholera, sixty of the ship's company having died and been cast overboard. Dr. Doremus applied chlorine gas by the decomposition of immense quantities of manganese binoxide and common salt with sulphuric acid. The outcome was most successful and his method of disinfection was made to supersede the forty-day detention at Quarantine previously practiced, a most important matter for a commercial port like New York. It was at Dr. Doremus's instigation that the obelisk (Cleopatra's Needle) in Central Park was successfully preserved by the use of melted paraffin wax. Dr. Doremus was a lover of music and was for several terms president of the Philharmonic Society. At the funeral services on Sunday, March 25, a number of members volunteered to play. The services were extremely beautiful and every participant was deeply impressed with their beauty and grandeur.

Dr. Doremus never fully recovered from his wife's death in 1905, which brought to him a deep and abiding sorrow. Dr. and Mrs. Doremus had eight children born to them, and he is survived by one daughter, Miss Estelle E., and three sons, Dr. Charles A., and Messrs. Thomas C. and Arthur L. Doremus.

JACOB C. LYONS, NEW ORLEANS.

Jacob C. Lyons, manager of the wholesale and retail drug house of I. L. Lyons & Co., of New Orleans, succumbed to an attack of pneumonia on March 21, after having been ill only five days. Mr. Lyons was born in Columbia, S. C., October 16, 1849, and was the son of J. C. Lyons and Louisa Hart. He moved to New Orleans in 1868 from Philadelphia, to which place his family had moved at the close of the Civil War.

When he arrived in New Orleans he secured employment in the wholesale drug store of his uncle, E. J. Hart. In the early seventies, after a thorough schooling in the drug business under the tutelage of his uncle, Mr. Lyons associated himself with the firm of which his elder brother, I. L. Lyons, was the head. He continued with this firm until his death, seeing it grow to be one of the largest drug houses in the South. On the retirement of I. L. Lyons from the active direction of the business fifteen years ago this responsibility fell to J. C. Lyons. He is survived by a widow and two children, J. Clifford and Miss Elizabeth.

FREDERICK ASCHENBACH.

Frederick Aschenbach, of Aschenbach & Miller, died at his residence in Germantown, near Philadelphia, on March 26, aged sixty-eight years. Mr. Aschenbach was born in Saxony, Germany. He came to this country with his parents at quite an early age and served his apprenticeship in the drug business with Dr. Lindsey, at the corner of Eleventh and Master streets. Afterward he entered the employ of Henry O. D. Banks at the corner of Fourth and Callowhill streets. After having had chief charge of this establishment for several years, the new firm of Henry O. D. Banks & Co. was formed by the admission of Frederick Aschenbach and Adolph W. Miller, in May, 1862. About three years later Mr. Banks withdrew from active business and the remaining partners associated themselves together under the title of Aschenbach & Miller. The firm is incorporated and the business will suffer no interruption.

EUGENE GRASSELLI.

Eugene Grasselli, vice-president and director of the Grasselli Chemical Company, died at Albuquerque, N. M., March 20, aged forty-six years. Mr. Grasselli was born in Cincinnati, a son of the founder of the company that bears his name. In 1867 his family moved to Cleveland, which city was his home until his death. He was married, his wife dying six years ago. He is survived by a son, Edward, and a daughter, Lucretia. Two brothers are living, C. A. Grasselli, president of the Grasselli Chemical Company, at Cleveland, and A. G. Grasselli, of Kansas, and four sisters.

DIED.

AARON.—In Mt. Olive, N. C., on Friday, February 16, Dr. Leonard P. Aaron, aged thirty-two years.

ASCHENBACH.—In Philadelphia, on Monday, March 26, Frederick Aschenbach, aged sixty-eight years.

BRANDRETH.—In Ossining, N. Y., on Sunday, March 18, William Brandreth, aged sixty-four years.

BROWN.—In Atlanta, Ga., on Wednesday, February 21, Dempsey Brown.

BOOTH.—In Bridgeport, Conn., on Wednesday, March 28, Frederick D. Booth, aged forty-three years.

BUNNELL.—In Bridgeport, Conn., on Sunday, March 25, Hubert W. Bunnell, aged sixty-seven years.

CHERRY.—In Boston, Mass., on Friday, February 23, Dr. James B. Cherry.

DAVIS.—In Brooks, W. Va., on Monday, March 5, Daniel Webster Davis, aged thirty-five years.

DEBOW.—In New Orleans, La., on Wednesday, February 14, Ellsworth R. DeBow, aged 45 years.

ENNIS.—In Newburgh, N. Y., on Wednesday, February 14, Richard Ennis, aged fifty-eight years.

FREEMAN.—Recently, in California, Simon A. Freeman, formerly of Everett, Mass., aged sixty-three years.

GREVE.—In New Orleans, La., on Wednesday, March 7, Mrs. Josephine Greve.

HAHNE.—In Dayton, Ohio, on Sunday, March 11, John A. Hahne, aged forty-nine years.

HATTIE.—In Halifax, N. S., on Friday, March 2, H. B. Hattie, aged forty-four years.

HEMM.—In Kirkwood, St. Louis, Mo., on Friday, February 23, Louis P. Hemm, aged forty-seven years.

JELLISON.—In Boston, Mass., on Sunday, February 18, Dr. J. M. Jellison.

KELLY.—In Cincinnati, Ohio, on Wednesday, March 7, Joseph H. Kelly, aged thirty-five years.

KINGSLEY.—In Stamford, Conn., on Monday, March 26, Harry Kingsley.

McCOLLUM.—In Waterbury, Conn., on Thursday, March 15, Robert J. McCollum, aged thirty-three years.

McMAKIN.—In Cincinnati, Ohio, on Thursday, March 8, Robert J. McMakin, aged sixty-five years.

MORRISEY.—In Bath Beach, Brooklyn, N. Y., on Sunday, March 18, Frank J. Morrisey, aged forty-three years.

O'BRIEN.—In Coney Island, N. Y., on Sunday, February 25, Christopher O'Brien.

PUNCH.—In Montgomery, Ala., on Saturday, March 10, William F. Punch, aged sixty-six years.

PUTNAM.—In East Nassau, N. Y., on Monday, March 12, Charles Putnam, aged forty-five years.

RIKER.—In New York, on Thursday, February 22, William B. Riker, aged eighty-five years.

SCHOETTLE.—In St. Louis, Mo., on Sunday, February 25, John F. Schoettle, aged thirty-five years.

STILWELL.—In New York, on Tuesday, March 20, Arthur A. Stilwell, aged fifty-two years.

WESLEY.—Recently, in Boston, Mass., Charles M. Wesley, aged sixty-four years.

ZEILE.—In San Francisco, Cal., on Monday, February 19, Carl David Zeile, aged sixty-eight years.

Greater New York News.

W. H. McGarrah, a retail druggist, of Scranton, Pa., was seen in town last week.

Samuel Felt, of the Samuel Felt Drug Company, of Watertown, N. Y., visited the local wholesale and manufacturing trade during the first week in April.

Frederick D. Booth, a prominent retail druggist, of Bridgeport, Conn., who was also well known in this city, died at his home on March 28.

George H. Harding, of Derby, Conn., visited the local wholesale trade recently to purchase pharmaceuticals and toilet articles.

Herman Hartz, senior partner in the wholesale drug firm of Hartz & Bahnsen, of Rock Island, Ill., visited the local manufacturing and jobbing trade during the last week in March.

A. B. Henderson, of the Dominion Drug Company, wholesale drug dealers of Hamilton, Ontario, visited the local manufacturing and jobbing trade on March 27, 28 and 29.

Justin Keith, Western sales representative of J. L. Hopkins & Co., drug importers of 100 William street, visited the local offices of his company during the last week in March.

Representatives of all of the leading perfumery houses in this country attended the annual meeting of the Manufacturing Perfumers' Association, which was held in this city on Tuesday, Wednesday and Thursday, April 3, 4 and 5.

George Reynard, secretary and treasurer of Magnus & Lauer, Incorporated, of 257 Pearl street, has just purchased a 40 horse-power Panhard automobile with which he expects to enjoy frequent spins about town and on Long Island.

Joseph Robb, Jr., of the Henry B. Gilpin Company, wholesale druggists of Baltimore, Md., was among the prominent visitors in the local manufacturing and wholesale trade during the last week in March.

Walter J. Krappe, formerly in charge of the 149th street branch of Hegeman & Co., at Third avenue and 149th street, has just been chosen manager of the new Kalish pharmacy, at Madison avenue and Fifty-ninth street.

L. L. Walton, a retail druggist of Williamsport, Pa., who visited the local wholesale district recently, is planning to remodel his store in Williamsport by erecting a new front to the building and making several interior alterations which will add materially to the attractiveness of the place.

The stock and fixtures of the Phœnix Drug Company, at 275 Water street, have been placed in the hands of the sheriff, on two executions for a total of $1,085. The company was incorporated in 1904, with a capital of $100,000, to manufacture specialties for the wholesale drug trade.

Joseph Weinstein was nominated by the New York Retail Druggists' Association for member of the State Board of Pharmacy, to succeed himself, at the regular monthly meeting of that association, which was held Friday evening, March 30, in the Herrnstadt Restaurant, at 27 West 115th street.

J. Maxwell Pringle, Jr., the retail druggist whose store was formerly located at 977 Eighth avenue, has vacated his old premises and opened a new pharmacy at Fifty-fifth street and Eighth avenue. Mr. Pringle has also started a small branch store at 982 Eighth avenue, directly opposite his original pharmacy.

Local members of the American Association for the Advancement of Science have received from the local secretary, J. McKeen Cattell, a circular directing attention to the fact that the annual meeting of the association will be held in New York during Christmas week and urging the recipients to make an effort to secure a large increase in membership in view of that event.

Owing to the fact that his health is not at present sufficiently robust to undertake his contemplated trip through the Mediterranean Sea, Col. Edward W. Fitch has decided to abandon this project and return immediately to his former home in Louisville, Ky., with Mrs. Fitch. After resting for several weeks in Louisville it is the colonel's intention to retire permanently to Pasadena, Cal.

W. B. Duryea, formerly a partner in the retail drug firm of Duryea & Johnson, of Freehold, N. J., has just purchased the interest of G. V. Johnson in the business and will hereafter conduct the store under his own name. Mr. Johnson, as previously mentioned in the AMERICAN DRUGGIST, has opened a new store in Highlands, N. J., about a mile from Atlantic Highlands.

Frank A. Weed, for the past 30 years well and favorably known throughout the State of New York and the New England territory as the traveling representative of the Whitall Tatum Company, last month severed his connection with the firm. Mr. Weed makes his home at Charlotte, a suburb of Rochester, N. Y., and intends to take a respite for a time from active business.

Members of the Chevron Council of the Royal Arcanum, most of whom are druggists and doctors, held their anniversary dinner in the Cafe Moretti, 51 West Thirty-fifth street, Thursday evening, March 29. Invitations were sent to the Supreme Regent of the Royal Arcanum, to Mayor McClellan and many others. Patrick McGowan, President of the New York City Board of Aldermen, was among those present at the banquet.

S. V. B. Swann, secretary of the Metropolitan Association of Retail Druggists and Manhattan Pharmaceutical Association, has been chosen manager of the New York Consolidated Drug Company at 188 First avenue to succeed Felix Hirseman, who has already tendered his resignation to take effect on May 1. In order to assume his duties as manager of the Consolidated Drug Company Mr. Swann will be compelled to resign his position as salesman for Eli Lilly & Co., of 203 Fulton street, as well as his association secretaryships.

Among the recent visitors to New York, most of whom registered at the New York Drug Club, were: J. W. Johnson, Manchester, N. H.; T. M. Hoover, Washington, D. C.; W. G. Todd, Secaucus, N. J.; E. B. Wilson, Newark, N. J.; E. G. Wilson, Menominee, Mich.; M. Fahere, St. Louis, Mo.; Edwin Isham, London, Eng.; George Devoll, London, Eng.; G. P. Finnigan, Greene, N. Y.; S. C. Irving, San Francisco, Cal.; George Rocke, London, Eng.; L. S. McPhail, London, Eng.; H. I. Hall, Boston; C. H. Morrill, St. Louis, Mo.; D. D. Kimball, Boston; M. Wightman, Hartford, Conn.; Jean Siebert, Hanover, Germany; M. Wendell, Chicago; L. Tollamsen, Frankfort-on-the-Main, Germany; O. E. Edwardy, Constantinople, Turkey; Frank L. Parker, Seattle, Wash.; J. L. Collins, Bayonne, N. J.; William B. Curtis, Tonopah, Nev.; F. W. Mihlhop, Chicago; J. L. Vandeveer, Philadelphia; Justin Keith, Chicago, M. F. Roberts, Philadelphia, and S. E. Locke, Hartford, Conn.

A joint meeting of the Eighth and Tenth District branches of the Metropolitan Association of Retail Druggists was held Friday afternoon, March 30, in Heinebund Hall, on Eighth avenue near Thirty-fourth street, for the purpose of promoting the organization of the M. A. R. D. and N. A. R. D. in all sections of Greater New York. The fact that two new organizers, in addition to Mr. Bohan, will soon arrive in this city to assist William De Shetley, manager of the Eastern territory of the N. A. R. D., was mentioned as one reason for the necessity of hastening the collection of the 1906 dues for the local and national associations. The expense of one of the new organizers is to be borne by the M. A. R. D., while the national organization will defray the expense of the other. Upon the arrival of the organizer destined to assume the duties of Mr. Bohan in the M. A. R. D. as well as in the N. A. R. D., Mr. Bohan will devote himself entirely to the affairs of the national association. W. B. Montgomery, chairman of the Eighth District, and William Weiss, chairman of the Tenth District, both of whom attended the joint meeting, urged that all members also assist the organization work of both associations in every way possible.

Fighting the Telephone Company.

Druggists in this city who have been fighting for the installation of telephone slot machines in their stores by the New York and New Jersey Telephone Company are greatly annoyed by the dilatory tactics of the company, which has postponed taking any action upon the subject indefinitely. U. N. Bethell, formerly general manager of the New York and New Jersey Telephone Company, who has recently been elected vice-president of that corporation, has referred the application framed by the Metropolitan Association of Retail Druggists to H. F. Thurber, the general superintendent, who has up to date done nothing to assist the cause of the druggists.

Representatives of the New York and New Jersey Telephone Company appeared recently before the Assembly committee in Albany in charge of the 5-cent telephone rate bill and opposed the passage of this measure most vigorously, asserting that they would never consent, if they could prevent it, to granting a 5-cent toll in the Borough of Manhattan, though they were willing to grant such a rate in the Borough of the Bronx. Whether the 5-cent toll bill passes or not, however, the druggists interested in the slot machine 'phones are determined to fight for them until the telephone company is compelled to grant their request.

The Phi Chi Banquet.

The annual banquet of the Gamma Chapter of the Phi Chi Fraternity was held at Reisenwebers' on Tuesday evening, March 27. Some forty-odd members were present, including several members of the faculty of the New York College of Pharmacy and alumni members of the fraternity. The plans for the after dinner speechmaking were somewhat disarranged by the lateness of the hour at which the dinner was served, and Prof. John Oehler and Professor Coblentz were compelled to cut short both their dinners and their speeches. In introducing Professor Oehler the toastmaster, Caswell A. Mayo, intimated that the professor would tell the members in confidence something about the examinations which they were to undergo in a week or so. Professor Oehler very cleverly followed this lead and talked about the examinations in a most tantalizing way, which gave the undergraduates no clew as to the particular troubles which were in store for them. Professor Coblentz made a few remarks in lighter vein on synthesis, with one eye on his watch, as he belongs to the colony of commuters. D. E. Driscoll, Worthy Chief Counsellor, formally welcomed the guests and members. Other speakers were F. N. Pond, '94, one of the charter members of the chapter; William P. Maher and Wallace Sabine, of the dinner committee; Richard L. Pierce, Clarence H. Eggleston, Charles K. Brown, F. Leslie Everson, of the undergraduate members; Henry D. Swain, '02; A. J. Bauer, '04, and W. C. Bradley.

A committee was appointed to take into consideration the method for providing for a chapter house.

William Brandreth Dead.

William Brandreth, for many years interested in the drug business and a prominent citizen of Ossining, N. Y., died of heart disease at his home in that city, March 18. Mr. Brandreth was a son of Dr. Benjamin B. Brandreth, the celebrated manufacturer of pills and plasters. He was born October 22, 1842, and became interested in the drug business at an early age. After traveling through the Western States, South America and the West Indies for several years, he entered the real estate and insurance business in 1868, but in 1878 abandoned this field and engaged in the sale of mines and mining properties.

Professor La Wall Is Promoted.

For the course of lectures in the Philadelphia College of Pharmacy beginning in October, 1906, Professor Remington has announced that, with the approval of the Board of Trustees, he has appointed Prof. Charles H. LaWall associate professor of theory and practice of pharmacy, who will lecture to the second year class for the next term and continue his duties as instructor and assistant to Professor Remington for the first year and third year lectures. The whole department of theory and practice of pharmacy remains in charge of Professor Remington, as heretofore. Professor LaWall receives an increase in salary for the additional work.

C. H. Davidson,

Manager of the Beef Extract Department of Armour & Co.

We present herewith a portrait of C. H. Davidson, successor to Robert Cabell as manager of the beef extract department for Armour & Co. Mr. Davidson has been for seven years connected with the Kansas City branch, in charge of the advertising and canned meat department. He says that he welcomes the change that brings him to Chicago, as it will give him an opportunity to show his ability, and that he will continue to furnish the world with the best beef extract on the market and the high standard of excellence will be maintained. He will be assisted in this department by J. A. Cass, for ten years Mr. Cabell's confidential man. Mr. Cabell will leave the employ of Armour & Co. and engage in business in New York, but when seen by a representative of the AMERICAN DRUGGIST he said he was not at that time ready to give out information, but the readers of the AMERICAN DRUGGIST would hear from him later.

Apollinaris Founder Dead.

The death is announced in England at Lyndhurst, Hayward's Heath, on February 28, of Edward Steinkopff, aged sixty-eight. Mr. Steinkopff was the founder of the great Apollinaris business, from which he retired in 1897. He was born in Frankfort, and in due course started on a commercial career which took him as a comparatively young man to Glasgow, where he joined a German house, and was afterward in business for himself as a merchant. The failure of the City of Glasgow Bank ruined him, as it did many more; but he faced his misfortunes boldly, and coming to London he, in 1874, with the support of George Smith (Smith, Elder & Co.), founded the Apollinaris business and took the chief charge of its affairs during the period of its development, with the assistance of Julius Prince, till it attained an unparalleled position, Apollinaris becoming the leading natural table water in the world. Mr. Steinkopff sold his share of the business in 1897 to the late Frederick Gordon for nearly ten million dollars, and since then Mr. Prince has been at the head of it. Mr. Steinkopff was for some time the owner of the *St. James' Gazette*. In 1897 he purchased the charming estate of Lyndhurst, in Sussex, and enjoyed his retirement there, with occasional brief periods of residence at his beautiful London house in Berkeley Square, which was at one time the residence of Prime Minister Pitt. Mrs. Steinkopff died a few months ago. Their only child is the wife of Colonel Stewart Mackenzie, of Seaforth, brother of the Marchioness of Tweeddale.

WESTERN NEW YORK.

A Dull Month for Retailers—All Stores Registered or Accounted for—State Association Meets at Niagara Falls in Last Week in June—Buffalo Bowls Out Rochester.

(From our Regular Correspondent.)

Buffalo, April 5.—"March was a 'dub' month in the retail trade," assented the most sanguine member of the Buffalo trade. "I hear that the wholesalers are reporting the usual activity or more, but it did not come to us. Somehow it seems that good trade with them does not always mean anything to us. Either their cheerful moons do not rise with ours or the good wholesale trade does not correspond with the same thing down the line."

THE WESTERN BRANCH OF THE STATE BOARD OF PHARMACY has finished its registry of stores, turning a very few names over to the authorities for action, and now, or at least after the April examination on the 18th, there will be a resumption of the store-to-store inspection. It is found that there are not stores enough in the section to keep an inspector busy all the time, so it is arranged to "borrow" one or two as needed from the other sections. A more or less continual round is needed, though, in order to keep the whole list in line.

DATE FIXED FOR STATE MEETING.

There was a meeting on the 3d between President Lockie, of the State Pharmaceutical Association, and President Laurier, of the Niagara Falls Association, at the former's store in Buffalo, at which the date of the annual convention of the State Association was definitely fixed for the last week in June, beginning on the 26th and lasting four days. It was expected that that time would be taken, but there was nothing official about it till now. The headquarters and local committees will be settled upon as soon as possible. A great meeting is assured, for there is business to do and the list of entertainments will be long and attractive.

ROCHESTER ROUTED.

The return game between the Buffalo and Rochester druggists' bowling clubs was played in Rochester on March 29 and resulted in the complete rout of the Rochester men. In fact they seemed to be quite "off" on that day, as a team from Syracuse took part in the closing game and also outplayed Rochester. Buffalo sent down 17 men, from which players in the afternoon and evening games were selected. They were most royally received by the Rochester druggists and every attention was shown them that could be given an honored guest. The banquet in the evening was a very pleasant affair, showing that Rochester can entertain at all times, even when not at her best as a bowler. The best of feeling prevailed throughout the meeting, and the annual visits will be kept up.

MORE OPTIONS FOR THE OCTOPUS.

The retail druggists of Buffalo are much exercised over the report that the Cahoon-Lyon Drug Company has obtained options on two more retail drug stores in the city, one on the East Side and one on the West Side. After absorbing the store of Dr. Gregory, which is located in the center of the business district, this is looked on as an attempt to control the business in the city, just as the company under other names is doing in certain Eastern cities. The effect is of course to depress the feelings of the city retailers generally. They speak of the company as composed of fine people, but they are sharp competitors.

BUFFALO NEWS NOTES.

Dr. Henry S. Ellwood, one of the oldest druggists in Buffalo, died March 22, at the age of 68. He was born in London, Canada, and graduated in 1868 from the Medical College in Buffalo, where he located and remained for the succeeding 38 years of his life. Besides conducting his drug store he had a large medical practice. He leaves a widow and a son, Dr. Grant T. Ellwood.

Druggist Horace P. Hayes, of Buffalo, is letting others look after his two drug stores and is spending a great part of his time in the Isle of Pines, as he is president of a land and development company there that is showing great activity at present.

The abolition of the age qualification for graduation and the establishment of a course in analytical chemistry has been pretty definitely settled upon by the Buffalo College of Pharmacy, only the Council of the University of Buffalo having to pass upon it now.

J. A. Lockie, the popular druggist of upper Main street, Buffalo, and president of the State Pharmaceutical Association, is putting in a new $2,300 soda fountain. When it is in position it will be taking no second place in the city or the country for appearance or the goods it turns out. And the proprietor knows how to get the crowd, too.

W. W. Hayden, lately of the Buffalo drug firm of Hayden & Twohey, has taken the drug store building in the new block at Main and Utica streets, Buffalo, and will soon be ready for business.

H. E. Smith, of Scranton, who represents in the Buffalo territory the Philadelphia drug house of Smith, Kline & French Company, covered the houses in his line lately and went his way rejoicing.

The two new drug stores facing each other at the corner of Delaware avenue and Chippewa street, Buffalo, are in operation. That of H. M. Wise adds drugs to a restaurant and employs Michael Harris as pharmacist. That of C. E. Clark is run by the proprietor, who left Samuel Rudin as pharmacist in charge in his Clinton street store.

CANADIAN NEWS.

Department Stores Oppose Registration Bill—Proprietors Protest Against Formula Measure—Commercial Travelers' Tax Modified.

(From our Regular Correspondent.)

Toronto, Canada, April 4.—The bill introduced into the Ontario Legislature by James Downey requiring every director of a corporation engaged in the sale of drugs to be a qualified pharmacist has passed a second reading and was considered by a special committee on the 29th of March. It was strongly opposed by representatives of the Eaton & Simpson department stores. F. S. Mearns, representing the Ontario College of Pharmacy, urged that the measure was necessary for the preservation of the retail trade. Dr. J. H. Preston said that 6,000 druggists were supporting the bill. The bill was unanimously reported by the committee and is altogether likely to pass.

PROTESTING AGAINST FORMULA BILL.

At Ottawa on the 22d of March a large deputation representing manufacturers and agents of patent medicines interviewed Hon. W. Templeman, protesting against proposed legislation to compel them to print the formulæ of their goods as an unjust interference with their rights as manufacturers. The deputation was headed by Henry Miles, of Montreal.

THE TAX ON COMMERCIAL TRAVELERS MODIFIED.

The tax on commercial travelers for firms outside of Canada has recently been modified. The law as it now stands provides for a semiannual license on nonresident travelers for firms having no place of business in Canada, on which the fee is as follows: For those dealing with the wholesale trade only, $50; dealing with retail trade, $100; dealing with consumer, $200.

CANADIAN NEWS ITEMS.

Charles H. Green, of Toronto, traveler for Henry K. Wampole & Co., of Perth, Ont., fell 14 feet over a staircase at the Tecumseh House, London, Ont., on March 28, as the result of a fainting fit, and died of his injuries the following day. He was 43 years of age and well known in trade circles. He leaves a wife and family.

G. S. Borrowman, druggist of Leamington, Ont., has removed to Guelph.

The business of G. E. Learmontie, High River, Alberta, is offered for sale.

P. H. Coad, druggist of Lindsay, Ont., has disposed of his business to L. A. Murphy.

Ezra Haist, druggist of Crediton, Ont., has sold out his business.

NEW ENGLAND.

A Clash on Prices—Big Cutters Cut Off—Suits Threatened—Plans for the State Meeting—Wildest Demonstration for Boston Druggists—Tinkering with the License Bill—Patent Medicine Bills All Postponed—Proposed Change in Screen Law.

(*From our Regular Correspondent.*)

Boston, April 3.—Four firms of this city, namely, William B. Hunt & Co., Houghton & Dutton, Lewis & Co., and the Jaynes companies, have refused to sell goods at the schedule set and sent out on the 23rd of last month by the B. A. R. D. In consequence of the rejection of this list these firms have been blacklisted by the N. A. R. D., and wholesalers have been notified not to sell them the serial numbered and direct contract goods. This move precipitates what promises to be a great cut rate war. The local work for the N. A. R. D. is in good hands, being looked after personally by Agent J. F. Keiser. One of the above firms in a published interview stated that if annoyed by the N. A. R. D. they would enlist the Federal laws against the association. An endeavor is being made in this newspaper campaign to give the impression that these four firms are selling goods at very much lower prices than those demanded by B. A. R. D. members.

THE MASSACHUSETTS STATE MEETING.

President McCormick has announced that the annual M. S. P. A. meeting will be held at the New Magnolia, Magnolia, Mass., June 19, 20 and 21. His committees are now at work endeavoring to make this a record breaking meeting. A large attendance is anticipated.

THE MONTHLY MEETING OF THE B. D. A.

The March meeting of the Boston Druggists' Association was held at Young's Hotel, on the evening of March 27. At the business meeting the subject of retaining connection with the Boston Associated Board of Trade was discussed at length. The matter was finally left to the April meeting for settlement. After dinner the members were entertained by an insight into the mysteries of wireless telegraphy. The subject was explained by Prof. John Stone and illustrated by appropriate apparatus. President Bartlet is considering some entertainment novelties for the delectation of the members at the meeting of April 24.

LICENSE LEGISLATION ADVANCED.

In the House last Friday the bill relative to the sale of intoxicating liquors by registered pharmacists was discussed. An attempt was made to so amend the bill that certificates of fitness could not be revoked or suspended by the Board of Pharmacy unless "for cause." The amendment was defeated, as it was argued that it would not give the licensing board the power to control the business. An attempt was then made to amend the bill so that the licensing authority could suspend certificates of fitness at pleasure. This likewise met defeat. It was then argued, by those in charge of the bill, that the House evidently was opposed to vesting the revocation powers in the Board of Pharmacy and that it would be better to kill the bill, but this idea did not prevail, as it was advanced to the engrossment stage.

PATENT MEDICINES.

All patent medicine bills relating either to labels for poison or alcohol or to cocaine have been referred to another executive session.

The Public Health Committee has voted to repeal two unnecessary sections of the revised laws, leaving the penalty for the sale of adulterated drugs at not less than $100 nor more than $500. The same committee voted "leave to withdraw" upon the bill relating to publishing bulletins by the State Board of Health.

The Committee on Liquor Law has just reported a bill relating to screens in hotels and drug stores, which if adopted should be satisfactory to the drug trade. It simply prohibits obstructing the view of a room or premises in which liquor is sold over a public bar.

THE WEST.

Druggists the Victors in License Fight—Miscellaneous Sales o Liquor by Druggists Condemned—Booming the Drug Club.

(*From our Regular Correspondent.*)

Chicago, April 4.—The battle over the $250 license has resulted in a victory for druggists. The plan to compel the owners of retail drug stores to pay a license fee of $250 for the privilege of dispensing liquors has been killed in one of the council committees after a hard fight, and the retailers are therefore happy over their escape from this attack, especially as their case seemed desperate for a long time. The saloon element was angry over the passage of the ordinance demanding a $1,000 fee of saloons and determined to even up matters by hitting back at the druggists. The saloon men had the upper hand for a long time and the druggists were not even able to get the committeemen to listen to them, but steady, organized effort had its effect, the committee listened and at last decided to kill the measure. There will, however, be more rigid supervision of druggists' records in the future. This supervising should be done by the police, but the officers often neglect it. It would, of course, please the trade to have the books carefully watched and to have every other possible precaution taken to prevent illicit sales of liquor. It can truthfully be said that there are only a few who really need to be watched, and to have these few compelled to walk straight would suit the others perfectly. It was the druggists themselves who called the attention of the chief of police to the fact that his officers have been remiss in this part of their duty. In pursuance of this policy the C. R. D. A. executive board has passed the following resolution:

Resolved, That it is the sense of this board that members of this association discontinue selling such malt preparations as are sold or dispensed in saloons.

OPPOSED TO MISCELLANEOUS SALE OF LIQUORS.

There has been a great deal of feeling in regard to such sales in drug stores. It was this feeling, in fact, that came near causing the high license to be passed. The C. R. D. A. officials have announced that they trust that retail druggists will heed the advice of the resolution, as they believe the best interests of the trade will be thus conserved.

A new peril has just come to the notice of the trade. This danger is in the shape of an ordinance restricting sales of liquor to prescriptions only. This is, of course, being fought. The matter is to be settled by the new council after election, and there is no telling at present what the result may be.

AN ICE CREAM LICENSE PROPOSED.

Another ordinance against which a fight is being waged by druggists is that demanding a fee of $25 for a license from every fruit store, ice cream parlor or other place where ice cream is sold. This ordinance has been recommended for passage, but has not yet been acted upon by the council. The interest which the druggists are taking in local politics just now can easily be understood.

TO BUILD UP THE DRUG CLUB.

A brochure that has been sent to members of the Drug Trade Club by President L. A. Becker contains his ideas in regard to what should be done to advance the interests of the organization. Among the statements made by him are the following:

How can we hope to occupy quarters in a future building, known as the Drug Trade Building, unless we strive through united action at the present time to build up our membership and increase the daily attendance in a marked degree? The quarters occupied by our institution are central, convenient, comfortable and cheerful, and based on the nominal dues, are all that members can rightfully expect. Our menu is large and the food excellent, the prices reasonable and the service fairly good. In all of these latter conditions our club equals or excels the New York institution, where the prices are fully 20 per cent. higher, the food barely as good and the service no better.

Our lease in the present quarters extends to August next. Arrangements are in process for the renewal of the present lease for at least a period of one year further. Messrs. Eitel Bros., the proprietors of the Bismarck, propose extensive alterations and additions to their entire premises. These changes will afford the club an opportunity for securing approximately a 75-foot rear addition to the present quarters, and with this addition your officers are afforded the opportunity of making desirable changes of value and benefit to all members. Let it be understood, however, that a larger daily attendance is required in order that the club can support larger quarters.

It is needless to state that unless we grow (and we should easily double our membership this coming year) that we cannot hope to occupy larger and more expensive quarters, to say nothing of occupying in the future our own quarters in a Drug Trade Building, which has been the ambition and hope of many of the members since the inception of the institution.

Let the Chicago spirit, "I will," assert itself in each individual member of this club—let each member pledge himself to secure at least two new members, and the Chicago Drug Trade Club will be what it is deserving of and what rightfully belongs to it—a power to the city of Chicago and throughout the United States, and a credit to each member of the institution.

I have a plan in mind that is logical and practical, involving the future welfare of this institution, especially pertaining to the occupancy of larger quarters and the financial considerations necessary thereto. When presented it will be deserving of your consideration and will require your co-operation. I do not present it now because the first consideration at present is your co-operation for the increase of the membership necessary.

NOTES.

The Social Drug Club's "Evening in Bohemia" was well attended and proved to be a highly enjoyable affair.

The syndicate system does not seem to work well in Chicago if an insolvency petition filed by Healy & Renner, who operated five stores in Chicago, is any evidence.

The Chicago branch of the A. Ph. A. had a successful meeting in the Northwestern University building in the latter part of last month. Plans for checking the assaults of "yellow journalism" occupied much of the members' attention.

E. H. Nichols, formerly a druggist at Lexington avenue and Fifty-fifth street, died recently, in a hospital, of pneumonia. Mr. Nichols' store had been sold to his devoted wife and he had many troubles during his last months.

Chicago druggists are anxious to know the identity of a man who signs himself "Wangermann." He has a letter in the daily press every few days on some pharmaceutical topic. His name does not appear among the R. P.'s of Illinois.

Some of the local druggists, while they give Mr. Voegeli full credit for coming out into the open in regard to the National cigar stands and United Drug Company, are still somewhat skeptical as to whether Liggett's plans and N. A. R. D. doctrines can live under one and the same roof.

J. R. Kathrens, former manager of the advertising department of the Pabst Brewing Company, Milwaukee, has severed his connection with the firm, and is now associated with the J. Walter Thompson Company, advertising agents, with headquarters in Chicago.

Some of the ardent supporters of the Mann bill say they are greatly disapointed in the explanation of that measure which appeared in the issue of N. A. R. D. Notes for March 29. These men say they fail to see why the desired changes are not made so as to get the bill through Congress.

Among those who were recently heard in the course of lectures on business topics at the Chicago College of Pharmacy were I. Giles Lewis, of Robert Stevenson & Co., who spoke on "Olive Oil," and F. H. Hertle, whose subject was "Druggist's Printing, Labels and Boxes."

The telephone situation in Chicago has been attracting a great deal of attention of late. The Illinois Manufacturers' Association, which is fighting the Chicago Telephone Company, is making an effort to obtain an independent franchise for operating 'phones. It is promised that the service will be at the rate of 2 or 3 cents instead of the present 5-cent rate. Whatever happens, the promised competition can hardly harm the druggists.

Edward Long, manager of the sales department for W. J. Bush & Co., of New York, was in Chicago recently for a week for a conference with the Chicago branch. Mr. Long was the first manager of this branch when it was opened by the house of Bush & Co., seven years ago, and he reports the same in a flourishing condition, showing an increase over previous years of over 50 per cent. Mr. Long made such a record in the West that he was transferred to the New York office, a position which was a couple of rounds up the ladder.

It appears that the single-line druggist is getting wise after the manner of the generation of grocers and department store people. These large dealers have a pleasant way of advertising in the city papers how low they are selling this or that well-known drug specialty and then quoting prices that everybody charges. It creates a diversion in favor of the advertiser for all that and it hurts the non-advertiser, so he is learning to try the plan too. This is really a proof that the agreement is holding.

THE SOUTH.

Southern Wholesalers Meet—Ready for State Meeting—Business Prospers.

(From our Regular Correspondent.)

New Orleans, La., April 2.—The annual convention of the Southern Wholesale Druggists' Association will take place in New Orleans April 17, 18 and 19, simultaneously with the convention of the Louisiana State Pharmaceutical Association, and it is indicated that there will be considerable going on in the drug line in this particular corner of the globe. Probably 50 or 60 members of the association will attend the convention, and according to the programme a great many important matters will be handled. Local members of the association have begun laying plans for properly receiving and entertaining the delegates who will represent St. Louis, Louisville, Indianapolis, Memphis, Pine Bluff, Fort Smith, Little Rock, Atlanta, Montgomery, Mobile, Houston, Galveston, Forth Worth, San Antonio, Waco and other cities. The last convention of the association was held in Memphis last year. The present officers of the association are E. D. Phillips, of Berry Demoville & Co., of Nashville, president; A. M. Reed, Lamar-Rankin Drug Company, of Atlanta, vice-president; F. A. Dicks, of Finlay, Dicks & Co., New Orleans, secretary and treasurer, and Charles S. Martin, of Nashville, chairman of the Advisory Board.

The convention will be held in the Banquet Hall of the St. Charles Hotel.

READY FOR THE STATE MEETING.

Practically all preliminaries for the convention of the Louisiana State Pharmaceutical Association, which will be held here April 17, 18 and 19 have been arranged and all will be in readiness for the opening at Odd Fellows' Hall on the morning of the 17th. A large number of delegates from all parts of the State and a good many visitors are looked for. The programme has not yet been completed, but it is understood that Mayor Behrman will deliver the address of welcome and will be followed by the Rev. Dr. Beverley Warner, the eloquent rector of Trinity Church.

As is usually the case the morning hours will be devoted to business, such as the hearing of the president's annual address, the reading of reports, etc., and the transacting of any business brought before the convention. It is being held this year in April, having been advanced from May, because of the fact that the General Assembly of the State is assembling in May. It was regarded as probable that the convention would have some legislation to recommend, but the present outlook is that the pharmacy laws will be allowed to stand just as they are and that no recommendations will be made by the association.

The business of the meeting will of course be interspersed with entertaining and amusing features, and everything possible will be done to insure the visitors a pleasant three days' visit. In this respect the wholesale houses are contributing largely and several of these will entertain at luncheon, etc.

The election of officers on the morning of the 19th will close the convention in the regular manner.

Trade here continues good and there is at present no indications of a let-up or depression. All of the houses are finding business in good shape and no one is complaining.

Louisiana Licentiates.

Following are the announced results of the examination conducted February 2 and 3 at New Orleans by the Board of Pharmacy of the State of Louisiana:

Registered Pharmacists—H. G. Legarde, Thibodaux; M. B. Lemaire, New Iberia; E. L. King, Henry Welsche, P. D. O'Donnell, W. J. Gagnet, Walter Poynot, New Orleans; W. H. Wellman, Shreveport.

Qualified Assistants—C. A. Desport, jr., E. B. Scott, J. C. Richards, H. J. Naquin, New Orleans; J. J. Dubourg, Union Post Office; R. H. Chargrain, Lafayette; A. J. Laiche, Lutcher.

Two failed to complete their applications to show the experience required by law and seven failed in the examinations, there having been 24 applicants. The members of the board that conducted the examination were F. C. Godhold, William M. Levy, Adam Wirth and C. D. Sauvinet. The next examination will be held at New Orleans on May 4.

Suggestions for Papers.

The Pennsylvania Pharmaceutical Association succeeds in getting members to present numerous and excellent papers at the annual meetings. One of the methods by which the Committee on Papers get so many papers is to formulate a number of questions and send them to each of the 950 members of the association. The questions for this year's meeting, which takes place at Glen Summit Springs, June 26, 27 and 28, are given below, in the hope that they may prove suggestive for the members of other State Associations:

1. Many pharmacists buy concentrated nitrous ether with which to make spirit of nitrous ether, instead of making it by the U. S. P. process. Does the spirit thus prepared usually meet the pharmacopœial requirements for strength? What special precautions must be taken to insure getting a full strength spirit?
2. Wanted: A formula for headache powders which will not add to the already long list of those who "died after taking."
3. Wanted: A formula for the preparation of a solution of sulphurous acid extemporaneously; one which does not require distillation.
4. Is the liquor chlori compositus of the new Pharmacopœia a satisfactory substitute for the aqua chlori of the preceding edition? Does it contain the required amount of free chlorine?
5. In making liquor chlori compositus by the U. S. P. VIII process are any oxides of chlorine produced? If so, how may the operation be conducted so as to insure the maximum amount of chlorine and the minimum amount of oxides of chlorine?
6. Is it not the duty as well as the interest of the pharmacist to bring to the attention of physicians U. S. P. preparations of definite formula, such as cataplasma, kaolini for antiphlogistine and liquor cresolis compositus for lysol?
7. Does the modern pharmacy represent real pharmacy as fully as the apothecary shop of a half century ago?
8. Have pharmacists who prepare their own perfumery found the business satisfactory and profitable?
9. It is admitted that great changes have occurred in the practice of both pharmacy and medicine; is the condition not largely due to the spirit of commercialism?
10. In the conduct of a successful pharmacy, does not the personal equation of the pharmacist count for more than any other influence?
11. Is not the pharmaceutical manufacturer the real exponent of scientific progress in medicine?
12. What are the merits and demerits of the Mann bill?
13. Is a law possible which will require the coroner to issue death certificates in the cases where physicians have dispensed their own medicines?
14. How does the free distribution of antitoxin by the State Board of Health affect the druggist?
15. Solid meat extracts range in price from $2 to $4.50 per dozen two-ounce jars. Is the cost an index of nutritive value?
16. What are the advantages of calcium dioxide as a dentifrice?
17. What is the real source of the various floral oils (so called) as sold on the market for the manufacture of perfumery?
18. Does the work of collecting vital statistics as carried on by pharmacists in various parts of the State, under the direction of the State Board of Health, interfere with their other work to any great extent, or is it an advantage to them?
19. The U. S. P. VIII has admitted formulas for a number of preparations which are imitations of well-known proprietary preparations. Is this policy conducive to the best interests of pharmacy, and is it strictly in harmony with the ethics of the profession?
20. Does the question of ethics influence the business policy of many pharmacists?
21. Is it proper to refuse to sell on Sunday such patent medicines as are strongly alcoholic and which are often professedly purchased for the alcohol which they contain?
22. If it is wrong to sell alcoholic patent medicines on Sunday, is it any more justifiable to sell them on week days?
23. Has not the pharmacist of the past few decades sold his birthright for a mess of pottage in joining hands with the manufacturers of proprietaries in helping them to further their interests at the ultimate expense of his own?
24. Should the pharmacists not welcome the attitude of certain lay journals toward patent medicines, as affording them an opportunity to free themselves from the shackles which have bound them for so long?
25. Is it true that the U. S. P. VIII is more of a manufacturer's handbook than a pharmacist's guide?
26. Do the physicians in your neighborhood keep up with the changes in strength in official preparations?
27. Do the physicians in your neighborhood use the new official nomenclature for synthetics?
28. Wanted: Window display ideas which are out of the ordinary.
29. What new or unusual incompatibilities have you noticed during the past year?
30. Is the popular use of headache powders increasing or decreasing?
31. What formula can be suggested for a perfumed liquid toilet soap, suitable for use on the most delicate skin?
32. Give the formula for a satisfactory tooth paste which can be easily made on a small scale.
33. How may collapsible tubes be filled with thick or jelly-like preparations?
34. Is the Basham's mixture of the U. S. P. VIII as permanent a preparation as that of the 1890 edition?
35. What method can be suggested for the popularisation of the metric system among the laity?
36. What is the best Druggist's Library?
37. How can the State Association be made most useful to the retail druggist, and how can the latter be persuaded to give it his support?
38. How can the physician be made acquainted with the U. S. P. and N. F. preparations?
39. What is the best method of filing prescriptions, for permanence, convenience of filing and reference, and keeping the prescriptions clean?
40. What is the value of a set of A. Ph. A. Proceedings to an average retail druggist?
41. What are some preventable sources of waste and loss in the drug store?
42. What is the most effective method of advertising for the retail druggist?
43. Can a powdered extract of sumbul be made that will be of the same therapeutic value as the solid extracts?
44. Elixir of calisaya is much used by physicians and pharmacists. Should it not have been made official?
45. Are show windows an advantage in suburban sections?
46. Is the compound tincture of cardamon, U. S. P. VIII, as satisfactory as that of the 1890 edition?
47. Is the use of purified talcum in the making of medicinal waters as satisfactory as other substances which have been used for this purpose?
48. Is the eighth revision tincture of strophanthus as satisfactory as the 1890 preparation?
49. What cause can be ascribed for the success of various combinations of digestive principles in proprietary preparations?
50. Are the vegetable digestive ferments displacing the enzymes of animal origin? If so, why?

Co-operative Fire Insurance for Druggists.

For the purpose of securing for retail druggists in all sections of the country a much lower rate of fire, tornado and explosion insurance than that now offered by regular insurance companies several prominent retail drug interests have formed and incorporated the American Druggists' Fire Insurance Company, in Columbus, Ohio. While the headquarters of this new insurance concern will be in Cincinnati the business of the corporation will be transacted in every State. As there are about 42,000 retail druggists in the country it now appears that the success of the company is assured. It is expected that the concern will begin active operations within the next two or three months.

The incorporators are C. H. Avery, Chicago; G. B. Kaufman, Columbus, Ohio; L. C. Hopp, Cleveland; Prof. J. H. Beal, Scio; E. B. Tainter, Carrel, Iowa; Samuel C. Davis, Nashville, Tenn.; M. A. Burkhardt, Dayton, Ohio; I. M. Helms, Indianapolis; T. B. Huston, Toledo; Walter Rothwell, Hatboro, Pa.; T. B. Cartwell, Wilmington, Del.; Edward Voss, Jr., A. O. Zwick, Frank H. Freericks, Cincinnati, and L. G. Heinritz, Holyoke, Mass.

The new organization will cover the same field for the entire country that the Ohio Mutual Druggists' Fire Association does for Ohio. The American Druggists' Fire Insurance Company, however, will be a stock company, while the Ohio organization is a mutual concern. A meeting of the incorporators of the American Company will be held in Cincinnati within the near future to complete the organization and elect officers. J. H. Beal, of Scio, one of the incorporators, is professor of pharmacy at Scio University and is an ex-president of the American Pharmaceutical Association in the Pittsburgh College of Pharmacy and is well known by his writings, while Charles H. Avery, of Chicago, is president of the Chicago Retail Druggists' Association and vice-president of the National Association of Retail Druggists.

Though the new concern is a stock company it is intended as nearly as possible to afford the advantages of a mutual company without any of its disadvantages, and the incorporators intend to accomplish this result by placing the stock with retail druggists, thereby giving them an opportunity to obtain a much lower rate of insurance and also to share in the actual profits of the company. The par value of the shares of stock has been fixed at $25, so that they may be within the reach of all retailers, but an advance of $1 per share will be asked to cover the initiatory expense of organization and license fees.

As the formation of the company was an outgrowth of a movement started at the last convention of the National Association of Retail Druggists, which was held in Boston, the stock will first be offered to those who manifested an interest in the undertaking in writing at this convention. The next offering of stock will be made to those who attended the convention of the N. A. R. D. and the A. Ph. A. and then stock will be offered to all retail druggists throughout the country.

The company will write policies only on retail drug stores and will limit its individual risks so that they will not exceed $5,000 each. It is asserted by the incorporators that stockholders will probably receive a dividend of from 15 to 20 per cent. annually on their stock investment after the first year, so that the value of the stock will soon be much greater than the price originally paid. At first a premium reduction of 25 per cent. is contemplated, so that a dealer who is now insuring his property at the rate of $10 per $1,000 will have a reduction to $7.50 per $1,000.

Opportunities *for* Export Trade

(Written for the American Druggist.)

A JOURNEY THROUGH SOUTHERN PERU.

By John M. Draper.

When leaving Lima, Peru, to travel southward the traveler learns that the red tape and expense is much greater than when entering the city. All the bother and expense is entailed because the bubonic plague still lingers along the coast, and the rules of the sanitary boards require a close inspection of all outgoing baggage and the disinfection of all baggage, personal or otherwise, should the medical examiner deem such a course necessary. This year the authorities are not so exacting as they were on former occasions, and I had to spend only half a day going from the hotel to the disinfection station, await there the judgment of the medico, and then, aided by lazy truck drivers, finally get to the "Muelle" for embarking. Here is where trouble almost invariably arises, for the police guard every gateway to see that no piece of baggage is passed to the steamers unless it bears the label of the sanitary department and the stamp of the doctor. The "fletero" who had charge of my dozen or more trunks and grips had neglected in the hurry to see that all were marked, and the inspector found one small grip without a label. Instantly all became confusion and profanity, with the result that I was compelled to send this one

The Volcano at Arequipa; Elevation of 19,200 Feet.

piece back to the station and get a label placed upon it. The disinfection station was three miles away, but I had to obey, and two hours later got into a small boat with all my traps and was rowed out to the steamer.

MOLLENDO, THE GATEWAY TO SOUTHERN PERU.

Leaving Callao, which is the seaport of Lima, we sailed southward for two days before disembarking at Mollendo, the gateway for all the southern part of the republic. Mollendo is known from one end of the coast to the other as being one of the most difficult ports to land in. It possesses no harbor whatever, and landing is always attended with considerable danger. This disagreeable impression is not greatly changed when one finally does land, for the city is a miserable little place, made up principally of commission firms and agents of the customs. It possesses one small drug store, whose owner does most of his buying in Lima.

CLIMBING THE ANDES.

Leaving Mollendo next morning at half past eight, our journey to Arequipa began. This city lies inland 107 miles and is some 7,500 feet above the sea level. The day was spent climbing the Andes till late in the afternoon, when, coming over a range of mountains, we saw the first green spot during our whole trip. This was the little valley of Arequipa, where the waters of two small rivers irrigate a narrow stretch of land about ten miles long by three wide. Outside of this little oasis all was barren soil because of the lack of rain for the past three years.

THE ENTERPRISING DRUGGISTS OF AREQUIPA.

Arequipa, a city of some 20,000 people, has several drug stores, three of which do both a retail and a wholesale business, supplying the smaller places in the interior. The Botica del Pueblo of Jose F. Portugal is the largest pharmacy and has the

Mountains Between Sicuani and Cusco.

largest trade in Southern Peru. The pharmacists of Arequipa buy the major portion of the stock from Europe, but each year more and more is being purchased from the United States, and they are keenly alive and progressive. The son and namesake of Senor Portugal is now studying at the Philadelphia College of Pharmacy and has become thoroughly imbued with American ideas which he will carry back with him to Arequipa.

The Botica Cosmos of Sres. Castillo & Vinelli is one of those small corner drug stores whose large business cannot be represented in any way by the size of their store. Being young and energetic, Senor Vinelli has built up a good business in and around Arequipa. They desire good American agencies, and will take much interest in pushing such goods.

The Botica Central, conducted by Senor Moron y Hijo, is a drug store established over fifty years ago and conducted on

Breakfast on the Road to Cusco.

conservative principles. The store has a good financial standing and buys largely in the United States.

Valdivia Hnos. and Senor G. Bindernagel both own small drug stores in the city.

CONGESTION OF FREIGHT AT PANAMÁ.

At present, owing to the congested conditions of the Panama Railroad, all druggists recommend the shipping of their goods via the Straits of Magellan, as that route at present is both cheaper and quicker. American shippers must not forget that

Lake Titicaca, the Highest Navigable Body of Water in the World.

both the net and the gross weights must be marked on all cases. They should also remember that as advertising matter calendars and almanacs are the most popular things down here and are highly appreciated.

"SAMPLING THE DOCTORS."

In sending samples of preparations to the physicians it is always better and safer to address each package with the doctor's name and then inclose all in one case and consign it to one of the druggists in Arequipa. They will forward to the shipper a receipt from each doctor who has received a package; thus the shippers will know for certain who has and who has not received their goods. The expense of this method is not large, and the druggist is glad to assist in the building up of such sales as follow this propaganda.

ACROSS THE ROOF OF THE WORLD.

More important even than Arequipa in the extent of territory it supplies is the city of Cuzco, Peru. Leaving Arequipa by

Market Scene in Plaza, Cusco.

train on a Tuesday morning at 7 o'clock, we spend the day climbing to the very summit of the western chain of the Andes, 14,660 feet above sea level, and then descending to the 12,500-foot level we arrived at a small station to spend the night. Next morning from this little station we took a branch line running along the plateau of the Andes northward to a small Indian town called Sicuani, the whole day being consumed in reaching this little place at the end of the railway. Finding the hotel, I was told that the stage leaving next morning was entirely filled and that I must therefore wait five days for the next regular stage. Of course this is impossible. How much does a special stage cost? Eighty Bolivianos ($38.00). We decide at once to go by the special, and at eight the next morning my baggage was aboard the stage, the mule drivers were in place and I began my two days' race to Cusco, the ancient capital of the Incas, the most historic city in all South America, which I reached on the afternoon of the second day.

From a business point of view it would be useless to write of the beautiful scenery met with en route. No valley I have ever visited equals in charm the valley of the Incas. The abundance of rain gives these Indians a country that it would be difficult to find the equal of in the United States. Grain grows in every nook and cranny of the valley, barley and corn being the principal products. Potatoes, peas, tomatoes, etc., are also grown. No dirtier race exists than the Indians, who till the soil and cultivate their small farms up to the very top of the mountains. From the small children to the oldest Indian, they all chew the coca leaves from which we make cocaine, and we see them, as the train stops at some small station, gathered about a tiny market, trading a handful of coca leaves for some other commodity, while the receiver of the leaves invariably chucks the whole lot into his mouth. None escape its influence,

Llamas Used in Carrying Freight Between Cusco and the Southern Railroad.

for among the older Indians we find the majority helpless cripples, twisting and shaking like the genuine cocaine fiend of our own Tenderloin. Perhaps the very high altitude demands some stimulant, for the plateau is 12,000 feet above the sea, and work such as plowing, etc., is done in the most primitive manner.

THE CAPITAL OF THE INCAS.

Cuzco, Peru, has a population of 15,000, mostly Indians, and was a city of several times that size some three centuries ago, being then the capital of the Incas, whose works, such as fortresses, excavations, etc., still stand as monuments to their wonderful skill. To-day this place depends for its large business upon the eastern slope of the Andes, where we find the richest part of the whole republic. The population supplied from this city of Cuzco numbers 250,000. The drug stores do not supply this vast area alone, because many of the large general mer-

Thatched Roofs of Cusco, with Cathedral in the Background.

chants carry supplies of drugs and patent medicines, and though I only make note in this paper of four drug stores in the city at least four other depots for drugs and medicines may be counted. In fact, it is a very good plan to sell specialties to some house, such as a large importer who distributes to the drug stores and stands upon neutral ground.

The drug stores of Cuzco are: M. Tello y Valderrama, Botica Italiana; Andreas C. Velazco, Drogueria del Pueblo; Vargas Hnos., Botica del Progreso, and Manuel Domingo Pegasa, Botica de los Andes.

The first two are the leading stores and worthy of good credit. Sres. Ces Lomellini & Cia. and Sres. Antonio Calvo y Cia. are general merchants of high standing who purchase drugs and specialties.

ADVICE TO EXPORTERS.

How to Extend and Hold United States Trade.

Consul Gaulin, of Havre, furnishes to the Department of Commerce and Labor a very interesting and instructive article on how to secure and extend American trade, which is published in *Daily Consular and Trade Reports*, for January 15. He deprecates the useless and obsolete methods generally adopted by American exporters, especially as to their manner of soliciting trade in non-English speaking countries. His advice, if closely followed, would no doubt add greatly to the sales of American products abroad. He says:

The consulate at this port receives in the course of each year a great number of letters from houses in the United States desirous of finding in France a market for their goods. It may be taken for granted that the firms in question, especially if they are important ones, give in their own country the greatest possible attention and make the most systematic efforts to secure business. It is probable that they have a number of salesmen constantly traveling and soliciting orders and that these salesmen are provided with a full line of samples, when it is possible for them to carry samples, of the article or articles in which they deal. Yet these same firms, in spite of the fact that they know competition the world over to be keen, and in spite of their experience and knowledge of the difficulty in getting orders, expect to sell goods in Europe with very little effort, relying, as a rule, upon a list of names of possible purchasers sent to them, at their request, by the American consul. To the persons whose names are thus furnished the American merchant or manufacturer sends catalogues printed in English (a language which comparatively few Frenchmen can read), with measurements in feet and inches, weights in pounds, capacities in gallons, and prices in dollars and cents, all of which are as unintelligible to the average Frenchman as shakus, bongkals, almudes, sols, yens, and rubles would be to an American. Indeed if an American merchant were offered by a firm in Canton 10,000 piculs of rice at so many Haikwan taels a picul, with freight to San Francisco at so many Chefoo taels per 100 cubic li, it is doubtful if he would at once see the advantages or disadvantages of the offer.

It is true that the American might, if he took the time and pains to do so, reduce these unfamiliar weights, measurements, and prices to bushels, feet and dollars. But the Chinaman's chances of doing business would be much greater if he offered his merchandise in a manner and on a basis which would be understood at once by the person to whom the offer was made, for the reason that in these days, when the seller seeks the buyer rather than the buyer the seller, it is advisable to avoid anything that tends to confuse the possible purchaser or befog him in the transaction. But the average American business man who desires to establish a trade in France not only imagines that it can be done with far less effort than at home, but that it can be done by sending out catalogues and circular letters. He does not seem to reflect nor to take into consideration the fact that English, German, and other manufacturers and merchants who make and sell the same articles that he does and who, in a word, are competitors, send competent commercial travelers at regular intervals to visit the trade in France and elsewhere—travelers who speak French and other languages, who are provided with samples and whose employers, knowing that over 445,000,000 people in the world use the metric system when transacting business with customers who know no other, make it a point to use it also. Moreover, the German, English, French, Austrian, Italian and Swiss business men are ready to give credit of thirty, sixty or ninety days to houses of good standing, for the reason that the firms to which the latter sell also ask for credit and because credit is customary in Europe. The American exacts cash before the goods are shipped.

BAD BUSINESS METHODS.

In addition to the American business man who imagines that he can do a large trade by sending catalogues printed in English to France is the merchant who seeks a European market, not because he has any idea of systematically establishing and building up a trade, but because business happens to be dull for the time being in the United States. He writes, let us say, to the consul at Havre (and hundreds of letters at this office go to attest the fact) asking to be put in communication with a reputable firm desirous of buying a certain kind and quality of lumber at a certain price. The consul, acting practically as the American's agent, finds a firm ready, and perhaps eager, to purchase an important lot, and an order is sent to America. A cash payment is agreed upon, and a sufficient credit deposited in a New York bank to be drawn by the shipper upon presentation of the invoice and bill of lading. Everything is satisfactory, the importer is to receive the lumber he wants, and the American merchant has secured the order he sought. The moment for shipment arrives, but in the meantime business, which was dull in America, has revived. The lumber merchant has more orders at home than he can fill, and he decides not to ship to Havre the lumber for which he solicited, received and accepted an order. In other words, he has simply been looking for a foreign trade because business at home was temporarily depressed, and it was not his intention to either establish a foreign trade or develop it. Sometimes this failure to fill an order ends in no serious consequences; or, again, if the merchant in Havre has agreed to deliver to certain customers on this side the wood which he counts upon receiving and finds that he is unable to do so, the situation becomes a very embarrassing one for him and a thoroughly disheartening one for the consul. All of this annoyance could have been avoided and would be avoided had the American, upon discovering an outlet for his merchandise, determined upon nursing and developing it as he does at home. As it is, the dealer in Havre sends future orders to Norway, and will have nothing more to do with America.

SUCCESSFUL METHODS.

We now come to another category of the American business man. He comes in person to France, examines and investigates the demand for the product or article in which he deals, ascertains what nations are already filling this demand, sees if he can supply the same article at a lower price, but of as good quality, sets to work proving to the trade that he can do so, gets orders, fills them, determines to hold the business he gets and to increase it, does not trust solely to catalogues, meets his competitors on their own ground and—succeeds. I can name fifty or more firms of this description in France, while those who might have done a large business, but who have given up after a faint-hearted effort, are innumerable; all of which would tend to establish the fact that whenever our manufacturers, who now furnish France with only 12 per cent. of the manufactured articles which she imports, will make an earnest effort to secure that market they will succeed, but not until then. Their real indifference has been the chief cause of their relative failure.

Health Exhibition at Lima.

The Institute of Hygiene, Lima, Peru, is planning the establishment there of a permanent health exhibition, with a view to instructing the Peruvian public in the latest methods of hygiene, sanitation, etc. The institute would be glad to receive samples or printed descriptions of such articles as patent foods, meat extract, surgical appliances, disinfectants, hygienic clothing, electrotherapeutic devices, hospital equipment, etc.

FRENCH PHARMACY IN 1905.

Patent Medicine Troubles in France—A Factional Fight in the General Association—British Pharmacists Visit Gay Paris—The Changes and the Chief Incidents of the Year.

(*From our Regular Correspondent.*)

Paris, January 2, 1906.—The year that has just closed was a comparatively uneventful one, so far as French pharmacy was concerned, but few occurrences being worthy of record. The General Association of French Pharmacists, a body which may be likened to the N. A. R. D. and including in its ranks about half the men who hold the French diploma, held its annual meeting at Lyons. The second city of France has the advantage of a fairly central position, and besides the usual meetings and banquets, the ceremony of unveiling a bust of the late Professor Crolas took place at the Mixed Faculty of Pharmacy and Medicine in presence of the pharmacists assembled. But from a business point of view the meeting was not a success. The old feud between "specialists" and "anti-specialists," on the question of patent medicines" (a burning one, in these cutting days, in France as elsewhere), ran high. The new president, elected at Lyons, M. Weil, only held office a few months. At a meeting held at Paris last month he was replaced by M. Vaudin, a Parisian whose views on the "patent" question appear to be more in harmony with those of a somewhat powerful and very active section of the association, and a composite "bureau" was formed of "specialists" and "anti-specialists." It is fervently to be hoped, for the sake of the future of the profession, that they will definitely bury the hatchet, and by mutual concessions arrive at some compromise which will satisfy alike the Parisians (who mostly prepare some proprietary article of their own) and the Southerners (many of whom make no secret of their desire to see the sale or advertisement of patent medicines prohibited by law). If so, brighter days may yet be in store for French pharmacy.

THE VISIT OF THE BRITISH PHARMACISTS

to Paris was one of the interesting developments of the recent "entente cordiale" between England and France. A small but representative body of pharmacists from all parts of the United Kingdom came over to the French capital at the close of the British Pharmaceutical Conference. Besides "doing" the stock "sights" of the French capital, a "pharmaceutical day" was arranged for them by a London drug journal; they were "personally conducted" over the Pasteur Institute by Dr. Roux, of antidiphtheric serum fame. M. Bourquelot (secretary of the French Pharmacopœia Revision Committee and professor of galenics at the School of Pharmacy) showed them over the Laennec Hospital, and the School of Pharmacy was visited. Unfortunately it was the long vacation, but the president of the Pharmacy Students' Association, M. Oudin, acted as *cicerone*, and finally carried them off to the Students' Club for brief rest and refreshment. A glimpse of the Faculty of Sciences and a stroll through the large manufacturing premises of the Central Pharmacy of France wound up a most interesting but terribly "strenuous" day. It is to be hoped that this interesting corporative visit will one day be imitated by some American pharmaceutical body.

NEW LAWS.

The new pharmacy law seems as far off as ever. The recent army act makes all pharmacy students liable to serve two years with the colors, like the rest of their fellow citizens, and one of its consequences has been to depopulate the benches of pharmacy schools of that not particularly interesting class of students whose chief object in obtaining a diploma was to do one year's service instead of three. The medical students will do two years also, but will principally be engaged in hospital work. The petition of the pharmacy students for the same privilege seems likely to be fruitless. The new adulteration act should be carefully studied by firms exporting to France. Some of its clauses are sufficiently stringent, but it bears more on foodstuffs than drugs.

THE 1905 OBITUARY

is not a lengthy one, but two well-known men have passed away. M. Marc Boymond was a leading Parisian pharmacist, who long held "Hottot's" pharmacy in the Faubourg St. Honoré, and was chairman of the Paris Society of Pharmacy in 1894; while M. George Thomas, of Agen, was a wholesale druggist in southwestern France, whose propositions for the regulation of the "cutting" of prices of patent medicines attracted some attention of late years, though his scheme never really obtained a fair hearing. The death of Professor Rietsch, of the Marseilles Faculty of Pharmacy, may also be mentioned, while M. Alfred Radiguet's name will be familiar to those who have studied the X-rays.

CHANGES.

One or two well-known faces are still with us, but not where we have been accustomed to see them. M. Balland, so long head army pharmacist at the Invalides, Paris, has been pensioned off, and M. Lextreit, after 20 years' service, has retired from the direction of the practical chemistry classes at the Paris School of Pharmacy.

On the other hand, M. John Jarvis, jr., the English pharmacist at Chantilly (son of the Mr. Jarvis who has so long operated a store at Pau), has come to Paris and is now one of the heads of Swann's Anglo-American Pharmacy, in the Rue Castiglione. The Rue de la Paix, which is merely the continuation of the same street, is more than ever the home of pharmacy and perfumery. Roger & Gallet, the well-known French firm, have just opened new premises here, and a big "perfumery palace" has been inaugurated a few doors nearer the boulevards, while all the old houses—Guerlain's, Fay's, Botot's and one or two English agencies—still cling in and around this street. A well known landmark has, however, disappeared rom the Rue de la Paix by the removal of the Pharmacie Beral to the Rue de Rivoli. The old house, now pulled down, was just a hundred years old, and was the last survivor of the buildings which lined the "Rue Napoleon," when it first opened.

SCIENTIFIC EVENTS.

The sensation of the year was Dr. Behring's announcement at the Tuberculosis Congress, in October, of his new remedy. Pharmacists and others, warned by experience, "lie low and say nuffing" till matters seem more conclusive.

M. Pierre Curie, discoverer of radium, and Dr. Gilbert, a member of the French Pharmacopœia Revision Committee, were elected members of the Academy of Sciences during 1905.

The King of Portugal's visit to the Museum, to hear lectures on chemistry and physical science, was a refreshing contrast to the reviews and banquets which usually form the programme of royal state visits.

Dr. Calmette, director of the Pasteur Institute of Lille, was awarded the Audiffred prize ($3,000) for his bacteriological researches. The offer of a $2,000 prize by the Parisian daily paper *Le Matin* for a really scientific and certain method of destroying flies (without the use of any patent apparatus) may also be noted. It was prompted by Dr. Chantemesse's declaration that flies are one of the principal agents in spreading cholera, etc.

Hegeman Corporation Buys J. N. Hegeman & Co.'s Store.

The corporation of Hegeman & Co. has purchased from George J. Seabury, of Seabury & Johnson, all of the capital stock of J. N. Hegeman & Co., whose store at 21 Park row has frequently attracted public attention by its clever window exhibitions. The Hegeman Corporation has also bought the fixtures and all the drugs, toilet articles and other goods in the store and will hereafter operate it as one of its numerous branches. George Ramsay, manager of the main store of the Hegeman Corporation, at 200 Broadway, announces that he will close the Park row branch for a week while a general cleaning and repairing of the premises is being effected. It is Mr. Ramsay's intention to install a much larger soda fountain than that now in the store. The deal whereby the title to the business and store of J. N. Hegeman & Co. passed to the Hegeman Corporation was effected on Saturday, March 31.

The Drug and Chemical Market

The prices quoted in this report are those current in the wholesale market, and higher prices are paid for retail lots The quality of goods frequently necessitates a wide range of prices.

Condition of Trade.

NEW YORK, April 7, 1906.

The market for most lines of drugs and chemicals has been exceedingly dull during the fortnight just closed, and the business results of the month of March have been, upon the whole, unsatisfactory. The actual price changes during the interval have been mostly in the interests of buyers, but the shrinkages in values have not appreciably aided in the distribution. It is doubtful if trade could be stimulated by further concessions, as interior dealers appear to be well supplied with articles currently inquired for. The patent on phenacetin having expired, manufacturers have begun to offer acetphenetidin, which is the pharmacopœial name of the substance, at $1.35 per lb. Holders of the Bayer product are offering at a considerable reduction from previous prices, down to $3.50 being named, it is reported, for pound lots. Apart from this, actual price changes are somewhat inconsequential. There has been an advance of 2c per lb. in manufacturers' quotations for citric acid and all citrates. Opium continues on the downward grade, and the alkaloids are cheaper. The new crop of Norwegian codliver oil is expected to more than double the yield for the preceding year, the catch so far this season being more than one-half of the entire yield for 1905.

HIGHER.	LOWER.
Citric acid,	Opium,
Blue vitriol,	Codeine,
Menthol,	Ergot,
Gentian root,	Japan wax,
Oxalic acid,	American saffron,
Pink root,	Phenacetin,
Decorticated cardamons.	Elm bark, select,
	Cubeb berries,
	Colocynth apples,
	Citronella oil.

Drugs.

Acetanilid maintains its firmness and the tone of the market is strong on the basis of 24c to 25c, as to quality.

Acetphenetidin, the United States Pharmacopœial preparation of phenacetin, is being offered to the trade at the range of $1.30 to $1.45 in bulk, as to quantity; 1-ounce cartons are quoted at 15c.

Alcohol is maintained steadily by the combination of producers at $2.45 to $2.47, as to terms of sale. Wood is actively inquired for, and values are well sustained at the range of 70c to 75c for 95 and 97 per cent. grades, respectively.

Balsam copaiba is less freely inquired for, but the tendency of values is steady under the influence of light supplies. It is reported that an arrival of 16 boxes of Central American offered at 34c was refused. On spot the quotation ranges from 29c to 32c, as to quality and quantity. Para is in better supply and prices are somewhat irregular, though 38c to 45c is generally quoted.

Balsam fir and Peru remain quiet at nominally unchanged prices.

Balsam Peru is in improved supply and the market is easier in tone, though quotations remain at the basis of 20c to 21c.

Barks.—Cascara sagrada is not meeting with any active inquiry, but holders show no lack of firmness at the quoted range of 5½c to 9c, as to quality and quantity. Elm has offered more freely during the interval, and we hear of sales of select at a reduction to 10c to 18c. Sassafras continues in good consuming request, with prime grades steadily held at 12c to 14c. Bayberry is offered at 12c, but in most quarters 13c to 14c is maintained. Waboo continues scarce and for the small available supply, which is closely concentrated, 45c is named.

Buchu leaves are coming to hand in small quantities, and command steady prices, or, say, 18c to 20c, though yellowish leaves are available at 17c.

Cacao butter is characterized by an active consuming demand and values are well sustained at the range of 28½c to 30c for bulk, and 34c to 35c for 12-lb. boxes.

Cantharides are characterized by an active jobbing demand and prices are firmly maintained at the range of $1.20 to $1.25 for whole Russian and $1.25 to $1.30 for powdered Russian. The supply of Chinese is under good control and 75c to 77c is named for whole and powdered, respectively.

Chamomile flowers are well maintained at current prices, especially for new crop Roman, which are reported higher abroad; though some dealers have advanced prices to 20c. to 25c stock is yet available at 18c to 22c; German are offered more freely and the market is easier at 8c to 10c.

Codeine and its salts have been reduced by the manufacturers to correspond with the decline in price of opium, and current quotations are on the basis of $3.05 to $3.25 for pure in bulk, as to quantity; sulphate and hydrochloride are 25c per oz. less than the alkaloids, and phosphate 50c per oz. less. The inside quotations are for lots of 10 ounces in one delivery.

Codliver oil does not improve in position with the receipt of cable advices indicating a heavy yield in the fishing now in progress. The favorable indications for the new crop of oil have brought the f.o.b. shipment price down to $13.50. Meanwhile sales on spot are making at unchanged quotations, or, say, $20.00 to $25.00, as to brand and quality.

Colocynth apples, Trieste, are in better supply and values are easier to the extent that 28c to 30c is now named as acceptable.

Cubeb berries are a shade easier, dealers showing more disposition to urge sales by price concessions, and 8½c to 9½c is now named for prime grades.

Cuttlefish bone is firmer under the influence of strong primary markets and prime Trieste has been advanced to 17c.

Ergot has developed an easier turn in sympathy with weaker markets abroad, and quotations show declines to 29c to 30c. for Russian and 34c to 35c for Spanish.

Gurana has been in good demand and values are firmly maintained at the range of 75c to 80c.

Menthol is again higher, and only a limited quantity appears available at $2.50. The tendency is upward, and everything below the figure quoted appears to be out of market.

Opium remains exceedingly dull and weak, and quotations are irregular and unsettled owing to competition. Buyers appear to be indifferent to future wants, the tendency of the market being regarded as favorable to a policy of limiting operations to actual necessities. Jobbing sales only are reported at prices within the range of $2.75 to $2.80, while cases are obtainable at $2.72½. Powdered is held and selling in a limited way at $3.25 to $3.30.

Quinine does not improve in position and the movement appears limited to deliveries on old contract. Some interest was lent to a rather dull market by the announcement of a falling off in bark shipments for March, the amount being said to be considerably below that for the corresponding period of the previous year. Local manufacturers continue to quote 18c to 21c, and foreign brands are maintained at a parity with this, though there are offerings from second hands of German and Java at 17½c to 18c.

Saw palmetto berries are scarce and wanted and the market is firmer in tone at 14c to 20c.

Touka beans are in active request and firm at 62¼c to 65c for jobbing quantities.

Vanilla beans have sold actively in a jobbing way since our last, Bourbons being in especially good demand, and an advance in this variety would not surprise the market. We quote the range at $2.75 to $3.00 for whole Mexican, $2.00 to $2.50 for cut, $1.00 to $3.25 for Bourbon, and 40c to $1.00 for Tahiti.

Chemicals.

Acetate of lime is maintained steadily, with sales of brown at 1.60c to 1.65c and gray at 2.35c to 2.40c.

Alum is maintained firmly at manufacturer's quotations, and numerous sales are reported at 1.75c to 1.80c for lump and 1.85c to 1.90c for ground.

Arsenic, white, is offered in instances at a shade under 6c, but the position of the article at primary sources is said not to justify the reduction.

Blue vitriol has developed a firmer tone and 6¼c is generally named for less than carload lots.

Carbolic acid is in active demand and the tone of the market for bulk is decidedly firmer; holders of the limited supply in large drums decline to shade 15c to 16c. The supply of stock in pound bottles is ample and quotations do not vary from 20c to 22c.

Chlorate of potash is in improved jobbing inquiry and spot lots have changed hands during the interval at 9½ to 9¾c for crystals and powdered, respectively.

Citric acid is maintained firmly at an advance to 43c to 43½c in sympathy with the strong position of crude material abroad. All citrates are correspondingly higher.

Cream tartar offers more freely at current quotations, though an advance is generally looked for.

Nitrate of soda is firmer owing to temporary scarcity, and quotations show an advance to $2.30 for 96 per cent. and $2.27½ for 95 per cent.

Oxalic acid is in light supply and for the limited available stock 5¾c is named.

Quicksilver is passing out actively into channels of consumption at prices within the quoted range of 55½c. to 57c.

Tartaric acid sells in a limited jobbing way only, small lots being taken at 28¼c to 28½c for crystals and powdered.

Essential Oils.

Anise has developed an easier feeling, and sales were made at $1.32½ for 15 degrees and at $1.27½ for 14 degrees.

Camphor, light gravity Japanese, is in upward tendency, and current quotations are firmly maintained at 17½c to 18c.

Citronella has developed no action of consequence, either as regards price or demand, and only jobbing sales are reported at the recently lowered range of 38c to 39c for drum, and 39c to 40c for cans.

Clove has not responded to the advance in spice, and quotations remain at the previous range of 80c to 82½c for cans and 82½c to 85c for bottles.

Pennyroyal has developed a firmer feeling, and up to $1.50 is asked in some instances for American, though most sales were at $1.35; French oil is offered at $1.10 to $1.20.

Peppermint has been rather quiet since our last, but the article has lost none of its strength in view of the repeated intimations that the next crop would show a smaller yield than the one previously harvested. Sellers are somewhat cautious in their operations, as it seems to be impossible to duplicate supplies at primary sources at current values. While $2.60 will buy in instances, the popular quotation for bulk oil is $2.75 to $3.00.

Sassafras, natural, is held and selling in a jobbing way at 50c to 55c.

Wintergreen, natural, is somewhat irregular, there being sellers at $1.45, while some holders insist on $1.75.

Gums.

Aloes, of the various grades, are without quotable change, either as regards price or demand. For Curacao, which is in rather limited supply, 6c to 6¼c is named, while Barbadoes and Cape are maintained at 17c to 15c and 7c to 8c, respectively.

Asafœtida is quiet and nominally steady at 14c to 18c, the outside figure being for prime.

Benzoin, Sumatra, is held with increased firmness in consequence of diminishing spot supplies, and sales were made during the interval of 34c to 36c; Siam is held and selling at 50c to $1.00, as to quality and quantity.

Camphor abates none of its strength, though the distribution does not reach very large proportions. Japan refined ounces is quoted at 98c to $1.00, but American refined is held and selling at $1.00 to $1.00½.

Chicle, Mexican, is offered more freely at 34c, but efforts to cut this figure have not been successful.

Gamboge is slightly easier in consequence of reports from London indicating a decline there. Meanwhile whole pipe is not available at under $1.05.

Tragacanth is in fair inquiry and quotations are maintained on the basis of 30c to 65c for Aleppo and 35c to 80c for Turkey.

Roots.

A firm market prevails for most druggists' roots and actual price changes are few and unimportant. Jamaica ginger maintains its firm position, bleached being held at 17c to 18c and natural at 14c to 15c. Golden seal is not inquired for to any extent and quotations are largely nominal at $1.20 to $1.25. Ipecac maintains its firmness, with Rio quoted at $1.75 to $1.80 and Cartagena at $1.70 to $1.75. Squill has been in good demand and values are steadier at 11c to 12c. Doggrass is a shade easier, 4¾c being now named as acceptable.

Seeds.

Few new features of interest have developed in this market since our last. Cardemoms have maintained their upward course and decorticated is now quoted at 32c to 34c. Canary is slow of sale and the market is easier in tone at 4½c to 5c. Caraway is in better supply and offers at a reduction at 5¾c to 6c. Russian hemp has developed increased firmness and is quoted at 3⅛c to 3¼c. Strophanthus, Kombe, is in better supply and offers more freely at a decline at 89c to 90c.

Bentonite.

Bentonite clay, which is chiefly known to pharmacists as the material from which "antiphlogistine" is made, has a vast variety of uses which are described by C. E. Siebenthal, of the United States Geological Survey. It occurs in many localities in Wyoming, but particularly in the Laramie basin.

When freshly exposed it varies in color from a light yellow to a light olive green with a waxy luster. On exposure it assumes a dull cream color. In freshly uncovered outcrops it appears as a bedded joint clay, the blocks varying from roughly rectangular or conchoidal shape to long slender pieces. The joints are more or less open and occasionally contain crystals and plates of gypsum and sodium sulphate.

In texture the clay is very fine grained. It develops no grit to the touch and very little when ground between the teeth. The microscope shows that it is made up of extremely minute, more or less rounded, particles of fairly uniform size and apparently of the same mineral nature, with here and there particles of undecomposed labradorite.

The clay has a soft, unctuous or soapy feeling, but it is brittle and is easily quarried. It clings strongly to the tongue. In weathering it absorbs a great amount of water and increases much in volume, forming a network mantle an inch thick, but later melting down, under the effects of rainfall and frost, to a white powder. Mixed with the proper amount of water, it is exceedingly plastic, and with the addition of more water becomes a perfect paste. Tests show that it completely absorbs over three times its weight, or seven times its volume, of water and twice as much glycerin as diatomaceous earth will absorb.

The chief use of the clay so far developed is as a material to give body and weight in the manufacture of paper. Practically the whole output of the clay for the last few years has been taken by a paper mill in Denver. It is also used as an adulterant in the manufacture of candies and drugs. Its first use was as a material for hoof packing, a dressing or poultice for the inflamed hoofs of horses.

Though highly plastic, it is unsuitable, on account of its low fusibility, for the manufacture of fire clay products. If mixed with ground feldspar, it could possibly be used in the manufacture of pottery. It is a good retarder for use with the hard cement plasters. Its high absorption of glycerin, as compared with diatomaceous earth, suggests its substitution for that material in the manufacture of dynamite.

Ionone Case Decided in Favor of George Lueders & Co.

After a litigation extending over six years, the celebrated Ionone, or artificial violet, infringement suit brought against George Lueders & Co., manufacturers of essential oils, of 218 Pearl street, by the Haarmann-DeLaire-Schaefer Company, of Maywood, N. J., has at last been decided in favor of Lueders & Co. Judge Ray, in the United States Circuit Court, handed down this decision, together with his opinion on the merits of the case, on Tuesday, March 27.

In his opinion Judge Ray held that Lueders & Co. had not infringed the patent by making the article in question and therefore dismissed the bill of complaint filed by the Haarmann-DeLaire-Schaefer Company with costs. Mr. Lueders says he owes the successful termination of the suit entirely to Arthur von Briesen and his son, Hans von Briesen, of the law firm of Briesen & Knauth, of 49-51 Wall street, who appeared for him in this tedious litigation.

The suit against Lueders & Co. for the infringement of the Ionone patent was begun in July, 1900, by Haarmann & Reimer, of Holzminden, Germany, who had secured the patent, known as United States patent 556,943, for the manufacture of an aromatic ketone and the process of making the same, by an assignment fromthe inventor, Johann Carl Wilhelm Ferdinand Tiemann, of Berlin. It was not until March, 1902, however, that the Haarmann-DeLaire-Schaefer Company, which had meanwhile secured the patent rights from Haarmann & Reimer, entered into the litigation as the complainant. Testimony was taken by the Haarmann-DeLaire-Schaefer Company on and after March, 1902, and George Lueders & Co. began to take its expert testimony in February, 1903.

The Haarmann-DeLaire-Schaefer Company complained that Lueders & Co. had imported from a Swiss manufacturer of essentials oils a preparation of Ionone, which constituted an infringement upon the Tiemann patent. Prof. Peter D. Austen, formerly professor of chemistry in Dartmouth College and later in Rutgers College, submitted to the Circuit Court testimony which showed that the citrolene, which formed the chief constituent in the Lueders importation of Ionone, possessed a much greater specific gravity than that described in and made according to the Tiemann patent, while its index of refraction was considerably less than that of the Haarmann-DeLaire-Schaefer Company. Professor Austen also showed that the boiling point of the citrolene in the Lueders preparation corresponded more closely to that of beta ionone than that of the patent. In tabulated form the professor compared the two preparations of ionone, as follows:

	Specific gravity.	Index of refraction.	Boiling point.
The special ionone prepared according to the Tiemann patent	0.935	1.507	120 degrees at 12 mm.
Lueders & Co.'s importation of ionone	0.939	1 50113	144 degrees at 16 mm.

The formula for ionone is in both cases $C_{13}H_{20}O$.

Having demonstrated to the court the marked variation in the two preparations, Lueders & Co., through its attorneys, claimed that it had not infringed the patent rights of the Haarmann-DeLaire-Schaefer Company and this contention was subsequently sustained.

Advertising matter for counter distribution and window display of the line of licorice specialties manufactured by the National Licorice Company, of 106 John street, Brooklyn, may be had on application. In writing for this, please state which of the brands is used. The advertisement of the company will be found in this issue, and this embodies the line of specialties.

In ordering chemicals it is safe to specify "P., W. & R." The Powers, Weightman, Rosengarten Company, of Philadelphia, was established in 1818. The line embraces everything medicinal, technical and for the arts, and is generally considered as standard in point of purity. The goods are sold only to the wholesale drug trade, but by specifying, may be obtained anywhere.

Hints to Buyers.

A sample of Dentacura may be obtained by addressing the Dentacura Company, Newark, N. J. This is in all respects a first-class tooth paste, possessing such prophylactic qualities as commend it to the consideration of dentists and the public generally.

Gilpin Langdon & Co., of Baltimore, Md., invite our readers to write them for a price-list of their assayed drugs. These goods are labeled with alkaloidal strength, as determined by the average of many tests, and consequently are invaluable in prescription work. One of the prominent features in the line is granulated opium.

The sum of $10,000 was distributed to the retail drug trade in 1905 by a special offer on Eskay's Albumenized Food by the manufacturers, Smith, Kline & French Company, of Philadelphia. This special price protecting offer still holds good and particulars regarding it may be obtained by addressing the company.

The house of Justus Brauer & Son, 248 North Front street, Philadelphia, was established in 1865, and has ever since maintained a first-class reputation for its excellent machine cut corks. We can conscientiously recommend this house to our readers as one supplying goods fully up to sample and of full count.

We invite the attention of our readers to the announcement of the Dalley Mfg. Company, of 12 Duane street, New York, which applies equally to both American and foreign readers. Dalley's Magical Pain Extractor, or as it is more familiarly called, Dalley's Salve, has been so long in the American market that it needs no commendation at our hands. It is one of the very few old proprietaries still surviving. It has been made and sold through three successive generations of the Dalley family, and despite the fact that no advertising whatever has been done, the sale has steadily grown. It is also one of the very few proprietary articles in America that has received the unequivocal indorsement of the first-class American physician. Dalley's Salve is something which every druggist should carry in stock, and which all could very well afford to recommend to customers.

Registered in Kansas.

At the meeting of the Kansas State Board of Pharmacy, held at Atchison, Kan., February 15, there were 56 applicants present to take the examination, 21 of whom passed the examination and were registered. The following are the names of those who passed as pharmacists:

B. W. McFall, Salina; Julius F. Graf, Atchison; F. J. McAuliffe, Leavenworth; R. M. Campbell, North Topeka; Homer T. Clifton, Paola; R. W. Coppedge, Topeka; Leonard A. Doan, Chanute; S. M. Dotterer, Leavenworth; August Fleckenstein, Atwood; Henry J. De Vries, Helper; Frank E. Potter Anthony; Stacy A. Haines, Columbus; Fred. L. Strohwig, Athol; Frank Sheets, Parsons; J. Leslie Reed, Belleville; G. W. Murden, Ellis; Guy Miller, Topeka; John T. Burke, West Mineral; Albert H. Thielen, St. Paul; Albert R. Hatcher, Allen, and William B. Mellenbruch, Fairview.

The following were registered as assistant pharmacists:

Claude Hiltabidel, Atwood; Aubrey G. Pilcher, Winfield; Francis I. E. Monley, Wellington, and G. W. Sourk, Goffs.

The following were registered since the last meeting of the board by virtue of being graduates of recognized colleges of pharmacy:

Judah J. Drisk, Abilene; M. B. Ford, Viola; Claude C. Bacon, Iola, and L. F. Gramley, Clay Center.

Since the last meeting of the board duplicate certificates were issued to the following:

R. Stewart, Powhattan; J. A. Winkler, Caney; R. O. Constable, Herndon; Allan T. Stewart, Powhattan, and S. R. Swan, Gas City.

Following are the names of those who were restored to the register during the last quarter:

L. A. Baugh, Kansas City; LeRoy M. Williams, Topeka; C. E. Vest, Kansas City; J. F. Anderson, Coffeyville; Robert C. Wright, Wichita; W. R. Shumate, Goodland, and C. C. Moore, Galena.

Temporary certificates were issued during the past quarter to the following:

J. A. Bermingham, Chanute; T. J Hinton, Scammon; M. K. Ingraham, Caney, and August Fleckenstein, Atwood.

Licenses were issued to about 160 merchants during the past quarter.

AMERICAN DRUGGIST

and PHARMACEUTICAL RECORD

PHILADELPHIA. NEW YORK, APRIL 23, 1906. CHICAGO

ISSUED SEMI-MONTHLY BY

AMERICAN DRUGGIST PUBLISHING CO.

62-68 WEST BROADWAY, NEW YORK.

CHICAGO, 221 Randolph St. PHILADELPHIA, 3713 Walnut St.

A. R. ELLIOTT, President.

CASWELL A. MAYO, Ph.G. .... Editor.
THOMAS J. KEENAN .... Associate Editor.

ROMAINE PIERSON .... Manager Chicago Office.

$1.50 a year. 15 cents a copy.

ADVERTISING RATES QUOTED ON APPLICATION.

THE AMERICAN DRUGGIST AND PHARMACEUTICAL RECORD is issued on the second and fourth Mondays of each month. Changes of advertisements should be received ten days in advance of the date of publication.

Remittances should be made by New York exchange, post office or express money order or registered mail. If checks on local banks are used 10 cents should be added to cover cost of collection. The publishers are not responsible for money sent by unregistered mail, nor for any money paid except to duly authorized agents. All communications should be addressed and all remittances made payable to American Druggist Publishing Co., 62-68 West Broadway, New York.

Entered at New York as Second-Class Matter.

TABLE OF CONTENTS.

EDITORIAL COMMENT.

A CASE FOR SYMPATHY. We are sure that the deep sympathy of the pharmacists of the country will go out to Albert E. Ebert, the veteran pharmacist of Chicago, who has suffered a sad affliction in the loss of his wife, the helpmeet of many years, who died on the morning of Wednesday, April 11. This, we are grieved to learn, is but the culmination of several misfortunes of a lesser character which have combined to put a heavy load on him in his declining years, and we can only hope that under his afflictions he will be comforted by the sympathetic messages of his professional brethren.

FOR A NEW YORK BRANCH OF THE A. PH. A. A praiseworthy movement in the direction of forming local sections of the American Pharmaceutical Association is in progress throughout the country and it is to the credit of the cities of Chicago, Philadelphia, Baltimore and Boston that such sections or branches have been actually established since the plan was mooted about a year ago. It has always been a matter of great difficulty to get the pharmacists of Greater New York to come together in one body which should represent the entire city. Since the formation of a Greater New York, including within its boundaries five separate boroughs—some of which existed previously as separate counties—the difficulty has been increased rather than lessened. At the time of the organization of the Manhattan Pharmaceutical Association no distinct drug trade organization was in existence and the need for a local association, which should devote special attention to trade matters, was greatly felt at a time when labor agitators were seeking by a passage of legislative acts to bring pharmacy under the control of the labor unions and otherwise interfere with the regulation of pharmacy by pharmacists. Since New York has been organized by the National Association of Retail Druggists and district branches have been established in many places throughout the city, the need for existence of an association like the Manhattan Pharmaceutical Association has become correspondingly less. Dr. Alpers, who resigned the presidency of the association last week, had come to realize this and gave expression to his views on the subject in resigning his office. These will be found in our report of the meeting on another page. We trust that Dr. Alpers will not allow the matter to rest, but will take steps to arouse the enthusiasm and enlist the co-operation of every member of the American Pharmaceutical Association residing in the greater city. There is room for an association formed as a branch of the American Pharmaceutical Association, in which subjects of a scientific and technical nature might receive the attention which they deserve and would get in a city like New York.

The Earthquake.

The beautiful and prosperous city of San Francisco has in a moment's time been reduced to a waste of ashes, its commerce paralyzed, its citizens killed, wounded or fleeing. In the awful calamity from which they are suffering the citizens of the Pacific Coast have the sincerest sympathy and most profound commiseration of the remainder of the United States. Immediately upon receipt of the news of the disaster which has resulted in the wiping out of this prosperous metropolis the public officers of States, municipalities and of the general government took prompt and energetic action to diminish as much as lies within human power the suffering entailed by the catastrophe. Every wholesale drug house in the city of San Francisco has been completely obliterated, and the very large majority of the retail stores have also been destroyed or irreparably damaged. To the members of the drug trade, both wholesale and retail, who have suffered through this visitation, we extend our profound sympathy and can assure them that they have the sympathy of their professional brethren in the East, who will gladly lend a helping hand where this is possible toward the rehabilitation of the fortunes of the sufferers.

It is gratifying to record that the wholesale and manufacturing drug trade outside of the stricken area have responded nobly to the needs of the hour, several houses having to our knowledge advised their customers that settlements might be put off indefinitely. Other interests have responded in an equally generous and noble spirit and out of these circumstances we may derive a crumb or two of comfort. The calamity is a national one, and should call for aid and succor from every citizen of our broad country. In this work of relief we know that pharmacists will not lag behind.

Government by Bureau.

The essential spirit of American law is opposed to bureaucracy, but there seems to exist a tendency on the part of the unthinking to develop a system of bureaucratic government which, if unchecked, will lead to a condition of affairs as deplorable as that which has driven thousands of Russians into exile and brought that country to the verge of anarchy. This tendency has manifested itself in an amendment of the Stevens-Wainwright bill, now before the Legislature of the State of New York, which proposes to grant to the State Board of Health authority to add to the list of dangerous drugs at its own discretion and without any reference either to the legislative, judicial or executive authority. However lofty the motives which have prompted this proposal it is fraught with such danger to the liberty of the individual and so opposed to the basic principles of our form of government that it seems difficult to believe that such a proposition would receive favorable consideration at the hands of the Legislature. The only possible excuse that the legislator could offer for voting in favor of a measure so subversive of all law and precedent is, that being ignorant of the subject matter he was willing to delegate to some one else the authority which should rest with him alone, for such an amendment would in effect delegate full legislative power to the Board of Health, and place that board in a position to propose and enforce regulations which would bring absolute ruin to some of the legitimate branches of the drug business without any corresponding public advantage.

The Stevens-Wainwright law in its aim to bring about a millennium first included drugs which could by no stretch of the imagination be regarded as dangerous or likely to bring about the establishment of a narcotic habit, then introduced a blanket clause regarding classes of drugs which no three physicians would interpret in exactly the same way, and it is now finally proposed to take away from the legislature its legislative functions and vest them in the hands of a small bureau which is not subject to checks from either the legislative, judiciary or executive branches of the government.

We earnestly urge our readers to second the efforts of the Legislative Committee of the State Association to defeat the Stevens-Wainwright bill, and we feel sure that if a concerted and vigorous movement were undertaken the measure would be killed and the measure proposed by the Chicago Conference, which is known as the Hill bill, be substituted for it, with advantage to the physician, the public, and the pharmacist alike.

A Pharmaceutical Encyclopaedia.[1]

We have for some time past, indeed ever since receiving in April, 1904, the first volume of that great encyclopædia of pharmacy, *Real-Enzyklopädie der gesamten Pharmazie*, contemplated the idea of giving American pharmacists who are unaware of the existence of the volumes some inkling of the scope and contents of the work, which reflects so much credit on the industry and pharmaceutical knowledge of the two chief editors and their able corps of assistants, to mention the names of which would be but to call the honor roll of German botanists, chemists, pharmacologists, pharmacognoscists and therapeutists. It is at the same time most creditable to German publishers that a firm could be found to make possible the publication of so extensive a work, and Urban & Schwarzenberg, the scientific book publishers of Berlin, are entitled to a warm place in the hearts of pharmacists for the liberality they have displayed in undertaking the publication of a work which in the nature of things cannot be much of a success financially.

The first edition of the encyclopædia of pharmacy was published in 1886 under the editorship of Dr. Ewald Geissler and Dr. Josef Moeller, from Vienna, where the main establishment of the publishers was then located. Dr. Geissler, who was for many years editor of the *Pharmazeutische Zentralhalle*, of Dresden, died shortly before the new edition was planned, and his place was filled by Professor Thoms, the director of the Pharmaceutical Institute of the University of Berlin, who is justly regarded as the foremost pharmaceutical chemist in Germany to-day. Professor Moeller is an eminent pharmacologist, being director of the Pharmacological Institute of the University of Gratz, Austria. The completed work will number ten volumes, and in form and typography will not differ essentially from the first edition, though it is evident that the number of pages must be increased to accommodate mention of recent progress in pharmacy and the allied sciences. Four volumes have been issued thus far, and judging by their contents the revised edition, when completed, will constitute a repository of the entire art and science of pharmacy, such as is not available in any other single work devoted to the subject.

It is impossible with the space at our command to do more than give the barest outline of what the pharmacist will find in the volumes. In the first place the work is a dictionary of words and terms used in pharmaceutical, chemical and botanical literature—English words that have passed into and become a part of German pharmaceutical literature are defined, both the Latin and German synonyms being given, while the extended descriptions are, of course, written in German. The same applies to Latin terms and titles which are in more familiar use than the corresponding German titles The editors have adopted the new Prussian governmental regulations for the spelling of words; hence we find the old form "Encyclopädie" replaced by "Enzyklopädie," and "gesammten Pharmacie" by "gesamten Pharmazie."

Besides describing the individual drug, the best method of dispensing it in prescriptions is indicated, and the process of manufacture of galenical compounds is fully illustrated in the text. Methods of detecting adulterations and of estimating the quality of preparations are given in detail, while the legal regulations governing the practice of pharmacy by German apothecaries are to find appropriate place in the finished work. The work will contain formulas for special preparations of which the formula has been at some time published.

A valuable feature of the encyclopædia is the bibliographical references, giving the names of works which can be consulted by the student or practising pharmacist who wishes to pursue the study of a given subject at greater length than is afforded by the encyclopædia, making it invaluable as a reference book for college libraries.

[1] Real-Enzyklopädie der Gesamten Pharmazie. Handwörterbuch für Apotheker, Artze und Medizinalbeamte. Begrundet von Dr. Ewald Geissler und Dr. Josef Moeller Zweite, Gänzlich umgearbeitete Auflage. Herausgegeben von Prof. Dr. Josef Moeller, Vorstand des Pharmakologischen Institutes an der Universität Graz, und Prof. Dr. Hermann Thoms, Vorstand des Pharmazeutischen Institutes an der Universität Berlin. Mit zahlreichen Illustrationen. Berlin: Urban & Schwarzenberg, 1904. Erscheint in zirka 10 Bänden von je 45 Druckbogen. (Preis pro Band broschiert: 18 M. = 21 K. 60 h, eleg. geb.: 20 M. 50 Pf. = 24 K 60 h.)

(*Written for the American Druggist.*)

DESERVED CRITICISM IS NOT ALWAYS A GOOD EXCUSE.

By Joel Blanc.

There are among those who have thus far declined to ally themselves with the N. A. R. D. many energetic, intelligent, generous men, and it is to these, whose criticisms of the N. A. R. D. are at least partly based upon fact, that the following is addressed.

What are the criticisms which are used as excuses for not joining the national association? The most common, the best of them, consist of complaints running somewhat as follows:

"The N. A. R. D. has not benefited, cannot or will not benefit me.

"I cannot afford to pay the dues; or, I cannot get adequate return if I do.

"The men in the organization are not the right kind of men; they do not practice what they preach, and my self-respect will not permit me to accept them as my leaders."

The N. A. R. D. being a delegate organization, it in itself is simply a representative body with constantly changing representation, and as all criticism must be of comparative deduction, criticisms of the organization must be, and always are, based upon comparisons between individuals, or, at least, between locals or groups of individuals. As every excuse for not joining the national organization must find its basis in at least semi-local conditions, the only ground upon which to combat the criticisms must be either local or semi-local. In this, the only rational point of argument, it must be conceded that each of the criticisms noted above is based upon limited truth, if not invariable fact. As is shown in the following, the last of the criticisms noted is the strongest, and yet the very portrayal therein of the organization's greatest weakness is the strongest argument why every intelligent man should become a member.

Now my friend, not as the confession of a fact, but for the sake of argument, we will consider that the reasons advanced by you for not joining the N. A. R. D. are in the abstract good reasons.

Let us suppose that the N. A. R. D. has been of no benefit to you. If that is so, it must be that either it has refused to benefit you because you are not a member or because it lacks the power to benefit you. If it has refused to help you, you must concede that it has the power to restrict its benefits to its friend-members, and you thereby acknowledge its strength and justice, and show why you should be a member. If you say that it has not the power to help you, it must be that either your condition is above improvement or that you are confronted by problems that the N. A. R. D. has not attempted to solve. If your condition is all that you desire, if you have reached a commercial position that is your ideal, does not your manliness, your pride, demand that you tell your fellows how you won success? Can you make your voice heard except through the megaphone of organization?

On the other hand, let us grant that you are confronted by problems that the N. A. R. D. has not attempted to solve. As the purpose of the N. A. R. D. is to solve every commercial problem of the trade *for its members*, it will become its business to solve yours when you are a member, but you have no right to expect it to know of your troubles until you tell them, and tell them *as a member*. To say that your troubles are beyond solution is to put yourself in a position of ridiculous pre-eminence, because any problem that men can create men can solve, and if your problems are beyond solution you are a mere unit, must be more than man, more than all men. Surely you do not put yourself in a position where you see your shadow so great that others can see nothing to make the shadow.

Perhaps your argument is that it will cost you in combined dues from six to twelve dollars per year and that the greatest possible benefits to be received are not worth that. This cannot be true unless your business is so small that it is not worth having unless it can be developed into something better. Of course you desire to so develop it. If you positively cannot afford to pay your dues *now*, no one wants you to, but you can give service that will be accepted in lieu thereof, which will be gladly accepted by your fellows until you can afford to pay in dollars. The reason that the N. A. R. D. cannot give you full return for your dollars now is because the volume of your business is so small and it therefore follows that as your business increases your problems will increase, and the more rapid the increase the sooner the N. A. R. D. will become a necessity to you and make you not only willing, but able to pay your dues.

I will wager, however, that you make one of the foregoing excuses. I am sure that you base your criticisms of the organization upon the action or lack of action of individuals who are members. Now, perhaps you are one of those who accuse me of calling hard names in my writings. Reconsider such of my work as you have ever read and see if I do not speak truly when I say that I have attacked types and characteristics of classes and never individuals. Are you not working injustice to yourself by failing in your own judgment to distinguish between the personality and character of men as represented in classes. Let me illustrate:

A friend whom I very much respect once accused me of "calling names" of the classes I criticised, and a moment later he personally criticised a proprietor whose gifts have more than once saved the N. A. R. D from bankruptcy. He assumed that it was wrong for me to criticise a class for lack of self-interest, while it was right for him to criticize an individual for what he termed self interest, even when that self-interest was only achieved by benefiting thousands. Do you not sometimes make this mistake, my brother? Do you not lose sight of the value of the service merely because you have forgotten that "the laborer is worthy of his hire"? Suppose that hire is only a little prominence, a little praise; suppose even, that the fleeting fame does make its recipient a little lordly and pompous; does it make the good he has done any less?

But now (we are getting closer together) you say that your local—and therefore the N. A. R. D.—does not command your respect, and that in your own town the local is apathetic; the officials are dead wood and that you see no use in joining an organization that is accomplishing nothing. If you are located in a large city I will not acknowledge the right of this criticism, because members invariably force the mere figureheads to the background. But if you are in one of the many smaller places I must acknowledge the force of your argument and have only to say that your hypothesis is at fault.

It is unhappily true that among the locals some presidents have been elected merely because they were old and dignified; some secretaries because of a family tree, and executive committee men merely on account of their geographical distribution over the town or county.

Too often has a "knocker" been put in office in the hope that the honor would stop his "knocking"; too often the reformed cutter has been made an official merely to keep him "reformed," or the snail been honored in the foolish belief that the honor would turn him into a racehorse. Is it any wonder that a dark pall of apathy falls over such locals? But are you not indirectly to blame? Are not you one of the ultra-purists, who hold the mediæval theory that the office should seek the man? When a group of men, having hustled for offices, and having secured them, put energy and enthusiasm in their labors, do you not call them a "Machine?" Is your position tenable if you one day criticise your local because it is dead and the next day because it is too lively? You consider it presumptuous for an outsider to tell you how to run your business and say that is only a partner's privilege. Have you a right to criticise an organization in which you are not a partner?

Let us concede that all the criticisms you make are deserved: why not make them effective by uttering them as an interested party? Why not secure the *right* to make them? Do you expect to put mere figureheads and drones out of office when you are but a drone, and even less than a figurehead? Suppose there is a "machine," do you expect to block its cogs by long distance putty balls of speech? The way to break a machine is with your own works, and nine times out of ten when you get right among the wheels you will find that so-called machines is only a body of sincere, enthusiastic, self-sacrificing men to whose efforts you add your own and are proud of being part of a machine that works for the accomplishment of good.

On the other hand, I will acknowledge that your criticisms deal with lamentable facts; I will acknowledge that you clearly show where the weakness is; that you know what remedy is needed and how to administer it; that you are one of the many non-members I have met who know just what should be done, how to do it and have the ability to do it. Yes; YOU have the ability to do all that is needed, to make your local all that it should be; to lead others and thus make a worthy leader of yourself; YOU have the intelligence, the strength and energy to carry out those reforms that would assure success, but you simply WILL NOT.

As an outsider your criticisms are worthless, your words powerless, and your energy wasted. All that you make of your ability is to offer yourself to less intelligent, less worthy men to use as a shield to strike their fellows over your shoulder.

Because organization men pay some attention to you and attempt to combat some of your arguments you think that you are accomplishing something, when in fact you are but being used as a buffer by those unworthy ones who fear to fight in the open. You may feel that you have a following because a few hang on your words as well as your neck. Try to start a rival organization and see how far your followers will follow. Try to collect dues from them and see them take to the tall fodder.

My friend, you are unjust to yourself, belittling your own ability, wasting your energy, sacrificing deserved honor and, above all, losing true happiness, that real manly self-respect that comes from accomplishing great things with great men and thus realizing your own greatness.

OUTLINES FOR THE SAMPLING OF DRUGS AND CHEMICALS.[1]

BY LYMAN F. KEBLER.

The importance of procuring representative samples for analytical work is overlooked and underestimated only by those who have never had any practical experience. Its value, however, is known to those who have had the pleasure of seeing their results confirmed by a referee because sampling was properly performed and those who have been unfortunate enough to find that their results were "off" because of careless sampling. Probably many of us have experienced both. The observations embodied in this paper are gleaned from practice and are presented here with the view of assisting in bringing about some uniform system of sampling and, if possible, to save some of the younger chemists many trying and at times embarrassing experiences.

The procuring of uniform samples is the first important step in securing uniformity in chemical analysis. So long as we are not certain of obtaining samples which represent the total average of the material of a given consignment we can never be positive that the analytical results can be relied on as truly setting forth the quality of the goods delivered. Non-representative samples are worse than worthless.

Recommendations for the sampling of butter, cheese and soils are contained in Bulletin No. 45 of the Bureau of Chemistry, entitled "Methods of Analysis." The general principles involving the proper sampling of ores have been thoroughly treated by several writers.[2]

One of the factors that contributes largely to the uncertainty of obtaining average samples is the practice in commerce of entrusting most of the sampling to workmen, who do not realize the importance of this duty, are frequently indifferent and exercise little judgment. For example, the containers in which the material is placed, after preparing the samples, have not been well cleaned, thus detracting from the physical appearance of the article; or rinsing a bottle out with water and neglecting to dry the same before taking a sample of oil; or placing a sample of bleaching powder in a wet bottle, or allowing the uncorked bottles containing effervescing or deliquescing material to stand around several days before the same are transmitted to the chemical laboratory, or disregarding instructions relative to the manner in which the samples should be taken, etc. It can readily be seen that it does not require any discriminating intelligence to minimize the above disturbing factors, but this nevertheless demands definite plans of procedure. To accomplish this it is imperative for the chemist himself to learn how to take samples properly, and when the chemist is accomplished in the art then he can instruct a reliable person, in detail, by example, how to collect samples. The analyst himself should take samples in person from time to time and at unexpected moments when samples are being taken "turn up" and make a careful inspection.

The second and most important part to consider is the method of sampling and the number of samples to be taken from each delivery or purchase. The procedure which will reduce the disputes that may arise to a minimum is to adopt definite schemes for sampling (such as are outlined below), sample each package and analyze each sample. Such a procedure, however, is in the vast majority of transactions a commercial impossibility. Yet it is at present the common practice with a commodity like opium. In the writer's experience no hard-and-fast rules can be laid down to govern all sampling. Good judgment plays an important part. Points that should be duly considered are: the brand, the manufacturer or producer, serial numbering of the packages, physical appearance of several successive samples taken and previous experience with the goods in hand. The writer experienced very little friction by taking samples from every fifth package with such goods as acetanilide, benzoic acid, calomel, carbolic acid, citric acid, copper sulphate, copperas, fixed oils, flaxseed meal, formaldehyde, glycerine, milk sugar, nux vomica beans, oxalic acid, petrolatum, quinine sulphate, soda ash, sodium phosphate, etc.

The containers holding the samples and the original packages must be carefully marked for identification. The amount taken from each package was about 200 Gm. The samples were then carefully examined physically, and if no difference could be detected approximately one-half of each sample was removed to form a single composite sample. After thoroughly mixing this composite sample a sufficient amount was taken for analysis and a suitable amount set aside for future use. If, on the other hand, any difference was detected, several of the samples were tested, and if any abnormality was noted either the entire consignment was rejected or each sample was tested separately. Before either of the above procedures was put into effect the consignor was informed as to the findings and was usually given the option of having the goods rejected en masse or paying for having the samples tested individually.

It is self-evident that where only every fifth package is sampled the possibility of accepting some inferior goods is greater than when every package is tested, but even the latter procedure does not ensure positively against this, when the usual methods of sampling are followed. For example, on examining a carload of flaxseed meal it was found that a goodly number of barrels contained an A No. 1 product in the marked end of the barrel, but the unmarked end was filled with a mineral-oil-saturated product. Such a reprehensible method is not often met with, and it was only by exercising eternal care and vigilance that it was discovered.

The "one in five plan" of sampling has its defects. For example, if 25 per cent. of a delivery of olive oil is adulterated to the extent of 25 per cent., it is in the first place possible to miss the adulterated goods entirely, and in the second place it is quite probable, even if a fair proportion of the adulterated goods are sampled and a composite sample is made, for the analyst to miss such a small per cent. of foreign material.

In the case of high-priced goods such as opium and some of the essential oils and chemicals to be used in quantities proportionate to their strength, in the manufacture of other com-

[1] Contribution No. 8 from the Drug Laboratory, Bureau of Chemistry, U. S. Department of Agriculture, read at the annual meeting of the American Pharmaceutical Association.

[2] A. N. Tate, J. Soc. Chem. Ind., 1884, 3, 330; E. Keller, J. Am. Chem. Soc., 1897, 19, 243; Wm. Glen, Trans. Am. Inst. Min. Eng., 1891, 20, 155.

modities, every container should be tested. The reasons are obvious.

Other essential points to be considered are: first, the physical properties of the goods, whether viscid or semi-viscid, crystalline, powdered, whole or partly broken or cut, such as roots, leaves, barks and beans; liquids and products that become liquefied on raising the temperature; second, the containers in which the goods are handled commercially, such as barrels, bags, bales, pockets, boxes, carboys, open and sealed iron drums, etc. In order to meet these condition the following classification based on the average commercial package may be followed:

1. Gums and Gummy Substances: Asafetida, benzoin, Curacoa aloes, myrrh, opium, etc.

2. Large Crystals and Crystalline Masses: Ammonium carbonate, copper sulphate, corrosive sublimate, potassium cyanide, sodium carbonate, etc.

3. Powders and Small Crystals: Acetanilide, arsenious oxide, bismuth subnitrate, bleaching powder, charcoal, cinchona bark, ipecac root, gum arabic, wild cherry bark, etc.

4. Crude Vegetable Drugs: Aconite root, belladonna leaves, bloodroot, cocoa leaves, cubeb berries, nux vomica beans, vanilla beans, etc.

5. Liquids: Acetone, alcohol, ammonia water, balsam copaiba, glycerine, sulphuric acid, turpentine, etc.

6. Articles that congeal in part or as a whole : ι moderately low temperatures: Oils of anise seed, eucalyptus, peppermint, sassafras, glacial acetic acid, etc.

7. Solid at ordinary temperatures but liquefy on warming: Carbolic acid crystals, beeswax, ceresin, Japan wax, petrolatum, paraffin, spermaceti, etc.

This classification will not be taken up seriatim.

1. Gum opium comes in globular or subglobular lumps packed with Rumex seeds in tin-lined wooden boxes, and the sampling should be conducted as follows: The cases containing the lumps of opium should be carefully opened and the tin lining the same should be cut and bent with as little mutilation as possible, so that it can be returned to its original position and soldered if necessary. From every fifth lump a conical section should be taken in such a manner that the apex of the cone approximately comes from the centre of the lump, and the amount of the surface of the cone should approximately bear the same proportion to the entire surface of the lump that the whole cone bears to the sphere. With a little practice these samples can be cut very accurately. The size of the cones should be such as to approximately give the desired amount of material necessary for analysis, and at the same time sufficient should be left so that the chemist can retain a portion for future use, if necessary. For duplicate analysis, according to the present U. S. Pharmacopœia process, 20 Gm. will be necessary. In order to have a sufficient amount left for the chemist's reserve sample and to provide for contingencies, it is desirable to take from each package approximately 120 Gm.

Aloes, Curacao, comes in tin cans holding about 50 pounds, two cans being packed in one case. Samples should be taken from both cans of every fifth case by cutting a 2-inch circular hole at the top near a corner formed by three planes. Through this opening the contents are thoroughly mixed by means of a strong, smooth stirring rod, then the sample is withdrawn either by pouring off or by using the stirrer; at times, though, aloes is too stiff to mix in this manner, then it becomes necessary to warm the cans; even then the contents of some packages will not liquefy sufficiently to thoroughly mix. In such cases it is best to take one sample through the center of the can by means of a tryer.

Asafœtida is delivered in 400-pound cases in lumps, more or less massed together. Small pieces must be taken from many separate lumps and all parts which show some difference in physical appearance. The size of the pieces should approximately be proportionate to the size of the lumps from which they are taken. In sampling, the finer material, if present, should be remembered. The pieces must then be thoroughly broken up, either in an iron mortar or in a strong iron mill, thoroughly mixed and about 1 pound placed in a bottle for a sample.

The cases of gum benzoin usually contain about 140 pounds and the sampling should be conducted as for asafetida. The fine portion should, however, not be forgotten.

2. Large Crystals and Crystalline Masses come in boxes, barrels and sealed iron drums. In every case each package sampled should be fully opened for inspection. This gives a much better idea of the physical appearance than could be obtained from a small sample. About 1 pound of material should be taken from each package sampled and finely powdered before testing.

3. Powders and Small Crystals. With this form of material it is necessary to take into consideration the kind of containers, such as barrels, boxes, bins, sealed drums, and at times heaps must be sampled. Barrels, sealed iron drums and boxes should be sampled by taking not less than 1 pound from both ends of the container. The two places of sampling should be as far from each other as possible. The material thus withdrawn must be thoroughly mixed and a suitable amount of this mixture taken for a sample. The number of packages to be sampled in this manner will depend on the size of the consignment, the value of the article to be tested and other factors enumerated above. One of the best ways of taking samples from packages of this character is to bore or cut a 2-inch hole into the ends and through this opening introduce a tryer, such as is used in sampling cheese, give the same a circular turn and withdraw the material by having the convex portion of the tryer at the bottom of the opening. The openings are to be closed with suitable stoppers or small pieces of tin nailed over them. Heaps can best be sampled by horizontally thrusting a 2-inch tin tube, of suitable length, into the material at about a half-dozen different places, removed as far from one another as possible, thoroughly mixing the several withdrawals and taking such an amount of the mixture for a sample as may be necessary. The proper sampling of bins presents numerous difficulties, chiefly on account of inaccessibility. The procedure must be governed by the conditions that obtain in each case. Sometimes it is possible to bore holes in the bins, but frequently this is neither possible nor feasible.

4. Crude Vegetable Drugs usually come in bales, pockets, barrels, bags, kegs and boxes. In the case of bales, pockets and bags, about half-pound samples should be taken from the top, bottom and near the middle, mixed and placed in receptacles carefully numbered. Barrels, kegs and boxes must be opened by removing the heads or covers and thoroughly inspecting their contents as to physical appearance and foreign odors, such as mustiness. It is at times desirable to take out both heads of a barrel or empty it entirely. One end is at times materially different from the other end. The number of packages to be sampled must be determined by their size and the nature of the material to be examined. Packages containing from 300 to 400 pounds should all be sampled, especially potent remedies. With drugs that are liable to considerable variation every package should be sampled and tested. With some goods it is sufficient to sample every fifth package. If the samples are sufficiently dry they should be coarsely ground with an iron mill, completely dried at 100° C. and reduced to a number 40 powder. This procedure ensures a uniform sample.

5. Liquids are delivered in barrels, iron drums and carboys. There is usually no difficulty in taking samples from these containers by pouring, but it should be borne in mind that liquid preparations often contain sediments or suspended material due to recent agitation, either present in the original material or derived from a dirty container. It frequently happens that the upper portion is perfectly satisfactory, but the bottom is contaminated with foreign material, and, therefore, is not salable, but a source of loss. Before taking samples from liquid preparations the containers, opening at the top, should be allowed to remain quiet from 24 to 48 hours, depending on the nature of the material. The sample should then be withdrawn from the bottom by means of a siphon, which is started by using a portion of the liquid at the top of the container. Conditions at times and the nature of the substance (glycerine), sometimes preclude this procedure, then it becomes necessary to remove the material from the bottom of the package by using a glass tube, from ¾ to 1 inch in diameter, constricted at one end so that a rubber tube with a pinchcock can be slipped on. When

ready to take the sample close the pinchcock, lower the open end of the tube to the bottom of the container, open pinchcock, allow the tube to fill, either by gravity or suction, close the pinchcock, withdraw the tube, and carefully place its contents in a suitable receptacle. Repeat the operation until a sufficient amount is collected.

6. Articles that congeal in part or as a whole at moderately low temperatures. Considerable care should be exercised in taking samples from this class of goods to see that the contents of a package are completely liquefied and thoroughly mixed. For example, if a can of sassafras oil has congealed, the heavier portions are usually at the bottom and it is not sufficient to liquefy the oil, but it becomes imperative to thoroughly mix the same by mechanical means, such as stirring. If shaking is resorted to the containers must be partially emptied before so doing, otherwise unsatisfactory results will be arrived at. Pouring from one can to another is a good procedure. In the case of sassafras oil it frequently becomes necessary to examine every can, but usually the testing of every fifth container gives satisfactory results. What has been said about oil of sassafras holds for the other oils, but is not so conspicuous in some cases. On allowing congealed glacial acetic acid to liquefy slowly the first portion liquefied is usually more dilute and contains a larger proportion of the impurities than the portion still congealed. Unless this point is borne in mind unreliable results may be obtained.

7. Goods solid at ordinary temperatures but liquefy on warming. Of this class carbolic acid crystals form a good example. This chemical is usually collected in tin or galvanized cans, holding about 300 pounds, and allowed to cool. In so doing the portion of lowest melting point is forced to the centre, where it finally congeals, or sometimes remains liquid. To secure a representative sample it will be necessary to melt the contents of the cans by placing them in a hot room or hot water above 50° C. for several days. A circular hole about 8 inches in diameter is then cut into one end, the liquefied carbolic acid thoroughly mixed with a strong glass or brass rod and the sample taken.

Petrolatum comes in barrels. In order to get a representative sample it is best to remove one head, introduce a galvanized iron coil and pass steam until completely liquefied, and then remove the material. The packages can be sampled in the solid form with an ordinary tryer, but it is then desirable to take samples from both ends, because "toppings" are occasionally practiced.

Waxes and similar products are sampled by cutting numerous small pieces from different portions of the package and making a homogeneous mixture by melting and subsequently cooling. Any dirt will settle to the bottom and can be seen on inspection.

The above notes treat the many-sided subject of sampling only in a limited manner. Many details could be added, but the general principles are set forth, and if others will add of their experience a fair amount of material will soon be at hand to place the matter on a good basis.

To Color Incandescent Globes.

Frosted effects may be obtained by dipping the globe in a saturated solution of alum. The lamp must be held in the hand while the crystallization takes place on the surface of the globe. If it is laid down or even hung up the coating will be unevenly done and the result unsatisfactory. Repeated dippings will make a heavier deposit.

The alum solution may be colored by the use of some of the dyes which are to be purchased ready prepared for use. A red effect may be secured by the use of logwood or cochineal. Turmeric added while the alum solution is cooling will give a yellow tinge.

Where these globes are to be exposed to the weather, a transparent solution of white shellac should be applied. Shellac dissolved in wood alcohol and colored with an aniline dye of some kind will be found appropriate.

MISLEADING TRADE NAMES.[1]

BY CHARLES A. HILL.

The tendency to give definite names to articles of trade, the production in fresh localities of commodities hitherto associated with a particular place and the frequent and increasing substitution of artificial for natural products, together with the growth of a happy distaste for false descriptions, as evidenced by some recent prosecutions under the Merchandise Marks act, such as those relating to butter, linen, wine and spirits—these and other considerations have led me to the conclusion that a communication indicating the sort of inaccuracy of nomenclature that tends to obtain, and calling attention to some of the most common instances of pharmaceutical trade misnomers, might usefully be made at the present time.

I think that it may be said at once that no one dislikes false descriptions of any kind more cordially than many of those whose lot it is to trade in products which habitually pass under such pseudonyms, and many have doubtless noticed in wholesale price-lists that certain names are printed between inverted commas, or with a marginal note, the purpose being to direct attention to such courtesy titles.

Names of commercial products may be inaccurate from a variety of causes. A large number of cases arise, however, from the fact that the name which originally indicated either the method or the locality of production has since become obsolete. How far a name obsolete from one or other of these causes should control the product (possibly an improved one) of a later period—the whole subject, in fact, of the importance and true meaning of such original names—leads one on to a large and rather vexed question quite beyond the scope of this paper.

Without being controversial, however, I think it may safely be said that narrowing down the nature of a product so as to make it correspond precisely with the etymological meaning of an ancient and obsolete name is a principle which may very easily be carried too far. How untenable the principle may be is easily seen by the consideration of extreme cases—to take only two instances (the one etymological, the other geographical). Pomade is not always made from apples, nor do Bath buns emanate exclusively from Bath. The contention that anything which takes its name from its original source of production should ever after be produced from that same source is easily seen to be untenable in the case of chemical substances, such as benzoic acid, which on this principle would have to be made exclusively from gum benzoin. With products of variable composition (*e.g.*, whiskey) the difficulty arises of proving that different methods of production can give rise to perfectly similar products. In these cases, however, it would seem that a rigid interpretation of the principles above referred to is calculated to impede progress.

Although inaccurate trade names cannot be classified into strictly rational groups, it will be convenient to deal with some of them in sections.

GEOGRAPHICAL MISNOMERS.

This class, made up largely of crude drugs, is fairly numerous, even though one excludes the names of drugs derived not from their habitat, but from the port from which they are actually shipped. There may be some who will learn with surprise that we do not obtain aloes from Barbados, the so-called Barbados aloes coming from Curacao. "Turkey" colocynth comes from Cyprus and Jaffa, while all the "Turkey" and "East Indian" rhubarb, of course, comes from China. An interesting case is that of sarsaparilla: "Jamaica" sarsaparilla comes from Bocos del Toro, near Panama, the "Lima" variety also coming from Panama, while the only sarsaparilla which comes from Jamaica does not bear the name of its habitat. Gum acacia (gum arabic), ordinarily known as "Turkey" gum, comes from the Soudan, and "Malabar" cardamoms are grown in Ceylon and not on the Malabar coast of India. It is seen that sometimes the name of the habitat seems to get inseparably connected with a particular variety of drugs; this, however, scarcely excuses a false description, and it may not be out of place to point out here that pods of *Cassia obovata*

[1] *Chemist and Druggist.*

from plants cultivated in Arabia are not correctly described as "Alexandrian" merely because to an inexpert observer they resemble the pods of *Cassia angustifolia*.

The name "Venice turpentine" indicates the place from which this article was formerly obtained, while "Burgundy pitch" is a name given to a product which used to come via Burgundy. The so-called "true" variety of the latter product is now obtained from Finland and the Black Forest, but in each of these cases (Venice turpentine and Burgundy pitch) the names are also applied to factitious products. The name "Petroleum barbadense" no longer indicates the source of this tar, and it may be doubted whether "grains of Paradise" were ever obtained from the locality from which they take their name. Tallow, the useful fat to which the epithet "Russian" clings so tenaciously, now comes from Australia.

Jordan almonds, French chalk, Naples soap and a host of others may be dismissed as pious frauds, along with such old friends as Bath buns and Banbury cakes; but the piety is lacking in the case of arrowroot, which is sold at an enhanced price, on account of the prenomen "Bermuda," notwithstanding the fact that it has never seen that island. A somewhat similar thing occurs with eucalyptus oil sent from Australia to Tasmania, there to be mixed with the genuine product and the whole reshipped as Tasmanian Globulus oil.

BOTANICAL AND PHARMACEUTICAL MISNOMERS.

Under this head I refer to the very common practice of classing rhizomes, corms, etc., as roots, and fruits as seeds. It is not necessary to take up time by giving instances of these, but another case may be mentioned—that of the alga *Chondrus crispus* (Irish moss), which is often mistermed "lichen hybern." By pharmaceutical misnomers I mean such things as balsam copaiba and Canada balsam, which are not balsams but oleoresins. Passing now to the more purely

TRADE MISNOMERS,

one may consider miscellaneous errors of nomenclature separated for convenience sake from the previous sections. The term "carbolic acid" must be considered a misnomer when applied to liquid mixtures of cresols and allied compounds more or less innocent of phenol.

Calamine is a name well known in pharmacy, yet the native ore is now, I believe, practically unobtainable. The name is sometimes applied to zinc carbonate without any indication of the artificial nature of the latter. Sometimes it is applied to barium sulphate containing zinc carbonate. To apply the term "lapis calaminæ" to an artificial product, colored so as to represent the native ore, must be regarded as misleading, though no exception can be taken to the description "calamina præparata."

The oils are a class fertile in names which are, from one cause or another, questionable. Among the fixed oils we find the oil expressed from peach or apricot kernels still referred to by some firms by a compound name containing the word "amygdalæ"; colza and rape are confused; while the essential oils afford examples of various kinds of misnomers. We have "oleum cedrat," "oleum rhodii," "oleum juniper. lig." and oleum pini sylvestris," all factitious oils; "oleum organi" confused with and even sold as oil of thyme. "Oleum succini" is not made from amber. A sample of so-called "Russian turpentine" examined in the writer's laboratory consisted of light oil of tar.

The difficulty of deciding what constitutes falsity in a name is illustrated by a consideration of the practice of separating one or more constituents and selling the residue as the oil itself; thus, dementholized oil of peppermint is sold in large quantities as oil of peppermint, and essential oil of camphor reaches the market after having been deprived both of its safrol and of its camphor. From these cases it would not be such a great step to eucalyptus oil deprived of at least a portion of its eucalyptol, while the final stage might be the marketing of lemon oil terpene as oil of lemon, and though this stage has happily not—so far as I am aware—been realized, yet large quantities of oils of lemon and bergamot are bought and sold which are heavily adulterated with such terpenes.

CHEMICAL MISNOMERS.

Here is a subject too great to grapple with, so that one has to pass over all the minor inaccuracies, such as classing phenol and pyrogallol as acids, and as ethers bodies which are not ethers. A protest, however, may perhaps be entered against the antiquated nomenclature which survives with chemical brokers and dealers, and also against the use which has been made by a German firm of the chemical name "resorcinol" to denote a mixture of resorcinol (resorcin) and iodoform.

In the drug trade proper we have the purely fanciful "citrate of magnesia" and such interesting survivals as "ferri carb.," and even "ferri subcarb." for ferric oxide; and attention may be called to the curious habit of referring to acetic anhydride as "acid. acetic. anhydros.," which is, of course, very apt to mislead. "Stearine" to denote stearic acid is common but noteworthy. A pharmaceutical name which if not misleading ought to be is "pulv. violæ." The Latin form of violet powder (which is itself a misnomer unless violets be present in some form) is, of course, "pulvis violaris."

The Massage Cream Problem.

As the result of many experiments and practical tests of products prepared from casein, employing various methods of coagulation and treatment of the coagulum, we are finally in position to offer a fairly good solution of the problem. At least three barbers who do a large massage business, and who have been testing products for us, agree that the last "batch" is all right. Thus says B. C. Cooban in the April *Bulletin of Pharmacy*.

Hydrochloric acid was found to give the best results, giving a larger yield of casein. Glycerin cannot be used in softening up the dried mass—it is too hard to "rub out," and it is essential that the finished product be ground in a paint mill, for otherwise it will soon become grainy and unsatisfactory. Running it through the mill gives a better mixed and smoother product that it is possible to obtain with a mortar. There is an inherent stickiness in the product that makes it hard to rub out and it leaves a starchy feeling on the face; this may be overcome by the addition of a small amount of sweet almond oil and by the use of dilute alcohol in softening the dried casein. After ascertaining these points the following formula was constructed. It works well, but as we intend adding massage cream to our own list of specialties, experience may make necessary some changes in manipulation. Therefore we do not claim the product to represent perfection, but, as the barber says, "It's the best I have seen and it's O. K." The formula:

Skimmed milk	1 gallon.
Hydrochloric acid	1 fluidounce.
Boric acid	1 ounce.
Oil of bitter almond	20 drops.
Oil of rose geranium	30 drops.
Oil of sweet almond	½ fluidounce.
Solution of carmine	sufficient to tint.

Add to the milk one gallon of hot water—hot enough to raise the temperature to about 80 degrees Fahrenheit. Mix the hydrochloric acid with one pint of water and add this to the diluted milk slowly, with constant stirring sufficient to completely coagulate the casein, which separates in a finely divided condition. Allow to stand for an hour, collect the precipitate on cheese-cloth, and after draining return the mass to the vessel and add two gallons of water. Stir the coagulum, breaking up any masses that may form; pour off the water and wash again. It is necessary that all of the acid and whey be washed out of the casein. Collect on strainer and squeeze out all the water possible, then transfer to a mortar or other suitable vessel and incorporate the boric acid. Transfer to a cheesecloth bag, suspend this from a shelf or other suitable place and allow it to hang for 36 to 48 hours, squeezing the bag occasionally. The mass contracts and forces water from itself and it will take about two days to get it all out.

The casein will then be found quite dry and granular. Transfer it to a mortar, rub it as fine as possible, put in about one ounce of dilute alcohol (enough to moisten) and then add the oil of sweet almonds and perfume. Tint the product with the solution of carmine. Add sufficient water to form a soft paste, beat all together until uniformly mixed and then run through a paint mill and bottle it at once, or else put it up in collapsible tubes. It dries out very rapidly and must be put into packages immediately.

Cream *of* Current Literature

A summary of the leading articles in contemporary pharmaceutical periodicals.

A New Plant Containing Hydrocyanic Acid.—*Sambucus nigra* was some time ago described as a plant containing hydrocyanic acid. Guignard (*Archiv der Pharm.*, 1905, p. 553) adds to the list of plants containing this acid, *Thalictrum aquilegifolium*, which contains hydrocyanic acid in the shape of a glucoside chiefly found in the leaves of this plant. The root does not contain any of the acid, and the stem contains but a slight amount. The plant also contains an enzyme, which can decompose and furnish amygdalin.

The Use of Solution of Formaldehyde in the Treatment of Burns.—Camus (*Scalpel*, February, 1906, quoted in *Répertoire de pharmacie*, March 10, 1906) recommends the use of formaldehyde solution in burns. Applications of a 40 per cent. solution are made twice daily, or, if advisable, the solution may be diluted with equal parts of water. The ulcerated parts should not be touched. The pain and burning disappear rapidly, the tension and redness quickly subside and the burn heals within a few days.

Assay of Nitroglycerin Tablets.—The following method is proposed by E. Sautesson for the assay of nitroglycerin tablets: One hundred tablets are powdered and extracted with ether in a Soxhlet extraction apparatus. The residue obtained on evaporating the ethereal solution consists of cacao butter and nitroglycerin; it is saponified with alcoholic potash and the potassium nitrate yielded by the nitroglycerin reduced by nascent hydrogen to ammonia. Excess of caustic soda is then added and the ammonia distilled off and determined in the usual way.—*Phar. Jour.*

Poisoning with Veronal.—The pharmacist must be on his guard against the ever-increasing number of accidents with the new hypnotics. Veronal, which is so popular nowadays, has contributed its share to the list of fatalities, although it must be admitted that large doses of this remedy have been taken without ill effects. A case was recently reported by Held (*Répertoire de pharmacie*, March 10, 1906, p. 117), in which a woman swallowed 9 Gm. of veronal for suicidal purposes. She became unconscious, with rapid breathing, her head being bent back, and she was seized with a series of convulsions. A number of blisters appeared over the joints of her fingers and her urine was very dark. The treatment consisted of washing the stomach and of administering hot baths and cold douches, while the patient was fed through the rectum.

Some Incompatibilities.—A paragraph in a recent issue of *Pharmazeutische Zentralhalle* calls attention to the following incompatibilities: Oil of cade when mixed with liquid petrolatum gives rise to a dirty opaque fluid from which the oil of cade rapidly separates, while the liquid petrolatum becomes slightly discolored with a brown ring on its surface. Liquid petrolatum is also incompatible with liquid styrax. Stovaine, the new anæsthetic, which has been quite extensively used instead of cocaine, is incompatible with alkaline solutions and with solutions of mercuric chloride. For this reason alkalis and mercuric chloride should be avoided in the disinfection and cleaning of hypodermic syringes used for stovaine, unless the syringe be afterward thoroughly cleaned with distilled water or with physiological salt solution.

Some Hints in Compounding Pills are given by Wiegand in December number of the *American Journal of Pharmacy*, of which the following extracts are of interest: For the accurate preparation of phosphorus pills it is best to make a solution of the phosphorus in cacao butter by dissolving the weighed amount of phosphorus in a test tube provided with a stopper, adding a little carbon disulphide, and by gradually adding small amounts of cacao butter, until five times the weight of phosphorus has been reached. The tube is then heated by immersing it in warm water until the mixture is homogeneous. The necessary amount of this mass is then taken for the preparation of the pills.

In making pills containing volatile oils a small amount of soap should be added, and in making pills containing camphor a small amount of resin should be incorporated. Pills containing potassium permanganate are best prepared by triturating the drug with cacao butter and adding enough white wax to form the mass.

The Estimation of Alkaloids in Belladonna Leaves.—Forsberg (*Pharm. Post*, 1906, p. 2) tried four different methods of determining the amount of alkaloids in belladonna leaves. In the first process he employed the method recommended by the German Pharmacopœia, involving the use of 20 Gm. of the powdered leaves; in the second and third methods he used milk of lime and ammonia respectively as the alkali, while in the fourth, which closely resembles that of the German Pharmacopœia, he dried the finely powdered leaves on the water bath in the presence of equal parts of a 20 per cent. solution of sodium carbonate. He treated the product with a mixture of ether, chloroform and caustic soda. The ethereal solution thus obtained was distilled until its volume was reduced to three-quarters of the original. The small amount of ammonia in this solution need not be determined, and the resulting liquid is clear, colorless and ready for trituration. [As we know, the U. S. P. VIII prescribes ammonia as the alkali in the process of assay of belladonna.]

A Practical Hint in Cases of Poisoning.—Triboulet (*Union Pharmaceutique*, March, 1906, p. 112) speaks of the great difficulty often met with in introducing the stomach tube into the mouths of patients unwilling or unable to relax their jaws. In people with strong teeth it is impossible at times to separate the jaw sufficiently to introduce the large stomach tube usually employed. In persons with false teeth or dental plates there is a grave danger of dislodging these artificial dental appliances into the throat in our efforts to pass the stomach tube. In such cases Triboulet has found two simple expedients of value—namely, first the employment of a small sized stomach tube, such as is used in children, and which can be much more readily passed, oftentimes through breaches in the teeth; and, second, the use of a soft rubber catheter of the ordinary size, introduced through the nose. Either of these smaller tubes provided with a funnel at the distal end can serve as a means of introducing ipecac or other emetics, or of washing the stomach with plain water. It is well to remember this simple expedient when called to attend cases of poisoning.

The Presence of Arsenic in Presumably Pure Glycerin.—Gallmard (*Journal de pharmacie et de chimie*, February 16, 1906) calls attention to the fact that commercial glycerins very frequently contain quantities of arsenic, which can be detected by means of chemical reactions, and what is still more important, that so-called pure glycerins contain traces of arsenic in such form that they cannot be directly detected by means of Marsh's apparatus. Gallmard believes that the arsenical compound which is present in these pure glycerins and which has hitherto escaped observation is an arsenous ether and is derived from the sulphuric acid used in the manufacture of crude glycerins. In order to detect the presence of arsenic in glycerin the glycerin is mixed with twice its volume of distilled water to which 1 per cent. of pure sulphuric acid is added. The mixture is boiled for ten hours, the apparatus being provided with a refrigerating coil. After cooling the mixture gives the characteristic ring with Marsh's test. This shows that the arsenic is present in the form of a compound which does not become dissociated by the ordinary method of Marsh, but must be previously decomposed by the method described by Gallmard.

Liquid Antiseptic Soap.—Wilbert, pharmacist to the German Hospital, Philadelphia, recommends the following formula for a liquid antiseptic soap:

Cottonseed oil	Cc. 300
Alcohol	Cc. 300
Water	Cc. 325
Sodium hydrate	Gm. 45
Sodium carbonate	Gm. 10
Sulphuric ether	Gm. 15
Carbolic acid	Gm. 25

The oil is placed in a flask, 100 Cc. of alcohol added, as well as the sodium hydrate. The mixture is heated on a water bath until it is completely saponified. It is then cooled, and the rest of the alcohol and the sodium carbonate dissolved in water are added. Finally, the carbolic acid and the ether are added and the whole is shaken and filtered. This soap is a yellowish liquid, with an ethereal odor and an alkaline reaction.

The Strength of Alcohol Used in the Preparation of Tincture of Opium.—According to Buttner (*Journal suisse de chimie et pharmacie*, 1905, p. 542) it is useless to employ alcohol in the strength of 70 degrees in the formula for tincture of opium, as adopted by the International Conference for the Unification of the Formulas of Potent Remedies. An alcohol of the strength of 50 degrees gives just as good results as one of 70 degrees, so far as the percentage of morphine in the tincture is concerned. Buttner also objects to percolation as the method of preparing tincture of opium, and finds that maceration gives as satisfactory results. Percolation, in his opinion, gives excellent results in the preparation of other tinctures but is not adapted for tincture of opium, for the reason that opium can never be exhausted, even if ten times its weight of alcohol be used. On the other hand, a larger quantity of alcohol cannot be employed, as is done in the case of fluid extracts, save if the product is afterward reduced to a convenient volume, and this requires heat, which would change the active principles of opium. [United States Pharmacopœia VIII prescribes diluted alcohol as the menstruum in the percolation of tincture of opium, the strength of the official diluted alcohol being about 41.5 per cent. by weight. During the preliminary maceration which is prescribed for 60 hours before the percolation is begun, equal parts of water and alcohol are employed, so that practically 50 per cent. alcohol is then used. In the process of the Pharmacopœia, therefore, the strength of alcohol used in the preparation of opium does not exceed 50 per cent. Both maceration and percolation are used in the process.]

Purified Benzin as a Dressing for Wounds.—Crouzel, in an article in *Répertoire de pharmacie*, for March 10, 1906, page 10, strongly advocates the employment of pure benzin as a dressing for cut or abraded surfaces, as favoring the removal of poisonous products and promoting healing. In his opinion the ideal dressing for a wound is a substance which dissolves the elements of pus—that is, the fatty products which accumulate on the surface of infected wounds and which serve as a culture ground for germs. Pure benzin is not toxic, but is antiseptic, as it counteracts decomposition and suppuration. By its rapid, spontaneous evaporation benzin cools the surface and thus counteracts inflammation, and with its aid all disintegrated portions of tissues, blood, etc., can be removed very readily from a wound. The objection to the use of benzin in surgical dressings is its disagreeable odor; the best deodorant for it is nitrobenzin or artificial oil of almonds, which is frequently used in perfumery, hair oils, etc. A variety of medicinal substances may be dissolved in benzin which is employed for surgical purposes, as, for example, camphor, quinine, morphine, iodine, sulphur and phosphorus. Solutions of paraffin or of rubber in benzin can be employed for hermetically sealing wounds, while benzin can be mixed with alcohol and ether when this is advisable. Benzin thus can be employed as a vehicle for the application of curative substances, as well as a means of washing and disinfecting the wound.

The treatment of wounds by benzin is absolutely harmless, is extremely inexpensive, and by adding menthol to benzin one can obtain a very fair anæsthesia in painful wounds. The addition of 5 per cent. of petrolatum to benzin offers an excellent means of preventing surgical instruments from rusting, and all that is necessary is to dip the instrument in the liquid.

Cocaine Formate.—Vigier, in a communication to the Pharmaceutical Society of Paris, January 10, 1906, gave the results of his investigations on the preparation and properties of the formate of cocaine. This compound was prepared by Vigier for the purpose of obtaining the anæsthetic properties of cocaine in combination with a vaso-dilator, such as formic acid, with the view of counteracting the vaso-constrictive action of the older compounds of cocaine. Formic acid combines with cocaine in the proportion of 46 to 303, and the formate is prepared by saturating one molecule of pure cocaine dissolved in distilled water with one molecule of formic acid in the pure and crystalline form. The latter slowly dissolves and on evaporating the product at low temperature a slightly yellowish syrupy liquid is obtained, which on cooling deposits long silky needles, which must be quickly washed in distilled water, so as to redissolve as little as possible. The solution obtained with this washing deposits shiny, silky white needles of pure cocaine formate. The crystals are slightly bitter in taste, melt at a low temperature and rapidly decompose. Watery solutions are neutral to litmus paper and the salt is soluble in the proportion of 1 part to 41 of distilled water, increasing in solubility with any increase of temperature.

Liquor Cresolis Compositus.[1]—The recent revision of the Pharmacopœia admits a compound solution of cresol under the name of Liquor Cresolis Compositus, the formula of which is as follows:

Cresol	Gm. 500
Linseed oil	Gm. 350
Potassium hydroxide	Gm. 80
Water, a sufficient quantity to make	Gm. 1,000

La Walle and Cook (*American Journal of Pharmacy*, April, 1906, page 169) complain that the quality of the commercial cresol on the market and the practicability of the process recommended by United States Pharmacopœia, VIII, were such that considerable difficulty is experienced in preparing the compound solution in a satisfactory manner. The commercial samples of cresol varied particularly as regards solubility and specific gravity. Not one of the samples made a perfectly bright, clear solution, but all contained varying proportions of a flocculent material, which was not dissolved even after the addition of a large excess of water. When the cresol solutions were made up according to the U. S. P., the preparation was not soluble in water, but acquired solubility after standing for three weeks.

The authors suggest that the formula of the U. S. P. be modified, so as to complete the reaction between the linseed oil and the potassium hydroxide, before adding the cresol. By this method they succeeded in obtaining a preparation which is transparent as soon as completed and mixes clear with all proportions of water without any delay. The following is the process used:

A soft soap is first prepared, using the same amounts of linseed oil and potassium hydroxide as directed for the preparation of the official compound solution of cresol. The details of this process on the small scale may be the same as that directed for the U. S. P. soft soap.

Heat the linseed oil (350 Gm.) in a deep, capacious vessel on a water bath to a temperature of about 70 degrees C. Dissolve the potassium hydroxide (80 Gm.) in 450 Cc. of water, warm the solution to about 70 degrees C.; add it to the linseed oil and mix thoroughly. Then incorporate 40 Cc. of alcohol and continue to heat without stirring until a small portion of the mixture is found to be soluble in boiling water without the separation of oily drops. The soap thus prepared is now dissolved in 500 Gm. of cresol and a sufficient quantity of water added to make the solution weigh 1,000 Gm.

This solution may be immediately mixed with water in any proportion, forming a clear liquid, and will correspond with the official solution in strength and contents.

[1] Compare Wilbert's formula for antiseptic soap, above.

Queries and Answers

We shall be glad, in this department, to respond to calls for information on all pharmaceutic matters.

The Taste of Lecithin.—A. M. M. asks how the taste of solution of lecithin may be improved. As supplied by the principal American manufacturer solution of lecithin has a cloyingly sweet taste and a heavy odor which is objected to by some patients.

An inquiry of the manufacturer brought the following information: "Lecithin itself has a markedly disagreeable taste, which it is difficult to mask. Personally, we should have preferred to make it rather bitter than sweet, but the American palate seems so given to sweets that if we had done so we would probably have had many more complaints on this score. It is easy enough, of course, to make an elixir containing a mere trifling amount of lecithin—a combination of a whole lot of other drugs, but a pure lecithin preparation is a difficult matter to deal with. We have two new products of this now which we are about ready to bring out, because we have every reason to believe that lecithin is a valuable contribution to medicine of far more importance than is generally understood. For the particular case mentioned by you we should suggest the addition of about four drachms of compound tincture of gentian to an eight-ounce bottle of lecithin solution, or in that proportion."

"Acamulsia."—J. F. writes: "Kindly give the formula for acamulsia, or any other good emulsifying agent for oils."

The emulsifying agent known as acamulsia is a compound acacia powder, of which the following is the formula:

Acacia.	
Tragacanth.	
Starch.	
Sugar	āā ℥v.
Boric acid	℥i.

The ingredients named are reduced to a fine powder and mixed thoroughly. The mixed powder is then used in the proportion of half an ounce to the pint of completed emulsion. Eight ounces of oil is put into a quart bottle and shaken up, then half an ounce of acamulsia is added and the whole again well shaken, finally eight ounces of water and the whole shaken vigorously for a few minutes.

Another emulsifying agent of recent introduction is emulgen. This is said to form good emulsions with oil in the proportion of 1 part of emulgen to 5 parts of oil. The composition of emulgen is not definitely known, but a formula which we have seen calls for tragacanth, 10 parts; acacia, 5 parts; gluten, 5 parts; glycerin, 20 parts; alcohol, 10 parts; water, 50 parts. For the preparation of emulsion of codliver oil 400 Gm. of the oil is shaken with 80 Gm. of emulgen, 125 Gm. of glycerin, 20 Gm. of alcohol and the required amount of flavoring and solutions of hypophosphites mixed with 400 Gm. of distilled water.

Silver Polish.—L. R. asks for a process of resilvering a silver plated article by the application of a powder on a wet cloth.

A good preparation of this kind is represented by the following:

	Parts.
Silver chloride	3
Potassium bitartrate	20
Sodium chloride	15

Mix in a mortar to a very fine powder. This powder is commonly applied by mixing it to a thin cream with water and allowing it to dry on the article to be polished, the dry deposit being afterward removed with a polishing rag. The silver chloride is best made by precipitating a solution of silver nitrate, 3.6 Gm. in 100 Cc. of water, with hydrochloric acid. The solution of silver nitrate should be previously acidulated with nitric acid. The precipitate of silver chloride obtained in this way is separated on a filter and washed and dried.

Lotion for Itch.—C. T. S.—There is nothing so generally useful in the treatment of scabies or itch, as the old fashioned sulphur ointment, though thymol in alcoholic solution has come largely into use in recent years. The following formulas are suggested:

I.

	Parts.
Thymol	10
Alcohol	100

II.

	Parts.
Thymol	10
Ether	20
Alcohol	80

Used as a lotion thrice daily.

Menthol, parts 5, may be added to either lotion when itching is severe, but this is usually perfectly controlled by the thymol.

A general lotion for the various forms of dermatitis simulating scabies is pink sulphur lotion made as follows:

Pink Sulphur Lotion.

Calamine	℥i.
Zinc oxide	℥i.
Sulphur	℥ij.
Carbolic acid	℥ss.
Glycerin	℥iss.
Water to make	Oi.

M. sig.: Shake well before using. Pour out in a saucer and dab on the skin with a bit of cloth both night and morning.

This "pink lotion" has many uses as a soother of cutaneous inflammation. It may be applied every half hour in acute eczemas with good results. After dabbing on the inflamed parts the areas may be covered with thin cloth, or bits of cheesecloth may be sopped in the lotion and often applied.

The Market Price of Radium.—F. T. H. inquires as to the market price of radium preparations.

Pure radium bromide is quoted at the source of supply in Paris, at $80 a milligramme, the smallest size of vial put up. In this market importers quote 20,000 activity at $150 a decigramme and 200,000 at $250. There is an import duty of 25 per cent. ad valorem on radium preparations which would make the lay down cost of the pure French preparation the equivalent of $5,000 a grain.

Iodine in Oily Combination.—H. W. N. submits the subjoined prescription, saying he has had considerable trouble with it as the lanolin would not mix, but remained in small particles at the bottom of the bottle. He asks for advice as to how the difficulty may be overcome and a homogeneous mixture obtained. The prescription:

Iodine	gr. xxv.
Lanolin	ℨiv.
Olive oil	q. s. ad. ℥vi.

M. sig.: Apply externally as directed.

We should advise our correspondent to dissolve the iodine in the least possible amount of alcohol and incorporate the solution with the wool fat before adding the olive oil. It is very difficult to powder iodine sufficiently fine to permit of incorporation with an ointment vehicle, and solution must first be effected, either with alcohol or by means of water and potassium iodide. In the present case either alcohol or chloroform should be used.

To Color Sweet Oil Red.—C. T. S. asks how he may color sweet oil or a mixture of sweet oil, bay rum and alcohol a red color.

Sweet oil may be readily colored red by the use of alkanet root. Two ounces of the bruised root to a pint of oil will make a concentrated red oil which can be used in any proportion to give the tint of color desired with fresh lots of oil. The root should be macerated in the oil for a fortnight with occasional agitation and afterward strained. This coloring is also adapted for use with a mixture of the oil and bay rum and alcohol.

Window Dressing Literature.—J. F. D. wishes the addresses of publishers of literature pertaining to window dressing for pharmacies, and letters sent to him in our care will be forwarded.

Book on the Manufacture of Sulphuric Ether on a Commercial Scale.—G., Mexico, asks for information regarding books treating of the manufacture on a commercial scale of sulphuric ether, saying he desires a work printed in either French, Spanish or English, which will give him descriptions of apparatus.

The book which will best answer our correspondent's requirements is "Les Produits Chimiques Employés en Médecine, Chimie Analytique et Industrielle," by A. Trillat. This work gives a full account of the production of ether on a commercial scale. It is published by J. B. Balliere et fils, Paris, at 3 francs, 50 centimes.

Book Reviews.

OUR NATIVE ORCHIDS. A Series of Drawings from Nature of All the Species Found in the Northeastern United States. By William Hamilton Gibson. With descriptive text elaborated from the author's notes, by Helena Leeming Jelliffe. New York: Doubleday, Page & Co., 1905. Pp. xxxv-158. (Price, $1.35.)

A most fascinating subject, charmingly treated in a book of unusual typographical excellence, Mrs. Jelliffe's work will have a special appeal to all lovers of the woodland, swamp, and field. To pharmacists who cultivate the study of botany this study of a special branch of the subject will be most welcome, since Mrs. Jelliffe will be known to many as the brilliant and accomplished wife of Dr. Smith Ely Jelliffe, Professor of Pharmacognosy, College of Pharmacy, and Instructor in Materia Medica and Therapeutics in Columbia University, New York. The often dry-as-dust details of botanical description are absent from *Our Native Orchids*, though nothing is lacking which the student should know. Much of the matter contained in the book is prose poetry and one might quote paragraph after paragraph to illustrate the beauties of the author's style. The book starts off with the description of an orchid which is familiar to pharmacists everywhere—the cypripedium or lady's-slipper. Ten species of this orchid grow in North America and six of them form the loveliest of the native orchids.

The peculiar forms, colorings and secretions of different orchids and the purpose of these in the life of the flower are charmingly described.

Orchids would never mature their seeds did they not receive pollen from neighboring plants through the medium of insect visitors, and the devices of the plants to woo certain insects are clearly and attractively set forth by means of text and illustrations. The orchids have each their one or few bidden guests whose coiled tongues are of exactly the same length as the spur that holds the honey which they come to sip and whose heads are adapted to the space between the pollen sacs of the particular flower visited. Where the goldenrod swarms with the common striped bugs and flies, the queenly orchid attracts choicer company. The pollen of the orchids is not the dry and dusty sort that characterizes most flowering plants. It is of a waxy consistency, and it is this which makes the flowers dependent upon insects for their perpetuation through seed. Certain insects, as has been said, haunt certain flowers, their attention to a particular flower being determined by a "display of stripes and fringes of brilliant colors and the long horns of nectar swung beneath the lip to entice the useful visitors."

The book is beautifully illustrated from drawings by William Hamilton Gibson, 58 plates being used to embellish 158 pages of large sized type printed on heavy paper. The book is bound very attractively and should make an acceptable gift for any one who is at all interested in the branch of botanical study of which it treats.

HANDBUCH DER DROGISTEN-PRAXIS. Ein Lehr- und Nachschlagebuch für Drogisten. Farbwarehändler, u.s.w. In Entwurf von Drogisten-Verband preisgekrönte Arbeit von G. A. Buchheister. Mit einem Abriss der allgemeinen Chemie von Dr. Rob. Bahrmann. Achte Auflage. Mit 234 in den Text gedruckten Abbildungen. Berlin: Verlag von Julius Springer, 1906. Pp. xii-948. (Price, 10 marks [$2.50].)

The eighth edition of Buchheister's druggists' practical handbook appeared shortly before the lamented death of the author, who was held in great esteem by German "Drogisten." The book is comprehensive in its scope. Part I, consisting of some 850 pages, treats of botanic materia medica, the subject being divided into 28 groups, comprising dried plants, roots, stems, woods, barks, buds, leaves, herbs, flowers, fruits, seeds, spores, gums, gum resins, balsams, oils, liquid and solid fats, plant juices, sponges and animal substances, such as are dealt in by Drogisten. The last group also contains certain mineral substances which are found in the natural state, such as plumbago, gypsum, talcum, calamine, pumice and asbestos. Part II of the book gives an outline of general chemistry and treating substances of both organic and inorganic origin. This part was prepared by Dr. Rob. Bahrmann. The cuts of apparatus printed with the text are unusually good, the drawings being in fine perspective and well printed. Part III is devoted to a comprehensive survey of the dye-stuffs, three principal groups being considered—dyes for dyers, dyes for painters and printers, and dryers, varnishes and lacquers; the poisonous dye-stuffs are indicated by a cross placed in front of the name. The text of this part is embellished with cuts of the apparatus used in the industry concerned. The geographical source of crude drugs is given in seven pages immediately preceding Part IV, which is devoted to commercial practice and contains a mass of information pertaining to the transaction of business, including a dictionary of commercial terms.

The German "Drogist" is not permitted to compound prescriptions and, unlike the "Apotheker," may establish stores without regard to the official concession. This work of Buchheister's is specifically intended for the "Drogist" rather than the "Apotheker," and hence the descriptions of botanic drugs are limited to such drugs as may be carried in these stores and are couched in more general and popular terms than would be descriptions intended for the "Apotheker" who, under the German system, is a university man.

THE MODERN MATERIA MEDICA. The Source, Chemical and Physical Properties, Therapeutic Action, Dosage, Antidotes and Incompatibles of All Additions to the Newer Materia Médica That Are Likely to be Called for on Prescriptions. New York: The Druggists' Circular, 1906. Pp. 306. (Price, $1.50.)

Undoubtedly a useful reference book of remedies of comparatively recent introduction, this somewhat pretentiously named book is far from being the ideal work on the subject. Many of the substances enumerated within its 306 pages of text are rather out of date. As examples we may name abrin, agaricin, agathin, aleuronat, aluminum acetotartrate (the compiler apparently favors the English spelling of aluminum, *i.e., aluminium*), amylene hydrate, anthrarobin, antikamnia, antiseptol, exalgin, and so on through to starch iodide, strychnine nitrate, xeroform and zinc cyanide. A large number of the articles enumerated are to be found described in the Dispensatories at greater length, and some of the articles are even official in the latest edition of the United States Pharmacopœia. The book will suffer by comparison with "The Newer Remedies" of Coblentz.

WHYS IN PHARMACY. A Compilation of Reasons Underlying the Principles of Pharmacy, Supplemented by a Table of Equations. By Edsel A. Ruddiman, Ph.M., M.D., Professor of Pharmacy and Materia Medica in Vanderbilt University. Author of "Incompatibilities in Prescriptions." New York: John Wiley & Sons, 1906. Pp. vi-196. (Price, $1.)

This is a very practical little volume, one that should be of considerable use to members of boards of pharmacy who have to do with the preparation of sets of examination questions. As the matter is presented in question and answer form, the book should also find favor at the hands of candidates for examination. The only fault to be found with it is the arrangement of the subjects and the typographical disposition of the paragraphs. Owing to the character of the subject matter, it is difficult to suggest any improvement in these respects. The faulty arrangement is relieved considerably by a useful index. The table of contents is helpful, too, in this regard. Some of the answers to questions are dangerously terse, as instance the following: "Why does sulphuric acid when dropped on such organic matter as wood blacken it?" The answer is: "The acid abstracts the elements of water and leaves carbon." The book can be heartily commended to beginners in pharmacy.

A TREATISE ON PHARMACY FOR STUDENTS AND PHARMACISTS. By Charles Caspari, Jr., Professor of Pharmacy and Director of the Pharmaceutical Laboratory in the Maryland College of Pharmacy, Department of Pharmacy, University of Maryland. Third edition, enlarged and thoroughly revised. Illustrated with 301 engravings. Philadelphia and New York: Lea Brothers & Co., 1906. Pp. xi-834. (Price, $4.25.)

A large part of the text of Caspari's Pharmacy has been rewritten to bring the book in accord with the new Pharmacopœia and the advance of scientific pharmacy in general. The plan of the work is the same as has characterized preceding editions, and while the book has been considerably enlarged by added matter, it yet remains of convenient size. Professor Caspari has been eminently successful in his efforts to answer the many questions of why and wherefore with which students and practicing pharmacists are almost daily confronted, and this faculty of making difficult subjects plain and understandable to the student is seen at its best in the chapter on the Assay of Alkaloidal Drugs and in that on Mixtures, pages 325-339, which latter gives the student in concise form an admirable review of the different forms of incompatibility of medicinal substances. We confess to a fondness for Caspari's work which has grown with the successive issues. There is no superfluous matter in it, and the student who pursues his studies along the lines laid down by the author will acquire a solid foundation for the prosecution of more advanced work.

POTTER'S CYCLOPAEDIA OF BOTANICAL DRUGS AND PREPARATIONS. By R. C. Wren. London: Potter & Clarke, 1906. Pp. iv-208. (Price, 2s. 6d.)

This book is at once a book of plant synonyms, a guide to the therapeutic action of botanical drugs and a complete herbalist. The drugs are described under their common names, the botanical title being printed alongside. The order is to give the synonyms, part used, therapeutic action and preparations employed. In addition to this, a brief formulary of medical compounds favored by herbalists is given. In this section is found what we must suppose to be the original formula for "Thompson's No. 6; or, Rheumatic Drops." It calls for African pepper, 1 oz.; myrrh (powdered), 1 lb.; brandy (fourth proof), 1 gal. The directions for preparing the drops are: "Put these into a stone jug and boil it for half an hour in a kettle of water, the jug to be uncorked." The volume closes with a selection of formulas for household remedies, a therapeutical index and an index of medical, botanical and eclectic works. It is doubtful if a work of this kind would be popular among pharmacists in this country, except such as cultivate a herbal practice.

A SYSTEMATIC COURSE OF QUALITATIVE CHEMICAL ANALYSIS OF INORGANIC AND ORGANIC SUBSTANCES, WITH EXPLANATORY NOTES. By Henry W. Schimpf, Ph.G., M.D., Professor of Analytical Chemistry in the Brooklyn College of Pharmacy. New York: John Wiley & Sons, 1906. Pp. vii-166. (Price, $1.25.)

In the preface of this book the author states that it has been prepared for students in pharmacy, and that it is based mainly on the lectures on analytical chemistry and on the "hectographed notes" on the laboratory exercises which have been delivered to the students of the Brooklyn College of Pharmacy during the past few years. This statement fully explains the limitations of the work. It doubtless will serve the author's purpose in connection with his teaching work, but we cannot conceive of the book being generally useful to teachers of chemistry or to students in institutions where chemistry is taught as a science and not as a branch of practical pharmacy.

ELEMENTS OF VEGETABLE HISTOLOGY. For the Use of Students of Pharmacy, Preparatory to the Study of Pharmacognosy. With 62 illustrations. By Daniel Base, Ph.D., Professor of Chemistry and Vegetable Histology in the Maryland College of Pharmacy. Second edition, revised and enlarged. Baltimore: The author, 1905. Pp. 112.

This little book is another of that class of works published by teachers primarily for the use of their own classes, but, unlike many of its type, is a really excellent compilation because the author has taken pains to treat his subject in a scientific manner. Commencing with a few general physical principles and a description of the action of a compound microscope the author takes the student by graduated steps from the simplest type of vegetable cell, as found, for instance, in the yeasts and bacteria, up to the more highly differentiated structures of the flowering plants, carefully instructing the reader how to prepare his specimens and examine them under the microscope with the aid of the usual microscopical reagents and stains. In the selection of his specimens the author has shown a wise discretion, and has avoided the use of too many technical terms and hair-splitting distinctions, treating the subject in a broad but yet strictly scientific manner. We commend the book to the study of those teachers who may be inclined to the production of textbooks for a similar purpose. The present volume is the second edition, the first having been published by the author in 1897. It deserves a wide recognition among teachers of pharmacognosy.

METHODS OF ORGANIC ANALYSIS. By Henry C. Sherman, Ph.D., Adjunct Professor of Analytical Chemistry in Columbia University. New York: The Macmillan Company, 1905. Pp. 245. (Price, $1.75.)

The greater portion of this work is devoted to qualitative methods for food materials and similar substances; processes for the determination of alcohols, carbohydrates, fatty acids, oils and fats, soaps and lubricants, proteids and cereals and milk being given at length. The book is well and concisely written, and is increased in volume by numerous references to other textbooks and to recent literature in the various publications dealing with organic analysis. As a work of reference and as a guide to analysts in carrying out special processes the work will prove of undoubted value, but we should hesitate to recommend it as a textbook for the students who purpose to take up analytical chemistry as a means of livelihood, for the reason that the author does not appear to be any too familiar with what we may term the commercial side of organic analysis. In other words, he appears to us to treat his subject too much from the point of view of the pure chemist, and, in his description of processes for determining the purity or otherwise of commercial natural products not to devote sufficient attention to the limitations of these processes when applied to such products. Familiarity with the commercial side is to our mind one of the requisites of the analytical chemist. Manufacturers and dealers have suffered too long from the *ipse dixit* of analysts whose commercial knowledge was not commensurate with their technical training.

We do not wish to be construed as condemning this work, for the author's position and published papers are sufficient guarantee of the sufficiency of his knowledge as a chemist. As a work of reference, particularly for recent improvements in methods of organic analysis, we consider it excellent. The book is well printed and strongly bound in cloth.

A MANUAL OF PHARMACOLOGY. By Walter E. Dixon, M.A., Cantab., M.D., B.S., B.Sc, Lond., D.P.H. Camb., etc., assistant to the Downing Professor of Medicine in the University of Cambridge, Examiner in Pharmacology in the Universities of Cambridge and Glasgow. London: Edward Arnold, 1906. Pp. vii-451. (Price, $4.)

It may be said without any fear of contradiction that this work is not one for the student of pharmacy. This is not because of any deficiencies that it may possess, but by reason of its chief interests lying in a field that is not so extensively cultivated by our students of pharmacy.

The pharmacology that Dr. Dixon presents is an experimental pharmacology, rich in the details of recorded facts of animal experimentation—classified in the typical pharmacological method of Schmiedeberg—and adapted to the needs of second or third year medical students, working in a laboratory. For this latter class of students it is to be highly recommended, although be it said throughout that it regards the science from its own point of view rather than that of its applicability in the treatment of disease.

The Manual should be particularly helpful and informing to the pharmacist who would know the most plausible detailed technical action of a drug, particularly of a special drug's effect on the heart's action.

FORMULAIRE DES MÉDICAMENTS NOUVEAUX POUR 1906, par H. Bocquillon-Limousin, docteur en pharmacie de l'Université de Paris. Introduction par le Dr. Huchard, médecin des hôpitaux. 1 vol. in-18 de 322 pages, cartonné. Paris: Librairie J.-B. Baillière et Fils, 19 rue Hautefeuille. (Price, 3 francs.)

This valuable compendium of new remedies has been brought well up to date by the inclusion of descriptions of the numerous medicaments introduced during 1905. A distinguishing feature of Bocquillon-Limousin's formulary is the exact information which it supplies regarding the therapeutic action of the remedies enumerated.

SAN FRANCISCO DESTROYED.

Every Wholesale Drug House Wiped Out—Large Quantities of Crude Drugs Destroyed—'Frisco Offices of Eastern Firms Burned—Cascara, Grindelia and Damiana Likely to Advance on Account of Destruction of Stock.

With the arrival in this city of more definite reports concerning the devastation and damage worked by the terrific earthquake and fire in the city of San Francisco, many of the leading manufacturing and wholesale drug houses in New York are learning of the total destruction of their warehouses, home and branch offices in that fated city on the Pacific Coast. Seven large drug concerns in this city have already received private despatches from their officers and managers in 'Frisco, announcing that their properties have been utterly ruined, and other large establishments are expecting similar news within the next few days. Practically the entire wholesale drug district in the metropolis has been wiped out, but the full extent of the damage will not be realized for several days.

The seismic disturbance alone hurled down almost all of the drug house buildings on Market and Mission streets, while those on Third, Montgomery, Second, First and Freemont streets which escaped the earthquake were destroyed by the flames. Redington & Co.'s warehouse and store and offices at 25 Second street are known to have been completely destroyed. This concern has local offices at 30 Cliff street, where the firm is known as Coffin, Redington & Co., wholesale druggists and agents for the California Fig Syrup Company and its product "Syrup of Figs." The Pacific Coast Borax Company's warehouse and offices, at 101 Sansome street, and its factory at Alameda, have been obliterated, according to a private wire received at the local offices of that company at 100 William street. The despatch received at the local offices was sent by C. B. Zabriskie, the eastern manager, who happened to be in the doomed city when the calamity occurred. Mr. Zabriskie in his message, which he sent from Oakland, across the bay from Frisco, announced that President F. M. Smith and all the officers and employees of the company had escaped unharmed from the city with their families.

The Celluloid Company, of 30 Washington place, this city, has received word that its stores and offices in 'Frisco are totally destroyed. Johnson & Johnson has been notified that their warehouse and offices are also in ruins. Seabury & Johnson has also received similar intelligence concerning their stock depot, salesrooms and offices, at 513 Market street, between First and Second streets. Mack & Co.'s properties have also been reduced to a mass of charred ruins, and although Langley, Michaels & Co., have not been heard from directly by their local agents, Samuel G. McCotter & Co., at 16 Platt street, this city, reports on the general destruction of property include the 'Frisco offices of that concern as among those wholly or in part consumed in the conflagration.

While it is understood that the loss of the properties of the Pacific Coast Borax Company will not affect in any way the cost of this merchandise there is no doubt that the destruction of the warehouses containing large stocks of cascara, grindelia robusta and damiana will cause a decided upward movement in the prices of these drugs, as it will be 30 to 60 days before the merchants engaged in this business can hope to resume shipments and re-establish communication with their eastern agents.

Registered in Florida.

At the semiannual meeting of the Florida Board of Pharmacy, held in Ocala, Fla., on January 17, 13 applicants were present for examination. The following were successful: H. H. Bearce, Ormond; G. B. Young, St. Augustine; W. Y. Hunter, Madison; J. C. Moore, Welborne, and H. P. Bitting, Ocala.

The next meeting of the board will be in Orlando, June 13, during the meeting of the Florida State Pharmaceutical Association.

THE PURE FOOD AND DRUG BILL.

Bill Satisfactory to Drug Interests if Proposed Amendment Is Adopted.

The National Wholesale Druggists' Association is taking special interest in the pure food and drug bill that is now before the House of Representatives at Washington. M. N. Kline, chairman of the Committee on Legislation, is keeping a careful watch on all matters pertaining to pure food and drugs, and recently he sent the following letter to the members of the National Wholesale Drug Association:

Following my circular letter of recent date asking your influence to secure some modification in the Pure Food and Drug bill now pending in the House of Representatives, S. 88, I am informed that the inclosed amendment is to be inserted by the committee having it in charge when it comes up for consideration in the House.

This amendment meets all the objections we can reasonably urge against the misbranding portion of this bill, and I hope now that you will address your member of Congress upon the subject expressing your approval of the proposed amendment and expressing the hope that the Pure Food bill will now be passed, provided this amendment is made a part of it, because this protects our interests as far as we can reasonably hope that any bill that may be considered will protect them, and it will be a decided advantage to get this national legislation enacted so as to secure a settlement of this question, which has been before us for about fifteen years in various forms, some of which threatened great annoyance to the wholesale and retail drug interests of this country.

I sincerely hope, therefore, that for the above reasons you will use your influence to secure the insertion of this amendment, and the passage of the bill when it has been made a part of it.

The following is the proposed amendment to the Pure Food bill:

Second. If the contents of the original package shall have been removed, in whole or in part, and other contents shall have been placed in such package; or if when the article contained be not described in the United States Pharmacopœia or National Formulary and be not the prescription of a regularly licensed physician, in the District of Columbia and the Territories, the package fails to bear a statement on the label of the quantity or proportion of any alcohol, morphine, opium, cocaine, heroin, alpha or beta eucaine, or chloral hydrate, or any preparation of any of such substances contained therein; provided, that the quantity or proportion of alcohol need not be stated when not more than the quantity or proportion prescribed by the United States Pharmacopœia or the National Formulary as a solvent or preservative of the active constituents of the medicine or preparation in such package is used. And further provided, that the quantity or proportion of opium or morphine need not be stated unless the proportion in such package contain more than 2 grains of opium of ¼ grain of morphine to a fluid ounce, or if a solid preparation to an avoidupois ounce.

ANTI-COCAINE LAW FOR MARYLAND.

(From Our Regular Correspondent.)

Baltimore, April 19.—Of all the various measures designed to regulate the practice of pharmacy or to abolish abuses in the business, offered at the last meeting of the Maryland General Assembly, only one became a law, this being the bill introduced by Delegate Blank, of the city delegation, and named after him. This bill aims to stop the promiscuous sale of cocaine, the vending of which drug as well as opium it prohibits outright, while the sale of other habit-forming substances is surrounded with restrictions. They cannot be dispensed except on the prescription of a regular practicing physician, and prescriptions cannot be renewed except on the written order of the physician. The bill was based on the Beal model, and had the indorsement of the druggists throughout the State.

The radical Godwin bill, which provided that manufacturers of proprietary medicines must print the formulas on the label or wrapper, and the measure drawn by Attorney General Bryan, regulating the sale of poisons and narcotics, failed because of their drastic provisions, which made them objectionable to many pharmacists. The former would have virtually destroyed all property values in medicinal compounds.

THE PATENT MEDICINE AGITATION IN CANADA.

Thirty Samples of Headache Powders Examined—Fifteen Patent Medicines Analyzed by the Canadian Government—A Formula Bill to Be Introduced.

(From our Regular Correspondent.)

Toronto, April 19.—The question of regulating the sale of patent and proprietary medicines is receiving much attention at present. The Canadian Department of Inland Revenue has just issued a bulletin containing the report of Thomas Macfarlane, Chief Government Analyst, and giving analyses of 30 samples of headache powders and similar preparations and 15 patent medicines. The report commented on the large percentage of alcohol found in some of the proprietary medicines, and in this connection referred to the order issued by the Revenue Department of the United States requiring dealers in certain specified remedies to pay a revenue tax as liquor dealers. The report also called attention to the large proportion of acetanilide in some of the headache powders as likely to be injurious to those using them.

Another drastic measure for the regulation of the sale of patent medicines has been presented in the Ontario Legislature by A. C. Pratt. It provides that where any patent medicine shall contain more than 6 per cent. of alcohol or more than 1-20 of 1 per cent. of morphine heroin, cocaine or of the salts or equivalents or derivatives of the same the package or bottle shall be labeled with the ingredients and their percentages in red ink. Where poisons are ingredients the word "poison" must be printed upon the label in red ink letters ¼ inch deep. Every firm manufacturing patent medicines is required to file samples with the Provincial Board of Health before November 1, 1906, with affidavits that the article offered for sale is the same as the sample. Other proprietary preparations must be filed with the board before February 1. The Board of Health is authorized to make periodical analyses of samples and goods offered for sale. Firms violating these provisions may be fined $50 for the first and $100 for the second offense. The filing of false samples or making false affidavits entails a penalty of $1,000. A schedule to the bill contains a long list of drugs considered dangerous, the presence of which in the proportion indicated will make it necessary to label the package or the bottle with the ingredients.

There appears to be some uncertainty as to whether legislation dealing with this subject falls constitutionally within the scope of the Federal or the Provincial Government. As it is clearly within the jurisdiction of the Province to deal with the sale of liquor, it is contended that the regulation of all medicines containing alcohol falls within the scope of the Provincial Government.

Registered in South Dakota.

As a result of the examination of the State Board of Pharmacy at its recent meeting in Canton the following candidates were registered:

As Licentiates.—O. C. Koelle, Sioux City; G. C. McCullen, Canton; T. D. Kriebs, Beresford; G. J. Brushler, Beresford; Mrs. Bena Mitchell, Artesian; J. W. Brackett, Sturgis; F. L. Mitchell, Artesian; H. D. Jehu, Geddes; T. W. Lalley, Montrose; W. L. Sackett, Corsica; G. Tillman Thompson, Dell Rapids; J. B. Dickey, Iroquois.

Assistants.—C. A. Hubbard, Des Moines; Hubert Faust, Parkston; Clyde Kellar, Viborg; Adolph Barke, Wagner.

The next meeting of the board will be held at Aberdeen, in April. E. C. Bent, of Dell Rapids, the secretary of the board, will furnish blanks for intending applicants.

The Prescott Memorial Scholarship.

The committee of the Michigan Pharmaceutical Association appointed to secure funds for the establishment of a scholarship in memoriam of Dr. A. B. Prescott has issued an appeal for subscriptions and would be pleased to receive any amount from $5 upward. The members of the committee are Charles F. Mann, Frederick W. R. Perry and Arthur F. Parker.

BOSTON DRUGGISTS MEET.

Sale of Alcoholic Tonics Discussed—Organizers Report—Mineral Water on Serial Numbering Plan.

(From our Regular Correspondent.)

Boston, April 19.—The Boston Association of Retail Druggists held its regular monthly meeting at the Massachusett College of Pharmacy building on the evening of April 11, with Professor La Pierre in the chair. The secretary and treasurer submitted the usual reports, which were accepted. The by-laws having been modified to conform to the new charter were next presented by Mr. Ernst, for the Committee on By-Laws. This matter will be again considered at the next meeting.

THE SALE OF ALCOHOLIC TONICS FROM A LICENSE STANDPOINT.

In response to the query submitted by the association: Can (old) Peruna and Hostetters' Bitters be sold by druggists in this State without a sixth class license? Counsel for the organization gave an opinion, holding that the presence of alcohol did not determine the question, but that the inquiry must be as to whether it was sold and used as a beverage.

D. C. S. N. PLAN COMMENDED.

Letters were then read from manufacturers to whom had been sent the association's resolution favoring the sale of all articles on the $2, $4 and $8 basis; also one from the E. C. Dewitt Company, Chicago, commending the Direct Contract and Serial Numbering plan.

LEGISLATION FOR THE DRUGGISTS.

Henry Canning gave an account of pending legislation, speaking upon the following bills: That providing for the sale of liquor in no-license towns upon physicians' prescriptions; a general bill which will provide screens for open bars only; a formula bill which is fairly satisfactory so far as druggists are concerned, as long as some bill must be offered. He mentioned the "reformers'" absurdity of having omitted from their bills the complete suppression of the sale of cocaine preparations except on physicians' prescriptions, and said it was the "wicked" pharmacists who were attempting amendments by the insertion of this provision, notwithstanding that it would entail monetary loss on Bay State dealers.

MINERAL WATER ON THE D. C. AND S. N. PLAN.

Mr. Parks, of Philadelphia, representing the Consolidated Mineral Water Company, explained the firm's serial numbering contract. He was told that the B. A. R. D. did not indorse or accept contracts unless they were approved by the Chicago office.

It was voted to have a smoke-talk for the May meeting.

ORGANIZERS REPORT ON LOCAL CONDITIONS.

Before the gathering adjourned Mr. Burroughs, the new N. A. R. D.'s organizer outside of Boston, was introduced, and spoke briefly.

Mr. Keiser, representing the Chicago headquarters, has opened an office for New England at 35 Court street, Room 11, Boston. His latchstring is always out for N. A. R. D.'s members.

The Tampa Drug Company.

E. Berger, who has been in the drug and merchandise brokerage business in Tampa, Fla., for the last ten years, and who prior to that time was in the retail business there, is secretary and manager of the recently organized Tampa Drug Company, which has been incorporated with a capital of $100,000. This company proposes to do a strictly wholesale drug business and has no retail connections whatever, being the only wholesale drug house in that section of the State, and they have every prospect of doing a large and very flourishing business. Mr. Berger is very well and widely known, having attended several meetings of the American Pharmaceutical Association and having been active in association work in Florida for some years. He has all the qualities, both of head and heart, that go to make success.

NEW YORK STATE LEGISLATION.

Many Amendments of the Stevens-Wainwright Bill—Spirited Opposition from the Entire Drug Trade—Hill Bill to Be Pushed by Drug Trade—Other Measures in Suspense.

Led by the energetic members of the Legislative Committee of the New York State Pharmaceutical Association the representatives of the Manhattan Pharmaceutical Association, Kings County Pharmaceutical Society, Metropolitan Association of Retail Druggists and German Apothecaries' Society are making strenuous and unceasing efforts to kill the Wainwright bill which in its amended form is now before the State Assembly and likely to be passed unless this determined opposition of drug interests proves successful. The Senate Committee on Public Health has favorably reported the Stevens bill, as the measure is called in the Senate, and the bill is now in shape to be passed by that body.

In its amended form the Stevens-Wainwright bill, as the two measures are familiarly called, provides that the State Department of Health and not the local departments of health, as originally specified, shall appoint public analysts, chemists and inspectors for the execution of the proposed law, and shall make regulations in addition to the provisions already outlined in the bill, as may seem necessary to enforce or facilitate the enforcement of the proposed law, and shall also have authority to add to the list of drugs whenever it shall deem such action necessary for public health. All such regulations, declarations and additions to the drug list made in any year shall be filed in the office of the Secretary of State and published in the session laws, first published after the expiration of thirty days from such filing, and also that all additions to the drug list shall take effect sixty days after the publication of the same in the session laws.

Still another amendment to the bill eliminates from the list of proprietary and other medicinal preparations containing alcohol or narcotic or other potent drugs which must be labeled, "any other hypnotic, anæsthetic, analgesic or cardiac, circulatory, respiratory or nerve depressant"; but as the State Department of Health is empowered in the amended bill to make regulations in addition to the regular provisions and extend the number of drugs which are to be labeled, this amendment does not relieve the proprietary manufacturer or druggist of any responsibility. The measure also contains a further amendment whereby the stock on hand of any retail druggist or dealer on July 1 of this year is exempted from the provisions of the labeling measure, which, even if passed, will not become effective until October 1.

In the hope that retail druggists, whether associated with any pharmaceutical organization or not, will do their utmost to defeat the bill, the Legislative Committee of the State Pharmaceutical Association has sent out a general appeal to every regularly licensed pharmacist in Greater New York urging them to address strong personal letters or telegrams to the Senators and Assemblymen in their respective districts protesting against the measure as destructive of the drug business and pharmacy in general. In part this general appeal for assistance in the fight against the bill reads as follows:

> The bill confers extraordinary powers upon the State Board of Health, and it is not easy to grasp its main purpose unless it be regarded as a first step toward the overthrow of the whole system of pharmacy legislation in this State and as evidencing a determination to subject the profession of pharmacy and the entire drug trade to the arbitrary rule of such physicians as may hereafter be fortunate enough to secure positions in the Department of Health. No other State has ever subjected the profession of pharmacy to such unmerited and uncalled for humiliation as this bill contemplates for the State of New York. The present law puts the sale of drugs and poisons at retail under the direct supervision and control of the State Board of Pharmacy. The division of authority provided by this bill would lead to constant conflict and confusion.

This appeal is signed by J. A. Lockie, of Buffalo, chairman of the committee; Dr. William Muir, of Brooklyn; William H. Rogers, of Middletown; R. K. Smither, of Buffalo; Warren L. Bradt, of Albany; George Kleinau, of New York, and W. B. Bissel, of Syracuse.

THE HILL BILL.

So determined are the proponents of the Stevens-Wainwright bill to secure the passage of their measure that it is now feared there is little chance of persuading the State Senate to pass in its place the substitute measure known as the Hill bill, Senate bill 1,118, which would accomplish a much better result in protecting the public health. The Hill bill is also known as the Chicago conference bill because it was prepared at a conference held last year by representatives of the American Pharmaceutical Association, the National Wholesale Druggists' Association, the Proprietary Association of America and the National Association of Retail Druggists. This measure makes it unlawful for any person, firm or corporation to sell, furnish or give away any cocaine, alpha or beta eucaine, opium, morphine, heroin, chloral hydrate or any salt or compound of any of the foregoing substances, except upon the original written order or prescription of a lawfully authorized practitioner of medicine, dentistry or veterinary medicine, but these provisions are not to apply to preparations containing not more than 2 grains of opium or not more than ¼ grain of morphine, or not more than ¼ grain of heroin, or not more than ⅛ grain of cocaine, or not more than ⅛ grain of alpha or beta eucaine, or not more than 10 grains of chloral hydrate in 1 fluid or avoirdupois ounce. A few other exceptions are also made in the cases of mild preparations. The manufacture and sale of stronger compounds are, however, wholly prohibited. The Harawitz bill, which is now before the Assembly, is identical with the Hill measure. The Sammon bill, or Assembly bill 1920, has been killed. This bill made it a misdemeanor for any person, copartnership or corporation to compound, manufacture, give, sell or expose for sale any preparation containing morphine, opium, cocaine or similar preparations. Dr. Muir and Messrs. Kleinau and Bradt pointed out at the hearing before the Assembly Committee on Codes, which was held on Wednesday, April 11, that the bill did not make any provision against the sale of the drugs in their crude state, but only prohibited the sale of their preparations.

THE PAGE ANTISUBSTITUTION BILL AMENDED.

Dr. Muir, who also attended a recent hearing on the Page, or Antisubstitution, bill before the Senate Committee on Codes, persuaded Senator Page to accept an amendment to his measure which limits the antisubstitution clause to drugs. This amendment reads: "No licensed pharmacist shall deviate from the terms of a prescription or order or demand by using one drug for another." A. Clayton Searles, chairman of the Legislative Committee of the Manhattan Pharmaceutical Association, and Mr. Kleinau also attended the hearing on the Page bill and urged the adoption of this amendment.

THE HASTINGS BILL,

which is now before the Senate, provides that the holder of a pharmacy license granted by any local board of pharmacy, whether after an examination or without such an examination, shall upon the payment of a fee of $5 receive a regular license from the State Board of Pharmacy without any further examination. This bill has already been passed by the Assembly.

LUPTON BILL PROBABLY SCOTCHED IN SENATE.

The Lupton bill, providing for the granting of permits to all classes of merchants to deal in numerous drugs not classified as household remedies, has been passed by the Assembly, but is believed to have been killed in the Senate Committee on Public Health, before which Dr. Muir and Mr. Bradt appeared on Thursday, April 12. Both of these representatives of drug interests opposed the measure vigorously on the ground that it would tend to work an injury to public health by permitting unskilled merchants to deal in remedies about which they know practically nothing.

SANTEE ANTICOCAINE BILL IN SUSPENSE.

Though the Santee bill for the regulation of the sale of cocaine is still before the Senate it is feared that some secret opposition has developed among cocaine interests to prevent its passage. The State Pharmaceutical Association and other retail drug associations have sent representatives to all the hearings to assist in its passage, but though there has been no public opposition at any of these hearings it is generally believed that some influence is being brought to bear upon the Senate Committee on Public Health, which is restraining it from reporting the bill favorably.

Formula Bill Favorably Reported in the Massachusetts Legislature.

(From our Regular Correspondent.)

Boston, April 19.—The following is the Patent Medicine bill reported by the Committee on Public Health; it has already received preliminary action in the House:

Section 1. Upon every package, bottle or other receptacle, holding any proprietary or patent medicine, or any proprietary or patent food preparation, which contains alcohol to an amount in excess of the amount shown to be necessary by the United States Pharmacopœia or the National Formulary as a solvent or preservative of the active constituents of the drugs contained therein, shall be marked or inscribed a statement of the percentage of alcohol by volume contained therein; and the provisions of section 19 of chapter 75 of the Revised Laws shall apply to the manner and form in which such statements shall be marked or inscribed.

Sec. 2. Every package, bottle or other receptacle holding any proprietary or patent medicine or any proprietary or patent food preparation shall bear a label containing a statement of the quantity of any opium, morphine, heroin or chloral-hydrate contained therein, provided that the package contains more than two grains of opium, or more than one-fourth grain of morphine, or more than one-sixteenth grain of heroin, or more than eight grains of chloral-hydrate in one fluid ounce, or if a solid preparation, in one avoirdupois ounce; and the provisions of section 19 of chapter 75 of the Revised Laws shall apply to the manner and form in which such statements shall be marked or inscribed.

Sec. 3. It shall be unlawful for any person to sell, or to expose or offer for sale, or to give or exchange, any patent or proprietary medicine or article containing cocaine or any of its salts, or alpha or beta eucaine or any synthetic substitute of the aforesaid.

Sec. 4. It shall be unlawful for any person to sell, or to expose or offer for sale, or to give or exchange any cocaine or alpha or beta eucaine or any synthetic substitute of the aforesaid or any preparation containing the same, or any salts or compounds thereof, except upon the written prescription of a physician, dentist or veterinary surgeon registered under the laws of the commonwealth; and no such prescription shall be filled more than once.

Sec. 5. The provisions of sections 3 and 4 shall not apply to sales at wholesale made to retail druggists or dental depots, nor to sales made to physicians, dentists or regularly incorporated hospitals.

Sec. 6. Whoever manufactures, sells or offers for sale any medicine or food preparation in violation of the provisions of this act shall be punished by a fine of not less than $5 nor more than $100. It shall be the duty of the State Board of Health to cause the prosecution of all persons violating the terms of this act; but no prosecution shall be brought for the sale at retail, or for the gift or exchange of any patent or proprietary medicine containing any of the drugs or preparations, the sale of which is prohibited or restricted as aforesaid, unless the said board has, prior to such sale, gift or exchange, given public notice in such trade journals or newspapers as it may select that the sale of the said medicine at retail would be contrary to law.

Local, Philadelphia and Baltimore Bowling Experts to Meet.

Another interesting bowling match has been arranged by the expert pin topplers of the drug house teams in Philadelphia and Baltimore as well as those in this city. This contest of alley skill, which will be held in Atlantic City on May 4 and 5, will be known as the Intercity Wholesale Drug Trade Bowling League games. The members of the teams, representing all three cities, will be chosen from among the bowlers of the local teams who have won honors making the highest individual scores.

It is probable that seven men will be picked from among the crackerjacks on the Parke, Davis & Co., Dodge & Olcott, Colgate & Co., Whitall, Tatum Company, Seabury & Johnson and Lazell, Dalley & Co. teams to fight for the New York Wholesale Drug Trade Bowling Association, for although only five men are needed to compose the team for this city it is thought to be desirable to have at least two substitutes on hand. The Philadelphia and Baltimore associations will also make up their teams in a similar manner, and it is expected that the contest will attract a large audience of bowling enthusiasts.

Dr. Lovis, "Lou" Burgess, "Mat" Judge, William J. Carr, Oldershaw, Gooding and Ruddiman, who are likely to be selected for the local team, are continuing their practice games at the Albion alleys.

The New York team will make its headquarters in the Hotel Strand at Atlantic City.

Registered in Vermont.

At the meeting of the Vermont Board of Pharmacy, held at Montpelier, April 4, seven candidates appeared for examination, and certificates were issued to C. B. Hazen, Bradford, Vt., and Hibbard Campbell, Springfield, Vt. The board adjourned to meet at Montpelier, Vt., June 27. The secretary of the board is J. G. Bellrose, of Burlington.

Commencement at the Albany College of Pharmacy.

The twenty-fifth annual commencement exercises of the Albany College of Pharmacy, which took place at Odd Fellows' Hall, in Albany, on Tuesday evening, April 10, were in the nature of a silver celebration, and all the speakers made reference to the anniversary character of the occasion.

MISS MABEL DICKINSON.

Dr. Willis G. Tucker, professor of chemistry and dean of the faculty, opened the exercises with an address of welcome, taking as the basis of his remarks an outline of the history of the institution, which was founded in 1881 as a department of Union University. Of those active in the organization of the college, only two are now living, namely, Dr. Alfred B. Huested and Professor Tucker, the latter of who alone of the original faculty remains on the active list. Professor Tucker pointed out the great improvement which had been wrought in the institution. The course of instruction has been lengthened, the hours of instruction quadrupled, the laboratory work increased and the requirements for graduation materially elevated. Special reference was made to the effect of the prerequisite law, which Dr. Tucker expected to exert a very powerful influence for good in the cause of pharmacy. The alumni of the institution now number 481, and a special appeal was made to the alumni to aid in the erection of a building for the institution and for the upholding of the high standing which had been inculcated in their minds by the faculty.

After the formal conferring of the degrees by the Rev. Dr. Raymond, Chancellor of the University, an address to the graduates was delivered by Dr. J. H. Mitchell, of Cohoes.

In his address Dr. Mitchell urged the graduates to establish high ideals of duty and to keep true to those ideals under the most adverse circumstances, and exhorting them to remember that not only would the individual pharmacist suffer should he fail to live up to the full measure of his duty, but that his shortcomings would be charged against the profession at large. He counselled his hearers to obey all laws, whether the laws be good or bad, but also admonished them that it was part of their duty as citizens to secure the repeal of bad laws, and that in order to be in a position to do this it would be necessary for them to take an active part in politics in certain limits. He said that the retailer who dispensed an alcoholic proprietary as a harmless tonic was just as guilty as the man who made it. In conclusion, he urged the graduates never to forget their alma mater, to which they owed their professional education.

The valedictory address by Joseph D. Beavan was next on the order on the programme, after which came the presentation of prizes by Prof. Alfred B. Huested, as follows: A prize of $25 for the best examination in all branches was awarded to Joseph Dudley Beavan, with honorable mention of Harmon S. Van Patten, H. S. Bertrand and W. C. Bartram. A prize of $25 offered by the alumni association for the best examination in pharmaceutical laboratory work was awarded to H. D. Mudge, with honorable mention of J. H. Christopher and C. W. Strong. A prize of $15 offered by Dr. John M. Bigelow, a member of the board of trustees, for the best examination in microscopy, was awarded to J. D. Beavan, with honoroble mention of W. C. Barton. A prize of $15 for the best junior examination in all branches was awarded to C. G. Clifford, with honorable mention of W. D. Foody, A. Shoemaker and L. E. Carey. A prize of $10, offered by Professor Tucker to the junior student passing the best examination in chemistry, was awarded to Miss Ida L. Moore, with honorable mention of

L. E. Carey and C. G. Clifford. A prize of $10 offered by the director of the pharmaceutical laboratory for the best set of pharmaceutical preparations was awarded to C. G. Clifford, with honorable mention of L. E. Carey and W. D. Foody. The exercises were interspersed with music by Holding's Orchestra.

Among the graduates was Miss Mabel Dickinson, of Warrensburg, N. Y., who was the only lady in the class. Miss Dickinson's father, G. W. Dickinson, in whose store she received her first training in pharmacy, is a well-known druggist. Miss Dickinson says that her first attempt to take up seriously the study of pharmacy was in connection with the Quiz questions which were published in the AMERICAN DRUGGIST for some years, and that interest thus engendered in study has been the most important factor in deciding her future. We present a portrait of Miss Dickinson herewith.

A list of the graduates follows:

F. G. Atwell, Cohoes; W. C. Barton, Ballston Spa; J. W. Beavan, Greenwich; H. S. Bertrand, Tupper Lake; J. H. Christopher, Schenectady; E. J. Corte, Canajoharie; Mabel Dickinson, Warrensburgh; J. L. Everleth, Plattsburgh; F. T. Heyman, Albany; L. S. Horton, Albany; E. A. Hoyt, Deposit; G. W. Jewett, Watervliet; J. T. Kelly, Albany; A. L. Kincade, Johnstown; H. H. Mather, Clayton; J. F. Mitchell, Jr., Cooperstown; C. E. Montanye, Saratoga Springs; R. C. Mowitt, Massena; H. D. Mudge, Schenectady; J. J. O'Keefe, Hadley; E. M. Parker, Waterbury, Conn.; C. I. Place, Catskill; F. W. Rice, Troy; S. J. Sanford, Nicholville; C. M. Scoville, Hadley; C. R. Silvernail, Dalton, Mass.; E. B. Spalding, Portland, Conn.; C. W. Strong, Albany; W. I. Van Arnum, Waterford; W. C. Van Hoesen, Schenevus; H. S. Van Patten, Schenectady; H. Waltermire, Chatham; A. H. Wears, Madrid; I. L. Williams, Herkimer; L. E. Wray, Altona; J. P. White, Delanson.

CASWELL-MASSEY COMBINE.

To Operate a Chain of Drug Stores in New York—A Colossal Undertaking.

Following closely upon the announcement of the incorporation of the well-known firm of Caswell, Massey & Co., with a capital of $500,000, comes the astonishing news that the Caswell-Massey Company has been acquired by George C. Lyon and John C. Knight, of the Hall & Lyon Company, of Providence, R. I., who purpose to operate not only the three high class stores formerly owned by Caswell, Massey & Co., but also seven additional stores, and eventually a long chain of such establishments throughout various sections of this city. It is also the intention of Messrs. Lyon and Knight, who have secured an almost unlimited financial backing, to market a big list of special preparations and proprietary remedies, to be prepared by the new corporation, through the medium of its numerous stores and those of the Hall & Lyon Company. Although the directors of the Caswell-Massey Company have not yet discussed the question, it is generally believed that they will also decide to handle the products of the United Drug Company and the National Cigar Stands Company, of which Louis K. Liggett, who is likewise associated with Messrs. Lyon and Knight in the business of the Hall & Lyon Company, is president.

Though it would appear likely that the new Caswell-Massey Company, with its powerful backing and chain of retail stores, would prove a formidable rival of the corporation of Hegeman & Co. and the Drug Merchants' Association, neither Mr. Lyon nor Mr. Knight are inclined to fear a titanic struggle for supremacy with the Hegeman interests, as they believe that their field of business will be wholly different from that of the big corporation at 200 Broadway and its various branches. Mr. Knight, who has just been elected secretary and treasurer of the Caswell-Massey combine, asserts that the new corporation will establish its branch stores almost entirely in the wealthy and fashionable districts and will not indulge in any price cutting on its drugs, proprietary articles or other goods, confining itself to marketing the highest class of merchandise rather than those most attractive from the viewpoint of low prices. With the question of price cutting and quick selling articles eliminated by the stand which it has taken in regard to its trade, the new corporation does not expect any determined opposition on the part of any other large drug interest in this city, although it is probable that the new stores of the Caswell-Massey Company will be compelled to purchase or surpass by their excellence the retail stores already located in the sections which they will invade.

Great progress is now reported by Messrs. Lyon and Knight in concluding the business of the old firm of Caswell, Massey & Co. Every outstanding obligation of the old partnership is being paid as speedily as possible and all affairs of the former concern are being settled with creditors and debtors alike. William M. Massey, who has been elected vice-president of the corporation, will continue the active operation of the big store at Twenty-fifth street, Broadway and Fifth avenue, which has been a prominent landmark for many years, while the branch establishments at Fifth avenue and Forty-seventh street and at Columbus avenue and Seventy-second street, formerly owned by Caswell, Massey & Co., will be conducted by the same managers, who have been in charge for some time. Mr. Caswell, senior partner in the old firm, has retired permanently from active participation in the drug business.

The Board of Directors in the Caswell-Massey Company is at present only temporary because of the fact that its personnel will undoubtedly be changed within a month by the entrance of several other interests who are now arranging for the purchase of large blocks of the preferred stock offered by J. Craig Havemeyer, of 43 Exchange place, who has been appointed fiscal agent of the corporation. The names of the men who are to become members of the new Board of Directors are already known by Messrs. Lyon, Knight and Massey, but have not yet been made public. Mr. Knight, however, announces positively that they do not include any representatives of the National Cigar Stands Company nor of the United Drug Company, but it is likely that they will include W. C. Bolton, of the Riker Drug Company; E. D. Cahoon, treasurer of the same concern; John Haigney, also of that company; Major Hall, of the firm of Hall & Lyons, of Providence, R. I.; Edward Dodge, of the Cahoon-Lyon Drug Company, of Buffalo, and other interests associated with Hall & Lyon.

Mr. Lyon, who is also treasurer of the Hall & Lyon Company, has just been selected president of the Caswell-Massey Company by the temporary directors of that corporation, who have also chosen Mr. Massey as vice-president, and Mr. Knight, who is assistant secretary-treasurer of the Hall & Lyon Company, as secretary and treasurer.

The first step in the establishment of the new chain of retail branch stores for the Caswell-Massey Company has already been taken by Messrs. Lyon, Knight and Massey, who have secured a long term lease on a store in the old Astor House, on Broadway, at the Vesey street corner. These premises are now being renovated, redecorated and furnished with a big soda fountain and all the fixtures required in a drug store. The sites of four more branch stores have also been selected by the president, vice-president and secretary-treasurer of the new corporation, but because of some uncertainty regarding the desirability of their location these officers have not yet deemed it advisable to close the options which they hold on the places in question, and therefore do not consider it best to disclose at present the locations of the first four new stores in their proposed chain. There is no doubt, however, that these additional places of business will soon be opened by the Caswell-Massey Company, while at least two more in this city and probably one in Providence or Newport will also be included in its scheme of acquisition and operation.

In a prospectus issued by Mr. Havemeyer, the fiscal agent of the new corporation, who is now offering some of the stock which has not been purchased by Messrs. Lyon and Knight, the volume of business and profits of the big combine are demonstrated and estimated to be as follows:

	Volume.	Net profit.
The present Caswell-Massey stores....	$200,000	$20,000
Vesey street store, almost ready......	100,000	10,000
Four other stores....................	500,000	50,000
Totals	$800,000	$80,000
Laboratory profits..................................		20,000
Total profits..................................		$100,000

It will be perceived that the prospectus includes only the eight stores originally decided upon by the corporation, but with the addition of the other contemplated stores the volume of business and profits may be swelled to even greater proportions.

The prospectus issued by Mr. Havemeyer describes the issue of capital stock by the corporation as consisting of $250,000 in 7 per cent. cumulative stock and $250,000 in common stock. Each subscription of $1,000 carries with it 10 shares of preferred stock, with a bonus of five shares of common stock. The present profits from the three Caswell-Massey Company stores, formerly owned by Caswell, Massey & Co., will pay 7 per cent. dividend on the preferred stock, while it is estimated that the sale of the Caswell-Massey preparations in the other stores controlled by Messrs. Lyon and Knight will insure a profit in their manufacture of more than $20,000 annually, which will probably result in causing the common stock to pay 10 per cent. in dividends.

Of the money required to purchase the old business of Caswell, Massey & Co., Messrs. Lyon and Knight have furnished $75,000, for which they have received new securities upon the same basis as that now offered to the subscribers. The money subscribed has been and will be used as follows:

For the purchase of the Caswell-Massey business....	$150,000
For the purchase of the Vesey street store..........	10,000
For establishing four more stores..................	50,000
For working capital.................................	40,000
Total	$250,000

If, as estimated, the business of the Caswell-Massey Company shows net profits of 10 per cent., in addition to the 7 per cent. on the preferred stock, these profits will be used for the extension of the business, as a surplus, or to be paid as dividends on the common stock.

When interviewed recently by an AMERICAN DRUGGIST representative relative to the plans of the new corporation, Mr. Knight said:

"This big combine of drug interests, which is to be known as the Caswell-Massey Company, will be the largest concern of its kind in this city. The corporation is planning to establish a long chain of stores in many of the fashionable sections of this city and maintain the excellent reputation of Caswell-Massey as dealers in the highest class of goods.

"The business is to be controlled by Mr. Lyon, myself and a few associates, but the National Cigar Stands Company and the United Drug Company will have nothing whatever to do with the management of its affairs. Mr. Liggett himself, although president of these two concerns, had no idea that the Caswell-Massey Company was to be formed until after the company had been incorporated and the officers elected. I cannot say whether we will handle the products of these corporations. That subject has not yet been discussed by us, but I can say that we intend to deal only in the highest class of drugs, proprietary articles and merchandise. Mr. Massey is going abroad within a few days to purchase stock and we expect to be able to offer the best that can be procured in our numerous establishments in this city. The success of the corporation is assured."

The Indian Territory Association.

The 12th annual meeting of the Indian Territory Pharmaceutical Association will be held in Sulphur, Ind. Ter., May 22, 23 and 24, 1906. Sulphur is a Government reservation of 640 acres and is celebrated as a great health resort of the Indian Territory. The convention will be called to order at 2 o'clock P.M. on the 22d day of May, 1906, and will close at noon, Thursday, May 24, 1906. A cordial invitation is extended to all pharmacists and other friends of the Indian Territory Pharmaceutical Association to be present, and especially a hearty invitation is extended by the secretary to every member of the Oklahoma Pharmaceutical Association.

Edward J. Smith, manufacturer of perfumes and extracts in Danbury, Conn., died suddenly of heart trouble on Friday, April 6, at his home in that city. Mr. Smith, who had been engaged in the perfumery business for more than a quarter of a century, was born in Rome, N. Y.

Parke, Davis & Co. Wins Bowling Tournament Cup.

In one of the most closely contested sets of games ever rolled in the Albion alleys the Parke, Davis & Co. team scored a sweeping victory over the Dodge & Olcott pin destroyers at the last competitive struggle for first place in the great bowling tournament of the Wholesale Drug Trade Bowling Association of New York, which was held Monday evening, April 9. The Parke, Davis & Co. team is therefore the acknowledged winner of the tournament, and the big silver trophy cup will remain for another year in its accustomed place in the offices of Superintendent William J. Carr, at 90 Maiden lane. This is the third year that Parke, Davis & Co. has captured first honors.

The last games bowled by the Parke, Davis & Co. and Dodge & Olcott knights of the pin were deemed necessary for the proper awarding of first honors in the tournament, as both teams were tied for first place at the conclusion of the regular match games, which occurred Monday evening, April 2. With sixteen games to their credit and only four to their discredit, the presumptive champions of the alley were forced to bowl three deciding games, with the understanding that the team winning two out of the three games should be declared the victor for the season.

In addition to securing the right to hold the trophy cup another year, the Parke, Davis & Co. team will also receive the first prize, consisting of a $25 present, to be selected by the members of the team themselves. The Dodge & Olcott bowlers, who are entitled to second place, will receive the second prize, a present to cost $15, while the third prize, which is to cost $10, will be awarded to the Colgate & Co. contingent.

In the supplementary games between Parke, Davis & Co. and Dodge & Olcott, "Ed" Conway, of the Parke, Davis & Co. team, made the highest individual record, scoring 212 in the second game, with six strikes, one spare and one split spare. During the first game Conway experienced some difficulty in making himself acquainted with the championship alley upon which the rivals were compelled to roll off the tie, but he more than compensated for his early deficiency in the second and last trials. Second only to Conway's individual score was that of William J. Carr, of the Parke, Davis & Co. crew, who chalked up 211, with six strikes and three spares. "Lou" Burgess, the winner of highest individual average prize in the tournament, also made a good showing by reaching 200, with four strikes and an equal number of spares, but "Johnny" Ruddiman went Burgess a few better in this last contest by scoring 205, with six strikes and one split spare and one straight spare.

In fact, the average scores of Carr, Burgess, Blake, Conway and Bruun on April 9 all deserve special mention, as they reached 186, 181, 166, 165 and 160, respectively.

The Dodge & Olcott team won the first of the match games in the last contest with the Parke, Davis & Co. men, with a score of 833 to 797. The superior bowling of Carr and Burgess, however, won the second game for the Parke, Davis & Co. team by 918 to 797, but in the third and deciding game the Parke, Davis & Co. men were only seven pins ahead of their rivals at the eighth frame, and it required all the skill of every member of the team to win the victory by 64 pins, the score of the final game being 859 to 795.

The judges of the tournament will make their final awards before the end of this month, giving to the first three teams the prizes to which they are entitled. To Burgess, moreover, a special high individual average prize, consisting of a $15 present, will also be awarded, while an additional $10 prize will also be presented to the highest individual score man on each of the other ten teams.

Gilbert-Cook.

The marriage is announced of Dr. Frank J. Gilbert and Miss Florence, daughter of Mr. and Mrs. Charles Cook, of Portland, Maine. Miss Cook has many friends among the members of the National Wholesale Druggists' Association, as she has attended several of the meetings of the association, having been one of the California party.

MANHATTAN ASSOCIATION ELECTS OFFICERS.

Interest in Pending Legislation—Agitation for Slot Telephones to Be Urged.

While the chief feature of interest at the last regular monthly meeting of the Manhattan Pharmaceutical Association, held Monday evening, April 16, in the lecture room of the New York College of Pharmacy, was the annual election of officers, several other matters of great importance to the members of this organization and druggists in general were also discussed. The association declared itself as unalterably opposed to the passage of the Lupton bill, providing that merchants other than licensed druggists be permitted to deal in many drugs and medicines besides ordinary household remedies, and took steps to secure the assistance of the Assemblymen of Greater New York in an effort to kill the measure. A committee of three members was also appointed to conduct the campaign for the installation of slot telephone machines with a 40 per cent. commission for retail druggists in this city. A suggestion by President Alpers that increased interest would be aroused in the work of the association if it would affiliate with the American Pharmaceutical Association as a local branch seemed to be well received. It was not put as a motion or directly advocated, but he said he deemed it worthy of the attention of the incoming officers.

PRESIDENT ALPERS DECLINES RE-ELECTION.

President William C. Alpers presented his resignation from that office, stating that he found his business affairs so pressing that he would hereafter be unable to devote sufficient time to his duties as head of the association. His resignation was accepted only after an expression of profound regret had been tendered to him by all the members. Jacob Diner was thereupon unanimously elected to the presidency, to assume his new duties at the next regular meeting. Gilbert P. Knapp was chosen first vice-president, and Michael Rafter, formerly third vice-president, was selected as second vice-president, while Thomas Latham was elected third vice-president to fill the place left vacant by Mr. Rafter.

SECRETARY SWANN RELINQUISHES OFFICE.

S. V. B. Swann tendered his resignation as secretary on the ground that he would hereafter be compelled to give all his time to the New York Consolidated Drug Company, of which he has recently been made manager. Upon the acceptance of Mr. Swann's resignation Bruno R. Dauscha was chosen as secretary of the association. G. H. Hitchcock was re-elected treasurer. All of these officers will serve throughout the ensuing year.

In his annual address to the members President Alpers reviewed briefly the work accomplished by the organization during the last year, and mentioned especially the success which had attended the giving of a series of lectures on professional pharmacy by druggists, physicians and chemists prominent in their various lines. He expressed the hope that the Manhattan Association would continue to represent only the professional side of the business, leaving most of the subjects of trade interest to the M. A. R. D. and the N. A. R. D., which have proved themselves capable of dealing with these matters and accomplishing the desired results.

President-elect Diner replied to Dr. Alpers' speech later in the evening by promising the members that the same policy which had been adopted by his predecessor would be continued under his leadership. Interesting lectures, like those arranged for the association by the Executive Committee during the last year, Mr. Diner assured his auditors, would be among the main features of that body's work in the ensuing year.

TO ADVOCATE INSTALLATION OF SLOT MACHINES.

After a lengthy discussion on the prospect of persuading the officers and directors of the New York & New Jersey Telephone Company to install in their stores slot telephone machines, from the profits of which the proprietors would receive a 40 per cent. commission, the members voted to empower President Alpers to appoint a committee of three to accomplish this much desired end. A. Clayton Searles, Edward F. Pfaff and Edward H. Schaaf were selected as the members of this committee, with instructions to report all action taken by them to the Executive Committee.

TO ACTIVELY OPPOSE THE LUPTON BILL.

When the report of the Legislative Committee on the status of the Lupton bill had been read, a unanimous vote condemning this measure was passed by the members on the ground that the bill, which has already been reported favorably by the State Senate Committee on Public Health and is now before the Assembly, would nullify to a great extent the full power of the State Pharmacy law, which prohibits the sale of drugs specified in the measure by persons without a license. After some discussion as to the best ways and means of fighting the bill, the members present at the meeting requested Secretary Dauscha to write to all the members of the association asking them to appeal individually to the Assemblymen representing their districts in Albany and make a direct call upon them for assistance in killing the bill.

The executive and other committees of the association will be appointed at the next monthly meeting, which will be held in the College of Pharmacy Building on Monday evening, May 21.

New Officers for M. A. R. D.

Several changes were made in the officers of the Metropolitan Association of Retail Druggists at the last general meeting of that organization, which was held Friday evening, April 6, in the lecture room of the New York College of Pharmacy Building. S. V. B. Swann resigned as secretary and Jacob Diner, formerly vice-president of the association, was elected to succeed him. W. B. Montgomery was chosen vice-president to succeed Mr. Diner in that office.

Owing to the resignation from the treasurership of A. H. Bischof, A. B. Baltzley was selected to fill this place. The resignation of William C. Alpers, who announced that his business was so pressing that he could no longer afford the time to attend the meetings and forward the interests of the association, left a vacancy among the members of the Executive Committee, which was filled by A. Clayton Searles.

The two new organizers, who have been engaged by the National Association of Retail Druggists to assist William De Shetley, manager of the Eastern territory of the N. A. R. D., and Organizer G. S. Bohan in their efforts to increase the membership of the M. A. R. D. and that of the national body, were introduced to the members. These two new organizers, G. H. Sanborn and R. H. Clark, have had long experience in this kind of work and will undoubtedly render material assistance in their new field. The cost of the services of one of them will be defrayed by the National Association, while the salary of the other will be paid by the M. A. R. D.

Mr. Pollock, representing the St. Louis club plan or limited contract scheme for the marketing of proprietary remedies, explained to the members of the M. A. R. D. the advantages offered to the retail druggist by the terms of this agreement with the jobbers, irrespective of the manufacturing interests. No action was taken, however, regarding the new contract plan.

A representative of the Great Eastern Telephone Company, which is now offering to establish a 5-cent toll rate in every borough of this city if the municipal authorities will grant to it conduit privileges for $2,000,000, told the members that his company would willingly install in their stores nickel in the slot telephones, which should be controlled by the druggists, on a liberal commission basis. After some discussion the members referred the advisability of accepting this offer to the Executive Committee.

The Manufacturing Chemists' Registration Bureau.

The following titles have been received for registration in the Manufacturing Chemists' Registration Bureau: "Fringe Tree Alterative," by Nelson, Baker & Co.; "Narco," by Hance Brothers & White, and "Dentozone," by Frederick Stearns & Co., Detroit, Mich.; "Confect," by Eli Lilly & Co.

Greater New York News.

F. M. Sames has bought the fittings and stock of the store formerly owned by F. Kahlenberg, at 3206 Third avenue.

C. Succhi has purchased the fixtures and stock of the drug store until recently owned by Charles M. Du Gay, at 508 Third avenue, corner of Thirty-fourth street.

George G. Jacks, owner of several retail drug stores in Chicago, was among the recent visitors in the local manufacturing trade.

Harry B. Skillman, of Detroit, business manager of the Parke, Davis & Co. house publications, visited the local offices of that concern and the AMERICAN DRUGGIST last week.

Chester Estes, a prominent retail druggist in Rockland, Mass., visited friends in the local wholesale and manufacturing trade on April 9 and 10.

Harry Thornton, manager of Parke, Davis & Co.'s Boston offices, spent the Easter holidays with relatives and friends in this city.

James F. Ballard, of St. Louis, is making a tour of the establishments in this city through which he markets his proprietary medicines.

E. J. Edwards, a prominent retail druggist of Easthampton, L. I., recently made a trip through the local wholesale trade for the purpose of buying toilet articles.

Carl Schneitzer, president of the Compania Morana, manufacturing perfumers of Zurich, Switzerland, visited the offices of Magnus & Lauer, the American agents of the company, at 257 Pearl street, on April 17 and 18.

Dr. George Rosengarten, of the Powers-Weightman-Rosengarten Company, has just returned with his wife from a three months' trip through Continental Europe and is now at the local offices of the corporation, at 145 Front street.

A fire, which threatened for some time to prove very disastrous, damaged slightly the stock and building occupied by W. J. Bush & Co., at 5 Jones lane, on Thursday, April 12. The business of the firm is being conducted as usual, however.

A. H. Gilmer, of Houston, Tex., president of the newly incorporated wholesale drug house known as the Southern Drug Company, of that city, visited the local manufacturing trade recently for the purpose of purchasing stock for his company.

For the purpose of opening a retail drug store at Sixty-fifth street and Broadway, David Wallace Rintels, formerly buyer for the Simpson-Crawford Company and the Fourteenth Street Store, has resigned these positions. Mr. Rintels is already the proprietor of the Walker-Rintels pharmacy, on Dewey square, in Boston.

A. Bretzfeld, manager of the J. Linde & Son's pharmacy, of New Haven, Conn., called upon his friends in this city on April 9 while on his way home from Washington, Baltimore and Philadelphia, where he had been spending his honeymoon.

Dr. Richard Thonet, a well-known Vienna chemist, is in this city making a thorough investigation and study of the most recent chemical processes used by the manufacturing drug trade in this city.

Edward Ziegler, formerly a partner in the wholesale and retail drug firm of Lyons & Ziegler, of Jersey City, has purchased the interest in the business hitherto owned by Frederick W. Lyons and has therefore become sole proprietor of the store at 746 Bergen avenue, in that city.

James E. Lilly, vice-president of Eli Lilly & Co., of Indianapolis, is now making a tour of southern Spain, Algiers, Italy, France, central Europe and England with his wife. Mr. and Mrs. Lilly sailed for the Mediterranean on Saturday, April 7, on the steamship *Princess Irene* and expect to remain abroad until the early fall.

Plans have been filed for the remodeling of the old five-story loft and store building at 183 Broadway, known as the Milhau Building. It was the first iron front store building erected on Broadway and is reproduced in a noted historic print of old New York as a Broadway landmark. The interior will be made over into stores on all five floors.

Stuart Cohen, representing Elliott Brothers, Limited, manufacturing and wholesale drug merchants in Sydney, New South Wales, Australia, is making a tour of the United States, stopping at all the principal cities in the Eastern as well as in the Central and Pacific Coast States. Mr. Cohen came by steamship from Melbourne to San Francisco, and arrived in this city on Monday, April 16.

The commencement exercises of the graduating class of the Brooklyn College of Pharmacy will be held Thursday evening, May 3, at 8 o'clock, in the Baptist Temple at Third avenue and Schermerhorn street, Brooklyn. Adrian F. Paradis, jr., has been chosen valedictorian, and a splendid entertainment has been arranged by the committee, which includes F. Milton Martin, chairman; Hyman Felder, Matthew R. Newstead and Augustus A. Reynolds, advisory member.

The annual banquet and reception of the Alumni Association of the college will be held commencement night at the conclusion of the exercises in the Imperial, 360 Fulton street.

Members of the senior class of the New York College of Pharmacy who are now assured that they have successfully passed the final examinations are planning to make the class day exercises, which will be held in the college building on Wednesday, April 25, of greater interest to their relatives and friends than they have ever been in previous years. The commencement, as already mentioned in the AMERICAN DRUGGIST, will be held in Carnegie Hall on Thursday, April 26.

S. V. B. Swann assumed his new duties as manager of the New York Consolidated Drug Company, at 188 First avenue, on April 16, having resigned his position as salesman for Eli Lilly & Co. during the first week of the month. In addition to resigning from the secretaryship of the Metropolitan Association of Retail Druggists and the Manhattan Pharmaceutical Association, Mr. Swann also intends to resign as secretary of the New York State Pharmaceutical Association at its next meeting, which will be held at Niagara Falls early in June. Felix Hirseman, formerly manager of the New York Consolidated Drug Company, has opened a retail drug store in the Bronx.

A routine business meeting of the Twelfth District Branch of the Metropolitan Association of Retail Druggists was held Tuesday evening, April 17, in Turnverein Hall, at Eighth avenue and Fifty-fourth street. A. Schlosser, who has succeeded Reuben R. Smith as president of the branch, presided at the gathering, at which Secretary E. J. Emelin and 12 other members were also present. The main topic of discussion at the meeting was the necessity for the spread of the direct contract serial numbering plan among manufacturers and retailers not yet interested in this scheme, and also for the strict maintenance of the terms of the contract among those who have bound themselves to observe its provisions.

Among recent visitors to this city, most of whom registered at the Drug Trade Club, of New York (the new corporate and legal title of the New York Drug and Chemical Club), were: Henry Weber, Goldfield, Nev.; D. F. Dickson, Philadelphia; W. G. Marshall, Grimsby, England; A. B. Mitchell, New Haven, Conn.; Ludwig Schmalcher, San Francisco, Cal.; F. E. Johnson, St. Louis, Mo.; James F. Ballard, St. Louis, Mo.; W. Crocker, Albany, N. Y.; F. L. Barnes, Rochester, N. Y.; Gen. R. M. J. Reed, Philadelphia; Charles S. Crosby, Providence, R. I.; A. J. Ayer, Montreal, Canada; H. M. Larter, Newark, N. J.; Charles Bludan, New Brunswick, N. J.; H. M. Voorhis, Philadelphia; D. Mitchell, New Orleans, La.; W. H. Ridley, Burlington, Vt.; Eugene Saxe, Boston, Mass.; S. Saxe, Bradford, Pa.; M. F. Banjamin, Riverhead, L. I.; A. H. Wightman, Hartford, Conn.; Dr. T. S. K. Morton, Philadelphia; C. H. Thornton, Duluth, Minn.; L. C. Haughey, Bound Brook, N. Y.; H. S. Bailey, Denver, Col.; A. M. Fode, Kalamazoo, Mich.; Franklin Phillips, Newark, N. J.; Dr. W. C. Abbot, Chicago; E. R. Grier, Bridgeport, Conn.; C. A. Reed, Plainfield, N. J.; Frederick Roth, San Francisco, Cal., and J. B. Fallman, Grand Rapids, Mich.

Parke, Davis & Co. Forms Another Bowling Team.

A new bowling team has just been formed among the men in the local offices of Parke, Davis & Co., for the purpose of playing the team which has just carried off first honors in the tournament of the New York Wholesale Drug Trade Bowling Association. A challenge has already been issued by the novices and the old team has accepted it. In accordance with the terms of this challenge the old and new teams will contest for supremacy in three games, the team winning the first two games to be declared the victor, while the losing team is to defray the expense of a banquet to be held in the Café Martin. The games will be rolled in the Albion Alleys on some date within the near future. The newly organized contingent includes "Charley" Nale, "Eph" Plummer, Dr. Tuthill, "Jack" Doran and Frank Tupper, while, as already known, the old team consists of "Lou" Burgess, William Carr, "Chris" Bruun, Blake and Conway.

Unless some unforeseen obstacle presents itself to prevent the rolling of these games the contest will be held on Tuesday evening, April 24.

James E. Lilly Sails for Europe.

On the evening of March 31 the officers of Eli Lilly & Co., Indianapolis, and the heads of the departments gave a dinner in honor of James E. Lilly, vice-president of the company. After many years of close application to business Mr. Lilly decided to take a protracted vacation and realize a long cherished ambition to make a European tour. The eve of his departure was made the occasion of a handsome testimonial to him from his associates and friends. Mr. and Mrs. Lilly sailed from New York Saturday, April 7, on the Princess Irene. They will visit southern Spain, some of the northern African coast cities, Italy, France, central Europe and England before their return in the autumn. The midsummer will be spent in the Alpine countries.

German Apothecaries Will Hold Outing in Jamaica.

The annual outing of the German Apothecaries' Society will take place this year on June 14 in Morningside Park, Hoffman boulevard, Jamaica. The time and place for this outdoor entertainment of the society were selected by the Entertainment Committee of that body, which made its report on the subject at the meeting held Thursday evening, April 5, in Allaire's Restaurant and Café, at 190 Third avenue. The report of the Entertainment Committee, of which Paul Arndt is chairman, was unanimously approved by all the members present.

At this meeting, moreover, George Kleinau, the corresponding secretary of the society, presented to the members a letter from the Austrian Apothecaries' Society which announced that that body was sending to the German Apothecaries' Society a copy of the new Austrian Pharmacopœia in acknowledgment of the copy of the United States Pharmacopœia which the New York organization recently presented to the Austrian body. Announcement was also made at the meeting that George Goetting and Otto Seifert had both resigned from the society, the former because of his retirement from the drug business and the latter because of his intention to leave this city. Dr. R. Dénig, the guest of the evening, delivered an interesting lecture on conjunctivitis.

Proprietary Men Meet Next Month.

The twenty-fourth annual meeting of the Proprietary Association of America will be held in this city at the Hotel Astor on Tuesday, Wednesday and Thursday, May 8, 9 and 10. The first session will begin at 11 o'clock on Tuesday morning, when as soon as the preliminary work is attended to, the question of amending article VII of the by-laws will be discussed. This amendment provides that, by the unanimous vote of all the members present at any annual meeting, the by-laws may be amended without the necessity for sending out any previous notice.

We have received the Fifth Annual Report of the New York State Board of Pharmacy, a neatly printed and bound brochure of 56 pages, containing an account of the transactions of the annual meeting at Albany on January 2, together with the text of the pharmacy law and the by-laws and rules and regulations.

PERUNA CUT IN NEW YORK.

Milhau Leads Off, Others Follow—Agent Denies that Cut Was Authorized by Manufacturers—President Hartman Promise to Cut Off Cutters.

Instead of replying directly to Secretary Thomas V. Wooten, of the National Association of Retail Druggists, who asked him to make a definite statement as to whether he had authorized a cut of 9c. per bottle in the price of Peruna, President Hartman, of the Peruna Drug Manufacturing Company, has cut off the list of that concern's retail agents all the druggists which recently indulged in such price cutting. The news that Dr. Hartman and the Peruna Company had taken this action has been received by the wholesale drug trade in this city, but the retailers themselves have not been officially notified that they have been dropped from the list.

The firms which have been cut from the Peruna Company's list are: J. Milhau's Son, William B. Riker & Sons' Company, Hegeman & Co., J. Jungmann, Kinsman & Co., Reid, Yeomans & Cubit, and the Kalish Pharmacy, of this city, and Eugene Hartnett and J. E. Williams, of Jersey City.

Frank Ennis, manager of the Milhau store, which is now located at 205 Broadway, who is said to have consented to make the initial cut, refuses to make any statement regarding what Mr. Evans said to him about the prevailing price of Peruna, though he admits he had an interview with that representative. The managers of William B. Riker & Son Company and Hegeman & Co. maintain that they merely made the cut because they were forced to take such action in order to compete with the house which made the first move in this direction.

William De Shetley, manager of the Eastern territory of the National Association of Retail Druggists, received an unofficial reply from Dr. Hartman a week ago, to the effect that two officers of the Peruna Company were in New York at that time and that they could answer all questions relating to the authenticity of the reported cut. The officers referred to in this answer were F. E. Schumacher, vice-president of the Peruna Company, and W. E. Baker, representing the product in Ohio, but both of these gentlemen left this city, after a brief conference with Mr. Evans, who was then in town, before Mr. De Shetley or any other representative of the N. A. R. D. or M. A. R. D. could see them.

Before departing for Dutchess County, where he expects to take a long rest, Mr. Evans denied that the Peruna Company has authorized the cut from 83 to 74 cents, but asserted that he had notified the concern at its home offices in Columbus, Ohio, and expected that the offending druggists would be cut off the customers' list.

The big drug houses, which have followed the action of J. Milhau's Son in cutting the price of Peruna, have not violated their contracts with the Peruna Company, as this agreement distinctly specifies that they are to maintain the price of the product only as long as their competitors.

Portraits of Deceased Members.

A most commendable innovation is noted in the published proceedings of the New York meeting of the National Wholesale Druggists' Association, which we have just received through the courtesy of Secretary Toms. This consists of portraits of deceased members, which are printed in the report of the Committee on Memorials of Deceased Members. This is a feature which should be very welcome to the members, as serving with the text to recall the personalities of departed associates. The volume as a whole is a very creditable one as regards the editing and arrangement of the matter contained in it, as well as from the mechanical end, the book being substantially bound, and printed on a good quality of paper. The frontispiece of the volume consists of well executed portraits of the president, secretary and treasurer.

WESTERN NEW YORK.

Business Dull in Buffalo—Prices Stand Unchanged—Prerequisite Law Affects Applications—The Rigor of the Law for Offenders.

(*From our Regular Correspondent.*)

Buffalo, April 19.—Again we have slow trade in the Buffalo retail drug stores, possibly a little better than it was last month, but not good enough to satisfy the average member of the trade. There is, though, one notable exception to the general report of poor business, and that is of Secretary George Reimann, of the Western branch of the State Board of Pharmacy, who finds everything to his liking, but then he is making money enough so that he has lately spent six weeks in California with his family and is excusable for seeing everything in the large for a while.

PRICES MAINTAINED.

There is no giving up of the uniform price-list, which has now held so long that it may be said to have taken a firm root. These prices are by no means high, and there are those who would like to see them advanced again, but there is a sign of resistance from certain big stores downtown, where it is held that the prices are too high now, so the Retail Drug Association has concluded to be discreet and let the prices remain where they are.

DR. GREGORY TO RETIRE FROM THE STATE BOARD.

Dr. W. G. Gregory, who has been a member of the Board of Pharmacy so many years, being in the Erie County Board till it was merged into the State Board, announces that he shall retire from it with the expiration of his term in June. He has also declined to stand for re-election to the presidency of the Buffalo Drug Merchants' Exchange, a position he has held since its organization. The primary reason for this course is without doubt his becoming a part of the Cahoon-Lyon Drug Company, so that he does not consider himself a strictly individual retail druggist any longer. He has done the State and county great service, and every one will be sorry to see him give up his old positions. It is expected that J. A. Lockie, of Buffalo, president of the State Pharmaceutical Association, will be elected to fill Dr. Gregory's place in the State Board. So far there does not appear to be any other candidate. Mr. Lockie seems to be the logical candidate anyhow, and ought to be elected.

DRUGGISTS SEEK TO RESTRAIN SALE OF CARBOLIC ACID AND COCAINE.

The Buffalo druggists are pleased to find no opposition from the City Council to their measure restricting the sale of carbolic acid and cocaine in the city. It was taken up very vigorously by Health Commissioner Greene, which made the matter easy. The ordinance, now on its way to become a city enactment, provides for only a 5 per cent. solution of carbolic acid, unless prescribed by a physician, and no sale whatever of cocaine unless prescribed by a physician or a dentist. It is really the cocaine restriction that is most desired by the druggists, as it was becoming alarmingly common as a tipple.

EFFECT OF THE PREREQUISITE LAW.

The April examination held in Buffalo by the Western branch of the State Board of Pharmacy was very significant, as there were 35 candidates, every one of them for a druggist's license. It is held that the new prerequisite law has now taken up all who are qualified for a pharmacist's license. At the former examination there were only a few candidates for the higher license, and all of them failed. So hereafter there will be seekers for that position only on the part of pharmacy college graduates. These will appear in clouds for the June examination, and then it will be druggists only for the rest of the year.

The annual meeting of the Buffalo Drug Merchants' Exchange was not so very harmonious a gathering as it might have been, for there was no report of the retiring board prepared, and, when it was demanded, there was a discussion.

COLLEGE NOTES.

University Day was recently celebrated by the different departments of University of Buffalo, the dean and faculty of the College of Pharmacy being represented. The faculty in pharmacy has requested the council to rescind the age requirement for graduation. A course in analytical chemistry has been outlined. The final junior examination closes on April 25. The following directors were elected: E. H. Breckon, F. S. Cushing, of Hamburg; J. P. Diehl, E. C. Field, C. H. Gauger, J. S. Greey, S. A. Grove, A. J. Keller, H. A. Scheck and P. M. Lockie. The officers have not been elected yet, but the following choice is expected to go through: President, C. H. Gauger; treasurer, J. S. Greey; secretary, E. H. Breckon. The exchange is in a very prosperious condition, and its membership includes nearly all the retail druggists in the city.

THE REGISTRATION OF DRUG STORES

in the Western section of the State has developed the fact that there are still people who cannot be brought into line by any sort of persuasion. One or two druggists had been presented to the district attorney as delinquents every year since the law went into effect. It was seen that they were again waiting for the district attorney to write them a letter, but he refused this time and ordered them prosecuted.

NEWS NOTES FROM WESTERN NEW YORK DRUG STORES.

Frank L. Crandall has sold his drug store on Forest avenue, Buffalo, to George J. Wheeler.

Edgar H. Lincoln, a Buffalo College of Pharmacy graduate from Warsaw, has opened a new drug store in his home town.

The drug firm of Wilson & Parker at Warsaw has been dissolved, Earl H. Parker buying out his partner and Mr. Wilson going into other business in Buffalo.

Arthur F. Humbert, who has a general store at Clarence, Erie County, has put in a stock of drugs and applied for a license.

Andrew J. Kramer, formerly with Pierce's World's Dispensary, is now manager of the drug store of Hubbard & Co., Herkimer street, Buffalo.

Charles A. Chiarra, who has a drug store on the Terrace, Buffalo, has opened a second one on Canal street, with Louis Scharrino as pharmacist in charge.

Carl E. Freeman has been engaged as pharmacist in charge of the new drug store of Harry M. Wise, at Delaware avenue and Chippewa street, Buffalo.

Samuel Rudin, who was in charge of the Kehr, later Moore, drug store, at 117 Jefferson street, Buffalo, has lately bought the property.

A. W. Mapes & Co. have bought the drug store of W. S. Thomas, at Angelica. Mr. Mapes was formerly pharmacist with A. M. Palmer in Olean.

The pharmacy of C. M. Burrows, of Albion, has been sold to Jackson & McChain, who will call it the Central Drug Store. They are not pharmacists, and have placed Irving L. Gifford in charge.

A. C. Heegaard is preparing to open a new drug store at Genesee and Jefferson streets, Buffalo. He has one at Genesee and Johnson streets, and is preparing to manage one and give the management of the other to his brother, O. E. Heegaard.

Otto Moehlau, who is out of health and talks of locating in Texas, has sold his Genesee street pharmacy, Buffalo, to Mrs. E. M. Cable, who has engaged H. M. Rhodes as licensed manager.

H. M. Groves, the Batavia member of the State Board of Pharmacy, is recovering from his attack of typhoid fever and will return to board work soon. Charles T. Mann is in charge of his store.

Edward H. Leadley, the active and licensed member of the Batavia drug firm of Leadley & Buell, has bought out his partner, Edward G. Buell, and is forming a $20,000 stock company and will run the store under the name of the Leadley Drug Company.

The new National cigar stands are now becoming numerous in Buffalo, about 25 going in lately. Some like them and appear to be making money by them, while others object to what they call catering to the enemy of the retail druggist, especially as it includes the selling of cheap cigars.

NEW ENGLAND.

Massachusetts Alumni Dine and Elect Officers—License Troubles in Peabody—A Hundred and Sixty Dollars for Coaching.

(From our Regular Correspondent.)

Boston, April 18.—The annual meeting and dinner of the Alumni Association of the Massachusetts College of Pharmacy was held at the Parker House on the evening of April 12, with President Perley B. Thompson, Ph.G., in the chair. Routine reports of the secretary and treasurer were received and accepted. The Committee on Alumni Journal submitted a report advising the discontinuance of the journal. It was voted to adopt the committee's suggestion.

It was proposed to change the date of the annual meeting to the first Thursday in February. The idea was considered favorably, and it will be acted upon finally at the May meeting. The following officers were elected: President, Arthur Tripp, Ph.G.; vice-presidents, George L. Burrough, Ph.G., and Florence Eichorn, Ph.G.; secretary, F. S. Schmidt, Ph.G., M.D.; treasurer, William R. Acheson, Ph.G., and auditor, Prof. Elie H. La Pierre, Ph.G. The retiring officers were made a committee to make arrangements for the annual dinner, scheduled for next month, complimentary to the graduating class.

THE BOARD OF PHARMACY

has recently been very busy considering subjects appertaining to the license question. This matter is a live issue in Peabody, and it was recently stated that the certificates of the druggists of that town will not be approved by the board, for the reason that some of those who conduct stores in that town destroyed the books in which the sales of liquor were recorded after the alleged discovery that liquor was being retailed at these establishments.

HE WAS COACHED FOR THE BOARD EXAMINATION.

At Cambridge, on April 12, in the Superior Court, Joseph C. Stammers, of Boston, was awarded $162.64 against Edward H. Callahan, of Woburn, on a contract whereby the plaintiff was to prepare Callahan to pass the Board of Pharmacy examinations. Callahan passed, and is a registered pharmacist.

REGISTERED IN MASSACHUSETTS.

The board recently held three examinations, at which the following candidates were successful:

Harry Belin, Boston; John W. Cuff, Braintree; Clinton B. Davis, Fall River; James P. Lawrence, Salem; James H. Riley, Salem; Thomas W. Somers, Boston; Raymond P. Young, No. Grafton; James F. Doherty, Cambridge; Carroll A. Hanson, Medford; Timothy E. Murphy, jr., Newton; John W. Rawnsley, Methuen; Charles F. Wright, Waltham; John T. Collins, Milford; Thomas H. Nabb, Fall River, and Bernard B. Merten, Boston.

TIT FOR TAT—THE DRUGGIST WINS.

Gilbert J. Healey, of Gainsboro street, has recently been awarded a jury verdict of $300 against a Brookline resident. In 1904 the latter made a criminal complaint against Healey for assault by alleged elbowing his way through a crowded car. Healey was acquitted by the Court, and then he brought suit against the complainant for $2,000, alleging malicious prosecution. The jury found for Healey, but discounted his claim for damages.

FINED FOR ILLEGAL LIQUOR SALES.

A heavy fine was recently imposed upon Allyn E. Hone, of Stoughton, for alleged violation of the liquor law. He was ordered to pay $50 on a charge of maintaining a liquor nuisance and the same amount on the charge of illegal keeping. He appealed and was put under bonds of $600.

John H. Welch, of Quincy, has just been fined $50 for keeping and exposing liquor for sale. He also appealed and furnished bonds to the amount of $300.

E. Walter Faulkner, the Malden druggist, and Miss Mannie L. Thomas, his former clerk, who were arrested in January on a charge of passing bad checks, were defaulted in the Charlestown court, April 2, when their cases came up for continuance. Capiases were issued for their arrest.

PENNSYLVANIA.

Increased Interest in the Philadelphia Association of Retail Druggists—P. A. R. D. to Dance—Bright Prospects for the State Association Meeting—Quaker City Bowlers—Retail Druggists' Prices Unaffected by Loder Decision.

(From our Regular Correspondent.)

Philadelphia, April 20.—The officials of the Philadelphia Association of Retail Druggists are doing everything that lies in their power to make the association more of a power among druggists. Since the suit between it and Loder instead of there being a falling off in the membership, it has increased, and there has been a general "rally around the flag" at each meeting. Many members who were only connected with the association in name are now taking a prominent part in its affairs, and the future of the organization is brighter than ever. During the past few months there has been a steady increase in the applications for membership and it is said that the members who have been delegated to look up all druggists who are not members are meeting with more success than ever. There is a feeling that the association has done much good, and with every druggist in the city a member further good results will be obtained. The Loder decision was somewhat of a setback, but as yet this case is far from settled, and even if a verdict is secured against the association there will be future agreements made by which the druggists who desire to live up to contracts will have an opportunity to do so.

QUAKER CITY DRUGGISTS TO DANCE.

Believing that the interests of the retail drug trade will be promoted by the bringing together of its members, socially as well as commercially, the Philadelphia Association of Retail Druggists, through its Entertainment Committee, has arranged for the holding of a musical and dance on Tuesday evening, May 8, in Lu Lu Temple. An effort is being made to eclipse this year the successes of former years. With this in mind President Charles Rehfus has chosen the following well-known pharmacists as a committee to arrange for the affair: Chairman, Clarence H. Campbell; vice-chairman, S. C. Henry; secretary, Frank M. Apple; treasurer, Dr. E. K. Boltz; John H. Bailey, William Hilpert, J. E. Marsden, C. G. Neely, H. A. Nolte, N. S. Steltzer, W. E. Supplee and W. H. Sutton.

AMONG THE BOWLERS.

There is more interest being taken in the bowling match between the various teams of the Wholesale Drug League than ever before. While the J. Ellwood Lee Company's team is a sure winner, there is considerable rivalry between the rest of the teams. The matches are played every Tuesday evening, and the alleys of the Central Bowling Club are utilized by this club. The standing of the teams on April 16 was as follows:

	Won.	Lost.
J. Ellwood Lee Company	60	12
Wanderers	35	31
Smith, Kline & French Company	33	36
Philadelphia College of Pharmacy, white	34	38
Geo. D. Feldt & Co.	28	48
Philadelphia College of Pharmacy, blue	22	47

High one game: Boltman, 247.
High three games: Donnel, 641.
High one game, team: J. Ellwood Lee Company, 997.
High three games, team: J. Ellwood Lee Company, 2,781.

The bowling season is drawing to a close, and toward the end of the month it will wind up with a banquet. The time and place where the dinner will be given has not been definitely decided upon. Preparations are being made for the national tournament which will be held at Atlantic City the first week in May. The Philadelphia League will be represented by a team made up of two bowlers from the J. Ellwood Lee Company, two from Smith, Kline & French Company, two from the Wanderers and one from George D. Feldt & Co.

NO EFFECT YET FROM LODER SUIT.

So far the decision in the Loder suit has not had any material effect on retail prices of drugs and proprietary medicines. There have been in a few isolated cases reductions made, but, as a rule, the retailer has not made any material change. As yet there has been no rush to patronize the cut rate druggists, and it is said that until this becomes apparent the retailers, especially those who are members of the Philadelphia Association of Retail Druggists, will not take any drastic action. Some of the large retail stores in close proximity to Sixteenth and Chestnut streets have made the reductions in proprietary goods necessary to conform to the prices published by Loder. It was demonstrated last week that the department stores that handle drugs and proprietary goods do not always sell as low as some of the druggists. One of the largest department stores in the country advertised to sell a certain article at 25 cents. This same article has been sold by a Chestnut street druggist for months at 20 cents. And this was done without any advertising.

A NEW PRICE SCHEDULE PROMULGATED.

Recently a new price schedule was sent out by the officers of the association. This schedule makes a reduction of about 2 cents on all 25 cent articles, also on 45 cent goods, and 4 cents on 83 cent medicines. The placing of these articles on a reduced scale was to meet the competition set by Mr. Loder. However, it is optional as to whether they are put into effect, and in many cases the druggists have made no change. The meeting last Friday was well attended and there were a number of speeches made which were of vital interest to the drug trade. The reports submitted were of a favorable nature and the best of good will prevailed. The sentiment among the members of the association is that the outlook is decidedly encouraging, and it is believed that by the end of this year there will be a large increase in the membership.

THE CO-OPERATIVE JOBBERS.

Under the management of President Rohrman the Philadelphia Wholesale Drug Company, Limited, is flourishing. This company has recently secured the adjoining building and even with this increased space it is hampered for room. Nearly all the leading druggists in this city are members of the company and it is said that there is likely to be a further increase in the manner of doing business which will necessitate the securing of larger quarters. The latter no doubt will be done as soon as the lease for the present buildings expires. The proposition which was made some time ago to form a National Association of all the wholesale drug companies which were conducted in the interest of the retail druggists is still hanging fire. It is said that greater headway could be made if some of the smaller companies were not desirous of securing a greater representation. This association is the desire of the Brooklyn druggists, but for some reason there is not the same feeling all over the country. It is thought that within a short time the committee that has the matter in charge will agree upon a plan which will be acceptable to all the various companies.

PREPARING FOR THE STATE MEETING.

The approaching meeting of the Pennsylvania Pharmaceutical Association, which is to be held at Glen Summit from June 26 to 28, inclusive, promises to be the largest gathering of druggists ever held in this State. It is likely that there will be a good increase in the attendance, as it is the desire of the officers to have as near as possible the full membership on hand. It is likely that some sort of an agreement will be made with the National Association of Retail Druggists, so that there can be united efforts made to prevent any legislation being enacted which will be detrimental to the retail druggists. At the last session of the Legislature the association was successful in having killed a number of measures that if they had been passed would have been injurious to all reputable druggists.

HEARING ON THE LODER APPEAL.

On Monday last the hearing of the appeal from the decision of the verdict rendered in favor of Druggist Loder against the N. R. D. A. and others was begun in the United States Court of Appeals. This case has attracted great interest throughout the country. Loder sued various wholesale druggists as well as the N. W. D. A. and the N. A. R. D., claiming that they had bound themselves together to restrict him from securing the various proprietary goods. The jury rendered a verdict in his favor. An appeal was taken and the Court of Appeals heard the testimony. No matter what decision is reached the case will go higher until a decision is reached by the court of last resort.

WHOLESALE TRADE GOOD.

While the wholesale drug houses report trade as being quiet, the retail druggists state that business is exceedingly good. Naturally, if the retailers are doing a good business it will not be long before the wholesale firms will be receiving new orders. The feeling in the drug trade in this city is inclined to be optimistic, and the dealers look for a continuance of prosperity for some time to come. During the past few years there has been more of an effort on the part of the wholesale houses to secure some of the Southern trade. At one time the bulk of the business with the South was done by Philadelphia houses, but of recent years this trade has been diverted to other places. It is thought that most of it legitimately belongs here, and an effort is being made to regain it. The efforts have met with great success. All of the large wholesale houses here now have representatives in the South, and the men who are traveling in that section of the country are receiving many orders.

The fear of a coal strike has caused a falling off in orders from the anthracite region. The drug stores in that section of Pennsylvania are holding back their orders, and during the past month the sales have greatly declined. There is considerable sickness in this city and the retail druggists are reaping a harvest in preparing prescriptions.

BOTANICAL EXCURSIONS OF THE PHILADELPHIA COLLEGE.

During the spring of 1906 a series of five botanical excursions will be conducted by Prof. Henry Kraemer. These excursions are open not only to matriculates and graduates of the college, but to any who may desire to join in the work. This year attention will be given not only to the recognition of the early spring plants, but their succession in development and the mutual relations of plants in a community will also be considered. The excursions will be on Wednesday afternoons, as follows:

April 25, Castle Rock, Pa.: Meet at Sixty-third and Market streets at 2 p.m.

May 2, Swarthmore, Pa.: Take Angora cars on Walnut street and meet at Angora Junction at 2 p.m.

May 9, West Chester Road, Pa.: Meet at Sixty-third and Market streets at 2 p.m.

May 16, Crum Creek, Pa.: Take Angora car on Walnut street, and meet at Angora Junction at 2 p.m.

May 23, Haddonfield, N. J.: Meet at Market Street Ferry at 2 p.m.

PHILADELPHIA NEWS NOTES.

T. Neal, the popular city salesman for Smith, Kline & French Company, is confined to his home with an attack of typhoid fever.

C. P. Donald, of bowling fame and one of the most popular representatives of Smith, Kline & French Company, will sail for Europe early in May, to be away for three months.

J. Ellwood Lee has returned from a trip to Mexico much improved in health and spirits.

E. D. Quickel, formerly with H. Fisher, of Richmond, has opened a store in York, Pa.

R. Bleaker has relinquished his position with George B. Evans, and has returned to the Miller Drug Company as an assistant buyer.

The business of the Walter F. Ware Company has increased so rapidly that President Ware has been compelled to send an expert machinist to Europe to purchase additional machinery for the manufacture of elastic goods. This plant has been working night and day for the past two years, and the company is still unable to catch up with its orders.

The business of Farrow Brothers at the corner of Twenty-ninth street and Columbia avenue has increased so materially of late that they are tearing out the entire interior of the building preparatory to enlarging their floor space.

H. H. Mentzer, who owns and operates one of the finest and most lucrative drug stores in Germantown, has purchased the store at the corner of Broad and Girard avenue.

E. R. Gatchell, Tenth and Spring Garden streets, is placing a new preparation on the market called Elixir Peprhiza, and is meeting with surprising success. Specifications are now under way for a new laboratory.

OHIO.

The New Law on Liquors—Arrested for Sale of Cocaine—A New Co-operative Jobbing House.

(From our Regular Correspondent.)

Cleveland, April 17.—All the wholesale houses and many of the retail stores report a continuance of good business. Since the weather moderated somewhat a good soda business has been done.

EFFECT OF THE SEARCH AND SEIZURE LAW.

It is claimed that the Search and Seizure law, passed by the Legislature in February, has resulted in the prosecution of many druggists who have been handling liquor without a State license at points that have voted "dry." In all, more than fifty suits have been instituted, but a large number of these were private clubs.

ARRESTED FOR THE ILLEGAL SALE OF COCAINE.

Samuel Klein, a druggist on East Sixth street, was arrested a few days ago for selling cocaine illegally. It is claimed that he has been selling to habituals, notwithstanding the fact that the officers have been keeping a close watch upon all drug stores.

A CO-OPERATIVE JOBBING HOUSE AT CONNEAUT.

The Consolidated Drug Co., of Conneaut, has been incorporated with a capital stock sufficient to control the purchases for twenty stores. These stores are in Conneaut, Ashtabula, Youngstown, Warren, Geneva, Painesville and several smaller places in the northern part of Ohio, and Erie and Meadville, Pa. The Conneaut Drug Co., of Conneaut, will act as purchasing agents. The idea of the company is to purchase goods for all these stores through one medium and thus reduce the expenses of buying and get better prices, because of the amount of business controlled. In all probability there will be some pretty lively bidding for the business of the combination.

Maxwell G. Teilke, of Cleveland, was one of the fortunate appointees of former Governor Herrick, as the Senate confirmed him as a member of the State Board of Pharmacy before it adjourned. Many others of his recess appointments were turned down. Mr. Teilke is considered an excellent man for the place.

Registered in Ohio.

Out of a class of 72 applicants before the State Board of Pharmacy at the last examination 24 were granted certificates as pharmacists. Seventeen passed the examination as assistants and 9 of the applicants in the first class may have certificates as assistants if they desire. The following were successful in the class for pharmacists:

Arthur J. Curtis, Cleveland; Harry S. Kendrick, Dayton, Ky.; Bert Gassman, Norwalk; Jay Meek, Braden; Walter A. Braunlin, Portsmouth; Fred. Fruechtemeyer, Cincinnati; Charles F. Keller, Mechanicsburg; Max Rosenfeld, Cleveland; Robert A. Schultz, Cincinnati; Howard C. Rempes, Akron; J. E. Engleken, Versailles; George P. Wennes, Sandusky; Fred. E. Rathbun, Gallipolis; Frank Bolles, Columbus; O. H. Stringer, Phillippi, W. Va.; John J. Kenninger, Toledo; James S. Reed, Lancaster; W. M. Whitacre, Springfield; J. E. Calhoun, Wellsville; William H. Lints, Kenton; Kyle George, Lisbon; G. W. Dankworth, Bellaire.

Applicants who may receive assistants' certificates on their pharmacists' examination are as follows:

George J. Vortkamp, Lima; Edward Vogler, Canton; Warren E. Hickman, Delaware; Bert E. Shay, East Liverpool; Clayton Zeluff, Toledo; Philip H. Obly, Sandusky; F. A. Morris, Leetonia; A. C. Steckel, Wauseon ;Charles A. Wingard, Montpelier.

Those who passed the examination as assistants are:

John M. Combs, Columbus; W. C. Pate, Montgomery; Ralph R. Roebuck, Washington C. H.; D. Jay Cooke, Kent; Edward Lindeman, Cincinnati; Ralph H. Christmas, Zanesville; S. C. Conrad, Lancaster; James Kelso, Corning; Leon Tuholske, Akron; Grover Schlenk, Columbus; Robert Ludwig, Cleveland; William F. Walter, Cleveland; George A. Paler, Ludlow, Ky.; Walter Stokes, Cincinnati; L. N. Beck, Zanesville; Clifford R. Lewis, Granville; Warner O. Rogers, Zanesville.

The Indian Territory Board of Pharmacy.

The next meeting of the Territorial Board of Pharmacy for the Indian Territory will be held in Ada, Ind. Ter., April 17, 1906.

THE WEST.

Tobacco Trust Condemned—The Tribune Forced to Make Better Terms—The Pringle License Ordinance Adopted by Council but Vetoed by Mayor.

(From our Regular Correspondent.)

Chicago, April 19.—The cigar "Trust" got some hard knocks at the last C. R. D. A. meeting. The following resolution, which showed the temper of the druggists, was passed with a hurrah:

Whereas, The steady encroachments made by the Tobacco Trust upon the business of independent dealers in tobacco and cigars has affected the retail druggist by lessening his profits in this part of our business: and

Whereas, Members of our association have been forced to give up locations in which they had established themselves, owing to the covetousness of the United Cigar Stores Company; and

Whereas, The sale by druggists of brands of cigars manufactured by the Tobacco Trust has a tendency to seriously affect our future business interests; therefore be it

Resolved, That we, the members of the C. R. D. A. in regular meeting assembled, deem it of great importance that our members should encourage the sale of only such cigars as are made by independent manufacturers and that such trust goods as we are required to keep in stock should be kept in places not in view of our customers.

With reference to the National Cigar Stands Company, it was recommended that druggists exercise great care in signing contracts with any corporation seeking control of their cigar business. It was ordered that every druggist in Chicago be informed of the action of the C. R. D. A. and urged to act in harmony with the organization. A letter embodying these points has been sent out by Secretary S. C. Yeomans to all the trade. It is the belief of the local trade that systematic efforts are being made in various ways to get control of the stands in both cigar stores and drug stores and thus ruin the independent cigar manufacturers.

During the long meeting some lively attacks were made on the *Tribune*, and that paper finally agreed to raise the percentage paid for advertisements and to make other concessions. As one druggist put it, "You cannot serve two masters—in other words, you cannot preach N. A. R. D. doctrine and practice Rexall methods."

The Hydrox Company was rapped for alleged double dealing. It was charged that after the druggists got customers the company took them away and made direct sales. The session lasted until long after midnight and it was therefore necessary to defer action on narcotic legislation problems until later.

The Common Council passed the Pringle ordinance with a rush and the Mayor vetoed it with equal promptness. This ordinance provided that:

No dramshop license shall be issued to any person engaged in the business of selling drugs or keeping what is commonly known as a drug store. No person or corporation conducting any such drug store shall be permitted to place in show windows or in show cases, or in any other public or conspicuous place about the premises in which the drug store is located, for the purpose of advertisement or for any other purpose whatever, any bottles or signs or any other things to advertise the sale of any vinous, spirituous, ardent, intoxicating or fermented liquors, under a penalty of not less than one hundred dollars nor more than two hundred dollars for each offense.

The veto was based on the statement that this represented arbitrary legislation against a particular branch of business. The Corporation Counsel first passed favorably upon the measure and later informed the Mayor that it was defective; the veto was the result.

WARNING REGARDING LIQUOR SALES.

Druggists have again been warned by officials of the C. R. D. A. that they must exercise great care in registering liquor sales, for the ordinances bearing on that point will hereafter be enforced strictly. They are especially warned to keep all bottled goods out of sight. The Liquor Dealers' Association is irritated by the passage of the big saloon license and the failure to get a license levied against druggists, and is believed to be watching for a chance to even up matters.

THE DEATH OF MRS. EBERT.

Mrs. Albert E. Ebert died April 11 and was buried April 13. Many members of the C. V. D. A. attended the funeral and sent floral tributes, others acted as pallbearers. A funeral oration on "Immortality" was delivered by G. P. Engelhard. One of the members of the Klio Association spoke of Mrs. Ebert's many kind acts as a member of that organization. Mrs. Ebert had been ill for some time, but had borne up while Mr. Ebert was at a hospital. Upon his recovery the devoted wife gave out. Expressions of the most heartfelt sympathy have been made to Mr. Ebert by his hundreds of friends.

CHICAGO NEWS NOTES.

Miss Ottilie Bodemann, daughter of W. Bodemann, was married April 11 to A. Wilder Eichenberger.

The ordinance providing for a $10 license fee from all who sell ice cream has been held over.

Mrs. M. S. Hall, Thirty-first street and Forrest avenue, has decided to sell her store and to retire from business.

The Girten store, at 3046 Wentworth avenue, has been bought by Frank Senft, Jr., formerly a clerk of Mr. Girten's.

Smucker's Pharmacy, at 1620 Madison street, has been bought by W. M. Smale.

There has been a rumor of a combination of all the local jobbing houses, but those alleged to be in it have made emphatic denials.

The fine drug store in the new Brevoort Hotel Building, on Madison street, just east of Lasalle, is to be occupied by the new Standard Drug Company.

Members of the local trade have received due warning that spring is here and that they will be expected to appear on the baseball diamond within a short time.

The United Cigar Stores Company has acquired control of the building at Monroe and State streets, now occupied by the Colbert Drug Company, and that concern will have to move May 1.

Drug clerks, full, registered and assistant, are to meet at 2.30 P. M. Thursday, April 26, in the assembly room of Northwestern University Building, Lake and Dearborn streets, for the purpose of forming a permanent organization of the Drug Clerks' Auxiliary of the C. R. D. A.

Judson S. Jacobus, one of the old-time druggists of Chicago, died April 14 at his residence, 4146 Berkeley avenue. Mr. Jacobus was born in Chicago September 20, 1847, and started in the drug business in the spring of 1864 in the store of E. H. Sargent. He was with them for six years, then with T. C. Borden & Co. for two years, and then went to another of Sargent's stores. He went into business on his own account in 1874. During his career he had been associated with many of the best known druggists and had a wide acquaintance. He was a member of the Veteran Druggists' Association.

They Do Not Know How to Study.

Such is the observation of the AMERICAN DRUGGIST in a recent editorial dealing with the pharmaceutical student problem. Such is also the experience of every teacher of pharmacy in this country. The average scholar passes rapidly through grammar and high schools learning an immense number of facts without learning how to use them, and, above all, without learning how to study in a comprehensive manner. It is not uncommon to find students in colleges of pharmacy who can work problems in percentage if they relate to dollars and cents, but are utterly at a loss if grains or ounces are substituted. While this is a criticism on our public schools, it evidently applies with equal force to higher education. We believe that Dr. Harry P. Morse, Professor of Physics, at Harvard University, is not an exception to the average student. Professor Morse says: "After an experience of 20 years in studying chemistry I believe I could safely forget nearly all the facts which I was required in school to memorise, provided I remembered the fundamental relations which held them together." The difference between the safe pharmacist and the quiz book for college made man is that the safe man understands a sufficient number of the fundamental relations in pharmacy to be able to safely conduct his business. The quiz book applicant for registration may be brimful of facts committed to memory.

Will it ever be possible for a Board of Pharmacy to conduct an examination along such lines that the man versed in fundamental relations will pass and the one with the load of quiz book facts will fail?—*Meyer Brothers' Druggist.*

THE SOUTH.

Poor Business Follows Bad Weath-r—The State Meeting—Southern Jobbers Convene.

(From our Regular Correspondent.)

New Orleans, La., April 16.—Trade conditions in New Orleans have not been exceptionally good during the last fortnight, and the same applies generally throughout this section. Heavy rains have affected all lines of business, and in this particular the drug lines have not proven an exception to the rule.

THE STATE ASSOCIATION MEETING.

A large attendance is expected at the twenty-fourth annual convention of the Louisiana State Pharmaceutical Association, which will open in Odd Fellows' Hall at 10.30 o'clock to-morrow morning. The session will last three days, and it is indicated that it will prove a record breaker in the history of the association.

The delegates will be well entertained during their stay here, the conspicuous features of the entertainment programme being a children's May ball on Wednesday night and a banquet at West End Thursday night. There will also be other entertainments. The committee having charge of this is composed of George W. McDuff, chairman; C. C. Johnston, F. A. Dicks, L. E. Lyons, W. J. Sbisa, John E. Scott and George S. Humphreys.

WHOLESALERS TO MEET.

Simultaneously with the opening of the convention of the State Pharmaceutical Association to-morrow will come the beginning of the three days' session of the Southern Wholesale Druggists' Association, which has been called to assemble here. A number of prominent drug men from various parts of the country have been requested to take part in the convention, and already they have begun to arrive here. Several came in today, and the remainder are due to-morrow morning. It is believed that between fifty and sixty drug men will be here for the meeting.

REGISTERED IN MISSISSIPPI.

The Mississippi State Board of Pharmaceutical Examiners recently closed one of the largest examinations ever held in the State of Mississippi. There were fifty-six applications, and of these thirty-three passed successfully. The successful ones were:

C. C. Chatham, Centreville, Miss.; H. C. Thomas, New Orleans; W. L. Holmes, New Orleans; S. C. Williams, Shrop; W. S. Moore, Ackerman; W. B. Johnson, Waynesboro; E. L. Toler, Centreville; E. O. Marper, Quitman; Miss S. P. Bowen, Bayhalia; W. R. Smith, Enterprise; W. W. Anderson, Hattiesburg; J. W. Whitley, Dodson; R. D. Marsales, Roxie; L. G. Salter, Columbia; G. S. Stovall, Vicksburg; G. M. Knight, Oxford; Henry Weston, Bay St. Louis; M. A. Tate, Picayune; L. H. Barnett, Florence; J. W. Harding, Vicksburg; D. W. Goldstein, Greenville; A. J. Laichet, Lutcher, La.; A. P. Smith, Brookhaven; Platt McDonald, Laurel; F. S. Gayden, Brandon; G. L. Miller, West Point; C. A. Hammack, Priddens; H. M. Scroggins, Jonesboro; L. H. Ferrington, Booksville; R. D. Marco, Natches; G. W. Nicholson, Durant; M. J. Nye, Valden; R. L. Bouton, New Albany.

MINOR NEWS NOTES.

Marion's Pharmacy, at St. Charles and Napoleon avenues, in which place Station No. 7, of the Post Office Department is located, was broken into last Thursday night. Nothing in the store was touched, the thieves devoting themselves entirely to the post office branch, where they stole cash and stamps worth considerable money. Two men have been arrested here in connection with the crime and are now held by the Federal authorities.

Covington, La., will shortly boast a new and enterprising drug establishment, which will occupy an excellent location on its main street. The promoters have secured the site formerly occupied by Richard's grocery and are now putting in a good stock. The new place will in all probability be one of the most attractive in that part of the State.

Employees Give Memorial Tablet.

The 500 employees of the Meyer Brothers Drug Company, of St. Louis, Mo., have presented the officers and directors of that corporation with a bronze memorial tablet in honor of Christian F. G. Meyer, the founder and late president of the house.

THE AMERICAN PHARMACEUTICAL ASSOCIATION.

Announcement of the Philadelphia Branch—The Chicago Branch Has a Lively Meeting—Opposes Tax-Free Alcohol—Favors the Heyburn Bill.

CHICAGO BRANCH.

At the meeting of the Chicago Branch on the evening of April 3 the relation of the U. S. Pharmacopœia and the National Formulary to the Pure Food bill was discussed and the following resolution was adopted:

Whereas, There is now pending in Congress a bill, S. 86, entitled "An act for preventing the manufacture, sale or transportation of adulterated or misbranded or poisonous or deleterious food, drugs and medicines and for regulating traffic therein, and for other purposes," which said bill is most heartily approved; and

Whereas, Three amendments have been proposed on which pharmacists should express themselves; therefore be it

Resolved, That the amendment be approved, eliminating the requirement that in medicines containing alcohol the percentage be stated on the label of package; be it further

Resolved, That the amendment be approved exempting preparations of United States Pharmacopœia and the National Formulary, and physicians' prescriptions from the requirement that the amount and proportion of potent ingredients be stated on the label or package, but that the amendment exempting proprietary medicines when containing not more than two grains of opium to the fluid, or avoirdupois, ounce, or one-fourth grain morphine to the fluid, or avoirdupois, ounce, be not approved; that it be

Resolved, That proprietary medicines containing opium, morphine or other potent or habit-forming drugs should be required to state on the label or package what may be the quantity.

GREATER PUBLICITY FOR PHARMACOPŒIAL WORK.

The following resolution was offered by A. B. Thorburn and adopted:

Whereas, In proposed legislation before Congress and State Legislatures it is intended that the United States Pharmacopœia and National Formulary shall be made authoritative publications fixing legal standards for crude drugs and preparations; and

Whereas, These publications are now controlled by bodies whose appointment and conduct is not provided for in any of our food or drug laws, but whose acts will have the authority of laws; therefore be it

Resolved, By the Chicago Branch of the American Pharmaceutical Association, that the Pure Food bill now pending in Congress should be amended to require that the bodies controlling the United States Pharmacopœia and National Formulary should give frequent public hearings before there be made any changes in, withdrawals from, or additions to, these standards.

Resolutions were also adopted favoring the reduction of the tax on alcohol, but protesting against the bill for providing for denatured alcohol as a delusion and a snare.

After some discussion as to the best method for advertising the National Formulary and the pharmacopœial preparations to the medical profession a committee was appointed to report upon the matter. Resolutions were also adopted favoring the enactment of the bill now before Congress providing for the adoption of the metric weights and measures.

PLANS FOR THE NEXT MEETING OF THE PHILADELPHIA BRANCH.

The second meeting of the Philadelphia Branch will be held on the evening of April 24 at the College of Physicians and will have for its special subject the discussion of the immediate objects and aims of the branch.

Suggestions have been promised by Messrs. Lemberger, Remington, Cliffe, LaWall, Apple, Osterlund, Westcott and others, and it is expected that an efficient programme for the coming year's work may be evolved from the suggestions thus received. The preamble of the local branch will be open for the signatures of active members at this meeting.

PLANS FOR A BRANCH IN NEW YORK.

At the annual meeting of the Manhattan Pharmaceutical Association, held on April 16, President Alpers proposed that the association be converted into a branch of the American Pharmaceutical Association, a proposal that met with approval.

Distinguished Honors for Dr. Takamine.

A cablegram from Tokio announces that His Majesty the Emperor of Japan has conferred upon Dr. Jokichi Takamine, a well-known Japanese chemist, residing in New York, the decoration of the Order of the Rising Sun, which signifies high distinction of merit. The doctor is well known among the medical and pharmaceutical profession throughout the world for his original work, particularly as being the first to isolate the active principle of the suprarenal gland in crystalline form, known as adrenalin, and also as the inventor of taka-diastase, a remarkable starch digesting ferment.

Hostetter's Bitters Taken from Liquor Tax List.

Commissioner John W. Yerkes, of the Department of Internal Revenue, has just issued a new ruling on the list of alcoholic medicines subject to the special liquor license tax, which instructs revenue agents that "as the preparation known as 'Hostetter's Stomach Bitters,' as now prepared, is unfit for beverage purposes, it shall be classed as a proprietary medicine and not as an alcoholic medicine." The Hostetter Company, manufacturers of Hostetter's Stomach Bitters, have sent out a new circular to the drug trade in which they assert that they have revised their formula and that their new method of preparing their product has exempted it from the special liquor tax.

From One of Our Oldest Subscribers.

Edwin McManus, of Randolph, N. Y., is an esteemed friend of the AMERICAN DRUGGIST, having been a subscriber to the journal for a period extending over many years. In renewing his subscription for the ensuing year he notes that the day on which he writes is his eighty-first birthday, and fears that he may not be able to take the paper for many more years, an expression which prompts the hope on our part that he may long be spared to enjoy the AMERICAN DRUGGIST, along with the few other good things which tend to gladden the otherwise trying life of a druggist.

Mr. McManus was first master of Randolph Lodge, No. 359, F. & A. M., which celebrated its golden jubilee in June, 1905, and he attended the anniversary celebration.

Prof. P. Curie Accidentally Killed.

Paris, April 19.— Professor Curie, the discoverer of radium, was run over and killed by a wagon on the Place Dauphine this afternoon.

DIED.

CARPENTER.—In Burlington, Vt., on Wednesday, March 20, B. W. Carpenter, aged seventy years.

FARROW.—In Baltimore, on Wednesday, April 4, Joseph Henry Farrow, aged seventy-five years.

GATES.—In Toledo, Ohio, on Saturday, March 17, Joseph Gates, aged seventy years.

LYONS.—In New Orleans, La., on Wednesday, March 21, Jacob C. Lyons, aged fifty-seven years.

MILLER.—In Albany, N. Y., on Thursday, March 22, James H. Miller.

ROSS.—In Baltimore, Md., on Thursday, April 5, Oscar E. Ross, aged thirty-nine years.

RUPPERT.—In Cincinnati, Ohio, on Tuesday, March 20, John Ruppert, aged fifty-seven years.

SCHLEIFER.—In Rochester, N. Y., on Saturday, April 7, John Schleifer, aged fifty-three years.

SIMMONS.—In Gloversville, N. Y., on Friday, March 30, Dr. Andrew M. Simmons, aged sixty-six years.

SMITH.—In Thompsonville, Conn., on Sunday, April 8, Edward N. Smith, aged fifty-one years.

SMITH.—In Brooklyn, N. Y., on Friday, March 23, Paul Gustave Smith, aged sixty-seven years.

Gustav Adolph Buchheister, the fifth edition of whose *Vorschriftenbuch für Drogisten* was reviewed in the AMERICAN DRUGGIST for January 22, died in Hamburg on January 14 at the age of 70. He studied under Wöhler at the University of Göttingen and under Liebig at Munich. Dr. Buchheister was held in the greatest esteem among German "Droguisten."

The World's Production of Essential Oils.

The production of essential oils in the entire world is an important fact, according to the *American Perfumer*, and may be summed up as follows: Cannes-Grasse, 20,000 to 30,000 kilos of cassie, 300,000 to 400,000 kilos of violets, 1,500,000 kilos of roses, 2,000,000 of orange flowers, 500,000 to 600,000 kilos of jasmin. Here is manufactured also 80,000 kilos of oil of lavender, 30,000 kilos of aspic, 20,000 of thyme, 20,000 of rosemary, etc., representing a value of more than 30,000,000 francs.

Sicily and Calabria in 1904 produced 1,600,000 kilos of oil of bergamot, lemon and orange, valued at 14,758,000 francs; Bulgaria produced 4,000 to 5,000 kilos of oil of rose, valued at 3,500,000 francs; Algeria produced about 30,000 kilos of oil of geranium; Zanzibar produced 4,000,000 to 7,000,000 kilos of cloves; the Island of Bourbon, 30,000 kilos of oil of geranium and some vetiver; India, 1,500,000 kilos of oil of sandal-wood, 500,000 kilos of oil of citronella, oil of palmarosa, lemongrass, cinnamon; the Peninsula of Malacca, about 150,000 kilos of leaves of patchouly and vetiver roots; Central China, thyme, anise and cassia; the Philippines, ylang-ylang to the value of 500,000 francs; Java, oil of kananga and citronella; Japan, about 200,000 kilos oil of peppermint, a considerable amount of camphor; the United States, 100,000 kilos oil of peppermint; Mexico, oil of linaloe; Guyana, 3,000 kilos oil of rosewood; Paraguay, 3,000 kilos oil of petit grain.

Change in Place of Meeting of Georgia Association.

The Executive Committee of the Georgia Pharmaceutical Association announce that the annual meeting will be held at Atlanta instead of at Valdosta, as formerly proposed, on May 22 and 23.

Recent Decisions by Board of Appraisers.

GINSENG FREE OF DUTY.

Protesting against the imposition of the duty for ground or refined seeds upon his importation of "one case of ginseng," S. H. Kim, of Boston, has won his case before the Board of Appraisers at this port by claiming that ginseng in its crude state is entitled to free duty, according to paragraph 548 or paragraph 617 of the act of 1897, which provides that all crude drugs, seeds, etc., shall be admitted free of duty. The duty originally assessed on this case of ginseng was at the rate of ¼ of 1 cent per pound and 10 per cent. ad valorem. After an official examination of the merchandise it was discovered that the ginseng was in its crude state and therefore exempt from duty.

FIR BALSAM FREE AS CRUDE DRUG.

John Reeve, an importer, has succeeded in persuading the Board of Appraisers that fir balsam is entitled to free entry into this country as a crude drug. The balsam had been assessed for duty by the Collector of Customs at the port of Newport, Vt., at the rate of ¼ of 1 cent per pound and 10 per cent. ad valorem, under the provisions of paragraph 20 of the tariff act of 1897, and Mr. Reeve protested against this assessment, claiming that it was entitled to free entry, under the provisions of paragraph 548, above referred to. He asserted that the balsam was in the crudest condition known to commerce. The Assistant Appraiser and official examiner connected with the drug department of the United States Appraisers' office at the port of New York expressed the opinion that the merchandise was in the crude form, but stated that they had seen it in less pure condition, containing in some instances pieces of the bark of the tree. Mr. Reeve admitted that the balsam had been submitted to a process of straining for the purpose of eliminating bits of sticks, bark, chips and dirt, but as such a process of purification is not considered as a refining of the merchandise, but is regarded by the trade as leaving it in the crude condition, the Board of Appraisers decided to admit the drug free of duty.

BELLADONNA EXTRACT DUTIABLE AS ALCOHOLIC PREPARATION.

The Board of Appraisers has refused to sustain the claim of J. M. Blanco, of San Juan, Porto Rico, that belladonna extract should not be assessed as an alcoholic medicinal preparation, dutiable at 55 cents per pound, under paragraph 67 of the tariff act of 1897. Blanco maintained that the belladonna extract should be dutiable as a nonalcoholic medicinal preparation at 25 per cent. ad valorem, under paragraph 68 of the 1897 act. A sample of the drug in question was analyzed and reported to contain traces of alcohol. The board therefore decided that it had been properly classified as an alcoholic medicinal preparation, dutiable at 55 cents per pound, under paragraph 67.

Powdered opium, produced by evaporating extract of opium, then grinding and sifting the article, is dutiable under the tariff provision for opium, crude or manufactured, and not as a drug advanced in value or condition by refining, grinding or other process. Such, in brief, is the decision of the U. S. Circuit Court in the case of Merck & Co. against the United States over an importation of powdered opium at New York, which was assessed for duty by the collector at the rate of $1 per pound. Merck & Co. claimed it dutiable at a less amount as a drug advanced in value by refining or grinding. The collector's action was affirmed by the court.

The U. S. Circuit Court has ruled that oleic acid or red oil, which was shown to have other uses than as soap stock, is excluded from the tariff provision for "oils commonly used in soap making, fit only for such uses," and is dutiable as an acid not specially provided for. The decision was in the case of Edward Hill's Sons & Co., who appealed from a decision of the Board of U. S. General Appraisers. The importers claimed the article should be allowed free entry as "crude soap stock." The court affirms the decision of the General Appraisers and holds the merchandise properly dutiable at 25 per cent. ad valorem.

The Berlin Aniline Works imported merchandise at this port invoiced as extract of Persian berries. The article was returned by the appraiser of the port as a color, and the collector assessed duty at the rate of 30 per cent. ad valorem. The importers protested against this assessment, claiming the article was properly dutiable at ⅝ cent per pound under paragraph 22 of the tariff act, which provides this rate of duty for "extracts and decoctions of logwood and other dyewoods, and extracts of barks, such as are commonly used for dyeing and tanning, not specially provided for in this act." The testimony before the Board of General Appraisers was to the effect that although the merchandise in question may be exclusively used for the purpose of staining foodstuffs, nevertheless Persian berry extract is recognized as a dyestuff for coloring wool and calico with mordants. The board overruled the importers' protest, without affirming the action of the collector.

One of the most important customs decisions of interest to the drug trade was rendered recently by the U. S. Circuit Court of Appeals for the first circuit. The decision thwarted the attempt of the Treasury Department to collect a duty equivalent to 400 per cent. on extract of nutgalls, by sustaining the contention of the importers for assessment under the drug provision of the Dingley tariff law at the rate of ¼ cent per pound and 10 per cent. ad valorem. The litigation has extended over a period of more than two years, and while the case just decided stands in the name of W. N. Proctor & Co., the issue is of vital importance to the drug trade in general, and particularly to the nutgall trade. The Government contended that the article should be classified as "tannic acid, or tannin," with duty at 50 cents a pound. The Board of U. S. General Appraisers affirmed the collector's assessment at this rate. The importers carried the fight to the Federal Circuit Court and won, but the Treasury Department carried it up to the U. S. Circuit Court of Appeals. The question of the proper classification of nutgall extract is a very complex one, and it is possible that the U. S. Supreme Court may grant the Treasury Department's request for a writ of certiorari, in order that the tribunal of last resort may decide the points involved.

A candidate before a board of pharmacy had a drug for identification, but for the life of him could not think whether it was buchu or senna. Strategy came to his rescue. Stepping up to one of the board, he said: "I believe senna is mixed with the specimen I am now examining." The board member answered "No," and the candidate at once knew that he had buchu.

The Drug and Chemical Market

The prices quoted in this report are those current in the wholesale market, and higher prices are paid for retail lots
The quality of goods frequently necessitates a wide range of prices,

Condition of Trade.

NEW YORK, April 21, 1906.

Although the month thus far shows some slackening in the demand the general movement of drugs and chemicals into channels of consumption is of average volume. Prices are characterized by fair strength, and most fluctuations during the period under review have favored sellers, there being further appreciations in some of the leading staples. The most important price change since our last was a decline in cocaine, which is commented on below. Codliver oil, opium and quinine are dull, and camphor has not changed. An improvement in the demand for naphthalin balls, coupled with some scarcity, has resulted in a fractional advance in quotations. The outlook for peppermint oil is more encouraging, firmer views being generally maintained at primary sources of supply. Powdered Chinese cantharides are higher, while Russian flies and Russian ergot are in freer offering at somewhat lower values. A new schedule of prices has been issued by the manufacturers of Paris green and the revised range is higher than that of the preceding season. There has been no speculative movement calling for special comment since our last, but despite the somewhat tame and uninteresting appearance which the market presents the undertone is steady, and the indications point to a satisfactory and profitable trade during the season.

HIGHER	LOWER.
Pink root.	Ergot,
Nitrate of soda.	Cocaine,
Peppermint oil,	Lycopodium,
Naphthalin balls,	Gamboge,
Para copaiba balsam,	Russian cantharides,
Caraway seed,	White arsenic,
Menthol.	Buchu leaves,
Carnauba wax,	Golden seal root.
Cajuput oil.	

Drugs.

Acetphenetidin, the official preparation of phenacetin, is being offered in bulk at $1.15 per lb., special prices being made for large quantities to manufacturers of specialties and headache remedies; 1-oz. packages are quoted at $1.60 per lb., and 1-lb. cartons at $1.17.

Alcohol is maintained by the combination of producers on the basis of $2.45 to $2.47 net, as to terms of sale. Wood has remained quiet, but values appear well sustained at 70c for the 95 per cent. and 75c for the 97 per cent.

Arnica flowers have remained quiet; while some grades are available at 9c 9½c is generally named.

Balsams.—Copaiba continues extremely scarce, and for the limited available supply 35c to 38c is asked; Central American has been received in small amounts only since our last, and holders continue firm in their views at 29c to 32c, as to quality and quantity. Tolu is in somewhat better supply, but holders decline to shade 20c to 21c, at which range a fair distribution is reported.

Barks.—Cascara sagrada is receiving increased attention, and there has been a good jobbing movement since our last. Large dealers are expressing some apprehension over the fate of the stock available in the San Francisco warehouses. Sassafras is meeting with a good inquiry, and values are well sustained at 12c. to 15c. Cut soap is in good seasonable demand, but prices show no change from the previous range of 5½c to 6c. Cottonroot is maintained at 8½c to 10c, and a good jobbing movement is reported at this range.

Buchu leaves, long, are in better supply, and the market has eased off to the range of 29c to 30c. Short are maintained at 17c to 20c.

Cacao butter has not varied since our last, and the limited jobbing demand is being met at the range of 28½c to 30c.

Cantharides, Chinese, are offered with more reserve, and holders are firmer in their views at an advance to 75c to 80c for both the whole and powdered.

Cocaine prices have been reduced by the manufacturers, who now name $3 to $3.20 for bulk, as to quantity, a reduction of 25c.

Codliver oil continues inactive, and the market is easier in consequence, with quotations more or less nominal. New oil for prompt shipment offers in some quarters at $16 f.o.b., though upward to $18 is named in others. Meanwhile spot quotations for Norwegian are maintained at $20 to $25, as to brand, and Newfoundland at $19 to $20.

Ergot is quiet on spot, and Russian has declined to 27c to 28c; Spanish offers at 36c.

Haarlem oil continues in good demand, and dealers occasionally experience difficulty in meeting consuming requirements, so that prices are well sustained at the range of $3 to $3.25.

Lycopodium does not gain in strength, though conditions abroad would seem to favor higher values, and sales during the interval were at 46c to 48c, the outside figure being for Pollitz.

Menthol is held with firmness, despite an absence of an important demand, quotations being well sustained at $2.60 to $2.75, as to quality and quantity, and only a limited quantity being available at the inside range.

Naphthalin is finding increased inquiry with the advance of the season, and a firmer tone has developed for balls, which are in limited supply and held at 2¼c; flake is nominally unchanged at 1.95c to 2c.

Opium has shown no action of any consequence since our last. Cases are still quoted at $2.72, though reports of lower quotations are not infrequent, and holders are not entertaining offers at under $2.70; for jobbing lots $2.75 to $2.77½ is yet named. Powdered is finding a moderate jobbing outlet at prices within the quoted range of $3.25 to $3.30.

Quinine has met with rather less inquiry since our last, and we have little new or interesting to report, the bulk of the business transacted being on contract orders at manufacturers' prices, or, say, 18c for bulk in 100-ounce tins; German from second hands offers at 17½c, while Java is obtainable from the same source at 17c.

Saffron, American, continues in steady, moderate demand, and sales were made at $1.25, the scarcity of spot stock serving to harden the views of holders, though prospective buyers are holding off awaiting the arrival of new crop goods, when it is expected that the prices will return to a normal basis.

Vanilla beans show increasing firmness, and quotations for cut Mexican have been advanced to $2.15 to $2.50, as to quality and quantity. Tahiti is reported scarce on the coast, and values are firm at 40c. to $1.00, which figures are likely to be advanced if the reports of damage done to stocks in San Francisco are substantiated.

Wax, Brazil, is extremely scarce, and quotations for No. 2 have been advanced to 44c to 47c, and No. 3 to 37c.

Chemicals.

Arsenic, white, is less actively inquired for, and quotations have dropped to the range of 5½c to 8c, while red is held and selling at 6½c to 6¾c.

Blue vitriol is held with increased firmness, the best makes being well under control of orders and nothing offering at under 6c.

Cream tartar has offered more freely in instances since our last, second hands showing more disposition to urge the distribution at the range of 22½c to 22¾c for crystals.

Chlorate potash is quiet, but the market is firm at previous prices. Some jobbing sales are reported at 9½c to 9¾c for crystals and powdered.

Glauber's salt has sold actively during the interval and quotations for crystals are maintained at 45c to 65c.

Nitrate of soda has developed an upward tendency and spot quotations have been advanced to $2.35 for 96 per cent. and $2.30 for 95 per cent.

Oxalic acid is scarce on spot and supplies are difficult to obtain at under 6c, with up to 6¼c paid.

Paris green prices have been revised by the combination of the producers to the following range: ½ barrels of 200 to 400 lbs., 20c; small kegs of 100 to 200 lbs., 20½c; 14-28-56-lb. kits or 2 to 5 lb. paper boxes, 21½c; 1-lb. paper boxes, 22c; ½-lb. paper boxes, 23c; ¼-lb. paper boxes, 24c. Lots of 5,000 to 10,000 lbs. ½c per lb. additional, 1,000 to 5,000 1c additional, 500 to 1,000 lbs. 2c additional and less than 500 lbs. 3c additional.

Essential Oils.

Anise has not been inquired for to any extent, but supplies have not been urged, importers quoting the range at $1.25 to $1.30.

Cajuput is in reduced supply, and holders are firm in their views at an advance to 54c to 55c.

Camphor is in better supply, and offers a shade more freely at 10c to 12c, as to quality and quantity.

Cassia is a shade easier, recent offerings being at 75c to 77½c for 75 to 80 per cent., and 80c to 82½c for 80 to 85 per cent.

Citronella has slackened in demand, owing to the high level of current values, but prices are unchanged at 38c to 40c for drums and cans, respectively.

Clove is finding a satisfactory jobbing sale, and dealers continue to quote on the basis of 80c. to 82½c in cans, and 82½c to 85c in bottles, though they believe that an advance is warranted, as it would be impossible to distill oil at this basis on the present parity of the spice. Prices have since advanced.

Pennyroyal is in limited supply only and prices are in upward tendency, though domestic is yet obtainable at $1.35 to $1.40 and French at $1.20 to $1.25.

Peppermint does not find a very active outlet at present prices, though holders are not disposed to abate any of their firmness and inquiries for round lots at prevailing prices are known to have been declined. Advices from the growing sections continue favorable to holders, the outlook for the new crop being considered decidedly discouraging, as the weather has been unfavorable and damage to the roots is reported. Meanwhile sales on spot are making on the basis of $2.75 to $3.00 for bulk. Case oil has sold during the interval at $3.25. Japanese is firmer in sympathy, desirable grades having been marked up to $1.75 to $1.80.

Wintergreen, natural, is in good consuming demand, and while $1.50 to $1.65 is generally named supplies are obtainable at $1.45.

Gums.

Aloes are quiet, but supplies do not offer at less than full previous prices, or, say, 14c to 15c for Barbadoes, 8c to 9c for Curacao and 6c to 6¼c for Socotrine.

Arabic sorts are somewhat scarce on spot, but quotations are nominally unchanged, there being sales at 6c to 11c.

Benzoin, Sumatra, of the choicer grades is held and selling at 34c to 35c, while stock of a less desirable quality offers at 32c.

Camphor, American refined, maintains its strong position and the demand continues of good seasonable proportions at the range of $1.00 to $1.00½ for American refined in barrels and cases, respectively. For the limited available supply of Japanese in ounce cakes 97c to 98c is named.

Gamboge is maintained in firm position, though only jobbing sales are reported at $1.05 to $1.15 for whole pipe, as to holder.

Mastic is jobbing freely at nominally unchanged prices, or, say, 46c to 48c.

Tragacanth has been in rather better demand and the inside price of Aleppo is fractionally higher. We quote the range at 63c to 67c for first Aleppo, 45c to 55c for second Aleppo; 75c to 85c for first Turkey and 40c to 50c for second Turkey.

Roots.

Gentian is finding increased outlet and the tendency is upward, though 4c to 4½c will yet buy.

Ginger, Jamaica, is held with increased firmness, with bleached quoted at 17c to 18c and natural at 14c to 16c.

Golden seal is somewhat easier in tone and holders are more free to offer at $1.18 to $1.20.

Ipecac has sold more freely and the present range of $1.75 to $1.80 appears well sustained; Carthagena is held at 5c under this figure.

Pink has dropped a notch or two since our last, supplies being offered at 80c to 85c without, however, appreciably stimulating the demand.

Rhubarb, high dried, is in reduced supply and the inside quotation has been marked up to 24c, though some lots might be picked up at 22c.

Sarsaparilla, Mexican, is in reduced supply and prices are well maintained on the basis of 9¾c to 10c.

Squill is somewhat neglected at the moment, the season for its use being about over, and quotations have dropped to 11c to 12c.

Seeds.

Anise, Russian, offers more freely, with sellers at 6c to 6½c, as to quantity.

Canary is held with increased firmness at, say, 4¾c to 5c for Sicily and 4⅝c to 4¾c for Smyrna.

Caraway, Dutch, is in improved request and the market is firmer and fractionally higher at 6c to 6¾c.

Cardamoms, decorticated, are firmly maintained at 32c to 34c, with sales at this range.

Strophanthus, Kombe, has developed an easier tendency owing to recent heavy arrivals and 75c will now buy. Hispidus is unchanged at 50c.

Radium Prices.

Elmer & Amend, Third avenue and Eighteenth street, New York, quote as follows on radium salts, prices being net:

Radium bromide 20,000 activity 1-10 Gm., $150; 1 Gm. vial, $1,200; 50,000 activity 1-10 Gm., $375; 200,000 activity 10 milligrammes, $150; 500,000 activity 10 milligrammes, $375; 1,800,000 activity 1 milligramme, $125; one vial German radium bromide of 1,000,000 activity, containing 20 milligrammes, $400.

Even if more than the minimum quantity is ordered, but put up in fractions of a gramme, the price of the minimum quantity will be charged and not the gramme price, on account of loss in filling.

Aluminum vials, with silver caps and silver protecting tube: Original pattern, $15; E. & A. pattern, $10. Spinthariscopes, showing the scintillations of radium, each $9. Spinthariscope slides for use under the microscope, each $4.50. Zinc sulphide phosphorescent "very strong," for making sulphide screens, per bottle of 25 grammes, $3.

Chloral Hydrate Dutiable as an Alcholic Compound.

On the ground that chloral hydrate should be classified under the head of "medicinal preparations containing alcohol, or in the preparation of which alcohol is used," as defined in paragraph 67 of the traiff act of 1897, the New York Board of Appraisers has just decided to overrule the protest of Emil Levi, who contended that a recent importation of this drug was not dutiable at 55 cents per pound. Mr. Levi asserted that the drug should be dutiable at the rate of 25 per cent. ad valorem, under the provision of paragraph 3, which fixes the duty on "all chemical compounds," or under paragraph 68, as "a medicinal preparation not containing alcohol or in the preparation of which alcohol is not used."

The Board of Appraisers, however, decided, in accordance with several former decisions, that the drug was a medicinal preparation in the preparation of which alcohol is used and that it was therefore dutiable at 55 cents per pound.

AMERICAN DRUGGIST
and PHARMACEUTICAL RECORD

PHILADELPHIA. NEW YORK, MAY 14, 1906. CHICAGO

ISSUED SEMI-MONTHLY BY

AMERICAN DRUGGIST PUBLISHING Co.,

62-68 West Broadway, New York.

CHICAGO, 221 Randolph St. PHILADELPHIA, 871 Walnut St.

A. R. ELLIOTT, President.

CASWELL A. MAYO, Ph.G. .... Editor.

THOMAS J. KEENAN .... Associate Editor.

ROMAINE PIERSON .... Manager Chicago Office.

$1.50 a year. 15 cents a copy.

ADVERTISING RATES QUOTED ON APPLICATION.

THE AMERICAN DRUGGIST AND PHARMACEUTICAL RECORD is issued on the second and fourth Mondays of each month. Changes of advertisements should be received ten days in advance of the date of publication.

Remittances should be made by New York exchange, post office or express money order or registered mail. If checks on local banks are used 10 cents should be added to cover cost of collection. The publishers are not responsible for money sent by unregistered mail, nor for any money paid except to duly authorised agents. All communications should be addressed and all remittances made payable to American Druggist Publishing Co., 62-68 West Broadway, New York.

Entered at New York as Second-Class Matter.

TABLE OF CONTENTS.

EDITORIAL COMMENT.

AID FOR SAN FRANCISCO DRUGGISTS.

The appalling catastrophe which afflicted San Francisco so recently has evoked demonstrations of charity, generosity and all the other human virtues such as have never been called out before, and it is a source of sincere gratification to note that the retail druggists of the country have responded promptly and liberally to the appeal for aid, issued in behalf of their fellow druggists in the stricken city by the National Association of Retail Druggists. Elsewhere in this issue will be found details of the losses incurred by the drug trade, together with particulars of the relief afforded, perhaps the most complete account printed in any periodical. Any of our readers who may feel disposed to contribute to the fund may do so by sending contributions in care of the AMERICAN DRUGGIST, or direct to Secretary Thomas V. Wooten, 79 Dearborn street, Chicago.

THERE IS A LESSON IN THIS.

The experience of New York druggists with the Stevens-Wainwright bill, which has been so frequently commented upon in these columns, should lead them to take steps to prevent the introduction of similar obnoxious measures at future sessions of the Legislature. This could be done best by the organized druggists of the State coming to an agreement on the draft of a law which should be satisfactory to them and at the same time secure the end to which the Stevens-Wainwright bill was aimed, without that bill's bad features. It would also be well for the druggists of the State to take some means of getting in touch with the interests which were behind the Stevens-Wainwright bill, in order that a conference may be arranged at which conflicting opinions might be harmonized and a bill satisfactory to all interests concerned agreed upon.

ATTACKING IT AT ITS SOURCE.

Not long ago when New York druggists were being subjected to all sorts of vilification in the lay press, and at gatherings of reformers, chemical and otherwise, for their alleged crimes of adulteration and substitution, the suggestion was made to one of the head reformers in the Department of Health by the editor of this journal that the pollution of drugs and chemicals, if it existed, should be remedied at its source. The point was made that if one wholesale druggist could be detected in the act of selling pharmacopœial preparations which were below standard, and made an example of, it would have the effect of remedying conditions in several hundred pharmacies. It now appears that the suggestion offered has been acted on, and an expert has been employed by the Department of Health to examine and report upon the character of the pharmacopœial preparations sold by jobbing druggists to retailers. For two months past a rigid investigation has been conducted and various galenical compounds, including fluid extracts and tinctures, have been examined. The results in some instances were startling. According to private information which we have received, several of the so-called fluid extracts were found to be almost completely devoid of alkaloidal constituents. The retailer who depends, in large measure, upon the manufacturer and wholesaler of drugs and chemicals has been too often made the scapegoat of the really responsible parties, and it is gratifying to know that this has been recognized and the blame put where it properly belongs. Interesting developments may be shortly looked for.

Government Trust Baiters.

The United States Attorney General has brought suit in the United States Circuit Court for the district of Indiana against the National Wholesale Druggists' Association, the Proprietary Association of America and the National Association of Retail Druggists, on the grounds that these associations and their members have been engaged in a combination in restraint of trade. The statement made public by the Attorney General reflects with a remarkable degree of accuracy the sentiments expressed by the attorneys in the Loder suit, and the results in that suit are cited as evidence of the existence of such a trust.

It will be remembered that substantial damages were awarded to C. G. A. Loder in a suit brought by him, under section 7 of the Sherman Antitrust act, against these three associations. The Attorney General claims that the evidence adduced in that trial establishes a case substantially the same as that charged in the Government's bill, and the Circuit judge in that case held that the evidence was sufficient to prove a combination in restraint of trade within the meaning of the first section of the Federal Antitrust act.

The defendants in the Loder suit are by no means convinced that their case has been lost, for they feel confident that when the case comes up for trial upon the appeal which has been taken the verdict of the Supreme Court will be in their favor.

We present in our news columns the results of interviews with leading members of the three associations involved, all of whom are quite confident that both the Loder suit and the Government suit will eventually be decided in favor of the defence.

In retail drug circles the action taken by the Attorney General is ridiculed as being merely a political play to the galleries. Whatever may be the result, the bringing of this suit will furnish excellent capital for the administration politicians, who can, and no doubt will, loudly proclaim on the hustings that the administration is the original "trust buster" and will point with pride to the ferocious vigor with which this frightful trust monster has been attacked by the fearless Government. The organizations in question have comparatively little influence, either financial or political, and they may be attacked with entire safety and entire immunity, so far as any political ill consequences may be concerned. The immunity with which avowed trusts of immense means and vast influence can carry on machinations universally condemned as being in restraint of trade makes the attack on the so-called Drug Trust open to all kinds of imputations. In view of all the circumstances it would appear natural that the members of the trade should feel inclined to question the origin of this movement and feel confident that its ultimate result will be nil.

Druggists' Fire Insurance.

The present agitation by insurance companies for a 25 per cent. increase in premium rates adds to the problem which for years has been a subject for serious consideration by the drug trade. Unfair apportionment in rating drug store risks has been, and is now, the rule with these companies, and, doubtless, druggists have been made to pay a large portion of the loss incurred on other classes of property. In view, therefore, of the proposed additional increase to affect druggists in common with others, it would seem that the present is an opportune time to consider the long existing injustice.

It cannot be successfully denied that drug store fires are of infrequent occurrence. There seems to be no possible comparison between the premiums collected from druggists and the losses paid to them. The annual average tribute levied is probably not less than $1,250,000, while not more than $400,000 was required to meet the losses occurring in a period of 12 months. The claim that an average excess of about 50 per cent. is exacted seems well founded from experience and observation, and this without other reason than that such conditions are simply allowed to exist. Next to residence property no class of property is a safer risk, for few drug stores but do not constantly have some one around by day and night. All drug stores are under watchful care for at least 16 hours out of the 24, yet the drug store risk is regarded as hazardous!

The present method of estimating risks seems to be founded on a wrong basis. Certainly something is radically wrong with drug store rates and a change is indicated. It seems reasonable to conclude that the owners of a hundred risks of the same kind are better prepared to insure each other on a basis of equality than the owners of a hundred risks each substantially differing in nature and subjected to peculiar conditions of its own. That this is being more and more realized is plainly evidenced by the number of special insurance companies which are being organized by those engaged in different branches of trade. The effort of the American Druggists' Fire Insurance Company to provide specialty insurance for druggists is a case in point. Opportunity for such a company to provide equitable insurance rates should not be wanting. The success of such a company would not alone relieve the present anxiety regarding a further increase in rates, but would do away for all time with the existing unfairness toward the drug trade on the part of insurance companies.

The Physician Must Be Explicit.

It will be remembered that some months ago suit was brought against a Brooklyn druggist by a patient who claimed that she had been damaged to the extent of $7,000 by a pharmacist's error in dispensing a prescription written by Dr. William J. Cruikshank. This prescription called for compound elixir of white pine with heroin. The pharmacist not having this preparation as made up by the manufacturer, but having the elixir of white pine, added the requisite amount of heroin, not being aware of the fact that as the manufacturer put out the preparation he omitted the morphine, which is a constituent of the compound syrup of white pine, when he added the heroin. The case attracted a great deal of attention on account of the attitude of the physician, who published statements in medical journals to the effect that the decision rendered by Justice Gaynor granted the pharmacist the right of altering prescriptions at will. This statement was denied by Justice Gaynor most vigorously, in the following words:

> My attention is called to the fact that the doctor has published in a medical journal and otherwise the false and invented statement that it was decided in this case that a pharmacist may change a doctor's prescription, or substitute some other medicine than that it calls for, without liability. I regret to feel obliged to say that he is so well known in our courts, where he has been for many years connected with litigations of an unsavory character, to say the least, that no notice needs to be taken of his false statement so far as the legal profession is concerned, and I understand that to be so of the medical profession also. But lest any drug clerk may be misled by such false statement to the danger of others, it seems proper that I say that not only was no such thing said or decided, but it was not presented or even mooted. Where would counsel be found to present and argue such an absurd proposition?

The Appellate Division of the New York Supreme Court has now handed down a unanimous decision supporting the decision of Justice Gaynor in declaring that the pharmacist had made no error in dispensing the "elixir pinus comp. cum heroin" by adding 1-24 of a grain of heroin to each teaspoonful of the ordinary "elixir pinus comp."

The result of this controversy is of interest to pharmacists and to physicians alike, teaching to the physicians the necessity of understanding clearly what they want and of being explicit in their orders. It is also interesting to pharmacists in that it is so rarely that the pharmacist is treated with such fairness and such complete comprehension of his functions and responsibilities as he was in the decision of Justice Gaynor.

(*Written for the American Druggist.*)

THE PHARMACEUTICAL SPECIALIST.

By J. Diner.

The general tendency at present is toward a better understanding between the professions of pharmacy and medicine. This is as it should be. But in order to firmly establish these relations a clear understanding must be had regarding the relative positions of the adherents of the two professions.

Theoretically the pharmacist should occupy the same position to the general practitioner as does the specialist in medicine.

The general practitioner has neither time nor facility to treat diseases of the eye. Therefore he sends his eye cases to the oculist. Surgical cases requiring special treatment, or major operations, are referred to the surgeon, and so on down the line of medical specialization. Now pharmacy, in the abstract, is really only another specialty of medicine, and matters pertaining to pharmacy should be referred to the specialist in that line, the pharmacist, in the same manner in which other cases are referred to the respective specialists, that is without specification. When a physician refers a case to the oculist he does not presume to tell him how to treat the case, nor does he undertake to prescribe to the surgeon how to perform his operation. Theoretically, therefore, the physician should not interfere with the specialist in that branch of medicine known as pharmacy, and after diagnosing his case and indicating the drugs needed, he should leave it to the pharmacist to use his own judgment, both as to the selection of the quality and the manner of compounding and mixing said drugs.

Why, then, is this position of specialist not accorded to us? And why does the physician insist on specifying certain makes of goods, relegating the pharmacist to the position of a mere handler of drugs? The answer is very easy indeed. Simply because the average pharmacist has done nothing to merit the title of specialist. He has neither the mechanical nor the mental equipment necessary for that position.

The oculist fits up an office containing all the paraphernalia necessary for his special work; so does the surgeon; but the druggist cuts down on his laboratory and prescription room equipments as much as possible, until it hardly deserves the name of laboratory or prescription department, so prominently displayed on his sign. The pharmacist will invest thousands of dollars in a soda water apparatus, spend plenty of money on beveled mirrors and hard wood fixtures, but will cavil at the expense of an accurate prescription balance; will get along with a pharmacopœia antiquated 20 years ago, and certainly not invest any more than he can possibly help on other laboratory and prescription room equipments.

But these are only the external qualifications which he lacks. When we strike his mental outfit we find, if possible, an even more destitute condition. To make himself a specialist the pharmacist must keep posted on the advances made in his profession. The therapeutic action of the newer remedies must be studied carefully, and he must be ready to give his medical friend any desired information in the field of pharmacy.

Chemical reactions and incompatibilities must be as familiar to him as the wholesale price of "St. Louis chemicals." The art and science of preparing palatable and elegant looking preparations must be an open book to him. And when he is prepared to furnish all this there still remains a good deal to be done in order to place the pharmacist on the footing of a specialist in his branch of medicine.

The other specialists—the eye, ear, nose and throat men, the surgeon, etc.—would not get very far if they attempted to practice general medicine along with their specialty. To build up a name and clientele as specialists they must abandon all secondary pursuits, and devote all their time and energy to the one branch chosen.

The pharmacist must do likewise. If he wants to be a specialist in pharmacy he must abandon his soda water fountain, give up his cigar case, relegate his toilet article department to a secondary position, if not close it out entirely, and certainly he must divorce himself from the most unprofessional of all side lines, the patent or proprietary medicine. Furthermore, he must abandon the most pernicious of all practices, counter prescribing. It is not within the scope of the pharmacist to prescribe. It is unjust to our medical friends and, above all, it is a great wrong committed against the trusting and suffering public.

The prescription department, which now occupies the smallest possible space with the poorest possible equipment, should be made the main part of the pharmacist's outfit; his laboratory supplied with the latest and best mechanical devices and chemical ware; a good pharmaceutical library should be at his command, and last, but not least, his mental furnishing should be brought up to date. Fitted out thus, physically and mentally prepared to assume the place of pharmacy specialist, he can go to his brethren in general medicine and demand recognition, and I am sure he will be welcomed by them with open arms.

THE INDEPENDENCE OF MEDICINE AND PHARMACY.[1]

By Augustus A. Eshner, M.D.

The province of the physician is the alleviation of suffering and so far as possible the prevention and cure of disease. In the fulfillment of these functions he has at his command divers agencies, some of a medicinal, others of a nonmedical character. Over certain of these he can exercise entire control. In the application of others he requires the aid of experts in other departments of science and art. For purposes of diagnosis, for example, he must have instruments of precision, such as the microscope, apparatus for blood counting, hæmoglobin estimation, study of blood pressure, urea estimation and the like. In treatment he may avail himself of various physical agencies, such as light and heat, water, air, electricity, manual procedures and mechanical appliances. Some of these he may himself devise and apply. For others he depends upon workers in other spheres of activity. So also with regard to the articles of the materia medica. The primitive physician was himself able to gather the simple herbs needed in the preparation of the infusions and decoctions through whose aid he sought to bring relief. With the evolution of medicine and the gradual increase in the number and complexity of medicinal agents the practitioner of medicine has become dependent upon the pharmacist.

On the former reposes the obligation of familiarizing himself with disease for the purpose of its recognition and appropriate treatment, while upon the latter devolves the duty of preparing and providing in most convenient, most palatable and most reliable form the drugs prescribed by the physician. The physician should know more or less intimately the sources of the preparations he uses and their general chemical composition, but he cannot be expected to be able to construct them for himself. The pharmacist, however, must be master of all these things, but he is exempt from the obligation of directing the employment of the remedies; it is his function to prepare. The duty of diagnosis and treatment belongs to the sphere of the physician, that of drug preparation and dispensing to the sphere of the pharmacist. Physician and pharmacist are thus mutually dependent on each other, and a spirit of friendly and helpful co-operation must subsist between them for the attainment of the fullest measure of success in the direction of the end in view that both have in common—namely, the healing of the sick.

Fire Caused by a Chemical Reaction.—Namias reports (*Annali della Societa Chimica di Milano*, 1905, p. 293), an accident which occurred in a drug house as the result of the contact of a barrel containing potassium permanganate with some glycerin which had trickled from an adjoining receptacle. When concentrated glycerin is brought into contact with potassium permanganate there is a burst of bright flame due to the reduction of the permanganate to an incandescent mass of manganese dioxide. Druggists should take care to prevent the contact of these two chemicals which may give rise to a fire.

[1] Read before the Philadelphia Branch of the American Pharmaceutical Association, March 28, 1906.

THE ORGANIZATION AND WORKING OF THE DRUG LABORATORY.[1]

By L. F. Kebler, Chief.

The Drug Laboratory, which is an integral part of the Bureau of Chemistry, United States Department of Agriculture, has been in active operation for a little over two years, and in view of the fact that this association has taken so much interest in its establishment and progress, and encouraged it in so many ways, it seems but right and proper to give an account of its entrusted work at this time.

By an act of Congress approved June 30, 1902, the Secretary of Agriculture was authorized to investigate the adulteration of drugs in the United States. Among the chief reasons why the Drug Laboratory was delegated to the United States Department of Agriculture were undoubtedly the following: First, because a large number of drugs of known utility are derived from the farms, gardens and forests of this country, and these interests are all centered in the Department of Agriculture. Second, because most of the work connected with the adulteration of drugs is of a chemical character, for which a bureau is established in this Department. Agricultural industries interested in the production of drugs are seriously retarded, hindered and threatened by the importation into this country of adulterated and inferior goods, which diminish legitimate profits and tend to destroy interest in the production of these commodities.

Under the act mentioned above, the Secretary of Agriculture took steps to establish the Drug Laboratory. The Civil Service Commission held an examination for the purpose of establishing an eligible list from which appointments could be made to fill the various positions created in this laboratory. From this list a chief was appointed, who assumed active charge March 1, 1903. The demands on the laboratory have been very great, and the personnel of its working force has been increased until there is at present a chief, three assistant chemists and a stenographer and typewriter. In addition to this we have the co-operation of the various laboratories organized in the Bureau of Chemistry for the purpose of prosecuting certain lines of investigation. For example, one laboratory is devoted exclusively to the determination of nitrogen; when technical reasons do not prevent doing so this laboratory makes all nitrogen determinations for the Drug Laboratory, and in all events makes checks. On the same basis all sugar determinations are made by the Sugar Laboratory. Under these conditions the actual available working force of the Drug Laboratory is much greater than indicated above. The work of the laboratory is also much facilitated by the arrangement which obtains in the Department of Agriculture relative to the workings of the library. For example, the current numbers of periodicals that are of interest to the Drug Laboratory are brought to this laboratory for reading and review. The librarian of the Bureau also secures all books of reference that are needed for consultation, reading and verification. This feature alone is very time saving and valuable.

The work now in progress in the laboratory reaches out in many directions, some of which will be enumerated below.

CHEMICAL REAGENTS.

When active duties were assumed in this laboratory, the examination of chemical reagents was delegated to it. The objects of these examinations were: First, to insure reliable chemicals for analytical work; second, to secure data from which standards of purity can be constructed, and, last, to place competitors on an equal footing. The qualities usually specified in placing orders and letting contracts are the best grades of the several respective types. Some very interesting examples have been met with, but it is encouraging to note that the number of inferior and mislabeled goods received during the past year is less than when this work was first instituted. For example, when an article is purchased that is to comply with the regulations of the Pharmacopœia, the vendor does at times either mark it as of the quality requested or leave it unlabeled entirely, and it frequently happens that these goods do not comply with the standards set. There are now available in the Drug Laboratory the data of about 700 analyses of chemicals, and a bulletin is in preparation giving these results and setting forth the standards under which these goods were accepted or rejected.

[1] Presented at the last annual meeting of the American Pharmaceutical Association.

PLANT DRUGS.

This is one of the most interesting lines of work connected with this laboratory. It involves a systematic study and improvement of the analytical methods at present available. The general principles to be followed are similar to those that have been utilized by the Association of Official Agricultural Chemists for many years. It also includes a study of the influence of time on the active constituents contained in many potent plants. At the twenty-first annual meeting of the Association of Official Agricultural Chemists the first report was presented by the referee, appointed a year previous, on plants and drugs, giving the results of co-operative work, which was confined to the methods of opium assay.

CODLIVER OIL INVESTIGATIONS.

It is a well-known fact that physicians consider Norwegian codliver oil superior to the American codliver oil, and so far as we can judge there does not appear to be a good reason for this discrimination. Such a discrimination places an important American industry in a very disadvantageous position. The object of this investigation is to determine by comparative study of American and Norwegian codliver oils, chemically, medicinally and commercially, whether there is any good reason for this preference, and if so what it is and how it could be remedied. In order to make the investigation as complete as possible the chief of the Drug Laboratory secured the assistance of the Division of Foods of the Bureau of Chemistry, and the Bureau of Fisheries was asked to co-operate in this undertaking, with the result that those in charge expressed an earnest willingness to assist us in every possible way, guaranteeing to provide us with oils of authentic quality. This work has been carried out to a certain extent, and we have now in possession at the Bureau of Chemistry a large number of oils with full histories as to the method of manufacture, the condition of the fish from which the oils were taken and the locality in which the fish were caught. The Fish Commission is also making a study of the methods of preparing the oils commercially, both in Norway and in this country. The results obtained by us so far tend to show that the American codliver oils are equal to the Norwegian oils in every respect chemically. This line of work will be prosecuted during the coming year, and a large number of samples of authentic purity will be secured, and these will be compared with the commercial articles generally available.

PROPRIETARY MEDICINAL AGENTS.

By authority of Congress any department of the Government may secure the service of the Bureau of Chemistry by making application to the Secretary of Agriculture for assistance. It is under this authorization that the Drug Laboratory was requested to assist the Post Office Department by analyses and other means in arriving at fair and just conclusions relative to the fraudulent and dangerous nature of certain products that are enjoying the privileges of the mail. The fraudulent representations and impossible cures set forth by many of these remedies are certainly interesting.

Claim Originality.—Some base their claims on originality. For example, one concern set forth in its advertising literature that they were the orginators of hyoscine hydrogenbromide (hyoscine hydrobromate) and were the first to introduce it into medicine. This company was organized nearly 20 years after hyoscine hydrobromate had been thoroughly studied and recognized as a medicinal agent of great value. Another firm dealt in a commodity which it called by the name of "Paris Food." This remedy resembled closely the ordinary cold cream of the Pharmacopœia and was a good product, but the claims made for it were highly extravagant. The company stated in its literature that this remedy was largely used by European physicians and was doing marvelous things. On investigation it was found that this remedy had never been used by any physician in Europe, except possibly by representatives of the firm itself. Another general principle taken advantage of by these firms is that the remedies they are using are *rare* and expensive, when as a matter of fact they are usually among the most ordinary well-known medicinal agents.

New Methods of Application.—This has been claimed by a number of firms that are at present no longer doing business. One claim was that they were the originators of what is commonly known in medicine as bougies. On investigation it was found that the use of the bougies antedated the existence of the company by at least a score of years. This same company also claimed by literature and cuts to deliver to the prospective patient agents that had been electrified. Such a product (bougie) it was believed to be impossible of production and, at the hearing, the physician in charge admitted that nothing of this kind was done; neither was it possible in general, but he stated that this electrifying may mean something similar to what is generally meant when a speaker is spoken of as electrifying his audience. We hardly believe that an electrification of this character could have any very great medicinál virtue.

Coined Names.—A common practice followed by a number of firms dealing in goods of this character is to advertise a prescription which is heralded as being efficacious in the cure of many diseases, and in this prescription will be found a number of coined or absolutely ambiguous names which cannot be found in ordinary medical and pharmaceutical literature available in the best regulated drug stores. The prospective patient on taking this prescription to the drug store to have the same filled is usually informed that certain drugs cannot be supplied. The advertisement connected with this prescription usually anticipates this and makes provision by informing the patient that if he is unable to secure the ingredients called for in this prescription at his local drug store the advertising firm will be pleased to comply with his request on forwarding the prescription and price. The price charged is usually exorbitant.

Radium Fraud.—Since the discovery of radium a number of cures have apparently been effected by its use. This fact, coupled with the popular interest aroused in radium, has been taken advantage of by a number of firms to the disadvantage of many patients. A number of these products have been examined and not a single one has been found to contain a trace of radium. One consisted of a pyrophosphorescent ore composed of sulphides of lead and zinc.

Standard Remedies but Exaggerated and Fraudulent Claims.—Many of these firms use some of the well-known ethical combinations of standard drugs commonly employed by all physicians in their practice and nothing could be urged against the use of these remedies if it were not for the fact that these people through these remedies claim to do marvelous things bordering on the miraculous. For example, one firm with a very good remedy stated that there was nothing that their remedy would not cure. Such a statement as this is known by any one who has the remotest knowledge of medicines to be false. Many ridiculous claims of a similar character are met with.

Some Marvelous Remedies.—The Post Office Department asked for the investigation of certain remedies which through their advertising literature were heralded as being capable of curing all ills that human flesh is heir to, especially lost manhood, lost vitality, the production of fine complexions, and turning a black skin white by means of complexion powders, tablets and lotions; removing wrinkles and taking kinks out of hair. One of the lost vitality restorers consisted of flavored vaseline. One of the complexion lotions consisted of a solution of corrosive sublimate mixed with tincture of benzoin and glycerine. A complexion powder was ordinary Rochelle salt.

In this connection it might be desirable to call attention to another practice common with the firms dealing in goods of the above character. As an example may be cited the case of a prospective patient who was sent an envelope on which it was stated that it contained medicated papers, and that when these medicated papers were dipped in the urine of the patient and forwarded to the office of the sender these papers would be analyzed microscopically and chemically and the nature of the diseases with which the patient was suffering would be diagnosed. The envelope contained only a single slip of litmus paper. Such a procedure we know is false in every detail, because there is no chemist or microscopist who could under these conditions give any information relative to the nature of a disease under which the patient may be suffering.

DRUG LEGISLATION.

For the past year numerous requests have come from legislative bodies all over the United States relative to present existing laws regulating the adulteration of drugs and the proper labeling of the same. It was therefore considered expedient to collect into bulletin form all Federal and State laws bearing on this subject, so that these inquiries could be fully and completely answered in the shortest possible time. It is hoped that this bulletin will be available by the first of next year.

AUTHORITY TO EXAMINE SAMPLES.

Numerous requests come to the Bureau of Chemistry asking that investigations be made of certain medicinal remedies. In general the Bureau of Chemistry is unable to make such examinations, especially when they are of value only to an individual or a small group of individuals. On the other hand, such investigations may be taken up for the general public welfare. The Drug Laboratory is authorized by the Secretary of Agriculture to co-operate with the American Pharmaceutical Association and the American Medical Association.

Ointment of Yellow Mercuric Oxide.

Dufaut (*Répertoire de pharmacie*, February 10, 1906) takes a hand in the controversy as to the best method of preparing the ointment of yellow mercuric oxide, which has been going on for some time past in the foreign journals. Some years ago the author published a process for preparing by the moist method a pure yellow mercuric oxide, to which the name of "orange colored oxide" was given. The advantage of this product over the ordinary yellow oxide and the red oxide is that it can be more easily purified by washing and more readily divided into an impalpable powder. The official ointment of yellow mercuric oxide, as prescribed by the French *Codex*, proves frequently irritating when introduced into the eye, owing to the fact that it contains minute particles of gritty oxide. On the other hand, some manufacturers make by secret formula ointments of the same substance which are not at all irritant to the eye and which do not contain any anæsthetic substances. Purification of the mercuric oxide does not seem to remedy the difficulty, as even the purest oxide sometimes causes violent pain in the eye.

The author found that this irritation was due to the action of the mercuric oxide upon the sodium chloride of the tears, the reaction giving rise to the formation of mercuric chloride. If a piece of red litmus paper be placed under a small quantity of the oxide to which a drop of water has been added, and if at some distance from this a few crystals of sodium chloride be dissolved in water upon the litmus paper, the color of the paper is not changed; but if the two drops be mixed with a glass rod the paper changes immediately to blue. It seems that the curative action of the ointment is dependent on the formation of this chloride and that the fatty substances in the ointment in reality go far toward neutralizing the caustic action of the mercuric chloride thus formed. A variety of fatty substances has been used in preparing the mercuric oxide ointment, including fresh butter, lard, cold cream and even codliver oil and castor oil to which wax had been added. The trouble with all these was that they did not resist the oxidizing action of mercuric oxide, and thus the ointments became darker with age and lost much of their efficacy.

The formula given by Carles obviates all this difficulty, but an equally satisfactory result may be obtained with the following formula:

℞ Orange colored mercuric oxide.........gm. 1
Petrolatum (white?)..................gm. 9
Wool-fat (hydrous?) ....gm. 10

In this process the mercuric oxide should be triturated with one part of the petrolatum after liquefying the latter, and the rest of the ingredients should be added. In this way a very, smooth, nonirritating ointment is obtained. In the forthcoming edition of the French *Codex* petrolatum alone is recommended as a vehicle for the ointment. (The formula of the U. S. P., 1900, provides for the employment of equal parts of wool fat and petrolatum as vehicles and specifies the addition of a little water to the oxide in order to render the mixture smooth and free from gritty particles.

THE LATEST REMEDIES.

(*Continued from page 102.*)

Almateine is a condensation product of formaldehyde and hæmatoxylin obtained by the action of formaldehyde on a decoction of campechy wood. It is a reddish powder without taste or odor, almost insoluble in water, but soluble in alcohol, ether and glycerin. Used both internally and externally as a substitute for iodoform for antiseptic and disinfectant purposes.

Anthraquinone cholalate is put up in tablet form and represents a combination of colalin and cascara sagrada, the bark being extracted with a solution of cholalic acid which is said to combine with the anthraquinone principle contained in it. Made by T. Morson & Son, London, Eng.

Antirheumatin is a name applied to crayons of salocreol (creosote salicylate), which are used in the same way as menthol cones. Made by W. Newiger, Berlin.

Arsenferratose is a solution of ferratin in syrup form (syrupus ferratini arseniati) containing 0.3 per cent. of iron and 0.003 per cent. of arsenic. Used as a hæmatopoietic and alterative, in doses of a tablespoonful three or four times a day for adults, and for children, a teaspoonful to a dessertspoonful. It is put up by C. F. Boehringer & Soehne, Mannheim, Germany, and New York, in 250 Gm. bottles, selling wholesale at 55 cents each.

Benzosalin-Roche is the methyl ester of benzoyl salicylic acid, and being a salicylic and benzoic acid derivative is an analogue of acetylsalicylic acid and is employed similarly with the last named in the treatment of rheumatism and neuralgia, in doses of from 3½ to 15 grains, several times a day. It forms white, faintly aromatic, almost tasteless, needle-shaped crystals, soluble in alcohol, benzol and chloroform, but insoluble in water. It is put up in tablet form only by the makers, the Hoffmann-La Roche Chemical Works, Basel, Switzerland and New York.

Brom-Protylin (Bromated phosphorus-albumin). Faintly yellowish powder; slight bromine odor and taste, not perceptible when mixed with food. Contains 2.6 per cent. phosphorus and 4 per cent. bromine organically combined with albumin. Employed as a nerve nutrient and sedative in hysteria, epilepsy and other neuroses. Dose, 8 to 16 grains three time daily. In 1-oz. carton, 50 cents oz.; 4-grain tablets in cartons of 100, 55 cents each. Made and marketed by the Hoffmann-LaRoche Chemical Works, Basel, Switzerland, and New York.

Cascoferrin is stated to be a compound of triferrin and a tasteless extract of cascara sagrada, and intended for use as a ferruginous laxative. Made by E. Weigert, Breslau, Germany.

Callaquol, a thick, milky-looking fluid of aromatic odor, consists of an ester of oxytricarballylic acid, combined with a soapy solution of oil of thyme, and it is to the latter that it owes its odor. It is used as a vulnerary. Made by Friedrich Braun, Würnberg, Germany.

Ciba is a new trade name for creosote carbonate and represents any article which is said to be cheaper in price.

Colalin is the name applied to a purified preparation of cholalic acid from bile, containing a trace of magnesium carbonate. Introduced by T. Morson & Son, London, Eng.

Cypress Oil distilled from *Cupressus sempervirens* has been brought forward of late as a remedy for whooping cough. Schimmel & Co., of Leipsic, who are the only manufacturers, have exploited the medicinal properties of the oil, and it is marketed in the United States by their branch house, Fritzsche Brothers, New York, at $9 per lb.; 1-oz. bottles, 70 cents.

Dolonephran is a dental anæsthetic, the chief constituents of which are reported to be alypin and adrenalin. Introduced by Chemische Institute, Berlin.

Eutonicin is a liquid preparation of German origin, consisting of a mixed percolate of condurango bark, cinchona bark, gentian root, orange peel and rhubarb root, with aromatics, iron, manganese and peptone.

Fer-Protylin (Ferrated phosphorus-albumin). Yellowish-white, odorless, tasteless powder; soluble in alkaline fluids. Prescribed as a conservative and hæmatinic in anæmia, chlorosis and other wasting diseases. Contains 2.6 per cent. phosphorus and 2.3 per cent. iron, organically combined with albumin. Dose, 8 to 16 grains thrice daily. In 1-oz. cartons, 50 cents oz. Four-grain tablets in cartons of 100, 55 cents each. Manufactured by the Hoffmann-LaRoche Chemical Works, Basel, Switzerland, and New York.

Fluotal is a brand name of recent adoption for bismuth fluorbromphenyl, a powerful antiseptic.

Haemosoter is an insoluble mercurial compound of German origin, the exact composition of which has not been disclosed.

Iodferratose is a liquid preparation in the form of a syrup containing 0.3 per cent. of iron and 0.3 per cent. of iodine, put up in 250 Gm. bottles (55 cents, wholesale) by C. F. Boehringer & Soehne, Mannheim, Germany, and New York.

Iodoglobin is a coined term for a kaolin poultice mass.

Kasucolum is a brand name for potassium guaiacol sulphonate.

Maltocrystal is the name given to a crystalline form of malt extract made by C. Brunnengräber, Rostock, Germany.

Mercurial compound, new. Subcutine (anæsthesine paraphenol sulphonate) in combination with mercuric iodide furnishes a painless hypodermatic injection of mercury. The solution is composed of mercuric iodide, 0.01 Gm.; sodium iodide, 0.01 Gm.; subcutine, 0.005 Gm.; sodium chloride, 0.002 Gm.; dissolved in sterilized hydrogen dioxide water, 1 Mil.

Migrol is a headache remedy stated by the manufacturers to consist of a mixture in equal parts of caffeine and sodium pyrocatechinmonoacetate.

Mucogene is a new purgative compound, the chemical name of which is dimethyl-phenyl-para-ammonium-beta-oxynaphthoazine hydrochloride. It forms blue crystals, almost insoluble in water, but dissolved by alkalies and alkaline solutions. It derives its name from its property of exciting an abundant excretion of intestinal mucus. Dose, 1½ to 3 grains in colic and other intestinal disorders.

Neuraemin is a lecithin compound made by dissolving lecithin, 20 Gm., in ether, 100 Gm., and adding in portions while shaking, hæmatin, 10 Gm.; smilacin, 10 Gm., dissolved in alcohol, 2 Lt. The volatile ingredients are recovered by distillation *in vacuo* at 30 degrees C., and the remaining mass dried on a porcelain evaporating dish. It forms a light, homogeneous, wax-like brown substance, readily soluble in alcohol, ether and acetone. Made and marketed by Gablin & Co., Paris, France.

Pittylene, a tar-formaldehyde condensation product, is a light-brown powder of slightly tarry odor, which is used in the treatment of eczema, applied either as a dusting powder, soap or plaster.

Protylin (Phosphorus-albumin). White, odorless, tasteless powder; contains 2.6 per cent. phosphorus. Insoluble in water; soluble in alkaline liquids. Reported to be an assimilable, nontoxic form of phosphorus. Nerve tonic and reconstructive in neurasthenia, rickets, scrofula, etc. Dose, 8 to 16 grains in soup broth, etc. Must not be boiled with food. One-oz. carton, 50 cents oz.; 4-grn. tablets, 55 cents per 100. Manufactured by the Hoffmann-LaRoche Chemical Works, Basel, Switzerland, and New York.

Quinine phytin occurs as a yellowish crystalline powder, soluble in water to a fluorescent solution. It is the acid quinine salt of anhydrooxymethylenediphosphoric acid. Tonic and antimalarial in doses of 5 to 10 grains. Made by the Society for Chemical Industry, Basel, Switzerland.

Renastyptin is the brand name for a solution of the active hæmostatic principle of the suprarenal bodies as put up by Willows, Francis, Butler & Thompson, London, Eng.

Saiodin is a mono-iodide compound of one of the higher fatty acids, and is referred to as calcium mono-iodobehenate, or iodosebacic acid, the name being derived from *sapo* and *iodum*. It is a colorless, almost odorless and tasteless powder, insoluble in water, which is intended as a tasteless substitute for potassium iodide. It contains 26 per cent. of iodine and 4.1 per cent. of calcium. Dose, 15 grains once to thrice daily. Marketed by the Continental Color and Chemical Company, New York.

Salene is a preparation similar to mesotan, being a mixture of methylglycol and ethylglycol salicylates. It is used as a liniment or embrocation mixed with equal parts of castor oil or alcohol.

Secacornin, formerly known as ergotin-Keller, is made by the Hoffmann-LaRoche Chemical Works, Basel, Switzerland, and New York. It is a standardized sterile liquid preparation of ergot, 1 Cc. being equal to 4 Gm. of the drug.

Spermathanaton is stated to be a compound of sodium tetraborate and oxygen in stable combination. It is put up in tablet form and, as its name implies, has for its purpose the prevention of conception. Put on the market by Fr. J. Reusch, Wiesbaden, Germany.

Styptogan is a paste composed of definite quantities of potassium permanganate and petrolatum, which has been recommended as a styptic application for bleeding surfaces. It is made by J. D. Riedel, Berlin.

Thephorin is a double salt of theobromine and sodium formate, being a diuretin in which the salicylic acid is replaced by formic acid. It forms a white powder, soluble in 10 parts of water. It contains 62½ per cent. of theobromine as against 50 per cent. in diuretin, and is administered in the same way and in similar doses as diuretin. Made by the Hoffmann-LaRoche Chemical Works, Basel, Switzerland, and New York.

Vesipyrin is acetylsalol, being to salol what aspirin is to salicylic acid. Occurs as white crystals, insoluble in water, but soluble in alcohol and other volatile solvents. Recommended in articular rheumatism in 15-grain doses.

Veseptol is a vanadium preparation which has been recommended as a useful antiseptic and healing application to wounds and abraded surfaces.

Xaxa is a brand name for acetylsalicylic acid.

Zymphene is sodium metaoxycyanocinnamate. It forms yellowish tabular crystals, soluble in water and alcohol. Used in anorexia (loss of appetite) as a tonic and digestive stimulant in doses of 0.5 gm. (7½ grains).

Origin of the Word Menstruum.

The words of pharmaceutical connotation in the *Historical Medical Dictionary*, which is now being issued in parts in England, are receiving attention in the columns of our London contemporary, *The Chemist and Druggist*. Regarding the word "menstruum," it is noted that this, which is one of the most interesting of pharmaceutical words, means simply monthly, and the connection of this idea with that of a chemical solvent has been a puzzle to many etymologists. Richardson explains it by the theory that the action of a solvent was, "as we are told, assisted by a moderate fire during the month!" Dr. Johnson's explanation of how it came to acquire the meaning of a solvent, and this is the idea which has been usually adopted, is that it "originated in some notion of the old chemists about the influence of the moon in the preparation of dissolvents." The *Historical English Dictionary* tracks the development of the sense more exactly. "Menstruum," it says, "was a mediæval Latin term used in alchemy to express the belief that the base metal undergoing transmutation into gold corresponded with the seed within the womb which was being acted upon by the agency of the menstrual fluid."

GATHERED FORMULAS.

PHOSPHORESCENT PHOTOGRAPHS.

A sheet of card paper, slightly warmed, is covered with the following solution:

	Parts.
Potassium dichromate	4
Gum arabic	8
Glucose	6
Glycerin	12
Water, distilled	100

After drying, it is placed under a negative and exposed to the light. As soon as the details appear the copy is put in some damp place. The parts not lit up absorb the dampness and get sticky and seize and hold fast calcium, strontium or zinc sulphide, in fine powder dusted on it. The picture, after being exposed to a powerful light for a short time and then taken into a darkened room emits a light, the strength of which depends on the length of exposure to the source of light, and the time that has since elapsed—the phosphorescent quality gradually waning as time progresses.

EMULSION OF PETROLEUM AND GLYCEROPHOSPHATES.

(Bournemouth Formulary.)

Liquid petrolatum	fl. oz. 2
Powdered gum acacia	oz. 1
Calcium glycerophosphate	grains 24
Magnesium glycerophosphate	grains 12
Sodium glycerophosphate	grains 12
Citric acid	grains 5
Spirit of chloroform	fl. dr. 2
Tincture of lemon	fl. dr. 1
Elixir of saccharin	min. 24
Distilled water sufficient to produce 6 fl. oz.	

Triturate the petroleum with the gum and emulsify with 1½ oz. of water added all at once. Dissolve the glycerophosphates and acid in 1 oz. of water and add to this solution the other ingredients, then add gradually to the emulsion and adjust the volume to 6 oz. with water.

Dose: 1 to 4 fl. dr.

GLYCEROLE OF GLYCEROPHOSPHATES WITH RED MARROW.

(Bournemouth Formulary.)

Calcium glycerophosphate	grains 80
Potassium glycerophosphate	grains 40
Sodium glycerophosphate	grains 40
Magnesium glycerophosphate	grains 40
Iron glycerophosphate	grains 20
Manganese glycerophosphate	grains 20
Citric acid	grains 15
Dissolve in	
Distilled water	fl. oz. 10
Filter and add—	
Chloroform	min. 5
Alcohol	min. 40
Orange flower water	dr. 1
Cherry laurel water	dr. 1½
Glycerin extract of red bone marrow	fl. oz. 10

Dose: 1 to 2 fl. dr.

GLYCEROLE OF HYPOPHOSPHITES.

(Bournemouth Formulary.)

Potassium hypophosphite	grains 160
Calcium hypophosphite	grains 160
Manganese hypophosphite	grains 80
Quinine hypophosphite	grains 80
Strychnine hypophosphite	grains 2½
Strong solution of iron hypophosphite (B. P. C.)	fl. oz. 4
Hypophosphorous acid	fl. dr. 2
Distilled water	fl. oz. 3
Glycerin to produce	fl. oz. 20

Mix. (Each fluid drachm contains 1-64 grain strychnine hypophosphite, ½ grain quinine hypophosphite.)

Dose: 1 dr.

PHENOLPHTHALEIN LAXATIVE LOZENGES.

Phenolphthalein	grains 2
Chocolate basis	q. s.
To make one lozenge.	

Dose: 1 to 4 lozenges.

CODLIVER OIL AND IRON.

(Formula of the Deutscher Apotheker-Verein.)

Iodine ....Gm. 6
Almond oil ....Gm. 50
Iron, powdered ....Gm. 1
Codliver oil, enough to make......Gm. 1,000

Triturate the iodine to fine powder and rub with the almond oil; when dissolved add the iron, and then the cod liver oil. Shake vigorously and repeatedly; set aside to deposit, and filter.

NEW PERFUMES.

Bouquet d'Irlande.

Essence of white rose ....℥xx.
Essence of vanilla ....℥ij.

Mix.

Bouquet du Japon.

Essence of rose ....℥x.
Essence of neroli ....℥x.
Essence of patchouli ....℥iiss.
Essence of verbena ....℥v.
Essence of vetivert ....℥v.
Essence of civet ....℥j.
Essence of musk ....ʒj.

Mix.

WITCHHAZÉL CREAM.

I.

Stearic acid ....oz. 2
Glycerin ....fl. dr. 2
Sodium carbonate ....grains 180
Water to ....fl. oz.10

Melt the stearic acid and add to it the hot solution of sodium carbonate and glycerin. Keep on a water bath with frequent stirring for one hour, and make up to 10 fluid ounces with water. Add

Hamamelis water ....fl. oz. 10

Transfer to hot mortar and agitate very thoroughly with an egg whisk; continue agitation till quite thick. Let stand twelve hours, stir well and bottle.

II.

Stearin ....grains 360
Oil of theobroma ....grains 360
Sodium carbonate ....grains 240
Distilled water ....fl. oz. 12

Heat these together on a water bath, stir until chemical action ceases, then transfer to a large jar and whip up thoroughly with a solution made as follows:

Agar agar ....grains 80
Distilled water ....fl. oz. 8
Hamamelis water ....fl. oz. 12

Allow to stand a few days, with occasional stirring until dissolved, then strain through muslin.

SHAMPOO PASTE.

Castile soap ....℥iv.
Curd soap ....℥ij.
Potassium carbonate ....℥i.
Honey ....℥i.
Perfume ....q. s.

With sufficient hot water make a homogeneous paste.

HAIR TONICS.

I.

	Parts.
Extract of cinchona, aqueous............	3
Resorcin	1
Essence of violets	20
Alcohol	150
Distilled water	200
Olive oil	25
Extract of elder	10

Mix.

II.

	Parts.
Alcohol	600
Distilled water	1900
Spirit of soap	30
Tincture of cinchona	30
Tincture of nut gall	15
Heliotropin	5

Mix.

CHURCH INCENSE.

	Parts.
Gum olibanum, best tears..............	500
Gum olibanum, ordinary	500
Gum benzoin, Sumatra	100
Styrax	100

Mix.

ANTISEPTIC POWDER.

Pulv. boracis ....℥iss.
Pulv. alum. exsicc.............................℥iss.
Thymolis ....gr. xj.
Mentholis ....gr. ¾
Phenoli ....gr. viiss.
Eucalyptoli ....gtt. x.
Ol. gaultheriæ ....gtt. ij.
Carmini ....q. s. ad color.

M. ft. pulv.

For perspiring feet the following, used in conjunction with a warm foot bath of a weak solution of potassium permanganate, has been found very beneficial:

Potass. permangan ....℥iss.
Pulv. aluminis ....ʒj.
Pulv. cretæ gallicæ ....℥viss.
Zinci oxidi ....℥iiss.
Calcii hydrat. ....℥iiss.

M. ft. pulv.

CURE-ALL LINIMENT.

Sassafras oil ....℥iij.
Origanum oil ....℥iij.
Tincture of arnica ....℥ij.
Tincture of camphor ....℥ij.
Tincture of opium ....℥ij.
Tincture of valerian ....℥ij.
Tincture of guaiac ....℥i.
Ammonia water ....℥iss.
Chloroform ....℥ij.
Alcohol (95 per cent.) ....Cong. i.
Tincture of cochineal...............................q. s.

"LIQUID SMOKE."

Rectified spirit of tar...............................℥ij.
Alcohol ....℥iv.

Mix and add

Crude pyroligneous acid ....℥xx.

Shake well and filter through a filter wetted with the acid.

Directions: Let the meat dry well after salting, then apply the liquid smoke with a brush to one side of meat; let dry few hours and then apply to other side; after drying for few hours hang up for several days. Then repeat the process and in another week the meat is ready to be eaten.

CLOTHES CLEANSING BALLS.

I.

Pipe clay 16
Fuller's earth 2
Prepared chalk 2
White pepper 1
Ox-gall sufficient to make a paste.

Mix.

II.

Pipe clay 24
White pepper 1
Starch 1
Orris powder 1½
Ox-gall .... q. s.

Mix.

III.

Pipe clay 8
Bath brick 4
Pumice powder 1
Soft soap 1
Ox-gall .... q. s.

Mix.

BED BUG POISON.

Naphthol, crude ....℥ss.
Gasoline ....Oi.
Cedar oil ....℥i.

Shake well when using.

BAKING POWDER.

	Parts.
Sodium bicarbonate	2
Tartaric acid	1
Cream of tartar	1
Powdered Indian corn starch	4

Mix thoroughly and pass through a fine sieve.

Cream of Current Literature

A summary of the leading articles in contemporary pharmaceutical periodicals.

Red Cabbage as an Indicator.—According to *Union pharmaceutique*, April, 1906, a new indicator for titrating is furnished by red cabbage. Ordinary red cabbage is cut into minute pieces and is soaked in water, then boiled for a time and allowed to stand for a day. The extract is evaporated and dissolved in alcohol. This indicator turns red in the presence of acids and green in the presence of alkalies. A small amount of the indicator turns from red to green with a single drop of the decinormal solution of sodium hydrate. When the indicator is present in large quantity the neutral color is blue, but this disadvantage may be obviated by adding a few drops of a yellow color, such as tincture of saffron. The new indicator is not influenced by heat and can be used with artificial light.

Lactobacillin.—Metchnikoff *(Rousky Vratch*, March 18, 1906), recommends a pure culture of certain lactic acid bacteria for the manufacture of curdled milk which is used as an article of diet, especially for patients with diseases either of the intestines or kidneys. This ferment is marketed in sealed tubes in both liquid and powdered form. A sufficient amount of the ferment is added to boiled skimmed milk, which is allowed to stand in a warm place for a few hours to form the refreshing junket known in Russia as *próstokvásha* and in France as *lait caillé*. This soured milk prevents intestinal fermentation, improves digestion and promotes the action of the kidneys. As an article of diet it is recommended to persons who have grown tired of milk, and especially for the aged. Metchnikoff even goes so far as to say that persons who consume a sufficient quantity (a pint or more daily) of this food can avert in a measure the changes incident to old age. (See Lactoserve in New Remedies Price List.)

Hypodermic Injections of Veronal.—Guyot *(Répertoire de pharmacie*, April 10, 1906), found that by combining veronal with a solution of caustic soda he was able to produce a compound of sodium and veronal which had so slightly an alkaline reaction that it could be used for hypodermic administration, the more so because it was perfectly soluble in water. Hypodermic injections of veronal have been tried with success in patients who have become so used to taking the drug by mouth that it no longer produced the desired effect when thus administered. Ordinary solutions of veronal cannot be used for hypodermic injection for the drug is soluble in water only in the proportion of 1 in 145 parts. The formula employed by Guyot consisted of 2 Gm. of veronal; 20 drops of a solution of sodium hydrate, sp. gr. 1,032; and 10 Cc. of distilled water. Each Cc. of this solution corresponds to 0.20 Gm. of veronal.

It would seem, at first thought, that the caustic soda would prevent the employment of this solution for hypodermic injection, but it appears that the veronal combines with the sodium, so that the combination is very slightly alkaline. The resulting compound, veronal-sodium, was isolated by Guyot in the form of shining crystals very readily soluble in water. Compounds of veronal can also be obtained with ammonia and with piperazine.

A Color Reaction of Morphine.—Raduleско (*Bulletin de la Société des sciences de Bucharest*) describes a reaction of morphine which is applicable not only in the solution of this drug, but also in infusions containing this alkaloid, without any preliminary procedures. Exceedingly minute quantities of morphine may be readily detected with it. If a filtered solution of some colorless or slightly colored decoction containing an amount of morphine equal or superior to one part in 800,000 be treated with a crystal of sodium nitrate, and with enough of any acid to liberate the nitrous acid; and if when the effervescence ceases a concentrated alkali be added, a red color will appear, which varies in depth according to the concentration of the solution, from a pale pink to a dark red. The color disappears again when an acid is added. When small amounts of a very dilute solution are available the following method is used: Half a cubic centigramme of the solution is placed in a very small test tube. A fragment of sodium nitrite is added, and a single drop of glacial acetic acid dropped into the tube. One drop of concentrated solution of caustic potash is then added to neutralize the solution. This color reaction is characteristic for morphine and its salts and is not affected by the presence of organic matter. [This test should prove useful in determining the presence of morphine in complicated mixtures, for example, in proprietary medicines.—Ed.]—*Union pharmaceutique*, April, 1906, p. 159.

Cresol and Its Solutions.—C. S. N. Hallberg opened the discussion on this subject before the Section on Practical Pharmacy and Dispensing of the American Pharmaceutical Association (*Bulletin of the A. Ph. A.*, April 1, 1906), and gave an interesting account of the various preparations of cresol used for antiseptic purposes. The subject has of late received considerable attention in the pharmaceutical press on account of the introduction of a solution of cresol into U. S. P., viii. Cresol—or cresylic acid, as it was known—is contained in crude carbolic acid which is supposed to be made up of about equal parts of phenol and cresol. Owing to the sparing solubility of cresol in water it was difficult to use it as an antiseptic until a Hamburg firm made a watery solution of cresol in soap, calling it "creolin." The impure cresol which goes into this preparation and the resin soap which is used in the manufacture of creolin, produce a milky mixture with water. The next step was the manufacture of a solution of cresol which made a clearer solution with water, namely, lysol, which is said to be made with a soft soap. Since then the number of preparations of these two types has steadily increased. A difficulty in making preparations of cresol is the price of the product, which about a year ago was $2.25 a pound. A cresol which corresponds to the requirements of the Pharmacopœia as to specific gravity and boiling point is now made at Niagara Falls by the Schoellkopf, Hartford & Hanna Company, and is sold by the barrel at a reasonable figure.

Some Reactions of Veronal.—Guyot (*Répertoire de pharm.*, April 10, 1906), contributes an important study of the reactions of veronal to our knowledge of this hypnotic. Veronal or diethylbarbituric acid is a feeble acid which forms salts with alkalies, which have been obtained in crystalline form. The sodium salts of veronal crystallize in rhomboidal plates which rapidly lose their lustre and become covered with a white powder, as the result of the action of the carbonic acid of the air upon the sodium. Veronal, as we know, is soluble in alcohol, ether, chloroform and acetone. With mercuric sulphate a white precipitate is obtained with a watery solution of veronal or of sodium veronal. This reaction was discovered by Lemaire, who also found that veronal blackens calomel when the two are brought into contact, owing to the fact that a small amount of mercury is thus liberated. Veronal, as we know, is a compound of urea, and Guyot found that urea also reduces calomel.

Another reaction observed in a solution of veronal containing 1 part in 150, is the green color, which turns yellow, and which appears on the addition of one or two drops of tincture of iodine. Urea is decomposed by sodium hypobromite, forming nitrogen and carbonic acid. If veronal is decomposed by means of concentrated alkali and heat, this decomposition of urea may also be obtained and thus still another reaction is added to the list.

An interesting fact is that veronal is decomposed by the micrococcus ureæ, a germ which grows in the urine, decomposing it and producing the characteristic fermentation which occurs on standing. When this germ is added to solutions of veronal urea is formed, and the solution beomes more acid as the result of the liberation of diethylmalonic acid. If the action of the germ continues, ammonia is formed and the solution becomes alkaline.

Queries and Answers

We shall be glad, in this department, to respond to calls for information on all pharmaceutic matters.

Orders Difficult to Decipher.—From two esteemed subscribers we have received copies of orders received over the counter recently, and we present photographic reproductions

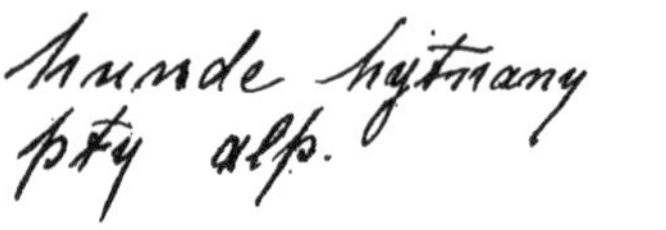

Fig. 1.

of them herewith. To the subscriber who sends the first correct interpretation of the order in Fig. 1. We will award a book to the value of $2, and to the subscriber from whom we receive

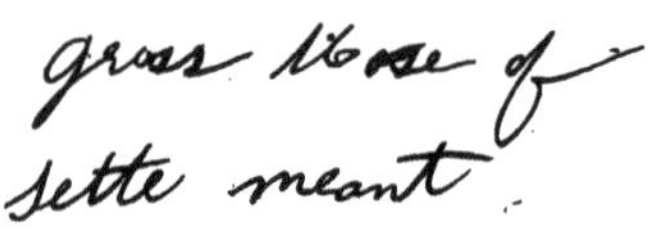

Fig. 2.

the first interpretation of the order in Fig. 2 one year's extension of his subscription for the AMERICAN DRUGGIST will be awarded.

Stamping Ink.—F. T. B. writes: "Please publish a formula for a stamping ink to use with a steel die. We have been trying to prepare such an ink for a customer who uses considerable of it, but the regular stamping inks do not seem to work well. The base should be oily, as the ink he is now using has the appearance of having an oily base. I have found it difficult to get a satisfactory color."

Oily stamp inks are in a class by themselves. The most satisfactory preparations are made according to the following formulas, which we take from MacEwan's "Pharmaceutical Formulas":

Blue.

I.

Ultramarine ....ʒv.
Olive oil ....℥xvj.

Reduce the ultramarine to an impalpable powder and mix with the olive oil.

II.

Paris blue ....ʒj.
Ultramarine ....ʒss.
Olive oil ....℥ix.

Mix the solids, and when reduced to an impalpable powder gradually add the olive oil, with constant stirring.

Green.

Verdigris ....ʒvj.
Oleic acid ....ʒj.
Olive oil ....℥viij.

Rub the verdigris to very fine powder, mix the oleic acid with it, and, after a few minutes, the olive oil.

Red.

Vermilion ....ʒiij.
Olive oil ....℥v.

Prepare as above.

Black.

Gas-black ....ʒiss.
Olive oil ....℥ix.

Prepare as above.

All these inks should be well shaken before pouring on the pad. Heavy petroleum oil may be used instead of olive oil.

The Deodorization of Benzin.—F. H.—Your query presupposes ignorance on your part of the contents of the latest revision of the United States Pharmacopœia. Under *Benzinum Purificatum*, page 69, a process is given for freeing benzin of its objectionable odor. A modified form of this process has already been printed in the AMERICAN DRUGGIST. It leaves the benzin with an ethereal or faint petroleum-like odor. If a perfumed benzin is desired, the following formula will be found satisfactory:

Benzin ....℥xx.
Oil of lavender............................♏l.
Potassium bichromate ....ʒi.
Sulphuric acid ....ʒi.
Water ....℥xx.

This is directed to be treated as follows: Dissolve the bichromate in the water, add the acid, and when the solution is cold shake up the benzin with it. Shake every hour during the day, allow to stand all night, decant the benzin, wash with a pint of water, and again decant; lastly, add the oil of lavender.

To Make a Chemical Globe.—B. D. C. asks how he can make a stalactite formation in a globe containing a liquid?

This effect can be produced by suspending a clean cut crystal of copper sulphate over a solution of potassium silicate so that the crystal will just touch the fluid. The solution of potassium silicate should have a density of 1.065. Within a few minutes after contact with the solution a hollow green column will drop from the crystal to the bottom of the globe. While copper sulphate gives the best results, ferrous, manganous or nickle sulphate may be used, with changes in the shape and, of course, in the color of the stalactites. The solution may be neutralized with sulphuric acid, hydrochloric acid, or acetic acid, and it is well to note that if the solution has a density less than 1.06 no growth will occur. The tubes or stalactites seem to be composed of silicon with a small proportion of the metal used.

Paper Bottles for Milk.—Dr. W. A. B., Philadelphia, writes: "In answer to G. B., Italy, who makes inquiry concerning paper milk bottles, I would advise that all information concerning these bottles, which are O. K., can be obtained from Mr. Heyl, president, the Union Paper Cap Company, 3951 Market street, Philadelphia."

Quantitative Estimation of Chloral Hydrate.—A number of methods have been recommended for the estimation of chloral hydrate in solutions, but all of them give only approximate results. Wallis (*Pharmaceutical Journal*, 1906, Vol. 1, page 162) recommends a process based on the transformation of the entire amount of chloral into sodium chloride by the action of sodium hydrate and heat, which is said to be very active. One gramme of chloral hydrate corresponds to 18.27 Cc. of a decinormal solution of silver nitrate. The test is carried on as follows: 0.1 Gm. of chloral hydrate is dissolved in 10 Cc. of alcohol, and to this is added 10 Cc. of normal sodium hydrate. The mixture is heated on a water bath for three hours in a well-stoppered flask, which is preferably closed by means of a rubber stopper held in place with a cork. The resulting combination is accurately neutralized with normal sulphuric acid, and the neutral solution is titrated with a decinormal solution of silver nitrate.

CONDUCTED BY FRANK FARRINGTON.

Under this head will appear suggestions and plans for increasing trade, advertising experiences, information, and notes of interest useful to the pharmacist in the preparation of his advertising matter. Specimens of current advertising will be reproduced, with suggestive analysis and criticism, and queries relative to advertising matters will be answered. To avoid delay address communications to Department of Business Building, AMERICAN DRUGGIST, 66 West Broadway, New York.

THE STORE'S INFLUENCE.

For the druggist seeking a spot in which to locate a store there is more than simply to find an empty store in the right neighborhood and then to stock it up with so many dollars' worth of goods. After the choice of a location is made, whether for a new store or for a removal, there is much to be considered in regard to the shape, size and internal arrangement of the premises.

Most druggists know the sort and size of stock that must be carried, and also know the amount of room it will take and what kind of an arrangement is best suited to the purpose. It is important to get near to actual requirements in the first place and thus avoid the necessity for future changes with the hope of making things more convenient.

The store should fit the stock. The stock should fit the store. A $3,000 stock in a hole-in-the-wall sort of a drug store is likely to make a place look like a junk shop. A $1,000 stock in a mirrored, pretentious, plate-glass pharmacy would make it look like one pill in a box. It would be a lonesome and dismal place to repel anybody.

It is difficult to make a crowded store look neat and clean. A store that does not look neat and clean cannot hope to succeed. An almost empty store can be made to look clean, but who wants to trade at a store where they don't have any goods to sell?

To the druggist already located and doing business at a satisfactory stand, the consideration of the above principles may be of use in leading him to consider whether his present conditions are satisfactory. Are the inside arrangement and make-up of the store such as will yield the best results?

In the first place, is the finish of the wood work of a light and clean color? White or very light paint makes a decidedly more cheerful looking store, and, as for keeping the paint clean, unless there is an unusual amount of gingerbread work in the way of trimmings, etc., it should not be a difficult matter to apply a fresh coat of paint as often as the old one gets dull. Keep it scrubbed clean as long as possible, and when that gets to be a difficult matter, paint it over. Paint is cheap and can be put on without stopping business. It makes business better as soon as it is on.

If part of the walls or of the ceiling is papered, have the paper renewed as often as it gets dull and dirty. It is some trouble to put on new paper, but it is worth while.

Every merchant ought to walk into his store once a week or oftener with the eye of a stranger and notice how the paint and the wood work look. It will do no harm if he looks at other things as well with the unbiased eye. A man gets so used to the appearance of his own store that he does not notice the soiled paint and the fly-specked wall paper.

The floor must be of some kind of material that will be easily mopped clean or scrubbed when too dirty. An oiled floor is the terror of all women whose gowns touch it, for it makes clothes absolutely filthy whenever oil touches. If a tile floor is not wanted, hardwood can be used. Maple makes about as satisfactory a floor as any. It wears forever and is not as slippery as certain other woods. It does not sliver up. It is easily cleaned.

With the store kept well painted and papered inside and out, it is made attractive to womankind to quite an extent, for there is inherent in every feminine breast a liking for bright cleanliness. Add to that a clean floor, and a good setting for the goods displayed is at once made.

A dark store is an unpleasant place to enter, and it is a store that will not show the goods. There should be light enough to show everything that is on exhibition, so that any goods that are kept in sight can be seen and their appearance considered without having to take them out on the front steps.

What a difference between the store where the goods stand out on the shelves, the glassware brilliant, scintillating—and the store where it is just possible to distinguish the packages on the shelves and where you can only see the back of the store by the slight reflected light in the mirror or the prescription case! It doesn't take a man with a very keen intellect to see the advantages of a light store. Why is it then that so many are dark? Lots of stores that take pains to make everything particularly light at night go through the day with awning darkened windows through which there comes scarcely enough light by which to count money.

Another thing that needs to be let into a store besides light is air. With oxygenless air the whole force is liable to get sleepy and groggy, and customers will be greeted and served in a way that will prevent them from buying anything more than what they absolutely need. The sales force cannot be speeded up on devitalized air.

In the summer season there is no lack of air in the store, but while enjoying the open weather it is just as well to consider ways in which the store can be made more habitable for the winter. In times of peace prepare for war.

The floor case is the best display furniture at the druggist's command. Of course, thousands of drug stores have them already. The druggist who is behind the times will find that with the old-fashioned cases he is not only failing to sell a lot of goods that he could sell if he showed them, but is losing trade by letting people think that some one else is a more progressive man. If the money to equip the store properly is not available it should be borrowed.

If there isn't room in the store for a surplus stock of goods without taking up space that ought to be given over to the things that will sell better for being right in sight, a nearby cellar or loft that will give store room should be rented. The druggist can't afford to fill up valuable space with surplus original cases and other more or less unsightly packages.

The part of the selling room that is open and visible to customers ought to be kept in attactive condition and entirely devoted to the display of the things in demand—the things that people buy faster for seeing them.

For making goods sell there is nothing like keeping them where they will be seen. Hundreds of times customers say, "Oh, yes, I see you have so-and-so. I will take some of that, but I wouldn't have thought of it if I hadn't seen it." The goods themselves are a constant reminder to any one who comes in. They are more than that; they show visitors what the things look like that have been advertised in the newspapers.

Showing the goods helps sell them by reminding people, by showing them what they are like and by creating in them a desire. To make them do the most work in the last named way, the goods must be made to look as attractive as possible. That means clever arrangement of the articles themselves and a good setting for them. The goods come to the druggist looking as well as those particular goods can look. It is up to him to make the setting one that will add to the attractiveness of the stock and then arrange it to add all that is possible to that.

With a too small store, one that will not hold enough stock to enable the druggist to supply the demands of the neighborhood without narrowing the items down to a twelfth of a dozen or so each, he is not in a position to do any business at all, beyond supplying a few first calls. Better a store a little too large than one at all too small.

A store of regular shape inside is most desirable, but the most irregular shape obtainable would be better than too little room.

THE PROPRIETARY ASSOCIATION OF AMERICA.

Twenty-fourth Annual Meeting—Promises of Cordial Support for the N. A. R. D.—Resolutions Approving of the Direct Contract and Serial Numbering Plan—News of the Government Action Against the Drug Trust Received with Equanimity.

By their action in passing two resolutions whereby they agreed to grant the requests of both wholesale and retail drug interests throughout the country the members of the Proprietary Association of America, who held their twenty-fourth annual convention in the Hotel Astor, in this city, on May 8, 9 and 10, showed that they appreciated and wished to continue the friendly relationship between themselves and the two branches of the trade through which they market their products. In several other ways, moreover, the Proprietary Association expressed its gratitude to the wholesalers and retailers alike for their arduous labors in opposing all legislation hostile to the interests of the manufacturers.

In the resultion favoring the wholesale drug trade the Proprietary Association recommended that the members confine their sales at best discounts to the legitimate wholesale drug distributers; refuse to make similar concessions to large retail or catalogue houses, and also recognize all just claims for breakage, and in the resolution benefiting the retailers the committee urged upon the members of the association the necessity for adhering strictly to wholesale prices on the basis of $2, $4 and $8 a dozen for goods to retail at 25c., 50c. and $1 per package or bottle, and for maintaining the Direct Contract and Serial Numbering Plan.

The annual election resulted, with one or two exceptions, in the re-election of the officers and members of the Executive Committee which have served the association so faithfully throughout the past year. The Orrine Company of Washington, D. C., was elected a member of the organization, and the resignation of one member was accepted.

The meeting was opened with the usual congratulatory interchange of greetings between the different branches of the trade, in the Pompeiian room of the Hotel Astor, in this city, on Tuesday morning, May 8. The president, Frank J. Cheney, of Toledo, opened the proceedings by the introduction of delegates from the N. W. D. A. Albert Plaut, of New York, speaking as chairman of the association, assured the proprietors of the cordial co-operation and good will of the wholesale trade and expressed a hope for a still closer agreement upon various lines of policy between the two branches. W. P. Ritchey made a few remarks in a similar vein, and Frank E. Holliday vice-chairman of the Committee on Proprietary Goods, said that he might take occasion at a later date to address the members on a purely business interest. William H. Gove, president of the Lydia E. Pinkham Medicine Company, made a suitable response on behalf of the Proprietary Association.

THE RETAILER'S POINT OF VIEW.

Charles A. Rehfuss, of Philadelphia, made a few remarks on behalf of the delegation from the N. A. R. D., followed by J. C. Gallagher, of Jersey City, who read a formal address on behalf of the retail association. In this address Mr. Gallagher gave assurance of the good will which existed for the proprietors on behalf of the retailers, and expressed a hope that this meeting would prove a particularly successful one. The identity of interests between proprietor and the retailer was pointed out and the hope expressed that any criticism that might be offered would be taken in the friendly spirit in which it was conceived. Mr. Gallagher said that the N. A. R. D. had "nothing in common with those representatives of the manufacturing interests who want only to take advantage of the ignorance, the gullibility and the immorality of the people. We take it that the Proprietary Association does not represent that class of manufacturer, except in so far as it has been unable as yet to purge itself of their unwanted and contaminating presence." Referring to the campaign against proprietary medicines Mr. Gallagher said:

THE AGITATION AGAINST PROPRIETARY MEDICINES.

Since the last annual meeting of your association a great deal has been said in the magazines and elsewhere regarding the doubtful, not to say pernicious, practices to which some proprietary manufacturers have resorted in order to create and to maintain a demand for their preparations. Coming into immediate personal contact with the consumer, as our people do, these criticisms have been poured into our ears many times, and the members of our associations, along with the other druggists of our country, have often been compelled to declare themselves as being opposed to the methods to which we have referred. As good citizens we could do nothing less than to take our places on the side of right, and inasmuch as right has not always been with the proprietors, but, on the contrary, has frequently been with their censors, we druggists have learned what we never before fully realized—the seriousness of the proprietary medicine situation, the hurtful character of the methods that have been employed by some proprietors, and the extent to which these proprietors have carried their extremely questionable practices.

We have but little patience with the hysterical outcry against all proprietary medicines which contain alcohol or which embody other agents, the excessive use of which or the long continued use of which, tend to debauch the public but the moderate and sane use of which is only helpful. On the contrary, we have the keenest sympathy with the criticism which differentiates between deserving and undeserving proprietaries, between those whose manufacturers make reasonable claims for them and those preparations the makers of which deliberately attempt to deceive the public and to profit by their blind confidence. It is because we believe your organization represents those manufacturers who want to deal justly by the afflicted that we have year after year sent delegates to your annual meetings.

THE LEGAL REGULATION OF THE PROPRIETARY MEDICINE TRAFFIC.

During the past year efforts have been made in a number of Legislatures to pass laws regulating the sale of medicines, which proposed laws we believed would be injurious alike to our own members who manufacture household remedies and to the proprietary manufacturers. Such bills as imposed unreasonable restrictions upon the makers of ready-to-take medicines, or the effect of which would have been to hamper those druggists and manufacturers to the use of whose preparations no reasonable objection could be made, have been opposed by us. For the most part these measures have been proposed and championed by those who know nothing of the drug business and extremely little, if anything, of the manufacturing of medicines, otherwise some of the provisions upon which they have strenuously insisted would never have been thought of. While we have opposed and shall continue to oppose measures that needlessly hamper druggists or other manufacturers without any compensating advantage to the public, we have not in the past nor do we intend hereafter to oppose the passage of bills that do in reality safeguard the welfare of the public, preventing, as is expected of them, the use of habit-producing drugs and the debauchment of the public by unscrupulous men who shamelessly ignore all other considerations than those of sordid personal gain.

THE CHICAGO CONFERENCE BILLS.

During the past winter a delegation representing our association conferred in Chicago with certain representatives of your organization and of the American Pharmaceutical Association in relation to provisions which may be embodied in pharmacy laws without disadvantage to the public, to the retail drug trade or to the proprietors, but, on the contrary, to the advantage of all interests. It is the intention of our association to favor, wherever changes are to be made in the pharmacy laws of the various States, the provisions of the bill which was the outcome of that conference, the essential features of which, as we understand it, have been embodied in the law recently passed by Congress for the District of Columbia. To the extent that the public welfare demands further restrictions than those which are imposed by that measure we stand ready to assist in making the needed changes.

Mr. Gallagher admitted that the average druggist had been accustomed to sell proprietary medicines as mere merchandise, not concerning himself with the intrinsic value of the preparation or with the truth or falsity of the claims made for it. He said that this condition of affairs was not wholly creditable to the retail drug trade, and he believed that hereafter the trade must take cognizance of the advertising claims that are made by the manufacturers and act in accordance with what they believed to be the best interests of their patrons.

Mr. Gallagher said that taking the entire country as a basis, the cost of doing a retail business amounts to 25 per cent. of the gross receipts. If the cost of proprietaries is higher than $2, $4, and $8, respectively, for the three sizes, the druggist cannot make any profit whatever in handling them, and for that reason the retailers again appeared before the proprietors, urging a reduction of the wholesale price to $2, $4, and $8, respectively, per dozen, or less.

THE DIRECT CONTRACT SERIAL NUMBERING PLAN.

Mr. Gallagher pointed out that the weak point in most of the plans for the betterment of the price conditions lay in the fact that they depended upon the good faith of the several branches of the trade, and experience had demonstrated that this could not be uniformly reckoned upon. Experience had further shown that the only safe method for insuring the maintenance of prices was the adoption of the direct contract between the retailer and the wholesaler. The serial numbering of goods was an essential element of the plan, and offered the only means of detecting violations. The animus of the cutter in the matter of substitution was pointed out, and the fact accentuated that the profit of the cutter lay in his substitutions. In regard to the working of the plan, Mr. Gallagher said:

Not only is the plan effective in preventing price demoralization, its legality has been sustained by a number of sweeping court decisions. So numerous and so powerful are the arguments in favor of this plan that the retail druggists of the country are beginning to suspect the sincerity of those proprietors who do not adopt it and yet profess to be genuine friends of the price-maintaining retailer. There are throughout the country many thousands of druggists who say, "The proprietors know how the selling price of their articles can be protected, the means to that end are easily within their reach; if they do not adopt these means why should we give their preparations any consideration?"

While Mr. Gallagher realized the fact that the association could not obligate its members to any concerted course of action, he urged the adoption of two resolutions, one bringing the favorable consideration of the association to the desirability of reducing the wholesale prices of their preparations to a basis which will yield a living profit to the retailer, and another recommending the adoption of the direct serial numbering plan, which would insure the selling of the goods at the stipulated price.

J. Diner, of New York; S. L. Hilton, of Washington, D. C., and T. H. Potts, of Philadelphia, also made brief addresses on behalf of the N. A. R. D.

J. W. Kennedy, of the E. C. DeWitt Company, Chicago, chairman of the Committee on Legislation, responded, assuring the retailers of the desire of the association to comply as far as possible with the wishes expressed in the addresses. Mr. Kennedy moved that the discussion of this proposition be made a special order of business at 2 o'clock on Wednesday afternoon. A. H. Beardsley, of the Dr. Miles Medical Company, moved as an amendment that a committee be appointed to confer with the retailer, which was agreed to.

David Watson, president of the Proprietary Articles' Trade Association of Canada, made a brief address on the Canadian situation, devoting the major portion of his remarks to the legislative phase of the proprietary medicine situation. He reviewed in detail the legislation which had been proposed in Canada during the last year, and spoke of the difficulties that had confronted the Legislative Committee in their efforts to prevent the enactment of unfavorable legislation. He referred to the expense involved in such a way as to create what he afterward pointed out was a wholly erroneous impression, for he later gave the most positive assurance that while the sums expended were considerable, they had been expended only in legitimate channels, and that not one cent had been used for corruption.

D. M. Newbro, of the Herpicide Company, responded on behalf of the association.

MEXICO HEARD FROM.

Juan Reichman, of Monterey, Mexico, proprietor of the establishment of Edward Bremer & Co., was extended the privileges of the floor and, speaking on behalf of the pharmacists of Mexico, he outlined the opportunities for American trade which existed in that republic and urged his hearers to study the whole question of export. He was responded to by F. W. Schumacher, of the Peruna Drug Manufacturing Company.

LOCAL RETAILERS APPEAR.

The Metropolitan Association of Retail Druggists was represented by A. Clayton Searles, who acted as spokesman of the delegation; A. B. Baltzly and Peter Diamond, who also represented the New York Retail Druggists' Association.

W. S. Douglas, of the Douglas Manufacturing Company, responded to Mr. Searles on behalf of the proprietors, and after a few remarks from Mr. Cheney, the president of the association, concerning an explanation of the misrepresentation which had been created by Mr. Watson's remarks concerning the expenditure of money, and a vigorous statement of the case by Mr. Watson denying absolutely the expenditure of any money for corrupt purposes, the session was adjourned.

The afternoon was devoted to an executive session, during which a committee was appointed to confer with the retailers. The report of the treasurer showed a favorable balance and the report of the secretary showed a membership of 257.

The joint committee, which met with the retailers in executive session on Wednesday morning, was composed of the following members: A. H. Beardsley, of the Dr. Miles Medical Company; Ira B. Clark, of the Paris Medicine Company; A. H. Kennedy, of the Charles N. Crittenton Company; W. H. Gove, of the Lydia E. Pinkham Medicine Company; A. C. Meyer, of A. C. Meyer & Co., and J. W. Kennedy, chairman, of E. C. De Witt & Co. The entire delegation of retailers discussed with this committee the recommendation contained in the address of Mr. Gallagher, and after various tentative resolutions had been drafted the phraseology was altered to suit all concerned and the resolutions adopted, to be submitted to a later session of the general association.

The Wednesday morning session was also executive in character and consisted of a conference with the delegates of the N. W. D. A., who presented their claims for a pledge from the proprietors that they would hereafter give their best terms only to the recognized wholesale distributers. The assurance was given on Thursday morning to the wholesalers in the form of a resolution, which read as follows:

Resolved, That the Proprietary Association of America recommends to its members that they confine their sales at best discounts to the legitimate wholesale drug distributers and that they recognise all just claims for breakage.

This resolution, which was drafted and proposed by A. H. Beardsley, H. B. Foley and A. C. Meyer, the special committee appointed by President Cheney to this duty, was unanimously passed by the delegates.

At the session held Wednesday afternoon a conference was held with the N. A. R. D. representatives on the adoption of the $2, $4 and $8 wholesale price basis and also on the D. C. S. N. plan. The resolution adopted by the proprietors' committee read in part as follows:

Resolved, That the maintenance of cordial relations between the manufacturers and retail druggists is of highest importance, and that we earnestly recommend to our members to study and seriously consider the means of bringing about the cordial and hearty co-operation so much to be desired, and we especially urge the consideration of the request of the retail druggists in regard to the $2, $4 and $8 wholesale prices of proprietary goods and the benefits to be derived therefrom, and we earnestly commend to every proprietor the consideration of the adoption of the direct contract and serial numbering plan as the most effective means of saving the retail druggist from the injury and disaster caused by the cut-rate evil.

This resolution was also passed by the association.

At the session held Thursday morning the Committee on Nominations, consisting of E. C. DeWitt, chairman; D. M. Newboro, A. H. Beardsley, Harry H. Good, W. H. Gove, O. E. Foster and W. A. Talbott, reported unanimously the following candidates, who were elected by a unanimous vote: Frank J. Cheney, of Toledo, O., president; John W. Kennedy, of Chicago, vice-president; A. H. Beardsley, of Elkhart, Ind., second vice-president; Orient C. Pinkney, of New York, secretary, and W. S. Douglas, of New York, treasurer. The following members were chosen for the Executive Committee: H. H. Good, of this city; Joseph F. Hines, of Baltimore; William H. Gove, of Lynn, Mass.; H. E. Bucklen, of Chicago; R. R. Land, of Binghamton, N. Y., and D. M. Newboro, of Detroit, Mich.

Among those who were registered as being in attendance we note the following names:

REGISTER OF ATTENDANCE.

William H. Gove and Arthur W. Pinkham, Lydia E. Pinkham Medicine Company; Lester H. Green, Green Syrup of Tar; O. Merrill, Dr. B. J. Kendall Company; Nicholas Newlin, George B. Evans; Geo. L. Douglass and C. H. McLean, the Dr. J. H. McLean Drug Company; T. W. Schumacher, Peruna Drug Manufacturing Company; David Watson, Kerry Watson & Co.; W. R. Davidson, Viavi Company; A. H. Beardsley, Dr. Miles Medical Company; W. E. Weiss, the J. W. James Company; E. H. Parker, Foley Medicine Company; D. M. D. Newbro, the Herpicide Company; H. B. Foley, Foley & Co.; W. A. Talbott, Micajah & Co.; A. F. Moore, Pepsin Syrup Company; Edward P. Vail, Dr. Peter Fahrner & Son Company; N. H. Evans, the Evans Chemical Company; James Sharp, Eastern Viavi Company; E. K. Hyde, the Yucca Company; E. P. Merty, the Orrine Company; Benj. Weir, Chattanooga Med. Company; John W. Kennedy, E. C. DeWitt & Co.; F. E. Holliday, New York; John H. Bell, the Hostetter Company; E. C. De Witt, E. C. DeWitt & Co.; E. T. Kemp, Chicago; D. T. Mathers, G. G. Green, Woodbury, N. J.; Charles Benji, Kickapoo Med. Company; Edward J. Schall, Meyer Bros. Drug Company; A. G. Pike, J. J. Pike & Co., Chelsea Sta., Boston; W. S. Douglass, Douglass Manufacturing Company; C. J. Searles, the Athlophoros Company, New Haven; Wm. Hardham, Philo Hay Specialty Company; Chas. Alcott, E. E. Southerland Med. Company, Paducah, Ky.; J. F. Hiscox, Hiscox Chemical Works; Chas. H. Thayer, Ripans Chemical Company; Wm. V. Carlin, Wright's Indian Vegetable Pills Company; Robt. A. Brown, Lyman Bros.; W. H. Comstock, Norristown, N. Y.; W. P. Ritchey, New York; H. H. Good, Carter Med. Company; H. Poliff Planten, H. Planten & Son; Ira M. Clarke, Paul Med. Company; Albin L. Page, Vapo Cresoline Company; A. L. Jaros, Mariani & Co.; Lee M. Evans, Jno. C. Gallegher and John A. Yakel, Kohler Manufacturing Company; Frank J. Cheney, Cheney Medicine Company; Orient C. Pinckney, Himrod; W. Holloway, Johnston Holloway & Co.; O. E. Foster, Foster-Milburn Company; A. C. Myers, Myers & Co., Baltimore; A. H. Kennedy, Chas. N. Crittenton Company; P. J. Brady, Cleveland; H. M. Clarke, M. M. Fenners & Co.; E. Robert Kopp, Mrs. J. A. Kopp; J. Nelson Clark, McNeil Med. Company, Harrisburg, Pa.; C. G. Panter, Garfield Tea Company, Brooklyn; R. J. Peltert, Van Stan's Stratena; E. L. Andrews, Andrews Manufacturing Company, Bristow, Tenn.; Gilbert F. Kennedy, Dr. David Kein & Son.

TRIPARTITE PLAN IN PERIL.

Government Starts Injunction Proceedings Against Parties to Tripartite Agreement.

On May 9 Attorney General Moody announced that the Government had filed in the United States Circuit Court for the District of Indiana a petition for an injunction against the associations which are parties to the tripartite agreement for the regulation of the selling price of proprietary medicines. The text of the statement made public by the Attorney General follows:

The Government has to-day filed in the Circuit Court of the United States for the District of Indiana a petition for an injunction against certain associations, corporations and individuals comprising what is commonly known as the "Drug Trust of the United States." The parties defendant specifically named in the bill have voluntarily combined together to control the prices at which proprietary medicines and drugs shall be sold to the consumer through the retail druggists, in violation of the Sherman Anti-Trust law. The parties to the combination include the Proprietary Association of America, the National Wholesale Druggists' Association and the National Association of Retail Druggists.

Each of these three associations has officers who are charged with the transaction of the business of the respective associations. These officers are made parties defendant to the suit, as well as certain other individuals, firms and corporations who are members of the respective associations.

The bill charges in substance that these associations, their officers, delegates and members are duly engaged in a common undertaking, to wit, the business of manufacturing, buying and selling patent medicines and drugs and proprietary articles throughout the United States; that these associations and the members thereof have entered into a conspiracy to arbitrarily fix and regulate the price at which such articles shall be sold to the consumer, and that they have established rules and regulations to enforce such an unlawful agreement by restricting the purchase and sale of such commodities to those members of the several associations who shall live up to and observe the rules and regulations thus arbitrarily prescribed by the respective associations.

There is but one ultimate object of the conspiracy, viz., to fix the price which shall be observed by all retail druggists in selling to the consumer the various commodities manufactured by the several members of the Proprietary Association. The plan by which such object is effected is in brief as follows:

"No retail druggist can obtain goods from a wholesale druggist or a manufacturer of a proprietary medicine unless such retail druggist becomes a member of the National Association of Retail Druggists, and in order to become such member he must agree to observe the established price at which such proprietary medicines shall be sold to the consumer. If such retail druggist after becoming a member of the National Association of Retail Druggists cuts prices in the sale of such articles to the consumer he is immediately placed upon the list of what is known as "aggressive cutters," and thereafter such retail druggist is unable to obtain from any manufacturer who is a member of the Proprietary Association, or from any other wholesale druggist who is a member of the Wholesale Druggists' Association, any of the commodities which may be manufactured and sold by them or any of them.

"Henry W. Loder, of Philadelphia, recently brought suit in the United States Circuit Court for the Eastern District of Pennsylvania, under section 7 of the Sherman Anti-Trust act, against these three associations. The evidence produced upon the trial, for the purpose of showing the existence of a conspiracy, established a case substantially the same as that charged in the Government's bill. Judge Holland, before whom that case was tried, in his charge to the jury, held that such evidence was sufficient to show a combination in restraint of trade within the meaning of the first section of the Federal Anti-Trust act.

"The plaintiff obtained a substantial verdict. The court pointed out that the evidence showed a conspiracy between several manufacturers to fix the price of their manufactured articles to wholesalers, and a conspiracy among the wholesalers inter se and with the manufacturers to fix the price at which they should sell to retail dealers, and a conspiracy among the retail dealers inter se and with the wholesale druggists and manufacturers to fix and maintain prices which such retail dealers should observe in making sales to the general public—that is, to the consumer.

"For several months prior to the trial of the Loder case in Philadelphia the Department of Justice had been engaged in the investigation of this conspiracy. The Attorney General having reached the conclusion that the combination is one prohibited by the terms of the Sherman Anti-Trust act, has directed the district attorney for the District of Indiana to file this bill. An injunction is prayed for prohibiting these associations from acting in concert for the purpose of maintaining prices, and the individuals, firms and corporations who are members of the respective associations from acting together for the purpose of maintaining uniform prices to the consumers throughout the United States."

Views of Those Interested.

When Frank J. Cheney, president of the Proprietary Association, was interviewed at the meeting of the Proprietary Association in regard to the announcement by the Attorney General he said: "Our organization has nothing whatever to fear from this threatened action, for there is no truth in the statements contained in the report. Further than emphatically denying the truth of the charges as outlined, there is nothing more that I can say."

George L. Douglass, counsel for the Proprietary Association, expressed himself as follows: "This association is not in any sense a combination to control prices; neither has it ever fixed them high or low. Before we can state what action we may take we will, of course, have to find out just what allegations the bill of complaint contains. The matter, however, is not one to cause us much concern."

Thomas V. Wooten, Chicago, the secretary of the National Association of Retail Druggists, when informed of the action taken by the Attorney General, said to a representative of the AMERICAN DRUGGIST: "We are entirely unterrified by the Attorney General's action. We have nothing to conceal and the Government is welcome to all information regarding our methods. We are not enemies of society. Our whole aim is to maintain the drug business as an honorable calling. We are trying to prevent the selling of cheap drugs and the substitutions that are sometimes made when the business is unprofitable and the retailer impoverished. We feel that whatever we do to prevent sales at ruinous prices is to the best interest of the public. If we have committed an illegal act in trying to protect the honor of the calling, then the sooner we find it out the better, for we want to get on a sound footing as soon as possible. But at present we do not admit that there is anything illegal in our plan. The Government knows our objects, for these are printed openly. We do not fear the outcome of this suit, as we are confident of the justice and correctness of our methods, as far as the public is concerned. We doubt if the present action will prove formidable. The direct contract plan is again brought up. That has already been adjudicated, a number of decisions favoring that plan having been handed down."

A. H. Beardsley, of Elkhart, Ind., newly elected second vice-president of the Proprietary Association, when questioned about the attitude of that organization toward the Attorney General's action said:

"It is only a waste of time to consider the groundless charges made in this petition now before the United States Circuit Court in Indiana. Every one knows that the Proprietary Association has never entered into any combination to control prices or fix them at any level. The manufacturer of a proprietary remedy, like the holder of a patent, has a right to sell arbitrarily his product wherever and at whatever price he likes, and it has been my experience that this is just what the proprietary medicine manufacturer does. The Proprietary Association will not take any action in the matter unless some further step is taken by the Attorney General, in which event, however, it is prepared to fight for its rights."

H. B. Foley, a prominent member of the Proprietary Association, said:

"The association will not notice the Attorney General's action in any way. The statements contained in the petition are false and deserve derision rather than serious consideration. We are not worrying about the matter."

George L. Douglas, counsel for the Proprietary Association, said:

"I can see no reason for the assertion that the Proprietary Association constitutes in any sense a combination to fix prices high or low. I will have to see the bill of complaint, however, before I can say positively whether the association will adopt any course to rebut its allegations."

AS VIEWED BY THE N. W. D. A.

Clayton F. Shoemaker, of Philadelphia, formerly president of the National Wholesale Druggists' Association, said to our Philadelphia representative: "The action of the Attorney General in regard to the 'drug trust,' so called, is unwise and uncalled for, because utterly inappropriate. The object of a trust is to protect the few at the expense of the many. The object of the work done by drug associations is to protect the many from the greed and rapacity of the few. The bill of information filed by the Attorney General is almost a verbatim copy of a part of the plaintiff's brief in the Loder case. This is humiliating. The bill claims that the object of the so-called drug trust is to restrict the purchase and sale of articles in our line to members of the several associations. This, as well as other statements made in the bill, is absolutely untrue. When the power of our Government is used as a lever to back up a private prosecution it seems to me that it is time for us to consider where we are drifting."

A LEGAL OPINION.

Edward J. Newell, of 50 Pine street, New York, an attorney who has heretofore represented large drug interests in litigation in the United States courts, said to a representative of the AMERICAN DRUGGIST, who asked him for an expression of his opinion regarding the announcement of the Attorney General:

"The essence of the 'Sherman Antitrust law,' under which the suit is brought, lies in the first section of the act, which reads: "Every contract, combination in the form of a trust or otherwise, or conspiracy, or restraint of trade or commerce among the several States or with foreign nations, is hereby declared to be illegal." The subsequent sections of the law deal with the punishment to be inflicted for violating the first section, the procedure to obtain convictions and the civil remedies of those injured by such violations.

"Whether or not the great drug associations named by the Attorney General in his petition for an injunction, filed on the 9th inst. in the United States Circuit Court for the District of Indiana, are guilty is simply a question of fact. To succeed in its prosecution the Government must prove that there is some agreement, or even some secret understanding actually carried into effect, between the associations or their members, which has for its object the control of prices of drugs or medicines sold in the drug stores of the several States, or which aims in some way to limit the freedom of druggists to sell goods in such quantities, at such prices and to such persons as they may desire. Whether the associations are incorporated or not cuts no figure. All the members of an unincorporated association who take part in or who passively assent to and permit themselves to be bound by any such agreement or understanding fall within the law.

"There must, however, be two or more persons or corporations acting under the agreement to constitute it such a "contract" or "combination" as is intended by the law. What is perfectly lawful for one individual to do may be unlawful for two or more to combine to do. Any proprietor or wholesaler may make such terms regarding the sale of his own wares as may suit his fancy. But if he brings another into combination with him (his employees and agents, of course, excepted) in an effort to direct, control or limit any part of the business of tradesmen or merchants throughout the country generally, or in certain States, that act constitutes an illegal combination or conspiracy, and may be enjoined and punished, and any individual who suffers loss thereby may recover treble damages, besides the reasonable expense of the legal proceedings.

DETAILED REPORT ON SAN FRANCISCO LOSSES.

Ninety Per Cent. of Manufacturing, Wholesale and Retail Drug Business in That City Destroyed—Six Pharmacists Killed and at Least Two Injured—Proprietary Houses Tell How Much They Suffered and Where They Are Now Located.

As more detailed and complete dispatches and letters are received from the manufacturing, wholesale and retail drug trade of San Francisco and other towns on the Pacific Coast, the magnitude and extent of the losses suffered by the drug interests on the Pacific Coast is beginning to be appreciated. A special telegram received by the AMERICAN DRUGGIST from our regular correspondent just as this issue was going to press, summarizes the frightful results of the catastrophe as follows:

> No less than 90 per cent. of the drug business in San Francisco and almost all of the drug properties in Santa Rosa have been totally destroyed. In San Francisco three prominent retail druggists, Abraham Levin, of the German Druggists' Benevolent Society; L. J. Hicks and Dr. T. F. Bacon, were killed, while in Santa Rosa an equal number, including Harry F. Newman, M. H. Digman and Al Truggen, died as the result of injuries received during the seismic disturbance and fire.
>
> At 'Frisco the injured include Aug. Zeig, chief chemist of the National Pharmacy Company, and at Santa Rosa F. S. Gray was also seriously injured. A brief résumé of the losses sustained involves that of the Langley, Michaels Company, wholesalers, $300,000, of which $200,000 is covered by insurance; that of Redington & Co., wholesalers, $350,000, of which $330,000 is covered by insurance; that of Mack & Co., a complete loss, which has rendered the firm unwilling to continue in the drug business and induced it to engage in the oil trade.

Our San Francisco correspondent states in an earlier letter that more than three-quarters of the entire wholesale and retail drug business of San Francisco has been wholly ruined. The wholesale and retail druggists throughout the city, the special correspondent says, "responded liberally to the appeals of the emergency hospitals for bandages, stimulants and other supplies. As soon as it became apparent that their places of business would be destroyed by the flames, Redington & Co. opened its doors to the hospitals so that they could secure all the supplies they needed temporarily, and other wholesalers and retailers quickly followed this example.

WHOLESALERS ALL WIPED OUT.

"As most of the wholesalers were situated in the business district where the fire commenced, their places of business were soon consumed. Three-quarters of the retail drug stores were reduced to ashes, including the best equipped and handsomest pharmacies on the Pacific Coast. The druggists whose stores were not destroyed assisted the sufferers by filling prescriptions for them and attending to the injured. The few druggists who would otherwise have been able to continue in business, could not secure supplies to replenish their rapidly depleted stocks for many days. The Department of Pharmacy of the University of California, fortunately, was not touched by the flames and suffered only slightly from the effects of the earthquake. Most of the records and stock of the Alumni Association, which were in the hands of Secretary Musante, were destroyed, but Prof. William M. Searby, dean of the college, whose store was destroyed by fire, saved most of his records by removing them to Berkeley, Cal. The department of pharmacy connected with the College of Physicians and Surgeons was completely destroyed by the fire.

"Almost without exception the wholesalers and retailers who were forced to leave the burning city located as quickly as possible in Oakland. Drug interests in Sacramento, Cal., Portland, Ore., and Seattle, Wash., helped to supply the wholesalers and retailers of 'Frisco with goods. Redington & Co have located at 731 Fourteenth street, Oakland, and the San Francisco Chemical Company, whose works were uninjured, at 1020 Fourteenth street, Oakland. The California State Board of Pharmacy is located in the Sather Building, in Oakland. Seabury & Johnson's depot is at present situated at Sutter street near Broderick street, in Oakland, while druggists from Santa Rosa and San Jose who also suffered from the earthquake and fire, have likewise taken up temporary quarters on the outskirts of Oakland.

Bowman & Co., of Oakland, is receiving all contributions from surrounding druggists, and applications for relief are being made to this concern.

The AMERICAN DRUGGIST has just secured statements from all the leading manufacturing drug houses, which had warehouses and stores on the Pacific Coast, stating in detail the extent of their losses and their plans for the immediate future. These reports follow:

The Alcock Mfg. Company suffered a very small loss, and immediately shipped goods to Sacramento and Los Angeles to supply the expected demand following the rehabilitation of the city.

The Apollinaris Agency.—Large stocks of Apollinaris, Apenta and Johannis-Lithia waters which had been shipped direct to San Francisco from the springs in Europe, were destroyed by the fire, but fresh stock was immediately forwarded by rail from warehouses in New York and other points in the United States. J. S. Anderson, the Pacific Coast representative of the agency, whose temporary address is 1425 Fruit Vale avenue, Fruit Vale, a part of Oakland, has already secured storage facilities not only in Oakland but also in San Francisco, and a shipment of 22,600 bottles of Apollinaris which had just arrived from Europe on the ship Uarda is to be stored in San Francisco.

The Whitall, Tatum Company lost its entire stock of glassware and druggists' sundries carried at the San Francisco branch at 55 Stevenson street. The amount of the loss has not yet been determined. Quarters have been secured by them at 1348 Park street, Alameda, where they propose to carry a stock of glassware and druggists' sundries for supplying the trade in that section.

The Pasteur Vaccine Company lost all the stock carried at their San Francisco branch, 409 Market street, but made immediate arrangements to supply customers on the coast from their Chicago office.

The Ammonol Chemical Company lost their entire San Francisco stock, but had at once forwarded supplies from New York City.

The Welch Grape Juice Company had about 200 cases of Welch's Grape Juice in the hands of their brokers, John H. Spohn Company, and this stock was entirely destroyed. Supplies were shipped at once, however, to the John H. Spohn Company, who have opened temporary quarters in Oakland.

Frederick Stearns & Co. report that its losses will amount to less than $5,000, but that "these are offset entirely by the good news that our resident representative, W. D. Briggs, is safe, uninjured and his home intact." They have ample stock in Los Angeles, Portland, Seattle and Sacramento, and also en route to San Francisco to supply immediate demands.

The H. K. Mulford Company carried a stock of goods in San Francisco before the earthquake amounting to $20,000 to $25,000. Arrangements have been made for a depot to supply San Francisco and the surrounding trade. The Langley & Michaels Company at Second and Townsend streets, San Francisco, office 207-208 Blake Block, Oakland, are their distributers.

The Norwich Pharmacal Company's large office and warerooms were completely destroyed, but the business of the concern has been resumed in Los Angeles.

Johnson & Johnson's entire stock of goods at 144 Second street, 'Frisco, was wholly destroyed. They fear that their records were destroyed by the falling of the building containing the safe in which such records were placed. The firm, however, has duplicates of the records in New Brunswick, N. J. The destruction of the stock entails a loss of $40,000. Supplies were quickly sent to assist in the relief work by hospitals. The company has now secured a warehouse at Thirty-seventh street and San Pablo avenue, Oakland, and has reopened for business and is now taking orders. The firm, together with the J. Ellwood Lee Company, has subscribed $2,000 in cash and has also contributed numerous supplies and 200 barrels of antiseptic solution.

Borden's Condensed Milk Company reports that it has lost everything in its 'Frisco offices except the contents of one safe. It has opened temporary offices in Oakland. The day after the disaster the company donated two carloads of condensed milk and cream to the sufferers, shipping it from points near San Francisco.

The Wells & Richardson Company suffered but slight loss, which was fully covered by insurance. It has temporary quarters at 944 Jefferson street, Oakland.

The New York Pharmacal Association reports its loss of stock at $21,000, part of which, however, was covered by insurance. Its books and records were saved.

Seabury & Johnson lost $25,000 worth of stock at 513 Market street. The company has established temporary quarters for a stock depot at 2482 Sutter street, San Francisco, where a moderate amount of stock has already been received, while more is on its way there.

The Chattanooga Medicine Company's branch office and warehouse in San Francisco were destroyed, entailing a loss of about $6,000 through the destruction of stock of medicine, advertising material, office and warehouse equipment. The company expects to fill orders from its St. Louis branch for some time to come.

Merck & Co. reports that they have sent a large quantity of Creolin-Pearson, or enough to make over 500,000 pounds of disinfectant. The shipment was accompanied by instructions regarding the most effective use, printed in several languages, including Chinese.

Armour & Co. reports that its branch house and stocks of special preparations were completely wiped out. It has temporary quarters in Oakland.

William R. Warner & Co. report a loss of stock amounting to $15,000. They have made arrangements with the Richardson & Erlin Company, their former representatives, who have established temporary quarters in Oakland, to continue the distribution of their goods.

Runkel Brothers report that the warehouses and places of business of their agents in 'Frisco were completely destroyed. They have, however, made temporary quarters in Oakland. They have also distributed chocolate to the sufferers. They report their loss at about $500.

The Cudahy Packing Company reports that it sustained losses of about $75,000 on building and stock. It will take care of its Pacific Coast trade temporarily from its branch houses in Portland, Ore., and Los Angeles, Cal., as well as through temporary quarters in Sacramento, Cal.

The Davidson Rubber Company reports a loss of $4,000 on stock of goods in the hands of its agents, the Richardson & Erlin Company, formerly located at 421 Mission street, which is now at 116 Broadway, Oakland.

Horlick's Malted Milk Company reports that its stock was uninjured and was distributed to the amount of $25,000 by the Federal Government to the sufferers. The company later sent additional supplies to the unfortunates.

John Wyeth & Brother report that they suffered a complete destruction of stock, but have established temporary quarters in Oakland.

The Searle & Hereth Company reports that its loss was completely covered by insurance, and that it has established temporary quarters in Oakland.

Bauer & Black report that they lost $2,500 in the fire.

The J. Hungerford Smith Company reports that it lost a large stock of goods which was in the place of business of the De Martini Supply Company, but is resuming business in 'Frisco through J. H. Newbauer & Co. and the De Martini Supply Company, as well as through Castle Bros., whose store was destroyed, but which has re-established itself at 2402 Steiner street.

The National Licorice Company reports that, though its

stock of goods was destroyed by fire, several consignments in transit at the time of the catastrophe are now available at the temporary quarters of W. M. Duval & Co., at 1168 Jackson street, Oakland.

The Tilden Company reports that $2,000 worth of its stock, carried by the Langley & Michaels Company, was totally destroyed, but that the loss is merely nominal, inasmuch as the stock was insured.

The William S. Merrell Chemical Company reports that its entire stock at 67 Stevenson street was destroyed, but was partly insured. It has established temporary quarters at 820½ Eighteenth street, Oakland.

The C. I. Hood Company reports that its loss was approximately $10,000. It has made arrangements with the John H. Spohn Company at 944 Jefferson street, Oakland, for a new supply depot.

Schieffelin & Co. report that their stocks carried by their agents, Waldron & Dietrich, were wholly destroyed. They have opened new quarters with Waldron & Dietrich in Oakland.

The Smith, Kane & French Company, of Philadelphia, reports that it had on consignment to three wholesale drug houses in 'Frisco and in its warehouse about $5,250 worth of goods, of which only $1,500 were insured.

The San Francisco office of the Denver Chemical Mfg. Company, at 162 New Montgomery street, was entirely destroyed, with a stock approximating $25,000 in value. The resident manager of the office escaped with his life, but lost all his personal effects.

A steamship from New York, carrying 35,000 pounds of Antiphlogistine, was within a short distance of San Francisco when the earthquake occurred, and as soon as the Government removed the embargo from shipping in the harbor the consignment of Antiphlogistine was unloaded by orders from New York and was distributed gratis in large quantities to all the emergency hospitals in the affected districts.

THE SUBSCRIPTIONS FOR SAN FRANCISCO SUFFERERS.

Though manufacturers of proprietary medicines and all descriptions of drugs, wholesale houses and retail druggists and clerks in all sections of the country have responded magnificently to the call of the National Association of Retail Druggists to assist the unfortunate pharmacists in San Francisco, whose stores and stocks were wholly destroyed in the earthquake and fire which devastated that city, the total subscriptions received by Secretary Thomas V. Wooten up to date reach only $36,500, of which $25,000 is in actual cash.

As more than 300 retail druggists in 'Frisco were rendered virtually destitute by the catastrophe which befell that city, the necessity for additional contributions will readily be perceived. Even if the $100,000 which the N. A. R. D. still hopes to raise is realized within the next few weeks, this vast sum will only provide each of the stricken druggists with $333 with which to resume business—a small capital when the difficulties of starting anew in a desolated city are considered.

Secretary Wooten in a special dispatch to the AMERICAN DRUGGIST, however, gives an encouraging report on the subscriptions, which are still pouring in with every mail, and it is to be hoped that druggists who have not yet contributed will do so promptly and as liberally as their circumstances permit.

From manufacturers, wholesalers and retailers in the drug trade of New York State alone a vast sum has already been raised for the N. A. R. D. fund, and drug interests in other cities, townships, villages and counties in all parts of the United States have also aided in proportion. The retail druggists of this city expect to contribute $10,000. A list of the subscriptions received by Secretary Wooten from New York drug houses follows:

Johnson & Johnson, $1,000; Merck & Co., $1,000; Solon Palmer, $500; Allcock Manufacturing Company, $500; Farbenfabriken of Elberfeld Company, $500; Sharp & Dohme, $250; Pond's Extract Company, $250; Scott & Bowne, $500; Carter Medicine Company, $200; Omega Chemical Company, $100; Vapo-Cresoline Company, $100; Centaur Company, $250; *Druggists' Circular*, $100; R. H. Nestle, $100; Maltine Company, $100; Metropolitan Drug Company, $1,000; F. M. Prindle & Co., $50; National Licorice Company, $50; Garfield Tea Company, $200; H. W. Warner, Albany, N. Y., $10; Chemung County Ph. Asso., $20; J. Allen Rice, $10; Robertson & Best, Amsterdam, N. Y., $5; Ed. Henderson, Amsterdam, N. Y., $5; D. B. Van Aken, Amsterdam, N. Y., $3; N. Y., $5; F. Adams & Bros., Amsterdam, N. Y., $5; Hugh Barkhuff, Am-
$5; F. Adams & Bros., Amsterdam, N. Y., $5; Hugh Barkhuff, Amsterdam, N. Y., $1; D. M. Priest, $10; Kutnow Bros., Ltd., $25; John L. Thompson's Sons Company, Albany, N. Y., $50; Kress & Owen Company, $25; Crown Cordial & Extract Company, $25; Anthony Wall, $5; Schenectady Association, $15; R. J. Lindsey, Amsterdam, N. Y., $5; A. J. Sherbourne, Amsterdam, N. Y., $5; Frank J. Adams & Bros., Amsterdam, N. Y., $5; Saratoga Drug Association, $25; Robert R. Cronyn, of Colgate & Co., $2; N. W. Tupper, *Pharmaceutical Era*, $5; John A. Proben, $10; Seven Sutherland Sisters, $25.

Many of the big manufacturers, wholesalers and retailers in this city sent their contributions to the general sufferers' relief funds, which were gathered by the New York Chamber of Commerce, New York Merchants' Association, Red Cross Society and the Mayor. Among such subscriptions were the following:

Lanman & Kemp, $1,000; American Hard Rubber Company, $1,000; Elmer & Amend, $1,000; William H. Nichols, $1,000; Union Sulphur Company, $1,000; H. A. Metz & Co., $1,000; Huyler's, $1,000; Mississippi Glass Company, $1,000; Lehn & Fink, $500; Maltine Company, $500; McKesson & Robbins, $500; F. W. Devoe & C. T. Raynolds Company, $500; Schieffelin & Co., $500; Continental Glass Company, $500; Nat. Aniline & Chemical Company, $250; Parfumerie E. Pinaud, $500; Chas. N. Crittenton Company, $250; Peerless Rubber Manufacturing Company, $200; Alfred H. Smith & Co., $300; Bristol-Myers Company, $200; J. Talsamine, $100; R. Hudnut's Pharmacy, Inc., $250; Denver Chemical Manufacturing Company, $200; Fred. E. Himrod, $100; National Remedy Company, $500; E. Fougera & Co., $100; California Wine Association, $100; Geigy Aniline & Extract Company, $50; Puritan Pure Food Company, $25; Gum & Sweetmeat Company, $2.50; Yates Drug & Chemical Company, $10; Friday Bowling Club, $10; Continental Color & Chemical Company, $500; H. J. Barker & Bro., $300; Heyden Chemical Works, $75; employees of Whitall, Tatum Company, $55; National Sponge & Chamois Company, $50; office force and employees of Powers-Weightman-Rosengarten Company, $177.40; Richard Young Company, $250; Fairchild Bros. & Foster, $500; employees of Church & Dwight Company, $269; H. Planten & Son, $100; Marx & Rawolle, $500; National Lead Company, $5,000.

Seabury & Johnson have also wired their manager in San Francisco, where their properties were wholly destroyed, that they have appropriated a fund of $1,000, to be used upon his recommendation in relieving the suffering of the homeless.

By a unanimous vote the members of the Metropolitan Drug Club, which represents the leading jobbers and wholesale drug interests of this city, decided at their meeting on Tuesday evening, April 24, to contribute $1,000 to the fund of the National Association of Retail Druggists, which is to be used for the relief of the druggists in San Francisco whose stores have been utterly destroyed by the earthquake and fire. This subscription is entirely independent of the individual donations of the wholesale drug houses.

Massachusetts Aids California.

(From our Regular Correspondent.)

Boston, May 9.—The druggists of this section have opened up their purses in aid of the San Francisco sufferers in a praiseworthy manner. The Mellin's Food Company was one of the first in the field. The concern wired its agent at San Francisco to distribute through physicians free to starving babies and other earthquake sufferers an entire shipment of over 12,000 bottles of Mellin's Food, due to arrive at San Francisco April 23. At the request of President Wooten, of the A. R. D., a meeting at the M. C. P. was recently held by the B. A. R. D. to assist in raising a fund of $100,000. About $250 was subscribed, and the local association pledged itself to raise $2,500. It is expected that $15,000 will be raised in New England. It was voted to send a call to all members of the National Druggists' Association and all affiliated with that organization inviting subscriptions. This call was sent by Mr. Keizer, the N. A. R. D. agent, by telephone all over New England, the telephone company donating the use of its lines for this purpose. The faculty and students at the M. C. P. are enthusiastically engaged in raising a fund for the students of the San Francisco College of Pharmacy and also for the use of that institution. The Dry Salters' Club, embracing all of the chemical concerns in this city, are also collecting money to be sent to San Francisco.

North Carolina Board of Pharmacy.

The next meeting of the North Carolina Board of Pharmacy for the examination of candidates to practice pharmacy will be held in the Sea Shore Hotel at Wrightsville Beach, on Tuesday, June 12, 1906, at 9 A. M. All applicants must make application to the secretary at least ten days before the date of examination for blanks and necessary instructions. The examinations will be based upon the new Pharmacopœia. For full information address F. W. Hancock, secretary, Oxford, N. C.

THE AMERICAN PHARMACEUTICAL ASSOCIATION.

Eighty-seven Applicants for Membership—The Committee on Publicity—Two Sessions for the Commercial Section—Work of the Local Branches in Detail.

The general council of the association has under advisement a resolution providing for two sessions of the commercial section, and it seems probable that this will be arranged for at the next meeting. The local committees at Indianapolis have been appointed and are making arrangements for elaborate entertainment features.

Subcommittees on publicity are being appointed by the chairman of that committee, E. H. Gane, of New York, with a view to meeting local emergencies. The instructions sent out by this committee to subcommittees will, if followed, undoubtedly prove beneficial to the cause of pharmacy in general.

SECTION OF PRACTICAL PHARMACY AND DISPENSING.

The officers of the Section of Practical Pharmacy and Dispensing have issued an address inviting co-operation in the work of the section. They point out that ever since the establishment of the section great interest has been manifested in the presentation and discussion of difficult and odd prescriptions. The committees, therefore, have decided to continue this work and make the participation in it as broad and general as possible, and ask pharmacists to send to the secretary of the section, H. A. B. Dunning, 423 North Charles street, Baltimore, Md., from three to six prescriptions, taken from prescription files, the discussion of which will probably prove of interest.

From the prescriptions thus received will be selected 30 or 40 for discussion at the next meeting of the association. The prescriptions must be forwarded to the secretary before June 1.

The committee further believe that a discussion of some of the new preparations of the Pharmacopœia would be of interest and benefit, and therefore invite the members to bring to the next meeting samples of the following preparations coming from their own laboratories: Cataplasm of kaolin, elixir adjuvans, elixir and glycerite of the phosphates of iron, quinine and strychnine, antiseptic solution, compound cresol solution, compound solution sodium phosphate, effervescing sodium phosphate, compound syrup of hypophosphites, or any other preparation not mentioned.

They also invite the members to write and present papers on any subject relating to the practice of pharmacy and dispensing. Manuscripts must be sent to the chairman of the section at least six weeks before the meeting, in order to have them printed in time. The members should recall that for the best paper or collection of notes read before this section Enno Sander offers the yearly prize of $50.

The activity of the several local branches has resulted in a very considerable augmentation of the list of applicants for membership, a total of 87 having applied since the last meeting. Some details of the work of the local branches appear below:

AUXILIARY OF THE A. PH. A. FORMED IN BALTIMORE.

Following the example of other cities, the druggists of Baltimore on May 4 organized a branch of the American Pharmaceutical Association, the meeting being held at the rooms of the Maryland Medical and Chirurgical Faculty, on North Eutaw street. John F. Hancock was elected president; Charles H. Ware, vice-president, and E. F. Kelly, secretary-treasurer. Joseph Lemberger, of Lebanon, Pa., president of the national association, was present and made an address on the aims and purposes of such auxiliaries and the good they accomplish. Dr. S. T. Earle, former president of the Medical and Chirurgical Faculty, also spoke.

THE PHILADELPHIA BRANCH.

The second stated meeting of the Philadelphia Branch of the American Pharmaceutical Association was held on the evening of Tuesday, April 24, 1906, the first vice-president, Mr. Wm. McIntyre, presiding.

The discussion on "The immediate object and the aims of the Philadelphia Branch of the American Pharmaceutical Association" was opened by Jos. L. Lemberger, of Lebanon, the president of the association. Mr. Lemberger spoke of the value of the association in fostering fraternal relations between members of the pharmaceutical profession. In this connection Mr. Lemberger referred to the imperative need for association and expressed the opinion that the development of the idea of local branches of the American Pharmaceutical Association will have a tendency to bring local pharmacists together to discuss matters relating to the professional side of their calling and will in turn serve to impress physicians with the abilities and accomplishments of the younger generation of pharmacists.

Wm. L. Cliffe, in support of his suggestion that the immediate object was "to endorse and to assist in the present movement for higher educational requirements for pharmacists," said that in his capacity as a member of the State Board of Pharmacy, he deeply felt that the education of the pharmacist had not progressed in the same ratio as the need for education. The demand for increasing the educational qualifications of prospective pharmacists was therefore an imperative one and one that should be recognized and provided for.

Franklin M. Apple, the next speaker, suggested that it would be desirable to co-operate with physicians to prevent the indiscriminate renewal of prescriptions. This practice he believed had been productive of much misunderstanding and had no doubt led to abuses that should be corrected.

O. W. Osterlund suggested the cultivation of friendly relations between physicians and pharmacists and expressed the opinion that in the greater number of instances suggestions and corrections would be kindly received by physicians and would in turn serve to impress on the latter a recognition of the need of practical assistance and advice.

John K. Thum expressed the belief that the most desirable way of promoting the welfare of the average pharmacist would be found in fostering and developing the professional side of pharmacy. This he asserted could be best accomplished by securing the co-operation of all reputable pharmacists to work together for the common good.

Additional suggestions were made by Messrs. England, Peacock and Hunsberger, Dr. Weidemann and Professor Kraemer.

Professor Kraemer suggested the advisability of giving publicity to the deliberations of the local branch and of taking an active interest in matters of public concern that might in any way improve the professional standing of members of the pharmaceutical profession. In this connection he called attention to the need for endorsing and assisting the Council on Pharmacy and Chemistry of the American Medical Association.

The several suggestions that had been made in the course of the evening, with some additional ones that had been offered in writing, were referred to a committee of three, to report at the next meeting.

PROGRAMME FOR THE NEXT MEETING.

The third stated meeting of this branch will be held on the evening of Monday, May 21, 1906, at 8 o'clock, in the lower lecture hall of the College of Physicians, northeast corner Thirteenth and Locust streets. The meeting will be devoted to the discussion of Self Medication and the evils of counter prescribing, and will include the following contributions: "Counter Prescribing and Its Relation to the Public Health," by Dr. W. M. L. Coplin, director of the Department of Public Health and Charities, Philadelphia; "Limitations to Self Medication," by Dr. Thos. R. Neilson, clinical professor of genito-urinary diseases, University of Pennsylvania; "The Duty of the Pharmacist to Aid in the Elimination of Irregular Practices," by Charles H. Lawall, Ph.M., associate professor of the theory and practice of pharmacy, Philadelphia College of Pharmacy.

PHARMACOPŒIA TRUSTEES MEET.

Progress on the Spanish Edition—Additional Honoraria for Workers —Prizes for Papers on the Pharmacopœia—Officers Elected.

The sixth annual meeting of the Board of Trustees of the United States Pharmacopœial Convention was held at Washington, D. C., April 28, with Dr. J. H. Beal, Chairman Charles E. Dohme, Professor J. P. Remington, S. A. D. Sheppard, and Dr. H. M. Whelpley present. Progress was reported on a Spanish translation of the pharmacopœia, but no date was set for its appearance.

The By-Laws provide that "the Committee of Revision shall receive such nominal compensation for their services as the board of trustees shall direct." At a previous meeting the board had voted the sum of $200 for each member of the Committee of Revision. The board decided that certain members of the committee, having performed exceptional services in connection with the work of revision, should receive additional payments of honoraria, the list being as follows: Charles Caspari, Jr., V. Coblentz, C. Lewis Diehl, Alfred R. L. Dohme, Walter S. Haines, C. S. N. Hallberg, Henry Kraemer, Edward Kremers, A. B. Lyons, H. H. Rusby, Samuel Sadtler, W. L. Scoville, E. H. Squibb, and A. R. Stevens. The By-Laws provide that the members of the board of trustees shall not receive compensation for their services.

The Public Health and Marine Hospital Service, which published a bulletin giving the changes in the pharmacopœia, may also publish a bulletin embodying a digest of comments on the pharmacopœia.

One hundred dollars was appropriated for advertising in the bulletin of the A. Ph. A.

Dr. Edward Kremers was authorized to make an exhibit of pharmacopœias at the Boston meeting of the American Medical Association.

It was decided to distribute the remaining copies of the Rice memorial among the colleges represented in the American Conference of Pharmaceutical Faculties.

The request of the Chicago branch of the A. Ph. A. for an epitome of the U. S. P. was discussed, and the branch requested to furnish more definite information on the subject.

A telegram was sent to Albert E. Ebert, an absent trustee, expressing the sympathy of the board in his bereavement.

A number of publishers were given permission to use the text of the U. S. P. in their books, the rate of compensation being fixed by the board.

It was decided to send the president of each State pharmaceutical association a copy of the pharmacopœia, to be awarded as a prize for a meritorious paper presented at the 1906 meeting. An additional copy will be presented to each association next year, as a prize for the best paper on "How to Increase the Interest of the Medical Profession in the United States Pharmacopœia."

It was decided to prepare an abstract of the proceedings of the board of trustees from the date of organization. The following officers were elected for the ensuing year: Chairman, Charles E. Dohme, Baltimore; Executive Committee, Messrs. Beal, Wood, and Dohme; Auditing Committee, Messrs. Whelpley, Sheppard, and Ebert. Dr. Murray Galt Motter, of Washington, was re-elected secretary of the board.

The Associated Drug Companies of America.

For the purpose of securing all the advantages possible for retailers in purchasing their drugs, proprietary remedies and other goods, a new buyers' organization, known as the Associated Drug Companies of America, has just been formed by representatives of the various buying clubs of Brooklyn, Philadelphia, Providence, Hartford and Buffalo. The organization of this body was effected Tuesday evening, May 8, by 50 retail druggists interested in this movement, who held a meeting at the Hotel Astor and elected the following officers: Dr. William C. Anderson, of Brooklyn, president; James O'Hare, of Providence, vice-president; John G. Wischerth, of Brooklyn, secretary, and S. A. Grove, of Buffalo, treasurer.

THE DOHMES ORGANIZE A THREE MILLION DOLLAR CHEMICAL COMPANY.

Special Products Company to Manufacture Chemicals and Specialties—A Large Factory Site Purchased in Baltimore—European Capital Interested.

(From our Regular Correspondent.)

Baltimore, May 12.—This city is to have a new industry in the shape of a large plant for the manufacture of heavy chemicals. This much has been determined, though the details of the enterprise still remain to be worked out. Just what chemicals are to be produced and the precise dimensions of the plant are matters to be settled in the future after some of those interested have had another opportunity to confer with certain European investors, who will be represented in the undertaking. One of the foremost figures in the projected laboratory is Louis Dohme, of Sharp & Dohme, manufacturers of pharmaceuticals here, though the proposed factory will be an independent venture and have no connection whatever with the old establishment. Another participant is Dr. A. R. L. Dohme, a nephew of Louis Dohme, and also a member of Sharp & Dohme, being one of the vice-presidents, while a third Baltimorean identified with the project is Angus Cameron, an Englishman who has made this city his home for a number of years and who purchased the Thomsen Chemical Works at Locust Point upon the retirement of the Messrs. Thomsen some years ago, and afterward disposed of them to the United States Chemical Company.

The new company will be known as the Special Products Company, and has been incorporated under the laws of New Jersey with a capital of $3,000,000. The preliminaries were arranged very quietly, and the first information to get out was the transfer of a one-half undivided interest in a large piece of property on Boston and Patuxent streets, this city, from Mr. Cameron to Louis Dohme. The deed was recorded the latter part of last week, and inquiry started thereby brought out the announcement of the proposed chemical works. The Boston street property has railroad track connection on Boston street and runs back to the water front, thus enabling direct shipment of the products by either rail or by vessel. It fronts 287 feet on Boston street and its depth is 702 feet.

Mr. Dohme, when seen last Saturday, stated that no further particulars about the enterprise could be given at the present time, and that the details remained to be determined. With the exception of the fact that heavy chemicals and spcialties would be manufactured, nothing was settled, he said, and nothing further could be said until Dr. Dohme and Mr. Cameron returned from Europe, whither they had gone to consult with associates.

Dr. Dohme and Mr. Cameron sailed from New York last Saturday. They will be gone about one month or six weeks. The former had only recently returned from London and Paris after a stay of several months. During this time, it is said, the first steps in the projected enterprise were taken. Dr. Dohme spent some of his time in various laboratories investigating diverse processeses, and it is supposed then managed to interest the foreign capitalists in the undertaking.

Two Companies Out of One.

In the belief that it would be more advantageous to handle the regular jobbing business of the R. W. Robinson & Son Company, of 186 Greenwich street, in other quarters and under a new corporate title, Charles S. Littell, president of the corporation, has established, with Theodore W. Day and George Thompson, the new house of Charles S. Littell & Co., which is now located at 228 Fulton street. The old corporation of R. W. Robinson & Son Company will continue its business in laboratory products and specialties, and will also conduct a wholesale business on a cash basis; but the new concern, which has bought a large portion of the stock of the Robinson Company, will handle a general jobbing line as well as the special products of the parent corporation. The R. W. Robinson & Son Company has been in business under various titles since 1840. The property at 228 Fulton street, now occupied by Littell & Co., was originally leased by the Robinson company, which has effected a transfer of the lease to the new concern.

1906 NEW YORK COLLEGE GRADUATES.

Address by Attorney-General Mayer—The Prize Winners and List of Graduates.

Hundreds of relatives and friends of the 1906 graduates of the University of Columbia College of Pharmacy of the City of New York attended the seventy-sixth annual commencement exercises, held Thursday evening, April 26, in Carnegie Music Hall. In the absence of President Nicholas Murray Butler, who was unable to preside at the ceremonies because of pressing business connected with the university, Vice-President Charles F. Chandler conferred the degree of Ph.G. on 144 graduates and the degree of Ph.D. on 15 post-graduates.

Four alumni prizes were awarded to the graduates whose examination papers showed the highest percentages, and three special prizes of $100 each were presented for the greatest proficiency in materia medica, pharmacognosy and chemistry. Attorney-General Julius M. Mayer, the guest of honor, delivered an interesting and instructive address to the graduates, and musical selections were furnished between the numerous features of the programme by the Seventh Regiment Band.

Although the exercises were scheduled to begin promptly at 8 o'clock, the faculty of the college did not conclude its arrangements for the entrance of the graduating class until three-quarters of an hour later. By 9 o'clock, however, the members of the faculty had taken their places upon the flag-draped stage and were ready to receive the members of the graduating class, led by A. Clayton Searles, and the members of the post-graduate class, conducted by William H. Ebbitt.

After a selection by the band the Rev. Nathan A. Seagle delivered a prayer and Dr. Chandler addressed the graduates, giving a brief history of the college.

After Secretary Thomas F. Main had read the rolls of those entitled to degrees these were conferred by Dr. Chandler.

ATTORNEY GENERAL MAYER ADVISES GRADUATES TO CULTIVATE CIVICS.

In the course of his address to the graduates Attorney General Mayer said: "Twenty years ago, when I was graduating from the Columbia Law School, I was compelled to listen to a gentleman who insisted upon giving advice to the graduating class of that institution of learning. I had to sit still and drink it all in, and I thereupon determined that some day I would get square for the awful punishment I had to suffer. This is my opportunity. In more serious vein, let me say it is indeed an admirable profession that you have chosen. It combines the highest knowledge of science and skill in pharmacy with up-to-date progressiveness in business matters, and knowledge of men and of the world. I admire the combination, and let me say that not the least of the characteristics of a successful professional man is this knowledge of men and of the world. In the practice of your profession you must learn to become acquainted with men at large, with human nature and human knowledge. Busy as you may become in the pursuance of your work, you should find time to think about public affairs. A government is always just as good or as bad as you, the people, choose to make it."

The trustees' special prizes of $100 each, given for special proficiency in materia medica, pharmacognosy and chemistry, were awarded by William J. Gies to Charles Krepela, Orest S. Ghirardi and Eide F. Thode. Victor L. Peirce then delivered the valedictory address, which was followed with the concluding feature of the evening, the distribution of the floral tributes sent by relatives, friends and admirers of the happy graduates.

GRADUATES OF 1906.

NEW YORK: Isaac Abrams, Charles Alder, George Alexion, Samuel J. Allison, Harry Aronovic, Morris Bimstein, Pierre Clark Bingham, Alexander Block, Leo Boeder, Frank George Bradtke, Alexander Brooks, Harry Brundage, Ulderich Ciani, Morris Cohen, Harry Davidson, Walter S. Dean, Hugo Elwyn, Frank Eusner, Harry Edward Faleila, Morris Feinstein, Leonard J. Finkle, George L. Freer, Leo Goldlust, Israel Goulko, Francis Joseph Grimm, Achilles Aeneas Guarnier, Robert Hahn, William George Heddesheimer, Robert K. Henry, William Arthur Holley, Herman William Kaiser, Louis Klein, Louis A. Klein, George Kobrick, Maurice A. Kopel, Charles Krepela, George William Krause, Anthony Landi, Diana Leibson, Alexander Levinsohn, Harry David Levy, Elias Litsky, Charles Joseph A. Lund, Charles Lutz, jr., William Margowitz, Emil Matthiessen, Joseph Anthony Mauro, Morris Meyers, Isidore Moss, Samuel Moretsky, Erwin W. Nicolai, Samuel Ogus, Leo Reich, Julius Robbins, Charles Rubano, Morris J. Sandor, Abraham Seiger, Nathan Snyder, Frederick Ferdinand Sontag, Henry Spindler, Charles Morris Stein, Morris Abraham Taft, Frederick Thimble, Eide Frederick Thode, Morris Tobias, Mayer Herman Touster, John Trivigno, Morris Uhler, Bernard Warlyn, Joseph C. Weiler, Nathan Winter, John Theodore Zimmerman and Isidor Nathaniel Zlinkoff.

NEW YORK STATE: Nathanial J. Alexander, Utica; Charles Whittington Bock, Utica; Alexander Bonnymann, Warwick; James C. Brault, Brooklyn; Emmett Broderick, Rome; Arthur C. Brown, Brooklyn; Charles K. Brown, Deposit; Theodore Calderara, Mt. Vernon, N. Y.; Theodore A. Crolly, Mt. Vernon, N. Y.; Clarence E. Cutting, Staten Island; Everett C. De La Vergne, Woodhaven; Arthur F. Dold, Port Chester; D. Eugene Driscoll, Binghamton; George A. Eden, Brooklyn; Francis L. Everson, Utica; Raymond W. Fish, Mount Kisco; Isidore Flanzer, Brooklyn; Max Frindel, Brooklyn; William H. Gaul, Yonkers; Tobias Ginsberg, Brooklyn; Harold Van W. Goring, Wappingers Falls; Edward A. Grogan, jr., Rome; Charles J. Haman, Long Island City; Sydney Kirby Hunt, Middletown; Louis W. Irmisch, Lindenhurst, L. I.; Corral W. M. Johnson, jr., Plattsburgh; William Klein, Rockaway Beach; Arthur Lawrence Lahey, Laurel Hill; Henry W. Lehmkuhl, Middletown; Edward Mackey, Port Jervis; William P. Maher, Little Falls; William J. Mahoney, Canton; Edmund T. Maloney, Camden; William R. Masten, Chester; William F. Miller, Peekskill; Walter C. Overton, Brooklyn; Charles Parker, Ludlow-on-Hudson; Victor L. Pierce, Brooklyn; Charles F. Perthou, Brooklyn; Charles E. Phelps, Middletown; Leopold Rein, Brooklyn; Wallace G. Sabine, Utica; Maurice M. Schlesinger, Brooklyn; Samuel Schoenfeld, Yonkers; Ignatz Schwartz, Brooklyn; Aaron Spanier, Brooklyn; Horace Sullivan, Brooklyn; Nicholas Trombo, Brooklyn; Morris Uihlein, Astoria; Ralph L. Washburn, Peekskill; Samuel A. Weiss, Yonkers; Howard J. White, McGraw.

FROM OTHER PARTS: George A. Albach, West Hoboken, N. J.; William D. Ashton, Piqua, Ohio; Nittert Bakker, Haledon, N. J.; Clarence L. Ballou, East Haven, Conn.; George S. Bangert, East Orange, N. J.; Bernard N. Basson, Jersey City, N. J.; Robert J. Benham, Waterbury, Conn.; Harry E. Bischoff, West Hoboken, N. J.; Andrew A. Brown, Scranton, Pa.; George H. Buteau, Baltic, Conn.; William C. Driscoll, Bridgeport, Conn.; Charles W. Flint, St. Johnsbury, Vt.; Orest S. Ghirardi, Montclair, N. J.; Frank Guagliardo, Hoboken, N. J.; Edward H. Hartnett, Jersey City, N. J.; Earl G. Hastings, North Adams, Mass.; Frank H. Hickling, Lisbon, O.; Charles W. Holzhauer, Newark, N. J.; Henry T. Hopkins, Keyport, N. J.; Arthur A. Kahn, Long Branch, N. J.; Samuel E. Karp, Scranton, Pa.; Walter S. Kennedy, Woodbridge, Conn.; William H. Koch, Collinsville, Conn.; William A. Lowell, Portland, Me.; Wilbur B. Meachem, Elizabeth, N. J.; Edmund Mercier, Taftville, Conn.; Benjamin Meyer, Newark, N. J.; Offim Myerson, West Hoboken, N. J.; John G. Neil, Dunedin, New Zealand; Charles A. Otto, Villingen Baden, Germany; Napoleon Parent, Taftville, Conn.; Clarence C. Perdoe, Phillipsburg, N. J.; Peter Angelo R. Pra, Passaic, N. J.; Rae Safier, Newark, N. J.; Joseph S. Scheuer, Berryville, Va.; Bruno H. Schubert, Town of Union, N. J.; Ralph E. Seaman, Perth Amboy, N. J.; Oscar H. W. A. Stachmann, Jersey City, N. J.; Ernest F. Stovall, Vienna, Ga.; Isador Tessler, Bridgeport, Conn.; William E. Thomas, Priceburg, Pa.; Everett C. Ward, Westbrook, Me.; Lester B. Westcott, Danbury, Conn.; William L. Wolfson, Key West, Fla.

GRADUATED DOCTORS OF PHARMACY.

NEW YORK: Joseph Cohen, Fermin Ferrer, Frederick E. Jorgensen, Julius Kaplan, William G. Norton, Abraham J. Seid, Nathan Siegel, Joseph Weinstein, John W. Wurthmann.

NEW YORK STATE: John H. Crowe, Richfield Springs; Charles H. Ellis, jr., Port Chester; John J. A. Voelker, jr., Lindenhurst, L. I.; Hassow O. van Wedel, Dobbs Ferry.

William A. Holley, Greensboro, N. C.; John M. Williams, Perth Amboy, N. J.

GRADUATES OF THE BROOKLYN COLLEGE.

Graduation of a Large Class Witnessed by a Great Assemblage—The Close of a Successful Year.

The commencement exercises of the Brooklyn College of Pharmacy were held in the Baptist Temple, Brooklyn, on the evening of Thursday, May 3. The seating capacity of this building, the largest now available in Brooklyn, was packed to its utmost and the aisles and passageways could not accommodate the overflow. The graduates marched on the stage in cap and gown under the direction of Secretary Andrew E. Hegeman. Occupying the center of a large platform, which had been erected around the pulpit, were the faculty and trustees. The front of the platform was banked high with floral offerings for the graduates from relatives and admiring friends. Professor Anderson acted as master of ceremonies and introduced the Rev. Edward Niles, who opened the exercises with prayer. Prof. A. Percival Lohness read the list of graduates and distributed the diplomas. The following received diplomas and the degree of graduate in pharmacy was conferred on them by Prof. W. C. Anderson:

GRADUATES OF PHARMACY.

John B. Adatte, Peter V. Ahlborn, Walter H. Albert, Sydney Arensberg, E. E. Ashley, Hermann B. Barteld, Lewis Bailey, Morris Behm, Edwin Bensen, Morris E. Berkowitz, Israel I. Berow, Joseph Boll, Samuel Bookstaber, Max Brandes, Isidore Broadman, Abraham Burstein, Paul Buss, William H. Clinton, Charles Cohen, David Cohen, Max Corn, Viva Dahlberg, James F. A. Dawson, Harry A. Dobromilsky, Joseph A. Driscoll, Philip Duckman, Benjamin J. Elysowitz, Theodore Fallmesger, Abram Farber, Hyman Felder, Julius I. Feigelman, Sophia Feiginow, Meyer A. Feinberg, Isaac A. Feldberg, William S. Finkelstein, Louis Freidman, Solem Gaer, Leon L. Gawurin, C. G. Geffen, Herman Gerdes, jr., John J. Gerlinger, Nicholas S. Gesoalde, Thomas F. Gilmartin, Harry Glucksman, Katherine Goldberg, Nathan Goldberg, Samuel Goodman, Mandel Greenberg, Joseph Grubman, Charles D. Guarini, George F. Hamann, Charles Hecht, Morris I. Horney, William Horni, Merton A. Hunsinger, Joseph Ingoglia, Halsted James, John Karussa, Oscar J. Kahn, Samuel Katz, Isaac Kaufman, Nathan Kaufman, Herbert

W. Kimball, Henry G. Lammers, Barnet Landau, Blaine R. Lehman, Louis P. Lesoine, Anna Leritt, Robert Levine, Abraham Ludwig, Abraham S. Margulis, Theodore Margulis, Benno H. Mark, F. Milton Martin, Edward J. Miller, Samuel Mesnicoff, Frank William Meyer, Charles Clark Neff, John F. Neumann, Matthew R. Newstead, Anthony L. Palma, Adrian F. Paradis, Perry Pick, George Andrew Rauh, Anthony G. Reif, Augustus A. Reynolds, Vincenzo L. Rizzuto, Max M. Rosenberg, Morris Rosenberg, Joseph Rosenthal, Edward Rothman, George F. Ruffrage, Jacob Saltman, Fred. A. Sandman, Israel J. Sasmorsky, Frank M. Saxton, Morris Schubert, Arthur O. Schwencke, Henry A. Segall, Isidor Sherman, Abraham S. Silverman, Gustave G. Smith, Rosalie Sookne, Bertha C. Squire, Morris Steinberg, Samuel D. Strawgate, Eric A. J. Tietse, Matilda M. Toscano, Frederick J. Wiericks, William R. Wilkens, Henry M. Woessner.

DOCTORS OF PHARMACY.

The degree of doctor of pharmacy was conferred on the following:

Edwin Bensen, Alice J. Kunkel, Emil A. Lauer, Manasseh A. B. Levy, William Levine, Barnett Miller, Jacob Mirsky, Joseph Ostrewicz, William H. Weygandt.

A FINE VALEDICTORY ADDRESS.

The valedictory address was delivered by Adrian F. Paradis, jr., who succeeded in holding the interested attention of the large audience during the entire recital of a well constructed and logical account of the debt of agriculture and the arts and industries to chemistry and pharmacy.

Supreme Court Justice Burr was the guest of honor and addressed the graduates. His remarks contained much sound advice and were enlivened with several humorous references, as when he told what happened to "a king of early days who had turned from God to the physician for the alleviation of his ills, and was gathered to his fathers." The keynote of Justice Burr's address was the safety to the public that comes through education, and the success of the Brooklyn College of Pharmacy was referred to as an instance of the sacrifice of individualism to organization.

THE PRIZE WINNERS.

Adrian Paradis, president of the college, announced the award of prizes. The first prize, the college gold medal, went to Hyman Felder, for the highest general standing in class work. The second prize, the college silver medal, was awarded to Benjamin J. Elysowitz. The third prize, a bronze medal, was captured by Theodore Margulis, while the Anderson gold medal went to Frank W. Meyer. The alumni prize of a silver medal was won by a lady graduate, Miss Rosalie Sookne. Dr. Alice J. Kundel was the recipient of the special alumni prize of a fully equipped microscope. The postgraduate prize of a gold medal was won by Dr. Barnett Miller. The senior honor roll was announced by Professor Lohness, as follows:

SENIOR HONOR ROLL.

Lewis Bailey, Morris Behm, Max Brandes, David Cohen, Benjamin J. Elysowitz, Hyman Felder, Barnet Landon, Theodore Margulis, F. Milton Martin, Frank Wm. Meyer, John F. Neumann, Adrian F. Paradis, Max M. Rosenberg, Joseph Rosenthal, Jacob Saltman, Israel J. Sasmorsky, Rosalie Sookne.

JUNIOR HONOR ROLL.

The junior honor roll contained the following names, the junior prize, a silver medal, being won by Joseph S. Goldwag:

Clarisse Anghel, Rafael Abelsky, Isidore Blumenkranz, Adolph Eisenbud, Hinrich Ghiterman, Benzion Giventer, Joseph S. Goldwag, Frank L. R. Guernsey, Max Kaufman, Martin H. Kleine, Isaac Lazaroff, Joseph A. Ortolan, Charles J. W. Reid, Louis Rosenbluth, Julius Sallerup, Benjamin Scheinfinkel, Theodore Strimling, Tobias B. Weaver, Frederick G. Wunderlich, Philip Zubrinsky.

THE ALUMNI BANQUET.

At the close of the exercises some 200 graduates and members of the college adjourned to the Imperial, where they enjoyed a banquet and reception and listened to remarks by different speakers. The Dinner Committee was composed of William H. Weygandt, Phar.D., chairman; William C. Anderson, Phar.D.; William G. Meister, Ph.G., and Edward Kleine, Phar.D. A feature of the evening proceedings, which was much enjoyed by everybody, was the presentation to Dr. Weygandt of a microscope. Dr. Weygandt, as toastmaster, had called upon Dr. Edward Kleine to respond to the toast, "The Alumni Association." Dr. Kleine dodged the toast and sprung a surprise on the toastmaster by presenting him with the microscope, which he said was the gift of an anonymous donor and was intended as a testimonial of the esteem in which Dr. Weygandt was held for his great work in the association. Another interesting feature was the presentation to the Alumni Association by Adrian F. Paradis, jr., of a large college flag on behalf of the class of 1906. Frank L. R. Guernsey responded for the class of 1907.

ELECTION AT THE KINGS COUNTY MEETING.

Annual Meeting—Legislative Committee Reviews Work of the Year—Growth of Drug Legislation Pointed Out.

The May meeting of the Kings County Pharmaceutical Society was the annual meeting of the organization, at which the yearly reports of officers and committees were received and new officers elected for the ensuing year. The meeting was called to order by President Adrian Paradis, Tuesday, May 8, at 3 o'clock p.m. The minutes of the previous meeting having been read by Secretary Hegeman and adopted, applications for membership were received, and five candidates for election to membership who were favorably reported on by the Committee on Membership were admitted. The new members are: Eli Rosenstein, Phar. D., 155 Glenmore avenue; Charles H. Gaer, 115 Nostrand avenue; Meyer Sambur, 550 Bushwick avenue; C. F. Schoenherr, 1044 Broadway, and Berthold Gerson, 167 Monroe street.

The annual report of Dr. Peter W. Ray, the veteran treasurer of the society, showed a balance of $698.27 in the society's treasury, and $1,437.61 in the treasury of the college. After his reports were received Dr. Ray gave an interesting review of the history of the college, from its earliest beginnings as a class for drug clerks in the Pratt Institute in 1888. The picture he drew of conditions as they were then was a graphic one, his reminiscences conjuring up more than one ghost of the past to set the older members thinking.

As supplementary to Dr. Ray's report, Dr. Muir read a communication from the society's accountant, giving a financial statement of the year's business, in which the officers were greatly complimented on their management of the affairs of the college and society. The value of the college property was estimated in this statement at $49,000.

Secretary Hegeman reported a total membership of 459, with an average attendance at the monthly meetings of 35. During the past year 31 new members were elected, 5 died, 5 resigned and 31 were dropped from the roll for nonpayment of dues.

THE LEGISLATIVE RECORD OF THE YEAR

was reviewed by Dr. William Muir in his report as chairman of the Legislative Committee, the other members of which were Thomas J. France, O. C. Kleine, Andrew E. Hegeman and William H. Bussenschutt. The report opened with a statement regarding the increasing number of pharmacy bills introduced year after year in the Legislature. The session of 1906 had the distinction of producing the largest number of measures having application to pharmacy, eighteen distinct and separate bills having made their appearance. The Stevens-Wainwright bill received special attention from the committee. Concerning this bill the report said:

The bill that created the greatest amount of interest and excitement was known as the Stevens-Wainwright bill, which was drafted by representatives of the Prohibition element and aimed to compel publicity where a compound contained alcohol or drugs of specific character, regardless of the quantity or purposes of such ingredients. This bill did not prohibit and would have no deterrent effect upon the use of cocaine or opium or other habit-forming drugs, and all arguments in favor of the bill based upon the assumed desire to correct these evils were totally irrelevant, as the measure had scarcely any bearing upon the subject except that it might possibly tend to facilitate and encourage the evil of the drug habit by publishing to the world the quantities contained in the preparations. Most of the drugs named in the bill are never used in proprietary medicines, and the long list of drugs enumerated was evidently used to confuse the public and to convey an exaggerated impression of the importance of the measure as greatly needed legislation in the interest of public morals. Nowhere in the bill was any restriction placed upon the sale or use of the drugs specified; the restriction was only upon medicines containing the drugs named, and then only if the percentage of the drug was not printed upon the label.

Continuing, the report said:

Your committee is more than ever impressed with the fact that thoroughly organized effort alone can promote the welfare of the pharmacists. The work, however, cannot be left entirely to the men who constitute your Committee on Legislation. They are willing to give of their time and talents in the discharge of the duty imposed upon them, but they must have the personal, interested support of every member of the association to accomplish results. During the session just closed several appeals were made to the druggists of Brooklyn to reach their representatives in the Legislature. The response to these appeals was not all that was expected and hoped for by your committee. It seems eminently fair that members who have great pecuniary and professional interests at stake should be willing to take the trouble to write a letter or to visit their Senator or Assemblyman upon the simple request of your Committee on Legislation. We therefore urge that each member should acquaint himself at least with the names of the legislators from the district in which he resides or does business, and we recommend that they take a greater interest in their own affairs by prompt communication with their representatives in the halls of legislation when requested so to do. Such requests are not frequently made and are only made when absolutely essential to success. Immediate response is not too much to expect and should be given freely when necessary.

On motion the report was received, placed on file and the recommendations contained in it adopted. The committee was thanked for their services to the society during the past year. In connection with the adoption of the report, ex-President Kleine took occasion to express regret that pharmacists did not respond more readily to appeals by the Legislative Committee to send letters to their representatives at Albany. His own district was, however, an exception to the general rule of apathy, as the druggists there had been so persistent in bombarding their Assemblymen and Senators with messages that one Assemblyman had appealed to Mr. Kleine to call off his dogs of war.

On motion of Dr. William Muir, the society passed a special vote of thanks to Assemblyman Geo. H. Whitney, of Mechanicsville, Saratoga County, who had rendered valuable services to the Legislative Committee and had actually made many sacrifices to safeguard the interests of pharmacists in the Legislature.

PRESIDENT'S ADDRESS.

President Paradis then called Vice-President Rehfuss to the chair and read his annual report, in which he reviewed the work of the year and paid a glowing tribute to Dr. Muir for his work as chairman of the Legislative Committee. Mr. Paradis reiterated what he said last year, that it would be a blessing if the Legislature met at intervals of only two or three years instead of annually. He also submitted a separate report as president of the college, praising the faculty for their success in raising the institution to its present high standing. Much of the success was due, he said, to the fact that faculty and trustees worked hand in hand without friction.

John G. Wischerth reported for the Committee on Trade Matters and asked for a larger appropriation than the $150 granted last year to carry on the work of the committee in distributing reading matter and samples of National Formulary preparations among physicians. He suggested that lecturers competent to describe and discuss N. F. preparations be hired to talk on them at joint meetings of physicians and pharmacists.

Reports were received from the Committee on Papers and the Library Committee. The first named hoped to offer the same prizes for papers this year as last, while the Library Committee announced that the library now contained 3,500 volumes, 500 more than last year. The members were invited to make use of the books. It was announced by the Committee on the Pharmacopœia that information had been received from the publishers of the United States Dispensatory that that work would not be ready for sale for six months to come.

DONATION FOR THE N. A. R. D. FUND.

On motion of Dr. Muir, the society made an appropriation of $100 for the relief of the suffering druggists of San Francisco, the amount to be paid into the relief fund of the National Association of Retail Druggists.

RETAIL DRUGGISTS' FIRE INSURANCE PROJECT.

Frank H. Freericks, of Cincinnati, who is in New York in the interests of the American Druggists' Fire Insurance Company, was accorded the privileges of the floor, on motion of Prof. W. C. Anderson, who introduced him as one of the original workers on the D. C. S. N. plan. Mr. Freericks expressed himself as proud of the privilege of appearing before the society. He said the Kings County Pharmaceutical Society was favorably known throughout the entire country, because of the standing of the society's representatives at the annual conventions of the N. A. R. D. and the active part they took in the discussions. He then described the organization and operation of his company, which was for retail druggists only. In the short time the company had been in operation $55,000 worth of stock had been subscribed for through correspondence. Much of this business had come from the States of Ohio, Massachusetts, Pennsylvania, Illinois and Indiana, but New York and Brooklyn had paid hardly any attention to the subject. For this reason it was determined to put a solicitor in the field, as it was the intention of the company to get the business of at least one-fifth of the entire retail drug trade of the country. The rates in the new company were considerably lower than the old-line companies and the security was the same, if not better.

A recess was then taken before proceeding to the election of officers, in order to give members an opportunity to pay their annual dues. Most of the old officers were re-elected, the only new man being Charles Heimerzheim, who was elected to the Board of Censors. The officers for the ensuing year are:

NEW OFFICERS.

President, Adrian Paradis; first vice-president, Jacob H. Rehfuss; second vice-president, Clarence O. Douden; third vice-president, William F. Maas; secretary, Andrew E. Hegeman; treasurer, Peter W. Ray. Elective trustees for 1906-1910: Thomas J. France, William J. Hackett, J. H. Droge. Censors: William P. Wuest, chairman; John G. Wischerth, C. Heimerzheim. Librarian: Joseph L. Mayer. Counsel: William L. Perkins.

Delegates to the American Pharmaceutical Association: William C. Anderson, Frederic P. Tuthill, Thomas J. Keenan, Andrew E. Hegeman and Joseph L. Mayer.

Delegates to the National Association of Retail Druggists: William C. Anderson and William Muir.

Announcement was made that two visitors from sister associations were present, and James O'Hare, of Providence, and Henry C. Blair, of Philadelphia, were accorded the privileges of the floor. Both gentlemen addressed the meeting, saying they had experienced profit and pleasure in attending, and felicitating the society on its success. The meeting then adjourned.

Peruna Loyal to the Contract Plan.

A representative of the American Druggist, in conversation with one of the officials of the Peruna Drug Mfg. Company, during the meeting of the Proprietary Association last week, asked him for his opinion on the contract plan and as to whether the company purposed to continue marketing its goods on the basis of its present contracts. In reply he said:

"In view of the attacks which have been made on the good faith of the Peruna Drug Mfg. Company, in connection with the D. C. S. N. plan, we are glad to reaffirm most emphatically, through the American Druggist, our allegiance to and belief in this plan. We have been to much trouble and expended considerable money in establishing and maintaining this system. We believe in it as a legal and reasonable method of protecting our interests, holding our trade and securing a fair and legitimate profit for all who handle our medicines, and insinuations against our honesty of purpose are absolutely unfounded. We shall certainly continue this system."

Italian Pharmacists Celebrate.

At a banquet held at a well-known Italian restaurant in this city Wednesday evening, April 25, the Italian Pharmaceutical Association of the State of New York gave good evidence of its strength since reorganizing and incorporating. About 75 members and guests attended and a fine feeling of good fellowship prevailed. A Neapolitan quartette sang and played during the repast. The menu was distinctively Italian, the guests being regaled before the soup was served with Italian delicacies in the form of salami, tunny in oil, anchovies and other tit-bits. The spirit of the gathering was lightened with some of the wines for which Italy is famed, Capri Bianco and red Chianti being served lavishly. Frank Avignone, president of the association, acted as toastmaster, and his speech and that of the representatives of the William R. Warner & Co.

and H. K. Mulford Company were the only speeches in English. Giovanni Scavo, secretary of the association, responded to a toast in the name of the association and gave a brief historical account of its progress. Others who responded to toasts were Prof. Giacinto Vetere, of the University of Naples; Ludwig Ferrara, N. Caliva, Dr. Di Darrio and Pio Mari. Signor Calcano, the representative of H. K. Mulford Company, sent a beautiful floral horseshoe. The following was the menu:

Blue Point Oysters.
Capri Bianco.
Salame, Prosciutto, Mortadella, Acciughe, Tonno,
Peperoni, Rossi, Sedani Radici.
Consommé di Pollo.
Salmone Bollito. Salsa Olandese.
Patate alla Parigina.
Chianti.
Tagliarini alla Bolognese.
Scaloppine al Pomodoro. Piselli Francese.
Punch alla Romana.
Piccione al forno con crostino.
Insalata Lattuga.
Cognac.
Frutta. Formaggio. Caffé.

The Committee of Arrangements comprised J. Aquaro, chairman; N. Caliva, L. Ferrara, G. Scavo and Frank Avignone. Some others present were J. D'Anna, J. Scaturo, M. Cerone, Prever, Beccari, P. Agnaro, J. Marin, C. Maufredi, F. Caliva, F. Perilli, Gandolfi, E. Trippitelli, O. Abbamonte, R. Santangelo, N. Stella, F. Discepolo, J. Grassi, Biondi, F. Fitus, A. Midalini, Guagliardo, J. Zito, D. Villamena, Ferro, Fabbri, Maffia, Cocaro, Torina, R. Grassi, A. Caccisig and D. Peville.

D. S. Dunning.

The New York Representative of the Peruna Drug Mfg. Company.

After some seven years spent in the service of the Peruna Drug Mfg. Company Mr. Dunning comes to New York City full of energy and enthusiasm, a firm believer in the direct contract plan and with the benefit of a wide and varied experience to guide him in his work as local representative of the Peruna Drug Mfg. Company. Mr. Dunning is a native of New York State and was engaged in business in Rochester until he went on the road for the Peruna company, for whom he traveled all over the United States. About three years ago he was put in charge of the Indianapolis territory in carrying out "the Washington promise," and about 18 months ago was transferred to the Chicago office, looking after the interests of the company in and around that city. He won a high place in the esteem of the Chicago trade as an energetic, resourceful and tactful man and will undoubtedly meet a cordial reception at the hands of the New York trade.

Greater New York News.

Dominick F. Corrigan, a well-known druggist of Fall River, Mass., was in town on Monday and Tuesday, May 7 and 8.

Charles A. West, of the Eastern Drug Company, of Boston, visited the local wholesale trade the last week in April.

R. A. Carson, of Brannon & Carson, of Columbus, Ga., is taking a rest from business cares in this city.

A. G. Rosengarten, treasurer of the Powers-Weightman-Rosengarten Company, called at the local offices of that corporation, at 145 Water street, on May 1.

William O. Hale, of Hale, Justis & Co., of Cincinnati, Ohio, who has just recovered from a severe illness, is now in this city on a pleasure trip.

Maas & Waldstein, manufacturing chemists, formerly located at 107 Murray street, have removed their offices to 100 William street.

E. B. Rickey has bought the stock, fixtures and good will of the business formerly owned by H. J. Reel, the popular retail druggist of 616 Monroe street.

James R. Owen, of the wholesale drug house of Morrisson, Plummer & Co., of Chicago, visited the local manufacturing trade on May 8.

Francis X. Lynch has purchased the business, stock and fixtures of J. T. Lennon, a retail druggist, at 177 Asburton avenue, Yonkers.

The Fetter Drug Company, a newly incorporated concern, has opened a store at One Hundred and Forty-first street and Edgecombe avenue.

Francis W. Leonard has purchased the fixtures and stock of the drug store formerly owned by Carl Bendendorfer, at Eighty-fourth street and East End avenue.

J. C. Eliel, of the Jerman, Eliel Drug Company, of Minneapolis, Minn., has just returned from a trip through continental Europe with Mrs. Eliel and is now spending a few days in this city.

Simeon Nauheim, formerly proprietor of the S. Nauheim Pharmacy, at 750 Lexington avenue, has sold the business, stock and fixtures of the store at that address to James Lurie and Abraham M. Stoller.

Charles F. Zeitfuss, a well-known retail druggist of South Norwalk, Conn., has sold his store at 8 North Main street to Edward W. Kelley, Jr., who was formerly associated with the Stillson-Powell Corporation, of that place.

The marriage is announced of Miss Georgiana M. Parks, daughter of the Rev. Dr. and Mrs. Parks, of New York, to J. Percy Remington, son of Prof. J. P. Remington. The marriage took place on Wednesday, May 9.

Granden V. Johnson, partner in the retail drug firm of Duryea & Johnson, of Freehold, N. J., has opened a pharmacy of his own at Atlantic Highlands, N. J. It is reported that Mr. Johnson will sell his interest in the Duryea & Johnson firm, but he has not yet taken any steps in this direction.

H. W. Chambers, another popular druggist of South Norwalk, has sold his store to Platner & Bradley, a firm which already owns a large business there. It is the intention of Platner & Bradley to operate the new store as a branch pharmacy.

Lester H. Carragan, representing Parke, Davis & Co. in Cuba and the West Indies, returned to this city from Havana on May 1, and reported an unusually successful trip. Mr. Carragan was in Santiago when two slight earthquakes shook that city and terrified its inhabitants.

James F. Ballard, of St. Louis, Mo., has just purchased the business of the Dr. Herrick's Family Medicine Company, of 69 Murray street, which was established in Albany, N. Y., almost 70 years ago, and has been located in its present quarters since 1860. The stock and fixtures of the company will be moved to St. Louis within the next few weeks.

Louis Cohen, 10 Amsterdam avenue, New York, who for many years was apothecary at Gouverneur Hospital, retired recently from this position, and on the occasion of his retirement was the recipient of a dinner given him by the prominent men of the neighborhood in recognition of his services. The guests at the dinner embraced many men prominent in commercial and political circles.

W. H. Judson, who has for some years covered New Jersey and the western part of New York for William R. Warner & Co., has been assigned to the metropolitan territory tributary to New York to take the place of E. Milburn, Jr., who recently sailed for Rio Janeiro, where he will be associated with P. J. Christoph, the Brazilian agent for a number of American pharmaceuticals and specialties.

Because his landlord raised the rent on his drug store at 146 Delancey street, Dr. Riedel, the veteran pharmacist of the East Side, decided on April 25 to abandon his business at that place, which he had occupied for more than a quarter of a century. He had been paying $130 a month, but refused to consider the increased rental of $225 per month asked of him by the agents of the property.

Theodore Buhl, of Detroit, president of Parke, Davis & Co., visited the local offices on April 30 and 31. C. N. Anderson, of Detroit, head of the animal industry department, also paid a call upon the local manager and superintendent, and George Hargreaves, treasurer of the corporation, held his usual spring conference with the men in the local financial department, during the last week of April.

A crowded street car on the Ocean avenue line created havoc in the pharmacy of George Christ, at 39 Grant Square, Brooklyn, on Sunday afternoon, April 29, by jumping from its tracks and plunging headlong into the store, which was thronged with customers. The conductor of the car, the motorman and two boy patrons of Christ's soda fountain were all injured and taken to St. Mary's Hospital.

Ten members of the financial department in the local offices of Parke, Davis & Co. held their annual banquet Monday evening, April 23, in Lüchow's restaurant, at 110 East Fourteenth street. After the dinner the entire party attended the evening performance at the Hippodrome. The participants included C. N. Bruun, John J. Doran, H. C. Rollinson, J. Budelman, A. M. Bourne, W. J. Dunham, John Mincke, John McBride, Joe Tucker and Sumner Canfield.

Having regained some of his former vigor and strength by indulging in complete rest for several weeks at Atlantic City, Colonel Edward W. Fitch found himself able to take his contemplated trip abroad on Wednesday, April 18. With Mrs. Fitch and Mr. and Mrs. Hartwell, of Louisville, Ky., Colonel Fitch sailed on the steamship *Noordam* for Rotterdam, Holland. Because of his severe illness, Colonel Fitch was compelled to postpone his proposed foreign tour several times, and it was at one time feared that he would have to retire to his former home in Louisville, Ky., and recuperate there, before taking a Mediterranean trip.

Frank Richardson, of Cambridge, N. Y., the treasurer of the New York State Pharmaceutical Association, was a welcome visitor in New York drug circles last week. During his short stay here in attendance upon the State Masonic gathering he was a guest at the New York Drug Club. Mr. Richardson anticipates a most interesting session of the State Pharmaceutical Association at the forthcoming convention in Niagara Falls, the last week in June. A stiff contest for representation on the middle branch of the State Board of Pharmacy is expected, three candidates being in the field. Arrangements for the meeting are progressing actively, some particulars of which will be found in our Buffalo news letter.

Instead of selecting a new site for his business in the immediate vicinity of his well-known City Hall Pharmacy, at 263 Broadway, which he has been compelled to vacate because the building is to be pulled down, George Kneuper has sold the stock and fixtures of his store at public auction and has decided to retire permanently from the retail trade. The auction sale of Mr. Kneuper's stock and fixtures was held Friday and Saturday, April 27 and 28. The old building in which his store was located, as previously mentioned in the AMERICAN DRUGGIST, will be razed to clear the site for the eighteen-story Smith, Gray & Co. Building.

Additional support was promised in the campaign for the re-election of Joseph Weinstein as member of the New York State Board of Pharmacy at the regular monthly meeting of the New York Retail Druggists Association, which was held Friday evening, April 27, in Odd Fellows' Hall, at 67 St. Mark's place. At this meeting all the members pledged their assistance in the campaign and were greatly pleased to learn of the endorsement of Mr. Weinstein by the members of the Alumni Association of the New York College of Pharmacy and the Manhattan Pharmaceutical Association. The members of the N. Y. R. D. A. also reported at this meeting that they had generally written to their assemblymen, urging them to oppose the passage of the Stevens-Wainwright measure.

The golden wedding anniversary of Mr. and Mrs. I. C. Chapman, of Newburgh, was celebrated on Tuesday evening, April 10. Mr. Chapman is an honored citizen of Newburgh, in which city he was born July 31, 1833. For 52 years he has been continuously in business at his pharmacy in Water street. Mr. and Mrs. Chapman have one son, John H., who is the proprietor of a pharmacy at West Newburgh. Mr. and Mrs. Chapman have received many remembrances of the regard of their friends, including a silver loving cup from the trustees of the Union Presbyterian Church, of which he has been an honored officer for many years. Mr. Chapman was one of the original members of the New York State Pharmaceutical Association and was first vice-president in 1894, after serving as second vice-president the preceding year.

Mrs. Charles L. Gesell, who is associated with her husband in the management of the pharmacy at 709 Manhattan avenue, Brooklyn, and is herself a graduate in pharmacy, had a narrow escape from the San Francisco earthquake and fire. She had been visiting the Coast the week previous and stayed some time in San Francisco before returning East, which she was fortunate enough to do two days before the catastrophe occurred. Since her return Mrs. Gesell has been the recipient of numerous heartfelt congratulations from her many friends in pharmacy circles in Brooklyn. She has of late been a regular attendant at the annual meetings of the State Pharmaceutical Association, the social affairs of which have been always rendered more attractive and interesting by her participation, and it is hoped that nothing will prevent her attendance at the Niagara Falls meeting in June.

George J. Seabury and the J. N. Hegeman & Co. Stores.

Mention was made in our last issue of the fact that the J. N. Hegeman & Co.'s last store was sold to the Corporation of Hegeman & Co. and that it was sold by Mr. Seabury. It is well known in New York that when J. Niven Hegeman was secretary of the New York College of Pharmacy Mr. Seabury befriended him; at the same time he had no interest whatever in the five stores carried on by the J. N. Hageman & Co. Corporation. It happened that when Mr. Hegeman passed away, Mr. Seabury, to protect himself, was obliged to take the assets of J. N. Hegeman & Co. From the time he came into their possession he advertised them for sale, as he had no desire or disposition to continue them. Four were closed up as the leases expired, leaving only the pharmacy in the Park Row Building, which Hageman & Co. purchased, as stated in the preceding issue. This bit of history is given in order to correct false rumors, to the effect that Mr. Seabury had engaged in the retail drug business, for he has at no time ever considered such a thing.

Keeps Him Posted.

Inclosed find money order for renewal of subscription for AMERICAN DRUGGIST AND PHARMACEUTICAL RECORD. Although not now actively engaged in the drug business, I continue my interest in your journal, which keeps me posted as to what is going on in the drug line. JNO. WENDELL FRECH, PH.G.

ATLANTA, GA., April 12, 1906.

WESTERN NEW YORK.

Providing for the Niagara Falls Meeting—Bonding Companies' Exorbitant Demands—Bowlers' Final Meet Only Druggists Registered—A Special Fund for the California Sufferers.

(From our Regular Correspondent.)

Buffalo, May 9.—Details of the arrangements for the Niagara Falls meeting will be found in a special article in another column.

PRICE SCHEDULE WELL MAINTAINED.

It is a cold spring in Buffalo, but the retail druggist gets now and then a pleasant evening or a mild Sunday and finds that there is a disposition to return to the soda water habit. There is besides, a little better trade in regular druggists' articles, so that the complaints that have been pretty common most of the year are not so numerous now. The price list is held to without a break, so that the evidence of good faith is also an item in the direction of good feeling.

PRICE OF BONDS GO UP.

Buffalo retail druggists are not inclined to say much that is pleasant of the insurance companies that sell excise bonds this year. The companies have long been at loggerheads on the subject, and have practically given away their bonds to all comers—hotels and saloons—as well as any one. Often the charge to the worst saloon was only $8 or so, when the license fee was $1,150, and was quite too often forfeited. So this year eight companies combined, put the regular price up to $50 and $40 and made it impossible for any saloon to get a lower rate. There was squirming, but it had to be paid. The druggists proceeded to cut down their full $450 licenses to five—Stoddart Bros., Cahoon-Lyon, Faxon and R. K. Smithers' two stores. The regular prescription licenses were also reduced in number, but as the rate was only $7.50, it was thought that a very small fee for bond would be charged, and when it was made $20 there was rebellion, and they all went out and got individual bonds, besides vowing that they would never deal with the grasping insurance companies again. So their bonds cost nothing, and overreaching defeated itself.

THE BUFFALO DRUGGISTS' BOWLING CLUB

invited the ladies to be present on the closing night of the season, May 4, and had a very fine time. They offered a long list of prizes and served lunch, but they stuck to bowling all the evening. The ladies joined in the bowling with zest, and sometimes made bigger scores than the men did. The club as a whole is stronger than ever, as the old members keep up their records and several new ones have done especially well, as for instance, H. M. Anthony and John W. Kellner. William Waugh is also a new "high roller," and with J. A. Lockie forms a two-man team in a city club, where they stand at the top.

REGISTERED BY THE BOARD.

At the April examination of the applicants for license by the Western branch of the State Board of Pharmacy only prospective druggists appeared, of whom the following were successful: C. A. Anderson, George H. Grimes, E. F. Bachmann, Jay L. Harnish, Mark P. Barry, Charles V. Hawley, Grover E. Massage, Clarence L. Heath, Charles W. Bullock, Walter J. Heegaard, Carl R. Brooks, Luther H. Roper, Arthur G. Davis, Garnet A. Siple, Arthur G. Drefs, Nealy Stafford, Lew R. Dunfee, John B. Sumner, Le Roy W. Farnam, Charles H. Van Brocklin, Lum D. Fuller, William R. Wheeler, William E. Gallagher, all of Buffalo; James E. Cooney, Bradford, Pa.; Edward R. Jones, Niagara Falls.

PRESENTATION TO DR. GREGORY.

There was a very pleasant gathering of Buffalo druggists, directors of the Drug Merchants' Exchange, and their wives, at the home of Manager S. A. Grove, of the company, on the evening of April 26. Refreshments were served, and Dr. W. G. Gregory, the retiring president of the Exchange, was presented with an elegant coffee set of five pieces, President F. A. Darrin, of the City Retail Druggists' Association, making the presentation speech. The Exchange is in a very flourishing condition, and includes in its members nearly all of the retail druggists in the city.

SPECIAL FUND FOR SAN FRANCISCO SUFFERERS.

The Buffalo retail druggists are getting up a special fund to send to the druggists of San Francisco, who seem to have suffered fully as much as any one in the ill-fated city, many of them having lost everything. The Buffalo druggists had already contributed considerably to the regular relief fund before the special appeal was made, but it is found that it is quite an easy matter to do a little in a special way also.

BUFFALO NEWS NOTES.

The Cahoon-Lyon Drug Company of Buffalo is opening a special East Side store on Fillmore avenue. The store lately bought of Dr. Gregory on Main street will soon be refitted and enlarged, great pains being made to put it in the best possible shape. The company gave a spring opening at the central store lately and attracted a great crowd by the displays of specialties. Manager Drake has made a success of the new venture.

J. A. Lockie is very proud of the fine new soda fountain lately installed in his store on upper Main street, Buffalo. It is so elegant and serviceable at the same time without being in any way gaudy or bulky. He is now to have a new front, and then proposes to give an opening, providing music and other attractions.

PREPARING FOR THE NEW YORK STATE MEETING.

Headquarters at the International Hotel, Niagara Falls—Outline of Entertainments—Buffalo to Do Its Full Share.

(From our Regular Correspondent.)

Buffalo, May 9.—President Lockie and the local committees at Niagara Falls have about completed the arrangements for the annual convention of the State Pharmaceutical Association, which is to be held in that city June 26-29. President Eugene Laurier, of the Retail Druggists' Association at Niagara Falls, is chairman of the General Committee, and Harry Stein of the Entertainment Committee. The International Hotel has been selected as headquarters, and all the sessions will be held in the hotel assembly room. This hotel is now under the same management as the Cataract House, which adjoins it, and both are included in the arrangement. Rooms on the American plan will be provided at $3 to $5, according to location.

It is promised that the business of the convention shall be of a specially interesting and important character, though it is not the plan to give out any details beforehand. Such subjects as legislation, excise, State board and the like will be taken up.

THE ENTERTAINMENT PROGRAMME IS LONG AND VARIED.

On Tuesday afternoon the visiting ladies will be taken in charge by the Ladies' Committee and a suitable outing will be given. In the evening there will be the president's reception and dance. On Wednesday the outings will include a visit to the Shredded Wheat Biscuit factory. It was at one time arranged to hold the meetings there, but it was felt that it was too far away from the hotel and the falls. On Wednesday evening the commercial travelers give their entertainment, which is promised to be one of especial interest. F. W. Buescher, Buffalo representative of Parke, Davis & Co., is chairman of this committee.

On Thursday the convention will be turned over to the Buffalo retail druggists for entertainment. The plan is not worked out yet, but the visitors will be taken to Buffalo for a lunch, theater party or something of the sort. Probably there will be more than one feature of it besides the ride. The committee to manage the matter is to be appointed by President Darrin, of the city retail association.

Friday's outing will consist of an excursion to Toronto by lake from Lewiston, taking in all of the Gorge route, going and returning. A long stay in Toronto is planned, and the day ought to be a very acceptable one. For those who remain Friday night there will be dancing on the return from Toronto.

NEW ENGLAND.

License or No License the Question of the Hour—A Silver Wedding—Charged with Illegal Sale of Liquor—The State Board of Health Brings Charges Against a Druggist.

(From our Regular Correspondent.)

Boston, May 9.—This is the time of year when the license question is an important issue in the Bay State. The Board of Aldermen of Malden voted 5 to 2 against granting licenses to druggists in that city. One of the aldermen said he believed the new law, which gives druggists the right to sell liquors on doctor's prescriptions, was sufficient. In Cambridge the Committee on Licenses reported against issuing any permits. The report was tabled. This action disturbed the druggists of that city, and a meeting was subsequently held in Boston to consider the question. Since then the Aldermen have agreed to give a hearing on the druggists' petitions. The Somerville Aldermanic Board has voted to license thirty druggists. One application is still pending. Before the granting of these licenses considerable of a flurry was created by the Aldermen requesting a conference at one of their meetings with several of the petitioners, and a report was circulated, which subsequently proved erroneous, that a number of applications were to be refused. In Framingham the feeling over this subject is intense. In March the town voted no license, but this did not deter the druggists from petitioning for licenses, and their request is backed up by petitions bearing the names of several hundred signers favoring the idea. To add fuel to the flames, a no-license organization of the town has registered an emphatic protest against granting a single license. At Fitchburg, where a "no" vote was registered in December, the License Commissioners have voted 2 to 1 against granting any licenses. As the above two are favorable to license it is thought that their action in making the town "extra dry" is an attempt to make license votes for the coming December.

A SILVER WEDDING.

On the evening of April 27, Mr. and Mrs. Fred A. Hubbard, of Newton, celebrated the twenty-fifth anniversary of their wedding, and they were the recipients of many congratulations and gifts from their numerous friends. They were assisted in receiving by their two children, E. Florence and G. Whitney Hubbard. The ushers were Burdett Mansfield, Henry C. Nutting and William H. Whitcomb. The Rev. Thomas W. Bishop, of Auburndale, who married the couple, was present. Mr. Hubbard is prominently identified with the Board of Pharmacy and has held many positions of trust in druggists' organizations.

SALE OF ADULTERATED ALCOHOL CHARGED.

The State Board of Health recently complained of Allyn E. Howe and Dr. William H. Jackson, both of Stoughton, for the alleged sale of adulterated alcohol.

LIQUOR TROUBLES.

Three druggists of Dorchester were recently before the court charged with a violation of the liquor law. They were Thomas A. Bishop, of 1522 Dorchester avenue; Frank W. Proctor, of 212 Bowdoin street, and William H. Cole, of 1876 Dorchester avenue. Two Malden dealers, Joseph P. Kerrigan and John A. Quigley, were in the court in that city a few days ago charged with keeping and exposing liquor without a license. They were fined $100; the two men are partners and run a store at 274 Main street.

HONOR FOR A MANUFACTURING DRUGGIST.

James E. Wetherald, the president of Chester Kent & Co., has been appointed one of the five sinking fund commissioners, who have the control and the distribution of the permanent funds of the city of Boston, which amount to over $30,000,000. The position is one of the highest honor, carries no salary with it, and the selection of Mr. Wetherald is a well-deserved compliment. Mr. Wetherald is widely and favorably known in the wholesale trade through his connection with the Vinol Company and is well known in newspaperdom through his proprietorship of the advertising agency which bears his name.

PENNSYLVANIA.

No Ill Effect from the Loder Verdict—P. A. R. D. Grows Steadily—P. A. R. D. Have Mammoth Entertainment—A Move Against Counter Prescribing—Wm. McIntyre to Retire.

(From our Regular Correspondent.)

Philadelphia, May 7.—The monthly meetings of the Philadelphia Retail Drug Association are becoming more attractive, and there is a larger attendance each month. The meeting on May 4 was largely attended, and there were a number of important things done that kept the attention of those present until the session was adjourned. Three new members were elected. The committee that was appointed to secure funds for the San Francisco druggists reported that it had collected $800, which amount was sent forward to assist their fellow druggists. A number of visitors were present and they were greatly interested in the work that the local association is doing. Mr. Bottume, the organizer who is looking after the druggists throughout the city, reported that the business was in better shape than it has been for a long time and that the druggists are pulling together better than they have ever before. Many had been of the opinion that the Loders verdict would cause general cutting throughout the city. Such, however, has not been the case, and while there has been some reduction made on certain articles, prices have been well maintaind, as a rule.

MORE COMMISSION ON ADVERTISEMENTS.

The retail druggists who are acting as branch advertising agencies for the newspapers have demanded a larger commission on the business they take. Heretofore the papers have been paying the druggists 10 per cent., but they now ask 25 per cent. commission. It is understood that some of the papers are willing to grant this concession, but the dailies which do the greater business through these stores are not inclined to grant the request. It is said if the newspapers do not pay 25 per cent. commission that the retail druggists will refuse to handle their business. This action has been brought about in a great measure through the fact that all the leading druggists being members of the retail drug association. Here again is another example that in union there is strength and that without this organization the retailers could not combine together to compel the newspapers to accede to their request.

THE ANNUAL P. A. R. D. ENTERTAINMENT.

The musicale and dance given by the members of the Philadelphia Association of Retail Druggists on May 8 at the Lulu Temple was a pronounced success. As part of the funds realized from this festive affair were to be devoted to assisting fellow druggists in San Francisco, the attendance was very large, and there were many present from out of town. It is not often that the druggists have an opportunity to indulge in any gayety, and they did not fail to grasp the opportunity. While some of the two steps looked more like side stepping at a prize fight than like the fashionable measure, there was an enthusiasm displayed which added zest to the occasion. The affair was a most enjoyable one. Every one was in his or her best mood, and there was nothing left undone by the committee to make things pleasant. Nearly every owner of a drug store in the city was present, and many clerks who were lucky enough to get a night off were also there with their best girls. The programme included musical numbers by a large orchestra and solos by Mrs. H. A. Nolte and Edward Shippen, vocalists; Fritz Ulrich, violinist; Mrs. Ray Daniel-Jones, organist, and H. Gruhler, pianist. The second part of the programme included vaudeville numbers by some of the best professional talent appearing at the local theatres. After 11 o'clock dancing commenced, and liquid refreshments consisting of the most popular beverages were dispensed to the thirsty from real soda water counters. Great credit for the success of the affair is due to the energetic work of the chairman, Clarence H. C. Campbell, of the Entertainment Committee, and the following well-known pharmacists who assisted him: Samuel C. Henry, vice-chairman; Frank M. Apple, secretary; Dr. E. K. Boltz, treasurer, and William Hilpert, J. E. Marsden, H. A. Nolte, J. H.

Bailey, C. G. Neely, William H. Sutton, W. E. Supplee, and N. S. Steltzer.

THE WEIGHTMAN ESTATE STILL INTERESTED IN CHEMICALS.

Mrs. Anne M. Weightman Walker, one of the leading women financiers of the country and the daughter of the late W. W. Weightman, has lately taken a prominent part in the merger of three big chemical companies in this city and Baltimore. They were controlled by the sons of Henry Bower, who owed his start in business to the friendship of William Weightman. The interests united are the Baltimore Chrome Works Company, of Baltimore; the Kaolin Chemical Company and the Ammonia Company, of Philadelphia. These companies have been merged and will be conducted by the Henry Bower Chemical Manufacturing Company, with a capital of $2,000,000 common, $500,000 first preferred and $150,000 second preferred stock.

PHARMACY BOARD TO PROSECUTE FOR THEFT OF EXAMINATION PAPERS.

There will shortly be something doing which will be of great interest to all retail druggists of this city and the State of Pennsylvania. The State Pharmaceutical Examining Board has been quietly working on the stealing of the examination questions, and it is said that within a few weeks that further arrests will be made. It is the intention of the board to press this matter to the end, and every effort is to be made to punish all those who were in any way connected with the theft of the papers. The members of the board have placed the matter in the hands of detectives, and it is understood that valuable information has been secured, which will enable the board to further press the suits and to have arrested several who were connected in the stealing of the papers. On May 19 there will be an examination of druggists at Harrisburg and Pittsburgh. It is safe to say that the examination questions will not get beyond the members of the board before they are submitted to the applicants for certificates. It is understood that a large class will come up for examination.

The good business that the retail druggists have had during the winter is letting up. This is mainly on account of the more pleasant weather and the amount of illness being less than it has been. Besides this, many people have begun to move out of the city for the summer, and this always means a falling off in business. There are some druggists who follow their customers up, no matter where they go, and manage to hold their trade throughout the year. More are doing this than ever.

WILLIAM M'INTYRE TO RETIRE.

William McIntyre, of Frankford avenue and Adams street, has decided to retire from the drug business and has sold his story to Q. Hoch. Mr. McIntyre is one of the best known druggists in this State and will be missed from the different associations. He is a member of the Board of Education and is very active in educational matters and will devote a large part of his time to public affairs of that kind.

PHILADELPHIA NEWS NOTES.

The graduating exercises of the Philadelphia College of Pharmacy will be held on May 17. It is understood that the class will be a large one and comprises members from nearly every section of the country. On May 11 the Board of Trustees passed on the examination papers, and arrangements were made to have the usual preliminaries preceding the commencement. This week the prizes will be announced and the regular dinner to the commencement class will be given by the faculty.

John L. Curty, who has been ill for some time, has sold his store, at Twenty-second and Callowhill streets, to Joseph S. Clair, his former clerk.

A co-operative drug sundry house is in process of formation in this city. The value of the stock has been placed at $100 per share, and the success of the Philadelphia Wholesale Drug Company has acted as an incentive for druggists to join. There is no reason why the new enterprise should not be a success, as the drug company does not handle sundries and the two concerns will not conflict.

THE WEST.

Lively Meeting of the Chicago Association—Resolutions Opposing Trust Brands of Cigars—Sellers of Cocaine Censured—Medical Society Seeks Co-operation of Druggists on Pure Food Bill—The N. A. R. D. Relief Fund.

(From our Regular Correspondent.)

Chicago, May 9.—So many important matters came up for discussion at the last meeting of the C. R. D. A. that the session lasted until 1 o'clock in the morning. So much business was then unfinished that an adjourned meeting became necessary. The Chicago manager of the National Cigar Stands Company had been invited to be present to state his side of the matters now in dispute, but he failed to put in an appearance. After a short discussion these resolutions were adopted:

Whereas, The steady encroachments made by the Tobacco Trust upon the business of independent dealers in tobacco and cigars has affected the retail druggist by lessening his profits in this part of our business; and

Whereas, Members of our association have been forced to give up locations in which they had established themselves, owing to the covetousness of the United Cigar Stores Company; and

Whereas, The sale by druggists of brands of cigars manufactured by the Tobacco Trust has a tendency to seriously affect our future business interests; therefore, be it

Resolved, That we, the members of the C. R. D. A., in regular meeting assembled, deem it of great importance that our members should encourage the sale of only such cigars as are made by independent manufacturers, and that such trust goods as we are required to keep in stock should be kept in places not in view of our customers.

President Avery told the druggists what had been accomplished in their behalf with regard to measures pending before the Council, and I. M. Light called attention to the fact that representatives of the Saloonkeepers' Association are keeping close watch of drug stores in the hope that they can discover violations of the ordinances. A partnership proposition from the Sanitol Company, which offered a profit-sharing plan, was rejected. Resolutions threatening A. and Joseph Monaco with expulsion from the organization because they had been fined for selling cocaine were adopted.

The adjourned meeting was made notable by the presence of Dr. Bacon, president of the Chicago Medical Society, and Dr. Gilmore, a member. As this marks the beginning of relations between the Chicago Medical Society and the C. R. D. A. the event was of more than ordinary importance. It is believed that the results of united action will be far-reaching. Drs. Bacon and Gilmore asked druggists to go on record as being opposed to amending the Senate bill in such a way as not to require patent medicine to be labeled "poison," when they contain poisonous ingredients. It was argued that druggists have to use such labels, and that it was not logical to exempt patent medicines. A motion in opposition to the proposed amendment was adopted by an unimous vote.

TWENTY-NINE THOUSAND DOLLARS FOR 'FRISCO SUFFERERS.

A generous response has been made to the appeal from National Headquarters for funds to be used in relieving the condition of druggists in San Francisco who have suffered because of the earthquake and fire. Up to the time of the last report the sum of $29,000 had been subscribed.

NOTES.

Albert E. Ebert has moved his stock around the corner from his old stand on State street. He is now at 9 Polk street.

John Krone will soon reopen a store at his old stand on Clark street.

Parke, Davis & Co. have begun operations on the handsome building they are to erect on Franklin street, across the alley from their present quarters. It will be six stories high, cover a space 60 x 100 feet and will be of modern construction. The material will be brick, with a stone front.

The botanical excursions of the students of the University of Illinois School of Pharmacy, announced for May and June, will be held as follows: First excursion, Thursday, May 10, to Glencoe, Ill. Take C. & N. W. R. R., Wells street depot. Train leaves on Milwaukee division at 10.30 A. M. Second excursion, Thursday, May 24, to Hinsdale, Ill. Train leaves on C., B. & Q., Union depot, at 10.15 A. M. Third excursion, Thursday,

June 7, to Glencoe, Ill. Same hour and place as for the first excursion. Fourth excursion, Thursday, June 21, to Gibson, Ind. Announcement of time will be made later.

The Social Drug Club gave a May party on the evening of May 4. The members played progressive cinch and then danced.

Robert Stevenson, Jr., formerly of the firm of Robert Stevenson & Co., drug importers and wholesale dealers in chemicals, announces his connection with the Chicago office of Messrs. Lee, Higginson & Co., bankers, of Boston, who are large dealers in conservative bonds. Mr. Stevenson's offices are in the Rookery.

John S. Cass, of the house of Armour & Co., who looks after the beef extract department, has made a successful tour of the East, calling on their branch houses at Toronto, Montreal, Boston, New York, Philadelphia and Baltimore. He reported that the house of Armour & Co. were getting their share of the Eastern business, and the future looks very promising.

The new Briggs House Pharmacy, opened May 1 by the Allen R. Fellows Company, will prove a winner and is greatly appreciated by the business men in that locality. There has been no drug store in this hotel since the removal of the pharmacy conducted by the late Louis Waldron, and this one started by Allen R. Fellows Company should be a colossal success.

The Oklahoma Board of Pharmacy.

The Oklahoma Board of Pharmacy met in Guthrie, Okla., on January 9. A class of 32 was present and took the examination, of whom the following passed and received certificates of registration:

Sidney B. Buchanan, Mangum; W. E. Bailey, Carnegie; Carl W. Denney, Lawton; J. L. Fink, Blackwell; E. W. Hiatt, Edmond; C. Le Roy Hunt, Oklahoma City; D. G. Kilburn, Quincy, Ill.; Edw. Lieurance, Neosha Falls, Kan.; Henry Ozanne, Woodward; Chas. A. Ridley, Davenport; Wm. F. Wylde, Perry; Jno. B. C. Worley, Cache; Earl D. Walker, Meeker, and Wm. Ziegler, Pond Creek.

The following were registered upon diplomas from colleges:

Edw. S. Arnold, Davenport, Ia., Highland Park College of Pharmacy.
H. G. Agner, Ottawa, Ohio, Ohio Northern University.
Jno. H. Bonton, Enid, Okla., Oklahoma University, Norman.
W. A. Blaesser, Cherokee, Iowa, Northwestern University, Chicago.
G. G. Curry, Greenville, Pa., Ohio Northern University.
M. S. Caldwell, Jonesborough, Ark., Atlanta College of Pharmacy.
Geo. C. Diekman, New York City, New York College of Pharmacy.
Chas. W. Davis, Tecumseh, Okla., Oklahoma University.
Jno. R. Elson, Wellsburg, W. Va., Scio College of Pharmacy.
Jno. P. Eckers, Oklahoma City, Chicago College of Pharmacy.
Jno. H. Frost, Rockford, Ill., University of Michigan.
N. E. Hawkins, Scio, O., Scio College of Pharmacy.
E. W. Hammond, Sparks, Okla., Detroit College of Pharmacy.
Jno. C. Inman, Bradner, O., Ohio Northern University.
Chas. E. Kirschner, Davenport, Ia., Highland Park College of Pharmacy.
Jno. E. Mertes, Prague, Okla., University of Oklahoma.
Perry O. Sheer, Kingfisher, Okla., Highland Park College of Pharmacy.
Wm. H. Selig, Cherokee, Okla., Northwestern University.
Arthur T. Schieder, Lena, Ill., Chicago College of Pharmacy.
E. R. Thorson, Rock Island, Ill., Highland Park College of Pharmacy.
Hite Watson, Oklahoma City, Philadelphia College of Pharmacy.
Chas. M. Wagner, McLean, Ill., Ohio Northern University.

The date of the next regular meeting was set for April 10, 1906, at Oklahoma City, Okla. T.

F. B. Lillie, Guthrie, Okla., who is secretary of the board, recently celebrated the twenty-fifth anniversary of his wedding and was the recipient of many handsome presents on that occasion.

Mr. Kathrens Enters the Advertising Field.

Joseph R. Kathrens, who has long been a prominent figure in the proprietary medicine world, has resigned his position as manager of the Best Tonic department and the general advertising department of the Pabst Brewing Company and has associated himself with the advertising agency known as the J. Walter Thompson Company, of New York and Chicago. When he announced his intention of leaving Milwaukee to take up his residence in Chicago the Milwaukee Press Club tendered him a farewell supper, which brought out a large and brilliant gathering of men, who wished to join in doing honor to Mr. Kathrens.

THE SOUTH.

Busy with Conventions in New Orleans—Hopeful Situation—Wholesalers as Well as Retailers Co-operate—Help for 'Frisco Sufferers.

(From our Regular Correspondent.)

New Orleans, La., May 7.—The recent convention of the State Pharmaceutical Association, the meeting of the Southern Drug Club, which took place during the convention of the pharmacists, the efforts of the druggists to secure funds for the sufferers in San Francisco, and the existing trade conditions in New Orleans, are giving the druggists, both retail and wholesale, ample food for thought and consideration. Fruits of the work of the State pharmacists' convention are beginning to show, and the druggists locally are taking advantage of existing conditions.

WHOLESALERS ALSO IN SESSION.

The session of the Southern Drug Club, composed of wholesalers of the South, was held here during the meeting of the State Association, in order that the members of the former might form the acquaintance of the representatives and delegates of the latter. In this respect the meeting of the Drug Club was very successful.

THE SAN FRANCISCO RELIEF COMMITTEE.

A competent committee, headed by William M. Levy, is representing the local druggists in getting subscriptions for the relief of the San Francisco pharmacists who suffered as a result of the disastrous earthquake and fire. This committee has already raised a good sized sum and is still busy securing contributions. It is composed of William M. Levy, chairman: George V. Claren, John E. Scott, Joseph T. Balter, A. Di Trapani, C. D. Sauvinet, and George W. McDuff. Among the subscribers are all the members of the committee and the following others: M. T. Breslin, F. C. Godbold, E. W. Vacher, R. F. Grace, Dr. Richard Angel, Adam Wirth, Dr. E. S. Kelly, and R. L. Villere.

GRADUATES IN PHARMACY.

Eighteen pharmacists were graduated from the medical department of Tulane University of Louisiana, at the annual exercises, held at the Tulane Theater last Wednesday. At the same time 102 doctors of medicine were also graduated. These are the names of the pharmaceutical graduates: Miss R. Buisslerre, C. H. Drake, George W. Faivre, Walter S. Fossier, T. S. Jones, A. J. Laiche, W. W. Leake, R. H. Moers, E. H. Morgan, J. T. Moss, P. D. O'Donnell, W. D. Phillips, J. H. Pridgen, J. C. Richards, H. M. Scroggins, A. P. Smith, E. C. Vocke and H. Weston.

Maryland Board Pass List.

The Maryland Board of Pharmacy held a meeting at the Hotel Rennert on May 2 to elect officers for the ensuing year and to pass upon candidates who took the April examination. The following were successful:

Pharmacists—Miss Emma Grace Lotz, William Stichel, Edwin A. Schmidt, Stanley A. Pentz, Thomas F. A. Stevens, George P. Hetz, Benjamin D. Benfer, James E. Hancock, Charles Rossberg, William Van Vorst Parramore, Joseph T. Wallace, Joseph Porembsky, Franklin D. Wilson, Samuel B. Downes, Alfred S. Williams.

Assistant Pharmacists—Thomas W. Ritch, John C. Eby, Amil K. Parks, Normon E. Shakespeare, Frank C. Balmert, Fred. L. Henry, D. C. Pharr, Moore R. Garland, John William Bauth, James W. Thompson, Howard Ruff, George O. Sharrett, Francis O. Barrett, Merker N. Buppert.

The officers were elected as follows:

President, William C. Powell, Snow Hill, Md.; secretary, Ephraim Bacon, Roland Park; treasurer, John A. Davis, Baltimore. The other members are J. Lionel Meredith, Hagerstown, Md., and Louis Schulz, of Baltimore.

The Manufacturing Chemists' Registration Bureau.

The following title has been received for registration in the Manufacturing Chemists' Registration Bureau: "Dulcissa," by Frederick Stearns & Co., Detroit, Mich., and "Trikresin," "Anticongestus Compound" and "Anticongestus," by William R. Warner & Co., Philadelphia, Pa.

The Drug and Chemical Market

The prices quoted in this report are those current in the wholesale market, and higher prices are paid for retail lots. The quality of goods frequently necessitates a wide range of prices.

Condition of Trade.

NEW YORK, May 12, 1906.

Comparatively little has transpired in the general market for drugs and chemicals during the period under review to excite any unusual interest. About the usual number of variations in prices are to be noted, and while the market has not been characterized by any show of activity, a fairly good tone prevails all along the line and sufficient business is passing to cause a cheerful feeling. A good proportion of the orders received by local houses have come from the Pacific Coast, where the demand for disinfectants especially is heavy. It is expected that values on certain lines will be improved if local stocks are much depleted by orders from San Francisco. Alcohol was advanced, and quinine lowered in value. Peppermint oil maintains its firm position, and the position of clove and pennyroyal oils has been strengthened, a sharp advance being recorded for the last named. Spermaceti is higher, while American saffron shows a sharp decline. There is little new or interesting to report on botanical drugs, and chemicals are without noteworthy interest. Prices are firm as a rule, and the majority of changes are in favor of buyers, as will be seen by the subjoined table:

HIGHER.	LOWER.
Alcohol,	Opium,
Castor oil,	Quinine,
Peppermint oil,	Balsam fir, Canada,
Pennyroyal oil,	Pulsatilla herb,
Balsam, Para,	Arsenic, white,
Clove oil,	Saffron, American,
Cubeb berries,	Wahoo bark,
Calamus root,	Juniper berries,
Jalap root,	Menthol,
Guarana,	Wax, Japan.
Silver nitrate,	
Cardamon seeds,	
Liquid styrax,	
Lycopodium,	
Spermaceti,	
Tartar emetic.	

Drugs.

Alcohol has been advanced in the interval, the distillers of grain now asking $2.47 to $2.49 for 95 per cent. quality. Wood is held and selling at 70c to 75c for 95 per cent. and 97 per cent., respectively.

Balsams.—Copaiba, Para, is in light supply and firmer, with some holders asking 50c for prime, though supplies are obtainable down to 45c. Central American has been received in fair volume since our last, but almost all of the available supply has been taken, at the current range of 29c to 32c. Fir, Oregon, has developed some scarcity, and holders are firmer in their views, at the quoted range of 75c to 80c; Canada is without change of consequence, either as regard price or demand; quoted, $3 to $3.10. Peru and Tolu are dull, at nominally unchanged prices.

Buchu leaves, short, are maintained with firmness, at the quoted range of 18c to 20c, in view of cable advices from primary sources of supply reporting that the new crop had all been sold for Hamburg and London interests, and that new crop would not be available until next January.

Burgundy pitch has eased off a trifle in the interval and sales are reported at 4c to 4¼c.

Cantharides, Chinese whole, are held with marked firmness, in view of concentration of stocks, and we hear of no sales at under 75c; powdered is available at 76c to 77c.

Cascara sagrada is offered sparingly from the coast, and values show a hardening tendency, though supplies are still obtainable at 5½c to 8c.

Castor oil has been advanced by the refiners, owing to a reported scarcity of beans; No. 1 is now quoted at 11¼c to 12½c and 12c to 13c in barrels and cases, respectively, while No. 3 is held at 10½c to 11½c and 11c to 12c.

Codliver oil is seasonably quiet and we have no important features to chronicle. Business is confined for the most part to jobbing transactions, at unchanged quotations, or, say, $21.00 to $25.00 for Norwegian and $19.00 to $20.00 for Newfoundland. Cable advices reported the Finmarken catch of oil to the end of last week as 3,100,000 fish, equal to 2,150 barrels of oil. The Finmarken season will last until the early part of June, and as it may add considerably to the catch of Lofoten and other districts, now practically at an end, buyers will probably continue their waiting tactics until the final result is known. Cable advices on April 30 reported the close of the Lofoten codfishing season, with a result of 18,600,000 fish, or 14,615 barrels, and the total for entire Norway was given as 36,100,000 fish, or 28,600 barrels of oil.

Cubeb berries are maintained with more firmness, owing to the tenor of foreign advices, and spot quotations are fractionally higher, at 9½ to 10c., as to quality and quantity.

Cuttlefish bone is finding a moderate outlet only, but prime grades of Trieste are firmly held at 17c to 17½c, owing to stronger advices from primary sources of supply; French is held at 12c to 12½, while jewelers' large and small are quoted at 70c for the former and 40c to 50c for the latter.

Grindelia robusta is in good demand and the tone of the market is stronger, owing to reduced stocks. An offer of 8½c on a lot of 1,000 pounds has been turned down by one holder, though a lesser quantity might be released at this figure, despite the quoted range of 9c to 9½c. It is reported that 3,000 pounds had been offered to a local dealer from San Francisco before the catastrophe, and this was said to represent the principal holdings in that quarter.

Haarlem oil is reported as jobbing fairly and meeting with a good consuming inquiry as well; quoted, $3.00 to $3.25.

Lycopodium is finding increased seasonable demand, and recent sales of unlabeled in cases were 48c, with the tendency upward.

Menthol has eased off a trifle since our last, single cases being obtainable in instances at $2.55, though $2.60 to $2.75 is a more popular quotation.

Naphthalin balls have declined in the interval, owing to heavy arrivals and lack of important demand; quoted 1.80c to 1.95c, as to quantity.

Opium is selling in a jobbing way only, there being little inquiry for quantity lots. The continued lack of interest in the article has served to further depress value, and cases now are offered $2.72½ to $2.75 and broken packages at $2.75 to $2.77½. Powdered is finding a moderate consuming outlet only at prices within the quoted range of $3.20 to $3.25.

Pulsatilla herb is in a dull and unsatisfactory condition, with offerings at 7c to 7½c.

Quinine was reduced on the 4th inst. by domestic and foreign manufacturers to the uniform level of 17c for bulk in 100-ounce cans, but the demand has not been stimulated by the reduction and the tone of the market has not strengthened in the interval, only a limited jobbing business being reported at the new range of values. The decline was unexpected and took second hands unawares, though they are now quoting at 16¾c; Java is held and selling at 16½c to 16¾c.

Saffron, American, has suddenly dropped in price and the market is now in a very unsettled condition. Keen competition, stimulated by the approach of new crop goods, is attributed as the cause. Sales were reported last Wednesday at $1.25, but the flowers are now obtainable at $1.05. Other varieties are unchanged, Valencia being quoted at $7.50 to $8.00 and Alicante at $4.50 to $5.00.

Wax, Japan, is lower as the result of recent arrivals and keen local competition, 11c to 12c being now quoted. Bayberry is also lower and supplies are obtainable at 42c to 45c. Brazil maintains its firm position, with No. 1 quoted 50c to 52½c, No. 2, 42½c to 45c, and No. 3 at 36c to 37c.

Chemicals.

Acetate of lime has been in better demand since the month opened, but prices show no change from the previous range of 1.60c to 1.65c for brown, and 2.35c to 2.40c for gray, as to quantity and terms.

Ammonium carbonate is in moderate demand and steady, with sales reported at 7¾c to 8c, in barrels, as to quantity; powdered is held and selling at 8¾c to 9c.

Arsenic, white, offers freely at 5¼c to 5¾c, a practical decline, but the reduction in price has not stimulated trade to any extent.

Chlorate of potash has receded in the interval, on account of pressure to sell from second hands, and 9¼c to 9½c is now asked for crystals in jobbing quantities; powdered is also easier, at 9½c to 9¾c.

Citric acid maintains its firmness, in view of the advance of the season, and manufacturers' quotations remain at the previous range of 43c to 43½c. It is not expected that prices will further advance, except in the event of corresponding improvement abroad, since under existing conditions importations of foreign might be encouraged.

Cream tartar is in improved demand, and the market is quoted firm, at 22½c for crystals and 23¼c for powdered.

Nitrate of silver has been advanced since our last, manufacturers now quoting 42¼c to 45¾c, as to quantity, the inside figures being for lots of 1,000 ounces or more.

Oxalic acid has weakened in the interval, owing to competition, and the revised quotations are 6c to 6½c.

Tartaric acid is in improved jobbing request and values are well sustained, at the range of 27¾c to 28¼c for crystals and 28c to 28½ for powdered.

Essential Oils.

Almond, expressed sweet, is higher at primary sources, and spot quotations have been advanced to 41c. to 43c.

Citronella remains quiet, but the quotations of the market are maintained at 38c. to 40c.

Clove is in strong upward tendency in sympathy with the spice, and dealers offer sparingly at the quoted range of 90c. to 92½c. in cans and 92½c. to 95c. in bottles.

Cubeb is held with more confidence, in view of the stronger position of the berries, but quotations show no change from 85c. to 90c.

Lemon has developed increased firmness, and 70c. to 75c. is quoted for the leading brands, though supplies are available at 65c.

Pennyroyal continues scarce and values have advanced. French oil is in better supply than the domestic, but is held at $1.60 to $1.75; domestic quoted $2 to $2.25.

Peppermint maintains its firm position, and dealers are confident of a further early advance, sales being made with reserve in view of the depletion of spot stocks and the unfavorable outlook for the new crop. The market for case oil shows an advance to $3.35 to $3.50. Bulk is also in firmer tendency, with several holders asking $3, though $2.75 will yet buy.

Gums.

Aloes, Curacao, is in better supply, but only a limited inquiry is experienced and values show no change from 5¾c to 6c. Barbados is in light supply and holders are firmer in their view, with sales at 16c to 17c.

Asafœtida continues inactive and the tendency of the market favors buyers, at the quoted range of 14c to 18c, for good to prime.

Arabic sorts is not coming forward in any quantity, and dealers complain of difficulty in meeting requirements.

Camphor is held steadily at the recently established range of $1 to $1.00½ for refined in bbls. and cases, respectively. Crude is reported scarce and higher in Europe, and local refiners are experiencing some difficulty in getting sufficient supplies to operate their plants.

Gamboge is in better supply and offers more freely, but at unchanged prices. Broken pipe is obtainable at 95c, but for the whole pipe $1.05 is named.

Tragacanth has sold more actively in the interval and values are firmer, especially for the Aleppo variety, which is held at 64c to 68c for first, and 40c to 45c for thirds.

Roots.

Calamus, bleached, is in light supply and firmer, with quotations for desirable grades advanced from 25c to 30c.

Ginger, Jamaica, is in improved demand, and the tendency of the market is firmer, with sales at 17c to 18c for bleached and 14c to 16c for unbleached.

Gentian is maintained steadily, in the face of an increased demand; we hear of jobbing sales at 4½c., though less would be named on a quantity order.

Golden seal continues inactive and quotations reflect the easier condition of the market, the price having dropped to 3c since our last, the range now standing $1.15 to $1.18.

Ipecac, Carthagena, is a shade easier, owing to lack of inquiry, and offerings were made in some quarters at $1.65, though $1.67½ was generally named. Rio is held with more firmness at $1.75 to $1.80.

Jalap continues in demand and values are maintained firmly at 12c to 13c, with sales at this range.

Pink is in better supply and sales were made since our last at 70c.

Seeds.

Canary is offered more freely at a fractional decline, there being sales of Smyrna at 4c. to 4¼c., and of Sicily at 4½c. to 4¾c.

Caraway appears well sustained at 6c. to 6¼c. for Dutch, and we hear of numerous jobbing sales at this range.

Cardamoms, decorticated, have developed increased strength, and the course of the market continues upward in sympathy with the position of the seeds abroad. The prevailing range of quotations at 35c. to 36c., with comparatively little offered at the lower figure.

Celery continues dull, and sales were made at 7½c., though some holders declined to shade 7¾c.

Hemp, Russian, has continued in demand, and the tone of the market is firmer, with sales at 2⅞c. to 3c.

Mustard is selling fairly at unchanged prices, or say 4c. to 4¼c. for California yellow and German yellow, and 6c. to 6¼c. for California brown; Bari brown is unchanged at 5½c. to 6c.

Poppy is in good demand, and values are maintained firmly at 5¼c. to 5½c.

Wormseed is well maintained at 7c. to 8c. for American, and 17½c. to 18c. for Russian, though at present there is no inquiry for quantity.

An Opening for American Proprietaries in Peru.

Abelardo B. Indacochea, proprietor of the Drogueria y Farmacia "Indacochea," calle del Comercio No. 38, Huacho, Peru, writes us that he is in a position to establish relations, although it may be only in a small way, with manufacturers of drugs and specifics and other goods from the United States, and I would be glad to get into communication with these houses in order that they may send him prices and terms of sale, which should be in Spanish and as clear as possible. He would like to have correspondents advise him at the same time if they have representatives or agents in Lima, or if not, how he can make payment. He does business for cash—that is to say, 30 days after receipt of the goods.

Opportunities *for* Export Trade

(Written for the American Druggist.)

ALONG THE WEST COAST OF SOUTH AMERICA.

Glimpses of the Coast Cities of Chile—Antofagasta a Busy City—Iquique a City of Fine Pharmacies—Cheapness the Curse of the Chilean Republic.

By John M. Draper.

Antofagasta, Chile, is one of the busiest ports on the whole west coast of South America, for with its immense forwarding trade to Bolivia and the shipping of saltpetre from this port, which has grown to immense proportions, it is no uncommon sight to see twelve or fifteen vessels waiting to load this product for Europe. The absence of a harbor here is a great drawback, and delays because of bad weather in the loading and unloading of a vessel lasting sometimes five days are not uncommon.

The druggists here are generally direct importers, though in this port, where one would expect to find at least one large wholesale firm, there are no large dealers. The Botica del Virginia, V. de Brunswig is the principal pharmacy and also boasts a branch store. This store is well managed and progressive in all its work. They are about to install an American soda fountain, and when we realize that not half a dozen of these are to be found from Cape Horn to Panama, we can see that they are bold in making the experiment, which will undoubtedly convert the people to an American drink which pays well. The Botica Germania, of Señor Blanco, is another very progressive pharmacy, whose large stock of articles of American origin, as well as French and other foreign goods, is indicative of a large clientele. Several smaller Boticas may be found in this city, whose entire trade is outside the realm of proprietary medicines.

Iquique, Chile, lying two days north of Antofagasta, via steamer, is about midway between Lima, Peru, and Valparaiso, Chile. This city of 100,000 supports some excellent pharmacies, the Botica de Valparaiso being the principal one, enjoys a very large wholesale and retail business, and its credit is considered very good. Boticas de Alemania are found in several parts of the city, as also are the Boticas de Italia, for these names are popular in every way, though we find also the Botica Inglesia, whose manager, or owner, is almost invariably a German, and may not speak a word of English. Of the German pharmacies the Botica Aleman of C. Lehmann is an excellent store, and enjoys a large trade, with good credit. All the stores in this city are very large places, and entirely different from the pharmacies in the tropical countries of Ecuador, Columbia, etc., their interiors being of much the same style as the American pharmacy. The newspaper is freely used as an advertising medium in the city, the French proprietors having the majority of ads. The publishers are very chary about the American ads. at the present time owing to the fact that they have recently been beaten out of six months' advertising by two or three fake "regenerator" medicine firms doing business from New York. I saw several accounts and returned drafts during my visit here and also in Antofagasta, therefore, as the publishers told me, the American houses do not now find the same welcome that was formerly accorded, though those houses whose products are well known and advertised are a great contrast to these fake remedy men.

Wholesale and Retail Establishment of Daube y Cie., One of the Most Enterprising Houses of Valparaiso, Chile.

THE GREAT SEAPORT OF THE WEST COAST.

In Valparaiso, Chile, the great seaport of the west coast and another port without the semblance of a harbor, the principal drug firms of the country are centered. Of the wholesale concerns to interest Americans, the firm of Baube y Cia, whose large business extends to all parts of the Republic of Chile, comes first. This house, founded by Italians in 1857, has come down the years to its present name of Daube y Cie enjoying great prosperity, and is virtually in control of the drug trade in Chile to-day. Weidmayer y Cia and Aristazabel y Cia are the two other wholesale firms doing business in Valparaiso, and like Daube y Cia, they have branch offices in Santiago.

The firm of Hochstetter y Cia are the largest retailers in the city and own six branch drug stores in various parts of the city. Besides drugs, they also carry hospital supplies, and in general are very Teutonic in their stock and buying. Señors G. Ortiz y Cia, in Calle Condell, do a large prescription trade and push new goods of promise with great vigor. Griffiths y Cia have an English pharmacy in Calle Esmeralda which is well equipped in every way. This firm tried ten years ago to introduce the soda water drinks to the Chilenos by importing a small fountain from Boston, but their efforts were not successful. The women do not go to the drug store for buying other articles than drugs and medicines, and the supplying of ice cream and soft drinks is left entirely to the confectionery shop, though there can be no doubt, were the American fountains installed and run even a short while as they ought to be run and the equipment was such as to draw attention, the Chilean women would readily take the fashion which Americans follow. We notice in this republic the term American, as we use it generally at home, is not applied here to people from the United States, but we are designated as North Americans, while the more generally used term is "Yanqui."

Valparaiso, with a population estimated at 180,000, has about thirty-two pharmacies. It has excellent newspapers, whose columns are well filled with advertising, the rates for which are quite reasonable. The European houses have the trade almost entirely, and those well known preparations from the United States, which we even meet in Peru, are not seen at all in Chile, and I note articles on the invoice from English and French firms which I well know they buy first in the United

Example of Defective Packing of American Goods.

States, and these American firms lose order after order because they are not represented in this market by active men. I have recently had an opportunity to send orders direct to an American concern whose goods were formerly bought through a London firm, but the buyer here had to abandon the article because of the high price charged by London.

Santiago is a fine city with a population of 350,000. It is well lighted, has electric cars, etc., and the señoritas are charming. German competition is extremely strong here, with the rankest prices I ever ran against, and the whole republic asks for cheapness and not quality—get it cheap and you cannot fail to do business.

Consul Brittain, of Kehl, writes to the Department of Commerce and Labor at Washington that, notwithstanding the advice given by consuls, every mail brings to hand circulars which the German cannot read, and to add to his discomfiture, he is frequently obliged to pay penalty postage for the privilege of receiving from the postman circulars which are useless to him.

DEFECTIVE PACKING OF AMERICAN GOODS.

Lack of Discrimination by American Exporters in Packing—Goods Ruined in Transit—Lack of Care in Addressing Packages.

We present herewith two illustrations which furnish the most convincing evidence of the deficiencies of American manufacturers when it comes to the matter of packing goods. We have frequently had occasion to refer to the carelessness displayed by our American manufacturers in this important particular, and are glad to reinforce these arguments with a

The Condition in Which American Goods Reached Tientsin.

note taken from the report of Special Consular Agent Crist who, writing from Tientsin, the great commercial depot of North China, criticises severely the faulty packing of American exporters. Mr. Crist says: "There is probably no one thing to which American exporters can give their attention that would bring better returns than that of packing. As a general proposition the wood of which they construct their cases is too light in weight. Where ½-inch stuff is required they will use ⅜. If 1-inch stuff will insure safe delivery English and German exporters use that thickness, while many Americans select a three-quarters or seven-eighths thickness. Two cases in point have been brought to my attention within the past few days which showed that the utmost thought, attention and care had been expended upon the details of packing, but with an evident lack of complete understanding of the strain to which breakable goods are subjected in transit to this market. In one instance, by a slight oversight, an automatic piano player barely escaped complete destruction."

In one instance cited by Mr. Crist a Western manufacturer sent eight packages of opaque or figured window glass in cases the sides of which were made of boards ⅜-inch thick, while the end boards were only ⅝-inch thick, and moreover were of soft pine, which could stand no strain or jar of any kind without fracture. The glass was laid in the cases with loose hay, each box was wrapped in more hay and the whole incased in sacking. The result was that the packers, thinking the package to be merely a sack of some nondestructible material, packed it at the bottom of a ship's cargo and every piece of glass in the shipment was broken into little bits, not a single piece being left larger than 4 x 8 inches. In another case, an automatic piano player was packed in boxes that were so light that they could not stand the strain to which they were subjected. In this case the packing was properly constructed, but was not sufficiently heavy.

The English make it a practice to line their packing boxes with tin and solder this tin water tight wherever the contents are such as to be injured by water.

In relation to the matter of addresses, Mr. Crist says that the addresses upon bales and boxes arriving from Europe and England are always in large, bold-faced letters.

AMERICAN DRUGGIST

and PHARMACEUTICAL RECORD

PHILADELPHIA. NEW YORK, MAY 28, 1906. CHICAGO

ISSUED SEMI-MONTHLY BY

AMERICAN DRUGGIST PUBLISHING CO.,

62-68 WEST BROADWAY, NEW YORK.

CHICAGO, 221 Randolph St. PHILADELPHIA, [illegible] Walnut St.

A. R. ELLIOTT, President.

CASWELL A. MAYO, Ph.G. .... Editor.

THOMAS J. KEENAN .... Associate Editor.

ROMAINE PIERSON .... Manager Chicago Office.

$1.50 a year. 15 cents a copy.

ADVERTISING RATES QUOTED ON APPLICATION.

THE AMERICAN DRUGGIST AND PHARMACEUTICAL RECORD is issued on the second and fourth Mondays of each month. Changes of advertisements should be received ten days in advance of the date of publication.

Remittances should be made by New York exchange, post office or express money order or registered mail. If checks on local banks are used 10 cents should be added to cover cost of collection. The publishers are not responsible for money sent by unregistered mail, nor for any money paid except to duly authorized agents. All communications should be addressed and all remittances made payable to American Druggist Publishing Company, 62-68 West Broadway, New York.

Entered at New York as Second-Class Matter.

TABLE OF CONTENTS.

EDITORIAL COMMENT.

WRITE NOW! It would be a pity if the Mann drug patent bill were to die in committee owing to any apathy on the part of the retail druggists of the country. It is distinctly a retail druggists' measure, fathered by the National Association of Retail Druggists, and should be pushed to a passage by the united efforts of the trade everywhere. No retail pharmacist should allow his representative in Congress to rest until he has received the assurance of his support for the measure. The influence of retail pharmacists should be exerted unceasingly in this direction and such influence can be brought to bear most effectively by correspondence with their representatives in Congress. Let each druggist constitute himself a committee of one to procure the passage of the Mann bill and the bill is as good as passed.

PRIZES FOR PUZZLING ORDERS. In the preceding number prizes were offered to subscribers who would most promptly submit correct interpretations of two badly scrawled orders received by druggists over the counter, and the awards are announced in this issue. Some difficulty was experienced in awarding the prizes, owing to the calculations that had to be made regarding the time of receipt of the paper by the contestants and the time of mailing the reply, but we feel we have succeeded in being entirely fair to all who participated in the contest. The interest taken in this contest was widespread and encourages us to offer prizes for chirographically puzzling orders, the prize to be awarded to readers who submit scrawls which, in the judgment of the editor, are most suitable for publication and calculated to arouse the greatest interest. The accepted order will be reproduced in *facsimile*, and both the name of the contributor and the name of the successful decipherer will be published in connection with the award of the prize in a subsequent issue. Contributions should be addressed to Queries and Answers.

JUBILAEUMS FEIER. The issue of the *Pharmazeutische Zeitung*, of Berlin, for March 31, completed the fiftieth year of the existence of that admirable journal, and the number which was issued in commemoration of this important event contained several interesting and valuable contributions to the history of pharmacy in Germany. The number opened with a history of the *Pharmazeutische Zeitung*, by Dr. E. Werncke, illustrated with a reproduction of the first page of the first number, issued at Bunzlau, on March 31, 1856, the whole of the front page being devoted to an announcement signed by Hermann Mueller, the founder of the journal. Excellent portraits were presented of Mr. Mueller and Dr. J. T. Boettger, the present editor of the periodical. This historical sketch was followed by an article by H. Schelenz, a well-known writer on historical pharmacy, on the co-operation of the *Pharmazeutische Zeitung* in the advancement of both the technical and scientific aspects of pharmacy during the past fifty years. Dr. E. Mylius, himself a prominent figure in European pharmacy, discussed pharmacy and pharmacists for the past fifty years, and the future of the pharmacist was outlined by E. Sonnenberg, of Friedenau. We heartily congratulate our esteemed contemporary on its long and flourishing career and hope that it will continue to flourish and grow strong with age.

THE ORIGIN OF THE WORD MENSTRUUM. It has remained for a correspondent of the AMERICAN DRUGGIST to set the modern lexicographers right in regard to the etymology of the word "menstruum," a word which has been the subject of numerous connotations by the dictionary makers. In the *Encyclopædic Medical Dictionary* of Dr. Frank P. Foster, editor of the *New York Medical Journal*, the derivation is given as "from menstruus, belonging to a month." The *Standard Dictionary* makes no attempt to trace the origin of the word and rests with citations from Skeat, who himself was indebted to Richardson for the explanation that the action of a solvent was assisted by a moderate fire during the month. Dr. Johnson's explanation is the one found in most medical dictionaries, which is that the word menstruum "originated in some notion of the old chemists about the influence of the moon in the preparation of dissolvents." The new *Historical English Dictionary* attempted a more scientific explanation of the term, saying "menstruum was a mediæval Latin term used in alchemy to express the belief that the base metal undergoing transmutation into gold corresponded with the seed within the womb, which was being acted upon by the agency of a menstrual fluid." Mr. Carrington, of Brooklyn, has discovered a reference in a work written in mediæval French which convinces him that the dictionary makers have failed to carry their researches far enough, and that in their explanations they have put the cart before the horse. It is shown by his citation that up to the fifteenth century at least the belief prevailed that the menstrual fluid was a potent solvent, as bitumen used to cement together pieces of wood could only be dissolved by it, and this glue, it is noted, was "*si fort et si tenant*." We are much indebted to Mr. Carrington for his informing note, which we are sure our readers will peruse with interest.

GETTING TOGETHER. The steps about to be taken by the Manhattan Pharmaceutical Association of this city toward bringing about a conference of doctors, druggists, retail and manufacturing pharmacists, and pharmaceutical editors for the discussion of the ethics of pharmacy and the allied profession should be cordially supported. It is a significant sign of the time that the old attitude of hostility between druggists and doctors is passing away, and that the relations of druggists with medical men are becoming more cordial. In these days of collectivism it is not so easy to discern those who maintain the old fashioned friendly relations between doctors and druggists. This is no contradiction of what we have just said, because the few eminent pharmacists of the late 60's and 70's who were noted for the intimate friendly relations which they sustained toward medical men carried on business at a time when the stress of competition was not felt so severely as in these strenuous days of trusts and syndicates, and consequently stood out more prominently. There was much more counter prescribing done in those days than at present, and for the voluntary discontinuance of this practice, which was such a good source of revenue for the druggist, what has the physician done in return? Judging by recent events, he has occupied himself principally in efforts to deprive the retail druggist, through legislative enactment, of one of his remaining sources of income—the manufacture and sale of his own proprietary compounds. It is most reassuring to know that a joint meeting of doctors and druggists will soon be held, at which some of the subjects that now divide the two professions, will be discussed and obstacles in the way of a more perfect *rapprochement* be removed.

The Hearing on the Mann Bill.

In another column we present a complete report of the hearing on the Mann drug patent bill, which is intended to amend the patent laws so as to deny patents on products intended for medicinal use. This bill is familiar to our readers, as it is identical with the measure which was introduced at the last session of Congress, and which has had the earnest and active support of every drug trade organization in the United States. The most interesting feature of the hearing was the announcement by the chairman of the committee of his views favoring the enactment of a law requiring reciprocity on the part of every foreign country the citizens of which desire to take out patents in the United States. This reciprocity feature has been much dwelt upon by pharmacists conscious of the evils of our existing patent laws, but every proposal that a reciprocity feature be incorporated in the patent laws has been met by the argument that the adoption of such an amendment to the patent laws would be in contravention of the treaty bearing upon the existence of patents and trade marks now existing between the United States and various foreign powers. This contention was answered by Mr. Currier, chairman of the House committee, by the statement that the acts of Congress were above all treaties, and that where treaties conflicted with acts of Congress the acts would take precedence. Whatever may be the outcome of this agitation, therefore, it seems quite sure that some law will be enacted embracing the reciprocity idea in the issuance of patents.

Another interesting feature of the hearing was the volteface of Prof. Charles F. Chandler, who had brought down upon himself a storm of protest by the attitude assumed by him last Fall at the Senate hearing on this bill. In his remarks at that time he referred to the retail druggist in terms far from complimentary and dwelt at some length upon the fact that he had devoted a great deal of his valuable time to teaching retail druggists without receiving any compensation therefor. At the present hearing he went out of his way to laud the retail druggist as a long-suffering martyr, a prodigy of learning, a miracle of kindness, and a good samaritan for all the world, in addition to being a poorly paid worker. The retail drug trade will be much pleased, no doubt, to learn of this change of heart upon the part of Professor Chandler, and it is to be hoped that the sentiments expressed by him are as genuine as they are creditable. It is certainly unfortunate that, despite Professor Chandler's high opinion of druggists, he is constrained to differ with them as to the desirability of the passage of the Mann bill.

Tax-Free Alcohol for the Industries.

Nothing but the strongest kind of pressure could have forced the Senate to pass the Free Alcohol bill at this session of Congress. The question has been before the country for more than 25 years, and Congress passed a relief measure in connection with the Wilson act when John G. Carlisle was Secretary of the Treasury, but the measure was so badly drafted that it could not be made effective. The bill which passed the Senate last Thursday differs in many respects from any bill of the kind heretofore introduced, for it provides for the withdrawal "from bond, tax free, of domestic alcohol when rendered unfit for beverage or liquid medicinal uses by mixture with suitable denaturing material" when such alcohol is intended for use in the arts and industries and for fuel, light and power. The chief opposition to the bill came from the manufacturers of wood alcohol, who indeed succeeded in having the operation of the act postponed to January, 1907, on the plea that they had a supply of their product on hand that would be valueless if the law went into effect at once. As this and one other minor amendment were made to the bill as received from the House of Representatives, it will have to be considered again by the House, but it is the general impression in Washington that nothing will be done to prevent the bill becoming law.

It is felt that the operation of the act will give an enormous impetus to the chemical and pharmaceutical industries of this country, as it is well known that the uses to which denatured alcohol can be applied in these industries are many and various. It is not likely that the retail pharmacists of the country will benefit to any extent through the operation of the act for a good deal of time to come, but its benefits will be felt indirectly, and those retailers and co-operative societies of retailers who do any considerable manufacturing for their own consumption will derive immediate benefit, and these will undoubtedly hail the passage of the act with acclaim. While not pertinent to the pharmaceutical aspect of the subject, one advantage to the public from the operation of the act may be pointed out, and that is the use of denatured alcohol in place of the odoriferous gasoline in motor cars, which will serve to restore to the *Mephitis mephitica* the pre-eminence in its field which it formerly held alone and undisputed.

(Written for the American Druggist.)

MAIL ORDER COMPETITION.

By Frank Farrington,
Delhi, N. Y.

What a great big bugaboo the mail order house has become to the retailer, to be sure! The druggist in the country town sits behind his prescription case, with his feet up in the air, and wonders what business is coming to, anyway. The city druggist has less time to sit and think it over, but the competition is there just the same and it eats into his profits.

There seems to be a prevalent idea among the druggists that the mail order business is not exactly fair; that the big catalogue houses have no right to be taking trade away from them. There is a tendency to sulk and to say sarcastic things about people sending their money out of town for goods that could be bought at home.

Well, now, that is a rather foolish way to act under the circumstances. As druggists, we or our families are sending to the cities for things that our merchants are selling. We buy out of town ourselves to some extent, but in each case we know the reason for doing it and think it a good one. In the case of the other fellow, we do not know the reason and consequently think it unfair.

HERE TO STAY.

The mail order man is doing business in a square way and he is doing a lot of it. He has built up his trade on the same principles that make success along any line. He is a good advertiser and he treats people as they want to be treated, and he has a right to business wherever he can get it. If he gets it away from us, that is his good fortune. He is a condition and a fair one. We cannot argue or reason or legislate him out of business. He has come to stay. We might as well make up our minds to that and see what we can do to keep up our end of the competition.

The chief reason why our customers keep sending to the mail order man for goods is that he keeps asking them to do so. They are bombarded constantly with advertising, in some form or other, asking for business. They get a complete catalogue once or twice a year, and that lies there before them ready for inspection, a constant temptation to make up an order and get the special price that they offer on some leader.

They receive mail order papers containing ads. of the mail order man, and they get folders and circulars from him galore. He is a busy fellow and determined that no one shall have time to forget him.

HOW TO OFFSET IT.

What are the druggists doing to offset this constant stream of advertising that is being poured upon their customers?

Most of them are probably running newspaper ads. unless they live in too large a city. These ads. are in exceptional cases carefully prepared, and in the majority of cases made up in a hurry at the last minute, when it occurs to them that the copy has not been changed for three weeks.

Some exceptional men go further, and besides good newspaper advertising get out other matter, in the way of folders, booklets, counter slips, etc., which do them a great deal of good. These are the successful men, and though there are a great many successful druggists in the 45,000 in the country, the percentage is very low when the possibilities are considered. Few go as far as they might.

Advertising in the way that nine druggists in ten do, it pays but a fair or small return for the investment. It costs just as much for space in which to run a worthless ad. as it does for the same space filled with the best ad. that brains can compose.

CARE IN ADVERTISEMENT CONSTRUCTION.

If one wishes his ads. to be of the top notch order there must be work on them. Nothing worth while is done in a hurry, at the last moment. The advertisement writing of the store should have a special time and should be made up with careful thought as to the best goods to talk about at the time and the best way of telling about them. There should be a price for every article mentioned and a sufficient description to make the reader want that article. Plan to write your newspaper ads. on a certain day and to have them in the printer's hands early. Always do the work on time and never shirk it just because it is not compulsory.

When the newspaper ads. are systematized, then it is time enough to go after some additional form of publicity. My idea is that every druggist who wants to get a lot of business ought to have a good mailing list of his actual and possible customers and send to that list at least once a year a complete catalogue of the staple things in his stock, with many specials and leaders at very attractive prices.

This catalogue ought to be supplemented by sheets of additions, or by folders, calling attention to the catalogue, these latter to be sent out regularly once a month, once in two, three or four months, as the conditions warrant and the dealer can afford.

The catalogue is not an expensive thing and can be made the basis for a great variety of following up. A small mail order business can be planned on it, and premiums and special discounts may be offered on certain lines or pages of goods from time to time. The expense of an edition of 5,000 catalogues, 5 x 7 page, 16 pages and cover, would be about $100, and a much smaller book would answer for many druggists.

THE MAIL ORDER MAN'S DECOY.

The next great hit that the mail order houses make in going after business is the impression they give that they are selling so very cheap. They harp constantly upon their low prices. They talk quality but little. They get their business because they ask for it and because they say that they are selling cheaper than any one else.

Now, the good druggists like to sell a high class of goods, the sort that will wear well and give satisfaction. They do not want to recommend cheap plunder. They like to cater to the "best trade." They say, "If we go ahead and advertise cheap things people will think that we are running a cheap John store and will not come."

I call that poor logic. The mail order house is getting the business that the druggists object to their having by just those "cheap John" methods. They are drawing trade, nine times in ten, just on the price, nothing else.

If the druggists are not willing to use any honest methods by which their competitors succeed, how can they object to the business going where the inducements lie that appeal most strongly to the people?

TALK PRICES.

The most susceptible spot in a customer is his pocketbook. An argument that scores in that direction will win where a dozen others fail. Of course the best trade does not think so much of the price—and that is the class to get—but it must be remembered that where there are four hundred of the "best class" there are four million of the masses, and the masses are the customers who keep the business of the country going.

However, it must not be thought that because it is a good thing to advertise cheap goods or low prices it is necessary to sell that kind altogether, or even to those whom the cheap prices allure.

Low prices get people into the store where all else would fail. When once in it is a very simple thing to sell them a better grade of goods than they came to buy. Why, I know of a druggist who sold a lot of hot water bottles last winter at $1.50 each and did it by advertising, "Two-quart hot water bottles, 48 cents."

AN EXAMPLE.

How? Why, every one who came in to look at hot water bottles was shown the 48-cent one (he only had one or two of them), and then the dollar one (a similar stock of those), and then the $1.50 article. The customer was told that in regard to the 48-cent one, "The less said, the better. It is a hot water bottle and that is all we guarantee." The dollar one was said to be a first-class article for the money, and the good one, the $1.50 bag, was recommended, the difference explained and a guarantee for a year offered with it. Only one 48-cent one was sold all winter and two or three of the dollar ones.

That's the principle upon which one ought to work. Advertise the low-priced goods and then sell the good ones.

Of course, there are plenty of times for the advertising of the high-grade goods, too. They need it as much as the others, but I was talking more especially about going after the trade that the mail order people have been getting.

The druggists will do well to send to such houses as Sears, Roebuck & Co. and Montgomery, Ward & Co., of Chicago, and get their catalogues. This will show how and where the enemy are attacking and give one an inkling as to what line to follow in returning the fire.

If one would make leaders at low prices, let them be made with a view to beating the mail order prices. Every druggist has some leaders that he can offer at lower figures than the outside competition makes. If the home dealers hustle as hard as the out of town contingent there will be much less money sent away. The trouble is as much with the local dealers as anywhere. The people are at liberty to buy where they will.

THE RELATION OF THE MANUFACTURING PHARMACIST TO THE MEDICAL PROFESSION.[1]

By Joseph W. England, Ph. G.,

Philadelphia.

In a recent paper upon the subject of the Secret Nostrum Evil[2] Dr. Frank Billings condemns the use of nostrums or secret proprietary medicinal preparations, and incidentally claims that while the reputable manufacturing pharmacists deserve great credit for the improvement they have made in pharmaceutical products, they have manufactured their own special mixtures, which are just as objectionable as the products of the special manufacturers. They, too, have been active with their agents in visiting physicians and in distributing literature. This encourages drug-giving in specific mixtures for special symptoms, and is wrong. With the one hand they do good work, with the other much evil is done.

If this criticism means anything at all it means that reputable manufacturing pharmacists have done much harm by marketing "specific mixtures for special symptoms." As a matter of fact what they have done has been to market special mixtures for specific or pathologic conditions. Every one knows that the specific drugs can be counted, almost, on the fingers of one hand—iodine, mercury, iron, quinine, diphtheria antitoxin, and possibly a few more; and it would be folly for manufacturers to claim specific action for special mixtures where specific action cannot possibly be obtained. If some physicians have chosen, on their own responsibility, to use special mixtures as specifics for special symptoms, it is rather disingenuous, to say the least, to blame the manufacturers for it. The manufacturers have simply met the demands of medical men, and in no sense have dictated their policies.

Few outside of those directly concerned have any conception of the wonderful development that has taken place in the pharmaceutical and chemical industries of this country since the Civil War. It parallels the advance of the medical profession. New methods for the extraction of vegetable drugs and the manufacture and purification of chemical compounds have been devised, and large numbers of products have been developed. In fact, as Zeig states:[3] "A new era in manufacture has been born which, for its scope, the number and character of products manufactured, the mechanical devices and machinery employed, exceeds all the efforts of the preceding centuries." As he further points out: The modern laboratory contains tablet machines capable of compressing 200,000 tablets in ten hours; pill cutting machines and vacuum gelatin-coating machines, which, by means of vacuum tubes and two operators, can coat 75,000 to 100,000 pills a day; vacuum stills for concentrating extracts, by means of which the injurious heat-effects to vegetable drugs, occurring during the evaporation of percolates, can be obviated; centrifugal extractors and centrifugal filters, in place of the unsightly filter presses and filter stands of the past; power suppository machines; collapsible tube-closing machines; mass mixers; granulators; pulverizers; and scores of other labor-saving devices.

It is obvious that with such machinery, and the technical skill necessary to use it, together with improved processes, and a command of the best markets of the world, the modern manufacturer can make products that are cheaper and better in every way than was possible half a century ago, when such conditions did not exist, and that the retail pharmacist of to-day can buy such products at a less cost than he can make them. The manufacturer has not usurped the work of the retail pharmacist and deprived him of his revenues, as has been claimed, but instead, has worked to the interest of the latter, by relieving him of the necessity of making his own products, with just as much profit to himself, or more. A return to the old-time methods is impossible; evolutions, like revolutions, never work backward.

It would be strange if, in view of these advances, there had not come a corresponding advance in the manufacture of medicinal products for the use of physicians; and such an advance is exactly what has taken place. In appearance, in palatability, and in effectiveness, the American pharmaceutical preparations, as a class, lead the world.

It has been questioned whether or not the proprietary system of non-secret medicinal preparations, as followed by reputable manufacturers, has been for the best interests of the medical profession, but a careful study of the question will show that it has come as a logical necessity, because it ensures a reliability and uniformity of product that can be had in no other way. E. R. Squibb & Son's choloroform and ether; Powers, Weightman & Rosengarten Co.'s quinine and morphine salts; Parke, Davis & Co.'s cascara preparations; Fairchild Bros. & Foster's ferment products, and numerous other preparations are specific examples of the wisdom of such a system. Many manufacturers have sought to duplicate these products and have failed, because they did not possess the special knowledge and skill acquired by these firms after years of painstaking study and the expenditure of thousands of dollars. The products named, chemical and pharmaceutical alike, are all non-secret, and they are all equally proprietary in character, because the specific knowledge and skill required for their production has not been divulged, but is held as a property right. Similarly other proprietary products, not so well known, and having in some cases a few more ingredients, but non-secret also, may be fairly placed in the same class. The difference, if any, is simply in the number of ingredients.

The proprietary medicinal preparations are protected by the use of the firm's name attached to their titles, or by means of trademarks, or both. In the past the use of the firm name alone was sufficient for protection; to-day this does not suffice. Unfair competition compels manufacturers in many cases to use trademarks, in order to protect the consumer as well as themselves.

Perhaps the best illustration of the value of the proprietary system may be found in the one recently used by the editor of *Medicine* in an editorial on Patenting Instruments by the Profession. He referred to the famous Murphy button, which, as originally devised by Dr. John B. Murphy, contained a spring adjusted to a certain tension, so that when placed in position it produced sufficient pressure on the opposite edges of the peritoneum to cause pressure-atrophy, but without cutting through the tissues and causing necrosis. Dr. Murphy very carefully worked out the problem, but did not patent the button. What has been the result? The button has been copied by instrument makers who, observing that the two halves of the button were connected by a spring, simply used one about the same strength and size, with the result that a number of imperfect buttons were and are upon the market. There is no telling how many lives have been lost by the failure of Dr. Murphy to patent his button.

Other examples could readily be given of apparatus devised by medical men and copied by instrument makers, wherein

[1] From *Monthly Cyclopædia of Practical Medicine*, Vol. IX, page 51, 1906.

[2] *Journal of the American Medical Association*, December 2, 1905.

[3] The Manufacture of Pharmaceutical Preparations, by H. C. Zeig, Ph.C., *American Journal of Pharmacy*, 1905, 405.

the cost has been cheapened at the expense of the quality. These cheaper patterns gradually displace the dearer, and untold harm results. The fine humanitarian impulse which impels a medical man to give his discoveries to the world "without money and without price" should command the highest of respect, but the old world does not appreciate the sacrifice, and in the end the phyisican and the world both suffer.

As the editorial further states: "The trademark not only protect the original inventor and maker of the article in the enjoyment of his reasonable reward for the invention, and for his expenditure in making the same known to the profession, but protects as well the physician in the quality of the products furnished—in purity and uniformity and strength—and, if an article of real worth, in its perpetuity; the trademark protecting the same against displacement and final loss to the practice by cheap imitation, cheapened owing to competition, at the expense of quality in the product. The trademark protection also enables its wide publicity and distribution, and at a lower cost to the patient than a like quantity and quality of medicine under any other method, thus securing the greatest good to the greatest number."

However much medical scientists may wish the development of rational therapeutics, the fact remains that to-day a large majority of physicians are broadly empirical in their methods of treatment. They follow the teachings of physiological actions as far as they dare, but they recognize the fact that the physiological actions of drugs are not pathological actions, and that in the end the individuality of each patient must be reckoned with. Hence if the physician can call to his aid when necessary the trained technical skill of the modern manufacturer, in devising new preparations, and in perfecting old ones, to meet individual conditions, it would seem to be the height of unwisdom to repel such assistance.

In the final analysis the vital question to the work-a-day phyisician is not whether a given preparation is proprietary in character—because all medicinal preparations are, in a broad sense, proprietary—but what is its composition; what are its clinical possibilities and limitations; will it yield the results clamed, and will it yield the results better than can be obtained in any other way?

The interests of reputable manufacturing pharmacists and physicians are mutual. They are both working for the same end—the common good of humanity. That the manufacturing pharmacist, as well as the physician, is in sympathy with high ideals is shown by the research laboratories he has founded and maintained, and the work these laboratories have done for pure science, without any thought of commercial gain. It has been the habit of a certain class of medical men to sneer at pharmaceutical commercialism, as they term it, and assume that the manufacturing pharmacist has no interest in humanity, except that of dollars and cents. Such a view is most unjust. Whether a man is in commercial life or in medical life "a man's a man for a' that and a' that," as dear old Bobby Burns put it; or as Wycherly expresses the thought, "I weigh the man, not his title; 'tis not the king's stamp can make the metal better." A man is honest or dishonest, he has high ideals or low ones, and he works for the right or wrong irrespective of his vocation. The quality of a man's work does not depend upon the nature of his vocation; it depends upon his fitness for the work, and his character as a man.

Physicians in Support of Pharmacists

It is refreshing to find a medical journal taking the part of the pharmacist and demonstrating the falsity of the wholesale charges of adulteration and substitution which are sometimes made against him by medical men as well as yellow journalists, and it is accordingly a pleasure to reprint the following editorial article from the *Medical Times* for May:

DRUGGISTS AND SUBSTITUTION.

Whenever we hear people talk about druggists and substitution we like to recall a man by the name of Diekman—George C. Diekman, M.D., Ph.G., Professor of Dispensing Pharmacy in the Columbia University and Member of the New York State Board of Pharmacy. We once heard some observations which this gentleman made in a public meeting; and we reached the conclusion that he is the kind of man who, whenever he says a thing, there is no need for him to add to his statements an affidavit signed and sworn to.

Dr. Diekman has been in a position to collect data, which he presented in the *Medical News*, June 17, 1905; these data demonstrate that statements accusing druggists of fraudulent and sordid substitution and adulteration are absolutely false concerning at least 90 per cent. of these professional men. What other calling could make a better showing than this? In his official relations with the State Board of Pharmacy he has had collected during the year 1904 more than 2,000 samples from pharmacists carrying on business in and about New York City. Analyses of these samples showed that 87.37 per cent. were standard or nearly so. One hundred and seventeen samples, representing 5.51 per cent. of the total number collected, were found to contain methyl alcohol; most of such preparations were intended for external use. Besides, these samples were not taken from 117 different sources; three, and sometimes four of them were in many instances taken from the same store. One hundred and fifty-one samples, representing 7.12 per cent. of the total number collected, were found to be deficient in strength, but containing no ingredients except such as constitute the pharmacopœial formula. Such violations are usually the result of a careless supervision during the process of manufacture of such preparations; they may well be classed as errors of omission rather than of commission. In some instances it was found that the pharmacist sold to the public preparations deficient in strength, while if a physician's prescription were presented for the same preparations they were dispensed of a quality strictly in accord with the official standard.

Some of the samples were collected from stores not classified as pharmacies, which are, nevertheless, under the Pharmacy act, permitted to sell such "household remedies" as cream of tartar, borax and the like. Every adulterated sample of cream of tartar was purchased from a grocer, while every sample of drug store origin was found to be pure.

We pass from much other equally convincing statistical matter to the observation that the druggists have had enacted a law which requires that an apprentice possess a much higher degree of education than heretofore; the course which he must now pursue if he would practice pharmacy in New York State is certainly a difficult and arduous one. It is thus evident that pharmacists are endeavoring to develop the professional side of their business rather at the expense of the commercial side; as one result a greater outlay for hire of assistants is necessitated. The ultimate object is to elevate the profession of pharmacy to the same level with our own, so far as educational requirements are concerned.

What we want to emphasize, however is that he who makes sweeping assertions of dishonesty concerning any calling is utterly ignorant or oblivious of human conditions. Human nature is to the good; more than 50 per cent. to the good. If one reflects for a moment he must conclude that civilization were impossible on any other basis. Most men are honest; if they were not, the world's business could not be done. We recall a conversation between a physician and a druggist in which the advantage, so far as good temper is concerned, was certainly with the latter. The physician declared: "Oh, well; all you druggists are substitutors." "Yes, and all you doctors are ab——" (we don't like to print the word). "But you know very well," continued the druggist, smiling genially, "that neither statement is true." And this the physician had the grace to admit. There are exceptions, of course, but as a rule the druggists make up our prescriptions faithfully and accurately.

A NEW LABEL PASTE.

	Parts.
Tragacanth, powdered	2
Boiling water	16

Add the water to the tragacanth, stirring vigorously the while.

In another vessel mix the following:

	Parts.
Cold water	4
Rye flour	6
Dextrin	1

Add the paste thus made to the tragacanth paste and mix to a homogeneous mass. To the mixed paste is then added, with constant stirring, 24 parts of boiling water, and later 1 part of glycerin and 1 part of salicylic acid, the whole being lastly boiled three to four minutes under constant stirring.

Cream of Current Literature

A summary of the leading articles in contemporary pharmaceutical periodicals.

Suicide from Bitter Almonds.—The *Therapeutische Monatshefte* (1906, No. 1) records the case of a young drug clerk who committed suicide by eating a handful of bitter almonds. Despite the use of the stomach pump and other measures he succumbed to the toxic action of the almonds.

Belloform.—This is a condensation product of various high-boiling hydrocarbons (poor in cresols) with formaldehyde in soap solution, which forms a cherry red fluid of aromatic odor and is readily soluble in both water and alcohol. The weak aqueous solution of this product is transparent, with a yellowish opalescence, while the stronger solutions are nearly opaque. The antiseptic effect of belloform is said to be quite equal to those produced by either creolin or lysoform; it is said to have no irritant or caustic effect on the skin and, without making it slippery, to soften it.

Corosuccin, a New Antiseptic.—Babesh and Begnesco (*Journal de pharm. et de chimie*, April 16, 1906, p. 389) describe a new antiseptic, consisting of mercuric chloride, with a rather concentrated solution of succinic acid, which they have named corosuccin. According to the authors, a 1 to 20,000 solution of mercuric chloride, to which 2.5 Gm. per hundred of succinic acid is added, has the same antiseptic power as a simple 1 to 50 solution of mercuric chloride. Each liter of corosuccin therefore contains only 50 Mg. of mercuric chloride. In order to prepare an efficient and inexpensive solution of this antiseptic it should be made in the proportion of equal parts of a 1.5 per cent. solution of succinic acid and a 1 in 10,000 solution of mercuric chloride.

Eugatol, a New Hair Dye.—Tomacheffsky and Erdmann (*Apotheker Zeitung*, 1906, p. 153) describe a new organic hair dye, which they style eugatol and which has recently been placed on the market in Berlin. It is claimed that this hair dye is absolutely harmless. Of late years efforts have been made to employ synthetic products for dyeing haid, but all attempts hitherto have been unsuccessful. Either the tint obtained was unstable, or it did not correspond to the shade desired, or the dye was found to be injurious. In most cases these dyes contained pyrogallic acid or phenylenediamin, both of which are far from harmless. The authors call attention to the irritation of the skin produced by such basic substances as metol, paraaminophenol, etc. By introducing a sulphon group into the molecules of these basic substances the irritating action and their toxicity may be removed. Thus by mixing salts of sodium and of oxyaminophenylsulphonic acid and of para-aminodiphenylaminosulphonic acid the proper tints may be obtained. Eugatol is such a mixture to which one-half volume of a 3 per cent. solution of hydrogen dioxide has been added. The authors report that they have tested the new dye in 90 cases and found it slightly irritating only in one instance.

The Adulteration of Phenacetin with Parachloroacetanilid. Mannich (*Ber. der pharm. Ges.*, 1906, p. 57) examined a sample of phenacetin, the use of which had been followed by symptoms of poisoning. He found that this sample differed in many ways from pure phenacetin. The melting point of the product was found to be about 120 instead of 134 or 135 degrees C., the melting point of phenacetin. Moreover, the suspected sample contained a 5.89 per cent. of chlorine, while phenacetin does not contain even a trace of this element. It was found that the chlorine was present in the form of an organic compound, and the chlorine compound was isolated in pure state by treating the sample repeatedly with ether and then repeatedly crystallizing the portion soluble in ether by treating it with boiling water. The substance thus isolated melted at from 175 to 177 degrees and possessed all the characteristics of parachloroacetanilid. On boiling with sulphuric acid it gave a bluish violet color, in contrast with that of phenacetin, which is a dirty reddish brown. The suspected phenacetin was therefore found to be a mixture of 72 per cent. of phenacetin and 18 per cent. of parachloroacetanilid. The presence of this chlorine compound cannot be considered an impurity, since it is not used in the preparation of phenacetin. The author believes that this is the first time that this particular adulteration has been noted. Mannich points out the importance of testing the products which are purchased at wholesale as to their purity. He dwells especially upon the value of the melting point, as giving a clue to the purity of a product such as phenacetin. If the melting point is found to be that given in the pharmacopœia the product may be assumed to be pure with fair certainty.

The Decomposition of Some Pharmaceutical Preparations Under the Influence of Air and Light.—Schoorl and Van den Berg (*Ber. pharm. Ges.*, 1905, p. 387) have made a study of the decomposition of chloroform, bromoform, iodoform and chloral hydrate under the influence of light and air. They exposed samples of these products to light and to a stream of oxygen, and the following is a summary of the results which they obtained:

Chloroform under the influence of light and in the presence of oxygen is almost completely decomposed after an exposure of six hours daily for 32 days. The products resulting from the oxidation are carbonic acid, water and chlorine. If a smaller quantity of oxygen is present the decomposition takes place differently, the larger part of the chloroform remaining unaltered, while the presence of a certain amount of carbon oxychloride or of hydrochloric acid may be detected. This reaction is the decomposition which takes place in the pharmacy where chloroform is kept in bottles which are half filled and exposed to light. The addition of alcohol in sufficient proportion almost completely prevents the decomposition.

Iodoform is very easily decomposed, both by heat and by sunlight, especially when it has been placed in solution. Free iodine is given off, and at the same time carbonic acid and water. A small amount of acetylene is also formed. The present authors have confirmed this fact and show that carbon dioxide as well as carbon oxide are formed in the decomposition of iodoform.

Bromoform is known to be easily decomposed, and the authors found that the products of decomposition were water, carbon dioxide, hydrobromic acid and bromine.

Chloral hydrate in the presence of oxygen and sunlight is entirely decomposed into chlorine, carbon dioxide and water. Sunlight alone decomposes it partly, forming hydrochloric acid and carbon dioxide.

Mixtures of Castor Oil and Balsam of Peru.—Sorber (*Pharm. Weekblad*, 1905) calls attention to the fact that balsam of Peru mixes very slowly with most fixed oils and that resin deposits at the bottom of the container from such mixtures. Castor oil alone mixes with the balsam to form a tenacious, sticky fluid which does not precipitate on standing. Croton oil also mixes well with the balsam, and linseed oil gives less resinous precipitate than the non-drying oils. According to the author, this is due to the fact that castor oil does not contain any triolein. Pure triolein produces a resinous precipitate with balsam of Peru, and the various fixed oils precipitate resin from the balsam in proportion as they contain triolein. Another reason for the stability of the mixture of balsam of Peru and castor oil is the fact that there is but a slight difference in the specific gravity of these two fluids. An adulteration of the balsam with a fixed oil is only possible with the aid of castor oil; as much as 15 per cent. of the oil can be added without producing any cloudiness.

A few practical hints are given by Sorber as to preparations containing these two ingredients. Thus, an ointment consisting of four parts of boric acid, two parts of balsam of Peru, twenty parts of petrolatum and three parts of glycerin becomes lumpy and separates resin, on account of the presence of boric acid. On adding from ten to twenty drops of castor oil, the mixture makes a smooth ointment, without any lumps. Ointments containing boric acid, olive oil and balsam of Peru also tend to become lumpy, but if instead of the olive oil castor oil be employed the ointment becomes perfectly homogeneous. The fat that is capable of taking up the largest amount of balsam of Peru is lanolin, while other fats on being mixed with the balsam deposit lumps of resin, which, however, may be removed upon the addition of castor oil. By adding castor oil to liquid petrolatum the latter becomes miscible with balsam of Peru.

The Saponins.—Schneider presented an interesting communication to the Algemeiner Oesterreichischer Apotheker Verein (*Pharm. Rundschau*, 1905, No. 50) on the saponins, in which he dealt with the various uses of these substances as constituents of foods and beverages. Saponins are found in about 46 families of the vegetable kingdom. They are colloidal bodies and foam when mixed with water, even in alcoholic solutions. The technical value of the saponins, depending upon this foaming property, has been known to the natives of South America from time immemorial. A special advantage of the saponins is that they do not injure even the most delicate colors and that in solutions of one part in 10,000 they produce foam when added to carbonated beverages. The saponins are excellent emulsifying agents for a variety of oils. Saponin was discovered in 1808 by Schrader in the root of *Saponaria officinalis*. It was believed that saponin was a soap existing as such in nature, but further chemical investigations, especially those of Kobert, showed this to be erroneous. There are no general reactions to which all saponins respond, but most of them turn red on the addition of concentrated sulphuric acid. On the addition of alcoholic sulphuric acid and of a drop of ferric chloride saponin solutions turn a bluish green. Some of them turn a cherry red on the addition of selenic acid and of concentrated sulphuric acid. Mercuric acetate, to which a drop of potassium nitrite has been added, gives a red color, the latter reaction serving for the demonstration of saponin in foods, beverages and emulsions, as this test can be obtained in almost all the impure saponins. Some of the saponins are very toxic, for they are protoplasmic poisons which irritate the nose, producing sneezing, besides irritating the eye and throat and causing an increase of saliva. They promote the action of the intestines.

A variety of solutions are on the market which contain saponin and which are intended to be added to ice cream, soda syrups, etc. They are sold under various fanciful names, such as cremolin, spumatalin, etc. A substitute for these may be prepared by making an infusion of 250 Gm. of quillaja bark in 1 litre of 70 per cent. alcohol. The addition of saponin to carbonated waters should be prohibited. The following test may be employed for the detection of this substance: The water is concentrated by evaporation and enough pure carbolic acid is added to allow 5 Cc. of the latter to remain undissolved. The addition of some ammonium sulphate facilitates the separation of the phenol. The carbolic acid which is separated by means of a separating funnel is shaken with water and with a mixture of equal parts of ether and of petroleum ether. On evaporating the watery solution the saponin is obtained and can be recognized by its tendency to foam as well as by the reddish-blue color which is produced on the addition of a drop or two of concentrated sulphuric acid and some water.

Determination of Uric Acid in the Urine.—One of the most difficult quantitative tests in the urine, on account of the complicated nature of the process, is the determination of the uric acid. The estimation of the amount of this substance, however, is frequently asked for by physicians, especially in cases suspected to be suffering from rheumatism, gout, etc. There are several short-cut methods for the estimation of uric acid, but none of them are accurate enough for practical purposes. A method which obviates the difficulties of the more complex processes, and which, according to the author, is sufficiently accurate, was recently presented to the Société de Biologie by Ronchese (*Union Pharmaceutique*, April, 1906). This author conducted a series of experiments to determine the methods of estimating the quantity of uric acid with the aid of iodine. He found that at ordinary temperatures uric acid is regularly oxidized by iodine, provided the operation be conducted in a medium rendered alkaline with some substance which has no effect upon the iodine (potassium bicarbonate, borax). Under these conditions one molecule of uric acid requires two atoms of iodine, and this proportion is independent of the dilution and of the amount of the liquid to be tested. One Cc. of the decinormal solution of iodine corresponds to 0.0084 Gm. of uric acid. In order to apply this reaction to the urine the various substances which might be affected by the iodine must first be eliminated. The uric acid must be precipitated in the form of ammonium urate and the following method of procedure followed:

One hundred Cc. of urine is treated with 15 Cc. of ammonia and 15 Gm. of ammonium chloride. The mixture is allowed to remain standing for half an hour and the precipitate of ammonium urate collected on a filter and washed with the following solution: Ammonia, 150 Cc.; ammonium chloride, 150 Gm.; water enough to make 1 Lt. The precipitate is suspended in 300 Cc. of water and is dissolved with the aid of a little dilute acetic acid. To this solution is then added either a mixture of potassium bicarbonate and of borax until a noticeably alkaline reaction is obtained, or else 20 Cc. of a saturated solution of these two salts may be used. A decinormal solution of iodine is next added through a Mohr's burette until the end reaction is heralded by the less rapid discoloration of the iodine. A few cubic centigrammes of starch solution are then added, and the iodine solution is dropped slowly until a markedly blue color permeates the entire liquid. If any discoloration occurs within a few minutes no attention should be paid to it, as it is not due to uric acid. If the number of Cc.'s of decinormal iodine employed is multiplied by 0.084, and to this product is added 0.01 Gm., the result is the amount of uric acid in a litre of urine. It is not necessary in practice to remove the albumin from the urine before applying this test.

The Origin of the Word Menstruum.

The paragraph on The Origin of the Word Menstruum, printed in the AMERICAN DRUGGIST for May 14, page 257, has attracted a great deal of attention. Among other communications which have been received on the subject, one by Charles S. Carrington, Brooklyn, is especially interesting. Mr. Carrington thinks that most of the writers quoted in the paragraph in question have placed the cart before the horse, and submits the subjoined note as "a bit of copy which may perhaps throw some light on the matter":

"In the year 1404 Pierre Bontier, a monk, and Jean le Verrier, a priest, '*assez bons clercs*,' by the direction of their patron, Jehan de Bethencourt, conqueror of the Canary Islands, drew up an 'introduction' for the preparation of the pagan islanders for Christianity and the instruction and guidance of those already baptized.

"This very interesting document can be found in chapters 47 to 52 of the narrative of the conquest and conversion of the Canarians, written by the two chaplains and published by the Hakluyt Society.

"Chapitre LXVIII treats 'de l'Arche de Nouel.' After describing how Noah was warned of the approaching flood, it proceeds: 'Et luy commanda qu'il fist vne arche de bois carré, poly, et qu'il l'oindroit dedant et dehors de Betun; Betun est vn glu si fort et si tenant, qui quand deur pieces de fait en sont assemblées et ioinctes, on ne les peut par nul art des-assembler sinon par sang naturel de fleurs de femmes.'

"It is very evident from the interpolation of this definition of bitumen in their description of the ark by the two learned clerics that in their day the menstrual fluid was supposed to be a most potent solvent.

"The extended use of the word from a particular to a general signification is in accordance with the known laws of linguistics."

Queries and Answers

We shall be glad, in this department, to respond to calls for information on all pharmaceutic matters.

Indecipherable Orders Deciphered.—An astonishingly large number of solutions of the two scrawled orders printed in the preceding issue have been received from all parts of the country. We again reproduce the two figures and accompany them with some of the odd interpretations submitted. We may as well inform our readers at the start that Fig. 1 is a *fac-simile* reproduction of an order written by a Hungarian physician on the bottom of a prescription, and it was only the pharmacist's knowledge of Hungarian prescriptions and the demands of Hungarian customers that enabled him to translate the order into pharmaceutical Latin and supply the desired ointment. The Latin translation of the order is Unguentum Hydrargyri Præcipitati Albi, which in ordinary English is white precipitate ointment.

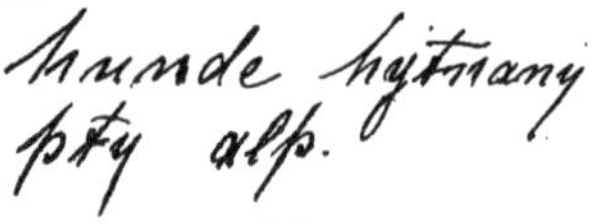

Fig. 1.

The first correct translation of Fig. 1 was received from O. B. Epstein, 1060 Dawson street, Borough of the Bronx, New York, and he is accordingly awarded the prize of a book to the value of $2, the selection of book to be his own. Correct answers were received from a number of other subscribers, but Mr. Epstein was the first to mail his interpretation, judging by the postmark on the envelope of his letter. In order to be perfectly fair to all participants in this contest pains were taken to ascertain the time of delivery of the AMERICAN DRUGGIST in the respective localities from which answers were received, allowance being made for the time taken in transmission of replies.

It is a curious thing in this connection that one prize winner should be located in New York and the other as far away as Wisconsin, for the subscriber who interpreted Fig. 2 and was first to mail his interpretation was H. T. Eberle, of 204 Main street, Watertown, Wis., whose subscription has been extended one year.

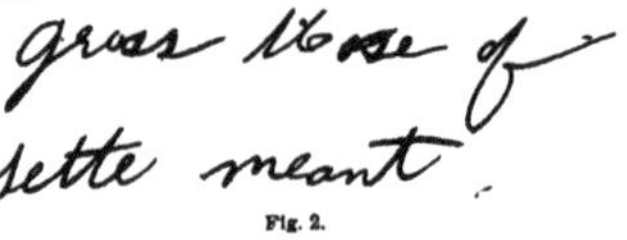

Fig. 2.

Fig. 2 offered little difficulty to any of the hundred or more subscribers who sent in interpretations of the scrawl, but some curious readings were submitted, ingenious readings, such as to excite wonder at the mental workings of those who could read such strange things into a comparatively simple and easily decipherable order. For the edification of our readers we tabulate below some of the different interpretations of the two orders which were received. Hunjadi water and soda mint outnumbered all others:

Fig. 1. (*White precipitate ointment.*)	Fig. 2. (*Corrosive sublimate.*)
A bottle of hunyadi water janos.	Large dose of soda mint.
One kidney plaster.	Glass bottle of soda mint.
Hunyadi Arpad bitter water.	Large measure of soda mint.
Dog has bitten Annie, please help.	Large dose of peppermint.
	Gross troches of sodium bicarbonate, with peppermint.
	Permanganate of potash.

Replies were received from the following places, the larger number coming from Chicago and New York:

Alton, Ill.	McAdoo, Pa.
Ashland, Wis.	Milton, Pa.
Auburn, N. Y.	Mobile, Ala.
Bancroft, Neb.	Nashville, Tenn.
Brooklyn, N. Y.	Newark, N. J.
Buffalo, N. Y.	New York, N. Y.
Chicago, Ill.	Norwich, N. Y.
Durand, Wis.	Ocean Grove, N. J.
East Liverpool, O.	Paterson, N. J.
Elkland, Pa.	Philadelphia, Pa.
Evansville, Ind.	Saginaw, Mich.
Geneseo, Ill.	Somerville, Mass.
Grand Rapids, O.	Syracuse, N. Y.
Hackensack, N. J.	Terre Haute, Ind.
Huntington, N. Y.	Thomasville, Ga.
Jersey City, N. J.	Trenton, N. J.
Jonesboro, Ill.	Union Hill, N. J.
Kansas City, Mo.	Watertown, N. Y.
Kent, O.	Watertown, Wis.
Keyport, N. J.	Weehawken, N. J.
Lakewood, N. J.	West Lynn, Mass.
Lewisburg, Pa.	Wilkes-Barre, Pa.

Questions on Phenol Prescriptions.—L. L. writes: "Kindly inform me how you would dispense the subjoined prescriptions, as I have asked several pharmacists and received different answers." The prescriptions are:

" (1) Saturated solution of carbolic acid. . fl. ℥i
" (2) Carbolic acid, liquid. . . . . fl. ℥i

"What percentage of acid does each contain? When carbolic acid is called for what strength should be dispensed?"

It is customary to consider a 1 in 20, or 5 per cent., solution of phenol in water a saturated solution, and a solution of the crystals of this strength is as near to a saturated solution as one can get. Prescription No. 2 calls for the liquefied phenol of the Pharmacopœia, made by adding 1 Gm. of distilled water to 9 Gm. of phenol crystals melted by the heat of a water bath. Before the introduction into the Pharmacopœia of *Phenol liquefactum*, a so-called 95 per cent. solution of phenol, made by adding 5 parts of water to 95 parts of phenol, was usually dispensed as liquid carbolic acid. It was the practice in the laboratory of Roosevelt Hospital to make liquid carbolic acid by standing the pound bottles of acid as received from the jobber in hot water until the acid liquefied, when the empty space in the bottles was filled with water, which was mixed with the acid by shaking.

It is generally understood that when carbolic acid is ordered the liquid preparation is desired, and unless the crystalline acid is specified the liquefied phenol should be dispensed.

It should be known that there is no such thing now recognized in the United States Pharmacopœia as "carbolic acid." Phenol and liquefied phenol are the official titles of what were formerly popularly known as carbolic acid crystals and liquefied carbolic acid, respectively.

Evidently a Depilatory.—J. T. B. was presented with the subjoined prescription, but could not dispense it, as the exact nature of the ingredients ordered was not known to him. He asks for a translation. The prescription as submitted by J. T. B. reads as follows:

Sodi hydr. Sulph. . . . . ℥iv
Solv in aq. Calc. . . . . ʒx
Calc hydr. pulv. . . . . ℥iss

There is nothing very cryptic about this prescription. The spelling, capitalization and punctuation are a little "off," to be sure, but otherwise it offers no special difficulty. We should read it as follows:

Sodium sulphide. . . . . ℥iv
Dissolve in Lime water. . . . . ʒx
And incorporate Powdered quicklime. . . . . ℥iss

Preparations of this character are occasionally prescribed as applications for the removal of superfluous hair.

Trouble with Stokes's Liniment.—B. J. says he has had trouble in making Stokes's liniment of the National Formulary so as to obtain a good creamy emulsion which would not separate. Upon standing the liniment as made by him separates with the formation of lumpy particles.

If fresh eggs are used and the acetic acid is of proper strength no difficulty should be experienced in the manufacture of this liniment. In fact, the mixture should grow more homogeneous and creamy with age. It has been suggested to eliminate the oil of lemon completely, as the odor of this is masked by the turpentine, and to use only one-half of the white of the egg. Try making the liniment in a bottle by shaking together the oil and egg mixture, adding the water and acid mixture and incorporating in small quantities at a time by vigorous shaking. In this way it will be found possible to make a thick creamy emulsion which will not separate.

Substitute for Cacao Butter in Suppositories.—A. W. D. asks if we can suggest a substance for use in place of cacao butter in suppositories, or name some ingredient that can be added to the cacao butter to mask the odor of the butter, as it is disagreeable to the patient.

For rectal suppositories there is nothing that answers so well as cacao butter. The odor can be covered to some extent by using a mixture of cacao butter, 5 parts; castor oil, 1 part, and yellow wax, 1 part; or, cacao butter, 2 parts; hydrous wool fat and white wax, of each 1 part.

The glycerinated jelly of the Pharmacopœia is used as a vehicle for suppositories, diluted with water and glycerin, as it is too firm for use by itself. Suppositories made from glycerinated jelly are obviously not adapted for use in the rectum and are intended for urethral or vaginal use.

Coconut oil has been suggested as a substitute for cacao butter. The melting point of coconut oil is lower than that of cacao butter and it is therefore necessary to add a small amount of white wax, about 85 grains of wax to 1 ounce of coconut oil being sufficient.

Glycerin in a Tooth Paste.—F. R. asks us to state how the glycerin contained in a tooth paste may be prevented from working through the tube and soiling the outer wrapper.

It is almost an impossibility to keep glycerin from penetrating the ordinary collapsible tube, and the real solution of the difficulty is to avoid the use of glycerin and employ honey in its stead.

The Ammonia Refrigerating Process.—F. P. G. writes: "In the AMERICAN DRUGGIST of March 26, in speaking of Evans's drug store, you mention the ammonia refrigerating process. Can you give estimates of the cost of refrigerating machinery or give the names of manufacturers from whom information may be obtained?"

The cost will vary with the size of plant installed. The cheapest form of apparatus would call for an expenditure of nearly $2,000. The new Hegeman pharmacy in the Times Square Building, New York, operates an ammonia ice machine made by the Brunswick Mfg. Company, of New Brunswick, N. J., and a Thomas ice cream freezer, the invention of the head of the soda department of the Siegel Cooper Company, New York. The principal manufacturers of refrigerating machinery known to us are the Case Refrigerating Machinery Company, 31 Main street, Buffalo, N. Y.; Buffalo Refrigerating Machine Company, 126 Liberty street, New York; Allen Ice Machine Company, 33 Degraw street, Brooklyn; American Linde Refrigerating Company, 120 Liberty street, New York; Pennsylvania Iron Works Company, 277 Broadway, New York, and J. F. Maynard, 122 Geyer avenue, St. Louis, Mo.

The Zonite Mfg. Company, East Orange, N. J., make an apparatus in which air is compressed and then released from pressure in the storage room where the refrigeration is desired, thus doing away with some of the piping which is a necessary part of the ammonia process. In the Zonite process the walls of the storage room are hollow and they, too, are filled with the expanding air. This process has been only recently placed on a commercial basis, but we do not think it has yet been adjusted for use at the soda fountain.

What Is Mistura Bismuthi?—A subscriber in New York asks us to state what we would dispense on a prescription calling for "mistura bismuthi."

There is no official preparation of this name either in the *United States Pharmacopœia* or the *National Formulary*. The preparation is, however, familiar enough to hospital apothecaries, and if it was ordered by a physician attached to a neighboring hospital we should not hesitate to dispense it according to the formula followed in that hospital. If situated where our correspondent is, in the vicinity of Roosevelt Hospital, we should make the mixture according to the following formula:

Sodii bicarb. .... ʒss
Bismuth submit. .... gr. xlviii
Aquæ menth. pip. .... ℥i
Mist. cretæ, q. s. ad. .... ℥iv

M. Dose, ʒij.

At the Demilt Dispensary, Twenty-third street and Second avenue, the following is dispensed for *mistura bismuthi:*

Bismuth subnit. .... ʒij
Glycerini .... ʒij
Mistura cretæ, ad .... ℥iv

M. Dose, ʒi.

In the absence of specific directions the druggist would be justified in dispensing either one of the foregoing formulas. The Roosevelt Hospital formula is the more preferable, in our opinion.

The First Souvenir Postal Card.

In the AMERICAN DRUGGIST for April 9 was printed a note on the origin of the illustrated postal card, in which the story was told that it was a custom of a small circle of painters, authors and a certain art publisher to take luncheon together in a well-known café in Munich. In June, 1878, this coterie, including the elder Kaulbach, determined to write postal cards to one of their number, whom they recently heard from, who was in the Alps. A chance drop of coffee running across one end of the card lying before Kaulbach, he absentmindedly began to draw lines with the coffee by means of a toothpick while engaged in animated conversation and being apparently entirely unconscious of the drawing. In fact, when it was completed he dropped the toothpick without observing that he had completed a very striking sketch of a bearded Tyroleian. The other members of the party, however, were delighted with the results, and thereupon each member of the group set about the preparation of an illustrated card, to be sent to the absent member, and shortly after this the art publisher placed upon the market a series of cards, reproducing pen and ink sketches of scenes about Munich. Thus, according to the story, was born the illustrated post card, the sale of which constitutes a large and rapidly growing industry.

The Original Souvenir Postal Card.

Our Paris correspondent disputes the German origin of the fad, and produces the subjoined reproduction of a card issued in 1870 during the Franco-Prussian War in support of his contention that the souvenir postal card is of French and not German origin.

THE DRUG SITUATION IN SAN FRANCISCO.

Business Being Resumed in the Burned District—Mack & Co. Retire from the Drug Field - Other Wholesalers Carrying On Business—View of the Ruins Photographed by Our Correspondent.

(From our Regular Correspondent.)

San Francisco, May 18.—The ruins of the wholesale and retail drug houses tell as vividly as anything else the story of the destruction caused by the earthquake and fire. Stores that were once scenes of active pharmacies and laboratories that formerly were running day and night are now no more. The charred remains of three-fourths of the retail stores and the tons of broken bricks, with here and there a brick wall that refused to submit to the elements, representing all that is left of the wholesale houses that formerly supplied this and surrounding cities, force one to the conclusion that the restoration of the drug business to its former normal condition is impossible. One must go among the ruins and speak with the unfortunate victims of the catastrophe, who will be found digging among the debris for fireproof valuables, or, dressed in the unassuming cos-

The Picture Shows All that Remains of Redington's Magnificent Building at 27 Second Street.

tumes of the carpenters, helping, hurrying on the latter's work of reconstruction, because of the comparative scarcity of builders, and gaze upon the many temporary one-story structures that are already being put up to house drug stores of former grandeur, to be convinced that the pharmacist will be in the lead in the forward movement that has been instituted in this unfortunate city.

In the unburned districts things are quite different. Stores that formerly barely furnished a living to their owners are now filled with new faces and prosperity has also entered. "It's an ill wind that blows no one some good."

CHANGES AMONG THE WHOLESALERS.

Many of the wholesalers are returning to the city. Redington & Co.'s men have donned carpenters' aprons and are at work helping build at the new location at Third and Brannan streets. The firm will continue to publish the *San Francisco and Pacific Druggist.* While at Oakland the firm was situated at 731 Fourteenth street. Langley & Michaels Company obtained temporary quarters six days after the fire at Second and Townsend streets, San Francisco. They have also secured additional quarters at Second street and South Park. Mack & Co., who have decided to retire from the wholesale business to engage

Langley & Michaels' Former Stand. They Are Not Disheartened by the Disaster.

in the oil business, have arranged to have all their shipments transferred to Langley & Michaels Company. F. S. Kellog and J. H. Coult, formerly with Mack & Co., are now associated with Langley & Michaels Company. The National Pharmacy Company, formerly of Townsend street, near Third, are situated temporarily at 957 Broadway street, Oakland. Waldron & Dietrich, agents for Johnson & Johnson and Schieffelin & Co., are occupying offices at Thirty-seventh street and San Pablo avenue, Oakland. Richard & Erin, agents of Warner Company's goods, are also in Oakland. The San Francisco Chemical Company are still at 1020 Fourteenth street, Oakland. The Carisa Chemical Company has moved to 108 Bacon Block, Oakland. Seabury & Johnson's agents are now at Sutter street, near Broderick. Cutter Vaccine and Serum Company, of San Francisco, are now at Grayson and Sixth streets, Oakland.

SOME RETAIL LOSSES.

The Owl Drug Company lost their five stores and laboratory and the damage is placed at $200,000, which is fairly well cov-

The Destroyed Building of Mack and Co., Who Have Decided to Retire from the Wholesale Business, is Seen in the Middle of the Left Side of the Photograph.

ered by insurance. The Union Drug Company lost four stores and their damage is placed at $40,000, with insurance of about $27,000. Wakelee & Co. and Leipuitz's Snake Drug Company, two of the oldest of the better equipped stores, are both complete losses. The World Drug Company, operating four stores; S. A. McDounell, Gleason & Ruggles, E. W. Joy, the Ferry Drug Company, and Bowman & Co. are some of the heavier losers

All that Remains of Professor Searby's Pharmacy, 400 Sutter Street. Professor Searby Will Not Re-enter Business, but Will Devote Himself to Teaching.

among the retailers. J. J. Mahoney's two stores, at Tenth and Folsom streets and 1800 Market street, were destroyed, the damage to the latter amounting to $8,500, with an insurance of $3,500. Bowman & Co. place their damage at $20,000 and carried $12,000 insurance. W. Haman's loss is about $15,000, while R. W. Coffin's is $10,000, with insurance at $3,000.

STORES RETURN TO FORMER SITES.

Among the stores which have already returned to the burned districts are the Owl Drug Company, at Sutter and Van Ness and Market, near Third streets; the Ferry Drug Company and the Edward L. Baldwin Company, of Market street; Perrone,

Removing the Ruins of the National Pharmacy Company on Townsend Street.

The Former Location of Wakelee & Co., Who Have Withstood Since 1850 Everything Except the Recent Earthquake and Fire.

Fervier & Zabaldano, at Montgomery avenue and Jones street; Garibaldi & Oliva, at Montgomery avenue and Green street.

RELIEF WORK EFFECTIVE.

Thanks to the efforts of the N. A. R. D., as well as of the individual help of Johnson & Johnson and the California Fig Syrup Company, the retail druggists will have but little trouble in starting again, on a small scale, of course. The fund of the N. A. R. D. is already nearing the $40,000 mark.

W. B. Cheatham, the local N. A. R. D. representative, in an interview with the AMERICAN DRUGGIST correspondent, thus

This Building Formerly Housed Joseph Calegaris' Pharmacy, Montgomery Avenue and Pacific Street.

sizes up the situation: "The local association has appointed a Relief Committee to take charge of funds and to distribute same among the needy. The personnel of the committee is: Prof. F. T. Green, chairman; E. L. Baldwin, J. A. Boyson, D. H. Wulzen, C. F. Fuller, A. J. Brannagan, K. B. Bowerman, Felix Lengfeld, and W. B. Cheatham, secretary. About $36,500 has already been contributed, according to last reports, and about 75 druggists have already applied for relief. We have

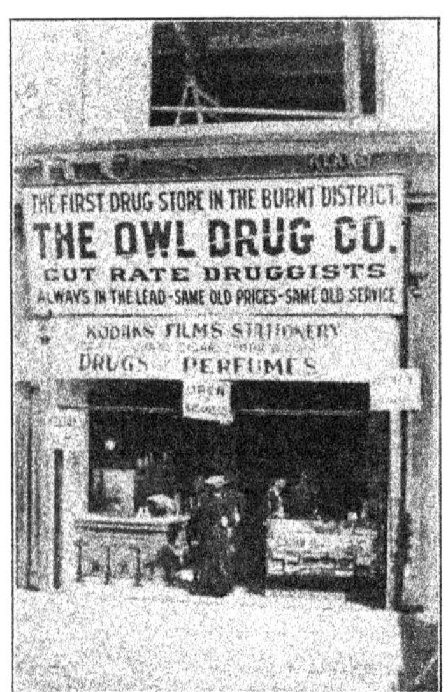

The Owl Drug Company Has Already Returned to the Site of Its Former Store, Acquired Just Prior to the Disaster.

estimated that between 160 and 170 stores were burned and that about one-third of the losses will be covered by insurance. The druggists sacrificed much in caring for the injured. Dr. C. S. Morgan was taking care of a woman in his store, and so earnest was he in his help that he stuck until death overtook the victim in the doctor's store. The relief work will be extended to the drug clerks as well. I understand that the California Fig Syrup Company has donated $100 to the drug clerks' fund and that the national organization of the clerks has given $1,000. We have estimated that 400 drug clerks are out of employment, 85 per cent. being almost destitute. The Syracuse Druggists' Association and other local bodies are also raising a fund for the drug clerks.

Indiana's Contribution to the California Sufferers.

(From our Regular Correspondent.)

Indianapolis, May 7.—The drug companies of Indianapolis contributed their full share to the fund obtained here for the relief of the San Francisco sufferers. The Hoosier capital altogether subscribed more than $100,000, which is certainly a most liberal response for this "no mean city," as ex-President Howison once characterized Indianapolis, his home city. The State of Indiana contributed another $100,000, so that almost a quarter of a million dollars were given by the people of Hoosierdom in answer to humanity's call for aid for the California earthquake victims. Among the Indianapolis drug companies that contributed were the following: A. Keifer Drug Company and employees, wholesale druggists, $250; Eli Lilly & Co., manufacturing chemists, $250; Daniel Stewart & Co., wholesale druggists, $100; Mooney-Mueller Drug Company, wholesale druggists, $100; employees of Eli Lilly & Co., $95; employees of Ward Bros. Drug Company, $20; Novin's Pharmacy, $10, and the Eichroat Drug Company, $10.

HEARING ON THE MANN BILL.

Influential Delegations Appear Both For and Against the Measure—N. A. R. D. Representatives Open the Argument—The Chairman of the Committee Intimates Possibility of Introducing a Reciprocity Feature—Professor Chandler Opposes the Measure but Attempts to Conciliate Retailers—Farbenfabriken Represented by Counsel.

Washington, D. C., May 24.—The House Committee on Patents has given a hearing on the Mann bill, devoting May 16, 17 and 23 to this subject. A further hearing is to be given next week. At the hearing on the 16th and 17th the following retail druggists appeared in favor of the measure: J. C. Gallagher, of Jersey City, representing the National Association of Retail Druggists; George M. Beringer, of the New Jersey Pharmaceutical Association; S. L. Hilton, chairman of the Legislative Committee of the N. A. R. D.; B. E. Pritchard, Louis Emanuel and Charles W. Rehfuss, of Pennsylvania, and Joseph W. Errant, of Chicago, attorney for the N. A. R. D. The measure was opposed by Arthur P. Greeley, of the Washington Patent Bar Association, formerly Commissioner of Patents; Frank L. Freeman, a patent attorney, representing unnamed companies; Prof. Charles F. Chandler, of the School of Pharmacy of Columbia University, and Anthony Gref, attorney for the Farbenfabriken of Elberfeld Company.

The most important feature of the hearing was a suggestion by Representative Currier, chairman of the committee, that a reciprocity clause be included in the bill, reading substantially as follows:

> Be it enacted, etc., That no patent shall be granted to a subject or citizen of a foreign country unless such country will grant a similar patent upon the application of a citizen of the United States: Provided, however, that this act shall not apply to any citizen or subject of a foreign country domiciled in this country who has declared his intention under the United States naturalization laws to become a citizen of the United States.

At the hearing yesterday the only person to appear was Livingston Gifford, a patent attorney of New York City, who presented before the committee the same argument which he had presented before the Senate committee at the hearing given last year.

The hearing on the 16th was opened on behalf of the supporters of the bill with a brief address from J. C. Gallagher, supplemented by a lengthy written argument, the main features of which are given below.

Mr. Gallagher said that his committee appeared as representatives of more than 28,000 retail druggists, divided into over 900 local associations, located in every State and Territory

The Ruins of the Snake Drug Store, One of the Most Costly Drug Stores West of Chicago.

of this country; that the bill had been indorsed by every State and local pharmaceutical organization in the United States. He briefly outlined the history of the bill and contrasted the conditions existing in foreign countries with those existing in the United States as regards patents on medicinal substances, and pointed out that the following countries exclude from the protection of their patent laws medicines, pharmaceutical preparations and chemicals: Argentine Republic, Austria, Denmark, Finland, France, Germany, Hungary, Italy, Japan, Luxemburg, Norway, Peru, Portugal, Russia, Spain, Sweden, Switzerland, Tunis, Turkey, Uruguay, Venezuela and Mexico. The following countries grant a patent on the process of manufacture only as applied to medicinal remedies: Austria, Finland, Germany, Hungary, Luxemburg, Norway, Peru, Portugal, Sweden, Tunis and Mexico. Switzerland will only grant a patent on an invention that can be shown by a model.

The citizens of these countries could therefore obtain in the United States a form of monopoly which was denied them in their own country.

Mr. Gallagher said that the granting of a patent on a product was wrong in principle, as it put an effectual estoppal upon all inventive ingenuity which might otherwise be expended in an effort to improve upon the process of production of some wholly new product. He then gave the prices asked for phenacetin before and after the expiration of the product patent and made lengthy quotations from Bulletin No. 80 of the United States Department of Agriculture. He reviewed the work of the commission to revise the statutes relating to patents, trade and other marks, etc., and summed up as follows:

None of the proposed amendments to the patent laws will interfere with or violate any treaty now in existence between this country and any other, or with any statute of the United States, and they will make our patent laws conform to those of other countries in regard to granting patents on medicines.

This bill will not interfere with the present system of the Patent Office, but it is believed that it will tend to increase the number of patents granted on curative agents.

The relief asked from your committee and the United States Congress will be a benefit to science and the medical and pharmaceutical professions.

This bill does not apply to remedies commonly known as patent medicines; they are not patented, but derive their protection from copyright and trade-marks. The socalled patent medicines are known in the drug trade as proprietary remedies.

This bill does not apply to chemicals used in the arts, sciences, or for agricultural purposes. The amendments proposed apply to drugs, medicines and medicinal chemicals only.

In conclusion we would request the Committee to give due consideration to the following facts in regard to this bill:

First, That foreign patentees will not receive greater privileges here than is accorded them in their own country, in regard to protecting medicinal remedies; privileges that our citizens cannot obtain abroad.

Second, That it will make our patent laws conform to those of other countries in regard to medicinal remedies.

Third, That medicinal and chemical science in the United States will be encouraged to do research work for the improvement of processes and thereby produce better remedial agents for the cure of disease.

We ask the passage of this bill in the name of the retail druggists of the United States, who realize more than any one else the abuses that have existed under our patent laws, abuses that will increase as the years go on, and may become so great that no remedy can be applied to correct it. We, therefore, most respectfully ask of your Honorable Committee a favorable report on the Mann Bill, and the speedy passage of same through the United States Congress at this session.

George M. Beringer, Camden, dwelt particularly upon the effect of the present law in virtually discriminating against American citizens. It was brought out that the estimated amount of phenacetin imported was about 600,000 ounces annually. When Mr. Beringer touched upon the lack of reciprocity under the present conditions he was interrupted by Representative Currier, chairman of the committee, who said:

"I might say, so far as I know, the foreign nations are forever expressing great admiration for our system and refusing to follow it wherever it serves to give their citizens an undue advantage here; they are forever getting ready to wipe out their working laws, forever getting ready to do this, that and the other, and never doing it."

In conclusion, Mr. Beringer said that the amendment proposed would create an increased demand for American chemicals, would encourage research and develop the chemical industry of the United States. He denied emphatically that the Mann bill would in any interfere with the legitimate results of the labors of any chemist or inventor.

THE ARGUMENT FOR THE OPPOSITION.

Arthur P. Greeley, formerly a member of the Commission to Revise the Patent and Trade Mark Laws, made a lengthy argument in opposition to the Mann bill, on the ground that its enactment would deprive American chemists of the benefit of protection for their ideas.

B. E. Pritchard made a strong plea for the passage of the bill, closing the hearing for May 16.

PROFESSOR CHANDLER VERY POLITE TO PHARMACISTS.

At the second day's hearing, on May 17, Prof. Charles F. Chandler, of Columbia University, appeared and occupied most of the time in opposing the bill. Professor Chandler was evidently smarting under the criticism to which he had been subjected by his remarks at the hearing before a committee of the Senate last winter, for he opened his remarks with the express statement that he had not been hired to appear before the committee in opposition to the bill. He introduced his argument as follows:

I appear here as an individual chemist. I am not here sent by anybody or paid by anybody to come here. I appeared before the Senate committee last year in opposition to the Mann bill under the same circumstances. I have never been employed by any one, nor shall I ever receive any compensation for appearing before you. I appear here because I am a chemist, and I think I have a right to represent the chemical profession. I have been twice president of the American Chemical Society; I have been president of the Society of Chemical Industry; I have been president of the Chemists' Club, and I have been engaged nearly fifty years in educating chemists. When my attention was called to this Mann bill I saw at once that it was an effort to rob the chemists of the rights which are offered to every inventor in the United States, whether he invents a machine or a process or a new product, and when I looked further into this bill I discovered that, while this bill is nominally for the benefit of the public, that is not the legitimate object of it, and can never, if the bill becomes a law, be the result of the bill.

After setting forth the evils which in his opinion would befall chemistry by the enactment of the measure, he occupied some time in expressing the high regard in which he held pharmacists, in the endeavor to make it perfectly clear that he regarded the druggist as indispensable to the community. He concluded his remarks by saying that every druggist in the community was a refuge for people who had suffered from accidents or who were taken sick in the streets, and he didn't want his friends, the representatives of the pharmacists, to think that he came there to say anything disrespectful of the pharmaceutical profession. "I have the highest respect for the profession," said he, "and I do not think they are half paid for their services. I know they work long hours; they never get rich. But at the same time I am not in sympathy with them in this particular project, because it is aimed to rob my particular profession, that of the chemist, of the remuneration which the patent law contemplates for every person who by his ingenuity and industry confers a benefit on the human race."

In the course of his remarks Professor Chandler stated that he did not believe that 50 druggists in the United States had even seen the Mann bill, a statement which was immediately controverted by both Mr. Pritchard and Mr. Gallagher.

A SPECIAL HEARING FOR MR. GIFFORD.

Anthony Gref having requested the committee to set a date for a hearing when Livingston Gifford, an attorney of New York, might be heard, the committee named May 23 as a suitable date. Mr. Gifford appeared on that date and submitted an article which was practically identical with that submitted by him at the Senate hearing last year. He appeared as representing a number of manufacturers of chemicals. While Mr. Hilton, of the Legislative Committee of the N. A. R. D., was present, the whole of the hearing on May 23 was taken up by Mr. Gifford's argument, which has already been presented to our readers.

Lebanon Druggists Dine with President Lemberger.

J. L. Lemberger, president of the American Pharmaceutical Association, and also of the Lebanon County (Pa.) Association of Retail Druggists, entertained the members of the latter association at dinner on Thursday, May 10, on the occasion of the annual meeting. The officers of the association are: President, Joseph L. Lemberger, Ph.M., Lebanon; vice-president, George H. Bender, of Jonestown; treasurer, George W. Schools, Lebanon, and the acting secretary, Eli Mader, Lebanon.

DELAWARE PHARMACISTS' ANNUAL MEETING.

Interesting Address by Members and Visitors.

The Delaware Pharmaceutical Society held its twentieth annual meeting in New Castle on May 16. Joseph P. Williams, of Wilmington, presided and made a short address, followed by Secretary F. W. Fenn's report, which showed a loss by death of two members—Dr. J. B. Butler, of Newark, and Edward S. Collins, of Wilmington. Suitable memorial resolutions were made and adopted.

Thomas Donaldson, of Wilmington, submitted a report for the Committee on Trade Interests, which was well received. John M. Harvey reported for the Executive Committee. Theodore Campbell, of Philadelphia, spoke on behalf of the Pennsylvania Association. William F. Dunn, secretary of the Board of Pharmacy, submitted a report which caused considerable discussion and showed that the board has been active during the year. Strong resolutions were adopted endorsing the work and policy of the National Association of Retail Druggists and supporting the Mann bill now before Congress.

The principal address of the day was delivered by Prof. E. Fullerton Cook, of the Philadelphia College of Pharmacy, on Commercial Training for Pharmacists. He showed how the subject was taught in his college and gave many valuable hints on advertising, bookkeeping, taking stock and commercial law.

The election for new officers resulted as follows: President, Levi Scott, of Dover; vice-presidents, New Castle County, N. J. Ferris, New Castle; for Kent County, E. L. Clarke, Dover; for Sussex County, Benjamin H. Matthews, of Milford; secretary, Frederick W. Fenn, of Wilmington; treasurer, John O. Bosley, Wilmington; Executive Committee, H. Pierce Brown, Robert Megee, William F. Dunn.

For candidates for the vacancy which will occur July 1 in the Board of Pharmacy the following were nominated: Albert Dougherty, Herbert J. Watson, T. H. Cappeau, all of Wilmington.

Dover was selected as the place of meeting next year, on the second Thursday in May.

The following new members were elected: Walter L. Morgan, Walter A. Grant, B. W. T. Tobin, Robert Megee, H. Pierce Brown, E. C. Robbins, Dr. Horace Bradley, Samuel W. Fox, John F. Floyd, all of Wilmington; J. Gaylord Bragdon, of Middletown; P. C. Murry, Lewes; Dr. J. Martin, Selbyville; F. W. Wilson, Pocomoke City.

After adjournment the usual annual dinner was served to the members and invited guests.

Reciprocal Registration.

The National Association of Boards of Pharmacy announces that the following active members have agreed to carry out reciprocal registration:

South Dakota, Louisiana, Florida, Georgia, Ohio, Arizona, Alabama, Indiana, Oregon, Indian Territory and Kentucky.

Uniform application blanks for interchange with the various States are obtainable from the secretary of any of the above mentioned boards, the usual fee being $1 for obtaining certificates from the secretary before whom the applicant passed his first examination and $10 from the board issuing the new certificate. Fees vary somewhat, according to board rulings and State laws. All active members of the association will now be glad to entertain applications from any druggists wishing to interchange with some other State.

The following boards are associate members of the association, which means that they are not as yet prepared to exchange registration:

Oklahoma, Massachusetts, District of Columbia, Maryland, New York, Vermont, North Dakota, New Mexico and Illinois.

The next meeting of the association will be held in Indianapolis during the meeting of the American Pharmaceutical Association. Any one desiring further information concerning the association should apply to E. Berger, secretary-treasurer, Tampa, Fla.

THE OKLAHOMA MEETING.

Prof. Sayre and Dr. Whelpley Guests of Honor—Doctors and Druggists Confer—To Boom N. F. Preparations.

Guthrie, Okla., May 19.—The sixteenth annual meeting of the Oklahoma Pharmaceutical Association was held in this city on May 9, 10 and 11. The sessions were held in the council chamber of the courthouse. The exhibits were attractive and were made quite a feature of the occasion.

The initial meeting was opened by the usual formalities. Orville Frantz, who is brother and private secretary to the Governor, represented the latter in a very effective address, which indicated that he was familiar with the problems of the drug trade and the peculiar relation existing between the pharmacists and the public. Dr. J. W. Duke, Mayor of the city, in his address of welcome referred to the question of adulteration and naturally made a drive at the quacks who are wandering into the Territory, and whom, he said, should be driven across the border. He also referred to the one thing in the minds of Territory people—that of Statehood. Responses were made to these addresses. Prominent among these speakers was Dr. Edwin DeBarr, of the Pharmacy School of the University of Oklahoma. In the address of President Clark reference was made to the organization, the work of the N. A. R. D. and to the creation of local organizations in the different counties of the Territory, which were multiplying in number and increasing in size in a gratifying manner. It was evident from his address that the cutter was not much feared in the Territory, but nevertheless in looking toward the future the maintenance of organization was considered the only salvation of the druggists. The remainder of the morning was consumed by matters of business and the reading and discussion of papers.

A communication from the Executive Committee of the N. A. R. D. was read, tendering fraternal greetings and requesting that the Mann bill be indorsed, which suggestion was adopted.

In the afternoon of the first day a large part of the time was devoted to a lecture by Prof. L. E. Sayre, University of Kansas, on the extraction of alkaloidal drugs and drug assay. The lecture was demonstrated by chemical experiments showing the processes of extraction and assaying. There were also exhibited some 30 alkaloids, and charts were displayed showing the relative strength of alkaloidal drugs and preparations.

On Thursday, the following day, various papers were read. Among them was a paper entitled Purity Rather than Price a Prime Condition. Two competitive papers were presented on this subject, one by W. S. Samuel and the other by J. S. Moore; another was, Should the Druggists of the New State of Oklahoma Have the Right to Sell Liquor for Medicinal, Mechanical and Scientific Purposes? by Vernon L. Pendleton. Dr. H. M. Whelpley, of St. Louis, gave a talk on the National Formulary. In the evening of the first day an entertainment was given in the palatial Masonic Temple, and later a reception and dance at the Elks' clubroom.

At the second day's session C. E. Potts, of Wichita, was called to the floor as a delegate from Kansas, and gave a vigorous and wholesome talk with regard to the association work and to the work of the National Wholesale and other large associations affiliated with the Retail Drug Associations.

A communication from the conference of pharmaceutical faculties bearing upon the subject of uniform title for degrees was presented, and the consensus of opinion seemed to be that one title or degree should be used in all parts of the United States and this title should refer to and require a uniform quantity and quality of educational training and work.

One of the features of the morning was a paper read by Mr. Wickmiller, of Kingfisher, who gave a humorous account of How I Started the First Drug Store in Oklahoma. Mr. Wickmiller came to the Territory at the time of the opening, driving a wagon pulled by two oxen. The oxen became exhausted and fell by the wayside. It was then necessary for Mr. Wickmiller to secure a team of horses to pull his supply wagon into town. He now owns one of the finest drug stores in Oklahoma. His pioneer drug store was started in a tent. Miss Stone, of Jones City, before the adjournment of the morning session read a paper relating to the State pharmaceutical laws.

In the afternoon a talk was given by Dr. H. M. Whelpley on the revision of the United States Pharmacopœia and the Pharmacopœia itself.

One of the features of the afternoon session was a paper by Dr. A. L. Blesh, a practicing physician of Guthrie, on Dispensing Physicians. His paper took the M. D.'s point of view and was an explanation of the situation of the practitioner of to-day who is surrounded by fierce competition, not least among the competitors being the prescribing druggist and the vender of quack remedies.

After the programme of business was completed the festivities and sports began, one of the features of the entertainment being an illustrated lecture on the Mammoth Cave, given by Dr. Whelpley at the Opera House on Thursday evening.

CONVENTION WEEK IN NEW ORLEANS.

Retailers Hold a Successful and Enthusiastic Meeting—"Collier's" and the "Ladies' Home Journal" Endorsed.

The twenty-fourth annual convention of the Louisiana State Pharmaceutical Association adjourned in this city at 1.30 o'clock on the afternoon of April 19, after having elected the following officers:

President, C. D. Sauvinet, New Orleans; first vice-president, E. L. McClury, Natchitoches; second vice-president, Adam Wirth, New Orleans; treasurer, George S. Brown, New Orleans; recording secretary, George W. McDuff, New Orleans; corresponding secretary, W. J. Sbisa New Orleans.

Executive Committee—William M. Levy, chairman; J. E. Scott, A. di Tripani, T. J. Balter, George V. Claren.

Delegates to the National Association of Retail Druggists—M. Bernstein, Shreveport; George W. McDuff, New Orleans.

Delegates to American Pharmaceutical Association—T. J. Labbe, F. C. Godbold, M. Samson, William M. Levy and O. A. Kaczodoski.

Delegates to National Wholesale Druggists' Association: A. D. Parker, Lucien E. Lyons, F. A. Dicks, A. di Tripani and A. de Lanzac.

A brilliant banquet at West End that night, at which the members of the association were the guests of Finlay, Dicks & Co., I. L. Lyon & Co. and the Parker-Blake Company, concluded the very successful meeting, and the following morning the delegates dispersed to their homes. Covers were laid for 150 guests and nearly every seat was occupied. G. W. McDuff officiated as toastmaster.

THE PROCEEDINGS.

Generally speaking, the convention was one of the most successful ever held by the association. It was well attended, close attention was paid to business, and the results were exceedingly gratifying. The first day's session was signalized by the adoption of a report from the Legislative Committee, presented by its chairman, P. A. Capdau, recommending the enactment of a law by the Legislature prohibiting the sale of carbolic acid at retail, except when ordered by prescription of a licensed physician. A violation of the purposed act is to be considered a misdemeanor, punishable by a fine of not more than $25, or imprisonment for 30 days, or both.

NEW MEMBERS ELECTED.

The following new members were elected:

Warren E. Scott, Crowley; Harry Cohen, Woodville, Miss.; Edward Thompson, Anchor; W. M Halle, New Roads; Henry Knecht, Albert Graner, Plaquemine; Clarence E. Schonberg, St. James; Florian Brignac, Jr., Lutcher; George Pourceau, New Roads; W. J. Babin, Torras; L. E. Bergeron, Oscar; Charles Heno, Napoleonville; Albert H. Waguespack and Joseph Waguespack, Oubre; Dugald M. Monroe, Harold E. Welck, Phil. P. Cusachs, Henry Welsch, P. A. Culotta, New Orleans; David M. Tomb, Daniel M. Brunbury, Jackson.

THE SECOND DAY'S SESSION.

During the second day's session the association, after a protracted discussion, placed itself on record as indorsing the *Ladies' Home Journal* and *Collier's Weekly* in their warfare on deleterious patent medicines.

EIGHTY-FIFTH COMMENCEMENT EXERCISES AT THE PHILADELPHIA COLLEGE.

One Hundred and Twenty-four Graduates Receive Diplomas—A Girl Takes the Highest Honors—One of the Largest Classes in the History of the Institution.

(From our Regular Correspondent.)

Philadelphia, May 23.—The eighty-fifth annual commencement of the Philadelphia College of Pharmacy was held in the Academy of Music, in this city, on May 17. The graduating class consisted of 124, one of the largest classes that this old institution has ever turned out. Prof. J. P. Remington, the dean of the college, highly complimented the class for the excellent showing it had made, not only in the senior year, but in the earlier years as well. The first honors were won by Miss Berta Whaland, of 4401 Market street, Philadelphia. She was awarded the prize for the highest average in the three years' course offered by the Alumni Association, the pharmacy prize offered by Dean Remington, the microscopical research prize offered by Prof. Henry Kraemer and the Kappa Psi Fraternity prize, as well as receiving honorable mention in several other conditions. As Miss Whaland stepped on the stage it was a signal for a general uprising of the students, and a cheer which fairly shook the foundation of this old building was given with a will. The members of the class and the profession, as well as the lady's friends, were proud of her. The speaker of the occasion was Congressman Robert Adams, Jr. In the course of his remarks he stated that the growth of pharmacy in this country was something phenomenal, and urged his hearers not to think that their education, while completed in one respect, could now be neglected. He declared that broad minded men were never more in demand by the country than they are now, and that it was to young men like the present graduates that the Republic was looking for its preservation and advancement. Besides the prizes awarded to Miss Whaland prizes were also awarded to George S. Du Bois, Franklin A. Butter, William R. Shearer, Herbert L. Richards, Hamilton Russell, Robert B. Anawalt, José A. Portugal and Herbert L. Flack.

Following is a list of the graduates:

GRADUATES WHO RECEIVED THE DEGREE OF DOCTOR IN PHARMACY.

H. C. Albert, J. H. Allen, R. B. Anawalt, J. C. Andrews, Wilmot Ayres, A. L. Baskin, Frances R. Bell, W. L. Bender, J. A. Betts, P. T. Bienkowski, F. J. Bilnzig, C. E. Bragdon, Elam Brubaker, W. D. Bursoon, Helen R. Burns, S. S. Butler, F. A. Butter, F. W. Carl, F. L. Cheney, C. S. Coles, E. D. Cook, G. F. Crouse, M. H. Cunningham, G. C. Davy, J. D. Dawson, G. S. Du Bois, Erma D. Eadie, F. W. Earl, C. W. Eckenroth, C. W Evans, H M. Fahr, H. P. Feigley, Manuel Fernandez, H. L. Flack, F. C. Fogg, F. G. Fogg, R. A. Forrest, W. W. Foster, Jr., W. B. Goodyear, L. E. Goss, C. R. Grammer, F. Green, C. P. Greyer, H. C. Grim, G. B. Haley, G. O. Hancock, J. W. Haws, H. A. Henry, J. A. Herr, J. C. Hoenstine, W. C. Hoffman, H. C. Hughes, B. R. Hurst, S. M. Irvin, J. F. Irwin, B. H. Jenkins, W. Jessup, E. A. Jones, F. B. Kelty, R. M. Kettl, E. J. Laubach, H. A. Lloyd, O. B. McClements, Charles Mann, C. A. Mehring, J. H. Medrano, J. B. Metz, C. A. Monaghan, J. K. Moore, O. I. Olewiler, W. H. Orrick, H. F. Peters, G. L. Pfeiffer, G. H. Platt, J. A. Portugal, C. H. Reese, W. H. Reisch, H. G. Reuwer, Jr., H. L. Richards, W. G. Riley, J. T. Roach, P. P. Robinson, Hamilton Russell, E. E. Scatchard, W. F. Schlitzer, C. C. Schomo, C. F. Schrader, C. W. Schwenzer, Raymond Sharp, L. M. Shear, W. R. Shearer, A. M. Shiffer, A. E. Shirer, J. A. Shrom, E. E. Slayton, E. W. Silfer, G. Staver, J. C. Stouffer, H. J. Sunday, F. C. Taylor, E. S. Thomas, F. W. Thomas, W. S. Thompson, S. E. Thorley, G. E. Traul, R. J. Walther, H. W. Whitacre, E. E. Wilkins, H. D. Wilkinson, R. J. Wolf, F. R. Yost.

GRADUATES WHO RECEIVED THE DEGREE OF PHARMACEUTICAL CHEMIST.

G. H. Broadbelt, W S. Camp, W. H. Haines, Harry Seidman, Berta Whaland.

GRADUATES WHO RECEIVED THE CERTIFICATE OF PROFICIENCY IN CHEMISTRY.

J. C. Carlin, F. C. Handwork, C. J. Heinle, M. B. Hile, W. H. King, J. G. Roberts, F. W. Steigerwalt, J. E. McCambridge, Jr.

Annual Meeting of W. J. Bush & Co., Limited.

The ninth annual general meeting of this concern was held May 10 in London. The chairman showed that the gross profit amounted to $414,302.78, as against $390,103.16 for the preceding year. After deducting all expenses a net profit of $98,784.60 was shown, as against $73,865.83 for the year preceding, an increase in net profits of $24,918.77. A dividend of 5 per cent. on the ordinary shares was declared.

1.—Ladies' Dining Room.
2.—Main Dining Room.
3.—Reception Room.
4.—Entrance Hall.
5.—Dutch Grill Room.
6.—J. L. Hopkins, president.

THE DRUG AND CHEMICAL CLUB OF NEW YORK.

THE DRUG CLUB'S NEW QUARTERS.

Successful Career of the Pioneer Drug Trade Club—Good Work of the Presiding Officers—Views of the Interior.

Although the formal opening of the new quarters of the Drug and Chemical Club did not take place until the latter part of the month, the club in reality opened for the accommodation of the members on Monday, April 30, and the number in attendance showed the keen interest felt in the undertaking.

The club was organized in 1894 and occupied rather restricted quarters in the second floor of a building on John street, above a restaurant, whence the members were served. At the end of two years arrangements were made by which the top floor of the Woodbridge Building, in William street, was secured for the use of the club, on very favorable terms.

The new quarters occupy three stories of an addition to the Woodbridge Building, at 100 William street, and these rooms being especially designed for the purposes of the club it was possible to make a home which for convenience of arrangement and beauty of design is probably not equalled by any of the downtown clubs. This is sufficiently evidenced in the interior views shown on the opposite page.

The entrance to the club quarters from the elevator on the fourteenth floor is through a short hallway which leads into a corridor, in the floor of which is inlaid the seal of the club, consisting of a caduceus, with a branch of flowers and a scroll, bearing the name of the club, surrounded by a circle. This corridor opens into a Dutch grillroom, with square red brick floors and weathered oak furniture. The windows of this and of all the main rooms look out on the East River and give a panoramic view of the graceful Brooklyn Bridge and of the more massive Williamsburg Bridge beyond.

On the left of the entrance is the reception room, with windows facing east and south. The furniture is finished in red leather and velours, green being the prevailing color of the hangings. On one side of this room is a large oak fireplace, and one of the walls furnishes space for low book shelves, which so far have not been filled. Rising from the entrance corridor is a marble stairway leading to the two main dining rooms on the fifteenth floor, the northernmost of which is intended for ladies and nonsmokers, while the room to the south, the larger of the two, is the general dining room, in which will be found the familiar groupings at the tables, which was a feature of the club in its old quarters.

To the east of the ladies' room are three small dining rooms, which can be used for special dinners, meetings, etc. The sixteenth floor is devoted to the kitchen, refrigerators, pantries and servants' quarters. Each of these departments is complete in every detail, the kitchen in particular being fitted with all the latest appliances for facilitating the work of the culinary artist.

The rapid growth of the club has necessitated enlargement of the former limit of membership of 300 to 500, and this latter limit has been already almost reached. The financial history of the club has been quite remarkable, in that it is one of the few downtown dining clubs which has never had any debts and which has never had to issue any bonds. A large portion of the credit for this is due to the two men who have been president of the club since it moved from the old John street quarters. The first of these, Thomas P. Cook, conducted the arrangements which led to making a very favorable lease of the building when the club first moved into the Woodbridge Building from their old John street quarters. Jesse L. Hopkins, who succeeded Mr. Cook, has been a most successful official and his régime has been distinguished by this latest move, which is the most convincing evidence of his success as president of the club.

The Connecticut Pharmaceutical Association.

The next annual meeting of the Connecticut Pharmaceutical Association will be held at New London on Wednesday and Thursday, June 20 and 21.

BOSTON RETAILERS MEET.

Final Review of the Legislation of the Year—The Objectionable Screen Law Knocked Out—Interchange of Registration Permitted.

(From our Regular Correspondent.)

Boston, May 9.—The May meeting of the Boston Association of Retail Druggists was held at the American Legion of Honor Hall to-night. This evening was a "smoker," with entertainment and a little business thrown in.

The secretary submitted the usual report and also one of the special meeting for the N. A. R. D. San Francisco relief fund. Treasurer Godding stated that he had received subscriptions for this fund amounting to $1,154.50 and that he had forwarded a check for $1,000 to the N. A. R. D. treasurer, leaving a balance for the fund of $154.50.

Henry Canning for the Legislative Committee gave it as his opinion that the drug trade was to be congratulated on the outcome of the various legislative problems. It was true they had failed to prevent the increase of the maximum penalty for the adulteration of drugs, which had been placed at $100, to $500, but as the fraud clause still remained the penalty change ought not to be seriously felt. He said the screen law as applied to druggists had been repealed, the effort to have the salaries of the Board of Pharmacy members increased would undoubtedly result in success, a law had been adopted permitting the interstate exchange of certificates, the sale of liquor in no license towns on physicians' prescriptions had been legalized, the measure removing the proof of fraud in cases of drug adulteration had been killed, the anti-narcotic bill had been adopted, and the 3 per cent. alcohol scheme buried. He spoke also of the untiring efforts of Representative Edward F. Leonard, of Springfield, a druggist, in behalf of pharmacists, and said the latter were under a debt of gratitude to Mr. Leonard for his services during the present session. The new by-laws and constitution were adopted.

To Determine Status of Trademark Rights to the Use of the Word Sulfonal.

Though nominally the defendants in a suit brought by the Farbenfabriken of Elberfeld, Germany, for an alleged infringement of the trademark "Sulfonal," which that foreign corporation claims as its exclusive property, Lehn & Fink, the wholesale and manufacturing druggists of this city, are actually the aggressors in the pending contest to establish the right of all drug interests to market medicinal chemicals no longer protected by patents under their popular and trade designations.

The Farbenfabriken corporation, formerly Friedrich Bayer & Co., has begun its infringement suit in the United States Circuit Court for the Southern District of New York, and Lehn & Fink have answered the bill of complaint by asserting the legality of their use of the word "Sulfonal" on the product of that name with their own label and name, on the ground that the patent on Sulfonal expired many years ago.

Through their attorneys, Frederick W. and Alfred E. Hinrichs, of 76 William street, Lehn & Fink maintain that they are justified by trade usage and because the monopoly of manufacture and sale claimed by the Farbenfabriken corporation ended with the expiration of the patent rights. The New York company also asserts that the foreign corporation should not be permitted to prolong this monopoly, and likewise proclaims the belief that the medical fraternity and all patients should profit by the establishment of the general right of manufacturing drug concerns to make products upon which the patent rights have expired, as the competition which will follow will result in much lower selling prices.

Although the patent for "Sulfonal" expired March 23 of this year, the Farbenfabriken corporation, through its attorney, Anthony Gref, of 128 Duane street, maintains that the trademark has not thereby become public property.

"There have been cases," says Mr. Gref, "where it has

been held by the United States courts that a trademark name became public upon the expiration of a patent, but the rule is not universal. In my opinion trademarks, of which 'Sulfonal' is an example, do not become public property. It is the intention of the Farbenfabriken corporation to protect its trademarks, and suits will be commenced against any infringements of those rights."

MANHATTAN PHARMACEUTICAL PLANS BIG "CONFAB."

Will Invite Physicians, Retail and Manufacturing Druggists to Join in Discussion on June 18—Members Elect Delegates to Conventions and Favor Establishment of Local A. Ph. A. Branch.

The May meeting of the Manhattan Pharmaceutical Association, held in the New York College of Pharmacy Building on Monday evening, May 21, was notable because of the fact that its members decided to consider the advisability of establishing a local branch of the American Pharmaceutical Association. The proposal that the Manhattan association should become a branch of the national organization was made by Prof. Henry P. Hynson, of Baltimore, who is chairman of the American Pharmaceutical Association committee for establishing local branches. After a communication from him, relating to this subject, had been read by Secretary Bruno R. Dauscha, President Jacob Diner called for a general discussion. As the consensus of opinion appeared to favor such a move, provided that the separate identity of the Manhattan association be preserved, Mr. Diner appointed a committee of five to consider the question further and report their findings at the general meeting of members in October. The members of this committee are George H. Hitchcock, chairman; J. L. Lascoff, Dr. W. C. Alpers, Thomas Latham and Joseph Weinstein.

A UNIFORM TITLE FOR PHARMACISTS.

Following closely upon the discussion of the local branch of the American Pharmaceutical Association question, another letter from Professor Hynson was read to the members. In this communication he suggested the establishment and general recognition in professional circles of a degree or title for pharmacists. Inasmuch as physicians, dental surgeons and similar professional men have long been entitled to the degree of "doctor," it was suggested that a similar degree or title be adopted for all graduated and licensed pharmacists holding the college degree of Ph.G. or Ph.D. President Diner appointed A. C. Searles, chairman, and Dr. W. C. Alpers and George H. Hitchcock members of a committee to consider the suggestion and report later to the main body.

The announcement was then made that all the members of the Manhattan association were expected to participate in the election of a successor to Joseph Weinstein as member of the eastern branch of the New York State Board of Pharmacy, which will be held on Thursday, June 7. The voting will be done in the New York College of Pharmacy Building from 9 a.m. to 3 p.m. on that date.

The Telephone Committee reported that it had made arrangements to hold another conference next week with General Suprintendent H. F. Thurber and Contract Agent W. F. Baker, of the New York Telephone Company, relative to securing the long needed slot telephones and the required commission on all tolls. The committee promised to make a report on the success or failure of their efforts at the June meeting.

AGAINST THE LUPTON BILL.

In view of the fact that the obnoxious Lupton bill has passed both the New York State Senate and Assembly and is now only awaiting the signature of Governor Higgins to make it a law, A. Bakst proposed that the members adopt a resolution instructing the secretary to prepare and send a telegram of disapprobation to the Governor, explaining to him the injustice which this measure would work in the legitimate retail drug trade and urging him to veto the bill. This resolution was unanimously adopted.

President Diner, in addressing the meeting, told of the plans which, with the assistance of Mr. Hitchcock and Mr. Dauscha, he had prepared to make the June meeting especially attractive. The feature which has been arranged for that meeting consists of a symposium on the Ethics of Pharmacy and the Allied Professions, and it is the intention of the officers and Executive Committee to invite as participants in this discussion several eminent physicians, the most prominent retail pharmacists and manufacturing druggists and representatives of all of the pharmaceutical and medical publications.

The appointment of members of the Board of Trustees, which is composed of the members of the various committees, resulted in the following selections: Committee on Legislation, A. C. Searles, chairman; J. Weinstein and Charles S. Erb. Committee on Finance, E. J. Emelin, chairman; A. Bakst and A. Baltzly. Committee on Trade Interests, C. H. Lowe, F. J. Congleton and W. H. Porr. Committee on Grievances, H. H. Biomeier, chairman; Charles O. Grube and J. M. Pringle. Committee on Membership, R. Timmerman, chairman; Ed. F. Pfaff and F. Wichelns. Committee on Press, John M. Tobin, chairman; J. L. Lascoff and H. Spriggs. Committee on Entertainment, A. Klingmann, chairman; W. H. Ebbitt and L. Berger.

The five delegates appointed for the meeting of the New York State Pharmaceutical Association are George H. Hitchcock, A. C. Searles, Albert Baltzly, J. L. Lascoff and S. V. B. Swann. Delegates to the New Jersey Pharmaceutical Association, Dr. William C. Alpers, C. O. Bigelow and Reuben R. Smith. Delegates to the Connecticut Pharmaceutical Association, Michael Rafter, Ed. Pfaff and Max Marlamson. American Pharmaceutical Association, Jacob Diner, Dr. George C. Diekman and Otto Boeddiker.

Topics for the Ohio Meeting.

The announcement of the twenty-eighth annual meeting of the Ohio State Pharmaceutical Association has been issued with commendable promptitude by permanent Secretary Wetterstroem, of Cincinnati. The place of meeting is Cedar Point, a delightful summer resort on Lake Erie, headquarters being the Breakers' Hotel. The sittings will be held June 26, 27, 28 and 29. The Committee on Papers and Queries offers the following subjects for papers and discussion:

1. How can the Ohio State Pharmaceutical Association be of more benefit to its members, financially and morally?

2. What forms of printing can be run off in quantity at minimum cost and be used to advantage by our members?

3. What is the best method for filing prescriptions, for convenience, permanence and cleanliness?

4. What is the best method for advertising and selling seasonable goods—disinfectants, polishes, etc.?

5. Soda water or other side lines—how to make them profitable.

6. For the best exhibit of any selected finished preparations of the new U. S. P. VIII.

7. Wanted—Formula for a headache powder free from the deleterious effects of acetanilid or similar depressing coal tar products; formula for toothpaste, for toothwash, for compound resorcin ointment, or other remedy that may suggest itself.

The following topics are suggested for discussion:

1. What prescription difficulties have you met with during the year that would interest the profession generally?

2. Are the physicians using the new nomenclature for synthetics of the U. S. P. VIII?

3. What experiences or criticisms have you to offer on any of the U. S. P. VIII preparations?

4. Have you any criticisms to offer on any of the assay processes or indicators used for strength of the potent preparations of the U. S. P. VIII?

5. Do the sales on alcohol or prescriptions for spiritus frumenti justify you in taking out the retail liquor dealer's license?

6. What has been the saving in money in your fire insurance premium since you have been insured in the Retail Druggists' Fire Insurance Company, as compared with other general fire insurance rates?

7. Do you notice any decrease in the sale of such patent medicines, the composition of which has been recently given to the public, viz.: Bromo Seltzer, Pierce's preparations, Peruna, Hostetter's Bitters, wines of extract of codliver oil? Is this decrease offset by an increase in the number of prescriptions for U. S. P. and N. F. preparations from your physicians?

Philadelphia Bowlers Win Inter-City Tournament.

RESULT OF THE CONTEST BY GAMES.

	Won.	Lost.
Philadelphia	9	3
Baltimore	7	5
New York	3	9

A crushing defeat on the alleys befell the picked team sent to Atlantic City by the New York Wholesale Drug Trade Bowling Association to wrest the honors of the ninth annual tournament of the American Drug Trade Bowling League from their Philadelphia and Baltimore rivals. The inter-city contest resulted in a sweeping victory for the Philadelphia team, which won first prize by capturing nine games and losing only three. The Baltimore contingent cinched second honors, with seven games to its credit and only five to its discredit, but, sad to relate, the local team came out third best, with only three games to its credit and nine to its discredit. As each team played twelve games, it was expected that the New York contingent would make a much better showing.

The games were held in the mornings, afternoons and evenings of Friday and Saturday, May 4 and 5, in Sweeney's Casino, on the boardwalk at Virginia avenue, but the members of the teams made their headquarters at the Strand Hotel. The New York men found some consolation for their defeat in the fact that William J. Carr won a special prize, consisting of a set of gold shirt buttons, for making the highest individual score of 200 and over, while John Ruddiman received a diamond scarf pin for his prowess in split spare bowling.

At the conclusion of the games the rollers celebrated the occasion of their meeting with a banquet at the hotel, and followed this function by breakfasting together on Sunday morning, May 6, before departing for their respective homes.

The bowlers selected to represent the New York association were the high score men from the teams of that body who had proved themselves most capable of defending the title against all comers. To quote the language of the alleys, however, "they fell down on themselves" when the greatest need for their expert work presented itself. Besides William J. Carr, the local contingent included John Ruddiman, "Matt Judge, William Malsch and William Norris and Dr. H. C. Lovis, who substituted in six of the games.

At a meeting held Saturday evening, May 5, after the last game had been played, the bowlers representing the three teams elected the following officrs to serve during the ensuing year: J. Elwood Lee, president; John Ruddiman, vice-president, and William Armour, secretary and treasurer. The Executive Committee, chosen by the members, included L. W. Davis, of Baltimore; Samuel Wright, of Philadelphia, and William J. Carr, of New York. Unless the Executive Committee changes its mind, the next annual tournament of the American Drug Trade Bowling Association will also be held in Atlantic City.

New Jersey Association.

The thirty-sixth annual meeting of the New Jersey Pharmaceutical Association will be held at the Hotel Chelsea, Atlantic City, June 6, 7 and 8, 1906. The local committee, comprising G. M. Hayes Deemer, H. H. Deakyne, W. F. Ridgway, M.D., A. D. Cuskaden, M.D., and Harry B. Leeds, are now completing arrangements for an elaborate programme. They have secured accommodations at the Hotel Chelsea, one of the largest and handsomest hotels in Atlantic City, and having an unparalleled location. It occupies a square from Morris to Brighton avenue and from Pacific avenue to the ocean. It is just away from the business and amusement centers and nearer the water than any other hotel in Atlantic City. A special rate of $3.50 per diem has been secured.

The general programme follows:

Wednesday Evening, June 6.—Meeting of Executive Committee and officers: president's reception.

Thursday Morning Session.—Address of welcome; address of president; appointment of Credential Committee; reception of delegates; report of the secretary; report of the treasurer; report of the Membership Committee; report of the secretary of the Board of Pharmacy; report of the treasurer of the Board of Pharmacy; appointment of Nominating Committee: appointment of Committee on Place of Meeting: appointment of Committee on Publication, and reading of communications.

Thursday Afternoon Session (at call of chair).—Report of Membership Committee; report of the delegates: report of the Legislative Committee, report of Query Committee, and reading and discussion of papers.

Friday Morning Session (at 9 a.m.)—Report of Trade Interest Committee; report of Committee on President's Address; report of Committee on Place of Meeting; report of Executive Committee; election of new members; miscellaneous business; report of Nominating Committee; election of officers.

Friday Evening Session (at call of chair).—Installation of officers; appointment of delegates and local committee by newly elected president, and meeting of Auxiliary Association for entertainment.

The American Pharmaceutical Association Local Committees Appointed.

Frank H. Carter, Indianapolis, secretary of the American Pharmaceutical Association, which will hold its annual meeting at the Claypool Hotel, in Indianapolis, during the first week in September, has appointed his committees to make preparations for the meeting. It is expected that the attendance will be 500. The committees appointed are as follows:

Arrangements.—F. H. Carter, chairman; J. K. Lilly, treasurer; J. E. Toms, secretary.
Finance.—William J. Mooney, chairman; H. J. Huder, J. K. Lilly, F. E. Walcott, Minor T. Waddell.
Souvenirs.—I. N. Helms, chairman.
Transportation and Hotels.—G. B. Moxley, chairman.
Reception at Trains and Hotels.—A. Timberlake, chairman.
Monday Night Reception.—John N. Hurty, chairman.
Local Intesests.—Maurice Schwartz, chairman.
Attendance from Indiana.—Leo Eliel, South Bend, chairman.
Press.—John N. Hurty, chairman; Lannes McPhetridge and Charles Dennis.
Commercial Travelers.—Michael P. Lynch, chairman.
Ladies.—Mrs. F. H. Carter, chairman.

How to See Europe.

George W. Voss, the well-known pharmacist of Cleveland, will make his fourth annual tour of Europe, conducting a special party which will sail from New York on Saturday, June 28, on the steamer *Koenigin Luise*, of the North German Lloyd line. The party will visit Gibraltar, spend five days in Naples and vicinity, six days in Rome, two in Florence, two in Venice, several on the Italian lakes, and then journey through Switzerland and Germany by way of Munich, Heidelberg and Mayence, down the Rhine to Cologne, through Holland and Belgium to Paris, where a week will be spent, thence to London, and from London, by way of Dover, back to New York, arriving on September 6. Mr. Voss has made such a success of these tours in the past that each year the number participating increases materially, and many pharmacists have either taken part in these outings or have sent members of their families, being assured on account of Mr. Voss' reputation and standing that they will be properly cared for while abroad.

A Retail Firm's Anniversary Celebration.

Reid, Yeomans & Cubit, the enterprising druggists of 140 Nassau street, New York, celebrated their sixth anniversary in business at their present location on Monday, May 7. General invitations to all their old and prospective customers and friends were issued several days before the event, and more than 30,000 persons made the circuit of the store during the day. Manufacturers of proprietary medicines, toilet preparations and other articles with whom Reid, Yeomans & Cubit have been dealing for several years and many new proprietors exhibited their products and gave away more than 100,000 souvenirs. An orchestra of eight pieces, mostly stringed instruments, furnished music for the crowds, and three negroes sang plantation and popular songs. Six thousand glassfuls of soda water were served during the day.

Registered in New Jersey.

Henry A. Jorden, of Bridgeton, secretary of the board, has been reappointed by Governor Stokes as a member of the New Jersey Board of Pharmacy for the full term of five years.

The following candidates passed the April examination, and have been duly registered:

As Registered Pharmacists.—Rafael Abelsky, New York; Nittert Bakker, Haladon; F. A. Coleman, Woodstown; J. E. Dubell, Columbus; J. H. Dolan, Jersey City; Joseph Danzis, Newark; O. S. Ghirardi, Montclair; Minnie R. Gold, Harrison; E. H. Harnett, Jersey City; J. M. H. Hain, Newark; H. W. Lehmkuhl, Bronxville, N. Y.; J. J. Monigan, New Brunswick; Charles Mann, Frankford, Pa.; Otto Neubert, Asbury Park; M. D. Olshin, Newark; A. A. Philo, Perth Amboy; C. O. Riede, Newark; B. A. Reynolds, Englewood; A. B. Richert, Brooklyn; Lodovico Santangelo, Paterson; Jacob Saltman, New York, N. Y.; I. J. Sasmorsky, New York, N. Y.; F. H. Scholz, Newark, and M. A. Taft, New York, N. Y.

As Registered Assistants.—G. M. Conwell, Vineland; M. A. Harris, Paterson; A. A. Kahn, Long Branch; Max Kraemer, Newark; Max Lapat, Paterson; W. H. McNeill, Paterson; W. C. McLeer, Bayonne; J. F. Mair, Elizabeth; A. A. B. Schectman, Newark; Albert Van Eerde Paterson, and S. M. Wojciechowski, Newark.

Obituary.

M. PIERRE CURIE.

(By our Paris Correspondent.)

The discoverer of radium met with his death on April 20 in the streets of Paris. He had just left the book store of Gauthier-Villars, a scientific publisher on the Quai des Grands-Augustins and was crossing the Rue Dauphine when he was knocked down by a heavy two-horse goods wagon. The wheel passed over his head, and death was instantaneous. The driver was arrested, but acquitted, as it seemed evident that M. Curie had been hidden from his view by a cab and only came into view at the very moment the accident occurred.

The news was broken to the savant's father, and Madame Curie, who was absent from Paris, was sent for. It will be remembered that this lady took a leading part in the now historical series of experiments by which radium was discovered. They were a very united and unassuming couple, to whom publicity of any kind was always distasteful, and although the French Government would certainly have honored the late savant by a public funeral, Madame Curie's one request, to be left alone in her grief, was implicitly respected, so the interment took place in the most unobtrusive and discreet manner, all the usual accompaniments of wreathes and speeches and even the usual and invariable formality of *lettres de faire part* (mailed notices of death and invitations to funeral sent to friends) being dispensed with.

PROF. PIERRE CURIE.

Born in Paris, May 15, 1859, Pierre Curie was counted among the youngest of great French savants. His election as member of the Academy of Sciences was recently noted in the AMERICAN DRUGGIST, and the biographical sketch and portraits published in 1904 will have made our readers familiar with the simple life story of the Curies.

The irony of fate was perhaps never more tragically evident than in the case of this gifted and worthy couple. Almost the whole of their married life was one long struggle, carrying out difficult and often expensive experiments on the most modest means. Then at last came a brief period of worldwide glory and financial prosperity, and all seemed to smile upon them till the most shockingly sudden yet essentially commonplace of street accidents cut short a career on which such high hopes were founded. The truckman's wheel, like the "brute bullet" of Lucknow "crashed through the brain that could think for the rest," and deprived France of one of her national glories and the scientific world of a savant whose name is familiar in every corner of the civilized universe.

CHARLES H. LESTER.

Charles H. Lester, general manager and also a member of the Whitall Tatum Company at the New York office, 46 Barclay street, is dead of pneumonia in the forty-seventh year of his age. He complained of feeling ill about a week before his death, went home, and despite the best skill that could be summoned he grew weaker, and finally succumbed to pneumonia on Monday, April 16.

Mr. Lester's career with the firm of Whitall, Tatum & Co. was an inspiring one. Starting in as post office boy in 1878, he attracted the favorable notice of his superiors by his industry, faithfulness and integrity and was rapidly advanced. Mr. Lester had a wide acquaintance among the drug trade and was highly esteemed for his genial ways. He was a member of the Hardware Club, of this city; of the Masonic (Blue) Lodge, of Montclair; Knight Templar Commandery and Masonic Chapter, of Orange, N. J., and Mystic Shrine, of Newark. He is survived by his widow and two children, a boy and a girl, aged respectively four and ten years.

Th funeral was held at his late residence, 209 Orange road, Montclair, Wednesday, April 18.

DIED.

BAILY.—In Baltimore, Md., on Wednesday, May 2, James Baily, aged seventy-five years.

BRANDT.—In Barron, Wis., on Monday, May 14, W. H. Brandt, aged fifty years.

COCHRAN.—In Baltimore, Md., on Monday, April 30, Dr. J. Forrest Cochran, aged thirty-five years.

HILFERT.—In Milwaukee, Wis., on Monday, April 30, H. O. Hilfert.

JACKSON.—In Freeport, N. Y., on Sunday, April 23, Philo Jackson, aged seventy-four years.

KACHLINE.—In Nazareth, Pa., on Friday, April 13, Paul Kachline, aged thirty-three years.

KENT.—In Jamestown, N. Y., on Sunday, May 20, Walter H. Kent, formerly professor of chemistry in the Brooklyn College of Pharmacy, aged sixty-four years.

LINCOLN.—In Middletown, Conn., on Monday, April 16, Remington R. Lincoln, aged thirty-two years.

MARCHISI.—In Utica, N. Y., on Monday, April 23, Henry N. Marchisi, aged eighty-two years.

MEYER.—In Brooklyn, N. Y., on Sunday, April 24, George Charles Meyer, aged forty-five years.

MURPHY.—In Springfield, Mass., on Tuesday, April 10, Timothy F. Murphy, aged thirty-six years.

O'DONNELL.—In Topeka, Kan., on Sunday, April 8, Martin O'Donnell, aged thirty-five years.

PILSON.—In Baltimore, Md., on Friday, April 13, Dr. A. O. Pilson, aged fifty-seven years.

RODRIQUEZ.—In Brooklyn, N. Y., on Monday, May 14, Andrew C. Rodriquez, aged sixty-four years.

ROSS.—In Baltimore, Md., on Thursday, April 5, Dr. Oscar E. Ross, aged forty years.

RYER.—In Flatbush, Brooklyn, N. Y., on Monday, May 21, Alfred Lawrence Ryer.

SHORT.—In St. John, N. B., on Tuesday, May 15, C. K. Short, aged fifty years.

VON WALTHAUSEN.—In Bay City, Mich., on Saturday, May 12, George L. Frederick Von Walthausen, aged seventy-five years.

WALKER.—In Carmel, N. Y., on Sunday, May 13, J. M. Walker, aged fifty-two years.

WILBUR.—In Fisher's Island, N. Y., on Wednesday, April 11, Henry A. Wilbur, aged sixty years.

Henrik Ibsen Dead.

The death of Henrik Ibsen, the Norwegian dramatist, which occurred on May 22, plunged the whole of Norway into mourning, for he held a peculiarly high place in the esteem of his fellow countrymen. His fame in English speaking countries rested solely on his social dramas, the most popular of which were "A Doll's House; or, "Nora," "Ghosts" and "Hedda Gabler." As a youth Ibsen served as an apprentice to an apothecary in his native village of Grimstad and prepared to study medicine, but just as he was about to enter the university a play by him was successfully produced. This determined his future as a purely literary worker. He died at the age of 78.

Greater New York News.

A new store has been recently opened by the Fetter Drug Company, at 128 Edgecombe avenue, corner of 141st street.

The Zagat Drug Company, of 2117 Eighth avenue, are fitting up a new store at the corner of Eighth avenue and 115th street, where they expect to move shortly.

Charles W. Snow, of C. W. Snow & Co., wholesale druggists of Syracuse, N. Y., visited the local manufacturing trade on May 14, 15 and 16.

Charles West, of the Eastern Drug Company, drug jobbers, of Boston, Mass., called upon friends in local wholesale and manufacturing houses on May 16.

C. Bischoff & Co., importers of synthetic chemicals and manufacturers of aniline dyes, have just removed their place of business from 88 Park place to 451-453 Washington street.

L. M. Jones, M.D., a retail druggist of Port Jervis, N. Y., visited the local manufacturing and wholesale trade on May 22 for the purpose of purchasing stock.

Charles H. Hubbard, of Charles Hubbard's Son & Co., wholesale druggists, of Syracuse, N. Y., visited many of the local manufacturing houses on May 16 and 17.

T. P. Gillespie, of T. P. Gillespie & Co., retail pharmacists of New Haven, Conn., made a tour of the wholesale drug houses in this city on May 14 and 15.

Charles Weisz, of McKesson & Robbins, has just returned to his duties after an illness of two weeks' duration. Mr. Weisz suffered from a severe attack of rheumatism, but asserts that he now feels better than before his illness.

Howard Miller has disposed of his pharmacy at Eighty-third street and Amsterdam avenue to L. Scarneo, who in turn has sold his store at 112th street and Second avenue to Dr. Fornuato.

The New Jersey Pharmaceutical Association will hold its annual convention in Atlantic City, N. J., on June 6, 7 and 8. The headquarters of the delegates to the convention will be in the Hotel Chelsea.

A. A. Burgess, of the wholesale drug house of Strong, Cobb & Co., of Cleveland, Ohio, made a tour of inspection through the factories and laboratories of many of the local manufacturing companies on May 18 and 19.

C. G. Euler, of Antoine Chiris, manufacturer and dealer in essential oils at 20 Platt street, sailed Tuesday, May 22, on the steamship *Kaiser Wilhelm II*, for an extended tour of continental Europe. Mr. Euler was accompanied by his daughter.

Charles Miller, the new organizer for the N. A. R. D. and M. A. R. D., who is to take the place of R. H. Clark as assistant to Eastern Manager William De Shetley and Organizers Bohan and Sanborne, has just arrived in this city from Chicago. Mr. Clark has resigned his position.

G. E. Taylor, president of the Taylor Bros. Company, manufacturer of clinical and other scientific thermometers, Rochester, N. Y., sailed on May 24 for his regular annual visit to the London branch. Mr. Taylor expects to be absent from this country about three months.

A. Defour, senior partner in the firm of E. Sachsse & Co., of Leipzig, Germany, manufacturers of essential oils, visited last week his American representatives, Magnus & Lauer, Incorporated, of 257 Pearl street, and returned to Germany on Thursday, May 24, on the steamship *Kaiserin Auguste Victoria*.

In referring to the retirement of William Cohen, of 476 Grand street, from the Gouveneur Hospital to accept a position with the Board of Health in our last issue, we inadvertently gave his name as Louis, having confused his name with that of his brother on Amsterdam avenue.

Adolph Stahl will not preside at this year's meeting of the Commercial Travelers' Auxiliary to the New York State Pharmaceutical Association, since it is his intention to sail for Europe on June 21, in the week preceding the meeting. There is no more wholesouled or jollier traveler in the association than "Dolph" Stahl, and he will be missed.

P. E. Anderson, the importing and exporting drug merchant of 7 Gold street, New York, sailed on May 12 for a European tour, accompanied by his wife. Mr. Anderson will visit all the great drug markets of Europe, London, Hamburg, Marseilles and Trieste, and expects to still further strengthen his foreign connections while abroad.

Members of the Drug and Chemical Club of New York have drafted and placed on record a minute expressive of their sorrow over the recent death of Arthur A. Stilwell. They have also forwarded a copy, attested by the president and secretary, to the family of the deceased member in testimony of the sympathy extended by them to the bereaved relatives.

The first copy of the new publication edited by the officers and members of the Metropolitan Association of Retail Druggists, and entitled *M. A. R. D. Notes*, was issued on May 15 to the members of that organization and other retail druggists in this city. It is now the intention of the M. A. R. D. to publish *Notes* every fortnight, although originally its backers had planned to issue on the 15th of every month.

D. R. Holmes, representing Parke, Davis & Co. in Australia, has returned to this city for a vacation and rest from business cares. Mr. Holmes makes his headquarters for the Australian trade in Sidney, New South Wales, where he has represented Parke, Davis & Co. for more than six years. He intends to visit the home offices of the company, in Detroit, and then take a vacation of at least a month before returning to Australia. Conditions in the drug trade on that island, Mr. Holmes asserts, are excellent, despite the keen competition offered by the English, French and German houses.

Colonel Edward W. Fitch, formerly manager of the local offices of Parke, Davis & Co., who is now making a tour of continental Europe for the benefit of his health, is reported to be recovering rapidly from the illness which assailed him just prior to his departure. Edward Morkill, a relative of Colonel Fitch, who is now in the city, says he met the Colonel in London recently and that his condition was greatly improved. William J. Carr, superintendent of the local Parke, Davis & Co. offices, has also received a letter informing him that Colonel and Mrs. Fitch had made a trip to the ancestral Fitch estate, in Barking, England, and that they were now on their way to Naples.

Another extraordinary accident, in some respects similar to that which befell the pharmacy of George R. Christ, of 39 Grant square, Brooklyn, into which a trolley car plunged last month, happened to the drug store of Vincent & Seymour, 982 Fulton street, Brooklyn, on Wednesday, May 16, when a heavy touring car automobile crashed into the front windows, breaking the plate glass and terrifying the soda customers. The automobile was empty at the time of the accident and no one knows how it started itself. The fact remains, however, that it did wreck the front of the Vincent & Seymour store without causing injury to any one in the place.

The feature of the meeting of the New York Section of the Society of Chemical Industry, held last Friday evening, was an address on the subject of color photography. Prof. Charles F. Chandler told of The Older Processes of Producing Colored Pictures by Mechanical Means. Others who had prepared papers on this subject were Hoyt Miller, who read a paper on Three-Color Photography; Maximilian Toch, who told of Present Practical Methods of Photography in the Colors of Nature; F. E. Ives, who explained, with exhibits, The Ives System of Kromscop Color Reproduction, and Controller Herman A. Metz, who demonstrated Hoechst's New Process of Color Photography.

George C. Reynard, secretary of Magnus & Lauer, Incorporated, who has returned from San Francisco, where he went immediately after the disaster which devastated that city, reports that most of the leading manufacturers and wholesalers of drugs, essential oils and allied products are already established in temporary quarters and are making speedy preparations to rebuild the stores, offices and warehouses which were burned to the ground in the terrific fire which swept the city. Magnus & Lauer have rented a private house in 'Frisco and are receiving and filling orders from this place as well as from a temporary warehouse and store in Oakland. The company is already making plans to rebuild its warehouse and offices in San Francisco.

George C. Reynard, secretary and treasurer of Magnus & Lauer, Inc., of 257 Pearl street, has just returned from San Francisco, with the encouraging report that business is being rapidly resumed by all drug and chemical manufacturers and jobbers in that city. The Magnus & Lauer store and warehouse, at 215 Battery street, San Francisco, was totally destroyed by the fire which swept that portion of the city, but as the building and all the stock were insured, the corporation suffered no material loss. Mr. Reynard says that almost all of the leading wholesalers and manufacturers have located in temporary quarters and are suffering but little inconveniece in the transaction of their regular business.

The Caswell-Massey Company, of New York City, one of the oldest and best known drug firms in the country, naturally represent the conservative element in the drug trade more than do their younger brethren. When considering the question of a soda fountain for their new store in the Astor House, corner of Broadway and Vesey street, Caswell-Massey made a radical departure from old-time methods, however, by deciding upon the Innovation, of the American Soda Fountain Company, although this style of construction embodies the latest and best ideas. The apparatus will be of white Italian marble, with trimmings of green marble, and with a beautiful mahogany superstructure inlaid with onyx. It will be installed in May. W. J. McCahill secured President Lyon's signature to the contract.

The Greater New York Drug Clerks' Association is an East Side organization of which comparatively little has been heard outside of the New York Retail Druggists' Association and the Drug Clerks' Circle. It is to some extent a rival of the last named society, which it has almost succeeded in outnumbering in point of membership. Some 300 licensed and unlicensed drug clerks are enrolled as members, and the organization has attracted the interested attention of the Central Federated Union, who have an idea that they can induce the drug clerks to enroll the association as a branch labor union. A mass meeting of the Greater New York Drug Clerks' Association for the discussion of this and other topics will take place at Odd Fellows' Hall, 69 St. Mark's place, New York, on Wednesday evening, June 6, at 10.30 o'clock, when prominent speakers will make addresses. The association was organized last August with a membership of 75, under the presidency of J. Kramer, and meetings are held on the first and third Wednesdays of each month at the place named above.

Recent visitors to New York, many of whom registered at the Drug and Chemical Club of New York, include: Lloyd Batre, Vice-Consul to the Argentine Republic; B. H. Seward, of London, Eng.; Dr. F. L. Humphreys, Morristown, N. J.; R. E. Desmond, St. Louis, Mo.; Charles Eamesman, Boston; Albert Dufour, Leipzig, Germany; H. A. Riker, Para, Brazil; Wallace Flanders, Boston; F. M. Piker, Mansfield, Pa.; Charles Markell, Sydney, New South Wales, Australia; Charles M. Logue, Pittsburgh; A. E. Meyer, Whitehall, N. Y.; Charles S. Brown, St. Louis, Mo.; V. S. Mulford, Montclair, N. J.; George W. Cummings, Boston; O. J. Garlock, Palmyra, N. Y.; E. J. Schall, St. Louis, Mo.; Harry B. Foley, Chicago; William G. Whedon, Sea Gate, L. I.; T. D. Barlow, London, Eng.; R. V. Scudder, St. Louis, Mo.; J. McGill Walker, Baltimore, Md.; E. L. Kemp, Chicago; Albert T. Suydam, Closter, N. Y.; A. Allan Graham, Newton Center, Mass.; W. P. Titter, Philadelphia; G. G. Achenon, Hackensack, N. J.; John C. Pennie, Washington, D. C.; E. Ruh, Sydney, Australia; John Travers, Palmyra, N. Y.; D. R. Taylor, Philadelphia; Guy Foke, Rutherford, N. J.; Dr. Henry Straesser, Union Course, L. I.; James Chalmers, Jr., Williamsville, N. Y.; L. L. Wood, Schenectady, N. Y.; D. E. Breinig, New Milford, Conn.; W. H. Oat, Norwich, Conn.; C. G. Robb and C. E. Hoover, Toledo, Ohio; J. A. Richardson, Baltimore; M. Dennison, Grand Rapids, Mich.; John C. Wallace and A. A. Burgess, Cleveland, Ohio; F. A. Applin, Albany, N. Y.; D. M. Lockerly, Montreal, Can., and Thomas Nelson, jr., New Brunswick, N. J.

S. P. Nickells.

Manager of the New York Branch of Wm. R. Warner & Co.

S. P. Nickells, who has been for some years manager of the New Orleans branch of Wm. R. Warner & Co., of Philadelphia, has been made manager of the New York branch, succeeding J. W. Pennock, who has resigned.

Although recently from the South, Mr. Nickells' experience has not been confined entirely to that section of the country, as he is well known in pharmaceutical circles throughout the entire Middle West, Northwest and South.

Born in Ohio in 1866, Mr. Nickells, of whom the above is an excellent portrait, went West in 1881 and entered the pharmaceutical profession in 1884 in Kansas City, Mo. After a business experience of six years in that city he spent four years covering the principal Western cities in the interest of one of the larger pharmaceutical houses, and in 1895 was assigned to New Orleans, La., to establish a branch house for his firm. He met with immediate success and continued in that capacity for several years.

Entering Wm. R. Warner & Co.'s service in 1903 as manager of their New Orleans branch, Mr. Nickells increased the business of that field many fold and brought it to its present enormous volume. He continued in that capacity until the present time, and, in fact, still retains control of the sales and traveling service branch of that department while occupying the post of New York manager.

Twenty-two years of pharmaceutical experience fits Mr. Nickells for his present assignment, and the trade and profession of Gotham and vicinity may expect that liberal and courteous treatment that has made Mr. Nickells and his employers, Wm. R. Warner & Co., prominent factors in pharmaceutical circles. Mr. Nickells' Western and Southern friends will be pleased to learn of his promotion to his present important post and will wish him continued success.

The time of meeting of the Minnesota State Pharmaceutical Association has been changed to June 26. The place of meeting is Lake Minnetonka.

The thirteenth annual meeting of the Vermont Pharmaceutical Association will be held in Burlington, July 11 and 12, and we are asked by Secretaries Bellrose and Churchill to announce the fact.

The New Hegeman Pharmacy a Beauty.

On of the most elaborately equipped drug stores in this city is that of the corporation of Hegeman & Co., recently opened in the *Times* Building, at Forty-second street, Broadway and Seventh avenue. Unlike almost any other pharmacy in town, this new branch of Hegeman & Co. has its drug, surgical and prescription departments in the basement, which is on the same level as the Times square station of the Subway, so that customers may enter the store below ground as well as above.

Broadway Front of the Hegeman Corporation's Times Square Pharmacy.

The main room, on the first or street floor of the building, contains an unsually handsome equipment. The walls hold shelving behind plate glass sliding doors, and below the shelving are hundreds of drug drawers, cupboards and other storage arrangements. About 10 feet from the flooring, on all sides of the room, is a wrought and cast iron balcony, about 3 feet wide,

Mr. Schroeder and Mr. Gardiner at the Instrument Counter of the Subway Floor of the Times Square Pharmacy.

which is reached by two ornamental wrought iron staircases. The balustrade of this balcony is also made of wrought iron, and from the balcony depend several ornamental electroliers in the form of sprays. Above the balcony the walls are covered with cases behind glass doors, in which the proprietary medicines are kept.

The most attractive feature of the main room, however, is located in front of a column a trifle to the west of the Forty-second street entrance, where a showcase with a revolving display is operated and lighted by electricity. This showcase is modeled after the Ferris Wheel, with carriers of nickel and plate glass, upon which the goods to be exhibited are placed. The revolving display is inclosed in a plate glass box, the back of which is lined with mirrors.

The Patent Medicine Department, with Revolving Electrical Showcase in the Foreground, Times Square Pharmacy.

The color scheme of that portion of the main room under the balcony is white enamel, the dazzling purity of which is intensified by mirrors placed on all the available wall space and also in back of the cases. The walls above the balcony are decorated with gold leaf. The main room also contains a beautiful onyx

Drug Sales Counter on the Subway Floor of the Times Square Pharmacy.

soda fountain and departments for cigars, candy, fancy goods, perfumery and proprietary medicines. More than 500 electric lamps are used to light the room, the under side of the balcony being lined with 16 candle-power bulbs about 9 inches apart, while the shelving in the gallery is decorated with rows of bulbs projecting from the cornice, and still further lighting apparatus is located on the beams in the ceiling. The decoration of the ceiling is in cream color, with a gold border around the panels. The ornamental plastering on the soffit and the sides of the beams has its high lights touched with gold leaf.

In addition to the drug, surgical and prescription departments, the basement also contains the cashier's room, into which the pneumatic cash carrier tubes enter. The partitions inclosing all of the separate rooms are lined with mirrors, and the shallow wall cases are lined with mirror backing and plate glass shelves and doors. The fixtures in the basement, moreover, are finished in natural oak, and each individual showcase has its own electric lighting.

In the sub-basement is a large storeroom and an elaborate soda water apparatus, with equipment for refrigeration and the preparation of ice cream, syrups and flavors. The equipment and decoration of the new Hegeman store was designed and

Mr. Marco and Mr. Steinheuer at the Dispensing Counter of the Times Square Pharmacy.

superintended by John E. Nitchie, architect, of 150 Nassau street, while the decorations in the show windows were designed by J. H. Guerin, of 2542 Seventh avenue.

THE SODA FOUNTAIN.

When Hegeman & Co. determined to take the entire ground floor and basement of the *Times* Building, at Broadway and Seventh avenue, the soda fountain was one of the great questions. The location of this store, coupled with the energy of the firm who would operate it, promised to make it the greatest drug store in the world. As the *Times* Building marks the heart of the theater district of the city the importance of the

Mr. Lee and Mr. Johnson at the Soda Fountain of the Times Square Pharmacy.

soda fountain can readily be seen. J. H. Fredericks, the New York sales manager of the American Soda Fountain Company, who had already secured contracts from the Hegeman Corporation for the five "Innovation" fountains now installed in its other stores, was commissioned to put an "Innovation" into the Times Square store. He was instructed to design the handsomest and most costly apparatus ever constructed. The complete plant was to include mechanical refrigeration and embody every modern feature permitting the dispensing of soda water rapidly and in the most attractive and cleanly manner. The result is the fountain illustrated herewith.

WESTERN NEW YORK.

A Full Class to Graduate—Dr. Gregory in Charge—For the San Francisco Sufferers—Automobiles for Druggists—Election of Board Member—Arrangements for Buffalo Day.

(From our Regular Correspondent.)

Buffalo, May 24.—The Buffalo College of Pharmacy, as a branch of the but partly fledged University of Buffalo, but a very efficient branch for all that, will hold its annual commencement June 1 with the usual ceremonies. The faculty is pleased to state that the class is the best and largest in the history of the college. The number at present is 55, and it is not expected that it will be reduced much, possibly not at all.

DR. GREGORY IN FULL CHARGE OF THE CAHOON-LYON INTERESTS.

The resignation of Arthur Kelsey from the assistant management of the Cahoon-Lyon Drug Company to take charge of one of the stores of the Caswell-Massey drug stores in New York places Dr. W. G. Gregory in the vacated position in the Buffalo store, though there is said to be no particular appointment, as he was already a member of the company. The company will soon have the Gregory Pharmacy refitted in elegant shape. It is stated that the report that it has other stores in the city besides is a mistake, as none are desired at present. The business is growing fast in its present form and it would be poor policy to increase it faster than can be done thoroughly.

LOCKIE LOSES FAITH—AND SIXTEEN DOLLARS.

President J. A. Lockie of the State Pharmaceutical Association has less faith in young human nature than he once had. He lately hired a boy of 15 to do errands, and on the first day sent him to the post office with $16 and lent him a bicycle. The boy did not return and the police had a long search for him, as he had hired out under an assumed name. The wheel and part of the money were recovered, and the boy is now paying for the good time he had with the rest of the money.

FOR THE SAN FRANCISCO RELIEF FUND.

The Buffalo retail druggists, not satisfied with the sum of nearly $50,000 raised in the Mayor's general fund for the San Francisco sufferers, and learning that the druggists in the earthquake and burned district of the doomed city were especially destitute, have so far raised $125 for them and will probably add to the sum.

DRUGGISTS AS AUTOMOBITES.

Buffalo retail druggists are showing that some of them at least can make money by coming out lately with new automobiles. The list includes Fred. Seisser, George Reimann and H. A. Scheck. One of them says the excitement of learning to run a "machine" is so great that one is all a-tremble for some days and quite unfitted for any sort of fine work in the dispensing line.

DATE FIXED FOR BOARD ELECTION.

The Buffalo Retail Druggists' Association held a special meeting on the 18th and fixed Wednesday, June 6, as the day for electing a member of the State Board of Pharmacy to succeed Dr. W. G. Gregory, who retires from the board. The place of election will be the University of Buffalo, as usual. It is reported that the candidacy of J. A. Lockie for the position is opposed by A. J. Keller, a well-known Buffalo druggist.

It was arranged at the meeting that President Darrin of the association name a local committee to take charge of the entertainment of the attendants of the State pharmaceutical meeting at Niagara Falls on the day set off as Buffalo day. The committee has not been announced, but will be in active operation in a few days, as it is the intention to give the visitors a very fine time in Buffalo.

THE NEXT EXAMINATION TO BE HELD BY THE WESTERN BRANCH OF THE NEW YORK STATE BOARD OF PHARMACY

will be in Buffalo June 22, when the candidates from the colleges of pharmacy are expected to present themselves. A list of about 45 is looked for. The Western Branch held a special executive meeting at Lockport May 22, to take up some cases of violation of the law which have come up in that vicinity of late.

MASSACHUSETTS.

Massachusetts College Graduates—Alumni Participate in Festivities—Illegal Sales of Liquor Cause Trouble for Several Druggists.

(From our Regular Correspondent.)

Boston, May 23.—The M. C. P. '06 graduating exercises were inaugurated on the evening of May 16 by a reception and dance tendered by the members of the class to their friends. These latter were numerous this year and Howe Hall, where the event was held, was not large enough to comfortably accommodate the crowd. Every one was in a merry mood, however, and consequently there was much enjoyment. The affair continued until a late hour and was matronized by Mrs. J. G. Godding, Miss Smith and Mrs. Bardwell. Refreshments were served and the music was by the Salem Cadet Orchestra.

THE COMMENCEMENT AND CLASS DAY EXERCISES

were held at the college building on the afternoon of May 17. Pharmacy Hall and the whole building was prettily decorated for the event. The class day exercises came first. William H. Doherty, president of the class, presided, and introduced Roland R. Moxley, who recited the class history. Robert A. Newton then delivered the class oration. Raoul J. B. Verina read the class will, which provoked much merriment. George E. Vose gave a reading and Samuel M. Best delivered the class prophecy. Irving R. Howatt closed with a brief farewell address. Vocal selections were given by Miss Florence M. Reilly, a student, and music was furnished by an orchestra. An intermission followed, during which refreshments were served. This was followed by the graduating exercises, which were opened by Irving P. Gammon, Ph.G., president of the college. The Rev. William W. Bustard delivered the address on "The Characterization of True Greatness, or The Way to Win." After this President Gammon conferred degrees upon the following:

Degree of Doctor of Pharmacy.—James Holmes Adams, Hyman Alkon, Samuel M. Best, Harry Braconier, Charles Parker Brown, Arthur Odilon Burque, Edmund Joseph Collette, William Henry Doherty, John Augustine Donahoe, William English, Mary Cecelia Gorman, William Hamilton, Irving Richard Howatt, Charles Cleophas Martel, Otto Frederick Morgner, Edward Joseph Morin, Roland Rufus Moxley, William John Murnane, Robert Albro Newton, Everett Augustus Nichols, Romeo Tancrede Robillard, Avery George Smith, Franklin Horton Stacey, William Lafayette Stokes, Raoul Jean Baptiste Verina, George Ellery Vose, Daniel Isidor Weston, Warren Bremner Wilson.

Degree of Pharmaceutical Chemist.—Edward Perry Bigelow, Frederick Goss Cushing, Herman Francis Hawthorne, Edward Woodbury Luques, Bernard Benedict Merten.

DINNER AT THE COPLEY SQUARE.

In the evening, at the Copley Square Hotel occurred the annual dinner complimentary to the graduating class, tendered by the Alumni Association. This event was largely attended and many ladies were also present. President Perley B. Thompson, Ph.G., of Norwood, occupied the chair. The speakers were Rev. William W. Bustard, Capt. J. Stearns Cushing, Fred A. Hubbard and President William H. Doherty, of the class of '06. Florence C. White, reader, gave several selections, and there was also much music. Prior to the dinner a business meeting was held, at which the constitution was so amended that the annual meetings will in the future be held on the first Thursday in February instead of on the "second Thursday in April," as hitherto.

WHOLESALE EMPLOYEES' BENEFIT ASSOCIATION.

The Mutual Benefit Association, composed of the employees of the Eastern Drug Company, gave a musical and dance to their friends in Howe Hall on the evening of May 4. The con-

DRUGGISTS FINED FOR ILLEGAL SALES OF LIQUORS.

Several Amesbury druggists recently paid liquor fines of $50 each, after entering pleas of guilty. This action followed police raids upon stores of the above. The list follows: Harris Chadwell, H. Duffault, E. S. Davis and Bahan & Maloney.

Dr. William H. Jackson, of Stoughton, and Joseph H. Hart, of Canton, were each fined $25 a few days ago for selling adulterated liquors. Hart appealed and furnished $100 bonds for his appearance in the Superior Court. Dr. Jackson pleaded guilty to a complaint charging him with practicing medicine without a physician's certificate and the case was continued for sentence.

A FIGHT OVER LICENSE QUESTION IN CAMBRIDGE.

The question of licensing Cambridge druggists is still evoking much comment. A few days ago the License Committee of the Board of Aldermen gave a hearing to the druggists who had filed applications for sixth class license permits. A suggestion was made by the presiding officer that it might be possible to grant licenses to five or six druggists. Those who favored granting all of the licenses argued that the new law would make it very difficult for persons to procure liquor in cases of sudden emergency. The matter was taken under advisement, and later it was decided not to grant the licenses.

SODA FOUNTAINS IN MAINE.

W. B. Berry, sales manager in northern New England for the American Soda Fountain Company, reports that recent sales continue to show that Maine dispensers appreciate the new Innovation construction, the following druggists having recently ordered Innovation fountains: Louis H. Hamm, Bangor; John H. Shaw, Portland; the Essex Pharmacy, Bangor; John D. Henry, Presque Isle. F. H. Beck, a confectioner of Norway, Maine, has also ordered an Innovation. Among Mr. Berry's customers for other apparatus are: T. Hilton, Portland; W. R. McDonald Drug Company, Rumford Falls; C. W. Prescott, Monmouth; J. H. Montgomery, Searsport; Wm. G. Treat, Stockton Springs; Wright & Lodge, Eastport; S. G. Cushman, Steuben, and J. H. Foley, Bangor. In Kennebunkport W. F. Goodwin, a leading confectioner, has ordered a beautiful solid onyx wall apparatus.

AMERICAN GROWN DRUGS ON EXHIBIT.

Practical Papers Presented at the Philadelphia College Meeting—England Criticises U. S. P. viii Formula for Syrup of Wild Cherry—The Procter Monument.

Philadelphia, May 16.—The last of the series of pharmaceutical meetings of the Philadelphia College of Pharmacy for 1905-'06 was held on Tuesday afternoon, May 15, with M. I. Wilbert in the chair.

William G. Toplis, a pharmacist of Germantown, presented a paper on Pasting Labels on Tin, in which he stated that the reason that labels curl from metal surfaces is the contracting of the paste consequent upon its drying. In order to prevent this he recommended the coating of the label with pure glycerin previous to the application of the paste.

Joseph W. England read a paper on Syrup of Wild Cherry U. S. P., VIII, in which he asserted that the present formula yields a product which is inferior to that made according to the formula of the previous pharmacopœia. He suggested a slight modification of the formula of 1890, as yielding more satisfactory results.

AMERICAN GROWN DRUGS.

Prof. Henry Kraemer exhibited 25 samples of crude drugs from plants grown in the United States by Dr. Rodney H. True, of the United States Department of Agriculture. The specimens included serpentaria, echinacea, convallaria, belladonna, digitalis, conium, pyrethrum flowers, etc. The specimens presented a fine appearance, for the most part, and showed what can be done by cultivation and care in collection.

M. I. Wilbert presented a report on recent advances in pharmacy, and Prof. Clement B. Lowe and E. M. Boring presented some notes of practical pharmaceutical interest. There was considerable discussion on the various subjects, and among those who took part were O. W. Osterlund, Ambrose Hunsberger, Dr. C. A. Weidemann and the authors of the several papers.

THE PROCTER MONUMENT.

Professor Kraemer stated that the Committee on Procter Memorial of the American Pharmaceutical Association were now ready to begin an active campaign for the collection of funds and said that he was ready to receive subscriptions, and several subscriptions were handed in. Professor Kraemer stated that there was no question in his mind but that the monument would be erected.

PENNSYLVANIA.

A Telephone Swindler Touches the Jobber—Commencement Week at the College—The Drug Trust Suit—Philadelphia Branch of the American Pharmaceutical Association.

(From our Regular Correspondent.)

Philadelphia, May 22.—The eighty-fifth annual commencement of the Philadelphia College of Pharmacy was held in the Academy of Music on May 17, 124 men graduating, this being the largest class ever turned out from this institution. The highest honors were won by a woman, Miss Berta Whaland, of Philadelphia, who took three prizes and won honorable mention in connection with several others. Details of the exercises appear in another column.

A NEW PHASE OF THE TELEPHONE SWINDLE.

Wholesale druggists of this city are somewhat chary about receiving orders for delivery to bearer over the telephone. This has been brought about by a sharper who has victimized two of the leading houses here. He called up the wholesale house and told the clerk who answered the "phone" that he was "So and so" and that he would send his boy after certain goods, which he would then order. This system worked a couple of times, and one of the orders delivered to the boy who called for the goods amounted to over $100. Now when a druggist calls up a wholesaler and wishes goods to be delivered to bearer a return call is immediately made to the retailer to ascertain whether the retail druggist has really ordered the goods.

PLANS FOR DEFENSE IN THE DRUG TRUST SUITS.

The suit brought by the United States Attorney-General against the manufacturers and wholesale and retail dealers in proprietary articles has attracted widespread attention. While those attacked are not afraid of the results of the suit there is considerable guessing being done as to the outcome. The suite of Loder, from which this one had emanated, has not been concluded by a long way. An appeal has been taken and the case argued. The decision is now being awaited. No matter what is decided, the case will eventually be taken to the highest court. It has been decided on the part of the manufacturers and wholesale and retail dealers in proprietary articles that they will arrange with Messrs. Reed & Rogers, of Chicago, to enter an appearance on June 4 for each of the defendants, and that what action shall be taken by the proprietors and wholesalers will be determined at a conference to be held soon after June 4 between H. G. Ward, of New York, Messrs. H. La Barre Jayne and John G. Johnson, of Philadelphia, and Messrs. Reed & Rogers, of Chicago. It is likely that these attorneys will be authorized to file an answer on or before July 1 in behalf of the defendants belonging to the above classes. This suit promises to be the most important one in the history of the drug trade. It is of vital interest to all dealers in proprietary articles, and the best legal talent of the country will be pitted against the attorneys representing the Government.

It is thought that the case will be eventually taken before a court which will consist of Judges as the ones to give a final decision.

THE PHILADELPHIA BOARD OF THE A. PH. A.

The monthly meeting of the American Pharmaceutical Association, held in the Philadelphia College of Pharmacy on May 21, was an exceedingly interesting one, and the remarks of the speakers attracted considerable attention. Serious menace to public health and a false sense of security, declared Director Coplin, of the Department of Health, was the result of the indiscriminate prescribing by druggists to the ills of the public. Dr. Coplin took as his subject Counter Prescribing and Its Relation to Public Health. He treated the subject particularly in connection with the treatment of communicable diseases. During the course of his remarks he said that immigration was introducing thousands of cases of diseases of the scalp, which, according to the reports of the school inspectors in this city, were being treated by druggists as though they were cases of excessive dandruff. He cited instances where smallpox, diphtheria, measles and other diseases had been wrongly treated by pharmacists. It was explained by Dr. Coplin that many symptoms of serious afflictions in the first stages resembled trifling complaints, and that while it might often seem a hardship to turn what might be a trifling complaint away with instructions to hunt up a physician, it was better than any chance being taken of affecting a whole community. Dr. Thomas R. Neilson, of the University of Pennsylvania, discussed The Limitations of Self Medication, and C. H. La Wall on The Duty of the Pharmacist to Aid in the Elimination of Irregular Practices. The meeting was well attended.

PHILADELPHIA NEWS NOTES.

Ross A. Walker will open a new store at Oil City.

Charles P. Phipps has purchased the Joseph Reesenman branch of the Franklin Drug & Chemical Company, at Franklin.

Mary A. Clark has sold her store at Jamestown to C. E. J. Crawford.

John B. Haley has opened a store at Newcastle.

H. G. Clark has purchased the store of the late F. T. Griffith at Oil City.

There are still rumors going around to the effect that a syndicate has been formed to buy up the retail drug stores in this city. The reports are to the effect that several of the large retail stores have been sought, but as yet no sale has been made.

Now that the bowling season has ended the retail druggists are paying more attention to outdoor exercise. Baseball is the rage now, and at every chance the hard working clerk hies himself to the grounds of the association.

Henry C. Blair has purchased a beautiful home at Edgewater Park and is now making alterations to the property, which when completed will make it a very handsome suburban residence.

John Gleichman, who was formerly connected with the traveling staff of Rosengarten & Sons, has secured a position with the General Chemical Company and is doing a big business for his new concern.

Clarence Nichols, who was with the house of David E. Green & Co., of New York, up to the time that that concern went out of business, has obtained a position with the National Aniline Company as the resident agent in this city. Mr. Nichols has an immense personal following, and his employers are to be congratulated on obtaining his services.

William B. Burk, the senior member of the sponge firm of W. B. Burk & Co., Sixth and Arch streets, will sail for Europe on June 21 and will be gone until about the middle of September. Mr. Burk will be accompanied by his wife and they intend to make a tour of Norway, Sweden, Denmark and Russia. The trip is strictly for pleasure.

J. J. McFadden, the druggist of many stores, has added another to his already long list. He has purchased the new building at 501 South Fifty-second street, and as soon as the store can be fitted up he intends to open one of the most attractive drug stores west of the Schuylkill River. This is a newly built up section of the city, and most of the buildings are being taken by newly married couples.

Walter F. Ware, president of the Walter F. Ware Company, who has been seriously ill, has recovered and is now able to again attend to business. Mr. Ware says that during the past few weeks there has been a large increase in the demand for all kinds of elastic hosiery, abdominal supporters and other goods of like description. The orders come from all over the country, and he has been compelled to purchase more machinery to be able to meet the demand.

Richard V. Mattison, Jr., the vice-president of the Keasbey & Mattison Company and the son of the senior member of that firm, has surprised his friends by announcing that he is a married man, having married Miss Nancy Cruikshank, a chorus girl in the "Social Whirl" company, a play now running at the New York Casino. It is said that Mr. Mattison met Miss Cruikshank in England about eighteen months ago and married her abroad. His family, scandalized by the unconventional marriage, insisted that he should announce his engagement and be married over again more formally.

MARYLAND.

Preparation of Galenicals by Pharmacists Discussed—One Druggist Gets a Sunday Holiday—Views on the Drug Trust Suit—One Hundred Per Cent. Dividend from the Emerson Company.

(From our Regular Correspondent.)

Baltimore, May 24.—At a meeting of the Maryland College of Pharmacy, held last Thursday evening at the Eutaw House, there was discussed, among other things, the making of preparations such as galenicals by the druggists themselves, instead of depending upon the manufacturers. The discussion was started by Prof. Charles Caspari, Jr., who deplored the indisposition of pharmacists to prepare articles in general use in their own laboratories, and expressed the belief that the druggist was thus neglecting an important source of profit. On the other hand, it was pointed out that the complaint, so far from being new, had been heard for at least fifty years, and in support of this statement a paper written by A. P. Sharp as far back as the middle of the last century was read, which, apart from reference to certain obsolete institutions, such as omnibuses and other things, might be applied without a change to present day conditions. Then, as now, pharmacists were urged to make their own preparations instead of getting them from the manufacturers, the situation being apparently much the same.

It was also pointed out that home manufacture might not be quite as profitable as it seems, and that the clerk who gave his time to the preparation of compounds could perhaps more advantageously devote it to other purposes, aside from the question of uniformity in the quality of the product. Two of the most important factors in causing the deterioration of drugs are air and heat. The manufacturer on a large scale has appliances to guard against both which are not available to the ordinary druggist. He has big vacuum pans for evaporation and other appliances that enable him to turn out a perfect product at the lowest possible cost. There are various products which cannot be profitably made advantageously in small quantities. The waste and loss, it was said, would soon absorb the possible saving.

JOINT OUTING IN JULY.

The Entertainment Committee was empowered to co-operate with the newly formed branch of the American Pharmaceutical Association and arrange an excursion in July, when a president and two members of the Board of Examiners are to be elected. Dr. John F. Hancock presided at the meeting, and among those present was Dr. Richard Sappington, who is regarded as the oldest druggist in Baltimore.

As the Maryland College of Pharmacy is no longer identified with the teaching of pharmacy and has no connection with the department of pharmacy, University of Maryland, with which the College of Pharmacy was merged one year ago, it was decided that two meetings annually would suffice. The association is now entirely confined to scientific discussion of pharmaceutical subjects.

SUNDAY LAW STRICTLY OBSERVED IN LAUREL.

One of the dryest places in the country is the town of Laurel, Prince George's County, Maryland, where the sale of cigars and cigarettes on the Sabbath is strictly prohibited, and where even the seductive soda water may not be dispensed. Such a sharp lookout is kept on all places which have these articles on sale that there is no chance to keep a side door open, and the one druggist in the place has, therefore, decided to assist in making the law odious by strict compliance with its provisions. Accordingly, he locks up his place and goes away, generally to Washington, taking the view that people who can do without cigars and soda water ought to be able to get along without prescriptions as well during one day in the week.

THAT ALLEGED DRUG TRUST.

Baltimore druggists do not entertain a very high opinion either of the effectiveness of the action taken by the United States Government to prosecute the alleged drug trust or of the motives behind the instructions given to the United States District Attorney for St. Louis. It is the common impression here that the whole proceeding is nothing more than political clap trap, intended mainly to create the belief that the Government is doing something to relieve the dear public from the supposed exactions of a conscienceless monopoly, when, as a matter of fact, the trust exists only in the imagination of the uninformed and of those who seek to make capital out of the movement. It has not escaped attention that every cut rate druggist in the city has seized upon the action taken by the Federal authorities with avidity to advertise himself and pose as a public benefactor, who is only prevented from doing incalculable good by a vast combination of bloated capitalists.

Of course, every one at all familiar with conditions knows that there is no drug trust, no powerful combination of moneyed interests, no stockholding corporation, no board of directors and no division of profits, as in the case of the Standard Oil Company and other monopolies. As a matter of fact, the druggists have done nothing more than to form an association for self-protection, such as exists among grocers, undertakers, candy men, dry goods merchants and concerns engaged in other lines of business. Each house retains the fullest measure of independence, and nothing more is aimed at than to prevent the complete demoralization in prices which the cutters so zealously seek to bring about.

The Baltimore druggists are, furthermore, of the opinion that the movement inaugurated against the alleged trust will prove abortive in so far as the promised results are concerned, and that the agitation was inaugurated chiefly for political effect.

DECLARES 100 PER CENT. STOCK DIVIDEND.

The stockholders of the Emerson Drug Company were called together in extra session on May 19 at the headquarters of the company, 308 West Lombard street, Baltimore, to ratify the action of the directors in declaring a stock dividend of 100 per cent., to be paid by a new issue of preferred shares. The total amount to be issued is $250,000, and the proposition was promptly approved. This will give the company a capital of $500,000, and furnish one more proof of the great success of the company, which manufactures bromo seltzer and other preparations. Each stockholder will get preferred stock to the amount of his holdings of common. The Board of Directors includes Isaac E. Emerson, president; Philip L. Heuisler, John F. Waggaman, Parker Cook and Joseph F. Hinds.

NOTES.

The pharmacy of W. H. Moore, at Fort avenue and Cooksie street, has been sold to Charles Weber.

The pharmacy of the late Oscar E. Ross, at Park avenue and McMechen street, will be sold at public auction on June 6.

The drug store of J. Forrest Cochran, who died recently, at St. Paul and Twenty-first streets, Baltimore, has been sold to J. J. Chidester.

J. J. Bowersox has purchased the pharmacy formerly conducted by Thomas Wildsmith, on East Baltimore street, near Ann.

The Klein & Fox Company has been incorporated in Baltimore to manufacture drugs, chemicals and toilet articles, with a capital stock of $10,000, divided into 200 shares. The incorporators are Samuel Fox, B. F. Klein, Louis D. Wiedman, Bertha Wiedman and Albert Wiedman.

Miss Whaland, who got her diploma as a graduate in pharmacy from the Philadelphia College recently, taking high honors, is a Maryland girl. She comes from Chestertown, Kent County, Md., and her father was the late Albert Constable Whaland, a lawyer. She is a cousin of H. P. Hynson, of the Baltimore firm of Hynson, Westcott & Co.

Theodore Rohrbach, a druggist at 1822 Pennsylvania avenue, was fined $5 and costs recently for selling strychnine without registering the name and address of the purchaser. The man who bought the poison committed suicide, and the coroner's investigation brought out the fact that no record of the sale had been made. Rohrbach pleaded that other druggists ignore the law on the subject.

OHIO.

President Hall, of the N. W. D. A., on the Drug Trust Suit—Abuse of Liquor Privileges Charged—Business Good.

(From our Regular Correspondent.)

Cleveland, May 22.—President Lucien B. Hall, of the National Wholesale Druggists' Association, says that he cannot understand why the Government should attack the organization in a suit at law, as it has been the constant endeavor of the officers to conduct it in a perfectly legal manner. In fact, the best legal talent has given opinion to the effect that the work of the association is entirely within the pale of the law. The same might be said of the Proprietary Association and the National Association of Retail Druggists. So far as the organizations of the wholesalers and retailers are concerned, however, he says that they are conducted especially for the purpose of protecting the small druggist from the larger ones, who are able to cut prices and often run them out of business. This is especially true of department stores which have drug departments. They make a practice of shading the prices on proprietary articles. As the small druggist does business on a very small margin he cannot stand the opposition of the big fellows. It would seem, therefore, that the fights against the railroads and the druggists are directly opposed to each other, so far as principle is concerned.

DEFENSE IN THE HANDS OF THE COMMITTEE ON SUITS.

President Hall says that nothing will be done by the association and that he has called no meeting. The Committee on Suits will have the matter of preparing a defense in hand. They are good men and will have able legal talent to aid them. Of course no one knows just what will come of an attack of this kind, but the belief is that when the ideas and work of the organization are made plain that there will be no reason to carry the suit further.

THE POINT AT ISSUE.

The principles upon which the suit is based are well known, and it is the belief that manufacturers of proprietary medicines have a right to fix a retail price on them, just the same as the manufacturers of many other kinds of goods who not only do this, but enforce it. The only question is regarding the association of manufacturers and the manner of making contracts with retailers through the wholesale houses.

DRUGGISTS ACCUSED BY SALOON KEEPERS.

An association of saloon keepers has been organized in the east end of the city for the purpose of bringing about a better condition in their business and enforcing the State and city laws. One of the objects of the association is to get the retail druggists into line. Some of them are accused of selling liquor illegally and this organization will endeavor to put a stop to it. With the stricter laws regarding the saloon business the dealers have found it necessary to protect their interests in every way possible.

Both the wholesale and retail druggists here report a fairly good business for the past two or three weeks. Both the prescription and sundry business has been satisfactory. For a time the weather was so cool that the soda fountains did but little business, but with the advent of warm days they are again busy.

CLEVELAND NEWS NOTES.

L. A. Lesser has opened a new store at 1095 Woodland avenue.

H. W. Dickere will open a new drug store at the corner of Lorain avenue and Twenty-eighth street within a short time.

Charles A. Siebel has purchased Smithnight's pharmacy at 200 Cedar avenue.

OHIO ITEMS.

J. B. Kathe has opened a new store at Elyria.

Eshelman & Hicks have bought the Hauck drug store at Fostoria.

The firm of Pancoast & Spencer has succeeded Duff Pancoast at Ashland.

E. B. Hubbard, who has operated a drug business at Tiffin for some time, has sold out to Weidling & Son.

G. G. Ralston & Co., of Martin's Ferry, has been succeeded by Ralston & Parker.

H. A. Dykeman has sold his store at Elyria to A. E. Frost, formerly of Mantua, Ohio. Mr. Dykeman owns an opera house at Elyria and will give his entire attention to it in the future.

J. D. Price, of the wholesale drug firm of Orr, Brown & Price, has been chosen as one of the delegates to the annual meeting of the National Association of Credit Men, at Baltimore, by the local association at Columbus.

The report of the Committee on Statistics of the Columbus Board of Trade shows that the four wholesale drug houses do a business estimated at $2,550,000 a year, while the 112 retail stores do an aggregate business of about $1,120,000 a year.

The Kauffman-Lattimer Company, wholesale druggist at Columbus, will shortly enlarge its business house, either by adding two or three stories or securing additional frontage on West Spring street and building an addition. The business has outgrown the present building.

Thomas H. Plummer, of Cincinnati, who filed a voluntary petition in bankruptcy some time ago, has asked that a receiver be appointed for the business at the corner of Richmond street and Central avenue, as he is not a practical druggist and the business will not stand the expense of a registered clerk.

W. H. Syfert & Co. have opened a general brokerage and commission business and will act as manufacturers' agents, with offices and warehouse in Columbus, Ohio. W. H. Syfert, of this firm, has been actively engaged in the wholesale and retail drug business for over 20 years and has a large personal knoweldge of the trade.

George W. Lattimer, of the wholesale drug house of the Kauffman-Lattimer Company, has been elected president of the Columbus Board of Trade, Columbus, over a very strong opponent, J. F. Firestone, of the Columbus Buggy Company. Mr. Lattimer is an eminently public spirited man and will prove a success as the head of that body. He is active and prominent in the affairs of the N. W. D. A.

Registered by the Maryland Board of Pharmacy.

Baltimore, May 9.—The Maryland Board of Pharmacy, which has just begun a new year, held a meeting on Tuesday of last week and organized by electing William C. Powell, of Snow Hill, president; Ephraim Bacon, of Roland Park, secretary, and John A. Davis, of Baltimore, treasurer. The other members are H. Lionel Meredith and Louis Schulze, the latter having been appointed recently by Governor Warfield to fill the vacancy caused by the expiration of the term of J. Webb Foster. On the afternoon of the day of organization the board held a session to examine over fifty applicants for registration as competent pharmacists and assistants. The following passed:

Pharmacists.—Miss Emma Grace Lotts, William Stichel, Edwin A. Schmidt, Stanley A. Pentz, Thomas F. A. Stevens, George P. Hetz, Benjamin D. Benfer, James E. Hancock, Charles Rossberg, Wm. V. V. Parramore, Joseph T. Wallace, Joseph Porembsky, Franklin D. Wilson, Samuel B. Downes, Alfred S. Williams.

Assistant Pharmacists.—Thomas W. Ritch, John C. Eby, Amil K. Parks, N. E. Shakespeare, Frank C. Balmert, Fred. L. Henry, D. C. Pharr, Moore R. Garland, John W. Rauth, James W. Thompson, Howard Ruff, George O. Sharrett, Francis O. Barrett, Merker N. Buppert.

James E. Hancock is the son of John F. Hancock, one of the most prominent druggists in Baltimore, who for years conducted a retail store in East Baltimore and has been long engaged in the manufacture of medicated lozenges. Mr. Hancock, though not a graduate of any college of pharmacy, passed with flying colors, attaining a percentage near the 90 mark.

Daube & Co., of Valparaiso, Purchase the Brunswig Pharmacy.

Notice has just come to hand from our representative in Chile that the well-known firm of Daube & Co., of Valparaiso, a photograph of whose store was reproduced in our last issue, has recently acquired the wholesale and retail drug establishment of Virginia v. de Brunswig. It is understood that they contemplate conducting this establishment separately, as heretofore.

THE WEST.

The City Council Again Threatens the Drug Trade—A Special Train for the New Orleans Meeting of the N. A. R. D.—Doctors Ask Co-operation of Druggists on Telephone Franchise.

(From our Regular Correspondent.)

Chicago, May 23.—Local druggists are once more menaced by council action aimed at liquor sales, but at the present moment it is believed that the attack will fail. The new assault comes through Alderman Hoffman, who has introduced into the council an ordinance which prohibits sales of liquor in drug stores, except on a physician's prescription. The ordinance was passed over to the License Committee and from this body to a subcommittee, with Alderman Hoffman at its head. It is thought that efforts made by the representatives of the druggists to kill the obnoxious measure in committee will prove successful. At one hearing the entire Executive Committee of the Chicago Liquor Dealers' Association was present attended by its attorney. The druggists were represented by President Avery and Field Representative White. In reply to the attacks made upon them Messrs. Avery and White informed the saloon men that they would have to stop dispensing bromo-seltzer and other things meant to produce medicinal effects. It was suggested that the Board of Pharmacy could make a lot of trouble for the barkeepers and saloon owners if the matter should be pressed. It was suggested that as a compromise the druggists might be permitted to sell not to exceed half a pint for medicinal purposes.

THE N. A. R. D. SPECIAL.

At the last regular monthly meeting of the executive board of the C. R. D. A. plans for visiting the N. A. R. D. annual convention in October were discussed. It is the intention to run a special train as usual. The rate will be about one fare for the round trip, provided that 100 persons take advantage of the offer. There will be a large number of attractions along the road and it is believed many will avail themselves of the opportunity.

DOCTORS APPEAL TO DRUGGISTS.

The views of the Chicago Medical Society in regard to the city's granting a new franchise to the Chicago Telephone Company were presented by Dr. W. A. Evans, who asked the assistance of the organization in obtaining greater privileges for doctors. The Hoffman ordinance, mentioned above, came up for discussion and numerous suggestions were made as to how it could be defeated.

PREPARING FOR THE STATE MEETING.

The twenty-seventh annual convention of the Illinois Pharmaceutical Association and the travelers' auxiliary will be held at Peoria, Tuesday, Wednesday and Thursday, June 19, 20 and 21. For the past three years the entertainment features have been in the hands of the Pharmaceutical Travelers' Association, which has resulted in making these conventions very successful both from an entertainment and attendance standpoint. The programme this year includes a reception and dance, launch rides, band concert and field sports. It is confidently expected that this convention will have the largest attendance of any convention held in many years. A rate of a fare and one-third has been obtained from the Western and Central Passenger associations from all points in Illinois, and the Chicago contingent have planned for a special train, to be known as the Pharmaceutical Special, leaving Chicago at 9 a. m. over the Chicago & Alton Railroad, Tuesday morning, June 19, reaching Peoria at 1 p.m., in ample time for the opening ceremony. The train will have the finest equipment and run on express schedule. The complete programme is now in the press and will shortly be mailed to every druggist in the State.

NOTES.

The Chicago Veteran Druggists' Association held its regular meeting May 21.

The Morton Safety Razor Company has moved from 1197 Tacoma Building to 1207 Tacoma Building.

A. C. Williams has bought the Englewood Pharmacy at Sixty-third and Halsted streets.

The next meeting of the Illinois State Board of Pharmacy will take place July 18.

The druggists' baseball season opened with a game Thursday, May 17, between the North and West Side clubs and the South and Southwest siders.

A Chicago druggist asserts that the State Board makes a great mistake by accepting affidavits from Russian drug stores regarding the time experience of apprentices. It is said the affidavits can be purchased.

C. N. Anderson, manager of the department of animal industry for Parke, Davis & Co., was a guest at the Chicago Drug Trade Club on May 15 and stated that he was making one of his regular trips over the West, conferring with the branch managers and agents. Mr. Anderson has made a colossal success of the department which he is in charge of.

F. G. Waiss will open a new drug store about June 15 at 1224 West Harrison street, at the corner of Kinzie street. Alexander Harris, the hustling representative for Johnson & Johnson, secured a stock order from Mr. Waiss for his plasters and surgical dressings. Mr. Waiss is not new to the drug trade of Chicago, as he at one time conducted a store at 335 West Harrison street.

The Sherer-Gillett Company, 1705 South Clark street, Chicago, have issued a handsome and instructive booklet on the subject of saffron, which they offer to send free to druggists on request. It seems that the firm have succeeded in cultivating true Spanish saffron by the selection of soil and surroundings for its propogation. In the booklet it is shown by text and illustrations from photographs how saffron is planted, cultivated, harvested and prepared for the market.

C. P. Van Schaack, vice-president and secretary of the old Salamander Drug House, is spending two weeks in Mexico with a party of friends. They journeyed southward in a private car and the party was strictly a stag affair. Mr. Van Schaack is one of the few wholesale druggists in the city who is so rich in the world's goods that he can frequently take trips of this kind. When he is in Chicago he is one of the first to get down in the morning, and he is a hustler and untiring in his efforts. He will be missed at the Chicago Drug Trade Club, where he is a regular attendant, and up to a short time ago was president of this club.

The Kentucky Board.

At the meeting of the Kentucky Board of Pharmacy, held in Louisville, April 10, the following, out of a class of 61, passed the examination: Charles F. Baird, Louisville; Jas. W. Coleman, Paducah; Thos. C. Dedman, Harrodsburg; Mrs. V. G. Donan, Three Springs; Daniel Fortune, Ashland; Albert F. Griffith, Memphis, Tenn.; Clyde C. Best-Isthman, Cincinnati, Ohio; John H. Jones, Hopkinsville; James S. Lee, Paducah; Lyman T. Reber, Louisville; R. C. Saufley, Somerset; Sam'l L. Sterett, Hawesville; Henry J. Ullrich, Ironton, Ohio; Frank L. Velten, Newport; Conrad P. Weber, Henderson; A. B. Whitehead, Carrollton; James Witherspoon, Louisville; L. B. St. Sayer, Louisville.

The next meeting will be held at Dawson Springs, July 10, and applications should be filed with the secretary of the board at least ten days before that time.

No Advertisements for A. Ph. A. Programme.

Chas. Caspari, Jr., the general secretary of the association, has sent out the following circular notice to the pharmaceutical press:

"I beg to inform you that at the forty-seventh annual meeting of this association, held at Put-in-Bay, Ohio, September, 1899, the general secretary was directed annually to inform the local secretary and the pharmaceutical press of the following resolution adopted at that meeting:

"'Resolved, That no advertisements shall be solicited or accepted for any of the publications or programmes issued by or in the name of the American Pharmaceutical Association.'"

The Drug and Chemical Market

The prices quoted in this report are those current in the wholesale market, and higher prices are paid for retail lots
The quality of goods frequently necessitates a wide range of prices.

Condition of Trade.

New York, May 26, 1906.

The past fortnight has not been characterized by any special show of activity, the volume of trade, indeed, showing a slight falling off. During the last few days, however, trade has picked up a little, and while the market is still backward the fluctuations are mostly in sellers' favor. In some lines values are decidedly firm and supplies offer sparingly. While mail orders for small parcels have been fairly numerous, interest in round lots is still an absent feature, and dealers appear to be resigned to the trade quietude usual at this season. Opium and quinine are given very little consideration, and conditions have undergone no change of importance during the interval. An upward tendency for cubeb berries is noted, and clove oil is firmer and higher. Chinese cantharides are maintained at a higher level, and silver nitrate has advanced twice in the interval in sympathy with the position of the metal. Despite the absence of important demand the tendency on prices generally is upward, and no disposition is apparent in the way of stimulating attention by price concessions.

HIGHER.	LOWER.
Peppermint oil,	Saffron, American,
Clove oil,	Cajuput oil,
Phosphoric acid,	Ginger root, bleached,
Lycopodium,	Gum gamboge,
Lemon oil,	Oil of turpentine.
Senna leaves,	
Tartaric emetic,	
Chinese cantharides,	
Cascara sagrada,	
Anise oil,	
Cassia oil,	
Chamomile flowers,	
Cadmium salts,	
Laurel leaves,	
Cubeb berries,	
Silver nitrate,	
Pink root,	
Damiana leaves,	
Guarana,	
Balsam fir, Oregon.	

Drugs.

Alcohol is meeting with about the usual demand at the advance reported in our last, the sales being at $2.47 to $2.49 for grain. Wood is held and selling at the previous range of 70c to 75c for 95 and 97 per cent., respectively.

Arnica flowers have remained quiet, though the market appears steady at 9c to 10c.

Balsams.—Copaiba, Central American, is firmer, and prices, though not quotably higher, tend in sellers' favor, 30c to 32c being generally named; Para is in limited supply, and values are steady at 40c to 45c. Fir, Oregon, is scarce on spot, and holders are firmer in their views at 80c to 85c for bbls., and 90c to 95c for cans. Peru is held about as before, though in better supply; sales at $1.00 to $1.05. Tolu is in moderate demand only at the moment and nominally quoted at 20c to 21c.

Barks.—Cascara sagrada is maintained firmly on spot, in view of the stronger tenor of advices from the coast, but prices are unchanged from 6c to 8c; 7c was quoted a few days ago on a carload lot of two-year old bark. Cottonroot is offered freely in a small way at 8½c to 9c, with, however, a very moderate trade. Elm continues inactive, though the market appears steady at 16c to 18c for select. Sassafras continues held at the range of 12c to 15c, as to quantity and quality. Orange peel has developed some scarcity, especially in the better grades, the limit of which has been advanced to 5c.

Buchu leaves, short, have developed increased firmness, and numerous sales were made during the interval at 18c to 20c.

Calendula flowers are held with increased firmness, owing to scarcity, and recent sales were at 26c to 30c for German.

Cantharides, Chinese, are scarce and the limited available stock is under good control, with the principal holder maintaining 85c for whole and powdered flies; sales of Russian are reported within the range of $1.20 to $1.25, but the tone of the market for this variety is easier.

Chamomile flowers, Roman, are held with increased confidence, owing to the clearing up of some of the cheaper lots, which were disturbing the market; nothing now seems to be obtainable under 22c to 25c; old crop is unchanged at 16c to 17c and German at 8c to 10c.

Codliver oil remains seasonably quiet, at unchanged quotations. Dealers report sales of Norwegian at $20.00 to $25.00. The best quotation obtainable in Norway is $18.00.

Cubeb berries are maintained firmly, in the face of stronger advices from primary sources and diminishing spot supplies. While natural are still offered at 9c, and 10c is named for some, holders ask at an advance on these figures; powdered quoted at 12c to 14c.

Cuttlefish bone is maintained steadily, in the face of a limited demand, and some sellers decline to shade the outside figure of 17½c for prime Trieste.

Damiana leaves are firmer and higher, in sympathy with other Pacific Coast products, and quotations now range from 8¾c to 10c, as to quality and quantity. Some 10,000 lbs. are reported destroyed in the San Francisco fire.

Ergot is attracting slightly increased attention, though the market is still dull and spiritless, and only jobbing sales are reported, at the quoted range of 26c to 28c for Russian and 34c to 36c for Spanish. It is explained by *The Chemist and Druggist* that the recent heavy offerings of Russian ergot was the result of a circular sent out by the Government, in which peasants were advised that the value of rye would be increased by picking out the ergot, for which good prices could be obtained.

Guarana is in reduced supply and wanted, with the result that values are more firmly maintained, at an advance to $1.00.

Laurel leaves are attracting a good deal of attention at present, and the increased demand has hardened the views of holders, who now name 4¼c. to 4½c. as acceptable.

Lycopodium maintains its upward tendency, and sales have been made during the interval at higher prices, both here and in Hamburg. Sales are reported at 50c. to 51c.

Menthol has remained dull during the interval, and values do not respond to the advancing tendency at primary sources of supply, $2.50 to $2.75 being yet named in the face of the limited seasonable demand.

Opium continues neglected, and we have no new feature of interest to report either as regards price or demand. The market is dull and spiritless, with quotations barely steady at $2.72½ for cases and $2.75 to $2.77½ for broken lots; powdered is held and selling in a moderate jobbing way at $3.20 to $3.25.

Quinine is selling in a dull routine way only, and the market is tame to a degree, most of the distribution into consuming channels being on old contract orders. A moderate jobbing inquiry is experienced and manufacturers' prices appear well sustained at 17c. to 19c., as to quantity.

Saffron flowers, American, have receded in the interval, values being easier to the extent that sales are making down to 95c., and the tendency is still downward.

Senna, Alexandria, has developed an upward movement owing to the stronger tenor of advices from primary markets. The new crop is reported to be disappointing and higher prices are named. Most holders decline to shade 10c for half leaf, though some is yet available at 9½c. Siftings are maintained at 5½c to 6c.

Tartar emetic reflects the advance in price of raw material, and 28¼c to 28¾c is now quoted.

Vanilla beans are in good supply, both Tahiti and Mexican having been received in fair quantities since our last. Sales of the former are making at 60c to $1.25, and of the latter at $2.75 to $5 for whole, and $2 to $2.25 for cut; Bourbons are steady at $1.15 to $3.

Chemicals.

Arsenic, white, is weak and neglected, with quotations further reduced to 5½c to 5¾c, as to brand and quantity.

Benzoic acid is to be sold under a new schedule of prices beginning July 1, and this will mark a reduction of 4c. on the artificial variety. On lots of 1,000 lbs. the quotations will be 26c, and for larger quantities a shade less will probably be named; the outside figure will stand at 28c.

Bleaching powder is firmer, under the influence of diminishing spot supplies, and 1¼c to 1¾c is named, as to make, quantity and time of delivery.

Blue vitriol is scarce and wanted, with 6c to 6¼c generally quoted.

Cadmium salts have been advanced by the manufacturers, owing to the increased cost of the metal, and the revised range is $1.10 for bromide, $2.60 for iodide, $1.50 for chloride and $4.50 for carbonate.

Carbolic acid is now in better supply, and crystals offer more freely, at 14c to 15c in drums, while bottles are held at 20c to 22c.

Oxalic acid is scarce and firmer, and up to 6⅝c has been paid in the interval for domestic, while English acid has sold at 6½c.

Phosphoric acid has advanced in the interval, and the revised range for U. S. P. is 19c to 23½c, and for 1.750, 19½c to 24c, as to quantity.

Prussiate of potash, yellow, is maintained in firm position, and holders offer with reserve at the quoted range of 14⅝c to 14¾c.

Quicksilver is in good demand and values are well sustained at 56c to 58c.

Tartaric acid is in good seasonable demand, the jobbing movement being fully up to that of the corresponding period of previous years. There is also a good movement into channels of consumption, and values are sustained at 28¼c to 28½c for crystals and powdered.

Essential Oils.

Anise has developed increased firmness, and primary conditions are favorable to higher values. For the better grades of oil $1.35 to $1.37½ is named, and holders offer sparingly at this range.

Bergamot abates none of its firmness, and such sales as come to the surface are making within the range of $2.15 to $2.25.

Cajuput is in better supply, and values have eased off to the range of 53c to 54c.

Clove is held with increased firmness, owing to the stronger markets for the spice, and quotations for bulk now range to $1.00, with nothing offering below 92½c.

Lemon is offered with some reserve in view of the stronger tenor of advices from Messina, and 70c to 77½c is now generally named, as to brand.

Pennyroyal is in improved condition, and up to $2.25 is named for domestic, while French is firmer at $1.75.

Peppermint is meeting with increased inquiry, but the views of holders appear slightly above those of prospective buyers, and only small sales are reported at the present high range of $2.80 to $3 for tins, and $3.40 to $3.50 for cases. Reports are numerous regarding the expected curtailment of stock through adverse weather conditions, but it should be said that some of these reports are taken in the same spirit as the annual reports of the failure of the Delaware peach crop, though it is undeniably true that planting has been retarded on account of the difficulty in obtaining roots.

Rose.—The winter has been extremely severe in Bulgaria and Turkey, with the result of markedly impairing the present crop of roses. The number of flowers and their quality have been considerably impaired, and altogether the crop has been very much inferior to that of the preceding year. There is, therefore, a prospect of a rise in price of rose oil and the various products derived from roses.

Sassafras remains quiet at 50c to 60c for natural and 26c to 28c for artificial.

Wintergreen is unchanged at $1.50 to $1.60 for natural and 37c to 40c for artificial, with sales at this range.

Gums.

A moderate demand is reported for all varieties of druggists' gums, without any special feature to report. The demand for new Barbadoes aloes is exceptionally good, and the same may be said of camphor, especially for Japanese in ounces, which is obtainable at 97c, or about 5c below the parity of domestic values. There is nothing new or interesting to report so far as the mucilaginous gums are concerned.

Roots.

Echinacea has been in demand, and the prevailing scarcity has induced holders to raise their limit, and the former price of 25c is no longer quoted, recent sales being at 27c.

Gentian maintains its firm position, and we hear of nothing offering at under 4¼c to 4½c.

Ginger, Jamaica, bleached, has receded a trifle in the interval, with quotations reduced to 16c to 17c.

Golden seal is in moderately active demand, but spot values show no change from the previous range of $1.15 to $1.20.

Ipecac is in improved request and the market has a firmer undertone, with Rio quoted at $1.75 to $1.80 and Carthagena at $1.65 to $1.70.

Jalap is held with increased firmness, and some holders decline to shade 12½c, though 12c will yet buy.

Spigelia (pink) has advanced several times during the interval, and is now maintained at $1.00 owing to scarcity. Supplies are reported exhausted at primary sources.

Seeds.

Cardamoms, decorticated, maintain their firm position, and we note a further advance to 36c to 38c, and some holders hold out for 40c; bleached are held and selling within the range of 30c to 75c. Nothing of special interest is to be noted in other seeds, which are maintained generally at current quotations.

High Class Soda Fountain Supplies.

Dispensers who have not heretofore used "Liquid" fruits, diamond brand crushed fruits and diamond brand liquid gas will at once be interested upon investigating these splendid mediums for producing high-grade soda beverages. "Liquid" fruits and diamond brand crushed fruits are products of The Liquid Carbonic Company's high standards of excellence and modern methods. The original fruits are grown by contract in a dozen States, and prepared in three of the largest fruit laboratories in the world. They represent—from start to finish of preparation—a perfected system of hygienic cleanliness and are prepared by "The Liquid's" own special cold process, which maintains the full life and flavor of the ripe, fresh fruit. The dispenser who is interested in the maintenance of a reputation for thoroughly high-grade fountain beverages will do well to communicate with "The Liquid" with reference to these products. They have branches in all the leading cities. Write to the nearest branch.

Arisen from Its Ashes.

The plant of the Clinic Publishing Company, which was entirely destroyed by fire in November of last year, has been rebuilt and occupied in ninety days. The May number of the new *American Journal of Clinical Medicine* (formerly *The Alkaloidal Clinic*) was printed in this new building on new presses and new equipment throughout. The building is larger and better than before, and the *Journal*, with several new departments and additional talent on its editorial staff, is stronger than ever. Copies of the May number will be sent free to druggists on request.

Souvenir Booklet of New York Scenes Free.

Druggists can secure free of charge ample supply of attractive booklets illustrating over a hundred of the most attractive scenes in New York City free of all cost by applying to The Centaur Company, New York City. The booklets come in a series of five. Write for a supply, sending your business card or label, so as to have this printed on the booklets for free distribution. Address The Centaur Company, New York City, mentioning the AMERICAN DRUGGIST.

Leather Post Cards Are All the Rage.

Vacation time is post card time. Leather post cards are novel and attractive. Write to James D. Anderson, 417 Sixth avenue, New York, for quotations on these and other post card novelties. Have you seen the post card pillows? Write him for particulars and quotations, mentioning the AMERICAN DRUGGIST.

The Path of the Innovation.

Ten new "Innovations," all sold this season, are helping to quench the public's thirst in Norfolk, Va. Eight of them are within two blocks. The "Innovation" and R. H. Thomas, Virginian representative of the American Soda Fountain Company, were a combination Norfolk dispensers found hard to resist. And Buffalo, too, has fallen under the spell of the "Innovation" and a Thomas—this time C. B. Thomas, Western New York State representative. A large number of new "Innovations" will draw nickels this summer from the throngs on Buffalo's most crowded thoroughfare—Main street.

The "Innovation" is no less a trade puller in the handsome city store than in the summer resort. Mr. McCahill, New England sales manager of the American Soda Fountain Company, reports a sale of a 50-foot "Innovation" as well as three other large "American apparatus to the Spring Water Carbonating Company for use at Wonderland Park, Revere Beach, Mass. The fact that this sale was made after the Spring Water Carbonating Company had carefully observed the service given by other makes of apparatus at seaside resorts reflects considerable additional honor on the "American" fountains.

Five of the "Innovations" used by the Hegeman Corporation in its New York stores are shown in the American Soda Fountain Company's advertisement on another page. The almost unparalleled success of this drug corporation as a dispenser of soda water is a good thought to consider in connection.

Digitalis—Physiological Standardization.

Since the discovery of digitoxin, which is regarded as the active constituent of digitalis leaves, numerous endeavors have been made to standardize digitalis preparations on the basis of their digitoxin content. H. F. Moschkowitsch, referring to this (*Arch. de Phar., No. 5*) remarks that more recently experiments have been directed to the determination of the digitoxin by physiological methods. This, in nearly all cases, depended on the susceptibility of the heart of the frog to the action of this constituent of digitalis, and the belief that by this means a direct quantitive estimation of digitoxin in different preparations could be effected. The author gives an account of the experiments undertaken with the object of ascertaining the availability of such a method, depending upon the greater or less rapidity in which the systolis of the heart of frogs is effected by digitoxin and by preparations which he made himself. As a result of his experiments, the author is of the opinion that standardizing digitalis preparations by the physiological method is not sufficient.

It is because of the uncertainties of the therapeutics of digitalis that physicians are evincing a decided interest in Digalen-Digitoxinum Solubile Cloetta. It gives the full effect of digitalis leaves, produces no gastric disturbance and allows of exact dosage. Pharmacists who wish to acquaint themselves with the merits and advantages of Digalen should address The Hoffman-LaRoche Chemical Works, 51-53 Maiden lane, New York.

Abbott Specialties.

There is an increasing demand for Abbott's Saline Laxative among physicians and druggists. It is used in large quantities by the medical profession the year around, and particularly during the summer season. Druggists would do well to get stocked before warm weather, so as to take care of the orders. The containers, either tin or glass, are sealed and packed in such a way as to insure practically no deterioration in the effervescent qualities of Abbott's Saline Laxative. Every package is guaranteed against loss by the Abbott trademark.

Salithia, Calcalith, have always been popular with the medical profession, and Carbenzol, the new remedy for skin diseases, continues to receive unlimited praise for the effective work it does. Carbenzol soap should be carried in stock. Send for literature to the Abbott Alkaloidal Company, Chicago, if you are not familiar with these preparations.

A Convenience to Physicians.

As a great convenience in office practice, and especially to the country doctor who is not in close touch with a druggist, the Gibbs hollow suppositories are much appreciated. Any doctor who has ever made suppositories, even with the latest molds for the purpose, will agree that it is difficult to get them firm, smooth and evenly medicated, and that cocoa butter, which forms the base of nearly all suppositories, is by no means easy to manipulate. The Gibbs hollow suppositories, which have held their popularity for more than twenty years, overcome these difficulties. These cocoa butter shells, which are provided with conoidal self sealing stoppers, are all made from the purest cocoa butter procurable. They are firm and smooth, may be easily and quickly filled with any medicine, and are hermetically sealed by the stoppers. The hollow suppositories assure even medication and perfect solubility, and are of such a shape that when the large, or stoppered, end is inserted the contraction of the sphinter aul forces them up into the rectum without the use of a suppository syringe or any other appliance whatever. The Gibbs hollow suppositories are made in eight sizes, and are adapted for anal, nasal, urethral, cystic, vaginal and intra-uterine medication. The suppositories are put up in wooden boxes, each suppository standing upright in a compartment by itself, convenient for filling and sealing with the stoppers without handling or removing from the box, thus furnishing a most convenient means of easily and quickly preparing a firm, smooth and evenly medicated suppository. The suppositories may be obtained from any druggist or direct from the agents, Schieffelin & Co., New York.

Effective Advertising.

Some unusually striking and effective advertising has been put out by the American Soda Fountain Company this season. An odd little booklet came to our desk this week that gave us a pleasant tingle of surprise, inasmuch as the cover is a perfect representation of a bank book inclosing some checks. The soda water dispenser who opens its pages will find that they are as good as "money in the bank" to him, as each page shows some genuine bargains in rebuilt fountains at such prices that the dispenser can make a big saving in money, while getting a fountain that is practically as good as new.

The illustrations show a wide variety of styles, in prices ranging from $100 to $300, up to some magnificent fountains in onyx and mahogany for $1,300 to $2,400. On many of these the prices have been cut exactly in half. Lucky the dispenser who gets one of these.

These semiannual sales of the American Soda Fountain Company are important events in the soda water world. Such low prices are bound to move even a large stock quickly, and the dispenser who wants first choice must act quickly in getting in his application.

The booklet shows typographical work of a high standard.

AMERICAN DRUGGIST
and PHARMACEUTICAL RECORD

PHILADELPHIA. NEW YORK, JUNE 11, 1906. CHICAGO

ISSUED SEMI-MONTHLY BY

AMERICAN DRUGGIST PUBLISHING CO.,

62-68 West Broadway, New York.

CHICAGO, 221 Randolph St. PHILADELPHIA, 3713 Walnut St.

A. R. ELLIOTT, President.

CASWELL A. MAYO, Ph.G. .... Editor.
THOMAS J. KEENAN .... Associate Editor.

ROMAINE PIERSON .... Manager Chicago Office.

$1.50 a year. 15 cents a copy.

ADVERTISING RATES QUOTED ON APPLICATION.

THE AMERICAN DRUGGIST AND PHARMACEUTICAL RECORD is issued on the second and fourth Mondays of each month. Changes of advertisements should be received ten days in advance of the date of publication.

Remittances should be made by New York exchange, post office or express money order or registered mail. If checks on local banks are used 10 cents should be added to cover cost of collection. The publishers are not responsible for money sent by unregistered mail, nor for any money paid except to duly authorized agents. All communications should be addressed and all remittances made payable to American Druggist Publishing Company, 62-68 West Broadway, New York.

Entered at New York as Second-Class Matter.

TABLE OF CONTENTS.

EDITORIAL COMMENT.

NEW YORK DRUGGISTS SLOW. Much to the surprise of those in charge of the matter, the contributions by New York druggists to the fund being raised for the relief of San Francisco druggists have been coming in very slowly. Up to a few days ago only about $200 had been received. It is hoped that those who have not done so will send in their contributions without delay.

BOARD REFORMS. Increasing interest is being taken by pharmacists in the reform of board methods, and the list of subjects to be discussed by the members of boards of pharmacy and the faculties of colleges, printed elsewhere in this issue, is commended to the perusal of those who are dissatisfied with present conditions.

NOSTRUMITIS. From reports to hand of the transactions of the American Medical Association at the meeting held in Boston last week it would seem that the leaders in the association have fallen victims to a disease which may properly be termed nostrumitis. There is a general tendency nowadays to regulate men and matters from centers of authority, real or imaginary, and the tendency is deplorable. The manufacturer of proprietary remedies, and by this we do not mean preparations advertised to the laity, is being hard pressed on all sides. His former friends, the physicians, are deserting him, and the dispensing pharmacists are at war with him. It is difficult to predict the outcome of all the agitation now going on for the reform of the proprietary medicine business, but there is no doubt that, at the present juncture, the position of the manufacturer is a critical and unenviable one. A special report of the proceedings of the Section on Pharmacology and Therapeutics of the American Medical Association is printed elsewhere, and this should prove interesting reading for all manufacturers of specialties and many retail pharmacists.

STATE ASSOCIATIONS ACTIVE. State pharmaceutical associations were never so active as at present, and there is no period of the year in which so many meetings are held synchronously as in the last week in June. Ohio, Pennsylvania and New York will witness gatherings of pharmacists in that week, to mention only a few of the June meetings. Interest in subjects of a technical and scientific nature has been stimulated by the committees of the various associations through the award of prizes for papers, and this should result in some notable contributions to the literature of pharmacy. We have always urged attendance upon the meetings of the local, State and national associations for the benefit such attendance brings with it. In the paper by Mr. Gable, on another page, some of the advantages of attendance on pharmaceutical meetings are eloquently set forth, and all that Mr. Gable says with regard to the American Pharmaceutical Association applies equally to the State associations. The local and State associations should be supported and developed in more ways than can be enumerated, for they are bulwarks of strength for the retail pharmacist. Through papers presented and discussed at these meetings members keep informed of the progress of pharmacy and improved methods of conducting business, and by the social contact their characters are sweetened and they are enabled to forget for a time the dull routine of store life.

The Trademark Right in Names.

The suit which has been brought by the Farbenfabriken of Elberfeld Company against the firm of Lehn & Fink to restrain the latter from using the word sulfonal, on the ground that this is a copyright word, will be welcomed by pharmacists generally, as affording a means for determining a point upon which there has long been a serious difference of opinion. In common with other manufacturers of synthetic preparations the Farbenfabriken Company have held that the expiration of the patent upon the product does not affect the copyright name under which that product is most generally known. Many pharmacists, on the other hand, have held that while there is another name than sulfonal for this substance, this other name is so little known and has been so little used that it can scarcely be termed a true descriptive title of sulfonal to the exclusion of the word sulfonal itself, as this is the term which has been almost exclusively used in medical literature, and that this practically exclusive use of the word sulfonal in medical literature has made that term a descriptive name and that therefore the exclusive rights of the manufacturers to that name terminate with the life of the patent upon the product.

At the Boston meeting of the American Medical Association, Dr. Solomon Solis-Cohen, of Philadelphia, in discussing the limits of proprietorship in medicines, went into the subject at some length and set forth very clearly the views held by the major portion of the medical profession and, we believe, by the majority of pharmacists on this particular point, when he said that if the law now permits the perpetuation of a monopoly after the expiration of a product patent through the copyright on the name of the product, then the law is wrong and must be changed.

While Dr. Cohen referred to phenacetin as a case in point, his remarks apply with equal force to the entire series of patented products bearing what are claimed to be copyrighted names.

It is possible, of course, that under the present law, or under the construction which may be put upon that law by our judiciary, the contention of the Farbenfabriken Company for exclusive right in the name sulfonal may be maintained. If the courts so decide, then, in the language of Dr. Cohen, "the law must be changed." But we do not believe that any change in the law is required, for the term sulfonal has been so largely used in medical literature in a descriptive way that we are confident the courts of highest authority will rule that the term is a descriptive one and therefore not subject to copyright.

The Physician and the Pharmacopoeia.

> However successful the new Pharmacopœia may be from a scientific standpoint, it is a flat failure from the standpoint of the teacher of therapeutics.—DR. O. T. OSBORNE, *before the American Medical Association.*

This is a severe arraignment from a teacher of much experience and undoubted ability, and it behooves the reviewers of the Pharmacopœia to ask Dr. Osborne for a bill of particulars, with a view to making improvement where possible. Other speakers before the section of Pharmacology and Therapeutics at the Boston meeting of the American Medical Association were more specific and hardly less caustic in their criticisms. Mr. Wilbert objected to the steady increase in the number of medicaments listed in the book. The irrepressible Dr. Robinson characterized the dosage as a mass of misstatements, and Dr. Solis-Cohen also took a shy at the matter of dosage, being particularly caustic in his criticism of the translations of the metric system.

In such a chorus of dispraise it was reassuring to hear one strong voice lifted in defence, and Dr. Reid Hunt's point that the Pharmacopœia was becoming increasingly important as a standard for the administration of law was an argument in favor of completeness in the statements of purity standards for which no refutation was forthcoming.

Let us not be cast down that the physician criticises the Pharmacopœia, but let us rather be overjoyed that he has at last awakened to the consciousness of the existence of such a work. If the Pharmacopœia is not what the physician needs the fault is his own. Every regularly chartered body of physicians in the United States was not only given an opportunity to formulate suggestions for the revision of the Pharmacopœia before the calling of the last convention, but was specifically urged to do so. Only three of these bodies performed their duty in this respect. If, therefore, there is any warrant for the criticism that the Pharmacopœia is a pharmacist's and not a physician's book the fault lies with the physician himself.

No one regrets the lack of interest in the Pharmacopœia on the part of the physician so much as does the pharmacist, and we, therefore, welcome these criticisms—whether ill or well founded—as evidence of an awakening on the part of the physician to the importance of the work, which should belong to both professions alike and express the best work of both.

Foreign Pharmacists and Proprietary Medicines.

It would seem that the question of the sale, advertising, etc., of proprietary medicines is agitating drug circles in foreign countries as well as in this country. Swiss pharmacists make bitter complaint of the increasing number of proprietary medicines and the injury done to their business through the increasing demand for these articles. In an article on this subject in the *Journal suisse de chimie et de pharmacie* Kuster bewails the present condition of the drug business in his country and attempts to place the blame for the flood of proprietaries which has poured over Swiss pharmacists during the past few years. The Swiss pharmacist, he acknowledges, is powerless under the circumstances; for he cannot discriminate between the proprietaries of true merit and those without any real value, and must sell whatever is asked for. The authorities seem to be totally indifferent to the situation.

Many pharmacists, in order to protect themselves against the encroachment of proprietary medicines, have resorted to the expedient of preparing their own specialties, but even this is not sufficient to stem the tide. Kuster suggests that the Swiss pharmacists should organize a syndicate of their own for manufacturing and advertising the various specialties. In this way the pharmacist could use his influence for the promotion of articles of true merit, could interest the physicians in these articles, and regain some of the lost profits from the constant sale of proprietaries. He believes that such an association should not be a stock company, but should have a governing body which should have charge of the advertising. It is proposed that similar syndicates of pharmacists be organized in other countries, and that the various associations be united in an international body. Switzerland, Kuster thinks, would be a favorable center for this body, inasmuch as that country has been the home of a number of international movements. The Swiss pharmacist does not seem to have a National Formulary to aid him in stemming the flood of proprietaries, and it might be a good idea for the American Pharmaceutical Association to confer with their Swiss confrères with a view to the production of an International Formulary, so as to accomplish in an international way what it is hoped the National Formulary may be able to accomplish for American pharmacy.

The New Remedies Compendium and Price List is printed in every other issue of the AMERICAN DRUGGIST. This is the most trustworthy guide to the Newer Materia Medica published.

DETERMINATION OF CAMPHOR IN CAMPHORATED OIL, B. P.

By John Lothian,

Principal of the Glasgow School of Pharmacy, Glasgow, Scotland.

In a communication made last year to the Pharmaceutical Society (American Druggist, June 26, 1905), I advocated the method of assay by volatilization, 3 to 5 Gm. of the camphorated oil being heated on a water bath for one hour. A shallow porcelain evaporating basin was used.

The following table shows the work that has been done in this direction, and it is at once seen that a considerable diversity of opinion exists as to the proper temperature to employ, the time required for complete volatilization of the camphor, and the corrections to be applied.

Temperature.	Time allowed.	Corrections applied.	Authority.
120° C.	2 hours.	0.16 per cent. for gain of olive oil.	Leonard & Smith.
150° C.	30-40 min.	Comparison experiment made with olive oil.	Cowle & Dickson.
Water bath.	3 hours.	None.	Liverseege.
Water bath.	3 hours.	½ per cent. allowed for camphor unvolatilized.	Fullerton Cook.
Water bath.	1 hour.	None.	Lothian.

Conflicting statements especially have appeared as to the time required for complete volatilization by the water bath method. Fullerton Cook (American Druggist, June 26, 1905) stated that in half an hour only 33 per cent. of the camphor was evaporated, and that after three hours apparently one-half per cent. of the camphor still remained. Messrs. Cowle and Dickson (*Pharmaceutical Journal*, March 10, 1906) state that the time required to expel the camphor at water bath temperature exceeds five hours. In order to settle these points I have made a fresh series of experiments; a very large number of determinations have been carried out, some of which are described below, in order to determine the rate of volatilization and the most suitable vessel to employ. I can thoroughly confirm the statement I made last year—namely, that in one hour practically all the camphor is driven off, in half an hour on an average 95 per cent. is expelled, and under favorable conditions as much as 98.4 per cent. The low figures obtained by others indicate that the operation has not been carried out under the most favorable conditions.

Instead of a shallow porcelain basin I use now a shallow cylindrical glass dish 1 Cm. in height and 8 Cm. inside diameter. The cover of a culture dish answers well. The superficies of such a dish is 50 sq. Cm., and when 5 Cc. of oil are placed in it there is a layer of oil 1 Mm. deep. It is better to use half that quantity—that is a layer of half a millimeter in depth. The dish is supported on a copper ring of the same inside diameter, placed on the water bath and levelled, so as to obtain a uniform layer, by propping up the legs of the tripod. The bath should be nearly filled with water, which is kept boiling briskly, no further attention being required until an hour has elapsed, when the dish is taken off, quickly cooled, weighed and the loss determined.

The results obtained by using a deep cylindrical dish dipping in the water were not so good, obviously owing to the difficulty of maintaining a layer of oil of uniform depth.

In order to ascertain the rate of volatilization, 4.1838 Gm. of a camphorated oil—*i. e.*, a layer of about 0.8 Mm. deep—containing 21.79 per cent. of camphor was heated as above described for 5 minutes at a time, cooled, weighed and the loss noted.

The above quantity of oil contained .9116 Gm. of camphor.

After 5 minutes, 0.3522 camphor was expelled.
After 10 minutes, 0.5460 camphor was expelled.
After 15 minutes, 0.7230 camphor was expelled.
After 20 minutes, 0 8060 campher was expelled.
After 25 minutes, 0.8328 camphor was expelled.
After 30 minutes, 0.8790 camphor was expelled.
After 35 minutes, 0.8975 camphor was expelled.
After 40 minutes, 0.9026 camphor was expelled.
After 45 minutes, 0.9068 camphor was expelled.
After 60 minutes, 0.9082 camphor was expelled.

The above results show that the rate of volatilization is proportional to the amount of camphor present at any given instant, following what is termed the "compound interest law" expressed in the following formula: $Y=Y.e^{-kt}$ where Y is the amount of camphor originally present, Y the amount present at time *t* in minutes that the oil has been on the water bath and *k* the logarithmic decrement or rate of decrease per minute, which is a constant for a layer of oil of constant depth. The mean value of *k* calculated from the above figures is 10.6 per cent. of camphor per minute. This is rather too high, as camphor is lost during the repeated coolings, and calculating from the mean results of half an hour's heating in similar experiments 10 per cent. would be nearer the mark, though with thinner layers the rate is much greater.

At the rate of 10 per cent. per minute decrease (.8 Mm. layer).

After 7 minutes, 50 per cent. of the camphor present is expelled.
After 30 minutes, 95 per cent. of the camphor present is expelled.
After 60 minutes, 99.75 per cent. of the camphor present is expelled.
After 69 minutes, 99.9 per cent. of the camphor present is expelled.

These figures agree remarkably well with the experimental results.

The behavior of the olive oil, however, must be taken into account, and in practice it was not found advantageous

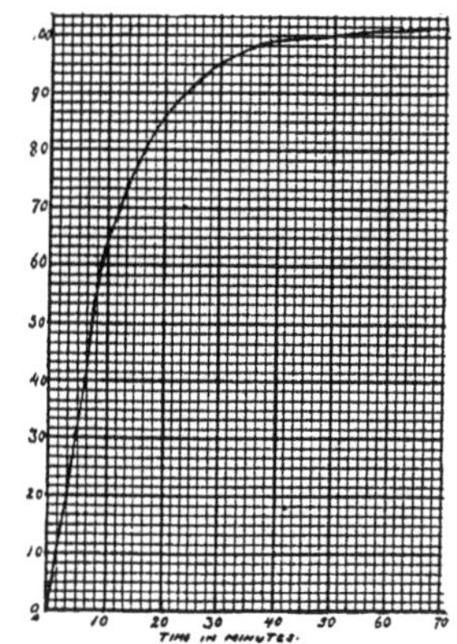

The Vertical Ordinates of This Curve Show the Percentage of Camphor Volatilized at Any Given Time on a Water Bath Using a Layer of 0.8 Mm. in Depth.

to continue the heating beyond one hour, as after the camphor is expelled the olive oil assumes a bleached appearance and begins to gain weight, as much as 2 Cgm. may be gained on heating for another hour. This is apt to give one the impression that the whole of the camphor has not been expelled if a previous weighing has not been made. The olive oil itself heated under the same conditions did *not* gain weight, but lost 0.07 per cent. (No corrections need be applied for this trifling loss.) It is evident that the olive oil is affected in some way by the camphor, and, therefore, I place no reliance on correction figures obtained by heating the plain olive oil under similar conditions to the camphorated oil, as is usually done.

The following results prove the accuracy of the method, which has the merit of great simplicity, requires no expensive apparatus and enables the ordinary pharmacist to make his own determinations, an important desideratum at the present time, when there are so many prosecutions for selling camphorated oil of deficient strength.

The samples of oil were made by weighing the camphor and olive oil in a stoppered weighing bottle on the chemical balance so as to obtain rigidly accurate percentages of camphor.

TABLE 2.

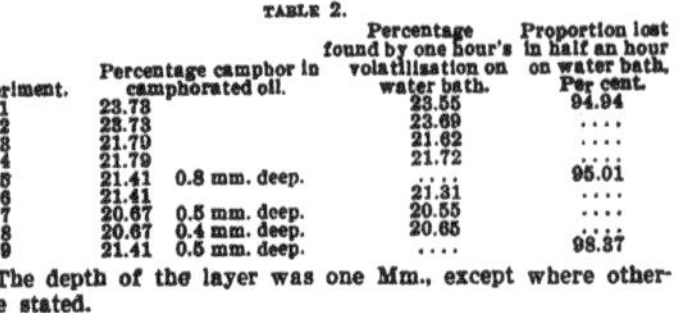

Experiment.	Percentage camphor in camphorated oil.		Percentage found by one hour's volatilisation on water bath.	Proportion lost in half an hour on water bath. Per cent.
1	23.78		23.55	94.94
2	23.73		23.69	....
3	21.79		21.62	....
4	21.79		21.72	....
5	21.41	0.8 mm. deep.	....	95.01
6	21.41		21.31	....
7	20.67	0.5 mm. deep.	20.55	....
8	20.67	0.4 mm. deep.	20.65	....
9	21.41	0.5 mm. deep.	....	98.37

The depth of the layer was one Mm., except where otherwise stated.

(Written for the American Druggist.)

DRUGGISTS AND LINGUISTICS.

By J. A. Sanford.

Stockton, Cal.

A letter published in the American Druggist for February 12, 1906, p. 73, directed attention to the advantages of a knowledge of foreign languages on the part of drug clerks. The possession or knowledge of a foreign language is compared by the editor in the same issue to a savings bank account. I have never seen it put this way before, but the comparison seems apt and correct.

The drug clerk in almost any place in the United States can obtain a position more quickly and at better pay if he has a knowledge of or familiarity with one or more of the foreign languages, such as German, Spanish, French or Italian. The locality will govern as to which language would be the most useful to acquire in a particular place. The local prestige of the druggist very often depends upon his ability to converse in the language of a customer, and while this applies with peculiar directness to the retail drug trade, the knowledge of foreign languages, especially that of Spanish, opens up a wider and more profitable field to those having a knowledge of the general drug business, due to our growing relations with the Spanish-speaking countries to the south of us. In many parts of the country, particularly in the seacoast ports, where most of the exporting is done, there is a constant demand for men trained in the drug business who at the same time have a knowledge of one or more foreign languages. This demand is also felt by an increasing number of proprietary medicine houses, who are looking more and more to the different foreign countries for their trade, due to the agitation on this subject throughout the United States.

There are as many ways to learn a foreign language as there are cures for rheumatism. Select some method or plan and stick to it, because as time goes on it will become easier and you will be able to notice your own progress day by day. In beginning the study of a foreign language do not worry about the errors you are sure to make or about very correct speaking or the imperfections attendant upon the beginning of anything which we undertake to master. Strike out, and if you make small errors, as you will, do not be discouraged or frightened. Remember one can never learn to walk until he first learns to creep. As a rule, when the student shows a real desire to learn a language the foreigner is glad to help him correct an error rather than laugh at him for making it.

My first language study was German. From my teacher in this I also took my first Latin studies, the text-book being a very elementary one, printed in German. I boarded at a restaurant where many of the patrons were German, and at each meal I had an opportunity to hear the language spoken. A little later I went to a German church, which practice, together with a German newspaper, accustomed me to both sound and sight of the then strange language, and very soon I was well on the way toward helping myself, until now I am just as much at home in the German language as in English, and have sufficient Spanish to make me feel comfortable in any conversation, and this knowledge has come in handy on numerous occasions.

The beginner should start with an elementary grammar such as Whitney's "Brief German Grammar," price 60 cents (Henry Holt & Co., New York), which is not very technical, and then when he falls in love with the language, as he will, a more complete grammar should be procured, as Whitney's "Compendious German Grammar, $1.30 (Henry Holt & Co.) For French, Whitney's "Brief French Grammar," 65 cents (Henry Holt & Co.), followed by the same author's "Practical French Grammar," $1.30, can be recommended. For Spanish, "De Tornes' Combined Method" or Ollendorff's Spanish Grammar can be recommended.

It is advisable to master a small vocabulary and just as soon as newspaper reading can be taken up this should be done, as the language of the newspaper is the everyday language, its words are the words of everyday life expressions, it uses the words ordinarily heard and the words needed for colloquial expression, and because it deals with practical subjects it will prevent talking over the heads of people later on. Then besides, the newspaper treats of everyday subjects with which the student is already more or less familiar.

The drug clerk must very often do his studying late in the day and perhaps when tired. On such occasions I found that it was best and less fatiguing to study in parallel books. I was often very much fatigued when study time came, but did not allow that to dampen my ardor or to cloud the object I always held before me. A good English novel, of which there are plenty, will furnish diversion to the beginner. Then later on a novel printed in any of the four important languages should be obtained, the language which is being studied, of course, but the student should be sure to get a good translation from some reliable publishing house. Many of the translations are poorly made; they are very much abridged and are worthless for parallel reading. The New Testament can be had in German, French, Italian or Spanish, in parallel columns, at small cost, perhaps 30 or 40 cents for the volume. These parallel readings obviate to a very great extent the tedious delay of looking up words in the dictionary; besides, a word met with in the body of a sentence gives its meaning in a clearer way than the dictionary can very often give.

In recent years the phonograph, or language phone method, has become an important factor in the study of languages. There is one in particular that is eminently practical and can be recommended. It supplies the grammar, vocabulary and the teacher. By this plan the instructor is ready at all times and the first expense is the whole expense, so far as money outlay is concerned. The rest depends simply upon one's disposition to learn and inclination to stick to a thing until it is accomplished, if for no other reason than to succeed.

In conclusion let me enjoin again on the ambitious druggist to take up this fascinating and profitable study. There is no novel in the world so pleasing to read as the French novel and there is no language more easy to learn or more pleasant to hear than the Spanish, unless it be the Italian, while a knowledge of German to the serious mind enables one to delve deeply into modern chemistry, pharmacy and other branches intimately associated with the general drug business.

(Written for the American Druggist.)

THE FLAVOR OF WORDS.

By Ralph B. Gable.

When Keats for the first time read the phrase "sea-shouldering whales" he shouted with delight. The picture presented was so vivid that he never quite forgot the impression the words created. One of our noted Shakespearean scholars speaks of the phrase, "death's dateless night!" "How it catches the breath! The night when there shall be no more time." Whittier, with all his calm confidence, was saddened by the connotation of those words which recur in so many lives—"It might have been." Poe, brilliant, erratic, scholarly beyond his years and time, was haunted by the sonority of a single word—"Nevermore."

The ability to extract flavor from words does not necessarily reside with the poetic or artistic temperament. If it did, I should not be enjoying that fine phrase, "a patent of honor," used by A. E. Ebert in the *Western Druggist* some months ago. He was writing of membership in the American Pharmaceutical Association, and he characterized it as mentioned above. There have been many fine things said of the A. Ph.

A., but I know of nothing finer than the words I quote from the pen of the genial veteran of Chicago.

Imagination has been aptly defined as "getting at the truth beneath the surface." So I am going to ask you to let your imagination dwell earnestly on the words, "A patent of honor." I shall not attempt at this point to fire your imagination by entering into a comprehensive discussion as to the potential value of membership in the A. Ph. A.; the subject is too broad and has so many phases. I want to remind you, however, that words as instruments of thoughts are freighted with a double mission. Sometimes they are more deeply significant in what they connote than in what they denote. Having said this I leave "A patent of honor" to your reflections.

And now I ask you to spend your vacation this year in attending the annual meeting of the American Pharmaceutical Association. It occurs in Indianapolis and begins on the first Monday in September.

Lottridge, whose charming work, "Animal Snapshots," shows that he has spent much time with the children of field and forest, has this to say of vacations:—"My ideal vacation is one that affords healthful pleasure not only for the time being, but for the remainder of the year; that furnishes something to which I can turn for recreation and enjoyment after the working day is over."

If you come with us to Indianapolis I can promise you healthful pleasure for the time being; I can tell you your experiences will be of a character that will be pleasing to dwell on in retrospect. More than this, no earnest pharmacist can attend a meeting of the A. Ph. A. without having benefits conferred on him which will materialize perhaps a score of times during the following year.

First of all, you enjoy a bit of travel. When I mention the word "travel" in this connection I am reminded of a pharmacist with whom I talked a few months ago. He is located near New York. He joined the American Pharmaceutical Association in 1892. That year he attended the meeting held in the White Mountains. Since then he has been at meetings in Chicago, Asheville, N. C.; Denver, Montreal, Lake Minnetonka, Minn.; Baltimore, Put-in-Bay, O.; Richmond, St. Louis, Philadelphia, Mackinac Island, Kansas City, Atlantic City. After the meeting in the White Mountains he went to Boston. He there visited numerous buildings and localities which are associated with historic events or noted personages in political and literary life. He went to Cambridge and Concord. When the meeting at Denver closed he journeyed on to Salt Lake City and then to San Francisco and Los Angeles. After the farewells had been said at Minnetonka he visited that Wonderland of the Northwest—The Yellowstone Park. There is hardly an important city in the country that he does not know something about, and his traveling has broadened him immeasurably. In the eyes of neighborhood physicians and his public this particular pharmacist is deemed a cultivated gentleman as well as a highly successful pharmacist. He smiled in a quizzical way as he said: "Paradoxical as it may seem, I have made new business and professional friends at home by going away from home. I know more people hereabouts now since I regularly take a vacation of ten days or two weeks than when I was in the store practically all the time."

Just at this point I want to remind you that the railroads always make a special rate relative to the A. Ph. A. convention. You pay full fare to the city where the convention is held. For the return trip you pay one-third of that amount. Then again, there are always certain hotels at the place of meeting which allow special rates. I mention these two matters particularly to offset the cry sometimes raised that attendance at the annual meeting is too expensive.

Make your plans, then, to go with us to Indianapolis. If you start from some large city you will meet others going. At the meeting you may see, hear and meet makers of pharmaceutical history; you will come face to face with men whose names appear on the title pages of Dispensatories; with men who have assisted in the revision of the U. S. P.; with those who have written text books on pharmacy, botany, chemistry, materia medica. You will come in contact with the editors of the pharmaceutical journals, and a genial group you will find them. And you will meet the leaders in actual, practical pharmacy from every part of the country. Aside from the papers and the discussions, you may participate in various entertainments and enjoy numberless chats with congenial spirits. If you want to go through a pharmaceutical laboratory you can visit the plant of Eli Lilly & Co. If you have never visited a large manufacturing establishment, a trip through the house which bears the "Sign of the Red Lilly" will be a memorable feature of your vacation. You will come back to your pharmacy with a distinct sense of physical and intellectual refreshment.

Some months later you will receive the "Proceedings," a volume containing all the addresses, reports, papers and discussions of the entire meeting. To be familiar with the "Proceedings" from year to year means that you will keep abreast of progress in pharmacy and cognate sciences.

Of course, there is a proviso about receiving the "Proceedings." You must be a member of the association.

Applications for membership can be secured by writing to the following :—

Dr. H. M. Whelpley, 2342 Albion place, St. Louis; William Mittelbach, Boonville, Mo.; or to the writer, whose address is 51 Maiden Lane, New York.

I should like to take a hundred applications to Indianapolis. May I have yours?

THE OLD AND NEW CHEMISTRY.[1]

By Prof. Sir James Dewar.

In giving a brief sketch of the evolution of chemistry from the earliest times up to the present day the lecturer divided the history of chemistry into five periods. The first of these, which extends from the earliest times to the first centuries of the present era, may be divided into three sections, and comprises, first, what little is known of the chemical arts of the Indians, Egyptians, and Hebrews down to the seventh century, and can only be judged by the metals, glass, colors, and other antiquities left by these peoples; secondly, the philosophic studies and speculations of the Greeks and Romans; and, thirdly, the rise and progress of mysticism of the later Alexandrian schools, in which chemistry first appears as a branch of occult learning. The second period, which corresponds to the Middle Ages of European history, is the period of alchemy associted with the names of Rhazes. Avicenna, and Geber in the East, and of Aluertus Magnus, Roger Beacon, Lully, and Basil Valentine in the West. With the third period, which extends over the two centuries after the Rerformation, is associated the rise of medical chemistry as developed by Paracelsus, Glauber, Agricola, and others. The fourth period falls within the seventeenth and eighteenth centuries, and is the first in which chemistry stands out as a definite subject with a special field of investigation apart from applications; it was inaugurated by Boyle, and was concluded by the brilliant discoveries of Black, Cavendish, Priestley, and Scheele. The fifth period, that of modern chemistry, in which the subject is raised to the rank of an exact science, was inaugurated by Lavoisier.

The Egyptians' knowledge of metallurgy appears to have been confined to the metals gold, silver, copper, iron, lead, and tin, the latter being used, together with copper or even copper and iron, in the form of bronze. With the discovery of mercury the number of metals known was brought to seven, and as this number was sacred to the Egyptians and Persians, all things which amounted to this number were supposed to have some connection with each other, and thus arose the relationship between the names and symbols of the metals with the names of the gods and the planets. During the alchemistic period this connection with astrology and the occult sciences was largely developed by the unscrupulous, while on the part of the more serious workers an earnest search was made after three principles: First, a universal medicine, the elixir of life; secondly, a universal solvent; and, thirdly, the transmutation of metals.

[1] An abstract of a lecture delivered at the Royal Institution, printed in *The Pharmaceutical Journal*.

A SYMPOSIUM ON COLOR PHOTOGRAPHY.

The Present Status of the Art.

A symposium on color photography formed the principal feature of the regular monthly meeting of the New York Section of the Society of Chemical Industry held at the Chemists' Club on Friday evening, May 25.

The most interesting paper of the evening was contributed by Herman A. Metz, of the firm of H. A. Metz & Co., who besides being a chemist is the Comptroller of the City of New York. Mr. Metz described in detail the two processes which have recently been invented by Dr. Koenig, of Hoechst, and which are known respectively as pinachromy and pinatype.

An abstract of this description follows:

The fact was brought out that practically all attempts to reproduce colors photographically are based on the fact that all the various shades and colors may be reproduced by a proper blending of three basic colors, generally red, yellow and blue, or some modification of those colors. Some workers use blue, orange, red and purple, others green, yellow and red. Three different negatives are taken, each through a colored screen, which screen may be composed of glass of the proper shades of color or of a box with glass sides containing a solution of a dye of the desired shade. Each of these negatives is then used in printing—not with the color of the screen used in making it, but with the complementary color.

PINACHROMY.

In the process known as pinachromy paper is covered with three films of prepared collodion, one imposed above the other, the specially prepared negatives (one for each color), being printed on each successive film as it is prepared, the necessary colors being brought out in each of the superposed films by the action of light on the different chemicals employed in each film. The process depends upon the light sensitiveness of certain leuco-bases of organic dyestuffs. This sensitiveness is much enhanced in the presence of collodion, a fact attributed to the presence in that body of nitric acid esters.

The blue color is produced with leucosteo-cyanine, which is ortho-chlor-tetra-ethyl-diamido-triphenyl-methane; the green with leucomalachite green, or with meta-nitro or meta-amido tetra-ethyl-diamido-triphenyl-methane; red with para-leuco aniline, which is a leucobase of para-fuchsine, or leucorhodamine violet with hexamethy-para-leuco aniline, which is a leucobase of violet 6 B-crystals, and yellow with leucofluoresceine or leucoflavaniline. The fixing of the picture is accomplished with dilute organic acids, mono-chloracetic acid being the best medium to employ. Neither acetic acid, nor di- or tri-chlor acetic acid can be used.

The practical application of this process is carried out as follows: A sheet of paper is coated with the blue collodion mixture and exposed under its corresponding negative, a separate negative being taken for each color. When the blue picture appears sufficiently strong it is fixed in a 10 per cent. solution of mono-chloracetic acid, washed, coated with thin gelatin film, and dried. This gelatin film serves to protect the first collodion coating from dissolving when the second coating is put on.

The dry blue picture is then flowed with the yellow collodion mixture and exposed under its corresponding negative, care being taken that the pictures register accurately. After exposure it is fixed, washed and dried, and the yellow picture produced. The final red picture is obtained in a corresponding manner. On account of the complete transparency of these very thin films and the brilliancy of the colors produced, the prints appear very uniform, and give faithful reproductions of the natural color.

The permanency of pinachromy pictures is naturally not absolute, but the dyestuffs used are relatively fast. The most fugitive is the blue, but even this surpasses the so-called blue prints (cyanotypes) in permanency. The quantity of the leuco bodies necessary is extremely small, hence pictures composed of the three color films cost but a trifle more to produce than do the ordinary gum or pigment prints.

THE PINATYPE.

In pinatype, the second process, on the other hand, a single gelatin film is so treated that a succession of prints on paper may be obtained from the colored plate as often as desired. This makes pinatype especially adapted to three color work, and it is now being carefully tested by those interested in that line.

If a bichromate plate covered with a coating of gelatin with an admixture of bichromate be exposed to light under a photographic negative, those parts exposed to the action of the light are hardened and the negative loses its solubility in water to a greater or less extent. If the undecomposed bichromate, still contained in the gelatin layer, is then removed by washing, a picture in relief is obtained visible to only a very slight extent, consisting of partly hardened and partly unhardened gelatin.

Pinatype dyes have, however, the property of dyeing the unhardened gelatin very strongly, whereas the hardened portions are colored either not at all or very slightly. If most paper, coated with specially prepared gelatin, is now brought into intimate contact with the gelatin layer, colored by means of a pinatype dye, in short time a colored paper picture with all the half tones is obtained, which appears strongly colored on those parts not affected by light, while the most exposed parts remain white. From this it is evident that in order to obtain a positive picture the bichromate gelatin layer must be exposed under a diapositive.

The facility with which enlarged copies can be made is especially important for three color photography, as the direct production of large sized plates in three colors offers many technical difficulties.

THE PINATYPE PROCESS.

The print plates for pinatype, which are not sensitive to light, are steeped with the film side uppermost in shaded daylight or lamplight, for three or four minutes, in a sensitizing solution composed of 2 grams of chromic acid dissolved in 110 Cc. of cold water. The solution must not be warmer than 20 degrees C. Any bubbles of air should be removed with the finger or a brush. A great number of plates may be sensitized, one after the other, in the same bath. After the plates have been sensitized, they are well drained and dried in a dark and not too warm place free from dust.

The diapositives to be copied are laid in a frame with the film side in contact with the film side of a sensitized print plate, the frame is then closed with a good spring and exposed to either direct electric light or sunlight, the exposure required for a print plate being about the same as that for collodion paper. After copying the pictures should be distinctly seen in a brown color on a yellow background. The print plate is now washed in running water until all undecomposed chromic acid has been removed, which usually requires about ten minutes. The plates may now be dried or placed directly in the dye solution.

The well washed print plate, either dry or moist, which corresponds to the red filter negative, is steeped in the blue dye solution composed of five grams of pinatype blue dissolved in 250 Cc. of water and the dish rocked from time to time. The first dyeing takes about 15 minutes. The plate is then washed and rinsed until the water running off from it is no longer colored.

When the dyed plate is finished a piece of transfer paper of the size of the plate is softened in cold water, until the paper has become completely pliable and fully stretched. The paper is now attached to the plate, preferably under water, with the film side against the film side of the printed plate, and both removed from the bath, at the same time draining off the excess of water by a gentle motion of the hand.

The plate is then laid upon a table, paper uppermost, and protected with a piece of oiled silk or the like, and the paper firmly smoothed over with a rubbber squeegee, from the middle outward, using moderate pressure. The operation is similar to that used in the pigment process. When the paper adheres satisfactorily it is covered with a damp sheet and a glass plate, in order to prevent evaporation, and the whole allowed to stand ten to fifteen minutes, under a light weight. At the end of this time the picture will be found transferred to the paper with sufficient strength. The paper is now removed and hung up to dry.

The print plate is now again placed for about five minutes in the dyebath, rinsed and the picture again transferred to a fresh sheet of prepared paper as above directed. These operations may be repeated as often as desired.

By repeated immersion in the dyebath the print plate becomes darker. Nevertheless the prints from the plate are quite uniform, as only the exterior surface of the dyed plate acts on the paper.

The dyed plates may be kept for any length of time after use, and can be again employed after a fresh immersion in the dyebath.

The dyeing of the print plate corresponding with the green filter negative is done in the same manner.

For the dyebath five grams of pinatype red are stirred with a little water to a paste and then three to five Cc. concentrated ammonia solution added. Sufficient ammonia must be used to completely dissolve the dye to a clear deep red liquid. After about five minutes the solution is diluted with cold water to 250 Cc.

After the red plate has been washed free from the excess of dyestuff, the blue picture is softened in water and laid under water upon the red print plate. The operation is carried out in the same way as before described, the blue picture being easily shifted under water, so as to exactly correspond to the red print plate. When the adjustment is perfect, the paper is held firmly against the plate with suitable clamps, leaving the film free. The film is then withdrawn, water is again run over the plate and the paper pressed firmly down with the squeegee. It is allowed to stand for ten to fifteen minutes and the paper then removed from the plate.

About thirty minutes should be allowed for the first immersion of the print plate, corrresponding to the blue filter negative, in a dyebath composed of five grams of pinatype yellow dissolved in 200 Cc. of hot water; for subsequent immersions five to ten minutes. The yellow transfer upon the blue and red picture takes about thirty minutes.

To increase the picture's permanency and to harden the gelatin layer, the paper is now immersed for about one to two minutes in a fixing bath of two grams of fixative Chromium salt and 100 Cc. water. After fixing the picture is washed for about five minutes in clean water and hung up to dry.

The principal advantage of pinatype lies in the use of print plates, which are prepared in a simple manner with the aid of light; allowing the preparation of a large number of paper copies therefrom by a purely mechanical process, without further recourse to light. The print plates can be kept and used again at any time, without the aid of light, for the preparation of paper copies. In consequence of the intensity of the pinatype dyestuffs and the immunity from spoiled pictures pinatypes are very cheap. Pinatypes are extremely fast to light. A three colored pinatype is not composed of different films. A single thin film carries all of the colors, which therefore blend harmoniously.

THE EARLIER PROCESSES OF MECHANICAL PRODUCTIONS.

Prof. Charles S. Chandler of the New York College of Pharmacy opened the symposium by an address in which he outlined the first attempts made at mechanical reproduction of photographs, illustrating his remarks with numerous specimens of prints produced by the several methods described. Dr. Chandler said that the first attempt to reproduce photographs mechanically was by what is known as the Woodbury type method, the results being very beautiful, though so expensive as not to be available for very large editions. This, as well as the Albertype, which was brought out later, belongs to what is known as the collotype class, their reproduction involving the use of gelatin or some similar substance, the method being given its name from the Latin word for gelatin. The principle involved in all the collotype processes is practically the same, the results depending upon the fact that when gelatin or a similar body is mixed with a bichromate the mixture becomes sensitive to light; that part on which the light shines becoming hard and insoluble even in warm water. In the Woodbury type the thick solution of gelatin in which the bichromate is dissolved is flowed on a plate of glass which has been previously wiped off with some oleaginous substance. This coating of gelatin is dried in the dark, leaving a film about 1-100 of an inch in thickness. This film is placed under the negative, exposed to light, then taken into a dark room and gently washed with a sponge and warm water until a certain portion of the gelatin which has not been acted upon by the light has been dissolved out. The film is then allowed to dry, becoming as hard as glass and almost as strong as steel. The result of this process is a reproduction in the gelatin of the photograph in relief. When thoroughly dried this plate of gelatin is laid on a plate of lead and subjected to a pressure of 2,000 to 3,000 pounds to the square inch, practically molding the lead into a reversed reproduction of the negative. This process, of course, reverses the lights and shades, producing an intaglio plate instead of a relief plate. On attempting to print from this on the method usually followed by engravers—that is by inking the whole surface and then wiping off the ink from the smooth parts where the high lights are—it was found that the ink failed to adhere to the surface of the gelatin. This difficulty was solved by adding a considerable quantity of powdered glass' to the gelatin solution, with the result that when the gelatin plate was "fixed" by washing with warm water and then dried and, when thoroughly dry, pressed against lead plate as before, the protruding bits of glass gave just the necessary degree of "tooth" to the lead plate to retain the ink when it was applied. The colored prints made by the Woodbury type method are produced by first stenciling the desired color flat on the paper on which the print is to be made. Numerous specimens of both the colored and uncolored Woodbury type in various stages were shown.

PHOTOGRAVURE.

Prof. Chandler explained that what was ordinarily called photogravure by the publishers was not a photogravure, as this name could be restricted to a print made from a copper intaglio plate produced by the same method as are the lead plates from the Woodbury type. In the photogravure the colored inks are applied to the plates literally by hand. Each workman has before him a plate and a colored print and has in one hand a palette of colored inks such as is used by artists. He takes up a small bit of the ink on his finger, applies this on the proper portion of the plate, and when he has finished with the application of this particular color wherever it appears in the picture, he carefully wipes off the surplus ink and proceeds to apply to the other portions of the plate the other colors as required. Finally a print is taken and then the entire plate must be carefully washed and the process repeated. For an ordinary photogravure a workman would require about two hours to apply colors to an 8 x 10 plate. When asked whether this was not rather expensive, a Parisian publisher informed Professor Chandler that since they paid the workmen about 2 francs a day and sold the prints at 20 francs each they were fairly well satisfied with the results.

Albumen and gum arabic act in much the same way as does gelatin and can be used in lieu of gelatin if desired.

Another variation of this method described briefly by Prof. Chandler is effected by coating metal plate with chromated gelatin, washing off the unacted on gelatin and etching by the application of corrosive liquids which will not affect the gelatin left on the plate but will erode the uncovered surface.

This method is used very largely in Paris in illustrating newspapers and is known as "chromo typographie." In this method different plates are used for printing different colors, as many as seven different plates being used for one print.

THE ALBERTYPE.

The Albertype was next described by Prof. Chandler. This process owed its name to Prof. Albert, of Berlin, the inventor, but has been very much improved by the American artist, Bierstadt, a close friend of Prof. Chandler, who had given him many specimens interesting from a historical point of view. In the original process a plate of glass one-third of an inch thick was coated with a layer of chromatized gelatin which was exposed to the light and hardened uniformly all over the surface. When this has been thoroughly hardened and dried a second layer of chromatized gelatin was applied and this was dried in a dark room. This plate was then exposed under a negative and the unacted on portions of the gelatin moistened with warm water. The surface was then wiped dry and the whole inked by a roller bearing an ink with an oleaginous base. The portions of the gelatin which had been not acted on by light having absorbed water would not "take" the ink, but the hard portions would take the ink. After inking the plate was printed in the same way as an ordinary engraving, the ink wiped off, the plate reinked and another print taken. The artotype was referred to as an improved form of Albertype. Prof. Chandler then touched briefly upon the nature of light and the various color processes which were described later by other speakers.

THE IVES KROMOSCOPE.

F. E. Ives, the inventor of the kromoscope process of color production, read a paper which was concerned chiefly with setting forth his claims to having been much in advance of the times as the inventor of the half tone process and of the three color half tone process. He dwelt with particular emphasis on his kromoscope process which consists in reproduction of photographs in natural colors by interposing colored screens between the eye and the transparent positive, and transmitting light through the positive and the colored screen, the results being much more vivid and natural than that obtained by any other process.

THE KOENIG PROCESS OF COLOR PHOTOGRAPHY.

H. A. Metz here read his interesting paper describing the two new processes invented by Dr. E. Koenig, of Hoechst, known respectively as pinachromy and pinatype, which paper is presented in abstract above.

Maximilian Toch briefly described the processes now used in a practical way for reproducing photographs. Commercial photography in the colors of nature was based, he said, on three-color work, the pigments of the positive being red, yellow and blue, and the screens for the negatives being orange, green and violet. He showed three screens which are used, and three prints made by the half-tone process. The mechanical process did not differ, he said, from that of the Albert-type, excepting that the plates were half-tone zinc plates, and these were then electrotyped for further use. Much depended upon the orthochromatism of the plates used as negatives, for all silver bromide plates, unless properly prepared, stained and screened, were sensitive only to the blue end of the spectrum and not at all sensitive to the red.

Another factor in the successful process for the production of prints in the colors of nature was the proper tone value, or tinctorial value, of the three pigments finally used in the positive. A mixture of the three primary pigments tends to make a black, while a mixture of the three primary colors tends to make a white.

The Lumiere single plate process was based on the coloring of the grains of potato starch—orange, green and violet. These are carefully laid on the plates so they do not superimpose, and the opaque interstices filled up—followed by a varnish having the same refractive index, which fastens them to the plate; finally a translucent emulsion is poured over this. A photograph is then taken and developed with the glass side facing the lens. A similar plate is then prepared of colored starch, the grain colors being red, yellow and blue, and an emulsion sensitive to each of these colors. A positive is then made from the negative plate and on fixation a photograph in the colors of nature is produced with marvelous effect.

After this Mr. Toch showed on the screen the Joly process, consisting of three line color screens and three line positives superimposed, and likewise the Lumiere process of three dyed positives of red, yellow and blue superimposed, some of which were remarkably true to life.

Hoyt Miller also described certain processes in color photography, very briefly illustrating his remarks with colored lantern slides showing the results obtained.

Illinois Antinarcotic Law.

The following is the draft of a bill to regulate the sale of certain narcotic drugs, which has been prepared by the Committee on Legislation of the Illinois Pharmaceutical Association for discussion at the annual meeting in Peoria next week:

A Bill to provide against the evils resulting from the traffic in certain narcotic drugs, and to regulate the sale thereof.

Section 1. Be it enacted by the People of the State of Illinois, represented in the General Assembly:

That it shall be unlawful for any person, firm or corporation to sell, furnish or give away any cocaine, alpha or beta eucaine, opium, morphine, heroin, chloral hydrate or any salt or compound of any of the foregoing substances, or any preparation or compound containing any of the foregoing substances, or their salts or compounds, except upon the original written order or prescription of a lawfully authorized practitioner of medicine, dentistry or veterinary medicine, which order or prescription shall be dated and shall contain the name of the person for whom prescribed, or if ordered by a practitioner of veterinary medicine, shall state the kind of animal for which ordered, and shall be signed by the person giving the prescription or order. Such written order or prescription shall be permanently retained on file by the person, firm or corporation who shall compound or dispense the articles ordered or prescribed, and it shall not be again compounded or dispensed, except upon the written order of the original prescriber for each and every subsequent compounding or dispensing. No copy or duplicate of such written order or prescription shall be made or delivered to any person, but the original shall at all times be open to inspection by the prescriber and properly authorized officers of the law.

Provided, however, that the above provision shall not apply to preparations containing not more than two grains of opium or not more than one-fourth grain of morphine, or not more than one-fourth grain of heroin, or not more than one-eighth grain of cocaine, or not more than one-eighth grain of alpha or beta eucaine, or not more than ten grains of chloral hydrate, in one fluid ounce, or if a solid preparation, in one avoirdupois ounce. Provided also that the above provision shall not apply to preparations containing opium and recommended and sold in good faith for diarrhœa and cholera, each bottle or package of which is accompanied by specific directions for use, and a caution against habitual use, nor to powder of ipecac and opium commonly known as Dover's Powder, nor to liniments or ointments when plainly labeled "for external use only." And provided further that the above provision shall not apply to sales at wholesale by jobbers, wholesalers and manufacturers to retail druggists or qualified physicians, or to each other, nor to sales at retail by retail druggists to regular practitioners of medicine, dentistry or veterinary medicine, nor to sales made to manufacturers of proprietary or pharmaceutical preparations for use in the manufacture of such preparations, nor to sales to hospitals, colleges, scientific or public institutions.

Sec. 2. It shall be unlawful for any practitioner of medicine, dentistry or veterinary medicine to furnish to or to prescribe for the use of any habitual user of the same any cocaine, heroin, alpha or beta eucaine, opium, morphine, chloral hydrate, or any salt or compound of any of the foregoing substances, or any preparation containing any of the foregoing substances or their salts or compounds. And it shall also be unlawful for any practitioner of dentistry to prescribe any of the foregoing substances for any person not under his treatment in the regular practice of his profession, or for any practitioner of veterinary medicine to prescribe any of the foregoing substances for the use of any human being.

Provided, however, that the provisions of this section shall not be construed to prevent any lawfully authorized practitioner of medicine from furnishing or prescribing in good faith for the use of any habitual user of narcotic drugs who is under his professional care such substances as he may deem necessary for their treatment, when such prescriptions are not given or substances furnished for the purpose of evading the provisions of this act.

Sec. 3. Any person who shall violate any of the provisions of this act shall be deemed guilty of a misdemeanor, and upon conviction, for the first offense shall be fined not less than $25.00 nor more than $50.00, and upon conviction for a second offense shall be fined not less than $50.00 nor more than $100.00, and upon conviction for a subsequent offense shall be fined not less than $100.00 nor more than $200.00, and shall be imprisoned in the county jail for not more than six months, and if a licensed pharmacist, physician, dentist or veterinary surgeon, his license shall be revoked. It shall be the duty under this act of all judges of the courts of common pleas in this State, at every regular term thereof, to charge all regularly impaneled grand juries to diligently inquire into and investigate all cases of the violation of the provisions of this act and to make a true presentment of all persons guilty of such violations. It shall be the duty of the Board of Pharmacy to cause the prosecution of all persons violating the provisions of this act. No prosecution shall be brought for the sale of any patent or proprietary medicine containing any of the drugs or preparations hereinbefore mentioned until the Board of Pharmacy shall certify that such medicine contains any of the said drugs or preparations in excess of the maximum percentages hereinbefore mentioned.

Sec. 4. In any proceedings under the provisions of this act the charge may be brought against any or all of the members of a partnership, or against the directors or executive officers of a corporation, or against the agent or any person, partnership or corporation.

Sec. 5. All laws and parts of laws in conflict with this act are hereby repealed.

It might be well to in some way call attention of all the State boards of health to the pharmacopœial statements that "The purity standard requirements, which limit the quantity of innocuous impurities, are, unless otherwise specified, to be understood as applying to chemical substances which are free from adherent moisture, but an allowance not exceeding 3 per cent. of moisture is permitted in nonhygroscopic crystallized chemical salts. Chemical substances in the form of powder or capillary crystals, and all hygroscopic salts, are to be dispensed in a condition of sensible dryness. As long as this condition is fulfilled the moisture present is not to be regarded as an impurity."

Cream *of* Current Literature

A summary of the leading articles in contemporary pharmaceutical periodicals.

Charcoal as an Antidote to Mushroom Poisoning.—The *Bulletin général de thérapeutique*, April 15, 1906, states that pulverized wood charcoal, or preferably animal charcoal, is an efficient antidote to the poison of mushrooms, acting almost miraculously. Several spoonfuls of animal charcoal, mixed with water, are sufficient to relieve or check the most severe cases of poisoning, according to this authority.

Festoform is a solid formaldehyde which is obtained by mixing three parts of a 40 per cent. solution of formaldehyde with one part of soda soap, or by passing formaldehyde gas into a solution of soap. It forms a white mass, dissolving in water to make a feebly opalescent neutral fluid, which is used for disinfection. It is offered in tablet and pastil form, prepared by a patent process. It is said to be useful in the form of smelling salts, in inflammation of the mucus lining of the nasal passages.

Protosal is a salicylic ether of glycerin, occurring as an oily liquid, devoid of color, having a specific gravity of 1,344, boiling at 200 degrees C., and partly decomposing at that temperature. It is soluble in alcohol, ether, chloroform, benzin, castor oil, and less soluble in olive oil and sesame oil. It is insoluble in water, petroleum-ether, glycerin and liquid petrolatum, and is decomposed by alkalies and by acids. It is used as a local application in mixtures of equal parts with olive oil containing 10 per cent. of alcohol. Salicylic acid can be detected in the urine twelve hours after these applications.

Reactions for Identifying Veronal.—Tagliarini mentions the following characteristic points about veronal which will help to identify it (*Bollettino chimico farmaceutico*, 1906, p. 105): The shape of the crystals of veronal obtained with the aid of ether is identical to the shape of the crystals of the pure product. The salt is very soluble in ether and soluble in alkaline fluids, but is insoluble in water. With mercuric nitrate it forms a gray precipitate, soluble in dilute nitric acid. It reduces the sulphuric acid solution of potassium bichromate in the cold and also reduces solutions of potassium permanganate in the presence of sulphuric acid.

Sodium Nitrate in the Preservation of Meat.—Andouard (Bulletin Commercial, April, 1906) examined certain samples of meat products which had been eaten by a number of persons who had contracted a form of poisoning in consequence. He found that the chemical which had been employed to color the meat a bright pink color consisted of sodium arsenate and sodium nitrate, together with traces of sodium sulphate, etc. The arsenical salt was present in these meat products in alarming amounts. The samples were obtained from one butcher many of whose customers had been affected by symptoms of poisoning. The author urges that sodium nitrate and other nitrates be prohibited as additions to meat products.

The Treatment of Vomiting.—A review of this subject which is of interest to pharmacists in emergency work appeared recently in *Répertoire de therapeutique*, May 1906. Ice is often used, but it should not be sucked. The small pieces should be swallowed continuously. The vomiting of consumptives is often arrested by swallowing some pieces of ice after each meal. Sometimes iced or carbonated drinks are of benefit, including champagne. Small doses of morphine or of cocaine in solution are among the most successful remedies for vomiting, as are also chloroform water and extract of cannabis indica. Menthol is also employed in persistent vomiting. Tincture of iodine has given excellent results in the hands of some physicians, the dose being 12 to 15 drops daily. Mustard plasters and other means of counter irritation have been used over the stomach and are especially valuable in cases of nervous vomiting. Galvanic or faradic electricity applied to the stomach also gives good results.

Protocetraric Acid, the New Antemetic.—The therapeutic action of Iceland moss in arresting vomiting was first described by Brissemoret and Deguy, and is due to the protocetraric acid contained in it. This acid, which crystallizes with difficulty, is found in the form of white needles insoluble in water and in ether, but soluble in alcohol, especially in hot alcohol. It usually occurs as a greyish white powder, with a peculiar aromatic odor, and in the presence of acids and alkalies it is split up into cetraric and fumaric acids. Most writers who have studied cetrarin have worked with cetrarates and not with protocetraric acid. The latter is quite abundant in the lichen, and usually the plant contains from sixteen to twenty grammes of it per kilogramme. It is slightly poisonous to dogs and to rabbits when injected in sufficient doses into the veins of these animals. Poisoning produces excitement and convulsions, followed by a stage of depression and of paralysis, first of the front, later of the hind legs. In a man a saturated alcoholic solution of the acid was used in doses of from 20 to 100 drops without ill effect, and this solution was found to be an excellent remedy against vomiting.

The Preparation of Syrup of Tolu.—Astruc and Cambe (*Journal de pharmacie et de chimie*, May 1, 1906) discuss the best and most practical methods of preparing syrup of tolu. They review the various methods recommended in the different editions of the French Codex and complain that the official French method is too long; that six or eight hours are usually needed to prepare the syrup, and that the method of preparation is not sufficiently described to enable a pharmacist to prepare the syrup without any other directions. They offer a formula, which they say is more practical, more efficient and more rapid of execution than the formula of the official French Codex. For the purpose of obtaining an excellent syrup of tolu they recommend the process used for the preparation of coffee as practiced in every family in France, namely, lixiviation with hot water. The solvent power of a substance upon a solid is in proportion to the surface of the substance exposed. If then the balsam of tolu be so divided that a very large surface of it is presented to the solvent a concentrated solution will result. The method of lixiviation, moreover, offers the best means of exhausting such a substance as balsam of tolu. The process which they recommend is as follows: First, a granulated balsam of tolu is prepared by mixing 50 Gm. of the balsam, 100 Gm. of alcohol and 450 Gm. of purified sand. The balsam of tolu is dissolved in the alcohol, the solution is poured into the sand, and the whole is thoroughly mixed by triturating in a mortar. The mixture is then exposed to the air until the alcohol has evaporated, and shaken from time to time to avoid agglomeration. The granulated substance is kept in well-stoppered bottles in a cool place. Of this 10 per cent. granulate of balsam of tolu, 500 Gm. are poured into a glass flask stoppered with cotton, and enough hot water is poured into the percolator to make 1,000 Gm. of percolate. The liquid is then allowed to cool and is filtered. Sugar is added and a solution of syrup made, according to the usual method, using gentle heat and a closed vessel. This gives a clear and strongly aromatic syrup, which corresponds to all requirements of the Codex and is even superior in quality. The authors acknowledge that the Belgian Pharmacopœia has a similar process of lixiviation, with the aid of heat, for the syrup of tolu, but claim that their method gives better results and is simple and rapid.

Queries and Answers

We shall be glad, in this department, to respond to calls for information on all pharmaceutic matters.

Comment on Answers to Queries.—O. R. is kind enough to comment on the reply to J. T. B., as printed in the AMERICAN DRUGGIST for May 28, page 290. He does not agree with us that the abbreviation "calc. hydr. pulv." means powdered quicklime, and if he had the prescription to dispense he would use slaked lime—powdered calcium hydrate. If, however, quicklime is used and slaked in contact with the water, the mixing should be done in an open vessel, not in a bottle, or there will be trouble.

Our interpretation of "mistura bismuthi" is not accepted by O. R., who asserts that the term mistura bismuthi is a synonym for the cream of bismuth mentioned in the second edition of the National Formulary. We are unable to agree with our correspondent in this, as we find nothing in the literature to support his contention. Further correspondence on this subject would be welcomed, and if any readers have a better explanation of the term to offer we trust they will not hesitate to send it in for publication.

Interchange of Certificates.—M. H. asks if he can exchange his New York certificate of registration in pharmacy for a Massachusetts certificate. He says he has read in the AMERICAN DRUGGIST that a law had been passed in the State of Massachusetts which permits reciprocal registration of this kind.

Our correspondent is in error regarding the passage of a new pharmacy law for Massachusetts. Steps are being taken by the members of the National Association of Boards of Pharmacy to effect the interchange of certificates among the States, but thus far only a few of the Southern and Western States have agreed to the proposition. The following States are carrying out reciprocal registration: Alabama, Arizona, Georgia, Indiana, Indian Territory, Kentucky, Florida, Louisiana, Ohio, Oregon and South Dakota.

A Formula for Aristol.—L. H. L.—The substance sold under this name is official in the new edition of the United States Pharmacopœia, under the title thymol iodide, but no formula is given for its preparation, the description being confined to the statement that it is a product of the condensation of two molecules of thymol, with the introduction of two atoms of iodine into the phenolic groups of the thymol.

There is hardly another definite chemical product for which so many different formulas exist. By the two solution process the following method will yield aristol in small quantities:

Solution A.

Thymol	Gm. 1
Sodium hydroxide	Gm. 1
Potassium iodide	Gm. 1
Distilled water	Cc. 10

Dissolve.

Solution B.

Solution of chlorinated soda	Cc. 50

Solution A is poured into Solution B and the whole shaken vigorously. The aristol precipitates in about fifteen minutes. The precipitate is transferred to a filter, washed with distilled water and dried. The whole operation should be conducted in a dark room.

Beringer's formula differs from the foregoing, as will be perceived by the following:

Thymol	Gm. 15
Sodium hydroxide	Gm. 20
Iodine	Gm. 6.35
Potassium iodide	Gm. 8.3
Solution of chlorinated soda	q.s.

The thymol and soda are dissolved in 250 Cc. of water. The iodine and potassium iodide are also dissolved in 250 Cc. of water, and the two solutions mixed, resulting in an opalescent solution with distinct green tint, the slight precipitate first formed being redissolved. Solution of chlorinated soda is now added gradually while stirring, until no further precipitate is produced, a slight excess being indicated by the odor. About 650 or 700 Cc. will be required. The precipitate, a light red brown in color, is collected, washed and dried, by spreading on bibulous paper in a suitable room, where it can be protected from the light, at a temperature not exceeding 50 degrees C. The filtrate showed the absence of iodides in any quantity, and a portion acidified and extracted with ether yielded no thymol. The yield by this formula was about 29 Gm. of aristol, corresponding in color, melting point and solubilities with the aristol in the market and closely approximating the theoretical yield, Gm. 29.285.

Freckle and Moth Lotion.—H. K. & Co. ask for a formula for a preparation thus designated by them.

One of the most effective preparations of this kind, as well adapted for the removal of pimples as for beautifying the complexion, is the following:

Acid nitric. dil	ʒij
Alcoholis	℥iij
Ext. rosæ alb	℥ss
Ol. neroli	mx
M. et. adde.	
Hydrogen. dioxidi	℥ij
Glycerin	℥iij
Liquor. coccinel	q.s.
Aqua	ad ℥xl

The mixture should be allowed to stand for three weeks before filtering and bottling. For use the following directions should be printed on the label:

"Wet a piece of soft cloth with the lotion and apply to the face, neck, arms and hands each time after washing, then dry."

Other freckle lotions and complexion bleaches are represented by the following formulas:

I.

Zinci oxidi	ʒj
Calamin	ʒj
Hydrarg. ammon. chlor	gr. xv
Glycerini	ʒij
Aq. rosæ ad	℥vj

II.

Zinc sulphocarbolate	ʒj
Glycerin	℥iij
Alcohol	℥ij
Rose water	℥x

III.

Zinc oxide	ʒiij
Bismuth subiodide	gr. xxx
Dextrin	ʒiiss
Glycerin	ʒiij

Nos. 1 and 2 are to be used as a wash night and morning, while the face is to be anointed at night and washed off in the morning with No. 3.

Buttermilk or sour milk was considered an effective complexion wash in days gone by, but in these modern times the chemist's substitute for buttermilk is employed in a preparation containing lactic acid, as represented by the following formula, for which we are indebted to "Pharmaceutical Formulas":

IV.

Acid. lactic. (10 per cent.)	ʒij
Glycerini	℥ss
Ess. rosæ alb	ʒiss
Tinct. benzoin	ʒj
Aquæ	ad ℥vj

Mix the acid and glycerin with the water and add the rose extract and tincture, previously mixed.

From the same source we take an alkaline lotion, which is intended to be applied to the face with a piece of soft cloth twice daily:

V.

Potass. carbonat	ʒiiss
Boracis	℥ss
Aq. coloniensis	℥iss
Aq. rosæ	ad ℥xxiv

Dissolve and after two days filter.

CONDUCTED BY FRANK FARRINGTON.

Under this head will appear suggestions and plans for increasing trade, advertising experiences, information, and notes of interest useful to the pharmacist in the preparation of his advertising matter. Specimens of current advertising will be reproduced, with suggestive analysis and criticism, and queries relative to advertising matters will be answered. To avoid delay address communications to Department of Business Building, AMERICAN DRUGGIST, 66 West Broadway, New York.

TALCUM POWDER ADVERTISING.

At this time of year the talcum powder business begins to pick up. Talcum is a steady seller all the year around, but the summer is the best season for it, and in the summer its sale ought to be pushed hardest.

Every druggist ought to keep all the standard brands that he has calls for and ought to sell them at the prices other stores ask, but, at the same time, he will make most money by keeping the cut price kinds in the background, and—except where they are particularly asked for—selling his own make.

If he has not the time nor the facilities for making a talcum or for putting up one, he can buy first-class brands under his own name, talcum that is pure and fine grade, daintily perfumed, for $9.00 per gross or less.

PUT YOUR OWN LABEL ONLY ON HIGH GRADE GOODS.

The talcum that bears the name of the store ought to be of good quality, and it ought to be sold at a fairly high price. It is better policy for a store to recommend something that commands a fair price than an article that is so cheap as to make a person doubt its quality.

The druggist's own brand can be sold at nineteen cents and be high enough in price to establish the quality principle, and yet it will be low enough to be below the higher priced advertised articles.

If all the advertised brands that a store sells come in cans or in paper, the store brand will appear more distinctive in glass. Glass gives one a little talking point on the impossibility of contamination from the container.

Of course it is possible to make a good business on talcum without an individual brand, but if a store is to spend its money on window displays and printer's ink for talcum sales, it might just as well have all the results as to be obliged to divide them, giving the lion's share to the proprietor of some outside kind.

Talcum packages are always attractive and lend themselves well to making attractive window exhibitions. The use of crepe tissues and ribbons or anything that will add richness to the display helps to get a good effect, and it is necessary to use plenty of good, plain price cards, which should read somewhat like those shown herewith.

The main thing to remember in making the show cards is to have them give the price so that even he who runs may read, and at the same time indicate the kind of article and the quality as concisely as possible.

AN EFFECTIVE WINDOW DISPLAY.

A simple window for the smaller dealer can be arranged with one or two circular pillars of the powder, which may be made as follows: Cover two sound empty ten gallon cans with paper and place talcum packages all the way around, first a row around the bottom, then a second row on top of those, and so on. Around each row tie a piece of twine the color of the packages and going around the whole pillar. This holds the packages tight to the can. With the one or two pillars for a basis it is easy to make up the balance of the display to fit the window. A gross will make one pillar and leave plenty for the rest of a small window, but for a two-pillar display a gross and a half or two gross would be needed.

The window display should, of course, properly be timed to be concurrent with any mailed advertising of the goods, and newspaper ads should be run at the same time.

SAMPLING THE MOST PROFITABLE METHOD OF ADVERTISING.

As sampling is the most profitable form of advertising, a sample of the talcum sent out with a little folder telling about it will bring the best results of anything.

Samples of the powder can be put up in small envelopes properly labelled and so sealed as to keep in a maximum of the perfume. A dainty parchment paper envelope may be gotten up in a very effective manner.

The advertisement sent with the samples need not be elaborate or expensive, but it must be well printed, and ought to be done on very good paper. It should be so written as to attract a woman's attention and should give strong and cogent reasons why your talcum will do more toward adding to woman's attractiveness than other kinds.

The druggist should not let it appear that he is urging his own talcum so strongly that he does not keep or does not want to sell the other sorts. There are many people who are closely wedded to some one talcum and could not be induced to try any other. He who would keep their trade must make it evident that he can and will comply with their wishes and that he is as willing to sell any special talcum they may want as he is to sell his own.

DAINTY TALCUM, 19c.

19c. TALCUM. NONE BETTER

VIOLET TALCUM, 19c.

NO PRICE COULD BUY BETTER

VERRYBEST TALCUM, 19c.

In advertising his own brand the dealer should, therefore, make it a rule to mention regularly that all the standard brands are kept in stock at the lowest prices. This statement places the advertiser on a better footing with his public. It makes his statement that his is the best talcum sound stronger; it will be believed more often and he will not look so much as if he were simply trying to supplant the cut price kinds.

A CAMPAIGN OF INSTRUCTION

May be undertaken on the subject of talcums with advantage to the dealer. A folder that tells the public what it is that makes a talcum a good talcum, and what are the adulterants that go into cheap talcums, will add to the number of people who eschew the ten cent article. The circular should explain that the fineness of the powder, the absence of adulterant, the lack of contamination from container, the use of a perfume that is a good perfume and one that will not disappear as soon as the box is first opened, are all requisites of a good talcum powder. It is easy to tell the difference between the quantity of powder in a ten cent box and that in a nineteen cent container. But the public must be educated up to the point of discriminating as to quality. The mere statement that one sells a better talcum for nineteen cents than is to be had for fifteen is not necessarily convincing, especially when the people have been buying the fifteen cent kind right along and have found it eminently satisfactory. The reason why comes in at this juncture, and the advertiser must show the consumer wherein lies the difference between one grade and another. The people in general judge any article by what they can see for themselves. Not knowing of further factors, they look for nothing further. This condition should be the cue to much of the druggist's advertising, not only of talcum powder, but of his stock generally.

If folders are mailed with samples of the talcum enclosed in smaller envelopes, the envelopes containing the sample ought to be tough enough so that the post office cancelling stamp will not break them open. The powder must not sift out when the receiver opens the outer envelope or she will be prejudiced against the sender at the start.

Samples in abundance can be put up and inserted in parcels going out of the store. The envelope should bear the name of the talcum, the price and the store name, all plainly printed.

A package slip telling about this talcum will help to give it publicity and can be had with very trifling expense if the ad. that is run in the best newspaper is used, having the newspaper job office take it just as it is set up and print the slips from it without alteration, thus saving all cost of composition. If this further use of the ad. is borne in mind in writing it, it can be made entirely suitable for the purpose.

COUNTER DISPLAY EFFECTIVE.

At all times a dozen or more of the dealer's special talcum should be kept displayed in a prominent position upon the show case with a neat price card upon it. Talcum is one of the things that often sells on sight. If properly displayed it sells itself to a great many people who do not come into the store for the purpose of getting it, but who, when seeing it, remember their need for it. Then, too, if it is particularly attractive, it will create some demand for itself among people who are always ready to try any new kind of an article.

The advertising of talcum is, of course, like the advertising of anything else. It must be kept up if the best results are to be obtained.

SPORADIC ADVERTISING IS A POOR PROPOSITION.

When once a talcum has been introduced to the public it should be pushed continually. It is entitled to a good share of the advertising space in the hot weather because it responds readily to advertising and is a thing that will bring people in who may make other purchases.

Sometimes these little things that do not count up fast of themselves do more to help the business of a store than the articles which sell for large prices. The little things that are bought often bring the people in often. It pays to push them for that reason, as well as for their own profits, for it doesn't take many nineteen cent sales to make a dollar.

Edible Soils.

It has long been known, says *The Chemist and Druggist*, that many native races in Central Africa, the Eastern and Western Soudan, India, Bolivia, Peru, New Caledonia, and elsewhere are habitual eartheaters. Various views have been held as to the object with which earth is eaten by these races. Humboldt was of opinion that the Indians of the Orinoco districts ate earth to appease hunger, and a similar statement has recently been made in respect of the New Caledonian eartheaters. Other travelers have advanced the view that the earth serves as a mechanical aid to digestion and defæcation, while in the case of the natives inhabiting some parts of the Soudan the soil habitually eaten is impregnated with sodium salts, and probably serves to appease the natural craving for salt; salt, it may be mentioned, is scarce all over northern Africa. Balland has recently analyzed two samples of soil eaten by natives—one from the Gaboon district, and the other from New Caledonia. The first contains silica 95, alumina and ferric oxide 4.20, magnesia 0.28, and water 0.55 per cent. The second is composed of silica 97.9, magnesia 0.43, and water 0.80 per cent. The second sample differs markedly from a specimen of New Caledonian edible soil analyzed by Vauquelin in 1801, in which he found silica 36, magnesia 37, ferric oxide 17, lime and cupric oxide 2, and water 3 per cent.

Correspondence.

More About Menstruum.

To the Editor:

Sir—The complicated explanation of the origin of the word menstruum by Charles J. Carrington, of Brooklyn, in your issue for May 28, has excited my curiosity. I did not know that there could be any doubt as to the origin of the good and correct Latin word menstruus, a, um, meaning monthly or lasting a month and the noun menstruum, i, a neuter meaning provisions for one month. The noun menstruum can mean the menstruation, the monthly period; although it is more often named menses (plural) or menstruation. During the Middle Ages under menstruum was understood by the alchemists a third extradirum, a preparation for dissolving; there was also a menstruum universale, a universal medicine. When I shall have opportunity I will examine the preceding correspondence on the word in question in your esteemed journal. A. Rose.

126 East Twenty-ninth Street, New York, June 2, 1906.

A Druggist's Faulty Latin.

To the Editor:

Sir,—A country drug store keeper once reprimanded me for writing "*fiant pilulæ*" and produced his U. S. Dispensatory, in which, to my surprise, *fiat* = *make* was given. This happened over twenty-five years ago, but the same atrocity is to be found in recent books on materia medica.

Facio, feci, factum, facere (active), to make. Imperative: *fac* = make.

Fio, factus sum, fieri (passive) to be made; *fiat* is the conjunctive present singular, third person of this passive, and means that he, she or it may be made or become; *fiant* is conjunct. pres. plural third person and means that they may be made, that they may become. Let us see in which awkward position the *fiat* = make man will be when he recites the pater noster: *Fiat voluntas tua*. This would then be "make thy will," but, again, that would me impossible if *fiat* meant make; he would have to say *fiat voluntatem tuam*. Again, how would it sound if in the translation of the Genesis God said: *Fiat lux*, or in other words, acording to *fiat* = make, *fiat lucem*. To whom did he give this order "Make light"?

"A. Doctor."

Book Reviews.

Proceedings of the American Pharmaceutical Association at the fifty-third annual meeting, held at Atlantic City, N. J., September, 1905. Also the Constitution, By-laws and Roll of Members. Baltimore: Published by the American Pharmaceutical Association, 1905, Charles Caspari, jr., secretary. Pp. x—957.

This valuable compilation of original and selected articles fully maintains the high reputation of its predecessors. Membership in the American Pharmaceutical Association costs $5 a year, and if members derived no other benefit from membership than the bound volume of proceedings the investment would be a profitable one. But the advantages of social contact with fellow pharmacists throughout the country at the annual meetings cannot be overestimated. One may know the leaders of the craft through mention of their names in the pharmaceutical press and yet not get into the same touch with them as through contact at one of the annual gatherings. The interchange of ideas and experiences possible at these meetings is valuable, both as a means of keeping pace with progress in technics as well as trade relations, and when to this is added the annual volume of proceedings, replete as it is with information touching on every phase of pharmacy, from prescription compounding to apparatus and formulas, too much cannot be said in favor of the advantages of membership.

The present volume has not been so carefully proofread as preceding issues, as we find many printed names misspelled. Professor Diekman's name, for example, has the added "c" of the newspapers, the contraction of *Repertoire* is given as "Rip.," though the paper still lives, and animal is spelled with two "n's," only to mention a few of the numerous typographical errors noted in a cursory inspection of the volume.

THE AMERICAN MEDICAL ASSOCIATION.

The Fifty-Seventh Annual Meeting Carries Thousands to Boston—N. A. R. D. Delegates Recognized for the First Time—Pharmacists Active in the Section on Pharmacology and Therapeutics.

(*Editorial Correspondence.*)

Boston, June 7, 1906.—The Fifty-seventh annual meeting of the American Medical Association which is just drawing to a close in this city brought together the largest number of physicians ever assembled at one place in America, and probably in the world. The assemblage embraced many practitioners of distinction from abroad, as well as the majority of the leaders of the medical profession in the United States. The foreign visitors included Baron Takaki, surgeon general of the Imperial Japanese Navy; Prof. Frederick Trendelnburg, of Leipsig; Prof. Alfonse von Rosthorn, of Heidelberg; Prof. Alfred Duhrssen, of Berlin; Prof. Max von Frey, of Wurtzburg; Prof. Krehl, of Strassburg; Prof. Wesley A. Mills, of McGill University, and Dr. Richard A. Reeve, of Toronto, president of the British Medical Association.

The interests of pharmacy naturally centered in the attack on proprietary medicines which has been made by the association and in which the aid of the pharmacists has been invoked through the Council on Chemistry and Pharmacy, and through the Section on Pharmacology and Therapeutics, to which section the American Pharmaceutical Association sends delegates.

The matter of proprietary remedies was referred to frequently in the course of the proceedings of the House of Delegates, the governing body of the general association, and also came up in the Section on Pharmacology and Therapeutics.

The bitter feelings engendered by the aggressive attitude of the *Journal of the Association* found vent in the meetings of the House of Delegates, where at one time the air was full of protest. But as point after point of the criticisms offered was taken up and answered seriatim, the critics were silenced—if not convinced—and in the end resolutions were adopted fully endorsing the work of the administration. In one instance only—that of the severe criticisms of the action of Dr. Vaughan, of Ann Arbor, which had appeared in the *Journal of the Association* did the administration show any tendency to make concessions. In that case apologies were extended from both sides and the breach healed.

AS TO PROPRIETARY REMEDIES.

In regard to the question of proprietary remedies the House of Delegates adopted the resolutions, fully endorsing the work of the Council on Chemistry and Pharmacy.

PACKING HOUSE METHODS CONDEMNED—THE PURE FOOD BILL COMMENDED.

In the House of Delegates the packing house disclosures were referred to in connection with the Pure Food bill in the following preamble and resolutions, which were adopted without opposition:

Whereas, The revolting methods recently revealed by both private and Governmental inquiry to exist in connection with the selection and preparation of meat for the American and foreign markets are a serious menace to the public health; and

Whereas, The impurities demonstrated by Government experts and by the Bureau of Chemistry and Pharmacy of the American Medical Association to exist in numerous other food products, in nostrums purveyed to the public and in remedies prescribed for the sick ,comprise even more serious menaces to the public welfare; therefore, be it

Resolved, That the American Medical Association, with an affiliated membership of more than 60,000 physicians, and representing the organized medical profession in 2,400 of the 2,830 counties of the United States, views with satisfaction the efforts of the Administration and of Congress to protect the American public against adulterated foods and impure drugs, and to purge our commerce, domestic and foreign, of fraudulent products:

Resolved, That the House of Representatives be and is hereby earnestly petitioned to place the pending pure food and drug bill on its passage during the present week.

The special interests of pharmacists centered in the

SECTION ON PHARMACOLOGY AND THERAPEUTICS.

The first meeting of the section was called to order in the lecture room of Tufts Medical College by the chair, Dr. Thomas F. Reilly, of New York, on Tuesday afternoon, June 5. The secretary, Dr. C. S. N. Hallberg, read a latter from the President of the American Pharmaceutical Association, naming the following delegates: Henry P. Hynson, Baltimore; Thomas P. Cook, New York; C. S. N. Hallberg, Chicago; John F. Hancock, Baltimore; Chas. F. Nixon, Boston; Elie H. La Pierre, Boston, and S. P. Sadtler, Philadelphia. The delegates were extended the courtesy of the floor.

Henry P. Hynson, of Baltimore, speaking as chairman of the delegation from the American Pharmaceutical Association, called attention to the vast field of usefulness in co-operation between the physician and pharmacist and instanced the results of the joint meetings of the Chicago Branch of the American Pharmaceutical Association with the physicians of that city, at which the following propositions were set forth:

1st. "That an effort should be made to clearly define the limitations and respective functions of the practice of medicine and the practice of pharmacy; differentiating as to the rights and privileges to be accorded each, with special reference to dispensing by physicians and prescribing by pharmacists"—

2nd. "That the popular demand for medicines should be met with preparations of the United States Pharmacopœia and National Formulary in preference to proprietary medicines"—

3rd. "That the physician and pharmacist should have joint control of the prescription and that, when the prescriber orders the prescription not to be refilled, such instructions should be observed by the pharmacist"—

4th. "That physicians should discriminate, as far as possible, in favor of reputable pharmacists and against drug stores which make use of cut rate methods for imposing on the public."

Mr. Hynson reviewed the history of the agitation against abuses in medicine and pharmacy, quoting liberally from the proceedings of the American Pharmaceutical Association to show that that organization had always been active in its efforts to improve the status of pharmacy and to place on a higher plane the relations between the pharmacists and the physicians.

The chairman of the section announced that, in accordance with custom, he would appoint the executive committee of the section to act as a committee on nominations, the committee named being composed of Dr. S. S. Cohen, of Philadelphia, Dr. O. T. Osborne, of New Haven, and Dr. Heinrich Stern, of New York.

A REVIEW OF RECENT THERAPEUTICS.

Dr. O. T. Osborne, of New Haven, taking the chair, Dr. Reilly, the chairman of the section, presented his address, which comprised a succinct review of the therapeutic advances and tendencies developed during the past year. He said that very few new remedies had been launched during the past year, the flood of synthetics which has deluged medicine during the past decade having had a slight recession. Ethylchloride anæsthesia has grown in popularity during the year. Scopolamine—morphine anæsthesia—from which so much had been expected, had fallen flat. Hypodermic injection of soluble mercury for the treatment of syphilis had come to be accepted as a routine treatment, and was rapidly growing in popularity. Therapeutic nihilism in the treatment of pneumonia still prevailed. The tendency toward the utilization of substance of animal origin still continued.

A warning was sounded by Dr. Reilly against indiscriminate use of the suprarenal glands. The field of usefulness for the x-ray was becoming more limited and more clearly defined. Antitoxin was being administered in larger doses.

Dr. Reilly urged that the curative action of indigenous drugs be studied, as he believed that double the result could be obtained for one half the effort expended on the production of new synthetic products.

He said that medical men were paying more attention to the Pharmacopœia than ever before, and suggested that the association should take a more active interest in its revision than it has heretofore.

Dr. Reilly said that there was a legitimate field for some proprietary remedies, and that some will stay, but that others must and will go. The address was referred for consideration to a committee composed of Dr. Heinrich Stern, of New York, Dr. H. C. Wood, Jr., of Philadelphia, and Dr. Reilly himself.

The secretary, Dr. Hallberg, of Chicago, made a brief oral report pending the arrival of his report, which had been left in Chicago.

SCIENTIFIC PAPERS.

Dr. O. T. Osborne, of New Haven, read a paper on the Therapeutics of Thyroid Preparations, and Dr. Robert A. Hatcher, of New York, followed with a Study of the Pharmacology of Digitalis. Both papers were discussed at some length, as was also a paper on the Pharmacolgy of Veratrum, by H. C. Wood, Jr., of Philadelphia, when the section adjourned to meet on Wednesday morning.

The morning of the second day's session of the Section on Pharmacology and Therapeutics was devoted to papers which had no pharmaceutical interest. The afternoon's proceedings were opened by a paper by William F. Waugh, of Chicago, on solanine, in which he took occasion to commend the use of this drug in the treatment of epilepsy of all kinds. In discussing this paper Dr. Thresh, of Philadelphia, stated that he had his attention first called to solanine in a purely empirical manner, having observed that the negroes of West Virginia secured very favorable results in the treatment of epileptic convulsions by the administration of the alcoholic infusion of a certain plant which, upon investigation, turned out to be solanum carolinense. Dr. Max Einhorn, of New York, read a paper on the dietetic treatment of diabetes mellitus.

Martin I. Wilbert, of Philadelphia, presented a paper on the Revision of the United States Pharmacopœia, in which he made a plea for the more active co-operation of the medical profession in the work of revision. He reviewed briefly the history of pharmacopœial revision, showing how the interest of the medical profession in the work of revision had gradually died out, and how as the interest of physicians had abated, the number of preparations included in the work had increased, until now something like 1,000 articles were listed. He urged that steps be taken by the Section to ensure a more active co-operation of the medical profession in the work of revision.

In discussing the paper of Mr. Wilbert, Dr. Oliver T. Osborne, of New Haven, said that while the Pharmacopœia might be all that could be desired from a purely scientific standpoint it was certainly a flat failure from the standpoint of the medical teacher. He believed that the criticism of Mr. Wilbert as to the undue expansion of the pharmacopœial list was well grounded, and moved that a committee be appointed to study the whole situation and to propose some means of remedying the evils set forth by Mr. Wilbert, a suggestion which was approved by the Section, the chairman appointing Dr. Osborne, Dr. W. J. Robinson, and Dr. H. E. Lewis, of New York, as such a committee.

Dr. Reid Hunt, of the United States Public Health and Marine Hospital Service, pointed out that in this discussion the members of the Section had overlooked one of the important functions of the Pharmacopœia, namely, its use as a legal standard. It would be impossible to materially decrease the volume of matter in the Pharmacopœia without seriously affecting its value in this direction, a fact which physicians should by no means overlook, as there was a constantly growing tendency to depend more and more upon the Pharmacopœia for the determination of legal points.

Prof. C. Lewis Diehl, of Louisville, presented a paper on the attitude of the National Formulary to pharmaceutical proprietaries, a subject upon which he was eminently fitted to discuss, since his work as editor of the Formulary entitled him to speak with authority. He said that the committee were not inclined to question proprietary rights based upon real discoveries, or to do anything which might tend to diminish the value of such rights, but that where claims of proprietorship were set up as to medicines or preparations which were already well known, the committee did not feel bound to accept any such claims as valid, and for that reason felt at liberty to make and publish formulas regardless of any such proprietary claims.

He referred to a class of preparations which seemed to have, in fact, been called into being by the inroads made by the National Formulary on their successful exploitation, saying: "Leaving out of consideration the modern synthetics, which are a host in themselves, and which are taken care of by the Council on Pharmacy and Chemistry of the American Medical Association, there is a large number of preparations, exploited under brief, fanciful titles, which consist of simple drugs or chemicals, such as are on the shelves of every pharmacy and uniformly obtainable in a condition of acceptable purity in the form of pills, capsules, tablets or powder; others that are simply solutions of one or more salts, for which exceptional purity is claimed, and all of these are claimed to be products resulting from the application of prolonged investigation, diligent study or unusual facilities and skill. Then, again, under similarly coined titles, the attention of physicians is invited to pharmaceutical compounds of a more intricate nature, compounded from drugs of 'rare quality' or representing the 'essential principles' of this, that and the other drug—quantities (if given) pertaining to the drug, but not to the 'essential principle' involved—the development of which have required years of study or which are the outcome of vast experience, not to speak of occult divination, and so on, *ad nauseam*. All these claims are, of course, subservient to the pharmacological import of the article exploited, which is rarely 'just as good,' but always superior, in one direction or the other, to other medicaments that have stood the test of time in similar cases, the literature accompanying these trade-named pharmaceutical proprietaries teeming with fulsome and extravagant claims, so preposterous as to leave it doubtful what is the more amazing, the unparalleled effrontery of the exploiter or his confidence in the gullibility of the physician.

"It would be passing strange if among the many trade-named 'pharmaceutical proprietaries' there were not some of intrinsic value as remedial agents, and certainly there are others which, whatever may be the estimate of their worth, are presented with sufficient frequency to call for representation in the National Formulary in a form in which such products may be intelligently tested. While, therefore, the first edition of the Formulary was comparatively free from formulas representing trade-named preparations, a number of such have been admitted into the revised editions that have since been made, without, however, referring in any way to the trade-named title. In this respect the compilers of the work have the precept of the revisers of the Pharmacopœia, who, in the recent edition (U. S. P., VIII, 1900), have included formulas for a number of preparations which have been heretofore, and still are being, exploited under fanciful names. Indeed, some of these have been appropriated either from the text of the National Formulary or from the text of the reports in which they were proposed for admission into that work. The Committee on National Formulary has been criticised in some quarters, probably by interested parties, for having constructed and included formulas for certain trade-named preparations. On the grounds indicated this committee will doubtless not be discouraged from so appropriating or constructing formulas for any preparation so long as the formula is not vested in private ownership by right of patent, if the frequency of its use shall justify such action."

Dr. C. S. N. Hallberg, of Chicago, presented his report as Secretary of the Section, in which he referred to the "muck-rakers" of medicine, who had rendered most valuable service by their exposure of the evils involved in the indiscriminate use and sale of proprietary medicines. He said, however, that this was a subject of so delicate a character, involving so much special knowledge, that the lay publications which had engaged in this "debut der siecle reform" had overstepped the bounds of their usefulness and posed as sponsors for "formula" legislation which was harmful, as it produced a false and misleading sense of security. Dr. Hallberg said that "the formula on the label requirement is a delusion and a snare." He recommended the establishment of a National Department of Health as the only means for relief from the dangers surrounding the public in the matter of medication.

This recommendation was referred to the same committee to which the recommendations of Mr. Wilbert had been referred, to be reported on at the next annual convention.

L. F. Kebler, Chief of the Drug Laboratory of the Bureau of Chemistry of the Department of Agriculture, exhibited a number of nostrums which had been denied the use of the mails as a result of examinations made for the Post Office Department by the Drug Laboratory. He also referred the members to the exhibit of the Laboratory as shown in the buildings of the new Harvard Medical School, stating that the exhibits embrace some preparations of so disgusting a character that he hesitated to refer to them more specifically even before an audience composed of medical men.

THE LIMITS OF PROPRIETORSHIP IN MEDICINE.

Dr. Solomon Solis Cohen, of Philadelphia, then spoke at some length on the limit of proprietorship in materia medica. He entered a strong protest against proprietary rights based upon the "trademark" word, using phenacetin as an instance. He said that there was no objection whatever to exclusive proprietary rights based upon patents under existing laws, but that an effort to perpetuate those rights by the use of a copyrighted designation such as phenacetin was essentially wrong in principle, and that if the law permitted it, the law should be changed.

He said that the right to exclusive ownership was not an inherent right, but one based upon the permission of society. Not a great while ago it was considered eminently proper to recognize proprietary rights in human beings. Certain cranks, agitators and abolitionists took the matter up and as a consequence this right is no longer recognized. We still recognize individual rights, proprietary rights in land, but already there is a considerable body of reformers, cranks and single taxers who deny the right of the individual to exclusive ownership of land. So in medicine the time may come when any exclusive ownership will be denied, though that time has not yet arrived. Dr. Cohen believed, however, the time had arrived when the perpetual exclusive ownership through word trademarks should no longer be accorded. Individual rights of manufacturers should be amply protected, he said, by the legitimate trademark use of the manufacturer's name applied to the article, as phenacetine Bayer, or Squibb's ether. He insisted, however, that where a new article is brought into the world it needs a name; the name given to it by its producer and by which it is known generally in medical literature is practically the only name it has, even though it might have some systematic title, from a chemical standpoint.

He said that when the manufacturer made a mixture and honestly told the actual ingredients, only reserving information regarding the diluents and inactive adjuvants, he had no criticism to offer to that particular form and extent of secrecy, but unfortunately the temptation was very strong on the part of the manufacture to add some such corrective, as a small quantity of cocaine, omitting to mention this fact on the label. Such an omission constituted an essential fraud, and he felt that such evasion should not be too severely condemned.

As a matter of fact, the claims that the only secret rested in the flavor and water were rarely true, for there is very little money in merely water and flavor.

Dr. William J. Robinson, of New York, arose to set forth his claims to the credit for having inaugurated the present era of reform as regards patent medicines, and took occasion to criticise the advertisements of Labordine, taken from a recent issue of *American Medicine*, in which, after warning the readers of the dangers of coal tar derivatives in general, and acetanilid in particular, the advertiser went on to state that Labordine itself contained 15 per cent. of acetanilid, but disguising the systematic name by an inversion of the syllables.

He also criticised the *Journal of the Association* as still containing two or three preparations which should not be admitted to its columns. He particularly criticised the appearance of the advertisement of Buffalo Lithia Water, saying that the committee of which he was a member, in formulating a rule under which the advertising of mineral waters was permitted, had in mind only such advertisement as the ordinary table waters used, and not advertising to the public as is done by the Buffalo Lithia Water, in which advertising the most extravagant claims are made for its curative action in dangerous diseases.

M. I. Wilbert, of Philadelphia, said that he thought it was much more important to turn the attention of the Section to the future than it was to endeavor to set up claims for originating the movement now in progress, and he directed the attention of Dr. Robinson to the fact that as long ago as 1817, the President of the New York State Medical Society had taken up this question of the nostrum evil, and that two years later, in 1819, the New York County Medical Society had issued a pamphlet on the subject. He refered to other instances in which this evil had been condemned publicly by various pharmaceutical and medical organizations.

Dr. Robinson replied with some heat that the subject was even older than Mr. Wilbert intimated, as some 2,000 or more years ago it had been dealt with in Egypt, but that his claim referred only to the present movement, which he was firmly convinced had originated with his paper presented at New Orleans.

Dr. H. E. Lewis, of New York, said that he deprecated a certain over-critical and even dictatorial attitude on this matter on the part of pharmacists, and he even feared that the council on pharmacy and chemistry were too exclusively pharmaceutical. To be effective, he was convinced, this campaign must be educative and not coercive. The mere fact of proprietorship was of itself not offensive, he thought. The essential element was the honesty of the claims of the proprietor.

In closing the discussion Mr. Kebler said that Dr. Cohen had intimated that the physician had no interest in the low class of frauds which had been treated of by him, but he wished to point out the fact that the fraudulent dealers did not make their own preparations, but had them made by the eminently respectable manufacturers.

Dr. Cohen said that he was glad that Mr. Kebler had brought out this fact, for he felt it was incumbent upon the medical profession and the pharmacists as well to impress upon these manufacturers the fact that it was impossible for them to be dishonest on one side and honest on the other.

He said that honesty was, after all, the final test. He hoped that there would be a close affiliation, not only between the individual pharmacist and the physician, but between the honest manufacturer and the physician, for he realized the debt which medicine owed even to commercial exploitation. In 1858 Sir Benjamin Ward Richardson published practically everything that we now know about the therapeutics of hydrogen dioxide, but this drug never came into general use until it was exploited commercially in 1880, and even then physicians did not recall the careful work done by Richardson, and it was not until many a bladder and an ear drum had been bust before its use was understood. "For bust," said he, "is the only word that expressed what happened when the ignorant physician filled the bladder with hydrogen peroxide in the presence of pus."

Appreciating, therefore, the debt of medicine to exploitation, he was not averse to giving the commercial manufacturer his just due.

This discussion closed the proceedings of the Section for Wednesday.

The first paper presented at the opening of the Section on Pharmacology and Therapeutics on Thursday morning was a rather lengthy one on Palatable Medication, by H. B. Sheffield, of New York. This was followed by a clear and concise summary of the Chemistry of the Organic Silver Compounds, by W. A. Puckner, of Chicago. The other papers presented at the morning session were of no particular pharmaceutical interest.

At the afternoon session on Thursday the Committee on Resolutions, to which various matters had been referred for consideration, submitted the following report, which was adopted without discussion:

1. The Section of Pharmacology and Therapeutics of the American Medical Association welcomes every endeavor to advance the status of pharmacy as a learned profession, and expresses its full sympathy with the efforts of the American Pharmaceutical Association in this direction. The pharmacist, whether he be a dispenser or a manufacturer, must work hand in hand with the physician to consummate the results so urgently desired by both. We recognise that physicians as prescribers must rely upon the fidelity of the pharmacist and of the pharmaceutical manufacturer. Therefore it is highly desirable that more cordial relations and more thorough understanding should be fos-

tered between both professions in order that the limits of legitimate pharmaceutical manufacturing may be more clearly defined.

We believe in regard to pharmaceutical preparations that secrecy concerning any substance possessing the slightest physiologic activity is improper and intolerable. The doctor has a right, and it is his duty, to insist upon the most complete and exact information obtainable concerning the active agents which exist in any preparation he uses.

We deprecate fanciful and inaccurate trade names and titles, and recommend a more rational and scientific nomenclature in the naming of pharmaceutical preparations and products. We believe that by a system of process patenting a closer approach to ideal conditions can be reached and that it would obviate many of the present features of the pharmaceutical industry to which just objection has been taken. Such tangible protection as is necessary can be given in most instances by the addition of the manufacturer's name to the proper and intelligible title of the pharmaceutical product, thus insuring a recognized grade of accuracy and quality.

2. The Section believes that the Council of Pharmacy and Chemistry can do much to bring about this desirable state of affairs; and, to the end that its work may be broadened and the results become of as great benefit as possible to the medical profession whose interests it must primarily serve, the Section earnestly recommends that a larger representation be given to clinical therapeutics by the election annually from the working membership of this Section of two members of the Council to serve for one year.

3. The Section is heartily in favor of and strongly urges the establishment of a National Department of Health, with representation in the Cabinet.

4. The Section learns with regret that certain manufacturing pharmacists have practically placed the facilities of their plants at the disposal of venders of some of the worst and vilest nostrums by which the people of the United States have been defrauded. It is obvious that such practices cannot be too severely condemned, especially if the patronage and confidence of the medical profession is to be retained.

5. The Section strongly condemns the revolting evils which have been shown to exist in regard to foods and food supplies, especially the meat packing industry. In the fundamental interests of the people such evils must be controlled by appropriate and adequate legislation, which we strongly urge as a paramount duty of our National Congress.

In connection with the question we wish to emphasize the fact that antiseptics and preservatives cannot mitigate in any degree the dangers from decayed or decaying meat. Antiseptics may destroy putrefactive organisms, but they cannot neutralize toxines or ptomaines. Any contention to the contrary is unsound, and meat that requires such treatment is totally unfit for food, inasmuch as it still contains poisons of virulent and dangerous character.

6. The Section notes with regret, in examining the commercial exhibit, that the degree of selection which the members of the association have a right to expect and demand has not been exercised. As a prevention of further abuse in this directin, at future meetings we would recommend that all pharmaceuticals be indiscriminately excluded from the commercial exhibit, or that provisions be made for a committee on exhibit from this Section, which committee shall be empowered to exercise full supervision in the matter and co-operate with the local committee.

H. EDWIN LEWIS, New York.
S. SOLIS-COHEN, Philadelphia.
HEINRICH STERN, New York.
Committee.

Dr. Heinrich Stern, of New York, representative of the Section in the House of Delegates, said that he had come to the meeting inclined to assume a critical attitude toward the administration, but that what he had learned of the work of the general secretary in the reports submitted to the House of Delegates had convinced him that he was a master of detail, and he proposed the passage of resolutions of thanks to Dr. Simmons by the Section, which proposal was agreed to.

OFFICERS ELECTED.

The following officers were elected by the Section to act for the ensuing year: Chairman, Dr. H. C. Wood, Jr., of Philadelphia; vice-chairman, Dr. Henry R. Slack, of Atlanta; secretary, Dr. C. S. N. Hallberg, of Chicago; representative in the House of Delegates, Dr. Solomon Solis-Cohen, of Philadelphia.

Dr. C. S. N. Hallberg, of Chicago, presented an oral abstract of a paper on the External Preparations of the United States Pharmacopœia. He explained that as chairman of the subcommittee on this particular portion of the Pharmacopœial revision he had first gotten into touch with the leading dermatologists, both of Europe and America, and consulted them as to the objects which they desired to accomplish. The subcommittee had then undertaken an attempt to accomplish these objects. He referred to the several classes of preparations, giving a general outline of the processes used in preparing them. The plasters, he said, were made of a base composed of equal parts of rubber and petrolatum, this making a plaster which penetrated into but not through the skin, differing vastly in its effects from those rubber plasters which are made simply by the mechanical admixture of rubber with various gums and gum resins and for which he expressed the most severe condemnation.

The suppositories of the Pharmacopœia are made with cacao butter as a base where they are to be used for rectal administration; where they are to be used for urethral or vaginal administration a glycero-gelatin base is substituted, owing to the acidity of the secretions met with. Since only a small quantity of oilic acid is required to make the oleates of the alkaloid, the oleates are first made and then diluted with an equal quantity of olive oil, with the exception of the oleate of quinine, which is not so diluted.

In the selection of a base for ointments a careful study of the relative absorbability of the various ointment bases led finally to the adoption of a mixture of lanolin and petrolatum, as presenting a base which was of about the same degree of absorbability as lard, but had the great advantage of stability. This was shown by the stability of the various mercurial ointments, which when made according to previous Pharmacopœia were speedily decomposed. The only exception made to the use of this base was in the preparation of the ointment of nitrate of mercury, in which, in deference to the conservatism of some of the Eastern members who still clung to the belief in the increased efficacy of the ointment due to the presence of elaidin, lard was retained in this particular preparation.

He explained that the forthcoming National Formulary contained several general formulas which would be found useful.

Dr. Wm. J. Robinson, of New York, at the conclusion of this paper and its discussion, asked, "Where are the fakirs? It was generally reported that they were going to be on hand at this meeting and would do up Dr. Hallberg, swab up Simmons and lay me out, but they seem not to have materialized at all."

THE TREATMENT OF INOPERABLE CANCER.

Abraham Jacobi, of New York, made a brief verbal report on the treatment of inoperable cancer by the internal administration of methyl thimion hydrochloride or methylene. He gives it in doses of from 2 up to 6 grains daily, adding ¾ of a grain of belladonna extract to the daily dose. He sometimes found it advisable to add from 1-40th to 1-20th of a grain of arsenic trioxide, and sometimes combined with this an equal quantity of strychnine. This was given usually divided into four doses, one before each meal and one at bed-time. He said that while he had been pursuing this course of treatment, for a period of some 14 years, he had never published anything on it for fear that the results might prove disappointing. He had himself not effected any cures with it, but through this means he had frequently prolonged the life of patients for several years, and he thought that it should be adopted as a routine treatment, not only in inoperable cancers, but after operations in which there was great probability of the recurrence of the cancer, such, for instance, as cancer of the breast and of the uterus. He further said that quite recently he had had his attention drawn to the possible influence of fluorescence as a curative factor in the use of this drug, and since that time had been exposing the patients to sunlight, but was unable to make any report as to results of this particular modification of the treatment. He cautioned his hearers as to the appearance of the color in the urine and said the patient should always be informed of this lest they should be unduly alarmed.

Dr. William James Morton, of New York, made some remarks on the subject of the therapeutics of fluorescent material, apropos of the reference to fluorescence by Dr. Jacobi.

The session closed with a series of papers on the therapeutic uses of the Roentgen Rays, all the authors taking occasion to caution the profession as to the need for accurate knowledge of the technique in doses. This closed the work of the Section.

THE GENERAL OFFICERS OF THE ASSOCIATION.

Atlantic City was selected as the next place of meeting of the association, and the following general officers of the association were elected by the House of Delegates:

President, Dr. Joseph D. Bryant, New York.

Vice-presidents, Dr. Herbert L. Burrell, Boston; Dr. Andrew C. Smith, Portland, Ore.; Dr. E. S. Fairchild, Des Moines, Ia.; Dr. W. S. Foster, Pittsburgh, Pa.

Treasurer, Dr. Frank Billings, Chicago, Ill.

Secretary, Dr. George H. Simmons, Chicago, Ill.

Resident trustee, Dr. M. L. Harris, Chicago, Ill.

Trustees, Dr. W. H. Welch, Baltimore, Md.; Dr. Miles M. Porter, Fort Wayne, Ind.

The meeting place for the next annual session is Atlantic City, N. J.

ANNUAL MEETING OF THE NEW JERSEY PHARMACEUTICAL ASSOCIATION.

Topics Discussed by the Pharmacists of New Jersey at the Thirty-Sixth Annual Meeting—To Urge An Antinarcotic Law—Beal Model Law Favored—Proposal to Control the Sale of Proprietary Medicines—Other New Legislation Proposed.

(*Special Correspondence.*)

Atlantic City, June 8.—The instructions to the Legislative Committee to have a law framed regulating the sale of habit-forming drugs and present it to the next session of the State Legislature was the most important matter accomplished at the thirty-sixth annual meeting of the New Jersey Pharmaceutical Association, held at the Hotel Chelsea, Atlantic City, on Wednesday, Thursday and Friday, June 6, 7 and 8.

Several hundred delegates, together with their wives and families, arrived in Atlantic City on Wednesday and tendered President William M. Davis, of East Orange, a reception in the parlors of the headquarters hotel in the evening. On the following morning the assembly gathered in the auditorium at 10 o'clock for the first business session.

The meeting was opened with an invocation by the Rev. Edward E. Tyson, of Atlantic City. This was followed by an entertaining address of welcome by Mayor Franklin P. Stoy. President Davis then read his annual address. In part he said:

"Many things of interest to our profession have happened since our last meeting. The new Pharmacopœia has been issued and has caused a deal of discussion. The N. A. R. D., in which we are all interested, has been busy working for the betterment of the trade. Like all great movements instituted for the improvement of man's condition it has been obliged to fight for justice and fair play. Bills have been introduced in our State Legislature which, if they had become laws, would have crippled the business not a little.

"Pure food bills are now before Congress that are of vital importance to the pharmacist. The Denatured Alcohol Bill has passed both houses of Congress, despite the fact that we were told that corporation interests would defeat it.

"There have been several hearings on the Mann bill. It will not be the fault of the association if the bill does not become a law, as it has been ably advocated by some of our brightest and most earnest representatives.

"The Pure Food Bill, now being considered by the House Committee on Interstate and Foreign Commerce, has provisions affecting pharmacy, one of which, as an example, would punish for misbranding, if it be an imitation of or offered for sale under the name of another article. This provision might involve serious complications."

During the course of his address President Davis recommended the appointment of a Publicity Committee, the duties of which should be to correctly inform the pharmaceutical press regarding matters of interest to the trade and happenings therein. He also recommended the forming of a Committee of Necrology, composed of one delegate from the north, one from the south, and one from the middle of the State, the duties of which should be to record the deaths during the year and have notices of such properly appear in the report of the proceedings.

Secretary Frank C. Stutzlen's report for the year showed that the large increase in the membership of the association had necessitated an increase in the number of copies of proceedings. There had been an issue of 672 copies. The membership was averaged in the report as follows: Total net membership last year, 458; joined at 1905 meeting, 155; loss by dropping out and by death, 42; balance, net active members 1905, 571, associate members, 45; honorary members, 12; grand total, 628, being an increase of 158 over the last report.

Treasurer James C. Field, of Somerville, stated in his report that up to June 7, 1906, the receipts of the association were $3,196.72, the balance on hand $1,551.81, and the balance in the Monmouth Trust Company $947.70.

The report submitted by Treasurer G. W. Parisen, of the Board of Pharmacy, showed that the receipts of the secretary and fines during the past year had been $3,738.90; expenditures, $3,433.43; by check to State Treasurer, $305.47.

After the reports of the various committees delegates were received and reported from the Pennsylvania, Maryland, Kings County and Essex County associations. Dr. Fred. P. Tuthill and Charles Heimerzheim, who represented the Kings County Pharmaceutical Society, both expressed the hope that pharmacy would be generally uplifted by organized effort and reported that students now applying for membership to colleges in New York are of higher quality than ever before. The delegate from the Maryland Association said that there was need of reform in the pharmaceutical profession all through, and that a more practicable pharmacy law would only be obtained through a recognition of the commercial status of the trade and a steering clear of the radical view.

The secretary of the Board of Pharmacy reported that several violations of the pharmacy laws had been noted during the year, mostly arising from the neglect of employees to register and be properly licensed. "During the year ahead," he concluded, "we will make a systematic canvass of the State and try to see that the laws are enforced."

Charles Holzhauer, of Newark, objected to the report on the grounds that it suggested no reform for present violations. "Very few assistants are registered," he said, "and pharmacists are experiencing much difficulty in getting clerks. It is my idea that no man should be allowed to apply for registration as pharmacist until he has served for a certain length of time as an assistant. And another thing, I think the danger of suicide would be reduced if carbolic acid and other poisons were sold in a diluted form—say one-quarter the original strength."

But Mr. Holzhauer's objections were overruled on the ground that they had to do more with the Legislative Committee, the report of which was to immediately follow.

Henry A. Jorden, of Bridgeton, read the report of the Legislative Committee, the feature of which was the following: "We suggest that this committee be empowered to draft a bill to be presented to the Legislature concerning the sale of habit-forming drugs, or medicines, that will protect the pharmacist and also the general public; also to include in such bill to regulate the manufacture and to govern the inspection and analysis of certain 'patent' or 'proprietary' medicines, not to amend our present pharmacy law, but a separate and distinct law, and we would suggest that the president enlarge the Legislative Committee for this purpose and work."

It was moved to adopt this suggestion immediately, but after much heated discussion pro and con a motion prevailed to lay it over until the afternoon session.

As the "Beal law" was considered a good model for the intents and purposes of the Legislative Committee in carrying out the proposed legislation the motion was finally amended to read as follows: "That the 'Beal law' be referred to the Legislative Committee as a model for framing a new bill, to be presented to the Legislature, governing narcotics."

For a time it seemed that even this would not meet the favor of the association, but an able address by George M. Beringer, of Camden, father of the motion, changed the sentiment and resulted in its passage unanimously.

Chairman Beringer, in reply to the query, What Should be the Proper Attitude of the State Pharmaceutical Association toward Legislation destined to control the sale of proprietary medicines? said in part:

"The public mind is aroused against the sale of proprietary medicines and aware of the false claims and deception practiced by the patent medicine men. The gravity of the evil is realized by this association and the pharmacist will continue to agitate the matter until some remedial action is found.

"This association should not make war against patent medicines in the same spirit as the *Ladies' Home Journal*, *Colliers'* and numerous other magazines of the day, but rather from a standpoint of ethics. We should continue to make an effort against the unrestricted sale of patent medicines and favor bills looking to reform in this matter.

"All proprietary medicines containing poisonous ingredients should be labeled with a complete formula, so as to give the druggist an idea of the antidote that should be applied in case of necessity. Or the formulas should be placed in the hands of a National Board of Health, which could make frequent investigations to see that the medicine was always manufactured in conformity to the original formula.

"The public is demanding reform in the matter of patent medicine sales and it is incumbent upon this association to take a hand in the reforming."

Charles Holzhauer, delegate to the N. A. R. D. in Boston, suggested affiliation with the N. A. R. D., and when the meeting adjourned it looked as if a resolution to this effect would be introduced during the concluding session.

An interesting paper in reply to the query, Why does the U. S. P. VIII, direct alcohol as a menstruum for making oleoresin of Cubebs and Acetone for ether Oleoresons? was read by Professor Charles H. Lawall, of Philadelphia. He said in part:

"The change from ether to acetone as the official menstruum for the class of oleoresins was a distinct advance in pharmacy, as exemplified by the eighth decennial revision of the U. S. P., but the fact that the change did not apply to oleoresin of cubeb, which is to be prepared by percolation with alcohol, has led to the query to which I am listed to answer."

After several described experiments Professor Lawall concluded as follows:

"The conclusions to be drawn from the above experiments are confirmatory of the wisdom of the Revision Committee in selecting alcohol as a menstruum for oleoresin of cubeb, for it yields a finer preparation than is possible with acetone, the solvent which is used in all the other official oleoresins, or ether, which had been used as the official solvent for this preparation during the two previous revisions."

No less important than the business transacted at the sessions was the lengthy and enjoyable pleasure program arranged through the local committee, including Dr. D. M. H. Deemer, Dr. A. D. Cuskaden, Dr. H. H. Deakyne, and Dr. William F. Ridgeway.

This program included a progressive euchre, at which six prizes were awarded; a matinee rolling chair parade the entire length of the famous Atlantic City Boardwalk, an evening ball at the Hotel Chelsea, a special trolley excursion to the Inoet Wharf, followed by a beautiful sailing trip ten miles to sea and return, and a brilliant smoker given by the Traveling Men's Auxiliary during the last night of the convention. This latter event was a most enjoyable one, most of the delegates agreeing that it far surpassed the "Night in Bohemia," given during the convention here in 1905.

THE OKLAHOMA ASSOCIATION MEETING.

The Oklahoma Pharmaceutical Association held a successful three days' convention at Guthrie, May 8, 9 and 10. A representative of the Governor of the Territory made a welcoming speech, and he was followed by the Mayor of Guthrie. Robert Scott, of Oklahoma, and H. D. Kneisley, of Cheotah, I. T., responded for the association. Several interesting papers were read and the meeting was addressed by Professors Sayre and Whelpley. The list of papers included the following titles: Pioneer Pharmacy in Oklahoma, by C. B. Haley, Oklahoma City; The Druggist in Politics, by W. T. Barrett, Carmen; The Experience of a Druggist, Compared with That of a Traveling Salesman, by A. C. Fitschen, Hobart; How I Started the First Drug Store in Oklahoma, by C. P. Wickmiller, Kingfisher; Early Day Reminiscences of a Druggist in Guthrie and Chandler, by A. M. McElhaney, Chandler; The Druggist as a Game Catcher, by Eugene Watrous, Enid; My Experience Abroad, by John A. Bilan, Lexington, and Dispensing Physicians, by Dr. A. L. Blesh, Guthrie.

The social features of the meeting were unusually attractive, there being ball games, foot races, nail driving and target shooting contests, etc.

The following officers were elected: President, Robert Scott, Oklahoma City; first vice-president, C. A. Frasier, Red Rock; second vice-president, H. O. Hixon, Elk City; secretary and treasurer, F. M. Weaver, Oklahoma City.

BENJAMIN FRANKLIN DISCUSSED AT THE PHILADELPHIA COLLEGE OF PHARMACY.

Franklin a Dealer in Drugs as Well as a Philosopher and a Statesman—The First Medical Publisher in America.

Philadelphia, June 6.—The regular monthly pharmaceutical meeting of the Philadelphia College of Pharmacy was held last month, with J. C. Peacock in the chair.

M. I. Wilbert, Ph.M., apothecary at the German Hospital, Philadelphia, read a paper on Benjamin Franklin and His Influence on Medicine and Pharmacy in America. Mr. Wilbert said that "while the political, philosophical, literary, mechanical and philanthropic achievements of Benjamin Franklin have been generally recognized, it does not appear to be so commonly known that this same Benjamin Franklin probably had a more direct and a more lasting influence on the progress of the science of medicine in these United States than any one other individual; certainly more than any other one layman." Franklin not only assisted in the formation of the University of Pennsylvania, the American Philosophical Society and the Pennsylvania Hospital, but he was also a dealer in drugs and medicines, and did all he could to introduce the use of native medicinal plants. He was an ardent advocate of hygienic measures of all kinds, and took an active part in the work of introducing and popularizing the practice of inoculation in the cure of smallpox. He was one of the first, if not the first, publishers of medical books and pamphlets in the Colonies.

The paper was discussed by Thomas S. Wiegand, librarian of the college, who called attention to the fact that Benjamin Franklin was the first secretary of the Pennsylvania Hospital, and that the present secretary of the hospital, James T. Shinn, is the treasurer of the Philadelphia College of Pharmacy. Dr. C. A. Weidemann called attention to the bust of Franklin, which is in the museum of the college, and wondered how long it had been in the institution, saying that it had been in the possession of the college at least 40 years. Prof. Henry Kraemer referred briefly to the career of Franklin, and said that his genius seemed to consist in being entirely himself. The paper was also discussed by Prof. C. B. Lowe and E. M. Boring.

North Carolina Meeting.

Wrightsville Beach has been selected as the meeting place for the twenty-seventh annual convention of the North Carolina Pharmaceutical Association, which will begin on Thursday, June 14. This beach is one of the most popular seaside resorts in North Carolina, and is situated near Wilmington, from which it may be reached by trolley cars. The Seashore Hotel, which will be the headquarters of the association, has offered special rates of $1.50 per day for two in a room, and $2.00 per day for one in a room. The meeting of the Board of Pharmacy will be held at the same place at 10 o'clock on June 12 and 13. Applications for examinations should be filed in advance of the date of meeting with the Secretary of the Board, F. W. Hancock, Oxford, N. C.

Further information regarding the meeting may be obtained by addressing the Secretary of the Association, P. W. Vaughan, Durham.

New National Formulary Ready.

It will be welcome news to the pharmacists of the country that the new revised edition of the National Formulary will be shortly on sale. In a communication received from Charles Caspari, Jr., the general secretary of the American Pharmaceutical Association, who has charge of the distribution of the work and has kindly supplied us with advance pages, we are informed that the work will be ready for delivery in a few days at the following prices: Cloth, plain, $1; interleaved, $1.25; sheep, $1.35; interleaved, $1.50. The book can be ordered direct from Mr. Caspari, University of Maryland, Baltimore, Md., or through the American Druggist Publishing Company.

Subjects to Be Discussed by Boards and Schools of Pharmacy.

The Joint Committee on Arrangement and Programme of the National Association of Boards of Pharmacy and the American Conference of Pharmaceutical Faculties have issued a report and proposed programme of a joint conference, to be held at Indianapolis during the meeting of the American Pharmaceutical Association in September. The following is the programme of propositions suggested for discussion and action, which we reproduce at the request of Professor Oldberg, the chairman of the committee:

First. All laws and regulations governing the licensing of pharmacists should make due distinction between apprentices, clerks and principals, and should establish definite minimum qualifications and indicate the rights and duties of each of these three classes of pharmaceutical workers.

Second. The age of seventeen years and a preliminary general education of one year's satisfactorily completed high school work, or its full educational equivalent, should be the minimum prerequisites to the practical pharmaceutical experience or apprenticeship demanded by the laws, and no drug store experience acquired at an earlier age or before the attainment of the preliminary education prescribed should be accepted as sufficiently effective to satisfy the intent of the law.

[The adoption of this rule does not prevent the employment of children under seventeen years or with less than one year's high school education in drug stores; it only prevents the recognition or acceptance of their employment as legally admissible evidence of fit preparation for license to practice pharmacy.]

Third. The age and preliminary general education prescribed for legally sufficient drug store training should also be minimum prerequisites for admission to schools of pharmacy.

Fourth. Special education for the practice of pharmacy is in this age a necessity and should as rapidly as possible be made compulsory, and the rules of the Boards of Pharmacy should be such as to promote and encurage it in all practicable ways.

The special pharmaceutical education required should include substantial laboratory courses.

Fifth. Persons who have not given sufficient time and attention to the study of the subjects included in the board examinations in pharmacy should not be admitted to said examinations. All applicants for admission to such examinations should be required to submit proper evidence that they have satisfactorily completed systematic courses of study in the subjects upon which they are to be examined, which subjects should be named and described in public announcements issued by the boards.

Sixth. A syllabus of pharmacy examinations should be prepared by a committee of this conference which shall indicate the subjects to be included in the board examinations as well as in the courses of instruction in the pharmaceutical schools, with the view to the attainment of a reasonably uniform standard of minimum requirements which may be adopted by all boards and schools.

Seventh. A National Committee on Examination Questions should be appointed by the National Association of Boards of Pharmacy, which committee should consist of —— members, including experienced specialists in the subjects mentioned in the syllabus of pharmacy examinations, who shall, under the direction of the said association, prepare questions suitable for the examinations to be held by such State Boards of Pharmacy as may avail themselves of the services of said committee.

Eighth. Definite and uniform conditions of efficiency should be adopted which all pharmaceutical schools must comply with in order to receive recognition by the Boards of Pharmacy in all cases where students and graduates of such schools receive credit in any form for the courses they have completed or for the time of attendance at such schools, these conditions of efficiency to be made public and to be applied equally to all schools.

The conditions of efficiency prescribed for the recognition of schools of pharmacy should relate solely to matters directly affecting the character of their educational work.

Ninth. In the determination of the fitness of any applicant to receive a license to practice pharmacy all important facts of his educational history, practical experience and technical services should be taken into account, including his preliminary general education, his special education in pharmaceutical and other related technical schools, his practical experience in pharmacy and the results of the examinations he has passed, and an average of these several factors, each assigned its appropriate value, should be adopted as the passing grade. Substantial credit should be given each candidate for any satisfactorily completed courses of education in pharmaceutical schools according to their extent and character.

Tenth. Graduates of schools of pharmacy registered by the boards as fulfilling the prescribed conditions of efficiency should be exempt from the board examinations, except in prescription reading and dispensing, upon presentation of satisfactory evidence that they have successfully completed systematic courses of instruction in such schools extending thrugh two school years of not less than eight months each, with not less than twenty-five hours' instruction weekly, of which not less than sixteen hours shall be laboratory work, the evidence of their graduation being accepted as a sufficient equivalent to the passing of the board examination, provided all other legal requirements for license shall be fulfilled, and provided further the candidate shall have had two years' high school education; but no person should be granted a license to practice pharmacy unless he shall have successfully passed a practical examination in the proper reading of prescriptions and the art of dispensing.

Eleventh. No person should be licensed as a pharmacist or given the right to conduct a pharmacy on his own account, or as manager, who has not reached the age of legal responsibility.

Twelfth. The laws and the rules of the Boards of Pharmacy should be so framed and construed as to require sufficient practical experience in pharmacies independently of courses of study, but to the end that substantial courses in the pharmaceutical schools may not be discouraged the laws and the board rulings should not require persons who take longer courses to wait a correspondingly longer time before they are enabled to secure their licenses. The minimum total period prescribed for both college education and practical experience in pharmacies should, therefore, be the same for all persons without reference to the length of the college courses they may have completed, and should be sufficient to include a full two years' course in a pharmaceutical school.

Thirteenth. We recommend to all concerned that the foregoing principles and standards be adhered to in any amendments to the pharmacy laws hereafter proposed, in order that national uniformity may be ultimately attained. The minimum requirements indicated, and especially the preliminary general education, should be increased from time to time as circumstances permit.

The proposed programme is signed by the committee, consisting of I. A. Keith, George B. Kauffman, Z. B. Hopkins, F. B. Lillie and Oscar Oldberg.

Ohio State Association Offers Prizes for Meritorious Papers.

Cincinnati, June 6.—The Committee on Papers and Queries of the Ohio State Pharmaceutical Association, which meets in twenty-eighth annual convention in the Breakers Hotel, Cedar Point, Lake Erie, coincidentally with the meeting of the New York State Pharmaceutical Association, June 26, 27, 28 and 29, have prepared an elaborate programme, and it is expected that numerous papers of technical and business value will be presented in competition for the various prizes offered, every one of the manufacturing pharmacists who were solicited for prizes having responded favorably. The list of queries prepared by the committee was printed in full in the AMERICAN DRUGGIST for May 28 at page 300. For replies to query No. 1 Wm. S. Merrell Chemical Company, Cincinnati, offer ¼ pound Merrell's sodium salicylate from oil of wintergreen, ¼ dozen akaralgia (granular effervescing powder); ¼ dozen alkarhein (pints), 2 dozen talborate, 2 dozen boronaphthol soap. The Mallinckrodt Chemical Works have contributed 20 one-eighth ounce bottles of morphine sulphate. For responses to query No. 5, the Lime Fruit Juice Company, of Lima, O., offer five gallons of Allen's tame cherry phosphate; Upjohn & Company, five pints caripeptic liquid; Sharp & Dohme, 1,000 lapactic pills and 3 dozen salt sal laxa; William R. Warner & Company, 1 dozen bromo soda; Parke, Davis & Company, 3 dozen euthoymol dentrifice; Nelson Baker & Company, 3 dozen euderme cream; Eli Lilly & Company, case of hypodermic tablets; Armour & Company, Chicago, 1 dozen 1 ounce bottles of suprarenal solution; Solon Palmer, New York, ¼ dozen 4 ounce satin lined extracts, consisting of assorted violet leaves, rose leaves and apple leaves; Frederick Stearns & Company, 5 pints kasagra; Merck & Company, $10 worth of Merck's chemicals; Johnson & Johnson, one gross Lister's tooth soap; E. R. Squibb & Sons, New York, 1 dozen Squibb's talcum toilet powder. The Board of Trustees of the United States Pharmacopœia Convention, one copy of U. S. Pharmacopœia VIII for the best paper on any subject connected with the Pharmacopœia.

The Kansas Board of Pharmacy.

At a quarterly meeting of the Kansas State Board of Pharmacy held at Emporia, May 24, 1906, the following officers were elected for the ensuing year: C. L. Becker, Ottawa, president; W. E. Sheriff, Ellsworth, secretary; W. W. Naylor, Holton, treasurer; F. A. Snow, Topeka, and L. Ardery, Hutchinson, Finance Committee. There were 76 applicants in attendance to take the examination, 42 of whom were successful and were registered. The following are the names of those who passed: Emil D. Brenker, Bern; W. C. Fleming, Burlington; R. M. Vliet, Lawrence; Lloyd B. Foster, Kansas City; William A. McDaniel, Valley Falls; W. C. Johnston, Manhattan; L. D. Shambaugh, LeRoy; Nelson Wolcott, Oakley; George Holden, Herington; C. D. Vermillion, Tescott; W. N. Kelsey, Linwood; H. B. Leach, jr., Alton; R. E. Lake, Erie; Omie H. Davis, Wichita; J. M. Craig, Garnett; Alvin R. Snapp, McPherson; Charles A. P. Mosher, Kinsley; Harry L. Riley, Wichita; Howard D. McAdams, Salina; Elizabeth Martin, Wichita; J. A. Bermingham, Chanute; Dollie Ball, Longton; J. R. Brogan, St. Paul; Clarence R. Helper, Wisley; B. J. Patterson, Rexford; Dale L. North, Parson; C. W. Bowen, Kansas City; Fred G. Beanlien, Sabetha; Joseph Henry Haska, Holyrood; William Post, Altoona; J. E. Clark, Eureka; M. L. Klinck, Hutchinson; Bert R. Hazen, Horton; J. H. Powers, Little River; F. W. Wedel, Moundridge; Lulu Kelly, Topeka; H. J. B. Evans Lombe, Edan; Will Robertson, Coyville; D. C. Cashman; F. B. Forrester, Wakeeney; J. H. Benson, Salina; Claude R. Moore, Delphos.

Dr. Joseph Weinstein Succeeds Himself on Board of Pharmacy.

The election for a member of the Board of Pharmacy to succeed Joseph Weinstein in the Eastern Branch was held at the New York College of Pharmacy on Thursday, June 7, and passed off uneventfully. It was at first feared that a contest would be made that might lead to considerable discord and friction. Some overzealous friends of Charles S. Erb made a candidate of him, but Mr. Erb announced his refusal to run on the morning of the election. Three votes were cast for him out of a total of 509, of which Dr. Weinstein received 477, and S. L. Schlesinger, the candidate of the Westchester County Association, polled 29.

As noted elsewhere, Dr. Weinstein will receive the degree of Phar. D. from Columbia University at the commencement exercises, June 13. He took the postgraduate course at the New York College of Pharmacy and received the degree of Phar. D. there. Mr. Weinstein is the first and only postgraduate student of the college to receive the degree from Columbia this year. Mr. Weinstein is a native of Russia, having been born in Courland in 1860. He entered a pharmacy as an apprentice in Vilna in 1878, after having completed the required course in the high school. His first pharmaceutical degree, that of *Pharmacopæi auxiliarius*, was taken at the Imperial University of Kharkoff, Russia. He engaged in the drug business there, both as clerk and proprietor, and in 1887 took a four semesters' course in pharmacy at the Imperial University of Moscow and was graduated with the degree of *provisor*.

JOSEPH WEINSTEIN, PHAR.D.

Dr. Weinstein came to New York fifteen years ago and established himself in business at 75 East Broadway, where he still conducts a prosperous pharmacy. His colleagues in the Eastern Branch of the State Board of Pharmacy speak admiringly of Dr. Weinstein's ability as secretary, and his dealings with the pharmacists of this city have been characterized by a constant regard for the maintenance of just and friendly relations with all.

Board of Pharmacy to Enforce Part of Sanitary Code.

In the notices of the regular meeting of the Kings County Pharmaceutical Society Tuesday for June 12, mention is made of the fact that the Board of Pharmacy is now enforcing section 67 of the Sanitary Code of the Board of Health. The entire chapter of the Sanitary Code relating to drugs, medicines, adulterations and poisons will have special interest for our readers at this time, in view of the many attempts which are being made to "regulate" the drug business, and this is our excuse for printing the section herewith:

DRUGS, MEDICINES, ADULTERATIONS AND POISONS.

Sec. 65. No person shall make, prepare, put up, administer or dispense any prescription, decoction, or medicine under any deceptive or fraudulent name, direction or pretence; nor shall any ingredient be substituted for another in any prescription; nor shall any false or deceptive representation be made by any person to any other, as to the kind, quality, purpose, or effect of any such drug, medicine, decoction, drink, or other article offered or intended to be taken as food or medicine.

Sec 66. No poison shall be sold at retail by any person in the City of New York without having affixed to the bottle, box, parcel or receptacle containing such poison, a label bearing the word "Poison" distinctly shown, printed or written in red ink, together with the name and place of business of the seller and the name of the poison, printed or written upon such bottle, box, parcel or receptacle in plain, legible characters.

Sec. 67. No phenol, commonly known as carbolic acid, shall be sold at retail by any person in the City of New York, except upon the prescription of a physician, when in a stronger solution than five per cent.

Sec. 68. No person shall have, sell or offer for sale in the City of New York any food which is adulterated. The term food, as herein used, shall include every article of food and every beverage used by man, and all confectionery. Food, as herein defined, shall be deemed adulterated:

(a). If any substance or substances has or have been mixed with it so as to reduce or lower or injuriously affect its quality or strength.

(b). If any inferior or cheaper substance or substances have been substituted wholly or in part for the article.

(c). If any valuable constituent of the article has been wholly or in part abstracted.

(d). If it be an imitation or be sold under the name of another article.

(e). If it consists wholly or in part of diseased or decomposed or putrid or rotten animal or vegetable substance, whether manufactured or not, or in the case of milk, if it is the product of a diseased animal.

(f). If it be colored, or coated or polished, or powdered, whereby damage is concealed, or it is made to appear better than it really is, or of a greater value.

(g). If it contains any added poisonous ingredient, or any ingredient which may render such article injurious to the health of the person consuming it; or if it contains any antiseptic or preservative not evident and not known to the purchaser or consumer.

Spirituous, fermented and malt liquors shall be deemed adulterated if they contain any substance or ingredient not normal or healthful to exist in spirituous, fermented or malt liquors, or which may be deleterious or detrimental to health when such liquors are used as a beverage.

Confectionery shall be deemed adulterated if it contains terra alba, barytes, talc or other mineral substances or poisonous colors or flavors or other ingredients deleterious or detrimental to health.

Sec. 69. No person shall manufacture, produce, compound, brew, distill, have, sell or offer for sale in the City of New York any drug which is adulterated. The term drug, as herein used, shall include all medicine for external or internal use, or both. Drugs, as herein defined, shall be deemed adulterated:

(a). If, when sold by or under a name recognized in the United States Pharmacopœia, it differs from the standard of strength, quality or purity laid down therein.

(b). If, when sold by or under a name not recognized in the United States Pharmacopœia, but which is found in some other pharmacopœia, or other standard work on materia medica, it differs materially from the standard of strength, quality, or purity laid down in such work.

(c). If its strength or purity fall below the professed standard under which it is sold.

It should be understood by druggists in this city that the provisions of the Sanitary Code have the force of law and Health Department officers are empowered to execute them. It is a new departure, however, for the Board of Pharmacy to undertake the enforcement of the Sanitary Code.

TO ATLANTA BY BOAT.

Planning to Charter a Boat to Take Eastern Delegates to N. A. R. D. Meeting.

William De Shetley, manager of the Department of the East of the N. A. R. D., is planning a big excursion, by a chartered steamer from this city, to the N. A. R. D. convention at Atlanta, Ga., next October. The plan is to get druggists of New York, New Jersey, New England and other nearby sections to co-operate and charter a steamer. The project has been enthusiastically received, and Mr. De Shetley has already entered into negotiations with various steamship lines with regard to securing a boat for that occasion. The boat would land the delegates at Savannah, and the trip thence to Atlanta would be made by rail. The trip would take two or three days, but it is figured that the cost to the members of the party would be less than the regular fare. The party would "own the boat" and undoubtedly would have a most delightful salt water outing. All the arrangements for the affair, which has the sanction of the N. A. R. D. headquarters in Chicago, are in the hands of Manager De Shetley, whose office is in the Woodbridge Building, 100 William street.

Local Branch of the N. A. R. D. Holds Executive Session.

The Executive Committee of the M. A. R. D. held a meeting at the New York College of Pharmacy May 31. President Reuben R. Smith was in the chair and called the meeting to order at 9.30 p. m. Others present were Messrs. Searles, Klein, Maas, Diamond, Rafter, Montgomery and Chairman Weiss, of the Tenth District.

The treasurer's report showed that about $1,200 had been collected, and that there was a balance in the treasury of $900 approximately.

Secretary Diner reported that three organizers are working in Greater New York, namely, Mr. Bohan in Brooklyn, Mr. Miller in The Bronx and Mr. Sanbren in Manhattan. Collections, the secretary said, have been coming in fairly, and there had been but few complaints of violations of the D. C. S. N. plan.

The reports were received and placed on file.

Mr. Weiss reported that nearly all of the members in the Tenth District had paid their 1906 dues.

The Committee on Incorporation reported progress.

A communication was received from the American Druggists' Syndicate, acknowledging the receipt of the M. A. R. D.'s resolution regarding the direct contract and serial number plan submitted by the Syndicate. This plan, it will be recalled, was drafted by the Syndicate, and, as it embodies the salient features of the D. C. S. N. plan, was accepted by the M. A. R. D. It has yet to be formally approved by the Syndicate. The latter also sent a contribution of $100 to the fund that has been started by New York pharmacists for the relief of their fellow druggists in San Francisco.

Mr. Pennock with Arthur Stillwell & Co.

EDWARD PENNOCK.

Edward Pennock, who has been manager of the New York branch of William R. Warner & Co. for the past four years, has taken charge of the Southern and Philadelphia territory of Arthur Stillwell & Co., dealers in essential oils, perfumers' materials, etc. Mr. Pennock will look after the trade in Philadelphia, Baltimore, Washington and surrounding territory, and through his intimate personal acquaintance with the trade in that section will undoubtedly be able to add materially to the business of his house.

EXTENDING THE CHAIN.

Caswell-Massey Company Buys Out Alpers—Hegeman Corporation Absorbs Rosenzweig.

Two notable changes in ownership of Greater New York pharmacies have taken place within the past week or two, namely, those of the Alpers Pharmacy in Manhattan, and the Rosenzweig Pharmacy in Brooklyn. They are both among the leading and most prominent stores in the respective boroughs. The Caswell-Massey Company has added the pharmacy of Dr. William C. Alpers at Broadway and Thirty-first street and took possession June 2, Dr. Alpers being retained as manager. The pharmacy, for the present at least, will be conducted practically on the same lines as heretofore.

The Caswell-Massey Company also intends to open a branch store this summer on Sixth avenue near Sixteenth street; another is to be opened soon at One Hundred and Twenty-fifth street and Madison avenue, and one at Broadway and One Hundred and Sixth street, besides the pharmacy in the Astor House, which will be ready for business as soon as the new soda fountain is installed. It is understood that the company intend to open other branches in this city as soon as business warrants.

New York Retail Druggists' Association Meets.

A regular meeting of the New York Retail Druggists' Association was held at the "Herrnstadt," 27 West One Hundred and Fifteenth street, May 25, with Mr. Marmor in the chair. The minutes of the previous two meetings were read and approved, as well as the minutes of the meeting of the Executive Committee. Morris Perla, Henry Levitas and Isadore Rosenblum were duly elected to membership in the association.

The following four members were proposed, and upon motion, elected: Wolf Krimmerman, 322 Rivington street; Edward Sanpagata, 1 Mott street; Charles Hitsch, 1 Mott street; Anthony Ofrias, 198 First avenue.

Mr. Diamond reported for the Legislative Committee that the Lupton bill had passed and was now before the Governor for signature; that every effort was being made by committees on legislation of the various associations to have the bill vetoed, but that the individual action of all pharmacists would be necessary to accomplish that end. He urged the members to write to the Governor without further delay. He further reported that a lengthy telegram was sent by him to the Governor in the name of the association, and that a reply acknowledging the receipt of it had been received.

Mr. Beck, Mr. Epstein, Mr. Herzenberg, A. Weinstein, and Mr. Rosenthal volunteered to canvass various districts in the city and have the pharmacists write letters to the Governor.

The Committee of Election reported that they had decided to issue a circular to the pharmacists of Manhattan in general, and follow the same up a week later with another circular to the members of the association, also to send a postal to all pharmacists three days before election, urging upon them the necessary to vote. The question of a mass meeting before election was submitted by the committee to the association and was voted down.

The Telephone Committee reported that no definite conclusions were as yet reached with the telephone company.

Communications were read from the Interborough Pharmaceutical Association and the Deutsche Apotheker Verein, endorsing the nomination of Mr. Weinstein.

A communication from the Board of Pharmacy was read, naming June 7 as the day of election.

The following five delegates were elected to the meeting of the State Pharmaceutical Association June 26 next:

P. Diamond, Charles Bernstein, Jesse K. Bernhardt, Aaron Siegel, and Louis B. Epstein. Substitutes: Joe Beck, Jacob Pick, Joseph Herzenberg, Moses Naumoff, and Mr. Shapiro.

Pure nitrogen forms a colorless, oxygen a bluish, ozone a deep blue fluid, on compression to the liquefied state.

New York Retailers Want Slot 'Phones.

A delegation of New York druggists had a conference on Friday, June 1, with General Manager Thurber of the New York Telephone Company, regarding the druggists' agitation for slot telephones in their stores, in place of the present system. Those present at the conference were William C. Anderson, Jacob Diner, Albert Baltzly, F. H. Plump, Peter Diamond, Joseph Weinstein and A. C. Searles.

The situation was fully discussed and the important position occupied by drug stores in the telephone company's service was clearly pointed out. Mr. Thurber at first made the familiar argument that only about 15 per cent. of the pay stations were in drug stores, and that the company, therefore, could not discriminate in favor of that small percentage. The druggists present, however, made the argument that people generally preferred to telephone from a drug store rather than from a grocery, saloon, butcher shop or cigar store, where a great many of the pay stations are located, and that pharmacies were open at all hours. It was also pointed out that while the number of pay stations in drug stores is relatively small, these stations in reality do a very large percentage of the company's total pay station business, because drug store 'phones are patronized more extensively than other stations. The druggists requested slot machines, with an allowance or commission of 25 per cent. of the gross receipts from the slot 'phones placed in their stores.

Manager Thurber seemed favorably impressed with the arguments advanced by the druggists, and promised to consider the matter carefully and give an early decision.

New York City Board Pass List.

At the examination on May 16 last the following candidates for registration as pharmacists passed the Eastern Section of the New York State Board of Pharmacy:

W. H. Albert, N. J. Alexander, G. J. Alexion, N. Bakker, M. Behm, R. J. Benham, C. W. Bock, L. Boeder, S. Bookstaber, E. P. Broderick, A. A. Brown, H. Brundage, A. Burstein, P. Buss, Charles Cohen, David Cohen, Joseph Cohen, V. Dahlberg, S. Dancis, J. F. Dawson, W. S. Dean, H. A. Dobromilsky, A. F. Dold, D. E. Driscoll, William C. Driscoll, C. H. Ellis, jr., H. Elwyn, A. Farber, H. Felder, M. Feinstein, I. A. Feldberg, R. W. Fish, C. W. Flint, S. W. Fraser, L. Freidman, L. Gawurin, N. S. Gesoalde, T. F. Gilmartin, H. Glucksman, N. Goldberg, L. Goldlust, H. V. Goring, I. Goulko, M. Greenberg, F. J. Grimm, E. A. Grogan, jr., J. Grubman, F. Guagliardo, A. A. Guarnier, R. K. Henry, F. H. Hickling, N. R. Hirsch, W. Horni, E. H. Hartnett, C. W. M. Johnson, jr., O. J. Kahn, S. Katz, N. Kaufman, W. S. Kennedy, H. W. Kimball, Louis Klein, M. A. Kopel, C. Krepela, A. L. Lahey, A. Landi, B. R. Lehman, H. W. Lehmkuhl, R. Levine, B. N. Levy, A. Ludwig, C. J. A. Lund, W. P. Maher, W. J. Mahoney, A. S. Margulis, T. Margulis, B. H. Mark, F. M. Martin, F. Matthiessen, J. A. Mauro, L. E. Mercier, W. F. Miller, C. E. Neff, M. R. Newstead, E. W. Nicolai, G. H. Opper, C. A. Otto, N. Parent, C. C. Perdoe, C. F. Perthou, G. A. Rauh, L. Reich, J. Robbins, M. M. Rosenberg, L. Rosenstein, J. Rosenthal, E. A. Rothman, W. G. Sabine, M. J. Sander, I. Sasmorsky, M. M. Schlesinger, S. Schoenfeld, M. Schubert, I. Schwartz, A. O. Schwencke, R. E. Seaman, A. Seiger, I. Sherman, N. Seigel, A. S. Silverman, G. G. Smith, N. Snyder, F. F. Sontag, R. Sookne, C. M. Stein, S. D. Strawgate, H. Sullivan, I. Tessler, F. N. Thimble, W. E. Thomas, M. Tobias, J. Trivigno, H. O. von Wedel, B. Warlyn, H. J. White, H. M. Woessner, I. N. Zlinkoff, P. W. Barry, I. Heifler, A. Mueller, S. Coller, E. Mackey, C. E. Phelps. A druggist's license was issued to W. H. Dippel.

Arrangements for the New York State Meeting.

The arrangements for the annual meeting of the New York State Pharmaceutical Association, to be held at Niagara Falls, June 26, 27, 28 and 29, are described in a folder issued by S. V. B. Swann, secretary. The meeting will open at 10 o'clock Tuesday morning, June 26, when the members will be welcomed by the Hon. O. W. Cutler, Mayor of Niagara Falls, and by Eugene Laurier, President of the Niagara Falls Retail Druggists' Association. The usual business of the association will then go on from day to day, the final sitting taking place on board the boat which will take the visitors to Toronto. The entertainment features have been already described in the AMERICAN DRUGGIST and it only remains to say that Niagara Falls may be reached by five lines of railroads, the New York Central, round trip $12.35; Erie Railroad, $10.70; Lehigh Valley, $10.70; West Shore, $10.70, and D., L. & W., $10.70. On limited trains an extra fee is charged for the return trip. M. R. Mandelbaum, New York representative of Committee on Transportation, expects to take a party over the D., L. & W. by the 10 o'clock a. m., train on Monday, June 25.

Obituary.

HENRY D. RIDGLEY.

Henry D. Ridgley, secretary of Eli Lilly & Co., manufacturing pharmacists, of Indianapolis, died June 1 at a sanitarium in Biloxi, Miss., where he went last February in the hope of improving his health. His death was due to arterial sclerosis. He had been connected with Lilly & Co. for the last twenty years, and through his long association there he formed a very wide personal acquaintance with the drug trade of Indiana. He was a graduate of the Purdue School of Pharmacy at Lafayette, Ind. He leaves a wife and two children.

JOEL S. ORME.

Joel S. Orme, a well-known and highly respected citizen of Cambridge, died at his home, 429 Massachusetts avenue, May 27, after a brief illness. Mr. Orme was a native of Cambridge, and was born on August 12, 1825. At the age of 13 years he entered the drug store of Isaac H. Snow, of Boston, for whom he worked three years. When 16, together with his brother, a business was established; their partnership lasted eight years. Then Mr. Orme branched out for himself and since August 1, 1841, he conducted business at the same place and in the same building, now 427 Massachusetts avenue. This building was over 100 years old and Mr. Orme had owned it since 1856. Deceased had attended to his business up to a few weeks of his death; he was a pleasant man to meet, and his reminiscences were most interesting; he was a gentleman of the old school. Modern business methods were repugnant to him and he took much pride in stating that he had never cut prices. He had membership in many organizations and had served in a large number in official capacities. He was connected with the Cambridge Veteran Firemen's Association, the Boston Druggists' Association and the Massachusetts State Pharmacists' Association. He was also a member of the Essex Institute of Salem, the Sons of the American Revolution, the American Pharmaceutical Association, the Massachusetts College of Pharmacy, the Massachusetts State Druggists' Alliance, and was a member of Amicable Lodge of Masons. He was married in 1850; a son and daughter survive him.

The funeral took place at his late residence, on May 31, and was attended by many prominent druggists. Representatives were present from the Boston Druggists' Association and from the Massachusetts College of Pharmacy.

DIED.

COTTERREL.—In Waynesburg, Pa., on Monday, June 4, John F. Cotterrel, aged forty years.

FIELDS.—In Pikesville, Md., on Saturday, May 19, William C. Fields, aged thirty-four years.

ORNE.—In Cambridge, Mass., on Monday, May 28, Joel S. Orne, aged eighty years.

PHILLIPS.—In Beckley, W. Va., on Saturday, May 26, Blake Phillips, aged twenty-two years.

A New Auditor for Parke, Davis & Co.

H. D. Allee, who has been appointed auditor for Parke, Davis & Co. to succeed Philo E. Hall, was formerly connected with the auditing department of the C. B. & Q. Railroad.

In Honor of Professor Sayre.

On June 4 the twentieth anniversary of the Shool of Pharmacy of the University of Kansas, and of Professor Sayre's connection with that institution, was celebrated by a banquet given by the University and the Alumni at the Eldridge House, Lawrence.

The Mississippi Pharmaceutical Association's convention will be held in Chrystal Springs, Miss., on Monday and Tuesday, July 23 and 24.

The Iowa Pharmaceutical Association will hold its twenty-seventh annual convention in Cedar Rapids, Iowa, on Tuesday, Wednesday and Thursday, July 10, 11 and 12.

Greater New York News.

A. G. Rosengarten, treasurer of the Powers-Weightman-Rosengarten Company, was a recent visitor to New York.

Pond, Bowes & Carthwright have succeeded the Sherman Square Pharmacy at Seventieth street and Amsterdam avenue.

A new drug store is being fitted up at the corner of Lenox avenue and One Hundred and Fourteenth street by E. A. Denicke, formerly of Tenth street.

Extensive alterations have been made in the establishment of the Caswell Massey Company, at Seventy-seventh street and Columbus avenue.

Wm. A. Sherry, traveling representative for the Stallman & Fulton Company, spent a few days at the home office a week or so ago.

Unless a special call is issued there will be no more meetings of the Drug Trade Section of the New York Board of Trade and Transportation until next fall.

The Schoellkopf, Hartford & Hanna Company is now located on the twelfth floor of the Woodbridge Building, occupying the former quarters of the Drug and Chemical Club.

Dr. J. B. Maloney, of the Key West Drug Company, Key West, Fla., was in town recently on his way to Boston to attend the annual meeting of the American Medical Association.

A petition in bankruptcy has been filed against the Ada-Surlem Medicine Company, of No. 1135 Broadway. F. C. McLaughlin has been appointed receiver. The liabilities are placed at $10,000 and assets $5,000.

S. P. Nickells, who for some time past has been manager of Wm. R. Warner & Co.'s branch in New Orleans, has been appointed New York manager, succeeding Edward Pennock, who has gone to Arthur Stillwell & Co.

J. W. Folsom, formerly with Metcalf & Company, of Boston, and later with W. B. Riker, Son & Company, of this city, has purchased the store of B. A. Walton & Company, at Seventieth street and West End avenue.

The Lupton Bill, which was the only one of several measures affecting the drug trade to pass the New York State Legislature, was not signed by Governor Higgins and therefore the bill will not become a law.

Geo. Andrews and C. Mitchell, Parke, Davis & Co.'s representatives in eastern Pennsylvania; G. E. Reid, manager of the company's Philadelphia branch, and P. Matty, the Massachusetts representative, were callers at the New York branch recently.

W. S. Sindey, until recently a clerk in Joseph Weinstein's pharmacy, at No. 75 East Broadway, has gone to Hunter, N. Y., to take charge of the Flag Pharmacy, a new store, in which Mr. Weinstein and C. H. Bernstein, of New York, are interested.

The new pharmacy opened at 771 Ninth avenue, bearing the name Milerick's Pharmacy, is under the management of John Milerick, a New York College graduate. The neighborhood is tenanted by numerous families and the venture should prove a successful one.

Rudolph Theiss, formerly at the southwest corner of Seventh avenue and Twenty-fifth street, moved May 1 to the opposite side of the avenue into a more spacious establishment, a finely equipped store and having a large prescription department and laboratory in the rear.

Jacob Weiss, formerly of Eighty-second street and Second avenue, has purchased the store of Leon Cohen, at One Hundred and Twelfth street and Lenox avenue. C. L. Doty, formerly with Kalish, is now manager for Mr. Weiss. Mr. Cohen has purchased a pharmacy at One Hundred and Fifty-first street and Edgecomb avenue.

The annual outing of the Alumni Association of the New York College of Pharmacy will take place on Wednesday, June 13, at Donnelly's Grove, College Point. The boat leaves the foot of East Ninety-ninth street at 2 p. m. An interesting programme, including dancing, shooting, bowling, with prizes for both ladies and gentlemen, has been arranged.

Joseph Weinstein enjoys the distinction of having received the degree of Doctor of Pharmacy from Columbia University—the first ever awarded by that institution. Mr. Weinstein was the only one of the graduates who received their degree of Phar. D. from the New York College of Pharmacy to get the degree of Doctor of Pharmacy from Columbia.

The next general meeting of the M. A. R. D. will be held on the evening of June 22, at the New York College of Pharmacy. At that meeting a representative of the American Druggists' Fire Insurance Company will be present and will speak on the benefits to be derived by druggists from a fire insurance company of their own.

We are advised by Frank H. Freericks, secretary of the American Druggists' Fire Insurance Company, Cincinnati, Ohio, of the appointment of Dr. W. C. Anderson, of Brooklyn, as a representative of the company in Greater New York to take charge of a stock subscription book for the entry of subscriptions from druggists throughout the State. It is believed by the incorporators of the company that Dr. Anderson's interest in the undertaking will do much toward enlisting the support of druggists. There are less than 1,000 shares now to be placed in New York State, and an effort is to be made to secure subscriptions for this amount by personal letters to a selected list of druggists.

President Diner, of the Manhattan Pharmaceutical Association, has sent out notices for the next meeting on June 18, calling special attention to the features arranged for that meeting. There will be among other subjects a discussion on the ethics of pharmacy and the allied professions, and an invitation has been extended to prominent physicians, retail and manufacturing pharmacists and representatives of the pharmaceutical and medical publications to be present and participate in the discussions. An elaborate collation is also being planned for the occasion, and the affair promises to be one of the most interesting and instructive meetings held by the Manhattan this year.

A great deal of interest centers in the forthcoming annual convention of the New York State Pharmaceutical Association, but particularly in the election of officers for the ensuing year, since different men have been suggested for each of the various offices. The prevailing sentiment of pharmacists in this section seems to be that whatever men the association selects the offices should be distributed throughout the State; in other words, all the offices, or most of them, it is pointed out, should not be filled by pharmacists of one particular section. "The honors should be distributed as evenly as possible throughout the State," said a well-known pharmacist the other day, "and Greater New York certainly should receive recognition and be represented in the official family of the State Association. All the offices should not be filled by pharmacists of any one section; if they should, there is bound to be retaliation on the part of the interests or sections that are ignored, which is not conducive to harmony. The best interests of the State Association demand a fair distribution of the offices."

H. A. Woolnough, of Bowen & Co., pharmacists, Melbourne, Australia, passed through New York last week on his way home. Mr. Woolnough left Melbourne last February and has been traveling pretty constantly ever since. He is the president of the Victorian Board of Pharmacy and his firm is the leading concern of its kind in the great city of Melbourne, maintaining four branches. In a chat with a representative of the AMERICAN DRUGGIST, Mr. Woolnough gave an interesting account of the condition of pharmacy in Australasia. The five States forming the commonwealth of Australia preserve a certain degree of autonomy so far as pharmacy matters are concerned, each State having its own pharmacy laws. The pharmacists of Australia are beginning to feel the pressure of proprietary prescribing, just as their American confreres do, and much complaint is heard of the tendency on the part of physicians to neglect the Pharmacopœia in favor of the cleverly worded advertising matter of the specialty manufacturer. During his stay in this city Mr. Woolnough established a buying connection with a prominent firm in order to make direct purchases of American preparations.

WESTERN NEW YORK.

J. A. Lockie, President of the State Pharmaceutical Association, Elected a Member of the State Board of Pharmacy Vote was 48 to 26—A. J. Keller the Defeated Candidate—Buffalo College Commencement—Buffalo to Entertain Members of the State Association at the Annual Meeting.

(*From our Regular Correspondent.*)

Buffalo, June 6.—The election for a member of the State Board of Pharmacy to succeed Dr. Willis G. Gregory, who was not a candidate for re-election, took place to-day and J. A. Lockie, the popular President of the State Pharmaceutical Association and President of the National Association of Retail Druggists, was successful over his competitor, A. J. Keller, of Buffalo, by a vote of 48 to 26.

BUFFALO COLLEGE COMMENCEMENT.

The College of Pharmacy carried off the honors, for numbers at least, in the Sixtieth Annual Commencement of the University of Buffalo, which took place June 1, for of the 157 graduates in the four departments, law, medicine, pharmacy and dentistry, there were 59 degrees conferred on students in pharmacy.

There were the usual forensic and presentation ceremonies, the candidates for graduation in pharmacy being presented to Vice-Chancellor Norton by Dr. John R. Gray, of the faculty, as follows: Ray V. Agrelius, Youngsville, Pa.; Victor H. Bargar, Buffalo; Arthur D. Barnes, Buffalo; Joseph C. Belle-Isle, Campbellton, N. B.; Roselle U. Blackney, Angola; Henry U. Brown, Bradford, Pa.; John Buettner, Buffalo; Peter R. Buettner, jr., Buffalo; Charles W. Bullock, Louisville, Ky.; John Calhoun, Sherman; Charles E. Cerwinka, Buffalo; J. Raymond Clark, Waterloo; Harold G. Dobson, Buffalo; Genevieve M. Driscoll, Dayton, O.; Lew R. Dunfee, Mawverton, Pa.; Homer E. Dyke, Buffalo; LeRoy W. Farnham, Buffalo; John M. Frost, Buffalo; Lum Fuller, Elmira; William E. Gallagher, Oxford; Charles S. Glenn, Clyde; Moses H. Goodwin, Springvale, Me.; Julius W. Gregory, Buffalo; Jay L. Larish, Honeoye Falls; Charles V. Hawley, Hornell; Walter J. Heegaard, Buffalo; Charles G. Heise, Dunkirk; Neil J. Hughey, Buffalo; William D. Hulse, Sodus; Frank M. Inglis, Buffalo; Charles W. Janke, Tonawanda; Charles W. Jeffers, Buffalo; Harry G. Jewett, Buffalo; Peter C. Jezewski, Buffalo; Louis A. Keiser, Buffalo; George H. Knapp, Sodus; Delwin A. La May, Buffalo; Lewis N. McCauley, Buffalo; Owen W. McShane, Bristol, Vt.; Thomas H. Meredith, Jamestown; Pierre B. Merrill, Homer; Benjamin F. Miles, Rochester; Mabel I. Miller, Colden; Alvah H. Radder, Buffalo; Charles E. Reeves, Dexter; Walter S. Redfield, Penn Yan; Luther H. Roper, Candor; Joseph J. Ross, Buffalo; Hattie May Seely, Rochester; Mrs. Mary G. Shaw, Lestershire; Arthur H. Sherburne; Milo, Me.; William H. Short, Camden; Walter W. Siegel, Erie, Pa.; Garnet A. Siple, Rochester; John B. Sumner, Buffalo; Walter C. Tomczak, Buffalo; C. H. Van Brocklin, Manlius; Jay M. Ward, Albion; Alfred C. Wilkins, Buffalo.

The honor list of the graduating class was composed of Lew R. Dunfee, who carried off the $50 Peabody prize, Roselle U. Blackney, C. H. Van Brocklin, Hattie May Seely, and Moses H. Goodwin. Homer E. Dyke was made Master in Pharmacy, a degree seldom conferred.

At the meeting of the Alumni Association the following officers were elected: President, Ernest B. Walker, '92; vice-president, Rudolf C. Miller, both of Buffalo; second vice-president, Mary E. Kelly, of Victor Hill; third vice-president, Joseph T. W. Coble, of Colorado Springs, Col.; secretary, William E. Lemon; treasurer, Charles H. Gauger; historian, Herbert D. Atwater, all of Buffalo.

The annual banquet of the Alumni Association, held at the Niagara Hotel, was largely attended and many excellent speakers were present. The members contributed $100 to the University Extension Fund.

TO SUPPRESS VITRIOL THROWING.

Buffalo has concluded to make an example of the vitriol throwers and County Judge Emery has just sentenced Cora Greenwood to Auburn for two to five years for the crime of disfiguring a rival in that way. The judge said such practices must stop. When the new cocaine and carbolic acid city ordinance was urged by the druggists, some one asked why sulphuric acid was not included so that jealous girls could not get it, but the reply was that it was in too common use to be tied up in any such way.

FOR BUFFALO DAY ENTERTAINMENT AT STATE MEETING.

President F. A. Darrin of the Buffalo Retail Druggists' Association has appointed the following committee to take charge of the Buffalo day's entertainment of the visiting druggists during the meeting of the National Association at Niagara Falls: George Reimann, chairman, Thomas Stoddard, George C. Dykeman, T. W. Tyson, J. L. Perkins. The committee is trying to get the use of Olympic Park for a ball game, as that would be something new on the list. If that is done the ladies will be given an automobile ride and there will also be something doing in the evening. The date is June 28th. President Lockie, of the State Association, and President Laurier, of the Niagara Falls Association, are in frequent conference over details, but no new announcements have been made.

NEWS AND NOTES.

Clarence N. Reese, a graduate of the Buffalo College of Pharmacy, but of late on the road for some concern, has bought the drug store of John F. Mayer on Jefferson street, Buffalo. Mr. Mayer expects to locate in the same business in Jersey City.

The next examination of candidates for license by the Western Branch of the State Board of Pharmacy, which takes place on the 20th, will have about 40 people on the list, practically all college graduates. At the late meeting of the branch in Lockport several delinquent cases were taken up, but none of them was brought to a conclusion.

Dr. Edmund B. Reimann, of the Buffalo General Hospital, underwent an operation for appendicitis a few days ago and is doing quite well. He is the son of Secretary Reimann, of the Western Branch of the State Board of Pharmacy, and was always a druggist till going into medicine a few years ago.

William Fletcher, who some years ago was transferred from the Buffalo headquarters of the Empire State Drug Company to the company's New York office, has returned to Buffalo and will take charge of city canvassing for the company.

Buffalo druggists do not boast of business much yet, though they agree that it is improving. June has already betrayed the fact that it has a lot of soda water days in waiting, to make up for a very cold spring.

NEWS OF THE TRAVELING MEN.

Richsecker's perfumes took another step forward lately on the visit here of the regular salesman of that house, Arthur E. Allbright, late in May, in his usual round.

B. L. Lambert, of the Detroit house of Lambert & Lowman, closed May in Buffalo and sold our druggists a long list of pharmaceuticals and other specialties of his manufacture.

W. P. Smith still sells on the road the guns and other specialties of Thurston & Braidich, and he closed May in Buffalo looking after his good customers here.

H. P. Snow, one of the regular salesmen in this district for the Red Cross firm of Johnson & Johnson, gave us the usual welcome call lately with the usual welcome results.

Alfred Wright, the Rochester perfumer, sends us on the usual errand his trusted and trusty salesman, W. H. Mook, who always covers his territory with satisfaction to all concerned.

Mullens & Kropff are still covering the Buffalo district in the person of R. S. Arcularius, who has always been able to sell our druggists a supply of cologne and toilet soaps, as he did on his May visit here.

W. J. Bush & Co., manufacturing chemists of New York, send us for the closing of May, their special salesman for this district, J. McKnight, who is always able to take a good list of orders here.

The trademark of the "New Skin," otherwise the Douglas Manufacturing Company, of New York, were in this market lately in the person of W. Luke, who never comes this way for nothing.

NEW ENGLAND.

The Price of Ice Cream Soda a Live Issue in Everett—Mr. Gilman's Eighty-fourth Birthday Celebration—Fire in Cellar Burns Druggist—Sixth-Class Liquor License Still a Source of Trouble.

(From our Regular Correspondent.)

Boston, June 6.—There is a live issue out in Everett over the price of ice cream sodas, with Kilby P. Sargent, Fred A. Spencer and Mitchell & Gaynor for participants. The latter firm put the price at 5 cents per serving, while the first named dealers felt that 10 cents was the right charge. Messrs. Sargent and Spencer called upon Mitchell & Gaynor and endeavored to convert them to the 10 cent idea by argument. They met with non-success and it is asserted that threats were then made that unless Mitchell & Gaynor acceded to the 10 cent figure they would be stopped from using the ice cream of a well known manufacturer. This proved unavailing and so the ice cream dealer came upon the scene with the alleged statement that unless the price of this soda-ice cream mixture was increased to 10 cents Mitchell & Gaynor could no longer use his goods. Even this proved unavailing and a contest involving the participants is on, with court proceedings. The case was tried June 1, Mitchell & Gaynor alleging criminal conspiracy against Sargent, Spencer and the ice cream dealer. The prosecution failed, however, as conspiracy and attempt to injure complainants' business could not be proven.

A BIRTHDAY CELEBRATION.

Hon. Gorham D. Gilman, of Gilman Bros., Franklin street, celebrated his eighty-fourth birthday May 29, at his home in Newton. He received many friends on that day who called to offer congratulations. Mr. Gilman has led an active and useful life and occupied many positions of trust. He is still actively engaged in business in partnership with his brother, J. A. Gilman.

DRUGGIST BADLY BURNED.

The store of Thomas Joyce & Co., 141 West Broadway, South Boston, was the scene of a fire on May 25, which will long be remembered by the partners in this concern. Patrick J. Cuddyer, one of the firm, on the day in question had occasion to attend to some work in the cellar in connection with a preparation of ginger. He had been gone but a short time when he shouted for aid. His partner, Mr. Joyce, believing it to be a prank, did not respond until he saw smoke issuing from the stairway. Then he went into the cellar and discovered his partner with hair and clothing on fire. The burning man was frantic with pain and Joyce had difficulty in getting him up the stairway. Thence Joyce forced him to the doorway, tore off the burning clothing and extinguished Cuddyer's blazing hair with his bare hands. Cuddyer was taken to a hospital and later removed to his home, from which, owing to his condition, he was sent to the City Hospital. The fire department was called out for the blaze in the cellar, which burned briskly. The flames were confined to the cellar but the contents of the building were damaged by smoke. It is thought the loss will not exceed a few hundred dollars.

NEW TRUSTEES FOR M. C. P.

The annual meeting of the Massachusetts College of Pharmacy was held on June 4, President Gammon in the chair. Routine reports were made by the officers and committees and then William F. Sawyer, C. Herbert Packard, Ph. G., and William H. Glover, Ph. G., were elected trustees, each for terms of five years.

THE SIXTH-CLASS LICENSE PROBLEM.

In Cambridge the sixth-class license problem is still agitating the drug trade, and it is said that there is a possibility of a change in the recent refusal to grant licenses. At least one alderman who voted against granting the permits is known to have experienced a change of heart and thinks the best interests of the city demand that licenses should be granted. A largely signed petition has been handed the board asking that the recent vote be rescinded. The temperance people fear that the failure to grant licenses will be an important factor in increasing the license vote in Cambridge.

PENNSYLVANIA.

Trade Not So Brisk—The Government Trust Prosecution—Points in the N. A. R. D. Memorial to President Roosevelt—Doings of the Local Association—Plan to Meet in a Boat on the River—Delegates Chosen for N. A. R. D. Meeting in Atlanta.

(From our Regular Correspondent.)

Philadelphia, June 7.—The retail drug trade in this city is not as brisk as it has been. This is in a measure due to the fact that many of the regular customers have gone out of the city and that the health of the residents here is better now than it has been for a long time. The number of colds have declined and there has also been a decrease in the number of cases of typhoid fever. Generally in Summer the retail drug trade is considerably less than it is in the colder months. This year it is thought it will be fully as dull as it has been heretofore. On this account it is said that a number of the druggists have planned to take long vacations and it is rumored that several have made preparations for a trip to the Northern Pacific Coast. Besides this there will be a number of improvements made to some of the stores here. Orders have been issued to the builders for several large additions.

THE FEDERAL INJUNCTION SUIT.

The attitude the Government is taking against trusts is causing considerable comment among druggists in this city. The recent suit against the manufacturers and members of the N. W. D. A. and others has been freqently discussed, and members of the association involved are of the opinion that a mistake has been made in this suit. The memorial submitted to the President and referrred to the Department of Justice is an apt one and gives the druggist side of the controversy. In the memorial there were three paragraphs that attracted the atttention of the leading wholesale druggists here and they say that it shows that the N. W. D. A. is doing just what is required by law and is assisting the Government to carry out its plans for the suppression of unfair means and no favors to the large dealers. The paragraphs are as follows:

THE N. A. R. D. MEMORIAL.

A few years ago you, sir, took a most distinguished part in the settlement of the great coal strike in Pennsylvania. You might have said: "Let the fight go on to a finish; it is their matter; it is the business of no one else." But there was a third factor to be taken into consideration. That factor was the public welfare, and representing that third factor you entered into the situation and compelled a settlement of the strike. It is true that the result of your efforts was to increase the price of coal to every one of us, but humanity demanded that the miner should have wages sufficient for himself and family, and the people are cheerfully paying.

In your battle, sir, for a railroad rate law you have proclaimed against secret rates and special privileges for any one, because you realized that if some men had special rebates it was foolish to speak of others competing on any sort of fair terms with them.

Now the plans which the National Association of Retail Druggists have worked out means nothing more than that which you are endeavoring to secure for the shipper, namely, equality of opportunity for all. From this equality of opportunity no one is shut out, and for the community from every point of view the advantages are enormous.

TO MEET ON THE RIVER.

Arrangements are being made to hold the next monthly meeting of the Philadelphia Retail Druggist Association on one of the large excursion boats on the Delaware river. Now that the College of Pharmacy is closed for the Summer the meetings are to be held in Odd Fellows' Temple each month. It is thought that plans can be arranged for holding the meeting on the water in July. This will afford an outing not only to the members of the association but for the members of their family as well, and all at a slight expense. A committee has been appointed to look into the matter. The regular monthly meeting on June 1 was a largely atttended and enthusiastic one, the best of good fellowship prevailing. Four new members were elected and it is understood that there is a large waiting list.

DELEGATES TO N. A. R. D. MEETING.

Considerable interest was manifested in the selection of delegates and alternates for the annual meeting of the N. A. R. D., which is to be held at Atlanta, Ga., in October. The delegates and alternates selected are: Alternates: Charles Rehfus, T. H. Potts, H. C. Blair, Charles Leedom, N. A. Cozens, Clarence Campbell, William E. Lee, A. T. Pollard, Warren H. Poley, D. J. Reese, D. G. Potts, F. Apple, Walter Rophwell, William L. Cliffe, Joshua Marsden, R. H. Lakey, William E. Supplee, George Fehr, C. W. Shull, Frank Fluck, S. P. Henry, Otto Kraus, N. S. Seltzer, H. K. Nolte, E. K. Boltz, William Morrison, O. Osterlund, P. G. Neeley, John M. G. Long and S. W. Strump. Besides this aggregation of representative druggists, it is understood that there will also be a number of the members who will attend the convention as individuals.

MR. KLINE'S PROMINENCE IN CIVIL LIFE.

M. N. Kline, of the firm of Smith, Kline & French Company, is one of the most talked of business men of this city. Mr. Kline is not only the head of one of the largest wholesale drug houses in this city, but he seems to find time to work for the interest of the city. Some time ago it was rumored that a movement was on foot to make him the next Mayor, but he soon put a stop to this report. He is one of the Mayor's confidential advisers and there is hardly a day passes that he is not in communication with the head of the city. At the recent convention of delegates to the Lincoln Party he took a prominent part and succeeded in having his choice placed on the ticket for Governor. Now it is proposed to give him more honor. There will be elections held for three Congressmen this Fall and it is likely that some unexpected candidate will be placed in the field. It is rumored that many of the most prominent citizens of this city are in favor of sending M. N. Kline to Washington. It is a question whether he will accept as he prefers to take the part of the people in having reforms executed.

A PERTINENT QUERY.

"What has become of the million dollar trust that was recently formed to put up various drug stores in the different cities?" is the question that is being asked by many druggists. This so-called drug trust was going to try to corner the retail drug business. It had a charter granted and from the reports sent out it would not be long before the retail stores that did not deal in a certain brand of cigars would feel the iron hand of this new company. So far there have been no reports of any retail drug store in this city having been compelled to close down owing to the inroads of the new company. No wireless reports have been received to the effect that this company has in any way begun to do business. There were rumors that offers had been made for several stores here, but so far no option has been taken.

ITEMS OF NEWS.

Samuel B. Davis, who conducts the drug store at Sixth street and Snyder avenue, was married on June 4. His friends wish him joy and prosperity.

Dr. Holland, the well-known druggist, of Grays Ferry avenue, is now in Europe and writes back that he is thoroughly enjoying himself. This is the doctor's seventh trip abroad.

Charles Leedom, 1403 Filbert street, who has lately returned from a hunting trip through the wilds of Virginia, has been elected president of the East Magnolia Gold Placer Mining Company.

Lincoln McNeil, Front and York streets, will shortly sail for Europe, and will remain away until September 5th. He will travel pretty much all over the continent, but pass most of his time in the quiet town of Paris.

L. J. Ringer will be married on June 5th. Mr. Ringer has many friends, and it will be very surprising if they do not see to it that the ceremony will not be known as a "quiet affair." He will reside at Sixth and Poplar streets, where his principal store is located.

Charles H. Snyder, manager of the Walter F. Ware Company, has returned from a successful business trip to the Pacific Coast. Mr. Snyder combined business with pleasure. He visited nearly all of the prominent cities of the West and was in San Francisco after the earthquake. He succeeded in securing a number of large orders for his house.

Charles W. Hancock, who is now retired from the drug business, but who for years was located at Thirty-fourth and Spring Garden streets, has gone through this world a bachelor, or for 72 years, but now the word comes to us that he is shortly to be married, and he and his bride will reside at Langhorne, Pa.

James A. Ferguson, Howard and Thompson streets, has been seriously ill with pneumonia, and for a time his life was despaired of, but later reports from the sick room indicate that he is now improving, which will be welcome news for his many friends. Mr. Ferguson is one of the most genial men in the drug business, and though he has been an unusually successful druggist he remains one of the most modest gentlemen in the trade.

OUR CANADIAN LETTER.

The Government to Supervise Production and Sale of Proprietary Remedies—New Companies Doing Business in Ontario—Canadian Imports and Exports of Drugs.

(From our Regular Correspondent.)

Toronto, June 4.—The Special Committee of the Dominion Parliament appointed to inquire into the sale of fraudulent or deleterious medicines are practically unanimous as to the need of stringent legislation for the protection of the public. Dr. Dube, professor of Lavel University, testified before the committee that about 75 per cent. of standard drugs were adulterated, owing to the keen competition in business. The Department of Inland Revenue will prepare a draft bill providing for the analysis and registration of all patent and proprietary medicines. The committee will summon prominent medical men to advise them as to the extent to which the medicines of this class which are harmless in prescribed doses would be injurious if used continuously for prolonged periods.

The following companies have been incorporated under the laws of Ontario: Sovereign Perfumes, Ltd., head office, Toronto; capital, $40,000; provisional directors, Thomas Kennedy, Alex. Nelson, John Nelson, William F. Scott, John F. Nelson and William D. Corson.

Sutherlands, Ltd., head office, Hamilton, Ont.; capital, $150,000; provisional directors: James W. Sutherland, Harvey Little, H. Sutherland, Alex. J. Douglas and Elizabeth Wynn; to manufacture soda water fountain supplies, extracts, etc.

The Garfield Tea Company, incorporated under the laws of New York, has been authorized to do business in Ontario on a capital not exceeding $25,000.

The monthly report of the Canadian Department of Trade and Commerce for February, just issued, shows total imports of drugs, dyes, chemicals and medicines for the month amounting to $566,142, of which $400,443 were from the United States, as against total imports of $374,007 and American imports $243,219 in February, 1905. Exports of drugs, dyes, chemicals and medicines of home production amounted to $90,679, of which $44,788 went to the American market, as compared with total shipments of $51,356 and American shipments of $29,178 for February, 1905.

Thomas J. Leitch has purchased the drug business of H. A. Clemens, Hamilton, Ont.

A. T. Embury, druggist, of Bancroft, Ontario, was recently burned out.

D. Nairn & Co., druggists, of Enderby, B. C., are succeeded by W. T. Broderick.

Among the losers by an extensive fire which destroyed a large portion of the business section of Woodstock, N. B., May 30, are Garden Bros. and the I. E. Sheasgreen Drug Company, both establishments being burned out.

ILLINOIS.

Hepburn Pure Food and Drug Bill Discussed by Druggists—Chicago Retail Druggists' Association Favor Amendments Proposed by Interstate Commerce Committee—Medical Men Oppose While Proprietary Medicine Men Support Them—Another Antinarcotic Bill.

(From our Regular Correspondent.)

Chicago, June 7.—The Hepburn Pure Food and Drug bill was discussed at length at a special meeting of the C. R. D. A., which took place May 25 in the Northwestern Building. The gist of the discussion is to be found in the following resolution which was adopted:

Wheras, At the April meeting of the Chicago Retail Druggists' Association action was taken favoring the elimination from the Hepburn Pure Food and Drug bill, now before Congress, of a clause exempting (from the provision that amounts of all poisonous substances contained in proprietary preparations be published) those preparations containing minimum quantities of narcotics; and

Whereas, It appears that many of our members have signed petitions to Congress favoring the change just menitoned, as well as other changes not contemplated in the action referred to; and

Whereas, It has come to our knowledge that the proposed changes in the amendments would impose serious hardship upon druggists doing business in the District of Columbia, in the Territories and in the insular possessions, who would have no protection from *State* legislation; and also that insistence now upon changing the proposed amendments would jeopardize the adoption of *any* amendments affording retail druggists protection from a measure which, if unamended, would be unjust and seriously hurtful to the retail drug business; therefore, by the Chicago Retail Druggists' Association in special session assembled, be it

Resolved, That we urge upon the Congressmen from Cook County that they support the amendments to this bill that were recommended by the Interstate Commerce Committee.

The discussion was started by John W. Kennedy, of the Proprietary Association, who asked support for the amendments to the Hepburn bill. Dr. Gilmore, as the representative of the Chicago Medical Society, opposed the portion of the amendments that allows minimum quantities of morphine and alcohol in medicinal preparations without labelling. Attorney George Douglass, of the P. A. of A., did not agree with Dr. Gilmore. In the general talk that followed Albert E. Ebert, Charles Havery, W. Bodemann, T. V. Wooten, V. H. Chantler, J. J. Boehm, C. M. Carr, L. P. Larsen, J. P. Crowley and I. M. Light were heard from. Some of the speakers referred to articles which have appeared recently in a Chicago paper to the effect that it is the intention to sidetrack the Pure Food bill and thus prevent its passage. It was alleged in these articles that the enemies of the measure had gained the upper hand at Washington.

PROPOSED NEW ANTINARCOTIC LAW.

The Legislative Committee of the Illinois Pharmaceutical Association has drafted a bill to prevent the sale of narcotics or habit producing drugs without prescriptions from licensed physicians. This measure is to be submitted for approval at the meeting in Peoria that opens June 19. The sessions will last three days. The measure will be much broader than that now in force and will not be limited to cocaine. It is provided that the name of the person applying must be made a matter of record. The prescriptions are to be retained and must not be refilled without a new order from a licensed practitioner. The prosecutions for violations are to be carried out by the State Board of Pharmacy. No prosecutions are to be started against patent medicines until the State Board certifies that they contain narcotics. Violations are to be punished with fines, and for the third offense the defendant may be sent to jail for a term of not more than six months.

NOTES OF THE TRADE.

S. M. Elliott has opened a store at Halsted and Eighty-seventh street, South Englewood.

The W. O. N. A. R. D., chapter II, gave its first social at the home of Mrs. Geo. Bollinger. The thirty-six in attendance played euchre all evening.

H. W. Matthews, father of Charles E. Matthews, of Sharp & Dohme, is reported to be seriously ill from blood poisoning, due primarily to a corn or bunion.

Vincenzo Coletta and Gaetano Celestino, druggists in the levee district, have been indicted by the Grand Jury for selling cocaine. The State's Attorney says he will try to make examples of these men by having penitentiary sentences imposed.

Thomas Voegeli, of Minneapolis, has resigned from the National Executive Committee of the N. A. R. D. Mr. Voegeli says that his personal affairs have suffered so much because of his attention to N. A. R. D. affairs that he felt the step to be imperative.

The Chicago Veteran Druggists' Association had its "Ebert Day" May 21. T. H. Patterson was elected president; T. N. Jamieson, vice-president; H. Biroth, treasurer. J. Blocki, the present corresponding secretary, and W. Bodemann, the recording secretary, were made permanent officers. The "Jamieson Day" of the organization will take place June 21.

Charles Havery, representing the C. R. D. A., and W. Bodemann, representing the State Board of Pharmacy, attended a meeting of the Social Hygiene Association which was held here recently for the purpose of forming a local branch. In order to aid in the work it is suggested that druggists should refuse to treat venereal diseases.

A special meeting of 25 doctors and the same number of druggists is to take place June 21 at Vogelsang's restaurant. In the fall there is to be an enormous banquet to which all doctors and druggists in good standing will be invited. Preliminaries for the special meeting were gone through with at a luncheon attended by Messrs. Avery, Bodemann, Chantler, Forsyth, Light and Yoemans, who met Drs. Bacon, Gilmore, Greene and Webster. Efforts are bein made, with every prospect of success, to bring druggists and physicians together.

L. E. Gauss, superintendent of the sales department of Eli Lilly & Co., has just returned from a trip to San Francisco. He started for the West directly after the earthquake and spent some time on the Coast arranging for stock orders with the jobbers in that locality. He returned to the Hoosier city and was in Chicago again June 5, leaving for New York the same night on the Twentieth Century Limited train. Mr. Gauss is a Chicago boy, spent his earlier days here and has made many friends, who are proud of his success.

B. T. Van Allen, who looks after the Western trade for C. F. Boehringer & Soehne, has been ill at his home here, but it is hoped that he will be able to call on the trade in this locality again in about ten days. Mr. Van Allen was one of the commercial tourists who journeyed to San Francisco after the upheaval, but the strain on his nervous system and the hardships of railroad travel were too much for him, and since his return he has been confined to his home. Mr. Van Allen is one of the best known men in the West and has a host of friends, who will be glad to know when he is able to be about his duties.

Allen R. Fellows has turned his back on Chicago and embarked for Sioux Falls, S. D., where he has accepted the position of manager for the Brown Drug Company. Mr. Fellows has had a brilliant career here and is a man of no small ability. He learned the wholesale drug business with Hartz & Bahnsen, Morrisson, Plummer & Co., and Humiston, Keeling & Co. He first attracted attention as manager for the Ross-Flowers Company. Later, when this concern was absorbed by the Searle & Hereth Company, he was one of the assets and in one year worked himself up to general manager. He is a man of good ideas and sterling qualities and will be missed by his many friends here.

THE ANNUAL VISIT TO PARKE, DAVIS & CO.'S LABORATORIES.

The annual visit of the physicians and pharmacists from Chicago and surrounding territory to the laboratories of Parke, Davis & Co. has come to be considered an established institution. This year June 6th was the date selected for making the start, and a full train load left on a special train of the Michigan Central at 10 o'clock on that date for a two days' visit to Detroit under the care of James E. Bartlett, manager of the Chicago branch. The programme laid out insures the party having a busy and an agreeable time. All expenses save the railroad fare are borne by Parke, Davis & Co. The first day, Thursday, will be devoted to a visit to the laboratories, and the second, Friday, to a trip up the river to the St. Clair Flats.

INDIANA.

Proceedings Begun in Government Suit Against Drug Associations—Papers Read at the Chemical Society—Maintaining Prices in Terre Haute—New Indiana Corporations.

(From our Regular Correspondent.)

Indianapolis, June 4, 1906.—A number of attorneys representing various defendants in the case of the United States against the National Association of Retail Druggists *et al.*, now on the docket of the Federal Court at Minneapolis, have filed written appearances. The bill of complaint was originally filed a couple of weeks ago by Joseph B. Kealing, United States District Attorney for this district, by direction of Attorney-General W. H. Moody, in an effort to break up the alleged illegal combination of what is known as the "drug trust." The case promises to be bitterly contested on both sides when it comes up for trial. The defendants, whose attorneys filed their appearances to-day, (June 4), must file their answers by the first Monday of July. Among the attorneys who filed their appearances in the Federal Court were the following:

Ferdinand Winter, for the National Wholesale Druggists' Association; D. P. Williams, for the Milks Emulsion Company and Charles C. Bombaugh; James W. Noel, for Seabury & Johnson and Searle & Herth; Norris & Morey, Buffalo, for D. Ransom, Son & Co.; Baker & Daniels, for the Eli Lilly Company; Ryan & Ruckelshaus and Frank H. Fredericks, for William D. Freeman; Wilson & Townley and Joseph Errant, for the National Association of Retail Druggists; Williams & Lancaster, Chattanooga, Tenn., for the Chatttanooga Medicine Company; Charles M. Woodruff, Detroit, for Parke, Davis & Co.

PAPERS READ AT THE CHEMICAL SOCIETY.

The Indiana section of the American Chemical Society met at Lafayette, Ind., on the night of May 12. Several important subjects were discussed, the programme being headed by a discussion of Sulphuric Acid and Calcium Chloride as Drying Agents, by Dr. Percy N. Evans, of Purdue University. Some Applications for the Ionic Theory in Physiology was the subject treated by Dr. E. G. Martin, of Lafayette. Other papers read and discussed were: A Rapid Method of Determining Carbon in Iron and Steel, by Mr. Aupperne, of Indianapolis, and Analysis of London Purple, by E. H. Mahin, of Purdue.

MAINTAINING PRICES IN TERRE HAUTE.

Recently the drug trade of Terre Haute, Ind., has been having a lively experience with the method by which prices for proprietary articles are maintained. Wholesale dealers have been heavily penalized more than once for selling to cut price retailers, and in one instance which was of public nature a wholesale house lost nearly all its retail customers because it sold to a cut price store, the requirement of the National Association of Retail Druggists being that retailers should not buy from this wholesale house.

NEW INDIANA DRUG COMPANIES

incorporated during the past fortnight include the following: The Alford Drug Company, of Richmond, with a capital stock of $10,000, to conduct a general drug business, and directors, William H. Alford, Harry G. Alford and George E. Kemper.

The Brown Drug Company, of Lafayette, with $4,000 capital stock, to conduct a retail drug business, and incorporators, Albert A. Wells, Ernest A. Brown, Emory J. Yeager, and Frank W. Best.

THE SOUTH.

A Campaign Against Unlicensed Druggists—A New Anticocaine Law Proposed—Sixteen Graduates from the New Orleans College—Pure Food Law Endorsed.

(From our Regular Correspondent.)

New Orleans, La., May 21, 1906.—With F. C. Godbold, one of the city's best known pharmacists, at its head, a crusade against all pharmacists not registered under the State act has been launched in this city and bids fair to stir up a considerable sensation. The first affidavits in this connection were made in the First City Criminal Court, when Mr. Godbold, as the representative of the Louisiana State Board of Pharmacy, charged John F. Krumpfur, a druggist of Washington avenue and Howard street, with several violations of the State law. Six affidavits were preferred against Krumpfur, and it was alleged in all of these that he was guilty of compounding drugs without having the necessary license to do so. On the same day affidavits were filed charging Otto Lyncker, who conducts a drug store at 361 South Rampart street, with selling poisonous drugs without a physician's prescription. Lyncker's wife made the alleged sale, but Lyncker has assumed the responsibility. This practically opens a campaign which has as its object the strict enforcement of all laws providing against the evil practices which, it is alleged, exist here.

TO ENACT A MORE EFFECTIVE ANTINARCOTIC LAW.

War on the selling of cocaine has been opened in the Louisiana Legislature, which is now in session, and efforts are now being made to amend the law so as to provide a much heavier punishment for the sellers of this article. It is argued that the punishment provided by the statute for the unlawful retailing of cocaine is inadequate, and that inasmuch as many crimes are directly traceable to the effects of this drug its sellers should be severely punished.

GRADUATES FROM THE NEW ORLEANS COLLEGE OF PHARMACY.

Sixteen young pharmacists were graduated from the New Orleans College of Pharmacy at the annual commencement exercises, held Monday, May 14, at the Tulane Theatre, which marked the close of the sixth season of the successfully conducted institution. Those graduated were: Samuel W. Hills, Lerrier P. Blanchard, C. A. Desporte, Jr., R. H. Chargrois, R. H. Rawlings, H. J. Lagarde, Y. V. Terrebonne, L. W. Holmes, J. F. Whitley, E. J. Naquin, J. O. Ferrier, Miss Alice Louapre, P. F. Dastugue, J. J. Dubourg, J. G. Hirsch and W. J. Gagnet. The alumni medal offered to the member of the class having the highest general average in his studies and examinations was won by Mr. Hirsch. Dr. Charles Chassaignac delivered the annual address, which was chiefly devoted to an expose of the patent medicine evil. This he termed one of the burning questions now before the public for settlement. Dr. Chassaignac appealed to the graduates just entering upon the practice of their profession to join in the movement for the annihilation of the evil. The druggist could do much toward this end, he said, for it was he who stood between the manufacturer and the consumer.

Dr. Philip Asher, dean of the college, read his annual report to the Board of Trustees, showing the excellent progress of the school in the few years which have elapsed since its establishment. Each year showed a healthy increase in the attendance. The enrollment at the session just closed was 55. President George D. Feldner conferred the degrees and awarded the diplomas. Ferrier P. Blanchard was salutatorian and Samuel Willard Hills the valedictorian. Arthur E. Breslin made the presentation address conferring the alumni medal upon J. G. Hirsch. On the stage with the graduates were the Board of Directors and the members of the faculty.

LOUISIANA CHEMISTS INDORSE PURE FOOD BILL.

At a recent meeting held in this city the Louisiana Chemical Society declared itself to be unanimously in favor of pure food laws. This action came at the conclusion of an address delivered by Prof. Charles E. Coates, in which he said that conditions in this State were deplorable. A resolution was passed asking the Legislature to memorialize Congress to pass the bill now pending before that body.

The Drug and Chemical Market

The prices quoted in this report are those current in the wholesale market, and higher prices are paid for retail lots
The quality of goods frequently necessitates a wide range of prices.

Condition of Trade.

NEW YORK, June 9, 1906.

The volume of trade in drugs and chemicals during the past fortnight has been rather light and an absence of features is to be noted, though conditions are not of a character to cause uneasiness considering the season of the year. The usual summer exodus of heads of firms to seashores, mountain and foreign resorts has begun, and buying in excess of current necessities is apparently suspended for the moment, round lots being almost neglected. The aggregate volume of business is, however, of seasonable proportions, and dealers show no disposition to complain. The fluctuations in values are limited to a few articles only and are not of particular interest. American saffron continues on the downward grade, and opium remains featureless, with only a hand to mouth demand experienced. Quinine has not varied in the interval, and the bark sale at Amsterdam on the 7th instant did not affect the situation, the unit value being identical with that of the previous sale, while seven-eighths of the bark offered was disposed of. Manufacturers have reduced the price of silver nitrate, and the lithia salts are lower. Lemon and peppermint oils are held with increased firmness, the first-named at an advance. Among the chemicals oxalic acid and blue vitriol are maintained in strong position. Arsenic has developed an easier tendency, though values are as yet nominally unchanged. Strontium nitrate has advanced in value, but to a limited extent only. A good seasonable demand for powdered hellebore root, coupled with scarcity, has served to advance values on this insecticide, and camphor is in good request, with values firmly maintained for both domestic and Japanese refined. Other changes noted and commented on below include a further decline in American saffron, and advances in lemon oil, cassia oil and beeswax.

HIGHER.	LOWER.
Beeswax,	Saffron, American,
Lemon oil,	Silver nitrate,
Cassia oil,	Haarlem oil,
Cardamom seed,	Golden Seal root,
Cubeb berries,	Wormseed, American,
Oxalic acid,	Lithia salts,
Hellebore root (powdered),	Belladonna leaves,
Agar-agar,	Tonka beans,
Chamomile flowers, Roman,	Canary seed,
Yerba santa,	Condurango bark.
Guarana,	

Drugs.

Acetanilid has improved in tone somewhat, owing to the strength of raw materials, and bulk stock does not offer below 24c.

Acetone continues in good request, with current sales at the range of 15c to 17c, as to quantity.

Agar-agar is finding an increased consuming outlet, and holders are firmer in their views, at 50c.

Alcohol, grain, remains in steady position, and the passage of the Denatured Alcohol bill has had no apparent effect on values, quotations being maintained on the basis of $2.47 to $2.49, as to quantity. Wood is steady, at 70c to 75c.

Balsam copaiba, Central American, continues scarce, and holders are firmer in their views, at 30c to 31c; Para is held and selling at 45c to 50c.

Balsam Peru is in better supply, but holders abate none of their firmness, $1.00 to $1.05 being still asked.

Balsam tolu is more freely offered, in view of recent heavy arrivals, but values are apparently unaffected, 20c to 21c being yet named.

Bayberry bark is likely to be scarce this year, according to the London *Chemist and Druggist*, which says that practically no new crop will be forthcoming, but values in this market are easier, with sales at 11c to 13c.

Belladonna leaves are offered more freely, owing to the market being better supplied, and 8½c to 9c will now buy, according to quality and quantity.

Buchu leaves, short, are in good request, numerous sales of prime green leaf being reported at 18c to 20c. The season's supply is about at an end, arrivals at the Cape having ceased, according to reports.

Cacao butter is unchanged in price, importers quoting Dutch bulk at 28c to 28¾c, and 12-lb. boxes at 34c to 35c, but sales are unimportant.

Cantharides, Chinese, are in better supply, but prices are unchanged, the stock being closely concentrated. It is difficult to shade 85c, the price named by the principal holder, for both whole and powdered.

Cascara sagrada is in good demand and values are steadily maintained at the recent advance to 6½c to 9c, as to age, the first figure being for 1905 bark and the second for three-year-old.

Chamomile flowers are in demand, and Roman have advanced in the interval to 25c, owing to scarcity of spot supplies. Cable advices are to the effect that new crop German for shipment is held at figures above those quoted for old on the spot.

Codliver oil is seasonably dull, but values appear well sustained at the previous range of $18 to $24 for Newfoundland and $23 to $27 for Norwegian. According to cable advices the Finmarken fishing to date is 8,000,000 fish, yielding 5,763 barrels of oil, a gain for the past week of 1,445 barrels. More inquiry is noted on the part of local dealers to cover their requirements for next season, as primary values are believed to be in firmer tendency.

Condurango bark is in better supply and offered more freely at lower prices, or, say, 10c to 11c.

Cramp bark has eased off a trifle in the interval, and holders are now free to offer at 7c to 8c, according to quality.

Cubeb berries have improved in price, though business has not been noticeably active, inquiries being mostly confined to jobbing parcels of whole, for which 10½c to 11½c has been paid. The revised range for powdered is 12c to 16c, as to quality and quantity.

Cuttlefish bone, jewelers', is held with increased firmness, in consequence of reports of advancing primary markets, and local holders ask 70c for large bone and 40c for small.

Ergot is cabled firmer abroad, but the local market is very dull; spot quotations are nominally unchanged at 20c to 29c for German.

Grindelia robusta is in moderately active demand and values are well maintained, at the range of 4½c to 4¾c.

Guarana has hardened in value during the interval, and $1.35 to $1.50 is now firmly maintained for the small available supply, which is closely concentrated.

Haarlem oil is easier, to the extent that sales of uncapped have been made at $2.75, though $3.00 is yet asked for capped bottles.

Isinglass, Japanese, is in limited supply, and dealers offer with reserve at the range of 42c to 48c.

Lycopodium is dull and neglected, at the quoted range of 48c to 50c, as to grade and quantity.

Menthol is dull and neglected, to the extent that there have been sellers at $2.50.

Opium continues weak and neglected, and there is no change of consequence to report. Only small jobbing sales are reported, though quotations are nominally steady, at $2.72½ for cases and $2.75 to $2.80 for broken packages. Powdered is finding a moderate consuming outlet, at $3.20 to $3.25.

Quinine is rather dull and uninteresting at the moment, though the tone of the market has improved. The Amsterdam sale of bark on Thursday last resulted in a unit of 4¼ Dutch cents, at which seven-eighths of the offerings of 8,122 packages were disposed of. This is regarded as encouraging to holders of quinine, and more inquiry was reported in some quarters. Quotations from second hands remain more or less nominal, at 16c to 16½c, while manufacturers' prices are unchanged at 17c for bulk in 100-oz. tins.

Saffron, American, has dropped in price, and the tendency is still downward, with 85c named as acceptable for either bales or broken lots.

Saffron flowers, American, are offered more freely, in consequence of keen competition among dealers, and 85c is now named as acceptable for bales and 87½c to 90c for broken lots.

Senna, Alexandria, is maintained in firm position, with a good demand reported at the current range of 17c to 20c for whole leaf, 9½c to 11c for half leaf and 5½c to 6c for clippings.

Soap bark, cut, has sold freely in the interval at 5½c, though some grades command 6c to 6½c.

Tonka beans reflect the influence of competition among holders, and values have eased off to the range of 60c to 62½c for prime.

Vanilla beans are maintained in firm position, though no considerable inquiry is reported. The season's crop has turned out larger than was expected; quoted $2.75 to $5.00 for whole and $2.00 to $2.25 for cut.

Wax, bees, is meeting with increased inquiry, and the tone of the market is firmer at an advance to 33½c to 34c for ordinary and 34½c to 35c for selected. Japan is maintained at 11½c to 11¾c.

Chemicals.

There are few new features of special interest to report in this department. Oxalic acid is in better supply, and business was done at 6½c. Blue vitriol is firmer, owing to increased demand, and 6c to 6½c is named as to quantity. Silver nitrate is fractionally lower, in sympathy with the decline in the price of metal, and quotations are now 41⅞c to 45¼c, as to quantity. Arsenic is in improved position, though sales are yet making at 5¼ to 5½c. Strontium nitrate is in light supply, and the tone of the market is firmer, with quotations advanced to 8c to 8½c. Quicksilver is finding a good consuming outlet, and jobbing sales are reported at 55c to 56c. There is nothing new to report as regards the respective positions of citric acid, tartaric acid or cream tartar.

Lithium carbonate and other salts of lithia are easier, owing to keen competition, and sales of carbonate are reported at $1.05 to $1.10.

Phosphoric acid has hardened in the interval, owing to scarcity, and dealers now quote U. S. P. at 10c to 24c.

Essential Oils.

Anise is in steady moderate demand and quotations during the interval fluctuated from $1.27 to $1.32½ and back again to $1.30 to $1.35, at which range sales are now making.

Cassia is in good seasonable demand and held at full previous prices, or, say, 80c to 82½c.

Citronella is in limited demand and quotations have not varied in the interval from 38c to 40c.

Clove is offered a shade more freely, there being sellers at 92½c for bulk, though others hold out for 97½c.

Coriander is inquired for more freely, and the quotations of the market are steadily maintained at $9.00 to $13.00.

Hemlock is scarce and wanted, and the inside quotation has been advanced to 52½c.

Messina essences are maintained in firm position, lemon being especially strong, though quotations cover a wide range; while small lots are obtainable at 70c, up to 80c is named for the leading brand.

Pennyroyal, French, has been in better demand during the interval, and this, coupled with slight scarcity, has led to firmer views on the part of holders, who now quote $1.75 to $1.85.

Peppermint is maintained in firm position and the market is steady at $2.80 to $3.00 for bulk oil. Reports from producing centers point to a shortage of crop, it being asserted in some quarters that the crop in Wayne Conty would be nearer an absolute failure than ever known before.

Wintergreen, natural, is now coming forward in the usual volume and the market is irregular and unsettled in consequence, with quotations ranging from $1.45 to $1.75.

Gums.

About the usual inquiry is experienced for the mucilaginous gums, on which values are firmly maintained for all varieties, arabics being noticeably strong and likely to go higher. Camphor continues held and selling, and values on which, firmly maintained, are at the range of $1.00 to $1.50.

Roots.

Calamus, bleached, is in reduced supply and holders do not offer at under 30c.

Golden seal is firmer and holders express more confidence in the situation, sales being made at the close at $1.25.

Hellebore, white, powdered, is maintained with more firmness at 6c to 7c, in consequence of a shortage of whole.

Ipecac is maintained steadily at $1.75 to $1.80 for Rio, and $1.65 to $1.70 for Carthagena. Stocks in first hands are reported exhausted.

Jalap has moved into firmer position owing to scarcity, and nothing now offers at 13c to 14c.

Pink continues to attract attention, but there is no visible supply and the quotation of $1.25 is merely nominal.

Senega offers more freely with the advent of new crop and spot quotations have been reduced to 55c to 56c.

Serpentaria continues in fair consuming demand, but supplies are freer and quotations are reduced to 40c to 42c.

Squill is not inquired for to any extent and offers freely in a jobbing way at 10c.

Seeds.

Canary is lower, owing to recent heavy arrivals of South American seed, Smyrna being held at 3¾c to 4c and Sicily at 4¼c to 4½c.

Cardamoms, decorticated, are maintained in firm position in the face of continued strong advices from abroad, and recent sales were at 36c.

Coriander is firmer, owing to the strong tenor of advices from primary markets, but spot quotations remain unchanged at 6c to 10¾c.

Sunflower is in good consuming demand and holders have advanced their range of prices, foreign being held at 4¼c and domestic at 4½c to 5c.

Wormseed, American, has developed an easier tendency and sales were made at 6c to 7c; Russian is firmer, quotations being well maintained at 17½c to 18c.

Medicine or Knife in Appendicitis ?

A statistical study of the subject has been completed by Dr. Chauvel, Medical Inspector of the French army. It shows conclusively the difference between the medical and the surgical method of dealing with appendicitis and similar troubles with the intestines.

Notwithstanding the theory that there is no such thing as medical treatment for this disease, the investigation proved it to be successful in ninety-nine cases in every hundred. It also shows fatalities of over twenty per cent. where the knife is resorted to in the place of well-known medicines. This information is highly valuable to the lay mind, for when in trouble one wants to be able to decide intelligently what to have done. To the agony of the situation must be added his decision whether to take the chances of an operation with the knife or rely upon medicine.

Merck & Co., of New York and St. Louis, have issued their June price-list of chemicals, alkaloids, new remedies and specialties in a most conveniently arranged pamphlet of 48 pages. With this in his possession no druggist should be at a loss for information regarding the kind of containers and prices of chemicals and new remedies. Copies can be had for the asking from Merck & Company, University place and Eighth street, New York.

Opportunities *for* Export Trade

(Written for the American Druggist.)

THE PROFESSION OF PHARMACY IN THE ISLAND OF PORTO RICO.

By Joaquin Duran Cottes,
Pharmacist, Curabo, Porto Rico.

In the "noble and loyal city of San Juan de Puerto Rico," by virtue of a Royal Decree of March 14, 1839, there was established a Royal Governmental Sub-delegation of the Faculty of Medicine. This Sub-delegation was subordinate to the General Administration of Studies of the Kingdom at Madrid, and was composed of three members, which on the nomination of the Governor Captain General of Porto Rico was named by her majesty the Queen of Spain. Of these three members one acted as President, another as First Member and the other as Secretary, and they composed the tribunal or board to examine those who aspired to the title of pharmacist.

In order to become a licentiate it was necessary to possess the title of Bachelor or to have acquired a knowledge in a recognized educational institution of the branches of Latin, logic and mathematics equivalent to that required for the degree of Bachelor.

Four years' instruction under the direction and practice of an intelligent pharmacist was also required, the first year being devoted to natural history, the second to chemistry, the third to theoretical pharmacy, and the fourth to practical pharmacy and toxicology.

After passing a rigorous examination in the four above named courses, the student was required to take two other examinations as a last test.

The work of this organization was carried on with regularity and success until December, 1898, at which time the Royal Governmental Sub-delegation of the Faculty of Medicine ceased to exist.

Must organizations which have been so useful to the country be totally annulled? I am of the opinion that advancement is not found in destruction, but in modifying and improving existing conditions, making use of new ideas and materials. What would happen to the science of to-day if we destroyed the scientific principles of yesterday?

The scientific body alluded to rendered great benefits to the country, and its members could show their diplomas with pride; its effect was certainly felt in the Island most advantageously for the space of more than half a century, being seconded and helped by self-sacrificing pharmacists who worked for the progress of pharmacy.

Pharmacy of Sr. Joaquin Durán Cottes, Gurabo, Puerto Rico.

There exists now another organization, a "Boaro." The men who are at the head of this belong to the old school. That which is really new is the plan of study of to-day; the old method gave brilliant results. Will this do the same? I believe so, and such is the desire of the small part of suffering humanity constituting the pharmacists of the Island of Porto Rico.

As will be seen by the accompanying illustration of the store of Senor Cottes, he has one of the best equipped pharmacies on the Island, and one which is conducted on the most scientific lines. Senor Cottes is much interested in educational questions and has done much to maintain the professional status of pharmacy on a lofty plane.

Consul Brittain, of Kiehl, gives four leading reasons why German merchants are succeeding in extending their foreign trade, which are as follows: (1) The training of men especially for the business, who shall know every detail, and who are able to speak several languages. (2) Disposition to please the purchaser with styles and prices and giving long credits. (3) Determination to hold a customer once won. (4) Their ability, by government aid, to deliver goods in their own ships.

(*Written for the American Druggist.*)

THE CONDITION OF PHARMACY IN THE UNITED STATES OF COLOMBIA.

By J. A. Gonzalez,
Barranquilla, United States of Colombia.

The laws regulating the practice of pharmacy in the United States of Colombia are far from being in a satisfactory condition, the only regulations of any kind, up to last year, having to do solely with what might be termed the political aspect of pharmacy, that is the relations of the pharmacist to the State as a business man in regard to taxation, etc. Last year, however, the National Assembly did draft and enact certain regulations bearing on the practice of pharmacy, but these are far from being satisfactory.

One of the results of this lack of proper governmental supervision of the practice of pharmacy is that many of those who are actively engaged as managers of the various "boticas" have no scientific knowledge or training whatever. As a matter of fact, nearly every physician conducts his own dispensary, having some person in charge, whose knowledge of pharmacy, materia medica and toxicology is limited to such superficial instruction as his employer may choose to give, supplemented, possibly, by a study of such books of formulæ, etc., as the physician may chance to have in the store.

In view of this ignorance and lack of training on the part of those who conduct the majority of the drug stores in this country, one is agreeably surprised to learn of the comparative immunity from serious accidents in the dispensing of drugs.

LOCAL REGULATIONS FOR BARRANQUILLA.

The present intelligent mayor of Barranquilla has recently issued a decree prohibiting the sale of medicine in grocery stores, a much needed step toward the safeguarding of the handling of drugs. The fact that such an edict was necessary is the best—or rather the worst—possible comment on existing conditions.

There are, it is true, a few independent pharmacies conducted by men who have a high degree of scientific knowledge of all branches of pharmacy, and it is all the more to the credit of these men that they should have taken the trouble and the time to study the scientific aspects of their calling, since they were not required to do so by law.

It is to be hoped that this scientific element in pharmacy may eventually become so powerful as to bring about the enactment of a general pharmacy law which will place the practice of pharmacy in this country on a higher plane, will provide for the teaching of pharmacy in the universities, and will establish adequate educational requirements.

COMMERCIAL AFFILIATIONS.

Commercially we are affiliated almost equally with Europe and the United States. From the latter country we obtain our fluid extracts and galenicals and a large number of proprietary preparations which have a considerable sale here. The alkaloids and fine chemicals used come almost exclusively from Germany and France, the latter country also supplying several popular specifics. Italy supplies us direct with castor oil, alum, sulphur and various roots and herbs, while our heavy chemicals come largely from the United Kingdom.

Toilet articles, perfumes, etc., have been drawn mostly from France, but of late the American products have made some headway in popular favor.

[Barranquilla, the city from which Senor Gonzalez writes, has a population of 90,000, and is one of the most important cities, commercially, of the United States of Colombia. Owing to the lack of all restrictions there are a large number of very small drug stores in which business is carried on on a very small scale indeed. The Farmocia Nacional, however, of which Gonzalez & Co. are the proprietors, is a large and well-appointed store, and carries a large and well assorted stock, embracing French, English and American perfumes and toilet articles, optical goods, rubber goods, surgical instruments and supplies, such as bandages, dressings, etc., and druggists' sundries generally. Mr. Gonzalez having been educated in the United States retains a warm intent in everything of American origin and informs us that he will be glad to co-operate with American firms who wish to secure the introduction of their goods into Colombia.—Ed.]

To Promote Trade with Chile.

Promotion of trade between Chile and this country is deemed so important that the South American republic has appointed Count Julian de Ovries as Commercial Commissioner to the Unted States. He arrived last week from England.

Count de Ovries is also accredited as a consul of his government at Pittsburgh, where he was sent on account of the interest which the Chileans feel in the important industrial developments which are centered about the iron and steel industries. The new repersentative was seen by representatives of the newspaper press shortly after his arrival.

"All classes in Chile," he said, "are so thoroughly convinced that mutual benefits would be the result of a closer commercial union between the United States and Chile that the government is making every preparation to meet this country half way. The fact that Secretary Root is to represent the Government of the United States at the conference in Brazil shows that North and South America are drawing more closely together. The Chilean Government has recently offered a subsidy of $150,000 a year for a steamship line which shall connect Panama with Valparaiso and thus insure the delivery of American goods across the isthmus; or the government, for that matter, is willing to subsidize a line between New York and Chile by way of the Straits of Magellan.

"It must be recognized by all Americans that it is the natural thing for the South American republics to be supplied from this market with many things which they require. Few realize how great are the natural resources of Chile. The chief article for export trade just now is nitrates. There is always a demand for fertilizer in this country, and such material is certainly required in the eastern part of the United States. The exports of this commodity from Chile amount to millions of dollars, the principal trade being with Germany and England.

"Germans probably understand how to handle the Chilean trade better than any other nation, for they are diplomatic and easily adapt themselves to the methods of the Latin Americans. They are indeed very plausible, and the South Americans like them. But some of the things they sell us! I have seen cars made of boards which have been painted without even having been planed. The Americans, on the other hand, furnish cars for our railroads which are well made and so equipped that it is a pleasure and a comfort to ride in them.

"I have heard some persons say that the Chileans were not good pay. This is absolutely false. It is their custom to send 25 per cent. of the price with an order and the balance on the receipt of the goods or of a bill of lading. There is a demand in Chile for American locomotives, rails, automobiles, mining machinery, pumps and artesian well outfits. In return Chile offers copper nitrates and many other things.

"Chile is desirous of entering into closer relations with the United States and it is believed that such an arrangement will be of the greatest advantage to both parties. I have already had correspondence with leading merchants of this country, and I believe that soon the two republics will come to a better understanding."

Full information regarding the druggists and physicians in Chile can be obtained by addressing the Foreign Department of the American Druggist.

AMERICAN DRUGGIST
and PHARMACEUTICAL RECORD

PHILADELPHIA. NEW YORK, JUNE 25, 1906. CHICAGO

ISSUED SEMI-MONTHLY BY

AMERICAN DRUGGIST PUBLISHING CO.,

62-68 West Broadway, New York.

CHICAGO, 221 Randolph St. PHILADELPHIA, 3718 Walnut St.

A. R. ELLIOTT, President.

CASWELL A. MAYO, Ph.G....................Editor.
THOMAS J. KEENAN................Associate Editor.

ROMAINE PIERSON...........Manager Chicago Office.

$1.50 a year. 15 cents a copy.

ADVERTISING RATES QUOTED ON APPLICATION.

The American Druggist and Pharmaceutical Record is issued on the second and fourth Mondays of each month. Changes of advertisements should be received ten days in advance of the date of publication.

Remittances should be made by New York exchange, post office or express money order or registered mail. If checks on local banks are used 10 cents should be added to cover cost of collection. The publishers are not responsible for money sent by unregistered mail, nor for any money paid except to duly authorized agents. All communications should be addressed and all remittances made payable to American Druggist Publishing Company, 62-68 West Broadway, New York.

Entered at New York as Second-Class Matter.

TABLE OF CONTENTS.

EDITORIAL COMMENT.

Victory for New York Druggists. The New York Telephone Company has bowed to the inevitable and New York druggists are to be supplied with slot telephones, from the gross receipts of which they will receive a commision of 25 per cent. The American Druggist has constantly supported the agitation in favor of such telephones, and if what has been said in these columns has had the effect of stirring the druggists of New York to action in order to obtain an honest division of profits from the telephone monopoly we are correspondingly pleased; but the druggists of the city must not halt here, for 25 per cent. is a poor measure of compensation for all the trouble and inconvenience caused by the installation of telephones in drug stores. Under the operation of a 5-cent telephone toll in Chicago the druggists are paid a commission of 40 per cent., and while this seems proportionately less, the increased business resulting from the low tariff makes it possible for our Chicago brethren to net a handsome profit. The agitation should be continued until a proper measure of relief is obtained.

The Mann Bill Goes Over. It has been definitely announced by the chairman of the Committee on Patents of the House of Representatives that neither the Mann Drug Patent bill nor any substitute for it will be presented for final action in Congress during the present session. This will be disappointing to the retail drug trade generally, and the disappointment will be the keener when it becomes known that the failure to bring about final action on the measure at the present session of Congress was due to dilatoriness on the part of the officers of the National Association of Retail Druggists in arranging for hearings. This charge is brought by the usually well informed and accurate correspondent of the *Oil, Paint and Drug Reporter.* The measure was introduced by Representative Mann last December, but no hearing was had until May 16, and it is charged that the bill was before the House five months before the N. A. R. D. authorities decided to push it. This decision was reached just as Mr. Mann was about to leave Washington for a month's absence, and on his return he was unable to give the matter the personal attention he could have given it earlier in the session, on account of his engagements in connection with the Railroad Rate bill, the Pure Food and Drug bill and other equally important measures. Whatever the cause of the postponement, it is certainly much to be regretted, for the prospects of the passage of the bill were at one time very favorable.

Look to Your Soda Beverages! It would be well for New York druggists to exercise care in the preparation of elixirs and similar decoctions intended for sale at the soda fountain, in order not to unwittingly lay themselves open to proceedings by the officers of the Department of Internal Revenue for the sale of liquors as a beverage. One or two druggists in the lower part of the city have been already visited by the department officials who have taken samples of elixir of calisaya and forwarded them to Washington for analysis and report. The department's ruling is that any druggist who adds to syrups, extracts or elixirs used in the manufacture of soda beverages alcohol or compounds thereof in excess of the amount necessary for the preservation of the syrups and elixirs shall be held liable to special tax as a rectifier and wholesale or retail liquor dealer, or both, according to the quantity sold at one time. It appears that a certain make of elixir of calisaya now sold to druggists is rather heavily charged with alcohol, and it is against the sale of this elixir as a beverage over the soda counter that the department is proceeding. The ruling under which the local officers of the department are working is contained in Internal Revenue Circular No. 640, issued by the Treasury Department. Our readers are familiar with Circular No. 676, in which it is announced that the department intends to examine proprietary medicines from time to time and to brand such as contain alcohol in excess of the quantity required for preserving them as liquors, and retail pharmacists selling the same will be regarded as retail liquor dealers, subject to tax as such. The importance of complying with the regulations of this department need not be emphasized, and if some druggists are caught napping they cannot blame the AMERICAN DRUGGIST.

The Centralization of Power.

In every form of popular government, whether republican or ostensibly monarchical, there are ever at war two sets of factors, one tending toward a greater centralization of power and the other toward its decentralization. In the American Government the tendency toward centralization has grown steadily —or with but a few temporary recessions in the movement— from the time when Jefferson relinquished his office. This tendency toward centralization has never been more marked than at the present period. We have in the White House a strong, resourceful, competent and aggressive man who has won the personal regard of a great majority of the American people regardless of political affiliations. More than any other President of the United States he has been active in initiating legislation, and, indeed, the most serious criticism which has been made of the President is based upon his activity in matters which his predecessors have deemed beyond the limits of the Executive prerogative. The leader of the minority in the House of Representatives, when discussing the attitude of Representative Wadsworth of New York on the meat inspection measure, referred with rather bitter sarcasm to the fact that when the President and the Speaker of the House were agreed as to the fate of a measure the wishes or convictions of individual members of the House did not count.

A consideration of the measures which have been enacted during the present session of Congress and of those which have attracted the largest share of public attention indicates that the tendency toward centralization in government has received an impetus which if unchecked will before many years practically obliterate State lines and reduce State governments to a condition of practical vassalage.

The Railroad Rate bill, the Meat Inspection bill, the Pure Food and Drug bill all add materially to the power and the prestige of the central Government, and all in effect, though not under a strictly literal interpretation, usurp those functions of government which the founders of our nation considered as purely State functions.

The judiciary is also being utilized, and the suits which have been brought under the Sherman Anti-Trust act all accentuate the constantly growing power of the central Government. Nor do the Government officials balk at considerations of propriety. In their efforts to still further aggrandize the Federal power the officials of the Attorney-General's office, in commencing action against the National Drug Association, did not hesitate to copy verbatim a large portion of the presentation made by the attorneys for the prosecution in the Loder case, a civil suit between private individuals. This fact was adverted to in an able address delivered by Clayton F. Shoemaker, of Philadelphia, before a recent meeting of the National Association of Credit Men. This act on the part of Government officers certainly shows a lamentable lack of the ordinary considerations for decency which keep public and private matters on separate planes.

In discussing the tendency shown by the Government in this as in similar suits, Mr. Shoemaker characterized it as a "dangerous tendency toward national interference in private affairs." This tendency has never been so marked as under the present Administration, and it is one which it behooves the thinking men of the country, regardless of party affiliations, to consider carefully and wisely. It is predicted by some observers that complete federalization is a matter of only a comparatively short time, and some publicists openly favor acceleration of the process. Certain it is that this process is going steadily on, and it is also certain that a large proportion of the citizens of the United States agree with us in deprecating a tendency which has already given us practically a one-man power in Congress and which if it goes on unchecked may result, as above intimated, in the practical abdication of all State authority in favor of a central Government. Already the President of the United States has greater authority than has the King of England, and with every session of Congress that authority is being added to.

The Pure Food and Drug Bill.

As we go to press the Pure Food and Drug bill is up for discussion in Congress, and will possibly be pushed to final passage before this issue reaches our readers. The measure is one which has been long needed, and if some branches of the drug interests should suffer through its enactment the trade as a whole would, we are confident, be benefited in one form or another. This measure has been before the people of the United States for the last 15 years. The recent exposures in connection with the meat packing industries have so stirred the public mind and so aroused public sentiment that whatever pressure may be brought to bear by individual interests to prevent the passage of the bill will be far outweighed by the thoroughly aroused public sentiment in favor of rigid and careful inspection of all food and drug products.

It is somewhat unfortunate that this measure failed of enactment when presented at the last session of Congress, and those members of the drug trade who favored its passage may now have the sad consolation of being able to say, "I told you so," to such of the trade as had opposed any measure of this kind. Under the pressure of the sentiment aroused by the wholesale attacks upon proprietary remedies of all sorts it is highly probable that proprietary interests will suffer in the final roundup, or at least that the form which the measure will finally take will be one that shall not be approved by the proprietary interests.

As a matter of fact we believe that the alarm felt by proprietors over the idea of having to publish a statement as to the potent ingredients in their remedies is based upon a misapprehension of the results which would accrue from such publication, save in those instances, and happily they are few, in which potent drugs are wrongfully used. We are of the opinion that the public will be but little more influenced by such publication than it has been by the publication of the facts concerning the presence of preservatives in catsups, etc., in accordance with the laws of several of the States. On almost every restaurant table in this city will be found bottles of tomato catsup, bearing labels setting forth the fact that they contain a certain small percentage of sodium benzoate, used as a preservative. This does not seem to have materially affected the sale of these goods. In the same way we believe that the announcement of the presence of opium in sedative mixtures will not materially affect their sale, save possibly in the case of so-called soothing syrup, the sale of which has already been curtailed by the present agitation.

While the retail drug trade has not been given any special consideration in the Pure Food bill we feel confident that the intelligent, well-informed pharmacist will in the end be benefited by any legislation which curtails the opportunities for adulteration and which puts a penalty upon this practice.

THE ETHICS OF THE ALLIED PROFESSIONS OF MEDICINE AND PHARMACY.[1]

BY H. EDWIN LEWIS, M. D.,
New York.

Apropos of the trend of some parts of the discussion which has preceded these remarks, let me state that I am glad that I have not as yet been infected, or affected, with the evidently prevalent diseases of nostrumitis and proprietophobia. There are probably those who will attribute my immunity to the fact that I am the editor of a medical journal that accepts advertisements of proprietary remedies. But I emphatically resent this imputation, for I know that a medical journal can accept advertisements and derive a considerable portion of its income from them without being subsidized in any particular whatsoever. To me the most unfortunate phase of the campaign we have been witnessing during the past few years is the indiscriminate attack that has been made on everything and everybody.

Right here I wish to state that in the practice of my profession I write a considerable number of extemporaneous prescriptions, I dispense some, and I use such proprietary preparations as come up to my requirements of honesty, worth and efficiency. I shall certainly continue to do so, for I maintain that it is my right, and I relegate to no one the privilege of dictating to me in these matters. Therefore, if what I may say later on does not coincide with your views, I trust you will at least give me credit for sincerity and honesty.

In speaking for the medical press in a general discussion of the Ethics of the Allied Professions of Medicine and Pharmacy, I assume that the relations of the medical press to the question are no different than those of the medical profession. Certainly, since a river never rises higher than its source, the medical press, having its inception in the needs, duties and opportunities of the medical profession, can take no other part in a discussion involving the ethics of medicine than as an integral or subsidiary factor. The ethics of the medical press must necessarily be those of the medical profession, and what concerns the medical profession must necessarily concern the medical press.

In this connection let me express just one private opinion in regard to this word "ethics." If any word in the English language is offensive to me it is this etymological prostitute—ethics. It has been used so promiscuously, and to my knowledge has been so often caught in illicit relations with cant and hypocrisy that to me its reputation for virtue has been sadly smirched.

Like many another young medical man, I entered upon the practice of medicine believing myself far removed from the laity and ordinary mortals—in fact, only a little lower than the angels—not because of any superior knowledge, but because of the higher ethics of my profession. I believed that medical men were in a class by themselves because of their ethical relations to each other and to the public. To me medical ethics was something real, tangible and altogether beautiful. It took me a little longer than the proverbial nine days to get my eyes opened, but I finally did, and soon found out that medical ethics as an institution, or as pictured in my mind's eye, did not exist. It was not exactly a myth, but hardly more tangible than a good thick shadow. I noticed, however, that medical men were much given to criticising the ethical standing of their colleagues, and the most damnatory statement a doctor could make about another was, "Oh, he is not ethical!" The thought and investigation I gave to the matter led me to conclude that the situation was false and unreal, and very far from what I had been led to believe. Naturally I was disappointed.

But so is every one when they find clay where gold was expected. Fortunately I had just enough common sense left after the shock of my awakening to see that I was the one most to blame, for I was foolishly seeking to build up my conduct on doctrines and customs, rather than on principles. In other words, I was taking elaborate rules and usages as the length and breadth of medical ethics, and completely losing sight of the real underlying truths.

Gradually it dawned upon me that the medical profession had no ethics aside from those common to all mankind, that there was one great basic principle—the principle of right at all times and in all places, which must justify my motives and acts as a physician just as it must those of any other man, irrespective of calling, profession or anything else. This conclusion was the salvation of the situation for me at least, and it has been of immeasurable personal benefit to realize that there can be but one standard of human action—the standard of *right*—which is as distinct from its antithesis *wrong* as white is from black. Rules and usages are arbitrary things evolved to meet certain arbitrary requirements. It is apparent that they are subject to modifications of time, place, manners and conditions. But the principle of right is unchangeable and irrevocable.

This, then, has finally become my conception of what ethics should imply—to know the right and to do the right. It is the "square deal" in human conduct, whether you are a doctor, a lawyer, a clergyman, a druggist, a merchant, a bricklayer, or whatever you may be. It requires no argument, for it is axiomatic that right is always right and wrong is never right.

If this is conceded, and I do not see how it can be denied, the only occasion for a discussion of the ethics of the allied professions is the presence of abuses or evils. From the acrimonious discussions I have heard between druggists about doctors, and between doctors about druggists, as well as among doctors about doctors and among druggists about druggists, I am reminded of the story that is told about the man out West who was left hanging to a tree by some of his loving friends with the epitaph pinned on his breast, "This man was very bad in some respects, and a damned sight worse in others."

I hardly think this applies to our allied professions, for while we may be bad in some respects, we are certainly good in others.

To be a little more serious, let me say I believe that the druggist and the doctor bear very important relations to each other. If we have grown apart and seemed to care less for each other during the past few years, the fault can probably be laid at both our doors. But what is the use of spending our time in idle recriminations? Why not let us get closer together and cultivate a crearer idea of each other's rights, privileges and duties?

Frankly, I am one of those individuals who are absolutely opposed to this present day spirit of unbridled criticism. The three C's—conference, consultation and counsel—can accomplish more in solving problems and correcting abuses than ruthless condemnation ever can, and the time will come when people will learn, doubtless at much unnecessary cost, that our present day custom of doing our laundry work in public is as disastrous to ourselves as it is injurious to what we wish to clean. Cleanliness is all right, but we can clean up without destroying the fabric if we go at it right, without hysteria and sensationalism. It is always easy enough to say what we might have done in the past, or what we ought to do in the future, but what about now? for the way to the future is through the doorway of the present.

In regard to the relations of our allied professions, I therefore earnestly believe that we must get together, and by association, conference and precept emphasize the value of the doctor and the druggist to the public, to each other and to themselves—the doctor as diagnostician, adviser and prescriber—the pharmacist as chemist, compounder and dispenser. Everything that increases the efficiency of either should be fostered, and every step or effort toward higher constructive education of both the doctor and the pharmacist should be encouraged.

You will note that I have said nothing about sanitation, counter prescribing, the piracy of private formulas, the dispensing doctor, the commission seeking doctor, the subsidized doctor, etc. It is not necessary. We all have pretty well defined ideas as to the right or wrong of these things, and what's the use of threshing over husks? There are too great opportunities along constructive lines to warrant this waste of time, if nothing else, in useless directions.

[1] An address delivered before the Manhattan Pharmaceutical Association, June 18, 1906.

The one great need for all of us is greater efficiency. To me this is the secret of success, to do something a little better than some one else. This means work, study and time. When such endeavor is coupled with honesty, plain every-day Simon pure honesty, the result is ethical enough for me. The world asks no more, and has no right to ask any more, for there is nothing more to give.

A few years ago it was my privilege to know a man who was one of the brightest, broadest and bravest doctors this country has ever known. He was I. N. Love, of St. Louis, and later of New York, and any words of mine are entirely too inadequate to properly describe him.

One night at a little luncheon at the Lotus Club, after we had been attending a medical meeting, he spoke these words in reply to a personal tale of woe I had poured into his ear:

"My boy, never mind the meanness of half the men you meet. Set your course with your conscience for a compass and let your professional brethren go hang. Wherever you go you will find dishonesty, deceit and—dirt, and if you are at all successful and try to do things, you will be a mark for jealousy, lies and slander. But there will be flowers and birds and sunshine, and the world will be just as beautiful when the mean men of our day are lined up in hell on the point of a darning needle. Therefore, work, play when you can, look up at the stars and remember that there is more good than bad in the world if you will only look for it."

In leaving the subject I commend these words to your attention, "there is so much bad in the best of us, and so much good in the worst of us, that all of us should be very careful in speaking ill of any of us."

THE LEGAL CONTROL OF PROPRIETARY MEDICINES.[1]

By George M. Beringer.
Camden, N. J.

There can be no doubt that the public mind has been aroused against the sale of injurious proprietary medicines and also against the extravagant claims regarding efficacy made by many of the proprietors. As the druggist is generally the intermediary between the manufacturer and the consumer, we are well aware of the fraudulent and ridiculous claims that are frequently made and the specious deceptions practiced by the "patent medicine men."

We know that many of the extensively advertised remedies contain so little drug content and such a high percentage of alcohol that they have become popular beverages, enjoying in some localities a very large sale, especially on Sundays. Others contain cocaine, morphine, chloral or other drug that possesses the power of enslaving the users with a "drug habit." Investigations tend to show that the number of drugs that possess such a controlling influence over users is quite large. The encouragement of self-medication by proprietaries is undoubtedly responsible for many "dope fiends" and inebriates. The gravity of the evil has been realized and is receiving careful consideration by those who regard the ethics of our calling as important, and it must soon engross the attention of the entire drug trade.

The agitation to control the sale of proprietaries by legal restrictions and to require the publication of the formulas on all such packages is becoming popular. The influences promulgating this agitation are strong, determined and sincere and, being well entrenched on moral grounds, will continue to wage this warfare until at least a large measure of the reform demanded has been secured. Their arguments against the deception practiced, the misrepresentation and extravagant claims and the evils resulting from indiscriminate self-medication are based upon established facts, with many of which we as pharmacists are cognizant. Led by resourceful men skilled in argument and in molding public opinion, who have at their command the proper avenues to create sentiment, they will continue their determined efforts until remedial legislation is secured.

[1] Read at the meeting of the New Jersey Pharmaceutical Association. Atlantic City, June 7, in reply to the question, What should be the proper attitude of the State Pharmaceutical Association toward legislation destined to control the sale of proprietary medicines?

It behooves us as professional gentlemen to take neither stock nor part in the counter attacks that are being made against the American Medical Association and certain popular magazines for engaging in this agitation for a needed reform. On the contrary, it should appeal to us as based on ethical principles and should merit our indorsement and support.

I conceive it to be the duty of the State Pharmaceutical Association to represent and protect the interests of the drug trade. Druggists should take a lively interest in the making of laws relating to these subjects. Those who know the existing trade conditions of medicine and pharmacy should frame, or at least shape, legislation so as not to work unnecessary injury to the trade interests involved, while at the same time securing to the public the largest amount of desired benefit.

During the last session of the New Jersey Legislature bills designed to regulate the sales of proprietary medicines and providing for published formulas were introduced in both houses, and the Legislative Committee of the association was compelled to oppose these vigorously, not because of opposition to the ethical principles involved, but because of their imperfections and crudities. The wording gave evidence that they were drawn by persons not acquainted with trade conditions, and their enactment would have proved destructive of the proper interests of the druggists. That these efforts will be renewed at each succeeding session is assured, and in my mind the correct attitude for the State Pharmaceutical Association to assume is to encourage such legislation and to assist in the framing and enactment of a just and a comprehensive law that shall meet the demands of the public and do no injustice to our trade interests. This appears to me to be our plain duty as good citizens and as representatives of a profession.

At present the drug trade is not united in favoring the publication of all formulas of proprietary medicines on the packages. The advocates of such publication claim that the consumer has a right to know what are the constituents of the remedy he purchases and that the State should adopt police regulations to protect its citizens from unsafe medication and from petty robbery by deception in advertising.

On the proposition of the desirability of having such police regulations, I believe that pharmacists are not only ready to join hands but to go a step further and insist that these regulations apply with equal force to proprietaries introduced to the medical profession and prescribed by physicians.

I confess that, after giving considerable thought to the subject, I am not convinced that it is desirable to publish all formulas. The knowledge of the public regarding medicines is very limited, and even with a statement of the contents of a package of proprietary medicine before him the average purchaser could not determine the remedial action. With this want of discrimination on the part of the public, from lack of special knowledge, I fail to see how the plan would protect from self-medication. On the other hand, it would become an excellent method of advertising to the dope fiends and inebriates what "patent" medicines they can purchase to satisfy their cravings. However, I am prepared to advocate that all proprietaries containing poisonous ingredients should have the name of such and the content per dose or ounce stated on the label along with the word POISON printed in bold face capitals. This provision of the English law is commended, as it gives at once to physician or druggist an idea of the proper antidote or treatment in the event of an accident or untoward effect being observed. I would, therefore, recommend that any such act of legislation should contain a list of drugs, or a schedule of drugs, which, if used in proprietary medicines, would require such a statement on the label.

In the hearing before the committees of the Legislature during the past session, the writer suggested a plan that would compel the manufacturer of a "patent" or proprietary medicine who proposed to advertise and sell his remedy in the State to file with the State Board of Health an exact copy of his formula, which should be recorded and protected as a confidential communication, and likewise copies of the label and advertised claims of remedial action. If these met with the approval of the board they should issue, at a nominal fee, a license permitting the sale of such medicine. Any change made in the formula must be immediately filed with the board and receive its approval. The board should be empowered to examine from time to time samples of such medicines in the market, and if satisfied that deception had been practiced in compounding or marketing same, then said proprietor's license should be revoked and the sale of his remedy be proscribed under a penalty.

This plan has many advantages over the mere publication of the formula. It gives to the manufacturer a certain amount of protection for his private formula, and some of them claim that these secrets are valuable property rights. It gives to the public a measure of real effective protection against the evils of self-medication in that experts with the necessary technical knowledge and special education will pass discriminating judgment upon the safety of such medicines. It gives to the intermediary, the drug trade, protection against improper censure and prosecution.

From a recent issue of a trade journal I learn that a similar plan has been proposed in Canada by Mr. Bole, of Winnipeg, who suggested to the special committee of the House of Commons, appointed to inquire into the composition of deleterious patent medicines, "a law that would compel a maker of a patent medicine to take out a license and register his formula with the Department of Inland Revenue. If that formula was approved, license to sell the medicine could be issued, and an analysis from time to time would determine whether the medicine was being made according to the license."

In other directions this plan is being taken up as a possible solution of this problem, and I hope it will receive your careful consideration and if it meets with your approval that the Legislative Committee will be authorized to frame a law along the lines proposed.

It is admitted that our system of State jurisdiction places a limitation on this plan, but this is not a serious objection. An ideal situation would be the establishment of a National Board of Health, with the control of proprietary medicines and foods as one of their specific duties. The establishment of such a national board is contemplated and should receive the indorsement of the pharmaceutical profession.

CHEMICAL EXAMINATION OF A EUCALYPTUS OIL, AN OVERDOSE OF WHICH CAUSED DEATH.[1]

By F. A. Upsher Smith.

The relative therapeutic values of the two classes of eucalyptus oil, known respectively as cineol oils and phellandrene oils, is not at present precisely known. The Pharmacopœia gives preference to the former class of oil, as typified by *Eucalyptus globulus*, but it was the latter class of oil—*e. g.*, the oil of *E. amygdalina*—whereby the therapeutic properties of eucalyptus were first established in Australia, and until 1898 the oil of *E. amygdalina* was official in the British Pharmacopœia. When a case of poisoning by an overdose of eucalyptus oil took place at Derby at the end of last December it occurred to me that it would be of interest, and perhaps of value, to make a chemical examination of the oil, with a view of determining whether it was composed chiefly of cineol or of phellandrene. Accordingly, I obtained by the courtesy of H. G. Toy, of Derby, a sample of the same oil as he supplied for the deceased. The oil was pale yellow in color; its specific gravity at 15.5 degrees C. was 0.919. It rotated the plane of a ray of polarized light 4.47 degrees to the right in a 100 Mm tube. A semi-solid mass was obtained on adding to 10 Gm. of the oil phosphoric acid of specific gravity 1.75 until a red coloration appeared, the whole being well stirred during the operation. The mass was then subjected to great pressure and weighed. The weight of pressed cineol phosphate was 8.62 Gm., corresponding to 52.7 per cent. cineol; a duplicate test gave 52.6 per cent. of cineol. On applying the official test for phellandrene with glacial acetic acid and sodium nitrite no crystalline mass was obtained, showing the absence of phellandrene. The results may thus be summarized:

Specific gravity, 0.919.
Optical rotation in 100 Mm. tube + 4.47 degrees.
Cineol, 52.65 per cent.
Phellandrene absent.

The oil was, therefore, an excellent sample of the cineol class, and complied in every way with the official requirements. It follows from this that the official oil, when taken in excessive doses, may cause a fatal result. In the case in question 6 fl. drachms of the oil were supplied, and, according to the evidence, about half a wineglass full was taken by the deceased with a similar quantity of warm water.

[1] From the *Pharmaceutical Journal.*

Fluidextract of Cinchona Bark.

The formulas recently published for making a liquid extract of cinchona to resemble Nanning's, a much advertised Dutch preparation, yield an extract that is distinctly different from the one that they profess to imitate. According to P. van der Widen (*Schweiz, Wochenschr.*, 44, 244), the following is the best method of procedure: Determine first the quantity of hydrochloric acid necessary to convert the alkaloidal compounds into soluble salts. For this purpose mix 10.0 Gm. of the powdered bark with 100.0 Gm. of water, to which have been added 1.0 Gm. of phenol and hydrochloric acid in the proportion of 0.071 Gm. of HCl for every 0.310 Gm. of alkaloid, 310 being the mean molecular weight of the alkaloids in red cinchona bark. Macerate for twenty-four hours, add 3.5 Ml. of decinormal acid and repeat the maceration; continue this treatment until the liquid is acid to Congo paper. Calculate the quantity of hydrochloric acid that has been employed. Macerate 100 of bark for four hours with 400 of water, 10 of glycerin and three-fourths of the calculated quantity of hydrochloric acid. Transfer to a percolator, and when the liquid ceases to pass continue the percolation with a second 400 of water to which the remainder of the acid has been added. Percolate finally with water until the liquid ceases to precipitate with solution of sodium carbonate (which is preferable to sodium hydroxide). Evaporate the percolate on a water bath at a temperature not exceeding 70° C. (or in a vacuum) until reduced to 90. In this determine the alkaloid and add alcohol, water and glycerin until the fluid extract contains 5 per cent. of alkaloid, 10 per cent. of glycerin, and 10 per cent. of 90 per cent. alcohol. If less hydrochloric acid is used the exhaustion is imperfect, if more the extract acquires an unpleasant taste. A good liquid extract should be reddish-brown in color and clear. It should become only slightly turbid when diluted with water, and should clear again on the addition of a little acid. Diluted with 10 parts of water it should not be acid to Congo paper. The assay of the liquid extract is easily accomplished as follows: Weigh 6.0 Gm. into a bottle, add 60 of chloroform and 10 Ml. of a 10 per cent. solution of caustic soda. Shake vigorously at intervals during two hours. Add 3.0 Gm. of powdered tragacanth, shake until agglomeration has taken place, and stand until the chloroformic solution is quite clear. Filter an aliquot portion of the chloroformic solution through a small filter, evaporate, dry and weigh. The residue may be titrated in the usual way. Experiments undertaken by the author showed that exhaustion was in eight cases out of nine practically completed, the ninth yielding 7.3 Gm. of alkaloid instead of 8.4 Gm.

HONEY-GLYCERIN JELLY.

	No. 1.	No. 2.
Gelatin	ʒj	ʒvj
Honey	ʒiv	ʒv
Glycerin	℥iij	℥j
Salicylic acid		ʒj
Oil of rose	gtt. ij	
Oil of bergamot		ʒj
Oil of neroli, artificial		ʒj
Water	ʒxj	
Rosewater		℥xij

FORGED PRESCRIPTIONS FOR POISONS.

Curious Verdict by a French Jury.

(*By our Regular Correspondent.*)

Paris, June 1, 1906.—Madame Canaby was acquitted last Sunday by a Bordeaux jury on the charge of attempting to poison her husband, but was found guilty of forgery of prescriptions. The startling facts of the case have aroused general attention in France, and some very delicate medical and pharmaceutical questions are raised by this singular domestic drama. Madame Canaby was particularly well educated, her studies including a sufficient knowledge of chemistry, and both she and her husband were well known and respected in Bordeaux.

Her uncle, M. Henri Fouries, pharmacist, rue Fondaudege, deposed that on April 27, 1905, Madame Canaby's cook handed him a prescription for aconitine, digitaline and chloroform signed "Dr. Gaube." This was accompanied by a letter in which his niece explained that the doctor, who lives some way out of Bordeaux, needed these poisons to carry out certain scientific experiments. The servant asked him to return the prescription, which he did, after duly copying same, and delivered the drugs as required. But he wrote Madame Canaby that had he known he would have kept the paper, and he could execute no more prescriptions of this character. He also handed her letter to the head of the police.

M. Joseph Erny, of Bordeaux, who appears to be the Canabys' regular pharmacist, stated that on May 1 the servant brought in a prescription, signed "Dr. Gaube," for a large quantity of digitaline "for a scientific experiment." The envelope bore the inscription, "Office of the Procureur of the Republic." Three days later he executed a second prescription, "1 gramme aconitine, 5 centigrammes digitaline," as "the first experiment had not succeeded," he was told. A third prescription—the signature was always "Gaube"—was for "potassium cyanide 1 gramme, digitaline 1 gramme," and his assistant supplied the poison.

The evidence of this witness was accompanied by one of the many exciting incidents of the trial. The presiding judge and the procureur both severely blamed the pharmacist for thus delivering such dangerous drugs, and the latter threw out a broad hint that had he been less anxious after profit he might have prevented regretable incidents. The pharmacist retorted that his business was to execute prescriptions when properly drawn up and signed, not to criticise them. Now that Dr. Gaube had stated that the signatures were forged, it was easy enough to blame his conduct, but it should be remembered that he was not an expert in handwriting. Were he in the same position again he would act in the same manner.

The procureur declared this last statement to be impertinent on the part of a man who had made a grave error in judgment, and repeated his remark about mercenary motives. The sympathies of the audience were with the pharmacist thus gratuitously attacked by a Government official, and the protest of the public was only silenced by the threat of the president to have the court cleared. His honor made a half apology to M. Erny, who then left the box.

Three bottles of Fowler's solution were purchased by Madame Canaby at other pharmacies, Domenjole's and Couraud's. Two more pharmacists deposed that about the end of March, 1905, they received the visit of a young man who presented a prescription signed "Dr. Lafforgue," calling for abnormal quantities of toxic substances. M. Roussel (one of the pharmacists) called up Dr. Lafforgue on the telephone to make inquiries, and while he was doing this the would-be purchaser disappeared. (Dr. Lafforgue replied he had never signed such a prescription.) The other pharmacist also found a means of avoiding the dispensing of the drugs inquired for.

All this was, of course, purely circumstantial evidence, but coupled with the fact that between May 2 and May 12 the state of M. Canaby's health—unsatisfactory for some days previously—became very grave, it seemed to call for some action. The pharmacist had given some account of these extraordinary prescriptions to the Canaby's family doctor, and he decided to call a consultation of four fellow physicians. The upshot of this was that M. Canaby was conveyed to the private clinic of Dr. Villar. Here he was kept a practical prisoner, only receiving the briefest visits from those who had formerly surrounded him, and his health improved. His state, as he came into the witness box to testify to his wife's innocence, was still pitiable, but it was stated he may still regain his health. His hair and beard, analyzed, gave respectively 40 and 20 grammes of arsenic per kilo. The evidence of the analysts and medical men was lengthy but not conclusive.

Madame Canaby's defense was that she handed the poisons to a young man whom she understood to be Dr. Gaube's messenger. (This person was not presented as a witness and the defendant had no idea as to his identity.) She defended herself stoutly and indignantly, though frequently fainting under the ordeal, and her own family's evidence was all in her favor. The spectacle of four doctors in the witness box, called upon by Madame Canaby to give evidence, and unanimously replying that "neither she nor any one else could free them from the obligations of professional secrecy," was the medical sensation of this most sensational case. The jury's verdict may be considered as a very merciful, if not a very logical, solution of the mystery.

The Estimation of Morphine in Toxicological Works.

Georges and Gascard (*Journal de pharmacie et de chimie*, June 1, 1906), describe a colorimetric method of determining the amount of morphine contained in the stomach, etc., in cases of poisoning, claiming that their method has marked advantages over the tedious procedures hitherto employed for this purpose, which lack precision, and this is all-important in cases in which the question is, Was the dose of morphine ingested sufficient to have killed this person? In the Staas-Otto method the product is fixed with a considerable amount of impurities, which add markedly to its weight. Mayer's process, which is based upon the amount of Mayer-Valser's reagent needed to precipitate the entire amount of morphine in the substances under investigation, is also unsatisfactory, because the solubility of the precipitate obtained with this method varies considerably, according to temperature and other conditions. Girard's method is inaccurate, as it is based upon the amount of iodine absorbed by the morphine when in contact with a solution of potassium iodide and iodine. This amount is very variable, and is not proportionate to the amount of morphine in the solution used.

The principles underlying the new method described by the present authors are as follows: When iodic acid is added to neutral or slightly acid solutions of morphine, a yellow or reddish-yellow color results. On the addition of some ammonia a brownish-yellow color is obtained. In both instances the color reaction is intense in proportion to the amount of morphine in the solution. The differences in tint can be read with the aid of Dubosq's colorimeter. If this instrument cannot be had, one can construct colorimetric scales in proper test tubes, by simply using definite weights of the alkaloid and adding the reagents.

The necessary solutions for this method of analysis are: (1) A solution of morphine hydrochloride, containing 1.256 grains per litre, equivalent to 0.001 Gm. of morphine per cubic centimetre; (2) A solution of iodic acid, 5 per cent. and (3) A solution of ammonia, 10 per cent., or the official solution properly diluted. With Dubosq's colorimeter the procedure consists in measuring 5, 10, or 20 Cc. of the solution of morphine, which must be either neutral or faintly acid, and whose amount of morphine has been carefully weighed previously into one beaker. Into the second beaker a similar amount of the unknown solution is poured, and to each beaker 5 Cc. of solution of iodic acid are now added. The development of the color reaction is now carefully noted, and when the color has become constant, the scale of the apparatus is read in correspondence with each of the beakers. The same method is also pursued when ammonia is used in addition to the iodic acid. The results of this method were always accurate.

Cream of Current Literature.

Calcium Bromoborates.—Ouvard (*Union pharmaceutique*, May, 1906), obtained calcium bromoborate by fusing one molecule of boric anhydride with two molecules of calcium bromide, cooling, and adding cold water. The bromoborate crystallizes in needles or in prisms, which dissolve slowly in hot water or dilute acetic acid.

Differentiation of Codeine and Dionin.—Rodionoff (*Union pharmaceutique*, May, 1906), finds the following method useful in testing a substance which may be either codeine or dionin. Two Cc. of a 1 per cent. solution of codeine are treated with ten drops of Wagner's reagent, which immediately gives a reddish-brown precipitate. This deposit does not change color on shaking the tube vigorously. On the other hand, with dionin, while a precipitate of the same color is formed, it turns an orange-brown on shaking, and rises to the surface of the liquid. Wagner's reagent is a decinormal solution of iodine in potassium iodide.

Disinfectant Solution for Stables, Railway Cars, Etc.—The French Government has just adopted the following disinfecting solution, which is prescribed for the disinfection of stables, carriages, railway cars, etc. The formula has been adopted for the forthcoming edition of the French Codex:

Cresol ....1,000 parts
Solution of sodium hydroxide....................1,000 parts

The ingredients are to be mixed in an appropriate vessel. The reaction develops considerable heat, and thus glass vessels should not be employed. This stock solution, known as "liquid cresol sodium hydrate," is used in various dilutions as a disinfectant.

Incompatibilities of Digitalis.—According to a writer in *Bulletin mensuel de l'association des docteurs en pharmacie de France* (quoted in *Union pharmaceutique*, May, 1906), the incompatibilities of digitalis are of two kinds—physiological and chemical. The chemical incompatibilities are the metallic salts and the astringent decoctions. The physiological incompatibilities are of three kinds: First, remedies which "close the kidneys" and prevent the elimination of digitalis, such as antipyrine, belladonna and opium. Second, those which weaken the heart's action—quinine and its salts. Third, those which dilate the blood vessels and lower the blood pressure, such as the nitrites and the iodides.

Mergal, a New Preparation of Mercury.—This is the mercuric salt of cholic acid, and has the formula $(C_{24} H_{39} O_5)_2 Hg$. It occurs as a yellowish-gray powder, almost insoluble in water and soluble in solutions of the alkaline salts. Mergal is especially soluble in salt water, though the solutions thus obtained are never perfectly clear. Mergal is decomposed by alcohol, as well as by acids and alkalies. In order to identify this new product a small amount of mergal is heated in a test tube with some dilute hydrochloric acid on the water bath. The mercury dissolves and forms a chloride, while the cholic acid remains. The latter is separated and is identified by means of Pettenkofer's reagent. Cholic acid, when heated with sulphuric acid, 50 per cent in strength, and then treated with a small amount of sugar, gives an intense purple color.—*Journal de pharm, et de chemie*, June, 1906.

The Dangers of Carbolic Acid.—This antiseptic is so commonly used by the laity, as well as by physicians and pharmacists, that the warning as to its dangers when locally applied, which is uttered by two Swiss authors, Veyrassat and Richner (*Revue medicale de la Suisse romande*, 1906, p. 209), should be heeded more generally than is at present the case. Carbolic acid was first proposed for the treatment of wounds by Jules Lemaire in 1860, and ever since then the evidence as to its danger, when used locally, has been accumulating. The authors mentioned relate seven cases of gangrene or tissue death caused by the application of carbolic acid, even in dilute forms, that is to say, in solutions of ½ part to 100. It is very important, indeed, for those who are often brought face to face with surgical accidents, which they must treat as best they know, to bear in mind that above all things they should do no harm, and should wash wounds, etc., with clean boiled water; perhaps with the addition of hydrogen peroxide, but should avoid the use of carbolic washes.

Medical Students' Examination in Pharmacy.

Prof. M. F. DeLorme, of the Long Island College, Brooklyn, has kindly favored us with copies of the examination papers in pharmacy and materia medica given at the last examination, May 19 to 28. The papers are reproduced below, as they may prove suggestive to examiners and students in pharmacy:

EXAMINATION IN PHARMACY.

1. (*a*) Define pharmacology, pharmacy, therapeutics, synergist.
   (*b*) How many teaspoonfuls in 50 Cc.?
   (*c*) How many wineglassfuls in eight fluid ounces of infusion of buchu?
   (*d*) Describe the National Formulary.
2. (*a*) State in metric terms the approximate width of the sheet of paper upon which your answers are written.
   (*b*) How many 10-grain powders can be made from ʒij soda bicarb.?
   (*c*) How many Cc. in half litre of normal saline solution (0.6 per cent.)?
   (*d*) How much NaCl is required to prepare the above quantity of solution?
3. (*a*) State distinguishing features of fluid extracts, tinctures, infusions and spirits.
   (*b*) Mention four tinctures that are immiscible with water.
   (*c*) State difference between an ointment and a cerate; a water and a solution.
   (*d*) Give percentage drug strength of the following: Donovan's solution, tinct. iodine, Dover's powder, tinct. digitalis, syrup iodide of iron.
4. Arrange following drugs in regular prescription form: Order a four-ounce mixture for Mary Jones, aged 12 years. Give teaspoonful doses. Complete directions according to your own judgment. Employ unabbreviated Latin.
   (*a*) Tr. red pepper, sulphate strychnine, rhubarb and soda mixture, syrup tolu, bromide of soda.
   (*b*) Bismuth subnitrate, pepsin, pancreatin, bicarbonate of soda, powdered ginger, charcoal. (Order 12 powders for an adult. In other particulars follow above general instructions.)
5. (*a*) Give official Latin titles of the following: Laudanum, chalk mixture, Lugol's solution, phenacetin, white precipitate, flaxseed, Hoffman's anodyne, mustard, Basham's mixture, hive syrup.
   (*b*) Mention any incompatibilities that may exist in prescriptions forming question No. 4. How many drugs incompatible with tannin can you mention?

EXAMINATION IN MATERIA MEDICA.

1. Define the following classes of medicines, mentioning two typical drugs under each class: Sedatives, anodynes, expectorants, hypnotics, antispasmodics, carminatives, mydriatics, narcotics, cathartics, with subclasses; diuretics, with subclasses.
2. (*a*) Mention the several routes employed in administering medicine.
   (*b*) State essentials for the successful use of the hypodermic syringe.
   (*c*) Name in order of rapidity of action the several forms in which medicines are administered.
   (*d*) Define idiosyncrasy.
3. Divide the following drugs into two groups: (1) Those that are soluble in or miscible with water, and (2) those that are insoluble and immiscible with water. Indicate with an X any that are poisonous: Sodium iodide, acid salicylic, tinct. iodine, calcium chloride, potass. citrat., syr. iron iodide, wine of antimony, fl. ext. cannab. ind., sp. ether comp., tinct. hyoscyamus, phenacetin, tannin, phenyl. salicylas, quinine sulphate, oleores. capsicum, tinct. iron chloride, pilocarpine muriate, zinc oxide, manganese dioxide, ammonium carbonate.
4. Supply common names of the following, indicating those intended for external use only with an X: Gaultheria, oleum tiglii, thymolis iodidum, ol. theobromatis, potass. sulphurata, ol. ricini, liq. sodii boratis co., plumbi acetas, ol. morrhuæ, aq. mentha virid, magnesii sulphas, hydrastis, lotio hydrarg. nigra, fl. ext. glycyrrhiza, caryophyllus, liq. plumbi subacetatis dil., pil. ferri carbonatis, tr. benzoini comp., aconitum, adeps lanæ, oleores. aspidium.
5. State average adult doses of the following, indicating those that are liquids with an X: Ac. gallicum, aconitina, ac. sulph. arom., liq. potass. arsen., emuls. asafœtida, sp. ammon. arom., syr. pruni virg., hydrarg. iodid., flav. ext. belladonna, potass. citras, inf. digitalis, res. podophylli, ammon. valerianas, codeinæ sulph., ant. et potass. tart., mist. cretæ, acetanilid, cocaine hydrochlor., argenti nitras, tr. ferri chlor.

THE NEWER REMEDIES.

Being Notes on the Composition, Therapeutic Properties, Style of Container and Source of Non-Pharmacopoeial Remedies of Recent Introduction.

Acetal, ethylidene diethylether, is a colorless, volatile liquid, soluble in 18 parts of water, very soluble in alcohol. Used as a sedative and hypnotic in doses of 2 to 3 fluid drachms, usually in form of emulsion. Pure medicinal, per oz., $1.00; commercial, oz., 65c.

Acetozone, benzoyl-acetyl peroxide, forms a white powder, containing a mixture of an equal weight of an inert soluble powder; soluble in water (1 : 1,000). Bactericide; used internally and externally in diseases of germ origin. Dose, 1 to 3 grains in solution. Boxes containing 6 vials of 15 grains each, per box, $1.25; ¼ oz. bot., $1.40; ½ oz. bot., $2.70; 1 oz. bot., $5.25. Made and marketed by Parke, Davis & Co.

Acet-theocin-sodium, a white crystalline powder, readily soluble in water, is a powerful diuretic; used in dropsy, in doses of 5 to 7 grains, two to three times daily. ½ and 1 oz. bot., $1.90 to $2.30 per oz. Marketed by the Continental Color & Chemical Company.

Acetysal is a trade name adopted for acetylsalicylic acid, as made by G. and R. Fritz, Vienna.

Acoine, chemically di-para-anisyl-monophenethyl guanidine hydrochloride, is a white crystalline powder, soluble in 17 parts of water. Local anæsthetic like cocaine, used hypodermatically in eye surgery; dental anæsthetic in normal saline solution, 2 per cent. 15 grain vials, each, 30c.; capsules, 2½ grains, 28 in box, 75c. Marketed by the Heyden Chemical Works.

Adrenalin forms a grayish-white powder, difficultly soluble in water. It is the blood-pressure-raising principle of the suprarenal glands. 1 grain vials, 85c. Chloride solution, 1 : 1,000, a solution of 1 part of adrenalin chloride in 1,000 parts of physiologic salt solution, with 0.5 per cent. of chloretone. Powerful astringent, hæmostatic and cardiac stimulant. Used for the control of hemorrhages, internal and superficial, for the reduction of congestion and inflammation of mucous membranes, as a heart stimulant in collapse, and as an adjuvant to the local anæsthetic action of cocaine. Internal dose, 5 to 30 minims. 1 oz. bot., 85c.; inhalant, 1 oz. bot., 85c.; ointment, ½ oz. tubes, 48c.; suppositories, boxes of 1 doz., 38c.; tablets, vials of 25, 85c. Made and marketed by Parke, Davis & Co.

Adrin, epinephrin hydrate, is a whitish nonhygroscopic powder, the active principle of the suprarenal gland. 1 grain vials, each, 75c.; 1-1,000 solution, 1 oz. vials, each, 75c.; in tubes of 12 tablets, each tablet q. s. to make 15 minims of 1-1,000 solution, each, 40c.; in 100's, each, $3.10; inhalant, 1 oz. vials, 75c.; ointment, ½ oz. tubes, 40c.; suppositories, box of 1 doz., 30c. Made and marketed by H. K. Mulford Company.

Adnephrin solution is a 1-1,000 solution of the active principle of the suprarenal gland in physiological salt solution containing ½ of 1 per cent. of methaform. Used chiefly as a hæmostatic, also for treatment of inflammations, congestions and tumefactions of the mucous membranes, and as a cardiac stimulant. 1 oz. vials, 60c.; emollient, tubes, each, 30c.; oil spray, 1 oz. vials, each, 60c. Made and marketed by Frederick Stearns & Co.

Aethrol is a name applied to a series of water-soluble antiseptic and cosmetic preparations which find a wide range of usefulness, being employed for spraying in sick rooms and for rendering the hands aseptic and as a mouth wash. Aethrol can be combined with eau de cologne, eucalyptol, peppermint and other flavoring agents. It is also put up in powder form, *e. g.*—aethrol powder B is a borax compound for the bath and toilet. It is made and marketed by H. Noerdlinger, Flörsheim on Main, Germany.

Agurin, acet-theobromine-sodium, is a white hygroscopic powder, soluble in water; incompatible with acids. Diuretic in dropsy. Dose, 7 to 15 grains, twice daily. ½ and 1 oz. bot., $1.55 to $1.70. Marketed by Continental Color & Chemical Company.

Airol, a grayish-green powder, insoluble in water or alcohol, is bismuth oxyiodogallate. On admixture with water airol partly decomposes and turns red. Should be mixed with water only with intervention of glycerin. Used externally as application to wounds, burns, skin diseases, eye, nose, gonorrhœa, either pure, in 10 per cent. suspension, equal parts glycerin and water, or 10 to 20 per cent. ointment. 1 oz. cartons, $1.00. Marketed by the Hoffmann-La Roche Chemical Works.

Albargin, gelatose silver, forms a light brown powder, readily soluble in water. Contains 15 per cent. of silver. For gonorrhœa a 2 per cent. solution is injected 4 or 5 times daily. 1 oz. vials, $1.10; tubes of 50 tablets, 0.2 Gm. each, per tube, 50c. Marketed by Victor Koechl & Co.

Alcho is a trade name for aluminum carbonate, made by A. Gawalowski, which is beginning to find uses in medicine and chemistry. It is a white, tasteless powder, containing 40 to 45 per cent. of aluminum.

Alcohol-Silver Ointment consists of 0.5 parts of collargol, 96 parts of alcohol and 70 parts of soda soap, some wax and some glycerin. It is a soft and smooth brown ointment, which keeps well in an air-tight receptacle and is made by the chemical works at Helfenberg, formerly E. Dietrich. It is said to be excellent for sprains, contusions, burns, inflammations of the skin, infected wounds, felons, etc.

Aldol is a colorless liquid of characteristic odor and sweetish taste, soluble in two parts of water and in corresponding portions of ether and alcohol. When exposed to the air it gradually crystallizes, forming a polymer called paraldol. Chemically aldol is an aldehyde corresponding to butanediol. To make it a cold mixture of ethyl aldehyde and diluted hydrochloric acid is set aside until the whole assumes a yellow color. After then neutralizing with sodium bicarbonate, the mixture is shaken with ether and the aldol finally obtained by evaporating the ether in a vacuum. It is said to possess hypnotic properties and has been used in the treatment of insomnia.

Almateine is a condensation product of formaldehyde and hæmatoxylin obtained by the action of formaldehyde on a decoction of campechy wood. It is a reddish powder without taste or odor, almost insoluble in water, but soluble in alcohol, ether and glycerin. Used both internally and externally as a substitute for iodoform for antiseptic and disinfectant purposes.

Alphozone, succinic peroxide, is a white fluffy powder, quickly soluble in 60 parts of water. Germicide and antiseptic, internally and externally. Dose, 3 to 5 grains. 1 oz. bot., $4.50; ½ oz., $2.30; ¼ oz., $1.20; 1 grain tablets, bot. of 90, $1.00. Made by Frederick Stearns & Co.

Alumnol, aluminum naphthol disulphonate, forms a whitish powder, very soluble in water, slightly soluble in alcohol and glycerin; astringent and antiseptic; dissolves in pus and penetrates tissues. Used in 1 per cent. solution in gonorrhœa: 10 to 20 per cent. mixture with talcum as a dusting powder. 1 oz. tins, per oz., 50c. Marketed by Victor Koechl & Co.

Alypin, benzoyltetramethyldiaminoethyldimethylcarbinohydrochloride, which has been recommended by Dr. E. Impens, of Elberfeld, Germany, as an anæsthetic, forms a white crystalline powder, easily soluble in water and alcohol, but dissolving very sparingly in ether. Watery solutions have a neutral reaction and can be sterilized by boiling for a short period. Local anæsthetic, substitute for cocaine. The strength of the solutions ordinarily employed varies from 1 to 5 and even up to 10 per cent. It can be combined with adrenalin and antipyrine. Alypin should not be used in connection with silver nitrate, owing to the formation of a precipitate. This objection, however, does not apply to protargol solutions, which, although they become slightly turbid at first, soon clear up. 15 grain vials, each, 20c.; 10 grain vials, per vial, 16c.; ¼ and ½ oz. bots., per oz., $4.20; 1 oz. bots., per oz., $4.10. Marketed by the Continental Color & Chemical Company.

Aminoform is a trade name for ammonium formaldehyde (hexamethylenetetramine). Forms white granular crystals. Used as antiseptic for urinary passages, diuretic and solvent in uric acid concretions; dose, 5 to 10 grains, well diluted, three times daily. 1 oz. bot., 60c.; 7½ grain tablets, oz., 70c. Marketed by C. Bischoff & Co.

Anaesthesin is a white crystalline powder, almost insoluble in cold water, but easily soluble in ether, alcohol, benzin and fatty oils. Local anæsthetic and used internally in gastric ulcer, nervous dyspepsia, etc. Dose, internally, 5 to 8 grains several times daily. Used externally pure or in ointment, 5 to 20 per cent., and in suppositories containing 3 grains each. 1 oz. bot., $1.00. Marketed by Victor Koechl & Co.

Analgine is a powder composed of acetanilid, 50 parts; sodium bicarb., 5 parts; sodium salicylate, 5 parts; camphor monobrom., 5 parts; caffeine citrated, 2½ parts; ext. cannabis indica, 2½ parts; aromatic powder, q. s. 100 parts. Recommended as an analgetic, antipyretic and nerve sedative in neuralgia, migraine, headache, rheumatism, gout, sciatica, etc. Dose, 5 to 10 grains. 1 oz. screw cap bot., 40c. Made and marketed by H. K. Mulford Company.

Anthraquinone cholalate is put up in tablet form and represents a combination of colalin and cascara sagrada, the bark being extracted with a solution of cholalic acid, which is said to combine with the anthraquinone principle contained in it. Made by T. Morson & Son, London, Eng.

Anthrasol is a yellow, oily liquid, with a distinctive tarry odor; soluble in alcohol, acetone, fats and petrolatum. A distillate from coal tar, used in diseases of the skin where coal tar is employed. 1 oz. vials, 55c. Marketed by Knoll & Co. and Merck & Co.

Anticilloids are urethral bougies composed of oil of theobroma containing 10 per cent. of protargol. Used as a prophylactic against gonorrhœa.

Antidiabetic is the name given by the maker, W. M. Stock, Düsseldorf, Germany, to a mixture composed of aqueous fluidextract of *Senecio fuchsi*, 97.78 per cent.; salicylic acid, 0.2 per cent. (as a preservative); trypsin, 0.02 per cent., and 2 per cent. of an alkali, the nature of which is not disclosed. It is given in doses of one tablespoonful three times daily after meals.

Antirheumatin is a name applied to crayons of salocreol (creosote salicylate), which are used in the same way as menthol cones. Made by W. Newiger, Berlin.

Antisclerosin forms tablets, consisting of a compound of inorganic blood salts, used in treatment of arteriosclerosis and its sequelæ. Dose, 2 tablets three times daily. Carton of 4 tubes of 24 tablets, $1.50. Marketed by Schering & Glatz.

Antisudor is a disinfectant solution in which salicylic acid is present, but no formaldehyde. As its name implies, it is used as a remedy against offensive perspiration, being applied as a paint over the parts affected twice daily and allowed to dry. It should not be confounded with antisudorin. Made by C. Fr. Haussmann, St. Gall, Switzerland.

Antitranspirin is the name applied to an external application for the relief of excessive perspiration of bromidrosis. It is said to consist of a 5 per cent. solution of formaldehyde perfumed with spirit of lavender.

Antitussin, difluordiphenyl ointment, is an ointment containing lanolin, 85 per cent.; petrolatum, 10 per cent., and difluordiphenyl, 5 per cent. A whooping cough remedy applied as inunction to patient's neck, chest and back once a day, in doses of 5 Gm. 20 Gm. collapsible tubes, 40c.; 40 Gm., 75c. Marketed by C. Bischoff & Co.

Anusol suppositories form a compound of bismuth iodoresorcin sulphonate, used in hæmorrhoids, etc. Dose, 1 to 2 daily. Box of 12, $1.00. Marketed by Schering & Glatz.

Apicin, the chief constituent of which is calcium guaiacolphosphate, and which is used in the treatment of pulmonary disorders, is marketed as a chocolate covered pastil by the makers, G. and R. Fritz, Vienna.

Argentamine is a colorless, alkaline liquid representing a solution of silver nitrate, 10 per cent., and ethylenediamine, 10 per cent.; soluble in water. Used in all cases where silver nitrate is used, mostly in gonorrhœa, in strength of 1 in 2,000-4,000 solution. 1 oz., g. s. bot., 75c. Marketed by Schering & Glatz.

Argonin is marketed as a white powder, very slightly soluble in cold, but freely so in hot water. A compound of silver nitrate and sodium casein. Antiseptic, germicide and gonococcicide, less caustic than silver nitrate. Solutions of 2 to 10 per cent. strength recommended for injection in gonorrhœa and 3 per cent. solutions for use in the eye. 1 oz. vials, 65c. Marketed by Victor Koechl & Co.

Arhovin, an addition product of diphenylamine and esterified thymyl-benzoic acid, is a fluid of aromatic odor and slightly burning taste, soluble in oil. Gonocide for internal and topical use. Given by mouth in capsules of 4 grains (1 or 2 capsules, three to six times daily); in urethral bougies (1 bougie, two to four times daily); in vaginal globules (1 globule, two to four times daily), and injected in 2 per cent. to 5 per cent. oily solution. 1 oz. vials, 90c.; box of 50 capsules, 65c.; box of 12 bougies, 50c.; box of 12 globules, 50c. Marketed by Schering & Glatz.

Aristochin, the carbonic ester of quinine, is a white powder, tasteless, insoluble in water. Decomposes in the system to yield 96.1 per cent. of quinine. Prescribed like quinine, but in somewhat larger doses. ½ and 1 oz. cartons, per oz., $2.20. Marketed by the Continental Color & Chemical Company and Merck & Co.

Arsenferratose is a solution of ferratin in syrup form (syrupus ferratini arseniati) containing 0.3 per cent. of iron and 0.003 per cent. of arsenic. Used as a hæmatopoietic and alterative, in doses of a tablespoonful three or four times a day for adults, and for children, a teaspoonful to a dessertspoonful. It is put up by C. F. Boehringer & Soehne, Mannheim, Germany, and New York, in 250 Gm. bottles, selling wholesale at 55c. each.

Asaprol, or abrastol, is a whitish powder, freely soluble in water and alcohol. It is the calcium salt of betanaphtholsulphonic acid. Antipyretic and antirheumatic, in doses of 5 to 15 grains. Used also as test for albumin in urine. 1 oz. bot., $1.25.

Aspirin, acetyl salicylic acid, is a white crystalline powder, insoluble in water, incompatible with alkalies. Used instead of the salicylates in articular and muscular rheumatism and other therapeutic indications for the salicylates. Dose, 5 to 15 grains, three to five times daily. 1 oz. bot., per oz., 33c. to 43c. Marketed by the Continental Color & Chemical Company.

Atoxyl, meta-arsenous anilide, is a white powder, containing 37.69 per cent. of arsenic in organic combination. Soluble in 6 parts of water and used in this strength solution for hypodermic injection; relatively nontoxic. Dose, 1 to 3 grains. 1 oz. vials, $3. Marketed by Victor Koechl & Co.

Belloform is a condensation product of various high-boiling hydrocarbons (poor in cresols) with formaldehyde in soap solution, which forms a cherry red fluid of aromatic odor and is readily soluble in both water and alcohol. The weak aqueous solution of this product is transparent, with a yellowish opalescence, while the stronger solutions are nearly opaque. The antiseptic effect of belloform is said to be quite equal to those produced by either creolin or lysoform; it is said to have no irritant or caustic effect on the skin and, without making it slippery, to soften it.

Benzonaphthol is a white crystalline powder, soluble in alcohol and chloroform; insoluble in water. Employed as intestinal antiseptic in doses of 5 to 15 grains. 1 oz. vials, 22c.; ¼ lb. bottles, $2.20; ½ lb., $2.10; 1 lb., $2. Marketed by Schering & Glatz.

Benzosalin-Roche is the methyl ester of benzoyl salicylic acid, and being a salicylic and benzoic acid derivative is an analogue of acetylsalicylic acid and is employed similarly with the last named in the treatment of rheumatism and neuralgia, in doses of from 3⅓ to 15 grains, several times a day. It forms white, faintly aromatic, almost tasteless, needle-shaped crystals, soluble in alcohol, benzol and chloroform, but insoluble in water. It is put up in tablet form only by the makers, the Hoffmann-La Roche Chemical Works, Basel, Switzerland, and New York.

(*To be continued.*)

Queries and Answers

We shall be glad, in this department, to respond to calls for information on all pharmaceutic matters.

Another Puzzling Prescription.—C. F. H. submits a prescription in competition for the prize offered in a previous issue, and it is reproduced in fac-simile below:

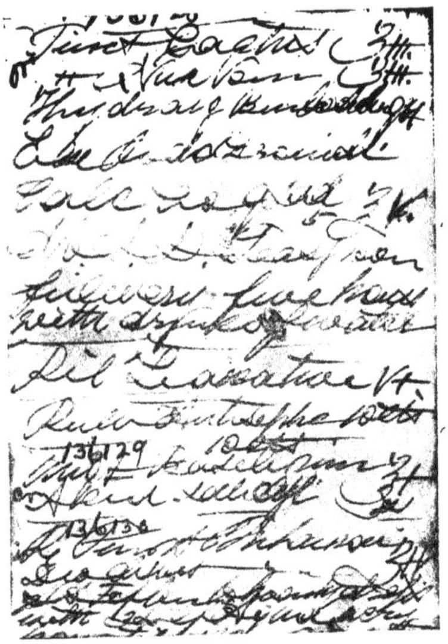

To the subscriber who is the first to mail a correct interpretation of this prescription we shall award a book to the value of $2, and we may award consolation prizes to contestants in cases where there is any doubt about the time of receipt of the paper and the mailing of the interpretation.

We invite readers to submit the originals of puzzling prescriptions for possible reproduction, with the assurance on our part that the prescriptions will be returned in good order and with the least possible delay to the senders. The acceptance of a prescription for reproduction will entitle the sender to a paid-up subscription for the AMERICAN DRUGGIST for one year.

Aristol (Thymol Iodide).—Replying further to L. H. L., whose query regarding the manufacture of aristol, and the answer thereto, was printed on page 324 of the preceding issue, we print herewith the method of preparing aristol given in the new Spanish Pharmacopœia:

SOLUTION I.

Iodine	60
Potassium iodide	80
Water to	300

SOLUTION II.

Thymol	15
Sodium hydroxide	15
Water to	300

Solution No. 1 is poured, little by little, into No. 2, with constant shaking. The precipitate is collected, washed and dried at ordinary temperature. The preparation contains 46 per cent. of iodine, but varies according to the method of preparation.

Prescription for Criticism.—A. S. asks us to criticise the subjoined prescription:

Tr. ferri. chloridi	ʒiv.
Quinin sulp.	ʒi.
Gray's glycerin tonic	q. s. ad ℥iv.

A. S. concludes by asking "what do you think of the druggist that put this up? Do you think him capable of taking charge of a pharmacy?"

We fail to see what the putting up of this prescription has to do with the capacity of the druggist to conduct a pharmacy. The question should rather be directed at the doctor who wrote the prescription. The composition of Gray's Glycerin tonic is generally well known, and we think it contains sufficient phosphoric acid to prevent the formation of ink through the action of the iron on the gentian and other vegetable ingredients in the compound. Apart from this we see nothing in the prescription to call for special comment.

Regulation of Liquor Sales by Pharmacists in New York.—A. A. C. submits the following queries:

"(1) What are the New York city laws governing the sale of grain alcohol by druggists?

"(2) Is a city license, a State license and a Federal license required?

"(3) Is a druggist holding the alcohol license permitted to sell bottled liquors?"

The sale of alcohol and traffic in liquor generally is regulated by a State law, the enforcement of which is left to State officials.

It is necessary to take out a Federal or U. S. Government license, costing $25 annually, if alcohol or spirituous liquors are to be sold. This is entirely independent of the State license, which costs $7.50 and permits licensed pharmacists to sell liquors upon the prescriptions of regularly licensed physicians. The holder of such a license is privileged to sell alcohol for medicinal or mechanical purposes without a prescription, except during prohibited hours.

Foam for Soda Syrups.—J. R., Mexico. Various substances are employed for the manufacture of foaming compounds for soda syrups, the most widely used being soapbark, though objection has been made to the use of this substance on account of its supposed poisonous properties, and many pharmacists of our acquaintance prefer the white of egg, made into a solution by special manipulation. There is certainly no better or more wholesome article to use than this. The whites of four eggs are sufficient for two gallons of syrup. T. D. McElhenie, of Brooklyn, breaks up the white of egg by shaking it in a tin of his own construction. Taking two of the square, screw capped, half pound tins used for Huyler's cocoa, he had the top cut off one and the bottom off the other, the second one was soldered on the top of the first with a diaphragm of wire netting between, so that by putting in two or three ounces of water, dropping in the whites and replacing the cap a slight shaking up and down is sufficient to break up the albumen and make a solution.

A soapbark foam may be made as follows:

Soapbark	℥ij.
Alcohol	℥ij.
Glycerin	℥ij.
Water, enough to make	℥viij.

Macerate the bark in the mixed liquids and filter after three days, passing sufficient water through the filter to make eight ounces, as directed. Two drachms of this foam is sufficient for one gallon of syrup. Some pharmacists use fluid extract of licorice, U. S. P., in the proportion of one drachm to one gallon of syrup, and say they can get nothing else to equal it as a foam producer.

A Solvent for Mica.—G. C. F. asks what he can use as a solvent for mica.

Mica varies so greatly in its chemical composition that it would be difficult to name a solvent for any given specimen without experimentation. The mineral is regarded as a double silicate of aluminum and various alkali earths, its composition being seldom constant. We suppose that it might be dissolved by any strong acid or combination of acids, such as nitric or nitro-hydrochloric. In the preparation of alum from aluminum silicate the shale is extracted by hot sulphuric acid, and hot sulphuric acid might dissolve mica.

Correspondence.

Fiat and Fiant.

To the Editor:

SIR,—Since I learned from you that you had accepted for publication my remarks on the confusion which exists in regard to the meaning of *fiat* and *fiant*—in current pharmaceutical and medical literature, I noticed in the *Pharmaceutical Journal* for June 2, page 23, some new confusion, which is indeed the climax of nonsense. The writer in the *Pharmaceutical Journal* translates *fiant pulvis* as "let them—*i. e.*: the ingredients named—become a powder." *Fiat pulvis*, now, means "let there be a powder." There is no plural of *pulvis* in Latin. The Romans as well as the Greeks must have considered it awkward to speak of powder in the plural. If there exists a plural of *pulvis* in monk's Latin, of which I am not aware, it will be *pulveres*, and if any one has bad taste enough to write monk's Latin in serious literature, he must write *fiant pulveres*. *Fiant pulvis*, whether composed of one substance or more ingredients, is an atrocity, a crime against grammar. Indeed, I never have seen "*fiant pulveres*." It would be bad taste. I was instructed to write *divide in —partes æquales*, but never divide in *pulveres æquales*. Whoever objects to criticism of the faulty use of Latin in current pharmaceutical literature should read the beautiful language of Lavoisier, to whom we are indebted for our scientific chemical nomenclature. "A DOCTOR."

"A Patent of Honor."

To the Editor:

SIR,—In reading Ralph B. Gable's article on the Flavor of Words, one cannot but admire the sentiment, but when it comes to membership in the A. Ph. A. as a patent of honor, is not that a strained construction? I take it that the membership depends on payment of dues, and the more who join, the better —but at $5 per, and not as a patent of honor! The writer mistook the phrase likely for the roll of honor—as understood by the U. S. Pension Office, but that depends on patriotic service, not on $5 per. H. C. CLARENDON.

EAGLE LAKE, WIS., June 14, 1906.

A Rejoinder by Mr. Gable.

To the Editor:

SIR,—I much appreciate your courtesy in permitting me to see the letter of H. C. Clarendon, in which he gently derides me for designating membership in the A. Ph. A. as "A patent of honor." I am constrained first of all, however, to remind Mr. Clarendon that the expression is not original with me; that it was first used by my friend, A. E. Ebert, of Chicago. When I cite this fact I do not do so because I fear I have been guilty of a strained construction. I do so because Mr. Ebert was a student of Liebig and for upwards of a half century has been associated with men of scholarly minds, men of broad attainments, men of eminence in various fields of science. Since he is willing to subscribe to the belief that membership in the A. Ph. A. is "A patent of honor," I, assuredly, do not hesitate to employ the phrase.

If one takes Vol. 50 of the *Proceedings of the American Pharmaceutical Association*, and turns to the end of the book, he will find a series of portraits. They are the pictures of the officers of the association during the first fifty years of its existence—Chas. Ellis, Wm. Procter, Jr., Edward Parrish, E. R. Squibb, John M. Maisch, Chas. Rice—why should I name others? Every man who has really contributed to advance pharmacy in America has been a member of the A. Ph. A. Is it not an honor to belong to an association which has had on its rolls the names of such men? Is there nothing in inspiration—nothing in ideals? I am inclined to believe there is. The soldier on the field of battle does prodigious feats of valor when he has before him a captain, a colonel or a general who has won his admiration. And so in the field of pharmacy; there are pharmacists who have been stimulated in research by the work of those who have gone before us. There are processes used in our laboratories which were devised by members of the A. Ph. A. There are appliances that we employ at the prescription counter which were first made by members of the A. Ph. A. There are formulas that we follow in making both official and unofficial preparations, which are the result of long hours of work of members of the A. Ph. A.

We cannot all win honor. We cannot all accomplish something which makes our names stand out prominently. But we can all be "soldiers of the common good"; we can have a share in the progress of the world by being members of the A. Ph. A.

We are standing on the shoulders of past generations. As individuals we should be willing to contribute to the heritage which our time leaves to succeeding generations.

RALPH B. GABLE.

NEW YORK, June 20, 1906.

Jobbers Only.

To the Editor:

SIR,—We notice your courteous reference to our house in a recent issue of your periodical and beg to ask you that in case you have occasion to refer to us in the future you omit the "retail" in connection with our firm. It is one of our strongest points that we do not retail and have no retail or prescription department, being strictly jobbers, avoiding in every possible way any competition with our customers, the retail druggists.

THE CHARLES W. WHITTLESEY COMPANY.

NEW HAVEN, CONN.

Deficient Postage on Foreign Mail.

The negligence of American business houses in the matter of postage on foreign mail is so general that at least one firm of pharmacists having considerable dealings with the United States has a printed postal card form calling attention to this fault in American correspondents, which we reproduce herewith:

SAN JOSE, COSTA RICA,................,1906.

Gentlemen,—We wish to inform you that your letter of the.... inst. was sent short postage.

In spite of the efforts of the consuls throughout these countries and the frequent notices in the different trade journals relative to short postage, we find that this practice, indulged in only by American houses, has not in the least decreased.

Please instruct your mailing clerk that letters to Costa Rica require a 5 cent stamp for every ½ ounce or fraction. Besides the annoyance and expense of having to pay short postage and fines, it delays the delivery of the letter one day, which frequently means a delay of one week before it can be answered.

Last year the amount we paid in short postage fines amounted to nearly $50.

Hoping this will have your best attention, we are

Yours truly,

HERMAN & ZELEDON.

This firm is one of the largest, most enterprising and most successful concerns connected with the drug business in Costa Rica. They import in a large way and are practically the only distributors of drugs in the city of San Jose. Senor Zeledon speaks English fluently and has visited the United States several times. An extended interview with him was published in our columns on the occasion of his last visit to this country, which occurred about two years ago. He is a man of very considerable scientific attainments, takes an active part in the affairs of the College of Pharmacy, and is one of the most progressive citizens of our sister republic. His warning should certainly be heeded by American exporters.

CONDUCTED BY FRANK FARRINGTON.

Under this head will appear suggestions and plans for increasing trade, advertising experiences, information, and notes of interest useful to the pharmacist in the preparation of his advertising matter. Specimens of current advertising will be reproduced, with suggestive analysis and criticism, and queries relative to advertising matters will be answered. To avoid delay address communications to Department of Business Building, AMERICAN DRUGGIST, 66 West Broadway, New York.

ATTRACTING ATTENTION.

It is easy enough to attract attention. It is easy enough to become notorious, but to attract favorable attention and to become noted is quite another thing.

Some people achieve notoriety through infamous or through criminal conduct, but at its best notoriety is undesirable. Some people attain a position in which they are neither noted nor notorious, but simply conspicuous.

Some years ago a young New Yorker with an itching for celebrity attained conspicuousness by a very simple method. Every morning he went through the elevated train, upon which he regularly rode down town, and bade each passenger a pleasant "Good morning."

At first people were only mildly surprised, but thought little of the proceeding. Soon, however, they began to get curious and take notice, and before long every regular traveller on that particular train knew the name of the young man, and inquiring strangers were met with the remark, "What, don't you know ———?" From that it was but a step to a city-wide reputation, which the chap proceeded to use to his own manifest advantage.

Few druggists perhaps become noted, and I hope that still less become notorious, but it would be to the advantage of most of them to be noticed, and to be noticed one must do something noticeable.

There is a part of the advertising of a store which aims not so much at creating a demand for some particular article as at keeping the name of the store before the public in a general way. This general publicity is more like that accomplished by that modern institution the press agent. It calls for new plans, new methods and actual changes and alterations for the better in store and management as often as possible. As for the practical ways of accomplishing this favorable conspicuousness, they are as varied as the schemes of the press agent.

The druggist may, to advantage, study the advertising of the department store, or the bargain store, which sees to it that there is always something special doing within its walls to make people think of the store.

The bulk of the store's advertising must, of course, concern itself with the actual goods to be sold, but the advertiser's ingenuity must not stop there. The druggist can have special sales as well as the big store. He can have bargain counters and he can make special offers.

It requires but a slight pretext to make a peg upon which to hang a special sale, and the druggist has as many of those pretexts as his more ostentatious neighbor.

Fresh paint is one of the things that always attracts attention to a store, and the store which has just been "done over," either outside or in, is looked upon as keeping up to date. The man who keeps his property well painted is considered progressive and it makes people think that business is good.

It pays to keep people thinking that business is good in a store. There are druggists who seem to think that it pays to look "down in the mouth" so that they will get business from sympathy, but all the business that a fellow gets from sympathetic motives as a rule won't pay the interest on what it will cost him in loss of the trade of people who like to take part in a successful man's advancement.

A new show case or two in the store ought to make a news item for the local papers, and the new cases should be filled with some attractive bargains, so that the advertising may tell the people that Smith has been improving his facilities for showing his brush stock and his new, big line is now being exhibited in modern cases, where every article can be plainly seen and the price noted without having to ask a question.

The store improvements that are really rather unimportant can be made to sound important in print, and they can be made to appear worthy of notice to the people who see them, if enough pains are taken to get up something attractive and even elaborate in the way of display to set off the new show case or the different arrangement of things.

Suppose a partition is cut out, or the store enlarged a little in some inexpensive way. That fact ought to be made public so that every one will know that you are enlarging. Everything that tends to spread the news that a store is doing more business than it did, enlarges its number of patrons.

A man may have an up to date drug store and run it in an up to date manner, increasing his business every year, but even so, unless he keeps the public posted as to his continual gain, the majority of people will not know whether he is doing well or just scraping along. It pays in real money to have the general public know that one's store is getting to be the popular store. Business follows the crowd, and people like to go where every one else is going.

It does not call for a very great change in a prescription desk to make it possible to get an item in the local paper to the effect that Smith is increasing his facilities for handling his growing prescription business. A new set of scales that is sensitive to the one hundred and twenty-eighth of a grain will make a nice groundwork for a newspaper note on the skill and care required in compounding. The newspaper that a druggist advertises in generously will do quite a bit for him if it gets the chance. If such notices won't go in free as news items, then they can be paid for, and be run as "readers" and be valuable at that.

A new cigar case, or simply a new plan of keeping the old case moistened, can be made to call attention to the fact that one has added a new line of cigars, or is going to devote especial care to that branch of the business.

Whenever a little improvement is made, extra displays, changes in arrangement, special offers, etc., grouped about that little change, will make it look like a big change. The small improvement can be made to appear great by judicious use of goods in its vicinity.

There are always chances to get the store before the public on account of the doings of the personnel of the management or the working force. Such opportunities ought to be seized. It may be merely the vacations of the clerks or of the proprietor, but if nothing more it is news, and the newsgatherer will, as a rule, not be averse to tagging a puff for the store on the end of the item.

If the pharmacist goes to a state convention, he is not doing his duty unless his newspapers state that "Our up to date druggist, Mr. J. Smith, is attending the meeting of tht state Association of Pharmacists in search of anything new in the way of methods for improving the service of his store." If it is regular vacation that he is on, then he has gone for "A much needed rest on account of the strain of the last few months of particularly heavy business."

All these are rather trite statements, but the modern newspaper is not materially different from its predecessor, though it will find new ways of saying these things. If a man wants to keep his store before the public in every possible way, he must not shrink from the lime light himself.

People, the public, are more interested in people than in things. They will read personal news items when they are tired of advertisements. If they are kept thinking about one store and its workers, while another store is seldom mentioned, the store that they think about is pretty apt to get them sooner or later.

In every store there is a frequent accumulation of articles that become unsalable through being shop-worn or getting out of date. The druggist has not been in the habit of having sales that will get rid of such accumulations as the general merchants have them.

It is good business for the drug store to work off its old stock whenever possible, and even patents that are dead will start up a little if the price is low enough. The best chances for having these cleaning up sales are anything in the way of changes in the management of the store or in the inside arrangement of it.

If a partner comes into the store; if one leaves; if there is a change from a cash to a credit basis; if the store changes its location; if there is a damage by fire or by water; if the town experiences a set back or a noticeably dull season for any reason. These all make excuses for a sale that gives one a chance to clean up the old stock.

The live man is on the lookout for such opportunities and seizes them at once. He seizes the smaller chances, too, and makes capital out of everything that happens to him or to his business. This sort of publicity is a little out of the line of straight advertising, but it pays and costs comparatively nothing.

PURE FOOD BILL AGAIN BEFORE THE HOUSE.

Representative Mann Attacks the Proprietary Associations—Borrows Material from "Collier's Weekly" for Insertion in the "Record"—Charges of Bad Faith Against the Proprietary Medicine Interests—Drastic Arraignment of Manufacturing Grocers.

(*From our Regular Correspondent.*)

Washington, D. C., June 21.—Representative Mann, of Chicago, spoke on the Pure Food bill for nearly an hour to-day, illustrating his remarks by a very full and interesting display of adulterated foods and fraudulent products. He referred to the crusade of *Collier's Weekly* against the use of patent medicines, and asked leave to print as part of his speech the articles which have appeared in that journal on this subject. He vigorously attacked the Proprietary Association of America and charged its members with having resorted to unfair means to prevent the inclusion in the Pure Food bill of provisions requiring a statement as to the content of opium, cocaine and other poisons. He said that the members of Congress have been urged to support the Senate bill because it was stronger than the House bill, whereas, as a matter of fact, it does not contain a line on the subject of opium. Mr. Mann said he had received letters from Chicago physicians, and among others from the secretary of the American Medical Association, urging him to support the Senate bill on the ground that it prohibited the use of opium. He said: "It is plain what is behind this widespread movement. The Proprietary Association has in some manner falsified the situation about this bill and given to the country the impression that the Senate bill has the clause and the House bill has it not, whereas, it is in the House bill,, which puts in the clause the Senate left out.

'The great mass of our foods is not adulterated," Mr. Mann went on, "and since the pure food agitation began there has been a marked reduction in the quality of adulteration and the number of cases. Yet everywhere the honest dealer is met with competition by adulterated or short weight goods."

Mr. Mann then took up the question of adulterated food stuffs and cited statistics to prove the wholesale practice of adulteration in this line. He exhibited specimens of various foods and food stuffs which upon examination had proved to be other than they were represented to be, and among other things showed a specimen of glucose masquerading as honey, in which the verisimilitude was carried out by having a dead bee in the container. The bill will be discussed further before final action is taken.

THE ETHICS OF MEDICINE AND PHARMACY.

Doctors, Druggists and Editors Confer—A Notable Display of Good Feeling at the Manhattan Meeting—A Large Number in Attendance.

Under the auspices of the Manhattan Pharmaceutical Association a joint discussion on the ethics of the allied professions of medicine and pharmacy was held at the College of Pharmacy of the City of New York on Monday evening, June 18. In introducing the speakers Jacob Diner said that the primary object of the Manhattan Association was the elevation of the professional side of pharmacy, and that for this reason the officers had arranged for the symposium on "the ethics of the allied professions." He then introduced as the first speaker Dr. Reynold Webb Wilcox, Professor of Medicine at the New York Post-Graduate Medical school.

Dr. Wilcox said that he did not feel that in appearing before a gathering of pharmacists he was appearing before strangers, but rather that he was appearing before friends, and that if any of his hearers felt that they were really strangers this was all the more reason for such a conference.

THE PHYSICIAN'S POINT OF VIEW.

He said that in regard to the relations of the physician and the pharmacist and the use of proprietary preparations and ready made prescriptions he was frankly willing to assume that a large share of the blame for these untoward conditions rested upon the physician. He said that the tendency toward the use of ready made prescriptions was due principally to the ignorance of therapeutics on the part of the new fledged graduates.

"It is a lamentable fact," he said, "that the young doctor of to-day is less fitted to practice his profession than was the young doctor of ten years ago. The theoretical work in the medical schools is enormously out of proportion to the practical. Instruction should not stop at diagnosis. More time should be devoted to therapeutics, and the student should learn the properties of drugs and their application to disease.

"The average student when he comes out of college to practice his profession knows little or nothing about compounding prescriptions. He has never been taught this thoroughly. He goes into the hospitals and comes away with the nauseous formulas used there—nauseous chiefly because they can be made up in bulk without much expense to the hospitals. He has not been taught to prescribe, but merely to write orders for A in cases of typhoid fever, for B in cases of bronchial cough and for C in some other specific complaint. When he leaves college with such an equipment he either becomes a kind of a carpenter keeping a doctor's shop with an array of ready made prescriptions, falling an easy prey to the detail man, or, failing to get the results which he expected to get, becomes a therapeutic nihilist. I have a supreme contempt for the therapeutic nihilist, whom in my heart I look upon as a therapeutic ignoramus."

Dr. Wilcox said the medical profession itself was largely to blame for the failing interest in drug therapeutics. The fault lay, he said, with the curriculum, which had spread over so much ground and had become so ultra scientific as to leave no time to instruct the student in the application of medicine. He believed that the students should be made to learn their materia medica and pharmacy just as they are made to learn anatomy, and should be made to compound prescriptions, so as to learn something of the practical difficulties of dispensing. He said that he was happy to say that he had no part in turning out the new crop of physicians, but that he was kept busy in instructing and trying to make better physicians of men who were already graduates.

THE PHARMACOLOGICAL SOCIETY.

Dr. F. E. Stewart, the next speaker, said that the pharmacist was constantly asked as to what was good for a cough, a cold, a pain or an ache, and that it was practically impossible for the pharmacist to refrain from giving some advice over the counter. The standard by which his acts were to be judged could not be established definitely along hard and fast lines, but the general attitude of each individual toward the question of right and wrong would have to determine the limit to go in each case. Dr. Stewart outlined the organization of the Pharmacological Society, which had been founded with a view to furnishing a means for the independent and authoritative investigation of new pharmaceutical products, and which proposed to act in conjunction with and under the guidance of the Council on Pharmacy and Chemistry of the American Medical Association. He recited the rules adopted by that council, and pointed out the good results which would follow the application of those rules in conjunction with the investigations carried on by the Pharmacological Society. The most important results, he said, would be to bring into closer affiliation the pharmacist and physician, who were natural allies. In closing Dr. Stewart referred to the patent medicine business as a disturbing factor in the relations of the pharmacist and physician, saying: "Whom God hath joined together let no patent medicine man put asunder."

COMMERCIAL THERAPEUTICS.

Dr. John P. Davin, of New York, presented an interesting paper under the title of "Commercial Therapeutics," which had been written some 21 years ago as an inaugural thesis and which no medical journal would publish at that time, but which was published in a drug journal. The essay was most interesting, as it was so appropriate to the existing conditions that it might well have been written within the last few weeks. He sketched the growth of the commercial therapeutics under the guidance of the large manufacturing pharmacists, who, he said, not only exploited their own goods, but "harnessed the U. S. Pharmacopœia to a pill compressor," turning out pills which the druggist was compelled to carry in stock and which were hermetically sealed by a glaze which only came off in the stomach, if it came off then. He spoke of the flood of literature supporting the ready made prescription idea, and said that St. Louis had become so well known as the headquarters for this sort of thing that some of the medical journals heretofore published there had been transferred to New York. He said that the pseudo-ethical proprietary was much more objectionable than the plain patent medicine; that when the physician would call on his patient the patient would hide the patent medicine, but would bring out with pride the pseudo-ethical proprietary which he had been prescribing for himself.

THE MANUFACTURER'S STANDPOINT.

Dr. Frederick P. Tuttle, of Parke, Davis & Co., was introduced to speak on behalf of the manufacturing pharmacist. Dr. Tuttle explained that he was not prepared to undertake this serious task, as it had been expected that Mr. Helfman would come on from Detroit to act as the spokesman of the firm. He said that he frankly acknowledged a strong prejudice in favor of Parke, Davis & Co., with whom he had been actively engaged for the past 20 years. He believed that this house had done whatever could be done for the investigation and study of pharmaceutical and pharmacological problems, and for the dissemination of the knowledge thus gained for the medical and pharmaceutical profession. He said that the products of this house were always prepared in a thoroughly ethical manner, that their labels were accurate, full and descriptive, and that even in their specialties they gave all the necessary information to keep the physician fully enlightened as to the medicinal character of the substances they were using.

DR. SCHIEFFELIN DEFENDS THE STEVENS-WAINWRIGHT BILL.

Dr. William Jay Schieffelin was also called upon by the president, Mr. Diner, to speak on behalf of the manufacturing pharmacists. Dr. Schieffelin opened his remarks by saying: "I cannot stand here and say we are strictly ethical, for I don't think we are. I think it does not matter what line of business a person is engaged in, he will occasionally find out that he had made mistakes; but so long as he finds this out and rectifies the mistakes himself he should receive some credit. When I was a student at the School of Mines the professor of metallurgy was accustomed to say: 'Gentlemen, you are going to make mistakes in your work—everybody does. These mistakes will entail loss of time and money. Be sure that you discover and rectify your own mistakes—that is the most that can be asked of any man.' I have been finding out our mistakes and trying to rectify them, and if you gentlemen find something of ours that you think unethical I ask you to suspend judgment until you ascertain whether the error is not being corrected. I do not think it is right for a man to do one thing with one hand and another thing with the other. I don't think that we ought to put up under our own label only those things which are prepared and marketed in an ethical manner, and at the same time put up other preparations under labels of other persons which are marketed in a manner which constitutes a fraud. The private formula business presents many serious problems to the manufacturer of pharmaceuticals, and if the manufacturer is not careful as to the person he is dealing with and does not investigate carefully as to the uses to which a private formula is put, he may find himself involved in a business the prosecutor of which may be and ought to be put in jail." Dr. Schieffelin said that the question of protection by trademark was a very serious one from the manufacturer's standpoint. He said that his own firm had prepared and placed on the market an excellent elixir of heroin and terpin hydrate. This proving successful was widely advertised, and the firm did a large business in it for the first year. The next year, however, the business rather fell off, for Parke, Davis & Co., Sharpe & Dohme, Ely Lilly & Co. and probably half a dozen other manufacturing pharmacists were also selling elixir of heroin and terpin hydrate. If a trademark name such as heroterpin had been given to the elixir instead of a simple descriptive name he believed that his own firm would have continued to lead in the sale and would have been able to "make a little money honestly." In connection with this question of trademark protection Dr. Schieffelin said that he had heard a point brought out in the discussion of the phenacetin trademark rights at the Boston meeting which had suggested a wholly new idea to him. This was that in the scientific descriptions of the drug phenacetin and in the clinical reports upon its use which were used in the introduction of the drug the true scientific descriptive name, acetphenetidin, should have been used. Had this been done and the trade name phenacetin having been reserved for use as a "word mark," there would have been no question raised now as to whether phenacetin was really a descriptive word or whether it was a trademark.

Dr. Schieffelin then took up the Stevens-Wainwright bill and discussed the objections that had been raised to it by the pharmacists. He said that the bill was in reality divisible into three parts and it was unfortunate that it had not been so divided, for in that case some parts of the bill would have no doubt been enacted. He said that the arguments advanced in favor of placing the administration of the bill in the hands of the Board of Health by the doctors and lawyers who were interested in drafting it seemed to him to be unanswerable. One of these was that it was bad policy to place in the hands of one druggist, as a member of the Board of Pharmacy, the power to annoy a rival druggist who might be guilty of a technical violation of the law.

Mr. Diner, the president of the association, replying to this particular objection, said that the pharmacists having themselves selected the members of the Board of Pharmacy it was fair to assume that they were willing to entrust to them full power to administer law.

THE POINT OF VIEW OF THE MEDICAL EDITOR

was set forth by Dr. H. Edwin Lewis, editor of the *International Journal of Surgery*, whose remarks we print in full in another column. Dr. Lewis's paper was received with frequent applause and many evidences of approval.

THE PHARMACEUTICAL JOURNALIST.

Caswell A. Mayo was introduced as a representative of the pharmaceutical press, and made a brief address reviewing the relations at present existing between physician and pharmacist. He said that the leaders in the present reform movement, like leaders in all such movements, had in some instances been too radical, but that one of the most hopeful indications of a possibility for permanent benefit was the noticeable modification of the views of extremists and the very marked change in the attitude of the physicians toward the pharmacists. This change in attitude of physicians had been signalized by the tone of the addresses made by Dr. Willcox, Dr. Stewart and Dr. Lewis on the present occasion, but had been no less marked in the discussions which took place among the physicians attending the sessions of the section on pharmacology and therapeutics of the American Medical Association at the recent meeting in Boston.

E. C. Goetting, editor of the *Deutsch-Amerikanische Apotheker Zeitung*, read an address on behalf of the pharmaceutical press, reviewing the relations of the physician and the pharmacist. He defended the pharmacists at large from the charge of promiscuous counter prescribing, but said that in this calling, as in every other, there was a certain number of black sheep, and asked that physicians should not hold the profession at large responsible for the shortcomings of a few. He said that it was impossible for the pharmacist to always decline to give advice in the minor ailments, and he thought that the giving of such advice was wholly justifiable where the ailment was evidently of a simple character, and provided always that the pharmacist recommended some ready made preparation and did not undertake to compound a mixture for the specific case under treatment. This act he looked upon as being wholly inadmissible. He regarded the prescription as being the property of the physician and condemned the miscellaneous refilling of prescriptions calling for potent remedies, but he said he believed that physicians generally overrated the damage done by the refilling of ordinary prescriptions and also overrated the financial loss entailed on the physician by such practice. He believed that in most cases the patient who had a prescription refilled would, if cut off from this privilege, not return to the physician for a prescription, but resort to a household remedy or patent medicine.

FROM THE RETAILER'S STANDPOINT.

William C. Alpers, speaking for the retailer, said that there seemed to be two kinds of ethics, one for association use and the other for private consumption. The average member of an association subscribed to a very charming and altogether delightful system of ethics as propounded in the association, and then went home and acted upon a wholly different basis. He said that he had formerly opposed the manufacturing pharmacist bitterly, but was now convinced that the manufacturing pharmacist was a logical, necessary and even beneficent evolution. He said that the manufacturing pharmacist could not be held to strict accountability for the final disposition of all his products by others, but he did think that they should be held up to a very high standard of ethics in their relations to each other. He instanced the manufacture by the large dealer of imitations of copyrighted preparations as a reprehensible practice, contravening ethical relations between the manufacturers themselves. He had only to-day received a prescription calling for "Pepto-mangan, P., D. & Co." Now the question was what should the druggist dispense? Should he dispense the original pepto-mangan, in which case he would not send out the P. D. & Co.'s product, or should he dispense P. D. & Co.'s solution of iron peptonate and manganese? He said that in the effort to produce better ethical conditions it was necessary to interest and educate the public. The public has no idea that there is any impropriety whatever in the druggist's prescribing. Mr. Alpers cited an instance in which he had been soundly rated by a customer for declining to prescribe. He said that it was necessary for the pharmacist to love and honor his profession and to magnify it in the eyes of the public by his attitude to his own calling, and that unless a pharmacist did show his respect for his calling he could not command for it the respect of the medical profession or of the public at large.

William C. Anderson, of Brooklyn, closed the discussion on behalf of the pharmacist, saying that in all the reforms that the druggist was called upon to participate in the first step in the reform involved sacrifice on the part of the pharmacist, and in fact the pharmacist was always the first man who had to give up something. He said it was useless to contemplate the abandonment by the pharmacist of the sale of household remedies and patent medicines, as the pharmacist's calling was largely a commercial one and this branch of the business was too important to be thrown over. He believed, though, that much could be accomplished by constant and intelligent work in exploiting the preparations of the National Formulary and United States Pharmacopœia.

On motion of R. R. Smith the speakers of the evening were tendered a rising vote of thanks.

In dismissing the meeting the president, Mr. Diner, congratulated the members upon the large attendance and upon the interesting matter which had been placed before them for discussion, and expressed the hope that similar occasions might be arranged for in the future. After the adjournment, which took place near 1 o'clock, the members partook of a bountiful collation which was served in the library of the college.

THE AMERICAN PHARMACEUTICAL ASSOCIATION.

Subscriptions for the Procter Monument Fund Received—The Chicago Branch Takes Up Educational Questions.

Professor Henry Kraemer, of Philadelphia, has issued a letter to the pharmaceutical press, as secretary of the Committee on the Wm. Proctor, Jr., Monument Fund of the American Pharmaceutical Association, announcing the receipt of subscriptions amounting to over $200. The letter follows:

To the Editor:

SIR.—Now that the Procter Monument Fund Committee of the American Pharmaceutical Association have begun systematically to solicit subscriptions to the Fund, the drug journals will be in a position to help the movement to a very great extent by publishing the names of subscribers and giving such other information as may be forthcoming, and by commenting editorially on the work.

I began soliciting subscriptions here in Philadelphia this week, and have already received $219, of which nearly $50 is in cash. The following is a list of subscribers, together with the amount subscribed by each:

J. B. Moore	$25	J. H. Stein	$5
J. C. Peacock	5	Jos. A. Heintzelman	10
Lorne E. Hastings	2	Florence Yaple	5
Edwin L. Newcomb	5	Wm. R. Warner, jr	50
Henry P. Thorn	5	Henry Kraemer	10
Ambrose Hunsberger	5	J. Warren Worthington	2
Joseph P. Remington	100		

Information will be furnished you from time to time as the work progresses.

HENRY KRAEMER.

PHILADELPHIA, June 16, 1906.

THE CHICAGO BRANCH.

The largest meeting so far held by the Chicago Branch of the American Pharmaceutical Association was that held at the Northwestern University Building on Tuesday evening, June 12.

The subject for discussion had been announced as "How to Bring About More Satisfactory Educational Requirements for Pharmacy in Illinois."

The Committee on Education and Legislation presented a report which caused a lively discussion. After some amendments and eliminations the report of the committee, embracing the following preamble and resolutions, was adopted:

"*Whereas*, The only distinguishing characteristic of the pharmacist's vocation is his professional work, and

"*Whereas*, The rights of the public as well as the prosperity of the pharmacist demand that proper pharmaceutical education be effectively fostered and the admission of educationally unfit persons to the apothecary's business prevented, and

"*Whereas*, Examinations cannot take the place of systematic education, and

"*Whereas*, These truths are now given practical recognition in several States, as follows: In Michigan a preliminary education amounting to two years of high school work is required of candidates for license as registered pharmacists; in New York, Ohio, South Dakota and Wisconsin one year of high school work is required; in New York and Pennsylvania candidates for license must also be graduates of a recognized school of pharmacy, and in Wisconsin applicants for certificates as registered pharmacists must have a technical education amounting to two years of not less than 32 weeks' instruction annually in a recognized school of pharmacy, and

"*Whereas*, Our great State of Illinois should not be permitted to fall behind other States in necessary educational reform. Therefore, be it

"*Resolved*, By the Chicago Branch of the American Pharmaceutical Association, that the preliminary general education required for apprentices in pharmacy, under Section 7 of the

Pharmacy law, should be not less than one year of high school work or its equivalent, and we request the Board of Pharmacy of Illinois to so order, under the ample authority conferred upon it by said section, and be it further

"*Resolved*, That the Board of Pharmacy of our State be and is hereby requested to accept the standards of efficiency of the American Conference of Pharmaceutical Faculties, to be applied to all schools of pharmacy to whose students and graduates any credit is extended for courses of study in any school not conforming to such standards, and be it further

"*Resolved*, That the board be and is hereby requested to make the scope of the examinations for the licensing of registered pharmacists commensurate with the courses of education given in schools of pharmacy registered by the board as conforming to its standards of efficiency, and be it further

"*Resolved*, That we request the Board of Pharmacy of Illinois to take into account all direct evidence of effective training for the practice of pharmacy which any candidate may present in his behalf, and especially satisfactorily completed courses of study and laboratory practice in schools of pharmacy, in the determination of his fitness for registration and license, and be it further

"*Resolved*, That the Pharmacy law of Illinois should be so amended as to require two years' practical experience in pharmacies, independently of courses of study, but to the end that substantial courses in the pharmaceutical schools may not be discouraged, the laws and board rulings should not require persons who take longer courses to wait a correspondingly longer time before they are enabled to secure their licenses; and that the minimum total time prescribed for both college education and practical experience in pharmacies should be the same for all persons, without reference to the length of the college course they may have completed, and should be sufficient to include a full two years' course in a pharmaceutical school, and be it further

"*Resolved*, That the secretary of the branch be instructed to communicate this set of resolutions to the Board of Pharmacy of the State of Illinois and to the Illinois State Pharmaceutical Association."

Twenty-five new members were received. The next meeting will be held September 11.

President Stahl Sails.

Adolph Stahl has joined the rush of seagoers, having sailed on the steamship *Kaiserin Auguste Victoria* last Thursday for a two months' vacation in Europe. Mr. Stahl is known to a host of readers of the AMERICAN DRUGGIST in the New England States, New York and Pennsylvania through his connection with the Manhattan Drug Company and as president of the Commercial Travelers' Auxiliary of the New York State Pharmaceutical Association. It is safe to say that few more energetic, genial and altogether charming representatives of the traveling fraternity can be found than Mr. Stahl, and be will have the heartiest good wishes of his many friends for a pleasant sojourn abroad. It is his intention to spend a short time in London, and from there visit Amsterdam, The Hague, Brussels, Cologne, Mayence, Heidelberg and Munich (his stay in Munich may extend over a longer period than at any other place, this city being famous for its breweries, although his next stopping place, Leipzig, may claim an equal share of his attention, for Mr. Stahl is fond of music, and Leipzig is a place where he may indulge his fancy to the limit); Berlin and Paris will be visited, not to mention cities of lesser note, and he will set his face homeward from Cherbourg on the steamship *Deutschland*, August 8.

The South Dakota Board of Pharmacy Raises the Grade.

Notice has been issued that the South Dakota Board of Pharmacy has raised the rating required in the examinations, as follows: For licentiate, full registration, 75 per cent. and not below 60 per cent. in any one branch.

For assistant certificate 60 per cent. and not below 50 per cent. in any one branch.

E. C. Bent, secretary of the board, Dell Rapids, will furnish application blanks on request.

THE PURE FOOD BILL FOR LOUISIANA.

Drug Interests Involved in the State Law—Details of the Provisions—Orleans and State Associations Both Take a Hand.

(*From our Regular Correspondent.*)

New Orleans, June 18.—The fight for a Pure Food and Drug law for the State of Louisiana is now at its height, and drug men throughout the State have memorialized the General Assembly in an effort to secure a law that will be in accord with their ideas and wishes. A bill has already been introduced in the Legislature and will be taken up for final action within the next few days. It has passed the committee successfully, even though a hard fight was necessary to secure its passage, and will before very long be put to a final vote.

CITY AND STATE ASSOCIATIONS ACT JOINTLY.

Last Saturday night the Louisiana State Pharmaceutical Society, acting in conjunction with the Orleans Pharmaceutical Association, went on record as favoring the bill which was introduced by the State Board of Health, with amendments which would provide "the highest standards of the United States Pharmacopœia, the National Formulary, the standard of the Association of Official Agricultural Chemists and the Committee of Standards of the Association of State Dairy and Food Departments, for the guidance and control of those intrusted with the execution of such laws." In order to acquaint members of the association with what was proposed the committee having the matter in charge on Saturday wired every druggist in Louisiana, asking his support of the proposed amendments submitted.

AMENDMENTS OFFERED BY THE DRUG TRADE.

Here are the amendments offered to those sections affecting drugs and their introduction into the State:

Provided, That the introduction into the State of Louisiana, from any other State or Territory, or from any foreign country, of any article of food, liquor, water or drugs which is adulterated or misbranded, within the meaning of this act, is hereby prohibited; and any person who, having received, shall deliver, in original, unbroken packages, for pay or otherwise, or offer to deliver to any person, any such article so adulterated or misbranded, within the meaning of this act, or any person who shall sell or offer for sale in the State of Louisiana any such adulterated or misbranded foods, liquor, water or drugs, shall be guilty of a misdemeanor. Provided, however, that no person shall be liable to the penalty of imprisonment as provided herein unless he knowingly committed the offense charged.

Sec. 2. Be it further enacted, etc., that the examinations of specimens of foods, liquors, water and drugs shall be made in the laboratory of the State Board of Health, or under the direction and supervision of such board, for the purpose of determining from such examinations whether such articles are adulterated or misbranded within the meaning of this act, and if it shall appear from any such examination that any of such specimens are adulterated or misbranded, within the meaning of this act, the president of the State Board of Health shall cause notice thereof to be given to the party from whom such sample is obtained. Any party so notified shall be given an opportunity to be heard, under such rules and regulations as may be prescribed as aforesaid, and if it appears that any of the provisions of this act have been violated by such party, then the president of the State Board of Health shall at once certify the facts to the proper district attorney with a copy of their results of the analysis or the examination of such articles, duly authenticated by the analyst or officer making such examination, under the oath of such officer. After judgment of the court notice shall be given by the publication in such manner as may be prescribed by the rules and regulations aforesaid.

Sec. 3. Be it further enacted, etc., that the term "drug," as used in this act, shall include all medicines and preparations recognized in the United States Pharmacopœia, or National Formulary, for internal or external use, and any medicine or preparation of medicine intended to be used for the cure, mitigation or prevention of disease of either man or other animals. The term "food," as used herein, shall include all articles used for food, drink, confectionery or condiment by man or other animals, whether simple, mixed or compound.

Sec 4. Be it further enacted, etc., that for the purpose of this act an article shall be deemed adulterated in case of drugs:

First—If, when a drug is sold under the standard recognized in the United States Pharmacopœia, or National Formulary, it differs from the standard of strength, quality or purity, as determined by the test laid down in the United States Pharmacopœia, or National Formulary, official at the time of the investigation.

Second—If its strength or purity differ from any other professed standard or quality under which it is sold.

Sec. 5. Be it further enacted, etc., that the term "misbranded," as used herein, shall apply to all drugs, liquors, waters or articles of food, or articles which may enter into the composition of food, the package or label of which shall bear any statements regarding the ingredients or substances contained in such article, which statement shall be false or misleading in any particular, and to any food or drug product which is falsely branded as to the State, Territory or country in which it is manufactured or produced.

That for the purpose of this act an article shall also be deemed misbranded.

In case of drugs:

First—If it be an imitation of or offered for sale under the name of another article.

Second—If the contents of the original package shall have been removed, in whole or in part, and other contents shall have been placed in such package, or if, when the article contained be not described in the United States Pharmacopœia or National Formulary, and be not the prescription of a regular licensed physician, and the package fail to bear a statement on the label of the quantity or proportion of any alcohol, morphine, opium, cocaine, heroin, alpha or beta eucaine, or chloral hydrate, or any preparation of any of such substances contained therein; provided, however, that the quantity or proportion of alcohol need not be stated when not more than the quantity or proportion prescribed by the United States Pharmacopœia, or the National Formulary, as a solvent or preservative of the active constituents of the medicine or preparation in such package and used. And provided further, that the quantity or proportion of opium or morphine need not be stated when the contents of the package contain not more than two grains of opium or one-quarter grain of morphine, or one-eighth grain cocaine, or ten grains of chloral hydrate to the fluid ounce, or, if a solid preparation, to the avoirdupois ounce.

NEW JERSEY PHARMACEUTICAL ASSOCIATION.

Report of the Meeting Concluded—Officers Elected—Motion to Admit Wives of Members to Associate Membership Voted Down—Will Meet Next Year at Asbury Park.

The conclusion of our correspondent's report of the annual meeting of the New Jersey Pharmaceutical Association, sent by telegraph on June 9, reached us too late for publication in our issue of June 11. Our correspondent reports the following officers elected to serve during the ensuing year: President, Philemon E. Hommell, 859 Bergen avenue, Jersey City; first vice-president, H. H. Deakyne, Atlantic City; second vice-president, Louis E. Feindt, South Orange; secretary, Frank C. Stutzlen, 231 Third street, Elizabeth; treasurer, James C. Field, Somerville; Executive Committee, William F. Ridgway, Atlantic City; George M. Andrews, Woodstown; Eugene Hartnett, Jersey City, and H. P. Thorn, Medford.

Kings County Delegates to the Annual Meeting of the New Jersey Pharmaceutical Association, June, 1906.
Dr. Fred. P. Tuthill and Charles Helmersheim, Standing; W. H. Bussenschutt, Sitting.

The association voted down a proposition to admit the wives of members to associate membership and took no action on a resolution to contribute to the relief of the druggists who have lost their homes and property in San Francisco.

Prof. H. J. Lohman took occasion to berate the pharmaceutical press for what he alleged to be neglect of New Jersey in their news reports on trade and scientific matters, but his objection was not sufficient to prevent the passage of a resolution to appoint a special State Press Committee.

A somewhat acrimonious debate arose over the question of meeting next year at Atlantic City, the upshot of which was that Asbury Park was selected.

The Parmele Pharmacal Company.

The officers of this company are Charles Roome Parmele, president; Adelrich Benziger, treasurer, and A. W. Hallett, secretary, and they succeed to the business of Charles Roome Parmele Company in the manufacture and sale of arsenauro, mercauro, manganauro, calcauro and hypotone. The arrangement whereby Sharp & Dohne were sole distributers has been terminated by friendly agreement.

Minnesota College Graduates.

The commencement exercises of the College of Pharmacy of the University of Minnesota took place on Thursday morning, June 14, at the University Armory. Dr. H. Pratt Judson, acting president of the University of Chicago, delivered the commencement address. The following nineteen students graduated: H. J. Barnett, W. H. Bockhoven, Mrs. Charlotte E. Caton, Joseph P. Cutting, E. G. Carlson, Emmet R. Desmond, Leonard Granberg, Dottie Curtis Frise, John Abner Handy, Edward Philip Kennedy, George Thrall Kermott, Miss Koyla Myrtle Ketcham, Leo Daniel Madden, Robert North, Henry Ellis Peterson, Sumner Amos Peterson, Le Roy Sweet, Norman C. Schreiter and Miss Carolyn H. Smith.

The baccalaureate sermon was delivered by President Northrup at the University Armory on Sunday. The class play occurred on Saturday, and afternoon and evening performances were given at the Metropolitan Theatre. Monday was devoted to class day exercises on the campus and to an excursion to historic Minnehaha Falls. Tuesday was devoted to class reunions and the senior promenade. Wednesday was Alumni Day. The general alumni picnic was an innovation. Lunch was served at 12 o'clock, and a general good time was had until 3, when the alumni meeting was called. In the evening the annual banquet of the Alumni Association was given at the West Hotel.

All of the graduates who desired positions are already placed. A few will take a summer's vacation.

Charles J. Lynn.

Eli Lilly & Co. announce the promotion of Charles J. Lynn, present manager of the New York office, to manager of the sales division of the business. He will assume his new duties with headquarters at Indianapolis, July 1.

Mr. Lynn, whose portrait is shown herewith, was born in 1874 and received his education in the Indianapolis public schools. His first experience in drug lines was obtained in the wholesale house of the Daniel Stewart Company, of Indianapolis, which he entered when about 16 years of age. His first experience selling drugs was with Lord Owen & Co., of Chicago, whom he represented in Colorado and Utah.

In 1895 Mr. Lynn engaged with Eli Lilly & Co. as a salesman, and in this work his results were such that when they started their New York branch in 1902 he was placed in charge. His success in the management of the Eastern business has in turn brought him promotion to the head of the sales division of the company.

Obituary.

JOSEPH LEEMING.

Joseph Leeming, for many years secretary of the Proprietary Association of America, died at his late home in Summit, N. J., on June 21, at the age of thirty-seven. Less than two years ago Mr. Leeming, who had previously enjoyed excellent health, became afflicted with tuberculosis of the larynx and moved at once with his family to Colorado Springs, where he seemed to steadily improve to such an extent that his physician sanctioned his returning home this spring. Consequently he brought his family East early in May and took up his residence in Summit, N. J. The disease took a sudden turn for the worse a week ago and he failed rapidly until the end.

Mr. Leeming was born in Montreal in 1869 and came with his father to New York when a boy. At the age of fourteen he entered the drug business in the service of the old firm of Lazell, Marsh & Gardner, and three years later entered the employ of his father, who did business as an importer of drug specialties under the firm name of Thomas Leeming & Co. When twenty-one years old he was admitted to partnership. Mr. Leeming and his brother Thomas, on the death of their father, succeeded to the business of Thomas Leeming & Co., who had been for many years agents for Nestlé's Food in this country. In 1900, when Henri Nestlé, of Vevey, Switzerland, the maker of Nestlé's Food, decided to establish a branch house in the United States, Mr. Leeming and his brother Thomas were made managers of the American branch.

The intelligence of his death will be received with sincere sorrow by the large number of manufacturers of proprietary medicines to whom he was personally known through his long term of service as secretary of the Proprietary Association of America, an office to which he was elected in 1891 at the early age of twenty-two, and which he filled most acceptably for more than twelve years, when he was compelled to resign on account of his failing health. The relations of Mr. Leeming to the association were such that upon his retirement the officers and members of the Executive Committee presented him with a handsome silver loving cup as a token of their esteem and friendship and in appreciation of his faithful and efficient services as secretary. Mr. Leeming was for a time treasurer of the Association of American Advertisers and was a member of the Canadian Proprietary Association, as well as of the American organization. He was also a member of the Sphinx, the Salmagundi, the Nassau Country, the Montauk and the Hardware clubs.

Mr. Leeming was a gentleman of charming presence, an artist of no mean ability, having painted several pictures which attracted considerable attention in art circles, and an ardent sportsman, having many trophies of his hunting trips in New Brunswick and the Eastern Provinces.

RALPH BRANDRETH.

Gen. Ralph Brandreth, vice-president and general manager of the Allcock Manufacturing Company, died on June 12 at his home in Bellport, L. I., after an illness of several weeks. He was forty-six years old and was born in Ossining, N. Y. He was prominent in the public affairs of that place and always took an active interest in Democratic politics. He was commissioned a brigadier-general on the staff of David B. when the latter was Governor of the State. Gen. Brandreth was a member of the Proprietary Association and a vestryman in Trinity parish.

DIED.

BRANDRETH.—In Bellport, L. I., N. Y., on Tuesday, June 12, Gen. Ralph Brandreth, aged forty-six years.

COLLIER.—In Salisbury, Md., on Wednesday, June 13, Dr. Levin D. Collier, aged seventy-six years.

EMMERT.—In Beloit, Kan., on Saturday, June 9, Martin Emmert, aged seventy years.

LEEMING.—In Summit, N. J., on Thusday, June 21, Joseph Leeming, aged thirty-seven years.

SCHWEITZER.—In Cambridge Springs, Pa., on Friday, June 8, Henry B. Schweitzer, aged forty-seven years.

VARDEMAN.—In Sparta, Ga., on Wednesday, June 6, Dr. Albert G. Vardeman, aged twenty-seven years.

WEISHENKER.—In Baltimore, Md., on Sunday, June 3, Dr. Abraham Weishenker, aged twenty-three years.

Georgia Pharmaceutical Association.

Atlanta, June 8.—The annual meeting of the Georgia Pharmaceutical Association, held during the week ended May 26, was characterized by a degree of harmony and attention to business that was unusual. The association agreed to appropriate a sum of money to be placed to the credit of the Atlanta local association to aid in defraying the expenses of entertainment of the delegates to the National Association of Retail Druggists, which meets here in October. The only discordant note in the whole proceedings was heard in the election for the nomination of members to serve on the Board of Pharmacy. A successor to Dr. George F. Payne, who retires this year, is to be appointed, and among the list of names from which the Governor of the State was to select an appointee was that of Amos W. Braselton. The nomination was declared illegal by President Morris on the ground that the nominee had not been licensed three years, as required by law. Mr. Braselton accordingly withdrew his name, but not until after some heated words had been passed. The following five members were then elected: T. F. Burbank, Cedartown; M. H. Taylor, Macon; M. D. Hodges, Marietta; W. S. Elkins, Jr., Atlanta, and C. T. King, Macon.

The election of officers for the ensuing year resulted as follows: President, W. B. Freeman, Atlanta; first vice-president, J. B. Persse, Savannah; second vice-president, L. S. Brigham, Columbus; third vice-president, M. D. Hodges, Marietta; secretary, Max Morris, Macon. There was no election for treasurer, the term of J. T. Shuptrine not having expired.

The Kansas Association.

The Kansas Pharmaceutical Association, in session at Emporia during the last week in May, elected the following officers: President, M. W. Friedenburg, Winfield; vice-president, A. R. Holzchurer, Junction City; second vice-president, W. R. Irwin, Emporia; secretary, A. E. Topping, Overbrook; assistant secretary, Matt Weightman, Topeka; treasurer, W. H. Hemion, Wichita; librarian, L. E. Sayre, Lawrence; Executive Committee, Louis Loeb, Junction City; E. C. Fritche, Leavenworth; Harry Higginson, Wichita; Harry W. Taylor, Kansas City, Kan.; Ed B. Mallott, Abilene.

Kansas City, Kan., was selected as the place for the convention next year.

Greater New York News.

M. Sieger, of the Amsterdam Quinine Factory, was a visitor to the local drug trade recently.

The American Druggists' Syndicate has leased the five story building at No. 67 Murray street, this city, and will occupy the entire building as soon as alterations are completed.

Fred J. Stock, well known in pharmaceutical circles, has purchased the drug store formerly owned by H. B. Smith at 937 Third avenue.

Dr. William Muir, of Brooklyn, will spend the summer abroad. He has made arrangements to sail on July 7 for Glascow, Scotland, the land of his birth, and expects to visit London and Paris, and possibly, Berlin. He will be accompanied by his daughter and his sister-in-law, Mrs. Whitten.

Romaine Pierson, Western manager of the AMERICAN DRUGGIST, sailed last Saturday for Liverpool on the Cunard steamship *Campania* for a stay of several weeks' duration in Europe. Among other places, Mr. Pierson will visit London, Dublin, Paris, Berlin and Munich.

H. Dubois, of the Roessler & Hasslachler Chemical Company, sailed for Europe recently on a business and pleasure trip combined. He expects to return the latter part of August.

J. H. Z. Stallman, vice-president of the Stallman-Fulton Company, and who has charge of the company's London office, has been calling on friends in the New York market. During his stay in this country J. H. Stallman, president of the company, is looking after the firm's European business.

On July 1, Charles S. Erb will move from his present location at Amsterdam avenue and Sixty-fifth street to a new store at 108 Amsterdam avenue, between Sixty-fourth and Sixty-fifth streets. The building now occupied by Mr. Erb is to be torn down to make room for a public school.

Among the recent visitors to the New York drug market were Adolph Lange, Jr., of Leavenworth, Kan.; W. F. Peterson, of Minneapolis; Mr. Thurston, of Smither & Thurston, Buffalo; A. N. Doerschut, of St. Louis; W. E. Jenkins, of Baltimore, Southern representative of Schieffelin & Co., and T. Benjamin, of M. F. Benjamin's Sons, of Riverhead, N. Y.

F. A. Moore, vice-president of the R. Hillier's Son Company, has retired from active business after some 40 years' service. V. S. Hillier succeeds Mr. Moore as vice-president in addition to his duties as treasurer. George R. Hillier is still the president of the company. Wm. C. Moore has been promoted to the position of secretary.

The Drug Club Golf Association, which is composed of members of the Drug and Chemical Club, this city, has resumed its series of semi-monthly tournaments, the first tournament being held the early part of this month, and the second on Wednesday of last week, at the Garden City links. At the opening series, the trophy—a cup in the form of a barrel, with a suitable crest—was won by E. D. Congdon.

Two more stores are to be added to the chain of pharmacies in this city controlled by the Caswell-Massey Company, if present plans are carried out, which seems likely. Negotiations, it is understood, are practically completed for the purchase of the Daggett & Ramsdell pharmacy on West Thirty-fourth street, near Fifth avenue. The deal, it is said, will also include the branch store in the Waldorf-Astoria.

Fred Idler, who made many friends among the wholesale manufacturing trade during his connection with the Drug and Chemical Club of New York as steward a few years ago, is now the proprietor of a successful café and restaurant at Coney Island, his place being one door west of Luna Park. Those who know Mr. Idler need not be told that his menu and service are both excellent, and if the visitor is a drug man he is assured of a hearty welcome and the best attention of the proprietor.

The German Apothecaries' Society held a very successful outing at Morningside Park, Jamaica, L. I., on Thursday, June 14, about 300 persons being present. The afternoon was pleasantly spent in games for the ladies and children, and prize bowling contests for both sexes. Dinner was served at 7 p.m. President Hirseman welcomed the guests in a few remarks that were roundly applauded. About 9 p.m. dancing began and continued until time for the last trolley car homeward bound. The Entertainment Committee, which performed its duties "to the queen's taste," consisted of S. V. B. Swann, Paul Arndt, H. F. Albert, George Lienecker and Hugo Kantrowitz.

P. E. Anderson, of the drug importing firm of P. E. Anderson & Co., 7 Gold street, New York, sailed for the United States from Hamburg on the *Amerika* on June 21 after a two months' visit to the principal European drug markets. While Mr. Anderson's connections have been established for years, he makes frequent visits to the principal drug markets of the world so as to keep in close personal touch with the original sources of the crude drugs which he imports in such large quantities.

Charles M. Brooke, a well-known retail pharmacist of Christchurch, New Zealand, has been visiting in the States for business purposes. Mr. Brooke conducts a cordial factory in Melbourne and has been gathering ideas for the improvement of his plant, at the same time making connections for the sale of some of his products in the United States. Like many other visiting foreigners, Mr. Brooke made his headquarters at the office of the AMERICAN DRUGGIST, the foreign department of which was glad to be in a position to bring him in touch with leading firms with whom he placed contracts for bottles, labels, cartons, etc. Mr. Brooke sailed for London last Tuesday on *S. S. Kaiser Wilhelm II.*

Frank A. Bean is to take the road for the Manhattan Drug Company, of New York, early in July and will cover an extensive territory, comprising Ohio, Indiana and Michigan, with side trips into Massachusetts, Rhode Island and Connecticut. Mr. Bean was formerly in the retail drug business at South Framingham, Mass., and is a graduate of the Massachusetts College of Pharmacy, class of '90. For the last two years he has represented the Beach & Clarridge Company, of Boston. The Manhattan Drug Company evidently believe with Cæsar in having men of goodly proportions around them, for Mr. Bean, like his friend, Mr. Stahl, looks like a man who slept well o' nights and more need not be said.

KINGS COUNTY MEETING.

Routine Business Transacted—Dr. Muir Sails for Scotland July 7—Presented with a Remembrance from the Society.

The June meeting of the Kings County Pharmaceutical Society, held at the Brooklyn College of Pharmacy on the 12th inst., was largely routine in character. President Adrian Paradis was absent, and his place was taken by Vice-President J. H. Rehfuss. The usual reports of officers were received, after which Charles E. Brennan, of 562½ Fifth avenue, Brooklyn, was elected to membership. Treasurer Ray reported a balance of $451.42 in the treasury of the society and $1,910.28 to the credit of the college.

In the report of the Committee on Legislation, presented by Dr. Wm. Muir, considerable attention was paid to the efforts made to pass the Stevens-Wainwright bill, and the necessity of the pharmacists of the State taking action to secure the passage of some measure agreeable to them was emphasized. On motion, it was resolved to instruct the delegates from the society to the State meeting to favor the introduction of the Chicago Conference bill, which was the measure introduced by Senator Hill this year and which failed of passage.

The announcement of the willingness of the New York Telephone Company to install slot telephones in Manhattan drug stores was made by Professor Anderson, who stated at the same time that for Brooklyn a two-coin machine would be preferable, since a good many of Brooklyn messages are sent to Manhattan.

The following committees were named:

Legislative—William Muir, Thos. J. France, O. C. Kleine, W. H. Bussenschutt, A. E. Hegeman. Pharmacy—A. P. Lohness, W. F. Morgan, Charles Heimerzheim. Trade Matters—J. G. Wischerth, F. E. Kalkbrenner, Charles Heimerzheim. Revision of the Pharmacopœia—Wm. C. Anderson, D. C. Mangan, H. W. Schimpf, F. P. Tuthill, J. H. Droge. Library—Wm. C. Anderson, W. J. Hackett, C. A. Kunkel, C. L. Gesell, J. L. Mayer.

Doctor Muir, who reported for the Committee on Legislation, was lured out of the room on some pretext or other at this point, and Professor Anderson announced that the doctor intended to sail for his old home in Scotland July 7, and moved that the society appropriate the sum of $10 for the purchase of a basket of fruit. Professor Anderson later presented Doctor Muir with a small American flag of silk and a copy of the new prospectus of the college bearing the autographs of all present.

The Hudson River Association to Stop Sampling Physicians for the Summer.

At the June meeting of the Hudson River branch of the M. A. R. D., held recently, Peter Diamond, one of the guests, informed the members that the fight for slot telephones in drug stores in this city had been won, the demands having been acceded to by the telephone company. This proved very welcome news to the members present, who have had the same objectionable features of the old system to complain about as their fellow druggists in other sections of the city. At this meeting several gross lots of goods were distributed. The branch has a plan for co-operative buying from the wholesalers which, so far, has worked very satisfactorily. Those who participate pool their orders, thus entailing only one delivery on the part of the jobber and securing the extra discount allowed for the larger quantity.

As many physicians are out of town this month the Committee on Standard Preparations reported that the work of sending samples to physicians had been temporarily suspended. Attention was called to the plan for a special boat to convey druggists from this section to the N. A. R. D. convention in Atlanta next fall. The plan was well received.

The New York Retail Druggists' Association.

An unusually enthusiastic meeting of the N. Y. R. D. A. was held on Friday night, June 15, at Westminster Hall, No. 72 Lenox avenue. It was designed largely to commemorate the re-election of Joseph Weinstein to the Board of Pharmacy. Much gratification was expressed on every side over the successful campaign conducted by the association. Music, dancing and an elaborate collation were features of the evening's entertainment. At the business meeting nine new members were elected, and all the committees were thanked for their efficient work during the year. A proposal was made to amend the by-laws so as to provide for annual instead of semi-annual election of officers, and the proposition will be acted on at the next meeting. The following officers were elected:

President, W. Marmor; first vice-president, Aaron Segall; second vice-president, S. B. Epstein; treasurer Joseph Weinstein; recording secretary, Wm. J. Larkin; financial secretary, J. K. Bernhard.

SLOT TELEPHONES FOR NEW YORK.

A Victory for the Drug Trade—Twenty Per Cent. Profit for the Druggist—Auxiliary Instruments for Out of Town Calls.

The druggists of New York City have won a notable victory in their fight for slot telephones in their stores—a victory that means for them a much more satisfactory and sensible arrangement with the telephone company, increased and assured revenue from this feature of their business, and the elimination of all the trouble and annoyance they were subjected to under the old system. The New York Telephone Company, through General Manager H. F. Thurber, has informed Albert Baltzly, chairman of the joint delegation that waited on the company and presented the druggists' case, that the company will install slot machines in drug stores and allow a commission of 20 per cent. The druggists had asked for 25 per cent., but the company compromised on 20.

The announcement created no little favorable comment in the trade, and while it will require some time to put the new order into general operation, the work will be expedited as rapidly as possible. It is estimated that the change will entail an outlay of about $100,000 to the telephone company.

The new arrangement provides for a uniform pay station commission of 20 per cent. on calls used over the regular auxiliary 'phone, as well as over the slot 'phone. The latter will be of the one-coin style, and will be used only for borough calls, which cost 5 cents. For other calls the auxiliary instrument will be used. Druggists still have the option of having a slot 'phone or of taking out a contract for the message system. The commissions under the latter are higher than 20 per cent., but such contracts are usually for a larger number of messages than the average druggist can afford. It is, therefore, more than likely that the great majority of the trade will install the slot 'phone, which has the distinct advantage of giving the druggist no trouble or annoyance, besides assuring him of no discrepancies or shortages in the matter of collections.

Peter W. Ray, Ph.G., M.D.

In his eighty-first year, Dr. Peter W. Ray, the treasurer of the Kings County Pharmaceutical Society and of the Brooklyn

DR. PETER W. RAY.
Treasurer of the Kings County Pharmaceutical Society.

College of Pharmacy, is as upright and sturdy looking as a well preserved man in the early forties. Dr. Ray, who was elected treasurer of the Kings County Pharmaceutical Society for the fifteenth time at the recent annual meeting, has conducted a pharmacy at the northeast corner of Second and Hooper streets, Brooklyn, for fifty-six years, or, to be exact, from August 4, 1850; and his managing clerk, P. R. Morse, has been in Dr. Ray's service continuously for thirty-five years—surely a record that is creditable alike to employer and employee. The portrait of Dr. Ray, which is shown herewith, was taken during the administration of Mayor Strong, when the doctor was appointed a member of the city committee for the collection of funds to raise a monument to General Grant. He has not changed much since then, and the picture is still a striking likeness. Dr. Ray served his apprenticeship in medicine and pharmacy with the late Dr. James McCune Smith, a graduate of Edinburgh University, and one of the foremost practitioners of his time. After six years' service with Dr. Smith, attending lectures at the New York College of Pharmacy meanwhile, Dr. Ray attended a course of lectures at Bowdoin College, Brunswick, Me., and in 1849 took his degree in medicine at Castleton College, Vermont. In commemoration of his fifty years' connection with pharmacy the members of the Kings County Pharmaceutical Society six years ago presented him with a gold medal suitably engraved. Another medal which he cherishes was the gift of President Grover Cleveland on the occasion of the Ninth International Medical Congress held at Washington in 1887. Dr. Ray was a delegate to the congress from the County Medical Society.

The existence of "The Ray Medical Society" may not be generally known. This is a society of medical men who bear the name of Ray, and Dr. P. W. Ray, the subject of this sketch, is one of its honored vice-presidents, and he happens to be the only colored man in the organization, though he possesses the consanguinity requirement for membership. The society was organized at the World's Fair in St. Louis, on September 20, 1904, and numbers 145 members. Meetings are held annually, usually in connection with the meeting of the American Medical Association. The objects of the society are concerned mostly with the development of sociability and for the reunion of members of the Ray family.

WESTERN NEW YORK.

Buffalonians Preparing for the Visiting Druggists—Plans for Entertainment—Athletics Taken Up by the Drug Trade The Gregory Store Reopened.

(*From our Regular Correspondent.*)

Buffalo, June 20.—Some big soda water days in June have put the Buffalo retail druggists in a decidedly better humor than they have confessed to in quite a long while, for the winter and early spring were not periods of big trade. There are no complaints of prices. They are low, but they are much higher than they were, and the price cutter is now content with pretending to undersell his competitors, just as the department store pretends to do in the big advertisements it sends out.

TO WELCOME STATE DRUGGISTS.

Buffalo will do everything possible to make the visiting druggists comfortable when they come up from the Falls for Buffalo Day, June 28, during the meeting of the State Association. It is arranged to run a special train from Niagara Falls, starting after noon. For the ladies there will be a trip about the city, and for the more athletic division of the party there will be a very solid baseball game at Olympic Park, the meeting place of the professional nines. The plan is to pit all Buffalo against a nine of all-State players, and it looks as if the game would be a sharp one. The Buffalo nine has been picked by J. A. Lockie, and Alderman Stine, of Niagara Falls, will pick the opposition team. Each side is constantly hearing that the other has found a lot of professionals who are regular druggists, and at once there is a rush for better men to meet them. The evening will be devoted to a dinner at the Ellicott Club.

BUFFALO FANS HAVE NEW FIELD.

The Buffalo druggists are now playing ball every Tuesday and Friday, and they are just now rejoicing in a new diamond out near the new drug store of R. K. Smither, on upper Main street. The park meadow had its drawbacks, one of them being that a permit had to be taken out for every game, and besides there is no car line running near the spot. The idea of regular exercise of some sort is now well fixed in the convictions of the druggists as a thing that is much needed. One of the players said lately that he was no wtaking from 1 to 5 p.m. off every day in the week for athletic exercise. If he were to stay in the store all day he would get so peevish he would ruin his trade in a short time.

DRUGGIST SHRINERS.

The gathering of Shriners at Jamestown, N. Y., on June 15, made a good showing for the druggist as a member of the Order of Masons. Among the druggists in the list were H. A. Sloan, Dr. A. I. Drake, George Reimann, Walter Nichols and H. C. Deuel, of Buffalo; W. H. Parsons, of Forestville; N. B. Allen, of Gowanda; W. H. Thayer, of Sherman, and G. W. Ross, of Olean. Tending drug store next day was a standoff between going to sleep and waking up.

THE POST OFFICE ADDRESS OF THE BOARD.

There is complaint from the Western Branch of the State Board of Pharmacy that between the faulty addressing of letters intended for that body and the stupidity of the Buffalo post office distributers there is much delay in a great part of its mail. Letters that come addressed to the "State Board of Pharmacy" and ought to be delivered to Secretary Reimann, who is well known in Buffalo, are sent to the dead letter office. As there are about 1,500 letters in that mail every year the loss and inconvenience are no small matter.

The new store of the Cahoon-Lyon Drug Company in Buffalo, so long known as Gregory's Genesee Pharmacy, was formally opened June 16, with gay decorations, an orchestra and all the accessories that usually attend such affairs. The store has been closed since the end of May and is now enlarged and much improved, with a new soda fountain and other attractions.

DR. GREGORY ADDRESSES THE RHODE ISLAND COLLEGE.

Dr. W. G. Gregory, of Buffalo, lately made a tour of the New England States in connection with the delivery of an address before the graduating class of the Rhode Island College of Pharmacy at Providence. He took as his subject "Pay Your Debts," which is a short way of saying that the educated man or woman owes something to society that other people do not, or, as the Frenchman would say, "Noblesse Oblige."

WHO WILL SUCCEED MR. LOCKIE?

President J. A. Lockie, of Buffalo, announces that he is not a candidate for re-election to the position he has held during the past year in the State Pharmaceutical Association. It has been the rule, especially with Buffalo druggists who have held that office, and they have been quite numerous—R. K. Smither, W. G. Gregory, C. O. Rano, Thomas Stoddart—to accept a second election, but President Lockie, having been elected to the State Board of Pharmacy, thinks it would be poor taste to remain at the head of the State Association another year. So who takes it?

Among the recent visitors to Buffalo in the interest of the drug trade was E. O. Norte, who is well known as the regular representative of Eli Lilley & Co., pharmaceutical manufacturers.

G. M. Jost, who has been selling the specialties of Bruen, Ritchey & Co. in the Buffalo drug trade, was with us about the middle of June, paying his visits to the retailers as well as the wholesalers.

The popular New York house of John M. Maris & Co. again sends to this market their trusty salesman, H. J. Baringer, who is as able as usual to dispose of large amounts of druggists' sundries and glassware.

J. S. Marvin we often have with us as a salesman and always as a resident, so he is able to make a special drive at the Buffalo perfumery trade in the interest of Lundborg.

Registered in Nebraska.

At an adjourned meeting held at Hastings, June 5, the Board of Examiners to the Nebraska Board of Pharmacy held an examination for the benefit of those applicants who wished to attend the State Association, it being in session at the same time. A class of 35 presented themselves, of which the following 26 passed:

Mark L. Atchison, Omaha; Bernice W. Barnes, Nelson; Chas. A. Brown, Omaha; Myra Cock, Red Cloud; Richard J. Drewelow, Stanton; Clarence E. Jaques, Omaha; Lewis Walter, Omaha; Clyde W. Martin, Omaha; Clarence P. Moores, Ansley; Fred. C. O'Donnell, Kearney; J. Earle Russell, Lincoln; Jas. B. Summers, Macon; W. B. Walter, Beatrice; J. S. Baird, Omaha; Benj. W. Barth, Lincoln; H. E. Callahan, Omaha; W. A. DeMay, Danbury; Albert Fricke, Omaha; J. B. Klotz, Exeter; Lee B. Liliodol, Waco; Edna L. Melvin, Lincoln; Tom E. O'Conner, Allen; Chas. M. Redman, Kenesaw; W. Earl Shields, Hildreth; A. L. Wagoner, Wood River, and F. H. Ware, Norfolk.

This class was above the average, a larger percentage passing than usual. The next examination will be held in Omaha, August 8, commencing at 8 a.m. sharp. D. J. Fink, Holdrege, secretary of the board, will furnish application blanks.

NEW ENGLAND.

New Officers for the Massachusetts College—Severe Sentences for Transgressions of Liquor Tax Law—Women Elect Delegates to Atlanta.

(From our Regular Correspondent.)

Boston, June 20.—The annual meeting of the trustees of the Massachusetts College of Pharmacy was held at the college building, June 11. Officers were elected as follows: President, J. P. Gammon, Ph.G.; vice-president, Linville H. Smith, Ph.G., and William W. Bartlett, Ph.G.; secretary, George E. Coleman, Ph.G.; treasurer, John G. Godding, Ph.G., and auditor, Thomas B. Nichols. The teaching force remains the same as last year, excepting that R. A. Newton, Ph.G., is to be instructor in analytical and organic chemistry in place of Steadman G. Bixby, Ph.C. Mr. Bixby recently accepted a position with a firm of milk contractors in this city and is now engaged in the bacteriological examination of milk and milk products.

A HORSE IN A SHOW WINDOW.

At Wakefield recently, a horse wrecked the front of Ryder's drug store. The animal became frightened and ran, gaining such headway that he not only broke all of the glass, but bent some of the ironwork connected with the plate glass front. Proprietor Ryder also had a narrow escape. He was standing near the plate glass window talking to an acquaintance when he fortunately saw the horse plunging down the street and ran to the rear of the store. Although 30 feet away when the crash came he was showered with broken glass.

SENT TO JAIL FOR THE SALE OF LIQUOR.

Alexander Fox, a druggist of Nonantum, was sentenced on June 15, in the Superior Court at Cambridge, to three months in jail, and fined $100. Fox was charged with selling liquor to an intoxicated person. This was after a jury trial, at which evidence had been introduced by the defence to prove that the sale was made by Fox's sister during his absence. When Miss Fox heard the sentence pronounced, she shrieked and rushed toward the dock where Fox was sitting. She was stopped by a court officer and then ran screaming from the room; in the hallway she almost collapsed. After she became calm, Fox's attorney asked the judge to hear the girl's story. This request was granted and the girl made an earnest plea that sentence be rescinded. This the court declined to do, whereupon the girl had another attack of hysteria and had to be led from the room by a court officer. On the same day John A. Quigley and Joseph B. Kenigan of Malden were fined $100 for illegally selling liquor.

THE WOMEN'S AUXILIARY MEETS.

The last meeting of the W. O. B. A. R. D., until October, was recently held at the home of Mrs. E. H. La Pierre in Cambridge. This was a monetary occasion, the members being expected to bring at least $1 which they had personally earned. A part of the fun came during the "experience meeting," when the members related the schemes by which they acquired their contributions. This covered a wide range of devices, from pressing trousers to shampooing, manicuring and walking to save electric car fares. Delegates to the Atlanta convention were chosen as follows: Mrs. C. H. Davis and Mrs. E. H. La Pierre; alternates, Mrs. F. W. Archer and Mrs. C. A. Stover. The members were urged to attend the M. S. P. A. meeting at Magnolia.

POLITICAL STRAWS POINT TO MANY PHARMACISTS.

Thus early is the political pot boiling. Announcement has just been made in Salem that William H. Gove of that city will contest the senatorial seat from that district with present occupant. The caucuses are three months away, but a lively battle is anticipated. Mr. Gove is president of the Lydia E. Pinkham Medicine Company, although by profession he is a lawyer. He is a native of Maine, but came to Lynn in 1866 as a boy, and on graduation from the Lynn high school studied law and was admitted to the bar in 1872. He later entered Harvard and was graduated in 1876, second in his class. Later he took a degree from the Harvard law school. He served on the Lynn school committee, but, moving to Salem in 1881, entered Salem politics. In 1894 and 1895 he served in the Salem board of aldermen, and was one year president of the board. He represented the 17th district in the Legislature in 1904 and 1905. He has been secretary of the Republican city committee and is a member of the Salem Republican Club.

BOSTON NEWS ITEM.

Assignment has just been made for the benefit of creditors by the Frank I. Pierson Drug Company, Washington and Essex streets, to Charles F. Cutler and Joseph P. Manning.

BOSTON RETAILERS ELECT DELEGATES TO ATLANTA.

New Formula Bill Goes Into Effect September 1—A Summer Outing Planned.

(From our Regular Correspondent.)

Boston, June 13.—The monthly meeting of the B. A. R. D., Inc., was held this evening at the M. C. P. Building. The reports of the secretary and treasurer were read and accepted.

Henry Canning, for the legislative committee, stated that the new formula bill takes effect September 1 and that it applied to preparations made by druggists. He also said that the State Board of Health would notify the trade in relation to any proprietary articles of general sale which fail to conform to the law in amounts of alcohol and narcotics.

It was decided to hold the summer outing July 24, at which time the monthly meeting will occur. It was voted that the organization spend no money in connection with this picnic, for which tickets will shortly be on sale.

Delegates and alternates to the Atlanta convention of the N. A. R. D. were elected as follows: Delegates, F. F. Ernst, Henry Canning, Elie H. La Pierre, J. G. Godding, J. F. Finneran, C. H. Davis, J. A. Bean, W. D. Wheeler, S. V. Rintels; alternates, I. P. Gammon, Frank Tucker, A. H. Tripp, B. G. McCormick, Paul Klein, L. W. Griffin, D. L. Burroughs, J. W. Lowe, F. W. Archer, J. M. O'Brien, J. J. Naughton. J. F. Keiser, organizer for New England, will be one of the party.

Mr. Van Horn, of the Peruna Company, addressed the members and emphasized the faith of his concern in the contract plan.

Henry Canning, Paul C. Klein and Elie H. La Pierre were selected to present the greetings of the association to the Massachusetts State Pharmaceutical Association at the coming meeting at Magnolia.

Graduates from the Winona College.

The Winona College of Pharmacy held its second annual commencement exercises on the college grounds at Indianapolis, Ind., on June 8, the class being addressed by Hon. Frank A. Vanderlip, of New York City. Previous to the commencement exercises a banquet was held at the English Hotel, the guests of the class being Dr. S. C. Dickey, president of the institute, and Prof. W. C. Smith, general director. The school enrolled 98 students and graduated 43. The following is a list of the names of the graduates:

From Indianapolis.—H. W. S. Carter, W. S. Edwards, A. L. Turner, Gustav Hitzelberger, Harry Knannlein, Miss M. B. McCord, Lawrence I. Mills, Edward Arnold, Fred Binzer, Harry Neimeyer, C. S. Merrick, Howard McAllister, Royal L. W. McClain, Carl Vanzant, Louis Twente, Edward Wagener.

From Indiana outside of Indianapolis.—Louis Carnefix, Middletown; W. E. Durkes, Eden; W. S. Duesterburg, Vincennes; H. P. Rager, Silver Lake; Oscar Passmore, W. Newton; A. F. Miller, Vincennes; John W. Cade, Covington; Columbus Talbott, New Marion.

From Ohio.—H. M. Rathbun, Monroeville; J. E. Ogle, Woodsfield; W. G. Rathbun, Monroeville; E. W. Ohl, Pavonia; L. C. Rush, E. Germantown; J. V. Riesbeck, Woodsfield; W. W. Evans, Woodsfield; A. F. Haller, Taylorsville; P. H. Miller, Wash. Court House; L. M. Saladin, Lorraine.

From other States.—L. L. Alexander, Cottage Grove, Tenn.; R. T. Carnefix, Bedford City, Va.; Urie Howard, Cottage Grove, Tenn.; J. T. Moss, Mayfield, Ky.; Owen Rice, Rushville, Ill.; Shan S. Rose, Blu-field, Va.; John R. Ankron, Middleburn, W. Va.; B. V. Beck, Chicago; R. M. Eppstein, Slonin, Russia.

PENNSYLVANIA.

All Quiet Along the Delaware—Business Better in the Coal Regions—Plans for the State Meeting—The Associated Drug Companies Organizing.

(From our Regular Correspondent.)

Philadelphia, July 20.—There is a lull in the wholesale as well as the retail drug trade in this city at the present time. This was expected, as it is between seasons and the druggists are now able to take a breathing spell. There is very little complaint heard from the retail druggists over the business done so far this year. It has been in almost every case ahead of what it was in 1905, and it looks as if it will be a record breaking year. For the next two months there will be many improvements made to the different drug stores in this city. However, the changes will be mostly in the shape of additions. With the beginning of fall there will be several retail drug stores opened up in various sections of the city. In the western and northwestern part, as well as in the southern, many hundred new dwellings have been erected, and in some cases the builders have made special offers to retail druggists to open stores in the vicinity. During the early months of the year the wholesale druggists here did little business with the druggists of the anthracite coal region. Now that the miners have gone back to work the business has greatly improved, and it is believed that this month there will be more business done in the anthracite towns than ever before; the miners have received their first pay since April and they will be anxious to lay in a stock of medicines and sundries.

SUMMER PLANS OF THE P. A. R. D.

There will be no steamboat ride for the members of the Philadelphia Association of Retail Druggists as a body next month. At the last meeting in June a committee was appointed to sound the members about holding the next meeting, which will take place on July 6. Now that the Philadelphia College of Pharmacy is closed for the summer, the meetings of this association are held in the Odd Fellows' Temple. The last meeting was a record breaking one, and it was thought by some that if a steamboat could be chartered it would afford the members, as well as their families, a day's outing. The plan was considered a good one, and the committee started in to work it up. But there were too many obstacles in the way. The first was the annual meeting of the Pennsylvania State Pharmaceutical Association, which is held the latter part of this month, then the Fourth of July, and lastly that many of the drug clerks were away on their vacations and the employers could not find the time to get away. There were other objections. Some members were preparing papers to be read at the annual convention of the State Association, while others were endeavoring to get the doctors in line so that they will adhere more strictly to the U. S. P. in writing their prescriptions. One of the secretaries of the local retail association said that he had this work well under way, and to stop it now would mean that he would have to begin all over again. This he declined to do, and after a few more members had been seen the committee decided to give up the idea of holding the next meeting on the Delaware River. The meeting is likely to be a slim one, as many of the members will have just returned from the annual meeting of the State Association.

THE ANNUAL MEETING OF THE PENNSYLVANIA STATE PHARMACEUTICAL ASSOCIATION,

which begins at Glen Summit on June 26, is likely to prove one of the most interesting meetings that this association has ever held. All the plans for a gala time have been prepared, the regular fun makers have been hard at work, and it is reported that they have prepared a programme that far exceeds anything of the like that has ever been gotten up by the Entertainment Committee of the association. Glen Summit is a beautiful spot. It is situated on the line of the Lehigh Valley Railroad Company and is on the top of one of the ranges of the Blue Mountains. The Glen Summit House is one of the best summer hotels in Pennsylvania. There are lovely drives, besides giving to the visitors a magnificent view of the country. A few miles up the line can be seen the beautiful Wyoming Valley. It is only a short distance from Wilkes-Barre and Scranton. A large delegation will leave from this city.

THE ASSOCIATED DRUG COMPANIES OF AMERICA

is now in course of incorporation. This association, as exclusively told by the AMERICAN DRUGGIST several months ago, is composed of the wholesale drug companies of the United States. All the leading buying associations of retail druggists are members of the new association. Philadelphia, Brooklyn and New York have taken a prominent hand in the formation of the company. It is understood that about fifteen cities are represented, and that as soon as all the by-laws are prepared a movement will be made to establish a central buying agency. This is really what the Associated Drug Companies of America is for. During the recent year there has been considerable trouble between these retail buying companies and the members of the National Wholesale Druggists' Association. So great has been the breach between these two bodies that the retail associations were compelled to look out for themselves. It is proposed to have the buying done by one company, and it is believed that by buying in such large quantities a considerable saving can be made to the retail druggists who are members of the associations.

PHILADELPHIA NEWS NOTES.

L. J. Ringer, who was recently married and started on his wedding trip, getting as far as Montreal, was called home on account of the death of his father-in-law.

A. S. Hollopeter has accepted a position with J. F. Ely at Ninth and Filbert streets as night clerk. Mr. Ely has decided to keep his store open all night.

C. H. Bauman, of Glauzler & Co., druggists' sundries, of New York, was in this city last week visiting his many customers.

A. P. Conger, the representative of the Celluloid Company, of New York, is going around among the trade. He reports business good.

E. Fuller, of Ed Pinaud, of New York, is here again. Mr. Fuller has no trouble in getting orders for his house. Every drug store keeps some of their goods on hand.

John B. Reynolds, who conducts the drug store at Front and Norris streets, had a small fire recently. The prompt arrival of the Fire Department soon put out the blaze. The damage was trifling.

President Rohrman, of the Philadelphia Wholesale Drug Company, Limited, has gone to St. Louis on business for the house of which he is the head. Since he became the manager of this company it has made rapid strides.

The Walter F. Ware Company, since its formation a few years ago, has made rapid advances in the manufacture of elastic hosiery, abdominal supporters, etc. Twice the establishment has been enlarged, and this year he was compelled to send to England for more machinery. This machinery has arrived and is now being put together.

Now that the overworked society people are going away for the summer there is naturally a good demand for playing cards. So as to have all the dealers keep their stock up and be able to supply the demand, R. Neibeck, representing the United States Playing Card Company, is here looking after the interests of his house.

The Druggists' Co-operative Fire Insurance Company.

In view of the recent advance in fire insurance rates in this city druggists are manifesting an increased interest in the new American Druggists' Fire Insurance Company, and there is every indication that the new enterprise will receive substantial support from pharmacists in this section. Dr. William C. Anderson, of Brooklyn, has taken charge of the stock subscription books for New York City and State. Of the stock allotted for this State there are less than 1,000 shares unsubscribed for, which shows the advisability of an early application by those who wish to participate in the enterprise.

MARYLAND.

Twenty-Three New Druggists Get Degrees—Alumni Officers for Maryland—A Day's Soda Sales for Charity—A Baltimore Local Branch Organized by N. A. R. D.

(*From our Regular Correspondent.*)

Baltimore, June 19.—Twenty-three young druggists, among them two women, received diplomas and honors at the commencement of the Department of Pharmacy, Maryland University, which was held jointly with that of the Medical and Law schools on the 4th inst. at the Academy of Music. Francis K. Carey, a Baltimore attorney, delivered the address to the graduates, and Prof. Charles Caspari, jr., conferred the degrees, while Bernard Carter, provost of the university, awarded the prizes, the recipients of the latter being as follows:

First general prize, Miss E. Grace Lotz, of Maryland; second general prize, E. Reynolds Thorne, of Pennsylvania; prize for best averages, Frank G. Balment, Ohio; prize for best practical pharmacy manipulations, Alfred S. Williams, of Maryland; William Simon prize for practical chemistry, William V. Parranmore, Georgia; Pharmacy Alumni Association prize for work in histology, William G. Harper, South Carolina; honorable mention, William V. Parranmore, Alfred S. Williams, Benjamin D. Benfer, S. Bradford Downes and W. Trueheart Bodiford.

The graduates, in addition to those mentioned, were: Maryland, M. N. Buppert, William Devan, G. P. Hetz, S. A. Pentz, Charles Rosenberg, T. F. A. Stevens, William Stichel; Pennsylvania, Anna F. Clancy and E. R. Thome; Florida, W. T. Bodiford; South Carolina, W. G. Harper, Malcolm Gondelock and L. N. Patrick; North Carolina, M. S. Morrison and H. A. Shepherd; Tennessee, J. J. Peeler; West Virginia, Dabney C. Pharr.

THE ALUMNI ASSOCIATION

held a business meeting and banquet at the Stafford Hotel on Friday evening before the commencement and elected these officers: Franz Naylor, president; Ephraim Bacon, first vice-president; C. M. Hornbrook, second vice-president; H. L. Troxel, secretary; J. W. Westcott, treasurer; W. J. Lowry, jr., J. J. Barnett, F. L. McCartney and J. C. Wolf, Executive Committee. Addresses were made by President Naylor, Dr. Gorsuch, Dr. D. M. R. Culbreth, William C. Smith, Prof. H. P. Hynson, B. D. Benfer and E. F. Kelly. J. Emery Bond acted as toastmaster.

EMERSON DRUG COMPANY INCREASES STOCK.

A certificate of the increase of the capital stock of the Emerson Drug Company, manufacturers of bromo-seltzer and other compounds, from $250,000 to $500,000 was filed for record in the court last Tuesday. The increase is to consist of 10,000 shares of the par value of $25 each, and is to be entitled to a guaranteed dividend of 8 per cent. a year. The decision to make the increase was reached some time ago and ratified by the stockholders. Isaac E. Emerson is president of the company.

SODA WATER FOR CHARITY.

George A. Bunting, a retail druggist at 6 West North avenue, recently decided to devote one day's receipts at his soda water fountain to the Fresh Air Fund, which organization provides outings down the bay for poor people. The occasion was the first anniversary of the installation of the new fountain. The store was handsomely adorned with flowers and an orchestra discoursed music. Crowds of people, many of them from a distance, visited the pharmacy, and by purchasing soda water contributed to the fund.

ORGANIZING THE RETAILERS.

The retail druggists need to be stirred up every now and then, and in furtherance of this purpose several organizers of the N. A. R. D. have been at work in Baltimore for some weeks with a view to getting all the pharmacists in line for maintenance of prices and other efforts designed to improve the condition of the trade. On Thursday of last week an association was formed with these officers: Samuel Nattans, president; George A. Bunting, vice-president; R. E. Lee Williamson, secretary. About fifty druggists were present and much confidence in the effectiveness of the new body to attain the objects set forth was expressed. It is a noteworthy fact that while the cutters usually held aloof from previous movements, they now seem to be in line for averting demoralization.

Two calls for the meeting were sent out, one of them signed by Charles H. Ware, Hess Bros., Charles F. Freyer, Quandt Bros. and George A. Bunting, and the other by M. S. Kann, The Read Drug & Chemical Company, J. S. Hopkins, Thomas & Thompson and Williamson & Watts.

MARYLAND NEWS NOTES.

William C. Fields, a druggist of Pikesville, Baltimore County, died there recently, after an illness of about three weeks, in the thirty-fifth year of his age. He left a widow and two children. He had conducted a pharmacy at Pikesville for fourteen years.

Albert E. Thompson, of the widely known Baltimore drug firm of Thomas & Thompson, Light and Baltimore streets, has been very ill for some time past, and was taken to Atlantic City in the hope that the salt air would do him good.

Druggist E. C. Esslinger has installed a handsome onyx Italian marble and wood soda water fountain of the Puffer Constellation type in his pharmacy, Fulton and Woodbrook avenues. The improvement cost $2,400.

The drug store of the late Oscar E. Ross, Park avenue and McMechen street, was sold last week at public auction to John R. Riggs for $1,100. There was a mortgage on the property for $8,500.

A fire which broke out in the window of the drug store of Fred Ulman, Druid Hill avenue and Biddle street, last week, caused considerable excitement, but was put out before much damage had been done. The blaze was presumably caused by a defective electric wire.

Druggist William H. Stewart, North avenue and Payson street, has been sued for $5,000 damages by Miss Alice Killmond, who alleges that the druggist mixed up the labels on two bottles so that she used a preparation intended for internal use on her face and was permamently disfigured. This is contrary to the usual experience, when persons claim damages for injuries alleged to have resulted from taking inwardly a medicine intended for external use.

Trusted Employee of Lanman & Kemp Accused of Defalcation.

Raoul Auerbach, for more than 30 years a trusted employee of Lanman & Kemp, of this city, and its predecessor, is accused by the firm of having misappropriated a large amount of the company's funds. Auerbach was an invoice clerk, and his accounts were found to fall short in his custom house transactions. It is alleged that he drew on the firm's funds for consular fees on the making of invoices for exports far in excess of the actual figures in the receipts and pocketed the surplus.

The expert accountant questioned Auerbach and the next day the latter disappeared. An attachment for $29,615 was placed in the sheriff's hands, but detectives failed to find any trace of the missing invoice clerk. A deputy sheriff served the attachment on two savings banks and a trust company in which Auerbach is said to have funds.

Edward Kemp and George Massey, members of the firm, have sworn to an affidavit setting forth the allegations against Auerbach. The charges cover only the missing clerk's alleged peculations during the existence of the present firm, hence the amount in the attachment is $29,615, but it is said that the evidence given by the expert accountant reveals a much larger defalcation, extending over many years and under the management of the old firm.

THE WEST.

Chicago Doctors and Druggists Get Closer Together—Antinarcotic Legislation Discussed—Bodemann Criticises Physicians—The Board of Health to Let Up on Drug Trade.

(*From our Regular Correspondent.*)

Chicago, June 20.—Doctors and druggists, to the number of about 50, sat at meat together one evening last week and discussed matters of mutual interest. The dinner had been planned for a considerable time, and was significant in that it showed an increase of intimacy in the relations of prescribers and dispensers. The meeting took place at Vogelsang's. It was presided over by Dr. Bacon, who was ably seconded by Chas. Havery, president of the C. R. D. A. The chief topic of the evening's discussion was the new antinarcotic law, which was printed in the last issue of the AMERICAN DRUGGIST. All of the doctors present said they approved most emphatically of the resolution adopted by the State Medical Association, to the effect that all patent medicines containing habit producing drugs should bear a label announcing this fact. A number of druggists said they were of the same opinion. Mr. Bodemann took advantage of his opportunity to administer a good-natured "roast" to the doctors becase of their frequently manifested penchant for prescribing proprietaries, the formula of which they do not know. Mr. Bodemann expressed himself in the following manner: "You fellows want us to help you frame a law compelling makers of patent medicines containing narcotics to put on a suitable label, yet you often go it blindly yourselves. Your patients take it for granted that you know what you are giving them,, but, as a matter of fact, you don't know a thing about it when you prescribe this unknown dope. Is this because of ignorance or laziness? In either case, oh Father in heaven, forgive them, for they know not where they are at." Mr. Wooten then advised, in a conservative talk, that too radical action with regard to patents be avoided. Drs. Gilmore, Webster, Johnson and others spoke, and Druggists Chandler, Forsyth, Boehm and others were heard. Mr. Bodemann scored those who have been guilty of causing the Board of Health to prosecute druggists for alleged counter prescribing, and Dr. Webster promised, on behalf of the board, that the practice would be stopped. A number of other matters likely to cause friction between those present were also touched upon. A motion that a harmony conference of doctors and druggists be appointed was carried. It is believed that a good start has been made toward better relations and that the benefit will be permanent.

NOTES.

J. Goodman has started a new store at 4135 Vincennes avenue.

The Standard Drug Company has opened a new store at 145 Madison street.

C. A. Montgomery, 233 Twenty-second street, and J. H. Montgomery, 2506 State street, have been again arrested on the charge of selling cocaine. The arrests were due to information given by a victim to representatives of Hull House.

A. C. Musselwhite has moved his downtown store from the Old Colony Building, at Van Buren and Dearborn streets, to the Pontiac Building, on Harrison street. He has also opened a new store in Englewood, opposite the Sixty-third street station of the elevated.

This has been a busy month for the Chicago Veteran Druggists' Association. June 6 two of the members had a birthday luncheon, F. M. Schmidt, forty-seventh, and W. Bodemann, sixtieth. J. Blocki was the recipient of hearty congratulations at the regular meeting, June 15.

The Alumni Association of the Northwestern School of Pharmacy has elected the following: H. F. Schaper, president; G. H. Adamick, first vice-president; Bert Tyler, second vice-president; P. E. Finninger, third vice-president; George D. Oglesby, secretary; Maurice A. Miner, treasurer; George Hanson, Wm. F. Egler and A. F. Kasper, trustees.

THE SOUTH.

A Third Term for Mr. Breslin—Comments of the State Association.

(*From our Regular Correspondent.*)

New Orleans, June 18.—At the annual meeting of the Orleans Pharmaceutical Association, held last Friday night, M. T. Breslin, a well-known and popular druggist, was unanimously elected for a third term as the president of that organization. The other officers named for the ensuing year were: M. Stolzenthaler, first vice-president; F. C. Godbold, treasurer; R. L. Villere, secretary; Executive Committee, George W. McDuff, George McNulty, E. D. Sauvinet, A. O. Kaczoroski and John E. Scott. The meeting was executive, and lasted sevral hours, many matters of importance being discussed. The association went on record as opposed to any change in the present pharmacy law.

NEW COMMITTEES OF THE LOUISIANA ASSOCIATION.

C. D. Sauvinet, of New Orleans, president of the Louisiana State Pharmaceutical Association, has announced that the next convention of that body will be held in New Orleans, May 14, 15 and 16, 1907. At this convention the twenty-fifth anniversary of the association will be fittingly observed. President Sauvinet has appointed the following committees to serve during the coming year:

Executive Committee.—William M. Levy, John E. Scott, George V. Claren, A. Di Trapani, T. J. Baltar.

Trade Interests.—F. C. Godbold, George McNulty, A. T. Wainright, Eugene Daste, R. M. Phillips, A. P. Irwin, Albert Estorge, V. B. Richard.

Pharmacy and Queries.—Philip Asher, Adam Wirth, J. F. Code, A. S. Brand, R. L. Villere, Joseph N. Richard, John T. Norman.

Legislation.—C. G. Peters, George S. Humphreys, M. T. Breslin, P. A. Capdau, M. Bernstein, T. J. Labbe, J. S. Claverie, P. L. Blanchard.

Adulteration and Deterioration of Drugs.—George S. Brown, Henry P. Kenny, Joseph H. Dunn, Miss Cora Wright, L. J. Fournet, G. U. Rybiski, H. C. Lynch.

Pharmaceutical Education.—George D. Feldner, E. J. Marion, J. N. W. Otto, Mrs. S. L. Wagner, Paul Fleming, J. L. Watkins, A. Villeret.

Membership.—Atal A. Sarradet, Joseph Ipser, J. Fuerstenberg, A. DeLanzac, Ed. F. Guste, Harry J. Cockburn, C. C. Rybiski, Victor H. Jones, Charles A. McDonald.

Entertainment.—George W. McDuff, C. C. Johnston, Lucien E. Lyons, F. A. Dicks, John E. Scott, George S. Humphreys, W. J. Sbisa.

Memorial.—L. Szabary, W. P. Duplantis, A. Noha, H. W. Roelling, J. A. Bourg, L. L. Heureux, L. E. Richard.

Transportation.—P. A. Capdau, J. W. Hirsch, A. D. Parker, Alf. Levy, A. F. Belanger, F. H. Carruth, W. Danseran, A. S. Tomb.

Exhibit.—George S. Humphreys, W. J. Sbisa, A. Di Trapani, T. J. Baltar, G. O. Bergeron, A. M. Dietrich, W. E. Allen, Van A. Woods.

REGISTERED IN LOUISIANA.

The result of the examinations held by the Louisiana Board of Pharmacy, May 4 and 5, has been announced. There were 27 applicants and over 50 per cent. passed, as follows:

Registered Pharmacists' Certificates.—Louis F. Bruznae, Lutcher; R. E. Moers, New Orleans; J. G. Hirsch, New Orleans; F. A. Johnson, Amite City; Y. B. Terrebonne, Morgan City; S. W. Hills, Amite City; C. A. Desport, jr., New Orleans; E. B. Scott, Winsboro; P. A. Calotta, New Orleans.

For Qualified Assistant Certificates.—M. E. Toorean, St. Francisville; Miss Alice L. Lanapre, New Orleans; F. W. Raggio, Natchitoches; C. A. Walsdorf, New Orleans; L. E. Carruth, Kentwood; E. C. Webre, New Orleans; J. J. Dejois, New Orleans.

The Examining Committee was: William M. Levy, C. D. Sauvinat, Adam Wirth and F. C. Godbold.

The next examination will be held August 3 and 4, when the board expects a large class, on account of the decision of the Supreme Court settling the question of the constitutionality of the pharmacy law.

NEWS ITEMS.

The Retail Drug Clerks' Association of Louisiana has indorsed the bill of Dr. Joseph A. O'Hara, which provides for a law restricting the sale of carbolic acid.

John Clapper, sr., has been awarded the contract for building the new drug store of the Poplarville Drug Company, a new enterprise of Poplarville, Miss. The building is to be of concrete blocks and two stories in height. This drug company was only recently organized with a capital of $10,000. D. W. C. Hunnicut, W. L. Arledge, B. Franklin Nimmocks and associates are the organizers. The drug company will occupy the lower floor of the building, while the upper story will be used as physicians' offices.

THE PACIFIC COAST.

Insurance Settlements Unsatisfactory—The Work of Relief—Retailers Find Difficulty in Securing Supplies—Commencement Day at the University—Registered in California—Proposed Regulation of the Sale of Narcotics, etc.

(From our Regular Correspondent.)

San Francisco, June 12.—Although the stringent orders of military rule are things of the past (and *spiritus frumenti* can now be dispensed *per se* in a prescription), all is not serene in the domain of the pharmacist of San Francisco. It has been a difficult matter for the retailer to have even a reasonable fraction of his orders supplied by the wholesaler. Touching upon the scarcity of chemicals for blondes, a local newspaper aptly remarks: "The blonde of yesterday, who was a brunette the day before, is a blonde-brunette of to-day." So it is with the pill roller—druggists whose ambition it was never to be "out" of even rare articles must now face the embarrassing predicament of being without the commonest remedies.

RELIEF WORK OF THE N. A. R. D.

The Relief Committee of the local N. A. R. D. is taking steps for the protection of the rights of burned out druggists, and is watching closely the treatment accorded the members of the association at the hands of the adjusters of the insurance companies. The secretary of the committee, W. B. Cheatham, has written to the local drug men, including clerks, urging them to make no unsatisfactory compromises of their losses without first consulting the attorney engaged by the committee.

With regard to the publication of an insurance blacklist, Secretary Cheatham says:

"Through our National Association we will be able to make sworn statements of those who receive injustice in the settlement of drug losses and have same printed and displayed in the windows of 40,000 drug stores in this country and Canada." Already several attempts at unjust methods have been brought to light.

DRUG CLERKS REFUSE INDIVIDUAL HELP FROM N. A. R. D.

Owing to their sensitive pride, the stranded drug clerks of San Francisco have refused to accept individual funds from the Relief Committee of the local N. A. R. D. The Drug Clerks' Association is quite anxious to have a lump sum turned over to them for distribution among their needy members, but the latter refused to sign personal receipts and have their names transcribed upon the relief books of the proprietors. There is some bitter feeling at the refusal of the N. A. R. D. committee to turn over a portion of the relief fund to the clerks' organization, and as a result Messrs. Fetz, Gay and Whilden, composing the Relief Committee, have started a separate fund for the clerks. Almost $1,000 has been contributed to this new fund, while nearly $50,000 has been raised for the N. A. R. D. members.

COMMENCEMENT AT UNIVERSITY OF CALIFORNIA SCHOOL OF PHARMACY.

The most solemn exercises marked Commencement Day at the University of California on May 16. Even the gait of the successful pharmaceutical candidates, who headed the procession of the professional graduates of the university, spoke of the sorrow of the city across the bay that had been wrecked by the earth's convulsions.

Degrees in pharmacy were conferred upon the following:

Phar. B.—J. R. Lindsay, Ph. C., San Francisco; G. M. Nelson, Ph. C., Gilroy; F. W. Nish, Ph. G., San Francisco.

Ph. C.—J. A. Abreu, Oakland; T. J. Armstrong, Arroyo Grande; R. S. Baker, Oakland; C. N. Bichard, San Francisco; A. L. Cuneo, San Francisco; R. G. Duffey, San Rafael; N. S. Elder, Pomona; F. D. Fleming, San Jose; E. P. Genochio, Redwood; E. M. Hale, Placerville; J. G. Harrington, San Francisco; E. E. Johnson, Mountain View; J. L. Justice, Hollister; M. P. Kaufman, San Francisco; H. W. Law, San Francisco; A. R. Maas, Los Angeles; E. H. MacGilvray, Mobile, Ala.; W. D. Osgood, Oakland; P. M. Nolan, San Francisco; H. G. Parsons, Bakersfield; H. H. Patterson, Wheatland; G. Q. Pease, Geyserville; V. A. Renfro, Downey; J. H. Seaton, San Luis Obispo; J. W. Tuttle, Petaluma; W. C. Williams, Dinuba.

FACULTY CHANGES.

The regents of the University of California met on the 11th inst. and appointed Dr. Henry B. Carey to succeed Dr. Albert Schneider, who lately resigned as professor of botany, materia medica, pharmacognosy and physiology in the Department of Pharmacy. Dr. Carey was formerly Dr. Schneider's assistant at the Northwestern University School of Pharmacy. Dr. Schneider still retains the chair of bacteriology at the California College of Pharmacy.

NEWLY REGISTERED PHARMACISTS.

The following candidates were successful in the last examinations held by the Board of Pharmacy in Los Angeles and San Francisco:

Licentiates.—Joseph A. Abreu, C. Fred. Barnes, Benj. C. Belden, Ralph M. Bellows, H. W. Brayton, Z. E. Burgess, J. R. Cajacob, H. Whitfield Clarkson, Joseph G. Clayworth, Michael E. Crete, Robt. E. Davenport, Herbert T. Fricke, Alfred J. Fredrichs, John Guehring, jr., John G. Harrington, Wm. J. Hewes, W. Alton Irwin, Demas Lafrance, Albert J. Lewek, D. C. Linebaugh, Chas. A. Lutz, Edward L. Marshall, James W. McCoubrey, Benj. J. Miller, Will. E. Murphy, Fred. G. Nopel, Owen Overman, Emile J. Pierron, V. A. Renfro, Albert T. Renner, John Wesley Salter, E. E. Schroeder, John E. Siebold, Elliott E. Seiser, Frank G. Shepherd, Leon Shulman, Horace D. Stewart, A. E. Syverson, Paul Tholl, Al. C. Tienken, Willis H. Alpers, Bert C. Ansley, John Taylor Ball, Chas. S. Battey, Elmer E. Berglund, Herman A. Brandner, Leander W. Burtt, Chas. N. Cortright, A. D. Campbell, Herman Todd Davis, John E. Davis, John A. Erickson, Louis Josephs, E. H. Kennard, Fredric W. Kruger, A. V. McComb, G. H. McKenzie, J. R. Memmel, Wm. F. Passer, Ray T. Prettyman, F. H. Seery, R. L. Shinker, George Raymond Smith, Walter H. Stout, Jay W. Swain, Carl A. Swenson, Frederick W. Tilton, Lawrence B. Waggoner, Herbert V. Williams, Joseph F. Zika, Edward W. Vogel, A. C. Kurrasch, J. R. Hafford, Wm. W. Wilson, A. B. Smith, Edward B. McAllister, Thos. L. Parker, W. T. Strother, Chas. M. McKelvey, Auguste E. Charbonneaux, Victor Dupont, Ansel Woodworth, R. C. Logan, K. J. Slaughter, Geo. D. Zeile, H. Kielhorn.

Assistants.—Clinton B. Afflerbaugh, James M. Beazell, Louis J. Bernell, O. F. Dietz, Frank B. Fleming, F. E. Gassaway, Henry C. Johnson, Eugene B. Kemper, Fred. W. Korman, Adolph W. Leman, Cyrus Lesinsky, Wm. McKinlay, M. C. Smith, Joseph H. Tupling, James E. Dougherty, Herbert L. Fulton, L. R. Leslie, George A. Lewis, B. C. Lytle, W. H. Sanders, Frederick W. Wengenroth.

The next meetings of the board will be July 19 at Los Angeles and the following week at San Francisco. Secretary Whilden announces that registration fees become due July 1.

TO LEGISLATE AGAINST NARCOTICS AND ADULTERATED DRUGS.

The Board of Supervisors of San Francisco on the 11th inst. passed to print two ordinances of interest to pharmacists. One forbids the sale of adulterated drugs or medicines containing wood alcohol, while the other is intended to regulate the sale of cocaine, alpha or beta cocaine, opium, morphine, heroin, chloral hydrate or any salt or compound of such substances by requiring a prescription for every sale.

COAST BREVITIES.

At the special session of the State Legislature, necessitated by the earthquake and fire of San Francisco and vicinity, $2,500 was appropriated for the restoration of the property of the State Board of Pharmacy.

The trustees of Chico, Cal., have passed an ordinance prohibiting the distribution of samples of medicine.

The first result on this Coast of the passage of the "denaturized alcohol" bill by Congress is the notification sent by the Agnews (Cal.) distillery to Special Agent of the Internal Revenue Department B. M. Thomas, to the effect that they intend to engage in the manufacture of the spirit. By utilizing the by-products produced in the manufacture of beet sugar it is thought that the project will cause an increased demand for beets in this State.

The Mississippi Medical College.

The first session of this institution will open on October 1 in a new building being erected for that purpose on Fifth street, between Twenty-fourth and Twenty-fifth avenues, Meridian. The officers of the college are: Dr. W. W. Hamilton, president; Dr. T. A. Barber, vice-president; O. W. Bethea, Ph. G., secretary; Dr. T. J. Houston, treasurer, and Dr. L. N. Clarke, dean. Mr. Bethea, who is well known through his activity in the affairs of the American Pharmaceutical Association, besides being secretary of the college, will occupy the chair of pharmacology.

The Drug and Chemical Market

The prices quoted in this report are those current in the wholesale market, and higher prices are paid for retail lots
The quality of goods frequently necessitates a wide range of prices.

Condition of Trade.

NEW YORK, June 23, 1906.

The usual summer dullness has set in and there is an entire absence of important demand for nearly all lines included in the department of drugs and chemicals. Little of special interest is to be noted as regards price changes. Manufacturers have advanced the price of phosphoric acid, and golden seal root is enhanced in value, while a stronger tendency is evident among the essential oils, most of which are held at higher figures, cloves, citronella, neroli and peppermint being among the list which show actual advances, but price changes generally appear to favor sellers, despite a generally quiet market. At this period of the year jobbers are engaged in stock taking and naturally show small disposition to add to their holdings, the rule with the majority being to cover current requirements as they develop.

HIGHER.	LOWER.
Oil of cloves,	Oil of cedar leaf,
Safrol,	Canary seed,
Powdered cantharides,	Saffron flowers, American.
Citronella oil,	Squills.
Golden seal root,	
Phosphoric acid,	
Jalap,	
Buchu leaves,	
Oil of almond.	

Drugs.

Alcohol has been in steady consuming demand since our last, and values are well sustained at the range of $2.47 to $2.49 for grain, though $2.46½ is named on quantity orders. Wood is steady and in moderate request at 70c to 75c for 95 to 97 per cent. respectively.

Amyl acetate is held with increased firmness and manufacturers generally are naming a higher figure, though $1.50 will yet buy.

Balm of Gilead buds are not quotably lower, but the market is easier in the absence of important demand.

Balsams.—Copaiba is in better supply and the market for Central American is easy at the quoted range of 30c to 32c; Para is held and selling at 40c to 45c. Fir, Peru and tolu are without quotable change.

Barks.—Buckthorn is in better supply and offers more freely at 4¾c. Cascara sagrada continues to monopolize interest among the barks and values are firmly maintained at 6½c to 9c as to age and quantity, a sale of two year old bark being reported at inside figure. Soap, cut, is offered a shade more freely, 5½c being named in some quarters, though 6c is being realized on other. White pine and white cherry are dull and neglected as usual at this season, with only small lots changing hands at current prices, or say 4½c to 6c for the former and 6c to 9c for the latter.

Buchu leaves, short, are held with increased firmness in view of the tenor of advices from primary sources; foreign markets are reported very strong, sales of prime picked green leaf being made in London at 9d. On spot sales were reported at 18c to 22c, the outside figure being for fancy green. The new crop is said to be disappointing as to size, and the outlook consequently favors higher prices.

Cacao butter appears well sustained at 28½c to 29c for prime Dutch and German brands, and at 30c for Van Houten and Cadbury, with jobbing sales reported at this range.

Cantharides, Chinese, has developed increased strength, some holders declining to shade 90c, though sales were made in other quarters at 85c near the close. Russian are not inquired for to any extent, and, while whole flies offer at $1.20, powdered are available at $1.25.

Castor oil is held with more firmness in the face of strong reports from the seed producing districts, but prices are as previously quoted, or, say, 11½c to 12½c and 12c to 13c for No. 1 in barrels and cases, respectively, and 10½c to 11½c and 11c to 12c for No. 3.

Chamomile flowers, Hungarian, of the new crop have offered in the interval at 15c, but 7½c will yet buy old. Roman offers in some quarters at 24c, but there is little available at this figure.

Cocaine is held and selling from manufacturers at $3.00 to $3.25; the market is easier in the absence of important demand.

Codliver oil is seasonably dull and prices are unchanged at $21.00 to $25.00 for Norwegian and $19.00 to $20.00 for Newfoundland.

Colocynth apples have met with a fair inquiry during the interval and quotations are maintained steadily at 28c to 30c for prime Trieste and 22c to 24c for Spanish.

Cuttlefish bone remains quiet, though without quotable change in price. We hear of sales of prime Trieste at 17c to 17½c and of French at 12c to 12½c, while 70c is named for jewelers' large and 40c to 50c for small.

Elder flowers have developed some scarcity and dealers are firmer in their views of 10c to 11c.

Ergot attracts little attention, though reports from primary sources indicate the likelihood of improved values for Russian, which is now quoted at 26c to 27c, with 36c named for Spanish.

Eserine is lower in sympathy with the beans, manufacturers having reduced prices to the basis of 6c a grain in 5-grain vials, for both sulphate and salicylate.

Juniper berries have continued in moderate jobbing demand and values are sustained at the full quoted range of 3½c to 4c.

Laurel leaves are in improved demand and the tone of the market is firmer, owing to diminished spot supplies; quoted 4½c to 4¾c.

Menthol remains in about the same position as noted in our last, though the market is a shade firmer, if anything, there being nothing now obtainable at under $2.50, with up to $2.75 named, according to size of lot.

Opium is not meeting with any special inquiry, and the market retains the dull and spiritless appearance that has characterized it for some time past. Speculative interest is yet an absent feature, though there are evidences in some quarters of a disposition to urge sales. Meanwhile the quoted range remains at $2.72½ to $2.80 for cases, $2.75 to $2.80 for broken packages and $3.20 to $3.25 for powdered.

Quinine shows no improvement, and the market is, if anything, quieter, owing to the absence of speculative interest. Manufacturers continue to quote on the old basis of 17c for bulk in 100-ounce tins, while second hands name 16½c to 16¾c; Java is held and selling at 16c to 16½c.

Saffron, American, owing to arrivals and competitive influence, has declined in the interval, and 80c is now named as acceptable, a figure which is said to be on a parity with the price of new crop goods.

Tonka beans are not finding any special demand, but supplies are somewhat restricted, and quotations for desirable grades of Tonka have been advanced to 22½c to 25c. Most of the demand is for Angostura, which is maintained at 60c to 62½c.

Vanilla beans are in better supply, but some recent arrivals of cuts have not been up to the standard of quality owing, it is supposed, to haste in curing, and some lots have been disposed of at a fractional decline. Sales of whole are reported at $2.75 to $5.00 and of cut at $2.00 to $2.25, while Bourbon are held at $1.15 to $3.00 and Tahiti at 60c to $1.35.

Chemicals.

Arsenic, white, is not in active demand, but quotations are maintained at 5c to 5½c. Red is held and selling at 6½c to 6¾c, as to quantity.

Bleaching powder is offered a shade more freely, owing to recent heavy arrivals, and is now quoted at 1.25c to 1.30c.

Blue vitriol is held with increased firmness, but quotations are as previously reported, or, say, 6c to 6¼c for jobbing parcels.

Carbolic acid is in good demand, and values are ruling steady at the previous range of 14c to 15c for drums and 20c to 22c for pound bottles.

Citric acid is in steady seasonable demand, and values are firmly maintained at 43c to 43½c.

Cream tartar has sold actively during the interval, especially in a jobbing way, and values are well sustained at 22½c to 22¾c for crystals and 22¾c to 23c for powdered.

Oxalic acid continues scarce on spot, and 6¼c to 6½c is the present range of quotations.

Phosphoric acid is fractionally higher, manufacturers having raised the outside limit to 24c, and the revised range stands at 20c to 24c for 1.710 and 20½c to 24½c for 1.750, the inside figures being for carboys.

Quicksilver is finding a steady jobbing outlet at the range of 55c to 56c.

Silver nitrate is in advancing tendency, owing to the increased cost of bullion, and the revised range of manufacturers is 42c to 45c.

Sodium benzoate has receded in the interval, owing to competition among manufacturers, with the sales at 28c to 29c.

Sodium nitrate is firmer for future deliveries, up to $2.37½ being named for 96 per cent. and $2.32½ for 95 per cent. Spot parcels are generally quoted at $2.30.

Stearic acid has hardened in the interval in consequence of an advance in the price of crude material. Single pressed is quoted at 9¾c, double pressed at 10½c to 11c, and extra quality at 11½c to 12c.

Strontium nitrate is in seasonable demand, and values are firm at the range of 8c to 9c.

Tartaric acid is in good seasonable demand, and quotations are steadily maintained at the previous range of 28¼c to 28½c for crystals and powdered, respectively.

Essential Oils.

Almond, expressed, is higher in foreign markets and holders here have advanced their range to 43c.

Anise has moved into firmer position, most of the chief lots having been taken up, and $1.32½ is now quoted inside.

Cajuput has eased off since our last, quotations having been reduced to 52c to 53c.

Cedar leaf is in better supply and quotations have declined to 55c to 65c.

Citronella is held with increased strength and confidence, and recent sales were at 40c to 42c.

Clove has advanced in the interval, in sympathy with the spice, and there is little obtainable at under $1.00.

Lemon, for future delivery, is quoted at an advance of 2½c per pound and the general tendency of Messina essences is upward, though quotations for spot goods are nominally unchanged.

Neroli has developed some scarcity, and higher prices are generally named, some dealers naming $75.00 and $85.00 for Bigarade and petale respectively, though the oils are obtainable in some quarters at $55.00 and $60.00.

Peppermint maintains its upward tendency, and while parcels are obtainable at $2.80, $3.00 is more generally asked for bulk oil; cases are quoted at $3.40 to $3.50.

Safrol is held with more firmness, and dealers decline to shade 35c to 37½c.

Gums.

Aloes are without quotation change. The outlook for Cape is said to be unfavorable owing to drought in South Africa. Recent sales of Curacao on spot were at 5¾c to 6c, and Barbadoes in gourds is held at 16c to 17c.

Arabic sorts has sold in a limited way during the interval at 6c, but 6½c is generally named; up to 11c is named for the choicer white grades.

Camphor continues in good demand, and values are firmly maintained at $1.00 to $1.50 for barrels and cases respectively.

Gamboge is easier in sympathy with conditions at primary sources and mass and broken are now quoted down to 87½c, though prime whole pipe commands 92½c to 95c.

Tragacanth is in upward tendency, and quotations on the choice grades of Aleppo show an advance of 5c, No. 1 being quoted at 70c. There is some scarcity in the better grades of gum, and the market is generally firmer in consequence.

Roots.

Alkanet is quiet, but the market is steady at 7¼c to 7½c.

Ginger, Jamaica, is attracting more attention, and there have been jobbing sales at 13c to 16c for unbleached and bleached, respectively.

Golden seal is in upward movement, prices having climbed to the $1.50 limit since our last. Prospective buyers are holding off, as the views of holders are considered too high. It is thought, however, that if inquiries for export continue at the present high level, a further stimulus will be given to values.

Ipecac is in slightly better supply, owing to an arrival of some 500 pounds of Rio, but prices are maintained steadily at $1.75 to $1.80; Carthagena is held and selling at $1.65 to $1.70.

Jalap of the better grades is scarce and wanted. Such sales as came to the surface were at an advance of 1c.

Squill is less actively inquired for, and holders show more disposition to urge sales at 10c, or even a shade lower.

Stillingia is meeting with increased inquiry, and the tone of the market is firm at 5¾c.

Seeds.

There has been a fairly active business in the general line of druggists' seeds since our last, but no price changes of special importance are to be reported. Canary is lower, with Sicily offering at 3¾c and Symrna at 3½c. Cardemoms maintain their firm position, but little business is passing, owing to the divergent views of the buyers and sellers. The latter hold out for 37c, while the former bid 35½c for decorticated.

Desirable Opening for a Druggist in New York City.

A high class apartment house has been completed at the northeast corner of Fifth avenue and 126th street, the ground floor of which is intended for the use of a druggist. The store has a floor space of 24 x 35 feet, has two store entrances, three show windows and a commodious private space in the cellar. This is a rapidly growing neighborhood and there are an unusual number of doctors' offices in the two blocks between Madison and Lenox avenues. The store will be finished to suit the requirements of the tenant. The rent is $1,200 per annum, a low figure considering the advantages. Prospective tenants should apply to Porter & Co., 159 West 125th street, New York.

Laboratory Appliances.

The old house of Eimer & Amend, at 205 Third avenue, New York, makes a specialty of all appliances used for pharmaceutical, chemical and physical work. The concern is also an extensive dealer in drugs and chemicals. Druggists who are in the market for such goods would do well to communicate with Eimer & Amend before placing their orders.

AMERICAN DRUGGIST

and PHARMACEUTICAL RECORD

NUEVA YORK y CHICAGO: 8 DE ENERO DE 1906

«The American Druggist» es un periódico bimensual del que se publica cada mes un suplemento español con anuncios en el mismo idioma

AMERICAN DRUGGIST PUBLISHING COMPANY

62-68 WEST BROADWAY, NEW YORK, U. S. A.

Dirección cablegráfica «Amdruggist, New York.» Clave A B C

A. R. ELLIOTT, *Presidente*

CASWELL A. MAYO, Ph. G..................*Director*

THOMAS J. KEENAN, Lic. en Farm., *Director Asociado*

PRECIOS DE SUSCRIPCION

Pago adelantado, Estados Unidos, Canadá, México, Cuba, Puerto Rico, Hawaii y las Filipinas .. ..(oro americano) $1.50

Otros países (franco de porte).................. » » $3.00

Las suscripciones pueden empezar en cualquier tiempo.

«THE AMERICAN DRUGGIST AND PHARMACEUTICAL RECORD» sale el segundo y cuarto lunes de cada mes. Todo cambio de anuncios debe ser recibido diez días antes de la fecha de salida.

Remesas deben hacerse con libranzas sobre Nueva York, giros postales internacionales ó por expreso ó correo en carta certificada. Toda correspondencia debe dirigirse á la AMERICAN DRUGGIST PUBLISHING Co., 62-68 West Broadway, New York, U. S. A.

EDICION ESPAÑOLA DE LA FARMACOPEA AMERICANA

LA decisión de los administradores de la Farmacopea de los Estados Unidos, de traducir al español la última edición de la misma para el uso de los farmacéuticos de los países anexados á los Estados Unidos que hablan aquella lengua, será recibida con júbilo por los mismos y de igual manera por los farmacéuticos de México, Centro y Sud-América. Como hemos dicho en números anteriores, por algún tiempo se hicieron esfuerzos cerca del Gobierno federal para que en la imprenta nacional se imprimiese una versión española de nuestra Farmacopea para los fines expresados arriba; pero el lento expedienteo hizo imposible llevar á la práctica la idea, y abandonóse la esperanza de recibir el apoyo oficial que se buscaba.

Dado el comercio en general, y en particular el de drogas que se hace entre este país y los del Sur, es natural el creciente interés que allí se siente por los asuntos farmacéuticos americanos, por las fórmulas emanadas aquí, como también por los procedimientos mecánicos. Hasta aquí en la mayoría de las farmacias de Centro y Sud-América el libro de medicina oficial que sirve de pauta para todas las labores, es la Farmacopea española y el Códex francés. Estas obras se tienen en mucha estima. En el Brasil se emplea además la Farmacopea portuguesa.

Un distintivo de la nueva edición de la Farmacopea española — la obra se revisó casi simultáneamente con la americana, aunque se publicó algunos meses antes que la última — es la alusión á la acción terapéutica y al empleo de las drogas y compuestos, informe que precede á la dosis. Como podía esperarse, los revisores del libro español fueron más conservadores que los nuestros en la cuestión de excluir y añadir artículos. Aquellas preparaciones de origen animal como los folículos prepuciales desecados del castor, el coral, las raspaduras de cuerno de ciervo, la colapez y huesos calcinados, se retienen en la Farmacopea española, por más que entre las adiciones vemos la antitoxina para la difteria, la grasa de lana y el suero artificial de Hayem.

Al traducir la obra americana al idioma español, la comisión encargada no debería adoptar con rigor el estilo tipográfico característico de la Farmacopea de los Estados Unidos. Los apretados renglones que permiten agrupar una buena cantidad de materia en poco espacio relativamente, no serían del agrado de los lectores españoles, acostumbrados como están al tipo de letra grande, con los renglones bien espaciados. Con todo, nuestra Farmacopea, si bien traducida, está llamada á producir buena impresión entre los farmacéuticos inteligentes de la América española, é indirectamente habrá de contribuir al fomento de una educación farmacéutica superior en los países en que circule.

La cuestión de la versión española de la Farmacopea, se ha puesto en manos de una comisión compuesta de los Sres. Joseph P. Remington, Charles E. Dohme y el Dr. H. C. Wood, quienes activarán los trabajos para que la nueva edición vea la luz dentro de un año á más tardar.

Para Distinguir las Fibras de Algodón de las de Hilo

Hertzog nos recuerda (*L'Union Pharm.*, octubre, 1905), que la mejor manera de distinguir el algodón del hilo, es tomando un trozo del tejido, de unos cuatro centímetros cuadrados, y después de sacar algunas de las fibras, sumergirlas en una solución alcohólica de cianino caliente. Después que este tinte ha compenetrado bien la fibra se enjuaga ésta en agua y se trata con ácido sulfúrico diluído. Esta fibra descolora el algodón completamente mientras que el hilo conserva un color azul muy distinto después de aquel tratamiento. Este color azul de la tela de hilo se aviva si se enjuaga otra vez la muestra y se sumerge en amoníaco.

Los Amargos como Auxiliar de la Digestión

En estos últimos años ha adelantado tanto la medicina con motivo de las pesquisas y ensayos llevados á cabo en el laboratorio, que en muchos casos quizás hayamos aceptado con demasiada prisa datos emanados de experiencias en contravención de las enseñanzas empíricas, desviándonos hasta cierto-punto de la «sabiduría de nuestros antepasados,» como diría Dickens. Pero realmente y haciendo justicia á los hechos, lo que nos extravía es la investigación incompleta. Un ejemplo por vía de ilustración: es un hecho que los amargos se tratan con indiferencia por la razón de que por las experiencias verificadas con ellos se ha demostrado que carecen de aquella acción que se suponía ser un auxiliar de la digestión.

Se ha averiguado, en efecto, que los amargos no aumentan la secreción del jugo gástrico; pero, después de todo, resulta que sí obran de esa manera, si después de su ingestión se toma el alimento inmediatamente. Habiendo Straschenko llevado á cabo varias experiencias con perros, ha visto confirmarse la aseveración anterior, la cual además ha sido comprobada por otros. Es, pues, evidente que la simple omisión en las experiencias de tiempos anteriores de administrar alimento tan luego de tomar los amargos, viciaba el valor de las investigaciones. Y todo esto se expone en un informe leído recientemente en una junta de la Sociedad Médica de Hospitales de París, de que eran autores J. Nano y F. Mironesco, de Bucharest, cuyo informe fué presentado por M. Roger (*Bulletins et mémoires de la Société Médicale des Hôpitaux de Paris*, nov. 23).

Los experimentadores de Bucharest, agregaban á la memoria una observación muy interesante, y es que los amargos por ellos empleados al hacer las experiencias con un sujeto, y que eran en su mayor parte tintura de cincona, no tan sólo produjeron un aumento marcado en el flujo de jugos gástricos cuando á su administración seguía la alimentación, sino que también dieron lugar á un notable aumento en la cantidad de ácido hidroclórico en la secreción. De lo dicho podemos llegar á la conclusión que en la forma de insuficiencia gástrica llamada hipocloridria, los amargos desempeñan un importante papel, y además podemos inferir de todo lo dicho que las propiedades de los amargos están comprobadas hoy día por las observaciones llevadas á cabo en el laboratorio por varios investigadores. — *New York Medical Journal.*

Observaciones de un Químico Americano en París

El Dr. H. H. Fries, de la casa Fries Bros., de Nueva York, quien regresó recientemente de un prolongado viaje á Europa, ha comunicado al *Oil Paint and Drug Reporter* las siguientes impresiones:

«Hace ahora algunas semanas, estando yo en París, encontré al profesor Auguste Behal, de l'Ecole de Pharmacie y secretario general de la Sociedad Química de Ciencias de Francia, quien tiene la reputación de ser uno de los químicos más notables del mundo, y fué el representante de Francia en la Exposición Universal de St. Louis. Entre los inventos suyos más valiosos é interesantes á que hubo de referirse, es el alcanfor sintético fabricado en el laboratorio y en pequeña escala para el comercio, de 50 á 100 libras diarias, con toda regularidad, y cuya planta visité. El alcanfor, según explicó él, es un producto sintético en absoluto, poseyendo todas las cualidades del de Formosa. Con motivo del bajo costo de la producción, puede considerarse el primer proceso fructuoso para la fabricación del alcanfor en grande escala.

» Otro asunto altamente interesante es el descubrimiento por un químico eminente asociado con el profesor Behal, y el cual consiste en un proceso, que ha merecido privilegio, para producir terpinol á un costo muy bajo, y en relación con el mismo otro proceso para disolver gomas vegetales. Parece que aun las gomas más duras pueden ponerse en solución por medio de este proceso sin tener que hervir, y al mismo tiempo da á las gomas brillantez y elasticidad y muchas otras ventajas que ningún otro solvente realiza.

» Entre otros asuntos que me interesaron fué el descubrimiento por el Dr. Robert Cambien, de París, miembro del Instituto Bacteriológico del Departamento de Sanidad, de la esterilización del agua por un procedimiento frío, de cuyas resultas perecen todos los bacilos. El agua queda esterilizada y puede usarse para beber sin hervirla. También se llamó la atención á un proceso para hacer comestibles los aceites animales neutros, tales como el aceite de pescado, el de aceitunas y el sésame; y en general todos los aceites vegetales y animales. El rendimiento de estos aceites, exentos de ácido libre, aunque el coste es pequeño, en muchos casos duplica ó triplica el valor de los aceites. Por este procedimiento el aceite de linaza se hace sin ácido libre, de modo que se pone blanco cual el agua, y el litopono cuando se mezcla con este aceite de color blanco permanece blanco á la luz del sol, no se descolora ni se ennegrece, como sucede de ordinario.»

Un Consejo á los Farmacéuticos

Las medicinas que receta el médico deben ser dispensadas por el farmacéutico. Si el farmacéutico cree que alguna droga, que no sea la que aquel tiene el hábito de prescribir, fuese tan buena ó mejor para el enfermo, el médico y para él mismo, tiene el privilegio y al mismo tiempo el deber de presentarle sus razones al médico, porqué piensa de aquella manera.

El *St. Paul Medical Journal* dice que es tanto más fácil para el médico prescribir un específico por su nombre eufónico, fácil de recordar, que escribir una receta, motivo para que prefieran hacer lo primero muchos médicos. El periódico citado recomienda que en los colegios de medicina se dedique menos tiempo á la instrucción espectacular, y por contra que enseñen á los estudiantes la manera de escribir una receta por valor de veinticinco centavos de medicina y que tenga que prepararla el farmacéutico, en lugar de prescribir un paquete de específico por valor de un peso.

Pero mejor sería que los farmacéuticos no aguardasen hasta que los colegios adopten el consejo del periódico de St. Paul y los estudiantes hagan uso del nuevo conocimiento que obtienen con el cambio; deberían hacer algo de por sí en la parte educativa, aunque tuviesen que acuñar algunos nombres eufónicos, y proporcionar á los médicos muestras de los efectos hechos por ellos. Si las «medicinas hechas en casa» son tan buenas — y así lo opina el médico — como las que se traen de distancia, y sus nombres son tan fáciles de recordar, sólo falta acercarse con discreción al médico, y probablemente recetará menos específicos adoptando la fórmula del farmacéutico. Por supuesto, que el farmacéutico ha de tener la aptitud y competencia para ello, y siempre que no tenga negocio más provechoso. — *Drug. Circ.*

NOTAS PRACTICAS

INGESTION DE ALGODON ABSORBENTE PARA EXPELER CUERPOS EXTRAÑOS DEL CUERPO.—A menudo se llevan á la farmacia niños de pocos años, al parecer en un estado precario, por haber engullido algún objeto agudo, como es un alfiler. Por lo regular es difícil en tales casos hallar los medios de expeler el objeto, y en otros imposible. Por este motivo es interesante el informe de un cirujano á que alude el *Medical Press and Circular*, del 4 de junio de 1905. En efecto, el profesor puso en práctica un método original en un niño de 18 meses que había tragado un broche. El Dr. Bell, el cirujano en cuestión, pensó que haciendo engullir al niño una cantidad de algodón absorbente éste rodearía el broche dentro del estómago, verificándose la expulsión sin peligro. El algodón se dió en parte con leche y en parte con un emparedado que tenía jalea extendida. Pocas horas después administróse al niño una dosis de aceite de ricino. El broche se halló en una de las deposiciones de tal modo rodeado con algodón, que fuera imposible lesionar los intestinos.

El éxito obtenido en este caso indujo al mismo cirujano á probar el método mencionado en un niño de cuatro años que había tragado un botón de cobre de buen tamaño. El cuerpo extraño estaba completamente envuelto en el algodón y fué expelido de la misma manera que en el caso precedente. Parece, por consiguiente, que la ingestión de algodón puede ayudar la expulsión de cuerpos extraños del intestino, no tan sólo rodeándolos, sino que también atrayendo materias fecales. Mr. Johnson, médico de Dublin, parece haber sido el autor de este método, habiendo dado un poco de algodón á un niño que tragó un juego de dientes artificiales, cuyo hecho ocurrió antes que el cirujano Bell hubiese dado á conocer los dos casos citados arriba.

Si bien la administración de algodón en tales casos puede ser fructuosa, como se ha demostrado arriba, no debería perderse de vista de que al dar esta forma de celulosa purificada, estamos realmente introduciendo otro cuerpo extraño. Por supuesto, el algodón ha de ser aséptico; pero existe siempre el peligro de que forme un centro para una masa fecal que el recto puede que no pase, y en este caso endurecería cada vez más hasta formar una verdadera obstrucción en el intestino. Este peligro en parte se evita administrando aceite de ricino, pero, como es sabido, este aceite no siempre vacía todo el tubo intestinal, y hay la posibilidad de que se quede algún algodón, que más tarde causará no poca dificultad. — ED.

AMASAMIENTO PARA EL TRATAMIENTO DE GRANOS. — Este procedimiento es el mejor para el tratamiento del acné facial en los jóvenes, especialmente el que se origina de desarreglos en las funciones de la piel acompañados de secreción excesiva de material grasoso. El objeto del amasamiento es estimular las funciones perezosas de la piel aumentando la circulación de la sangre, mejorando el tono de los tejidos y estimulando la descarga de las glándulas cebáceas que son la causa del desarreglo. Sabemos que en el primer período del grano es este una masa pequeña llamada puntos negros ó espinillas, y que consisten en una acumulación de secreciones en una de las glándulas sebáceas dichas. Si se deja que la espinilla se quede en la piel, los tejidos de su alrededor empiezan á inflamarse de cuyas resultas sale el grano. En el primer tiempo de su aparición la espinilla es fácil de sacar con sólo apretando la piel de alrededor. La mejor manera de impedir que salgan las espinillas, y por consiguiente los granos ó diviesos, es aplicar el amasamiento á la cara todas las noches después de calentar las manos sumergiéndolas en agua muy caliente y lubricándolas con vaselina esterilizada.

Pospepon (aludido en el *Répertoire de Thérapeutique*, pág. 214, oct. de 1905), describe la mejor manera de aplicar amasamiento al semblante para aquel objeto. Primeramente se amasará la frente desde la línea del medio hacia las sienes, después las mejillas en el mismo sentido, siguiendo su curvatura y paralelamente á la quijada inferior; sucesivamente el arranque y puente de la naríz, de arriba abajo y hacia fuera, el labio superior desde la línea del medio hacia las esquinas, y finalmente la barba de arriba abajo siguiendo sus propias curvas.

UNTURAS DE MERCURIO CON BASE DE JABON. — Una parte repugnante del tratamiento de unturas tratándose de una afección sifilítica y en aquellos casos en que el enfermo no puede tomar más mercurio en el estómago, es la naturaleza grasienta de los ungüentos que se usan de ordinario. El enfermo siente una repugnancia natural por el ungüento gris-obscuro con el cual se unta en días alternados y le ensucia la ropa interior. Para obviar esta dificultad, el médico francés Ivon ha sustituido la manteca por jabón que generalmente se emplea en preparar la untura. La mejor combinación que pudo hacer fué una masa consistente en 10 partes de mercurio y 1,000 partes de jabón negro que deberá ser tan neutro como posible. Todo exceso de álcali que pudiera contener se elimina al contacto con el aire mientras se prepara el ungüento. El jabón se mezcla bien con el mercurio y puede guardarse indefinidamente sin despedir ningún olor. La gran ventaja de esta preparación y que permite emplearla en tiempo caliente, es que no se resblandece bajo la acción del sol. No irrita en lo más mínimo la piel y puede lavarse con sólo agua ordinaria.

PREPARACION DE LAPICES DE IODOFORMO. — Uno de los mejores medios para emplear el cloroformo en el tratamiento de ciertas clases de fístulas, es en la forma de lápices, cuya preparación exige mucho cuidado. El farmacéutico que se tome el trabajo necesario se granjeará el aprecio del médico. Un colaborador del *Répertoire Thérapeutique* (1905, pág. 219), recomienda el siguiente procedimiento: Disuélvanse 15 grm. de gelatina pura en 50 grm. de agua, y 7.5 grm. de glicerina al baño-maría. Evapórese hasta que la mezcla mida 54 grm.; añádense 27 grm. de iodoformo en polvo fino; sacúdese la mezcla para que se incorpore bien el iodoformo y en este estado viértase en un molde ligeramente calentado; inmediatamente se enfriará ésta en agua helada. Importa que esto se haga sin pérdida de tiempo, á fin de evitar el depósito de partículas de iodoformo. Los lápices que resultan se guardan en un lugar seco hasta perder dos terceras partes de su peso. En este estado son blandos y flexibles. Se puede disminuir el olor del iodoformo añadiendo café quemado en polvo fino.

UNGÜENTO INSIPIDO DE IODOFORMO. Oppler ha dado una fórmula de un ungüento de iodoformo sin olor como sigue:

Lanolina	20.	partes
Iodoformo	2.5	»
Café tostado en polvo	1.25	»
Manteca de puerco	2.05	»

PROBLEMAS SOBRE RECETAS

OPINIONES VARIAS

En la asamblea de la Asociación Farmacéutica Americana llevada á cabo en Atlantic City, el miembro de la misma, Wm. F. Kaemmerer, de Columbus (Ohio), presentó para discutirse copias de 20 recetas tomadas de sus colecciones, conteniendo cada una de ellas algún punto de interés. Las recetas se escribieron con tiza sobre papel azul de polvos de seidlitz, y expusiéronse á la vista de los presentes, prácticos dispensadores interesados en esta rama.

Para que este asunto reuniera todo el interés que se merece, se sometieron copias de las citadas recetas á un número de farmacéuticos de diferentes partes del país á fin de que hicieran los consiguientes comentarios, los cuales se hallarán al pié de cada receta con el nombre del autor.

Agradecemos á esos caballeros la molestia que se han tomado, no obstante ser tantas sus ocupaciones, y esperamos que sus opiniones llevarán algún peso, y que nuestros lectores de fuera podrán apreciarlas, no obstante de existir diferencias entre esas mismas opiniones autorizadas.

Los comentarios que siguen á las recetas son del mismo señor Kaemmerer, como también lo es la siguiente introducción:

«Se presentan las siguientes recetas con la esperanza de que se dilucidarán puntos que puedan servir de guía á los demás, caso de que fueran llamados á poner recetas de una naturaleza semejante. No se ha intentado clasificarlas, sino que se dan en el mismo orden en que fueron recibidas en el establecimiento. En algunas de estas recetas se observarán puntos nuevos. Llamaré la atención á dos de ellas sobre cosas que generalmente se pasan por alto. En otras recetas no tengo la seguridad de haber hecho lo más acertado. Tómese como ejemplo la receta No 1.

I

Sulfato ferroso....................	5 granos
Magnesia	10 granos
Agua de menta piperita...	11 dr. fl.
Espíritu de nuez moscada..........	1 dr. fl.

» Mézclese. Hágase una pinta de tal dosis.

» INSTRUCCIONES: — Una cucharadita dos veces al día.

» Esta receta era del extranjero y al ponerla tuve que ejercer mi propio criterio. Llegué á la conclusión que el autor se había olvidado escribir la palabra «sulfato» antes de la palabra «magnesia,» y parece que así sería, porque la receta se repitió varias veces sin que se hiciera queja alguna. También es interesante por la manera inusitada como estaba escrita, al decir «hagase una pinta de tal dosis.»

El Sr. HYNSON: No teniendo de antemano experiencia con las recetas de ese médico, hubiese empleado óxido magnésico. Debería hacerse una solución de la sal de hierro en cosa de la mitad del agua de la menta piperita, vertiéndola en un frasco apropiado. Mójese el mortero con la solución de hierro y añadese espíritu de nuez moscada. Al dispensarse se pondrá en la rotulata la recomendación de «sacúdase bien.» Caso de haberse puesto un número de recetas semejantes del mismo médico, y habiendo prescrito en ocasiones anteriores sulfato magnésico, sólo entonces estaría justificado el acto del Dr. Kaemmerer.

El Sr. WILBERT: Este es un ejemplo para el farmacéutico llamar la atención á los males que podrían resultar de una medicinación propia. Caso de que sus observaciones fuesen desatendidas, es su deber preparar la fórmula como está prescrita. La dispensación de sulfato magnésico en lugar de magnesia, sin más explicaciones, sería considerado por muchos de nuestra profesión puramente como una contra-prescripción.

El Sr. DUNNING: En esta receta opino que la magnesia (ligeramente calcinada) debería de haberse empleado, á menos de que el dispensador no tuviese ocasión de asesorarse de sus parroquianos que cuando primeramente se puso la receta, se recibió una solución y no una mezcla.

El Sr. NIXON: Esta receta no es cosa nueva en nuestro establecimiento: lo que se quiere siempre es el sulfato de magnesia, y esto mismo debió ser en el caso que se somete.

El Sr. HANKEY: No me creería justificado emplear en esta receta el sulfato de magnesia. Me imagino que el autor tenía en vista que se administrase el hierro en la forma de un hidróxido flojo en lugar del sulfato astringente como habría de resultar si en su lugar se emplease el sulfato magnésico. Por consiguiente hubiese hecho el compuesto según lo escrito, empleando la magnesia oficinal — á saber, *magnesii oxidum.*

El Sr. SIMMS: Opino que en la receta de que se trata el autor tenía en vista el óxido magnésico y no el sulfato magnésico.

El Sr. BERINGER: En mi opinión, la intención del médico que redactó la receta es aparente: magnesia (óxido magnésico) está llanamente escrito, y debería haberse dispensado. Si bien se prescriben con frecuencia mezclas conteniendo sulfato ferroso y sulfato magnésico, la cantidad del último es generalmente de mas de 10 granos. Por otra parte, se receta con frecuencia la *magnesia,* habiendo yo visto un número de recetas semejantes, pidiéndola en combinación con el sulfato ferroso.

El Sr. CLIFFE: El sulfato ferroso y el sulfato de magnesia se emplean de ordinario en solución como ferruginoso salino, y, faltando la necesaria instrucción del autor de la receta, supondríamos que lo que tenía en vista era el sulfato de magnesia, puesto que la preparación resultante sería ciertamente más eficaz terapéuticamente que el insoluble óxido férrico que se formaría rápidamente según la prescripción escrita.

El Sr. RAPELYE: Procediendo del extranjero la receta de que se trata, y siendo imposible pedir explicaciones al autor, la manera de dispensarla depende del buen criterio del dispensador. Interpretándola literalmente debió haber usado óxido magnésico; pero al dispensarla fundóse en que se había omitido el sulfato, y dispensó la mezcla del sulfato ferroso y sulfato magnésico — que es lo que se usa comunmente — y quizás en esto ejerció buen sentido.

El Sr. SCOVILLE: Probabl...... era el sulfato magnesico, que es l[illegible] Kaemmerer.

El Sr. MCELHENIE: No opino q[illegible] que hacer en la manera como el Sr. Kaem[illegible] la receta; pero tengo mis dudas de si el médico e[illegible] jero quiso que se hiciera una pinta [illegible] que se daban — *i. e.*, sobre diez veces la cantidad. De otra manera la dosis sería insignificante.

II

Ungüento de bromo, 10 por ciento...... 1 onza

Úsese según instrucciones.

No se expresa la base que ha de emplearse. A fin de hacer un ungüento de plomo que sea satisfactorio, es necesario hacer una solución de bromo en agua con la ayuda de algún bromuro de potasa, á guisa de lo que hacemos con el iodo al preparar un ungüento de iodo, en el que empleamos ioduro de potasa y agua para disolver el iodo; pero en el caso del bromo fué necesario usar mucha mayor cantidad de agua para disolver el bromo. Preparé el ungüento en cuestión de la siguiente manera: En un pequeño frasco pesé 150 granos de agua, 100 granos de bromuro de potasio y 50 granos de bromo. Los sacudí bien hasta que el bromo y el bromuro de potasio quedaron disueltos. Luego puse doscientos granos de lanolina anidrosa en un mortero, añadiendo gradualmente la solución de bromo y agitando constantemente, dándome por resultado un ungüento hermoso, algo cremoso y sin gases de bromo.

El Sr. HYNSON: A falta de experiencia con ungüentos de bromo y sin conocer la base que se desea, creo que el procedimiento puesto en práctica por el Sr. Kaemmerer habría de dar resultados muy satisfactorios. Conviene, por supuesto, impedir el escape del bromo, lo que parece haber realizado el dispensador. Pudieran quizás llevarse á cabo algunas experiencias provechosas con relación á las cantidades de bromuro de potasa y agua necesarios.

El Sr. BERRINGER: La aplicación externa del bromo en la forma de aceites brominatados y ungüentos, ha sido recomendada, y ahora hace algunos años que se prescribía comunmente un ungüento de bromo con una base de petrolatum para el envenenamiento del toxicondendrón Yo no hubiese hecho una solución del bromo, sino dispensado un ungüento preparado frotando el bromo y el petrolatum, para tener el bromo en un estado tan libre como posible y en una forma en que pueda liberarse con facilidad al aplicarse.

El Sr. DUNNING: A menos de que uno no esté familiarizado con una receta de esta clase, lo mejor sería hacer experiencias con ella. Por vía de ensayo rodeé un tablero de cristal para ungüentos, con cuatro platos de porcelana que contenían amoníaco líquido, procediendo luego á hacer los ungüentos, frotando una cantidad pesada de bromo directamente con la base, empleando vaselina, lanolina y manteca de cerdo. También hice tres lotes con vaselina, lanolina y manteca de cerdo respectivamente habiendo mezclado el bromo con agua y bromuro de potasa en esta proporción, á saber: bromo, 48 granos; bromuro de potasa, 48 granos; agua, 60 mínimos. Cualquiera de estos seis ungüentos debería dar satisfacción. El bromo y manteca de puerco, directamente era el mejor, aunque la solución de bromo con bromuro y agua facilita más el trabajo.

El Sr. SIMMS: Con motivo de la insolubilidad del bromo en manteca de cerdo ó petrolatum, me negaría á componer la receta citada, á menos de que el médico me permitiese emplear suficiente bromuro de potasa y agua para poder hacer un ungüento perfecto.

El Sr. CLIFFE: Lo prepararíamos de la misma manera que un ungüento de iodo de igual fuerza, pero empleando solamente un bromuro en lugar de un ioduro para efectuar la solución. La mejor base de un ungüento debería ser la lanolina con motivo de la perfecta miscibilidad con las soluciones acuosas.

El Sr. RAPELYE: Yo disputaría el empleo de lanolina á menos de que el objeto del autor de la receta no fuese la absorción del bromo. La mezcla directa del bromo y ungüento simple fuera mejor, aunque el dispensador tenía un buen precedente para proceder de la manera como lo hizo.

El Sr. MCELHENIE: El modo como procedió el Sr. Kaemmerer fué para mí de lo más acertado. No creo que pudiera mejorarse.

El Sr. NIXON: Yo hubiese dispensado la receta como lo hizo el Sr. Kaemmerer Si el bromo se incorpora directamente con una base de ungüento, se deshará en gases. La lanolina anhidrosa es la única base que retendrá la cantidad necesaria de solución acuosa.

III

Sulfuro de calcio.................. 15 granos

Háganse 60 píldoras.

He averiguado que la glucosa es el mejor excipiente para hacer píldoras de sulfuro de calcio. Las píldoras no se desintegran y son tan pequeñas como las producidas por diferentes establecimientos de farmacia. No es necesario añadir nada para dar el tamaño á las píldoras.

El Sr. SIMMS: Yo añadiría 20 granos de azúcar de leche al sulfuro de calcio, empleando como excipiente mucílago o glicerina de tragacanto. Opino que una píldora con capa de gelatina sería aceptable á la mayoría de los médicos

El Sr. HYNSON: Pienso que los médicos prefieren generalmente tales substancias como sulfuro de calcio, valeratos, sumbul, asafétida, etc., dispensadas en la forma de píldoras con capa. Cuando las recetan en forma de píldora, es indudable que el excipiente que debería usarse es la glucosa aunque buena miel es tan apropiada para píldoras prietas.

El Sr. BERINGER: Tales píldoras deberían cubrirse con una solución etérea de tolú para resguardarlas de la acción del aire.

El Sr. WILBERT: Ha habido siempre y probablemente habrá discrepancia en las opiniones con respecto al excipiente más generalmente aceptable: algunos farmacéutas á lo menos, y yo me cuento entre ellos, prefieren gliceritos de tragacanto con motivo de sus cualidades higroscópicas.

El Sr. CLIFFE: Haría píldoras de $\frac{1}{4}$ grano con una mezcla de azúcar de caña 10 por ciento; acacia 5 por ciento, y azúcar de leche 85 por ciento, empleando jarabe como excipiente.

El Sr. SCOVILLE: Añadiría un peso igual de azúcar de leche y masa con glucosa.

El Sr. DUNNING: Me parece que hubiese sido acertado haber añadido un peso igual de azúcar de leche.

El Sr. NIXON: Considero un error dispensar píldoras que pesen menos de 1 grano. Yo añadiría 15 granos de altea pulverizada con cuya y la necesaria glucosa se formaría una píldora de un tamaño presentable.

NOTAS TERAPEUTICAS

VENDAJE PARA VENAS VARICOSAS

Un vendaje de cola de cinc puede hacerse de gelatina, glicerina, óxido de cinc y agua calentado al baño-maría, aplicándolo así á la piel desnuda con una brocha de pintor Luego se aplica un vendaje de gasa, muy por igual, pero no demasiado apretado. Este se pinta con cola de cinc, y por el exterior se le aplica un nuevo vendaje. El vendaje dispuesto de esta manera puede llevarse de cinco á ocho semanas sin cambiar. El Dr. H. Keogh, dice en el *Northwestern Lancet*, que docenas de sus pacientes que estaban sujetos á molestias por efecto de las venas varicosas se han sentido confortados con este vendaje.—*Journal American Medical Association.*

ASMA

Lo siguiente es casi un específico para el alivio y curación final del asma:

℞	Tintura de Gelsemio	℥j
	Tintura de lobelina	℥j
	Bromuro de potasio	℥ss

M Sig.: Dosis, veinte gotas en agua, cada tres horas. — Barnett, *The Medical Summary.*

PARA DERMATITIS VENENATA DEL TOXICODENDRO

℞	Sodii hyposulphitis	℥j
	Glicerini	℥ss
	Aquæ, c. s. añádese	℥viij

M. Sig.: Aplíquese constantemente. — *Medical News.*

OPINION SOBRE LAS INSOLACIONES

Dunkin asevera que la insolación es causada por los rayos químicos y no por los rayos calientes, como generalmente se cree. Su aserto está basado en el hecho de que nadie es víctima de insolación por efecto de exposición á un origen oscuro de calor y cuando faltan los rayos químicos. Los rayos actínicos son los peligrosos. Pasan á través de cualquier cosa, excepto un filtro de color interpuesto. Es, pues, necesario á fin de poder evitar los ataques de insolación, tratar el cuerpo como el fotógrafo trata sus placas, y rodearlo de amarillo ó rojo. Menciona el caso de un oficial del ejército egipcio, que había sufrido de varios ataques de insolación, y evitó nuevas dificultades de esta naturaleza durante cinco años de exposición, forrando el yelmo y casaca de amarillo. — *Modern Medicine.*

ULCERAS EN LAS PIERNAS

Wörner recomienda la aplicación de un vendaje ligero cubierto con una capa de gelatina, consistente en tragacanto, 0.5; gelatina, 10.0; glicerina, 5.0; ácido bórico, 5.0; borato sódico, 5.0; y agua c. s. 1000, y esto se cubre á su vez por otro vendaje tenue para el tratamiento de úlceras de la pierna. — *Lancet-Clínica.*

TRATAMIENTO RACIONAL PARA EL MAL DE OIDO

Sobre este asunto Frank W. Miller se expresa así: «Para tratar inteligentemente el mal de oído, convendrá servirse del espéculum. En las manifestaciones flojas y congestivas, las aplicaciones locales resultarán á menudo beneficiosas, pero si aquellas duraren más de doce horas, debería practicarse la paracentesis. La paracentesis temprana, una vez que se practica como corresponde, es un procedimiento inofensivo del que obtiene el mayor beneficio el enfermo, corriendo el mínimo de riesgo y sufrimiento. Se anticipa á la naturaleza, alivia el dolor y reduce la posibilidad de complicaciones mastoides é intracraniales. Como preliminar á la operación, el médico rinde aséptico el canal exterior con una solución de bicloruro de 1 á 10,000, valiéndose para ello de una jeringuilla, y secando después con algunas gotas de alcohol. Puede evitarse que el dolor acompañe el procedimiento, aplicando primeramente sobre la línea de la incisión una mezcla de partes iguales de mentol, fenol y cocaína, hecho siruposo con alcohol.—*Southern California Practitioner.*

TRATAMIENTO DE LOS CALLOS (BROCQ.)

Por la noche se ablandará el callo cubriéndolo con una pieza de flanela saturada con espíritu de vino y con una capa de jabón; el callo se raspa después con una cucharita ó cuchillo. En los ocho días sucesivos se aplica una capa del siguiente colodión:

℞	Extracto alcohólico de cannabis indica	gr.	v
	Acido salicílico	»	j
	Alcohol (90 por ciento)	»	j
	Eter	»	ij
	Colodión flexible	»	v

M. f. s. a.

Al octavo día, después de bañarse el pié por bastante tiempo con agua caliente, se raspará con una cucharita ó cuchillo la masa de colodión, y al mismo tiempo la mayor parte del callo. Si fuese necesario se repetirá el tratamiento.

Un remedio común y á menudo eficaz, es el colocar sobre el callo un cachito redondo de limón, una ó varias noches sucesivas. También se emplea colodión cantaridal ó ungüento salicílico. Tratándose de cáusticos, deberían usarse con suma cautela. Rodéese el callo doloroso con un anillo de lana ó un parche para callos. Cuando el callo se halla entre los dedos manténganse éstos separados con una muñequita de tela suave, y espolvoréese el callo con polvo de tanino, alumbre ú óxido de cinc.

Algunos autores recomiendan: (1) Se humedece el callo con una solución concentrada de ácido salicílico en alcohol; (2) cúbrese con ácido salicílico en polvo, y se hace una cubierta con una pequeña cantidad de algodón de rellenar; cada cuatro ó cinco días se renueva el apósito, y si hubiese inflamación se suspenderá el tratamiento. Al octavo día sácase el callo remojándolo. —*Medical News.*

INCOMPATIBILIDAD DEL CLORAL CON LA EXALGINA Y EL PIRAMIDON

Los farmacéuticos están familiarizados con las propiedades licuantes de las mezclas de cloral con alcanfor, salol, antipirina y otras substancias de esta clase. Con todo, parece que no se había advertido que el mismo proceso licuante tiene efecto cuando el cloral
se pone en contacto con exalg
Esto es un descubrimiento re
Laval (*Bulletin Commercial*, julio
y otro de estos remedios el cloral
sos, sin color ni transparentes; p
han anunciado aun si estos pro
nuevos compuestos ó sólo mezcl
la atención á la incompatibilidad
naftol y varios fenoles.

NOTAS FARMACEUTICAS

PASTILLAS DE PARAFINA PERFUMADAS

La última novedad parisiense. Un diseminador de perfume universal. Por doquiera se frota brota el perfume.

Mata la polilla, perfuma el guardaropa. Se restriega por la ropa y el pañuelo.

Parafina	1 onza
Petrolatum blanco	2 onzas
Heliotropina	10 granos
Aceite de bergamota	5 gotas
Aceite de espliego	5 »
Aceite de clavos	2 »

Derrítanse las dos primeras substancias.

PARA CALMAR EL DOLOR DE LAS PAROTIDAS

A menudo no se sabe lo que hacer para calmar el dolor que acompaña la hinchazón de las parótidas. La afección no es peligrosa y no exige tratamiento heróico; pero precisa no emplear anodinos en los niños afectados. El guayacol es en sí un eficaz é inofensivo remedio, el cual, si aplicado externamente á la hinchazón, noche y mañana, cubriéndolo con un tejido de goma (gutta percha) y una ligera venda de gasa, alivia el dolor rápidamente y reduce la hinchazón. Este tratamiento es muy sencillo, y la mejor manera de aplicar el guayacol en esta afección es en la siguiente mezcla:

Guayacol	1 grm.
Petrolatum	10 »
Lanolina	10 »

Los farmacéuticos pueden recomendar esta aplicación á los médicos amigos.

TABLETA EFERVESCENTE

La siguiente fórmula habrá de hallarse muy aceptable para una tableta no medicinada:

Acido cítrico	480 granos
Bicarbonato de sosa	304 »
Azucar pulverizado	276 »
Agua	bastante

Redúzcase á polvo el ácido cítrico y deséquese bien, mezclándolo después con 96 granos de azúcar, luego se humedece con agua, se pasa por un tamiz y vuélvese á desecar bien. Mézclese el bicarbonato y el resto del azúcar, granúlese y séquese; mézclense los dos polvos y háganse las tabletas.

POLVOS DE VIOLETA AFELPADA

Raíz de lirio	2 oz.
Almidón de maíz	12 oz.
Licopodio	1 oz.
Aceite de flores de azaar	½ dr.
Aceite de bergamota	½ dr.
Aceite de flores de espliego	½ dr.
Aceite de clavos	15 gotas
Aceite de canela	15 »

Mézclense todos los polvos y todos los aceites, y luego, añádense gradualmente los últimos á los primeros.

Linimentos Medicinales

LINIMENTO FEBRIFUGO.—Esencia de trementina, 120 gramos; láudano de Rousseau, 4. H. s. a.
Dos cucharadas para fricciones sobre el raquis por mañana y noche. - *Bellencontre.*

LINIMENTO FORTIFICANTE.—(a) Tintura de quina, 15 gramos; alcohol alcanforado, 15; bálsamo de Fioraventi, 15; agua carmelitana, 30; tintura etérea de digital, 60. Mézclense.
Se emplea con buen éxito en los casos de inercia muscular y de los esfínteres, en especial de la vejiga con incontinencia de orina.

(b) Bálsamo de Fioraventi, 15 gramos; tintura de quina, 15; alcohol, 15; aguardiente alcanforado, 15; agua carmelitana, 30; tintura etérea de digital, 60. Disuélvanse. — *Double.*

LINIMENTO FOSFORADO. — (a) Aceite animal de Dippel, 10 gramos; fósforo, 0 30. Disuélvase.
Contra las parálisis parciales, á la dosis de 1 gramo en dos ó tres fricciones diarias. — *Gerdeesen.*

(b) Aceite de almendras, 100 gramos; nafta, 25; fósforo, 0.20.
Para dar fricciones por la noche sobre la frente, en las parálisis musculares del ojo. — *Tavignot.*

(c) Aceite fosforado, 75 gramos; aceite de nafta, 25. Mézclese.
En las parálisis de los músculos de los ojos, en fricciones sobre la frente. — *F. V. M. F.*

LINIMENTO FUNDENTE. — Hiel de vaca, 12 gramos; extracto de cicuta, 4; jabón de sosa, 8; aceite de olivas, 30.
Cuatro fricciones diarias contra los tumores hipertróficos de las glándulas mamarias. — *Bonarden.*

LINIMENTO HIDROIODADO. — Jabón de sebo, 40 partes; alcohol concentrado, 430. Disuélvase el jabón raspado en el alcohol, fíltrese y añádase: ioduro potásico, 30 partes; esencia de cidra, 3. H. s. a. — *F. Helv.*
También se denomina *bálsamo de Opodeldoch iodurado.*

LINIMENTO HIDROSULFURADO. — Jabón blanco, 500 gramos; aceite de adormideras, 1.000; súlfuro de potasio seco y pulverizado, 96. Mézclense. — *Jadelot.*

LINIMENTO DE HIPNONA. — Hipnona, 5 gramos; aceite de almendras, 10. — *Vigier.*

LINIMENTO HUNGARO. — Alcanfor pulverizado, 40 gramos; pimienta pulverizada, 20; mostaza pulverizada, 40; ajo machacado, 20; cantáridas pulverizadas, 10. Digiérase por veinticuatro horas en vinagre, 86 gramos; alcohol rectificado, 160.
Se usa en fricciones en el colera.

LINIMENTO HUNGARO CONTRA EL COLERA. — Alcanfor pulverizado, 40 gramos; pimienta en polvo, 20; harina de mostaza, 40; ajo machacado, 20; cantáridas en polvo, 10. Se hace digerir por veinticuatro horas en vinagre, 85 gramos; alcohol rectificado, 100.
Para fricciones á todo el cuerpo.

LINIMENTO DE ICTIOL.—Ictiol, 50 gramos; manteca, 35; aceite de almendras, 15. Mézclese.
En las darmatosis. — *F. V. M. F.*

NOTAS COMERCIALES

El periodo de agotamiento. — En el tratamiento de alcoholismo y dipsomania se llama al médico en el período de agotamiento ó postración, existiendo entonces una perturbación general de casi todas las funciones. La neurosis, congestión cerebral, aceleramiento cardíaco, trastorno gástrico y mesentérico, náusea, intolerancia del alimento, irritación intensa, insomnio y una variedad sin fin de secuelas mórbidas exigen pronta atención. Se hallará que la antikamnia en combinación con codeina ejerce una acción rápida y satisfactoria aliviando toda la retahila de síntomas tan aflictivos y usualmente tan pertinaces que desafían toda intervención terapéutica ordinaria. El mejor método consiste en administrar una tableta de Antikamnia y Codeina (antikamnia, gr. 4¾, codeina gr. ¼), cada quince minutos á media hora, hasta haber tomado tres; entonces se distanciará el intervalo á una y media hasta dos horas, según sea la urgencia de los síntomas. Bajo este tratamiento la circulación se modificará, cesarán los dolores cardíacos, el temblor, la ansiedad y mórbida vigilancia se trocarán en un sueño reposado, sosegado y conciliador. También desaparecerán la náusea y vómitos, juntamente con las toses irritantes que con tanta frecuencia caracterizan estos casos. Los resultados tan completos que se obtienen con las Tabletas de Antikamnia y Codeina, débense en buena parte al hecho de que los fabricantes refinan y purifican toda la codeina que entra en estas tabletas, y por este medio se impide el estreñimiento, la depresión de ánimo y el hábito que se contrae frecuentemente con la administración de preparaciones que contienen codeina comercial ordinaria.

Producto alimenticio. — Acertada combinacion quimico-agricola. — Está admitido en general que la enseñanza agrícola y las investigaciones llevadas á cabo en este ramo, han dado muy buenos frutos en combinación con los trabajos de las varias estaciones experimentales creadas por el Gobierno. De todos los Estados de la Unión, el de Wisconsin considérase uno de los más adelantados en la cuestión de popularizar la enseñanza agrícola, contando con una de las estaciones citadas, con un personal muy activo, y con varias escuelas llamadas á resolver prácticamente los más arduos problemas agrícolas. La naturaleza del suelo del Estado y los grandes pastos de que dispone, son los más apropiados seguramente para hacer toda clase de experiencias, y esto está demostrado por los trabajos fructuosos llevados á cabo con las materias primas por los químicos fabricantes, transformándolas en productos de consumo universal, entre ellos el de la leche, trigo y malta de cebada combinadas, que ha despertado altísimo interés no tan sólo entre los químicos de este país, sino que también entre los del extranjero. Este producto ya tiene un consumo universal, y nos referimos á la Leche Malteada de Horlick, fabricada en Racine, Estado de Wisconsin. Es indudable que las ventajas de ese suelo privilegiado, de pastos ricos y abundantes, llamaría la atención de esos fabricantes y dedicáronse con ahinco á su explotación, produciendo un alimento que no sólo es ideal para los niños, sino que para las personas crecidas, y cuya bondad se debe á la excelencia de las primeras materias, como también á los procesos empleados y vigilados con escrupulosidad.

Damos aquí cabida al método adoptado en la preparación de la Leche Malteada de Horlick:

Constituyentes sólidos de leche pura y rica de vacas pasteurizada	50.00
Trigo, rico en gluten	26.25
Malta de cebada	23.00
Bicarb. de sosa y bicarb. de potasa	0.75

Con una acertada manipulación el trigo y la malta, en unión con el agua, se someten al calor por cuyo medio el almidón se convierte en dextrina y dextrosa, y la mezcla se licúa, con excepción de las cáscaras. A esto sigue una compresión gradual, y la coladura, dando por resultado un líquido claro que pasa luego á unos tachos de vacío. Añádese una cantidad de leche pura, que se toma de las haciendas vecinas sometidas á inspección oficial, cuya leche se hace pasar por caños de platino. Luego se practica un nuevo tratamiento que impide que la leche se coagule, y el procedimiento termina con la evaporación, que da por resultado la leche malteada en polvo. Es obvio que se ejerce la mayor vigilancia sobre los constituyentes, en comprobación de lo cual hemos de citar el hecho, que nos consta, de que los Sres. Horlick no se fían de la malta comercial del mercado, sino que maltean la cebada en su fábrica. La presencia de los bicarbonatos en la fórmula, es, por supuesto, para impedir la acidez, y en relación con una controversia reciente por una parte de la facultad médica de que todos los alimentos específicos tienden á iniciar el escorbuto con motivo de la disminución de la acción vitalizante de los constituyentes durante la fabricación, puede señalarse que el carbonato potásico es un preventivo del escorbuto, y que la leche que se emplea es pasteurizada (no esterilizada), y por consiguiente no ha pasado por el proceso de la «desvitalización.»

Que el producto que nos ocupa merece la confianza de la profesión médica, está establecido sin ningún género de duda por la correspondencia especial que poseen los fabricantes. La Leche Malteada de Horlick, es excelente para los niños y los inválidos y para las personas en general; vigoriza la musculatura y nutre el cerebro, ayuda las digestiones difíciles. Beneficia en las fiebres tifoideas y otros muchos estados febriles en los cuales se necesita un régimen alimenticio de esta clase.

No se altera en los países cálidos, pues la importa la India, Birmania, Estados del Oriente, como también la Argentina, el Brasil y otros países de Sud-América. Su consumo acrecienta diariamente.

Las Lamparas mas nuevas. — La moderna industria en estos pasados tiempos ha mejorado mucho los medios de iluminación, presentando modificaciones sorprendentes de las lámparas de gas y las eléctricas (*Pharm. Centralhalle*, julio 27, pág. 603). Una nueva lámpara eléctrica que lleva el nombre de Auer-Os-Lamp, está dispuesta con un hilo de osmio, que á fuerza de experimentos se ha llegado á preparar de tal modo que llena ahora todos los requisitos para producir una luz incandescente. Los ensayos hechos anteriormente con el mismo material habían fracasado por no poseer éste suficiente resistencia y flexibilidad. El nuevo hilo de osmio crudo es poroso y contiene carbono; se somete á un tratamiento de vapor para que adquiera las propiedades necesarias. Después de llevar á cabo varias investigaciones, se cree que existe bastante osmio para poder fabricar estas lámparas en mayor escala.

La Lámpara Zirconium no se ha popularizado mucho todavía. Después que las primeras experiencias llevadas á cabo en 1903 demostraron que respondía á las esperanzas que se habían formado, se obtuvo privilegio de invención para la Lámpara Tantalum, de que son propietarios Siemens & Halske. El hilo para la producción de luz se fabrica ahora de material puro. La luz que da esta lámpara es muy agradable, de color blanco, siendo la duración de estas lámparas de 800 á 1,000 horas. Con un kilogramo de tántalo pueden prepararse cuarenta y cinco mil lámparas de esta clase. Con el consumo que se hace de este material, el mercado está abastecido. La Lámpara Magnetite es de arco, en el cual el carbón positivo está reemplazado por una placa de cobre para evitar su rápida destrucción con el gran calor que desarrolla. El carbón negativo es el único que se consume, y se prepara de una mixtura especial de hierro magnético. Se quema tan lentamente, que la lámpara dura tanto como las peras de la luz incandescente.

AMERICAN DRUGGIST

and PHARMACEUTICAL RECORD

NUEVA YORK Y CHICAGO: 12 DE FEBRERO DE 1906

«The American Druggist» es un periódico bimensual del que se publica cada mes un suplemento español con anuncios en el mismo idioma

AMERICAN DRUGGIST PUBLISHING COMPANY

62-68 WEST BROADWAY, NEW YORK, U. S. A.

Dirección cablegráfica «Amdruggist, New York.» Clave A B C

A. R. ELLIOTT, *Presidente*

CASWELL A. MAYO, Ph. G. .... *Director*

THOMAS J. KEENAN, Lic. en Farm., *Director Asociado*

PRECIOS DE SUSCRIPCION

Pago adelantado, Estados Unidos, Canadá, México, Cuba, Puerto Rico, Hawaii y las Filipinas .. ..(oro americano) $1.50

Otros países (franco de porte).................. » » $3.00

Las suscripciones pueden empezar en cualquier tiempo.

«THE AMERICAN DRUGGIST AND PHARMACEUTICAL RECORD» sale el segundo y cuarto lunes de cada mes. Todo cambio de anuncios debe ser recibido diez días antes de la fecha de salida.

Remesas deben hacerse con libranzas sobre Nueva York, giros postales internacionales ó por expreso ó correo en carta certificada. Toda correspondencia debe dirigirse á la AMERICAN DRUGGIST PUBLISHING Co., 62-68 West Broadway, New York, U. S. A.

DISPOSICION DE EFECTOS COMO RECLAMO

ESTE es un asunto de la mayor importancia, y uno de los puntos más prácticos del negocio, que, si manejado convenientemente, facilita muchísimo el trabajo y acrecienta el negocio.

1. — Empezando con los remedios llamados específicos, deberían clasificarse agrupando todos aquellos que curan una afección ú otra semejante, agregando, por supuesto, nuestro remedio para igual fin.

Algunos establecimientos de farmacia tienen reservada una sección especial para las preparaciones que se componen en la botica, esto es, las mantienen separadas de las que adquieren por compra. El autor cree que esto es un error, pues si las nuestras están juntas con las demás preparaciones de su clase, con frecuencia podeis coger vuestro propio remedio, y con sólo una palabra dirigida al cliente que ha hecho la demanda, lérselo; pero, si por lo contrario, vais á otro sección de la tienda, el parroquiano se forma que cogeis una cosa diferente de lo que el lo dicho me refiero más bien á los parro- le tránsito, puesto que los regulares, cuya merecemos, están dispuestos por lo regular á nosotros la elección de lo que piden ó que

2. — Para el arreglo de artículos varios, y de efectos que consignamos á las vitrinas, creo que el método que en general se sigue aquí es el más conveniente y debería por consiguiente adoptarse; el aparato de aguas carbónicas y gaseosas, caso de tener uno en el establecimiento, debería ocupar el primer puesto á un lado; la vitrina de los cigarros, boquillas, etc., debería ser la primera emplazada en el lado opuesto, y junto á ella los perfumes, preparaciones del tocador, jabones, cepillos, peines en otras vitrinas; como también artículos de papelería, dulces y otros efectos menos vendibles, los que generalmente se colocan en la parte más interior del mostrador. Esto último me parece una equivocación, pues yo opino, además de lo dicho arriba, que ciertos artículos convendría cambiar de cuando en cuando de vitrina para llamar la atención del parroquiano, con lo cual se venderían más efectos de aquellos que son menos vendibles. Esta aseveración queda comprobada: al colocar un día jabones de lavar ordinarios en una vitrina que regularmente contenía los perfumados, me dijo un cliente al advertirlo, «que ignoraba que nosotros vendiésemos aquella clase de jabones, que acostumbraba comprar en otra tienda.»

Por lo regular los parroquianos no van más adentro que el centro de la tienda; al entrar se dirigen al mostrador donde se expenden los artículos; hacen la compra y se marchan sin haber tenido ocasión de ver los efectos que encierran las vitrinas de más al interior, y es por esta razón que el cambio de efectos se impone (con excepción de los cigarros), si es que se intenta sacar partido de todo.

Algunos de nuestros establecimientos han descartado las grandes ampollas llenas de sales cristalizadas, y también botellas de tinturas de los estantes; pero yo considero esencial para conservar la apariencia llamativa del establecimiento tener esos vasos á la vista. Al trasladar á la parte del fondo los frascos de drogas, se menoscaba la intención y naturaleza del establecimiento, aun suponiendo que otros artículos tomen el puesto de los frascos trasladados.

Como complemento de estos apuntes, he de añadir que el establecimiento de farmacia que aspira al favor del público, ha de estar bien surtido de efectos y de substancias de clase superior. El servicio también habrá de ser de lo mejor, pues el público se paga de estas cosas y no hay para que regateárselas.

Crítica de la Farmacopea Española

Por un Español

Durante el período de revisión de la Farmacopea española, se presentó la cuestión de por qué no se consultaban los principales colegios. En Francia existe lo que podría llamarse un sistema formal de centralización de la opinión de todos los cuerpos farmacéuticos organizados, acerca de lo que ha de añadirse, omitirse ó modificarse. De fecha reciente el sistema en voga en los Estados Unidos se ha dado á conocer al público inglés y se consulta regularmente la Sociedad Farmacéutica. A tal pregunta, cual la de arriba expresada, la contestación oficial sería que la farmacia estaba bien representada en la Comisión Revisora. Pero los miembros farmacéuticos ocupan una posición excepcional — un farmacéutico regio y varios profesores de la facultad. Las opiniones que abrigaban acerca de los requisitos profesionales no están basadas en la práctica diaria de las preparaciones recetadas. Veamos ahora la crítica del libro.

UN ERROR DE CANTIDAD

En la página 463 de la séptima (nueva) edición la fórmula para píldoras de cinoglosa:

Azúcar en polvo	5	gramos
Extracto de opio en polvo	10	»
Goma arábiga en polvo	10	»
Azafrán en polvo	15	»
Castóreo en polvo	15	»
Recortes de raíz de cinoglosa en polvo	45	»

Mézclese y háganse 100 píldoras.

Cada gramo contiene 0.10 de extracto de opio.

Acción terapéutica: Calmante y antiespasmódica; se usan especialmente para toses espasmódicas.

Dosis: Diez á veinticinco centígramos.

El error está en el número de píldoras que podían hacerse de la masa; por un error tipográfico se puso 100 en lugar de 1,000.

LOS NUEVOS DISTINTIVOS

de la Farmacopea habían de ser naturalmente objeto de crítica en un país conservador. Una de esas novedades es la introducción de los algodones lanas medicinados. Las instrucciones son de disolver 50 gramos de ácido (borácico, fénico, etc., según el caso) en 2,000 gramos de alcohol, y mezclarlo con 20 gramos de glicerina; luego se impregnan 930 gramos de algodón hidrofílico en esta mixtura hasta que el líquido está distribuído por igual por la masa. Se seca al aire ó en un hornillo calentado á 20° ó 25° (centígrados).

¿Por qué 2 por ciento de glicerina? se pregunta; no ayuda á arreglar la mezcla en el algodón-lana, y por otra parte hace la disecación imposible. Un farmacéutico no puede poner en práctica el proceso en su laboratorio, á menos de que no tenga el aparato especial que emplean los fabricantes para fijar la mezcla en el algodón-lana, y por encima de esto para cardar el algodón. ¿No hubiese sido mejor dar un buen proceso para probar el valor antiséptico del artículo comercial?

LA FORMULA DE ACEITE ALCANFORADO

encuentra oposición por incompleta. La Farmacopea dice que ha de usarse para inyecciones hipodérmicas— ¿no debiera haberse añadido que en caso tal el aceite de olivas debería haberse lavado en alcohol y esterilizado?

LAS OMISIONES

en algunos casos se consideran deplorables. Los practicantes de Madrid y Barcelona se dan la mano para decir que el *syrupus ratanhiæ* y el *syrupus cydonii* se emplean aun de ordinario en puntos rurales y también en algunas plazas comerciales. El hecho de que tiene uno que acudir á la cuarta edición (1817) para hallar la fórmula para la preparación del jarabe de rosas blancas, demuestra simplemente—dice el crítico—que hace 90 años los revisores de la Farmacopea ejecutaban su trabajo con más cuidado que en el tiempo presente.

LA NUEVA TABLA PARA CALCULAR GOTAS

también es blanco de crítica. ¿Por qué (ya que el calculador de gotas empleado es el mismo) no corresponden las cifras españolas á las del Códex francés ó con Bourriez?

Aceite de Croton	Esencia de Menta Piperita	Amoniaco	Cloroformo	Creosota	Eter	
48	50	22	56	43	90	Bourriez
48	50	22	56	43	90	Códex
44	52	24	60	42	91	Farm. española

Mucho más útil que esa tabla de gotas (continúa diciendo el crítico) hubiese sido la tabla de solubilidades de los principales cuerpos. Esta última figuraba en la Farmacopea de 1884; debiera de haberse reinsertado y aumentado; en lugar de hacer lo cual queda suprimida del todo en la séptima edición.

LAS TABLAS

en efecto, son objeto de severos comentarios. El título «Corrección de la Temperatura del Aerómetro de Gay Lussac» se considera incorrecto, y sugiérese en su lugar «Correcciones de las Indicaciones del Alcoholómetro Centesimal de Gay Lussac á Temperaturas Distintas de + 15° (centígrados).

Según la nueva fórmula internacional para tinturas se necesita alcohol de 70°, pero en las tablas alcohólicas de la Farmacopea se dan 30°, 60°, 80°, 85° y 90° y se omite, sin poder explicarse, el 70°.

El proceso para obtener alcohol anhidroso se impugna por inexacto. La siguiente solución, se nos asegura, no realiza lo que la Farmacopea expresa — determinar la cantidad de hierro libre.

Iodo	4.535	gramos
Ioduro potásico	3.000	»
Agua destilada	90.000	»

Disuélvense el iodo y el ioduro en agua. Añádese más agua para hacer 100 centímetros cúbicos. Cada solución cúbica corresponde á 1 centígramo de hierro puro.

EL ARREGLO ALFABETICO

es también objeto de crítica no muy severa que digamos. ¿Por qué, se pregunta, mezclar las drogas crudas y las preparaciones farmacéutica[illegible]
cuando el Codex francés no tan [illegible]
separadas, sino que hasta lle[illegible]
ciones químicas de las galénica[illegible]

Pero lo singular es que es[illegible]
se abandonará en la próxima edicion
cés adoptándose un orden más senci[illegible]
ple forma alfabética que es c[illegible]
de la F. de los E. U.

PARA REMATAR

el crítico español dice: « Inyecciones hipodérmicas de cloruro de cocaína, deberían, dice la Farmacopea, esterilizarse cual las de bromuro de quinina, *i. e.*, el tubo que las contiene debería ponerse en un baño-maría hirviendo por cinco minutos. Pero yo, dice el crítico, tengo entendido que la solución de cocaína puede sólo esterilizarse por « tindalización » á 60° (centígrados), porque la proximidad al agua hirviendo descompone los alcaloides y les priva de sus propiedades anestésicas; pero atendida la ilustración de los señores de la Comisión yo debo ser un chillado. Con todo he de confesar con franqueza no haber leído nunca en libros ó revistas nada que pruebe la incertidumbre de la descomposición de la solución de cocaína á una temperatura de cerca de 100° (centígrados).

Asistencia Farmacéutica

Por D. H. Neil

Muchos son los servicios profesionales que pueden prestar los farmacéuticos, pero en ningún caso pueden rendir mayor servicio que en poner recetas cuyos resultados son tan trascendentales. Al recibir una receta es deber del farmacéutico leerla con suma atención y calcular las dosis de todos los ingredientes activos, luego ver si hay incompatibilidades y los medios de salvarlas si las hubiese.

Si el público en general pudiese estar presente diariamente detrás del mostrador de prescripciones, y darse cuenta por completo del trabajo del farmacéutico, en muchos casos incurriría los riesgos del farmacéutico más bien que del hombre que ha redactado la prescripción. Esto, no obstante, no falta gente que llame al farmacéutico un boticario en tono de desprecio, como si fuese un ordinario fabricante de específicos; mas ¡cuán pronto se desvanece este pensamiento cuando ocurre un accidente! El primer pensamiento es de acudir á la botica en demanda de auxilio. Apenas si transcurre un día en cualquiera vecindad en que el farmacéutico no sea llamado á mitigar algún dolor ó aliviar algún herido. Muchas veces en localidades nutridas de habitantes se reclaman sus servicios para algún caso de intoxicación ó envenenamiento. Tengo memoria de haber sido llamado dos veces á tratar casos de envenenamiento por ácido oxálico tomado en lugar de sal de Epsom. De igual manera son frecuentes los casos de desvanecimiento, de mujeres en particular, que presa de excitación no saben lo que hacer. Luego podemos citar espasmos, insolaciones, ataques epilépticos, etc., en cuyos casos podemos hacer bastante antes de que llegue el médico.

Algunas veces, no muchas en toda la vida, puede requerirse los servicios del farmacéutico para algún ahogado; los momentos son apremiantes si es que ha de salvarse la vida de la víctima. También puede requerirse al farmacéutico en exámenes póstumos, particularmente en pueblos pequeños donde no hay expertos y es de suponerse que el médico ú hombre profesional sería el llamado á hacer el trabajo.

Póngase cuidado en tomar notas, en que las fechas sean exactas. Véase que cuando se abandona el cuarto de operaciones la puerta esté bien cerrada, pues más de un caso se ha perdido ante los tribunales á causa de puntos frívolos.

Si teneis en vista llegar á obtener la confianza de vuestras parroquianas, á lo menos de la mayoría de las mismas, convendrá que estudiéis todas las preparaciones destinadas á alimento de los niños, poniéndoos en condiciones, para en ausencia del médico poder dar el consejo más conveniente.

Cuanto á recetar desde el mostrador, he de decir que no es ni debería ser el deber del farmacéutico, y no obstante, no pocas veces se ve obligado á hacerlo como si se hallase entre dos fuegos. Se presenta el parroquiano, como que cree posee vuestra confianza, espera que daréis el consejo que se os pide. ¿Qué vais á hacer entonces? Si os negais no tan sólo ofendeis al parroquiano, si no que entregais vuestro negocio en manos de vuestro colega, que se aprovechará de la ocasión. Si recetais, los amigos de vuestro médico se ofenden; si las razones que alegan están fundadas, entonces el farmacéutico no vale para recetar para un enfermo; este podrá ponerse peor, pero la práctica de aquel en lugar de perder habrá aumentado.

A parte las consideraciones expuestas, el público viene dándose cuenta diariamente de que el farmacéutico es algo más que un comerciante de específicos. Tanto es así que el especialista ya se da cuenta de que el farmacéutico, cual el practicante ordinario, está abandonando su legítima labor para entrar en la especialidad.

Pero hay un servicio mucho mayor que el que podamos prestar en casos de urgencia á nuestros parroquianos, y es de no ser desleales á la confianza depositada en nosotros, la cual no es menor que si se tratara del médico de familia.

NOTAS TERAPEUTICAS

TRATAMIENTO DE LLAGAS ANTIGUAS

El tratamiento de antiguas úlceras por medio de agua caliente, por el que aboga el profesor P. Reclus, lo ha mejorado recientemente M. A. Veyrassett, sustituyéndolo por una solución de sal normal (*Journal de Médecine de Paris et Bulletin Médical*). El método que se recomienda consiste en irrigar la úlcera una vez al día al principio, y más tarde cada dos ó tres días con una solución de cloruro de sodio (7 g. por litro) á una temperatura de 50° C., y bajo presión de 1.50 m. Se emplean cuatro ó cinco litros en una jeringa de depósito, ó bien se vierten de un jarro á cada irrigación, dirigiendo el chorro particularmente á los bordes de la úlcera. Caso de que el paciente ó la úlcera fuesen muy sensibles, podrá verterse la solución en chorros sucesivos. Con la misma solución se emplea como apósito un trozo de gasa humedecida en ella; tratándose de úlceras en las piernas, se aplica un vendaje arrollado desde los dedos del pié para arriba; también se emplea un vendaje de caucho. — *New York Med. Jour.*

NUEVO PROCESO PARA CONSERVAR LA LECHE

A los métodos conocidos hasta la fecha para conservar la leche hay que agregar otro descubierto por dos médicos italianos, y el cual consiste en conservar la leche por medio de una atmósfera de gas ácido carbónico bajo presión. La leche permanece sin alterarse durante algunos días, tanto en su naturaleza física como química, é igualmente en los constituyentes biológicos y en los fermentos. Algunos de los gérmenes presentes perecen mientras que el desarrollo de otros queda atajado. La leche cruda por este proceso puede conservarse por ocho ó doce días á una temperatura de 12° á 14° C. La leche hervida se conserva indefinidamente. El gas se genera con poca ó ninguna dificultad. Los inventores pretenden que por este medio queda resuelta la cuestión del alimento de los niños. La leche conservada de esta manera debería ser ciertamente superior á la leche esterilizada al calor, porque por este proceso la leche puede conservarse por un largo período sin la presencia de gérmenes patogénicos, mientras que sus funciones bioquímicas permanecen intactas, lo que no sucede cuando se emplea la esterilización al calor.—*Medical Age.*

TRATAMIENTO DE ALMORRANAS INTERNAS

C. F. Martin, de Filadelfia, recomienda el método inyectivo para el tratamiento de hemorroides. Su técnica consiste en la inyección de 7 á 10 mínimos de una solución de fenol al 50 por ciento en cada tumor de almorrana, á intérvalos de dos á siete días dependiente de los efectos producidos. Como preliminar de la inyección el autor recomienda la divulsión de los esfínteres bajo la anestesia óxida nitrosa, atribuyendo á este procedimiento buena parte del éxito obtenido. Concluye diciendo que las recurrencias no exceden de 15 por ciento, y que los accidentes y complicaciones no son en modo alguno tan frecuentes como cuando se acude á las operaciones de cauterización y compresión. Con este método no surge dolor y el paciente no interrumpe sus negocios. — *Medical News.*

GASES DEL CUERPO

L. H. Watson, en el *Medical Record*, expone que este asunto no es muy bien comprendido. Algunos de los gases tales como el oxígeno, el nitrógeno y el dióxido de carbono son esenciales á nuestra existencia, mientras que otros son productos superfluos, pudiendo incitar la apendicitis, obstrucción intestinal, afecciones del ovario y afecciones del corazón, cuando están presentes en el canal intestinal. Son gases principales del cuerpo el nitrógeno, el oxígeno, el dióxido de carbono, el hidrógeno sulfuratado y carburatado y también el gas formeno. El dióxido de carbono desplaza el mayor volumen y es el que está más difundido. De ordinario se le ha designado como gas venenoso; pero la química fisiológica moderna nos ha revelado un nuevo conocimiento, según el cual puede solamente considerarse venenoso cuando es una obstrucción de la respiración. Puede hallarse en cantidad considerable en el estómago y en los intestinos en estado de salud, pero más en estados neuróticos; pero el coeficiente de absorción es alto, causando muy poca inconveniencia los resultados. La acumulación de gas en los intestinos, puede dar lugar á trastornos diagnósticos; el autor cita algunos de estos casos. Los gases que de ordinario se hallan son hidrógeno carburatado y sulfuratado y gas formeno, como también oxígeno y dióxido de carbono. La fermentación de ácido bútrico, acético y lácteo como también la descomposición de grasas, materia proteida y celulosa, están todos relacionados con la formación de gases intestinales. Cuando los anillos de tripa están estrangulados primeramente aparece agua y después gases, dando lugar al meteorismo. Los tumores simulados tienen esta naturaleza. El dolor de cabeza, vértigo, náuseas son á menudo el resultado de la presencia de hidrógeno sulfuratado en el intestino. La formación de gases intestinales debe de atenderse por medio del régimen alimenticio.

TRATAMIENTO DE LA COMEZON EN EL RECTO

Un médico americano que hace una especialidad de las afecciones del recto, el Dr. J. P. Tuttle, de Nueva York, hace hincapié en la existencia de reumatismo, gota ó diabetes como causa de la comezón rectal. Algunas veces la indigestión, ó por haber comido especias tales como pimienta, mostaza, ó ciertas carnes saladas ó salsas está relacionado con ese desarreglo molesto. Algunas bebidas, por ejemplo el café, también originan á veces la comezón en el ano. Por consiguiente, lo primero que debería hacerse en tales casos, es regularizar el régimen alimenticio, y huir de aquellos artículos. Otras causas que pueden ejercer influencia en estos estados, como son lombrices, almorranas, grietas, etc., deberían tratarse por separado.

El tratamiento local de la enfermedad no es fácil, aunque el Dr. Tuttle ha ensayado un remedio con excelentes resultados, y el cual consiste en:

℞	Acido fénico	7.12 gramos
	Acido salicílico	3.75 »
	Glicerina	30. »

Mézclese para uso externo.

Esto se emplea como aplicación local. Cuando hay grietas, prefiere una solución de argitol, 50 por ciento, que permite secarse en la superficie agrietada, y luego cubre la misma con una capa de ictiol. Al principio se procede diariamente con lo prescrito, y después cada dos ó tres días. Entre estas aplicaciones emplea el siguiente ungüento:

℞	Acido fénico	0.2 de gm.
	Resorcina	0.2 de gm,
	Ictiol, puro	1. gramo
	Vaselina	10. gramos

ECZEMA EN LOS NIÑOS

En el eczema que ataca de ordinario á los niños, y en que hace falta estimular la piel, Starr recomienda la siguiente fórmula, que parece da buen resultado:

℞	Zinci oxid	℥ ij
	Ungt. picis liq	℥ ss
	Ungt. aq. rosæ	℥ ss
	Lanolin	℥ j

— *The Southern Clinic.*

PALUDISMO. — TRATAMIENTO SUBSIGUIENTE

El Dr. B. F. Bell, de Taylor (Texas), afirma que lo siguiente es una receta excelente para el tratamiento subsiguiente de la malaria.

℞	Jr. ferri mur	℥ j
	Strych. sulph	gr. j
	Liq. potass. arsen	ʒ ij
	Tr. capsici	ʒ iij
	Acid phcs. dil	℥ iij
	Glycerine, q. s. ad	℥ viij

M. Sig.: Una cucharadita en agua, tres veces al día. Los dientes se resguardarán con una lavadura alcalina ó empleando el monda-dientes.

Para niños disminuyo el hierro y estricnina según la edad, y para niños tiernos, el ácido ha de ser una mitad. Manténgase la exoneración del vientre, y la piel activa, limpiándola con frecuencia. Si volvieren los escalofríos mientras se toma el tónico, suspéndase éste, y atájense aquellos con quinina; después se continúa con el tónico. En la infección palúdica crónica no puede prometerse alivio antes de tres meses con el tratamiento *regular*. La combinación descrita la he usado por espacio de quince años, y no se había publicado antes. — *Medical Summary.*

DISENTERIA AGUDA

R. J. Windle recomienda la siguiente combinación:

No. 1

℞ Chloral hydrat	gr. xx-xxx
Liq. opii. sed	m. xx
Aq., ad	ʒ j
Syrup. aurant	ʒ ij

No. 2

℞ Pulv. ipecac	gr. xx-xxx
Aq. chloroformi	℥ j
Mucilag. Tragacanto, q. s.	

Se administra la bebida No. 1, la que regularmente tiene efecto en el tiempo de diez á quince minutos. Cuando el paciente acaba de dormirse, se le despierta lo suficiente para tomar el No. 2. Debe sacudirse en una redomita y verterse antes de tomarse. En muchos casos el paciente, después de este tratamiento, dormirá de tres á seis horas, despertándose sin experimentar ningún inconveniente. En algunos casos la ipecacuana produce malestar, no obstante la bebida de cloral; pero el autor no tiene experiencia de que el malestar haya sobrevenido en menos de una hora y media; pero en ningún caso los vómitos contenían ipecacuana, lo que es evidencia de que ya había sido absorbida.—*Journal of the Royal Army Medical Corps.*

MAL DE OIDO EN LOS NIÑOS

℞ Acid carbolici	mvij.
Ext. opii fl.	mvj.
Cocainæ hydrochlor	gr. vj.
Atropinæ sulph	gr. iij.
Aq.	miij.
Gelatine	gr. xviij.
Glycerine	ʒ iij.
M. div. in bougies no.	xlvii.

Sig.: Introdúzcase una candelilla en el canal auditivo cada dos horas.

Nota. — Deberá usarse antes de que ocurra la exhudación timpánica. — *The Practitioner.*

Cemento para Mangos de Manos Almirez

Se han empleado numerosos cementos para trabar las dos partes de que se componen las manos de almirez, y entre ellos el yeso, del cual se hace un amasijo muy delgado con agua; yeso con resina, partes iguales y derretidas juntas; yeso con arena y agua; cera de lacrar derretida; goma laca derretida; laca y guttapercha derretidas juntas; litargirio y glicerina, y una mezcla de dos partes de resina, una parte de cera amarilla y tres partes de tierra morena derretidas juntas. Una cantidad suficiente del cemento debería colocarse en el hueco comprimiendo fuertemente en él la otra parte, después de lo cual la mano de almirez debería cogerse en un sitio apropiado, como entre dos estantes, y dejarse allí el tiempo suficiente para que el cemento seque y endurezca. — *Drug. Circular.*

NOTAS FARMACEUTICAS

SOLUCION DE TIMOL COMPUESTA

Timol	2 dracmas
Acido benzoico	6 »
Eucaliptol	½ »
Aceite de gaulteria	20 mínimos
Menthol	1 dracma

Disuélvese en:

Alcohol (90 por ciento)	20 onzas
Agua bastante para hacer	100 »
Biborato sódico	1 »
Acido bórico	1 »

Déjese reposar por algunos días, y fíltrese á través de talco.

ESENCIA DE CUAJALECHE

Cuajaleche libre de sales, picado fino.	6 onzas
Sal	4 »
Alcohol (90 por ciento)	10 »
Agua bastante para hacer	40 »

Macérese cuatro días y añádese luego:

Vino de Jeréz	5 onzas

Después de un día ó dos se colará, añadiendo entonces:

Glicerato de ácido tánico	10 gotas
Tierra de batán	1 onza

Sacúdese y déjese en reposo una semana. Decántese la solución clara y fíltrese el sedimento.

LINIMENTO

Aceite de trementina	1 oz. fl.
Aceite de alquitrán	2 »
Acido fénico	½ »
Aceite de pescado, bastante para hacer	1 pinta

Tiene fama de ser un buen linimento en general y es eficaz particularmente para cortaduras de alambre, y para heridas á que está sujeto el ganado de las haciendas. Después de lavar bien la cortadura ó llaga con agua caliente y jabón de Castilla, aplíquese el linimento una ó dos veces á la semana.

POLVOS PARA LAS UÑAS

Cera blanca	8 onzas
Alcohol	8 oz. fl.
Eosina	6 granos
Creta francesa	32 onzas
Electro-silicón	24 cajas

Derrítase la cera, caliéntese 7 onzas fluídas del alcohol y viértase lentamente en la cera caliente. En un mortero grande de *wedgewood* se pondrán 12 cajas de electro silicón, vertiendo gradualmente la mezcla de alcohol y cera sobre aquél, frotando constantemente; entonces se añade gradualmente el remanente del electro silicón y la creta francesa. Disuélvase la eosina en 1 onza fluída del alcohol y añádese la solución á los polvos; luego se cierne, primeramente en un cedazo No. 40, y finalmente por uno del No. 60.

JALEA DE PLANTA DEL SORTILEGIO

Gelatina francesa	1 onza
Agua de hamamelis	20 oz fl.
Glicerina	3 »

Disuélvase la gelatina en la glicerina y el hamamelis al baño maría. Si se desea puede añadírsele perfume. Dispénsese en frascos ó en tubos flexibles.

EMULSION DE ACEITE DE RICINO CON CHOCOLATE

Aceite de ricino	30.	c.c.
Acacia en polvo	6 5	grm.
Tragacanto en polvo	0.25	»
Cacao soluble	1.	»
Tintura compuesta de vanillina, N. F.	1.	c.c.
Solución de sacarina, N. F.	4 ó 5	gotas
Agua bastante para hacer	60.	c c.

Disuélvase el cacao (cualquiera apropiado para jarabe de sosa) en 15 c.c. de agua hirviendo y enfríese. Cuando esté frío añádese la tintura de vanillina compuesta y la solución de sacarina; empléese esta mezcla, como emulsión núcleo, poniendo en práctica el método continental. Finalmente añádese bastante agua para hacer 60 c.c.

TONICO DE CALISAYA

Escamas de fosfato de hierro	1024	granos
Sulfato de estricnina	6	»
Sulfato de quinina	128	»
Sulfato de cinconidina	64	»
Sulfato de cinconina	64	»
Elixir de naranja, bastante p. hacer	1	galón

Disuélvanse los alcaloides (escepto la estricnina) revolviendo en un medio galón de elixir. Añádese la estricnina, la cual se habrá disuelto previamente en agua caliente. Disuélvase la sal en una pequeña cantidad de agua haciéndolo hervir en un flasco ó cápsula, empleando tan poca agua como posible y añadiéndolo á la mezcla susodicha. Luego se añade bastante elixir para hacer un galón, color rojo obscuro con caramelo y solución de rojo anilina.

FLUIDO PARA LIMPIAR

Amoníaco, del más fuerte	1	onzas
Tintura de jabón verde	3	»
Carbonato sódico	2	drac.
Borato sódico	2	»
Eter	1	onza
Alcohol	1	»
Agua, bastante para hacer	32	»

PASTA PARA FOTOGRAFIAS

Dextrina blanca	8	onzas
Borax	1	»
Glucosa	1	»
Agua	6	»

Disuélvase el borax en el agua al calor, añadiendo luego la dextrina y glucosa, continuando el calor hasta disolverse. Cuélese á través de una tela.

POLVOS PARA MEZCLAS DE CRETA

Creta preparada	50	granos	5.0	gm.
Tragacanto en polvo	7	»	0.7	»
Azucar en polvo	100	»	10.0	»

Mézclense los polvos y guárdense en una botella con tapón esmerilado.

Cuando se necesiten para hacer una mezcla de creta empléense 40 granos (2.6 gm.) de los polvos por cada onza fluída (28.4 c.c.) de agua de canela.

Pepsina Vegetal

Se ha descubierto que es posible obtener una clase excelente de pepsina del llamado melón papilla que crece en abundancia en el distrito de Tuxpám, México. Según noticias fidedignas un americano que posee una hacienda cerca de Tampico ha hecho ensayos fructuosos para extraer la pepsina. La leche obtenida de la fruta se somete á un proceso de desecación y la pepsina resultante redúcese a polvo. El artículo se ha venoido va a bnen orecio en los Estados Unidos.

Linimentos Medicinales

LINIMENTO DE ICTIOL PARA LA CIATICA.—Ictiol, 20 gramos; bálsamo tranquilo, 30; cloroformo, 30. H. s. a. embrocaciones sobre la parte dolorida. *Crock.*

De 20 ciáticas rebeldes á todos los demás tratamientos, 14 curaron, 4 consiguieron mejoría hasta el punto de reanudar sus ocupaciones habituales, y únicamente en 2 no se notó mejoría.

De estos casos deduce Crock que si bien este remedio no es infalible, no por eso deja de ser el medio más eficaz de que disponemos en la actualidad para esta afección. Esta medicación no excluye el uso simultáneo de analgésicos destinados á calmar momentáneamente las sensaciones dolorosas, esperando que la acción del ictiol, más lenta, pero más radical, tenga tiempo de obrar.

LINIMENTO DE IODO.—(a) Iodo, 5 partes; ioduro potásico, 2; glicerina, 1; alcohol rectificado, 40. — *F. Brit.*

(b) Iodo, 1 gramo; aceite de olivas, 30.

Una ó dos aplicaciones en el vientre á los niños, y algunas más á los adultos, para las diarreas y otras afecciones abdominales. — *Mac Diarmid.*

(c) Iodo, 56 gramos; ioduro potásico, 23; glicerina, 14; agua, 28; alcohol, c. s. Mézclense 300 gramos de alcohol, la glicerina y el agua, y disuélvanse en la mezcla el iodo y el ioduro. Complétese después con más alcohol para obtener 450 gramos. — *F. N.*

LINIMENTO DE IODO COMPUESTO. — Tintura de iodo, 5 partes; amoníaco líquido, 2; linimento común, 5. — *H. St. George.*

LINIMENTO DE IODO CON BELLADONA. — Linimento de iodo, 1 parte; linimento de belladona, 1. Mézclense. — *H. Women.*

LINIMENTO DE IODOFORMO. — (a) Iodoformo, 1 gramo; bálsamo del Perú, 3; alcohol ó glicerina, 12. Disuélvase. — *Gallois.*

(b) Alcohol de 36°, 30 gramos; jabón animal, 4; iodoformo, 1. Disuélvase en baño-maría, fíltrese por papel la solución y consérvese en un frasco bien tapado. — *Maitre.*

(c) Alcohol de 85°, 30 gramos; jabón animal, 4; iodoformo, 1; esencia de menta, 1. Disuélvase en baño-maría.

Para combatir los dolores reumáticos.

LINIMENTO IODURADO VESICANTE. — Iodo, 10 gramos; ioduro potásico, 4; alcanfor, 2; alcohol, 6.

Debe aplicarse con precaución, porque goza de una propiedad vesicante enérgica. Podrá usarse en la pleuresía con derrame cuando se tema la acción de un vejigatorio de cantáridas sobre los riñones. — *Néligan.*

LINIMENTO DE IODURO DE POTASIO. — Amoníaco líquido fuerte, 7 gramos; linimento de jabón, 50; ioduro de potasio, 3.50. Méz[illegible]nse — *H. [illegible]*

LINIMENTO DE IODUR[illegible]
Jabón duro, 16 partes; ioduro potás[illegible]
8; esencia de limón, 1; agua destilad[illegible],
el jabón mezclado con el agua y la glice[illegible]
de porcelana y baño-maría, y viértase en
sobre el ioduro pulverizado, agitando
hasta que se enfríe. Pasada una hor[illegible]
esencia. — *F. Brit.*

Cultivo y Recolección de la Cáscara Sagrada

Esta importante droga americana ha sido objeto de un extenso informe en uno de los periódicos de farmacia que publica todos los años una noticia de la producción de la cáscara. La exportación de la misma en 1901 comprendía 1.000,000 de libras y en 1902 sobre 960,000. No se tienen todavía datos exactos de la exportación en 1903, ó á lo menos no se han publicado. La cantidad de cáscara producida en ese año fué muy pequeña, de aquí que su precio subiera. Como resultado de los altos precios en el año que siguió hubo un aumento en la producción, y en 1904 alcanzó la imponente cifra de 1.500,000 libras. Dícese que la recolección total de cáscara este año no llegará á aquella cantidad, porque los mayoristas están pagando ahora 4½ á 6 centavos por libra de la corteza y, por consiguiente, el cultivo y recolección de la planta no es tan provechoso como lo era el año precedente.

Desgraciadamente las noticias llegadas de algunas localidades parecen indicar que la corteza va haciéndose cada día más escasa porque los árboles no forman ninguna nueva corteza después de haber sido descortezados y por consiguiente están condenados á morir. Un árbol, por término medio, rinde diez libras de corteza, y, por consiguiente, una producción anual de un millón de libras significa una destrucción de unos 100,000 árboles. También se destruyen un número considerable de árboles jóvenes al desmontar los bosques para ensanchar el área cultivable en aquellas regiones, así es que llegará el día en que la cáscara sagrada sea una droga rara, á menos de que el Gobierno no adopte medidas para defender los árboles.

Debería consagrarse más cuidado á la desecación de la corteza. Las lonjas de la cáscara deberían colgarse de alambres y exponerse con su cara exterior al sol, porque el interior de la misma es de un amarillo claro. en la cáscara fresca, y pierde valor en el mercado cuando aquélla se vuelve prieta bajo la influencia de los rayos solares. Después de completado el proceso de la desecación la corteza se corta en trozos pequeños como viene al mercado. La grande cosecha de 1904 ha dado lugar á precios muy bajos para la cáscara durante el presente año, pero es probable que suba el precio en el año entrante porque en apariencia la cosecha se presenta corta.

Luz del Día Artificial

En una de las exhibiciones eléctricas recientes que el público ha tenido ocasión de admirar en el Madison Square Garden de la ciudad de Nueva York, el alumbrado de una parte del gran salón procedía de un larguísimo tubo de vidrio lleno al parecer de un humo lumínico que á voluntad puede tomar diferentes colores. De ordinario la luz que emite es clara, caliente y blanca, sin destello ó intensidad ofensiva á la vista.

La luz eléctrica emanada de tubos llenos de substancias químicas no es nueva entre nosotros por estar [illegible]ico familiarizado desde hace algún tiempo con [illegible]os azules-verduscos de la luz Cooper Hewitt; [illegible] luz que nos ocupa, cuyo inventor es D. Mc [illegible] generada llenando un tubo, en el que se ha [illegible] vacío, con vapores químicos que conducen [illegible]d, dando por resultado una iluminación ma[illegible]illosa. La dificultad con que tropezó el inventor al [illegible]er sus ensayos, no era en obtener un gran volumen [illegible] luz del d[illegible] en regularizarla para producir una luz normal al mismo tiempo que conservase el valor y la armonía del color.

Según parece, el campo de utilidad para este sistema de luz es ilimitado, pues tanto sirve para tiendas como talleres, trenes al igual que tranvías, y hasta para el alumbrado de la vía pública. El tubo que iluminaba de una manera tan suntuosa el salón llamado Madison Square Garden — donde se llevan á cabo casi todas las exhibiciones — medía más de 150 piés de largo, sin comparación en todo el mundo. Estaba formado en secciones de siete piés, unidas por soldaduras. Habiéndose el vacío en todo el tubo, se inyectan en él ciertas substancias químicas y se introduce la corriente eléctrica que culmina en un gas lumínico; aquella se toma de los alambres de la calle.

Refiriéndose Mr. McFarlan, el inventor, á la luz en cuestión, dijo, que podría producirse á la mitad del costo de la luz incandescente, mientras que su fuerza lumínica es veinticinco veces mayor que la luz eléctrica ordinaria.

¿Quién Descubrió el Calomelano?

El alquimista Theodore Turquet, inventor del calomelano en el siglo XVII, y quien se supone haber dado el nombre á la droga (*Kalos, hermoso; melas, negro*) para honrar á un criado muy fiel de color moreno, se ha dicho en varias crónicas que murió en Mayerne cerca de Ginebra. *La Gaceta Médica de París* publicó recientemente un artículo atribuyendo á Turquet el haber descubierto el calomelano é introducídolo en la terapéutica, pero negando que hubiese muerto en aquella ciudad, en donde había nacido el 28 de septiembre de 1573, sino en Chelsea (Londres), en 1655. En un número más reciente del periódico, un colaborador que se firma «Xrayer,» sostiene que Theodore Turquet no tiene derecho á la pretensión del descubrimiento de la droga en cuestión, alegando de que apenas si era alquimista. Como médico alcanzó lisongero éxito, pues desempeñó aquel cargo oficial cerca de los reyes Jaime I y Carlos I, y en calidad de tal cerca del Rey de Francia. «Krayser» conviene en que Turquet empleaba en el ejercicio de su profesión cantidades de calomelano, y por esta causa y por pertenecer á la fé protestante, se vió obligado á salir de Francia. El calomelano lo habían descritos varios escritores de temas medicinales, particularmente Crollius que vivió y murió antes de que el ciudadano de Mayerne hubiese nacido. La droga era conocida por el nombre de dragón mitigado, de mercurio dulce, de panquimagogo mineral y águila blanca. La parte que tuvo Turquet en la fama de la droga, fué al parecer, de haberla popularizado y de haberla dado el nombre, pues no se ha podido hallar este último en escritos de fecha anterior á los de Turquet. Pero cómo formó el nombre no se sabe con exactitud. Hooper, en su *Diccionario de Medicina*, dice, que «calomel» era el nombre del mineral negro, y que después fué traspasado al blanco, pero cuando se efectuó esto no se precisa.

— Como nuevos remedios que tienen buena aceptación tanto en los Estados Unidos como en Europa hemos de citar la Nervita, ó sean los Glicero Fosfatos de Huxley, la Sal Sanitaria de Huxley para lavados quirúrgicos, enjuagatorios, gárgaras, heridas, úlceras, etc., y los «Küglofds» para la gripe, faringitis catarral, bronquitis, etc. Para estos remedios hay ya buena demanda en la América española, y á medida que se conozcan más se extenderá su aplicación. Los fabrica la Anglo-American Pharmaceutical Co. de Londres, Paris y Nueva York.

NOTAS COMERCIALES

— El ramo de perfumería es delicioso y tiene por esta causa muchos admiradores, particularmente entre el bello sexo. El farmacéutico que tiene la suerte de explotar perfumes que tienen el favor del público gana dinero; quizás los perfumes más acreditados son los que salen del establecimiento de Solón Palmer, de Nueva York; son en efecto perfumes exquisitos, de aquí que tengan tanta demanda. Doquiera se ofrecen tienen buena salida. El Sr. Palmer, que cuenta ya con parroquianos en la América española, desea extender sus negocios á aquellos países, y para ello dará toda clase de facilidades á los compradores.

— Hemos de permitirnos llamar la atención especial á nuestros lectores sud-americanos y otros al anuncio de Mead Johnson & Company, de Jersey City, E. U. A., cuya casa ha venido á reemplazar, como sucesora, á la American Ferment Company, del mismo lugar. Su renglón de píldoras fabricadas de polvos es un gran adelanto sobre la antigua forma de amasijo de píldora y representa un grado mayor de solubilidad y de acción terapéutica. La píldora se deshace fácilmente en polvo á la menor presión del pulgar y el índice. La capa es enteramente soluble y de tal naturaleza que puede resistir la acción de cualquier clima. El anuncio de la casa está en español, y probablemente despertará suficiente interés para que nuestros lectores hagan alguna solicitud á los fabricantes.

— Como hay tantos droguistas y boticarios que también están interesados en el negocio de bebidas gaseosas y aguas minerales, creemos que lo siguiente será leído con interés por una gran mayoría de nuestros lectores. El prohombre de los fabricantes de aparatos de agua de soda y bebidas gaseosas en los Estados Unidos fué Mr. John Matthews, quien en 1832 vino á New York y comenzó á fabricar Agua de Soda. Mr. Matthews fué discípulo y amigo de Bramah, el eminente ingeniero inglés que inventó la bomba hidráulica. Aunque su negociación en un principio era muy limitada, su carácter inventivo y enérgico, ayudado por lo productivo del negocio de aguas gaseosas y bebidas carbonatadas, lo puso en circunstancias de fabricar ya no agua de soda, sino aparatos para fabricar agua de soda á cuyo negocio dedicó toda su energía y experiencia. Su pequeño negocio creció con tal rapidez que á su muerte dejó la inmensa fábrica de seis edificios que en 1891 los nietos de Mr. Matthews vendieron á la American Soda Fountain Co., cuya compañía ha dado un gran impulso á este negocio, reteniendo su posición como principales fabricantes en el ramo como lo prueba el hecho de haber recibido el «Grand Prize» y muchas Medallas de Oro en la Exposición Universal de St. Louis, 1904. El grabado que acompaña representa el carbonatador «Baby Cataract» que es probablemente la máquina más sorprendente é ingeniosa que se ha inventado para fabricar agua de soda y bebidas geseosas. Esta máquina ha prácticamente sustituído á todas las de su género en los Estados Unidos y está siendo recibida con mucho entusiasmo en el extrangero. Sus principales característicos son: economía de gas, simplicidad de mecanismo y solidez de construcción, combinadas con un moderado precio. Su mecanismo es continuo y automático y no requiere más atención que el que se le aceite diariamente. Tanto el sistema de regar como el de agitar están comprendidos en dicha máquina de modo que se obtiene como resultado una agua carbonatada de superior calidad, sin desperdicio alguno de gas. Su capacidad es 1,000 galones de agua de soda carbonatada á 100 por ciento de saturación en 10 horas. Este es uno de los muchos aparatos que fabrica la American Soda Fountain Co., Export Department «A» Boston (Mass.), U. S. A., quien tendrá gusto en remitir catálogos y adicional información á quien esté interesado en máquinas, aparatos, accesorios ó ingredientes para fabricar aguas gaseosas.

— Lo bueno, lo exquisito, lo seguro es siempre apreciado con justicia, lo cual está comprobado con el ya tan conocido artículo que bajo el nombre de Creta Inglesa Preparada de Thomas, fabrica la Thomas Manufacturing Company, de Baltimore, E. U. A. Es un producto tipo para fines farmacéuticos y del tocador, y en la actualidad tiene demanda en países de la América Central y del Sur. La Compañía proporcionará muestras y cotizaciones al solicitarlo.

ALIVIO EN LA NEURALGIA Y DOLORES OPRESIVOS. — La eficacia de las tabletas de Antikamnia para el alivio de la neuralgia, es indisputable como está ilustrado por el caso siguiente: Una enfermera anciana que por muchos años y á intervalos había padecido de neuralgia, habiéndosele puesto gris el cabello de un lado de la cabeza por aquella causa, manifestó que había obtenido más alivio de las tabletas susodichas que de todas las medicinas que le habían recetado. Para dolores en la cabeza, de cualquier clase que sean, las tabletas de Antikamnia han sido siempre preferidas á todas las preparaciones de coaltar. Constituyen un auxiliar útil en el tratamiento de jaqueca, y los dolores de cabeza que padecen los niños que van á la escuela, pronto ceden á dosis moderadas. Tratándose de enfermedad especial orgánica, han demostrado poseer mucho valor. Una mujer de 52 años enferma de mielitis de través (paraplegia completa) halló estas tabletas seguras para subyugar los dolores opresivos molestos. Dos ó tres dosis, de una tableta cada una, dentro de veinticuatro horas, fueron suficientes para hacer el dolor llevadero. En otro caso en que existía la opresión y parestesia de las extremidades inferiores, se administró una tableta de Antikamnia tres veces al día al tiempo en que se daba el tratamiento regular de ioduro de potasio. Este caso ha estado observándose durante 18 meses, progresando el restablecimiento de una manera visible durante las seis últimas semanas en que tomó la enferma con regularidad las pastillas de Antikamnia. Para mayores informes dirigirse á la Antikamnia Chemical Co., St. Louis, E. U. A.

GERINGA DE LUBRICACION MECANICA. — La Becton-Dickinson Company de Nueva York, llama la atención á los grandes adelantos llevados á cabo en la fabricación de jeringas hipodérmicas. Uno de los cambios más importantes efectuados en años recientes, es el émbolo hueco para cuyo invento tiene la Compañía un privilegio. Este émbolo es de metal de aluminio, que no se corroe y todo el interior es hueco formando una cámara para contener el aceite lubricante, teniendo la extremidad exterior un casquete de tornillo que permite la cámara de aceite llenarse sin quitar el émbolo del cañón de la jeringa. Este arreglo puede verse en la ilustración que acompaña. No tan sólo es el émbolo hueco en toda su longitud, sino que está hecho más grande que de ordinario á fin de poder retener mayor cantidad de aceite. Esta disposición, dícese, no tan sólo mantiene la empaquetadura húmeda y elástica, sino que por ser tan grande la cantidad de aceite, permite á la jeringa funcionar con tanta suavidad y facilidad, después de largo uso como al principio; la empaquetadura no se gasta ni se pone reseca como sucede con otras jeringas que no tienen esta mejora.

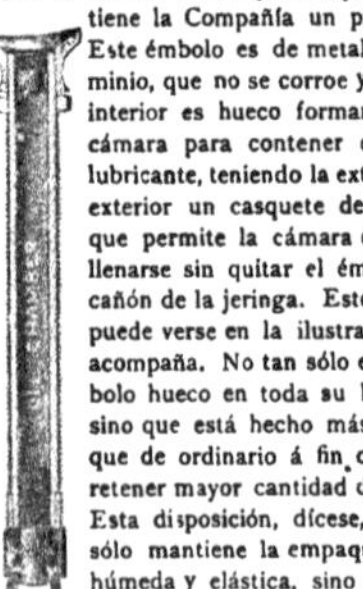

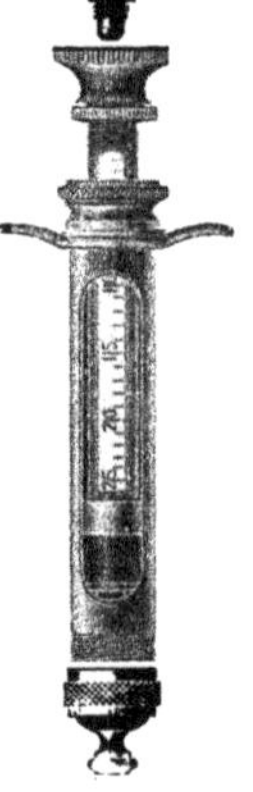

AMERICAN DRUGGIST

and PHARMACEUTICAL RECORD

NUEVA YORK Y CHICAGO: 12 DE MARZO DE 1906

«The American Druggist» es un periódico bimensual del que se publica cada mes un suplemento español con anuncios en el mismo idioma

AMERICAN DRUGGIST PUBLISHING COMPANY

62-68 WEST BROADWAY, NEW YORK, U. S. A.

Dirección cablegráfica «Amdruggist, New York.» Clave A B C

A. R. ELLIOTT, *Presidente*

CASWELL A. MAYO, Ph. G.................*Director*

THOMAS J. KEENAN, Lic. en Farm., *Director Asociado*

PRECIOS DE SUSCRIPCION

Pago adelantado, Estados Unidos, Canadá, México, Cuba, Puerto Rico, Hawaii y las Filipinas... ....(oro americano) $1.50

Otros países (franco de porte).................. » » $3.00

Las suscripciones pueden empezar en cualquier tiempo.

«THE AMERICAN DRUGGIST AND PHARMACEUTICAL RECORD» sale el segundo y cuarto lunes de cada mes. Todo cambio de anuncios debe ser recibido diez días antes de la fecha de salida.

Remesas deben hacerse con libranzas sobre Nueva York, giros postales internacionales ó por expreso ó correo en carta certificada. Toda correspondencia debe dirigirse á la AMERICAN DRUGGIST PUBLISHING CO., 62-68 West Broadway, New York, U. S. A.

DISCRECION EN LA DISPENSACION DE RECETAS

SE tendrá presente que en el número del AMERICAN DRUGGIST, correspondiente al mes de noviembre del año próximo pasado, publicamos un número de recetas sobre cuyo método de dispensarlas surgieron diferencias de opinión, como lo demuestra el hecho de haberlas sometido á diez farmacéuticos de posición reconocida en el ramo, sin que recayera unanimidad en este asunto. En este número presentamos un extracto de las observaciones que ha emitido el profesor Hynson, de Baltimore, en el Colegio de Farmacia de Nueva York, estando presente la Asociación Farmacéutica Manhattan.

El profesor Hynson ha llamado muy apropiadamente el tal estudio de los problemas que envuelve la dispensación de recetas, «una clínica farmacéutica,» porque de esta manera el farmacéutico en general posee una idea previa de tales recetas ú otras semejantes, que un día ú otro puede ser llamado á poner para sus parroquianos. Hay en esto una cuestión latente, y es el límite de discreción que ha de ejercer el farmacéutico al dispensar prescripciones facultativas que pueden dar lugar á discrepancia de opiniones.

Sobre esta fase problemática, uno de nuestros más distinguidos colaboradores, el profesor Wilbert, de Filadelfia, insta á los farmacéuticos á que cuando una receta envuelva la posibilidad de interpretaciones distintas, se consulte desde luego al facultativo. Sostiene que bajo ninguna circunstancia debería asumir el farmacéutico responsabilidad alguna si puede obtener el parecer explícito del recetante. El profesor Wilbert hace hincapié en el hecho de que desde el momento en que una receta se presta á diferentes interpretaciones, surge la necesidad de llamar la atención del médico á la falta de claridad en la redacción. Si el farmacéutico corrigiese de por sí lo que á él le parece un error palpable de la prescripción, el médico podría muy bien continuar indefinidamente duplicando la tal receta, y como consecuencia natural, duplicando el error. Si el dispensador, por otra parte, llama la atención del autor de la receta á la falta, real ó aparente, que ha advertido, el último tendrá ocasión de rectificar en conciencia la falta, con lo que quedarán beneficiados el médico y el público.

Debe quedar sentado, ó cuando menos admitirse, que el primer deber del farmacéutico es de consultar al médico en el acto de abrigar una duda. Esto, sin embargo, no es posible siempre, y además se presentan también ocasiones en que la receta, aun brillando por su claridad, puede dar lugar á dudas razonables acerca del modo de dispensarla, y en tales casos, lo que el profesor Hynson ha llamado «prescripción clínica,» es particularmente valiosa. Nosotros nos permitimos recomendar á nuestros lectores del ramo esta forma de estudio, y habríamos de apreciar que se nos sometiesen espécimens de recetas de carácter dudoso para discutirlos en los números subsiguientes del AMERICAN DRUGGIST.

MATERIALES NATURALES Y ARTIFICIALES PARA PERFUMERIA (*)

Por EDWIN H. BURR, Nueva York

La historia de la perfumería está íntimamente asociada con la historia de la civilización. Si bien los materiales de perfumería se contaban entre los primeros productos de comercio, los artículos preparados por los antiguos eran necesariamente muy crudos, determinándose en la forma de aguas perfumadas, y mezcladas á menudo con cuerpos grasosos; pero el arte de combinar olores para formar perfumes homogéneos y originales es de creación reciente. Como quiera que no hay reglas fijas y establecidas para la combinación de materiales oloríferos, el fabricante de perfumes debe necesariamente depender de su imaginación é inspiración para obtener los mejores resultados. El arte del perfumista es prácticamente cual el del pintor

(*) Leído ante el Colegio de Farmacia de la Universidad Columbia, el 16 de enero de 1906.

y músico. Se conciben primeramente los efectos artísticos y armónicos los cuales se desarrollan después á fuerza de estudio. Deseo hacer hincapié en este hecho porque de llevarlo á la práctica fielmente depende el mejor éxito.

A parte del genio artístico é inspiración necesaria en la composición de perfumes, es también de la mayor importancia y absolutamente esencial que el perfumista posea el conocimiento más inteligente y comprehensivo de todas las substancias que entran en tal composición. Y en este particular es ciertamente un hecho que el farmacéutico instruido del presente se halla en situación de emprender la industria perfumista, estando convencido que entre los alumnos graduados del Colegio de Farmacia de la Universidad Columbia y de otras instituciones de igual índole, se reclutarán los mejores perfumistas del futuro. La industria perfumista se extiende considerablemente en los Estados Unidos, y se hallarán seguramente en los laboratorios de los perfumistas plazas lucrativas para los graduados farmacéuticos que posean un ancho conocimiento técnico de los materiales y les guie el verdadero espíritu artístico tan esencial en el arte.

LA INDUSTRIA DE PERFUMES NATURALES

ha existido en Francia por mucho tiempo. Está concentrada en el Departamento de los Alpes Marítimos, y ciertos productos especiales para la misma proceden de varios Departamentos vecinos. El centro principal es Grasse, donde están situadas las fábricas á que afluyen los abastos de las fincas florales enclavadas en el distrito. Tanto Grasse como su distrito se hallan en una situación excepcional con respecto al clima. Los habitantes que han sabido crear esta industria, y que á través de toda clase de peripecias la han sostenido marchando siempre al compás de los adelantos en los procedimientos y en los aparatos de trabajo, están dispuestos á resistir toda tentativa encaminada á despojarles de la supremacía que han adquirido.

Una industria que prepara productos como los que os voy á enseñar no está estacionaria y menos en

VISTA GENERAL DE LA CIUDAD DE GRASSE

decadencia. El desarrollo considerable, y notable adelanto en el método de los solventes volátiles en el sur de Francia, es prueba manifiesta del cuidado con que los perfumistas de los Alpes Marítimos ponen en mejorar constantemente sus productos. Grasse abastece al comercio de perfumería con los productos extraídos de las flores que crecen en su suelo: como son rosas, flores de azahar, violetas, jazmines, casia mimosa y tuberosa. Me es imposible entrar en detalles de los procedimientos empleados en la extracción y sólo haré de ellos somera descripción. Son tres en número:

DESTILACION AL VAPOR

El primero y el más antiguo es la destilación al vapor. Practícase hoy con un aparato perfeccionado en alto grado calentado por vapor. Rinde aceites esenciales que son generalmente líquidos oleosos casi insolubles en agua, y que no siempre se asemejan al perfume de la flor, pero que no obstante poseen propiedades especiales principalmente de tenacidad, por cuya circunstancia pueden entrar en todas las preparaciones de perfumería.

EMPLEO DE SOLVENTES FIJOS

El segundo procedimiento para la extracción de olores de las flores envuelve el empleo de solventes fijos, y se ha puesto en práctica también por mucho tiempo. Consiste en colocar las flores en contacto con cuerpos grasosos, sólidos y líquidos, que absorben el perfume. De este modo se obtienen pomadas de grasas perfumadas, las cuales se tratan por medio del alcohol que extrae el perfume que entonces puede utilizar el perfumista. Generalmente se emplea manteca de puerco como cuerpo grasoso sólido, se derrite y mezcla con las flores. Después de permanecer por algún tiempo en contacto se separa la grasa perfumada de las flores agotadas por filtración y compresión. Con las flores frescas se efectúan sucesivamente varias maceraciones. A este se le llama el proceso de maceración caliente. Tratándose de jazmines y tuberosas, se colocan estas flores en contacto con la grasa á la tempera-

RECOGIENDO VIOLETAS EN LA VECINDAD DE GRASSE

tura ordinaria en unas armazones de madera con fondos de cristal en los cuales se deposita un paño basto empapado con la grasa ó aceite. Este es el proceso de *enfleurage* al frío.

EMPLEO DE SOLVENTES VOLATILES

El tercer procedimiento envuelve el procedimiento de solventes volátiles y es más moderno que el precedente. Atribúyese su descubrimiento á un químico llamado Robiquet. Después de numerosas experiencias los fabricantes de Grasse han logrado recientemente resolver el problema de la extracción exacta, con todos sus distintivos de los aromas sutiles de las flores. Los *parfums solides* extraídos de esta manera por la digestión de las flores con espíritu ligero de petróleo y la evaporación del último al vacío, se presentan en la forma de masas cerosas con frecuencia coloreadas. El solvente se carga no solamente con la materia odorífera, pero también con la materia vegetal grasosa parecida á la cera de abejas, y con materias colorantes. Los fabricantes que han tenido éxito, particularmente en esta rama de la industria, han concebido la idea de preparar en una forma más utilizable los cuerpos olorosos extraídos de esta manera. Sus «esencias líquidas,» de las que pongo ante vosotros una colección, contie-

RECOGIENDO FLORES DE AZAHAR EN GRASSE

nen la misma cantidad de perfume que un peso igual del *parfum solide*. Yendo todavía más allá han preparado por medios no divulgados aún, y sin ningún vehículo, la verdadera materia olorosa de la flor. Aquí veréis una colección de estas esencias absolutas de las flores. Algunas de las mismas poseen un valor intrínsico considerable. La esencia absoluta de la flor de violeta cuesta no menos de 15,000 francos por kilógramo.

PRODUCTOS TROPICALES

Juntamente con estos productos emanados del suelo francés, el perfumista emplea también una multitud de materiales importados de fuera, procedentes en su mayoría del lejano Oriente. Mencionaré aquí los aceites esenciales de las linaloas de México, del palorosa hembra de Guayana, de los ylang-ylarg de las Filipinas y el cananga de Java, los varios aceites de las Indias inglesas, los varios aceites de canela de la China y Ceilán, y de clavos y patchulí. Para la mayoría de estos productos somos deudores á las Colonias británicas.

PERFUMES ARTIFICIALES

Sería interesante seguir desde un principio el maravilloso desarrollo de estos productos; pero me veda hacerlo el poco tiempo de que dispongo. Por otra parte, tampoco me encuentro con capacidad para intentar tal problema científico ante esta reunión de caballeros cada uno de los cuales es más conocedor de la química y de los problemas químicos que yo. Con todo, no vacilo en decir que la síntesis empieza donde el análisis cesa, y que la primera depende de los progresos del último. Hoy día el fabricante de perfumes artificiales tiene en vista un doble objeto. Primero: la reproducción de los perfumes naturales por medio de procedimientos químicos; y, Segundo: la preparación de productos poseyendo olores hasta aquí desconocidos, lo que podrá aumentar los recursos del perfumista, y puede decirse que en la actualidad existe el empeño de extender principalmente la serie de perfumes sin esforzarse en imitar en absoluto los productos de la naturaleza. Desde este punto de vista la industria de perfumes artificiales es susceptible de un vasto desarrollo, por la razón de que de esta manera aporta un auxiliar muy útil á la originalidad del perfumista. Al principio se presentaba la cuestión de si el descubrimiento de los perfumes químicos no podría paralizar el desenvolvimiento natural de la industria de perfumería. Ha acontecido lo contrario, la prosperidad de la industria de materiales naturales crudos no ha cesado de aumentar desde que se dieron á conocer los perfumes artificiales. La única consecuencia, afortunadamente, ha sido un formidable aumento en la producción de perfumería. Gracias á los productos químicos el perfumista y el fabricante de jabón han podido producir artículos á precios muy bajos que han hallado desde luego nuevos consumidores. Una de las características más distintivas de la historia social de nuestro tiempo, es el hábito progresivo contraído por las clases inferiores en la adquisición de una comodidad, podríamos decir de un lujo hasta aquí reservado á las clases pudientes. Esta tendencia se halla muy extendida en cuanto se relaciona con el empleo de los productos de la perfumería. En el presente, el artesano más pobre usa jabón perfumado que le cuesta un precio insignificante. El empleo de agua de Colonia, de vinagres aromáticos, de aguas del tocador y perfumes para el pañuelo, se ha generalizado. Este aumento de consumo y producción débese al empleo de productos artificiales que ponen á la disposición del perfumista, á un precio moderado, un perfume de considerable fuerza. Al mismo tiempo, y guardando paso con este desenvolvimiento, ha aumentado el consumo de productos naturales, lo cual es fácil de comprender.

Por otra parte, el producto químico definido no puede en ningún caso ser suficiente para la composi-

CLASIFICACION DE ROSAS PARA PERFUMERIA EN GRASSE

ción de un perfume homogéneo; son indispensables para ellos los productos naturales, aunque sea en pequeña cantidad. En apoyo de esta aseveración citaré algunos típicos ejemplos. Desde que se descubrió la vanillina, la vainilla no ha cesado de cultivarse, la importación no ha disminuido y los precios se han mantenido. La vanillina artificial ha hallado una enorme salida en la confitería para aromar los productos de venta diaria, al paso que en la fabricación de artículos de clase superior, se han continuado utilizando las habas de vainilla. También se hubiese creído que el descubrimiento del ionono causaría la ruina del cultivo del iris y la violeta. Precisamente ha sucedido todo lo contrario, teniendo que extender considerablemente el cultivo de aquella flor; los fabricantes del producto natural se han hallado en una situación apurada para hacer frente á la demanda. La razón de esto es que el empleo del ionono, por el cual el perfumista reproduce con mayor facilidad la fragrancia de la flor, ha dadó lugar á la preparación de un número de artículos que han gozado y gozan de merecida popularidad. La verdad es que el ionono no puede usarse solo para producir esos artículos, sino que tiene que combinarse con la raíz de lirio de Florencia. Puede todavía citarse el caso del almizcle, cuyo consumo ó precio no han bajado desde la aparición del almizcle de Baur.

Ahora me permitireis que diga algunas palabras acerca de los principales productos artificiales.

ALMIZCLE ARTIFICIAL

Hace ya mucho tiempo que se observó que la nitración de ciertos cuerpos rerdía productos compenetrados por un tenue olor de almizcle, mas ninguna de las substancias poseedoras de tales propiedades hubo de emplearse en perfumería. En 1888, A Baur obtuvo privilegio por un sustituto de almizcle obtenido por la nitración de butil tolueno.

IONONO

La historia química del ionono se remonta á una década atrás cuando empezaron á recogerse datos acerca del linalool, gernaiol y citral. Lo descubrió Tiemann, en 1893. Es un derivado del citral, aldehido que contienen los aceites esenciales del limón y el andropogón esquenanto. Sacudiendo el citral con la acetona, en presencia de un agente alcalino débil, como por ejemplo agua de barita, rinde por la reacción Claisen un ketono que encierra triple unidad de potencia combinada, pero sin olor característico. Cuando se calienta con un ácido diluido, tal como el ácido sulfúrico, sufre un cambio isómero peculiar, en la serie geránica dando por resultado el ionono. Este compuesto posee propiedades tan favorables, que desde luego fué admitido con entusiasmo por el comercio de perfumería. Y á la verdad que en un estado de dilución extremada desarrolla un olor característico de violetas.

CAMPO DE JAZMINES — CERCA DE GRASSE

VANILLINA

La reproducción sintética de la vanillina, principio odorífero predominante del haba de vainilla, débese á los trabajos de Tiemann y sus colaboradores. Después de llevar á cabo experiencias de poco interés práctico con coniferina, la preparación de vanillina entró en el campo industrial en 1876, en cuyo año Tiemann y Nagai establecieron el hecho de que podía producirse por la oxidación del acetil-eugenol por medio del permanganato de potasio. El segundo paso progresivo que se dió en la manufactura de este producto, fué el descubrimiento, también por Tiemann, en 1890, del isoeugenol. En la actualidad la producción de la vanillina constituye una inmensa industria, y su precio,

RECOGIENDO TUBEROSAS EN GRASSE

bajo la influencia de una concurrencia activa, ha bajado de una manera asombrosa.

Si bien debe reconocerse que los perfumes artificiales han contribuido mucho en extender la demanda de perfumes entre las clases pobres de la sociedad, con todo, debe añadirse que estos perfumes artificiales no se emplean exclusivamente en la preparación de perfumes de los llamados baratos, puesto que también tienen un puesto en la perfumería superfina cuya originalidad desarrollan en manos hábiles. En efecto, con su ayuda se avalora más la delicadeza de los perfumes más elegantes; pero siempre que sea con una grande proporción de los productos naturales; así es que se considera imposible en el tiempo presente el empleo de una clase de productos con exclusión de la otra.

ENSAYOS DE DISPENSACION

Por LEONARD A. SELTZER

Deseo ocuparme de lo que podría llamarse un tropiezo en la preparación de jarabe de regaliz, que con frecuencia se receta, y es además una preparación de suma importancia, porque á parte de las propiedades terapéuticas que indudablemente posee, está á la cabeza de la lista de todas las preparaciones que tenemos para enmascarar el gusto amargo ó el salino de las medicinas. Desgraciadamente el Formulario Nacional no contiene sugestión alguna por la cual la preparación puede hacerse estable ó elegante en apariencia.

Toda la dificultad estriba en el primer paso del procedimiento. Después de disolver la masa de regaliz en agua, queda un residuo insoluble que no puede separarse por la manera ordinaria de filtración. Dado el caso que se haga una tentativa de filtración, la primera porción que se escurre, ó más bien la porción que pasa no es clara, y tan pronto como parece que se pone clara, cesa de pasar ó colar por pegarse el residuo fino al papel y lo vuelve impermeable. Si el farmacéutico quiere emitir la filtración y acomodarse á una preparación desmedrada, resulta que la materia inerte inicia inmediatamente la fermentación y echa á perder el jarabe.

Para vencer esta dificultad he puesto en práctica el siguiente método: después de desintegrar la masa de regaliz al baño-maría, con toda la cantidad de agua que se necesita para preparar el jarabe, añadiendo de cuando en cuando suficiente amoníaco líquido para mantener en solución la glicerizina, pero evitando con cuidado suficiente exceso, de modo que pueda descubrirse bien por el olor ó el sabor, la quito del baño-maría y la dejo enfriar. Entonces añado el blanco de un huevo, lo mezclo bien y lo caliento otra vez al baño maría hasta que la albúmina se ha coagulado. De esta manera mucha de la materia insoluble está rodeada por la albúmina en coagulación, pero queda todavía bastante para hacer la filtración difícil. Llegado á este punto, el método que empleo es el siguiente: tomo unas verutillas limpias y las coloco en el fondo del colador, haciendo la superficie tan desigual como posible. Luego majo algún papel de filtrar en un mortero hasta quedar reducida la solución á una pulpa, después, aquella y el remanente de la solución se traspasan al colador, devolviendo el filtrado hasta que pasa claro. Toda la solución entonces pasará en un tiempo razonable. Puede ahora añadirse el azúcar disolviéndole bien al frío, ó bien con la ayuda de calor. Caso de emplearse este último, será necesario reemplazar de cuando en cuando el amoníaco que se echa.

El jarabe hecho de esta manera es estrictamente de acuerdo con la fórmula oficial, es de atractiva apariencia y se conservará tanto tiempo como los jarabes más estables.

Perfeccionamiento Importante en la Fotografía de las Bacterias

La ciencia médica contará dentro de poco tiempo, y será anunciado oficialmente, con uno de los más importantes descubrimientos realizados en años recientes. El profesor H. C. Ernst, de la Escuela Médica de Harvard, está para completar las investigaciones que ha hecho con un nuevo método de fotografiar las bacterias, por el cual es posible estudiar sus movimientos vitales, celar el efecto que hacen en ellas las medicinas y recoger nuevos hechos respecto á su forma y desarrollo, que en lo pasado había sido imposible conseguir.

El profesor Ernst emplea los rayos ultra-violeta del espectrum para fotografiar los gérmenes. El antiguo procedimiento consistía en someter las bacterias á un tratamiento con varios productos químicos, por cuyo medio se averiguaba alguna propiedad peculiar de cada bacilo. Un ácido volvía un germen de cierto color, al paso que otros no quedaban afectados, ó se volvían de otro color. Los gérmenes de la tuberculosis se ponían rojos al ser tratados químicamente, mientras que nada más quedaba afectado. A cada germen se le reservaba un tratamiento.

Este método se había considerado un maravilloso adelanto, pues permitía sacar fotografías y al mismo tiempo estudiar el germen; pero tenía sus desventajas. Empleábanse substancias químicas fuertes que, naturalmente, mataban el germen y lo encogían ó arrugaban, y con este cambio quedaban ocultos los esporos ó partes vitales de la bacteria. En consecuencia era difícil obtener la naturaleza exacta del germen. Por el método que emplea el profesor Ernst, el germen queda con vida y puede fotografiarse á medida que crece. Fotografiándolo repetidas veces, por espacio de algunos minutos, puede apreciarse fácilmente su desarrollo rápido y la manera cómo se extiende y acciona. Entonces puede aplicarse el tratamiento, mientras el germen está sometido á la lente, y sacarse fotografías á medida que la medicina hace efecto. Por este procedimiento los esporos no están afectados, al paso que el efecto de la medicina es visible. No efectúa ningún cambio en la vida del bacilo. Es, pues, el descubrimiento de mucho alcance, destinado como está á ensanchar nuestros conocimientos de la vida de los gérmenes.

El proceso consiste simplemente en utilizar los rayos ultra-violeta del espectro (en lo que han hecho también experiencias los profesores de Harvard). Bajo la acción de los rayos ultra-violeta, invisibles á simple vista, la bacteria se revela en el negativo sin ninguna coloración artificial. El espectro se fija de modo que los rayos ultra-violeta se proyectan sobre el sujeto que ha de fotografiarse y el aparato. Cada germen se destaca en su propia forma, mientras que con el antiguo procedimiento nada era visible hasta introducir la materia colorante. Había alguna cualidad en la luz blanca que dejaba el germen invisible; lo contrario sucede con la ultra-violeta.

Otra ventaja consiste en el ahorro de tiempo. Antes se consumía bastante tiempo en el tratamiento con la materia colorante para descubrir lo qué era el germen. Ahora puede fotografiarse éste inmediatamente y aplicarse el tratamiento en un tiempo más corto.

El profesor Ernst ha dado cuenta de su descubrimiento á la Sociedad de Medicina de Boston. Las experiencias por él llevadas á cabo han durado tres años; trató, aunque en vano, de obtener la cooperación de los científicos de Europa; pero gracias á la asistencia de sus colegas de la Universidad de Harvard, se halla á la víspera de poner en conocimiento del público científico el resultado de sus labores.

¿Son Inofensivos el Acido Bórico y el Borax?

No obstante las muchas y muy detenidas investigaciones llevadas á cabo para conocer los efectos del ácido bórico y del borax sobre el sistema, no se ha podido llegar á conclusiones definitivas. Durante los dos años pasados el gobierno de los Estados Unidos ha hecho continuos ensayos con el borax tomado con el alimento para averiguar los efectos en el sistema. Un número de jóvenes se presentaron en Washington y pusiéronse á las órdenes del director de la sección química del departamento de Agricultura encargado de la investigación, quien desde luego les trazó el plan que habían de seguir con respecto al consumo de borax.

Pero para el farmacéutico ha de tener mayor interés el conocimiento de los efectos del borax y del ácido bórico tomado en dosis mayores que el hallado de ordinario en las conservas alimenticias. Según E. Rost, el ácido bórico, aunque no sea más que una sola dosis produce un efecto diurético. Las preparaciones de este ácido se eliminan muy lentamente y pueden producir erupciones de la piel y dar lugar también á diarreas. Después de tomar borax ó ácido bórico, los intestinos pierden parte de su poder absorbente de cuyo efecto el alimento no se utiliza como debiera, y aquel que lo toma enflaquece. Se ha observado con las experiencias hechas con irracionales que esas substancias les provocan vómitos.

NOTAS PRÁCTICAS

PARA LIMPIAR EL MOHO DE LOS INSTRUMENTOS. — El *Pharmaceutische Zentralblatt* publica un procedimiento eficaz para quitar el moho de los instrumentos quirúrgicos. Los instrumentos se colocan por toda una noche en una solución saturada de cloruro estánnico, que hace desaparecer las manchas por reducción. Los instrumentos se enjuagan después en agua, se ponen en una solución caliente de jabón de sosa y se secan. Será conveniente restregarlos con alcohol absoluto y creta preparada. Otro medio conveniente para quitar el moho es poner los instrumentos en petróleo.

El aceite de parafina es el mejor preservativo contra el moho y el mejor modo de aplicarlo, sin que la capa sea demasiada espesa; es como sigue: Se disuelve una parte del aceite en 200 partes de bencina, y los objetos después de haberlos secado bien y estando aun calientes se sumergen en la solución. Aquellos instrumentos que tienen articulaciones, como son tijeras y portagujas, se ponen en el fluído, haciéndolo penetrar bien en todos los intersticios, y luego se deja evaporar la bencina en un cuarto seco.—*Medical Standard.*

FORMATO DE QUININA. — En octubre de 1905, Lacroix pasó un informe á la Sociedad Terapéutica de París sobre la acción de una combinación de quinina y ácido fórmico, según la cual se forman dos compuestos de estas dos drogas, siendo el uno un formato neutro consistente en dos moléculas del ácido por una de quinina; el otro es un formato básico consistente en una molécula de cada uno de los ingredientes mencionados. El formato neutro cristaliza, formando largas agujas blancas, brillantes, solubles en agua, y contiene 77.8 por ciento de quinina. Es inestable y pierde alguna cantidad de ácido fórmico á temperaturas aun más bajas que 56 grados. Sus soluciones son ácidas.

El formato básico se obtiene saturando la quinina diluída con cierta cantidad de agua, con la cantidad necesaria de ácido fórmico puro. Cristaliza en hermosos cristales blancos lustrosos, formando masas sedosas de agujas. Su gusto es mucho menos amargo que el de sulfato de quinina. Es muy estable, y contiene 87.56 por ciento de quinina. Es también muy soluble, y sus soluciones son neutras en la reacción. Puede emplearse en inyecciones hipodérmicas sin que cause dolor. Su solución acuosa no fluorece. Hemos dicho que es estable y no se descompone estando en reposo.

El formato básico de quinina, conocido también como quiniforme, es la combinación más rica que se conoce hasta aquí, y es también la más soluble de las sales básicas de este alcaloide. Es especialmente ventajoso en inyecciones hipodérmicas. Los efectos irritantes de inyecciones hipodérmicas de otras sales de quinina débense á la acción cáustica de estas sales. Por no descomponerse el formato en la solución acuosa, esta solución cáustica no está presente cuando se emplea la combinación.

SOLUBILIDAD DEL ACIDO PICRICO.— Según el *Apotheker Zeitung* (1905, página 1031), uno de sus colaboradores examinó la solubilidad del ácido pícrico en varios solventes, habiendo averiguado que á 15° c., 1 parte de ácido pícrico es soluble en 86 partes de agua, en 9 partes de alcohol, en 44 partes de éter, en 50 partes de cloroformo, en 13 partes de benzol, en 3000 partes de éter de petróleo. El autor añade que la relación publicada en el *Merck's Index*, de que 1 parte de ácido pícrico es soluble en 6.5 de éter, no es correcta. Según Cobet (página 1046 del *Apotheker Zeitung*), el ácido pícrico se disuelve en esta proporción de éter cuando se le añade una gota de agua.

TINTURA DE IODO CLOROFORMICA. — Chassavant, en un artículo leído ante la Sociedad de Terapéutica (*Bulletin Commercial* de enero 31, 1906), recomienda eficazmente el empleo de una tintura de iodo hecha con cloroformo. Las soluciones de iodo en alcohol, éter, acetona y ioduro de potasio son de color obscuro. Soluciones de iodo en cloroformo, bencina y bisulfuro de carbono son de color violeta. Las soluciones de iodo obscuras son con contrairritantes, pero además causan, más ó menos, la destrucción de la epidermis, especialmente de personas que tienen la piel delicada. Los enfermos susceptibles por esta razón temen más las aplicaciones de iodo que el empleo del cauterio. Por otra parte, los soluciones violetas de iodo no producen efectos cáusticos al paso que producen los efectos contrairritantes avalorados en la tintura de iodo ordinaria. La tintura clorofórmica de iodo puede aplicarse al cutis más delicado que no tolera la aplicación de la tintura ordinaria. La solución de cloroformo se aplica de la misma manera que la tintura alcohólica, evaporándose el cloroformo al instante, mientras que la capa de iodo permanece en la piel y es absorbida rápidamente. La acción contrairritante de esta solución es muy marcada, y su aplicación es mucho menos dolorosa que la de la tintura de iodo hecho con alcohol. Una solución al 10 por ciento de iodo sublimado en cloroformo puede prepararse extemporáneamente, porque el iodo es muy soluble en cloroformo. Debería dispensarse en frascos con tapón de vidrio esmerilado. La solución clorofórmica puede usarse internalmente, siendo la dosis para este caso de 2 á 4 gotas durante las comidas.

Linimentos Medicinales

LINIMENTO IRRITANTE. — Aceite de croton, 1 gramo; aceite de hipericón, 60. Mézclense.

LINIMENTO DE JABON. — (a) Jabón blando, 5 partes; alcanfor, 2; alcohol metílico, 20; agua hirviendo, 20. — *H. Gt. Nord.*

(b) Jabón blando, 12 partes; alcanfor, 3; alcohol rectificado, 12; esencia de trementina, 2.—*H. Lond.*

(c) Jabón blando, 1 parte; agua caliente, 10. — *H. Middl.*

LINIMENTO DE JABON Y ACEITE DE CADE. — Jabón blando, 1 parte; aceite de cade, 1; alcohol rectificado, 1. — *H. Westm.*

LINIMENTO DE JABON AMONIACAL. — (a) Linimento de jabón, 3 partes; amoníaco, 1. — *H. E. Lond.*

(b) Esencia de mejorana, 6 gotas; esencia de trementina, 4.25 gramos; solución de amoníaco, 3.50; alcohol metílico, 10.50; jabón blando, 14: agua hirviendo, c. s. para 112. — *H. St. Barth.*

LINIMENTO DE JABON COMPUEST... blando, 27 partes; alcanfor, 7; alcohol m... vino, 272; agua, c. s. para 454. — *H. Roy.* ...

LINIMENTO DE JABON CON ALCANFO... animal, 15 partes; alcohol, 125; alcanfor, 12; e... de romero, 5; amoniaco, 5. H. s. a. — *F. R. I.*

También se llama *bálsamo de Opodel...*

LINIMENTO DE JABON CON OPIO. — Tintura de opio, 1 parte; linimento de jabón, 3. Mézclense. — *H. Middl.*

LINIMENTO JABONOSO. — (a) Alcohol de 90°, 48 partes; jabón de sosa, seco y raspado, 8; alcanfor, 3. Disuélvanse. — *F. Esp.*

Llámase también *alcohol alcanforado jabonoso* y *solución alcohólica de jabón alcanforada.*

(b) Jabón duro, 16 partes; alcanfor, 8; esencia de romero, 3; alcohol rectificado, 128; agua, 32. Mézclese agua y alcohol, y añádanse la esencia, el jabón y el alcanfor. Ténganse en digestión durante siete días á un calor que no exceda de 70°, y fíltrese. — *F. Brit.*

(c) Jabón, 10 partes; alcanfor, 5; esencia de romero, 1; alcohol rectificado, 70; agua, c. s. Disuélvase el jabón en 14 partes de agua, y por parte el alcanfor y la esencia en el alcohol; mézclense ambas soluciones; fíltrese el líquido y agréguese el agua suficiente para completar 100 partes. — *F. E. U.*

(d) Tintura de jabón, 10 partes; aceite de almendras, 1; alcohol de 80°, 9. Mézclense, agítese y consérvese en frasco. — *F. Franc.*

Se prepara el *linimento jabonoso alcanforado* reemplazando en la preparación el alcohol de 80° por alcohol alcanforado.

(e) Jabón blando, 70 gramos; alcanfor, 28; alcohol rectificado, 56; agua hirviendo, 500.—*H. Gt. North.*

(f) Jabón blando, 42 gramos; alcanfor, 14; alcohol rectificado, 227; esencia de orégano, 3.50.—*H. Guy.*

(g) Jabón blando, 6 gramos; esencia de tramentina, 1; agua, 25; alcanfor, 1.50; alcohol rectificado, 4.25. — *H. Lond.*

(h) Tintura de jabón, 50 gramos; aceite de cacahuete, 10. Mézclense en frasco tapado. — *H. M. F.*

NOTAS TERAPEUTICAS

TRATAMIENTO DEL RESFRIADO EN LA CABEZA

Maget (*Presse médicale*, 1905, página 803), recomienda la inhalación de los vapores del peróxido de hidrógeno, tres ó cuatro veces al día, por espacio de cinco minutos cada vez para el tratamiento del resfriado ordinario en la cabeza. Debe hervirse el líquido para que emita vapor. Caso de que la nariz estuviese obstruida, convendrá rociarla primeramente con una solución de adrenalina al 1.1000, preparándola de este modo para la recepción del vapor. Dícese que este tratamiento cura la renitis aguda en veinticuatro horas.

TRATAMIENTO DE QUEMADURAS

Lo primero que ha de hacerse como tratamiento general, es aliviar el dolor por medio del opio, bien internalmente ó por medio de morfina empleada hipodérmicamente en pequeñas dosis. Caso de ser las quemaduras de alguna extensión, se han de estimular los riñones por medio de inyecciones de suero artificial. Más tarde estarán indicados los tónicos.

Cuanto al tratamiento local, comprende una variedad de procedimientos, dándose la preferencia al tratamiento húmedo consistente en la aplicación de una compresa de gasa permanente empapada en una solución de cloruro de mercurio al 1.2000; ó con una solución saturada de nitrato de potasio. La primera es antiséptica mientras que la último alivia el dolor haciendo bajar la temperatura. También ha dado resultado esta solución de nitrato lavando con ella la herida continuamente por dos ó tres horas.

Pero el tratamiento más popular para las quemaduras son las soluciones oleosas y onturas, no obstante que la cirugía moderna es más bien parca en el empleo de ungüentos y aceites en esta clase de heridas. Hasta ha habido ya quien ha rechazado por ineficaces la mezcla del agua de cal y el aceite de linaza, que con tanta frecuencia emplean los profanos. El siguente ungüento recomendado por Reclus, considérase una aplicación muy útil para quemaduras:

℞ Vaselina	50 gramos
Acido bórico	5 »
Antipirina	5 »
Iodoformo	1 »

La desventaja de la mayoría de los ungüentos, incluyendo aquellos que contienen naftol, salol, etc., son de que retardan la cicatrización, causan irritación de la piel, y mantienen la supuración.

Los polvos secos son á menudo mejores en el tratamiento de heridas, como son el subnitrato de bismuto, el iodoformo, el aristol, traumatol, y una mezcla de iodoformo, carbón vegetal y quinina. Muchos de estos polvos puede que sean tóxicos y pueden resultar dañinos para los niños, y también cuando se traten quemaduras que ocupan mucha superficie.

El tratamiento más racional y el más fructuoso para las quemaduras, consiste en lavar perfectamente las partes afectadas con buen jabón y agua, administrando al herido cloroformo mientras se efectúa el lavado. Si se levantase vejigas se punzonarán, aplicando un vendaje seco después de tratada la quemadura con alguna solución que propenda á cicatrizar, considerándose para el caso el ácido pícrico como el mejor. El itiol es también útil y puede emplearse líquido, ó bien una mezcla de tiol, talco y subnitrato de bismuto para espolvorear. El ácido pícrico se emplea en solución saturada, conteniendo sobre 12 partes en 1000; mas este tratamiento no debería emplearse para los niños, ni para quemaduras profundas y antiguas que supuran La parte afectada se lava con una solución de ácido pícrico por espacio de media hora, y luego se venda con gasa embebida en ácido pícrico. Sobre este vendaje no convendrá emplear ningun tejido de gutta-percha, porque mantiene la humedad y el ácido pícrico constituye un apósito seco. Después de permanecer éste por seis ú ocho días, la costra se habrá puesto tan dura que la gasa se hallará adherida á la piel. La parte se lava entonces con una solución caliente de ácido pícrico, y de este modo podrá quitarse el vendaje sin dolor. Si las manos quedaren manchadas con el ácido, se limpiarán con una solución saturada de carbonato de litio ó de borax, ó bien con agua á la que se le habrá añadido un álcali. Para evitar el mancharse las manos con el ácido pícrico, mientras se pone el vendaje se untarán aquéllas de antemano con vaselina.

DE COMO ADMINISTRAR LA QUININA Y EL RUIBARBO A LOS NIÑOS

En un número reciente de la *Presse médicale* (1905, página 336), Ivon sugiere varios medios para enmascarar el gusto de la quinina y el ruibarbo, especialmente cuando han de administrarse estas drogas á los niños. Dice que en Argel la quinina se consume en cantidad considerable distribuyéndola en el zumo de limón, así la toman los jóvenes, pues á los niños no parece gustarles el zumo de limón; para este caso se les da la quinina en un aceite al que se añade un poco de bicarbonato de sosa. Prepárase una masa consistente en 90 gramos de quinina y 10 gramos de aceite de almendras dulces disuelto en éter. Después de añadir un poco de bicarbonato de sosa, se aroma la masa con un poco de limón ó de menta piperita; tragándolo con rapidez no deja sabor de quinina. El ruibarbo puede disfrazarse de idéntica manera.

Envenenamiento por Fenacetina

Despierta siempre tanto interés la lectura de envenenamientos con drogas que se consumen de ordinario, que á menudo se olvidan los peligros en que se incurre con algunas que son muy populares, como por ejemplo la fenacetina, que tanto se emplea hoy día, sin parar mientes á sus efectos venenosos, quizás por falta de un conocimiento exacto de la droga Esto no obstante, los periódicos técnicos publican de cuando en cuando casos de envenenamiento que merecen copiarse en la prensa diaria para divulgar entre el pueblo los riesgos que envuelve el uso de la fenacetina.

En una publicación alemana (*Deutsch Med. Wochen*, 1905, No. 2), el médico de Berlín Hirshfeld hace el relato de una mujer que durante dos meses había estado padeciendo de una erupción cutánea, principalmente manchas en las piernas, que en algunas partes formaban zonas grandes negruzcas, ó negro obscuras, muy dolorosas al tacto, trocándose finalmente en úlceras con orillas ásperas y gruesas. Por algún tiempo el tratamiento no dió resultado, siendo difícil descubrir la causa del mal. Observando el médico con más atención la enferma, halló vestigios de envenenamiento crónico de fenacetina. En efecto, la mujer había usado la droga por algún tiempo como remedio para fuertes dolores de cabeza. Tan luego como cesó de tomarla las manchas desaparecieron, empezaron á cicatrizar las úlceras y la enferma se restableció al cabo de un mes. Transcurrido algún tiempo volvió á tomar cosa de 1.5 gramos de fenacetina en el curso de un día, y una semana después aparecía otra erupción y una nueva úlcera.

Se conocen muchos otros casos de erupciones cutáneas nacidas del consumo de fenacetina. De su estudio se desprende que hay personas predispuestas á estos resultados en virtud de alguna peculiaridad de su sistema.

NOTAS COMERCIALES

— El Sr. J. R. González, Apartado 2261, México, es el representante de los Sres. Armour & Company, de Chicago. Todos los pedidos para Pepsina, Pancreatina, Solución Suprarenalina, etc., como también para Manteca Benzoinatada ó cualquiera de los productos del Laboratorio Armour, que se envíen al Sr. González, serán objeto de pronta atención.

— La Pasteur Vaccine Company, de París, Francia, y de Nueva York, E. U. A., con muchos puntos de distribución en todo el mundo, llama la atención de nuestros lectores españoles á sus productos, particularmente aquellos que se emplean para combatir el ántrax, la morriña negra y otras enfermedades del ganado. Esta Compañía es la única que distribuye los productos á que ha dado nombre el insigne Pasteur.

— Hay medios muy legítimos de llamar la atención del público, y, valiéndose de los mismos, E. S. Wells, de Jersey City (N. J.), U. S. A., ofrece una interesante y divertida litografía en siete colores, midiendo 14 x 21 pulgs., á quien se la pida, haciendo á la vez mención del AMERICAN DRUGGIST. E. S. Wells ha creado una venta considerable en los Estados Unidos y en muchos otros países para su «veneno para matar ratas, y sus exterminadores de insectos,» tan útiles doquiera esa plaga infecta los establecimientos. En su vista, estos productos deberían expenderlos todos los farmacéuticos, pues siempre hay demanda por ellos.

— Es indudable que por la fama que los acompaña, los Emplastos de Alcock y las Píldoras de Brandreth, anunciados en este número del AMERICAN DRUGGIST por la Alcock Manufacturing Company, de Nueva York, habrán de despertar sumo interés entre nuestros lectores del ramo situados en la América española. Estos dos artículos específicos, tan antiguos ya, se venden en todas partes del mundo, y particularmente en la América Meridional, donde son tan apreciados. Debido á su constante excelencia y propiedades curativas, se hallan algunas imitacions espúreas en el mercado, y los señores de la Compañía Alcock agredecerían á sus amigos que les diesen cuenta de cualquiera imitación con que tropiecen.

— Los productos americanos de excelencia reconocida son muchos, mereciendo citarse entre ellos, por el buen nombre que se han aquistado, el Glyco-Heroina (Smith) y el Ergoapiol (Smith); ambos artículos son fabricados por la Martin U. Smith Company, del 105 Chambers Street, Nueva York, y tienen muy buen acogida en todas partes de México y Centro-América, al igual que en la América del Sur. El Glyco-Heroina es para toses y afecciones del aparato respiratorio, y el Ergoapiol es para la amenorrea, dismenorrea, etc. No obstante el hecho de que el Ergoapiol no contiene narcóticos, opiatos ni analgésicos, posee propiedades muy notables para el alivio del dolor. Nuestros lectores pueden obtener muy valiosos informes de esos dos preparados dirigiéndose á los fabricantes, mencionando nuestro periódico.

PUNIBLE IMITACION DE MEDICINAS. — Habiendo tenido noticia la Antikamnia Chemical Co., de St. Luis, que se falsificaban sus celebrados productos, ha enviado un aviso á la prensa extranjera concebido en esta forma:

« Recientemente ha llegado á nuestro conocimiento que en esa República se han vendido y se venden, como Tabletas ó Pastillas de Antikamnia legítimas, *Tabletas de Antikamnia*, por las Droguerías y Farmacias otras Pastillas ó Tabletas que llevan impresa la letra « A,» las letras « A. C.,» las letras « qp » y también tabletas sin marca alguna.

» Lamentamos sinceramente ese estado de cosas, que lastima la reconocida integridad de droguistas y farmacéuticos. El mérito real y la justa popularidad de las *Tabletas de Antikamnia* han hecho posible para personas poco delicadas, el expendio fraudulento de pastillas ó tabletas de distintas marcas, en sustitución de las legítimas y verdaderas.

» Somos enemigos acérrimos de toda sustitución ó falsificación de medicinas, y por consiguiente, deseamos informar á nuestros lectores y á los consumidores, que las legítimas pastillas ó *Tabletas de Antikamnia* llevan siempre el monograma « AK » y estas dos letras se encuentran siempre unidas y nunca separadas. Por consiguiente, todas las tabletas que lleven separadas dichas letras, otras distintas ó distinto monograma, ó ningún distintivo, no son *Tabletas de Antikamnia*, y el Droguista ó Farmacéutico que las expende con tal nombre, vende en realidad positivamente *Tabletas de Antikamnia* falsificadas.

» Conocida, pues, la fraudulenta sustitución de nuestras tabletas para prevenir la imposición hecha á Médicos y enfermos de productos distintos del solicitado, esperamos que en cada caso de éstos se haga conocer el nombre de la Droguería ó Farmacia que así proceda á *La Compañía Química de la Antikamnia, St. Louis, E. U. A.*»

Es interesante para todo Médico y Farmacéutico el insistir en obtener las únicas « *Tabletas de Antikamnia* » genuinas, porque no puede lograr los mismos resultados satisfactorios por la administración de todas sus imitaciones.

AMERICAN DRUGGIST

and PHARMACEUTICAL RECORD

NUEVA YORK y CHICAGO: 9 DE ABRIL DE 1906

«The American Druggist» es un periódico bimensual del que se publica cada mes un suplemento español con anuncios en el mismo idioma

AMERICAN DRUGGIST PUBLISHING COMPANY

62-68 WEST BROADWAY, NEW YORK, U. S. A.

Dirección cablegráfica «Amdruggist, New York.» Clave A B C

A. R. ELLIOTT, *Presidente*

CASWELL A. MAYO, Ph. G.................... *Director*

THOMAS J. KEENAN, Lic. en Farm., *Director Asociado*

PRECIOS DE SUSCRIPCION

Pago adelantado, Estados Unidos, Canadá, México, Cuba, Puerto Rico, Hawaii y las Filipinas .. ..(oro americano) $1.50

Otros paises (franco de porte).................... » » $3.00

Las suscripciones pueden empezar en cualquier tiempo.

«THE AMERICAN DRUGGIST AND PHARMACEUTICAL RECORD» sale el segundo y cuarto lunes de cada mes. Todo cambio de anuncios debe ser recibido diez días antes de la fecha de salida.

Remesas deben hacerse con libranzas sobre Nueva York, giros postales internacionales ó por expreso ó correo en carta certificada. Toda correspondencia debe dirigirse á la AMERICAN DRUGGIST PUBLISHING Co., 62-68 West Broadway, New York, U. S. A.

EL CONGRESO PAN-AMERICANO

SE anuncia en las esferas del gobierno que además del delegado nombrado para asistir con carácter oficial á las sesiones del Congreso Pan-Americano, el secretario de Estado Hon. Elihu Root, estará igualmente presente, y en tiempo oportuno visitará oficialmente á todas las repúblicas sudamericanas, con cuyo paso se espera se estrechen más las relaciones entre aquellas países y los Estados Unidos.

Aunque el Congreso indudablemente se dedicará á la ventilación de asuntos de carácter comercial y financiero que conduzcan á estrechar los lazos de todas las partes interesadas, se ha sugerido en círculos militares que tal vez se aproveche la ocasión para tratar de la formación de una alianza defensiva que conduzca al establecimiento sobre una anche base de la doctrina de Monroe. Cierto es que el secretario Root está bien capacitado por su experiencia para presentar al Congreso los aspectos militares y políticos de la situación de una manera que llame la atención de las autoridades con quienes vendrá en contacto durante su visita oficial. El secretario Root antes de desempeñar el presente cargo había sido ministro de la Guerra, cuya cartera desempeñó á satisfacción de la nación. Con todo, el Gobierno no ha intimado oficialmente que la doctrina de Monroe haya de ser parte del programa que se discuta en el Congreso. Hay que convenir en que el establecimiento de una inteligencia ó alianza de las naciones americanas habría de ser beneficiosa; equivaldría á una protección moral cuando menos, contra la invasión de este continente por las potencias europeas ó asiáticas. Un acercamiento cordial entre las Repúblicas de este continente, norte y sur, constituiría una formal intimación á las potencias del mundo que la integridad de la doctrina Monroe sería mantenida por la acción concertada de las repúblicas continentales contra cualquier agresor. Si bien la cooperación militar y naval que pudieran ofrecer esas repúblicas quizás no fuera muy formidable, el efecto de la inteligencia intercontinental tendría mucho alcance, no siendo probable en este caso que ninguna nación europea tratase de engrandecerse con la apropiación de territorios que la alianza estaría llamada á defender.

En la cuestión de negocios, todos los países continentales habrían de salir gananciosos por el acercamiento de relaciones. Durante el año 1905 los Estados Unidos vendió á los países de la América del Sur por valor de $90.000,000 de efectos, ó una quinta parte del total que importaron de Europa; solamente la República Argentina importó de aquel continente durante el año pasado, por valor de $180.000,000, en lo cual habrán salido perjudicados no tan sólo los países del Sur sino que también los Estados Unidos, convencidos como estamos de que la mayoría de efectos tomados de Europa hubiesen podido comprarse en este país con gran economía tanto en el precio como en la calidad.

De la conferencia que se celebrará en el mes de julio en Río Janeiro, esperamos excelentes resultados, tanto si se adopta ningún acuerdo sobre la cuestión política intercontinental, tomando como base la doctrina de Monroe, como si se discuten cuestiones puramente comerciales, monetarias, aduaneras, etc., y creemos un buen augurio que el secretario Root esté presente durante el tiempo en que duren las sesiones.

Cloruro de Etilo Peligroso

Ante una de las sociedades médicas de Londres, se leyó recientemente un interesante informe referente á la administración de anestésicos en la práctica de la cirugía dental. Este estudio revestía especial interés con motivo de un caso que resultó fatal, hace poco tiempo, en manos de un dentista de la gran metrópoli. En el informe está demostrado de una manera palmaria que la droga en cuestión, que se había venido empleando con sobrada confianza en los tres años pasados, es mucho más peligrosa de lo que el público se imagina, pues de una investigación detenida resulta que después de un estímulo temporal sobreviene una baja notable en la presión de la sangre del cuerpo humano, por efecto de lo cual se recomienda en el informe que no se emplee más el cloruro de etilo.

En los casos de personas de edad ó de otras que

padezcan de trastornos cardíacos, se condena en absoluto el empleo de un vapor fuerte. En los trabajos dentales deberían emplearse invariablemente el oxígeno y el gas de óxido nitroso, á menos que no se trate de niños.

Venenos en Nuestros Alimentos

Una variedad sorprendente de los venenos vegetales más poderosos tales como morfina, estricnina, digitales y nicotina, están íntimamente asociados á las tomaínas Muchos de estos productos tomaínicos que obran cual venenos, en su origen se conocían con el nombre de «alcaloides cadavéricos,» porque al describirse por primera vez averiguóse que eran producidos por la descomposición de substancias animales. Después hallóse que procedían de la actividad animal durante la vida, y en su vista sería más apropiado llamar las dos clases de tomaínas alcaloides animales, para poder incluir en ellas tanto las que resultan de procesos de descomposición, como las procedentes de la acción fisiológica.

Muchas de las dolencias más ordinarias de la vida, tales como dolores de cabeza, sensaciones de fatiga, al igual que los trastornos nerviosos más graves, se originan á menudo del fracaso de los procesos excretorios ordinarios para eliminar estos productos tóxicos de la vitalidad La relación de las bacterias á los alcaloides animales, ó tomaínas, es de que obran en la molécula compleja de la albúmina, que es el antecesor común de los alcaloides, animales ó vegetales, y la dividen en varias moléculas menos complejas, entre las cuales se hallan las tomaínas. Este es el proceso de la putrefacción; la clase de tomaína que de él se forma, depende de la clase particular de bacteria existente, de la naturaleza del material en que se desarrollan, y de las condiciones tales como la temperatura, etc., en las cuales procede la putrefacción.

En un informe de trece casos el material de las experiencias era como sigue: Carne de puerco, en alguna forma, nueve casos, carne de carnicero (sin expresar clase) dos casos, ternera un caso, y vaca otro caso. El pescado y el queso pueden ser igualmente atacados; más los cangrejos, langostas, mejillones son los más expuestos, siendo el origen de la infección la bacteria introducida por el medio de las aguas corrompidas y cuando los mismos se dejan en el mar abierto por algunos meses, todas las propiedades venenosas son eliminadas. Por supuesto, otros venenos además de las tomaínas se desarrollan en alimentos de todas clases por la agencia de las bacterias.

No se ha decidido todavía, por qué ciertas clases de alimentos, por ejemplo, la caza, pueden comerse impunemente en un estado de descomposición avanzada, mientras que el puerco, estando aun tan ligeramente infectado, que apenas si puede descubrirse, causa envenenamiento.

Hay otro peligro, por cierto muy curioso, derivado de la formación de tomaínas en el cuerpo humano. Se conocen casos en que se ha declarado que la muerte fué causada por la administración maliciosa de alcaloides vegetales, que los toxicólogos clasifican como casos de envenenamiento por tomaínas. Es posible, en vista de esto, que muchas personas inocentes hayan sufrido por esta causa y que otras sufran en lo futuro, aunque los médicos llamados á atender tales casos, están más sobre aviso que en tiempo atrás, cuando no se había adelantado tanto en los estudios de bacteriología.

La dificultad estriba en el hecho de que no hay reacciones químicas por cuyo medio las tomaínas como clase puedan distinguirse de los alcaloides vegetales. Como las tomaínas se hallan presentes, en más ó menos cantidad, probablemente en cada uno de los órganos sometidos al toxicólogo para su examen, claro es que podrían cometerse graves errores si los químicos no estuviesen alerta contra toda precipitación en declarar de buenas á primeras como compuestos tomaínicos los alcaloides vegetales venenosos. Estos habrán de haber sido administrados deliberadamente con alimento ó bebida como vehículo, mientras que los primeros se habrán administrado bien como alimento tomado como de ordinario, siendo el alimento el veneno y no meramente el vehículo; ó pueden hallarse en el cuerpo después de la muerte como resultado de las condiciones ó estado del mismo en producir su propio veneno durante la vida, ó pueden haberse originado del proceso de putrefacción después de la muerte.

La química por sí misma no puede determinar cuál es la solución, por consiguiente se habrían de buscar otras pruebas en síntomas específicos que pudieran producirse solamente por algún veneno particular conocido y en las circunstancias generales en que ocurrió la muerte. Más inocentes personas han perecido por el envenenamiento positivo de tomaínas, que por equivocación se han juzgado ser alcaloides vegetales, de lo que es posible imaginarse.

¡Alerta con Ciertos Tintes!

Muchos de los tintes para el cabello de los que se usan ordinariamente, contienen sustancias que si llegan á penetrar en los ojos habrán de causar suma molestia y probablemente mucho daño. Cuanto al peróxido, que en tal cantidad lo emplean las mujeres para obtener tintas caprichosas de color rubio, si invade los ojos no causa ningún serio resultado, por más que ataca y deteriora el cabello, y eventualmente impide su crecimiento; pero en cuanto á afectar á la salud en general, lleva la ventaja á muchos de los tintes orgánicos y metálicos en extremo nocivos.

De los tintes de anilina, empleados para dar color al cabello distinto del natural, algunos producen irritación cutánea mortificante, no tan sólo en el cuero cabelludo, sino hasta en la cara y cejas. Uno de estos productos en particular, el parafenilendiamina, usado en los tintes para el cabello, debe evitarse, porque á veces produce manifestaciones graves de envenenamiento. Está probado que el mismo producto, que en la industria se emplea para teñir calcetería, ha dado lugar, sin ningún género de duda, á casos de envenenamiento, irritación del cutis, eczemas, vómitos y parálisis de los miembros.

En un artículo que ha visto recientemente la luz pública en el *Science, Art, Nature*, rev
autor, M. Berger, relata el caso de
quien acostumbraba á emplear un prod
para el cabello no tardó mucho en expe
tornos de la visión, acompañados de fuertes do
cabeza; examinada, descubriéronse señales visi
envenenamiento causado por la anilina. Cesó l
de aplicarse al cabello el nocivo p
gradualmente la salud.

LA PLANTA PATCHULI

El patchulí es indígena de la India y la China en cuyos países es muy común. También crece y prospera en Ceilán, Paraguay y la isla francesa La Reunión. Las hojas y ramas de esta planta poseen un perfume parecido al almizcle y al destilarse dan la esencia de patchulí. Se asemeja á la salvia por su alto, al igual que por su forma; pero sus hojas tienen menos pulpa. Nuestro primer conocimiento de esta planta data del año 1850 cuando se importó por primera vez en Londres. En aquel entonces los chales de la India legítimos se vendían á precios extravagantes por lo altos, y los compradores reconocían los verdaderos por su olor por estar perfumados con el patchulí. Los fabricantes franceses, para poder imitar á la perfección los chales de la India, importaban la planta y perfumaban los artículos con la esencia, vendiéndolos después como genuinos. Desde entonces los perfumistas han tomado por su cuenta la industria.

El cultivo de la planta patchulí se ha llevado á cabo durante siglos en China y la Península Malaca. Necesita un suelo ligero, y más ó menos á nivel, ó formado de pequeñas colinas. Durante la estación de las lluvias se transplantan las plantas, colocándose á una distancia de 18 pulgadas entre sí cubriéndose de hojas. Seis meses después se lleva á cabo el primer corte. Cada hectárea (2,471 acres) rinde en cada recolección sobre 344 libras de hojas secas y ramas, y 185 libras de tallos.

Las ramas secas están valoradas en unos 11 centavos por libra, y como se verifican dos cortes al año, los cosecheros reciben en bruto sobre $25.00 el acre, y á veces tanto como $40.00.

La cosecha se clasifica de tres modos: (1) Hojas; (2) hojas mezcladas con retoños tiernos y un poco de palo; (3) tallos grandes. En Java las hojas de patchulí se mezclan á menudo con un 25 por ciento de hojas de dilem. Las hojas de aquel que se importan de Catuill y Bombay contienen 75 por ciento de tallos, y rinden una esencia menos valiosa que las plantas de la Península de Malaca. El patchulí de Java es de fina apariencia, pero es pobre de aroma. La esencia se extrae á veces en los países que se origina; pero la destilación en grande escala de las hojas se lleva á cabo solamente en Europa. Las hojas se cortan primeramente, luego se hidatran dejándose así por 12 horas y después se destilan al vapor. El rendimiento de aceite es de 1¾ á 3 por ciento. Es un líquido amarillo verdoso que con el tiempo se vuelve de color obscuro; es más bien espeso y posee un olor penetrante que es desagradable en estado concentrado; pero agradable ó á lo menos característico cuando está diluído y se asocia á otros perfumes. La densidad del aceite á 29,4° C., es como sigue: aceite verde de Penang, 0.957; aceite oscuro de Penang, 0.958; aceite oscuro francés, 1.012; aceite ordinario comercial, 1.0119.

[illegible] ceite de patchulí es soluble en 10 ó 12 par- [illegible]cohol. El material se falsifica á veces con esen- [illegible]edro.

[illegible]olor del aceite de patchulí es tan fuerte que [illegible]oca gente puede resistirlo. De aquí que se em- [illegible] siempre en forma diluída. Cuando se mezcla con [illegible] aceite, éste es imperceptible. A menudo se pulzan las hojas secas, se pone el polvo en *sachets* que [illegible]uardan contra la polilla puestos en cómodas ó [illegible]os.

NOTAS FARMACEUTICAS

CILINDROS DE MENTOL CLORAL

Siguiendo la fórmula siguiente puede el farmacéutico preparar un cilindro excelente para el tratamiento de la jaqueca, neuralgia, dolores de cabeza, etc.:

Cloral de hidrato	1 parte
Mentol	1 »
Manteca de cacao	2 partes
Spermaceti	4 »

Se derrite la manteca de cacao con el espermaceti añadiendo á la masa derretida el cloral hidrato y el mentol, y cuando ya esté suave se vierte la masa en moldes para enfriarse. Estos cilindros pueden fijarse en mangos apropiados de madera.

MODO DE EVITAR LA CRISTALIZACION DEL JARABE SIMPLE

Es á menudo difícil impedir que se formen cristales en el jarabe simple, no obstante las precauciones tomadas en la preparación de este artículo. Alcock, droguista inglés, recomienda la adición de pequeñas cantidades de carbonato de potasio, sobre 2 granos por pinta de jarabe. Se ha averiguado que la cristalización del jarabe se presenta en la proporción de la acidez del mismo, y que esta preparación es por lo regular ácida en la reacción, aunque algunas veces es alcalina, y con menos frecuencia neutra. Con la adición del carbonato de potasio queda contrarrestada la acidez, impidiéndose la cristalización y no alterándose el gusto del jarabe.

DESAGREGACION DE TABLETAS

Una de las condiciones esenciales en la preparación de tabletas, es la obtención de un excipiente que las permita deshacerse con prontitud para que se disuelvan fácilmente en agua. Desde que se adoptó la forma de tableta en la farmacia americana, ha llegado á generalizarse de tal manera, que no sorprende ver que hayan hecho tantos esfuerzos en perfeccionar la maquinaria y los procedimientos empleados en la manufactura del artículo. El farmacéutico que observe la apariencia y la condición de estos productos en diferentes circunstancias, hallará seguramente la diferencia en la solubilidad de los que proceden de fabricantes distintos. El problema consiste en preparar una tableta que sea dura y seca lo suficiente para no pegarse ni perder peso con el manoseo, y que se deshaga casi al instante de usarse. En los comienzos de la manufactura de tabletas se halló que había de añadirse algo á la tableta que está formada á menudo de substancias insolubles, como el calomelano, el bismuto, etc., para que pudiera deshacerse fácilmente en agua. La adición de almidón de maíz á los polvos de que se componen las tabletas, produce la desintegración al poco tiempo cuando se echa le tableta en agua; pero si cuando se fabricaron las tabletas el tiempo era húmedo, entonces se deshacen con dificultad. O bien si se hubiese añadido almidón con exceso la tableta se pone quebradiza, se hiende y causa sinnúmero de molestias al farmacéutico. Si añadimos almidón en polvo fino al polvo granulado que se emplea para hacer las tabletas, las últimas que se hagan de una partida resultarían deficientes en almidón y más fuertes en ingredientes medicinales.

William J. Lowry, de Baltimore, considerado farmacéutico práctico y observador minucioso, en una discusión reciente acerca la desagregación de la tableta, dijo haber hallado que la pasta de harina ordinaria sin ningún ácido ó alumbre, era mejor excipiente para tabletas, aunque esto todavía deja que desear para la desintegración que se busca en las tabletas insolubles. El almidón de maíz hecho pasta con agua caliente, es también un excipiente excelente, y se le puede añadir algunas veces un poco de almidón sin cocer, mezclándolo con los gránulos antes de colocar la masa en los moldes. Las observaciones del Sr. Lowrey fueron discutidas, dando lugar á que uno de los discursantes dijese que el empleo de agentes adhesivos en las tabletas tiende á hacerlas tan duras que no se deshacen cuando se ponen en agua. Otro farmacéutico dijo que, según su experiencia, no es posible prever el resultado de la fabricación de una partida de tabletas. Algunas veces con la añadidura de un poco de almidón la tableta mejora; pero á menudo es causa de que aquella se asiente y se deshaga más tarde. En otros casos, cuando la mezcla de pasta de almidón, goma de acacia y glicerina, etc., cuya mezcla se hace con objeto de granular los polvos al hacer las tabletas, está conforme, no será necesario añadir más almidón para que las tabletas se desagreguen. Mas tratándose de ciertas tabletas, como las de salol, que es difícil desmenuzar, convendrá añadir un poco de almidón extra.

Hay que poner ciertos reparos al empleo de pasta de almidón al preparar tabletas solubles, pues cuando las tabletas se secan en la hornilla el almidón se vuelve insoluble, y esto entorpece la solubilidad de la tableta. De todos modos la solución se presenta muy turbia.

PRECAUCIONES CON EL AGUA DE CAL

Pritchard, conocido farmacéutico de Pennsylvania, leyó una interesante memoria, el año pasado, ante la Asociación Farmacéutica de aquel Estado, en la que exponía varios extremos valiosos acerca de la manera de manejar el agua de cal en la botica. Hace algún tiempo, dijo, ponía el agua de cal en vasijas de un galón, y para dispensarla se servía de una botella con pico. Como se sabe, es de mucha importancia dispensar un agua clara y límpida, de otra manera la reputación del farmacéutico quizás sufriría. Esto no obstante, sabido es de todo el mundo cuán difícil es mantener siempre clara esa agua. Cada vez que se saca una parte del líquido de la vasija, lo restante queda en una condición turbia, y si sucediese entonces que hubiese de tomarse alguna agua más, hállase el agua turbia. Al servirse de un número de vasijas no se sabe cuantas se han vaciado, y algunas veces las existencias se agotan inesperadamente. Esto causa mucho embarazo en algunas estaciones del año, cuando las labores de enyesado ó la construcción de casas escasean, pues no es fácil entonces el procurarse un trozo de cal viva, con que se hace el agua.

Sugiere que se empleen vasijas ó botes de cinco galones, que á veces se reciben conteniendo otros productos; se practica entonces un agujero en un costado usando un taladro de maquinista con un poco de trementina. Luego se toma un corcho de buen tamaño y se hace en él un agujero para poner una llave de latón en cuyo extremo interior hay un tubo de cristal sujetado por medio de una unión de caucho de modo que sobresalga varias pulgadas del cuello de la vasija. Se pone entonces un taponcito en el orificio que sirve de respiradero, y se llena por último la vasija con agua de cal, hecha según prescribe la Farmacopea. Se afirma bien el tapón con la llave, y habiendo hecho en un estante un agujero bastante grande para introducir el cuello de la vasija, inviértese aquella, llave abajo haciendo pasar el cuello por el agujero y sujetando con una correa al estante el cuerpo de la vasija. La cal que se ha disuelto se asienta en el cuello, mientras que el tubo de latón se extiende á través del precipitado hacia arriba donde está clara el agua. Cuando se necesita una cantidad de agua de preparación reciente, se da vuelta á la llave y se abre el respiradero. De este modo se tendrá siempre agua clara y se sabrá qué existencia hay de ella en la botica.

MEZCLAS INCOMPATIBLES

El aceite de enebro y la parafina líquida cuando se mezclan producen un líquido sucio, opaco, del que se precipita después de algún tiempo el aceite, mientras que la parafina permanece arriba formando un anillo obscuro en la superficie.

Cuando se mezclan salol, benzonaftol y timol, resulta un líquido siruposo con motivo de la unión del salol y el timol. Un líquido semejante sobreviene de la adición de salol á una solución alcohólica de timol, en cuyo caso se precipitan al fondo del vaso gotas oleosas.

La estovaina rinde precipitados al añadírsele soluciones alcalinas de alcaloides y soluciones de cloruro de mercurio. De aquí que el empleo del cloruro de mercurio debería evitarse en la desinfección de jeringas que se hayan usado para inyecciones de estovaina.

El estoraque líquido y la parafina líquida son incompatibles.

HISTORIA DE LA BALANZA

Tiene tal importancia este instrumento en la farmacia, que probablemente habrá de interesar la relación que hace la *Revista Farmacéutica* de Crandel & Kramer, en sus números de noviembre y diciembre de 1905, que es como sigue: «La Balanza (*Bilanx, Bilancis*, que tiene dos platillos; de *bis* dos, y *lanx*, platillo) fué conocida en los primeros tiempos de la civilización, habiéndose hallado alusiones á ella en manuscritos egipcios y en vasos griegos. La forma más sencilla de la balanza consistía en una barra sustentada por su centro, y más tarde suspendida por una cinta ó cadena, también por el centro. De cada extremo de la barra colgaba un platillo. La primera mejora que se introdujo en esa forma primitiva fué la añadidura de un índice afirmado en ángulo recto á la barra. En la antigua Roma se usaban balanzas con este apéndice. En Pompeya se empleaba una pesa corrediza en la barra, que estaba graduada.

En Roma se conocían con un brazo, con el nombre de *staterae*, y este estilo de balanzas todavía es corriente en Italia y otros países del mediodía de Europa. Estas balanzas no tienen sino un platillo y un gancho del cual se suspenden los objetos. Están provistas con doble brazo, uno para el platillo y el otro para el gancho teniendo los dos brazos escala graduada, por los cuales se podía correr un pilón

De esta forma aproximadament
últimos del siglo dieciocho, cuando la
químicas llevadas á cabo por Lavois
sarias balanzas de más precisión p
reacciones cuantitativas, y en consec..
de precisión fué entonces un instrumen
ble para el químico. Por lo cual
Wochler, en sus cartas, observ

encargado á un relojero que le hiciera una balanza de conformidad con las instrucciones de Gahn (J. G. Gahn, químico sueco, fallecido en Stockolmo en 1745). Estas instrucciones para fabricar balanzas las considera de tal importancia Berzelius en su *Lehrbuch der Chimie*, que en el libro se citan en detalle. Las balanzas de precisión de los tiempos presentes están calcadas en aquellas que acabamos de citar.

Podría decirse que no se conoce un solo inventor de la balanza de precisión, pues ha llegado á nosotros por un proceso de evolución desde los egipcios.

NUEVOS REMEDIOS

ACETAL. (*Eter Etelideno Dietílico*). — Líquido incoloro, volátil, soluble en 18 partes de agua, y muy soluble en alcohol. Se emplea como sedante é hipnótico. En dosis de 2 á 3 dracmas fluídas, y de ordinario como emulsión. Puramente medicinal, la onza, $1.00; comercial, la onza, 65 centavos.

ACETOZONO. (*Peróxido Benzoilacetil*). — Polvo blanco, ligeramente soluble en agua (1:1000), poco soluble en alcohol. Bactericida. Se emplea interna y externalmente en enfermedades derivadas de gérmenes. Se halla en el mercado como mezcla de un 50 por ciento con polvo inerte absorbente. Dosis de 1 á 3 granos en solución. Cajas conteniendo 6 tubos ó 15 granos, cada una, la caja, $1.25; frascos de ¼ de onza, $1.40; frascos de ½ onza, $2.70; frascos de 1 onza, $5.25.

(Parke, Davis & Cía.)

ACET-THEOCINO-SODIO. — Polvo blanco, cristalino, soluble fácilmente en agua. Diurético poderoso. Se emplea en la hidropesía, en dosis de 5 á 7 granos, dos ó tres veces al día. Frascos de ½ y 1 onza, $1.90 y $2.30.

(Continental Color & Chemical Cía.)

ACOINA. Hidrocloruro de Guanidina, Diparoanisilmonofenitil. — Polvo blanco cristalino, soluble en 17 partes de agua. Anestésico local cual la cocaína, empleado hipodérmicamente en la cirugía del ojo; anestésico dental, en solución normal salina, 2 por ciento, tubos de 15 granos, cada tubo, 30 cents.; cápsulas de 2½ granos, 28 en una caja, 75 centavos.

(The Heyden Chemical Work)

SOLUCION ADNEFRINA. — Solución al 1.1000 del principio activo de la glándula suprarrenal, en solución salina fisiológica, conteniendo ½ de 1 por ciento de metaformo. Se emplea principalmente como hemostático, y también para el tratamiento de inflamaciones, congestiones y tumefacciones de las membranas mucosas, igualmente como estimulante cardíaco. Tubo de 1 onza, 60 centavos.

EMOLIENTE. — Tubos, cada uno, 30 cent.

.VERIZACION DE ACEITE. — Tubos de 1 onza, ents.

Frederick Stearns & Co.)

...NA. — Polvo blanco grisáceo, soluble cultad en el agua. Principio elevador de la pre- de la sangre de las glándulas suprarrenales. Tubos 1 gr cents. Se emplea invariablemente en la

SOLUCION DE CLORURO, 1:1000; solución de 1 parte de cloruro de adrenalina en 1,000 partes de solución salina fisiológica, con 0.5 por ciento de cloretona. Astringente poderoso, hemostático y estimulante cardíaco. Empléase para dominar hemorragias internas y superficiales, para la reducción de la congestión é inflamación de las membranas mucosas, como estimulante del corazón en el colapso, y como auxiliar de la acción anestésica local de la cocaína. Dosis interna, de 5 á 30 mínimas. Frascos de 1 onza, 85 cents.

UNGÜENTO. — Tubos de ½ onza, 43 cents.

INHALANTE. — Frasco de 1 onza, 85 cents.

SUPOSITORIOS. — Caja de 1 docena, 38 cents.

TABLETAS. — Tubos de 25, 85 cents.

(Parke, Davis & Co.)

ADRIN (*Hidrato Epinofrino*). — Polvo blanquizco, nonhigroscópico; principio de la glándula suprarrenal. Tiene las mismas propiedades que la adrenalina. Tubos de 1 grano, cada uno, 75c.; solución al 1-1000, tubos de 1 oz., cada uno, 75c.; tabletas en tubos de 12, c. s. para hacer 15 mínimos de la solución del 1 1000, cada una, 40c.; en tubos de 100, cada uno, $3.10.

(H. K. Mulford & Co.)

AGURIN (*Acet. Teobromino Sódico*). — Polvo blanco higroscópico, soluble en agua, incompatible con ácidos. Diurético en hidropesía. Dosis, 7 á 15 granos, dos veces al día. Frascos de ½ y 1 oz., $1.55 á $1.70.

(Continental Color and Chemical Co.)

AIROL (*Oxiodogalato de Bismuto*). — Polvo verde gris, insoluble en agua ó en alcohol. Mezclado con agua el airol se descompone parcialmente y vuélvese rojo. Debería mezclarse con agua solamente con la intervención de la glicerina. Usado externalmente como aplicación á heridas, quemaduras, enfermedades de la piel, del ojo, nariz, gonorrea. Bien puro, en 10 por ciento en suspensión, con iguales partes de glicerina y agua, ó 10 á 20 por ciento; ungüento. Cartones de 1 oz., $1.00.

(Hoffman La Roche Chemical Works.)

ALBARGIN (*Plata Gelatose*) — Polvo ligeramente prieto, soluble en agua con facilidad. Contiene 15 por ciento de plata. Para genorrea se inyecta una solución al 2 por ciento cuatro ó cinco veces al día. Tubos de 1 oz., $1.10; tubos de 50 tabletas, 0.2 grm, cada uno, el tubo, 50c.

(Victor Koechl & Co.)

ALFOZONO (*Peróxido Succítico*). — Polvo blanco, blando, soluble rápidamente en 60 partes de agua, Germicida y antiséptico, interna y externalmente. Dosis, 3 á 5 granos. Frascos de 1 oz., $4 50; de ½ oz., $2.30; de ¼ oz., $1.20; tabletas de un grano, frascos de 90, $1.00.

(Frederick Stearns & Co.)

ALIPIN. — Polvo blanco cristalino, soluble fácilmente en agua y alcohol; pero en éter se disuelve con dificultad. Las soluciones acuosas poseen una reacción neutra, y puede eterilizarse haciéndolas hervir por corto tiempo. Anestésico local, sustituto de la cocaína. La fuerza de las soluciones que se emplean de ordinario varía de 1 á 5 y hasta 10 por ciento. Puede combinarse con adrenalina y antipirina. No debería emplearse el alipín en relación con nitrato de plata con motivo de formarse un precipitado. Este reparo, sin embargo, no se refiere á las soluciones de protargol, las cuales aunque se presentan ligeramente turbias al principio pronto se aclaran.

(*Continuará*)

La Zarzaparrilla que se halla en los Mercados de Francia

Fleury (*Bulletin des Sciences Pharmacologiques*, octubre 1905), ha publicado en este periódico un buen artículo nutrido de informes acerca de las diferentes variedades de zarzaparrilla que se consumen en general, y en especial de las que se encuentran en los mercados de Francia. Según él la zarzaparrilla es hoy día una droga mucho menos importante que antes, con motivo de la denuncia de las estafas que se perpetraban en relación con ciertos compuestos de zarzaparrilla cuyos autores pretendían que curaban todos los males. No obstante lo dicho, hay todavía una regular demanda de parte de los médicos y del público por la zarzaparrilla legítima como alterante, cuyas virtudes se han demostrado por muchos años.

Las variedades á que alude Fleury comprenden las zarzaparrillas de México, Honduras, Jamaica y Pará, las cuales se consumen en Francia, entrando todos esos productos por el gran puerto del Havre.

La zarzaparrilla mexicana la considera la más importante de las clases descritas. De esta hay una variedad procedente de Tampico que se considera de segunda clase, y se importa vía de Nueva York al Havre y Hamburgo. Se embala en fardos de forma cúbica que miden 60 cm. de ancho y sobre 1 m. de alto. Cada fardo está compuesto de un número de paquetes aplanados sujetos con alambre. El peso de éstos, por término medio, es de 300 gramos cada uno. Consisten en rizomas y raíces, estando estas últimas retorcidas y dobladas una sobre otra en las balas. Las rizomas y tallos son de un color blanco amarillento, y las raíces de un color rojo gris. Estas están muy arrugadas con motivo del proceso seco á que se las somete, y tienen en algunos puntos placas de tierra negruzca. La corteza de la raíz se desprende fácilmente del palo interior que es de color gris y tiene un meollo blanco.

La zarzaparrilla de Honduras se coloca en el mercado de Londres y procede de Belisa y de varios lugares de la bahía de Honduras. Véndese en fajos cilíndricos pequeños de unos 75 cm. de largo y 5 ó 6 cm. de diámetro. Estas raíces también se doblan una sobre otra y se aseguran con otras raíces arrolladas en espiral en el fajo. Estos se embalan en fardos envueltos en cuero, cuya medida es de 45 cm. de ancho por 75 cm. de alto. Las raíces son de un color gris oscuro y rojo-oscuro, y las acanaladuras de la superficie varían según la cantidad de almidón que contienen. La raíz de Honduras llega al mercado más limpia que la de México; es más costosa que esta última, y quizás por este motivo se han hecho tentativas para hacer pasar la mexicana por hondureña sin lograr ningún éxito.

La zarzaparrilla de Jamaica va á Londres y se embarca para el Havre. Se conoce bajo el nombre de zarzaparrilla roja, si bien la variedad mexicana se vende también con el nombre de zarzaparrilla roja. Está puesta en fajos de varios tamaños, consistentes en raíces solamente, cubiertas de diminutas radículas que produce el efecto de un alambre de púas. Son de un color gris-obscuro, pero más á menudo rojo ó de color anaranjado; son muy desiguales y arrugadas. La caña central está muy desarrollada, mucho más que en las demás variedades.

La zarzaparrilla de Pará es del Brasil y proviene de diferentes variedades de esmilax. Viene en fajos grandes cilíndricos formados de raíces cortadas de un mismo largo, bien alisadas y atadas juntas con fibras vegetales. Estas raíces son de un color negro rojizo; son más delgadas que plumas de ganso, pero menos arrugadas que las demás variedades. Dícese que la raíz del Pará ya no llega al mercado del Havre. Hace algunos años que se vendía en una forma algo diferente. Las raíces estaban bien estiradas en todo su largo y atábanse en fajos largos que á su vez eran atados formando unos paquetes cónicos.

Curioso é Importante Descubrimiento

El profesor Elmer Gates, conocido científico de Washington, ha anunciado en una conferencia, haber descubierto rayos de luz ultra violeta, en ondas de cierta extensión, por cuyo medio opina el autor será posible resolver algunos de los misterios fundamentales de la vida, de la muerte, las enfermedades y la traslación del pensamiento.

Sujetos vivientes colocados al alcance de estos rayos extraños, proyectan una sombra que existe solamente en tanto que hay vida en el sujeto. Cuando éste muere, se vuelve trasparente y aquella sombra se disipa.

Los nuevos rayos, según el profesor Gates, ofrecen probablemente el primero y único método exacto de determinar si una persona está realmente muerta. Por estos rayos quedan revelados los procesos más recónditos del pensamiento humano. Con sólo dirigir los rayos sobre una persona un científico puede medir los pensamientos de aquella, puede hallar si está más afligida hoy que ayer, ó si está pensando más hondo en el acto de ser examinada que no media hora antes.

Cuando se proyectan estos rayos maravillosos sobre dos personas que están sentadas juntas, revelarán cual de las dos posee más fuerza mental.

Revela la aproximación de la enfermedad

Por medio de estos rayos es también posible descubrir cómo se aproxima una enfermedad antes de que puedan descubrirla los médicos ó cirujanos, y por este motivo presentan un método cierto y rápido de hallar si existe la menor huella de enfermedad en cualquiera parte en las profundidades del cuerpo, meramente por el grado de transparencia de éste á los rayos.

«Estaba experimentando,» dijo el profesor Gates, «con una luz invisible y ondas eléctricas, cuando hallé que ciertas extensiones de la luz extra violeta y ciertas ondulaciones eléctricas frecuentes atravesaban más completamente el cuerpo de un animal muerto que él de un animal vivo. Tenemos aquí, pues, una nueva prueba de la muerte, y también un nuevo medio de diagnosis, que nos revela tejidos enfermos y en parte muertos en la organización viviente.

»Se ha sugerido que la transparencia del organismo muerto y la disipación de la sombra pudieran atribuirse á que el alma abandona el cuerpo ó se extingue; pero esta conclusión no está justificada por haber descubierto subsiguientemente que la opacidad (la sombra) de los cuerpos vivientes era debida á la presencia de corrientes eléctricas en los nervios y músculos. Mientras la vida existe, el cuerpo es un haz de corrientes eléctricas á través de las cuales no pueden pasar las ondas eléctricas.

MEDICION DE LAS ONDAS ELECTRICAS HUMANAS

»Todos los organismos vivientes emiten ondas eléctricas en proporción al grado de actividad muscular ó mental que poseen. Esto lo he medido en mi laboratorio por medio de un delicado aparato eléctrico. Esta es, por consiguiente, la primera medida cuantitativa de estados subjetivos, y la cual nos sirve de pauta para apreciar el volumen del pensamiento de un hombre y compararlo con el de otro, permitiéndonos además el apuntar el esfuerzo mental que el hombre apronta hora tras hora, día tras día.

»Cuando las mediciones acusan cualquiera disminución mental de las tomadas como tipo anteriormente, es indicación de la aproximación de alguna enfermedad, cuyos primeros síntomas el enfermo tarda aun en sentir, y sin que exista ningún otro medio de diagnosis para revelarla.

»Estos experimentos nos proporcionarán probablemente algún dato importante sobre el problema de la traslación del pensamiento. Por ejemplo, las ondas eléctridas emitidas por un organismo viviente, cuando se posan sobre otro organismo viviente, aceleran ó retardan de un modo apreciable la actividad del mismo.»

Son, pues, dos las agencias que se han descubierto —una por medio de la acción de los nuevos rayos, revelando la intensidad de la «sombra» del cuerpo compenetrado de vida, la otra por medio de las ondulaciones eléctricas, enseñando el estado de la mentalidad y el estado físico del cuerpo. Si estos fenómenos quedan bien comprobados la ciencia habrá dado un gran paso.

Métodos de Anunciar

Pocas localidades pueden emplear los mismos métodos de anunciar por ser las condiciones diferentes. En pequeños pueblos rurales generalmente se acude al único periódico que suele publicarse en el pueblo, y que todo el mundo lee por contener los anuncios de las tiendas. Hay quien para anunciar se sirve de circulares repartidas profusamente, otros distribuyen muestras, quien emplea rótulos, quien tarjetas y también listones.

Hay, en efecto, muchos medios á los que acude el farmacéutico para anunciar sus artículos ó su botica. Para obtener patrocinio de recetas, algunos farmacéuticos visitan á los médicos y les hacen regalos, otros los convidan á dar alguno que otro paseo en coche, ó los convidan al teatro. Todo lo cual es muy bueno para ciertas localidades; pero yo no tengo fe en aquellos métodos que sirven para ponernos en contacto con los médicos.

Hay un método indirecto de anunciar, que según mi entender, podría aplicarse á todas las localidades, y es, el empleo de auxiliares ó dependientes aptos y listos, la limpieza de la tienda, buen servicio al público acompañado de modales obsequiosos. A todo esto hay que agregar habilidad y esmero en hacer los paquetes. Luego precisa tener siempre presente que los efectos de primera calidad son siempre los más baratos. Esta es, en verdad, la manera más juiciosa de anunciar y hacer propaganda que podría adoptarse para cualquier localidad. El autor ha empleado una serie de listones ó tarjetas enviándolas con la cuenta pendiente á fin de mes. Bastará con poner un listón y una tarjeta en el sobre que va la cuenta. La inscripción ó contenido de las tarjetas puede aludir á algo que sea de estación, por ejemplo en el verano se referirá á bebidas gaseosas ó aguas carbónicas, á perfumes, cigarros, etc. Este plan de reclamo nos ha dado buen resultado.

También hago uso de una guía de negocios; cada dos ó tres años compilo una guía que abraza los establecimientos de dentro de un radio de una milla ó tres cuartos de ella. A cada familia enviamos una ó más de estas guías.

Cuanto á los médicos no sé que haya visitado á ninguno con referencia á negocios. No lo he hecho nunca ni lo apruebo. Si vuestro establecimiento merece ser visitado no tardarán en averiguarlo, y más pronto ó más tarde recibireis su patrocinio. Atención, suma atención, buenos artículos y tendreis parroquianos.

LINIMENTOS MEDICINALES

LINIMENTO JABONOSO ALCANFORADO. — Jabón medicinal, 30 partes; alcanfor, 10; alcohol, 405; glicerina, 25. Hágase solución en caliente; fíltrese en la vasija que haya de contenerlo, habiendo mezclado previamente: esencia de tomillo, 2 partes; esencia de romero, 3; solución amoniacal cáustica, 25. — *F. Aust*

LINIMENTO JABONOSO AMONIACAL ALCANFORADO. — (a) Jabón medicinal, 10 partes; alcohol de romero, 48; alcanfor, 1. Disuélvanse en baño-maría, fíltrese y añádase: amoníaco, 1 parte. — *F. Neerl*

Denomínase también *bálsamo de Opodeldoch líquido.*

(b) Jabón blando, 30 partes; alcohol de 80°, 400; alcanfor, 12; esencia de romero, 3; esencia de tomillo, 3; amoníaco líquido, 12. H. s. a. *F. Mej.*

LINIMENTO JABONOSO AMONIACAL ALCANFORADO LIQUIDO. — (a) Jabón de Venecia, 8 partes; jabón común, 16; esencia de espliego, 1; esencia de romero, 1; amoníaco, 4; alcanfor, 2; alcohol de vino, 100. Disuélvanse. *F. Aust.*

También se denomina *bálsamo de Opodeldoch.*

(b) Jabón de sosa, 50 gramos; alcanfor, 25; alcohol de 85°, 500; esencia de romero, 8; esencia de tomillo, 4; amoníaco de 22°, 20. Disuélvase el jabón raspado en el alcohol al calor del baño maría; añádase el alcanfor pulverizado; déjese enfriar; fíltrese y añádanse las esencias y el amoníaco. Consérvese en un frasco bien tapado.

Pr. terap.: Excitante y antiespasmódica. En fricciones. — *F. Esp.*

Como otras muchas, ha sufrido está fórmula variaciones de cierta importancia en sus componentes, pues, comparándola con la de la quinta edición, resulta contener más alcanfor, en la proporción de 3 á 5; algo menos de esencia de romero (2 á 1.60) y de tomillo (1 á 0.80) y una tercera parte menos de amoníaco (6 á 4). También se ha rebajado un poco la concentración del alcohol, pues de 90° ha disminuido á 85°. El método de preparación ha sufrido igualmente cambio, pues, en la vigésima edición, se ha suprimido la destilación de las esencias con el alcohol.

Llámase también *bálsamo Opodeldoch líquido.*

(c) Jabón medicinal raspado, 10 partes; alcanfor pulverizado, 9; esencia de romero, 2; esencia de tomillo, 1; amoníaco, 2; alcohol de 80°, 100.—*F. Franc.*

(d) Alcohol alcanforado, 60 partes; alcohol jabonoso, 170; amoníaco, 17; esencia de romero, 2; esencia de tomillo, 1. Mézclense. — *F. Helv.*

También se denomina *Opodeldoch líquido.*

NOTAS COMERCIALES

UNA COMBINACION ELIGIBLE. — Hace años que el doctor James J. Sullivan (Colegio Médico de la Universidad de Nueva York) hizo la aplicación de la observacion de «Una Combinación Eligible» á lo que entonces era una nueva preparación de muy conocidos agentes curativos sinergéticos. Es casi ocioso manifestar que la preparación á que aludía el citado facultativo es hoy ventajosamente conocida con el nombre de Tabletas de Antikamnia y Codeína, conteniendo cada tableta ¼ de grano de codeína y 4¾ grs. de antikamnia.

Un hecho que no debería pasar inadvertido es que la codeína usada en estas tabletas ha sido especialmente preparada y purificada, no es constipante y no provoca el hábito. Estos son algunos distintivos ventajosos de la codeína de la Antikamnia Chemical Company, y bien vale la pena que se tengan presente.

En la tos tan acongojante de la tisis ó en el dolor de pleuritis, en la sensación dolorosa que acompaña la bronquitis, cuando los tubos están resecos é irritables—como lo están de ordinario—con el desdoblamiento de las dos drogas que componen las Tabletas de Antikamnia y Codeína, se hallará que poseen acción, obteniéndose resultados que habrán de halagar al médico como al enfermo. Esta tableta obra cual sedante de los centros respiratorios en los desarreglos agudos y crónicos de los pulmones. La tos en la inmensa mayoría de los casos disminuye al poco tiempo y á veces cesa por completo. En las enfermedades del aparato respiratorio, el dolor y la tos son síntomas que exigen algo para aliviarlos, y esta tableta es la que realiza este trabajo, á parte de que subyuga los espasmos violentos que acompañan la tos y que tanto afligen al enfermo.

RELOJES PARA EL TRUST DEL TABACO EN AUSTRALIA. — Un ejemplo notable de la superioridad de los efectos americanos sobre los de fabricación extranjera, está demostrado por el hecho de que Robt. H. Ingersoll & Bro., de Nueva York, han embarcado durante un período de 18 meses, más de 138,000 relojes á Cameron, Bros. & Co., Ltd. de Melbourne, considerados los tratantes en tabaco más importantes de Australia, quienes los emplean como premio para sus marcas de tabaco fabricado. Los relojes llevan sobre la esfera el impreso «Havelock.»

El hecho de que los compradores, entre tantos relojes, demostraron preferencia por el renglón Ingersoll sobre los relojes baratos alemanes y suizos, y las imitaciones del Ingersoll, es testimonio suficiente de su mérito.

La razón de la superioridad de la marca Ingersoll es muy simple; la fábrica, que es la mayor del mundo, está destinada exclusivamente á la manufactura de relojes, cuyo número asciende diariamente á unos ocho mil, gracias á la perfección de la delicada maquinaria empleada.

Y es solamente debido á este enorme rendimiento y á los privilegios inapreciables de que es dueña la Compañía, que le permiten poner en el mercado, á un precio tan notablemente bajo, una máquina que por su exactitud duración y elegancia no puede ser igualada por ninguna otra de precio igual, de factura nacional ó extranjera.

Todos los años se hacen á miles de estos relojes con mascarillas especialmente impresas para anunciantes emprendedores que tienen en vista aumentar sus ventas, y el favor general con que estos souvenirs son recibidos, es la mejor prueba de su conveniencia y utilidad.

En estos días, cuando el tiempo es uno de los más apreciados factores, un buen reloj es absolutamente indispensable, y el reloj Ingersoll puede usarlo cualquiera. La demanda para ellos ha aumentado constantemente durante los pasados diez años, y continuará aumentando á medida que la gente sepa que un buen reloj puede comprarse por una pequeña fracción de lo que antes costaba.

Los relojes Ingersoll prestan servicio en todo el mundo, y puede decirse de ellos, aplicándoles una frase histórica, que son los únicos relojes en que el sol jamás se pone.

BOMBILLAS ARTIFICIALES ACANALADAS—Nos permitimos llamar la atencion de nuestros lectores al anuncio de la New Jersey Paper Tube Company que aparece en otro lugar de este periódico. Estas bombillas, que en algunos países son también conocidas con el nombre de pajuelas, están puestas en número de 500 en una caja especial a prueba de polvo. Pueden obtenerse muestras dirigiéndose al efecto á la Compañía. Para tomar bebidas frías como también para usarse en las habitaciones de los enfermos, estas bombillas poseen ventajas importantes sobre las pajuelas naturales. Son perfectamente limpias y enterizas, siendo su precio insignificante.

ZUMO DE FRUTAS AMERICANAS PARA LA EXPORTACION. — Boericke & Tafel, 145 Grand street, Nueva York, por su atención extremada á los detalles de la fabricación y con el empleo de materiales de clase superior, han establecido un enorme negocio de zumo de uvas en toda la América española. La producción de este zumo ha llegado á ser una industria muy importante en los Estados Unidos; pero relativamente se exporta una cantidad pequeña, porque para resistir bien los cambios de clima envueltos en la exportación, el zumo ha de prepararse con el mayor cuidado y esmero. La experiencia que los señores Boericke & Tafel han adquirido en la producción de este zumo, les permite ofrecer un artículo que puede cruzar el ecuador y llegar á su destino sin sufrir deterioro alguno, y estando esto comprobado, recomendamos este producto á nuestros lectores, pues en él hallarán un zumo de uvas rico y sabroso, que se conserva bajo todas circunstancias. Diríjanse á los fabricantes, á las señas expresadas arriba, quienes cotizarán precios especiales para la exportación.

PIES PARA LA EXHIBICION DE NOVEDADES. — Muchos artículos vende el farmacéutico cuya venta podría aumentarse considerablemente si estuviesen convenientemente expuestos á la vista del público. Por ejemplo, la venta de tarjetas postales ilustradas ha llegado á ser un importante renglón entres los artículos

varios que se despachan en las farmacias americanas, tanto es así que hoy día no hay ninguna que no tenga expuesta una serie selecta. De entre los medios más eficaces [illegible] de tales tarjetas pueden citarse los «piés» f[illegible] Western Fixture Works, de Chicago (Illino[illegible] ilustramos una forma de estos «piés,» y com[illegible] rece en la sección correspondiente el anuncio de[illegible] pero éstos hacen además una variedad de esta c[illegible] que constan en el catálogo ilustrado de la casa, obtenerse gratis dirigiéndose á The Great [illegible] 195 Fifth Avenue, Chicago (Ill.), [illegible]

AMERICAN DRUGGIST

and PHARMACEUTICAL RECORD

NUEVA YORK Y CHICAGO: 14 DE MAYO DE 1906

«The American Druggist» es un periódico bimensual del que se publica cada mes un suplemento español con anuncios en el mismo idioma

AMERICAN DRUGGIST PUBLISHING COMPANY

62-68 West Broadway, New York, U. S. A.

Dirección cablegráfica «Amdruggist, New York.» Clave A B C

A. R. ELLIOTT, *Presidente*

CASWELL A. MAYO, Ph. G.....................*Director*

THOMAS J. KEENAN, Lic. en Farm., *Director Asociado*

PRECIOS DE SUSCRIPCION

Pago adelantado, Estados Unidos, Canadá, México, Cuba, Puerto Rico, Hawaii y las Filipinas... ....(oro americano) $1.50

Otros países (franco de porte).................. » » $3.00

Las suscripciones pueden empezar en cualquier tiempo.

«The American Druggist and Pharmaceutical Record» sale el segundo y cuarto lunes de cada mes. Todo cambio de anuncios debe ser recibido diez días antes de la fecha de salida.

Remesas deben hacerse con libranzas sobre Nueva York, giros postales internacionales ó por expreso ó correo en carta certificada. Toda correspondencia debe dirigirse á la American Druggist Publishing Co., 62-68 West Broadway, New York, U. S. A.

DESTRUCCION DE LA CIUDAD DE SAN FRANCISCO

La hermosa y próspera ciudad de San Francisco, que anidaba en su seno cerca de medio millón de habitantes, ha sido inesperadamente reducida á cenizas por la violencia de un terremoto y las llamas alimentadas por el gas del alumbrado. Su comercio está paralizado, un número de sus emprendedores hijos sepultados en las ruinas, muchos miles sin casa ni hogar acampados en los parques y otros huyendo despavoridos en todas direcciones. En esta hora aciaga el pueblo americano abriga las más profundas simpatías por sus desventurados hermanos del Pacífico y con la generosidad que le distingue se ha apresurado á enviar en el acto socorros de todas clases y millones de pesos.

Todas las casas de drogas al por mayor en San Francisco han sido arrasadas y pocas boticas quedan en pie en estado de servir al público. Con el terremoto se vinieron abajo los establecimientos de drogas de las
ca [illegible] y Mission, al paso que aquellos situados en
la [illegible] ird, Montgomery, Second, First y Fremont,
fu [illegible] esa de abrasadoras llamas. El almacén, tienda
y [illegible] s de Redington & Co., de la calle Second,
n [illegible] han sido totalmente destruidos. Esta compa-
ñí [illegible] oficinas en la calle de Cliff, núm, 30, con el
n [illegible] e Coffin, Redington & Co., droguistas al por
m [illegible] ntes de la California Fig Syrup Company
y su producto «Jarabe de Higos.» La Pacific Coast Borax Company, con almacén y oficinas en la calle Sansome, núm. 101, y su fábrica en Alameda, ha visto desaparecer como el humo toda esa propiedad y su contenido, según un telegrama que acaba de recibirse en las oficinas locales de esta compañía, calle William, núm. 100, de la ciudad de Nueva York. El despacho fué trasmitido por C. B. Zabriskie, administrador de la compañía en el Este, quien se hallaba en San Francisco al ocurrir la catástrofe, y pudo llegar salvo á Oakland, del otro lado de la bahía, desde donde telegrafió que el presidente de la compañía, F. M. Smith, y demás oficiales y empleados, se habían salvado con sus familias.

La tan conocida casa de Johnson & Johnson ha recibido aviso que su almacén y oficinas están en ruinas. Seabury & Johnson tienen informes de que el depósito de sus existencias, almacenes de venta y oficinas, situados en la calle Market, núm. 513, entre las calles First y Second, se han perdido. La propiedad de Mack & Co. está igualmente convertida en un montón de escombros. Aunque de Langley, Michaels & Co. no han sabido nada directamente sus agentes de la calle Platt, núm. 16, Nueva York, se sabe que el incendio devoró en todo ó en parte las oficinas y dependencias de San Francisco.

Aunque parece que la pérdida de las propiedades de la Pacific Coast Borax Company no habrá de afectar el costo de este producto, no cabe dudar que la destrucción de los almacenes conteniendo tan grandes existencias de cáscara, grindelia robusta y damiana, creará una tendencia al alza en el precio de estas drogas, pues habrán de pasar de 30 á 60 días antes que los comerciantes dedicados á este negocio puedan reanudar los embarques y volver á establecer relaciones con sus agentes del Este.

Peligros de la Vibración

La población de Londres se preocupa seriamente en estos momentos acerca de la seguridad de la mayoría de edificios y paredes. Con motivo del enorme tráfico de la vía pública, y especialmente el de los vehículos de motor, y los trabajos que se verifican en la abertura de túneles para los ferrocarriles subterráneos, muchos edificios y obras de desagüe corren peligro por efecto de las incesantes vibraciones. Atribúyese á esta causa el desmoronamiento de varias paredes en el recinto de la ciudad.

Son relativamente pocos los arquitectos y maestros de obras que reconozcan la fuerza maravillosa de las vibraciones. Se reirían si se les dijese que la pared más sólidamente construida podría sufrir detrimento con sólo las vibraciones del arco al raspar las cuerdas del violín. Por supuesto, habría de tocarse aquel instrumento por muchos años antes de que se aflojase la obra de mortero, ó que el hierro se pusiese quebradizo; pero existen hechos para demostrar que han ocurrido tales resultados. En un buque acorazado un hombre puede sentir las vibraciones por efecto de tocarse en alguna parte el violín, aunque no pueda oir la música. Es la regularidad de las vibraciones que produce efecto. Al tocador del instrumento no lo afectan, porque el hombre es un objeto flexible y cede al movimiento.

Es un hecho generalmente conocido que cualquier cuerpo de tropas al momento de ir á pasar por un puente altera el paso de marcha, pues de otro modo la estructura sufriría muchísimo con la consiguiente vibración. Hasta las mismas pisadas de un perro hacen sacudir un puente, de aquí que en muchos de los puentes colgantes esté prohibido el tránsito de los perros á menos que sus dueños no los lleven en brazos.

Como ilustración de los efectos inequívocos de la fuerza de la vibración, mencionaremos lo que sucede en el Observatorio de Greenwich. Está situado en la parte superior de una colina en cuyas laderas juegan en las tardecitas plácidas centenares de muchachos, quienes desde el punto más alto y dándose las manos arrancan á correr hacia el pie de la ladera donde generalmente caen amontonados. Esto inicia la vibración en el cerro, hasta el punto que los científicos del Observatorio no pueden proceder con las observaciones, que se llevan á cabo con el estado inmóvil de una bandeja de mercurio. Tal es el temblor que conmueve y sacude la colina, que las vibraciones duran hasta pasada medianoche, hora en que los muchachos que las causaron hace tiempo están durmiendo.

Otro ejemplo de la vibración maravillosa, lo tenemos en la garganta humana, que para producir un sonido necesita el auxilio de sesenta vibraciones por segundo. Este sonido no se emplea para hablar, pero se halla en la voz de aquellos hombres de muy bajo registro. El sonido más alto emitido por la voz humana — que es E en altísimo — es causado por 1,024 vibraciones por segundo. Esto es excepcional, por obtenerse solamente con la voz cultivada de la mujer ó la de ciertos muchachos.

Realmente son las cuerdas vocales las que vibran, y no la garganta. En las notas más bajas se emplea todo el largo y espesor de las cuerdas vocales, las orillas afiladas se emplean en las notas más altas. De modo que al hablar por un minuto ó dos, se genera bastante vibración en la garganta para quebrarla y destruirla, si las paredes de la misma en lugar de ser blandas y flexibles fuesen de naturaleza sólida. Cada minuto que hablamos las cuerdas vocales vibran de 20,000 á 40,000 veces.

Cultivo de Cinconas en los Estados Unidos

En el reciente Congreso Farmacéutico de Lewis and Clark, Albert Schneider leyó una memoria sobre el cultivo de la cincona en varios países, señalando la posibilidad de llevarse á cabo tal cultivo en los Estados Unidos, especialmente en la costa del Pacífico. En otros países, fuera del Perú, se ha emprendido en fecha relativamente reciente. Los primeros ensayos los llevaron á cabo los holandeses en Java en 1854. En 1860 el gobierno inglés hizo las primeras tentativas para introducir el cultivo en la India con plantas obtenidas por Markman en Bolivia, juntamente con plantas y semillas de las plantaciones holandesas de Java y Nueva Granada. La primera finca dedicada á este cultivo radicaba en el suroeste de la Presidencia de Madras, entre los cerros de Nilgiri. La corteza apareció en el mercado de Londres en 1867, y desde entonces se ha vendido allí.

Tan luego como pudo apreciarse el buen resultado obtenido por los holandeses é ingleses en la preparación de la especie cincona, en sus colonias respectivas, pensó en cultivarse en los Estados Unidos. En 1879, hallándose en Bagotá W. Weaver, sugirió este cultivo, haciéndose en consecuencia ensayos en California, dirigidos por la Universidad de California, habiéndose importado las plantas de la India inglesa. La experiencia demostró lo difícil que era cultivar la cincona bajo condiciones ordinarias. Faltaban estufas apropiadas y condiciones apropiadas de desagüe, motivo para que la mayoría de las plantas pereciesen aunque pudo apreciarse que la especie de más resistencia era aparentemente la *C. succirubra.* El mayor enemigo de las cinconas eran las heladas, que las destruían con rapidez. Pero en California hay comarcas cuyo clima es semejante al de los Andes, y teoricamente parece que la cincona habría de prosperar en ellas. De todos modos, es un hecho que las más ligeras variaciones de temperatura interrumpen el desarrollo de estas plantas; por este motivo opina el doctor Rusby que la cincona no puede prosperar en este país, y que el cultivo, todo lo más, sería artificial.

Solubilidad del Hidrocloruro de Apomorfina

Por D. B. Dott Ph. C., F. T. C., F. R. S. E.

Obsérvase notable discrepancia en la opinión de diferentes autoridades respecto á la solubilidad de esta sal, motivada indudablemente por los varios métodos de determinación empleados. Si el agua se satura á una temperatura más bien alta, se enfría la solución á 60° F., apreciándose entonces la proporción de la sal, el resultado será alto, con motivo del grado apreciable de supersaturación. Tampoco cabe dudar de que algunas determinaciones á la «temperatura ordinaria,» se han efectuado realmente á una temperatura de 60° F. Otro punto en que conviene fijarse es el hecho de que el hidrocloruro de apomorfina que se ha expuesto al baño-maría para que se desprendiera la humedad higroscópica, se vuelve en consecuencia ligeramente básico, aumentándose perceptiblemente su solubilidad. Squire da la solubilidad en agua en la proporción de 1 en 56 á 60, lo que es bastante exacto; yo la hallé 1 en 59. La solubilidad en alcohol (90 por ciento) la da Squire como 1 en 50, *i. e.*, 1 gm. en 50 ml. Yo la he hallado 1 en 51. La Farmacopea de los Estados Unidos fija la solubilidad del cloruro de apomorfina á 25° C., como 1 en 39.5 partes d[illegible]
debería ser 1 en 49 ó cosa a[illegible]

No cabe duda de que r[illegible]
necesitan revisarse desde el punto de v[illegible]
sador. Deberían representar la c[illegible]
que pueda disolverse sacudien[illegible]
estado de finura) con el solver[illegible]
un espacio de tiempo razonable. O[illegible]
en sí parecerán correctos, no son sa[illegible]
el punto de vista práctico d[illegible]

Tipificación de Preparaciones Galénicas

Por CHARLES ALEXANDER HILL, B. Sc., F. T. C.

Hasta que llegue el momento en que todas las preparaciones galénicas hayan de ser sustituidas por otras, su tipificación continuará ocupando la atención de los farmacéuticos, y esto es más cierto ahora especialmente cuando está en curso de preparación una nueva edición de la Farmacopea (B. P.). Por todas partes se concede que á medida que nuestro conocimiento de drogas se ensancha, debería también aumentarse el número de preparaciones galénicas que están tipificadas, por cuyo motivo se propone aquí estudiar nuestra posición brevemente para averiguar hasta donde podemos ir sin riesgo, dado el estado actual de nuestros conocimientos; pero antes de hacerlo convendrá considerar lo que significa en farmacia tipificación.

Parece evidente que cuando esta palabra se aplica á preparaciones galénicas, tiene un significado diferente y menos definido que el que posee en química; tampoco es equivalente al vocablo «ensaye» en química. En esta ciencia, todo lo que se desea saber respecto á una preparación química se determina por las experiencias directas. Por ejemplo, la determinación del cloro presente como cloruro en una solución de cloruro de sodio tipo, determina el constituyente del cual depende solamente la utilidad. La tipificación de una preparación galénica, por otra parte, consiste en la determinación de un factor ó factores, los cuales, tomados en unión con otro conocimiento, se considera aseguran uniformidad: uniformidad, esto es, de valor medicinal ó fisiológica.

Las preparaciones de opio se tipifican determinando su contenido de morfina. Pero si el valor medicinal de las preparaciones de opio fuese apreciado con exactitud por la proporción de morfina presente, no habría necesidad de retenerlas en la farmacia. A semejanza de lo dicho, si las preparaciones de nuez vómica para su utilidad dependen enteramente de la estricnina que contienen, entonces puede dispensarse de ellas enteramente, empléandose en su lugar el alcaloide. Cuanto á este último caso, creo haberse sugerido formalmente la exclusión de la nuez vómica y sus preparaciones de la Farmacopea, y si se incluyen meramente con el fin de suministrar estricnina lista para entregarse en varias formas diluidas, esto no parecería ser razón suficiente para retenerse. Cuanto al primer caso, es obvio que la morfina no puede reemplazar enteramente el opio.

Estos dos ejemplos sirven para ilustrar el significado más bien limitado del vocablo «tipificación» aplicado á una preparación galénica. En efecto, para llevar estas consideraciones á su lógica conclusión, puede decirse que tan pronto como es posible tipificar completa y satisfactoriamente por medios químicos una preparación galénica, tal preparación deja de tener razón de ser.

[illegible]tivo de la gran importancia que tiene en n[illegible] química de la digital ha sido objeto de c[illegible]siderables investigaciones; con todo, estamos aun s[illegible] los medios para tipificar químicamente las prepar[illegible]ones de esta droga, por cuyo motivo se ha acudido á [illegible]s métodos fisiológicos de ensaye. Por cierto que t[illegible] recientemente como agosto de 1904, los doctores E[illegible]ger y Shaw, después de una serie de experiencias, ll[illegible]aron á la conclusión de que «en la actualidad el ú[illegible]o método de ensaye de confianza de la tintura d[illegible]ico.» No hay duda de que es factible el medir la actividad de una tintura de digital, determinando el aumento en la presión de la sangre que una cantidad determinada es capaz de producir, pero deberá tenerse presente que á menos de que tales pruebas no se ejecuten debidamente son en absoluto inútiles, y que para efectuarlas como corresponde, para que sean cuantitativas, son esenciales, no sólo un cuidado excesivo, sino una práctica especial en esta clase de trabajo muy por encima de la enseñanza fisiológica en general. Además es limitado el número de casos en que está indicado el método fisiológico, y también la naturaleza de los métodos los coloca fuera del alcance del farmacéutico ordinario.

En la mayoría de los casos la tipificación, bien por medios químicos ó fisiológicos, es en la actualidad imposible. Con todo, es altamente de desear que aun en estos casos hubiese alguna uniformidad. Como ha de obtenerse ésta con el conocimiento imperfecto que poseemos, es asunto importante merecedor de la atención más concentrada de los farmacéuticos científicos.

Durante años recientes, la publicación, de procedencias distintas, de datos analíticos, principalmente las cantidades, por término medio, de materia extractiva sólida hallada en tinturas, extractos fluídos, etc., ha tenido muy buena acogida. Estos datos son de indudable utilidad *per se* en algunos casos, y poseen cierto valor en todos aquellos en que también se toman en cuenta otras consideraciones. Pero tomar tales datos analíticos y establecer por ellos tipos arbitrarios en la creencia de que por este medio se fomentan los intereses de la farmacia es una ilusión, y en algunos casos, en más ó menos grado, hasta constituyen un peligro positivo. Es casi imposible dentro de los límites de este artículo, discutir en detalle el porcentaje de extracto sólido de las varias preparaciones galénicas fluídas, y el valor de este factor en cada caso; pero tomando algunos casos típicos, bastará para ilustrar los varios grados de utilidad.

Tomemos, por ejemplo, la tintura de asafétida. Aquí tenemos indudablemente un buen factor, por cuanto como la droga comercial está expuesta á ser mezclada con materia mineral, la determinación de materia extractiva sólida (si pasamos por alto la posibilidad de la adulteración deliberada) es una medida positiva de la cantidad de droga usada. Cuanto al extracto fluído de cáscara sagrada, nace un reparo; después de poner en ejecución las instrucciones de la Farmacopea para esta preparación galénica, puede decirse que el extracto está oficinalmente acabado; pero todos los farmacéuticos prácticos saben bien que, como cuestión de hecho, no está «acabado,» pues continuará por semanas y aun meses soltando un depósito. Si en el proceso de la fabricación se separa este cuerpo extractivo, obtiénese entonces un producto que es de la fuerza B. P., por contener los principios activos de la proporción de la droga prescrita, y constituye una preparación clara y estable por haberse eliminado una parte de la materia inútil é inactiva. Es seguramente intolerable que este producto perfeccionado del farmacéutico hábil haya de condenarse porque deja de conformarse con un tipo mal concebido y arbitrario.

En opinión del autor, la determinación de la cantidad de materia extractiva en las preparaciones galénicas fluídas, considerada como norma de la calidad de tales preparaciones, posee un grado diferente de importancia en casi cada caso. Alcanza quizás el mayor valor en manos del fabricante; pero, *prima facie*, no está justificado en alterar su producto acabado, con el fin meramente de hacerlo conformar con un tipo arbitrario, y esto es especialmente cierto tratándose de drogas tan importantes y activas como el cornezuelo de centeno y la digital.

Plantas Utiles en Togo y los Camerones

W. Busse, en una publicación que publica el *Pharm. Journ.*, No. 3506, pág. 910, da noticia de una planta de las más útiles de aquellas colonias, la *Butyrospermum Parkii*, cuyas simientes rinden sobre 30 por ciento de una grasa sólida parecida á la manteca de cacao por su olor, gusto y apariencia, y también por no ponerse rancia fácilmente. Se hacen panes semejantes á los de azúcar, pesando de 2 á 3 kilos, siendo su costo en el punto de producción, cosa de seis peniques por kilo. Esta grasa, conocida por el nombre de «shea butter,» es una substancia alimenticia importante para los negros, y juntamente con las semillas del *Bassia Parkii*, debería ser un valioso artículo de exportación para Europa. La corteza contiene zumo lácteo en abundancia, del que se obtiene una guttapercha parecida á la de Borneo.

En vista de lo dicho, no solamente debería cultivarse el árbol *Bassia Parkii*, sino que también las especies aliadas. Otro árbol valioso es el kapok (*ceiba pentandra*). En adición á la borra sedosa que rinden las simientes, la madera que es muy blanda y liviana se emplea mucho en la construcción de canoas. Es muy común en terrenos bajos y encharcados. Cuando las simientes maduran, el terreno queda cubierto de una lana sedosa que se desprende de ellas. La corteza se quema y el álcali obtenido de las cenizas empléase para hacer jabón de aceite de palmera. Las flores se secan, machacan, hierven, y en este estado se comen. En los Camerones el árbol momangi (*Chlorophora Excelsa*) rinde una madera muy preciosa. El árbol cola (*Cola Acuminata*), cuyas semillas poseen cuatro cotiledones es común en los Camerones. Las semillas se mascan y dan alivio. Para el cultivo es preferible la *Cola vera*, que da semillas con dos cotiledones y se venden á precios más altos en Africa; pero las de la *C. acuminata* desecadas convenientemente forman un valioso artículo para la exportación. La corteza del *Erythrophlœum guineensis* tiene mucha aplicación, y la madera á su vez es muy apreciada. Pero el aceite de palmera es el más importante de los productos vegetales. La palmera (*Elœis guineensis*) está muy distribuida, hallándose muchas variedades que rinden grasa. Para desarrollar el comercio del aceite de palmera en Togo y los Camerones, convendría, según el autor, aumentar las facilidades de transporte de las nueces y del aceite del interior á la costa.

Nueva Navaja de Seguridad

La última novedad en el renglón de navajas de afeitar de seguridad, es un instrumento de sencillez de construcción, consistente en solo tres piezas, el mango, la hoja y el guarda-hoja. Las hojas se fijan automáticamente al mango, haciendo de esta manera innecesarios los muelles, charnelas y tornillos. Los dientes del guarda-hoja están en dirección de la hoja, dejando libre el filo de ésta y un espacio para que la jabonadura pueda pasar arriba de la hoja, de la misma manera y con igual ventaja que con una navaja ordinaria.

Emulsión sin Sabor de Aceite de Ricino

Los ingredientes que se expresan á continuación matan casi por completo el gusto peculiar del aceite de ricino y conservan éste:

Aceite de ricino	24	partes
Glicerina	24	»
Tintura de corteza de naranja	8	»
Tintura de serpentaria	2	»
Agua de canela, c. s. para hacer	100	»

Mézclese y hágase una emulsión. Dosis para un niño, una cucharada.

Con lo siguiente puede hacerse un aceite de ricino casi agradable al paladar, si tal cosa es posible:

Goma arábiga, escogida	64	partes
Agua de flor de azahar	142	»
Agua de canela	8	»
Aceite de ricino	148	»
Azúcar pulverizada	196	»

Hágase un mucílago espeso de la goma y parte del agua de la flor de azahar, póngase en un mortero caliente y añádese el aceite poco á poco y agitando constantemente. Mézclese el residuo del agua de la flor de azahar con el agua de canela, y disuélvase en la mezcla el azúcar con la ayuda del calor. Mézclense las dos soluciones y sacúdanse bien juntas, pónganse entonces en el baño-maría y llégase al hervor gradualmente, espumándose á medida que se forma la espuma. Hágase hervir por un minuto, quítese del fuego, déjese enfriar, decántese y embotéllese. Esto permanece inalterable indefinidamente, tomándolo sin reparo los niños y adultos. No se sabe generalmente, aunque es un hecho, que el aceite de ricino puede lavarse, agitándolo con numerosos cambios de agua clara hasta que pierde todo su sabor y olor nauseabundo, sin por esto menoscabarse en lo más mínimo sus propiedades medicinales. Convendrá que el agua que se emplee sea caliente, y se cambiará con frecuencia. Cuando se trate de una cantidad considerable convendrá servirse de una máquina agitadora. Para una pequeña cantidad bastará una botella ordinaria. El aceite de ricino tratado de esta manera con cuidado, endulzado con sacarina y aromado con aldehido cinámico, hace una preparación que puede compararse con la primera aunque no la supera.

Enfermedades Infecciosas y Gérmenes

El Dr. Robertson, médico de Sanidad de la ciudad de Birmingham (Inglaterra), ha dado recientemente una conferencia ante la Universidad local acerca de enfermedades infecciosas y propagación de gérmenes, de la cual entresacamos los siguientes párrafos:

«La lista de enfermedades infecciosas, dijo el conferenciante, está aumentando continuamente, esto no obstante, nadie que se sepa ha podido averiguar el germen de la viruela y de la fiebre escarlatina, al paso que otros gérmenes son tan diminutos, que si se multiplicasen hasta alcanzar el tamaño de una pulgada y se multiplicase en proporcion el sér humano, éste aparentaría tener de veinticinco á treinta millas de alto.»

También, dijo el conferenciante, que no sabía de ningún caso en que los gérmenes de la fiebre escarlatina hubiesen pasado de una casa á otra por medio del aire, pues la luz solar bastaría para matarlos; pero un orador hablando podía proyectar gérmenes á una distancia de treinta á cuarenta pies; el toser y estornudar eran también poderosos distribuidores de los gérmenes. Cuanto á la tisis, aquellas personas que están bien nutridas y habitan locales de condiciones higiénicas, no son susceptibles á esa terrible enfermedad.

LINIMENTOS MEDICINALES

LINIMENTO JABONOSO AMONIACAL ALCANFORADO SOLIDO. — (a) Jabón animal raspado, 15 partes; alcanfor, 12; alcohol de 90°, 125; esencia de romero, 3; esencia de tomillo, 1; amoníaco de 22°, 5; carbón animal, 5. Disuélvase el jabón, colocado con el alcohol en un matraz, al calor del baño-maría; añádase el alcanfor pulverizado y las esencias; en seguida el carbón animal, agitando para que se descolore el líquido, y, por fin, el amoníaco; fíltrese rápidamente antes que se enfríe, y recíbase el líquido caliente en frascos pequeños de boca ancha, que se taparán con corchos envueltos en papel de estaño.

Pr. terap. y usos: Iguales que el bálsamo Opodeldoch. — *F. Esp. Franc. y Mej.*

También se llama *bálsamo Opodeldoch sólido.*

(b) Jabón de sebo, 20 partes; alcanfor, 5; alcohol concentrado, 210; esencia de romero, 2; esencia de tomillo, 1; licor amoniacal cáustico, 12. — *F. Helv.*

(c) Acido asteárico, 2 partes; carbonato de sosa, 1; alcohol rectificado, 50. Digiérase esta mezcla en baño-maría, hasta que no dé reacción ácida; fíltrese y, aun caliente, añádase: amoníaco, 2 partes; alcanfor, 1; esencia de bergamota, 2. — *F. Neerl.*

Como los anteriores, se denomina también *bálsamo Opodeldoch sólido.*

LINIMENTO JABONOSO COMPUESTO. — Agua hirviendo, 90 gramos; jabón blando, 17.50; amoníaco líquido, 3.50; alcohol rectificado, 10.50; esencia de trementina, 4.50; esencia de mejorana, 6 gotas. — *H. St. Barth.*

LINIMENTO JABONOSO FENICADO. — Jabón de estearina dializado, 4 gramos; jabón medicinal, 1; alcohol, 90; ácido fénico, 5. Disuélvanse y fíltrese.

Eficaz contra el prurito, el eczema, el herpe tonsurante, etc. También se sirven de él los operadores para lavarse las manos.

LINIMENTO JABONOSO DE GOULARD. — Jabón animal blanco, 50 partes; agua, 200; aceite de sésamo, 25; acetato de plomo líquido, 12. Disuélvase el jabón en el agua á un suave calor; se bate con una mano de madera hasta que se enfríe, y se incorpora la mezcla del aceite y el acetato de plomo.

Añadiendo á 60 gramos de este líquido 4 de alcohol alcanforado, se obtiene el *linimento de jabón alcanforado.*

Pr. terap.: Resolutiva. — *F. Mej.*

LINIMENTO JABONOSO IODADO. — Tintura de iodo, 1 parte; linimento de jabón, 7. — *H. City Ch.*

LINIMENTO JABONOSO OPIADO. — Tintura de opio, 1 parte; linimento de jabón, 5. — *H. Consumpt.*

LINIMENTO DE LADY FORD. — Esencia de trementina, 15 gramos; alcohol alcanforado, 30; vinagre, . para 360; huevo, núm. 1. H. s. a. Para friccionar es y la nuca en el reumatismo de la cabeza.

NIMENTO MAGICO DE LESLIE. — Tintura de parte; linimento de acónito, 1; linimento de ona, 1; linimento de jabón, 1.

e emplea contra los dolores musculares, neural-tc.

NIMENTO MAGISTRAL. — Pomada de albayalde, mos; aceite de solano, 70. Mézclese. — *F. V. M. F.*

Pitileno

El pitileno es el producto de la condensación de alquitrán de pino y el formaldehido, que tiene por objeto reemplazar las preparaciones usuales de alquitrán en varias enfermedades de la piel. Es un polvo fino amarillo obscuro, con un tenue olor, pero no del alquitrán. Es soluble en soluciones de álcalis; los ácidos resinosos, los fenoles y otras substancias presentes en la preparación dan, con el álcali, compuestos solubles acuosos. La preparación es también soluble en alcohol, acetona, colodión y terpineol. Cual el alquitrán, no es una substancia simple, sino una mezcla de las varias substancias siempre presentes en el alquitrán de pino. La combinación con el formaldehido da por resultado el dominio de la acción irritante y cáustica de estas substancias, de modo que se previene toda irritación local.

La preparación la ha empleado el Dr. Max Joseph (*Wien. Klin. Therap. Wochenschr*, XIII, pág. 64) en eczemas agudos y subagudos, como también en los crónicos é igualmente en un número considerable de otras afecciones cutáneas, aplicándose al efecto un ungüento que contiene de 2 á 10 por ciento. También puede emplearse en la forma de polvo para espolvorear, en la de jabón (sólido y líquido) y como emplasto.

Acción de la Acacia en la Morfina

Bourquelet, que ha hecho un estudio del asunto, dice que la acción de la acacia en la morfina consiste en una oxidación de esta última en oximorfina, resultado que naturalmente podía esperarse y puede que tenga alguna significancia práctica, cuando el opio y la morfina están en contacto con la acacia por algún tiempo, particularmente en presencia de la humedad, como acontecerá en mezclas, extractos, etc. Esta acción, por supuesto, pudiera evitarse destruyendo las oxidasas presentes en la acacia, calentando al efecto la última. Firbas (*Pharm. Ztg.*, l. p. 1906), ha demostrado que la acacia en solución se obtiene en la mayoría de los casos sin contener oxidasas; pero calentando por una hora en el baño-maría la acacia en polvo, no se desprenden tan fácilmente las que contiene, y sólo en el caso de someterse á un calor de 160° C. por varias horas, desarrollará el polvo un color amarillo y olor á caramelo; entonces por la prueba de la tintura de guayaco, se revelará la ausencia de oxidasas. Esto no obstante, como ha demostrado el autor por sus experiencias, las oxidasas que están presentes en mezclas pulverulentas de acacia, no ejercen influencia apreciable en la morfina; y aun en las soluciones acuosas, la conversión de la morfina en oximorfina procede muy lentamente. — MERCK.

Manchas de Acido Pirogárico en los Dedos

Como medio eficaz de impedir las manchas de pirogálico, Harold Hood (*Photo-Am.*) recomienda restregarse un poco de grasa de lana antes de empezar el trabajo. Un medio eficaz de excluir las manchas procedentes del revelador es de sumergir las puntas de los dedos, de cuando en cuando, en el baño durante un trabajo prolongado de revelación. Es mucho mejor emplear el líquido, friccionando bien las partes manchadas antes de acudir al jabón, pues parece que el último más bien fija que quita las manchas. También puede tenerse junto á la cubeta, para el mismo objeto un cachito de corteza de limón.

CONSULTAS FARMACEUTICAS

Por WILLIAM DUNCAN, Ph. C., F. C. S.

(1) — ¿Por qué sobreviene un precipitado inmediatamente después de añadir alcaloide á la solución mercuriosa en la siguiente mezcla?

℞ Sol Hydrarg. Bichlor................
Glycerini............................aa 1 oz.
Cocain. Hydrochlor.................. 2 p. %

El cloruro de mercurio es un precipitante general de alcaloides, que son con dificultad solubles en agua, y los cuales desprenden un precipitado cuando la solución es bastante fuèrte. En el caso particular que se cita puede evitarse, disolviendo la sal alcaloide en la glicerina previamente mezclada con el líquido. Con cloruro mercurioso, 1 en 100, el precipitado no puede impedirse.

(2) — ¿En qué consiste el precipitado color verde-oliva que se separa en esta mezcla?

℞ Ferri et Quin. Citrat................ 2 drac.
Tinct. Nucis Vom...................
Tinct. Rhei Co......................aa 1 »
Aquam...........................ad 8 onzas

El precipitado, aunque voluminoso, pesa solamente cosa de 1¼ grano, y consiste principalmente en resinas neutras de la diluición de la tintura de nuez vómica, con huellas de tannato de quinina, del citrato de hierro y quinina y el tanino del ruibarbo.

(3) — ¿Qué es Magnes Carb.?

La B. P. de 1867, tenía «Magnesiæ Carbonas» como título de carbonato fuerte. En 1888, la B. P. añadió el adjetivo «ponderosa,» el cual se ha retenido en la B. P. de 1898. Yo dispensaría carbonato bien cargado bajo la suposición de que el autor estaba más familiarizado con el título de 1867 que con el de la Farmacopea de 1898.

(4) — ¿Debería añadirse ioduro de potasio para ayudar la solución en lo siguiente?

℞ Iodi.......................... 4 granos
Glycerini......................... 1 onza
Solve

No es necesario porque el iodo es soluble en unas 65 partes de glicerina. El ioduro de potasio no aumenta la solubilidad del iodo en todos los solventes, sino solamente en aquellos que contienen agua. Aumenta la solubilidad, por ejemplo, en espíritu rectificado, pero no en alcohol absoluto.

(5) — ¿Qué es lo que se forma en la siguiente mezcla?

℞ Bismuth Salicylat................ 40 granos
Sodii Iodidi...................... 6 »
Pulv. Tragacanth. Co.............. 15 »
Syr. Codein....................... 6 drac.
Aquam............................ 6 onzas

Es imposible informar bien sin examinar el producto. Probablemente los primeros dos reaccionan para formar ioduro de bismuto y salicilato de sodio. El ioduro de bismuto es un precipitante de alcaloides, y probablemente se continuará con la codeina, al paso que también hidrolisa en agua, dejando libre ácido hidriódico. Esto puede oxidarse con la liberación de iodo libre, el cual combinando con el almidón del polvo de tragacanto compuesto imprimirá á la mezcla un color azul.

(6) — ¿Qué es lo que causa la liberación de iodo en lo siguiente?

℞ Aspirin...........................
Potass. Iodid....................aa 2 drac.
Glycerini......................... ½ onza
Aquam.......................ad 6 »

Siendo aspirín ácido salicílico acetil, deja en libertad ácido hidriódico, el cual con la acción combinada de aire y luz, se desdobla en iodo y agua.

(7) — ¿Cuál es la causa de no permanecer medianamente clara la siguiente mezcla?

℞ Magnes. Sulph.................... 3 drac.
Magnes. Calcin.................... 2 »
Ferri Sulph....................... 16 granos
Tinct. Nucis Vom.................. 1 drac.
Syr. Aurantii..................... 1 onza
Tinct. Card Co.................... 4 drac.
Aquam........................ad 8 onzas

Siendo la magnesia calcinada ligeramente soluble en agua, precipitará hidróxido ferroso del sulfato de hierro, y esto oxidándose al estado férrico, rendirá el color negro usual con el tanino de las tinturas.

(8) — ¿Cuál es el mejor método de dispensar esto así como está?

℞ Zinci Oleat.......................
Calamin.......................aa 1 dracma
Acid. Carbolic.................... 20 granos
Lin. Calcis....................... 4 dracmas
Adipis Lanae...................... 1 oz.

Es perder el tiempo intentar dispensarlo así como está dispuesto. Se obtiene un ungüento excelente colocando el equivalente de grasa de lana anhidrosa y aceite de oliva en un mortero calentado. Se frotan hasta quedar suaves el oleato y la calamina con los equivalentes de agua de cal y agua, en los cuales se habrá disuelto previamente el ácido fénico, y combínase con las grasas blandas por trituración.

(9) — ¿Debería añadirse goma, como agente de suspensión en lo siguiente?

℞ Tinct. Quin. Ammon.................
Agua Aurant. Flor.................aa 2 oz.

Aunque no es absolutamente necesaria, la adición es una ventaja por cuanto el hidrato de quinina tiende á ponerse cristalino y adherirse al vidrio.

(10) — ¿Qué es el precipitado en este compuesto?

℞ Liq. Bismuthi.................... 3 oz.
Magnes. Sulph..................... 1 »
Sodii Salicyl..................... 2 dracmas
Syr. Aurant....................... 1 oz.
Aq. Menth. Pip.................... 12 »

No he logrado obtener un precipitado. La B. P. permite el Liquor Bismuthi que sea levemente acalino, pero el exceso precipitará el hidróxido magnésico del sulfato magnésico. El solicitante debería examinar su Liquor Bismuthi.

(11) — ¿Puede impedirse el precipitado en lo siguiente?

℞ Sodii Salicylat................... 4 dracmas
Caffein. Cit...................... 24 granos
Tinct. Capsici.................... 30 mínimas
Sp. Chloroformi................... 30 »
Infus. Gentian................ad. 4 oz.

No se puede, aferrándose á la fórmula. El precipitado del ácido salicílico puede impedirse, sustituyendo el citrato de cafeina por un equivalente de alcaloide puro.

(12)—¿Cuál es la rázon de reventar la botella la siguiente mezcla?

℞ Tinct. Digitalis.......... ......
Tinct. Hyosciam................aa 1 dracma
Spirit. Aether. Nit... .... 4 dracmas
Infus. Caryoph.................ad. 6 oz.

Es probable que el resultado pueda atribuirse al ácido nitroso del espíritu actuando sobre el tanino de la infusión. He observado un fenómeno igual dos ó tres veces con infusión de gayuba, y es posible que acontezca con otras medianamente ricas en tanino. Al diluir espíritu de nitro dulce con una infusión fresca de gayuba, el nitrito de etilo queda muy descompuesto por el agua en alcohol y ácido nitroso, y el último obrando en el tanino libera gas igual á lo menos dieciseis veces al volumen de la infusión usada. Pocas botellas podían resistir esto. De que el tanino es la causa, pruébase por el hecho de que si la infusión fuese detannatada por medio de la colapez no ocurriría tal dificultad.

NUEVOS REMEDIOS

ALUMNOL (*Disulfonato Naftol Aluminio*).—Polvo blanquizco muy soluble en agua; ligeramente soluble en glicerina y alcohol; astringente y antiséptico; disuelve el pus y penetra los tejidos. Empléase en una solución al 1 por ciento en gonorreas: una mezcla del 10 al 20 por ciento con talco sirve para espolvorear.

AMINOFORMO (*Hexametil Enetretamina*).—Cristales blancos granulares, solubles con facilidad en agua, preparados combinando amoníaco y formaldehído. Antiséptico para las vías urinarias, diurético y solvente en las concreciones de ácido úrico. Dosis, de 5 á 10 granos, bien diluído, tres veces al día. Un frasco de 1 onza, 60 centavos; en tabletas de 7½ granos, onza, 70 centavos.

(C. Bischoff & Co.)

AMILOFORMO. — Polvo blanco insoluble en agua: producto de la condensación de almidón y formaldehído. Antiséptico quirúrgico. Se usa puro ó con talco y ácido bórico. Cartón de 1 onza, 25 centavos.

(Stallman & Fulton)

ANÆSTESINA. — Polvos blancos cristalinos, casi insolubles en agua fría, pero solubles con facilidad en éter, alcohol, bencina y aceites crasos. Anestésico local; úsase internalmente en úlcera gástrica, dispepsia nerviosa, etc. Dosis, de 5 á 8 granos, varias veces al día. Usado externalmente puro ó en ungüento de 5 á 20 por ciento, y en supositorios, conteniendo 3 granos [illegible] Frascos de 1 onza, $1.00.

(Victor Koechi & Co.)

— Líquido amarillo, aceitoso, con un rceptible á alquitrán; soluble en alcohol, acea, grasas y petrolatum. Es destilado del coaltar, y ısa en afecciones de la piel en las que se emplea el -rán de carbón. Tubos de 1 onza, 55 centavos.

(Knoll & Co. y Merck & Co.)

NINA (*Potasio Orthodinitro-Cresol*). — Pasta de un color naranjo brillante, soluble en agua; posee olor tenue de jabón, no volátil. Desdorizante, desinfectante; impide el crecimiento de las fungosidades, la formación del moho y de la carcoma en los pisos de los sótanos y habitaciones humanas. Usase en forma de solución, 1 lb. por 5 á 15 galones de agua. Latas, ¼ lb., $1.10 la lb.; latas de 1 lb., 95 centavos; latas de 50 libras, la lb. 77 centavos.

(Continental Color & Chemical Co.)

ANTINOSINA (*Sal Sódica de Nosofeno*). — Polvo azul, soluble en agua, alcohol y glicerina. Se emplea en solución de 1 al 5 por ciento como antiséptico en enfermedades de los ojos y oídos, en afecciones génitourinarias, y como polvo cicatrizante en úlceras crónicas de la pierna. Frascos de 1 onza, $2.10.

(Stallman & Fulton Co.)

ANTITUSINA (*Ungüento Difluordifenil*). — Ungüento conteniendo lanolina, 85 por ciento; petrolatum, 10 por ciento, y difluordifenil, 5 por ciento. Remedio para la tos ferina, aplicado como untura al cuello del enfermo, pecho y espalda, una vez al día; en dosis de 5 grm. Tubos flexibles, 40 centavos; 40 grm., 75 cts.

(Schering & Glatz)

SUPOSITORIOS ANUSOL. — Compuesto de sulfonato iodo-resorcino de bismuto, empleado en las hemorroides, etc. Dosis, 1 ó 2 diariamente. Caja de 12, $1.00.

(Shering & Glatz)

ARGENTAMINA. — Líquido incoloro, alcalino formando una solución de nitrato de plata 10 por ciento y etileno diamina 10 por ciento; soluble en agua. Es útil para todos aquellos casos en que se usa el nitrato de plata, y más particularmente en la gonorrea, en una solución de fuerza de 1 en 2000 á 4000. Frasco de 1 oz. con tapón de vidrio esmerilado, 75 centavos.

(Schering & Glatz)

ARGONINA.— Polvo blanco, apenas soluble al frío, pero mucho en agua caliente. Compuesto de nitrato de plata y caseina sódica. Antiséptico, germicida y gonococcida, menos cáustico que el nitrato de plata. Soluciones de 2 al 10 por ciento de fuerza, se recomiendan para inyecciones, y en soluciones de al 3 por ciento, para aplicarse á los ojos. Tubos de 1 oz., 65 centavos.

(Victor Koechi & Co.)

ARHOVINA. — Producto adicional de difenilamina y ácido tímico benzoico esterilizado. Fluído de un olor aromático y gusto ligeramente mordiente, soluble en aceite. Gonococcida para uso interno y tópico. Administrándose por la boca en cápsulas de 4 granos (1 ó 2 cápsulas, tres á seis veces al día), en candelillas uretrales, dos á cuatro veces al día); en glóbulos vaginales (1 glóbulo, dos á cuatro veces al día); inyectada en solución oleosa del 2 al 5 por ciento.

ASAPROL (*Abrastol*).—Polvo blanquizco, muy soluble en agua y alcohol. Es la sal cálcica del ácido sulfónico benaftol. Antipirético y antireumático en dosis de 5 á 15 granos. Se emplea también como prueba para la albúmina en la orina. Frasco de 1 oz., $1.25.

ARISTOCHINA (*Eter Carbónico de Quinina*).—Polvo blanco, insípido, insoluble en el agua. Se prescribe cual la quinina, pero en dosis algo más grandes. En cartones de ¼ y 1 oz., la onza, $2.20.

(Continental Color & Chemical Co. y Merck & Co.)

ASPIRINA (*Acido Salicilico Acetil*).— Polvo blanco cristalino insoluble en el agua, incompatible con álcalis. Se emplea en lugar de los salicilatos en el reumatismo articular y muscular y otras indicaciones terapéuticas para salicilatos. Dosis, 5 á 15 granos, tres á cinco veces al día. Frasco de 1 oz., la onza, 33 á 43 centavos.

(Continental Color & Chemical Co.)

ATOXYL (*Anilido Meta-Arsenoso*).— Polvo blanco, conteniendo 37.69 por ciento de arsénico en combinación orgánica. Soluble en 6 partes de agua, empleándose en solución de esta fuerza para inyección hipodermica. No tóxico relativamente. Dosis, 1 á 3 granos. Tubos de 1 oz., $3.00.

ANTISCLEROSINA.— Tabletas de un compuesto de sales inorgánicas para el tratamiento de la arterioesclerosis y sus secuelas. Dosis, 2 tabletas tres veces al día. Cartones de 4 tubos á 24 tabletas, $1.50.

(Schering & Glatz)

BENZONAFTOL.— Polvo blanco cristalino, soluble en alcohol y cloroformo, insoluble en agua. Empleado como antiséptico intestinal en dosis de 5 á 15 granos. En tubos de 1 oz., 22 centavos; en frascos de ¼ lb., $2.20; ½ lb., $2.10; 1 lb., $2.00.

(Schering & Glatz)

BENZOSOL (*Benzoato de Guayacol*). — Pequeños cristales descoloridos, casi insolubles en agua. Contiene 54 por ciento de guayacol, y por el hecho de ser saponificado lentamente por los jugos gástricos, liberándose el guayacol gradualmente, se recomienda como antiséptico intestinal y como substituto agradable de la creosota en la tisis incipiente. Dosis, 4 á 8 granos.

HIDROCLORURO DE BETA EUCAINA.— Polvo blanco cristalino, soluble en 30 partes de agua. Compuesto sintético aliado químicamente á la cocaina, siendo el hidrocloruro de benzoil-vinil-diacetón-alkamina. Es de acción más lenta que la cocaina, pero la anestesia se prolonga más, y es una tercera parte menos tóxica que aquella. Se emplea generalmente en soluciones de al 2 por ciento, en operaciones dentales y oftálmicas. En ⅛ de onza y en ½ onza, la oz., $3.60; ¼ y 1 oz., $3.50.

(Schering & Glatz)

NOTAS QUIMICAS

BALSAMO DE COPAIBA NEUTRO

Según un privilegio obtenido en el extranjero, la acción irritante del bálsamo de copaiba queda anulada por medio de la acilación y esterificación del mismo. Por ejemplo, calentando bálsamo de copaiba con anhidrido acético al baño-maría por algunas horas, y apartando después el ácido acético que se haya formado, bien por la destilación al vacío, bien tratándolo con una solución de carbonato de sodio diluído, se obtendrá un producto siruposo de la apariencia y consistencia de bálsamo de copaiba, el cual es soluble fácilmente en alcohol, éter, benceno, cloroformo y ligroina, y no contiene ácidos libres. Su gravedad específica es sobre 0.984, la cual varía según el bálsamo que se use. La preparación puede emplearse en todos aquellos casos en que se usa el copaiba ordinario. — *Chem. Zeit.* y *Merks Report.*

NUEVA FORMA DE CALOMELANO

Por conducto de la *Pharmazeutische Zeitung*, J. Meyer nos da á conocer una nueva forma de calomelano por él obtenida reduciendo el cloruro de mercurio con sulfito de litina. Mezcla una solución de sublimado corrosivo de 27 grm. con una solución tibia de 12 grm. del sulfito, de cuyas resultas sobreviene inmediatamente la precipitación del calomelano. Al filtrar y calentar la filtración á 70° C. fórmanse escamas lustrosas que al depositarse ocupan un espacio considerable. Al calentar estas escamas se subliman en la forma usual del calomelano, asumiendo entonces un volumen de sólo una sexta parte del que tenía antes. Se ha hallado que la gravedad específica de esta forma de calomelano era de 4.5 á 5. Parece ser idéntica con la preparación japonesa obtenida por el procedimiento seco, que ha descrito Lunge.

NUEVA REACCION PARA EL AZUCAR DE LECHE Y LA MALTOSA

Por el siguiente ensayo se obtiene: Disolviendo 0.5 á 0.7 grm. de azúcar de leche en 10 cc. de amoníaco en un tubo de prueba, y colocando éste en un baño-maría hasta que hierva, se evapora el amoníaco sin que llegue á hervir el líquido del tubo, formándose en 15 ó 20 minutos un color rojo muy semejante al que se desarrolla cuando se hierve por algunos minutos ácido hidroclórico resorcinol con una solución floja de azúcar de caña. La maltosa da también esta reacción, pero no los demás carbohidratos.

MODIFICACIONES NEGRAS Y AMARILLAS DEL ANTIMONIO

Stock y Siebert (*Pharm. Ztg. li.*, pág. 117) las han obtenido de la manera siguiente: El antimonio negro (no la muy conocida modificación gris cristalina) se obtiene por medio de la oxidación de hidruro de antimonio por el oxígeno, y también por la conversión espontánea de la modificación amarilla. El antimonio amarillo se obtiene haciendo pasar gas oxígeno á un anhidruro de antimonio licuado á 90° C. También puede obtenerse de conformidad con la reacción $S6H_3+3Cl=S6+3HCl$. Los autores obtuvieron antimonio amarillo puro por la acción de soluciones de cloro en hidruro de antimonio en etano líquido á 100° C. Esta preparación es, no obstante, muy inestable, y al traspasar 90° C. se vuelve negra.

NUEVO METODO PARA DETERMINAR LA GLICERINA

A. Buisine informa que una mezcla de potasa cáustica y cal de potasa reacciona con glicerina á una temperatura de 350°, como sigue:

$$C_3H_8O_3+4KOH=2K_2CO_3+8H+CH$$

Durante la reacción se forma un acetato que es estable á 300° C., pero que á 350° C. se descompone en carbonato y metano. 1 grm. de glicerina rinde á 350° C., 967 cc. de gas (á 0°C y 760 mm. de presión). Para la determinación de la glicerina se mezclan 0.2 á 0.3 grm. con 4 á 5 grm. de hidróxido de potasio en polvo, y 15 á 20 grm. de cal de [illegible] calienta la mezcla por una hora á [illegible] de mercurio.

GOMA ARTIFICIA

El musgo irlandés, en la propor[illegible] á 80-90° C. con agua 1,000, hasta que se [illegible] todo el mucílago. Después de quitar toda [illegible] suspendida, la solución se mezcla con alm[illegible] 200, que deberá haberse frotado ant[illegible] se esparce la mezcla en capas delgadas sobre placas de metal aceitadas, y se deseca á 100° C., á cuya temperatura forma un producto sin color, que se quiebra fácilmente. Se ablanda en agua fría, y al calentarse forma en mucílago espeso, que puede emplearse como sustituto del mucílago de acacia ó base para colores.—*Journ. and Merck's Report.*

DETERMINACION DIRECTA DE LA GLICERINA EN SOLUCION

Cuando el líquido sea alcalino, se acidula con ácido sulfúrico, y si fuese necesario se filtra, y entonces se hace levemente alcalino con potasa. Pero si la solución original es ácida, luego se concentra á una temperatura que no exceda 80° C. para evitar pérdida de glicerina Si el líquido contiene sales disueltas, se procede á la evaporación para obtener un residuo semisólido, éste se mezcla con sulfato de sosa anhidroso en polvo, luego se transfiere á una cápsula de extracción, y se extrae por espacio de cuatro horas en un Soxhlet con acetona anhidrosa, obtenida destilando acetona sobre carbonato de potasa desecado. Luego se destila la acetona, y caso de observarse algún aceite en el residuo de glicerina, se elimina tratándolo con éter de petróleo. En este estado desécase la glicerina entre 70–80° C. por espacio de cuatro ó cinco horas y se pesa; pero habrá de cuidarse de no exceder aquella temperatura. Las soluciones que contengán más de 40 por ciento de glicerina no es necesario evaporarlas, sino que pueden tratarse directamente con sulfato de sodio anhidroso.

PEROXIDO ANISOIL

Se obtiene tratando una solución, de cloruro de anisol en acetona con peróxido de hidrógeno. El peróxido de anisoil se separa al principio en la forma de un líquido aceitoso, que, no obstante, no tarda en solidificarse, formando un precipitado blanco granular, cuya fórmula es $OCH_3.C_6.H_4.CO.O.O.OC.C_6.H_4OCH_3$, y el que se derrite á 128° C. Al calentarse en una lámina de platino ó tubo capilar, arde ligeramente; pero, no obstante, es estable bajo presión y choque. Es perfectamente insípido y sin olor. Al tratarse con ácido sulfúrico concentrado arde, asumiendo un color verde. —*Apoth. Zeitung and Merks Report.*

Notas Prácticas

PROCEDIMIENTO RAPIDO PARA PREPARAR OXIGENO.— El *Bulletin Commercial* de enero 31, 1906, contiene un artículo en que se describe un procedimiento rápido para obtener oxígeno puro. Los farmacéuticos situados á distancias de los centros de población donde puede obtenerse oxígeno preparado, apreciarán la sen- [illegible] procedimiento, la falta de peligro para el [illegible] pureza del producto obtenido por este [illegible] ha reciente, el mejor proceso empleado [illegible] que era el del dióxido de sodio que exige un [illegible] rato especial. Pero Bridon sugiere un método para [illegible] xido de sodio sin aparato, que es como sigue: [illegible] ponen tabletas de sodio en una cápsula de por- [illegible] con fondo plano, de cabida de 100 á 150 c.c., la [illegible] ca en el fondo de una olla de barro que contenga de 5 á 6 litros. Esta cápsula se cubre con un embudo de cristal de un litro puesto sobre aquella invertido. El diámetro de la olla debe ser, por supuesto, mayor que el del embudo. Luego se fija un tubo de goma al extremo del embudo, y se vierte alguna agua en el espacio entre la olla y aquel hasta que el nivel del agua llegue á la orilla de la cápsula. La adición de agua se efectúa ahora muy poco á poco, y tan pronto como aquella penetra en la cápsula, el oxígeno empieza á formarse. Las primeras burbujas empujan el aire fuera del embudo y el tubo de goma se enlaza con el receptáculo que ha de contener el oxígeno. Va formándose el gas gradualmente, y para regular su formación se añadirá agua con más ó menos rapidez en el espacio de la olla. Cuando cesa de emitirse gas, lo que se demuestra por el hecho de que no escapan más burbujas, toda la cantidad de oxígeno que todavía queda en el aparato puede salvarse llenando la olla de agua y comprimiendo así el gas en la dirección del receptáculo. En cosa de 10 minutos, puede manufacturarse 30 litros de oxígeno. Mejor será lavarlo ó purificarlo después de recogido en el receptáculo, haciéndolo pasar por las soluciones necesarias, y de un receptáculo á otro. El oxígeno obtenido por medio de este proceso es muy puro y no contiene ningún compuesto de cloro, como sucede con el oxígeno preparado con clorato de potasa. El oxígeno puede lavarse con una solución de sosa al 5 por ciento y una solución de permanganato de potasio al 1 por ciento, después de lo cual es absolutamente puro.

Fuerza del Alcohol Empleado en la Preparación de Tintura de Opio

Por las declaraciones del químico Buttner (*Journal Suisse de Chimie et Pharmacie*, 1905, p. 542) parece que es inútil emplear alcohol de la fuerza de 70 grados en la fórmula para tintura de opio, que es la adoptada por la Conferencia Internacional para la Unificación de Fórmulas de Remedios Potentes. Alcohol de fuerza de 50 grados da precisamente tan buenos resultados como el de 70 grados en cuanto se refiere al porcentaje de morfina en la tintura. Buttner es también opuesto á la coladura, como método de preparar la tintura de opio, por haber hallado que la maceración da resultados tan satisfactorios. Opina que la coladura rinde resultados excelentes en la preparación de otras tinturas; pero no es apropiada para la tintura de opio, por la razón de que el opio no puede agotarse nunca, aunque se use diez veces su peso en alcohol. Por otra parte, tampoco puede emplearse mayor cantidad de alcohol come se hace con los extractos fluídos, á menos de que el producto no sea después reducido á un volumen conveniente, para lo cual se necesita calor, lo que cambiaría los principios activos del opio.

[La Farmacopea de los Estados Unidos prescribe alcohol diluído como menstruo en la percolación de tintura de opio, siendo la fuerza oficial del alcohol diluído sobre 41.5 por ciento, por peso. Durante la maceración preliminar que se prescribe por espacio de 60 horas antes de que se empiece la percolación, se emplean partes iguales de agua y alcohol, de modo que, prácticamente, se usa entonces 50 por ciento de alcohol. En el proceso de la Farmacopea, la fuerza del alcohol usado en la preparación de opio no excede 50 por ciento. En el proceso se emplean ambos, la maceración y la percolación.]

A NUESTROS LECTORES

Es tan halagüeña la acogida que ha merecido en el comercio de farmacia hispano-americano el «Suplemento» español del AMERICAN DRUGGIST, y tantas son las promesas para el porvenir en relación con nuestra publicación, que hemos creído conveniente publicar un número extraordinario que esperamos sea del agrado de nuestros favorecedores. Si en lo futuro se ofrece una oportunidad favorable como la presente repetiremos esta edición grande sin reparar en los gastos.

En obsequio á nuestros favorecedores, publicaremos en el «Suplemento» toda novedad relacionada con el ramo que se nos envíe, ó daremos noticia de cualquiera especialidad que prepare cualquiera de nuestros suscritores, y enviaremos el periódico con la noticia marcada á aquellos miembros de la facultad médica que les conviniera tener conocimiento de tal especialidad. Igualmente daremos cabida en nuestro «Suplemento» de vistas fotográficas de establecimientos de farmacia acreditados, acompañando suscinta descripción de los mismos.

Plantas Descubiertas Recientemente

Por E. M. HOLMES

PALO KALAMETO

En el *Journal of the Linnean Society* han visto la luz recientemente pormerores interesantes concernientes al Palo Kalameto de Birmania, según los cuales tan atrás como el año 1878 fué examinado por Sir D. Brandis, Mr. J. S. Gamble y Mr. A. Smithies, un espécimen de Palo Kalameto de Tavoy llegando á la conclusión de que se parecía á la madera de sándalo y difería en los rayos medulares que se destacaban mucho más. Esta opinión aparece en el *Manual of Indian Timbers.* Al prepararse la segunda edición del Manual, Mr. Gamble escribió á Mr. Menson, custodio de bosques en Tenasserim, pidiendo ejemplares mejores de Kalameto, recibiendo en 1900 un trozo del palo procedente de Theingôn Choung, cerca de la frontera siamesa del distrito de Mergui.

En 1901, después de haber enseñado á Sir D. Brandis un espécimen de Kalameto que Mr. Smith había donado al museo de la sociedad, Sir Brandis, en carta dirigida al *Indian Forester* (octubre, 1901), solicitó ejemplares de flores y fruta del árbol citado para poder clasificarlo, habiendo averiguado que tanto por su estructura como por su olor difería del Toungkalanet (*Cordia fragrantissima*, Kurz), P. J. [4], XIII, 552.

En 1903 obtuvo Mr. Manson, custodio de bosques, espécimens de fruta del árbol Kalameto; pero con motivo de las dificultades nacidas del hecho de que los bosques de Kalameto están situados en los cerros de la frontera siamesa, más de cien millas arriba el viejo pueblo de Tenasserim, no encontrándose aldea alguna en las últimas cuarenta millas de la jornada, y la circunstancia de que el período en que esos árboles florecen es aparentemente del 15 de marzo al 15 de abril, cuando los caudales de los ríos están reducidos haciendo el viajar muy fastidioso, de aquí que hasta noviembre de 1904 no pudiera Mr. Manson enviar espécimens de flores, comprendiendo dos especies de árboles llamados ambos Kalameto, aunque ninguno de los dos es la *Cordia fragrantissima*, Kurz. Uno de ellos, que crece en pequeños cerros y espolones salientes de la cordillera principal de Mawdoung, fué examinado en el Herbario de Calcutta por J. R. Drummond. El doctor Prain ha dado el nombre de *Mansonia* á uno de estos espécimens y lo incluye en el *Sterculaceæ* N. O., aunque Mr. Right coloca la planta en una *Triplochitomaceæ N. O.* distinta, que fué descrita por el difunto doctor Schumann para aceptar el género muy aliado *Triplochiton*. Estos dos géneros, *Triplochiton* y *Mansonia*, el doctor D. Prain los coloca ahora en una nueva tribu, *Mansonieæ* de la *N. O. Sterculiaceæ*.

J. R. Drummond ha dado el nombre de *Mansonia Gagei* al árbol Kalameto, en honor del capitán Gage, curador del Herbario de Calcutta, quien fué el primero en señalar su afinidad á la *Sterculiaceæ* por la aparencia del fruto.

Cuanto á la madera, Mr. J. S. Gamble la describe así: Corteza, ¼ de pulgada de espesor, color gris prieto, con hendiduras verticales someras; la parte exterior se desprende en láminas delgadas, irregulares. La madera es muy dura; el corazón es de color oliva obscuro, el alburno obscuro claro, textura compacta y homogénea. Anillos anuales dudosos, pero los anillos se perciben aunque es difícil seguir su formación. Si son anillos anuales verdaderos hay catorce por pulgada de radio, lo que denuncia crecimiento lento. Los poros pequeños, numerosos, dispuestos, más ó menos definidos, á menudo en líneas oblicuas concéntricas; distribuidos con igualdad; tocando los poros á los rayos medulares adyacentes de cada lado. Rayos medulares finos, muy numerosos, regulares, largos, sobre 300 por pulgada, sección radial, enseñando un grano plateado finamente marcado; peso sobre 70 libras por pie cúbico.

Sir Dietrich Brandis (P. J. [4], XIII, p. 552), dice que los rayos medulares consisten en sola una ó dos hileras de células, y los vasos miden solamente 0.05 en diámetro.

Estos árboles miden de circunferencia de 5 á 7 pies; los recolectores no los hacen cortar porque en su estado verde despiden un olor acre, desagradable; pero después de tumbados por años en los bosques, el olor se vuelve fragrante. Los naturales temen cortar estos árboles por creer que en ellos se anidan demonios. Esto, no obstante, la madera de los Kalametos abatidos por los vientos se encuentra en cantidad inagotable (*Journ. Lin. Soc.*, l. c., p. 253), y durante la estación fría se organizan expediciones para ir en su busca.

La cantidad de palo Kalameto exportado de Merqui en el período de 1887–1903, según cálculos del teniente-coronel Prain, basados en tablas aprontadas por Mr. Manson, ha sido por término medio de 28,296 lbs. por año, valuadas en £192 2s, á razón de 5½d. la libra. Mas el precio al por menor del palo en Rangoon varía de 12 annas á 3 rupias, *i. e.*, 1s. á 4s. por viss de 3 0857 libras, según la abundancia ó escasez de los abastos.

No se expresa si lo anterior se refiere al *Mansonia Gagei* ó incluye la otra especie de Kalameto, cuyo origen botánico no se ha averiguado aún. T...
sabe es que tiene hojas más grandes,
rente, y hasta el presente no está rep
Herbario de Calcutta. Mr. Manson describe l
como de un color de oro pálido, y, cual la del
sonia Gagei, despide un olor delicioso. Se ha reci
de Tavoy, y cree Mr. Manson que está id
con la B. 4,921 decrita por Mr. J. S. Gam
segunda edición del *Manual de Maderas de l*
Pharm. Journ.

Aire Liquido en la Medicina y Cirugía

Se han verificado importantes experiencias acerca del valor terapéutico del aire líquido. Sobre este particular, un conocido especialista se ha expresado así: « Todo proceso inflamatorio en que las aplicaciones frías son parte esencial del tratamiento, pueden éstas hacerse en alguna forma de aire líquido más satisfactoriamente que de otra manera. Por ejemplo, una rodilla inflamada ú otra articulación pueden exponerse al vapor seco, frío emanado de un vaso de aire líquido hirviendo, siendo posible graduarse su temperatura, y también reducirse la temperatura de la articulación ó parte afectada al grado que se desea. Otro método, más rápido en los efectos ulteriores es remojar una tohalla en el líquido, aplicándola con prontitud é intermitentemente hasta que la parte ha sido enteramente enfriada. También hay otro medio eficaz de obtener este resultado, y consiste en llenar una pera de vidrio con el líquido y hacerla rodar por la superficie de la articulación. Puede enviarse una corriente de aire por el carrete helado, siempre que haya la defensa correspondiente entre aquel y la piel, siendo los efectos muy ventajosos, cuando el frío es una condición apetecible, como sucede con los trastornos abdominales agudos, por ejemplo, la apendicitis.

» Para producir una inflamación ó efecto estimulante, el aire líquido se aplica directa é intermitentemente á la piel. El mejor ejemplo de este efecto obsérvase en las superficies ulcerantes indolentes crónicas, cuando con la pulverización, aquí y allá, en la superficie suficiente para helarla por un segundo, obtiénese después de algunas veces de esta aplicación una superficie granulante sana.

» Se comprenderá fácilmente que cualquier crecimiento de materia extraña que desgarre la piel puede extirparse con el aire líquido; quizás sean necesarias para ello dos ó tres aplicaciones. El único peligro, que debe evitarse, es la congelación excesiva, que podría dar lugar á la inflamación. Pero la inflamación de esta naturaleza cesa con prontitud aplicando al efecto fomentos calientes de ácido borácico ó fénico. Si la excrecencia consistiese en verrugas ó marca de nacimiento ó tumor, tratándolo con precaución se extirpa con más prontitud y menos dolor que por cualquier otro método. Una vez que la operación no se hace atropelladamente, no deja cicatriz ó señal local.

» En el tratamiento de carbuncos que no estén muy avanzados, y de no más de tres pulgadas de circunferencia, el aire líquido parece obrar como un específico En todos los casos tratados del tamaño dicho, la actividad mórbida ha abortado á la hora de helarse. Si el aire líquido pudiese ser útil solamente en el tratamiento del carbunco, el éxito obtenido en estas lesiones sería bastante compensación por su descubrimiento.»

Producción de Aceites Esenciales en el Mundo

ı producción de aceites esenciales en todo el es asunto de importancia, según el *American fumer*, que publica los siguientes cálculos: Cannes-ısse, 20.000 á 30,000 kilos de casia; 300,000 á 400,000 ›s de violetas; 1.500,000 kilos de rosas; 2.000,000 flores de azahar; 500,000 á 600,000 kilos de jazmi-. También se fabrican en ese punto 80,000 kilos de ite de espliego; 30,000 kilos de alhucema; 20,000 ›s de tomillo; 20,000 de romero, etc., representando en conjunto un valor de más de 30.000,000 de francos.

Sicilia, Calabria, en 1904, produjo 1.600,000 kilos de aceite de bergamota, limón y naranja, valuados en 14.758,000 francos. Bulgaria, produjo de 4,000 á 5,000 kilos de aceite de rosa, valuados en 3.500,000 francos; Argelia, produjo sobre 30,000 kilos de aceite de geranio; Zanzíbar, produjo 4.000.000 á 7.000,000 kilos de clavos; la Isla de Borbón, 30,000 kilos de aceite de geranio y algún vetiver; la India, 1.500,000 kilos de madera de sándalo, 500,000 kilos de aceite de nardo, aceite de palmarosa, esquenanto, canela; la península Malaca, sobre 150,000 kilos hojas de patchulí y raíces de vetiver; la China Central, tomillo, anís, casia; las Filipinas, ylang-ylang por valor de 500,000 francos; Java, aceite de kananga y nardo; Japón, sobre 200,000 kilos de aceite de menta piperita, una cantidad considerable de alcanfor; los Estados Unidos, 100,000 kilos de aceite de menta piperita; México, aceite de linaloa; Guayana, 3.000 kilos de aceite de palo de rosa; Paraguay, 3,000 kilos de aceite de petit grain.

EDIFICIO FULLER

Llamado el « Edificio Plancha,» Quinta Ave., Broadway y calles 22ª y 23ª, con vista á la Plaza Madison. Construcción atrevida, armadura de acero, levantado en un solar de solamente 7,690 pies cuads.; 300 pies de altura; 120,000 pies cuads. espacio de los pisos; 13,340 pies cuads. debajo de las aceras. Edificio de los más notables de los Estados Unidos.

Crema para Amasamiento

Experimentando á menudo y haciendo pruebas prácticas de productos preparados con caseina, empleando varios métodos de coagulación y tratamiento del coágulo, nos hallamos finalmente en estado para ofrecer una solución bastante aceptable del problema. Hay en esta ciudad tres peluqueros á lo menos que hacen un buen negocio con el amasamiento, y han tenido ocasión de ensayar varios productos, conviniendo todos ellos en que la crema á que nos referimos valía ciertamente la pena de probarla.

En el curso de las experiencias referidas, hallóse que para dar los mejores resultados nada superaba al ácido hidroclórico, puesto que es el que rinde más caseina. La glicerina no puede usarse para ablandar la masa desecada. Es demasiado dura para frotarse, y además es esencial que el producto acabado se muela en un molinillo exprofeso de los de pinturas, de otra manera no tardaría en ponerse granulosa, y, por consiguiente, inservible. Haciéndola pasar por el molino da un producto mejor mezclado y más suave de lo que es posible obtenerlo de un mortero. Hay cierta pegajosidad inherente al producto que hace difícil el quitarla, á parte de que deja en el rostro una sensación como de almidón; pero esto puede reducirse con el aditamento de una pequeña cantidad de aceite de almendras dulces y el empleo de alcohol diluído para resblandecer la caseina desecada. Una vez comprobados estos puntos, se preparó la siguiente fórmula. Su ejecución es satisfactoria, pues siendo nuestro objeto dar á conocer esta crema para amasamientos, la experiencia quizás sugiera algunos cambios en la manipulación. Por lo cual no pretendemos que el producto sea la misma perfección, mas queda en pie lo dicho por uno de los principales barberos: «Es lo mejor que he visto hasta aquí.» Esta es la fórmula:

Leche	1 galón
Acido hidróclorico	1 onza fluída
Acido bórico	1 onza
Aceite de almendras amargas	20 gotas
Aceite de geranio rosa	30 »
Aceite de almendras dulces	½ onza fluída
Solución de carmín	suficiente para colorearlo

A la leche se añadirá un galón de agua caliente, bastante para elevar la temperatura á unos 80 grados Fahrenheit. Mézclese el ácido hidroclórico con una pinta de agua, y añádese esto lentamente á la leche diluida, agitando constantemente lo bastante para coagular completamente la caseina, que se reposa en un estado de finura. Déjese reposar por una hora; recójase el precipitado en una tela y después de comprimirse, devuélvase la masa al vaso y añádese dos galones de agua. Agítese el coágulo, rompiendo los grumos que se formen; viértase el agua y lávese otra vez. Es necesario que todo el ácido y el suero se desprendan de la caseina lavándola. Recójase en un colador y escúrrase todo el agua posible; pásese luego á un mortero ú otro vaso apropiado é incorpórese el ácido bórico. Trasládese á un saco de tela; suspéndase del andén de un armario ú otro lugar apropiado, por espacio de 36 á 48 horas, comprimiendo el saco de cuando en cuando. La masa se contrae y expele el agua y se necesitarán unos dos días para desprenderse de toda ella.

Se hallará entonces que la caseina estaba bien desecada y granulosa. Traspásese á un mortero, frótese tan fina como posible; póngase cosa de una onza de alcohol diluido (bastante para humedecer) y añádese entonces aceite de almendras dulces y perfumes. Coloréese el producto con solución de carmín. Añádese entonces agua suficiente para formar una pasta blanda; bátese todo junto hasta que esté mezclado por igual, luego hágase pasar por un molino de los de pinturas, y embotéllese inmediatamente, ó bien póngase en tubos flexibles. Se seca muy rápidamente, y debe ponerse en paquetes desde luego.

Fallecimiento del Fundador de la Apollinaris

Se anuncia en Inglaterra el fallecimiento de Mr. Edward Steinkopff, ocurrido en Lyndhurst, Hayward's Heath, el 28 de febrero próximo pasado. El difunto fué el fundador del vasto negocio del agua Apollinaris, del cual se retiró en 1897. Steinkopff había nacido en Frankfort, y andando el tiempo dedicóse á la carrera del comercio, siendo todavía joven, empezando á desarrollar su actividad en la ciudad de Glasgow donde entró en una casa alemana. Más tarde estableció un negocio por su cuenta. La quiebra del Banco de la Ciudad de Glasgow lo dejó arruinado, y en este estado pasó á Londres el año 1874, donde, con el apoyo de George Smith (Smith, Elder & Co.) fundó el negocio del agua Apollinaris, poniéndose al frente de la empresa durante el período de su desenvolvimiento y contando con la cooperación de Julius Prince hasta alcanzar una posición sin paralelo, habiendo logrado que la Apollinaris fuese aceptada como el agua natural de la mesa en todo el mundo. Steinkopff vendió la parte que tenía en el negocio en 1897 á Frederick Gordon, importando casi diez millones de pesos, desde cuya fecha Prince ha estado á la cabeza. Por algún tiempo Steinkopff fué el propietario de la *St. James Gazette*. En 1897 compró la hermosa quinta de Lyndhurst, en Sussex, gozando el retiro que le brindaba. También hacía alguna estancia en su suntuosa casa de Londres, en Berkeley Square, que en un tiempo era la residencia del presidente del Consejo de Ministros, Pitt. Madama Steinkopff falleció hace cosa de algunos meses, habiendo tenido una sola hija que es la esposa del coronel Stewart Mackenzie, de Seaforth, hermano de la marquesa de Tweedale.

CRUCE DE BROADWAY Y LA QUINTA AVENIDA

Punto de la ciudad, llamado anteriormente el «Gran Distrito de las Luces Blancas,» y en lenguaje policíaco el «Tenderloin.» Vista también de la Avenida de la moda, invadida hoy por el comercio hasta más arriba de la Catedral de San Patricio. En las calles adyacentes hay suntuosos hoteles, grandes teatros, museos artísticos, bibliotecas, etc. A la izquierda se ve el Hotel de la Quinta Avenida, á la derecha la Plaza Madison, y la bifurcación de Broadway y la Avenida.

«The Liquid» y lo que este Nombre Significa

El personal, el método y los productos que han contribuido al desarrollo de esta Compañía, y establecido una reputación que es sinónima de excelencia en todo lo concerniente á bebidas gaseosas.

La Liquid Carbonic Company, hoy una de las más grandes de su clase en el mundo, es, sin embargo, una institución relativamente nueva, pues su fundación legal data del año de 1888, en cuya fecha debe su nacimiento, ó mejor dicho, su incepción en la mente del que hoy es aún su Presidente-Tesorero, don Jacobo Baur, quien ha sido desde su fundación, su paladín incansable cuya incesante energía, entusiasmo constante han sido y son una de las causas del éxito obtenido por la Compañía «The Liquid.»

Esto que decimos de su jefe y cabeza principal, puede con verdad decirse de todos los otros jefes y subalternos de la Directiva de esta joven industria, pues son bien conocidos como hombres emprendedores y de cualidades comerciales. Este personal incluye en su número hombres tales como don Carlos Minshall, Vice-Presidente, don Oscar Baur, que es el encargado en jefe, y don C. F. Rauchfuss, Secretario de la Compañía y jefe del departamento general de ventas.

En el cortísimo período de diez y siete años, «Liquid» se ha desarrollado de un modo asombroso; las graciosas espirales de humo que arrojan, día y noche, las chimeneas de sus diez y siete inmensas fábricas, anuncian un trabajo constante en la producción cuantiosa de todos y cada uno de los innumerables y necesarios artefactos del ramo á que se dedican, los que se envían á todas partes del mundo por conducto de los once grandes almacenes ó depósitos que dicha Compañía mantiene con este solo fin en once de las más populosas y principales ciudades de este rico é industrioso país, á saber: Chicago, Nueva York, Pittsburg, Saint Louis, Milwaukee, Cincinnati, Baltimore, Minneapolis, Kansas City, Atlanta y Dallas, con un sin número de sucursales y agencias en todos los puntos civilizados del globo.

La nueva oficina central de esta Compañía, construída hace sólo dos años en Chicago, debido á la necesidad de un tal centro y al éxito obtenido, constituye uno de los más imponentes edificios en dicha ciudad. Es de estructura moderna, consta de ocho pisos, de material á prueba de fuego, de cualidades sanitarias y de ventilación; cubre un área grande en la intercepción de las calles Michigan y Wells, de casi tres cuartas partes de la manzana, circunvalada por las calles antedichas al sur y este, y por las calles Illinois y Franklyn al norte y oeste. El área total es de unos 10,000 pies cuadrados, destinados exclusivamente á las oficinas generales, imprenta y contaduría. Para la fabricación de los aparatos dispensatorios de gaseosas, ó como se les llama comunmente Fuentes, ha construído esta Compañía un edificio enorme en la misma calle de Wells, un poco hacia el norte de las oficinas generales, que ocupa toda una manzana.

El ver las ventas obtenidas para los productos insignificantes usados en los primeros años de la historia de las bebidas gaseosas en este país, bastó para demostrar á personas tan despiertas como las de esta Compañía, la inmensa posibilidad del negocio que podía hacerse tanto con los tratantes como con el público, en las gaseosas que fueran de rico sabor, bien carbonatadas, ables, variadas y apetecibles; así como también no tardaron preciar, la importante necesidad de mejorar la calidad de las osas por medio de maquinarias útiles y accesorios perfecsiendo este el principio y base de que partió para el éxito o.

dvenimiento de la Liquid Carb. Co. al campo industrial o de bebidas gaseosas, tanto en el terreno del consumo o en el de la fabricación, marca una época en dicha industria; olución hacia la adquisición de todo aquello que sea lo más moderno, eficiente, práctico é higiénico en la construcción de aparatos y artefactos anexos á dicho ramo, así como el empeño en producir lo más selecto, le he dado el nombre prestigioso que hoy goza.

Jugos de Frutas, Jarabes, Extractos, etc., de la «Liquid»

Se planteó esta rama de fabricación de la «Liquid» hará como unos diez años; y era por consiguiente en una escala comparativamente pequeña; y al contemplarla hoy, se ve como prueba fidedigna de la verdad innegable de que el verdadero mérito no depende del tiempo para establecer una reputación envidiable.

La preparación de los Jugos de Frutas, Jarabes, Extractos, etc., de la «Liquid» (conocidos en el comercio como Frutas Liquid y Frutas en Almíbar, «Marca Diamante,» etc.) se lleva á cabo en el edificio central, y se destina para este efecto los pisos tercero y cuarto del mismo, habiéndosele dedicado un almacén refrigeratorio exclusivamente para este ramo en un edificio adyacente; dichos pisos tercero y cuarto están equipados con los aparatos y utensilios más modernos que se conocen, á fin de producir y fabricar estos Jarabes y Almíbares por el mejor y más perfecto sistema. En este departamento hay también un laboratorio químico aprestado completamente con todos aquellos aparatos necesarios y bajo la dirección de un jefe perito y de un número de ayudantes. Como adición á este departamento de Chicago, hay en los edificios de Nueva York y St. Louis, sucursales que por su magnitud é importancia podrían considerarse centrales, pues que se les dedica la misma cantidad de lugar y superficie.

No hace muchos años que la mayoría de los fabricantes y traficantes en bebidas gaseosas usaban como componente, jarabes y siropes que pueden llamarse artificiales por estar hechos con extractos y productos del laboratorio *químico que á su vez*, era lo mejor hasta entonces conocido; pero el público demandó bebidas gaseosas que contuviesen como componente sólo aquellos jarabes hechos con los jugos de las frutas en almíbar, y por lo tanto, estos han superado y eliminado los productos químicos ó de laboratorio por completo.

La Compañía «Liquid» se apercibió bien pronto de la necesidad de suplir el mercado con las buenas clases de jarabes y almíbares, siendo la consecuencia natural de este conocimiento la instalación de los tres centros de fabricación de estos ingredientes en Chicago, St. Louis y Nueva York, ciudades que por su posición y condiciones especialmente favorables, se prestaban más á ello.— Con los anchurosos locales, los equipos perfectos y otras muchas circunstancias favorables, «The Liquid» posee hoy tres vastas fábricas de jarabes y sus productos son usados en cantidades en todo el hemisferio occidental, siendo un hecho innegable que las ventas en este ramo el año pasado, excedieron el triple de las anteriores; la clase de trabajos antecitados está en manos de peritos, hombres de conocimientos técnicos adquiridos en colegios y escuelas de nombradía, pues unen á su carrera comercial los títulos de Farmacéuticos y Peritos químicos. Don Jacobo Baur, el presidente de esta Compañía, es él mismo un farmacéutico con revàlida del Colegio de Farmacia de Filadelfia (en el año 1881), es miembro de la Sociedad de Industrias Químicas de Inglaterra, y de la Asociación de Farmacéuticos Americanos; así como también miembro honorario y de número de varias sociedades científicas.

Los Jarabes y Almíbares de frutas, conocidos en el comercio bajo los nombres ingleses de «liquid fruit» (frutas líquidas) y «Diamond Brand crushed fruits» (frutas en almíbar) se hacen solamente de las mejores y más selectas frutas, absolutamente sanas y maduras, cogidas directamente de las cepas y de los árboles, teniendo que llevar todos y cada uno de los lotes recibidos el visto bueno de varios inspectores que los sujetan á riguroso examen antes de permitirlos pasar á los diferentes departamentos para su preparación y evolución en ricos dulces. Aunque las frutas en general sufren muy poco manoseo, aquel que es absolutamente indispensable se lleva á efecto bajo las más escropulosas condiciones de higiene y limpieza en las bien ventiladas y claras estancias destinadas á este trabajo por la Compañía « Liquid. »

Los suelos de estas piezas, son todos de asfalto para poder baldearlos y limpiarlos tan á menudo como se necesite, asegurando así un grado de pulcritud insuperable. Nada entra en la preparación de estos productos que no sea las frutas más frescas, sanas y deliciosas y el puro azúcar de caña.

En la preparación de las frutas en conserva de la marca «Diamante» ó «Diamond Brand,» se observa el más escrupuloso cuidado en retener la forma natural de las frutas; ambos, los jarabes y almíbares de frutas frescas, se embotellan en frascos de 1 galón (4 litros) y medio galón (2 litros).

Creemos indispensable al referirnos á consumidores y traficantes, el hacer las aclaraciones precisas para conocimiento de aquellos que no han visto aun ninguno de los adelantos en el sistema de despacho de bebidas gaseosas; el traficante es aquel que despacha bebidas al público, no embotelladas como ha sido la costumbre inmemorial, sino al día, procedente de los aparatos más modernos y mezclando el jarabe ó la fruta en almíbar delante del consumidor que la va á beber.

Las frutas que se utilizan en la elaboración de dichos productos, tales como fresas, frambuesas, cerezas, damascos, etc., etc., se compran bajo contrato en los Estados de Michigan, Indiana, Illinois, Nueva Jersey, teniendo además contratos en otros Estados de la Unión, pues el consumo que hace de frutas la Compañía, no puede ser suplido por un sólo Estado. En cuanto á las piñas y ananás se suplen de ellas en las Bahamas, teniendo allí un representante especial que cuida de inspeccionar su calidad y estado antes del embarque, así que las piñas en almíbar en trozos, raspadas y en ruedas son de calidad superior.

Durante la estación de la fruta, este departamento emplea un número de muchachas, como auxiliares que varía entre 300 y 400, para el trabajo de escoger, mondar, etc., teniendo que ceñirse extrictamente al «Lema» de esta Compañía, y muy particularmente de este departamento, que es

«El aseo es á la salud
Lo que al alma á la virtud.»

Bajo reglas tan estrictas como lo que antecede, y una inspección rigida, es vano el repetir que la preparación de estas frutas se hace bajo las más regurosas condiciones de aseo y salubridad en todas sus detalles, desde el principio al fin.

En adición al grupo que antecede ó sea de frutas en almibar y jarabes de la «Liquid» para su uso en unión con las bebidas gaseosas, se preparan también un cierto número de especialidades en el ramo, que gozan del mismo grado de excelencia y que por su carácter especial las nombraremos en inglés y daremos entre paréntesis las traducciones más aproximadas, y que son: *Grape-Kola* (compuesto de uvas y kola), *Xola-Mint* (compuesto de kola y menta), *Chocolate-Mint* (de cacao y menta), *Peach-Blow* (una composición de duraznos), *Nut Confections* (una variedad en que entran como componentes diferentes clases de nueces, avellanas, piñones y azúcar), así como también ciertas bebidas ó componentes que se usan con agua caliente y que en momento de apuro pueden suplir á los caldos que con tanta paciencia y trabajo se preparan en las casas. Como los anteriores los nombraremos en inglés y daremos sus traducciones entre paréntesis, á saber: *Liquid Tomato Bouillon* (preparación ó extracto de carne de vaca y tomates para usarse en forma liquida como caldo espeso), *Liquid Clam Bouillon* (preparación de extracto de almejas para ser usado como el anterior), *Liquid Fluid and Solid Extract of Beef* (esta preparación no necesita explicación pues su uso es muy general desde hace años bajo el nombre de extracto de carne, la única diferencia que existe es que el *Fluid* está en estado líquido sin perder ninguna de sus virtudes), Bromuro Baur, etc.

En cuanto á los extractos, «The Liquid» hace solo una clase consideraba bajo el punto de vista de la calidad, esto es, hace solo lo mejor. Los «Extractos Solubles Baur» son ya bien conocidos entre los fabricantes de bebidas gaseosas en general y su venta por lo tanto no tiene hoy quien le aventaje. Este departamento está también bajo la dirección de un químico de gran experiencia que es también farmacéutico titular, quien con un numeroso personal de ayudantes, se ocupa constantemente en probar, examinar y ensayar cada una de las aromas y esencias que entran á componer los extractos «Liquid,» y esto se refiere tanto á cada componente del extracto como al producto completo una vez terminado y listo. Estos análisis así como esta clasificación de extractos para uso de los fabricantes de bebidas gaseosas, constituye un rasgo distintivo de la fabricación de esta clase de productos.

LOS APARATOS DISPENSATORIOS O FUENTES

Antes de entrar de lleno en la cuestión de la fabricación de estos modernísimos aparatos, daremos á vuela pluma una explicación al lector del porqué le vamos á llamar fuente en adelante, en todos nuestros escritos, así adoptando una palabra que si bien ha existido por muchos años en la lengua castellana nunca se le dió tal acepción, como es la de brotar agua carbónica ó mineral artificialmente carbonatada.

En los países latinos, y aun en los europeos, el negocio del despacho de bebidas gaseosas difiere radicalmente del sistema norteamericano y salvo en algunas capitales latinas y europeas en donde hombres emprendedores, que están haciendo una ganancia colosal, al mismo tiempo que deleitando al consumidor, porque han adoptado el despacho que puede llamarse directo, poco ó ningun progreso se ha hecho en el sentido de mejorar el ramo.

El sistema norteamericano, sin perjudicar en nada, sino muy al contrario ayudar, al ramo de fabricantes de bebidas gaseosas, lo redondea, si así puede decirse, ofreciendo al público un sinnúmero de bebidas gaseosas preparadas en el momento que se desean, y que por su confección y carácter especial es imposible despacharlas de una botella ó sifón.

No nos referimos, pues, á las aguas gaseosas que están hechas con almíbares ó jarabes, porque estos en su carácter fluído y limpio pueden pasar por el cuello de la botella ó la llave del sifón. Nos referimos á quellos refrescos gaseosos en que se emplean las frutas en almíbar de que hicimos mención anteriormente.

Los refrescos combinados de helado y agua carbónica que tanto deleitan al consumidor en los países en que se han introducido, no se pueden despachar por botellas, y para obviar este vacío para complacer á todos, el ingenio norteamericano inventó los ahora suntuosos aparatos dispensatorios ó fuentes que no son más que la traslación de un manantial carbónico (en este caso artificial) á la respotería del club, al mostrador del farmacéutico ó de la tienda ó de la confitería; como verá el lector más adelante, todo cuanto el genio inventivo del norteamericano ha podido propinar, y todo en lo que el capital ha podido ayudarle, se ha hecho on el sentido de avanzar este ramo; resultando de esto, unos negocios productores, no solo de cuantiosas fortunas á los fabricantes y comerciantes sino de un bienestar y comodidades sin número al consumidor en general.

La gran fábrica de Fuentes para gaseosas que tiene la Compañía «Liquid» está ubicada en Chicago, y sus trabajos son exclusivamente Fuentes y sus accesorios, desde el croquis hasta su consumación. El trabajo de madera es completo, comenzando por aserrar los trozos vírgenes, que vienen muchos de ellos de los países tropicales, y se sigue el cepillado, la talla y el barnizado; con el onix y mármoles, que importa esta Compañía directamente de México y Italia, se hace lo mismo; comenzando por tablear las grandes masas, siguiéndolo con la talla, el pulido y el pareo; el formarlos en un conjunto artístico, en una palabra. Todo el trabajo de metal y de hierro — tales como grifos verticales, grifos horizontales, canillas, armazones, lámparas de luz eléctrica y las innumerables piezas necesarias á los anteriores — se funden, pulen y platean; en fin, se convierte todo clase de la materia prima necesaria para todos los detalles de la fabricación de Fuentes para gaseosas en piezas componentes de las mismas, hasta convertirlos en un conjunto artístico y armonioso que ha dado al negocio de la «Liquid» el ímpetu que tiene, contándose esta Compañía entre las de su clase en el mundo, que construyen fuentes en tal escala, también la esta Compañía construye sus fuentes de una manera completa y exclusiva, desde el croquis, como hemos dicho, hasta sus accesorios. En la fabricación de los aparatos ó fuentes para gaseosas, la «Liquid» tomó en consideración siempre y ante todas las cosas, la importantísima cuestión de la salud del público, una salubridad completa y una limpieza que raya en pulcritud, son los modelos que no se separan jamás en lo más mínimo, ninguna de los aparatos «Liquid.»

Es un hecho que las Fuentes «Liquid» difieren muy materialmente de todas las hechas por otras compañías, por razón de su estructura peculiar y partes componentes propias, que abrazan peculiaridades como son los jarros de blanca porcelana tan aseados y salúbricos para los jarabes; las canillas de caucho endurecido para los mismos, y otras muchas particularidades que parecen pequeñeces á primera vista, pero que tienden de un modo poderoso á evitar en un todo, cualquier posibilidad de contagio, á causa de los infusorios, acumulación de suciedad de cualquier clase que esta sea, filtraciones, goteos, etc. Está hoy admitido de una manera general que el sano y práctico sistema de construcción adoptado por la «Liquid» para sus fuentes es verdaderamente excelente.

La «Liquid» por el mero hecho de operar, como lo hace, una de las fábricas grandes de aparatos de gaseosas en el mundo, en lo cual se hacen los mismos en todas y cada de sus partes constituyentes, y además por emplear un crecido personal de ingenieros, mecánicos y peritos en construcción técnica, y un número de obreros mecánicos hábiles, constituye de por sí una clase especial de fabricación. Una fuente para gaseosas de la «Liquid» figura entre los modelos perfectos, por su belleza, fortaleza, durabilidad, facilidad en el manejo, ahorro de hielo, salubridad, limpieza y economía en general. El distribuidor al comprar una fuente de la «Liquid» sabe que compra directamente del fabricante y á precios de fábrica.

El renglón de aparatos distribuidores de aguas gaseosas de la «Liquid» abraza todos los varios estilos en uso, é incluye desde el bien conocido equipo ó fuente de onix para el testero hasta el «dispensador de mostrador» «Liquid,» ambos poseen muchos puntos de excelencia. Haciendo mención especial del «distribuidor de mostrador» «Liquid,» puede decirse que los vasos que contienen el jarabe son de porcelana blanca, de una pieza, no habiendo pues tazas de cristal que puedan romperse, despegarse ó derramarse en las junturas, con el uso. Estos vasos ó tarros de jarabe son de recambio é independientes unos de otros, y no pueden salirse de línea.

El aparato para medir ó graduar la salida de los jarabes, es muy seguro en su acción y de una exactitud absoluta, no teniendo muelles que se descompongan ó aflojen, ni hay posibilidad de ninguna clase de contaminación metálica en los jarabes. Como las espitas de los siropes son estacionarias, el que despacha ó distribuye las gaseosas no puede romper los vasos ni derramar sus contenidos á causa de choques ó enredos al sacar los jarabes. Estos así como las frutas en almíbar están constantemente en contacto con el hielo, asegurando de esta manera refrescos bien fríos. Los mostradores están construidos con un cuádruple aislamiento para que no rezumen las maderas; las mesas ó tableros de labor y los escurridores de los vasos, son espaciosos y completos en todos sus detalles; considerándolos en un todo, el conjunto proporciona un aparato completo.

APARATOS CARBONATADORES

Los carbonatadores, desde hace mucho tiempo han probado su eficacia, no solo como una necesidad en el negocio de fabricación de aguas gaseosas, sino también como un anexo productor de los aparatos distribuidores. Los carbonatadores fabricados por la Liquid Carbonic Company son máquinas tan perfectas como pueden resultar de la unión de elementos tan esenciales y poderosos como son, inteligencia, larga experiencia, materiales de lo mejor obtenible y el trabajo material de hábiles mecánicos. Estos carbonatadores no son sólo muy fuertes en su construcción y de una durabilidad extrema, sino que son en todo tiempo perfectamente continuos y automáticos, en su trabajo mecánico, (requiriendo casi ninguna atención ó cuidado) y se garantizan de carbonatar las aguas á un grado de saturación de 100 por ciento. En esta máquina se combinan, afortunadamente, todos aquellos métodos de saturación conocidos que son tres, á saber: rocío, absorción y agitación.

El hecho existe de que no hay máquina que pueda mezclar de una manera perfecta el agua con el gas carbónico, á menos que no abrace su construcción el total de los tres distintos y separados métodos de carbonización antes mencionados. Según hemos expuesto anteriormente, el mecanismo completo del carbonatador «Liquid» es lo más sencillo que puede imaginarse; no hay válvulas flotantes ú otras piezas complicadas que puedan descomponerse; y como sucede que toda la fuerza expansiva del gas carbónico se utiliza, se requiere muy poca fuerza operativa, relativamente. Puede muy bien decirse que un carbonatador «Liquid» prácticamente se maneja el mismo, pues arranca y se para por sí mismo sin necesidad de atención ó cuidado; supliendo una cantidad constante de agua perfectamente saturada á un costo que no excede de un cuarto de centavo (americano) por litro. Estas máquinas están hechas para aguantar un largo y continuo uso y servicio y sus dueños se reembolsan de su valor en muy corto tiempo. El éxito obtenido por estas máquinas entre fabricantes y distribuidores de aguas gaseosas, ha sido feliz; y hoy se encuentran en uso en todos los Estados Unidos y muchas partes del Canadá, México, Centro y Sud América, así como en países europeos.

Una sola Compañía en los Estados Unidos, posee y opera casi 200 de estos carbonatadores, todos de una misma clase.

GAS CARBONICO «LIQUID» MARCA «DIAMOND»

Este producto es el resultado final y perfecto de estudios y experimentos científicos de las condiciones existentes, emanando de la convicción de que es un hecho incontestable, que para obtener y surtir al público, con un renglón de bebidas gaseosas puras y saludables, hay que tener á mano, como componente primordial, un gas carbónico que sea absolutamente puro y saludable. Las bebidas gaseosas preparadas con dicho gas carbónico, se distinguen por su sin igual efervescencia, brillantez y exquisito gusto. Por razón de la perfecta pureza de este artículo (como son sus propiedades anhídricas ó de sequedad y la ausencia de aire atmosférico) su uso es mucho menos costoso que el de otras marcas que ordinariamente contienen aire comprimido ó humedad. La Compañía Liquid Carbonic tiene fábricas de gas carbónico en todos los centros comerciales de importancia de los Estados Unidos, poniéndose así en posición para efectuar prontos envíos y rápidas entregas á cualquier punto dado. También se observa un cuidado especial en que este artículo sea en todos sus detalles de uniformidad perfecta, así como todos los cilindros contensores de peso completo.

PREMIOS AL MERITO

Aunque no se preste más que una ligera atención á los diferentes renglones que fabrica esta Compañía, pronto se revela aun al más desinteresado observador, el anchísimo campo é infinita practicabilidad de los métodos y productos de la «Liquid.»

La calidad actual de los productos de esta Compañía debe constituir una prueba fidedigna de la perfecta familiaridad de dicha Compañía con las necesidades del ramo y del público, no habiendo la menor duda del discernimiento é inteligencia de las personas que están á su cargo.

La «Liquid» se ha acreditado por la perfecta fabricación de gaseosas, mereciendo la más alta consideración, tanto la fabricación como el personal, no sólo de aquellos que desean mejorar el ramo por ser partes interesadas, sino del público en general cuyo natural deseo es obtener bebidas gaseosas en todo puras, sanas y deliciosas.

NOTAS COMERCIALES

— Para tener un conocimiento exacto del artículo y poder apreciarlo, la Dentacura Company, de la ciudad de Newark (N. J.) enviará muestras de su Dentacura, que es una pasta dentífrica antiséptica, á quien lo solicite. El artículo goza ya de buena popularidad entre el público y los dentistas.

— La excelencia de ciertos efectos es tal que vale ciertamente la pena de llamar la atención del público hacia ellos, y en este caso nos referimos al anuncio de la Dalley Manufacturing Company del No. 12 Duane Street, Nueva York, cuyo Mata-Dolor Mágico de Dalley es un ungüento que ha estado en el mercado durante tres generaciones de la familia Dalley, de modo que es muy conocido del público. Los fabricantes se proponen introducirlo en la América española para lo cual solicitan correspondencia para hacer arreglos satisfactorios.

— Las cosas se aprecian cuando se conocen y así no hay engaño. Por si acaso fuese aun nueva para alguien la tan acreditada Creta Francesa preparada por Thomas, bastará con dirigirse á Thomas Manufacturing Company, de Baltimore (Md.), para recibir una muestra del producto que se halla muy útil para usos farmacéuticos, y para la manufactura de artículos de tocador.

— La introducción de sillas y muebles de alambre ha efectuado una revolución en los enseres de las boticas. Estas sillas y mesas son livianas, ocupan poco espacio; son duraderas, artísticas y poco costosas. Para pormenores de este estilo de muebles, muy apropósito para climas cálidos, nuestros lectores podrán dirigirse á los fabricantes Chicago Wire Chair Company, Chicago, 66 N. Jefferson street, E. U. A.

— El mundo adelanta y la ciencia descubre nuevos campos de investigación y se elaboran cada día nuevos productos. Ahora se trata de dar á conocer á los países hispano-americanos el afamado anestésico francés somoformo, de que son agentes en este país E. De Trey & Son, del 109 West 42d Street, Nueva York. En el anuncio que la Compañía despliega en este número se hallará una excelente descripción de este notable producto.

— Uno de los renglones más antiguos de medicinas cuyos fabricantes tienen privilegio y se manufacturan en los Estados Unidos, es el de la Allcock Manufacturing Company, de Nueva York. Estos efectos han sido de tal modo adoptados por las familias, que muchos fabricantes sin escrúpulos, aprovechándose de su fama, han tratado de colocar en el mercado artículos contrahechos, motivo porque esa Compañía apreciará que se le denuncien las imitaciones de sus medicinas que circulen.

— Acercándose la estación de los calores en que tantas bebidas frescas se consumen, es oportuno referirnos á las bombillas, ó pajuelas artificiales que la New Jersey Paper Tube Company, de Nueva York, fabrica y cuyo anuncio se hallará entre las páginas de este número. Estas bombillas son perfectamente higiénicas y llegan al público sin haberlas tocado mano humana. Son de apariencia hermosa y poco costosas. Son á propósito para bebidas calientes y frías y también para la estancia de los enfermos. La Compañía enviará muestras de estas pajuelas artificiales á quien se lo pida.

— Dícese que lo bueno nunca harta, de aquí que nuestros lectores con seguridad se interesarán en el anuncio de la Martin H Smith Company, de Nueva York, que entre otros orna la sección correspondiente del periódico. Esta Compañía es la propietaria del Glico-Heroina (Smith) y el Ergo-Apiol (Smith), productos que hallarán seguramente salida en los países españoles como en los demás donde se han dado á conocer. La Compañía desea entablar relaciones con los tratantes con el fin de efectuar arreglos mutuamente ventajosos.

— Por más que no pretendemos sorprender al público tratándose de los tan populares Remedios Garfield, la verdad es que la demanda por ellos aumenta todos los días y ha llegado el momento de los fabricantes establecer nuevas agencias en la América española, y con tal objeto ofrecen incentivos á los farmacéuticos dispuestos á aprovecharse de esta ocasión. Anunciarán en grande escala y tendrán sumo gusto en comunicar á sus corresponsales el plan y condiciones para dar á conocer sus remedios.

— El Big G es un remedio no venenoso para todas las manifestaciones de inflamación catarral, incluyendo gonorrea, catarro nasal, coriza aguda, cólera morbo, conjuntivitis, gota militar, etc., de aquí que su venta sea considerable. Como medio para dar á conocer el remedio, los fabricantes The Evans Chemical Company, de Cincinnati, E. U. A., proporcionarán interesante materia anunciadora en español. Esta especialidad considérase muy provechosa y por esta razón muy válida, los farmacéuticos que no la tienen aun deberían procurarse existencias. Los fabricantes han hecho un precio especial de $86.40 neto en partidas de gruesas, aunque una sola docena cuesta $8.00.

HIGADO ACTIVO CABEZA DESPEJADA. — Hace ya, como todo el mundo sabe, setenta años que las Píldoras Hepáticas de Mandrágora Schenck se venden en el mercado. Los fabricantes garantizan que son de productos vegetales en absoluto y un sustituto perfecto del calomelano como colagogo. Obran directa y prontamente en el tubo digestivo y en el hígado, y son inapreciables en todas las formas de paludismo. Los fabricantes Dr. J. H. Schenck & Son, de Filadelfia, tienen en vista establecer agencias en puntos donde todavía no están representados y están inclinados á hacer arreglos satisfactorios. Al escribírseles, sírvanse mencionar el AMERICAN DRUGGIST.

— Casi tres cuartos de siglo hace que un joven inglés llamado John Matthews vino á Nueva York. Mr. Matthews, aunque joven, era de un carácter emprendedor y enérgico y poseía profundos conocimientos de ingeniería mecánica. A su llegada á Nueva York, procedió á hacer una indagación de las perspectivas que los negocios en esta Metrópoli le presentaban para decidir á cuál de ellos le sería más conveniente dedicar sus conocimientos y energías. El no tardó en descubrir el vasto campo que le presentaba el negocio de Agua de Soda, Bebidas Carbonatadas y Aguas Minerales por lo que prontamente se dedicó á la manufactura de aparatos para fabricar estas bebidas, estableciendo su pequeña fábrica en lo que es ahora Primera Avenida de Nueva York. A la inventiva de Mr. Matthews, los Estados Unidos deben la producción del «Sistema Americano» de maquinaria para fabricar aguas gaseosas y la hoy famosa Fuente de Soda Americana fué también una de sus invenciones. Los negocios de Mr. Matthews se desarrollaron con tal rapidez, que él no tardó en sentir la necesidad de agrandar su fábrica la que ensanchó hasta llegar á ocupar un edificio entero al que más tarde añadió otro y otros, hasta terminar por construir una gran fábrica que comprendía seis edificios. Para las fechas en que estos trabajos fueron concluidos, ya eran los hijos de Mr. Matthews quienes con juvenil energía atendían al negocio, el cual recibió un nuevo y notable impulso. En 1901, una poderosa compañía denominada la American Soda Fountain Co., con un capital de $3.750,000 oro, compró de los nietos de Mr. Matthews la grandiosa fábrica que setenta y cuatro años hace, modestamente estableció en este mismo sitio el joven inglés John Matthews. La American Soda Fountain Co. con excelente recursos y hecha ya dueña de la situación en los Estados Unidos se dedicó desde luego á extender sus negocios á países extranjeros, con tan alhagadores resultados, que sus más marcados esfuerzos en la actualidad son dirigidos á aumentar su negocio de exportación. El negocio de la fabricación de agua de soda y su expendio al detall, es muy lucrativo en este y otros países, pero particularmente lo es en países cálidos como México, Cuba, las Antillas y las Américas Central y del Sur. Muchos son los droguistas y farmacéuticos en esos países que comprendiendo esto han anexado á su negocio principal una planta para fabricar y despachar al mostrador agua de soda, gaseosas y minerales, y si usted piensa que este negccio pudiera convenirle, ncsotros aconsejaríamos que usted se ccmunique cuanto antes con la American Soda Fountain Co., de Boston, U. S. A., quienes tendrán gusto en prcporcicnar cualquier información concerniente al ramo.

AMERICAN DRUGGIST

and PHARMACEUTICAL RECORD

NUEVA YORK Y CHICAGO: 11 DE JUNIO DE 1906

«The American Druggist» es un periódico bimensual del que se publica cada mes un suplemento español con anuncios en el mismo idioma

AMERICAN DRUGGIST PUBLISHING COMPANY

62-68 West Broadway, New York, U. S. A.

Dirección cablegráfica «Amdruggist, New York.» Clave A B C

A. R. ELLIOTT, *Presidente*

CASWELL A. MAYO, Ph. G.................*Director*

THOMAS J. KEENAN, Lic. en Farm., *Director Asociado*

PRECIOS DE SUSCRIPCION

Pago adelantado, Estados Unidos, Canadá, México, Cuba, Puerto Rico, Hawaii y las Filipinas... ....(oro americano) $1.50

Otros países (franco de porte).................. » » $3.00

Las suscripciones pueden empezar en cualquier tiempo.

«The American Druggist and Pharmaceutical Record» sale el segundo y cuarto lunes de cada mes. Todo cambio de anuncios debe ser recibido diez días antes de la fecha de salida.

Remesas deben hacerse con libranzas sobre Nueva York, giros postales internacionales ó por expreso ó correo en carta certificada. Toda correspondencia debe dirigirse á la American Druggist Publishing Co., 62-68 West Broadway, New York, U. S. A.

EL RADIUM.—EL PROFESOR CURIE

EL fallecimiento reciente en París del profesor Curie nos trae á la memoria el momento de expectación en todo el mundo científico que siguió al descubrimiento del radium. Este elemento posee propiedades que al principio se creían ser subversivas de toda la fábrica levantada por la ciencia física moderna sobre los principios de conservación y correlación de la energía. El radium emite luz, que es una forma de energía; pero no parecía generar calor, que es una forma correlativa de aquélla. Aquellos que llevaron á cabo experiencias con él, no hubieron de tardar en experimentar sus tendencias destructoras semejantes á las características de la exhibición del calor. No fueron, por consiguiente, subvertidos los principios, sino más firmemente establecidos. Casi tan estupendo como este descubrimiento inicial fué otro derivado de él — el de que los ochenta elementos varios de que trata la quí[illegible] nada más que variedades de un solo [illegible] es la base de toda la materia, lo que [illegible]er aceptado por la opinión científica. Sir Wil[illegible]amsey, entre otros, lo demostró cuando descom[illegible] «elemento» radium para producir de él otro [illegible],» el helium. (Parece como si ahora tuvié[illegible] poner la palabra entre comillas, porque con [illegible] conocimiento adquirido, no denota en reali[illegible]ncia elemental). Se han inventado nuevas voces para definir ciertas formas de materia que antes se describían como átomos, elementos y otros parecidos; y á las voces antiguas se les han de añadir nuevos significados. La presente unidad de la materia no es el átomo, sino el *electrón*, que es realmente la unidad de la electricidad negativa. Electricidades semejantes tienden á rechazarse una á otra, y lo que estábamos acostumbrados á llamar átomo, es una entidad mantenida unida por un núcleo de electricidad positiva, al que se le da ahora el nombre de *ion*.

El descubrimiento del profesor Curie dió un impulso fabuloso á la ciencia física y á la química, de que era eminente exponente el difunto, quien había sido admitido en la Academia de Ciencias de París. Nacido el profesor Curie el 15 de mayo de 1859, era uno de los jóvenes sabios de que podía alabarse Francia. Dedicado á los estudios desde su juventud, y no obstante las contrariedades de su posición, proseguía sus experiencias con expectación anhelosa. Más tarde cooperó con él su esposa, entusiasta también de las ciencias físicas y coopartícipe con su esposo en el descubrimiento del radium, hecho culminante en su larga serie de investigaciones, que había de cambiar su posición social y desahogarla, á parte de la fama universal que el descubrimiento alcanzó para sus autores. La parca cruel impidió que se ciñiese á sus sienes nuevos laureles el ilustre científico, decretando su trágica muerte con el atropello de pesado vehículo, que aplastó aquel cerebro luminoso.

Nuevo Remedio para Resfriados

El cónsul general Guenther, estacionado en Frankfort (Alemania), anuncia el descubrimiento de un nuevo remedio para resfriados, consistente en una mezcla de cocaína y paranfrina aplicada á la nariz con una mota de algodón. Con varias aplicaciones las secreciones mucosas quedan suprimidas y curado el resfriado nasal.

Como los resfriados conducen á veces á enfermedades graves ó peligrosas, es muy acertado atajar su desarrollo. Tratándose de niños afectados por la dolencia, el doctor Vohsen aconseja á las madres cortar un tubito de goma oblicuamente, introduciendo en la nariz el extremo apuntado, y luego por medio de una pera de goma introducir aire en el tubo. De este modo las secreciones de un lado se expulsan con la fuerza del aire por el otro. Esto alivia la dificultad nasal en los niños y les permite respirar libremente. Este medio se aplica á todos los casos en que la nariz y la garganta están afectadas.

Teoría Corpuscular de la Materia

Por el Prof. J. J. THOMPSON

Al presentar una nueva teoría de la materia precisa explicar de una manera satisfactoria todas las propiedades químicas, ópticas y eléctricas de la materia misma. Según la teoría que acaba de enunciarse, lo que acostumbrábamos describir como un átomo, supónese ahora que está compuesto de electricidad positiva y negativa, consistiendo la última en pequeñas partículas á las que se da el nombre de «corpúsculos.» En un principio había demostrado el profesor Crookes que cuando una descarga eléctrica se hace pasar por un tubo del cual se ha extraído bien el aire, se produce inmediatamente una fluorescencia verde en el extremo opuesto del catodo, ó sea el polo negativo, al chocar contra el vidrio un haz de rayos luminosos á los que se dió el nombre de rayos catodos. Demostróse también que estos rayos se movían en línea recta, para probar lo cual se interponía en su dirección una lámina de mica cortada cual una cruz, y la sombra de la misma aparecía sobre el vidrio. La mayoría de los físicos de la Europa continental contendían que los rayos catodos eran otras tantas vibraciones del éter, mientras que los físicos ingleses favorecían la teoría de que eran partículas materiales ó corpúsculos, cuya ha sido últimamente confirmada por los tres hechos siguientes: *Primero*, los rayos pueden ser desviados por medio de un imán; *segundo*, cuando se desvían dirigiéndolos con el tubo de vacío contra una cacerola de metal hueca, el metal se carga negativamente, lo que se demuestra enlazando la misma á un electroscopio; *tercero*, los rayos son desviados por fuerzas electrostáticas de atracción y repulsión.

Wehnelt ha demostrado recientemente, que los rayos catodos también se producen cuando se calientan hasta la incandescencia en una lámina de platina al vacío los óxidos de calcio ó bario. Los rayos obtenidos de este modo, al hacerlos proyectar sobre una superficie metálica en el tubo de vacío, fácilmente se demuestra que se desvían de su curso normal para trazar una órbita parabólica. Como resultado de mediciones cuantitativas cuidadosamente practicadas, se ha averiguado que la velocidad de los corpúsculos varía considerablemente en diferentes casos, estando afectada tanto por la forma del tubo como por el grado del vacío. Los corpúsculos generados del óxido de calcio incandescente, muévense menos aprisa que los producidos por medio del carrete de inducción. La proporción de la carga eléctrica (e) á la masa (m) de los corpúsculos, se ha averiguado ser una cualidad constante independiente de su velocidad ó de los materiales de que están hechos los electrodos, ó de la naturaleza del gas restante en el tubo. De esto se arguye que todas las substancias emiten los mismos corpúsculos. Esta proporción e/m es de 1.7×10^7C.G.S. unidades — *i. e.*, 1,700 veces tan grandes como el valor correspondiente para el átomo de hidrógeno en la electrolisis que es de 10^4C.G.S. unidades. La diferencia debe atribuirse á una ó dos causas—ya sea que el corpúsculo lleve una carga mayor que el átomo de hidrógeno en la electrolisis, ya que su masa sea mucho menor. Esto, no obstante, desde que el profesor C. T. R. Wilson ha probado que las cargas que llevan los dos son idénticas, la diferencia en la magnitud de la proporción e/m, debe explicarse por la suposición de que la masa del corpúsculo es la 1.1700 parte de la masa del átomo de hidrógeno.

Breve Idea de Cómo se Hacen las Botellas

Todas las botellas se hacen por una «tanda de manos» que puede consistir en cuatro ó cinco. Las botellas «medicinales» necesitan cuatro y las de whiskey y otras hasta cinco manipulaciones. Estando el vidrio acabado de derretir, en unas vasijas ó tanques, el operario recoge al extremo de un tubo largo de hierro llamado el soplete, una cantidad de vidrio que considera suficiente para el objeto. Esta operación necesita mucha práctica porque la cabida interior de la botella acabada depende de la correspondiente cantidad de vidrio recogida desde un principio. El operario toma entonces el soplete con el vidrio adherido, sopla en él un momento, lo rueda por un hierro liso ó piedra, lo que hace tomar á la botella en ciernes una forma cónica. Luego se dirige al costado de la casa del vidrio, pone el vidrio en un hueco, tira de golpe de una varilla de hierro, y sopla á través del soplete; después hay otra sacudida y sale la botella formada. El hueco contenía el molde, que está dividido por su largo y acharnelado en su base. Lo sucedido es que con la primera sacudida queda el vidrio encerrado en el molde; con el soplo del operario toma la forma la botella, y con la segunda sacudida queda suelta. El molde enfría el vidrio lo suficiente para hacerle perder su plasticidad; la botella está aun á la extremidad del soplete; es pequeña cual las medicinales; golpea el tubo en el canto de una artesa y la botella se desprende, cayendo en ella. Si la botella fuese grande, cual las de whiskey, el operario la pasa entonces á un muchacho quien en aquel instante remoja en el agua una cuña de hierro, hace voltear el tubo por el canto de una artesa y hace pasar la cuña alrededor del gollete de la botella, la cual se desprende del soplete. Aun no tiene labio formado la botella. La boca del cuello está contraída ó enseña los bordes agudos y cortantes.

Habráse observado que los botellas son más grandes en el hombro que en el fondo y que se adelgazan hacia abajo. Esto se ve en las botellas de whiskey. Esta peculiaridad se distingue, poniendo en línea media docena de botellas. Esta forma permite á otro operario coger la botella de la artesa, ponerla otra vez en el horno, calentar el gollete y formarle los labios; en este estado se deja caer aún en otra artesa, de donde la saca con una varilla un muchacho y la pone en un agujero en el horno para después hacer la última operación y queda concluida la botella. Todo el procedimiento es rápido, pues un operario ordinario, trabajando diez horas al día, hace unas 130 botellas concluidas.—*Bottlers' Gazette.*

Quinina en Batavia

El cónsul general Rairden, de Batavia, envía una relación del resultado de la segunda venta de quinina en aquel punto, el 21 de febrero próximo pasado, que fué como sigue:

Se pusieron á la venta 3,084.48 kilógramos (6,786 libras) de sulfato de quinina, una parte del cual estaba puesto en cajas de 400 onzas, y otra parte empaquetada á opción del comprador. De toda la partida sólo 96 kilógramos (sobre 211 libras) de la quinina de la opción se vendieron á 17.55 francos ($7,135) por kilógramo (sobre 2.2 libras).

Refiriéndose á lo nada satisfactorio de las ventas este año, un comerciante observó que no obstante la pobreza de las ventas en esta ciudad, la situación del mercado no era tan mala, especialmente al tener presente que á fines de 1905 había existencias en Londres calculadas en 78,943 kilógramos (sobre 173,674 libras), 27,000 kilógramos (sobre 59,400 libras) de existencias y en vía de preparación en las fábricas, 8,000 kilógramos (sobre 17,600 libras) en las droguerías, 186,057 kilógramos (sobre 409,314 libras) existencias de corteza en Londres y Amsterdam; en conjunto 300,000 kilógramos (sobre 659,988 libras) para abastecer cosa de 900.000,000 de consumidores, esto es, apenas lo suficiente para el consumo ordinario de nueve meses.

Sorprende que en vista de estos guarismos y de los hechos con ellos relacionados, que ninguna casa de los Estados Unidos se haya mostrado directa ó visiblemente interesada en el artículo. Todas las existencias podrían obtenerse por $2.500,000, pudiendo sacarse unos $3.000,000. Hubo un tiempo en que la quinina se vendía á $120.00 el kilógramo.

Extracto de Vainilla

Una de las fórmulas más satisfactorias que conocemos, es la de que dió cuenta Oscar Kalish en una de las juntas del Colegio de Farmacia de Nueva York. El primer paso que ha de darse en el proceso es la obtención de habas de vainilla de primera calidad. Las habas se cortan en trozos pequeños, de tres cuartos de pulgada de largo y longitudinalmente, por medio de una cuchilla de cortar hierba. La fórmula é instrucciones para la preparación del extracto están concebidas en los siguientes términos:

Habas de vainilla mexicana	3½	av. lb.
Azúcar granulado	7	» »
Alcohol desdorizado	4	gals.
Agua	3	»

Por encima de las habas cortadas, que se habrán puesto en un tarro de porcelana, viértase siete pintas de agua hirviendo y se cubre entonces el vaso, dejándolo reposar por 24 horas, siendo el objeto de esta maceración el devolver la haba en cuanto sea posible al estado natural de cuando era verde. Después de esta maceración el líquido que sobrenada se vierte, y se pasan las habas á una máquina que las desmenuza ó muele tan fino como es posible, empleándose para ello un cortador de cuatro discos de acero que revuelven alrededor de un bloque de madera. Es de la mayor importancia que las habas no se pongan en contacto con el hierro. Una vez molida la vainilla se traspasa á un tarro de porcelana, añadiendo siete libras de azúcar granulado y después el liquido con que había sido previamente macerada y ocho pintas adicionales de agua. La mezcla se ag ta con frecuencia durante 24 horas, después de cuyo tiempo se añade un galón de acohol desdorizado, permitiendo que el todo macere durante siete días, cuando se agrega otro galón de alcohol, y la maceración continúa por una semana, añadiendo en el entretanto cuatro pintas más de alcohol. Evítese la filtración. Hasta el momento de añadir las cuatro últimas pintas, el líquido tiene una apariencia turbia, pero el alcohol que se le añade finalmente precipita la albúmina, dejando una solución clara. La mezcla, tal como está formada ahora, se permite macerar por espacio de 30 días más, al cabo de los cuales el todo se traspasa á un percolador Squibb, que se cubre con un diafragma de muselina. Después de haber pasado el líquido con el cual ha estado la vainilla, se continúa la filtración con un menstruo consistente en nueve pintas de agua y 12 pintas de alcohol. Se hallará que el percolado forma un extracto excelente de vainilla. No se conoce procedimiento por cuyo medio pueda obtenerse un producto satisfactorio sólo en pocos días, y por este motivo el farmacéutico tiene que anticiparse á lo menos 70 días para poder tener á mano el extracto que se necesite.

Raíz Zabou

En los bazares de Beyrout, se vende con el nombre de arriba, una raíz á la que se atribuyen virtudes afrodisíacas, la cual se recoge en una región pequeña de las montañas del Líbano, y lleva el nombre botánico de *Ferula Hermonii*, Boiss. Según P. Guiges, esta raíz es de textura esponjosa, color castaño, y está cubierta con papyraceus lamellæ, teniendo arriba los restos de numerosas hojas, y muchas fibras largas, que están arrolladas (cual en la angélica y otras raíces umbelíferas). Las raíces sencillas las llaman los labradores «machos,» y las que tienen ramificaciones hembras.

Tiene una corteza espesa que forma una tercera parte de la raíz, la corteza se desprende con frecuencia del parénquima cortical. El gusto es acre y aromático á la vez, muy parecido al del gálbano. La raíz fresca rinde 6.68 de una resina blanda, una pequeña cantidad de aceite volátil y una pequeña proporción de goma. La resina difiere de la del gálbano en que con el ácido hidroclórico da una coloración verde, que desaparece al aplicarle calor, y en el hecho de que el ácido nítrico no altera el color de una solución alcohólica de la resina, y también en no producir una fluorescencia azul cuando se la trata con agua y amoníaco. Esta resina exhuda en la raíz á la línea de separación, entre la madera y la corteza, y se percibe desde luego en una sección trasversal de la raíz.

Depresión en el Comercio de Quinina

Y ahora el tan nombrado alcaloide quinina, atraviesa un período de verdadera humillación. No parece que sea de fecha tan atrasada desde que la quina nos llegaba exclusivamente de la América del Sur. La corteza del Perú estaba entonces en sus glorias, y la quinina se vendía á $2.50 le onza, y $1.50 la onza la corteza roja. Por aquel entonces se inició en Java el cultivo de la cincona, pidiendo débilmente ser admitida en el comercio la quinina de aquel país. No hubo de tardar en darse á conocer invadiendo los mercados, bajando al mismo tiempo con rapidez el precio de la corteza sudamericana, y estrellándose por consecuencia el monopolio de este artículo que tan fuertemente atrincherado estaba. Los golpes demoledores venían de Java, el quino que allí se cultivaba era riquísimo, y la corteza batía en brecha la peruana. Bajaba el precio de la quinina, y cuando llegó á 75 centavos, el Dr. R. V. Mattison predijo entonces que descendería todavía más, hasta 25 centavos.

Pero el ariete que tumbó por el suelo el monopolio gigante, á su vez ha perdido su potencia, pues tal es la depresión que experimentan los cosecheros de quina en Java, que como alivio se han destruido millones de quinos, por ser ruinoso el cultivo; las fincas se replantan con te que promete aun algún provecho. El consumidor de quinina es el que ha salido ganancioso. — JOHN URI LLOYD, en el *Eclectic Medical Gleaner*.

NOTAS QUIMICAS

FORMATO DE COCAINA

Esta sal se obtiene en la forma de agujas brillantes, sedosas, algo amargantes, m. p. sobre 42° C. sobreviniendo descomposición inmediata, neutralizando un peso molecular de cocaina alcalóidea con un peso molecular de ácido fórmico. Los cristales que deposita el licor madre siruposo se lavan rápidamente con agua destilada y se desecan. La solubilidad en el agua es relativamente ligera 1 : 41 á temperaturas ordinarias, y aumenta hasta 80° C. Pero á 90° la combinación se desune y la base sepárase en gotas oleosas que se solidifican al enfriarse. La sal es mucho más soluble en alcohol de 95 por ciento en la extensión de 45 : 100. Las soluciones son neutras con el papel tornasol. El formato de cocaina es insoluble en aceite de olivas y en vaselina. —*Journ. Pharm. Chim.*

PREPARACION DE ACIDO HIDROCLORICO DE ARSENICO LIBRE

A 1,500 ml. de ácido hidroclórico artificial, siendo 11 su gravedad específica, se añaden sobre 40 ml. de nafta de madera rectificada en un frasco Wurtz de 2 litros, y 5 á 10 grm. de ácido de arsénico libre. En este estado se enlaza el frasco con un condensador de reflujo y el mismo tapón que lleva el condensador lleva una varilla de vidrio con una hoja de cobre electrolítico, siendo su superficie de 120 pulgadas cuadradas. El tubo lateral del frasco habiendo sido obturado, el condensador se pone en relación con una bomba de agotamiento, iniciándose la ebullición en un vacío parcial. Con un ácido que contenga de 0.5 á 1 grano de arsénico por galón, serán suficientes tres horas de digestión suave, retirándose el cobre, el cual se habrá limpiado á lo menos una vez. Entre la bomba y el condensador se interpone un vaso para recoger un líquido fumante, negro, embreado que pasa por encima, y también debería emplearse otra vasija conteniendo agua para absorver cualquier vapor acidulado que pase por encima. Luego se destila el ácido de la manera acostumbrada sobre cobre electrolítico. —*Analist*, 1906, 31, 38.

ACEITE DE EUCALIPTO Y CLOROFORMO COMO VERMIFUGO

Aceite de eucalipto y cloroformo combinados con aceite de ricino, como recomendó por primera vez Hermann, según L. P. Phillips considérase el antihelmíntico más eficaz para expeler el anquilostomo. La fórmula original de Hermann era: Aceite de eucalipto, 2 grm.; cloroformo, 3 grm.; aceite de ricino, 40 grm. Habiendo averiguado que esto era bien soportado, el autor aumentó la dosis á: Aceite de eucalipto, 25 grm.; cloroformo, 35 grm.; aceite de ricino, 40 grm. El enfermo adulto toma la mitad de esta mezcla por la mañana, en ayunas, y la otra mitad dentro de media hora después. Si sobreviniese alguna depresión después de la primera mitad, se omitirá la segunda dosis. Tratándose de muchachos, pacientes anémicos y débiles, la dosis se administra por terceras partes á intervalos de veinte y cinco minutos. Después, si fuese necesario, se repite en días salteados. Será ventajoso administrar un purgante salino la noche antes del tratamiento. En algunos casos la primera dosis no produce efecto, mientras que en otros es suficiente. Considérase más eficaz que el timol para igual objeto, como lo prueba el hecho de que en cuarenta y cuatro casos el tratamiento dió buenos resultados, y apenas si causa depresión cardiaca. Con este tratamiento los oxiuros son expelidos en cantidad considerable, y también podemos citar un caso de tenia en que el parásito fué expelido. — D. P. PHILLIPS.

Reacción Alcohólica

El renombrado químico J. Kossa, da lo siguiente como una nueva reacción de alcohol: Póngase con precaución algunos centímetros cúbicos de ácido nítrico al 50 por ciento en un tubo de prueba, y un volumen igual de alcohol al 90 por ciento, dejándolo reposar por varios minutos. En el punto de contacto de los dos líquidos aparece primeramente una capa blanca, lanudosa y opaca, y un poco más tarde por debajo de ella una capa verde. No tarda en bajar la capa verde, arrojando espuma, y á medida que se desarrolla calor, se hace cada vez más perceptible un olor de aldehido. Cuando se sacude el líquido desaparece desde luego la capa verde, aunque la espuma se mantiene visible algunas horas. Colocando el tubo de prueba en agua enfriada á 0°C, cesa la espumación, la capa verde toma un color más obscuro, y, finalmente azul. La reacción que depende de la formación de trióxido nitrógeno, también se obtiene cuando en lugar de ácido nítrico se mezclan un volumen de una solución saturada de nitrato de potasio y cuatro volúmenes de ácido sulfúrico concentrado, y cuando ha enfriado se le pone por encima el alcohol. Como una gota de alcohol es suficiente para colorear 20 cc. de ácido nítrico, la reacción parece ser muy sensible. El aldehido, la acetona, el éter y el cloroformo no dan la reacción. — *Pharm. Zeitung.*

Origen de las Tarjetas Postales Ilustradas

El profesor Oswald Schroeder, en el primer número del *Post Card Dealer*, publica una interesante relación del origen de la tarjeta postal ilustrada. Parece haber sido la costumbre entre un pequeño círculo de pintores, autores y un editor de publicaciones artísticas, tomar juntos un tente en pie en un establecimiento muy conocido de Munich. En junio de 1878 esta cotérie, incluyendo el mayor Kaulbach, determinó escribir varias tarjetas postales á uno de sus colegas que se hallaba en los Alpes, y de quien habían tenido noticias recientemente. Mientras tomaban el café se cayó una gota en el extremo de una de esas tarjetas, que Kaulbach tenía en la mesa delante de sí, y sin parar mientes en lo que hacía, absorto como estaba en la conversación con los demás amigos, con un palito de dientes empezó á trazar líneas por la tarjeta mojando el palito en la gota de café. Después de haberse entretenido de esta manera se le fué el palillo de entre los dedos. observando entonces que había dibujado la cabez lés con barba. Este dibujo casual regocijó amigos presentes y cada uno de ello ilustrada para enviarlo al amigo ause después el editor artístico á quien se caba en el mercado una serie de tarje pluma y tinta, representando escenas d fué el nacimiento de la tarjeta post el profesor Schroeder.

LINIMENTOS MEDICINALES

LINIMENTO MAGNETICO.—Esencia de trementina, 18 partes; tintura de pimiento, 24; alcohol alcanforado, 192; alcohol rectificado, 36; amoníaco líquido fuerte, 18; esencia de sasafrás, 1. H. s. a.

LINIMENTO MAYET.—Amoníaco líquido, 15 gramos; cloroformo, 10; alcanfor, 10; tintura de opio, 5; alcohol de 90°, 60. Mézclese. Rubefaciente y calmante.

Embébase un pedazo de franela en el linimento y aplíquese sobre la piel durante quince minutos.—*F. V. M. F.*

Esta fórmula fué deducida del análisis. La verdadera composición del renombrado *linimento de Mayet*, tan usado en Inglaterra, aun no se conoce.

También se denomina *linimento amoniacal con cloroformo.*

LINIMENTO DE MENTOL.—(a) Mentol, 1 parte; aceite de olivas, 5. Disuélvase.—*H. St. George.*

(b) Mentol, 1 parte; aceite de olivas, 10; lanolina, 10. Interpóngase.—*Eloy.*

(c) Mentol, 1 parte; aceite de olivas, 9; agua de cal, 10.

Util en las quemaduras.—*Langnard.*

(d) Mentol, 4 gramos; cloroformo, 20; bálsamo tranquilo, 30.

Aplicaciones contra los dolores neurálgicos y reumáticos.—*Debove.*

(e) Mentol, 3 partes; cloroformo, 4; alcohol rectificado, 16. Mézclese.

LINIMENTO DE MENTOL COMPUESTO. (a) Mentol, 3 partes; tintura de acónito, 4; cloroformo, 4; linimento de jabón, 5. H. s. a.—*H. Samar.*

LOCIONES MEDICINALES

LOCION AMARILLA.—Cloruro mercúrico, 1.50 gramos; agua hirviendo, c. s.; solución de cal, c. s. Disuélvase el cloruro mercúrico en 14 gramos de agua y añádase la solución á cantidad suficiente de la solución de cal para tener 450 gramos. Agítese al usarlo.—*F. N.*

Se denomina también *loción de mercurio amarillo* y *agua fagedénica amarilla.*

LOCION AMONIACAL ALCANFORADA.—Amoniaco de 22°, 17 partes; alcohol alcanforado, 3; cloruro sódico, 17; agua común, 300. Disuélvase en frío la sal en el agua; añádase el alcohol alcanforado y el amoníaco, y agítese bien la mezcla.

Para el segundo grado de esta agua, auméntese la cantidad de amoníaco hasta 24 partes, y para el tercero 30 partes.

terap.: Excitante, resolutiva y antiespasmó- fomentos.—*F. Esp.*

nase también *agua sedativa de Raspail.*

:ION AMONIACAL PLUMBICA.—Carbonato amó- parte; acetato plúmbico, 2; agua de rosas, 60. la urticaria.—*Aitken.*

ta misma preparación, en las proporciones de 'o, emplea *E. Wilson* como calmante de las a piel.

LOCION ANDEER.—Agua, 28 gramos; resorcina, 2.80. Disuélvase.

Antiséptico y estimulante en las ulceraciones sifilíticas, y para evitar las irritaciones en el eczema crónico y psoriasis.—*H. Brit. Sk.*

Denomínase también *loción de resorcina.*

Panorama de la Vida en Nueva York

De tal manera se precipitan los acontecimientos en Gotham, que parece casi imposible registrarlos todos. De los más importantes nos da una idea el periódico *La Tribuna* de Nueva York, y vale por cierto la pena de reproducirlos. Véanse:

Cada 40 segundos llega un inmigrante.
Cada 3 minutos alguien es arrestado.
Cada 6 minutos nace un niño.
Cada 7 minutos hay un funeral.
Cada 13 minutos se casa una pareja.
Cada 42 minutos empieza negocios una empresa mercantil.
Cada 48 minutos se incendia un edificio.
Cada 48 minutos sale del puerto un buque.
Cada 51 minutos se erige un nuevo edificio.
Cada 1¼ horas alguien perece por accidente.
Cada 7 horas quiebra una casa de comercio.
Cada 8 horas se atenta á la vida de alguien.
Cada 8¼ horas alguna pareja se divorcia.
Cada 10 horas hay un suicidio.
Cada 2 días alguien es asesinado.

Se explica este corolario de acontecimientos, con sólo tener presente que recientemente y en una sola semana, han llegado á Nueva York, procedentes del extranjero, cuarenta y cinco mil inmigrantes cuya mayoría se quedará aquí.

MUSEO DE ARTES

Parque Central, con vista á la Quinta Avenida en la calle 82ª. El ala del este forma el Salon Escultórico, 166 x 4 pies. Gabinetes y Galería destinados á objetos de porcelana. Edificios anexos cubren un área de 233 x 344 pies cuads. Fundado en 1869. Planos de Richard N. Hunt, comprendían 18¼ acres, á un costo de $20.000,000. Desarrollados por Henry G. Marquand y el difunto general Louis P. di Cesnola. Curadores: J. Pierpont Morgan, presidente; Sir C. Purdon Clarke, Director.

NUEVOS REMEDIOS

BISOL (*Fosfato de Bismuto Soluble*). — Polvo blanco, soluble en agua; reacción alcalina débil. Antiséptico intestinal y astringente en el catarro gástrico y entérico. Dosis, 3 á 7½ granos. En tubos de 1 oz., 70 centavos.

(C. Bischoff & Co.)

BROMETONE. — Polvo ligeramente soluble en agua. Compuesto de bromoformo y acetona; recomendado como sustituto de los bromuros. Contiene 77 por ciento de bromo. Dosis, 3 á 5 granos; frascos de 1 oz., 85 centavos. Cápsulas de 5 granos, en frascos de 100, $1.25.

(Parke, Davis & Co.)

BROMIPIN (*Aceite de Sésame Brominizado*). — Fluído amarillo, oleoso, empleado como nervino y sedativo en la epilepsia. Sucedáneo de bromuros. Dosis, una cucharadita. Tubos de 1 oz., 18 centavos; la libra, $2.10 á $2.35.

(Merck & Co.)

ACIDO CACODILICO (*Acido Arsénico Dimetil*). — Cristales pequeños, sin color delicuescentes. Producto de la oxidación arsenio-dimetil (cacodilo) y óxido cacodilo. Contiene 54.4 por ciento de trióxido de arsénico; pero es relativamente no tóxico. Dosis, 1 á 3 granos; tubos de 1½ oz., la oz., $4.00.

UNGÜENTO CALOMELOL. — Ungüento mecurioso blanco hecho del calomelano coloidal para el tratamiento de inunción de la sífilis, y especialmente para la curación de sus manifestaciones cutáneas. Tubos graduados de 2 oz., el tubo, 55 centavos.

(Heyden Chemical Works)

POLVOS DE CALOMELOL. — Polvo blanco gris de reacción neutra, insípido y sin color. Rinde una solución lechosa cuando se añade á agua fría en la proporción de 1 á 50. Empléase para espolverear en el tratamiento de las erupciones papulosas y ulceraciones, y como aplicación externa para chancros ulcerados, en una solución de al 2 por ciento. Tubos de 1 oz., 70c.

(Heyden Chemical Works)

ACIDO CAMFORICO. — Escamas cristalinas sin color, ligeramente solubles en agua. Formadas por la oxidación del alcanfor y el ácido nítrico. Empléase en sudores nocturnos de la tisis, y también en la cistitis como antiséptico intestinal, en dosis de 10 á 20 granos. Tubos de 1 oz., 45c.; bot. de 1 lb., $7.00.

(Merck & Co.)

CALLAQUOL. — Fuído lechoso espeso, de olor aromático y consistente en un éter de ácido oxitricarbalílico, combinado con una solución jabonosa de aceite de tomillo, al que debe el olor. Empléase como vulnerario. Lo fabrica Friedrich Braun, Wurenberg (Alemania).

CEROLIN. — Píldoras de una substancia grasosa aislada de la levadura. Obra cual la levadura en la furunculosis, el acné, etc., pero más como catártico.

QUINAPENIN (*Ester Carbónico de Quinina de Fenitidina*). — Polvo blanco sin sabor que representa la quinina fenacetina sintética, poseyendo propiedades medicinales de ambas. Insoluble en agua, pero soluble fácilmente en alcohol, éter y cloroformo. Dosis, 5 á 10 granos, tres veces al día. Cartones de ½ y 1 oz., la oz., $1.25 á $1.30.

QUINOTROPINA (*Quinato de Urotropina*). – Combinación de ácido quínico y urotropina (hexmetilenetetramina), empléase como solvente de ácido úrico en las varias manifestaciones de la diátesis de ácido úrico. Dícese que libera formaldehido internalmente y forma compuestos solubles en ácido úrico. Dosis, 10 á 30 granos. Tubos de ½ y 1 oz., $1.75; tabletas, 7½ granos, 25 en un tubo, 2 tubos en una caja, $1.75.

(Schering & Glatz)

CHLORETONE. — Cristales blancos, ligeramente solubles en agua (1 : 125), hipnótico, anestésico local y antiséptico. Dosis, 5 á 20 granos, en cachet, en tableta ó cápsula. Externalmente como polvo espolvoreador para heridas combinado con 23 partes de zinc, óxido 120, y creta francesa 90. Tubos de ½ oz., la onza, 90c.; 1 oz., 85c.

(Parke, Davis & Co.)

ACIDO CINNAMICO (*Acido Cinnamílico*). — Cristales transparentes micáceos, ligeramente solubles en el agua; solubles en alcohol y éter. Inyectado intravenosamente en la tuberculosis en dosis de ¼ á ½ de grano, dos veces por semana. Tubos de 1 oz., 35c.; frascos de 1 lb., la libra, $5.00.

(Merck & Co.)

CITARIN (*Anhidrometilencitrato de Sodio*). — Polvo blanco cristalino, soluble fácilmente en agua. Antilitémico para los estados gotosos y reumático crónicos; libera formaldehido en la sangre. Dosis, 15 á 30 granos, tres veces al día. Frascos de 1 oz, la onza, 70c. á 75c.

(Continental Color & Chemical Co.)

Jarabe de Regaliz Estable

L. A. Seltzer, recomienda el siguiente método para preparar el jarabe de regaliz del Formulario Nacional, á fin de obtener un producto que sea presentable en apariencia y se conserve tanto tiempo como el jarabe más estable. Después de desintegrar el extracto de regaliz al baño-maría con toda el agua necesaria para preparar el jarabe, y añadiendo de tiempo en tiempo bastante amoníaco para retener la glicirizina en solución (pero evitando un exceso), quítese ésta del baño-maría y póngase á un lado á enfriar. Añádese entonces el blanco de un huevo, mézclese bien, bátese otra vez en el baño-maría hasta que toda la albúmina esté coagulada.

Mucha de la materia insoluble la rodea la albúmina coagulada; pero permanece bastante para dificultar la filtración. Tómese ahora algún excelsior claro, colocándolo en el fondo de un colador, haciendo la superficie tan desigual como posible. Macháquese algún papel de filtrar en un mortero con la solución hasta dejarlo hecho una pasta, y traspásese la mezcla al colador, repitiendo la filtración hasta que pase perfectamente clara. Toda la solución pasará entonces en un espacio de tiempo razonable. Añádese ahora el azúcar y disuélvase bien al frío ó con la ayuda de calor. En este caso será necesario reponer de cuando en cuando e amoníaco que queda desplazado.

Una Profecía de Edison

Siendo Thomas A Edison, hombre de un genio tan brillante, cuanto dice reviste interés, de aquí que reproduzcamos una entrevista de fecha reciente. Refiriéndose á la electricidad, dijo: «Estamos acercándonos á otra grande época en la historia del mundo. No me asombraría despertar una mañana y saber que alguno de los 300,000 hombres científicos que están investigando por toda la tierra, ha hallado por último el secreto de producir electricidad por un proceso directo, lo que constituiría una revolución en los asuntos humanos. Lo que insinuo puede realizarse. Se realizará, y yo espero verlo antes de morir.

» El primer gran cambio en la producción de electricidad, suprimirá el transporte de carbón para aquel objeto. En lugar de excavar material grueso de las entrañas de la tierra, cargarlo en carros y conducirlo, digamos 500 millas, para ponerlo allí debajo de una caldera y quemarlo, montaremos instalaciones en las bocas de las minas, generaremos allí la fuerza para transmitirla por cable doquiera se necesite.

» Ya parece ridículo poner minas de carbón sobre ruedas, y además es muy costoso; no hay ya necesidad para ello. Más fácil es llevar la vibración molecular en millones de ondas por segundo que wagones de carga llenos de la materia prima. Podemos «embarcar» con más rapidez 100,000 caballos de fuerza por los alambres, y también con más economía, que enviar el equivalente en carbón por la vía férrea.

» De este problema vamos á descartar por completo el ferrocarril. ¿De qué nos sirve? De todos modos ¿para qué queremos carbón? No nos beneficia mirándolo. Lo que buscamos es el resultante de la mayor energía que pueda producirse. No parece que haya buen sentido en ir conduciendo de aquí para allí millones de toneladas de materia prima, cual es el carbón, cuando podemos disponer de un producto que se nos entregará por los alambres.

» Todo parece dirigirse al hecho culminante de que en un porvenir cercano se producirá electricidad para el consumo general por medio de grandes casas de fuerza motriz situadas en las bocas de las minas. Este parece será el resultado lógico de los acontecimientos que se desarrollan.

» La verdad es que costará una tercera parte menos transportar fuerza eléctrica por alambre que llevarla en la forma de carbón en vagones de los ferrocarriles. Suponiendo que el precio del carbón sea de $1 á la boca de la mina, y que el flete importe $1.90, nosotros podemos convertir el carbón en electricidad en la mina y conducirlo por alambre á menos de la mitad del costo del flete del carbón.

» La electricidad tomará el puesto de los caballos; resolverá el problema de los vehículos y del tráfico en las ciudades. Mi nueva batería eléctrica de acumulación hará la electricidad más barata que los caballos. Estas baterías no tardarán en colocarse en el mercado. No sólo tomarán la mitad del tráfico caballar, sino que irán dos veces más aprisa. Pueden almacenarse en los pisos altos por medio de ascensores. Con la economía que se realizará en el espacio ocupado con establos en Nueva York, dejará una propiedad disponible valuada en 200.000,000 de pesos.

» No sólo la fuerza eléctrica se generará y distribuirá en las minas de carbón en lo futuro, sino que toda la fuerza hidráulica del mundo se empleará en la producción de electricidad. Este movimiento ha empezado y avanza con rapidez. En California, con la energía que distingue á aquellos hombres, están transmitiendo fuerza eléctrica por alambre á 275 millas, poniendo en movimiento tranvías y alumbrando ciudades. Este espíritu de empresa despertará en todo el mundo. No tardaremos en presenciarlo.»

NOTAS FARMACEUTICAS

SHAMPOO DE HUEVO

Jabón de coco	4 onzas
Carbonato de potasio	1 »
Agua	1 galón

Disuélvase el jabón en el agua con la ayuda de calor y añádese el carbonato de potasio; coloréese con amarillo de anilina y perfúmese con aceites de espliego y de limón, ú otro olor apropiado. Dícese que esta fórmula representa la composición de los llamados «shampoos de huevo» del mercado.

FLUIDO PARA RIZAR EL CABELLO

Borax	1 onza
Goma arábiga	1 dracma
Espíritu de alcanfor	1 oz. fluida
Agua, bastante para hacer	16 oz. fluidas

Disuélvase el borax y la goma en agua caliente y cuando haya enfriado añádese el alcanfor. Instrucciones: Humedézcase el cabello con el fluido y arróllese en rizos, prendiéndolo con ganchitos.

CREMA DE ALMENDRAS PARA EL TOCADOR

Tragacanto en polvo	½ onza
Borax	½ »
Cloruro de amonio	1 »
Glicerina	10 oz. fluidas
Tintura de benzoin	1 dracma fl.
Aceite de almendras amargas	10 gotas
Agua	54 oz. fluidas

Tritúrese la goma con la glicerina hasta obtener una pasta suave; disuélvase el borax y el cloruro de amonio en una cantidad de agua; fíltrese esta solución; mézclense los dos líquidos; añádese el remanente del agua é incorpórese la tintura de benzoin y aceite esencial por medio de la agitación.

BARNIZ DE CELULOIDE

Celuloide	10 gramos
Alcanfor	4 »
Eter	30 »
Acetona	30 »
Acetato de amilo	30 »

POLVOS PARA DESCANSAR LOS PIES

Timol	20 granos
Almidón	2½ onzas
Acido salicílico	½ onza
Acido bórico	2 onzas
Talco, polvo fino	15 »

LINIMENTO DE MENTOL COMPUESTO

Mentol	30 granos
Alcanfor	60 »
Tintura de iodo descolorido	1 oz. fluida
Glicerina	1 oz. »
Alcohol, 90 por ciento, bastante para hacer	4 oz. fluidas

UNGÜENTO DE RESORCINA COMPUESTO

Resorcina................	80 granos
Agua destilada..................	80 mínimas
Aceite de Abedul blanco.........	80 »
Oxido de zinc....................	80 granos
Vacelina........................	4 dracmas
Lanolina anhidrosa..............	4 »
Ungüento de resina.........	160 granos

Disuélvase la resorcina en el agua y mézclese con los demás ingredientes.

BALSAMO DE COLUMBIA

Borax.........................	1 onza
Glicerina......................	1½ »
Aceite de romero..............	15 mínimas
Alcohol........................	2 onzas
Agua..........................	14 »

Disuélvase el borax en el agua y el aceite en alcohol y mézclese.

NOTAS COMERCIALES

—Con el *Somnóforo* aquellos pacientes que acuden á los dentistas quedan anestesiados sin necesidad de ninguna preparación especial, se levantan del sillón y caminan sin ayuda de nadie. Los pacientes recuperan el conocimiento y su estado normal sin pérdida de tiempo, y manifiestan sorpresa al ver con la gran facilidad que perdieron y recobraron el conocimiento.—Del *British Medical Press*, abril de 1903.

—Han llegado á nuestras manos varios números de *Estudios de Medicina*, revista mensual de ciencias médicas, que ve la luz en la ciudad de Quito. Su lectura nos ha gustado mucho, por estar nutrida de materia excelente y provechosa. Observamos que ha alcanzado el año sexto de su publicación, de cuyo hecho puede deducirse con seguridad que el periódico es bien quisto del público profesional. Agradecemos al distinguido colega la mención que hace de nuestro periódico, y le deseamos toda clase de prosperidades.

—Todas las enfermedades de la visión debidas á deficiencias musculares, pueden mejorarse con el empleo del Restaurador de la Vista Ideal, fabricado por The Ideal Company, 239 Broadway, Nueva York, E. U. A. Este restaurador de la vista depende en lo que podría llamarse amasamiento neumático de los múculos oculares, el cual se efectúa por medio de dos copas que se ajustan á los ojos, de los cuales se agota y devuelve alternativamente el aire, causando de este modo movimientos de los globos de los ojos, de lo cual quedan muy beneficiados los músculos. Los fabricantes proporcionarán los pormenores más satisfactorios del aparato á quien esté interesado.

—El comercio emplea muchos aparatos ingeniosos y eficaces, pero pocos son tan útiles como las balanzas. Los Sres. Herman Kohlbusch, del No. 193 Broadway, Nueva York, fabrican un renglón de balanzas para prescripciones, conocidas del público desde hace cincuenta años. Las pruebas á que han estado sometidas durante este dilatado espacio de tiempo, hacen estas balanzas acreedoras á la mayor confianza de los farmacéuticos. Aquellos de nuestros lectores del ramo que establezcan inteligencias con los fabricantes y mencionen el AMERICAN DRUGGIST, se les enviará gratis un lindo catálogo instructivo.

DIEZ TONELADAS DE QUININA ANUALMENTE.—¡Hay motivo para maravillarse! Diez toneladas de quinina, ó 20,000 libras, ó 320,000 onzas, que son cosa de 9.600,000 gramos, se emplean anualmente en la manufactura de las 7.000,000 de cajas de bromo quinina laxante que salen anualmente del acreditado establecimiento de la Paris Medicine Company. Este remedio tiene por objeto «curar un resfriado en un día,» y esta aseveración la hace la Compañía 165.000,000 de veces cada semana durante la estación de anunciar. Con anuncios tan extensos y eficaces en la prensa americana y en la extranjera, no es de sorprender que se consuma tanto bromo quinina laxante. Aquellos de nuestros lectores que no tuviesen existencias de este tan útil remedio, les tendrá cuenta pedir precios y condiciones para su introducción á la Paris Medicine Company, de St. Louis (Mo.), E. U. A. Propone condiciones muy favorables á sus agentes.

INNOVACION EN MAQUINAS DE ESCRIBIR.—LA «AMERICAN» SE OFRECE A LA MITAD DE PRECIO, $50.—PRINCIPIOS QUE HAN HECHO ESTO POSIBLE.—VENTAJAS PARA LOS FARMACEUTICOS.

La necesidad de una máquina de escribir es más sentida entre los farmacéuticos, porque con ella se salvan errores que en el ramo son peligrosos. Si se escriben las etiquetas y rotulatas en Máquina American, queda establecido un antecedente permanente que no se borra ó palidece aunque se moje con substancias químicas. Con la «American» se escriben rotulatas de tamaño corriente, sin necesidad de apéndices. Otra ventaja, con la lindeza del trabajo atrae parroquianos. Comunica cierto tono á la correspondencia escrita con esta máquina, pues representa un adelanto. Antes de aparecer el «American» en el mercado, el precio de $100 fijado por el trust prohibía el uso universal de las máquinas de escribir. El ahorro del precio con esta máquina débese á una tecla de una sola pieza con privilegio, á la barra de tipo con cuyo empleo se han economizado 1,200 piezas, que resultan inútiles. Las piezas excluídas son los cojinetes endebles que se hallan en las barras de tipo complicadas de las máquinas de $100. Y estas son las piezas que primeramente se descomponen, siendo difícil reajustarlas. La Máquina American de $50 con sólo 325 piezas, que produce una carta insuperable en hermosura y es de construcción sólida y compacta y posee resistencia, halla mucho favor en los mercados de la América Meridional. La «American» es conocida en el mercado desde hace cinco años. Los fabricantes se han abstenido de hacer propaganda hasta que el público apreciase las cualidades de la máquina; siendo ahora el veredicto favorable ha llegado la hora de establecer agencias, con la exclusiva de territorio. Los agentes tendrán una máquina que halla mucha salida.

ESPIRITU DE EMPRESA.—Nelson L. Martin, propietario del establecimiento Oak Grove Dairy, del No. 1310 Massachusetts Avenue, de la ciudad de Cambridge, decidió instalar un aparato-fuente para la expendición de bebidas gaseosas, enviando el pedido á la American Soda Fountain á las cinco de la tarde de un martes. Dos horas más tarde, desde el depósito de la Compañía en Boston, se enviaba una fuente «Innovation,» camino de Cambridge; antes de abrir el establecimiento al público, en la mañana siguiente, el aparato habíase instalado, hechos todos los enlaces de tubería, y el propietario Mr. Martin estaba listo para servir á sus parroquianos. La novedad y elegancia de la fuente atrajo temprano sinnúmero de aquellos, llegando á aumentar de tal modo el número, que Mr. Martin se vió obligado á llamar la policía para que hiciese mover á la multitud.

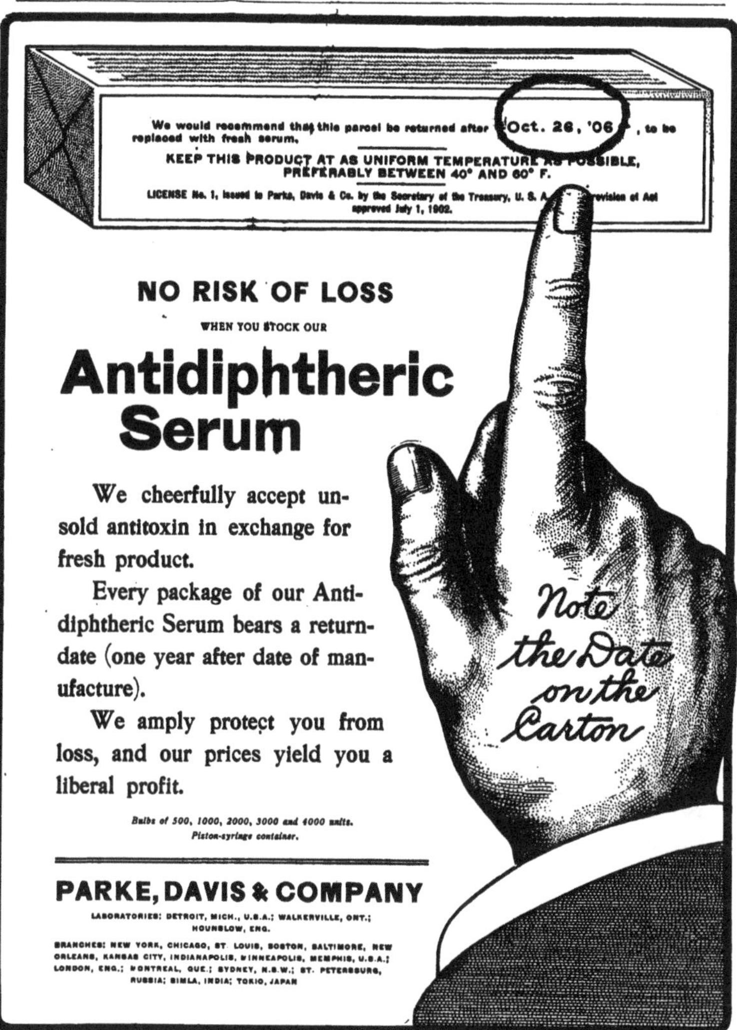
We would recommend that this parcel be returned after Oct. 26, '06, to be replaced with fresh serum.
KEEP THIS PRODUCT AT AS UNIFORM TEMPERATURE
PREFERABLY BETWEEN 40° AND 60° F.
LICENSE No. 1, issued to Parke, Davis & Co. by the Secretary of the Treasury, U. S. A.
approved July 1, 1902.
NO RISK OF LOSS
WHEN YOU STOCK OUR
Antidiphtheric Serum
We cheerfully accept unsold antitoxin in exchange for fresh product.
Every package of our Antidiphtheric Serum bears a return-date (one year after date of manufacture).
We amply protect you from loss, and our prices yield you a liberal profit.
Bulbs of 500, 1000, 2000, 3000 and 4000 units.
Piston-syringe container.
PARKE, DAVIS & COMPANY
LABORATORIES: DETROIT, MICH., U.S.A.; WALKERVILLE, ONT.; HOUNSLOW, ENG.
BRANCHES: NEW YORK, CHICAGO, ST. LOUIS, BOSTON, BALTIMORE, NEW ORLEANS, KANSAS CITY, INDIANAPOLIS, MINNEAPOLIS, MEMPHIS, U.S.A.; LONDON, ENG.; MONTREAL, QUE.; SYDNEY, N.S.W.; ST. PETERSBURG, RUSSIA; SIMLA, INDIA; TOKIO, JAPAN
Note the Date on the Carton

Bennedetti Hnos have placed a line of stationery in their drug store and report excellent business along that line.

In the Botica of Stanley Simmons, H. A. Lewis and Señor Baranano we find also the confidence in business enjoyed by

Offices of U. S. Government, Panama.

the larger stores, each enjoying the good times now on the isthmus.

Pharmacy and Patent Medicines in Honduras.

United States Consul Alger, of Tegucigalpa, reports that there are no regulations or restrictions in Honduras as to the sale of patent medicines. With regard to pharmacy, articles that may be used are specified in the penal code and police regulations under which business must be done. The consul sends

Botica del Globo of Sr. Y. Preciado, Panama.

to the State Department the substance of these regulations, which follow:

No prescription shall be filled unless clearly written in the Spanish language, without abbreviations, except those in common use as regards the method of preparation, and must be signed by a regular doctor of medicine.

All prescriptions that are filled must be sealed and numbered, with number corresponding to that of the register kept by the pharmacist, returning to the interested party the original prescription or a sealed and numbered copy of the same.

When in the judgment of the pharmacist the filling of a prescription calls for the largest doses of a drug that

Botica of Sr. Arturo Kophcke, Panama.

might be prejudicial in taking, he will return the same under seal to the physician who issued it, calling on him to accept over his signature all responsibility.

No prescription shall be filled a second time. The physician ordering its repetition shall state how many times repetion is necessary. The prescriptios is to be dated each time

Botica of Sr. Manuel Espinosa B., Panama.

it is put up, adding initials—Rp-a-i (recipe ad integran).

Violation of any regulation is punished with a fine of from $30 to $500, and closing of the pharmacy in case of further offense.

The commission is constituted or composed of the inspector of hygiene, one pharmacist, and the agent of police, to revise the books and inspect the condition and quality of drugs and medicines. The medical faculty is informed of the result of revision and inspection.

The sale of medicines is positively forbidden at any place except an authorized pharmacy.

AKARALGIA MERRELL

A new and most attractive form of exhibiting the valuable properties of pure Sodium Salicylate, (From Natural Wintergreen Oil) overcoming chronic migraine by single daily doses.

Send for Literature: "A New Remedy and Cure for Migraine."

Generally prescribed: "Akaralgia, 1 bot."

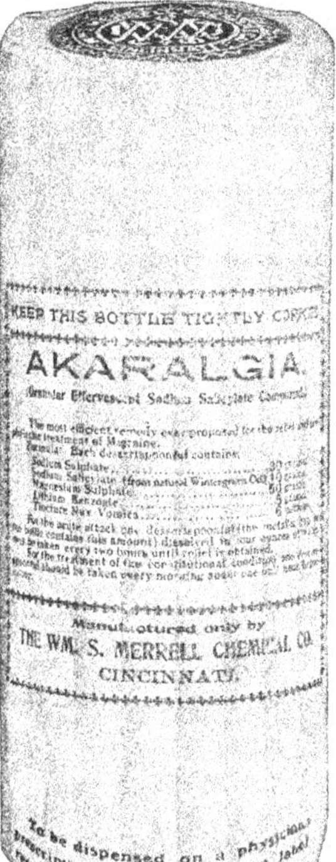

The demand for Akaralgia will steadily increase as it is advertised in the leading Medical Journals. If you do not have it in stock order from your Jobber one-quarter dozen or more and be prepared to fill your Physicians prescriptions promptly.

$6.75 net—dozen. Broken dozen same rate.

SIMPLICITY PALATABILITY EFFICACY

Your Jobber Supplies MERRELL "LINE" Goods at 40% discount, regardless of quantity.

Fluid Extracts, Tablets, Pills, Elixirs, Granular Effervescent Salts, &c, &c.

WRITE

"Merrell" and the results will please you.

ON YOUR ORDERS

THE WM. S. MERRELL CHEMICAL CO.

New York. Cincinnati. San Francisco.

The Possibilities of Increasing American Trade Abroad.

The Sphinx Club is an association of men who have to do with advertising in various ways, which is known to the public chiefly through the reports of the speeches made at its monthly dinners. The club numbers many bright men among its members and the speeches are frequently of great interest. It is customary to select some one topic for discussion, the topic selected for the dinner given at Delmonico's on November 14 being The Possibilities of Increasing American Trade Abroad.

The guest of the evening on that occasion was J. Hampden Moore, of Philadelphia, former chief of the Bureau of Manufactures, Department of Commerce and Labor.

FAULTS OF AMERICAN METHODS.

Mr. Moore made a powerful plea for a greater effort toward the upbuilding of our foreign trade, and indulged in some clear cut criticism of the methods frequently pursued by American manufacturers and merchants in their dealings with foreigners. In this connection Mr. Moore said: "The Yankee wants to drop into a town one day and expects to leave it the next with orders for his goods, just as he does here in the United States. One of the great problems that business men have to solve is the problem of geographical education, as well as of commercial education. If the young men of this country can be made to understand that when there is no opportunity for them in the congested cities of New York, Boston, Philadelphia and Chicago there is a great world open to them in South America, in Africa, in China, in Japan, and that a few years' training for a business or a commercial career will bring them honor, fame and wealth, then the United States will begin to ship its goods abroad, and will begin to establish that commercial foothold that the older nations have already established.

"Before I left Washington an appropriation of $30,000 had been made by Congress to send commercial agents into foreign lands. The reports of these agents are coming in from South America, China, Europe and Japan. These reports show, for instance, how people in Germany are using American-made shoes, and how the people of China and Japan are being imposed upon by an inferior article which bears the American label; how some goods are so poorly packed that the consignees refuse to accept them; how those goods are being shipped in utter ignorance of the conditions which prevail in foreign countries, and how the American manufacturer is trying to shove American ideas down the foreigner's throat, instead of packing and shipping them as the buyer wishes, and observing the tariff regulations, customs requirements, etc. America can control the foreign trade of the world if her manufacturers, merchants and advertising men will only unbend bemselves a little, get the idea out of their heads that they w it all, and that whatever is good enough for an American ıt to be good enough for a foreigner. You must study, pend a little money in investigation and be willing to do a little in Rome as the Romans do, if you would succeed in pushing your goods in other countries. That whole Consular Service, which is not diplomatic, should be constructed for the promotion of American trade and should be placed absolutely under the control of the Department of Commerce and Labor. Great agencies are now at work in this country to bring the consular system under the Department of Commerce. When the Consular Service shall have been enlarged and improved, through larger and more adequate appropriations from Congress, then you will begin to get valuable information which will tell you just when, how and where to strike for any particular market for your products."

A GREAT AMERICAN ADVERTISER.

President Patterson, of the National Cash Register, who has but recently returned from a tour round the world, gave testimony to the soundness of Moore's criticism of American methods as contrasted with those of other sections after foreign trade. Mr. Patterson dwelt upon the need for a more intimate knowledge of the foreign countries with which we desire to do business, saying: "I do not believe that we are able to judge of foreign countries unless we send out our representatives, or go there ourselves and ascertain just what the conditions are in those countries. The American tries to crowd down the throats of the foreigners the American methods of business, and it cannot be done. Foreign people have customs of their own, and their own way of doing things, which they will not change any more than we will ours. Like China, we have believed all along that ours is the only country on earth, and that we can't learn anything from any other country or people. If we are going to be a greater nation we must go into foreign countries for trade."

FOR AN AMERICAN MERCHANT MARINE.

An eloquent and forceful argument was made by Mr. Hunziger for the establishment of conditions which would enable us to again have an adequate American merchant marine.

American Patent Medicines from a Chinese View Point.

The following letter to an American manufacturer of proprietary medicines will be found of interest, both in respect to the information conveyed and the phraseology, which we present unedited and unchanged. The few slight departures from idiomatic English but serve to accentuate the general excellence and clarity of the English used:

MAN YU TONG, LIMITED.

Stationers, Printers, Publishers, Type Founders, &c., &c.
Proprietors of "China" News.
Nos. 92 AND 94, HOLLYWOOD ROAD,
HONGKONG, 10th October, 1904.

Dear Sirs: We have much pleasure in acknowledging the receipt of your favor of the 20th August, for which we are exceedingly obliged.

We regret to learn that your advertisement in our daily news has not produced the expected results in the way that your patented medicines were not sold more than what were sold prior to the appearance of the advertisement—the cause of which you seem to attribute to the non-appreciation of your medicines by the readers of "China." For a solution of this we respectfully beg to submit the following for your consideration:

FIRST—THE SOCIAL CONDITION OF THE CHINESE PEOPLE AND THEIR FINANCIAL STATUS.

It is an indisputable fact that the Chinese as a nation are the most conservative people in the world. They do not readily take to things that are new and novel, but when they see that the new things are good and have found them to be so by experience, they will stick to them with all the tenacity and fervor of a hero-worshipper. This is the same in the case of medicines which are being flooded into China of every kind and description and at prices ranging from very cheap to very expensive. You can then well understand that in the matter of medicines the credulity of the Chinese is being imposed upon.

Again, your medicines being of the very best quality command prices too high for the consumption of the average Chinaman. Your preparations are put up with a view to satisfying the most fastidious, which is no consideration to the Chinese. For instance, ——— ———; it is well known throughout the world—that is, it is the best preparation of its kind in existence, but the price of it, which is $2.75 per flacon from the local dispensers here, is too much for an ordinary Chinese to pay. When he can get a mixture of Copaibe and Santal wood oil made for $1.00 per 8 oz. bottle, which will answer the same purpose, his financial status will at once tell him to take this mixture instead of the ——— ———.

So in the case of your ———, which is undoubtedly the best ever made and which has given the most efficacious results in all cases I have known of Chinese ladies who have taken it. But again the price of it is a great barrier for the middle class to avail themselves of it. In the pharmaceutical line, patented medicines do not appeal to the better or wealthy class, who generally have their own family doctors or who will cling to the Chinese medicines. It is only those very few who live in the treaty ports who take to Western medical science. The point then is that if you desire to do business in China you must be prepared to offer a class of medicine which will be compatible with their means and not at the prices now charged.

SECOND—THE ESTABLISHMENT OF YOUR OWN OFFICES IN SHANGHAI AND HONGKONG.

This point is advanced for various obvious reasons. First, that you would push the sale of your medicines with better effects yourselves than if you left it to the local pharmacies who have many of their own preparations to place before the Chinese consumer. Second, you will deal direct with the Chinese, which is a great advantage in itself. In placing your medicines

in the hands of a pharmacy you are not only at the mercy of the pharmaceutist, but also his compradore and staff. Third, you will be able to acquire accurate knowledge of the requirements of the Chinese people. Fourth, the Chinese retailers do not like to buy from the local pharmacy medicines which are not their own make, thinking such patented medicines are sold to them at the same high profit as those of their own make.

In submitting the above points for your consideration we well recognize that you have already given your careful attention to them. But the reason that prompted us to do so is that we desire simply to place before you the views of a Chinese in the hope that they may be of some service to you.

We observe that you are advertising in the "Chinese Mail," which is a very popular paper in Hongkong. You are certainly doing the right thing and it is a course which any practical man would follow, since "China" has failed to produce any results. But at the same time we may be permitted to say that in the event of a certain amount of success attending on this trial it cannot be entirely attributable to the influence of the "Chinese Mail," inasmuch as the "China" was the first medium through which your advertisement passed.

In China things go very much slower than in Europe, so that now the advertisement in "China" for the last year is in all likelihood bearing fruit. We have been the planters and probably the "Chinese Mail" will be the reapers. We wish you heartily all success, and whatever may attend you we hope that you will carry a pleasant remembrance of "China," the pioneer of your advertising in the South of the Chinese empire.

As we wrote you, we have allowed your advertisement to remain in the columns of our paper until we hear definitely from you. We have now taken out the advertisement, giving you the benefit of three months' circulation without further charge from us.

In conclusion we heartily reciprocate your kind sentiment expressed in regard to our paper and trust that we may have further opportunity to renew our very pleasant associations to the mutual benefit of us all. If at any time we can be of a service to you, please command us. Yours faithfully.

MAN YU TONG, LIMITED (YUNG HIR, Manager).
Proprietors of "China."

Trade in Chili.

A correspondent at Coquimbo writes to the London *Pharmaceutical Journal* that trade with Great Britain in drugs and chemicals is stationary. The United States and Germany are doing well in these goods with Chili, while France is making headway as regards toilet articles. Proprietary medicines form more than half the total imports under the heading of drugs and medicines. Another correspondent, writing from Iquique (the principal export port for saltpetre) says that owing to the large number of workmen employed in the manufacture of nitrate of soda in this district (estimated at 12,000 to 15,000 in the immediate neighborhood alone) and to the fact that these are for the most part attended by English doctors the trade in high-class drugs is necessarily large and is increasing owing to the extension of the nitrate factories. The Germans are making most headway, their success being undoubtedly due to the fact that the principal retail druggists are of German nationality. There is not an English druggist in the district. Drugs used in the preparation of febrifuges have the largest sale. Iodine is, of course, bought locally.

An Unusual Method of Avoiding Import Duty.

According to the *Australasian Journal of Pharmacy*, a customs' case possessing interesting features was heard before Mr. Justice O'Connor in the High Court of Australia on November 6. The Crown sued Albert C. Lyon, the local manager of the W. H. Comstock Company, the proprietors of Dr. Morse's Indian Root Pills, to recover a penalty for an alleged breach of the Customs Act in making a false entry and declaration as to the value of six cases of pills imported by him in bulk in October, 1902. The duty on them was 15 per cent. ad valorem—£23 2s. was paid—the value being given as £154. Counsel for the Crown alleged that the price of the pills in America was £4 7s. 6d. per gross, and the value of the six cases should have been £2,100. Deducting £136 for labor locally in bottling and labeling and adding 10 per cent. it made £2,160, the amount on which the customs department contended duty should have been paid. That at 15 per cent. ad valorem gave £324 1s. 3d., leaving an alleged underpayment of £300 19s. Defendants' papers showed that the pills were invoiced as "American cathartic" pills and were not "Dr. Morse's Indian Root" pills until bottled and labeled here; it was the trade name which gave them their much higher value, and the demand for them was created by enormous advertising. Counsel for the defence claimed that the only duty payable was on the price of the American cathartic pills. The case was referred to the Full Court.

Commercial Travelers in Costa Rica.

The regular customs duties of Costa Rica are levied on a traveling man's samples, but refunded to him upon leaving the country, if he takes the samples with him. A wharfage of 3 centavos per kilo is also levied. This is equivalent in United States currency to six-tenths of 1 cent per pound, and is not refunded. All the important points or towns in the country are easily accessible by railroad. San Jose, the capital and commercial center, is situated 103 miles from Port Limon, and reached in six hours. Spanish and English, in the commercial world of Costa Rica, are spoken in the proportion of probably 60 to 40. Naturally, the traveler speaking the two languages will have the advantage, but it is possible for an active man speaking English only to do a fair amount of business.

Honduras.

A correspondent of the *Pharmaceutical Journal* at Amapala says there is a very limited trade between Honduras and the United Kingdom in drugs and chemicals. These are chiefly imported from the United States and Germany, and also from France. This is probably due to the fact that prominent houses in these countries make use of travelers and agents visiting regularly their customers in Central America and also to the fact that American and French manufacturers of proprietary medicines advertise freely.

Vienna.

Business in drugs is increasing in Vienna, while on the other hand the trade in chemicals is not advancing. Surgical instruments of British manufacture, as far as the finest qualities are concerned, are in better demand, but toilet articles of foreign origin are threatened by the new tariff bill. Germany is the country which is making most headway in the chemical and general surgical instrument trade, while America has been doing well in toilet articles. There is a good sale for compressed drugs, but "patent" medicines are for the most part forbidden.

The United States Gains Ground in San Salvador.

Writing from the chief town of the Republic of Salvador in Central America, a correspondent of the *Pharmaceutical Journal* says that in past years a large business was done with the United Kingdom in drugs and chemicals, but it has gradually dwindled down and is now very small, owing to the comparative dearness of English goods. The United States are the most successful competitors as far as proprietary medicines are concerned, while Germany is making great headway in chemical products on account of cheapness and suitability to this particular market. Proprietary medicines are in large demand.

Our Naval Contemporary.

The *Mortar and Pestle* is the appropriate title of the official organ of the association of the hospital corps of the United States Navy. It is published at the U. S. Naval Hospital, Chelsea, Mass., with the following staff: Editor-in-chief, A. L. Eldridge; associate editors, P. J. Waldner and J. P. Mahneke; business manager, S. Wierzbicki. The paper is bright and interesting and will no doubt prove of signal service in building up an *esprit de corps* in the association.

FRANK S. BETZ CO.

(Incorporated)

CAPITAL, SEVEN HUNDRED AND FIFTY THOUSAND DOLLARS

Drugs
Pharmaceuticals
Chemicals
Tablets
Fluid Extracts
Oils
Wines
Syrups
Capsules

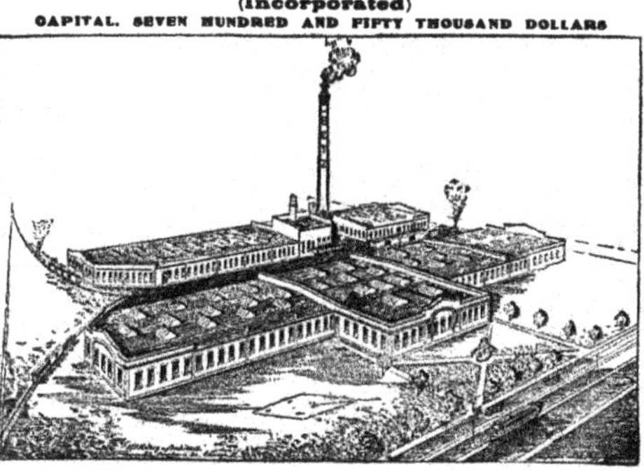

Surgical Instruments
Apparatus
Appliances
Dressings
Rubber Goods
Glassware
Trusses
Sundries

MANUFACTURING PHARMACISTS

Surgical and Hospital Supplies of Every Description

LARGEST PLANT OF ITS KIND IN THE WORLD

SURGEON'S GREEN SOAP,	10 lb. jars, net, $1.00;	20 lb. jars, net, $1.90
	Barrel, 400 lbs.	lb., 6c.
STRONGER AMMONIA, C. P., Sp. Gr. 90°,	8 lb., gal., $1.00;	16 lb., 2 gal., $1.90
	Carboys,	lb., 8½c.
CHLOROFORM, Strictly Pure,	5 lb. bottle, $1.60;	12 lb. bottle, $4.25
	100 lb. bulk,	$31.00
DISTILLED EXTRACT WITCH HAZEL,	Gal. jugs, 80c;	5 gal. jugs, $3.90
	Barrel,	60c. gallon
AMBER PETROLATUM,	5 lb. cans, 45c;	doz. cans, $5.00
	Barrel,	per lb., 3½c.
SNOW WHITE PETROLATUM (Russian),	5 lb. cans, $1.00;	doz. cans, $11.00
	Barrel,	per lb., 14c.
NITRIC ACID, C. P., Sp. Gr. .84	7 lb. bottle,	$1.20
	Carboy,	per lb., about 8½c.
HYDROCHLORIC ACID (Muriatic),	Strictly Pure, 7 lb. bottle,	$1.10
	Carboy,	per lb., about 7½c.
SULPHURIC ACID, C. P	7 lb. glass bottle,	$1.10.
	Carboy,	per lb., 6½c.

BETZ' SANITARY FLUID, Saponified Coal Tar Creosote. 1 gal. makes 100 gals. of strong, efficacious disinfectant - - - gal., $3.00
HYDROGEN PEROXIDE, U. S. P. (Medicinal), - - - 1 gal. bottle, $1.65
FORMALDEHYDE, 40% Solution, Guaranteed to be of highest purity, per lb, 25c; 5 lbs., $1.25; gal. bot., $1.60; 5 gal., $7.25; 10 gal., $12.75; barrels of about 400 lbs, per lb., 12c.
SOLIDIFIED FORMALDEHYDE, Powdered, - lb., $1.50; 5 lbs., $6.00; 10 lbs., $11.00
PARAFORMALDEHYDE, Paste, - - - lb., $1.50; 5 lbs., $6.00; 10 lbs., $11.00

We are headquarters for everything used for municipal sanitation and that of ship factories, railroads, etc. We supply in the smallest or largest quantities.

THERMOMETERS, Clinical, 60 sec., Magnifying with certificate, - - - doz., $4.00
HYPODERMIC SYRINGE, glass or metal barrel, doz., $4.00
MEDICINE DROPPERS, either bent or straight or assorted, - - - gross, $1.40
RUBBER GLOVES, any size, - - doz., $6.00

WOOD ALCOHOL STOVES (Reform), nickel plated on brass, - - - doz., $6.00
GLASS GONORRHŒAL SYRINGES, French Make, gross, $3.00
SUSPENSORIES, J. P. Silk Knit Sack, - - doz., $1.50
SUSPENSORIES, Army and Navy Lisle Thread, doz., $2.00
FINGER COTS FOR SURGEONS, - - gross, $1.75

TERMS, CASH WITH ORDER

CHICAGO SALESROOM, 90 WABASH AVENUE

GENERAL OFFICES AT WORKS, HAMMOND, INDIANA

Where All Communications Should be Addressed

The History of Artificial Salts of Mineral Waters.

The business of manufacturing artificial salts imitating the composition of mineral waters recently celebrated its twenty-fifth anniversary, for on November 20, 1880, Dr. Ernest Sandow began to manufacture substitutes for the natural mineral waters in a dry state. This work was done on a very small scale in his pharmacy in Hamburg, and later on was enlarged and transferred to a special factory. Sandow undoubtedly was the founder of the important industry of manufacturing artificial mineral water salts, but the manufacture of artificial mineral waters was first begun in Germany in the sixteenth century, although the attempts did not seem to be very successful.

In 1820, 1823 and 1824 Struve, of Dresden, founded factories for the manufacture of artificial mineral waters in Dresden, in Leipsig and in Berlin, and thus laid the corner stone of one of the greatest industries connected with pharmacy. Struve remained almost the sole representative of this special branch of business for thirty years, but gradually the analyses upon which he worked were improved, and a number of waters were added to the list of those which could be imitated. Active competition between the natural and the artificial mineral water began about that time and has continued ever since.

A further development of this industry came in the forties of the past century, when the proprietors of natural springs began to sell the salts obtained by evaporating their mineral waters. The manufacturers of artificial mineral waters began then to imitate the products just mentioned and sold artificial salts which imitated the residues of natural mineral waters. The first attempts to produce these salts were unsuccessful because the residues of various springs were very hygroscopic, or else the solutions of these residues were found to be cloudy. By changing the composition of these salts slightly Sandow succeeded in producing dry and stable preparations which were soluble in water, making clear solutions. The artificial Carlsbad salt was introduced into the German Pharmacopœia as early as 1882. Sandow's effervescent salts were an improvement upon his artificial mineral water salts, and he has found a great number of imitators within the last twenty years, so that now a substitute for almost every natural mineral water can be obtained in the form of artificial salts. It is of course open to question whether these artificial products are satisfactory.

A Good New Year's Resolution.

A good resolution for the soda water dispenser has been framed by the Liquid Carbonic Company in the following words:

"*Resolved*, That on and after this date, I, A. Soda-Water Dispenser, will bend every energy, spare neither time nor money, and leave no stone unturned, in placing my soda water business on a paying basis, and in developing it into the most lucrative department of my establishment, ere my fountain closes for 1906. I intend to overhaul my soda fountain, and, if needs be, install one of modern construction; one that is down-to-the-minute in every respect. I will buy the best carbonator on the market, to insure against flat, lifeless beverages; also to reduce the cost of production to a minimum. My service will be faultless; my soda a little better than my competitors. With these facilities, I will control the cream of the trade and pocket the 'Lion's share' of the fat profits that rightfully belong to me."

But three short months are left before the soda fountain will again be running at full blast. If you have not as yet made your calculations and placed your order, it is high time that you should do so. The machinery is beginning to hum in the soda fountain and carbonator factories, and the quicker the manufacturer receives your order the better for all parties concerned. Don't overlook the fact that the output of The Liquid Carbonic Company is practically unlimited, and they can fill all your requirements in the shortest possible time. When you buy from this firm you can secure terms which practically enable you to pay for your fountain and carbonator out of the profits accruing from future business.

A postal or letter requesting full information, addressed to any of their eleven branch establishments, Chicago, New York, Pittsburg, St. Louis, Milwaukee, Cincinnati, Baltimore, Kansas City, Minneapolis, Dallas or Atlanta, will receive prompt and courteous attention.

Easter Comes on April 15.

The "White Rabbit" reminds the progressive druggist that Easter will be here soon, and he should prepare for the demand that is sure to come for the White Rabbit Easter Dyes. The White Rabbit and Easter Egg are inseparable.

In choosing a satisfactory brand of Easter Dye for the coming season no mistake will be made in buying the well known White Rabbit brand. These Dyes have been on the market for many years and always give satisfaction.

The old German myth, familiar to all, that the White Rabbit is responsible for the colored Easter Egg is utilized and combined with a most attractive line of White Rabbit Easter Dyes, which have become exceedingly popular with the children as well as with the older persons and also with the trade, on account of their easy sale and the further fact that the retailer's profit is large.

They are packed in handsome display boxes which contain attractive advertising matter for the dealer.

They are the best advertised dyes as well as the best in quality. Get the best. Order from your jobber.

A Heavy Demand Expected.

The trade hardly needs to be reminded of the fact that this is the season when Scott's Emulsion is in the greatest demand, and from all indications it is evident that this excellent remedy will have a very large sale this winter. Advance orders bear out this impression, and despite the many new preparations of codliver oil, Scott's Emulsion continues to lead the market for such goods, the sales each year showing a great increase over the preceding year. The absolute purity and uniform quality of Scott's Emulsion, together with the satisfactory results that always follow its use, have made this preparation a household article all over the world. As Scott's Emulsion has been on the market thirty years it is reasonable to suppose that something besides extensive advertising has secured for it the position it occupies. It's the quality and value of the preparation that have made it outlive so many imitations and competitors.

The Best Color for Weak Eyes.

"Why blue glasses?" asks Dr. Motais. The real color for fatigued eyes is yellow. The statement may seem odd, but it is said to be clearly demonstrated that what tires the eye are the heat and chemical rays of the spectrum. The yellow glass modifies both, and at the same time gives the clear outline to objects which are apt to be blurred by dark colored glasses. For the reasons above stated yellow glasses are specially recommended to those who read or write by arc lamps or acetylene light.

Hints to Buyers.

The Wells & Richardson line of price-protected proprietaries has the friendship of all N. A. R. D. men, says *N. A. R. D. Notes*. This firm wants the retailers to make a good profit on their goods and are helping them to do it.

From William R. Warner & Co., manufacturing pharmaceutists, Philadelphia, we are in receipt of a handsome plaque bearing a Titianesque portrait of a woman in all the wealth of coloring which the adjective connotes. It forms a most artistic desk ornament.

We call special attention to the advertisement of British Lanolin in this issue. The American agency of Evans & Sons, Limited, the makers, is at 133 William street, New York. This product has been found very satisfactory wherever used and has the added advantage of cheapness.

A sample of Dentacura may be obtained by addressing department A, Dentacura Company, Newark, N. J. This celebrated tooth paste has obtained a wide vogue in many parts of the world, notably in the United States, by reason of the fact that it is a remarkable preservative of the teeth and gums and has the general endorsement of the dental profession.

The offices and stock departments of E. R. Squibb & Sons are now fully installed in their New York building at 78 and 80 Beekman street. All orders and communications should henceforth be addressed to New York. The Squibb plant at Brooklyn is entirely given over to the rapidly extending manufacturing departments of the house.

The granular effervescent salt, which is similar to the celebrated bitter waters of Bohemia, is marketed under the trademark name of Sal Hepatica, by the Bristol-Myers Company, of 277 Greene avenue, Brooklyn, N. Y. This preparation has gained a very wide sale in all parts of the country owing to its qualities as a saline laxative, uric acid solvent and eliminent. It is for sale by all jobbers.

We call special attention to the new advertisement of White's Fluted Straws. The New Jersey Paper Tube Company is turning out a better straw than ever before, and one feature of marked advantage is that it is not touched by human hands in the manufacture and is in addition sterilized by heat so that it comes to the consumer perfectly clean and sweet. With the approach of the soda water season druggists will be interested in this announcement. The Coe Mfg. Company, of New York, are the distributing agents.

A "Christmas Line" in the American Soda Fountain Company's Mailing Room.

Some of the after echoes of the Christmas cheer are just reaching us, in the way of reports of the day's doings among our business friends. It is pleasant to note that the Christmas spirit reached through all the rank and file of workers.

At the American Soda Fountain Company, one of the pleasantest celebrations of the day was in the mailing room of the advertising department, where some 30 young women gathered about the "Christmas Tree," which in this case was a "Gift Line," the presents, in mysterious looking packages, being suspended by strings from a line across one end of the room. There was a great amount of fun and shouts of merriment as the young people, one by one, were blindfolded, turned about and then groping their way to the line, made a "grab" for one of the pretty presents.

The celebration was under the direction of Miss Foye, who for some years has had charge of the mailing department of the company. It is pleasant to record that the spirit of kindness and helpfulness among women workers has always been in evidence in Miss Foye's department, and that her earnest and untiring efforts for the good of her "girls" have won appreciation and a loving loyalty from those under her charge. A practical testimony of this was shown in the handsome silver toilet set that was presented to Miss Foye as a Christmas remembrance from the workers in her department.

That this genuine interest and co-operation pays in a business sense is also noted by the officers of the company, who find that more willing, efficient and intelligent service is obtained as a result.

The Best Thing in Physics.

The following story is told by a former superintendent of public schools in a Maine town:

A young girl came to the superintendent, saying that she wished to enter the high school. She passed the entrance examinations successfully. Then the superintendent asked, "What have you taken in physics?"

"Well," she replied, "I've never taken much in physics, but I've always heard that salts were about the best."—*Boston Herald.*

Not the Same Army.

An amusing incident in connection with the annual Thanksgiving collection made on the streets of Boston by the members of the Salvation Army is mentioned by the *Mortar and Pestle* as follows: "Two hospital stewards in uniform stopped for a moment one evening in the vicinity of a member of the army, when a gentleman passing by thrust a dollar bill into the hands of one of them, with the request that they 'use it for the Thanksgiving dinner.' What became of the dollar is unknown, but we trust it reached its proper destination. We have heard of members of the corps being taken for street car conductors, etc., but this is the first instance that has come to our notice where a hospital steward resembled a Salvation Army laddie.' '

Profit in Handling View Post Cards.

Collecting souvenir post cards started as a "fad," but has outgrown that term long ago. The dictionary declares this by describing a fad as something which temporarily engages the attention and interest, as a passing fancy. The steady growth of the post card industry, for such it has become both in this country and abroad, extends over such a long space of time—years, in fact—as to entirely eliminate the expression "temporary attention" from the definition.

The use of post cards, view, fancy and other kinds, is now literally an international habit. Very few are the drug stores which do not prominently display some such notice as this:

WE SELL VIEW POST CARDS.

And all find it to pay them well for more than one reason. While profitable in itself the display of cards attracts customers to the store and other purchases result.

The Souvenir Post Card Company of New York City are among the leaders manufacturing and importing these cards and carry in stock many millions of view, fancy and comic post cards. In fact, they handle all varieties and import direct from abroad as well as manufacture, and are constantly engaged in turning out vast quantities to meet the trade that has come to them, as up to this time they have never placed an advertisement of any kind. Now, however, having increased their facilities so largely, they invite orders for any kind and quantity of goods. Recently this company opened its new and large salesrooms, situated at 50-52 Franklin street, and will have in stock an immense selection ready for instant shipment to any part of the world. They have made a good reputation for the care and skill with which they handle cards made after original photographs.

With the shrewd druggist it is no longer a question of putting in post cards to sell. The active demand of the public and the eager buying when the stock is right, has left no doubt. The Souvenir Post Card Company has certainly the largest stock and variety of kinds of goods, and the dealer has but to communicate with their office to learn as to how to obtain postals of any kind. The factories of the company are at 268-270 Canal street, New York City, and in Berlin and Leipsic, Germany, but its business offices and salesroom are at 50-52 Franklin street, where all interested in this line are welcome and will receive courteous treatment and any information regarding the post card business they may be seeking.

BUY A GROSS AND SAVE 5 and 2½ PER CENT.

THE KIND YOU HAVE ALWAYS HANDLED

IT PAYS TO HANDLE RELIABLE GOODS

$33.60 Per Gross. | Jobbers Sell in Gross Lots, 5 Per Cent. and 2½ Per Cent. OFF. | $2.80 Per Dozen.

THIS IS THE GENUINE.

Send for Cards, Cartons and Counter Wrappers.

THE CENTAUR COMPANY,
77 MURRAY STREET, NEW YORK CITY. Chas. H. Fletcher, *President,*

BUY A GROSS AND SAVE 5 and 2½ PER CENT.

——Who can't sell 12 dozen per annum?——

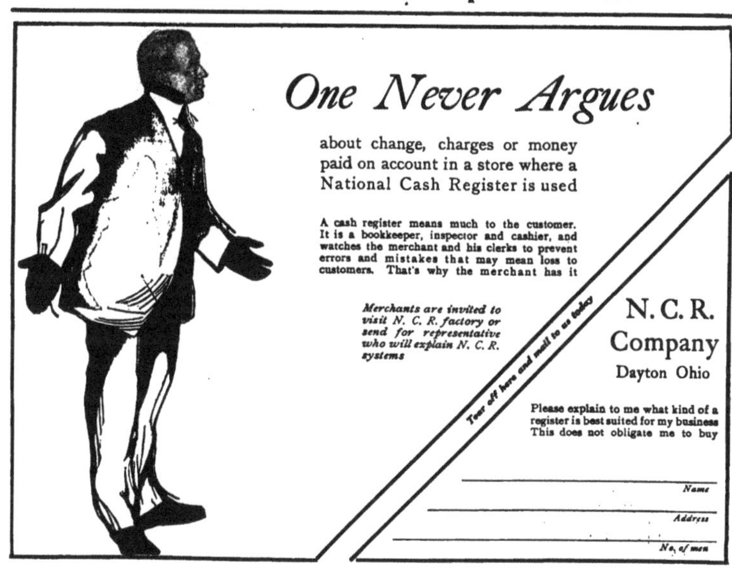

Fairchild Scholarship and Prizes.

According to the London *Chemist and Druggist* A. E. Holden, Bath House, Holborn Viaduct, E. C., London, England, secretary to the Committee of Trustees, of the scholarship for pharmaceutical students at the School of Pharmacy of the Pharmaceutical Society of Great Britain, has issued the syllabus for 1906, which was ready for distribution to applicants on December 1. Several changes and additions have been made as the result of the first year's experience, and these are thus summarized:

1. The examination will be held at the same five centers as before during the last week of June, 1906. Candidates are strongly advised to register as students under the Pharmacy act not later than April, 1906, otherwise they may not be eligible for the 1906 competition.

2. Candidates to whom prizes have been awarded in one year shall not be eligible for prizes in any subsequent year, but may compete for the scholarship, if otherwise eligible.

3. The object of the founders of the scholarship and prizes being to encourage study during the period of apprenticeship, and thus materially facilitate and enhance the chances of success of the diligent student on entrance for the qualifying examination, it necessarily follows that no student already qualified can compete for or obtain either the scholarship or any of the prizes.

4. The ground of the subject, elementary materia medica, has been enlarged to include drugs of animal origin.

We may recall the fact that the scholarship is of the value of £50, and is obtainable by any registered apprentice or student (male or female) in England, Ireland, Scotland or Wales. The prizes are £5 each. The subjects of examination are elementary chemistry, elementary materia medica, practical pharmacy and prescription reading and elementary business knowledge. The scholarship is supported by S. W. Fairchild, of Fairchild Bros. & Foster, of New York.

The Popular Bee Brand Insect Powder.

The constantly increasing demand for Bee Brand Insect Powder, the product of the well-known house of McCormick & Co., of Baltimore, attests to the fact that a real insect powder is appreciated by both the trade and the consumer. The main reason for the superiority of Bee Brand over the many so-called "insect powders" is the fact that McCormick & Co. do not import any insect powder, but instead have their agent on the field buying up the choicest grades of flowers from which the powder is ground, grinding same in their own mills, the largest and finest in this country, and hence avoiding all chance of adulteration. Bee Brand Insect Powder is sold strictly on its merits and it will cost you nothing to find out how good it is, as McCormick & Co. will send you generous samples for the asking. Their popular wooden bottle package overcomes all the objections of other containers, as the powder will not get moist and cake as it does in tin nor affected by the light as is the case when packed in glass; it will not break, and weighs less than glass. The bottle has a sprinkler top and thus requires no gun. It is a popular 10 cent seller with the trade.

A Very Practical Premium.

Every druggist realizes that in compounding prescriptions a set of absolutely accurate weights is of the greatest value. First, because poisons and dangerous drugs can only be safely handled when the weights are correct, and second, because expensive drugs may be overweighed—a profit-losing operation. The Chichester Chemical Company, of Philadelphia, are now giving free with every dozen of their regular size Chichester's Pills a set of standard prescription weights, guaranteed by "Troemner" to be hand adjusted, and absolutely accurate. This company also announces that in accordance with the "Two-Four-Eight" resolution adopted by the N. A. R. D. at the Boston Convention, the price of Chichester's Pills is now $16 per dozen. Also that the New Trial Size are on the market at $8 per dozen. Everyone of our readers should read Chichester's full-page advertisement which appears elsewhere in this issue.

The Rapid Fire Soda Fountain.

The Herron Soda Fountain Company have named their perfected counter dispensing system the "Rapid Fire" on account of the rapidity with which the dispenser can hand out satisfactory beverages from it. Their other fountains have always had a good sale, being satisfactory both on account of their reliability and of their "style." For illustrations and quotations address the Herron Soda Fountain Company, 2509 to 2517 State street, Chicago.

To Prevent Freezing in the Cooling Tank of Automobiles.

Druggists are frequently asked by automobilists for something to add to the cooling tank of the machine to prevent freezing in very cold weather. Glycerine has been recommended, but is expensive and not altogether satisfactory, while salt and similar alkali salts are not efficient at low temperatures and, moreover, rapidly attack brass and iron connections or tubes. Calcium chloride is the most useful addition and exerts the least action upon the metal parts, while giving a very low freezing point. A 10 per cent. solution of calcium chloride freezes about 22 degrees F., a 15 per cent. about 12 degrees F., a 20 per cent. about 1 degree F., and a 25 per cent. about 20 degrees F., which last is sufficient to stand the cold prevalent in most sections of the country.

Work Standing Up.

You can work standing up with a "Sanitas" Counter Fountain. Soda serving was never meant to be back-breaking drudgery. The soda dispenser with aching back, grown tired and weary with the constant twisting, turning and stooping incident to a "rush" day at the ordinary soda fountain, hails with delight the "Sanitas" Counter Fountain. With this fountain you can work all day without bending your back; no twisting or turning; everything right in front of you: syrups, crushed fruits, ice cream, carbonated water, chipped ice, glasses, sugar, cutting board, towel, slop chute, all right at hand in front of you. No wonder it's a popular soda fountain. Yet, with all its advantages we would not call it a wonderful soda fountain. It's so plain, clean and simple in appearance that any claim for "marvelousness" would appear an exaggeration. But add to this plain, practical, "built-for business" soda fountain a wall display structure of say L'Art Nouveau design, using in construction a combination of two such rich woods as Mexican mahogany and silver finished bird's-eye maple. To this combination add the effectiveness of mirrors reflecting the brilliant tints of the Tiffany electric hood shades that surmount the draught stands, and the effect of reflected colors of fruits and syrups; then add the brilliancy of uniquely distributed illumination and you have an effect well calculated to arouse the æsthetic nature of any man, woman or child. Taken as a whole, it can truthfully be said that you have a fountain that appeals to both the eye and the intellect, to the taste and the appetite.

This "Built-for-Business" soda fountain is one of the five types of "20th Century Sanitary" Fountains manufactured by the L. A. Becker Company, the largest independent soda fountain manufacturing concern in the world. General offices and factory located at 911 Halsted street, Chicago; branches, 27 East Twenty-second street, New York; 72 Portland street, Boston; 19 North Liberty street, Baltimore; 82 Marietta street, Atlanta; Thirteenth and Lawrence streets, Denver; 211 Second avenue, Seattle.

The offices of the Marvel Company, manufacturer of the Marvel Syringe, have been moved to East Twenty-third street, New York City. The syringe is carried in stock by most of the jobbing druggists of the United States, but where it cannot be obtained orders may be sent to the New York address. The syringe may be described as first-class in every respect and to embody many advantages over the ordinary form. As it is something which is endorsed and prescribed by physicians and is also in popular demand it should be carried in stock by every retail druggist.

We would recommend that this parcel be returned after Oct. 26, '06, to be replaced with fresh serum.
KEEP THIS PRODUCT AT AS UNIFORM TEMPERATURE AS POSSIBLE, PREFERABLY BETWEEN 40° AND 60° F.
LICENSE No. 1, issued to Parke, Davis & Co. by the Secretary of the Treasury, U. S. A.
approved July 1, 1902.
NO RISK OF LOSS
WHEN YOU STOCK OUR
Antidiphtheric Serum
We cheerfully accept unsold antitoxin in exchange for fresh product.
Every package of our Antidiphtheric Serum bears a return-date (one year after date of manufacture).
We amply protect you from loss, and our prices yield you a liberal profit.
Bulbs of 500, 1000, 2000, 3000 and 4000 units.
Piston-syringe container.
PARKE, DAVIS & COMPANY
LABORATORIES: DETROIT, MICH., U.S.A.; WALKERVILLE, ONT.; HOUNSLOW, ENG.
BRANCHES: NEW YORK, CHICAGO, ST. LOUIS, BOSTON, BALTIMORE, NEW ORLEANS, KANSAS CITY, INDIANAPOLIS, MINNEAPOLIS, MEMPHIS, U.S.A.; LONDON, ENG.; MONTREAL, QUE.; SYDNEY, N.S.W.; ST. PETERSBURG, RUSSIA; SIMLA, INDIA; TOKIO, JAPAN
Note the Date on the Carton

THE WEST.

Ladies' Day at the C. R. D. A.—Old Officers Re-elected—Social Affairs to the Fore—Two Vacancies on the Illinois Board.

(From our Regular Correspondent.)

Chicago, January 17.—At the annual meeting of the Chicago Retail Druggists' Association last week all of the old officers were re-elected and general good feeling was manifested. A number of annual reports were read and other routine matters were disposed of. The social side of the meeting came into more than usual prominence because of the presence of a number of ladies. The regular proceedings were more quiet than usual on this account. After the regular session there was a luncheon that was much enjoyed. Short speeches were then made by officers and members, who pointed out the benefits of the work of the organization.

THE CHAIN OF STORES.

There is considerable mystery in regard to the plan of the Ideal Drug Company to control a chain of drug stores. Such work is usually done in secret, and it is difficult to get at all of the facts, for the reason that the promoters are silent, but in this case there has been a leaning in the opposite direction, for it is now intimated that some one has been drawing the long bow. Out of ten stores which the new organization is said to control only three admit the truth of the sale. Fred A. Shayer has made an open denial of the reported sale of his place at Madison street and Ogden avenue.

VACANCIES ON THE BOARD.

There are two vacancies on the Illinois State Board of Pharmacy that have not yet been filled. Mr. Dyche's term expired at the close of the last year and Mr. Schwartz's period in office also reached its limit at that time. Governor Deneen has not yet appointed their successors.

A NEW CHEMICAL FIRM.

The Hawkes & Bowen Company announce the formation of their offices at 79 Dearborn street, Chicago, which will make a specialty of handling a complete line of chemicals suitable for all industrial and technical purposes. The members of the company have been identified with the chemical trade for a great many years, some of them through a long connection with the General Chemical Company, and are thoroughly equipped in every way to serve buyers of chemicals advantageously. The members of the firm are A. W. Hawkes, B. C. Hawkes and Henry Bowen.

CHICAGO NOTES.

Peter J. Roth, formerly with Burroughs Bros., has become manager of Hance Bros. & White's Chicago office. Mr. Roth was with Searle & Hereth for ten years.

Albert E. Ebert will be forced to give up his old store May 1. The building where his stand has been located for so many years has been rented to a cigar store syndicate at $600 a month.

The Chicago Retail Druggists' Association has endorsed the candidacy of Congressman Mann because of what he has done in behalf of the Mann bill for correcting the statute relating to patent medicines.

A movement looking toward the formation of a Chicago branch of the Society of Chemical Industries was started at the annual meeting of the Chicago section of the American Chemical Society.

Efforts to stop the selling of narcotics have received a hard blow. Judge Walker has held that eucaine, not being mentioned in the State poison law, is therefore exempt from its rulings. Louis Re, 438 Dearborn street, who was charged with selling eucaine, was therefore acquitted. City Chemist Jones says this makes it impossible to prosecute such druggists.

James E. Bartlett has just returned from a tour of inspection of the branches of Parke, Davis & Co. in St. Louis, Memphis and New Orleans. Mr. Bartlett tendered 60 of the Western representatives of Parke, Davis & Co. a banquet at the Voglesang, January 29. A number of chiefs from the parent house in Detroit were present.

THE SOUTH.

Trade Brisk in the Crescent City—Arrangements for the State Meeting—More New Stores Planned.

(From our Regular Correspondent.)

New Orleans, La., January 15.—Trade conditions in New Orleans and throughout this section are in good shape and the druggists are satisfied. Both retailers and wholesalers are finding considerable difference in the existing conditions now and those which obtained when the visitation of the yellow fever began to show its effect. Consequently there is much satisfaction among the trade and all are looking for still greater improvements.

PREPARING FOR THE STATE MEETING.

Secretary George W. McDuff is busy with the preliminary arrangements for the annual convention of the Louisiana State Pharmaceutical Association which will open here about the middle of April. Though the convention is still nearly three months off there are many arrangements to be made and it is with these that Mr. McDuff is busying himself. A number of especial features, which will be unusually attractive, will be introduced at the coming session and there are many important matters to be discussed.

MORE NEW STORES ON CANAL STREET.

Rumor has it that the proprietors of Cusachs' Pharmacy, at Canal and Baronne streets, are negotiating for the control of the Katz's place at St. Charles and Jackson avenues. They will, it is understood, operate both places if they succeed in getting the uptown drug store. Katz's place is in a splendid location and offers an opportunity for a good paying business.

Crouere and Sauvinet, two progressive young druggists of the Crescent City, to-day opened to the public their handsome new store at Canal and Villere streets. The establishment is well stocked and its fixtures are very attractive and entirely above those found in the average drug store. Success is predicted for the young men at their new location.

Stewart's Pharmacy, at Philip and Baronne streets, a well known drug house, recently changed hands and is now being operated as Fears' Pharmacy. Mr. Fears has a good location and has improved the place to a large degree. He is catering to a good class and indications are that success will attend his efforts to build up the trade in that part of the city.

About January 20, the new St. Charles street drug store, The Orpheum, which will occupy one half of the Rathskellar building, will be ready for the opening. One of the handsomest soda fountains in the South is being installed and some very pretty and attractive fixtures will be used. Announcement is made that the stock of the new establishment will be second to none in the South.

SOUTHERN NEWS NOTES.

The Palmer Drug Company, of Shreveport, La., was recently sold out by the receiver into whose hands it passed some time ago. The fate of the concern is still in doubt.

Trouilly & Oplatek, well known druggists, of Gretna, La., which is directly across the river from New Orleans, are making arrangements to open a new store at Covington, La. They expect to complete their new store before long. If the same success attends their efforts in Covington as has attended them in Gretna there can be little doubt that the Covington store will rank among the best in this part of the State.

Lucius E. Lide & Co. have opened a handsome new drug store at Columbus, Miss. They have secured a good location and have stocked their establishment with the best that could be obtained. Progressive citizens of Columbus are behind the enterprise and there is little doubt that it will be successful. Mr. Lide is a graduate of the Philadelphia College of Pharmacy and has been for many years with Mayo & Weaver, of Columbus.

THE PACIFIC COAST.

Drug Clerks Entertain—Professor Searby Discusses Pharmacy from an Historical Standpoint—The New Board Elects Officers—Changes in Schedule of Prices.

(*From our Regular Correspondent.*)

San Francisco, January 13.—The San Francisco Drug Clerks' Association have elected the following officers to serve for the first six months of the year: President, A. D. Fretz; first vice-president, J. H. Flint; second vice-president, Charles Bucher; recording and corresponding secretary, Philip Weiss; treasurer, G. M. Sutherland; guide, J. M. Eitel, guardian, J. P. Zipf; advocate agent, J. H. Hubachek; grievance committee, E. J. Molony, C. B. Whilden and W. H. Adair; trustees, A. H. Hoag, Fred Driscoll and C. F. Holman, and delegates to the San Francisco Labor Council, J. H. Hubachek, Charles Bucher and J. J. Crowley.

In accordance with their usual custom, the drug clerks held "open house" on New Year's Day, from 10 A. M. to 10 P. M., in the banquet hall of the Pioneer Building. The "pill rollers" have gained an enviable reputation for their hospitality, and as a result they were overwhelmed by friends, who were given the glad hand and other more substantial refreshments. To make things more lively, a running entertainment was also supplied.

PROFESSOR SEARBY OPENS DRUG CLERKS' LECTURES.

The first of a series of lectures on scientific topics arranged by the local Drug Clerks' Association was delivered on the 12th inst. by Professor W. M. Searby, dean of the California College of Pharmacy, University of California, on the subject "From Alchemy to Bacteriology." Chairman J. H. Flint, Ph.G., stated that the association was as much interested in the intellectual improvement of its members as it was in the matter of more satisfactory hours and salaries. Professor Searby was then introduced as the "dean of California pharmacists." The lecturer explained that there had existed two kinds of alchemists—one, a set of charlatans, and the other, a class of philosophers, the latter being really the founders of chemistry. He reviewed the working hours and salaries of past and present pharmacists, as well as the difficulties that the would-be pharmacist encountered in the time of his apprenticeship, in the '49's. Pharmaceutical education of the past and present centuries was also compared, and the pharmacist's business methods of earlier days described. Many old processes formerly used were mentioned, to the delight of the audience. While Professor Searby contended that many of the old-time elements of the profession had been discarded, he thought that the gain in other directions, notably as regards pharmaceutical education, more than compensated for the loss. A brief survey of the development of pharmacopœias and the dispensation of a goodly amount of advice to the impatient student of modern times brought to a close this highly interesting lecture.

THE PHARMACY BOARD HAS A SURPLUS.

The annual report of the last State Board of Pharmacy is as follows: Total receipts, $11,537.80; total expenditures, $9,185.74, leaving a balance of $2,352.06. Adding the balance from last year and that from the itinerary account, the total amount in the State treasury belonging to the board is stated as $3,752.08.

The new Pharmacy Board, the personnel of which was given in these columns in November, held their initial examinations in Los Angeles during the week commencing January 3. E. Off, of Los Angeles, was elected president and C. B. Whilden secretary.

COAST NEWS ITEMS.

Mrs. F. M. Smith, wife of the borax king, died at her home in East Oakland, Cal., on January 1.

The D. D. Johnson Drug Company, at Mountain View, Cal., was destroyed by fire on the night of December 25. The insurance of $2,000 covers less than one-third of the damage.

PRICE SCHEDULE CHANGED.

The San Francisco Bay Counties Association of Retail Druggists announces the following changes in the price schedule: Fletcher's Castoria, 25 cents, a reduction of three cents; Fellows' syrup, $1,15, a reduction of 10 cents; Stewart's dyspepsia cure (50 cent size), 39 cents, an advance of five cents; antiphlogistine (50 cent size), 39 cents, an advance of five cents, and Shoop's restorer, 82 cents, an advance of five cents.

'FRISCO BREVITIES.

City Chemist Gibbs found that 55 of 275 samples of beer analyzed by him contained salicylic or sulphurous acid.

The newly appointed Pharmacy Board has just concluded its first examination in this city. About 100 candidates appeared for certificates. The office of the board has been changed to the Callaghan Building, in this city.

Hints to Buyers.

We call special attention to the new advertisement of the Gillette Safety Razor appearing in this issue. This is an article which druggists have found to be a valuable side line, as it leads to the sale of shaving soaps and brushes and other accessories.

A. H. Wirz, of Philadelphia, manufactures a line of bottle stoppers for cork and screw neck liquid and powder bottles as well as collapsible tubes, hand pill machines, hand pill compressors, suppository and bougie molds and metal syringes. These goods are all for sale by the wholesale and retail trade.

Some of the most artistic post cards which have been made in America are the output of the Albertype Company, 250 Adams street, Brooklyn, N. Y. It has received many letters in commendation of its cards from the retail druggists who have handled them. It makes a specialty of reproducing local views which always sell well. Write it for specimen and quotation, with special trade discount.

A Marvel in Steel.

The Gillette Safety Razor plant, which is located in Boston, Mass., is the largest factory devoted exclusively to the manufacture of razors in the world. It employs over six hundred people and has one of the model business systems of the United States.

The fusion of the steel used in the Gillette safety razor blades is a scientific marvel in steel work. It is made by a process that frees it absolutely from natural impurities, removing all manganese, sulphur and phosphorus, and yet retains the carbon in just the right proportion. The blades are as flexible and resilient as a Damascus sword. The hardening, tempering, grinding and sharpening of the blade to secure the desired edge are an invention or process which the visitor to the plant looks upon as one of the twentieth century wonders in working steel.

Until this blade was created it was not thought possible to make steel to possess such a fine degree of tensile strength; it was looked upon as one of the lost arts. Perhaps the greatest difficulty that formerly troubled workers in steel was the tempering of such thin steel without hardening to a degree of useless brittleness. The flexibility of the Gillette blade as shown in the accompanying illustration proves how perfectly the secret and patented process has been developed and accomplished after a long series of experiments.

Another peculiar and interesting feature of this blade is its two cutting edges, keen as lightning, sharpened to perfect uniformity. It has always been considered an unsolved problem to produce a double edged instrument of such thin steel because of the inability to uniformly perfect the edges. The accuracy with which these blades are made by automatic machinery proves that the genius of invention still has undiscovered realms.

Cod Liver Oil in Capsules.

The efficacy of cod liver oil in the treatment of coughs and wasting diseases is universally conceded by the medical profession but, unfortunately, the taste of cod liver oil is so disagreeable that it is difficult to make patients take it except under the compulsion of severe illness. The Crystal Capsule Company of 15 North Eleventh street, Philadelphia, Pa., have placed on the market packages of capsules containing pure Norwegian cod liver oil put up in such form that the patient will not object to taking them. This new departure is sure to prove successful and druggists who want to be up to date should write at once for samples and prices to the Crystal Capsule Company, at the above address, mentioning THE AMERICAN DRUGGIST.

A Handsome Display Case Free of Charge.

We illustrate herewith a very attractive display case for clinical thermometers, which will be given away free of charge by Becton, Dickinson & Co., of New York, who are leading manufacturers in this line, with an assortment of their goods. In connection with this assortment they have an ingenious advertising plan which will place the goods prominently before the public. The laity are just beginning to appreciate the value of clinical thermometers and the importance of having a kind which is thoroughly reliable. Heretofore a thermometer has been used indiscriminately by the whole family or a whole community; but there is a growing appreciation of a certain nicety which tends to individualize in such matters, and many fastidious patients would as soon use a borrowed tooth brush as a borrowed thermometer. This idea it would do well to cultivate. For details regarding the advertising plan address Becton, Dickinson & Co., New York, mentioning the AMERICAN DRUGGIST.

A Handsome Soda Fountain for Louisville.

What is claimed to be the finest fountain in Louisville, Ky., is the handsome "Innovation" recently installed in the T. P. Taylor Company's new drug store. This fountain was built by the American Soda Fountain Company and was especially designed for this store. The superstructure is a magnificent creation of solid mahogany, with Moorish domes of Tiffany art glass, supported by onyx columns.

The refrigerator base and the dispensing counter are of Pavanazzo marble, with onyx trimmings and base of Verd Antique. The draft stands are of beautiful Pedrara onyx, each crowned with a gracefully shapen canopy of art glass, brilliantly illuminated and hung with beaded fringe.

Every part of the mechanical appointments of this fountain is of the latest and best design in soda fountain construction. There are many features which make the serving of delicious ice-cold drinks an easy matter. The dispensers are enabled t serve deftly and rapidly, and customers find an added piquai to the flavors and a smoother deliciousness to the drinks serv... amid such attractive surroundings.

The American Soda Fountain Company is said to be the largest manufacturer of soda fountains in the world. It may well be a matter of gratification to the friends of the T. P. Taylor Company and to residents of Louisville that one of the finest soda fountains ever built by the "American" has been placed in a Louisville pharmacy.

Praise of Tobacco.

"Here," said a Chicago antiquary, "is a tract that should interest you—a rare tract in praise of tobacco. It is dated 1665 and it deals with the pestilence. The price is $14."

The dusty little book was called "A brief treatise of the Nature, Causes, Signs, Preservation from and Cure of the Pestilence." The author was given as "W. Kemp, Mr. of Arts." The passage about tobacco which came among a list of devices for purifying the air, said eloquently:

"The American Silver-weed, or Tobacco, is very excellent for this Purpose, and an excellent Defence against bad Air, being smoked in a Pipe, either by itself, or with Nutmegs shred, and Rawseeds mixed with it, especially if it be nosed; for it cleanseth the Air, and choketh, suppresseth and disperseth any venemous Vapor; it hath singular and contrary effects; it is good to warm one being cold, and will cool one being hot.

"All Ages, all Sexes, all Constitutions, young and old, Men and Women, the sanguine, the cholerick, the melancholy, the plegmatick, take it without any manifest Inconvenience; it abates Hunger, and yet will get one a good stomach; it is agreeable with Mirth or Sadness, with Feasting and with Fasting; it will make one Rest that wants Sleep, and will Keep one waking that is drowsie."—*Detroit Journal.*

Riker Repeats.

A good part of the success of the Wm. B. Riker & Son Company of New York is due to their belief that large investments of capital bring correspondingly large profits.

About two years ago they installed a fine "Innovation" fountain in one of their drug stores. This proved such a trade winner that in a few months they ordered a second and a third for other stores under their charge.

"Nothing succeeds like success," and having found the direct highway to profitable soda water selling, Messrs. Riker & Son have now further testified to their faith in the "Innovation" by placing an order with the American Soda Fountain Company for an "Innovation" fountain of large size, to be specially built for their Sixth avenue and Twenty-third street store in New York. The order was placed through J. H. Fredericks, the genial and popular representative of the American Soda Fountain Company.

This magnificent apparatus will cost $20,000. The dispensing counter will be 36 feet long, built of Pavonazzo or Rose Sienna Marble, trimmed with onyx, and with onyx pilasters having solid bronze bases and bronze capitals. The slabs of both the dispensing counter and of the display section are to be of Mexican onyx from the quarries of the New Pedrara Onyx Company, from which come large blocks of the choicest onyx of wonderful coloring and perfect soundness.

The display, or wall section, with its large French plate beveled mirrors, its gleaming onyx, with electrical illumination revealing the rich colors of the art glass and of the fine paintings above the mirrors, will be indeed a marvel of beauty. The refrigerator at the base of the wall section is to be of white Italian and Pavonazzo marble, relieved by onyx trimmings, and with silver-plated door frames enclosing panels of fine French plate glass. The refrigerator is thoroughly insulated and equipped for cooling and storage purposes.

The mechanism of the fountain—its working parts—of draft tubes, coolers, syrup jars, work-boards, etc., embody all that is latest and best in the soda fountain construction of the American Soda Fountain Company.

Sample Needles Sent Free to Physicians at the Request of the Druggist.

The Randall-Faichney Company, the makers of the Pyrotometer and other lines of standard clinical thermometers, have moved their offices from the second floor to much more commodious and convenient ones on the fifth floor of the Sudbury Building, Boston. This puts them in close proximity to their assembling and testing rooms, which occupy the sixth floor of the same building.

This progressive firm are also manufacturers of high-grade hypodermic goods of every description, and for years have made a specialty of marketing the R. & B. hypodermic needle, which they claim to be decidedly better than any other hypodermic needle on the market, in that it is tested and guaranteed not to leak, not to break, and from some other claims they make with reference to the sharpness of the point, one would think that professional hypodermic injections were a pleasure.

In this connection they are making a special offer to supply the best professional customers of our readers with samples of this needle, if the druggists will send them the names of the ten such doctors as they wish favored in this way.

In that the R. & B. needle is so thoroughly guaranteed, it would indicate that it is a profitable adjunct for any druggist to handle.

What Yields the Druggists the Greatest Profit?

A personal friend of the corner druggist dropped in, and as he lit a cigar at the counter he looked about the store and remarked:

"Lots of things in a drug-store stock, ain't there?"

"Yes," answered the owner, with a smile. "But there isn't a stupendous profit now in most of them."

"Used to be more in drugs, didn't there?"

"Yes."

"What pays you best to handle nowadays?"

"Well," replied the druggist, "you'd probably laugh if I said View and Comic Post Cards, wouldn't you?"

"No, I wouldn't; because I happen to know some one up in the office of the biggest manufacturer and importer in the world."

"Foreign firm?"

"Foreign nothing. It's the Souvenir Post Card Company, in New York City—No. 50 Franklin street, I think, is the address."

"Why, that's the company I buy of!"

"So much the better for you. That company is It, all right, and I know it."

"Well, I make good money handling their lines, that's straight enough. They help a chap to make sales, too. It pays to have a lot of people visiting the store. I constantly make new business friends by it."

"You're right there, but I'm surprised that selling Souvenir Post Cards is such a profitable branch."

"It is, when you buy of the Souvenir Post Card Company," and the druggist had sold his friend to the tune of $1.15 before he went out of the store!

Other druggists can do as well.

California Tours.

The Southern Railway offers two high class tours to and through California and return under personal escort from Washington, the tours being in charge of an agent whose frequent trips over the entire route enable him to describe with interesting detail every feature pertaining thereto either while traveling or at stopover points. Opportunity to see the National Capital with its diplomatic, social or legislative functions two days at New Orleans, one day at San Antonio, one at El Paso to see Juarez, Old Mexico; then California from Redlands to San Francisco in the green season, when it is most attractive in climate and flora; the California coast line, with its exquisite marine views; old missions and an infinity of interesting detail. The return is through Salt Lake, Colorado, and Chicago, with appropriate stops. Tickets may be purchased from eastern points for round trip, joining the tour at Washington. Apply to Southern Railway offices, 271 and 1185 Broadway. Alexander S. Thweatt, Eastern Passenger agent.

Thweatt's Snowstorm.

Alexander Southern Thweatt's snowstorm arrived at the precise moment of the departure of the Palm Limited for Miami, Palm Beach, Aiken, Augusta, Nassau, Havana, Savannah, Jacksonville, Ormond and St. Augustine, on Monday. I was inveigled into going to Jersey City to inspect the new train, and found a St. Regis on trucks, says Victor Smith in the New York *Press* for January 10. Too fine for my blood—now that everybody must pay. Thweatt took as much pride in that train as if it had been a new baby on Washington Heights—the coldest part of New York. Male passengers gave a satisfied grunt, and the females said "Ah!" This is the train that arrives at Jacksonville and St. Augustine on time.

The New United States Pharmacopœia

makes many changes in the strength of drugs and preparations, reducing some, increasing others as much as double. The law recognizes the current U. S. Pharmacopœia as the standard. To avoid accidents and damage suits on the one hand, and puzzling lack of results on the other, both the druggist and doctor must follow the same standard. As a convenient pocket reminder of these changes, the importance of which must be at once obvious to every physician and pharmacist, Messrs. Lea Brothers & Co., the medical publishers, of 706-8-10 Sansom street, Philadelphia, and 111 Fifth avenue, New York, have issued for free distribution a carefully prepared leaflet giving an alphabetical list of the important changes. The strength of each preparation listed is given as in both the old and the new U. S. P.

To aid in preventing untoward or negative results in the use of powerful drugs this leaflet will prove handy and valuable.

A postal card request will bring a copy to any physician, druggist, student or nurse.

A Metal Edge Box for Mailing Purposes.

We call the attention of our readers to the advertisement of the National Metal Edge Box Company, of Eighth and Willow streets, Philadelphia, appearing in this issue. The box advertised is not only quite strong enough for the purpose, but is sightly, and is sold at a moderate price. Many retail druggists who have occasion to mail samples of their own manufacture could use these boxes to advantage. In writing the concern please mention the American Druggist.

A Notable Catalogue.

We have received the annual price list and catalogue for 1906 of Whitall Tatum Company, manufacturer of druggists', chemists' and perfumers' glassware and druggists' sundries, 46 Barclay street, New York. The firm has purchased the business of Meinecke & Co., of New York, and the consolidation of this business with its own has enabled the Whitall Tatum Company to add a number of new and desirable articles to its line of druggists' sundries and hospital and sickroom specialties. The price-list forms a valuable reference catalogue for pharmacists, and remains the handsomest publication of its kind.

Druggists who are looking for a reliable, ethical article which will give satisfaction to patrons and will bring renewal orders should write to Hudson & Co., New York City, for full information concerning Lythol. This is an antiseptic lotion which has a variety of uses, which gives satisfaction to the physician and to the patient and which is marketed on terms which leave a very substantial margin of profit for the retailer. Liberal inducements are offered to retailers by the manufacturer.

Hints to Buyers.

Machine-cut prescription corks are the specialty of Justus Brauer & Son, of 248 North Front street, Philadelphia. First-class corks of full count can be expected from this old reliable house.

A special compliment for Gilpin, Langdon & Co., of Baltimore, is conveyed in the fact that the last revision of the United States Pharmacopœia contains most of the assayed drugs placed upon the American market by that house 20 years ago. A price list of the line may be had upon application.

Our readers are invited to specify the Lanolines marketed by Victor Koechl & Co., of New York, which are to be recognized by the "Dartring" trademark. Their Lanoline "Liebreich" and Adeps Lanae "B. J. D." are official in both the United States and British Pharmacopœias.

Progressive druggists will note the clever advertising of the Rubberset Shaving Brush, running in this paper. By addressing Rubberset Brush Company, of 61 Ferry street, Newark, N. J., and asking for catalogue K, much valuable information on the subject of shaving brushes may be obtained.

We invite the attention of our readers to the new advertisement of Runkel Brothers, of New York, which appears in this issue. This house has made a specialty of its soluble chocolate for soda fountain use, and this, together with other items of its line, should make its announcements to the trade of both interest and profit to our readers.

Cudahy's Nutritive Beef Extract is sold only by the drug trade. It is indorsed by thousands of the leading druggists as one of the best sellers on the market. This extract has a fine flavor, is uniform in quality and is guaranteed to keep in any climate. The extract is scientifically prepared and is claimed to be "soluble beef," containing all the nutriment of fresh, lean meat. For literature and quotations address Cudahy Packing Company, Omaha, Neb., mentioning the AMERICAN DRUGGIST.

Lautier Fils Olive Oil is continually increasing in favor, and the imports show a remarkable growth during the last year. This oil received two grand prizes in one year, one at St. Louis and the other at Vienna, besides many gold medals and first awards in previous years. This oil remains the only one in the market which is placed before the public by the firm which grows the olives, presses the oil and fills the original containers as they are sold. George Lueders & Co. are the sole agents for the wholesale trade.

The old-fashioned remedy for coughs and colds which still stands high in popular esteem is licorice. At this season of the year we take pleasure in calling the attention of our readers to the National Licorice Company, manufacturer of Y. & S. licorice, Scudder, and the M. & R. licorice specialties. It also puts up the powdered extract and the powdered root in convenient packages for the drug trade. Our readers may obtain a supply of good advertising matter for counter and window display by addressing the advertiser and stating which of the brands are used.

The Lock Stub Check System.

The new advertisement of the Lock Stub Check Company will be found in this issue and will no doubt be interesting to our readers, who are preparing for the forthcoming soda water season. This is one of the best systems we know for getting all of the profit obtained through soda water sales, and we take pleasure in commending it to the consideration of our readers.

One Thousand Dollars Reward.

This reward is offered by Mariani & Co., of 52 West Fifteenth street, New York, for information leading to the arrest of any person spreading malicious falsehoods, libelous or defamatory reports intended to discredit the old established reputation of the house of Mariani or of the integrity of Vin Mariani. They state in the most positive manner that Vin Mariani is not a cocaine preparation, as has been clearly shown by numerous tests at the hands of pure food commissioners, boards of health and others; and any statement to the contrary will be combatted by criminal prosecution as suggested by the above offer of a reward. This tonic cocoa of wine has been on the market for 50 years and has met with practically universal endorsement by physicians.

Profitable and Satisfactory to Handle.

The line of mixed paints and varnishes, manufactured by the Buckeye Paint & Varnish Company, of Toledo, Ohio, is a profitable one for the druggist to handle, for it pays a liberal margin of profit and gives satisfaction to the user. This company has behind it 31 years' of success in its special field, and it guarantees every gallon of paint that it sends out. The paint is ready for use without any further preparation, gives complete satisfaction and is durable and economical. The manufacturer will be glad to send our readers interesting advertising matter for free distribution. For sample color cards, etc., address the Buckeye Paint & Varnish Company, Toledo, Ohio, mentioning the AMERICAN DRUGGIST.

1874-1906.

Thirty years ago codliver oil had to be forced down the patient's throat. Invalids couldn't take it, and the children wouldn't. But the doctors prescribed it and it had to be taken. Yet it cured people, for it has ever been the greatest of all tissue-builders and reconstructives.

About 1874 came the change. It was then that Scott's Emulsion first appeared. The days of dreading the dose ceased. Codliver oil taking became easy. The palate was pleased, the stomach was satisfied, the patient prospered and the doctor was delighted. Druggists everywhere commenced to order the old remedy in its new dress. And from those early days began the enormous demand of to-day for codliver oil.

Scott & Bowne are responsible, to a great extent, for the present extensive use of codliver oil either plain or as an emulsion. They first made it palatable, first made it popular, first extensively told of its therapeutic value, first brought out a permanent, pleasant emulsion of the oil with hypophosphites.

Thirty years have passed and, notwithstanding the countless thousands of imitations, Scott's Emulsion is known to be the standard preparation and the stable and reliable emulsion.

A Good Advertising Idea.

The cold weather which we have been having of late offers a suggestion for a valuable advertising idea. Everybody wants to know what the temperature is. The druggist can make sure that his advertisements will be read in the cold weather by distributing to his prospective patrons the attractive advertising thermometers, made by the Taylor Brothers Company, of Rochester, who are among the largest thermometer makers in the world. We illustrate herewith one of these advertising thermometers of which they make a large variety, and which they sell at a very moderate price. They have barometers also and can furnish either the barometers or thermometers, or the two combined on suitable advertising cards, at a very low cost. For instance, they can furnish 100 thermometers, already printed in one color at from $7.50 to $20.00, or in lots of 1,000 at a relatively much cheaper price. They also furnish wood thermometers, either in natural finish or white enamel, printed to suit the needs of customers, at prices ranging from $10.00 to $30.00 per hundred. For further information write the Taylor Brothers Company, Rochester, for a copy of their pamphlet on the profitable uses of advertising thermometers.

"Squibb's Materia Medica."

From E. R. Squibb & Sons, manufacturing chemists, New York, with offices and stockrooms at 78 to 80 Beekman street, Borough of Manhattan, and laboratories and works at 24 to 42 Doughty street, Borough of Brooklyn, we have received a well-bound volume of 394 pages, exclusive of a 14 page introductory chapter, dealing with the Squibb line of products, as well as the non-official and newer remedies which are used in medicine to-day. While the book is primarily intended to serve as a list of prices, it also constitutes a valuable work of reference in which may be found all the more important data concerning the nature, source, physical and therapeutical properties, doses, antidotes, etc., of the drugs recorded. The names of the articles enumerated are arranged in alphabetical order, the titles employed being those in most common use. The English name is followed by the chemical term, indicating the composition of the substance, while the doses of articles official in U. S. Pharmacopœia viii are given according to that authority and the doses of other products are in accordance with those given by recognized authorities.

A departure for the house of E. R. Squibb & Sons is found in the introduction of compressed tablets. Tablet triturates or moulded tablets are not favored by E. R. Squibb & Sons, though exception is made in a few cases where the moulded form of tablet offers some mechanical advantage.

The establishment of a laboratory for the manufacture of digestive ferments and animal products also marks a departure for the firm of E. R. Squibb & Sons, who are now prepared to supply diastase, hæmoglobin, meat peptone, ox-gall, pancreatin, pepsin, rennin, suprarenal glands dried and thyreoid glands under the well-known Squibb guarantee of purity.

Squibb's Materia Medica is published at the beginning of each year in a new and carefully revised edition and constitutes an invaluable book of reference—a veritable *Vade Mecum* for the dispensing pharmacist *Verb. Sap.*

"Making Business."

A great many dealers in post cards have discovered that they can create new business in that line by getting out a set of local views and advertising them to the people of their own town and vicinity.

The way to go about it is to have good glossy prints prepared from excellent negatives of the views desired, about 6½ x 8½ inches, or not less than 5 x 7 inches.

The "sollo finish" is the desirable one, as yielding the best effects in subsequent processes. These prints, mailed to a concern like the Souvenir Post Card Company of New York City (their street address is 50-52 Franklin street) will do the business. Nothing more is necessary except an order for such quantity as the dealer believes he can probably dispose of. There is, of course, a minimum number below which it doesn't pay to go, if cards are to yield a fair profit. In some varieties, it is not possible to order less than 2,000 of a subject; in others 500 constitutes the smallest "wise" order. Gelatin cards give fine effects in one color when but a few choice views are desired. The "Green Graphure" process cards, especially offered by the Souvenir Post Card Company, are cheaper, though elegantly printed in an art shade of green ink. These cards have achieved a decided hit with the trade, and the company offers samples and prices to any one interested. Its colored cards represent, it claims, the supreme point of excellence in the view post card. The "made-to-order" view card gives some special advantages appreciated by all dealers, and the Souvenir Post Card Company claims to be "it" in making them. Samples of all will be sent on request.

The R. Hoehn Company states that the Red Cross Aseptic Clinical Thermometer, which it is now advertising, has proved a big success. These are diffierent from the ordinary clinical thermometers that have been on the market so long, and being made with the accuracy that the R. Hoehn Company is noted for, it is easy to understand why the repeat orders are pouring in for them.

Why Did He Do Himself All This Damage?

We sold a customer a small bill, writes John A. Walker, vice-president of Joseph Dixon Crucible Company, and when due it was not promptly paid.

We reminded him by statement, and no answer.

We wrote a letter and still no answer.

We, after giving him notice, sent a draft to his local bank which was returned, marked "Refused." We called his attention to this by letter and not a word.

We then wrote a friendly letter explaining a forced collection was the only alternative and would be used in case he did not pay by a given date.

The given date passed, and no response. It then went to his local attorney and immediately thereafter he sent his check.

Now, why did he do it this way?

His method is understandable if he had made up his mind never to pay; but intending, some day, to pay, as he finally did, why did he go—

First, through the process of disgrace with us?

Second, of disgrace with his local bank?

Third, of disgrace with his local attorney?

This we don't understand.

Post Card Display.

One of the most important features in handling post cards is their proper display. Other things being equal, the man who makes the best displays sells the largest number of cards. The American News Company, of New York, manufactures what it calls the "paragon post card" display stand, which is certainly one of the best on the market. It is made entirely of gun metal and beautifully lettered, so that the finish will last a lifetime. The stand will hold over 2,000 cards, exposing to view 72 different kinds, and still takes up little more than a square foot of counter space. The stand is illustrated herewith.

Few lines are so profitable in proportion to the investment as post cards, and druggists will find that a well-selected stock well displayed will prove a very profitable investment. The investment will be profitable not alone directly but also indirectly in bringing additional patrons to the store. The American News Company is making an offer on another page which will enable the druggist to put in a satisfactory stock on very easy terms indeed, and such of our readers as are not already stocked up on this line or as may not have a satisfactory display stand should write the American News Company, mentioning the AMERICAN DRUGGIST, for particulars regarding this offer.

Misunderstood.

"My husband is so poetic," said one lady to another on a trolley car. Whereupon an honest looking woman, with a big market basket at her feet, interjected with "Excuse me, mum, but have you ever tried rubbing his joints with mustard oil?"

The Romance of the Drug Trade.

Probably no other commercial field has so much of romance, so much of world-wide interest, as has the drug trade. The little corner drug store has gathered within its walls the products of all quarters of the globe. The importing druggist is coming to deal more and more directly with the original sources of supply, and firms like P. E. Anderson & Co., of 7 Gold street, New York, have agents in every crude drug market in the world filling their orders and keeping them in touch with conditions. We present herewith a reproduction of a photograph taken in Egypt for this firm, showing the process of selecting the choice grades of Alexandria senna, which are imported by Anderson & Co., direct. The bales in the background, bearing a diamond A mark, are ready to be shipped direct from Alexandria to P. E. Anderson & Co., whose customers get the benefit of this direct dealing without having to pay tribute to London drug brokers.

A large proportion of our crude drugs reach New York through London, but P. E. Anderson & Co. have succeeded in establishing direct touch with the original market for many of the drugs which are largely consumed in this country. On buchu leaves, for instance, this firm has been enabled to obtain

Native Experts in Alexandria, Egypt, Selecting Choice Grades of Senna for Direct Shipment to P. E. Anderson & Co., of New York.

direct shipments from the Cape of very handsome and high grade long buchu leaves. It will be remembered that these leaves were practically out of the market during the late unpleasantness with the Boers, but since the settlement of that trouble the supplies have gradually increased until now the market has gotten into a normal condition. P. E. Anderson, the head of the firm, was for many years associated with A. E. Andrus & Co., who in turn succeeded to the importing and exporting business of Lazell, Dalley & Co. when that firm retired from the jobbing trade to devote itself exclusively to the manufacture of perfumery. The connections of Messrs. Anderson & Co. are therefore not matters of recent date, but have been established either by themselves or their predecessors by years of careful study of market conditions.

This firm does not devote itself exclusively to imported drugs, but is a large buyer of drugs of domestic origin, both for distribution in the United States and for exportation. Druggists and manufacturers who wish to deal with first hands should correspond with P. E. Anderson & Co. before making contracts, as they will find this firm in a position to offer exceptional bargains on round lots of crude drugs of high quality.

Eusoma (Echinacea compound) is a perfected form of Echinacea, adapted to both internal and external administration, which is being extensively and persistently advertised in the medical press. As the remedy possesses great intrinsic merit and is a perfect antiseptic, alterative and antipurulent, all prescription pharmacists should place this preparation in stock in order to be able to promptly supply the demand which is sure to be created for it. There is no danger that Eusoma will become dead stock. For literature address the manufacturer, the Eusoma Pharmacal Company, Cincinnati.

Merck's New Price List.

Merck's Price List for 1906 has just been received from the publishers, Merck & Co., New York. It gives the wholesale price of chemicals, alkaloids, new remedies and specialties, and calls attention prominently to three winter specialties, on which the druggist should specify "Merck's" in ordering. These are beechwood creosote, U. S. P. VIII; codeine sulphate, which "dissolves instantly," and terpin hydrate, which "gives a perfect solution." The price list is of handy size and is printed from a very readable font of type, condensed gothic caps being used for titles, while the price figures are in a similar large faced type. If any of our readers has been overlooked in the distribution of this price list, they will thank us for the reminder.

Makes Money While You Sleep.

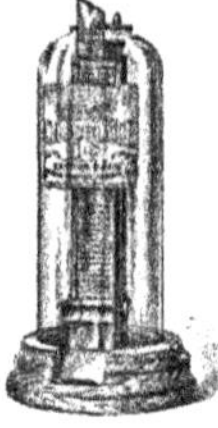

We illustrate herewith a salesman who neither eats, drinks nor smokes, who does not believe in "shorter hours," who works Sundays and holidays, and who works on a commission basis entirely, charging a very small commission for services rendered. This salesman is the automatic vendor of the National Vending Machine Company, 32 South Canal street, Chicago. It is loaned to a retailer on terms which insure its being very profitable. For full particulars address the National Vending Machine Company, 32 South Canal street, Chicago, mentioning the AMERICAN DRUGGIST.

The Magnet of Trade.

Perhaps the most notable feature in the development of modern retail business has been the inventing and perfecting of devices and schemes to draw people into the store. The more progressive the merchant, the more he will expend upon a trade magnet. There are plate glass windows and cases costing small fortunes, and "bargain sales" where goods are sold at actual loss; there are many famous proprietary articles sold at cost; all these just to attract customers. The man who does not draw new people every day is surely falling behind. No matter what it costs, customers must be attracted.

The greatest trade magnet for the drug store happens to be also the greatest profit maker. This is a modern soda fountain, generally conceded to be a necessity to the popular store to-day.

The wonderful improvement in the soda fountain, both in architectural beauty and in cleanliness, makes it the most ornamental and thoroughly pleasing part of the store. It pleases every sense and appeals to every possible buyer in the strongest kind of way.

But while it is making the store popular it is also coining money. Managers of the largest drug stores in Boston and New York testify that there is no department of their stores so profitable in direct returns, reckoned by the square foot of floor space used, as the modern soda fountain. The same is true of small drug stores. Notice how frequently that adjective "modern" creeps in. This is necessary because our commendation of the soda fountain as a trade magnet of the highest pulling power applies especially to the latest development of the fountain.

One of the latest developments is called The Innovation, and is made by the American Soda Fountain Company. All progressive business men will enjoy noting the points of attractiveness and economy this "Innovation" fountain has to distinguish it.

A line to the American Soda Fountain Company will bring a large portfolio of views of handsome fountains, as well as exact figures of the profits produced by the "Innovation" in several department stores.

The American Soda Fountain Company can give applicants the latest news about soda sundries, too. It pays to keep abreast of the times on these matters.

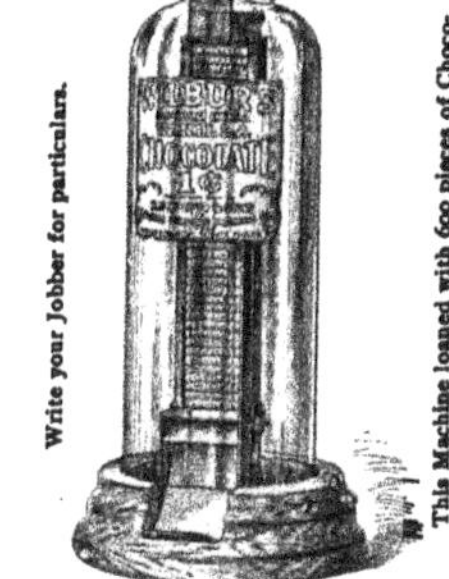

In Memoriam.

A very clever little pamphlet with comic lines and illustrations is issued under the title of "In Memoriam" by the Gillette Safety Razor Company. The lines are in memoriam of the barber's pole, whose reign has been cut short by the introduction of the Gillette Safety Razor. This razor is provided with thin blades, which are so inexpensive that they may be thrown away when dull. The razor can be handled as freely as an ordinary table knife and shaving with it ceases to be a terror and becomes a pleasure. It is simple in construction and cannot be put together wrong. Its use saves time, trouble and suffering. These razors form a profitable side line for the druggist, who will be furnished an ample supply of these little booklets for distribution. If you have not seen this booklet write to the Gillette Safety Razor Company, Boston, Mass., for a supply, mentioning the AMERICAN DRUGGIST.

An Unprecedented Demand for Post Cards.

The American News Company reports a very large response to its special offer, as contained in its advertisement on page 20. It gives a total of 950 cards as a premium with each Paragon stand, and inasmuch as the stand itself sells for $10, dealers will do well to take advantage of this exceptional opportunity for starting in the post card business at a very small outlay of money. Dealers who are already handling post cards will appreciate even more the value of this special proposition.

Although the American News Company is headquarters for everything pertaining to post cards, it makes a specialty of publishing cards for dealers with their (the dealers') own imprint. The advantage of this to the dealer is obvious. It enables him to provide his own photographs, thereby giving him absolute control over those subjects, as the American News Company will not publish cards from the same photographs for any one else.

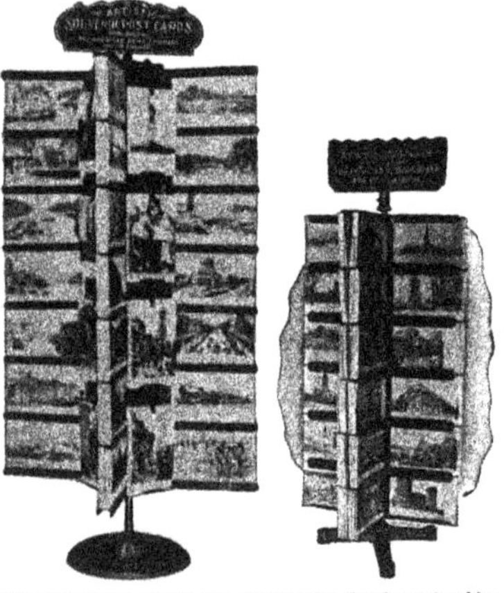

Then, again, the dealer's name and address appearing as publisher on cards of such high quality attracts the most favorable attention to that dealer's establishment. As the cards are mailed all over the country, so is the dealer's name carried, and it is not unusual for a dealer to receive inquiries from people located thousands of miles from his place of business, due to the wide circulation of these high grade cards.

The stands here shown are supplied with their cards.

Full particulars, including samples, will be sent you upon request by the American News Company, 39-41 Chambers street, New York.

Vegetable Colors Which Comply with Pure Food Laws.

The food laws, both Federal and State, are now becoming more and more an important factor to be considered by every manufacturer of food products. Recently the laws passed about colors have been very severe, and manufacturers of candy, extracts, syrups and fruit products must be very careful not to use any but vegetable colors in their products. For many years it has been difficult to produce colors of an absolutely vegetable origin low enough in price to enable the manufacturer to use them. Many liquid colors have been placed on the market. The guarantees given in most instances are not reliable and are dangerous to the consumer, because very often the words "non-poisonous," "healthful," or even "vegetable," are used by manufacturers, particularly in Europe, without giving an actually reliable guarantee as to the origin. The reading of the guarantee on the label is so framed that in most cases this guarantee would not hold the manufacturer before the law, and the consumer would have no redress. George Lueders & Co. now place before the public a line of vegetable colors in powder which are soluble in water and which have been tested by renowned chemists in this country and by different food law commissions and have in all instances been pronounced absolutely vegetable, or, in the language of the food commissioners, "legal." These colors may therefore be used with entire safety. Moreover, George Lueders & Co. stand ready to take up any case in which the vegetable origin of these colors should be doubted or attacked.

Elixir of Enzymes.

Elixir of Enzymes is the name given by Armour & Co. to a palatable and highly efficient preparation of the soluble enzymes. It is an aid to digestion and is found of value in diseases of the alimentary tract. Elixir of Enzymes is a splendid vehicle for potassium iodide, potassium bromide and the salicylates. The patient's digestive apparatus is saved a great deal of distress by giving these chemicals in the Elixir of Enzymes. A favorite prescription is to make a saturated solution of potassium iodide in Elixir of Enzymes, using enough to give the desired dose and making a junket out of lukewarm milk, which is very acceptable. Large doses of potassium iodide may be given for long periods in this way. Elixir of Enzymes is put in 1-pint and 5-pint bottles and 1-gallon jugs.

Pond's Extract Company Protects Prices.

On January 21 the Pond's Extract Company issued a new price-list and increased its discounts to the jobbing trade from the former rate of 12½ per cent. to 10 and 5 per cent. In its new order form, which must be signed by each purchaser, there is a clause protecting retail prices which reads as follows: "The purchaser of this order hereby agrees not to sell nor permit the goods to be sold at retail at less than list retail prices, except that Pond's Extract may be sold at not less than 21 cents, 42 cents, 83 cents and $1.45 for 25 cent, 50 cent, $1 and $1.75 sizes, respectively."

No order will be accepted which deviates from these terms. The year 1905 was the most successful of the 60 years of success which this company has known and the company by its new terms indicates its appreciation of the co-operation of the drug trade of the United States, which has made this success possible, and hopes that this co-operation will be extended in quite as full measure during 1906.

An interesting and unique advertisement has been designed by the Pacific Coast Borax Company, which is sending through the country the famous Twenty Mule Team, which was formerly used to haul borax out from Death Valley. This company is making liberal offers to the retail drug trade to stock its line of specialties, which are good sellers and which offer a liberal margin of profit. A list of special discounts can be obtained by addressing the Pacific Coast Borax Company, 100 William street, New York City.

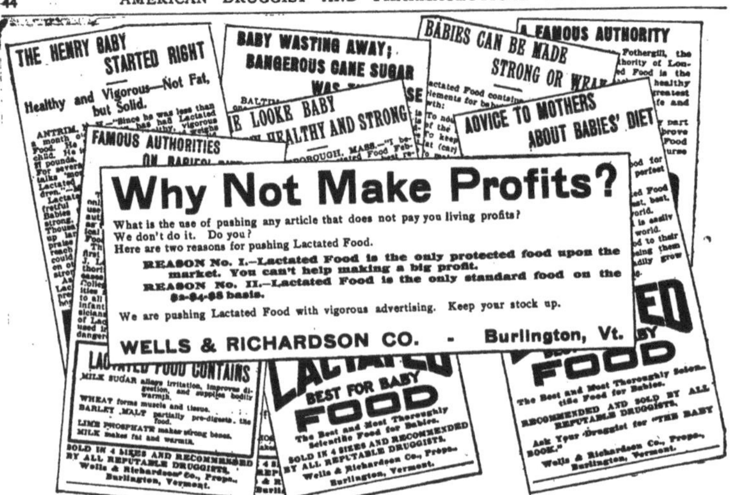

AMERICAN CAN COMPANY

Manufacturers of

Standard Druggist Tinware

We carry in stock a **full assortment** of **Miller, Taite, Gill** and **Norton** styles of Boxes. These Boxes have an **established reputation** among **Druggists**. **Seamless Boxes** of all sizes, styles and designs carried in stock by every leading jobber in the country.

Principal Offices: **New York, Baltimore, Chicago, San Francisco.**

LOCAL SALES OFFICES

Boston, Philadelphia, Buffalo, Detroit, Pittsburg, Richmond, Atlanta, Cleveland, Toledo, Cincinnati, St. Louis, New Orleans, Kansas City, Denver, Los Angeles, Portland, Seattle, St. Paul, Milwaukee, Havana

---

A The STANDARD PRESORIPTION -CORKS- ...OF... THE WORLD B

ARMSTRONG CORK CO.

There is a Sparkle and Dash to a Drug Store equipped with

Andrews Steel Rod Furniture

that makes it attractive to customers and secures and holds their trade—Cheerful people, the kind who spend money, like cheerful surroundings and go where they are to be found. Andrews Steel Rod Furniture for Drug Stores is cheerful, bright and attractive—Cleanly, convenient, inexpensive—The modern equipment for Drug Stores—Send for Catalogue.

The A. H. Andrews Co., 174 Wabash Ave., Chicago

SAL HEPATICA

The Original Effervescing

SALINE LAXATIVE, URIC ACID SOLVENT and ELIMINANT

A Combination of Tonic, Alterative and Laxative Salts

similar to the celebrated Bitter Waters of Bohemia, fortified by the addition of Lithium and Sodium Phosphates.

$2.00, $4.80 and $10.20 per doz.
All Jobbers.

BRISTOL-MYERS CO.
Manufacturing Chemists
277-279 Greene Ave.
BROOKLYN, - - - NEW YORK.

ORIGINAL PACKAGE PRICES.

It should be understood that the prices quoted in this column are strictly those current in the wholesale market, and that higher prices are paid for retail lots. The quality of goods frequently necessitates a considerable range of prices.

Drugs, Chemicals, &c.

Acetanilid	lb.	.23 @ .24
Acetate of Lime:		
Brown	100 lb.	1.80 @ 1.85
Gray	100 lb.	2.35 @ 2.40
Acetone	lb.	.15½ @ .16
Acid:		
Acetic Com'l	100 lb.	2.60 @ 2.75
Acetic C. P.	lb.	.21 @ .25
Acetic, Glacial		.30 @ .33½
Aquafortis, 36°	lb.	.03½ @ .04½
" 40°	lb.	.. @ .06½
Benzoic, Ger	lb.	.32½ @ .33
" Eng	oz.	.10 @ .10½
Boric, Cryst	lb.	.10 @ .10½
powd	lb.	.10 @ .10½
Carbol. cryst., blk	lb.	.14 @ .15
lb. bottles	lb.	.20 @ .22
Chrysophanic		2.50 @ 2.65
Citric, dom	lb.	.33 @ .33½
" Sicilian	lb.	.. @ ..
Gallic	lb.	.53 @ .55
Muriatic C. P.	lb.	.07 @ .09
Nitric C. P.	lb.	.09½ @ .11½
Oxalic, English	lb.	.05½ @ .05¾
Phosphoric	lb.	.19 @ .21½
Picric	lb.	.33 @ .35
Pyrogallic	lb.	1.60 @ 1.70
Salicylic	lb.	.31 @ .31
Sulphuric, 66°	lb.	.01½ @ .02
Tartaric, crystals	lb.	.27½ @ .28½
powdered	lb.	.28½ @ .29½
Tannic, cryst	lb.	.54 @ .65
Alcohol, grain	gal.	2.49 @ 2.51
Molasses		2.47 @ 2.49
wood, 95-97%	gal.	.70 @ .73
Aloin	lb.	.45 @ .50
Alum, Lump	100 lb.	1.75 @ 1.85
Ground	100 lb.	1.85 @ 1.95
Ammon. carb		.07½ @ .09½
" bromide, bulk		.20 @ .21
" iodide, bulk		4.75 @ 4.80
Aniline Oil		.09 @ .09½
Salt		.08½ @ .08½
Antipyrine (New)	oz.	.. @ .18
Arrowroot, Bermuda	lb.	.38 @ .40
St. Vincent, in bbl	lb.	.05½ @ .08
Arsenic: Red Saxon	lb.	.06½ @ .07
White	lb.	.10 @ .12
Balm of Gilead Buds	lb.	.35 @ .38
Balsam Copaiba, Cent. Amer	lb.	.. @ .30
Para	lb.	.30 @ .37
Fir, Canada	gal.	3.10 @ 3.20
Fir, Oregon	gal.	.70 @ .80
Peru	lb.	1.00 @ 1.05
Tolu	lb.	.20 @ .22
Bark, Angostura	lb.	.38 @ .40
Buckthorn	lb.	.05 @ .05½
Cascara Sag	lb.	.06½ @ .10
Cascarilla	lb.	.10 @ .14
Cotton root	lb.	.08½ @ .10
Cramp	lb.	.07 @ .09
Elm, select	lb.	.19 @ .20
Pine, white	lb.	.05 @ .08
Prickly Ash	lb.	.12 @ .15
Sassafras	lb.	.10 @ .12
Soap—whole	lb.	.05 @ .05½
Crushed	lb.	.05½ @ .08
Wild Cherry	lb.	.05½ @ .10
Bismuth, citrate	lb.	1.75 @ 1.80
" ammon cit	lb.	1.85 @ 1.90
" subnit	blk.	1.50 @ 1.55
" subcarb	lb.	1.75 @ 1.80
" subgallate	lb.	1.85 @ 1.90
Bleaching Powder, Eng		.01½ @ .01½
German B		.01½ @ .01½
Domestic		.01 @ .01½
Blue Vitriol	lb.	.05½ @ .06
Borax, Refined	lb.	.07½ @ .07¾
powd. conc	lb.	.07½ @ .08
crystals	lb.	.07½ @ .07½
Brimstone, crude 2d	ton	22.00 @ ..
Brucine, bulk	lb.	.. @ .50
Burgundy Pitch	lb.	.04 @ .04½
Cacao Butter, blk		.28 @ .30
" " 12 lb. boxes		.34 @ .35
Caffeine	lb.	.. @ 2.65
Calcium hypophosphite	lb.	.60 @ .64
Cantharides, Chinese	lb.	.52½ @ .58
" powd	lb.	.54 @ .56
Russian, whole	lb.	1.25 @ 1.30
Cassia Buds	lb.	.20 @ .20½
Castor Oil, No. 1, bbl	lb.	.11 @ .12
" " No. 1, cases	lb.	.11½ @ .12½
" " No. 3, bbl	lb.	.10½ @ .11½
" " No 3, cases	lb.	.10½ @ .11½
Caustic Soda	100 lb.	1.70 @ 1.75
Chalk, Eng. Precip., bulk	lb.	.06 @ ...
Chloral Hydrate, crystals, bulk	lb.	... @ 0.23
crusts, blk	lb.	... @ 0.93
Chloroform, bulk	lb.	.25 @ .30
Cinchonidine Sulph	oz.	.12 @ .15
Cocaine Muriate	oz.	3.25 @ 3.50
Codeine Sulph	oz.	3.20 @ 3.40
Cod Liver Oil, Norweg	bbl.	25.00 @ 40.00
Newfoundland	bbl.	24.00 @ 25.00
Colocynth, Trieste	lb.	.30 @ .32
Spanish	lb.	.25 @ .28
Copperas, car lots	100 lb.	.47½ @ .52
single bbls	100 lb.	.65 @ .80
Creosote, Beechwood		.83 @ .90
Cream Tartar lb	powd.	.22½ @ .23
Cubeb berries, xx	lb.	.18 @ .20
Powdered	lb.	.11 @ .13
Cutch, bales	lb.	.07½ @ .08
boxes	lb.	.05 @ .05½
Cuttle Bone, Trieste	lb.	.16 @ .16½
French	lb.	.13 @ .13
Jewelers', large	lb.	.70 @ ...
" small	lb.	.40 @ .45
Dextrin	lb.	.05½ @ .08
Divi Divi	ton.	30.00 @ 45.00
Dragon's Bl'd, lump	lb.	.15 @ .18
In reeds	lb.	.50 @ .55
Epsom Salts	100 lb.	.85 @ 1.00
Ergot, German	lb.	.41 @ .43
Spanish	lb.	.45 @ .48
Ergotine, Dom	lb.	4.25 @ 5.00
Flowers, Arnica	lb.	.09 @ .10
Flowers—cont'd		
Calendula	lb.	.28 @ .33
Chamomile, Roman	lb.	.16 @ .22
German	lb.	.15 @ .25
Hungarian	lb.	.09½ @ .11
Insect, open	lb.	.15 @ .17
Half closed	lb.	.26 @ .23
Closed	lb.	.26 @ ..
Powder	lb.	.11 @ .22
Lavender	lb.	.12 @ .13
Select	lb.	.15 @ .20
Saffron, Amer	lb.	1.25 @ ....
Spanish Alicante	lb.	4.75 @ 6.00
" Valencia	lb.	8.00 @ 8.50
Formaldehyde	lb.	.08½ @ .09½
Glauber Salt	per 100 lb.	.50 @ .60
Glycerin, C. P. drums	lb.	.11½ @ .11¾
" cans	lb.	.12½ @ .12¾
Grains of Paradise	lb.	.11½ @ .15
Guarana	lb.	.62 @ .65
Gums: Aloes, Cape		.08 @ .10
" Barbadoes	lb.	.14 @ .16
" Curacoa		.06½ @ .06½
" Socot	lb.	.18 @ .20
Arabic, 1st pkd	lb.	.25 @ .35
" 2d pkd	lb.	.17 @ .23
" sorts	lb.	.06½ @ .11
Asafoetida	lb.	.14 @ .14
Benzoin, Sumatra	lb.	.32 @ .35
Siam	lb.	.90 @ 1.00
Camphor, ref'd. blk	lb.	.94 @ ..
cases	lb.	.94½ @ ..
Chicle	lb.	.36 @ .38
Gamboge	lb.	.85 @ .90
Guaiac	lb.	.19 @ .33
Kino	lb.	.25 @ .28
Mastic	lb.	.46 @ .48
Myrrh	lb.	.23 @ .28
Olibanum	lb.	.06 @ .15
Sandarac	lb.	.14 @ .18
Senegal, pkd	lb.	.11 @ .13
Tragacanth, Aleppo	lb.	.30 @ .65
Tragacanth, Turkey	lb.	.35 @ .80
Haarlem Oil		3.00 @ 3.25
Hypophosphite lime	lb.	.48 @ .50
" potash	lb.	.48 @ .50
" soda	lb.	.48 @ .51
Ichthyol	lb.	4.00 @ 4.25
Indigo	lb.	.90 @ 1.75
Insect Pwd, pure	lb.	.14 @ .25
Iodine, resub		4.15 @ 4.20
Iodoform	lb.	4.40 @ 4.45
Iron citrate, U. S. P	lb.	..... @ .41
" and ammon. cit	lb.	..... @ .33
and ammon. citrate (green scales)		
and quinine citrate	lb.	1.15 @ 1.20
phosphate, scales	lb.	.... @ .38
pyrophosphate, scales	lb.	.... @ .38
quinine and strychnine citrate	lb.	1.65 @ 1.70
Isinglass, Amer	lb.	.75 @ .80
Russian	lb.	4.00 @ 4.10
Juniper Berries	lb.	.04 @ .04½
Lanoline	lb.	.60 @ .65
Leaves: Aconite		.09 @ .10
Belladonna	lb.	.09 @ .11
Buchu, short	lb.	.14 @ .17
" long	lb.	.45 @ .50
Cannabis Indica, tops	lb.	1.00 @ ....
Coca, Truxillo	lb.	.18 @ .19
" Huanuco	lb.	.32 @ .35
Damiana	lb.	.08 @ .10
Digitalis	lb.	.07½ @ .09
Grindelia robusta	lb.	.08 @ .09
Horehound	lb.	.04½ @ .06
Hyoscyamus	lb.	.07 @ .08
Jaborandi	lb.	.11 @ .15
Pulsatilla		.07½ @ .11
Rose, Red	lb.	.65 @ .70
Senna, pkd, whole	lb.	.17 @ .20
Alexandria, natural	lb.	.10 @ .11
garbled and sifted	lb.	.15 @ .16
Tinnevelly	lb.	.06½ @ .14
Alexandria, siftings	lb.	.05½ @ .08
Stramonium	lb.	.08 @ .08½
Uva ursi	lb.	.05½ @ .08
Yerba Santa	lb.	.07 @ .07½
Liquorice—mass	lb.	.08 @ .10
Spanish	lb.	.14 @ .20
Imported mass Spanish	lb.	.19 @ .24
Stick, Calabria	lb.	.23 @ .26
Domestic	lb.	.18½ @ .23½
Lithia, carbonate	lb.	1.50 @ 1.75
" citrate	lb.	1.15 @ 1.25
Lupulin, Ger	lb.	.19 @ .25
Lycopodium	lb.	.51 @ .53
Magnesia, carb	lb.	.12 @ .15
Manna, large flk	lb.	.45 @ .50
Small flake	lb.	.33 @ .35
Menthol, Japanese	lb.	2.20 @ 2.25
Mercurials:		
Blue Pill	lb.	.43 @ .45
Calomel	lb.	.77 @ .79
Corr. Sublim	lb.	.70 @ .72
Mercury and Chalk	lb.	.33 @ .34
Ointment, ½	lb.	.47 @ .48
Ointment, ⅓	lb.	.33 @ .39
Red Precip	lb.	.87 @ .89
White "	lb.	.92 @ .94
Morphine, bulk	oz.	2.25 @ 2.50
Eighths	oz.	2.45 @ 2.50
Moss, Iceland	lb.	.05 @ .06
Irish	lb.	.06½ @ .08
Irish, bleached	lb.	.09½ @ .10
Naphthaline, flake	lb.	.02 @ .02½
Ball	lb.	.... @ .02
Nux Vomica	lb.	.02½ @ .03
Oil, Anise	lb.	1.30 @ 1.35
Almonds, bit, Eng	lb.	5.50 @ 5.75
French	lb.	3.55 @ 3.60
bit., artificial	lb.	.65 @ 1.50
sweet, true	lb.	.37 @ .40
Peach kernels		.19 @ .22
Bay	lb.	2.10 @ 2.25
22 oz. bots	bot.	3.21 @ 3.35
Bergamot	lb.	2.15 @ 2.20
Cajuput	lb.	.50 @ .52
Camphor	lb.	.12 @ .18
Caraway	lb.	1.18 @ 1.40
Cassia 75@80%	lb.	.50 @ .53
Oils—cont'd.		
Cedar, pure	lb.	.60 @ 1.65
red	lb.	.21 @ .25
Citronella	lb.	.40 @ .42
Clove, bud		.85 @ .87½
Copaiba	lb.	.60 @ .70
Coriander	lb.	8.00 @ 11.00
Croton	lb.	.75 @ .80
Cubeb	lb.	.85 @ .90
Eucalyptus	lb.	.40 @ .60
Geranium	lb.	1.60 @ 4.75
Lavender, flowers	lb.	2.00 @ 2.25
Lemon	lb.	.70 @ .71
Lemongrass	lb.	2.90 @ 3.00
Mustard	lb.	4.25 @ 5.25
Myrbane	lb.	.06½ @ .07½
Neroli	lb.	22.00 @ 60.00
Nutmeg	lb.	.80 @ 0.90
Orange, sweet	lb.	2.10 @ 2.30
Orange, bitter	lb.	2.15 @ 2.50
Origanum	lb.	.19 @ .22
Pennyroyal	lb.	1.15 @ 1.25
Peppermint	lb.	2.40 @ 2.50
Cases	lb.	3.10 @ 3.20
Petit, grain, French	lb.	4.00 @ 4.50
" " So. Amer	lb.	1.90 @ ....
Pimento	lb.	1.90 @ 1.90
Rose	oz.	3.50 @ 4.50
Rosemary	lb.	.62½ @ .80
Sandalwood	lb.	3.25 @ 3.50
Sassafras	lb.	.50 @ .55
" Artificial	lb.	.21 @ .25
Safrol		.35 @ .36
Spearmint	lb.	4.75 @ 5.00
Tansy	lb.	3.75 @ 4.00
Thyme		1.00 @ 1.20
Winterg'n, sweet birch		1.65 @ 1.85
" Synthetic	lb.	.37 @ .40
Wood (Chinese)		.08 @ .09
Wormwood		3.25 @ 3.50
Wormseed	lb.	3.00 @ 3.25
Opium, Nat cases	lb.	2.95 @ 2.97½
" Ordinary, Job-		2.97½ @ 3.00
" powdered	lb.	3.47 @ 3.50
Orange peel, bit	lb.	.03 @ .04
Sweet	lb.	.04½ @ .10
Petrolatum		.03 @ .08
Phenacetine	oz.	.85 @ .95
Potassium acetate	lb.	.17 @ .18
" bromide		.16 @ .17
" bottles		.23 @ .30
bichromate		.08½ @ .08¾
chlorate, cryst		.09 @ .09½
" powd		.09½ @ .09½
cyanide		.21 @ .23
hypophosphite		.60 @ .64
iodide bulk		3.15 @ 3.20
permanganate	lb.	.09½ @ .10½
Prickly Ash berries		.14 @ .16
Quicksilver flasks	lb.	.56 @ .60
Quinine Sulph., Domestic bulk	oz.	.17 @ .20
German, bulk	oz.	.17 @ .20
German, outside	oz.	.17 @ .18
Java, bulk	oz.	.17 @ .19
Rochelle Salts	lb.	.20½ @ .21
Root, Aconite	lb.	.09½ @ .10
Alkanet	lb.	.08 @ .09
Althea, cut	lb.	.17 @ .19
Arnica	lb.	.08½ @ .09
Belladonna, Atropa	lb.	.10 @ .12
Blood	lb.	.10 @ .12
Calamus	lb.	.07 @ .08
Calamus, bleached	lb.	.23 @ .25
Colchicum	lb.	.12 @ .13
Calumba	lb.	.04 @ .05
Dandelion, Ger	lb.	.07½ @ .08
Galangal	lb.	.05 @ .05½
Gentian	lb.	.04 @ .04½
Ginger, Ja., blcd	lb.	.11½ @ .14
unbleached	lb.	.08 @ .09
Ginseng	lb.	6.25 @ 7.75
Golden Seal	lb.	1.25 @ 1.30
Hellebore, pwd	lb.	.06 @ .07
Helonias	lb.	.42 @ .45
Ipecac, Rio	lb.	1.60 @ 1.65
Carthagena	lb.	1.60 @ 1.65
Jalap	lb.	.08½ @ .11
Kava Kava	lb.	.11 @ .12
Liquorice, ord	lb.	.03½ @ .04
Select	lb.	.06½ @ .11
Lovage	lb.	.45 @ .85
Mandrake	lb.	.04½ @ .04½
Musk, Russian	lb.	.13 @ .14
Orris, Florentine	lb.	.06 @ .07
Orris, Verona	lb.	.04 @ .06
Pariera Brava	lb.	.10 @ .11
Pink	lb.	.80 @ .85
Rhatany	lb.	.10 @ .12
Rhub., Canton	lb.	.35 @ .40
Shensi	lb.	.65 @ .70
Sars'p'la, Hond	lb.	.35 @ .40
Mexican	lb.	.09½ @ .09½
Senega	lb.	.55 @ .60
Snake Virgina	lb.	.42 @ .45
Texas	lb.	.39 @ .42
Canada	lb.	.13 @ .25
Squill	lb.	.13 @ .15
Valerian, Belg	lb.	.08 @ .08½
German	lb.	.12 @ .14
English	lb.	.12 @ .15
Salicine	lb.	3.75 @ 4.00
Sal Ammon, lump	lb.	.09½ @ .09½
Granulated	lb.	.05½ @ .06
Sal Soda, Eng	100 lb.	.67½ @ .72½
American	100 lb.	.75 @ .80
Salol	lb.	.80 @ .85
Saltpetre, crude	lb.	.04 @ .04½
Refined	lb.	.04½ @ .05½
Santonin, crystals	lb.	9.50 @ 9.70
Powdered	lb.	9.70 @ 9.90
Saw Palmetto Berries	lb.	.15 @ .20
Seed, Anise Ital	lb.	.08½ @ .10½
German	lb.	.06½ @ .07
Star	lb.	.20 @ .21
Canary, Smyrna	lb.	.04 @ .04½
Sicily	lb.	.05 @ ...
Caraway	lb.	.06½ @ .07½
Celery	lb.	.07½ @ .08
Cardamom blchd		.30 @ .70
" Decorticated	lb.	.30 @ .31
Colchicum	lb.	.21 @ .25
Coriander	lb.	.07½ @ .08
Seeds—cont'd.		
Bleached	lb.	.08½ @ .10½
Cummin	lb.	.06½ @ .07½
Fennel, Ger	lb.	.09 @ .10
" Italian	lb.	.05 @ .05½
Flax, whole	lb.	6.50 @ 6.75
" ground	lb.	.03½ @ .03¾
Foenugreek	lb.	.03 @ .03½
Hemp, Rus	lb.	.03 @ .03½
Millet, nat	lb.	.01½ @ .03
" shld	lb.	.04½ @ .04½
Mustard, Cal. brown	lb.	.04½ @ .05½
Trieste, brown	lb.	.07 @ .07½
Bari, brown	lb.	.04½ @ .05
German, brown	lb.	.03½ @ .05
Western, brown	lb.	.01½ @ .03
Cal. yellow	lb.	.04½ @ .04½
Eng. yellow	lb.	.05 @ .05½
Ger. yellow	lb.	.05½ @ .05½
Poppy, blue	lb.	.04½ @ .05
Quince, Ger	lb.	.32 @ .34
Rape, Ger	lb.	.03½ @ .05
" Eng	lb.	.04 @ .05
" Amer	lb.	.03½ @ .03
Strophanthus		.42 @ .43
Kombé		.80 @ 1.25
Sunflower		.04½ @ .05
Wormseed, American	lb.	.07 @ .08
" Levant	lb.	.17 @ .17½
Seidlitz Mixture	lb.	.17 @ .17½
Silver, Nitrate	oz.	.41 @ .44½
Soap, Castile, white	lb.	.10 @ .10½
" green	lb.	.08 @ .10½
" mottled	lb.	.05½ @ .07
Sodium bicarb, Eng		1.37½ @ 1.75
" domestic	100 lb.	1.50 @ 1.60
" benzoate	lb.	.40 @ .41
" brom. blk	lb.	.31 @ .33
" carb., cryst	100 lb.	1.60 @ 1.75
" citrate	lb.	... @ .33
" hypophosphite		.60 @ .64
" iodide		3.50 @ 3.55
" nitrate	100 lb.	2.30 @ 2.35
" phosphate	lb.	.02½ @ .03
" salicylate	lb.	.32 @ .34
Spermaceti	lb.	.27 @ .28
Spts. Nitre, U. S. P.		.46 @ .48
Spts. Ammonia Aromat	lb.	.44 @ .45
Strontium, nitrate	lb.	.08 @ .08½
Strychnine, Sulph	oz.	.95 @ 1.05
Sugar of Milk	lb.	.15 @ .30
Sugar, Lead, white	lb.	.09½ @ .10
" brown	lb.	.07½ @ .08
Sulphur, Roll	lb.	1.85 @ 2.15
Flowers	lb.	2.15 @ 2.50½
Sulphuric Ether	lb.	.63 @ .65
Sumac, Sicily	ton	42.00 @ 47.00
" Virginia	ton	23.00 @ 25.00
Tar, Barbadoes	gal.	... @ .35
Thymol		1.85 @ 2.05
Tonka B'ns, Para	lb.	.17½ @ .20
" Angostura	lb.	.60 @ .65
" Surinam	lb.	.25 @ .27
Turmeric		.04½ @ .05
Turpentine	gal.	.67½ @ .65
Vanilla Beans	lb.	3.75 @ 6.50
" Cut, Mex	lb.	1.75 @ 2.00
" Tahiti	lb.	.45 @ 1.25
" Bourbon		1.25 @ 2.50
Vanillin	oz.	.24 @ .27½
Venice Turps, bbls	lb.	.14 @ .17
" " cans	lb.	.19 @ .20
Wax, Bayberry	lb.	... @ .20
" Bees, ord. pur	lb.	.28½ @ .30
" " sel	lb.	.32½ @ .34
" " blch	lb.	.40 @ .45
" Brazil, No. 1	lb.	.48 @ .50
" " No. 2	lb.	.44 @ .45
" " No. 3	lb.	.31 @ .33
" Ceresin, yel	lb.	.14 @ .18
" " white	lb.	.16 @ .20
" Japan	lb.	.13½ @ .14
" Paraffin	lb.	.08 @ .08½
Zinc Oxide	lb.	.07 @ .08½

Heavy Oils, &c.

Bank, Menhaden	gal.	.27 @ .30
Coconut, Ceylon	lb.	.06½ @ .08½
Cochin	lb.	.07½ @ .07½
Cuban	lb.	.05½ @ ...
Cod, Domestic	gal.	.35 @ .36
" Newfoundland	gal.	.38½ @ .40
Corn	gal.	3.90 @ ...
Cottonseed, crd. prime		.27½ @ .28
Summer Yellow, prime		.29½ @ .30
" " Butter		.30 @ .31
Old, off grade		... @ ...
White, Winter		.30 @ .31
Winter Yellow, prime		.30 @ .31
Salad Oil		.40 @ .41
Gasoline, 86°	gal.	.14 @ ...
" 88°	gal.	.16 @ ...
" 90°	gal.	.18 @ ...
Lard, Extra Prime	gal.	.63 @ .64
Lard, Extra No. 1	gal.	.43 @ .53
Lard, No. 1	gal.	.38 @ .40
Linseed, Raw City	gal.	.44 @ .45
" Boiled	gal.	.45 @ .46
Naphtha, 68°	gal.	.12 @ ...
" Deodorized, 76°	gal.	.13½ @ ...
Neatsfoot, prm	gal.	.49 @ .50
White		.97 @ ...
Olive Oil, tap	tins	1.50 @ 2.25
" Com., bbls	gal.	.53½ @ .58
Palm, prm., L'gos	lb.	.06½ @ .06¼
Peanut	lb.	.61 @ .62
Rapeseed	gal.	.67 @ .71
Red Elaine	gal.	... @ .49
" Saponified	lb.	.06½ @ .06½
Salad Oil	gal.	.46 @ .46
Sesame	gal.	.55 @ .60
Sperm, Crude	gal.	.63 @ .65
" Nat. Win	gal.	.62 @ .63
" Blch. Win	gal.	.64 @ .65
Straits	gal.	... @ .32
Tallow, prime	gal.	.62 @
Whale, Crude	gal.	... @ ...
Crude, Nat. Win	gal.	.42 @ .44
Bleached Win	gal.	.44 @ .46

New Remedies Compendium and Prices Current.

In this list, which is intended for the use of dispensing druggists, and not for analytical chemists, chemical formulas, melting points and other data of no immediate use to the dispenser are omitted. While additions will be made from time to time as new remedies make their appearance on the market, and the list thus kept fully up to date, remedies falling into disuse will be dropped as expediency may determine.

Corrected to February, 1906.

ACETAL. (ETHYLIDENE DIETHYL ETHER.) Colorless, volatile liquid, soluble in 18 parts of water, very soluble in alcohol. Used as a sedative and hypnotic in doses of 2 to 3 fluid drachms, usually in form of emulsion. Pure medicinal, per oz., $1.00; commercial, oz. ....65c.

ACETOZONE. (BENZOYL-ACETYL PEROXIDE). White powder, very slightly soluble in water (1:1000); slightly soluble in alcohol. Bactericide; used internally and externally in diseases of germ origin. Marketed as 50 per cent. mixture with inert absorbent powder. Dose, 1 to 3 grains in solution. Boxes containing 6 vials of 15 grains each, per box, $1.25; ¼ oz. bot., $1.40; ½ oz. bot., $2.70; 1 oz. bot. $5.25
(Parke, Davis & Co.)

ACET - THEOCIN - SODIUM. White crystalline powder, readily soluble in water. Powerful diuretic; used in dropsy, in doses of 5 to 7 grains, two to three times daily. ½ and 1 oz. bot.......$1.90 to $2.30 per oz.
(Continental Color & Chemical Co.)

ACOINE. (DI-PARA-ANISYL-MONO-PHENETHYL GUANIDINE HYDROCHLORIDE). White crystalline powder, soluble in 17 parts of water. Local anæsthetic like cocaine, used hypodermatically in eye surgery; dental anæsthetic in normal saline solution, 2 per cent. 15 grain vials, each, 40c.; capsules, 2½ grains, 28 in box.................75c.
(The Heyden Chemical Works.)

ADNEPHRIN SOLUTION. A 1-1000 solution of the active principle of the suprarenal gland in physiological salt solution containing one-half of 1 per cent. of methaform. Used for treatment of inflammations, congestions and tumefactions of the mucous membranes, also as a cardiac stimulant. 1 oz. vials ....60c.

EMOLLIENT. Tubes, each...30c.

OIL SPRAY. 1 oz. vials, each.60c.
(Frederick Stearns & Co.)

ADRENALIN. Grayish-white powder; with difficulty soluble in water. The blood-pressure-raising principle of the suprarenal glands. 1 grain vials.85c. Invariably employed in the form of

CHLORIDE SOLUTION, 1:1000, a solution of 1 part of adrenalin chloride in 1000 parts of physiologic salt solution, with 0.5 per cent. of chloretone. Powerful astringent, hemostatic and cardiac stimulant. Used for the control of hemorrhages, internal and superficial, for the reduction of congestion and inflammation of mucous membranes, as a heart stimulant in collapse, and as an adjuvant to the local anæsthetic action of cocaine. Internal dose, 5 to 30 minims. 1 oz. bot...................85c.

INHALANT, 1 oz. bot.........85c.

OINTMENT, ½ oz. tubes.....48c.

SUPPOSITORIES, boxes of 1 doz. 88c.

TABLETS, vials of 25.........85c.
(Parke, Davis & Co.)

ADRIN. (EPINEPHRIN HYDRATE). Whitish nonhygroscopic powder; the active principle of the suprarenal gland, same properties as adrenalin. 1 grain vials, each, 75c.; 1-1000 solution, 1 oz. vials, each, 75c.; tablets in tubes of 12, tablet, q. s. to make 15 minims of 1-1000 solution, each, 40c.; in 100's, each $3.10
(H. K. Mulford & Co.)

AGURIN. (ACET-THEOBROMINE-SODIUM.) White hygroscopic powder, soluble in water; incompatible with acids. Diuretic in dropsy. Dose, 7 to 15 grains, twice daily. ¼ and 1 oz. bot..............$1.55 to $1.70
(Continental Color & Chemical Co.)

AIROL. (BISMUTH OXYIODOGALLATE.) Grayish-green powder, insoluble in water or alcohol. On admixture with water airol partly decomposes and turns red. Should be mixed with water only with intervention of glycerin. Used externally as application to wounds, burns, skin diseases, eye, nose, gonorrhœa, either pure, in 10 per cent. suspension, equal parts glycerin and water, or 10 to 20 per cent. ointment. 1 oz. cartons $1.00
(Hoffmann-La Roche Chemical Works.)

ALBARGIN. (GELATOSE SILVER.) Light brown powder, readily soluble in water. Contains 15 per cent. of silver. For gonorrhœa a 2 per cent. solution is injected 4 or 5 times daily. 1 oz. vials, $1.10; tubes of 50 tablets, 0.2 gm. each, per tube ....50c.
(Victor Koechl & Co.)

ALPHOZONE. (SUCCINIC PEROXIDE.) White fluffy powder, quickly soluble in 60 parts of water. Germicide and antiseptic, internally and externally. Dose, 3 to 5 grains. 1 oz. bot., $4.50; ½ oz., $2.30; ¼ oz., $1.20; 1 grain tablets, bot. of 90 ....$1.00
(Frederick Stearns & Co.)

ALYPIN. White crystalline powder, easily soluble in water and alcohol, but dissolving very sparingly in ether. Watery solutions have a neutral reaction and can be sterilised by boiling for a short period. Local anæsthetic, substitute for cocaine. The strength of the solutions ordinarily employed varies from 1 to 5 and even up to 10 per cent. It can be combined with adrenalin and antipyrine. Alypin should not be used in connection with silver nitrate, owing to the formation of a precipitate. This objection, however, does not apply to protargol solutions, which, although they become slightly turbid at first, soon clear up. 15 grain vials, each, 20c.; 10 grain vials, per vial, 16c.; ½ and ¼ oz. bots, per oz., $4.20; 1 oz. bots., per oz.........$4.10
(Continental Color & Chemical Co.)

ALUMNOL. (ALUMINUM NAPHTHOL DISULPHONATE.) Whitish powder, very soluble in water; slightly soluble in alcohol and glycerin; astringent and antiseptic; dissolves in pus and penetrates tissues. Used in 1 per cent. solution in gonorrhœa; 10 to 20 per cent. mixture with talcum as a dusting powder. 1 oz. tins, per oz..50c.
(Victor Koechl & Co.)

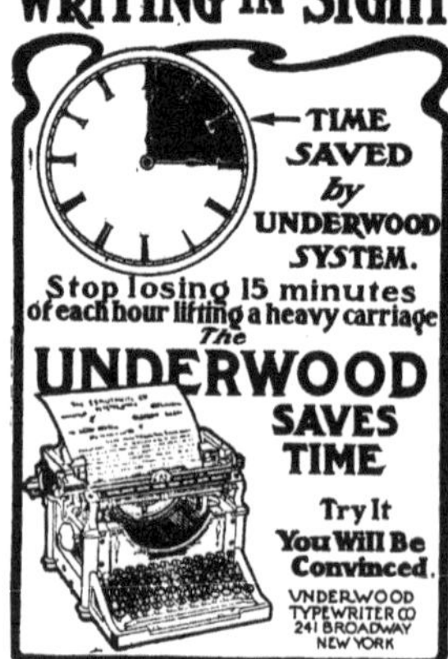

AMINOFORM. (HEXAMETHYLENETETRAMINE.) White granular crystals, readily soluble in water, prepared by combining ammonia and formaldehyde. Antiseptic for urinary passages, diuretic and solvent in uric acid concretions; dose, 5 to 10 grains, well diluted, three times daily. 1 oz. bot., 60c.; 7½ grain tablets, oz..........70c.
(C. Bischoff & Co.)

AMYLOFORM. White powder, insoluble in water; condensation product of starch and formaldehyde. Surgical antiseptic, used pure or with talcum and boric acid. 1 oz. carton..........25c.
(Stallman & Fulton.)

ANAESTHESIN. White crystalline powder, almost insoluble in cold water, but easily soluble in ether, alcohol, benzin and fatty oils. Local anaesthetic, and used internally in gastric ulcer, nervous dyspepsia, etc. Dose, internally, 5 to 8 grains several times daily. Used externally pure or in ointment 5 to 20 per cent., and in suppositories containing 8 grains each. 1 oz. bot....$1.00
(Victor Koechl & Co.)

ANTHRASOL. Yellow, oily liquid, with a distinctive tarry odor; soluble in alcohol, acetone, fats and petrolatum. A distillate from coal tar, used in diseases of the skin where coal tar is employed. 1 oz. vials..........55c.
(Knoll & Co. and Merck & Co.)

ANTINONNIN. (POTASSIUM ORTHODINITRO-CRESOL.) Paste of brilliant orange color, soluble in water, slight soapy odor, nonvolatile. Deodoriser, disinfectant, prevents the growth of fungi, mildew and dry rot in cellars and human habitations. Used in form of solution. 1 lb. to 5 to 15 gallons of water. Cans, ¼ lb., $1.10 per lb.; 1 lb. cans, 95c.; 50 lb. cans, per lb..........77c.
(Continental Color & Chemical Co.)

ANTINOSINE. (SODIUM SALT OF NOSOPHEN.) Blue powder, soluble in water, alcohol and glycerin. Used in solution of 1 to 5 per cent. as an antiseptic in diseases of the eye and ear, genito-urinary diseases, and as a healing powder on chronic leg ulcers. 1 oz. bot..........$2.10
(Stallman & Fulton Co.)

ANTISCLEROSIN. Tablets, consisting of a compound of inorganic blood salts, used in treatment of arteriosclerosis and its sequellæ. Dose, 2 tablets three times daily. Carton of 4 tubes, 24 tablets.....$1.50
(Schering & Glatz.)

ANTITUSSIN. (DIFLUORDIPHENYL OINTMENT.) Ointment containing lanolin, 85 per cent.; petrolatum, 10 per cent., and difluordiphenyl, 5 per cent. A whooping cough remedy applied as inunction to patient's neck, chest and back once a day, in doses of 5 Gm. 20 Gm. collapsible tubes, 40 c.; 40 Gm..........75c.
(C. Bischoff & Co.)

ANUSOL SUPPOSITORIES. A compound of bismuth iodoresorcin sulphonate, used in hemorrhoids, etc. Dose, 1 or 2 daily. Box of 12..........$1.00
(Schering & Glatz.)

ARGENTAMINE. A colorless, alkaline liquid representing a solution of silver nitrate, 10 per cent., and ethylenediamine, 10 per cent.; soluble in water. Used in all cases where silver nitrate is used, mostly in gonorrhœa, in strength of 1 in 2000-4000 solution. 1 oz., g. s. bot..........75c.
(Schering & Glatz.)

ARGONIN. White powder, very slightly soluble in cold, but freely so in hot water. A compound of silver nitrate and sodium casein. Antiseptic, germicide and gonococcicide, less caustic than silver nitrate. Solutions of 2 to 10 per cent. strength recommended for injection in gonorrhœa and 3 per cent. solutions for use in the eye. 1 oz vials..........65c.
(Victor Koechl & Co.)

ASAPROL. (ABRASTOL.) Whitish powder, freely soluble in water and alcohol. It is the calcium salt of betanaphthol-sulphonic acid. Antipyretic and antirheumatic in doses of 5 to 15 grains. Used also as test for albumin in urine. 1 oz. bot..........$1.25

ARISTOCHIN. (CARBONIC ESTER OF QUININE.) White powder, tasteless, insoluble in water. Decomposes in the system to yield 96.1 per cent. of quinine. Prescribed like quinine, but in somewhat larger doses. ¼ and 1 oz. cartons, per oz.....$2.20
(Continental Color & Chemical Co. and Merck & Co.)

ASPIRIN. (ACETYL SALICYLIC ACID.) White crystalline powder, insoluble in water; incompatible with alkalies. Used instead of the salicylates in articular and muscular rheumatism and other therapeutic indications for the salicylates. Dose, 5 to 15 grains, three to five times daily. 1 oz. bot., per oz..........38c. to 48c.
(Continental Color & Chemical Co.)

ATOXYL. (META-ARSENOUS ANILIDE.) White powder, containing 37.69 per cent. of arsenic in organic combination. Soluble in 6 parts of water and used in this strength solution for hypodermic injection; relatively nontoxic. Dose, 1 to 3 grains, 1 oz. vials..........$8.00
(Victor Koechl & Co.)

BENZONAPHTHOL. White, crystalline powder, soluble in alcohol and chloroform; insoluble in water. Employed as intestinal antiseptic in doses of 5 to 15 grains. 1 oz. vials, 22c.; ¼ lb. bottles, $2.20; ½ lb., $2.10; 1 lb..........$2.00
(Schering & Glatz.)

BENZOSOL. (GUAIACOL BENZOATE.) Small colorless crystals, nearly insoluble in water. Contains 54 per cent. of guaiacol and, as it is slowly saponified by the gastric juice, the guaiacol being liberated gradually, it is recommended as an intestinal antiseptic and as an agreeable substitute for creosote in incipient phthisis. Dose, 4 to 8 grains. 1 oz. tins.....$1.25
(Victor Koechl & Co.)

BETA-EUCAINE HYDROCHLORIDE. White, crystalline powder, soluble in 30 parts of water. A synthetic compound chemically allied to cocaine, being the hydrochloride of benzoyl-vinyl-diaceton-alkamine. It is slower in action than cocaine, but anæsthesia is more prolonged, and a third less toxic. Used generally in 2 per cent. solutions in dental and ophthalmic work. ⅛ oz. and ¼ oz., per oz., $3.60; ½ oz. and 1 oz..........$3.50
(Schering & Glatz.)

BETA-EUCAINE LACTATE. White powder, possessing the same properties as the hydrochloride, but is more soluble in water (about 1 in 5). Prices and containers same as for beta-eucaine hydrochloride.
(Schering & Glatz.)

BISOL. (SOLUBLE BISMUTH PHOSPHATE.) White powder, soluble in water, faint alkaline reaction. Intestinal antiseptic and astringent in gastric and enteric catarrh. Dose, 3 to 7½ grains. 1 oz. vials..........70c.
(C. Bischoff & Co.)

BROMETONE. Powder; slightly soluble in water. Compound of bromoform and acetone; recommended as a substitute for bromides; contains 77 per cent. of bromine. Dose, 3 to 5 grains. 1 oz. bot., 85c.; 5 grain capsules in bot. of 100..........$1.25
(Parke, Davis & Co.)

BROMIPIN. (10 % BROMINIZED SESAME OIL.) Yellow, oily fluid, used as a nervine and sedative in epilepsy; succedaneum for bromides. Dose, 1 teaspoonful. 1 oz. vial, 18c.; per lb..........$2.10 to $2.25
(Merck & Co.)

CACODYLIC ACID. (DIMETHYL ARSENIC ACID.) Small colorless deliquescent crystals, the ultimate product of oxidation of arsenium-dimethyl (cacodyle) and of cacodyle oxide. Contains 54.4 per cent.

of arsenic trioxide, but is relatively nontoxic. Dose, 1 to 3 grains. ½ oz. vials, per oz. $4.00

CALOMELOL OINTMENT. White mercurial ointment made from colloidal calomel for the inunction treatment of syphilis and especially for the cure of its cutaneous manifestations. 2 oz. graduated tubes, per tube ....65c.
(Heyden Chemical Works.)

CALOMELOL POWDER. Grayish-white powder of neutral reaction, tasteless and odorless. Yields a milky solution when added to cold water in the proportion of 1 to 50. Used as a dusting powder in the treatment of papular eruptions and ulcerations, and as external application to ulcerated chancres in 2 per cent. solution. 1 oz. vials ....70c.
(Heyden Chemical Works.)

CAMPHORIC ACID. (Colorless crystalline scales, very slightly soluble in water; formed by the oxidation of camphor with nitric acid. Used in night sweats of phthisis, also in cystitis and as an intestinal antiseptic in doses of 10 to 20 grains. 1 oz. vials, 45c.; 1 lb. bot. $7.00
(Merck & Co.)

CEROLIN. Pills of a fatty substance isolated from yeast. Acts same as yeast in furunculosis, acne, etc., but more cathartic. Pills containing 0.1 Gm., box of 100, each.....50c.
(C. F. Boehringer & Soehne.)

CHINAPHENIN. (QUININE CARBONIC ESTER OF PHENETIDINE.) White tasteless powder, representing synthetic quinine-phenacetin and having medicinal properties of both. Insoluble in water, but easily soluble in alcohol, ether and chloroform. Dose, 5 to 10 grains, thrice daily. ½ and 1 oz. cartons, per oz..........
$1.25 to $1.30
(Continental Color & Chemical Co.)

CHINOTROPINE. (UROTROPINE QUINATE.) A combination of quinic acid and urotropine (hexamethylenetetramine) used as uric acid solvent in the various manifestations of the uric acid diathesis. Is said to liberate formaldehyde freely internally and to form soluble compounds with uric acid. Dose, 10 to 30 grains. ¼ oz. and 1 oz. vials, $1.75; tablets, 7½ grains, 25 in tube, 2 tubes in box.........................$1.75
(Schering & Glatz.)

CHLORETONE. White crystals, slightly soluble in water (1:125); hypnotic, local anesthetic and antiseptic. Dose, 5 to 20 grains, in cachet, tablet or capsule. Externally as a dusting powder for wounds, combined 33 with zinc oxide, 120, and French chalk, 90 parts. ½ oz. vials, per oz., 90c.; 1 oz.....................85c.
(Parke, Davis & Co.)

CINNAMIC ACID. (CINNAMYLIC ACID.) Transparent micaceous crystals, very slightly soluble in water; soluble in alcohol and ether. Injected intravenously in tuberculosis in doses of ¼ to ¾ of a grain, twice a week; per os., 1-20 to ¼ grain twice daily. 1 oz. vial, 85c.; 1 lb. bot, per lb. $5.00
(Merck & Co.)

CITARIN. (SODIUM ANHYDROMETHYLENCITRATE.) White, crystalline powder, easily soluble in water. Antilithæmic for gouty and chronic rheumatic conditions; liberates formaldehyde in the blood. Dose, 15 to 30 grains, thrice daily. 1 oz. bot., per oz...70c. to 75c.
(Continental Color & Chemical Co.)

COLLARGOL. (COLLOIDAL SILVER.) Shining, black scales, soluble in 1 in 20 of water. Used as a bactericide, 1 in 100 to 10,000 in water or glycerin. Internally a 1 to 500 or 1 to 100 solution may be added to the food in teaspoonful doses. ½ oz. and 1 oz. vials, $2.75; tablets, 1 grain each, tubes of 50...60c.
(Schering & Glatz.)

COTARNINE HYDROCHLORIDE. See Stypticin.

CREOSOTE CARBONATE. (CREOSOTAL.) Yellow, transparent viscous liquid, insoluble in water, but miscible with alcohol; contains 92 per cent. of creosote combined with 8 per cent. of carbon dioxide. Used in tuberculosis and pneumonia in doses of 5 to 60 drops several times daily. 1 oz. vials, 35c.; ¼ lb. bot., per lb., $9.25; ½ lb. $9.10; 1 lb....................$9.00
(Schering & Glatz and Continental Color & Chemical Co.)

CUPROL. Green powder, readily soluble in water; a chemical combination of nucleinic acid and copper; solution does not coagulate albumen. Applied locally as an astringent; of use in granular ophthalmia in the form of 5 per cent. instillations, or may be applied in the dry form with a brush. ¼ oz. vials, $1.30 per oz.; 1 oz. vials $1.20
(Parke, Davis & Co.)

DERMATOL. (BISMUTH SUBGALLATE.) Yellow, insoluble powder; nonirritant antiseptic, especially serviceable in burns, ulcers and moist eczema. Used internally in diarrhœa, dysentery, intestinal fermentation and gastric ulcers, in doses of 10 to 30 grains three times daily. 1 oz. tins, 19c.; 1 and 5 lb. tins, per lb.........$2.50
(Victor Koechl & Co.)

DIATHESIN. White crystalline leaflets, soluble in 15 parts cold water, freely soluble in hot water or alcohol. Is ortho-oxybenzylalcohol, or synthetic saligenin. Used in place of salicin in rheumatism, neuralgia, pleurisy, etc., in doses of 7½ to 15 grains. 1 oz. cartons $2.40
(C. Bischoff & Co.)

DIFLUORDIPHENYL. White crystalline powder of pleasant aromatic odor, insoluble in water, soluble in alcohol, ether, chloroform and oils. Used as antiseptic dusting powder mixed with talc in proportion of difluordiphenyl, 10 parts; talc, 90 parts, or in 10 per cent. ointment with lanolin as dressing for burns. Dose, 1-16 to ¼ grain. 5 Gm. envelopes, each $1.50
(C. Bischoff & Co.)

DIGALEN. (CLOETTA'S SOLUBLE DIGITOXIN.) Marketed only in solution in 15 Cc. (½ oz.) vials, on account of infinitesimal dosage. Active principle of digitalis leaves, nonaccumulative heart tonic and diuretic. 1 Cc. of solution represents 0.0003 Gm. (0.0045 grain) of digitoxin, which is the average dose, by the mouth, hypodermatically, or by enema; intravenously the dose is from 3 to 10 Cc. ½ oz. vials....................$1.00
(Hoffmann-La Roche Chemical Works.)

DIONIN. (ETHYL MORPHINE HYDROCHLORIDE.) White crystalline powder, very soluble in water and alcohol. Recommended to replace codeine and morphine in bronchitis, emphysema and asthma. Dose, ¼ to ½ grain. 1 oz. vials, $6.00; ⅛ oz. vials, per oz., $6.25; 15 grain vials, each, 35c.; tablets, ¼ grain, bot. of 50, 35c.; bot. of 100 ....60c.
(Merck & Co.)

DIURETIN. (THEOBROMINE SODIUM SALICYLATE.) White powder, soluble in water, decomposed by acids. Must be kept dry and air-tight. Diuretic, antiasthmatic and vascular stimulant. Dose, 15 grains four to six times daily. 1 oz. bot., per oz....................$1.75
(Knoll & Co.)

DORMIOL. (AMYLENE CHLORAL.) Oily, colorless liquid, with a camphoraceous odor, insoluble in water, soluble in alcohol and ether. Hypnotic in mania; 50 per cent. solution supplied commercially. Dose, 5 to 60 minims. 1 oz. vials, 28c.; ½ lb. bot., per lb.............$4.00
(Merck & Co.)

DUOTAL. (GUAIACOL CARBONATE.) White, crystalline powder, soluble in alcohol, insoluble in water. Same therapeutic action as Creosotal, which see.

Dose, 5 to 20 grains, gradually increased. 1 oz. vials, $1.50; tablets, 7½ grains, 50 tablets in box, $1.50; 4½ grains, 50 tablets in box.............90c.
(Schering & Glatz and Continental Color & Chemical Co.)

DUOTONOL. White powder; a mixture, equal parts of the lime and sodium glycerophosphates. Nerve nutrient in doses of 5 to 10 grains three times daily. 1 oz., 50c.; 1 lb., $6.00; tablets, 5 grains, 100 tablets in bottle..........65c.
(Schering & Glatz.)

DYMAL. (DIDYMIUM SALICYLATE.) Pinkish powder, odorless. Applied as powder and ointment in skin diseases, notably dry and weeping eczema. 1 oz. cartons, each, 35c.; 4 oz. cartons, each.............$1.20
(C. Bischoff & Co.)

EKA-IODOFORM. A chemically pure iodoform, prepared by electrical synthesis, and sterilised with paraform. 1 oz. vials ....50c.
(Schering & Glatz.)

EMPYROFORM. Brown powder; condensation product of birch tar and formaldehyde; insoluble in water, readily soluble in acetone, chloroform and solutions of caustic alkalies. Used like tar in ointment, paste and tincture. 1 oz. vials..65c.
(Schering & Glatz.)

EPICARIN. (CONDENSATION PRODUCT OF BETANAPHTOL AND CRESOLIC ACID.) Colorless or yellowish needles, difficultly soluble in hot water, easily soluble in alcohol, ether and oils. Nontoxic substitute for naphthol in parasitic skin diseases. Employed chiefly in ointments (5 to 10 per cent.) 1 oz. cartons, per oz..60 to 70c.
(Continental Color & Chemical Co.)

EUDOXINE. (BISMUTH SALT OF NOSOPHEN.) Reddish-gray powder, insoluble in water, but soluble in alkaline fluids. Used as an intestinal antiseptic in doses of 3 to 5 grains. 1 oz. bot., $2.10; 3 grain tablets, per oz., $2.60; 5 grain tablets, per oz. $2.50
(Stallman & Fulton Co.)

EUGALLOL. (PYROGALLOL MONOACETATE.) Yellowish, syrupy liquid, marketed in 66 per cent. acetone solution. Soluble in water and acetone; applied pure or diluted with acetone as paint in skin diseases, especially psoriasis, and deemed superior to pyrogallol. 1 oz. vials $1.00
(Knoll & Co. and Merck & Co.)

EUMYDRIN. White crystalline powder, obtained from atropine; easily soluble in water. Powerful mydriatic, less poisonous than atropine. Dose, internally, about 1-70 grain. 1 or 2 per cent. solution dilates the pupil after 10 to 25 minutes. 1 grain tubes, 45c. to 55c. per box of 10 tubes; ¼ oz. and ½ oz. packages, per oz.. $16.50
(Continental Color & Chemical Co.)

EUNATROL. (SODIUM ACID OLEATE.) Light yellow substance, readily soluble in water and alcohol; supplied as powder and chocolate-coated pills. Recommended in treatment of gallstones, being excellent cholagogue. Dose, four pills, 4 grains each, three times daily, or in solution, 25 Gm. bot., each, 75c.; bot. of 50 pills, 70c.; 100 pills..........$1.30
(C. Bischoff & Co.)

EUPHORIN. (PHENYL-URETHANE.) White, acicular crystals, slightly soluble in water, freely in alcohol. Energetic antipyretic and analgetic in doses of 7½ to 15 grains, 2 to 3 times daily. 1 oz. vials.$1.00
(Schering & Glatz.)

EUPHTHALMINE HYDROCHLORIDE. White crystals; a synthetic derivative of beta-eucaine; soluble in water; 2 to 5 per cent. solutions dilate the pupil, without causing discomfort or accommodation disturbances. ½ and 1 Gm. vials, per Gm. $1.25
(Schering & Glatz.)

EUPYRINE. (PARA-PHENETIDINE VANILLIN ETHYLCARBONATE.) Light yellow crystals, sparingly soluble in water, readily in alcohol, chloroform and ether. Stimulant antipyretic in doses of 7½ to 15 grains. 1 oz. cartons, each...................$1.50
(C. Bischoff & Co.)

EUQUININE. (QUININE CARBONIC ESTER.) Tasteless, fleecy crystals, slightly soluble in water; soluble in alcohol, ether and chloroform. Succedaneum for quinine sulphate, reported not to disturb stomach or produce cindionism. Dose, same as quinine. Tablets, 5 grains, 100 in bot., $1.75; 2 grain, 100 in bot.........................75c.
(Merck & Co.)

EUROPHEN. Yellow light powder, containing 25 per cent. of iodine, insoluble in water and glycerin. Iodoform substitute used in dry powder and in ointment. 1 oz. bot., per oz. $1.65 to $1.80
(Continental Color & Chemical Co.)

EUZONE. (PURE SODIUM PERBORATE.) White, odorless powder, containing about 7.1 per cent. boron, 15 per cent. sodium, 31.2 per cent. oxygen and 46.2 per cent. water; represents 22 per cent. by weight of hydrogen dioxide, equivalent to 10.4 per cent. by weight of nascent oxygen. Soluble in water 1 in 10, such a solution being taken to represent a 2 per cent. solution of hydrogen dioxide. Tablets, 2½ Gm. each, boxes of 20, 40c.; powder, in 100 Gm. cartons, 85c.; 500 Gm. boxes $1.20
(Schering & Glatz.)

EXODIN. Yellowish powder; a synthetic oxyanthraquinone derivative; tasteless, mild aperient in doses of 7½ to 15 grains. 1 oz. vials, $1.40; tablets, 7½ grains each, 10 tablets in box, 30c.; 50 in bottle.......$1.40
(Schering & Glatz.)

FERRATIN. Reddish-brown powder, slowly soluble in ordinary liquids, but readily in hot beverages. Used in anemia and chlorosis in doses of 7½ grains three times daily. 1 oz. vials, 85c.; tablets, 7½ grains, 50 in box, per box.........85c.
(C. F. Boehringer & Soehne.)

FERRATOGEN. (IRON NUCLEINATE.) Grayish-yellow powder, obtained by growing yeast in a ferruginous medium; insoluble in water. Used in chlorosis and anemia in doses of 5 grains, three times daily. 1 oz. cartons, each...........90c.
(C. Bischoff & Co.)

FERRIPYRIN. (FERRIC CHLORIDE ANTIPYRIN.) Orange-red powder, soluble in 5 parts of water, very soluble in alcohol, but insoluble in ether. A compound of ferric chloride and antipyrine. Styptic and analgetic when applied in solution or powder. Given internally in chlorosis and anæmia as a hæmatinic in doses of 7½ grains. 1 oz. tins........$1.50
(Victor Koechl & Co.)

FERROPYRIN. (Same as Ferripyrin, but made by Knoll & Co. and sold in 1 oz. cartons, $1.40.)
(Knoll & Co. and Merck & Co.)

FIBROLYSIN. Solution of thiosinamine and sodium salicylate, sterilised. Put up in sealed tubes, each containing 2.3 Cc. solution (= 0.2 Gm. thiosinamine). Same uses as thiosinamine, but specially adapted for hypodermic use. Dose, contents of 1 tube every 1, 2 or 3 days, as required. 2.3 Cc. tubes, each.........15c.
(Merck & Co.)

FLUOROFORMOL. (FLUORYL.) Colorless, tasteless liquid, a 2.8 per cent. solution of fluoroform. Used in phthisis, internally and externally; also in pneumonia, acting as an antiseptic. Dose, 1 tablespoonful four times daily. 1 lb. bot....$1.00
(C. Bischoff & Co.)

FLUORRHEUMIN. Ointment composed of petrolatum, 10; lanolin, 85; difluordiphenyl, 4; fluorphenetol, 1. Used in rheumatism, sciatica and lumbago; dose by inunction, 4 to 5 Gm.

Collapsible tubes, 20 Gm., 40c.; 40 Gm. ....75c.
(C. Bischoff & Co.)

FORTOINE. (METHYLENEDICOTOINE.) Yellow crystals, with slight cinnamon flavor, obtained through action of formaldehyde on cotoine; insoluble in water, sparingly soluble in alcohol, ether and benzol; easily soluble in chloroform, acetone and alkaline liquids. Astringent antiseptic in protracted diarrhœas of consumptives. Dose, 4 grains three times daily. 10 Gm. envelopes, each $2.00
(C. Bischoff & Co.)

GALLOGEN. (ELLAGIC ACID.) Yellowish, tasteless powder, insoluble in all acid and neutral media, but soluble in alkaline solutions. Resembles tannic acid, being the astringent principle of divi-divi. Used in dysentery and diarrhœa. Dose, 10 to 15 grains for adults, 5 to 8 grains for children. 1 oz. cartons, 80c.; chocolate coated tablets, 3 grains each, 24 in box ....35c.
(C. Bischoff & Co.)

GAULTHERINE. Pinkish powder, slowly soluble in cold water, more readily so in hot water; insoluble in ether and chloroform, but very soluble in alcohol. It is the sodium salt of methyl salicylate prepared from natural oil of wintergreen. Antiseptic, antifermentative and soothing antiputrefactive. Used internally and externally. 4 oz. bot., per lb., $6.30; ¼ lb. bot, per lb., $6.60; 1 lb. bot., ...$6.50
(The Wm. S. Merrell Chemical Company.)

GEOSOTE. See Guaiacol Valerate.

GLUTOL. (FORMALDEHYDE GELATIN.) Whitish, granular, insoluble powder; recommended as an antiseptic dressing for burns, cavities and suppurating ulcers. 1 oz. tins, 65c.; vials of ⅓ oz., with sprinkler top, each ....25c.
(Schering & Glatz.)

GUAETHOL. (AJACOL; THANATOL.) Oily liquid, or purer in crystals resembling thymol, insoluble in water. Succedaneum for guaiacol. Allays pain by direct application. Dose, 4 to 8 minims. 1 oz. vials....$1.40

GUAIACOL VALERATE. (GEOSOTE.) Yellow, oily liquid; a combination of guaiacol and valerianic acid, having the characteristic odor of the latter. Insoluble in water, soluble in alcohol and ether. Said to be useful in tuberculosis and chlorosis and as intestinal antiseptic in doses of 3 to 10 minims three times daily. 3 minim capsules, per 100.........$2.10

GUAIACETIN. (SODIUM PYROCATECHIN-MONOACETATE). White odorless powder, soluble in water. A succedaneum for guaiacol and creosote, used in tuberculosis. Dose, 8 grains, preferably in tablet form. Powder in 1 oz. tins, $3.30; bot. containing 100 tablets, 8 grains each, $3.50; 50, $2.00; 25.....$1.17
(Fuerst Bros. & Co.)

GUIASANOL. (DIETHYLGLYCOCOLL-GUAIACOL.) Crystalline powder, readily soluble in water. Indications same as for creosote and guaiacol. Used internally in doses of from 45 to 180 grains a day. 25 Gm. bot. $1.00
(Victor Koechl & Co.)

HEDONAL. White, crystalline powder, insoluble in water, but soluble in alcohol, chloroform and ether; best administered as a dry powder. Given in mild forms of insomnia as a hypnotic in doses of 15 to 30 grains. 1 oz. bot.$1.50 to $1.60
(Continental Color & Chemical Co.)

HELMITOL. (HEXAMETHYLENETETRAMINE-ANHYDROMETHYLENE CITRATE.) Colorless crystals, freely soluble in water; insoluble in alcohol and ether. Urinary antiseptic in cystitis, phosphaturia, urethritis, etc., in doses of 15 grains, three or four times daily; liberates formaldehyde in the urinary tract. 1 oz. bot.......................60c.
(Continental Color & Chemical Co.)

HEMICRANIN. White powder; a mixture of 5 parts phenacetin, 1 part caffeine and 1 part citric acid, used in migraine, headaches, intercostal neuralgia and sciatica, in doses of 5 to 10 grains. 1 oz. cartons, per oz. 90c.
(Continental Color & Chemical Co.)

HEROIN. White, crystalline powder, difficultly soluble in water, but readily so in alcohol and in water to which a little acetic acid has been added; incompatible with alkali carbonates. Substitute for morphine, of which it is the diacetic acid ester, in doses of 1-24 to 1-12 grain; used for relief of cough and dyspnœa in phthisis, pneumonia, etc. 15 grain vials, 23c. per vial; ¼ oz. vials, per oz., $5.15; 1 oz. vials, per oz..$4.85
(Continental Color & Chemical Co.)

HEROIN HYDROCHLORIDE. (WATER SOLUBLE SALT OF HEROIN.) White, crystalline powder, used in same indications as heroin, but is adapted for hypodermatic injections. The dose and prices are the same as those of hero'n.
(Continental Color & Chemical Co.)

HIPPOL. (METHYLENE HIPPURIC ACID.) Colorless, prismatic crystals; sparingly soluble in water; urinary antiseptic in bacterial diseases of the urinary tract. Dose, 22½ grains. 1 oz., $1.50; 20 tablets in box $1.10
(Schering & Glatz.)

HIRUDIN. Grayish, glittering plates and scales, representing a dried extract of the head, pharyngeal rings and lips of the leech (*Sanguisuga medicinalis*); readily soluble in water. Used in the treatment of certain diseases of women and in experiments to prevent coagulation of blood on exposure to air. Tubes, 0.01 Gm., 75c.; 0.1 Gm., $3.75; 1 Gm....$30.00
(C. Bischoff & Co.)

HISTONSAN. (GUAIACOL ALBUMINATE.) Light brown powder of faintly aromatic odor and taste; soluble in water. Used in pulmonary tuberculosis and in diarrhœa in doses of 7½ grains three times daily. 1 oz. cartons $1.30
(C. Bischoff & Co.)

HOLOCAINE HYDROCHLORIDE. White, crystalline powder, difficultly soluble in cold (1 in 75), but readily so in hot water. Chemically para-diethyoxyethenyl-diphenyl-amidine hydrochloride, produced by combination of phenacetin and para-phenetidin. Antiseptic and germicidal in 1 per cent. solution. Used entirely as anæsthetic for operations on the eye, a 1 per cent. solution being equal to 2 per cent. cocaine solution. 1 Gm. vials, 35c.; 5 Gm. vials, per Gm., 30c.; 1 oz. vials, per oz. $7.00
(Victor Koechl & Co.)

HYDRONAL. (POLYMERIZED CHLORAL.) White powder, a polymeric form of anhydrous chloral, known in Germany as viferral. It dissolves slowly in cold, but readily in boiling water. Used as hypnotic in simple sleeplessness and in the insomnia of mania in doses of 15 grains. Tubes of 15 tablets, 1 Gm. each.......................35c.
(C. Bischoff & Co.)

HYRGOL. (COLLOIDAL MERCURY.) Dark, solid body, fairly soluble in cold water, insoluble in alcohol and ether; used in syphilis as 10 per cent. ointment by inunction, and pills and tablets internally. Dose, ⅓ to ⅝ grain thrice daily. 1 oz. vials.......................80c.
(Schering & Glatz.)

ICHTHALBIN. (ICHTHYOL ALBUMINATE.) Grayish-brown powder, odorless and tasteless; combination of ichthyol and albumin, containing 40 per cent. of the former. Used internally for skin diseases and gastrointestinal affections in doses of 5 to 30 grains three times daily. 1 oz. cartons,

85c.; 5 grain tablets, 100 in bottle $1.00
(Knoll & Co. and Merck & Co.)

ICHTHARGAN. (ICHTHYOL SILVER; SILVER ICHTHYOLSULPHONATE; SILVER THIO-HYDROCARBUROSULPHONATE.) Brown powder containing 30 per cent. silver; soluble in water and glycerin. Bactericide and astringent in urinary diseases in injections of 1 to 500 and 1 to 3000 in water; in diseases of the eye, as trachoma, by brush applications of 1 to 3 per cent. solutions. Dose, 1-24 to 1-12 grain in water. 1 oz. vials, $3.00; ½ oz.....$3.10
(Merck & Co.)

ICHTHOFORM. (ICHTHYOL FORMALDEHYDE.) Blackish-brown powder, insoluble in water. Used externally as succedaneum for iodoform. Internally as intestinal antiseptic in the diarrhœa and intestinal disorders occurring in tubercular diseases, and in typhoid fever and dysentery. Dose, 15 to 30 grains three or four times daily, in powder or capsules. 1 oz. vials..................$1.00
(Merck & Co.)

IODIPIN. (IODIZED SESAME OIL; IODINOL.) Thick, yellow oil, odorless and of oily taste, made similarly to bromipin by repeated iodization of sesame oil by means of iodine monochloride in alcoholic solution; insoluble in water and alcohol, soluble in ether and chloroform. Made in two strengths, 10 per cent iodine and 25 per cent. iodine, respectively, the former for internal and the latter for hypodermic use. Succedaneum for iodide in syphilis, scrofula, etc. Dose, 10 per cent., 1 to 3 fl. drachms; hypodermically (25 per cent.), 30 to 90 minims. On unspecified orders the 10 per cent. strength is supplied. Used in all cases where iodine and iodides are indicated; hypodermically in syphilis. 10 per cent. strength, 1 lb. bottles, $3.65; ¼ lb., $3.90; 1 oz. vials, 28c.; 20 per cent., 1 lb. bottles, $8.25; ¼ lb., $8.30; 1 oz. vials.....85c.
(Merck & Co.)

IODOFORMOGEN. Light yellow powder, odorless in use; combination of iodoform and albumin, insoluble in water; used like iodoform as a dressing for wounds. 1 oz. cartons ....55c.
(Knoll & Co. and Merck & Co.)

IODOZEN. Yellowish-white powder, a chemical combination of methyl salicylate and iodine; insoluble in water, soluble in 2 parts of alcohol, in 3 parts of ether and in 10 parts of chloroform. Antiseptic application, applied as solution or ointment. Marketed in sprinkler top cans, 1 oz.........................75c.
(The Wm. S. Merrell Chemical Co.)

IODOTHYRINE. Whitish powder, representing the active principle of the thyroid gland, combined with sugar of milk. Alterative in goitre, myxœdema, obesity, psoriasis, menstrual disorders of women, etc., in daily doses of 15 to 30 grains. Powder, in ¼ oz. vials, per oz., $3.90; 1 oz. vials, $3.40. Tablets, 5 grains, each, vials of 25, per vial, $1.00; 100 ....$3.90
(Continental Color & Chemical Co.)

IOTHION. Syrupy, yellowish-brown liquid, difficultly soluble in water, easily soluble in alcohol, ether, benzol and chloroform; miscible with petrolatum and with anhydrous lanolin, which takes up twice its weight of iothion. Organic compound of iodine, of which it contains 79 to 80 per cent. Applied in form of ointment by inunction as a substitute for potassium iodide in doses of 30 to 60 grains a day. 1 oz. bot., per oz......................$1.10
(Continental Color & Chemical Co.)

IRON TONOL. (IRON GLYCEROPHOSPHATE.) Powder; soluble in water; tonic, nerve nutrient. Dose, 3 to 10 grains. 1 oz., 35c.; 1 lb....................$3.50
(Schering & Glatz.)

IRON TROPON. Brownish powder; albuminoid food preparation composed of tropon (pure albumen) and iron in an assimilable form. Contains 2½ per cent. of iron. Used as a tonic food in treatment of anæmia, chlorosis, impoverished conditions of the system generally, and in convalescence. Tins, 100 Gm., 75c.; 1 doz. tins $6.75
(Tropon Works.)

ISOPRAL. White crystals, soluble in water up to 3 per cent. and easily in alcohol and ether. A nondepressing substitute for chloral in doses of 7 to 15 grains, indicated in all forms of sleeplessness in which chloral is employed. Powder, in 1 oz. bot., per oz., $1.40; 3 grain tablets, bottles of 100, $3.00; 8 grain tablets, tubes of 20 ....75c.
(Continental Color & Chemical Co.)

KRESAMINE. Clear, watery liquid, representing a solution of trikresol, 25 per cent., and ethylenediamine, 25 per cent.; soluble in 3 parts of water, and in all proportions of glycerin; antiseptic and sedative to inflammed tissues. 1 oz...$1.00
(Schering & Glatz.)

KRYOFINE. White, granular crystals, sparingly soluble in cold water (1 in 600); freely soluble in alcohol and ether. A compound of paraphenetidin and methylglycolic acid. Antipyretic and antineuralgic in doses of 4 to 7½ grains. 1 oz. cartons, powd., $1.00; tablets, 4 or 7½ grains, per oz....$1.00
(C. Bischoff & Co.)

LACTOPHENIN. (LACTYL-PARA-PHENETIDIN.) Small, white crystals, soluble in 330 parts of water. Differs from phenacetin in containing a molecule of lactic acid in place of acetic. Antipyretic and analgetic in doses of 4 to 8 grains. 1 oz. cartons, each......$1.00
(C. F. Boehringer & Soehne.)

LARGIN. (SILVER PROTALBIN.) Gray powder containing 11 per cent. of silver; soluble in 10 parts of water. Bactericide and astringent application in gonorrhœa in ¼ to 1½ per cent. injections. 1 oz. vials...$1.75
(Merck & Co.)

LENIGALLOL. (PYROGALLOL TRIACETATE.) White, crystalline powder, insoluble in water, possessing the same reducing properties as pyrogallol and used in acute and chronic eczema as ointment. 1 oz. vials $1.00
(Knoll & Co. and Merck & Co.)

LEVULOSE. (FRUIT SUGAR.) Crystalline powder, soluble in water. Sweetening agent used in diabetes, tuberculosis, malnutrition and marasmus of children. Dose, 3 drachms to 2 ounces daily. 1 lb. jars..$1.60
(Schering & Glatz.)

LYCETOL. (DIMETHYLENEDIAMINE TARTRATE.) White powder, readily soluble in water. Uric acid solvent, antiarthritic and diuretic in doses of 5 to 10 grains three times daily. 10 Gm. vials, $1.50; ¼ oz., ½ oz., 1 oz. cartons, per oz...
$4.25 to $4.40
(Continental Color & Chemical Co. and Schering & Glatz.)

LYGOSINE. (SODIUM LYGOSINATE.) Glossy, greenish crystals; a condensation product of salicylaldehyde and acetone; readily soluble in water, forming ruby red solutions. Non-irritant substitute for silver as urethral injection in gonorrhœa, 5 per cent. strength. 10 Gm. vials......................85c.
(C. Bischoff & Co.)

LYSIDIN. (ETHYLENE-ETHENYLDIAMINE HYDROCHLORIDE.) Pale yellowish liquid, containing 50 per cent. of pure lysidin, the substance itself being very hygroscopic. Used in acute gout and uric acid diathesis in doses of 10 to 30 minims. 1 oz. vials $1.75
(Victor Koechl & Co.)

MARETIN. White, glistening crystals, very sparingly soluble in water (1 to 1050). Antipyretic, being a methyl acetanilid with a urea nucleus in place of the acetyl group. Dose, 3 to 5 grains. 1 oz. cartons, per oz..........$1.25 to $1.40 (Continental Color & Chemical Co.)

METHAFORM. (DIMETHYLCARBINOL CHLOROFORM.) White, shiny, needle-like crystals, with a slightly camphoraceous taste and odor, sparingly soluble in water, but readily so in chloroform, alcohol, ether and glacial acetic acid. It is hypnotic, analgetic, anæsthetic and antiseptic, somewhat resembling chloral in physiological action. 1 oz. vials, 60c.; 3 grain capsules, bot. of 100, 50c.; 5 grain, 100 ....75c.
(Frederick Stearns & Co.)

MERCUROL. (Brownish powder, soluble in water; insoluble in alcohol; a chemical combination of nucleinic acid and mercury, containing 10 per cent. of the metal. Does not coagulate albuminous liquids. Applied to ulcers and suppurating mucous membranes in from ½ to 5 per cent. solution, or in ointment. ¼ oz. vials, per oz., $1.60; 1 oz. vials $1.50
(Parke, Davis & Co.)

MESOTAN. (METHYLOXYMETHYLESTER OF SALICYLIC ACID.) Clear, yellow fluid, insoluble in water, but miscible with alcohol, ether and fixed oils. External application mixed with equal parts of olive oil in muscular and articular rheumatism, pleuritis and gout. 1 oz. bot., 47c.; 25 oz. lots 42c. (Continental Color & Chemical Co.)

MIGRAININ. (PHENAZONE CAFFEINE CITRATE.) Small white crystals, readily soluble in water and alcohol. Analgetic and antipyretic. Used in migraine, headaches of influenza, neuralgia, sciatica, etc., in doses of 17 grains. 1 oz. tins....$1.50
(Victor Koechl & Co.)

NARGOL. Brownish powder, readily soluble in warm water. Compound of silver and nucleinic acid containing 10 per cent. of the former; does not coagulate albumen. Used in gonorrhœa, conjunctival and other pyogenic inflammations. ¼ oz. vials, per oz., $1.80; ½ oz., per oz., $1.75; 1 oz..$1.70
(Parke, Davis & Co.)

NEODERMIN. Ointment containing lanolin, 85; petrolatum, 10; difluordiphenyl, 4; fluorpseudocumol, 1. For ulcerated surfaces, burns, etc. Collapsible tubes, Gm. 20 and Gm. 40, each..............40c. and 75c.
(C. Bischoff & Co.)

NOSOPHEN. (TETRAIODOPHENOLPHTHALEIN.) Grayish powder, odorless, slightly anæsthetic, insoluble in water, alcohol or ether, but soluble in alkaline fluids. Antiseptic dusting powder in wounds, burns, ulcers; substitute for iodoform. ¼ oz. bot., per doz......$4.50
(Stallman & Fulton Co.)

NOVARGAN. (SILVER PROTEINATE). Fine yellow powder containing 10 per cent. of metallic silver, readily soluble in water. Used as injection in gonorrhœa; is very penetrating and free from irritating effects upon mucous membrane. 1 oz. vials, $1.40
(Heyden Chemical Works.)

OLEOCREOSOTE. Pale brown, oily liquid combination of beechwood creosote, 88 per cent., with oleic acid. Used in affections of the respiratory organs, tuberculosis, etc. Dose, 10 to 30 minims. 1 oz...65c.
(Schering & Glatz.)

OREXINE. (PHENYLDIHYDROQUINAZOLINE TANNATE.) Yellowish powder, tasteless and odorless; insoluble in water, slightly soluble in dilute acid solutions, readily so in hydrochloric acid. Should not be prescribed with preparations of iron. Used in anorexia (lack of appetite) as stimulant of gastric secretion; in seasickness and vomiting of pregnancy. Orexine base is no longer on the market. Dose, 8 to 12 grains two times daily, in powder or in tablets. 1 oz. vials, $1.00; orexoids, Merck's tablets, 4 grains, 50 in bottle ....55c.
(Merck & Co.)

ORPHOL. BISMUTH BETANAPHTHOLATE.) Odorless and tasteless fawn colored powder, insoluble in water; consists of 80 per cent. bismuth oxide and 20 per cent. beta-naphthol. Intestinal antiseptic in doses of 5 to 15 grains three or four times daily. 1 oz., 80c.; tablets, 5 grains, 50 tablets in vial, per vial ....60c.
(Schering & Glatz.)

ORTHOFORM. White crystalline powder, the methyl ester of metaamidoparaoxybenzoic acid; slightly soluble in water; local anæsthetic and antiseptic. Forms a hydrochloride salt soluble in 9 parts of water. 10 per cent. solution of the hydrochloride salt, or 10 to 20 per cent. in ointment used to alleviate pain in sores or burns. Orthoform, 1 oz. vials, $1.40; orthoform hydrochloride, 1 oz. vials $1.80
(Victor Koechl & Co.)

OVARADEN. Tasteless and odorless powder consisting of the active substance of pigs' ovaries. Used in dysmenorrhœa and neurasthenia in doses of 15 to 30 grains daily. 1 oz. vials, $1.30; 4 grain tablets, bottles of 100..........$1.30
(Knoll & Co. and Merck & Co.)

OVARIIN. Powder representing 1 part in 8 of fresh cow's ovary, being the desiccated substance of the ovary. Used in chlorosis, affections of the heart, and menstrual troubles. 1 oz. vials, $2.00; ¼ oz., $2.10; 3 grain tablets, 100 in bottle $1.50
(Merck & Co.)

PANKREON. Grayish-red powder; a tannin-pancreatin compound; insoluble in water, obtained from the pancreas; used in pancreatic diabetes, gastritis and apepsia in doses of 7½ grains three times daily. Box of 25 Gm., $1.50; tablets of 0.25 Gm., 50 in box, $1.00; sugar tablets (⅝ grain), 100 in box........................50c.
(Merck & Co.)

PHENOCOLL HYDROCHLORIDE. White, crystalline powder, with sharp, saline taste; soluble in 16 parts of water; very soluble in hot water and alcohol. Similar to phenacetin, and used in malaria, pneumonia, influenza, rheumatism, etc. Dose, 7 to 15 grains. 25 Gm. vials....................$1.50
(Schering & Glatz.)

PIPERAZINE. Crystalline powder, readily soluble in water. Solvent of uric acid and insoluble urates in the system; used in gout, rheumatism and urinary calculi. Dose, 5 to 15 grains thrice daily. 10 Gm. vials, per vial, $1.50; lots of 60, per vial, $1.25. Tablets, tubes of ten 15 grain tablets, $1.50; 60 tubes, per tube, $1.25; ½ and 1 oz. bot., per oz. $4.25
(Continental Color & Chemical Co. and Schering & Glatz.)

POLLANTIN. Liquid and powder; antitoxic serum for hay fever, autumnal catarrh, rose fever and June cold. Package of powder and brush, $1.75; liquid, per package of serum and pipette...............$1.75
(Fritzsche Brothers.)

PROBILIN PILLS. Composed of salicylic acid, acid sodium oleate, phenolphthalein and menthol; used in gallstone affections. Dose, 3 to 4 pills twice daily for twenty days. Vials of 60, per vial......$1.25
(Schering & Glatz.)

PROFERRIN. (IRON NUCLEOPROTEID.) Reddish-brown powder, insoluble in water and acid solutions; contains 10 per cent. of iron and 1 per cent. of phosphorus, in organic combination; is absorbed from the duodenum, being unaffected by the gastric juice. Used in blood impoverishment in doses of 5 grains three times daily. 1 oz. cartons, per doz., $6.00; 5 grain

WHEN YOU have a vacancy for a clerk use the AMERICAN DRUGGIST "Want" column. Notices inserted one time free of charge for subscribers.

tablets, bottle of 100, 60c.; 2½ grain, bottle of 100........40c.
(H. K. Mulford Co.)

PROTAN. (TANNIN NUCLEO-PROTEID.) Light brown powder, insoluble in water; formed by the synthesis of tannic acid with nucleo-proteid. Used in all forms of diarrhœa in doses of from 20 to 30 grains; is astringent and acts in the intestines, being unaffected by the gastric juice. 1 oz. cartons, per doz., $6.00; 7½ grain tablets, bottle of 100, 85c.; 5 grain, per 100.............60c.
(H. K. Mulford Co.)

PROTARGOL. Yellowish, light powder, easily soluble in water. A proteid compound containing 8 per cent. of silver; not precipitated by albumen or salt solutions. Bactericide in gonorrhœa; antiseptic in eye, ear, nose and throat affections. 0.25 to 1 per cent. solutions for gonorrhœa; 0.5 to 5 per cent. for eye, and 2 to 10 per cent. for ear, nose and throat. Internally in doses of 1 to 3 grains. ½ oz. and 1 oz vials, per oz.........$1.10 to $1.85
(Continental Color & Chemical Co.)

PURGATIN. (PURGATOL; ANTHRAPURPURIN ACETATE.) Yellow crystalline powder; a synthetic oxyanthraquinone, having mild aperient properties; insoluble in water; decomposed in contact with alkalies. Dose, 10 to 30 grains. 1 oz. cartons, 85c.; 5 grain tablets, 100 in bottle $1.00
(Knoll & Co. and Merck & Co.)

PYRAMIDON. (DIMETHYL-AMIDO-ANTIPYRIN.) White powder, soluble in 9 parts of water and 2 parts of alcohol. Used as antipyretic in treatment of asthma, pulmonary tuberculosis and abdominal typhus, and as anodyne in headaches and neuralgic pains in doses of 8 to 12 grains. 1 oz. cartons, $2.15; pyramidon camphorate, acid, 1 oz. bot., $1.50; camphorate, neutral, 1 oz. bot., $1.75; salicylate, 1 oz. bot.$1.50
(Victor Koechl & Co.)

QUARTONOL. Tablets consisting of a compound of duotonol, quinine tonol and strychnine tonol. Blood and nerve tonic. Dose, 1 to 2 tablets three times daily. Bottle of 100 5-grain tablets ....75c.
(Schering & Glatz.)

QUININE LYGOSINATE. Orange-yellow, amorphous powder, containing 70.8 per cent. of quinine; difficultly soluble in water, readily soluble in alcohol, chloroform and benzin. Nontoxic antiseptic and styptic, employed as a dusting powder, gauze or suppository. 10 Gm. vials, each...............70c.
(C. Bischoff & Co.)

RENADEN. Powder obtained from extract of pigs' kidneys; used in uræmia and nephritis in doses of 1 to 2 drachms daily. 1 oz. vials, $1.30; 4 grain tablets, bottles of 100 ....$1.30
(Knoll & Co. and Merck & Co.)

RUBIDIUM IODIDE. Colorless, cubical crystals; soluble in less than 1 in 1 of water; bitter, saline taste. Used in place of potassium iodide in polyarthritis and syphilis. Dose, 5 to 20 grains. 1 oz. vial.$1.00
(Merck & Co.)

SAL-ETHYL. A colorless, transparent, volatile fluid; chemically pure ethyl salicylate. A substitute for methyl salicylate or oil of wintergreen. Globules, 5 min., in bot. of 50, per doz. bot...........$5.00
(Parke, Davis & Co.)

SALIT (SALICYLIC ACID ESTER). Oily fluid, insoluble in water, slightly soluble in glycerin and readily soluble in alcohol, ethers and oils. Used in muscular and articular rheumatism, lumbago, neuralgia and rheumatic pains following colds. 1 oz. bot.................22c.
(Heyden Chemical Works.)

SALOCREOL (SALICYLIC ACID ESTER OF CREOSOTE). Oily fluid of neutral reaction, almost odorless, insoluble in water, readily soluble in alcohol, ether, chloroform and oils. Used in facial erysipelas, acute and chronic inflammation of the lymph glands and chronic arthritis. 1 oz. bot........45c.

SALOPHEN. White, crystalline powder, containing 51 per cent. of salicylic acid; almost insoluble in water; soluble in alcohol and ether; incompatible with alkalies, which decompose it. Antipyretic, analgetic and antiseptic in rheumatism and neuralgia. Dose, 10 to 15 grains 3 to 4 times daily. 1 oz. cartons..............85c. to $1.00
(Continental Color & Chemical Co.)

SALOQUININE. (SALICYLIC ACID ESTER OF QUININE.) Whitish powder, insoluble in water, with difficulty soluble about 1 in 120 of alcohol and ether. Tasteless quinine substitute, used in malaria, tropical fevers, neuralgia and rheumatism. Dose, 15 to 30 grains, one to three times daily. ½ and 1 oz. cartons, $1.25 to $1.30
(Continental Color & Chemical Co. and Merck & Co.)

SCOPOLAMINE HYDROBROMIDE is identical with hyoscine hydrobromide, but lower in price. 15 grain tubes, each, $3.00; 10 grain tubes, $2.10; 5 grain tubes.....$1.05
(Merck & Co.)

SEXTONOL. Tablets consisting of a compound of duotonol, quinine tonol, iron tonol, manganese tonol and strychnine tonol. Blood and nerve nutrient. Dose, 1 to 2 5-grain tablets three times daily. Bottle of 100................75c.
(Schering & Glatz.)

SIDONAL. (PIPERAZINE QUINATE.) White amorphous powder, readily soluble in water. Uric acid solvent in gout and allied affections in doses of 75 to 120 grains a day in divided doses, well diluted with water. 1 oz. bot.................$2.75
(Victor Koechl & Co.)

SIDONAL NEW. (QUINIC ACID ANHYDRIDE.) Same properties and uses as above. 1 oz. bot. $2.00
(Victor Koechl & Co.)

SILVER CITRATE. (ANTISEPTIC CREDE; ITROL.) White powder, soluble about 1 in 4000 of water. Recommended in Credé's treatment as an antiseptic for wounds, in lotion, ointment, or powder. For disinfection of hands, skin and instruments, 1 to 1000-5000 watery solution; as gargle 1 to 5000 to 10,000; in gonorrhœa, 1 to 8000. Oz. ....$1.20 to $1.25
(Schering & Glatz and Merck & Co.)

SILVER LACTATE. (ACTOL.) Whitish powder, soluble in 15 parts of water; recommended in solution 1 in 200 to 1000 as an antiseptic for surgical use. ¼ oz. and 1 oz. vials, per oz., $1.30; tablets, 3 grains, boxes containing 5 vials of 10 tablets, per box.............$1.15
(Schering & Glatz and Merck & Co.)

SOMATOSE. Light yellow almost tasteless powder, easily soluble in water, prepared from meat and consisting of deutero and hetero albumoses. Nitrogenous food product for the sick and convalescent. Dose for adults, 90 to 180 grains daily; for children, 50 to 100 grains. 2 oz. tins, per doz., $8.25; ¼ lb. tins, per lb., $5.25; ½ lb. tins, per lb.........$5.00
(Continental Color & Chemical Co.)

SOMNOS. (CHLORMETHANAL ALCOHOLATE.) Clear liquid, miscible with water, produced by the synthesis of chlormethanal with a polyatomic alcohol radical. Hypnotic and cerebral sedative in doses of from 2 to 4 fluid drachms. Pint bottles, $1.10 per pint; $12.00 per doz.; 4 oz. bottles, per doz..........$4.00
(H. K. Mulford Co.)

STOVAINE. (AMYLENE HYDROCHLORIDE.) White, crystalline powder, readily soluble in water and in methyl alcohol; less soluble in ethyl alcohol and almost insoluble in ether. A substitute for cocaine, approximately one-fifth as toxic. Aqueous solutions are slightly acid and bitter to the taste.

Put up in solutions of various strengths, ¾ per cent., 1 per cent., 10 per cent., in tubes; tablet triturates, 1¼ grains each; pastilles, 3-100 grain each. Original packages, 1 oz., ½ oz. and ¼ oz. bottles, per. oz. $4.00
(Walter F. Sykes & Co.)

STYPTICIN. (COTARNINE HYDROCHLORIDE.) Yellow amorphous powder, the salt of an opium base (cotarnine is a product of the oxidation of narcotine), soluble in water and alcohol. Because of its chemical resemblance to hydrastinine, it being methoxylhydrastine, it is recommended in all forms of uterine hæmorrhage. Used in functional dysmenorrhœa and in the menorrhagia of puberty and the climacteric. Dose as styptic, 1½ to 4 grains, as needed, per os or by injection (10 per cent. solution). Sugar coated tablets, ¾ grain, per tube of 20, 25c.; 1 oz. bottles, per oz., $6.50; ½ oz. bottles, per oz., $6.60; ⅛ oz., per oz., $7.00; 15 grain vials, each, 85c.; hypodermic tablets, ¾ grain, per box of 40 (4 tubes)......60c.
(Merck & Co.)

STYPTOL. (COTARNINE PHTHALATE.) Yellow, crystalline powder, readily soluble in water. It is the phthalate salt of an opium base. Recommended in uterine hæmorrhage in doses of ¼ to ½ grain; externally in 10 per cent. solution. 1 oz. vials, $6.50; ¼ oz., per oz., $6.75; ⅛ oz., $7.00; 15 grain vials, per vial, 85c.; ¾ grain tablets, bottles of 100, per bot...$1.20
(Knoll & Co. and Merck & Co.)

STYRACOL. (GUAIACOL CINNAMIC ESTER.) White granular crystals, insoluble in water, readily soluble in alcohol; contains 85 per cent. of guaiacol. Given in phthisis, catarrh of the stomach and intestines and in gonorrhœa in doses of 5 to 15 grains thrice daily. 1 oz. cartons, $1.20; 5 grain tablets, bot. of 100.............$1.40
(Knoll & Co. and Merck & Co.)

SUBLAMINE. MERCURIC ETHYLENE-DIAMINE SULPHATE.) Crystalline powder, containing 43 per cent. of mercury; very soluble in water. Used in solutions of 1 to 1000 as a substitute for corrosive sublimate. 1 oz. vials, 50c.; tablets, 15 grains, 100 tablets in bottle, $1.10; 20 tablets in tube, 5 tubes in box..............$1.30
(Schering & Glatz.)

TANNALBIN. (TANNIN ALBUMINATE.) Pale brown, insoluble, tasteless powder, containing about 50 per cent. of tannin. It is not affected by the gastric juice, but is split up in the intestinal canal; hence is used as intestinal astringent and for diarrhœa. Dose, 15 to 30 grains three to five times daily. 1 oz. cartons, 85c.; 5 grain tablets, bot. of 100......$1.00
(Knoll & Co. and Merck & Co.)

TANNIGEN. (ACETYLTANNIN.) Grayish powder, insoluble in water, soluble in alcohol; incompatible with alkalies which decompose it. Intestinal astringent in chronic diarrhœa and intestinal diseases of children. Adult dose, 3 to 10 grains, three to six times daily; children, 1-3 to ½ that quality. 1 oz. bot., per oz....55c. to 75c.
(Continental Color & Chemical Co.)

TANNOPINE. (HEXAMETHYLENETETRAMINE TANNIN.) Brownish powder, insoluble in water, decomposed by alkalies; compound of tannin and urotropine, containing 87 per cent. of tannic acid. Intestinal astringent and disinfectant. Adult dose, 10 to 15 grains; children, 3 to 8 grains four times daily. 1 oz. cartons, per oz..................55c. to 75c.
(Continental Color & Chemical Co.

TESTADEN. Powdered extract of the testicle juice of animals. Used in impotency, neurasthenia and spinal irritation. Dose, 15 grains three to four times daily. 1 oz. vials, $1.30; 4 grain tablets, bot of 100.$1.30
(Knoll & Co. and Merck & Co.)

THEOBROMINE. White crystalline powder, soluble in ether, but almost insoluble in cold water or alcohol; organic base obtained from seeds of *Theobroma cacao*. Diuretic in dropsy of cardiac and renal affections. Dose, 5 to 8 grains. 1 oz. bot., per oz..........90c.
(Continental Color & Chemical Co. and Merck & Co.)

THEOBROMINE - SODIUM - SALICYLATE. White powder, very soluble in water, decomposed by acid solutions. Diuretic in dropsy of cardiac and renal origin. Dose, 7 to 15 grains. 1 oz. bot., per oz. ....60c.
(Farbenfabriken of Elberfeld Co. and Merck & Co.)

THEOCIN. Fine, colorless crystals; synthetic alkaloid of tea (theophylline); difficultly soluble in alcohol and cold water, more easily in warm water; forms salts with alkalies. Powerful diuretic in doses of 3 to 6 grains, two to three times daily. ½ and 1 oz. bot., per oz...............$2.50 to $2.70
(Continental Color & Chemical Co.)

THEOPHYLLIN. White crystalline needles, soluble in 226 parts of water. Identical with theocin, being the synthetic alkaloid of tea. Diuretic in doses of 4 to 8 grains. 1 oz. vials, $1.40. Theophyllin sodium, 1 oz. vials, $1.50. Theophylline sodium salicylate, 1 oz. vials $1.10
(C. F. Boehringer & Soehne.)

THIGENOL. Dark brown, thick liquid; odorless on use; slight empyreumatic taste; soluble in water, diluted alcohol, glycerin and collodion; same uses as ichthyol. It is the sodium salt of the sulphonic acid of a synthetic sulpho oil. Dose, 3 to 10 grains. 1 oz. boxes, per oz., 32c; 1 lb. tins, per lb.....$4.00
(Hoffmann-La Roche Chemical Works.)

THIOCOL. (POTASSIUM GUAIACOL SULPHONATE.) White crystalline powder, soluble in water, slightly in alcohol and ether. Used in phthisis and similar diseases which require the creosote or guaiacol treatment; nonirritating and readily assimilable. Dose, 5 to 20 grains three times daily. 1 oz. bot., per oz., $1.40; tablets, 5 grains each, 100 in bot....$1.75
(Hoffmann-La Roche Chemical Works.)

THIOSINAMIN. Colorless crystals, soluble in water, alcohol and ether; used hypodermically for lupus and uterine affections in doses of 1 to 3 grains in 15 per cent. alcoholic or 10 per cent. glycerinated water solution, one injection being given every three days; by the mouth, in capsules containing ⅛ to 3 grains. 1 oz. vials, per oz. 60c.
(Schering & Glatz and Merck & Co.)

THYMOXOL. Alcoholic 1 per cent. solution of thymol containing 3 per cent. of hydrogen dioxide; miscible with water. Used in 5 or 10 per cent. solutions as antiseptic and bactericide. ¼ lb. bot., per lb....$2.40
(C. Bischoff & Co.)

THYRADEN. Brownish powder; dried extract of sheep's thyroid, containing all the constituents of the gland. Used in myxœdema, obesity, goitre, psoriasis, eczema, menorrhagia and rickets. Dose, 15 to 30 grains daily. 1 oz. vials, $1.80; 2 grain tablets, bot. of 100.75c.
(Knoll & Co. and Merck & Co.)

THYREOIDECTIN. Reddish powder obtained from the blood of animals deprived of the thyreoid gland. A remedy for exophthalmic goitre. Dose, 5 to 10 grains. Capsules, 5 grains each, bot. of 50...$1.00
(Parke, Davis & Co.)

THYROIDIN. Dried extract of sheep's thyroid, 1 part equaling 6 parts of fresh gland. Used in myxœdema, cretinism, psoriasis, obesity, lupus, etc. Dose, ½ to 1 grain, increased to 2 grains three times daily. 1 oz. bot..................$1.25
(Merck & Co.)

TONOLS. Trade name adopted by Schering & Glatz for the

glycerophosphate salts. See under the name of the alkali earth or metallic base.

TRIFERRIN. (IRON PARANUCLEINATE.) Brownish-yellow powder, soluble in alkaline solutions, insoluble in water. Said to contain 22 per cent. of iron, 9 per cent. of nitrogen and 2.5 per cent. of phosphorus. Used in anæmia, chlorosis and debility in dose of 5 grains three times daily. 1 oz. cartons, $1.00; 5 grain tablets, bot. of 50, 75c.; solution (Triferrol), 8 oz. bot., per bot..55c.
(C. Bischoff & Co. and Knoll & Co.)

TRIKRESOL. Clear, colorless liquid; a mixture of ortho, meta and para cresols in the proportion of 35, 40 and 25 per cent., respectively. Corresponding to Creosol, U. S. P., viii; soluble in 40 parts of water. Said to have three times the germicidal power of carbolic acid. Solutions of from ½ to 1 per cent. strength are recommended for surgical use; for internal use 1 to 2 minims three times a day. 1 oz. vials, 15c.; 1 lb. bot. ....60c.
(Schering & Glatz.)

TRIPHENIN. (PROPIONYLPHENETIDIN.) White crystalline powder obtained by the action of propionic acid on paraphenetidine; almost insoluble in water (1 in 2000), more readily in alcohol and ether. Is a strong antipyretic, used in neuralgias and rheumatism in doses of 5 to 15 grains three or four times daily. Tablets, 5 grains, bot. of 50, 65c.; 1 oz. cartons..50c.
(Merck & Co.)

TROPACOCAINE HYDROCHLORIDE. (BENZOYLPSEUDOTROPEINE HYDROCHLORIDE.) Colorless crystals, soluble in water. Local anæsthetic like cocaine, but said to be less depressing to the heart. Used hypodermically in 3 to 10 per cent. solutions in 0.6 per cent. solution of sodium chloride. 5 grain vials, 40c.; 15 grain vials ....95c.
(Merck & Co.)

TUMENOL. Reddish-brown, oily paste, obtained from a bituminous rock deposit. Consists of a mixture of sulphonized hydrocarbons similar to ichthyol, and possessing similar properties, being antiseptic and healing in skin diseases, applied either as attenuated powder, 5 per cent. ointment, or dissolved in ether and alcohol or water and glycerine.

AMMONIUM. Black, viscid, oily liquid, odorless; soluble in water and miscible with oils and fats. Used as antiseptic application in skin diseases, in form of ointment, paste or glycerin-ethereal solution painted on surface. 1 oz. bottles.........25c

OIL is a dark yellow fluid of thick consistency, having the same application as the foregoing.

POWDER. (SULPHOTUMENOLIC ACID.) Dark yellow powder, readily soluble in water. Used with equal parts of zinc starch paste in treatment of skin diseases. Paste, 1 oz. vials, 55c.; ¼ lb. jar, $1.75; ½ lb. jar, $3.25. Oil, 1 oz. vials, 65c.; ¼ lb. bottles, $3.25; 1 lb. bottles, $6.30. Powder, 1 oz. tin, $1.10; 2 oz. tins, per tin. $1.85
(Victor Koechl & Co.)

URITONE. White crystalline powder; a product of formaldehyde and ammonia of the same composition and properties as hexamethylenetetramine; used in treatment of purulent conditions of the urine, cystitis, etc., in doses of 5 to 15 grains. 1 oz. vials, 60c.; 5 grain capsules, per bot. of 100....85c.
(Parke, Davis & Co.)

UROSINE. (LITHIUM QUINATE.) Colorless crystals, readily soluble in water. Used in gout, cystitis and uric acid diathesis. Supplied in effervescent tablets containing quinic acid, 7½ grains; lithium carbonate, 1½ grains; sugar, 4½ grains. Vial of 10, 50c.; 25, $1.20. Powder, 1 oz. vial........................95c.
(C. Bischoff & Co.)

UROTROPIN. (HEXAMETHYLENETETRAMINE.) Colorless granular crystals, with an alkaline reaction; readily soluble in water. Urinary antiseptic in cystitis, bacteruria, phosphaturia, gout, rheumatism, irritable bladder, etc., used also before and after instrumentation to forestall urinary infection. Dose, 5 to 15 grains. 1 oz. vials, 60c.; lb., $7.50; tablets, 7½ grains each, 20 tablets in box, 25c.; 5 grains each, 30 tablets in box..........25c.
(Schering & Glatz.)

UROTROPIN METHYLENE CITRATE. (NEWUROTROPIN.) Crystals resembling urotropin and having same therapeutic indications, though dose is double, being 15 grains three times daily. 1 oz. vials, 60c.; tablets, 7½ grains, 20 tablets in box, per box..........25c.
(Schering & Glatz.)

VALIDOL. (VALERIC ACID MENTHYL ESTER.) Colorless liquid, a combination of valeric acid and menthol; insoluble in water, readily soluble in alcohol. Used in hysteria and neurasthenia in doses of 10 to 15 drops three times daily. Vials, 10 Gm., 50c.; 25 Gm., $1.20; pills, 25 in bot., each......50c.
(C. Bischoff & Co.)

VALIDOL CAMPHORATE. Colorless liquid, insoluble in water, readily soluble in alcohol and oils. A 10 per cent. solution of camphor in validol. Used in toothache by local application and internally in same indications and dose as validol. Vials, 10 Gm. each, 50c.; 25 Gm. $1.20
(C. Bischoff & Co.)

VALYL. (VALERIC ACID DIETHYLAMIDE.) Colorless, oily liquid, with a valerian odor and burning taste, supplied only in gelatin capsules, each containing 2 grains. Nerve sedative used in hysteria, neurasthenia, hypochondriasis, and in neuralgia and menstrual disturbances in doses of 2 or 3 capsules two or three times daily. Bot. of 50 capsules........90c.
(Victor Koechl & Co.)

VERONAL. White crystalline powder, soluble in 150 parts of cold and 12 parts of boiling water. Hypnotic in simple sleeplessness and the insomnia of mania. Dose, 5 to 15 grains, dissolved in hot fluids. 1 oz. bot. and cartons, per oz., $1.60; tablets, 5 grains each, tube of 10, 30c.; bot. of 100 ....$2.25
(Merck & Co. and Continental Color & Chemical Co.)

VIOFORM. (IODOCHLOROXYCHINOLINE.) Greenish-yellow powder, insoluble in water. Used in same way as iodoform, than which it is six times lighter and bulkier. 1 oz. cartons $1.15
(C. Bischoff & Co.)

XEROFORM. (TRIBROMPHENOL-BISMUTH.) Greenish-yellow, insoluble powder, containing bismuth oxide and tribromphenol in nearly equal proportions. A powerful bactericide recommended especially for cholera. Dose, 5 to 20 grains. 1 oz. ....50c.
(Schering & Glatz.)

American Druggist "WANTS" Page.

THIS Department is intended to be used as a medium for the exchange or sale of stores, the employment of clerks, and the securing of situations. Suitable notices of moderate length under this heading inserted one time free for subscribers; for each additional insertion Fifty Cents will be charged. Advertisements not in the foregoing classification Forty Cents per line.

SITUATIONS VACANT.

WANTED.—A young man who has had experience in the manufacture of food products, toilet articles, perfumes, &c., for premium trade. Address, stating salary and experience. Cash Papworth Premium Co., Syracuse, N. Y.

SALESMAN WANTED.—An unusual opportunity for salesmen visiting the regular drug trade to make money. Address promptly the G. S. O. Company, Lancaster, Pa.

WANTED.—Drug employees, wholesale and retail. Vacancies now open in New York, Illinois, Iowa, Arkansas, Alabama, Florida and other States. Salary $50 to $100. Diplomas recognized. If you would accept a better position now or later, send us your name at once. Employers referred to competent men free. National Pharmaceutical Agency, 616 Holland Bldg., St. Louis, Mo.

WANTED.—Licensed clerk at retail drug store. Good position. E. L. Schmitt, 812 North street, Rochester, N. Y.

WANTED, LICENSED CLERK at retail drug store; steady position for right party. Best of references required. Address J. F. S., care of AMERICAN DRUGGIST.

SITUATIONS WANTED.

SALESMAN, PHYSICIAN, also Ph.G., at present employed as manager by a large foreign concern, seeks new position; first-class salesman and specialty introducer; clever ad. writer; can prepare literature in French, German, Italian and Spanish; can superintend a traveling force or manage a business in all its details; has personal acquaintance with the wholesale and retail drug and grocery trade and department stores, physicians, hospitals, their superintendents and trained nurses; quite familiar with all kinds of electrical, medicinal, surgical appliances; have been "at it" nearly twenty years and have references that are gilt edged; a fluent talker, with wide-awake, live ideas; not afraid of being interviewed; small salary, but large commission and steady occupation desired; offers considered from all parts of the world. Address, for ten days, "Dr. A.," 300 Fourth avenue, New York City.

BUSINESS OPPORTUNITIES.

SHEEP DIP, ETC.—A gentleman with special knowledge of the trade and an extensive connection in South Africa wishes to represent a manufacturer of sheep dip in that country; 11 years' experience. Address "Dip," Box 671, Sells Advertising Offices, London, England.

Materia Medica of India

A book full of interest and value for students of pharmacy and medicine. It is entitled,

The indigenous Drugs of india

By KANNY LALL DEY and WILLIAM MAIR

The American Druggist Publishing Company

Offers this authoritative work at the reduced price of 50 cents.

I WISH TO BUY BOOKS of formulas of all kinds. Dr. J. A. Oyster, Paola, Kan.

WANTED—To purchase, a copy of Vol. XXXVI, No. 2, AMERICAN DRUGGIST, 1900. Address Apothecary, Buffalo State Hospital, Buffalo, N. Y.

A BARGAIN.—A Morris Tablet Machine, Style B. Direct Driver. Includes dies and punches; this machine is practically new, having only been in use about three months. ANOTHER BARGAIN.—A 60-Gallon Drug Still, including rectifier, condenser, and low wine still. The still can be operated independent of the rectifier. This set is in splendid condition, being practically good as new. Address Dept A, 212 S. Seventh Street, St. Louis, Mo.

FOR SALE.—Paying drug store in Honolulu, Hawaii. Langley & Michaels Co., 34 First street, San Francisco.

PARTNER WANTED.—I want as an equal partner a good pharmacist and business man who can command $2,000 or $3,000 in real money. I have a store that has a stock of nearly $6,000 in clean, fresh goods, most of it bought in the last eight months, and a business that is too big for one man to handle. It is capable of a vast development, as it is a suburb of New York that may increase its population five fold in the next five years. Would sell out, but am forming a stock company to operate a chain of stores in this section and want this store in the combination. I must have time to attend to this company matter and do not want to lose this store, as it will be an important link in our chain of stores. If I can find the right man I have a good thing for him, as the store will go into the combination as soon as the company is incorporated. Or I will make a contract to sell all my interest to my partner in case he doesn't want to go into the company. In short, I want to hold and continue the building up of this business by some one that I can absolutely depend upon. Apply by letter only to Dawson, care AMERICAN DRUGGIST.

FOR RENT in a flourishing borough of 1,200 population, located in the heart of slate and cement region, a large dwelling house with store room. Building is on Main street and in business center. An A1 opportunity with practically no opposition to drug business. For further information address F. Geise, 235 Berkley street, Germantown, Phila.

DRUG STORE FOR SALE.—Business established over 25 years; best location on Jersey Coast. Profits over 100 per cent. each season on money invested. Address Bargain, care of AMERICAN DRUGGIST.

WHAT OFFERS?

Mrs. G. C. de Lessing, 945 Park Avenue, New York, wishes to dispose of the library of her late husband and invites offers on the following books:

Dick, William B. Encyclopædia of Practical Receipts and Processes. 6,422 receipts. Third edition, 1879.

Stille and Maisch. The National Dispensatory, 1880.

The National Formulary of Unofficial Preparations. Revised edition, 1896.

Merck's Index. Second edition. An encyclopedia for the physician and the pharmacist, 1896.

Merck's Manual of the Materia Medica. A ready reference pocket book for the physician and surgeon. 1899.

Coblentz. The Newer Remedies, 1896.

Nelson, John H. Druggists' Handbook of Private Formulas. Revised edition, 1882.

Bonney, G. E. The Electroplater's Handbook, 1894.

Lieber, Hugo. The Use of Coal Tar Colors in Food Products, 1904.

Snively, John H., Ph.D. A Treatise on the Manufacture of Perfumes and Kindred Toilet Articles, 1890.

THE following Advertisement is one of a series now being run in all the important Horse and Farm Papers in United States, Canada and England.

Your demand for ABSORBINE will be greatly increased. Regular Jobbers can supply you. Mail me your card so I can place it on file and refer inquiries from your section to you for supplies.

FOR cleansing everything about a drug store or a soda fountain there is nothing equal to Hoffman's

Barkeeper's Friend

Marble, Glass, Nickel, Brass, Copper, Tin and German Silver

can all be cleaned and polished with it easier than with anything else. Let us send you a FREE SAMPLE.

Highest Award, Chicago World's Fair, 1893, Louisiana Purchase Exposition, St. Louis, Mo., 1904.

GEO. WM. HOFFMAN, 295 E. Washington St. Indianapolis, Ind.

FOR SALE BY JOBBING TRADE

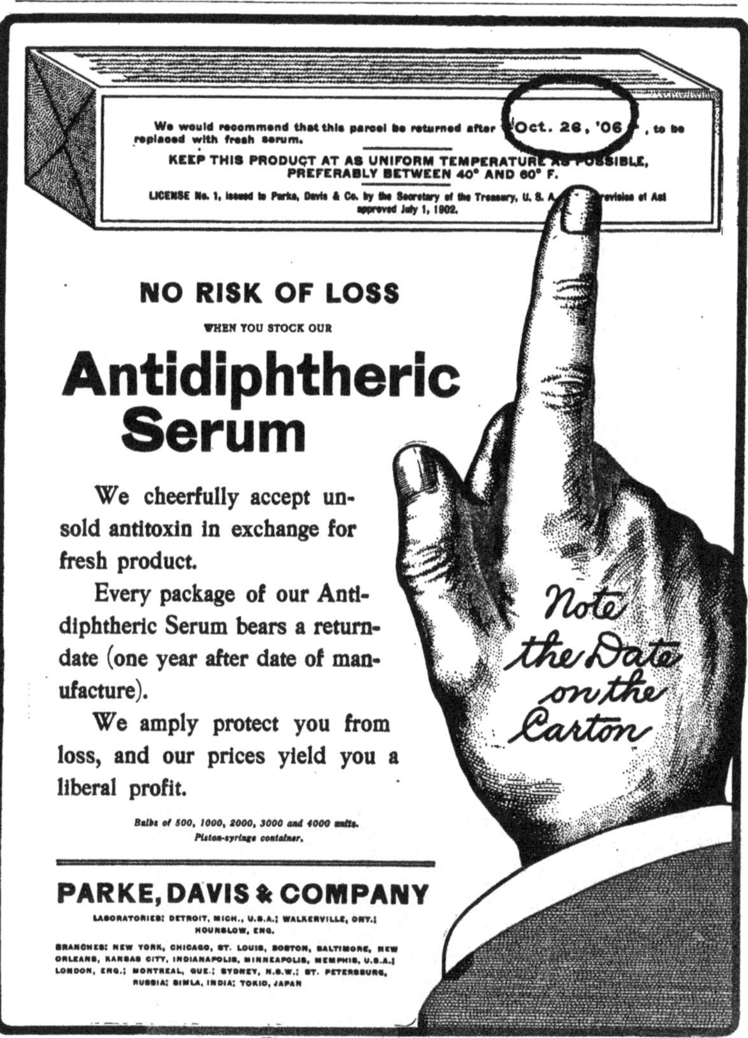
We would recommend that this parcel be returned after Oct. 26, '06, to be replaced with fresh serum.
KEEP THIS PRODUCT AT AS UNIFORM TEMPERATURE AS POSSIBLE, PREFERABLY BETWEEN 40° AND 60° F.
LICENSE No. 1, issued to Parke, Davis & Co. by the Secretary of the Treasury, U. S. A.
approved July 1, 1902.
NO RISK OF LOSS
WHEN YOU STOCK OUR
Antidiphtheric Serum
We cheerfully accept unsold antitoxin in exchange for fresh product.
Every package of our Antidiphtheric Serum bears a return-date (one year after date of manufacture).
We amply protect you from loss, and our prices yield you a liberal profit.
Bulbs of 500, 1000, 2000, 3000 and 4000 units.
Piston-syringe container.
PARKE, DAVIS & COMPANY
LABORATORIES: DETROIT, MICH., U.S.A.; WALKERVILLE, ONT.; HOUNSLOW, ENG.
BRANCHES: NEW YORK, CHICAGO, ST. LOUIS, BOSTON, BALTIMORE, NEW ORLEANS, KANSAS CITY, INDIANAPOLIS, MINNEAPOLIS, MEMPHIS, U.S.A.; LONDON, ENG.; MONTREAL, QUE.; SYDNEY, N.S.W.; ST. PETERSBURG, RUSSIA; SIMLA, INDIA; TOKIO, JAPAN
Note the Date on the Carton

The Changes in the Pharmacopœia.

The new United States Pharmacopœia makes many changes in the strength of drugs and preparations, reducing some, increasing others as much as double. The law recognizes the *current* U. S. Pharmacopœia as the standard. To avoid accidents and damage suits on the one hand, and puzzling lack of results on the other, both the druggist and doctor must follow the *same* standard. As a convenient pocket reminder of these changes, the importance of which must be at once obvious to every physician and pharmacist, Messrs. Lea Brothers & Co., the medical publishers, of 706-8-10 Sansom street, Philadelphia, and 111 Fifth avenue, New York, have issued for *free* distribution a carefully prepared leaflet giving an alphabetical list of the important changes. The strength of each preparation listed is given as in both the old and the new U. S. P.

To assist in preventing untoward or negative results in the use of powerful drugs this leaflet will prove handy and valuable.

A postal card request will bring a copy to any physician, druggist, student or nurse.

A Handsome Soda Fountain for a Toronto Druggist.

George A. Bingham of 100 Yonge street, Toronto, has one of the largest and finest drug stores in Canada. In the rear is a most attractive palm garden, under cover, 50 by 25 feet, decorated with handsome growing palms. Here customers may sit at the little tables and enjoy the egg phosphates, sundaes, college ices and other popular soda fountain drinks.

W. J. Cahill, manager of sales at the home office of the American Soda Fountain Company, Boston, has secured an order from Mr. Bingham for a handsome Innovation fountain of latest design, having a dispensing counter 30 feet in length. This will be of fine white Italian marble, set off by green marble pilasters and top and base mouldings. The slab will be of white Italian marble. There are three onyx draft stands, two of them with the usual soda water and mineral water draft arms, the other arranged for hot soda. Each of these is surmounted by a handsome electric light fixture. The superstructure of the display, or wall section, is to be finished in white enamel and gold, inlaid with onyx. The refrigerator base of the wall section is of white Italian marble.

The fountain is to be installed early in March, and Mr. Bingham expects to have the distinction of owning the handsomest fountain in the Dominion. We are glad to have American goods in Canada such as reflect credit on American manufacturers, and the American Soda Fountain Company may be depended upon to uphold our national reputation in this line. The Toronto people are sure to be delighted with this beautiful and artistic fountain.

Kymo Makes Delicious Ice Cream.

Ice cream which possess richness, smoothness and a good body is far superior to the same delicacy when it is lacking in both body and richness. It is also a safe bet that the high grade ice cream will sell much more rapidly and produce better results for the dealer. The only objection to the production of rich, smooth cream with a good body and proper expansion has formerly been the increased cost, but when this is eliminated the acme of perfection in cream making and the consequent money making appear to be within the reach of all. Kymo, a preparation which will produce delicious ice cream from milk alone, is therefore a very desirable article. It is manufactured by the Kymo Company, 6 Mill street, Little Falls, N. Y., which will supply complete directions, so simple that they can be followed with the best of results by a youngster as well as by an experienced cream maker. The Kymo Company is so confident that its product will be appreciated by every ice cream manufacturer that it offers to send a free sample of Kymo to all such so that it may be thoroughly tested.

It would be a good time to try Kymo before the ice cream season opens. If you desire, a 50-cent package will be sent to you for 25 cents or a 75-cent package for 40 cents; the postage will be prepaid by the Kymo Company, which will also send you a booklet on the cost, quality and healthfulness of Kymo ice cream, showing how to save 25 to 50 per cent. in production.

Lilly & Co.'s Pharmaceuticals.

Druggists who desire to make sure of obtaining quality in the purchase of your pharmaceuticals, it will pay you to investigate the virtues of those manufactured by Eli Lilly & Co., of Indianapolis, New York, Chicago, St. Louis, Kansas City and New Orleans, unless you have, like many other druggists, been using them regularly for many years, in which case you do not need to have them recommended to you. As every druggist knows, no field of manufacture is more exacting and possessed of graver responsibilities than the making of supplies for physicians' prescriptions, and it is equally true that Lilly & Co.'s products show that a constant effort has been made to manufacture supplies which shall make the name of Lilly a guarantee and sign of goods honestly made with fullest knowledge and highest skill. In its advertisement in this issue the company pledges itself to continue its policy of helping the dealer to build up and maintain a profitable prescription business.

A Large Demand for Sanitol.

The Sanitol Chemical Laboratory Company is spending $200,000 this year in advertising. Fourteen of the largest magazines in the country are to-day carrying large spaces each month. In addition to this Sanitol is carrying on the most unique newspaper advertising campaign ever conducted for a dentifrice. All the newspapers in about 50 of the largest cities in the United States are being used, the illustrations for them being in black and white, silhouette, all of them beautifully executed. In the city of St. Louis, where the newspaper campaign first began, the Sanitol sales jumped in two weeks 33 per cent., and to-day it is claimed that there are more of the Sanitol tooth and toilet preparations sold in St. Louis than any other. With this advertising the company is sending out beautiful window display screens, showing the Sanitol Girl, reproduced in 12 colors. Special propositions now being given to the retail drug trade in the United States by the Sanitol Company have enabled the retail druggist to make more profit on Sanitol than ever before, profits for the small as well as large purchasers being proportionate. This company, too, is carrying out special plans which protect the price of its goods in the market. We have no doubt that this mammoth advertising campaign will put Sanitol in the front rank as a seller by all retail druggists, and the retailer is sure to respond by giving Sanitol the first call in his store. The new advertising matter, lithographed cards, counter displays and window displays can be secured by writing the Sanitol Chemical Laboratory Company, St. Louis, Mo.

Apollinaris and lager are the choice of drinks for breakfast at the Hôtel Métropole, Sekondi, West Africa, built by Sir Alfred Jones, of Liverpool. Water is so scarce that tea is not to be had for love or money, and after a bit they find that "Polly" suits them better than the hot drinks.—*The Chemist and Druggist.*

PHARMACEUTICAL RESEARCH BY A COMMERCIAL HOUSE.

A Sketch of the House of Merck—Its Contributions to Pharmacology—Dates of Historical Interest.

An interesting sketch of the House of Merck appears in a recent issue of the *British & Colonial Druggist* which traces the history of the house from the days of Cromwell and the Thirty Years War when Frederich Jacob Merck, an ancestor of the present E. Merck, is mentioned as the owner of the "Engelapotheke" in Darmstadt. This "Engel" pharmacy has remained in the uninterrupted possession of the Merck family for 237 years and furnished the nucleus of the chemical house of E. Merck.

The idea of developing from this pharmacy an independent manufacturing concern did not, however, fructify until 1831, when the actual founder of the firm, Heinrich Emanuel Merck, in his attempts, in conjunction with Liebig, of Giessen, and Geiger, of Heidelberg, to establish an association for the exchange of pharmaceutical and purely chemical preparations failed for want of support on the part of the German apothecaries. Four years previously, in 1827, H. E. Merck had prepared morphine—with which Serturner had enriched science but a few years—and shortly afterwards received a Paris Exhibition award for his products.

SANTONIN AND MORPHINE.

In 1830 Kahler, a Düsseldorf apothecary, and Augustus Alms, a druggist's assistant at Penzlin, in Mecklenburg-Schwerin, working apart, almost simultaneously discovered santonin, and this, in conjunction with morphine, was one of the first preparations made on a commercial scale by Merck. In this connection Robert Mayer, the celebrated propounder of the mechanical theory of heat, who had used Merck's santonin in carrying out the experiments which were to furnish material for his graduation thesis ("Das Santonin: Inaugural Dissertation zur Erlangung der Doctorwürde." Printed 1838, by Maximilian Müller, Heilbronn), made the following observations with regard to the preparation of this body: "Mr. Apothecary Merck, of Darmstadt, who since 1833 has been the first to prepare santonin commercially, employs for this purpose the best Levant santonica, which he digests with alcohol and calcium hydrate. The alcohol is then evaporated, the extract decomposed by acetic acid, and the resulting impure santonin crystals purified by repeated recrystallization. By this means he derives from 1 pound of seed, according to its quality, ½ to 2 drachms of dazzling white crystals of santonin."

PHARMACEUTICALS AS WELL AS CHEMICALS.

This was followed by the preparation of emetine, strychnine, picrotoxin, later that of codeine, and in 1836 that of narceine and amorphous veratrine, whereas the crystallized alkaloid (cevadine) discovered by Dr. George Merck was not prepared until 1855. The preparation in large quantities of jalapin was begun in 1840, that of atropine and its salts some 10 years later. The preparation of alkaloids went hand in hand with that of extracts, and gradually the manufacture of articles used in the trade associated itself with that of purely pharmaceutical preparations. Later operations embraced hippuric acid, chrysophanic acid, arbutin, cantharidin, theobromine, caffeine, colchicin, solanine, digitalin and bromoform. It was also about this time, the middle of the last century, that the manufacture of pyrogallic acid, gallic acid, tannin and nitrate of silver was taken up.

In 1853 the firm was awarded a medal for its exhibits at the New York Exposition. Cocaine, which had been isolated by Lossen, was first prepared in 1862, but 22 years elapsed before it was introduced into therapeutics by Koller and Freud. It is interesting to note that it was cocaine prepared by Merck which was used in these classical experiments. Of other pharmaceutical preparations belonging to this period we hear mentioned for the first time: aloin, podophyllin, koussein, physostigmine, hyoscyamine, oxalate of cerium, and a few important cæsium and rubidium compounds.

The year 1870 saw an extension of the manufacture of preparations intended for purely chemical, microscopic and industrial purposes, and in this year we read of the manufacture of apomorphine, crystallized aconitine, pilocarpine and some of its salts, as well as various bismuth and lithium preparations. The preparation of sparteine and its salts dates from 1872, then followed cotoin preparations, and in 1874 salicylic acid. Salicylate of eserine was originated by the firm towards the end of the seventies, and 10 years later the rarer opium alkaloids became the subject of comprehensive investigations. Shortly after the works produced in commercial quantities the two poisonous proteids, abrin and ricin.

THE MORPHINE DERIVATIVES.

In 1898 the establishment underwent a considerable expansion by the incorporation of the chemical works of H. Trommsdorff in Erfurt, which were practically taken over in their entirety inclusive of the scientific staff. After this influx of fresh blood the firm proceeded to introduce several now well-known preparations. Dionin made its appearance as a substitute for morphine and codeine, and became highly valued and largely employed as a pectoral and analgesic, especially in gynæcology. About the same time iodipin and bromipin entered the arena as substitutes for iodides and bromides. Iodipin has excited the liveliest interest, and has found extensive and most beneficial application in human and veterinary medicine, especially as an agent in hypodermic therapy.

A few years ago perhydrol was introduced in deference to the wishes of eminent surgeons. After lengthy and laborious experiments a preparation was at last produced which contained 30 per cent. by weight of absolutely pure, and hence also quite acid-free, peroxide of hydrogen. This was a quality by which perhydrol differed very markedly from ordinary peroxide of hydrogen.

The same applies to another preparation, the new hypnotic veronal, which was first prepared commercially and introduced into therapeutics by this firm. Despite its many competitors this hypnotic has made its presence felt in a manner which is almost without a parallel in the history of pharmacology. Though introduced but two years ago, it has with little dissent come to be widely praised as a safe and reliable hypnotic.

Some two years ago, when the works had expanded as far as its central situation rendered it possible, a new site was secured, and an entirely new concern planned and erected on a more favorable site. This new establishment, being the result not of gradual evolution but of a harmonious design, is entirely modern, and provided with buildings, appliances, and well-equipped laboratories of the most advanced type.

In America the firm of Merck & Co. have grown so rapidly that some years ago they purchased a large chemical plant in St. Louis entire, that of Herf & Frerichs. Besides they have also erected a very large plant occupying some forty acres at Rahway, N. J. One distinctive feature of the history of E. Merck & Co. is the attention which it has always paid to scientific investigations which have no immediate and direct bearing on commercial aspects of the business, but it is this scientific work which has served to make the name of Merck a power in the commercial world as well as in that of science.

Send Ten Names.

The Randall-Faichney Company, Boston, will be pleased to mail with your compliments a sample of their non-leakable, non-breakable hypodermic needles to any ten physicians whose addresses you may furnish. This is an opportunity for special advertising which you should not neglect. Send the names of ten of your best physicians. It will cost you nothing. Write the D. L. Bates & Brother Company, Dayton, O., for their catalogue of fans and ice shavers, both of which are a necessity at every well-regulated soda fountain.

The fourteenth edition of Fenner's Twentieth Century Formulary and International Dispensatory, comprising the changes in the new U. S. P.—1,868 pages—is announced by the publishers, The Fenner Press, Westfield, N. Y.

Seabury on a Merchant Marine.

An interesting addition to Seaburyana has appeared in the form of a pamphlet entitled "My Last Plea for an Oversea Merchant Marine," the title page of which shows a "Jackie" nailing a star spangled banner to the mast. This is a subject on which George J. Seabury has been long and ardently interested and upon which he has made addresses on various occasions and has written copiously. He thus summarizes the "Four Paramount and Patriotic Motives for Restoring an American Oversea Merchant Marine":

"(1.) American independence in times of peace for the transportation of our great exports, imports, passengers and mails, and in time of war for conveying our army, navy and war materials.

"(2.) For establishing oversea steamship and clipper ship construction co-operatively, involving the utilization of American crude materials, grown products and multifarious manufactures and establishing new labor fields that will create additional national prosperity.

"(3.) It is the only unprotected American industry. The reasons why our flag on the high seas remains unfurled are not openly explainable at this time, nor is the absence of a merchant marine wrapt in mystery. Its suppression may be discussed if the Congressional Marine Commission's Shipping bill, or one equally effective, fails to receive President Roosevelt's signature in 1906.

"(4.) The creation of an adequate force of American navigators and seamen is a vital need in time of war. This will be a natural sequence of a restored merchant marine. At present the trade of sailoring on the high seas in the United States is practically among the 'lost arts.' It is one of the neglected gainful occupations. The power of Congress to provide us with the ships will naturally develop a great force of trained navigators and seamen to meet any demand needed for naval war exigencies."

Mr. Seabury says in the introduction to his pamphlet that "Americans have attained commercial supremacy. Our chief industrial competitors for export trade are Great Britain and Germany. They maintain and promote their commerce through a great merchant marine service. They have established regular lines to all the commercial seaports by granting to their shipping lines subventions or liberal subsidies for the expansion of their commerce and the employment of their labor field. If such a Governmental enterprise were not remunerative in the forms and for the purposes named, their statesmen and legislators would not have consented to indorse such acts. A powerful nation like our own, having great natural resources, all the constructive forces—capital, diversified manufactured wares, skilled and unskilled labor in great abundance—should no longer permit a liberal National Shipping Act to be defeated! It is absolutely necessary for our great and growing commerce! It is high time that equal competitive subventions were granted to American shipping lines. Oversea shipbuilding will become a permanent national industry of great value in peace or war."

Must Not Accept Gratuities.

The *New York Journal of Commerce*, asked to quote the New York law recently enacted, "making it a punishable offense against the law for a buyer to accept a commission or other payment from those from which he purchases for his employer," replies:

The act to which our correspondent refers is chapter 136 of the Laws of 1905. It adds to the Penal Code a new section, to be known as 384r. It declares to be guilty of a misdemeanor any one of the four following classes of persons:

(1) Any one who "gives, offers or promises to an agent, employee or servant any gift or gratuity whatever, without the knowledge and consent of the principal, employer or master of such agent, employee or servant, with intent to influence his action in relation to his principal's, employer's or master's business";

(2) An agent, employee or servant who, without the knowledge and consent of his principal, etc., requests or accepts a gift or gratuity or a promise to do an act beneficial to himself, under an agreement or with an understanding that he shall act in any particular manner in his employer's business;

(3) An agent, employee, etc., authorized to procure materials, supplies or other articles, either by purchase or contract, for his employer, or to employ service or labor for his employer, who receives, directly or indirectly, for himself or for another, a commission, discount or bonus from the person who makes such sale or contract, or furnishes such materials, etc., or from a person who renders such service or labor;

(4) Any person who gives or offers to such an agent or employee such commission or bonus.

The punishment is a fine of not less than $10 nor more than $500, or such fine and imprisonment for not more than one year. The act became effective on September 1, 1905.

New Customs Decisions.

A customs decision of much importance to drug importers was handed down last week by United States General Appraiser McClelland, sustaining the claim of Schering & Glatz. The merchandise involved was invoiced as crude camphor, but was returned by the appraiser of the port as refined camphor, and duty was accordingly assessed at the rate of 6 cents a pound. The importers claimed free entry, or, as an alternative, duty at the rate of ¼ of one cent a pound and 10 per cent. ad valorum. The decision says in part: "There seems to be no merit whatever in the said alternative claim made under paragraph 20, and it is therefore overruled." The question is "narrowed down to whether the merchandise is crude or refined camphor, but from the testimony taken on the hearing there arises the further question as to whether the merchandise is either the crude or refined camphor of commerce, it having been stated and, as a matter of fact, conceded on the record, that the merchandise is not produced from the gum of the camphor tree but is a synthetic product, the result of a partially secret process covered by letters patent issued by the United States. In view of the concession on the part of the protestant and the contention made in the brief of counsel for the Government, it may be accepted that the article in question is synthetic camphor. It thus appears that the merchandise is neither crude nor refined camphor—the product of the camphor tree, but an artificial product which counsel for the Government contends should be classified as a chemical compound under paragraph 3. The board has made numerous decisions wherein it has been held that articles of merchandise, which, through changes in manufacturing processes, the result of new discoveries, are artificial in character and are known in trade as substitutes for natural products, are entitled to the same classification as the natural product or the article which originally was known by a name which had a much narrower significance. The official examiner in the appraiser's office at the port of New York, experienced in appraising camphor, was unable to say whether the official sample was gum camphor or a synthetic product. We are of the opinion, therefore, that the merchandise before us must be considered to be camphor within the meaning of the term as used in the tariff act. To hold otherwise would be in effect, in innumerable cases doubtless, an abridgement of the opportunity for carrying out new discoveries in manufacturing processes. We find the merchandise to be crude camphor and sustain the claim for free entry under paragraph 513, the decision of the collector being reversed accordingly."

The Board of General Appraisers held that dried pods or fruit of the red pepper (genus capsicum) are dutiable under the provision in the tariff for "capsicum or red pepper, or Cayenne pepper," and not as vegetables in their natural state, at a lower rate of duty. The importers, J. R. Dagnino & Co., had protested against the assessment of duty by the collector at Boston.

Ginseng root, imported at New York by Yee Hing, was classified as a drug advanced in value. The importer claimed free entry on the ground that the merchandise was a crude drug. The Board did not allow this claim.

THE IDEAL SIGHT-RESTORER

Is Your Sight Failing?

All refractive errors, muscular trouble and chronic diseases of the Eye successfully treated by scientific MASSAGE.

"I am in my seventy-ninth year, and have the Sight Restorer and yourselves to thank for renewed eye-sight." (Testimonial 177)

"I wish I could impress every one afflicted so they would give the Restorer a trial." (Testimonial 944)

English, German or Spanish pamphlet mailed free. Address

THE IDEAL COMPANY, 239 Broadway, New York.

WHY NOT SEND US A TRIAL ORDER FOR

MEXICAN NATIONAL PILLS?

They say they are the greatest of Antimalarials !! If you do not want a gross, try a dozen.
We can send them by mail.

Your profit on a dozen will be . . . . 41 per cent. . . . . Dozen $4.25
Your profit on a gross will be . . . 59 per cent. . . . . Gross 46.00

THE NATIONAL PILL CO. Apartado 2357. Mexico, D. F., Mex.

OR

MEYER BROTHERS DRUG CO., St. Louis, Mo.

Paints, Varnishes, Mixed Paints, Brushes, Etc.

In Every Variety

Largest and oldest manufacturers in the world.

Finest Quality

We use only raw material of superior class and guarantee that our products will give perfect satisfaction, having proven successful in every test to which they have been subjected.

Once Tried Always Used

Cheap paints and varnishes of other makes in which materials of inferior grade have been used, invariably crack, split, wear out quickly, and are not to be recommended. There is no economy in buying anything but the *very best*; they are cheapest in the end.

We make only this kind.

Barnices, Pinturas y Mezcladas, Brochas, Etc.

En Todas las Variedades

Los más grandes y más antiguos manufactureros en el mundo.

Las Calidades más Finas

Usamos solamente materias primas de la clase más superior y garantizamos que nuestros productos dan perfecta satisfacción, saliendo victoriosos en cualquier prueba á que se les someta.

Una Vez Probadas Siempre Usadas

Pinturas baratas y barnices de otras fábricas, en las que materiales de clase inferior se han usado, invariablemente se cuartean, descascaran, se acaban pronto ó quedan sin uso, no siendo por ningún respecto recomendadas. No hay economía alguna en comprar otras excepto cuando se adquieren las *muy mejores*, son al fin las más baratas.

Nosotros fabricamos solamente esta clase.

Catálogo Español completo enviado franco al hacer aplicación.

F. W. DEVOE & C. T. RAYNOLDS CO., 101 Fulton Street, NEW YORK, U. S. A.

Cucumber and Elder Flower Cream. ✤ Quick Hair Restorer.

Tomorrow Is the Day That People Order Things That Never Get them

THIS must be so or we wouldn't be saying it—and perhaps you know of some things you were sure you were going to order "tomorrow" that haven't showed up yet. We would like to suggest that TODAY you write us asking for a trial package of our handsome and impressive advertising matter that sells the goods. We've been offering this trial package of expensive printed matter which, together with the express, costs us over a dollar, for one cent—the price of a postal card—and we'll keep on offering it in the hope that we'll catch you tomorrow if not today. Our advertising matter in your store will increase your sales; it positively will; and you won't have to order a penny's worth of our goods till you want to. We're doing a lot of high-class magazine advertising, and the counter advertising supplements this and adds to its value. Let us send you the package today—to increase your business.

MRS. GERVAISE GRAHAM,

1262 Michigan Ave., Chicago, Ill.

MRS. GERVAISE GRAHAM

Kindly mention AMERICAN DRUGGIST when writing to Advertisers.

Alphabetical Index to Advertisers.

Where numbers are omitted, the advertisement appears in alternate issues.

(For Classified Index see pages IO *and* II.)

ORIGINAL PACKAGE PRICES.

It should be understood that the prices quoted in this column are strictly those current in the wholesale market, and that higher prices are paid for retail lots. The quality of goods frequently necessitates a considerable range of prices.

Drugs, Chemicals, &c.

Acetanilid	lb.	.28	@	.34
Acetate of Lime:				
Brown	100 lb.	1.60	@	1.65
Gray	100 lb.	2.35	@	2.40
Acetone	lb.	.15½	@	.16
Acid:				
Acetic Com'l	100 lb.	2.60	@	2.73
Acetic C. P.	lb.	.21	@	.25
Acetic, Glacial		.30	@	.33½
Aquafortis, 36°	lb.	.05½	@	.05½
" 40°	lb.	...	@	.05½
Benzoic, Ger	lb.	.30	@	.31
" Eng	oz.	.10	@	.10½
Boric, Cryst	lb.	.10	@	.10½
" powd	lb.	.10	@	.10½
Carbol. cryst., blk	lb.	.15	@	.15½
lb. bottle	lb.	.20	@	.22
Chrysophanic		2.50	@	2.65
Citric, dom	lb.	.32	@	.35½
" Sicilian	lb.	...	@	...
Gallic	lb.	.53	@	.65
Muriatic C. P.	lb.	.07½	@	.08½
Nitric C. P.	lb.	.07½	@	.10
Oxalic, English	lb.	.05½	@	.06½
Phosphoric	lb.	.18	@	.22½
Picric	lb.	.30	@	.33
Pyrogallic	lb.	1.35	@	...
Salicylic	lb.	.31	@	.31
Sulphuric, 66°	lb.	.01½	@	.02
Tartaric, crystals	lb.	.27½	@	.28½
powdered	lb.	.28	@	.29½
Tannic, cryst	lb.	.58	@	.63
Alcohol, grain	gal.	2.47	@	2.49
Molasses		2.45	@	2.47
wood, 95-97%	gal.	.70	@	.75
Aloin	lb.	.45	@	.50
Alum, Lump	100 lb.	1.75	@	1.85
Ground	100 lb.	1.85	@	1.95
Ammon, carb		.08½	@	.08½
" bromide, bulk		.23	@	.21
" iodide, bulk		4.75	@	4.80
Aniline Oil		.09	@	.09½
Salt		.08½	@	.08½
Antipyrine (New)	oz.	...	@	.18
Arrowroot, Bermuda	lb.	.38	@	.40
St. Vincent, in bbl	lb.	.06½	@	.08
Arsenic: Red Saxon	lb.	.06½	@	.07
White	lb.	.09½	@	.10
Balm of Gilead Buds	lb.	.32	@	.33
Balsam Copaiba, Cent. Amer	lb.	.30	@	.32
Para	lb.	.40	@	.42
Fir, Canada	gal.	3.10	@	3.20
Fir, Oregon	gal.	.70	@	.80
Peru	lb.	1.00	@	1.05
Tolu	lb.	.20	@	.22
Bark, Angostura	lb.	.35	@	.40
Buckthorn	lb.	.05	@	.05½
Cascara Sag	lb.	.06½	@	.10
Cascarilla	lb.	.10	@	.14
Cotton root	lb.	.08½	@	.10
Cramp	lb.	.07	@	.09
Elm, select	lb.	.18	@	.20
Pine, white	lb.	.05	@	.06
Prickly Ash	lb.	.11	@	.15
Sassafras	lb.	.13½	@	.14
Soap—whole	lb.	.05	@	.05½
Crushed	lb.	.05½	@	.06
Wild Cherry	lb.	.05½	@	.10
Bismuth, citrate	lb.	1.75	@	1.80
" ammon cit	lb.	1.85	@	1.90
" subnit	blk.	1.50	@	1.55
" subcarb	lb.	1.75	@	1.80
" subgallate	lb.	1.85	@	1.90
Bleaching Powder, Eng		.01½	@	.01½
German B.		.01½	@	.01½
Domestic		.01	@	.01½
Blue Vitriol	lb.	.05½	@	.06
Borax, Refined	lb.	.07½	@	.07½
powd. conc	lb.	.07½	@	.08
crystals	lb.	.07½	@	.07½
Brimstone, crude 2d	ton.	22.00	@	...
Bromine, bulk	lb.	.22	@	.25
Burgundy Pitch	lb.	.04	@	.04½
Cacao Butter, blk		.29	@	...
" " 12 lb. boxes		.35	@	.40
Caffeine	lb.	...	@	2.65
Calcium hypophosphite	lb.	.60	@	.64
Cantharides, Chinese	lb.	.52½	@	.55
" powd	lb.	.54	@	.56
Russian, whole	lb.	1.25	@	1.30
Cassia Buds	lb.	.18½	@	.19½
Castor Oil, No. 1, bbl	lb.	.11	@	.12
" " No. 1, cases	lb.	.11½	@	.12½
" " No. 3, bbl	lb.	.10½	@	.11½
" " No 3, cases	lb.	.10½	@	.11½
Caustic Soda	100 lb.	1.70	@	1.75
Chalk, Eng. Precip., bulk	lb.	.06	@	...
Chloral Hydrate, crystals, bulk	lb.	...	@	0.95
crusts, blk	lb.	...	@	0.98
Chloroform, bulk	lb.	.25	@	.30
Cinchonidine Sulph	oz.	.12	@	.15
Cocaine Muriate	oz.	3.25	@	3.50
Codeine Sulph	oz.	3.20	@	3.40
Cod Liver Oil, Norweg.	bbl.	28.00	@	28.00
Newfoundland	bbl.	24.00	@	25.00
Colocynth, Trieste	lb.	.30	@	.32
Spanish	lb.	.25	@	.28
Copperas, car lots	100 lb.	.47½	@	.52
single bbls	100 lb.	.57½	@	.65
Creosote, Beechwood		.85	@	.90
Cream Tartar lb.	powd.	.22½	@	.23
Cubeb berries, xx	lb.	.09	@	.10
Powdered	lb.	.11	@	.13
Cutch, bales	lb.	.07½	@	.08
boxes	lb.	.06	@	.06½
Cuttle Bone, Trieste	lb.	.16½	@	.17
French	lb.	.12	@	.13
Jewelers', large	lb.	.70	@	...
" small	lb.	.40	@	.45
Dextrin	lb.	.05½	@	.05
Divi Divi	ton.	30.00	@	45.00
Dragon's Bl'd, lump	lb.	.15	@	.18
In reeds	lb.	.50	@	.55
Epsom Salts	100 lb.	.85	@	1.00
Ergot, German	lb.	.35	@	.40
Spanish	lb.	.45	@	.48
Ergotine, Dom	lb.	4.25	@	5.00
Flowers, Arnica	lb.	.09	@	.10
Flowers—cont'd				
Calendula	lb.	.25	@	.30
Chamomile, Roman	lb.	.16	@	.22
German	lb.	.10	@	.18
Hungarian	lb.	.09½	@	.11
Insect, open	lb.	.15	@	.17
Half closed	lb.	.16	@	.25
Closed	lb.	.26	@	...
Powder	lb.	.14	@	.22
Lavender	lb.	.12	@	.13
Select	lb.	.15	@	.20
Saffron, Amer	lb.	1.25	@	...
Spanish Alicante	lb.	4.75	@	5.00
" Valencia	lb.	8.00	@	8.50
Formaldehyde	lb.	.09	@	.09½
Glauber Salt	per 100 lb.	.40	@	.80
Glycerin, C. P. drums	lb.	.11½	@	.11½
" cans	lb.	.12½	@	.12½
Grains of Paradise	lb.	.11½	@	.15
Guarana	lb.	.62	@	.65
Gums: Aloes, Cape		.08	@	.10
" Barbadoes	lb.	.14	@	.16
" Curacoa		.05	@	.08½
" Socot	lb.	.18	@	.20
Arabic, 1st pkd	lb.	.30	@	...
" 2d pkd	lb.	.19	@	.22
" sorts	lb.	.06½	@	.11
Asafoetida	lb.	.15	@	.22
Benzoin, Sumatra	lb.	.34	@	.38
Siam	lb.	.90	@	1.08
Camphor, ref'd. blk	lb.	.94	@	..
cases	lb.	.94½	@	...
Chicle	lb.	.36	@	.38
Gamboge	lb.	.85	@	.86
Guaiac	lb.	.17	@	.23
Kino	lb.	.25	@	.28
Mastic	lb.	.46	@	.48
Myrrh	lb.	.25	@	.28
Olibanum	lb.	.10	@	.15
Sandarac	lb.	.14	@	.18
Senegal, pkd	lb.	.11	@	.13
Tragacanth, Aleppo	lb.	.30	@	.85
Tragacanth, Turkey	lb.	.35	@	.80
Haarlem Oil		3.00	@	3.25
Hypophosphite lime	lb.	.48	@	.50
" potash	lb.	.48	@	.50
" soda	lb.	.48	@	.50
Ichthyol	lb.	4.00	@	4.25
Indigo	lb.	.90	@	1.25
Insect Pwd. pure	lb.	.14	@	.25
Iodine, resub		2.70	@	2.75
Iodoform	lb.	3.00	@	3.05
Iron citrate, U. S. P.	lb.	.....	@	.41
" and ammon. cit	lb.	.....	@	.38
and ammon. citrate (green scales)				
and quinine citrate	lb.	1.15	@	1.20
phosphate, scales	lb.	....	@	.38
pyrophosphate, scales	lb.	....	@	.38
quinine and strychnine citrate	lb.	1.65	@	1.70
Isinglass, Amer	lb.	.75	@	.80
Russian	lb.	4.00	@	4.10
Juniper Berries	lb.	.03½	@	.04
Lanoline	lb.	.60	@	.65
Leaves: Aconite		.09	@	.10
Belladonna	lb.	.10	@	.11
Buchu, short	lb.	.17	@	.20
" long	lb.	.45	@	.50
Cannabis Indica, tops	lb.	1.00	@	1.10
Coca, Truxillo	lb.	.17	@	.18
" Huanuco	lb.	.30	@	.33
Damiana	lb.	.08	@	.10
Digitalis	lb.	.08½	@	.09
Grindelia robusta	lb.	.08	@	.09
Horehound	lb.	.04½	@	.05
Hyoscyamus	lb.	.07	@	.08
Jaborandi	lb.	.14	@	.15
Pulsatilla		.07½	@	11
Rose, Red	lb.	.65	@	.70
Senna, pkd. whole	lb.	.17	@	.20
Alexandria, natural	lb.	.10	@	.11
garbled and sifted	lb.	.15	@	.16
Tinnevelly	lb.	.06½	@	.14
Alexandria, siftings	lb.	.05½	@	.06
Stramonium	lb.	.08	@	.08½
Uva ursi	lb.	.08½	@	.08½
Yerba Santa	lb.	.07	@	.07½
Liquorice—mass	lb.	.08	@	.10
Spanish	lb.	.14	@	.20
Imported mass Spanish	lb.	.18	@	.24
Stick, Calabria	lb.	.23	@	.26
Domestic	lb.	.18½	@	.23½
Lithia, carbonate	lb.	1.50	@	1.75
" citrate	lb.	1.15	@	1.25
Lupulin, Ger	lb.	.18	@	.25
Lycopodium	lb.	.51	@	.53
Magnesia, carb	lb.	.12	@	.15
Manna, large flk	lb.	.45	@	.50
Small flake	lb.	.33	@	.35
Menthol, Japanese	lb.	2.20	@	2.25
Mercurials:				
Blue Pill	lb.	.43	@	.45
Calomel	lb.	.77	@	.79
Corr. Sublim	lb.	.70	@	.72
Mercury and Chalk	lb.	.33	@	.34
Ointment, ½	lb.	.47	@	.48
Ointment, ⅓	lb.	.38	@	.39
Red Precip	lb.	.87	@	.89
White "	lb.	.92	@	.94
Morphine, bulk	oz.	2.25	@	2.50
Eighths	oz.	2.45	@	2.50
Moss, Iceland	lb.	.05	@	.06
Irish	lb.	.06½	@	.08
Irish, bleached	lb.	.09½	@	.10
Naphthaline, flake	lb.	.02	@	.03
Ball	lb.	.02	@	.03½
Nux Vomica	lb.	.02½	@	.03
Oil, Anise	lb.	1.30	@	1.35
Almonds, bit, Eng	lb.	5.50	@	5.75
French	lb.	3.55	@	3.60
bit., artificial	lb.	.85	@	1.50
sweet, true	lb.	.37	@	.40
Peach kernels		.19	@	.22
Bay	lb.	2.10	@	2.25
22 oz. bots	bot.	3.25	@	3.35
Bergamot	lb.	2.15	@	2.30
Cajuput	lb.	.50	@	.52
Camphor	lb.	.17½	@	.19
Caraway	lb.	1.15	@	1.40
Cassia 75@80%	lb	.80	@	.85
Oils—cont'd.				
Cedar, pure	lb.	60.	@	1.65
red	lb.	.21	@	.25
Citronella	lb.	.40	@	.42
Clove, bud		.52½	@	.55
Copaiba	lb.	.60	@	.70
Coriander	lb.	5.00	@	11.00
Croton	lb.	.75	@	.80
Cubeb	lb.	.90	@	1.00
Eucalyptus	lb.	.40	@	.60
Geranium	lb.	1.60	@	4.75
Lavender, flowers	lb.	2.00	@	2.25
Lemon	lb.	.73	@	.75
Lemongrass	lb.	3.00	@	3.10
Mustard	lb.	4.25	@	5.25
Myrbane	lb.	.07	@	.08
Neroli	lb.	28.00	@	60.00
Nutmeg	lb.	.80	@	0.90
Orange, sweet	lb.	2.10	@	2.30
Orange, bitter	lb.	2.15	@	2.50
Origanum	lb.	.18	@	.22
Pennyroyal	lb.	1.15	@	1.25
Peppermint	lb.	2.40	@	2.60
Cases	lb.	3.10	@	3.20
Petit, grain, French	lb.	4.00	@	4.50
" " So. Amer.	lb.	1.90	@	...
Pimento	lb.	1.80	@	1.90
Rose	oz.	3.50	@	4.50
Rosemary	lb.	.62½	@	.80
Sandalwood	lb.	3.25	@	3.50
Sassafras	lb.	.50	@	.55
" Artificial	lb.	.24	@	.25
Safrol		.35	@	.36
Spearmint	lb.	4.75	@	5.00
Tansy	lb.	3.75	@	4.00
Thyme		1.00	@	1.20
Winterg'n, sweet birch		1.65	@	1.85
" Synthetic	lb.	.37	@	.40
Wood (Chinese)		.08	@	.09
Wormwood		3.25	@	3.50
Wormseed	lb.	3.00	@	3.25
Opium, Nat	cases, lb.	2.87½	@	2.95
" Ordinary, Job-		2.90	@	3.00
" powdered	lb.	3.40	@	3.45
Orange peel, bit	lb.	.03	@	.04
Sweet	lb.	.01½	@	.10
Petrolatum		.03	@	.08
Phenacetine	oz.	.85	@	.95
Potassium acetate	lb.	.17	@	.18
" bromide		.15	@	.16
" bottles		.23	@	.30
bichromate		.08½	@	.08½
chlorate, cryst		.09½	@	.09½
" powd		.10	@	.10½
cyanide		.20	@	.21
hypophosphite		.60	@	.64
iodide bulk		2.15	@	2.20
permanganate	lb.	.09½	@	.10½
Prickly Ash berries		.14	@	.16
Quicksilver	flasks, lb.	.56	@	.60
Quinine Sulph., Domestic bulk	oz.	.18	@	.20
German, bulk	oz.	.17	@	.20
German, outside	oz.	.17	@	.18
Java, bulk	oz.	.17	@	.18
Rochelle Salts	lb.	.20½	@	.21
Root, Aconite	lb.	.09½	@	.10
Alkanet	lb.	.08	@	.09
Althea, cut	lb.	.17	@	.18
Arnica	lb.	.08½	@	.09
Belladonna, Atropa	lb.	.10	@	.12
Blood	lb.	.10	@	.12
Calamus	lb.	.07	@	.08
Calamus, bleached	lb.	.23	@	.25
Colchicum	lb.	.12	@	.13
Calumba	lb.	.04	@	.06
Dandelion, Ger	lb.	.07½	@	.08
Galangal	lb.	.05	@	.05½
Gentian	lb.	.04	@	.04½
Ginger, Ja., blcd	lb.	.11½	@	.14
unbleached	lb.	.09	@	.10
Ginseng	lb.	6.00	@	7.50
Golden Seal	lb.	1.25	@	1.30
Hellebore, pwd	lb.	.06	@	.07
Helonias	lb.	.42	@	.45
Ipecac, Rio	lb.	1.50	@	1.60
Carthagena	lb.	1.50	@	1.60
Jalap	lb.	.10½	@	.11
Kava Kava	lb.	.11	@	.12
Liquorice, ord	lb.	.03½	@	.04
Select	lb.	.06½	@	.11
Lovage	lb	.55	@	.85
Mandrake	lb.	.04½	@	.05½
Musk, Russian	lb.	.13	@	.14
Orris, Florentine	lb.	.06	@	.07
Orris, Verona	lb.	.04	@	.06
Pariera Brava	lb.	.10	@	.11
Pink	lb.	...	@	.75
Rhatany	lb.	.10	@	.12
Rhub., Canton	lb.	.35	@	.40
Shensi	lb.	.65	@	.70
Sars'p'la, Hond	lb.	.26	@	.30
Mexican	lb.	.09½	@	.09½
Senega	lb.	.55	@	.60
Snake Virgina	lb.	.42	@	.45
Texas	lb.	.39	@	.42
Canada	lb.	13	@	.25
Squill	lb	.13	@	.15
Valerian, Belg	lb.	.08	@	.08½
German	lb.	.12	@	.14
English	lb.	.12	@	.15
Salicine	lb.	3 75	@	4.00
Sal Ammon, lump	lb.	.09½	@	.09½
Granulated	lb.	.05½	@	.06
Sal Soda, Eng	100 lb	.67½	@	.72½
American	100 lb.	.75	@	80
Salol	lb.	.90	@	.95
Saltpetre, crude	lb.	.04½	@	.04½
Refined	lb.	.04½	@	.05½
Santonin, crystals	lb.	9.50	@	9.70
Powdered	lb.	9.70	@	9.90
Saw Palmetto Berries	lb.	.15	@	.20
Seed, Anise Ital	lb.	.08½	@	.10½
German	lb.	.06½	@	.07
Star	lb.	.20	@	.21
Canary, Smyrna	lb.	.04	@	.04½
Sicily	lb.	.04½	@	.05
Caraway	lb.	.06	@	.06½
Celery	lb.	.07½	@	.08
Cardamom blchd		.30	@	.70
" Decorticated	lb.	.30	@	.31
Colchicum	lb	.21	@	.25
Coriander	lb.	.0	@	10½
Seeds—cont'd.				
Bleached	lb.	[illegible]	@	.10½
Cummin	lb.	.06½	@	.07½
Fennel, Ger	lb.	.09	@	.10
" Italian	lb.	.05	@	[illegible]
Flax, whole	lb.	6.50	@	6.75
" ground	lb.	.03½	@	[illegible]
Foenugreek	lb.	.03	@	[illegible]
Hemp, Rus	lb.	.03	@	[illegible]
Millet, nat	lb.	.01½	@	[illegible]
" shld	lb.	.04½	@	.04½
Mustard, Cal. brown	lb.	.04½	@	[illegible]
Trieste, brown	lb.	.08	@	[illegible]
Bari, brown	lb.	.04½	@	[illegible]
German, brown	lb.	.02½	@	[illegible]
Western, brown	lb.	.01½	@	[illegible]
Cal. yellow	lb.	.04½	@	[illegible]
Eng. yellow	lb.	.06	@	[illegible]
Ger. yellow	lb.	.03½	@	[illegible]
Poppy, blue	lb.	.05½	@	[illegible]
Quince, Ger	lb.	.32	@	[illegible]
Rape, Ger	lb.	.02½	@	[illegible]
" Eng	lb.	.04	@	[illegible]
" Amer	lb.	.02½	@	[illegible]
Strophanthus		.45	@	.50
Kombe		1.00	@	1.25
Sunflower		.01½	@	[illegible]
Wormseed, American	lb.	.07	@	[illegible]
" Levant	lb.	.17	@	[illegible]
Seidlitz Mixture	lb.	.17	@	.17½
Silver, Nitrate	oz.	.41½	@	.45½
Soap, Castile, white	lb.	.10	@	.10½
" green	lb.	.08	@	.10½
" mottled	lb.	.05½	@	.07
Sodium bicarb, Eng		1.37½	@	1.75
" domestic	100 lb.	1.50	@	1.59
" benzoate	lb.	.40	@	.41
" brom. blk	lb.	.21	@	.22
" carb., cryst	100 lb.	1.00	@	1.75
" citrate	lb.	...	@	.32
" hypophosphite		.60	@	.64
" iodide		3.50	@	3.55
" nitrate	100 lb.	2.20	@	2.25
" phosphate	lb.	.02½	@	.03
" salicylate	lb.	.32	@	.34
Spermaceti	lb.	.27	@	.28
Spts. Nitre, U. S. F.		.46	@	.48
Spts. Ammonia Aromat.	lb.	.44	@	.45
Strontium, nitrate	lb.	.07½	@	.08
Strychnine, Sulph	oz.	.95	@	1.05
Sugar of Milk	lb.	.15	@	.18
Sugar, Lead, white	lb.	.09½	@	.10
" brown	lb.	.07½	@	.08
Sulphur, Roll	lb.	1.85	@	2.15
" Flowers	lb.	2.15	@	2.25½
Sulphuric Ether	lb.	.63	@	.65
Sumac, Sicily	ton	42.00	@	47.00
" Virginia	ton	33.00	@	35.00
Tar, Barbadoes	gal.	...	@	.35
Thymol		1.90	@	2.05
Tonka B'ns, Para	lb.	.18	@	.20
" Angostura	lb.	.85	@	.87½
" Surinam	lb.	.30	@	.32
Turmeric		.04½	@	.06
Turpentine	gal.	.67½	@	.68
Vanilla Beans	lb.	2.75	@	6.50
" Cut. Mex	lb.	1.75	@	2.00
" Tahiti	lb.	.45	@	1.25
" Bourbon		1.25	@	3.50
Vanillin	oz.	.32	@	.37½
Venice Turps, bbls	lb.	.14	@	.17
" " cans	lb.	.19	@	.20
Wax, Bayberry	lb.	...	@	.30
" Bees, ord. pur	lb.	.30½	@	.32
" " sel	lb.	.32½	@	.34
" " blch	lb.	.40	@	.45
" Brazil, No. 1	lb.	.48	@	.50
" " No. 2	lb.	.42	@	.43
" " No. 3	lb.	.31	@	.32
" Ceresin, yel	lb.	.14	@	.18
" " white	lb.	.15	@	.20
" Japan	lb.	.13½	@	.14
" Paraffin	lb.	.06	@	.08½
Zinc Oxide	lb.	.07	@	.08½

Heavy Oils, &c.

Bank, Menhaden	gal.	.27	@	.30
Coconut, Ceylon	lb.	.06½	@	.06½
Cochin	lb.	.07½	@	.07½
Cuban	lb.	.05½	@	...
Cod, Domestic	gal.	.35	@	.36
" Newfoundland	gal.	.38½	@	40
Corn	gal.	3.80	@	...
Cottonseed, crd. prime		.32½	@	.33
Summer Yellow, prime		.32½	@	.33
" " Butter		.30	@	.31
Old, off grade		...	@	...
White, Winter		.30	@	.31
Winter Yellow, prime		.30	@	.31
Salad Oil		.40	@	.41
Gasoline, 86°	gal.	.14	@	...
" 88°	gal.	.16	@	...
" 90°	gal.	.18	@	...
Lard, Extra Prime	gal.	.63	@	.64
Lard, Extra No. 1	gal.	.49	@	.52
Lard, No. 1	gal.	.38	@	.40
Linseed, Raw City	gal.	.44	@	.45
" Boiled	gal.	.45	@	.46
Naphtha, 68°	gal.	.12	@	...
" Deodorized, 76°	gal.	.13½	@	...
Neatsfoot, prm	gal.	.45	@	.50
White		.97	@	...
Olive Oil, tap	tins	1.50	@	2.75
" Com., bbls	gal	.53½	@	.58
Palm, prm., L'gos	lb	.06½	@	.06½
Peanut	lb	.40	@	.52
Rapeseed	gal.	.67	@	.71
Red Elaine	gal.	...	@	.49
" Saponified	lb.	.06½	@	.06½
Salad Oil	gal.	.46	@	.48
Sesame	gal.	.55	@	.60
Sperm, Crude	gal.	.63	@	.65
" Nat. Win	gal.	.62	@	.63
" Blch. Win	gal.	.64	@	.65
Straits	gal.	...	@	.38
Tallow, prime	gal.	.63	@	
Whale, Crude	gal.	...	@	...
Crude, Nat. Win.	gal.	.43	@	
Bleached Win	gal.	.44	@	.46

Prices Current.

The outside prices quoted are for such quantities as retailers usually purchase. When purchasing original packages the inside quotations should be expected, while a slight advance over the outside quotations given may be demanded for very small lots. Current commercial quality is understood unless otherwise indicated. For extra quality or for specified makes a slightly higher price will have to be paid.

Corrected to February 24

Article	Unit	Price
Acetanilid, 5 lbs., .30	lb.	.32-34
Acetone, lb., .22; Medicinal	lb.	.85
Acid, Acetic, U. S. P., carboys, .6	lbs.	.8-9
No. 2, carboy, .5; lb., .7; Glacial	lb.	.28-30
Arsenous, fused, lb., .18	oz.	.5
Benzoic, English, 50-oz. boxes, .10	oz.	.13-16
Benzoic, from Toluol, lbs., .58	oz.	.11-12
Boric, crystals, 25 lbs., .14	lb.	.15
Boric, Po., 25 lbs., .14	lb.	.16
Cacodylic, 1/8ths	ozs.	4.00
Camphoric	oz.	.50
Carbolic crystals, 10 lbs., .23	lb.	.23-27
Calvert's No. 1, lb., 1.95; No. 2	lb.	1.40
Solution, 10 gals., .45	gal.	.50
Chromic, lb., .55	ozs.	.11
Chrysophanic, 1-oz. cartons	ozs.	.31-33
Cinnamic	oz.	.35-40
Citric, crystals, 10 lbs., .40	lb.	.42-44
Gallic, lbs., .70	ozs.	.9
Hydrochloric, carboys, .2½	lb.	.4-5
C. P.	lb.	.11-12
Hydrocyanic, dil., lbs., .30	ozs.	.10
Hydrobromic, dil.	lb.	.28
Hypophosphorus, 50 per cent. sol.	lb.	1.65
Lactic, concentr., lbs., .70	ozs.	.12
Nitric, carboys, 5½lbs., .8; C. P.		.14
Oleic, purified, U. S. P.	lbs.	.40
Oxalic, 10 lbs., .9	lb.	.10-12
Phosphoric, glacial	lbs.	.85
U. S. P., 85 per cent. syrupy	lb.	.33-35
Picric	lb.	.55
Pyrogallic, lbs., 2.35	ozs.	.24-27
Pyroligneous, pure	lb.	.30
Salicylic, white, 10 lbs., .40	lb.	.42-44
Stearic, hard	lb.	.18
Succinic	oz.	.37
Sulphuric, carboys, .2	lb.	.4
" C. P., carboys, .10	lb.	.12
Sulphurous	lb.	.10
Tannic, lbs., .85	oz.	.12-15
Tartaric, powdered, 10 lbs., .34	lbs.	.35-38
Valerianic	ozs.	.20
Aconitine, Amorphous, 1/8 oz.	oz.	1.40
Adeps Lanae, B. J. D.	lb.	.28
Adnephrin, solution	oz.	.60
Adonidin, 15-gr. vials	gr.	.15
Agaricin, 15-gr. vials, each, .10	ozs.	.90
Agaric, white	lb.	.40
Agathin	oz.	3.25
Agurin	ozs.	1.70
Airol, ozs.	oz.	1.00
Albumen, Egg	lb.	.70
Alcohol, 10 gals., 2.70	gal.	2.80-2.85
Alcohol, Columbia Spirit, 10 gals., 1.85	gal.	1.50
Cologne Spirit, 10 gals., 2.75	gal.	2.85
Wood, 10 gals., .80	gal.	.85-90
Alizarin	oz.	.15
Allspice, 10 lbs., .11	lb.	.12
powdered, 5 lbs., .18	lb.	.20
Almonds, bitter, shelled	lb.	.40
Sweet, shelled	lb.	.35
Almond Meal, true, 10 lbs., .45	lb.	.50
Aloin, lb., .70	oz.	.7-9
Alpha-Eucaine	oz.	3.50
Alphozone	oz.	4.50
Alum, cryst., bbls., .2¼	lb.	.3-4
powdered, bbls., .3½	lb.	.6-8
burnt, 10 lbs., .10	lb.	.12-14
Aluminum, Acetate	oz.	.15
Sulphate, lb., .10; Wire	lb.	2.25
Aluminol	oz.	.50
Amber, rasped	lb.	.35
Ambergris, gray, oz., $30.00	dram.	4.00
Ammonia (See Water and Spirit.)		
Ammonium, Bromide, 5-lb. bot., .35	lb.	.40
Carbonate, 25 lbs., .11	lb.	.12-14
Iodide, lbs., 6.15	oz.	.47
Muriate, gran. com.	lb.	.10
purified, lb., .17; powdered	lb.	.18
Salammoniac, muriate, cryst.	lb.	.12-14
Nitrate, crystals, 10 lbs., .22	lb.	.25
Valerianate, lb., 1.50	oz.	.15-22
Ammonol	oz.	1.05
Amygdalin, ½-oz. vials	oz.	2.40
Amyl, Nitrite	oz.	.28
Amylene, Hydrate	oz.	.40
Anaesthesin	ozs.	1.00
Aniline, Red, crystals	lb.	1.25
Black	lb.	.75
Crystals for ink	lb.	1.50
Blue, Deep, No. 1	lb.	2.00
Sol., reddish, No. 1	lb.	2.50
Crimson	lb.	1.50
Brown, Bismarck	lb.	1.25
soluble	lb.	1.00
Green, crystals	lb.	1.50
Orange	lb.	1.00
Purple, B. B.	lb.	1.75
Scarlet....lb. 1.50. Yellow	lb.	1.25
Annatto	lb.	.45-50
Anodyne, Hoffman's	lb.	.60
" " U. S. P.	lb.	.88
Anthrax Vaccine, "Pasteur," double tubes	doz.	18.00
Antiarthrin	oz.	1.65
Antikamnia, powdered or tablets	oz.	1.00
Combination tablets	oz.	1.00
10-oz. lots, assorted to order		9.25
Tablets, "vest-pocket boxes"	doz.	1.75
In 1 gross lots, 5 per cent. discount.		
Antimony Sulphuret, powd., pure, 10 lbs., .16	lb.	.17-20
Antinosine	oz.	2.10
Antiphthisin, Klebs', 15-Cc. vials, ea.		2.75
Antipyretic Liquid, Tilden's	doz.	2.50
Antipyrine, Dr. Knorr's	oz.	.31
New Grade	oz.	.28
Antistreptococcic Serum (Veterinary), "Pasteur," 10-Cc. vial	doz.	9.00
Antitetanic Serum (Veterinary), "Pasteur," 10-Cc. vial	doz.	9.00
Antithyroidin, 10-Cc. vials	ea.	1.50
Antitoxin, Diphtheria, Stearns':		
No. 0, per 500 units		1.10
No. 1, per 1,000 units		1.05
No. 2, per 2,000 units		1.80
No. 3, per 3,000 units		2.40
No. 4, per 4,000 units		6.50
Antivom. Ritsert, Pills, .80 ea.	doz.	9.50
Apiol, Fluid Green	oz.	.25
Capsules, Joret's	doz.	6.25
Apolysin	oz.	.65
Apomorphine, Hydrochlor, Cryst.	oz.	7.50
" " Amorphous	oz.	2.80
Areca, Nuts, powd.	lb.	.25-28
Argentamine	oz.	.75
Argols, Red, powdered	lb.	.13
Argonin	oz.	.65
Aristol, 25 ozs., 1.65	oz.	1.80
Aristochin, ozs.	oz.	2.20
" ½ ozs.	oz.	2.25
Arrowroot, Bermuda, true	None in market	
St. Vincent, 30 lbs., .14	lb.	.18
Taylor's, ½-lb., 24 lbs., .28	lb.	.32
Arsenauro, 1-oz. bots.	doz.	8.50
Arsenic, Donovan's Sol.	lb.	.30
Fowler's Sol.	lb.	.16
White	lb.	.12
Aspirin, 50 ozs., .38	oz.	.42
Atropin, Sulph., ⅛-oz.	oz.	5.65
Balsam, Copaiba, Para, 5 lbs., .45	lb.	.47-50
Fir, Canada	lb.	.50-55
Oregon	lb.	.35-50
Peru	lb.	1.35
Tolu, 10-lb. can, .33	lb.	.35
Barbadoes Tar	gal.	.60
Barium, Acetate	oz.	.15
Carbonate	lb.	.60
Chloride	lb.	.17
Nitrate	lb.	.15
Oxide, pure	oz.	.10
Bark, Angostura	lb.	.55
Barberry	lb.	.28
Berberis Aquifol.	lb.	.30
Buckthorn	lb.	.18
Canella	lb.	.30
Cascara, Sagrada	lb.	.18-20
Cascarilla, select	lb.	.25
Cassia, in mats	lb.	.14
Saigon	lb.	.65
Cinchona, Red, E. I.	lb.	.36
powdered, 10 lbs., .32	lb.	.32-35
Cinchona Calisaya	lb.	.36
powdered	lb.	.40
pale, lb., .30; powdered	lb.	.35
Cinnamon, Ceylon	lb.	.35

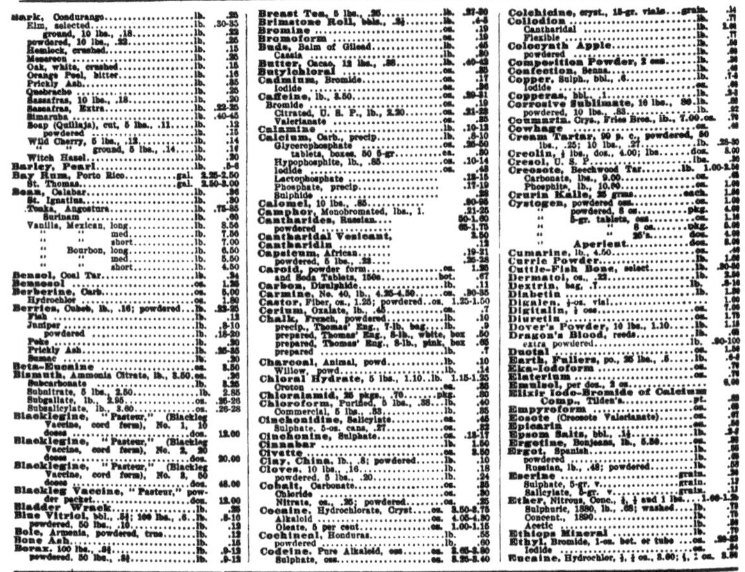

Article	Unit	Price
Bark, Condurango	lb.	.25
Elm, selected	lb.	.30-35
ground, 10 lbs., .18	lb.	.22
powdered, 10 lbs., .22	lb.	.25
Hemlock, crushed	lb.	.15
Mezereon	lb.	.25
Oak, white, crushed	lb.	.15
Orange Peel, bitter	lb.	.16
Prickly Ash	lb.	.35
Quebracho	lb.	.25
Sassafras, 10 lbs., .18	lb.	.20
Sassafras, Extra	lb.	.22-25
Simaruba	lb.	.40-45
Soap (Quillaja), cut, 5 lbs., .11	lb.	.12
powdered	lb.	.15
Wild Cherry, 5 lbs., .12	lb.	.14
" " ground, 5 lbs., .14	lb.	.16
Witch Hazel	lb.	.20
Barley, Pearl	lb.	.5-6
Bay Rum, Porto Rico	gal.	2.25-2.50
St. Thomas	gal.	2.50-3.00
Bean, Calabar	lb.	.36
St. Ignatius	lb.	.30
Tonka, Angostura	lb.	.75-85
Surinam	lb.	.60
Vanilla, Mexican, long	lb.	8.50
" " med	lb.	7.50
" " short	lb.	7.00
" Bourbon, long	lb.	6.50
" " med	lb.	5.50
" " short	lb.	4.50
Benzol, Coal Tar	lb.	.24
Benzosol	oz.	1.25
Berberine, Carb	oz.	5.00
Hydrochlor	oz.	1.80
Berries, Cubeb, lb., .16; powdered	lb.	.22-25
Fish	lb.	.12
Juniper	lb.	.8-10
powdered	lb.	.18-20
Poke	lb.	.30
Prickly Ash	lb.	.25-35
Sumac	lb.	.20
Beta-Eucaine	oz.	3.50
Bismuth, Ammonia Citrate, lb., 3.50	oz.	.26
Subcarbonate	lb.	2.25
Subnitrate, 5 lbs., 2.50	lb.	2.85
Subgallate, lb., 2.95	oz.	.25-26
Subsalicylate, lb., 3.60	oz.	.26-28
Blacklegine, "Pasteur," (Blackleg Vaccine, cord form), No. 1, 10 doses	doz.	12.00
Blacklegine, "Pasteur," (Blackleg Vaccine, cord form), No. 2, 20 doses	doz.	20.00
Blacklegine, "Pasteur," (Blackleg Vaccine, cord form), No. 3, 50 doses	doz.	48.00
Blackleg Vaccine, "Pasteur," powder packet	doz.	12.00
Bladder Wrack	lb.	.25
Blue Vitriol, bbl., .5½; 100 lbs., .6	lb.	.8-10
powdered, 50 lbs., .10	lb.	.12
Bole, Armenia, powdered, true	lb.	.12
Bone Ash	lb.	.15
Borax, 100 lbs., .8½	lb.	.9-12
powdered, 50 lbs., .8½	lb.	.9-12
Breast Tea, 5 lbs., .25	lb.	.27-30
Brimstone Roll, bbls., .3½	lb.	.4-5
Bromine	oz.	.19
Bromoform	oz.	.19
Buds, Balm of Gilead	lb.	.45
Cassia	lb.	.30
Butter, Cacao, 12 lbs., .38	lb.	.40-42
Butylchloral	oz.	.85
Cadmium, Bromide	oz.	.17
Iodide	oz.	.36
Caffeine, lb., 3.50	oz.	.30-31
Bromide	oz.	.19
Citrated, U. S. P., lb., 2.20	oz.	.21-23
Valerianate	oz.	.25
Calamine	lb.	.10-12
Calcium, Carb., precip	lb.	.8-10
Glycerophosphate	oz.	.25-50
tablets, boxes, 50 5-gr.	ea.	.30
Hypophosphite, lb., .85	oz.	.10-14
Iodide	oz.	.48
Lactophosphate		.13-15
Phosphate, precip		.17-19
Sulphide		.28
Calomel, 10 lbs., .85		.90-95
Camphor, Monobromated, lbs., 1.		.21-25
Cantharides, Russian		50-1.60
powdered		65-1.75
Cantharidal Vesicant,		2.50
Cantharidin		.12
Capsicum, African		.19-21
powdered, 5 lbs., .23		.25-28
Caroid, powder form	oz.	1.25
and Soda Tablets, 150s	bot.	.67
Carbon, Disulphide	lb.	.11
Carmine, No. 40, lb., 4.25-4.50	oz.	.30-35
Castor, Fiber, oz., 1.25; powdered	oz.	1.25-1.50
Cerium, Oxalate, lb., .45	oz.	.7
Chalk, French, powdered	lb.	.10
precip., Thomas' Eng., 7-lb. bag	lb.	.9
prepared, Thomas' Eng., 8-lb., white, box		.50
prepared, Thomas' Eng., 8-lb., pink, box		.65
prepared	lb.	.7
Charcoal, Animal, powd	lb.	.10
Willow, powd	lb.	.14
Chloral Hydrate, 5 lbs., 1.10	lb.	1.15-1.25
Croton	oz.	.85
Chloralamid, 25 pkgs., .70	pkg.	.80
Chloroform, Purified, 5 lbs., .38	lb.	.40
Commercial, 5 lbs., .33	lb.	.35
Cinchonidine, Salicylate	oz.	.45
Sulphate, 5-oz. cans, .27	oz.	.32
Cinchonine, Sulphate	oz.	.12-17
Cinnabar	lb.	1.50
Civette	oz.	3.50
Clay, China, lb., .8; powdered	lb.	.10
Cloves, 10 lbs., .16	lb.	.18
powdered, 5 lbs., .20	lb.	.24
Cobalt, Carbonate	oz.	.25
Chloride	oz.	.30
Nitrate, oz., .25; powdered	oz.	.25
Cocaine, Hydrochlorate, Cryst	oz.	3.50-3.75
Alkaloid	oz.	4.05-4.30
Oleate, 5 per cent	oz.	1.00-1.15
Cochineal, Honduras	lb.	.55
powdered	lb.	.60
Codeine, Pure Alkaloid, ozs	oz.	3.65-3.90
Sulphate, ozs	oz.	3.25-3.40
Colchicine, cryst., 15-gr. vials	grain.	.14
Collodion	lb.	[illegible]
Cantharidal	lb.	[illegible]
Flexible	lb.	[illegible]
Colocynth Apple	lb.	[illegible]
powdered	lb.	[illegible]
Composition Powder, 2 ozs	lb.	[illegible]
Confection, Senna	lb.	[illegible]
Copper, Sulph., bbl., .6	lb.	[illegible]
Iodide	oz.	[illegible]
Copperas, bbl., .1	lb.	[illegible]
Corrosive Sublimate, 10 lbs., .80	lb.	[illegible]
powdered, 10 lbs., .83	lb.	[illegible]
Coumarin, Crys., Fries Bros., lb., 7.00	oz.	[illegible]
Cowhage	oz.	[illegible]
Cream Tartar, 99 p. c., powdered, 50 lbs., .25; 10 lbs., .27	lb.	.28-30
Creolin, ½ lbs., doz., 4.00; lbs	doz.	8.00
Cresol, U. S. P	lbs.	[illegible]
Creosote, Beechwood Tar	lb.	1.00-2.50
Carbonate, lbs., 9.00	oz.	[illegible]
Phosphite, lb., 10.00	oz.	1.00
Crurin Kalle, 25 grms	each.	[illegible]
Cystogen, powdered ozs	oz.	1.00
" powdered, 8 oz	pkg.	[illegible]
" 5-gr. tablets, ozs	oz.	[illegible]
" " 8 oz	pkg.	[illegible]
" " 25's	doz.	[illegible]
" Aperient	doz.	[illegible]
Cumarine, lb., 4.50	oz.	.45
Currie Powder	lb.	[illegible]
Cuttle-Fish Bone, select	lb.	[illegible]
Dermatol, oz., .22	lb.	[illegible]
Dextrin, bag, .7	lb.	.8-10
Diabetin	lb.	[illegible]
Digalen, ½-oz. vial		1.00
Digitalin, ⅛ ozs	oz.	[illegible]
Diuretin	oz.	1.75
Dover's Powder, 10 lbs., 1.10	lb.	1.15
Dragon's Blood, reeds	lb.	[illegible]
extra powdered	lb.	.90-100
Duotal	oz.	[illegible]
Earth, Fullers, po., 25 lbs., .5	lb.	[illegible]
Eka-Iodoform	oz.	.75
Elaterium	oz.	[illegible]
Emulsol, per doz., 2 oz.		[illegible]
Elixir Iodo-Bromide of Calcium Comp., Tilden's	pt.	[illegible]
Empyroform	oz.	[illegible]
Eosote (Creosote Valerianate)	oz.	[illegible]
Epicarin	oz.	[illegible]
Epsom Salts, bbl., .1½	lb.	[illegible]
Ergotine, Bonjeans, lb., 5.50	oz.	[illegible]
Ergot, Spanish	lb.	[illegible]
powdered	lb.	[illegible]
Russian, lb., .48; powdered	lb.	[illegible]
Eserine	grain.	[illegible]
Sulphate, 5-gr. v.	grain.	.12
Salicylate, 5-gr. v.	grain.	.12
Ether, Nitrous, Conc., ¼, ½ and 1 lbs.		[illegible]
Sulphuric, 1880, lb., .68; washed	lb.	[illegible]
Concent., 1890	lb.	[illegible]
Acetic	lb.	[illegible]
Ethiops Mineral	lb.	[illegible]
Ethyl, Bromide, 1-oz. bot. or tube	oz.	[illegible]
Iodide	oz.	[illegible]
Eucaine, Hydrochlor, ⅛, ¼ oz., 3.60; ½, 1 oz.		[illegible]

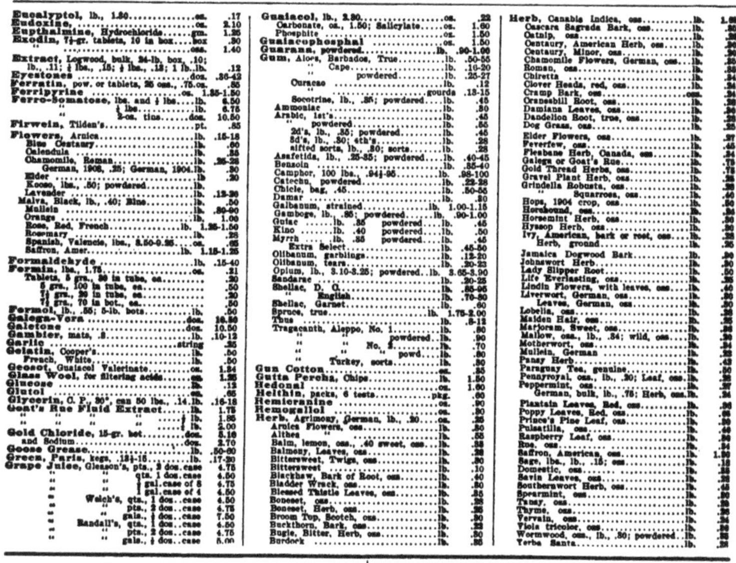

Article	Unit	Price
Eucalyptol, lb., 1.80	oz.	.17
Eudoxine,	oz.	2.10
Eupthalmine, Hydrochloride	gm.	1.25
Exodin, 7½-gr. tablets, 10 in box	box	.30
"	ozs.	1.40
Extract, Logwood, bulk, 24-lb. box, .10; lb., .11; ¼ lbs., .15; ½ lbs., .13; 1 lb.	lb.	.12
Eyestones	doz.	.36-42
Ferratin, pow. or tablets, 25 ozs., .75	oz.	.85
Ferripyrine	oz.	1.35-1.50
Ferro-Somatose, lbs. and ½ lbs.	lb.	6.50
" ¼ lbs.	lb.	6.75
" 2-oz. tins	doz.	10.50
Firwein, Tilden's	pt.	.85
Flowers, Arnica	lb.	.15-18
Blue Centaury	lb.	.60
Calendula	lb.	.35
Chamomile, Roman	lb.	.25-28
German, 1903, .25; German, 1904	lb.	.30
Elder	lb	.20
Kooso, lbs., .50; powdered	lb.	
Lavender	lb.	.12-20
Malva, Black, lb., .40; Blue	lb.	.50
Mullein	lb.	.80-90
Orange	lb.	1.00
Rose, Red, French	lb.	1.25-1.50
Rosemary	lb.	.28
Spanish, Valencia, lbs., 8.50-9.25	oz.	.65
Saffron, Amer.	lb.	1.15-1.25
Formaldehyde	lb.	.15-40
Formin, lbs., 1.75	oz.	.21
Tablets, 5 grs., 30 in tube, ea.		.30
5 grs., 100 in tube, ea.		.50
7½ grs., 20 in tube, ea.		.30
7½ grs., 70 in bot., ea.		.50
Formol, lb., .55; 5-lb. bots	lb.	.50
Galega-Vera	doz.	10.50
Galetone	doz.	10.50
Gambier, mats, .8	lb.	.10-12
Garlic	string	.35
Gelatin, Cooper's	lb.	.50
French, White	lb.	.50
Geosot, Guaiacol Valerinate	oz.	1.24
Glass Wool, for filtering acids	oz.	1.25
Glucose	lb.	.12
Glutol	oz.	.65
Glycerin, C. P., 30°, can 50 lbs., .14	lb.	.16-18
Goat's Rue Fluid Extract	lb.	1.75
" " " " ½	lb.	1.85
" " " " ¼	lb.	2.00
Gold Chloride, 15-gr. bot.	doz.	5.10
and Sodium	doz.	2.70
Goose Grease	lb.	.50-60
Green, Paris, kegs, .13½-15	lb.	.17-20
Grape Juice, Gleason's, pts., 2 doz.	case	4.75
" " qts. 1 doz.	case	4.50
" " ½ gal.	case of 8	4.75
" " 1 gal.	case of 4	4.50
" Welch's, qts., 1 doz.	case	4.50
" " pts., 2 doz.	case	4.75
" " gals., ½ doz.	case	7.50
" Randall's, qts., 1 doz.	case	4.50
" " pts., 2 doz.	case	4.75
" " gals., ½ doz.	case	5.00
Guaiacol, lb., 2.80	oz.	.22
Carbonate, oz., 1.50; Salicylate	oz.	1.60
Phosphite	oz.	1.50
Guaiacophosphal	oz.	1.50
Guarana, powdered	lb.	.90-1.00
Gum, Aloes, Barbados, True	lb.	.50-55
" Cape	lb.	.10-20
" powdered	lb.	.25-27
Curacao	lb.	.12
"	gourds	.13-15
Socotrine, lb., .35; powdered	lb.	.45
Ammoniac	lb.	.30
Arabic, 1st's	lb.	.45
" powdered	lb.	.55
2d's, lb., .35; powdered	lb.	.45
3d's, lb., .30; 4th's	lb.	.28
sifted sorts, lb., .30; sorts	lb.	.28
Asafetida, lb., .25-35; powdered	lb.	.40-45
Benzoin	lb.	.35-40
Camphor, 100 lbs., .94½-95	lb.	.98-100
Catechu, powdered	lb.	.22-28
Chicle, bag, .45	lb.	.50-55
Damar	lb.	.30
Galbanum, strained	lb.	1.00-1.15
Gamboge, lb., .85; powdered	lb.	.90-1.00
Guiac ... lb. .35 powdered	lb.	.45
Kino ... lb. .40 powdered	lb.	.50
Myrrh ... lb. .35 powdered	lb.	.45
Extra Select	lb.	.45-50
Olibanum, garblings	lb.	.12-20
Olibanum, tears	lb.	.20-23
Opium, lb., 3.10-3.25; powdered	lb.	3.65-3.90
Sandarac	lb.	.20-25
Shellac, D. C.	lb.	.85-95
" English	lb.	.70-80
Shellac, Garnet	lb.	.60
Spruce, true	lb.	1.75-2.00
Thus	lb.	.8-12
Tragacanth, Aleppo, No. 1	lb.	.80
" " powdered	lb.	.90
" " No. 2	lb.	.70
" " " powd	lb.	.80
" Turkey, sorts	lb.	.30
Gun Cotton	oz.	.25
Gutta Percha, Chips	lb.	1.50
Hedonal	oz.	1.60
Helthin, packs, 6 tests	pkg.	.60
Hemicranine	oz.	.90
Hemogallol	oz.	.30
Herb, Agrimony, German, lb., .20	oz.	.25
Arnica Flowers, ozs	lb.	.30
Althea "	lb.	.55
Balm, lemon, ozs., .40 sweet, ozs.	lb.	.33
Balmony, Leaves, ozs	lb.	.28
Bittersweet, Twigs, ozs	lb.	.30
Bittersweet	lb.	.10
Blackhaw, Bark of Root, ozs	lb.	.40
Bladder Wrack, ozs	lb.	.30
Blessed Thistle Leaves, ozs	lb.	.35
Boneset, ozs	lb.	.28
Boneset, Herb, ozs	lb.	.25
Broom Top, Scotch, ozs	lb.	.30
Buckthorn, Bark, ozs	lb.	.22
Bugle, Bitter, Herb, ozs	lb.	.30
Burdock	lb.	.35
Herb, Canabis Indica, ozs	lb.	1.88
Cascara Sagrada Bark, ozs	lb.	.35
Catnip, ozs	lb.	.28
Centaury, American Herb, ozs	lb.	.20
Centaury, Minor, ozs	lb.	.30
Chamomile Flowers, German, ozs	lb.	.25
Roman, ozs	lb.	.35
Chiretta	lb.	.24
Clover Heads, red, ozs	lb.	.24
Cramp Bark, ozs	ozs.	.24
Cranesbill Root, ozs	lb.	.28
Damiana Leaves, ozs	lb.	.20
Dandelion Root, true, ozs	lb.	.25
Dog Grass, ozs	lb.	.25
Elder Flowers, ozs	lb.	.27
Feverfew, ozs	lb.	.45
Fleabane Herb, Canada, ozs	lb.	.24
Galega or Goat's Rue	lb.	.75
Gold Thread Herbs, ozs	lb.	.75
Gravel Plant Herb, ozs	lb.	.28
Grindelia Robusta, ozs	lb.	.28
" Squarrosa, ozs	lb.	.40
Hops, 1904 crop, ozs	lb.	.50
Horehound, ozs	lb.	.24
Horsemint Herb, ozs	lb.	.30
Hyssop Herb, ozs	lb.	.20
Ivy, American, bark or root, ozs	lb.	.28
Herb, ground	lb.	.25
Jamaica Dogwood Bark	lb.	.20
Johnswort Herb	lb.	.30
Lady Slipper Root	lb.	.50
Life Everlasting, ozs	lb.	.35
Lindin Flowers, with leaves, ozs	lb.	.40
Liverwort, German, ozs	lb.	.30
Leaves, German, ozs	lb.	.30
Lobelia, ozs	lb.	.25
Maiden Hair, ozs	lb.	.35
Marjoram, Sweet, ozs	lb.	.28
Mallow, ozs., lb., .34; wild, ozs	lb.	.30
Motherwort, ozs	lb.	.24
Mullein, German	lb.	.22
Pansy Herb	lb.	.43
Paraguay Tea, genuine	lb.	.50
Pennyroyal, ozs., lb., .30; Leaf, ozs.	lb.	.28
Peppermint, ozs	lb.	.27
German, bulk, lb., .75; Herb, ozs.	lb.	.24
Plantain Leaves, Red, ozs	lb.	.26
Poppy Leaves, Red, ozs	lb.	.68
Prince's Pine Leaf, ozs	lb.	.30
Pulsatilla, ozs	lb.	.40
Raspberry Leaf, ozs	lb.	.30
Rue, ozs	lb.	.24
Saffron, American, ozs	lb.	1.30
Sage, lbs., lb., .15; ozs	lb.	.18
Domestic, ozs	lb.	.25
Savin Leaves, ozs	lb.	.28
Southernwort Herb, ozs	lb.	.45
Spearmint, ozs	lb.	.30
Tansy, ozs	lb.	.28
Thyme, ozs	lb.	.35
Vervain, ozs	lb.	.24
Viola tricolor, ozs	lb.	.26
Wormwood, ozs., lb., .30; powdered	lb.	.28
Yerba Santa	lb.	.28

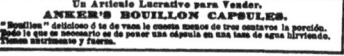

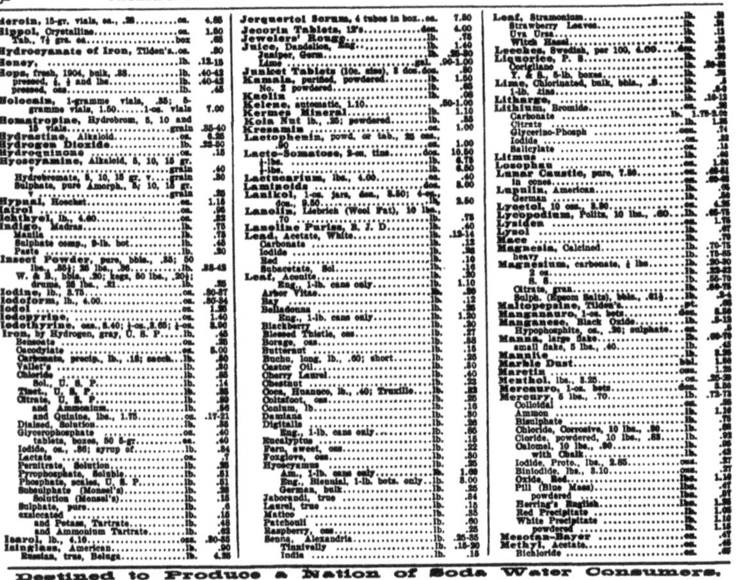

Article	Unit	Price
Heroin, 15-gr. vials, ea., .28	oz.	4.85
Hippol, Crystalline	oz.	1.60
Tab., 7½ grs. ea.	box	.65
Hydrocyanate of Iron, Tilden's	oz.	.80
Honey,	lb.	.12-15
Hops, fresh, 1904, bulk, .38	lb.	.40-42
pressed, ¼, ½ and lbs	lb.	.40-42
pressed, ozs	lb.	.45
Holocain, 1-gramme vials, .85; 5-gramme vials, 1.50	1-oz. vials	7.00
Homatropine, Hydrobrom, 5, 10 and 15 vials	grain	.35-40
Hydrastine, Alkaloid	oz.	6.25
Hydrogen Dioxide	lb.	.22-50
Hydroquinone	oz.	.15
Hyoscyamine, Alkaloid, 5, 10, 15 gr. v	grain	.40
Hydrobromate, 5, 10, 15 gr. v	grain	.30
Sulphate, pure Amorph., 5, 10, 15 gr. v	grain	.25
Hypnal, Hoechst	oz.	1.15
Iatrol	oz.	.95
Ichthyol, lb., 4.60	oz.	.32
Indigo, Madras	lb.	.75
Manila	lb.	.75
Sulphate comp., 9-lb. bot	lb.	.45
Paste	lb.	.30
Insect Powder, pure, bbls., .35; 50 lbs., .35½; 25 lbs., .36	lb.	.38-43
W. & B., bbls., .20; kegs, 50 lbs., .20½; drums, 25 lbs., .21	lb.	.25
Iodine, lb., 3.75	oz.	.30-37
Iodoform, lb., 4.00	oz.	.30-34
Iodol	oz.	1.35
Iodopyrine,	oz.	1.40
Iodothyrine, ozs., 3.40; ½-oz., 3.65; ¼-oz.		3.90
Iron, by Hydrogen, gray, U. S. P	lb.	.45
Benzoate	oz.	.25
Cacodylate	oz.	5.00
Carbonate, precip., lb., .18; sacch.	lb.	.30
Vallet's	lb.	.80
Chloride	lb.	.65
Sol., U. S. P	lb.	.14
Tinct., U. S. P	lb.	.38
Citrate, U. S. P	lb.	.60
and Ammonium	lb.	.56
and Quinine, lbs., 1.75	oz.	.17-21
Dialsed, Solution	lb.	.55
Glycerophosphate	oz.	.40
tablets, boxes, 50 5-gr.	ea.	.40
Iodide, oz., .36; syrup of	lb.	.34
Lactate	oz.	.7
Pernitrate, Solution	lb.	.25
Pyrophosphate, Soluble	lb.	.51
Phosphate, scales, U. S. P	lb.	.51
Subsulphate (Monsel's)	lb.	.38
Solution (Monsel's)	lb.	.15
Sulphate, pure	lb.	.6
exsiccated	lb.	.15
and Potass, Tartrate	lb.	.48
and Ammonium Tartrate	lb.	.63
Isarol, lb., 4.10	ozs.	.30-35
Isinglass, American	lb.	.90
Russian, true, Beluga	lb.	4.35
Jerquertol Serum, 4 tubes in box	ea.	7.50
Jecorin Tablets, 12's	doz.	4.00
Jewelers' Rouge	lb.	.75
Juice, Dandelion, Eng	lb.	1.40
Juniper, Germ	lb.	.35-50
Lime	gal.	.90-1.00
Junket Tablets (10c. size), 3 doz.	doz.	.80
Kamala, purified, powdered	lb.	1.50
No. 2 powdered	lb.	.65
Kaolin	lb.	.08
Kelene, automatic, 1.10		.50-1.00
Kermes Mineral	lb.	1.10
Kola Nut lb., .25; powdered	lb.	.35
Kresamin	oz.	1.00
Lactophenin, powd. or tab., 25 ozs., .90	oz.	1.00
Lacto-Somatose, 2-oz. tins	doz.	10.50
¼-lbs.	lb.	6.75
½-lbs.	lb.	6.50
Lactucarium, lbs., 4.00	oz.	.40
Laminoids	doz.	3.00
Lanikol, 1-oz. jars, doz., 3.50; 4-oz., doz., 9.50	lb.	2.50
Lanolin, Liebrich (Wool Fat), 10 lbs., .70	lb.	.75
Lanoline Puriss, B. J. D	lb.	.40
Lead, Acetate, White	lb.	.12-14
Carbonate	lb.	.12
Iodide	lb.	.38
Red	lb.	.10
Subacetate, Sol	lb.	.16
Leaf, Aconite	lb.	.30
Eng., 1-lb. cans only	lb.	1.10
Arbor Vitae	lb.	.38
Bay	lb.	.12
Belladonna	lb.	.35
Eng., 1-lb. cans only	lb.	1.20
Blackberry	lb.	.30
Blessed Thistle, ozs	lb.	.27
Borage, ozs	lb.	.58
Butternut	lb.	.16
Buchu, long, lb., .60; short	lb.	.25
Castor Oil	lb.	.80
Cherry Laurel	lb.	.40
Chestnut	lb.	.23
Coca, Huanuco, lb., .40; Truxillo	lb.	.32
Coltsfoot, ozs	lb.	.35
Conium, lb	lb.	.16
Damiana	lb.	.30
Digitalis	lb.	.38
Eng., 1-lb. cans only	lb.	.65
Eucalyptus	lb.	.15
Fern, sweet, ozs	lb.	.22
Foxglove, ozs	lb.	.30
Hyoscyamus	lb.	.35
Am., 1-lb. cans only	lb.	1.60
Eng., Biennial, 1-lb. bots. only	lb.	3.00
German, bulk	lb.	.25
Jaborandi, true	lb.	.34
Laurel, true	lb.	.15
Matico	lb.	.85
Patchouli	lb.	.60
Raspberry, ozs	lb.	.25
Senna, Alexandria	lb.	.25-35
Tinnivelly	lb.	.15-20
India	lb.	.15
Leaf, Stramonium	lb.	[illegible]
Strawberry Leaves	lb.	[illegible]
Uva Ursa	lb.	.12
Witch Hazel	lb.	.15
Leeches, Swedish, per 100, 4.00	doz.	.60
Liquorice, P. S	lb.	.35
Corigliano	lb.	.30-35
Y. & S., 5-lb. boxes	lb.	.35
Lime, Chlorinated, bulk, bbls., .3	lb.	.4
1-lb. tins	lb.	.8-9
Litharge,	lb.	.10-12
Lithium, Bromide	oz.	.28
Carbonate	lb.	1.75-2.00
Citrate	lb.	1.35
Glycerino-Phosph	ozs.	.74
Iodide	oz.	.32
Salicylate	oz.	.18
Litmus	lb.	.40
Losophan	oz.	1.35
Lunar Caustic, pure, 7.50	oz.	.48-51
in cones	oz.	.50-53
Lupulin, American	lb.	.65
German	lb.	.85
Lycetol, 10 ozs., 3.90	oz.	4.25
Lycopodium, Politz, 10 lbs., .60	lb.	.65-75
Lysiden	oz.	1.75
Lysol	lb.	.47
Mace	lb.	.70
Magnesia, Calcined	lb.	.70-75
heavy	lb.	.75-85
Magnesium, carbonate, ¼ lbs	lb.	.20-30
2 oz	lb.	.32-42
S. S	lb.	.55-70
Citrate, gran	lb.	.58-75
Sulph. (Epsom Salts), bbls., .01½	lb.	2-4
Maltopepsine, Tilden's	pt.	.65
Manganauro, 1-oz. bots	doz.	2.50
Manganese, Black Oxide	lb.	.8-12
Hypophosphite, oz., .30; sulphate	oz.	[illegible]
Manna, large flake	lb.	.60-70
small flake, 5 lbs., .40	lb.	.45
Mannite	lb.	2.25
Marble Dust	bbl.	1.50
Maretin	ozs.	1.25
Menthol, lbs., 3.25	oz.	.25-29
Mercauro, 1-oz. bots	doz.	2.50
Mercury, 5 lbs., .70	lb.	.72-73
Colloidal	oz.	.85
Ammon	lb.	1.10
Bisulphate	lb.	.75
Chloride, Corrosive, 10 lbs., .80	lb.	.88
Cloride, powdered, 10 lbs., .83	lb.	.92
Calomel, 10 lbs., .90	lb.	.98
with Chalk	lb.	.48
Iodide, Proto., lbs., 2.85	ozs.	.37
Biniodide, lbs., 3.10	ozs.	.27
Oxide, Red	lbs.	1.14
Pill (Blue Mass)	lbs.	.47
powdered	lbs.	.57
Herring's English	lbs.	1.35
Red Precipitate	lb.	1.05
White Precipitate	lb.	1.10
powdered	lb.	1.15
Mesotan-Bayer	oz.	.47
Methyl, Acetate	oz.	.45
Bichloride	oz.	[illegible]

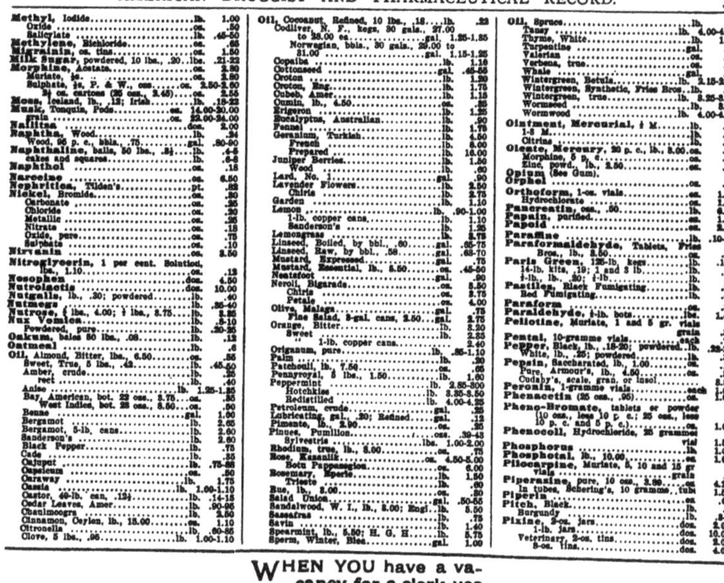

Article	Unit	Price
Methyl, Iodide	lb.	1.00
Oxide	oz.	.50
Salicylate	lb.	.45-50
Methylene, Bichloride	oz.	.65
Migrainin, oz. tins	oz.	1.50
Milk Sugar, powdered, 10 lbs., .20	lbs.	.21-22
Morphine, Acetate	oz.	2.80
Muriate, ⅛s	oz.	2.80
Sulphate, ⅛s, P. & W., ozs.	oz.	2.50-2.60
2½ oz. cartons (25 ozs., 2.45)	oz.	2.55
Moss, Iceland, lb., .12; Irish	lb.	.18-22
Musk, Tonquin, Pods	oz.	14.00-20.00
grain	oz.	22.00-24.00
Nallitsa	doz.	2.00
Naphtha, Wood	lb.	.24
Wood, 95 p. c., bbls., .75	gal.	.80-90
Naphthaline, balls, 50 lbs., .3½	lb.	.4-5
cakes and squares	lb.	.6-8
Naphthol	oz.	.18
Narceine	oz.	6.50
Nephritica, Tilden's	pt.	.82
Nickel, Bromide	oz.	.80
Carbonate	oz.	.25
Chloride	oz.	.20
Metallic	oz.	.25
Nitrate	oz.	.18
Oxide, pure	oz.	.75
Sulphate	oz.	.10
Nirvanin	oz.	2.50
Nitroglycerin, 1 per cent. Solution, lbs., 1.10	oz.	.12
Nosophen	doz.	4.50
Nutrolactis	doz.	10.00
Nutgalls, lb., .30; powdered	lb.	.40
Nutmegs	lb.	.35-40
Nutrose, ¼ lbs., 4.00; ½ lbs., 3.75	lb.	2.25
Nux Vomica	lb.	.8-10
Powdered, pure	lb.	.20-25
Oakum, bales 50 lbs., .08	lb.	.12
Oatmeal	lb.	.6
Oil, Almond, Bitter, lbs., 6.50	oz.	.55
Sweet, True, 5 lbs., .42	lb.	.45-50
Amber, crude	lb.	.25
rect	lb.	.40
Anise	lb.	1.25-1.35
Bay, American, bot. 22 ozs., 3.75	oz.	.35
West Indies, bot. 23 ozs., 5.50	oz.	.50
Benne	gal.	1.00
Bergamot	lb.	2.65
Bergamot, 5-lb. cans	lb.	2.60
Sanderson's	lb.	2.60
Black Pepper	lb.	.75
Cade	lb.	.35
Cajuput	lb.	.75-85
Capsicum	oz.	.50
Caraway	lb.	1.75
Cassia	lb.	1.00-1.10
Castor, 40-lb. can, .12½	lb.	.14-15
Cedar Leaves, Amer.	lb.	.90-95
Chaulmoogra	lb.	2.50
Cinnamon, Ceylon, lb., 15.00	oz.	1.10
Citronella	lb.	.60-65
Clove, 5 lbs., .95	lb.	1.00-1.10
Oil, Cocoanut, Refined, 10 lbs., .18	lb.	.22
Codliver, N. F., kegs, 30 gals., 27.00 to 28.00 ea.	gal.	1.25-1.35
Norwegian, bbls., 30 gals., 29.00 to 31.00	gal.	1.15-1.25
Copaiba	lb.	1.18
Cottonseed	gal.	.45-55
Croton	lb.	1.20
Croton, Eng.	lb.	1.75
Cubeb, Amer.	lb.	1.15
Cumin, lb., 4.50	oz.	.35
Erigeron	lb.	1.25
Eucalyptus, Australian	lb.	.90
Fennel	lb.	1.75
Geranium, Turkish	lb.	4.50
French	lb.	8.00
Prepared	lb.	16.00
Juniper Berries	lb.	1.50
Wood	lb.	.60
Lard, No. 1	gal.	.90
Lavender Flowers	lb.	2.50
Chiris	lb.	2.75
Garden	lb.	1.10
Lemon	lb.	.90-1.00
1-lb. copper cans	lb.	1.10
Sanderson's	lb.	1.25
Lemongrass	lb.	2.75
Linseed, Boiled, by bbl., .60	gal.	.65-75
Linseed, Raw, by bbl., .58	gal.	.63-70
Mustard, Expressed	gal.	.75
Mustard, Essential, lb., 5.50	oz.	.45-50
Neatsfoot	gal.	.90
Neroli, Bigarade	oz.	5.50
Chiris	oz.	3.75
Petale	oz.	4.00
Olive, Malaga	gal.	.75
Fine Salad, 3-gal. cans, 2.50	gal.	2.75
Orange, Bitter	lb.	3.20
Sweet	lb.	2.35
" 1-lb. copper cans		2.40
Origanum, pure	lb.	.85-1.10
Palm	lb.	.20
Patchouli, lb., 7.50	oz.	.65
Pennyroyal, 5 lbs., 1.50	lb.	1.60
Peppermint	lb.	2.85-300
Hotchkiss	lb.	3.35-3.50
Redistilled	lb.	4.00-4.25
Petroleum, crude	gal.	.25
Lubricating, gal., .20; Refined	gal.	.12
Pimento, lb., 2.90	oz.	.25
Pinues, Pumilion	ozs.	.39-43
Sylvestris	lbs.	1.00-2.00
Rhodium, true, lb., 5.00	oz.	.75
Rose, Kazanlik	oz.	4.50-5.00
Botu Pappazoglou	oz.	6.00
Rosemary, Hperie	lb.	1.50
Trieste	lb.	.60
Rue, lb., 3.00	oz.	.30
Salad Union	gal.	.50-55
Sandalwood, W. I., lb., 3.00; Engl.	lb.	5.50
Sassafras	lb.	.75
Savin	lb.	1.40
Spearmint, lb., 5.50; H. G. H.	lb.	5.75
Sperm, Winter, Blea.	gal.	1.00
Oil, Spruce	lb.	.60
Tansy	lb.	4.00-4.50
Thyme, White	lb.	1.35
Turpentine	gal.	.75
Valerian	oz.	.65
Verbena, true	oz.	.50
Whale	gal.	.75
Wintergreen, Betula	lb.	2.15-2.25
Wintergreen, Synthetic, Fries Bros.	lb.	.75
Wintergreen, true	lb.	3.25-3.50
Wormseed	lb.	3.50
Wormwood	lb.	4.00-4.50
Ointment, Mercurial, ½ M.	lb.	.48
1-3 M.	lb.	.46
Citrine	lb.	.46
Oleate, Mercury, 20 p. c., lb., 3.00	oz.	.25
Morphine, 5 p. c.	oz.	.46
Zinc, powd., lb., 2.50	oz.	.20
Opium (See Gum).		
Orphol	oz.	.80
Orthoform, 1-oz. vials	oz.	1.40
Hydrochlorate	oz.	1.80
Pancreatin, ozs., .50	lb.	6.50
Papain, purified	oz.	1.00
Papoid	oz.	2.00
Paraffine	lb.	.10-12
Paraformaldehyde, Tablets, Fries Bros., lb., 3.50	oz.	.35
Paris Green, 125-lb. kegs	lb.	.16½
14-lb. kits, .19; 1 and 3 lb.	lb.	.20
½-lb., lb., .20; ¼-lb.	lb.	.22
Pastiles, Black Fumigating	lb.	.35
Red Fumigating	lb.	.40
Paraform	oz.	.35
Paraldehyde, ¼-lb. bots.	lbs.	1.40
Pellotine, Muriate, 1 and 5 gr. vials	grain	.35
Pental, 10-gramme vials	each	.75
Pepper, Black, lb., .18-20; powdered	lb.	.22-25
White, lb., .25; powdered	lb.	.30
Pepsin, Saccharated, lb., 1.00	oz.	.12
Pure, Armour's, lb., 4.50	oz.	.36
Cudahy's, scale, gran. or insol.		3.50
Peronin, 1-gramme vials	each	1.05
Phenacetin (25 ozs., .95)	oz.	1.00
Pheno-Bromate, tablets or powder (10 ozs., less 10 p. c.; 25 ozs., less 10 p. c. and 5 p. c.)	oz.	1.00
Phenocoll, Hydrochloride, 25 grammes	vial	1.50
Phosphorus	lb.	1.00
Phosphotal, lb., 10.00	oz.	1.00
Pilocarpine, Muriate, 5, 10 and 15 gr vials	grain	.6
Piperazine, pure, 10 ozs., 3.90	oz.	4.25
In tubes, Schering's, 10 gramme	tube	1.50
Piperin	oz.	.65
Pitch, Black	lb.	.6
Burgundy	lb.	.5-6
Pixine, 2-oz. jars	doz.	2.00
1-lb. jars	doz.	10.00
Veterinary, 2-oz. tins	doz.	2.00
8-oz. tins	doz.	4.00

WHEN YOU have a vacancy for a clerk use the AMERICAN DRUGGIST "Want" column. Notices inserted one time free of charge for subscribers.

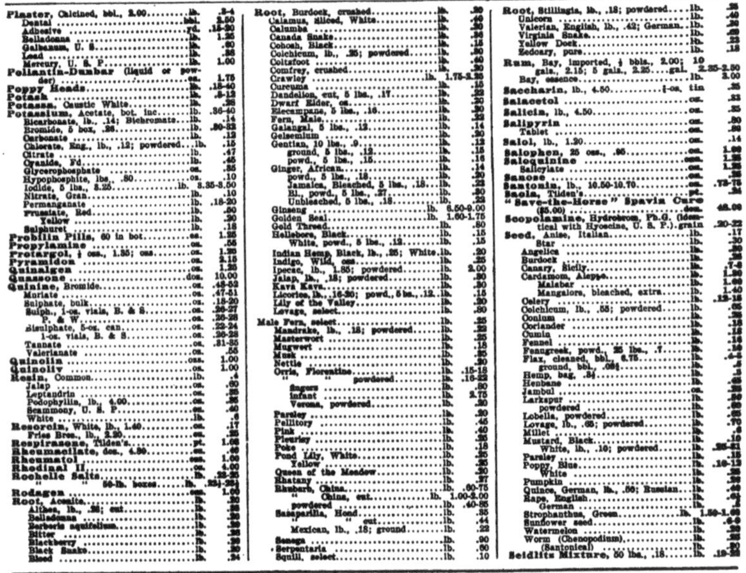

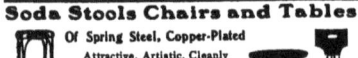

Article	Unit	Price
Plaster, Calcined, bbl., 2.00	lb.	.3-4
Dental	bbl.	2.50
Adhesive	yd.	.15-30
Belladonna	lb.	1.25
Galbanum, U. S.	lb.	.60
Lead	lb.	.25
Mercury, U. S. P.	lb.	1.00
Pollantin-Dunbar (liquid or powder)	oz.	1.75
Poppy Heads	lb.	.15-40
Potash	lb.	.9-12
Potassa, Caustic White	lb.	.28
Potassium, Acetate, bot. inc.	lb.	.36-40
Bicarbonate, lb., .14; Bichromate	lb.	.14
Bromide, 5 box, .28	lb.	.30-32
Carbonate	lb.	.12
Chlorate, Eng., lb., .12; powdered	lb.	.15
Citrate	lb.	.47
Cyanide, Fd	lb.	.45
Glycerophosphate	oz.	.35
Hypophosphite, lbs., .80	oz.	.10
Iodide, 5 lbs., 3.25	lb.	3.35-3.50
Nitrate, Gran.	lb.	.10
Permanganate	lb.	.18-20
Prussiate, Red	lb.	.50
Yellow	lb.	.30
Sulphuret	lb.	.18
Probilin Pills, 60 in bot.	ea.	1.25
Propylamine	oz.	.55
Protargol, ¼ ozs., 1.35; ozs.	oz.	1.20
Pyramidon	oz.	2.15
Quinalgen	oz.	1.25
Quassone	doz.	10.00
Quinine, Bromide	oz.	.48-52
Muriate	oz.	.47-51
Sulphate, bulk	oz.	.18-20
Sulph., 1-oz. vials, B. & S.	oz.	.26-27
P. & W.	oz.	.26-28
Bisulphate, 5-oz. can	oz.	.22-24
1-oz. vials, B. & S.	oz.	.26-28
Tannate	oz.	.31-35
Valerianate	oz.	.55
Quinolin	ozs.	1.00
Quinoliv	oz.	1.00
Resin, Common	lb.	.4
Jalap	oz.	.60
Leptandrin	oz.	.35
Podophyllin, lb., 4.00	oz.	.35
Scammony, U. S. P.	oz.	.40
White	lb.	.6
Resorcin, White, lb., 1.40	oz.	.17
Fries Bros., lb., 2.20	oz.	.25
Respirazone, Tilden's	pt.	1.08
Rheumacilate, doz., 4.80	ea.	.45
Rheumatol	ozs.	1.00
Rhodinal II	oz.	4.00
Rochelle Salts	lb.	.22-25
" " 50-lb. boxes	lb.	.23½-25½
Rodagen	ozs.	1.00
Root, Aconite	lb.	.30
Althea, lb., .28; cut	lb.	.28
Belladonna	lb.	.26
Berberis aquifolium	lb.	.20
Bitter	lb.	.25
Blackberry	lb.	.20
Black Snake	lb.	.20
Blood	lb.	.24
Root, Burdock, crushed	lb.	.20
Calamus, Sliced, White	lb.	.40
Calumba	lb.	.20
Canada Snake	lb.	.35
Cohosh, Black	lb.	.15
Colchicum, lb., .35; powdered	lb.	.30
Coltsfoot	lb.	.40
Comfrey, crushed	lb.	.20
Crawley	lb.	1.75-2.25
Curcuma	lb.	.15
Dandelion, cut, 5 lbs., .17	lb.	.22
Dwarf Elder, oz.	lb.	.20
Elecampane, 5 lbs., .16	lb.	.20
Fern, Male	lb.	.22
Galangal, 5 lbs., .12	lb.	.14
Gelsemium	lb.	.20
Gentian, 10 lbs., .9	lb.	.12
ground, 5 lbs., .12	lb.	.15
powd., 5 lbs., .15	lb.	.16
Ginger, African	lb.	.14
powd., 5 lbs., .18	lb.	.20
Jamaica, Bleached, 5 lbs., .18	lb.	.22
Bl., powd., 5 lbs., .27	lb.	.30
Unbleached, 5 lbs., .18	lb.	.22
Ginseng	lb.	6.50-9.00
Golden Seal	lb.	1.60-1.75
Gold Thread	lb.	.80
Hellebore, Black	lb.	.15
White, powd., 5 lbs., .12	lb.	.15
Indian Hemp, Black, lb., .25; White	lb.	.20
Indigo, Wild, ozs.	lb.	.25
Ipecac, lb., 1.85; powdered	lb.	2.00
Jalap, lb., .18; powdered	lb.	.30
Kava Kava	lb.	.30
Licorice, lb., .16-20; powd., 5 lbs., .12	lb.	.15
Lily of the Valley	lb.	.30
Lovage, select	lb.	.80
Male Fern, select	lb.	.25
Mandrake, lb., .18; powdered	lb.	.22
Masterwort	lb.	.25
Mugwort	lb.	.18
Musk	lb.	.35
Nettle	lb.	.20
Orris, Florentine	lb.	.15-18
" " powdered	lb.	.16-22
fingers	lb.	.50
infant	lb.	2.75
Verona, powdered	lb.	.20
Parsley	lb.	.20
Pellitory	lb.	.45
Pink	lb.	.40
Pleurisy	lb.	.25
Poke	lb.	.18
Pond Lily, White	lb.	.25
Yellow	lb.	.35
Queen of the Meadow	lb.	.20
Rhatany	lb.	.27
Rhubarb, China	lb.	.60-75
" China, cut	lb.	1.00-2.00
powdered	lb.	.40-85
Sarsaparilla, Hond.	lb.	.35
" " cut	lb.	.44
Mexican, lb., .18; ground	lb.	.22
Senega	lb.	.90
Serpentaria	lb.	.60
Squill, select	lb.	.10
Root, Stillingia, lb., .18; powdered	lb.	.25
Unicorn	lb.	.40
Valerian, English, lb., .42; German	lb.	.20
Virginia Snake	lb.	.40
Yellow Dock	lb.	.22
Zedoary, pure	lb.	.18
Rum, Bay, imported, ½ bbls., 2.00; 10 gals., 2.15; 5 gals., 2.25	gal.	2.35-2.50
Bay, essence	lb.	3.00
Saccharin, lb., 4.50	⅛-oz. tin	.35
Salacetol	oz.	.82
Salicin, lb., 4.50	oz.	.35
Salipyrin	oz.	.80
Tablet	oz.	.89
Salol, lb., 1.20	oz.	.14
Salophen, 25 ozs., .95	oz.	1.00
Saloquinine	ozs.	1.25
Salicylate	oz.	1.25
Sanose	oz.	.25
Santonin, lb., 10.50-10.70	oz.	.73-75
Saola, Tilden's	pt.	.84
"Save-the-Horse" Spavin Cure ($5.00)	doz.	48.00
Scopolamine, Hydrobrom, Ph.G. (identical with Hyoscine, U. S. P.)	grain	.20-22
Seed, Anise, Italian	lb.	.17
Star	lb.	.30
Angelica	lb.	.30
Burdock	lb.	.25
Canary, Sicily	lb.	.7-8
Cardamom, Aleppo	lb.	1.20
Malabar	lb.	1.00
Mangalore, bleached, extra	lb.	1.40
Celery	lb.	.13-15
Colchicum, lb., .55; powdered	lb.	.65
Conium	lb.	.25
Coriander	lb.	.15
Cumin	lb.	.15
Fennel	lb.	.15
Fenugreek, powd., 25 lbs., .7	lb.	.10
Flax, cleaned, bbl., 6.75	lb.	.4-5
ground, bbl., .08½	lb.	.5
Hemp, bag, .3½	lb.	.5
Henbane	lb.	.65
Jambul	oz.	.25
Larkspur	lb.	.50
powdered	lb.	.65
Lobelia, powdered	lb.	.55
Lovage, lb., .65; powdered	lb.	.70
Millet	lb.	.6
Mustard, Black	lb.	.10
White, lb., .10; powdered	lb.	.25-21
Parsley	lb.	.15
Poppy, Blue	lb.	.10-12
White	lb.	.25
Pumpkin	lb.	.25
Quince, German, lb., .56; Russian	lb.	.60
Rape, English	lb.	.6
German	lb.	.5
Strophanthus, Green	lb.	1.50-1.60
Sunflower seed	lb.	.6-8
Watermelon	lb.	.25
Worm (Chenopodium)	lb.	.25
(Santonica)	lb.	.20
Seidlitz Mixture, 50 lbs., .18	lb.	.19-22

Article	Unit	Price
Silver, Nitrate, cryst., lb., 7.50	oz.	.50-55
67 per cent., oz., .37; 50 per cent.	oz.	.30
Cones	oz.	.60-63
Soap, Castile, Marseilles, box, .7	lb.	.10
Mottled, pure, box, .8	lb.	.10
White, Conti's, box, .12	lb.	.14
powdered, 25 lbs., .28	lb.	.35
Green (Sapo Vir.), 10 lbs., .12	lb.	.10-15
Eng. Blue Mottled Soap, cases, 112 lbs.		5.50-6.50
Soda, Chlor. Sol	doz.	2.25
Sodium, Acetate, pure, gran	lb.	.15
Bicarbonate, Eng., keg, .03	lb.	.4-5
" Natrona, keg, .2½	lb.	.3-5
Bromide	lb.	.35-37
Carbonate, bbl., .1	lb.	.2½
Citrate	lb.	.47
Glycerophosphate	oz.	.35
Hypophosphite, lbs., .85	lb.	.10-14
Hypophosphite, kg., .2½	lb.	.5
Hyposulphite	keg	.02½
Iodide, lb., 3.45	oz.	.38-40
Phosphate, cryst	lb.	.10
Salicylate	lb.	.44
Silicate, Syrupy, bbl., .2½	lb.	.5-10
Sulphate	lb.	.3
Somatose, 2 ozs	doz.	8.25
Somnal	oz.	.80
Sozoiodol	oz.	1.15
Sparteine, Sulph., B & S	oz.	.75-1.00
Spermaceti	lb.	.28-30
Spermine, Poehl, box 4 tubes	ea.	3.00
Spirit Ether Nit., U. S. P	lb.	.52
Streptolytic Serum, Stearns', 20 Cc., in two sero-bulbs of 10 Cc. each		3.00
Discount, 25 per cent.		
Strontium, Nitrate	lb.	.16
Bromide, lb., .55	oz.	.12
Iodide	oz.	.41
Lactate, lb., 1.25	oz.	.16
Salicylate, lb., .75	oz.	.13
Strophanthin, c. p. cryst	grain	.6
Strychnine, Crystals, ⅛-oz. vials	oz.	1.20
powdered, ⅛-oz. vials	oz.	1.20
Sulphate, ⅛-oz. vials	oz.	1.20
Glycerophosphate, ozs	oz.	2.50
Sulfonal, 25 ozs., 1.25	oz.	1.35
Sulphur, Flowers, bbls., .2½	lb.	.4-5
Precipitate, pure	lb.	.16-18
Suprarenal Glands, Dessicated, powd., oz., 2.00; Tablets	oz.	1.00
Saccharated	oz.	1.20
Tablets, 1 grain, per 100		.40
Capsules, 1 grain, per 100		.65
Sycose, 2-oz. package	each.	1.00
Takadiastase	oz.	1.70
Liquid, 8-oz. bots	doz.	6.00
Tannigen, 25 ozs., .65	oz.	.75
Tannopine	oz.	.75
Tar, N. C. pine, Diamond brand, pts.	doz.	.95
Tartar Emetic, powdered	lb.	.36
Terebene	lb.	.65
Terpin Hydrate, cryst	oz.	.10
in bulk	lb.	.45
Theocin-Bayer	ozs.	2.70
Theophyllin, B. & S	oz.	1.40
sodium, oz., 1.50; sodium salicylate	oz.	1.10
Thigenol, lbs., 4.00	oz.	.32
Thiocol	oz.	1.40
Thiocol Tablets, 100 in vial		1.75
Thioform, 25-gramme pkgs	each	.59
Thiol, liquid, oz., .40; powdered	oz.	.75
Thymol (Thymic Acid), lbs., 2.25	oz.	.27
Thyroids, dessicated, Cudahy's	lb.	7.00
Tinct. Simulo, Christy's, lbs	lb.	4.25
½ lbs., lb., 4.35; ¼ lbs	lb.	4.50
Trional, 25 ozs., 1.40	oz.	1.50
Tuberculinum Kochii, "Pasteur," 1 Cc	doz.	3.30
Tuberculin (Veterinary), "Pasteur," 1 Cc	doz.	3.20
Tuberculin Solution (Veterinary), "Pasteur," 10 Cc	doz.	4.00
Turpentine, Spirits, bbls., .72½	gal.	.80-90
Chian, oz., .45; Venice	lb.	.30
Tussol	oz.	1.65
Urethane, C. P	oz.	.54
Uricedin, 5 ozs	doz.	15.00
Urotropin	oz.	.60
Urotropin Tablets, 5 or 7½ grs.	doz.	3.00
Vaccine, Mulford's (Discount, 40 per cent.), 1 pkg. Glycerinized Lymph, containing 10 tubes		1.00
1 vial Glycerinized Lymph, containing sufficient for 50 vaccinations		4.50
1 pkg. Ivory Points, containing 10 points		.95-1.85
Glycerinated, F. Stearns & Co., Points (10 in a package)		1.00
Tubes (10 tubes in one wooden box, accompanied by one needle, rubber bulb and 10 temporary shields)		1.00
Discount, 40 per cent.		
Vanillin (various brands)	oz.	.60-75
Veratrine, ⅛-oz., 2.75; Sulph., ⅛ths.	oz.	2.90
Veronal, ¼-oz., oz., 1.60; 1-oz	oz.	1.60
Veronal Tablets, 5 grs., tubes, .15	ea.	.40
" " bots. 50	ea.	1.15
" " " 100	ea.	2.25
Water, Ammonia, 16 deg., carboy, .3½	lb.	.6
20 deg., carboys, .4½	lb.	.8
26 deg. (Conct.), carboy, .8½	lb.	.10-12
Wax, Bayberry	lb.	.60-65
Carnauba, No. 1	lb.	.55-60
Ceresin, yellow, cases, .18	lb.	.22
" white, cases, .21	lb.	.25-28
Japan, cases, .15	lb.	.18-20
White, Star Brand, 60 lbs., .50	lb.	.55
White, S. B	lb.	.85
Leonard's T. L. Brand, 60 lbs., .47½	lb.	.55
" " 60 lbs., .42½	lb.	.50
Yellow, select	lb.	.38
White Lead, Dry, pure	lb.	.10
Zinc, American, lb., .10; French	lb.	.15
Whiting, bbls., .¾	lb.	.3
Witch Hazel Ext., 10 gals., .70	gal.	.85
Wood, Guaiac, rasped	lb.	.6
Quassia Chips, bbl., .6	lb.	.7-12
Red Saunders, bbl., .4	lb.	.6-8
Sandal, ground	lb.	.40
Yohimbin Hydrochlor, ⅛-gramme vials	each.	5.00
Tablets, 1-12 gr., 10 in tube	each.	1.00
Zinc, Acetate	lb.	.25-30
Carbonate, Precip	lb.	.22
Chloride, granular, lbs., .22	oz.	.6
Iodide	oz.	.40
Oxide	lb.	.10
Hubbuck's, 7-lb. boxes, .35	lb.	.38-40
Zinc, Sulphate, bbls., .8½	lb.	.5-6
Sulphocarbolate, lbs., .50	oz.	.7-9
Valerianate, lbs., 1.75	oz.	.20

PAINTS AND COLORS.

Article	Unit	Price
Black, Coach, in oil	lb.	.18-25
dry	lb.	.15-20
Drop, in oil	lb.	.15-25
dry, in oil	lb.	.12-20
Ivory, in oil, lb., .18-25; dry	lb.	.12-18
in Japan	lb.	.22-25
Lamp, Germantown, ass'd papers, ¼-lb., ½-lb., 1-lb	lb.	.12
in oil	lb.	.10
Black Lead, E. I., 25 lbs., .6½	lb.	.8
German, 15 lbs., .4½	lb.	.6
Blue, Celestial, dry	lb.	.10
Chinese, dry	lb.	.60
in oil	lb.	.55
Paint, in oil	lb.	.9
Prussian, dry	lb.	.50
in oil	lb.	.45
Soluble, 10 lbs., .45	lb.	.50
Ultramarine, dry	lb.	.15
in oil	lb.	.20
Brown, Sienna, burnt, dry	lb.	.4
in oil	lb.	.10-15
Raw, dry	lb.	.4
in oil	lb.	.10-15
Spanish, dry, bbls., .1	lb.	.3
Vandyke, dry	lb.	.6
in oil	lb.	.12
Chalk, lump, bbls., .¾	lb.	.2
Green, Chrome, powd., 6-lb. cans, .10	lb.	.12
in oil	lb.	.12-16
Paris, bulk, lbs., .16-17; 1-lbs., .18-20; ½-lbs., .20-22; ¼-lbs., .22-25; in oil	lb.	.22-27
Litharge	lb.	.10
Pumice Stone, bbl., .6	lb.	.8
powdered, bbl., .3	lb.	.4
Putty, in bladders, bbls., .2½	lb.	.3½
in oil	lb.	
Red, Indian, Eng., dry	lb.	.8
in oil	lb.	.10-12
Lead	lb.	.8-10
Orange Mineral	lb.	.12
Rose Lake, Eng., dry	lb.	.5
Pink, Eng., dry	lb.	.15
Tuscan, Eng., dry	lb.	.4
in oil	lb.	.22
Venetian, dry, American, bbls., .1	lb.	.3½
Vermilion, American	lb.	.20
Chinese	lb.	.90
English	lb.	.80
Rotten Stone, bbl., .6	lb.	.8
Umber, Burnt, bbls., .1½	lb.	.3
Raw, bbls., .1½	lb.	.3
White, China, dry	lb.	.20
Flake, dry	lb.	.15
Lead, dry	lb.	.10
oil	lb.	.9-10
Paris, English	lb.	.2
Whiting, bbls., .¾	lb.	.2
Yellow, Chrome, dry	lb.	.10-15
in oil	lb.	.10-20
Golden, in oil	lb.	.16
Ochre, French, dry, bbls., .1½	lb.	.2½
American, dry, bbls., .1	lb.	.2
Zinc, White, dry, American	lb.	.6
in oil	lb.	.16

American Druggist "WANTS" Page.

THIS Department is intended to be used as a medium for the exchange or sale of stores, the employment of clerks, and the securing of situations. Suitable notices of moderate length under this heading inserted one time free for subscribers; for each additional insertion Fifty Cents will be charged. Advertisements not in the foregoing classification Forty Cents per line.

SITUATIONS VACANT.

WANTED. — Ambitious young drug clerk for pleasant position; must be a good salesman and able to take full charge; registered in New Jersey; also assistant; all replies answered confidential; must have good reference. E. A. Travero, 172 Hamilton street, New Brunswick, N. J.

WANTED.—Competent registered assistant for a high class pharmacy in a family neighborhood. Particulars as to salary, etc., can be obtained by addressing Clayton, care of AMERICAN DRUGGIST.

WANTED.—Drug employees, wholesale and retail. Vacancies now open in New York, Illinois, Iowa, Arkansas, Alabama, Florida and other States. Salary $50 to $100. Diplomas recognized. If you would accept a better position now or later, send us your name at once. Employers referred to competent men free. National Pharmaceutical Agency, 616 Holland Bldg., St. Louis, Mo.

WANTED.—Licensed clerk at retail drug store. Good position. E. L. Schmitt, 812 North street, Rochester, N. Y.

WANTED, LICENSED CLERK at retail drug store; steady position for right party. Best of references required. Address J. F. S., care of AMERICAN DRUGGIST.

DRUG CLERK WANTED FOR MEXICO.—Young graduate in pharmacy, with knowledge of Spanish preferred, who can be trusted in important position in well-known Mexican drug store; must be qualified in every particular; chance of advancement good; send references and state salary expected. Mexico, care Foreign Department, AMERICAN DRUGGIST.

REGISTERED PHARMACISTS and drug employees, if you would accept a better position, now or later, send us your name at once; fine openings in all States; salaries, $600 to $2,000 a year; employers referred to competent men free. NATIONAL PHARMACEUTICAL AGENCY, 616 Colonial Security Building, St. Louis, Mo.

BUSINESS OPPORTUNITIES.

SHEEP DIP, ETC.—A gentleman with special knowledge of the trade and an extensive connection in South Africa wishes to represent a manufacturer of sheep dip in that country; 11 years' experience. Address "Dip," Box 671, Sells Advertising Offices, London, England.

FOR $25,000, a working interest in a fine wholesale drug business. Address Drugs, care Stringer & Seymour, St. Paul, Minn.

FOR SALE.—An old established drug store in a manufacturing town in Connecticut, one hour from New York; reason for selling, poor health of owner; a good store; $4,500 inventory. Address Lysol, care of AMERICAN DRUGGIST.

FOR SALE OR EXCHANGE.—Only drug store for sale in town of about 800; $8,000 stock; have been in the business thirty-four years; wish a change; will exchange for small farm in western New York. Address George U. Saxton, Delevan, N. Y.

CIRCULARS, BOOKLETS, LETTERS and advertising matter of any description designed and prepared; high-grade medical advertising a specialty. C. L. Mueller, M. D., Advertising Counselor, Wapakoneta, Ohio.

FOR SALE.—San Juan, Porto Rico; only American drug store; established seven years; good business; inventory about $7,500; reason, sickness. P. O. Box 226, San Juan, Porto Rico.

PARTNER WANTED.—I want as an equal partner a good pharmacist and business man who can command $2,000 or $3,000 in real money. I have a store that has a stock of nearly $6,000 in clean, fresh goods, most of it bought in the last eight months, and a business that is too big for one man to handle. It is capable of a vast development, as it is a suburb of New York that may increase its population five fold in the next five years. Would sell out, but am forming a stock company to operate a chain of stores in this section and want this store in the combination. I must have time to attend to this company matter and do not want to lose this store, as it will be an important link in our chain of stores. If I can find the right man I have a good thing for him, as the store will go into the combination as soon as the company is incorporated. Or I will make a contract to sell all my interest to my partner in case he doesn't want to go into the company. In short, I want to hold and continue the building up of this business by some one that I can absolutely depend upon. Apply by letter only to Dawson, care AMERICAN DRUGGIST.

FOR SALE.—The controlling interest in a manufacturing business that has an exceedingly bright future; must be sold by April 1. Address B. O. Company, care of AMERICAN DRUGGIST.

FOR SALE.—One of the finest drug stores in western New York; cement block; building new; steel ceiling; all fixtures new; everything up to date; hot water, heat, gas or electric lights; insurance, 1 per cent; will sell with or without building. Address V. C. Armes, Gowanda, N. Y.

FOR SALE.—Wishing to retire from business on account of age, I offer a large and prosperous business at a liberal discount from the inventory to a cash customer; when answering this state how much capital you have to invest. Address Filmore, care of AMERICAN DRUGGIST.

WHAT OFFERS?

Mrs. G. C. de Lessing, 945 Park Avenue, New York, wishes to dispose of the library of her late husband and invites offers on the following books:

Piesse, G. W. Septimus, Ph.D. The Art of Perfumery and the Method of Obtaining the Odours of Plants; the growth and general flower farm system of raising fragrant herbs. 1880.

Fenner's Formulary, containing formulæ for the preparation of all the elixirs, emulsions, essences, flavoring extracts, glycerites, solutions, syrups, wines, etc. Fifth edition, 1879.

Parsons, Samuel B. A Treatise on the Propagation, Culture and History of the Rose. Illustrated. 1888.

Power, Frederick B., Ph.G., Ph.D. Descriptive Catalogue of Essential Oils and Organic Chemical Preparations.

Harrop, Joseph, Ph.G. Monograph on Flavoring Extracts, with Essences, Syrups and Colorings. 1891.

Reduction in Price of Koenig Remedies.

The Koenig Medicine Company, of 100 Lake street, Chicago, announce that on April 1 the price for Pastor Koenig's Nerve Tonic will be reduced to $8 a dozen, price for the other preparations being reduced in proportion. This tonic is a great seller, one Baltimore druggist, A. C. Huthwelker, having sold 49 bottles at retail one day. Write makers at 100 Lake street, Chicago, for special proposition, mentioning the AMERICAN DRUGGIST.

Pretty Windows.

While there are a number of ornamental possibilities in the ordinary daily dressing of drug store windows from stock they are nearly always "druggy." People glance at the display much as they might at goods on the shelf. There is very little of real beauty in sight. One druggist we know used Souvenir Post Cards in brilliant assortment merely to introduce the eye-catching quality of beauty.

Much to his surprise the quick demand from appreciative card buyers forced a new purchase of the stock, and this was repeated again and again until the truth dawned on him—for he was slow to admit it—that it pays to carry lines of good view cards for sale in a drug store. Where preferred a card rack can be used exclusively and in very small space.

Realizing these conditions one of our enterprising advertisers (the Souvenir Post Card Company, 50 Franklin street, New York) is making a special "combination" offer of a first-class card display rack—one that holds 2,000 cards—together with 1,200 cards for "even money" ($10), a low price. The privilege extended to purchasers of "full sample lines" permits the return of any cards not desired. Send for the samples. Any dealer may safely trust "the biggest manufacturers of post cards in the world."

The New Edition of Remington.

The publishers inform us that the first large issue of the fourth edition of Remington's Practice of Pharmacy has been oversold. The books of the second issue and the plates are now being shipped, and the third printing, a still larger issue, is now under way. This is the best evidence of the appreciation of this valuable work shown by the retail drug trade. If you have not already bought a copy write for descriptive circular to J. B. Lippincott Company, Philadelphia, Pa.

The Rapid Growth of the Souvenir Post Card Business.

When the post card business was first introduced into the United States from abroad it was principally exploited by people who cared more for the immediate profits than for the permanent success, and as a natural result the cards that were first offered to the trade were generally of most inferior quality. For the greater part they were made up of cheaply printed cards, produced by the half-tone process, and scores of printing shops throughout the country started to turn out souvenir post cards the quality of which was in every way inferior to that of the imported cards.

Fortunately for the success of the post card business in the United States, reputable concerns saw its big possibilities and took it in hand. Among these was the American News Company, who at first handled the business through their regular stationery department, but it was soon found that the superior quality of its cards brought in such a tremendous volume of orders that it became necessary to establish a special department, in charge of experts in that branch of the business, to give it special and exclusive attention.

The American News Company now offers the trade in view cards three different styles of souvenir post cards. Of the miscellaneous cards, such as comic, leather, novelty and fancy post cards, they have an endless variety. They make it a specialty to always have an elaborate edition of cards appropriate for each particular season. For instance, now Easter cards are to the front. Their line of these cards is very complete. These cards are put up principally in sets. One set consists of six (6) different cards, beautifully illuminated in many colors. A unique feature about these cards is that they are transparent when held to the light. Easter eggs, rabbits, chickens and many other beautiful symbols of the joyous season show upon these cards in illuminated form. These cards retail at 5 cents, with a very liberal margin of profit to the trade.

The unsolicited testimonials which the American News Company is constantly receiving from satisfied customers would fill a large volume, and when the best dealers in the trade take the trouble to write, as they do, using words of the highest praise, the American News Company feels amply repaid for the special effort and expense made necessary in order to supply the trade with these high art post cards. On another page of the AMERICAN DRUGGIST appears the American News Company's advertisement, which makes special mention of their Improved Paragon Revolving Post Card Display Stand. To introduce the stand they are giving a valuable and desirable assortment of cards as a premium with each stand, and making no charge for the post cards. This makes it easy for every dealer to start in the post card business at once at little expense.

Enterprising dealers will do well to send at once to the American News Company, 39-41 Chambers street, New York, for samples, price-list and full particulars with reference to their entire line of post cards.

Keep Your Store Cool.

When a woman drinks a glass of soda water (and women are the most generous patrons of the bubbling beverage) and feels cool and comfortable afterward she does not analyze the means by which this delectable state was reached. All she knows, and all she needs to know, is that she drank a delicious glass of soda at Blank's fountain. Blank will know that the coolness was due to the rotary fans which he bought from D. L. Bates & Bro., Dayton, Ohio. We illustrate one of these fans herewith, and such of our readers as have not already installed these fans should write to the manufacturer for descriptive catalogue, mentioning the AMERICAN DRUGGIST.

Of all the improvements to which the modern soda counter is heir there is none more valuable than the lightning tumbler washer made by the Whiteman Mfg. Company, of Canton, Ohio. Write them for a descriptive circular of the machine with two sets of rapidly revolving brushes, which washes the inside and outside of the glass at the same time—and does it well. Don't wait until after the season has begun to write about this, but write to the manufacturer. Write now.

The Pharmacopœial Standard for Witch Hazel Too Low?

The pharmacopœial standard adopted in the Eighth Revision for what is popularly known as witch hazel extract, but is given the official title of aqua hamamelidis, or hamamelis water, provides that 10,000 Gm. of hamamelis bark be macerated in 20,000 Cc. of water for 24 hours, and that from this 8,500 Cc. be distilled off, and that to this distillate 1,500 Cc. be added. This means that 8 pounds of bark should be used for each gallon of witch hazel extract produced, and that the finished product should contain 15 per cent. of alcohol. E. E. Dickinson & Son, of Essex, Conn., who are among the largest, if not the largest, distillers of this product in the world, say that an extract made according to this formula is very unsatisfactory. They use in their double distilled extract 20 pounds of green witch hazel twigs for every gallon of extract produced, and they claim that by their process of double distillation they obtain a cleaner, sweeter, better flavored witch hazel than can be obtained in any other way and one that is free from any precipitate. The labels of E. E. Dickinson & Co. are frequently imitated, and their containers are filled with inferior brands, but druggists who wish to secure a thoroughly satisfactory preparation would do well to make sure that they are securing the Dickinson distillate. For quotations and further particulars address E. E. Dickinson & Co., Essex, Conn.

Metcalf's Air Tight Sachet Tins.

A novelty in sachet powder packages is being introduced by Theo. Metcalf Company, the well-known druggists of Boston. This package is an elegant affair, hermetically sealed, thus retaining the full strength of the sachet powder indefinitely.

The druggist retails this package at 50 cents. There is a liberal profit for him in handling it.

Two of the latest successful odors packed in this way are Metcalf's Yale Violette and Metcalf's Harvard Crimson.

We would suggest that our readers write to the Theo. Metcalf Company, Boston, for its special proposition as advertised in another part of this issue.

Vanilla Bean Production.

Although so large a percentage of the so-called vanilla extract sold in the United States is a cheap imitation, composed usually of tonka bean and cold-tar products, enormous quantities of the genuine bean are actually imported, but the distribution of this expensive article is restricted. During the past year $1,424,647 represented the value of vanilla beans imported by the United States, two-thirds of which came from Mexico, at a valuation of $1,053,813, and weighing 177,301 pounds. France came second, with her exportation valued at $265,456. So says the *Monthly Bulletin* of the Industrial Bureau of the American Republics for December, 1905.

Queen City Special.

The Big Four Route of the New York Central lines has recently added two new trains to the passenger schedule which will be greatly appreciated by the traveling public, and especially by commercial men, as it will enable them to spend the evening with friends, or at the theatre in Chicago or Cincinnati, and take the "Queen City Special," arriving at their destination early in the morning. These two new trains carry Pullman's latest designed open buffet sleeper and compartment car, with special service between Chicago and Indianapolis and Chicago and Louisville. The new service leaves Chicago and Cincinnati at 11.30 P.M., arriving at destination at 7.45 A.M., connecting at Union Depot with all Southern roads for the South. Sleepers will be ready for occupancy at 9.30 P.M. Further particulars regarding this new effective service will be gladly furnished by I. P. Spining, general Northern Passenger Agent, Chicago.

An Accommodating Pharmacist.

Under the heading, At the Drug Store, the New York *Sun* prints the following, credited to the Irrigon *Irrigator*:

"For a nice mint julep, a Tom Collins, or a highball, or a nice, clean shave, or a haircut, or anything in the grocery, hardware, dry goods, or millinery line, call at the City Drug Store. Also drugs for sale."

If the *Sun* would say in what part of the country Irrigon is situated it would relieve us of a doubt regarding the actual existence of the place, which is not named in the latest Postal Guide.

Where True Quality is Shown.

The excellence of Scott's Emulsion is recognized by the highest authority. The London *Lancet* said of it: "The value of the hypophosphites combined with codliver oil, especially in wasting diseases and debilitated conditions, is well known. In addition to these constituents, Scott's Emulsion also contains glycerin, which is well recognized as assisting very materially in the absorption of oils and fats. We have examined the preparation with care and find that it fulfills all the requirements and presents all the conditions of a very satisfactory emulsion. In appearance and consistence it is not unlike cream and under the microscope the fat globules are seen to be of perfectly regular size and uniformly distributed. In fact, the preparation, microscopically examined, presents the appearance of cream. So well has the oil been emulsified that even when shaken with water the fat is slow to separate, the liquid then looking like milk. The taste is decidedly unobjectionable and is pleasantly aromatic and saline. We had no difficulty in recognizing the presence of the hypophosphites in an unimpaired state. The emulsion keeps well even when exposed to wide changes of temperature. Under the circumstances just described the emulsion should prove an excellent food as well as a tonic."

Catarrhal Conditions.

Just at this season of the year we are especially called upon to consider the advantages to be found in Glyco-Thymoline for the treatment of acute catarrhal diseases of the nose and throat.

Coryza, naso-pharyngitis, tonsillitis and laryngitis are now most common. After exposure to cold the mucous membrane, with its delicate cell structure and fine capillary net work, takes on a turgid appearance. The minute blood vessels or capillaries become congested and their function practically suspended. The blood cells, through lack of nourishment, die and are thrown off. The glandular secretions are altered; instead of excreting a bland, nonirritating mucus, we have present an acid discharge most irritating in type. This is about the condition we find in all catarrhal inflammation.

How does Glyco-Thymoline apply here? What are its special advantages?

Glyco-Thymoline in a 25 per cent. solution, being approximately of the same alkalinity and specific gravity as blood serum, causes by its exosmotic action (the passage outwardly through the tissues of normal secretions and products of inflammation), a rapid depletion of the engorged tissue, thus aiding nature after her own manner in restoring capillary circulation, normal glandular action and fostering cell nourishment, which soon brings about a general normal condition of the membrane.

Glyco-Thymoline quickly dissolves all accumulations of thick, ropy mucus, crust formations, and, due to the anæsthetic or anodyne effect, gives a soothing sensation to the inflamed membrane.

Pure Almond Oil.

The question of what is meant by almond oil is not clearly settled in the minds of some dealers, though the health authorities in most States are very clear on the subject. One result of this is that the reports of investigations by health authorities frequently show that the article dispensed as almond oil is not what it purports to be. As a matter of fact, much of the so-called almond oil is the fixed oil expressed from the peach kernels. In the wholesale trade this is frequently known as "French" oil of almonds. Druggists who want to get the true oil of sweet almonds can do this by specifying "Allen's." We illustrate the package in which Allen's oil is placed on the market. It is prepared by Stafford Allen & Son, of England, the oldest oil men in the drug trade, and its purity can be absolutely relied upon. Allen's oil can be had from the leading jobbers everywhere and is well worth the slight increase in cost which is charged above that asked for the ordinary commercial or "French" oil, which, as stated above, is merely the expressed oil of peach kernels.

A man dropped his wig on the street and a boy who was following close behind the loser picked it up and handed it to him. "Thanks, my boy," said the owner of the wig. "You are the first genuine hair restorer I have even seen."

ORIGINAL PACKAGE PRICES.

It should be understood that the prices quoted in this column are strictly those current in the wholesale market, and that higher prices are paid for retail lots. The quality of goods frequently necessitates a considerable range of prices.

Drugs, Chemicals, &c.

Acetanilid	lb.	.24	@	.25
Acetate of Lime:				
Brown	100 lb.	1.60	@	1.65
Gray	100 lb.	2.35	@	2.40
Acetone	lb.	.15½	@	.16
Acid:				
Acetic Com'l	100 lb.	2.60	@	2.65
Acetic C. P.	lb.	.21	@	.25
Acetic, Glacial		.20	@	.23½
Aquafortis, 36°	lb.	.03½	@	.04½
" 40°	lb.	..	@	.06½
Benzoic, Ger	lb.	.30	@	.33
" Eng	oz.	.10	@	.10½
Boric, Cryst	lb.	.10	@	.10½
powd	lb.	.10	@	.10½
Carbol. cryst., blk	lb.	.14	@	.15
lb. bottle	lb.	.20	@	.22
Chrysophanic		2.60	@	2.65
Citric, dom	lb.	.41	@	.41½
Gallic	lb.	.53	@	.55
Muriatic C. P.	lb.	.07½	@	.08½
Nitric C. P.	lb.	.07½	@	.10
Oxalic, English	lb.	.05½	@	.05½
Phosphoric	lb.	.19	@	.22½
Picric	lb.	.36	@	.35
Pyrogallic	lb.	1.65	@	..
Salicylic	lb.	.31	@	.34
Sulphuric, 66%	lb.	.01½	@	.02
Tartaric, crystals	lb.	.27½	@	.28½
powdered	lb.	.29	@	.29½
Tannic, cryst	lb.	.56	@	.65
Alcohol, grain	gal.	2.47	@	2.49
Molasses		2.45	@	2.47
wood, 95-97%	gal.	.70	@	.75
Aloin	lb.	.45	@	.50
Alum, Lump	100 lb.	1.75	@	1.80
Ground	100 lb.	1.80	@	1.85
Ammon, carb.		.08½	@	.08½
" bromide, bulk		.23	@	.24
" iodide, bulk		4.75	@	4.80
Aniline Oil		.09	@	.09½
Salt		.08½	@	.08½
Antipyrine (New)	oz.	...	@	.18
Arrowroot, Bermuda	lb.	.38	@	.40
St. Vincent, in bbl	lb.	.06½	@	.08
Arsenic: Red Saxon	lb.	.06½	@	.07
White	lb.	.07	@	.10
Balm of Gilead Buds	lb.	.32	@	.33
Balsam Copaiba, Cent. Amer	lb.	.30	@	.32
Para	lb.	.40	@	.42
Fir, Canada	gal.	3.10	@	3.20
Fir, Oregon	gal.	.70	@	.80
Peru	lb.	1.00	@	1.05
Tolu	lb.	.20	@	.22
Bark, Angostura	lb.	.35	@	.40
Buckthorn	lb.	.05	@	.05½
Cascara Sag	lb.	.05½	@	.09
Cascarilla	lb.	.10	@	.14
Cotton root	lb.	.08½	@	.10
Cramp	lb.	.07	@	.09
Elm, select	lb.	.18	@	.20
Pine, white	lb.	.05	@	.06
Prickly Ash	lb.	.11	@	.15
Sassafras	lb.	.13½	@	.14
Soap—whole	lb.	.05	@	.05½
Crushed	lb.	.05½	@	.06
White Pine	lb.	.04½	@	.06
Wild Cherry	lb.	.06	@	.09
Bismuth, citrate	lb.	1.75	@	1.80
" ammon cit	lb.	1.85	@	1.90
" subnit	blk.	1.50	@	1.55
" subcarb	lb.	1.75	@	1.80
" subgallate	lb.	1.85	@	1.90
Bleaching Powder, Eng		.01½	@	.01½
German B		.01½	@	.01½
Domestic		.01	@	.01½
Blue Vitriol	lb.	.05½	@	.06
Borax, Refined	lb.	.07½	@	.07½
powd. conc	lb.	.07½	@	.08
crystals	lb.	.07½	@	.07½
Brimstone, crude 2d	ton.	22.00	@	...
Bromine, bulk	lb.	.23	@	.25
Burgundy Pitch	lb.	.01	@	.01½
Cacao Butter, blk		.27½	@	.30
" " 12 lb. boxes		.31	@	.35
Caffeine	lb.	....	@	2.75
Calcium hypophosphite	lb.	.60	@	.64
Cantharides, Chinese	lb.	.52½	@	.55
" powd	lb.	.54	@	.56
Russian, whole	lb.	1.25	@	1.30
Cassia Buds	lb.	.18½	@	.19½
Castor Oil, No. 1, bbl	lb.	.11	@	.12
" " No. 1, cases	lb.	.11½	@	.12½
" " No. 3, bbl	lb.	.10½	@	.11½
" " No 3, cases	lb.	.10½	@	.11½
Caustic Soda	100 lb.	1.70	@	1.75
Chalk, Eng. Precip., bulk	lb.	.06	@	...
Chloral Hydrate, crystals, bulk	lb.	...	@	0.95
crusts, blk	lb.	...	@	0.95
Chloroform, bulk	lb.	.25	@	.30
Cinchonidine Sulph	oz.	.12	@	.15
Cocaine Muriate	oz.	3.25	@	3.50
Codeine Sulph	oz.	3.20	@	3.40
Cod Liver Oil, Norweg.	bbl.	21.00	@	25.00
Newfoundland	bbl.	....	@	20.00
Colocynth, Trieste	lb.	.30	@	.32
Spanish	lb.	.25	@	.26
Copperas, car lots	100 lb.	.47½	@	.52
single bbls	100 lb.	.57½	@	.65
Creosote, Beechwood		.85	@	.90
Cream Tartar lb	powd.	.22½	@	.23
Cubeb berries, xx	lb.	.09	@	.10
Powdered	lb.	.11	@	.13
Cutch, bales	lb.	.07½	@	.08
boxes	lb.	.05	@	.05½
Cuttle Bone, Trieste	lb.	.16½	@	.17
French	lb.	.12	@	.13
Jewelers', large	lb.	.70	@	...
" small	lb.	.40	@	.45
Dextrin	lb.	.05½	@	.05
Divi Divi	ton.	30.00	@	45.00
Dragon's Bl'd, lump	lb.	.15	@	.18
In reeds	lb.	.50	@	.55
Epsom Salts	100 lb.	.85	@	1.00
Ergot, German	lb.	.32	@	.33
Spanish	lb.	.35	@	.37
Ergotine, Dom	lb.	4.95	@	5.00
Flowers, Arnica	lb.	.09	@	.10

Flowers—cont'd				
Calendula	lb.	.25	@	.30
Chamomile, Roman	lb.	.16	@	.22
German	lb.	.10	@	.18
Hungarian	lb.	.09½	@	.11
Insect, open	lb.	.15	@	.17
Half closed	lb.	.25	@	.23
Closed	lb.	.26	@	..
Powder	lb.	.14	@	.22
Lavender	lb.	.12	@	.13
Select	lb.	.15	@	.20
Saffron, Amer	lb.	1.25	@	....
Spanish Alicante	lb.	4.75	@	6.00
" Valencia	lb.	8.00	@	8.50
Formaldehyde	lb.	.09	@	.09½
Glauber Salt	per 100 lb.	.40	@	.60
Glycerin, C. P. drums	lb.	.11½	@	.11½
" cans	lb.	.12½	@	.12½
Grains of Paradise	lb.	.11½	@	.15
Guarana	lb.	.62	@	.65
Gums: Aloes, Cape		.08	@	.10
" Barbadoes	lb.	.14	@	.16
" Curacoa		.06	@	.06½
" Socot	lb.	.18	@	.20
Arabic, 1st pkd	lb.	.30	@	...
" 2d pkd	lb.	.19	@	.23
" sorts	lb.	.06½	@	.11
Asafoetida	lb.	.15	@	.22
Benzoin, Sumatra	lb.	.34	@	.38
Siam	lb.	.90	@	1.00
Camphor, refi'd. blk	lb.	.96	@	..
cases	lb.	.96½	@	..
Chicle	lb.	.36	@	.38
Gamboge	lb.	1.05	@	1.10
Guaiac	lb.	.17	@	.23
Kino	lb.	.25	@	.26
Mastic	lb.	.46	@	.48
Myrrh	lb.	.25	@	.28
Olibanum	lb.	.10	@	.15
Sandarac	lb.	.11	@	.18
Senegal, pkd	lb.	.11	@	.13
Tragacanth, Aleppo	lb.	.30	@	.65
Tragacanth, Turkey	lb.	.35	@	.90
Haarlem Oil		3.00	@	3.75
Hypophosphite lime	lb.	.48	@	.50
" potash	lb.	.48	@	.50
" soda	lb.	.48	@	.50
Ichthyol	lb.	4.00	@	4.25
Indigo	lb.	.90	@	1.25
Insect Pwd. pure	lb.	.14	@	.25
Iodine, resub		2.70	@	2.75
Iodoform	lb.	3.00	@	3.05
Iron citrate, U. S. P.	lb.	.....	@	.44
" and ammon. cit	lb.	.....	@	.41
and ammon. citrate (green scales)				
and quinine citrate	lb.	1.18	@	1.23
phosphate, scales	lb.	....	@	.38
pyrophosphate, scales	lb.	....	@	.38
quinine and strychnine citrate	lb.	1.68	@	1.73
Isinglass, Amer	lb.	.75	@	.80
Russian	lb.	4.00	@	4.10
Juniper Berries	lb.	.03½	@	.04
Lanoline	lb.	.60	@	.65
Leaves: Aconite		.08	@	.10
Belladonna	lb.	.10	@	.11
Buchu, short	lb.	.17	@	.20
" long	lb.	.45	@	.50
Cannabis Indica, tops	lb.	1.00	@	1.10
Coca, Truxillo	lb.	.17	@	.18
" Huanuco	lb.	.30	@	.32
Damiana	lb.	.08	@	.10
Digitalis	lb.	.08½	@	.09
Grindelia robusta	lb.	.08	@	.09
Horehound	lb.	.04½	@	.08
Hyoscyamus	lb.	.07	@	.08
Jaborandi	lb.	.14	@	.15
Pulsatilla		.07½	@	.11
Rose, Red	lb.	.65	@	.70
Senna, pkd. whole	lb.	.20	@	.22
Alexandria, natural	lb.	...	@	...
garbled and sifted	lb.	.15	@	.16
Tinnevelly	lb.	.04	@	.09
Alexandria, siftings	lb.	.05½	@	.06
Stramonium	lb.	.08	@	.08½
Uva ursi	lb.	.08½	@	.08½
Yerba Santa	lb.	.07	@	.07½
Liquorice—mass	lb.	.08	@	.10
Spanish	lb.	.14	@	.20
Imported mass Spanish	lb.	.18	@	.24
Stick, Calabria	lb.	.23	@	.28
Domestic	lb.	.16½	@	.23½
Lithia, carbonate	lb.	1.50	@	1.75
" citrate	lb.	1.15	@	1.25
Lupulin, Ger	lb.	.18	@	.25
Lycopodium	lb.	.51	@	.53
Magnesia, carb	lb.	.12	@	.15
Manna, large flk	lb.	.45	@	.50
Small flake	lb.	.33	@	.35
Menthol, Japanese	lb.	2.20	@	2.25
Mercurials:				
Blue Pill	lb.	.43	@	.45
Calomel	lb.	.77	@	.79
Corr. Sublim	lb.	.70	@	.72
Mercury and Chalk	lb.	.32	@	.34
Ointment, ¼	lb.	.47	@	.48
Ointment, ⅓	lb.	.38	@	.39
Red Precip	lb.	.87	@	.89
White "	lb.	.92	@	.94
Morphine, bulk	oz.	2.25	@	2.50
Eighths	oz.	2.45	@	2.50
Moss, Iceland	lb.	.06	@	.08
Irish	lb.	.06½	@	.08
Irish, bleached	lb.	.09½	@	.10
Naphthaline, flake	lb.	.02	@	.03
Ball	lb.	.02	@	.02½
Nux Vomica	lb.	.02½	@	.05
Oil, Anise	lb.	1.30	@	1.35
Almonds, bit, Eng	lb.	5.50	@	5.75
French	lb.	3.55	@	3.60
bit., artificial	lb.	.85	@	1.50
sweet, true	lb.	.37	@	.40
Peach kernels		.19	@	.22
Bay	lb.	2.10	@	2.25
22 oz. bots	bot.	3.25	@	3.35
Bergamot	lb.	2.15	@	2.50
Cajuput	lb.	.50	@	.55
Camphor	lb.	.17½	@	.19
Caraway	lb.	1.15	@	1.40
Cassia 75@80%	lb.	.80	@	.85

Oils—cont'd.				
Cedar, pure	lb.	60.	@	1.65
red	lb.	.21	@	
Citronella	lb.	.40	@	
Clove, bud		.82½	@	.25
Copaiba	lb.		@	.90
Coriander	lb.	5.	@	11.
Croton	lb.	.60	@	
Cubeb	lb.	.90	@	1.
Eucalyptus	lb.		@	
Geranium	lb.	1.40	@	4.
Lavender, flowers	lb.	2.00	@	2.00
Lemon	lb.	.70	@	.80
Lemongrass	lb.	3.00	@	3.10
Mustard	lb.	4.25	@	5.
Myrbane	lb.	.07	@	
Neroli	lb.	45.00	@	57.
Nutmeg	lb.	.80	@	0.
Orange, sweet	lb.	2.00	@	2.25
Orange, bitter	lb.	2.20	@	2.30
Origanum	lb.	.18	@	.22
Pennyroyal	lb.	1.15	@	1.25
Peppermint	lb.	2.60	@	2.75
Cases	lb.	3.20	@	3.25
Petit, grain, French	lb.	4.00	@	4.50
" " So. Amer	lb.	2.00	@	2.05
Pimento	lb.	1.80	@	1.90
Rose	oz.	3.50	@	4.50
Rosemary	lb.	.62½	@	.90
Sandalwood	lb.	3.25	@	3.50
Sassafras	lb.	.50	@	.55
" Artificial	lb.	.25	@	.28
Safrol			@	.36
Spearmint	lb.	.85	@	5.00
Tansy	lb.	3.75	@	4.00
Thyme		1.00	@	1.20
Winterg'n, sweet birch		1.65	@	1.85
" Synthetic	lb.	.37	@	.40
Wood (Chinese)		.08	@	.09
Wormwood		3.25	@	3.50
Wormseed	lb.	3.00	@	3.25
Opium, Nat cases	lb.	2.85	@	2.87½
" Ordinary, Job-		2.87½	@	2.90
" powdered		3.40	@	3.43
Orange peel, bit	lb.	.03	@	.04
Sweet	lb.	.04½	@	.10
Petrolatum		.03	@	.08
Phenacetine	oz.		@	.93
Potassium acetate	lb.	.85	@	.14
" bromide		.13	@	.14
" bottles		.23	@	.30
bichromate		.08½	@	.08½
chlorate, cryst		.09½	@	.09½
" powd		.10	@	.10½
cyanide		.20	@	
hypophosphite		.68	@	
iodide bulk		2.15	@	2.21
permanganate	lb.	.09½	@	.09½
Prickly Ash berries		.14	@	.16
Quicksilver flasks	lb.	.56	@	.60
Quinine Sulph., Domestic bulk	oz.	.18	@	
German, bulk	oz.	.17	@	.20
German, outside	oz.	.17	@	.30
Java, bulk	oz.	.17	@	.18
Rochelle Salts	lb.	.20½	@	.21
Root, Aconite	lb.	.09½	@	.10
Alkanet	lb.	.08	@	.09
Althea, cut	lb.		@	.18
Arnica	lb.			.09
Belladonna, Atropa	lb.		@	.12
Blood	lb.		@	.12
Calamus	lb.		@	.08
Calamus, bleached	lb.		@	.25
Colchicum	lb.	.17	@	.18
Calumba	lb.	.05½	@	.06
Dandelion, Ger	lb.	.07½	@	.08
Galangal	lb.		@	.05½
Gentian	lb.	.06	@	.04½
Ginger, Ja., blcd	lb.	.18½	@	
unbleached	lb.	.09	@	
Ginseng	lb.	6.00	@	7.14
Golden Seal	lb.	1.25	@	1.30
Hellebore, pwd	lb.	.06	@	.07
Helonias	lb.	.42	@	.45
Ipecac, Rio	lb.	1.75	@	1.80
Carthagena	lb.	1.75	@	1.80
Jalap	lb.	.10½	@	.11
Kava Kava	lb.	.11	@	.12
Liquorice, ord	lb.	.03½	@	.04
Select	lb.	.10½	@	.11
Lovage	lb.	.53	@	.83
Mandrake	lb.	.04½	@	.05½
Musk, Russian	lb.	.13	@	.14
Orris, Florentine	lb.	.06	@	.07
Orris, Verona	lb.	.04	@	.05
Pariera Brava	lb.	.10	@	.11
Pink	lb.	...	@	.75
Rhatany	lb.	.10	@	.12
Rhub., Canton	lb.	.35	@	.40
Shensi	lb.	.65	@	.75
Sars'p'la, Hond	lb.	.26	@	.30
Mexican	lb.	.09½	@	.09½
Senega	lb.	.55	@	.60
Snake Virgina	lb.	.42	@	.45
Texas	lb.	.39	@	.42
Canada	lb.	.13	@	.25
Squill	lb.	.13	@	.15
Valerian, Belg	lb.	.08	@	.08½
German	lb.	.12	@	.14
English	lb.	.12	@	.15
Salicine	lb.	3.75	@	4.00
Sal Ammon, lump	lb.	.09½	@	.09½
Granulated	lb.	.05½	@	.06
Sal Soda, Eng	100 lb.	.67½	@	.72½
American	100 lb.	.75	@	.80
Salol	lb.	.90	@	.95
Saltpetre, crude	lb.	.04½	@	.04½
Refined	lb.	.04½	@	.05½
Santonin, crystals	lb.	9.50	@	9.70
Powdered	lb.	9.70	@	9.90
Saw Palmetto Berries	lb.	.15	@	.20
Seed, Anise Ital	lb.	.08½	@	.10½
German	lb.	.06½	@	.07
Star	lb.	.20	@	.21
Canary, Smyrna	lb.	.04½	@	.04½
Sicily	lb.	.04½	@	.05
Caraway	lb.	.06	@	.06½
Celery	lb.	.07½	@	.08
Cardamom blchd		.30	@	.70
" Decorticated	lb.	.30	@	.31
Colchicum	lb.	.21	@	.23
Coriander	lb.	9	@	10½

Seeds—cont'd.				
Bleached	lb.	.09½	@	.10½
Cummin	lb.	.06½	@	.07½
Fennel, Ger	lb.	.09	@	.10
" Italian	lb.	.05	@	.05½
Flax, whole	lb.	6.50	@	6.75
" ground	lb.	.03½	@	.03½
Foenugreek	lb.	.02	@	.02½
Hemp, Rus	lb.	.03	@	.03½
Millet, nat	lb.	.01½	@	.02
" shld	lb.	.04½	@	.04½
Mustard, Cal. brown	lb.	.04½	@	.04½
Trieste, brown	lb.	.08	@	.08½
Bari, brown	lb.	.04½	@	.05
German, brown	lb.	.03½	@	.06
Western, brown	lb.	.01½	@	.02
Cal. yellow	lb.	.04½	@	.04½
Eng. yellow	lb.	.05	@	.05½
Ger. yellow	lb.	.05½	@	.06½
Poppy, blue	lb.	.05½	@	.05½
Quince, Ger	lb.	.32	@	.34
Rape, Ger	lb.	.03½	@	.03
" Eng	lb.	.04	@	.05
" Amer	lb.	.03½	@	.05
Strophanthus		.45	@	.50
Kombé		1.00	@	1.25
Sunflower		.04½	@	.05
Wormseed, American	lb.	.07	@	.08
" Levant	lb.	.17	@	.20
Seidlitz Mixture	lb.	.17	@	.17½
Silver, Nitrate	oz.	.41½	@	.45½
Soap, Castile, white	lb.	.10	@	.10½
" green	lb.	.08	@	.10½
" mottled	lb.	.05½	@	.07
Sodium bicarb, Eng		1.57½	@	1.75
" domestic	100 lb.	1.50	@	1.60
" benzoate	lb.	.40	@	.41
" brom. blk	lb.	.21	@	.22
" carb., cryst	100 lb.	1.60	@	1.75
" citrate	lb.	...	@	.32
" hypophosphite		.60	@	.64
" iodide		3.50	@	3.55
" nitrate	100 lb.	2.20	@	2.25
" phosphate	lb.	.02½	@	.03
" salicylate	lb.	.32	@	.34
Spermaceti	lb.	.27	@	.29
Spts. Nitre, U. S. P.		.46	@	.48
Spts. Ammonia Aromat	lb.	.44	@	.45
Strontium, nitrate	lb.	.07½	@	.08
Strychnine, Sulph	oz.	.95	@	1.05
Sugar of Milk	lb.	.15	@	.20
Sugar, Lead, white	lb.	.09½	@	.10
" brown	lb.	.07½	@	.08
Sulphur, Roll	lb.	1.85	@	2.15
" Flowers	lb.	2.15	@	2.59½
Sulphuric Ether	lb.	.62	@	.68
Sumac, Sicily	ton	.00	@	47.00
" Virginia	ton	[illegible]	@	35.00
Tar, Barbadoes	gal.	...	@	.38
Thymol		1.90	@	2.05
Tonka B'ns, Para	lb.	.18	@	.20
" Angostura	lb.	.55	@	.57½
" Surinam	lb.	.30	@	.32
Turmeric		.04½	@	.06
Turpentine	gal.		@	.73½
Vanilla Beans	lb.	2.75	@	6.50
" Cut, Mex	lb.	1.75	@	2.00
" Tahiti	lb.	.45	@	1.25
" Bourbon		1.25	@	3.50
Vanillin	oz.	.32	@	.37½
Venice Turps, bbls	lb.	.14	@	.17
" " cans	lb.	.19	@	.20
Wax, Bayberry	lb.	....	@	.50
" Bees, ord. pur	lb.	.30½	@	.32
" " sel	lb.	.32½	@	.34
" " blch	lb.	.40	@	.45
" Brazil, No. 1	lb.	.49	@	.50
" " No. 2	lb.	.44	@	.45
" " No. 3	lb.	.31	@	.32
" Ceresin, yel	lb.	.14	@	.18
" " white	lb.	.15	@	.20
" Japan	lb.	.13½	@	.14
" Paraffin	lb.	.06	@	.08½
Zinc Oxide	lb.	.07	@	.08½

Heavy Oils, &c.

Bank, Menhaden	gal.	.27	@	.30
Coconut, Ceylon	lb.	.06½	@	.06½
Cochin	lb.	.07½	@	.07½
Cuban	lb.	.05½	@	...
Cod, Domestic	gal.	.35	@	.36
" Newfoundland	gal.	.38½	@	.40
Corn	gal.	3.60	@	...
Cottonseed, crd. prime		.25	@	...
Summer Yellow, prime		.32	@	.33
" " Butter		.33	@	.34
Old, off grade		.32	@	...
Winter Yellow, prime		.33	@	.34
Salad Oil		.40	@	.41
Gasoline, 86°	gal.	.14	@	...
" 88°	gal.	.16	@	...
" 90°	gal.	.18	@	...
Lard, Extra Prime	gal.	.63	@	.64
Lard, Extra No. 1	gal.	.49	@	.52
Lard, No. 1	gal.	.38	@	.40
Linseed, Raw City	gal.	.42	@	.43
" Boiled	gal.	.43	@	.44
Naphtha, 68°	gal.	.12	@	...
" Deodorized, 76°	gal.	.12½	@	...
Neatsfoot, prm	gal.	.49	@	.50
White		.97	@	...
Olive Oil, tap	tins	1.50	@	2.75
" Com., bbls	gal.	.55½	@	.58
Palm, prm., L'gos	lb	.06½	@	.06½
Peanut	lb	.40	@	.52
Rapeseed	gal.	.67	@	.71
Red Elaine	gal.	...	@	.48
" Saponified	lb.	.05½	@	.05½
Salad Oil	gal.	.46	@	.48
Sesame	gal.	.55	@	.60
Sperm, Crude	gal.	.63	@	.65
" Nat. Win	gal.	.62	@	.63
" Blch. Win	gal.	.64	@	.65
Straits	gal.	...	@	.33
Tallow, prime	gal.	.62	@	
Whale, Crude	gal.	...	@	...
Crude, Nat. Win	gal.	.48	@	
Bleached Win	gal.	.46	@	5

125% PROFIT

This beautiful and conveniently arranged Mahogany Show Case **GIVEN FREE** with your first order for Six Dozen of our Certified **FEVER THERMOMETERS.**

Half of which must be shipped with case. Balance may be taken within four months.

Our line of Thermometers is made to retail at 75 cents to $1.75, with more than 100 per cent. profit to the dealer.

TO THE DEALERS WHO TAKE ADVANTAGE OF OUR

FREE DISPLAY CASE OFFER

With each Display Case we furnish 500 Free Booklets for Distribution to your patrons.

THIS HELPS TO SELL THE GOODS

We give **an absolute guarantee** that every thermometer will meet the Government requirements.

Our reputation protects you against everything except breakage.

Write for "Display Case Booklet," which contains full particulars.

BECTON, DICKINSON & CO., - New York, U. S. A.

Makers of Thermometers, Hypodermic Syringes, Needles, etc.

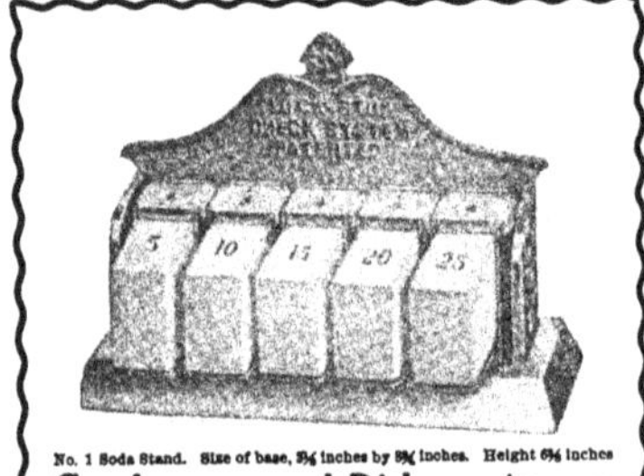

No. 1 Soda Stand. Size of base, 9¾ inches by 8¾ inches. Height 6¾ inches

Carelessness and Dishonesty are Frailties of Human Nature

They exist in almost every business; they exist in the soda fountain and ice cream business. Out of these two human weaknesses—and the necessity for guarding against them—has grown the

Lock-Stub Check System of Controlling Soda Fountain and Ice Cream Receipts

It detects dishonesty where it exists; it prevents it where it would exist without a proper system of control. Throw out your celluloid checks and other antiquated checking systems and get the most modern system.

This is the original system, fully covered by letters patent. Don't buy an infringing system and court a law suit. We hereby give notice that we will promptly and vigorously prosecute all infringers. Imitations lack the essential features of the Lock-Stub Check System. Full particulars in our interesting booklet. Write for it. We have an interesting proposition for large users.

THE LOCK-STUB CHECK COMPANY

136-138 W. 34th Street, NEW YORK

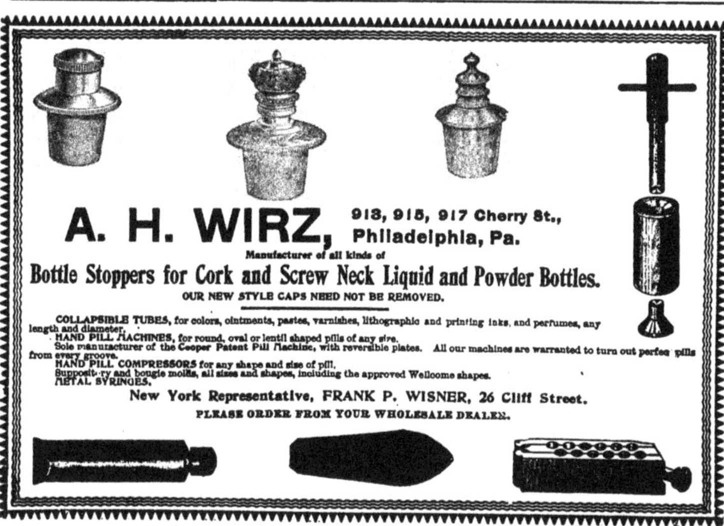

HOME MADE CANDIES

An attractive and up-to-date book, entitled "Hood's Book of Home Made Candies No. 2," a supply of which will be sent to any retail druggist upon request.

These Candy Books are gotten up in fine style, and are recommended very highly for counter distribution. Inasmuch as we print the dealer's name on each book, it is a winner.

If requested will also send novelties for making a

WINDOW DISPLAY.

C. I. HOOD CO., Lowell, Mass.

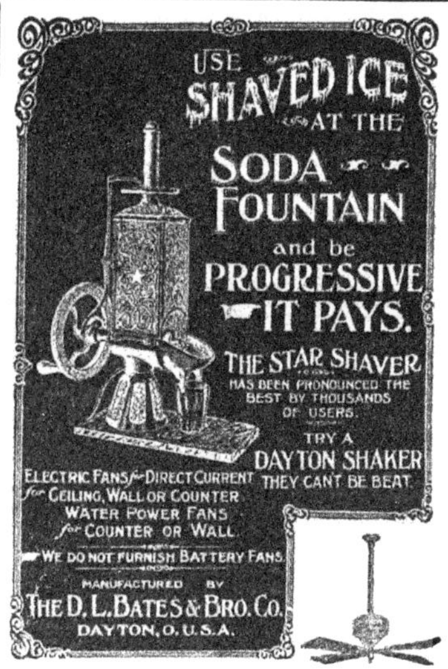

USE SHAVED ICE AT THE
SODA FOUNTAIN
and be
PROGRESSIVE
IT PAYS.
THE STAR SHAVER
HAS BEEN PRONOUNCED THE BEST BY THOUSANDS OF USERS.
TRY A
DAYTON SHAKER
THEY CAN'T BE BEAT.
ELECTRIC FANS for DIRECT CURRENT
for CEILING, WALL OR COUNTER
WATER POWER FANS
for COUNTER OR WALL
WE DO NOT FURNISH BATTERY FANS.
MANUFACTURED BY
THE D. L. BATES & BRO. CO.
DAYTON, O. U.S.A.

A Satisfied Customer

is a good asset. The patron who gets what he wants and ask for is satisfied. Unless you can get along on transient trade it is necessary for you to cultivate the patronage of people who will come again. Scott's Emulsion customers are satisfied customers—give them what they ask for. No "money back if unsatisfactory." If the goods are right and fulfill all promises buyers won't want their money back. Scott's Emulsion is right and will do all that is claimed for it. Your customers know this, so don't side-track them. We do the advertising and bring the customers to your store—the rest is easy. The demand for Scott's Emulsion this season has been very large; perhaps your stock has run low and you have neglected replenishing it. It might be well to have enough on hand to meet the demands for the balance of the season.

SCOTT & BOWNE

Manufacturing Chemists, - 409 Pearl Street, New York

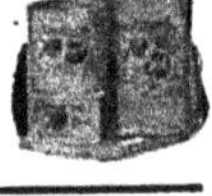

has been on the market 25 years, and is the Best Blood Purifier Known. It cures Cancer, Eczema, Salt Rheum, Rheumatism, Blood Poison and Constipation. PUT UP IN THREE FORMS: Blossoms, $4.00; Fluid Extract, $8.00; Solid Extract, $90.00 per dozen.

Order of your jobber. Attractive advertising matter, on application, from the manufacturers.

D. NEEDHAM'S SONS, Chicago

HAVE YOUR LOCAL VIEWS MADE INTO

Finest American Made

From 250 up of a subject

THE ALBERTYPE CO., - Brooklyn, N. Y.

The LENOX HOTEL

IN BUFFALO

North St., at Delaware Ave.

Modern. Highest Grade. Absolutely Fireproof. Unexcelled Service Throughout.

Most charming location in the city.

EUROPEAN PLAN.

Rates, $1.50 per day and upward.

Wire Reservations at Our Expense.

GEO. DUCHSCHERER, Prop.

Destined to Produce a Nation of Soda Water Consumers.

"Perfecto"

FRUIT JUICES *and* CRUSHED FRUITS, The Standard of Excellence.

MANUFACTURED BY

THE CRANDALL & GODLEY COMPANY,

The New Perfecto Ice Cream Soda Dishing Spoon, $1.50. Send for Catalogue of Ice Cream Utensils and Machinery. 185-187-189 Franklin St., New York

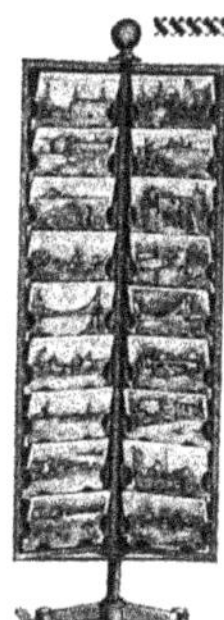

OUR COMBINATIONS IN

POST CARDS and RACKS

interest every dealer. Write for circular and get full information. Racks and Cards from $5.00 up. FOUR DIFFERENT OFFERS to select from, comprising Leather, Birthday, Fancy Comic Post Cards.

"WE ARE HEADQUARTERS"

JOSEPH KOEHLER

— DEPT. A —

150 Park Row, NEW YORK

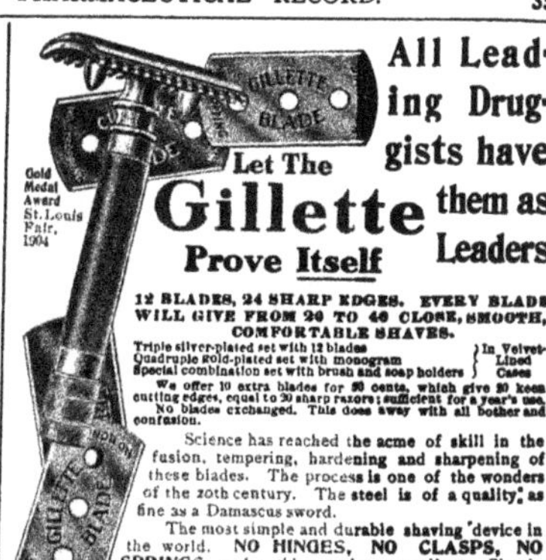

All Leading Druggists have them as Leaders

Gold Medal Award St. Louis Fair, 1904

Let The

Gillette

Prove Itself

12 BLADES, 24 SHARP EDGES. EVERY BLADE WILL GIVE FROM 20 TO 40 CLOSE, SMOOTH, COMFORTABLE SHAVES.

Triple silver-plated set with 12 blades
Quadruple gold-plated set with monogram
Special combination set with brush and soap holders } In Velvet-Lined Cases

We offer 10 extra blades for 50 cents, which give 20 keen cutting edges, equal to 20 sharp razors; sufficient for a year's use.
No blades exchanged. This does away with all bother and confusion.

Science has reached the acme of skill in the fusion, tempering, hardening and sharpening of these blades. The process is one of the wonders of the 20th century. The steel is of a quality as fine as a Damascus sword.

The most simple and durable shaving device in the world. NO HINGES, NO CLASPS, NO SPRINGS, and nothing to learn or adjust. Simply lather and shave in four minutes' time.

Our new combination set, with razor, soap and brush holders in same box, is now ready.

SOLD BY ALL LEADING DRUG, CUTLERY AND HARDWARE DEALERS

Ask to see them, and for our booklet, or write us for our special trial offer.

Gillette Sales Company,
TIMES BUILDING, NEW YORK CITY.

EXAMINATION QUESTIONS: I have collected and bound in a 64-page pamphlet (6 x 9 inches, fine print), the PHARMACY EXAMINATION QUESTIONS of the various states and territories; also the Pharmacy Laws of the different states. All of the questions are recent, many based on new U. S. P. They are intended for those who wish to prepare for State Board or other examinations.

A candidate about to take an examination can have no better preparation than a thorough drill on the questions that have been asked by State Board Examiners.

This pamphlet will be sent post paid to any address upon receipt of 75cts. Address:

J. A. HYNES, 292 S. Marshfield Avenue, Chicago, Ill.

PRESCRIPTION FILES

THE RELIANCE

The Only Practical Device on the Market

Cabinet has perforator for top. Each drawer has our patented arch file. Capacity of each drawer is 800 prescriptions. File is quick and handy, and saves time and labor in referring to old numbers. Transfer cases have removable arch wires. Capacity is 1,000 prescriptions.

Send for testimonials and our catalogue of our line of druggists' filing devices and specialties.

RELIANCE CABINET FILE CO., 206 Longworth Street Cincinnati, O.

WARNING NOTICE

to the world of my proprietary rights to the trade-mark names of Satin, Satin Skin, Satin-Skin (hyphenated), Satin Scent, etc., as applied to toilet preparations, soaps, perfumes, etc., is given by U. S. patent office registrations No. 21,618, 24,186, 27,854, 37,669, 42,297. Canadian 399,444. I promptly prosecute infringers, imitators, and sellers of substitutes. (Signed)

ALBERT F. WOOD, Detroit, Mich., Mfr. and Propr. of Satin Skin Cream, Satin Toilet and Talcum Powders, Satin-Skin Soaps, Satin Tooth Preparations, Satin Scents, etc.

GARROD

Spa Lithia Water

For Gout, Gravel and Rheumatism.

WHOLESALE

DISTRIBUTING AGENTS,

CHARLES N. CRITTENTON CO.

Mount Washington

IMPERVIOUS

BOXES for DRUGGISTS

In strength, lightness, and beauty of finish, superior to all others. ¼ oz. to 16 oz., Black Walnut and Silver Poplar.

Specify "Mt. Washington" in ordering of wholesaler.

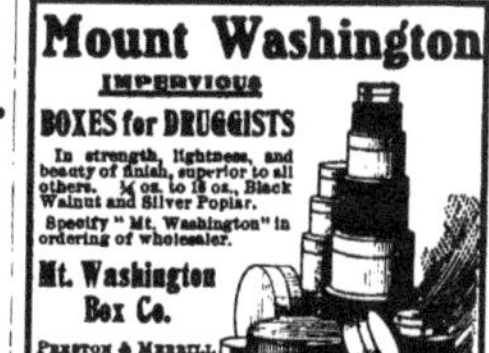

Mt. Washington Box Co.

PRESTON & MERRILL, PROPRIETORS,

BOSTON.

Kindly mention AMERICAN DRUGGIST when writing to Advertisers.

Prices Current.

The outside prices quoted are for such quantities as retailers usually purchase. When purchasing original packages the inside quotations should be expected, while a slight advance over the outside quotations given may be demanded for very small lots. Current commercial quality is understood unless otherwise indicated. For extra quality or for specified makes a slightly higher price will have to be paid.

Corrected to March 10

Acetanilid, 5 lbs., .30 .... lb. .32-34
Acetone, lb., .22; Medicinal .... lb. .85
Acid, Acetic, U. S. P., carboys, .6 ... lbs. .8-9
No. 2, carboy, .5; lb., .7; Glacial . lb. .28-30
Arsenous, fused, lb., .18 .... oz. .8
Benzoic, English, 50-oz. boxes, .10 .. oz. .18-16
Benzoic, from Toluol, lbs., .58 ...... oz. .11-13
Boric, crystals, 25 lbs., .14 .... lb. .15
Boric, Po., 25 lbs., .14 .... lb. .16
Cacodylic, ⅛ths .... ozs. 4.00
Camphoric .... oz. .50
Carbolic, crystals, 10 lbs., .23 ...... lb. .23-27
Calvert's No. 1, lb., 1.95; No. 2 .. lb. 1.40
Solution, 10 gals., .45 .... gal. .50
Chromic, lb., .55 .... ozs. .11
Chrysophanic, 1-oz. cartons .... ozs. .18-20
Cinnamic .... oz. .35-40
Citric, crystals, 10 lbs., .43 .... lb. .45-47
Gallic, lbs., .70 .... ozs. .9
Hydrochloric, carboys, .2¼ .... lb. .4-5
C. P. .... lb. .11-13
Hydrocyanic, dil., lbs., .30 .... ozs. .10
Hydrobromic, dil. .... lb. .28
Hypophosphorus, 50 per cent. sol .... lb. 1.65
Lactic, concentr., lbs., .70 .... ozs. .12
Nitric, carboys, 5½lbs., .8; C. P. .... .14
Oleic, purified, U. S. P .... lbs. .40
Oxalic, 10 lbs., .9 .... lb. .10-12
Phosphoric, glacial .... lbs. .85
U. S. P., 85 per cent. syrupy .... lb. .30-35
Picric .... lb. .55
Pyrogallic, lbs., 2.35 .... ozs. .24-27
Pyroligneous, pure .... lb. .30
Salicylic, white, 10 lbs., .40 .... lb. .42-44
Stearic, hard .... lb. .18
Succinic .... oz. .27
Sulphuric, carboys, .3 .... lb. .4
" C. P., carboys, .10 ...... lb. .12
Sulphurous .... lb. .10
Tannic, lbs., .85 .... oz. .12-15
Tartaric, powdered, 10 lbs., .34 .... lbs. .35-38
Valerianic .... ozs. .30
Aconitine, Amorphous, ⅛ ozs. .... oz. 1.40
Adeps Lanae, E. J. D .... lb. .28
Adnephrin, solution .... oz. .60
Adonidin, 15-gr. vials .... gr. .15
Agaricin, 15-gr. vials, each, .10 .... ozs. .90
Agaric, white .... lb. .40
Agathin .... oz. 3.25
Agurin .... ozs. 1.70
Airol, ozs .... oz. 1.00
Albumen, Egg .... lb. .70
Alcohol, 10 gals., 2.70 .... gal. 2.80-2.85
Alcohol, Columbia Spirit, 10 gals., 1.35 .gal. 1.50
Cologne Spirit, 10 gals., 2.80 ...... gal. 2.90
Wood, 10 gals., .85 .... gal. .90
Alizarin .... oz. .15
Allspice, 10 lbs., .11 .... lb. .12
powdered, 5 lbs., .18 .... lb. .20
Almonds, bitter, shelled .... lb. .40
Sweet, shelled .... lb. .55
Almond Meal, true, 10 lbs., .45 .... lb. .50
Aloin, lb., .70 .... oz. .7-9
Alpha-Eucaine .... oz. 3.50
Alphozone .... oz. 4.50
Alum, cryst., bbls., .2¼ .... lb. .3-4
powdered, bbls., .3¼ .... lb. .6-8
burnt, 10 lbs., .10 .... lb. .13-14
Aluminum, Acetate .... oz. .15
Sulphate, lb., .10; Wire .... lb. 2.25
Aluminol .... oz. .50
Amber, rasped .... lb. .85
Ambergris, gray, oz., $30.00 .... dram. 4.00
Ammonia (See Water and Spirit.)
Ammonium, Bromide, 5-lb. bot., .35 . lb. .40
Carbonate, 25 lbs., .11 .... lb. .12-14
Iodide, lbs., 6.15 .... oz. .47
Muriate, gran. com .... lb. .10
purified, lb., .17; powdered ...... lb. .18
Salammoniac, muriate, cryst ..... lb. .12-14
Nitrate, crystals, 10 lbs., .22 ...... lb. .25
Valerianate, lb., 1.50 .... oz. .15-22
Ammonol .... oz. 1.05
Amygdalin, ¼-oz. vials .... oz. 2.40
Amyl, Nitrite .... oz. .35
Amylene, Hydrate .... oz. .49
Anaesthesin .... ozs. 1.00
Aniline, Red, crystals .... lb. 1.25
Black .... lb. .75
Crystals for ink .... lb. 1.50
Blue, Deep, No. 1 .... lb. 2.00
Sol., reddish, No. 1 .... lb. 2.50
Crimson .... lb. 1.50
Brown, Bismarck .... lb. 1.25
soluble .... lb. 1.00
Green, crystals .... lb. 1.50
Orange .... lb. 1.00
Purple, B. B .... lb. 1.75
Scarlet .... lb. 1.50. Yellow .... lb. 1.25
Annatto .... lb. .45-50
Anodyne, Hoffman's .... lb. .60
" " U. S. P .... lb. .88
Anthrax Vaccine, "Pasteur," double tubes .... doz. 18.00
Antiarthrin .... oz. 1.65
Antikamnia, powdered or tablets ... oz. 1.00
Combination tablets .... oz. 1.00
10-oz. lots, assorted to order 9.25
Tablets, "vest-pocket boxes" ..... doz. 1.75
In 1 gross lots, 5 per cent. discount.
Antimony Sulphuret, powd., pure, 10 lbs., .16 .... lb. .17-20
Antinosine .... oz. 2.10
Antiphthisin, Klebs', 15-Cc. vials, ea. 3.75
Antipyretic Liquid, Tilden's .... doz. 3.50
Antipyrine, Dr. Knorr's .... oz. .81
New Grade .... oz. .39
Antistreptococcic Serum (Veterinary), "Pasteur," 10-Cc. vial .. doz. 9.00
Antitetanic Serum (Veterinary), "Pasteur," 10-Cc. vial .... doz. 9.00
Antithyroidin, 10-Cc. vials .... ea. 1.50
Antitoxin, Diphtheria, Stearns':
No. 0, per 500 units 1.10
No. 1, per 1,000 units 1.05
No. 2, per 2,000 units 1.80
No. 3, per 3,000 units 2.40
No. 4, per 4,000 units 6.50
Antivom. Ritsert, Pills, .30 ea ... doz. 9.50
Apiol, Fluid Green .... oz. .28
Capsules, Joret's .... doz. 6.25
Apolysin .... oz. .65
Apomorphine, Hydrochlor, Cryst ... oz. 7.50
" " Amorphous . oz. 2.80
Areca, Nuts, powd .... lb. .25-28
Argentamine .... oz. .75
Argols, Red, powdered .... lb. .12
Argonin .... oz. .65
Aristol, 25 ozs., 1.65 .... oz. 1.80
Aristochin, ozs .... oz. 2.30
" ⅛ ozs .... oz. 2.35
Arrowroot, Bermuda, true ..... None in market
St. Vincent, 30 lbs., .14 .... lb. .18
Taylor's, ¼-lb., 24 lbs., .28 .... lb. .32
Arsenauro, 1-oz. bots .... doz. 8.50
Arsenic, Donovan's Sol .... lb. .30
Fowler's Sol .... lb. .16
White .... lb. .12
Aspirin, 50 ozs., .38 .... oz. .42
Atropin, Sulph., ⅛-oz .... oz. 5.65
Balsam, Copaiba, Para, 5 lbs., .45 .. lb. .47-50
Fir, Canada .... lb. .50-55
Oregon .... lb. .25-30
Peru .... lb. 1.35
Tolu, 10-lb. can, .33 .... lb. .35
Barbadoes Tar .... gal. .60
Barium, Acetate .... oz. .15
Carbonate .... lb. .46
Chloride .... lb. .17
Nitrate .... lb. .15
Oxide, pure .... oz. .10
Bark, Angostura .... lb. .55
Barberry .... lb. .28
Berberis Aquifol .... lb. .30
Buckthorn .... lb. .15
Canella .... lb. .28
Cascara, Sagrada .... lb. .15-20
Cascarilla, select .... lb. .35
Cassia, in mats .... lb. .14
Saigon .... lb. .65
Cinchona, Red, E. I .... lb. .36
powdered, 10 lbs., .32 .... lb. .32-35
Cinchona Calisaya .... lb. .36
powdered .... lb. .40
pale, lb., .30; powdered .... lb. .35
Cinnamon, Ceylon .... lb. .35

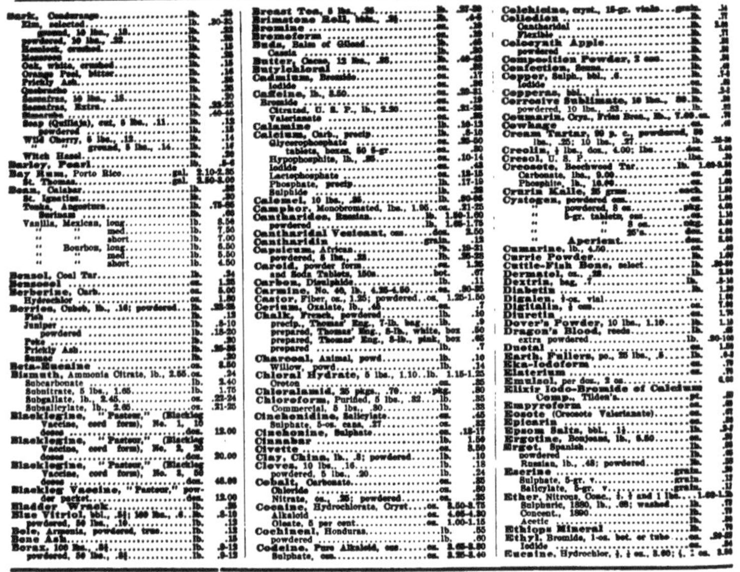

Article	Unit	Price
Bark, Condurango	lb.	[illegible]
Elm, selected	lb.	.30-35
ground, 10 lbs., .18	lb.	[illegible]
powdered, 10 lbs., .22	lb.	[illegible]
Hemlock, crushed	lb.	.15
Mezereon	lb.	[illegible]
Oak, white, crushed	lb.	.15
Orange Peel, bitter	lb.	.16
Prickly Ash	lb.	[illegible]
Quebracho	lb.	[illegible]
Sassafras, 10 lbs., .18	lb.	.20
Sassafras, Extra	lb.	[illegible]
Simaruba	lb.	.40-45
Soap (Quillaja), cut, 5 lbs., .11	lb.	.12
powdered	lb.	.15
Wild Cherry, 5 lbs., .12	lb.	.14
" " ground, 5 lbs., .14	lb.	.16
Witch Hazel	lb.	[illegible]
Barley, Pearl	lb.	.5-6
Bay Rum, Porto Rico	gal.	2.10-2.35
St. Thomas	gal.	2.50-3.00
Bean, Calabar	lb.	[illegible]
St. Ignatius	lb.	.30
Tonka, Angostura	lb.	.75-85
Surinam	lb.	.65
Vanilla, Mexican, long	lb.	8.50
" " med	lb.	7.50
" " short	lb.	7.00
" Bourbon, long	lb.	6.50
" " med	lb.	5.50
" " short	lb.	4.50
Benzol, Coal Tar	lb.	.24
Benzosol	oz.	1.25
Berberine, Carb.	oz.	5.00
Hydrochlor	oz.	1.80
Berries, Cubeb, lb., .16; powdered	lb.	[illegible]
Fish	lb.	.12
Juniper	lb.	.8-10
powdered	lb.	.15-20
Poke	lb.	.30
Prickly Ash	lb.	[illegible]
Sumac	lb.	.30
Beta-Eucaine	oz.	8.50
Bismuth, Ammonia Citrate, lb., 2.55	oz.	.24
Subcarbonate	lb.	2.40
Subnitrate, 5 lbs., 1.65	lb.	1.75
Subgallate, lb., 2.45	oz.	.22-24
Subsalicylate, lb., 2.65	oz.	.21-25
Blacklegine, "Pasteur," (Blackleg Vaccine, cord form), No. 1, 10 doses	doz.	12.00
Blacklegine, "Pasteur," (Blackleg Vaccine, cord form), No. 2, 20 doses	doz.	20.00
Blacklegine, "Pasteur," (Blackleg Vaccine, cord form), No. 3, 50 doses	doz.	40.00
Blackleg Vaccine, "Pasteur," powder packet	doz.	12.00
Bladder Wrack	lb.	[illegible]
Blue Vitriol, bbl., .5½; 100 lbs., .6	lb.	.8-10
powdered, 50 lbs., .10	lb.	.12
Bole, Armenia, powdered, true	lb.	.12
Bone Ash	lb.	.15
Borax, 100 lbs., .8½	lb.	.9-12
powdered, 50 lbs., .8½	lb.	.9-12
Breast Tea, 5 lbs., .25	lb.	.27-30
Brimstone Roll, bbl., .3½	lb.	.4-5
Bromine	oz.	[illegible]
Bromoform	oz.	[illegible]
Buds, Balm of Gilead	lb.	[illegible]
Cassia	lb.	[illegible]
Butter, Cacao, 12 lbs., .35	lb.	[illegible]
Butylchloral	oz.	[illegible]
Cadmium, Bromide	oz.	.17
Iodide	oz.	[illegible]
Caffeine, lb., 3.50	oz.	[illegible]
Bromide	oz.	.19
Citrated, U. S. P., lb., 2.30	oz.	[illegible]
Valerianate	oz.	[illegible]
Calamine	lb.	.10-12
Calcium, Carb., precip	lb.	.8-10
Glycerophosphate	oz.	[illegible]
tablets, boxes, 50 5-gr.	oz.	.30
Hypophosphite, lb., .85	oz.	.10-14
Iodide	oz.	[illegible]
Lactophosphate	oz.	.12-15
Phosphate, precip	lb.	.17-19
Sulphide	lb.	[illegible]
Calomel, 10 lbs., .85	lb.	.90-95
Camphor, Monobromated, lbs., 1.95	oz.	.21-25
Cantharides, Russian	lb.	1.50-1.60
powdered	lb.	1.65-1.75
Cantharidal Vesicant, cans	doz.	2.50
Cantharidin	grain	.12
Capsicum, African	lb.	[illegible]
powdered, 5 lbs., .23	lb.	[illegible]
Caroid, powder form	oz.	1.35
and Soda Tablets, 150s	bot.	.67
Carbon, Disulphide	lb.	.11
Carmine, No. 40, lb., 4.25-4.50	oz.	[illegible]
Castor, Fiber, oz., 1.25; powdered	oz.	1.25-1.50
Cerium, Oxalate, lb., .65	oz.	.7
Chalk, French, powdered	lb.	.10
precip., Thomas' Eng., 7-lb. bag	lb.	.9
prepared, Thomas' Eng., 8-lb., white, box		.50
prepared, Thomas' Eng., 8-lb., pink, box		.65
prepared	lb.	.7
Charcoal, Animal, powd	lb.	.10
Willow, powd	lb.	.14
Chloral Hydrate, 5 lbs., 1.10	lb.	1.15-1.25
Croton	oz.	[illegible]
Chloralamid, 25 pkgs., .70	pkg.	.80
Chloroform, Purified, 5 lbs., .32	lb.	.35
Commercial, 5 lbs., .30	lb.	.33
Cinchonidine, Salicylate	oz.	.45
Sulphate, 5-oz. cans, .27	oz.	.32
Cinchonine, Sulphate	oz.	.12-17
Cinnabar	lb.	1.50
Civette	oz.	3.50
Clay, China, lb., .8; powdered	lb.	.10
Cloves, 10 lbs., .16	lb.	.18
powdered, 5 lbs., .20	lb.	.24
Cobalt, Carbonate	oz.	[illegible]
Chloride	oz.	[illegible]
Nitrate, oz., .25; powdered	oz.	[illegible]
Cocaine, Hydrochlorate, Cryst	oz.	3.50-3.75
Alkaloid	oz.	[illegible]
Oleate, 5 per cent	oz.	1.00-1.15
Cochineal, Honduras	lb.	.55
powdered	lb.	.60
Codeine, Pure Alkaloid, ozs	oz.	[illegible]
Sulphate, ozs	oz.	[illegible]
Colchicine, cryst., 15-gr. vials	grain	[illegible]
Collodion	lb.	[illegible]
Cantharidal	lb.	[illegible]
Flexible	lb.	[illegible]
Colocynth Apple	lb.	[illegible]
powdered	lb.	[illegible]
Composition Powder, 3 cans	lb.	[illegible]
Confection, Senna	lb.	[illegible]
Copper, Sulph., bbl., .6	lb.	[illegible]
Iodide	oz.	[illegible]
Copperas, bbl., 1	lb.	[illegible]
Corrosive Sublimate, 10 lbs., .80	lb.	[illegible]
powdered, 10 lbs., .83	lb.	[illegible]
Coumarin, Crys., Fries Bros., lb., 7.00	oz.	[illegible]
Cowhage	oz.	[illegible]
Cream Tartar, 99 p. c., powdered, 50 lbs., .25; 10 lbs., .27	lb.	[illegible]
Creolin, ¼ lbs., doz., 4.00; lbs	doz.	[illegible]
Cresol, U. S. P.	lbs.	[illegible]
Creosote, Beechwood Tar	lb.	[illegible]
Carbonate, lbs., 9.00	oz.	[illegible]
Phosphite, lb., 16.00	oz.	[illegible]
Crurin Kalle, 25 grams	each	[illegible]
Cystogen, powdered ozs	oz.	[illegible]
" powdered, 8 oz.	pkg.	[illegible]
" 5-gr. tablets, ozs	oz.	[illegible]
" " 8 oz.	pkg.	[illegible]
" " 25's	doz.	[illegible]
" Aperient	doz.	[illegible]
Cumarine, lb., 4.50	oz.	[illegible]
Currie Powder	lb.	[illegible]
Cuttle-Fish Bone, select	lb.	[illegible]
Dermatol, oz., .22	lb.	[illegible]
Dextrin, bag, .7	lb.	[illegible]
Diabetin	lb.	[illegible]
Digalen, ½-oz. vial		[illegible]
Digitalin, ⅛ ozs	oz.	[illegible]
Diuretin	oz.	[illegible]
Dover's Powder, 10 lbs., 1.10	lb.	[illegible]
Dragon's Blood, reeds	lb.	[illegible]
extra powdered	lb.	[illegible]
Duotal	oz.	[illegible]
Earth, Fullers, po., 25 lbs., .5	lb.	[illegible]
Eka-Iodoform	oz.	[illegible]
Elaterium	oz.	[illegible]
Emulsol, per doz., 2 oz.		[illegible]
Elixir Iodo-Bromide of Calcium Comp., Tilden's	pt.	[illegible]
Empyroform	oz.	[illegible]
Eosote (Creosote Valerianate)	oz.	[illegible]
Epicarin	oz.	[illegible]
Epsom Salts, bbl., 1½	lb.	[illegible]
Ergotine, Bonjean, lb., 6.50	oz.	[illegible]
Ergot, Spanish	lb.	[illegible]
powdered	lb.	[illegible]
Russian, lb., .48; powdered	lb.	[illegible]
Eserine	grain	[illegible]
Sulphate, 5-gr. v.	grain	[illegible]
Salicylate, 5-gr. v.	grain	[illegible]
Ether, Nitrous, Conc., ¼, ½ and 1 lbs.		[illegible]
Sulphuric, 1880, lb., .68; washed	lb.	[illegible]
Concent., 1890	lb.	[illegible]
Acetic	lb.	[illegible]
Ethiops Mineral	lb.	[illegible]
Ethyl, Bromide, 1-oz. bot. or tube	oz.	[illegible]
Iodide	oz.	[illegible]
Eucaine, Hydrochlor, ⅛, ¼ oz., 3.00; ⅛, ¼ oz.		[illegible]

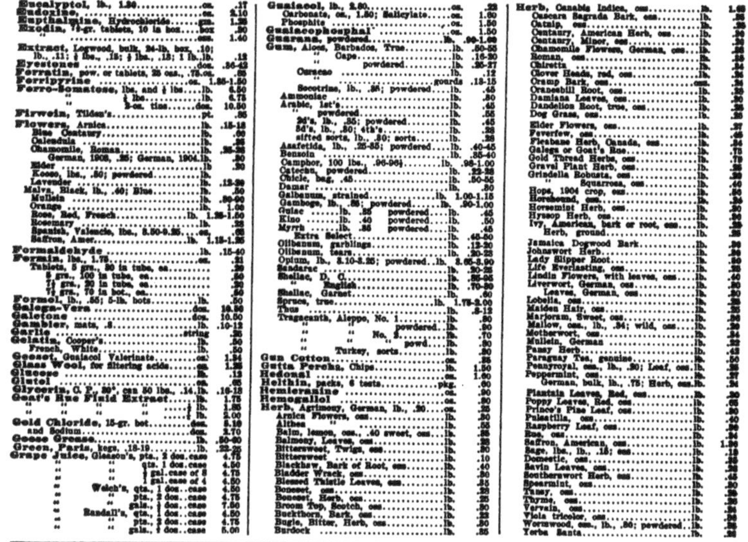

Item	Unit	Price
Eucalyptol, lb., 1.30	oz.	.17
Eudoxine,	oz.	2.10
Eupthalmine, Hydrochloride	grn.	1.35
Exodin, 7½-gr. tablets, 10 in box	box	.30
"	oss.	1.40
Extract, Logwood, bulk, 24-lb. box, .10; lb., .11; ½ lbs., .12; ¼ lbs., .13; 1 lb.	lb.	.12
Eyestones	doz.	.36-42
Ferratin, pow. or tablets, 25 ozs., .75	oz.	.85
Ferripyrine	oz.	1.25-1.50
Ferro-Somatose, lbs. and ½ lbs.	lb.	6.50
" ¼ lbs.	lb.	6.75
" 2-oz. tins	doz.	10.50
Firwein, Tilden's	pt.	.85
Flowers, Arnica	lb.	.15-18
Blue Centaury	lb.	.60
Calendula	lb.	.35
Chamomile, Roman	lb.	.35-38
German, 1903, .25; German, 1904	lb.	.30
Elder	lb	.30
Kosso, lbs., .80; powdered	lb.	
Lavender	lb.	.12-20
Malva, Black, lb., .40; Blue	lb.	.50
Mullein	lb.	.80-90
Orange	lb.	1.00
Rose, Red, French	lb.	1.25-1.50
Rosemary	lb.	.28
Spanish, Valencia, lbs., 8.50-9.25	oz.	.65
Saffron, Amer.	lb.	1.15-1.35
Formaldehyde	lb.	.15-40
Formin, lbs., 1.75	oz.	.21
Tablets, 5 grs., 30 in tube, ea.		.30
5 grs., 100 in tube, ea.		.60
7½ grs., 20 in tube, ea.		.30
7½ grs., 70 in bot., ea.		.60
Formol, lb., .55; 5-lb. bots	lb.	.50
Galega-Vera	doz.	10.50
Galetone	doz.	10.50
Gambier, mats, .8	lb.	.10-12
Garlic	string	.35
Gelatin, Cooper's	lb.	.50
French, White	lb.	.50
Geoset, Guaiacol Valerinate	oz.	1.24
Glass Wool, for filtering acids	oz.	1.35
Glucose	lb.	.12
Glutol	oz.	.65
Glycerin, C. P., 30°, can 50 lbs., .14	lb.	.16-18
Goat's Rue Fluid Extract	lb.	1.75
" " " " ½	lb.	1.85
" " " " ¼	lb.	2.00
Gold Chloride, 15-gr. bot	doz.	5.10
and Sodium	doz.	3.70
Goose Grease	lb.	.50-60
Green, Paris, kegs, .18-19	lb.	.22-25
Grape Juice, Gleason's, pts., 2 doz.	case	4.75
" " qts. 1 doz.	case	4.50
" " ½ gal. case of 8		4.75
" " 1 gal. case of 4		4.50
" Welch's, qts., 1 doz.	case	4.50
" " pts., 2 doz.	case	4.75
" " gals., ½ doz.	case	7.50
" Randall's, qts., 1 doz.	case	4.50
" " pts., 2 doz.	case	4.75
" " gals., ½ doz.	case	5.00
Guaiacol, lb., 2.60	oz.	.22
Carbonate, oz., 1.80; Salicylate	oz.	1.80
Phosphite	oz.	1.50
Guaiacophosphal	oz.	1.50
Guarana, powdered	lb.	.90-1.00
Gum, Aloes, Barbados, True	lb.	.50-55
" Cape	lb.	.16-20
" powdered	lb.	.25-27
Curacao	lb.	.12
"	gourds	.13-15
Socotrine, lb., .35; powdered	lb.	.45
Ammoniac	lb.	.30
Arabic, 1st's	lb.	.45
" powdered	lb.	.55
2d's, lb., .35; powdered	lb.	.45
3d's, lb., .30; 4th's	lb.	.28
sifted sorts, lb., .30; sorts	lb.	.28
Asafetida, lb., .25-35; powdered	lb.	.40-45
Benzoin	lb.	.35-40
Camphor, 100 lbs., .96-96½	lb.	.98-1.00
Catechu, powdered	lb.	.22-28
Chicle, bag, .45	lb.	.50-55
Damar	lb.	.30
Galbanum, strained	lb.	1.00-1.15
Gamboge, lb., .85; powdered	lb.	.90-1.00
Guiac ......lb. .35 powdered	lb.	.45
Kino ......lb. .40 powdered	lb.	.50
Myrrh ......lb. .35 powdered	lb.	.45
Extra Select	lb.	.45-50
Olibanum, garblings	lb.	.12-20
Olibanum, tears	lb.	.20-23
Opium, lb., 3.10-3.25; powdered	lb.	3.65-3.90
Sandarac	lb.	.20-25
Shellac, D. C.	lb.	.55-65
" English	lb.	.70-80
Shellac, Garnet	lb.	.60
Spruce, true	lb.	1.75-2.00
Thus	lb.	.8-12
Tragacanth, Aleppo, No. 1	lb.	.80
" " powdered	lb.	.90
" " No. 2	lb.	.70
" " " powd.	lb.	.80
" Turkey, sorts	lb.	.30
Gun Cotton	oz.	.35
Gutta Percha, Chips	lb.	1.50
Hedonal	oz.	1.60
Helthin, packs, 6 tests	pkg.	.60
Hemieranine	oz.	.90
Hemogallol	oz.	.80
Herb, Agrimony, German, lb., .20	ozs.	.25
Arnica Flowers, ozs	lb.	.30
Althea "	lb.	.55
Balm, lemon, ozs., .40 sweet, ozs.	lb.	.35
Balmony, Leaves, ozs	lb.	.35
Bittersweet, Twigs, ozs	lb.	.30
Bittersweet	lb.	.10
Blackhaw, Bark of Root, ozs	lb.	.40
Bladder Wrack, ozs	lb.	.30
Blessed Thistle Leaves, ozs	lb.	.35
Boneset, ozs	lb.	.23
Boneset, Herb, ozs	lb.	.25
Broom Top, Scotch, ozs	lb.	.30
Buckthorn, Bark, ozs	lb.	.23
Bugle, Bitter, Herb, ozs	lb.	.30
Burdock	lb.	.35
Herb, Canabis Indica, ozs	lb.	1.65
Cascara Sagrada Bark, ozs	lb.	[illegible]
Catnip, ozs	lb.	[illegible]
Centaury, American Herb, ozs	lb.	[illegible]
Centaury, Minor, ozs	lb.	[illegible]
Chamomile Flowers, German, ozs	lb.	[illegible]
Roman, ozs	lb.	[illegible]
Chiretta	lb.	[illegible]
Clover Heads, red, ozs	lb.	[illegible]
Cramp Bark, ozs	ozs.	[illegible]
Cranesbill Root, ozs	lb.	[illegible]
Damiana Leaves, ozs	lb.	[illegible]
Dandelion Root, true, ozs	lb.	[illegible]
Dog Grass, ozs	lb.	[illegible]
Elder Flowers, ozs	lb.	[illegible]
Feverfew, ozs	lb.	.45
Fleabane Herb, Canada, ozs	lb.	[illegible]
Galega or Goat's Rue	lb.	.75
Gold Thread Herbs, ozs	lb.	.75
Gravel Plant Herb, ozs	lb.	[illegible]
Grindelia Robusta, ozs	lb.	[illegible]
" Squarrosa, ozs	lb.	.40
Hops, 1904 crop, ozs	lb.	[illegible]
Horehound, ozs	lb.	[illegible]
Horsemint Herb, ozs	lb.	[illegible]
Hyssop Herb, ozs	lb.	[illegible]
Ivy, American, bark or root, ozs	lb.	[illegible]
Herb, ground	lb.	[illegible]
Jamaica Dogwood Bark	lb.	[illegible]
Johnswort Herb	lb.	[illegible]
Lady Slipper Root	lb.	[illegible]
Life Everlasting, ozs	lb.	[illegible]
Lindin Flowers, with leaves, ozs	lb.	.40
Liverwort, German, ozs	lb.	[illegible]
Leaves, German, ozs	lb.	[illegible]
Lobelia, ozs	lb.	[illegible]
Maiden Hair, ozs	lb.	[illegible]
Marjoram, Sweet, ozs	lb.	[illegible]
Mallow, ozs., lb., .34; wild, ozs	lb.	[illegible]
Motherwort, ozs	lb.	[illegible]
Mullein, German	lb.	[illegible]
Pansy Herb	lb.	.42
Paraguay Tea, genuine	lb.	.50
Pennyroyal, ozs., lb., .20; Leaf, ozs.	lb.	[illegible]
Peppermint, ozs	lb.	[illegible]
German, bulk, lb., .75; Herb, ozs.	lb.	[illegible]
Plantain Leaves, Red, ozs	lb.	[illegible]
Poppy Leaves, Red, ozs	lb.	[illegible]
Prince's Pine Leaf, ozs	lb.	[illegible]
Pulsatilla, ozs	lb.	.40
Raspberry Leaf, ozs	lb.	[illegible]
Rue, ozs	lb.	[illegible]
Saffron, American, ozs	lb.	1.35
Sage, lbs., lb., .15; ozs	lb.	[illegible]
Domestic, ozs	lb.	[illegible]
Savin Leaves, ozs	lb.	[illegible]
Southernwort Herb, ozs	lb.	.45
Spearmint, ozs	lb.	[illegible]
Tansy, ozs	lb.	[illegible]
Thyme, ozs	lb.	[illegible]
Vervain, ozs	lb.	[illegible]
Viola tricolor, ozs	lb.	[illegible]
Wormwood, ozs., lb., .80; powdered	lb.	[illegible]
Yerba Santa	lb.	[illegible]

Heroin, 15-gr. vials, oz., .23 ....oz.	4.85
Hippol, Crystalline ....oz.	1.50
Tab., 7½ grs. ea. ....box	.65
Hydrocyanate of Iron, Tilden's..oz.	.80
Honey, ...lb.	.13-15
Hops, fresh, 1904, bulk, .38 ....lb.	.40-42
pressed, ¼, ½ and lbs ....lb.	.40-42
pressed, ozs ....lb.	.45
Holocain, 1-gramme vials, .35; 5-gramme vials, 1.50......1-oz. vials	7.00
Homatropine, Hydrobrom, 5, 10 and 15 vials ....grain	.30-85
Hydrastine, Alkaloid ....oz.	6.25
Hydrogen Dioxide ....lb.	.25-50
Hydroquinone ....oz.	.15
Hyoscyamine, Alkaloid, 5, 10, 15 gr. v ....grain	.40
Hydrobromate, 5, 10, 15 gr. v....grain	.30
Sulphate, pure Amorph., 5, 10, 15 gr. v ....grain	.25
Hypnal, Hoechst ....oz.	1.15
Iatrol ....oz.	.95
Ichthyol, lb., 4.00 ....oz.	.32
Indigo, Madras ....lb.	.75
Manila ....lb.	.75
Sulphate comp., 9-lb. bot ....lb.	.45
Paste ....lb.	.20
Insect Powder, pure, bbls., .35; 50 lbs., .35½; 25 lbs., .36 ....lb.	.38-42
W. & B., bbls., .20; kegs, 50 lbs., .20½; drums, 25 lbs., .21 ....lb.	.25
Iodine, lb., 3.75 ....oz.	.30-37
Iodoform, lb., 4.00 ....oz.	.30-34
Iodol ....oz.	1.25
Iodopyrine, ...oz.	1.40
Iodothyrine, ozs., 3.40; ½-oz., 3.65; ¼-oz.	3.90
Iron, by Hydrogen, gray, U. S. P....lb.	.45
Benzoate ....oz.	.25
Cacodylate ....oz.	5.00
Carbonate, precip., lb., .18; sacch...lb.	.50
Vallet's ....lb.	.80
Chloride ....lb.	.35
Sol., U. S. P. ....lb.	.14
Tinct., U. S. P. ....lb.	.35
Citrate, U. S. P. ....lb.	.59
and Ammonium ....lb.	.56
and Quinine, lbs., 1.75 ....oz.	.17-21
Dialsed, Solution ....lb.	.55
Glycerophosphate ....oz.	.40
tablets, boxes, 50 5-gr ....ea.	.40
Iodide, oz., .36; syrup of ....lb.	.34
Lactate ....oz.	.7
Pernitrate, Solution ....lb.	.25
Pyrophosphate, Soluble ....lb.	.51
Phosphate, scales, U. S. P. ....lb.	.51
Subsulphate (Monsel's) ....lb.	.23
Solution (Monsel's) ....lb.	.15
Sulphate, pure ....lb.	.6
exsiccated ....lb.	.15
and Potass, Tartrate ....lb.	.48
and Ammonium Tartrate ....lb.	.62
Isarol, lb., 4.10 ....ozs.	.30-35
Isinglass, American ....lb.	.90
Russian, true, Beluga ....lb.	4.35
Jerquertol Serum, 4 tubes in box..ea.	7.50
Jecorin Tablets, 12's ....doz.	4.00
Jewelers' Rouge ....lb.	.75
Juice, Dandelion, Eng ....lb.	1.40
Juniper, Germ ....lb.	.25-30
Lime ....gal.	.90-1.00
Junket Tablets (10c. size), 3 doz. doz.	.80
Kamala, purified, powdered ....lb.	1.50
No. 2 powdered ....lb.	.65
Kaolin ....lb.	.08
Kelene, automatic, 1.10	.80-1.00
Kermes Mineral ....lb.	1.10
Kola Nut lb., .26; powdered ....lb.	.35
Kresamin ....oz.	1.00
Lactophenin, powd. or tab., 25 ozs., .90 ....oz.	1.00
Lacto-Somatose, 2-oz. tins ....doz.	10.50
¼-lbs. ....lb.	6.75
½-lbs. ....lb.	6.50
Lactucarium, lbs., 4.00 ....oz.	.40
Laminoids ....doz.	8.00
Lanikol, 1-oz. jars, doz., 3.50; 4-oz., doz., 9.50 ....lb.	2.50
Lanolin, Liebrich (Wool Fat), 10 lbs., .70 ....lb.	.75
Lanoline Puriss, B. J. D. ....lb.	.40
Lead, Acetate, White ....lb.	.12-14
Carbonate ....lb.	.12
Iodide ....lb.	.28
Red ....lb.	.10
Subacetate, Sol ....lb.	.16
Leaf, Aconite ....lb.	.20
Eng., 1-lb. cans only ....lb.	1.10
Arbor Vitae ....lb.	.30
Bay ....lb.	.12
Belladonna ....lb.	.25
Eng., 1-lb. cans only ....lb.	1.20
Blackberry ....lb.	.20
Blessed Thistle, ozs ....lb.	.27
Borage, ozs ....lb.	.88
Butternut ....lb.	.15
Buchu, long, lb., .60; short ....lb.	.25
Castor Oil ....lb.	.30
Cherry Laurel ....lb.	.40
Chestnut ....lb.	.23
Coca, Huanuco, lb., .40; Truxillo ....lb.	.32
Coltsfoot, ozs ....lb.	.25
Conium, lb ....lb.	.16
Damiana ....lb.	.30
Digitalis ....lb.	.26
Eng., 1-lb. cans only ....lb.	.65
Eucalyptus ....lb.	.15
Fern, sweet, ozs ....lb.	.22
Foxglove, ozs ....lb.	.30
Hyoscyamus ....lb.	.25
Am., 1-lb. cans only ....lb.	1.08
Eng., Biennial, 1-lb. bots. only ..lb.	5.00
German, bulk ....lb.	.25
Jaborandi, true ....lb.	.34
Laurel, true ....lb.	.15
Matico ....lb.	.35
Patchouli ....lb.	.60
Raspberry, ozs ....lb.	.25
Senna, Alexandria ....lb.	.25-35
Tinnivelly ....lb.	.15-20
India ....lb.	.15
Leaf, Stramonium ....lb.	[illegible]
Strawberry Leaves ....lb.	[illegible]
Uva Ursa ....lb.	.13
Witch Hazel ....lb.	[illegible]
Leeches, Swedish, per 100, 4.00 ....doz.	[illegible]
Liquorice, P. S. ....lb.	[illegible]
Corigliano ....lb.	.30-35
Y. & S., 5-lb. boxes ....lb.	[illegible]
Lime, Chlorinated, bulk, bbls., .3 ....lb.	.4
1-lb. tins ....lb.	.8-9
Litharge, ...lb.	.10-13
Lithium, Bromide ....oz.	[illegible]
Carbonate ....lb.	1.75-2.00
Citrate ....lb.	1.35
Glycerino-Phosph ....ozs.	.74
Iodide ....oz.	[illegible]
Salicylate ....oz.	.15
Litmus ....lb.	.44
Losophan ....oz.	1.80
Lunar Caustic, pure, 7.50 ....oz.	.48-51
in cones ....oz.	[illegible]
Lupulin, American ....lb.	.65
German ....lb.	.50
Lycetol, 10 ozs., 3.80 ....oz.	4.35
Lycopodium, Politz, 10 lbs., .60...lb.	.65-75
Lysidan ....oz.	1.75
Lysol ....lb.	.67
Mace ....lb.	.78
Magnesia, Calcined ....lb.	.70-75
heavy ....lb.	.75-85
Magnesium, carbonate, ¼ lbs ....lb.	.20-30
2 oz ....lb.	.23-33
S. S ....lb.	.53-70
Citrate, gran ....lb.	.50-75
Sulph. (Epsom Salts), bbls., .01½....lb.	3-4
Maltopepsine, Tilden's ....pt.	.63
Manganauro, 1-oz. bots ....doz.	8.50
Manganese, Black Oxide ....lb.	.8-12
Hypophosphite, oz., .20; sulphate...oz.	.8
Manna, large flake ....lb.	.60-75
small flake, 5 lbs., .40 ....lb.	.45
Mannite ....lb.	2.35
Marble Dust ....bbl.	1.50
Maretin ....ozs.	1.25
Menthol, lbs., 3.25 ....oz.	.25-29
Mercauro, 1-oz. bots ....doz.	8.50
Mercury, 5 lbs., .70 ....lb.	.72-75
Colloidal ....oz.	.85
Ammon ....lb.	1.10
Bisulphate ....lb.	.75
Chloride, Corrosive, 10 lbs., .80....lb.	.85
Cloride, powdered, 10 lbs., .83....lb.	.92
Calomel, 10 lbs., .90 ....lb.	.95
with Chalk ....lb.	.45
Iodide, Proto., lbs., 2.85 ....ozs.	.27
Biniodide, lbs., 3.10 ....ozs.	.37
Oxide, Red ....lbs.	1.10
Pill (Blue Mass) ....lbs.	.67
powdered ....lbs.	.57
Herring's English ....lbs.	1.35
Red Precipitate ....lb.	1.05
White Precipitate ....lb.	1.10
powdered ....lb.	1.15
Mesotan-Bayer ....oz.	.47
Methyl, Acetate ....oz.	.45
Bichloride ....oz.	.85

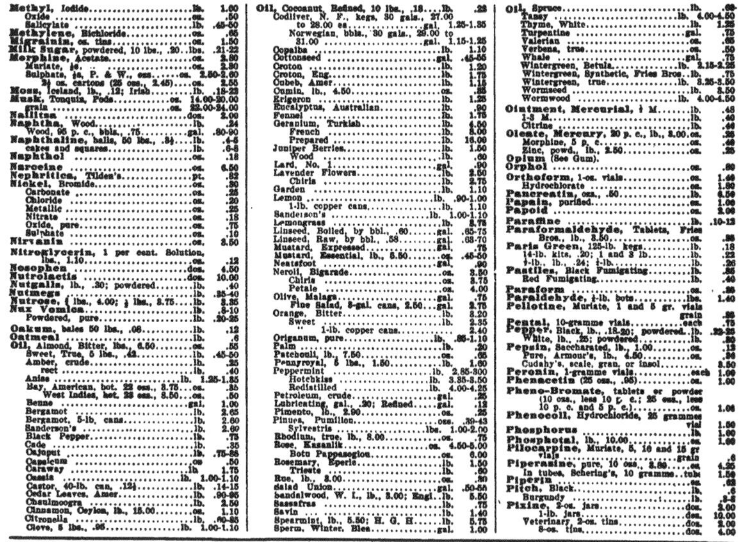

Article	Unit	Price
Methyl, Iodide	lb.	1.00
Oxide	oz.	.50
Salicylate	lb.	.45-50
Methylene, Bichloride	oz.	.65
Migrainin, oz. tins	oz.	1.50
Milk Sugar, powdered, 10 lbs., .20	lbs.	.21-22
Morphine, Acetate	oz.	2.80
Muriate, ⅛s	oz.	2.80
Sulphate, ⅛s, P. & W., ozs.	oz.	2.50-2.60
2½ oz. cartons (25 ozs., 2.45)	oz.	2.55
Moss, Iceland, lb., .12; Irish	lb.	.18-22
Musk, Tonquin, Pods	oz.	14.00-20.00
grain	oz.	22.00-24.00
Nalitisa	doz.	2.00
Naphtha, Wood	lb.	.24
Wood, 95 p. c., bbls., .75	gal.	.80-90
Naphthaline, balls, 50 lbs., .3½	lb.	.4-5
cakes and squares	lb.	.6-8
Naphthol	oz.	.18
Narceine	oz.	6.50
Nephritica, Tilden's	pt.	.82
Nickel, Bromide	oz.	.30
Carbonate	oz.	.25
Chloride	oz.	.20
Metallic	oz.	.25
Nitrate	oz.	.18
Oxide, pure	oz.	.75
Sulphate	oz.	.10
Nirvanin	oz.	3.50
Nitroglycerin, 1 per cent. Solution, lbs., 1.10	oz.	.12
Nosophen	doz.	4.50
Nutrolactis	doz.	10.00
Nutgalls, lb., .30; powdered	lb.	.40
Nutmegs	lb.	.35-40
Nutrose, ¼ lbs., 4.00; ½ lbs., 3.75	lb.	3.35
Nux Vomica	lb.	.8-10
Powdered, pure	lb.	.20-25
Oakum, bales 50 lbs., .08	lb.	.12
Oatmeal	lb.	.6
Oil, Almond, Bitter, lbs., 6.50	oz.	.55
Sweet, True, 5 lbs., .42	lb.	.45-50
Amber, crude	lb.	.25
rect	lb.	.40
Anise	lb.	1.25-1.35
Bay, American, bot. 22 ozs., 3.75	oz.	.35
West Indies, bot. 23 ozs., 3.50	oz.	.50
Benne	gal.	1.00
Bergamot	lb.	2.65
Bergamot, 5-lb, cans	lb.	2.60
Sanderson's	lb.	2.60
Black Pepper	lb.	.75
Cade	lb.	.35
Cajuput	lb.	.75-85
Capsicum	oz	.50
Caraway	lb	1.75
Cassia	lb.	1.00-1.10
Castor, 40-lb. can, .12½	lb.	.14-15
Cedar Leaves, Amer	lb.	.90-95
Chaulmoogra	lb.	2.50
Cinnamon, Ceylon, lb., 15.00	oz.	1.10
Citronella	lb.	.60-65
Clove, 5 lbs., .95	lb.	1.00-1.10
Oil, Cocoanut, Refined, 10 lbs., .18	lb.	.22
Codliver, N. F., kegs, 30 gals., 27.00 to 28.00 ea	gal.	1.25-1.35
Norwegian, bbls., 30 gals., 29.00 to 31.00	gal.	1.15-1.25
Copaiba	lb.	1.10
Cottonseed	gal.	.45-55
Croton	lb.	1.20
Croton, Eng	lb.	1.75
Cubeb, Amer	lb.	1.15
Cumin, lb., 4.50	oz.	.35
Erigeron	lb.	1.25
Eucalyptus, Australian	lb.	.90
Fennel	lb.	1.75
Geranium, Turkish	lb.	4.50
French	lb.	5.00
Prepared	lb.	16.00
Juniper Berries	lb.	1.50
Wood	lb.	.60
Lard, No. 1	gal.	.90
Lavender Flowers	lb.	2.50
Chiris	lb.	2.75
Garden	lb.	1.10
Lemon	lb.	.90-1.00
1-lb. copper cans	lb.	1.10
Sanderson's	lb.	1.00-1.10
Lemongrass	lb.	2.75
Linseed, Boiled, by bbl., .60	gal.	.65-75
Linseed, Raw, by bbl., .58	gal.	.63-70
Mustard, Expressed	gal.	.75
Mustard, Essential, lb., 5.50	oz.	.45-50
Neatsfoot	gal.	.90
Neroli, Bigarade	oz.	3.50
Chiris	oz.	3.75
Petale	oz.	4.00
Olive, Malaga	gal.	.75
Fine Salad, 5-gal. cans, 2.50	gal.	2.75
Orange, Bitter	lb.	3.20
Sweet	lb.	2.35
" 1-lb. copper cans		2.40
Origanum, pure	lb.	.85-1.10
Palm	lb.	.20
Patchouli, lb., 7.50	oz.	.65
Pennyroyal, 5 lbs., 1.50	lb.	1.60
Peppermint	lb.	2.85-300
Hotchkiss	lb.	3.35-3.50
Redistilled	lb.	4.00-4.25
Petroleum, crude	gal.	.25
Lubricating, gal., .20; Refined	gal.	.12
Pimento, lb., 2.90	oz.	.25
Pinues, Pumilion	ozs.	.39-43
Sylvestris	lbs.	1.00-2.00
Rhodium, true, lb., 8.00	oz.	.75
Rose, Kazanlik	oz.	4.50-5.00
Botu Pappazoglou	oz.	6.00
Rosemary, Eperle	lb.	1.50
Trieste	lb.	.60
Rue, lb., 3.00	oz.	.30
Salad Union	gal.	.50-55
Sandalwood, W. I., lb., 3.00; Engl	lb.	5.50
Sassafras	lb.	.75
Savin	lb.	1.40
Spearmint, lb., 5.50; H. G. H	lb.	5.75
Sperm, Winter, Blea	gal.	1.00
Oil, Spruce	lb.	.60
Tansy	lb.	4.00-4.50
Thyme, White	lb.	1.25
Turpentine	gal.	.75
Valerian	oz.	.65
Verbena, true	oz.	.50
Whale	gal.	.75
Wintergreen, Betula	lb.	2.15-2.25
Wintergreen, Synthetic, Fries Bros	lb.	.75
Wintergreen, true	lb.	3.25-3.50
Wormseed	lb.	3.50
Wormwood	lb.	4.00-4.50
Ointment, Mercurial, ½ M	lb.	.48
1-3 M	lb.	.40
Citrine	lb.	.44
Oleate, Mercury, 20 p. c., lb., 3.00	oz.	.35
Morphine, 5 p. c.	oz.	.48
Zinc, powd., lb., 2.50	oz.	.35
Opium (See Gum).		
Orphol	oz.	.80
Orthoform, 1-oz. vials	oz.	1.40
Hydrochlorate	oz.	1.50
Pancreatin, ozs., .50	lb.	6.50
Papain, purified	oz.	1.00
Papoid	oz.	2.00
Paraffine	lb.	.10-12
Paraformaldehyde, Tablets, Fries Bros., lb., 3.50	oz.	.35
Paris Green, 125-lb. kegs	lb.	.18
14-lb. kits, .20; 1 and 3 lb.	lb.	.22
½-lb., lb., .24; ¼-lb.	lb.	.26
Pastiles, Black Fumigating	lb.	.85
Red Fumigating	lb.	.40
Paraform	oz.	.35
Paraldehyde, ½-lb. bots	lbs.	1.40
Pellotine, Muriate, 1 and 5 gr. vials	grain	.35
Pental, 10-gramme vials	each	.75
Pepper, Black, lb., .18-20; powdered	lb.	.22-25
White, lb., .25; powdered	lb.	.30
Pepsin, Saccharated, lb., 1.00	oz.	.12
Pure, Armour's, lb., 4.50	oz.	.36
Cudahy's, scale, gran. or insol		3.50
Peronin, 1-gramme vials	each	1.00
Phenacetin (25 ozs., .95)	oz.	1.00
Pheno-Bromate, tablets or powder (10 ozs., less 10 p. c.; 25 ozs., less 10 p. c. and 5 p. c.)	oz.	1.06
Phenocoll, Hydrochloride, 25 grammes	vial	1.50
Phosphorus	lb.	1.00
Phosphotal, lb., 10.00	oz.	1.00
Pilocarpine, Muriate, 5, 10 and 15 gr vials	grain	.6
Piperazine, pure, 10 ozs., 3.80	oz.	4.25
In tubes, Schering's, 10 grammes	tube	1.50
Piperin	oz.	.62
Pitch, Black	lb.	.6
Burgundy	lb.	.3-5
Pixine, 2-oz. jars	doz.	2.00
1-lb. jars	doz.	10.00
Veterinary, 2-oz. tins	doz.	2.00
8-oz. tins	doz.	4.00

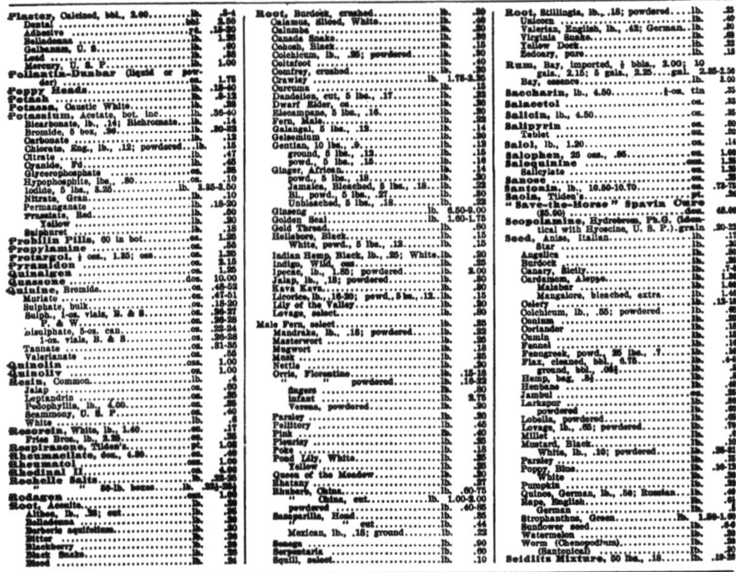

Article	Unit	Price
Plaster, Calcined, bbl., 2.00	lb.	.3-4
Dental	bbl.	2.50
Adhesive	yd.	.15-20
Belladonna	lb.	1.25
Galbanum, U. S.	lb.	.60
Lead	lb.	.55
Mercury, U. S. P.	lb.	1.00
Pollantin-Dunbar (liquid or powder)	oz.	1.75
Poppy Heads	lb.	.18-40
Potash	lb.	.9-12
Potassa, Caustic White	lb.	.58
Potassium, Acetate, bot. inc.	lb.	.36-40
Bicarbonate, lb., .14; Bichromate	lb.	.14
Bromide, 5 box, .30	lb.	.30-32
Carbonate	lb.	.12
Chlorate, Eng., lb., .12; powdered	lb.	.15
Citrate	lb.	.47
Cyanide, Fd	lb.	.45
Glycerophosphate	oz.	.35
Hypophosphite, lbs., .80	oz.	.10
Iodide, 5 lbs., 3.25	lb.	3.35-3.50
Nitrate, Gran.	lb.	.10
Permanganate	lb.	.18-20
Prussiate, Red	lb.	.50
Yellow	lb.	.20
Sulphuret	lb.	.18
Probilin Pills, 60 in bot.	ea.	1.25
Propylamine	oz.	.55
Protargol, ¼ ozs., 1.35; ozs.	oz.	1.30
Pyramidon	oz.	2.15
Quinalgen	oz.	1.25
Quassone	doz.	10.00
Quinine, Bromide	oz.	.48-52
Muriate	oz.	.47-51
Sulphate, bulk	oz.	.18-20
Sulph., 1-oz. vials, B. & S.	oz.	.26-27
P. & W.	oz.	.26-28
Bisulphate, 5-oz. can	oz.	.22-24
1-oz. vials, B. & S.	oz.	.26-28
Tannate	oz.	.31-35
Valerianate	oz.	.55
Quinolin	ozs.	1.00
Quinoliv	oz.	1.00
Resin, Common	lb.	.4
Jalap	oz.	.60
Leptandrin	oz.	.35
Podophyllin, lb., 4.00	oz.	.35
Scammony, U. S. P.	oz.	.40
White	lb.	.6
Resorcin, White, lb., 1.40	oz.	.17
Fries Bros., lb., 2.25	oz.	.25
Respirazone, Tilden's	pt.	1.00
Rheumacilate, doz., 4.50	ea.	.45
Rheumatol	ozs.	1.00
Rhodinal II	oz.	4.00
Rochelle Salts	lb.	.22-25
" " 50-lb. boxes	lb.	.22½-23½
Rodagen	ozs.	1.00
Root, Aconite	lb.	.30
Althea, lb., .22; cut	lb.	.25
Belladonna	lb.	.35
Berberis aquifolium	lb.	.30
Bitter	lb.	.28
Blackberry	lb.	.20
Black Snake	lb.	.25
Blood	lb.	.24
Root, Burdock, crushed	lb.	.20
Calamus, Sliced, White	lb.	.40
Calumba	lb.	.20
Canada Snake	lb.	.35
Cohosh, Black	lb.	.15
Colchicum, lb., .25; powdered	lb.	.30
Coltsfoot	lb.	.40
Comfrey, crushed	lb.	.20
Crawley	lb.	1.75-2.25
Curcuma	lb.	.15
Dandelion, cut, 5 lbs., .17	lb.	.22
Dwarf Elder, cs.	lb.	.30
Elecampane, 5 lbs., .16	lb.	.20
Fern, Male	lb.	.22
Galangal, 5 lbs., .12	lb.	.14
Gelsemium	lb.	.20
Gentian, 10 lbs., .9	lb.	.12
ground, 5 lbs., .12	lb.	.15
powd., 5 lbs., .15	lb.	.16
Ginger, African	lb.	.14
powd., 5 lbs., .18	lb.	.20
Jamaica, Bleached, 5 lbs., .18	lb.	.22
Bl., powd., 5 lbs., .27	lb.	.30
Unbleached, 5 lbs., .18	lb.	.22
Ginseng	lb.	6.50-9.00
Golden Seal	lb.	1.60-1.75
Gold Thread	lb.	.80
Hellebore, Black	lb.	.15
White, powd., 5 lbs., .12	lb.	.15
Indian Hemp, Black, lb., .25; White	lb.	.20
Indigo, Wild, ozs.	lb.	.25
Ipecac, lb., 1.85; powdered	lb.	2.00
Jalap, lb., .18; powdered	lb.	.30
Kava Kava	lb.	.30
Licorice, lb., .16-20; powd., 5 lbs., .12	lb.	.15
Lily of the Valley	lb.	.20
Lovage, select	lb.	.30
Male Fern, select	lb.	.25
Mandrake, lb., .18; powdered	lb.	.22
Masterwort	lb.	.25
Mugwort	lb.	.18
Musk	lb.	.25
Nettle	lb.	.20
Orris, Florentine	lb.	.15-18
" " powdered	lb.	.16-22
fingers	lb.	.80
infant	lb.	2.75
Verona, powdered	lb.	.20
Parsley	lb.	.30
Pellitory	lb.	.45
Pink	lb.	.40
Pleurisy	lb.	.25
Poke	lb.	.18
Pond Lily, White	lb.	.25
Yellow	lb.	.25
Queen of the Meadow	lb.	.20
Rhatany	lb.	.27
Rhubarb, China	lb.	.60-75
" China, cut	lb.	1.00-2.00
powdered	lb.	.40-85
Sarsaparilla, Hond.	lb.	.35
" " cut	lb.	.44
Mexican, lb., .18; ground	lb.	.22
Senega	lb.	.90
Serpentaria	lb.	.60
Squill, select	lb.	.10
Root, Stillingia, lb., .18; powdered	lb.	.25
Unicorn	lb.	.40
Valerian, English, lb., .42; German	lb.	.30
Virginia Snake	lb.	.40
Yellow Dock	lb.	.22
Zedoary, pure	lb.	.15
Rum, Bay, imported, ½ bbls., 2.00; 10 gals., 2.15; 5 gals., 2.25	gal.	2.25-2.50
Bay, essence	lb.	2.00
Saccharin, lb., 4.50	⅛-oz. tin	.35
Salacetol	oz.	.33
Salicin, lb., 4.50	oz.	.35
Salipyrin	oz.	.30
Tablet	oz.	.30
Salol, lb., 1.20	oz.	.14
Salophen, 25 ozs., .95	oz.	1.00
Saloquinine	ozs.	1.25
Salicylate	oz.	1.35
Sanose	oz.	.35
Santonin, lb., 10.50-10.70	oz.	.73-75
Saola, Tilden's	pt.	.50
"Save-the-Horse" Spavin Cure ($5.00)	doz.	48.00
Scopolamine, Hydrobrom, Ph.G. (Identical with Hyoscine, U. S. P.)	grain	.20-22
Seed, Anise, Italian	lb.	.17
Star	lb.	.30
Angelica	lb.	.30
Burdock	lb.	.35
Canary, Sicily	lb.	.7-8
Cardamom, Aleppo	lb.	1.20
Malabar	lb.	1.00
Mangalore, bleached, extra	lb.	1.40
Celery	lb.	.12-15
Colchicum, lb., .55; powdered	lb.	.65
Conium	lb.	.25
Coriander	lb.	.15
Cumin	lb.	.12
Fennel	lb.	.16
Fenugreek, powd., 25 lbs., .7	lb.	.15
Flax, cleaned, bbl., 6.75	lb.	.4-5
ground, bbl., .06½	lb.	.7
Hemp, bag, .5¼	lb.	.6
Henbane	lb.	.45
Jambul	oz.	.25
Larkspur	lb.	.25
powdered	lb.	.30
Lobelia, powdered	lb.	.65
Lovage, lb., .65; powdered	lb.	.75
Millet	lb.	.6
Mustard, Black	lb.	.15
White, lb., .10; powdered	lb.	.20-21
Parsley	lb.	.15
Poppy, Blue	lb.	.10-12
White	lb.	.25
Pumpkin	lb.	.25
Quince, German, lb., .50; Russian	lb.	.60
Rape, English	lb.	.6½
German	lb.	.7
Strophanthus, Green	lb.	1.50-1.60
Sunflower seed	lb.	.6-8
Watermelon	lb.	.20
Worm (Chenopodium)	lb.	.20
(Santonica)	lb.	.20
Seidlitz Mixture, 50 lbs., .18	lb.	.19-22

"SQUIBB'S" has been to physicians for half a century a synonym for Quality, Efficiency and Reliability. Are yon giving SQUIBB products a conspicuous place in your Prescription Department?

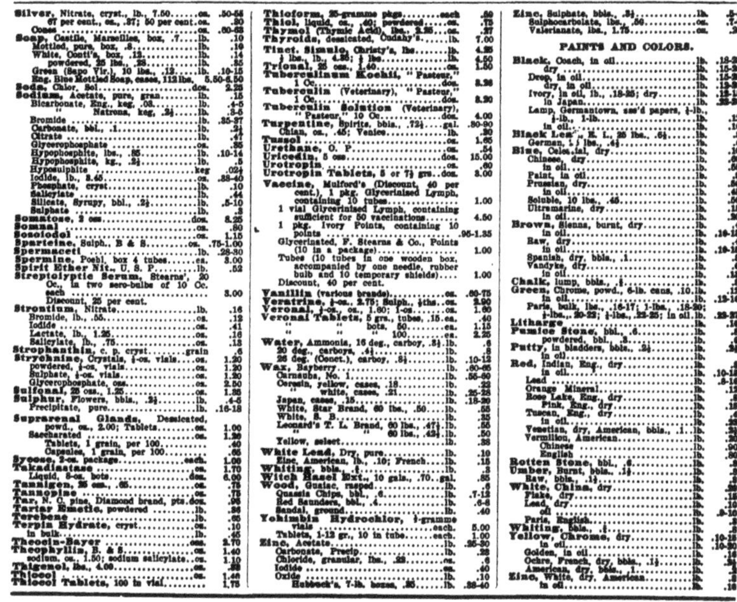

Silver, Nitrate, cryst., lb., 7.50......oz. .50-55
67 per cent., oz., .37; 50 per cent..oz. .30
Cones......oz. .60-63
Soap, Castile, Marseilles, box, .7....lb. .10
Mottled, pure, box, .8......lb. .10
White, Conti's, box, .13......lb. .14
powdered, 25 lbs., .28......lb. .35
Green (Sapo Vir.), 10 lbs., .13.....lb. .10-15
Eng. Blue Mottled Soap, cases, 112 lbs. 5.50-6.50
Soda, Chlor. Sol......doz. 2.25
Sodium, Acetate, pure, gran......lb. .15
Bicarbonate, Eng., keg, .03......lb. .4-5
" Natrona, keg, .2½....lb. .3-5
Bromide......lb. .35-37
Carbonate, bbl., .1......lb. .2½
Citrate......lb. .47
Glycerophosphate......oz. .35
Hypophosphite, lbs., .85......lb. .10-14
Hypophosphite, kg., .2½......lb. .5
Hyposulphite......keg .02½
Iodide, lb., 2.45......oz. .38-40
Phosphate, cryst......lb. .10
Salicylate......lb. .44
Silicate, Syrupy, bbl., .2½......lb. .5-10
Sulphate......lb. .3
Somatose, 2 ozs......doz. 8.25
Somnal......oz. .80
Sozoiodol......oz. 1.15
Sparteine, Sulph., B & S......oz. .75-1.00
Spermaceti......lb. .28-30
Spermine, Poehl, box 4 tubes......ea. 3.00
Spirit Ether Nit., U. S. P......lb. .52
Streptolyptic Serum, Stearns', 20 Cc., in two sero-bulbs of 10 Cc. each...... 3.00
Discount, 25 per cent.
Strontium, Nitrate......lb. .16
Bromide, lb., .55......oz. .12
Iodide......oz. .41
Lactate, lb., 1.25......oz. .16
Salicylate, lb., .75......oz. .13
Strophanthin, c. p. cryst......grain .6
Strychnine, Crystals, ⅛-oz. vials....oz. 1.20
powdered, ⅛-oz. vials......oz. 1.20
Sulphate, ⅛-oz. vials......oz. 1.30
Glycerophosphate, ozs......oz. 2.50
Sulfonal, 25 ozs., 1.25......oz. 1.35
Sulphur, Flowers, bbls., .2½......lb. .4-5
Precipitate, pure......lb. .16-18
Suprarenal Glands, Desiccated, powd., oz., 2.00; Tablets......oz. 1.00
Saccharated......oz. 1.25
Tablets, 1 grain, per 100...... .40
Capsules, 1 grain, per 100...... .65
Sycose, 2-oz. package......each. 1.00
Takadiastase......oz. 1.70
Liquid, 8-oz. bots......doz. 6.00
Tannigen, 25 ozs., .65......oz. .75
Tannopine......oz. .75
Tar, N. C. pine, Diamond brand, pts.doz. .95
Tartar Emetic, powdered......lb. .36
Terebene......lb. .65
Terpin Hydrate, cryst......oz. .10
in bulk......lb. .45
Theocin-Bayer......oz. 2.70
Theophyllin, B. & S......oz. 1.40
sodium, oz., 1.50; sodium salicylate..oz. 1.10
Thigenol, lbs., 4.00......oz. .33
Thiocol......oz. 1.40
Thiocol Tablets, 100 in vial...... 1.75

Thioform, 25-gramme pkgs......each .60
Thiol, liquid, oz., .40; powdered......oz. .75
Thymol (Thymic Acid), lbs., 2.25...oz. .27
Thyroids, dessicated, Cudahy's......lb. 7.00
Tinct. Simulo, Christy's, lbs......lb. 4.25
½ lbs., lb., 4.50; ¼ lbs......lb. 4.50
Trional, 25 ozs., 1.40......oz. 1.50
Tuberculinum Kochii, "Pasteur," 1 Cc......doz. 8.26
Tuberculin (Veterinary), "Pasteur," 1 Cc......doz. 8.30
Tuberculin Solution (Veterinary), "Pasteur," 10 Cc......doz. 4.00
Turpentine, Spirits, bbls., .72½....gal. .80-90
Chian, oz., .45; Venice......lb. .30
Tussol......oz. 1.65
Urethane, C. P......oz. .54
Uricedin, 5 ozs......doz. 15.00
Urotropin......oz. .60
Urotropin Tablets, 5 or 7½ grs...doz. 3.00
Vaccine, Mulford's (Discount, 40 per cent.), 1 pkg. Glycerinised Lymph, containing 10 tubes...... 1.00
1 vial Glycerinised Lymph, containing sufficient for 50 vaccinations...... 4.50
1 pkg. Ivory Points, containing 10 points...... .95-1.35
Glycerinated, F. Stearns & Co., Points (10 in a package)...... 1.00
Tubes (10 tubes in one wooden box, accompanied by one needle, rubber bulb and 10 temporary shields).... 1.00
Discount, 40 per cent.
Vanillin (various brands)......oz. .60-75
Veratrine, ⅛-oz., 2.75; Sulph., ⅛ths..oz. 2.90
Veronal, ¼-oz., oz., 1.80; 1-oz......oz. 1.60
Veronal Tablets, 5 grs., tubes, .15.ea. .40
" " bots. 50......ea. 1.15
" " " 100......ea. 2.25
Water, Ammonia, 16 deg., carboy, .3½.lb. .6
20 deg., carboys, .4½......lb. .8
26 deg. (Conct.), carboy, .8½......lb. .10-12
Wax, Bayberry......lb. .60-65
Carnauba, No. 1......lb. .55-60
Ceresin, yellow, cases, .18......lb. .22
" white, cases, .21......lb. .25-28
Japan, cases, .15......lb. .18-20
White, Star Brand, 60 lbs., .50....lb. .55
White, S. B......lb. .35
Leonard's T. L. Brand, 60 lbs., .47½.lb. .55
" " 60 lbs., .42½.lb. .50
Yellow, select......lb. .38
White Lead, Dry, pure......lb. .10
Zinc, American, lb., .10; French....lb. .15
Whiting, bbls., .⅞......lb. .3
Witch Hazel Ext., 10 gals., .70..gal. .85
Wood, Guaiac, rasped......lb. .6
Quassia Chips, bbl., .6......lb. .7-12
Red Saunders, bbl., .4......lb. .6-8
Sandal, ground......lb. .40
Yohimbin Hydrochlor, ⅛-gramme vials......each. 5.00
Tablets, 1-12 gr., 10 in tube......each. 1.00
Zinc, Acetate......lb. .25-30
Carbonate, Precip......lb. .25
Chloride, granular, lbs., .23......oz. .6
Iodide......oz. .40
Oxide......lb. .10
Hubbuck's, 7-lb. boxes, .35......lb. .38-40

Zinc, Sulphate, bbls., .3½......lb. .5-6
Sulphocarbolate, lbs., .56......oz. .7-9
Valerianate, lbs., 1.75......oz. .20

PAINTS AND COLORS.

Black, Coach, in oil......lb. .18-25
dry......lb. .15-20
Drop, in oil......lb. .15-25
dry, in oil......lb. .12-20
Ivory, in oil, lb., .18-25; dry......lb. .12-15
in Japan......lb. .22-25
Lamp, Germantown, sse'd papers, ¼-lb., ½-lb., 1-lb......lb. .12
in oil......lb. .10
Black Lead, E. L., 25 lbs., .6½......lb. .8
German, 1½ lbs., .4½......lb. .6
Blue, Celestial, dry......lb. .16
Chinese, dry......lb. .60
in oil......lb. .55
Paint, in oil......lb. .9
Prussian, dry......lb. .50
in oil......lb. .45
Soluble, 10 lbs., .45......lb. .50
Ultramarine, dry......lb. .15
in oil......lb. .20
Brown, Sienna, burnt, dry......lb. .4
in oil......lb. .10-15
Raw, dry......lb. .4
in oil......lb. .10-15
Spanish, dry, bbls., .1......lb. .3
Vandyke, dry......lb. .6
in oil......lb. .12
Chalk, lump, bbls., .⅞......lb. .3
Green, Chrome, powd., 6-lb. cans, .10.lb. .13
in oil......lb. .12-16
Paris, bulk, lbs., .16-17; 1-lbs., .18-20; ½-lbs., .20-22; ¼-lbs., .22-25; in oil.lb. .23-27
Litharge......lb. .10
Pumice Stone, bbl., .6......lb. .8
powdered, bbl., .3......lb. .6
Putty, in bladders, bbls., .2½......lb. .3½
in oil......lb.
Red, Indian, Eng., dry......lb. .8
in oil......lb. .10-15
Lead......lb. .8-16
Orange Mineral......lb. .12
Rose Lake, Eng., dry......lb. .8
Pink, Eng., dry......lb. .15
Tuscan, Eng., dry......lb. .4
in oil......lb. .23
Venetian, dry, American, bbls., .1..lb. .3½
Vermilion, American......lb. .20
Chinese......lb. .90
English......lb. .80
Rotten Stone, bbl., .6......lb. .8
Umber, Burnt, bbls., .1½......lb. .3
Raw, bbls., .1½......lb. .3
White, China, dry......lb. .20
Flake, dry......lb. .15
Lead, dry......lb. .10
oil......lb. .9-10
Paris, English......lb. .3
Whiting, bbls., .⅞......lb. .3
Yellow, Chrome, dry......lb. .10-15
in oil......lb. .10-20
Golden, in oil......lb. .16
Ochre, French, dry, bbls., .1½......lb. .3½
American, dry, bbls., .1......lb. .3
Zinc, White, dry, American......lb. .8
in oil......lb. .10

American Druggist "WANTS" Page.

THIS Department is intended to be used as a medium for the exchange or sale of stores, the employment of clerks, and the securing of situations. Suitable notices of moderate length under this heading inserted one time free for subscribers; for each additional insertion Fifty Cents will be charged. Advertisements not in the foregoing classification Forty Cents per line.

SITUATIONS VACANT.

WANTED.—Young pharmacist who is posted in retail drug business. Good opening. Rocky Mountain town on new transcontinental railroad line now building. Address City Drug Store, Steamboat Springs, Colo.

SALESMAN WANTED.—An unusual opportunity for salesmen visiting the regular drug trade to make money. Address promptly the G. S. O. Company, Lancaster, Pa.

REGISTERED PHARMACISTS and drug employees, if you would accept a better position, now or later, send us your name at once; fine openings in all States; salaries, $600 to $2,000 a year; employers referred to competent men free. NATIONAL PHARMACEUTICAL AGENCY, 616 Colonial Security Building, St. Louis, Mo.

WANTED, LICENSED CLERK at retail drug store; steady position for right party. Best of references required. Address J. F. S., care of AMERICAN DRUGGIST.

WANTED.—A first-class tablet man with executive ability and understanding the manufacturing of tablets on a large scale. In answering give age, experience, references and salary expected. P. O. Box 1404, Philadelphia, Pa.

DRUG CLERK WANTED FOR MEXICO.—Young graduate in pharmacy, with knowledge of Spanish preferred, who can be trusted in important position in well-known Mexican drug store; must be qualified in every particular; chance of advancement good; send references and state salary expected. Mexico, care Foreign Department, AMERICAN DRUGGIST.

BUSINESS OPPORTUNITIES.

FOR SALE.—One of the finest drug stores in western New York; cement block; building new; steel ceiling; all fixtures new; everything up to date; hot water, heat, gas or electric lights; insurance, 1 per cent; will sell with or without building. Address V. C. Armes, Gowanda, N. Y.

FOR SALE.—Wishing to retire from business on account of age, I offer a large and prosperous business at a liberal discount from the inventory to a cash customer; when answering this state how much capital you have to invest. Address Filmore, care of AMERICAN DRUGGIST.

SHEEP DIP, ETC.—A gentleman with special knowledge of the trade and an extensive connection in South Africa wishes to represent a manufacturer of sheep dip in that country; 11 years' experience. Address "Dip," Box 671, Sells Advertising Offices, London, England.

FOR $25,000, a working interest in a fine wholesale drug business. Address Drugs, care Stringer & Seymour, St. Paul, Minn.

WANTED.—A drug store doing a moderate business, "no paints or oils," within 35 miles of New York. It must bear the closest examination or please do not waste your time or mine by noticing this. Address Geo. Kempton, 197 Fulton street, New York.

A BARGAIN.—A Morris Tablet Machine, Style B. Direct Driver. Includes dies and punches; this machine is practically new, having only been in use about three months. ANOTHER BARGAIN.—A 60-Gallon Drug Still, including rectifier, condenser, and low wine still. The still can be operated independent of the rectifier. This set is in splendid condition, being practically good as new. Address Dept A, 212 S. Seventh Street, St. Louis, Mo.

WANTED.—An experienced manager of travelers to take charge of sales department in a prominent pharmaceutical specialty house. One who has executive ability and can act as assistant manager. State salary expected and full particulars to New York, care of AMERICAN DRUGGIST.

PARTNER WANTED.—I want as an equal partner a good pharmacist and business man who can command $2,000 or $3,000 in real money. I have a store that has a stock of nearly $6,000 in clean, fresh goods, most of it bought in the last eight months, and a business that is too big for one man to handle. It is capable of a vast development, as it is a suburb of New York that may increase its population five fold in the next five years. Would sell out, but am forming a stock company to operate a chain of stores in this section and want this store in the combination. I must have time to attend to this company matter and do not want to lose this store, as it will be an important link in our chain of stores. If I can find the right man I have a good thing for him, as the store will go into the combination as soon as the company is incorporated. Or I will make a contract to sell all my interest to my partner in case he doesn't want to go into the company. In short, I want to hold and continue the building up of this business by some one that I can absolutely depend upon. Apply by letter only to Dawson, care AMERICAN DRUGGIST.

CIRCULARS, BOOKLETS, LETTERS and advertising matter of any description designed and prepared; high-grade medical advertising a specialty. C. L. Mueller, M. D., Advertising Counselor, Wapakoneta, Ohio.

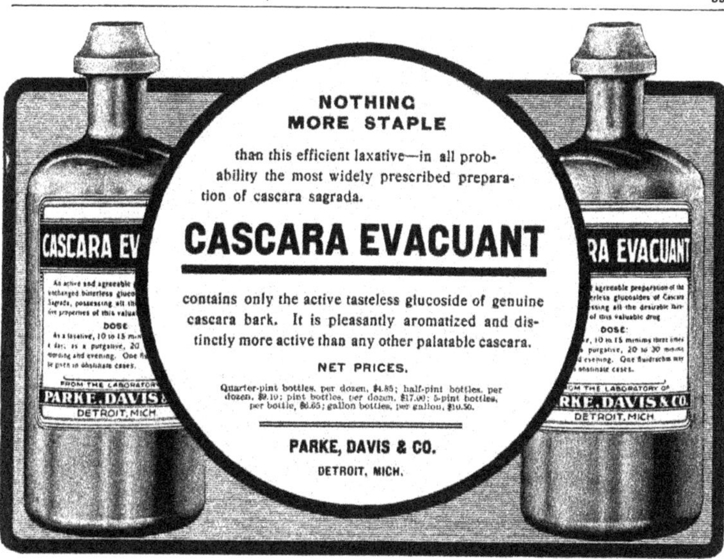
NOTHING MORE STAPLE
than this efficient laxative—in all probability the most widely prescribed preparation of cascara sagrada.
CASCARA EVACUANT
contains only the active tasteless glucoside of genuine cascara bark. It is pleasantly aromatized and distinctly more active than any other palatable cascara.
NET PRICES.
Quarter-pint bottles, per dozen, $4.85; half-pint bottles, per dozen, $9.10; pint bottles, per dozen, $17.00; 5-pint bottles, per bottle, $8.65; gallon bottles, per gallon, $10.50.
PARKE, DAVIS & CO.
DETROIT, MICH.
CASCARA EV
PARKE, DAVIS &
DETROIT, MICH
RA EVACUANT
RKE, DAVIS & CO.
DETROIT, MICH

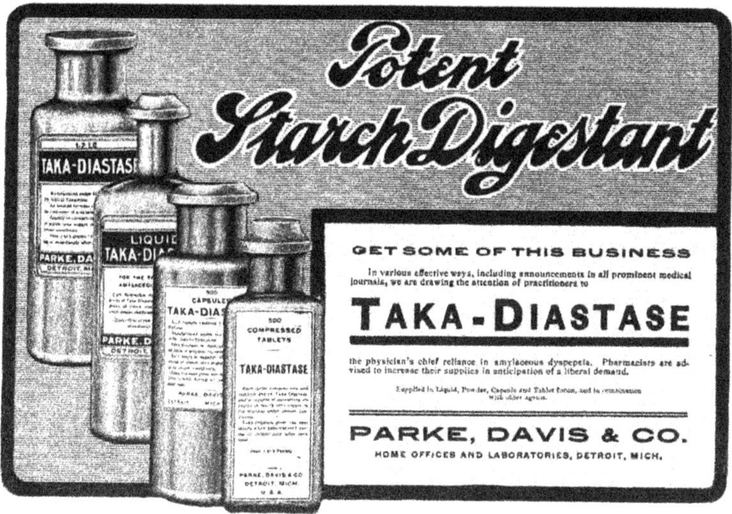
Potent Starch Digestant
GET SOME OF THIS BUSINESS
In various effective ways, including announcements in all prominent medical journals, we are drawing the attention of practitioners to
TAKA-DIASTASE
the physician's chief reliance in amylaceous dyspepsia. Pharmacists are advised to increase their supplies in anticipation of a liberal demand.
PARKE, DAVIS & CO.
HOME OFFICES AND LABORATORIES, DETROIT, MICH.
TAKA-DIASTASE
LIQUID
TAKA-DIASTASE

An Anticocaine Crusade in Indianapolis.

Indianapolis, March 20.—An active war is to be waged against certain Indianapolis druggists who have been selling morphine and cocaine without a physician's prescription. Among the indictments found by the March Grand Jury, it is said, are several against prominent druggists who are said to have been violating the law continually.

"Radiumite."

The Radiumite Display Stand, embracing an assortment of radiumite razors and radiumite strops, is furnished free of charge and will undoubtedly sell the goods. Write to the Radiumite Company, 97 South Clinton street, Chicago, for a booklet on salesmanship, which contains many valuable pointers and will cost you nothing. An illustration of the Radiumite Display Stand, which is given absolutely free to the dealer, appears on page 48 of this issue.

$500 for a Formula.

A thoroughly reliable capitalist offers $500 for a formula for a pharmaceutical preparation suitable for sale through the medical profession. Full details of the offer appear in the advertisement which is printed on page 45a of this issue. We can guarantee to our readers that any communication made to the advertiser in question will be treated with perfect fairness and in the strictest confidence.

A Captivating Postal Card Offer.

For an investment of $7 the enterprising druggist can obtain an effective display stand, in the form of a revolving rack, together with 625 cards, retailing at $15.75, making a net profit of $8.75 on the investment. Druggists who will guarantee transportation charges may have one of these sent on approval by applying to Joseph Koehler, Department A, 150 Park Row, New York. Mr. Koehler has also four other combination offers, involving an outlay of from $5 to $50, which he would like to lay before our readers. Write him for particulars.

"Listen to Petz."

This is the cabalistic title of the clever little booklet describing the Petz corner post and transom bar, patents for which are owned by the Detroit Show Case Company, of which Mr. Petz is the president. These devices enable the maker to present a show case or a show window which has the largest possible amount of uninterrupted glass surface consistent with stability. If you have not already received a copy of this little booklet write at once for one to the Detroit Show Case Company, Detroit, Mich. It is an interesting study in clever advertising.

May the Best Man Win.

A drug journal deprecating "the inability of the N. A. R. D. to hold its members in line" on various resolutions wails because it has seen in drug store windows a malted milk product not made by the malted milk company which gave the N. A. R. D. $1,000 or such a matter a year or two ago. With great severity it quotes the N. A. R. D. committee on trademarks to the effect that druggists should refuse to handle the "imitation" article.

To *The New Idea* malted milk would appear very much like cheese or pianos or sarsaparilla in that any one who has sense enough and knows how has a right to make and sell it; and it is just as foolish to call one malted milk an imitation of another as to say that a colt is an imitation of a horse because the horse is older. Doubtless it would be conceded that other things being equal the colt has a right to exist. And you can bet your old straw hat that if malted milk company No. 1 could establish in court the imitation so glibly talked about, it would get a judgment for damages and an injunction that would put malted milk company No. 2 out of the running in double-quick time. *The New Idea* doesn't care a straw one way or the other, but the inconsistency of the proprietary attitude is so plain as to make all this talk about "imitations" tiresome. Add to that the fact that the courts have had a say and the further fact that it is no drug journal's business if a druggist chooses to handle a legitimate product, and it makes us feel like saying something. So we have.—*The New Idea.*

A New Capsule Plant.

The mechanical department of Eli Lilly & Co. is now designing and contracts will soon be let for the construction of an additional building to the plant at Indianapolis. A portion of this new building will be especially arranged for the manufacture of empty gelatine capsules. The present plant will be moved to the new building and additional machinery placed to increase the output severalfold. As heretofore, the product of the capsule department will be limited strictly to prescription capsules. The cheaper grades will not be made.

Other portions of this new building, together with the quarters vacated by the old capsule plant, will make it possible to enlarge a number of other departments to meet the increasing demands for the products of the Red Lilly laboratories.

Signs of Spring.

One of the unfailing signs of spring in the drug trade is the blossoming of the Gem Spoon Company, of Troy, N. Y., into verse. The latest effusion, which forms part of the little valentine they sent out to the trade, reads thus:

Can cherished memories be forgot
And need I say forget-me-not,
When each fond impulse felt for you
You've met with impulse warm and true?

Tho' the skies o'ercast have been,
Thou hast ever proved a frien',
Since first we met thou'st been a boon
To comfort me, my old Gem Spoon.

A companion piece to the Gem Ice Cream Spoon is an ice cream scraper, which is intended to remove the surplus cream from the bowl of the spoon. This can be readily adjusted to any position in the can or packer. For descriptive matter write the Gem Spoon Company, Troy, N. Y., mentioning the AMERICAN DRUGGIST.

A Vest Pocket Lighter.

The International Auto and Yacht Agency, 119-121 Nassau street, New York City, which has been marketing a line of imported French automobile accessories, is now placing for sale a novel and practical vest pocket lighter which is ignited by air and is guaranteed to answer all purposes of general use.

The construction of the perpetual Le Radium Lighter, model No. 3, is simple, consisting of a highly polished metal tube, 2¼ inches in length, with a screw cap. Upon removing the cap a metal standard is exposed to view. Fastened to the under side of this is an igniting pellet, or "pilole," and suspended from this are several fine platinum wires. When this is exposed to the air (by the simple act of removing the cap) the ignited apparatus will glow with heat, and the "glowing stone" will cause the wires to flame the wick and immediately burst into a small, strong, steady flame. Upon simply replacing the cap, thus cutting off the air, the flame and all the heat will instantly die out and can be immediately and safely replaced in the vest pocket.

The above sole importer of this practical novelty is now delivering trade orders to druggists and will mail a single one complete, postpaid, to any individual upon receipt of 50 cents, which sum will be refunded if the lighter is not as represented.

The Le Radium Lighter is a great convenience to sportsmen, canoeists, yachtsmen, autoists, etc., as it is not affected by rain, snow or strong wind. Testimonials to this effect will be sent upon request.

It is of great convenience to any one who uses matches, as it will light lamps, gas, give light as a night lamp in the dark, etc. As a novelty it is supreme, for it will mystify every one, because of being ignited by simple air without any mechanical help. With ordinary care it is indestructible and perpetual.

The International Auto and Yacht Agency, 119-121 Nassau street, New York City, solicits correspondence from all interested.

Hints to Buyers.

Nearly all cough syrups have a tendency to produce constipation, owing to the fact that they contain opiates or astringent drugs. Kennedy's Laxative Honey and Tar contains no opium, morphine, codeine or heroine and is a gentle yet an effective laxative. It expels all cold from the system, relieves coughs and stimulates the bronchial tubes. Write for introductory terms to the E. C. De Witt Company, 203 La Salle avenue, Chicago.

J. A. Hynes, 292 South Marshfield avenue, Chicago, has collected and published in a 64-page pamphlet the pharmacy examination questions of the various States and territories, together with the laws of the respective States. This pamphlet will be an invaluable guide to students about to take the State examinations. A copy will be sent by Mr. Hynes, postage prepaid, on receipt of 75 cents.

A. H. Wirz, of 913 Cherry street, Philadelphia, manufactures a large line of metal goods for the drug trade, including bottle stoppers for cork and screw-neck liquid and powder bottles, collapsible tubes, hand pill machines, hand pill compressors, suppository and bougie molds and metal syringes. These goods are all carried in stock by wholesale druggists. The New York representative is Frank P. Wisner, with offices at 26 Cliff street.

The thing that assures the druggist a good profit nowadays always appeals to him. Abbott's Effervescent Saline Laxative, made by the Abbott Alkaloidal Company, of Chicago, belongs to the category of money makers. Thousands of druggists are dispensing it at a big profit. One thing should be borne in mind—namely, this article is being advertised constantly in the best medical journals and has the confidence of the medical profession. Every druggist knows what that means and should keep a supply on hand. The retail prices are 25 cents, 50 cents and $1. It is supplied by all leading jobbers. For particulars address the Abbott Alkaloidal Company, Ravenswood, Chicago.

Lythol is an antiseptic mouth wash free from acid. Druggists are frequently requested to furnish such a preparation and they can recommend this particular preparation with safety. It is made by Hudson & Co., 489 Fifth avenue, New York, and is invaluable in catarrhal conditions of the mucous membranes. Write to the makers for introductory terms and descriptive literature mentioned in the AMERICAN DRUGGIST.

An Attractive Window Display of Borden's Malted Milk.

We illustrate herewith a window display of Louis P. Horning, Elizabeth, N. J., which has attracted a great deal of favorable attention. This display consisted mainly of cartons, fastened together with small staples in such a way that the structure is quite substantial. In making the arch the base of the carton is fastened with the staples and one of the top flaps is left out and inserted under the top of the adjoining carton, where it is fastened with a pin. Red cheese-cloth furnishes an excellent and effective background for the cartons and the cutouts, both of which are furnished by the Borden's Condensed Milk Company free of cost to druggists who carry their malted milk in stock. Write them for full description of the display.

"Freezing the Summer."

In writing of the hot weather the American Soda Fountain Company says that the soda water dealer who is far-sighted enough to "freeze the summer" and "thaw the winter" in his store is sure to win a high rating in Bradstreet's. There is no question but that a soda counter can either draw or drive away trade, according to the manner in which it is operated.

In winter the steaming broth, the hot cup of chocolate and the warm atmosphere near the door will put the customer in a pleased purchasing frame of mind quicker than anything else; and in the hot summer time a sweet, cool air and sanitary marble counter and fixtures, coupled with plenty of ice and the sight of cold drinks, will so refresh and stimulate the heat-tired flow of customers that other departments, as well as the soda counter, will be benefited.

If proof of this is desired nothing more convincing could be found than the success of the American Soda Fountain Company in their work along this line.

While they have devoted a wonderful amount of attention to the perfecting of high-type labor and material-saving machines and fixtures, perhaps the greatest reason for their unusual success is the keen appreciation of things that attract the public, aside from good service and high quality of drinks.

The summer days are coming quickly and it would be well to think these things over in planning for summer business. The more you can attract people who come into your store, the more you are doing to increase business.

Popularity and Price Protection

POPULARITY

LAXATIVE BROMO QUININE originated as the first product of its kind and through merit and continuous extensive advertising it has become an absolutely staple article.

PRICE PROTECTION

The terms and discounts on LAXATIVE BROMO QUININE from the beginning have afforded a most liberal profit, and now, by the adoption of the DIRECT CONTRACT AND SERIAL NUMBERING PLAN, this profit is absolutely insured to the retail dealer. The support of this Plan by the Retail Drug Trade demands, simply, that EVERY INDIVIDUAL Druggist shall sign the contract. Those who have not done so should sign and have the contract properly recorded without further delay.

LAXATIVE BROMO QUININE

Price $1.75 per dozen.

6 dozen lots,	1 dozen free,	. . . .	Cost $10.50 or	$1.50 per dozen
12 dozen lots,	2 dozen free,	5 per cent. trade discount,	" 19.95 or	1.43 " "
36 dozen lots,	6 dozen free,	8 per cent. trade discount,	" 57.96 or	1.38 " "
60 dozen lots,	10 dozen free,	10 per cent. trade discount,	" 94.50 or	1.35 " "

WHOLESALE DRUGGISTS WILL ACCEPT ORDERS UNDER THIS DATING OFFER.

PARIS MEDICINE COMPANY,

SAINT LOUIS AND LONDON.

An Attractive Novelty Display Case.

John Phillips & Co., Limited, of Detroit, have devised a novelty display case which is intended for use on top of other showcases and which is most effective for displaying those little novelties which form so profitable a branch of the average druggist's stock. It is 13½ inches wide, 13½ inches high and 25¾ inches long and is finished with oxidized copper frames, glass top, front, sides and shelf, and with mirror back. It costs only $6.50 and pays for itself in a very short time. Write for full description to John Phillips & Co., Limited, mentioning the AMERICAN DRUGGIST.

Wire Furniture for the Soda Department.

Wire furniture is just the thing for the soda department. Alexander H. Revell & Co., Rees and Hawthorne streets, Chicago, make many attractive designs in wire furniture and those of our readers who have not seen Revell's catalogue should write to them at once for a copy. When writing for it please mention the AMERICAN DRUGGIST.

Business Magnets.

The New England Confectionery Company, of Boston, makes a line of specially high class goods for sale to the retail drug trade. A line of these business magnets will not only make your candy counter a good paying department, but will add to the popularity of your establishment with that large portion of the community which has a sweet tooth. Some of their specialties are: Lenox chocolates, Peerless wafers, 5-lb. and 5c. packages; druggist gum drops, violet pastilles, 5c. packages; violet pastilles, 10c. packages; carnation pastilles, 5c. packages; carnation pastilles, 10c. packages.

For full particular regarding these business magnets address the New England Confectionery Company, of Boston, Mass., mentioning the AMERICAN DRUGGIST.

"Goods with a Conscience."

The old house of E. R. Squibb & Sons is thoroughly justified in describing its products as "goods with a conscience." Its line of pharmaceutical preparations, medicinal chemicals and drugs and medicinal tablets represents goods of the highest quality manufactured in the most scientific manner. That these are facts thoroughly appreciated by both physician and druggist is shown by the fact that the house has constantly had to increase its manufacturing facilities.

Mason's Essence of Beef

is an English preparation that has been successfully prescribed by the medical profession of Great Britain and used in the leading English hospitals for many years. It is now being made in this country by the Mason Concentrated Food Company, and several of New York's prominent physicians indorse it as being the purest and most nourishing beef preparation ever brought to the notice of the medical world. For introductory terms address the Mason Concentrated Food Company, 1906 Broadway, New York, mentioning the AMERICAN DRUGGIST.

Only the Best Will Do.

The standing of any particular soda fountain in the estimation of the consumer of this cooling and healthful beverage is determined for all time by the first glass drunk. There are always new people dropping in at every soda counter, and it is therefore essential that every glass that is dispensed should be up to the highest possible standard and should be served in the best possible manner. The public has been educated in the matter of soda water drinks so that they know and appreciate good soda. This field is one in which you cannot hope to fool the public, even for a portion of the time. Therefore the druggist must take good care to get and serve only the best supplies and to serve them from the best and most artistic fountain obtainable. The American Soda Fountain Company, of Boston, puts forth vigorous claims that their "Innovation" fountain is the "last word" in fountain improvement. Certain it is that this fountain is a beauty and that many of its purchasers are enthusiastic in its praises as a business getter and a money maker. The American Soda Fountain Company will be glad to send to our readers some interesting facts about different styles in soda fountains and to offer help and suggestions as to how others have won great successes and how our readers may follow their example. Their new catalogue should be in every druggist's business library. Write to them for a copy.

Lehn & Fink Buy Another Building.

Albert Plaut, partner in the firm of Lehn & Fink, has announced the purchase by his company of the property at 118 William street, adjacent to its present offices, at 120 William street and 79 John street. The new property includes a three-story stone and brick building, on a lot 25 x 127 feet, adjoining Lehn & Fink's whitestone building in William street and abutting on the extension of the same structure which faces on John street.

The newly acquired building is now occupied by Benedict & Highet, paper and twine dealers, and several sign painting concerns. The property was bought of the McCrea estate, and it is understood that the entire structure will soon be altered to suit the purposes of Lehn & Fink. Mr. Plaut says that part of the present building will be immediately used as a storage warehouse, but adds that the firm is considering the advisability of making extensive alterations in the structure within the near future. It is expected that such alterations will include tearing down the walls separating the building now occupied by the firm and that which it has just acquired, but Mr. Plaut says the plans of the firm have not yet matured sufficiently to admit that such a change is contemplated.

The Kismet Tumbler Holder.

There is shown in this connection a cut of the latest soda fountain novelty. It is known as the "Kismet" holder and is the newest thing in holders. It is being put on the market by the Kismet Specialty Company, 21 Park Row, New York.

The Kismet holder is suitable for soda glasses, ginger ale bottles, coffee and chocolate cups, etc. Made in one piece, there is nothing to come apart. The manufacturer claims for it that it is the most durable holder, because there is no soldering or brazing, no joints, pins or rivets. It is a thoroughly up-to-date holder. It is easy to clean, there being no pockets or corners for the dirt to lodge in.

In these days, when so much is being said and written about the necessity for absolute cleanliness as the first essential in conducting a soda fountain, the Kismet holder should at once appeal to every soda water man in the country. The Kismet Specialty Company claims that its holder is the only sanitary holder made. Another good point is that it is light in weight and still strong—it is impossible to break it. Another feature which should commend itself to the soda water trade is that it is instantly adjustable to a glass of any shape or size. Write for prices to the Kismet Specialty Company, 21 Park Row, New York.

Check Your Soda Fountain Sales.

The Lock-Stub Check Company, of 136 West Thirty-fourth street, New York, offers its first-class checking system to the consideration of the readers of the AMERICAN DRUGGIST in this issue. This system is considered the best possible means of checking soda fountain and ice cream receipts. As the advertiser says "carelessness and dishonesty are frailties of human nature," which statement is borne out by the experience of very many druggists. To many thoughtful druggists the soda fountain has become almost the measure of success in pharmacy, and if carelessness and dishonesty in its administration are not eliminated the success will be of doubtful commercial value and the failure be all the more intensified. We earnestly commend the attention of our readers to the company's advertisement in this issue.

BUY A GROSS AND SAVE 5 and 2½ PER CENT.

THE KIND YOU HAVE ALWAYS HANDLED

IT PAYS TO HANDLE RELIABLE GOODS

$33.60 Per Gross — Jobbers Sell in Gross Lots, 5 Per Cent. and 2½ Per Cent. OFF. — **$2.80 Per Dozen**

THIS IS THE GENUINE

Send for Cards, Cartons and Counter Wrappers.

THE CENTAUR COMPANY,
77 Murray Street, New York City.

Chas H. Fletcher President.

BUY A GROSS AND SAVE 5 and 2½ PER CENT.

——Who can't sell 12 dozen per annum?——

A BAG OF GOLD

IN the magic of the day's performance of business it is Gold we want. But gold sometimes comes in the shape of Opportunity. Take this one on our guarantee of satisfaction: We offer to send you our full line of Souvenir Post Cards with privilege to return all cards not wanted, after examination. Address:

The Souvenir Post Card Company
80 Franklin Street New York City

SYRINGE BOXES

Of White Wood, Bass, Oak, Ash, &c.

Fine Work Low Prices Prompt Shipments. — *Estimates and Samples Furnished on Application*

Also any other kind of fancy wood boxes made to order. Extensive facilities enable us to guarantee satisfaction.

HENRY H. SHEIP MFG. CO.,
529-35 Columbia Avenue. PHILADELPHIA.
Cable Address—Sheip, Phila., Western Union Code.

THE "KISMET" HOLDER

LATEST

SODA FOUNTAIN NOVELTY.

The Kismet Holder is the newest thing in holders. It is suitable for Soda Glasses, Ginger Ale Bottles, Coffee and Chocolate Cups, etc.

Being all in one piece there is nothing to come apart. This holder is the most durable because there is **no soldering or brazing; no joints, pins or rivets.** It is the only **up-to-date** holder made—**easiest to clean**—no pockets for dirt to gather in.

THE ONLY SANITARY HOLDER MADE

THE "KISMET" HOLDER

Yet it is **light in weight and so strong**—you can't break it. Instantly **adjustable** to a glass of any shape or size. **Unique design,** and **cannot** be **surpassed** in **simplicity, efficiency** and **low cost.**

Heavily Nickel Plated	$4.50 a Doz.
" Silver "	7.00 "
" Gold "	12.00 "

Money back if you want it, but you wont want it. Remit by express or money order to Kismet Specialty Co. References: R. G. Dun & Co., New York.

KISMET SPECIALTY COMPANY,
21 Park Row, NEW YORK.

Another Reason or Two Why.

An unusually clever circular reaches us from the press of the Liquid Carbonic Company which we would commend to the careful study of every enterprising druggist. It embraces several novel features, the most taking of which is a detachable post card, giving instructions to the Liquid Carbonic Company to forward estimates on a Liquid carbonator. Write for one of these if you have not already received one to the Liquid Carbonic Company, Chicago, mentioning the AMERICAN DRUGGIST. Both in form and manner it offers valuable suggestions to advertisers.

Hypodermic Needles Free of Cost.

We are advised by the Randall-Faichney Company, maker of the R. & B. hypodermic needles, that it will extend the time for distribution of sample needles to doctors for a limited season. This enterprising manufacturer has undoubtedly done much to place the hypodermic trade on a high professional basis, and where years ago "any old thing" would do, through its energy and the actual merits of its goods, its best hypodermic needle has forced itself into a position where nothing will do but the R. & B. It will be good policy for druggists to get in touch with the Randall-Faichney Company on its free sampling proposition. Address it at Boston, Mass., asking for details of its free distribution offer.

Contains No Dangerous Drugs.

The agitation against all proprietary medicines during the past year has decreased the sale of a number of popular remedies. However, the business of Foley & Co. is a notable exception, as they are one of the large proprietors whose business shows an increase this season. They attribute this to the fact that their remedies do not contain opiates or injurious drugs of any kind, and notwithstanding their enormous sale, have not been attacked. This firm's advertising is unusually effective, and they have among other things a very attractive lithographed window display, which they are pleased to send to druggists prepaid upon request.

A Bag of Gold.

If some one should hand you a bag of gold, would you take it? Of course you would. If the gold was not handed to you, but was within easy reach, wouldn't you be willing to exert yourself to obtain it? Of course you would. We call your attention to the advertisement of the Druggists' Own Paper Company, 170 South Canal street, Chicago, in this issue. They are not going to hand you a bag of gold, but they would like to assist you in obtaining the gold that is within your reach, but which you will never get unless you go after it. They have just issued an advertising text-book for progressive retail druggists, entitled "Push the Sale of Your Own Preparations." It tells you how to obtain more business and increased profits and, therefore, a bag of gold. If you will attach one of your labels to a postal and mention AMERICAN DRUGGIST they will send you a copy of the book free. Send for it to-day; you may be too busy to-morrow and forget it by the day after. The book is well worth reading.

The Men and the Methods of the "Liquid."

Though its corporate existence only dates back as far as 1888, the Liquid Carbonic Company has grown during its 17 years to proportions which it is hard for the average retail druggist to appreciate. The president and moving spirit of the company, Jacob Baur, is an old druggist, having graduated from the Philadelphia College of Pharmacy in the year 1881. He has shown his interest in scientific affairs by maintaining his membership in the American Pharmaceutical Association, the Society of Chemical Industry and various other scientific associations. Associated with Mr. Baur in the enterprise are Charles Minshall, vice-president; Oscar Baur, general superintendent; C. F. Rauchfauss, secretary and sales manager, and a host of bright, energetic men. Though so comparatively young, the Liquid Carbonic Company has upward of 17 factories and has active sales establishments in 11 different cities. Only two years ago the company erected as a home office building an eight-story structure, covering 110 x 118 feet and occupying nearly three-fourths of the block inclosed by Wells, Michigan, Franklin and Illinois streets, Chicago, and have still further added to their productive capacity by the erection of a soda fountain factory on North Wells street, which covers an entire city block. Their products embrace everything "touchin' on and appertainin' to" the sale of soda water, from the most elaborate onyx fountain to the spoon that stirs the beef tea. Their fresh fruit products embrace many novelties, and the druggist whose business library does not include a "Liquid" catalogue may count himself poor indeed.

Photographing Kittens.

Every amateur photographer must at some time have fallen under the charm which a graceful kitten exercises for photographers and artists. We illustrate herewith one of a very attractive series of post cards in which kittens constitute the models. These picture cards are unusually lifelike and natural and will undoubtedly prove very profitable sellers. The value of these post cards is enhanced by appropriate and humorous titles printed on each. The series will undoubtedly prove very profitable sellers, particularly among the young folk, and our readers would do well to write to the Rotograph Company, 684 Broadway, New York, for samples, which will be sent free of charge if the AMERICAN DRUGGIST is mentioned in writing.

The Free Sample Bottle Nuisance.

So many complaints have been made by druggists in regard to the way in which some proprietary medicine houses are imposing on the druggists with their sample campaigns that we are particularly glad to-day to call the attention of the retail trade to the methods pursued by the D. D. D. Company, of Chicago. This company, manufacturing a reliable remedy for eczema, D. D. D. Prescription, is now conducting a sweeping sample bottle campaign which extends from one end of the country to the other. Instead of asking the druggists to help them in any way they are shouldering all the work and expense themselves by sending the bottles direct postpaid to the patients, then referring customers to the druggists, thus helping the retailer. In fact, the sample bottle campaign is creating a demand for D. D. D. Prescription in every town and hamlet in the United States and the live druggist will be quick to appreciate this and foster its sales.

D. D. D. Prescription is an especially good article in stock, because when it is once introduced it is a con[illegible] peater and the sales on it become easier and easier. [illegible] heard of many cases where a druggist secured eczema [illegible] on D. D. D. Prescription and sold them from 50 to 1[illegible] at a profit to himself of $16.66 to $33.33. This was in [illegible] chronic cases. But the great majority are cured w[illegible] bottles and then tell their friends, so that a steady s[illegible] secured. The real reason for this success is the gen[illegible] of the remedy itself. Retailers may secure this re[illegible] their jobbers on a maintenance of price basis. Write [illegible] the D. D. D. Company, 116 Michigan street, Chicago f[illegible]

In China eggs are considered a delicacy only when [illegible] decidedly "ancient." They reach perfection when [illegible] become almost completely green, the result of several [illegible] burial in chalk or sawdust. The price for such eggs ri[illegible] given in this country for the choicest wines.

Alphabetical Index to Advertisers.

Where numbers are omitted, the advertisement appears in alternate issues.

For Classified Index see pages 24 and 25.)

ORIGINAL PACKAGE PRICES.

It should be understood that the prices quoted in this column are strictly those current in the wholesale market, and that higher prices are paid for retail lots. The quality of goods frequently necessitates a considerable range of prices.

Drugs, Chemicals, &c.

Acetanilid	lb.	.24	@	.25
Acetate of Lime:				
Brown	100 lb.	1.60	@	1.65
Gray	100 lb.	2.35	@	2.40
Acetone	lb.	.15½	@	.16
Acid:				
Acetic Com'l	100 lb.	2.40	@	2.63
Acetic C. P.	lb.	.21	@	.23
Acetic, Glacial		.30	@	.33½
Aquafortis, 36°	lb.	.03½	@	.04½
" 40°	lb.	...	@	.05½
Benzoic, Ger	lb.	.30	@	.38
" Eng	oz.	.10	@	.10½
Boric, Cryst	lb.	.10	@	.10½
powd	lb.	.10	@	.10½
Carbol, cryst., blk	lb.	.11	@	.15
lb. bottle	lb.	.20	@	.22
Chrysophanic		2.50	@	2.63
Citric, dom	lb.	.41	@	.41½
Gallic	lb.	.53	@	.55
Muriatic C. P.	lb.	.07½	@	.08½
Nitric C. P.	lb.	.07½	@	.10
Oxalic, English	lb.	.06½	@	.15½
Phosphoric	lb.	.18	@	.22½
Picric	lb.	.30	@	.35
Pyrogallic	lb.	1.63	@	...
Salicylic	lb.	.31	@	.34
Sulphuric, 66%	lb.	.01½	@	.02
Tartaric, crystals	lb.	.27½	@	.28½
powdered	lb.	.28	@	.28½
Tannic, cryst	lb.	.58	@	.65
Alcohol, grain	gal.	2.47	@	2.49
Molasses		2.45	@	2.47
wood, 95-97%	gal.	.70	@	.75
Aloin	lb.	.45	@	.50
Alum, Lump	100 lb.	1.75	@	1.80
Ground	100 lb.	1.80	@	1.85
Ammon, carb.		.08½	@	.08¾
" bromide, bulk		.23	@	.24
" iodide, bulk		4.75	@	4.80
Aniline Oil		.09	@	.09½
Salt		.08½	@	.08¾
Antipyrine (New)	oz.	...	@	.18
Arrowroot, Bermuda	lb.	.38	@	.40
St. Vincent, in bbl.	lb.	.05½	@	.06
Arsenic: Red Saxon	lb.	.06½	@	.07
White	lb.	.07	@	.10
Balm of Gilead Buds	lb.	.33	@	.35
Balsam Copaiba, Cent. Amer	lb.	.30	@	.33
Para	lb.	.40	@	.42
Fir, Canada	gal.	3.10	@	3.20
Fir, Oregon	gal.	.70	@	.80
Peru	lb.	1.00	@	1.05
Tolu	lb.	.20	@	.23
Bark, Angostura	lb.	.35	@	.40
Buckthorn	lb.	.05	@	.05½
Cascara Sag	lb.	.05½	@	.09
Cascarilla	lb.	.10	@	.14
Cotton root	lb.	.08½	@	.10
Cramp	lb.	.07	@	.09
Elm, select	lb.	.18	@	.20
Pine, white	lb.	.05	@	.06
Prickly Ash	lb.	.11	@	.12
Sassafras	lb.	.13½	@	.14
Soap—whole	lb.	.05	@	.05½
Crushed	lb.	.05½	@	.06
White Pine	lb.	.04½	@	.05
Wild Cherry	lb.	.06	@	.08
Bismuth, citrate	lb.	1.75	@	1.80
" ammon cit.	lb.	1.85	@	1.90
" subnit	blk.	1.50	@	1.55
" subcarb	lb.	1.75	@	1.80
" subgallate	lb.	1.85	@	1.90
Bleaching Powder, Eng		.01½	@	.01¾
German R.		.01½	@	.01¾
Domestic		.01	@	.01¼
Blue Vitriol	lb.	.05½	@	.06
Borax, Refined	lb.	.07½	@	.07¾
powd. conc	lb.	.07½	@	.08
crystals	lb.	.07½	@	.07¾
Brimstone, crude 2d	ton.	22.00	@	...
Bromine, bulk	lb.	.22	@	.25
Burgundy Pitch	lb.	.01	@	.01½
Cacao Butter, blk		.24½	@	.30
" " 12 lb. boxes		.34	@	.35
Caffeine	lb.	...	@	2.75
Calcium hypophosphite	lb.	.60	@	.64
Cantharides, Chinese	lb.	...	@	.75
" powd	lb.	.75	@	.77
Russian, whole	lb.	1.25	@	1.30
Cassia Buds	lb.	.18½	@	.19½
Castor Oil, No. 1, bbl.	lb.	.11	@	12
" " No. 1, cases	lb.	.11½	@	.12½
" " No. 3, bbl.	lb.	.10½	@	.11½
" " No 3, cases	lb.	.10½	@	.11¾
Caustic Soda	100 lb.	1.70	@	1.75
Chalk, Eng. Precip., bulk	lb.	.06	@	...
Chloral Hydrate, crystals, bulk	lb.	...	@	0.85
crusts, blk	lb.	...	@	0.93
Chloroform, bulk	lb.	.25	@	.30
Cinchonidine Sulph	oz.	.12	@	.15
Cocaine Muriate	oz.	3.25	@	3.50
Codeine Sulph	oz.	3.20	@	3.40
Cod Liver Oil, Norweg.	bbl.	20.00	@	25.00
Newfoundland	bbl.	...	@	20.00
Colocynth, Trieste	lb.	.30	@	.32
Spanish	lb.	.25	@	.28
Copperas, car lots	100 lb.	.47½	@	.52
single bbls	100 lb.	.57½	@	.65
Creosote, Beechwood		.85	@	.90
Cream Tartar lb.	powd.	.22½	@	.23
Cubeb berries, xx	lb.	.09	@	.10
Powdered	lb.	.11	@	.13
Cutch, bales	lb.	.07½	@	.08
boxes	lb.	.05	@	.05½
Cuttle Bone, Trieste	lb.	.16½	@	.17
French	lb.	.12	@	.13
Jewelers', large	lb.	.70	@	...
" small	lb.	.40	@	.45
Dextrin	lb.	.05½	@	.06
Divi Divi	ton.	30.00	@	45.00
Dragon's B'l'd, lump	lb.	.15	@	.18
In reeds	lb.	.50	@	.55
Epsom Salts	100 lb.	.85	@	1.00
Ergot, German	lb.	.31	@	.32
Spanish	lb.	.34	@	.35
Ergotine, Dom	lb.	4.95	@	5.00
Flowers, Arnica	lb.	.09	@	.10

Flowers—cont'd	Unit	Price		Price
Calendula	lb.	.25	@	.30
Chamomile, Roman	lb.	.16	@	.22
German	lb.	.10	@	.15
Hungarian	lb.	.09½	@	.11
Insect, open	lb.	.15	@	.17
Half closed	lb.	.28	@	.33
Closed	lb.	.26	@	...
Powder	lb.	.14	@	.22
Lavender	lb.	.12	@	.13
Select	lb.	.13	@	.20
Saffron, Amer	lb.	1.25	@	...
Spanish Alicante	lb.	4.75	@	6.00
" Valencia	lb.	8.00	@	8.50
Formaldehyde	lbs.	.09	@	.09½
Glauber Salt	per 100 lb.	.40	@	.60
Glycerin, C. P. drums	lb.	.11½	@	.11¾
" cans	lb.	.12½	@	.12¾
Grains of Paradise	lb.	.11½	@	.15
Guarana	lb.	.70	@	.75
Gums: Aloes, Cape		.08	@	.10
" Barbadoes	lb.	.14	@	.16
" Curacoa		.06	@	.06½
" Socot	lb.	.18	@	.20
Arabic, 1st pkd	lb.	.30	@	...
" 2d pkd	lb.	.19	@	.23
" sorts	lb.	.06½	@	.11
Asafoetida	lb.	.15	@	.22
Benzoin, Sumatra	lb.	.34	@	.38
Siam	lb.	.90	@	1.00
Camphor, ref'd, blk	lb.	1.00	@	..
cases	lb.	1.00½	@	...
Chicle	lb.	.36	@	.38
Gamboge	lb.	1.15	@	1.20
Guaiac	lb.	.17	@	.23
Kino	lb.	.35	@	.38
Mastic	lb.	.46	@	.48
Myrrh	lb.	.25	@	.28
Olibanum	lb.	.10	@	.15
Sandarac	lb.	.14	@	.18
Senegal, pkd	lb.	.11	@	.13
Tragacanth, Aleppo	lb.	.50	@	.65
Tragacanth, Turkey	lb.	.35	@	.90
Haarlem Oil		3.00	@	3.75
Hypophosphite lime	lb.	.48	@	.50
" potash	lb.	.48	@	.50
" soda	lb.	.48	@	.50
Ichthyol	lb.	4.00	@	4.25
Indigo	lb.	.90	@	1.75
Insect Pwd. pure	lb.	.14	@	.25
Iodine, resub		2.70	@	2.75
Iodoform	lb.	3.00	@	3.05
Iron citrate, U. S. P.	lb.	...	@	.44
" and ammon. cit.	lb.	...	@	.41
and ammon. citrate (green scales)				
and quinine citrate	lb.	1.18	@	1.23
phosphate, scales	lb.	...	@	.38
pyrophosphate, scales	lb.	...	@	.38
quinine and strychnine citrate	lb.	1.68	@	1.73
Isinglass, Amer	lb.	.75	@	.80
Russian	lb.	4.00	@	4.10
Juniper Berries	lb.	.03½	@	.04
Lanoline	lb.	.60	@	.65
Leaves: Aconite		.09	@	.10
Belladonna	lb.	.10	@	.11
Buchu, short	lb.	.17	@	.20
" long	lb.	.45	@	.50
Cannabis Indica, tops	lb.	1.00	@	1.10
Coca, Truxillo	lb.	.17	@	.18
" Huanuco	lb.	.30	@	.32
Damiana	lb.	.08	@	.10
Digitalis	lb.	.08½	@	.09
Grindelia robusta	lb.	.08	@	.09
Horehound	lb.	.04½	@	.06
Hyoscyamus	lb.	.07	@	.08
Jaborandi	lb.	.14	@	.15
Pulsatilla		.07½	@	11
Rose, Red	lb.	.65	@	.70
Senna, pkd whole	lb.	.30	@	.32
Alexandria, natural	lb.	...	@	...
garbled and sifted	lb.	.15	@	.16
Tinnevelly	lb.	.04	@	.09
Alexandria, siftings	lb.	.05½	@	.06
Stramonium	lb.	.08	@	.08½
Uva ursi	lb.	.06½	@	.06¾
Yerba Santa	lb.	.07	@	.07½
Liquorice—mass	lb.	.08	@	.10
Spanish	lb.	.14	@	.20
Imported mass Spanish	lb.	.18	@	.24
Stick, Calabria	lb.	.25	@	.26
Domestic	lb.	.16½	@	.22½
Lithia, carbonate	lb.	1.50	@	1.75
" citrate	lb.	1.15	@	1.25
Lupulin, Ger	lb.	.18	@	.25
Lycopodium	lb.	.51	@	.53
Magnesia, carb	lb.	.12	@	.15
Manna, large flk	lb.	.45	@	.50
Small flake	lb.	.33	@	.35
Menthol, Japanese	lb.	2.40	@	2.60
Mercurials:				
Blue Pill	lb.	.43	@	.45
Calomel	lb.	.77	@	.79
Corr. Sublim	lb.	.70	@	.72
Mercury and Chalk	lb.	.33	@	.34
Ointment, ¼	lb.	.47	@	.48
Ointment, ½	lb.	.38	@	.39
Red Precip	lb.	.87	@	.89
White "	lb.	.92	@	.94
Morphine, bulk	oz.	2.25	@	2.50
Eighths	oz.	2.45	@	2.50
Moss, Iceland	lb.	.05	@	.06
Irish	lb.	.06½	@	.08
Irish, bleached	lb.	.09½	@	.10
Naphthaline, flake	lb.	.02	@	.02
Ball	lb.	.02	@	.02¼
Nux Vomica	lb.	.02½	@	.03
Oil, Anise	lb.	1.30	@	1.35
Almonds, bit, Eng	lb.	5.50	@	5.75
French	lb.	3.55	@	3.60
bit., artificial	lb.	.65	@	1.30
sweet, true	lb.	.37	@	.40
Peach kernels		.19	@	.22
Bay	lb.	2.10	@	2.25
22 oz. bots	bot.	3.25	@	3.35
Bergamot	lb.	2.15	@	2.30
Cajuput	lb.	.50	@	.52
Camphor	lb.	.17½	@	.19
Caraway	lb.	1.18	@	1.40
Cassia 75@80%	lb	.77½	@	.78

Oils—cont'd.	Unit	Price		Price
Cedar, pure	lb.	60.	@	1.65
red	lb.	.21	@	.25
Citronella	lb.	.40	@	.42
Clove, bud		.82½	@	.85
Copaiba	lb.	.60	@	.70
Coriander	lb.	5.00	@	11.00
Croton	lb.	.75	@	.80
Cubeb	lb.	.90	@	1.00
Eucalyptus	lb.	.40	@	.60
Geranium	lb.	1.60	@	4.75
Lavender, flowers	lb.	2.00	@	2.25
Lemon	lb.	.60	@	.75
Lemongrass	lb.	3.00	@	3.10
Mustard	lb.	4.25	@	5.25
Myrbane	lb.	.07	@	.08
Neroli	lb.	45.00	@	57.50
Nutmeg	lb.	.80	@	0.90
Orange, sweet	lb.	2.00	@	2.15
Orange, bitter	lb.	2.30	@	2.40
Origanum	lb.	.18	@	.22
Pennyroyal	lb.	1.15	@	1.25
Peppermint	lb.	2.60	@	2.75
Cases	lb.	3.20	@	3.25
Petit, grain, French	lb.	4.00	@	4.50
" " So. Amer.	lb.	2.00	@	2.05
Pimento	lb.	1.80	@	1.90
Rose	oz.	3.50	@	4.50
Rosemary	lb.	.62½	@	.80
Sandalwood	lb.	3.25	@	3.50
Sassafras	lb.	.50	@	.53
" Artificial	lb.	.23	@	.24
Safrol		.35	@	.36
Spearmint	lb.	4.75	@	5.00
Tansy	lb.	3.75	@	4.00
Thyme		1.00	@	1.20
Winterg'n, sweet birch		1.65	@	1.85
" Synthetic	lb.	.37	@	.40
Wood (Chinese)		.08	@	.09
Wormwood		3.25	@	3.50
Wormseed	lb.	3.00	@	3.25
Opium, Nat cases	lb.	2.80	@	2.85
" Ordinary, Job-		2.87½	@	2.90
" powdered	lb.	3.30	@	3.35
Orange peel, bit	lb.	.03	@	.04
Sweet	lb.	.04½	@	.10
Petrolatum		.05	@	.08
Phenacetine	oz.	.85	@	.95
Potassium acetate	lb.	.17	@	.18
" bromide		.15	@	.16
" bottles		.23	@	.30
bichromate		.08½	@	.08¾
chlorate, cryst		.09½	@	.09¾
" powd.		.10	@	.10½
cyanide		.20	@	.21
hypophosphite		.60	@	.64
iodide bulk		2.15	@	2.20
permanganate	lb.	.09½	@	.10½
Prickly Ash berries		.14	@	.16
Quicksilver flasks	lb.	.56	@	.60
Quinine Sulph., Domestic bulk	oz.	.18	@	.20
German, bulk	oz.	.17	@	.20
German, outside	oz.	.17	@	.18
Java, bulk	oz.	.17½	@	.18
Rochelle Salts	lb.	.20½	@	.21
Root, Aconite	lb.	.09½	@	.10
Alkanet	lb.	.08	@	.09
Althea, cut	lb.	.17	@	.18
Arnica	lb.	.08½	@	.09
Belladonna, Atropa	lb.	.10	@	.12
Blood	lb.	.10	@	.12
Calamus	lb.	.07	@	.08
Calamus, bleached	lb.	.22	@	.25
Colchicum	lb.	.12	@	.13
Calumba	lb.	.04	@	.05
Dandelion, Ger	lb.	.07½	@	.08
Galangal	lb.	.05	@	.05½
Gentian	lb.	.04	@	.04½
Ginger, Ja., blcd	lb.	...	@	.14
unbleached	lb.	.12	@	.14
Ginseng	lb.	6.00	@	7.50
Golden Seal	lb.	1.25	@	1.30
Hellebore, pwd	lb.	.05	@	.07
Helonias	lb.	.42	@	.45
Ipecac, Rio	lb.	1.75	@	1.80
Carthagena	lb.	1.75	@	1.80
Jalap	lb.	.10½	@	.11
Kava Kava	lb.	.11	@	.12
Liquorice, ord	lb.	.03½	@	.04
Select	lb.	.06½	@	.11
Lovage	lb	.55	@	.85
Mandrake	lb.	.04½	@	.05½
Musk, Russian	lb.	.13	@	.14
Orris, Florentine	lb.	.06	@	.07
Orris, Verona	lb.	.04	@	06
Pariera Brava	lb.	.10	@	.11
Pink	lb.	...	@	.75
Rhatany	lb.	.10	@	.12
Rhub., Canton	lb.	.35	@	.40
Shensi	lb.	.65	@	.75
Sars'p'la, Hond	lb.	.26	@	.30
Mexican	lb.	.09½	@	.09¾
Senega	lb.	.55	@	.60
Snake Virgina	lb.	.42	@	.45
Texas	lb.	.39	@	.42
Canada	lb.	13	@	.25
Squill	lb.	.13	@	.15
Valerian, Belg	lb.	.08	@	.08½
German	lb.	.12	@	.14
English	lb.	.12	@	.15
Salicine	lb.	3.75	@	4.00
Sal Ammon, lump	lb.	.09½	@	.09¾
Granulated	lb.	.05½	@	.06
Sal Soda, Eng	100 lb.	.67½	@	.72½
American	100 lb.	.75	@	.80
Salol	lb.	.90	@	.95
Saltpetre, crude	lb.	.04¼	@	.04½
Refined	lb.	.04½	@	.05½
Santonin, crystals	lb.	9.50	@	9.70
Powdered	lb.	9.70	@	9.90
Saw Palmetto Berries	lb.	.15	@	.20
Seed, Anise Ital	lb.	.08½	@	.10½
German	lb.	.06½	@	.07
Star	lb.	.20	@	.21
Canary, Smyrna	lb.	.04½	@	.04¾
Sicily	lb.	.04½	@	.05
Caraway	lb.	.06	@	.06¼
Celery	lb.	.07¾	@	.08
Cardamom blchd		.30	@	.70
" Decorticated	lb.	.30	@	.31
Colchicum	lb.	.21	@	.25
Coriander	lb.	9	@	10½

Seeds—cont'd.				
Bleached	lb.	.09½	@	.10½
Cummin	lb.	.06½	@	.07½
Fennel, Ger	lb.	.09	@	.10
" Italian	lb.	.05	@	.15½
Flax, whole	lb.	6.50	@	6.75
" ground	lb.	.03½	@	.03¾
Foenugreek	lb.	.02	@	.02½
Hemp, Rus	lb.	.03	@	.03½
Millet, nat	lb.	.01½	@	.02
" shld	lb.	.04½	@	.04½
Mustard, Cal. brown	lb.	.04½	@	.04½
Trieste, brown	lb.	.08	@	.08½
Bari, brown	lb.	.04½	@	.05
German, brown	lb.	.02½	@	.03
Western, brown	lb.	.01½	@	.02
Cal. yellow	lb.	.04½	@	.04½
Eng. yellow	lb.	.05	@	.05½
Ger. yellow	lb.	.05½	@	.05¾
Poppy, blue	lb.	.05½	@	.06
Quince, Ger	lb.	.32	@	.34
Rape, Ger	lb.	.02½	@	.03
" Eng	lb.	.04	@	.05
" Amer	lb.	.02½	@	.03
Strophanthus		.45	@	.50
Kombé		1.00	@	1.25
Sunflower		.04½	@	.05
Wormseed, American	lb.	.07	@	.08
" Levant	lb.	.17	@	.20
Seidlitz, Mixture	lb.	.17	@	.17½
Silver, Nitrate	oz.	.41	@	.44½
Soap, Castile, white	lb.	.10	@	.10½
" green	lb.	.06	@	.10½
" mottled	lb.	.05½	@	.07
Sodium bicarb, Eng		1.37½	@	1.75
" domestic	100 lb.	1.50	@	1.80
" benzoate	lb.	.40	@	.41
" brom. blk	lb.	.31	@	.32
" carb., cryst.	100 lb.	1.60	@	1.75
" citrate	lb.	...	@	.32
" hypophosphite		.60	@	.64
" iodide		3.50	@	3.55
" nitrate	100 lb.	2.20	@	2.75
" phosphate	lb.	.02½	@	.03
" salicylate	lb.	.32	@	.34
Spermaceti	lb.	.27	@	.29
Spts. Nitre, U. S. P.		.46	@	.48
Spts. Ammonia Aromat.	lb.	.44	@	.45
Strontium, nitrate	lb.	.07½	@	.08
Strychnine, Sulph	oz.	.95	@	1.05
Sugar of Milk	lb.	.15	@	.20
Sugar, Lead, white	lb.	.09½	@	.10
" brown	lb.	.07½	@	.08
Sulphur, Roll	lb.	1.85	@	2.15
" Flowers	lb.	2.15	@	2.59½
Sulphuric Ether	lb.	.63	@	.68
Sumac, Sicily	ton	42.00	@	47.00
" Virginia	ton	25.00	@	35.00
Tar, Barbadoes	gal.	...	@	.38
Thymol		1.80	@	1.90
Tonka B'ns, Para	lb.	.18	@	.20
" Angostura	lb.	.65	@	.67½
" Surinam	lb.	.30	@	.32
Turmeric		.04½	@	.05
Turpentine	gal.	...	@	.72½
Vanilla Beans	lb.	2.75	@	6.50
" Cut. Mex	lb.	2.00	@	2.25
" Tahiti	lb.	.45	@	1.25
" Bourbon		1.00	@	3.00
Vanillin	oz.	.32	@	.37½
Venice Turps, bbls	lb.	.14	@	.17
" " cans	lb.	.19	@	.20
Wax, Bayberry	lb.	...	@	.50
" Bees, ord. pur	lb.	.32½	@	.33
" " sel	lb.	.33½	@	.34
" " blch	lb.	.40	@	.45
" Brazil, No. 1	lb.	.48	@	.50
" " No. 2	lb.	.41	@	.43
" " No. 3	lb.	.31	@	.32
" Ceresin, yel	lb.	.14	@	.18
" " white	lb.	.15	@	.20
" Japan	lb.	.13½	@	.14
" Paraffin	lb.	.06	@	.06½
Zinc Oxide	lb.	.07	@	.08½

Heavy Oils, &c.

Bank, Menhaden	gal.	.27	@	.30
Coconut, Ceylon	lb.	.06½	@	.06¾
Cochin	lb.	.07½	@	.07¾
Cuban	lb.	.05½	@	...
Cod, Domestic	gal.	.35	@	36
" Newfoundland	gal.	38½	@	40
Corn	gal.	3.60	@	...
Cottonseed, crd. prime		.35	@	...
Summer Yellow, prime		.33	@	.33
" " Butter		.33	@	.34
Old, off grade		.32	@	...
Winter Yellow, prime		.33	@	.34
Salad Oil		.40	@	.41
Gasoline, 86°	gal.	.14	@	...
" 88°	gal.	.16	@	...
" 90°	gal.	.18	@	...
Lard, Extra Prime	gal.	.63	@	.64
Lard, Extra No. 1	gal.	.49	@	.52
Lard, No. 1	gal.	.38	@	.40
Linseed, Raw City	gal.	.42	@	.43
" Boiled	gal.	.43	@	.44
Naphtha, 62°	gal.	.12	@	...
" Deodorized, 76°	gal.	.13½	@	...
Neatsfoot, prm	gal.	.49	@	.50
White		.97	@	...
Olive Oil, tap	tins	1.50	@	2.75
" Com., bbls	gal	.53½	@	.58
Palm, prm., L'gos	lb	.05½	@	.05¾
Peanut	lb	.40	@	.52
Rapeseed	gal.	.67	@	.71
Red Elaine	gal.	...	@	.40
" Saponified	lb.	.06½	@	.06¾
Salad Oil	gal.	.46	@	.48
Sesame	gal.	.55	@	.60
Sperm, Crude	gal.	.65	@	.66
" Nat. Win	gal.	.62	@	.63
" Blch. Win	gal.	.64	@	.65
Straits	gal.	...	@	.32
Tallow, prime	gal.	.62	@	
Whale Crude	gal.	...	@	...
Crude, Nat. Win.	gal.	.43	@	[illegible]
Bleached Win	gal.	.46	@	48

New Remedies Compendium and Prices Current.

In this list, which is intended for the use of dispensing druggists, and not for analytical chemists, chemical formulas, melting points and other data of no immediate use to the dispenser are omitted. While additions will be made from time to time as new remedies make their appearance on the market, and the list thus kept fully up to date, remedies falling into disuse will be dropped as expediency may determine.

Corrected to March, 1906.

ACETAL. (ETHYLIDENE DIETHYL ETHER.) Colorless, volatile liquid, soluble in 18 parts of water, very soluble in alcohol. Used as a sedative and hypnotic in doses of 2 to 3 fluid drachms, usually in form of emulsion. Pure medicinal, per oz., $1.00; commercial, oz. ....65c.

ACETOZONE. (BENZOYL-ACETYL PEROXIDE.) White powder, very slightly soluble in water (1:1000); slightly soluble in alcohol. Bactericide; used internally and externally in diseases of germ origin. Marketed as 50 per cent. mixture with inert absorbent powder. Dose, 1 to 3 grains in solution. Boxes containing 6 vials of 15 grains each, per box, $1.25; ¼ oz. bot., $1.40; ½ oz. bot., $2.70; 1 oz. bot. $5.25
(Parke, Davis & Co.)

ACET - THEOCIN - SODIUM. White crystalline powder, readily soluble in water. Powerful diuretic; used in dropsy, in doses of 5 to 7 grains, two to three times daily. ½ and 1 oz. bot......$1.90 to $2.30 per oz.
(Continental Color & Chemical Co.)

ACOINE. (DI-PARA-ANISYL-MONO-PHENETHYL GUANIDINE HYDROCHLORIDE.) White crystalline powder, soluble in 17 parts of water. Local anæsthetic like cocaine, used hypodermatically in eye surgery; dental anæsthetic in normal saline solution, 2 per cent. 15 grain vials, each, 30c.; capsules, 2½ grains, 28 in box ....75c.
(The Heyden Chemical Works.)

ADNEPHRIN SOLUTION. A 1-1000 solution of the active principle of the suprarenal gland in physiological salt solution containing one-half of 1 per cent. of methaform. Used chiefly as a hæmostatic, also for treatment of inflammations, congestions and tumefactions of the mucous membranes, also as a cardiac stimulant. 1 oz. vials ....60c.
EMOLLIENT. Tubes, each...30c.
OIL SPRAY. 1 oz. vials, each.60c.
(Frederick Stearns & Co.)

ADRENALIN. Grayish-white powder; with difficulty soluble in water. The blood-pressure-raising principle of the suprarenal glands. 1 grain vials.85c. Invariably employed in the form of
CHLORIDE SOLUTION, 1:1000, a solution of 1 part of adrenalin chloride in 1000 parts of physiologic salt solution, with 0.5 per cent. of chloretone. Powerful astringent, hemostatic and cardiac stimulant. Used for the control of hemorrhages, internal and superficial, for the reduction of congestion and inflammation of mucous membranes, as a heart stimulant in collapse, and as an adjuvant to the local anæsthetic action of cocaine. Internal dose, 5 to 30 minims. 1 oz. bot........85c.
INHALANT, 1 oz. bot.......85c.
OINTMENT, ½ oz. tubes.....43c.
SUPPOSITORIES, boxes of 1 doz. 38c.
TABLETS, vials of 25........85c.
(Parke, Davis & Co.)

ADRIN. (EPINEPHRIN HYDRATE.) Whitish nonhygroscopic powder; the active principle of the suprarenal gland, same properties as adrenalin. 1 grain vials, each, 75c.; 1-1000 solution, 1 oz. vials, each, 75c.; tablets in tubes of 12, tablet, q. s. to make 15 minims of 1-1000 solution, each, 40c.; in 100's, each $3.10
(H. K. Mulford & Co.)

AGURIN. (ACET-THEOBROMINE-SODIUM.) White hygroscopic powder, soluble in water; incompatible with acids. Diuretic in dropsy. Dose, 7 to 15 grains, twice daily. ½ and 1 oz. bot..............$1.55 to $1.70
(Continental Color & Chemical Co.)

AIROL. (BISMUTH OXYIODOGALLATE.) Grayish-green powder, insoluble in water or alcohol. On admixture with water airol partly decomposes and turns red. Should be mixed with water only with intervention of glycerin. Used externally as application to wounds, burns, skin diseases, eye, nose, gonorrhœa, either pure, in 10 per cent. suspension, equal parts glycerin and water, or 10 to 20 per cent. ointment. 1 oz. cartons $1.00
(Hoffmann-La Roche Chemical Works.)

ALBARGIN. (GELATOSE SILVER.) Light brown powder, readily soluble in water. Contains 15 per cent. of silver. For gonorrhœa a 2 per cent. solution is injected 4 or 5 times daily. 1 oz. vials, $1.10; tubes of 50 tablets, 0.2 gm. each, per tube ....50c.
(Victor Koechl & Co.)

ALPHOZONE. (SUCCINIC PEROXIDE.) White fluffy powder, quickly soluble in 60 parts of water. Germicide and antiseptic, internally and externally. Dose, 3 to 5 grains. 1 oz. bot., $4.50; ½ oz., $2.30; ¼ oz., $1.20; 1 grain tablets, bot. of 90 ....$1.00
(Frederick Stearns & Co.)

ALYPIN. White crystalline powder, easily soluble in water and alcohol, but dissolving very sparingly in ether. Watery solutions have a neutral reaction and can be sterilized by boiling for a short period. Local anæsthetic, substitute for cocaine. The strength of the solutions ordinarily employed varies from 1 to 5 and even up to 10 per cent. It can be combined with adrenalin and antipyrine. Alypin should not be used in connection with silver nitrate, owing to the formation of a precipitate. This objection, however, does not apply to protargol solutions, which, although they become slightly turbid at first, soon clear up. 15 grain vials, each, 20c.; 10 grain vials, per vial, 16c.; ¼ and ½ oz. bots., per oz., $4.20; 1 oz. bots., per oz.........$4.10
(Continental Color & Chemical Co.)

ALUMNOL. (ALUMINUM NAPHTHOL DISULPHONATE.) Whitish powder, very soluble in water; slightly soluble in alcohol and glycerin; astringent and antiseptic; dissolves in pus and penetrates tissues. Used in 1 per cent. solution in gonorrhœa; 10 to 20 per cent. mixture with talcum as a dusting powder. 1 oz. tins, per oz...50c.
(Victor Koechl & Co.)

AMINOFORM. (HEXAMETHYLENETETRAMINE.) White granular crystals, readily soluble in water, prepared by combining ammonia and formaldehyde. Antiseptic for urinary passages, diuretic and solvent in uric acid concretions; dose, 5 to 10 grains, well diluted, three times daily. 1 oz. bot., 60c.; 7½ grain tablets, oz. . . . . .70c.
(C. Bischoff & Co.)

AMYLOFORM. White powder, insoluble in water; condensation product of starch and formaldehyde. Surgical antiseptic, used pure or with talcum and boric acid. 1 oz. carton. . .25c.
(Stallman & Fulton.)

ANAESTHESIN. White crystalline powder, almost insoluble in cold water, but easily solubl in ether, alcohol, benzin and fatty oils. Local anæsthetic, and used internally in gastric ulcer, nervous dyspepsia, etc. Dose, internally, 5 to 8 grains several times daily. Used externally pure or in ointment 5 to 20 per cent., and in suppositories containing 3 grains each. 1 oz. bot. $1.00
(Victor Koechl & Co.)

ANTHRASOL. Yellow, oily liquid, with a distinctive tarry odor; soluble in alcohol, acetone, fats and petrolatum. A distillate from coal tar, used in diseases of the skin where coal tar is employed. 1 oz. vials . . . . .55c.
(Knoll & Co. and Merck & Co.)

ANTINONNIN. (POTASSIUM ORTHODINITRO-CRESOL.) Paste of brilliant orange color, soluble in water, slight soapy odor, nonvolatile. Deodorizer, disinfectant, prevents the growth of fungi, mildew and dry rot in cellars and human habitations. Used in form of solution. 1 lb to 5 to 15 gallons of water. Cans, ¼ lb., $1.10 per lb.; 1 lb. cans, 95c.; 50 lb. cans, per lb. . . . . .77c.
(Continental Color & Chemical Co.)

ANTINOSINE. (SODIUM SALT OF NOSOPHEN.) Blue powder, soluble in water, alcohol and glycerin. Used in solution of 1 to 5 per cent. as an antiseptic in diseases of the eye and ear, genito-urinary diseases, and as a healing powder on chronic leg ulcers. 1 oz. bot. $2.10
(Stallman & Fulton Co.)

ANTISCLEROSIN. Tablets, consisting of a compound of inorganic blood salts, used in treatment of arteriosclerosis and its sequellæ. Dose, 2 tablets three times daily. Carton of 4 tubes @ 24 tablets. . .$1.50
(Schering & Glatz.)

ANTITUSSIN. (DIFLUORDIPHENYL OINTMENT.) Ointment containing lanolin, 85 per cent.; petrolatum, 10 per cent., and difluordiphenyl, 5 per cent. A whooping cough remedy applied as inunction to patient's neck, chest and back once a day, in doses of 5 Gm. 20 Gm. collapsible tubes, 40c.; 40 Gm. . . . . .75c.
(C. Bischoff & Co.)

ANUSOL SUPPOSITORIES. A compound of bismuth iodoresorcin sulphonate, used in hæmorrhoids, etc. Dose, 1 or 2 daily. Box of 12. . . . .$1.00
(Schering & Glatz.)

ARGENTAMINE. A colorless, alkaline liquid representing a solution of silver nitrate, 10 per cent., and ethylenediamine, 10 per cent.; soluble in water. Used in all cases where silver nitrate is used, mostly in gonorrhœa, in strength of 1 in 2000-4000 solution. 1 oz., g. s. bot. . . . . .75c.
(Schering & Glatz.)

ARGONIN. White powder, very slightly soluble in cold, but freely so in hot water. A compound of silver nitrate and sodium casein. Antiseptic, germicide and gonococcicide, less caustic than silver nitrate. Solutions of 2 to 10 per cent. strength recommended for injection in gonorrhœa and 3 per cent. solutions for use in the eye. 1 oz. vials. . . . . .65c.
(Victor Koechl & Co.)

ARHOVIN, an addition product of diphenylamine and esterified thymyl-benzoic acid, is a fluid of aromatic odor and slightly burning taste, soluble in oil. Gonocide for internal and topical use. Given by mouth in capsules of 4 grains (1 or 2 capsules, three to six times daily); in urethral bougies (1 bougie, two to four times daily); in vaginal globules (1 globule, two to four times daily), and injected in 2 per cent. to 5 per cent. oily solution. 1 oz. vials, 90c.; box of 50 capsules, 65c.; box of 12 bougies, 50c.; box of 12 globules. . . . . .50c.
(Schering & Glatz.)

ASAPROL. (ABRASTOL.) Whitish powder, freely soluble in water and alcohol. It is the calcium salt of betanaphthol-sulphonic acid. Antipyretic and antirheumatic in doses of 5 to 15 grains. Used also as test for albumin in urine. 1 oz. bot. $1.25

ARISTOCHIN. (CARBONIC ESTER OF QUININE.) White powder, tasteless, insoluble in water. Decomposes in the system to yield 96.1 per cent. of quinine. Prescribed like quinine, but in somewhat larger doses. ½ and 1 oz. cartons, per oz. $2.20
(Continental Color & Chemical Co. and Merck & Co.)

ASPIRIN. (ACETYL SALICYLIC ACID.) White crystalline powder, insoluble in water; incompatible with alkalies. Used instead of the salicylates in articular and muscular rheumatism and other therapeutic indications for the salicylates. Dose, 5 to 15 grains, three to five times daily. 1 oz. bot., per oz. . . . . .33c. to 43c.
(Continental Color & Chemical Co.)

ATOXYL. (META-ARSENOUS ANILIDE.) White powder, containing 37.69 per cent. of arsenic in organic combination. Soluble in 6 parts of water and used in this strength solution for hypodermic injection; relatively nontoxic. Dose, 1 to 3 grains. 1 oz. vials. $3.00
(Victor Koechl & Co.)

BENZONAPHTHOL. White, crystalline powder, soluble in alcohol and chloroform; insoluble in water. Employed as intestinal antiseptic in doses of 5 to 15 grains. 1 oz. vials, 22c.; ¼ lb. bottles, $2.20; ½ lb., $2.10; 1 lb. $2.00
(Schering & Glatz.)

BENZOSOL. (GUAIACOL BENZOATE.) Small colorless crystals, nearly insoluble in water. Contains 54 per cent. of guaiacol and, as it is slowly saponified by the gastric juice, the guaiacol being liberated gradually, it is recommended as an intestinal antiseptic and as an agreeable substitute for creosote in incipient phthisis. Dose, 4 to 8 grains. 1 oz. tins. $1.25
(Victor Koechl & Co.)

BETA - EUCAINE HYDROCHLORIDE. White, crystalline powder, soluble in 30 parts of water. A synthetic compound chemically allied to cocaine, being the hydrochloride of benzoyl-vinyl-diaceton-alkamine. It is slower in action than cocaine, but anæsthesia is more prolonged, and a third less toxic. Used generally in 2 per cent. solutions in dental and ophthalmic work. ⅛ oz. and ¼ oz., per oz., $3.60; ½ oz. and 1 oz. $3.50
(Schering & Glatz.)

BETA-EUCAINE LACTATE. White powder, possessing the same properties as the hydrochloride, but is more soluble in water (about 1 in 5). Prices

and containers same as for beta-eucaine hydrochloride.
(Schering & Glatz.)

BISOL. (SOLUBLE BISMUTH PHOSPHATE.) White powder, soluble in water, faint alkaline reaction. Intestinal antiseptic and astringent in gastric and enteric catarrh. Dose, 3 to 7½ grains. 1 oz. vials......70c.
(C. Bischoff & Co.)

BROMETONE. Powder, slightly soluble in water. Compound of bromoform and acetone; recommended as a substitute for bromides; contains 77 per cent. of bromine. Dose, 3 to 5 grains. 1 oz. bot., 85c.; 5 grain capsules in bot. of 100 ....$1.25
(Parke, Davis & Co.)

BROMIPIN. (10 % BROMINIZED SESAME OIL.) Yellow, oily fluid, used as a nervine and sedative in epilepsy; succedaneum for bromides. Dose, 1 teaspoonful. 1 oz. vial, 18c.; per lb..........$2.10 to $2.85
(Merck & Co.)

CACODYLIC ACID. (DIMETHYL ARSENIC ACID.) Small colorless deliquescent crystals, the ultimate product of oxidation of arsenium-dimethyl (cacodyle) and of cacodyle oxide. Contains 54.4 per cent. of arsenic trioxide, but is relatively nontoxic. Dose, 1 to 3 grains. ¼ oz. vials, per oz.........$4.00

CALOMELOL OINTMENT. White mercurial ointment made from colloidal calomel for the inunction treatment of syphilis and especially for the cure of its cutaneous manifestations. 2 oz. graduated tubes, per tube ....55c.
(Heyden Chemical Works.)

CALOMELOL POWDER. Grayish-white powder of neutral reaction, tasteless and odorless. Yields a milky solution when added to cold water in the proportion of 1 to 50. Used as a dusting powder in the treatment of papular eruptions and ulcerations, and as external application to ulcerated chancres in 2 per cent. solution. 1 oz. vials ....70c.
(Heyden Chemical Works.)

CAMPHORIC ACID. (Colorless crystalline scales, very slightly soluble in water; formed by the oxidation of camphor with nitric acid. Used in night sweats of phthisis, also in cystitis and as an intestinal antiseptic in doses of 10 to 20 grains. 1 oz. vials, 45c.; 1 lb. bot. $7.00
(Merck & Co.)

CEROLIN. Pills of a fatty substance isolated from yeast. Acts same as yeast in furunculosis, acne, etc., but more cathartic. Pills containing 0.1 Gm., box of 100, each.....50c.
(C. F. Boehringer & Soehne.)

CHINAPHENIN. (QUININE CARBONIC ESTER OF PHENETIDINE.) White tasteless powder, representing synthetic quinine-phenacetin and having medicinal properties of both. Insoluble in water, but easily soluble in alcohol, ether and chloroform. Dose, 5 to 10 grains, thrice daily. ½ and 1 oz. cartons, per oz.........
$1.25 to $1.30
(Continental Color & Chemical Co.)

CHINOTROPINE. (UROTROPINE QUINATE.) A combination of quinic acid and urotropine (hexamethylenetetramine) used as uric acid solvent in the various manifestations of the uric acid diathesis. Is said to liberate formaldehyde freely internally and to form soluble compounds with uric acid. Dose, 10 to 30 grains. ¼ oz. and 1 oz. vials, $1.75; tablets, 7½ grains, 25 in tube, 2 tubes in box...................$1.75
(Schering & Glatz.)

CHLORETONE. White crystals, slightly soluble in water (1:125); hypnotic, local anæsthetic and antiseptic. Dose, 5 to 20 grains, in cachet, tablet or capsule. Externally as a dusting powder for wounds, combined 23 with zinc, oxide, 120, and French chalk, 90 parts. ⅞ oz. vials, per oz., 90c.; 1 oz................85c.
(Parke, Davis & Co.)

CINNAMIC ACID. (CINNAMYLIC ACID.) Transparent micaceous crystals, very slightly soluble in water; soluble in alcohol and ether. Injected intravenously in tuberculosis in doses of ¼ to ¾ of a grain, twice a week; per oz., 1-20 to ¾ grain twice daily. 1 oz. vial, 85c.; 1 lb. bot., per lb. $5.00
(Merck & Co.)

CITARIN. (SODIUM ANHYDROMETHYLENCITRATE.) White; crystalline powder, easily soluble in water. Antilithæmic for gouty and chronic rheumatic conditions; liberates formaldehyde in the blood. Dose, 15 to 30 grains, thrice daily. 1 oz. bottle, per oz. .70c. to 75c.
(Continental Color & Chemical Co.)

COLLARGOL. (COLLOIDAL SILVER.) Shining, black scales, soluble in 1 in 20 of water. Used as a bactericide, 1 in 100 to 10,000 in water or glycerin. Internally a 1 to 500 or 1 to 100 solution may be added to the food in teaspoonful doses. ½ oz. and 1 oz. vials, $2.75; tablets, 1 grain each, tubes of 50...60c.
(Schering & Glatz.)

COTARNINE HYDROCHLORIDE. See Stypticin.

CREOSOTE CARBONATE. (CREOSOTAL.) Yellow, transparent viscous liquid, insoluble in water, but miscible with alcohol; contains 92 per cent. of creosote combined with 8 per cent. of carbon dioxide. Used in tuberculosis and pneumonia in doses of 5 to 60 drops several times daily. 1 oz. vials, 65c.; ¼ lb. bot., per lb., $9.25; ½ lb., $9.10; 1 lb.......$9.00
(Schering & Glatz and Continental Color & Chemical Co.)

CUPROL. Green powder, readily soluble in water; a chemical combination of nucleinic acid and copper; solution does not coagulate albumen. Applied locally as an astringent; of use in granular ophthalmia in the form of 5 per cent. instillations, or may be applied in the dry form with a brush. ¼ oz. vials, $1.30 per oz.; 1 oz. vials $1.20
(Parke, Davis & Co.)

DERMATOL. (BISMUTH SUBGALLATE.) Yellow, insoluble powder; nonirritant antiseptic, especially serviceable in burns, ulcers and moist eczema. Used internally in diarrhœa, dysentery, intestinal fermentation and gastric ulcers, in doses of 10 to 30 grains three times daily. 1 oz. tins, 19c.; 1 and 5 lb. tins, per lb........$2.50
(Victor Koechl & Co.)

DIATHESIN. White crystalline leaflets, soluble in 15 parts cold water, freely soluble in hot water or alcohol. Is ortho-oxybenzylalcohol, or synthetic saligenin. Used in place of salicin in rheumatism, neuralgia, pleurisy, etc., in doses of 7½ to 15 grains. 1 oz. cartons $2.40
(C. Bischoff & Co.)

DIFLUORDIPHENYL. White crystalline powder of pleasant aromatic odor, insoluble in water, soluble in alcohol, ether, chloroform and oils. Used as antiseptic dusting powder mixed with talc in proportion of difluordiphenyl, 10 parts; talc, 90 parts, or in 10 per cent. ointment with lanolin as dressing for burns. Dose, 1-16 to ¼ grain. 5 Gm. envelopes, each $1.50
(C. Bischoff & Co.)

DIGALEN. (CLOETTA'S SOLUBLE DIGITOXIN.) Marketed only in solution in 15 Cc. (½ oz.) vials, on account of infinitesimal dosage. Active principle of digitalis leaves, nonaccumulative heart tonic and diuretic. 1 Cc. of solution represents 0.0003 Gm. (0.0045 grain) of digitoxin, which is the average dose, by the mouth, hypodermatically, or by enema; intravenously the dose is from 3 to 10 Cc. ½ oz. vials..................$1.00
(Hoffmann-La Roche Chemical Works.)

DIGITALIN VERUM. White powder, the active constituent of digitalis, free from impurities and noxious principles. Almost insoluble in water. Dose, 0.002 Gm. to 0.006 Gm., three times daily, increasing to not over 0.02 Gm. (1-3 grain). 1 Gm. vials......................$7.25
(C. F. Boehringer & Soehn.)

DIONIN. (ETHYL MORPHINE HYDROCHLORIDE.) White crystalline powder, very soluble in water and alcohol. Recommended to replace codeine and morphine in bronchitis, emphysema and asthma. Dose, ¼ to ½ grain. 1 oz. vials, $6.00; ⅛ oz. vials, per oz., $6.25; 15 grain vials, each, 85c.; tablets, ¼ grain, bot. of 50, 35c.; bot. of 100......................60c.
(Merck & Co.)

DIURETIN. White powder, soluble in water, decomposed by acids. Must be kept dry and air tight. It is a chemical compound of theobromine sodium and sodium salicylate. Diuretic, antiasthmatic and vascular stimulant. Dose, 15 grains four to six times daily. 1 oz. bot., per oz..............$1.75
(Knoll & Co.)

DORMIOL. (AMYLENE CHLORAL.) Oily, colorless liquid, with a camphoraceous odor, insoluble in water, soluble in alcohol and ether. Hypnotic in mania; 50 per cent. solution supplied commercially. Dose, 5 to 60 minims. 1 oz. vials, 28c.; ½ lb. bot., per lb..............$4.00
(Merck & Co.)

DUOTAL. (GUAIACOL CARBONATE.) White crystalline powder, soluble in alcohol, insoluble in water. Same therapeutic action as Creosotal, which see. Dose, 5 to 20 grains, gradually increased. 1 oz. vials, $1.50; tablets, 7½ grains, 50 tablets in box, $1.50; 4½ grains, 50 tablets in box.............90c.
(Schering & Glatz and Continental Color & Chemical Co.)

DUOTONOL. White powder; a mixture, equal parts of the lime and sodium glycerophosphates. Nerve nutrient in doses of 5 to 10 grains three times daily. 1 oz., 50c.; 1 lb., $6.00; tablets, 5 grains, 100 tablets in bottle......................65c.
(Schering & Glatz.)

DYMAL. (DIDYMIUM SALICYLATE.) Pinkish powder, odorless. Applied as powder and ointment in skin diseases, notably dry and weeping eczema. 1 oz. cartons, each, 35c.; 4 oz. cartons, each..............$1.20
(C. Bischoff & Co.)

EKA-IODOFORM. A chemically pure iodoform, prepared by electrical synthesis, and sterilized with paraform. 1 oz. vials......................50c.
(Schering & Glatz.)

EMPYROFORM. Brown powder; condensation product of birch tar and formaldehyde; insoluble in water, readily soluble in acetone, chloroform and solutions of caustic alkalies. Used like tar in ointment, paste and tincture. 1 oz. vials..65c.
(Schering & Glatz.)

EPICARIN. (CONDENSATION PRODUCT OF BETANAPHTOL AND CRESOLIC ACID.) Colorless or yellowish needles, difficultly solube in hot water, easily soluble in alcohol, ether and oils. Nontoxic substitute for naphthol in parasitic skin diseases. Employed chiefly in ointments (5 to 10 per cent.) 1 oz. cartons, per oz..............60c. to 70c.
(Continental Color & Chemical Co.)

EUCASIN. Casein compound, containing 95 per cent. albumin and 5 per cent. water. Prepared from cow's milk. Dietetic for convalescents, invalids or persons afflicted with lung, stomach or kidney trouble; also in anæmia and typhoid. 1 lb. tins, $3.00; ½ lb., $1.50; ¼ lb.......................80c.
(Fuerst Bros. & Co.)

EUDOXINE. (BISMUTH SALT OF NOSOPHEN.) Reddish-gray powder, insoluble in water, but soluble in alkaline fluids. Used as an intestinal antiseptic in doses of 3 to 5 grains. 1 oz. bot., $2.10; 3 grain tablets, per oz., $2.60; 5 grain tablets, per oz......................$2.50
(Stallman & Fulton Co.)

EUGALLOL. (PYROGALLOL MONOACETATE.) Yellowish, syrupy liquid, marketed in 66 per cent. acetone solution. Soluble in water and acetone; applied pure or diluted with acetone as paint in skin diseases, especially psoriasis, and deemed superior to pyrogallol. 1 oz. vials......................$1.00
(Knoll & Co. and Merck & Co.)

EUMYDRIN. White crystalline powder, obtained from atropine; easily soluble in water. Powerful mydriatic, less poisonous than atropine. Dose, internally, about 1-70 grain. 1 or 2 per cent. solution dilates the pupil after 10 to 25 minutes. 1 grain tubes, 45c. to 55c. per box of 10 tubes; ¼ oz. and ½ oz. packages, per oz......................$16.50
(Continental Color & Chemical Co.)

EUNATROL. (SODIUM ACID OLEATE.) Light yellow substance, readily soluble in water and alcohol; supplied as powder and chocolate-coated pills. Recommended in treatment of gallstones, being excellent cholagogue. Dose, four pills, 4 grains each, three times daily, or in solution. 25 Gm. bot., each, 75c.; bot. of 50 pills, 70c.; 100 pills..............$1.30
(C. Bischoff & Co.)

EUPHORIN. (PHENYL - URETHANE.) White, acicular crystals, slightly soluble in water, freely in alcohol. Energetic antipyretic and analgetic in doses of 7½ to 15 grains, 2 to 3 times daily. 1 oz. vials...$1.00
(Schering & Glatz.)

EUPHTHALMINE HYDROCHLORIDE. White crystals; a synthetic derivative of beta-eucaine; soluble in water; 2 to 5 per cent. solutions dilate the pupil, without causing discomfort or accommodation disturbances. ½ and 1 Gm. vials, per Gm......................$1.25
(Schering & Glatz.)

EUPYRINE. (PARA-PHENETIDINE VANILLIN ETHYLCARBONATE.) Light yellow crystals, sparingly soluble in water, readily in alcohol, chloroform and ether. Stimulant antipyretic in doses of 7½ to 15 grains. 1 oz. cartons, each..................$1.50
(C. Bischoff & Co.)

EUQUININE. (QUININE CARBONIC ESTER.) Tasteless, fleecy crystals, slightly soluble in water; soluble in alcohol, ether and chloroform. Succedaneum for quinine sulphate, reported not to disturb stomach or produce cinchonism. Dose, same as quinine. Tablets, 5 grains, 100 in bot., $1.75; 2 grain, 100 in bot......................75c.
(Merck & Co.)

EURESOL. (RESORCINE MONOACETATE.) Oily, yellow liquid, soluble in alcohol and acetone. Succedaneum for resorcin, externally. Used in skin and scalp diseases, as paint pure or diluted with acetone. 1 oz. vials......................$1.00
(Knoll & Co. and Merck & Co.)

EUROPHEN. Yellow light powder, containing 25 per cent. of iodine, insoluble in water and

glycerin. Iodoform substitute used in dry powder and in ointment. 1 oz. bot., per oz.... $1.65 to $1.80
(Continental Color & Chemical Co.)

EUZONE. (PURE SODIUM PERBORATE.) White, odorless powder, containing about 7.1 per cent. boron, 15 per cent. sodium, 31.2 per cent. oxygen and 46.2 per cent. water; represents 22 per cent. by weight of hydrogen dioxide, equivalent to 10.4 per cent. by weight of nascent oxygen. Soluble in water 1 in 10, such a solution being taken to represent a 2 per cent. solution of hydrogen dioxide. Tablets, 2½ Gm. each, boxes of 20. 40c.; powder, in 100 Gm. cartons, 35c.; 500 Gm. boxes $1.20
(Schering & Glatz.)

EXODIN. Yellowish powder; a synthetic oxyanthraquinone derivative; tasteless, mild aperient in doses of 7½ to 15 grains. 1 oz. vials, $1.40; tablets, 7½ grains each, 10 tablets in box, 30c.; 50 in bottle........$1.40
(Schering & Glatz.)

FERRATIN. Reddish - brown powder, slowly soluble in ordinary liquids, but readily in hot beverages. Used in anæmia and chlorosis in doses of 7½ grains three times daily. 1 oz. vials, 85c.; tablets, 7½ grains, 50 in box, per box..............85c.
(C. F. Boehringer & Soehne.)

FERRATOGEN. (IRON NUCLEINATE.) Grayish-yellow powder, obtained by growing yeast in a ferruginous medium; insoluble in water. Used in chlorosis and anæmia in doses of 5 grains, three times daily. 1 oz. cartons, each..............90c.
(C. Bischoff & Co.)

FERRATOSE. (LIQUOR FERRATINI.) Fluid preparation of ferratin, containing 0.3 per cent. iron. 250 Gm. bottles.....45c.
(C. F. Boehringer & Soehn.)

FERRIPYRIN. (FERRIC CHLORIDE ANTIPYRIN.) Orange-red powder, soluble in 5 parts of water, very soluble in alcohol, but insoluble in ether. A compound of ferric chloride and antipyrine. Stypic and analgetic when applied in solution or powder. Given internally in chlorosis and anæmia as a hæmatinic in doses of 7½ grains. 1 oz. tins........$1.50
(Victor Koechl & Co.)

FERROPYRIN. (Same as Ferripyrin, but made by Knoll & Co. and sold in 1 oz. cartons, $1.40.)
(Knoll & Co. and Merck & Co.)

FILMARON OIL 1:10. A 10 per cent. solution of filmaron, the active principle of malefern, in castor oil. Used in removal of tapeworm. 10 Gm. bot....35c.
(C. F. Boehringer & Soehn.)

FIBROLYSIN. Solution of thiosinamine and sodium salicylate, sterilized. Put up in sealed tubes, each containing 2.3 Cc. solution (= 0.2 Gm. thiosinamine). Same uses as thiosinamine, but specially adapted for hypodermic use. Dose, contents of 1 tube every 1, 2 or 3 days, as required. 2.3 Cc. tubes, each....................15c.
(Merck & Co.)

FLUOROFORMOL. (FLUORYL.) Colorless, tasteless liquid, a 2.8 per cent. solution of fluoroform. Used in phthisis, internally and externally; also in pneumonia, acting as an antiseptic. Dose, 1 tablespoonful four times daily. 1 lb. bot..................$1.00
(C. Bischoff & Co.)

FLUORRHEUMIN. Ointment composed of petrolatum, 10; lanolin, 85; difluordiphenyl, 4; fluorphenetol, 1. Used in rheumatism, sciatica and lumbago; dose by inunction, 4 to 5 Gm. Collapsible tubes, 20 Gm., 40c.; 40 Gm.......................75c.
(C. Bischoff & Co.)

FORTOINE. (METHYLENEDICOTOINE.) Yellow crystals, with slight cinnamon flavor, obtained through action of formaldehyde on cotoine; insoluble in water, sparingly soluble in alcohol, ether and benzol; easily soluble in chloroform, acetone and alkaline liquids. Astringent antiseptic in protracted diarrhœas of consumptives. Dose, 4 grains three times daily. 10 Gm. envelopes, each $2.00
(C. Bischoff & Co.)

GALLOGEN. (ELLAGIC ACID.) Yellowish, tasteless powder, insoluble in all acid and neutral media, but soluble in alkaline solutions. Resembles tannic acid, being the astringent principle of divi-divi. Used in dysentery and diarrhœa. Dose, 10 to 15 grains for adults, 5 to 8 grains for children. 1 oz. cartons, 80c.; chocolate coated tablets, 3 grains each, 24 in box ....35c.
(C. Bischoff & Co.)

GAULTHERINE. Pinkish powder, slowly soluble in cold water, more readily so in hot water; insoluble in ether and chloroform, but very soluble in alcohol. It is the sodium salt of methyl salicylate prepared from natural oil of wintergreen. Antiseptic, antifermentative and soothing antiputrefactive. Used internally and externally. 4 oz. bot., per lb., $6.30; ½ lb. bot., per lb., $6.60; 1 lb. bot. $6.50
(The Wm. S. Merrell Chemical Co.)

GEOSOTE. See Guaiacol Valerate.

GLUTOL. (FORMALDEHYDE GELATIN.) Whitish, granular, insoluble powder; recommended as an antiseptic dressing for burns, cavities and suppurating ulcers. 1 oz. tins, 65c.; vials of ⅓ oz., with sprinkler top, each ....25c.
(Schering & Glatz.)

GUAETHOL. (AJACOL; THANATOL.) Oily liquid, or purer in crystals resembling thymol, insoluble in water. Succedaneum for guaiacol. Allays pain by direct application. Dose, 4 to 8 minims. 1 oz. vials......$1.40

GUAIACOL VALERATE. (GEOSOTE.) Yellow, oily liquid; a combination of guaiacol and valerianic acid, having the characteristic odor of the latter. Insoluble in water, soluble in alcohol and ether. Said to be useful in tuberculosis and chlorosis and as intestinal antiseptic in doses of 3 to 10 minims three times daily. 3 minim capsules, per 100..........$2.10

GUAIACETIN. (SODIUM PYROCATECHIN-MONOACETATE.) White odorless powder, soluble in water. A succedaneum for guaiacol and creosote, used in tuberculosis. Dose, 8 grains, preferably in tablet form. Powder in 1 oz. tins, $3.30; bot. containing 100 tablets, 8 grains each, $3.50; 50, $2.00; 25.....$1.17
(Fuerst Bros. & Co.)

GUIASANOL. (DIETHYLGLYCOCOLL - GUAIACOL.) Crystalline powder, readily soluble in water. Indications same as for creosote and guaiacol. Used internally in doses of from 45 to 180 grains a day. 25 Gm. bot. $1.00
(Victor Koechl & Co.)

HEDONAL. White, crystalline powder, insoluble in water, but soluble in alcohol, chloroform and ether; best administered as a dry powder. Given in mild forms of insomnia as a hypnotic in doses of 15 to 30 grains. 1 oz. bot. $1.50 to $1.60
(Continental Color & Chemical Co.)

HELMITOL. (HEXAMETHYLENETETRAMINE-ANHYDROMETHYLENE CITRATE.) Colorless crystals, freely soluble in water; insoluble in alcohol and ether. Urinary antiseptic in cystitis, phosphaturia, urethritis, etc., in doses of 15 grains, three or four times daily; liberates formaldehyde in the urinary tract. 1 oz. bot..................60c.
(Continental Color & Chemical Co.)

HEMICRANIN. White powder; a mixture of 5 parts phenacetin, 1 part caffeine and 1 part citric acid, used in migraine, headaches, intercostal neuralgia and sciatica, in doses of 5 to 10

grains. 1 oz. cartons, per oz. ....90c.
(Continental Color & Chemical Co.)

HEROIN. White, crystalline powder, difficultly soluble in water, but readily so in alcohol and in water to which a little acetic acid has been added; incompatible with alkali carbonates. Substitute for morphine, of which it is the diacetic acid ester, in doses of 1-24 to 1-12 grain; used for relief of cough and dyspnœa in phthisis, pneumonia, etc. 15 grain vials, 23c. per vial; ¼ oz. vials, per oz., $5.15; 1 oz. vials, per oz. . $4.85
(Continental Color & Chemical Co.)

HEROIN HYDROCHLORIDE. (WATER SOLUBLE SALT OF HEROIN.) White, crystalline powder, used in same indications as heroin, but is adapted for hypodermatic injections. The dose and prices are the same as those of heroin.
(Continental Color & Chemical Co.)

HIPPOL. (METHYLENE HIPPURIC ACID.) Colorless, prismatic crystals; sparingly soluble in water; urinary antiseptic in bacterial diseases of the urinary tract. Dose, 22½ grains. 1 oz., $1.50; 20 tablets in box $1.10
(Schering & Glatz.)

HIRUDIN. Grayish, glittering plates and scales, representing a dried extract of the head, pharyngeal rings and lips of the leech (*Sanguisuga medicinalis*); readily soluble in water. Used in the treatment of certain diseases of women and in experiments to prevent coagulation of blood on exposure to air. Tubes, 0.01 Gm., 50c.; 0.1 Gm., $2.75; 1 Gm. . . . $19.00
(C. Bischoff & Co.)

HISTOSAN. (GUAIACOL ALBUMINATE.) Light brown powder of faintly aromatic odor and taste; soluble in water. Used in pulmonary tuberculosis and in diarrhœa in doses of 7½ grains three times daily. 1 oz. cartons $1.30
(C. Bischoff & Co.)

HOLOCAINE HYDROCHLORIDE. White, crystalline powder, difficultly soluble in cold (1 in 75), but readily so in hot water. Chemically para-diethyoxyethenyl-diphenyl-amidine hydrochloride, produced by combination of phenacetin and para-phenetidin. Antiseptic and germicidal in 1 per cent. solution. Used entirely as anæsthetic for operations on the eye, a 1 per cent. solution being equal to 2 per cent. cocaine solution. 1 Gm. vials, 35c.; 5 Gm. vials, per Gm., 30c.; 1 oz. vials, per oz. $7.00
(Victor Koechl & Co.)

HYDRONAL. (POLYMERIZED CHLORAL.) White powder, a polymeric form of anhydrous chloral, known in Germany as viferral. It dissolves slowly in cold, but readily in boiling water. Used as hypnotic in simple sleeplessness and in the insomnia of mania in doses of 15 grains. Tubes of 5 tablets, 1 Gm. each.......................35c.
(C. Bischoff & Co.)

HYRGOL. (COLLOIDAL MERCURY.) Dark, solid body, fairly soluble in cold water, insoluble in alcohol and ether; used in syphilis as 10 per cent. ointment by inunction, and pills and tablets internally. Dose, ⅓ to ⅝ grain thrice daily. 1 oz. vials . . . 80c.
(Schering & Glatz.)

ICHTHALBIN. (ICHTHYOL ALBUMINATE.) Grayish-brown powder, odorless and tasteless; combination of ichthyol and albumin, containing 40 per cent. of the former. Used internally for skin diseases and gastro-intestinal affections in doses of 5 to 30 grains three times daily. 1 oz. cartons, 85c.; 5 grain tablets, 100 in bot. . $1.00
(Knoll & Co. and Merck & Co.)

ICHTHARGAN. (ICHTHYOL SILVER; SILVER ICHTHYOLSULPHONATE; SILVER THIO-HYDROCARBUROSULPHONATE.) Brown powder containing 30 per cent. silver; soluble in water and glycerin. Bactericide and astringent in urinary diseases in injections of 1 to 500 and 1 to 3000 in water; in diseases of the eye, as trachoma, by brush applications of 1 to 3 per cent. solutions. Dose, 1-24 to 1-12 grain in water. 1 oz. vials, $3.00; ¼ oz.......................$3.10
(Merck & Co.)

ICHTHOFORM. (ICHTHYOL FORMALDEHYDE.) Blackish-brown powder, insoluble in water. Used externally as succedaneum for iodoform. Internally as intestinal antiseptic in the diarrhœa and intestinal disorders occurring in tubercular diseases, and in typhoid fever and dysentery. Dose, 15 to 30 grains three or four times daily, in powder or capsules. 1 oz. vials.......................$1.00
(Merck & Co.)

IODIPIN. (IODIZED SESAME OIL; IODINOL.) Thick, yellow oil, odorless and of oily taste, made similarly to bromipin by repeated iodization of sesame oil by means of iodine monochloride in alcoholic solution; insoluble in water and alcohol, soluble in ether and chloroform. Made in two strengths, 10 per cent. iodine and 25 per cent. iodine, respectively, the former for internal and the latter for hypodermic use. Succedaneum for iodide in syphilis, scrofula, etc. Dose, 10 per cent., 1 to 3 fl. drachms; hypodermically (25 per cent.), 30 to 90 minims. On unspecified orders the 10 per cent. strength is supplied. Used in all cases where iodine and iodides are indicated; hypodermically in syphilis. 10 per cent. strength, 1 lb. bottles, $3.65; ¼ lb., $3.90; 1 oz. vials, 28c.; 20 per cent., 1 lb. bottles, $8.25; ¼ lb., $8.30; 1 oz. vials ....65c.
(Merck & Co.)

IODOFORMOGEN. Light yellow powder, odorless in use; combination of iodoform and albumin, insoluble in water, capable of sterilization; used like iodoform as a dressing for wounds. 1 oz. cartons ....55c.
(Knoll & Co. and Merck & Co.)

IODOZEN. Yellowish-white powder, a chemical combination of methyl salicylate and iodine; insoluble in water, soluble in 2 parts of alcohol, in 3 parts of ether and in 10 parts of chloroform. Antiseptic application applied as solution or ointment. Marketed in sprinkler top cans, 1 oz.......................75c.
(The Wm. S. Merrell Chemical Co.)

IODOTHYRINE. Whitish powder, representing the active principle of the thyroid gland, combined with sugar of milk. Alterative in goitre, myxœdema, obesity, psoriasis, menstrual disorders of women, etc., in daily doses of 15 to 30 grains. Powder, in ¼ oz. vials, per oz., $3.90; 1 oz. vials, $3.40. Tablets, 5 grains, each, vials of 25, per vial, $1.00; 100 ....$3.90
(Continental Color & Chemical Co.)

IOTHION. Syrupy, yellowish-brown liquid, difficultly soluble in water, easily soluble in alcohol, ether, benzol and chloroform; miscible with petrolatum and with anhydrous lanolin, which takes up twice its weight of iothion. Organic compound of iodine, of which it contains 79 to 80 per cent. Applied in form of ointment by inunction as a substitute for potassium iodide in doses of 30 to 60 grains a day. 1 oz. bot., per oz.......................$1.10
(Continental Color & Chemical Co.)

IRON TONOL. (IRON GLYCERO PHOSPHATE.) Powder; soluble in water; tonic, nerve nutrient. Dose, 3 to 10 grains. 1 oz., 35c.; 1 lb.......................$3.50
(Schering & Glatz.)

IRON TROPON. Brownish powder; albuminoid food preparation composed of tropon (pure albumen) and iron in an assimilable form. Contains 2½

per cent. of iron. Used as a tonic food in treatment of anæmia, chlorosis, impoverished conditions of the system generally, and in convalescence. Tins, 100 Gm., 75c.; 1 doz. tins $6.75
(Tropon Works.)

ISOPRAL. White crystals, soluble in water up to 3 per cent. and easily in alcohol and ether. A nondepressing substitute for chloral in doses of 7 to 15 grains, indicated in all forms of sleeplessness in which chloral is employed. Powder, in 1 oz. bot., per oz., $1.40; 8 grain tablets, bottles of 100, $3.00; 8 grain tablets, tubes of 20 ....75c.
(Continental Color & Chemical Co.)

KRESAMINE. Clear, watery liquid, representing a solution of trikresol, 25 per cent., and ethylenediamine, 25 per cent.; soluble in 8 parts of water, and in all proportions of glycerin; antiseptic and sedative to inflammed tissues. 1 oz...$1.00
(Schering & Glatz.)

KRYOFINE. White, granular crystals, sparingly soluble in cold water (1 in 600); freely soluble in alcohol and ether. A compound of paraphenetidin and methylglycolic acid. Antipyretic and antineuralgic in doses of 4 to 7½ grains. 1 oz. cartons, powd., $1.00; tablets, 4 or 7½ grains, per oz....$1.00
(C. Bischoff & Co.)

LACTOPHENIN. (LACTYL-PARAPHENETIDIN.) Small, white crystals, soluble in 330 parts of water. Differs from phenacetin in containing a molecule of lactic acid in place of acetic. Antipyretic and analgetic in doses of 4 to 8 grains. 1 oz. cartons, each......$1.00
(C. F. Boehringer & Soehne.)

LACTOSERNE. Buttermilk in powder form, scientifically prepared from fresh milk, free from bacteria. Used as infant food. 250 Gm. bot.........25c.
(C. F. Boehringer & Soehn.)

LARGIN. (SILVER PROTALBIN.) Gray powder containing 11 per cent. of silver; soluble in 10 parts of water. Bactericide and astringent application in gonorrhœa in ¼ to 1½ per cent. injections. 1 oz. vials...$1.75
(Merck & Co.)

LENIGALLOL. (PYROGALLOL TRIACETATE.) White, crystalline powder, insoluble in water, possessing the same reducing properties as pyragallol and used in acute and chronic eczema as ointment. 1 oz. vials $1.00
(Knoll & Co. and Merck & Co.)

LEVULOSE. (FRUIT SUGAR.) Crystalline powder, soluble in water. Sweetening agent used in diabetes, tuberculosis, malnutrition and marasmus of children. Dose, 3 drachms to 2 ounces daily. 1 lb. jars..$1.60
(Schering & Glatz.)

LYCETOL. (DIMETHYLENEDIAMINE TARTRATE.) White powder, readily soluble in water. Uric acid solvent, antiarthritic and diuretic in doses of 5 to 10 grains three times daily. 10 Gm. vials, $1.50; ¼ oz., ½ oz., 1 oz. cartons, per oz... $4.25 to $4.40
(Continental Color & Chemical Co. and Schering & Glatz.)

LYGOSINE. (SODIUM LYGOSINATE.) Glossy, greenish crystals; a condensation product of salicylaldehyde and acetone; readily soluble in water, forming ruby red solutions. Nonirritant substitute for silver as urethral injection in gonorrhœa, 5 per cent. strength. 10 Gm. vials....................35c.
(C. Bischoff & Co.)

LYSIDIN. (ETHYLENE-ETHENYLDIAMINE HYDROCHLORIDE.) Pale yellowish liquid, containing 50 per cent. of pure lysidin, the substance itself being very hygroscopic. Used in acute gout and uric acid diathesis in doses of 10 to 30 minims. 1 oz. vials $1.75
(Victor Koechl & Co.)

MARETIN. White, glistening crystals, very sparingly soluble in water (1 to 1050). Antipyretic, being a methyl acetanilid with a urea nucleus in place of the acetyl group. Dose, 3 to 5 grains. 1 oz. cartons, per oz............$1.25 to $1.40
(Continental Color & Chemical Co.)

METHAFORM. (DIMETHYLCARBINOL CHLOROFORM.) White, shiny, needle-like crystals, with a slightly camphoraceous taste and odor, sparingly soluble in water, but readily so in chloroform, alcohol, ether and glacial acetic acid. It is hypnotic, analgetic, anæsthetic and antiseptic, somewhat resembling chloral in physiological action. 1 oz. vials, 60c.; 3 grain capsules, bot. of 100, 50c.; 5 grain, 100 ....75c.
(Frederick Stearns & Co.)

MERCUROL. Brownish powder, soluble in water; insoluble in alcohol; a chemical combination of nucleinic acid and mercury, containing 10 per cent. of the metal. Does not coagulate albuminous liquids. Applied to ulcers and suppurating mucous membranes in from ⅛ to 5 per cent. solution, or in ointment. ¼ oz. vials, per oz., $1.60; 1 oz. vials $1.50
(Parke, Davis & Co.)

MESOTAN. (METHYLOXYMETHYLESTER OF SALICYLIC ACID.) Clear, yellow fluid, insoluble in water, but miscible with alcohol, ether and fixed oils. External application mixed with equal parts of olive oil in muscular and articular rheumatism, pleuritis and gout. 1 oz. bot., 47c.; 25 oz. lots, 42c.
(Continental Color & Chemical Co.)

MIGRAININ. (PHENAZONE CAFFEINE CITRATE.) Small white crystals, readily soluble in water and alcohol. Analgetic and antipyretic. Used in migraine, headaches of influenza, neuralgia, sciatica, etc., in doses of 17 grains. 1 oz. tins.........$1.50
(Victor Koechl & Co.)

MIGROL. White powder, composed of equal parts of sodium pyrocatechinmonoacetate and caffein pyrocatechinmonoacetate. Effective and harmless remedy in headache, toothache, neurasthenia, etc. 1 oz.......$4.00
(Fuerst Bros. & Co.)

NARGOL. Brownish powder readily soluble in warm water. Compound of silver and nucleinic acid containing 10 per cent. of the former; does not coagulate albumen. Used in gonorrhœa, conjunctival and other pyogenic inflammations. ¼ oz. vials, per oz., $1.80; ½ oz., per oz., $1.75; 1 oz............$1.70
(Parke, Davis & Co.)

NEODERMIN. Ointment containing lanolin, 85; petrolatum, 10; difluordiphenyl, 4; fluorpseudocumol, 1. For ulcerated surfaces, burns, etc. Collapsible tubes, Gm. 20 and Gm. 40, each..................40c. and 75c
(C. Bischoff & Co.)

NOSOPHEN. (TETRAIODOPHENOLPHTHALEIN.) Grayish powder, odorless, slightly anæsthetic, insoluble in water, alcohol or ether, but soluble in alkaline fluids. Antiseptic dusting powder in wounds, burns, ulcers; substitute for iodoform. Bottles containing about ⅙ oz., per doz....................$4.50
(Stallman & Fulton Co.)

NOVARGAN. (SILVER PROTEINATE.) Fine yellow powder containing 10 per cent. of metallic silver, readily soluble in water. Used as injection in gonorrhœa; is very penetrating and free from irritating effects upon mucous membrane. 1 oz. vials, $1.40

(Heyden Chemical Works.

OLEOCREOSOTE. Pale brown, oily liquid combination of beechwood creosote, 33 per cent., with oleic acid. Used in affections of the respiratory organs, tuberculosis, etc. Dose, 10 to 30 minims. 1 oz...65c.

(Schering & Glatz.)

OREXINE. (PHENYLDIHYDRO-QUINAZOLINE TANNATE.) Yellowish powder, tasteless and odorless; insoluble in water, slightly soluble in dilute acid solutions, readily so in hydrochloric acid. Should not be prescribed with preparations of iron. Used in anorexia (lack of appetite) as stimulant of gastric secretion; in seasickness and vomiting of pregnancy. Orexine base is no longer on the market. Dose, 8 to 12 grains two times daily, in powder or in tablets. 1 oz. vials, $1.00; orexoids, Merck's tablets, 4 grains, 50 in bottle ....55c.

(Merck & Co.)

ORPHOL. (BISMUTH BETANAPHTHOLATE.) Odorless and tasteless fawn colored powder, insoluble in water; consists of 80 per cent. bismuth oxide and 20 per cent. beta-naphthol. Intestinal antiseptic in doses of 5 to 15 grains three or four times daily. 1 oz., 80c.; tablets, 5 grains, 50 tablets in vial, per vial ....60c.

(Schering & Glatz.)

ORTHOFORM. White crystalline powder, the methyl ester of metaamidoparaoxybenzoic acid; slightly soluble in water; local anæsthetic and antiseptic. Forms a hydrochloride salt soluble in 9 parts of water. 10 per cent. solution of the hydrochloride salt, or 10 to 20 per cent. in ointment used to alleviate pain in sores or burns. Orthoform, 1 oz. vials, $1.40; orthoform hydrochloride, 1 oz. vials $1.80

(Victor Koechl & Co.)

OVARADEN. Tasteless and odorless powder consisting of the active substance of pigs' ovaries. Used in dysmenorrhœa and neurasthenia in doses of 15 to 30 grains daily. 1 oz. vials, $1.30; 4 grain tablets, bottles of 100............$1.30

(Knoll & Co. and Merck & Co.)

OVARIIN. Powder representing 1 part in 8 of fresh cow's ovary, being the desiccated substance of the ovary. Used in chlorosis, affections of the heart, and menstrual troubles. 1 oz. vials, $2.00; ¼ oz., $2.10; 3 grain tablets, 100 in bottle $1.50

(Merck & Co.)

PANKREON. Grayish-red powder; a tannin-pancreatin compound; insoluble in water, obtained from the pancreas; used in pancreatic diabetes, gastritis and apepsia in doses of 7½ grains three times daily. Box of 25 Gm., $1.50; tablets of 0.25 Gm., 50 in box, $1.00; sugar tablets (¾ grain), 100 in box......................50c.

(Merck & Co.)

PHENOCOLL HYDROCHLORIDE. White, crystalline powder, with sharp, saline taste; soluble in 16 parts of water; very soluble in hot water and alcohol. Similar to phenacetin, and used in malaria, pneumonia, influenza, rheumatism, etc. Dose, 7 to 15 grains. 25 Gm. vials...............$1.50

(Schering & Glatz.)

PIPERAZINE. Crystalline powder readily soluble in water. Solvent of uric acid and insoluble urates in the system; used in gout, rheumatism and urinary calculi. Dose, 5 to 15 grains thrice daily. 10 Gm. vials, per vial, $1.50; lots of 60, per vial, $1.25. Tablets, tubes of ten 15 grain tablets, $1.50; 60 tubes, per tube, $1.25; ½ and 1 oz. bot., per oz. $4.25

(Continental Color & Chemical Co. and Schering & Glatz.)

POLLANTIN. Liquid and powder; antitoxic serum for hay fever, autumnal catarrh, rose fever and June cold. Package of powder and brush, $1.75; liquid, per package of serum and pipette.............$1.75

(Fritzsche Brothers.)

PROBILIN PILLS. Composed of salicylic acid, acid sodium oleate, phenolphthalein and menthol; used in gallstone affections. Dose, 3 to 4 pills twice daily for twenty days. Vials of 60, per vial.....$1.25

(Schering & Glatz.)

PROFERRIN. (IRON NUCLEO-PROTEID.) Reddish-brown powder, insoluble in water and acid solutions; contains 10 per cent. of iron and 1 per cent. of phosphorus, in organic combination; is absorbed from the duodenum, being unaffected by the gastric juice. Used in blood impoverishment in doses of 5 grains three times daily. 1 oz. cartons, per doz., $6.00; 5 grain tablets, bottle of 100, 60c.; 2½ grain, bottle of 100.......40c.

(H. K. Mulford Co.)

PROTAN. (TANNIN NUCLEO-PROTEID.) Light brown powder, insoluble in water; formed by the synthesis of tannic acid with nucleo-proteid. Used in all forms of diarrhœa in doses of from 20 to 30 grains; is astringent and acts in the intestines, being unaffected by the gastric juice. 1 oz. cartons, per doz., $6.00; 7½ grain tablets, bottle of 100, 85c.; 5 grain, per 100.............60c.

(H. K. Mulford Co.)

PROTARGOL. Yellowish, light powder, easily soluble in water. A proteid compound containing 8 per cent. of silver; not precipitated by albumen or salt solutions. Bactericide in gonorrhœa; antiseptic in eye, ear, nose and throat affections. 0.25 to 1 per cent. solutions for gonorrhœa; 0.5 to 5 per cent. for eye, and 2 to 10 per cent. for ear, nose and throat. Internally, in doses of 1 to 3 grains. ½ oz. and 1 oz. vials, per oz.........$1.10 to $1.35

(Continental Color & Chemical Co.)

PURGATIN. (PURGATOL; ANTHRAPURPURIN ACETATE.) Yellow crystalline powder; a synthetic oxyanthraquinone, having mild aperient properties; insoluble in water; decomposed in contact with alkalies. Dose, 10 to 30 grains. 1 oz. cartons, 85c.; 5 grain tablets, 100 in bottle $1.00

(Knoll & Co. and Merck & Co.)

PYRAMIDON. (DIMETHYL-AMIDO-ANTIPYRIN.) White powder, soluble in 9 parts of water and 2 parts of alcohol. Used as antipyretic in treatment of asthma, pulmonary tuberculosis and abdominal typhus, and as anodyne in headaches and neuralgic pains in doses of 8 to 12 grains. 1 oz. cartons, $2.15; pyramidon camphorate, acid, 1 oz. bot., $1.50; camphorate, neutral, 1 oz. bot., $1.75; salicylate 1 oz. bot. $1.50

(Victor Koechl & Co.)

PYRENOL, a white, crystalline, slightly hygroscopic powder of aromatic odor and sweetish taste, is an addition product of

salicylic and benzoic acids with thymol. Antiseptic, expectorant, analgetic, sedative, antipyretic and cardiotonic. Indicated in the treatment of asthma, bronchitis, pertussis, pneumonia, influenza, typhoid fever and in rheumatic and neuralgic affections. Dose, 7½ to 15 grains, thrice daily, dry or in cold liquids. 1 oz. vial, 70c.; tube of 20 tablets..............30c.
(Schering & Glatz.)

QUARTONOL. Tablets consisting of a compound of duotonol, quinine tonol and strychnine tonol. Blood and nerve tonic. Dose, 1 to 2 tablets three times daily. Bottle of 100 5-grain tablets ....75c.
(Schering & Glatz.)

QUININE LYGOSINATE. Orange-yellow, amorphous powder, containing 70.8 per cent. of quinine; difficultly soluble in water, readily soluble in alcohol, chloroform and benzin. Nontoxic antiseptic and styptic, employed as a dusting powder, gauze or suppository. 10 Gm. vials, each..................70c.
(C. Bischoff & Co.)

RENADEN. Powder, obtained from extract of pigs' kidneys; used in uræmia and nephritis in doses of 1 to 2 drachms daily. 1 oz. vials, $1.30; 4 grain tablets, bottles of 100 ....$1.30
(Knoll & Co. and Merck & Co.)

RUBIDIUM IODIDE. Colorless, cubical crystals; soluble in less than 1 in 1 of water; bitter, saline taste. Used in place of potassium iodide in polyarthritis and syphilis. Dose, 5 to 20 grains. 1 oz. vial..$1 00
(Merck & Co.)

SAL-ETHYL. A colorless, transparent, volatile fluid; chemically pure ethyl salicylate. A substitute for methyl salicylate or oil of wintergreen. Globules, 5 min., in bot. of 50, per doz. bot. $5.00
(Parke, Davis & Co.)

SALIT. (SALICYLIC ACID ESTER OF BORNEOL.) Oily fluid, insoluble in water, slightly soluble in glycerin and readily soluble in alcohol, ethers and oils. Used in muscular and articular rheumatism, lumbago, neuralgia and rheumatic pains following colds. 1 oz. bot......22c.
(Heyden Chemical Works.)

SALOCREOL. (SALICYLIC ACID ESTER OF CREOSOTE.) Oily fluid of neutral reaction, almost odorless, insoluble in water, readily soluble in alcohol, ether, chloroform and oils. Used in facial erysipelas, acute and chronic inflammation of the lymph glands and chronic arthritis. 1 oz. bot........45c.

SALOPHEN. White, crystalline powder, containing 51 per cent. of salicylic acid; almost insoluble in water; soluble in alcohol and ether; incompatible with alkalies, which decompose it. Antipyretic, analgetic and antiseptic in rheumatism and neuralgia. Dose, 10 to 15 grains 3 to 4 times daily. 1 oz. cartons..............85c. to $1.00
(Continental Color & Chemical Co.)

SALOQUININE. (SALICYLIC ACID ESTER OF QUININE.) Whitish powder, insoluble in water, with difficulty soluble about 1 in 120 of alcohol and ether. Tasteless quinine substitute, used in malaria, tropical fevers, neuralgia and rheumatism. Dose, 15 to 30 grains, one to three times daily. ½ and 1 oz. cartons.
$1.25 to $1.30
(Continental Color & Chemical Co. and Merck & Co.)

SANTYL. Yellowish, oily liquid, tasteless and nonirritant. Salicylic ester of pure sandalwood oil. Used in acute gonorrhœia and its complications. Dose, 30 drops, thrice daily. Bottle of ½ oz.....................$1.00
(Knoll & Co. and Merck & Co.)

SCOPOLAMINE HYDROBROMIDE is identical with hyoscine hydrobromide, but lower in price. 15 grain tubes, each, $3.00; 10 grain tubes, $2.10; 5 grain tubes.....$1.05
(Merck & Co. and C. F. Boehringer & Soehn.)

SEXTONOL. Tablets consisting of a compound of duotonol, quinine tonol, iron tonol, manganese tonol and strychnine tonol. Blood and nerve nutrient. Dose, 1 to 2 5-grain tablets three times daily. Bottle of 100..................75c.
(Schering & Glatz.)

SIDONAL. (PIPERAZINE QUINATE.) White amorphous powder, readily soluble in water. Uric acid solvent in gout and allied affections in doses of 75 to 120 grains a day in divided doses, well diluted with water. 1 oz. bot..................$3.75
(Victor Koechl & Co.)

SIDONAL NEW. (QUINIC ACID ANHYDRIDE.) Same properties and uses as above. 1 oz. bot. $2.00
(Victor Koechl & Co.)

SILVER CITRATE. (ANTISEPTIC CREDE; ITROL.) White powder, soluble about 1 in 4000 of water. Recommended in Crédé's treatment as an antiseptic for wounds, in lotion, ointment or powder. For disinfection of hands, skin and instruments, 1 to 1000-5000 watery solution; as gargle 1 to 5000 to 10,000; in gonorrhœa, 1 to 8000. Oz...............$1.20 to $1.25
(Schering & Glatz and Merck & Co.)

SILVER LACTATE. (ACTOL.) Whitish powder, soluble in 15 parts of water; recommended in solution 1 in 200 to 1000 as an antiseptic for surgical use. ½ oz. and 1 oz. vials, per oz., $1.30; tablets, 3 grains, boxes containing 5 vials of 10 tablets, per box......................$1.15
(Schering & Glatz and Merck & Co.)

SOMATOSE. Light yellow almost tasteless powder, easily soluble in water, prepared from meat and consisting of deutero and hetero albumoses. Nitrogenous food product for the sick and convalescent. Dose for adults, 90 to 180 grains daily; for children, 50 to 100 grains. 2 oz. tins, per doz., $8.25; ¼ lb. tins, per lb., $5.25; ½ lb. tins, per lb.........................$5.00
(Continental Color & Chemical Co.)

SOMNOS. (CHLORÆTHANAL ALCOHOLATE.) Clear liquid, miscible with water, produced by the synthesis of chlorætbanal with a polyatomic alcohol radical. Hypnotic and cerebral sedative in doses of from 2 to 4 fluid drachms. Pint bottles, $1.10 per pint; $12.00 per doz.; 4 oz. bottles, per doz...........$4.00
(H. K. Mulford Co.)

SPIROFORM. White, crystalline powder, insoluble in water, but readily soluble in alcohol and other solvents. Odorless and practically tasteless. Antirheumatic, analgetic, uric acid solvent. Dose, 7½ to 15 grains, three to five times daily. 25 Gm. cartons, 75c.; 7½ grain tablets, cartons of 50.....75c.
(C. Bischoff & Co.)

STOVAINE. (AMYLENE HYDROCHLORIDE.) White, crystalline powder, readily soluble in wa-

ter and in methyl alcohol; less soluble in ethyl alcohol and almost insoluble in ether. A substitute for cocaine, approximately one-fifth as toxic. Aqueous solutions are slightly acid and bitter to the taste. Put up in solutions of various strengths, ⅝ per cent., 1 per cent., 10 per cent., in tubes; tablet triturates, 1⅙ grains each; pastilles, 3-100 grain each. Original packages, 1 oz., ½ and ¼ oz. bottles, per oz. $4.00
(Walter F. Sykes & Co.)

STYPTICIN. (COTARNINE HYDROCHLORIDE.) Yellow amorphous powder, the salt of an opium base (cotarnine is a product of the oxidation of narcotine), soluble in water and alcohol. Because of its chemical resemblance to hydrastinine, it being methoxyl-drastine, it is recommended in all forms of uterine hæmorrhage. Used in functional dysmenorrhœa and in the menorrhagia of puberty and the climacteric. Dose as styptic, 1½ to 4 grains, as needed, per os or by injection (10 per cent. solution). Sugar coated tablets, ⅝ grain, per tube of 20, 25c.; 1 oz. bottles, per oz., $6.50; ½ oz. bottles, per oz., $6.60; ⅛ oz., per oz., $7.00; 15 grain vials, each, 35c.; hypodermic tablets, ⅝ grain, per box of 40 (4 tubes).......60c.
(Merck & Co.)

STYPTOL. (COTARNINE PHTHALATE.) Yellow, crystalline powder, readily soluble in water. It is the phthalate salt of an opium base. Recommended in uterine hæmorrhage in doses of 1 to 3 grains; externally in 10 per cent. solution. 1 oz. vials, $6.50; ¼ oz., per oz., $6.75; ⅛ oz., $7.00; 15 grain vials, per vial, 35c.; ⅝ grain tablets, bottles of 100, per bot...$1.20
(Knoll & Co. and Merck & Co.)

STYRACOL. (GUAIACOL CINNAMIC ESTER.) White granular crystals, insoluble in water, readily soluble in alcohol. Given in phthisis, catarrh of the stomach and intestines in doses of 15 grains three to four times daily. 1 oz. cartons, $1.20; 5 grain tablets, bot of 100..$1.40
(Knoll & Co. and Merck & Co.)

SUBLAMINE. (MERCURIC ETHYLENE-DIAMINE SULPHATE.) Crystalline powder, containing 43 per cent. of mercury; very soluble in water. Used in solutions of 1 to 1000 as a substitute for corrosive sublimate. 1 oz. vials, 50c.; tablets, 15 grains, 100 tablets in bottle, $1.10; 20 tablets in tube, 5 tubes in box............$1.60
(Schering & Glatz.)

TANNALBIN. (TANNIN ALBUMINATE.) Pale brown, insoluble, tasteless powder, containing about 50 per cent. of tannin. It is not affected by the gastric juice, but is split up in the intestinal canal; hence is used as intestinal astringent and for diarrhœa. Dose, 15 to 30 grains three to five times daily. 1 oz. cartons, 85c.; 5 grain tablets, bot. of 100......$1.00
(Knoll & Co. and Merck & Co.)

TANNIGEN. (ACETYLTANNIN.) Grayish powder, insoluble in water, soluble in alcohol; incompatible with alkalies which decompose it. Intestinal astringent in chronic diarrhœa and intestinal diseases of children. Adult dose, 3 to 10 grains, three to six times daily; children, 1-3 to ½ that quantity. 1 oz. bot., per oz....55c. to 75c.
(Continental Color & Chemical Co.)

TANNOPINE. (HEXAMETHYLENETETRAMINE TANNIN.) Brownish powder, insoluble in water, decomposed by alkalies; compound of tannin and urotropine, containing 87 per cent. of tannic acid. Intestinal astringent and disinfectant. Adult dose, 10 to 15 grains; children, 3 to 8 grains four times daily. 1 oz. cartons, per oz..............55c. to 75c.
(Continental Color & Chemical Co.)

TESTADEN. Powdered extract of the testicle juice of animals. Used in impotency, neurasthenia and spinal irritation. Dose, 15 grains three to four times daily. 1 oz. vials, $1.30; 4 grain tablets, bot. of 100.$1.30
(Knoll & Co. and Merck & Co.)

THEOBROMINE. White crystalline powder, soluble in ether, but almost insoluble in cold water or alcohol; organic base obtained from seeds of *Theobroma cacao.* Diuretic in dropsy of cardiac and renal affections. Dose, 5 to 8 grains. 1 oz. bot., per oz.........90c.
(Continental Color & Chemical Co. and Merck & Co.)

THEOBROMINE - SODIUM - SALICYLATE. White powder, very soluble in water, decomposed by acid solutions. Diuretic in dropsy of cardiac and renal origin. Dose, 7 to 15 grains. 1 oz. bot., per oz..60c.
(Farbenfabriken of Elberfeld, Continental Color Works and Merck & Co.)

THEOCIN. Fine, colorless crystals; synthetic alkaloid of tea (theophylline); difficultly soluble in alcohol and cold water, more easily in warm water; forms salts with alkalies. Powerful diuretic in doses of 3 to 6 grains, two to three times daily. ½ and 1 oz. bot., per oz.............$2.50 to $2.70
(Continental Color & Chemical Co.)

THEOPHYLLIN. White crystalline needles, soluble in 226 parts of water. Identical with theocin, being the synthetic alkaloid of tea. Diuretic in doses of 4 to 8 grains. 1 oz. vials, $1.40. Theophyllin sodium, 1 oz. vials, $1.50. Theophylline-sodium salicylate, 1 oz. vials $1.10
(C. F. Boehringer & Soehne.)

THIGENOL. Dark brown, thick liquid; odorless on use; slight empyreumatic taste; soluble in water, diluted alcohol, glycerin and collodion; same uses as ichthyol. It is the sodium salt of the sulphonic acid of a synthetic sulpho oil. Dose, 3 to 10 grains. 1 oz. boxes, per oz., 32c.; 1 lb. tins, per lb....$4.00
(Hoffmann-La Roche Chemical Works.)

THIOCOL. (POTASSIUM GUAIACOL SULPHONATE.) White crystalline powder, soluble in water, slightly in alcohol and ether. Used in phthisis and similar diseases which require the creosote or guaiacol treatment; nonirritating and readily assimilable. Dose, 5 to 20 grains three times daily. 1 oz. bot., per oz., $1.40; tablets, 5 grains each, 100 in bot...$1.75
(Hoffmann-La Roche Chemical Works.)

THIOSINAMIN. Colorless crystals, soluble in water, alcohol and ether; used hypodermically for lupus and uterine affections in doses of 1 to 3 grains in 15 per cent. alcoholic or 10 per cent. glycerinated water solution, one injection being given every three days; by the mouth, in capsules containing ⅓ to 3 grains. 1 oz. vials, per oz. 60c.
(Scherin & Glatz and Merck & Co.)

THYMOXOL. Alcoholic 1 per cent. solution of thymol containing 3 per cent. of hydrogen dioxide; miscible with water. Used in 5 or 10 per cent. solutions as antiseptic and bactericide. ¼ lb. bot., per lb...$2.40
(C. Bischoff & Co.)

THYRADEN. Brownish powder: dried extract of sheep's thyroid, containing all the constituents of the gland. Used in myxœdema, obesity, goitre, psoriasis, eczema, menorrhagia and rickets. Dose, 15 to 30 grains daily. 1 oz. vials, $1.30; 2 grain tablets, bot. of 100.75c.
(Knoll & Co. and Merck & Co.)

THYREOIDECTIN. Reddish powder obtained from the blood of animals deprived of the thyreoid gland. A remedy for exophthalmic goitre. Dose, 5 to 10 grains. Capsules, 5 grains each, bot. of 50...$1.00
(Parke, Davis & Co.)

THYROIDIN. Dried extract of sheep's thyroid, 1 part equaling 6 parts of fresh gland. Used in myxœdema, cretinism, psoriasis, obesity, lupus, etc. Dose, ½ to 1 grain, increased to 2 grains three times daily. 1 oz. bot..................$1.25
(Merck & Co.)

TONOLS. Trade name adopted by Schering & Glatz for the glycerophosphate salts. See under the name of the alkali earth or metallic base.

TRIFERRIN. (IRON PARANUCLEINATE.) Brownish-yellow powder, soluble in alkaline solutions, insoluble in water. Said to contain 22 per cent. of iron, 9 per cent. of nitrogen and 2.5 per cent. of phosphorus. Used in anæmia, chlorosis and debility in dose of 5 grains three times daily. 1 oz. cartons, $1.00; 5 grain tablets, cartons of 50, 75c.; solution (Triferrol), 8 oz. bot., per bot..55c.
(C. Bischoff & Co. and Knoll & Co.)

TRIKRESOL. Clear, colorless liquid; a mixture of ortho, meta and para cresols in the proportion of 35, 40 and 25 per cent., respectively. Corresponding to Creosol, U. S. P., viii; soluble in 40 parts of water. Said to have three times the germicidal power of carbolic acid. Solutions of from ½ to 1 per cent. strength are recommended for surgical use; for internal use 1 to 2 minims three times a day. 1 oz. vials, 15c.; 1 lb. bot....................60c.
(Schering & Glatz.)

TRIOTONOL. Tablet consisting of 5 grains duotonol and 1-60 grain strychnine-tonol. Nerve tonic. Dose, 1 to 2 tablets, thrice daily. Bottle of 100 tablets ....75c.
(Schering & Glatz.)

TRIPHENIN. (PROPIONYLPHENETIDIN.) White crystalline powder obtained by the action of propionic acid on paraphenetidine; almost insoluble in water (1 in 2000), more readily in alcohol and ether. Is a strong antipyretic, used in neuralgias and rheumatism in doses of 5 to 15 grains three or four times daily. Tablets, 5 grains, bot. of 50, 65c.; 1 oz. cartons..50c.
(Merck & Co.)

TROPACOCAINE HYDROCHLORIDE. (BENZOYLPSEUDOTROPEINE HYDROCHLORIDE.) Colorless crystals, soluble in water. Local anæsthetic like cocaine, but said to be less depressing to the heart. Used hypodermically in 3 to 10 per cent. solutions in 0.6 per cent. solution of sodium chloride. 5 grain vials, 40c.; 15 grain vials ....95c.
(Merck & Co.)

TUMENOL. Reddish-brown, oily paste, obtained from a bituminous rock deposit. Consists of a mixture of sulphonised hydrocarbons similar to ichthyol, and possessing similar properties, being antiseptic and healing in skin diseases, applied either as attenuated powder, 5 per cent. ointment, or dissolved in ether and alcohol or water and glycerine.

AMMONIUM. Black, viscid, oily liquid, odorless; soluble in water and miscible with oils and fats. Used as antiseptic application in skin diseases, in form of ointment, paste or glycerin-ethereal solution painted on surface. 1 oz. bottles.....25c.

OIL is a dark yellow fluid of thick consistency, having the same application as the foregoing.

POWDER. (SULPHOTUMENOLIC ACID.) Dark yellow powder, readily soluble in water. Used with equal parts of zinc starch paste in treatment of skin diseases. Paste, 1 oz. vials, 55c.; ¼ lb. jar, $1.75; ½ lb. jar, $3.25. Oil, 1 oz. vials, 65c.; ½ lb. bottles, $3.25; 1 lb. bottles, $6.30. Powder, 1 oz. tin, $1.10; 2 oz. tins, per tin..$1.85
(Victor Koechl & Co.)

URITONE. White crystalline powder; a product of formaldehyde and ammonia of the same composition and properties as hexamethylenetetramine; used in treatment of purulent conditions of the urine, cystitis, etc., in doses of 5 to 15 grains. 1 oz. vials, 60c.; 5 grain capsules, per bot. of 100.....85c.
(Parke, Davis & Co.)

UROSINE. (LITHIUM QUINATE.) Colorless crystals, readily soluble in water. Used in gout, cystitis and uric acid diathesis. Supplied in effervescent tablets containing quinic acid, 7½ grains; lithium carbonate, 1½ grains; sugar, 4¼ grains. Vial of 10, 50c.; 25, $1.20. Powder, 1 oz. vial....................95c.
(C. Bischoff & Co.)

UROTROPIN. (HEXAMETHYLENETETRAMINE.) Colorless granular crystals, with an alkaline reaction; readily soluble in water. Urinary antiseptic in cystitis, bacteruria, phosphaturia, gout, rheumatism, irritable bladder, etc., used also before and after instrumentation to forestall urinary infection. Dose, 5 to 15 grains. 1 oz. vials, 60c.; lb., $7.50; tablets, 7½ grains each, 20 tablets in box, 25c.; 5 grains each, 30 tablets in box.........25c.
(Schering & Glatz.)

UROTROPIN METHYLENE CITRATE. (NEWUROTROPIN.) Crystals resembling urotropin and having same therapeutic indications, though dose is double, being 15 grains three times daily. 1 oz. vials, 60c.; tablets, 7½ grains, 20 tablets in box, per box..............25c.
(Schering & Glatz.)

VALIDOL. (VALERIC ACID MENTHYL ESTER.) Colorless liquid, a combination of valeric acid and menthol; insoluble in water, readily soluble in alcohol. Used in hysteria and neurasthenia in doses of 10 to 15 drops three times daily. Vials, 10 Gm., 50c.; 25 Gm., $1.20; pills, 25 in bot., each......50c.
(C. Bischoff & Co.)

VALIDOL CAMPHORATE. Colorless liquid, insoluble in water, readily soluble in alcohol and oils. A 10 per cent. solution of camphor in validol. Used in toothache by local application and internally in same indications and dose as validol. Vials, 10 Gm. each, 50c.; 25 Gm. $1.20
(C. Bischoff & Co.)

VALYL. (VALERIC ACID DIETHYLAMIDE.) Colorless, oily liquid, with a valerian odor and burning taste, supplied only in gelatin capsules, each containing 2 grains. Nerve sedative used in hysteria, neurasthenia, hypochondriasis, and in neuralgia and menstrual disturbances in doses of 2 or 3 capsules two or three times daily. Bot. of 50 capsules.......90c.
(Victor Koechl & Co.)

VERONAL. White crystalline powder, soluble in 150 parts of cold and 12 parts of boiling water. Hypnotic in simple sleeplessness and the insomnia of mania. Dose, 5 to 15 grains, dissolved in hot fluids. 1 oz. bot. and cartons, per oz., $1.60; tablets, 5 grains each, tube of 10, 30c.; bot. of 100 ....$2.25
(Merck & Co. and Continental Color & Chemical Co.)

VIOFORM. (IODOCHLOROXYCHINOLINE.) Greenish-yellow powder, insoluble in water. Used in same way as iodoform, than which it is six times lighter and bulkier. 1 oz. cartons $1.15
(C. Bischoff & Co.)

XEROFORM. (TRIBROMPHENOLBISMUTH.) Yellow, insoluble powder, containing bismuth oxide and tribromphenol in nearly equal proportions. A powerful bactericide used in place of iodoform as a dressing for wounds and internally as an intestinal antiseptic in doses of 5 to 20 grains. 1 oz. vials...50c.
(The Heyden Chemical Works.)

American Druggist "WANTS" Page.

THIS Department is intended to be used as a medium for the exchange or sale of stores, the employment of clerks, and the securing of situations. Suitable notices of moderate length under this heading inserted one time free for subscribers; for each additional insertion Fifty Cents will be charged. Advertisements not in the foregoing classification Forty Cents per line.

SITUATIONS VACANT.

THE PUBLISHER OF ONE OF THE LEADING DRUG JOURNALS (NOT IN NEW YORK) DESIRES THE SERVICES OF A CAPABLE MAN FOR EDITORIAL WORK. MUST BE THOROUGHLY QUALIFIED IN PHARMACY AND BE ABLE TO WRITE GOOD, STRONG ENGLISH. PRACTICAL EXPERIENCE IN THE DRUG BUSINESS, AND ABILITY TO TRANSLATE FROM GERMAN AND FRENCH WOULD BE VERY DESIRABLE QUALIFICATIONS. ADDRESS, STATING EXPERIENCE, ETC., JOURNALIST, CARE OF AMERICAN DRUGGIST.

REGISTERED PHARMACISTS and drug employees, if you would accept a better position, now or later, send us your name at once; fine openings in all States; salaries, $600 to $2,000 a year; employers referred to competent men free. NATIONAL PHARMACEUTICAL AGENCY, 616 Colonial Security Building, St. Louis, Mo.

WANTED, LICENSED CLERK at retail drug store; steady position for right party. Best of references required. Address J. F. R., care of AMERICAN DRUGGIST.

WANTED.—Licensed clerk at retail drug store. Good position. E. L. Schmitt, 312 North street, Rochester, N. Y.

SITUATIONS WANTED.

DRUGGIST.—First-class graduate and experienced, desires to change positions. No bad habits. In answering state salary. Address Druggist, Box 226, Meridian, Miss.

BUSINESS OPPORTUNITIES.

CIRCULARS, BOOKLETS, LETTERS and advertising matter of any description designed and prepared; high-grade medical advertising a specialty. C. L. Mueller, M. D., Advertising Counselor, Wapakoneta, Ohio.

FOR SALE.—One of the finest drug stores in western New York; cement block; building new; steel ceiling; all fixtures new; everything up to date; hot water, heat, gas or electric lights; insurance, 1 per cent; will sell with or without building. Address V. C. Armes, Gowanda, N. Y.

FOR $25,000, a working interest in a fine wholesale drug business. Address Drugs, care Stringer & Seymour, St. Paul, Minn.

FOR SALE.—$4,000 stock of drugs, wall paper and books; no fountain. Rent $235 per year. Sales about $8,000. Address F. D. Graves, Antwerp, Ohio.

DRUG BUSINESS OFFER.—Owing to other business, which demands my attention, I offer controlling interest in a good drug (stock company) business, which carries with it a salaried position as manager, with full control. This offering is located in a live, progressive N. C. town of 3,000 population; only one other drug store; good business; nicely located and convenient. Good investment. Price, $3,000. Terms cash. Address Manager, care of AMERICAN DRUGGIST.

DRUG STORE FOR SALE doing a good business in city of 50,000; the best business city in the State. Full prices. Write for particulars. Box 109, Pueblo, Col.

WANTED.—To correspond with wholesale druggists' sundries salesman with an established trade to handle on commission a new and extremely useful household novelty—a corkscrew and spoonholder combined. Designed to draw corks from medicine bottles and hold spoon in suspension. Sells well on sight and yields good profit. The right man can have exclusive sales privilege in his territory. Address A. M. Irvy, Norfolk, Va.

WANTED.—A drug store doing a moderate business, "no paints or oils," within 35 miles of New York. It must bear the closest examination or please do not waste your time or mine by noticing this. Address Geo. Kempton, 197 Fulton street, New York.

A BARGAIN.—A Morris Tablet Machine, Style B. Direct Driver. Includes dies and punches; this machine is practically new, having only been in use about three months. ANOTHER BARGAIN.—A 60-Gallon Drug Still, including rectifier, condenser, and low wine still The still can be operated independent of the rectifier. This set is in splendid condition, being practically good as new. Address Dept A, 212 S. Seventh Street, St. Louis, Mo.

FOR SALE.—An old established drug store in a manufacturing town in Connecticut, one hour from New York; reason for selling, poor health of owner; a good store; $4,500 inventory. Address Lysol, care of AMERICAN DRUGGIST.

FOR SALE.—Wishing to retire from business on account of age, I offer a large and prosperous business at a liberal discount from the inventory to a cash customer; when answering this state how much capital you have to invest. Address Filmore, care of AMERICAN DRUGGIST.

Acetylmorphine, Ethylmorphine hydrochloride

ICHTOSAN

The cheapest substitute of Ichthyol in its healing power, and of equal value. Glycerophosphates, phenolphtaleine silver salts and a great range of other pharmaceutical chemicals.

J. H. WOLFENSBERGER,
Basle, Switzerland.
Manufacturer of Pharmaceutical Specialties.

WARNING NOTICE

to the world of my proprietary rights to the trade-mark names of Satin, Satin Skin, Satin-Skin (hyphenated), Satin Scent, etc., as applied to toilet preparations, soaps, perfumes, etc., is given by U. S. patent office registrations No. 21,618, 24,186, 27,834, 37,662, 42,297. Canadian 899,444. I promptly prosecute infringers, imitators, and sellers of substitutes. (Signed)

ALBERT F. WOOD, Detroit, Mich., Mfr. and Propr. of Satin Skin Cream, Satin Toilet and Talcum Powders, Satin-Skin Soaps, Satin Tooth Preparations, Satin Scents, etc.

EXAMINATION QUESTIONS:

I have collected and bound in a 64-page pamphlet (6x9 inches, fine print), the PHARMACY EXAMINATION QUESTIONS of the various states and territories; also the Pharmacy Laws of the different states. All of the questions are recent, many based on new U. S. P. They are intended for those who wish to prepare for State Board or other examinations.

A candidate about to take an examination can have no better preparation than a thorough drill on the questions that have been asked by State Board Examiners.

This pamphlet will be sent post paid to any address upon receipt of 75 cts. Address:

J. A. HYNES,
292 S. Marshfield Avenue Chicago, Ill.

THE following Advertisement is one of a series now being run in all the important Horse and Farm Papers in United States, Canada and England.

Your demand for ABSORBINE will be greatly increased. Regular Jobbers can supply you. Mail me your card so I can place it on file and refer inquiries from your section to you for supplies.

ACCIDENTS will happen. The colts will get hurt. Any Soft Inflamed Bunch can be removed in a pleasing manner with

ABSORBINE

No blister. No hair gone. Comfort for the horse. Profit for you. $2.00 per bottle delivered. Book 4-B free.

ABSORBINE, JR., for mankind, $1.00 Bottle. Removes the black and blue from a bruise at once. Stop Toothache, Reduce Swellings. Genuine manufactured only by

W. F. Young, P.D.F., 49 Monmouth St., Springfield, Mass.

ONCE TRIED, ALWAYS USED.

THE BAR-KEEPER'S "FRIEND"

FOR ... BAR FIXTURES, DRAIN BOARDS AND ALL Tin, Zinc, Brass, Copper, Nickel and all Kitchen and Plated Utensils. Glass, Wood, Marble, Porcelain, Etc.

GEORGE WM. HOFFMAN.

THE BAR-KEEPERS' FRIEND.

FOR cleansing everything about a drug store or a soda fountain there is nothing equal to Hoffman's

Barkeeper's Friend

Marble, Glass, Nickel, Brass, Copper, Tin and German Silver can all be cleaned and polished with it easier than with anything else. Let us send you a FREE SAMPLE.

Highest Award, Chicago World's Fair, 1893. Louisiana Purchase Exposition, St. Louis, Mo., 1904.

GEO. WM. HOFFMAN, 295 E. Washington St. Indianapolis, Ind.

FOR SALE BY JOBBING TRADE

TANSY PILLS

Dozen Boxes, $3. Prepaid

Our French Tansy and Pennyroyal Pills are attractively put up in fancy decorated tin boxes and are of the very finest quality.

We guarantee the best grade at $8.00 per dozen boxes, PREPAID, or $7.50 per quarter gross.

Special prices for quantity orders.

Aetna Chemical Co., 38 Griswold St., Detroit, Mich.

A Mix-Up in Cuts.

Owing to inadvertence the cut intended to illustrate the article by the Beaton Drug Company, in the series of articles on Soda Fountain Beverages in our issue for March 26, was placed with the article by Frank A. Epstein. The Beaton Drug Company is proud of its L. A. Becker Twentieth Century Sanitary Fountain and would like to have seen it displayed with its article, but to paraphrase an old saying—where the editor proposes the printer often disposes—and the Becker apparatus went to illustrate what should have been an American Soda Fountain Company's "Innovation," which is shown herewith.

"Innovation" Apparatus in Frank A. Epstein's Pharmacy, Boston.

The Right to Use the Name "Liebig's" Restricted by the Courts.

The litigation instituted by Liebig's Extract of Meat Company, Limited, has finally resulted in the United States Circuit Court of Appeals enjoining Libby, McNeill & Libby from using the word "Liebig" in connection with the sale of extract of meat not of the Liebig Company's manufacture, or from using the name "Liebig" either alone or in association with the words "extract of meat" or the word "Company" or in any other association calculated to indicate to the public that the goods bearing such names emanate from Baron Justus von Liebig, or from the Liebig Company, when this is not the fact.

Most of our readers know that the Liebig Company was formed with the co-operation of Baron Justus von Liebig, and has built up an enormous trade all over the world in Liebig's Extract of Beef.

As a result of the association of the said Baron Justus von Liebig with the Liebig Company and by reason of the excellence of their product, the extract of meat manufactured by this company acquired a great reputation; to the end that Liebig's Extract of Meat is regarded as an indispensable article in the sick room and as a table delicacy.

During the prosecution of the above cause, and while the questions involved were unsettled, numerous imitators of the Liebig package have sprung up, and the Liebig Company has instructed its attorneys to immediately proceed to prosecute all who may be guilty of infringement of its marks. Cornelius David & Co., of 120 Hudson street, New York, agents in the United States of the Liebig Company, will appreciate the co-operation of the trade in assisting them to suppress all infringements of the Liebig Company's trademarks.

The American Perfumer.

Under the above title Ungerer & Co., of 15 Platt street, New York, have launched an "authoritative organ devoted to the odoriferous arts," this being, we are told, the only publication devoted exclusively to perfumery which is printed in the English language. The first issue is an interesting one, containing a number of practical notes from leading American perfumers and the translation of an article on the alpha and beta ionones from the French of Dr. Phillippe Chuit. The little magazine is gotten up in a tasteful manner and will no doubt prove an immediate success, filling a distinct place in technical literature.

A Drug Store "Fishing" Feature.

It's all right to "cut bait," but occasionally you've got to *fish*. The right "line' is to be considered, but we mustn't forget to use a good book.

The druggist who has tried it knows that a line of souvenir post cards is an eye-catching proposition; and the Souvenir Post Card Company, located at 50 Franklin street, New York, declares that good subjects from their stock will "book" the fish-dollars and keep up a merry jingle in your cash drawer. Recently the company made a special offer to those desiring to secure a handsome card rack at nominal price; and this week they renew the offer, for the benefit of any who may have overlooked it before. The sum of $10 brings you 1,200 assorted post cards, together with its best display rack. Two thousand cards may be kept in this rack. It also offers a full line of samples to dealers sending $3, with privilege to return any cards not wanted. A good chance to hook some good things.

Hand-I-Hold Babe Mits.

We are glad to call attention to a new invention, the "Hand-I-Hold" babe mits, which is clearly illustrated and described in the advertisement which appears on another page. The device is calculated to prevent a small child from scratching when afflicted with sore eyes or any form of irritable skin disease. It is so simple and, withal, so effective that we wonder that no one has ever thought of it before.

Each hand is inclosed in an aluminum ball, so highly polished as to clearly reflect the child's face and the objects in the background. Every movement produces a kaleidoscopic change of picture, which is very entertaining to the baby, and soon causes him to forget his troubles.

There are various uses to which "Hand-I-Hold" babe mits are put, all of which are referred to in an attractive booklet published by the manufacturers. We commend the article as one worthy of prompt and thorough investigation by all physicians who have eczema and kindred diseases in charge and to druggists as a profitable and useful side line.

Incongruous.

Nothing disturbs one's sense of harmony and proportion more than the appearance of an old-fashioned, sluggish counter scale, in a store with fixtures otherwise modern and artistic. No fixture is more conspicuous, and customers instinctively look for it. They have associated it with every counter transaction.

With few exceptions scale manufacturers have been indifferent to this requirement of the trade. The Torsion Balance Company, of New York, however, have proved themselves the exception. Their various styles of counter scales are not only unique and artistic in design, but they are also constructed to weigh with the same precision and sensitiveness as their celebrated prescription scales.

Soda Counter Requisites.

The up to date druggist no longer uses makeshifts on his dispensing counter. "Any old thing" won't do in these modern days. It is interesting to note the large and varied line of counter requisites now manufactured by the American Soda Fountain Company. Every need of the dispenser has been carefully studied, and soda and sundae glasses, spoons, spoonholders, crushed fruit bowls and countless other accessories are now specially designed for the modern soda fountain. It is good business policy to have your whole equipment thoroughly modern. The cold sundries catalogue just issued by the American Soda Fountain Company will give the druggist many a new idea for his soda service. The artistic and useful articles illustrated in this catalogue will make a soda fountain more attractive to the customers, and consequently more profitable to the druggist. We understand that the catalogue will be sent upon request.

Get Your Share.

Some pharmacists make a practice of notifying physicians about additions to their list of new remedies. The idea is a good one. To a certain extent, such a custom localizes the general advertising efforts of manufacturers. To illustrate: A pharmacist receives a prescription containing thigenol, the odorless soluble sulphur compound; or he gets one for digalen, the new digitalis derivative. It is pretty safe to predict that other physicians in the neighborhood, aside from the one who prescribed the remedy, have read of the same medicament. Perhaps some of the other doctors are really interested in the remedy which has just been stocked, but they hesitate to prescribe it for fear it will not be readily procurable. When these particular physicians receive a notice that the remedy is in stock in a nearby pharmacy there will be more prescriptions written for the drug. Of course, the pharmacist might ask, "But why should I take the trouble to do any advertising for a manufacturer?" Is it not a fact that you always have to stock the new remedies for some physician in your neighborhood? Isn't it better to have a dozen or twenty physicians prescribing a new remedy than to have only two or three leaders?

Then, again, the custom of regularly sending reminders of your prescription department to physicians gives you the reputation of being progressive; of having a complete stock of all the important additions to the newer materia medica. A good word from a physician is worth a good many dollars' worth of advertising.

Just now various leading products of the Hoffmann-La Roche Chemical Works are broadly advertised. Why not get your share of the local influence of that advertising?

The offices of the Hoffmann-La Roche Chemical Works are at 51-53 Maiden Lane, New York, and the products just now attracting especial attention are airol, digalen, thicol and thigenol.

Post Card Display Stand.

The American News Company is now in a position to promptly fill all orders for their Improved Paragon Revolving Post Card Display Stand. The great demand for this stand taxed to the utmost the facilities of the factories and made necessary the establishment of another factory for these stands. New tools had to be made and material of the proper quality ordered, all of which took time, but we are now advised that shipments from the new factory have begun, which puts the company in a position to fill all orders for this most desirable post card fixture promptly upon receipt. The trade will do well to make careful note of the advertisement on another page of this issue. You should send your order now, before the big summer rush sets in, as even with the increased facilities they may find it difficult to fill orders received later with the same promptness that they can at present. Descriptive catalogues, price lists, etc., will be sent upon request by the American News Company, Post Card Department, New York.

Johnson & Johnson Show Plasters in Court.

In an effort to recover $50,000 which, they assert, they were unjustly compelled to pay as a proprietary medicine war tax on plasters, Johnson & Johnson, of New Brunswick, N. J., are now submitting as evidence in the United States District Court in Newark, N. J., three trunks full of bunion plasters, corn plasters and many other varieties of adhesives. The Johnson & Johnson suit has been brought against former Internal Revenue Collector William D. Rutan, who held the office in 1898 and 1899, and Dr. Herman C. H. Herold, the present incumbent. The manufacturers maintain that such plasters were not taxable, and the hearing in the suit has been adjourned indefinitely to permit the Government to take the testimony of Dr. C. A. Crampton, chemist of the Internal Revenue Department in Washington, relating to the medicinal properties of the plasters in question.

American Fruit Juice for Export.

Boericke & Tafel, 145 Grand street, New York City, have by careful attention to the details of manufacture and by the use of a superior quality of material, built up an enormous business in the sale of American grape juice in foreign countries. The production of grape juice has become a very important industry in the United States, but only a comparatively small quantity of it is exported, for the reason that in order to stand the climatic changes involved in export trade, the grape juice must be prepared with the greatest skill and care.

The experience of years in this field has enabled Boericke & Tafel to produce a grape juice which will undergo the severe ordeal of crossing the equator without suffering any deterioration. We commend this preparation to the careful attention of our readers who wish to secure a rich, fruity grape juice which will keep under all conditions. Special export prices will be quoted on application by the manufacturers at the above address.

The Toxic Properties of Cocaine.

Unless properly prepared, cocaine hydrochlorate is liable to contain cinnamyl-cocaine and isatrophyl-cocaine, both of which have more or less toxic properties and modify the action of the cocaine. Absolute purity is therefore highly essential in this drug. The cocaine manufactured by the Mallinckrodt Chemical Works, is a chemically pure product, and may be relied upon to produce prompt and accurate therapeutic results. When the Mallinckrodt cocaine was first introduced physicians were quick to recognize its excellent quality, and it has become a standard and leading brand in this country.

Pharmacists comparing the present list of the Mallinckrodt Chemical Works with that issued a number of years ago, will observe that the firm is becoming an important factor in the manufacture of alkaloids. It is a fact that they are now, if not the largest, certainly among the largest manufacturers of cocaine in the world.

The Origin of the Illustrated Post Cards.

Prof. Oswald Schroeder, in the first issue of the *Post Card Dealer*, gives a highly romantic and interesting history of the origin of the illustrated post card. It seems that it was a custom of a small circle of painters, authors and a certain art publisher to take luncheon together in a well-known cafe in Munich. In June, 1878, this coterie, including the elder Kaulbach, determined to write postal cards to one of their number, whom they recently heard from, who was in the Alps. A chance drop of coffee running across one end of the card lying before Kaulbach, he absent mindedly began to draw lines with the coffee by means of a toothpick while engaged in animated conversation and being apparently entirely unconscious of the drawing. In fact, when it was completed he dropped the toothpick without observing that he had completed a very striking sketch of a bearded Tyrolian. The other members of the party, however, were delighted with the results, and thereupon each member of the group set about the preparation of an illustrated card, to be sent to the absent member, and shortly after this the art publisher placed upon the market a series of cards, reproducing pen and ink sketches of scenes about Munich. Thus, according to Professor Schroeder, was born the illustrated post card, the sale of which constitutes a large and rapidly growing industry.

In view of the increased protection of trademarks afforded by the new copyright law, a great many proprietors who have not heretofore taken out copyrights are doing so on their labels and trademarks. Full particulars regarding the application of the law may be had from Sheppard & Parker, trademark experts, 110 Revenue Building, Chicago.

Stamp Vending Machine.

A new application of the coin controlled vending machine has recently been directed to the sale of postage stamps by mechanical means. A slot machine intended for the selling of both postage stamps and postal cards has been placed in the stamp division of the Post Office Department at Washington for exhibition purposes and to demonstrate its use to the officials of the department. According to the *Washington Post*, the machines are after the pattern of the chewing gum machines and chocolate machines, worked by putting in a coin and receiving a stamp or postal card in return. It is expected that each machine will replace a stamp clerk.

These machines are in practical use by the postal authorities in Germany and France, where they have met with great success, and from the favorable impression they have so far made upon the postal authorities in this country it is likely that in a few months they will be adopted, and then at the various postoffices in the larger cities throughout the country two or more such machines will be placed for the selling of stamps and postal cards.

The machines are for the selling of one and two cent stamps and postal cards. A separate machine is used for each article. A powerful magnet plays an important part in the passing of the coin through the machine.

The inventor says the magnets and other mechanism make it impossible to use a counterfeit coin in the machines.

One point about the new machines which, as explained by the officials, is likely to prove unpopular is that it is impossible to buy less than ten cents' worth of the stamps, as the machine will only work by the insertion of a dime.

Fun with the Soda Clerk.

A despondent looking man rolled into a Times Square drug store recently, says the *New York Times*, and, calling for a glass of water, pulled from a pocket a small bottle, extracting a tablet which he dropped into the glass. Holding the water on a level with his eyes, he looked thoughtfully as the tablet slowly dissolved. Then with a sigh he turned to the young soda clerk, who was watching him narrowly.

"It's a hard life," he remarked, gloomily. "We'd best be out of it."

"What's that you put in the glass?" asked the boy nervously.

"Now, Willie," answered the other, "you're a sweet young thing all right, but I'd advise you to go back to the patchouli department for more." The boy reached over to examine the potion the man was arranging.

"None o' that," growled the disconsolate one. "That's corrosive sublimate, and it's my finish, see!" Then he raised the glass and drank its contents.

The boy jumped over the counter and ran out, yelling. He brought back a policeman and a crowd.

"What's all this?" demanded the policeman.

"Oh, just the mere trifle of the finish of a man who's tired," answered the rolling one indifferently. The policeman stuck his hand into the man's pocket and brought forth a bottle labeled:

| FIVE GRAIN LITHIA TABLETS. |

"What the divvle d'ye mean by throwing us this sort of a scare?" demanded the policeman.

"That's all right," responded the unsteady one, shambling out. "I jus' wanted to teach that squab over there not to be so darned new; that's all."

Then he walked off with a chuckle.

Examination Questions.

A 64-page pamphlet, 6 x 9 inches, with fine print, has been made up from the examination questions of the pharmacy boards of the various States and Territories. This, together with an abstract of the pharmacy laws. This pamphlet also contains an abstract of the pharmacy laws of the several States, both being published by J. A. Hynes, 292 South Marshfield avenue, Chicago, who will forward a copy postage paid on receipt of 75 cents. When writing for a copy kindly mention the AMERICAN DRUGGIST.

FRANK S. BETZ CO.

(Incorporated)

CAPITAL, SEVEN HUNDRED AND FIFTY THOUSAND DOLLARS

Drugs
Pharmaceuticals
Chemicals
Tablets
Fluid Extracts
Oils
Wines
Syrups
Capsules

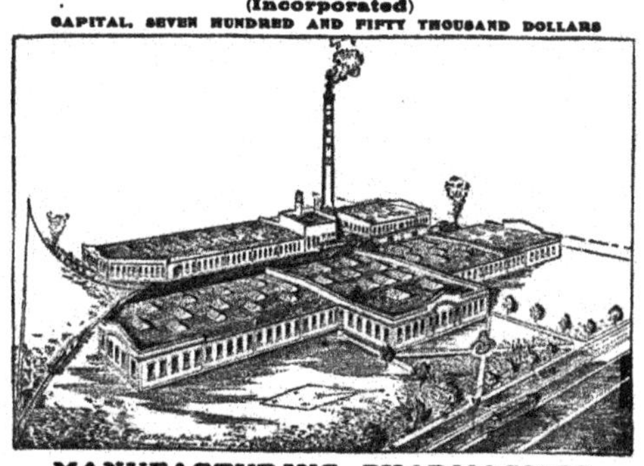

Surgical Instruments
Apparatus
Appliances
Dressings
Rubber Goods
Glassware
Trusses
Sundries

MANUFACTURING PHARMACISTS

Surgical and Hospital Supplies of Every Description

LARGEST PLANT OF ITS KIND IN THE WORLD

SURGEON'S GREEN SOAP,	10 lb. jars, net, $1.00;	20 lb. jars, net, $1.90
	Barrel, 400 lbs.	lb., 6c.
STRONGER AMMONIA, C. P., Sp. Gr. 90°,	8 lb., gal., $1.00;	16 lb., 2 gal., $1.90
	Carboys,	lb., 8½c.
CHLOROFORM, Strictly Pure,	5 lb. bottle, $1.60;	12 lb. bottle, $4.25
	100 lb. bulk,	$31.00
DISTILLED EXTRACT WITCH HAZEL,	Gal. jugs, 80c;	5 gal. jugs, $3.90
	Barrel,	60c. gallon
AMBER PETROLATUM,	5 lb. cans, 45c;	doz. cans, $5.00
	Barrel,	per lb., 3½c.
SNOW WHITE PETROLATUM (Russian),	5 lb. cans, $1.00;	doz. cans, $11.00
	Barrel,	per lb., 14c.
NITRIC ACID, C. P., Sp. Gr. .84	7 lb. bottle,	$1.20
	Carboy,	per lb., about 8½c.
HYDROCHLORIC ACID (Muriatic),	Strictly Pure, 7 lb. bottle,	$1.10
	Carboy,	per lb., about 7½c.
SULPHURIC ACID, C. P	7 lb. glass bottle,	$1.10.
	Carboy,	per lb., 6½c.

BETZ' SANITARY FLUID, Saponified Coal Tar Creosote. 1 gal. makes 100 gals. of strong, efficacious disinfectant - - - gal., $3.00

HYDROGEN PEROXIDE, U. S. P. (Medicinal), - - - 1 gal. bottle, $1.65

FORMALDEHYDE, 40% Solution, Guaranteed to be of highest purity, per lb., 25c; 5 lbs., $1.25; gal. bot., $1.60; 5 gal., $7.25; 10 gal., $12.75; barrels of about 400 lbs., per lb., 12c.

SOLIDIFIED FORMALDEHYDE, Powdered, - lb., $1.50; 5 lbs., $6.00; 10 lbs., $11.00

PARAFORMALDEHYDE, Paste, - - - lb., $1.50; 5 lbs., $6.00; 10 lbs., $11.00

We are headquarters for everything used for municipal sanitation and that of ship factories, railroads, etc. We supply in the smallest or largest quantities.

THERMOMETERS, Clinical, 60 sec., Magnifying with certificate, - - - doz., $4.00

HYPODERMIC SYRINGE, glass or metal barrel, doz., $4.00

MEDICINE DROPPERS, either bent or straight or assorted, - - - gross, $1.40

RUBBER GLOVES, any size, - - doz., $6.00

WOOD ALCOHOL STOVES (Reform), nickel plated on brass, - - - doz., $6.00

GLASS GONORRHŒAL SYRINGES, French Make, gross, $3.00

SUSPENSORIES, J. P. Silk Knit Sack, - - doz., $1.50

SUSPENSORIES, Army and Navy Lisle Thread, doz., $2.00

FINGER COTS FOR SURGEONS, - - gross, $1.25.

TERMS, CASH WITH ORDER

CHICAGO SALESROOM, 90 WABASH AVENUE

GENERAL OFFICES AT WORKS, HAMMOND, INDIANA

Where All Communications Should be Addressed

Long Island Codliver Oil.

The tremendous run of codfish off the Long Island coast this winter has, the *Brooklyn Daily Eagle* says, induced local fishermen to begin the manufacture of codliver oil. The livers from the millions of cod caught along the coast are tried out and the oil bottled. The plant is identical with those in operation in Norway and is in charge of a Norwegian, experienced in the business.

Keep Your Store Cool.

When a woman drinks a glass of soda water (and women are the most generous patrons of the bubbling beverage) and feels cool and comfortable afterward she does not analyze the means by which this delectable state was reached. All she knows and all she needs to know is that she drank a delicious glass of soda at Blank's fountain. Blank will know that the coolness was due to the rotary fans which he bought from D. L. Bates & Bro., Dayton, Ohio. We illustrate one of these fans herewith, and such of our readers as have not already installed these fans should write to the manufacturers for descriptive catalogues, mentioning the AMERICAN DRUGGIST.

Of all the improvements to which the modern soda counter is heir there is none more valuable than the lightning tumbler washer made by the Whiteman Mfg. Company, of Canton, Ohio. Write them for a descriptive circular of the machine with two sets of rapidly revolving brushes, which washes the inside and outside of the glass at the same time—and does it well. Don't wait until after the season has begun to write about this, but write to the manufacturer. Write now.

Hermetically Sealed Sachet Tins.

The Theo. Metcalf Company, of Boston, is now putting up its various sachet powders in a new air tight tin package. This is a great improvement over the old open jars which allowed the best value of the sachet powder to be lost. This new package prevents waste, the sachet doesn't lose its strength from constant opening, makes an elegant display and is a remarkably quick seller. The package is so convenient and practical that it appeals to the most fastidious trade.

Two of Metcalf's latest successes in sachet powders are Yale Violette and Harvard Crimson.

The sachet powder in these new packages retails at 50 cents, and can be had in all odors. There is a liberal profit for the druggist. See the advertisement in this issue. It will pay you to write for the special proposition which the firm is now making.

The Eli Dictionary.

Appendicitis—A modern pain, costing about $200 more than the old-fashioned stomach ache.

Automobile—From English "ought to," and Latin "moveo," to move. A vehicle which ought to move, but frequently can't.

Biliousness—A liver complaint often mistaken for piety.

Cauliflower—A cabbage with a college education.

Chauffeur—A man who is smart enough to operate an automobile, but clever enough not to own one.

Cinder—One of the first things to catch your eye when traveling.

Dock—A place for laying up.

Doctor—One who lays you up.

Earth—A solid substance much desired by the seasick.

Economy—Denying ourselves a necessity to-day in order to buy a luxury to-morrow.

Exposition—An overgrown department store, usually opened a year or two behind time.

Football—A clever subterfuge for carrying on prize fights under the guise of a respectable name.

Hotel—A place where a guest often gives up good dollars for poor quarters.

Hug—A roundabout way of expressing affection.

Kissing—Nothing divided by two, meaning persecution for the infant, ecstacy for the youth, fidelity for the middle-aged and homage for the old.

Tips—Wages we pay other people's hired help.

Vulgarity—The conduct of others.—*After Mark Twain.*

An Ideal Light.

A lamp that gives no shadow, that is safe, is handsome, is easy to keep in order, and above all is economical, must commend itself to every good business man. Druggists will find that the Angle Lamp, made by the Angle Mfg. Company, 78-80 Murray street, New York, answers all these requirements. Write the manufacturers for their little booklet, which has got a good story on William Rockefeller.

Whether for use in illuminating the store or for sale to discriminating patrons, the druggist will find that the Angle Lamp is a good investment.

A Soda Opening Offer.

A decidedly interesting proposition is made to our readers in this issue by the R. D. Cortina Company, of 44 West Thirty-fourth street, New York. This concern, whose business it is to teach foreign languages, offers to supply to druggists a very attractive invitation card bearing the date of the soda fountain opening day and the druggist's name, and a popular song entitled "The Soda Fountain Man," to be used as a gift to customers on the day named. The idea of a special day set for this purpose and to which customers are invited has proved a winning card with very many druggists who have tried it. Consequently this offer, which entails a very small expenditure on the part of the druggist, will likely be very well received by our readers. By addressing the company and mentioning this paper a sample of both the card and the song may be obtained free of cost, so that the druggist will not be purchasing in the dark.

Nutritive Beef Extract Sold Only Through the Drug Trade.

One of the most disagreeable things in the drug trade is to be brought into direct competition with the corner grocer. The druggist who handles Cudahy's Nutritive Beef Extract, a carton of which is illustrated herewith, is never confronted with this difficulty, as the sale of this extract is restricted entirely to the drug trade. Moreover, as this extract is prepared with the most scrupulous care in every respect, both as to the selection of material and the methods employed in producing the finished preparation, the druggist can feel assured of his ground when recommending it in preference to cheaper and less carefully prepared beef extracts, which are sold to the grocery trade. Write to the Pharmaceutical Department of the Cudahy Packing Company, South Omaha, Neb., for details regarding their plan for individual advertising for the druggists who stock this preparation.

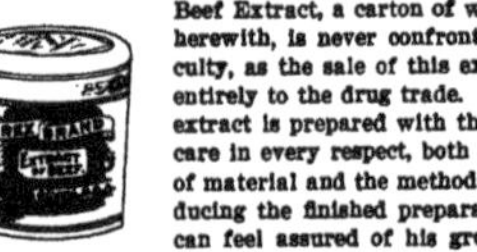

A Revolution in Pill Making.

All druggists who have their own special formulas in pills can do well by getting estimates from Mead, Johnson & Co., of Jersey City, N. J., a concern which has devoted itself to the preparation of what they correctly describe as "powder pills." They have succeeded in producing a line of highly soluble, friable pills of handsome appearance. A price-list and quotations for special orders will be forwarded on application.

In the spring the horseman's thoughts turn to the pleasures of the road, and he frequently finds that his favorite horse needs a little attention before being speeded again. The Lawrence-Williams Company, Cleveland, Ohio, agree to send some interesting circulars regarding the introduction of Gombault's Caustic Balsam to correspondents who mention the AMERICAN DRUGGIST when writing. This balsam is an invaluable aid to horsemen and should be carried in stock by every retail druggist.

ORIGINAL PACKAGE PRICES.

It should be understood that the prices quoted in this column are strictly those current in the wholesale market, and that higher prices are paid for retail lots. The quality of goods frequently necessitates a considerable range of prices.

Drugs, Chemicals, &c.

Acetanilid	lb.	.24	@	.25
Acetate of Lime:				
Brown	100 lb.	1.60	@	1.63
Gray	100 lb.	2.35	@	2.40
Acetone	lb.	.15½	@	.16
Acetphenetidin (U. S. P. Phenacetin	oz.	.15	@	...
Acid:				
Acetic Com'l	100 lb.	2.40	@	2.65
Acetic C. P.	lb.	.21	@	.23
Acetic, Glacial		.30	@	.32½
Aquafortis, 36°	lb.	.08½	@	.04½
" 40°	lb.	...	@	.06½
Benzoic, Ger	lb.	.30	@	.33
" Eng	oz.	.10	@	.10½
Boric, Cryst	lb.	.10	@	.10½
powd	lb.	.10	@	.10½
Carbol. cryst., blk	lb.	.14	@	.15
lb. bottle	lb.	.20	@	.22
Chrysophanic		2.50	@	2.65
Citric, dom	lb.	.43	@	.43½
Gallic	lb.	.55	@	.60
Muriatic C. P.	lb.	.07½	@	.08½
Nitric C. P.	lb.	.07½	@	.10
Oxalic, English	lb.	.05½	@	.06
Phosphoric	lb.	.18	@	.22½
Picric	lb.	.30	@	.33
Pyrogallic	lb.	1.65	@	...
Salicylic	lb.	.31	@	.31
Sulphuric, 66°	lb.	.01½	@	.02
Tartaric, crystals	lb.	.27½	@	.28½
powdered	lb.	.28	@	.29½
Tannic, cryst	lb.	.56	@	.65
Alcohol, grain	gal.	2.45	@	2.47
wood, 95-97%	gal.	.70	@	.75
Aloin	lb.	.45	@	.50
Alum, Lump	100 lb.	1.75	@	1.80
Ground	100 lb.	1.80	@	1.85
Ammon, carb		.08½	@	.08½
" bromide, bulk		.23	@	.24
" iodide, bulk		4.75	@	4.80
Aniline Oil		.09	@	.09½
Salt		.08½	@	.08½
Antipyrine (New)	oz.	...	@	.18
Arrowroot, Bermuda	lb.	.38	@	.40
St. Vincent, in bbl	lb.	.06½	@	.08
Arsenic: Red Saxon	lb.	.06½	@	.07
White	lb.	.07	@	.10
Balm of Gilead Buds	lb.	.28	@	.33
Balsam Copaiba, Cent. Amer	lb.	.30	@	.32
Para	lb.	.40	@	.42
Fir, Canada	gal.	3.10	@	3.20
Fir, Oregon	gal.	.70	@	.80
Peru	lb.	1.00	@	1.05
Tolu	lb.	.20	@	.22
Bark, Angostura	lb.	.35	@	.40
Buckthorn	lb.	.05	@	.05½
Cascara Sag	lb.	.03½	@	.09
Cascarilla	lb.	.10	@	.11
Cotton root	lb.	.08½	@	.10
Cramp	lb.	.07	@	.09
Elm, select	lb.	.18	@	.20
Pine, white	lb.	.05	@	.06
Prickly Ash	lb.	.11	@	.15
Sassafras	lb.	.13½	@	.14
Soap—whole	lb.	.05	@	.05½
Crushed	lb.	.05½	@	.06
White Pine	lb.	.04½	@	.06
Wild Cherry	lb.	.06	@	.09
Bismuth, citrate	lb.	1.75	@	1.80
" ammon cit	lb.	1.85	@	1.90
" subnit	blk.	1.50	@	1.55
" subcarb	lb.	1.75	@	1.80
" subgallate	lb.	1.85	@	1.90
Bleaching Powder, Eng		.01½	@	.01½
German B.		.01½	@	.01½
Domestic		.01	@	.01½
Blue Vitriol	lb.	.06	@	.06 1-10
Borax, Refined	lb.	.07½	@	.07½
powd. conc	lb.	.07½	@	.08
crystals	lb.	.07½	@	.07½
Brimstone, crude 2d	ton.	22.00	@	...
Bromine, bulk	lb.	.23	@	.25
Burgundy Pitch	lb.	.01	@	.01½
Cacao Butter, blk		.29½	@	.30
" " 12 lb. boxes		.34	@	.35
Caffeine	lb.	...	@	2.65
Calcium hypophosphite	lb.	.60	@	.64
Cantharides, Chinese	lb.	...	@	.75
" powd	lb.	.75	@	.77
Russian, whole	lb.	1.25	@	1.30
Cassia Buds	lb.	.18½	@	.19½
Castor Oil, No. 1, bbl	lb.	.11	@	.12
" " No. 1, cases	lb.	.11½	@	.12½
" " No. 3, bbl	lb.	.10½	@	.11½
" " No 3, cases	lb.	.10½	@	.11½
Caustic Soda	100 lb.	1.70	@	1.75
Chalk, Eng. Precip., bulk	lb.	.06	@	...
Chloral Hydrate, crystals, bulk	lb.	...	@	0.95
crusts, blk	lb.	...	@	0.91
Chloroform, bulk	lb.	.25	@	.30
Cinchonidine Sulph	oz.	.12	@	.15
Cocaine Muriate	oz.	3.25	@	3.50
Codeine Sulph	oz.	3.05	@	3.25
Cod Liver Oil, Norweg	bbl.	20.00	@	25.00
Newfoundland	bbl.	...	@	20.00
Colocynth, Trieste	lb.	.30	@	.32
Spanish	lb.	.25	@	.26
Copperas, car lots	100 lb.	.47½	@	.52
single bbls	100 lb.	.57½	@	.65
Creosote, Beechwood		.85	@	.90
Cream Tartar lb.	powd.	.22½	@	.23
Cubeb berries, xx	lb.	.09	@	.10
Powdered	lb.	.11	@	.13
Cutch, bales	lb.	.07½	@	.08
boxes	lb.	.05	@	.05½
Cuttle Bone, Trieste	lb.	.16½	@	.17
French	lb.	.12	@	.18
Jewelers', large	lb.	.70	@	...
" small	lb.	.40	@	.45
Dextrin	lb.	.03½	@	.05
Divi Divi	ton.	30.00	@	45.00
Dragon's Bl'd, lump	lb.	.18	@	.18
In reeds	lb.	.50	@	.55
Epsom Salts	100 lb.	.85	@	1.00
Ergot, German	lb.	.29	@	.30
Spanish	lb.	.34	@	.35
Ergotine, Dom	lb.	4.25	@	5.00
Flowers, Arnica	lb.	.09	@	.10
Flowers—cont'd				
Calendula	lb.	.25	@	.30
Chamomile, Roman	lb.	.16	@	.22
German	lb.	.10	@	.18
Hungarian	lb.	.09½	@	.11
Insect, open	lb.	.15	@	.17
Half closed	lb.	.18	@	.23
Closed	lb.	.26	@	...
Powder	lb.	.11	@	.21
Lavender	lb.	.12	@	.13
Select	lb.	.15	@	.20
Saffron, Amer	lb.	1.25	@	...
Spanish Alicante	lb.	4.75	@	6.00
" Valencia	lb.	8.00	@	8.50
Formaldehyde	lb.	.09	@	.09½
Glauber Salt	per 100 lb.	.40	@	.60
Glycerin, C. P. drums	lb.	.11½	@	.11½
" cans	lb.	.12½	@	.12½
Grains of Paradise	lb.	.11½	@	.15
Guarana	lb.	.70	@	.75
Gums: Aloes, Cape		.08	@	.10
" Barbadoes	lb.	.14	@	.16
" Curacoa		.06	@	.06½
" Socot	lb.	.18	@	.20
Arabic, 1st pkd	lb.	.30	@	...
" 2d pkd	lb.	.19	@	.23
" sorts	lb.	.06½	@	.11
Asafoetida	lb.	.15	@	.22
Benzoin, Sumatra	lb.	.34	@	.38
Siam	lb.	.90	@	1.00
Camphor, ref'd. blk	lb.	1.00	@	..
cases	lb.	1.00½	@	..
Chicle	lb.	.36	@	.38
Gamboge	lb.	1.15	@	1.20
Guaiac	lb.	.17	@	.23
Kino	lb.	.25	@	.26
Mastic	lb.	.46	@	.49
Myrrh	lb.	.25	@	.28
Olibanum	lb.	.10	@	.15
Sandarac	lb.	.14	@	.18
Senegal, pkd	lb.	.11	@	.13
Tragacanth, Aleppo	lb.	.30	@	.65
Tragacanth, Turkey	lb.	.35	@	.50
Haarlem Oil		3.00	@	3.75
Hypophosphite lime	lb.	.48	@	.50
" potash	lb.	.48	@	.50
" soda	lb.	.48	@	.50
Ichthyol	lb.	4.00	@	4.25
Indigo	lb.	.90	@	1.25
Insect Pwd. pure	lb.	.14	@	.23
Iodine, resub		2.70	@	2.75
Iodoform	lb.	3.00	@	3.05
Iron citrate, U. S. P.	lb.	.....	@	.44
" and ammon. cit	lb.	.....	@	.41
and ammon. citrate (green scales)				
and quinine citrate	lb.	1.18	@	1.23
phosphate, scales	lb.	....	@	.38
pyrophosphate, scales	lb.	....	@	.38
Quinine and strychnine citrate	lb.	1.68	@	1.73
Isinglass, Amer	lb.	.75	@	.80
Russian	lb.	4.00	@	4.10
Juniper Berries	lb.	.03½	@	.04
Lanoline	lb.	.60	@	.65
Leaves: Aconite		.08	@	.10
Belladonna	lb.	.10	@	.11
Buchu, short	lb.	.17	@	.20
" long	lb.	.45	@	.50
Cannabis Indica, tops	lb.	1.00	@	1.10
Coca, Truxillo	lb.	.17	@	.18
" Huanuco	lb.	.30	@	.32
Damiana	lb.	.08	@	.10
Digitalis	lb.	.08½	@	.09
Grindelia robusta	lb.	.08	@	.09
Horehound	lb.	.04½	@	.06
Hyoscyamus	lb.	.07	@	.09
Jaborandi	lb.	.14	@	.15
Pulsatilla		.07½	@	.11
Rose, Red	lb.	.65	@	.70
Senna, pkd. whole	lb.	.20	@	.22
Alexandria, natural	lb.	...	@	...
garbled and sifted	lb.	.15	@	.16
Tinnevelly	lb.	.04	@	.09
Alexandria, siftings	lb.	.05½	@	.06
Stramonium	lb.	.08	@	.08½
Uva ursi	lb.	.03½	@	.03½
Yerba Santa	lb.	.07	@	.07½
Liquorice—mass	lb.	.08	@	.10
Spanish	lb.	.14	@	.20
Imported mass Spanish	lb.	.18	@	.24
Stick, Calabria	lb.	.23	@	.26
Domestic	lb.	.18½	@	.23½
Lithia, carbonate	lb.	1.50	@	1.75
" citrate	lb.	1.15	@	1.25
Lupulin, Ger	lb.	.18	@	.25
Lycopodium	lb.	.51	@	.53
Magnesia, carb	lb.	.12	@	.15
Manna, large flk	lb.	.45	@	.50
Small flake	lb.	.33	@	.35
Menthol, Japanese	lb.	2.50	@	2.75
Mercurials:				
Blue Pill	lb.	.43	@	.46
Calomel	lb.	.77	@	.79
Corr. Sublim	lb.	.70	@	.72
Mercury and Chalk	lb.	.33	@	.34
Ointment, ¼	lb.	.47	@	.48
Ointment, ½	lb.	.38	@	.39
Red Precip	lb.	.87	@	.89
White "	lb.	.92	@	.94
Morphine, bulk	oz.	2.10	@	2.20
Eighths	oz.	2.45	@	2.50
Moss, Iceland	lb.	.05	@	.06
Irish	lb.	.06½	@	.08
Irish, bleached	lb.	.09½	@	.10
Naphthaline, flake	lb.	.02	@	.02
Ball	lb.	.02	@	.02½
Nux Vomica	lb.	.02½	@	.03
Oil, Anise	lb.	1.30	@	1.35
Almonds, bit, Eng	lb.	5.50	@	5.75
French	lb.	3.55	@	3.60
bit., artificial	lb.	.85	@	1.50
sweet, true	lb.	.37	@	.40
Peach kernels		.19	@	.22
Bay	lb.	2.10	@	2.25
22 oz. bots	bot.	3.25	@	3.35
Bergamot	lb.	2.15	@	2.30
Cajuput	lb.	.50	@	.52
Camphor	lb.	.17½	@	.19
Caraway	lb.	1.15	@	1.40
Cassia 75@80%	lb.	.77½	@	.78
Oils—cont'd.				
Cedar, pure	lb.	60.	@	1.55
red	lb.	.21	@	.25
Citronella	lb.	.40	@	.42
Clove, bud		.52½	@	.55
Copaiba	lb.	.64	@	.70
Coriander	lb.	8.00	@	11.00
Croton	lb.	.75	@	.80
Cubeb	lb.	.90	@	1.00
Eucalyptus	lb.	.40	@	.60
Geranium	lb.	1.60	@	4.75
Lavender, flowers	lb.	2.00	@	2.25
Lemon	lb.	.07	@	.75
Lemongrass	lb.	3.00	@	3.10
Mustard	lb.	4.25	@	6.25
Myrbane	lb.	.07	@	.09
Neroli	lb.	45.00	@	57.50
Nutmeg	lb.	.80	@	0.90
Orange, sweet	lb.	2.00	@	2.15
Orange, bitter	lb.	2.20	@	2.40
Origanum	lb.	.19	@	.22
Pennyroyal	lb.	1.15	@	1.25
Peppermint	lb.	2.60	@	2.75
Cases	lb.	3.20	@	3.25
Petit, grain, French	lb.	4.00	@	4.50
" " So. Amer	lb.	2.00	@	2.05
Pimento	lb.	1.80	@	1.90
Rose	oz.	3.50	@	4.50
Rosemary	lb.	.62½	@	.80
Sandalwood	lb.	3.25	@	3.50
Sassafras	lb.	.50	@	.55
" Artificial	lb.	.25	@	.28
Safrol		.25	@	.36
Spearmint	lb.	4.75	@	5.00
Tansy	lb.	3.75	@	4.00
Thyme		1.00	@	1.20
Winterg'n, sweet birch		1.65	@	1.85
" Synthetic	lb.	.37	@	.40
Wood (Chinese)		.08	@	.09
Wormwood		3.25	@	3.50
Wormseed	lb.	3.00	@	3.25
Opium, Nat	cases, lb.	2.72½	@	2.80
" Ordinary, Job-		2.75	@	2.80
" powdered	lb.	3.25	@	3.30
Orange peel, bit	lb.	.03	@	.04
Sweet	lb.	.01½	@	.10
Petrolatum		.03	@	.08
Phenacetin (see Acetphenetidin)				
Potassium acetate	lb.	.17	@	.18
" bromide		.15	@	.16
" bottles		.23	@	.30
bichromate		.08½	@	.08½
chlorate, cryst		.09½	@	.09½
" powd		.10	@	.10½
cyanide		.20	@	.21
hypophosphite		.60	@	.64
iodide bulk		2.15	@	2.20
permanganate	lb.	.09½	@	.10½
Prickly Ash berries		.14	@	.16
Quicksilver	flasks, lb.	.58	@	.60
Quinine Sulph., Domestic bulk	oz.	.18	@	.20
German, bulk	oz.	.17	@	.20
German, outside	oz.	.17	@	.18
Java, bulk	oz.	.17½	@	.18
Rochelle Salts	lb.	.20½	@	.21
Root, Aconite	lb.	.09½	@	.10
Alkanet	lb.	.08	@	.09
Althea, cut	lb.	.17	@	.18
Arnica	lb.	.08½	@	.09
Belladonna, Atropa	lb.	.10	@	.12
Blood	lb.	.10	@	.12
Calamus	lb.	.07	@	.08
Calamus, bleached	lb.	.23	@	.25
Colchicum	lb.	.12	@	.18
Calumba	lb.	.04	@	.06
Dandelion, Ger	lb.	.07½	@	.08
Galangal	lb.	.05	@	.05½
Gentian	lb.	.04	@	.04½
Ginger, Ja., blcd.	lb.	...	@	.14
unbleached	lb.	.12	@	.14
Ginseng	lb.	6.00	@	7.50
Golden Seal	lb.	1.25	@	1.30
Hellebore, pwd	lb.	.06	@	.07
Helonias	lb.	.42	@	.45
Ipecac, Rio	lb.	1.75	@	1.80
Carthagena	lb.	1.75	@	1.80
Jalap	lb.	.10½	@	.11
Kava Kava	lb.	.11	@	.12
Liquorice, ord	lb.	.03½	@	.04
Select	lb.	.06½	@	.11
Lovage	lb.	.55	@	.55
Mandrake	lb.	.04½	@	.05½
Musk, Russian	lb.	.13	@	.14
Orris, Florentine	lb.	.06	@	.07
Orris, Verona	lb.	.04	@	.06
Pariera Brava	lb.	.10	@	.11
Pink	lb.	...	@	.75
Rhatany	lb.	.10	@	.12
Rhub., Canton	lb.	.35	@	.40
Shensi	lb.	.65	@	.75
Sars'p'la, Hond	lb.	.26	@	.30
Mexican	lb.	.09½	@	.09½
Senega	lb.	.55	@	.60
Snake Virgina	lb.	.42	@	.45
Texas	lb.	.39	@	.42
Canada	lb.	.13	@	.25
Squill	lb.	.13	@	.15
Valerian, Belg	lb.	.08	@	.08½
German	lb.	.12	@	.14
English	lb.	.12	@	.15
Salicine	lb.	3.75	@	4.00
Sal Ammon, lump	lb.	.09½	@	.09½
Granulated	lb.	.05½	@	.06
Sal Soda, Eng	100 lb.	.67½	@	.72½
American	100 lb.	.75	@	.80
Salol	lb.	.90	@	.95
Saltpetre, crude	lb.	.04½	@	.04½
Refined	lb.	.04½	@	.05½
Santonin, crystals	lb.	9.50	@	9.70
Powdered	lb.	9.70	@	9.90
Saw Palmetto Berries	lb.	.15	@	.20
Seed, Anise Ital	lb.	.08½	@	.10½
German	lb.	.06½	@	.07
Star	lb.	.20	@	.21
Canary, Smyrna	lb.	.04½	@	.04½
Sicily	lb.	.04½	@	.05
Caraway	lb.	.06½	@	.06
Celery	lb.	.07½	@	.08
Cardamom blchd		.30	@	.70
" Decorticated	lb.	.33	@	.34
Colchicum	lb.	.21	@	.25
Seeds—cont'd.				
Coriander	lb.	.9	@	.17½
Bleached	lb.	.08½	@	.10½
Cummin	lb.	.05½	@	.07½
Fennel, Ger	lb.	.09	@	.10
" Italian	lb.	.05	@	.15½
Flax, whole	lb.	4.30	@	4.75
" ground	lb.	.03½	@	.03½
Foenugreek	lb.	.03	@	.03½
Hemp, Rus	lb.	.03	@	.03½
Millet, nat	lb.	.01¾	@	.02
" cbld	lb.	.04½	@	.04½
Mustard, Cal. brown	lb.	.04½	@	.04½
Trieste, brown	lb.	.06	@	.06½
Bari, brown	lb.	.04½	@	.05
German, brown	lb.	.05½	@	.06
Western, brown	lb.	.01½	@	.05
Cal. yellow	lb.	.04½	@	.04½
Eng. yellow	lb.	.05	@	.05½
Ger. yellow	lb.	.05½	@	.05½
Poppy, blue	lb.	.05½	@	.05½
Quince, Ger	lb.	.32	@	.34
Rape, Ger	lb.	.05½	@	.05
" Eng	lb.	.04	@	.05
" Amer	lb.	.03½	@	.05
Strophanthus		.45	@	.50
Kombé		1.60	@	1.65
Sunflower		.04½	@	.05
Wormseed, American	lb.	.07	@	.08
" Levant	lb.	.17	@	.20
Seidlitz, Mixture	lb.	.17	@	.17½
Silver, Nitrate	oz.	.41	@	.44½
Soap, Castile, white	lb.	.10	@	.10½
" green	lb.	.06	@	.10½
" mottled	lb.	.06½	@	.07
Sodium bicarb, Eng		1.37½	@	1.75
" domestic	100 lb.	1.50	@	1.60
" benzoate	lb.	.40	@	.42
" brom. blk	lb.	.21	@	.22
" carb., cryst.	100 lb.	1.00	@	1.75
" citrate	lb.	...	@	.22
" hypophosphite		.60	@	.64
" iodide		2.50	@	2.55
" nitrate	100 lb.	2.20	@	2.25
" phosphate	lb.	.02½	@	.03
" salicylate	lb.	.32	@	.34
Spermaceti	lb.	.27	@	.29
Spts. Nitre, U. S. P.		.46	@	.48
Spts. Ammonia Aromat	lb.	.44	@	.45
Strontium, nitrate	lb.	.07½	@	.08
Strychnine, Sulph	oz.	.95	@	1.05
Sugar of Milk	lb.	.15	@	.20
Sugar, Lead, white	lb.	.09½	@	.10
" brown	lb.	.07½	@	.08
Sulphur, Roll	lb.	1.85	@	2.15
" Flowers	lb.	2.15	@	2.52½
Sulphuric Ether	lb.	.60	@	.60
Sumac, Sicily	ton	42.00	@	47.00
" Virginia	ton	33.00	@	38.00
Tar, Barbadoes	gal.	...	@	.35
Thymol		1.80	@	1.90
Tonka B'ns, Para	lb.	.18	@	.20
" Angostura	lb.	.65	@	.67½
" Surinam	lb.	.30	@	.32
Turmeric		.04½	@	.08
Turpentine	gal.	.60	@	.60½
Vanilla Beans	lb.	2.75	@	6.50
" Cut, Mex	lb.	2.00	@	2.25
" Tahiti	lb.	.45	@	1.50
" Bourbon		1.00	@	2.00
Vanillin	oz.	.32	@	.37½
Venice Turps, bbls	lb.	.14	@	.17
" " cans	lb.	.19	@	.20
Wax, Bayberry	lb.	...	@	.20
" Bees, ord. pur	lb.	.28	@	.32½
" " sel	lb.	.34	@	.34½
" " blch	lb.	.40	@	.45
" Brazil, No. 1	lb.	.51½	@	.52
" " No. 2	lb.	.44	@	.45
" " No. 3	lb.	.35	@	...
" Ceresin, yel	lb.	.14	@	.18
" " white	lb.	.15	@	.20
" Japan	lb.	.12½	@	.14
" Paraffin	lb.	.06	@	.06½
Zinc Oxide	lb.	.07	@	.08½

Heavy Oils, &c.

Bank, Menhaden	gal.	.27	@	.30
Coconut, Ceylon	lb.	.08½	@	.08½
Cochin	lb.	.07½	@	.07½
Cuban	lb.	.06½	@	...
Cod, Domestic	gal.	.35	@	.36
" Newfoundland	gal.	.38½	@	.40
Corn	gal.	3.8	@	...
Cottonseed, crd. prime		.25	@	...
Summer Yellow, prime		.32	@	.33
" " Butter		.33	@	.34
Old, off grade		.32	@	...
Winter Yellow, prime		.33	@	.34
Salad Oil		.40	@	.41
Gasoline, 86°	gal.	.14	@	...
" 88°	gal.	.16	@	...
" 90°	gal.	.18	@	...
Lard, Extra Prime	gal.	.65	@	.64
Lard, Extra No. 1	gal.	.49	@	.52
Lard, No. 1	gal.	.38	@	.40
Linseed, Raw City	gal.	.42	@	.43
" Boiled	gal.	.43	@	.44
Naphtha, 62°	gal.	.12	@	...
" Deodorized, 76°	gal.	.13½	@	...
Neatsfoot, prm	gal.	.49	@	.50
White		.57	@	...
Olive Oil, tap	tins	1.50	@	2.75
" Com., bbls	gal	.55½	@	.58
Palm, prm., L'gos	lb	.05½	@	.05½
Peanut	lb	.40	@	.52
Rapeseed	gal.	.67	@	.71
Red Elaine	gal.	...	@	.42
" Saponified	lb.	.06½	@	.06½
Salad Oil	gal.	.46	@	.48
Sesame	gal.	.55	@	.60
Sperm, Crude	gal.	.53	@	.55
" Nat. Win	gal.	.62	@	.63
" Blch. Win	gal.	.64	@	.65
Straits	gal.	...	@	.35
Tallow, prime	gal.	.62	@	...
Whale, Crude	gal.	...	@	...
Crude, Nat. Win	gal.	.42	@	...
Bleached Win	gal.	.44	@	.44

Crystal Soft Elastic Gelatine Capsules

All Kinds. Machine and Hand Made.
All Sizes. Filled or Empty.

We make everything in the line of Soft Elastic Capsules and sell them at the very lowest prices. Special formulas and capsules in bulk filled at the most reasonable rates, either with material furnished or we will supply the same. Send for price list and estimates.

CRYSTAL CAPSULES OF PURE NORWEGIAN COD LIVER OIL

Sold on the Direct Contract Plan.

50 to 66 2-3 per cent. profit assured, according to quantities purchased. Three extra boxes on the first order for one dozen. Send for price list blank contract and two 25 cent. boxes free.

Crystal Capsule Company,

15 and 17 North Eleventh Street, - - - PHILADELPHIA.

RIPPEY'S

POWDERED FOAMOLINE

Specially Prepared for Manufacturers of

ICE CREAM,
SHERBETS,
FRUIT FROSTS
and WATER ICES

(Trade Mark Registered)

Rippey's Powdered Fbamoline not only enriches your Ice Cream and gives it that smooth, pasty appearance so much admired bv lovers of Ice Cream, but adds to its bulk and will remain firm and solid longer with less ice and less labor than any article ever before offered for that purpose.

No Heat or Eggs Required: you simply mix Rippey's Powdered Foamoline with the sugar while dry, add your cream or milk and it is ready for the Freezer.

For a limited time we will send by mail, postage paid, full half pound on receipt of 25 cents in stamps. Our formulas for Ice Cream, Sherbets, Fruit Frosts and Water Ices mailed free on receipt of your address.

CAUTION.—Rippey's Powdered Foamoline is packed in 1 pound boxes with registered trade mark and signature of William Rippey on every box. Never sold in bulk.

PRICE, 35 CENTS PER POUND.

WILLIAM RIPPEY

109 E. 2nd Street, - Cincinnati, O.

WALKER'S No.18
QUICK AND EASY
ICE CREAM
DISHER
1906 Model

COPPER SHELL
BRONZE HANDLE
NICKEL PLATED
WILL NOT RUST
NO PLACE FOR CREAM TO GATHER AND SOUR
TWO WEEKS' TRIAL FREE
MONEY REFUNDED IF NOT SATISFACTORY
SIZES: 5, 6, 8, 10, 12, 16, 20. PRICE: $2.00 EACH
ERIE SPECIALTY COMPANY, ERIE, PA.

Full Line of our Card Samples

Do you sell Souvenir Post Cards?

We want you to handle our taking, popular cards, and will send you complete sample line of all our varieties—Colored, Green Graphure, Black, Gelatine, Comic and Fancy—on receipt of $3 cash, giving you PRIVILEGE TO RETURN any cards not wanted. Order to-day.

SATISFACTION GUARANTEED.

NEW FLAG CARDS
in colors.

$10 for 1000 plain
15 for 1000 tinsel

SAMPLES ON REQUEST.

"NIAGARA" CARDS can be supplied in either colored or "Green Graphure" style. Only one of the thousands of fast sellers, superbly printed, and put into your hands at the bottom prices.

$10 brings you 1200 cards and handsome Rack. Ask to see illustration, and for particulars.

SPECIAL—Local scenes sell best. Send photos and get some splendidly printed cards. Price list and samples on request. Write to-day.

Souvenir Post Card Co.

50 Franklin St., Dept. D, New York City, N. Y.

Customers are Gained by

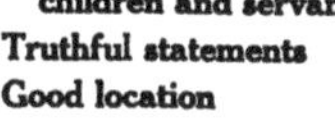

Accurate handling of cash
Correct credit charges
Never asking a customer to pay a bill twice
Attention to telephone orders
Tidy appearance of store
Quick service
Courteous clerks
Right change given to children and servants
Truthful statements
Good location

All these good features may be had by using a system that is of advantage to customers. An investigation of the system afforded by a National Cash Register will prove a good investment.

Drop a line to our nearest agency and our salesman will call and explain this system. It costs you nothing and places you under no obligation.

Tear off here and mail to us today

N.C.R. Company

Dayton Ohio

Please explain to me what kind of a register is best suited for my business. This does not obligate me to buy

________________ *Name*

________________ *Address*

________________ *No. of men*

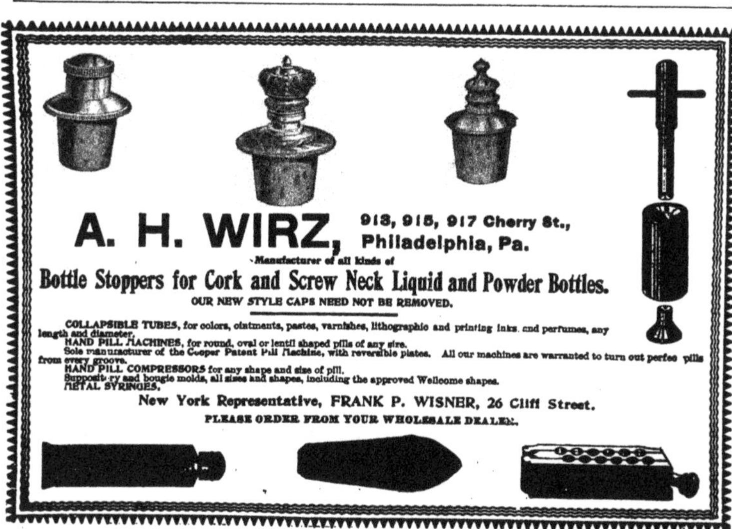

For Home Made Candies

No one in the trade needs to be told what the C. I. Hood Co. makes and markets, for all have sold Hood's Sarsaparilla and the other lines. But many may not know that this firm is offering free on request a book containing recipes for making candies. It is called "Hood's Book of Home-Made Candies, No. 2." A supply of these with the dealer's name printed on each book will be sent on request. They are recommended for counter distribution and are gotten up in style. If desired novelties for making a window display will also be sent.

C. I. HOOD CO., Lowell, Mass.

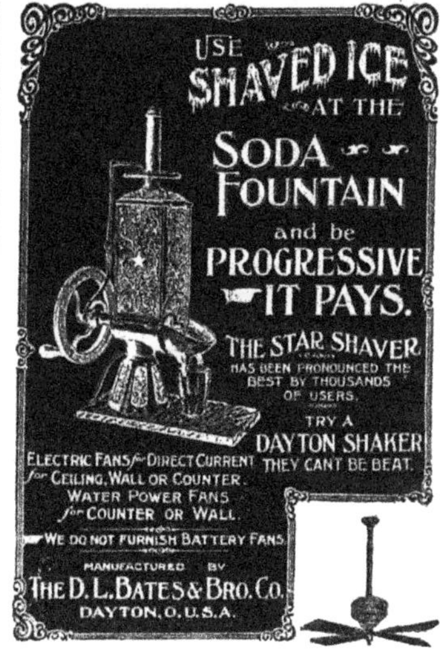

Prices Current.

The outside prices quoted are for such quantities as retailers usually purchase. When purchasing original packages the inside quotations should be expected, while a slight advance over the outside quotations given may be demanded for very small lots. Current commercial quality is understood unless otherwise indicated. For extra quality or for specified makes a slightly higher price will have to be paid.

Corrected to April 9

Acetanilid, 5 lbs., .30 .... lb. .32-34
Acetone, lb., .22; Medicinal .... lb. .85
Acetphenetidine .... oz. .15
Acid, Acetic, U. S. P., carboys, .6 .. lbs. .8-9
No. 2, carboy, .5; lb., .7; Glacial . lb. .28-30
Arsenous, fused, lb., .18 .... oz. .8
Benzoic, English, 50-oz. boxes, .10 .. oz. .13-16
Benzoic, from Toluol, lbs., .53 .... oz. .11-13
Boric, crystals, 25 lbs., .14 .... lb. .15
Boric, Po., 25 lbs., .14 .... lb. .16
Cacodylic, ¼ths .... ozs. 4.00
Camphoric .... oz. .60
Carbolic crystals, 10 lbs., .22 .... lb. .23-27
Calvert's No. 1, lb., 1.95; No. 2 .. lb. 1.40
Solution, 10 gals., .45 .... gal. .50
Chromic, lb., .55 .... ozs. .11
Chrysophanic, 1-oz. cartons .... ozs. .18-20
Cinnamic .... oz. .35-40
Citric, crystals, 10 lbs., .43 .... lb. .45-47
Gallic, lbs., .70 .... ozs. .9
Hydrochloric, carboys, .2½ .... lb. .4-5
C. P. .... lb. .11-13
Hydrocyanic, dil., lbs., .30 .... ozs. .10
Hydrobromic, dil .... lb. .28
Hypophosphorus, 50 per cent. sol .. lb. 1.65
Lactic, concentr., lbs., .70 .... ozs. .12
Nitric, carboys, 5½ lbs., .8; C. P. .... .14
Oleic, purified, U. S. P. .... lbs. .40
Oxalic, 10 lbs., .9 .... lb. .10-12
Phosphoric, glacial .... lbs. .55
U. S. P., 85 per cent. syrupy .. lb. .30-35
Picric .... lb. .55
Pyrogallic, lbs., 2.35 .... ozs. .24-27
Pyroligneous, pure .... lb. .30
Salicylic, white, 10 lbs., .40 .... lb. .42-44
Stearic, hard .... lb. .18
Succinic .... oz. .27
Sulphuric, carboys, .2 .... lb. .4
" C. P., carboys, .10 .... lb. .12
Sulphurous .... lb. .10
Tannic, lbs., .85 .... oz. .12-15
Tartaric, powdered, 10 lbs., .34 .. lbs. .35-38
Valerianic .... ozs. .20
Aconitine, Amorphous, ⅛ ozs .... ea. 1.40
Adeps Lanae, B. J. D. .... lb. .28
Adnephrin, solution .... oz. .60
Adonidin, 15-gr. vials .... gr. .15
Agaricin, 15-gr. vials, each, .10 .. ozs. .90
Agaric, white .... lb. .40
Agathin .... oz. 3.25
Agurin, ... ozs. 1.70
Airol, ozs .... oz. 1.00
Albumen, Egg .... lb. .70
Alcohol, 10 gals., 2.70 .... gal. 2.65-2.70
Alcohol, Columbia Spirit, 10 gals., 1.35. gal. 1.50
Cologne Spirit, 10 gals., 2.80 .... gal. 2.90
Wood, 10 gals., .85 .... gal. .90
Alizarin, ... oz. .15
Allspice, 10 lbs., .11 .... lb. .12
powdered, 5 lbs., .18 .... lb. .20
Almonds, bitter, shelled .... lb. .40
Sweet, shelled .... lb. .35
Almond Meal, true, 10 lbs., .45 .. lb. .50
Aloin, lb., .70 .... oz. .7-9
Alpha-Eucaine .... oz. 3.50
Alphozone, ... oz. 4.50
Alum, cryst., bbls., .2¼ .... lb. .3-4
powdered, bbls., .3¼ .... lb. .6-8
burnt, 10 lbs., .10 .... lb. .12-14
Aluminum, Acetate .... oz. .15
Sulphate, lb., 10; Wire .... lb. 2.25
Aluminol, ... oz. .50
Amber, rasped .... oz. .35
Ambergris, gray, oz., $30.00 .... dram. 4.00
Ammonia (See Water and Spirit).
Ammonium, Bromide, 5-lb. bot., .35. lb. .40
Carbonate, 25 lbs., .11 .... lb. .12-14
Iodide, lbs., 6.15 .... oz. .47
Muriate, gran. com .... lb. .10
purified, lb., .17; powdered .... lb. .18
Salammoniac, muriate, cryst .. lb. .12-14
Nitrate, crystals, 10 lbs., .22 .... lb. .25
Valerianate, lb., 1.50 .... oz. .15-22
Ammonol .... oz. 1.05
Amygdalin, ¼-oz. vials .... oz. 2.40
Amyl, Nitrite .... oz. .25
Amylene, Hydrate .... oz. .49
Anaesthesin .... ozs. 1.00
Aniline, Red, crystals .... lb. 1.25
Black .... lb. .75
Crystals for ink .... lb. 1.50
Blue, Deep, No. 1 .... lb. 2.00
Sol., reddish, No. 1 .... lb. 2.50
Crimson .... lb. 1.50
Brown, Bismarck .... lb. 1.25
Soluble .... lb. 1.00
Green, crystals .... lb. 1.50
Orange .... lb. 1.00
Purple, B. B. .... lb. 1.75
Scarlet .... lb. 1.50 Yellow .... lb. 1.25
Annatto .... lb. .45-50
Anodyne, Hoffman's .... lb. .60
" " U. S. P. .... lb. .88
Anthrax Vaccine, "Pasteur," double tubes .... doz. 18.00
Artiarthrin .... oz. 1.05
Antikamnia, powdered or tablets .. oz. 1.00
Combination tablets .... oz. 1.00
10-oz. lots, assorted to order 9.25
Tablets, "vest-pocket boxes" .... doz. 1.75
In 1 gross lots, 5 per cent. discount.
Antimony Sulphuret, powd., pure, 10 lbs., .16 .... lb. .17-20
Antinosine .... oz. 2.10
Antipyretic Liquid, Tilden's .... doz. 2.50
Antipyrine, Dr. Knorr's .... oz. .31
New Grade .... oz. .20
Antistreptococcic Serum (Veterinary), "Pasteur," 10-Cc. vial .. doz. 9.00
Antitetanic Serum (Veterinary), "Pasteur," 10-Cc. vial .... doz. 9.00
Antithyroidin, 10-Cc. vials .... ea. 1.50
Antitoxin, Diphtheria, Stearns':
No. 0, per 500 units 1.10
No. 1, per 1,000 units 1.05
No. 2, per 2,000 units 1.80
No. 3, per 3,000 units 2.40
No. 4, per 4,000 units 6.50
Antivom, Ritsert, Pills, .30 ea .. doz. 9.50
Apiol, Fluid Green .... oz. .38
Capsules, Joret's .... doz. 6.25
Apolysin .... oz. .65
Apomorphine, Hydrochlor, Cryst .. oz. 7.50
" " Amorphous . oz. 2.80
Areca, Nuts, powd .... lb. .25-28
Argentamine .... oz. .75
Argols, Red, powdered .... lb. .12
Argonin .... oz. .65
Aristol, 25 ozs., 1.65 .... oz. 1.80
Aristochin, ozs .... oz. 2.20
" ⅛ ozs .... oz. 2.25
Arrowroot, Bermuda, true .... None in market
St. Vincent, 30 lbs., .14 .... lb. .18
Taylor's, ¼-lb., 24 lbs., .28 .... lb. .32
Arsenauro, 1-oz. bots .... doz. 8.50
Arsenic, Donovan's Sol .... lb. .20
Fowler's Sol .... lb. .10
White .... lb. .12
Aspirin, 50 ozs., .38 .... oz. .43
Atropin, Sulph., ⅛-oz .... oz. 5.65
Balsam, Copaiba, Para, 5 lbs., .45 .. lb. .47-50
Fir, Canada .... lb. .50-55
Oregon .... lb. .25-30
Peru .... lb. 1.25
Tolu, 10-lb. can, .32 .... lb. .35
Barbadoes Tar .... gal. .60
Barium, Acetate .... oz. .15
Carbonate .... lb. .40
Chloride .... lb. .17
Nitrate .... lb. .15
Oxide, pure .... oz. .10
Bark, Angostura .... lb. .55
Barberry .... lb. .25
Berberis Aquifol .... lb. .20
Buckthorn .... lb. .18
Canella .... lb. .20
Cascara, Sagrada .... lb. .15-20
Cascarilla, select .... lb. .25
Cassia, in mats .... lb. .14
Saigon .... lb. .65
Cinchona, Red, E. I. .... lb. .36
powdered, 10 lbs., .32 .... lb. .32-35
Cinchona Calisaya .... lb. .36
powdered .... lb. .40
pale, lb., .20; powdered .... lb. .25
Cinnamon, Ceylon .... lb. .35

Item	Unit	Price
Bark, Condurango	lb.	.25
Elm, selected	lb.	.30-35
ground, 10 lbs., .18	lb.	.22
powdered, 10 lbs., .22	lb.	.25
Hemlock, crushed	lb.	.15
Mezereon	lb.	.25
Oak, white, crushed	lb.	.15
Orange Peel, bitter	lb.	.16
Prickly Ash	lb.	.35
Quebracho	lb.	.25
Sassafras, 10 lbs., .18	lb.	.20
Sassafras, Extra	lb.	.22-25
Simaruba	lb.	.40-45
Soap (Quillaja), cut, 5 lbs., .11	lb.	.12
powdered	lb.	.15
Wild Cherry, 5 lbs., .12	lb.	.14
" " ground, 5 lbs., .14	lb.	.16
Witch Hazel	lb.	.20
Barley, Pearl	lb.	.5-6
Bay Rum, Porto Rico	gal.	2.10-2.35
St. Thomas	gal.	2.50-3.00
Bean, Calabar	lb.	.36
St. Ignatius	lb.	.30
Tonka, Angostura	lb.	.75-85
Surinam	lb.	.60
Vanilla, Mexican, long	lb.	8.50
" " med	lb.	7.15
" " short	lb.	7.00
" Bourbon, long	lb.	6.50
" " med	lb.	5.50
" " short	lb.	4.50
Benzol, Coal Tar	lb.	.24
Benzosol	oz.	1.25
Berberine, Carb.	oz.	5.00
Hydrochlor	oz.	1.80
Berries, Cubeb, lb., .16; powdered	lb.	.22-25
Fish	lb.	.12
Juniper	lb.	.8-10
powdered	lb.	.18-20
Poke	lb.	.20
Prickly Ash	lb.	.25-35
Sumac	lb.	.20
Beta-Eucaine	oz.	3.50
Bismuth, Ammonia Citrate, lb., 2.55	oz.	.24
Subcarbonate	lb.	2.40
Subnitrate, 5 lbs., 1.65	lb.	1.75
Subgallate, lb., 2.45	oz.	.22-24
Subsalicylate, lb., 2.65	oz.	.21-25
Blacklegine, "Pasteur" (Blackleg Vaccine, cord form), No. 1, 10 doses	doz.	12.00
Blacklegine, "Pasteur" (Blackleg Vaccine, cord form), No. 2, 20 doses	doz.	20.00
Blacklegine, "Pasteur" (Blackleg Vaccine, cord form), No. 3, 50 doses	doz.	48.00
Blackleg Vaccine, "Pasteur," powder packet	doz.	12.00
Bladder Wrack	lb.	.25
Blue Vitriol, bbl., .5¾; 100 lbs., .6	lb.	.8-10
powdered, 50 lbs., .10	lb.	.12
Bole, Armenia, powdered, true	lb.	.12
Bone Ash	lb.	.15
Borax, 100 lbs., .8¾	lb.	.9-12
powdered, 50 lbs., 8¾	lb.	.9-12
Breast Tea, 5 lbs., .25	lb.	.27-30
Brimstone Roll, bbls., .2¼	lb.	.4-5
Bromine	oz.	.19
Bromoform	oz.	.19
Buds, Balm of Gilead	lb.	.45
Cassia	lb.	.30
Butter, Cacao, 12 lbs., .38	lb.	.40-42
Butylchloral	oz.	.35
Cadmium, Bromide	oz.	.17
Iodide	oz.	.36
Caffeine, lb., 3.50	oz.	.29-31
Bromide	oz.	.19
Citrated, U. S. P., lb., 2.20	oz.	.21-23
Valerianate	oz.	.35
Calamine	lb.	.10-12
Calcium, Carb., precip	lb.	.8-10
Glycerophosphate	oz.	.25-50
tablets, boxes, 50 5-gr.	ea.	.30
Hypophosphite, lb., .85	oz.	.10-14
Iodide	oz.	.43
Lactophosphate	oz.	.13-15
Phosphate, precip	lb.	.17-19
Sulphide	lb.	.28
Calomel, 10 lbs., .85	lb.	.90-95
Camphor, Monobromated, lbs., 1.95	oz.	.21-25
Cantharides, Russian	lb.	1.50-1.60
powdered	lb.	1.65-1.75
Cantharidal Vesicant, ozs.	doz.	2.50
Cantharidin	grain.	.12
Capsicum, African	lb.	.19-21
powdered, 5 lbs., .23	lb.	.25-28
Caroid, powder form	oz.	1.25
and Soda Tablets, 150s	bot.	.67
Carbon, Disulphide	lb.	.11
Carmine, No. 40, lb., 4.25-4.50	oz.	.30-35
Castor, Fiber, oz., 1.25; powdered	oz.	1.25-1.50
Cerium, Oxalate, lb., .45	oz.	.7
Chalk, French, powdered	lb.	.10
precip., Thomas' Eng., 7-lb. bag	lb.	.9
prepared, Thomas' Eng., 8-lb., white, box		.50
prepared, Thomas' Eng., 8-lb., pink, box		.65
prepared	lb.	.7
Charcoal, Animal, powd	lb.	.10
Willow, powd	lb.	.14
Chloral Hydrate, 5 lbs., 1.10	lb.	1.15-1.25
Croton	oz.	.35
Chloralamid, 25 pkgs., .70	pkg.	.80
Chloroform, Purified, 5 lbs., .30	lb.	.35
Cinchonidine, Salicylate	oz.	.45
Sulphate, 5-oz. cans, .27	oz.	.32
Cinchonine, Sulphate	oz.	.13-17
Cinnabar	lb.	1.50
Civette	oz.	3.50
Clay, China, lb., .8; powdered	lb.	.10
Cloves, 10 lbs., .16	lb.	.18
powdered, 5 lbs., .20	lb.	.24
Cobalt, Carbonate	oz.	.35
Chloride	oz.	.30
Nitrate, oz., .25; powdered	oz.	.25
Cocaine, Hydrochlorate, Cryst	oz.	3.50-3.75
Alkaloid	oz.	4.05-4.30
Oleate, 5 per cent	oz.	1.00-1.15
Cochineal, Honduras	lb.	.55
powdered	lb.	.60
Codeine, Pure Alkaloid, ozs.	oz.	3.65-3.80
Sulphate, ozs.	oz.	3.25-3.40
Colchicine, cryst., 15-gr. vials	grain.	.14
Collodion	lb.	.77
Cantharidal	lb.	2.00
Flexible	lb.	.77
Colocynth Apple	lb.	.50
powdered	lb.	.60
Composition Powder, 2 ozs.	lb.	.35
Confection, Senna	lb.	.40
Copper, Sulph., bbl., .6	lb.	.7-8
Iodide	oz.	.60
Copperas, bbl., .1	lb.	.2-3
Corrosive Sublimate, 10 lbs., .80	lb.	.88
powdered, 10 lbs., .83	lb.	.92
Coumarin, Crys., Fries Bros., lb., 7.00	oz.	.70
Cowhage	oz.	.40
Cream Tartar, 99 p. c., powdered, 50 lbs., .25; 10 lbs., .27	lb.	.28-30
Creolin, ¼ lbs., doz., 4.00; lbs.	doz.	8.00
Creosol, U. S. P.	lbs.	.80
Creosote, Beechwood Tar	lb.	1.00-2.50
Carbonate, lbs., 9.00	oz.	.65
Phosphite, lb., 10.00	oz.	1.00
Crurin Kalle, 25 grms	each.	1.50
Crystogen, powdered, ozs.	oz.	1.00
" powdered, 8 oz.	pkg.	4.00
" 5-gr. tablets, ozs.	oz.	1.10
" " 8 oz.	pkg.	5.00
" " 25's	doz.	4.00
" **Aperient**	doz.	8.00
Cumarine, lb., 4.50	oz.	.40
Currie Powder	lb.	1.00
Cuttle-Fish Bone, select	lb.	.30-50
Dermatol, oz., .22	lb.	2.50
Dextrin, bag, .7	lb.	.8-10
Diabetin	lb.	1.30
Digalen, ½-oz. vial		1.00
Digitalin, ⅛ ozs.	oz.	7.00
Diuretin	oz.	1.75
Dover's Powder, 10 lbs., 1.10	lb.	1.15
Dragon's Blood, reeds	lb.	.65
extra powdered	lb.	.90-1.00
Duotal	oz.	1.50
Earth, Fullers, po., 25 lbs., .5	lb.	.6-8
Eka-Iodoform	oz.	.70
Elaterium	oz.	.70
Emulsol, per doz., 2 oz.		6.00
Elixir Iodo-Bromide of Calcium Comp., Tilden's	pt.	.82
Empyroform	oz.	.65
Eosote (Creosote Valerianate)	oz.	.67
Epicarin	oz.	.30
Epsom Salts, bbl., .1¼	lb.	.2-3
Ergotine, Boujeans, lb., 5.50	oz.	.38
Ergot, Spanish	lb.	.55
powdered	lb.	.65
Russian, lbs., .48; powdered	lb.	.58
Eserine	grain.	.20
Sulphate, 5-gr. v.	grain.	.12
Salicylate, 5-gr. v.	grain.	.11
Ether, Nitrous, Conc., ¼, ½ and 1 lbs.		1.00-1.25
Sulphuric	lb.	.75-85
Acetic	lb.	.50
Ethiops Mineral	lb.	.70
Ethyl, Bromide, 1-oz. bot. or tube	oz.	.20-32
Iodide	oz.	.34
Eucaine, Hydrochlor, ⅛, ¼ oz., 3.60; ½, 1 oz.	oz.	3.50

Eucalyptol, lb., 1.30 ..... oz. .17
Eudoxine ..... oz. 2.10
Eupthalmine, Hydrochloride ..... gm. 1.23
Exodin, 7½-gr. tablets, 10 in box ..... box. .30
" ..... ozs. 1.40
Extract, Logwood, bulk, 24-lb. box, .10; lb., .11; ½ lbs., .15; ¼ lbs., .18; 1 lb. ..... lb. .12
Eyestones ..... doz. .36-42
Ferratin, pow. or tablets, 25 ozs., .75 ..... oz. .85
Ferripyrine ..... oz. 1.35-1.50
Ferro-Somatose, lbs. and ½ lbs. ..... lb. 6.50
" ¼ lbs. ..... lb. 6.75
" 2-oz. tins ..... doz. 10.50
Firwein, Tilden's ..... pt. .85
Flowers, Arnica ..... lb. .15-18
Blue Centaury ..... lb. .60
Calendula ..... lb. .35
Chamomile, Roman ..... lb. .25-28
German, 1903, .25; German, 1904 ..... lb. .30
Elder ..... lb. .20
Kooso, lbs., .50; powdered ..... lb.
Lavender ..... lb. .12-20
Malva, Black, lb., .40; Blue ..... lb. .50
Mullein ..... lb. .80-90
Orange ..... lb. 1.00
Rose, Red, French ..... lb. 1.25-1.50
Rosemary ..... lb. .28
Spanish, Valencie, lbs., 8.50-9.25 ..... oz. .65
Saffron, Amer. ..... lb. 1.15-1.25
Formaldehyde ..... lb. .15-40
Formin, lbs., 1.75 ..... oz. .21
Tablets, 5 grs., 30 in tube, ea. ..... .20
5 grs., 100 in tube, ea. ..... .50
7½ grs., 20 in tube, ea. ..... .20
7½ grs., 70 in bot., ea. ..... .50
Formol, lb., .55; 5-lb. bots ..... lb. .50
Galega-Vera ..... doz. 10.50
Galetone ..... doz. 10.50
Gambier, mats, .8 ..... lb. .10-12
Garlic ..... string. .25
Gelatin, Cooper's ..... lb. .50
French, White ..... lb. .50
Geosot, Guaiacol Valerinate ..... oz. 1.34
Glass Wool, for filtering acids ..... oz. 1.25
Glucose ..... lb. .12
Glutol ..... oz. .65
Glycerin, C. P., 30°, can 50 lbs., .14 ..... lb. .16-18
Goat's Rue Fluid Extract ..... lb. 1.75
" " " " ..... ½ lb. 1.85
" " " " ..... ¼ lb. 2.00
Gold Chloride, 15-gr. bot ..... doz. 5.10
and Sodium ..... doz. 2.70
Goose Grease ..... lb. .50-60
Green, Paris, kegs, .18-19 ..... lb. .22-25
Grape Juice, Gleason's, pts., 2 doz. case 4.75
" " qts., 1 doz. case 4.50
" " ½ gal. case of 8 4.75
" " 1 gal. case of 4 4.50
" Welch's, qts., 1 doz. case 4.50
" " pts., 2 doz. case 4.75
" " gals., ½ doz. case 7.50
" Randall's, qts., 1 doz. case 4.50
" " pts., 2 doz. case 4.75
" " gals., ½ doz. case 5.00

Guaiacol, lb., 2.30 ..... oz. .22
Carbonate, oz., 1.50; Salicylate ..... oz. 1.60
Phosphite ..... oz. 1.50
Guaiacophosphal ..... oz. 1.50
Guarana, powdered ..... lb. .90-1.00
Gum, Aloes, Barbados, True ..... lb. .50-55
" Cape ..... lb. .16-20
" powdered ..... lb. .25-27
Curacao ..... lb. .12
" ..... gourds. .13-15
Socotrine, lb., .35; powdered ..... lb. .45
Ammoniac ..... lb. .30
Arabic, 1st's ..... lb. .45
" powdered ..... lb. .55
2d's, lb., .35; powdered ..... lb. .45
3d's, lb., .30; 4th's ..... lb. .28
sifted sorts, lb., .30; sorts ..... lb. .28
Asafetida, lb., .25-35; powdered ..... lb. .40-43
Benzoin ..... lb. .35-40
Camphor, 100 lbs ..... lb. 1.00-1.10
Catechu, powdered ..... lb. .22-28
Chicle, bag, .45 ..... lb. .50-55
Damar ..... lb. .30
Galbanum, strained ..... lb. 1.00-1.15
Gamboge, lb., .85; powdered ..... lb. .90-1.00
Guaiac ..... lb. .35 powdered ..... lb. .45
Kino ..... lb. .40 powdered ..... lb. .50
Myrrh ..... lb. .35 powdered ..... lb. .45
Extra Select ..... lb. .45-50
Olibanum, garblings ..... lb. .12-20
Olibanum, tears ..... lb. .20-23
Opium, lb., 2.95-3.20; powdered ..... lb. 3.60-3.80
Sandarac ..... lb. .20-25
Shellac, D. C. ..... lb. .85-95
" English ..... lb. .70-80
Shellac, Garnet ..... lb. .60
Spruce, true ..... lb. 1.75-2.00
Thus ..... lb. .8-12
Tragacanth, Aleppo, No. 1 ..... lb. .80
" " powdered ..... lb. .90
" " No. 2 ..... lb. .70
" " " powd ..... lb. .80
" Turkey, sorts ..... lb. .30
Gun Cotton ..... oz. .35
Gutta Percha, Chips ..... lb. 1.50
Hedonal ..... oz. 1.60
Helthin, packs, 6 tests ..... pkg. .60
Hemicranine ..... oz. .90
Hemogallol ..... oz. .80
Herb, Agrimony, German, lb., .20 ..... oz. .25
Arnica Flowers, ozs ..... lb. .90
Althea " ..... lb. .55
Balm, lemon, ozs., .40; sweet, ozs ..... lb. .35
Balmony, Leaves, ozs ..... lb. .28
Bittersweet, Twigs, ozs ..... lb. .30
Bittersweet ..... lb. .10
Blackhaw, Bark of Root, ozs ..... lb. .40
Bladder Wrack, ozs ..... lb. .30
Blessed Thistle Leaves, ozs ..... lb. .85
Boneset, ozs ..... lb. .28
Boneset, Herb, ozs ..... lb. .25
Broom Top, Scotch, ozs ..... lb. .90
Buckthorn, Bark, ozs ..... lb. .22
Bugle, Bitter, Herb, ozs ..... lb. .30
Burdock ..... lb. .33

Herb, Canabis Indica, ozs ..... lb. 1.65
Cascara Sagrada Bark, ozs ..... lb. .35
Catnip, ozs ..... lb. .25
Centaury, American Herb, ozs ..... lb. .30
Centaury, Minor, ozs ..... lb. .20
Chamomile Flowers, German, ozs ..... lb. .35
Roman, ozs ..... lb. .35
Chiretta ..... lb. .34
Clover Heads, red, ozs ..... lb. .24
Cramp Bark, ozs ..... ozs. .24
Cranesbill Root, ozs ..... lb. .28
Damiana Leaves, ozs ..... lb. .30
Dandelion Root, true, ozs ..... lb. .28
Dog Grass, ozs ..... lb. .25
Elder Flows, ozs ..... lb. .27
Feverfew, ozs ..... lb. .45
Fleabane Herb, Canada, ozs ..... lb. .34
Galega or Goat's Rue ..... lb. .75
Gold Thread Herbs, ozs ..... lb. .75
Gravel Plant Herb, ozs ..... lb. .25
Grindelia Robusta, ozs ..... lb. .28
" Squarrosa, ozs ..... lb. .40
Hops, 1904 crop, ozs ..... lb. .50
Horehound, ozs ..... lb. .24
Horsemint Herb, ozs ..... lb. .30
Hyssop Herb, ozs ..... lb. .30
Ivy, American, bark or root, ozs ..... lb. .25
Herb, ground ..... lb. .25
Jamaica Dogwood Bark ..... lb. .30
Johnswort Herb ..... lb. .30
Lady Slipper Root ..... lb. .50
Life Everlasting, ozs ..... lb. .25
Lindin Flowers, with leaves, ozs ..... lb. .40
Liverwort, German, ozs ..... lb. .30
Leaves, German, ozs ..... lb. .30
Lobelia, ozs ..... lb. .28
Maiden Hair, ozs ..... lb. .25
Marjoram, Sweet, ozs ..... lb. .36
Mallow, ozs., lb., .34; wild, ozs ..... lb. .20
Motherwort, ozs ..... lb. .34
Mullein, German ..... lb. .22
Pansy Herb ..... lb. .42
Paraguay Tea, genuine ..... lb. .50
Pennyroyal, ozs., lb., .20; Leaf, ozs. ..... lb. .23
Peppermint, ozs ..... lb. .27
German, bulk, lb., .75; Herb, ozs. ..... lb. .24
Plantain Leaves, Red, ozs ..... lb. .30
Poppy Leaves, Red, ozs ..... lb. .65
Prince's Pine Leaf, ozs ..... lb. .30
Pulsatilla, ozs ..... lb. .40
Raspberry Leaf, ozs ..... lb. .30
Rue, ozs ..... lb. .34
Saffron, American, ozs ..... lb. 1.80
Sage, lbs., lb., .15; ozs ..... lb. .18
Domestic, ozs ..... lb. .35
Savin Leaves, ozs ..... lb. .28
Southernwort Herb, ozs ..... .45
Spearmint, ozs ..... lb. .30
Tansy, ozs ..... lb. .25
Thyme, ozs ..... lb. .26
Vervain, ozs ..... lb. .24
Viola tricolor, ozs ..... lb. .36
Wormwood, ozs., lb., .30; powdered ..... lb. .35
Yerba Santa ..... lb. .28

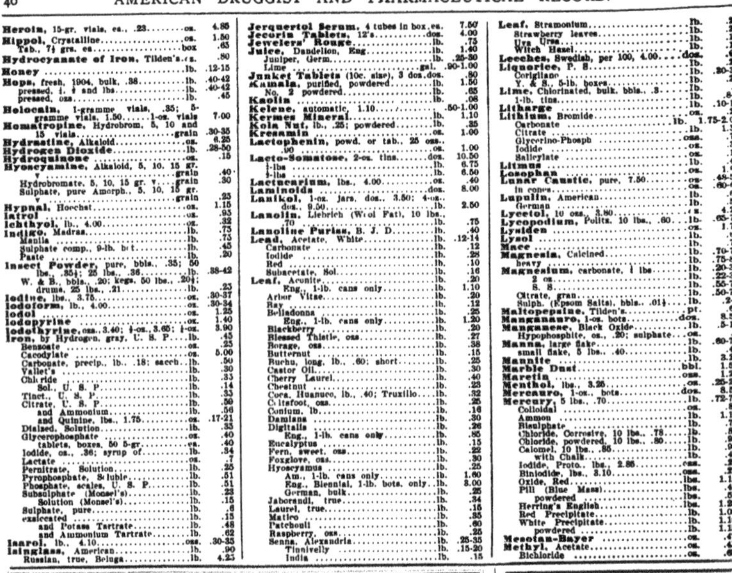

Article	Unit	Price
Heroin, 15-gr. vials, ea., .23	oz.	4.85
Hippol, Crystalline	oz.	1.50
Tab., 7½ grs. ea	box	.65
Hydrocyanate of Iron, Tilden's	oz.	.80
Honey	lb.	.12-15
Hops, fresh, 1904, bulk, .38	lb.	.40-42
pressed, ¼, ½ and lbs	lb.	.40-42
pressed, ozs	lb.	.45
Holocain, 1-gramme vials, .35; 5-gramme vials, 1.50	1-oz. vials	7.00
Homatropine, Hydrobrom, 5, 10 and 15 vials	grain	.30-35
Hydrastine, Alkaloid	oz.	6.25
Hydrogen Dioxide	lb.	.28-50
Hydroquinone	oz.	.15
Hyoscyamine, Alkaloid, 5, 10, 15 gr. v	grain	.40
Hydrobromate, 5, 10, 15 gr. v	grain	.30
Sulphate, pure Amorph., 5, 10, 15 gr. v	grain	.25
Hypnal, Hoechst	oz.	1.15
Iatrol	oz.	.95
Ichthyol, lb., 4.00	oz.	.32
Indigo, Madras	lb.	.75
Manila	lb.	.75
Sulphate comp., 9-lb. bot	lb.	.45
Paste	lb.	.20
Insect Powder, pure, bbls., .35; 50 lbs., .35½; 25 lbs., .36	lb.	.38-42
W. & B., bbls., .20; kegs, 50 lbs., .20½; drums, 25 lbs., .21	lb.	.23
Iodine, lbs., 3.75	oz.	.30-37
Iodoform, lb., 4.00	oz.	.30-34
Iodol	oz.	1.25
Iodopyrine	oz.	1.40
Iodothyrine, ozs., 3.40; ½-oz., 3.65; ¼-oz.		3.90
Iron, by Hydrogen, gray, U. S. P	lb.	.45
Benzoate	oz.	.25
Cacodylate	oz.	5.00
Carbonate, precip., lb., .18; sacch	lb.	.50
Vallet's	lb.	.30
Chloride	lb.	.35
Sol., U. S. P	lb.	.14
Tinct., U. S. P	lb.	.35
Citrate, U. S. P	lb.	.50
and Ammonium	lb.	.56
and Quinine, lbs., 1.75	oz.	.17-21
Dialzed, Solution	lb.	.35
Glycerophosphate	oz.	.40
tablets, boxes, 50 5-gr	ea.	.40
Iodide, oz., .36; syrup of	lb.	.34
Lactate	oz.	.7
Pernitrate, Solution	lb.	.25
Pyrophosphate, Soluble	lb.	.51
Phosphate, scales, U. S. P	lb.	.51
Subsulphate (Monsel's)	lb.	.23
Solution (Monsel's)	lb.	.15
Sulphate, pure	lb.	.6
exsiccated	lb.	.15
and Potass Tartrate	lb.	.48
and Ammonium Tartrate	lb.	.62
Isarol, lb., 4.10	ozs.	.30-35
Isinglass, American	lb.	.90
Russian, true, Beluga	lb.	4.25
Jerquertol Serum, 4 tubes in box	ea.	7.50
Jecorin Tablets, 12's	doz.	4.00
Jewelers' Rouge	lb.	.75
Juice, Dandelion, Eng	lb.	1.40
Juniper, Germ	lb.	.25-30
Lime	gal.	.90-1.00
Junket Tablets (10c. size), 3 doz.	doz.	.80
Kamala, purified, powdered	lb.	1.50
No. 2 powdered	lb.	.65
Kaolin	lb.	.08
Kelene, automatic, 1.10		.50-1.00
Kermes Mineral	lb.	1.10
Kola Nut, lb., .25; powdered	lb.	.35
Kresamin	oz.	1.00
Lactophenin, powd. or tab., 25 ozs., .90	oz.	1.00
Lacto-Somatose, 2-oz. tins	doz.	10.50
¼-lbs	lb.	6.75
½-lbs	lb.	6.50
Lactucarium, lbs., 4.00	oz.	.40
Laminoids	doz.	8.00
Lanikol, 1-oz. jars, doz., 3.50; 4-oz., doz., 9.50	lb.	2.50
Lanolin, Liebrich (Wool Fat), 10 lbs., .70	lb.	.75
Lanoline Puriss, B. J. D	lb.	.40
Lead, Acetate, White	lb.	.12-14
Carbonate	lb.	.12
Iodide	lb.	.28
Red	lb.	.10
Subacetate, Sol	lb.	.16
Leaf, Aconite	lb.	.20
Eng., 1-lb. cans only	lb.	1.10
Arbor Vitae	lb.	.20
Bay	lb.	.12
Belladonna	lb.	.25
Eng., 1-lb. cans only	lb.	1.20
Blackberry	lb.	.20
Blessed Thistle, ozs	lb.	.27
Borage, ozs	lb.	.38
Butternut	lb.	.15
Buchu, long, lb., .60; short	lb.	.25
Castor Oil	lb.	.30
Cherry Laurel	lb.	.40
Chestnut	lb.	.23
Coca, Huanuco, lb., .40; Truxillo	lb.	.32
Coltsfoot, ozs	lb.	.25
Conium, lb	lb.	.16
Damiana	lb.	.30
Digitalis	lb.	.26
Eng., 1-lb. cans only	lb.	.85
Eucalyptus	lb.	.15
Fern, sweet, ozs	lb.	.22
Foxglove, ozs	lb.	.30
Hyoscyamus	lb.	.25
Am., 1-lb. cans only	lb.	1.60
Eng., Biennial, 1-lb. bots. only	lb.	8.00
German, bulk	lb.	.25
Jaborandi, true	lb.	.34
Laurel, true	lb.	.16
Matico	lb.	.35
Patchouli	lb.	.60
Raspberry, ozs	lb.	.25
Senna, Alexandria	lb.	.25-35
Tinnivelly	lb.	.15-20
India	lb.	.15
Leaf, Stramonium	lb.	.20
Strawberry leaves	lb.	.25
Uva Ursa	lb.	.12
Witch Hazel	lb.	.15
Leeches, Swedish, per 100, 4.00	doz.	.60
Liquorice, P. S	lb.	.28
Corigliano	lb.	.30-33
Y. & S., 5-lb. boxes	lb.	.25
Lime, Chlorinated, bulk, bbls., .3	lb.	.5
1-lb. tins	lb.	.8-9
Litharge	lb.	.10-12
Lithium, Bromide	oz.	.23
Carbonate	lb.	1.75-2.00
Citrate	lb.	1.35
Glycerino-Phosph	ozs.	.74
Iodide	oz.	.38
Salicylate	oz.	.15
Litmus	lb.	.40
Losophan	oz.	1.50
Lunar Caustic, pure, 7.50	oz.	.48-51
in cones	oz.	.60-63
Lupulin, American	lb.	.65
German	lb.	.50
Lycetol, 10 ozs., 3.80	oz.	4.25
Lycopodium, Politz, 10 lbs., .60	lb.	.65-75
Lysiden	oz.	1.75
Lysol	lb.	.67
Mace	lb.	.70
Magnesia, Calcined	lb.	.70-75
heavy	lb.	.75-85
Magnesium, carbonate, ¼ lbs	lb.	.20-30
2 oz	lb.	.22-32
S. S	lb.	.55-70
Citrate, gran	lb.	.50-75
Sulph. (Epsom Salts), bbls., .01¼	lb.	.2-4
Maltopepsine, Tilden's	pt.	.62
Manganauro, 1-oz. bots	doz.	8.50
Manganese, Black Oxide	lb.	.5-12
Hypophosphite, oz., .20; sulphate	oz.	.5
Manna, large flake	lb.	.60-70
small flake, 5 lbs., .40	lb.	.45
Mannite	lb.	3.25
Marble Dust	bbl.	1.50
Maretin	ozs.	1.25
Menthol, lbs., 3.25	oz.	.25-29
Mercauro, 1-oz., bots	doz.	8.50
Mercury, 5 lbs., .70	lb.	.72-73
Colloidal	oz.	.85
Ammon	lb.	1.10
Bisulphate	lb.	.75
Chloride, Corrosive, 10 lbs., .78	lb.	.83
Chloride, powdered, 10 lbs., .80	lb.	.90
Calomel, 10 lbs., .85	lb.	.90
with Chalk	lb.	.42
Iodide, Proto., lbs., 2.85	ozs.	.27
Biniodide, lbs., 3.10	ozs.	.27
Oxide, Red	lbs.	1.10
Pill (Blue Mass)	lbs.	.47
powdered	lbs.	.57
Herring's English	lbs.	1.25
Red Precipitate	lb.	1.05
White Precipitate	lb.	1.10
powdered	lb.	1.15
Mesotan-Bayer	oz.	.47
Methyl, Acetate	oz.	.43
Bichloride	oz.	.65

Article	Unit	Price
Methyl, Iodide	lb.	1.00
Oxide	oz.	.50
Salicylate	lb.	.45-50
Methylene, Bichloride	oz.	.65
Migrainin, oz. tins	oz.	1.50
Milk Sugar, powdered, 10 lbs., .20	lbs.	.21-22
Morphine, Acetate	oz.	2.80
Muriate, ⅛s	oz.	2.80
Sulphate, ⅛s, P. & W., ozs.	oz.	2.50-2.60
2½ oz. cartons (25 ozs., 2.45)	oz.	2.55
Moss, Iceland, lb., .12; Irish	lb.	.18-22
Musk, Tonquin, Pods	oz.	14.00-20.00
grain	oz.	22.00-24.00
Nafalan	doz.	2.00
Naphtha, Wood	lb.	.24
Wood, 95 p. c., bbls., .75	gal.	.80-90
Naphthaline, balls, 50 lbs., .3½	lb.	.4-5
cakes and squares	lb.	.6-8
Naphthol	oz.	.18
Narceine	oz.	6.50
Nephritica, Tilden's	pt.	.82
Nickel, Bromide	oz.	.30
Carbonate	oz.	.25
Chloride	oz.	.25
Metallic	oz.	.25
Nitrate	oz.	.18
Oxide, pure	oz.	.75
Sulphate	oz.	.10
Nirvanin	oz.	3.50
Nitroglycerin, 1 per cent. solution lbs., 1.10	oz.	.12
Nosophen	doz.	4.50
Nutrolactis	doz.	10.00
Nutgalls, lb., .30; powdered	lb.	.40
Nutmegs	lb.	.35-40
Nutrose, ½ lbs., 4.00; ¼ lbs., 3.75	lb.	3.35
Nux Vomica	lb.	.8-10
Powdered, pure	lb.	.20-25
Oakum, bales 50 lbs., .08	lb.	.12
Oatmeal	lb.	.8
Oil, Almond, Bitter, lbs., 6.50	oz.	.55
Sweet, True, 5 lbs., .42	lb.	.45-50
Amber, crude	lb.	.25
rect	lb.	.40
Anise	lb.	1.25-1.35
Bay, American, bot. 22 ozs., 3.75	oz.	.33
West Indies, bot. 23 ozs., 3.50	oz.	.50
Benne	gal.	1.00
Bergamot	lb.	2.65
Bergamot, 5-lb. cans	lb.	2.60
Sanderson's	lb.	2.60
Black Pepper	lb.	.75
Cade	lb.	.35
Cajuput	lb.	.75-85
Capsicum	oz.	.50
Caraway	lb.	1.75
Cassia	lb.	1.00-1.10
Castor, 40-lb. can, .12½	lb.	.14-15
Cedar Leaves, Amer.	lb.	.90-95
Chaulmoogra	lb.	2.50
Cinnamon, Ceylon, lb., 15.00	oz.	1.10
Citronella	lb.	.60-85
Clove, 5-lbs., .95	lb.	1.00-1.10
Oil, Cocoanut, Refined, 10 lbs., .18	lb.	.22
Codliver, N. F., kegs, 30 gals., 27.00 to 28.00 ea.	gal.	1.00-1.20
Norwegian, bbls., 30 gals., 29.00 to 31.00	gal.	1.15-1.25
Copaiba	lb.	1.10
Cottonseed	gal.	.45-55
Croton	lb.	1.20
Croton, Eng.	lb.	1.75
Cubeb, Amer.	lb.	1.15
Cumin, lb., 4.50	oz.	.35
Erigeron	lb.	1.25
Eucalyptus, Australian	lb.	.90
Fennel	lb.	1.75
Geranium, Turkish	lb.	4.50
French	lb.	8.00
Prepared	lb.	16.00
Juniper Berries	lb.	1.50
Wood	lb.	.60
Lard, No. 1	gal.	.90
Lavender Flowers	lb.	2.50
Chiris	lb.	2.75
Garden	lb.	1.10
Lemon	lb.	.90-1.00
1-lb. copper cans	lb.	1.10
Sanderson's	lb.	1.00-1.10
Lemongrass	lb.	3.75
Linseed, Boiled, by bbl., .60	gal.	.65-75
Linseed, Raw, by bbl., .58	gal.	.63-70
Mustard, Expressed	gal.	.75
Mustard, Essential, lb., 5.50	oz.	.45-50
Neatsfoot	gal.	.90
Neroli, Bigarade	oz.	8.50
Chiris	oz.	3.75
Petale	oz.	4.00
Olive, Malaga	gal.	.75
Fine Salad, 3-gal. cans, 2.50	gal.	2.75
Orange, Bitter	lb.	3.20
Sweet	lb.	2.35
" 1-lb. copper cans		2.40
Origanum, pure	lb.	.85-1.10
Palm	lb.	.20
Patchouli, lb., 7.50	oz.	.65
Pennyroyal, 5 lbs., 1.50	lb.	1.60
Peppermint	lb.	2.85-3.00
Hotchkiss	lb.	3.35-3.50
Redistilled	lb.	4.00-4.25
Petroleum, crude	gal.	.25
Lubricating, gal., .20; Refined	gal.	.12
Pimento, lb., 2.90	oz.	.25
Pinus, Pumilio	ozs.	.39-43
Sylvestris	lbs.	1.00-2.00
Rhodium, true, lb., 8.00	oz.	.75
Rose, Kazanlik	oz.	4.50-5.00
Botu Pappazoglou	oz.	6.00
Rosemary, Eperle	lb.	1.50
Trieste	lb.	.60
Rue, lb., 3.00	oz.	.30
Salad Union	gal.	.50-55
Sandalwood, W. I., lb., 3.00; Engl.	lb.	5.50
Sassafras	lb.	.75
Savin	lb.	1.40
Spearmint, lb., 5.50; H. G. H.	lb.	5.75
Sperm, Winter, Blea.	gal.	1.00
Oil, Spruce	lb.	.60
Tansy	lb.	4.00-4.50
Thyme, White	lb.	1.25
Turpentine	gal.	.75
Valerian	oz.	.65
Verbena, true	oz.	.50
Whale	gal.	.75
Wintergreen, Betula	lb.	2.15-2.25
Wintergreen, Synthetic, Fries Bros.	lb.	.75
Wintergreen, true	lb.	3.25-3.50
Wormseed	lb.	3.50
Wormwood	lb.	4.00-4.50
Ointment, Mercurial, ½ M	lb.	.48
1-3 M	lb.	.40
Citrine	lb.	.46
Oleate, Mercury, 20 p. c., lb., 3.00	oz.	.25
Morphine, 5 p. c.	oz.	.40
Zinc, powd., lb., 2.50	oz.	.25
Opium (see Gum).		
Orphol	oz.	.80
Orthoform, 1-oz. vials	oz.	1.40
Hydrochlorate	oz.	1.80
Pancreatin, ozs., .50	lb.	6.50
Papain, purified	oz.	1.00
Papoid	oz.	2.00
Paraffine	lb.	.10-12
Paraformaldehyde, Tablets, Fries Bros., lb., 3.50	oz.	.35
Paris Green, 125-lb. kegs	lb.	.18
14-lb. kits, .20; 1 and 3 lb.	lb.	.22
½-lb., lb., .24; ¼-lb.	lb.	.26
Pastiles, Black Fumigating	lb.	.35
Red Fumigating	lb.	.40
Paraform	oz.	.85
Paraldehyde, ¼-lb. bots	lbs.	1.40
Pellotine, Muriate, 1 and 5 gr. vials,	grain	.85
Pental, 10-gramme vials	each	.75
Pepper, Black, lb., 18-20; powdered	lb.	.22-25
White, lb., .25; powdered	lb.	.30
Pepsin, Saccharated, lb., 1.00	oz.	.12
Pure, Armour's, lb., 4.50	oz.	.38
Cudahy's, scale, gran. or insol.		3.50
Peronin, 1-gramme vials	each	1.00
Phenacetin (see Acetphenetidin).		
Pheno-Bromate, tablets or powder (10 ozs., less 10 p. c.; 25 ozs., less 10 p. c. and 5 p. c.)	oz.	1.00
Phenocoll, Hydrochloride, 25 grammes,	vial	1.50
Phosphorus	lb.	1.00
Phosphotal, lb., 10.00	oz.	1.00
Pilocarpine, Muriate, 5, 10 and 15 gr. vials	grain	.6
Piperazine, pure, 10 ozs., 3.80	oz.	4.25
Piperin	oz.	.62
Pitch, Black	lb.	.6
Burgundy	lb.	.3-8
Pixine, 2-oz. jars	doz.	2.00
1-lb. jars	doz.	10.00
Veterinary, 2-oz. tins	doz.	2.00
8-oz. tins	doz.	4.00

Article	Unit	Price
Plaster, Calcined, bbl., 2.00	lb.	.3-4
Dental	bbl.	2.50
Adhesive	yd.	.15-20
Belladonna	lb.	1.25
Galbanum, U. S	lb.	.80
Lead	lb.	.33
Mercury, U. S. P	lb.	1.00
Pollantin-Dunbar (liquid or powder)	ea.	1.75
Poppy Heads	lb.	.18-40
Potash	lb.	.8-12
Potassa, Caustic White	lb.	.28
Potassium, Acetate, bot. inc	lb.	.36-40
Bicarbonate, lb., .14; Bichromate	lb.	.14
Bromide, 5 box, .26	lb.	.30-32
Carbonate	lb.	.12
Chlorate, Eng., lb., .12; powdered	lb.	.15
Citrate	lb.	.47
Cyanide, Fd	lb.	.45
Glycerophosphate	oz.	.35
Hypophosphite, lbs., .80	oz.	.10
Iodide, 5 lbs., 3.25	lb.	3.35-3.50
Nitrate, Gran	lb.	.10
Permanganate	lb.	.18-20
Prussiate, Red	lb.	.50
Yellow	lb.	.20
Sulphuret	lb.	.18
Probilin Pills, 60 in box	ea.	1.25
Propylamine	oz.	.55
Protargol, ¼ ozs., 1.35; ozs	oz.	1.25
Pyramidon	oz.	2.13
Quinalgen	oz.	1.25
Quassone	doz.	10.00
Quinine, Bromide	oz.	.48-52
Muriate	oz.	.47-51
Sulphate, bulk	oz.	.18-20
Sulph., 1-oz. vials, B. & S	oz.	.26-27
P. & W	oz.	.26-28
Bisulphate, 5-oz. can	oz.	.22-24
1-oz. vials, B. & S	oz.	.26-28
Tannate	oz.	.31-35
Valerianate	oz.	.55
Quinolin	ozs.	1.00
Quinoliv	oz.	1.00
Resin, Common	lb.	.4
Jalap	oz.	.60
Leptandrin	oz.	.35
Podophyllin, lb., 4.00	oz.	.35
Scammony, U. S. P	oz.	.40
White	lb.	.6
Resorcin, White, lb., 1.40	oz.	.17
Fries Bros., lb., 2.20	oz.	.25
Respirazone, Tilden's	pt.	1.03
Rheumacilate, doz., 4.80	oz.	.40
Rheumatol	ozs.	1.00
Rhodinal II	oz.	4.00
Rochelle Salts	lb.	.23-25
" " 50-lb. boxes	lb.	.22½-23½
Rodagen	ozs.	1.00
Root, Aconite	lb.	.20
Althea, lb., .28; cut	lb.	.35
Belladonna	lb.	.20
Berberis aquifolium	lb.	.20
Bitter	lb.	.28
Blackberry	lb.	.20
Black Snake	lb.	.20
Blood	lb.	.24
Root, Burdock, crushed	lb.	.20
Calamus, Sliced, White	lb.	.40
Calumba	lb.	.20
Canada Snake	lb.	.36
Cohosh, Black	lb.	.15
Colchicum, lb., .25; powdered	lb.	.30
Coltsfoot	lb.	.40
Comfrey, crushed	lb.	.20
Crawley	lb.	1.75-2.25
Curcuma	lb.	.15
Dandelion, cut, 5 lbs., .17	lb.	.22
Dwarf Elder, oz	lb.	.20
Elecampane, 5 lbs., .16	lb.	.20
Fern, Male	lb.	.22
Galangal, 5 lbs., .12	lb.	.14
Gelsemium	lb.	.20
Gentian, 10 lbs., .9	lb.	.12
ground, 5 lbs., .12	lb.	.15
powd., 5 lbs., .15	lb.	.16
Ginger, African	lb.	.14
powd., 5 lbs., .18	lb.	.20
Jamaica, Bleached, 5 lbs., .18	lb.	.22
Bl., powd., 5 lbs., .27	lb.	.30
Unbleached, 5 lbs., .18	lb.	.22
Ginseng	lb.	6.50-9.00
Golden Seal	lb.	1.50-1.60
Gold Thread	lb.	.80
Hellebore, Black	lb.	.15
White, powd., 5 lbs., .12	lb.	.15
Indian Hemp, Black, lb., .25; White	lb.	.20
Indigo, Wild, ozs	lb.	.25
Ipecac, lb., 1.85; powdered	lb.	2.00
Jalap, lb., .18; powdered	lb.	.30
Kava Kava	lb.	.30
Licorice, lb., .16-20; powd., 5 lbs., .12	lb.	.15
Lily of the Valley	lb.	.20
Lovage, select	lb.	.80
Male Fern, select	lb.	.25
Mandrake, lb., .18; powdered	lb.	.22
Masterwort	lb.	.25
Mugwort	lb.	.18
Musk	lb.	.35
Nettle	lb.	.20
Orris, Florentine	lb.	.15-18
" " powdered	lb.	.16-22
fingers	lb.	.80
infant	lb.	2.75
Verona, powdered	lb.	.20
Parsley	lb.	.20
Pellitory	lb.	.45
Pink	lb.	.40
Pleurisy	lb.	.25
Poke	lb.	.18
Pond Lily, White	lb.	.25
Yellow	lb.	.25
Queen of the Meadow	lb.	.20
Rhatany	lb.	.27
Rhubarb, China	lb.	.60-75
" China, cut	lb.	1.00-2.00
powdered	lb.	.40-85
Sarsaparilla, Hond	lb.	.85
" " cut	lb.	.44
Mexican, lb., .18; ground	lb.	.22
Senega	lb.	.90
Serpentaria	lb.	.55-60
Squill, select	lb.	.10
Root, Stillingia, lb., .18; powdered	lb.	.25
Unicorn	lb.	.40
Valerian, English, lb., .42; German	lb.	.30
Virginia Snake	lb.	.60
Yellow Dock	lb.	.22
Zedoary, pure	lb.	.18
Rum, Bay, imported, ½ bbls., 2.00; 10 gals., 2.15; 5 gals., 2.25	gal.	2.35-2.50
Bay, essence	lb.	3.00
Saccharin, lb., 4.50	½-oz. tin	.35
Salacetol	oz.	.33
Salicin, lb., 4.50	oz.	.35
Salipyrin	oz.	.80
Tablet	oz.	.80
Salol, lb., 1.20	oz.	.14
Salophen, 25 ozs., .95	oz.	1.00
Saloquinine	ozs.	1.25
Salicylate	oz.	1.25
Sanose	oz.	.25
Santonin, lb., 10.50-10.70	oz.	.73-75
Saola, Tilden's	pt.	.24
"Save-the-Horse" Spavin Cure ($5.00)	doz.	48.00
Scopolamine, Hydrobrom, Ph.G. (identical with Hyoscine, U. S. P.)	grain	.20-22
Seed, Anise, Italian	lb.	.17
Star	lb.	.30
Angelica	lb.	.30
Burdock	lb.	.25
Canary, Sicily	lb.	.7-8
Cardamom, Aleppo	lb.	1.30
Malabar	lb.	1.00
Mangalore, bleached, extra	lb.	1.40
Celery	lb.	.12-15
Colchicum, lb., .55; powdered	lb.	.65
Conium	lb.	.25
Coriander	lb.	.18
Cumin	lb.	.18
Fennel	lb.	.16
Fenugreek, powd., 25 lbs., .7	lb.	.10
Flax, cleaned, bbl., 6.75	lb.	.4-5
ground, bbl., .05½	lb.	.5
Hemp, bag, .3½	lb.	.5
Henbane	lb.	.45
Jambul	oz.	.25
Larkspur	lb.	.50
powdered	lb.	.60
Lobelia, powdered	lb.	.65
Lovage, lb., .65; powdered	lb.	.70
Millet	lb.	.6
Mustard, Black	lb.	.10
White, lb., .10; powdered	lb.	.25-31
Parsley	lb.	.15
Poppy, Blue	lb.	.10-12
White	lb.	.20
Pumpkin	lb.	.30
Quince, German, lb., .50; Russian	lb.	.40
Rape, English	lb.	.6½
German	lb.	.5
Strophanthus, Green	lb.	1.50-1.60
Sunflower seed	lb.	.6-9
Watermelon	lb.	.30
Worm (Chenopodium)	lb.	.25
(Santonica)	lb.	.30
Seidlitz Mixture, 50 lbs., .18	lb.	.19-22

Article	Unit	Price
Silver, Nitrate, cryst., lb., 7.50	oz.	.50-55
67 per cent., oz., .37; 50 per cent.	oz.	.30
Cones	oz.	.60-63
Soap, Castile, Marseilles, box, .7	lb.	.10
Mottled, pure, box, .8	lb.	.10
White, Conti's, box, .12	lb.	.14
powdered, 25 lbs., .28	lb.	.33
Green (Sapo Vir.), 10 lbs., .12	lb.	.10-15
Eng. Blue Mottled Soap, cases, 112 lbs.		5.50-6.50
Soda, Chlor. Scl	doz.	2.25
Sodium, Acetate, pure, gran	lb.	.15
Bicarbonate, Eng., keg, .08	lb.	.4-5
" Natrona, keg, .2½	lb.	.3-5
Bromide	lb.	.35-37
Carbonate, bbl., .1	lb.	.2½
Citrate	lb.	.47
Glycerophosphate	oz.	.35
Hypophosphite, lbs., .85	lb.	.10-14
Hypophosphite, kg., .2½	lb.	.5
Hyposulphite	keg	.02½
Iodide, lb., 3.45	oz.	.38-40
Phosphate, cryst	lb.	.10
Salicylate	lb.	.44
Silicate, Syrupy, bbl., .2½	lb.	.5-10
Sulphate	lb.	.3
Somatose, 2 ozs	doz.	8.25
Somnal	oz.	.80
Sozoiodol	oz.	1.15
Sparteine, Sulph., B & S	oz.	.75-1.00
Spermaceti	lb.	.28-30
Spermine, Poehl, box 4 tubes	ea.	3.00
Spirit Ether Nit., U. S. P	lb.	.52
Streptolyptic Serum, Stearns', 20 Cc., in two sero-bulbs of 10 Cc. each		3.00
Discount, 25 per cent.		
Strontium, Nitrate	lb.	.16
Bromide, lb., .55	oz.	.12
Iodide	oz.	.41
Lactate, lb., 1.25	oz.	.16
Salicylate, lb., .75	oz.	.13
Strophanthin, C. P. cryst	gr.	.6
Strychnine, Crystals, ⅛-oz. vials	oz.	1.20
powdered, ⅛-oz. vials	oz.	1.20
Sulphate, ⅛-oz. vials	oz.	1.20
Glycerophosphate, ozs	oz.	2.50
Sulfonal, 25 ozs., 1.25	oz.	1.35
Sulphur, Flowers, bbls., .2½	lb.	.4-5
Precipitate, pure	lb.	.16-18
Suprarenal Glands, Desiccated, powd., oz., 2.00; tablets	oz.	1.00
Saccharated	oz.	1.20
Tablets, 1 grain, per 100		.40
Capsules, 1 grain, per 100		.65
Sycose, 2-oz. package	each.	1.00
Takadiastase	oz.	1.70
Liquid, 8-oz. bots	doz.	6.00
Tannigen, 25 ozs., .65	oz.	.75
Tannopine	oz.	.75
Tar, N. C. pine, Diamond brand, pts.	doz.	.95
Tartar Emetic, powdered	lb.	.36
Terebene	lb.	.65
Terpin Hydrate, cryst	oz.	.10
in bulk	lb.	.45
Theocin-Bayer	ozs.	2.70
Theophyllin, B. & S	oz.	1.40
sodium, oz., 1.50; sodium salicylate	oz.	1.10
Thigenol, lbs., 4.00	oz.	.32
Thiocol	oz.	1.40
Thiocol Tablets, 100 in vial		1.75
Thioform, 25-gramme pkgs	each	.50
Thiol, liquid, oz., .40; powdered	oz.	.75
Thymol (Thymic Acid), lbs., 2.25	oz.	.27
Thyroids, desiccated, Cudahy's	lb.	7.00
Tinct. Simulo, Christy's, lbs	lb.	4.25
½ lbs., lb., 4.35; ¼ lbs	lb.	4.50
Trional, 25 ozs., 1.40	oz.	1.50
Tuberculinum Kochii, "Pasteur," 1 Cc	doz.	3.20
Tuberculin (Veterinary), "Pasteur," 1 Cc	doz.	3.20
Tuberculin Solution (Veterinary), "Pasteur," 10 Cc	doz.	4.00
Turpentine, Spirits, bbls., .72½	gal.	.80-90
Chian, oz., .45; Venice	lb.	.30
Tussol	oz.	1.65
Urethane, C. P	oz.	.54
Uricedin, 5 ozs	doz.	15.00
Urotropin	oz.	.60
Urotropin Tablets, 5 or 7½ grs.	doz.	3.00
Vaccine, Mulford's (Discount, 40 per cent.), 1 pkg. Glycerinised Lymph, containing 10 tubes		1.00
1 vial Glycerinised Lymph, containing sufficient for 50 vaccinations		4.50
1 pkg. Ivory Points, containing 10 points		.95-1.35
Glycerinated, F. Stearns & Co., Points (10 in a package)		1.00
Tubes (10 tubes in one wooden box, accompanied by one needle, rubber bulb and 10 temporary shields)		1.00
Discount, 40 per cent.		
Vanillin (various brands)	oz.	.60-75
Veratrine, ⅛-oz., 2.75; Sulph., ⅛ths.	oz.	2.90
Veronal, ¼-oz., oz., 1.60; 1-oz	oz.	1.60
Veronal Tablets, 5 grs., tubes, .15.	ea.	.40
" " bots. 50	ea.	1.15
" " " 100	ea.	2.25
Water, Ammonia, 16 deg., carboy, .3½	lb.	.6
20 deg., carboys, .4½	lb.	.8
26 deg. (Conct.), carboy, .8½	lb.	.10-12
Wax, Bayberry	lb.	.60-65
Carnauba, No. 1	lb.	.55-60
Ceresin, yellow, cases, .18	lb.	.22
" white, cases, .21	lb.	.25-28
Japan, cases, .15	lb.	.18-20
White, Star Brand, 60 lbs., .50	lb.	.55
White, S. B	lb.	.35
Leonard's T. L. Brand, 60 lbs., .47½	lb.	.55
" " 60 lbs., .42½	lb.	.50
Yellow, select	lb.	.33
White Lead, Dry, pure	lb.	.10
Zinc, American, lb., .10; French	lb.	.15
Whiting, bbls., .¼	lb.	.3
Witch Hazel Ext., 10 gals., .70.	gal.	.85
Wood, Guaiac, rasped	lb.	.6
Quassia Chips, bbl., .6	lb.	.7-12
Red Saunders, bbl., .4	lb.	.6-8
Sandal, ground	lb.	.40
Yohimbin Hydrochlor, ⅛-gramme vials	each.	5.00
Tablets, 1-12 gr., 10 in tube	each.	1.00
Zinc, Acetate	lb.	.25-30
Carbonate, Precip	lb.	.23
Chloride, granular, lbs., .22	oz.	.6
Iodide	oz.	.40
Oxide	lb.	.10
Hubbuck's, 7-lb. boxes, .35	lb.	.38-40
Zinc, Sulphate, bbls., .3½	lb.	.5-6
Sulphocarbolate, lbs., .60	oz.	.7-9
Valerianate, lbs., 1.75	oz.	.20

PAINTS AND COLORS.

Article	Unit	Price
Black, Coach, in oil	lb.	.18-25
dry	lb.	.15-20
Drop, in oil	lb.	.15-25
dry, in oil	lb.	.12-20
Ivory, in oil, lb., .18-25; dry	lb.	.12-18
in Japan	lb.	.22-25
Lamp, Germantown, ass'd papers, ½-lb., ¼-lb., 1-lb	lb.	.12
in oil	lb.	.10
Black Lead, E. I., 25 lbs., .6½	lb.	.3
German, 25 lbs., .4½	lb.	.6
Blue, Celestial, dry	lb.	.10
Chinese, dry	lb.	.60
in oil	lb.	.55
Paint, in oil	lb.	.9
Prussian, dry	lb.	.50
in oil	lb.	.45
Soluble, 10 lbs., .45	lb.	.50
Ultramarine, dry	lb.	.15
in oil	lb.	.20
Brown, Sienna, burnt, dry	lb.	.4
in oil	lb.	.10-15
Raw, dry	lb.	.4
in oil	lb.	.10-15
Spanish, dry, bbls., .1	lb.	.3
Vandyke, dry	lb.	.6
in oil	lb.	.18
Chalk, lump, bbls., .½	lb.	.3
Green, Chrome, powd., 6-lb. cans, .10.	lb.	.12
in oil	lb.	.12-16
Paris, bulk, lbs., .16-17; 1-lbs., .18-20; ½-lbs., .20-22; ¼-lbs., .22-25; in oil	lb.	.22-27
Litharge	lb.	.10
Pumice Stone, bbl., .6	lb.	.8
powdered, bbl., .3	lb.	.6
Putty, in bladders, bbls., .2½	lb.	.2½
in oil	lb.	
Red, Indian, Eng., dry	lb.	.8
in oil	lb.	.10-15
Lead	lb.	.8-10
Orange Mineral	lb.	.12
Rose Lake, Eng., dry	lb.	.5
Pink, Eng., dry	lb.	.15
Tuscan, Eng., dry	lb.	.4
in oil	lb.	.22
Venetian, dry, American, bbls., .1	lb.	.2½
Vermilion, American	lb.	.20
Chinese	lb.	.90
English	lb.	.80
Rotten Stone, bbl., .6	lb.	.8
Umber, Burnt, bbls., .1½	lb.	.3
Raw, bbls., .1½	lb.	.3
White, China, dry	lb.	.20
Flake, dry	lb.	.15
Lead, dry	lb.	.10
oil	lb.	.9-10
Paris, English	lb.	.3
Whiting, bbls., .½	lb.	.3
Yellow, Chrome, dry	lb.	.10-15
in oil	lb.	.10-20
Golden, in oil	lb.	.16
Ochre, French, dry, bbls., .1½	lb.	.2½
American, dry, bbls., .1	lb.	.2
Zinc, White, dry, American	lb.	.8
in oil	lb.	.10

American Druggist "WANTS" Page.

THIS Department is intended to be used as a medium for the exchange or sale of stores, the employment of clerks, and the securing of situations. Suitable notices of moderate length under this heading inserted one time free for subscribers; for each additional insertion Fifty Cents will be charged. Advertisements not in the foregoing classification Forty Cents per line.

SITUATIONS VACANT.

SALESMEN now calling on the drug trade in Greater New York can secure an advantageous side line on liberal commission; experienced men preferred; splendid opportunity for competent men. Address F. J. J., care AMERICAN DRUGGIST.

WANTED, LICENSED DRUG CLERK.—One who is capable, honest and a good salesman; a single man under 30 years of age and of good appearance preferred; position ready at any time; in answering state wages required; please give references. Address Box 812, Westfield, N. Y.

REGISTERED PHARMACISTS and drug employees, if you would accept a better position, now or later, send us your name at once; fine openings in all States; salaries, $600 to $2,000 a year; employers referred to competent men free. NATIONAL PHARMACEUTICAL AGENCY, 616 Colonial Security Building, St. Louis, Mo.

WANTED, LICENSED CLERK at retail drug store; steady position for ri[illegible] party; best of references required. Address J. F. S., care of AMERICAN DRUGGIST.

ADVERTISING WRITER, competent to construct high class retail druggist's advertising; applicant must be an experienced pharmacist with lofty ideals, a good command of English; original ideas, and competent to carry on a propaganda for retailers along the most enlightened lines; permanent and profitable employment for the right man. Address Pharmaceutical Advertiser, care AMERICAN DRUGGIST.

DRUG CLERK WANTED FOR MEXICO.—Young graduate in pharmacy, with knowledge of Spanish preferred, who can be trusted in important position in well-known Mexican drug store; must be qualified in every particular; chance of advancement good; send references and state salary expected. Mexico, care Foreign Department, AMERICAN DRUGGIST.

BUSINESS OPPORTUNITIES.

$14.40 for $1.00.—Send $1.00 for formula of "X—L" Headache Powders; guaranteed cure; 1 gross of 10-cent packages cost $1.00 to make. Address "C.," 212 Seventeenth avenue, Paterson, N. J.

FOR SALE.—Wishing to retire from business on account of age, I offer a large and prosperous business at a liberal discount from the inventory to a cash customer; when answering this state how much capital you have to invest. Address Filmore, care of AMERICAN DRUGGIST.

SHEEP DIP, ETC.—A gentleman with special knowledge of the trade and an extensive connection in South Africa wishes to represent a manufacturer of sheep dip in that country; 11 years' experience. Address "Dip," Box 671, Sells Advertising Offices, London, England.

FOR $25,000, a working interest in a fine wholesale drug business. Address Drugs, care Stringer & Seymour, St. Paul, Minn.

WANTED.—To correspond with wholesale druggists' sundries salesman with an established trade to handle on commission a new and extremely useful household novelty—a corkscrew and spoonholder combined. Designed to draw corks from medicine bottles and hold spoon in suspension; sells well on sight and yields good profit; the right man can have exclusive sales privilege in his territory. Address A. M. Irvy, Norfolk, Va.

PARTNER WANTED.—I want as an equal partner a good pharmacist and business man who can command $2,000 or $3,000 in real money. I have a store that has a stock of nearly $6,000 in clean, fresh goods, most of it bought in the last eight months, and a business that is too big for one man to handle. It is capable of a vast development, as it is a suburb of New York that may increase its population five fold in the next five years. Would sell out, but am forming a stock company to operate a chain of stores in this section and want this store in the combination. I must have time to attend to this company matter and do not want to lose this store, as it will be an important link in our chain of stores. If I can find the right man I have a good thing for him, as the store will go into the combination as soon as the company is incorporated. Or I will make a contract to sell all my interest to my partner in case he doesn't want to go into the company. In short, I want to hold and continue the building up of this business by some one that I can absolutely depend upon. Apply by letter only to Dawson, care AMERICAN DRUGGIST.

CALIFORNIA BUSINESS.—Chain of eight retail stores and wholesale house doing business of $400.000 annually, capable of indefinite expansion; book value of stock in this corporation in excess of 1.20 dividends, 8 per cent. annually and 10 per cent. to surplus: 65 per cent. of stock will be sold on basis of 105 per share; details furnished those giving assurance of satisfactory financial responsibility. F. A. Pollock, 413 Donohoe Building, San Francisco, Cal.

FOR SALE.—Drug store in lively Michigan town; sales average $500 per month; rent, $15; failing health the cause for selling; invoice, $2,200; will sell for $2,000. Address Libby, AMERICAN DRUGGIST.

WANTED.—A drug store doing a moderate business, "no paints or oils," within 35 miles of New York. It must bear the closest examination or please do not waste your time or mine by noticing this. Address Geo. Kempton, 197 Fulton street, New York.

A BARGAIN.—A Morris Tablet Machine, Style B. Direct Driver. Includes dies and punches; this machine is practically new, having only been in use about three months. ANOTHER BARGAIN.—A 60-Gallon Drug Still, including rectifier, condenser, and low wine still. The still can be operated independent of the rectifier. This set is in splendid condition, being practically good as new. Address Dept A, 212 S. Seventh Street, St. Louis, Mo.

FOR SALE.—An old established drug store in a manufacturing town in Connecticut, one hour from New York; reason for selling, poor health of owner; a good store; $4,500 inventory. Address Lysol, care of AMERICAN DRUGGIST.

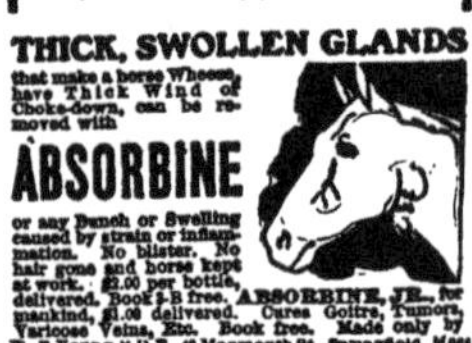

CERTAIN hypodermatic tablets go to pieces quickly enough when thrown into water, their undissolved particles settling to the bottom and solution proceeding slowly if at all. Unreliable agents at best—*worse than worthless in an emergency!*

PARKE, DAVIS & CO.'S

HYPODERMATIC TABLETS

dissolve promptly and thoroughly. Drop one into a syringe half filled with lukewarm water and shake vigorously. In five seconds (or less) it will have dissolved completely. There is never any delay, never any uncertainty.

SPECIFY "P., D. & CO." WHEN ORDERING FROM YOUR JOBBER.

PARKE, DAVIS & COMPANY

HOME OFFICES AND LABORATORIES, DETROIT, MICH.

The Bitter Principle of Cascara Sagrada

MINUS THE BITTER TASTE

BY many physicians the bitter extract of cascara is greatly preferred to aromatic preparations. But there has been one obstacle to its general use—its unpalatability.

CASCARA

TONIC-LAXATIVE GLOBULES

(P., D. & CO.)

meet this impediment squarely. The gelatin investment effectually masks the disagreeable taste. Our *Cascara Tonic-Laxative Globules* contain only the active bitter principle of Cascara Sagrada, each globule representing 3 grains of the bitter glucoside.

NET TRADE PRICES:

Boxes of 25, per dozen boxes, \$2 10 — Boxes of 100, per box, \$0 65

PARKE, DAVIS & CO.

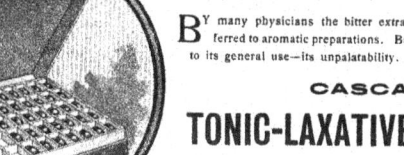

A Necessity for Every Household.

The F. A. Thompson Company, of Detroit, Mich., have solved the hitherto unsolvable problem of preparing an insecticide which is colorless, odorless, inexpensive, safe and absolutely certain in its action. This insecticide is Thompson's Rose Nicotine. It is put up in 25 and 50 cent cans and in 25-cent fumigators. The claims made for this insecticide are so wide and so convincing that a druggist cannot fail to see the advantages of carrying this remedy in stock and recommending it to every householder. It is a sanitary necessity in the house, as a means of killing off all sorts of insects, and is absolutely invaluable in the garden and yard. Write the F. A. Thompson Company, of Detroit, for their household hints on the use of insecticides.

Some New Post Cards.

The American News Company has just received a large importation of post cards—pictures of beautiful and rare flowers in their natural colors. The subjects are tastefully and exquisitely executed and are bound to be very popular. They have also added to their already large assortment of comic cards two new lines. To one of these they call particular attention, as it is a high-grade card of good, wholesome humor that the most sensitive would receive without offense. This line, comprising 14 subjects, will fill a long-felt want with the trade and meet a demand that has been made upon them by customers who wanted a humorous card, but one that was not trashy or offensive, and the company has been able to supply this by its close attention to the trade's requirements. An additional line which they offer of handsome colored cards, entitled "The American Beauty," consists of beautiful heads and figures of pretty women in various costumes, gowned to suit the seasons of the year—motoring, shopping, etc. To introduce the cards mentioned and others the company will supply the trade with their trial order, assortment No. 200—01, consisting of 250 cards, for $2.50, postage prepaid. To dealers handling or contemplating handling post cards this offer presents a splendid opportunity to secure an excellent assortment of good selling subects on which a large margin of profit is made.

The New S. A. R. D.

What promises to be the strongest individual move made by a proprietary article manufacturer to protect the retail druggists on the retail prices of its goods has just been inaugurated by the Sanitol Chemical Laboratory Company, St. Louis, for its Sanitol Tooth and Toilet Preparations.

A Sanitol Association of Retail Druggists has been formed and incorporated that will include in its membership every retail druggist in the United States.

The special features of the plan as announced are a price-protection, minimum retail selling schedule for the Sanitol products and an annual rebate of 5 per cent. on all purchases, either through the wholesaler or direct. The means thus taken to secure price-protection seem to be sound and logical, and the elaborate prospectus of the plan just issued by the Sanitol Company merits the earnest and careful consideration of every retail druggist.

In our next issue we hope to be able to present to our readers a detailed report of this plan, showing what it is and how it will affect the retail druggists.

American Chemicals.

The Albany Chemical Company, of Albany, N. Y., is one of the pioneer firms in the production of American chemicals, and its list embraces many important medicinal, photographic and technical chemicals of approved purity. The business of this company has grown rapidly and its output embraces a full line of fine chemicals which compare favorably both in quality and price with any on the market. Druggists who have no catalogue of this company in hand should not fail to write to the Albany Chemical Company, Albany, N. Y., mentioning the AMERICAN DRUGGIST.

Quinine at Batavia.

Consul General Rairden, of Batavia, reports the result [illegible] the second sale of quinine at that place on February 21, [illegible] follows:

There was put up for sale 3,084.48 kilograms (6,786 pounds) sulphate of quinine, part being packed in cases of 400 ounces and part packed at purchaser's option. Of the entire lot [illegible] 96 kilograms (about 211 pounds) of the option quinine [illegible] sold at 17.75 francs ($7.135) per kilogram (about 2.2 pounds).

Speaking of the unsatisfactory sales for this year, a merchant remarked that in spite of the poor showing at the sales in this city the situation is not so bad, especially when [illegible] calculates that at the close of 1905 there were 78,943 kilograms (about 173,674 pounds) in stock at London, 27,000 kilograms (about 59,400 pounds) in stock and in working at factories, 8,000 kilograms (about 17,600 pounds) at druggists, [illegible] kilograms (about 409,314 pounds) in bark in stock at London and Amsterdam; in all, 300,000 kilograms (about [illegible] pounds) to supply some 900,000,000 consumers, or scarcely sufficient for nine months' ordinary consumption.

It appears strange that, in view of these figures and the acceptance of the above facts, no American concern has directed its attention to this article. The entire stock could be had for about $2,500,000, and should bring a return of not less than $3,000,000. It is interesting to note that at one time quinine was selling at 300 francs ($120.60) per kilogram (2.2 pounds).

A Combination Offer on Postal Cards.

We illustrate herewith a display rack for post cards which offers special features of value. The rack, which holds a stock of 900 cards, will be given, together with 625 assorted post cards retailing at $15.75, for the sum of $7. The selection offered is as follows:

Revolving Rack Holding 900 Cards.

Cards.		Sell for
100	N. Y. Views (Black)	$1.00
100	N. Y. Views (Colored)	2.50
200	Comics (Colored)	5.00
25	N. Y. Views (Tinseled)	1.25
25	N. Y. Views (Transparent)	1.25
25	Leather	1.25
25	Birthday	1.25
100	Comics (Black)	1.00
25	Comics (Transparent)	1.25
	625 Cards retailing at	$15.75
	Cost,	7.00
	Profit and Rack,	$8.75

The liberal margin of profit provided in this offer insures the investment being a safe one. The illustrated post card fever appears to be increasing in intensity and is spreading to all classes, so that the druggist who has a good assortment can count on building up a trade which will prove steady and prosperous. Joseph Koehler, 146 Park Row, New York, who makes this offer, will also prepare special postal cards to order from photographs furnished by the customer, at a very low rate. The special combination offer made above is only one of the numerous special offers made by Mr. Koehler, one of which includes a rack and assortment of cards for the very small sum of $5. Details of this offer appear on another page of this issue. Write Mr. Koehler for his special offers, mentioning the AMERICAN DRUGGIST.

The Cleveland Fruit Juice Company, Cleveland, Ohio, has just issued a handsome little booklet of soda formulas. This goes to druggists all over the United States and should prove a valuable aid to the dispensers. This company makes a practice of issuing a booklet every year. At times it illustrates the goods in colors and at others follows other courses, but all are valuable to the druggist. The company is owned by the partners of the wholesale drug house of Benton, Hall & Co., and its goods are sold all over the United States. The business is growing from year to year and promises to become very extensive.

Hints to Buyers.

The lanolines for which Victor Koechl & Co., of New York, are agents, are official in both the United States and the British pharmacopœias. The packages will be recognized by the "dartring" trademark plainly stamped upon them.

High grade crude drugs and chemicals, together with a large line of chemical and physical apparatus, may be obtained of the old house of Eimer & Amend, of 205 Third avenue, New York. This house enjoys an enviable reputation for the quality of their goods and for their fair treatment of customers.

The druggist who does not read the advertisements of the C. I. Hood Company, of Lowell, Mass., is missing valuable trade opportunities which are constantly being offered by that enterprising concern. We would especially invite the attention of our readers to the advertisement appearing in this number.

The Marvel "Whirling Spray" Syringe was awarded the gold medal, diploma and certificate of approbation by the Société d'Hygiéne, of France, October 9, 1902. This syringe is patented in the United States and in other countries. It has particularly commended itself to physicians by reason of its peculiar and original action and become popular for the same reason. The Marvel Company, the patentee, has offices at 60 East Twenty-third street, New York.

Write to the Rubberset Brush Company, of 61 Ferry street, Newark, N. J., for a catalogue descriptive of the Rubberset Shaving Brush, which is certainly the most unique brush on the market. The bristles are set in soft rubber, which is then vulcanized, so that it is impossible afterward to dislodge them. The Rubberset is considered the handsomest and most durable shaving brush on the market, and druggists who have stocked it have found it a ready and profitable seller.

Enterprising druggists are making a good thing out of the sale of the Gillette razor, which is advertised in this issue. Very attractive hangers, signs and booklets are supplied to the trade upon application, and these means have proved fruitful in drawing custom wherever they have been used. The Gillette razor is of the "safety" class. The blades are made of fine flexible wafer steel. We refer our readers to the advertisement itself for further information upon an article which has undoubtedly obtained the interest and the confidence of the public.

"Perfecto" fruit juices and crushed fruits, manufactured by the Crandall & Godley Company, of 155 Franklin street, New York, seem to have given much satisfaction to both dispenser and user wherever introduced. The company has devoted much time and money to the perfection of its lines and really first-class products may be expected from it. The company also offers to the drug trade a new "Perfecto" ice cream soda dishing spoon at $1.50. A catalogue of ice cream utensils and machinery will be forwarded on application.

The query at the head of Runkel Brothers' advertisement is certainly interesting: "What do you say to chocolate syrup at 40 cents the gallon?" Runkel Brothers, of 445 West Thirtieth street, New York, have obtained widespread recognition for their soluble chocolate. Druggists who were a little shy of it in the beginning because of its remarkably low price have discovered by experience that it makes a pure, strong and finely flavored syrup. It is packed in 5-pound tins, and sold at the specially low price of 40 cents a pound. It may be had of jobbers or of the makers.

W. H. Young, P.D.F., of Springfield, Mass., is trying not only to create and maintain a demand for Absorbine, but to send customers to the nearby druggist with prescriptions to be filled. Mr. Young is spending $10,000 a year in advertising in all the important horse and farm papers in the United States and Canada. And from this advertising he receives many inquiries for advice touching horse sickness. It is his habit when so consulted to write a prescription and refer the horse's owner direct to the nearest druggist whose name is on the list. All druggists who carry Absorbine in stock should, if they have not already done so, inform Mr. Young of the fact, so that he may enter the name and properly direct the customer following his usual system. This is a case in which sensible co-operation on the part of the druggist will result in improved business.

How the Doctor Got His Cigarettes.

Whatever the law may be in Pennsylvania now regarding the sale of tobacco, it was very severe in Christmas week of 1889, so far as Sunday was concerned. Our friend, Dr. W., struck Pittsburg early Sunday morning in that year and, after an excellent breakfast at a restaurant, approached the inviting glass case near the cashier and asked for a package of cigarettes. He was informed that tobacco could not be sold on a Sunday.

The doctor blithely hied him to a druggist's and requested that twenty Straight Cuts should be handed over at the usual price. The urbane gentleman behind the counter informed him that his respect for the majesty of the Pennsylvania law forbade him to make any such sale. In vain the doctor pleaded that the transaction should be as secret as the grave; in vain he offered to purchase anything in the shop and have the cigarettes thrown in as a bargain; in vain he asked the druggist to drop the forbidden fruit on the floor and allow him to "find" them, at the same time dropping the price in an accessible place. Other subterfuges were suggested and met with equally ill success.

Finally the doctor said: "Look here, my friend, I am a duly qualified practitioner; I believe that if I write a prescription for those cigarettes, you will have to deliver them."

"I guess that's right," answered the druggist. "Hand over the prescription, and I'll hand over the goods."

After carefully scraping the rust off his highly oxidised Latin, Dr. W. was able to evolve the following:

℞ Foliarum nicotianæ................℥vi gr. xx.
Mitte in chartas.................. No. xx.
Sig.: Three to be inhaled every two hours.
——— W., M. D.

Jan. 20, 1889.

The druggist solemnly inspected the document, and eventually passed over the long desired cigarettes, forgetting, in the excitement of the moment, to write the directions on the package.

Life's Panorama in New York.

The whirligig of life in Gotham is so rapid that it seems impossible to check the pace. One must go with the crowd or be trampled on. To show just how people and things keep on the go, the *New York Tribune* summarizes the daily round in these expressive lines:

Every 40 seconds an immigrant arrives.
Every 3 minutes some one is arrested.
Every 6 minutes a child is born.
Every 7 minutes there is a funeral.
Every 13 minutes a couple get married.
Every 42 minutes a new business firm starts up.
Every 48 minutes a building catches fire.
Every 48 minutes a ship leaves the harbor.
Every 51 minutes a new building is erected.
Every 1¼ hours some one is killed by accident.
Every 7 hours some one fails in business.
Every 8 hours an attempt to kill some one is made.
Every 8½ hours some couple is divorced.
Every 10 hours some one commits suicide.
Every 2 days some one is murdered.

A Convenient Price-List.

One of the most conveniently arranged price-lists of plasters, cotton and surgical supplies is that issued by Johnson & Johnson, New Brunswick, N. J. Reference is facilitated by a thumb index and the book is interleaved with lithographed illustrations, which give an excellent idea of the form of packages, etc. Any druggist who may have been overlooked in the distribution of this list should write at once for a copy.

Students Urge Advancement for Naval Pharmacists.

The class of 1906 of the University of Illinois School of Pharmacy has adopted resolutions favoring an increase in the pay and elevation in the rank of the naval pharmacist, and has forwarded the resolutions to the Senators from Illinois.

Soda Fountain Supplies.

The Liquid Carbonic Company, of Michigan and Wells streets, Chicago, with branch establishments and factories in all the principal cities of the country, has issued catalogue No. 52, which supersedes all former issues. This catalogue will be a revelation to pharmacists who have not already seen it. Nearly every requisite for the soda fountain, from paper napkins, through soda clerks' coats to dispensing counters, are listed and illustrated, and no druggist in business should neglect to possess a copy of this book.

The Aesthetics of Perfumery.

Clothes do not make the man nor does the package make the perfume, but the effect of appearance is universally acknowledged. The time, attention and money expended upon tasteful and attractive bottles and labels goes far toward the salability of an extract. The designer who puts some human interest into the picture on the bottle helps to attract attention to the goods and is well worthy of his hire. The shapely receptacle, unusual but artistic, does its share toward making a sale, and when there is added to all the external graces really good material in the extract, the continued sale of the novelty must follow. As is the case with the man, the clothes may obtain consideration in the first instance, but he must have something to say to hold his friends. Many a man has been attracted by a pretty face, only to be disgusted by the silliness behind it. But other things being equal the attractive package goes far toward making sales and retaining custom.—*The American Perfumer.*

Satisfactory Lighting.

On another page of the AMERICAN DRUGGIST is an advertisement which we believe will interest nearly every reader of this paper. The advertisement referred to is that of the Angle Lamp. This lamp burns common kerosene or coal oil. It is entirely different from the ordinary oil lamp, for the flame instead of burning perpendicular above the oil fount burns at almost a right angle from the side of the oil fount and in this way the under-shadow created by all ordinary lamps is done away with. This is only one of the seven features, however, which have made the Angle lamp one of the most popular of all methods of lighting, not only in the United States, where it is manufactured, but in all parts of the world, for in almost every country of the world where people are looking for a good, satisfactory and economical method of illumination Angle lamps are daily being used.

We would strongly advise those of our readers who are interested in lighting their homes or stores better and more economically to write to the Angle Mfg. Company for their 24-page catalogue, which explains the new principle employed in this lamp and gives some very good illustrations of the lamp in use.

To Check Soda Sales.

With the present strong signs of spring in the air the druggist's mind will be turned more than ever to considerations of what plans it will be necessary to lay in order to successfully carry on the forthcoming soda season. In this connection the advertisement of the Lock Stub Check Company, of 136 West Thirty-fourth street, New York, will be of interest. This means of checking and correcting both carelessness and dishonesty on the part of clerks is one of the very best of its kind and has given perfect satisfaction wherever used. The system is an original one and is covered by patents. Full particulars may be had by writing for a booklet. A special proposition will be made to large users.

The Warner Glass Company, of McDonald, Pa., has issued an attractive catalogue of druggists' and perfumers' glassware and sundries, which will be found interesting and useful for druggists in business.

Afraid of Work!

Cleveland evidently has a kind of boy that courts the strenuous life, if the following by "W. R. R.," in the *Plain Dealer*, signifies:

"Did you advertise for a boy?" "Yes. Have you answered the advertisement?" "I have. But I'd like to know first what you mean by saying you want a boy who ain't afraid of work." "It's plain enough, isn't it?" "Maybe it is, but I should think you'd rather have a boy that was a little afraid of work. Just enough afraid of it to catch hold of it and rassle with it, and down it and jump on it, and get the best of it, and show it that it won't get a chance to prove too much for him. That's the kind o' boy I should think you'd like—instead o' the kind that isn't afraid of work. Why, I knew a boy once who wasn't the least mite afraid of it, and he'd rub up against it, and walk right into the cage where they kept it, and let it eat off his hand, and at the same time never meddle with it enough to soil his finger tips." "That's enough, young fellow, the job is yours."—*New York Commercial.*

Ingenious Advertising.

One of the most ingenious forms of advertising that we have seen in a long time belongs to the American Soda Fountain Company; 282 Congress street, Boston, Mass. It consists of a pad of what looks like telegrams, printed in the well-known blue ink of the Postal Telegraph Company, which has been mailed to all users of soda fountains. Sixteen sheets, each one bearing what looks like a telegraphic message in front and a cartoon on the back, serve to advertise the different specialties of the American Soda Fountain Company. The back cover is perforated to permit detaching a postal card which, when mailed to the company, will bring the sender a complete illustrated catalogue of carbonators' and bottlers' supplies. Advertising of this kind should be very effective.

The Depression in Quinine.

And now the conspicuous alkaloid quinine comes before us in its humiliation. It seems not so long since cinchona bark came altogether from South America; then the South American Peruvian bark was in the height of its glory. Quinine sold at about $2.50 per ounce, and redbark at about $1.50 per pound. Then came the cultivated cinchona of Java; it knocked feebly at the door of commerce. But soon it waxed strong; the South American bark dropped rapidly in price, and one of the greatest monoplies that the world has ever known, than which, possibly, none was ever more firmly entrenched, came rapidly to an end. Quinine responded. Down it went. Under the successful cultivation of the rich, quinine-bearing cinchona-tree in Java, the bark became more plentiful, and quinine still cheaper. Well do we remember, when it reached the 75-cent point, the prediction of Dr. R. V. Mattison, that it would decline to 25 cents. Fresh in mind are the criticisms he received for his "vagaries." Who in the glory of that great monoply could have forseen the present conditions. But alas, the club that broke the South American monoply is itself shattered. So great is the depression among the cinchona bark planters of Java, that millions of cinchona trees are being destroyed as unprofitable; the plantations are being replanted with tea. This indicates the unstableness of any man's position in the face of the world's opportunities, for possibly no monoply was ever more firmly entrenched than was the South American Peruvian bark in the day of its glory.—*John Uri Lloyd in Eclectic Medical Gleaner* for January.

So Say We All.

Though they affirm a deadly germ
   Lurks in the sweetest kiss,
Let's hope the day is far away
   Of antiseptic bliss.
To sterilize a lady's sighs
   Would simply be outrageous—
I'd much prefer to humor her
   And let her be contagious!

—*Atlanta Journal.*

BUY A GROSS AND SAVE 5 and 2½ PER CENT.

THE KIND YOU HAVE ALWAYS HANDLED

IT PAYS TO HANDLE RELIABLE GOODS

$33.60 Per Gross

Jobbers Sell in Gross Lots, 5 Per Cent. and 2½ Per Cent. OFF.

$2.80 Per Dozen

THIS IS THE GENUINE

Send for Cards, Cartons and Counter Wrappers.

THE CENTAUR COMPANY,
77 Murray Street, New York City.

Chas. H. Fletcher, *President.*

BUY A GROSS AND SAVE 5 and 2½ PER CENT.

——Who can't sell 12 dozen per annum?——

The American $50 Typewriter

This exclusive patent is the most distinctive improvement in many years. It has done more than reduce the cost of construction. It has reduced the chances for breakage and made possible a typewriter so simple that anyone can operate and understand it. It permits unlimited speed—no locking of type—nothing but the easy operation of a typewriter that has every essential of the modern writing machine at half the usual cost.

Write to-day for copy of "The American Way."

American Typewriter Co., Inc. 1893, 267½ Broadway, N. Y.

SYRINGE BOXES

Of White Wood, Bass, Oak, Ash, &c.

Fine Work
Low Prices
Prompt Shipments.

Estimates and Samples
Furnished on Application

Also any other kind of fancy wood boxes made to order. Extensive facilities enable us to guarantee satisfaction.

HENRY H. SHEIP MFG. CO.,
529-35 Columbia Avenue. PHILADELPHIA.

Cable Address—Sheip, Phila., Western Union Code.

LATEST

SODA FOUNTAIN

NOVELTY.

THE "KISMET" HOLDER

The Kismet Holder is the newest thing in holders. It is suitable for Soda Glasses, Ginger Ale Bottles, Coffee and Chocolate Cups, etc.

Being all in one piece there is nothing to come apart. This holder is the most durable because there is **no soldering or brazing; no joints, pins or rivets.** It is the only **up-to-date** holder made—**easiest to clean**—no pockets for dirt to gather in.

THE ONLY SANITARY HOLDER MADE

THE "KISMET" HOLDER

Yet it is light in weight and so strong—you can't break it. Instantly **adjustable** to a glass of any shape or size. **Unique design,** and **cannot** be **surpassed** in **simplicity, efficiency** and **low cost.**

Heavily Nickel Plated............$4.50 a Doz.
" Silver " .... 7.00 "
" Gold " ....12.00 "

Money back if you want it, but you won't want it.
Remit by express or money order to Kismet Specialty Co.
References: R. G. Dun & Co., New York

KISMET SPECIALTY COMPANY,
21 Park Row, NEW YORK

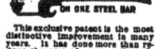

Where is "Dr." Fendler?

The New York *Press* asks, What has become of "Dr." Fendler? and proceeds to say that Dr. Fendler was a small man (of abnormal manual strength), a druggist and pharmacist, whose shop was at the junction of Forty-second street, Broadway and Seventh avenue. A hotel now occupies the site. In the days of the Tenderloin Club, about 1890, whenever the boys wanted a test of strength they would go to Fendler. Many braggadocios turned up from time to time at the club house in Thirtieth street, doing amazing stunts and defying all competition. Nothing was easier than to walk them up to Fendler's drug store and give the doctor the wink. In a jiffy Mr. Braggart was feeling worse than 80 cents and wondering "where he was at." And this modest young druggist used no "dope."

Soda Fountain Ordered at Night—Customers Served from It Next Morning.

Nelson L. Martin, proprietor of the Oak Grove Dairy, at 1310 Massachusetts avenue, Cambridge, opposite the main entrance to Harvard College, ordered a 10-foot "Innovation" from the American Soda Fountain Company the first week in April. He signed the order at 5 P.M. Tuesday. Two hours later the fountain had been taken from the Boston showroom and was on its way to Cambridge. Before opening hour the next morning the apparatus had been set up, all connections made and Mr. Martin was ready to serve customers. The customers came, attracted by the novelty and beauty of the fountain that had apparently grown up in a single night. In spite of the quick work of the dispensers in serving them the throng of customers increased so that by 10 o'clock in the morning Mr. Martin had to call in the police to keep the crowd moving!

Pretty quick work to buy a large soda fountain at 5 o'clock one night and to serve customers from it next morning!

A Postal Card Offer.

The American Historical Art Publishing Company, 111 East Fourteenth street, New York, makes a special offer to the drug trade of a very attractive assortment of picture postal cards, comprising scenes from the Yellowstone and reproductions from some of the celebrated paintings of the rotunda at Washington. For $3 they will send to any of our readers 300 of these cards and a metal rack for displaying them. This offer should be of interest to every progressive druggist, as it introduces a new line of goods which are steadily growing popular.

Applies to Druggists as Well.

Dr. Wm. Osler gives the following excellent advice to his brother practitioners: One cannot practice medicine alone and practice it early and late, as so many of us have to do, and hope to escape the malign influence of a routine life. The incessant concentration of thought upon one subject, however interesting, tethers a man's mind in a narrow field. The practitioner needs culture as well as learning. The earliest picture we have in literature of a scientific physician, in our sense of the term, is of a cultured Greek gentleman; and I care not whether the young man labors among the beautiful homes on Sherbrooke street, or in slums of Caughnawauga, or in some sparsely settled country district, he cannot afford to have learning only. In no profession does culture count for so much as in medicine, and no man needs it more than the general practitioner, working among all sorts and conditions of men, many of whom are influenced quite as much by his general ability, which they can appreciate, as by his learning, of which they have no measure. The day has passed for the "practicer of physic" to be like Robert Lever, Dr. Johnson's friend, "obscurely wise and coarsely kind." The wider and freer a man's general education the better practitioner is he likely to be, particularly among the higher classes, to whom the reassurance and sympathy of the cultivated gentleman of the type of Eryximachus may mean much more than pills and potions.

Changes in Nestlé's Food Formula.

An improved formula has been used for the Nestlé's Food on the American market since January 1, 1906. The improved formula was introduced in Switzerland and in England three years ago. As a result there has been a large increase in the sale of this popular product, and this change is now introduced in the United States. The manufacturers state that they would consider themselves behind the times if after studying the question of infant feeding for nearly 40 years they could not improve upon their original formula. The slight change made will result in a higher percentage of fats and less than half the amount of starch formerly present in Nestlé's Food. The package, wrapper and label remain just as before.

Customers may state that the food has a slightly different color and a sweeter taste than formerly. The makers affirm that you can assure your customers that you are giving the same Nestlé's Food as for the past 35 years, but with very slight modifications which make it more easily digested and more fattening than ever before.

They are willing to replace old stock with fresh. At the bottom of the label under the medals you will find a letter. If you will write what the letter is they can tell you the exact age of the food. You must also give the name of your jobber.

Their advertisement offers a large cut-out, 40 x 40, showing the familiar stork on the nest of babies, which makes a very handsome window display. This free advertisement they will send to druggists, accompanied by their "Book for Mothers." All you have to do is to send a postal card stating that you can use them. Address Henri Nestle, 73 Warren street, New York.

German Import Duty on Patent Medicines.

The proposals for the new German tariff include a duty of 500 marks on goods falling into class 389, which embraces "Geheimmittel," *i.e.*, proprietary medicines, the composition of which is not stated, whether they be designed for the prevention or cure of human ailments or of those of animals and in no matter what form they may be presented (solutions, liniments, powders, pills, pastilles, salves, suppositories, and so on). In the list of examples given—which extends the series of specially named patent medicines of a recent Government order—several well-known remedies are mentioned, such as Morrison's Pills, Mother Seigel's Syrup and Pills, Warner's Safe Cures, &c. The following classes of substances or preparations are excluded from the definition: "Geheimmittel":—Those which (1) are embodied in the German Pharmacopœia and are offered as such; (2) have acquired general recognition in medical science and practice as remedies; (3) are used as disinfectants, cosmetics, foods, condiments and the like. Where doubt arises as to the character of any preparation or the class to which it belongs a medical or pharmaceutical expert is to be consulted. Fruit juices and vegetable extracts for technical or medicinal purposes (Class 60) enter duty free. The duty on spirits in flask and on liqueurs (Class 178) is 240 mk.; on other spirit, 160 mk.; the like in other vessels (Class 179), 240 mk.; medicated wines in cask (Class 184), 24 mk.; in other vessels, 48 mk.; beer of all kinds and malt extract, medicated or not (Class 186), 6 mk.; medicated or non-medicated chocolate, &c. (Class 204), 80 mk.; liquorice extract, to which sugar, honey or medicament has been added (Class 385), 60 mk.; other raw or refined liquorice extract, duty free; artificial balsams and the like, free from ether or spirit (Class 386), 40 mk.; if containing either of those fluids, 60 mk.; prepared or other pharmaceutical goods not enumerated or included in above classes, 40 mk.—*British and Colonial Druggist.*

"What do you do for a living? What is your trade or profession?" asked the judge of a prisoner.

"I am, your honor, a pharmacocatagraphologist."

His honor threatened to fine him for contempt of court, but he proved that the word was all right, meaning a writer of prescriptions.

THE PURE-FOOD LAW

makes it prohibitory to sell any but

STRICTLY PURE Extract of VANILLA.

Wyeth's Extract Vanilla is prepared from the choicest variety of carefully selected and properly cured Vanilla Beans, and contains no coloring matter nor any of the artificial or synthetic principles so frequently employed.

The Delicate Aroma

a distinguishing feature of our preparation, is imparted by the natural flavor of the bean

SPECIAL PRICES IN BULK.

JOHN WYETH & BROTHER, Inc.,

Pharmaceutical Chemists, **PHILADELPHIA, PA.**

"BIG FOUR"

Operates in Ohio, Indiana, Illinòis and Kentucky,

2,600 Miles

of the best constructed and finest equipped railroad in America, and also maintains magnificent through train service in connection with Lake Shore, New York Central to New York, and Boston & Albany to Beston. Also with Michigan Central to Detroit, Mackinaw City and Intermediate Points, and with C. & O. to Washington, Baltimore and Richmond, Va.

WRITE FOR FOLDERS.

WARREN J. LYNCH, Gen'l Pass. and Ticket Agent, Cincinnati, O.

ARHOVIN

Addition-product of diphenylamine and thymyl-benzoic acid.

Aborts ACUTE GONORRHOEA or renders its course brief and painless. Soon improves and finally cures even CHRONIC FEMALE GONORRHOEA.

Given in CAPSULES, URETHRAL BOUGIES, VAGINAL GLOBULES or by INJECTION.

LITERATURE FROM

SCHERING & GLATZ, 58 Maiden Lane, New York.

CERTAIN hypodermatic tablets go to pieces quickly enough when thrown into water, their undissolved particles settling to the bottom and solution proceeding slowly if at all. Unreliable agents at best—*worse than worthless in an emergency!*

PARKE, DAVIS & CO.'S

HYPODERMATIC TABLETS

dissolve promptly and thoroughly. Drop one into a syringe half filled with lukewarm water and shake vigorously. In five seconds (or less) it will have dissolved completely. There is never any delay, never any uncertainty.

SPECIFY "P., D. & CO." WHEN ORDERING FROM YOUR JOBBER.

PARKE, DAVIS & COMPANY

HOME OFFICES AND LABORATORIES, DETROIT, MICH.

The Bitter Principle of Cascara Sagrada

MINUS THE BITTER TASTE

BY many physicians the bitter extract of cascara is greatly preferred to aromatic preparations. But there has been one obstacle to its general use—its unpalatability.

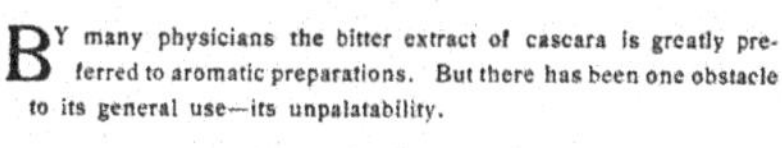

CASCARA

TONIC-LAXATIVE GLOBULES

(P., D. & CO.)

meet this impediment squarely. The gelatin investment effectually masks the disagreeable taste. Our *Cascara Tonic-Laxative Globules* contain only the active bitter principle of Cascara Sagrada, each globule representing 3 grains of the bitter glucoside.

NET TRADE PRICES:

Boxes of 25, per dozen boxes, $2 10 Boxes of 100, per box, $0 85

PARKE, DAVIS & CO.

$500 for a Formula

A THOROUGHLY responsible business man desires to introduce a meritorious medicinal or food preparation to the medical profession along strictly ethical lines. He believes that many ethical preparations have been devised by pharmacists and pharmaceutical chemists who have been unable to properly introduce same as their merits warrant. For the most practical and generally meritorious formula that may be placed at his disposal, the advertiser will pay the sum of Five Hundred Dollars ($500) provided any preparation that may hereafter be based upon the formula admits of strictly ethical presentation to physicians.

Preference will be given to

1 A liquid food for invalids and convalescents. (Preferably one *without alcohol*—with high percentage of nutritive matter.)
2. A Galactagogue liquid.
3. A Uterine tonic and sedative.

If more than one formula is accepted, the sum of $250 will be paid for each additional one purchased.

CONDITIONS:

1. The preparation must have undoubted keeping qualities and be of an agreeable taste.
2. Sample of the finished product, with full particulars, must accompany formula.
3. The advertiser reserves the right to reject any or all formulæ submitted.

¶ The financial responsibility and the absolute good faith of the advertiser are guaranteed by the publishers of the American Druggist. All information extended, and particulars of formulæ not purchased, will be treated as absolutely confidential, and such formulæ will be returned to the sender and will not be divulged to any one or used in any way whatsoever. Address all communications and samples to

"VODAX," care of the AMERICAN DRUGGIST
66 West Broadway, New York.

ORIGINAL PACKAGE PRICES.

It should be understood that the prices quoted in this column are strictly those current in the wholesale market, and that higher prices are paid for retail lots. The quality of goods frequently necessitates a considerable range of prices.

Drugs, Chemicals, &c.

Acetanilid	lb.	.24	@	.25
Acetate of Lime:				
Brown	100 lb.	1.80	@	1.85
Gray	100 lb.	2.35	@	2.40
Acetone	lb.	.15½	@	.16
Acetphenetidin (U. S. P. phenacetin)	lb.	1.15	@	...
Acid:				
Acetic Com'l	100 lb.	2.40	@	2.65
Acetic C. P.	lb.	.21	@	.25
Acetic, Glacial		.20	@	.23½
Aquafortis, 36°	lb.	.03¾	@	.04½
" 40°	lb.	..	@	.05½
Benzoic, Ger	lb.	.30	@	.33
" Eng	oz.	.10	@	.10½
Boric, Cryst	lb.	.10	@	.10½
powd	lb.	.10	@	.10½
Carbol. cryst., blk	lb.	.14	@	.15
lb. bottle	lb.	.20	@	.22
Chrysophanic		2.50	@	2.65
Citric, dom	lb.	.43	@	.43½
Gallic	lb.	.53	@	.55
Muriatic C. P.	lb.	.07½	@	.08½
Nitric C. P.	lb.	.07½	@	.10
Oxalic, English	lb.	.05½	@	.06
Phosphoric	lb.	.18	@	.22½
Picric	lb.	.26	@	.35
Pyrogallic	lb.	1.65	@	..
Salicylic	lb.	.31	@	.34
Sulphuric, 98%	lb.	.01½	@	.02
Tartaric, crystals	lb.	.27½	@	.28½
powdered	lb.	.28	@	.29½
Tannic, cryst	lb.	.58	@	.63
Alcohol, grain	gal.	2.45	@	2.47
wood, 95-97%	gal.	.70	@	.75
Aloin	lb.	.45	@	.50
Alum, Lump	100 lb.	1.75	@	1.80
Ground	100 lb.	1.80	@	1.85
Ammon, carb		.08½	@	.08½
" bromide, bulk		.23	@	.24
" iodide, bulk		4.75	@	4.80
Aniline Oil		.09	@	.09½
Salt		.08½	@	.08½
Antipyrine (New)	oz.	...	@	.15
Arrowroot, Bermuda	lb.	.38	@	.40
St. Vincent, in bbl	lb.	.06½	@	.08
Arsenic: Red Saxon	lb.	.06½	@	.06½
White	lb	.05½	@	.08
Balm of Gilead Buds	lb.	.32	@	.38
Balsam Copaiba, Cent. Amer	lb.	.29	@	.30
Para	lb.	.42½	@	.45
Fir, Canada	gal.	3.10	@	3.20
Fir, Oregon	gal.	.70	@	.80
Peru	lb.	1.00	@	1.05
Tolu	lb.	.20	@	.22
Bark, Angostura	lb.	.38	@	.40
Buckthorn	lb.	.05	@	.05½
Cascara Sag	lb.	.05½	@	.09
Cascarilla	lb.	.10	@	.14
Cotton root	lb.	.08½	@	.10
Cramp	lb.	.07	@	.09
Elm, select	lb.	.18	@	.20
Pine, white	lb.	.05	@	.06
Prickly Ash	lb.	.11	@	.15
Sassafras	lb.	.13½	@	.14
Soap—whole	lb.	.05	@	.05½
Crushed	lb.	.05½	@	.06
White Pine	lb.	.04½	@	.06
Wild Cherry	lb.	.06	@	.09
Bismuth, citrate	lb.	1.75	@	1.80
" ammon cit	lb.	1.85	@	1.90
" subnit	blk.	1.50	@	1.55
" subcarb	lb.	1.75	@	1.80
" subgallate	lb.	1.85	@	1.90
Bleaching Powder, Eng		.01½	@	.01½
German R		.01½	@	.01½
Domestic		.01	@	.01½
Blue Vitriol	lb.	.06	@	.06 1-10
Borax, Refined	lb.	.07½	@	.07½
powd. conc	lb.	.07½	@	.08
crystals	lb.	.07½	@	.07½
Brimstone, crude 2d	ton.	22.00	@	...
Bromine, bulk	lb.	.23	@	.26
Burgundy Pitch	lb.	.04	@	.04½
Cacao Butter, blk		.28½	@	.30
" " 12 lb. boxes		.34	@	.35
Caffeine	lb.	...	@	2.65
Calcium hypophosphite	lb.	.60	@	.64
Cantharides, Chinese	lb.	...	@	.75
" powd	lb.	.75	@	.77
Russian, whole	lb.	1.20	@	1.25
Cassia Buds	lb.	.18½	@	.19½
Castor Oil, No. 1, bbl	lb.	.11	@	.12
" " No. 1, cases	lb.	.11½	@	.12½
" " No. 3, bbl	lb.	.10½	@	.11½
" " No 3, cases	lb.	.10½	@	.11½
Caustic Soda	100 lb.	1.70	@	1.75
Chalk, Eng. Precip., bulk	lb.	.06	@	...
Chloral Hydrate, crystals, bulk	lb.	...	@	0.95
crusts, blk	lb.	...	@	0.93
Chloroform, bulk	lb.	.25	@	.30
Cinchonidine Sulph	oz.	.12	@	.15
Cocaine Muriate	oz.	3.00	@	3.25
Codeine Sulph	oz.	3.05	@	3.25
Cod Liver Oil, Norweg.	bbl.	20.00	@	25.00
Newfoundland	bbl.	19.00	@	20.00
Colocynth, Trieste	lb.	.30	@	.32
Spanish	lb.	.25	@	.26
Copperas, car lots	100 lb.	.47½	@	.52
single bbls	100 lb.	.57½	@	.65
Creosote, Beechwood		.85	@	.90
Cream Tartar lb.	powd.	.22½	@	.23
Cubeb berries, xx	lb.	.09	@	.10
Powdered	lb.	.11	@	.13
Cutch, bales	lb.	.07½	@	.08
boxes	lb.	.05	@	.05½
Cuttle Bone, Trieste	lb.	.16½	@	.17
French	lb.	.12	@	.13
Jewelers', large	lb.	.70	@	...
" small	lb.	.40	@	.45
Dextrin	lb.	.05½	@	.08
Divi Divi	ton.	30.00	@	45.00
Dragon's Bl'd, lump	lb.	.15	@	.18
In reeds	lb.	.50	@	.55
Epsom Salts	100 lb.	.85	@	1.00
Ergot, German	lb.	.27	@	.28
Spanish	lb.	...	@	.35
Ergotine, Dom	lb.	4.95	@	5.00
Flowers, Arnica	lb.	.09	@	.10
Flowers—cont'd				
Calendula	lb.	.25	@	.30
Chamomile, Roman	lb.	.16	@	.24
German	lb.	.10	@	.18
Hungarian	lb.	.09½	@	.11
Insect, open	lb.	.15	@	.17
Half closed	lb.	.18	@	.23
Closed	lb.	.25	@	...
Powder	lb.	.14	@	.22
Lavender	lb.	.12	@	.13
Select	lb.	.15	@	.20
Saffron, Amer	lb.	1.25	@	....
Spanish Alicante	lb.	4.75	@	6.00
" Valencia	lb.	8.00	@	8.50
Formaldehyde	lb.	.09	@	.09½
Glycerin, C. P. drums	lb.	.11½	@	.11½
" cans	lb.	.12½	@	.12½
Grains of Paradise	lb.	.11½	@	.15
Guarana	lb.	.70	@	.75
Gums: Aloes, Cape		.08	@	.10
" Barbadoes	lb.	.14	@	.16
" Curacoa		.06	@	.06½
" Socot	lb.	.18	@	.20
Arabic, 1st pkd	lb.	.38	@	...
" 2d pkd	lb.	.19	@	.23
" sorts	lb.	.06½	@	.11
Asafoetida	lb.	.15	@	.22
Benzoin, Sumatra	lb.	.34	@	.38
Siam	lb.	.90	@	1.00
Camphor, ref'd. blk	lb.	1.00	@	..
cases	lb.	1.00½	@	..
Chicle	lb.	.36	@	.38
Gamboge	lb.	1.05	@	1.10
Guaiac	lb.	.17	@	.25
Kino	lb.	.25	@	.36
Mastic	lb.	.46	@	.48
Myrrh	lb.	.25	@	.28
Olibanum	lb.	.10	@	.15
Sandarac	lb.	.14	@	.18
Senegal, pkd	lb.	.11	@	.13
Tragacanth, Aleppo	lb.	.30	@	.65
Tragacanth, Turkey	lb.	.35	@	.88
Haarlem Oil		3.00	@	3.25
Hypophosphite lime	lb.	.48	@	.50
" potash	lb.	.48	@	.50
" soda	lb.	.48	@	.50
Ichthyol	lb.	4.00	@	4.25
Indigo	lb.	.90	@	1.25
Insect Pwd. pure	lb.	.14	@	.25
Iodine, resub		2.70	@	2.75
Iodoform	lb.	3.00	@	3.05
Iron citrate, U. S. P.	lb.	.....	@	.44
" and ammon. cit	lb.	.....	@	.41
and ammon. citrate (green scales)				
and quinine citrate	lb.	1.15	@	1.23
phosphate, scales	lb.	....	@	.38
pyrophosphate, scales	lb.	....	@	.38
quinine and strychnine citrate	lb.	1.65	@	1.73
Isinglass, Amer	lb.	.75	@	.80
Russian	lb.	4.00	@	4.10
Juniper Berries	lb.	.03½	@	.04
Lanoline	lb.	.60	@	.65
Leaves: Aconite		.09	@	.10
Belladonna	lb.	.10	@	.11
Buchu, short	lb.	.17	@	.20
" long	lb.	.....	@	.30
Cannabis Indica, tops	lb.	1.00	@	1.10
Coca, Truxillo	lb.	.17	@	.18
" Huanuco	lb.	.30	@	.32
Damiana	lb.	.08	@	.10
Digitalis	lb.	.08½	@	.09
Grindelia robusta	lb.	.08	@	.09
Horehound	lb.	.04½	@	.06
Hyoscyamus	lb.	.07	@	.08
Jaborandi	lb.	.14	@	.15
Pulsatilla		.07½	@	.11
Rose, Red	lb.	.65	@	.70
Senna, pkd. whole	lb.	.20	@	.22
Alexandria, natural	lb.	..	@	..
garbled and sifted	lb.	.15	@	.16
Tinnevelly	lb.	.04	@	.09
Alexandria, siftings	lb.	.05½	@	.06
Stramonium	lb.	.08	@	.08½
Uva ursi	lb.	.05½	@	.06½
Yerba Santa	lb.	.07	@	.07½
Liquorice—mass	lb.	.08	@	.10
Spanish	lb.	.14	@	.20
Imported mass Spanish	lb.	.18	@	.24
Stick, Calabria	lb.	.23	@	.28
Domestic	lb.	.16½	@	.25½
Lithia, carbonate	lb.	1.50	@	1.75
" citrate	lb.	1.15	@	1.25
Lupulin, Ger	lb.	.18	@	.25
Lycopodium	lb.	.46	@	.48
Magnesia, carb	lb.	.12	@	.15
Manna, large flk	lb.	.45	@	.55
Small flake	lb.	.33	@	.35
Menthol, Japanese	lb.	2.60	@	2.75
Mercurials:				
Blue Pill	lb.	.43	@	.45
Calomel	lb.	.77	@	.79
Corr. Sublim	lb.	.70	@	.72
Mercury and Chalk	lb.	.32	@	.34
Ointment, ½	lb.	.47	@	.48
Ointment, ⅓	lb.	.38	@	.39
Red Precip	lb.	.87	@	.89
White "	lb.	.92	@	.94
Morphine, bulk	oz.	2.10	@	2.20
Eighths	oz.	2.45	@	2.50
Moss, Iceland	lb.	.05	@	.08
Irish	lb.	.06½	@	.08
Irish, bleached	lb.	.09½	@	.10
Naphthaline, flake	lb.	1.90	@	2.00
Ball	lb.	.02½	@	.....
Nux Vomica	lb.	.02½	@	.03
Oil, Anise	lb.	1.30	@	1.35
Almonds, bit, Eng	lb.	5.50	@	5.75
French	lb.	3.55	@	3.60
bit., artificial	lb.	.65	@	1.20
sweet, true	lb.	.37	@	.40
Peach kernels		.19	@	.22
Bay	lb.	2.10	@	2.25
[illegible] oz. bots	bot.	3.25	@	[illegible]
Bergamot	lb.	2.15	@	2.20
Cajuput	lb.	.54	@	.58
Camphor	lb.	.17½	@	.19
Caraway	lb.	1.18	@	1.40
Cassia [illegible]	lb.	.77½	@	.78
Oils—cont'd.				
Cedar, pure	lb	.80	@	1.85
red	lb.	.21	@	.25
Citronella	lb.	.40	@	.42
Clove, bud		.87½	@	.90
Copaiba	lb.	.61	@	.70
Coriander	lb.	8.00	@	11.00
Croton	lb.	.75	@	.80
Cubeb	lb.	.90	@	1.00
Eucalyptus	lb.	.40	@	.60
Geranium	lb.	1.60	@	4.75
Lavender, flowers	lb.	2.00	@	2.25
Lemon	lb.	.60	@	.75
Lemongrass	lb.	3.00	@	3.10
Mustard	lb.	4.25	@	5.25
Myrbane	lb.	.07	@	.08
Neroli	lb.	45.00	@	57.50
Nutmeg	lb.	.80	@	0.90
Orange, sweet	lb.	2.00	@	2.15
Orange, bitter	lb.	2.20	@	2.40
Origanum	lb.	.18	@	.22
Pennyroyal	lb.	...	@	1.50
Peppermint	lb.	2.70	@	2.75
Cases	lb.	3.25	@	3.35
Petit, grain, French	lb.	4.00	@	4.50
" " So. Amer.	lb.	2.00	@	2.05
Pimento	lb.	1.80	@	1.90
Rose	oz.	3.50	@	4.50
Rosemary	lb.	.62½	@	.80
Sandalwood	lb.	3.25	@	3.50
Sassafras	lb.	.50	@	.55
" Artificial	lb.	.25	@	.28
Safrol		.35	@	.36
Spearmint	lb.	4.75	@	5.00
Tansy	lb.	3.75	@	4.00
Thyme		1.00	@	1.20
Winterg'n, sweet birch		1.65	@	1.85
" Synthetic	lb.	.37	@	.40
Wood (Chinese)		.08	@	.09
Wormwood		3.25	@	3.50
Wormseed	lb.	3.00	@	3.25
Opium, Nat cases	lb.	2.72½	@	2.80
" Ordinary, Job-		2.75	@	2.80
" powdered	lb.	3.25	@	3.30
Orange peel, bit	lb.	.03	@	.04
Sweet	lb.	.04½	@	.10
Petrolatum		.05	@	.08
Phenacetin (see Acetphenetidin)				
Potassium acetate	lb.	.17	@	.18
" bromide		.15	@	.16
" bottles		.23	@	.30
bichromate		.08½	@	.09½
chlorate, cryst		.09½	@	.09½
" powd		.10	@	.10½
cyanide		.20	@	.21
hypophosphite		.60	@	.64
iodide bulk		2.15	@	2.20
permanganate	lb.	.09½	@	.10½
Prickly Ash berries		.14	@	.16
Quicksilver flasks,	lb.	.56	@	.60
Quinine Sulph., Domestic bulk	oz.	.18	@	.20
German, bulk	oz.	.18	@	.20
German, outside	oz.	.17½	@	.18
Java, bulk	oz.	.17½	@	.18
Rochelle Salts	lb.	.20½	@	.21
Root, Aconite	lb.	.09½	@	.10
Alkanet	lb.	.08	@	.09
Althea, cut	lb.	.17	@	.18
Arnica	lb.	.08½	@	.09
Belladonna, Atropa	lb.	.10	@	.12
Blood	lb.	.10	@	.12
Calamus	lb.	.07	@	.08
Calamus, bleached	lb.	.23	@	.25
Colchicum	lb.	.12	@	.13
Calumba	lb.	.04	@	.06
Dandelion, Ger	lb.	.07½	@	.08
Galangal	lb.	.05	@	.05½
Gentian	lb.	.04	@	.04½
Ginger, Ja., blcd	lb.	...	@	.14
unbleached	lb.	.12	@	.14
Ginseng	lb.	6.00	@	7.50
Golden Seal	lb.	1.18	@	1.25
Hellebore, pwd	lb.	.06	@	.07
Helonias	lb.	.42	@	.45
Ipecac, Rio	lb.	1.75	@	1.80
Carthagena	lb.	1.70	@	1.75
Jalap	lb.	.10½	@	.11
Kava Kava	lb.	.11	@	.12
Liquorice, ord	lb.	.03½	@	.04
Select	lb.	.05½	@	.11
Lovage	lb	.55	@	.85
Mandrake	lb.	.04½	@	.05½
Musk, Russian	lb.	.13	@	.14
Orris, Florentine	lb.	.06	@	.07
Orris, Verona	lb.	.04	@	.06
Pareira Brava	lb.	.10	@	.11
Pink	lb.	.50	@	.85
Rhatany	lb.	.10	@	.12
Rhub., Canton	lb.	.35	@	.40
Shensi	lb.	.65	@	.75
Sars'p'la, Hond	lb.	.26	@	.30
Mexican	lb.	.09½	@	.09½
Senega	lb.	.58	@	.60
Snake Virginia	lb.	.42	@	.45
Texas	lb.	.39	@	.42
Canada	lb.	.12	@	.25
Squill	lb.	.13	@	.15
Valerian, Belg	lb.	.08	@	.08½
German	lb.	.12	@	.14
English	lb.	.12	@	.15
Salicine	lb.	3.75	@	4.00
Sal Ammon, lump	lb.	.09½	@	.09½
Granulated	lb.	.05½	@	.06
Sal Soda, Eng	100 lb.	.67½	@	.72½
American	100 lb.	.75	@	.80
Salol	lb.	.90	@	.95
Saltpetre, crude	lb.	.04½	@	.04½
Refined	lb.	.04½	@	.05½
Santonin, crystals	lb.	9.50	@	9.70
Powdered	lb.	9.70	@	9.90
Saw Palmetto Berries	lb.	.15	@	.20
Seed, Anise Ital	lb.	.08½	@	.10½
German	lb.	.06½	@	.07
Star	lb.	.20	@	.21
Canary, Smyrna	lb.	.04½	@	.04½
Sicily	lb.	.04½	@	.05
Caraway	lb.	.06	@	.06½
Celery	lb.	.07½	@	[illegible]
Cardamom blchd		.30	@	.70
" Decorticated	lb.	.33	@	.34
Colchicum	lb.	.21	@	.25
Seeds—cont'd.				
Coriander	lb.	[illegible]	@	.10½
Bleached	lb.	.08½	@	.10½
Cummin	lb.	.06½	@	.07½
Fennel, Ger	lb.	.09	@	.10
" Italian	lb.	.05	@	.05½
Flax, whole	lb.	6.50	@	6.75
" ground	lb.	.03½	@	.03½
Foenugreek	lb.	.02	@	.02½
Hemp, Rus	lb.	.03	@	.03½
Millet, nat	lb.	.01½	@	.02
" sbld	lb.	.04½	@	.04½
Mustard, Cal. brown	lb.	.04½	@	.04½
Trieste, brown	lb.	.08	@	.08½
Bari, brown	lb.	.04½	@	.05
German, brown	lb.	.02½	@	.05
Western, brown	lb.	.01½	@	.02
Cal. yellow	lb.	.04½	@	.04½
Eng. yellow	lb.	.05	@	.05½
Ger. yellow	lb.	.03½	@	.03½
Poppy, blue	lb.	.05½	@	.05½
Quince, Ger	lb.	.32	@	.34
Rape, Ger	lb.	.02½	@	.03
" Eng	lb.	.04	@	.05
" Amer	lb.	.02½	@	.03
Strophanthus		.45	@	.50
Kombé		1.00	@	1.25
Sunflower		.04½	@	.05
Wormseed, American	lb.	.07	@	.08
" Levant	lb.	.17	@	.20
Seidlitz, Mixture	lb.	.17	@	.17½
Silver, Nitrate	oz.	.41	@	.44½
Soap, Castile, white	lb.	.10	@	.10½
" green	lb.	.06	@	.10½
" mottled	lb.	.05½	@	.07
Sodium bicarb, Eng		1.37½	@	1.75
" domestic	100 lb.	1.50	@	1.80
" benzoate	lb.	.40	@	.41
" brom. blk	lb.	.21	@	.22
" carb., cryst.	100 lb.	1.60	@	1.75
" citrate	lb.	...	@	.32
" hypophosphite		.60	@	.64
" iodide		3.50	@	3.55
" nitrate	100 lb.	2.30	@	2.35
" phosphate	lb.	.02½	@	.03
" salicylate	lb.	.32	@	.34
" sulphate	100 lb.	.40	@	.50
Spermaceti	lb.	.27	@	.30
Spts. Nitre, U. S. P.		.46	@	.48
Spts. Ammonia Aromat.	lb.	.44	@	.46
Strontium, nitrate	lb.	.07½	@	.08
Strychnine, Sulph	oz.	.95	@	1.05
Sugar of Milk	lb.	.15	@	.20
Sugar, Lead, white	lb.	.09½	@	.10
" brown	lb.	.07½	@	.08
Sulphur, Roll	lb.	1.95	@	2.15
" Flowers	lb.	2.15	@	[illegible]
Sulphuric Ether	lb.	[illegible]	@	[illegible]
Sumac, Sicily	ton	42.00	@	47.00
" Virginia	ton	32.00	@	35.00
Tar, Barbadoes	gal.	[illegible]	@	[illegible]
Thymol		1.80	@	1.90
Tonka B'ns, Para	lb.	.18	@	.20
" Angostura	lb.	.65	@	.67½
" Surinam	lb.	.30	@	.32
Turmeric		.04½	@	.05
Turpentine	gal.	.69½	@	.70
Vanilla Beans	lb.	3.75	@	6.00
" Cut, Mex	lb.	2.00	@	2.25
" Tahiti	lb.	.45	@	1.25
" Bourbon		1.00	@	5.00
Vanillin	oz.	.22	@	.27½
Venice Turps, bbls	lb.	.14	@	.17
" " cans	lb.	.19	@	.20
Wax, Bayberry	lb.	...	@	.20
" Bees, ord. pur	lb.	.28	@	.28½
" " sel	lb.	.24	@	.24½
" " blch	lb.	.40	@	.42
" Brazil, No. 1	lb.	.52½	@	.53
" " No. 2	lb.	.44	@	.47
" " No. 3	lb.	.25	@	...
" Ceresin, yel	lb.	.14	@	.18
" " white	lb.	.15	@	.20
" Japan	lb.	.13½	@	.14
" Paraffin	lb.	.06	@	.06½
Zinc Oxide	lb.	.07	@	.08½

Heavy Oils, &c.

Bank, Menhaden	gal.	.28	@	.30
Cocoanut, Ceylon	lb.	[illegible]	@	[illegible]
Cochin	lb.	.07½	@	.07½
Cuban	lb.	.05½	@	...
Cod, Domestic	gal.	.35	@	.36
" Newfoundland	gal.	.38½	@	.40
Corn	gal.	2.90	@	...
Cottonseed, crd. prime		.35	@	...
Summer Yellow, prime		.38	@	.39
" " Butter		.33	@	.34
Old, off grade		.33	@	...
Winter Yellow, prime		.33	@	.34
Salad Oil		.40	@	.42
Gasoline, 86°	gal.	.14	@	...
" 88°	gal.	.14	@	...
" 90°	gal.	.15	@	...
Lard, Extra Prime	gal.	[illegible]	@	[illegible]
Lard, Extra No. 1	gal.	[illegible]	@	[illegible]
Lard, No. 1	gal.	[illegible]	@	[illegible]
Linseed, Raw City	gal.	[illegible]	@	[illegible]
" Boiled	gal.	[illegible]	@	[illegible]
Naphtha, 68°	gal.	[illegible]	@	...
" Deodorized, 76°	gal.	[illegible]	@	[illegible]
Neatsfoot, prm.	gal.	[illegible]	@	[illegible]
White		[illegible]	@	[illegible]
Olive Oil, imp.		1.25	@	2.75
" Com., bbls.	gal.	[illegible]	@	[illegible]
Palm, prm., L'gos	lb.	[illegible]	@	[illegible]
Peanut	lb.	[illegible]	@	[illegible]
Rapeseed	gal.	[illegible]	@	.71
Red Elaine	gal.	[illegible]	@	[illegible]
" Saponified	lb.	[illegible]	@	[illegible]
Salad Oil	gal.	[illegible]	@	[illegible]
Sesame	gal.	[illegible]	@	[illegible]
Sperm, Crude	gal.	[illegible]	@	[illegible]
" Nat. Wtr.	gal.	[illegible]	@	[illegible]
" Blch. Wtr.	gal.	[illegible]	@	[illegible]
Straits	gal.	[illegible]	@	[illegible]
Tallow, prime	gal.	[illegible]	@	
Whale, Crude	gal.	[illegible]	@	...
Crude, Nat. Wtr.	gal.	[illegible]	@	[illegible]
Bleached Wtr.	gal.	[illegible]	@	.46

New Remedies Compendium and Prices Current.

In this list, which is intended for the use of dispensing druggists, and not for analytical chemists, chemical formulas, melting points and other data of no immediate use to the dispenser are omitted. While additions will be made from time to time as new remedies make their appearance on the market, and the list, thus kept fully up to date, remedies falling into disuse will be dropped as expediency may determine.

Corrected to April 23, 1906.

ACETAL. (ETHYLIDENE DIETHYL ETHER.) Colorless, volatile liquid, soluble in 18 parts of water, very soluble in alcohol. Used as a sedative and hypnotic in doses of 2 to 3 fluid drachms, usually in form of emulsion. Pure medicinal, per oz., $1.00; commercial, oz. .... 65c.

ACETOZONE. (BENZOYL-ACETYL PEROXIDE.) White powder, mixed with an equal weight of an inert soluble powder; soluble in water (1:1000). Bactericide; used internally and externally in diseases of germ origin. Dose, 1 to 3 grains in solution. Boxes containing 6 vials of 15 grains each, per box, $1.25; ¼ oz. bot., $1.40; ½ oz. bot., $2.70; 1 oz. bot. $5.25

ACET - THEOCIN - SODIUM. White crystalline powder, readily soluble in water. Powerful diuretic; used in dropsy, in doses of 5 to 7 grains, two to three times daily. ½ and 1 oz. bot...... $1.90 to $2.30 per oz. (Continental Color & Chemical Co.)

ACOINE. (DI-PARA-ANISYL-MONO-PHENETHYL GUANIDINE HYDROCHLORIDE.) White crystalline powder, soluble in 17 parts of water. Local anæsthetic like cocaine, used hypodermatically in eye surgery; dental anæsthetic in normal saline solution, 2 per cent. 15 grain vials, each, 30c.; capsules, 2½ grains, 28 in box................ 75c. (The Heyden Chemical Works.)

ADNEPHRIN SOLUTION. A 1-1000 solution of the active principle of the suprarenal gland in physiological salt solution containing one-half of 1 per cent. of methaform. Used chiefly as a hæmostatic, also for treatment of inflammations, congestions and tumefactions of the mucous membranes, also as a cardiac stimulant. 1 oz. vials .... 60c.
EMOLLIENT. Tubes, each... 30c.
OIL SPRAY. 1 oz. vials, each. 60c.
(Frederick Stearns & Co.)

ADRENALIN. Grayish - white powder; with difficulty soluble in water. The blood-pressure-raising principle of the suprarenal glands. 1 grain vials. 85c.
CHLORIDE SOLUTION, 1:1000, a solution of 1 part of adrenalin chloride in 1000 parts of physiologic salt solution, with 0.5 per cent. of chloretone. Powerful astringent, hemostatic and cardiac stimulant. Used for the control of hemorrhages, internal and superficial, for the reduction of congestion and inflammation of mucous membranes, as a heart stimulant in collapse, and as an adjuvant to the local anæsthetic action of cocaine. Internal dose, 5 to 30 minims. 1 oz. bot........ 85c.
INHALANT, 1 oz. bot....... 85c.
OINTMENT, ½ oz. tubes..... 48c.
SUPPOSITORIES, boxes of 1 doz. 38c.
TABLETS, vials of 25....... 85c.
(Parke, Davis & Co.)

ADRIN. (EPINEPHRIN HYDRATE.) Whitish nonhygroscopic powder; the active principle of the suprarenal gland. 1 grain vials, each, 75c.; 1-1000 solution, 1 oz. vials, each, 75c.; in tubes of 12 tablets, each tablet q. s. to make 15 minims of 1-1000 solution, each, 40c.; in 100's, each $3.10
INHALANT, 1 oz. vials...... 75c.
OINTMENT, ½ oz. tubes.... 40c.
SUPPOSITORIES, box of 1 doz. 30c.
(H. K. Mulford Co.)

AGURIN. (ACET-THEOBROMINE-SODIUM.) White hygroscopic powder, soluble in water; incompatible with acids. Diuretic in dropsy. Dose, 7 to 15 grains, twice daily. ½ and 1 oz. bot............... $1.55 to $1.70 (Continental Color & Chemical Co.)

AIROL. (BISMUTH OXYIODOGALLATE.) Grayish-green powder, insoluble in water or alcohol. On admixture with water airol partly decomposes and turns red. Should be mixed with water only with intervention of glycerin. Used externally as application to wounds, burns, skin diseases, eye, nose, gonorrhœa, either pure, in 10 per cent. suspension, equal parts glycerin and water, or 10 to 20 per cent. ointment. 1 oz. cartons .... $1.00 (Hoffmann-La Roche Chemical Works.)

ALBARGIN. (GELATOSE SILVER.) Light brown powder, readily soluble in water. Contains 15 per cent. of silver. For gonorrhœa a 2 per cent. solution is injected 4 or 5 times daily. 1 oz. vials, $1.10; tubes of 50 tablets, 0.2 gm. each, per tube .... 50c.
(Victor Koechl & Co.)

ALPHOZONE. (SUCCINIC PEROXIDE.) White fluffy powder, quickly soluble in 60 parts of water. Germicide and antiseptic, internally and externally. Dose, 3 to 5 grains. 1 oz. bot., $4.50; ½ oz., $2.30; ¼ oz., $1.20; 1 grain tablets, bot. of 90 .... $1.00
(Frederick Stearns & Co.)

ALYPIN. White crystalline powder, easily soluble in water and alcohol, but dissolving very sparingly in ether. Watery solutions have a neutral reaction and can be sterilized by boiling for a short period. Local anæsthetic, substitute for cocaine. The strength of the solutions ordinarily employed varies from 1 to 5 and even up to 10 per cent. It can be combined with adrenalin and antipyrine. Alypin should not be used in connection with silver nitrate, owing to the formation of a precipitate. This objection, however, does not apply to protargol solutions, which, although they become slightly turbid at first, soon clear up. 15 grain vials, each, 20c.; 10 grain vials, per vial, 16c.; ¼ and ½ oz. bots., per oz., $4.20; 1 oz. bots., per oz....... $4.10 (Continental Color & Chemical Co.)

ALUMNOL. (ALUMINUM NAPHTHOL DISULPHONATE.) Whitish powder, very soluble in water; slightly soluble in alcohol and glycerin; astringent and antiseptic; dissolves in pus and penetrates tissues. Used in 1 per cent. solution in gonorrhœa; 10 to 20 per cent. mixture with talcum as a dusting powder. 1 oz. tins, per oz... 50c.
(Victor Koechl & Co.)

AMINOFORM. (HEXAMETHYLENETETRAMINE.) White granular crystals, readily soluble in water, prepared by combining ammonia and formaldehyde. Antiseptic for urinary passages, diuretic and solvent in uric acid concretions; dose, 5 to 10 grains, well diluted, three times daily. 1 oz. bot., 60c.; 7½ grain tablets, oz.............. 70c.
(C. Bischoff & Co.)

ANAESTHESIN. White crystalline powder, almost insoluble in cold water, but easily solu-

bl in ether, alcohol, benzin and fatty oils. Local anæsthetic, and used internally in gastric ulcer, nervous dyspepsia, etc. Dose, internally, 5 to 8 grains several times daily. Used externally pure or in ointment 5 to 20 per cent., and in suppositories containing 3 grains each. 1 oz. bot..........$1.00
(Victor Koechl & Co.)

ANALGINE. A powder composed of acetanilid, 50 parts; sodium bicarb., 5 parts; sodium salicylate, 5 parts; camphor monobrom., 5 parts; caffeine citrated, 2½ parts; ext. cannabis indica, 2½ parts; aromatic powder, q. s. 100 parts. Recommended as an analgetic, antipyretic and nerve sedative in neuralgia, migraine, headache, rheumatism, gout, sciatica, etc. Dose, 5 to 10 grains. 1 oz. screw cap bottles..........40c.
(H. K. Mulford Company.)

ANTHRASOL. Yellow, oily liquid, with a distinctive tarry odor; soluble in alcohol, acetone, fats and petrolatum. A distillate from coal tar, used in diseases of the skin where coal tar is employed. 1 oz. vials ....55c.
(Knoll & Co. and Merck & Co.)

ANTINONNIN. (POTASSIUM ORTHODINITRO-CRESOL.) Paste of brilliant orange color, soluble in water, slight soapy odor, nonvolatile. Deodorizer, disinfectant, prevents the growth of fungi, mildew and dry rot in cellars and human habitations. Used in form of solution. 1 lb to 5 to 15 gallons of water. Cans, ½ lb., $1.10 per lb.; 1 lb. cans, 95c.; 50 lb. cans, per lb. ....77c.
(Continental Color & Chemical Co.)

ANTINOSINE. (SODIUM SALT OF NOSOPHEN.) Blue powder, soluble in water, alcohol and glycerin. Used in solution of 1 to 5 per cent. as an antiseptic in diseases of the eye and ear, genito-urinary diseases, and as a healing powder on chronic leg ulcers. 1 oz. bot. $2.10
(Stallman & Fulton Co.)

ANTISCLEROSIN. Tablets, consisting of a compound of inorganic blood salts, used in treatment of arteriosclerosis and its sequelæ. Dose, 2 tablets three times daily. Carton of 4 tubes @ 24 tablets...$1.50
(Schering & Glatz.)

ANTITUSSIN. (DIFLUORDIPHENYL OINTMENT.) Ointment containing lanolin, 85 per cent.; petrolatum, 10 per cent., and difluordiphenyl, 5 per cent. A whooping cough remedy applied as inunction to patient's neck, chest and back once a day, in doses of 5 Gm. 20 Gm. collapsible tubes, 40c.; 40 Gm. ....75c.
(C. Bischoff & Co.)

ANUSOL SUPPOSITORIES. A compound of bismuth iodoresorcin sulphonate, used in hæmorrhoids, etc. Dose, 1 or 2 daily. Box of 12...............$1.00
(Schering & Glatz.)

ARGENTAMINE. A colorless, alkaline liquid representing a solution of silver nitrate, 10 per cent., and ethylenediamine, 10 per cent.; soluble in water. Used in all cases where silver nitrate is used, mostly in gonorrhœa, in strength of 1 in 2000-4000 solution. 1 oz., g. s. bot. ....75c.
(Schering & Glatz.)

ARGONIN. White powder, very slightly soluble in cold, but freely so in hot water. A compound of silver nitrate and sodium casein. Antiseptic, germicide and gonococcicide, less caustic than silver nitrate. Solutions of 2 to 10 per cent. strength recommended for injection in gonorrhœa and 3 per cent. solutions for use in the eye. 1 oz. vials..........65c.
(Victor Koechl & Co.)

ARHOVIN, an addition product of diphenylamine and esterified thymyl-benzoic acid, is a fluid of aromatic odor and slightly burning taste, soluble in oil. Gonocide for internal and topical use. Given by mouth in capsules of 4 grains (1 or 2 capsules, three to six times daily); in urethral bougies (1 bougie, two to four times daily); in vaginal globules (1 globule, two to four times daily), and injected in 2 per cent. to 5 per cent. oily solution. 1 oz. vials, 90c.; box of 50 capsules, 65c.; box of 12 bougies, 50c.; box of 12 globules...................50c.
(Schering & Glatz.)

ASAPROL. (ABRASTOL.) Whitish powder, freely soluble in water and alcohol. It is the calcium salt of betanaphthol-sulphonic acid. Antipyretic and antirheumatic in doses of 5 to 15 grains. Used also as test for albumin in urine. 1 oz. bot. $1.25

ARISTOCHIN. (CARBONIC ESTER OF QUININE.) White powder, tasteless, insoluble in water. Decomposes in the system to yield 96.1 per cent. of quinine. Prescribed like quinine, but in somewhat larger doses. ½ and 1 oz. cartons, per oz......$2.20
(Continental Color & Chemical Co. and Merck & Co.)

ASPIRIN. (ACETYL SALICYLIC ACID.) White crystalline powder, insoluble in water; incompatible with alkalies. Used instead of the salicylates in articular and muscular rheumatism and other therapeutic indications for the salicylates. Dose, 5 to 15 grains, three to five times daily. 1 oz. bot., per oz...................33c. to 43c.
(Continental Color & Chemical Co.)

ATOXYL. (META-ARSENOUS ANILIDE.) White powder, containing 37.69 per cent. of arsenic in organic combination. Soluble in 6 parts of water and used in this strength solution for hypodermic injection; relatively nontoxic. Dose, 1 to 3 grains. 1 oz. vials......$3.00
(Victor Koechl & Co.)

BENZONAPHTHOL. White, crystalline powder, soluble in alcohol and chloroform; insoluble in water. Employed as intestinal antiseptic in doses of 5 to 15 grains. 1 oz. vials, 22c.; ¼ lb. bottles, $2.20; ½ lb., $2.10; 1 lb...........$2.00
(Schering & Glatz.)

BENZOSOL. (GUAIACOL BENZOATE.) Small colorless crystals, nearly insoluble in water. Contains 54 per cent. of guaiacol and, as it is slowly saponified by the gastric juice, the guaiacol being liberated gradually, it is recommended as an intestinal antiseptic and as an agreeable substitute for creosote in incipient phthisis. Dose, 4 to 8 grains. 1 oz. tins. $1.25
(Victor Koechl & Co.)

BETA-EUCAINE HYDROCHLORIDE. White, crystalline powder, soluble in 30 parts of water. A synthetic compound chemically allied to cocaine, being the hydrochloride of benzoyl-vinyl-diaceton-alkamine. It is slower in action than cocaine, but anæsthesia is more prolonged, and a third less toxic. Used generally in 2 per cent. solutions in dental and ophthalmic work. ⅛ oz. and ¼ oz., per oz., $3.60; ½ oz. and 1 oz...............$3.50
(Schering & Glatz.)

BETA-EUCAINE LACTATE. White powder, possessing the same properties as the hydrochloride, but is more soluble in water (about 1 in 5). Prices and containers same as for beta-eucaine hydrochloride.
(Schering & Glatz.)

BISMUTH FORMIC IODIDE. Yellowish, impalpable powder. A compound of formaldehyde and gelatin, with the addition of thymol iodide and bismuth subiodide. Bactericide, antiseptic and astringent. Employed as a dry dressing for wounds and ulcerations, suppurating surfaces and abscesses. Sprinkler-top boxes, 50c.; per dozen, $5.00

BISMUTH FORMIC IODIDE OINTMENT, per dozen ozs., $1.00; per lb., $1.00. Bismuth Formic Iodide Suppositories, per box of 1 doz.........................50c.
(H. K. Mulford Company.)

BISOL. (SOLUBLE BISMUTH PHOSPHATE.) White powder, soluble in water, faint alkaline reaction. Intestinal antiseptic and astringent in gastric and enteric catarrh. Dose, 3 to 7½ grains. 1 oz. vials......70c.
(C. Bischoff & Co.)

BROMETONE. Powder, slightly soluble in water. Compound of bromoform and acetone; recommended as a substitute for bromides; contains 77 per cent. of bromine. Dose, 3 to 5 grains. 1 oz. bot., 85c.; 5 grain capsules in bot. of 100 ....$1.25
(Parke, Davis & Co.)

BROMIPIN. (10 % BROMINIZED SESAME OIL.) Yellow, oily fluid, used as a nervine and sedative in epilepsy; succedaneum for bromides. Dose, 1 teaspoonful. 1 oz. vial, 18c.; per lb..........$2.10 to $2.35
(Merck & Co.)

CACODYLIC ACID. (DIMETHYL ARSENIC ACID.) Small colorless deliquescent crystals, the ultimate product of oxidation of arsenium-dimethyl (cacodyle) and of cacodyle oxide. Contains 54.4 per cent. of arsenic trioxide, but is relatively nontoxic. Dose, 1 to 3 grains. ½ oz. vials, per oz..........$4.00

CALOMELOL OINTMENT. White mercurial ointment made from colloidal calomel for the inunction treatment of syphilis and especially for the cure of its cutaneous manifestations. 2 oz. graduated tubes, per tube ....55c.
(Heyden Chemical Works.)

CALOMELOL POWDER. Grayish-white powder of neutral reaction, tasteless and odorless. Yields a milky solution when added to cold water in the proportion of 1 to 50. Used as a dusting powder in the treatment of papular eruptions and ulcerations, and as external application to ulcerated chancres in 2 per cent. solution. 1 oz. vials ....70c.
(Heyden Chemical Works.)

CAMPHORIC ACID. (Colorless crystalline scales, very slightly soluble in water; formed by the oxidation of camphor with nitric acid. Used in night sweats of phthisis, also in cystitis and as an intestinal antiseptic in doses of 10 to 20 grains. 1 oz. vials, 45c.; 1 lb. bot. $7.00
(Merck & Co.)

CEROLIN. Pills of a fatty substance isolated from yeast. Acts same as yeast in furunculosis, acne, etc., but more cathartic. Pills containing 0.1 Gm., box of 100, each.....50c.
(C. F. Boehringer & Soehne.)

CHINAPHENIN. (QUININE CARBONIC ESTER OF PHENETIDINE.) White tasteless powder, representing synthetic quinine-phenacetin and having medicinal properties of both. Insoluble in water, but easily soluble in alcohol, ether and chloroform. Dose, 5 to 10 grains, thrice daily. ½ and 1 oz. cartons, per oz.........
$1.25 to $1.30
(Continental Color & Chemical Co.)

CHINOTROPINE. (UROTROPINE QUINATE.) A combination of quinic acid and urotropine (hexamethylenetetramine) used as uric acid solvent in the various manifestations of the uric acid diathesis. Is said to liberate formaldehyde freely internally and to form soluble compounds with uric acid. Dose, 10 to 30 grains. ½ oz. and 1 oz. vials, $1.75; tablets, 7½ grains, 25 in tube, 2 tubes in box....................$1.75
(Schering & Glatz.)

CHLORETONE. White crystals, slightly soluble in water (1:125); hypnotic, local anæsthetic and antiseptic. Dose, 5 to 20 grains, in cachet, tablet or capsule. Externally as a dusting powder for wounds, combined 23 with, zinc oxide, 120, and French chalk, 90 parts. ½ oz. vials, per oz., 90c.; 1 oz....................85c. Capsules, 3 grs., bot. of 100, 80c.; 5 grs., bot. of 100..$1.25
(Parke, Davis & Co.)

CINNAMIC ACID. (CINNAMYLIC ACID.) Transparent micaceous crystals, very slightly soluble in water; soluble in alcohol and ether. Injected intravenously in tuberculosis in doses of ¼ to ¾ of a grain, twice a week; per os., 1-20 to ½ grain twice daily. 1 oz. vial, 85c.; 1 lb. bot., per lb. $5.00
(Merck & Co.)

CITARIN. (SODIUM ANHYDROMETHYLENCITRATE.) White, crystalline powder, easily soluble in water. Antilithæmic for gouty and chronic rheumatic conditions; liberates formaldehyde in the blood. Dose, 15 to 30 grains, thrice daily. 1 oz. bottle, per oz..70c. to 75c.
(Continental Color & Chemical Co.)

COLLARGOL. (COLLOIDAL SILVER.) Shining, black scales, soluble in 1 in 20 of water. Used as a bactericide, 1 in 100 to 10,000 in water or glycerin. Internally a 1 to 500 or 1 to 100 solution may be added to the food in teaspoonful doses. ½ oz. and 1 oz. vials, $2.75; tablets, 1 grain each, tubes of 50...60c.
(Schering & Glatz.)

CORNUTOL. A concentrated, preparation of ergot of rye, prepared for hypodermic and general use. Each Cc. represents 2½ Gm. of assayed Spanish ergot. Dose, hypodermically, 5 to 10 min. (or 0.3 to 2 Cc.). By mouth, 10 to 30 min. (or 0.6 to 2 Cc.). Marketed only in 1 oz. vials and in hermetically sealed aseptic bulbs, each bulb containing 2 Cc. (½ dr.). 1 oz. vials, 50c.; per package of 6 bulbs ....60c.
(H. K. Mulford Company.)

COTARNINE HYDROCHLORIDE. See Stypticin.

CREOSOTE CARBONATE. (CREOSOTAL.) Yellow, transparent viscous liquid, insoluble in water, but miscible with alcohol; contains 92 per cent. of creosote combined with 8 per cent. of carbon dioxide. Used in tuberculosis and pneumonia in doses of 5 to 60 drops several times daily. 1 oz. vials, 65c.; ¼ lb. bot., per lb., $9.25; ½ lb., $9.10; 1 lb.......$9.00
(Schering & Glatz and Continental Color & Chemical Co.)

CUPROL. Green powder, readily soluble in water; a chemical combination of nucleinic acid and copper; solution does not coagulate albumen. Applied locally as an astringent; of use in granular ophthalmia in the form of 5 per cent. instillations, or may be applied in the dry form with a brush. ¼ oz. vials, $1.30 per oz.; 1 oz. vials $1.20
(Parke, Davis & Co.)

DERMATOL. (BISMUTH SUBGALLATE.) Yellow, insoluble powder; nonirritant antiseptic, especially serviceable in burns, ulcers and moist eczema. Used internally in diarrhoea, dysentery, intestinal fermentation and gastric ulcers, in doses of 10 to 30 grains three times daily. 1 oz. tins, 19c.; 1 and 5 lb. tins, per lb.........$2.50
(Victor Koechl & Co.)

DIATHESIN. White crystalline leaflets, soluble in 15 parts cold water, freely soluble in hot water or alcohol. Is ortho-oxybenzylalcohol, or synthetic saligenin. Used in place of salicin in rheumatism, neuralgia, pleurisy, etc., in doses of 7½ to 15 grains. 1 oz. cartons $2.40
(C. Bischoff & Co.)

DIFLUORDIPHENYL. White crystalline powder of pleasant aromatic odor, insoluble in water, soluble in alcohol, ether, chloroform and oils. Used as antiseptic dusting powder mixed with talc in proportion of difluordiphenyl, 10 parts; talc, 90 parts, or in 10 per cent. ointment with lanolin as dressing for burns. Dose, 1-16 to ¼ grain. 5 Gm. envelopes, each $1.50
(C. Bischoff & Co.)

DIGALEN. (CLOETTA'S SOLUBLE DIGITOXIN.) Marketed only in solution in 15 Cc. (½ oz.) vials, on account of infinitesimal dosage. Active principle of digitalis leaves, nonaccumulative heart tonic and diuretic. 1 Cc. of solution represents 0.0003 Gm. (0.0045 grain) of digitoxin, which is the average dose, by the mouth, hypodermatically, or by enema; intravenously the dose is from 8 to 10 Cc. ½ oz. vials..............$1.00 (Hoffmann-La Roche Chemical Works.)

DIGITALIN VERUM. White powder, the active constituent of digitalis, free from impurities and noxious principles. Almost insoluble in water. Dose, 0.002 Gm. to 0.006 Gm., three times daily, increasing to not over 0.02 Gm. (1-3 grain). 1 Gm. vials....................$7.25 (C. F. Boehringer & Soehn.)

DIONIN. (ETHYL MORPHINE HYDROCHLORIDE.) White crystalline powder, very soluble in water and alcohol. Recommended to replace codeine and morphine in bronchitis, emphysema and asthma. Dose, ¼ to ½ grain. 1 oz. vials, $6.00; ⅛ oz. vials, per oz., $6.25; 15 grain vials, each, 35c.; tablets, ½ grain, bot. of 50, 35c.; bot. of 100.......................60c. (Merck & Co.)

DIURETIN. White powder, soluble in water, decomposed by acids. Must be kept dry and air tight. It is a chemical compound of theobromine sodium and sodium salicylate. Diuretic, antiasthmatic and vascular stimulant. Dose, 15 grains four to six times daily. 1 oz. bot., per oz..............$1.75 (Knoll & Co.)

DORMIOL. (AMYLENE CHLORAL.) Oily, colorless liquid, with a camphoraceous odor, insoluble in water, soluble in alcohol and ether. Hypnotic in mania; 50 per cent. solution supplied commercially. Dose, 5 to 60 minims. 1 oz. vials, 28c.; ½ lb. bot., per lb..............$4.00 (Merck & Co.)

DUOTAL. (GUAIACOL CARBONATE.) White crystalline powder, soluble in alcohol, insoluble in water. Same therapeutic action as Creosotal, which see. Dose, 5 to 20 grains, gradually increased. 1 oz. vials, $1.50; tablets, 7½ grains, 50 tablets in box, $1.50; 4½ grains, 50 tablets in box..............90c. (Schering & Glatz and Continental Color & Chemical Co.)

DUOTONOL. White powder; a mixture, equal parts of the lime and sodium glycerophosphates. Nerve nutrient in doses of 5 to 10 grains three times daily. 1 oz., 50c.; 1 lb., $6.00; tablets, 5 grains, 100 tablets in bottle.......................65c. (Schering & Glatz.)

DYMAL. (DIDYMIUM SALICYLATE.) Pinkish powder, odorless. Applied as powder and ointment in skin diseases, notably dry and weeping eczema. 1 oz. cartons, each, 35c.; 4 oz. cartons, each..............$1.20 (C. Bischoff & Co.)

EKA-IODOFORM. A chemically pure iodoform, prepared by electrical synthesis, and sterilized with paraform. 1 oz. vials.......................50c. (Schering & Glatz.)

EMPYROFORM. Brown powder; condensation product of birch tar and formaldehyde; insoluble in water, readily soluble in acetone, chloroform and solutions of caustic alkalies. Used like tar in ointment, paste and tincture. 1 oz. vials..65c. (Schering & Glatz.)

EPICARIN. (CONDENSATION PRODUCT OF BETANAPHTOL AND CRESOLIC ACID.) Colorless or yellowish needles, difficultly soluble in hot water, easily soluble in alcohol, ether and oils. Nontoxic substitute for naphthol in parasitic skin diseases. Employed chiefly in ointments (5 to 10 per cent.) 1 oz. cartons, per oz..............60c. to 70c. (Continental Color & Chemical Co.)

EUCASIN. Casein compound, containing 95 per cent. albumin and 5 per cent. water. Prepared from cow's milk. Dietetic for convalescents, invalids or persons afflicted with lung, stomach or kidney trouble; also in anæmia and typhoid. 1 lb. tins, $3.00; ½ lb., $1.50; ¼ lb........................80c. (Fuerst Bros. & Co.)

EUDOXINE. (BISMUTH SALT OF NOSOPHEN.) Reddish-gray powder, insoluble in water, but soluble in alkaline fluids. Used as an intestinal antiseptic in doses of 3 to 5 grains. 1 oz. bot., $2.10; 3 grain tablets, per oz., $2.60; 5 grain tablets, per oz........................$2.50 (Stallman & Fulton Co.)

EUGALLOL. (PYROGALLOL MONOACETATE.) Yellowish, syrupy liquid, marketed in 66 per cent. acetone solution. Soluble in water and acetone; applied pure or diluted with acetone as paint in skin diseases, especially psoriasis, and deemed superior to pyrogallol. 1 oz. vials......................$1.00 (Knoll & Co. and Merck & Co.)

EUMYDRIN. White crystalline powder, obtained from atropine; easily soluble in water. Powerful mydriatic, less poisonous than atropine. Dose, internally, about 1-70 grain. 1 or 2 per cent. solution dilates the pupil after 10 to 25 minutes. 1 grain tubes, 45c. to 55c. per box of 10 tubes; ¼ oz. and ⅛ oz. packages, per oz........................$16.50 (Continental Color & Chemical Co.)

EUNATROL. (SODIUM ACID OLEATE.) Light yellow substance, readily soluble in water and alcohol; supplied as powder and chocolate-coated pills. Recommended in treatment of gallstones, being excellent cholagogue. Dose, four pills, 4 grains each, three times daily, or in solution. 25 Gm. bot., each, 75c.; bot. of 50 pills, 70c.; 100 pills..............$1.20 (C. Bischoff & Co.)

EUPHORIN. (PHENYL - URETHANE.) White, acicular crystals, slightly soluble in water, freely in alcohol. Energetic antipyretic and analgetic in doses of 7½ to 15 grains, 2 to 3 times daily. 1 oz. vials...$1.00 (Schering & Glatz.)

EUPHTHALMINE HYDROCHLORIDE. White crystals; a synthetic derivative of beta-eucaine; soluble in water; 2 to 5 per cent. solutions dilate the pupil, without causing discomfort or accommodation disturbances. ⅕ and 1 Gm. vials, per Gm. ....$1.25 (Schering & Glatz.)

EUPYRINE. (PARA-PHENETIDINE VANILLIN ETHYLCARBONATE.) Light yellow crystals, sparingly soluble in water, readily in alcohol, chloroform and ether. Stimulant antipyretic in doses of 7½ to 15 grains. 1 oz. cartons, each..................$1.50 (C. Bischoff & Co.)

EUQUININE. (QUININE CARBONIC ESTER.) Tasteless, fleecy crystals, slightly soluble in water; soluble in alcohol, ether and chloroform. Succedaneum for quinine sulphate, reported not to disturb stomach or produce cinchonism. Dose, same as quinine. Tablets, 5 grains, 100 in bot., $1.75; 2 grain, 100 in bot.....................75c. (Merck & Co.)

EURESOL. (RESORCINE MONOACETATE.) Oily, yellow liquid, soluble in alcohol and acetone. Succedaneum for resorcin, externally. Used in skin and scalp diseases, as paint pure or diluted with acetone. 1 oz. vials......................$1.00 (Knoll & Co. and Merck & Co.)

EUROPHEN. Yellow light powder, containing 25 per cent. of iodine, insoluble in water and

glycerin. Iodoform substitute used in dry powder and in ointment. 1 oz. bot., per oz.... $1.65 to $1.80.
(Continental Color & Chemical Co.)

EUZONE. (PURE SODIUM PERBORATE.) White, odorless powder, containing about 7.1 per cent. boron, 15 per cent. sodium, 31.2 per cent. oxygen and 46.2 per cent. water; represents 22 per cent. by weight of hydrogen dioxide, equivalent to 10.4 per cent. by weight of nascent oxygen. Soluble in water 1 in 10, such a solution being taken to represent a 2 per cent. solution of hydrogen dioxide. Tablets, 2½ Gm. each, boxes of 20, 40c.; powder, in 100 Gm. cartons, 35c.; 500 Gm. boxes $1.20
(Schering & Glatz.)

EXODIN. Yellowish powder; a synthetic oxyanthraquinone derivative; tasteless, mild aperient in doses of 7½ to 15 grains. 1 oz. vials, $1.40; tablets, 7½ grains each, 10 tablets in box, 30c.; 50 in bottle.........$1.40
(Schering & Glatz.)

FERRATIN. Reddish - brown powder, slowly soluble in ordinary liquids, but readily in hot beverages. Used in anæmia and chlorosis in doses of 7½ grains three times daily. 1 oz. vials, 85c.; tablets, 7½ grains, 50 in box, per box..............85c.
(C. F. Boehringer & Soehne.)

FERRATOGEN. (IRON NUCLEINATE.) Grayish-yellow powder, obtained by growing yeast in a ferruginous medium; insoluble in water. Used in chlorosis and anæmia in doses of 5 grains, three times daily. 1 oz. cartons, each..............90c.
(C. Bischoff & Co.)

FERRATOSE. (LIQUOR FERRATINI.) Fluid preparation of ferratin, containing 0.3 per cent. iron. 250 Gm. bottles.....45c.
(C. F. Boehringer & Soehn.)

FERRIPYRIN. (FERRIC CHLORIDE ANTIPYRIN.) Orange-red powder, soluble in 5 parts of water, very soluble in alcohol, but insoluble in ether. A compound of ferric chloride and antipyrine. Styptic and analgetic when applied in solution or powder. Given internally in chlorosis and anæmia as a hæmatinic in doses of 7½ grains. 1 oz. tins........$1.50
(Victor Koechl & Co.)

FERROPYRIN. (Same as Ferripyrin, but made by Knoll & Co. and sold in 1 oz. cartons, $1.40.)
(Knoll & Co. and Merck & Co.)

FILMARON OIL 1:10. A 10 per cent. solution of filmaron, the active principle of malefern, in castor oil. Used in removal of tapeworm. 10 Gm. bot....35c.
(C. F. Boehringer & Soehn.)

FIBROLYSIN. Solution of thiosinamine and sodium salicylate, sterilised. Put up in sealed tubes, each containing 2.3 Cc. solution (= 0.2 Gm. thiosinamine). Same uses as thiosinamine, but specially adapted for hypodermic use. Dose, contents of 1 tube every 1, 2 or 3 days, as required. 2.3 Cc. tubes, each...................15c.
(Merck & Co.)

FLUOROFORMOL. (FLUORYL.) Colorless, tasteless liquid, a 2.8 per cent. solution of fluoroform. Used in phthisis, internally and externally; also in pneumonia, acting as an antiseptic. Dose, 1 tablespoonful four times daily. 1 lb. bot....................$1.00
(C. Bischoff & Co.)

FLUORRHEUMIN. Ointment composed of petrolatum, 10; lanolin, 85; difluordiphenyl, 4; fluorphenetol, 1. Used in rheumatism, sciatica and lumbago; dose by inunction, 4 to 5 Gm. Collapsible tubes, 20 Gm., 40c.; 40 Gm......................75c.
(C. Bischoff & Co.)

FORTOINE. (METHYLENEDICOTOINE.) Yellow crystals, with slight cinnamon flavor, obtained through action of formaldehyde on cotoine; insoluble in water, sparingly soluble in alcohol, ether and benzol; easily soluble in chloroform, acetone and alkaline liquids. Astringent antiseptic in protracted diarrhœas of consumptives. Dose, 4 grains three times daily. 10 Gm. envelopes, each $2.00
(C. Bischoff & Co.)

GALLOGEN. (ELLAGIC ACID.) Yellowish, tasteless powder, insoluble in all acid and neutral media, but soluble in alkaline solutions. Resembles tannic acid, being the astringent principle of divi-divi. Used in dysentery and diarrhœa. Dose, 10 to 15 grains for adults, 5 to 8 grains for children. 1 oz. cartons, 80c.; chocolate coated tablets, 3 grains each, 24 in box ....35c.
(C. Bischoff & Co.)

GAULTHERINE. Pinkish powder, slowly soluble in cold water, more readily so in hot water; insoluble in ether and chloroform, but very soluble in alcohol. It is the sodium salt of methyl salicylate prepared from natural oil of wintergreen. Antiseptic, antifermentative and soothing antiputrefactive. Used internally and externally. 4 oz. bot., per lb., $6.30; ½ lb. bot., per lb., $6.60; 1 lb. bot. $6.50
(The Wm. S. Merrell Chemical Co.)

GEOSOTE. See Guaiacol Valerate.

GLUTOL. (FORMALDEHYDE GELATIN.) Whitish, granular, insoluble powder; recommended as an antiseptic dressing for burns, cavities and suppurating ulcers. 1 oz. tins, 65c.; vials of ½ oz., with sprinkler top, each ....25c.
(Schering & Glatz.)

GUAETHOL. (AJACOL; THANATOL.) Oily liquid, or purer in crystals resembling thymol, insoluble in water. Succedaneum for guaiacol. Allays pain by direct application. Dose, 4 to 8 minims. 1 oz. vials......$1.40

GUAIACOL VALERATE. (GEOSOTE.) Yellow, oily liquid: a combination of guaiacol and valerianic acid, having the characteristic odor of the latter. Insoluble in water, soluble in alcohol and ether. Said to be useful in tuberculosis and chlorosis and as intestinal antiseptic in doses of 3 to 10 minims three times daily. 3 minim capsules, per 100.........$2.10

GUAIACETIN. (SODIUM PYROCATECHIN-MONOACETATE.) White odorless powder, soluble in water. A succedaneum for guaiacol and creosote, used in tuberculosis. Dose, 8 grains, preferably in tablet form. Powder in 1 oz. tins, $3.30; bot. containing 100 tablets, 8 grains each, $3.50; 50, $2.00; 25.....$1.17
(Fuerst Bros. & Co.)

GUIASANOL. (DIETHYLGLYCOCOLL-GUAIACOL.) Crystalline powder, readily soluble in water. Indications same as for creosote and guaiacol. Used internally in doses of from 45 to 180 grains a day. 25 Gm. bot. $1.00
(Victor Koechl & Co.)

HEDONAL. White, crystalline powder, insoluble in water, but soluble in alcohol, chloroform and ether: best administered as a dry powder. Given in mild forms of insomnia as a hypnotic in doses of 15 to 30 grains. 1 oz. bot. $1.50 to $1.60
(Continental Color & Chemical Co.)

HELMITOL. (HEXAMETHYLENETETRAMINE-ANHYDROMETHYLENE CITRATE.) Colorless crystals, freely soluble in water; insoluble in alcohol and ether. Urinary antiseptic in cystitis, phosphaturia, urethritis, etc., in doses of 15 grains, three or four times daily; liberates formaldehyde in the urinary tract. 1 oz. bot.....................60c.
(Continental Color & Chemical Co.)

HEMICRANIN. White powder: a mixture of 5 parts phenacetin, 1 part caffeine and 1 part citric acid, used in migraine, headaches, intercostal neuralgia and sciatica, in doses of 5 to 10

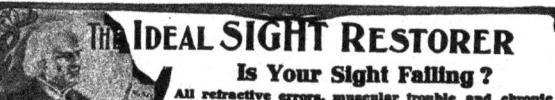

grains. 1 oz. cartons, per oz. ....90c.
(Continental Color & Chemical Co.)

HEROIN. White, crystalline powder, difficultly soluble in water, but readily so in alcohol and in water to which a little acetic acid has been added; incompatible with alkali carbonates. Substitute for morphine, of which it is the diacetic acid ester, in doses of 1-24 to 1-12 grain; used for relief of cough and dyspnœa in phthisis, pneumonia, etc. 15 grain vials, 23c. per vial; ¼ oz. vials, per oz., $5.15; 1 oz. vials, per oz...$4.85
(Continental Color & Chemical Co.)

HEROIN HYDROCHLORIDE. (WATER SOLUBLE SALT OF HEROIN.) White, crystalline powder, used in same indications as heroin, but is adapted for hypodermatic injections. The dose and prices are the same as those of heroin.
(Continental Color & Chemical Co.)

HIPPOL. (METHYLENE HIPPURIC ACID.) Colorless, prismatic crystals; sparingly soluble in water; urinary antiseptic in bacterial diseases of the urinary tract. Dose, 22½ grains. 1 oz., $1.50; 20 tablets in box $1.10
(Schering & Glatz.)

HIRUDIN. Grayish, glittering plates and scales, representing a dried extract of the head, pharyngeal rings and lips of the leech (*Sanguisuga medicinalis*); readily soluble in water. Used in the treatment of certain diseases of women and in experiments to prevent coagulation of blood on exposure to air. Tubes, 0.01 Gm., 50c.; 0.1 Gm., $2.75; 1 Gm....$19.00
(C. Bischoff & Co.)

HISTOSAN. (GUAIACOL ALBUMINATE.) Light brown powder of faintly aromatic odor and taste; soluble in water. Used in pulmonary tuberculosis and in diarrhœa in doses of 7½ grains three times daily. 1 oz. cartons $1.30
(C. Bischoff & Co.)

HOLOCAINE HYDROCHLORIDE. White, crystalline powder, difficultly soluble in cold (1 in 75), but readily so in hot water. Chemically para-diethyoxyethenyl-diphenyl-amidine hydrochloride, produced by combination of phenacetin and para-phenetidin. Antiseptic and germicidal in 1 per cent. solution. Used entirely as anæsthetic for operations on the eye, a 1 per cent. solution being equal to 2 per cent. cocaine solution. 1 Gm. vials, 35c.; 5 Gm. vials, per Gm., 30c.; 1 oz. vials, per oz. $7.00
(Victor Koechl & Co.)

HYDRONAL. (POLYMERIZED CHLORAL.) White powder, a polymeric form of anhydrous chloral, known in Germany as viferral. It dissolves slowly in cold, but readily in boiling water. Used as hypnotic in simple sleeplessness and in the insomnia of mania in doses of 15 grains. Tubes of 5 tablets, 1 Gm. each....................35c.
(C. Bischoff & Co.)

HYRGOL. (COLLOIDAL MERCURY.) Dark, solid body, fairly soluble in cold water, insoluble in alcohol and ether; used in syphilis as 10 per cent. ointment by inunction, and pills and tablets internally. Dose, ⅓ to ⅝ grain thrice daily. 1 oz. vials...80c.
(Schering & Glatz.)

ICHTHALBIN. (ICHTHYOL ALBUMINATE.) Grayish-brown powder, odorless and tasteless; combination of ichthyol and albumin, containing 40 per cent. of the former. Used internally for skin diseases and gastro-intestinal affections in doses of 5 to 30 grains three times daily. 1 oz. cartons, 85c.; 5 grain tablets, 100 in bot..$1.00
(Knoll & Co. and Merck & Co.)

ICHTHARGAN. (ICHTHYOL SILVER; SILVER ICHTHYOLSULPHONATE; SILVER THIO-HYDROCARBUROSULPHONATE.) Brown powder containing 30 per cent. silver; soluble in water and glycerin. Bactericide and astringent in urinary diseases in injections of 1 to 500 and 1 to 3000 in water; in diseases of the eye, as trachoma, by brush applications of 1 to 3 per cent. solutions. Dose, 1-24 to 1-12 grain in water. 1 oz. vials, $3.00; ¼ oz..............$3.10
(Merck & Co.)

ICHTHOFORM. (ICHTHYOL FORMALDEHYDE.) Blackish-brown powder, insoluble in water. Used externally as succedaneum for iodoform. Internally as intestinal antiseptic in the diarrhœa and intestinal disorders occurring in tubercular diseases, and in typhoid fever and dysentery. Dose, 15 to 30 grains three or four times daily, in powder or capsules. 1 oz. vials................$1.00
(Merck & Co.)

IODIPIN. (IODIZED SESAME OIL; IODINOL.) Thick, yellow oil, odorless and of oily taste, made similarly to bromipin by repeated iodization of sesame oil by means of iodine monochloride in alcoholic solution; insoluble in water and alcohol, soluble in ether and chloroform. Made in two strengths, 10 per cent. iodine and 25 per cent. iodine, respectively, the former for internal and the latter for hypodermic use. Succedaneum for iodide in syphilis, scrofula, etc. Dose, 10 per cent., 1 to 3 fl. drachms; hypodermically (25 per cent.), 30 to 90 minims. On unspecified orders the 10 per cent. strength is supplied. Used in all cases where iodine and iodides are indicated; hypodermically in syphilis. 10 per cent. strength, 1 lb. bottles, $3.65; ¼ lb., $3.90; 1 oz. vials, 28c.; 20 per cent., 1 lb. bottles, $8.25; ¼ lb., $8.30; 1 oz. vials ....65c.
(Merck & Co.)

IODOFORMOGEN. Light yellow powder, odorless in use; combination of iodoform and albumin, insoluble in water, capable of sterilization; used like iodoform as a dressing for wounds. 1 oz. cartons ....55c.
(Knoll & Co. and Merck & Co.)

IODOZEN. Yellowish-white powder, a chemical combination of methyl salicylate and iodine; insoluble in water, soluble in 2 parts of alcohol, in 3 parts of ether and in 10 parts of chloroform. Antiseptic application applied as solution or ointment. Marketed in sprinkler top cans. 1 oz..........................75c.
(The Wm. S. Merrell Chemical Co.)

IODOTHYRINE. Whitish powder, representing the active principle of the thyroid gland, combined with sugar of milk. Alterative in goitre, myxœdema, obesity, psoriasis, menstrual disorders of women, etc., in daily doses of 15 to 30 grains. Powder, in ¼ oz. vials, per oz., $3.90; 1 oz. vials, $3.40. Tablets, 5 grains, each, vials of 25, per vial, $1.00; 100 ....$3.90
(Continental Color & Chemical Co.)

IOTHION. Syrupy, yellowish-brown liquid, difficultly soluble in water, easily soluble in alcohol, ether, benzol and chloroform; miscible with petrolatum and with anhydrous lanolin, which takes up twice its weight of iothion. Organic compound of iodine, of which it contains 79 to 80 per cent. Applied in form of ointment by inunction as a substitute for potassium iodide in doses of 30 to 60 grains a day. 1 oz. bot., per oz........................$1.10
(Continental Color & Chemical Co.)

IRON TONOL. (IRON GLYCERO PHOSPHATE.) Powder; soluble in water; tonic, nerve nutrient. Dose, 3 to 10 grains. 1 oz., 35c.; 1 lb....................$3.50
(Schering & Glatz.)

IRON TROPON. Brownish powder; albuminoid food preparation composed of tropon (pure albumen) and iron in an assimilable form. Contains 2½

per cent. of iron. Used as a tonic food in treatment of anæmia, chlorosis, impoverished conditions of the system generally, and in convalescence. Tins, 100 Gm., 75c.; 1 doz. tins $6.75
(Tropon Works.)

ISOPRAL. White crystals, soluble in water up to 3 per cent. and easily in alcohol and ether. A nondepressing substitute for chloral in doses of 7 to 15 grains, indicated in all forms of sleeplessness in which chloral is employed. Powder, in 1 oz. bot., per oz., $1.40; 8 grain tablets, bottles of 100, $3.00; 8 grain tablets, tubes of 20 ....75c.
(Continental Color & Chemical Co.)

KRESAMINE. Clear, watery liquid, representing a solution of trikresol, 25 per cent., and ethylenediamine, 25 per cent.; soluble in 3 parts of water, and in all proportions of glycerin; antiseptic and sedative to inflammed tissues. 1 oz...$1.00
(Schering & Glatz.)

KRYOFINE. White, granular crystals, sparingly soluble in cold water (1 in 600); freely soluble in alcohol and ether. A compound of paraphenetidin and methylglycolic acid. Antipyretic and antineuralgic in doses of 4 to 7½ grains. 1 oz. cartons, powd., $1.00; tablets, 4 or 7½ grains, per oz....$1.00
(C. Bischoff & Co.)

LACTOPHENIN. (LACTYL-PARA-PHENETIDIN.) Small, white crystals, soluble in 330 parts of water. Differs from phenacetin in containing a molecule of lactic acid in place of acetic. Antipyretic and analgetic in doses of 4 to 8 grains. 1 oz. cartons, each......$1.00
(C. F. Boehringer & Soehne.)

LACTOSERNE. Buttermilk in powder form, scientifically prepared from fresh milk, free from bacteria. Used as infant food. 250 Gm. bot........25c.
(C. F. Boehringer & Soehn.)

LARGIN. (SILVER PROTALBIN.) Gray powder containing 11 per cent. of silver; soluble in 10 parts of water. Bactericide and astringent application in gonorrhœa in ¼ to 1½ per cent. injections. 1 oz. vials...$1.75
(Merck & Co.)

LENIGALLOL. (PYROGALLOL TRIACETATE.) White, crystalline powder, insoluble in water, possessing the same reducing properties as pyragallol and used in acute and chronic eczema as ointment. 1 oz. vials $1.00
(Knoll & Co. and Merck & Co.)

LEVULOSE. (FRUIT SUGAR.) Crystalline powder, soluble in water. Sweetening agent used in diabetes, tuberculosis, malnutrition and marasmus of children. Dose, 8 drachms to 2 ounces daily. 1 lb. jars..$1.60
(Schering & Glatz.)

LYCETOL. (DIMETHYLENEDIAMINE TARTRATE.) White powder, readily soluble in water. Uric acid solvent, antiarthritic and diuretic in doses of 5 to 10 grains three times daily. 10 Gm. vials, $1.50; ¼ oz., ½ oz., 1 oz. cartons, per oz... $4.25 to $4.40
(Continental Color & Chemical Co. and Schering & Glatz.)

LYGOSINE. (SODIUM LYGOSINATE.) Glossy, greenish crystals; a condensation product of salicylaldehyde and acetone; readily soluble in water, forming ruby red solutions. Nonirritant substitute for silver as urethral injection in gonorrhœa, 5 per cent. strength. 10 Gm. vials....................35c.
(C. Bischoff & Co.)

LYSIDIN. (ETHYLENE-ETHENYL-DIAMINE HYDROCHLORIDE.) Pale yellowish liquid, containing 50 per cent. of pure lysidin, the substance itself being very hygroscopic. Used in acute gout and uric acid diathesis in doses of 10 to 30 minims. 1 oz. vials $1.75
(Victor Koechl & Co.)

MARETIN. White, glistening crystals, very sparingly soluble in water (1 to 1050). Antipyretic, being a methyl acetanilid with a urea nucleus in place of the acetyl group. Dose, 3 to 5 grains. 1 oz. cartons, per oz..........$1.25 to $1.40
(Continental Color & Chemical Co.)

METHAFORM. (DIMETHYLCARBINOL CHLOROFORM.) White, shiny, needle-like crystals, with a slightly camphoraceous taste and odor, sparingly soluble in water, but readily so in chloroform, alcohol, ether and glacial acetic acid. It is hypnotic, analgetic, anæsthetic and antiseptic, somewhat resembling chloral in physiological action. 1 oz. vials, 60c.; 3 grain capsules, bot. of 100, 50c.; 5 grain, 100 ....75c.
(Frederick Stearns & Co.)

MERCUROL. Brownish powder, soluble in water; insoluble in alcohol; a chemical combination of nucleinic acid and mercury, containing 10 per cent. of the metal. Does not coagulate albuminous liquids. Applied to ulcers and suppurating mucous membranes in from ½ to 5 per cent. solution, or in ointment. ¼ oz. vials, per oz., $1.60; 1 oz. vials $1.50
(Parke, Davis & Co.)

MESOTAN. (METHYLOXYMETHYLESTER OF SALICYLIC ACID.) Clear, yellow fluid, insoluble in water, but miscible with alcohol, ether and fixed oils. External application mixed with equal parts of olive oil in muscular and articular rheumatism, pleuritis and gout. 1 oz. bot., 47c.; 25 oz. lots, 42c.
(Continental Color & Chemical Co.)

MIGRAININ. (PHENAZONE CAFFEINE CITRATE.) Small white crystals, readily soluble in water and alcohol. Analgetic and antipyretic. Used in migraine, headaches of influenza, neuralgia, sciatica, etc., in doses of 17 grains. 1 oz. tins........$1.50
(Victor Koechl & Co.)

MIGROL. White powder, composed of equal parts of sodium pyrocatechinmonoacetate and caffein pyrocatechinmonoacetate. Effective and harmless remedy in headache, toothache, neurasthenia, etc. 1 oz......$4.00
(Fuerst Bros. & Co.)

NARGOL. Brownish powder readily soluble in warm water. Compound of silver and nucleinic acid containing 10 per cent. of the former; does not coagulate albumen. Used in gonorrhœa, conjunctival and other pyogenic inflammations. ¼ oz. vials, per oz., $1.80; ½ oz. vials, per oz., $1.75; 1 oz......$1.70
(Parke, Davis & Co.)

NEODERMIN. Ointment containing lanolin, 85; petrolatum, 10; difluordiphenyl, 4; fluorpseudocumol, 1. For ulcerated surfaces, burns, etc. Collapsible tubes, Gm. 20 and Gm. 40, each................40c. and 75c
(C. Bischoff & Co.)

NOSOPHEN. (TETRAIODOPHENOLPHTHALEIN.) Grayish powder, odorless, slightly anæsthetic, insoluble in water, alcohol or ether, but soluble in alkaline fluids. Antiseptic dusting powder in wounds, burns, ulcers; substitute for iodoform. Bottles containing about ¼ oz., per doz....................$4.50
(Stallman & Fulton Co.)

NOVARGAN. (SILVER PROTEINATE.) Fine yellow powder containing 10 per cent. of metallic silver, readily soluble in water. Used as injection in gonorrhœa; is very penetrating and free from irritating effects upon mucous membrane. 1 oz. vials, $1.40
(Heyden Chemical Works.

OREXINE. (PHENYLDIHYDROQUINAZOLINE TANNATE.) Yellowish powder, tasteless and odorless; insoluble in water, slightly soluble in dilute acid solutions, readily so in hydrochloric acid. Should not be prescribed with preparations of iron. Used in anorexia (lack of appetite) as stimulant of gastric secretion; in seasickness and vomiting of pregnancy. Orexine base is no longer on the market. Dose, 8 to 12 grains two times daily, in powder or in tablets. 1 oz. vials, $1.00; orexoids, Merck's tablets, 4 grains, 50 in bottle ....55c.
(Merck & Co.)

ORPHOL. (BISMUTH BETANAPHTHOLATE.) Odorless and tasteless fawn colored powder, insoluble in water; consists of 80 per cent. bismuth oxide and 20 per cent. beta-naphthol. Intestinal antiseptic in doses of 5 to 15 grains three or four times daily. 1 oz., 80c.; tablets, 5 grains, 50 tablets in vial, per vial ....60c.
(Schering & Glatz.)

ORTHOFORM. White crystalline powder, the methyl ester of metaamidoparaoxybenzoic acid; slightly soluble in water; local anæsthetic and antiseptic. Forms a hydrochloride salt soluble in 9 parts of water. 10 per cent. solution of the hydrochloride salt, or 10 to 20 per cent. in ointment used to alleviate pain in sores or burns. Orthoform, 1 oz. vials, $1.40; orthoform hydrochloride, 1 oz. vials $1.80
(Victor Koechl & Co.)

OVARADEN. Tasteless and odorless powder consisting of the active substance of pigs' ovaries. Used in dysmenorrhœa and neurasthenia in doses of 15 to 30 grains daily. 1 oz. vials, $1.30; 4 grain tablets, bottles of 100..........$1.30
(Knoll & Co. and Merck & Co.)

OVARIIN. Powder representing 1 part in 8 of fresh cow's ovary, being the desiccated substance of the ovary. Used in chlorosis, affections of the heart, and menstrual troubles. 1 oz. vials, $2.00; ¼ oz., $2.10; 3 grain tablets, 100 in bottle $1.50
(Merck & Co.)

PANKREON. Grayish-red powder; a tannin-pancreatin compound; insoluble in water, obtained from the pancreas; used in pancreatic diabetes, gastritis and apepsia in doses of 7½ grains three times daily. Box of 25 Gm., $1.50; tablets of 0.25 Gm., 50 in box, $1.00; sugar tablets (⅝ grain), 100 in box....................50c.
(Merck & Co.)

PHENOCOLL HYDROCHLORIDE. White, crystalline powder, with sharp, saline taste; soluble in 16 parts of water; very soluble in hot water and alcohol. Similar to phenacetin, and used in malaria, pneumonia, influenza, rheumatism, etc. Dose, 7 to 15 grains. 25 Gm. vials..............$1.50
(Schering & Glatz.)

PIPERAZINE. Crystalline powder readily soluble in water. Solvent of uric acid and insoluble urates in the system; used in gout, rheumatism and urinary calculi. Dose, 5 to 15 grains thrice daily. 10 Gm. vials, per vial, $1.50; lots of 60, per vial, $1.25. Tablets, tubes of ten 15 grain tablets, $1.50; 60 tubes, per tube, $1.25; ½ and 1 oz. bot., per oz. $4.25
(Continental Color & Chemical Co. and Schering & Glatz.)

POLLANTIN. Liquid and powder; antitoxic serum for hay fever, autumnal catarrh, rose fever and June cold. Package of powder and brush, $1.75; liquid, per package of serum and pipette..............$1.75
(Fritzsche Brothers.)

PROBILIN PILLS. Composed of salicylic acid, acid sodium oleate, phenolphthalein and menthol; used in gallstone affections. Dose, 3 to 4 pills twice daily for twenty days. Vials of 60, per vial.....$1.25
(Schering & Glatz.)

PROFERRIN. (IRON NUCLEOPROTEID.) Reddish-brown powder, insoluble in water and acid solutions; contains 10 per cent. of iron and 1 per cent. of phosphorus, in organic combination; is absorbed from the duodenum, being unaffected by the gastric juice. Used in blood impoverishment in doses of 5 grains three times daily. 1 oz. cartons, per doz., $6.00; 5 grain tablets, bottle of 100, 60c.; 2½ grain, bottle of 100.......40c.
(H. K. Mulford Co.)

PROTAN. (TANNIN NUCLEOPROTEID.) Light brown powder, insoluble in water; formed by the synthesis of tannic acid with nucleo-proteid. Used in all forms of diarrhœa in doses of from 20 to 30 grains; is astringent and acts in the intestines, being unaffected by the gastric juice. 1 oz. cartons, per doz., $6.00; 7½ grain tablets, bottle of 100, 85c.; 5 grain, per 100..............60c.
(H. K. Mulford Co.)

PROTARGOL. Yellowish, light powder, easily soluble in water. A proteid compound containing 8 per cent. of silver; not precipitated by albumen or salt solutions. Bactericide in gonorrhœa; antiseptic in eye, ear, nose and throat affections. 0.25 to 1 per cent. solutions for gonorrhœa; 0.5 to 5 per cent. for eye, and 2 to 10 per cent. for ear, nose and throat. Internally, in doses of 1 to 3 grains. ½ oz. and 1 oz. vials, per oz.........$1.10 to $1.35
(Continental Color & Chemical Co.)

PURGATIN. (PURGATOL; ANTHRAPURPURIN ACETATE.) Yellow crystalline powder; a synthetic oxyanthraquinone, having mild aperient properties; insoluble in water; decomposed in contact with alkalies. Dose, 10 to 30 grains. 1 oz. cartons, 85c.; 5 grain tablets, 100 in bottle $1.00
(Knoll & Co. and Merck & Co.)

PYRAMIDON. (DIMETHYLAMIDO-ANTIPYRIN.) White powder, soluble in 9 parts of water and 2 parts of alcohol. Used as antipyretic in treatment of asthma, pulmonary tuberculosis and abdominal typhus, and as anodyne in headaches and neuralgic pains in doses of 8 to 12 grains. 1 oz. cartons, $2.15; pyramidon camphorate, acid, 1 oz. bot., $1.50; camphorate, neutral, 1 oz. bot., $1.75; salicylate 1 oz. bot.$1.50
(Victor Koechl & Co.)

PYRENOL, a white, crystalline, slightly hygroscopic powder of aromatic odor and sweetish taste, is an addition product of

salicylic and benzoic acids with thymol. Antiseptic, expectorant, analgetic, sedative, antipyretic and cardiotonic. Indicated in the treatment of asthma, bronchitis, pertussis, pneumonia, influenza, typhoid fever and in rheumatic and neuralgic affections. Dose, 7½ to 15 grains, thrice daily, dry or in cold liquids. 1 oz. vial, 70c.; tube of 20 tablets..............30c.
(Schering & Glatz.)

QUARTONOL. Tablets consisting of a compound of duotonol, quinine tonol and strychnine tonol. Blood and nerve tonic. Dose, 1 to 2 tablets three times daily. Bottle of 100 5-grain tablets ....75c.
(Schering & Glatz.)

QUININE LYGOSINATE. Orange-yellow, amorphous powder, containing 70.8 per cent. of quinine; difficultly soluble in water, readily soluble in alcohol, chloroform and benzin. Nontoxic antiseptic and styptic, employed as a dusting powder, gauze or suppository. 10 Gm. vials, each...............70c.
(C. Bischoff & Co.)

RENADEN. Powder, obtained from extract of pigs' kidneys; used in uræmia and nephritis in doses of 1 to 2 drachms daily. 1 oz. vials, $1.30; 4 grain tablets, bottles of 100 ....$1.30
(Knoll & Co. and Merck & Co.)

RUBIDIUM IODIDE. Colorless, cubical crystals; soluble in less than 1 in 1 of water; bitter, saline taste. Used in place of potassium iodide in polyarthritis and syphilis. Dose, 5 to 20 grains. 1 oz. vial..$1 00
(Merck & Co.)

SAL-ETHYL. A colorless, transparent, volatile fluid; chemically pure ethyl salicylate. A substitute for methyl salicylate or oil of wintergreen. Globules, 5 min., in bot. of 50, per doz. bot. $5.00
(Parke, Davis & Co.)

SALIT. (SALICYLIC ACID ESTER OF BORNEOL.) Oily fluid, insoluble in water, slightly soluble in glycerin and readily soluble in alcohol, ethers and oils. Used in muscular and articular rheumatism, lumbago, neuralgia and rheumatic pains following colds. 1 oz. bot......22c.
(Heyden Chemical Works.)

SALOCREOL. (SALICYLIC ACID ESTER OF CREOSOTE.) Oily fluid of neutral reaction, almost odorless, insoluble in water, readily soluble in alcohol, ether, chloroform and oils. Used in facial erysipelas, acute and chronic inflammation of the lymph glands and chronic arthritis. 1 oz. bot........45c.

SALOPHEN. White, crystalline powder, containing 51 per cent. of salicylic acid; almost insoluble in water; soluble in alcohol and ether; incompatible with alkalies, which decompose it. Antipyretic, analgetic and antiseptic in rheumatism and neuralgia. Dose, 10 to 15 grains 3 to 4 times daily. 1 oz. cartons.............85c. to $1.00
(Continental Color & Chemical Co.)

SALOQUININE. (SALICYLIC ACID ESTER OF QUININE.) Whitish powder, insoluble in water, with difficulty soluble about 1 in 120 of alcohol and ether. Tasteless quinine substitute, used in malaria, tropical fevers, neuralgia and rheumatism. Dose, 15 to 30 grains, one to three times daily. ½ and 1 oz. cartons, $1.25 to $1.30
(Continental Color & Chemical Co. and Merck & Co.)

SANTYL. Yellowish, oily liquid, tasteless and nonirritant. Salicylic ester of pure sandalwood oil. Used in acute gonorrhœia and its complications. Dose, 30 drops, thrice daily. Bottle of ½ oz..................$1.00
(Knoll & Co. and Merck & Co.)

SCOPOLAMINE HYDROBROMIDE is identical with hyoscine hydrobromide, but lower in price. 15 grain tubes, each, $3.00; 10 grain tubes, $2 10; 5 grain tubes.....$1.05
(Merck & Co. and C. F. Boehringer & Soehn.)

SEXTONOL. Tablets consisting of a compound of duotonol, quinine tonol, iron tonol, manganese tonol and strychnine tonol. Blood and nerve nutrient. Dose, 1 to 2 5-grain tablets three times daily. Bottle of 100...............75c.
(Schering & Glatz.)

SIDONAL. (PIPERAZINE QUINATE.) White amorphous powder, readily soluble in water. Uric acid solvent in gout and allied affections in doses of 75 to 120 grains a day in divided doses, well diluted with water. 1 oz. bot...............$3.75
(Victor Koechl & Co.)

SIDONAL NEW. (QUINIC ACID ANHYDRIDE.) Same properties and uses as above. 1 oz. bot. $2.00
(Victor Koechl & Co.)

SILVER CITRATE. (ANTISEPTIC CREDE; ITROL.) White powder, soluble about 1 in 4000 of water. Recommended in Credé's treatment as an antiseptic for wounds, in lotion, ointment or powder. For disinfection of hands, skin and instruments, 1 to 1000-5000 watery solution; as gargle 1 to 5000 to 10,000; in gonorrhœa, 1 to 8000. Oz............$1.20 to $1.25
(Schering & Glatz and Merck & Co.)

SILVER LACTATE. (ACTOL.) Whitish powder, soluble in 15 parts of water; recommended in solution 1 in 200 to 1000 as an antiseptic for surgical use. ½ oz. and 1 oz. vials, per oz., $1.30; tablets, 3 grains, boxes containing 5 vials of 10 tablets, per box..................$1.15
(Schering & Glatz and Merck & Co.)

SOMATOSE. Light yellow almost tasteless powder, easily soluble in water, prepared from meat and consisting of deutero and hetero albumoses. Nitrogenous food product for the sick and convalescent. Dose for adults, 90 to 180 grains daily; for children, 50 to 100 grains. 2 oz. tins, per doz., $8.25; ¼ lb. tins, per lb., $5.25; ½ lb. tins, per lb....................$5.00
(Continental Color & Chemical Co.)

SOMNOS. (TRICHLORETHIDENE PROPENYL ETHER.) [Elixir chlorethanal alcoholate.] Clear liquid, miscible with water, produced by the synthesis of Trichloraldehyde with a polyatomic alcohol radical. Hypnotic and cerebral sedative in doses of from 2 to 4 fluid drachms. Pint bottles, $1.10 per pint; $12.00 per doz.; 4 oz. bottles, per doz...........$4.00
(H. K. Mulford Co.)

SPIROFORM. White, crystalline powder, insoluble in water, but readily soluble in alcohol and other solvents. Odorless and practically tasteless. Antirheumatic, analgetic, uric acid solvent. Dose, 7½ to 15 grains, three to five times daily. 25 Gm. cartons, 75c.; 7½ grain tablets, cartons of 50.....75c.
(C. Bischoff & Co.)

STOVAINE. (AMYLENE HYDROCHLORIDE.) White crystalline powder, readily soluble in wa-

ter and in methyl alcohol; less soluble in ethyl alcohol and almost insoluble in ether. A substitute for cocaine, approximately one-fifth as toxic. Aqueous solutions are slightly acid and bitter to the taste. Put up in solutions of various strengths, $\frac{5}{8}$ per cent., 1 per cent., 10 per cent., in tubes; tablet triturates, $1\frac{1}{3}$ grains each; pastilles, 3-100 grain each. Original packages, 1 oz., $\frac{1}{2}$ and $\frac{1}{4}$ oz. bottles, per oz. $4.00
(Walter F. Sykes & Co.)

STYPTICIN. (COTARNINE HYDROCHLORIDE.) Yellow amorphous powder, the salt of an opium base (cotarnine is a product of the oxidation of narcotine), soluble in water and alcohol. Because of its chemical resemblance to hydrastinine, it being methoxyl-drastine, it is recommended in all forms of uterine hæmorrhage. Used in functional dysmenorrhœa and in the menorrhagia of puberty and the climacteric. Dose as styptic, $1\frac{1}{3}$ to 4 grains, as needed, per os or by injection (10 per cent. solution). Sugar coated tablets, $\frac{5}{8}$ grain, per tube of 20, 25c.; 1 oz. bottles, per oz., $6.50; $\frac{1}{2}$ oz. bottles, per oz., $6.60; $\frac{1}{4}$ oz., per oz., $7.00; 15 grain vials, each, 35c.; hypodermic tablets, $\frac{5}{8}$ grain, per box of 40 (4 tubes).......60c.
(Merck & Co.)

STYPTOL. (COTARNINE PHTHALATE.) Yellow, crystalline powder, readily soluble in water. It is the phthalate salt of an opium base. Recommended in uterine hæmorrhage in doses of 1 to 3 grains; externally in 10 per cent. solution. 1 oz. vials, $6.50; $\frac{1}{2}$ oz., per oz., $6.75; $\frac{1}{4}$ oz., $7.00; 15 grain vials, per vial, 35c.; $\frac{5}{8}$ grain tablets, bottles of 100, per bot...$1.20
(Knoll & Co. and Merck & Co.)

STYRACOL. (GUAIACOL CINNAMIC ESTER.) White granular crystals, insoluble in water, readily soluble in alcohol. Given in phthisis, catarrh of the stomach and intestines in doses of 15 grains three to four times daily. 1 oz. cartons, $1.20; 5 grain tablets, bot of 100..$1.40
(Knoll & Co. and Merck & Co.)

SUBLAMINE. (MERCURIC ETHYLENE-DIAMINE SULPHATE.) Crystalline powder, containing 43 per cent. of mercury; very soluble in water. Used in solutions of 1 to 1000 as a substitute for corrosive sublimate. 1 oz. vials, 50c.; tablets, 15 grains, 100 tablets in bottle, $1.10; 20 tablets in tube, 5 tubes in box..............$1.60
(Schering & Glatz.)

TANNALBIN. (TANNIN ALBUMINATE.) Pale brown, insoluble, tasteless powder, containing about 50 per cent. of tannin. It is not affected by the gastric juice, but is split up in the intestinal canal; hence is used as intestinal astringent and for diarrhœa. Dose, 15 to 30 grains three to five times daily. 1 oz. cartons, 85c.; 5 grain tablets, bot, of 100.......$1.00
(Knoll & Co. and Merck & Co.)

TANNIGEN. (ACETYLTANNIN.) Grayish powder, insoluble in water, soluble in alcohol; incompatible with alkalies which decompose it. Intestinal astringent in chronic diarrhœa and intestinal diseases of children. Adult dose, 3 to 10 grains, three to six times daily; children, 1-3 to $\frac{1}{2}$ that quantity. 1 oz. bot., per oz....55c. to 75c.
(Continental Color & Chemical Co.)

TANNOPINE. (HEXAMETHYLENETETRAMINE TANNIN.) Brownish powder, insoluble in water, decomposed by alkalies; compound of tannin and urotropine, containing 87 per cent. of tannic acid. Intestinal astringent and disinfectant. Adult dose, 10 to 15 grains; children, 3 to 8 grains four times daily. 1 oz. cartons, per oz................55c. to 75c.
(Continental Color & Chemical Co.)

TESTADEN. Powdered extract of the testicle juice of animals. Used in impotency, neurasthenia and spinal irritation. Dose, 15 grains three to four times daily. 1 oz. vials, $1.30; 4 grain tablets, bot. of 100.$1.30
(Knoll & Co. and Merck & Co.)

THEOBROMINE. White crystalline powder, soluble in ether, but almost insoluble in cold water or alcohol; organic base obtained from seeds of *Theobroma cacao*. Diuretic in dropsy of cardiac and renal affections. Dose, 5 to 8 grains. 1 oz. bot., per oz..........90c.
(Continental Color & Chemical Co. and Merck & Co.)

THEOBROMINE - SODIUM - SALICYLATE. White powder, very soluble in water, decomposed by acid solutions. Diuretic in dropsy of cardiac and renal origin. Dose, 7 to 15 grains. 1 oz. bot., per oz..60c.
(Farbenfabriken of Elberfeld, Continental Color Works and Merck & Co.)

THEOCIN. Fine, colorless crystals; synthetic alkaloid of tea (theophylline); difficultly soluble in alcohol and cold water, more easily in warm water; forms salts with alkalies. Powerful diuretic in doses of 3 to 6 grains, two to three times daily. $\frac{1}{2}$ and 1 oz. bot., per oz..............$2.50 to $2.70
(Continental Color & Chemical Co.)

THEOPHYLLIN. White crystalline needles, soluble in 226 parts of water. Identical with theocin, being the synthetic alkaloid of tea. Diuretic in doses of 4 to 8 grains. 1 oz. vials, $1.40. Theophyllin sodium, 1 oz. vials, $1.50. Theophylline sodium salicylate, 1 oz. vials $1.10
(C. F. Boehringer & Soehne.)

THIGENOL. Dark brown, thick liquid; odorless on use; slight empyreumatic taste; soluble in water, diluted alcohol, glycerin and collodion; same uses as ichthyol. It is the sodium salt of the sulphonic acid of a synthetic sulpho oil. Dose, 3 to 10 grains. 1 oz. bots., per oz., 32c.; 1 lb. tins, per lb....$4.00 Syrup, 6 oz. bots., per doz.$8.00
(Hoffmann-La Roche Chemical Works.)

THIOCOL. (POTASSIUM GUAIACOL SULPHONATE.) White crystalline powder, soluble in water, slightly in alcohol and ether. Used in phthisis and similar diseases which require the creosote or guaiacol treatment; nonirritating and readily assimilable. Dose, 5 to 20 grains three times daily. 1 oz. bot., per oz., $1.40; tablets, 5 grains each, 100 in bot...$1.75
(Hoffmann-La Roche Chemical Works.)

THIOSINAMIN. Colorless crystals, soluble in water, alcohol and ether; used hypodermically for lupus and uterine affections in doses of 1 to 3 grains in 15 per cent. alcoholic or 10 per cent. glycerinated water solution, one injection being given every three days; by the mouth, in capsules containing $\frac{1}{3}$ to 3 grains. 1 oz. vials, per oz. 60c.
(Scherin & Glatz and Merck & Co.)

THYMOXOL. Alcoholic 1 per cent. solution of thymol containing 3 per cent. of hydrogen dioxide; miscible with water. Used in 5 or 10 per cent. solutions as antiseptic and bactericide. $\frac{1}{4}$ lb. bot., per lb...$2.40
(C. Bischoff & Co.)

THYRADEN. Brownish powder; dried extract of sheep's thyroid, containing all the constituents of the gland. Used in myxœdema, obesity, goitre, psoriasis, eczema, menorrhagia and rickets. Dose, 15 to 30 grains daily. 1 oz. vials, $1.30; 2 grain tablets, bot. of 100.75c.
(Knoll & Co. and Merck & Co.)

THYREOIDECTIN. Reddish powder obtained from the blood of animals deprived of the thyreoid gland. A remedy for exophthalmic goitre. Dose, 5 to 10 grains. Capsules, 5 grains each, bot. of 50...$1.00
(Parke, Davis & Co.)

THYROIDIN. Dried extract of sheep's thyroid, 1 part equaling 6 parts of fresh gland. Used in myxœdema, cretinism, psoriasis, obesity, lupus, etc. Dose, ½ to 1 grain, increased to 2 grains three times daily. 1 oz. bot.....................$1.25
(Merck & Co.)

TONOLS. Trade name adopted by Schering & Glatz for the glycerophosphate salts. See under the name of the alkali earth or metallic base.

TRIFERRIN. (IRON PARANUCLEINATE.) Brownish-yellow powder, soluble in alkaline solutions, insoluble in water. Said to contain 22 per cent. of iron, 9 per cent. of nitrogen and 2.5 per cent. of phosphorus. Used in anæmia, chlorosis and debility in dose of 5 grains three times daily. 1 oz. cartons, $1.00; 5 grain tablets, cartons of 50, 75c.; solution (Triferrol), 8 oz. bot., per bot..55c. (C. Bischoff & Co. and Knoll & Co.)

TRIKRESOL. Clear, colorless liquid; a mixture of ortho, meta and para cresols in the proportion of 35, 40 and 25 per cent., respectively. Corresponding to Creosol, U. S. P., viii; soluble in 40 parts of water. Said to have three times the germicidal power of carbolic acid. Solutions of from ⅕ to 1 per cent. strength are recommended for surgical use; for internal use 1 to 2 minims three times a day. 1 oz. vials, 15c.; 1 lb. bot.....................60c.
(Schering & Glatz.)

TRIOTONOL. Tablet consisting of 5 grains duotonol and 1-60 grain strychnine-tonol. Nerve tonic. Dose, 1 to 2 tablets, thrice daily. Bottle of 100 tablets ....75c.
(Schering & Glatz.)

TRIPHENIN. (PROPIONYLPHENETIDIN.) White crystalline powder obtained by the action of propionic acid on paraphenetidine; almost insoluble in water (1 in 2000), more readily in alcohol and ether. Is a strong antipyretic, used in neuralgias and rheumatism in doses of 5 to 15 grains three or four times daily. Tablets, 5 grains, bot. of 50, 65c.; 1 oz. cartons..50c.
(Merck & Co.)

TROPACOCAINE HYDROCHLORIDE. (BENZOYLPSEUDOTROPEINE HYDROCHLORIDE.) Colorless crystals, soluble in water. Local anæsthetic like cocaine, but said to be less depressing to the heart. Used hypodermically in 3 to 10 per cent. solutions in 0.6 per cent. solution of sodium chloride. 5 grain vials, 40c.; 15 grain vials ....95c.
(Merck & Co.)

TUMENOL. Reddish-brown, oily paste, obtained from a bituminous rock deposit. Consists of a mixture of sulphonized hydrocarbons similar to ichthyol, and possessing similar properties, being antiseptic and healing in skin diseases, applied either as attenuated powder, 5 per cent. ointment, or dissolved in ether and alcohol or water and glycerine.

AMMONIUM. Black, viscid, oily liquid, odorless; soluble in water and miscible with oils and fats. Used as antiseptic application in skin diseases, in form of ointment, paste or glycerin-ethereal solution painted on surface. 1 oz. bottles.....25c.

OIL is a dark yellow fluid of thick consistency, having the same application as the foregoing.

POWDER. (SULPHOTUMENOLIC ACID.) Dark yellow powder, readily soluble in water. Used with equal parts of zinc starch paste in treatment of skin diseases. Paste, 1 oz. vials, 55c.; ¼ lb. jar, $1.75; ½ lb. jar, $3.25. Oil, 1 oz. vials, 65c.; ¼ lb. bottles, $3.25; 1 lb. bottles, $6.80. Powder, 1 oz. tin, $1.10; 2 oz. tins, per tin..$1.85
(Victor Koechl & Co.)

URITONE. White crystalline powder; a product of formaldehyde and ammonia, of the same composition and properties as hexamethylene tetramine; used in treatment of purulent conditions of the urine, cystitis, etc., in doses of 5 to 15 grains. 1 oz. vials, 60c.; 5 grain capsules, per bot. of 100, 85c.; compressed tablets, 7½ grs., each, per bot of 100.....$1.00
(Parke, Davis & Co.)

UROSINE. (LITHIUM QUINATE.) Colorless crystals, readily soluble in water. Used in gout, cystitis and uric acid diathesis. Supplied in effervescent tablets containing quinic acid, 7½ grains; lithium carbonate, 1½ grains; sugar, 4½ grains. Vial of 10, 50c.; 25, $1.20. Powder, 1 oz. vial.....................95c.
(C. Bischoff & Co.)

UROTROPIN. (HEXAMETHYLENETETRAMINE.) Colorless granular crystals, with an alkaline reaction; readily soluble in water. Urinary antiseptic in cystitis, bacteruria, phosphaturia, gout, rheumatism, irritable bladder, etc., used also before and after instrumentation to forestall urinary infection. Dose, 5 to 15 grains. 1 oz. vials, 60c.; lb., $7.50; tablets, 7½ grains each, 20 tablets in box, 25c.; 5 grains each, 30 tablets in box..........25c.
(Schering & Glatz.)

UROTROPIN METHYLENE CITRATE. (NEWUROTROPIN.) Crystals resembling urotropin and having same therapeutic indications, though dose is double, being 15 grains three times daily. 1 oz. vials, 60c.; tablets, 7½ grains, 20 tablets in box, per box..............25c.
(Schering & Glatz.)

VALIDOL. (VALERIC ACID MENTHYL ESTER.) Colorless liquid, a combination of valeric acid and menthol; insoluble in water, readily soluble in alcohol. Used in hysteria and neurasthenia in doses of 10 to 15 drops three times daily. Vials, 10 Gm., 50c.; 25 Gm., $1.20; pills, 25 in bot., each......50c.
(C. Bischoff & Co.)

VALIDOL CAMPHORATE. Colorless liquid, insoluble in water, readily soluble in alcohol and oils. A 10 per cent. solution of camphor in validol. Used in toothache by local application and internally in same indications and dose as validol. Vials, 10 Gm. each, 50c.; 25 Gm. $1.20
(C. Bischoff & Co.)

VALYL. (VALERIC ACID DIETHYLAMIDE.) Colorless, oily liquid, with a valerian odor and burning taste, supplied only in gelatin capsules, each containing 2 grains. Nerve sedative used in hysteria, neurasthenia, hypochondriasis, and in neuralgia and menstrual disturbances in doses of 2 or 3 capsules two or three times daily. Bot. of 50 capsules........90c.
(Victor Koechl & Co.)

VERONAL. White crystalline powder, soluble in 150 parts of cold and 12 parts of boiling water. Hypnotic in simple sleeplessness and the insomnia of mania. Dose, 5 to 15 grains, dissolved in hot fluids. 1 oz. bot. and cartons, per oz., $1.60; tablets, 5 grains each, tube of 10, 30c.; bot. of 100 ....$2.25
(Merck & Co. and Continental Color & Chemical Co.)

VIOFORM. (IODOCHLOROXYCHINOLINE.) Greenish-yellow powder, insoluble in water. Used in same way as iodoform, than which it is six times lighter and bulkier. 1 oz. cartons $1.15
(C. Bischoff & Co.)

XEROFORM. (TRIBROMPHENOLBISMUTH.) Yellow, insoluble powder, containing bismuth oxide and tribromphenol in nearly equal proportions. A powerful bactericide used in place of iodoform as a dressing for wounds and internally as an intestinal antiseptic in doses of 5 to 20 grains. 1 oz. vials...50c.
(The Heyden Chemical Works.)

American Druggist "WANTS" Page.

THIS Department is intended to be used as a medium for the exchange or sale of stores, the employment of clerks, and the securing of situations. Suitable notices of moderate length under this heading inserted one time free for subscribers; for each additional insertion Fifty Cents will be charged. Advertisements not in the foregoing classification Forty Cents per line.

SITUATIONS VACANT.

"TADS" are salted peanuts de luxe. Drug salesmen are now earning $10 to $30 weekly selling these goods as a side line. Write us if you are interested. Tads Food Confection Company, 661 Hudson street, New York City.

SALESMEN now calling on the drug trade in Greater New York can secure an advantageous side line on liberal commission; experienced men preferred; splendid opportunity for competent men. Address F. J. J., care AMERICAN DRUGGIST.

REGISTERED PHARMACISTS and drug employees, if you would accept a better position, now or later, send us your name at once; fine openings in all States; salaries, $600 to $2,000 a year; employers referred to competent men free. NATIONAL PHARMACEUTICAL AGENCY, 616 Colonial Security Building, St. Louis, Mo.

WANTED.—Correspondence invited with travelers calling regularly on physicians to take a new and interesting side line. One that appeals to every physician and pays a good profit. Address Chance, care of AMERICAN DRUGGIST.

WANTS COPIES of the *Pharmaceutical Record* for March 31, April 28 and May 5, 1892; also copies of the AMERICAN DRUGGIST for May 25 and June 22, 1893. Address F. L. D., care of AMERICAN DRUGGIST.

SITUATIONS WANTED.

LICENSED PHARMACIST (woman), desires position; registered in New York State, but will go to any State as general all-around clerk; careful prescriptionist, good saleswoman; 15 years' experience; good references. Ella A. Eaton, 708 Montgomery street, Syracuse, N. Y.

BUSINESS OPPORTUNITIES.

$14.40 for $1.00.—Send $1.00 for formula of "X—L" Headache Powders; guaranteed cure; 1 gross of 10-cent packages cost $1.00 to make. Address "C.," 212 Seventeenth avenue, Paterson, N. J.

FOR SALE.—One of the finest drug stores in western New York; cement block; building new; steel ceiling; all fixtures new; everything up to date; hot water, heat, gas or electric lights; insurance, 1 per cent; will sell with or without building. Address V. C. Armes, Gowanda, N. Y.

FOR $25,000, a working interest in a fine wholesale drug business. Address Drugs, care Stringer & Seymour, St. Paul, Minn.

FOR SALE.—$4,000 stock of drugs, wall paper and books; no fountain. Rent $285 per year. Sales about $8,000. Address F. D. Graves, Antwerp, Ohio.

CALIFORNIA BUSINESS.—Chain of eight retail stores and wholesale house doing business of $400,000 annually, capable of indefinite expansion; book value of stock in this corporation in excess of 1.20 dividends, 8 per cent. annually and 10 per cent. to surplus; 65 per cent. of stock will be sold on basis of 105 per share; details furnished those giving assurance of satisfactory financial responsibility. F. A. Pollock, 413 Donohoe Building, San Francisco, Cal.

BIG PAYING BUSINESS for sale; stock comprises drugs, wall paper, paint, books and stationery; sales, $30,000; want to sell and have a good reason for it. Address C. H. Mead, Gouverneur, N. Y.

WANTED.—To correspond with wholesale druggists' sundries salesman with an established trade to handle on commission a new and extremely useful household novelty—a corkscrew and spoonholder combined. Designed to draw corks from medicine bottles and hold spoon in suspension; sells well on sight and yields good profit; the right man can have exclusive sales privilege in his territory. Address A. M. Irvy, Norfolk, Va.

FOR SALE.—San Juan, Porto Rico; only American drug store; established seven years; good business; inventory about $7,500; reason, sickness. P. O. Box 226, San Juan, Porto Rico.

BACK NUMBERS of AMERICAN DRUGGIST for sale. Complete file covering a period of fourteen years in perfect condition and for five years previous to 1892 with a deficiency of six months during that period. What will you give for the entire lot? Address S. H. M., care of AMERICAN DRUGGIST.

WANTED.—To sell an International Correspondence School scholarship in chemistry and chemical tech.; 9 bound volumes, costing $180. Expect to go to resident school, so cannot work on course. Have not as yet started on course, so buyer can start at beginning. Write me what you will give. H. Brinkman, Napoleon, Ohio.

SPLENDID OPENING in health resort at the Berkshire Hills for a competent pharmacist. With capital of $500 a well established stand can be secured, including a small stock. Rental merely nominal. The opening is due to the death of the proprietor, who has made from $1,500 to $2,000 per year on an investment of a little over $500. Delightful location in one of the healthiest sections in the Berkshire Hills. Golden opportunity for a hustler. For particulars address "Gordon," care of AMERICAN DRUGGIST.

Granular Effervescent Salts
TWO
NEW FORMULAS
which we are directing to the attention of the physicians of the country and which are certain to be in large demand.
SALINE LAXATIVE.
Each drachm represents:
Sodium Phosphate, 20 grains.
Magnesium Sulphate, 25 grains.
Sodium Sulphate, 10 grains.
SODIUM PHOSPHATE, CONCENTRATED.
Each ounce contains:
Sodium Phosphate, 1 ounce.
Supplied in 2-oz. and 4-oz. bottles, with screw-cap measuring cup; also in pound bottles.
PUT THEM ON YOUR "WANT" LIST.
Our Granular Effervescent Salts are a triumph of manufacturing pharmacy. They dissolve with brisk effervescence, yielding snappy, refreshing draughts.
MILK OF BISMUTH
VALUABLE
Antacid and Gastric Sedative
Pharmacists who have not as yet stocked our Milk of Bismuth (a recent acquisition to our list) are advised to do so, and to notify their medical patrons of their ability to supply it.
Milk of Bismuth (P., D. & Co.) is of marked usefulness in the treatment of gastroenteric diseases, diarrheas, dysentery, etc.
NET PRICES.
Pint bottles, per dozen, $8.50. 5-pint bottles, each, $3.25.
Gallon bottles, each, $4.70.
PARKE, DAVIS & COMPANY
LABORATORIES: DETROIT, MICH., U.S.A.; WALKERVILLE, ONT.; HOUNSLOW, ENG.
BRANCHES: NEW YORK, CHICAGO, ST. LOUIS, BOSTON, BALTIMORE, NEW ORLEANS, KANSAS CITY, INDIANAPOLIS, MINNEAPOLIS, MEMPHIS, LONDON, ENG.; MONTREAL, QUE.; SYDNEY, N.S.W.; ST. PETERSBURG, RUSSIA; SIMLA, INDIA; TOKIO, JAPAN.
MILK OF BISMUTH
EACH FLUIDRACHM REPRESENTS THE BISMUTH EQUIVALENT OF 5 GRAINS BISMUTH SUBNITRATE.
DOSE:
ONE-HALF TEASPOONFUL TO ONE TABLESPOONFUL.
SHAKE THE BOTTLE
PARKE, DAVIS & CO
DETROIT, MICH., U.S.A.

A Visitor from Mexico Looking for American Connections.

Juan Reichmann, the principal partner of the firm of Edward Bremer & Co.'s Successors, Monterey, Mexico, was among the visitors in attendance at the twenty-fourth annual meeting of the Proprietary Association of America, a report of which appears in another column. Mr. Reichmann is a frequent visitor to the American markets, as he has very large and important connections with American manufacturers of proprietary preparations, his firm making a special feature of the manufacturing in Mexico of proprietary preparations of foreign origin, the importation of which into Mexico is rendered practically impossible, on account of the stringent tariff regulations. Among the accounts carried by Mr. Reichmann's firm are those of the Peruna Drug Mfg. Company, the J. C. Ayer Company, Hall & Ruckel, the Herpicide Company and other equally well-known American proprietors.

Mr. Reichmann is a thorough cosmopolitan, being a native of Hamburg, where he was for three years associated with the Hamburg house of Carlos Felix & Co., of Mexico City. About 23 years ago he went out to their main house in Mexico and after five years with that firm he became a partner in the firm of Edward Bremer & Co., with whom he has been associated ever since. Mr. Reichmann is here with the purpose of expanding his American connections, and has already added several important accounts to his list of proprietors, and hopes to add a number of others before his return to Mexico, and for that purpose will visit all the principal manufacturing centers in the United States before his return.

AS OTHER SEE US.

A Distinguished French Novelist on New York Window Dressing.

The tone of M. Paul Adam's recent work on America is generally appreciative, but there are exceptions. The following is from his description of the New York thoroughfares:

The appearance of the shop windows is similar to the Faubourg Montmartre. One often sees things negligently thrown in large heaps, as if, in his haste to offer his bargains to the passer-by, the shopkeeper had not had leisure to arrange his goods. This disorder accords with the character of the middle classes, who have no patience. It reveals to them the logical and practical spirit of the shopkeeper and inspires their confidence. At the pharmacist's—where one can stand and drink all the spirits, taste all the ices, choose writing paper, brushes, stamps and ointments, as well as remedies—the medley in the counter cases seems inextricable. Most of the shops, even in the finer streets, look like French "bazars," to which glass fronts have been added.

Neglect of Correspondence a Fault of American Exporters.

There is a blunt directness about business methods in America that does not meet with the approval of the Latin nations generally, with whom courtesy and politeness are carried into business as well as into social relations. This militates against the growth of our export trade. But aside from the mere question of politeness our exporters have been accused of many more serious faults in the matter of correspondence. In fact, if we may believe the reports that reach us from travelers, but few American houses make any serious effort to adjust their correspondence to the wishes or convenience of their foreign customers. When letters are received in a foreign language they should as a rule be answered in the same language.

It is also common for foreign importers to request quotations, including inland and ocean freight and marine insurance, in order that they may ascertain the cost of the goods delivered at their seaport. Probably in three-quarters of the cases this request for information is wholly ignored by the American, usually on the ground that he has not at hand the information which would enable him to estimate freight charges. This excuse is as ridiculous as it is shiftless, for correspondence with the steamship companies or forwarders could easily bring to hand the information, with which in his possession the foreign importer could form some adequate idea of the actual cost of the merchandise to him.

Another failing of the American, says the *Commercial*, is his negligence in the matter of explaining technical terms or trade phrases which may be well understood here, but meaningless abroad. This applies not only to statements of terms, discounts, etc., but also to catalogue announcements which, although plain to the man who makes the goods, might be entirely without sense to the man who might buy them. Contradictory statements as between catalogue and letter are also complained of frequently, as in the case of a firm which in its catalogue makes prices f. o. b. factory, and in its letter offers export figures f. o. b. seaport. Blunt and tactless statements of terms of payment are also very much too common in the letters of exporters. In his domestic business the manufacturer would know how to be polite when refusing to extend credit, and no reason appears why he should not be equally considerate of his foreign customer's feelings.

One item of information which would always interest the buyer very largely, and which would require but a brief paragraph in any business letter, is that with reference to export packing. If the manufacturer gives particular attention to this important detail, he could make it known to his prospective customer with great advantage both to himself and to the customer.

Foreign merchants are, as a class, much more punctilious in their observance of business etiquette than Americans, and for this reason their correspondence is usually much pleasanter reading. They are extremely quick to detect any lack of business courtesy on the part of their correspondents and even inclined to resent as a personal affront the somewhat brusque statements often found in American business letters. This goes a long way toward explaining why some export advertisers, although they may receive many replies to their advertisements, rarely succeed in establishing lasting business relations with those who answer their advertisements.

Sent to San Francisco.

枯裏都連杷臣
(CREOLIN-PEARSON)
用水攪勻
此藥專治傳染感
冒一切不潔之症
藥料一大玻璃杯
之一半能開四卡
倫水之多極有功
力謹佈

A large quantity of Creolin-Pearson, enough to make over half a million pounds of this ideal disinfectant, was donated and forwarded by Merck & Co. to the authorities of San Francisco immediately after the earthquake and fire had destroyed that beautiful city. The shipment was accompanied by instructions as to its most effective use, printed in several languages. The accompanying illustration, giving directions in Chinese for the use of Creolin, shows that the Celestials were not forgotten.

Declarations of Origin.

The secretary of the South African section of the London Chamber of Commerce recently addressed the Controller of Customs, Cape Town, on the subject of declarations of origin, stating that that department had refused to accept a supplier's certificate of origin, but demanded the actual manufacturers' certificate. In reply the controller says that under the British preferential tariff "it is stipulated that the certificate of origin must be signed either by the manufacturer or supplier. It very often happens, however, that persons who are not suppliers, but merely buy on commission, represent themselves as such, consequently the certificate signed by them is refused."

Cuticura People Lose.

The makers of the Cuticura remedies have been decided against in a suit for damages brought by them against the Williams Soap Company, of Indianapolis. It was charged that the "Hood's Cuticle Soap," made by the defendant, was a fraudulent imitation of Cuticura Soap.

The University of Illinois.

(From our Regular Correspondent.)

Chicago, May 9.—The forty-sixth commencement exercises of the School of Pharmacy of the University of Illinois took place April 26, in Steinway Hall. The principal address was delivered by Prof. Edward Kremers, Ph.D., of the University of Wisconsin. The salutory was delivered by Albert G. C. Ackermann and the valedictory by Claude E. Tilton. The degrees were conferred by President James. Prizes were awarded, as follows: Alumni medal, Claude E. Tilton; Biroth prize, F. M. F. Meixner; Scarle & Hereth prize, Claude E. Tilton; Becker prize, Charles D. Gauthier; Pharmacy prize, Ethelyn B. Arnold. A banquet followed at the Hamilton Club, at which Dr. A. W. Baer was toastmaster.

The following members of the class received the degree of Graduate of Pharmacy:

*A. G. C. Ackermann, Quincy; Emilio Alfaro, Barros, P. R.; W. E. Anderson, Kasson, Minn.; *Ethelyn B. Arnold, Watseka; Allen Beckett, Chicago; E. S. Bourne, Lewis, Ind.; F. E. Bucklin, Chicago; H. G. Carlson, Moline; D. T. Cropp, Chicago; G. G. Dale, Chicago; L. B. Fox, Chicago; N. G. Fry, Chicago; *C. D. Gauthier, Green Bay, Wis.; E. E. Grebel, Beaver Dam, Wis.; *W. Grimes, Clinton; L. M. Haeseler, Lisbon, Iowa; G. F. Haffner, Farmer City; C. E. Hoffman, Plymouth, Wis.; D. L. Holland, Chicago; L. G. Jacobs, Chicago; D. G. Knoblock, South Bend, Ind.; F. F. Krueger, Seymour, Ind.; H. J. Krueger, Chicago; J. E. Laats, Chicago; Hugh McCaslin, Nokomis; C. G. McDow, C. Juarez, Mexico; D. G. Machenheimer, Carmi; W. S. Mayhew, Kasson, Minn.; *F. M. F. Meixner, Chillicothe; *W. A. Murray, Traverse City, Mich.; *Rolf Reite, Cooperstown, N. D.; J. W. Robinson, Peru; G. W. Seifried, Chicago; *Paul Seyfert, Thiensville, Wis.; Otto Shatzkis, Chicago; L. L. Taylor, Havana; G. E. White, Chicago; J. P. Wiltgen, Chicago; E. J. Mercil (Class of '02), Chicago; C. Demes (Class of '04), Chicago; W. J. Leiner (Class of '04), Ottawa; H. J. Schumm (Class of '04), La Porte, Ind.; Charles Venn (Class of '04), Chicago; H. A. Watson (Class of '04), Chicago; C. W. Boyce (Class of '05), Chicago; J. R. Hall (Class of '05), Bloomington; W. M. E. Hawk (Class of '05), Kittanning, Pa.; J. M. Honsik (Class of '05), Chicago; E. A. Lukesek (Class of '05), Chicago; R. F. Mayfield (Class of '05), Mt. Vernon; J. K. Parker (Class of '05), Griggsville; James Patejdl (Class of '05), Chicago.

The following received a certificate of having finished the course successfully. They will receive the degree when the required age and practical experince are attained:

F. A. Crawford, Herscher; R. G. Mrazek, Chicago; Martin Schupmann, Chicago; Edward De Stefano, Chicago; *G. E. Tilton, Fairmount.

Class honors for excellence in scholarship were awarded those where names are starred.

Hints to Buyers.

Joseph Koehler, 146 Park Row, New York, makes a combination offer of 625 cards, retailing at $15.75, with a revolving rack, for $7 for the entire outfit. This offers an excellent opportunity for the druggist to make a trial in this field at a very small expenditure.

In ordering ointment boxes be sure to specify "Mount Washington." These goods are made in all sizes, from one-quarter ounce to sixteen ounces, and in black walnut and silver poplar. They possess a particularly desirable feature in the snug fitting of their covers and they are practically impervious, even to oils.

A useful catalogue of soda fountain supplies is issued by the Churchill Drug Company, of Burlington and Cedar Rapids, Iowa. It is fully illustrated and informing regarding prices. We presume that druggists doing business in the territory covered by this firm would be sent copies of the catalogue on request.

The Fischer Chemical Importing Company, of 14 Platt street, New York City, is the sole agent of the United States and Canada for a line of German chemicals and pharmaceuticals of peculiar value, among which may be named uricedin stroschein. Interesting and instructive literature on this line may be obtained by addressing the house.

The attention of our readers is invited to the pharmaceutical waxes prepared and marketed by W. H. Bowdlear & Co., of Boston, Mass. This concern has been manufacturing these goods for a great many years and has established for itself a reputation for first-class work. The advertisement of the company will be found on the front cover of the present issue.

Wire chairs and furniture have effected a revolution in store fittings, as these chairs and tables are light, take up but little space, are very durable and are artistic and inexpensive. For particulars regarding this style of furniture, which is particularly well adapted for warm climates, our readers should address the Chicago Wire Chair Company, 66 North Jefferson street, Chicago.

The Garfield remedies constitute a line of popular preparations which have a large and constantly growing sale. The manufacturers are desirous of establishing agencies, and with that object in view will offer unusual inducements to responsible pharmacists who will write them promptly. They will carry on a liberal campaign of advertising and will be pleased to furnish details of their scheme of introduction, with terms to agents.

A line of fine balances which has stood the test of nearly 50 years certainly deserves consideration at the hands of pharmacists who wish to secure the very best results in the purchase of a fine balance. A handsome and instructive catalogue of such a line will be sent free of cost to our readers who correspond with Herman Kohlbusch, 190 Broadway, New York, mentioning the AMERICAN DRUGGIST.

The Whitall-Tatum Company, of New York, are probably the largest manufacturers of druggists' sundries and glassware in the world. They certainly have a very complete line, and druggists can write them with assurance that they will get not only a full assortment to choose from, but will get a good article at a fair price. Write them for illustrated catalogue, which will be found to be very instructive.

$5.00 in Your Pocket.

This is the alluring title of a very clever advertising folder recently issued by the Liquid Carbonic Company. If you have not already received one write for a copy to the Chicago office, mentioning the AMERICAN DRUGGIST. It contains some valuable suggestions for the soda fountain counter.

Satisfactory Showcases.

Many druggists wish to purchase an extra showcase or two during the spring months and naturally are somewhat in doubt as to where they can be sure of being thoroughly suited in style, materials, finish, details of construction and price.

The showcases manufactured by John Phillips & Co., Limited, Detroit, Mich., have a guarantee of 43 years' reputation, and 43 years of satisfied customers throughout the country. Every detail of construction of the Phillips cases is just as it should be. Nothing is left to be desired. Their catalogue will be sent for the asking—a postal card will do. The case illustrated above, which is intended for the proper display of novelties, sells for $6.50. Is not that an attractive combination of quality and price?

A Revolving Post Card Display Stand.

The improved Paragon Revolving Post Card Display Stand is in great demand and has proved a great post card seller. Write to the American News Company, New York City, asking for special introductory terms on this stand, with a supply of cards.

A New Fountain for Caswell, Massey & Co.

Caswell, Massey & Co., of New York, have placed an order for a new "Innovation" soda fountain with W. J. McCahill, New England sales manager of the American Soda Fountain Company. While Hegeman & Co. are noted for the immense volume of their business the firm of Caswell, Massey & Co. has an equal reputation for doing perhaps the most exclusive business, having served since 1780 the elite of New York.

Stood the Test.

The investigations prompted by State and national measures have necessitated critical examinations of various proprietary preparations as to their purity and fitness. Notable instances of such work were the investigations of the Ohio Pure Food Commission, the State Board of Health of Pennsylvania and more recently the Illinois Pharmacy Board. In each instance Vin Mariani, analyzed from examples purchased in the open market, was proved to be precisely as represented and in conformity with the strict governmental analysis enacted in France, Germany, Russia and elsewhere in Europe.

This clearly indicated that the high standard of this preparation, established nearly half a century ago, continues unaltered, and is a justification for the distinctive endorsements which physicians everywhere have voluntarily accorded this restorative-tonic.

Worth Thinking About.

A farmer who has a good, profitable field doesn't let half of it lie idle. A merchant doesn't rent a store and leave half his showcases empty. But a good many druggists give a certain space to a soda fountain and make only half the profit they might. Suppose a druggist has a wall fountain in his store that he has had for eight or ten years. He sells a good many glasses of soda water, at a fair percentage of profit. But if he replaced the old apparatus with a thoroughly modern equipment the same would bring him in 100 per cent. more profit.

That these possibilities of increased sales with the modern equipment have become actual facts is proved by the reports of many druggists. The American Soda Fountain Company, the originators and manufacturers of the Innovation apparatus, stand ready at all times to give interested druggists proof of the practical profit power of their latest models. Write them for advice, stating the condition existing in your store.

The Right Way is Really the Cheapest.

The dispenser of soda water has in most cases by this time satisfactorily adjusted the question of apparatus for the soda season now opening. The next important matter is that of his fountain supplies. These should be as good as money and brains can make them. Some few dispensers prepare their own fruits and syrups, with more or less success, but to get the best results there are required years of practical experience in extract and fruit syrup making and close application to the production of a pure, wholesome and thoroughly high-grade article.

The large soda fountain supply manufacturers, who buy their fruits, sugar and other materials in carload lots, employ expert extract makers, and who have reduced this proposition to an absolute science, can usually furnish a superior product at less cost than the dispenser can make it himself. If you have not in your employ a practical syrup man the preparation of fruits and syrups for the fountain—buying the fruits, handling them, keeping a long list of necessary supplies on hand—is a slow process and quite apt to be not in any respect satisfactory. Liquid fruits and Diamond brand crushed fruits, prepared by the Liquid Carbonic Company, are the results of years of experience and careful consideration of the dispenser's needs. They are prepared in one of the finest equipped fruit laboratories in existence and are free from adulteration of any description. Valuable information concerning the "Liquid's" fruits and syrups or anything else needed at the fountain can be secured through a simple request on a postal card to one of the "Liquid's" branch houses, at Chicago, New York, Pittsburgh, St. Louis, Milwaukee, Cincinnati, Baltimore, Minneapolis, Kansas City, Atlanta and Dallas. Always write the nearest branch to insure prompt reply.

An Active Liver Means a Clear Head.

Schenck's Mandrake Liver Pills have enjoyed a large sale for the last 60 or 70 years. They are guaranteed to be purely vegetable and to be the most perfect substitute for calomel as a cholagogue. They act directly and promptly and are invaluable in all forms of malarial disease. The manufacturers, Dr. J. H. Schenck & Son, of Philadelphia, wish to introduce these pills wherever they are not sold and will make most satisfactory terms. Please mention the AMERICAN DRUGGIST when writing them.

A Practical Contribution.

On the day following the earthquake at San Francisco Borden's Condensed Milk Company contributed to the sufferers and had under way to the devastated city from one of its Pacific Coast factories two carloads of condensed milk and cream, aggregating 50,000 cans, the value of which was more than $5,000.

Borden's Condensed Milk Company has further authorized the Johnson-Locke Mercantile Company, who is its Pacific Coast representative, to donate and charge to its account $1,000 worth of Borden's malted milk for the benefit of the sufferers from earthquake and fire in the various devastated towns on the Pacific Coast.

Speaking of milk, the three-page illustrated article which appears in the April 26 issue of *Leslie's Weekly*, relating to the methods employed in the production of the products of Borden's Condensed Milk Company, is an article which every one should read who is interested in the problem of pure food.

Those Funny Cat Cards.

Among the inquiries concerning the series of cat pictures put upon the market by the Rotograph Company, 684 Broadway, New York, this has frequently occurred, "How did any one ever get those cats to pose?" A special request for an explanation was sent to the man who took the pictures, and this was his reply: "There are difficulties in connection with some of the pictures, but they are not what most people would anticipate. For instance, the picture, 'After the Battle,' necessitated my getting up at 5 o'clock in the morning. This was not the worst part, though. I had not slept a wink all night. Mr. Thomas Cat, our family pet, and Mr. John Puss, who lives next door, are rivals for the affections of Miss Kitty White, a charming young lady, who lives down the street. There had been bad blood between Tom and John for a long time, and they arranged to settle the affair on our back fence one night. They came armed to the claws, and through many long and weary hours, while every one in the block tossed sleeplessly in bed, they had it out. Oh, if they had only had it in! Behind closed doors, for instance, a padded cell would have been just the thing. Not that they were so awfully fierce to each other, though, excepting in their language. Which shows how much like human prize-fighters cats can be. Oh, yes, they were prize-fighters, all right. Miss Kitty White was the prize." The cat cards sell well wherever shown. Write for a free sample to the Rotograph Company, 684 Broadway, New York.

salicylic and benzoic acids with thymol. Antiseptic, expectorant, analgetic, sedative, antipyretic and cardiotonic. Indicated in the treatment of asthma, bronchitis, pertussis, pneumonia, influenza, typhoid fever and in rheumatic and neuralgic affections. Dose, 7½ to 15 grains, thrice daily, dry or in cold liquids. 1 oz. vial, 70c.; tube of 20 tablets..............30c.
(Schering & Glatz.)

QUARTONOL. Tablets consisting of a compound of duotonol, quinine tonol and strychnine tonol. Blood and nerve tonic. Dose, 1 to 2 tablets three times daily. Bottle of 100 5-grain tablets ....75c.
(Schering & Glatz.)

QUININE LYGOSINATE. Orange-yellow, amorphous powder, containing 70.8 per cent. of quinine; difficultly soluble in water, readily soluble in alcohol, chloroform and benzin. Nontoxic antiseptic and styptic, employed as a dusting powder, gauze or suppository. 10 Gm. vials, each...............70c.
(C. Bischoff & Co.)

RENADEN. Powder, obtained from extract of pigs' kidneys; used in uræmia and nephritis in doses of 1 to 2 drachms daily. 1 oz. vials, $1.30; 4 grain tablets, bottles of 100 ....$1.30
(Knoll & Co. and Merck & Co.)

RUBIDIUM IODIDE. Colorless, cubical crystals; soluble in less than 1 in 1 of water; bitter, saline taste. Used in place of potassium iodide in polyarthritis and syphilis. Dose, 5 to 20 grains. 1 oz. vial..$1 00
(Merck & Co.)

SAL-ETHYL. A colorless, transparent, volatile fluid; chemically pure ethyl salicylate. A substitute for methyl salicylate or oil of wintergreen. Globules, 5 min., in bot. of 50, per doz. bot. $5.00
(Parke, Davis & Co.)

SALIT. (Salicylic acid ester of borneol.) Oily fluid, insoluble in water, slightly soluble in glycerin and readily soluble in alcohol, ethers and oils. Used in muscular and articular rheumatism, lumbago, neuralgia and rheumatic pains following colds. 1 oz. bot......22c.
(Heyden Chemical Works.)

SALOCREOL. (Salicylic acid ester of creosote.) Oily fluid of neutral reaction, almost odorless, insoluble in water, readily soluble in alcohol, ether, chloroform and oils. Used in facial erysipelas, acute and chronic inflammation of the lymph glands and chronic arthritis. 1 oz. bot........45c.

SALOPHEN. White, crystalline powder, containing 51 per cent. of salicylic acid; almost insoluble in water; soluble in alcohol and ether; incompatible with alkalies, which decompose it. Antipyretic, analgetic and antiseptic in rheumatism and neuralgia. Dose, 10 to 15 grains 3 to 4 times daily. 1 oz. cartons............85c. to $1.00
(Continental Color & Chemical Co.)

SALOQUININE. (Salicylic acid ester of quinine.) Whitish powder, insoluble in water, with difficulty soluble about 1 in 120 of alcohol and ether. Tasteless quinine substitute, used in malaria, tropical fevers, neuralgia and rheumatism. Dose, 15 to 30 grains, one to three times daily. ⅛ and 1 oz. cartons, $1.25 to $1.30
(Continental Color & Chemical Co. and Merck & Co.)

SANTYL. Yellowish, oily liquid, tasteless and nonirritant. Salicylic ester of pure sandalwood oil. Used in acute gonorrhœia and its complications. Dose, 30 drops, thrice daily. Bottle of ½ oz..................$1.00
(Knoll & Co. and Merck & Co.)

SCOPOLAMINE HYDROBROMIDE is identical with hyoscine hydrobromide, but lower in price. 15 grain tubes, each, $3.00; 10 grain tubes, $2.10; 5 grain tubes.....$1.05
(Merck & Co. and C. F. Boehringer & Soehn.)

SEXTONOL. Tablets consisting of a compound of duotonol, quinine tonol, iron tonol, manganese tonol and strychnine tonol. Blood and nerve nutrient. Dose, 1 to 2 5-grain tablets three times daily. Bottle of 100................75c.
(Schering & Glatz.)

SIDONAL. (Piperazine quinate.) White amorphous powder, readily soluble in water. Uric acid solvent in gout and allied affections in doses of 75 to 120 grains a day in divided doses, well diluted with water. 1 oz. bot................$3.75
(Victor Koechl & Co.)

SIDONAL NEW. (Quinic acid anhydride.) Same properties and uses as above. 1 oz. bot. $2.00
(Victor Koechl & Co.)

SILVER CITRATE. (Antiseptic Credé; Itrol.) White powder, soluble about 1 in 4000 of water. Recommended in Credé's treatment as an antiseptic for wounds, in lotion, ointment or powder. For disinfection of hands, skin and instruments, 1 to 1000-5000 watery solution; as gargle 1 to 5000 to 10,000; in gonorrhœa, 1 to 8000. Oz..............$1.20 to $1.25
(Schering & Glatz and Merck & Co.)

SILVER LACTATE. (Actol.) Whitish powder, soluble in 15 parts of water; recommended in solution 1 in 200 to 1000 as an antiseptic for surgical use. ¼ oz. and 1 oz. vials, per oz., $1.30; tablets, 3 grains, boxes containing 5 vials of 10 tablets, per box..................$1.15
(Schering & Glatz and Merck & Co.)

SOMATOSE. Light yellow almost tasteless powder, easily soluble in water, prepared from meat and consisting of deutero and hetero albumoses. Nitrogenous food product for the sick and convalescent. Dose for adults, 90 to 180 grains daily; for children, 50 to 100 grains. 2 oz. tins, per doz., $8.25; ¼ lb. tins, per lb., $5.25; ½ lb. tins, per lb....................$5.00
(Continental Color & Chemical Co.)

SOMNOS. (Trichlorethidene propenyl ether.) [Elixir chlorœthanal alcoholate.] Clear liquid, miscible with water, produced by the synthesis of Trichloraldehyde with a polyatomic alcohol radical. Hypnotic and cerebral sedative in doses of from 2 to 4 fluid drachms. Pint bottles, $1.10 per pint; $12.00 per doz.; 4 oz. bottles, per doz..........$4.00
(H. K. Mulford Co.)

SPIROFORM. White, crystalline powder, insoluble in water, but readily soluble in alcohol and other solvents. Odorless and practically tasteless. Antirheumatic, analgetic, uric acid solvent. Dose, 7½ to 15 grains, three to five times daily. 25 Gm. cartons, 75c.; 7½ grain tablets, cartons of 50.....75c.
(C. Bischoff & Co.)

STOVAINE. (Amylene hydrochloride.) White crystalline powder, readily soluble in wa-

ter and in methyl alcohol; less soluble in ethyl alcohol and almost insoluble in ether. A substitute for cocaine, approximately one-fifth as toxic. Aqueous solutions are slightly acid and bitter to the taste. Put up in solutions of various strengths, ½ per cent., 1 per cent., 10 per cent., in tubes; tablet triturates, 1⅛ grains each; pastilles, 3-100 grain each. Original packages, 1 oz., ½ and ¼ oz. bottles, per oz. $4.00
(Walter F. Sykes & Co.)

STYPTICIN. (Cotarnine hydrochloride.) Yellow amorphous powder, the salt of an opium base (cotarnine is a product of the oxidation of narcotine), soluble in water and alcohol. Because of its chemical resemblance to hydrastinine, it being methoxyldrastine, it is recommended in all forms of uterine hæmorrhage. Used in functional dysmenorrhœa and in the menorrhagia of puberty and the climacteric. Dose as styptic, 1⅛ to 4 grains, as needed, per os or by injection (10 per cent. solution). Sugar coated tablets, ¾ grain, per tube of 20, 25c.; 1 oz. bottles, per oz., $6.50; ½ oz. bottles, per oz., $6.60; ⅛ oz., per oz., $7.00; 15 grain vials, each, 35c.; hypodermic tablets, ¾ grain, per box of 40 (4 tubes).......60c.
(Merck & Co.)

STYPTOL. (Cotarnine phthalate.) Yellow, crystalline powder, readily soluble in water. It is the phthalate salt of an opium base. Recommended in uterine hæmorrhage in doses of 1 to 3 grains; externally in 10 per cent. solution. 1 oz. vials, $6.50; ¼ oz., per oz., $6.75; ⅛ oz., $7.00; 15 grain vials, per vial, 35c.; ¾ grain tablets, bottles of 100, per bot....$1.20
(Knoll & Co. and Merck & Co.)

STYRACOL. (Guaiacol cinnamic ester.) White granular crystals, insoluble in water, readily soluble in alcohol. Given in phthisis, catarrh of the stomach and intestines in doses of 15 grains three to four times daily. 1 oz. cartons, $1.20; 5 grain tablets, bot of 100..$1.40
(Knoll & Co. and Merck & Co.)

SUBLAMINE. (Mercuric ethylene-diamine sulphate.) Crystalline powder, containing 43 per cent. of mercury; very soluble in water. Used in solutions of 1 to 1000 as a substitute for corrosive sublimate. 1 oz. vials, 50c.; tablets, 15 grains, 100 tablets in bottle, $1.10; 20 tablets in tube, 5 tubes in box............$1.60
(Schering & Glatz.)

TANNALBIN. (Tannin albuminate.) Pale brown, insoluble, tasteless powder, containing about 50 per cent. of tannin. It is not affected by the gastric juice, but is split up in the intestinal canal; hence is used as intestinal astringent and for diarrhœa. Dose, 15 to 30 grains three to five times daily. 1 oz. cartons, 85c.; 5 grain tablets, bot, of 100......$1.00
(Knoll & Co. and Merck & Co.)

TANNIGEN. (Acetyltannin.) Grayish powder, insoluble in water, soluble in alcohol; incompatible with alkalies which decompose it. Intestinal astringent in chronic diarrhœa and intestinal diseases of children. Adult dose, 3 to 10 grains, three to six times daily; children, 1-3 to ½ that quantity. 1 oz. bot., per oz....55c. to 75c.
(Continental Color & Chemical Co.)

TANNOPINE. (Hexamethylenetetramine tannin.) Brownish powder, insoluble in water, decomposed by alkalies; compound of tannin and urotropine, containing 87 per cent. of tannic acid. Intestinal astringent and disinfectant. Adult dose, 10 to 15 grains; children, 3 to 8 grains four times daily. 1 oz. cartons, per oz.................55c. to 75c.
(Continental Color & Chemical Co.)

TESTADEN. Powdered extract of the testicle juice of animals. Used in impotency, neurasthenia and spinal irritation. Dose, 15 grains three to four times daily. 1 oz. vials, $1.30; 4 grain tablets, bot. of 100.$1.30
(Knoll & Co. and Merck & Co.)

THEOBROMINE. White crystalline powder, soluble in ether, but almost insoluble in cold water or alcohol; organic base obtained from seeds of *Theobroma cacao*. Diuretic in dropsy of cardiac and renal affections. Dose, 5 to 8 grains. 1 oz. bot., per oz..........90c.
(Continental Color & Chemical Co. and Merck & Co.)

THEOBROMINE - SODIUM - SALICYLATE. White powder, very soluble in water, decomposed by acid solutions. Diuretic in dropsy of cardiac and renal origin. Dose, 7 to 15 grains. 1 oz. bot., per oz..60c.
(Farbenfabriken of Elberfeld, Continental Color Works and Merck & Co.)

THEOCIN. Fine, colorless crystals; synthetic alkaloid of tea (theophylline); difficultly soluble in alcohol and cold water, more easily in warm water; forms salts with alkalies. Powerful diuretic in doses of 3 to 6 grains, two to three times daily. ½ and 1 oz. bot., per oz...............$2.50 to $2.70
(Continental Color & Chemical Co.)

THEOPHYLLIN. White crystalline needles, soluble in 226 parts of water. Identical with theocin, being the synthetic alkaloid of tea. Diuretic in doses of 4 to 8 grains. 1 oz. vials, $1.40. Theophyllin sodium, 1 oz. vials, $1.50. Theophylline sodium salicylate, 1 oz. vials $1.10
(C. F. Boehringer & Soehne.)

THIGENOL. Dark brown, thick liquid; odorless on use; slight empyreumatic taste; soluble in water, diluted alcohol, glycerin and collodion; same uses as ichthyol. It is the sodium salt of the sulphonic acid of a synthetic sulpho oil. Dose, 3 to 10 grains. 1 oz. bots., per oz., 32c.; 1 lb. tins, per lb.....$4.00 Syrup, 6 oz. bots., per doz..$8.00
(Hoffmann-La Roche Chemical Works.)

THIOCOL. (Potassium guaiacol sulphonate.) White crystalline powder, soluble in water, slightly in alcohol and ether. Used in phthisis and similar diseases which require the creosote or guaiacol treatment; nonirritating and readily assimilable. Dose, 5 to 20 grains three times daily. 1 oz. bot., per oz., $1.40; tablets, 5 grains each, 100 in bot...$1.75
(Hoffmann-La Roche Chemical Works.)

THIOSINAMIN. Colorless crystals, soluble in water, alcohol and ether; used hypodermically for lupus and uterine affections in doses of 1 to 3 grains in 15 per cent. alcoholic or 10 per cent. glycerinated water solution, one injection being given every three days; by the mouth, in capsules containing ⅛ to 3 grains. 1 oz. vials, per oz. 60c.
(Scherin & Glatz and Merck & Co.)

THYMOXOL. Alcoholic 1 per cent. solution of thymol containing 3 per cent. of hydrogen dioxide; miscible with water. Used in 5 or 10 per cent. solutions as antiseptic and bactericide. ¼ lb. bot., per lb...$2.40
(C. Bischoff & Co.)

THYRADEN. Brownish powder; dried extract of sheep's thyroid, containing all the constituents of the gland. Used in myxœdema, obesity, goitre, psoriasis, eczema, menorrhagia and rickets. Dose, 15 to 30 grains daily. 1 oz. vials, $1.30; 2 grain tablets, bot. of 100.75c.
(Knoll & Co. and Merck & Co.)

THYREOIDECTIN. Reddish powder obtained from the blood of animals deprived of the thyreoid gland. A remedy for exophthalmic goitre. Dose, 5 to 10 grains. Capsules, 5 grains each, bot. of 50...$1.00
(Parke, Davis & Co.)

THYROIDIN. Dried extract of sheep's thyroid, 1 part equaling 6 parts of fresh gland. Used in myxœdema, cretinism, psoriasis, obesity, lupus, etc. Dose, ½ to 1 grain, increased to 2 grains three times daily. 1 oz. bot................$1.25
(Merck & Co.)

TONOLS. Trade name adopted by Schering & Glatz for the glycerophosphate salts. See under the name of the alkali earth or metallic base.

TRIFERRIN. (IRON PARANUCLEINATE.) Brownish-yellow powder, soluble in alkaline solutions, insoluble in water. Said to contain 22 per cent. of iron, 9 per cent. of nitrogen and 2.5 per cent. of phosphorus. Used in anæmia, chlorosis and debility in dose of 5 grains three times daily. 1 oz. cartons, $1.00; 5 grain tablets, cartons of 50, 75c.; solution (Triferrol), 8 oz. bot., per bot..55c.
(C. Bischoff & Co. and Knoll & Co.)

TRIKRESOL. Clear, colorless liquid; a mixture of ortho, meta and para cresols in the proportion of 35, 40 and 25 per cent., respectively. Corresponding to Creosol, U. S. P., viii; soluble in 40 parts of water. Said to have three times the germicidal power of carbolic acid. Solutions of from ½ to 1 per cent. strength are recommended for surgical use; for internal use 1 to 2 minims three times a day. 1 oz. vials, 15c.; 1 lb. bot....................60c.
(Schering & Glatz.)

TRIOTONOL. Tablet consisting of 5 grains duotonol and 1-60 grain strychnine-tonol. Nerve tonic. Dose, 1 to 2 tablets, thrice daily. Bottle of 100 tablets ....75c.
(Schering & Glatz.)

TRIPHENIN. (PROPIONYLPHENETIDIN.) White crystalline powder obtained by the action of propionic acid on paraphenetidine; almost insoluble in water (1 in 2000), more readily in alcohol and ether. Is a strong antipyretic, used in neuralgias and rheumatism in doses of 5 to 15 grains three or four times daily. Tablets, 5 grains, bot. of 50, 65c.; 1 oz. cartons..50c.
(Merck & Co.)

TROPACOCAINE HYDROCHLORIDE. (BENZOYLPSEUDOTROPEINE HYDROCHLORIDE.) Colorless crystals, soluble in water. Local anæsthetic like cocaine, but said to be less depressing to the heart. Used hypodermically in 3 to 10 per cent. solutions in 0.6 per cent. solution of sodium chloride. 5 grain vials, 40c.; 15 grain vials ....95c.
(Merck & Co.)

TUMENOL. Reddish-brown, oily paste, obtained from a bituminous rock deposit. Consists of a mixture of sulphonized hydrocarbons similar to ichthyol, and possessing similar properties, being antiseptic and healing in skin diseases, applied either as attenuated powder, 5 per cent. ointment, or dissolved in ether and alcohol or water and glycerine.

AMMONIUM. Black, viscid, oily liquid, odorless; soluble in water and miscible with oils and fats. Used as antiseptic application in skin diseases, in form of ointment, paste or glycerin-ethereal solution painted on surface. 1 oz. bottles.....25c.

OIL is a dark yellow fluid of thick consistency, having the same application as the foregoing.

POWDER. (SULPHOTUMENOLIC ACID.) Dark yellow powder, readily soluble in water. Used with equal parts of zinc starch paste in treatment of skin diseases. Paste, 1 oz. vials, 55c.; ¼ lb. jar, $1.75; ½ lb. jar, $3.25. Oil, 1 oz. vials, 65c.; ¼ lb. bottles, $3.25; 1 lb. bottles, $6.30. Powder, 1 oz. tin, $1.10; 2 oz. tins, per tin..$1.85
(Victor Koechl & Co.)

URITONE. White crystalline powder; a product of formaldehyde and ammonia, of the same composition and properties as hexamethylene tetramine; used in treatment of purulent conditions of the urine, cystitis, etc., in doses of 5 to 15 grains. 1 oz. vials, 60c.; 5 grain capsules, per bot. of 100, 85c.; compressed tablets, 7½ grs., each, per bot of 100....$1.00
(Parke, Davis & Co.)

UROSINE. (LITHIUM QUINATE.) Colorless crystals, readily soluble in water. Used in gout, cystitis and uric acid diathesis. Supplied in effervescent tablets containing quinic acid, 7½ grains; lithium carbonate, 1½ grains; sugar, 4¼ grains. Vial of 10, 50c.; 25, $1.20. Powder, 1 oz. vial....................95c.
(C. Bischoff & Co.)

UROTROPIN. (HEXAMETHYLENETETRAMINE.) Colorless granular crystals, with an alkaline reaction; readily soluble in water. Urinary antiseptic in cystitis, bacteruria, phosphaturia, gout, rheumatism, irritable bladder, etc., used also before and after instrumentation to forestall urinary infection. Dose, 5 to 15 grains. 1 oz. vials, 60c.; lb., $7.50; tablets, 7½ grains each, 20 tablets in box, 25c.; 5 grains each, 30 tablets in box..........25c.
(Schering & Glatz.)

UROTROPIN METHYLENE CITRATE. (NEWUROTROPIN.) Crystals resembling urotropin and having same therapeutic indications, though dose is double, being 15 grains three times daily. 1 oz. vials, 60c.; tablets, 7½ grains, 20 tablets in box, per box..............25c.
(Schering & Glatz.)

VALIDOL. (VALERIC ACID MENTHYL ESTER.) Colorless liquid, a combination of valeric acid and menthol; insoluble in water, readily soluble in alcohol. Used in hysteria and neurasthenia in doses of 10 to 15 drops three times daily. Vials, 10 Gm., 50c.; 25 Gm., $1.20; pills, 25 in bot., each.......50c.
(C. Bischoff & Co.)

VALIDOL CAMPHORATE. Colorless liquid, insoluble in water, readily soluble in alcohol and oils. A 10 per cent. solution of camphor in validol. Used in toothache by local application and internally in same indications and dose as validol. Vials, 10 Gm. each, 50c.; 25 Gm. $1.20
(C. Bischoff & Co.)

VALYL. (VALERIC ACID DIETHYLAMIDE.) Colorless, oily liquid, with a valerian odor and burning taste, supplied only in gelatin capsules, each containing 2 grains. Nerve sedative used in hysteria, neurasthenia, hypochondriasis, and in neuralgia and menstrual disturbances in doses of 2 or 3 capsules two or three times daily. Bot. of 50 capsules.......90c.
(Victor Koechl & Co.)

VERONAL. White crystalline powder, soluble in 150 parts of cold and 12 parts of boiling water. Hypnotic in simple sleeplessness and the insomnia of mania. Dose, 5 to 15 grains, dissolved in hot fluids. 1 oz. bot. and cartons, per oz., $1.60; tablets, 5 grains each, tube of 10, 30c.; bot. of 100 ....$2.25
(Merck & Co. and Continental Color & Chemical Co.)

VIOFORM. (IODOCHLOROXYCHINOLINE.) Greenish-yellow powder, insoluble in water. Used in same way as iodoform, than which it is six times lighter and bulkier. 1 oz. cartons $1.15
(C. Bischoff & Co.)

XEROFORM. (TRIBROMPHENOL-BISMUTH.) Yellow, insoluble powder, containing bismuth oxide and tribromphenol in nearly equal proportions. A powerful bactericide used in place of iodoform as a dressing for wounds and internally as an intestinal antiseptic in doses of 5 to 20 grains. 1 oz. vials...50c.
(The Heyden Chemical Works.)

ORIGINAL PACKAGE PRICES.

It should be understood that the prices quoted in this column are strictly those current in the wholesale market, and that higher prices are paid for retail lots. The quality of goods frequently necessitates a considerable range of prices.

Drugs, Chemicals, &c.

Acetanilid	lb.	.21	@	.25
Acetate of Lime:				
Brown	100 lb.	1.60	@	1.65
Gray	100 lb.	2.35	@	2.40
Acetone	lb.	.15½	@	.16
Acetphenetidin (U. S. P. phenacetin)	lb.	1.15	@	...
Acid:				
Acetic Com'l	100 lb.	2.40	@	2.65
Acetic C. P.	lb.	.21	@	.25
Acetic, Glacial		.30	@	.33¼
Aquafortis, 36°	lb.	.03½	@	.04¾
" 40°	lb.	..	@	.06¾
Benzoic, Ger	lb.	.50	@	.51
" Eng	oz.	.10	@	.10¼
Boric, Cryst	lb.	.10	@	.10¾
powd	lb.	.10	@	.10¾
Carbol. cryst., blk	lb.	.14	@	.15
lb. bottle	lb.	.20	@	.22
Chrysophanic		2.50	@	2.65
Citric, dom	lb.	.43	@	.43½
Gallic	lb.	.53	@	.55
Muriatic C. P.	lb.	.07½	@	.08½
Nitric C. P.	lb.	.07½	@	.10
Oxalic, English	lb.	.05½	@	.06
Phosphoric	lb.	.18	@	.21½
Picric	lb.	.30	@	.35
Pyrogallic	lb.	1.65	@	...
Salicylic	lb.	.31	@	.31
Sulphuric, 98%	lb.	.01½	@	.02
Tartaric, crystals	lb.	.27½	@	.28¼
powdered	lb.	.28	@	.28½
Tannic, cryst	lb.	.58	@	.63
Alcohol, grain	gal.	2.47	@	2.49
wood, 95-97%	gal.	.70	@	.73
Aloin	lb.	.45	@	.50
Alum, Lump	100 lb.	1.75	@	1.80
Ground	100 lb.	1.80	@	1.85
Ammon, carb		.08½	@	.08½
" bromide, bulk		.23	@	.24
" iodide, bulk		4.75	@	4.80
Aniline Oil		.09	@	.09¾
Salt		.08½	@	.08¾
Antipyrine (New)	oz.	...	@	.18
Arrowroot, Bermuda	lb.	.38	@	.40
St. Vincent, in bbl	lb.	.06½	@	.08
Arsenic: Red Saxon	lb.	.06½	@	.07¾
White	lb.	.05½	@	.08
Balm of Gilead Buds	lb.	.32	@	.33
Balsam Copaiba, Cent. Amer	lb.	.29	@	.32
Para	lb.	.42½	@	.45
Fir, Canada	gal.	3.00	@	3.10
Fir, Oregon	gal.	.70	@	.80
Peru	lb.	1.00	@	1.05
Tolu	lb.	.20	@	.21
Bark, Angostura	lb.	.35	@	.40
Buckthorn	lb.	.05	@	.05½
Cascara Sag	lb.	.05½	@	.09
Cascarilla	lb.	.10	@	.14
Cotton root	lb.	.08½	@	.10
Cramp	lb.	.07	@	.09
Elm, select	lb.	.16	@	.18
Pine, white	lb.	.05	@	.08
Prickly Ash	lb.	.11	@	.15
Sassafras	lb.	.13½	@	.14
Soap—whole	lb.	.05	@	.05½
Crushed	lb.	.05½	@	.08
White Pine	lb.	.04½	@	.06
Wild Cherry	lb.	.06	@	.09
Bismuth, citrate	lb.	1.75	@	1.80
" ammon cit	lb.	1.85	@	1.90
" subnit	blk.	1.50	@	1.55
" subcarb	lb.	1.75	@	1.80
" subgallate	lb.	1.85	@	1.90
Bleaching Powder, Eng		.01½	@	.01½
German B		.01½	@	.01½
Domestic		.01	@	.01½
Blue Vitriol	lb.	.06	@ .06	1-10
Borax, Refined	lb.	.07½	@	.07¾
powd. conc	lb.	.07½	@	.08
crystals	lb.	.07½	@	.07½
Brimstone, crude 2d	ton.	22.00	@	...
Bromine, bulk	lb.	.22	@	.25
Burgundy Pitch	lb.	.04	@	.04½
Cacao Butter, blk		.28½	@	.30
" " 12 lb. boxes		.34	@	.35
Caffeine	lb.	...	@	2.65
Calcium hypophosphite	lb.	.60	@	.64
Cantharides, Chinese	lb.	...	@	.75
" powd	lb.	.75	@	.77
Russian, whole	lb.	1.20	@	1.25
Cassia Buds	lb.	.18½	@	.19½
Castor Oil, No. 1, bbl	lb.	.11	@	12
" " No. 1, cases	lb.	.11½	@	.12½
" " No. 3, bbl	lb.	.10½	@	.11½
" " No 3, cases	lb.	.10¾	@	.11¾
Caustic Soda	100 lb.	1.70	@	1.75
Chalk, Eng. Precip., bulk	lb.	.06	@	...
Chloral Hydrate, crystals, bulk	lb.	...	@	0.95
crusts, blk	lb.	...	@	0.93
Chloroform, bulk	lb.	.25	@	.30
Cinchonidine Sulph	oz.	.12	@	.15
Cocaine Muriate	oz.	3.00	@	3.25
Codeine Sulph	oz.	3.05	@	3.25
Cod Liver Oil, Norweg.	bbl.	20.00	@	23.00
Newfoundland	bbl.	19.00	@	20.00
Colocynth, Trieste	lb.	.30	@	.32
Spanish	lb.	.25	@	.26
Copperas, car lots	100 lb.	.47½	@	.52
single bbls	100 lb.	.57½	@	.65
Creosote, Beechwood		.85	@	.90
Cream Tartar lb.	powd.	.22½	@	23
Cubeb berries, xx	lb.	.09½	@	.10½
Powdered	lb.	.11	@	.13
Cutch, bales	lb.	.07½	@	.08
boxes	lb.	.05	@	.05½
Cuttle Bone, Trieste	lb.	.16½	@	.17
French	lb.	.12	@	.13
Jewelers', large	lb.	.70	@	....
" small	lb.	.40	@	45
Dextrin	lb.	.05½	@	.06
Divi Divi	ton.	20.00	@	15.00
Dragon's Bl'd, lump	lb.	.15	@	.18
in reeds	lb.	.50	@	.55
Epsom Salts	100 lb.	.85	@	1.00
Ergot, German	lb.	.27	@	.28
Spanish	lb.	...	@	.36
Ergotine, Dom	lb.	4.95	@	5.00
Flowers, Arnica	lb.	.09	@	.10
Flowers—cont'd				
Calendula	lb.	.25	@	.30
Chamomile, Roman	lb.	.16	@	.23
German	lb.	.10	@	.18
Hungarian	lb.	.09½	@	.11
Insect, open	lb.	.15	@	.17
Half closed	lb.	.26	@	.28
Closed	lb.	.28	@	...
Powder	lb.	.14	@	.28
Lavender	lb.	12	@	.13
Select	lb.	.13	@	.20
Saffron, Amer	lb.	1.05	@	1.10
Spanish Alicante	lb.	4.75	@	6.00
" Valencia	lb.	8.00	@	8.50
Formaldehyde	lb.	.09	@	.09¼
Glycerin, C. P. drums	lb.	.11½	@	.11¾
" cans	lb.	.12½	@	.12¾
Grains of Paradise	lb.	.11½	@	.18
Guarana	lb.	.75	@	.80
Gums: Aloes, Cape		.07	@	.08
" Barbadoes	lb.	.16	@	.17
" Curacoa		.05½	@	.06
" Socot	lb.	.18	@	.20
Arabic, 1st pkd	lb.	.39	@	...
" 2d pkd	lb.	.11	@	.23
" sorts	lb.	.06½	@	.11
Asafoetida	lb.	.15	@	.23
Benzoin, Sumatra	lb.	.34	@	.38
Siam	lb.	.90	@	1.00
Camphor, ref'd. blk	lb.	1.00	@	..
cases	lb.	1.00½	@	..
Chicle	lb.	.36	@	.38
Gamboge	lb.	1.05	@	1.10
Guaiac	lb.	.17	@	.23
Kino	lb.	.25	@	.26
Mastic	lb.	.46	@	.48
Myrrh	lb.	.25	@	.28
Olibanum	lb.	.10	@	.15
Sandarac	lb.	.14	@	.18
Senegal, pkd	lb.	.11	@	.13
Tragacanth, Aleppo	lb.	.30	@	.65
Tragacanth, Turkey	lb.	.33	@	.80
Haarlem Oil		3.00	@	3.75
Hypophosphite lime	lb.	.48	@	.50
" potash	lb.	.48	@	.50
" soda	lb.	.48	@	.50
Ichthyol	lb.	4.20	@	4.35
Indigo	lb.	.90	@	1.75
Insect Pwd. pure	lb.	.14	@	.25
Iodine, resub		2.70	@	2.75
Iodoform	lb.	3.00	@	3.05
Iron citrate, U. S. P.	lb.	.....	@	.44
" and ammon. cit	lt.	.....	@	.41
and ammon. citrate (green scales)				
and quinine citrate	lb.	1.18	@	1.23
phosphate, scales	lb.	....	@	.38
pyrophosphate, scales	lb.	....	@	.38
quinine and strychnine citrate	lb.	1.68	@	1.73
Isinglass, Amer	lb.	.75	@	.80
Russian	lb.	4.00	@	4.10
Juniper Berries	lb.	.03½	@	.04
Lanoline	lb.	.60	@	.65
Leaves: Aconite		.05	@	.10
Belladonna	lb.	.10	@	.11
Buchu, short	lb.	.17	@	.20
" long	lb.	....	@	.30
Cannabis Indica, tops	lb.	1.00	@	1.10
Coca, Truxillo	lb.	.17	@	.18
" Huanuco	lb.	.30	@	.38
Damiana	lb.	.08	@	.10
Digitalis	lb.	.05½	@	.09
Grindelia robusta	lb.	.08	@	.09
Horehound	lb.	.04½	@	.06
Hyoscyamus	lb.	.07	@	.08
Jaborandi	lb.	.11	@	.15
Pulsatilla		.07½	@	11
Rose, Red	lb.	.65	@	.70
Senna, pkd, whole	lb.	.20	@	.22
Alexandria, natural	lb.	...	@	...
garbled and sifted	lb.	.15	@	.16
Tinnevelly	lb.	.04	@	.09
Alexandria, siftings	lb.	.05½	@	.06
Stramonium	lb.	.08	@	.08½
Uva ursi	lb.	.03½	@	.08½
Yerba Santa	lb.	.07	@	.07½
Liquorice—mass	lb.	.08	@	.10
Spanish	lb.	.14	@	.20
Imported mass Spanish	lb.	.18	@	.34
Stick, Calabria	lb.	.23	@	.36
Domestic	lb.	.16½	@	.22½
Lithia, carbonate	lb.	1.50	@	1.75
" citrate	lb.	1.15	@	1.25
Lupulin, Ger	lb.	.18	@	.25
Lycopodium	lb.	.47½	@	.50
Magnesia, carb	lb.	.12	@	.15
Manna, large flk	lb.	.45	@	.50
Small flake	lb.	.33	@	.35
Menthol, Japanese	lb.	2.55	@	2.70
Mercurials:				
Blue Pill	lb.	.43	@	.45
Calomel	lb.	.77	@	.79
Corr. Sublim	lb.	.70	@	.72
Mercury and Chalk	lb.	.33	@	.34
Ointment, ½	lb.	.47	@	.48
Ointment, ⅓	lb.	.38	@	.39
Red Precip	lb.	.87	@	.83
White "	lb.	.92	@	.94
Morphine, bulk	oz.	2.10	@	2.20
Eighths	oz.	2.45	@	2.50
Moss, Iceland	lb.	.06	@	.08
Irish	lb.	.06½	@	.08
Irish, bleached	lb.	.09½	@	.10
Naphthaline, flake	lb.	1.90	@	2.00
Ball	lb.	.02½	@	.....
Nux Vomica	lb.	.03½	@	.05
Oil, Anise	lb.	1.30	@	1.35
Almonds, bit, Eng	lb.	5.50	@	5.75
French	lb.	3.55	@	3.60
bit., artificial	lb.	.65	@	1.80
sweet, true	lb.	.37	@	.40
Peach kernels		.19	@	.22
Bay	lb.	2.10	@	2.35
22 oz. bots	bot.	3.25	@	3.35
Bergamot	lb.	2.15	@	2.30
Cajuput	lb.	.54	@	.55
Camphor	lb.	.17½	@	.19
Caraway	lb.	1.15	@	1.40
Cassia 75@80%	lb	77½	@	.78
Oils—cont'd.				
Cedar, pure	lb	60.	@	1.05
red	lb.	.21	@	.25
Citronella	lb.	.40	@	.42
Clove, bud		90	@	.95
Copaiba	lb.	.60	@	.70
Coriander	lb.	8.00	@	11.00
Croton	lb.	.75	@	.80
Cubeb	lb.	.90	@	1.00
Eucalyptus	lb.	.45	@	.60
Geranium	lb.	1.60	@	4.75
Lavender, flowers	lb.	2.00	@	2.25
Lemon	lb.	.65	@	.72½
Lemongrass	lb.	3.00	@	3.10
Mustard	lb.	4.25	@	5.25
Myrbane	lb.	.57	@	.67
Neroli	lb.	45.00	@	57.50
Nutmeg	lb.	.80	@	0.90
Orange, sweet	lb.	2.00	@	2.15
Orange, bitter	lb.	2.30	@	2.40
Origanum	lb.	.18	@	.22
Pennyroyal	lb.	1.70	@	2.25
Peppermint	lb.	2.75	@	3.00
Cases	lb.	3.35	@	3.50
Petit, grain, French	lb.	4.00	@	4.50
" " So. Amer	lb.	2.00	@	2.05
Pimento	lb.	1.80	@	1.90
Rose	oz.	3.50	@	4.50
Rosemary	lb.	.62½	@	.80
Sandalwood	lb.	3.25	@	3.50
Sassafras	lb.	.50	@	.55
" Artificial	lb.	.25	@	.28
Safrol		.35	@	.36
Spearmint	lb.	4.75	@	5.00
Tansy	lb.	3.75	@	4.00
Thyme		1.00	@	1.30
Winterg'n, sweet birch		1.63	@	1.83
" Synthetic	lb.	.37	@	.40
Wood (Chinese)		.08	@	.09
Wormwood		3.25	@	3.50
Wormseed	lb.	3.00	@	3.25
Opium, Nat cases	lb.	2.70	@	2.75
" Ordinary, Job-		2.75	@	2.80
" powdered	lb.	3.20	@	3.25
Orange peel, bit	lb.	.03	@	.04
Sweet	lb.	.04½	@	.10
Petrolatum		.03	@	.08
Phenacetin (see Acetphenetidin)				
Potassium acetate	lb.	.17	@	.18
" bromide		.15	@	.16
" bottles		.25	@	.30
bichromate		.08¼	@	.08¾
chlorate, cryst		.09½	@	....
" powd		.09½	@	....
cyanide		.20	@	.21
hypophosphite		.60	@	.64
iodide bulk		2.15	@	2.20
permanganate	lb.	.09½	@	.10½
Prickly Ash berries		.14	@	.16
Quicksilver flasks	lb.	.56	@	.60
Quinine Sulph., Domestic bulk	oz.	.17	@	.19
German, bulk	oz.	.17	@	.19
German, outside	oz.	.....	@	.17
Java, bulk	oz.	.....	@	.16½
Rochelle Salts	lb.	.20½	@	.21
Root, Aconite	lb.	.09½	@	.10
Alkanet	lb.	.08	@	.09
Althea, cut	lb.	.17	@	.18
Arnica	lb.	.08½	@	.09
Belladonna, Atropa	lb.	.10	@	.12
Blood	lb.	.10	@	.12
Calamus	lb.	.07	@	.08
Calamus, bleached	lb.	.25	@	.35
Colchicum	lb.	.12	@	.15
Calumba	lb.	.04	@	.08
Dandelion, Ger	lb.	.07½	@	.08
Galangal	lb.	.08	@	.08½
Gentian	lb.	.04	@	.04½
Ginger, Ja., blcd	lb.	...	@	.14
unbleached	lb.	.12	@	.14
Ginseng	lb.	6.00	@	7.50
Golden Seal	lb.	1.15	@	1.18
Hellebore, pwd	lb.	.06	@	.07
Helonias	lb.	.42	@	.45
Ipecac, Rio	lb.	1.75	@	1.80
Carthagena	lb.	1.70	@	1.75
Jalap	lb.	12	@	.13
Kava Kava	lb.	.11	@	.12
Liquorice, ord	lb.	.03½	@	.04
Select	lb.	.08½	@	.11
Lovage	lb	.55	@	.56
Mandrake	lb.	.04½	@	.05½
Musk, Russian	lb.	.13	@	.14
Orris, Florentine	lb.	.06	@	.07
Orris, Verona	lb.	.04	@	.08
Pareira Brava	lb.	.10	@	.11
Pink	lb.	.80	@	.85
Rhatany	lb.	.10	@	.12
Rhub., Canton	lb.	.35	@	.40
Shensi	lb.	.65	@	.75
Sars'p'la, Hond	lb.	.26	@	.30
Mexican	lb.	.09½	@	.09¾
Senega	lb.	.56	@	.60
Snake Virgina	lb.	.42	@	.45
Texas	lb.	.39	@	.42
Canada	lb.	13	@	.25
Squill	lb	.13	@	.15
Valerian, Belg	lb.	.08	@	.08½
German	lb.	.17	@	.14
English	lb.	.12	@	.15
Salicine	lb.	3.75	@	4.00
Sal Ammon, lump	lb.	.09½	@	.09¾
Granulated	lb.	.05½	@	.06
Sal Soda, Eng	100 lb	.67½	@	.72½
American	100 lb.	.75	@	.80
Salol	lb.	.90	@	.95
Saltpetre, crude	lb.	.04½	@	.04¾
Refined	lb.	.04½	@	.05½
Santonin, crystals	lb.	9.50	@	9.70
Powdered	lb.	9.70	@	9.90
Saw Palmetto Berries	lb.	.15	@	.20
Seed, Anise Ital	lb.	.08½	@	.10½
German	lb.	.06½	@	.07
Star	lb.	.20	@	.21
Canary, Smyrna	lb.	.04½	@	.04¾
Sicily	lb.	.04½	@	.06
Caraway	lb.	.06	@	.06½
Celery	lb.	.07½	@	.08
Cardamom blchd		.30	@	.75
" Decorticated	lb.	.36	@	.36
Colchicum	lb	.31	@	.36
Seeds—cont'd.				
Coriander	lb	9	@	1½
Bleached	lb.	.05½	@	.10½
Cummin	lb.	.05½	@	.07½
Fennel, Ger	lb.	.09	@	.10
" Italian	lb.	.05	@	.15½
Flax, whole	lb.	6.50	@	6.75
" ground	lb.	.03½	@	.05½
Foenugreek	lb.	.02	@	.02¾
Hemp, Rus	lb.	.03	@	.03½
Millet, nat	lb.	.01½	@	.02
" shld	lb.	.01½	@	.04½
Mustard, Cal. brown	lb.	.04½	@	.04½
Trieste, brown	lb.	.08	@	.08½
Bari, brown	lb.	.04½	@	.05
German, brown	lb.	.02½	@	.05
Western, brown	lb.	.01½	@	.02
Cal. yellow	lb.	.04½	@	.04½
Eng. yellow	lb.	.06	@	.06½
Ger. yellow	lb.	.05½	@	.06½
Poppy, blue	lb.	.05½	@	.05½
Quince, Ger	lb.	.32	@	.34
Rape, Ger	lb.	.02½	@	.03
" Eng	lb.	.04	@	.05
" Amer	lb.	.02½	@	.03
Strophanthus		.45	@	.50
Kombé		1.00	@	1.25
Sunflower		.04½	@	.05
Wormseed, American	lb.	.07	@	.08
" Levant	lb.	.17	@	.20
Seidlitz, Mixture	lb.	.17	@	.17½
Silver, Nitrate	oz.	.41½	@	.45½
Soap, Castile, white	lb.	.10	@	.10½
" green	lb.	.06	@	.10½
" mottled	lb.	.06½	@	.07
Sodium bicarb, Eng		1.37½	@	1.75
" domestic	100 lb.	1.50	@	1.80
" benzoate	lb.	.40	@	.41
" brom. blk	lb.	.21	@	.22
" carb., cryst	100 lb.	1.60	@	1.75
" citrate	lb.	...	@	.33
" hypophosphite		.60	@	.64
" iodide		3.50	@	3.55
" nitrate	100 lb.	2.30	@	2.35
" phosphate	lb.	.02½	@	.03
" salicylate	lb.	.32	@	.34
" sulphate	100 lb.	.40	@	.50
Spermaceti	lb.	.27	@	.29
Spts. Nitre, U. S. P.		.46	@	.48
Spts. Ammonia Aromat	lb.	.44	@	.45
Strontium, nitrate	lb.	.07½	@	.08
Strychnine, Sulph	oz.	.95	@	1.05
Sugar of Milk	lb.	.15	@	.27
Sugar, Lead, white	lb.	.09½	@	.10
" brown	lb.	.07½	@	.08
Sulphur, Roll	lb.	1.85	@	2.15
" Flowers	lb.	2.15	@	2.35
Sulphuric Ether	lb.	.62	@	.68
Sumac, Sicily	ton	42.00	@	47.00
" Virginia	ton	33.00	@	35.00
Tar, Barbadoes	gal.	...	@	.39
Thymol		1.80	@	1.90
Tonka B'ns, Para	lb.	.18	@	.20
" Angostura	lb.	.65	@	.67½
" Surinam	lb.	.30	@	.32
Turmeric		.04½	@	.06
Turpentine	gal.	.66	@	...
Vanilla Beans	lb.	2.75	@	5.00
" Cut. Mex	lb.	3.00	@	3.25
" Tahiti	lb.	.80	@	1.45
" Bourbon		1.00	@	3.00
Vanillin	oz.	.22	@	.27½
Venice Turps, bbls	lb.	.14	@	.17
" " cans	lb.	.19	@	.20
Wax, Bayberry	lb.	.42	@	.45
" Bees, ord. pur	lb.	.33	@	.33½
" " sel	lb.	.34	@	.34½
" " blch	lb.	.40	@	.46
" Brazil, No. 1	lb.	.52½	@	53
" " No. 2	lb.	44	@	.47
" " No. 3	lb.	.35	@	...
" Ceresin, yel	lb.	.14	@	.18
" " white	lb.	.15	@	.20
" Japan	lb.	.11	@	.12
" Paraffin	lb.	.06	@	.08½
Zinc Oxide	lb.	.07	@	.10½

Heavy Oils, &c.

Bank, Menhaden	gal.	.27	@	.30
Coconut, Ceylon	lb.	.08½	@	.08½
Cochin	lb.	.07½	@	.07¾
Cuban	lb.	.05½	@	...
Cod, Domestic	gal.	.35	@	36
" Newfoundland	gal.	38½	@	40
Corn	gal.	3.60	@	...
Cottonseed, crd. prime		.25	@	...
Summer Yellow, prime		.32	@	.33
" " Butter		.33	@	.34
Old, off grade		.32	@	...
Winter Yellow, prime		.33	@	.34
Salad Oil		.40	@	.41
Gasoline, 86°	gal.	.14	@	...
" 88°	gal.	.16	@	...
" 90°	gal.	.18	@	...
Lard, Extra Prime	gal.	.63	@	.64
Lard, Extra No. 1	gal.	.49	@	.52
Lard, No. 1	gal.	.38	@	.40
Linseed, Raw City	gal.	.42	@	.43
" Boiled	gal.	.43	@	.44
Naphtha, 62°	gal.	.12	@	..
" Deodorized, 76°	gal.	.13½	@	...
Neatsfoot, prm	gal.	.49	@	.50
White		.27	@	
Olive Oil, tap	tins	1.50	@	2.75
" Com., bbls	gal	.53½	@	.56
Palm, prm., L'gos	lb	.06½	@	.06¼
Peanut	lb	.60	@	.72
Rapeseed	gal.	.67	@	.71
Red Elaine	gal.	...	@	.49
" Saponified	lb.	.06½	@	.06½
Salad Oil	gal.	.66	@	.68
Sesame	gal.	.55	@	.60
Sperm, Crude	gal.	.56	@	.58
" Nat. Win	gal.	.62	@	.63
" Blch. Win	gal.	.64	@	.65
Straits	gal.	...	@	.32
Tallow, prime	gal.	.62	@	
Whale, Crude	gal.	...	@	...
Crude, Nat. Win	gal.	.42	@	
Bleached Win	gal.	.44	@	46

LACTATED FOOD

IS THIS YEAR'S BIG WINNER

The big magazine advertising and our work with the progressive retailers is showing wonderful results

BECAUSE WE BACK UP THE RETAILER

THE PROFIT SIDE

No other food is on the price protected basis and on the $2.00, $4.00 and $8.00 basis.

This means that the retailer can obtain a much larger profit on Lactated Food than upon any other food.

With a purchase of a $16.00 assortment of Lactated Food we will allow a discount of 5 per cent.; or you can buy Lactated Food with our $24.00 or $72.00 assortment discounts.

Select an assortment of Lactated Food, Paine's Celery Compound, Diamond Dyes, Wills' English Pills, etc., and make great big protected profits.

ORDER FROM YOUR JOBBER AT ONCE

WELLS & RICHARDSON CO., Burlington, Vermont

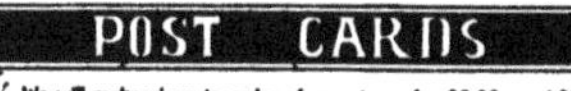

We will make views to order of your town for $5.00 per 1,000.

The same Card in color $1.00 per 100.

FREE SAMPLES ON APPLICATION.

Leather Post Cards a Specialty.

OVER 400 VARIETIES OF IMPORTED POST CARDS KEPT IN STOCK.

89 FULTON STREET, NEW YORK. **I. STERN,** 378 BUSHWICK AVENUE, BROOKLYN, N. Y.

THE DIRECT ROUTE TO MINERAL WELLS The Great Texas Health and Pleasure Resort

IS VIA

NO TROUBLE TO ANSWER QUESTIONS

Write for MINERAL WELLS BOOKLET and NEW BOOK ON TEXAS —*Free*

WM. E. HOYT,
General Eastern Pass. Agent,
385 Broadway, New York.

E. P. TURNER,
General Passenger Agent,
Dallas, Texas.

Post Cards of Quality

Our real photographic name and greeting cards are especially good for the summer trade. The summer girl likes to get them and likes to send them too.

PROPER NAME CARDS

These names are made of skeleton letters which frame pictures of beautiful women of the stage. The effect is very charming. Over fifty proper names to choose from—both men and women.

GREETING CARDS

Made the same as proper name cards, of skeleton letters framing beautiful women. The greetings include everything from the warmth of "My Dearest" to the friendly good-will of "Welcome." Are popular for the summer trade.

Price $2.50 per hundred. They retail at five cents each.

Remember! They are real photographs.

THE ROTOGRAPH COMPANY,
684D Broadway, New York.

Kindly mention AMERICAN DRUGGIST when writing to Advertisers.

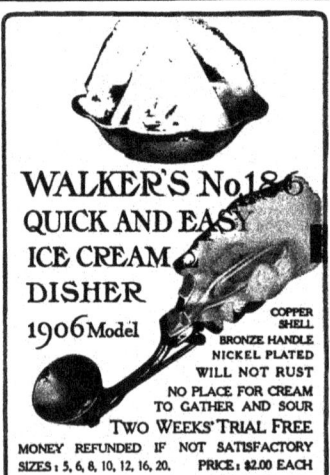

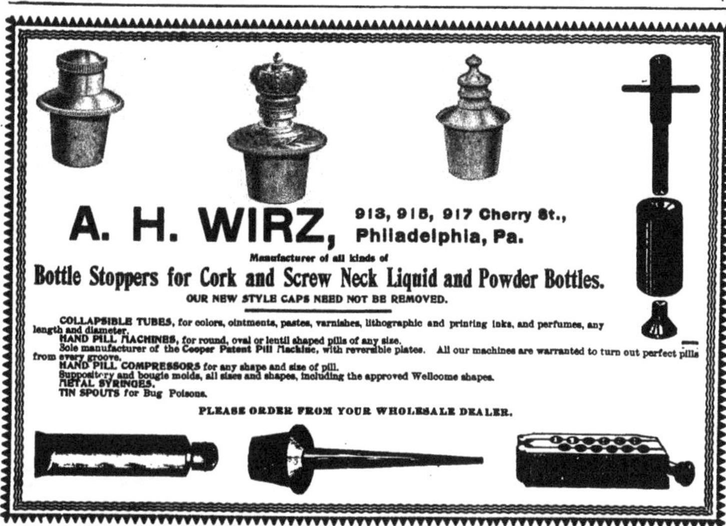

For Home Made Candies

No one in the trade needs to be told what the C. I. Hood Co. makes and markets, for all have sold Hood's Sarsaparilla and the other lines. But many may not know that this firm is offering free on request a book containing recipes for making candies. It is called "Hood's Book of Home-Made Candies, No. 2." A supply of these with the dealer's name printed on each book will be sent on request. They are recommended for counter distribution and are gotten up in style. If desired novelties for making a window display will also be sent.

C. I. HOOD CO., Lowell, Mass.

Prices Current.

The outside prices quoted are for such quantities as retailers usually purchase. When purchasing original packages the inside quotations should be expected, while a slight advance over the outside quotations given may be demanded for very small lots. Current commercial quality is understood unless otherwise indicated. For extra quality or for specified makes a slightly higher price will have to be paid.

Corrected to May 12

Article	Unit	Price
Acetanilid, 5 lbs., .30	lb.	.32-34
Acetone, lb., .22; Medicinal	lb.	.85
Acetphenetidine, lbs., 1.35	oz.	.10
Acid, Acetic, U. S. P., carboys, .6	lbs.	.8-0
No. 2, carboy, .5; lb., .7; Glacial	lb.	.28-30
Arsenous, fused, lb., .18	oz.	.8
Benzoic, English, 50-oz. boxes, .10	oz.	.13-14
Benzoic, from Toluol, lbs., .50	oz.	.11-13
Boric, crystals, 25 lbs., .14	lb.	.15
Boric, Po., 25 lbs., .14	lb.	.16
Cacodylic, ⅛ths	ozs.	4.00
Camphoric	oz.	.50
Carbolic crystals, 10 lbs., .22	lb.	.23-27
Calvert's No. 1, lb., 1.95; No. 2	lb.	1.40
Solution, 10 gals., .45	gal.	.50
Chromic, lb., .55	ozs.	.11
Chrysophanic, 1-oz. cartons	ozs.	.18-20
Cinnamic	oz.	.35-40
Citric, crystals, 10 lbs., .45	lb.	.46-48
Gallic, lbs., .70	ozs.	.11-13
Hydrochloric, carboys, .2½	lb.	.4-5
C. P.	lb.	.11-13
Hydrocyanic, dil., lbs., .30	ozs.	.10
Hydrobromic, dil	lb.	.28
Hypophosphorus, 50 per cent. sol	lb.	1.65
Lactic, concentr., lbs., .70	ozs.	.12
Nitric, carboys, 5½ lbs., .8; C. P.		.14
Oleic, purified, U. S. P.	lbs.	.40
Oxalic, 10 lbs., .9	lb.	.10-12
Phosphoric, glacial	lbs.	.55
U. S. P., 85 per cent. syrupy	lb.	.30-35
Picric	lb.	.55
Pyrogallic, lbs., 2.25	ozs.	.24-27
Pyroligneous, pure	lb.	.30
Salicylic, white, 10 lbs., .40	lb.	.42-44
Stearic, hard	lb.	.18
Succinic	oz.	.32-36
Sulphuric, carboys, .2	lb.	.4
" C. P., carboys, .10	lb.	.12
Sulphurous	lb.	.10
Tannic, lbs., .85	oz.	.12-15
Tartaric, powdered, 10 lbs., .34	lbs.	.35-38
Valerianic	ozs.	.20
Aconitine, Amorphous, ⅛ ozs	ea.	1.40
Adeps Lanae, B. J. D.	lb.	.28
Adnephrin, solution	oz.	.60
Adonidin, 15-gr. vials	gr.	.15
Agaricin, 15-gr. vials, each, .10	ozs.	.90
Agaric, white	lb.	.40
Agathin	oz.	3.25
Agurin,	ozs.	1.70
Airol, ozs	oz.	1.00
Albumen, Egg	lb.	.70
Alcohol, 10 gals., 2.70	gal.	2.65-2.70
Alcohol, Columbia Spirit, 10 gals., 1.35	gal.	1.50
Cologne Spirit, 10 gals., 2.80	gal.	2.90
Wood, 10 gals., .85	gal.	.90
Alizarin,	oz.	.15
Allspice, 10 lbs., .11	lb.	.12
powdered, 5 lbs., .18	lb.	.20
Almonds, bitter, shelled	lb.	.40
Sweet, shelled	lb.	.35
Almond Meal, true, 10 lbs., .45	lb.	.50
Aloin, lb., .70	oz.	.7-9
Alpha-Eucaine	oz.	3.50
Alphozone,	oz.	4.50
Alum, cryst., bbls., 2½	lb.	.3-4
powdered, bbls., .3½	lb.	.6-8
burnt, 10 lbs., .10	lb.	.12-14
Aluminum, Acetate	oz.	.13
Sulphate, lb., 10; Wire	lb.	2.25
Aluminol,	oz.	.50
Amber, rasped	oz.	.35
Ambergris, gray, oz., $30.00	dram.	4.00
Ammonia (See Water and Spirit).		
Ammonium, Bromide, 5-lb. bot., .35	lb.	.40
Carbonate, 25 lbs., .11	lb.	.12-14
Iodide, lbs., 6.15	oz.	.47
Muriate, gran. com	lb.	.10
purified, lb., .17; powdered	lb.	.18
Salammoniac, muriate, cryst	lb.	.12-14
Nitrate, crystals, 10 lbs., .22	lb.	.25
Valerianate, lb., 1.50	oz.	.15-19
Ammonol	oz.	1.03
Amygdalin, ½-oz. vials	oz.	2.40
Amyl, Nitrite	oz.	.25
Amylene, Hydrate	oz.	.49
Anaesthesin	ozs.	1.00
Aniline, Red, crystals	lb.	1.25
Black	lb.	.75
Crystals for ink	lb.	1.50
Blue, Deep, No. 1	lb.	2.00
Sol., reddish, No. 1	lb.	2.50
Crimson	lb.	1.50
Brown, Bismarck	lb.	1.25
Soluble	lb.	1.00
Green, crystals	lb.	1.50
Orange	lb.	1.00
Purple, B. B.	lb.	1.75
Scarlet....lb. 1.50 Yellow	lb.	1.25
Annatto	lb.	.45-50
Anodyne, Hoffman's	lb.	.60
" " U. S. P.	lb.	.88
Anthrasol	oz.	.55
Anthrax Vaccine, "Pasteur," double tubes	doz.	18.00
Artiarthrin	oz.	1.05
Antikamnia, powdered or tablets	oz.	1.00
Combination tablets	oz.	1.00
10-oz. lots, assorted to order		9.25
Tablets, "vest-pocket boxes"	doz.	1.75
In 1 gross lots, 5 per cent. discount.		
Antimony Sulphuret, powd., pure, 10 lbs., .16	lb.	.17-20
Antinosine	oz.	2.
Antipyretic Liquid, Tilden's	doz.	2.
Antipyrine, Dr. Knorr's	oz.	.10
New Grade	oz.	.86
Antistreptococcic Serum (Veterinary), "Pasteur," 10-Cc. vial	doz.	9.00
Antitetanic Serum (Veterinary), "Pasteur," 10-Cc. vial	doz.	9.00
Antithyroidin, 10-Cc. vials	ea.	1.50
Antitoxin, Diphtheria, Stearns':		
No. 0, per 500 units		1.10
No. 1, per 1,000 units		1.05
No. 2, per 2,000 units		1.80
No. 3, per 3,000 units		2.40
No. 4, per 4,000 units		6.50
Antivom, Ritsert, Pills, .30 ea.	doz.	9.50
Apiol, Fluid Green	oz.	.38
Capsules, Joret's	doz.	6.25
Apolysin	oz.	.65
Apomorphine, Hydrochlor, Cryst	oz.	7.50
" " Amorphous	oz.	2.80
Areca, Nuts, powd	lb.	.25-28
Argentamine	oz.	.75
Argols, Red, powdered	lb.	.12
Argonin	oz.	.65
Aristol, 25 ozs., 1.65	oz.	1.80
Aristochin, ozs	oz.	2.20
" ½ ozs	oz.	2.25
Arrowroot, Bermuda, true		None in market
St. Vincent, 30 lbs., .14	lb.	.18
Taylor's, ½-lb., 24 lbs., .28	lb.	.32
Arsenauro, 1-oz. bots	doz.	8.50
Arsenic, Donovan's Sol	lb.	.20
Fowler's Sol	lb.	.10
White	lb.	.12
Aspirin, 50 ozs., .38	oz.	.43
Atropin, Sulph., ⅛-oz	oz.	5.65
Balsam, Copaiba, Para, 5 lbs., .45	lb.	.47-50
Fir, Canada	lb.	.50-55
Oregon	lb.	.25-30
Peru	lb.	1.25
Tolu, 10-lb. can, .32	lb.	.35
Barbadoes Tar	gal.	.60
Barium, Acetate	oz.	.15
Carbonate	lb.	.40
Chloride	lb.	.17
Nitrate	lb.	.15
Oxide, pure	oz.	.10
Bark, Angostura	lb.	.55
Barberry	lb.	.25
Berberis Aquifol	lb.	.20
Buckthorn	lb.	.18
Canella	lb.	.20
Cascara, Sagrada	lb.	.15-20
Cascarilla, select	lb.	.25
Cassia, in mats	lb.	.14
Saigon	lb.	.65
Cinchona, Red, E. I.	lb.	.36
powdered, 10 lbs., .32	lb.	.32-35
Cinchona Calisaya	lb.	.36
powdered	lb.	.40
pale, lb., .20; powdered	lb.	.25
Cinnamon, Ceylon	lb.	.35

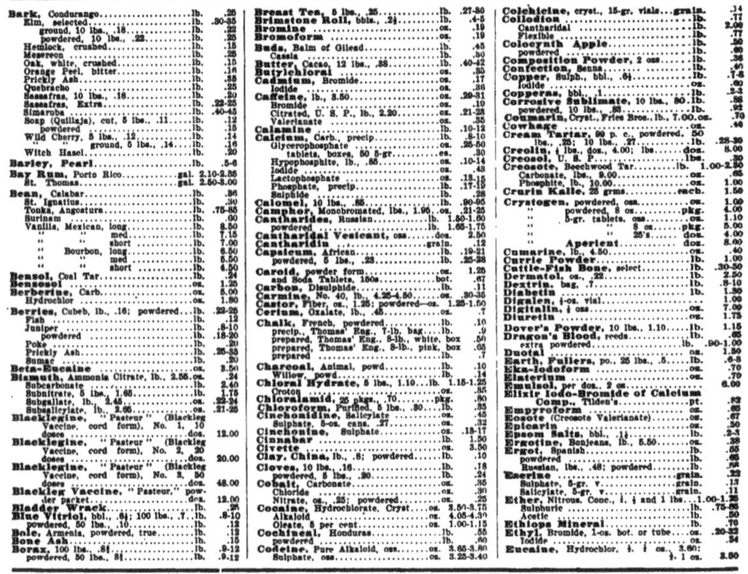

Article	Unit	Price
Bark, Condurango	lb.	.25
Elm, selected	lb.	.30-35
ground, 10 lbs., .18	lb.	.22
powdered, 10 lbs., .22	lb.	.25
Hemlock, crushed	lb.	.15
Mesereon	lb.	.25
Oak, white, crushed	lb.	.15
Orange Peel, bitter	lb.	.16
Prickly Ash	lb.	.35
Quebracho	lb.	.25
Sassafras, 10 lbs., .18	lb.	.20
Sassafras, Extra	lb.	.22-25
Simaruba	lb.	.40-45
Soap (Quillaja), cut, 5 lbs., .11	lb.	.12
powdered	lb.	.15
Wild Cherry, 5 lbs., .12	lb.	.14
" " ground, 5 lbs., .14	lb.	.16
Witch Hasel	lb.	.20
Barley, Pearl	lb.	.5-6
Bay Rum, Porto Rico	gal.	2.10-2.35
St. Thomas	gal.	2.50-3.00
Bean, Calabar	lb.	.36
St. Ignatius	lb.	.30
Tonka, Angostura	lb.	.75-85
Surinam	lb.	.00
Vanilla, Mexican, long	lb.	8.50
" " med	lb.	7.15
" " short	lb.	7.00
" Bourbon, long	lb.	6.50
" " med	lb.	5.50
" " short	lb.	4.50
Benzol, Coal Tar	lb.	.24
Benzosol	oz.	1.25
Berberine, Carb.	oz.	5.00
Hydrochlor	oz.	1.80
Berries, Cubeb, lb., .16; powdered	lb.	.22-25
Fish	lb.	.12
Juniper	lb.	.8-10
powdered	lb.	.18-20
Poke	lb.	.20
Prickly Ash	lb.	.25-35
Sumac	lb.	.20
Beta-Eucaine	oz.	3.50
Bismuth, Ammonia Citrate, lb., 2.55	oz.	.24
Subcarbonate	lb.	2.40
Subnitrate, 5 lbs., 1.65	lb.	1.75
Subgallate, lb., 2.45	oz.	.22-24
Subsalicylate, lb., 2.65	oz.	.21-25
Blacklegine, "Pasteur" (Blackleg Vaccine, cord form), No. 1, 10 doses	doz.	12.00
Blacklegine, "Pasteur" (Blackleg Vaccine, cord form), No. 2, 20 doses	doz.	20.00
Blacklegine, "Pasteur" (Blackleg Vaccine, cord form), No. 3, 50 doses	doz.	48.00
Blackleg Vaccine, "Pasteur," powder packet	doz.	12.00
Bladder Wrack	lb.	.25
Blue Vitriol, bbl., .6½; 100 lbs., .7	lb.	.8-10
powdered, 50 lbs., .10	lb.	.12
Bole, Armenia, powdered, true	lb.	.12
Bone Ash	lb.	.15
Borax, 100 lbs., .8½	lb.	.9-12
powdered, 50 lbs., 8½	lb.	.9-12
Breast Tea, 5 lbs., .25	lb.	.27-30
Brimstone Roll, bbls., .2½	lb.	.4-5
Bromine	oz.	.19
Bromoform	oz.	.19
Buds, Balm of Gilead	lb.	.45
Cassia	lb.	.30
Butter, Cacao, 12 lbs., .38	lb.	.40-42
Butylchloral	oz.	.35
Cadmium, Bromide	oz.	.17
Iodide	oz.	.38
Caffeine, lb., 3.50	oz.	.29-31
Bromide	oz.	.19
Citrated, U. S. P., lb., 2.20	oz.	.21-23
Valerianate	oz.	.35
Calamine	lb.	.10-12
Calcium, Carb., precip	lb.	.8-10
Glycerophosphate	oz.	.25-50
tablets, boxes, 50 5-gr.	ea.	.30
Hypophosphite, lb., .85	oz.	.10-14
Iodide	oz.	.43
Lactophosphate	oz.	.13-15
Phosphate, precip	lb.	.17-19
Sulphide	lb.	.28
Calomel, 10 lbs., .85	lb.	.90-95
Camphor, Monobromated, lbs., 1.96	oz.	.21-25
Cantharides, Russian	lb.	1.50-1.60
powdered	lb.	1.65-1.75
Cantharidal Vesicant, ozs.	doz.	2.50
Cantharidin	grain.	.12
Capsicum, African	lb.	.19-21
powdered, 5 lbs., .23	lb.	.25-28
Caroid, powder form	oz.	1.25
and Soda Tablets, 150s	bot.	.67
Carbon, Disulphide	lb.	.11
Carmine, No. 40, lb., 4.25-4.50	oz.	.30-35
Castor, Fiber, oz., 1.25; powdered	oz.	1.25-1.50
Cerium, Oxalate, lb., .45	oz.	.7
Chalk, French, powdered	lb.	.10
precip., Thomas' Eng., 7-lb. bag	lb.	.9
prepared, Thomas' Eng., 8-lb., white, box		.50
prepared, Thomas' Eng., 8-lb., pink, box		.05
prepared	lb.	.7
Charcoal, Animal, powd	lb.	.10
Willow, powd	lb.	.14
Chloral Hydrate, 5 lbs., 1.10	lb.	1.15-1.25
Croton	oz.	.85
Chloralamid, 25 pkgs., .70	pkg.	.80
Chloroform, Purified, 5 lbs., .30	lb.	.35
Cinchonidine, Salicylate	oz.	.45
Sulphate, 5-oz. cans, .27	oz.	.32
Cinchonine, Sulphate	oz.	.13-17
Cinnabar	lb.	1.50
Civette	oz.	3.50
Clay, China, lb., .8; powdered	lb.	.10
Cloves, 10 lbs., .16	lb.	.18
powdered, 5 lbs., .20	lb.	.24
Cobalt, Carbonate	oz.	.35
Chloride	oz.	.30
Nitrate, oz., .25; powdered	oz.	.25
Cocaine, Hydrochlorate, Cryst	oz.	3.50-3.75
Alkaloid	oz.	4.05-4.30
Oleate, 5 per cent	oz.	1.00-1.15
Cochineal, Honduras	lb.	.55
powdered	lb.	.60
Codeine, Pure Alkaloid, ozs.	oz.	3.65-3.80
Sulphate, ozs.	oz.	3.25-3.40
Colchicine, cryst., 15-gr. vials	grain.	.14
Collodion	lb.	.77
Cantharidal	lb.	2.00
Flexible	lb.	.77
Colocynth Apple	lb.	.50
powdered	lb.	.60
Composition Powder, 2 ozs.	lb.	.38
Confection, Senna	lb.	.45
Copper, Sulph., bbl., .6½	lb.	.7-8
Iodide	oz.	.60
Copperas, bbl., .1	lb.	.2-3
Corrosive Sublimate, 10 lbs., .80	lb.	.85
powdered, 10 lbs., .88	lb.	.92
Coumarin, Cryst., Fries Bros., lb., 7.00	oz.	.70
Cowhage	oz.	.46
Cream Tartar, 99 p. c., powdered, 50 lbs., .25; 10 lbs., .27	lb.	.28-30
Creolin, ¼ lbs., doz., 4.00; lbs.	doz.	8.00
Creosol, U. S. P.	lbs.	.30
Creosote, Beechwood Tar	lb.	1.00-2.50
Carbonate, lbs., 9.00	oz.	.65
Phosphite, lb., 10.00	oz.	1.00
Crurin Kalle, 25 grms.	each.	1.50
Crystogen, powdered, ozs.	oz.	1.00
" powdered, 8 oz.	pkg.	4.00
" 5-gr. tablets, ozs.	oz.	1.10
" " 8 oz.	pkg.	5.00
" " 25's	doz.	4.00
" **Aperient**	doz.	8.00
Cumarine, lb., 4.50	oz.	.40
Currie Powder	lb.	1.00
Cuttle-Fish Bone, select	lb.	.30-50
Dermatol, oz., .22	lb.	2.50
Dextrin, bag, .7	lb.	.8-10
Diabetin	lb.	1.30
Digalen, ½-oz. vial		1.00
Digitalin, ½ ozs.	oz.	7.00
Diuretin	oz.	1.75
Dover's Powder, 10 lbs., 1.10	lb.	1.15
Dragon's Blood, reeds	lb.	.65
extra powdered	lb.	.90-1.00
Duotal	oz.	1.50
Earth, Fullers, po., 25 lbs., .5	lb.	.6-8
Eka-Iodoform	oz.	.70
Elaterium	oz.	.70
Emulsol, per doz., 2 oz.		6.00
Elixir Iodo-Bromide of Calcium Comp., Tilden's	pt.	.82
Empyroform	oz.	.65
Eosote (Creosote Valerianate)	oz.	.67
Epicarin	oz.	.50
Epsom Salts, bbl., .1½	lb.	.2-3
Ergotine, Bonjeans, lb., 5.50	oz.	.38
Ergot, Spanish	lb.	.55
powdered	lb.	.65
Russian, lbs., .48; powdered	lb.	.58
Eserine	grain.	.22
Sulphate, 5-gr. v.	grain.	.13
Salicylate, 5-gr. v.	grain.	.11
Ether, Nitrous, Conc., ¼, ½ and 1 lbs.		1.00-1.25
Sulphuric	lb.	.75-85
Acetic	lb.	.50
Ethiops Mineral	lb.	.70
Ethyl, Bromide, 1-oz. bot. or tube	oz.	.20-32
Iodide	oz.	.54
Eucaine, Hydrochlor, ⅛, ¼ oz., 3.60; ½, 1 oz.		3.50

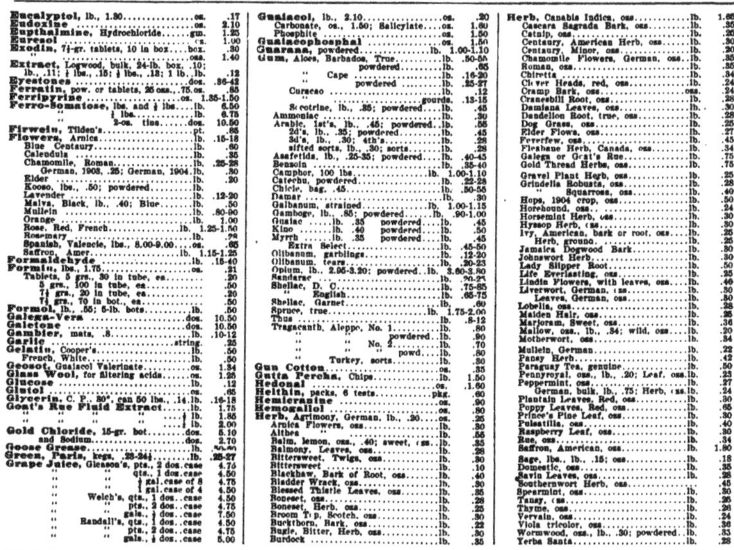

Eucalyptol, lb., 1.30 ... oz. .17
Eudoxine ... oz. 2.10
Eupthalmine, Hydrochloride ... gm. 1.25
Euresol ... oz. 1.00
Exodin, 7½-gr. tablets, 10 in box ... box. .30
" ... ozs. 1.40
Extract, Logwood, bulk, 24-lb. box, .10; lb., .11; ½ lbs., .15; ¼ lbs., .13; 1 lb. .lb. .12
Eyestones ... doz. .36-42
Ferratin, pow. or tablets, 25 ozs., .75 .oz. .85
Ferripyrine ... oz. 1.35-1.50
Ferro-Somatose, lbs. and ½ lbs. ... lb. 6.50
" ¼ lbs. ... lb. 6.75
" 2-oz. tins ... doz. 10.50
Firwein, Tilden's ... pt. .85
Flowers, Arnica ... lb. .15-18
Blue Centaury ... lb. .60
Calendula ... lb. .35
Chamomile, Roman ... lb. .25-28
German, 1903, .25; German, 1904 .lb. .30
Elder ... lb. .20
Kooso, lbs., .50; powdered ... lb.
Lavender ... lb. .12-20
Malva, Black, lb., .40; Blue ... lb. .50
Mullein ... lb. .80-90
Orange ... lb. 1.00
Rose, Red, French ... lb. 1.25-1.50
Rosemary ... lb. .78
Spanish, Valencia, lbs., 8.00-9.00 ... oz. .65
Saffron, Amer ... lb. 1.15-1.25
Formaldehyde ... lb. .15-40
Formin, lbs., 1.75 ... oz. .21
Tablets, 5 grs., 30 in tube, ea ... .20
5 grs., 100 in tube, ea ... .50
7½ grs., 20 in tube, ea ... .20
7½ grs., 70 in bot., ea ... .50
Formol, lb., .55; 5-lb. bots ... lb. .50
Galega-Vera ... doz. 10.50
Galetone ... doz. 10.50
Gambier, mats, .8 ... lb. .10-12
Garlic ... string. .25
Gelatin, Cooper's ... lb. .50
French, White ... lb. .50
Geosot, Guaiacol Valerinate ... oz. 1.34
Glass Wool, for filtering acids ... oz. 1.25
Glucose ... lb. .12
Glutol ... oz. .65
Glycerin, C. P., 30°, can 50 lbs., .14 .lb. .16-18
Goat's Rue Fluid Extract ... lb. 1.75
" " " " ... ½ lb. 1.85
" " " " ... ¼ lb. 2.00
Gold Chloride, 15-gr. bot ... doz. 5.10
and Sodium ... doz. 2.70
Goose Grease ... lb. [illegible]
Green, Paris, kegs, .23-24½ ... lb. .25-27
Grape Juice, Gleason's, pts., 2 doz. case 4.75
" " qts., 1 doz. case 4.50
" " ½ gal. case of 8 4.75
" " 1 gal. case of 4 4.50
" Welch's, qts., 1 doz. case 4.50
" " pts., 2 doz. case 4.75
" " gals., ½ doz. case 7.50
" Randall's, qts., 1 doz. case 4.50
" " pts., 2 doz. case 4.75
" " gals., ½ doz. case 5.00

Guaiacol, lb., 2.10 ... oz. .20
Carbonate, oz., 1.50; Salicylate ... oz. 1.60
Phosphite ... oz. 1.50
Guaiacophosphal ... oz. 1.50
Guarana, powdered ... lb. 1.00-1.10
Gum, Aloes, Barbados, True ... lb. .50-55
powdered ... lb. .65
" Cape ... lb. .16-20
" powdered ... lb. .25-27
Curacao ... lb. .12
" ... gourds. .13-15
Socotrine, lb., .35; powdered ... lb. .45
Ammoniac ... lb. .30
Arabic, 1st's, lb., .45; powdered ... lb. .55
2d's, lb., .35; powdered ... lb. .45
3d's, lb., .30; 4th's ... lb. .28
sifted sorts, lb., .30; sorts ... lb. .28
Asafetida, lb., .25-35; powdered ... lb. .40-45
Benzoin ... lb. .35-40
Camphor, 100 lbs ... lb. 1.00-1.10
Catechu, powdered ... lb. .22-28
Chicle, bag, .45 ... lb. .50-55
Damar ... lb. .30
Galbanum, strained ... lb. 1.00-1.15
Gamboge, lb., .85; powdered ... lb. .90-1.00
Guaiac ... lb. .35 powdered ... lb. .45
Kino ... lb. .40 powdered ... lb. .50
Myrrh ... lb. .35 powdered ... lb. .45
Extra Select ... lb. .45-50
Olibanum, garblings ... lb. .12-20
Olibanum, tears ... lb. .20-23
Opium, lb., 2.95-3.20; powdered ... lb. 3.60-3.80
Sandarac ... lb. .20-23
Shellac, D. C ... lb. .75-85
" English ... lb. .65-75
Shellac, Garnet ... lb. .60
Spruce, true ... lb. 1.75-2.00
Thus ... lb. .8-12
Tragacanth, Aleppo, No. 1 ... lb. .80
" " powdered ... lb. .90
" " No. 2 ... lb. .70
" " " powd ... lb. .80
" Turkey, sorts ... lb. .30
Gun Cotton ... oz. .35
Gutta Percha, Chips ... lb. 1.50
Hedonal ... oz. 1.60
Helthin, packs, 6 tests ... pkg. .60
Hemicranine ... oz. .90
Hemogallol ... oz. .80
Herb, Agrimony, German, lb., .20 ... oz. .25
Arnica Flowers, ozs ... lb. .30
Althea " ... lb. .55
Balm, lemon, ozs., .40; sweet, ozs ... lb. .35
Balmony, Leaves, ozs ... lb. .28
Bittersweet, Twigs, ozs ... lb. .30
Bittersweet ... lb. .10
Blackhaw, Bark of Root, ozs ... lb. .40
Bladder Wrack, ozs ... lb. .30
Blessed Thistle Leaves, ozs ... lb. .35
Boneset, ozs ... lb. .28
Boneset, Herb, ozs ... lb. .25
Broom Top, Scotch, ozs ... lb. .30
Buckthorn, Bark, ozs ... lb. .22
Bugle, Bitter, Herb, ozs ... lb. .30
Burdock ... lb. .35

Herb, Canabis Indica, ozs ... lb. 1.65
Cascara Sagrada Bark, ozs ... lb. .35
Catnip, ozs ... lb. .25
Centaury, American Herb, ozs ... lb. .30
Centaury, Minor, ozs ... lb. .20
Chamomile Flowers, German, ozs ... lb. .35
Roman, ozs ... lb. .35
Chiretta ... lb. .34
Clover Heads, red, ozs ... lb. .24
Cramp Bark, ozs ... ozs. .24
Cranesbill Root, ozs ... lb. .28
Damiana Leaves, ozs ... lb. .30
Dandelion Root, true, ozs ... lb. .28
Dog Grass, ozs ... lb. .25
Elder Flows, ozs ... lb. .27
Feverfew, ozs ... lb. .45
Fleabane Herb, Canada, ozs ... lb. .34
Galega or Goat's Rue ... lb. .75
Gold Thread Herbs, ozs ... lb. .75
Gravel Plant Herb, ozs ... lb. .25
Grindelia Robusta, ozs ... lb. .28
" Squarrosa, ozs ... lb. .40
Hops, 1904 crop, ozs ... lb. .50
Horehound, ozs ... lb. .24
Horsemint Herb, ozs ... lb. .30
Hyssop Herb, ozs ... lb. .30
Ivy, American, bark or root, ozs ... lb. .25
Herb, ground ... lb. .25
Jamaica Dogwood Bark ... lb. .30
Johnswort Herb ... lb. .30
Lady Slipper Root ... lb. .50
Life Everlasting, ozs ... lb. .25
Lindin Flowers, with leaves, ozs ... lb. .40
Liverwort, German, ozs ... lb. .30
Leaves, German, ozs ... lb. .30
Lobelia, ozs ... lb. .28
Maiden Hair, ozs ... lb. .25
Marjoram, Sweet, ozs ... lb. .36
Mallow, ozs., lb., .34; wild, ozs ... lb. .20
Motherwort, ozs ... lb. .34
Mullein, German ... lb. .22
Pansy Herb ... lb. .42
Paraguay Tea, genuine ... lb. .50
Pennyroyal, ozs., lb., .20; Leaf, ozs. lb. .23
Peppermint, ozs ... lb. .27
German, bulk, lb., .75; Herb, ozs. lb. .24
Plantain Leaves, Red, ozs ... lb. .30
Poppy Leaves, Red, ozs ... lb. .65
Prince's Pine Leaf, ozs ... lb. .30
Pulsatilla, ozs ... lb. .40
Raspberry Leaf, ozs ... lb. .30
Rue, ozs ... lb. .34
Saffron, American, ozs ... lb. 1.80
Sage, lbs., lb., .15; ozs ... lb. .18
Domestic, ozs ... lb. .35
Savin Leaves, ozs ... lb. .28
Southernwort Herb, ozs ... .45
Spearmint, ozs ... lb. .30
Tansy, ozs ... lb. .25
Thyme, ozs ... lb. .26
Vervain, ozs ... lb. .24
Viola tricolor, ozs ... lb. .36
Wormwood, ozs., lb., .30; powdered ... lb. .33
Yerba Santa ... lb. .28

Article	Unit	Price
Heroin, 15-gr. vials, ea., .23	oz.	4.85
Hippol, Crystalline	oz.	1.50
Tab., 7½ grs. ea	box	.65
Hydrocyanate of Iron, Tilden's	oz.	.80
Honey	lb.	.12-15
Hops, fresh, 1904, bulk, .25	lb.	.40-42
pressed, ¼, ½ and lbs	lb.	.40-42
pressed, ozs	lb.	.45
Holocain, 1-gramme vials, .35; 5-gramme vials, 1.50	1-oz. vials	7.00
Homatropine, Hydrobrom, 5, 10 and 15 vials	grain	.30-35
Hydrastine, Alkaloid	oz.	6.25
Hydrogen Dioxide	lb.	.28-50
Hydroquinone	oz.	.15
Hyoscyamine, Alkaloid, 5, 10, 15 gr. v	grain	.40
Hydrobromate, 5, 10, 15 gr. v	grain	.30
Sulphate, pure Amorph., 5, 10, 15 gr. v	grain	.23
Hypnal, Hoechst	oz.	1.15
Iatrol	oz.	.95
Ichthyol, lb., 4.00	oz.	.32
Indigo, Madras	lb.	.75
Manila	lb.	.75
Sulphate comp., 9-lb. bot	lb.	.45
Paste	lb.	.20
Insect Powder, pure, bbls., .35; 50 lbs., .35½; 25 lbs., .36	lb.	.38-42
W. & B., bbls., .20; kegs, 50 lbs., .20½; drums, 25 lbs., .21	lb.	.23
Iodine, lbs., 3.20	oz.	.28-35
Iodoform, lb., 3.75	oz.	.30-34
Iodol	oz.	1.25
Iodopyrine	oz.	1.40
Iodothyrine, ozs., 3.40; ½-oz., 3.65; ¼-oz.		3.90
Iron, by Hydrogen, gray, U. S. P	lb.	.50
Benzoate	oz.	.23
Cacodylate	oz.	5.00
Carbonate, precip., lb., .18; sacch	lb.	.50
Vallet's	lb.	.30
Chloride	lb.	.35
Sol., U. S. P	lb.	.14
Tinct., U. S. P	lb.	.35
Citrate, U. S. P	lb.	.64
and Ammonium	lb.	.60
and Quinine, lbs., 1.75	oz.	.17-21
Dialsed, Solution	lb.	.35
Glycerophosphate	oz.	.40
tablets, boxes, 50 5-gr	ea.	.40
Iodide, oz., .30; syrup of	lb.	.34
Lactate	oz.	.7
Pernitrate, Solution	lb.	.25
Pyrophosphate, Soluble	lb.	.51
Phosphate, scales, U. S. P	lb.	.51
Subsulphate (Monsel's)	lb.	.23
Solution (Monsel's)	lb.	.35
Sulphate, pure	lb.	.6
exsiccated	lb.	.15
and Potass Tartrate	lb.	.48
and Ammonium Tartrate	lb.	.62
Isarol, lb., 4.10	ozs.	.30-35
Isinglass, American	lb.	.90
Russian, true, Beluga	lb.	4.25
Jerquertol Serum, 4 tubes in box	ea.	7.50
Jecorin Tablets, 12's	doz.	4.00
Jewelers' Rouge	lb.	.75
Juice, Dandelion, Eng	lb.	1.40
Juniper, Germ	lb.	.25-30
Lime	gal.	.90-1.00
Junket Tablets (10c. size), 3 doz.	doz.	.80
Kamala, purified, powdered	lb.	1.50
No. 2 powdered	lb.	.65
Kaolin	lb.	.08
Kelene, automatic, 1.10		.50-1.00
Kermes Mineral	lb.	1.10
Kola Nut, lb., .25; powdered	lb.	.35
Kresamin	oz.	1.00
Lactophenin, powd. or tab., 25 ozs., .90	oz.	1.00
Lacto-Somatose, 2-oz. tins	doz.	10.50
¼-lbs	lb.	6.75
½-lbs	lb.	6.50
Lactucarium, lbs., 4.00	oz.	.40
Laminoids	doz.	8.00
Lanikol, 1-oz. jars, doz., 3.50; 4-oz., doz., 9.50	lb.	2.50
Lanolin, Liebrich (Wool Fat), 10 lbs., .70	lb.	.75
Lanoline Puriss, B. J. D	lb.	.40
Lead, Acetate, White	lb.	.12-14
Carbonate	lb.	.12
Iodide	lb.	.28
Red	lb.	.10
Subacetate, Sol	lb.	.16
Leaf, Aconite	lb.	.20
Eng., 1-lb. cans only	lb.	1.10
Arbor Vitae	lb.	.20
Bay	lb.	.12
Belladonna	lb.	.25
Eng., 1-lb. cans only	lb.	1.20
Blackberry	lb.	.20
Blessed Thistle, ozs	lb.	.27
Borage, ozs	lb.	.38
Butternut	lb.	.15
Buchu, long, lb., .60; short	lb.	.25
Castor Oil	lb.	.30
Cherry Laurel	lb.	.40
Chestnut	lb.	.23
Coca, Huanuco, lb., .40; Truxillo	lb.	.32
Coltsfoot, ozs	lb.	.25
Conium, lb	lb.	.16
Damiana	lb.	.30
Digitalis	lb.	.26
Eng., 1-lb. cans only	lb.	.85
Eucalyptus	lb.	.15
Fern, sweet, ozs	lb.	.22
Foxglove, ozs	lb.	.30
Hyoscyamus	lb.	.25
Am., 1-lb. cans only	lb.	1.60
Eng., Biennial, 1-lb. bots. only	lb.	3.00
German, bulk	lb.	.25
Jaborandi, true	lb.	.34
Laurel, true	lb.	.15
Matico	lb.	.35
Patchouli	lb.	.60
Raspberry, ozs	lb.	.25
Senna, Alexandria	lb.	.25-35
Tinnivelly	lb.	.15-20
India	lb.	.15
Leaf, Stramonium	lb.	.20
Strawberry leaves	lb.	.25
Uva Ursa	lb.	.12
Witch Hazel	lb.	.15
Leeches, Swedish, per 100, 4.00	doz.	.60
Liquorice, P. S	lb.	.28
Corigliano	lb.	.30-33
Y. & S., 5-lb. boxes	lb.	.25
Lime, Chlorinated, bulk, bbls., .3	lb.	.5
1-lb. tins	lb.	.8-9
Litharge	lb.	.10-12
Lithium, Bromide	oz.	.23
Carbonate	lb.	1.75-2.00
Citrate	lb.	1.35
Glycerino-Phosph	ozs.	.74
Iodide	oz.	.38
Salicylate	oz.	.15
Litmus	lb.	.40
Losophan	oz.	1.80
Lunar Caustic, pure, 7.50	oz.	.48-51
in cones	oz.	.60-63
Lupulin, American	lb.	.65
German	lb.	.50
Lycetol, 10 ozs., 3.80	oz.	4.25
Lycopodium, Politz, 10 lbs., .60	lb.	.65-75
Lysiden	oz.	1.75
Lysol	lb.	.67
Mace	lb.	.70
Magnesia, Calcined	lb.	.70-75
heavy	lb.	.75-85
Magnesium, carbonate, ¼ lbs	lb.	.20-30
2 oz	lb.	.22-32
S. S	lb.	.55-70
Citrate, gran	lb.	.50-75
Sulph. (Epsom Salts), bbls., .01½	lb.	.2-4
Maltopepsine, Tilden's	pt.	.62
Manganauro, 1-oz. bots	doz.	8.50
Manganese, Black Oxide	lb.	.5-12
Hypophosphite, oz., .20; sulphate	oz.	.5
Manna, large flake	lb.	.60-70
small flake, 5 lbs., .40	lb.	.45
Mannite	lb.	3.25
Marble Dust	bbl.	1.50
Maretin	ozs.	1.25
Menthol, lbs., 3.25	oz.	.25-29
Mercauro, 1-oz., bots	doz.	8.50
Mercury, 5 lbs., .70	lb.	.72-73
Colloidal	oz.	.85
Ammon	lb.	1.10
Bisulphate	lb.	.75
Chloride, Corrosive, 10 lbs., .78	lb.	.88
Chloride, powdered, 10 lbs., .80	lb.	.90
Calomel, 10 lbs., .85	lb.	.90
with Chalk	lb.	.42
Iodide, Proto., lbs., 2.85	ozs.	.27
Biniodide, lbs., 3.10	ozs.	.27
Oxide, Red	lbs.	1.10
Pill (Blue Mass)	lbs.	.47
powdered	lbs.	.57
Herring's English	lbs.	1.25
Red Precipitate	lb.	1.05
White Precipitate	lb.	1.10
powdered	lb.	1.15
Mesotan-Bayer	oz.	.47
Methyl, Acetate	oz.	.43
Bichloride	oz.	.65

Methyl, Iodide .... lb. 1.00
Oxide .... oz. .50
Salicylate .... lb. .45-50
Methylene, Bichloride .... oz. .65
Migrainin, oz. tins .... oz. 1.50
Milk Sugar, powdered, 10 lbs., .20 .. lbs. .21-22
Morphine, Acetate .... oz. 2.80
Muriate, ⅛s .... oz. 2.80
Sulphate, ⅛s, P. & W., ozs .... oz. 2.50-2.60
2½ oz. cartons (25 ozs., 2.45) .... oz. 2.55
Moss, Iceland, lb., .12; Irish .... lb. .18-22
Musk, Tonquin, Pods .... oz. 14.00-20.00
grain .... oz. 22.00-24.00
Nafalitza .... doz. 2.00
Naphtha, Wood .... lb. .24
Wood, 95 p. c., bbls., .75 .... gal. .80-90
Naphthaline, balls, 50 lbs., .3½ .... lb. .4-5
cakes and squares .... lb. .6-8
Naphthol .... oz. .18
Narceine .... oz. 6.50
Nephritica, Tilden's .... pt. .82
Nickel, Bromide .... oz. .30
Carbonate .... oz. .25
Chloride .... oz. .25
Metallic .... oz. .25
Nitrate .... oz. .18
Oxide, pure .... oz. .75
Sulphate .... oz. .10
Nirvanin .... oz. 3.50
Nitroglycerin, 1 per cent. solution lbs., 1.10 .... oz. .12
Nosophen .... doz. 4.50
Nutrolactis .... doz. 10.00
Nutgalls, lb., .30; powdered .... lb. .40
Nutmegs .... lb. .35-40
Nutrose, ½ lbs., 4.00; ¼ lbs., 3.75 .... lb. 3.35
Nux Vomica .... lb. .8-10
Powdered, pure .... lb. .20-25
Oakum, bales 50 lbs., .08 .... lb. .12
Oatmeal .... lb. .6
Oil, Almond, Bitter, lbs., 6.50 .... oz. .55
Sweet, True, 5 lbs., .42 .... lb. .50-55
Amber, crude .... lb. .25
rect .... lb. .40
Anise .... lb. 1.25-1.35
Bay, American, bot. 22 ozs., 3.75 .... oz. .35
West Indies, bot. 23 ozs., 3.50 .... oz. .50
Benne .... gal. 1.00
Bergamot .... lb. 2.65
Bergamot, 5-lb. cans .... lb. 2.60
Sanderson's .... lb. 2.60
Black Pepper .... lb. .75
Cade .... lb. .35
Cajuput .... lb. .75-88
Capsicum .... oz. .50
Caraway .... lb. 1.75
Cassia .... lb. 1.00-1.10
Castor, 40-lb. can, .12½ .... lb. .14-15
Cedar Leaves, Amer .... lb. .90-95
Chaulmoogra .... lb. 2.50
Cinnamon, Ceylon, lb., 15.00 .... oz. 1.10
Citronella .... lb. .60-85
Clove, 5-lbs., .95 .... lb. 1.00-1.10

Oil, Cocoanut, Refined, 10 lbs., .18 .... lb. .22
Codliver, N. F., kegs, 30 gals., 25.00 to 27.00 ea .... gal. 1.00-1.10
Norwegian, bbls., 30 gals., 27.00 to 29.00 .... gal. 1.15-1.25
Copaiba .... lb. 1.10
Cottonseed .... gal. .45-55
Croton .... lb. 1.20
Croton, Eng .... lb. 1.75
Cubeb, Amer .... lb. 1.15
Cumin, lb., 4.50 .... oz. .35
Erigeron .... lb. 1.25
Eucalyptus, Australian .... lb. .90
Fennel .... lb. 1.75
Geranium, Turkish .... lb. 4.50
French .... lb. 8.00
Prepared .... lb. 16.00
Juniper Berries .... lb. 1.50
Wood .... lb. .60
Lard, No. 1 .... gal. .90
Lavender Flowers .... lb. 2.50
Chiris .... lb. 2.75
Garden .... lb. 1.10
Lemon .... lb. .90-1.00
1-lb. copper cans .... lb. 1.10
Sanderson's .... lb. 1.00-1.10
Lemongrass .... lb. 3.75
Linseed, Boiled, by bbl., .60 .... gal. .65-75
Linseed, Raw, by bbl., .58 .... gal. .63-70
Mustard, Expressed .... gal. .75
Mustard, Essential, lb., 5.50 .... oz. .45-50
Neatsfoot .... gal. .90
Neroli, Bigarade .... oz. 3.50
Chiris .... oz. 3.75
Petale .... oz. 4.00
Olive, Malaga .... gal. .75
Fine Salad, 3-gal. cans, 2.50 .... gal. 2.75
Orange, Bitter .... lb. 3.20
Sweet .... lb. 2.50
" 1-lb. copper cans 2.65
Origanum, pure .... lb. .85-1.10
Palm .... lb. .20
Patchouli, lb., 7.50 .... oz. .65
Pennyroyal, 5 lbs., 1.50 .... lb. 1.60
Peppermint .... lb. 3.00-3.25
Hotchkiss .... lb. 3.50-3.65
Redistilled .... lb. 3.75-4.00
Petroleum, crude .... gal. .25
Lubricating, gal., .20; Refined .... gal. .12
Pimento, lb., 2.90 .... oz. .25
Pinus, Pumilio .... ozs. .39-48
Sylvestris .... lbs. 1.00-2.00
Rhodium, true, lb., 8.00 .... oz. .75
Rose, Kasanlik .... oz. 4.50-5.00
Botu Pappasoglou .... oz. 6.00
Rosemary, Eperle .... lb. 1.50
Trieste .... lb. .60
Rue, lb., 3.00 .... oz. .30
Salad Union .... gal. .50-55
Sandalwood, W. I., lb., 3.00; Engl .... lb. 5.50
Sassafras .... lb. .75
Savin .... lb. 1.40
Spearmint, lb., 5.50; H. G. H .... lb. 5.75
Sperm, Winter, Blea .... gal. 1.00

Oil, Spruce .... lb. .60
Tansy .... lb. 4.00-4.50
Thyme, White .... lb. 1.25
Turpentine .... gal. .75
Valerian .... oz. .65
Verbena, true .... oz. .50
Whale .... gal. .75
Wintergreen, Betula .... lb. 2.15-2.25
Wintergreen, Synthetic, Fries Bros .... lb. .75
Wintergreen, true .... lb. 3.25-3.50
Wormseed .... lb. 3.50
Wormwood .... lb. 4.00-4.50
Ointment, Mercurial, ½ M .... lb. .48
1-3 M .... lb. .40
Citrine .... lb. .46
Oleate, Mercury, 20 p. c., lb., 3.00 .... oz. .25
Morphine, 5 p. c. .... oz. .40
Zinc, powd., lb., 2.50 .... oz. .25
Opium (see Gum).
Orphol .... oz. .80
Orthoform, 1-oz. vials .... oz. 1.40
Hydrochlorate .... oz. 1.80
Pancreatin, ozs., .50 .... lb. 6.50
Papain, purified .... oz. 1.00
Papoid .... oz. 2.00
Paraffine .... lb. .10-12
Paraformaldehyde, Tablets, Fries Bros., lb., 3.50 .... oz. .35
Paris Green, 125-lb. kegs .... lb. .23½
14-lb. kits, .24½; 2 and 5 lb .... lb. .24½
1-lb., .25; ½-lb., lb., .28; ¼-lb .... lb. .27
Pastiles, Black Fumigating .... lb. .35
Red Fumigating .... lb. .40
Paraform .... oz. .35
Paraldehyde, ½-lb. bots .... lbs. 1.40
Pellotine, Muriate, 1 and 5 gr. vials, grain .35
Pental, 10-gramme vials .... each .75
Pepper, Black, lb., 18-20; powdered .... lb. .22-25
White, lb., .25; powdered .... lb. .30
Pepsin, Saccharated, lb., 1.00 .... oz. .12
Pure, Armour's, lb., 4.50 .... oz. .36
Cudahy's, scale, gran. or insol 3.50
Peronin, 1-gramme vials .... each 1.00
Phenacetin .... ozs. .33
Pheno-Bromate, tablets or powder (10 ozs., less 10 p. c.; 25 ozs., less 10 p. c. and 5 p. c.) .... oz. 1.00
Phenocoll, Hydrochloride, 25 grammes, vial 1.50
Phosphorus .... lb. 1.00
Phosphotal, lb., 10.00 .... oz. 1.00
Pilocarpine, Muriate, 5, 10 and 15 gr. vials .... grain .6
Piperazine, pure, 10 ozs., 3.80 .... oz. 4.25
Piperin .... oz. .62
Pitch, Black .... lb. .6
Burgundy .... lb. .3-8
Pixine, 2-oz. jars .... doz. 2.00
1-lb. jars .... doz. 10.00
Veterinary, 2-oz. tins .... doz. 2.00
8-oz. tins .... doz. 4.00

Article	Unit	Price
Plaster, Calcined, bbl., 2.00	lb.	.3-4
Dental	bbl.	2.50
Adhesive	yd.	.15-20
Belladonna	lb.	1.25
Galbanum, U. S.	lb.	.60
Lead	lb.	.38
Mercury, U. S. P.	lb.	1.00
Pollantin-Dunbar (liquid or powder)	ea.	1.75
Poppy Heads	lb.	.18-40
Potash	lb.	.8-12
Potassa, Caustic White	lb.	.28
Potassium, Acetate, bot. inc.	lb.	.36-40
Bicarbonate, lb., .14; Bichromate	lb.	.14
Bromide, 5 box, .28	lb.	.30-32
Carbonate	lb.	.12
Chlorate, Eng., lb., .12; powdered	lb.	.15
Citrate	lb.	.47
Cyanide, Fd	lb.	.45
Glycerophosphate	oz.	.35
Hypophosphite, lbs., .80	oz.	.10
Iodide, 5 lbs., 2.20	lb.	3.25-3.40
Nitrate, Gran.	lb.	.10
Permanganate	lb.	.18-20
Prussiate, Red	lb.	.50
Yellow	lb.	.20
Sulphuret	lb.	.18
Probilin Pills, 60 in box	ea.	1.25
Propylamine	oz.	.55
Protargol, ¼ ozs., 1.35; ozs	oz.	1.25
Pyramidon	oz.	2.13
Quinalgen	oz.	1.25
Quassone	doz.	10.00
Quinine, Bromide	oz.	.48-52
Muriate	oz.	.47-51
Sulphate, bulk	oz.	.18-20
Sulph., 1-oz. vials, B. & S.	oz.	.24-25
P. & W.	oz.	.25-26
Bisulphate, 5-oz. can	oz.	.20-22
1-oz. vials, B. & S.	oz.	.24-25
Tannate	oz.	.31-35
Valerianate	oz.	.55
Quinolin	ozs.	1.00
Quinoliv	oz.	1.00
Resin, Common	lb.	.4
Jalap	oz.	.60
Leptandrin	oz.	.35
Podophyllin, lb., 4.00	oz.	.35
Scammony, U. S. P.	oz.	.40
White	lb.	.8
Resorcin, White, lb., 1.30	oz.	.17
Fries Bros., lb., 2.20	oz.	.25
Respirazone, Tilden's	pt.	1.03
Rheumacilate, doz., 4.80	oz.	.40
Rheumatol	ozs.	1.00
Rhodinal II	oz.	4.00
Rochelle Salts	lb.	.23-25
" " 50-lb. boxes	lb.	.22½-23½
Rodagen	ozs.	1.00
Root, Aconite	lb.	.20
Althea, lb., .28; cut	lb.	.35
Belladonna	lb.	.20
Berberis aquifolium	lb.	.20
Bitter	lb.	.28
Blackberry	lb.	.20
Black Snake	lb.	.20
Blood	lb.	.24

Article	Unit	Price
Root, Burdock, crushed	lb.	.20
Calamus, Sliced, White	lb.	.40
Calumba	lb.	.20
Canada Snake	lb.	.36
Cohosh, Black	lb.	.15
Colchicum, lb., .25; powdered	lb.	.30
Coltsfoot	lb.	.40
Comfrey, crushed	lb.	.20
Crawley	lb.	1.75-2.25
Curcuma	lb.	.15
Dandelion, cut, 5 lbs., .17	lb.	.22
Dwarf Elder, oz.	lb.	.20
Elecampane, 5 lbs., .16	lb.	.20
Fern, Male	lb.	.22
Galangal, 5 lbs., .12	lb.	.14
Gelsemium	lb.	.20
Gentian, 10 lbs., .9	lb.	.12
ground, 5 lbs., .12	lb.	.15
powd., 5 lbs., .15	lb.	.16
Ginger, African	lb.	.14
powd., 5 lbs., .18	lb.	.20
Jamaica, Bleached, 5 lbs., .18	lb.	.22
Bl., powd., 5 lbs., .27	lb.	.30
Unbleached, 5 lbs., .18	lb.	.22
Ginseng	lb.	6.50-9.00
Golden Seal	lb.	1.50-1.60
Gold Thread	lb.	.80
Hellebore, Black	lb.	.15
White, powd., 5 lbs., .12	lb.	.15
Indian Hemp, Black, lb., .25; White	lb.	.20
Indigo, Wild, oss	lb.	.25
Ipecac, lb., 1.85; powdered	lb.	2.00
Jalap, lb., .18; powdered	lb.	.30
Kava Kava	lb.	.30
Licorice, lb., .16-20; powd., 5 lbs., .12	lb.	.15
Lily of the Valley	lb.	.20
Lovage, select	lb.	.30
Male Fern, select	lb.	.25
Mandrake, lb., .18; powdered	lb.	.22
Masterwort	lb.	.25
Mugwort	lb.	.18
Musk	lb.	.35
Nettle	lb.	.20
Orris, Florentine	lb.	.15-18
" " powdered	lb.	.16-22
fingers	lb.	.80
infant	lb.	2.75
Verona, powdered	lb.	.20
Parsley	lb.	.20
Pellitory	lb.	.45
Pink	lb.	.40
Pleurisy	lb.	.25
Poke	lb.	.18
Pond Lily, White	lb.	.25
Yellow	lb.	.25
Queen of the Meadow	lb.	.20
Rhatany	lb.	.27
Rhubarb, China	lb.	.60-75
" China, cut	lb.	1.00-2.00
powdered	lb.	.40-85
Sarsaparilla, Hond.	lb.	.35
" " cut	lb.	.44
Mexican, lb., .18; ground	lb.	.22
Senega	lb.	.90
Serpentaria	lb.	.55-60
Squill, select	lb.	.10

Article	Unit	Price
Root, Stillingia, lb., .18; powdered	lb.	.25
Unicorn	lb.	.40
Valerian, English, lb., .42; German	lb.	.20
Virginia Snake	lb.	.60
Yellow Dock	lb.	.22
Zedoary, pure	lb.	.18
Rum, Bay, imported, ½ bbls., 2.00; 10 gals., 2.15; 5 gals., 2.25	gal.	2.35-2.50
Bay, essence	lb.	3.00
Saccharin, lb., 4.50	¼-oz. tin	.35
Salacetol	oz.	.35
Salicin, lb., 4.50	oz.	.35
Salipyrin	oz.	.80
Tablet	oz.	.90
Salol, lb., 1.20	oz.	.14
Salophen, 25 ozs., .95	oz.	1.00
Saloquinine	ozs.	1.25
Salicylate	oz.	1.25
Sanose	oz.	.25
Santonin, lb., 10.50-10.70	oz.	.73-75
Saola, Tilden's	pt.	.24
"Save-the-Horse" Spavin Cure ($5.00)	doz.	48.00
Scopolamine, Hydrobrom, Ph.G. (identical with Hyoscine, U. S. P.)	grain	.20-22
Seed, Anise, Italian	lb.	.17
Star	lb.	.30
Angelica	lb.	.30
Burdock	lb.	.25
Canary, Sicily	lb.	.7-8
Cardamom, Aleppo	lb.	1.30
Malabar	lb.	1.00
Mangalore, bleached, extra	lb.	1.40
Celery	lb.	.12-15
Colchicum, lb., .55; powdered	lb.	.65
Conium	lb.	.25
Coriander	lb.	.18
Cumin	lb.	.18
Fennel	lb.	.16
Fenugreek, powd., 25 lbs., .7	lb.	.10
Flax, cleaned, bbl., 6.75	lb.	.4-5
ground, bbl., .03½	lb.	.5
Hemp, bag, .3½	lb.	.5
Henbane	lb.	.45
Jambul	oz.	.25
Larkspur	lb.	.50
powdered	lb.	.60
Lobelia, powdered	lb.	.65
Lovage, lb., .65; powdered	lb.	.70
Millet	lb.	.6
Mustard, Black	lb.	.10
White, lb., .10; powdered	lb.	.25-31
Parsley	lb.	.15
Poppy, Blue	lb.	.10-12
White	lb.	.20
Pumpkin	lb.	.20
Quince, German, lb., .50; Russian	lb.	.40
Rape, English	lb.	.6½
German	lb.	.5
Strophanthus, Green	lb.	1.50-1.60
Sunflower seed	lb.	.6-9
Watermelon	lb.	.20
Worm (Chenopodium)	lb.	.25
(Santonica)	lb.	.30
Seidlitz Mixture, 50 lbs., .18	lb.	.19-22

Article	Unit	Price
Silver, Nitrate, cryst., lb., 7.50	oz.	.50-55
67 per cent., oz., .37; 50 per cent.	oz.	.30
Cones	oz.	.60-63
Soap, Castile, Marseilles, box, .7	lb.	.10
Mottled, pure, box, .8	lb.	.10
White, Conti's, box, .12	lb.	.14
powdered, 25 lbs., .28	lb.	.33
Green (Sapo Vir.), 10 lbs., .12	lb.	.10-15
Eng. Blue Mottled Soap, cases, 112 lbs.		5.50-6.50
Soda, Chlor. Sol	doz.	2.25
Sodium, Acetate, pure, gran	lb.	.15
Bicarbonate, Eng., keg, .03	lb.	.4-5
" Natrona, keg, .2½	lb.	.3-5
Bromide	lb.	.35-37
Carbonate, bbl., .1	lb.	.2½
Citrate	lb.	.47
Glycerophosphate	oz.	.35
Hypophosphite, lbs., .85	lb.	.10-14
Hypophosphite, kg., .2½	lb.	.5
Hyposulphite	keg	.02½
Iodide, lb., 3.45	oz.	.38-40
Phosphate, cryst	lb.	.10
Salicylate	lb.	.44
Silicate, Syrupy, bbl., .2½	lb.	.5-10
Sulphate	lb.	.3
Somatose, 2 ozs	doz.	8.25
Somnal	oz.	.80
Sozoiodol	oz.	1.15
Sparteine, Sulph., B & S	oz.	.75-1.00
Spermaceti	lb.	.28-30
Spermine, Poehl, box 4 tubes	ea.	3.00
Spirit Ether Nit., U. S. P	lb.	.52
Streptolyptic Serum, Stearns', 20 Cc., in two sero-bulbs of 10 Cc. each		3.00
Discount, 25 per cent.		
Strontium, Nitrate	lb.	.16
Bromide, lb., .55	oz.	.12
Iodide	oz.	.41
Lactate, lb., 1.25	oz.	.16
Salicylate, lb., .75	oz.	.13
Strophanthin, C. P. cryst	gr.	.6
Strychnine, Crystals, ¼-oz. vials	oz.	1.20
powdered, ¼-oz. vials	oz.	1.20
Sulphate, ¼-oz. vials	oz.	1.20
Glycerophosphate, ozs	oz.	2.50
Sulphonmethane, U. S. P	ozs.	.60
" "	lbs.	8.00
Sulphur, Flowers, bbls., .2½	lb.	.4-5
Precipitate, pure	lb.	.16-18
Suprarenal Glands, Desiccated, powd., oz., 2.00; tablets	oz.	1.00
Saccharated	oz.	1.20
Tablets, 1 grain, per 100		.40
Capsules, 1 grain, per 100		.65
Sycose, 2-oz. package	each.	1.00
Takadiastase	oz.	1.70
Liquid, 8-oz. bots	doz.	6.00
Tannigen, 25 ozs., .65	oz.	.75
Tannopine	oz.	.75
Tar, N. C. pine, Diamond brand, pts.	doz.	.95
Tartar Emetic, powdered	lb.	.34
Terebene	lb.	.65
Terpin Hydrate, cryst	oz.	.10
in bulk	lb.	.45
Theocin-Bayer	ozs.	2.70
Theophyllin, B. & S	oz.	1.40
sodium, oz., 1.50; sodium salicylate	oz.	1.10
Thigenol, lbs., 4.00	oz.	.32
Thiocol	oz.	1.40
Thiocol Tablets, 100 in vial		1.75
Thioform, 25-gramme pkgs	each	.50
Thiol, liquid, oz., .40; powdered	oz.	.75
Thymol (Thymic Acid), lbs., 2.25	oz.	.27
Thyroids, desiccated, Cudahy's	lb.	7.00
Tinct. Simulo, Christy's, lbs	lb.	4.25
½ lbs., lb., 4.35; ¼ lbs	lb.	4.50
Trional, 25 ozs., 1.40	oz.	1.50
Tuberculinum Kochii, "Pasteur," 1 Cc	doz.	3.20
Tuberculin (Veterinary), "Pasteur," 1 Cc	doz.	3.20
Tuberculin Solution (Veterinary), "Pasteur," 10 Cc	doz.	4.00
Turpentine, Spirits, bbls., .72½	gal.	.80-85
Chian, oz., .45; Venice	lb.	.30
Tussol	oz.	1.65
Urethane, C. P	oz.	.54
Uricedin, 5 ozs	doz.	15.00
Urotropin	oz.	.60
Urotropin Tablets, 5 or 7½ grs.	doz.	3.00
Vaccine, Mulford's (Discount, 40 per cent.), 1 pkg. Glycerinized Lymph, containing 10 tubes		1.00
1 vial Glycerinized Lymph, containing sufficient for 50 vaccinations		4.50
1 pkg. Ivory Points, containing 10 points		.95-1.35
Glycerinated, F. Stearns & Co., Points (10 in a package)		1.00
Tubes (10 tubes in one wooden box, accompanied by one needle, rubber bulb and 10 temporary shields)		1.00
Discount, 40 per cent.		
Vanillin (various brands)	oz.	.60-75
Veratrine, ⅛-oz., 2.75; Sulph., ⅛ths	oz.	2.90
Veronal, ¼-oz., oz., 1.60; 1-oz	oz.	1.60
Veronal Tablets, 5 grs., tubes, .15	ea.	.40
" " bots. 50	ea.	1.15
" " " 100	ea.	2.25
Water, Ammonia, 16 deg., carboy, .3½	lb.	.6
20 deg., carboys, .4½	lb.	.8
26 deg. (Conct.), carboy, .8½	lb.	.10-12
Wax, Bayberry	lb.	.60-65
Carnauba, No. 1	lb.	.55-60
Ceresin, yellow, cases, .18	lb.	.22
" white, cases, .21	lb.	.25-28
Japan, cases, .15	lb.	.18-20
White, Star Brand, 60 lbs., .50	lb.	.55
White, S. B	lb.	.35
Leonard's T. L. Brand, 60 lbs., .47½	lb.	.55
" " 60 lbs., .42½	lb.	.50
Yellow, select	lb.	.38
White Lead, Dry, pure	lb.	.10
Zinc, American, lb., .10; French	lb.	.15
Whiting, bbls., .½	lb.	.3
Witch Hazel Ext., 10 gals., .70	gal.	.85
Wood, Guaiac, rasped	lb.	.6
Quassia Chips, bbl., .6	lb.	.7-12
Red Saunders, bbl., .4	lb.	.6-8
Sandal, ground	lb.	.40
Yohimbin Hydrochlor, ½-gramme vials	each.	5.00
Tablets, 1-12 gr., 10 in tube	each.	1.00
Zinc, Acetate	lb.	.25-30
Carbonate, Precip	lb.	.23
Chloride, granular, lbs., .22	oz.	.6
Iodide	oz.	.40
Oxide	lb.	.10
Hubbuck's, 7-lb. boxes, .35	lb.	.38-40
Zinc, Sulphate, bbls., .3½	lb.	.5-6
Sulphocarbolate, lbs., .50	oz.	.7-9
Valerianate, lbs., 1.75	oz.	.20

PAINTS AND COLORS.

Article	Unit	Price
Black, Coach, in oil	lb.	.18-25
dry	lb.	.15-20
Drop, in oil	lb.	.15-25
dry, in oil	lb.	.12-20
Ivory, in oil, lb., .18-25; dry	lb.	.12-18
in Japan	lb.	.22-25
Lamp, Germantown, ass'd papers, ¼-lb., ½-lb., 1-lb	lb.	.12
in oil	lb.	.10
Black Lead, E. I., 25 lbs., .6½	lb.	.8
German, 25 lbs., .4½	lb.	.6
Blue, Celestial, dry	lb.	.10
Chinese, dry	lb.	.60
in oil	lb.	.55
Paint, in oil	lb.	.9
Prussian, dry	lb.	.50
in oil	lb.	.45
Soluble, 10 lbs., .45	lb.	.50
Ultramarine, dry	lb.	.15
in oil	lb.	.20
Brown, Sienna, burnt, dry	lb.	.4
in oil	lb.	.10-15
Raw, dry	lb.	.4
in oil	lb.	.10-15
Spanish, dry, bbls., .1	lb.	.3
Vandyke, dry	lb.	.6
in oil	lb.	.18
Chalk, lump, bbls., .½	lb.	.3
Green, Chrome, powd., 6-lb. cans, .10	lb.	.12
in oil	lb.	.12-16
Paris, bulk, lbs., .16-17; 1-lbs., .18-20; ½-lbs., .20-22; ¼-lbs., .22-25; in oil	lb.	.22-27
Litharge	lb.	.10
Pumice Stone, bbl., .6	lb.	.8
powdered, bbl., .3	lb.	.6
Putty, in bladders, bbls., .2½	lb.	.2½
in oil	lb.	
Red, Indian, Eng., dry	lb.	.8
in oil	lb.	.10-15
Lead	lb.	.8-10
Orange Mineral	lb.	.12
Rose Lake, Eng., dry	lb.	.5
Pink, Eng., dry	lb.	.15
Tuscan, Eng., dry	lb.	.4
in oil	lb.	.22
Venetian, dry, American, bbls., .1	lb.	.2½
Vermilion, American	lb.	.20
Chinese	lb.	.90
English	lb.	.80
Rotten Stone, bbl., .6	lb.	.8
Umber, Burnt, bbls., .1½	lb.	.3
Raw, bbls., .1½	lb.	.3
White, China, dry	lb.	.20
Flake, dry	lb.	.15
Lead, dry	lb.	.10
oil	lb.	.9-10
Paris, English	lb.	.3
Whiting, bbls., .½	lb.	.8
Yellow, Chrome, dry	lb.	.10-15
in oil	lb.	.10-20
Golden, in oil	lb.	.16
Ochre, French, dry, bbls., .1½	lb.	.2½
American, dry, bbls., .1	lb.	.2
Zinc, White, dry, American	lb.	.8
in oil	lb.	.10

American Druggist "WANTS" Page.

THIS Department is intended to be used as a medium for the exchange or sale of stores, the employment of clerks, and the securing of situations. Suitable notices of moderate length under this heading inserted one time free for subscribers; for each additional insertion Fifty Cents will be charged. Advertisements not in the foregoing classification Forty Cents per line.

SITUATIONS VACANT.

DRUG CLERK WANTED.—A junior drug clerk of one or two years' experience; a country boy preferred; an all year drug store at a summer resort. J. Harrison Monroe, Ph.G., Guilford, Conn.

DRUG CLERK WANTED.—A permanent position is offered to competent man. Give experience and references. Address Samuel Davis, Boonton, N. J.

TRAVELING SALESMAN WANTED to sell specialties in Southern States; none but first-class man who is willing to start on a commission basis need apply; splendid line and good sellers; a first-class man can make a "good thing"; reference required. Address J. C. Simmons, Graham, N. C.

REGISTERED PHARMACISTS.—We are compiling a list of all drug employees in the United States who would accept better conditions. Every pharmacist should write at once for particulars. Employers referred to competent men, free. National Pharmaceutical Agency, 616 Colonial Security Building, St. Louis, Mo.

SALESMEN now calling on the drug trade in Greater New York can secure an advantageous side line on liberal commission; experienced men preferred; splendid opportunity for competent men. Address F. J. J., care AMERICAN DRUGGIST.

SITUATIONS WANTED.

LICENSED PHARMACIST (woman), desires position; registered in New York State, but will go to any State as general all-around clerk; careful prescriptionist, good saleswoman; 15 years' experience; good references. Ella A. Eaton, 708 Montgomery street, Syracuse, N. Y.

DRUG CLERK WANTED FOR MEXICO.—Young graduate in pharmacy, with knowledge of Spanish preferred, who can be trusted in important position in well-known Mexican drug store; must be qualified in every particular; chance of advancement good; send references and state salary expected. Mexico, care Foreign Department, AMERICAN DRUGGIST.

LICENSED PHARMACIST in Pennsylvania, licensed druggist in New York, graduate Albany College Pharmacy, good references, large experience, desires work. Joseph W. Beavan, 417 Larch street, Scranton, Pa.

BUSINESS OPPORTUNITIES.

FOR SALE.—Cleanest drug stock in Fort Wayne, Ind.; established store doing good business; located on principal street; no cutting; unusual opportunity. Address "Opportunity," care AMERICAN DRUGGIST.

FOR SALE.—Profitable drug business in town near New York; good prices; low rent; sales last year $4,500; will be $5,000 this year; can be doubled; $1,000 cash required; balance easy payments. Address "Pharmacist," care AMERICAN DRUGGIST.

FOR SALE.—San Juan, Porto Rico; only American drug store; established seven years; good business; inventory about $7,500; reason, sickness. P. O. Box 226, San Juan, Porto Rico.

FOR SALE.—Only drug store in good farming town of 800 population, with good neighboring territory; $2,500 stock; income about $8,000; rent, $100 per annum. Address David Letaw, Springville, Ala.

FINE INVESTMENT in a principal city of Texas; full prices; best corner drug store; good reasons for selling. Address "Importer," care AMERICAN DRUGGIST.

CALIFORNIA BUSINESS.—Chain of eight retail stores and wholesale house doing business of $400,000 annually, capable of indefinite expansion; book value of stock in this corporation in excess of 1.20 dividends, 8 per cent. annually and 10 per cent. to surplus; 65 per cent. of stock will be sold on basis of 105 per share; details furnished those giving assurance of satisfactory financial responsibility. F. A. Pollock, 418 Donohoe Building, San Francisco, Cal.

BIG PAYING BUSINESS for sale; stock comprises drugs, wall paper, paint, books and stationery; sales, $30,000; want to sell and have a good reason for it. Address C. H. Mead, Gouverneur, N. Y.

Granular Effervescent Salts
TWO
NEW FORMULAS
which we are directing to the attention of the physicians of the country and which are certain to be in large demand.
SALINE LAXATIVE.
Each drachm represents:
Sodium Phosphate, 20 grains.
Magnesium Sulphate, 25 grains.
Sodium Sulphate, 10 grains.
SODIUM PHOSPHATE,
CONCENTRATED.
Each ounce contains:
Sodium Phosphate, 1 ounce.
Supplied in 2-oz. and 4-oz. bottles, with screw-cap measuring cup; also in pound bottles.
PUT THEM ON YOUR "WANT" LIST.
Our Granular Effervescent Salts are a triumph of manufacturing pharmacy. They dissolve with brisk effervescence, yielding snappy, refreshing draughts.
MILK OF BISMUTH
VALUABLE
Antacid and Gastric Sedative
Pharmacists who have not as yet stocked our Milk of Bismuth (a recent acquisition to our list) are advised to do so, and to notify their medical patrons of their ability to supply it.
Milk of Bismuth (P., D. & Co.) is of marked usefulness in the treatment of gastroenteric diseases, diarrheas, dysentery, etc.
NET PRICES.
Pint bottles, per dozen, $8.50. 5-pint bottles, each, $3.25.
Gallon bottles, each, $4.70.
MILK OF BISMUTH
SHAKE THE BOTTLE
PARKE, DAVIS & CO.
DETROIT, MICH., U.S.A.
PARKE, DAVIS & COMPANY
LABORATORIES: DETROIT, MICH., U.S.A.; WALKERVILLE, ONT.; HOUNSLOW, ENG.
BRANCHES: NEW YORK, CHICAGO, ST. LOUIS, BOSTON, BALTIMORE, NEW ORLEANS, KANSAS CITY, INDIANAPOLIS, MINNEAPOLIS, MEMPHIS; LONDON, ENG.; MONTREAL, QUE.; SYDNEY, N.S.W.; ST. PETERSBURG, RUSSIA; SIMLA, INDIA; TOKIO, JAPAN.

Different Kinds of Glass.

The varieties of glass are described by *Drug Topics* as: Soluble glass, bottle glass, common window glass, crown glass, plate glass, flint glass, crystal glass, strass and enamel.

All other glasses are simply varieties of these. Soluble glass consists of an excess of an alkali with silica. This may be either soda, potash, or both.

Its uses are for stiffening fibrous substances, as a substitute for gum or starch, as a varnish for wood or cloth to render these fireproof, or as a coating for ancient monuments or buildings of stone, which may be thus preserved from decay or the action of the elements.

It is stated that the great obelisk in Central Park, New York City, was thus treated.

Bottle or green glass is composed of silica, soda, lime and alumina and receives its green color from the iron present as an impurity in the sand. The methods of making are by the blow pipe. Its uses are evident from its name and it is the substance from which the cheaper bottles are made.

Common window glass consists of silica, soda and lime, sometimes also of potash. This is a blow pipe glass, usually formed by the blow pipe in a cylinder and then cut and flattened while in a plastic state.

Its uses are evident and from which the cheaper windows are made.

Crown glass is a more aristocratic variety of common window glass, produced by a different manipulation of the blow pipe. This is a glass of great luster and beauty, but its use for windows has been superseded by other products, for the reason that only small panes can be cut from any piece of crown glass.

Plate glass, the purest silicate of soda or potash and lime, is made by casting the glass after fusion upon a table in sheets of any required size. This is an expensive glass. Its uses are chiefly for windows and mirrors.

Flint glass is so named as it is composed of a fine variety of pulverized flint, with potash and lead. It is to this latter substance that its brilliancy is due, which distinguishes this from all other varieties.

The use of lead is supposed to be a recent discovery in the manufacture of glass, but as the analysis of certain ancient glass shows lead in its composition, it must be conceded as known to the ancient glass makers.

Its uses include the great bulk of decorative glass, either blown or pressed. Its qualities are various, depending upon the grade of material in its composition.

French crystal glass is a variety of flint glass. This is the choicest material from which glass is made and is used for table service and for scientific instruments, as optical glasses, etc.

Bohemian glass is a lime variety of flint glass.

When more lead is added to flint glass the product is strass. This is a glass of brilliant luster, from which gems are produced by the addition before fusion of the oxides of various metals for desired colors. Thus, gold for the ruby, and so forth.

Enamel is a term given to glass which is rendered milk white opaque by the addition of the binoxide of tin to the silica, soda and lead of which it is composed. It is a variety of pure crystal glass and is a very ancient production.

Colored enamels are produced by the addition of the metallic oxides which produce the required colors.

The Diplomatic Druggist.

A certain druggist who does not like to answer night calls, especially as he has found by experience that he offends people who call him up at night by his displeased, abrupt manner, has devised a scheme by which he does not have to get up and at the same times does not lose customers. As described in the *Northwestern Druggist* by the druggist himself, he works the scheme in this way:

"I disconnect my bell so that it cannot ring. After waiting some time the person who wants to get in gives it up as a bad job and goes down the street to the next store. This man opens for him but is naturally very much displeased and, as I usually do, he shows that he is disgruntled and offends the customer. Early the next morning the customer calls at my store to inform me that my bell is out of order and tells me what a low opinion he has of the other druggist, whom he considers a very impolite man."

Hints to Buyers.

Such of our readers as have not studied carefully the price protective plans of the S. A. R. D. Association should write at once to the S. A. R. D. Association, H. C. G. Luytles, president. St. Louis, Mo., for full particulars. It means more money for the retailer.

A. H. Wirz, of 913 Cherry street, Philadelphia, manufactures bottle stoppers, collapsible tubes and pharmaceutical machinery. All his line is carried in stock by wholesale druggists and may be obtained upon specification. Write him for catalogue, mentioning the AMERICAN DRUGGIST.

When in the market for syringe boxes of white wood, bass, oak, ash, etc., be sure to obtain samples and quotations from the Henry H. Sheip Mfg. Company, of 529 Columbia avenue, Philadelphia. This old and reliable concern also manufactures any form of fancy wood boxes desired. Their facilities are so extensive that they can guarantee lowest prices and absolutely prompt shipment.

The Bee Brand of Insect Powder marketed by McCormick & Co., of Baltimore, Md., is a product upon which the reputation of this concern has been largely built. It is ground only from closed flowers purchased in the market of production by their own resident agent. A sample will be sent upon application. It is packed in airtight wooden bottles, retailing for 10 cents, and also in larger packages and in kegs and barrels.

Columbian Spirit, manufactured by the Wood Products Company, of Buffalo, N. Y., is the equal of grain alcohol for all purposes which do not involve internal application. In other words, Columbian Spirit is a wood product, and pharmacists must consider it from that point of view, but for all preparations designed for external application Columbian Spirit is to be recommended as taking the place of grain alcohol in a thoroughly satisfactory manner and, of course, at a much lower price.

The advertisement of the American Carbonate Company, of 434 East Nineteenth street, New York City, is entitled to the special consideration of our readers at this season. Retail druggists cannot be too often warned against buying the many inferior carbonic acid gases offered by unscrupulous manufacturers. The liquid carbonate manufactured and sold by the American Carbonate Company, on the other hand, has given invariable satisfaction wherever used. The success of the soda fountain business has to depend in a large measure upon the quality of the gas used. A poor gas at a low price is a bad investment. Send for an illustrated catalogue and price-list, mentioning the AMERICAN DRUGGIST.

It is important in buying goods to remember trademark rights and so avoid litigation at the hands of offended manufacturers. The Fellows Company, of New York, with offices at 26 Christopher street, is the sole owner of Fellows' Compound Syrup of Hypophosphites, one of the most sinned against of the old-time preparations. While the company has always been generous in its attitude towards the retail drug trade, it has had in self-defense to maintain a strict attitude regarding infringements. As the courts have held that even colorable imitations are liable as infringements, it behooves the careful pharmacist to avoid buying preparations which may be looked upon as infringements.

One Thousand Dollars Reward.

The above sum is offered by Mariani & Co., of 52 West Fifteenth street, New York City, and is designed to set at rest certain false and misleading statements which have been made regarding Vin Mariani. We invite the attention of our readers to the advertisement of the house, which appears in this issue. Vin Mariani has been on the American market for a great many years and has received the indorsement of some of the best physicians in the country.

Montserrat Lime Juice.

Evan's Sons, Lescher & Webb, of Liverpool and London, with a branch at 92 William street, New York City, invite the American drug trade to judge their Montserrat Lime Juice by scientific methods. The product is undiluted, and 30 to 50 per cent. less of it than of other brands may be used. If any of our readers should fail to obtain a supply of this famous product from their jobbers they are invited to correspond with the American branch.

Check Your Soda Sales.

We particularly invite the attention of our readers to the advertisement of the Lock-Stub Check Company, 136 West Thirty-fourth street, New York City. The system which this concern has devised is the most satisfactory method yet discovered for preventing either carelessness or dishonesty on the part of soda clerks. An interesting booklet on the subject will be sent upon application.

Special Offers Well Worth Attention.

On page 35 of this issue will be found listed a series of special offers on instruments and specialties, which is well worth the attention of every enterprising druggist. This offer comes from the Frank S. Betz Company, of Hammond, Ind., and Chicago, who has erected at Hammond one of the largest surgical instrument factories in the world. When writing the company for details kindly mention the AMERICAN DRUGGIST.

Ozone-Vanillin.

A new laboratory has been established at Niagara Falls for the manufacture of a new and valuable form of vanillin, which is being marketed under the name of Ozone-Vanillin. It is made from eugenol (the chief constituent of oil of cloves) oxidized by contact with electrically produced ozone. The product is several hundred times stronger than vanilla and it makes an extract with a very much finer and more persistent flavor. Any of our readers may obtain a sample of the extract by addressing the sales agents, Ferguson-Bedell Company, Board of Trade Building, Boston, Mass.

"Hand-I-Hold" Babe Mits.

A very ingenious method of disposing of a child's hands in cases of eczema and other skin diseases has been perfected by R. M. Clark & Co., of Boston, Mass. By addressing Department 6, 246 Summer street, Boston, an illustrated pamphlet may be obtained. The advertisement is running in the current issues of the AMERICAN DRUGGIST. The mits are being extensively advertised, and as they have the hearty approval of practicing physicians there is a growing demand for them. This is an article which it will pay druggists to push. The margin of profit is very satisfactory. Inquirers through the mail are referred to local druggists.

The Retail Mail Order Department.

A very interesting and instructive pamphlet has been issued with above title by Butler Brothers, of New York, Chicago and St. Louis. This pamphlet is intended to be practically helpful to the local retailer in the solution of what he certainly regards as his gravest problem.

Nothing could show more conclusively the intense interest in its subject than the fact that the first edition of 25,000 was wholly exhausted by advance requests for the book, and that to date the total of requests received for it is approximately 40,000—coming from every State in the Union and from "all sorts and conditions of" merchants, ranging from metropolitan department store to cross-roads general store owners.

It is all of three years ago since they began accumulating material for this booklet. Within that period and largely through the efforts of trade journals the retailer has passed from a state of paralyzing fear of retail mail order houses to a realization that they have created new and permanent conditions, which call for fighting instead of complaining.

Write Butler Bros. for a copy of this pamphlet and study the situation by its aid.

Welch Grape Juice Company Hurries Work on Additional Plant.

The Welch Grape Juice Company has decided that to take care if its very fast increasing business it must complete its No. 2 factory at Westfield, N. Y., this year. A three-story concrete factory, 110 x 160, fully equipped, and the new power plant will be erected in time for grapes this fall.

The enlargement of this already large concern means that the grape growers of Westfield and vicinity need not fear for the future of the grape business. According to the Westfield *Republican* the Welch Grape Juice Company can be credited with securing for the farmers from $1 to $3 per ton extra for every ton of grapes raised in the belt, whether sold to this company or not. There was used by Welch Grape Juice Company in 1903, 1,600 tons of grapes; in 1904, 2,200 tons; in 1905, 2,500 tons, and here the capacity of the No. 1 factory was crowded to its utmost. It is calculated that the first pressing in No. 2 factory will be more than 3,000 tons.

The Water Way Between Detroit and Buffalo.

Particular and experienced travelers habitually use the Detroit & Buffalo line en route between Eastern and Western States. Low rates and superior service attracts this class of travel. You can save $3 by purchasing your through tickets via the Detroit & Buffalo line. Send 2-cent stamp for illustrated pamphlet. Address Detroit & Buffalo Steamboat Company, 4 Wayne street, Detroit, Mich.

Removal Notice.

C. Bischoff & Co., importers of medicinal chemicals, announce their removal to 451 to 453 Washington street, corner of Watts street, New York, where all communications for the firm should now be addressed.

The Artificial Coloring of Flowers.

A recent issue of Torreya contains an interesting note by Prof. Henry Kraemer, of Philadelphia, on the artificial coloring of flowers, which is the outcome of a year's experimentation in the feeding of plants with certain chemicals. The results, however, have not been positive in their character, but in the course of this work Professor Kraemer made some interesting observations regarding the artificial coloring of cut flowers. He publishes a table of colors which can be produced in cut flowers, which are naturally white, by putting the stems in aqueous solutions of about ⅛ ounce of dye to a pint of water. We present below an abstract of this table, giving the common names of the dyes used and of the colors produced: Canary yellow: Acid yellow A. T. (C). Orange: Orange G. G. (C). Blue: Cyanole F. F. (C). Green: A mixture of equal parts of acid yellow A. T. and cyanole F. F. Purplish, red or magenta: Acid magenta C. Crimson: A mixture of equal parts of acid yellow A. T. and acid magenta. Purple: A mixture of equal parts of cyanole F. F. and acid magenta. Salmon pink: Brilliant croceine M. O. O. (C). Pale salmon pink: Crystal scarlet 6 R. (C). Dark gray or blackish: Naphtol black B. (C). When the desired effect has been produced, which is usually within an hour or less, the flowers may be put in plain water. The treatment does not affect the odor, and the color produced seems to be permanent, as the flowers may be dried without losing the color thus imparted.

An Assyrian Drink Cure.

The following is a translation of an inscription on one of the earliest Assyrian monuments in the British Museum: "The eggs of an owl given for three days in wine bring on a drunkard's weariness. The dried lung of sheep taken beforehand drives away drunkenness. The ashes of a swallow's beak ground up with myrrh and sprinkled in the wine which is drunk will make secure from drunkenness. Horus, King of the Assyrians, found this out."

Pure Nicotine for the Destruction of Plant Insects and Vermin.

It is a well-known fact that all vegetable and plant life is afflicted with some insect or parasite and something to destroy these parasites is much needed. In the case of plant insects and vermin pure nicotine is an agent that will cause their destruction. This is now produced from the refuse tobacco of large cigar and smoking tobacco factories. The alkaloid nicotine is described in chemical books as a colorless, oily, volatile liquid with a burning taste, which dissolves readily in water. Heretofore it has not been possible to obtain it save in a very limited way and then not pure. Now the pure product, known as rose nicotine, can be easily obtained in the leading drug stores. It has been brought out through the scientific research in the laboratories of F. A. Thompson & Co., Detroit. Tobacco stems, dust, etc., selected for their nicotine value, are gathered from the large tobacco and cigar manufacturers. Tons of the stems at a time are put through large drying ovens to remove moisture to permit grinding and then passed on to grinding mills having a capacity of 4 tons per day, where they are reduced to a fine powder. The coarse ground tobacco and the dust in going from the first mill to the second, which produces the proper fineness, pass over a magnetic attachment, which removes all metallic particles, nails, etc., leaving only the pure tobacco for treatment. From here the powder passes into large mixers, where the nicotine is liberated by a special process; the mixture is then put into exhausting tanks, where a special solvent is used to remove the pure nicotine only in a dilute form. This liquid is then transferred to large vacuum pans, where at about the temperature of the human body (98.50 degrees F.) it is reduced to a concentrated form. Before bottling or putting up in finished packages this pure concentrated nicotine solution is submitted to analytical assay and adjusted to a definite or uniform standard. Therefore the Thompson's Rose Nicotine used to-day and a year from to-day will be of the same strength and give the same results.

Nicotine is recognized by the United States Government, for the Bureau of Animal Industry demands that sheep and cattle infested with scab shall be dipped in a nicotine solution containing 0.05 per cent. nicotine.

Nicotine is a superior insecticide and parasiticide, as it is not only fatal to insects and parasites, but as it makes a colorless, odorless and stainless solution it can be used where strong smelling products would be prohibited.

The manufacturers of this pure nicotine issue a booklet entitled, "How to Destroy Plant Insects and Vermin," and every druggist should read it and see that his customers have one, as it interests every one. We refer our readers to F. A. Thompson & Co., of Detroit, for details of the special offer whereby every druggist can get the product free by paying express charges.

The Ideal Hair Brush.

The Ideal hair brush, which is illustrated herewith, has two unique features in its construction, as it consists of genuine Siberian bristles set singly instead of in tufts as in ordinary brushes in an elastic air cushion base. This peculiarity of construction enables the bristles to penetrate even the most luxuriant hair without undue pressure. It is particularly valuable in untangling the curly hair of children, as by its use the most matted tangles can be straightened out without injuring either the hair or scalp. The makers claim that it is the lightest hair brush ever made and that only the very best material is used in its construction. The military brush, which is illustrated herewith, has been placed upon the market for the first time in this form by the American agents and it is sure to prove a very prompt and profitable seller. For special introductory terms address the sole American agents, Henry L. Hughes, 78 Monroe street, Chicago.

New Advertising Energy for Pond's Extract.

According to *Printers' Ink* Pond's Extract is one of the clean, straightforward proprietary remedies, as far as composition is concerned, and also one of the most stable in point of sales. A harmless liquid, used chiefly for external application, it has none of the features that have raised the recent outcry against "patent medicines." And serving most of the purposes of a liniment, as well as having antiseptic character, it is used over and over in the average family many times a year and for many years, so that unlike a "cure-all," it is stable when once introduced.

With these obvious merits, Pond's Extract has one commercial disadvantage, and this has played havoc with its sales. A simple extract of the shrub *hamamelis virginica*, instead of a formula preparation, it has been extensively counterfeited, imitated and subjected to the competition of substitutes. Perhaps no other proprietary in the market has suffered so much from substitution. To add to the losses through this insidious channel the remedy has been handicapped by insufficient and poorly directed advertising until within the past year. But during 1905 a new, energetic campaign was started. More money was appropriated than had ever been spent before, new methods and mediums adopted, and after 11 months' work along these new lines the company had the satisfaction of learning that sales had been increased 80 per cent. and that it had done the largest business in its long history.

To thoroughly comprehend the advertising problem of Pond's Extract it is necessary to know something of its story, which goes back fully 60 years. The shrub *hamamelis virginica*, popularly known as "witch hazel," is native to North America alone, and found in quantities only in New Hampshire, Connecticut and New York State. Long before the white man came it was a medicinal herb valued by the Indians, and when New England was settled the whites soon learned to value it, too. For years "witch hazel" held a place among the home remedies, grandmother's "yarbs," being prepared by boiling in tea kettles. In the '40's this remedy was taken in hand by the Ponds at Utica, N. Y., a place where the shrub was then found in abundance, and converted into a stable liquid through distillation and the use of a preservative. For distilled witch hazel spoils after a few days unless fixed with alcohol, the preservative used in Pond's Extract. This commercial preparation of a favorite home remedy, put on the market as Pond's Extract, soon grew into a sale so wide that the shrubs around Utica gave out and it was necessary to move the distillery to Connecticut, where it is located to-day. Witch hazel blossoms late in autumn; the shrub can be distilled for medicinal purposes only when it is in flower.

The Ponds have been out of the Pond's Extract Company, which is a corporation, for more than 40 years. But they advertised their product from the first and early created a name for it that led to imitations. For 60 years practically Pond's Extract has been advertised. But there was never any defined policy. The advertising was chiefly general publicity—"Pond's cures" and "Good for cuts and bruises." People who knew the virtues of witch hazel bought Pond's sometimes, and again a bulk extract, which was cheaper. The advertising never told them the difference between bulk witch hazel and the proprietary article. The former is often a weak solution of the plant at its best, the company claims, while at its worst it may be adulterated with wood alcohol or formaldehyde, as many samples analyzed for the company have proved to be. Pond's has a high standard of strength and lives up to the United States Pharmacopœia. Again, the advertising was insufficient in volume and interest to keep witch hazel prominently before the new generations who had never heard of the old-time remedy. Population outgrew Pond's Extract and the new generation knew it not.

With this situation confronting it the company stirred itself over a year ago. W. T. Seagrave, an advertising man of 25 years' experience, mapped out a campaign with the idea of telling the public something about Pond's first, and telling people direct, or as nearly so as possible. A change of mediums was the initial step. The company had been using a good

deal of space in magazines. Mr. Seagrave is a newspaper man and believes in the daily papers. Daily papers, therefore, formed part of his plan. But not all.

"The company's former expenditure ran between $80,000 and $100,000 a year," he says. "But that for 1905 went a good deal higher. With the idea that people to-day know less about witch hazel than they did 30 years ago, and that those who do know about witch hazel are likely to know nothing about Pond's, we set out for a campaign of information. Pond's Extract is witch hazel, but witch hazel isn't Pond's Extract. Pond's is what Wanamaker calls 'that totally different kind.' There are ways of demonstrating this in print and we have taken them. We do it in our newspaper and other copy by telling the story of Pond's, and by securing samples of bulk witch hazel in certain territory we are covering and having them analyzed. Out of 70 samples bought this way on the Pacific Coast, for instance, 52 contained wood alcohol or formaldehyde, while none were of standard strength. Pond's therefore may mean safety from poisoning. It is sure to mean strength.

"In the way of mediums we are now using every daily paper on the Pacific Coast, except six that I had never heard of till our advertising started. These were not very prominent, it is true, but on general principles in covering a specified territory I believe in using the weak mediums, for they must reach some people, and are worth their price if the price is just. We are also using some daily papers in large cities elsewhere, but the Western coast is being covered because conditions out there make that inviting territory and because, as our appropriation is not large enough to cover the country nationally in dailies, we deem it best to concentrate. Our newspaper copy talks purity and strength, with the healing properties of Pond's as a secondary argument. We are after the users of witch hazel first and new converts second. The substitution problem is most important, and by attacking it and putting the public right we can make sales faster than with another line of argument. In all territory where daily newspaper advertising is running we have been working on the retail druggists through salesmen, not only enlisting their help in stocking up to meet demand, but in circularizing. Retailers furnish us lists of names and we send to these various sorts of literature, according to the size of the community.

"Here is a booklet that goes into small towns and the country. Probably it would be of little service in big cities. It is a handbook on first aid to the injured, made up of material compiled by the investigators of Johnson & Johnson, the makers of surgical supplies. All the information in this book is scientific and ethical, and in every line is emphasized the importance of sending for a physician. What to do till the doctor comes is its theme, and the advertising value is secured by specification of Pond's Extract for perfectly proper uses. In connection with this book we sell a Pond's Extract first-aid case for factories, farms and households. Such information is prized on farms and in small towns, where people must often act in emergencies, but in cities, where physicians are within a few minutes' call, it would not be valued. In such centers we distribute something like our book on 'Beauty,' which was written by Harriet Hubbard Ayer, and gives directions for massage, deep breathing, clearing the complexion, etc., in connection with Pond's Extract and our toilet essentials. As many as 30,000 or 40,000 booklets have been sent out of here in a day, and in the past six months the average has not been less than 10,000 a day.

"To stimulate sales in the country, where demand must be taken care of by jobbers, we have been using a list of agricultural and religious papers. I believe in both of these mediums, but particularly the farm papers. Our list of neither is large—more in the nature of experiment. That in the agricultural field, for example, comprises six mediums—*Wisconsin Agriculturist, Farm and Ranch, Country Gentleman, National Stockman, Practical Farmer* and *Farmer's Review*. The farm papers not only reach the best class in the country, but even when they go to towns and cities they are taken by people who read them thoroughly. We have printed in them a four-line reading notice in addition to our display advertisements, offering the first-aid book, about which nothing was said in the display ads. Requests for thousands of copies have come from these readers, showing that a very small ad. is seen and heeded in the farm publications. But our chief use of farm and religious mediums has been for general publicity thus far—advertising to create business that involves no such follow-up and personal work as does concentrated newspaper advertising in a territory where every retailer must be brought into line.

"Pond's Extract is also advertised in a large list of medical papers to reach physicians. The arguments here, too, are chiefly directed against substitutes. Pond's has been in the market so long that it is freely prescribed.

"Pond's offers many live advertising arguments on its merits as a remedy. Its advertising may be kept close to the almanac all the year round. In winter it is good for chilblains and rheumatism and in summer for insect bites, stings and sunburn. There is always the toilet argument, too. But the crux of the situation is substitution, and by attacking it in our advertising we have been able to show an 80 per cent. increase in sales from January 1 to December 1, 1905, at an increase in advertising expenditure that is, results considered, extremely moderate. During 1906 the company will make a still larger increase in its expenditure—I might say a big increase. And this money is to be spent principally for more advertising space in daily newspapers."

Supplementary campaign for a new article, Pond's Extract Soap, began in March. This product is being marketed by Armour and Co., Chicago, who make the soap and are the sole licensees from Pond's Extract Company for its manufacture and sale. Its publicity will be divided between newspapers and magazines, and alone will involve an expenditure of over $100,000 in 1906.

The New Building of the American Can Company.

The American Can Company removed its offices from Bowling Green on May 1 to its new eight-story steel frame, fireproof office and manufacturing building at 447 West Fourteenth street, New York City. This structure, fronting on Fourteenth street and extending through the block to Fifteenth street, is the largest building in the country devoted exclusively to the manufacture of tin cans. The basement and first five floors are devoted to manufacturing. On the three upper floors are located the executive and general offices; also those of the Atlantic sales district. The offices of the central sales district are located in Chicago and those of the Pacific sales district in San Francisco.

In addition to these district offices the company maintains 20 local sales offices and 39 factories, located at advantageous shipping points throughout the country. At 23 of these factories special attention is given to the manufacture of special cans used by meat, lard and fish packers, manufacturing druggists, paint and varnish manufacturers and all others using a tin package. These "specialty factories" are located at Lubec, Maine; Boston, Mass.; New York City (3); Newark, N. J.; Philadelphia, Pa.; Baltimore, Md.; Richmond, Va.; Atlanta, Ga.; New Orleans, La.; Savannah, Ga.; Cleveland, Ohio; Hamilton, Ohio; Toledo, Ohio; Detroit, Mich.; Maywood, Ill.; Chicago, Ill. (3); St. Paul, Minn.; Davenport, Iowa; St. Louis, Mo.; Kansas City, Mo.; San Francisco, Cal.; Portland, Ore.; Bellingham, Wash.

These factories being so widely distributed dealers are assured of a sure source of supply, as the disabling of one factory does not interfere with deliveries from the remaining 22. Another great advantage is the saving in freight because of the nearness of the delivery point to the purchaser.

The American Can Company is now better able than ever to handle with dispatch orders for any style of tin cans demanded by the various industries throughout the country using a tin package.

A special introductory offer on Ingersoll watches is made on another page. This offer includes four watches, each in a different finish, in a handsome plush and silk lined leatherette case, the whole being offered for $3.90. This case is illustrated on page 49. For further particulars address Robert H. Ingersoll & Brother, 53 Maiden lane, New York.

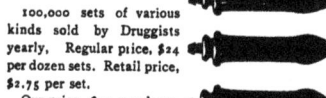

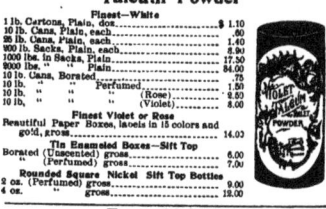

Alphabetical Index to Advertisers.

Where numbers are omitted, the advertisement appears in alternate issues.

For Classified Index see Pages 20 and 21.

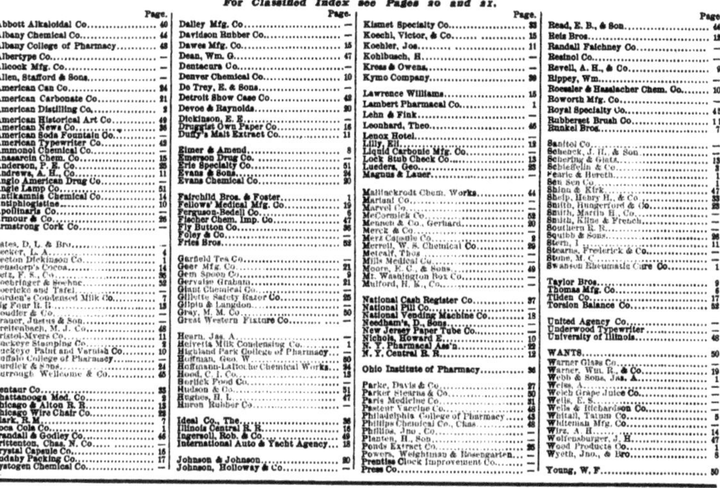

ORIGINAL PACKAGE PRICES.

It should be understood that the prices quoted in this column are strictly those current in the wholesale market, and that higher prices are paid for retail lots. The quality of goods frequently necessitates a considerable range of prices.

Drugs, Chemicals, &c.

Acetanilid lb. .24 @ .26
Acetate of Lime:
Brown 100 lb. 1.60 @ 1.65
Gray 100 lb. 2.35 @ 2.40
Acetone lb. .15½@ .16
Acetphenetidin (U. S. P. phenacetin) lb. 1.15 @ ...
Acid:
Acetic Com'l 100 lb. 2.40 @ 2.65
Acetic C. P. lb. .21 @ .25
Acetic, Glacial .20 @ .23¼
Aquafortis, 36° lb. .03½@ .04½
" 40° lb. .. @ .05½
Benzoic, Ger lb. .50 @ .58
" Eng oz. .10 @ .10½
Boric, Cryst lb. .10 @ .10½
powd lb. .10 @ .10½
Carbol. cryst., blk lb. .14 @ .15
lb. bottle lb. .20 @ .22
Chrysophanic 2.60 @ 2.65
Citric, dom lb. .43 @ .43½
Gallic lb. .53 @ .55
Muriatic C. P. lb. .07½@ .08½
Nitric C. P. lb. .07½@ .10
Oxalic, English lb. .05¾@ .06
Phosphoric lb. .20½@ .21½
Picric lb. .26 @ .35
Pyrogallic lb. 1.65 @ ..
Salicylic lb. .31 @ .34
Sulphuric, 98% lb. .01½@ .02
Tartaric, crystals lb. .27¾@ .28¼
powdered lb. .28 @ .28½
Tannic, cryst lb. .54 @ .65
Alcohol, grain gal. 2.47 @ 2.49
wood, 95-97% gal. .70 @ .75
Aloin lb. .45 @ .50
Alum, Lump 100 lb. 1.75 @ 1.80
Ground 100 lb. 1.80 @ 1.85
Ammon, carb .08½@ .08½
" bromide, bulk .23 @ .24
" iodide, bulk 4.75 @ 4.80
Aniline Oil .09 @ .09½
Salt .08¼@ .09½
Antipyrine (New) oz. ... @ .19
Arrowroot, Bermuda lb. .38 @ .40
St. Vincent, in bbl lb. .06½@ .08
Arsenic: Red Saxon lb. .06½@ .07½
White lb .05½@ .05
Balm of Gilead Buds lb. .37 @ .25
Balsam Copaiba, Cent. Amer lb. .29 @ .32
Para lb. .42½@ .45
Fir, Canada gal. 3.60 @ 3.10
Fir, Oregon gal. .70 @ .80
Peru lb. 1.10 @ 1.15
Tolu lb. .20 @ .21
Bark, Angostura lb. .38 @ .40
Buckthorn lb. .05 @ .05½
Cascara Sag lb. .06 @ .08
Cascarilla lb. .10 @ .14
Cotton root lb. .08½@ .10
Cramp lb. .07 @ .09
Elm, select lb. .16 @ .18
Pine, white lb. .05 @ .08
Prickly Ash lb. .11 @ .13
Sassafras lb. .17½@ .14
Soap—whole lb. .05 @ .05½
Crushed lb. .06½@ .08
White Pine lb. .04½@ .06
Wild Cherry lb. .06 @ .09
Bismuth, citrate lb. 1.75 @ 1.80
" ammon cit lb. 1.85 @ 1.90
" subnit blk. 1.50 @ 1.55
" subcarb lb. 1.75 @ 1.80
" subgallate lb. 1.85 @ 1.90
Bleaching Powder, Eng .01½@ .01¾
German R .01¾@ .01¾
Domestic .01 @ .01¾
Blue Vitriol lb. .06 @ .06 1-10
Borax, Refined lb. .07½@ .07¾
powd. conc lb. .07½@ .08
crystals lb. .07½@ .07¾
Brimstone, crude 2d ton. 22.00 @ ...
Bromine, bulk lb. .22 @ .23
Burgundy Pitch lb. .04 @ .04½
Cacao Butter, blk lb. .28½@ .30
" " 12 lb. boxes .34 @ .35
Caffeine lb. ... @ 2.65
Calcium hypophosphite lb. .60 @ .64
Cantharides, Chinese lb. ... @ .83
" powd lb. .75 @ .85
Russian, whole lb. 1.20 @ 1.25
Cassia Buds lb. .18½@ .19½
Castor Oil, No. 1, bbl lb. .11 @ .12
" " No. 1, cases lb. .11½@ .12½
" " No. 3, bbl lb. .11½@ .11½
" " No 3, cases lb. .10½@ .10½
Caustic Soda 100 lb. 1.70 @ 1.75
Chalk, Eng. Precip., bulk lb. .06 @ ...
Chloral Hydrate, crystals, bulk lb. ... @ 0.95
crusts, blk lb. ... @ 0.93
Chloroform, bulk lb. .25 @ .30
Cinchonidine Sulph oz. .12 @ .15
Cocaine Muriate oz. 3.00 @ 3.25
Codeine Sulph oz. 3.05 @ 3.25
Cod Liver Oil, Norweg. bbl. 20.00 @ 25.00
Newfoundland bbl. 19.00 @ 20.00
Colocynth, Trieste lb. .20 @ .27
Spanish lb. .25 @ .26
Copperas, car lots 100 lb. .47½@ .52
single bbls 100 lb. .57½@ .65
Creosote, Beechwood .85 @ .90
Cream Tartar lb powd. .22½@ .23
Cubeb berries, xx lb. .10 @ .11
Powdered lb. .12 @ .14
Cutch, bales lb. .07½@ .08
boxes lb. .16 @ .16½
Cuttle Bone, Trieste lb. .16½@ .17
French lb. .12 @ .18
Jewelers', large lb .70 @ ...
" small lb. .40 @ .45
Dextrin lb. .05½@ .06
Divi Divi ton. 30.00 @ 43.00
Dragon's Bl'd, lump lb. .18 @ .18
in reeds lb. .50 @ .55
Epsom Salts 100 lb. .85 @ 1.00
Ergot, German lb. .27 @ .28
Spanish lb. .. @ .38
Ergotine, Dom lb. 4.95 @ 5.00
Flowers, Arnica lb. .06 @ .10

Flowers—cont'd
Calendula lb. .25 @ .30
Chamomile, Roman lb. .22 @ .25
German lb. .15 @ .25
Hungarian lb. .09½@ .11
Insect, open lb. .15 @ .17
Half closed lb. .26 @ .28
Closed lb. .26 @ ...
Powder lb. .14 @ .22
Lavender lb. .12 @ .13
Select lb. .15 @ .20
Saffron, Amer lb. .95 @ ...
Spanish Alicante lb. 4.75 @ 6.00
" Valencia lb. 8.00 @ 8.50
Formaldehyde lb. .09 @ .09½
Glycerin, C. P. drums lb. .11½@ .11¾
" cans lb. .12½@ .12½
Grains of Paradise lb. .11½@ .15
Guarana lb. 1.00 @ ...
Gums: Aloes, Cape .07 @ .08
" Barbadoes lb. .16 @ .17
" Curacoa .05½@ .08
" Socot lb. .18 @ .20
Arabic, 1st pkd lb. .30 @ ...
" 2d pkd lb. .11 @ .23
" sorts lb. .06½@ .11
Asafoetida lb. .15 @ .22
Benzoin, Sumatra lb. .34 @ .38
Siam lb. .90 @ 1.00
Camphor, ref'd. blk lb. 1.00 @ ..
cases lb. 1.00½@ ..
Chicle lb. .35 @ .88
Gamboge lb. .95 @ 1.05
Guaiac lb. .17 @ .23
Kino lb. .25 @ .28
Mastic lb. .45 @ .48
Myrrh lb. .25 @ .28
Olibanum lb. .10 @ .15
Sandarac lb. .14 @ .18
Senegal, pkd lb. .1. @ .13
Tragacanth, Aleppo lb. .30 @ .65
Tragacanth, Turkey lb. .35 @ .80
Haarlem Oil 3.00 @ 3.75
Hypophosphite lime lb. .48 @ .50
" potash lb. .48 @ .50
" soda lb. .48 @ .50
Ichthyol lb. 4.00 @ 4.25
Indigo lb. .90 @ 1.45
Insect Pwd. pure lb. .14 @ .25
Iodine, resub 2.70 @ 2.75
Iodoform lb. 3.00 @ 3.05
Iron citrate, U. S. P lb. ..... @ .44
" and ammon. cit lb. ..... @ .41
and ammon. citrate (green scales)
and quinine citrate lb. 1.18 @ 1.23
phosphate, scales lb. .... @ .38
pyrophosphate, scales lb. .... @ .38
quinine and strychnine citrate lb. 1.68 @ 1.73
Isinglass, Amer lb. .75 @ .80
Russian lb. 4.00 @ 4.10
Juniper Berries lb. .03½@ .04
Lanoline lb. .60 @ .65
Leaves: Aconite .09 @ .10
Belladonna lb. .10 @ .11
Buchu, short lb. .17 @ .20
" long lb ..... @ .30
Cannabis Indica, tops lb. 1.00 @ 1.10
Coca, Truxillo lb. .17 @ .18
" Huanuco lb. .30 @ .32
Damiana lb. .08 @ .10
Digitalis lb. .07½@ .09
Grindelia robusta lb. .08 @ .09
Horehound lb. .04½@ .06
Hyoscyamus lb. .07 @ .08
Jaborandi lb. .14 @ .15
Pulsatilla .07½@ .11
Rose, Red lb .65 @ .70
Senna, pkd whole lb. .20 @ .22
Alexandria, natural lb. .08 @ .09
garbled and sifted lb. .15 @ .16
Tinnevelly lb. .04 @ .09
Alexandria, siftings lb. .05½@ .06
Stramonium lb. .06 @ .08½
Uva ursi lb. .08½@ .08½
Yerba Santa lb. .07 @ .07½
Liquorice—mass lb. .08 @ .10
Spanish lb. .14 @ .20
Imported mass Spanish lb. .19 @ .24
Stick, Calabria lb. .23 @ .28
Domestic lb. .16½@ .23½
Lithia, carbonate lb. 1.50 @ 1.75
" citrate lb. 1.35 @ 1.45
Lupulin, Ger lb. .18 @ .25
Lycopodium lb. .50 @ .51
Magnesia, carb lb. .12 @ .15
Manna, large flk lb. .45 @ .50
Small flake lb. .33 @ .35
Menthol, Japanese lb. 2.55 @ 2.70
Mercurials:
Blue Pill lb. .43 @ .46
Calomel lb. .77 @ .79
Corr. Sublim lb. .70 @ .72
Mercury and Chalk lb. .33 @ .34
Ointment, ½ lb. .47 @ .48
Ointment, ⅓ lb. .38 @ .39
Red Precip lb. .87 @ .89
White " lb. .92 @ .94
Morphine, bulk oz. 2.10 @ 2.20
Eighths oz. 2.45 @ 2.50
Moss, Iceland lb. .05 @ .06
Irish lb. .06½@ .08
Irish, bleached lb. .09½@ .10
Napthaline, flake lb. 1.90 @ 2.00
Ball lb. .02½@ .....
Nux Vomica lb. .02½@ .03
Oil, Anise lb. 1.25 @ 1.37½
Almonds, bit, Eng lb. 5.50 @ 5.75
French lb. 3.55 @ 3.60
bit., artificial lb. .65 @ 1.30
sweet, true lb. .37 @ .40
Peach kernels .19 @ .22
Bay lb. 2.10 @ 2.25
22 oz. bots bot. 3.35 @ 3.35
Bergamot lb. 2.15 @ 2.70
Cajuput lb. .45 @ .52½
Camphor lb. .17½@ .19
Caraway lb. 1.15 @ 1.40
Cassia 75@80% lb .80 @ .82½

Oils—cont'd.
Cedar, pure lb. .60 @ 1.85
red lb. .21 @ .25
Citronella lb. .40 @ .42
Clove, bud .97½@ 1.00
Copaiba lb. .65 @ .70
Coriander lb. 5.00 @ 11.00
Croton lb. .75 @ .80
Cubeb lb. .90 @ 1.00
Eucalyptus lb. .40 @ .60
Geranium lb. 1.90 @ 4.75
Lavender, flowers lb. 2.00 @ 2.25
Lemon lb. .67½@ .75
Lemongrass lb. 3.00 @ 3.10
Mustard lb. 4.25 @ 5.25
Myrbane lb. .07 @ .08
Neroli lb. 45.00 @ 57.50
Nutmeg lb. .80 @ 0.90
Orange, sweet lb. 2.00 @ 2.15
Orange, bitter lb. 2.20 @ 2.40
Origanum lb. .18 @ .22
Pennyroyal lb. 1.20 @ 2.25
Peppermint lb. 2.80 @ 3.00
Cases lb. 3.40 @ 3.50
Petit, grain, French lb. 4.00 @ 4.50
" " So. Amer lb. 2.00 @ 2.25
Pimento lb. 1.40 @ 1.50
Rose oz. 3.50 @ 4.50
Rosemary lb. .62½@ .80
Sandalwood lb. 3.25 @ 3.50
Sassafras lb. .50 @ .55
" Artificial lb. .25 @ .28
Safrol .30 @ .36
Spearmint lb. 4.75 @ 5.00
Tansy lb. 3.75 @ 1.00
Thyme 1.00 @ 1.20
Winterg'n, sweet birch 1.60 @ 1.95
" Synthetic lb. .37 @ .40
Wood (Chinese) .08 @ .09
Wormwood 3.25 @ 3.53
Wormseed lb. 3.00 @ 3.25
Opium, Nat cases lb. 2.75 @ 2.90
" Ordinary, Job- 2.75 @ 2.80
" powdered lb. 3.20 @ 3.75
Orange peel, bit lb. .05 @ .04
Sweet lb. .04½@ .10
Petrolatum .03 @ .09
Phenacetin (see Acetphenetidin)
Potassium acetate lb. .17 @ .18
" bromide .15 @ .16
" bottles .25 @ .30
bichromate .08½@ .08¾
chlorate, cryst .07½@ .
" powd .09½@ ...
cyanide .20 @ .21
hypophosphite .60 @ .64
iodide bulk 2.15 @ 2.20
permanganate lb. .09½@ .10½
Prickly Ash berries .14 @ .16
Quicksilver flasks, lb. .56 @ .60
Quinine Sulph., Domestic bulk oz. .17 @ .19
German, bulk oz. .17 @ .19
German, outside oz. .16½@ .17
Java, bulk oz. ..... @ .16½
Rochelle Salts lb. .20½@ .21
Root, Aconite lb. .09½@ .10
Alkanet lb. .08 @ .09
Althea, cut lb. .17 @ .18
Arnica lb. .08½@ .09
Belladonna, Atropa lb. .10 @ .12
Blood lb. .10 @ .12
Calamus lb. .07 @ .08
Calamus, bleached lb. .23 @ .25
Colchicum lb. .12 @ .13
Calumba lb. .04 @ .06
Dandelion, Ger lb. .07½@ .08
Galangal lb. .05 @ .05½
Gentian lb. .04 @ .04½
Ginger, Ja., blcd lb. .17 @ .18
unbleached lb. .14 @ .16
Ginseng lb. 6.00 @ 7.50
Golden Seal lb. 1.15 @ 1.18
Hellebore, pwd lb. .06 @ .07
Helonias lb. .42 @ .45
Ipecac, Rio lb. 1.75 @ 1.80
Carthagena lb. 1.70 @ 1.75
Jalap lb. .12 @ .13
Kava Kava lb. .11 @ .12
Liquorice, ord lb. .03½@ .04
Select lb. .05½@ .11
Lovage lb .55 @ .85
Mandrake lb. .04½@ .05½
Musk, Russian lb. .13 @ .14
Orris, Florentine lb. .06 @ .07
Orris, Verona lb. .04 @ .06
Pariera Brava lb. .10 @ .11
Pink lb. 1.25 @ ...
Rhatany lb. .10 @ .12
Rhub., Canton lb. .35 @ .40
Shensi lb. .65 @ .75
Sars'p'la, Hond lb. .26 @ .30
Mexican lb. .09½@ .09½
Senega lb. .55 @ .60
Snake Virgina lb. .42 @ .45
Texas lb .39 @ .42
Canada lb. .13 @ .25
Squill lb .13 @ .15
Valerian, Belg lb. .06 @ .08½
German lb. .17 @ .14
English lb. .12 @ .15
Salicine lb 3.75 @ 4.00
Sal Ammon, lump lb. .09½@ .09½
Granulated lb. .05½@ .06
Sal Soda, Eng 100 lb .67½@ .72½
American 100 lb. .75 @ .80
Salol lb. .80 @ .85
Saltpetre, crude lb. .04½@ .04½
Refined lb. .04½@ .05½
Santonin, crystals lb. 9.50 @ 9.70
Powdered lb. 9.70 @ 9.90
Saw Palmetto Berries lb. .15 @ .20
Seed, Anise Ital lb. .08½@ .10½
German lb. .06½@ .07
Star lb. .20 @ .21
Canary, Smyrna lb. .04½@ .04½
Sicily lb. .04½@ .06
Caraway lb. .08 @ .08½
Celery lb. .07½@ .08
Cardamom blchd .50 @ .75
" Decorticated lb. .35 @ .38
Colchicum lb. .21 @ .25

Seeds—cont'd.
Coriander lb. .. @ .17½
Bleached lb. .08½@ .11½
Cummin lb. .06½@ .07½
Fennel, Ger lb. .09 @ .10
" Italian lb. .05 @ .15½
Flax, whole lb. .06 @ .11½
" ground lb. .03½@ .03½
Foenugreek lb. .02 @ .02½
Hemp, Rus lb. .03 @ .03½
Millet, nat lb. .01½@ .02
" shld lb. .03½@ .04½
Mustard, Cal. brown lb. .04½@ .04½
Trieste, brown lb. .08 @ .07½
Bari, brown lb. .04½@ .05
German, brown lb. .02½@ .03
Western, brown lb. .03½@ .02
Cal. yellow lb. .04½@ .04½
Eng. yellow lb. .06 @ .05½
Ger. yellow lb. .05½@ .05½
Poppy, blue lb. .05½@ .05½
Quince, Ger lb. .32 @ .34
Rape, Ger lb. .02½@ .03
" Eng lb. .04 @ .05
" Amer lb. .02½@ .03
Strophanthus .45 @ .50
Kombé 1.00 @ 1.25
Sunflower .04½@ .05
Wormseed, American lb. .07 @ .08
" Levant lb. .17 @ .20
Seidlitz, Mixture lb. .17 @ .17½
Silver, Nitrate oz. .42½@ .46½
Soap, Castile, white lb. .10 @ .10½
" green lb. .08 @ .10½
" mottled lb. .05½@ .07
Sodium bicarb, Eng 1.37½@ 1.75
" domestic 100 lb. 1.50 @ 1.80
" benzoate lb. .40 @ .41
" brom. blk lb. .21 @ .22
" carb., cryst. 100 lb. 1.60 @ 1.75
" citrate lb. ... @ .22
" hypophosphite .60 @ .64
" iodide 3.50 @ 3.55
" nitrate 100 lb. 2.30 @ 2.35
" phosphate lb. .02½@ .03
" salicylate lb. .32 @ .34
" sulphate 100 lb. .40 @ .50
Spermaceti lb. .27 @ .29
Spts. Nitre, U. S. P. .46 @ .48
Spts. Ammonia Aromat lb. .44 @ .45
Strontium, nitrate lb. .07½@ .08
Strychnine, Sulph oz. .95 @ 1.05
Sugar of Milk lb. .15 @ .27
Sugar, Lead, white lb. .09½@ .10
" brown lb. .07½@ .08
Sulphur, Roll lb. 1.85 @ 2.15
" Flowers lb. 2.20 @ 2.60
" Flour lb. 2.00 @ 2.40
Sulphuric Ether lb. .62 @ .68
Sumac, Sicily ton 42.00 @ 47.00
" Virginia ton 33.00 @ 35.00
Tar, Barbadoes gal. ... @ .38
Thymol 1.80 @ 1.90
Tonka B'ns, Para lb. .18 @ .20
" Angostura lb. .65 @ .67½
" Surinam lb. .30 @ .32
Turmeric .04½@ .06
Turpentine gal. .61½@ ...
Vanilla Beans lb. 2.75 @ 5.00
" Cut, Mex lb. 2.00 @ 2.25
" Tahiti lb. .60 @ 1.25
" Bourbon 1.00 @ 3.00
Vanillin oz. .32 @ .37½
Venice Turps, bbls lb. .14 @ .17
" " cans lb. .19 @ .20
Wax, Bayberry lb. .42 @ .45
" Bees, ord. pur lb. .33 @ .33½
" " sel lb. .34 @ .34½
" " blch lb. .40 @ .45
" Brazil, No. 1 lb. .52½@ .53
" " No. 2 lb. .44 @ .47
" " No. 3 lb. .35 @ ....
" Ceresin, yel lb. .14 @ .18
" " white lb. .15 @ .20
" Japan lb. .11 @ .12
" Paraffin lb. .06 @ .08½
Zinc Oxide lb. .07 @ .08½

Heavy Oils, &c.

Bank, Menhaden gal. .27 @ .30
Coconut, Ceylon lb. .08½@ .08½
Cochin lb. .07½@ .07¾
Cuban lb. .05½@ ...
Cod, Domestic gal. .35 @ .36
" Newfoundland gal. .38½@ .40
Corn gal. 3.80 @ ...
Cottonseed, crd. prime .25 @ ...
Summer Yellow, prime .32 @ .33
" " Butter .33 @ .34
Old, off grade .30 @ ...
Winter Yellow, prime .33 @ .34
Salad Oil .40 @ .41
Gasoline, 86° gal. .14 @ ...
" 88° gal. .16 @ ...
" 90° gal. .18 @ ...
Lard, Extra Prime gal. .63 @ .64
Lard, Extra No. 1 gal. .49 @ .52
Lard, No. 1 gal. .38 @ .40
Linseed, Raw City gal. .42 @ .43
" Boiled gal. .43 @ .44
Naphtha, 63° gal. .12 @ ...
" Deodorized, 76° gal. .13½@ ...
Neatsfoot, prm gal. .49 @ .50
White .97 @ ...
Olive Oil, tap tins 1.50 @ 2.75
" Com., bbls gal .53½@ .58
Palm, prm., L'gos lb .06½@ .06½
Peanut lb .40 @ .52
Rapeseed gal. .67 @ .71
Red Elaine gal. ... @ .49
" Saponified lb. .05½@ .05½
Salad Oil gal. .66 @ .68
Sesame gal. .55 @ .60
Sperm, Crude gal. .62 @ .65
" Nat. Win gal. .62 @ .63
" Blch. Win gal. .64 @ .65
Straits gal. ... @ .32
Tallow, prime gal. .62 @
Whale, Crude gal. ... @ ...
Crude, Nat. Win gal. .42 @
Bleached Win gal. .44 @ .46

New Remedies Compendium and Prices Current.

In this list, which is intended for the use of dispensing druggists, and not for analytical chemists, chemical formulas, melting points and other data of no immediate use to the dispenser are omitted. While additions will be made from time to time as new remedies make their appearance on the market, and the list, thus kept fully up to date, remedies falling into disuse will be dropped as expediency may determine.

Corrected to May 24, 1906.

ACETAL. (ETHYLIDENE DIETHYL ETHER.) Colorless, volatile liquid, soluble in 18 parts of water, very soluble in alcohol. Used as a sedative and hypnotic in doses of 2 to 3 fluid drachms, usually in form of emulsion. Pure medicinal, per oz., $1.00; commercial, oz. .... 65c.

ACETOZONE. (BENZOYL-ACETYL PEROXIDE.) White powder, mixed with an equal weight of an inert soluble powder; soluble in water (1:1000). Bactericide; used internally and externally in diseases of germ origin. Dose, 1 to 3 grains in solution. Boxes containing 6 vials of 15 grains each, per box, $1.25; ¼ oz. bot., $1.40; ½ oz. bot., $2.70; 1 oz. bot. $5.25

ACET-THEOCIN-SODIUM. White crystalline powder, readily soluble in water. Powerful diuretic; used in dropsy, in doses of 5 to 7 grains, two to three times daily. ½ and 1 oz. bot...... $1.90 to $2.30 per oz. (Continental Color & Chemical Co.)

ACOINE. (DI-PARA-ANISYL-MONO-PHENETHYL GUANIDINE HYDROCHLORIDE.) White crystalline powder, soluble in 17 parts of water. Local anæsthetic like cocaine, used hypodermatically in eye surgery; dental anæsthetic in normal saline solution, 2 per cent. 15 grain vials, each, 30c.; capsules, 2½ grains, 28 in box................ 75c.
(The Heyden Chemical Works.)

ADNEPHRIN SOLUTION. A 1-1000 solution of the active principle of the suprarenal gland in physiological salt solution containing one-half of 1 per cent. of methaform. Used chiefly as a hæmostatic, also for treatment of inflammations, congestions and tumefactions of the mucous membranes, also as a cardiac stimulant. 1 oz. vials .... 60c.
EMOLLIENT. Tubes, each... 30c.
OIL SPRAY. 1 oz. vials, each. 60c.
(Frederick Stearns & Co.)

ADRENALIN. Grayish-white powder; with difficulty soluble in water. The blood-pressure-raising principle of the suprarenal glands. 1 grain vials. 85c.
CHLORIDE SOLUTION, 1:1000, a solution of 1 part of adrenalin chloride in 1000 parts of physiologic salt solution, with 0.5 per cent. of chloretone. Powerful astringent, hemostatic and cardiac stimulant. Used for the control of hemorrhages, internal and superficial, for the reduction of congestion and inflammation of mucous membranes, as a heart stimulant in collapse, and as an adjuvant to the local anæsthetic action of cocaine. Internal dose, 5 to 30 minims. 1 oz. bot........ 85c.
INHALANT, 1 oz. bot........ 85c.
OINTMENT, ½ oz. tubes..... 43c.
SUPPOSITORIES, boxes of 1 doz. 38c.
TABLETS, vials of 25........ 85c.
(Parke, Davis & Co.)

ADRIN. (EPINEPHRIN HYDRATE.) Whitish nonhygroscopic powder; the active principle of the suprarenal gland. 1 grain vials, each, 75c.; 1-1000 solution, 1 oz. vials, each, 75c.; in tubes of 12 tablets, each tablet q. s. to make 15 minims of 1-1000 solution, each, 40c.; in 100's, each.............. $3.10
INHALANT, 1 oz. vials...... 75c.
OINTMENT, ½ oz. tubes.... 40c.
SUPPOSITORIES, box of 1 doz. 30c.
(H. K. Mulford Co.)

AGURIN. (ACET-THEOBROMINE-SODIUM.) White hygroscopic powder, soluble in water; incompatible with acids. Diuretic in dropsy. Dose, 7 to 15 grains, twice daily. ½ and 1 oz. bot.............. $1.55 to $1.70
(Continental Color & Chemical Co.)

AIROL. (BISMUTH OXYIODOGALLATE.) Grayish-green powder, insoluble in water or alcohol. On admixture with water airol partly decomposes and turns red. Should be mixed with water only with intervention of glycerin. Used externally as application to wounds, burns, skin diseases, eye, nose, gonorrhœa, either pure, in 10 per cent. suspension, equal parts glycerin and water, or 10 to 20 per cent. ointment. 1 oz. cartons $1.00
(Hoffmann-La Roche Chemical Works.)

ALBARGIN. (GELATOSE SILVER.) Light brown powder, readily soluble in water. Contains 15 per cent. of silver. For gonorrhœa a 2 per cent. solution is injected 4 or 5 times daily. 1 oz. vials, $1.10; tubes of 50 tablets, 0.2 gm. each, per tube .... 50c.
(Victor Koechl & Co.)

ALPHOZONE. (SUCCINIC PEROXIDE.) White fluffy powder, quickly soluble in 60 parts of water. Germicide and antiseptic, internally and externally. Dose, 3 to 5 grains. 1 oz. bot., $4.50; ½ oz., $2.30; ¼ oz., $1.20; 1 grain tablets, bot. of 90 .... $1.00
(Frederick Stearns & Co.)

ALYPIN. White crystalline powder, easily soluble in water and alcohol, but dissolving very sparingly in ether. Watery solutions have a neutral reaction and can be sterilized by boiling for a short period. Local anæsthetic, substitute for cocaine. The strength of the solutions ordinarily employed varies from 1 to 5 and even up to 10 per cent. It can be combined with adrenalin and antipyrine. Alypin should not be used in connection with silver nitrate, owing to the formation of a precipitate. This objection, however, does not apply to protargol solutions, which, although they become slightly turbid at first, soon clear up. 15 grain vials, each, 20c.; 10 grain vials, per vial, 16c.; ¼ and ½ oz. bots., per oz., $4.20; 1 oz. bots., per oz....... $4.10
(Continental Color & Chemical Co.)

ALUMNOL. (ALUMINUM NAPHTHOL DISULPHONATE.) Whitish powder, very soluble in water; slightly soluble in alcohol and glycerin; astringent and antiseptic; dissolves in pus and penetrates tissues. Used in 1 per cent. solution in gonorrhœa; 10 to 20 per cent. mixture with talcum as a dusting powder. 1 oz. tins, per oz... 50c.
(Victor Koechl & Co.)

AMINOFORM. (HEXAMETHYLENETETRAMINE.) White granular crystals, readily soluble in water, prepared by combining ammonia and formaldehyde. Antiseptic for urinary passages, diuretic and solvent in uric acid concretions; dose, 5 to 10 grains, well diluted, three times daily. 1 oz. bot., 60c.; 7½ grain tablets, oz.............. 70c.
(C. Bischoff & Co.)

ANAESTHESIN. White crystalline powder, almost insoluble in cold water, but easily solu-

ble in ether, alcohol, benzin and fatty oils. Local anæsthetic, and used internally in gastric ulcer, nervous dyspepsia, etc. Dose, internally, 5 to 8 grains several times daily. Used externally pure or in ointment 5 to 20 per cent., and in suppositories containing 3 grains each. 1 oz. bot.........$1.00
(Victor Koechl & Co.)

ANALGINE. A powder composed of acetanilid, 50 parts; sodium bicarb., 5 parts; sodium salicylate, 5 parts; camphor monobrom., 5 parts; caffeine citrated, 2½ parts; ext. cannabis indica, 2½ parts; aromatic powder, q. s. 100 parts. Recommended as an analgetic, antipyretic and nerve sedative in neuralgia, migraine, headache, rheumatism, gout, sciatica, etc. Dose, 5 to 10 grains. 1 oz. screw cap bottles.........40c.
(H. K. Mulford Company.)

ANTHRASOL. Yellow, oily liquid, with a distinctive tarry odor; soluble in alcohol, acetone, fats and petrolatum. A distillate from coal tar, used in diseases of the skin where coal tar is employed. 1 oz. vials ....55c.
(Knoll & Co. and Merck & Co.)

ANTINONNIN. (POTASSIUM ORTHODINITRO-CRESOL.) Paste of brilliant orange color, soluble in water, slight soapy odor, nonvolatile. Deodorizer, disinfectant, prevents the growth of fungi, mildew and dry rot in cellars and human habitations. Used in form of solution. 1 lb to 5 to 15 gallons of water. Cans, ½ lb., $1.10 per lb.; 1 lb. cans, 95c.; 50 lb. cans, per lb. ....77c.
(Continental Color & Chemical Co.)

ANTINOSINE. (SODIUM SALT OF NOSOPHEN.) Blue powder, soluble in water, alcohol and glycerin. Used in solution of 1 to 5 per cent. as an antiseptic in diseases of the eye and ear, genito-urinary diseases, and as a healing powder on chronic leg ulcers. 1 oz. bot. $2.10
(Stallman & Fulton Co.)

ANTISCLEROSIN. Tablets, consisting of a compound of inorganic blood salts, used in treatment of arteriosclerosis and its sequelæ. Dose, 2 tablets three times daily. Carton of 4 tubes @ 24 tablets...$1.50
(Schering & Glatz.)

ANTITUSSIN. (DIFLUORDIPHENYL OINTMENT.) Ointment containing lanolin, 85 per cent.; petrolatum, 10 per cent., and difluordiphenyl, 5 per cent. A whooping cough remedy applied as inunction to patient's neck, chest and back once a day, in doses of 5 Gm. 20 Gm. collapsible tubes, 40c.; 40 Gm. ....75c.
(C. Bischoff & Co.)

ANUSOL SUPPOSITORIES. A compound of bismuth iodoresorcin sulphonate, used in hæmorrhoids, etc. Dose, 1 or 2 daily. Box of 12..............$1.00
(Schering & Glatz.)

ARGENTAMINE. A colorless, alkaline liquid representing a solution of silver nitrate, 10 per cent., and ethylenediamine, 10 per cent.; soluble in water. Used in all cases where silver nitrate is used, mostly in gonorrhœa, in strength of 1 in 2000-4000 solution. 1 oz., g. s. bot. ....75c.
(Schering & Glatz.)

ARGONIN. White powder, very slightly soluble in cold, but freely so in hot water. A compound of silver nitrate and sodium casein. Antiseptic, germicide and gonococcicide, less caustic than silver nitrate. Solutions of 2 to 10 per cent. strength recommended for injection in gonorrhœa and 3 per cent. solutions for use in the eye. 1 oz. vials..........65c.
(Victor Koechl & Co.)

ARHOVIN, an addition product of diphenylamine and esterified thymyl-benzoic acid, is a fluid of aromatic odor and slightly burning taste, soluble in oil. Gonocide for internal and topical use. Given by mouth in capsules of 4 grains (1 or 2 capsules, three to six times daily); in urethral bougies (1 bougie, two to four times daily); in vaginal globules (1 globule, two to four times daily), and injected in 2 per cent. to 5 per cent. oily solution. 1 oz. vials, 90c.; box of 50 capsules, 65c.; box of 12 bougies, 50c.; box of 12 globules..................50c.
(Schering & Glatz.)

ARISTOCHIN. (CARBONIC ESTER OF QUININE.) White powder, tasteless, insoluble in water. Decomposes in the system to yield 96.1 per cent. of quinine. Prescribed like quinine, but in somewhat larger doses. ½ and 1 oz. cartons, per oz.....$2.20
(Continental Color & Chemical Co. and Merck & Co.)

ARSENFERRATOSE. A solution of ferratin in syrup form (syrupus ferratini arseniati); contains 0.3 per cent. of iron and 0.003 per cent. of arsenic. Used as a hæmatopoietic and alterative, in doses of a tablespoonful three or four times a day for adults, and for children a teaspoonful to a dessertspoonful. 250 Gm. bottles......55c.
(C. F. Boehringer & Soehne.)

ASAPROL. (ABRASTOL.) Whitish powder, freely soluble in water and alcohol. It is the calcium salt of betanaphthol-sulphonic acid. Antipyretic and antirheumatic in doses of 5 to 15 grains. Used also as test for albumin in urine. 1 oz. bot. $1.25

ASPIRIN. (ACETYL SALICYLIC ACID.) White crystalline powder, insoluble in water; incompatible with alkalies. Used instead of the salicylates in articular and muscular rheumatism and other therapeutic indications for the salicylates. Dose, 5 to 15 grains, three to five times daily. 1 oz. bot., per oz................33c. to 43c.
(Continental Color & Chemical Co.)

ATOXYL. (META-ARSENOUS ANILIDE.) White powder, containing 37.69 per cent. of arsenic in organic combination. Soluble in 6 parts of water and used in this strength solution for hypodermic injection; relatively nontoxic. Dose, 1 to 3 grains. 1 oz. vials.......$3.00
(Victor Koechl & Co.)

BENZONAPHTHOL. White, crystalline powder, soluble in alcohol and chloroform; insoluble in water. Employed as intestinal antiseptic in doses of 5 to 15 grains. 1 oz. vials, 22c.; ¼ lb. bottles, $2.20; ½ lb., $2.10; 1 lb...........$2.00
(Schering & Glatz.)

BENZOSOL. (GUAIACOL BENZOATE.) Small colorless crystals, nearly insoluble in water. Contains 54 per cent. of guaiacol and, as it is slowly saponified by the gastric juice, the guaiacol being liberated gradually, it is recommended as an intestinal antiseptic and as an agreeable substitute for creosote in incipient phthisis. Dose, 4 to 8 grains. 1 oz. tins.$1.25
(Victor Koechl & Co.)

BETA-EUCAINE HYDROCHLORIDE. White, crystalline powder, soluble in 30 parts of water. A synthetic compound chemically allied to cocaine, being the hydrochloride of benzoyl-vinyl-diaceton-alkamine. It is slower in action than cocaine, but anæsthesia is more prolonged, and a third less toxic. Used generally in 2 per cent. solutions in dental and ophthalmic work. ⅛ oz. and ¼ oz., per oz., $3.60; ½ oz. and 1 oz.............$3.50
(Schering & Glatz.)

BETA-EUCAINE LACTATE. White powder, possessing the same properties as the hydrochloride, but is more soluble in water (about 1 in 5). Prices and containers same as for beta-eucaine hydrochloride.
(Schering & Glatz.)

BISMUTH FORMIC IODIDE. Yellowish, impalpable powder. A compound of formaldehyde and gelatin, with the addition of thymol iodide and bismuth

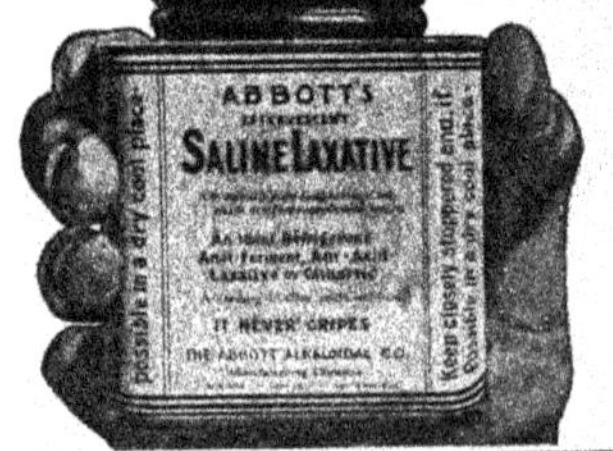

subiodide. Bactericide, antiseptic and astringent. Employed as a dry dressing for wounds and ulcerations, suppurating surfaces and abscesses. Sprinkler-top boxes, 50c.; per dozen, $5.00

BISMUTH FORMIC IODIDE OINTMENT, per dozen ozs., $1.00; per lb., $1.00. Bismuth Formic Iodide Suppositories, per box of 1 doz. ....50c.
(H. K. Mulford Company.)

BISOL. (SOLUBLE BISMUTH PHOSPHATE.) White powder, soluble in water, faint alkaline reaction. Intestinal antiseptic and astringent in gastric and enteric catarrh. Dose, 3 to 7½ grains. 1 oz. vials......70c.
(C. Bischoff & Co.)

BROMETONE. Powder, slightly soluble in water. Compound of bromoform and acetone; recommended as a substitute for bromides; contains 77 per cent. of bromine. Dose, 3 to 5 grains. 1 oz. bot., 85c.; 5 grain capsules in bot. of 100 ....$1.25
(Parke, Davis & Co.)

BROMIPIN. (10 % BROMINIZED SESAME OIL.) Yellow, oily fluid, used as a nervine and sedative in epilepsy; succedaneum for bromides. Dose, 1 teaspoonful. 1 oz. vial, 18c.; per lb...........$2.10 to $2.85
(Merck & Co.)

CACODYLIC ACID. (DIMETHYL ARSENIC ACID.) Small colorless deliquescent crystals, the ultimate product of oxidation of arsenium-dimethyl (cacodyle) and of cacodyle oxide. Contains 54.4 per cent. of arsenic trioxide, but is relatively nontoxic. Dose, 1 to 3 grains. ¼ oz. vials, per oz..........$4.00

CALOMELOL OINTMENT. White mercurial ointment made from colloidal calomel for the inunction treatment of syphilis and especially for the cure of its cutaneous manifestations. 2 oz. graduated tubes, per tube ....55c.
(Heyden Chemical Works.)

CALOMELOL POWDER. Grayish-white powder of neutral reaction, tasteless and odorless. Yields a milky solution when added to cold water in the proportion of 1 to 50. Used as a dusting powder in the treatment of papular eruptions and ulcerations, and as external application to ulcerated chancres in 2 per cent. solution. 1 oz. vials ....70c.
(Heyden Chemical Works.)

CAMPHORIC ACID. (Colorless crystalline scales, very slightly soluble in water; formed by the oxidation of camphor with nitric acid. Used in night sweats of phthisis, also in cystitis and as an intestinal antiseptic in doses of 10 to 20 grains. 1 oz. vials, 45c.; 1 lb. bot. $7.00
(Merck & Co.)

CEROLIN. Pills of a fatty substance isolated from yeast. Acts same as yeast in furunculosis, acne, etc., but more cathartic. Pills containing 0.1 Gm., box of 100, each.....50c.
(C. F. Boehringer & Soehne.)

CHINAPHENIN. (QUININE CARBONIC ESTER OF PHENETIDINE.) White tasteless powder, representing synthetic quinine-phenacetin and having medicinal properties of both. Insoluble in water, but easily soluble in alcohol, ether and chloroform. Dose, 5 to 10 grains, thrice daily. ½ and 1 oz. cartons, per oz..........
$1.25 to $1.30
(Continental Color & Chemical Co.)

CHINOTROPINE. (UROTROPINE QUINATE.) A combination of quinic acid and urotropine (hexamethylenetetramine) used as uric acid solvent in the various manifestations of the uric acid diathesis. Is said to liberate formaldehyde freely internally and to form soluble compounds with uric acid. Dose, 10 to 30 grains. ¼ oz. and 1 oz. vials, $1.75; tablets, 7½ grains, 25 in tube, 2 tubes in box.....................$1.75
(Schering & Glatz.)

CHLORETONE. White crystals, slightly soluble in water (1:125); hypnotic, local anæsthetic and antiseptic. Dose, 5 to 20 grains, in cachet, tablet or capsule. Externally as a dusting powder for wounds, combined 23 with, zinc oxide, 120, and French chalk, 90 parts. ⅛ oz. vials, per oz., 90c.; 1 oz.....................85c. Capsules, 3 grs., bot. of 100, 80c.; 5 grs., bot. of 100..$1.25
(Parke, Davis & Co.)

CINNAMIC ACID. (CINNAMYLIC ACID.) Transparent micaceous crystals, very slightly soluble in water; soluble in alcohol and ether. Injected intravenously in tuberculosis in doses of ¼ to ⅝ of a grain, twice a week; per oz., 1-20 to ¼ grain twice daily. 1 oz. vial, 85c.; 1 lb. bot., per lb. $5.00
(Merck & Co.)

CITARIN. (SODIUM ANHYDROMETHYLENCITRATE.) White, crystalline powder, easily soluble in water. Antilithæmic for gouty and chronic rheumatic conditions; liberates formaldehyde in the blood. Dose, 15 to 30 grains, thrice daily. 1 oz. bottle, per oz..70c. to 75c.
(Continental Color & Chemical Co.)

COLLARGOL. (COLLOIDAL SILVER.) Shining, black scales, soluble in 1 in 20 of water. Used as a bactericide, 1 in 100 to 10,000 in water or glycerin. Internally a 1 to 500 or 1 to 100 solution may be added to the food in teaspoonful doses. ½ oz. and 1 oz. vials, $2.75; tablets, 1 grain each, tubes of 50...60c.
(Schering & Glatz.)

CORNUTOL. A concentrated, preparation of ergot of rye, prepared for hypodermic and general use. Each Cc. represents 2½ Gm. of assayed Spanish ergot. Dose, hypodermically, 5 to 10 min. (or 0.3 to 2 Cc.). By mouth, 10 to 30 min. (or 0.6 to 2 Cc.). Marketed only in 1 oz. vials and in hermetically sealed aseptic bulbs, each bulb containing 2 Cc. (½ dr.). 1 oz. vials, 50c.; per package of 6 bulbs ....60c.
(H. K. Mulford Company.)

COTARNINE HYDROCHLORIDE. See Stypticin.

CREOSOTE CARBONATE. (CREOSOTAL.) Yellow, transparent viscous liquid, insoluble in water, but miscible with alcohol; contains 92 per cent. of creosote combined with 8 per cent. of carbon dioxide. Used in tuberculosis and pneumonia in doses of 5 to 60 drops several times daily. 1 oz. vials, 65c.; ¼ lb. bot., per lb., $9.25; ½ lb., $9.10; 1 lb.......$9.00
(Schering & Glatz and Continental Color & Chemical Co.)

CUPROL. Green powder, readily soluble in water; a chemical combination of nucleinic acid and copper; solution does not coagulate albumen. Applied locally as an astringent; of use in granular ophthalmia in the form of 5 per cent. instillations, or may be applied in the dry form with a brush. ¼ oz. vials, $1.30 per oz.; 1 oz. vials $1.20
(Parke, Davis & Co.)

DERMATOL. (BISMUTH SUBGALLATE.) Yellow, insoluble powder; nonirritant antiseptic, especially serviceable in burns, ulcers and moist eczema. Used internally in diarrhœa, dysentery, intestinal fermentation and gastric ulcers, in doses of 10 to 30 grains three times daily. 1 oz. tins, 19c.; 1 and 5 lb. tins, per lb.........$2.50
(Victor Koechl & Co.)

DIATHESIN. White crystalline leaflets, soluble in 15 parts cold water, freely soluble in hot water or alcohol. Is ortho-oxybenzylalcohol, or synthetic saligenin. Used in place of salicin in rheumatism, neuralgia, pleurisy, etc., in doses of 7½ to 15 grains. 1 oz. cartons $2.40
(C. Bischoff & Co.)

DIFLUORDIPHENYL. White crystalline powder of pleasant aromatic odor, insoluble in water, soluble in alcohol, ether, chloroform and oils. Used as

antiseptic dusting powder mixed with talc in proportion of difluordiphenyl, 10 parts; talc, 90 parts, or in 10 per cent. ointment with lanolin as dressing for burns. Dose, 1-16 to ¼ grain. 5 Gm. envelopes, each $1.50
(C. Bischoff & Co.)

DIGALEN. (Cloetta's soluble digitoxin.) Marketed only in solution in 15 Cc. (½ oz.) vials, on account of infinitesimal dosage. Active principle of digitalis leaves, nonaccumulative heart tonic and diuretic. 1 Cc. of solution represents 0.0003 Gm. (0.0045 grain) of digitoxin, which is the average dose, by the mouth, hypodermatically, or by enema; intravenously the dose is from 3 to 10 Cc. ½ oz. vials..............$1.00
(Hoffmann-La Roche Chemical Works.)

DIGITALIN VERUM. White powder, the active constituent of digitalis, free from impurities and noxious principles. Almost insoluble in water. Dose, 0.002 Gm. to 0.006 Gm., three times daily, increasing to not over 0.02 Gm. (1-3 grain). 1 Gm. vials $7.25
(C. F. Boehringer & Soehne.)

DIONIN. (Ethyl morphine hydrochloride.) White crystalline powder, very soluble in water and alcohol. Recommended to replace codeine and morphine in bronchitis, emphysema and asthma. Dose, ¼ to ½ grain. 1 oz. vials, $6.00; ½ oz. vials, per oz., $6.25; 15 grain vials, each, 35c.; tablets, ¼ grain, bot. of 50, 35c.; bot. of 100 ....60c.
(Merck & Co.)

DIURETIN. White powder, soluble in water, decomposed by acids. Must be kept dry and air tight. It is a chemical compound of theobromine sodium and sodium salicylate. Diuretic, antiasthmatic and vascular stimulant. Dose, 15 grains four to six times daily. 1 oz. bot., per oz..............$1.75
(Knoll & Co.)

DORMIOL. (Amylene chloral.) Oily, colorless liquid, with a camphoraceous odor, insoluble in water, soluble in alcohol and ether. Hypnotic in mania; 50 per cent. solution supplied commercially. Dose, 5 to 60 minims. 1 oz. vials, 28c.; ½ lb. bot., per lb..............$4.00
(Merck & Co.)

DUOTAL. (Guaiacol carbonate.) White crystalline powder, soluble in alcohol, insoluble in water. Same therapeutic action as Creosotal, which see. Dose, 5 to 20 grains, gradually increased. 1 oz. vials, $1.50; tablets, 7½ grains, 50 tablets in box, $1.50; 4½ grains, 50 tablets in box..............90c.
(Schering & Glatz and Continental Color & Chemical Co.)

DUOTONOL. White powder; a mixture, equal parts of the lime and sodium glycerophosphates. Nerve nutrient in doses of 5 to 10 grains three times daily. 1 oz., 50c.; 1 lb., $6.00; tablets, 5 grains, 100 tablets in bottle ....65c.
(Schering & Glatz.)

DYMAL. (Didymium salicylate.) Pinkish powder, odorless. Applied as powder and ointment in skin diseases, notably dry and weeping eczema. 1 oz. cartons, each, 35c.; 4 oz. cartons, each..............$1.20
(C. Bischoff & Co.)

EKA-IODOFORM. A chemically pure iodoform, prepared by electrical synthesis, and sterilized with paraform. 1 oz. vials ....50c.
(Schering & Glatz.)

EMPYROFORM. Brown powder: condensation product of birch tar and formaldehyde; insoluble in water, readily soluble in acetone, chloroform and solutions of caustic alkalies. Used like tar in ointment, paste and tincture. 1 oz. vials..65c.
(Schering & Glatz.)

EPICARIN. (Condensation product of betanaphtol and cresolic acid.) Colorless or yellowish needles, difficultly soluble in hot water, easily soluble in alcohol, ether and oils. Nontoxic substitute for naphthol in parasitic skin diseases. Employed chiefly in ointments (5 to 10 per cent.) 1 oz. cartons, per oz..............60c. to 70c.
(Continental Color & Chemical Co.)

EUCASIN. Casein compound, containing 95 per cent. albumin and 5 per cent. water. Prepared from cow's milk. Dietetic for convalescents, invalids or persons afflicted with lung, stomach or kidney trouble; also in anæmia and typhoid. 1 lb. tins, $3.00; ½ lb., $1.50; ¼ lb. ....80c.
(Fuerst Bros. & Co.)

EUDOXINE. (Bismuth salt of nosophen.) Reddish-gray powder, insoluble in water, but soluble in alkaline fluids. Used as an intestinal antiseptic in doses of 3 to 5 grains. 1 oz. bot., $2.10; 3 grain tablets, per oz., $2.60; 5 grain tablets, per oz. $2.50
(Stallman & Fulton Co.)

EUGALLOL. (Pyrogallol monoacetate.) Yellowish, syrupy liquid, marketed in 66 per cent. acetone solution. Soluble in water and acetone; applied pure or diluted with acetone as paint in skin diseases, especially psoriasis, and deemed superior to pyrogallol. 1 oz. vials $1.00
(Knoll & Co. and Merck & Co.)

EUMYDRIN. White crystalline powder, obtained from atropine; easily soluble in water. Powerful mydriatic, less poisonous than atropine. Dose, internally, about 1-70 grain. 1 or 2 per cent. solution dilates the pupil after 10 to 25 minutes. 1 grain tubes, 45c. to 55c. per box of 10 tubes; ¼ oz. and ½ oz. packages, per oz. $16.50
(Continental Color & Chemical Co.)

EUNATROL. (Sodium acid oleate.) Light yellow substance, readily soluble in water and alcohol: supplied as powder and chocolate-coated pills. Recommended in treatment of gallstones, being excellent cholagogue. Dose, four pills, 4 grains each, three times daily, or in solution. 25 Gm. bot., each, 75c.; bot. of 50 pills, 70c.; 100 pills..............$1.35
(C. Bischoff & Co.)

EUPHORIN. (Phenyl - urethane.) White, acicular crystals, slightly soluble in water, freely in alcohol. Energetic antipyretic and analgetic in doses of 7½ to 15 grains, 2 to 3 times daily. 1 oz. vials...$1.00
(Schering & Glatz.)

EUPHTHALMINE HYDROCHLORIDE. White crystals; a synthetic derivative of beta-eucaine; soluble in water; 2 to 5 per cent. solutions dilate the pupil, without causing discomfort or accommodation disturbances. ½ and 1 Gm. vials, per Gm. $1.25
(Schering & Glatz.)

EUPYRINE. (Para-phenetidine vanillin ethylcarbonate.) Light yellow crystals, sparingly soluble in water, readily in alcohol, chloroform and ether. Stimulant antipyretic in doses of 7½ to 15 grains. 1 oz. cartons, each....................$1.50
(C. Bischoff & Co.)

EUQUININE. (Quinine carbonic ester.) Tasteless, fleecy crystals, slightly soluble in water; soluble in alcohol, ether and chloroform. Succedaneum for quinine sulphate, reported not to disturb stomach or produce cinchonism. Dose, same as quinine. Tablets, 5 grains, 100 in bot., $1.75; 2 grain, 100 in bot....................75c.
(Merck & Co.)

EURESOL. (Resorcine monoacetate.) Oily, yellow liquid, soluble in alcohol and acetone. Succedaneum for resorcin, externally. Used in skin and scalp diseases, as paint pure or diluted with acetone. 1 oz. vials $1.00
(Knoll & Co. and Merck & Co.)

EUROPHEN. Yellow light powder, containing 25 per cent. of iodine, insoluble in water and

glycerin. Iodoform substitute used in dry powder and in ointment. 1 oz. bot., per oz.... $1.65 to $1.80
(Continental Color & Chemical Co.)

EUZONE. (PURE SODIUM PERBORATE.) White, odorless powder, containing about 7.1 per cent. boron, 15 per cent. sodium, 31.2 per cent. oxygen and 46.2 per cent. water; represents 22 per cent. by weight of hydrogen dioxide, equivalent to 10.4 per cent. by weight of nascent oxygen. Soluble in water 1 in 10, such a solution being taken to represent a 2 per cent. solution of hydrogen dioxide. Tablets, 2½ Gm. each, boxes of 20, 40c.; powder, in 100 Gm. cartons, 35c.; 500 Gm. boxes $1.20
(Schering & Glatz.)

EXODIN. Yellowish powder; a synthetic oxyanthraquinone derivative; tasteless, mild aperient in doses of 7½ to 15 grains. 1 oz. vials, $1.40; tablets, 7½ grains each, 10 tablets in box, 30c.; 50 in bottle.........$1.40
(Schering & Glatz.)

FERRATIN. Reddish - brown powder, slowly soluble in ordinary liquids, but readily in hot beverages. Used in anæmia and chlorosis in doses of 7½ grains three times daily. 1 oz. vials, 85c.; tablets, 7½ grains, 50 in box, per box..............85c.
(C. F. Boehringer & Soehne.)

FERRATOGEN. (IRON NUCLEINATE.) Grayish-yellow powder, obtained by growing yeast in a ferruginous medium; insoluble in water. Used in chlorosis and anæmia in doses of 5 grains, three times daily. 1 oz. cartons, each..............90c.
(C. Bischoff & Co.)

FERRATOSE. (LIQUOR FERRATINI.) Fluid preparation of ferratin, containing 0.3 per cent. iron. 250 Gm. bottles.....45c.
(C. F. Boehringer & Soehne.)

FERRIPYRIN. (FERRIC CHLORIDE ANTIPYRIN.) Orange-red powder, soluble in 5 parts of water, very soluble in alcohol, but insoluble in ether. A compound of ferric chloride and antipyrine. Stypic and analgetic when applied in solution or powder. Given internally in chlorosis and anæmia as a hæmatinic in doses of 7½ grains. 1 oz. tins.......$1.50
(Victor Koechl & Co.)

FERROPYRIN. (Same as Ferripyrin, but made by Knoll & Co. and sold in 1 oz. cartons, $1.40.)
(Knoll & Co. and Merck & Co.)

FILMARON OIL 1:10. A 10 per cent. solution of filmaron, the active principle of malefern, in castor oil. Used in removal of tapeworm. 10 Gm. bot....35c.
(C. F. Boehringer & Soehne.)

FIBROLYSIN. Solution of thiosinamine and sodium salicylate, sterilized. Put up in sealed tubes, each containing 2.3 Cc. solution (= 0.2 Gm. thiosinamine). Same uses as thiosinamine, but specially adapted for hypodermic use. Dose, contents of 1 tube every 1, 2 or 3 days, as required. 2.3 Cc. tubes, each..................15c.
(Merck & Co.)

FLUOROFORMOL. (FLUORYL.) Colorless, tasteless liquid, a 2.8 per cent. solution of fluoroform. Used in phthisis, internally and externally; also in pneumonia, acting as an antiseptic. Dose, 1 tablespoonful four times daily. 1 lb. bot....................$1.00
(C. Bischoff & Co.)

FLUORRHEUMIN. Ointment composed of petrolatum, 10; lanolin, 85; difluordiphenyl, 4; fluorphenetol, 1. Used in rheumatism, sciatica and lumbago; dose by inunction, 4 to 5 Gm. Collapsible tubes, 20 Gm., 40c.; 40 Gm.........................75c.
(C. Bischoff & Co.)

FORTOINE. (METHYLENEDICOTOINE.) Yellow crystals, with slight cinnamon flavor, obtained through action of formaldehyde on cotoine; insoluble in water, sparingly soluble in alcohol, ether and benzol; easily soluble in chloroform, acetone and alkaline liquids. Astringent antiseptic in protracted diarrhœas of consumptives. Dose, 4 grains three times daily. 10 Gm. envelopes, each $2.00
(C. Bischoff & Co.)

GALLOGEN. (ELLAGIC ACID.) Yellowish, tasteless powder, insoluble in all acid and neutral media, but soluble in alkaline solutions. Resembles tannic acid, being the astringent principle of divi-divi. Used in dysentery and diarrhœa. Dose, 10 to 15 grains for adults, 5 to 8 grains for children. 1 oz. cartons, 80c.; chocolate coated tablets, 3 grains each, 24 in box ....35c.
(C. Bischoff & Co.)

GAULTHERINE. Pinkish powder, slowly soluble in cold water, more readily so in hot water; insoluble in ether and chloroform, but very soluble in alcohol. It is the sodium salt of methyl salicylate prepared from natural oil of wintergreen. Antiseptic, antifermentative and soothing antiputrefactive. Used internally and externally. 4 oz. bot., per lb., $6.30; ½ lb. bot., per lb., $6.60; 1 lb. bot. $6.50
(The Wm. S. Merrell Chemical Co.)

GEOSOTE. See Guaiacol Valerate.

GLUTOL. (FORMALDEHYDE GELATIN.) Whitish, granular, insoluble powder; recommended as an antiseptic dressing for burns, cavities and suppurating ulcers. 1 oz. tins, 65c.; vials of ⅓ oz., with sprinkler top, each ....25c.
(Schering & Glatz.)

GUAETHOL. (AJACOL; THANATOL.) Oily liquid, or purer in crystals resembling thymol, insoluble in water. Succedaneum for guaiacol. Allays pain by direct application. Dose, 4 to 8 minims. 1 oz. vials......$1.40

GUAIACOL VALERATE. (GEOSOTE.) Yellow, oily liquid; a combination of guaiacol and valerianic acid, having the characteristic odor of the latter. Insoluble in water, soluble in alcohol and ether. Said to be useful in tuberculosis and chlorosis and as intestinal antiseptic in doses of 8 to 10 minims three times daily. 3 minim capsules, per 100.........$2.10

GUAIACETIN. (SODIUM PYROCATECHIN-MONOACETATE.) White odorless powder, soluble in water. A succedaneum for guaiacol and creosote, used in tuberculosis. Dose, 8 grains, preferably in tablet form. Powder in 1 oz. tins, $3.30; bot. containing 100 tablets, 8 grains each, $3.50; 50, $2.00; 25......$1.17
(Fuerst Bros. & Co.)

GUIASANOL. (DIETHYLGLYCOCOLL - GUAIACOL.) Crystalline powder, readily soluble in water. Indications same as for creosote and guaiacol. Used internally in doses of from 45 to 180 grains a day. 25 Gm. bot. $1.00
(Victor Koechl & Co.)

HEDONAL. White, crystalline powder, insoluble in water, but soluble in alcohol, chloroform and ether; best administered as a dry powder. Given in mild forms of insomnia as a hypnotic in doses of 15 to 30 grains. 1 oz. bot. $1.50 to $1.00
(Continental Color & Chemical Co.)

HELMITOL. (HEXAMETHYLENETETRAMINE-ANHYDROMETHYLENE CITRATE.) Colorless crystals, freely soluble in water; insoluble in alcohol and ether. Urinary antiseptic in cystitis, phosphaturia, urethritis, etc., in doses of 15 grains, three or four times daily; liberates formaldehyde in the urinary tract. 1 oz. bot......................60c.
(Continental Color & Chemical Co.)

HEMICRANIN. White powder; a mixture of 5 parts Phenacetin, 1 part caffeine and 1 part citric acid, used in migraine, headaches, intercostal neuralgia and sciatica, in doses of 5 to 10

grains. 1 oz. cartons, per oz. ....90c.
(Continental Color & Chemical Co.)

HEROIN. White, crystalline powder, difficultly soluble in water, but readily so in alcohol and in water to which a little acetic acid has been added; incompatible with alkali carbonates. Substitute for morphine, of which it is the diacetic acid ester, in doses of 1-24 to 1-12 grain; used for relief of cough and dyspnœa in phthisis, pneumonia, etc. 15 grain vials, 23c. per vial; ¼ oz. vials, per oz., $5.15; 1 oz. vials, per oz..$4.85
(Continental Color & Chemical Co.)

HEROIN HYDROCHLORIDE. (WATER SOLUBLE SALT OF HEROIN.) White, crystalline powder, used in same indications as heroin, but is adapted for hypodermatic injections. The dose and prices are the same as those of heroin.
(Continental Color & Chemical Co.)

HIPPOL. (METHYLENE HIPPURIC ACID.) Colorless, prismatic crystals; sparingly soluble in water; urinary antiseptic in bacterial diseases of the urinary tract. Dose, 22½ grains. 1 oz., $1.50; 20 tablets in box $1.10
(Schering & Glatz.)

HIRUDIN. Grayish, glittering plates and scales, representing a dried extract of the head, pharyngeal rings and lips of the leech (*Sanguisuga medicinalis*); readily soluble in water. Used in the treatment of certain diseases of women and in experiments to prevent coagulation of blood on exposure to air. Tubes, 0.01 Gm., 50c.; 0.1 Gm., $2.75; 1 Gm....$19.00
(C. Bischoff & Co.)

HISTOSAN. (GUAIACOL ALBUMINATE.) Light brown powder of faintly aromatic odor and taste; soluble in water. Used in pulmonary tuberculosis and in diarrhœa in doses of 7½ grains three times daily. 1 oz. cartons $1.30
(C. Bischoff & Co.)

HOLOCAINE HYDROCHLORIDE. White, crystalline powder, difficultly soluble in cold (1 in 75), but readily so in hot water. Chemically para-diethyoxyethenyl-diphenyl-amidine hydrochloride, produced by combination of phenacetin and para-phenetidin. Antiseptic and germicidal in 1 per cent. solution. Used entirely as anæsthetic for operations on the eye, a 1 per cent. solution being equal to 2 per cent. cocaine solution. 1 Gm. vials, 35c.; 5 Gm. vials, per Gm., 30c.; 1 oz. vials, per oz. $7.00
(Victor Koechl & Co.)

HYDRONAL. (POLYMERIZED CHLORAL.) White powder, a polymeric form of anhydrous chloral, known in Germany as viferral. It dissolves slowly in cold, but readily in boiling water. Used as hypnotic in simple sleeplessness and in the insomnia of mania in doses of 15 grains. Tubes of 5 tablets, 1 Gm. each....................35c.
(C. Bischoff & Co.)

HYRGOL. (COLLOIDAL MERCURY.) Dark, solid body, fairly soluble in cold water, insoluble in alcohol and ether; used in syphilis as 10 per cent. ointment by inunction, and pills and tablets internally. Dose, ½ to ¾ grain thrice daily. 1 oz. vials...80c.
(Schering & Glatz.)

ICHTHALBIN. (ICHTHYOL ALBUMINATE.) Grayish-brown powder, odorless and tasteless; combination of ichthyol and albumin, containing 40 per cent. of the former. Used internally for skin diseases and gastro-intestinal affections in doses of 5 to 30 grains three times daily. 1 oz. cartons, 85c.; 5 grain tablets, 100 in bot..$1.00
(Knoll & Co. and Merck & Co.)

ICHTHARGAN. (ICHTHYOL SILVER; SILVER ICHTHYOLSULPHONATE; SILVER THIO-HYDROCARBUROSULPHONATE.) Brown powder containing 30 per cent. silver; soluble in water and glycerin. Bactericide and astringent in urinary diseases in injections of 1 to 500 and 1 to 3000 in water; in diseases of the eye, as trachoma, by brush applications of 1 to 3 per cent. solutions. Dose, 1-24 to 1-12 grain in water. 1 oz. vials, $3.00; ¼ oz.............$3.10
(Merck & Co.)

ICHTHOFORM. (ICHTHYOL FORMALDEHYDE.) Blackish-brown powder, insoluble in water. Used externally as succedaneum for iodoform. Internally as intestinal antiseptic in the diarrhœa and intestinal disorders occurring in tubercular diseases, and in typhoid fever and dysentery. Dose, 15 to 30 grains three or four times daily, in powder or capsules. 1 oz. vials..............$1.00
(Merck & Co.)

IODIPIN. (IODIZED SESAME OIL; IODINOL.) Thick, yellow oil, odorless and of oily taste, made similarly to bromipin by repeated iodization of sesame oil by means of iodine monochloride in alcoholic solution; insoluble in water and alcohol, soluble in ether and chloroform. Made in two strengths, 10 per cent. iodine and 25 per cent. iodine, respectively, the former for internal and the latter for hypodermic use. Succedaneum for iodide in syphilis, scrofula, etc. Dose, 10 per cent., 1 to 3 fl. drachms; hypodermically (25 per cent.), 30 to 90 minims. On unspecified orders the 10 per cent. strength is supplied. Used in all cases where iodine and iodides are indicated; hypodermically in syphilis. 10 per cent. strength, 1 lb. bottles, $3.65; ¼ lb., $3.90; 1 oz. vials, 28c.; 20 per cent., 1 lb. bottles, $8.25; ¼ lb., $8.30; 1 oz. vials ....65c.
(Merck & Co.)

IODFERRATOSE. A syrup containing 0.3 per cent. of iron and 0.3 per cent. of iodine. 250 Gm. bottles...............55c.
(C. F. Boehringer & Soehne.)

IODOFORMOGEN. Light yellow powder, odorless in use, combination of iodoform and albumin, insoluble in water, capable of sterilization; used like iodoform as a dressing for wounds. 1 oz. cartons ....55c.
(Knoll & Co. and Merck & Co.)

IODOZEN. Yellowish-white powder, a chemical combination of methyl salicylate and iodine, insoluble in water, soluble in 3 parts of alcohol, in 3 parts of ether and in 10 parts of chloroform. Antiseptic application applied as solution or ointment. Marketed in sprinkler top cans. 1 oz....................75c.
(The Wm. S. Merrell Chemical Co.)

IODOTHYRINE. Whitish powder, representing the active principle of the thyroid gland combined with sugar of milk. Alterative in goitre, myxœdema, obesity, psoriasis, menstrual disorders of women, etc., in daily doses of 15 to 30 grains. Powder, in ¼ oz. vials per oz., $3.90; 1 oz. vials $3.40. Tablets, 5 grains, each, vials of 25, per vial, $1.00; 100 ....$3.90
(Continental Color & Chemical Co.)

IOTHION. Syrupy, yellowish-brown liquid, difficultly soluble in water, easily soluble in alcohol, ether, benzol and chloroform; miscible with petrolatum and with anhydrous lanolin, which takes up twice its weight of iothion. Organic compound of iodine, of which it contains 79 to 80 per cent. Applied in form of ointment by inunction as a substitute for potassium iodide in doses of 30 to 60 grains a day. 1 oz. bot., per oz....................$1.10
(Continental Color & Chemical Co.)

IRON TONOL. (IRON GLYCEROPHOSPHATE.) Powder; soluble in water; tonic, nerve nutrient. Dose, 3 to 10 grains. 1 oz., 35c.; 1 lb..............$3.50
(Schering & Glatz.)

IRON TROPON. Brownish powder; albuminoid food preparation composed of tropon (pure albumen) and iron in an assimilable form. Contains 2½ per cent. of iron. Used as a tonic food in treatment of anæmia, chlorosis, impoverished conditions of the system generally, and in convalescence. Tins, 100 Gm., 75c.; 1 doz. tins $6.75
(Tropon Works.)

ISOPRAL. White crystals, soluble in water up to 3 per cent. and easily in alcohol and ether. A nondepressing substitute for chloral in doses of 7 to 15 grains, indicated in all forms of sleeplessness in which chloral is employed. Powder, in 1 oz. bot., per oz., $1.40; 8 grain tablets, bottles of 100, $3.00; 8 grain tablets, tubes of 20 ....75c.
(Continental Color & Chemical Co.)

KRESAMINE. Clear, watery liquid, representing a solution of trikresol, 25 per cent., and ethylenediamine, 25 per cent.; soluble in 3 parts of water, and in all proportions of glycerin; antiseptic and sedative to inflammed tissues. 1 oz...$1.00
(Schering & Glatz.)

KRYOFINE. White, granular crystals, sparingly soluble in cold water (1 in 600); freely soluble in alcohol and ether. A compound of paraphenetidin and methylglycolic acid. Antipyretic and antineuralgic in doses of 4 to 7½ grains. 1 oz. cartons, powd., $1.00; tablets, 4 or 7½ grains, per oz.....$1.00
(C. Bischoff & Co.)

LACTOPHENIN. (LACTYL-PARA-PHENETIDIN.) Small, white crystals, soluble in 330 parts of water. Differs from phenacetin in containing a molecule of lactic acid in place of acetic. Antipyretic and analgetic in doses of 4 to 8 grains. 1 oz. cartons, each......$1.00
(C. F. Boehringer & Soehne.)

LACTOSERVE. Buttermilk in powder form, scientifically prepared from fresh milk, free from bacteria. Used as infant food. 250 Gm. box........25c.
(C. F. Boehringer & Soehne.)

LARGIN. (SILVER PROTALBIN.) Gray powder containing 11 per cent. of silver; soluble in 10 parts of water. Bactericide and astringent application in gonorrhœa in ¼ to 1½ per cent. injections. 1 oz. vials...$1.75
(Merck & Co.)

LENIGALLOL. (PYROGALLOL TRIACETATE.) White, crystalline powder, insoluble in water, possessing the same reducing properties as pyragallol and used in acute and chronic eczema as ointment. 1 oz. vials $1.00
(Knoll & Co. and Merck & Co.)

LEVULOSE. (FRUIT SUGAR.) Crystalline powder, soluble in water. Sweetening agent used in diabetes, tuberculosis, malnutrition and marasmus of children. Dose, 3 drachms to 2 ounces daily. 1 lb. jars..$1.60
(Schering & Glatz.)

LYCETOL. (DIMETHYLENEDIAMINE TARTRATE.) White powder, readily soluble in water. Uric acid solvent, antiarthritic and diuretic in doses of 5 to 10 grains three times daily. 10 Gm. vials, $1.50; ¼ oz., ½ oz., 1 oz. cartons, per oz... $4.25 to $4.40
(Continental Color & Chemical Co. and Schering & Glatz.)

LYGOSINE. (SODIUM LYGOSINATE.) Glossy, greenish crystals; a condensation product of salicylaldehyde and acetone; readily soluble in water, forming ruby red solutions. Nonirritant substitute for silver as urethral injection in gonorrhœa, 5 per cent. strength. 10 Gm. vials....................85c.
(C. Bischoff & Co.)

LYSIDIN. (ETHYLENE-ETHENYL-DIAMINE HYDROCHLORIDE.) Pale yellowish liquid, containing 50 per cent. of pure lysidin, the substance itself being very hygroscopic. Used in acute gout and uric acid diathesis in doses of 10 to 30 minims. 1 oz. vials $1.75
(Victor Koechl & Co.)

MARETIN. White, glistening crystals, very sparingly soluble in water (1 to 1050). Antipyretic, being a methyl acetanilid with a urea nucleus in place of the acetyl group. Dose, 3 to 5 grains. 1 oz. cartons, per oz...........$1.25 to $1.40
(Continental Color & Chemical Co.)

METHAFORM. (DIMETHYLCARBINOL CHLOROFORM.) White, shiny, needle-like crystals, with a slightly camphoraceous taste and odor, sparingly soluble in water, but readily so in chloroform, alcohol, ether and glacial acetic acid. It is hypnotic, analgetic, anæsthetic and antiseptic, somewhat resembling chloral in physiological action. 1 oz. vials, 60c.; 3 grain capsules, bot. of 100, 50c.; 5 grain, 100 ....75c.
(Frederick Stearns & Co.)

MERCUROL. Brownish powder, soluble in water; insoluble in alcohol; a chemical combination of nucleinic acid and mercury, containing 10 per cent. of the metal. Does not coagulate albuminous liquids. Applied to ulcers and suppurating mucous membranes in from ½ to 5 per cent. solution, or in ointment. ¼ oz. vials, per oz., $1.60; 1 oz. vials $1.50
(Parke, Davis & Co.)

MESOTAN. (METHYLOXYMETHYLESTER OF SALICYLIC ACID.) Clear, yellow fluid, insoluble in water, but miscible with alcohol, ether and fixed oils. External application mixed with equal parts of olive oil in muscular and articular rheumatism, pleuritis and gout. 1 oz. bot., 47c.; 25 oz. lots, 42c.
(Continental Color & Chemical Co.)

MIGRAININ. (PHENAZONE CAFFEINE CITRATE.) Small white crystals, readily soluble in water and alcohol. Analgetic and antipyretic. Used in migraine, headaches of influenza, neuralgia, sciatica, etc., in doses of 17 grains. 1 oz. tins........$1.50
(Victor Koechl & Co.)

MIGROL. White powder, composed of equal parts of sodium pyrocatechinmonoacetate and caffein pyrocatechinmonoacetate. Effective and harmless remedy in headache, toothache, neurasthenia, etc. 1 oz.......$4.00
(Fuerst Bros. & Co.)

NARGOL. Brownish powder readily soluble in warm water. Compound of silver and nucleinic acid containing 10 per cent. of the former; does not coagulate albumen. Used in gonorrhœa, conjunctival and other pyogenic inflammations. ¼ oz. vials, per oz., $1.80; ½ oz. vials, per oz., $1.75; 1 oz.......$1.70
(Parke, Davis & Co.)

NEODERMIN. Ointment containing lanolin, 85; petrolatum, 10; difluordiphenyl, 4; fluorpseudocumol, 1. For ulcerated surfaces, burns, etc. Collapsible tubes, Gm. 20 and Gm. 40, each................40c. and 75c
(C. Bischoff & Co.)

NOSOPHEN. (TETRAIODOPHENOLPHTHALEIN.) Grayish powder, odorless, slightly anæsthetic, insoluble in water, alcohol or ether, but soluble in alkaline fluids. Antiseptic dusting powder in wounds, burns, ulcers; substitute for iodoform. Bottles containing about ¼ oz., per doz....................$4.50
(Stallman & Fulton Co.)

NOVARGAN. (SILVER PROTEINATE.) Fine yellow powder containing 10 per cent. of metallic silver, readily soluble in water. Used as injection in gonorrhœa; is very penetrating and free from irritating effects upon mucous membrane. 1 oz. vials, $1.40

(Heyden Chemical Works.)

OREXINE. (PHENYLDIHYDROQUINAZOLINE TANNATE.) Yellowish powder, tasteless and odorless; insoluble in water, slightly soluble in dilute acid solutions, readily so in hydrochloric acid. Should not be prescribed with preparations of iron. Used in anorexia (lack of appetite) as stimulant of gastric secretion; in seasickness and vomiting of pregnancy. Orexine base is no longer on the market. Dose, 8 to 12 grains two times daily, in powder or in tablets. 1 oz. vials, $1.00; orexoids, Merck's tablets, 4 grains, 50 in bottle ....55c.

(Merck & Co.)

ORPHOL. (BISMUTH BETANAPHTHOLATE.) Odorless and tasteless fawn colored powder, insoluble in water; consists of 80 per cent. bismuth oxide and 20 per cent. beta-naphthol. Intestinal antiseptic in doses of 5 to 15 grains three or four times daily. 1 oz., 80c.; tablets, 5 grains, 50 tablets in vial, per vial ....60c.

(Schering & Glatz.)

ORTHOFORM. White crystalline powder, the methyl ester of metaamidoparaoxybenzoic acid; slightly soluble in water; local anæsthetic and antiseptic. Forms a hydrochloride salt soluble in 9 parts of water. 10 per cent. solution of the hydrochloride salt, or 10 to 20 per cent. in ointment used to alleviate pain in sores or burns. Orthoform, 1 oz. vials, $1.40; orthoform hydrochloride, 1 oz. vials $1.80

(Victor Koechl & Co.)

OVARADEN. Tasteless and odorless powder consisting of the active substance of pigs' ovaries. Used in dysmenorrhœa and neurasthenia in doses of 15 to 30 grains daily. 1 oz. vials, $1.30; 4 grain tablets, bottles of 100.............$1.30

(Knoll & Co. and Merck & Co.)

OVARIIN. Powder representing 1 part in 8 of fresh cow's ovary, being the desiccated substance of the ovary. Used in chlorosis, affections of the heart, and menstrual troubles. 1 oz. vials, $2.00; ¼ oz., $2.10; 3 grain tablets, 100 in bottle $1.50

(Merck & Co.)

PANKREON. Grayish-red powder; a tannin-pancreatin compound; insoluble in water, obtained from the pancreas; used in pancreatic diabetes, gastritis and apepsia in doses of 7½ grains three times daily. Box of 25 Gm., $1.50; tablets of 0.25 Gm., 50 in box, $1.00; sugar tablets (¾ grain), 100 in box.......................50c.

(Merck & Co.)

PHENOCOLL HYDROCHLORIDE. White, crystalline powder, with sharp, saline taste; soluble in 16 parts of water; very soluble in hot water and alcohol. Similar to phenacetin, and used in malaria, pneumonia, influenza, rheumatism, etc. Dose, 7 to 15 grains. 25 Gm. vials.............$1.50

(Schering & Glatz.)

PIPERAZINE. Crystalline powder readily soluble in water. Solvent of uric acid and insoluble urates in the system; used in gout, rheumatism and urinary calculi. Dose, 5 to 15 grains thrice daily. 10 Gm. vials, per vial, $1.50; lots of 60, per vial, $1.25. Tablets, tubes of ten 15 grain tablets, $1.50; 60 tubes, per tube, $1.25; ½ and 1 oz. bot., per oz. $4.25

(Continental Color & Chemical Co. and Schering & Glatz.)

POLLANTIN. Liquid and powder; antitoxic serum for hay fever, autumnal catarrh, rose fever and June cold. Package of powder and brush, $1.75; liquid, per package of serum and pipette.............$1.75

(Fritzsche Brothers.)

PROBILIN PILLS. Composed of salicylic acid, acid sodium oleate, phenolphthalein and menthol; used in gallstone affections. Dose, 3 to 4 pills twice daily for twenty days. Vials of 60, per vial.....$1.25

(Schering & Glatz.)

PROFERRIN. (IRON NUCLEOPROTEID.) Reddish-brown powder, insoluble in water and acid solutions; contains 10 per cent. of iron and 1 per cent. of phosphorus, in organic combination; is absorbed from the duodenum, being unaffected by the gastric juice. Used in blood impoverishment in doses of 5 grains three times daily. 1 oz. cartons, per doz., $6.00; 5 grain tablets, bottle of 100, 60c.; 2½ grain, bottle of 100.......40c.

(H. K. Mulford Co.)

PROTAN. (TANNIN NUCLEOPROTEID.) Light brown powder, insoluble in water; formed by the synthesis of tannic acid with nucleo-proteid. Used in all forms of diarrhœa in doses of from 20 to 30 grains; is astringent and acts in the intestines, being unaffected by the gastric juice. 1 oz. cartons, per doz., $6.00; 7½ grain tablets, bottle of 100, 85c.; 5 grain, per 100.............60c.

(H. K. Mulford Co.)

PROTARGOL. Yellowish, light powder, easily soluble in water. A proteid compound containing 8 per cent. of silver; not precipitated by albumen or salt solutions. Bactericide in gonorrhœa; antiseptic in eye, ear, nose and throat affections. 0.25 to 1 per cent. solutions for gonorrhœa; 0.5 to 5 per cent. for eye, and 2 to 10 per cent. for ear, nose and throat. Internally, in doses of 1 to 3 grains. ½ oz. and 1 oz. vials, per oz.........$1.10 to $1.35

(Continental Color & Chemical Co.)

PURGATIN. (PURGATOL; ANTHRAPURPURIN ACETATE.) Yellow crystalline powder; a synthetic oxyanthraquinone, having mild aperient properties; insoluble in water; decomposed in contact with alkalies. Dose, 10 to 30 grains. 1 oz. cartons, 85c.; 5 grain tablets, 100 in bottle $1.00

(Knoll & Co. and Merck & Co.)

PYRAMIDON. (DIMETHYLAMIDO-ANTIPYRIN.) White powder, soluble in 9 parts of water and 2 parts of alcohol. Used as antipyretic in treatment of asthma, pulmonary tuberculosis and abdominal typhus, and as anodyne in headaches and neuralgic pains in doses of 8 to 12 grains. 1 oz. cartons, $2.15; pyramidon camphorate, acid, 1 oz. bot., $1.50; camphorate, neutral, 1 oz. bot., $1.75; salicylate 1 oz. bot. $1.50

(Victor Koechl & Co.)

PYRENOL, a white, crystalline, slightly hygroscopic powder of aromatic odor and sweetish taste, is an addition product of

salicylic and benzoic acids with thymol. Antiseptic, expectorant, analgetic, sedative, antipyretic and cardiotonic. Indicated in the treatment of asthma, bronchitis, pertussis, pneumonia, influenza, typhoid fever and in rheumatic and neuralgic affections. Dose, 7½ to 15 grains, thrice daily, dry or in cold liquids. 1 oz. vial, 70c.; tube of 20 tablets..............30c.
(Schering & Glatz.)

QUARTONOL. Tablets consisting of a compound of duotonol, quinine tonol and strychnine tonol. Blood and nerve tonic. Dose, 1 to 2 tablets three times daily. Bottle of 100 5-grain tablets....................75c.
(Schering & Glatz.)

QUININE LYGOSINATE. Orange-yellow, amorphous powder, containing 70.8 per cent. of quinine; difficultly soluble in water, readily soluble in alcohol, chloroform and benzin. Nontoxic antiseptic and styptic, employed as a dusting powder, gauze or suppository. 10 Gm. vials, each................70c.
(C. Bischoff & Co.)

RENADEN. Powder, obtained from extract of pigs' kidneys; used in uræmia and nephritis in doses of 1 to 2 drachms daily. 1 oz. vials, $1.30; 4 grain tablets, bottles of 100 ....$1.30
(Knoll & Co. and Merck & Co.)

RUBIDIUM IODIDE. Colorless, cubical crystals; soluble in less than 1 in 1 of water; bitter, saline taste. Used in place of potassium iodide in polyarthritis and syphilis. Dose, 5 to 20 grains. 1 oz. vial..$1 00
(Merck & Co.)

SAL-ETHYL. A colorless, transparent, volatile fluid; chemically pure ethyl salicylate. A substitute for methyl salicylate or oil of wintergreen. Globules, 5 min., in bot. of 50, per doz. bot. $5.00
(Parke, Davis & Co.)

SALIT. (SALICYLIC ACID ESTER OF BORNEOL.) Oily fluid, insoluble in water, slightly soluble in glycerin and readily soluble in alcohol, ethers and oils. Used in muscular and articular rheumatism, lumbago, neuralgia and rheumatic pains following colds. 1 oz. bot......22c.
(Heyden Chemical Works.)

SALOCREOL. (SALICYLIC ACID ESTER OF CREOSOTE.) Oily fluid of neutral reaction, almost odorless, insoluble in water, readily soluble in alcohol, ether, chloroform and oils. Used in facial erysipelas, acute and chronic inflammation of the lymph glands and chronic arthritis. 1 oz. bot........45c.

SALOPHEN. White, crystalline powder, containing 51 per cent. of salicylic acid; almost insoluble in water; soluble in alcohol and ether; incompatible with alkalies, which decompose it. Antipyretic, analgetic and antiseptic in rheumatism and neuralgia. Dose, 10 to 15 grains 3 to 4 times daily. 1 oz. cartons.............85c. to $1.00
(Continental Color & Chemical Co.)

SALOQUININE. (SALICYLIC ACID ESTER OF QUININE.) Whitish powder, insoluble in water, with difficulty soluble about 1 in 120 of alcohol and ether. Tasteless quinine substitute, used in malaria, tropical fevers, neuralgia and rheumatism. Dose, 15 to 30 grains, one to three times daily. ½ and 1 oz. cartons.
$1.25 to $1.30
(Continental Color & Chemical Co. and Merck & Co.)

SANTYL. Yellowish, oily liquid, tasteless and nonirritant. Salicylic ester of pure sandalwood oil. Used in acute gonorrhœia and its complications. Dose, 30 drops, thrice daily. Bottle of ½ oz..................$1.00
(Knoll & Co. and Merck & Co.)

SCOPOLAMINE HYDROBROMIDE is identical with hyoscine hydrobromide, but lower in price. 15 grain tubes, each, $3.00; 10 grain tubes, $2 10; 5 grain tubes.....$1.05
(Merck & Co. and C. F. Boehringer & Soehn.)

SEXTONOL. Tablets consisting of a compound of duotonol, quinine tonol, iron tonol, manganese tonol and strychnine tonol. Blood and nerve nutrient. Dose, 1 to 2 5-grain tablets three times daily. Bottle of 100................75c.
(Schering & Glatz.)

SIDONAL. (PIPERAZINE QUINATE.) White amorphous powder, readily soluble in water. Uric acid solvent in gout and allied affections in doses of 75 to 120 grains a day in divided doses, well diluted with water. 1 oz. bot................$3.75
(Victor Koechl & Co.)

SIDONAL NEW. (QUINIC ACID ANHYDRIDE.) Same properties and uses as above. 1 oz. bot. $2 00
(Victor Koechl & Co.)

SILVER CITRATE. (ANTISEPTIC CREDE; ITROL.) White powder, soluble about 1 in 4000 of water. Recommended in Credé's treatment as an antiseptic for wounds, in lotion, ointment or powder. For disinfection of hands, skin and instruments, 1 to 1000-5000 watery solution; as gargle 1 to 5000 to 10,000; in gonorrhœa, 1 to 8000. Oz.............$1.20 to $1.25
(Schering & Glatz and Merck & Co.)

SILVER LACTATE. (ACTOL.) Whitish powder, soluble in 15 parts of water; recommended in solution 1 in 200 to 1000 as an antiseptic for surgical use. ½ oz. and 1 oz. vials, per oz., $1.30; tablets, 3 grains, boxes containing 5 vials of 10 tablets, per box.................$1.15
(Schering & Glatz and Merck & Co.)

SOMATOSE. Light yellow almost tasteless powder, easily soluble in water, prepared from meat and consisting of deutero and hetero albumoses. Nitrogenous food product for the sick and convalescent. Dose for adults, 90 to 180 grains daily; for children, 50 to 100 grains. 2 oz. tins, per doz., $8.25; ¼ lb. tins, per lb., $5.25; ½ lb. tins, per lb...................$5.00
(Continental Color & Chemical Co.)

SOMNOS. (TRICHLORETHIDENE PROPENYL ETHER.) [Elixir chlorœthanal alcoholate.] Clear liquid, miscible with water, produced by the synthesis of Trichloraldehyde with a polyatomic alcohol radical. Hypnotic and cerebral sedative in doses of from 2 to 4 fluid drachms. Pint bottles, $1.10 per pint; $12.00 per doz.; 4 oz. bottles, per doz...........$4.00
(H. K. Mulford Co.)

SPIROFORM. White, crystalline powder, insoluble in water, but readily soluble in alcohol and other solvents. Odorless and practically tasteless. Antirheumatic, analgetic, uric acid solvent. Dose, 7½ to 15 grains, three to five times daily. 25 Gm. cartons, 75c.; 7½ grain tablets, cartons of 50.....75c.
(C. Bischoff & Co.)

STOVAINE. (AMYLENE HYDROCHLORIDE.) White crystalline powder, readily soluble in wa-

ter and in methyl alcohol; less soluble in ethyl alcohol and almost insoluble in ether. A substitute for cocaine, approximately one-fifth as toxic. Aqueous solutions are slightly acid and bitter to the taste. Put up in solutions of various strengths, ¾ per cent., 1 per cent., 10 per cent., in tubes; tablet triturates, 1½ grains each; pastilles, 3-100 grain each. Original packages, 1 oz., ½ and ¼ oz. bottles, per oz. $4.00
(Walter F. Sykes & Co.)

STYPTICIN. (COTARNINE HYDROCHLORIDE.) Yellow amorphous powder, the salt of an opium base (cotarnine is a product of the oxidation of narcotine), soluble in water and alcohol. Because of its chemical resemblance to hydrastinine, it being methoxyl-drastine, it is recommended in all forms of uterine hæmorrhage. Used in functional dysmenorrhœa and in the menorrhagia of puberty and the climacteric. Dose as styptic, 1½ to 4 grains, as needed, per os or by injection (10 per cent. solution). Sugar coated tablets, ¾ grain, per tube of 20, 25c.; 1 oz. bottles, per oz., $6.50; ½ oz. bottles, per oz., $6.60; ⅛ oz., per oz., $7.00; 15 grain vials, each, 35c.; hypodermic tablets, ¾ grain, per box of 40 (4 tubes).......60c.
(Merck & Co.)

STYPTOL. (COTARNINE PHTHALATE.) Yellow, crystalline powder, readily soluble in water. It is the phthalate salt of an opium base. Recommended in uterine hæmorrhage in doses of 1 to 3 grains; externally in 10 per cent. solution. 1 oz. vials, $6.50; ¼ oz., per oz., $6.75; ⅛ oz., $7.00; 15 grain vials, per vial, 35c.; ¾ grain tablets, bottles of 100, per bot...$1.20
(Knoll & Co. and Merck & Co.)

STYRACOL. (GUAIACOL CINNAMIC ESTER.) White granular crystals, insoluble in water, readily soluble in alcohol. Given in phthisis, catarrh of the stomach and intestines in doses of 15 grains three to four times daily. 1 oz. cartons, $1.20; 5 grain tablets, bot of 100..$1.40
(Knoll & Co. and Merck & Co.)

SUBLAMINE. (MERCURIC ETHYLENE-DIAMINE SULPHATE.) Crystalline powder, containing 43 per cent. of mercury; very soluble in water. Used in solutions of 1 to 1000 as a substitute for corrosive sublimate. 1 oz. vials, 50c.; tablets, 15 grains, 100 tablets in bottle, $1.10; 20 tablets in tube, 5 tubes in box..............$1.60
(Schering & Glatz.)

TANNALBIN. (TANNIN ALBUMINATE.) Pale brown, insoluble, tasteless powder, containing about 50 per cent. of tannin. It is not affected by the gastric juice, but is split up in the intestinal canal; hence is used as intestinal astringent and for diarrhœa. Dose, 15 to 30 grains three to five times daily. 1 oz. cartons, 85c.; 5 grain tablets, bot, of 100......$1.00
(Knoll & Co. and Merck & Co.)

TANNIGEN. (ACETYLTANNIN.) Grayish powder, insoluble in water, soluble in alcohol; incompatible with alkalies which decompose it. Intestinal astringent in chronic diarrhœa and intestinal diseases of children. Adult dose, 3 to 10 grains, three to six times daily; children, 1-3 to ½ that quantity. 1 oz. bot., per oz....55c. to 75c. (Continental Color & Chemical Co.)

TANNOPINE. (HEXAMETHYLENETETRAMINE TANNIN.) Brownish powder, insoluble in water, decomposed by alkalies; compound of tannin and urotropine, containing 87 per cent. of tannic acid. Intestinal astringent and disinfectant. Adult dose, 10 to 15 grains; children, 3 to 8 grains four times daily. 1 oz. cartons, per oz.................55c. to 75c. (Continental Color & Chemical Co.)

TESTADEN. Powdered extract of the testicle juice of animals. Used in impotency, neurasthenia and spinal irritation. Dose, 15 grains three to four times daily. 1 oz. vials, $1.80; 4 grain tablets, bot. of 100.$1.80
(Knoll & Co. and Merck & Co.)

THEOBROMINE. White crystalline powder, soluble in ether, but almost insoluble in cold water or alcohol; organic base obtained from seeds of *Theobroma cacao*. Diuretic in dropsy of cardiac and renal affections. Dose, 5 to 8 grains. 1 oz. bot., per oz.........90c. (Continental Color & Chemical Co. and Merck & Co.)

THEOBROMINE - SODIUM - SALICYLATE. White powder, very soluble in water, decomposed by acid solutions. Diuretic in dropsy of cardiac and renal origin. Dose, 7 to 15 grains. 1 oz. bot., per oz..60c. (Farbenfabriken of Elberfeld, Continental Color Works and Merck & Co.)

THEOCIN. Fine, colorless crystals; synthetic alkaloid of tea (theophylline); difficultly soluble in alcohol and cold water, more easily in warm water; forms salts with alkalies. Powerful diuretic in doses of 3 to 6 grains, two to three times daily. ½ and 1 oz. bot., per oz..............$2.50 to $2.70 (Continental Color & Chemical Co.)

THEOPHYLLIN. White crystalline needles, soluble in 226 parts of water. Identical with theocin, being the synthetic alkaloid of tea. Diuretic in doses of 4 to 8 grains. 1 oz. vials, $1.40. Theophyllin sodium, 1 oz. vials, $1.50. Theophylline sodium salicylate, 1 oz. vials $1.10
(C. F. Boehringer & Soehne.)

THIGENOL. Dark brown, thick liquid; odorless on use; slight empyreumatic taste; soluble in water, diluted alcohol, glycerin and collodion; same uses as ichthyol. It is the sodium salt of the sulphonic acid of a synthetic sulpho oil. Dose, 3 to 10 grains. 1 oz. bots., per oz., 32c.; 1 lb. tins, per lb....$4.00 (Hoffmann-La Roche Chemical Works.)

THIOCOL. (POTASSIUM GUAIACOL SULPHONATE.) White crystalline powder, soluble in water, slightly in alcohol and ether. Used in phthisis and similar diseases which require the creosote or guaiacol treatment; nonirritating and readily assimilable. Dose, 5 to 20 grains three times daily. 1 oz. bot., per oz., $1.40; tablets, 5 grains each, 100 in bot...$1.75 Syrup, 6 oz. bots., per doz.$8.00 (Hoffmann-La Roche Chemical Works.)

THIOSINAMIN. Colorless crystals, soluble in water, alcohol and ether; used hypodermically for lupus and uterine affections in doses of 1 to 3 grains in 15 per cent. alcoholic or 10 per cent. glycerinated water solution, one injection being given every three days; by the mouth, in capsules containing ⅓ to 3 grains. 1 oz. vials, per oz 60c. (Schering & Glatz and Merck & Co.)

THYMOXOL. Alcoholic 1 per cent. solution of thymol containing 3 per cent. of hydrogen dioxide; miscible with water. Used in 5 or 10 per cent. solutions as antiseptic and bactericide. ¼ lb. bot., per lb...$2.40
(C. Bischoff & Co.)

THYRADEN. Brownish powder; dried extract of sheep's thyroid, containing all the constituents of the gland. Used in myxœdema, obesity, goitre, psoriasis, eczema, menorrhagia and rickets. Dose, 15 to 30 grains daily. 1 oz. vials, $1.30; 2 grain tablets, bot. of 100.75c.
(Knoll & Co. and Merck & Co.)

THYREOIDECTIN. Reddish powder obtained from the blood of animals deprived of the thyreoid gland. A remedy for exophthalmic goitre. Dose, 5 to 10 grains. Capsules, 5 grains each, bot. of 50...$1.00
(Parke, Davis & Co.)

THYROIDIN. Dried extract of sheep's thyroid, 1 part equaling 6 parts of fresh gland. Used in myxœdema, cretinism, psoriasis, obesity, lupus, etc. Dose, ½ to 1 grain, increased to 2 grains three times daily. 1 oz. bot. $1.25
(Merck & Co.)

TONOLS. Trade name adopted by Schering & Glatz for the glycerophosphate salts. See under the name of the alkali earth or metallic base.

TRIFERRIN. (IRON PARANUCLEINATE.) Brownish-yellow powder, soluble in alkaline solutions, insoluble in water. Said to contain 22 per cent. of iron, 9 per cent. of nitrogen and 2.5 per cent. of phosphorus. Used in anæmia, chlorosis and debility in dose of 5 grains three times daily. 1 oz. cartons, $1.00; 5 grain tablets, cartons of 50, 75c.; solution (Triferrol), 8 oz. bot., per bot. 55c. (C. Bischoff & Co. and Knoll & Co.)

TRIKRESOL. Clear, colorless liquid; a mixture of ortho, meta and para cresols in the proportion of 35, 40 and 25 per cent., respectively. Corresponding to Creosol, U. S. P., viii; soluble in 40 parts of water. Said to have three times the germicidal power of carbolic acid. Solutions of from ½ to 1 per cent. strength are recommended for surgical use; for internal use 1 to 2 minims three times a day. 1 oz. vials, 15c.; 1 lb. bot. .... 60c.
(Schering & Glatz.)

TRIOTONOL. Tablet consisting of 5 grains duotonol and 1-60 grain strychnine-tonol. Nerve tonic. Dose, 1 to 2 tablets, thrice daily. Bottle of 100 tablets .... 75c.
(Schering & Glatz.)

TRIPHENIN. (PROPIONYLPHENETIDIN.) White crystalline powder obtained by the action of propionic acid on paraphenetidine; almost insoluble in water (1 in 2000), more readily in alcohol and ether. Is a strong antipyretic, used in neuralgias and rheumatism in doses of 5 to 15 grains three or four times daily. Tablets, 5 grains, bot. of 50, 65c.; 1 oz. cartons .. 50c.
(Merck & Co.)

TROPACOCAINE HYDROCHLORIDE. (BENZOYLPSEUDOTROPEINE HYDROCHLORIDE.) Colorless crystals, soluble in water. Local anæsthetic like cocaine, but said to be less depressing to the heart. Used hypodermically in 3 to 10 per cent. solutions in 0.6 per cent. solution of sodium chloride. 5 grain vials, 40c.; 15 grain vials .... 95c.
(Merck & Co.)

TUMENOL. Reddish-brown, oily paste, obtained from a bituminous rock deposit. Consists of a mixture of sulphonised hydrocarbons similar to ichthyol, and possessing similar properties, being antiseptic and healing in skin diseases, applied either as attenuated powder, 5 per cent. ointment, or dissolved in ether and alcohol or water and glycerine.

AMMONIUM. Black, viscid, oily liquid, odorless; soluble in water and miscible with oils and fats. Used as antiseptic application in skin diseases, in form of ointment, paste or glycerin-ethereal solution painted on surface. 1 oz. bottles ..... 25c.

OIL is a dark yellow fluid of thick consistency, having the same application as the foregoing.

POWDER. (SULPHOTUMENOLIC ACID.) Dark yellow powder, readily soluble in water. Used with equal parts of zinc starch paste in treatment of skin diseases. Paste, 1 oz. vials, 55c.; ¼ lb. jar, $1.75; ½ lb. jar, $3.25. Oil, 1 oz. vials, 65c.; ¼ lb. bottles, $3.25; 1 lb. bottles, $6.30. Powder, 1 oz. tin, $1.10; 2 oz. tins, per tin .. $1.85
(Victor Koechl & Co.)

URITONE. White crystalline powder; a product of formaldehyde and ammonia, of the same composition and properties as hexamethylene tetramine; used in treatment of purulent conditions of the urine, cystitis, etc., in doses of 5 to 15 grains. 1 oz. vials, 60c.; 5 grain capsules, per bot. of 100, 85c.; compressed tablets, 7½ grs., each, per bot of 100 .... $1.00
(Parke, Davis & Co.)

UROSINE. (LITHIUM QUINATE.) Colorless crystals, readily soluble in water. Used in gout, cystitis and uric acid diathesis. Supplied in effervescent tablets containing quinic acid, 7½ grains; lithium carbonate, 1½ grains; sugar, 4¼ grains. Vial of 10, 50c.; 25, $1.20. Powder, 1 oz. vial .... 95c.
(C. Bischoff & Co.)

UROTROPIN. (HEXAMETHYLENETETRAMINE.) Colorless granular crystals, with an alkaline reaction; readily soluble in water. Urinary antiseptic in cystitis, bacteruria, phosphaturia, gout, rheumatism, irritable bladder, etc., used also before and after instrumentation to forestall urinary infection. Dose, 5 to 15 grains. 1 oz. vials, 60c.; lb., $7.50; tablets, 7½ grains each, 20 tablets in box, 25c.; 5 grains each, 30 tablets in box .... 25c.
(Schering & Glatz.)

UROTROPIN METHYLENE CITRATE. (NEWUROTROPIN.) Crystals resembling urotropin and having same therapeutic indications, though dose is double, being 15 grains three times daily. 1 oz. vials, 60c.; tablets, 7½ grains, 20 tablets in box, per box .... 25c.
(Schering & Glatz.)

VALIDOL. (VALERIC ACID MENTHYL ESTER.) Colorless liquid, a combination of valeric acid and menthol; insoluble in water, readily soluble in alcohol. Used in hysteria and neurasthenia in doses of 10 to 15 drops three times daily. Vials, 10 Gm., 50c.; 25 Gm., $1.20; pills, 25 in bot., each ...... 50c.
(C. Bischoff & Co.)

VALIDOL CAMPHORATE. Colorless liquid, insoluble in water, readily soluble in alcohol and oils. A 10 per cent. solution of camphor in validol. Used in toothache by local application and internally in same indications and dose as validol. Vials, 10 Gm. each, 60c.; 25 Gm. $1.20
(C. Bischoff & Co.)

VALYL. (VALERIC ACID DIETHYLAMIDE.) Colorless, oily liquid, with a valerian odor and burning taste, supplied only in gelatin capsules, each containing 2 grains. Nerve sedative used in hysteria, neurasthenia, hypochondriasis, and in neuralgia and menstrual disturbances in doses of 2 or 3 capsules two or three times daily. Bot. of 50 capsules .... 90c.
(Victor Koechl & Co.)

VERONAL. White crystalline powder, soluble in 150 parts of cold and 12 parts of boiling water. Hypnotic in simple sleeplessness and the insomnia of mania. Dose, 5 to 15 grains, dissolved in hot fluids. 1 oz. bot. and cartons, per oz., $1.60; tablets, 5 grains each, tube of 10, 30c.; bot. of 100 .... $2.25
(Merck & Co. and Continental Color & Chemical Co.)

VIOFORM. (IODOCHLOROXYCHINOLINE.) Greenish-yellow powder, insoluble in water. Used in same way as iodoform, than which it is six times lighter and bulkier. 1 oz. cartons $1.15
(C. Bischoff & Co.)

XEROFORM. (TRIBROMPHENOL-BISMUTH.) Yellow, insoluble powder, containing bismuth oxide and tribromphenol in nearly equal proportions A powerful bactericide used in place of iodoform as a dressing for wounds and internally as an intestinal antiseptic in doses of 5 to 20 grains. 1 oz. vials ... 50c.
(The Heyden Chemical Works.)

American Druggist "WANTS" Page.

THIS Department is intended to be used as a medium for the exchange or sale of stores, the employment of clerks, and the securing of situations. Suitable notices of moderate length under this heading inserted one time free for subscribers; for each additional insertion Fifty Cents will be charged. Advertisements not in the foregoing classification Forty Cents per line.

SITUATIONS VACANT.

WANTED.—TABLET MAKER and SUGAR COATER; permanent position with good prospects for strictly first-class, sober man; salary, $20. References and samples of coated work with reply. Tablets, care of AMERICAN DRUGGIST.

DRUG CLERK WANTED.—A junior drug clerk of one or two years' experience; a country boy preferred; an all year drug store at a summer resort. J. Harrison Monroe, Ph.G., Guilford, Conn.

REGISTERED PHARMACISTS.—We are compiling a list of all drug employees in the United States who would accept better conditions. Every pharmacist should write at once for particulars. Employers referred to competent men, free. National Pharmaceutical Agency, 616 Colonial Security Building, St. Louis, Mo.

WANTED.—Correspondence invited with travelers calling regularly on physicians to take a new and interesting side line. One that appeals to every physician and pays a good profit. Address Chance, care of AMERICAN DRUGGIST.

WANTED.—SALESMEN OF ABILITY TO CARRY THE MOST SALABLE, ATTRACTIVE AND RELIABLE LINE OF NON-SECRET PREPARATIONS, TOILET ARTICLES AND SPECIALTIES SOLD IN THIS COUNTRY. HOUSE ESTABLISHED FOR 50 YEARS. WE WANT BOTH LOCAL AND STATE REPRESENTATIVES. HOLLANDER-KOSHLAND & CO., BALTIMORE, MD.

SITUATIONS WANTED.

POSITION WANTED AS NEW YORK OR PHILADELPHIA MANAGER FOR A PHARMACEUTICAL MANUFACTURING HOUSE BY A MAN THOROUGHLY EXPERIENCED IN EVERY BRANCH OF THIS BUSINESS, WITH FULL KNOWLEDGE OF THE TRADE IN THE WHOLE EASTERN TERRITORY; P. C. P. GRADUATE; SPLENDID BUSINESS TRAINING, SOBER AND INDUSTRIOUS, AND CAN ANSWER EVERY NECESSARY REQUIREMENT. ADDRESS, WITH PARTICULARS, E. M., CARE OF AMERICAN DRUGGIST.

BUSINESS OPPORTUNITIES.

FOR SALE.—Only drug store in good farming town of 800 population, with good neighboring territory; $2,500 stock; income about $8,000; rent, $100 per annum. Address David Letaw, Springville, Ala.

FOR SALE.—Drug store in thickly populated German section doing fair business and steadily improving. Cash, $1,000, balance easy terms. Address Pharmacist, 222 Bushwick avenue, Brooklyn, N. Y.

FOR SALE.—San Juan, Porto Rico; only American drug store; established seven years; good business; inventory about $7,500; reason, sickness. P. O. Box 226, San Juan, Porto Rico.

FOR SALE.—Profitable drug business in town near New York; good prices; low rent; sales last year $4,500; will be $5,000 this year; can be doubled; $1,000 cash required; balance easy payments. Address "Pharmacist," care AMERICAN DRUGGIST.

GENUINE BOHEMIAN HOP LUPULINE. If you wish to purchase a real good quality of hop lupuline, apply to Joseph Pachmann, Saaz, Bohemia, who solely can meet your requirements to your satisfaction.

$1, FOR THE LAW on any legal proposition; U. S. Patents, $60; Designs, $50; Labels, $20; Trademarks, $25; Copyrights, $5; protect your inventions, writings and goods. Passports, $5; charters, $100 (foreign travel), (companies). Address The Hanlons, Attorneys, Washington, D. C., U. S. A.

FOR SALE.—One of the finest drug stores in western New York; cement block; building new; steel ceiling; all fixtures new; everything up to date; hot water, heat, gas or electric lights; insurance, 1 per cent; will sell with or without building. Address V. C. Armes, Gowanda, N. Y.

A reliable and progressive CHEMICAL FACTORY IN GERMANY desires to communicate with American importers and manufacturers with a view to secure orders for chemical and pharmaceutical articles to be manufactured in Germany and imported into this country ready for the market.

The Company would furthermore be able to excute orders for patent medicines, etc., on any given recipe.

Address for further particular, M. FRANKFURTER, Room 97, 25 Whitehall St., New York.

$250,000 Private Capital to Invest

Advertiser, who is a private capitalist, desires to invest $250,000, more or less, in an Eastern enterprise. Would prefer to invest in a business on the oil, paint, or drug order; must be an established business. Will confer only with party who can present sound investment in which $100,000 or more can be invested; correspondence strictly confidential and returned if desired. Party desiring to correspond with view to business, address, "SOLVENT."

FOR cleansing every thing about a drug store or a soda fountain there is nothing equal to Hoffman's

Barkeeper's Friend

Marble, Glass, Nickel, Brass, Copper, Tin and German Silver

can all be cleaned and polished with it easier than with anything else. Let us send you a FREE SAMPLE.

Highest Award, Chicago World's Fair, 1893, Louisiana Purchase Exposition, St. Louis, Mo., 1904.

GEO. WM. HOFFMAN.
295 E. Washington St
Indianapolis, Ind.

FOR SALE BY JOBBING TRADE

I am receiving inquiries and individual orders from your vicinity. As it is to our mutual advantage to supply a customer through his local Druggist I want to hear from you personally and ask you to fill out the coupon herewith and mail me at once.

ABSORBINE

is well advertised and I will see that it is not dead stock. Do you want advertising matter?

W. F. YOUNG, P. D. F.
49 Monmouth St.
Springfield, Mass.

TOWN OR CITY ______ POPULATION, COUNTY ______ STATE ______

FIRM NAME ______

STREET ______ BUSINESS ______

NEAREST SHIPPING POINT ______ EXPRESS CO. ______

What Drug Paper do you take? ______ What Horse or Farm Paper? ______

Do you carry ABSORBINE in stock? ______ If so, how long? ______

Do you carry ABSORBINE, JR., (mankind) in stock? ______ If so, how long? ______

If not, will you order a small quantity from your jobber? ______

Average sale per month? ______ What season do you sell most? ______

Give name of your jobber ______

What is the average Horse worth in your section? ______ Are many raised? ______

How can I help you sell more goods? ______

Kindly fill out the above and return for my files and I will refer inquiries from your section to you to our mutual benefit. W. F. YOUNG, P. D. F. 49 Monmouth St., Springfield, Mass.

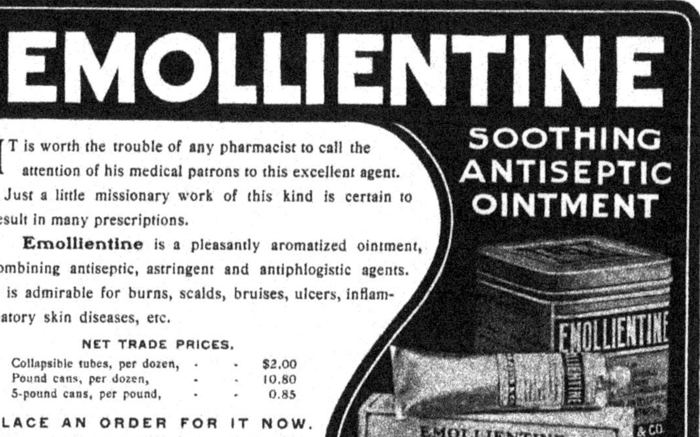
EMOLLIENTINE
SOOTHING
ANTISEPTIC
OINTMENT
IT is worth the trouble of any pharmacist to call the attention of his medical patrons to this excellent agent. Just a little missionary work of this kind is certain to result in many prescriptions.
Emollientine is a pleasantly aromatized ointment, combining antiseptic, astringent and antiphlogistic agents. It is admirable for burns, scalds, bruises, ulcers, inflammatory skin diseases, etc.
NET TRADE PRICES.
Collapsible tubes, per dozen, - - $2.00
Pound cans, per dozen, - - 10.80
5-pound cans, per pound, - - 0.85
PLACE AN ORDER FOR IT NOW.
PARKE, DAVIS & COMPANY
HOME OFFICES AND LABORATORIES, DETROIT, MICH.
EMOLLIENTINE
EMOLLIENTINE

SULPHUR TORCHES THAT BURN
SULPHUR candles that flutter, sputter and peter out are an unmitigated nuisance—to the seller no less than to the buyer. The druggist who supplies them isn't enhancing his reputation as a reliable merchandiser.
Our new Sulphur Torches are giving genuine satisfaction. We hear praise of them on every side. They are as different from the ordinary sulphur candle as day is from night. They burn, and burn steadily.
Our torch is molded in the form of a cube. It has a broad wick that projects from the lower edge at one side and runs diagonally through it. This wick is lighted at the bottom instead of at the top. The ascending flame causes the sulphur to burn freely.
NET TRADE PRICES.
Quarter-pound size, per dozen, $0.75; per gross, $8.00
One-pound size, per dozen, 1.75; per gross, 19.00
Put a Gross in Stock—You'll Sell Them Quickly
PARKE, DAVIS & CO.
HOME OFFICES AND LABORATORIES, DETROIT, MICH

Appeal by Greater New York Drug Clerks.

The Greater New York Drug Clerks' Association, with headquarters at 69 St. Mark's place, has issued a circular "to the drug clerks of Greater New York," of which the following is the text: "The Greater New York Drug Clerks' Association was organized twelve months ago in response to the growing sentiment among local clerks in favor of protective organization as a remedy for their industrial evils and in recognition of the following facts, which are the inevitable conclusions arrived at by all who make a casual study of the present day conditions in the drug store:

"(1) Considering the expensive preliminary requirements and the long apprenticeship necessary for legal qualification as a drug clerk, and the responsibilities he must consequently assume, the hours of service at present in vogue in the business are excessively long, and the remuneration he receives exceedingly inadequate. The long hours of service are not only detrimental to the welfare of the clerk himself, but also obviously dangerous to the public, since he is constantly called upon to handle poisonous chemicals and frequently human life depends upon his alertness and accuracy.

"(2) These unjust conditions to which the drug clerks have been forced to submit have been due to their failure to keep up with the modern progressive world, which has long since recognized *organization* as the watchword of commercial success, whether in the field of capital or labor. Nothing short of compact organization will avail in the struggle for better conditions. This is the era of organization, and everything comes to those who organze. The practicability of drug clerk organization has been shown in San Francisco and other Western cities, where the clerks, apparently more progressive than their Eastern colleagues, have perfected powerful organizations which succeeded in exacting favorable conditions from employers, besides securing legislative action in their favor, and gettng representation in the local boards of pharmacy.

"(3) That pharmacy in America has degenerated from the high professional standing it once held and still holds in most foreign countries, and its regeneration can only be acomplished by the drug clerks, who, by bettering their conditions and securing higher compensation for their services, will stop the opening of 'penny basis' stores on every street corner, and thus one evil besetting American pharmacy will be eradicated. The phenomenal success that the G. N. Y. D. C. has attained in the short time since its inception shows that the drug clerks are at last realizing what organization has in store for them. Ultimate success is bound to be the fruit of this movement, and the banner if the G. N. Y. D. C. A. will lead triumphantly towards the realization of its principles and win a victory that will be for the benefit of every man in the pharmaceutical profession.

"Mass meetings are being held in various parts of the city to familiarize the diverse elements with the work of the organization. We wish to annnounce a mass meeting which is to be held on Wednesday, June 6, 1906, at 10 o'clock p. m., at Odd Fellows' Hall, 69 St. Mark's place. The meeting will be addressed by such noted men as S. V. B. Swann, Dr. J. P. Bauerburg, and William Karlin. Do not fail to attend this mass meeting with your friends. If you are not already a member, we hope you will take the opportunity this meeting offers to become one, and if you are a member the meeting should stimulate you to greater efforts in promoting the propaganda of organization.

An Endless Chain.

A contributor sends in the following to the *Southern Druggist:* A man went into a drug store and asked the prescription clerk for something to warm him up. The druggist gave him, without charging him, a heavy dose of F. Capsicum. The man then had to buy an ice cold soda, and later a bottle of bismuth and pepsin mixture for his irritated stomach. This latter dose constipated him, which called for a dose of calomel; this nauseated him so that he bought a bottle of ess. pepsin. The fellow finally came to the druggist with the disgusted remark, "Say, Doc, let me pay for the first dose and stop this endless chain business."

Laboratory Girls.

The *Detroit News Tribune* for Sunday, March 25, devotes a special illustrated page to the laboratory girls of Detroit, outlining the character of the work done and presenting half a dozen very attractive portraits of different laboratory girls.

According to the *News Tribune* the hours in the laboratories are better than those in an average factory, being usually from 7.30 to 5 p.m., with an hour for luncheon, and Saturday afternoon free, and from two to four days holiday during the year with full pay. The work is healthy, cleanly and more prosperous than the average work.

As a general thing Detroit's laboratory girls do piece work, and for this reason the brighter and more alert a girl is the more she can earn. She starts in, however, on what is known as the "apprentice wage," which is from $2.50 to $3 a week. As soon as she has become educated in a certain kind of work she is allowed to take up piece work. Within three months, if she develops into an ordinarily good laboratory girl, the worker should be earning from $5 to $6 a week. From this time on her advance is slower, but after a year's work an enterprising girl almost invariably earns from $8 to $10 weekly. But this is by no means the limit. F. F. Ingram & Co. have girls who are earning as much as $18 a week, while F. K. Stearns & Co. have girls in their pill cutting department who make $20 a week. Similar cases may be found in the laboratories of Parke, Davis & Co., Nelson, Baker & Co., the Ray Chemical Company, and Lambert & Lowman. These firms have no restriction as to the amount of work a girl shall do, but they do not encourage a worker to earn more than $10 or $12 a week, for good laboratory girls are too valuable to lose through overwork.

All the various laboratories organize excursions for their employees during the summer, the firm bearing the full expense of the outing. F. F. Ingram also gives to his girls the privilege of spending their vacation on his large farm at Belleville.

The Executive and the Pharmacy Board.

Governor N. C. Blanchard, of the State of Louisiana, in his annual message to the Legislature, May 22, had the following to say regarding the operations of the State Board of Pharmacy:

"The report of the State Board of Pharmacy shows that professional standards have undergone appreciable improvement since the creation of a board having supervisory control of the practice of pharmacy in this State.

"'Pharmacy of to-day,' says the board in its annual report, 'is a combination of science and business, and the successful pharmacist must be both a business and professional man. The Board of Pharmacy has striven to keep up the professional end, which we are glad to say is progressing favorably. * * * The board accepts the United States Pharmacopœia as its standard and guide in examinations, and regrets, on account of the very limited income of the board, that it cannot make the examinations more practical.'

"The board recites at length, in its report, the progress made in elevating the practice of pharmacy in this State, and enumerates the benefits of the Federal pharmacy law recently enacted.

"It is a matter for general congratulation that the board successfully combated litigation intended to destroy its usefulness during the past year. A suit for damages for having refused to register an applicant was dismissed by the Supreme Court at plaintiff's cost, and an action attacking the constitutionality of the law creating the board was decided in favor of the defendant board.

"A complete list of the registered pharmacists of the State is attached to the report. N. C. BLANCHARD."

A pupil in a village school who had been requested to write an essay on the human body, handed in the following: "The human body consists of the head, thorax, abdomen and legs. The head contains the brains in case there are any. The thorax contains the heart and lungs, also the liver and lights. The abdomen contains the bowels, of which there are five—a, e, i, o, u and sometimes w and y. The legs extend from the abdomen to the floor and have hinges at the top and middle to enable a fellow to sit when standing or stand when sitting."—Kansas City *Star*.

Hints to Buyers.

Fries Bros., New York, are widely advertising their Kelene-pure chloride of ethyl, put up in automatic tubes for local and general anæsthesia. Clinical reports will be sent upon request.

All chemicals for medicinal, technical and other uses are manufactured by Powers, Weightman & Rosengarten Company, of Philadelphia, and sold by all wholesale druggists throughout the country. In ordering be sure to specify "P. W. & R."

The proprietor of the Long Island Ticket Agency, 500 Broadway, Long Island City, New York, advises us that he is prepared to visit at their residences individuals who are contemplating an European trip, and give all information regarding rates, routes and methods of travel.

The Warner Glass Company, of McDonald, Pa., has 67 varieties of bottles, and makes a specialty of lettered ware. Only the best materials are in the company's product, and special attention is paid to capacity. Send for catalogue showing the different styles.

Thousands of users testify to the value of the Star Ice Shaver, made by the D. L. Bates & Bro. Company, of Dayton, Ohio; it is a fine adjunct to any soda fountain and is a profitable instrument. The company can also supply wants in the line of electric fans for ceiling, wall or counter and water power fans for counter or wall.

"Something New" is the catchy and very appropriate description given to sparkling apenta splits (natural apenta carbonated) by the Apollinaris Agency Company, of New York, the sole agents. If any druggist hasn't this popular article in stock he should lose no time in getting prepared for the demand which he will undoubtedly be called upon to meet.

Magnus & Lauer, of New York, are one of the best sources of supply for all essential oils, vanilla beans and chemicals, and olive oils. The oils and chemicals are packed in small size containers suitable for the retail trade, in quantities of 1 ounce up. Write to the firm for descriptive price list, kindly mentioning the American Druggist.

Walker's ice cream disher, 1906 model, is one of the best on the market and will quickly prove its worth to any druggist who uses it. This disher has copper shell, bronze handle, and is nickel plated. It will not rust. Price $2.00. Two weeks' trial free. It is made by the Erie Specialty Company, Erie, Pa.

Many a time a druggist is puzzled as to just what he will feature in his window or what kind of a window display to make. The C. I. Hood Company, of Lowell, Mass., offers assistance in this direction. The company will send free to any retail druggist on request novelties suitable for a window display.

Torsion balance counter scales are so well known that they need no introduction. They possess the famous weighing qualities of the Torsion balance prescription scales and give to any pharmacy an air of prosperity which cannot fail to favorably impress customers. Write to the Torsion Balance Company, 92 Reade street, New York, for descriptive catalogue, prices, etc.

Ammonol, the well-known antipyretic, may be obtained in various forms, as Ammonol Salicylate, powdered and in tablets, Ammonol Lithiated Tablets, Ammonol Peptonate Tablets, Ammonol Bromide Tablets, Ammonol with Camphor and Codeine Tablets and Ammonol with Ipecac and Opium Tablets. All of these goods may be obtained from the wholesale drug trade.

Every druggist should take an active interest in any article that is sold by the drug trade only, and especially when that article has such real merit and is so well known as Armour's Soluble Beef. It is highly recommended as a food for invalids and convalescents. This is one of the articles that every pharmacy should have on hand at all times. Doesn't your stock need replenishing?

Manufacturers of ice cream, sherbets, fruit frosts and water ices will find Rippey's Powdered Foamoline a very valuable adjunct to their business. It enriches the ice cream and gives it a smooth, pasty appearance; it adds to the bulk and keeps the cream firm and solid, with a marked saving of ice and labor. Send 25 cents in stamps to William Rippey, 100 E. 2nd st., Cincinnati, Ohio, and get a half pound package. A trial will fully demonstrate its merits.

The Taylor Brothers Company, of Rochester, N. Y., has been advertising its clinical thermometers extensively among physicians, which in turn is bound to increase the demand on druggists for this particular clinical. For 50 odd years the company has been selecting and training men to make thermometers, and the clinicals are made by the most expert workmen. The druggist is sure of getting first-class reliable and high grade goods if he handles the products of this company.

All jobbers carry the Marvel "Whirling Spray" Syringe, which is advertised in the American Druggist. Of all the devices of the kind this article has received by far the largest measure of consideration at the hands of physicians, and because of its superior cleansing powers. It is well advertised and has obtained an established position for itself. It is consequently a ready and permanent seller, and it affords a good margin of profit to the dealer.

Smith, Kline & French Company's tubes of concentrated nitrous ether have proved to be of great utility to the dispenser who needs a small amount of spirit of nitrous ether and wishes to be exact as concerns its quality. These tubes are packed in single boxes at 10 cents each or $1.20 a dozen and in boxes holding a half dozen tubes at $1.00 a dozen. Sample and literature will be supplied upon application by addressing Smith, Kline & French Company, Philadelphia.

We invite the attention of our readers to the advertisement of the Chichester Chemical Company, of Philadelphia, which reappears in these pages after a temporary absence. The Chichester Chemical Company has always shown a strong inclination to maintain friendly and reciprocal relations with druggists. Their products are well advertised and have been on the market for a lifetime. They are of ready sale and afford a good margin of profit to the dealer.

One of the latest soda fountain novelties is the Kismet holder. It is made all in one piece, with no soldering or brazing, no joints, pins or rivets, and no pockets or corners for dirt to accumulate in. It is light in weight but at the same time strong and durable. It is suitable for soda glasses, ginger ale bottles, coffee and chocolate cups, etc., in fact, it is instantly adjustable to a glass of any size or shape. It is made by the Kismet Specialty Company, 21 Park Row, New York; prices $4.50 to $12.00 a dozen.

By addressing Gilpin, Langdon & Company, of Baltimore, an interesting list of assayed drugs, granulated opium, etc., may be obtained. Twenty years ago this house began to assay drugs for alkaloidal strength, and it is a substantial compliment to the accuracy and value of their work in this field that most of it has been incorporated in the last revision of the U. S. P. Druggists who pride themselves upon the accuracy of their prescription work will find these assayed drugs of the greatest possible service.

The "blue book," published by the L. A. Becker Company, Chicago, is an illustrated catalogue of soda fountain requisites, which should prove of much interest and practical usefulness to druggists who believe in pushing trade in soda water beverages. It contains 92 pages of reading matter, with illustrations on every page. No article, apparatus, implement or adornment for the druggist's soda fountain appears to have been overlooked, and the druggist who fails to secure a copy will miss a good thing.

Justus Brauer & Son, of 248 North Front street, Philadelphia, manufacturers of machine cut prescription corks, have been in business since 1865. As many druggists know to their sorrow, the cork business has fallen into bad hands of late. It consequently behooves the wary buyer to consider the reputation of the house quite as much as the price offered. This old house has an enviable reputation for goods fully up to

10 Tons of Quinine

This is our annual consumption—one thirtieth (1-30) of the entire Quinine production of the world.

7 Million Boxes of Laxative Bromo Quinine

This is the annual sale record. A box of LAXATIVE BROMO QUININE Tablets for every ounce and a third of Quinine used throughout the world.

To Cure a Cold in One Day

This phrase is reproduced in our advertising in the American and leading Foreign Press over one hundred and sixty-five million (165,000,000) times a week, during the season. Does its effectiveness appeal to you?

10 Toneladas de Quinina

Este es nuestro consumo actual, la trigésima parte (1-30) de la producción total de Quinina del mundo.

7 Millones de Cajas de Bromo Quinina Laxante

Es la cantidad de nuestras ventas anuales. Una caja de pastillas BROMO QUININA LAXANTE por cada onza y una tercera parte de Quinina consumida en todo el mundo.

Para Curar un Resfriado en Un Día

Esta frase se reproduce en nuestros anuncios en la Prensa Americana y la Extranjera más de ciento sesenta y cinco millones (165,000,000) de veces por semana durante la temporada. ¿No le llama su atención la eficacia del remedio?

El Comercio de Drogas de los Estados Unidos hace anualmente un provecho de unos $750,000.00 en la Bromo Quinina Laxante. Este producto ha sido conocido en el mercado por espacio de diez años. Pidánsenos muestras, materia-impresa, oferta para anunciar, condiciones y descuentos con los cuales nuestros favorecedores podrán vender la Bromo Quinna Laxante con un prevecho de más de ciento cuarenta (140) por ciento.

PARIS MEDICINE CO.

SAINT LOUIS, U. S. A.

sample and of full count. Our readers may place their orders with this concern with perfect assurance of proper treatment.

Not infrequently the druggist is asked for an antiseptic mouth wash that he can guarantee is entirely free from acid. He can safely recommend Lythol, made by Hudson & Company, Inc., New York City, and sold by all wholesale druggists. Lythol preserves the teeth by preventing decay; it allays inflammation and relieves catarrhal conditions of the mucous membranes of the eye, nose, mouth and throat. Druggists who have handled this preparation testify to its value and ready sale; those who have not included it in their stock should lose no time in ordering, for the demand is growing rapidly.

When ordering either digitalis or other narcotic herbs the druggist can make sure of securing the very best results by

Fac-Simile of Stafford, Allen & Sons' Label.

specifying Stafford, Allen & Sons' brand. These goods are kept in stock by the leading jobbers all over the United States, or if not in stock they can be easily secured through Lehn & Fink.

As was shown by the contribution of Fire Marshal Clarke, published recently in the AMERICAN DRUGGIST, the majority of city fires are traceable directly to naphtha. An unburnable naphtha is marketed by the Marshall Chemical Company, of 80 William street, New York, under the name "Carbona," and is advertised in this issue of the AMERICAN DRUGGIST. For all cleaning and household purposes Carbona offers marked advantages over naphtha, both in its efficacy and its non-inflammable character. Carbona is a product which is fully entitled to a fair trial at the hands of intelligent retail druggists, as it is certain in the end to completely supersede the use of the highly dangerous naphtha in the household. There are many parts of the United States where Carbona has not been introduced and in which our readers could probably find a market for it with very little effort. Any inquiries addressed to the Marshall Chemical Company will receive satisfactory attention.

The Whitall Tatum Company calls special attention to its offering of soda fountain accessories, which at this particular season should appeal to all druggists who cater to soda trade and wish to have up-to-date facilities. The Crown ice chipper, marketed by this company, is one of the best devices of the kind on the market for chipping ice for use in ice cream freezers, etc. One of the advantages of this chipper is that it quickly reduces the ice to small pieces without shaving it. The price is 40 cents each, net. The Whitall Tatum Company also carries an attractive line of tumbler holders of various designs, ranging in price from $3.50 per dozen net to $5.00, according to style, finish, etc. The assortment is so varied that any druggist will have no trouble in finding what he wants in this line. Nothing looks more cooling and refreshing on the soda counter than a handsome bowl filled with ice. The Whitall Tatum Company offers a handsomely decorated China bowl, with perforated bottom and hollow silver-plated base, at $4.00 each net. Any druggist in need of any of these articles will profit by an inspection of this company's line.

The Hegeman Corporation Invades Brooklyn.

The Hegeman Corporation, who conduct a chain of pharmacies in Manhattan, have now invaded Brooklyn by the purchase of the handsome pharmacy of Benj. Rosenzweig, 644 Fulton street, at the junction of Lafayette avenue and Fort Greene place. This would seem to mark the beginning of a great triangular trade duel, in which the firm named, the Wm. B. Riker Son's Company and the Caswell-Massey Company, of New York, are to figure.

The Pasteur Vaccines.

The selling department of the Pasteur Institute of Paris is the Pasteur Vaccine Company, Ltd., of the same city, with branches in most of the trade centers of the world. Headquarters for the American business is at 366 West Eleventh street, New York. Their anthrax vaccine and blackleg vaccine have obtained a remarkable vogue in all cattle raising districts in this country.

Dead Founder of Apollinaris Gave Millions to Charities.

By the will of the late Edward Steinkopff, at one time proprietor of the "*St. James's Gazette*," and founder with the late George Murray Smith of the business of the Apollinaris Company, charities will ultimately benefit to the extent of nearly $5,000,000.

Mr. Steinkopff left estate valued at $6,235,110, including $5,968,175 in net personalty. Subject to his daughter's life interests and to a number of bequests, the estate is left in trust for such charitable institutions as his daughter may appoint.

A Clever Announcement.

By all odds the most attractive and original announcement of a State meeting that has ever reached us has been sent out by Secretary Timberlake, of the Indiana Pharmaceutical Association. The announcement is in the form of a 16-page booklet with lithographed covers, measuring 9 inches high by 4 inches wide, and the front cover page is embellished with portraits of the officers, their figures rising from what are intended to represent wedgewood mortars of about No. 10 size, but which dangerously resemble another kind of utensil that need not be mentioned here. A graduated measuring glass, balance, pill tile and spatula complete the decorations of the cover page, which are printed on a background of rich corn color. The meeting takes place at Indianapolis, June 26, 27, and 28, headquarters being the Claypool Hotel.

Soluble Beef.

Comparatively speaking, the medical and chemical professions have been slow and backward in reaching their present high position in the world of science and invention, so far as the human anatomy is concerned, because of the fact they have been obliged to experiment with exceeding care and caution on life itself and not on inanimate objects. For instance, since the time of beef (bovines, also cattle, mentioned in Genesis 1:29, B. C. 4004, and in the Bible one hundred and fifty times, so that beef goes back to the earliest history), or at least from the inception of the doctor of medicine, there has been an absolute and positive need and requirement for a nutritious beef product in such form as to permit of its administration to the sick and likewise a food that could be retained and assimilated by the most delicate stomach.

Realizing through their own knowledge and entreaties made upon them by the medical profession the necessity for such a food, Armour & Company, of Chicago, set about some eight years ago to erect an experimental plant and engage scientists of world-wide reputation, with the latest machinery and devices known, for the purpose of giving to the world a product which would fulfill the pressing needs of the medical fraternity and a waiting public. After the expenditure of much time and money they were finally enabled to offer Armour's Soluble Beef, which has met with a hearty reception at the hands of the profession and public at large.

This product is made from fresh, lean meat (fibre and all), predigested by artificial methods to an albumose.

Soluble beef is not claimed to be a medicine, but a food for the convalescent and invalid, and by its use as a beef broth or in combination with eggs, milk, rice, etc., it enables the doctor or nurse to vary the diet of the patient. Among all diets beef in various forms is the product most frequently resorted to in the sickroom and hospital. Therefore, beef in a predigested form, which is Soluble Beef, is always in demand for the reason that it is assimilable and nutritious.

ORIGINAL PACKAGE PRICES.

It should be understood that the prices quoted in this column are strictly those current in the wholesale market, and that higher prices are paid for retail lots. The quality of goods frequently necessitates a considerable range of prices.

Drugs, Chemicals, &c.

Article	Unit	Price		Price
Acetanilid	lb.	.24	@	.26
Acetate of Lime:				
Brown	100 lb.	1.60	@	1.65
Gray	100 lb.	2.35	@	2.40
Acetone	lb.	.15½	@	.16
Acetphenetidin (U. S. P. phenacetin)	lb.	1.15	@	...
Acid:				
Acetic Com'l	100 lb.	2.40	@	2.65
Acetic C. P.	lb.	.21	@	.23
Acetic, Glacial		.20	@	.20½
Aquafortis, 36°	lb.	.03½	@	.04½
" 40°	lb.		@	.06½
Benzoic, Ger.	lb.	.30	@	.34
" Eng	oz.	.10	@	.10½
Boric, Cryst	lb.	.10	@	.10½
powd	lb.	.10	@	.10½
Carbol. cryst., blk.	lb.	.14	@	.15
lb. bottle	lb.	.20	@	.22
Chrysophanic		2.50	@	2.65
Citric, dom	lb.	.43	@	.43½
Gallic	lb.	.53	@	.55
Muriatic C. P.	lb.	.07½	@	.08½
Nitric C. P.	lb.	.07½	@	.10
Oxalic, English	lb.	.06½	@	.06¾
Phosphoric	lb.	.20½	@	.21½
Picric	lb.	.38	@	.38
Pyrogallic	lb.	1.65	@	...
Salicylic	lb.	.31	@	.34
Sulphuric, 66°	lb.	.01½	@	.02
Tartaric, crystals	lb.	.27¾	@	.28¼
powdered	lb.	.28	@	.28½
Tannic, cryst.	lb.	.58	@	.65
Alcohol, grain	gal.	2.47	@	2.49
wood, 95-97%	gal.	.70	@	.75
Aloin	lb.	.45	@	.50
Alum, Lump	100 lb.	1.75	@	1.80
Ground	100 lb.	1.80	@	1.85
Ammon, carb.		.08½	@	.08½
" bromide, bulk		.23	@	.24
" iodide, bulk		4.75	@	4.80
Aniline Oil		.09	@	.09¼
Salt		.08½	@	.08¾
Antipyrine (New)	oz.	...	@	.18
Arrowroot, Bermuda	lb.	.38	@	.40
St. Vincent, in bbl.	lb.	.06½	@	.08
Arsenic: Red Saxon	lb.	.06½	@	.06¾
White	lb.	.05½	@	.08
Balm of Gilead Buds	lb.	.32	@	.28
Balsam Copaiba, Cent. Amer.	lb.	.29	@	.32
Para	lb.	.43½	@	.45
Fir, Canada	gal.	3.00	@	3.10
Fir, Oregon	gal.	.70	@	.80
Peru	lb.	1.00	@	1.05
Tolu	lb.	.20	@	.21
Bark, Angostura	lb.	.35	@	.40
Buckthorn	lb.	.05	@	.05½
Cascara Sag	lb.	.06	@	.08
Cascarilla	lb.	.10	@	.14
Cotton root	lb.	.08½	@	.10
Cramp	lb.	.07	@	.09
Elm, select	lb.	.18	@	.18
Pine, white	lb.	.05	@	.06
Prickly Ash	lb.	.11	@	.13
Sassafras	lb.	.13½	@	.14
Soap—whole	lb.	.05	@	.05½
Crushed	lb.	.05½	@	.06
White Pine	lb.	.04½	@	.05
Wild Cherry	lb.	.06	@	.08
Bismuth, citrate	lb.	1.75	@	1.80
" ammon cit.	lb.	1.85	@	1.90
" subnit	blk.	1.50	@	1.53
" subcarb	lb.	1.75	@	1.80
" subgallate	lb.	1.85	@	1.90
Bleaching Powder, Eng.		.01½	@	.01¾
German S.		.01½	@	.01½
Domestic		.01	@	.01¼
Blue Vitriol	lb.	.06	@	.06½
Borax, Refined	lb.	.07½	@	.07¾
powd. conc	lb.	.07½	@	.08
crystals	lb.	.07½	@	.07½
Brimstone, crude 2d.	ton.	22.00	@	...
Bromine, bulk	lb.	.22	@	.25
Burgundy Pitch	lb.	.04	@	.04½
Cacao Butter, blk.		.28½	@	.30
" " 12 lb. boxes		.34	@	.35
Caffeine	lb.	...	@	2.65
Calcium hypophosphite	lb.	.60	@	.64
Cantharides, Chinese	lb.	...	@	.86
" powd.	lb.	.75	@	.85
Russian, whole	lb.	1.20	@	1.25
Cassia Buds	lb.	.18½	@	.19½
Castor Oil, No. 1, bbl.	lb.	.11	@	.12
" " No. 1, cases	lb.	.11½	@	.12½
" " No. 3, bbl.	lb.	.10½	@	.11½
" " No 3, cases	lb.	.10½	@	.11¾
Caustic Soda	100 lb.	1.70	@	1.75
Chalk, Eng. Precip., bulk	lb.	.06	@	...
Chloral Hydrate, crystals, bulk	lb.	...	@	0.95
crusts, blk	lb.	...	@	0.93
Chloroform, bulk	lb.	.25	@	.30
Cinchonidine Sulph.	oz.	.12	@	.15
Cocaine Muriate	oz.	3.10	@	3.25
Codeine Sulph.	oz.	3.05	@	3.25
Cod Liver Oil, Norweg.	bbl.	20.00	@	25.00
Newfoundland	bbl.	19.00	@	20.00
Colocynth, Trieste	lb.	.30	@	.32
Spanish	lb.	.25	@	.26
Copperas, car lots	100 lb.	.47½	@	.52
single bbls.	100 lb.	.57½	@	.65
Creosote, Beechwood		.85	@	.90
Cream Tartar lb.	powd.	.22½	@	.23
Cubeb berries, xx	lb.	.10½	@	.11½
Powdered	lb.	.12	@	.16
Cutch, bales	lb.	.07½	@	.08
boxes	lb.	.08	@	.08½
Cuttle Bone, Trieste	lb.	.16½	@	.17
French	lb.	.12	@	.13
Jewelers', large	lb.	.70	@	...
" small	lb.	.40	@	.45
Dextrin	lb.	.05½	@	.06
Dragon's Bl'd, lump	lb.	.15	@	.18
in reeds	lb.	.50	@	.55
Epsom Salts	100 lb.	.85	@	1.00
Ergot, German	lb.	.27	@	.28
Spanish	lb.	...	@	.36
Ergotine, Dom	lb.	4.25	@	5.00
Flowers, Arnica	lb.	.09	@	.10

Article	Unit	Price		Price
Flowers—cont'd				
Calendula	lb.	.25	@	.30
Chamomile, Roman	lb.	.25	@	.27
German	lb.	.15	@	.25
Hungarian	lb.	.09½	@	.11
Insect, open	lb.	.15	@	.17
Half closed	lb.	.25	@	.28
Closed	lb.	.26	@	...
Powder	lb.	.14	@	.22
Lavender	lb.	.12	@	.13
Select	lb.	.15	@	.20
Saffron, Amer.	lb.	.35	@	.37½
Spanish Alicante	lb.	4.75	@	6.00
" Valencia	lb.	8.00	@	8.50
Formaldehyde	lb.	.09	@	.09½
Glycerin, C. P. drums	lb.	.11½	@	.11¾
" cans	lb.	.12½	@	.12¾
Grains of Paradise	lb.	.11½	@	.15
Guarana	lb.	1.35	@	1.50
Gums: Aloes, Cape		.07	@	.08
" Barbadoes	lb.	.15	@	.17
" Curacoa		.05½	@	.06
" Socot	lb.	.18	@	.20
Arabic, 1st pkd.	lb.	.30	@	...
" 2d pkd.	lb.	.19	@	.22
" sorts	lb.	.08½	@	.11
Asafoetida	lb.	.15	@	.22
Benzoin, Sumatra	lb.	.24	@	.28
Siam	lb.	.80	@	1.00
Camphor, refi'd, blk.	lb.	1.00	@	...
cases	lb.	1.00½	@	...
Chicle	lb.	.36	@	.38
Gamboge	lb.	.95	@	1.05
Guaiac	lb.	.17	@	.23
Kino	lb.	.35	@	.38
Mastic	lb.	.45	@	.48
Myrrh	lb.	.25	@	.28
Olibanum	lb.	.10	@	.15
Sandarac	lb.	.14	@	.18
Senegal, pkd	lb.	.11	@	.13
Tragacanth, Aleppo	lb.	.30	@	.65
Tragacanth, Turkey	lb.	.35	@	.80
Haarlem Oil		3.00	@	3.75
Hypophosphite lime	lb.	.45	@	.50
" potash	lb.	.48	@	.50
" soda	lb.	.48	@	.50
Ichthyol	lb.	4.00	@	4.25
Indigo	lb.	.90	@	1.25
Insect Pwd. pure	lb.	.14	@	.25
Iodine, resub.		2.70	@	2.75
Iodoform	lb.	3.00	@	3.05
Iron citrate, U. S. P.	lb.	.....	@	.44
" and ammon. cit.	lb.	.....	@	.41
and ammon. citrate (green scales)				
and quinine citrate	lb.	1.18	@	1.23
phosphate, scales	lb.	....	@	.38
pyrophosphate, scales	lb.	....	@	.38
quinine and strychnine citrate	lb.	1.68	@	1.73
Isinglass, Amer.	lb.	.75	@	.80
Russian	lb.	4.00	@	4.10
Juniper Berries	lb.	.03½	@	.04
Lanoline	lb.	.60	@	.65
Leaves: Aconite		.09	@	.10
Belladonna	lb.	.08½	@	.09½
Buchu, short	lb.	.17	@	.20
" long	lb.	...	@	.20
Cannabis Indica, tops	lb.	1.00	@	1.10
Coca, Truxillo	lb.	.17	@	.18
" Huanuco	lb.	.20	@	.22
Damiana	lb.	.18	@	.19
Digitalis	lb.	.08½	@	.09
Grindelia robusta	lb.	.08	@	.09
Horehound	lb.	.04½	@	.06
Hyoscyamus	lb.	.07	@	.08
Jaborandi	lb.	.14	@	.15
Pulsatilla		.07½	@	.11
Rose, Red	lb.	.65	@	.70
Senna, pkd whole	lb.	.20	@	.22
Alexandria, natural	lb.	.08	@	.09
garbled and sifted	lb.	.15	@	.16
Tinnevelly	lb.	.04	@	.09
Alexandria, siftings	lb.	.05½	@	.06
Stramonium	lb.	.08	@	.08½
Uva ursi	lb.	.03½	@	.03¾
Yerba Santa	lb.	.07	@	.07½
Liquorice—mass	lb.	.08	@	.10
Spanish	lb.	.14	@	.20
Imported mass Spanish	lb.	.18	@	.24
Stick, Calabria	lb.	.22	@	.26
Domestic	lb.	.16½	@	.23½
Lithia, carbonate	lb.	1.50	@	1.75
" citrate	lb.	1.15	@	1.25
Lupulin, Ger.	lb.	.18	@	.25
Lycopodium	lb.	.50	@	.51
Magnesia, carb	lb.	.12	@	.15
Manna, large flk.	lb.	.45	@	.50
Small flake	lb.	.33	@	.35
Menthol, Japanese	lb.	2.55	@	2.70
Mercurials:				
Blue Pill	lb.	.54	@	.57
Calomel	lb.	.77	@	.79
Corr. Sublim	lb.	.68	@	.70
Mercury and Chalk	lb.	.32	@	.34
Ointment, ¼	lb.	.47	@	.48
Ointment, ½	lb.	.38	@	.39
Red Precip	lb.	.87	@	.89
White "	lb.	.92	@	.94
Morphine, bulk	oz.	2.10	@	2.20
Eighths	oz.	2.45	@	2.50
Moss, Iceland	lb.	.05	@	.08
Irish	lb.	.06½	@	.08
Irish, bleached	lb.	.09½	@	.10
Naphthaline, flake	lb.	1.90	@	2.00
Ball	lb.	.02½	@	.....
Nux Vomica	lb.	.02½	@	.03
Oil, Anise	lb.	1.30	@	1.35
Almonds, bit, Eng	lb.	5.50	@	5.75
French	lb.	3.55	@	3.60
bit., artificial	lb.	.85	@	1.50
sweet, true	lb.	.37	@	.40
Peach kernels		.19	@	.22
Bay	lb.	2.10	@	2.25
22 oz. bots	bot.	3.25	@	3.35
Bergamot	lb.	2.15	@	2.30
Cajuput	lb.	.45	@	.52½
Camphor	lb.	.17½	@	.19
Caraway	lb.	1.15	@	1.40
Cassia 75@80%	lb.	.82½	@	.85

Article	Unit	Price		Price
Oils—cont'd.				
Cedar, pure	lb.	60.	@	1.68
red	lb.	.21	@	.25
Citronella	lb.	.38	@	.40
Clove, bud		.97½	@	1.00
Copaiba	lb.	.60	@	.70
Coriander	lb.	8.00	@	11.00
Croton	lb.	.75	@	.80
Cubeb	lb.	.90	@	1.00
Eucalyptus	lb.	.40	@	.60
Geranium	lb.	1.60	@	4.75
Lavender, flowers	lb.	2.00	@	2.25
Lemon	lb.	.70	@	.80
Lemongrass	lb.	3.00	@	3.10
Mustard	lb.	4.25	@	5.25
Myrbane	lb.	.07	@	.08
Neroli	lb.	45.00	@	57.50
Nutmeg	lb.	.80	@	0.90
Orange, sweet	lb.	2.00	@	2.15
Orange, bitter	lb.	2.20	@	2.40
Origanum	lb.	.18	@	.22
Pennyroyal	lb.	1.70	@	2.25
Peppermint	lb.	2.80	@	3.00
Cases	lb.	3.40	@	3.50
Petit, grain, French	lb.	4.00	@	4.50
" " So. Amer.	lb.	2.00	@	2.05
Pimento	lb.	1.80	@	1.90
Rose	oz.	3.50	@	1.50
Rosemary	lb.	.02½	@	.50
Sandalwood	lb.	3.25	@	3.50
Sassafras	lb.	.50	@	.55
" Artificial	lb.	.35	@	.38
Safrol		.35	@	.36
Spearmint	lb.	4.75	@	5.00
Tansy	lb.	3.75	@	4.00
Thyme		1.00	@	1.20
Winterg'n, sweet birch		1.65	@	1.85
" Synthetic	lb.	.37	@	.40
Wood (Chinese)		.07½	@	.....
Wormwood		3.25	@	3.50
Wormseed	lb.	3.00	@	3.25
Opium, Nat cases	lb.	2.72½	@	2.80
" Ordinary, Job-		2.75	@	2.80
" powdered	lb.	3.20	@	3.25
Orange peel, bit	lb.	.03	@	.04
Sweet	lb.	.04½	@	.10
Petrolatum		.03	@	.08
Phenacetin (see Acetphenetidin)				
Potassium acetate	lb.	.17	@	.18
" bromide		.15	@	.16
" bottles		.23	@	.30
bichromate		.08½	@	.08¾
chlorate, cryst.		.09½	@	.....
" powd.		.09½	@	.....
cyanide		.20	@	.21
hypophosphite		.60	@	.64
iodide bulk		2.15	@	2.20
permanganate	lb.	.09½	@	.10½
Prickly Ash berries		.14	@	.16
Quicksilver	flasks, lb.	.55	@	.56
Quinine Sulph., Domestic bulk	oz.	.17	@	.19
German, bulk	oz.	.17	@	.19
German, outside	oz.	.16½	@	.17
Java, bulk	oz.	.....	@	.16½
Rochelle Salts	lb.	.20½	@	.21
Root, Aconite	lb.	.09½	@	.10
Alkanet	lb.	.08	@	.09
Althea, cut	lb.	.17	@	.18
Arnica	lb.	.08½	@	.09
Belladonna, Atropa	lb.	.10	@	.12
Blood	lb.	.10	@	.12
Calamus	lb.	.07	@	.08
Calamus, bleached	lb.	.23	@	.25
Colchicum	lb.	.12	@	.13
Calumba	lb.	.04	@	.06
Dandelion, Ger	lb.	.07½	@	.08
Galangal	lb.	.05	@	.05½
Gentian	lb.	.04	@	.04½
Ginger, Ja., blcd.	lb.	.17	@	.18
unbleached	lb.	.14	@	.16
Ginseng	lb.	6.00	@	7.50
Golden Seal	lb.	1.15	@	1.18
Hellebore, pwd	lb.	.06	@	.07
Helonias	lb.	.42	@	.45
Ipecac, Rio	lb.	1.75	@	1.80
Carthagena	lb.	1.70	@	1.75
Jalap	lb.	.12	@	.13
Kava Kava	lb.	.11	@	.12
Liquorice, ord	lb.	.03½	@	.04
Select	lb.	.05½	@	.11
Lovage	lb.	.55	@	.85
Mandrake	lb.	.04½	@	.05½
Musk, Russian	lb.	.13	@	.14
Orris, Florentine	lb.	.06	@	.07
Orris, Verona	lb.	.04	@	.06
Pariera Brava	lb.	.10	@	.11
Pink	lb.	1.25	@	...
Rhatany	lb.	.10	@	.12
Rhub., Canton	lb.	.35	@	.40
Shensi	lb.	.65	@	.75
Sars'p'la, Hond	lb.	.26	@	.30
Mexican	lb.	.09½	@	.09¾
Senega	lb.	.58	@	.60
Snake Virgina	lb.	.42	@	.45
Texas	lb.	.39	@	.42
Canada	lb.	.13	@	.25
Squill	lb.	.13	@	.15
Valerian, Belg	lb.	.08	@	.08½
German	lb.	.12	@	.14
English	lb.	.12	@	.15
Salicine	lb.	3.75	@	4.00
Sal Ammon, lump	lb.	.09½	@	.09¾
Granulated	lb.	.05½	@	.06
Sal Soda, Eng.	100 lb.	.67½	@	.72½
American	100 lb.	.75	@	.80
Salol	lb.	.90	@	.95
Saltpetre, crude	lb.	.04¼	@	.04½
Refined	lb.	.04½	@	.05½
Santonin, crystals	lb.	9.50	@	9.70
Powdered	lb.	9.70	@	9.90
Saw Palmetto Berries	lb.	.15	@	.20
Seed, Anise Ital	lb.	.08½	@	.10½
German	lb.	.06¼	@	.07
Star	lb.	.20	@	.21
Canary, Smyrna	lb.	.03½	@	.04
Sicily	lb.	.04¼	@	.04½
Caraway	lb.	.06	@	.06½
Celery	lb.	.07½	@	.08
Cardamom blchd		.30	@	.75
" Decorticated	lb.	.37	@	.40
Colchicum	lb.	.21	@	.25

Article	Unit	Price		Price
Seeds—cont'd.				
Coriander	lb.	.9	@	[illegible]
Bleached	lb.	[illegible]	@	[illegible]
Cummin	lb.	.08½	@	[illegible]
Fennel, Ger.	lb.	.09	@	[illegible]
" Italian	lb.	.05	@	[illegible]
Flax, whole	lb.	.04	@	[illegible]
" ground	lb.	.03½	@	[illegible]
Foenugreek	lb.	.03	@	[illegible]
Hemp, Rus.	lb.	.05	@	[illegible]
Millet, nat.	lb.	[illegible]	@	[illegible]
" shld.	lb.	[illegible]	@	[illegible]
Mustard, Cal. brown	lb.	[illegible]	@	[illegible]
Trieste, brown	lb.	[illegible]	@	[illegible]
Bari, brown	lb.	[illegible]	@	[illegible]
German, brown	lb.	[illegible]	@	[illegible]
Western, brown	lb.	[illegible]	@	[illegible]
Cal. yellow	lb.	[illegible]	@	[illegible]
Eng. yellow	lb.	[illegible]	@	[illegible]
Ger. yellow	lb.	[illegible]	@	[illegible]
Poppy, blue	lb.	[illegible]	@	[illegible]
Quince, Ger.	lb.	.22	@	[illegible]
Rape, Ger.	lb.	[illegible]	@	[illegible]
" Eng.	lb.	.04	@	[illegible]
" Amer.	lb.	[illegible]	@	[illegible]
Strophanthus		.45	@	[illegible]
Kombe		1.00	@	1.[illegible]
Sunflower		.04½	@	[illegible]
Wormseed, American	lb.	[illegible]	@	[illegible]
" Levant	lb.	.17	@	[illegible]
Seidlitz, Mixture	lb.	.17	@	.17½
Silver, Nitrate	oz.	.33½	@	[illegible]
Soap, Castile, white	lb.	.10	@	.16½
" green	lb.	.08	@	.10½
" mottled	lb.	.05½	@	.07
Sodium bicarb, Eng.		1.57½	@	1.75
" domestic	100 lb.	1.50	@	1.59
" benzoate	lb.	.40	@	.41
" brom. blk.	lb.	.21	@	.22
" carb., cryst.	100 lb.	1.60	@	1.75
" citrate	lb.	...	@	.32
" hypophosphite		.60	@	.64
" iodide		3.30	@	3.35
" nitrate	100 lb.	2.20	@	2.25
" phosphate	lb.	.02¾	@	.03
" salicylate	lb.	.32	@	.34
" sulphate	100 lb.	.40	@	.50
Spermaceti	lb.	.27	@	.29
Spts. Nitre, U. S. P.		.46	@	.48
Spts. Ammonia Aromat.	lb.	.44	@	.45
Strontium, nitrate	lb.	.07½	@	.08
Strychnine, Sulph	oz.	.95	@	1.05
Sugar of Milk	lb.	.15	@	.20
Sugar, Lead, white	lb.	.09½	@	.10
" brown	lb.	.07½	@	.08
Sulphur, Roll	lb.	1.85	@	2.15
" Flowers	lb.	2.20	@	2.60
" Flour	lb.	2.00	@	2.40
Sulphuric Ether	lb.	.62	@	.65
Sumac, Sicily	ton	42.00	@	47.00
" Virginia	ton	33.00	@	35.00
Tar, Barbadoes	gal.	...	@	.36
Thymol		1.80	@	1.90
Tonka B'ns, Para	lb.	.18	@	.20
" Angostura	lb.	.85	@	.87½
" Surinam	lb.	.30	@	.32
Turmeric		.04½	@	.06
Turpentine	gal.	.60½	@	.60¾
Vanilla Beans	lb.	2.75	@	5.00
" Cut, Mex.	lb.	2.00	@	2.25
" Tahiti	lb.	.60	@	1.25
" Bourbon		1.00	@	3.00
Vanillin	oz.	.32	@	.37½
Venice Turps, bbls.	lb.	.14	@	.17
" " cans	lb.	.19	@	.20
Wax, Bayberry	lb.	.42	@	.45
" Bees, ord. pur	lb.	.33	@	.33½
" " sel	lb.	.34	@	.34½
" " blch.	lb.	.40	@	.46
" Brazil, No. 1	lb.	.52½	@	.53
" " No. 2	lb.	.44	@	.47
" " No. 3	lb.	.35	@	...
" Ceresin, yel.	lb.	.14	@	.18
" " white	lb.	.15	@	.20
" Japan	lb.	.11½	@	.11¾
" Paraffin	lb.	.06	@	.06½
Zinc Oxide	lb.	.07	@	.08½

Heavy Oils, &c.

Article	Unit	Price		Price
Bank, Menhaden	gal.	.27	@	.30
Coconut, Ceylon	lb.	.06½	@	.07
Cochin	lb.	.06	@	.08½
Cuban	lb.	.05½	@	...
Cod, Domestic	gal.	.35	@	.36
" Newfoundland	gal.	.38½	@	.40
Corn	gal.	.14½	@	.04½
Cottonseed, crd. prime		.31	@	.31½
Summer Yellow, prime		.37½	@	.38
" " Butter		.41	@	.42
Old, off grade		.35½	@	.37
Winter Yellow, prime		.42	@	.44
Salad Oil		.40	@	.41
Gasoline, 86°	gal.	.14	@	...
" 88°	gal.	.16	@	...
" 90°	gal.	.18	@	...
Lard, Extra Prime	gal.	.62	@	.64
Lard, Extra No. 1	gal.	.49	@	.52
Lard, No. 1	gal.	.38	@	.40
Linseed, Raw City	gal.	.40	@	.41
" Boiled	gal.	.41	@	.42
Naphtha, 68°	gal.	.12	@	...
" Deodorized, 76°	gal.	.13½	@	...
Neatsfoot, prm.	gal.	.49	@	.50
White		.97	@	...
Olive Oil, tap	tins	1.50	@	1.75
" Com., bbls.	gal.	.53½	@	.56
Palm, prm., L'gos	lb.	.06½	@	.06¾
Peanut	lb.	.60	@	.62
Rapeseed	gal.	.67	@	.71
Red Elaine	gal.	...	@	.40
" Saponified	lb.	.05½	@	.05¾
Salad Oil	gal.	.46	@	.48
Sesame	gal.	.55	@	.60
Sperm, Crude	gal.	.58	@	.60
" Nat. Win.	gal.	.62	@	.63
" Blch. Win.	gal.	.64	@	.66
Straits	gal.	...	@	.38
Tallow, prime	gal.	.62	@	
Whale Crude	gal.	...	@	...
Crude, Nat. Win.	gal.	.42	@	
Bleached Win	gal.	.44	@	.46

BUFFALO COLLEGE OF PHARMACY, University of Buffalo.

Do you want a college education in a modern College of Pharmacy at a moderate expense?

Our course in every respect is up to date, thorough, practical, comprehensive, complete, and our students come in direct contact with the Faculty.

Extensive **laboratory courses** in manufacturing Pharmacy, Pharmaceutical Assaying, Dispensing, Analytical Chemistry, Bacteriology, Botany, Materia Medica, Pharmacognosy, and Microscopy constitute over one-half of the required course.

There are 160 drug stores in Buffalo in which to seek **employment** during and after the course. Students who desire employment are receiving from $5.00 to $10.00 per week, with college privileges.

No Examination is required except upon subjects in which students have been thoroughly drilled.

No drug store experience is required for graduation.

The Regular Course leads to the degree of Phar. B.

The Post-Graduate Courses lead to the degrees of Phar. M. and Phar. D.

Illustrated Announcement sent upon application. Address

DR. JOHN R. GRAY, Ph.G., Secretary, 423 Prospect Ave., **Buffalo, N. Y.**

THE BROOKLYN COLLEGE OF PHARMACY, 265-271 Nostrand Avenue BROOKLYN, N. Y.

Session of 1906-1907 **NEW COLLEGE BUILDING**

Fall Term begins September. LECTURE FEES FOR JUNIORS, SENIORS AND POST GRADUATES, EACH = **$90.00**

The Chemical, Pharmaceutical, Dispensing and Pharmacognosy Laboratories are thoroughly equipped for practical work. Library and Herbarium for use of the students.

For Prospectus and particulars, address WILLIAM HARLOE, Clerk of College, 265 Nostrand Ave., Brooklyn, N. Y.

University of Illinois School of Pharmacy,

(CHICAGO COLLEGE OF PHARMACY)

The forty-seventh session begins September 25th, 1906. The course comprises two terms of seven months each and leads to the degree of Graduate in Pharmacy. For announcement or further information, address

W. B. DAY, Actuary, Michigan Avenue and 12th Street, CHICAGO.

The Maryland College of Pharmacy

Department of Pharmacy of the University of Maryland

Sixty-third Annual Session will begin September 24, 1906.

Catalogue giving full information in regard to requirements for admission, courses of instruction, expenses, etc., will be mailed upon application. Address

CHARLES CASPARI, Jr., Dean, University of Maryland, Baltimore, Md.

PHILADELPHIA COLLEGE OF PHARMACY

The Oldest College of Pharmacy in America.

The laws of the States of Pennsylvania and New York compel every applicant for the State license to manage a drug store, to be a graduate of a college of pharmacy, and the diploma of this College is recognized in Pennsylvania and New York under the prerequisite laws, and throughout the world as a certificate of proficiency.

Next term begins September 27th, 1906. For further information and an Announcement, address

J. S. BEETEM, Registrar, 145 N. Tenth St., Philadelphia, Pa.

AMERICAN CAN COMPANY,

Manufacturers of

Standard Druggist Tinware

We carry in stock a **full assortment** of **Miller, Taite, Gill** and **Norton** styles of Boxes. These Boxes have an **established reputation** among Druggists. **Seamless Boxes** of all sizes, styles and designs carried in stock by every leading jobber in the country.

Principal Offices: New York, Baltimore, Chicago, San Francisco.

LOCAL SALES OFFICES

Boston, Philadelphia, Buffalo, Detroit, Pittsburg, Richmond, Atlanta, Cleveland, Toledo, Cincinnati, St. Louis, New Orleans, Kansas City, Denver, Los Angeles, Portland, Seattle, St. Paul, Milwaukee, Havana

ORIGINAL PACKAGE PRICES.

It should be understood that the prices quoted in this column are strictly those current in the wholesale market, and that higher prices are paid for retail lots. The quality of goods frequently necessitates a considerable range of prices.

Drugs, Chemicals, &c.

Article	Unit	Price	To
Acetanilid	lb.	.24	@ .25
Acetate of Lime:			
Brown	100 lb.	1.60	@ 1.65
Gray	100 lb.	2.35	@ 2.40
Acetone	lb.	.15½	@ .16
Acetphenetidin (U. S. P. phenacetin)	lb.	1.15	@ ...
Acid:			
Acetic Com'l	100 lb.	2.40	@ 2.65
Acetic C. P.	lb.	.21	@ .25
Acetic, Glacial		.30	@ .32½
Aquafortis, 36°	lb.	.03¾	@ .04½
" 40°	lb.	...	@ .05½
Benzoic, Ger	lb.	.30	@ .35
" Eng	oz.	.10	@ .10½
Boric, Cryst	lb.	.10	@ .10½
powd	lb.	.10	@ .10½
Carbol, cryst., blk	lb.	.14	@ .15
lb. bottle	lb.	.20	@ .22
Chrysophanic		2.50	@ 2.65
Citric, dom	lb.	.43	@ .43½
Gallic	lb.	.53	@ .55
Muriatic C. P.	lb.	.07½	@ .08½
Nitric C. P.	lb.	.07½	@ .10
Oxalic, English	lb.	.07½	@ .08¼
Phosphoric	lb.	.19½	@ .24
Picric	lb.	.25	@ .35
Pyrogallic	lb.	1.65	@ ...
Salicylic	lb.	.31	@ .34
Sulphuric, 66°	lb.	.01½	@ .02
Tartaric, crystals	lb.	.27¾	@ .28¼
powdered	lb.	.27	@ .27½
Tannic, cryst	lb.	.58	@ .65
Alcohol, grain	gal.	2.47	@ 2.49
wood, 95-97%	gal.	.70	@ .75
Aloin	lb.	.45	@ .50
Alum, Lump	100 lb.	1.75	@ 1.80
Ground	100 lb.	1.80	@ 1.85
Ammon, carb		.08½	@ .08¾
" bromide, bulk		.23	@ .24
" iodide, bulk		4.75	@ 4.80
Aniline Oil		.09	@ .09¼
Salt		.08½	@ .08½
Antipyrine (New)	oz.	...	@ .18
Arrowroot, Bermuda	lb.	.38	@ .40
St. Vincent, in bbl	lb.	.05½	@ .08
Arsenic: Red Saxon	lb.	.06½	@ .06¾
White	lb.	.05½	@ .06
Balm of Gilead Buds	lb.	.32	@ .35
Balsam Copaiba, Cent. Amer	lb.	.30	@ .32
Para	lb.	.43½	@ .45
Fir, Canada	gal.	3.00	@ 3.10
Fir, Oregon	gal.	.70	@ .80
Peru	lb.	1.00	@ 1.05
Tolu	lb.	.20	@ .21
Bark, Angostura	lb.	.35	@ .40
Buckthorn	lb.	.05	@ .05½
Cascara Sag	lb.	.06	@ .08
Cascarilla	lb.	.30	@ .14
Cotton root	lb.	.08½	@ .10
Cramp	lb.	.07	@ .09
Elm, select	lb.	.16	@ .18
Pine, white	lb.	.05	@ .06
Prickly Ash	lb.	.11	@ .18
Sassafras	lb.	.13½	@ .14
Soap—whole	lb.	.05	@ .05½
Crushed	lb.	.05½	@ .06
White Pine	lb.	.04½	@ .06
Wild Cherry	lb.	.08	@ .09
Bismuth, citrate	lb.	1.75	@ 1.80
" ammon cit	lb.	1.85	@ 1.90
" subnit	blk.	1.50	@ 1.55
" subcarb	lb.	1.75	@ 1.80
" subgallate	lb.	1.85	@ 1.90
Bleaching Powder, Eng		.01¼	@ .01½
German R.		.01¼	@ .01½
Domestic		.01	@ .01½
Blue Vitriol	lb.	.06	@ .06½
Borax, Refined	lb.	.07¼	@ .07½
powd. conc	lb.	.07½	@ .08
crystals	lb.	.07¼	@ .07½
Brimstone, crude 2d	ton.	22.00	@ ...
Bromine, bulk	lb.	.33	@ .35
Burgundy Pitch	lb.	.04	@ .04½
Cacao Butter, blk		.28½	@ .30
" " 12 lb. boxes		.34	@ .35
Caffeine	lb.	...	@ 2.65
Calcium hypophosphite	lb.	.60	@ .64
Cantharides, Chinese	lb.	..	@ .55
" powd	lb.	...	@ .60
Russian, whole	lb.	1.30	@ 1.35
Cassia Buds	lb.	.18½	@ .19½
Castor Oil, No. 1, bbl	lb.	.11	@ .12
" " No. 1, cases	lb.	.11½	@ .12¼
" " No. 3, bbl	lb.	.10½	@ .11½
" " No 3, cases	lb.	.10¾	@ .11½
Caustic Soda	100 lb.	1.70	@ 1.75
Chalk, Eng. Precip., bulk	lb.	.06	@ ...
Chloral Hydrate, crystals, bulk	lb.	...	@ 0.95
crusts, blk	lb.	...	@ 0.95
Chloroform, bulk	lb.	.25	@ .30
Cinchonidine Sulph	oz.	.12	@ .15
Cocaine Muriate	oz.	3.00	@ 3.25
Codeine Sulph	oz.	3.05	@ 3.25
Cod Liver Oil, Norweg.	bbl.	20.00	@ 25.00
Newfoundland	bbl.	19.00	@ 20.00
Colocynth, Trieste	lb.	.30	@ .32
Spanish	lb.	.25	@ .28
Copperas, car lots	100 lb.	.47½	@ .52
single bbls	100 lb.	.57½	@ .65
Creosote, Beechwood		.85	@ .90
Cream Tartar lb.	powd.	.22½	@ .23
Cubeb berries, xx	lb.	.10½	@ .11½
Powdered	lb.	.13	@ .16
Cutch, bales	lb.	.07½	@ .08
boxes	lb.	.05	@ .05½
Cuttle Bone, Trieste	lb.	.16½	@ .17
French	lb.	.12	@ .18
Jewelers', large	lb.	.70	@ ....
" small	lb.	.40	@ .45
Dextrin	lb.	.05½	@ .06
Dragon's Bl'd, lump	lb.	.15	@ .18
In reeds	lb.	.50	@ .55
Epsom Salts	100 lb.	.85	@ 1.00
Ergot, German	lb.	.27	@ .28
Spanish	lb.	...	@ .35
Ergotine, Dom	lb.	4.85	@ 5.00
Flowers, Arnica	lb.	.09	@ .10
Flowers—cont'd			
Calendula	lb.	.25	@ .30
Chamomile, Roman	lb.	.25	@ .27
German	lb.	.15	@ .25
Hungarian	lb.	.09½	@ .11
Insect, open	lb.	.15	@ .17
Half closed	lb.	.26	@ .28
Closed	lb.	.28	@ ...
Powder	lb.	.14	@ .22
Lavender	lb.	.12	@ .13
Select	lb.	.15	@ .20
Saffron, Amer	lb.	...	@ .80
Spanish Alicante	lb.	4.75	@ 8.00
" Valencia	lb.	7.50	@ 8.50
Formaldehyde	lb.	.19	@ .09½
Glycerin, U. P. drums	lb.	.11½	@ .11¾
" cans	lb.	.12½	@ .12¾
Grains of Paradise	lb.	.11½	@ .15
Guarana	lb.	1.35	@ 1.50
Gums: Aloes, Cape		.07	@ .08
" Barbadoes	lb.	.16	@ .17
" Curacoa		.06½	@ .08
" Socot	lb.	.18	@ .20
Arabic, 1st pkd	lb.	.30	@ ...
" 2d pkd	lb.	.17	@ .22
" sorts	lb.	.06½	@ .11
Asafoetida	lb.	.15	@ .22
Benzoin, Sumatra	lb.	.34	@ .35
Siam	lb.	.90	@ 1.00
Camphor, ref'd. blk	lb.	1.00	@ ..
cases	lb.	1.00½	@ ...
Chicle	lb.	.38	@ .38
Gamboge	lb.	.85	@ 1.05
Guaiac	lb.	.17	@ .23
Kino	lb.	.25	@ .28
Mastic	lb.	.46	@ .48
Myrrh	lb.	.25	@ .28
Olibanum	lb.	.10	@ .15
Sandarac	lb.	.14	@ .18
Senegal, pkd	lb.	.11	@ .13
Tragacanth, Aleppo	lb.	.30	@ .85
Tragacanth, Turkey	lb.	.35	@ .90
Haarlem Oil		3.00	@ 3.75
Hypophosphite lime	lb.	.48	@ .50
" potash	lb.	.48	@ .50
" soda	lb.	.48	@ .50
Ichthyol	lb.	4.00	@ 4.25
Indigo	lb.	.90	@ 1.25
Insect Pwd. pure	lb.	.14	@ .25
Iodine, resub		2.70	@ 2.75
Iodoform	lb.	3.00	@ 3.05
Iron citrate, U. S. P.	lb.	.....	@ .44
" and ammon. cit	lb.	.....	@ .41
and ammon. citrate (green scales)			
and quinine citrate	lb.	1.18	@ 1.23
phosphate, scales	lb.	....	@ .35
pyrophosphate, scales	lb.	....	@ .36
quinine and strychnine citrate	lb.	1.68	@ 1.73
Isinglass, Amer	lb.	.75	@ .80
Russian	lb.	4.00	@ 4.10
Juniper Berries	lb.	.03½	@ .04
Lanoline	lb.	.09	@ .85
Leaves: Aconite		.09	@ .10
Belladonna	lb.	.08½	@ .09½
Buchu, short	lb.	.14	@ .20
" long	lb.	.30	@ ...
Cannabis Indica, tops	lb.	1.00	@ 1.10
Coca, Truxillo	lb.	.17	@ .18
" Huanuco	lb.	.30	@ .32
Damiana	lb.	.18	@ .10
Digitalis	lb.	.04½	@ .09
Grindelia robusta	lb.	.18	@ .09
Horehound	lb.	.04½	@ .06
Hyoscyamus	lb.	.07	@ .08
Jaborandi	lb.	.14	@ .15
Pulsatilla		.10½	@ .11
Rose, Red	lb.	.65	@ .70
Senna, pkd. whole	lb.	.20	@ .22
Alexandria, natural	lb.	.13	@ .09
garbled and sifted	lb.	.15	@ .16
Tinnevelly	lb.	.04	@ .09
Alexandria, siftings	lb.	.05½	@ .06
Stramonium	lb.	.04	@ .48½
Uva ursi	lb.	.05½	@ .06½
Yerba Santa	lb.	.07	@ .07½
Liquorice—mass	lb.	.08	@ .16
Spanish	lb.	.14	@ .20
Imported mass Spanish	lb.	.18	@ .24
Stick, Calabria	lb.	.23	@ .25
Domestic	lb.	.16½	@ .22½
Lithia, carbonate	lb.	1.50	@ 1.75
" citrate	lb.	1.15	@ 1.25
Lupulin, Ger	lb.	.18	@ .25
Lycopodium	lb.	.50	@ .51
Magnesia, carb	lb.	.12	@ .15
Manna, large flk	lb.	.45	@ .50
Small flake	lb.	.38	@ .26
Menthol, Japanese	lb.	2.55	@ 2.70
Mercurials:			
Blue Pill	lb.	.34	@ .37
Calomel	lb.	.77	@ .79
Corr. Sublim	lb.	.66	@ .70
Mercury and Chalk	lb.	.32	@ .34
Ointment, ½	lb.	.47	@ .48
Ointment, ⅓	lb.	.36	@ .39
Red Precip	lb.	.87	@ .89
White "	lb.	.92	@ .94
Morphine, bulk	oz.	2.10	@ 2.20
Eighths	oz.	2.45	@ 2.50
Moss, Iceland	lb.	.05	@ .06
Irish	lb.	.08½	@ .08
Irish, bleached	lb.	.09½	@ .10
Naphthaline, flake	lb.	1.90	@ 2.00
Ball	lb.	.02½	@ ...
Nux Vomica	lb.	.02½	@ .08
Oil, Anise	lb.	1.32½	@ 1.35
Almonds, bit, Eng	lb.	5.50	@ 5.75
French	lb.	3.55	@ 3.60
bit., artificial	lb.	.65	@ 1.50
sweet, true	lb.	.40	@ .45
Peach kernels		.19	@ .22
Bay	lb.	2.10	@ 4.25
22 oz. bots	bot.	3.25	@ 3.35
Bergamot	lb.	2.15	@ 2.20
Cajuput	lb.	.52	@ .51
Camphor	lb.	.17½	@ .19
Caraway	lb.	1.15	@ 1.40
Cassia 75@80%	lb.	.82½	@ .85
Oils—cont'd.			
Cedar, pure	lb.	.55	@ .65
red	lb.	.20	@ .25
Citronella	lb.	.41	@ .42
Clove, bud		.97½	@ 1.00
Copaiba	lb.	.60	@ .70
Coriander	lb.	8.00	@ 11.00
Croton	lb.	.75	@ .80
Cubeb	lb.	.90	@ 1.00
Eucalyptus	lb.	.40	@ .60
Geranium	lb.	1.60	@ 4.75
Lavender, flowers	lb.	2.00	@ 2.25
Lemon	lb.	.75	@ .80
Lemongrass	lb.	3.00	@ 3.10
Mustard	lb.	4.25	@ 5.25
Myrbane	lb.	.07	@ .04
Neroli	lb.	45.00	@ 57.50
Nutmeg	lb.	.80	@ 0.90
Orange, sweet	lb.	2.00	@ 2.15
Orange, bitter	lb.	2.30	@ 2.40
Origanum	lb.	.18	@ .22
Pennyroyal	lb.	1.70	@ 2.25
Peppermint	lb.	2.80	@ 3.00
Cases	lb.	3.40	@ 3.50
Petit, grain, French	lb.	4.00	@ 4.50
" " So. Amer.	lb.	2.00	@ 2.05
Pimento	lb.	1.80	@ 1.90
Rose	oz.	3.50	@ 4.50
Rosemary	lb.	.62½	@ .80
Sandalwood	lb.	3.25	@ 3.50
Sassafras	lb.	.50	@ .55
" Artificial	lb.	.25	@ .32
Safrol		.35	@ .37½
Spearmint	lb.	4.75	@ 5.00
Tansy	lb.	3.75	@ 4.00
Thyme		1.00	@ 1.30
Winterg'n, sweet birch		1.65	@ 1.75
" Synthetic	lb.	.37	@ .40
Wood (Chinese)		.07½	@ .....
Wormwood		3.25	@ 3.50
Wormseed	lb.	3.00	@ 3.25
Opium, Nat. cases	lb.	2.72½	@ 2.80
" Ordinary, Job-		2.75	@ 2.80
" powdered	lb.	3.20	@ 3.75
Orange peel, bit	lb.	.03	@ .04
Sweet	lb.	.04½	@ .10
Petrolatum		.03	@ .08
Phenacetin (see Acetphenetidin)			
Potassium acetate	lb.	.17	@ .18
" bromide		.15	@ .16
" bottles		.23	@ .30
bichromate		.08½	@ .08¾
chlorate, cryst		.08½	@ ....
" powd		.09½	@ .....
cyanide		.20	@ .21
hypophosphite		.60	@ .64
iodide bulk		2.15	@ 2.20
permanganate	lb.	.09¾	@ .10½
Prickly Ash berries		.14	@ .16
Quicksilver, flasks	lb.	.55	@ .56
Quinine Sulph., Domestic bulk	oz.	.17	@ .19
German, bulk	oz.	.17	@ .19
German, outside	oz.	.16½	@ .17
Java, bulk	oz.	.....	@ .16½
Rochelle Salts	lb.	.20½	@ .21
Root, Aconite	lb.	.09½	@ .10
Alkanet	lb.	.08	@ .09
Althea, cut	lb.	.17	@ .18
Arnica	lb.	.08½	@ .09
Belladonna, Atropa	lb.	.10	@ .12
Blood	lb.	.10	@ .12
Calamus	lb.	.07	@ .08
Calamus, bleached	lb.	.23	@ .25
Colchicum	lb.	.12	@ .13
Calumba	lb.	.04	@ .06
Dandelion, Ger	lb.	.07½	@ .08
Galangal	lb.	.05	@ .05½
Gentian	lb.	.04	@ .04½
Ginger, Ja., blcd	lb.	.17	@ .18
unbleached	lb.	.14	@ .16
Ginseng	lb.	6.00	@ 7.50
Golden Seal	lb.	1.50	@ 1.55
Hellebore, pwd	lb.	.06	@ .07
Helonias	lb.	.42	@ .45
Ipecac, Rio	lb.	1.75	@ 1.80
Carthagena	lb.	1.70	@ 1.75
Jalap	lb.	.13	@ .14
Kava Kava	lb.	.11	@ .12
Liquorice, ord	lb.	.03½	@ .04
Select	lb.	.08½	@ .11
Lovage	lb.	.55	@ .58
Mandrake	lb.	.04¾	@ .05½
Musk, Russian	lb.	.13	@ .14
Orris, Florentine	lb.	.06	@ .07
Orris, Verona	lb.	.04	@ .06
Pareira Brava	lb.	.10	@ .11
Pink	lb.	1.25	@ ...
Rhatany	lb.	.10	@ .12
Rhub., Canton	lb.	.35	@ .40
Shensi	lb.	.65	@ .75
Sars'p'la, Hond	lb.	.28	@ .30
Mexican	lb.	.09½	@ .09¾
Senega	lb.	.58	@ .60
Snake Virgina	lb.	.42	@ .45
Texas	lb.	.39	@ .42
Canada	lb.	.13	@ .25
Squill	lb.	.10	@ .11
Valerian, Belg	lb.	.08	@ .08½
German	lb.	.12	@ .14
English	lb.	.12	@ .15
Salicine	lb.	3.75	@ 4.00
Sal Ammon, lump	lb.	.09½	@ .09¾
Granulated	lb.	.05½	@ .06
Sal Soda, Eng.	100 lb.	.67½	@ .72½
American	100 lb.	.75	@ .80
Salol	lb.	.90	@ .95
Saltpetre, crude	lb.	.04¼	@ .04½
Refined	lb.	.04½	@ .05½
Santonin, crystals	lb.	9.50	@ 9.70
Powdered	lb.	9.70	@ 9.90
Saw Palmetto Berries	lb.	.15	@ .20
Seed, Anise Ital	lb.	.08½	@ .10½
German	lb.	.06½	@ .07
Star	lb.	.20	@ .21
Canary, Smyrna	lb.	.03½	@ .04
Sicily	lb.	.03½	@ ...
Caraway	lb.	.06	@ .06½
Celery	lb.	.07½	@ .08
Cardamom blchd		.30	@ .75
" Decorticated	lb.	.37	@ .40
Colchicum	lb.	.21	@ .25
Seeds—cont'd.			
Coriander	lb.	[illegible]	@ [illegible]
Bleached	lb.	.05½	@ [illegible]
Cummin	lb.	.06½	@ [illegible]
Fennel, Ger	lb.	.09	@ [illegible]
" Italian	lb.	.05	@ [illegible]
Flax, whole	lb.	.04	@ [illegible]
" ground	lb.	.03½	@ [illegible]
Foenugreek	lb.	.02	@ [illegible]
Hemp, Rus	lb.	.03	@ [illegible]
Millet, nat	lb.	.01½	@ [illegible]
" shld	lb.	.04½	@ [illegible]
Mustard, Cal. brown	lb.	.04½	@ [illegible]
Trieste, brown	lb.	.08	@ [illegible]
Bari, brown	lb.	.04½	@ .05
German, brown	lb.	.03½	@ .05
Western, brown	lb.	.04½	@ .05
Cal. yellow	lb.	.04½	@ .05
Eng. yellow	lb.	.05	@ .05
Ger. yellow	lb.	.05½	@ .05
Poppy, blue	lb.	.05½	@ .06
Quince, Ger	lb.	.32	@ .34
Rape, Ger	lb.	.03½	@ .08
" Eng	lb.	.04	@ .05
" Amer	lb.	.03½	@ .08
Strophanthus		.45	@ [illegible]
Kombé		1.00	@ 1.25
Sunflower		.04½	@ .05
Wormseed, American	lb.	.06½	@ [illegible]
" Levant	lb.	.17	@ .20
Seidlitz, Mixture	lb.	.17	@ .17½
Silver, Nitrate	oz.	.43½	@ .45½
Soap, Castile, white	lb.	.10	@ .10½
" green	lb.	.08	@ .16½
" mottled	lb.	.05½	@ .07
Sodium bicarb, Eng		1.37½	@ 1.75
" domestic	100 lb.	1.50	@ 1.80
" benzoate	lb.	.40	@ .41
" brom. blk	lb.	.21	@ .22
" carb., cryst.	100 lb.	1.60	@ 1.75
" citrate	lb.	...	@ .32
" hypophosphite		.60	@ .64
" iodide		3.30	@ 3.35
" nitrate	100 lb.	2.20	@ 4.35
" phosphate	lb.	.02¾	@ .03
" salicylate	lb.	.32	@ .34
" sulphate	100 lb.	.40	@ .50
Spermaceti	lb.	.27	@ .29
Spts. Nitre, U. S. P.		.46	@ .48
Spts. Ammonia Aromat	lb.	.44	@ .46
Strontium, nitrate	lb.	.07½	@ .08
Strychnine, Sulph	oz.	.95	@ 1.00
Sugar of Milk	lb.	.15	@ .18
Sugar, Lead, white	lb.	.09½	@ .10
" brown	lb.	.07½	@ .08
Sulphur, Roll	lb.	1.85	@ 2.15
" Flowers	lb.	2.30	@ 2.60
" Flour	lb.	2.00	@ 2.40
Sulphuric Ether	lb.	.62	@ .68
Sumac, Sicily	ton	42.00	@ 47.00
" Virginia	ton	33.00	@ 35.00
Tar, Barbadoes	gal.	...	@ .38
Thymol		1.80	@ 1.90
Tonka B'ns, Para	lb.	.18	@ .20
" Angostura	lb.	.65	@ .67½
" Surinam	lb.	.20	@ .22
Turmeric		.04½	@ .06
Turpentine	gal.	.61	@ .61½
Vanilla Beans	lb.	2.75	@ 5.00
" Cut, Mex	lb.	2.00	@ 2.25
" Tahiti	lb.	.90	@ 1.25
" Bourbon		1.00	@ 3.00
Vanillin	oz.	.32	@ .37½
Venice Turps, bbls	lb.	.14	@ .17
" " cans	lb.	.19	@ .20
Wax, Bayberry	lb.	.42	@ .45
" Bees, ord. pur	lb.	.33	@ .33½
" " sel	lb.	.34	@ .34½
" " blch	lb.	.40	@ .45
" Brazil, No. 1	lb.	.52½	@ .53
" " No. 2	lb.	.44	@ .47
" " No. 3	lb.	.75	@ ...
" Ceresin, yel	lb.	.14	@ .15
" " white	lb.	.15	@ .9
" Japan	lb.	.11½	@ .11½
" Paraffin	lb.	.06	@ .06½
Zinc Oxide	lb.	.07	@ .08½
Heavy Oils, &c.			
Bank, Menhaden	gal.	.27	@ .30
Coconut, Ceylon	lb.	.06½	@ .07
Cochin	lb.	.06	@ .06½
Cuban	lb.	.06½	@ ...
Cod, Domestic	gal.	.35	@ .36
" Newfoundland	gal.	.38½	@ .4
Corn	gal.	.14½	@ .04½
Cottonseed, crd. prime		.31	@ .31½
Summer Yellow, prime		.37½	@ .38
" " Butter		.41	@ .42
Old, off grade		.36½	@ .37
Winter Yellow, prime		.42	@ .44
Salad Oil		.40	@ .41
Gasoline, 86°	gal.	.14	@ ...
" 88°	gal.	.16	@ ...
" 90°	gal.	.18	@ ...
Lard, Extra Prime	gal.	.62	@ .64
Lard, Extra No. 1	gal.	.49	@ .50
Lard, No. 1	gal.	.38	@ .40
Linseed, Raw City	gal.	.39	@ .40
" Boiled	gal.	.40	@ .41
Naphtha, 68°	gal.	.12	@ ...
" Deodorized, 76°	gal.	.12½	@ ...
Neatsfoot, prm	gal.	.49	@ .50
White		.57	@ ...
Olive Oil, tap	tins	1.20	@ 2.25
" Com., bbls	gal	.53½	@ .58
Palm, prm., L'gos	lb	.05½	@ .06
Peanut	lb	.60	@ .62½
Rapeseed	gal.	.67	@ .71
Red Elaine	gal.	...	@ .49
" Saponified	lb.	.06½	@ .06
Salad Oil	gal.	.66	@ .67½
Sesame	gal.	.55	@ .60
Sperm, Crude	gal.	.65	@ .66
" Nat. Win	gal.	.62	@ .63
" Blch. Win	gal.	.64	@ .65
Straits	gal.	...	@ .35
Tallow, prime	gal.	.62	@
Whale, Crude	gal.	...	@ ...
Crude, Nat. Win	gal.	.42	@
Bleached Win	gal.	.44	@ .44

New Remedies Compendium and Prices Current.

In this list, which is intended for the use of dispensing druggists, and not for analytical chemists, chemical formulas, melting points and other data of no immediate use to the dispenser are omitted. While additions will be made from time to time as new remedies make their appearance on the market, and the list, thus kept fully up to date, remedies falling into disuse will be dropped as expediency may determine.

Corrected to June 21, 1906.

ACETAL. (ETHYLIDENE DIETHYL ETHER.) Colorless, volatile liquid, soluble in 18 parts of water, very soluble in alcohol. Used as a sedative and hypnotic in doses of 2 to 3 fluid drachms, usually in form of emulsion. Pure medicinal, per oz., $1.00; commercial, oz............65c.

ACETOZONE. (BENZOYL-ACETYL PEROXIDE.) White powder, mixed with an equal weight of an inert soluble powder; soluble in water (1:1000). Bactericide; used internally and externally in diseases of germ origin. Dose, 1 to 3 grains in solution. Boxes containing 6 vials of 15 grains each, per box, $1.25; ¼ oz. bot., $1.40; ½ oz. bot., $2.70; 1 oz. bot. $5.25

ACET - THEOCIN - SODIUM. White crystalline powder, readily soluble in water. Powerful diuretic; used in dropsy, in doses of 5 to 7 grains, two to three times daily. ½ and 1 oz. bot......$1.90 to $2.30 per oz. (Continental Color & Chemical Co.)

ACOINE. (DI-PARA-ANISYL-MONO-PHENETHYL GUANIDINE HYDROCHLORIDE.) White crystalline powder, soluble in 17 parts of water. Local anæsthetic like cocaine, used hypodermatically in eye surgery; dental anæsthetic in normal saline solution, 2 per cent. 15 grain vials, each, 30c.; capsules, 2½ grains, 28 in box....................75c. (The Heyden Chemical Works.)

ADNEPHRIN SOLUTION. A 1-1000 solution of the active principle of the suprarenal gland in physiological salt solution containing one-half of 1 per cent. of methaform. Used chiefly as a hæmostatic, also for treatment of inflammations, congestions and tumefactions of the mucous membranes, also as a cardiac stimulant. 1 oz. vials ....60c.
EMOLLIENT. Tubes, each...30c.
OIL SPRAY. 1 oz. vials, each.60c.
(Frederick Stearns & Co.)

ADRENALIN. Grayish - white powder; with difficulty soluble in water. The blood-pressure-raising principle of the suprarenal glands. 1 grain vials.85c.
CHLORIDE SOLUTION, 1:1000, a solution of 1 part of adrenalin chloride in 1000 parts of physiologic salt solution, with 0.5 per cent. of chloretone. Powerful astringent, hemostatic and cardiac stimulant. Used for the control of hemorrhages, internal and superficial, for the reduction of congestion and inflammation of mucous membranes, as a heart stimulant in collapse, and as an adjuvant to the local anæsthetic action of cocaine. Internal dose, 5 to 30 minims. 1 oz. bot.........85c.
INHALANT, 1 oz. bot.........85c.
OINTMENT, ½ oz. tubes.....43c.
SUPPOSITORIES, boxes of 1 doz. 38c.
TABLETS, vials of 25.........85c.
(Parke, Davis & Co.)

ADRIN. (EPINEPHRIN HYDRATE.) Whitish nonhygroscopic powder; the active principle of the suprarenal gland. 1 grain vials, each, 75c.; 1-1000 solution, 1 oz. vials, each, 75c.; in tubes of 12 tablets, each tablet q. s. to make 15 minims of 1-1000 solution, each, 40c.; in 100's, each..............$3.10
INHALANT, 1 oz. vials.......75c.
OINTMENT, ½ oz. tubes....40c.
SUPPOSITORIES, box of 1 doz.30c.
(H. K. Mulford Co.)

AGURIN. (ACET-THEOBROMINE-SODIUM.) White hygroscopic powder, soluble in water; incompatible with acids. Diuretic in dropsy. Dose, 7 to 15 grains, twice daily. ½ and 1 oz. bot...............$1.55 to $1.70 (Continental Color & Chemical Co.)

AIROL. (BISMUTH OXYIODOGALLATE.) Grayish-green powder, insoluble in water or alcohol. On admixture with water airol partly decomposes and turns red. Should be mixed with water only with intervention of glycerin. Used externally as application to wounds, burns, skin diseases, eye, nose, gonorrhœa, either pure, in 10 per cent. suspension, equal parts glycerin and water, or 10 to 20 per cent. ointment. 1 oz. cartons ....$1.00 (Hoffmann-La Roche Chemical Works.)

ALBARGIN. (GELATOSE SILVER.) Light brown powder, readily soluble in water. Contains 15 per cent. of silver. For gonorrhœa a 2 per cent. solution is injected 4 or 5 times daily. 1 oz. vials, $1.10; tubes of 50 tablets, 0.2 gm. each, per tube ....50c.
(Victor Koechl & Co.)

ALPHOZONE. (SUCCINIC PEROXIDE.) White fluffy powder, quickly soluble in 60 parts of water. Germicide and antiseptic, internally and externally. Dose, 3 to 5 grains. 1 oz. bot., $4.50; ½ oz., $2.30; ¼ oz., $1.20; 1 grain tablets, bot. of 90 ....$1.00
(Frederick Stearns & Co.)

ALYPIN. White crystalline powder, easily soluble in water and alcohol, but dissolving very sparingly in ether. Watery solutions have a neutral reaction and can be sterilized by boiling for a short period. Local anæsthetic, substitute for cocaine. The strength of the solutions ordinarily employed varies from 1 to 5 and even up to 10 per cent. It can be combined with adrenalin and antipyrine. Alypin should not be used in connection with silver nitrate, owing to the formation of a precipitate. This objection, however, does not apply to protargol solutions, which, although they become slightly turbid at first, soon clear up. 15 grain vials, each, 20c.; 10 grain vials, per vial, 16c.; ¼ and ½ oz. bots., per oz., $4.20; 1 oz. bots., per oz.........$4.10 (Continental Color & Chemical Co.)

ALUMNOL. (ALUMINUM NAPHTHOL DISULPHONATE.) Whitish powder, very soluble in water; slightly soluble in alcohol and glycerin; astringent and antiseptic; dissolves in pus and penetrates tissues. Used in 1 per cent. solution in gonorrhœa; 10 to 20 per cent. mixture with talcum as a dusting powder. 1 oz. tins, per oz...50c.
(Victor Koechl & Co.)

AMINOFORM. (HEXAMETHYLENETETRAMINE.) White granular crystals, readily soluble in water, prepared by combining ammonia and formaldehyde. Antiseptic for urinary passages, diuretic and solvent in uric acid concretions; dose, 5 to 10 grains, well diluted, three times daily. 1 oz. bot., 60c.; 7½ grain tablets, oz...................70c.
(C Bischoff & Co.)

ANAESTHESIN. White crystalline powder, almost insoluble in cold water, but easily solu-

ble in ether, alcohol, benzin and fatty oils. Local anæsthetic, and used internally in gastric ulcer, nervous dyspepsia, etc. Dose, internally, 5 to 8 grains several times daily. Used externally pure or in ointment 5 to 20 per cent., and in suppositories containing 8 grains each. 1 oz. bot.........$1.00
(Victor Koechl & Co.)

ANALGINE. A powder composed of acetanilid, 50 parts; sodium bicarb., 5 parts; sodium salicylate, 5 parts; camphor monobrom., 5 parts; caffeine citrated, 2½ parts; ext. cannabis indica, 2½ parts; aromatic powder, q. s. 100 parts. Recommended as an analgetic, antipyretic and nerve sedative in neuralgia, migraine, headache, rheumatism, gout, sciatica, etc. Dose, 5 to 10 grains. 1 oz. screw cap bottles..........40c.
(H. K. Mulford Company.)

ANTHRASOL. Yellow, oily liquid, with a distinctive tarry odor; soluble in alcohol, acetone, fats and petrolatum. A distillate from coal tar, used in diseases of the skin where coal tar is employed. 1 oz. vials ....55c.
(Knoll & Co. and Merck & Co.)

ANTINONNIN. (POTASSIUM ORTHODINITRO-CRESOL.) Paste of brilliant orange color, soluble in water, slight soapy odor, nonvolatile. Deodorizer, disinfectant, prevents the growth of fungi, mildew and dry rot in cellars and human habitations. Used in form of solution. 1 lb to 5 to 15 gallons of water. Cans, ½ lb., $1.10 per lb.; 1 lb. cans, 95c.; 50 lb. cans, per lb. ....77c.
(Continental Color & Chemical Co.)

ANTINOSINE. (SODIUM SALT OF NOSOPHEN.) Blue powder, soluble in water, alcohol and glycerin. Used in solution of 1 to 5 per cent. as an antiseptic in diseases of the eye and ear, genito-urinary diseases, and as a healing powder on chronic leg ulcers. 1 oz. bot. $2.10
(Stallman & Fulton Co.)

ANTISCLEROSIN. Tablets, consisting of a compound of inorganic blood salts, used in treatment of arteriosclerosis and its sequelæ. Dose, 2 tablets three times daily. Carton of 4 tubes @ 24 tablets...$1.50
(Schering & Glatz.)

ANTITUSSIN. (DIFLUORDIPHENYL OINTMENT.) Ointment containing lanolin, 85 per cent.; petrolatum, 10 per cent., and difluordiphenyl, 5 per cent. A whooping cough remedy applied as inunction to patient's neck, chest and back once a day, in doses of 5 Gm. 20 Gm. collapsible tubes, 40c.; 40 Gm. ....75c.
(C. Bischoff & Co.)

ANUSOL SUPPOSITORIES. A compound of bismuth iodoresorcin sulphonate, used in hæmorrhoids, etc. Dose, 1 or 2 daily. Box of 12..................$1.00
(Schering & Glatz.)

ARGENTAMINE. A colorless, alkaline liquid representing a solution of silver nitrate, 10 per cent., and ethylenediamine, 10 per cent.; soluble in water. Used in all cases where silver nitrate is used, mostly in gonorrhœa, in strength of 1 in 2000-4000 solution. 1 oz., g. s. bot. ....75c.
(Schering & Glatz.)

ARGONIN. White powder, very slightly soluble in cold, but freely so in hot water. A compound of silver nitrate and sodium casein. Antiseptic, germicide and gonococcicide, less caustic than silver nitrate. Solutions of 2 to 10 per cent. strength recommended for injection in gonorrhœa and 3 per cent. solutions for use in the eye. 1 oz. vials..........65c.
(Victor Koechl & Co.)

ARHOVIN, an addition product of diphenylamine and esterified thymyl-benzoic acid, is a fluid of aromatic odor and slightly burning taste, soluble in oil. Gonocide for internal and topical use. Given by mouth in capsules of 4 grains (1 or 2 capsules, three to six times daily); in urethral bougies (1 bougie, two to four times daily); in vaginal globules (1 globule, two to four times daily), and injected in 2 per cent. to 5 per cent. oily solution. 1 oz. vials, 90c.; box of 50 capsules, 65c.; box of 12 bougies, 50c.; box of 12 globules.................50c.
(Schering & Glatz.)

ARISTOCHIN. (CARBONIC ESTER OF QUININE.) White powder, tasteless, insoluble in water. Decomposes in the system to yield 96.1 per cent. of quinine. Prescribed like quinine, but in somewhat larger doses. ½ and 1 oz. cartons, per oz......$2.20
(Continental Color & Chemical Co. and Merck & Co.)

ARSENFERRATOSE. A solution of ferratin in syrup form (syrupus ferratini arseniati); contains 0.3 per cent. of iron and 0.003 per cent. of arsenic. Used as a hæmatopoietic and alterative, in doses of a tablespoonful three or four times a day for adults, and for children a teaspoonful to a dessertspoonful. 250 Gm. bottles......55c.
(C. F. Boehringer & Soehne.)

ASAPROL. (ABRASTOL.) Whitish powder, freely soluble in water and alcohol. It is the calcium salt of betanaphthol-sulphonic acid. Antipyretic and antirheumatic in doses of 3 to 15 grains. Used also as test for albumin in urine. 1 oz. bot. $1.25

ASPIRIN. (ACETYL SALICYLIC ACID.) White crystalline powder, insoluble in water; incompatible with alkalies. Used instead of the salicylates in articular and muscular rheumatism and other therapeutic indications for the salicylates. Dose, 5 to 15 grains, three to five times daily. 1 oz. bot., per oz.................33c. to 43c.
(Continental Color & Chemical Co.)

ATOXYL. (META-ARSENOUS ANILIDE.) White powder, containing 37.69 per cent. of arsenic in organic combination. Soluble in 6 parts of water and used in this strength solution for hypodermic injection; relatively nontoxic. Dose, 1 to 3 grains. 1 oz. vials......$3.00
(Victor Koechl & Co.)

BENZONAPHTHOL. White, crystalline powder, soluble in alcohol and chloroform; insoluble in water. Employed as intestinal antiseptic in doses of 5 to 15 grains. 1 oz. vials, 22c.; ¼ lb. bottles, $2.20; ½ lb., $2.10; 1 lb...............$2.00
(Schering & Glatz.)

BENZOSOL. (GUAIACOL BENZOATE.) Small colorless crystals, nearly insoluble in water. Contains 54 per cent. of guaiacol and, as it is slowly saponified by the gastric juice, the guaiacol being liberated gradually, it is recommended as an intestinal antiseptic and as an agreeable substitute for creosote in incipient phthisis. Dose, 4 to 8 grains. 1 oz. tins..$1.25
(Victor Koechl & Co.)

BETA - EUCAINE HYDROCHLORIDE. White, crystalline powder, soluble in 30 parts of water. A synthetic compound chemically allied to cocaine, being the hydrochloride of benzoyl-vinyl-diaceton-alkamine. It is slower in action than cocaine, but anæsthesia is more prolonged, and a third less toxic. Used generally in 2 per cent. solutions in dental and ophthalmic work. ⅛ oz. and ¼ oz., per oz., $3.60; ½ oz. and 1 oz..............$3.50
(Schering & Glatz.)

BETA-EUCAINE LACTATE. White powder, possessing the same properties as the hydrochloride, but is more soluble in water (about 1 in 5). Prices and containers same as for beta-eucaine hydrochloride.
(Schering & Glatz.)

BISMUTH FORMIC IODIDE. Yellowish, impalpable powder. A compound of formaldehyde and gelatin, with the addition of thymol iodide and bismuth

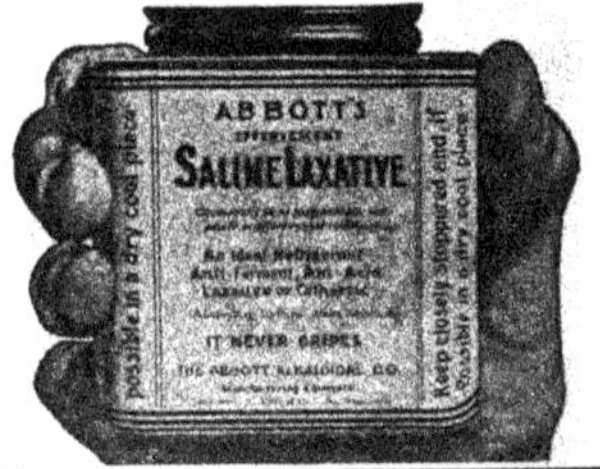

subiodide. Bactericide, antiseptic and astringent. Employed as a dry dressing for wounds and ulcerations, suppurating surfaces and abscesses. Sprinkler-top boxes, 50c.; per dozen, $5.00

BISMUTH FORMIC IODIDE OINTMENT, per dozen ozs., $1.00; per lb., $1.00. Bismuth Formic Iodide Suppositories, per box of 1 doz. .... 50c.
(H. K. Mulford Company.)

BISOL. (SOLUBLE BISMUTH PHOSPHATE.) White powder, soluble in water, faint alkaline reaction. Intestinal antiseptic and astringent in gastric and enteric catarrh. Dose, 3 to 7½ grains. 1 oz. vials...... 70c.
(C. Bischoff & Co.)

BROMETONE. Powder, slightly soluble in water. Compound of bromoform and acetone; recommended as a substitute for bromides; contains 77 per cent. of bromine. Dose, 3 to 5 grains. 1 oz. bot., 85c.; 5 grain capsules in bot. of 100 .... $1.25
(Parke, Davis & Co.)

BROMIPIN. (10 % BROMINIZED SESAME OIL.) Yellow, oily fluid, used as a nervine and sedative in epilepsy; succedaneum for bromides. Dose, 1 teaspoonful. 1 oz. vial, 18c.; per lb. .... $2.10 to $2.35
(Merck & Co.)

CACODYLIC ACID. (DIMETHYL ARSENIC ACID.) Small colorless deliquescent crystals, the ultimate product of oxidation of arsenium-dimethyl (cacodyle) and of cacodyle oxide. Contains 54.4 per cent. of arsenic trioxide, but is relatively non-toxic. Dose, 1 to 3 grains. ¼ oz. vials, per oz. $4.00

CALOMELOL OINTMENT. White mercurial ointment made from colloidal calomel for the inunction treatment of syphilis and especially for the cure of its cutaneous manifestations. 2 oz. graduated tubes, per tube .... 55c.
(Heyden Chemical Works.)

CALOMELOL POWDER. Grayish-white powder of neutral reaction, tasteless and odorless. Yields a milky solution when added to cold water in the proportion of 1 to 50. Used as a dusting powder in the treatment of papular eruptions and ulcerations, and as external application to ulcerated chancres in 2 per cent. solution. 1 oz. vials .... 70c.
(Heyden Chemical Works.)

CAMPHORIC ACID. (Colorless crystalline scales, very slightly soluble in water; formed by the oxidation of camphor with nitric acid. Used in night sweats of phthisis, also in cystitis and as an intestinal antiseptic in doses of 10 to 20 grains. 1 oz. vials, 45c.; 1 lb. bot. $7.00
(Merck & Co.)

CEROLIN. Pills of a fatty substance isolated from yeast. Acts same as yeast in furunculosis, acne, etc., but more cathartic. Pills containing 0.1 Gm., box of 100, each ..... 50c.
(C. F. Boehringer & Soehne.)

CHINAPHENIN. (QUININE CARBONIC ESTER OF PHENETIDINE.) White tasteless powder, representing synthetic quinine-phenacetin and having medicinal properties of both. Insoluble in water, but easily soluble in alcohol, ether and chloroform. Dose, 5 to 10 grains, thrice daily. ½ and 1 oz. cartons, per oz. .... $1.25 to $1.30
(Continental Color & Chemical Co.)

CHINOTROPINE. (UROTROPINE QUINATE.) A combination of quinic acid and urotropine (hexamethylenetetramine) used as uric acid solvent in the various manifestations of the uric acid diathesis. Is said to liberate formaldehyde freely internally and to form soluble compounds with uric acid. Dose, 10 to 30 grains. ½ oz. and 1 oz. vials, $1.75; tablets, 7½ grains, 25 in tube, 2 tubes in box $1.75
(Schering & Glatz.)

CHLORETONE. White crystals, slightly soluble in water (1:125); hypnotic, local anaesthetic and antiseptic. Dose, 5 to 20 grains, in cachet, tablet or capsule. Externally as a dusting powder for wounds, combined 23 with, zinc oxide, 120, and French chalk, 90 parts. ½ oz. vials, per oz., 90c.; 1 oz. .... 85c. Capsules, 3 grs., bot. of 100, 80c.; 5 grs., bot. of 100 .. $1.25
(Parke, Davis & Co.)

CINNAMIC ACID. (CINNAMYLIC ACID.) Transparent micaceous crystals, very slightly soluble in water; soluble in alcohol and ether. Injected intravenously in tuberculosis in doses of ¼ to ¾ of a grain, twice a week; per oz., 1-20 to ⅙ grain twice daily. 1 oz. vial, 35c.; 1 lb. bot., per lb. $5.00
(Merck & Co.)

CITARIN. (SODIUM ANHYDROMETHYLENCITRATE.) White, crystalline powder, easily soluble in water. Antilithæmic for gouty and chronic rheumatic conditions; liberates formaldehyde in the blood. Dose, 15 to 30 grains, thrice daily. 1 oz. bottle, per oz. .. 70c. to 75c.
(Continental Color & Chemical Co.)

COLLARGOL. (COLLOIDAL SILVER.) Shining, black scales, soluble in 1 in 20 of water. Used as a bactericide, 1 in 100 to 10,000 in water or glycerin. Internally a 1 to 500 or 1 to 100 solution may be added to the food in teaspoonful doses. ½ oz. and 1 oz. vials, $2.75; tablets, 1 grain each, tubes of 50 ... 60c.
(Schering & Glatz.)

CORNUTOL. A concentrated, preparation of ergot of rye, prepared for hypodermic and general use. Each Cc. represents 2½ Gm. of assayed Spanish ergot. Dose, hypodermically, 5 to 10 min. (or 0.3 to 2 Cc.). By mouth, 10 to 30 min. (or 0.6 to 2 Cc.). Marketed only in 1 oz. vials and in hermetically sealed aseptic bulbs, each bulb containing 2 Cc. (½ dr.). 1 oz. vials, 50c.; per package of 6 bulbs .... 60c.
(H. K. Mulford Company.)

COTARNINE HYDROCHLORIDE. See Stypticin.

CREOSOTE CARBONATE. (CREOSOTAL.) Yellow, transparent viscous liquid, insoluble in water, but miscible with alcohol; contains 92 per cent. of creosote combined with 8 per cent. of carbon dioxide. Used in tuberculosis and pneumonia in doses of 5 to 60 drops several times daily. 1 oz. vials, 65c.; ¼ lb. bot., per lb., $9.25; ½ lb., $9.10; 1 lb. $9.00
(Schering & Glatz and Continental Color & Chemical Co.)

CUPROL. Green powder, readily soluble in water; a chemical combination of nucleinic acid and copper; solution does not coagulate albumen. Applied locally as an astringent; of use in granular ophthalmia in the form of 5 per cent. instillations, or may be applied in the dry form with a brush. ¼ oz. vials, $1.80 per oz.; 1 oz. vials $1.20
(Parke, Davis & Co.)

DERMATOL. (BISMUTH SUBGALLATE.) Yellow, insoluble powder; nonirritant antiseptic, especially serviceable in burns, ulcers and moist eczema. Used internally in diarrhœa, dysentery, intestinal fermentation and gastric ulcers, in doses of 10 to 30 grains three times daily. 1 oz. tins, 10c.; 1 and 5 lb. tins, per lb. $2.50
(Victor Koechl & Co.)

DIATHESIN. White crystalline leaflets, soluble in 15 parts cold water, freely soluble in hot water or alcohol. Is ortho-oxybenzylalcohol, or synthetic saligenin. Used in place of salicin in rheumatism, neuralgia, pleurisy, etc., in doses of 7½ to 15 grains. 1 oz. cartons $2.40
(C. Bischoff & Co.)

DIFLUORDIPHENYL. White crystalline powder of pleasant aromatic odor, insoluble in water, soluble in alcohol, ether, chloroform and oils. Used as

antiseptic dusting powder mixed with talc in proportion of difluordiphenyl, 10 parts; talc, 90 parts, or in 10 per cent. ointment with lanolin as dressing for burns. Dose, 1-16 to ¼ grain. 5 Gm. envelopes, each $1.50
(C. Bischoff & Co.)

DIGALEN. (CLOETTA'S SOLUBLE DIGITOXIN.) Marketed only in solution in 15 Cc. (½ oz.) vials, on account of infinitesimal dosage. Active principle of digitalis leaves, nonaccumulative heart tonic and diuretic. 1 Cc. of solution represents 0.0003 Gm. (0.0045 grain) of digitoxin, which is the average dose, by the mouth, hypodermatically, or by enema; intravenously the dose is from 3 to 10 Cc. ½ oz. vials....................$1.00
(Hoffmann-La Roche Chemical Works.)

DIGITALIN VERUM. White powder, the active constituent of digitalis, free from impurities and noxious principles. Almost insoluble in water. Dose, 0.002 Gm. to 0.006 Gm., three times daily, increasing to not over 0.02 Gm. (1-3 grain). 1 Gm. vials $7.25
(C. F. Boehringer & Soehne.)

DIONIN. (ETHYL MORPHINE HYDROCHLORIDE.) White crystalline powder, very soluble in water and alcohol. Recommended to replace codeine and morphine in bronchitis, emphysema and asthma. Dose, ¼ to ½ grain. 1 oz. vials, $6.00; ⅛ oz. vials, per oz., $6.25; 15 grain vials, each, 35c.; tablets, ½ grain, bot. of 50, 35c.; bot. of 100 ....60c.
(Merck & Co.)

DIURETIN. White powder, soluble in water, decomposed by acids. Must be kept dry and air tight. It is a chemical compound of theobromine sodium and sodium salicylate. Diuretic, antiasthmatic and vascular stimulant. Dose, 15 grains four to six times daily. 1 oz. bot., per oz....................$1.75
(Knoll & Co.)

DORMIOL. (AMYLENE CHLORAL.) Oily, colorless liquid, with a camphoraceous odor, insoluble in water, soluble in alcohol and ether. Hypnotic in mania; 50 per cent. solution supplied commercially. Dose, 5 to 60 minims. 1 oz. vials, 28c.; ½ lb. bot., per lb....................$4.00
(Merck & Co.)

DUOTAL. (GUAIACOL CARBONATE.) White crystalline powder, soluble in alcohol, insoluble in water. Same therapeutic action as Creosotal, which see. Dose, 5 to 20 grains, gradually increased. 1 oz. vials, $1.50; tablets, 7½ grains, 50 tablets in box, $1.50; 4½ grains, 50 tablets in box....................90c.
(Schering & Glatz and Continental Color & Chemical Co.)

DUOTONOL. White powder; a mixture, equal parts of the lime and sodium glycerophosphates. Nerve nutrient in doses of 5 to 10 grains three times daily. 1 oz., 50c.; 1 lb., $6.00; tablets, 5 grains, 100 tablets in bottle ....65c.
(Schering & Glatz.)

DYMAL. (DIDYMIUM SALICYLATE.) Pinkish powder, odorless. Applied as powder and ointment in skin diseases, notably dry and weeping eczema. 1 oz. cartons, each, 35c.; 4 oz. cartons, each....................$1.20
(C. Bischoff & Co.)

EKA-IODOFORM. A chemically pure iodoform, prepared by electrical synthesis, and sterilised with paraform. 1 oz. vials ....50c.
(Schering & Glatz.)

EMPYROFORM. Brown powder; condensation product of birch tar and formaldehyde; insoluble in water, readily soluble in acetone, chloroform and solutions of caustic alkalies. Used like tar in ointment, paste and tincture. 1 oz. vials..65c.
(Schering & Glatz.)

EPICARIN. (CONDENSATION PRODUCT OF BETANAPHTOL AND CRESOLIC ACID.) Colorless or yellowish needles, difficultly soluble in hot water, easily soluble in alcohol, ether and oils. Nontoxic substitute for naphthol in parasitic skin diseases. Employed chiefly in ointments (5 to 10 per cent.) 1 oz. cartons, per oz....................60c. to 70c.
(Continental Color & Chemical Co.)

EUCASIN. Casein compound, containing 95 per cent. albumin and 5 per cent. water. Prepared from cow's milk. Dietetic for convalescents, invalids or persons afflicted with lung, stomach or kidney trouble; also in anæmia and typhoid. 1 lb. tins, $3.00; ½ lb., $1.50; ¼ lb. ....80c.
(Fuerst Bros. & Co.)

EUDOXINE. (BISMUTH SALT OF NOSOPHEN.) Reddish-gray powder, insoluble in water, but soluble in alkaline fluids. Used as an intestinal antiseptic in doses of 3 to 5 grains. 1 oz. bot., $2.10; 3 grain tablets, per oz., $2.60; 5 grain tablets, per oz. $2.50
(Stallman & Fulton Co.)

EUGALLOL. (PYROGALLOL MONOACETATE.) Yellowish, syrupy liquid, marketed in 66 per cent. acetone solution. Soluble in water and acetone; applied pure or diluted with acetone as paint in skin diseases, especially psoriasis, and deemed superior to pyrogallol. 1 oz. vials $1.00
(Knoll & Co. and Merck & Co.)

EUMYDRIN. White crystalline powder, obtained from atropine; easily soluble in water. Powerful mydriatic, less poisonous than atropine. Dose, internally, about 1-70 grain. 1 or 2 per cent. solution dilates the pupil after 10 to 25 minutes. 1 grain tubes, 45c. to 55c. per box of 10 tubes; ¼ oz. and ½ oz. packages, per oz. $16.50
(Continental Color & Chemical Co.)

EUNATROL. (SODIUM ACID OLEATE.) Light yellow substance, readily soluble in water and alcohol; supplied as powder and chocolate-coated pills. Recommended in treatment of gallstones, being excellent cholagogue. Dose, four pills, 4 grains each, three times daily, or in solution. 25 Gm. bot., each, 75c.; bot. of 50 pills, 70c.; 100 pills....................$1.30
(C. Bischoff & Co.)

EUPHORIN. (PHENYL - URETHANE.) White, acicular crystals, slightly soluble in water, freely in alcohol. Energetic antipyretic and analgetic in doses of 7½ to 15 grains, 2 to 3 times daily. 1 oz. vials... $1.00
(Schering & Glatz.)

EUPHTHALMINE HYDROCHLORIDE. White crystals; a synthetic derivative of beta-eucaine; soluble in water; 2 to 5 per cent. solutions dilate the pupil, without causing discomfort or accommodation disturbances. ½ and 1 Gm. vials, per Gm. $1.25
(Schering & Glatz.)

EUPYRINE. (PARA-PHENETIDINE VANILLIN ETHYLCARBONATE.) Light yellow crystals, sparingly soluble in water, readily in alcohol, chloroform and ether. Stimulant antipyretic in doses of 7½ to 15 grains. 1 oz. cartons, each....................$1.50
(C. Bischoff & Co.)

EUQUININE. (QUININE CARBONIC ESTER.) Tasteless, fleecy crystals, slightly soluble in water; soluble in alcohol, ether and chloroform. Succedaneum for quinine sulphate, reported not to disturb stomach or produce cindionism. Dose, same as quinine. Tablets, 5 grains, 100 in bot., $1.75; 2 grain, 100 in bot....................75c.
(Merck & Co.)

EURESOL. (RESORCINE MONOACETATE.) Oily, yellow liquid, soluble in alcohol and acetone. Succedaneum for resorcin, externally. Used in skin and scalp diseases, as paint pure or diluted with acetone. 1 oz. vials $1.00
(Knoll & Co. and Merck & Co.)

EUROPHEN. Yellow light powder, containing 25 per cent. of iodine, insoluble in water and

glycerin. Iodoform substitute used in dry powder and in ointment. 1 oz. bot., per oz.... $1.65 to $1.80
(Continental Color & Chemical Co.)

EUZONE. (PURE SODIUM PERBORATE.) White, odorless powder, containing about 7.1 per cent. boron, 15 per cent. sodium, 31.2 per cent. oxygen and 46.2 per cent. water; represents 22 per cent. by weight of hydrogen dioxide, equivalent to 10.4 per cent. by weight of nascent oxygen. Soluble in water 1 in 10, such a solution being taken to represent a 2 per cent. solution of hydrogen dioxide. Tablets, 2½ Gm. each, boxes of 20, 40c.; powder, in 100 Gm. cartons, 35c.; 500 Gm. boxes $1.20
(Schering & Glatz.)

EXODIN. Yellowish powder; a synthetic oxyanthraquinone derivative; tasteless, mild aperient in doses of 7½ to 15 grains. 1 oz. vials, $1.40; tablets, 7½ grains each, 10 tablets in box, 30c.; 50 in bottle.........$1.40
(Schering & Glatz.)

FERRATIN. Reddish-brown powder, slowly soluble in ordinary liquids, but readily in hot beverages. Used in anæmia and chlorosis in doses of 7½ grains three times daily. 1 oz. vials, 85c.; tablets, 7½ grains, 50 in box, per box..............85c.
(C. F. Boehringer & Soehne.)

FERRATOGEN. (IRON NUCLEINATE.) Grayish-yellow powder, obtained by growing yeast in a ferruginous medium; insoluble in water. Used in chlorosis and anæmia in doses of 5 grains, three times daily. 1 oz. cartons, each.............90c.
(C. Bischoff & Co.)

FERRATOSE. (LIQUOR FERRATINI.) Fluid preparation of ferratin, containing 0.3 per cent. iron. 250 Gm. bottles.....45c.
(C. F. Boehringer & Soehne.)

FERRIPYRIN. (FERRIC CHLORIDE ANTIPYRIN.) Orange-red powder, soluble in 5 parts of water, very soluble in alcohol, but insoluble in ether. A compound of ferric chloride and antipyrine. Styptic and analgetic when applied in solution or powder. Given internally in chlorosis and anæmia as a hæmatinic in doses of 7½ grains. 1 oz. tins.......$1.50
(Victor Koechl & Co.)

FERROPYRIN. (Same as Ferripyrin, but made by Knoll & Co. and sold in 1 oz. cartons, $1.40.)
(Knoll & Co. and Merck & Co.)

FILMARON OIL 1:10. A 10 per cent. solution of filmaron, the active principle of malefern, in castor oil. Used in removal of tapeworm. 10 Gm. bot....85c.
(C. F. Boehringer & Soehne.)

FIBROLYSIN. Solution of thiosinamine and sodium salicylate, sterilized. Put up in sealed tubes, each containing 2.3 Cc. solution (= 0.2 Gm. thiosinamine). Same uses as thiosinamine, but specially adapted for hypodermic use. Dose, contents of 1 tube every 1, 2 or 3 days, as required. 2.3 Cc. tubes, each...................15c.
(Merck & Co.)

FLUOROFORMOL. (FLUORYL.) Colorless, tasteless liquid, a 2.8 per cent. solution of fluoroform. Used in phthisis, internally and externally; also in pneumonia, acting as an antiseptic. Dose, 1 tablespoonful four times daily. 1 lb. bot....................$1.00
(C. Bischoff & Co.)

FLUORRHEUMIN. Ointment composed of petrolatum, 10; lanolin, 85; difluordiphenyl, 4; fluorphenetol, 1. Used in rheumatism, sciatica and lumbago; dose by inunction, 4 to 5 Gm. Collapsible tubes, 20 Gm., 40c.; 40 Gm.......................75c.
(C. Bischoff & Co.)

FORTOINE. (METHYLENEDICOTOINE.) Yellow crystals, with slight cinnamon flavor, obtained through action of formaldehyde on cotoine; insoluble in water, sparingly soluble in alcohol, ether and benzol; easily soluble in chloroform, acetone and alkaline liquids. Astringent antiseptic in protracted diarrhœas of consumptives. Dose, 4 grains three times daily. 10 Gm. envelopes, each $2.00
(C. Bischoff & Co.)

GALLOGEN. (ELLAGIC ACID.) Yellowish, tasteless powder, insoluble in all acid and neutral media, but soluble in alkaline solutions. Resembles tannic acid, being the astringent principle of divi-divi. Used in dysentery and diarrhœa. Dose, 10 to 15 grains for adults, 5 to 8 grains for children. 1 oz. cartons, 80c.; chocolate coated tablets, 3 grains each, 24 in box ....35c.
(C. Bischoff & Co.)

GAULTHERINE. Pinkish powder, slowly soluble in cold water, more readily so in hot water; insoluble in ether and chloroform, but very soluble in alcohol. It is the sodium salt of methyl salicylate prepared from natural oil of wintergreen. Antiseptic, antifermentative and soothing antiputrefactive. Used internally and externally. 4 oz. bot., per lb., $6.30; ½ lb. bot., per lb., $6.60; 1 lb. bot. $6.50
(The Wm. S. Merrell Chemical Co.)

GEOSOTE. See Guaiacol Valerate.

GLUTOL. (FORMALDEHYDE GELATIN.) Whitish, granular, insoluble powder; recommended as an antiseptic dressing for burns, cavities and suppurating ulcers. 1 oz. tins, 65c.; vials of ¼ oz., with sprinkler top, each ....25c.
(Schering & Glatz.)

GUAETHOL. (AJACOL; THANATOL.) Oily liquid, or purer in crystals resembling thymol, insoluble in water. Succedaneum for guaiacol. Allays pain by direct application. Dose, 4 to 8 minims. 1 oz. vials......$1.40

GUAIACOL VALERATE. (GEOSOTE.) Yellow, oily liquid; a combination of guaiacol and valerianic acid, having the characteristic odor of the latter. Insoluble in water, soluble in alcohol and ether. Said to be useful in tuberculosis and chlorosis and as intestinal antiseptic in doses of 3 to 10 minims three times daily. 3 minim capsules, per 100.........$2.10

GUAIACETIN. (SODIUM PYROCATECHIN-MONOACETATE.) White odorless powder, soluble in water. A succedaneum for guaiacol and creosote, used in tuberculosis. Dose, 8 grains, preferably in tablet form. Powder in 1 oz. tins, $3.30; bot. containing 100 tablets, 8 grains each, $3.50; 50, $2.00; 25......$1.17
(Fuerst Bros. & Co.)

GUIASANOL. (DIETHYLGLYCOCOLL-GUAIACOL.) Crystalline powder, readily soluble in water. Indications same as for creosote and guaiacol. Used internally in doses of from 45 to 180 grains a day. 25 Gm. bot. $1.00
(Victor Koechl & Co.)

HEDONAL. White, crystalline powder, insoluble in water, but soluble in alcohol, chloroform and ether; best administered as a dry powder. Given in mild forms of insomnia as a hypnotic in doses of 15 to 30 grains. 1 oz. bot. $1.50 to $1.60
(Continental Color & Chemical Co.)

HELMITOL. (HEXAMETHYLENETETRAMINE-ANHYDROMETHYLENE CITRATE.) Colorless crystals, freely soluble in water; insoluble in alcohol and ether. Urinary antiseptic in cystitis, phosphaturia, urethritis, etc., in doses of 15 grains, three or four times daily; liberates formaldehyde in the urinary tract. 1 oz. bot....................60c.
(Continental Color & Chemical Co.)

HEMICRANIN. White powder; a mixture of 5 parts phenacetin, 1 part caffeine and 1 part citric acid, used in migraine, headaches, intercostal neuralgia and sciatica, in doses of 5 to 10

Article	Unit	Price
Bark, Condurango	lb.	.25
Elm, selected	lb.	.30-35
ground, 10 lbs., .18	lb.	.22
powdered, 10 lbs., .22	lb.	.25
Hemlock, crushed	lb.	.15
Mezereon	lb.	.25
Oak, white, crushed	lb.	.15
Orange Peel, bitter	lb.	.18
Prickly Ash	lb.	.85
Quebracho	lb.	.25
Sassafras, 10 lbs., .18	lb.	.20
Sassafras, Extra	lb.	.22-25
Simaruba	lb.	.40-45
Soap (Quillaja), cut, 5 lbs., .11	lb.	.12
powdered	lb.	.13
Wild Cherry, 5 lbs., .12	lb.	.14
" " ground, 5 lbs., .14	lb.	.16
Witch Hazel	lb.	.20
Barley, Pearl	lb.	.5-6
Bay Rum, Porto Rico	gal.	2.10-2.35
St. Thomas	gal.	2.50-3.00
Bean, Calabar	lb.	.36
St. Ignatius	lb.	.30
Tonka, Angostura	lb.	.75-85
Surinam	lb.	.60
Vanilla, Mexican, long	lb.	8.50
" " med	lb.	7.15
" " short	lb.	7.00
" Bourbon, long	lb.	6.50
" " med	lb.	5.50
" " short	lb.	4.50
Benzol, Coal Tar	lb.	.24
Benzosol	oz.	1.25
Berberine, Carb.	oz.	5.00
Hydrochlor	oz.	1.80
Berries, Cubeb, lb., .16; powdered	lb.	.22-25
Fish	lb.	.12
Juniper	lb.	.8-10
powdered	lb.	.18-20
Poke	lb.	.20
Prickly Ash	lb.	.25-35
Sumac	lb.	.20
Beta-Eucaine	oz.	3.50
Bismuth, Ammonia Citrate, lb., 2.55	oz.	.24
Subcarbonate	lb.	2.40
Subnitrate, 5 lbs., 1.65	lb.	1.75
Subgallate, lb., 2.45	oz.	.22-24
Subsalicylate, lb., 2.65	oz.	.21-25
Blacklegine, "Pasteur" (Blackleg Vaccine, cord form), No. 1, 10 doses	doz.	12.00
Blacklegine, "Pasteur" (Blackleg Vaccine, cord form), No. 2, 20 doses	doz.	20.00
Blacklegine, "Pasteur" (Blackleg Vaccine, cord form), No. 3, 50 doses	doz.	48.00
Blackleg Vaccine, "Pasteur," powder packet	doz.	12.00
Bladder Wrack	lb.	.25
Blue Vitriol, bbl., .6½; 100 lbs., .7	lb.	.8-10
powdered, 50 lbs., .10	lb.	.12
Bole, Armenia, powdered, true	lb.	.12
Bone Ash	lb.	.15
Borax, 100 lbs., .8½	lb.	.8-12
powdered, 50 lbs., 8½	lb.	.9-12

Article	Unit	Price
Breast Tea, 5 lbs., .25	lb.	.27-30
Brimstone Roll, bbls., .2½	lb.	.4-5
Bromine	oz.	.19
Bromoform	oz.	.19
Buds, Balm of Gilead	lb.	.45
Cassia	lb.	.30
Butter, Cacao, 12 lbs., .38	lb.	.40-42
Butylchloral	oz.	.35
Cadmium, Bromide	oz.	.17
Iodide	oz.	.30
Caffeine, lb., 3.50	oz.	.29-31
Bromide	oz.	.19
Citrated, U. S. P., lb., 2.20	oz.	.21-23
Valerianate	oz.	.85
Calamine	lb.	.10-12
Calcium, Carb., precip	lb.	.8-10
Glycerophosphate	oz.	.25-50
tablets, boxes, 50 5-gr	ea.	.30
Hypophosphite, lb., .85	oz.	.10-14
Iodide	oz.	.43
Lactophosphate	oz.	.13-15
Phosphate, precip	lb.	.17-19
Sulphide	lb.	.28
Calomel, 10 lbs., .85	lb.	.90-95
Camphor, Monobromated, lbs., 1.95	oz.	.21-25
Cantharides, Russian	lb.	1.50-1.60
powdered	lb.	1.65-1.75
Cantharidal Vesicant, ozs	doz.	2.50
Cantharidin	grain.	.12
Capsicum, African	lb.	.19-21
powdered, 5 lbs., .23	lb.	.25-28
Caroid, powder form	oz.	1.25
and Soda Tablets, 150s	bot.	.67
Carbon, Disulphide	lb.	.11
Carmine, No. 40, lb., 4.25-4.50	oz.	.30-35
Castor, Fiber, oz., 1.25; powdered	oz.	1.25-1.50
Cerium, Oxalate, lb., .45	oz.	.7
Chalk, French, powdered	lb.	.10
precip., Thomas' Eng., 7-lb. bag	lb.	.9
prepared, Thomas' Eng., 8-lb., white, box		.50
prepared, Thomas' Eng., 8-lb., pink, box		.65
prepared	lb.	.7
Charcoal, Animal, powd	lb.	.10
Willow, powd	lb.	.14
Chloral Hydrate, 5 lbs., 1.10	lb.	1.15-1.25
Croton	oz.	.85
Chloralamid, 25 pkgs., .70	pkg.	.80
Chloroform, Purified, 5 lbs., .80	lb.	.85
Cinchonidine, Salicylate	oz.	.45
Sulphate, 5-oz. cans, .27	oz.	.32
Cinchonine, Sulphate	oz.	.13-17
Cinnabar	lb.	1.50
Civette	oz.	3.50
Clay, China, lb., .8; powdered	lb.	.10
Cloves, 10 lbs., .16	lb.	.18
powdered, 5 lbs., .20	lb.	.24
Cobalt, Carbonate	oz.	.35
Chloride	oz.	.30
Nitrate, oz., .25; powdered	oz.	.25
Cocaine, Hydrochlorate, Cryst	oz.	3.50-3.75
Alkaloid	oz.	4.05-4.30
Oleate, 5 per cent	oz.	1.00-1.15
Cochineal, Honduras	lb.	.55
powdered	lb.	.60
Codeine, Pure Alkaloid, ozs	oz.	3.65-3.80
Sulphate, ozs	oz.	3.25-3.40

Article	Unit	Price
Colchicine, cryst., 15-gr. vials	grain.	.14
Collodion	lb.	.11
Cantharidal	lb.	2.00
Flexible	lb.	.77
Colocynth Apple	lb.	.58
powdered	lb.	.60
Composition Powder, 2 ozs	lb.	.35
Confection, Senna	lb.	.45
Copper, Sulph., bbl., .6½	lb.	.7-8
Iodide	oz.	.60
Copperas, bbl., .1	lb.	.2-3
Corrosive Sublimate, 10 lbs., .80	lb.	.88
powdered, 10 lbs., .83	lb.	.92
Coumarin, Cryst., Fries Bros., lb., 7.00	oz.	.70
Cowhage	oz.	.40
Cream Tartar, 99 p. c., powdered, 50 lbs., .25; 10 lbs., .27	lb.	.28-30
Creolin, ¼ lbs., doz., 4.00; lbs	doz.	8.00
Creosol, U. S. P	lbs.	.30
Creosote, Beechwood Tar	lb.	1.00-2.50
Carbonate, lbs., 9.00	oz.	.65
Phosphite, lb., 10.00	oz.	1.00
Crurin Kalle, 25 grms	each.	1.50
Crystogen, powdered, ozs	oz.	1.00
" powdered, 8 oz	pkg.	4.00
" 5-gr. tablets, ozs	oz.	1.10
" " 8 oz	pkg.	5.00
" " 25's	doz.	4.00
" **Aperient**	doz.	8.00
Cumarine, lb., 4.50	oz.	.40
Currie Powder	lb.	1.00
Cuttle-Fish Bone, select	lb.	.30-50
Dermatol, oz., .22	lb.	2.50
Dextrin, bag, .7	lb.	.8-10
Diabetin	lb.	1.30
Digalen, ½-oz. vial		1.00
Digitalin, ⅛ ozs	oz.	7.00
Diuretin	oz.	1.75
Dover's Powder, 10 lbs., 1.10	lb.	1.15
Dragon's Blood, reeds	lb.	.65
extra powdered	lb.	.90-1.00
Duotal	oz.	1.50
Earth, Fullers, po., 25 lbs., .5	lb.	.6-8
Eka-Iodoform	oz.	.70
Elaterium	oz.	.70
Emulsol, per doz., 2 oz		6.00
Elixir Iodo-Bromide of Calcium Comp., Tilden's	pt.	.82
Empyroform	oz.	.65
Eosote (Creosote Valerianate)	oz.	.67
Epicarin	oz.	.50
Epsom Salts, bbl., 1¼	lb.	.2-3
Ergotine, Bonjeans, lb., 5.50	oz.	.38
Ergot, Spanish	lb.	.55
powdered	lb.	.65
Russian, lbs., .48; powdered	lb.	.58
Eserine	grain.	.22
Sulphate, 5-gr. v.	grain.	.13
Salicylate, 5-gr. v.	grain.	.11
Ether, Nitrous, Conc., ¼, ½ and 1 lbs.		1.00-1.25
Sulphuric	lb.	.75-85
Acetic	lb.	.50
Ethiops Mineral	lb.	.70
Ethyl, Bromide, 1-oz. bot. or tube	oz.	.30-32
Iodide	oz.	.54
Eucaine, Hydrochlor, ⅛, ¼ oz., 3.60; ½, 1 oz.		3.50

IRON TROPON. Brownish powder; albuminoid food preparation composed of tropon (pure albumen) and iron in an assimilable form. Contains 2½ per cent. of iron. Used as a tonic food in treatment of anæmia, chlorosis, impoverished conditions of the system generally, and in convalescence. Tins, 100 Gm., 75c.; 1 doz. tins $6.75
(Tropon Works.)

ISOPRAL. White crystals, soluble in water up to 3 per cent. and easily in alcohol and ether. A nondepressing substitute for chloral in doses of 7 to 15 grains, indicated in all forms of sleeplessness in which chloral is employed. Powder, in 1 oz. bot., per oz., $1.40; 8 grain tablets, bottles of 100, $3.00; 8 grain tablets, tubes of 20 ....75c.
(Continental Color & Chemical Co.)

KRESAMINE. Clear, watery liquid, representing a solution of trikresol, 25 per cent., and ethylenediamine, 25 per cent.; soluble in 3 parts of water, and in all proportions of glycerin; antiseptic and sedative to inflammed tissues. 1 oz...$1.00
(Schering & Glatz.)

KRYOFINE. White, granular crystals, sparingly soluble in cold water (1 in 600); freely soluble in alcohol and ether. A compound of paraphenetidin and methylglycolic acid. Antipyretic and antineuralgic in doses of 4 to 7½ grains. 1 oz. cartons, powd., $1.00; tablets, 4 or 7½ grains, per oz....$1.00
(C. Bischoff & Co.)

LACTOPHENIN. (LACTYL-PARAPHENETIDIN.) Small, white crystals, soluble in 330 parts of water. Differs from phenacetin in containing a molecule of lactic acid in place of acetic. Antipyretic and analgetic in doses of 4 to 8 grains. 1 oz. cartons, each......$1.00
(C. F. Boehringer & Soehne.)

LACTOSERVE. Buttermilk in powder form, scientifically prepared from fresh milk, free from bacteria. Used as infant food. 250 Gm. box........25c.
(C. F. Boehringer & Soehne.)

LARGIN. (SILVER PROTALBIN.) Gray powder containing 11 per cent. of silver; soluble in 10 parts of water. Bactericide and astringent application in gonorrhœa in ¼ to 1½ per cent. injections. 1 oz. vials...$1.75
(Merck & Co.)

LENIGALLOL. (PYROGALLOL TRIACETATE.) White, crystalline powder, insoluble in water, possessing the same reducing properties as pyragallol and used in acute and chronic eczema as ointment. 1 oz. vials $1.00
(Knoll & Co. and Merck & Co.)

LEVULOSE. (FRUIT SUGAR.) Crystalline powder, soluble in water. Sweetening agent used in diabetes, tuberculosis, malnutrition and marasmus of children. Dose, 3 drachms to 2 ounces daily. 1 lb. jars..$1.60
(Schering & Glatz.)

LYCETOL. (DIMETHYLENEDIAMINE TARTRATE.) White powder, readily soluble in water. Uric acid solvent, antiarthritic and diuretic in doses of 5 to 10 grains three times daily. 10 Gm. vials, $1.50; ¼ oz., ½ oz., 1 oz. cartons, per oz... $4.25 to $4.40
(Continental Color & Chemical Co. and Schering & Glatz.)

LYGOSINE. (SODIUM LYGOSINATE.) Glossy, greenish crystals; a condensation product of salicylaldehyde and acetone; readily soluble in water, forming ruby red solutions. Nonirritant substitute for silver as urethral injection in gonorrhœa, 5 per cent. strength. 10 Gm. vials..................35c.
(C. Bischoff & Co.)

LYSIDIN. (ETHYLENE-ETHENYLDIAMINE HYDROCHLORIDE.) Pale yellowish liquid, containing 50 per cent. of pure lysidin, the substance itself being very hygroscopic. Used in acute gout and uric acid diathesis in doses of 10 to 30 minims. 1 oz. vials $1.75
(Victor Koechl & Co.)

MARETIN. White, glistening crystals, very sparingly soluble in water (1 to 1050). Antipyretic, being a methyl acetanilid with a urea nucleus in place of the acetyl group. Dose, 3 to 5 grains. 1 oz. cartons, per oz...........$1.25 to $1.40
(Continental Color & Chemical Co.)

METHAFORM. (DIMETHYLCARBINOL CHLOROFORM.) White, shiny, needle-like crystals, with a slightly camphoraceous taste and odor, sparingly soluble in water, but readily so in chloroform, alcohol, ether and glacial acetic acid. It is hypnotic, analgetic, anæsthetic and antiseptic, somewhat resembling chloral in physiological action. 1 oz. vials, 60c.; 3 grain capsules, bot. of 100, 50c.; 5 grain, 100 ....75c.
(Frederick Stearns & Co.)

MERCUROL. Brownish powder, soluble in water; insoluble in alcohol; a chemical combination of nucleinic acid and mercury, containing 10 per cent. of the metal. Does not coagulate albuminous liquids. Applied to ulcers and suppurating mucous membranes in from ½ to 5 per cent. solution, or in ointment. ¼ oz. vials, per oz., $1.60; 1 oz. vials $1.50
(Parke, Davis & Co.)

MESOTAN. (METHYLOXYMETHYLESTER OF SALICYLIC ACID.) Clear, yellow fluid, insoluble in water, but miscible with alcohol, ether and fixed oils. External application mixed with equal parts of olive oil in muscular and articular rheumatism, pleuritis and gout. 1 oz. bot., 47c.; 25 oz. lots, 42c.
(Continental Color & Chemical Co.)

MIGRAININ. (PHENAZONE CAFFEINE CITRATE.) Small white crystals, readily soluble in water and alcohol. Analgetic and antipyretic. Used in migraine, headaches of influenza, neuralgia, sciatica, etc., in doses of 17 grains. 1 oz. tins.......$1.50
(Victor Koechl & Co.)

MIGROL. White powder, composed of equal parts of sodium pyrocatechinmonoacetate and caffein pyrocatechinmonoacetate. Effective and harmless remedy in headache, toothache, neurasthenia, etc. 1 oz......$4.00
(Fuerst Bros. & Co.)

NARGOL. Brownish powder readily soluble in warm water. Compound of silver and nucleinic acid containing 10 per cent. of the former; does not coagulate albumen. Used in gonorrhœa, conjunctival and other pyogenic inflammations. ¼ oz. vials, per oz., $1.80; ½ oz. vials, per oz., $1.75; 1 oz......$1.70
(Parke, Davis & Co.)

NEODERMIN. Ointment containing lanolin, 85; petrolatum, 10; difluordiphenyl, 4; fluorpseudocumol, 1. For ulcerated surfaces, burns, etc. Collapsible tubes, Gm. 20 and Gm. 40, each..............40c. and 75c
(C. Bischoff & Co.)

NOSOPHEN. (TETRAIODOPHENOLPHTHALEIN.) Grayish powder, odorless, slightly anæsthetic, insoluble in water, alcohol or ether, but soluble in alkaline fluids. Antiseptic dusting powder in wounds, burns, ulcers; substitute for iodoform. Bottles containing about ¼ oz., per doz..................$4.50
(Stallman & Fulton Co.)

NOVARGAN. (Silver Proteinate.) Fine yellow powder containing 10 per cent. of metallic silver, readily soluble in water. Used as injection in gonorrhœa; is very penetrating and free from irritating effects upon mucous membrane. 1 oz. vials, $1.40

(Heyden Chemical Works.)

OREXINE. (Phenyldihydroquinazoline Tannate.) Yellowish powder, tasteless and odorless; insoluble in water, slightly soluble in dilute acid solutions, readily so in hydrochloric acid. Should not be prescribed with preparations of iron. Used in anorexia (lack of appetite) as stimulant of gastric secretion; in seasickness and vomiting of pregnancy. Orexine base is no longer on the market. Dose, 8 to 12 grains two times daily, in powder or in tablets. 1 oz. vials, $1.00; orexoids, Merck's tablets, 4 grains, 50 in bottle .... 55c.

(Merck & Co.)

ORPHOL. (Bismuth Betanaphtholate.) Odorless and tasteless fawn colored powder, insoluble in water; consists of 80 per cent. bismuth oxide and 20 per cent. beta-naphthol. Intestinal antiseptic in doses of 5 to 15 grains three or four times daily. 1 oz., 80c.; tablets, 5 grains, 50 tablets in vial, per vial .... 60c.

(Schering & Glatz.)

ORTHOFORM. White crystalline powder, the methyl ester of metaamidoparaoxybenzoic acid; slightly soluble in water; local anæsthetic and antiseptic. Forms a hydrochloride salt soluble in 9 parts of water. 10 per cent. solution of the hydrochloride salt, or 10 to 20 per cent. in ointment used to alleviate pain in sores or burns. Orthoform, 1 oz. vials, $1.40; orthoform hydrochloride, 1 oz. vials $1.80

(Victor Koechl & Co.)

OVARADEN. Tasteless and odorless powder consisting of the active substance of pigs' ovaries. Used in dysmenorrhœa and neurasthenia in doses of 15 to 30 grains daily. 1 oz. vials, $1.30; 4 grain tablets, bottles of 100 .... $1.30

(Knoll & Co. and Merck & Co.)

OVARIIN. Powder representing 1 part in 8 of fresh cow's ovary, being the desiccated substance of the ovary. Used in chlorosis, affections of the heart, and menstrual troubles. 1 oz. vials, $2.00; ¼ oz., $2.10; 3 grain tablets, 100 in bottle $1.50

(Merck & Co.)

PANKREON. Grayish-red powder; a tannin-pancreatin compound; insoluble in water, obtained from the pancreas; used in pancreatic diabetes, gastritis and apepsia in doses of 7½ grains three times daily. Box of 25 Gm., $1.50; tablets of 0.25 Gm., 50 in box, $1.00; sugar tablets (¾ grain), 100 in box .... 50c.

(Merck & Co.)

PHENOCOLL HYDROCHLORIDE. White, crystalline powder, with sharp, saline taste; soluble in 16 parts of water; very soluble in hot water and alcohol. Similar to phenacetin, and used in malaria, pneumonia, influenza, rheumatism, etc. Dose, 7 to 15 grains. 25 Gm. vials $1.50

(Schering & Glatz.)

PIPERAZINE. Crystalline powder readily soluble in water. Solvent of uric acid and insoluble urates in the system; used in gout, rheumatism and urinary calculi. Dose, 5 to 15 grains thrice daily. 10 Gm. vials, per vial, $1.50; lots of 60, per vial, $1.25. Tablets, tubes of ten 15 grain tablets, $1.50; 60 tubes, per tube, $1.25; ½ and 1 oz. bot., per oz. $4.25

(Continental Color & Chemical Co. and Schering & Glatz.)

POLLANTIN. Liquid and powder; antitoxic serum for hay fever, autumnal catarrh, rose fever and June cold. Package of powder and brush, $1.75; liquid, per package of serum and pipette $1.75

(Fritzsche Brothers.)

PROBILIN PILLS. Composed of salicylic acid, acid sodium oleate, phenolphthalein and menthol; used in gallstone affections. Dose, 3 to 4 pills twice daily for twenty days. Vials of 60, per vial $1.25

(Schering & Glatz.)

PROFERRIN. (Iron Nucleoproteid.) Reddish-brown powder, insoluble in water and acid solutions; contains 10 per cent. of iron and 1 per cent. of phosphorus, in organic combination; is absorbed from the duodenum, being unaffected by the gastric juice. Used in blood impoverishment in doses of 5 grains three times daily. 1 oz. cartons, per doz., $6.00; 5 grain tablets, bottle of 100, 60c.; 2½ grain, bottle of 100 .... 40c.

(H. K. Mulford Co.)

PROTAN. (Tannin Nucleoproteid.) Light brown powder, insoluble in water; formed by the synthesis of tannic acid with nucleo-proteid. Used in all forms of diarrhœa in doses of from 20 to 30 grains; is astringent and acts in the intestines, being unaffected by the gastric juice. 1 oz. cartons, per doz., $6.00; 7½ grain tablets, bottle of 100, 85c.; 5 grain, per 100 .... 60c.

(H. K. Mulford Co.)

PROTARGOL. Yellowish, light powder, easily soluble in water. A proteid compound containing 8 per cent. of silver; not precipitated by albumen or salt solutions. Bactericide in gonorrhœa; antiseptic in eye, ear, nose and throat affections. 0.25 to 1 per cent. solutions for gonorrhœa; 0.5 to 5 per cent. for eye, and 2 to 10 per cent. for ear, nose and throat. Internally, in doses of 1 to 3 grains. ½ oz. and 1 oz. vials, per oz .... $1.10 to $1.35

(Continental Color & Chemical Co.)

PURGATIN. (Purgatol; Anthrapurpurin Acetate.) Yellow crystalline powder; a synthetic oxyanthraquinone, having mild aperient properties; insoluble in water; decomposed in contact with alkalies. Dose, 10 to 30 grains. 1 oz. cartons, 85c.; 5 grain tablets, 100 in bottle $1.00

(Knoll & Co. and Merck & Co.)

PYRAMIDON. (Dimethylamido-antipyrin.) White powder, soluble in 9 parts of water and 2 parts of alcohol. Used as antipyretic in treatment of asthma, pulmonary tuberculosis and abdominal typhus, and as anodyne in headaches and neuralgic pains in doses of 8 to 12 grains. 1 oz. cartons, $2.15; pyramidon camphorate, acid, 1 oz. bot., $1.50; camphorate, neutral, 1 oz. bot., $1.75; salicylate 1 oz. bot. $1.50

(Victor Koechl & Co.)

PYRENOL, a white, crystalline, slightly hygroscopic powder of aromatic odor and sweetish taste, is an addition product of

salicylic and benzoic acids with thymol. Antiseptic, expectorant, analgetic, sedative, antipyretic and cardiotonic. Indicated in the treatment of asthma, bronchitis, pertussis, pneumonia, influenza, typhoid fever and in rheumatic and neuralgic affections. Dose, 7½ to 15 grains, thrice daily, dry or in cold liquids. 1 oz. vial, 70c.; tube of 20 tablets..............30c.
(Schering & Glatz.)

QUARTONOL. Tablets consisting of a compound of duotonol, quinine tonol and strychnine tonol. Blood and nerve tonic. Dose, 1 to 2 tablets three times daily. Bottle of 100 5-grain tablets ....75c.
(Schering & Glatz.)

QUININE LYGOSINATE. Orange-yellow, amorphous powder, containing 70.8 per cent. of quinine; difficultly soluble in water, readily soluble in alcohol, chloroform and benzin. Nontoxic antiseptic and styptic, employed as a dusting powder, gauze or suppository. 10 Gm. vials, each................70c.
(C. Bischoff & Co.)

RENADEN. Powder, obtained from extract of pigs' kidneys; used in uræmia and nephritis in doses of 1 to 2 drachms daily. 1 oz. vials, $1.30; 4 grain tablets, bottles of 100 ....$1.30
(Knoll & Co. and Merck & Co.)

RUBIDIUM IODIDE. Colorless, cubical crystals; soluble in less than 1 in 1 of water; bitter, saline taste. Used in place of potassium iodide in polyarthritis and syphilis. Dose, 5 to 20 grains. 1 oz. vial..$1 00
(Merck & Co.)

SAL-ETHYL. A colorless, transparent, volatile fluid; chemically pure ethyl salicylate. A substitute for methyl salicylate or oil of wintergreen. Globules, 5 min., in bot. of 50, per doz. bot. $5.00
(Parke, Davis & Co.)

SALIT. (SALICYLIC ACID ESTER OF BORNEOL.) Oily fluid, insoluble in water, slightly soluble in glycerin and readily soluble in alcohol, ethers and oils. Used in muscular and articular rheumatism, lumbago, neuralgia and rheumatic pains following colds. 1 oz. bot......22c.
(Heyden Chemical Works.)

SALOCREOL. (SALICYLIC ACID ESTER OF CREOSOTE.) Oily fluid of neutral reaction, almost odorless, insoluble in water, readily soluble in alcohol, ether, chloroform and oils. Used in facial erysipelas, acute and chronic inflammation of the lymph glands and chronic arthritis. 1 oz. bot........45c.

SALOPHEN. White, crystalline powder, containing 51 per cent. of salicylic acid; almost insoluble in water; soluble in alcohol and ether; incompatible with alkalies, which decompose it. Antipyretic, analgetic and antiseptic in rheumatism and neuralgia. Dose, 10 to 15 grains 3 to 4 times daily. 1 oz. cartons............85c. to $1.00
(Continental Color & Chemical Co.)

SALOQUININE. (SALICYLIC ACID ESTER OF QUININE.) Whitish powder, insoluble in water, with difficulty soluble about 1 in 120 of alcohol and ether. Tasteless quinine substitute, used in malaria, tropical fevers, neuralgia and rheumatism. Dose, 15 to 30 grains, one to three times daily. ½ and 1 oz. cartons.
$1.25 to $1.30
(Continental Color & Chemical Co. and Merck & Co.)

SANTYL. Yellowish, oily liquid, tasteless and nonirritant. Salicylic ester of pure sandalwood oil. Used in acute gonorrhœa and its complications. Dose, 30 drops, thrice daily. Bottle of ½ oz., 75c.; capsules, box of 80, ...75c.
(Knoll & Co. and Merck & Co.)

SCOPOLAMINE HYDROBROMIDE is identical with hyoscine hydrobromide, but lower in price. 15 grain tubes, each, $3.00; 10 grain tubes, $2.10; 5 grain tubes.....$1.05
(Merck & Co. and C. F. Boehringer & Soehn.)

SEXTONOL. Tablets consisting of a compound of duotonol, quinine tonol, iron tonol, manganese tonol and strychnine tonol. Blood and nerve nutrient. Dose, 1 to 2 5-grain tablets three times daily. Bottle of 100................75c.
(Schering & Glatz.)

SIDONAL. (PIPERAZINE QUINATE.) White amorphous powder, readily soluble in water. Uric acid solvent in gout and allied affections in doses of 75 to 120 grains a day in divided doses, well diluted with water. 1 oz. bot................$3.75
(Victor Koechl & Co.)

SIDONAL NEW. (QUINIC ACID ANHYDRIDE.) Same properties and uses as above. 1 oz. bot. $2.00
(Victor Koechl & Co.)

SILVER CITRATE. (ANTISEPTIC CREDE; ITROL.) White powder, soluble about 1 in 4000 of water. Recommended in Credé's treatment as an antiseptic for wounds, in lotion, ointment or powder. For disinfection of hands, skin and instruments, 1 to 1000-5000 watery solution; as gargle 1 to 5000 to 10,000; in gonorrhœa, 1 to 8000. Oz.............$1.20 to $1.25
(Schering & Glatz and Merck & Co.)

SILVER LACTATE. (ACTOL.) Whitish powder, soluble in 15 parts of water; recommended in solution 1 in 200 to 1000 as an antiseptic for surgical use. ½ oz. and 1 oz. vials, per oz., $1.30; tablets, 3 grains, boxes containing 5 vials of 10 tablets, per box..................$1.15
(Schering & Glatz and Merck & Co.)

SOMATOSE. Light yellow almost tasteless powder, easily soluble in water, prepared from meat and consisting of deutero and hetero albumoses. Nitrogenous food product for the sick and convalescent. Dose for adults, 90 to 180 grains daily; for children, 30 to 100 grains. 2 oz. tins, per doz., $8.25; ¼ lb. tins, per lb., $5.25; ½ lb. tins, per lb....................$5.00
(Continental Color & Chemical Co.)

SOMNOS. (TRICHLORETHIDENE PROPENYL ETHER.) [Elixir chlorethanal alcoholate.] Clear liquid, miscible with water, produced by the synthesis of Trichloraldehyde with a polyatomic alcohol radical. Hypnotic and cerebral sedative in doses of from 2 to 4 fluid drachms. Pint bottles, $1.10 per pint; $12.00 per doz.; 4 oz. bottles, per doz..........$4.00
(H. K. Mulford Co.)

SPIROFORM. White, crystalline powder, insoluble in water, but readily soluble in alcohol and other solvents. Odorless and practically tasteless. Antirheumatic, analgetic, uric acid solvent. Dose, 7½ to 15 grains, three to five times daily. 25 Gm. cartons, 75c.; 7½ grain tablets, cartons of 50.....75c.
(C. Bischoff & Co.)

STOVAINE. (AMYLENE HYDROCHLORIDE.) White crystalline powder, readily soluble in wa-

ter and in methyl alcohol; less soluble in ethyl alcohol and almost insoluble in ether. A substitute for cocaine, approximately one-fifth as toxic. Aqueous solutions are slightly acid and bitter to the taste. Put up in solutions of various strengths, ¾ per cent., 1 per cent., 10 per cent., in tubes; tablet triturates, 1⅓ grains each; pastilles, 3-100 grain each. Original packages, 1 oz., ½ and ¼ oz. bottles, per oz. $4.00
(Walter F. Sykes & Co.)

STYPTICIN. (COTARNINE HYDROCHLORIDE.) Yellow amorphous powder, the salt of an opium base (cotarnine is a product of the oxidation of narcotine), soluble in water and alcohol. Because of its chemical resemblance to hydrastinine, it being methoxylhydrastine, it is recommended in all forms of uterine hæmorrhage. Used in functional dysmenorrhœa and in the menorrhagia of puberty and the climacteric. Dose as styptic, 1½ to 4 grains, as needed, per os or by injection (10 per cent. solution). Sugar coated tablets, ¾ grain, per tube of 20, 25c.; 1 oz. bottles, per oz., $6.50; ½ oz. bottles, per oz., $6.60; ⅛ oz., per oz., $7.00; 15 grain vials, each, 35c.; hypodermic tablets, ¾ grain, per box of 40 (4 tubes).......60c.
(Merck & Co.)

STYPTOL. (COTARNINE PHTHALATE.) Yellow, crystalline powder, readily soluble in water. It is the phthalate salt of an opium base. Recommended in uterine hæmorrhage in doses of 1 to 3 grains; externally in 10 per cent. solution. 1 oz. vials, $6.50; ½ oz., per oz., $6.75; ¼ oz., $7.00; 15 grain vials, per vial, 35c.; ¾ grain tablets, bottles of 100, per bot...$1.20
(Knoll & Co. and Merck & Co.)

STYRACOL. (GUAIACOL CINNAMIC ESTER.) White granular crystals, insoluble in water, readily soluble in alcohol. Given in phthisis, catarrh of the stomach and intestines in doses of 15 grains three to four times daily. 1 oz. cartons, $1.20; 5 grain tablets, bot of 100..$1.40
(Knoll & Co. and Merck & Co.)

SUBLAMINE. (MERCURIC ETHYLENE-DIAMINE SULPHATE.) Crystalline powder, containing 43 per cent. of mercury; very soluble in water. Used in solutions of 1 to 1000 as a substitute for corrosive sublimate. 1 oz. vials, 50c.; tablets, 15 grains, 100 tablets in bottle, $1.10; 20 tablets in tube, 5 tubes in box...............$1.60
(Schering & Glatz.)

TANNALBIN. (TANNIN ALBUMINATE.) Pale brown, insoluble, tasteless powder, containing about 50 per cent. of tannin. It is not affected by the gastric juice, but is split up in the intestinal canal; hence is used as intestinal astringent and for diarrhœa. Dose, 15 to 30 grains three to five times daily. 1 oz. cartons, 85c.; 5 grain tablets, bot, of 100......$1.00
(Knoll & Co. and Merck & Co.)

TANNIGEN. (ACETYLTANNIN.) Grayish powder, insoluble in water, soluble in alcohol; incompatible with alkalies which decompose it. Intestinal astringent in chronic diarrhœa and intestinal diseases of children. Adult dose, 3 to 10 grains, three to six times daily; children, 1-3 to ½ that quantity. 1 oz. bot., per oz....55c. to 75c.
(Continental Color & Chemical Co.)

TANNOPINE. (HEXAMETHYLENETETRAMINE TANNIN.) Brownish powder, insoluble in water, decomposed by alkalies; compound of tannin and urotropine, containing 87 per cent. of tannic acid. Intestinal astringent and disinfectant. Adult dose, 10 to 15 grains; children, 3 to 8 grains four times daily. 1 oz. cartons, per oz.....................55c. to 75c.
(Continental Color & Chemical Co.)

TESTADEN. Powdered extract of the testicle juice of animals. Used in impotency, neurasthenia and spinal irritation. Dose, 15 grains three to four times daily. 1 oz. vials, $1.30; 4 grain tablets, bot. of 100.$1.30
(Knoll & Co. and Merck & Co.)

THEOBROMINE. White crystalline powder, soluble in ether, but almost insoluble in cold water or alcohol; organic base obtained from seeds of *Theobroma cacao.* Diuretic in dropsy of cardiac and renal affections. Dose, 5 to 8 grains. 1 oz. bot., per oz...........90c.
(Continental Color & Chemical Co. and Merck & Co.)

THEOBROMINE - SODIUM - SALICYLATE. White powder, very soluble in water, decomposed by acid solutions. Diuretic in dropsy of cardiac and renal origin. Dose, 7 to 15 grains. 1 oz. bot., per oz..60c.
(Farbenfabriken of Elberfeld, Continental Color Works and Merck & Co.)

THEOCIN. Fine, colorless crystals; synthetic alkaloid of tea (theophylline); difficultly soluble in alcohol and cold water, more easily in warm water; forms salts with alkalies. Powerful diuretic in doses of 3 to 6 grains, two to three times daily. ½ and 1 oz. bot., per oz..................$2.50 to $2.70
(Continental Color & Chemical Co.)

THEOPHYLLIN. White crystalline needles, soluble in 226 parts of water. Identical with theocin, being the synthetic alkaloid of tea. Diuretic in doses of 4 to 8 grains. 1 oz. vials, $1.40. Theophyllin sodium, 1 oz. vials, $1.50. Theophylline sodium salicylate, 1 oz. vials $1.10
(C. F. Boehringer & Soehne.)

THIGENOL. Dark brown, thick liquid; odorless on use; slight empyreumatic taste; soluble in water, diluted alcohol, glycerin and collodion; same uses as ichthyol. It is the sodium salt of the sulphonic acid of a synthetic sulpho oil. Dose, 3 to 10 grains. 1 oz. bots., per oz., 32c.; 1 lb. tins, per lb....$4.00
(Hoffmann-La Roche Chemical Works.)

THIOCOL. (POTASSIUM GUAIACOL SULPHONATE.) White crystalline powder, soluble in water, slightly in alcohol and ether. Used in phthisis and similar diseases which require the creosote or guaiacol treatment; nonirritating and readily assimilable. Dose, 5 to 20 grains three times daily. 1 oz. bot., per oz., $1.40; tablets, 5 grains each, 100 in bot...$1.75 Syrup, 6 oz. bots., per doz.$8.00
(Hoffmann-La Roche Chemical Works.)

THIOSINAMIN. Colorless crystals, soluble in water, alcohol and ether; used hypodermically for lupus and uterine affections in doses of 1 to 3 grains in 15 per cent. alcoholic or 10 per cent. glycerinated water solution, one injection being given every three days; by the mouth, in capsules containing ½ to 3 grains. 1 oz. vials, per oz. 60c.
(Schering & Glatz and Merck & Co.)

THYMOXOL. Alcoholic 1 per cent. solution of thymol containing 3 per cent. of hydrogen dioxide; miscible with water. Used in 5 or 10 per cent. solutions as antiseptic and bactericide. ¼ lb. bot., per lb...$2.40
(C. Bischoff & Co.)

THYRADEN. Brownish powder; dried extract of sheep's thyroid, containing all the constituents of the gland. Used in myxœdema, obesity, goitre, psoriasis, eczema, menorrhagia and rickets. Dose, 15 to 30 grains daily. 1 oz. vials, $1.80; 2 grain tablets, bot. of 100.75c.
(Knoll & Co. and Merck & Co.)

THYREOIDECTIN. Reddish powder obtained from the blood of animals deprived of the thyreoid gland. A remedy for exophthalmic goitre. Dose, 5 to 10 grains. Capsules, 5 grains each, bot. of 50...$1.00
(Parke, Davis & Co.)

THYROIDIN. Dried extract of sheep's thyroid, 1 part equaling 6 parts of fresh gland. Used in myxœdema, cretinism, psoriasis, obesity, lupus, etc. Dose, ½ to 1 grain, increased to 2 grains three times daily. 1 oz. bot.....................$1.25
(Merck & Co.)

TONOLS. Trade name adopted by Schering & Glatz for the glycerophosphate salts. See under the name of the alkali earth or metallic base.

TRIFERRIN. (IRON PARANUCLEINATE.) Brownish-yellow powder, soluble in alkaline solutions, insoluble in water. Said to contain 22 per cent. of iron, 9 per cent. of nitrogen and 2.5 per cent. of phosphorus. Used in anæmia, chlorosis and debility in dose of 5 grains three times daily. 1 oz. cartons, $1.00; 5 grain tablets, cartons of 50, 75c.; solution (Triferrol), 8 oz. bot., per bot..53c. (C. Bischoff & Co. and Knoll & Co.)

TRIKRESOL. Clear, colorless liquid; a mixture of ortho, meta and para cresols in the proportion of 35, 40 and 25 per cent., respectively. Corresponding to Creosol, U. S. P., viii; soluble in 40 parts of water. Said to have three times the germicidal power of carbolic acid. Solutions of from ½ to 1 per cent. strength are recommended for surgical use; for internal use 1 to 2 minims three times a day. 1 oz. vials, 15c.; 1 lb. bot.......................60c.
(Schering & Glatz.)

TRIOTONOL. Tablet consisting of 5 grains duotonol and 1-60 grain strychnine-tonol. Nerve tonic. Dose, 1 to 2 tablets, thrice daily. Bottle of 100 tablets ....75c.
(Schering & Glatz.)

TRIPHENIN. (PROPIONYLPHENETIDIN.) White crystalline powder obtained by the action of propionic acid on paraphenetidine; almost insoluble in water (1 in 2000), more readily in alcohol and ether. Is a strong antipyretic, used in neuralgias and rheumatism in doses of 5 to 15 grains three or four times daily. Tablets, 5 grains, bot. of 50, 65c.; 1 oz. cartons..50c.
(Merck & Co.)

TROPACOCAINE HYDROCHLORIDE. (BENZOYLPSEUDOTROPEINE HYDROCHLORIDE.) Colorless crystals, soluble in water. Local anæsthetic like cocaine, but said to be less depressing to the heart. Used hypodermically in 3 to 10 per cent. solutions in 0.6 per cent. solution of sodium chloride. 5 grain vials, 40c.; 15 grain vials ....95c.
(Merck & Co.)

TUMENOL. Reddish-brown, oily paste, obtained from a bituminous rock deposit. Consists of a mixture of sulphonized hydrocarbons similar to ichthyol, and possessing similar properties, being antiseptic and healing in skin diseases, applied either as attenuated powder, 5 per cent. ointment, or dissolved in ether and alcohol or water and glycerine.

AMMONIUM. Black, viscid, oily liquid, odorless; soluble in water and miscible with oils and fats. Used as antiseptic application in skin diseases, in form of ointment, paste or glycerin-ethereal solution painted on surface. 1 oz. bottles.....25c.

OIL is a dark yellow fluid of thick consistency, having the same application as the foregoing.

POWDER. (SULPHOTUMENOLIC ACID.) Dark yellow powder, readily soluble in water. Used with equal parts of zinc starch paste in treatment of skin diseases. Paste, 1 oz. vials, 55c.; ¼ lb. jar, $1.75; ½ lb. jar, $3.25. Oil, 1 oz. vials, 65c.; ¼ lb. bottles, $3.25; 1 lb. bottles, $6.30. Powder, 1 oz. tin, $1.10; 2 oz. tins, per tin..$1.85
(Victor Koechl & Co.)

URITONE. White crystalline powder; a product of formaldehyde and ammonia, of the same composition and properties as hexamethylene tetramine; used in treatment of purulent conditions of the urine, cystitis, etc., in doses of 5 to 15 grains. 1 oz. vials, 60c.; 5 grain capsules, per bot. of 100, 85c.; compressed tablets, 7½ grs., each, per bot of 100....$1.00
(Parke, Davis & Co.)

UROSINE. (LITHIUM QUINATE.) Colorless crystals, readily soluble in water. Used in gout, cystitis and uric acid diathesis. Supplied in effervescent tablets containing quinic acid, 7½ grains; lithium carbonate, 1½ grains; sugar, 4½ grains. Vial of 10, 50c.; 25, $1.20. Powder, 1 oz. vial.....................95c.
(C. Bischoff & Co.)

UROTROPIN. (HEXAMETHYLENETETRAMINE.) Colorless granular crystals, with an alkaline reaction; readily soluble in water. Urinary antiseptic in cystitis, bacteruria, phosphaturia, gout, rheumatism, irritable bladder, etc., used also before and after instrumentation to forestall urinary infection. Dose, 5 to 15 grains. 1 oz. vials, 60c.; lb., $7.50; tablets, 7½ grains each, 20 tablets in box, 25c.; 5 grains each, 30 tablets in box..........25c.
(Schering & Glatz.)

UROTROPIN METHYLENE CITRATE. (NEWUROTROPIN.) Crystals resembling urotropin and having same therapeutic indications, though dose is double, being 15 grains three times daily. 1 oz. vials, 60c.; tablets, 7½ grains, 20 tablets in box, per box..............25c.
(Schering & Glatz.)

VALIDOL. (VALERIC ACID MENTHYL ESTER.) Colorless liquid, a combination of valeric acid and menthol; insoluble in water, readily soluble in alcohol. Used in hysteria and neurasthenia in doses of 10 to 15 drops three times daily. Vials, 10 Gm., 50c.; 25 Gm., $1.20; pills, 25 in bot., each.......50c.
(C. Bischoff & Co.)

VALIDOL CAMPHORATE. Colorless liquid, insoluble in water, readily soluble in alcohol and oils. A 10 per cent. solution of camphor in validol. Used in toothache by local application and internally in same indications and dose as validol. Vials, 10 Gm. each, 60c.; 25 Gm. $1.20
(C. Bischoff & Co.)

VALYL. (VALERIC ACID DIETHYLAMIDE.) Colorless, oily liquid, with a valerian odor and burning taste, supplied only in gelatin capsules, each containing 2 grains. Nerve sedative used in hysteria, neurasthenia, hypochondriasis, and in neuralgia and menstrual disturbances in doses of 2 or 3 capsules two or three times daily. Bot. of 50 capsules........90c.
(Victor Koechl & Co.)

VERONAL. White crystalline powder, soluble in 150 parts of cold and 12 parts of boiling water. Hypnotic in simple sleeplessness and the insomnia of mania. Dose, 5 to 15 grains, dissolved in hot fluids. 1 oz. bot. and cartons, per oz., $1.60; tablets, 5 grains each, tube of 10, 30c.; bot. of 100 ....$2.25
(Merck & Co. and Continental Color & Chemical Co.)

VIOFORM. (IODOCHLOROXYCHINOLINE.) Greenish-yellow powder, insoluble in water. Used in same way as iodoform, than which it is six times lighter and bulkier. 1 oz. cartons $1.15
(C. Bischoff & Co.)

XEROFORM. (TRIBROMPHENOLBISMUTH.) Yellow, insoluble powder, containing bismuth oxide and tribromphenol in nearly equal proportions A powerful bactericide used in place of iodoform as a dressing for wounds and internally as an intestinal antiseptic in doses of 5 to 20 grains. 1 oz. vials...50c.
(The Heyden Chemical Works.)

American Druggist "WANTS" Page.

THIS Department is intended to be used as a medium for the exchange or sale of stores, the employment of clerks, and the securing of situations. Suitable notices of moderate length under this heading inserted one time free for subscribers; for each additional insertion Fifty Cents will be charged. Advertisements not in the foregoing classification Forty Cents per line.

SITUATIONS VACANT.

WANTED.—DRUG CLERK licensed in New York State to work in country drug store with soda fountain; must have the right kind of references; sober, honest, not afraid of work; single man preferred. O. E. Shay's Pharmacy, Canaseraga, N. Y.

WANTED. — TRAVELING SALESMEN calling on the drug trade to carry popular proprietary remedy as side line; liberal commission. Address J. C., care AMERICAN DRUGGIST.

WANTED.—Licensed pharmacist, single man preferred; must be good salesman and of good appearance; state age, experience, salary required, and give references. Address Milton, care AMERICAN DRUGGIST.

WANTED.—TABLET MAKER AND SUGAR COATER. References and samples of coated work with reply. Address Sugar Coater, care AMERICAN DRUGGIST.

REGISTERED PHARMACISTS.—We are compiling a list of all drug employees in the United States who would accept better conditions. Every pharmacist should write at once for particulars. Employers referred to competent men, free. National Pharmaceutical Agency, 616 Colonial Security Building, St. Louis, Mo.

SITUATIONS WANTED.

POSITION WANTED AS NEW YORK OR PHILADELPHIA MANAGER FOR A PHARMACEUTICAL MANUFACTURING HOUSE BY A MAN THOROUGHLY EXPERIENCED IN EVERY BRANCH OF THIS BUSINESS, WITH FULL KNOWLEDGE OF THE TRADE IN THE WHOLE EASTERN TERRITORY; P. C. P. GRADUATE; SPLENDID BUSINESS TRAINING, SOBER AND INDUSTRIOUS, AND CAN ANSWER EVERY NECESSARY REQUIREMENT. ADDRESS, WITH PARTICULARS, E. M., CARE OF AMERICAN DRUGGIST.

GENUINE BOHEMIAN HOP LUPULINE. If you wish to purchase a real good quality of hop lupuline, apply to Joseph Pachmann, Saaz, Bohemia, who solely can meet your requirements to your satisfaction.

WANTED TO BUY DRUG BUSINESS doing $85 day or over; New York State only; in answer give full particulars. B. J. E., care AMERICAN DRUGGIST.

BUSINESS OPPORTUNITIES.

FOR SALE.—DRUG STORE in northern New York State: fine summer trade; will sell reasonable on account of other business. Address Store, care AMERICAN DRUGGIST.

CORRESPONDENCE SOLICITED from manufacturers, jobbers and importers desiring to establish a branch in Chicago; have had ten years' experience in the wholesale business and understand the Chicago market. Address Aristole, care AMERICAN DRUGGIST, 221 Randolph street, Chicago, Ill.

FOR SALE.—San Juan, Porto Rico; only American drug store; established seven years; good business; inventory about $7,500; reason, sickness. P. O. Box 226, San Juan, Porto Rico.

FOR SALE.—PERFECTION ELECTRIC CARBONATOR, because of closing of branch store; used only short time. Address J. B. Dakin, 59 Maiden lane, New York City.

DRUG STORES BOUGHT AND SOLD.—Drug men wanted. U. S. and Canada. F. V. Kniest, N. Y. L., Omaha, Neb.

WANTED.—SALESMEN OF ABILITY TO CARRY THE MOST SALABLE, ATTRACTIVE AND RELIABLE LINE OF NON-SECRET PREPARATIONS, TOILET ARTICLES AND SPECIALTIES SOLD IN THIS COUNTRY. HOUSE ESTABLISHED FOR 50 YEARS. WE WANT BOTH LOCAL AND STATE REPRESENTATIVES. HOLLANDER-KOSHLAND & CO., BALTIMORE, MD.

FOR SALE.—An up-to-date drug store in a manufacturing city of 20,000 population in Central New York will be disposed of owing to poor health of owner compelling him to retire from business. Will sell for less than inventory. This is a trade for a quick buyer. Particulars Box 285, Syracuse, N. Y.

DRUG STORE FOR SALE.—New York City; West Side; first-class location; good lease; well established; bargain for right man. Address Broadway, care AMERICAN DRUGGIST.

EXAMINATION QUESTIONS:

I have collected and bound in a 64-page pamphlet (6x9 inches, fine print), the PHARMACY EXAMINATION QUESTIONS of the various states and territories; also the Pharmacy Laws of the different states. All of the questions are recent, many based on new U. S. P. They are intended for those who wish to prepare for State Board or other examinations.

A candidate about to take an examination can have no better preparation than a thorough drill on the questions that have been asked by State Board Examiners.

This pamphlet will be sent post paid to any address upon receipt of 75 cts. Address:

J. A. HYNES,
292 S. Marshfield Avenue, Chicago, Ill.

ONCE TRIED, ALWAYS USED.

THE BAR-KEEPER'S "FRIEND"

FOR SCOURING, CLEANING AND POLISHING BAR FIXTURES, DRAIN BOARDS AND ALL Tin, Zinc, Brass, Copper, Nickel and all Kitchen and Plated Utensils. Glass, Wood, Marble, Porcelain, Etc.

GEORGE WM. HOFFMAN, Sole Manufacturer and Proprietor, 295 East Washington St., Indianapolis.

THE BAR-KEEPERS' FRIEND.

FOR cleansing everything about a drug store or a soda fountain there is nothing equal to Hoffman's

Barkeeper's Friend

Marble, Glass, Nickel, Brass, Copper, Tin and German Silver can all be cleaned and polished with it easier than with anything else. Let us send you a FREE SAMPLE.

Highest Award, Chicago World's Fair, 1893, Louisiana Purchase Exposition, St. Louis, Mo., 1904.

GEO. WM. HOFFMAN, 295 E. Washington St. Indianapolis, Ind.

FOR SALE BY JOBBING TRADE

JUST a word to say YOU can have by asking FREE of expense, our

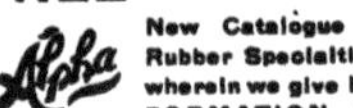

New Catalogue of Rubber Specialties: wherein we give INFORMATION OF IMPORTANCE TO YOU.

PARKER, STEARNS & CO.
Dept. K. 230 South St., New York

A reliable and progressive CHEMICAL FACTORY IN GERMANY desires to communicate with American importers and manufacturers with a view to secure orders for chemical and pharmaceutical articles to be manufactured in Germany and imported into this country ready for the market.

The Company would furthermore be able to excute orders for patent medicines, etc., on any given recipe.

Address for further particular, M. FRANKFURTER, Room 97, 25 Whitehall St., New York.

I am receiving inquiries and individual orders from your vicinity. As it is to our mutual advantage to supply a customer through his local Druggist I want to hear from you personally and ask you to fill out the coupon herewith and mail me at once.

ABSORBINE is well advertised and I will see that it is not dead stock. Do you want advertising matter?

W. F. YOUNG, P. D. F.
49 Monmouth St.
Springfield, Mass.

TOWN OR CITY ______ POPULATION, COUNTY ______ STATE ______

FIRM NAME ______

STREET ______ BUSINESS ______

NEAREST SHIPPING POINT ______ EXPRESS CO. ______

What Drug Paper do you take? ______ What Horse or Farm Paper? ______

Do you carry ABSORBINE in stock? ______ If so, how long? ______

Do you carry ABSORBINE, JR., (mankind) in stock? ______ If so, how long? ______

If not, will you order a small quantity from your jobber? ______

Average sale per month? ______ What season do you sell most? ______

Give name of your jobber ______

What is the average Horse worth in your section? ______ Are many raised? ______

How can I help you sell more goods? ______

Kindly fill out the above and return for my files and I will refer inquiries from your section to you to our mutual benefit. W. F. YOUNG, P. D. F. 49 Monmouth St., Springfield, Mass.

ource UK Ltd.
es UK
32280119
UK00011B/957/P

Lightning S
Milton Key
UKHW031
336340